DICTIONARY OF CANADIAN BIOGRAPHY

DICTIONARY OF CANADIAN BIOGRAPHY

DICTIONNAIRE BIOGRAPHIQUE DU CANADA

RAMSAY COOK GENERAL EDITOR

JEAN HAMELIN DIRECTEUR GÉNÉRAL ADJOINT

VOLUME XV

UNIVERSITY OF TORONTO

ROBERT L. FRASER executive officer

MARY P. BENTLEY executive editor
WILLADEAN T. LEO supervisory editor

DAVID ROBERTS senior manuscript editor
ELIZABETH HULSE manuscript editor

PHYLLIS CREIGHTON, HENRI PILON translations editors
SUSAN E. BÉLANGER, DIANE FERNS bibliographies editors
LORETTA M. JAMES, DEBORAH MARSHALL editorial assistants

UNIVERSITÉ LAVAL

ANNE CARRIER directrice de la rédaction

PAULETTE M. CHIASSON rédactrice-historienne principale
HUGUETTE FILTEAU rédactrice-historienne

JEAN-PAUL CORRIVEAU réviseur-traducteur et responsable administratif

MICHÈLE BRASSARD chargée de recherche
FRANCINE BOULET, CAROLE CARRIER, DENISE GAGNON, JOHANNE GIROUX,
DANIELLE JOLLY, ROSE-ALMA LACHANCE, LOUISE LÉPINE
secrétaires

TRANSLATORS
EDWARD BAXTER, DIANA BERRIS, GRAHAM FALCONER, DANIELLE HAMELIN

DICTIONARY
OF CANADIAN
BIOGRAPHY

VOLUME XV

1921 TO 1930

UNIVERSITY OF TORONTO PRESS

Toronto Buffalo London

© University of Toronto/Université Laval 2005
Printed in Canada

ISBN 0-8020-9087-7

Library and Archives Canada Cataloguing in Publication

Dictionary of Canadian biography. – Regular ed.

Issued also in French under title: Dictionnaire biographique du Canada.
Includes bibliographical references and indexes.
Contents: v. 15. 1921–1930.
ISBN 0-8020-9087-7 (v.15)
1. Canada – Biography.
FC25.D5 1966   920′.071   C66-003974-5 rev
F1005.D49 1966

Contents

JEAN HAMELIN
(1931–1998)

A Tribute to Jean Hamelin

JEAN HAMELIN passed away peacefully on 15 May 1998, in the night, after a few short weeks of illness. He was 66. The twin editorial teams of the *Dictionary of Canadian biography/Dictionnaire biographique du Canada* at the University of Toronto and the Université Laval wish to pay him tribute by dedicating this work, volume XV – for which he had laid the groundwork before his death – to him.

Jean Hamelin left inspiration as his legacy to this vast project of Canada's written history. Professor, historian, and great humanist, he infused a whole generation of researchers and the members of the two editorial teams of the DCB/DBC with his fine mind and his remarkable visionary spirit. A brilliant student in Quebec and in France, in 1957 he began an outstanding 36-year career in the department of history at the Université Laval. In 1987 the faculty of arts honoured him by naming him *professeur par excellence* of its first half-century. An erudite and rivetting teacher, he kindled a love of learning in hundreds of students who by the dozens subsequently undertook graduate studies. Many of them have taught in universities in Quebec and elsewhere in Canada, perpetuating the influence of their mentor. Innovative and unsparing in his efforts as a historian, Jean Hamelin left a rich and original treasure of works for a very diverse public. A pioneer in key areas of Quebec history, he never hesitated to take issue with traditions and methodologies, as he constantly sought new subjects and complex problems for research. He touched on politics, society, and the economy, as well as on culture, religion, and instruments of communication. He even took an interest in the tools of the historian's trade, producing reference works that are of great value to researchers. His clear, effective, fluid writing displayed his ability to "retell the mystery of man." As author or co-author, he produced 47 books and more than 75 scholarly articles focused, at times, on authoritative syntheses, of which he was the uncontested master in Quebec. His penultimate book, *Histoire de l'université Laval*, published in 1995, remains one of the finest examples of this gift. The subtitle he appended, *Les péripéties d'une idée* – that is, the university's idea of itself at the turning points in its long span of years – gave the work its character and power: the phrase revealed the mainspring for the development of the institution that the author had so treasured. Jean Hamelin received many honours, including on two occasions the Governor General's Literary Award for Non-Fiction. He was given the first, with Yves Roby, in 1972 for his *Histoire économique du Québec, 1851–1896*. The two volumes he wrote for the *Histoire du catholicisme québécois*, entitled *Le XXᵉ siècle: 1898–1940*, which was co-authored with Nicole Gagnon, and *Le XXᵉ siècle: de 1940 à nos jours*, earned him the second in 1985. Unquestionably Hamelin, as a man, professor, and historian, opened exciting avenues for the future and cast splendid light on great sweeps of Canadian and Quebec history.

Jean Hamelin brought all this intellectual wealth and experience to the DCB/DBC in

1973, when he accepted the position of *directeur général adjoint*. For 25 years, with almost daily dedication to the task, he helped imbue the scholarly undertaking with its standard of excellence, an indelible benchmark that distinguishes this project and that from the beginning has guided its editorial teams. Under his joint editorship, the DCB/DBC published ten volumes that often enlarged our knowledge of Canadian history and revealed many figures who, sometimes in obscurity, had carved out the paths of the country's development over time. Attentive to the researchers who gave so much to this epic work, he was often able to offer them much advice and judicious counsel. The quality of the articles forming the contents of these volumes assuredly has contributed to the strong upsurge in Canada in the genre of biography, which has regained its place in the elucidation of history. He himself, moreover, signed or co-signed 51 of these biographical sketches. In critical commentary, all the volumes of the DCB/DBC have received the highest praise: Jean-Michel Lacroix hailed them as a "marvellous work of bilingual synthesis" in 1982; Michael Bliss in 1986 acclaimed them as "the most important books published in Canada since 1966." These accolades surely must be seen as the fruit of the unceasing labour and the enlightened influence of the man who gave himself to this project for so many years. With the needed perceptiveness and wisdom, sometimes leavened by an irresistible sense of humour, he was a clear-sighted and unifying force leading the research and editorial teams to exceed their reach. He was able to help them develop their love of culture, explore the interest in pursuing questions integral to the scholarly task, enhance their respect for the men and women who were, indeed, the objects of their research but above all were the human beings who, in hardship and with effort, shaped Canada. This fine influence found its full meaning in the close collaboration between the teams at Laval and Toronto which he always enthusiastically encouraged. Our project, in which he made profound friendships, depends on this fruitful, frank, and amicable cooperation, the true pivot of our daily work. Drawing deeply on this spirit, Jean Hamelin helped make the DCB/DBC the work of reference in Canada for this type of bilingual publication.

Jean Hamelin will remain graven in our memories, as in the history and the very soul of our project. It is up to us to keep the work on the path beaten so magnificently, guided by the devotion he gave, which serves as our model.

RAMSAY COOK   RÉAL BÉLANGER

Introduction

GEORGE W. BROWN AND MARCEL TRUDEL, the founding general editors of the *Dictionary of Canadian biography/Dictionnaire biographique du Canada*, decided that the date of death would determine the appropriate volume for the biography of a chosen figure. This was a sensible choice since death dates are often more easily and accurately established than birth dates, but it inevitably results in some anomalies. The biographies of the long-lived – Sir Charles Tupper or Ambroise-Dydime Lépine, for example – sometimes appear in volumes covering periods long after the subjects' most active years. Perhaps only volume XIV (1911–20) contains descriptions of many Canadians whose adult lives began and ended during one tragic decade, in which World War I was the defining experience.

It is, then, the death-date rule that explains why this 15th volume, covering 1921 to 1930, presents the lives of many men and women who were the innovative pioneers of 20th-century Canada. Examples include Alexander Graham Bell, inventor of the telephone, and Cyrille Duquet, creator of a telephone receiver; Sir Adam Beck, father of Ontario Hydro, and Louis-Anthyme Herdt, innovator in electronics; Gordon Morton McGregor, manufacturer of automobiles, and Cléophas Fabien, maker of iceboxes. The biographies of professionals such as journalist Joséphine Marchand (Dandurand), lawyer Clara Brett Martin, nurse Isabel Johnstone, writers Sara Jeannette Duncan and Félicité Angers (known as Laure Conan), and teachers Jeanne Lajoie and Kate Mackintosh illustrate the expanding roles of women in the nation's life and in the DCB/DBC. The changing character of the population, a major theme in the country's development, can be seen in names like Peter Vasil'evich Verigin, Angelina Napolitano, Yip Sang, and Nestor Dmytriw. Among the politicians, Sir Clifford Sifton, Sir Lomer Gouin and Sir Robert Bond perhaps best exemplify the evolving mentality of the early part of the century, while Bishop Louis-Nazaire Bégin was one of the many church leaders who struggled with the questions that modernity has posed for organized religion. The account of the brilliant goaltender Georges Vézina forecasts the growth of professionalism in sport. The biographies of the Micmac (Mi'kmaw) hunter and guide Jerry Lonecloud, who realized the importance of preserving his people's traditions, Jules Jetté, who created a dictionary for the Koyukon, and Niaqutiaq, an Inuit trader, depict the challenges faced by native peoples. Sketches of farm families, including those of John Matheson and Joseph-Dominique Guay, outline some of the dilemmas confronted by agriculturalists, while the life of Alphonse Verville reveals the new political role of working people. In the arts, the career of Henry de Grandsaignes d'Hauterives shows the influence of the newly established cinematic medium, while the stories of James Wilson Morrice and Emma Lajeunesse (known as Emma Albani) document internationally acclaimed careers in painting and music. Of course, neither these figures, randomly chosen from a total of 619 biographies by 446 authors, nor a single volume of the DCB/DBC can fully reveal the social and cultural characteristics of a decade. A death date, like death itself, is arbitrary. Nevertheless, volume XV begins to describe, in rich and revealing detail, the origins of modern Canada.

If change and continuity represent a dominant theme in the biographies in this volume, then change and continuity have also been a major feature of our lives at the DCB/DBC in the first years of the 21st century. Nothing more satisfyingly portrays continuity than the appearance of volume XV under the sign of Johannes Gutenberg represented by the University of Toronto Press and Les Presses de l'Université Laval. Nothing more dramatically demonstrates change than the electronic versions of volumes I to XIV of the DCB/DBC. First, as a project to celebrate the millennium, a CD-ROM was created and distributed without charge to every high school, CEGEP, college, university, and public library in Canada, and to select university libraries around the world. Then, under an intellectual properties licensing agreement with the Department of Canadian Heritage, the texts of the 14 published volumes, together with some additional biographies, including those of 12 significant individuals whose death dates are post-1930, have been made available online through Library and Archives Canada, without the fees commonly required to use the online versions of major reference works. The staff of the DCB/DBC is extremely proud of this achievement – of both the print and the electronic versions. We are especially pleased that we have been able to make the results of the work done by hundreds of Canadian scholars, professional and non-professional, accessible to thousands of readers all over the world. With volume XV, we believe we have again fulfilled the mandate set for us by our original benefactor and patron saint, Mr James Nicholson, who declared that "the object [of the DCB/DBC] shall be not only to supply an acknowledged want in Canadian literature, but . . . it should compete with or even surpass works of a similar character produced elsewhere." Again, we have competed and surpassed.

Meeting this intellectual challenge has never been easy, but the effort has always been stimulating and enjoyable. In the last 15 years another challenge, a financial one, has often made our work more difficult, and sometimes threatened our future. While costs of production have risen, funds from traditional sources have declined. Mr and Mrs Nicholson's original generosity remains a partial insurance policy, but other institutions offering support have become increasingly important. In 2000, grants from the federal government's Millennium Bureau of Canada, the *National Post* and Hollinger Inc., and Historica, made the CD-ROM possible. We are very grateful to Taber M. James and his associates who presided over the creation of this digital miracle. For their generous support that year we wish to thank the Honourable Herb Gray, minister responsible for the Millennium Bureau of Canada, Mr Peter G. White of Hollinger Inc., and Mr Tom Axworthy of Historica. The Department of Canadian Heritage provided essential funding for both our print and online versions. We extend our deep appreciation to Dr Ian E. Wilson of Library and Archives Canada, Mr Alex Himelfarb, former deputy minister of Canadian Heritage, and Professor John English of the University of Waterloo for their assistance with the online project. We also thank many other donors for contributions both large and small whose grants and gifts encourage us to believe that, even in the worst of financial times, we have the confidence of agencies and individuals who know that Canadian history matters.

Finally, change and continuity have been experienced by our editorial team. In 1999, when Huguette Filteau retired from her position as *directrice de la rédaction* in Quebec, Anne Carrier, a highly qualified academic editor, was appointed to her position. In Toronto, Executive Editor Mary P. Bentley, having seen volume XV through its final stages, has retired; her many responsibilities have been assumed by another experienced editor, Willadean Thordis Leo. For more than 25 years Huguette Filteau and Mary Bentley, working with exceptional knowledge and skill as historians and editors, have ensured that the accuracy of the information and the quality of the prose provided by our contributors have met the highest standards. Moreover, they made certain that the editors under their supervision were well trained and confident, and that production schedules were kept. In short, they made the General Editors look extremely good. Their well-earned retirement from full-time editorial responsibilities is an opportunity for the General Editors and the staff in Quebec and Toronto to recognize their unlimited devotion to the scholarly and literary goals of the DCB/DBC and their importance in the creation of an effective, bilingual, and professional partnership founded on mutual respect and warm friendship. The contribution of Huguette Filteau and Mary Bentley to the esteemed scholarly reputation of the DCB/DBC is inestimable.

RÉAL BÉLANGER   RAMSAY COOK

Au Revoir to Ramsay Cook

AFTER SIXTEEN YEARS as general editor of the Dictionary of Canadian biography/Dictionnaire biographique du Canada, Ramsay Cook has decided to step down. As may be readily imagined, the staff members in the two offices of the DCB/DBC were saddened to learn of this decision; but, as they quietly resign themselves to it, they want to express their affection to this man who has made such an enormous contribution to the project. From 1989, this outstanding scholar, who, since the 1960s, has been closely involved in many of the leading issues of the day, threw himself wholeheartedly into this great undertaking, overseeing the publication of three volumes, always striving to bring new depth to the research aspects of the work while maintaining the highest standards of accuracy and editorial excellence. Ramsay Cook's effectiveness and acuity were particularly evident at certain crucial stages in the progress of the DCB/DBC as well as in the financial difficulties that arose in this period; his powerful analyses and stature as a scholar opened many doors, facilitating the continuity and the renewal of the project. Congenial, clear-sighted, determined, and courageous, Professor Cook is preparing to embark on another equally challenging course. The members of the staff in Toronto, with whom he worked most closely, will not forget his reassuring, supportive presence, his concern for their personal well-being, his sense of equity and justice, his irrepressible good spirits ever ready to overcome obstacles, his humanity, his unfailing generosity. For their part, the members of the *équipe* at Laval will remember the warm welcome he gave the *directeur général adjoint* on his appointment in 1998, the thoughtful courtesy he always showed them, particularly during joint meetings of the two offices, as well as the whole-hearted respect he displayed for the bilingual nature of the work, and his absolute candour. An outstanding general editor, then, and an outstanding man, one of those special people one hopes will always be around.

To Ramsay, we offer our most sincere thanks for everything you have accomplished in the project. As you set out on a new journey, we hope it will bring you the same joy you brought so effectively to the DCB/DBC.

RÉAL BÉLANGER

L'ÉQUIPE DE L'UNIVERSITÉ LAVAL
THE STAFF AT THE UNIVERSITY OF TORONTO

Acknowledgements

THE *Dictionary of Canadian biography/Dictionnaire biographique du Canada* wishes to recognize the encouragement it continues to receive from its parent institutions, the University of Toronto and the Université Laval, which formalized their long-standing relationship with regard to the DCB/DBC in January 2001. For their support over the course of this volume, we are pleased to recognize, at the University of Toronto, former presidents J. Robert S. Prichard and Robert Birgeneau, John Challis, vice-president – research and associate provost, former vice-president Heather Munroe-Blum – research and international relations, former vice-president Jon S. Dellandrea – chief advancement officer, Michael R. Marrus, former dean of graduate studies, Peter B. Munsche, former assistant vice-president – technology transfer, and Professor Ron Pruessen, former chair of the department of history. Special mention should be made here of Peter Munsche's unfailing support of the project through troubled times and better ones. At the University of Toronto Press we have benefited from the professional skills of Ani Deyirmenjian and the incomparable staff at the printing plant in Downsview. At the Université Laval, we would like to acknowledge the assistance of the late rector François Tavenas, Michel Pigeon, rector, Louise Filion and Christiane Piché, former vice-rectors – research, Raymond J. Leblanc, vice-rector – research, Jacques Desautels, former dean of the faculty of arts, and his successor, Jacques Mathieu, the former and current heads of the department of history, Claire Dolan and Alain Laberge, and their staffs, and at Les Presses de l'Université Laval, the director, Denis Dion, the administrative officer, Benoît Bernier, and their various associates.

The DCB/DBC owes its founding to the generosity of the late James Nicholson, whose estate continues to sustain the project. In the preparation of volume XV we have received substantial assistance as well from the Donors named in the next section, and to them we offer our sincere thanks. Their contributions reflect the liberality and public spiritedness of Mr Nicholson's original bequest. We should like to acknowledge in particular the long-standing support of the Social Sciences and Humanities Research Council of Canada as well as that of the Canadian Studies Program of the Department of Canadian Heritage. We also wish to recognize the numerous individuals, many of them contributors, who sustain our work through annual giving or special donations.

Throughout the preparation of volume XV we have benefited from the helpful cooperation of libraries and archives throughout Canada and elsewhere, whose assistance has helped us to maintain the scholarly standards of the DCB/DBC. We wish to express our gratitude to the staff especially of those institutions which we have most frequently consulted. The project achieved a milestone in its history when the CD-ROM versions of volumes I to XIV went online in 2003 followed by 200 biographies from volume XV the following year. In connection with this seminal development, it is important to mention the support of the

ACKNOWLEDGEMENTS

Canadian Culture Online Branch of Canadian Heritage and its programs. The staff of Library and Archives Canada has also figured prominently in the online project.

Of the numerous individuals who have helped in the production of volume XV we owe particular thanks to our contributors; they have made the project a truly collaborative effort. In addition, we are grateful for the special help we have received from a number of persons. In Toronto, Taber M. James assisted with computerization. In Quebec, Jean Benoit undertook preliminary research for the volume and helped choose the individuals to appear in it, and Réjean Banville and Claire Dussault assisted in the compilation of name lists and in the assignment of biographies.

DICTIONNAIRE BIOGRAPHIQUE DU CANADA   DICTIONARY OF CANADIAN BIOGRAPHY

Donors

Valerie Armstrong

Associated Medical Services, Incorporated

Margaret A. Banks

Bernard Bélanger, Premier Tech

Carl Berger

The Birks Family Foundation

Michael Bliss

R. Craig Brown

Susan Buggey

Jean Crowe

†Lois E. Darroch

Department of Canadian Heritage

Kenneth C. Dewar

Donner Canadian Foundation

Maurice Dupasquier in memory of Pierre Savard

Goldwin S. French

Francess G. Halpenny

David M. Hayne

Hollinger Inc.

Margaret Jean Houston

DONORS

Hudson's Bay History Foundation

Linda Hutcheon

Jackman Foundation

John C. Jones Estate, University of Toronto

Henry C. Klassen

Margaret A. MacAulay Estate

William A. Macdonald

Marcel Martel

Peter B. Munsche

James Nicholson Estate, University of Toronto

Noric Ltd. and Norman Webster

Stephen A. Otto

Margaret Prang

Ian Robertson

Royal Bank of Canada

Social Sciences and Humanities Research Council of Canada

Albert Tucker

Université Laval

University of Toronto

Peter Webb

R. Howard Webster Foundation

Subjects of Biographies

ADAMS, John Gennings Curtis (1839–1922)
Adamson, Agar Stewart Allan Masterton (1865–1929)
Aikins, Sir James Albert Manning (1851–1929)
Aikins, William Henry Beaufort (1859–1924)
Alba, Georges, known as Paul Cazeneuve (1871–1925)
Alderson, Sir Edwin Alfred Hervey (1859–1927)
Alikomiak (d. 1924)
Allison, David (1836–1924)
Alloway, William Forbes (1852–1930)
Amyot, Georges-Élie (1856–1930)
Anctil, Jeanne (1875–1926)
Anderson, Alexander (1836–1925)
Anderson, John (1855–1930)
Angers, Félicité, known as Laure Conan (1845–1924)
Angus, Richard Bladworth (1831–1922)
Appleby, Charles (1866–1929)
Arcand, Narcisse (1871–1927)
Archibald, Walter Palmer (1860–1922)
Armour, Edward Douglas (1851–1922)
Armstrong, James William (1860–1928)
Arsenault, Pierre-Paul (1867–1927)
Ashdown, James Henry (1844–1924)

BAILEY, Loring Woart (1839–1925)
Baillie, Sir Frank Wilton (1875–1921)
Baker, Percival (1867–1921)
Ball, Richard Amos (1845–1925)
Bancroft, James Frederick (d. 1929)
Barker, William George (1894–1930)
Barker, William Henry (1853–1929)
Barr, Annie Gardner (Brown) (1864–1921)
Barrington, Sibella Annie (1867–1929)
Barthe, Émilie (Lavergne) (1849–1930)
Beauchamp, Jean-Joseph (1852–1923)
Beck, Sir Adam (1857–1925)
Beck, Nicholas Du Bois Dominic (1857–1928)
Bégin, Louis-Nazaire (1840–1925)
Bélanger, Dina, named Marie Sainte-Cécile-de-Rome (1897–1929)
Bell, Alexander Graham (1847–1922)
Bell, Gordon (1863–1923)
Bell, John Howatt (d. 1929)
Belliveau, Alphée (1851–1927)
Bell-Smith, Frederic Marlett (1846–1923)
Bengough, John Wilson (1851–1923)
Bennett, Philip (d. 1922)

Benoit, Zéphirin (1850–1930)
Bernier, Arthur (1873–1928)
Bertrand, Julie, named Marie de Saint-Basile (1844–1923)
Bessette, Arsène (1873–1921)
Best, Edna May Williston (Sexton) (1880–1923)
Best, Thomas Henry (1850–1928)
Bibeau, Marie, named Marie-Anne-de-Jésus (1865–1924)
Bickerdike, Robert (1843–1928)
Bilsky, Moses (1829–1923)
Birge, Cyrus Albert (1847–1929)
Birks, Henry (1840–1928)
Blackburn, Victoria Grace (1865–1928)
Blackstock, George Tate (1856–1921)
Blain, Joseph (1859–1925)
Blaylock, Harry Woodburn (1878–1928)
Bond, Sir Robert (1857–1927)
Booth, John Rudolphus (1827–1925)
Borland, Robert (1839–1923)
Bostock, Hewitt (1864–1930)
Bourque, Edmond-Joseph (1843–1921)
Bower, James (1860–1921)
Boyle, Joseph Whiteside (1867–1923)
Braithwaite, Henry A. (1841–1927)
Breen, William Wright (1882–1927)
Brett, Robert George (1851–1929)
Briggs, William (1836–1922)
Bristol, Edmund James (1861–1927)
Brodeur, Louis-Philippe (1862–1924)
Brookfield, Samuel Manners (1847–1924)
Brown, Ada Mary (Courtice) (1860–1923)
Brunet, François-Xavier (1868–1922)
Brymner, William (1855–1925)
Bulyea, George Hedley Vicars (1859–1928)
Buote, François-Joseph (1861–1922)
Burchill, John Percival (1855–1923)
Burgess, Thomas Joseph Workman (1849–1926)
Burke, Alfred Edward (1862–1926)
Burke, John (1851–1930)
Burriss, Rufus Allen (1859–1930)
Burrows, Theodore Arthur (1857–1929)

CAIRNS, James Frederick (1870–1928)
Campbell, Archibald William (1863–1927)
Campbell, Catherine Anne, named Mother Ignatia (1840–1929)

St John, Thomas (fl. 1900–22)
Saunders, Dyce Willcocks (1862–1930)
Scallion, James William (1842–1926)
Scott, Agnes Mary (Davis) (1863–1927)
Scott, Benjamin Alexander (1859–1928)
Scott, David Lynch (1845–1924)
Scott, Henri-Thomas (1880–1926)
Scott, William Duncan (1861–1925)
Semlin, Charles Augustus (1836–1927)
Semmens, John (1850–1921)
Sganism Sm'oogit (d. 1928)
Shakespeare, Noah (1839–1921)
Sharpe, Thomas (1866–1929)
Shaughnessy, Thomas George, 1st Baron
    Shaughnessy (1853–1923)
Shaw, Flora Madeline (1864–1927)
Sheard, Charles (1857–1929)
Shearer, John George (1859–1925)
Sheppard, Edmund Ernest (1855–1924)
Shingwauk, George (d. 1920) (Appendix)
Shirreff, Jennie Grahl Hunter (Eddy) (1863–1921)
Shortt, Emily Ann McCausland (Cummings) (1851–
    1930)
Sifton, Arthur Lewis Watkins (1858–1921)
Sifton, Sir Clifford (1861–1929)
Sims, Louisa (Rogers) (fl. 1906–25)
Sinclair, Alexander MacLean (1840–1924)
Sinclair, David Volume (1864–1922)
Skill, Leonard James (1864–1923)
Sleeman, George (1841–1926)
Smith, George Robert (1860–1922)
Smith, George Washington (1845–1921)
Smith, Janet Kennedy (1902–24)
Smith, William Harley (1863–1929)
Snider, Elias Weber Bingeman (1842–1921)
Spencer, Joseph William Winthrop (1851–1921)
Springstead, Velma Agnes (1906–27)
Starkman, Besha (Tobin) (1889–1930)
States, Wellington Ney (1874–1927)
Staveley, Harry (1848–1925)
Stead, Hay Strafford (1871–1924)
Stephansson, Stephan Gudmundur (1853–1927)
Stephen, George, 1st Baron Mount Stephen (1829–
    1921)
Sterling, Alice Jane (Johnson) (1839–1921)
Stevenson, Alexander Patterson (1854–1922)
Stevenson, Frederick Joseph (1896–1928)
Stewart, Thomas (1855–1923)
Stewart, William James (1863–1925)
Stokes, Susannah Augusta (Maxwell) (1805–1923)
Strange, Thomas Bland (1831–1925)
Struthers, William Eugene (1869–1928)
Sugrue, James Leonard (1883–1930)
Sulte, Benjamin (1841–1923)
Sutherland, Hugh McKay (1843–1926)
Sutherland, Robert Franklin (1859–1922)
Symonds, Herbert (1860–1921)

TAILLON, Sir Louis-Olivier (1840–1923)
Tait, James Sinclair (1849–1928)
Tanguay, Georges-Émile (1858–1923)
Teit, James Alexander (1864–1922)
Tenass, John P. (1849–1928)
Tessier, Joseph-Adolphe (1861–1928)
Teyssèdre, Alexandrine, named Marie-Saint-David
    (1842–1921)
Thomson, William James (1857–1927)
Todd, Albert Edward (1878–1928)
Topley, William James (1845–1930)
Toupin-Fafard, Mathilde (1875–1925)
Tourigny, Paul (Napoléon) (1852–1926)
Townsend, Margaret (Fox; Jenkins) (1843–1923)
Townshend, Sir Charles James (1844–1924)
Trask, Catherine (Brown) (1857–1925)
Trémaudan, Auguste-Henri de (1874–1929)
Tupper, Sir Charles Hibbert (1855–1927)
Turgeon, Adélard (1863–1930)
Turner, John Herbert (1833–1923)
Turriff, John Gillanders (1855–1930)

ULOQSAQ (d. 1929)
Urry, Frederick (1863–1927)

VALLANCE, Margaret (Taylor, Lady Taylor) (1840–
    1922)
Vallée, Charles-Amédée (1850–1924)
Venne, Joseph (1858–1925)
Verigin, Peter Vasil'evich (1859–1924)
Verville, Alphonse (1864–1930)
Vézina, Georges (1887–1926)
Vézina, Joseph (1849–1924)
Vigneau, Placide (1842–1926)
Vogt, Augustus Stephen (1861–1926)

WADE, Frederick Coate (1860–1924)
Walker, Sir Byron Edmund (1848–1924)
Wallace, Francis Huston (1851–1930)
Wallace, William (1867–1928)
Warburton, Alexander Bannerman (1852–1929)
Warburton, George Augustus (1859–1929)
Warren, George Stephens (1846–1928)
Watson, Albert Durrant (1859–1926)
Watson, Sir David (1869–1922)
Webster, Ella Hobday (Bronson) (1846–1925)
Weldon, Isaac Hillock (1874–1928)
Weldon, Richard Chapman (1849–1925)
Wells, Emma Lucy (Dickson) (1854–1926)
Weston, George (1865–1924)
Wetmore, Edward Ludlow (1841–1922)
White, James (1863–1928)
White, James Francis (1857–1922)
Whitney, Henry Melville (1839–1923)
Whitty, Gerald Joseph (1896–1924)
Willison, Sir John Stephen (1856–1927)
Wilson, Erastus William (1860–1922)

Editorial Notes

Persons have been entered under family name rather than title, married name, pseudonym, stage name, popular name, nickname, or name in religion: George STEPHEN, 1st Baron Mount Stephen; Louisa SIMS (Rogers); Alexandrine TEYSSÈDRE, named Marie-Saint-David. Cross-references are provided in the text from alternative names to the main entry under the family name: e.g. from *Marie-Saint-David* to *Teyssèdre*. Where possible the form of the surname is based on the signature, although contemporary usage is taken into account. For francophones the signature also establishes the given name (sometimes followed in parenthesis by the names received at baptism). Common variant spellings are also included in parentheses.

In the case of French names, *La*, *Le*, *Du*, *Des*, and sometimes *De* are considered part of the name and are capitalized. When both parts of the name are capitalized in the signature, French style treats the family name as two words. However, with individuals who were integrated into an anglophone milieu, this rule of style has been applied only when it was confirmed by a signature. We have also respected the signatures of our contemporaries (the authors of biographies and especially the authors cited in bibliographies). Compound names occasionally appear: Marie HÉBERT de La Rousselière; Henry Charles Keith PETTY-FITZ-MAURICE. Cross-references are made in the text from the elements of the compound to the main entry for the name.

Where a signature was not available for a subject whose name begins with *Mc* or *Mac*, the form *Mac*, followed by a capital letter, has been used. Japanese and Chinese Canadian subjects have been entered under the romanized forms of their names used in Canada. Where possible and appropriate, the Pinyin romanization of Chinese characters has been included in parentheses. Persons from countries using the Cyrillic alphabet have been presented according to their signatures in the Roman alphabet when available, or according to the romanized form of their names most commonly used in Canada.

Names of indigenous peoples have presented a particular problem, since a person might be known by his/her own name (written in a variety of ways by people unfamiliar with native languages) and by a nickname or baptismal name. Moreover, some native families, such as the Tenasses [*see* John P. TENASS], were using family surnames. Indian and Inuit names have been used when they could be found, and, because it is impossible to establish original spellings, the form generally chosen is the one found in standard sources or the one linguists now regard as correct; variants are included in parentheses: PEYASIW-AWASIS (Thunderchild, also known as Kapitikow). Appropriate cross-references are included in the text. To assist readers who go back to contemporary documents, the names of tribal groupings have been given in a form likely to be found in those documents. In some instances, modern tribal names appear in parentheses: Micmac (Mi'kmaq); Sioux (Dakota).

Reference works useful in establishing the names of persons not receiving biographies in the DCB/DBC are listed in section C of the General Bibliography.

The first time the name of a person who has a biography in volume XV appears in another biography, his or her family name is printed in capitals and level small capitals: Alexander Graham BELL; Henry de GRANDSAIGNES d'Hauterives.

An asterisk following a name indicates either that the person has a biography in a volume already published – Honoré Mercier*; Mistahimaskwa* – or that he/she will receive a biography in a volume to be published – Marius Barbeau*; Lucy Maud Montgomery* (Macdonald). Birth and death (or floruit) dates for such persons are given in the index as an indication of the volume in which the biography will be found.

Place names are generally given in the form used at the time of reference; where necessary, the modern name and/or the present name of the province, territory, state, or country in which the place is located have been included in parentheses: Prince Arthur's Landing (Thunder Bay, Ont.), Baffin Island (Nunavut), Lemberg (Lviv, Ukraine). The English edition cites well-known place names in their present-day English forms: St Lawrence River, Montreal, Quebec, Geneva, Rome. Cities considered to be easily recognizable, such as Paris, Dublin, and Boston, have not been identified by country, though London, England, has been specified to prevent confusion with London, Ontario. Within Canada, provincial capitals and several well-known cities such as Montreal and Vancouver are not identified by province.

Many sources have been used as guides to establish 19th- and early-20th-century place names in Canada: *Atlas of Canada* ([Ottawa?], 1906); *Canadian encyclopedia*; *Encyclopedia Canadiana*, ed. K. H. Pearson *et al.* ([rev. ed.], 10v., Toronto, 1977); W. B. Hamilton, *Place names of Atlantic Canada* (Toronto, 1996); E. J. and P. M. Holmgren, *Over 2000 place names of Alberta* (3rd ed., Saskatoon, 1976); *Lovell's gazetteer of British North America . . .* (Montreal, 1881); Hormisdas Magnan, *Dictionnaire historique et géographique des paroisses, missions et municipalités de la province de Québec* (Arthabaska, Qué., 1925); *Manitoba historical atlas: a selection of facsimile maps, plans, and sketches from 1612 to 1969*, ed. John Warkentin and R. I. Ruggles (Winnipeg, 1970); *Manitoba, mosaic of place names*, comp. J. B. Rudnyc'kyj, intro. Watson Kirkconnell (Winnipeg, 1970); *Noms et lieux du Québec: dictionnaire illustré* (a project of the Commission de Toponymie du Québec, Sainte-Foy, Qué., 1994); *Place-names and places of Nova Scotia* (Halifax, 1967; repr. Belleville, Ont., 1976); *Places in Ontario: their name origins and history*, comp. Nick and Helma Mika (3v., Belleville, 1977–83); Alan Rayburn, *Geographical names of New Brunswick* (Ottawa, 1975), *Geographical names of Prince Edward Island* (Ottawa, 1973), and *Place names of Ontario* (Toronto, 1997); and E. T. Russell, *What's in a name: the story behind Saskatchewan place names* (3rd ed., Saskatoon, 1980).

Modern Canadian names are based whenever possible on the Canadian Geographical Names Data Base (*geonames.nrcan.gc.ca*), on the various digitized provincial equivalents, and on the *Canada gazetteer atlas* ([Ottawa], 1980).

For places outside Canada the following have been major sources of reference: *Bartholomew gazetteer of Britain*, comp. Oliver Mason (Edinburgh, 1977); *Dictionnaire universel des noms propres . . . le Petit Robert 2*, Paul Robert *et al.*, édit. (nouv. éd., Paris, 1993); *Grand Larousse universel* ([éd. révisée et corrigée], 15v., Paris, 1989); *National Geographic atlas of the world* (rev. 6th ed., Washington, 1992); *The new Encyclopædia Britannica* (16th ed., 32v., Chicago, 1989); and *Times atlas of the world* (9th ed., London, 1992).

INSTITUTIONS

Care has been taken to reproduce institutional names accurately. The titles of educational establishments, businesses, hospitals, philanthropical organizations, and government bodies have in many instances been confirmed in the statutes and other official records. In cases where institutions located in Quebec were incorporated under English names in the English-language statutes, the English form has been used. The names of institutions outside Canada that are in languages other than French or English have been translated into English.

TERMINOLOGY

The concise Oxford dictionary of current English, ed. Della Thompson (9th ed., Oxford, 1995), has been the standard guide for usage and spelling, but recourse has been had as well to *The shorter Oxford English dictionary on historical principles*, comp. William Little *et al.*, ed. C. T. Onions (3rd ed., 2v., Oxford, 1944; [rev. ed.], 1973), *The Oxford English dictionary . . .*, ed. J. A. H. Murray *et al.* (13v., Oxford, 1933; 4 supps., 1972–86), and *Canadian Oxford dictionary*, ed. Katherine Barber (2nd ed., Don Mills [Toronto], 2004). Reference works helpful in establishing contemporary, local, and particular usages are H. C. Black, *Black's law dictionary . . .* (5th ed., St Paul, Minn., 1979); *A dictionary of Canadianisms on historical principles*, ed. W. S. Avis *et al.* (Toronto, 1967); *Dictionary of Newfoundland English*, ed. G. M. Story *et al.* (Toronto, 1982); *Dictionary of Prince Edward Island English*, ed. T. K. Pratt (Toronto, 1988); Michael Greener, *The Penguin dictionary of commerce* (2nd ed., Harmondsworth, Eng., 1980); *The HarperCollins encyclopedia of Catholicism*, ed. R. P. McBrien *et al.* (San Francisco, 1995); and *The Oxford dictionary of the Christian Church*, ed. F. L. Cross and E. A. Livingstone (2nd ed., Oxford, 1974; repr. 1984). The *Vocabulaire général (glossaire anglais-français)*, Hector Carbonneau, compil. (7 fascicules, Ottawa, 1978), was useful in special areas of translation, as were *Budgetary, accounting and financial vocabulary/Vocabulaire budgétaire, comptable et financier* (Ottawa, 1987); *Dictionnaire du français plus, à l'usage des francophones d'Amérique* (Montréal, 1988); *Dictionnaire de la comptabilité et de la gestion financière*, Louis Ménard *et al.*, compil. (Toronto, 1994); and *Ontario English-French legal lexicon/Lexique anglais-français du droit en Ontario* ([Toronto], 1987).

QUOTATIONS

Quotations have been translated when the language of the original passage is different from that of the text of the biography. Readers of the DCB may consult the DBC for the original French of quotations that have been translated into English. When a passage is quoted from a work that has appeared in both languages, the published English version is generally used. The wording, spelling, punctuation, and capitalization of original quotations are not usually altered; adjustments are made only when it is necessary to do so for meaning, in which case the changes are placed within square brackets. A name appearing within square brackets has been substituted for the original in order to identify the person more precisely or to indicate that he/she has a biography within the volume or in another volume.

DATES

A date of baptism is not treated as a date of birth. If, in spite of assiduous enquiry, it is impossible to uncover a subject's birth and death dates, only the dates of his/her active career are documented. In the introductory paragraphs and in the various indexes the outside dates of activity are presented as floruit (fl.) dates.

NEWSPAPERS

Newspaper titles appearing in biographies are generally cited under the title in effect at the time of reference. Wherever possible, titles are determined from the issues themselves, but secondary reference works are also frequently used for this purpose. For a listing of these sources, the reader is referred to the General Bibliography. Because their titles frequently vary over time, some newspapers cited in individual bibliographies are placed under standardized uniform titles: *Manitoba Free Press*; *Montreal Herald*. Otherwise, when a range of years is cited, the title used is that of the latest issue.

BIBLIOGRAPHIES

Each biography is followed by a bibliography. Sources frequently used by authors and editors are cited in shortened form in individual bibliographies; the General Bibliography gives these sources in full. Many abbreviations are used in the individual bibliographies, especially for archival sources. A list of these may be found on p.2 and p.1100.

The individual bibliographies are generally arranged alphabetically according to the three sections of the General Bibliography: manuscript sources, newspapers, and printed or digitized works. These are preceded by details concerning the publications of the subject or any other annotation that may be applicable. Any special bibliographical comments by contributors appear within square brackets.

Wherever possible, manuscript material is cited under the location of the original documents; the location of copies used by contributors or editors is included in the citation. In general, the items in individual bibliographies are the sources listed by the contributors, but these items have often been supplemented by bibliographic investigation in the DCB/DBC offices.

Care has been taken to ensure the accuracy of bibliographic citations. Original documents and title pages of printed works have been examined where possible, or confirmed through enquiries to the archives or libraries in which they are held or through related websites. Numerous secondary reference works have also been used for bibliographic verification. Many of these are cited in the General Bibliography; additional information concerning Canadian reference sources is available in *Guide to reference materials for Canadian libraries*, ed. Kirsti Nilsen *et al.* (8th ed., [Toronto], 1992). Standards for citing websites are provided in Martin Crouse, "Citing electronic information in history papers": *cas.memphis.edu/~mcrouse/elcite.html.*

BIOGRAPHIES

List of Abbreviations

AC	Archives Civiles	GA	Glenbow Archives
AM	Archives of Manitoba	*GPQ*	*Guide parlementaire québécois*
AMLJH	Archives of Manitoba Legal-Judicial History	GRO	General Register Office
		HBCA	Hudson's Bay Company Archives
ANQ	Archives Nationales du Québec	LAC	Library and Archives Canada
AO	Archives of Ontario	MCQ-DSQ	Musée de la Civilisation (Québec), Dépôt du Séminaire de Québec
AVQ	Archives de la Ville de Québec		
BCA	British Columbia Archives	MCQ-FSQ	Musée de la Civilisation (Québec), Fonds du Séminaire de Québec
BCF	*Biographies canadiennes-françaises*		
BCM-G	Bibliothèque Centrale de Montréal, Salle Gagnon	MUA	McGill University Archives
		NSARM	Nova Scotia Archives and Records Management
BRH	*Le Bulletin des recherches historiques*		
CCHA	Canadian Catholic Historical Association	*OH*	*Ontario History*
		PAA	Provincial Archives of Alberta
CEF	*Canadian Expeditionary Force*	PANB	Provincial Archives of New Brunswick
CHA	Canadian Historical Association		
CHR	*Canadian Historical Review*	PANL	Provincial Archives of Newfoundland and Labrador
CIHM	Canadian Institute for Historical Microreproductions		
		PARO	Public Archives and Records Office (Prince Edward Island)
CPG	*Canadian parliamentary guide*		
DAB	*Dictionary of American biography*	QUA	Queen's University Archives
DALFAN	*Dictionnaire des auteurs de langue française en Amérique du Nord*	RBMB	Register of baptisms, marriages, and burials
DBC	*Dictionnaire biographique du Canada*	RBMS	Registre des baptêmes, mariages et sépultures
DBECC	*Dictionnaire biographique des évêques catholiques du Canada*		
		RHAF	*Revue d'histoire de l'Amérique française*
DCB	*Dictionary of Canadian biography*		
DHB	*Dictionary of Hamilton biography*	*RPQ*	*Répertoire des parlementaires québécois*
DNB	*Dictionary of national biography*		
DNLB	*Dictionary of Newfoundland and Labrador biography*	RSC	Royal Society of Canada
		TRL	Toronto Reference Library
DOLQ	*Dictionnaire des œuvres littéraires du Québec*	UCC	United Church of Canada
		UTA	University of Toronto Archives
DPQ	*Dictionnaire des parlementaires du Québec*	VM-DGDA	Ville de Montréal, Division de la Gestion de Documents et des Archives

2

Biographies

A

ADAMS, JOHN GENNINGS CURTIS, farmer, dentist, and reformer; b. 16 March 1839 in Adamsville (Acton), Upper Canada, son of the Reverend Ezra Adams and Amy Edmonds (Edmunds), widow of John Gennings Curtis; m. 18 Dec. 1861 Sarah Ann Fawcett (d. 1896) in Drayton, Upper Canada, and they had four sons and five daughters; d. 21 May 1922 in Burlington, Ont., and was buried in Mount Pleasant Cemetery, Toronto.

As a youth, John G. C. Adams farmed on the family homestead near Drayton. He drifted away in 1869 and the following year, at age 31, he moved to Toronto with his wife and children to study dentistry under his half-brother William Case Adams. His diary of 1871–73, kept during his indentureship, is a revealing record of his evangelical bent and dialogue with God, his visits to the sick and the poor, and his unswerving faith that Providence would send work his way (usually fillings) to pay for the next day's food and fuel. In 1872 he began performing free "Dental Hospital work" among the children of poor families. After receiving his LDS from the Royal College of Dental Surgeons of Ontario in 1874, he opened his own practice, which he moved in the 1880s to the corner of Elm and Yonge streets, in the core of the city.

Adams's Methodist and charitable convictions infused his dentistry to an extent that many deemed fanatical. He saw the dental care of children as a divine mission, and began acting aggressively on this belief in the 1890s. He was appalled by the wretched condition of children's teeth, the prevalence of related disease and deformity, and the degree of parental misunderstanding of dental development and oral hygiene. Examinations made by Adams and his son Dr Ezra Herbert Adams at Victoria Street School in 1893–94 revealed serious neglect in a stunning 98 per cent of the students.

At a time when the problem was a matter of no professional concern, Adams's efforts to help launch a dental infirmary for the poor in 1893 and his paper to the Ontario Dental Society in 1895, on the care of children's teeth, had little impact. Nonetheless, with the support of the Toronto Dental Society and the Toronto Trades and Labor Council, he travelled widely the following year to deliver his message, addressing such bodies as the Provincial Board of Health, the National Council of Women of Canada, its Local Council in Hamilton, and the Michigan State Dental Association. As well, he published and distributed *School-children's teeth: their universally unhealthy and neglected condition: the only practical remedy: dental public school inspection and hospitals for the poor* (Toronto, 1896).

Adams wrote there that to get needy children to his free clinic, which was next to his office, he had hired people to "hunt" them up. In 1896 he moved to expand his work by buying the Temperance Coffee House Association building on Elm at Teraulay Street. The following year he opened Christ's Mission Dental Hospital there, a free clinic combined with a mission hall, a coffee room, and an employment bureau. In April 1899 the RCDS agreed to his request that dental students be allowed to continue "to operate gratuitously in charitable institutions under the direction of a member." A month later, unable to pay back-taxes of $200, Adams was forced to close the mission hospital. City council refused an exemption on the grounds of charitable function.

Undaunted – Adams styled himself a "dental missionary" – he rechanneled his energy, lobbying municipal health and school officials for province-wide dental inspection and treatment. His attacks on physicians who mishandled tooth-related illness and his sweeping claims, as in his statement in 1901 to Premier George William Ross* that "there are not less than one million permanent teeth going to destruction in the mouths of the school children of Ontario," drew opposition as well as support. Undoubtedly Adams was pleased with the work of George K. Thomson and other dentists in Nova Scotia, where school inspections were instituted in 1908, the earliest in Canada. Adams's views, often expressed in such sympathetic forums as the *Dominion Dental Journal* (Toronto) and *Oral Health* (Toronto), gained momentum as they merged with the developing public health movement in Ontario. The Toronto Board of Education led the way in 1911 when it initiated inspections; two years later, in the spirit of Adams's hospital, the city's health department opened a dental clinic for the poor, the first free public clinic in Canada. (In the United States an experimental clinic had been set up in 1901 in Rochester, N.Y.)

Adams's public involvement was not limited to

preventive dentistry. He promoted window gardening as an element of civic pride. A Reformer in politics, he belonged to the Sons of Temperance, the Good Templars, the Ancient Order United Workmen, and the Select Knights of Canada, and was a steward and trustee of St Paul's Methodist Church in the Yorkville area of Toronto, where he had lived since the 1870s. His large family shared his religious and professional devotions. All of his sons followed him into dentistry; William Fawcett, who also earned degrees in medicine and divinity, spent many years in China as a medical missionary.

Adams retired in 1912 and he died in 1922. A visionary philanthropist, he had sparked an important movement. By the end of the 1920s most large municipalities across Canada had some form of dental inspection for children. Few dentists leave such a legacy.

ANNE CARLYLE DALE

[Materials concerning the Adams family, including copies of early letters to John Gennings Curtis Adams and his diary for 1871–73, were graciously provided by Joyce Pettigrew of Otterville, Ont., a great-granddaughter of the subject. A.C.D.]

A reprint of Adams's treatise, *School-children's teeth: their universally unhealthy and neglected condition*, appeared in Toronto in 1912. There were also apparently one or more pamphlets based on the larger work, as well as two articles published under the same title in the *Dental Register* (Cincinnati, Ohio), 50 (1896): 472–87 and the *Dominion Dental Journal* (Toronto), 24 (1912): 168–71, 209–12. Adams's writings on the subject also include "Systematic care of school children's teeth," *Dominion Dental Journal*, 12 (1900): 317–19.

AO, RG 22-305, no.12267; RG 80-8-0-198, no.25414; 871, no.14961; RG 80-27-2, 79: 71. Univ. of Toronto, Faculty of Dentistry Library, Dental Museum, "Adams family record" (typescript notes); framed copy of J. G. [C.] Adams, "Petition to the Honorable the Legislature of Ontario in session" (n.d.); J. J. Kelso, notice announcing meeting to establish a "Dental Infirmary, for the benefit of the poor, and principally for children," Toronto, 21 Sept. 1893; "Petition to the members of the School Board" (n.d.). *Toronto Daily Star*, 22–23 May 1922. G. M. Adam, *Toronto, old and new: a memorial volume . . .* (Toronto, 1891; repr. 1972), 112–13. T. L. Adams, *A dentist and a gentleman: gender and the rise of dentistry in Ontario* (Toronto, 2000). J. W. Bruce, "President's address," *Dominion Dental Journal*, 21 (1909): 246–60. J. J. Cassidy and P. H. Bryce, "Report of the committee on school hygiene on dental inspection," *Dominion Dental Journal*, 8 (1896): 177–85. *Commemorative biographical record of the county of York . . .* (Toronto, 1907). *Dental Practice* (Toronto), 10 (1911): 218–20. *Directory*, Toronto, 1871–1915. *Dominion Dental Journal*, 9 (1897): 266–68, 300; 34 (1922): 237–38, 245–46. D. W. Gullett, *A history of dentistry in Canada* (Toronto, 1971). *Oral Health* (Toronto), 3 (1913): 115–16. Royal College of Dental Surgeons of Ontario, *Report of the proc. of the annual meeting of the board of directors* (Toronto), 1898: 7, 20. Wallace Seccombe,

"J. G. Adams, dentist and philanthropist," *Oral Health*, 12 (1922): 265. J. W. Shosenberg, *The rise of the Ontario Dental Association: 125 years of organized dentistry* (Toronto, 1992), 81–91. G. K. Thomson, "The dental education of the public and school children," *Dominion Dental Journal*, 20 (1908): 255–74. "Toronto's municipal dental clinic," *Oral Health*, 3: 113–14. A. E. Webster, "Dental inspection of two schools in Toronto," *Dominion Dental Journal*, 22 (1910): 600–4.

ADAMSON, AGAR STEWART ALLAN MASTERTON, civil servant, militia and army officer, businessman, and bon vivant; b. 25 Dec. 1865 in Ottawa, second son of James Adamson and Mary Julia Derbishire; m. 15 Nov. 1899 Ann Mabel Cawthra* in Toronto, and they had two sons; d. 21 Nov. 1929 in London, England.

Without a war to fight, Agar Adamson would have lived out his days as an ageing Edwardian buck, memorable only for his charm and good looks. But the events of 1914 provided him with the opportunity to reinvent himself as a remarkable soldier. At 48, he was one of the oldest to enlist, and one of the first to go overseas. He survived nearly three years in the trenches, and became commanding officer of the legendary Princess Patricia's Canadian Light Infantry. Adamson's most remarkable memorial is the diary that he kept of his war, in the form of letters written daily to his wife. Unfailingly honest and direct, they are one of the best and most immediate personal Canadian accounts of World War I.

Adamson was born into the old Upper Canadian gentry; like many members of this class, he thought of himself as an overseas Englishman. His paternal grandfather, the Anglo-Irish sporting parson William Agar Adamson*, had immigrated in 1840 and became chaplain to Governor Lord Sydenham [Thomson*]. His maternal grandfather, Stewart Derbishire*, arrived in 1838 as a confidential agent in the service of Lord Durham [Lambton*] and later became an MLA for Bytown. Agar grew up in post-confederation Ottawa, where his father was a clerk in the Senate. Thanks to a rich maternal uncle in England, he spent several years at Cambridge. Though he did not shine academically, and left without a degree, he was a great success as a horseman, winning the prestigious Newmarket stakes. He returned to Ottawa and on 4 Feb. 1890 joined his father on the staff of the Senate as a junior clerk; he held the same position when he left the civil service. He applied himself much more enthusiastically to becoming one of the capital's most popular young bloods: he was gazetted a lieutenant in the No.1 Battalion of Infantry (Governor General's Foot Guards) in 1893 and became a favourite at the slightly louche vice-regal court presided over by Lord Minto [Elliot*] and Lady Minto. In 1899 he married Mabel Cawthra, a talented and strong-minded Toronto heiress. Taking leave from the Senate, in March 1900 he was commissioned a lieutenant in Lord Strathcona's Horse and set off for the war in South Africa.

Adamson's experiences on the veld were transformational. He served with distinction, winning a mention in dispatches. He had a natural gift for command, and an innate respect for his men. "He wore a uniform rather as a priest wears vestments," his younger son, Anthony, wrote in a family memoir. But a post-war attempt to become a regular officer in a British regiment proved unsuccessful, as did a plan to set up as a gentleman farmer. The Adamsons returned to Canada in 1903. Two years later Agar resigned from the Senate and moved to Toronto to become titular head of the Canadian branch, established by his wife, of the British decorating firm Thornton-Smith Company.

The outbreak of war on 4 Aug. 1914 found Adamson summering at Grove Farm in Port Credit, Ont., a property granted to the Cawthras in 1804. The following day he hastened to Ottawa. Though he was nearly blind in one eye, through connections at Rideau Hall he secured a commission as a captain in the newly formed Princess Patricia's Canadian Light Infantry, financed by the Montreal millionaire Andrew Hamilton Gault*. Adamson arrived in England with the regiment in October.

His first letters from the front date from early 1915, the Patricias having entered the line as part of the 27th British Division. He was most struck by the pounding sound of artillery and the stench of putrefying human and animal flesh. "I counted seven dead horses just outside my trench yesterday," he wrote on 3 March. "There is also a dead Frenchman there and has been for a long time. We got orders reading 'Keep the Shelley Farm on your right, and pass between the broken tree and the dead Frenchman on your right', so the poor fellow was being of some use in death." Adamson's most harrowing experience was recounted on 7 May, shortly before the PPCLI's "Old Originals" were virtually wiped out, during the second battle of Ypres. "Enemy in front of us advancing their line of trenches and sniping force in every direction, fire from Maxims and artillery come from 3 different directions. . . . Two men have gone mad and have had to be disarmed. . . . It seems certain that this line cannot be held, and that we are only making a bluff at it."

The line held and for his conspicuous bravery at Bellewaarde Ridge Adamson was awarded the Distinguished Service Order. After convalescing from a shoulder wound, he rejoined the Patricias in early 1916; a strong tactician, he was appointed commanding officer on 31 Oct. 1916 (somewhat to his discomfiture) and promoted lieutenant-colonel. "The isolation of a commanding officer is necessary," he wrote to Mabel, "but most trying to one of my disposition." Nevertheless, under him the regiment distinguished itself at both Vimy Ridge and Passchendaele, and in January 1918 it was singled out for its *esprit*

de corps by Lieutenant-General Sir Arthur William Currie*, commander of the Canadian Corps.

In March 1918 Adamson turned over his command to Charles James Townshend Stewart* in order to be with his ailing wife, who had spent the war years in London and behind the lines in Belgium, working with civilian refugees. She recovered quickly but, sadly, Agar, who had been assigned to divisional headquarters, soon became one of war's casualties. A delayed form of shell-shock, later known as post-traumatic stress syndrome, soured his judgement and his temperament. Soon after the armistice, his marriage disintegrated in all but name. He returned to Canada in March 1919; he spent much of the next decade visiting old friends in Ottawa and gambling in England.

In October 1929, having developed an interest in flying, he went up in an experimental airplane with a British aviator for a trip to Ireland. They crashed in the Irish Sea and although both survived, two hours in frigid water broke Adamson's exceptional constitution. He died in London a few weeks later in the presence of his wife and son Anthony; with a panache Agar would have relished, Anthony carried his father's ashes back to Canada in his own hatbox for a full-scale military funeral. He was buried at Trinity Anglican Church in Port Credit.

Among the many remembrances of Adamson, the ones he would have liked best were those of his military confrères. According to biographer Arthur Leonard Tunnell, "He was noted among his brother officers and friends as a most delightful dinner companion. He had a resonant voice, a good accent and an excellent vocabulary. His after-dinner speeches were not the less anticipated because he could indulge in pointed irony, and was not particular whose toes he trod on. . . . He refused to be bored."

SANDRA GWYN

Adamson's wartime correspondence has been published as *Letters of Agar Adamson, 1914 to 1919: lieutenant colonel, Princess Patricia's Canadian Light Infantry*, ed. N. M. Christie (Nepean, Ont., 1997).

AO, RG 80-5-0-298, no.2602. LAC, MG 30, E149. Anthony Adamson, *Wasps in the attic* ([Toronto, 1987]). Can., Parl., *Sessional papers*, 1906, no.30: 196. *Canadian men and women of the time* (Morgan; 1912). *Directory*, Toronto, 1905–13. Sandra Gwyn, *The private capital: ambition and love in the age of Macdonald and Laurier* (Toronto, 1984); *Tapestry of war: a private view of Canadians in the Great War* (Toronto, 1992). *Standard dict. of Canadian biog.* (Roberts and Tunnell).

AGATHA, Mother. *See* O'NEILL

AIKINS, Sir JAMES ALBERT MANNING, lawyer, politician, and lieutenant governor; b. 10 Dec. 1851 in Toronto Gore Township, Upper Canada, second son of James Cox Aikins* and Mary Elizabeth Jane Somerset; brother of WILLIAM HENRY BEAUFORT; m. first 10 Dec. 1884 Mary Bertha McLelan in Ottawa, and they had two sons; they divorced 9 July 1892; m. secondly 6 Sept. 1899 Mary French Colby (d. 1931) in Stanstead, Que., and they had three daughters, one of whom died shortly after birth; d. 1 March 1929 in Winnipeg and was buried there in St John's cemetery.

Of Irish extraction, James Aikins was born and raised on his parents' farm in Peel County, near Toronto. He was educated in public schools in Malton (Mississauga) and Brampton before attending Upper Canada College and the University of Toronto (BA 1875, MA 1876). On graduating in 1875, he "tried business" in the warehouse of the firm Macnab and Marsh, but he decided instead to become a student-at-law. He was articled to Matthew Crooks Cameron* of Cameron, McMichael, and Hoskin, a leading common law firm in Toronto. For practice in equity, he spent one year with Mowat, Maclennan, and Downey and then he returned to his original principal.

Aikins looked westward to practise his profession. In August 1878 he visited his brother John Somerset, who was in the real estate business in Winnipeg, and he decided he liked the opportunities available there. After his return to Toronto he was called to the Ontario bar on 19 Nov. 1878 and he was back in Winnipeg by February 1879. He was called to the Manitoba bar on the 15th of that month and began advertising legal services and mortgage loans four days later. His father had recently formed the Manitoba and North West Loan Company, which offered mortgages on urban and farm properties. The evaluation was undertaken by Somerset and the conveyancing was done by James. These transactions would provide a solid financial base for their careers.

A boost to Aikins's career was his appointment in 1879 as local counsel for the federal Department of Justice, a post he would hold for 17 years. In 1880 he was made a member of a royal commission to report on the administration of justice in the North-West Territories. Of greater significance was his nomination in 1881 as counsel for the western division of the Canadian Pacific Railway; he would retain this position until 1911.

By June 1879 Aikins had attracted sufficient work to be able to persuade Albert Monkman, a friend who had been practising in Ontario since 1875, to join him as a partner. Although this partnership was short-lived, it was the foundation of what would become one of the leading law firms in Canada, Aikins, MacAulay, and Thorvaldson, which at the beginning of the 21st century continues to use Aikins's name. His strong work ethic and assiduous attention to detail were recognized in his election as a bencher of the Law Society of Manitoba in May 1880. He served

until his death and held office as secretary (1883–85), treasurer (1885–88), and president (1889–91). He was appointed a dominion QC on 3 Nov. 1884.

"I know of no more powerful factor in the building up of any place than an industrious, upright and intelligent legal profession," Aikins once said. This belief in the strength of lawyers working together led him to form the Manitoba Bar Association in 1911 and to act as its first president. The idea of reviving the national bar association was planted when he attended a convention of the American Bar Association in Montreal in 1913. The first Canadian Bar Association had been formed in 1896, but it had lasted only a few years. Aikins acted as president of the new Canadian Bar Association from its beginnings in 1915 until 1927 and he was honorary president in his final years. According to his secretary, he hoped the organization would be "a great and powerful agency for the consolidation and benefit of Canada and for the profession which he loved." To foster its growth he set up an endowment fund in 1921, to which he added until his death. In his will he left $30,000 to improve the association's *Canadian Bar Review* and a smaller amount to promote the Conference of Commissioners on Uniformity of Legislation in Canada, which he had championed as its president from 1918 to 1923 and of which he was honorary president thereafter.

Aikins was tireless both in his profession and in the larger community. He had been secretary and later president of the first university Young Men's Christian Association, which had been formed at the University of Toronto in 1873, and he was president of the YMCA in Winnipeg from its formation in 1879 to 1882. Soon after he moved to Winnipeg he also became involved with Grace Methodist Church and the temperance movement. From a deeply religious Methodist family, he taught Sunday school for teenage boys and young adults at Grace Methodist for many years. The classes were well attended and well known in the city. As a student, he had committed passages of Scripture to memory and he later used them when speaking in public. The *Manitoba Free Press* considered him a "gifted orator," who had "established a reputation which transcends the bounds of country." Aikins was an early believer in the union of the Presbyterian, Congregational, and Methodist churches in Canada, and in his will he would leave his house, Riverbend, his property on the Assiniboine River, and $100,000 to the United Church of Canada to create and maintain a school for girls. In addition, he left funds for the church's home missions and for the Canadian Bible Society in the prairie provinces.

Education was a lifelong interest. In 1885 he joined with others to establish Wesley College [see Joseph Walter Sparling*]. He became a member of its first board of directors and was chairman from 1888 to

1908. As well, he was honorary bursar (1889–1915) and a member of the council (1881–1915) of the University of Manitoba. In 1901 he was appointed to a commission looking into establishing an agricultural college in Manitoba and in 1907 he was named chairman of the royal commission on the University of Manitoba. His abiding faith in the power of education was recognized by the federal government when he was named Canada's representative at the 2nd International Congress on Moral Education held at The Hague in 1912.

In the *Winnipeg Telegram* of 29 Jan. 1910 Aikins was described as being in the "somewhat unique position of being a millionaire lawyer." This comment was based not only on his large and lucrative law practice, but also on his acumen in investments, mostly in real estate in Winnipeg and elsewhere in Manitoba. Throughout his career he fostered both his legal and his business contacts by acting as solicitor for many companies, local and national, from the Westbourne and Northwestern Railway Company and the Northern Electric Light Company, both started in the early 1880s, to the Great-West Life Assurance Company, founded over a decade later. He acted as counsel in Winnipeg for the Imperial Bank of Canada, the Bank of Ottawa, and the Scottish American Investment Company, and as a director of the Northern Trusts Company, the Canadian Fire Insurance Company, and the Canadian Indemnity Company.

Politically, Aikins was a Conservative. During the early years of his career, apart from campaigning in the provincial election of 1879 when Somerset was elected to the Legislative Assembly as a follower of John Norquay*, Aikins had not played a public role in politics. In 1900 he was asked by Premier Hugh John MACDONALD to draft a bill introducing Prohibition. A founder and strong supporter of the Manitoba branch of the Dominion Alliance for the Total Supression of the Liquor Traffic, Aikins used the opportunity to write into legislation his views on the sale and consumption of liquor. Macdonald's successor as premier, Rodmond Palen Roblin*, had hopes that the Liquor Act would be declared unconstitutional when he referred it to the Judicial Committee of the Privy Council, but Aikins had drafted it so carefully that it was upheld. It was turned down by Manitobans, however, in a plebiscite held on 2 April 1902.

In 1911 Aikins agreed to run as the federal candidate in Brandon on the Conservative anti-reciprocity platform of Robert Laird Borden*. He won the seat with an overwhelming majority, but he did not find the role of government backbencher very rewarding. When asked by the provincial Conservative party to succeed Roblin as leader (Roblin had resigned on 12 May 1915 because of a scandal over the construction of a new legislative building), he left his seat in par-

liament and took up the post on 14 July. In the general election the following month, Aikins and his party were soundly defeated by the Liberals under Tobias Crawford Norris*, electing only five members. Aikins lost his seat in Brandon City. One of the planks of Aikins's platform had been to reintroduce temperance legislation. Norris agreed to another plebiscite, which was held on 13 March 1916 and decided in favour of Prohibition. The Manitoba Temperance Act, based largely on Aikins's Liquor Act of 1900, then went into effect. Aikins resigned as leader of the provincial Conservatives sometime in the spring or summer of 1916.

On 29 June 1914 Aikins had been created knight bachelor as a reward for his exemplary work in law and in the community. Further honours were his when he was sworn in as lieutenant governor of Manitoba on 7 Aug. 1916. His father had held the position for six years (1882–88) and he would enjoy it for ten. According to a biographical account written a few years after his death, "He discharged the social functions of the high office . . . with a grace and distinction rarely equalled" and "he entertained with lavish hospitality." Aikins was not averse to using the constitutional authority of his office if he felt it was necessary. In 1922 he denied defeated premier Norris a dissolution until essential supply orders had been passed. Later, he insisted that the legal functions of his office be both recognized and utilized by objecting to the fact that the government of John Bracken* had purchased securities before he had signed the orders in council.

After establishing himself in his profession in Winnipeg, Aikins had married Mary Bertha, the daughter of Archibald Woodbury McLelan*, federal minister of marine and fisheries. One of their sons, James Cox (Jamie), died when he was only six; the other, Gordon Harold, succeeded his father as head of the law firm. The marriage ended in divorce in 1892. Seven years later he married Mary French Colby, a granddaughter of Moses French Colby*. As well as the family home, Riverbend, Aikins owned and supervised the operation of a large farm at Elkhorn, Man. He was an avid outdoorsman, especially enjoying hunting and golf. To further interest in the arts, he established scholarships in English at the University of Manitoba and the University of Toronto and prizes for school choirs at the Manitoba Music Competition Festival. After his death his son, in his memory, donated the Aikins Memorial Trophy for senior instrumentalists, which is still presented at the festival.

To celebrate his 50 years at the Manitoba bar, Aikins gave a banquet for 450 members of the profession in Manitoba and from across Canada on 25 Feb. 1929. Congratulatory messages came from around the world. A sudden heart attack prevented him from attending the festivities, his condition worsened, and he died just after midnight on 1 March. After lying in state in the Legislative Building, he was accorded a state funeral during which Archbishop Samuel Pritchard Matheson* noted that he would be remembered as "a great and brilliant member of the legal profession, a magnetic and eloquent public speaker, a great legislator, a great educationalist, a great philanthropist, and above all, a great Canadian citizen."

LEE GIBSON

The unfinished memoirs which Sir James Albert Manning Aikins dictated to his secretary during 1926–27 are in the author's possession. The notes he prepared for his jubilee banquet were published in the *Canadian Bar Rev.* (Toronto), 7 (1929): 235–38; issue no.4 of that volume is almost entirely devoted to Aikins. His speeches as an MP can be found in Can., House of Commons, *Debates*, 1911–14. Numerous other speeches and remarks were quoted extensively in various newspapers. Two of his addresses are listed in the CIHM, *Reg.*

AM, AMLJH, M 1602; M 1603; P 1375–77, file A669, 1–3; P 1387, file A866; GR 393, I-2-8-4, file 19319, pt.2; P 474–77, 485–88. ANQ-E, CE501-S86, 6 sept. 1899. LAC, MG 28, I 169, 1. Man., Legislative Library (Winnipeg), Biog. scrapbooks. Manitoba Culture, Heritage and Recreation, Hist. resources branch (Winnipeg), D. R. M. Jackson, "Sir James Aikins (1851–1929), lieutenant-governor of Manitoba" (typescript, 1980). *Manitoba Free Press*, 14 Feb. 1879–31 Dec. 1886, 1 Oct. 1888–3 Oct. 1889, 1 May 1899–15 May 1902, 1904, 1906. *Manitoba Weekly Free Press*, 21 Jan.–28 Feb. 1894.

Lee Gibson, *A proud heritage: the first hundred years of Aikins, MacAulay and Thorvaldson* (Winnipeg, 1993). W. L. Morton, *One university: a history of the University of Manitoba, 1877–1952* ([Toronto], 1957). H. A. Robson, "The Honourable Sir James Albert Manning Aikins, K.C.; the lawyer in action," *Canadian Bar Rev.*, 7: 266–74. M. G. Ross, *The Y.M.C.A. in Canada: the chronicles of a century* (Toronto, 1951). *Saturday Night*, 26 Aug. 1916. F. H. Schofield, *The story of Manitoba* (3v., Winnipeg, 1913). *Standard dict. of Canadian biog.* (Roberts and Tunnell).

AIKINS, WILLIAM HENRY BEAUFORT, physician, medical editor, and founder of radiotherapy in Canada; b. 22 Aug. 1859 in Toronto Gore Township, Upper Canada, son of James Cox Aikins* and Mary Elizabeth Jane Somerset; m. 27 Dec. 1887 Augusta Hawkesworth-Wood in London, Ont.; they had no children; d. 2 Oct. 1924 in Toronto.

W. H. B. Aikins's family was prominent in Canadian politics and medicine. His father, James Cox Aikins, served as secretary of state under Sir John A. Macdonald* and in 1882 became lieutenant governor of Manitoba (a post later filled by another son, Sir James Albert Manning AIKINS). Two uncles, Moses Henry and William Thomas*, were well-known physicians.

Aikins received his early education at Upper Can-

ada College in Toronto, the Toronto School of Medicine (MB 1881), and Victoria College in Cobourg (MD, CM 1881). Like many physicians of his day, he pursued postgraduate studies in Europe, where he was exposed to the many pathological and surgical advances of the period. During this time he visited London (where he obtained his licentiate from the Royal College of Physicians in 1881), Edinburgh, Paris, and Vienna. In 1883 he established a general practice in Toronto, and he became prominent in Canadian medical circles. He was appointed to the staff at Toronto General Hospital, the Toronto Home (later Hospital) for Incurables, and Grace Hospital. On the editorial staff of the *Canadian Practitioner* from 1884 and co-editor of the *Dominion Medical Monthly* when it began in 1893, he became in 1895 the founding editor of the *Canadian Medical Review*; this journal merged with the *Canadian Practitioner* four years later to form the *Canadian Practitioner and Review*, with which Aikins would be associated until his death. In 1907 he was one of the charter members of the Academy of Medicine in Toronto, and in the years before World War I he represented Canada at several international medical congresses. In his private life he was a Methodist, a mason, and a senator of the University of Toronto.

Aikins's major contribution to Canadian medicine was the introduction and promotion of radium therapy. Radium had been discovered by Marie and Pierre Curie in 1898, but it was not until Henri Becquerel inadvertently inflicted a skin burn on himself in 1901 that the effect of its radiation on living tissue began to attract medical interest. Over the next decade radium was found to be an effective therapy for many diseases, particularly cancer where it held hope for treatment without the need for the mutilating operations then in vogue. Because of the limited sources of radium-bearing ore and the huge cost of refining it, however, radium remained scarce and expensive.

In 1907 Aikins visited the Laboratoire Biologique du Radium in Paris, a centre for the study of radium, and was impressed by the element's effects on various benign and malignant skin conditions. Like other doctors of the day, he marvelled at radium's ability to produce changes in tissues which could not be achieved by any other known substance and which resulted in "cures of a very surprising character." He returned from Paris convinced of its usefulness as a therapeutic agent. After visiting the Paris laboratory on two further occasions, he bought a small supply of radium in 1909, and soon opened a radium clinic, the Radium Institute of Toronto, at 134 Bloor Street West. Although small quantities of radium existed in other parts of Canada – it would not be refined here until the 1930s – Aikins's institute became the primary centre for radiotherapy. His many published case reports show that he treated over 3,000 patients referred from a wide area extending from Saskatchewan to Quebec. His equipment in 1914 included a radium plaque (a flat applicator coated with a varnish impregnated with radium) and a tube containing radium salts. With these instruments he treated patients suffering from a variety of cancerous and non-cancerous conditions. He became intrigued by the microscopic tissue changes which underlay the clinical effects of radium and carried out investigations into them with Dr Keith Myrie Benoit Simon, pathologist at Grace Hospital.

Aikins became particularly interested in the use of radiotherapy in thyroid disease. In 1920 he reported on 16 patients with "toxic goiter" (hyperthyroidism) who had been treated with a regime of quinine, ergotamine, and the application of ice-bags over the heart and radium over the thyroid. It is easy now to be shocked or amused by Aikins's use of radium to remedy benign conditions; at the time, however, there were no other effective treatments and there was limited awareness of the possible dangers of radiation. Patients and physicians alike were eager to try a new remedy for distressful or disfiguring diseases. To those who questioned the value of radium, Aikins replied, "I have several hundred living reasons on which my faith is founded, and they are walking about on two legs."

His continuing role as a medical editor gave him the opportunity to publicize the effects of radium in numerous articles. He became a leading proponent of the new medical science of radiotherapy and presented frequent papers and lectures to the Academy of Medicine, the Ontario Medical Association, and the Canadian Medical Association. His topics included the use of radium in gynaecological disorders, skin conditions, tuberculosis, and leukaemias. In October 1916 a group of North American physicians met in Philadelphia to establish the American Radium Society. It is a tribute to Aikins's reputation among his peers that he was unanimously elected its first president. As head of the premier North American organization for radiotherapy, he was in a unique position to synthesize the existing body of evidence about radium's efficacy in medicine. This he did masterfully in 1919 in an address before the society entitled "The value of radium in curing disease, in prolonging life, and in alleviating distressing symptoms." The three goals mentioned remain the primary goals of cancer treatment. Although he used radium to cure cancers, he was also interested in the purely palliative effects of radiotherapy. He felt that its greatest benefit was the relief it gave to "countless patients whose condition is absolutely hopeless from the point of view of cure." His case reports note numerous examples of its successful use in treating pain, bleeding, or discharge from advanced, incurable cancers to provide comfort to dying patients.

By the time of his sudden death from heart disease the avuncular Aikins was a respected and much liked figure in Canadian medicine. Although he made no original contributions to radiation science, he demonstrated radium's clinical effectiveness to Canadian doctors and eloquently articulated the role of radiation in medicine. He was a model of the clinician-experimenter who tested a new medical treatment empirically in the clinic rather than in the laboratory. His pioneering work stimulated Canadian interest in radium that led to such initiatives as the opening, under Joseph-Ernest Gendreau*, of the Institut du Radium in Montreal in 1923 and the various provincial cancer control programs of the 1930s. In his will Aikins left his medical books to the Academy of Medicine; his estate, worth over $90,000, included $9,950 in radium, described as his "stock in trade."

CHARLES HAYTER

William Henry Beaufort Aikins's papers on radium and radiotherapy include "Radium as a therapeutic agent," *Canadian Practitioner and Rev.* (Toronto), 32 (1907): 426–27; "Radium and its action in connection with certain diseases of the skin," *Canadian Practitioner and Rev.*, 34 (1909): 739–46; two reports co-written with F. C. Harrison, "Recent observations on the therapeutic use of radium" and "The present status of radium therapy," *Canadian Practitioner and Rev.*, 36 (1911): 1–10 and 465–79; an article co-written with K. M. B. Simon, "The histological and clinical changes induced by radium in carcinoma and sarcoma," *Dominion Medical Monthly* (Toronto), 43 (July–December 1914): 97–107; "Personal experiences with radium," *Canadian Practitioner and Rev.*, 39 (1914): 535–45; "President's address, Academy of Medicine, Toronto: the medical profession and the war; the cancer problem," *Canadian Practitioner and Rev.*, 40 (1915): 533–43; "The established value of radium as a therapeutic agent," *Canada Lancet* (Toronto), 50 (1917): 494–505; "The value of radium in curing disease, in prolonging life, and in alleviating distressing symptoms," *Canadian Practitioner and Rev.*, 44 (1919): 229–37 (also published in the *American Journal of Roentgenology* (New York), new ser., 6 (1919): 439–44); and "Radium in toxic goitre," *Canadian Practitioner and Rev.*, 45 (1920): 339–50.

AO, RG 22-305, no.51299; RG 80-5-150, no.7744. UTA, A1973-0026/3(46). *London Advertiser* (London, Ont.), 28 Dec. 1887. Canadian Medical Assoc., *Journal* (Toronto), new ser., 14 (1924): 1132. Canadienne [A. R. Gale Hunt], "Radium as a remedy," *Saturday Night*, 17 Jan. 1914: 29. J. T. Case, "The early history of radium therapy and the American Radium Society," *American Journal of Roentgenology* (Springfield, Ill.), new ser., 82 (July–December 1959): 574–85. *Commemorative biographical record of the county of York . . .* (Toronto, 1907). C. R. R. Hayter, "William H. B. Aikins: forgotten pioneer of Canadian radiotherapy," Royal College of Physicians and Surgeons of Canada, *Annals* (Ottawa), 31 (1998): 155–58. Douglas Quick, "William Henry Beaufort Aikins, M.D., C.M., L.R.C.P. (Lond.), F.A.C.P., 1859–1924," *American Journal of Roentgenology* (New York), new ser., 12 (July–December 1924): 490. *Standard dict. of Canadian biog.* (Roberts and Tunnell).

ALBA, GEORGES, known as **Paul Cazeneuve (Cazenuve)** (at birth he was given the names **Georges-Jean-François-Paul-Charles-Ludovic**), actor and theatre director; b. 11 May 1871 in Revel, France, son of Gabriel Alba, a teacher, and Augusta Grillières; m. Orpha Alba, a soprano; d. between 18 and 26 June 1925 in Hollywood (Los Angeles).

Georges Alba was said to be the godson of Joseph-Amédée-Victor Capoul, a famous French tenor who toured Quebec in 1883. He reportedly made his debut as an actor at the age of four and a half in Toulouse, France, his godfather's home town. Since his father moved to the United States to teach at Harvard University in Cambridge, Mass., in all probability as a professor of law, Paul Cazeneuve, as he would be called from then on, made his real debut in the United States in 1889 with a French troupe, the Maude Banks, which he accompanied to Montreal that year. He would be a member of the company for two years. At the same time, he was studying with Tomasso and Alessandro Salvini and the Shakespearean actor John A. Lane. During the 1891–92 season he accompanied actress Hortense Barbe-Loret, known as Mme Rhéa, on her tours. He shared the stage with the greatest celebrities of the day, including Edwin Thomas Booth and Helena Modjeska. In 1893 he returned to Montreal.

From 1896 to 1898 Cazeneuve performed in Canada and the United States at the head of his own company. In February 1899 he was in Montreal and Quebec with the Columbia Stock Company. His roles included Mephisto in an adaptation of Goethe's *Faust* and the Italian in *Melbourne*. The Montreal *Gazette* pointed out that although the young actor performed in English, he attracted to the theatre a large part of the French-speaking public which had already adopted him.

On 18 Feb. 1901 Cazeneuve again staged *Melbourne* at Her Majesty's Theatre in Montreal. Concurrently he was hired as an actor and artistic director by George Gauvreau, who wanted to raise his Théâtre National Français, built the previous year, to the standards of the English-language theatres. Cazeneuve opened on 11 March with his own French adaptation of *Faust* based on Lewis Morrison's version. His stage setting immediately won over both the public and the critics, who praised the magnificence of the sets and costumes and the daring use of electrical effects. The play ran for 28 consecutive performances and drew an audience of more than 12,000 in a single week. Cazeneuve continued to favour large-scale productions in the American style, and in June 1901 he added the future film-maker Léo-Ernest Ouimet* to his company as lighting engineer. Ouimet developed new systems to mount a stunning production of *Quo Vadis?* by Henryk Sienkiewicz. Cazeneuve built his repertoire from foreign playwrights, often taking French plays adapted into English, which he then translated back into French! He promoted local works, however, in particular those of Louis Guyon*. He would produce four of Guyon's plays: *Denis le Patriote* (1902), *Joe Montferrand* (1903), *Un mariage à la gaumine* (1904), and *Montcalm* (1907). In October 1903 *La Patrie* described *Joe Montferrand* as "a magnificent portrait of Canadian customs." In September 1904 Cazeneuve left the Théâtre National Français to organize a season at the Auditorium de Québec. He left the city in March 1905, having presented much the same repertoire as in Montreal. At the same time, he made several tours to a number of smaller centres, including Sorel and Trois-Rivières. On his return to Montreal, he undertook a summer season at the Théâtre Français from 29 May to 8 July, during which he produced the Montreal premiere of *Un fil à la patte* by Georges Feydeau, but the endeavour was not a great success.

In 1906 Cazeneuve returned to the Théâtre National Français as artistic director and co-owner of the establishment, which had undergone a relative decline since his departure. He rightly attributed this situation to too much repetition of the same repertoire and the overly cautious approach of his successors. His stroke of genius during his second term as director was to bring variety shows back into style with *Ohé! Ohé! Françoise!* by Ernest Tremblay, Léon May, and Gaston Dumestre; in January 1909 this show drew 40,000 spectators in three weeks, establishing a taste in the Quebec public for political revues. The Françoise of the title was none other than Robertine Barry*, a journalist and the editor of *Le Journal de Françoise* (Montréal). The revue was intended as an allegory of the problems facing Montreal at that time, when the municipal administration was being increasingly disparaged. It took on standards of political morality by putting the municipal council on stage, and attacked public utilities such as the tramways and electricity monopolies, and the problem created by the presence of both streetcars and automobiles on the streets. It was a sarcastic portrayal of a city on the verge of being put under trusteeship [*see* Lawrence John CANNON]. The revue was a success because it hit home: the townspeople recognized themselves in it.

Later in 1909 Cazeneuve again left the Théâtre National Français, but he would no longer enjoy the same success in his career. The growing popularity of the cinema was slowing the advance of theatre in Montreal. He tried his luck in other francophone theatres in the city and even renewed his association with the English-language stage by taking on, among other things, a season at the New Empire Theatre for a few weeks in 1917–18. Since the situation had not improved, he left Montreal for Hollywood around 1919 to begin a new career in motion pictures. Cazeneuve got a few small roles in silent films such as *The Queen of Sheba* (1921) and *The French doll* (1923).

In 1923 he and Ouimet, who had been living in Los Angeles since 1921, made *Why get married?*, which proved a failure. Cazeneuve also suggested scenarios for *Faust* and *Maria Chapdelaine*, by Louis Hémon*, but these plans did not materialize. A serious illness that would eventually prove fatal forced him to give up the cinema. At the beginning of 1925 he went to Montreal for treatment at the Royal Victoria Hospital. He then returned to Hollywood, but suffered a relapse from which he did not recover. He was so destitute when he died that actor William Farnum had to pay the expenses of his illness and funeral.

Paul Cazeneuve had had an impressive career, producing 300 French, English, and American plays and acting in some 200 roles. His use of American theatrical techniques would revitalize the Quebec stage to such a degree that he is considered one of the founders of French-language theatre in Montreal. Some critics would accuse him of sacrificing dramatic content for the sake of effect, of sometimes changing the structure of plays by blithely abbreviating them, and of ignoring an authentic French repertoire. However, he succeeded thereby in attracting to French theatre a public that had previously been too strongly influenced by the sensationalism of American companies. At a time when Quebec still had no theatre school, Cazeneuve made professionals of amateurs such as Elzéar Hamel, Jean-Paul Filion, Antoine Bailly (known as Antoine Godeau), and Joseph-Sergius Archambault (known as Palmieri). As a person, Cazeneuve was remembered by anglophone and francophone audiences alike for his charm and old-world courtesy. His passing marked the end of the old guard that had transformed the theatre in Montreal and Quebec at the beginning of the 20th century.

MIREILLE BARRIÈRE

Arch. Départementales, Haute-Garonne (Toulouse, France), État civil, Revel, 11 mai 1871. Bibliothèque Nationale du Québec (Montréal), Div. des coll. spéciales, Programmes de théâtre, 9.19 (Théâtre national français), semaine du 11 mars 1901. *Gazette* (Montreal), 7 Feb. 1899, 16 Feb. 1901. *Le Monde illustré* (Montréal), 30 mars 1901. *Montreal Daily Star*, 27 June 1925. *Le Passe-Temps* (Montréal), 1er juin 1907. *La Patrie*, 9 janv. 1909, 25 juin 1925. *La Presse*, 27 févr., 9 mars 1901; 27 mai, 1er juill. 1905; 12 janv. 1909; 6 août 1910; 25 juin 1925. *Quebec Daily Mercury*, 3 Feb. 1899. *Le Soleil*, 14 sept. 1904. Christian Beaucage, *Le théâtre à Québec au début du XXe siècle: une époque flamboyante!* ([Québec], 1996), 30–34, 70–73, 75–77. L.-H. Bélanger, *Les Ouimetoscopes: Léo-Ernest Ouimet et les débuts du cinéma québécois* (Montréal-Nord, 1978), 206–14. Jean Béraud, *350 ans de théâtre au Canada français* (Ottawa, 1958), 96. Brooks Bushnell, *Directors and their films: a comprehensive reference, 1895–1990* (Jefferson, N.C., 1993), 98, 203. Denis Carrier, "Le premier directeur artistique du National: Paul Cazeneuve," *L'Annuaire théâtral* (Montréal), automne 1987: 153–64. Franklin Graham, *Histrionic Montreal; annals of the Montreal stage . . .* (2nd ed., Montreal, 1902; repr. New York and London, 1969). Renée Legris *et al.*, *Le théâtre au Québec, 1825–1980: repères et perspectives* (Montréal, 1988), 53–58. *Magill's survey of cinema – silent films*, ed. F. N. Magill *et al.* (3v., Englewood Cliffs, N.J., 1982), 3: 892–95. David Ragan, *Who's who in Hollywood, 1900–1976* (New Rochelle, N.Y., 1976), 572. G.-É. Rinfret, *Le théâtre canadien d'expression française: répertoire analytique des origines à nos jours* (4v., [Montréal], 1975–78), 3: 176–79.

ALBANI, EMMA. *See* LAJEUNESSE, EMMA

ALDERSON, Sir EDWIN ALFRED HERVEY, army officer; b. 8 April 1859 in Capel St Mary, England, eldest son of Edward Mott Alderson and Catherine Harriett Swainson; m. 5 May 1886 Alice Mary Sergeant in Brackley, England, and they had a son; d. 14 Dec. 1927 at Lowestoft, England.

Edwin Alfred Hervey Alderson, whose father was a veteran of the Crimean War and a lieutenant-colonel of the 97th Foot, grew up in a family dedicated to hunting and field sports. At 17 he was a subaltern in the Norfolk militia artillery and two years later, in 1878, he was gazetted to his father's old unit, soon to become the Royal West Kent Regiment. Alderson joined it at Halifax, N.S., and followed it to Gibraltar and then to South Africa, where he was detached to the Mounted Infantry (MI) depot at Laing's Nek in the Drakensberg Mountains. Improvised for each campaign, the MI acquired a cadre of ambitious officers eager for service away from their regiments. Alderson saw action in Egypt in 1882 as an MI officer and in 1884–85, in the Sudan, he served with the Mounted Camel Regiment in the desperate but unsuccessful bid to save Major-General Charles George Gordon. For rescuing a soldier from the Nile in 1885 he won a medal from the Royal Humane Society.

Alderson was promoted captain in 1886 and appointed adjutant of the MI depot at Aldershot, England, which gave him sufficient status to marry a daughter of the vicar of Chesterton, in Oxford. He served with his old regiment as adjutant from 1890 until he entered the Staff College at Camberley in 1894. After passing out the next year as a major, he returned to southern Africa to command the MI in the suppression of the Matabele revolt of 1896 and, as a brevet lieutenant-colonel, he commanded all the troops in Mashonaland. He returned to Aldershot as deputy assistant adjutant-general, in charge of the MI.

Garrison duty gave Alderson the leisure and incentive to write *With the Mounted Infantry and the Mashonaland Field Force, 1896* (London, 1898). Mounted rifles, he argued, were not cavalry, but rather picked infantry who were good shots, "with extra means of locomotion." Having inherited his father's passion for the chase, he hunted with the Shorncliffe Drag, the Staff College Drag, and, in

Africa, the Cape Jackal and the Salisbury Hounds. In his most popular book, *Pink and scarlet: or hunting as a school for soldiering* (London, 1900), he insisted that hunting, with its demand for courage, quick decisions, and an eye for terrain, was ideal training for a young officer.

The South African War pitted a nation of mounted rifles against Britain's entire army. Alderson arrived in early 1900 to command a corps in the MI brigade of his friend and fellow MI enthusiast, Edward Thomas Henry HUTTON, former general officer commanding the Canadian militia. Two battalions of Canadian Mounted Rifles served under Alderson, and the commander of the 2nd CMR, Thomas Dixon Byron Evans, found him far preferable to the tactless Hutton. In 1901 Governor General Lord Minto [Elliot*] tried without success to bring Alderson to Canada as GOC. By the end of 1901, as a brevet colonel, Alderson was inspector-general of mounted infantry with the rank of brigadier-general, a CB, and an aide-de-camp to Queen Victoria. Promoted to the substantive rank of colonel in 1903, for four years he commanded the 2nd Infantry Brigade at Aldershot. In 1906 he was made major-general and from 1908 to 1912 he commanded the 6th (Poona) Division of the Indian army. Then placed on half pay, he could look forward to hunting and his new enthusiasm, yachting. He was about to become master of foxhounds in the South Shropshire Hunt when war broke out in Europe in August 1914.

Alderson was immediately given command of a division of yeomanry and of the troops in Norfolk and Suffolk, with responsibility for local defence. Because of his experience with Canadians, his name was included on a list of potential commanders of the division being mobilized at Valcartier, Que. If Colonel Samuel HUGHES, Canada's minister of militia and defence, could not command "his boys," Alderson, despite his age, seemed the best choice. His South African reputation led the Canadians to believe that he "would not get his troops into trouble."

Newly promoted lieutenant-general, Alderson met the Canadian Expeditionary Force as it disembarked in England in October. In dealing with the aggressive Hughes, who had preceded the CEF, his tact would be sorely tested. The minister insisted that his contingent was perfect; Alderson found it ill-equipped and untrained, with many weak officers. In a few cold, rain-sodden months on Salisbury Plain, he did what he could to put things right, dismissing some of Hughes's chosen officers and replacing useless Canadian-made equipment with British issue. Inadvertently he made an enemy of Hughes's representative in England. Appalled at conditions in the camps, Colonel John Wallace Carson persuaded the War Office to kick British troops out of their barracks and give them to Canadians. Opposed to such special

treatment, Alderson refused the privilege. Carson, who did not forgive this embarrassment, complained to Prime Minister Sir Robert Laird Borden* in January 1915 that Alderson "does not treat our men with a firm iron hand covered with the velvet glove which their special temperaments require." Although at the outset 70 per cent of Alderson's division was British-born, Canadian soldiers were different, largely because of their officers, who for the most part were not as powerful or as respected as was the case in British regiments, where class perhaps as much as competence served to maintain discipline.

In February the 1st Canadian Division moved to France. After a quick introduction to trench warfare, Alderson's division played a minor diversionary role at the battle of Neuve-Chapelle and then moved up to the Ypres (Ieper) sector in Belgium under another general who knew Canadians, Sir Horace Lockwood Smith-Dorrien of the British 2nd Army. They were between an Algerian division and the British 28th when the Germans unveiled poisonous chlorine gas on 22 April. In a few hours, as Algerian soldiers fled, choking, the Canadian left flank was exposed. The Germans hesitated, and Alderson sent what reserves he controlled to help Brigadier-General Richard Ernest William Turner*'s 3rd Canadian Infantry Brigade close the gap. Counter-attacks that night and the following morning were valiant disasters. More British troops were poured into the mêlée until Alderson struggled, from his chateau behind the Yser Canal, to manage as many as 33 battalions along a six-mile front. The French promised aid but it never came. On the 24th the Germans switched their attack to the Canadians. Turner's brigade was destroyed and Brigadier-General Arthur William Currie*'s brigade bore the brunt of holding the line. Alderson's efforts to organize support were contradicted by local British commanders. His headquarters was now farther back than that of the 27th British Division and was less in touch with the battle. By the time the Canadians were withdrawn, more than half their infantry strength had been lost as dead, wounded, and prisoners.

On his arrival in France, Alderson had told his men to reflect on the reputation of his old regiment, the West Kents, which had never lost a trench. The raw Canadians assumed that they too must never budge. At Ypres they had done their best but confusion, inexperienced leaders, and the horror of gas had been too much. Wisely, senior British commanders chose to praise the Canadians for their valour. Alderson, who might have lost his command for giving up ground, echoed the congratulations, but all had not been perfect. He had had a hard time with some of his Canadian officers. While Currie had been steadfast and effective, Turner had been brave and ineffective, and his brigade major, Hughes's son, Garnet Burk*, had sent back erratic and misleading reports. Moreover, the Canadian-made Ross rifle had jammed so regularly that a fifth of the infantry survivors had collected the British Lee-Enfield rifle from the battlefield. Carson held a different view: it was Alderson who had caused the huge losses while Turner and Hughes had performed brilliantly. When Alderson ignored Carson's suggestion that Canadian battalion commanders and brigade majors be promoted, Carson had another grievance. On 28 May 1915, echoing his son, Sam Hughes informed Borden that he could "see no hope with General Alderson in command of our boys."

Some days before, in the thick of the battle of Festubert, Sir Douglas Haig, commander of the 1st Army, had created a temporary corps ("Alderson's Force") from the 51st Highland and 1st Canadian divisions, and told Alderson to advance 600–1,000 yards against points almost two miles apart. Inadequate shelling, German machine-guns, and objectives that were hardly more than points on a map cost 2,468 Canadian casualties with little gain. At Givenchy-lez-La Bassée a month later, Alderson applied the lessons, but a heavy barrage warned the Germans, a mine destined for a German strong point did more damage to attackers than defenders, and, despite 366 casualties, no one got close to the clearly marked objective. This result did not harm Alderson at general headquarters. When Canada proposed to add a second contingent, to form a new corps of two divisions, the British commander-in-chief, Sir John Denton Pinkstone French, agreed, provided Alderson was corps commander. Borden too was pleased: in the summer of 1915 he found this dapper general with the bushy moustache to be honest, able, and popular with his men. In September the new corps commander opened his headquarters at Bailleul.

Meanwhile, Hughes acquired fresh grievances. To staff his headquarters Alderson favoured British veterans over untrained Canadians. Carson relayed the resulting complaints to Ottawa. For other commands, Hughes insisted on favourites, including his son. While Currie replaced Alderson in command of the 1st Division, Hughes's insistence that Turner have the new division was successfully resisted. To add to the minister's discomfiture Alderson was elevated to KCB on 14 Jan. 1916. Hughes's biggest complaint was the general's lack of faith in the Ross rifle, which Hughes had helped persuade the Canadian government to buy in 1902 and which, despite its faults, he savagely defended. Though more accurate than the Lee-Enfield, it was longer, heavier, worse made, and slightly too small for British ammunition. Rechambering made a little difference and allowed Hughes to denounce British bullets, not the Canadian rifle. Commenting coolly in a letter criticizing the Ross, Alderson offered ten reasons why, in his view, 85 per cent of the men in the corps disliked it. "I should not be fit for my position," he told Colonel Willoughby Garnons GWATKIN in February 1916, "if I passed

over anything which endangered men's lives or the success of our arms."

Stung to rage, Hughes accused Alderson of utter ignorance of rifles and commanded him to keep bad ammunition out of his men's hands. Then he sent 281 copies of his letter to officers in England and France. Alderson responded by asking brigade, battalion, and company commanders to report on the rifle. Two senior officers sent the request to Carson; one of them, Turner, complained that "action is being delayed too long as regards Alderson." Alderson's concerns would nonetheless be sustained in May, when Haig recommended to the War Office that the Canadian divisions be rearmed with the Lee-Enfield.

Turner had another reason to resent his superior. In a nasty battle in April, over mine craters near Saint-Eloi (Sint-Elooi), Belgium, the Germans had driven one of his brigades out of positions that had been painfully gained in a British attack. Neither Turner nor the Canadian commander of the brigade involved, Huntley Douglas Brodie Ketchen, had known where their men were located and most artillery support had been misdirected. Acting on instructions from Sir Herbert Charles Onslow Plumer, Smith-Dorrien's successor as commander of the British 2nd Army, Alderson took steps to fire Ketchen. Turner's pledge to resign if he did led Alderson to request that Turner be removed as well. Sir William Maxwell Aitken*, another of Hughes's agents, warned Haig (now commander-in-chief) that Canada would be furious over the removal of two senior Canadian officers. Faced with a crisis, Haig sacrificed Alderson on the promise that he would get a significant appointment in England. A feud would be worse than keeping "a couple of incompetent commanders," he concluded. On 26 April Borden and his cabinet agreed. Hughes, Carson, and Aitken, delighted to be rid of Alderson, were content to see him replaced by another British general, Sir Julian Hedworth George Byng*. On 28 May 1916 the public learned that Alderson had been named inspector-general of Canadian forces in England and France.

No one told him that the appointment was purely nominal until he asked for staff, assistants, even a car. The British insisted that he was a Canadian concern until they ended his embarrassment in September by making him an inspector of infantry. His Canadian appointment lapsed with the organization of Canada's Ministry of Overseas Military Forces in November. In 1920 Alderson retired. Though he would become colonel commandant of his old regiment in 1921, for the most part he resumed his main recreations, yachting and hunting. He returned to the South Shropshire Hunt and joined the Royal Norfolk and Suffolk Yacht Club; in the *Times* in April 1927 he complained, as commodore of the Broads Cruising Association, that its training for boys was menaced by the attractions of the automobile and motorcycle.

Alderson died of a heart attack in December and was buried at Chesterton.

"He was an Englishman of a fine type," claimed the *Times*, "and the affection which he inspired in all who knew him was great." In two wars, Canadians able to appreciate an energetic, conscientious English officer could echo that affection. At a Canadian dressing station in January 1916, a diarist described the "indefatigable" Alderson as a "kind, gentle, little man" who "spoke to the patients one by one, with a pleasant enquiry or a bit of banter for each." A decent, honourable, unimaginative man, he had been more faithful to the interests of Canadian soldiers than their own minister. "Canadian politics," Alderson had confessed to his friend Hutton in 1915, "have been too strong for all of us." They ended his career.

DESMOND MORTON

In addition to the publications mentioned in the biography, Alderson is the author of *The counter-attack* (London, [1898]) and *Lessons from 100 notes made in peace and war* (London, [1908]).

British Library (London), Add. MSS 50088 (Hutton papers). Church of Jesus Christ of Latter-day Saints, Geneal. Soc., International geneal. index. GRO, Reg. of marriages, Brackley, 5 May 1886. LAC, MG 26, H, 22813–14, 31777; RG 9, III, 29, file 8-1-28. *Times* (London), 14 Jan. 1916, 15 Dec. 1927. [J.] B. Burke, *A genealogical and heraldic history of the peerage and baronetage . . .* , ed. A. P. Burke (80th ed., London, 1921). *DNB*. A. F. Duguid, *Official history of the Canadian forces in the Great War, 1914–1919* (only 1v. in 2 pts. [1914–September 1915] was published, Ottawa, 1938), 1, pt.2, app.120: 18. G.B., War Office, *The official army list* (London), 1881–1921. W. A. Griesbach, "Lieut.-Gen. Sir Edwin Alderson, K.C.B., a brave commander who was sacrificed to the Ross rifle," *Khaki Call* ([Toronto]), February 1928. *Hart's annual army list . . .* (London), 1881–1921. Andrew Macphail, *Official history of the Canadian forces in the Great War, 1914–19: the medical services* (Ottawa, 1925). Carman Miller, *Painting the map red: Canada and the South African War, 1899–1902* (Montreal and Kingston, Ont., 1993). Desmond Morton, *A peculiar kind of politics: Canada's Overseas Ministry in the First World War* (Toronto, 1982). Nicholson, *CEF*.

ALEXIS, GERMAIN BARTLETT. *See* LONECLOUD, JERRY

ALEXIS LE TROTTEUR. *See* LAPOINTE, ALEXIS

ALIKOMIAK, convicted murderer; b. probably in the Bathurst Inlet–Coronation Gulf region (Nunavut); d. by hanging 1 Feb. 1924 at Herschel Island, Y.T.

The trials and executions of Alikomiak and Tatamigana were the last of three cases in which whites had been killed by Inuit in the western Arctic. In June 1912 two explorers, Harry V. Radford, an American, and Thomas George Street, a young man from Ottawa, were slain near the southern end of Bathurst Inlet because Radford had threatened and struck one of their Inuit guides. The Royal North-West Mounted Police investigated and, on the advice of the government, simply warned the killers that Canadian law must be obeyed in the future. Late in 1913 two Oblate priests, Jean-Baptiste Rouvière and Guillaume Le Roux, known as Ilogoak, were killed under similar circumstances near Bloody Falls on the Coppermine River. Again the police patrolled, and this time they arrested the perpetrators. Sinnisiak and ULOQSAQ were tried in Calgary in 1917 and convicted of murder, but the mandatory death penalty was immediately commuted to life imprisonment and they were in fact released after two years.

By then officials responsible for law in the north had come to believe that leniency had had the opposite effect to the one intended and that the Inuit thought murder was taken lightly by the government. Partly as a display of authority, therefore, and partly as a demonstration of Canadian sovereignty, a number of additional mounted police detachments were established on the Arctic coast and islands after World War I. The post at Tree River, in the Coppermine–Coronation Gulf region, was manned by Corporal William A. Doak and Constable D. H. Woolams. In December 1921 Doak patrolled to Kent Peninsula to investigate some killings of Inuit by other Inuit. He arrested Alikomiak, a man in his late teens, and Tatamigana, whose age is not known, and took them to Tree River. Because Inuit had always been cooperative in such cases, the two men were not confined. In the early morning of 1 April 1922, while Woolams was some miles distant, Alikomiak shot the sleeping Doak in the upper leg and sat watching him slowly bleed to death. Later the same morning he shot Otto Binder, the man in charge of the Hudson's Bay Company post nearby, who had come to visit the policeman. When Woolams learned what had happened, he seized and tied up the unresisting Alikomiak, and in the summer Alikomiak and Tatamigana, along with some other Inuit charged with serious crimes, were taken to the police post on Herschel Island for trial.

Alikomiak's statement, made freely to the police in the summer of 1923, showed that the motive for the killing was an echo of the fate of the two explorers and priests. He said that he was "scared of Doak. . . . I could not understand him and do not know whether he was angry with me. I was afraid he might use the dog whip on me though he never threatened or hit me with it. Doak gave me boots and lots of things to fix and I did not like it [such repairs were women's work]. One time he gave me seal skin long boots to fix the bottoms and I had done one when he told me that I had not done it right and for me not to fix the other boot. I was mad and did not feel good inside. The next day I think I like to kill that man." If this account is true, and there is no reason to think it is not, Doak showed poor judgement in his treatment of Alikomiak, particularly given the precedents of the two earlier cases.

Because the mounted police were the only representatives of the federal government on the Arctic coast, an attack on one of them could be viewed as an attack on Canadian sovereignty in the region – sovereignty which because it was based on some questionable foundations had to be carefully defended. It was for this reason, as well as to reverse the earlier policy of leniency, that the trial of Alikomiak was vigorously pursued; the trial of Tatamigana was to make it clear that the government was prepared to punish Inuit who killed their own people. In the summer of 1923 a judicial party was sent down the Mackenzie River to Herschel Island. It consisted of Lucien Dubuc of Edmonton, stipendiary magistrate for the Northwest Territories, Irving Brass Howatt, acting for the crown, and Thomas Lewis Cory, solicitor for the Northwest Territories and Yukon branch of the Department of the Interior, who acted for the defence. A jury, selected from the white residents of the Mackenzie valley, accompanied the court party, as did the hangman, Special Constable Gill, who brought with him a portable gallows.

On 17 July 1923 Alikomiak and Tatamigana were tried separately for the murder of the Inuk Pugnana; the two trials were finished in less than a day and resulted in guilty verdicts. The next day Alikomiak was tried for the murder of Doak and Binder in proceedings that also took less than a day. In his charge to the jury Dubuc urged them not to be swayed by pity or mercy and to remember their duty towards Canadian law and Corporal Doak, "lonely and fearless sentinels of Law and Order." The jury deliberated for 18 minutes and delivered a verdict of guilty. On 11 August Dubuc sentenced the two men to death.

These cases aroused great public interest, partly because of the exotic circumstances under which the events took place and partly because of a general fascination with the Inuit, many of whom had only recently been contacted by outsiders. There was considerable feeling that the sentences should be commuted, on the grounds that the Inuit were "simple," "primitive," and ignorant of the law. Wilfred Thomason Grenfell*, a medical missionary to Newfoundland and Labrador, commented that the Inuit as a people had the ethical sense of a child of seven and that it was therefore wrong to execute them. It was also widely believed that the Inuit would not understand death as a punishment. Yet this was precisely the punishment they meted out to their own people who killed others; thus hanging was neither unusual nor culturally inappropriate. It was further claimed, though the police denied it, that Alikomiak was only 16 at the time of the murders. The government, however, was determined to make an example, and the

two men went stoically to the gallows on 1 Feb. 1924.

WILLIAM R. MORRISON

LAC, RG 13, 1526, files 712A/CC207, 713A/CC207. S. L. Harring, "The rich men of the country: Canadian law in the land of the Copper Inuit, 1914–1930," *Ottawa Law Rev.*, 21 (1989): 1–64.

ALLISON, DAVID, professor, educational administrator, and author; b. 3 July 1836 in Newport, N.S., son of James Whidden Allison and Margaret Elder; m. first 18 June 1862 Elizabeth Powell (d. 1898) in Richibucto, N.B., and they had five sons; m. secondly 3 July 1902 Ellen Elizabeth Cummins in Montreal; d. 13 Feb. 1924 in Halifax.

Well connected both socially and politically, David Allison came from an Ulster Scottish family. His father was a substantial farmer and a magistrate who during David's childhood served a term as Conservative MHA for Newport Township. After receiving his early education at a local school and at the Dalhousie Collegiate School in Halifax, David Allison spent four years studying at the Wesleyan Academy in Sackville, N.B., which had been founded by his kinsman Charles Frederick Allison*. As other able Methodist young men from the Maritime colonies had done before him, he went on to Wesleyan University in Middletown, Conn., where he received his BA in 1859. He took an MA from the same institution three years later. By this time Allison was back in Sackville as classics teacher at the academy. He had been principal of the Stanstead Seminary in Lower Canada during 1859–60.

When Mount Allison Wesleyan College was established in Sackville in 1862, Allison immediately became professor of classics, but he also taught political economy, constitutional history, and international law. In 1869 he succeeded Humphrey Pickard* as president of the 21-student college. The nine years of his first term as president were eventful ones for the institution. Although enrolment increased only modestly, the college surmounted, through vigorous fundraising, the loss of its grant from the New Brunswick government in 1872 and agreed in 1876 to participate with other regional institutions in the confederated, though non-teaching, University of Halifax (which would ultimately fail in 1881). It also awarded, in 1875, a degree of bachelor of science and English literature to Grace Annie Lockhart, who thus became the first woman in the British empire to receive an undergraduate degree. It is unlikely that Allison himself was active in advocating the innovation of women's undergraduate education; this role seems to have been fulfilled primarily by his faculty colleague James Robert Inch*. Allison's opinion was that "any woman's best and highest sphere" was as helpmate to "some good, honest, faithful man," and he was known on occasion to show publicly his impatience with female student essayists who took a different view. Nevertheless, he also maintained that "any Education that differentiates between the sexes is wrong."

In November 1877 Allison was appointed superintendent of education for Nova Scotia, although he continued to discharge his Mount Allison duties until succeeded by Inch at the end of the 1877–78 academic year. While qualified for the superintendency by virtue of his educational and administrative experience, he was an attractive candidate to the Liberal government that appointed him for several other reasons. His already demonstrated support for the University of Halifax, an initiative of Premier Philip Carteret Hill*, was one recommendation. At a time of tension between Presbyterians and Roman Catholics, his Methodism promised impartiality, and his Conservative connections precluded the suggestion of a politically motivated appointment. Allison never made any secret of his Conservative leanings, although he endeavoured to avoid public partisanship. Reputedly he had argued against Maritime entry into confederation and had sympathized with the anti-confederate leader in New Brunswick, Albert James Smith*, but if this was indeed his position, he was soon reconciled with Conservative pro-confederates.

As superintendent of education, Allison favoured an academic orientation for the public schools of Nova Scotia and resisted the efforts of those who sought to make public education an instrument of progressivist reform. He was lukewarm towards the legislation of compulsory school attendance, and championed the traditional decentralization of decision-making. In all of these positions, as in his ill-concealed distaste for Prohibition, he struggled with limited success against the reformist tide. The opportunity to return to Mount Allison College in 1891 for a second term as president no doubt came as a relief to him, even though it meant abandoning public education in Nova Scotia to the reformists [see Alexander Howard MacKay]. The ensuing 20 years saw considerable expansion at Mount Allison, but by the time the 75-year-old Allison retired in 1911 he had come to be seen as a revered figure whose grip on matters such as student discipline and university finance was embarrassingly feeble.

In other respects, however, Allison retained a level of vitality that would sustain him through a lengthy retirement. His continuing reputation for impartiality had been shown in his participation in 1908 in a board of conciliation (which also included the political economist Adam Shortt*) that successfully resolved a dispute at Sydney Mines between the Nova Scotia Steel Company Limited and its striking miners. Residing in Halifax, he busied himself by marking provincial examination papers. Allison, who had already compiled an English grammar for Nova Scotia schools, also turned to writing a general history of the province. Historiographically undistinguished but handsomely produced, it was published in 1916.

David Allison was a large man with a booming voice. He enjoyed sports: an avid horse-racer in younger days, in later years he was not above using what was – for a prominent Methodist layman and preacher – risqué language in support of the Mount Allison rugby team. All of these traits led to mixed impressions recorded by contemporaries. For one former student, he was "a very bluff person, rough you know." For another, his oratory in the classroom – which was matched by his vigour in the pulpit – made him "a magnetic leader and a prince among teachers." Passionate and impulsive, Allison lacked the more patient and persistent skills of persuasion that might have made him a shrewder advocate of the conservative values he embraced in both education and religion. When old and ill, hearing his wife conversing at the front door with a journalist, he was reported to have summoned up the strength to shout down the stairs, "Tell him I'm a Tory and a Methodist!" Both in content and in delivery, it was apt enough as a self-chosen epitaph.

JOHN G. REID

[David Allison's career as president of Mount Allison College is documented chiefly in the collections of the Mount Allison Univ. Arch. in Sackville, N.B., although there is no systematic collection of his presidential papers, few of which seem to have survived. Some valuable letters can be found in Mount Allison Univ. Arch., 7508 (B. C. Borden fonds). Official records such as calendars and minutes of governing bodies provide details of institutional developments during Allison's terms of office. The crucial source for his period as superintendent of education for Nova Scotia is his *Annual report* (Halifax), 1879–91; indispensable in interpreting this phase of his career is R. N. Henley, "The transformation of common schooling in Nova Scotia, 1877–1896" (PHD thesis, Univ. of Toronto, 1997). Allison, along with Clyde Edwin Tuck, is the author of *History of Nova Scotia* (3v., Halifax, 1916). J.G.R.]

Mount Allison Univ. Arch., 5501 (R. C. Archibald papers); Biog. files, David Allison. *Argosy Weekly* (Sackville), 29 March 1924. *Chignecto Post and Borderer* (Sackville), 3 June 1880. *Morning Chronicle* (Halifax), 14 Feb. 1924. *Provincial Wesleyan* (Halifax), 1 Aug. 1860. *Sydney Daily Post* (Sydney, N.S.), 28–30 July, 3–4 Aug. 1908. *Wesleyan* (Halifax), 3, 10 Aug. 1898. *Canadian men and women of the time* (Morgan; 1898 and 1912). D. W. Johnson, *History of Methodism in Eastern British America* . . . ([Sackville], n.d.). *The Legislative Assembly of Nova Scotia, 1758–1983: a biographical directory*, ed. S. B. Elliott ([Halifax], 1984). L. A. Morrison, *The history of the Alison, or Allison family in Europe and America* . . . (Boston, Mass., 1893). J. W. O'Brien, *A parson reminisces: a mélange of recollections and reflections* (Sackville, n.d.). J. G. Reid, *Mount Allison University: a history, to 1963* (2v., Toronto, 1984). Benjamin Russell, *Autobiography of Benjamin Russell* (Halifax, 1932). *Standard dict. of Canadian biog.* (Roberts and Tunnell).

ALLOWAY, WILLIAM FORBES, businessman, politician, banker, and philanthropist; b. 20 Aug. 1852 in The Derries (Republic of Ireland), son of Arthur William Alloway, a veterinary surgeon, and Mary Frances Johnson; m. 3 Sept. 1878 Elizabeth MacLaren (d. 1926), daughter of James Maclaren*, in Buckingham, Que., and they had one son who died in infancy; d. 2 Feb. 1930 in Winnipeg.

In 1855, at age three, William Forbes Alloway immigrated to Hamilton, Upper Canada, with his family. There his father opened a veterinary surgery, a horse-shoeing establishment, and a riding school. Less than two years later his father moved the family and business to Montreal, where William attended the High School of Montreal.

Four days after his 18th birthday, Alloway arrived in Winnipeg as a private in the expeditionary force under Colonel Garnet Joseph Wolseley* sent to quell the Métis uprising led by Louis Riel*. Subsequently he was among the 19 persons selected to form the nucleus of a mounted constabulary force for Manitoba. Discharged from the militia in April 1871, he settled in Winnipeg, where he was, like his father, a veterinarian, as well as a tobacconist and an auctioneer of horses. In 1874 he went to work as foreman for the well-known freighter and politician James McKay* and the following year became his partner in the transportation business.

In 1876 Alloway struck out on his own. For the next four years forwarding and trading occupied his attention. He speculated in land and scrip on the side. Alloway obtained most of his work from Thomas Nixon, purveyor for the Department of the Interior at Winnipeg, with whom he developed a rather cosy relationship as Nixon's landlord. Later Nixon would be severely censured by a royal commission for his lack of diligence in business. On behalf of the dominion government, Alloway purchased horses for the surveying parties of the Canadian Pacific Railway. Buying principally from the Métis at the prevailing price of $50 for a good carthorse, he "reaped considerable advantage" by reselling them to the government at prices ranging on average from about $90 to $157. His enemies referred to him contemptuously as a "horse jockey."

Alloway also provided the surveyors with the common "bushed and banded" native carts (so called because of the iron boxing around the axles and the bands on the hubs) and shamelessly lined his pockets further by engaging with Nixon in the resale of abandoned government carts and harnesses. At one time he used Nixon to help him raise money on their joint liability. Alloway's questionable dealings with Nixon led to lucrative transportation contracts with the government, some of which were never advertised. He always subcontracted the work, which involved freighting supplies and carrying the mails to the construction crews of the CPR via the Dawson Road and Lake of the Woods, as well as supplying the various outposts of the North-West Mounted Police. Over the years his transactions with the government amounted to $40,000 or more.

Alloway's business ambitions led him into local politics. He served four year-long terms on the municipal council in 1876–77 and 1879–80. He also sat on the first two councils of the reinvigorated Winnipeg Board of Trade, which finally became fully functional in 1879. Alloway had an unshakeable faith that the west must "fill up with people" and that Winnipeg must grow in "importance, size, wealth and prestige." Photographs of him reveal a frank look and a fearless demeanour, characteristics which would earn him the respect and admiration of the business community in his efforts to help quicken the city's commercial pulse.

On 28 Nov. 1879 Alloway formed a partnership in Winnipeg with Henry Thompson Champion, an accountant with the Merchants' Bank of Canada, who had also come west with Wolseley's expedition. They formalized their partnership in March 1880 as Alloway and Champion, "bankers, brokers, commission merchants, freighters, traders, and real estate agents." The capital of the new firm was $7,000, of which Alloway contributed $5,000.

Starting in the unstable conditions incident to the building of the CPR, Alloway and Champion eschewed the real estate mania of 1881–82. As a private bank, the firm was free to deal in land and to lend money on its security, but the partners competed only for "legitimate business" rather than business connected with land speculation. Through Alloway's foresight, the firm acquired a large inventory of "well selected farm lands" in every township in the province as well as in the North-West Territories which were sold "at reasonable prices and on easy terms." The firm would also lend up to $25,000 on first mortgages.

By 1882 Alloway and Champion had increased its capital to some $175,000. About the same time, the firm became an agent for the CPR's lands. To its work as a real estate agency, it later added payments for pre-emptions of federal lands and transactions for the Canada North-West Land Company [*see* William Bain Scarth*]. Most of its dealings in land, however, were done indirectly through the purchase and resale of land- and money-scrip, military bounty warrants, and tax sale certificates. The acquisition of scrip was greatly facilitated by William's brother Charles Valentine, who would become a junior partner in the firm in 1885.

Alloway and Champion had opened in 1881 a branch in Portage la Prairie. That same year Alloway had become one of the founding directors of the Ogilvie Milling Company, the western subsidiary of A. W. Ogilvie and Company [*see* William Watson Ogilvie*]. In 1882 he helped establish the Manitoba Cartage and Warehousing Company and together with Champion and others he tried to organize a stock exchange. Although the exchange was not set up immediately because of the business collapse that spring, the firm soon turned its attention to the buying and selling of stocks on the Toronto, Montreal, New York, and Chicago exchanges. It also traded produce in the New York and Chicago markets.

In the early 1890s Alloway and Champion expanded its foreign exchange department to keep up with the demand of Manitoba's rapidly growing immigrant population, mainly from eastern Europe, to convert its gold, silver, and national currencies into Canadian dollars and to remit funds abroad. By 1904 the exchange business had reached such a volume that the partners decided to establish a branch in Winnipeg's north end. It opened the following year with five interpreters (later increased to ten). Acting generally as steamship and railway agents, Alloway and Champion helped to bring over many family members of those already established in the city. Alloway himself was extremely proud of the personal relationship which in large measure governed the branch's business dealings with these new Canadians. This intimacy was expressed by one of its first employees, a Romanian Jew, who – commenting on the branch's close connection with the Jewish community – fondly referred to it as the "Jewish Bank."

During the boom years following the turn of the century, the firm became involved with the promotion of local industrial capital through Champion's membership on the Winnipeg Stock Exchange, which opened in February 1909. Alloway and Champion's astonishing success is evident in its financial strength: it rose to over $1,000,000 by 1912. That September the firm was incorporated as Alloway and Champion Limited with an authorized capital stock of $3,000,000 and a reserve of $125,000. The paid-up capital of $1,025,000 was mostly held by the original partners. Alloway and Champion had now become the largest and strongest private bank in the dominion. In 1919, three years after Champion's death, Alloway sold the company to the Canadian Bank of Commerce, but he carried on as president until 1923. The business continued under the name Alloway and Champion Limited until his death in 1930.

The bank founded by William Forbes Alloway played an important role in the settlement and economic development of Manitoba and Winnipeg. Mindful, however, of the poverty and disadvantage wrought by unbridled growth, Alloway, a millionaire by 1910, was a generous supporter of many benevolent institutions through his annual contribution of $5,000 to the Federated Budget Board. He became a life governor of the Winnipeg General Hospital in 1884 and a member of its board of trustees from 1912 until his death. He was also a member for 25 years of the advisory board of the Margaret Scott Nursing Mission. His proudest achievement, however, was the incorporation in 1921 of Canada's first community trust, the Winnipeg Foundation, which he endowed with an initial gift of $100,000. His wife, Elizabeth, took a deep interest in the foundation as well, and together their donations amounted to $2,654,764. The trust has been mentioned in the wills of numerous Manitobans and its impressive record of service in advancing human welfare and knowledge stands as Alloway's abiding social testament.

PETER HANLON

ANQ-O, ZQ127/25, 3 sept. 1878. LAC, RG 9, II, A5, 3: 159; B4, 16: 1. Man., Dept. of Finance, Consumer and Corporate Affairs, Companies office (Winnipeg), Charter book A, 1880–90: 49–52, 144–45, 151–53; Letters patent, June–November 1912: 109; Partnership agreements, file no.83, 17 April 1880; file no.121, 3 April 1881. St John's Anglican Cathedral (Winnipeg), Reg. of burials. *Commercial* (Winnipeg), 22 July 1889. *Manitoba Free Press*, 1873–1930, esp. 3 Feb. 1930. *Winnipeg Tribune*, 1 Nov. 1912. Can., House of Commons, *Journals*, 1878, app.1; *Report of the Canadian Pacific Railway royal commission* (3v., Ottawa, 1882). *Canadian album* (Cochrane and Hopkins), vol.3. N. S. Garland, *Garland's banks, bankers and banking in Canada* ... (Ottawa, 1890). Peter Lowe, "All western dollars," Man., Hist. and Scientific Soc., *Papers* (Winnipeg), 3rd ser., no.2 (1945–46): 10–25. Helena Macvicar, *Margaret Scott: a tribute; the Margaret Scott Nursing Mission* ([Winnipeg 1947?]).

AMYOT, GEORGES-ÉLIE, manufacturer, businessman, politician, and philanthropist; b. 28 Jan. 1856 in Saint-Augustin-de-Desmaures, Lower Canada, son of Dominique Amyot (Amyot, *dit* Larpinière), a farmer, and Louise Nolin; m. 14 Nov. 1881 Joséphine Tanguay at Quebec, and they had six children, five of whom survived; d. 28 March 1930 in Palm Beach, Fla.

Georges-Élie Amyot lived on a farm in Saint-Augustin-de-Desmaures until he was ten years old. He then moved with his family to Sainte-Catherine (Sainte-Catherine-de-la-Jacques-Cartier), where he attended school for a short time and was taught English by the Irish curé of the parish. At the age of 14 he went to Quebec; there he learned the trade of saddler from Louis Girard and entered into partnership with the saddler Louis Tanguay, his future father-in-law. He joined his brother Bernard in New Haven, Conn., in 1874 and subsequently lived for a time in Springfield, Mass., engaged in his trade.

When he returned to his home province in 1877, he was employed in Montreal as a clerk in the wrought-iron business and the boot and shoe industry. In 1879 he began working as a clerk for his cousins Joseph and George-Élie Amyot, who were importers of novelty items in Quebec's Lower Town. He opened his own shop in the Upper Town in 1885, selling dry goods, fancy goods, and novelties. The following year, at the instigation of wholesaler Isidore Thibaudeau*, Amyot's retail business was forced into bankruptcy. In 1894, when he was better off financially, he would reimburse his creditors, a gesture that his contemporaries said was unusual.

On 11 Oct. 1886 Amyot entered into a five-year partnership with Léon Dyonnet, who had been led to start manufacturing corsets by the success of the corset shop run since 1882 by his French wife, Hélène Goullioud, and her sister Clotilde. Each contributed $2,000 in capital, was entitled to half the profits, and could withdraw $800 a year for his personal expenses. Their agreement also stipulated that the two partners would be involved in every aspect of the business and that Dyonnet was to initiate Amyot "into all the manufacturing details and secrets and let him benefit from the experience he had gained in the said production process." The question arises where Amyot had obtained this money so soon after his bankruptcy. It had probably come from his in-laws or from a fellow merchant, perhaps Pierre-Joseph Côté, to whom he owed an advance of $1,500 in the fall of 1887. In any case, in December 1886 Amyot's wife renounced community of property, and thus put the family assets out of the creditors' reach. On 26 March 1889, reportedly following Dyonnet's departure for Brazil, the partnership was dissolved; in its stead the Dominion Corset Manufacturing Company was set up. Amyot's partners were his sister Odile until her marriage in July 1890 and afterwards his older sister Marie-Louise until 9 Oct. 1897. He then continued in the Dominion Corset Company on his own.

The enterprise soon met with promising success, and rented larger and larger premises in the industrial section of Saint-Roch ward. In 1898 Amyot would purchase the bankrupt shoe factory of G. Bresse and Company [see Guillaume Bresse*] for $21,500. By November 1887 he was replacing the pedal-operated machines with steam-driven machinery, thereby substantially increasing his output and lowering the labour cost per unit. In his testimony to the royal commission on the relations of labour and capital in 1888, he said that he had about 60 employees, including 10 to 15 girls aged between 10 and 14. Most of the goods he produced went to markets outside Quebec City, in particular to the Montreal wholesale outlet, which opened in 1889, and then to the Toronto office, which was set up in 1892. Sales grew from $21,000 in 1887 to $58,000 in 1891 and $130,000 in 1895.

This expansion led Amyot to invest in related activities. From 1894, to ensure himself a steady and cheap supply of the cardboard boxes required for shipping his products, he manufactured them himself in a building adjacent to his corset factory. This operation was initially an integral part of Dominion Corset, but from 1906 it was carried on by a separate entity, the Quebec Paper Box Company. In 1916 Amyot would set up the Canada Corset Steel and Wire Corporation to manufacture the steel rods used in the corsets.

Amyot also went into the production of beer, opening a brewery in 1895. His partner, Pierre-Joseph Côté, contributed two-thirds of the capital and, in return for a basic salary, was to devote his full time to managing the enterprise. The partnership agreement had a clause allowing Amyot to buy back one-sixth of Côté's shares as well as to join him in working full-time in the business if its annual profits exceeded $10,000. This investment gave Amyot a contingency plan in the event that Dominion Corset failed. The brewery was located in Saint-Sauveur ward against the cliff where the spring water was drawn. On 12 Nov. 1896 beer merchant Michel Gauvin replaced Côté in the company, which became known as Amyot et Gauvin. It produced and distributed Fox Head beers, both ale and porter. In 1909, after buying Gauvin's share and engaging in a number of highly profitable financial transactions, Amyot sold the business to National Breweries Limited for $226,500 in shares and debentures of that company, which was in the process of amalgamating most of the province's breweries in Montreal and Quebec City.

From at least 1887, Amyot had been involved in politics. A member of the Liberal party, he focused mainly on finances and organization. He was particularly active in the debate on reciprocity with the United States, which by 1888 he supported. In 1897, a year after Wilfrid Laurier* came to power, a tariff reform was introduced that granted special concessions to Great Britain. In his dealings with Laurier, as well as in the Canadian Manufacturers' Association (he was a member of the Quebec section) and the Quebec Chamber of Commerce (he served as president in 1906 and 1907), Amyot tried in vain to defend his business interests. He complained that the duty on imported corsets (which mainly came from Britain) had been lowered, while the duty on his raw materials – cotton and steel – were as high as ever.

When Charles Fitzpatrick* was appointed chief justice of the Supreme Court of Canada in 1906, a by-election became necessary in the federal riding of Quebec. Seeking a businessman to represent the city's interests, Laurier offered the nomination to Amyot. His campaign, which was widely supported by the upper echelons of the Liberal party both federally and provincially, was organized by Cyrille-Fraser

Amyot

Delâge, the member of the Legislative Assembly for the same riding, and was financed by Amyot himself. Rebelling against the autocratic manner in which Laurier had chosen the candidate, a number of Liberals refused, however, to rally around Amyot. Lorenzo Robitaille, the 24-year-old son of a Beauport businessman, ran as an independent Liberal. He and his supporters attacked Amyot, calling him, among other things, a rich industrialist, an employer who treated his workers harshly, and Laurier's man. Robitaille won the backing of Armand La Vergne*, and then of Henri Bourassa*. The Nationalistes thus used the situation to enter the fray, in order to demonstrate their opposition to certain measures taken by the Laurier government and to embarrass the party leadership. Memorable mass meetings drew the protagonists of both camps, raising the level of the debate and transforming a by-election that should have been run off quietly into a popularity contest between Laurier and Liberals loyal to him and the Nationalistes clustered around Bourassa. Clearly overtaken by events, Amyot struggled on to the end, but on 23 October he had to concede defeat by 388 votes. In December 1911 the premier of Quebec, Sir Lomer GOUIN, with whom he was closely associated, appointed him legislative councillor for the division of La Durantaye.

Because of his success in industry and his political connections, Amyot was picked in January 1922 to take up the formidable challenge of saving the Banque Nationale, which had opened at Quebec in 1860, from bankruptcy. After a period of strong growth during World War I, the bank found itself in a precarious position, mainly because of the financial problems of the Machine Agricole Nationale Limitée, a company in Montmagny run by Charles-Abraham Paquet*. The firm had prospered as a result of the war economy, but when it tried to switch to producing farm implements, it experienced serious difficulties. In 1922 it had to obtain loans from the Banque Nationale totalling $5 million. This growing financial burden, along with a marked decrease in deposits from which the *caisses populaires* had in particular gained, posed a threat to the bank's survival. Such was the situation in 1922, when four new directors were elected: Amyot, who also became president of the bank, Joseph-Herman Fortier, Sir Georges Garneau*, and Charles-Edmond Taschereau, the brother of Premier Louis-Alexandre Taschereau*. Scarcely had Amyot taken up office when he was obliged, with Gouin's support, to make an urgent request to the federal minister of finance for a loan of $2.5 million. Unable to offer sufficient security, he received only $1 million, and he also failed in his bid for increased federal government deposits.

At the end of March, Amyot turned to the leading figures in the economic and political life of the province and the city of Quebec, inviting them to subscribe to a $1 million issue of capital shares. Despite the risks of double liability, Amyot himself took a block of $200,000 and got commitments from Olivier-Napoléon Drouin* and Fortier (for $100,000 each), as well as from a number of other businessmen and politicians, including Premier Taschereau (for amounts ranging from $10,000 to $50,000). The $1 million was officially subscribed within a few weeks and was in by the end of 1922. From 1922 to 1924, Amyot, whose face appeared on the newly printed bank notes, tried to recover as much of the assets of the Machine Agricole Nationale Limitée as possible and obtained large deposits from the provincial government. Despite his efforts, by the end of 1923 the situation had deteriorated to such an extent that a solution had to be found at once, in the form of a merger with the Banque d'Hochelaga. The premier persuaded it to absorb the Banque Nationale by guaranteeing it a reserve of $15 million in government bonds to balance the liquidity of the two banks. The bill providing for this assistance was passed on 24 Jan. 1924 and was vigorously defended by Taschereau, whom the opposition accused of trying to rescue Liberal friends threatened with sizeable losses, including Amyot. Once the merger was confirmed, Amyot became vice-president of the new Banque Canadienne Nationale, in which he maintained interests that were particularly useful to him in promoting his real estate and industrial endeavours.

Throughout this period Amyot had continued his cautious management of Dominion Corset. In 1901 it had about 320 employees and was producing 175 dozen corsets a day (in 125 different models) and 8,000 to 10,000 cardboard boxes. By the end of the first decade of the 20th century, its output had a total value of $500,000, of which roughly a third was sold in Ontario, 15 per cent in Montreal, 45 per cent in the rest of Quebec, the Maritimes, and western Canada, and 6 to 7 per cent in Australia and New Zealand. Sales rose from $560,000 in 1909 to more than $1 million in 1913, reaching $1.6 million in 1918 and $2.6 million the following year. This remarkable growth made it necessary in 1909 to expand the plant, but on 27 May 1911 it was devastated by a fire that destroyed part of the neighbourhood. Despite losses of $250,000, Amyot immediately rebuilt the factory, making it larger than ever. In the absence of internal accounting data, the company's performance in subsequent years is not clearly known. Information gathered by the Dominion Bureau of Statistics confirms, however, that Dominion Corset increasingly dominated an industry that was tending to level off.

At the turn of the century Amyot already had sizeable financial resources, which he invested in real estate, among other things. In 1897, for example, he paid $6,000 cash for a fine property on Chemin Sainte-Foy in the suburbs of Quebec. Over the years he had bought and speculated in real estate in other parts of the city (especially on the Grande Allée), in Montreal, and even in Saskatchewan and British Columbia. In the course of various subscriptions to Victory Loans, he himself, with $200,000 in 1917 and $500,000 in 1918, managed to come close to the amount contributed by the Price empire [*see* Sir William PRICE]. In the 1920s Amyot invested in and directed and promoted many projects, on his own, or through figureheads such as his son-in-law Henri Bray and his accountant Honoré-J. Pinsonneault, or as a member of some Canadian, British, or American politico-financial group. In addition to putting his money in real estate, he invested in numerous railway, shipping, and mining companies. During the winter he often spent time in resort areas in Europe (the French Riviera), the United States (Palm Beach, Fla), and Canada (Pointe-au-Pic, which would later become La Malbaie, in the Charlevoix region of Quebec), where he managed to make high-level personal and business connections. Direct and blunt, he did not skimp when it came to supporting causes dear to his heart, such as the church of Saint-Jean-Baptiste, the Asile du Bon-Pasteur, or the École Supérieure de Chimie at the Université Laval. In 1909 the minister of militia and defence, Sir Frederick William Borden*, appointed him honorary lieutenant-colonel of the 61st Regiment of Montmagny, a title he cherished.

Demanding but fair in his dealings with his employees, Amyot had brought his two sons into the business, beginning in 1906. Horatio, who had become deaf following surgery, was involved in the company's operations in Toronto, western Canada, and then Montreal. Adjutor, the elder, also worked at finding new markets, especially in Australia and New Zealand and later England. Georges-Élie's strong personality and thorough knowledge of the business world, however, left little room for Adjutor, who helped his father in the overall management but had little to do with day-to-day operations, which were entrusted instead to managers and accountants, including Pinsonneault. After putting in place an advantageous capital structure through various financial and legal transactions, Georges-Élie handed over control of Dominion Corset to Adjutor in 1924 through a private agreement. He transferred 11,499 of the 21,000 shares issued and subscribed, which were added to the 6,050 shares Adjutor already held, with the authority, however, to reduce the capital by selling them back to the company. In December of that year Adjutor conveyed all his shares except one to his father in trust, to be held until the latter's death, but this agreement was cancelled in 1929. These manoeuvres ensured that Adjutor would inherit the business.

In 1928, to guarantee the distribution and preservation of the capital investment, Amyot drew up a will reflecting his own image – all of a piece and absolutely solid – dividing among his heirs, with the exception of Adjutor, the usufruct from a capital that would amount to some $5.5 million, distributable on the death of the last of his grandchildren. Including Dominion Corset, the Amyot empire was worth, in 1930, at least $8 million in pre-Depression dollars and it constituted one of the great fortunes of Quebec City at that time.

Georges-Élie Amyot died suddenly in Palm Beach on 28 March 1930. In the ensuing days, the arrival of his body and the magnificent funeral attracted the political and commercial elite of Quebec City. Amyot was buried on 3 April in the cemetery of Notre-Dame de Belmont, in a marble mausoleum he had had prepared in 1908, as befitted the remarkable success of a French-speaking Quebec industrialist who had become a financier and entrepreneur on a continental scale.

MARC VALLIÈRES

The author wishes to thank Marc Paquet, Robert Amyot de Larpinière, and Pierre Amyot for their valuable assistance.

ANQ-Q, CE301-S17, 29 janv. 1856; S103, 14 nov. 1881; CN301-S292, 1886–1900; E53-S12, SS3/17; TP11, S1, SS20, SSS1, 13 oct. 1886, no.3688; 26 mars 1889, nos.4150–51; 23 juill. 1890, nos.4464–65; 13 nov. 1896, no.6036; 5 mai 1897, no.6073; 9 oct. 1897, no.6292; 20 avril 1918, no.339; janvier 1925, no.72. AVQ, P51, 1/1051-02; 2/1053-06; 4/1068-02. LAC, MG 26, G; MG 27, III, B4; MG 28, I 230. Qué., Bureau de la publicité des droits, Greffes, J.-É. Boily, 1886–1927; Joseph Sirois, 1925–34. *Le Devoir*, 28 mars 1930. *L'Événement*, 25 sept.–26 oct. 1906; 19 déc. 1911; 23 avril 1929; 29, 31 mars, 2, 4 avril 1930. *Le Soleil*, 7 déc. 1901; 28 sept.–25 oct. 1906; 29 mai, 19 déc. 1911; 18 janv. 1924; 28, 31 mars, 1er–3 avril 1930. Benjamin Demers, *Une branche de la famille Amyot-Larpinière: M. Georges-Élie Amyot, manufacturier et brasseur de Québec, ses ancêtres directs et ses enfants* (Québec, 1906). *Les grands débats parlementaires, 1792–1922*, Réal Bélanger et al., compil. (Sainte-Foy, Qué., 1994). *Les ouvrières de Dominion Corset à Québec, 1886–1988*, sous la dir. de Jean Du Berger et Jacques Mathieu (Sainte-Foy, 1993). Pierre Poulin, "Déclin portuaire et industrialisation: l'évolution de la bourgeoisie d'affaires de Québec à la fin du XIXe siècle et au début du XXe siècle" (mémoire de MA, univ. Laval, 1985); "Georges-Élie Amyot et la Dominion Corset," *Cap-aux-Diamants* (Québec), 1 (1985–86), no.1: 9–12. Ronald Rudin, "A bank merger unlike the others: the establishment of the Banque Canadienne Nationale," *CHR*, 61 (1980): 191–212; *Banking en français: the French banks of Quebec, 1835–1925* (Toronto, 1985). Robert Rumilly, *Henri Bourassa; la vie publique d'un grand Canadien* (Montréal, 1953); *Hist. de la prov. de Québec*. B. L. Vigod, *Taschereau*, Jude Des Chênes, trad. (Sillery, Qué., 1996).

ANCTIL, JEANNE (baptized **Marie-Jeanne-Antoinette**), teacher of household science and principal of the Écoles Ménagères Provinciales; b. 27 Dec. 1875 in Sainte-Anne-de-la-Pocatière (La Pocatière), Que., daughter of Barthelemi Anctil, a farmer, and Zélie Pelletier; d. unmarried 4 Dec. 1926 in Montreal.

In the province of Quebec the movement to promote the teaching of household science began in 1882 with the establishment of a school of domestic science in Roberval [see Malvina Gagné*]. Over 20 years would pass before similar initiatives materialized. Between 1905 and 1907 two schools would open in rural areas (in Saint-Pascal, near Kamouraska, and at Sainte-Anne-de-Bellevue), and one in Montreal – the only secular institution among them.

The Montreal school came about in the following way. In 1902 a handful of French-speaking middle-class women founded the women's section of the Association Saint-Jean-Baptiste de Montréal, with the aim at first of assisting the men (their husbands, for the most part) in their efforts to solve the society's financial problems. On 7 Nov. 1904 they were invited to a meeting – being held by Joseph-Xavier Perrault* – for a quite different purpose: to set up a school of household science in Montreal. The founding committee was chaired by Caroline Béïque [Dessaulles*], who would also be the school's president until 1936. Robertine Barry* (known as Françoise), Marie de Beaujeu, Joséphine Dandurand [MARCHAND], Marie Gérin-Lajoie [Lacoste*], and Marguerite Thibaudeau [Lamothe*] were among the other members of the committee, as were a group of men, including Raoul Dandurand*, Gaspard De Serres, Sir William Hales Hingston*, and Emmanuel-Persillier Lachapelle*, who dealt with financial matters. The project, which sought to offer public classes in home economics and train teachers for this purpose, was intended to meet a new need that had arisen because young women were now working outside the home. It was part of the movement to professionalize domestic work and of the growing movement to promote public health.

Since no French-language pedagogical training in household science was available at the time, it proved difficult to recruit teachers. The founders of the Montreal school immediately chose Jeanne Anctil and Marie de Beaujeu, and sent them to Europe for training in order to broaden their knowledge in this field. Marie de Beaujeu would come back to Canada in April 1905 after studying for five months. On her return to Montreal she would give lectures in schools and write a few articles for Le Journal de Françoise, a publication edited by Robertine Barry in order to publicize the institution that would soon open. Jeanne Anctil, a young woman of 28 who had attended the convent in Coaticook from 1886 to 1893, studied in Paris for a year and then went to Fribourg, Switzerland, where she was joined by a new student, Antoinette Gérin-Lajoie. In 1906 the two women returned to Canada, armed with diplomas from the Fribourg school of household science, where they had taken a course qualifying them for the position of principal of

such an establishment. In June of that year the Montreal institution obtained its charter and its corporate name, the Écoles Ménagères Provinciales, a title that, although plural, referred to only one school.

The official opening of the Montreal school of household science would take place on 9 Jan. 1907, with Lomer GOUIN, the premier of Quebec, as honorary chairman. Classes had begun, however, in December 1906 in premises for the Circuit Court of the District of Montreal on Rue Saint-Jacques that were on loan from the provincial government. The members of the Association Saint-Jean-Baptiste de Montréal and their friends provided most of the funding. There were also donations from various sources, as well as a grant of $1,000 from the provincial Department of Agriculture. Although it was a private school, it would continue to receive subsidies from this department until 1929. These financial contributions were evidently not sufficient to cover the operating costs, however, since Antoinette Gérin-Lajoie taught for two years without salary.

Jeanne Anctil and Antoinette Gérin-Lajoie were the school's co-principals. At first they shared the task of teaching the 36 students taking day courses and the 23 enrolled in evening classes. On 1 March 1907 a three-month teacher-training course was added. Thereafter Antoinette Gérin-Lajoie took charge of the public courses, which were designed for women of diverse backgrounds. Schoolgirls, for example, took classes on Saturday, working women attended evening classes, and women whose intention was to become housewives or domestic servants studied during the day. Jeanne Anctil was in charge of the teacher-training course, which was open to students who already had a teaching certificate. Advanced students, patronesses, and invited lecturers assisted the co-principals in carrying out their duties.

Also in 1907, on the initiative of Marie Gérin-Lajoie and Caroline Béïque, the women's section of the Association Saint-Jean-Baptiste de Montréal became the Fédération Nationale Saint-Jean-Baptiste. Although this organization took its inspiration from feminist thinking on social issues and the demand for equal rights, it was also influenced by clerical and nationalist ideology. In subsequent years it would lean more towards the stream of the European Christian feminist movement. It brought together 22 associations involved in three fields: charitable causes, social initiatives, and educational endeavours, including the Montreal school of household science. Although the federation's members campaigned in favour of higher education for girls, their work, at least as far as the teaching of home economics was concerned, was shaped by the concept of complementary roles, with women being defined first and foremost as wives and mothers. At the federation's first congress, held in May 1907, Jeanne Anctil gave a lecture on the importance of teaching household science and reported that 128 students were then attending the school.

The premises of the Circuit Court were soon too small, and in September of that year the school moved to 22 Rue Sherbrooke Ouest, which would be its home for the next three years. The curriculum was based on that of the Fribourg school. The students in the teacher-training course were given instruction in bookkeeping, housekeeping, the making and maintenance of clothing, the selection and preparation of food, hygiene, and the care of young children and the sick. "All that with sentiments of devotion to duty and of Christian self-sacrifice," Caroline Béïque had noted in *Le Journal de Françoise* on 20 Jan. 1906. The courses for the general public dealt more or less with the same subjects, but pedagogy and theoretical topics were reserved for future educators. The teacher-training course was of ten months' duration at that time. One could register as either a day or a residential student, for a monthly fee of $5.00 or $15.00 respectively, according to an advertisement in *Le Journal de Françoise* on 5 Oct. 1907. The same notice announced that the fees for public classes were between 10 and 50 cents for a two- or three-hour lesson. Enrolment in these courses, which were given mainly in French, but sometimes in English, would continue to increase until 1914–15, when it reached 906. From 1910 pedagogical training was also offered to qualified religious and lay teachers during the holidays. Since this was too short a period to provide adequate training, the experiment would come to an end in 1916. In 1917 Jeanne Anctil would note in the Montreal periodical *La Bonne Parole* – the organ of the Fédération Nationale Saint-Jean-Baptiste, to which she contributed occasionally – that training household science teachers "has been more difficult to achieve" than teaching the general public. The students were also offered special lectures on various topics. For instance, Benjamin SULTE came and spoke to them on the history of Canada, Abbé Henri Gauthier on the role of women in society, and Robertine Barry on "the feminine soul." By 1910 the premises were again too crowded, and the Montreal school of household science signed a nine-year lease for space in the newly constructed building of the Montreal Technical School, where it would in the end remain for some 15 years.

During World War I the school cooperated with various private and public agencies and thus reached a new clientele. From 1915 to 1917, for example, Jeanne Anctil gave weekly lectures in rural areas, while teachers trained in Saint-Pascal were hired by the Department of Agriculture to teach evening courses in 11 Montreal parishes that were affiliated with the Fédération Nationale Saint-Jean-Baptiste. These itinerant activities attracted thousands of women. The staff of the Montreal household science school also shared their knowledge at many schools in the city and in a number of places throughout the province (including Salaberry-de-Valleyfield, Sherbrooke, Quebec City, and the Lac-Saint-Jean region). In 1917–18, at the request of the management of the Laurentides Pulp Company in Grand-Mère and the Riordon Paper Mills in Hawkesbury, Ont., a bilingual teacher from the school organized courses in cooking, sewing, and hygiene, at the companies' expense, for their female employees. Changes in the school's board of directors over the years reflected its evolution. In 1917–18, for example, the woman who chaired the women's committee and the man who chaired the men's, the chaplain, and the representatives of the Montreal Technical School were joined on the board by female teachers and members of five Montreal school commissions.

In her capacity as co-principal, Jeanne Anctil performed numerous duties in return for an annual salary that, in 1919, reached $1,400. In addition to teaching students in various settings, giving lectures, bringing out the occasional publication, and participating in conventions, including one on the teaching of household science that was held in Atlantic City, N.J., in March 1921, she had to cope with many unforeseeable situations, such as the Spanish influenza epidemic of 1918–19, when the school had to close for five weeks. In 1918 the Department of Agriculture gave the school a grant of $3,000 and a special sum of $1,000 (to help provide housing for the teachers). It also received $2,000 from the city of Montreal. On 9 August Jeanne Anctil wrote a letter to De Serres, president of the Montreal Technical School and a member of the household science school board, telling him about the financial problems of the teacher-training course and expressing her weariness and dissatisfaction with the government, which refused to include home economics in the curriculum of the technical schools. "Our dear Premier seems to have ideas that are by no means favourable towards us. Yet in our country, as in every other country, *it is the women* who make society and . . . it is very important to give them fair and accurate ideas about everything. Secular instruction in household science meets these needs." At the meeting of the Fédération Nationale Saint-Jean-Baptiste in April 1921, Jeanne Anctil pointed out that, despite the problems encountered by her school, the teaching of household science had made significant progress in the province of Quebec. She suggested, however, that the Council of Public Instruction and the Department of Agriculture take a series of measures to encourage this kind of teaching. At the time of her death a few years later, following a brief illness, she was working to set up a program of studies in "maternal pedagogy." Antoinette Gérin-Lajoie would continue to run the school until 1936. It would be affiliated with the Université de Montréal the following year.

Jeanne Anctil was one of the first French Canadian women to receive a European education in the discipline of domestic economy. Under her direction, the teaching of household science not only took root in Montreal, an urban centre where this kind of education had not previously been seen as needed, but spread to other parts of the province. Although it perpetuated the traditional role of women, the Montreal household science school gave young women a chance to get professional training in a secular environment. Through Jeanne Anctil's determination, various levels of government offered their cooperation and support to sustain the institution.

LOUISE FRADET

Jeanne Anctil is the author of "Conférence sur l'enseignement ménager . . . ," in *Premier congrès de la Fédération nationale Saint-Jean-Baptiste (section des dames de l'Association Saint-Jean-Baptiste), tenu les 26, 27, 28, 29 et 30 mai à Montréal* (Montréal, 1907), 130–37; *Livret d'enseignement ménager: méthodologie spéciale à l'usage des normaliennes; résumé du cours donné à l'école ménagère de Fribourg (Suisse)* (Québec, 1915); *350 recettes de cuisine* ([Montréal?], 1912; réimpr., Montréal, 1915); "Comment former les maîtresses de l'enseignement ménager," *La Bonne Parole* (Montréal), 5 (1917), nos.2–3: 16–17; and "Rapports du congrès: les écoles ménagères provinciales, formation des maîtresses d'enseignement ménager et de leurs relations avec les commissions scolaires," *La Bonne Parole*, 10 (1922), no.6: 6–8.

ANQ-BSLGIM, CE104-S12, 29 déc. 1875. Arch. de l'Univ. de Montréal, E 81 (fonds École ménagère provinciale), B, 1B, 4, 5, 10; 3B, 1; C, 5C, 1; 6C, 1. *Le Devoir*, 6 déc. 1926. *La Presse*, 6 déc. 1926. Marie de Beaujeu, "L'utilité des écoles ménagères," *Le Journal de Françoise* (Montréal), 5 (1906–7): 166–68. Mme F.-L. Béïque [C.-A. Dessaulles], "Lettre de Mme la présidente de l'Association de la Saint-Jean-Baptiste," *Le Journal de Françoise*, 4 (1905–6): 314–15; *Quatre-vingts ans de souvenirs* (Montréal, 1939). "In memoriam," *La Bonne Parole*, 14 (1926), no.12: 8. Marie Lavigne et al., "La Fédération nationale Saint-Jean-Baptiste et les revendications féministes au début du 20ᵉ siècle," in *Travailleuses et féministes: les femmes dans la société québécoise*, sous la dir. de Marie Lavigne et Yolande Pinard (Montréal, 1983), 199–216. Hélène Pelletier-Baillargeon, *Marie Gérin-Lajoie: de mère en fille, la cause des femmes* (Montréal, 1985). "Prospectus des écoles ménagères provinciales," *Le Journal de Françoise*, 6 (1907–8): 206. [Sœur Sainte-Marie-Vitaline], *L'œuvre d'un grand éducateur: le chanoine Alphonse Beaudet* (2v., Montréal, 1947). Nicole Thivierge, *Histoire de l'enseignement ménager-familial au Québec, 1882–1970* (Québec, 1982).

ANDERSON, ALEXANDER, educator and office holder; b. 30 Sept. 1836 in Aberdeen, Scotland, son of Alexander Anderson and Margaret Imray; m. 11 Nov. 1862 Catherine Stewart Robertson in Alloa, Scotland, and they had three sons and a daughter; d. 13 Jan. 1925 in Halifax.

Alexander Anderson attended school in Aberdeen until 1854, when he led all of Scotland in the examinations for his year and won a scholarship to Moray House Training College for teachers in Edinburgh. He studied at this college for two years, was appointed a master in its training department, and later entered the University of Edinburgh. At the end of four years there, he won gold medals in mathematics and natural philosophy and a medal in chemistry.

In November 1862 Anderson and his bride sailed for Prince Edward Island, where he began teaching mathematics and science in Charlottetown at Prince of Wales College. A secular institution established by the government of Edward Palmer* in 1860, it was located in a dilapidated building formerly occupied by a boys' school, the Central Academy. The college, though basically a high school, also offered what was apparently the equivalent of first-year university. In 1868 Anderson was appointed principal when the founding principal, Alexander Inglis, resigned and returned to Scotland. His gifts soon became evident. As early as the 1870s, when enrolment stood at about 70, graduates were being accepted for second-year work at such colleges and universities as McGill, Dalhousie, Harvard, and Cornell, and many won scholarships and prizes.

Their accolades bear witness to Anderson's impact. One of his students in the 1870s was Jacob Gould Schurman of Freetown, who later attended universities in Edinburgh, London, and continental Europe, and would serve as a president of Cornell. "I have never yet met such a great teacher as Professor Anderson," he once said. "There is none to whom, all considered, I personally owe so much as to him." Sir Andrew Macphail*, a son of former school visitor William McPhail*, went to Prince of Wales in the 1880s before studying medicine at McGill. "Of the many teachers I have since known," he would recall, Anderson was "the best." In 1888 McGill awarded him an LLD, citing the "excellent training" he provided and his role in improving the Island's educational system.

What makes Anderson's success truly remarkable is the dismal state of elementary education in 19th-century Prince Edward Island. Year after year, inspectors' reports complained of vacant schools, poorly qualified and ill-paid teachers, no standard curriculum, and irregular attendance. In the two decades after Prince of Wales opened, students could enrol there or in the adjacent Normal School virtually by knocking on the doors. Consequently, Anderson had to devote much of his time to remedial work, spending five to seven hours a day in the classroom. He loved to teach. Of all her teachers, recalled Lucy Maud Montgomery*, a teacher-training student in 1893–94, "none was to be compared to Dr. Anderson. I can see him now, standing before us, making the dry bones of Roman History live, and clothing even Greek verbs with charm and 'pep.'" She knew him to be a hard marker who spared his praise, but he encouraged her to develop her writing talent. A stocky man with a beard and thick grizzled hair that stood up, the impeccably dressed Anderson presented a picture of dignity bordering on pomposity. He carried himself so ramrod straight that he almost leaned over backwards. Rarely known to rebuke a student, he established his authority effortlessly; he could quiet an unruly class simply by appearing in the room. He treated farm boys with esteem, as if they were destined for greatness. Some were. "Members of the government, of the judiciary, and of the professions had all passed through his school," Macphail wrote, "and they retained for him a respect and fear not unmixed with affection. In addition the best schools were taught by his pupils, and they helped to propagate the legend of his power."

Anderson's beneficial influence did not mean that his college was safe from criticism, underfunding, or even the threat of abolition. It was totally dependent on the government and was vulnerable to interminable disputes over religion, politics, and education [see Sir Louis Henry DAVIES]. Almost half of the Island's residents were Roman Catholics, and some of the fiercest fights centred on whether the government should give grants to public schools and Prince of Wales but not to Catholic schools and St Dunstan's College. Anderson, a Presbyterian, apparently did not become involved in these conflicts. Instead, he concentrated on promoting education, giving lectures across the Maritimes on topics such as Burns, Shakespeare, and Savonarola, and serving as a director of the Dominion Educational Association and a member of its dominion history committee.

In 1879 the government decided to save money by amalgamating Prince of Wales and the Normal School, which had failed to live up to its promise as a teacher-training institution. With union, women were admitted to the college for the first time and all pedagogical training was placed under Anderson's wing. With characteristic zeal, he immediately began reforming the Normal School. The next year Prince of Wales started screening students through entrance examinations. The failure rate was high; in 1893, for instance, fewer than half the 264 candidates passed. At the same time the entrance requirements encouraged the district schools to raise their standards, with Anderson constantly watching. In some of his annual reports, he spent as much time on the schools as on his college, praising and scolding the teachers and making suggestions for improving instruction. In 1896, for example, he noted that geography and history lessons seemed to be exercises in memorization. To foster a spirit of inquiry and "the faculty of attention," teachers should make history come alive by

reading adventure and travel stories to their classes and asking students to summarize them. More work on diction would improve spelling, he believed, and greater care should be paid to handwriting.

Toward the end of the century, Anderson added new courses to the curriculum, and enrolment continued to climb, reaching 246 by 1896. As well, he had attracted other forward-looking educators to his staff, among them Joseph-Octave Arsenault*, a professor of French, principal of the model school at Prince of Wales, and provincial inspector of French instruction in the Island's Acadian schools. The college building, however, remained in bad shape: it had dark, narrow halls, overcrowded, poorly ventilated classrooms, and no assembly hall or library. Anderson complained that the lack of space made it difficult to keep order and impossible to conduct the teacher-training program properly. When unprecedented outbreaks of headaches, colds, influenza, measles, and other ailments occurred in the 1890s, he blamed the cramped space and fetid air. Every year for almost two decades he begged the government for a new building, but nothing was done.

The province was chronically short of money. By the 1890s the shipbuilding boom was over and farm incomes were in decline. In the end, it was left to Anderson to come up with a solution: collecting tuition fees, to be set aside to pay the interest on erecting a new school. Previously, teacher-training students had been exempt from fees even though not all of them went on to teach. By 1896 the college had taken in $3,300, and construction began two years later. In February 1900 a three-storey brick structure, with six classrooms, an auditorium, and space for a library, opened to great fanfare. A reporter from the *Daily Patriot* pronounced it "a tribute to the untiring energy of Dr. Anderson, and, best of all, a source of pride to the intelligent inhabitants of this little Isle of the Sea."

Anderson had other ambitions for the college. For instance, he had been promoting degree-granting status for several years. He had seen many young Islanders leave the province for higher educations, including at least two of his children – his daughter studied in Paris and Hanover and a son went to the Royal Military College of Canada in Ontario. Unfortunately, he did not stay at Prince of Wales to press the issue. In March 1901, apparently satisfied that it was in good shape, he left to become the Island's chief superintendent of education. Then 64, he attacked his new tasks with vigour, travelling to dozens of one- and two-room schools, giving teachers advice, consulting with trustees, and writing forceful, often indignant reports to the government. In many districts, the school facilities shocked him, as did the low salaries. One district had never adequately compensated a good, long-serving teacher. "Such treatment is not only selfish and unjust, but ungrateful and cruel," he declared. Clearly ahead of his time, he promoted the consolidation of rural schools and argued that female teachers should be paid the same as male teachers. "Why . . . should such discrimination exist?" he asked in 1909. "*Surely the time has arrived when men and women, who do the same work, under the same exacting circumstances, shall be put on an equality by the school law.*"

It is difficult to measure Anderson's effect on the school system, aside from his reform of teacher training, but his superintendent's reports provide clues. In 1908 he expressed pleasure over the number of candidates who had performed well in the previous summer's entrance exams. School facilities had improved considerably, he claimed in 1910; the next year he observed that local ratepayers had increased their contributions to teachers' salaries every year since 1901. Teachers were showing readiness to adopt his suggestions, and he saw advances in penmanship, arithmetic, history, and geography. On the other hand, salaries were still so low by the time he retired that many good teachers had left the profession or the province. In addition, the experiment in 1905–11 in consolidating six school districts died when the financing from Sir William Christopher Macdonald* stopped.

Anderson retired in 1912 at age 76. In his eighties he moved to Halifax with his wife to live with their daughter, Helen Kingdon. He died in 1925 after a bout with pneumonia. Anderson did not live to see school consolidation, substantial improvements in teachers' salaries, or university status for Prince of Wales, but during his lifetime, and for decades afterwards, the college served as a lighthouse for education. In 50 years of service, he fostered the development of countless teachers, professors, and administrators, turned Prince of Wales into an institution recognized by some of the best universities on the continent, and earned the gratitude of many accomplished sons and daughters. "If there be today in Prince Edward Island a good school system, good machinery, good teaching, good scholars," J. G. Schurman declared, "it is all due, directly or indirectly to his genius for education."

MARIAN BRUCE

The author's history of Prince of Wales College is forthcoming.

Church of Jesus Christ of Latter-day Saints, Geneal. Soc., International geneal. index. LAC, MG 30, D150. *Examiner* (Charlottetown), 8 Nov. 1875. *Islander* (Charlottetown), 5 Dec. 1862. *Patriot* (Charlottetown), 15 May 1873, 8 July 1893, 5 Feb. 1900, 13 Jan. 1925. Duncan Campbell, *History of Prince Edward Island* (Charlottetown, 1875; repr. Belleville, Ont., 1972). G. E. MacDonald, *The history of St. Dunstan's University, 1855–1956* (Charlottetown, 1989). Frank MacKinnon, *Church politics and education in Can-ada: the P.E.I. experience* (Calgary, 1995). Andrew Macphail, *The master's wife*, intro. I. R. Robertson (facsimile ed., Charlottetown, 1994). M. O. McKenna, "The history of higher education in the province of Prince Edward Island," CCHA, *Study Sessions*, 38 (1971): 19–49. L. M. Montgomery Macdonald, "The day before yesterday," *College Times* (Charlottetown), 3 (1927), no.3: 29–34; *The selected journals of L. M. Montgomery*, ed. Mary Rubio and Elizabeth Waterston (4v., Toronto, 1985–98), 1. P.E.I., House of Assembly, *Journal* (Charlottetown), reports of the principal of Prince of Wales College, 1881, app.A: 33; 1882, app.A: 57–58; 1892, app.E: 70; reports of the superintendent of education, 1872, 1879; Legislative Assembly, *Journal* (Charlottetown), reports of the principal of Prince of Wales College, 1897, app.E: 66; 1898, app.E: 65; reports of the chief superintendent of education, 1901–12. *Past and present of Prince Edward Island . . .* , ed. D. A. MacKinnon and A. B. Warburton (Charlottetown, [1906]). I. R. Robertson, "Religion, politics, and education in Prince Edward Island from 1856 to 1877" (MA thesis, McGill Univ., Montreal, 1968).

ANDERSON, JOHN, businessman and politician; b. 27 Jan. 1855 in Saltcoats, Scotland, son of John Anderson and Agnes King; m. first 18 Nov. 1884 Amelia Murray in St John's, and they had two sons; m. there secondly 25 Dec. 1917 Clymena (Clymenia, Minnie) Kaye, widow of Dr John Edgar March, of Saint John; d. 8 Nov. 1930 in St John's.

Educated at the Saltcoats Academy, John Anderson came to St John's on 3 April 1875 to work as a draper's assistant with the firm of James Baird*. Nine years later he left to form a dry goods partnership with Andrew K. Lumsden under the name Anderson and Lumsden. Anderson was the senior partner in the firm, which was dissolved in 1887 when he went into business on his own under the name John Anderson. The firm popularly styled itself the "Great Provider" or the "Universal Provider," and by mid 1916 it was "Anderson's – The House of Quality." A general importing business, it dealt in dry goods, millinery, boots and shoes, and clothing. In 1917 the firm's credit was rated good, and it was judged to have a pecuniary strength of between $35,000 and $50,000.

During the early 1900s Anderson had been active in political life at both the national and the municipal levels. In 1900 he won election to the House of Assembly as a member of Robert BOND's Liberal party, which went on to form the government. He was one of three MHAs – all Liberals – returned for St John's West, a district controlled by the populist politician Edward Patrick Morris*. Anderson did not seek re-election in 1904 but in 1905 he accepted an appointment to the Legislative Council, of which he remained a member until his death.

In 1902 Anderson had considered seeking the mayoralty of St John's but instead he stood for election as a councillor. He was successful, and during his term the city reorganized its finances and initiated improved waterworks. In the next civic election, in

1906, Anderson ran for mayor, emphasizing conservative measures to preserve the financial health of the municipality, but he finished a distant third to the winner, Michael Patrick Gibbs*, who had strong labour support. Eight years later he accepted a government appointment to the municipal commission that administered the city from 1914 to 1916 under chairman William Gilbert GOSLING.

Anderson's name is probably most associated with daylight saving time, which Newfoundland, the first jurisdiction in North America to adopt it, has enjoyed since 1917. Anderson had first become fascinated with this idea in 1907 and later that year he met the London builder William Willett, who had been promoting it in England. Anderson would continue a correspondence with Willett until the latter's death in 1915. In 1910 the Legislative Council passed a daylight saving bill, but the assembly refused to accept it because of public misunderstanding about how the change would affect daily routines. Success came in 1917 following the recent adoption of daylight saving time in Great Britain, several European countries, and Australia. Anderson wanted the change to give residents an extra hour of daylight for recreational purposes, but it also enabled Newfoundlanders to limit their use of artificial light and coal during wartime conditions. The legislation provided for an extra hour of daylight each day between the months of June and September.

During World War I Anderson was a member of the Patriotic Association of Newfoundland, a government-appointed body under the chairmanship of Governor Sir Walter Edward Davidson which had responsibility for administering the colony's war effort. He was also a strong publicist for the Newfoundland Regiment; he visited members of the unit in Britain and, to boost morale at home, wrote regularly to the local press concerning the soldiers' living conditions there. His name was associated as well with Anderson's Houses, a range of residences constructed in 1920 on Merrymeeting Road in St John's by the Dominion Co-operative Building Association Limited. Anderson was the managing director and secretary of this company, which he had formed with the help of local business, labour, churches, and government to provide needed housing for the working poor and returning war veterans. Only 30 of the promised 600 houses were erected because the company experienced difficulty in raising sufficient capital. By 1924 some houses had been sold outright, others sold on an instalment basis, and the remainder left unsold.

Anderson was active in the St Andrew's Society and other organizations associated with the small but influential Presbyterian congregation in St John's. According to journalist Albert Benjamin Perlin*, he was "not a man to give in easily" to controversy and possessed "considerable oratorical gifts." He presented "a formidable appearance, big physically, with an arresting face whose most prominent features were his piercing eyes and aquiline nose that contributed to an imperious look."

MELVIN BAKER

Daily News (St John's), 26 Dec. 1917. Evening Telegram (St John's), 19 Nov. 1884, 12 Oct. 1900, 29 June 1906, 26 Dec. 1917. Mail and Advocate (St John's), 18 Aug., 16 Sept., 28 Oct., 25 Nov. 1916. Melvin Baker, "Municipal politics and public housing in St. John's, 1911–1921," in Workingmen's St. John's: aspects of social history in the early 1900s, ed. Melvin Baker et al. (St John's, 1982), 29–43. The mercantile agency reference book . . . (Montreal), July 1917. Nfld, General Assembly, Proc., House of Assembly, 28 Feb. 1910: 378–79; Legislative Council, 31 May 1917: 11. A. B. Perlin, "The origin of daylight saving time in Newfoundland," Newfoundland Quarterly (St John's), 73 (1977–78), no.2: 48. Who's who in and from Newfoundland . . . (St John's), 1927.

ANGERS, FÉLICITÉ (baptized **Marie-Louise-Félicité**), known as **Laure Conan**, novelist, biographer, journalist, and playwright; b. 9 Jan. 1845 in La Malbaie, Lower Canada, daughter of Élie Angers, a blacksmith, and Marie Perron; d. unmarried 6 June 1924 at Quebec.

Félicité Angers was one of a family of 12 children, of whom six survived to adulthood. The Angers had owned a general store and run the post office in La Malbaie since the end of the 18th century. All the children would get their higher education at Quebec. During her three years with the Ursulines, from 4 Oct. 1859 to 1 July 1862, Félicité was already attracting attention because of her literary talents. There were so many Irish Catholic girls at the convent that she lived in a naturally bilingual environment. She became fluent in English and in German as well. In 1861 she completed her literature course and won a number of prizes. The following year she was among five pupils enrolled in the higher class, which was optional and open only to the most gifted. She would be the only one to pursue a literary career. Some of her compositions and those of her close friend Suzanne Lauretta Stuart were published in the cahier d'honneur of the Papillon Littéraire, an academy whose director at the time was Abbé George-Louis Le Moine, the chaplain to the Ursulines. Le Moine criticized Félicité's earliest writing for its "almost total lack of punctuation" and its "style" which he thought "rather stiff." Nevertheless, Félicité's essays were among his favourites. Their historical and religious themes, featuring heroes whose strong personalities and tragic or patriotic actions were described in minute and intimate detail, clearly revealed what would characterize the form and content of the future Laure Conan's work.

Angers

When she returned home in the summer of 1862, Félicité apparently began seeing Pierre-Alexis Tremblay*, a surveyor and native of La Malbaie, who was then 34 years old. In January 1865 he became the MLA (of a Liberal stripe) for the united ridings of Chicoutimi and Saguenay. The romantic relationship ended sometime between 1867 and 1870, the year in which Pierre-Alexis married Mary Ellen Connolly. On 2 March 1871 Félicité had a mystical vision, another experience that would remain deeply engraved in her memory. "In receiving absolution, I received the application of the blood of Jesus Christ in the most tangible manner," she would write on 21 Feb. 1879 to her close confidante, Mother Catherine-Aurélie du Précieux-Sang [Caouette*], the founder of the Sisters Adorers of the Precious Blood in Saint-Hyacinthe.

Félicité would never recover from the break-up of her romance with Pierre-Alexis. Thinly veiled references to this relationship can be found in several of her novels, where she would reveal herself through the literary devices of letters and personal diary. According to a number of critics, the man she had loved and lost was the root cause of the world-weariness, low spirits, isolation, and bitter and fatalistic tone that would be found in the novelist's work and that, despite her use of a pseudonym, would lay bare her private and public life. Some researchers ascribe the parting of the lovers to a vow of chastity that Pierre-Alexis is thought to have taken in his youth; Félicité is believed to have refused her fiancé's offer of an unconsummated marriage. Mother Catherine-Aurélie's letter to Félicité dated 24 Jan. 1880 suggests quite the opposite. "Your *virginal dream* has not then as yet disappeared from your soul and your desires, my dear Félicité? I must admit that I am afraid the Friend who would suit you might be hard to find, but what I feel certain is that it is quite simply a divine Friend who might well meet your needs." Félicité would be unequivocal in her response. On 11 Nov. 1884 she wrote: "I have not the slightest inclination for the religious life – not the slightest for marriage either – that great Sacrament has no attraction for me. . . . Ah how I would suffer in it!"

In the space of a few years, death robbed Félicité of those closest to her: her father in 1875 and her mother in 1879. With the death of Pierre-Alexis, also in 1879, she lost all hope. She did, however, put together a network of acquaintances who would play a decisive role in her future. In the fall of 1877 and the winter of 1878 she had visited the Sisters Adorers of the Precious Blood, and thus met two women who would be her main correspondents, the founder of the community (letters from 1878 to 1905) and Sister Marie de Saint-François-Xavier, née Sophronie Boucher (letters from 1879 to 1918). In 1879 her brother Charles was a classmate and close friend of the future historian Thomas Chapais* when they were both studying law at the Université Laval at Quebec. They often arranged to meet at the presbytery of Narcisse Doucet, the curé of La Malbaie, where they joined other men of intellect, including Abbé Apollinaire Gingras, the curé of Saint-Fulgence, who would publish *Au foyer de mon presbytère* at Quebec in 1881, Abbé Paul Bruchési*, a young man spending his summer holidays there, and Félicité's older brother Élie Angers, a notary who wrote poetry when the spirit moved him and who had been a friend of Octave Crémazie*. Félicité also participated in the group's meetings. Chapais and Bruchési would become her chief patrons. Around 1880 Félicité discovered Father Louis Fiévez, a Redemptorist and brilliant preacher attached to the basilica of Sainte-Anne-de-Beaupré, her favourite place of pilgrimage. He would have to keep constantly reassuring her as to her choice of a literary vocation. Bruchési and Fiévez would serve as her spiritual directors, replacing Mgr Joseph-Sabin Raymond*, with whom she had kept up a correspondence until 1879.

It was in this context that Félicité Angers, at the age of 33, published her first work, a short story entitled "Un amour vrai," which appeared in the *Revue de Montréal* in 1878 and 1879. She used the pen name of Laure Conan, apparently after reading the works of Zénaïde Fleuriot, which contain a reference to Conan III, Duc de Bretagne. Since this "first effort has been noticed" and since "I absolutely must have activities that will absorb me [and] rescue me from the bitterness of my regrets," as she ventured to confide in Mother Catherine-Aurélie on 21 Feb. 1879, "I would like to begin writing. . . . If possible, I would like to use this talent to earn my livelihood." "Could you not," she beseeched her, using the English endearment "sweetest mother," "suggest a subject for a *short story or a novel*?" Now an orphan, Félicité was in a precarious financial position that year, living with her brother Élie and her then unmarried sisters, Marie-Marguerite (nicknamed Mary) and Adèle (who would marry in 1884). Except for marriage and the religious life, she would consider every possible means of supporting herself: taking over the post office, which Élie had run into debt, buying lottery tickets, praying, signing "partnership agreements" with God ("Once my debts are paid off," she would write to Mother Catherine-Aurélie on 11 Nov. 1884, "I will give him half the profits"), and writing. Only this last activity would enable her to earn a living, a rare privilege for writers of her time; she was the sole instance of a French Canadian woman doing so in this field. From then on literary works would follow in rapid succession.

"Angéline de Montbrun" appeared in the *Revue canadienne* (Montréal) in 1881 and 1882. From 1881 to 1919 this periodical would publish 38 articles (biographies and instalments of novels) by Laure Conan. The novelist was to bring out all her works, with but few exceptions, first in at least one periodical and then in book form. In 1882, eager to take advantage of her success with "Angéline de Montbrun" by publishing it as a book, she sought Bruchési's advice. He recommended that she contact Henri-Raymond Casgrain*. In a letter addressed to him on 4 March 1884, she referred to him as "the father of Canadian literature." She travelled to Rivière-Ouelle in 1882 and again in 1883 to visit her new patron. "Necessity alone has given me the extraordinary courage to get myself published," she confessed to him on 9 Dec. 1882. Everything possible was done to help the young novelist and make her better known. Casgrain was the only man who really took her financial and intellectual situation seriously. He sought the support of Pierre-Joseph-Olivier Chauveau* and Sir Hector-Louis Langevin* to get her a position as a librarian at the archives in Ottawa, but in vain. On 9 Oct. 1883, under the signature of Un Comité de Dames, Casgrain praised and promoted "Angéline de Montbrun" in the Quebec newspaper *Le Courrier du Canada*, since, as he had said to Chauveau the day before, "[women] must try to achieve their literary success in our country, just as men have had theirs." He managed to get Léger Brousseau* to publish the book, for which he himself wrote the preface, and to persuade Louis Fréchette*, Narcisse-Henri-Édouard Faucher* de Saint-Maurice, Chauveau, and the poet Alfred Garneau to write reviews of it. He did not succeed, however, in inducing Laure Conan to accept the part of his preface in which he revealed her true identity. "I have never allowed my name to be associated with my pseudonym," she told him on 14 Jan. 1884, after asking Garneau to intercede with him on her behalf. The hard-fought battle over her pseudonym led to a coolness between these two headstrong individuals, and they apparently exchanged no more letters from the time the book appeared, in 1884, until a few weeks before Casgrain's death in 1904.

Laure Conan was now definitely launched on her career. During a visit to Europe in 1884–85, Bruchési even took the opportunity to bring her to the attention of the writers Pauline de La Ferronnays (who wrote using her married name, Mrs Augustus Craven), Xavier Marmier, and René Bazin, with whom she would exchange a few letters. Because the intimist genres encouraged critics to reveal her identity against her will, and also because the subject of "À travers les ronces," a story published in the Quebec magazine *Les Nouvelles Soirées canadiennes* in 1883, had struck her as "tedious and unrewarding" (as she confessed to Sister Marie de Saint-François-Xavier on 20 April of that year), she now turned instead to historical novels and biography. Endowed with a prodigious

memory, she could recite passages from the many authors she had read and quote them in her works. Her reading included Dante, Jacques-Bénigne Bossuet, Jonathan Swift, Goethe, Alphonse de Lamartine, Victor Hugo, and Eugénie de Guérin, as well as the Bible and the church fathers. The Canadian works she referred to included those of Samuel de Champlain*, François-Xavier Garneau*, Crémazie, and Edmond de Nevers [Boisvert*], as well as the Jesuit *Relations*. In fact, critics would accuse her of alluding to these numerous sources of inspiration too frequently in her stories.

To document the work that would become *À l'œuvre et à l'épreuve*, which tells the story of the martyr Charles Garnier*, Laure Conan approached historians Louis-Édouard Bois*, Alfred DUCLOS De Celles (through Alfred Garneau's daughter Élodie), and Hospice-Anthelme-Jean-Baptiste Verreau*, as well as the Jesuit Joseph-Édouard Désy, but with little success. Since she could no longer depend on Casgrain, she herself began looking for a publisher and negotiated her financial terms. Offering her new novel to Mgr Thomas-Étienne Hamel for *Le Canada français*, a periodical published by the Université Laval at Quebec, she pointed out on 17 Feb. 1889: "Our poor Crémazie wanted Canadian writers who did their work carefully to be paid four or five dollars per page – regular size. This is what I would like for my novel." Through Father Désy, she eventually got *À l'œuvre et à l'épreuve* printed at Quebec in 1891. It was a novel for which the French government would award her the Ordre des Palmes Académiques in 1898. An edition commissioned by Marguerite d'Orléans, Princess Czartoryska, brought out in Paris in 1893, would give her a good deal of trouble because of the printer's refusal to pay the royalties in full. She encountered the same kind of problem in 1897, when the publishers J.-A. and M.-E. Leprohon marketed a pirated edition of *Un amour vrai* in Montreal under the title *Larmes d'amour*. She sued for damages, but unfortunately lost the case, which was closed in 1899.

At the time when Laure Conan began a career in journalism, after 1890, the mass-market newspapers served various interests (political, religious, social, and cultural) and readerships. Women were taking an increasingly important place in this field and making their contribution to it in many different ways. For example, in the December 1893 issue of the Montreal paper *Le Coin du feu*, she replied to Joséphine Dandurand [MARCHAND]: "I confess to you, madam, that it seems to me not very desirable for us [to have] the right to vote. But, if it were ever granted to us – and this is a matter I care little about – I am convinced that women could hardly make worse use of it than men [do]." It was only rarely, however, that the writer publicly expressed her political beliefs or her opinion on women's demands. As for her religious beliefs, that was quite another matter.

From 1894 to 1898 Laure Conan, who was living in Saint-Hyacinthe at the time, edited a periodical entitled *La Voix du Précieux Sang*, for $800 a year, plus room and board. She would contribute 90 articles to it, mostly religious biographies (including those of St Catherine of Siena, Jeanne Mance*, St Perpetua, St Felicity, and the Abbé de Rancé). In 1913 these would be collected into a volume brought out in Montreal under the title *Physionomies de saints*. In 1896–97 and again from 1903 to 1906 she contributed 20 biographies to *Le Rosaire et les autres dévotions dominicaines* (shortened in 1902 to *Le Rosaire*), a periodical published by the Dominicans of Saint-Hyacinthe. These articles and others (including a biography of Louis Hébert*) would make up a volume entitled *Silhouettes canadiennes*, which came out at Quebec in 1917 and again in 1922. From 1902 to 1907 Laure Conan wrote essays for the Montreal magazine *Le Journal de Françoise* [*see* Robertine Barry*], including in 1903 "La correspondance de Mme Julie Lavergne" – Lavergne was a French woman of letters whom she reputedly knew – and in 1904 "Un exemple aux femmes malheureuses en ménage" and "Vos morts," as well as stories and legends for children. Pieces by her can also be found in several other periodicals. She contributed 195 articles in all to Quebec publications.

In 1900 Laure Conan wrote an account of "Nos établissements d'éducation" for *Women of Canada: their life and work*, a collection prepared for the universal exposition in Paris and very probably published in Montreal, where she brought out (in serial form and as a book) *L'oublié*, a novel intended "to shed light on ... the beauty [and] the poetic grandeur of Montreal's early days," as she had told Verreau on 17 April 1899. But she was growing tired. "Mentally, I live in a terrible and very painful state of isolation," she confided to Abbé Henri-Arthur Scott on 1 Dec. 1900. Yet she had many faithful correspondents, even outside the country. It was, indeed, her French network that would arrange for her to receive a Prix Montyon from the Académie Française for *L'oublié* in June 1903. Joseph Lavergne (son of the late Julie Lavergne) and Hector Fabre* (the representative in Paris of the provincial and federal governments) in all likelihood had been behind this movement to recognize the first woman in French Canada to pursue a literary career. From then on the novelist's works were more widely circulated in schools, in both Quebec and Ontario. But Laure Conan had to endure many humiliations, in comparison, for example, to Louis Fréchette, who had been awarded a Prix Montyon in 1880. "Such gentlemen get everything, and I will always be the victim if you do not honour me with your patronage," she wrote to Prime Minister Sir Wilfrid Laurier* on 18

April 1904. On 6 April she had pointed out to him, "If I were a man, I would be treated very differently." In 1907, following the success of *L'oublié*, the novelist decided, on the advice of Father Edmond Rottot, to write a dramatized version of it, *Aux jours de Maisonneuve*.

Towards the end of her life, Laure Conan returned to intimist fiction. The open diary of a woman alienated by the emptiness of her life provides the framework for *L'obscure souffrance* and *La vaine foi*. The first was serialized in the *Revue canadienne* in 1915 and 1919 and published as a book at Quebec in 1919. The second came out in Montreal in 1921 in *La Revue nationale* and in book form. These works are not really novels, but rather collections of selected thoughts, bringing together the torments of a woman who, like Félicité Angers herself, was profoundly affected by existential, romantic, and religious crises. The writing is concise and strong, marked by a maturity lacking in *Angéline de Montbrun*. In a letter to her on 29 Feb. 1920, Albert LOZEAU commented on the "high moral value" of the thoughts expressed by Faustine in *L'obscure souffrance*. From 1910 to 2 July 1923 the novelist stayed regularly at the institute of the Little Daughters of St Joseph on Rue Notre-Dame-de-Lourdes in Montreal. In the fall of 1920 she sold her possessions at auction and left the family home. She spent the summers of 1922 and 1923 in Saint-André, near Kamouraska, with the Sisters of Charity, where no doubt she frequently saw her dear friend Thomas Chapais, with whom she had secretly fallen in love. She busied herself with her publications and the production of her play, *Aux jours de Maisonneuve*, which was finally staged in Montreal on 14 March 1921 under the auspices of the Société Saint-Jean-Baptiste de Montréal, thanks to its president, Victor Morin. Because of the indifferent reception it received, it was not put on again, and it would not be published until 1974, in Montreal. In 1886 Laure Conan published at Quebec *Si les Canadiennes le voulaient!*, a dramatic work that had never been performed. Her plays, in which descriptions and interior monologues steal the spotlight from the dialogue, do not have the solidity of her so-called psychological novels.

In the winter of 1923 Félicité Angers was preparing an historical novel to enter in competition for the Prix David. She would finish writing it at the Villa Notre-Dame des Bois, run by the Religious of Jesus and Mary in Sillery, where she had been living since September 1923. On 10 March 1924 she sought advice from Lionel Groulx*: "I am working on my novel. ... For the title, I am wavering between *Au tournant tragique*, *Au sombre tournant* and *Sur l'épave, 1760*." On 18 May she asked Chapais to send for Mgr Eugène Lapointe* to hear her confession. Although she was in pain, she completed her novel on 20 May at eleven o'clock in the morning. The deadline had passed, yet she believed it might still be accepted by the jury. Six days later, Dr Roland Desmeules, her grandnephew, diagnosed her condition as ovarian cancer. She was operated on by Dr Arthur Simard*, but died of heart failure on 6 June at the Hôtel-Dieu at Quebec. She bequeathed almost all her possessions and royalties to Mgr Ovide Charlebois*, a missionary whose courage she had always admired. Her last novel, which was finally given the title *La sève immortelle*, would be published in Montreal in 1925 by Chapais, the executor of her will. Félicité Angers was buried in La Malbaie, in a plot next to that of Pierre-Alexis Tremblay. In 1924, in *La Voix de Jésus-Marie*, her unidentified biographer from Sillery would sum up her life in these words: "She served three great loves: her God, her country, and her pen."

MANON BRUNET

[The author would like to thank Sister Éliane Angers, of the convent of the Sisters Adorers of the Precious Blood in Trois-Rivières, Qué., for her recollections.

The following archives hold documents by or about Félicité Angers: ANQ-M, P82/109–1574; P133; ANQ-Q, CE304-S3, 10 janv. 1845; P406; ANQ-SLSJ, P2, docs.725A–Q; dossier 35.27; Arch. de la Chancellerie de l'Archevêché de Montréal, 901.174 (Mgr Bruchési, corr. avec auteurs), .2.4 (Laure Conan); 990.070 (Élie Auclair, corr. avec auteurs), .2.6 (Laure Conan); RLBR (reg. des lettres de Mgr Bruchési), 5: 381–82. Arch. de la Chancellerie de l'Évêché de Saint-Hyacinthe, Qué., Reg. des lettres des évêques; Arch. de la Compagnie de Jésus, Prov. du Canada Français (Saint-Jérôme, Qué.), BO-165 (Émile Benoist), 3; Arch. de l'Univ. de Montréal, P56 (fonds Victor-Morin); Arch. de l'Univ. Laval, P225 (fonds Thomas-Chapais); Arch. des Religieuses de Jésus-Marie (Sillery, Qué.); Arch. des Religieuses Hospitalières de Saint-Joseph (Montréal); Arch. des Sœurs Adoratrices du Précieux-Sang (Saint-Hyacinthe), Chemise V.E.2 (Angers, Félicité, ou Laure Conan), 1879–85, 1895–1918, sans date. Arch. du Monastère des Ursulines (Québec); Arch. du Monastère des Ursulines (Trois-Rivières), III-C-2.13-277 (fonds sœur Marguerite-Marie [Eugénie Lasalle]); Arch. du Séminaire de Nicolet, Qué., F003 (L.-É. Bois); Arch. du Séminaire de Saint-Hyacinthe, AFG1 (fonds C.-P. Choquette); AFG2 (fonds Émile Chartier); AFG13 (fonds Rémi Ouellette); AFG34 (fonds F.-X. Solis); Bibliothèque Nationale du Québec (Montréal), MSS 231 (fonds L.-H. Fréchette); Centre de Recherche Lionel-Groulx (Outremont, Qué.), P1 (fonds Lionel Groulx), A, 845; LAC, MG 26, G; MG 29, D27, D40; MG 30, D56; LMS-0009; MCQ-DSQ, P8, P9, P14, P32, P40; MCQ-FSQ, SME 9/44/62, 66, 105, 116, 165; SME 9/165/86; Musée de Charlevoix (La Malbaie, Qué.), P1 (fonds Roland Gagné); P4 (fonds Famille Desmeules); P10 (fonds Laure Conan); Univ. of Ottawa, Morisset Library, Rare Books, Laure Conan, *L'oublié* (Montreal, 1900), in which two letters from Laure Conan to Henri d'Arles [Henri Beaudé] are enclosed; VM-DGDA, BM2, S10, D11.

No exhaustive bibliography for the life and works of Félicité Angers has been published. The author has drawn up a list that includes Angers's writings for periodicals, all the editions of her books, and reviews of her work, as well as articles in newspapers and magazines, theses, dissertations, chapters of books, and monographs written about her. A copy of this list, which completes and in some cases corrects the works mentioned below, is available at the DCB. M.B.]

Le Devoir, 7 juin 1924. Nicole Bourbonnais, "*Angéline de Montbrun*: à la jonction du vécu et du littéraire," in *L'aventure des lettres pour Roger Le Moine*, Michel Gaulin et P.-L. Vaillancourt, édit. (Orléans, Ont., 1999), 63–77. Laure Conan [Félicité Angers], *J'ai tant de sujets de désespoir: correspondance, 1878–1924*, J.-N. Dion, édit. (Montréal, 2002); *Œuvres romanesques*, Roger Le Moine, édit. (3v., Montréal, 1974–75). Renée Des Ormes [Léonide Ferland], "Glanures dans les papiers pâlis de Laure Conan," *La Rev. de l'univ. Laval* (Québec), 9 (1954–55): 120–35; "Laure Conan: un bouquet de souvenirs," *La Rev. de l'univ. Laval*, 6 (1951–52): 383–91. René Dionne et Pierre Cantin, *Bibliographie de la critique de la littérature québécoise et canadienne-française dans les revues canadiennes (1760–1899)* (Ottawa, 1992). *DOLQ*, vols.1–2. Micheline Dumont, "Laure Conan," Académie Canadienne-Française, *Cahiers* (Montréal), 7 (1963): 61–72. D. M. Hayne et Marcel Tirol, *Bibliographie critique du roman canadien-français, 1837–1900* ([Québec et Toronto], 1968). Annette Hayward, "Les religieuses ratées du roman québécois avant 1960," in *La vieille fille: lectures d'un personnage*, Lucie Joubert et Annette Hayward, édit. (Montréal, 2000), 51–82. Sœur Jean de l'Immaculée [Suzanne Blais], "*Angéline de Montbrun*," *Arch. des lettres canadiennes* (Montréal et Paris), 3 (1964): 105–22; "*Angéline de Montbrun*: étude littéraire et psychologique" (mémoire de MA, univ. d'Ottawa, 1962). Maurice Lemire, "Félicité Angers sous l'éclairage de sa correspondance," *Voix et images* (Montréal), 26 (2000–1): 128–44. Roger Le Moine, "Laure Conan et Pierre-Alexis Tremblay," *Rev. de l'univ. d'Ottawa*, 36 (1966): 258–71. P. de Lokieldo, "Laure Conan à N.-D. des Bois," *La Voix de Jésus-Marie* (Sillery), 4 (1924), no.4: 4. Gabrielle Poulin, "*Angéline de Montbrun* ou les abîmes de la critique," *Rev. d'hist. littéraire du Québec et du Canada français* (Montréal), no.5 (hiver–printemps 1983): 125–32. Louise Simard, *Laure Conan: la romancière aux rubans* (Montréal, 1995).

ANGUS, RICHARD BLADWORTH, banker, railway executive, and businessman; b. 28 May 1831 in Bathgate, Scotland, son of Alexander Angus, a merchant, and Margaret Forrest; m. 13 June 1857 Mary Anne Daniels (d. 1913) in Manchester, England, and they had six daughters and three sons; d. 17 Sept. 1922 in Senneville, Que.

The eighth of 12 children, Richard Bladworth Angus was educated at Bathgate Academy and then worked in Manchester as a clerk in the Manchester and Liverpool District Bank. He and his wife, the daughter of a wine merchant there, immigrated to Montreal in 1857. On his arrival, he secured employment with the Bank of Montreal as a bookkeeper-clerk at an annual salary of $600. Combining good looks with hard work and a mastery of figures and finance, he advanced rapidly. He was placed in charge of the bank's Chicago agency in 1861. Two years later he was promoted to second agent in New York at $2,400 a year. After returning to Montreal in 1864, he was appointed assistant manager and the following year he became interim manager of the Montreal office. On 2 Nov. 1869 he succeeded Edwin Henry King* as general manager with an annual salary of $8,000. He proved popular in the position, improving relations with the federal government, for which the Bank of Montreal was fiscal agent. In spite of the economic depression of the 1870s, the bank posted respectable profits during his tenure.

Angus's position provided him with opportunities for private investment at a time when conflict of interest regulations were virtually non-existent. In 1868 he had joined Montreal businessman George STEPHEN and Stephen's cousin Donald Alexander Smith* as investors in a textile mill, the Paton Manufacturing Company of Sherbrooke [see Andrew Paton*]. By the 1870s Stephen and Smith became interested in the development of railways in the Canadian northwest. Smith and Minnesota businessman James Jerome Hill* had decided to purchase the bankrupt St Paul and Pacific Railroad, but lacked financing for the scheme. In August 1877 Angus accompanied Stephen to see the line. Their meeting with Hill laid the foundation for the formation of the lucrative partnership George Stephen and Associates. Although Angus was not among the associates, he was closely involved in many of their ventures. In 1878 they purchased the St Paul line for $5,500,000. Unable to finance the deal with London investment banks, they provided cash and collateral and Stephen, now president of the Bank of Montreal, organized short-term financing from the bank.

The deal caused ripples in the financial community in Montreal, because of its audacity and because of rumours that Stephen had used his position to secure loans with preferred rates and limited collateral. Angus remained immune from the controversy until his resignation as general manager was announced on 15 Aug. 1879. The press hinted that he had left because of the excessive loans made to Stephen and his associates. The reports caused embarrassment for both Angus and the bank. His departure was also seen as a vote of no-confidence in the Canadian banking industry. Within two months the reason for his resignation became clear. Stephen confirmed that Angus had become vice-president of the railway, which had been renamed the St Paul, Minneapolis and Manitoba Railroad.

Late in 1879 Angus moved to St Paul, Minn., where he worked closely with Hill, constructing and improving the line. By 1880, however, he was spending as much time accompanying Stephen on numerous trips to Ottawa, New York, and London to negotiate the building of a Canadian transcontinental line. When the Canadian Pacific Railway contract was signed in October, Angus was listed as one of the members of the syndicate. He held the position of general manager until William Cornelius Van Horne* took office in 1882 and he sat as a member of the railway's executive committee. Angus would serve as a director and committee member for over 40 years. During the negotiations to secure additional land grants and cash subsidies for the CPR, he was often at Stephen's side. They proved to be a formidable team, with Stephen providing the acumen and Angus the analysis. As vice-president, Angus was entrusted with the creation of the eastern network, notably the extension of the Ontario and Quebec Railway and the purchase of the western section of the Quebec, Montreal, Ottawa and Occidental Railway in 1882.

By 1883 the CPR syndicate was showing increasing signs of strain. Hill resigned from the railway's board of directors in May, believing the advancement of the CPR and the St Paul line to be incompatible. Founding director Duncan McIntyre* resigned in May 1884. Author Pierre Berton* suggests that Angus was also tempted to abandon the syndicate and lost Stephen's confidence as a result. Although there is no evidence pointing to a rift of this magnitude, Angus's sang-froid was sorely tested by the fragility of the CPR's finances. The involvement of Stephen, Smith, and Angus with the St Paul railroad had made it increasingly difficult to lobby successfully for additional financial assistance to the CPR. Angus had finally resigned from the St Paul line in February 1884. Although the extent of his personal holdings in the company is unknown, they were at least in part responsible for his growing fortune. He remained vice-president of the CPR after Stephen resigned from an active role in 1888. Apparently never aspiring to the position, he supported Stephen's selection of Van Horne as president and, 11 years later, Van Horne's choice of Thomas George SHAUGHNESSY as his successor.

Angus's growing wealth had allowed him to invest in the empire of companies associated with the CPR or its directors, such as the Canada North-West Land Company, the Royal Trust Company, and the Dominion Bridge Company Limited. He joined Van Horne and former CPR contractors James Ross* and William MACKENZIE as an investor in street railways, in Winnipeg, Montreal, and Toronto. Prior to his death he would be the principal shareholder in Mackenzie's Toronto Power Company Limited. He also invested with Van Horne in the Laurentide Paper Company Limited, was among the founding financiers of Benjamin Tingley Rogers*'s British Columbia Sugar Refinery Limited, and was a principal backer of the Federal Telephone Company.

Angus also played a role in maintaining the close relationship between the CPR and the Bank of Montreal, whose growth in western Canada closely mirrored that of the railway. On 12 May 1891 he had returned to the bank as a director. After the death of Sir George Alexander Drummond*, he was elected president in July 1910. Two years later he was one of the bank's largest shareholders. He seemed content to work in the shadows, never aspiring to the perquisites which normally accompanied the presidency. It was widely reported that he had refused a knighthood in 1910. He continued as president until 1913 and would remain a director until his death.

By 1885 Angus and his large family were living in a sumptuous residence on Drummond Street. It would provide a suitable home for his art collection. He began actively buying from Montreal and London dealers in the late 1870s. His collection showed discernment, with fine examples of work by European masters. Angus served as president of the Art Association of Montreal in 1888–89. In 1889 he donated six paintings to the association, the most important gift since its foundation and its first major one in contemporary art. In 1886 he had built a home in the enclave of country estates at Senneville. Known as Pine Bluff, it was designed by John William Hopkins and his son Edward C. In 1898 he hired architect Edward MAXWELL to transform it into a Tudor Revival house. After it burned in 1899, Angus had it rebuilt to the designs of Maxwell and his brother William Sutherland.

A governor of McGill University, Angus was also president of the board of governors of the Royal Victoria Hospital. He was one of the founders of the Alexandra Hospital, opened in 1906, and he served on the board of the Montreal General Hospital and as vice-president of the Victorian Order of Nurses. He was involved in his community as well as a governor of the Numismatic and Antiquarian Society of Montreal, as president of the Fraser Institute's free library and the St Andrew's Society, and as a mason. A founder, in 1889, of the Mount Royal Club, he had more than a dozen club memberships in cities throughout Canada. He remained active until the end of his life, embarking on a European tour in 1921, at age 90.

An important figure in both banking and railways, Richard Bladworth Angus occupied one of the most prominent positions in Canadian banking at age 38. By abandoning this plum post for a highly speculative railway venture, he clearly illustrated the allure of railways and the riches they offered. When he died in 1922, he left an impressive estate, worthy of the railway magnate he had become. Although Stephen has generally been credited with the genius that created the railway empire, Angus was an indispensable lieutenant. His banking experience brought administrative expertise to the syndicate. He had been memorialized in 1904 by the CPR, which named its new repair complex the Angus Shops in his honour. On the day of his funeral, 19 Sept. 1922, the CPR stopped all trains for two minutes – a symbolic gesture to one of its founding partners.

ALEXANDER REFORD

James Jerome Hill Reference Library (St Paul, Minn.), J. J. Hill papers (mfm. at LAC). LAC, MG 29, A28. *Gazette* (Montreal), 16, 19–20 Aug. 1879; 18 Sept. 1922. *Globe*, 3 May 1922. *Montreal Daily Star*, 18 Sept. 1922. Christopher Armstrong and H. V. Nelles, *Monopoly's moment: the organization and regulation of Canadian utilities, 1830–1930* (Philadelphia, 1986). Bank of Montreal, *Annual general meeting* (Montreal), 1869–70, 1872, 1875, 1891–1900; *List of stockholders of the Bank of Montreal . . .* (Montreal), 1912. Pierre Berton, *The last spike: the great railway, 1881–1885* (Toronto and Montreal, 1971). Michael Bliss, *Northern enterprise: five centuries of Canadian business* (Toronto, 1987). J. M. Brooke, *Discerning tastes: Montreal collectors, 1880–1920* (exhibition catalogue, Montreal Museum of Fine Arts, 1989). *Canada collects: European painting, 1860–1960* (exhibition catalogue, Montreal Museum of Fine Arts, 1960). *Canadian Railway and Marine World* (Toronto), October 1922. Merrill Denison, *Canada's first bank: a history of the Bank of Montreal*, (2v., Toronto and Montreal, 1966–67), 2. *European paintings in Canadian collections*, essay and ed. R. H. Hubbard (2v., Toronto, 1956–62), 1 (*Earlier schools*). R. B. Fleming, *The railway king of Canada: Sir William Mackenzie, 1849–1923* (Vancouver, 1991). France Gagnon-Pratte, *Country houses for Montrealers, 1892–1924: the architecture of E. and W. S. Maxwell* (Montreal, 1987). Heather Gilbert, *The life of Lord Mount Stephen . . .* (2v., Aberdeen, Scot., 1965–77). *Land to energy, 1882–1982*, ed. C. S. Lee ([Calgary, 1982]). Gloria Lesser, "The homes, furnishings and collections of R. B. Angus (1831–1922)," in *Living in style: fine furniture in Victorian Quebec*, general ed. J. R. Porter (exhibition catalogue, Montreal Museum of Fine Arts, 1993). Albro Martin, *James J. Hill and the opening of the northwest* (New York, 1976; repr., intro. W. T. White, St Paul, 1991). *Standard dict. of Canadian biog.* (Roberts and Tunnell). B. J. Young, *Promoters and politicians: the north-shore railways in the history of Quebec, 1854–85* (Toronto, 1978).

APPLEBY, CHARLES, farmer; b. 25 Dec. 1866 in Jamaica; d. unmarried 12 March 1929 in Essondale (Port Coquitlam), B.C.

Of African descent, Charles Appleby immigrated to Canada in 1896, according to census records. After living for a time in British Columbia's lower mainland, he moved to Salt Spring Island, near the southern tip of Vancouver Island and the second largest of the Gulf Islands. He would reside there for more than 20 years, eking out an impoverished existence as a market gardener and farmer.

British Columbia's first black immigrants had arrived from San Francisco in 1858, part of the diverse population drawn by the Fraser River gold rush [*see* Mifflin Wistar Gibbs*]. Many also sought freedom from California's racially restrictive laws. Black settlers came to Salt Spring in 1859. Rich with game and good farming areas, it was part of the unsurveyed region opened by Governor James Douglas* in response to complaints about high land prices [*see* Joseph Despard Pemberton*]. On 26 July 1859, 29 settlers of different nationalities were given permission to pre-empt land on the island. The next day, black settlers Armstead Buckner, Abraham Copeland, and William Robinson were part of the initial group to set off for Salt Spring. Other blacks would follow, to brave the often perilous and isolated circumstances to create homes. Several would become involved in local civic and provincial affairs. By the end of the century a number of these early black settlers had left the island, some because of racial tensions and some because the end of the Civil War had made a return to the United States attractive. Others had relocated to explore economic opportunities elsewhere, and some had died. Descendants of several pioneer black families were still there, however, when Charles Appleby joined the community in 1896.

A photograph taken of Appleby around 1910 shows a thin, wiry man with greying hair and a pipe; in his forties, he looks over sixty. According to some islanders, he was a slightly mad but harmless person who possessed the gift of second sight. Leonard Tolson states in his memoirs that Appleby predicted the sinking of the steamship *Iroquois*, which on 10 April 1911 set out from Sidney, B.C., for the Gulf Islands, filled with freight and approximately 40 passengers. Less than a mile out, it encountered rough seas, some of the cargo shifted, and the ship sank with the loss of at least 21 lives. Tolson recalled that before the disaster Appleby had "stumbled up to a group of men, weeping and hysterical, and told them that he had just seen the *Iroquois* sinking and many people drowning. The men did not take this too seriously, knowing that his mind was unhinged."

Appleby lived on Salt Spring for almost ten more years, evidently with continuing problems. On 6 April 1921 he was admitted to the Provincial Hospital for the Insane at Essondale. Its intake file stated that "this patient's mental condition is such that no reliable family or personal history could be obtained from him. He will never give the same answer twice in succession." His physical examination found him to be 5 feet 6½ inches, 118 pounds, poorly nourished, and "showing marked advanced changes of senility." He had been committed by Dr Eva Maud Sutherland of Ganges Harbour on Salt Spring, whom he had told, among other stories, that he was the son of Queen Elizabeth I and that he had once gone out to catch his neighbour's horse, which was full of jewels. Appleby was not a source of trouble, except, as Sutherland and the provincial constable on Salt Spring noted, when he swore and was abusive towards children who teased him. He never left the asylum, and died in its farm annex.

SHERRY EDMUNDS-FLETT

BCA, GR-2880, 90, file 6815; GR-2951, no.1929-09-424334 (mfm.). LAC, RG 31, C1, 1901, New Westminster, B.C., div.2: 35. Salt Spring Island Hist. Soc. Arch. (Salt Spring Island, B.C.), Toynbee Coll. (photographs). Bea Hamilton, *Salt Spring Island* (Vancouver, 1969). *Snapshots of early Salt Spring and other favoured islands*, comp. R. M. Toynbee (Ganges, B.C., 1978), 56.

ARCAND, NARCISSE (baptized **Narcisse-Joseph-Philias**), carpenter and trade union leader; b. 24 April 1871 in Deschambault, Que., eighth child of Narcisse Arcand, a farmer, and Mélanie Belisle; m. 6 Oct. 1896 Marie-Anne Mathieu in Montreal; d. 14 Feb. 1927 in Montreal, and was survived by three sons and six daughters.

Narcisse Arcand moved to Montreal around 1895 and worked as a carpenter. By 1900 he had joined Local 134 of the United Brotherhood of Carpenters and Joiners of America, the local of French-speaking carpenters and joiners in that city. Originating in the United States, the brotherhood was one of the largest trade unions in Canada at the start of the 20th century. It practised a form of business unionism, based on negotiation of working conditions and on respect for the capitalist system, in the tradition of American Gomperism, and it claimed jurisdiction over virtually all the trades connected with the construction industry. In 1912 Arcand would even propose that the Amalgamated Society of Carpenters and Joiners, a British union in competition with the brotherhood, be expelled from the Trades and Labor Congress of Canada (TLC) in order to protect the monopoly of the United Brotherhood.

Arcand was soon playing an important role within his union. In 1902 he became its provincial organizer, a position he would hold for 23 years. He was active everywhere, both in Montreal and in outlying parts of the province. His work led to the creation of many locals of carpenters and joiners, including Thetford Mines Local 1554 in 1907 and Saint-Hyacinthe Local 1108 in 1915. Even in Trois-Rivières, where the Catholic unions were trying to stem the rise of the "international" unions, the majority of carpenters and joiners belonged to the United Brotherhood during World War I. In 1910 Arcand had been a delegate to its convention in the United States. From 1921 to 1927, during the last six years of his life, he was president of the union's provincial council, and in 1925 he was secretary of the Montreal district council. He also held other offices in the Canadian trade union movement. A member of the provincial executive committee of the TLC in 1913, 1914, and 1918, he became its president in 1917. For a few months in 1916 he had worked as a fair-wage officer in the Department of Labour in Ottawa, taking the place of Victor Dubreuil*, who had recently died. He resigned in a huff at the end of August, after responsibility for the miners in Thetford Mines was taken out of his hands.

Carpenters and joiners were not Arcand's only concern as a union organizer. In 1917, for instance, he supported the steps taken by the Western Federation of Miners to organize the miners of Thetford Mines into a militant union outside the Catholic fold. Interventions of this kind would make him a favourite target of Roman Catholic authorities, who denounced what they called the takeover of Canadian unionism by Americans.

In addition to his trade union activities, Arcand participated in the political life of Montreal, where he was involved in the political battles of the early 20th century. One of the first activists in the Labour party, which had been founded in Montreal in 1899 [*see* Joseph-Alphonse Rodier*], he was campaign manager for Alphonse VERVILLE, its candidate in the riding of Hochelaga in the provincial election of 1904. Verville was defeated but would be elected to the House of Commons for Maisonneuve in 1906. Arcand himself ran for the party in Montreal-Dorion in the 1912 provincial election. He received 912 votes, but the seat was won by Liberal Georges Mayrand. Arcand's platform included the eight-hour day, municipal ownership of public services such as street railways and street lighting, the nationalization of railways, abolition of child labour for those under 14 years of age, and numerous political measures such as the use of referendums. Arcand suffered another defeat in the provincial election of 1923, this time at the hands of Conservative Adolphe L'Archevêque in Montreal-Mercier. He had based his campaign on the need for "reasonable" wages for public works employees. In 1917, having been mandated by the TLC to reorganize the Labour party, whose central committee he chaired, he had helped set up the Quebec provincial section of the Canadian Labor party. He was a delegate to the founding convention of this section in November 1917, as well as to that of a local one, the Montreal Assembly, a few months later.

Arcand took an active interest in school questions early in the 20th century. He was one of the spokesmen for the Labour party when it submitted a brief to the royal commission set up in 1909 to look into the Montreal Catholic schools. Calling for free and compulsory education, he directly opposed the Montreal clergy, whom he accused of proscribing those wanting to discuss educational concerns. He declared himself in favour of annexing all the Catholic school boards on the island of Montreal to the Montreal Catholic School Commission, in order to ensure greater uniformity in school administration and the choice of textbooks.

From 1923 Narcisse Arcand devoted himself almost exclusively to his work as an organizer for the United Brotherhood of Carpenters and Joiners of America and gave much less attention to other struggles. He died at home on 14 Feb. 1927, at the age of 55. Of the nine children who survived him, his son Adrien*, leader of the Canadian fascist movement, is certainly the best known.

BERNARD DANSEREAU

ANQ-Q, CE301-S25, 26 janv. 1851, 24 avril 1871; CE601-S1, 6 oct. 1896. *Labor World* (Montreal), 9 Dec. 1916, 2 June 1917, 19 Feb. 1927, May–June 1950. *Le Pays* (Montréal), 14 mai 1910, 20 avril 1912. *La Presse*, 20 avril 1912; 7 févr., 27 avril 1916. *Le Soleil*, 8 juill. 1917. R. H. Babcock, *Gompers in Canada: a study in American continentalism before the First World War* (Toronto and Buffalo, N.Y., 1974), 146. Bernard Dansereau, "Congrès des métiers et du travail du Canada, comité exécutif, province de Québec, 1889–1937," RCHTQ [Regroupement des Chercheurs-Chercheures en Hist. des Travailleurs et Travailleuses du Québec], *Bull.* (Montréal), 23 (1997), no.1: 41–44. *Directory*, Montreal, 1897–1900. Robert Gagnon, *Histoire de la Commission des écoles catholiques de Montréal; le développement d'un réseau d'écoles publiques en milieu urbain* ([Montréal], 1996). *Résultats électoraux depuis 1867*.

ARCHIBALD, WALTER PALMER, Salvation Army officer, civil servant, and judge; b. 21 Sept. 1860 in Truro, N.S., son of William Pitt Archibald and Phœbe Ann Huestis; m. 25 Jan. 1893, in Hamilton, Ont., Captain Jessie Butler of the Salvation Army, and they had two daughters; d. 17 Jan. 1922 in Ottawa.

Walter Archibald was accepted as a cadet in the Salvation Army on 14 Dec. 1885 after being called to the army at a meeting in his home town. An athletic youth who was remembered as a "champion fancy skater of the Maritime provinces," he later described himself "as a wanderer from the word go" who had been born to Christian parents but "when quite young had learned the habits of drink and tobacco." His conversion reformed him. As a member of the Salvation Army, he was sent to Saint John, Moncton, and Charlottetown. He first went to Toronto in November 1886, and eventually involved himself in the army's rescue and training homes for men and in the Children's Shelter; about 1897 he became engaged in its Prison Gate movement, established in 1890 to help men released from jail. On 5 April 1900, a year after the federal parole system had been instituted, he was granted special leave to serve voluntarily as a parole officer while retaining his secretaryship of the Prison Gate program. Four months after his promotion to brigadier on 1 June 1904, he appeared at a conference under the title "commissioner of parole" for the Salvation Army.

With its permission, Archibald resigned his position (and likely gave up his commission) to assume a permanent appointment on 1 May 1905 as Canada's first dominion parole officer, in the penitentiary branch of the Department of Justice. He had to borrow the money to move his family from Toronto to Ottawa – after 20 years with the Salvation Army he had accumulated no financial assets. In his new post, which he would hold until his death at age 61, he was responsible for overseeing prisoners released under the terms of the Ticket of Leave Act of 1899, Canada's first parole legislation. He worked alone for the first eight years, travelling across the country to interview and supervise offenders. He described his work in a report in July 1911 to justice minister Sir Allen Bristol Aylesworth*. During the previous year he had interviewed 823 prisoners, visited 315 men out on parole, helped 67 of them find employment, and intervened in several family situations to reconcile separated partners. He claimed that the great majority of those released since the system's inception "have not betrayed their trust or honour." Discharge from penitentiary, he believed, should be gradual. "The man on parole is still a prisoner in the eyes of the law, and his release is simply a test of his ability and willingness to maintain himself as an honest citizen." He advocated stronger measures to prevent crime by improving social conditions, especially in Canadian cities, "which are producing a type of vicious criminality equal to any in quality (if not quantity) in the civilized world."

Although he questioned some proposals for reform, such as indeterminate sentencing and probation, Archibald carried on a steady campaign of speeches across Canada and abroad on the need for prison reform and the importance of the parole system. He gave addresses at the annual congresses of the National Prison Association of the United States. Speaking to the Empire Club of Canada in Toronto in 1908, he presented his recipe for reforming criminals: "good treatment, a strong and healthy discipline, fair dealing, the criminal's recognition of his own criminality, his desire and willingness to reform, a recognition of the criminal as a human being by outside society, and a recognition by the hand of justice that, while it is necessary and just to punish crime, yet the clemency of a parole is not to be withheld from any really hopeful case." Archibald, who never lost his Salvation Army missionary zeal, described his campaign to improve the climate for parolees as "his work in uplifting the fallen." He acknowledged that he and his wife used $200–300 of his annual salary of $2,650 to assist released prisoners who found themselves in financial trouble. Before he addressed the city council of Regina in 1912, the mayor introduced him as "the eyes, ears and the heart of justice as it is now administered in Canada." The *Moose Jaw Evening Times* (Moose Jaw, Sask.) saw him not as a man "paid to look after criminals, but rather as one who is in love with humanitarian work." In 1920 he was able to look back with pride on what had been accomplished. "The majority of people have been educated to give a man a fair chance coming out of prison to reclaim himself," he told the deputy minister of justice, Edmund Leslie Newcombe*.

Archibald's calls for penal reform and his Christian philanthropy were not universally applauded, however. Police officials intent on controlling and punishing criminals did not always agree with his emphasis on social conditioning as a factor in criminality and juvenile delinquency. John Taylor Gilmour, who as warden of Toronto's Central Prison had worked with Archibald in the Prison Gate program, came to oppose a parole system that had too few resources to provide effective supervision. In an unofficial letter to Newcombe in 1912, he referred to Archibald's "fondness for publicity and the amusing methods he resorts to in obtaining it." He further alleged that the parole officer had improperly solicited money from private individuals to assist prisoners. In rejecting the charges, Archibald responded that Gilmour had been trying for some time "to destroy my influence and character and in my estimation he ranks with any blackhand agency in the Dominion." Newcombe dismissed the allegations and Archibald carried on, unhindered by any other opponent. In 1919 he began to serve as an unpaid judge in Carleton County's Juvenile Court, where he was able to take a humanitarian approach to cases, in contrast to the strictly legal manner of the police magistrates who had tried juveniles formerly.

Archibald died suddenly of heart failure on the evening of 17 Jan. 1922 after leaving a quarterly board meeting at the Dominion Methodist Church, which he had attended since moving to Ottawa; he was survived by his wife and their daughters, Eva May and Frances Willard. He had been a freemason, a supporter of the Sailors' Mission, and a founder of the local Big Brothers and Big Sisters associations. The *Ottawa Evening Journal* described him as the father of the parole system in Canada. In commemoration, the Salvation Army named its first federal halfway house for discharged prisoners, which opened in Toronto in 1983, the W. P. Archibald Centre.

DAVID R. MURRAY

Walter Palmer Archibald is the author of "The parole system – an historical review," *Canadian Law Rev.* (Toronto), 6 (1907): 222–29.

AO, RG 22-354, no.10609; RG 80-5-0-210, no.13257; RG 80-8-0-863, no.9243. LAC, MG 29, D61, 1: 236; RG 13, 173, file 1001; 253, file 2315. Salvation Army, George Scott Railton Heritage Centre, Arch. and Museum (Toronto), W. P. Archibald Centre, hist. and description; W. P. Archibald personnel file. *Ottawa Evening Journal*, 18 Jan. 1922. *War Cry* (Toronto), 16 July 1887, 27 June 1891, 11 Feb. 1893. Can., Parl., *Sessional papers*, 1906, no.34: 15–21, app.A; 1906–7, no.30: 4; 1912, no.34: 9–13. *Canadian men and women of the time* (Morgan; 1912). D. O. Carrigan, *Crime and punishment in Canada: a history* (Toronto, 1991). *Directory*, Toronto, 1893, 1900. Greg Marquis, *Policing Canada's century: a history of the Canadian Association of Chiefs of Police* (Toronto, 1993). National Prison Assoc. of the United States, *Proc. of the annual congress*

(Pittsburgh), 1903: vi, 299–311; 1904: vii, 217–30; (Indianapolis), 1905: 218–19, 305–10. *Standard dict. of Canadian biog.* (Roberts and Tunnell).

ARMOUR, EDWARD DOUGLAS, lawyer, educator, journalist, and poet; b. 26 May 1851 in Port Hope, Upper Canada, son of Robert Armour and Marianne Burton; m. 30 March 1880 Alma Sarah Wossell Ponton (d. 1921) in Belleville, Ont., and they had three sons and three daughters; d. 3 Oct. 1922 in Toronto and was buried there in Prospect Cemetery.

Douglas Armour's Scots grandparents on his father's side immigrated in 1825 with the Robinson settlers [*see* Peter Robinson*] to Peterborough, Upper Canada, where the Reverend Samuel Armour founded the first Church of England parish. The family then turned to the law. Armour's father, Robert, was a barrister and Conservative party activist in Bowmanville and Port Hope, and his uncle John Douglas Armour became chief justice of Ontario before being appointed to the Supreme Court of Canada shortly prior to his death in 1903. Sons and grandsons of Robert and J. D. Armour followed them into the Ontario legal profession.

Having graduated from Trinity College School, Port Hope, in 1869, Douglas Armour enrolled at Trinity College, University of Toronto, but soon left to focus on legal studies. He was called to the bar and admitted as a solicitor in 1876. He practised in Toronto with Alexander Leith, a specialist in real-property law, and eventually succeeded Leith as a local authority on that subject. For most of his career Armour was head of his own firm in partnership with Henry Walter Mickle and other lawyers. D'Alton Lally McCarthy*, later a prominent Toronto counsel, described Armour as a litigator much respected in real-property matters, with "a keen mind but perhaps a rather bitter tongue."

Nineteenth-century law relied on self-education by lawyers, and Armour became a prolific member of the Ontario bar's text-writing fraternity. *A treatise on the investigation of titles to real estate in Ontario . . .* (known as "Armour on titles"), one of several works he wrote, went through four editions between 1887 and 1925. In 1881, with the support of the Toronto legal publisher Carswell and Company, Armour had launched the *Canadian Law Times*, a magazine that provided case reports, theoretical articles, professional news, and commentary. Armour contributed news and editorials to almost every issue, usually asserting Olympian standards and looking sceptically at innovations. Pressure of work obliged him to pass the journal to other editors in 1900; in 1923 it was merged into the Canadian Bar Association's *Canadian Bar Review*.

In his editorials Armour had advocated a centralized law school in Ontario run by the Law Society of Upper Canada. When the society opened such a school at Osgoode Hall in Toronto in 1889 [*see* William Albert Reeve*], he became one of its founding lecturers. Until 1910 he taught real-property law and constitutional law, while continuing his private practice and legal writing. He had been appointed a QC in 1890 and would receive an honorary DCL from Trinity College in 1902.

In 1889–90 Armour condemned Minister of Justice Sir John Sparrow David Thompson*'s refusal to disallow the Jesuits' Estates Act [*see* Honoré Mercier*]. He argued in the *Law Times* that the bill posed a fundamental challenge to crown sovereignty by authorizing the pope to arbitrate a settlement among contending Roman Catholics in Quebec. In the Ontario provincial election of 1890 Armour unsuccessfully ran in Toronto as an independent Conservative in support of the Equal Rights Association, founded to resist Catholic influence in Canada [*see* William Caven*; D'Alton McCarthy*].

As Osgoode Hall's lecturer in constitutional law, Armour taught students that the British North America Act established the central government's authority over the provinces. He opposed legislative interference with private contracts (which he deemed sacred), believed English was the "race language" of Canadians, and was sarcastic about the entry of women into the legal profession.

Soon after retiring from his lectureship (but not his practice) in 1910, Armour was elected a bencher of the Law Society. (His uncle J. D. Armour and his cousin Eric Norman Armour, a Toronto lawyer and crown attorney, served as benchers at other times.) As chairman of the society's legal education committee from 1915 to 1922, Armour was in effect the employer of his former colleagues at the law school. He supervised the waiving of educational requirements for law students who joined the military forces during World War I and helped initiate abbreviated summer courses to speed returned veterans into practice.

Late in life, Armour published two collections of poetry. *Law lyrics* (Toronto, 1918), which ingeniously recast long legal documents into rhyming couplets, satirized and celebrated the legal community. *Echoes from Horace in English verse* (Toronto, 1922) was a collection of rhymes inspired by the classical poet, some of which had first appeared in the new *Canadian Forum* (Toronto). They suggest cleverness more than substantial poetic gifts ("Achilles the haughty / Undoubtedly thought he . . ."). In 1921 Armour became a founding member of the Canadian Authors Association.

Armour had married Alma Ponton, from a Belleville legal family, in 1880. Their son Archibald Douglas joined the Armour and Mickle law firm and edited the 1925 posthumous edition of "Armour on titles." A devout Anglican but sceptical about rigid

Sunday-closing laws and other devotional extremes, Douglas Armour was a delegate to several synods of the Church of England in Canada. Upon his death in 1922 the Law Society honoured him as a man of strong will and a Christian gentleman.

CHRISTOPHER MOORE

The various editions of "Armour on titles" were published in Toronto in 1887, 1894, 1903, and 1925. Armour was also the author of *A treatise on the law of real property, founded on Leith & Smith's edition of Blackstone's commentaries on "The rights of things"* (Toronto, 1901; 2nd ed., 1916); *Essays on the devolution of land upon the personal representative and statutory powers relating thereto: with an appendix of statutes* (Toronto, 1903); and "Notes on Canadian statutes," in the 7th edition of H. S. Theobald, *A concise treatise on the law of wills* (London, 1908). In addition, he was the editor of *Reports of cases argued and determined in the Court of Queen's Bench in Manitoba both at law and in equity, and some cases determined in the county courts during the time of Chief Justice Wood, from 1875 to 1883: being principally judgments of the chief justice* (Toronto and Edinburgh, 1884).

AO, RG 80-5-0-89, no.4084; RG 80-8-0-858, no.5606. Law Soc. of Upper Canada Arch. (Toronto), 1-1 (Convocation, minutes), 1911–22, esp. 23 Nov. 1922; M259 (W. G. C. Howland fonds), D. L. McCarthy, draft autobiography; Curtis Cole, "A history of Osgoode Hall Law School, 1889–1989"; Ontario bar biog. research project database. Trinity College Arch. (Toronto), Student records, 1869–70. *Globe*, 4 Oct. 1922. *Toronto Daily Star*, 4 Oct. 1922. *The Canadian law list* (Toronto), 1876–1922. *Canadian Law Times* (Toronto), 4 (1884): 232; 8 (1888): 69, 276; 9 (1889): 231; 12 (1892): 111. *Canadian men and women of the time* (Morgan; 1912). *Directory*, Toronto, 1906–28. J. R. Miller, *Equal rights: the Jesuits' Estates Act controversy* (Montreal, 1979).

ARMSTRONG, JAMES WILLIAM, teacher, physician, and politician; b. 14 Jan. 1860 in Auburn, N.S., son of James Armstrong, a teacher and farmer, and Elizabeth Pearce; m. 7 April 1897 Mary Campbell in Winnipeg, and they had one son and two daughters; d. there 26 Feb. 1928 and was buried in Elmwood Cemetery.

James W. Armstrong attended Pictou Academy in Nova Scotia, taught school in the province to finance his higher education, and graduated from Acadia College, Wolfville, in 1888 with honours in political economy and history. After travelling west to Manitoba in 1889, he taught for one year at Brandon Collegiate Institute. He enrolled at the Manitoba Medical College and graduated in medicine and surgery in 1893. The next year he opened a practice in Gladstone.

Optimism and boosterism were rife in the west at the turn of the century as railways added branch lines, opening new areas for settlement. In Gladstone, Armstrong did what he could to help the town succeed. By 1899 he had an interest in a drugstore and the neighbouring jewellery store, behind which he had his office, and also in a variety of other businesses: the local newspaper, a livery stable, a boarding-house, and the Gladstone Electric Light and Telephone Company. He was involved in the building of a Baptist church which opened in 1900. The Board of Trade, of which he was treasurer, produced a booklet extolling the virtues of Gladstone.

In addition Armstrong had a busy medical practice. He took a keen interest in public health and served on the provincial Board of Health from 1897 to 1899. He also held a provincial appointment as district health officer. In this post he dealt with a serious outbreak of diphtheria in 1899, tracing contacts and ensuring that cases were isolated. The next year, to further his expertise in hygiene and infectious diseases, he studied at Guy's Hospital in London, England. In 1910 he was appointed inspector of health by the Department of Indian Affairs for the South Lake Manitoba area; in addition he served as health officer for the town and rural municipality of Westbourne. To meet the demands, he kept fast horses and had permission to use a velocipede car on the railway. He also made an agreement with the Canadian Northern Railway to obtain a pass in exchange for free advertising in the *Gladstone Age*. His first automobile was delivered on 12 June 1909.

In 1907 Armstrong had been elected to the Legislative Assembly for the Liberal party in the constituency of Gladstone. He would be re-elected in 1910, 1915, and 1920. Especially after the election of 1910, he took a major part in debates, in opposition to the administration of Rodmond Palen Roblin*. In 1915 the Liberals came to power during a scandal over the construction of the Legislative Building. Armstrong was appointed provincial secretary with responsibility for municipal affairs and the Board of Health in the government of Tobias Crawford Norris*. Among the many pieces of reform legislation brought in by the new government in 1916 were measures which he had supported while in opposition, such as the Manitoba Temperance Act and the School Attendance Act. Presenting amendments to the Public Health Act on 29 Jan. 1916, Armstrong announced that the Board of Health would be reorganized with a permanent staff in order to carry out an active campaign against tuberculosis and infant diseases, increasing prevention in the rural areas. With this extended mandate, the board hired public health nurses, the first in Canada. Speaking to the board's report during the session of 1918, Armstrong was able to point to favourable results after only one full year of operation. Deaths of children under two years caused by diarrhoea and enteritis had dropped from 424 to 277. The nurses had examined 12,179 children.

With the expanded services introduced by the government, the capital commitments made by its predecessor, and the demands of the war and its aftermath, the Norris regime risked unpopularity by raising taxes. Its majority was reduced in the election of 1920, it was defeated in the house in 1922, and in the election of 18 July it was swept away by candidates of the United Farmers of Manitoba. Armstrong did not run.

Curling and shooting were among Armstrong's favourite pastimes. In retirement he managed his business interests and enjoyed golfing. While in Victoria in early 1928 Armstrong took ill and returned to Winnipeg, where he passed away.

ROSEMARY MALAHER

AM, P 2187–92. Man., Legislative Library (Winnipeg), Biog. scrapbooks; Hansard scrapbooks, *Manitoba Free Press* (1907–20), *Winnipeg Telegram* (1907–20). Private arch., R. A. [Stevens] Malaher (Winnipeg), Family bible; Geneal. research done by Merle Armstrong of Waterloo, Ont. *Gladstone Age* (Gladstone, Man.), 21 Feb., 7 March 1907; 17 June 1909; 20 May 1915. *Manitoba Free Press*, 29 Jan. 1916, 9 Feb. 1918. *CPG*, 1907–22. *Gladstone's glory years, 1901–1910*, comp. A. E. MacLennan (Gladstone, 1981). Ross Mitchell, *Medicine in Manitoba; the story of its beginnings* ([Winnipeg, 1955?]). W. L. Morton, *Manitoba: a history* (Toronto, 1957). *Record of the graduates of Acadia University, 1843–1926, arranged by classes*, ed. A. C. Chute (Wolfville, N.S., 1926). F. H. Schofield, *The story of Manitoba* (3v., Winnipeg, 1913).

ARSENAULT, PIERRE-PAUL (baptized **Peter Arseneaux**), Roman Catholic priest, educator, farmer, and folklorist; b. 18 May 1867 in Tignish, P.E.I., son of Sylvain Arsenault and Tharsile Bernard; d. 22 Nov. 1927 in Mont-Carmel, P.E.I.

Pierre-Paul Arsenault was one of the prime movers of the Acadian community in Prince Edward Island early in the 20th century. One of ten children in a family of modest means, he grew up on a small farm and attended the local school. In 1884, through a bursary established in 1877 by Father Sylvain-Éphrem Perrey*, he was able to enrol at the Collège Saint-Joseph in Memramcook, N.B. While there, he distinguished himself not only by academic brilliance, but also by participation in sports and cultural activities. He was in turn treasurer, president, and secretary of the Société Saint-Jean-Baptiste, which promoted French language and culture within the bilingual institution. Having completed the classical program in 1889, he stayed on at the college, teaching and studying theology. He finished his theological course at the Grand Séminaire de Québec, where he was ordained on 5 Nov. 1893.

Immediately after his ordination, Arsenault returned to his native parish, where he remained for nearly a year as assistant priest. He then moved to St Dunstan's parish in Charlottetown; his service as assistant priest there lasted until October 1896, when he was appointed curé of the small Acadian parish of Notre-Dame-du-Mont-Carmel. He held this charge for the rest of his life. Because of his appealing and dynamic personality, he soon succeeded in bringing the parishioners together and carrying out major projects, including the erection of one of the most remarkable churches in the province, a neo-Gothic structure designed by Quebec architect René-Pamphile Lemay.

Like many parish priests of the time, Arsenault worked a farm where he put into practice the best techniques of the day, and it served as a model for the farmers of his parish. To promote the agricultural movement, Arsenault also took part in local organizations. He played a key role, for example, in setting up the Prince Edward Island Co-operative Egg and Poultry Association in 1914, and was its first president. This cooperative, which brought together the many Egg Circles throughout the Island, sought to maintain the quality of the produce and to obtain a good price for its members, for whom the sale of eggs represented an important supplementary income.

The causes dearest to Father Arsenault's heart were education for Acadians and promotion of the French language. At the local level, he ensured that the schools were well run and he personally helped the most promising students prepare for the provincial Board of Education examinations and continue their studies at college. In 1900 he set up a library of French books and, in order to emphasize the importance of speaking the language well, he produced plays.

Arsenault also was active as an educator within the Association des Instituteurs Acadiens de l'Île-du-Prince-Édouard [*see* Joseph-Octave Arsenault*]. From 1897 to 1927 he took part in its annual conventions, in particular by giving lectures on teaching methods, the benefits of reading, the art of public speaking, and the importance of having a thorough grasp of Acadian and Canadian history. Several times he served on its committee for choosing school textbooks in French, which then had to be submitted to the Board of Education for approval.

Father Arsenault is said to have been the chief founder of the Société Saint-Thomas d'Aquin, which was established in 1919 on the occasion of the annual convention of the Association des Instituteurs Acadiens. The new organization's primary aim was to raise money for promising candidates to study at college or university. Arsenault served as vice-president (1919–20) and president (1920–25) of this society, which played a preponderant role for the Island's Acadian and francophone community, becoming its chief institutional voice.

As a student at the Collège Saint-Joseph, Arsenault had associated with a few professors who were trying to make the history of the Acadians better known and who advocated the preservation of their oral and material heritage. One of these was Father Philéas-Frédéric Bourgeois*. It was probably through his influence that Father Arsenault, with the help of Father Théodore Gallant, a musician, collected traditional songs from older people in the Acadian community, including versions from the French repertoire as well as local compositions. These 130 pieces constitute the earliest collection of Acadian folk songs. In 1924 Senator Pascal Poirier*, to whom Arsenault had given his collection, turned it over to Marius Barbeau* of the Victoria Memorial Museum in Ottawa.

Arsenault also drew up the genealogies of the founding families of the parish of Notre-Dame-du-Mont-Carmel and published them in 1912. He preserved a number of farm implements and domestic appliances which are now part of the collection of the Acadian Museum of Prince Edward Island at Miscouche.

Pierre-Paul Arsenault's health had been deteriorating for several years and he died at the age of 60. An enlightened leader and pragmatist with widely varied interests, he was one of the outstanding leaders of the Acadian community in Prince Edward Island. With his engaging personality, he was able to win the respect and admiration not only of his compatriots, but of all Islanders. The Summerside *Pioneer*, announcing his death on its front page, commented, "The whole province has sustained a heavy loss." In the Mont-Carmel cemetery, where he was buried, parishioners erected a magnificent monument in the form of a chapel, a fitting memorial for this man "of far-ranging and lofty ideas."

GEORGES ARSENAULT

The manuscript of Pierre-Paul Arsenault's collection of Acadian folk songs is held by the Canadian Museum of Civilization, Canadian Centre for Folk Culture Studies, Hull, Que. Arsenault is the author of *Premier centenaire de la paroisse de Mont Carmel, Île du Prince Édouard, le 20 août, 1912* ([Moncton, N.-B., 1912?]).

Arch. paroissiales, Saint-Simon et Saint-Jude (Tignish, Î.-P.-É.), RBMS, 26 mai 1867. *L'Évangéline* (Moncton), 7 août 1912, 16 janv. 1919, 3 oct. 1921, 1 déc. 1927, 25 mars 1963. *Examiner* (Charlottetown), 24 June 1886; 30 March, 25 July 1899; 20 Jan. 1904. *L'Impartial* (Tignish), 2, 23 nov. 1893; 8 févr., 1 mars, 29 nov. 1900; 9 juill. 1903; 31 mai 1906, 7 févr. 1907; 23 mai 1911. *Le Moniteur acadien* (Shédiac, N.-B.), 23 août 1889, 10 août 1897. *Pioneer* (Summerside, P.E.I.), 26 Nov. 1927. Georges Arsenault, "Le père Pierre-Paul Arsenault: un pionnier en folklore acadien," *Canadian Folklore* (Nepean, Ont.), 18 (1996): 95–107; the same article also appeared in Soc. Hist. Acadienne, *Cahiers* (Moncton), 27 (1996): 19–32. J.-H. Blanchard, *Les Acadiens de l'Île-du-Prince-Édouard* (Charlottetown, 1956). Cécile Gallant, *Pierre-Paul Arsenault (1866–1927)* (Moncton, 1992). Ronald Labelle, "Philias-Frédéric Bourgeois: précurseur de l'ethnologie acadienne," *Francophonies d'Amérique* (Ottawa), no.2 (1992): 5–11. Ronnie LeBlanc, "Philias Bourgeois, historien acadien," Soc. Hist. Acadienne, *Cahiers*, 5 (1973–74): 55–67. David Le Gallant, *Histoire des Acadiens de Mont-Carmel* ([Summerside], 1998). *Livre-souvenir: soixante-quinze années de courage et de persévérance, 1919–1994; la Société Saint-Thomas-d'Aquin, société acadienne de l'Île-du-Prince-Édouard*, Georges Arsenault et Jacinthe Laforest, édit. ([Summerside], 1994). *La Petite Souvenance* (Wellington, Î.-P.-É.), no.6 (décembre 1981), numéro spécial consacré au père Arsenault. G. F. Robichaud, "The career of Father Pierre-Paul Arsenault, 1896–1927" (BA thesis, Univ. of P.E.I., Charlottetown, 1984).

ASHDOWN, JAMES HENRY, tinsmith, businessman, and politician; b. 31 March 1844 in London, England, eldest of at least six children of William Ashdown and Jane Watling; m. first 30 Nov. 1872 Elizabeth Allen (d. 1873) in Poplar Point, Man.; m. secondly 10 Feb. 1876 Susan Crowson in Winnipeg, and they had one son and three daughters; d. 5 April 1924 in Winnipeg.

William Ashdown brought his family to Upper Canada in 1852. They settled first in Etobicoke Township, but later moved to Weston (Toronto), where William taught school for a time and subsequently ran a store. Although James worked as clerk in the store from age 11, he continued to study at night school. When the store failed in 1862, the family moved to a bush farm in Brant County. At age 18 James left home and was apprenticed to John Zryd, a tinsmith in Hespeler (Cambridge), for three years. He kept the books of a local blacksmith to supplement his wages.

At the end of his apprenticeship, Ashdown headed west and worked for ten months on the construction of a blockhouse at Fort Zarah in Kansas. His experiences in the west left him restless and eager for new opportunities. In 1868 he set out for Upper Fort Garry (Winnipeg) in the Red River settlement (Man.). He arrived at the end of June and took on various jobs. In 1869 he signed on with the survey crew of John Stoughton Dennis*. His savings from these jobs and a loan of $1,000 from Dennis allowed him to set up a tinsmith business and on 14 September to purchase the hardware store of George Moser.

Ashdown had arrived in the Red River settlement at a time of increasing uncertainty over the implications of the transfer of the Hudson's Bay Company's territories to Canada. He felt that the actions of businessman John Christian Schultz* exacerbated tensions. Nonetheless, his sympathies were with Schultz's Canadian party, which favoured annexation to Canada. Reluctantly, he joined the small, armed group that attempted to keep Schultz's warehouse from falling into the hands of Louis Riel* and his supporters. On 7 Dec. 1869 Riel's men forced their surrender. Ashdown and some of the others were confined in Upper Fort Garry for 69 days.

With the establishment of Canadian governance, Ashdown concentrated on his business, meeting the growing demands of newcomers for stoves, stove-pipes, metal roofing, and all varieties of tinware and hardware. Because of the cost of transporting his goods into the region, he was one of several Winnipeg businessmen who operated the Merchants' Line of steamboats on the Red River from 1871 to 1873 in competition with those owned by James Jerome Hill*.

The demand for hardware and metal ware was considerable in the frontier market. In 1875, 1878, and 1880 Ashdown expanded his Winnipeg premises. In 1881 he opened branches in Portage la Prairie and Emerson and in 1889 in Calgary. The credit reports of R. G. Dun and Company charted his rapidly increasing business assets from less than $2,000 in 1870 to $25,000–$50,000 in 1876 and $75,000–$150,000 in 1881. Already the west's major hardware merchant with capital estimated at $200,000–$300,000 in 1891, he benefited even more during the boom of the late 1890s and first decade of the 1900s through his wholesale operation.

In 1896 Ashdown constructed a large warehouse in Winnipeg, which he expanded in 1902 and again in 1906. To advertise his business, on 6 March 1900 he dispatched from Winnipeg the Ashdown Special, a 40-car freight train pulled by three locomotives. Prominently displaying his name, the train travelled only during daylight to various prairie centres to fill orders for the current season. The train's length attested not only to Ashdown's sales, but also to the advantages that differential freight rates gave Winnipeg as a wholesale centre. The complaints of British Columbia and prairie boards of trade from 1907 persuaded the Board of Railway Commissioners, in a number of decisions up to 1914, to reduce Winnipeg's favoured position. Ashdown was already well positioned to respond to changing transportation costs. He had expanded his Calgary branch into wholesaling in 1909. In 1911 he transferred a branch operation set up in 1896 in Nelson, B.C., to Saskatoon (Sask.), where he had a large warehouse erected. By 1911 his assets exceeded $1,000,000 and by World War I he employed over 300 workers. In 1923 he opened a branch in Edmonton.

The importance of transportation policy for his business had drawn Ashdown to politics. He was a member of the Winnipeg City Council in 1874 and 1879 and was active on the Winnipeg Board of Trade from its founding in 1879. As its president in 1887, he prepared pamphlets that criticized the monopoly of the Canadian Pacific Railway and denounced the government of Sir John A. Macdonald* for "the abuse of the vice-regal veto power" during the controversy over the federal disallowance of provincial railway legislation [see John Norquay*]. He continued his opposition to the CPR, carrying the board of trade's complaints about rates to the railway committee in 1894 and pressuring the newly elected government of Wilfrid Laurier* in March 1897 to reduce rates. In 1903 he was appointed to represent the west on the royal commission on transportation.

Ashdown's prominence and advocacy of Winnipeg had led him to enter federal politics. In 1896 he ran unsuccessfully as a Liberal in Marquette. On the Manitoba school question he declared his position by sharing a platform with Joseph MARTIN and urging Manitobans to welcome D'Alton McCarthy*. In 1911 he again stood unsuccessfully for the Liberals, this time in Winnipeg, and he campaigned in favour of reciprocity. It was in the municipal arena, however, that he made his political mark.

In November 1906 Ashdown had agreed to enter the mayoralty election. The contest marked a departure for city government since it was the first to elect a board of control and to implement administration by commissioners. Ashdown had advocated municipal reform for two decades. In 1883 he had joined a citizen's committee to investigate the city's debt and irregularities in its tax assessment and collection system. In November 1895 he chaired a new citizen's committee on reform of municipal government. Both of these initiatives expressed the concerns of businessmen and property owners that municipal government, in which council initiated legislation and committee chairs expended funds, was too decentralized to be responsible to those with a stake in the city. The corporate model instituted through a board of control promised sound business management.

The major issue in the election of December 1906 was Ashdown himself. His main opponent, former alderman J. G. Latimer, sought election, "to represent the city as a whole – to see that the laboring man has a fair chance against the monied interests." The Independent Labor Party endorsed no candidate, although its chairman, Arthur W. Puttee*, favoured Latimer. His newspaper, the *Voice*, predicted that the trade unionists "most assuredly will not vote for Ashdown." Ashdown countered aggressively, proclaiming that he was not opposed to unions and that he favoured "paying a good fair day's wages for a fair day's work." Moreover, he had long been a critic of large corporations. He had fought the HBC's attempts to prevent municipal incorporation in 1872–73 and as a city councillor he had confronted the company's influence. As well, he charged that William MACKENZIE, Donald Mann*, and their Winnipeg Electric Railway Company controlled Latimer and he contended that the street railway franchise should never have been given to a private company. "What might be called the natural monopolies, water and light," should be owned and operated "by the people in the interest of the people." Ashdown won by the largest margin to that time in a Winnipeg civic election.

Ashdown

Although Ashdown had been a member of the Power Association, a group of prominent businessmen who had pressured the provincial government of Rodmond Palen Roblin* in 1905 to pass legislation permitting the city to sell electric power generated at its own plant, he shocked supporters not long after taking office by arguing that the construction of a municipal power utility be postponed. The state of the city's finances had surprised him. The city had overdrawn its account with the Canadian Bank of Commerce by $2,900,000 and owed another $1,300,000 to the Bank of Scotland. In January 1907 the Commerce, willing to hold only $750,000 of Winnipeg's debt, pressed Ashdown to refinance the city's obligations. He was turned down by eight major Canadian banks. He persuaded the Commerce to accept another $250,000 in debt and secured $1,150,000 from several British and American lenders, but at rates reaching seven per cent.

In this context, raising money for hydroelectric development was a daunting prospect. The advice Ashdown received in Canada and abroad was not encouraging and he recommended to council that the city postpone all non-essential expenditure until its finances were reorganized. In his view, improvements to the city's water supply should in any case receive a higher priority than hydroelectric development. His recommendation to delay the power project provoked controversy. When the matter came before the council and board of control on 5 Nov. 1907, few accepted Ashdown's reservations and some suspected his motives. Controller William Corston Watt Garson, who led the faction supporting immediate construction, asserted that "power is a necessity, and water . . . is not." The labour press had long supported hydroelectric development, hoping that the transformation of Winnipeg into a manufacturing centre would create jobs. Councillor A. H. Pulford later charged that "the financiers and the corporations were trying to beat out the power scheme. It was a fight between capital and the people." The council and board of control voted 13 to 5 to accept a financial arrangement from the Anglo-Canadian Engineering Company, the only firm that had tendered for the entire power project, but Ashdown vetoed their decision.

With the expiry of Anglo-Canadian's bid and in the absence of another contractor, the campaign for immediate construction lost its steam. Criticism of Ashdown persisted, but he had argued only to postpone, not cancel the scheme. His position was so widely accepted that in the election campaign which began not long after his veto the hydroelectric project was not an issue. He was acclaimed mayor late in 1907 for a second and uncontroversial term.

The controversy revealed that, regardless of his position, Ashdown was often perceived to represent capitalist interests and was criticized for it. His role in the dismissal of the Reverend Salem Goldworth Bland* as professor of church history at Wesley College provided another example of the opprobrium easily attached to business success. Ashdown had been a member of the college's board of directors from its founding in 1888, bursar from 1888 to 1890, and vice-chairman from 1890 to 1908; he would serve as chair from 1908 to 1924. In 1917 the college faced a difficult financial situation and needed to reduce expenses. In early June it informed Bland and two others that their services were no longer required. Because of Bland's social activism, the firings provoked controversy within the Methodist Church and among the public.

Bland charged that wealthy businessmen who had declined to contribute to the college's endowment fund while he was on faculty had pressured the college's board to fire him. Letters and articles in the local press echoed his interpretation. In response, the Saskatchewan Conference of the Methodist Church empowered a commission to investigate in September 1918. Ashdown chafed under the commission's questioning. He reiterated that the board sought only to reduce expenses, but admitted that he thought Bland's activism had hurt the college's fund-raising. The commission's report upheld the board's explanation of the dismissal, but also wondered why more consideration had not been shown to Bland.

In response to Bland's questions before the commission, Ashdown had declared that he had let go his own employees only for incompetence, never for financial reasons. Ashdown was a paternalistic employer, confident that he treated his workers fairly, and he was hence unlikely to be responsive to labour's demands for greater control over conditions of employment. As with other businessmen who were not directly involved in the Winnipeg General Strike of 1919 [see Mike Sokolowiski*], his exact role in that conflict is not clear. He no doubt sympathized with efforts to suppress what increasingly seemed to his class to be a revolutionary disruption of civil order. The conflict disturbed him, however. He conceded that some new basis had to be found for the relations between capital and labour.

Ashdown represented western Canadian wholesalers at the National Industrial Conference of Dominion and Provincial Governments in Canada, held in Ottawa in September 1919. The conference was a result of the royal commission on industrial relations. Whatever his position during the strike, he had felt no triumph afterwards and agreed that "a realizable *modus vivendi* [should] be evolved whereby interests apparently antagonistic, but in reality inter-dependent, shall continue to work in harmony." In a 50th anniversary history of his business, published just prior to the conference, he felt compelled to claim that "his relations with his own employees have been exceptionally cordial." At the conference he would look with sympathy on the demands of organized labour, "if kept within reasonable limits." He played only a minor role in the conference, however.

As a successful businessman, Ashdown participated in the affairs of several corporations, as a promoter of the Great-West Life Assurance Company, president of the Gold Pan Mining Company and the Canadian Fire Insurance Company, vice-president and director of the Northern Crown Bank, and director of the Bank of Montreal as well as of several mortgage and insurance companies. In addition, he contributed to a number of charities and was president of the Children's Aid Society, a director of numerous civic organizations, and a trustee of Grace Methodist Church. In his will he left to charities $300,000 from an estate valued at $1,634,000.

His business success made James Henry Ashdown a controversial public figure in Winnipeg, especially as social conflict increased through the first two decades of the 20th century. As class positions hardened, labour spokespersons easily associated him with the interests of capitalism. He was indeed a man of his class and his times. His views on a number of public issues, however – his criticism of monopolies, desire for a corporate model of government, support for the reformist provincial Liberal party, preference for safe water over public power, and willingness to reach some accommodation with the conservative elements of organized labour – revealed that he was much more of a progressive than many recognized. His public demeanour did little to promote understanding or sympathy. Accustomed as a businessman to making unchallenged decisions, he was impatient to the point of blustering anger when others did not readily accept his positions or explanations. Even the Reverend John Henry Riddell, principal of Wesley College and a friend, conceded, "We never met without a difference of opinion." Ashdown died unexpectedly and had remained actively involved in his business to the end.

DAVID G. BURLEY

As president of the Winnipeg Board of Trade, James Henry Ashdown prepared the board's pamphlet *An open letter to the shareholders of the Canadian Pacific Railway Co.* ... ([Winnipeg?], 1887). In addition, he is the author of "Winnipeg's board of control," *Canadian Municipal Journal* (Montreal), 4 (1908): 445–46.

City of Winnipeg, Arch. and records control branch, City council, communications, 1896, no.3312; 1907, nos.8154, 8162; 1908, nos.8284, 8307, 8455; Report of Marwick, Mitchell and Company on city of Winnipeg finances, 1908. Univ. of Winnipeg Library, "Proceedings of commission of Saskatchewan; [Methodist] Conference re Wesley College affairs, 1917–18" (typescript, 1918). *Manitoba Free Press*, 6 March 1900; 16 Oct. 1905; 29 June, 2 Nov., 6, 7, 12 Dec. 1906; 5, 9 Nov. 1907; 16 May, 1 July 1908; 1 Nov. 1915; 21 Sept. 1917; 17, 20 Sept. 1919. Edith Paterson, "It happened here: James H. Ashdown – tinsmith," *Winnipeg Free Press*, 28 June 1969, *Leisure Magazine*. *Voice* (Winnipeg), 7, 14, 28 Dec. 1906; 17 May, 1, 8, 15, 29 Nov., 7, 14 Dec. 1907; 8 June 1917. *Winnipeg Tribune*, 29 Jan. 1910; 2 May 1911; 13 June, 6 Aug. 1917; 25 June 1924; 6 April 1965. Richard Allen, "Salem Bland and the spirituality of the Social Gospel: Winnipeg and the west, 1903–13," in *Prairie spirit: perspectives on the heritage of the United Church of Canada in the west*, ed. D. L. Butcher *et al.* (Winnipeg, 1985), 216–32; *The social passion: religion and social reform in Canada, 1914–28* (Toronto, 1971). A. F. J. Artibise, *Winnipeg: a social history of urban growth, 1874–1914* (Montreal and London, 1975). J. H. Ashdown Hardware Company Limited, *Semi-centenary of the J. H. Ashdown Hardware Co., Limited, Calgary, Winnipeg, Saskatoon, established 1869* ([Winnipeg], 1919]). A. G. Bedford, *The University of Winnipeg: a history of the founding colleges* (Toronto and Buffalo, N.Y., 1976). *Canadian men and women of the time* (Morgan; 1912). D. J. Hall, *Clifford Sifton* (2v., Vancouver and London, 1981–85). Kenneth McNaught, *A prophet in politics: a biography of J. S. Woodsworth* (Toronto, 1959). *The mercantile agency reference book . . .* (Montreal), 1870, 1876, 1881, 1891. *Newspaper reference book. Pioneers and prominent people of Manitoba*, ed. Walter McRaye (Winnipeg, 1925). L. A. Shropshire, "A founding father of Winnipeg: James Henry Ashdown, 1844–1924," *Manitoba Hist.* (Winnipeg), no.19 (spring 1990): 23–26. *Winnipeg, Manitoba, and her industries* (Chicago and Winnipeg, 1882).

B

BAILEY, LORING WOART, educator, geologist, botanist, and author; b. 28 Sept. 1839 in West Point, N.Y., son of Jacob Whitman Bailey and Maria Slaughter; m. 19 Aug. 1863, in Fredericton, Laurestine Marie Marshall d'Avray, only child of Joseph Marshall* de Brett Maréchal, Baron d'Avray, and they had five sons and two daughters; d. 10 Jan. 1925 in Fredericton.

Loring Woart Bailey was introduced to scientific circles by his father, first professor of chemistry, mineralogy, and geology at the United States Military Academy in West Point. Eminent American and European scientists visited their home and as a youth he joined his father and brothers in botanical and geological field observations. He was educated at schools in Maryland and Rhode Island before entering Harvard

University in Cambridge, Mass., in 1855. There he studied under the geologist Louis Agassiz, the botanist Asa Gray, and the chemist Josiah Parsons Cooke. His AB degree in 1859 was followed by a period of further study in chemistry at Brown University in Providence, R.I. He then returned to Harvard, where he served as assistant to Cooke, who in 1861 recommended him, at the age of 21, for the post of professor of chemistry and natural science at the University of New Brunswick. He would receive his MA from Harvard the following year.

Arriving in Fredericton in the summer of 1861, Bailey found his prime duty was to teach, which he did with enthusiasm, skill, and devotion for 46 years. One of his early students, George Robert PARKIN, recalled later that "the introduction to Natural Science was like the opening of a new world to me, and it gave me just the intellectual stimulation I needed." Initially, Bailey was a one-man natural science faculty, covering the broad spectrum of physics, chemistry, zoology, botany, and geology, but in 1900 his sphere was reduced to biology and geology. To illustrate his lectures he collected geological and botanical specimens, and added them to the museum cabinets started by his predecessor, James Robb*. He valued museums as educational tools and lamented the attitudes of people who regarded them as "a mere collection of curiosities." His appeals for financial support from the provincial legislature, however, fell on deaf ears.

His enthusiasm for teaching was matched by his dedication to research; in New Brunswick's complex geology he found a pristine and potentially rich area for investigation. In 1863 Lieutenant Governor Arthur Hamilton Gordon*, anxious to promote the development of the province's resources, paid for him to carry out a mineralogical survey. After consulting the geological map prepared by Robb and partially based on Abraham Gesner*'s reports of 1839–43, he selected a wilderness route along the Saint John, Tobique, and Nepisiguit rivers in order to examine metalliferous rocks of the Cambrian series (which then included a portion of the Ordivician); en route he visited the mines in Woodstock and Bathurst. The following year he accompanied George Frederic MATTHEW and Charles Frederick Hartt* on a survey of the southern part of the colony including the complicated geological formations east of Saint John. Their discovery of a band of slates with embedded Cambrian fossils provided a key to the age of similar rocks in New England. Reports of these expeditions presented to the legislature in 1864 and 1865 are classics in New Brunswick's scientific literature.

In 1864 as well, Henry Youle Hind* was employed by the government to survey the northern part of the province. Although Bailey and Matthew received no pay, Hind, under the misapprehension that he was to be appointed provincial geological surveyor, viewed their activities as a threat and attacked them scurrilously in the press. He cited Bailey's youth, American nationality, and lack of experience as detrimental and suggested that Bailey should attend solely to his university duties. This acrimonious dispute led New Brunswick to abandon sponsorship of further geological surveys.

After confederation the director of the Geological Survey of Canada, Sir William Edmond Logan*, met with Bailey and Matthew in 1868 to discuss the survey's expansion to New Brunswick. Once again Bailey was employed in the summers. Accompanied by Matthew or by assistants such as Robert Wheelock Ells, he surveyed the southern half of the province and later the northern counties along the Saint John River, together with adjoining areas of Quebec and Maine, as well as southern Nova Scotia. Bailey's discovery of Silurian fossils in northern New Brunswick suggested that rocks of that region covered a wider range of geological time than had previously been supposed. His survey results were published in a series of GSC reports over the years 1872–1906. Together with Ells he also reported on the coalfields of central New Brunswick and mapped the area of bituminous shales in Albert and Westmorland counties. His philosophical bent is apparent in overviews of geological problems such as his 1897 paper entitled "The Bay of Fundy trough in American geological history." He was greatly admired for undertaking arduous field work in spite of having a lame leg, injured in a childhood accident.

The challenge of teaching and research and happiness in his marriage kept Bailey at the University of New Brunswick although he had tempting offers from American colleges. His home became a centre for students, visitors, and neighbours interested in science and literature, attracted by his wife's social gifts and Bailey's lively conversation. He also promoted science in the community, helping a neighbour, John Babbitt*, to experiment with new inventions, including the telephone and electric lighting. He lectured at the Mechanics' Institute in Saint John and was an honorary member of the Natural History Society of New Brunswick, giving an annual lecture to that body and contributing to its *Bulletin*. A charter member of the Royal Society of Canada, he was president of his section in 1888–89 and 1918–19.

While still a student, he had completed a scientific paper, started by his father, on the diatoms (plankton) of the Pará River in Brazil. In retirement he renewed this interest. Working sometimes in cooperation with the Biological Board of Canada and the Atlantic Biological Station at St Andrews, N.B., he identified diatoms of the Bay of Fundy, the coast of Prince Edward Island, and other parts of the east coast. His expertise became so widely recognized that he received specimens from the Pacific coast and

Alberta and Saskatchewan lakes. The results were published in various Canadian and American scientific journals and later brought together in "An annotated catalogue of the diatoms of Canada," issued a few months before his death. Altogether he was the author of around 100 scientific works, several of which were major publications.

Bailey's place among eminent geologists of the province was recognized in 1899 when fellow naturalist William Francis Ganong* named a northern New Brunswick mountain after him. His pioneering work in provincial geology enriched his teaching and his influence as a teacher is attested by the success of students such as Ganong and William Diller Matthew (G. F. Matthew's son), whose early training enabled them to undertake graduate work at prestigious universities; later they contributed to the broader world in botany and palaeontology. Honours bestowed on Bailey included a PHD from the University of New Brunswick in 1873 and an LLD from Dalhousie University in 1896.

C. MARY YOUNG

Loring Woart Bailey's writings are listed in the biography by Joseph Whitman Bailey mentioned below, as well as in *Science and technology biblio.* (Richardson and MacDonald). Among his publications is a tribute to his colleague George Frederic Matthew in RSC, *Trans.*, 3rd ser., 17 (1923), proc.: vii–x. His annotated catalogue of diatoms appears in Biological Board of Canada, *Contributions to Canadian biology, being studies from the biological stations of Canada* (Toronto), 2 (1925), no.2: [31]–67.

The main primary source for Bailey and his family is the Bailey family fonds at the Univ. of N.B. Library, Arch. and Special Coll. Dept. (Fredericton), MG H1. There are photographs of Bailey in the archives and in the university's department of biology. His botanical collections are preserved in the department's Connell Memorial Herbarium, and some of his geological specimens are in the department of geology.

Daily Evening Globe (Saint John), 25 April 1864. *Daily Gleaner* (Fredericton), 10 Jan. 1925. J. W. Bailey, *Loring Woart Bailey, the story of a man of science* (Saint John, 1925). R. A. Jarrell, "Science education at the University of New Brunswick in the nineteenth century," *Acadiensis* (Fredericton), 2 (1972–73), no.2: 55–79. Kenneth Johnstone, *The aquatic explorers: a history of the Fisheries Research Board of Canada* (Toronto, 1977). RSC, *Trans.*, 3rd ser., 19 (1925), proc.: xiv–xv. Morris Zaslow, *Reading the rocks: the story of the Geological Survey of Canada, 1842–1972* (Toronto and Ottawa, 1975).

BAILLIE, Sir FRANK WILTON, financier and industrialist; b. 9 Aug. 1875 in Toronto, son of John Baillie, a merchant, and Marion Wilton; m. there 8 June 1900 Edith Julia White, and they had three sons and two daughters; d. there 2 Jan. 1921.

Of Scottish-English parentage, Frank Baillie was educated in Toronto's public schools and began working about 1889 as a clerk with the Central Canada Loan and Savings Company, which by the 1890s was shifting its business from mortgage lending to bond dealing and underwriting. As private secretary to and a protégé of the company's founder, George Albertus Cox*, Baillie benefited from his employer's status as one of the country's most powerful financiers. He was made Central Canada's accountant in 1896, two years later its secretary, and in 1901 assistant manager. By this time his brother James W. had also joined the Cox network: he and Cox's son Herbert Coplin managed the eastern Ontario branch of the Canada Life Assurance Company. In addition to his work with Central Canada, in 1901 Frank became managing director of its new subsidiary, Dominion Securities Corporation, chartered to carry on bond trading. He must have impressed others within the Cox empire. When Cox's son-in-law and business associate Alfred Ernest Ames* decided to distance himself somewhat from the network and organized the Metropolitan Bank in 1902, Baillie, then in his mid twenties, became its general manager, reputedly the youngest man in Canadian history to run a chartered bank.

Banking evidently gave too little scope for Baillie's ambitions, however, and in 1903 he resigned to start up, with his brother and Frank Porter Wood, a brokerage firm, Baillie Brothers and Company (later Baillie, Wood, and Croft), which operated on the Toronto Stock Exchange. By this point, trading was expanding into new business sectors, especially resource development and manufacturing, spearheaded by a new generation of brokers, including Ames, Edward Rogers Wood* (Frank's brother and another Cox associate), Frederick Herbert Deacon, and William Maxwell Aitken*, who not only channelled investors' capital but also invested heavily themselves. Baillie prospered by putting his own money into the Cox group's transportation, utilities, and manufacturing projects, including the Dominion Coal Company Limited, out of which he earned a great deal of money. (At his death his estate would be worth more than two million dollars.) In 1912 he formed the Bankers' Bond Company Limited to succeed Baillie, Wood, and Croft.

As the Cox empire came under increasing criticism, Baillie had begun to strike out on his own as an industrialist. In 1910 he mobilized Toronto capital to create the Canada Steel Company Limited (renamed Burlington Steel in 1914), a large, specialized operation in Hamilton that employed about 300 men to roll bar products from scrap rails – the only such plant in Canada at the time. Baillie would be its president until his death. He also helped bring together Canadian capitalists and Clifton William Sherman*, the manager of the Pratt and Letchworth steelworks in Buffalo, N.Y., to create a syndicate in May 1912 to set up Hamilton's first steel-casting factory. Incorporated in September as the Dominion Steel Castings Company Limited, it erected a plant that winter and in 1913 merged with the recently created Hamilton Malleable Iron Company Limited to form the Dominion Steel Foundry Company. Both Canada Steel and Dominion Steel Foundry had state-of-the-art production facilities; Baillie would serve as vice-president of the latter briefly in 1916.

World War I gave new scope for his entrepreneurial energy. Late in 1914 he collaborated with the owners of the Chadwick Brass Company in Hamilton to set up the large Canadian Cartridge Company Limited, of which he became president and Frank Wood vice-president. Baillie began with about 200 workers but he would eventually employ 900 to manufacture brass cartridge cases for the British government. In August 1915 he won a lucrative contract to produce two million 18-pounder cases by promising to return any profits on the second million. By reorganizing production to cut costs drastically, he was able to turn over $758,248 in a well-publicized gesture in July 1916. Other manufacturers were "very disturbed" by this move, according to Joseph Wesley Flavelle*, chairman of the Imperial Munitions Board, the agency in Canada that contracted with the British government, and none took up his example. That year Baillie also made sure that the growing discontent among Hamilton's munitions workers did not disrupt production at either Canadian Cartridge or Burlington Steel by conceding the nine-hour day just before the outbreak of a bitter strike in most other metalworking plants in Hamilton.

Baillie's munitions work had brought him into regular contact with Flavelle, also a prominent member of the old Cox group, and Flavelle soon found a new job for him. The Royal Flying Corps had suffered heavy losses over European battlegrounds during 1916, and it now stepped up its efforts to secure recruits and training facilities in Canada. In December 1916 the IMB was mandated to provide buildings and equipment through an aviation department to be headed by E. R. Wood. When ill health led Wood to resign in January 1917, Flavelle persuaded Baillie and Toronto businessman George Andrew Morrow (another former Cox protégé and a director of Burlington Steel) to take over. Almost immediately they split their responsibilities: Morrow became director of aviation and Baillie president of the production company incorporated in December, Canadian Aeroplanes Limited. With a million-dollar advance from the federal government, it became one of the IMB's wholly owned "national factories."

Baillie moved quickly to start manufacturing. He acquired the small Toronto plant of Curtiss Aeroplanes and Motors Limited, and on 26 January signed a contract for a bigger plant. To the astonishment of most observers, within ten weeks he had a new, fully equipped factory operating on six acres on Dufferin Street, in Toronto's west-end industrial district. By November aircraft were leaving at a rate of more than 50 a week. Valued at nearly 14 million dollars, the aircraft produced were mostly slightly modified Canadian Curtiss JN-4s. (The number of JN-4s is estimated at 1,210 complete planes plus parts equal to about 1,600 more; 30 Felixstowe F-5-L flying boats were also built for the American government in 1918–19.) Baillie's effort was remarkable. Cotton for covering wings and fuselages had to be shipped in from Trois-Rivières and Sitka spruce for frames from British Columbia's coastal forests. Some 2,400 workers had to be assembled, ranging from skilled woodworkers and machinists to the many women needed to stitch the cotton.

Although Canadian Aeroplanes was a publicly owned company, Baillie ran it like a private enterprise, and, as in his other businesses, he made it a model of highly mechanized, tightly organized mass production. It was probably the most successful of the IMB's national factories. In fact, his costs of production dropped so far that Flavelle had to order him to cut his selling price before the end of 1917, though Baillie still made $1,000 on each plane. American aircraft manufacturers were so impressed that they brought him to Washington to provide advice and then asked him to take over the management of a plant in Buffalo, but he declined.

Baillie was thus one of several businessmen who, during World War I, brought the practices of corporate capitalism to the rapidly expanding state administration of economic and social life in Canada. With his steel plant in Hamilton producing steady profits, he was able to add to his record of public service by refusing to accept any remuneration for his work in aviation. On 9 Jan. 1918 he became the first Canadian to receive a knighthood of the Order of the British Empire, recently created to recognize wartime service. The manufacturing facilities he had created for the national effort were short-lived, however. When the federal government showed no interest in the post-war production of aircraft, the Toronto plant was closed some months after the armistice and sold to the Columbia Graphophone Company Limited. Although Baillie had hoped that Canadian Cartridge could produce forgings and steel barrels when munitions work ended, he had to close its plant too after the war.

Despite his heavy involvement in Hamilton's industrial life, Baillie continued to reside in Toronto. Unlike some other prominent businessmen, he showed little interest in charity, social reform, or high culture, though he had been a director of Wycliffe College and Grace Hospital in 1912. He seemed to prefer to spend his time away from business enjoying robust private pleasures in the exclusive social circles of his class. An Anglican in religion and reportedly independent in politics, he relaxed with male colleagues in several clubs in Toronto and Hamilton, and pursued his passion for outdoor sports in private golf and country clubs and in the Royal Canadian Yacht and Toronto Canoe clubs (he was a rear commodore of the latter). On his large Lisonally Farm near Oakville, he bred prize-winning Shorthorn cattle. By contrast, his wife, a daughter of Aubrey White*, Ontario's deputy minister of lands, forests, and mines, took "an active part in all forms of public-spirited work," serving as a president of the Women's Auxiliary of the Canadian National Institute for the Blind and as a board member of the Home for Incurable Children in Toronto.

When cancer and a pulmonary embolism ended Baillie's life abruptly in 1921, his skills and acumen as a promoter and an industrialist were widely praised. Among businessmen and politicians, he was known for facilitating the flow of capital to new industries and strengthening both the industrial base of Canada's premier steel-making centre and the country's wartime manufacturing capacity. The workers in his closely managed, technologically sophisticated factories might well have remembered him with mixed feelings for his contributions to a second Industrial Revolution. In all these ways, he typified the many ambitious financiers who directed their energies into the mainstream of Canada's industrial life in the early 20th century and helped to reshape the country's economy.

CRAIG HERON

AO, RG 22-305, no.42876; RG 80-5-0-276, no.1828; RG 80-8-0-800, no.1017. Dofasco Inc., Legal Services Dept. (Hamilton, Ont.), Articles of continuance, continuing Dominion Foundries and Steel Limited as Dofasco Inc., 1979; Library Resource Centre, Letters patent, incorporating Dominion Steel Castings Company Limited, 27 Sept. 1912; Hamilton Malleable Iron Company Limited, 17 Dec. 1912; Dominion Steel Foundry Company Limited, 1 March 1913; Hamilton Steel Wheel Company Limited, 7 Nov. 1916; and Dominion Foundries and Steel Limited, 15 May 1917 (microfiche). LAC, RG 31, C1, 1871, Toronto, St James' Ward, div.7: 1. *Daily Times* (Hamilton), 21 Sept. 1910; 16 March, 17 Dec. 1915. *Globe*, 3 Jan. 1921. *Hamilton Herald*, 25 March, 21 Dec. 1914; 18 May 1915; 10 June, 26 July 1916. *Hamilton Spectator*, 21 Jan. 1919. American Iron and Steel Institute, *Directory of the iron and steel works of the United States and Canada* (New York), 1916: 67. *Annual financial rev.* (Toronto and Montreal), 1916: 216. *Aviation in Canada, 1917–1918: being a brief account of the work of the Royal Air Force, Canada, the aviation department of the Imperial Munitions Board, and the Canadian Aeroplanes Limited*, comp. Alan Sullivan (Toronto, 1919). Michael Bliss, *A Canadian millionaire: the life and business times of Sir Joseph Flavelle, bart., 1858–1939* (Toronto, 1978), 53–82, 284, 310–11, 367–68, 370, 377, 388. *Canada Gazette*, 8 March 1913: 3287–88. *Canadian annual rev.*, 1913. *Canadian Foundryman and Metal Industry News* (Toronto), 8 (1917), no.1: 7. *Canadian Machinery and Manufacturing News* (Toronto), 7 (1911): 293–95; 11 (January–June 1914): 5–6; 16 (July–December 1916): 159. David Carnegie, *The history of munitions supply in Canada, 1914–1918* (London, 1925). *Cyclopædia of Canadian biog.* (Rose and Charlesworth), vol.3. *DHB*, vol.2. *Directory*, Toronto, 1893–1921. *Industrial Canada* (Toronto), 13 (1912–13): 858, 1002; 14 (1913–14): 1169. *Iron Age* (New York), 89 (January–June 1912): 1367, 1519. *Labour Gazette* (Ottawa), 11 (1910–11): 404; 15 (1914–15): 1389. K. M. Molson and H. A. Taylor, *Canadian aircraft since 1909* (Stittsville, Ont., 1982), 23, 227, app.2. *Monetary Times* (Toronto), 14 Jan. 1921. *National encyclopedia of Canadian biography*, ed. J. E. Middleton and W. S. Downs (2v., Toronto, 1935–37). P. E. Rider, "The Imperial Munitions Board and its relationship to government, business, and labour, 1914–1920" (PHD thesis, Univ. of Toronto, 1974). H. B. Ward, "Hamilton, Ontario, as a manufacturing centre" (PHD thesis, Univ. of Chicago, 1937). *Who's who and why*, 1919/20. *Women of Canada* (Montreal, 1930).

BAKER, PERCIVAL, preacher, farmer, and agrarian leader; b. 11 Jan. 1867 in York County, Upper Canada, son of Jacob Baker and Mary ——; m. 11 Sept. 1889 Susan Amanda Page in Vaughan Township, Ont., and they had two daughters and five sons; d. 19 July 1921 in Edmonton.

Percival Baker's father, a Canadian-born carpenter of German origin, was a Dunker in religion; his mother, of English origin, was a Methodist. Raised in Markham Township, Ont., for a time by the Klinck family, in 1889 Baker graduated from the College of the Bible (now Lexington Theological Seminary) in Lexington, Ky, after studying liberal arts and theology. He served as a Disciples of Christ minister, first in Rodney, Ont., next in Everton, Ont., and then for over ten years in the corn belt of east-central Illinois.

Smitten by the call of the Canadian west, Baker went to Alberta in 1908 and settled near Ponoka. Having had previous experience as a farmhand in Ontario, he built a successful and up-to-date mixed-farming operation. A former officer of the Ontario Disciples of Christ missionary body, he was a leading light in the Alberta Missionary Society of the Disciples of Christ, and he regularly preached in the Disciples church in Ponoka. Thus was he aptly called a "farmer-preacher."

Baker was a charter member of the Arbor Park local of the United Farmers of Alberta, the province's main agrarian organization, formed in 1909 [see Edwin Carswell*]. Destiny gripped him in 1916 when he was elected UFA director for the Strathcona constituency. In 1917 he was re-elected to this position, and in July of that year he was appointed third vice-president of the UFA. His leadership talents and "outstanding" contributions in its conventions led to his election from 1918 to 1921 as first vice-president, under President Henry Wise Wood*. In this capacity, he laboured tirelessly to protect the interests of livestock producers. Outside the UFA, he worked to improve public education, and he would become a director of the Western Canada Colonization Association, founded in 1920.

A Liberal in politics before 1919, Baker was on the resolutions committee at the 1917 Western Liberal Convention, which revealed the deep divisions within the party over conscription for overseas military service, soon imposed by Sir Robert Laird Borden*'s government in Ottawa, and over the need for a nonpartisan wartime government there. Baker faced a tough challenge in May 1918 after Borden's Union government had broken its promise to exempt young farmers from compulsory service. Under his guidance, in Wood's absence, the UFA executive grudgingly accepted the government's decision on the grounds that the need for more soldiers had become "imperative." Many Alberta and other farmers were incensed with this apparent endorsement of Ottawa's widening of the draft, but Baker successfully defended his position at the UFA secretaries' conventions later in 1918. He also mollified the opposition by issuing, along with two UFA board members, a statement that expressed farmers' anger over the government's policy.

Upset with the extension of conscription and other federal government policies, and suspicious of the old political parties, in 1919 Canadian farmers began taking independent and third-party action. At the UFA annual convention in January that year, Baker had presented the resolution that permitted such action. When the UFA executive met in March, he moved two resolutions that paved the way for the merger, later in 1919, of the UFA with the Non-Partisan League, a rival farmers' political movement. This amalgamation was crucial because it ensured that Alberta farmers entered politics united.

By early 1921 Percival Baker's star was rising. Ambitious – his gaze betrayed a steely determination – he had proved himself a dedicated and principled leader of sound judgement, a consensus builder, and an excellent orator. It was no surprise that he ran as a UFA candidate in the constituency of Ponoka when the reigning provincial Liberals called an election for 18 July 1921, and it was no surprise that he emerged victorious. But by then, disaster had struck. On 29 June Baker had been hit by a falling tree while clearing land on his farm; he passed away on 19 July, the day after the UFA won a majority government. Had he recovered, Baker would likely have been in the UFA cabinet and perhaps even have been offered the premiership, which in the event went to Herbert Greenfield*. A freak accident prevented him from shaping the political future of Alberta.

BRADFORD J. RENNIE

This biography is based in part on the author's interviews with Percy Baker (a grandson of the subject) and Janett [Pearson] Baker of Ponoka, Alta, and Robert Baker (another grandson) of Calgary. Although UFA and family sources indicate that the subject was born in York County, Ont., his marriage registration (AO, RG 80-5-0-174, no.13753) gives his place of birth as Ingersoll, in Oxford County, Ont.

GA, BR UFA, minutes and reports of annual conventions and of executive and board, 1916–21 (mfm.); M 1749, file 13. LAC, RG 31, C1, 1871, Markham Township, Ont., div.2: 50; 1881, Markham Township, div.4: 50. Private arch., Percy and Janett [Pearson] Baker, Birth record, marriage certificate, and other documents; Robert Baker, Documents and letters. *Calgary Herald*, 19–20 July 1921. *Edmonton Journal*, 20 July 1921. *Grain Growers' Guide* (Winnipeg), 22 May, 12, 26 June 1918; 17 Aug. 1921. *Manitoba Free Press*, 8 Aug. 1917. *Ponoka Herald*, 21 July 1921. Reuben Butchart, *The Disciples of Christ in Canada since 1830 . . .* (Toronto, 1949). Ponoka and District Hist. Soc., *Ponoka panorama* (Ponoka, 1973).

BALL, RICHARD AMOS, barber, British Methodist Episcopal minister, and musician; b. 30 Nov. 1845 in St Catharines, Upper Canada, son of Henry Ball and Sophia Hussey; m. there 7 Dec. 1864 Mary T. Jackson, and they had eight children; d. 22 Dec. 1925 in Windsor, Ont.

By the time of Richard A. Ball's death in 1925, the legend of the Underground Railroad had established itself firmly in the Canadian imagination. One of his obituaries constantly reminded readers that his family had come to Upper Canada fleeing slavery by this means. According to historian Robin W. Winks, his father was a fugitive slave from Virginia. Ball's death registration notes that his mother was a native of Liverpool, England, and Ball himself was born in St Catharines. By 1845 it had become a centre of black migration, for free persons as well as ex-slaves from the United States. Ball more than likely knew Harriet Tubman [Ross*], who used the town as her Canadian base, and abolitionist Hiram Wilson, who had set up a mission there for blacks. The public school he attended was no doubt segregated – de facto segregation did exist in St Catharines – and he would have known of the race riot of 1852, in which nearly every home in the black quarter was destroyed by a white mob.

Ball's first line of work was barbering, which occupied him from the 1860s to the 1880s. Following in the footsteps of his father, a British Methodist Episcopal lay preacher, he became active in the local BME church. (An offshoot of the American Methodist Episcopal Church, the denomination had been established in Upper Canada in 1856 [see Richard Randolph Disney*]). Ball's marriage in 1864, to 18-year-old Mary Jackson, a Pennsylvania-born black, was conducted by a BME minister, L. C. Chambers. At some point Ball became an elder in his church. In 1892, at the British Methodist Episcopal Church's annual conference in Windsor, he was ordained deacon. A minister by 1895 – one of about 25 in Canada – he took charge that year of the congregation in Brantford. At the BMEC annual conference held there in 1895, his son Richard R. was made an elder. No doubt the Balls took pride in the knowledge that ministry had thus become a family tradition. Ball Sr subsequently served congregations in Windsor, London, Toronto (1911–16, 1923–24), and Winnipeg (1919–21). In 1914 he and his wife celebrated their golden anniversary at his church on Chestnut Street in Toronto, surrounded, the Toronto *Canadian Observer* reported, "by their children and a host of friends, numbering 400, which filled the auditorium . . . and almost the balcony." The guests presented the couple with a purse containing $110 in gold. The chairperson for the evening was former city controller William Peyton Hubbard*.

Music was part and parcel of Ball's family life as well as of his religion. He and his wife, their children, and their grandchildren all sang and played instruments. This activity led to the formation of the Ball Family Jubilee Singers. Richard was the choral conductor of this gospel-music group, which achieved fame in the United States and Canada, where it toured several times.

Ball served the BMEC in several capacities: elder, deacon, pastor, general agent, temperance advocate, and president of its annual and general conferences. His dedicated involvement earned him tremendous prestige and respect. The colour bar was a fact of life in most of the towns and cities where he pastored. As Ball ministered to beleaguered blacks in these centres, it was common for him and his team to organize educational programs, help church members find jobs, run soup kitchens, and dispense counsel. Through these initiatives, many African Canadians were able to shore up their self-esteem. In the early 1920s Ball attacked any activist black ideology that diminished loyalty to British institutions – a strong feature of the BMEC's articles of faith – and he fervently resisted efforts to merge the BMEC with the American MEC. He retired at the end of 1924.

While in Windsor with his wife in December 1925 to celebrate his birthday and their anniversary and to visit their son Charles, Ball suffered heart problems and died. His funeral service was held at his church in Toronto. Interred there in Prospect Cemetery, he was survived by a daughter and three sons, among them the Reverend Richard R. Ball, then a BME minister in Rochester, N.Y.

AFUA COOPER

AO, RG 80-27-2, 33: 71; RG 80-8-0-991, no.13490. LAC, RG 31, C1, 1861, 1871, 1881, St Catharines, Ont. (mfm. at AO). TRL, SC, Black hist. file. UCC-C, 53, 96.031C (mfm.). *Canadian Observer* (Toronto), 14 Dec. 1914. *Globe*, 24 Dec. 1925. *St. Catharines Standard*, 23 Dec. 1925. Bee Allen, "Bee Allen, 1911," in *No burden to carry: narratives of black working women in Ontario, 1920s–1950s*, ed. Dionne Brand (Toronto, 1991), 105–27. R. R. Ball, "The British-Methodist Episcopal Church of Canada," *Canada, an encyclopædia* (Hopkins), 4: 136–37. British Methodist Episcopal Church, *The doctrine and discipline of the British Methodist Episcopal Church* (Toronto, 1892). *Directories*, St Catharines, 1875–93; Toronto, 1895–1924. Sheldon Taylor, "The black church in Canada, a rock on which they stood," *Akili* ([Toronto]), 2 (1994), no.2: 1–17; no.4: 22–23. R. W. Winks, *The blacks in Canada: a history* (2nd ed., Montreal and Kingston, Ont., 1997).

BANCROFT, JAMES FREDERICK, educator and office holder; baptized 5 Aug. 1855 in Chester, England, son of James Bancroft and Susannah Fleetcroft; m. August 1880, in St John's, Mary Jane Metcalfe (d. 1930) of Chamberlains, Nfld, and they had three sons and three daughters; d. 3 Sept. 1929 in St John's.

Educated in Chester, Frederick Bancroft moved to Newfoundland, where in 1877 he began teaching in the Methodist school at Little Bay Islands. He subsequently taught in Church of England schools at Pass Island, English Harbour, Chance Cove, and (for six years) Bay Roberts. By 1890 he held a first-class teaching certificate and earned an annual salary of $382. Though he had consistently received glowing reports from the superintendent of Church of England schools, the Reverend William Pilot*, his certificate was downgraded to second class in 1891 and his salary dropped to $332.

On 18 Oct. 1890, in Bancroft's school at Bay Roberts, a meeting of teachers had been held at which it was decided to work for the establishment of an association for "united action." Bancroft chaired the meeting, and it was likely he who had called the participants together. Other meetings followed, and on 22 November in Spaniard's Bay, with Bancroft again in the chair, the Newfoundland Teachers' Association was formed. When its constitution was approved and its first officers were elected in January, Bancroft became president. His activities in establishing an organization that had as its first goal "the protection of teachers" had thwarted the efforts of Pilot, who had been striving to organize the same group into a teachers' institute, aimed primarily at improving teaching methods and promoting professionalism. In Bancroft's view, such institutes, which flourished in England and Canada at the time, were designed to control teachers. In Canada, where they were often termed education associations, they typically included government officials and were under the aegis of provincial departments of education. In fact, of all the provincial teachers' associations operating in what is now Canada, only the Newfoundland and Labrador Teachers' Association was founded on trade union principles.

Barker

Since Bancroft had grown up in an area of England in which both the Industrial Revolution and labour unions had had their beginnings, it is not surprising that he followed trade union precepts and desired an association in which only practising teachers would be members and officers. Although the constitution of the NTA, in 1891 as today, listed among its objectives the improvement of education in general, the fledgling association, in its first petition to government that year, highlighted requests for salary increases, minimum salaries, and state-aided pension and insurance plans. This petition was heard sympathetically by the Liberal government of Prime Minister Sir William Vallance Whiteway*. According to MHA Alfred Bishop Morine*, Bancroft had worked well for the party in the election of 1889 and deserved well of the party in return. In 1892 a pension plan was set up and an increase was made in the grant for teachers' salaries.

Thirteen months after founding the NTA, Bancroft had quit the teaching profession. In December 1891 he left Bay Roberts en route to Bonne Bay, where he had obtained a position as sub-collector of customs at a salary of $600 plus 21 per cent of duties received (the total not to exceed $1,000). After his departure the NTA fell dormant and, an attempt to revive it as a teachers' institute in 1898–99 having failed, it remained inactive until 1908.

In 1904 Bancroft had been transferred to the customs service at St John's. There he worked until 1912, when he was retired because of poor health on a pension of $667, many times what he would have received on the teachers' pension plan. He subsequently worked as a land surveyor and, after World War I broke out, as a recruitment officer. Eventually, he withdrew to his estate at Topsail, The Hermitage, where he engaged in experimental farming until his death in 1929 at the General Hospital in St John's. He is buried in the Church of England cemetery in Topsail.

Bancroft's name is still well known in NLTA circles, and each year since 1980 this organization has bestowed Bancroft Awards on outstanding members.

HARRY CUFF

Cheshire Record Office (Chester, Eng.), Vital statistics for the Bancroft family. Newfoundland and Labrador Teachers' Assoc. (St John's), NTA minute-books. *Evening Telegram* (St John's), 28 Aug. 1880; 1899–1929. *Harbor Grace Standard* (Harbour Grace, Nfld), 1890–1900. H. A. Cuff, *A history of the Newfoundland Teachers' Association, 1890–1930* (St John's, 1985); "The Newfoundland Teachers' Association, 1890–1930: its founding; and its establishment as a stable, influential, and permanent professional organization" (MA thesis, Memorial Univ. of Nfld, St John's, 1971); "Prominent figures from our recent past: James Frederick Bancroft," *Newfoundland Quarterly* (St John's), 86 (1990–91), no.2: 27–28; "Recently-discovered information on the family of James Frederick Bancroft, 1855–1927, founder of the Newfoundland Teachers' Association," *Newfoundland Quarterly*, 73 (1977), no.4: 39–44. Christopher English, "A history of the Newfoundland Teachers' Association, 1890–1930" [book review], *Newfoundland Quarterly*, 82 (1986–87), no.4: 43–44. Newfoundland Teachers' Association, *NTA Journal* (St John's), 1909–80.

BARKER, WILLIAM GEORGE, soldier, air force officer, and businessman; b. 3 Nov. 1894 in Dauphin, Man., son of George William John Barker, a farmer, and Jane Victoria Alguire; m. 1 June 1921 Jean Kilbourn Smith, and they had one daughter; d. 12 March 1930 in Rockcliffe (Ottawa) and was interred in the Mount Pleasant Mausoleum, Toronto.

The eldest of nine surviving children, William Barker was born in a log house on the family farm and was educated at schools in or near Dauphin and Russell, Man. His sister Edna remembered Willie as a boy with innate poise and self-confidence as well as an intense personality. As a teenager, he displayed all the qualities that would later make him an exceptional military pilot. He was a kinaesthetic young man, attracted to risk, yet possessed of an analytical and independent mind. Gifted with exceptional eyesight, he was adept at shooting and was a skilled horseback rider. He served in the militia with the 32nd (Manitoba) Horse in 1913. After the outbreak of World War I, Barker, in his final year of high school at Dauphin Collegiate, volunteered for the Canadian Expeditionary Force, enlisting as a trooper in the 1st Canadian Mounted Rifles Regiment on 1 Dec. 1914. He trained as a machine-gunner and arrived in the United Kingdom in June 1915. About 26 September his regiment entered the Ypres (Ieper) salient in Belgium, where he served until late February 1916.

Weary of trench life, Barker volunteered for the Royal Flying Corps as a gunner; he received four weeks of field training with 9 Squadron. He was commissioned a temporary second lieutenant on 2 April 1916 and then joined 4 Squadron as an observer, undertaking artillery cooperation and photographic and visual reconnaissance for ground troops. In July he was transferred to 15 Squadron. Four months later he and his pilot received the Military Cross for their superior work in support of an assault on Beaumont-Hamel (Beaumont), France. In December he was sent to England for pilot training.

Barker completed all flying and ground school training in the brief period of four weeks, was graded a flying officer on 14 Feb. 1917, and returned to 15 Squadron. By the end of May he had been promoted captain and given command of C Flight, and had received a bar to his Military Cross. Wounded by artillery fire in August, he was sent to England for a rest as an instructor.

With no enthusiasm for teaching novices, Barker

frequently disobeyed regulations and on at least one occasion performed a low-level aerobatic display over Piccadilly Circus in London. He was transferred to 28 Squadron on 29 September and flew to France on 10 October. By the end of October he had logged at least 35 hours in combat in his Sopwith Camel, B6313, and was credited with destroying three enemy aircraft.

Barker's squadron was one of several units transferred to northern Italy in late October. On Christmas Day he and Lieutenant Harold Byrne Hudson completed an impromptu low-level attack against a German aerodrome, probably at San Fior, setting fire to one hangar and damaging four aircraft. In January 1918 he and Hudson were reprimanded by the commanding officer of 14 Wing for their successful but unauthorized attacks against enemy kite balloons. As a result of, or perhaps despite, his unauthorized patrols, Barker was awarded the Distinguished Service Order; the citation noted that "his splendid example of fearlessness and magnificent leadership have been of inestimable value to his squadron." In March he received a second bar to his Military Cross "for conspicuous gallantry and devotion to duty."

By the time he joined 66 Squadron on 10 April, Barker had 22 victories. As commander of its C Flight, he would be credited with another 16. In May 1918 Barker received the French Croix de Guerre. He was promoted temporary major in July and given command of 139 Squadron, equipped with two-seat Bristol Fighters. Unhappy with this aircraft, he was allowed to keep B6313 and added 8 more victories, bringing his total to 46, a unique achievement by one pilot with one machine. British historians would call B6313 "the single most successful fighter aircraft" in the history of the Royal Air Force.

On the night of 9–10 August, Barker and Captain William Wedgwood Benn dropped an Italian army agent by parachute behind enemy lines. For this flight Barker received the Silver Medal for Military Valour, one of Italy's highest military decorations. That same month he was awarded a bar to his DSO. Remarkably, in over 12 months of scout operations, from 9 or 10 Oct. 1917 to 27 Oct. 1918, he had never had a wingman killed in action and no aircraft he escorted had been shot down.

Prior to taking up a new command in late October, Barker was permitted to fly anywhere in France for a ten-day roving commission. He selected a Sopwith Snipe, E8102, and attached himself to 201 Squadron. On 27 October he attacked and shot down a German two-seater at around 22,000 feet and, in turn, was attacked by about 15 Fokker D-VIIs. He was wounded three times, but also shot down three more enemy aircraft. Bleeding profusely and barely conscious, he managed to crash-land and was evacuated to a field hospital. Awarded the Victoria Cross on 30

Nov. 1918, Barker now had 50 victories to his credit. Italy later conferred a second Silver Medal on him. While he struggled for survival in a French hospital, the *Canadian Daily Record* (London, England) declared that he held "the record among Canadians for fighting decorations won during the war."

Barker's wounds would cause him considerable physical and emotional pain for the remainder of his life. His legs were damaged and his left elbow was destroyed, effectively turning him into a one-armed pilot. While recovering in London, he met fellow VC recipient William Avery Bishop*. After the end of the war and Barker's release from hospital in April 1919, the two men first founded Bishop-Barker Company Limited in Ontario and then, in November 1919, a Toronto-based air charter and aircraft maintenance and sales firm, Bishop-Barker Aeroplanes Limited. Around this period they established an American importing firm, Interallied Aircraft Corporation, in New York City.

Barker tackled civil aviation with the same intensity he had shown in combat. Between 23 Aug. and 6 Sept. 1919 he led an aerial display team at the Canadian National Exhibition in Toronto, the first occasion on which formation flying was performed in Canada for a non-military audience. On 25–27 August he participated in an air race from Toronto to New York and back, becoming the first Canadian pilot to carry international airmail. He flew the first commercial cargo between the United States and Canada, from New York City via Montreal to Toronto in January 1921.

A commercial failure, like many other flying companies of this period, Bishop-Barker Aeroplanes ceased flying operations in 1922. On 3 June Barker was commissioned a wing commander in the Canadian Air Force, which had been created two years earlier [*see* Sir Willoughby Garnons GWATKIN]. His first permanent posting was as the commanding officer of the air station at Camp Borden, where he served from 1 Nov. 1922 to 15 Jan. 1924. He would be remembered for his highly innovative ideas and experiments in aircraft armament. He was then transferred to Ottawa and in mid February assumed the highest position within the CAF, acting director. He held this post on 1 April 1924, when the CAF was disbanded and the Royal Canadian Air Force was officially born [*see* Sir James Howden MacBrien*]. The following month he was posted to England as the RCAF's representative to the British Air Ministry. As a liaison officer, Barker witnessed RAF operations in Iraq in the spring of 1925 and in May he began advanced studies at the Royal Air Force Staff College in Andover; he graduated in March 1926.

Barker returned to Canada knowing that he would have to serve under Group Captain James Stanley Scott, the director of the RCAF and an officer he did not respect. Unwilling to compromise, he submitted his resignation in August 1926. He had struggled with the usual adjustments to civilian life of any wounded veteran and especially with the burden of being a much decorated hero. In these last years of his life he also suffered from alcoholism and possibly from post-traumatic stress disorder.

In 1927 the Toronto Maple Leafs' manager, Constantine Falkland Cary Smythe*, a former RAF pilot, had Barker appointed the first president of the hockey club, a symbolic gesture to help raise the losing team's profile. Smythe, a teetotaller, had no appreciation of the emotional challenges Barker faced and no sympathy for alcohol abuse; this situation led to public embarrassment for both men. Barker was also appointed general manager of an Ontario tobacco-growing company owned by his wife's father, Horace Bruce Smith. Oddly, Barker was a non-smoker with an antipathy to farming. As a sinecure offered by an unsympathetic father-in-law, the tobacco job was unrewarding, if not humiliating.

A much better post, suited to Barker's natural talents and experience, was secured when Fairchild Aircraft Limited of Canada in Montreal hired him in January 1930 as vice-president and general manager. While demonstrating a new biplane trainer, the Fairchild KR-21, at the RCAF air station in Rockcliffe, he lost control of the aircraft at the apex of a steep climb and was instantly killed when the aircraft struck the ice on the Ottawa River. His state funeral, held in Toronto on 15 March, included political and military leaders, six VC recipients, and an honour guard of 2,000 men.

On 6 June 1931 an airport in Toronto was renamed Barker Field in his memory and Bishop lauded his friend both then and later as "the deadliest air fighter that ever lived." Author Ernest Hemingway had another point of view. In a short story published in 1936, "The snows of Kilimanjaro," he portrayed Barker as a "bloody murderous bastard." Barker's character was in keeping with the tradition of the larger-than-life hero. He was driven above all else to excel – to be a figurehead was anathema to him. Because of his untimely death many of his war and post-war achievements would later be overlooked and he would be overshadowed by Bishop, who lived to 1956. The RCAF picked Barker as one of its role models for the recruitment of a new generation of flyers during World War II, but afterwards his legend, well known in Great Britain and the United States, faded in Canada. Few Canadians are aware that he was, and still is, Canada's most decorated war hero.

WAYNE RALPH

[This biography is based on the author's book *Barker VC: William Barker, Canada's most decorated war hero* (London and Toronto, 1997), which contains an exhaustive list of the documentation consulted: military files in the archives of Great Britain, Canada, and the United States, personal papers, logbooks, monographs, newspaper and magazine articles, and interviews with relatives and military personnel. W.R.]

BARKER, WILLIAM HENRY, businessman; b. 24 June 1853 in Manchester, England, one of the ten children of Ambrose Barker and Sarah Westerdale; m. Orpha Beard in Astoria, Oreg., and they had three sons and two daughters; d. 9 Jan. 1929 in Vancouver.

Following schooling in England, William Barker found employment in his father's Liverpool shipping business and later in the merchant navy. In 1872 he emigrated to the United States. He settled in Oregon just as the Columbia River fishery was gaining momentum and he quickly established a position within the pioneer canning business. He worked for several of the early canners in the state, including Robert Deniston Hume, whose interests he managed from 1878 to 1881 at the Kinney cannery in Astoria. In 1885, after a decade in managerial positions with different firms, he formed the George and Barker Packing Company on the Columbia River with George H. George; he was the junior partner. In 1895 this enterprise consolidated several rival canneries to form the Eureka and Epicure Packing Company. A further consolidation of nine separate businesses on the Columbia River occurred in 1897, creating the Columbia River Packers' Association with headquarters in Astoria. In all of these enterprises, Barker assumed significant administrative and managerial authority. The newly established CRPA, for example, retained him as its superintendent. In 1901, however, he resigned from the position to devote his attention to the George and Barker Company, which had been founded the previous year. He acted as the firm's president and manager, overseeing a program of expansion that included the establishment of a cannery at Point Roberts, Wash.

Barker was attracted to Vancouver in 1904 to carry forward the successful integration of canneries under the British Columbia Packers' Association. Two years earlier the BCPA, backed by eastern Canadian and American capital, had merged 22 firms and assumed control of over half the Fraser River's salmon pack; it operated with a capitalization of $4,000,000 and was the largest fish-packing business in the province. Barker was viewed favourably as a practical man, well acquainted with the business, who would ably conduct the BCPA's affairs. He assumed the position of general manager on 1 Oct. 1904. In the course of his duties he oversaw the day-to-day affairs of the association, represented its interests to federal and provincial governments, and sought to develop the labour and technological capacities of the business. In recognition of his success, he was appointed president of the BCPA in 1907, succeeding Alexander Ewen*. He continued to oversee operations as general manager, but gained greater authority within the association from his new appointment. In 1921 the British Columbia Fishing and Packing Company Limited took over the operation of the firm with the BCPA carrying on as a holding company. Barker served as president of the new firm until 1926, when he resigned because of his objections to further acquisitions by the firm.

Throughout his tenure Barker insisted that the BCPA follow business principles and inveighed against government regulation. In matters of conservation, he felt that Canadian packers suffered from reduced catches as a result of the pressure on Fraser-bound salmon exerted by packers in the United States. He tended to criticize conservation measures that affected the BCPA's interests, but supported action that might improve fish supplies, such as the establishment of hatcheries and the clearance of debris in the spawning grounds. With respect to ethnic conflict within the fishery, he displayed the racial biases of his time. He nonetheless felt that efficiency should triumph over racist attitudes or ethnic favouritism in the hiring of workers.

Barker did not play a significant role in the social or political life of Vancouver. He held membership in the Vancouver Club, but, as the *Vancouver Daily Province* would note at his death, he "had few interests outside his business and his home." This situation contrasted with his earlier years in Oregon, where he had been involved in the Republican party and municipal politics. Nevertheless, in the late 1920s he held high status in his adopted city because of his wealth and stature in the canning industry. Among the business leaders of Vancouver who had established themselves in the city before 1914 and who would die before 1940, Barker held the tenth largest estate, worth $551,909.

William Barker embodied the transnational flows of personnel and capital that shaped the early British Columbia fishery. In the late 19th and early 20th centuries the Fraser River fishery became, to some extent, the greatest and latest field of expansion for a class of cannery entrepreneurs and managers eager to develop large natural stocks in the wake of depletions in New England, California, and the American Pacific northwest. Like Henry Doyle, one of the founders of the BCPA, and John Pease Babcock*, the provincial assistant commissioner of fisheries, he had come to an important position in Canada in mid career as a result of his earlier experience in the United States. He represented the importation of human resources at a time when the growth and consolidation of the cannery business depended increasingly on the attraction of foreign capital from Britain and the United States.

MATTHEW EVENDEN

William Henry Barker is the author of "Reminiscences of the salmon industry," *Pacific fisherman yearbook* (Seattle, Wash.), 1919: 67–69.

BCA, GR-2951, no.1929-09-415205. City of Richmond Arch. (Richmond, B.C.), AN 2001 34 (British Columbia Packers fonds), Barker letter-books. Univ. of B.C. Library, Rare Books and Special Coll. (Vancouver), Henry Doyle papers; International Pacific Salmon Fisheries Commission coll. *Evening Telegram* (Portland, Oreg.), 10 Jan. 1929. *New Westminster Columbian* (New Westminster, B.C.), 10 Jan. 1929. *Oregon Daily Journal* (Portland), 21 March 1929. *Vancouver Daily Province*, 27 Aug. 1920, 10 Jan. 1929. *Victoria Daily Times*, 10 Jan. 1929. *The development of the Pacific salmon-canning industry: a grown man's game*, ed. Dianne Newell (Montreal and Kingston, Ont., 1989). Cicely Lyons, *Salmon: our heritage; the story of a province and an industry* (Vancouver, 1969). R. A. J. McDonald, *Making Vancouver: class, status, and social boundaries, 1863–1913* (Vancouver, 1996). *Portrait and biographical record of western Oregon, containing original sketches of many well known citizens of the past and present* (Chicago, 1904). D. J. Reid, "Company mergers in the Fraser River salmon canning industry, 1885–1902," *CHR*, 56 (1975): 282–302. "William H. Barker passes," *Pacific Fisherman* ([Portland]), 27 (February 1929): 22.

BARR, ANNIE GARDNER (Gardiner) (Brown), artist and social reformer; b. 29 July 1864 in Norwich, Upper Canada, daughter of James Barr and Beatrice Eadie; m. 10 Oct. 1895 George William Brown (d. 17 Feb. 1919) in Norwich, Ont., and they had a daughter and a son; d. 29 June 1921 in Regina.

In the 1871 census Annie G. Barr is listed as the youngest of six children (four sisters and one brother). Her parents were of Scottish heritage, and her father was then clerk of the Division Court in Norwich. Little is known about her childhood. A talented individual, she attended the Brantford Young Ladies' College. Upon graduation in 1883 she received rewards for excellence. She was also gifted in art and received formal training, including instruction at Alma Ladies' College in St Thomas. She graduated in 1893, and obtained a special mention for a still-life study exhibited at the Columbian exposition in Chicago that year.

She arrived in Regina on 17 Oct. 1895 as the 31-year-old bride of George W. Brown, and rose to a position of prominence in "the last best west." Her husband had been born and raised in Holstein, Ont., and had studied at the Brantford Collegiate Institute and the University of Toronto. In 1882 he moved to the North-West Territories, where he and his three brothers homesteaded. Several years later he settled in the territorial capital of Regina and studied law; he was called to the bar in 1892. His law firm prospered, his business interests expanded, and politics beckoned. Brown, a Liberal, served in the legislature from 1894 to 1905, and later was briefly a Regina alderman. His local interests included education. He served for over a decade on the public school board and would play a major role in establishing the Methodist-affiliated Regina College in 1910–11.

On 14 Oct. 1910 George W. Brown was sworn in as lieutenant governor of Saskatchewan, succeeding Amédée-Emmanuel FORGET. Until his retirement in 1915 his wife was his complement in this role. Press clippings describe her as "quiet and unassuming," "extremely popular," "exceedingly gracious and highly endowed intellectually and artistically." Also noted were her devotion to home, her social role, and her work in numerous women's organizations. As the chatelaine of Government House, she stepped into a position for which she had, in effect, been groomed, and a diary that she kept during these years illustrates in usually terse, descriptive fashion her many interests and talents. (She also kept a scrapbook but it focused more upon her husband's official activities.)

Although the mother of two young children – Beatrice Annie, born 8 March 1897, and Gordon Barr, born 15 May 1901 – Annie Brown had quickly become a prominent figure in Regina life. A devout Methodist (she had been a Presbyterian before her marriage), she attended Metropolitan Church and was active in its Ladies' Aid. It was this affiliation that apparently led to her initial involvement with the Local Council of Women, an umbrella group for most women's organizations, and one she served in an executive capacity.

Among the many organizations in which she was a member (and sometimes an office holder) were the Woman's Christian Temperance Union, the Young Women's Christian Association, the Imperial Order Daughters of the Empire, the Women's Musical Club, the Aberdeen Association, and the Hospital Aid. In 1913 she became active in the newly formed Women's Educational Club, an auxiliary for Regina College with a particular focus on the promotion of art, for her a lifelong pursuit. The organization most often mentioned in her diary, however, was the Kannata Club, a small group of Regina women of cultural and intellectual bent – with some interest in women's rights issues. Although she was not a major suffragist in Saskatchewan (which was to become the second province to grant the vote to women, in 1916), Annie Brown attended at least one local suffrage meeting, and she is listed as honorary president on the letterhead of the Provincial Equal Franchise Board of Saskatchewan, formed in 1915. Like so many "organization women," she did extensive war work during the Great War and participated in Red Cross activities. In fact, her obituary in the Regina *Morning Leader* states that in 1920 she received recognition from the Serbian king, government, and Red Cross for her work as president of the Saskatchewan Serbian Relief Committee.

At the time of her death she had been a widow for more than two years.

ANN LEGER-ANDERSON

AO, RG 80-5-0-227, no.9216. LAC, RG 31, C1, 1871, South Oxford County, Ont., North Norwich, div.3: 36. Saskatchewan Arch. Board (Saskatoon), S-1.20 (Annie G. Brown fonds) (mfm.). *Morning Leader* (Regina), 30 June 1921. N. F. Black, *History of Saskatchewan and the North-West Territories* (2v., Regina, 1913), 1: 307. *Who's who and why*, 1914. *Who's who in western Canada . . .* (Vancouver), 1912.

BARRINGTON, SIBELLA ANNIE, registered nurse and administrator; b. 4 Dec. 1867 in Sydney Mines, N.S., daughter of York Ainsley Walker Barrington and M. Matilda Mahon; d. unmarried 7 Dec. 1929 in Saint John and was buried at Barrington Park, Sydney Mines.

Sibella Barrington (also called Bay or Bey) was probably named after her father's sister Margaret Sibella, who had married Richard Brown, a mining agent and engineer in Cape Breton and the future author of three books. Her roots had been established on the island when her paternal grandfather, Charles Barrington, a captain in the British army, settled around 1825 near Sydney Mines. Charles's third son, York, was a gentleman farmer who filled a number of public offices and eventually inherited a baronetcy.

Little is recorded of Sibella's early life. In 1901, eight years after her father's death, she entered the Aberdeen Hospital School of Nursing in New Glasgow. Her work habits may have been influenced by its superintendent, Jessie Muir Sheraton, who had the reputation of being "very forceful, commanding and a great disciplinarian." Sibella, attired in a dark blue dress and white apron, would have gone directly to work on the wards, for 12-hour shifts, while living on the third floor of the hospital under the eaves. She graduated in 1904. She would become an RN when registration was introduced to Nova Scotia in 1922.

Evidence of her sincerity in her profession, she pursued postgraduate studies in Chicago and overseas. In Dublin she studied the public health and tuberculosis work that had been launched in 1907 by Lady Aberdeen [Marjoribanks*] and was carried on by caravan throughout the country; thus she learned about teaching people to combat illness. In London, England, she was associated with Dr Frederic Truby King, a pioneer of child welfare in New Zealand who believed in public participation in preventive medicine.

By 1917 Sibella was working in Halifax, where she apparently had a large private practice; she is credited with voluntary service during the massive explosion of 6 December that year and was awarded life membership in the British Red Cross Society. She had concentrated on obstetric cases since beginning her career, and from 1918 to 1923 she was superintendent of the Halifax Infants' Home, which took in unwanted children and also served as a women's hospital. She was noted particularly for her sympathy towards the unmarried mothers who made up the usual clientele of the maternity ward. She also served as vice-president of the Children's Aid Society for five years. In 1919 she became president of the Graduate Nurses' Association of Nova Scotia, having previously served as local vice-president, and with her colleagues she met with provincial health authorities to enquire about legislation on various health and professional issues. One of the councillors for Nova Scotia of the Canadian Nurses' Association by August 1924, she also served on its education committee. She was convenor of the public hospital committee of the Halifax Local Council of Women, and in the 1920s she would occasionally be a delegate to meetings of the National Council of Women of Canada, where she was a member of the public health committee. Her chief contribution, however, was with the Canadian Red Cross Society in New Brunswick.

At the close of World War I, the Red Cross had sought a role for itself in peacetime and had taken on a program of improvement of health, prevention of disease, and alleviation of suffering. One of its initiatives was the provision of classes to teach women how to identify illnesses and provide basic nursing care in the home. Dominion organizers of home nursing were appointed and fully paid for initially by the Central Council of the Red Cross. Lent to Saint John by the national society in December 1924, Sibella set to work with vigour. Her primary goal was saving children. In 1925 the work involved 101 personal visits, 119 addresses, and the organization of 62 home-nursing classes for 1,558 pupils. The following year she organized 77 classes. The home-nursing program depended on the voluntary service of graduate nurses to teach the classes, a contribution that the Red Cross gratefully acknowledged.

A brilliant speaker, Sibella used her gift to the full. She reached out to other organizations, including the Imperial Order Daughters of the Empire, of which she was a member, and to professional associations such as the New Brunswick Association of Registered Nurses and the Victorian Order of Nurses to support her campaign. She was skilled at arousing community spirit, travelling daily to various points in the province to speak under the auspices of the local councils of women, but she was particularly effective among nurses. Because of her efforts, New Brunswick's record of home-nursing classes completed from 1924 to 1928 was better than that of any other province except Ontario. She was also instrumental in establishing Red Cross outpost hospitals in St Leonard and St Clair (Clair) and the Red Cross nursing service in St George.

In 1928 the Central Council decided to eliminate grants for the home-nursing program. Perhaps as a consequence, in that year Sibella became port nurse for Saint John, where the first port nursery in the world had been established through another post-war initiative of the Red Cross. There nurses and local

volunteers combined to assist immigrants, initially the dependants of soldiers, on the last lap of their journey. The care provided by such nurses to mothers and children was complex and, although physicians were on call, their work resembled that of nurse practitioners. The following year Sibella did the Red Cross another service. With the New Brunswick Division at the end of its resources that spring, she accomplished "excellent work" in organizing communities to campaign for donations.

Sibella Barrington died suddenly in December 1929 following surgery at the Saint John General Public Hospital. She had apparently been unwell, one obituary noting that "she carried on her work with tireless energy in the face of tremendous handicaps of ill health." John Barrington accompanied the remains of his sister, an Anglican, to the family home, Barrington Park, where the funeral was held. An irreparable loss to New Brunswick, she was memorialized by glowing tributes in the Maritime press.

The contributions of women like Sibella Barrington are often ignored in the history of nation building; yet women, particularly nurses, were always in the forefront of shaping the direction of communities. Through the Canadian Red Cross, often among a populace far removed from health care, they undertook work that improved the lives of thousands. Sibella Barrington transformed her vision for New Brunswick's women and children into a workable plan. Her positive image, ability to link organizations to a cause, and skill at persuasion were crucial to the success of her goal.

ARLEE HOYT MCGEE

Beaton Institute, Univ. College of Cape Breton (Sydney, N.S.), Biog. and geneal. files, Barrington; Brown; MG 12.208, D (Elva Jackson papers), geneal. charts, Charles Barrington; Newspaper clippings. College of Registered Nurses of Nova Scotia (Halifax), Graduate Nurses' Assoc. of Nova Scotia, minutes, 1919. Nurses Assoc. of New Brunswick, Nursing Hist. Resource Centre (Fredericton), New Brunswick Assoc. of Graduate Nurses, minutes, 22 June 1927, 16 Oct. 1928; Scrapbooks. *Telegraph-Journal* (Saint John), 25 Jan. 1930. Canadian Red Cross Soc., *A history of Red Cross outposts in New Brunswick, 1922–1975* (Saint John, 1976). Faye Hoare et al., *90th anniversary booklet of the Aberdeen School of Nursing, 1987* ([New Glasgow, N.S., 1987]; copy in Aberdeen Hospital Nursing Alumni Arch., New Glasgow).

BARTHE, ÉMILIE (baptized **Marie-Louise-Émilie**) **(Lavergne)**, woman of the world; b. 26 March 1849 in Montreal, daughter of Joseph-Guillaume Barthe*, clerk of the Court of Appeal of Lower Canada, and Louise-Adélaïde Pacaud; m. 29 Nov. 1876 Joseph Lavergne, a lawyer, in Arthabaskaville (Victoriaville), Que., and they had one son and one daughter; d. 10 May 1930 in Montreal.

Émilie Barthe was the fourth child in her parents'

household, and it was soon clear that she would be as colourful, original, and talented as her father and uncles before her – including the famous Pacaud brothers, Édouard-Louis* and Philippe-Napoléon*. By the time she was four, she was living with her family in Paris, where it is thought that the Barthes were on visiting terms with such celebrities as Alphonse de Lamartine. Émilie's schooling began on her return to Lower Canada in 1855. Depending on her father's various postings, she studied initially with a tutor in Trois-Rivières, and then with the Ursuline sisters in Quebec City from 1 Oct. 1857 to 7 July 1862. After 1862 she probably continued to work for a couple of years with a tutor in Quebec City and between 1865 and 1869 she pursued her education in the Lévis region. By this point, Émilie Barthe had become a lively and witty young woman, a bilingual anglophile with cutting repartee and infectious cheerfulness. Although not herself a beauty, she had learned to appreciate beautiful things, fine clothes, English manners, and social gatherings. Ambitious, eager to reach new heights, and already highly cultured, she found great pleasure in reading widely – aside from the company of learned men, it was her chief interest.

It was at Arthabaskaville, from 1876, that Émilie Barthe shaped her future, for there, in the same year, she married Joseph Lavergne, a hard-working if rather lacklustre lawyer who was a partner of Wilfrid Laurier*. Although she had lived in Detroit around 1874–75, Émilie was happy in Arthabaskaville, where she had recently moved. In 1877 she gave birth to Gabrielle and in 1880 to Armand [La Vergne*], one of the future leaders of Henri Bourassa*'s Canadian nationalist movement, who, even as a child, was brought into the world of books and the arts by his mother. Émilie lost no time in winning over the leading citizens of the place who, besides visiting celebrities such as Louis Fréchette* and Hector Fabre*, included lawyers, politicians, and artists, some of whom, like Laurier and Marc-Aurèle de Foy Suzor-Coté*, were to become famous. Until 1897 the Lavergne home was the social hub of Arthabaskaville, where people gathered to enjoy fine cuisine and discuss Liberal politics, literature, and history, often to the accompaniment of music and singing. Émilie was an outstanding hostess. In the finery of her Parisian gowns, dutifully paid for by Joseph (though he could not manage to make ends meet), she reigned over her modest little realm. Her life was further brightened by visits to Murray Bay (La Malbaie) and by travel, with, for example, trips to Old Orchard Beach in Maine in 1888, New York in 1892, and Boston in 1894. In this period she also aspired to broaden her horizons and explore other worlds where her talents as a leading light in society would be appreciated. To this end, she developed special relationships with Premier Honoré Mercier* and with Edward Blake*, who had been

leader of the Liberal party. But it was Laurier who would show her the royal road ahead.

Émilie and Wilfrid had admired one another from 1876. They had the same literary interests, the same love of things English, the same desire to outdo themselves, and the same sensitivity. This mutual attraction grew into love and became the most celebrated liaison in Canadian political history. This woman, who would never have any official status, so captivated Laurier that at times, openly and with the full knowledge of their spouses, Zoé and Joseph, she was his confidante, go-between, and *éminence grise*. Already an established fact in 1878, the liaison became more intense in the 1880s and gave rise to a steady exchange of letters, at least at the beginning of the next decade. Émilie, whose library contained the volume of the collected *Lettres de Adrienne Le Couvreur* published by Georges Monval in Paris in 1892, was apparently the instigator of this correspondence. The 41 letters from Laurier discovered in 1963 by historian Marc La Terreur, which were written for the most part in English between 1891 and 1893, reveal the intimacy of their relationship. (Émilie's side of the correspondence has not, thus far, come to light.) Tender thoughts about Gabrielle and Armand are shared, as well as views on politics, religion, philosophy, and history. Opinions about literature in its many forms are also exchanged, though Émilie – whom Laurier compared to Mme de Staël and urged to become a writer herself – preferred historical biographies. In these letters, Laurier kept Émilie abreast of the undercurrents of politics in Ottawa, and in the summer of 1891 he made skilful use of her as a go-between in his dispute with Edward Blake over the issue of unrestricted commercial reciprocity with the United States. The opinions and advice she sent him helped transform Laurier into a sophisticated statesman. For his part, he at last would find the words to express his love openly, as in this letter of 23 Aug. 1891: "I would like to see you, my dear, dear, friend, not to have your explanations, but simply to see you, to hear you, to look in your eyes, to listen to your voice, to feel that it is you, to be sure of it, to enjoy the consciousness of it." Their love gave rise to gossip: some said that Laurier was the father of young Armand, who looked so like him. The letter writers, apparently, did not really care: they knew their love was "right," as Émilie would later declare.

Having become prime minister, Laurier exulted in this letter of 30 Sept. 1896: "How I long to see you in a milieu . . . more worthy of you." On 4 Aug. 1897 he appointed Joseph Lavergne, who until then had been an MP, a judge of the Superior Court for the district of Ottawa. The flamboyant Émilie lost no time in making her presence felt in the capital, organizing dazzling receptions, involving herself in charitable endeavours, and attending official dinners. However, at some point between 1899 and 1901, her star began to wane. Realizing the damage that the rumours about their relationship might cause, Laurier returned her letters to her and increasingly distanced himself from her. In addition, he moved her husband from Ottawa to Montreal in 1901. Henceforth it was through Joseph, Armand, or Gabrielle that he would send her his "best wishes." Émilie understood, but she would never be the same and never forgot Laurier, as her later correspondence with, for example, the librarian and historian Alfred DUCLOS De Celles reveals. Thus began what she referred to as her "dull years," during which she kept up certain social appearances in Montreal and Saint-Irénée (her summer residence). On 9 Jan. 1922 Joseph Lavergne died. On 15 Oct. 1924, at the age of 75, Émilie moved into the Foyer Saint-Mathieu of the Grey Nuns of Montreal, where she would spend the rest of her days. She lived as a recluse, sadder and lonelier than ever, always complaining about the lack of money and deeply affected by the loss of her daughter, Gabrielle, who died in 1928. It was then that she gave Laurier's 41 letters to her nephew, perhaps as a way of leaving her name attached to the man she had loved so deeply.

Émilie Lavergne died peacefully on 10 May 1930 and was buried in Arthabaska (Victoriaville). Described in 1903 as the most brilliant society woman in French Canada, she was a *mondaine* fitting for an exceptional period of Canadian history.

RÉAL BÉLANGER

[The Émilie Barthe Lavergne collection, held at the LAC, MG 27, I, I42, contains little information aside from copies of the 41 famous letters that Wilfrid Laurier wrote to her and some other correspondence. The author has a personal archival collection concerning the Lavergne family, including several unpublished letters written or received by Émilie, Armand, and his wife Georgette (née Roy), photographs, and a number of books, which offer remarkable insight into the private life of Émilie Barthe Lavergne. Among other useful collections are the papers of Sir Wilfrid Laurier (LAC, MG 26, G), Edward Blake (AO, F 2, mfm. at LAC), Armand La Vergne (LAC, MG 27, II, E12 and ANQ-Q, P487), and Ernest Pacaud (LAC, MG 29, D36). Worth mentioning as well are ANQ-M, CE601-S51, 29 mars 1849; ANQ-MBF, CE402-S2, 29 nov. 1876; Arch. des Sœurs Grises (Montréal), Foyer Saint-Mathieu, caisse recettes et déboursés, 1923–31; and Arch. du Monastère des Ursulines (Québec), Fonds de l'éducation, fichier des anciennes élèves; prospectus. The newspaper *L'Union des Cantons de l'Est* (Arthabaska [Victoriaville], Qué.), read for the period 1876–97, also provides interesting information.

There are no books or in-depth articles devoted exclusively to Émilie Barthe Lavergne. There are, however, some other articles and chapters, or excerpts, in books that concern her, especially the question of her relationship with Laurier: H.-A. Bizier, *Histoires d'amour* ([Montréal], 1987), 29–32;

[Sir Wilfrid Laurier], *Dearest Émilie: the love-letters of Sir Wilfrid Laurier to Madame Émilie Lavergne*, intro. Charles Fisher (Montreal, 1991); Sandra Gwyn, "The lady who loved Laurier," *Saturday Night*, 99 (1984), no.8: 18–26 and *The private capital: ambition and love in the age of Macdonald and Laurier* (Toronto, 1984), 243–72; Madeleine [A.-M]. Gleason-Huguenin, *Portraits de femmes* ([Montréal], 1938), 181; *Types of Canadian women . . .*, ed. H. J. Morgan (Toronto, 1903); Marc La Terreur, "Correspondance Laurier–Mme Joseph LaVergne, 1891–1893," CHA, *Report* (1964): 37–51 and "Sir Wilfrid Laurier écrit à Émilie Lavergne," *Le Magazine Maclean* (Montréal), 6 (1966), no.1: 14–15, 36–39, 41; [Armand La Vergne], *Armand Lavergne*, ed. Marc La Terreur (Montréal and Paris, 1968), and *Trente ans de vie nationale* (Montréal, 1934); and [Renaud La Vergne], *Histoire de la famille Lavergne*, comp. B. C. Payette (Montréal, [1970]). *Le Devoir*, 10 mai 1930, contains a very brief obituary. R.B.]

BARTLETT, JERRY. *See* LONECLOUD, JERRY

BATES, SARAH. *See* HYMAS

BEARDY, FANNY. *See* NICKAWA, FRANCES

BEAUCHAMP, JEAN-JOSEPH, lawyer and author; b. 18 Jan. 1852 in Montreal, son of Joseph Beauchamp, a tailor, and Marcelline Bayard; m. there 20 Feb. 1879 Marie-Éliza Décary, and they had seven children; d. there 14 Nov. 1923 and was buried 17 November in the Notre-Dame-des-Neiges cemetery.

Jean-Joseph Beauchamp was orphaned when he was seven years old. During his adolescence he spent a few years working in the United States. After returning to Montreal, he was tutored by a priest and received his graduation diploma from the Collège Sainte-Marie. Subsequently, probably in 1874, he began studying law at McGill College. Having obtained his degree in 1878, he was called to the bar of the province of Quebec the following year. He launched his career in Montreal, where over the years he would have many partners, including lawyers Edmund Barnard (1879–84), James George Aylwin CREIGHTON (1882–83), and Charles Bruchési (1895–98). The cases entrusted to him by clients attracted by his expertise would sometimes take him before the highest judicial authorities in the country and even the British empire.

The swift progress of industrialization and more efficient means of communication were transforming North American society as the 20th century began. Under the influence of these changes, the practice of law became more complex and speed came to be one of the qualities expected of a good legal practitioner. As a result, reference books became indispensable tools for quick access to information. Beauchamp's publications belonged in this category: they were basically catalogues providing summaries of judicial decisions and theoretical studies. His first work was published in Montreal in 1891 under the title *The jurisprudence of the Privy Council: containing a digest of all the decisions of the Privy Council. . . .* A second volume, bringing the digest up to date, would be issued in 1909, an indication that it had been well received both in Quebec and beyond the province. In 1904 and 1905 Beauchamp's *Le Code civil de la province de Québec annoté . . .* , in three volumes, was brought out at Montreal. An updated edition, completed by him before his death, would appear in 1924, after which the publishers would call on lawyer Joseph-Fortunat Saint-Cyr to prepare the supplement that followed in 1931. Beauchamp's most important work, however, is the *Répertoire général de jurisprudence canadienne . . .* , which summarizes the judicial decisions concerning the province of Quebec handed down by the courts in Quebec, Canada, and Great Britain from 1770 to May 1913. He said that this four-volume work, which was published in Montreal in 1914, was undertaken at the urging of many members in the legal profession. Three posthumous supplements would come out in succeeding decades (1927, 1935, and 1955). Beauchamp's contemporaries emphasized the quality of his works. Their praise shows a genuine admiration for the "painstaking labour" – to borrow the expression used by François Langelier* in the first volume of his *Cours de droit civil de la province de Québec* (Montréal, 1905) – to which the author had committed himself. The publication of updated versions and supplements bears witness to the merit of Beauchamp's various publications.

In 1895 Beauchamp also revived in Montreal *La Revue légale*, which had been founded in Sorel in 1869 by Adolphe Germain and Michel Mathieu* but had ceased publication in 1892. As its editor, a position he would hold until his death, Beauchamp hoped to make it a theoretical journal combining judicial science and the practice of law. He wrote many articles himself but depended also on the participation of judges, lawyers, and notaries. After some 12 years, and repeated appeals for articles to print, Beauchamp, like his predecessor Mathieu, decided to make *La Revue légale* simply a collection of legal judgements. In all likelihood it was because of his experience in this type of publishing that the general council of the Quebec bar chose Beauchamp in 1914 as editor of the *Rapports judiciaires de Québec*, an annual compendium of judgements handed down by the Court of King's Bench and the Superior Court. Beauchamp would hold this position for the rest of his life.

The work undertaken by Beauchamp helped create "a body of national law." He was not thinking, however, of a law in isolation from that in other jurisdictions. On the contrary, he took the view that this body of national law, despite its increasing originality, was bound to retain elements drawn from French, British,

and American law. During the same period, the development of uniform laws was a popular theme in American legal theory. Beauchamp took an interest in this question and advocated a similar exercise in Canada, pointing out, however, the necessity of respecting the traditions and homogeneity of the law in force in each province. The uniformity movement won followers in Canada, and by the end of the 1910s had triggered strong opposition from the conservative wing of the legal profession in Quebec.

Along with his professional career, Beauchamp showed an interest in activities of a religious, philanthropic, and patriotic nature. In 1893 he drew up the civil charter incorporating the apostolic syndics assigned by the Holy See to manage the temporal affairs of the Franciscans. He himself served as an apostolic syndic for some 30 years. His religious fervour also led him to write several works of piety and to help found in 1884 the *Petite Revue du Tiers-Ordre et des intérêts du Cœur-de-Jésus*, a Montreal periodical that in 1917 would become *La Revue franciscaine*, and to serve as editor of *Le Bulletin de l'Union Allet*, the voice of the papal Zouaves in Montreal. Beauchamp sat on the central council of the St Vincent de Paul Society of Montreal and in 1906 was vice-president of the Association Saint-Jean-Baptiste de Montréal. In recognition of his contribution to the legal community, he received a number of honours. He was made a QC in 1893 and the Université Laval conferred an honorary doctorate of laws on him in 1904.

Jean-Joseph Beauchamp was not one of the top-ranking members of the bar, but his editorial output gave him an opportunity to distinguish himself. Throughout his career, he remained somewhat contradictory. For example, he deplored his colleagues' lack of interest in theoretical studies, yet took on tasks that emphasized the utilitarian character of published materials on Quebec law. Beauchamp's work helped the legal community to become more competent, and it accurately reflects the changes that occurred in the practice of law at the beginning of the 20th century.

SYLVIO NORMAND

Most of the books written by Jean-Joseph Beauchamp can be consulted at CIHM and are listed in its *Reg.* In addition to the publications cited above, Beauchamp is the author of *Second general index of the Quebec judicial reports, 1898–1908* (Montreal, 1909) and *Supplément au Code civil annoté de la province de Québec* (2v., Montréal, 1924). The biography mentions various periodicals to which Beauchamp contributed; other articles by him can be found in *Bull. de la Caisse nationale d'économie* (Montréal) and in *La Famille* (Montréal).

ANQ-M, CE601-S51, 18 janv. 1852, 20 févr. 1879. *Le Devoir*, 15, 19–20 nov. 1923. *La Patrie*, 20 oct. 1902. *La Presse*, 16, 19 nov. 1923. *Canadian men and women of the time* (Morgan; 1898 and 1912). *Les Franciscains au Can-*

ada, 1890–1990, sous la dir. de Jean Hamelin (Sillery, Qué., 1990). J. Hamelin *et al.*, *La presse québécoise*, vols.2–4. Père Hugolin [Stanislas Lemay], *Bibliographie du Tiers-Ordre séculier de saint François au Canada (province de Québec)* (Montréal, 1921). "In memoriam: monsieur Jean Joseph Beauchamp, syndic apostolique," *La Rev. franciscaine* (Montréal), 40 (1924), no.1: 37–39. J.-J. Lefebvre, "Tableau alphabétique des avocats de la province, 1868–1899," *La Rev. du Barreau de la prov. de Québec* (Montréal), 22 (1962): 343–55. É.-Z. Massicotte, "L'escrime et les maîtres d'armes à Montréal," *BRH*, 29 (1923): 260–63. Sylvio Normand, "Une culture en redéfinition: la culture juridique québécoise durant la seconde moitié du XIXe siècle," in *Transformation de la culture juridique québécoise*, sous la dir. de Bjarne Melkevik (Sainte-Foy, Qué., 1998): 221–35; "Une lignée d'éditeurs-libraires montréalais, spécialisés en droit, au tournant du siècle," Biblio. Soc. of Canada, *Papers* (Toronto), 30 (1993): 7–55; "Un thème dominant de la pensée juridique traditionnelle au Québec: la sauvegarde de l'intégrité du droit civil," *McGill Law Journal* (Montreal), 32 (1986–87): 559–601. Siméon Pagnuelo, "La Cour suprême et le Barreau de Montréal," *La Thémis* (Montréal), 2 (1880–81): 353–66. Léo Pelland, "Me Jean-Joseph Beauchamp," *La Rev. du droit* (Québec), 2 (1923–24): 181–85. Robert Rumilly, *Hist. de la prov. de Québec*, vol.7; *Histoire de la Société Saint-Jean-Baptiste de Montréal: des patriotes au fleurdelisé, 1834–1948* (Montréal, 1975); *Hist. de Montréal.* Univ. Laval, Faculté de droit, *Annuaire*, 1942–43.

BECK, Sir ADAM, manufacturer, horseman, politician, office holder, and philanthropist; b. 20 June 1857 in Baden, Upper Canada, son of Jacob Friedrich Beck and Charlotte Josephine Hespeler; m. 7 Sept. 1898 Lillian Ottaway in Hamilton, Ont., and they had a daughter; d. 15 Aug. 1925 in London, Ont.

The Prometheus of Canadian politics during the first quarter of the 20th century, Sir Adam Beck brought the inestimable benefit of cheap electric light and power to the citizens of Ontario through a publicly owned utility, the Hydro-Electric Power Commission of Ontario. He had to fight continuously to build Hydro, as it came to be called, but supported by municipal allies he succeeded in creating one of the largest publicly owned integrated electric systems in the world. Brusque and overbearing, he made many enemies in the process, even amongst his friends, as he rammed his projects forward, frequently over the objections of the governments he notionally served. His ruthless determination to expand Hydro, with little regard to the cost, led eventually to a movement to rein him in. He spent his last years pinned down before three public inquiries as lawyers, accountants, and political adversaries picked over every Hydro expenditure. These public humiliations broke his spirit but failed to diminish his enormous popularity. Adam Beck more than any other public figure in Ontario reshaped the institutional life of the province by making electricity a public utility and legitimizing, through his accomplishments, public ownership

as an effective instrument of policy throughout Canada.

Beck came from an enterprising immigrant family of builders and makers. In 1829 Frederick and Barbara Beck had emigrated from the Grand Duchy of Baden (Germany) to upstate New York, and then had moved to the Pennsylvania Dutch community of Doon (Kitchener) in Upper Canada, where they settled on a farm and built a sawmill. Their son Jacob, who had stayed behind to work first as a doctor's apprentice and later in the mills and locomotive works of Schenectady, joined them in 1837. A few miles from his parents, in Preston (Cambridge), he opened a foundry. When fire destroyed it, his friends rallied and he was able to rebuild bigger than before. His first wife, Caroline Logus, whom he married in January 1843, died soon after the birth of a son, Charles. In 1843 Beck had recruited a skilled iron moulder from Buffalo, John Clare (Klarr), to join him; Clare would cement the alliance by marrying his sister in September 1845. With Clare and another partner (Valentine Wahn) running the business, Beck returned to tour his homeland, where he met Charlotte Hespeler, the sister of his Preston neighbour, merchant-manufacturer Jacob Hespeler. When Charlotte came out to Canada, she and Beck were wed, in October 1845; a daughter, Louisa, was born in 1847, followed by two sons, George and William. In a move typical of his venturing spirit, Jacob suggested relocating his company closer to the projected line of the Grand Trunk Railway, but Clare refused. So in 1854 Beck dissolved the partnership and bought 190 acres on the route of the railway ten miles west of Berlin (Kitchener). There he laid out a town-site, which he named Baden, and built a foundry, a grist mill, and a large brick house. Beck's businesses flourished on the strength of iron orders from the railway, and a brickyard and machine shop were eventually added. It was in this thriving hamlet that Adam Beck was born in 1857.

Adam passed a bucolic childhood exploring the edges of the millpond with his brothers, poking about the sooty recesses of the foundry with the workmen, and horseback-riding with his sister. He was sent off to attend William Tassie*'s boarding school in Galt (Cambridge), where he showed no particular distinction; a slow and indifferent student, he preferred riding to reading. His formal education ended at Rockwood Academy, near Guelph. On his return to Baden, his father, who abhorred idleness, set him to work as a groundhog (a moulder's apprentice) in the foundry. It was said by those who knew Adam that he inherited his enterprising spirit, his determination and visionary ability, and some of his sternness from his father, and a love of public service from his mother. Adam's career as a moulder came to an end with the failure of his father's businesses in 1879. At age 63

Jacob Beck, unbowed, started afresh once again, this time as a grain merchant in Detroit. Louisa and the youngest members of the family, Jacob Fritz and Adam, accompanied their parents; one of the older boys, William, stayed in Baden to run the cigar-box manufactory he had started in 1878. Adam returned to work briefly in Toronto as a clerk in a foundry and then as an employee in a cigar factory. With $500 in borrowed money, he joined William and their cousin William Hespeler in a cigar-box factory in Galt in 1881. Hespeler eventually left the partnership, but the two Becks persisted and built a modestly successful business. In 1884, with the inducement of a five-year tax exemption and free water, they moved their works to London, Ont., to be closer to the centre of the province's cigar-making industry. William left soon afterwards to open a branch in Montreal and for a time Adam worked in partnership with his brother George; from 1 Jan. 1888 Adam was the sole proprietor of William Beck and Company, which later became the Beck Manufacturing Company Limited.

Cigar boxes would appear to be a fragile basis on which to build a fortune or a political career. The smoking of cigars, however, was a major rite of male sociability during the Victorian era. Earlier in the century cigars consumed in Canada had originated in Germany and later they came from the United States. The imposition of the National Policy tariff of 25 per cent on rolled cigars but not on tobacco leaf led to the migration of the industry to Canada. London was one of the first major centres where the leaf grown in Ohio, Pennsylvania, and Wisconsin entered the dominion, and it was there and in Montreal [see Samuel Davis*] that the domestic cigar-making business took root. In London the industry would reach its peak around 1912, when 22 companies, employing 1,980 workers, produced more than 20 million cigars. Situated on Albert Street, the Beck factory was essentially a veneer plant. Cedar logs and specialty woods from Spain and Mexico arrived by rail, were stored in the yard for seasoning, and then were peeled into strips to make not only cigar boxes but also cheese boxes and veneer for furniture and pianos. Toiling side by side with his workers (25 in 1889, rising to 125 in 1919), Beck built a thriving business, taking orders, setting up equipment, manhandling logs, and wheeling the finished boxes to customers. (He himself was a non-smoker, an enduring fatherly influence.) Eventually the company supplied all of the main cigar makers with the boxes, labels, and bands in which their products were shipped. Until he was 40, business was Adam Beck's main preoccupation.

In the years after 1897 he emerged much more prominently in public life. He got out more, married, offered himself for public office, and turned the management of his firm over to his brother Jacob. An avid sportsman, he had played baseball as a boy; in Lon-

don he played tennis and lacrosse and, with a group of bachelors, organized a toboggan club. On the advice of his doctor he took up riding again for relaxation. But nothing with Adam Beck could ever be just a recreation – he quickly became a breeder of racehorses and a competitive jumper. His social life revolved around the London Hunt Club where, in 1897, he became master of the hounds, a post he would hold until 1922. A mutual love of horses and riding brought the muscular Beck and the slim, strikingly beautiful Lillian Ottaway together at a jumping meet; she was 21 years his junior. After a whirlwind courtship they were married in 1898 at Christ's Church Anglican Cathedral in Hamilton. Lillian, who had been raised in Britain, spoke with a slight English accent, had a lovely soprano voice, rode with gusto, and carried herself regally. Her mother, Marion Elizabeth Stinson*, from a wealthy Hamilton family, had married an English barrister, who died before Lillian was born. At 5 Lillian had returned to Canada when her mother married a prominent Hamilton lawyer. After a honeymoon tour of Europe, Beck triumphantly brought his bride to London, Ont., where they promptly acquired the most ostentatious house in the city, Elliston, the estate of Ellis Walton Hyman*, and proceeded to make it even grander, with his and hers stables, under a new name, Headley. From being a sporting, business-possessed bachelor, Beck, with his young wife on his arm, moved effortlessly into the very centre of London society. She sang in the cathedral choir, their house and grounds were the envy of the city, and they made a romantic and devoted couple at dinners and hunt club affairs. Winston Churchill stayed with them on his lecture tour of 1900–1, as did Governor General Lord Minto [Elliot*] and Lady Minto in 1903.

As Adam Beck came out into society, he developed an interest in public life. In provincial politics London had long been a Conservative fief – William Ralph MEREDITH held the seat from 1872 to 1894. The Liberals captured it in a by-election when Meredith was appointed to the bench. At the next general election, in March 1898, Beck entered the lists for the Conservatives, ultimately falling 301 votes short of beating the Liberal Francis Baxter Leys. Although he perhaps should not have expected a better result, having no previous political experience or strong organization, he left the field feeling slightly wounded. Nevertheless, his political energies were channelled into the Victoria Hospital Trust, to which he was appointed by the city in 1901. Here he scandalized supporters with his aggressive approach towards patients' rights, his attacks on hospital inefficiency, and his hands-on way of managing repairs economically. It is said that Beck, realizing that he was not likely to be reappointed, ran for mayor to outflank his opposition. In any case, he offered himself and was elected in January 1902. Making few promises, preferring instead to be judged by his works, he plunged into the first of what would be three one-year terms. His administration was marked by a vigorous, reforming tone that discomfited the aldermanic coterie. He promoted civic beautification by offering a prize from his own purse for a garden competition. He persuaded the city to take over the operation of the London and Port Stanley Railway when the private operator's lease expired. He cleaned out the fire department, promoted public health, and became involved in the leadership of the Union of Canadian Municipalities, whose annual convention he brought to London in 1904. Beck thus learned the political craft at the top of local politics, as a mayor without a long apprenticeship. He entered public life as an oppositionist, a critic who used his personal popularity to drive his reluctant colleagues forward and to cleanse the municipal stables. Despite his class position as a manufacturer, in politics he developed the style of a populist champion of the ordinary citizen against the establishment. Although one might have glimpsed intimations of his future in these London years, it would have required an extremely vivid imagination to see in this maverick local politician the system-building Napoleon of provincial politics that history would know as Sir Adam Beck.

In the election of May 1902 the leader of the Conservative party, James Pliny Whitney*, encouraged Beck to run again, with the offer of a cabinet post. Although the party as a whole was unsuccessful, the popular Beck beat Francis Leys by 131 votes and thus, for the next two and a half years, he would serve as both mayor and MPP of London. It was in his capacity as mayor of a southwestern Ontario industrial city that he came in contact with a group of activists from his home district of Waterloo County who had become agitated by the hydroelectric power question. Led by the manufacturer Elias Weber Bingeman SNIDER and the enthusiast Daniel Bechtel Detweiler, the anxious businessmen and municipal politicians of the industrial centres of the Grand River valley had begun to organize themselves to obtain Niagara power that they believed would otherwise go to Toronto and Buffalo. They had met in 1902 to study the situation, and then formed common cause with the politicians of Toronto concerned about private monopoly. At first they hoped the provincial government could be persuaded to undertake the distribution of cheap power to the municipalities. Talks with the Liberal premier, George William Ross*, who refused to take on the inevitable debt, convinced them that if they wanted control over electrical distribution they would have to do the job themselves. Beck went as an observer to the first meeting of this group, the Berlin Convention of February 1903, a gathering of 67 delegates representing all of the main towns and cities in southwestern Ontario; he came away an active convert to municipal intervention. In response to this public pressure, in June the Ross government passed legislation (drafted by Snider) authorizing a commission of investigation to explore the possibilities of cooperative municipal action and a statutory framework within which the municipalities could create a permanent commission to operate a distribution system. Snider was the obvious choice as chair of this Ontario Power Commission, which more frequently went by his name. Beck along with Philip William Ellis, a Toronto jewellery manufacturer and wholesaler, and William Foster Cockshutt, a Brantford farm-implements manufacturer, were chosen by the municipal delegates to serve with Snider as commissioners. Thus, in the fall of 1903, Beck began a crash course on the power question. It was a subject ideally suited to his developing temperament, and he could readily identify with the professed goals: economic electrical light and power, equity between the different manufacturing regions, and the welfare of the common people. The vision of sensible, non-partisan, and public-spirited businessmen and municipal leaders (such as himself) appealed to Beck. He could also subscribe to the implicit attack on monopoly, social privilege, and finance capitalism. This was a moral universe in which he felt right at home.

As the Snider commission began working out the details of a municipally owned hydroelectric distribution system in 1904, Beck sensed the weakness of the voluntary, cooperative structure. It lacked the authority to order the power companies to surrender sensitive information vital to the enterprise, and the municipalities could not agree on much for long. Financing a collective municipal enterprise without provincial backing would be fraught with difficulties. The more he studied the question the more he became convinced that the province would have to play a major role, not just facilitate municipal activity. This growing conviction coincided with a major shift in the political landscape. The Liberal party was losing its hold over the electorate. Rooted in rural Ontario, it had trouble coming to grips with issues important to the rapidly growing urban constituencies. The Conservatives had crept to within three seats of upsetting the Liberals in 1902. In January 1905 Whitney's Conservatives swept to a landslide victory, capturing 69 of the 98 seats. In London, the increasingly popular Adam Beck won with a plurality of 566 votes.

The hydroelectric question had not figured prominently in the campaign. The change in government, however, catapulted Beck into a position of some influence provincially. On 8 February he was made a minister without portfolio in the new administration. After the election, Whitney grandly promised that the water-power of Niagara "should be as free as air" and be developed for the public good. "It is the duty of the Government," Beck insisted in his populist fashion, "to see that development is not hindered by permitting a handful of people to enrich themselves out of these treasures at the expense of the general public." To that end Whitney cancelled an eleventh-hour water-power concession granted by the Ross government and on 5 July he appointed Beck to head a hydroelectric commission of inquiry. It was empowered to take an inventory of available water-power sites, gather information on existing companies in terms of their capital costs, their operating expenses, and the prices they charged, and recommend an appropriate provincial policy with respect to the generation and distribution of hydroelectricity. Beck continued to be a member of the Snider commission but clearly he had moved on to a broader conception of the power question; he now wielded a much more powerful regulatory and investigative instrument and could act with the authority of the province. Henceforth he would be the undisputed leader of the hydro movement.

The Snider commission, which reported first, in March 1906, recommended the construction of a cooperatively owned hydroelectric system linking the major municipal utilities to generating facilities at Niagara under the control of a permanent power commission financed and managed by the subscribing municipalities. In the weeks that followed, the Beck commission, in the first of its five regional reports, and more particularly the activities of Beck himself, superseded the Snider notion of a municipal cooperative. Beck's initial report, on Niagara and southwest Ontario, prepared the way instead for provincial action by pointing out the excessive rates charged by private power companies, and the inherent difficulties of government regulation. He gave an important speech in Guelph urging direct provincial intervention. He inspired a mass meeting of municipal representatives at Toronto city hall and, on 11 April, a demonstration on the lawn of the legislature demanding that the province empower a commission to generate, transmit, and sell power to the municipalities at the lowest possible cost, and regulate the prices charged by the private providers. Beck also orchestrated a deluge of petitions from the municipal councils. All of this effort was intended to soften up his colleagues in cabinet, most of whom harboured deep suspicions about public ownership in general and Beck's movement in particular. The strategy worked. The Whitney government hesitantly introduced legislation on 7 May (Act to provide for the transmission of electrical power to municipalities) which, in effect, created a three-member provincial crown corporation (though it was not called that), the Hydro-Electric Power Commission of Ontario. Operating outside the usual civil service constraints and with extensive powers of expropriation, this body would have full powers

to purchase, lease, or build transmission facilities financed by provincial bonds. Local utilities could buy power from the commission only after municipal voters had approved the contract and the enabling financial by-law. Astonishingly, Beck's extraparliamentary organization cowed even the opposition: the bill passed unanimously in less than a week.

In organizational terms Beck had pushed on beyond an unwieldy municipal cooperative to a provincial crown agency. In doing so he had alienated some of his friends, especially in the way he had shoved Snider aside and unilaterally appropriated studies done by the Snider commission for his own investigation. Nonetheless he had created a broad coalition of municipal activists behind his determination to build a publicly owned, provincial system. But there were many possible forms, involving different degrees of state intervention, that the organization might take. The government remained ambivalent, guarded, and internally divided. What eventually emerged as Ontario Hydro, however, was Beck's creation over the opposition of his cabinet colleagues. On 7 June 1906 Whitney appointed Beck chairman of the new commission, as expected. Needed engineering expertise would come from Cecil Brunswick Smith. And to balance Beck's populism and rein in his enthusiasms, Whitney also persuaded a reluctant John Strathearn HENDRIE of Hamilton to serve, Beck's peer as a horseman, a man of his wife's class, and a known supporter of the private power companies, among them the Hamilton Electric Light and Cataract Power Company Limited [see John Patterson*].

The private interests, especially the group promoting the only Canadian firm at Niagara, the Electrical Development Company of Ontario Limited from Toronto, having failed in their first attempts to derail Beck, now bent their minds to seeking some reasonable accommodation with the government. There were many in the cabinet, the premier included, who were sympathetic to this point of view. The Electrical Development Company was in a precarious financial position; a collapse would be a costly blot on the province. Whitney insisted that every consideration be given the company in negotiating the contract for power in early 1907 with the winning bidder, the American-based Ontario Power Company, and then with respect to the construction of the transmission line. In each case negotiations failed. The premier did not conceive of his policy as a *guerre à outrance* against the private interests. He believed in talking tough, but in the end was willing to come to terms. Unlike Beck, Whitney was a practitioner of brokerage politics. Beck, a newly formed ideologue, was not prepared to bargain away what had formed in his mind as a just alternative to private control. It was possible that neither of them knew the truth about themselves, though in time they came to a realization of their honest differences. For his part Beck had to manoeuvre against the wishes of his premier and colleagues in cabinet. From their point of view he could be unpleasant, ruthless, even unprincipled. He would change his mind without notice, withhold information, go back on deals, and alternately retreat in a sulk or play the rude bully.

Beck proved a formidable champion. The Toronto market was a key element in his grand scheme. Without access, which the city wanted, he could not deliver cheap electricity to southwestern towns, but Toronto's system was controlled by the Electrical Development Company. In the resulting contest over a proposed by-law to fund a municipal network powered by Hydro, Beck's emotional, simplistic rhetoric was a telling factor. He also profited from the ineptitude and arrogance of his corporate opponents in Electrical Development, Frederic Thomas NICHOLLS, Sir Henry Mill Pellatt*, and William MACKENZIE, whose financial reputations had already taken a beating from the royal commission on life insurance in 1906. During the winter of 1907–8 by-laws endorsing the contracts with Ontario Hydro were approved by municipal ratepayers with huge majorities in Toronto and elsewhere. Hydro policy also proved extremely popular in the election of June 1908, in which the government increased both its popular vote and its number of seats. Beck now had a dual mandate from the municipal and provincial electorates. When a desperate Mackenzie amalgamated several enterprises into one utility in 1908 and then belatedly attempted to forestall provincial ownership with a counterproposal to build the system and distribute power under government regulation, the offer came too late. The government had gone so far it could not safely turn back; a publicly owned transmission company would have to be created. Mackenzie and his colleagues had played the game badly and when they lost, after having been given every possible consideration, they turned viciously on Beck and the government. Their quixotic campaign to undermine provincial credit in British financial circles, and then to seek disallowance in Ottawa of key Hydro legislation, served only to bring Whitney and Beck closer together and solidify the political foundations of Ontario Hydro.

Using electricity generated by the Ontario Power Company, the Hydro-Electric Power Commission became an operating entity in a series of theatrical turning-on ceremonies that began in the fall of 1910 and continued into 1911 as successive towns and cities were wired into the grid. Each of these civic festivals became an opportunity for Beck to recount the triumph of public power over private greed. His hostility towards the private power companies, who were now his competitors, and his shameless self-promotion as the champion of "The People's Power," deeply troubled his colleagues. Moreover, his independent conduct raised awkward questions about the precise relationship between the management of Hydro and the government. Before the election of December 1911 Whitney floated a trial balloon, suggesting that the time had come to make Hydro a department of government, under the full control of the cabinet. Beck did not openly attack the proposal, but once he was acclaimed in his own seat and the government was re-elected, his municipal allies, acting through the Ontario Municipal Electric Association, formed in early 1912, launched an aggressive campaign on his behalf; it not only supported Beck as chairman of a quasi-independent commission, but also (in February) brought him a handsome $6,000 salary, without requiring his resignation from the legislature.

With this vote of confidence from the people and somewhat more reluctantly from the premier, Beck struggled within a competitive environment to build Hydro through dramatic price cutting and political showmanship. In his campaign to expand consumption Beck became an electrical Messiah: in speeches and publicity he extolled the power of abundant cheap light to brighten the homes of working people; cheap electricity would create more jobs in the factories of the province; hydro would lighten the drudgery of the barn and the household; and electric railways radiating out from the cities into the countryside would create more prosperous, progressive farms even as light and power made brighter, cleaner cities. With his famous travelling exhibits of the latest electrical appliances (popularly called circuses), rural tests, and local Hydro stores (where household appliances were on display), and in parade floats, newspaper and magazine advertisements, and a host of speeches, Beck presented public hydro as an elixir, but he was no snake-oil salesman. He understood the economics of the electric industry better than his competitors or his critics. Along with utilities magnate Samuel Insull of Chicago, Beck realized that the more electricity he could sell, the less it would cost to acquire. It was a difficult lesson to teach. He even had to browbeat some of the more fiscally conservative municipal utilities, most notably the Toronto Hydro-Electric Power Commission, to pass the lower rates on to consumers. In the process he continued to expand his publicly owned system at the expense of his private competitors.

In Toronto and across the province, Beck acquired a more ardent following than the government itself. At home he and his family continued to rise in public esteem. London's municipal electric utility, which received its first hydro from Niagara in 1910, became a model for progressive business promotion and Beck loyalism. Personally Beck maintained an active interest in civic politics. When the water commissioners proposed a treatment facility to take more water from the tainted Thames River, he boldly promised to find enough clean fresh water in artesian wells. The city took him up on this offer, voting $10,000 for the purpose. In 1910 Beck drilled the wells, installed electrical pumps, and brought the project in on time and on budget, or rather, he absorbed the excess costs himself. In two grand gestures Beck brought light and water to the growing city in the same year.

However, it was in the field of public health that the Becks made their greatest contribution. Sometime in 1907 or 1908 their young daughter, Marion Auria, contracted tuberculosis. Her worried parents sought out the best specialists in America and in Europe. Mercifully her case responded to treatment. But the Becks became concerned for those families in their community who lacked the means to provide their children with medical care. Everyone, they believed, ought to have close access to first-class tuberculosis facilities. Accordingly, in 1909 Adam and Lillian Beck organized the London Health Association to provide a sanatorium. From local individuals and organizations they raised $10,000 (led by their own donation of $1,200), the city contributed $5,000, and the province added $4,000. On 5 April 1910 Governor General Lord Grey* opened the Queen Alexandra Sanatorium in the village of Byron, west of the city. For the rest of their lives the Becks remained deeply attached to this sanatorium and made its maintenance and expansion their passion. As president from its inception to his death in 1925 and a sometimes overbearing physical presence on the weekends, Adam Beck personally oversaw all major and even many minor renovations.

A society beauty, Lillian Beck also continued to be a fiercely competitive horsewoman. The Beck stables produced a string of outstanding hunter-class horses that won Adam and Lillian international recognition. In 1907 they competed in the Olympia Horse Show in London, England, where Lillian's horse My Fellow won its class. To remain competitive, the Becks leased an estate in England in 1913 to maintain their equestrian operation at the highest international standards. From that time onward Lillian and Marion lived about half the year in England; Adam paid extended visits when his schedule permitted. In 1914 their prize-winning horses Melrose, Sir Edward, and Sir James were counted among the finest middleweight and heavyweight hunters in the world. The Becks also competed regularly at the National Horse Show in New York City where, in 1915, Lillian was named a judge over chauvinist protests, famously breaking down the barriers of this once exclusively male domain.

Adam Beck's contribution to London had been publicly recognized in an unprecedented dinner given in his honour on 25 Nov. 1913. At this glittering affair, attended by 500 in the Masonic Temple, Angli-

can bishop David Williams* proclaimed him "incorrupt and incorruptible"; Roman Catholic bishop Michael Francis Fallon* eulogized his vision, character, and charitable works; and the mayor and city council gave him a silver candelabra and tray. While the ladies looked on from the galleries, the head-table guests were served their dinners from a small electric railway. According to the *London Free Press*, this banquet was "the most remarkable and spontaneous demonstration of affection and regard ever tendered a public man in London." Visibly moved, Beck spoke briefly of his satisfaction at lightening the load of the poor, the housewife, the farmer, the merchant, and afflicted children, and pledged to carry on the fight to create a renewed citizenship based upon "service, progress and righteousness." These local honours were crowned the following year when he received a knighthood in the king's June honours list. He was now Sir Adam, the Power Knight, and Lillian formally became what she had long been in style, Lady Beck. Charging at fences on horseback, or driving the rapidly growing Hydro system forward, Sir Adam Beck was at the height of his power in 1914.

Re-elected by a large majority in the general election of 29 June 1914, Beck directed a major structural transformation of Hydro during his next term with fewer constraints than in the past. Whitney, who died in September, was replaced by a less adept premier, William Howard Hearst*. Beck's nemesis, John Hendrie, resigned from the Hydro-Electric Power Commission to become lieutenant governor. Beck thus had a much freer rein, though Hearst did not include him in his cabinet. Hydro's head set about expanding his organization with a powerful lobby, the Ontario Municipal Electric Association, zealously behind him. Beck and the regional municipalities fixed upon electric radial railways as a major force for modernization and rural reconstruction. In 1913 the Hydro Electric Railway Act and amendments to the Ontario Railway Act had prepared the way legislatively. A web of light lines that connected farms, towns, and cities and delivered transportation at cost under a public authority had enormous appeal and Beck became its most ardent hot gospeller. He managed to have the abject London and Port Stanley Railway electrified as a glowing prototype. Coincidentally the baseload of the proposed railways would greatly increase electric consumption and drive Hydro to a new stage of development as a fully integrated regional monopoly that provided hydroelectric generation, transmission, and distribution services as well as high-speed transportation. This grandiose vision of electrical modernization had commensurate costs, which Beck somewhat disingenuously managed to minimize.

In 1914 Hydro and the municipalities received legislative permission, subject to ratepayer approval, to enter into the inter-city electric railway business. By stages Hydro acquired the legal authority to generate power as well as distribute it through the purchase of a utility (Big Chute) on the Severn River and the construction of regional power stations in 1914–15 at Wasdell Falls, also on the Severn, and Eugenia Falls, near Flesherton. These were sideshows, however; the centrepiece of the proposed integrated system remained Niagara. In 1914 Hydro quietly began planning for a massive hydroelectric station there, but there was precious little water left at Niagara to turn the turbines. A treaty negotiated with the United States in 1908 limited the amount that might be diverted for power purposes; the three existing private companies at Niagara had already acquired, between them, the rights to most of the Canadian quota. Beck had made the development of the hydroelectric system into the central issue on the Ontario political agenda when conflict broke out in Europe in August 1914.

The Becks threw themselves wholeheartedly into the war effort. In 1912 the military authorities had cleverly put Adam's organizing talents and his knowledge of horses together by naming him to a remount committee. At the outset of the war he took charge of acquiring horses for the Canadian army in the territory from Halifax to the Lakehead. In June 1915 he assumed this responsibility for the British army as well, an appointment that brought him an honorary colonelcy. Inevitably, allegations arose that his agency either paid too much for horses or acquired unsuitable remounts, but the claims were not substantiated upon investigation. Together Adam and Lillian Beck also made personal contributions to the war effort, donating all of their champion horses to the cause. Lieutenant-General Edwin Alfred Hervey ALDERSON, for example, rode Sir James, Adam's most famous horse. Lady Beck, in England for most of the war, working with the Canadian Red Cross Society, devoted herself particularly to ensuring that wounded veterans were welcomed into British country homes for their convalescence. The Queen Alexandra Sanatorium in Ontario was expanded in 1917–18 to accommodate the rehabilitation of wounded returnees. The arrangement worked well, but in the later stages of the war battle-hardened veterans began to complain about the hospital's stern regimen, much of which was attributed to Sir Adam's "Germanic" direction. In 1916, for his local and patriotic help, Beck had received an LLD from the Western University of London, which he served as a director and later as chancellor.

At first the war had relatively little impact on Beck's plans for Hydro. The municipal elections of January 1917, for example, revolved around the approval of by-laws for Hydro radials and vague authorization for the future generation of power at Niagara. Then the rapidly increasing power demands of wartime industrialization provided the overriding

urgency, later in 1917, to overcome opposition to the purchase of one of the power companies at Niagara (Ontario Power) and forge ahead with the construction of a large diversion canal and a world-scale plant at Queenston, which would make much more efficient use of the available water. Shamelessly using the moral purpose of the war, Beck hemmed in his private competitors even more, setting the stage for their eventual acquisition, though the negotiations would be unduly drawn out, litigious, and embittered. However, war, inflation, railway nationalization, and the demands of automotive technology for better roads combined to damp enthusiasm for the radial railway project. Moreover, the problem for the Hydro-Electric Commission now was not finding ways of selling surplus power, but rather keeping up with galloping industrial, commercial, municipal, and domestic demand. When the war ended, Hydro's transformation into an integrated utility producing as well as transmitting its own power was much closer to realization. Its corresponding administrative growth had been grandly marked by the ornate office building begun on University Avenue in Toronto in 1914 and occupied in 1916. Sir Adam had a good war, but he emerged from it a wounded politician.

From the very beginning there had been critics of the Hydro project and Beck's management of it. Canadian private producers and British investors placed obstacles in the way during the early stages. As Hydro advanced, it attracted new opponents: private power advocates from the United States, who viewed the progress of public ownership in Ontario with alarm. In 1912 a New York State committee of investigation, the Ferris committee, issued a censorious report. A year later a prominent American hydroelectric expert, Reginald Pelham Bolton, denounced the unorthodox financing of Hydro in *An expensive experiment . . .* (New York). Between 15 July and 23 Dec. 1916 James MAVOR, a professor of political economy at the University of Toronto, published a devastating critique of Hydro's lack of accountability, dictatorial methods, and tendency to subvert democracy in a series of articles in the *Financial Post* (Toronto), later reprinted as *Niagara in politics . . .* (New York, 1925).

In the final analysis Beck was his own worst enemy. His authoritarian management style invited criticism. In 1916 the provincial auditor, James Clancy, threw up his hands at Hydro's accounting practices. Beck embarrassed his premier and government with surprises. He was not one to compromise, even with his friends. A scrapper and sometimes a bully, he intimidated his staff and his municipal allies, and regarded the government and the legislature with disdain. He was more popular and more powerful than the premier, and he acted as if he knew it. Hydro, in his mind, was bigger than any government and he was the personal embodiment of Hydro. Cautious people who wanted to know in advance how much projects would cost were battered into submission and put on his list of enemies; when the bills added up to two or three times the initial estimates, there were always convoluted exculpatory explanations. Dismissing his censors, Beck stormed ahead, fuming with rage at the conspiracies mounted against him and bristling with indignation at the slightest criticism. Even Beck's defenders tired of his haughty, domineering ways. A frustrated Hearst, when accused by Beck of hindering Hydro's development in the spring of 1919, rebuked Sir Adam for never taking him into his confidence, for his presumptuous attitude towards parliament, and for saddling others with responsibility for Hydro's mounting debt. Beck responded by withdrawing his support from the government and by announcing his intention to run independently in the upcoming election.

The election of October 1919 came as a devastating blow to Beck and, potentially, to his project. As an independent in London, he was defeated by his sole opponent, Dr Hugh Allan Stevenson, the Labour candidate, who benefited from disaffected Tory votes, some nastiness about Beck's ethnic background, and a vocal uprising amongst the returned soldiers in the Queen Alexandra Sanatorium. The timing could not have been worse. Beck's massive Queenston hydroelectric station lay only half completed and the radial railway scheme had stalled; however, Beck's enormous popularity, which transcended party lines, saved him. The victorious but leaderless United Farmers of Ontario initially sounded him out as a possible premier, but both sides quickly thought better of it. Although Labour strongly supported Hydro, the UFO were much more reserved, especially about Beck's radial-railway enthusiasms; they preferred improved roads. As chairman of the Hydro-Electric Power Commission, Beck had also been an MPP and, for much of the time, a minister without portfolio. The election broke that political connection with the government in power. The eventual premier, Ernest Charles Drury*, had little choice but to keep Beck on as chairman, but he appointed a tough ex-soldier, Lieutenant-Colonel Dougall Carmichael, to the commission to keep him in line.

Over the next four years the new government and the tempestuous Power Knight remained locked in combat. For much of the time William Rothwell Plewman, a reporter for the *Toronto Daily Star*, acted as unofficial mediator between Hydro and the premier, who was determined that Hydro do the government's bidding and not the other way around. On 6 July 1920 the government announced a royal commission to reconsider Beck's radial program in light of the rising costs, disappointing experience in other jurisdictions, and technological change. Beck imme-

diately orchestrated a campaign of resistance. In emergency meetings on the 8th at Toronto city hall and the Hydro building, for instance, the Hydro-Electric Radial Association registered its "strong disapproval" of the commission. Provincial treasurer Peter Smith responded for the government that it would not be stampeded. In July 1921 the commission, chaired by Robert Franklin SUTHERLAND, produced a report that was highly critical of radials and recommended construction of only a much reduced system. Meanwhile, Beck had wasted valuable political capital in an acrimonious takeover of Sir William Mackenzie's Toronto Power Company Limited and its related electric and radial companies and in fighting the City of Toronto over an eight-track entry corridor for a mammoth radial system. Characteristically, he condemned the Sutherland report in an intemperate pamphlet and urged the municipalities not to let up in their campaign. The adverse report, a hostile provincial government, and defeats for radial by-laws (particularly in Toronto) in the municipal elections of January 1922 effectively put an end to Beck's radial dream.

Drury, concerned at the spiralling costs of the Queenston hydroelectric plant, wanted an inquiry into this project as well. At first Beck agreed. However, when his hand-picked expert, Hugh Lincoln Cooper, questioned the design, recalculated the costs upward, and insisted upon changes in the power canal to enhance capacity, Beck rejected his advice and appointed another consulting engineer. The turbines had begun to turn on the first phase of this huge project on 29 Dec. 1921, but there seemed to be no relation between the estimates Beck presented and the mounting bills; in one year the difference amounted to $20 million. Unable to explain the situation, Colonel Carmichael offered his resignation, which the premier refused. The cost of the undertaking, now much larger, had ballooned from the initial $20 million to $84 million and counting. Drury, who had to guarantee the bonds for the over-budget project and take political responsibility for it, insisted upon a commission of inquiry with a sweeping mandate to examine the overall operations of Hydro, not just Queenston. This commission, appointed in April 1922 and chaired by Liberal lawyer Walter Dymond Gregory, became in effect an adversarial audit of Beck's management that involved scores of witnesses, produced thousands of pages of testimony, and ran into the middle of 1923.

These political setbacks were, in some respects, the least of his problems. On 17 Oct. 1921 his beloved wife had died from complications following surgery for pancreatitis. Sir Adam and Lady Beck had been a deeply devoted couple despite their often long absences from one another. Living in the Alexandra apartments next to the Hydro building, they had only just begun to settle into life together in Toronto society. Moreover, she had been the one mellowing influence in his life. He was devastated by the loss. A widower, he was now also the single parent of a fiercely independent teenager. With the check upon his temper in a Hamilton grave, he became more difficult and erratic in the face of his daughter's defiance and the ascendancy of those he considered to be his political enemies. These were the years of Beck's towering, black rages.

Beck had run Hydro as a private corporation. Honest and incorruptible personally, he nevertheless paid scant attention to the niceties of accounting. He would routinely spend funds authorized for one purpose on any project he deemed in the interests of Hydro, including local by-law campaigns. For Beck the ends justified the means. Meanwhile, his vision of a provincial, publicly owned hydroelectric monopoly that served the municipal utilities and provided power at the lowest possible cost had been largely realized. In 1923 Hydro served 393 municipalities and distributed 685,000 horsepower using facilities in which over $170 million had been invested. Beck was a magnificent builder. There could be no denying his accomplishments, though, as the hearings of the Gregory commission showed, his management style, planning, political methods, and accountability to the legislature could be questioned.

The vexations suffered at the hands of the UFO government eventually drew Beck back to the bosom of the Conservative party in self-defence. In the election of June 1923 he stood as a Conservative in his old London riding. The irony of a civil servant running as a candidate in opposition to the government was not lost on Drury or the *Farmers' Sun* (Toronto), but Beck managed to get away with it. This time he won with a plurality of more than 7,000 votes – a wonderful personal vindication. George Howard Ferguson*'s Conservatives swept the province, and Beck returned to cabinet in July as a minister without portfolio. Ferguson brought the Gregory inquiry to an abrupt conclusion and made much of the fact that Sir Adam's general stewardship of Hydro had been supported in the commission's voluminous evidence and summary reports. Beck's probity could be stressed while quietly the government used the critical aspects of Gregory's reports to bring Hydro more fully within the framework of financial and political accountability.

Then, just when it seemed these clouds had passed over, Beck's personal integrity came under attack from an unexpected source. Hydro secretary E. Clarence Settell absconded with $30,000 in Hydro funds and left a blackmailing letter itemizing Sir Adam's alleged misdeeds. When he was apprehended in October 1924 heading for the border with his mistress, he added further charges to the indictment. Wounded by Settell's treachery, and by now a very sick man, Beck had to endure yet another inquiry as judge Colin George Snider conducted an investigation of more

than 40 specific allegations having to do with the private use of automobiles, misappropriation of public money, unauthorized expenditures, conflicts of interest in tendering, and irregularities in expense records. Issued in December, Snider's report condemned Isaac Benson Lucas's management of Hydro's legal department and Frederick Arthur Gaby's conflict of interest in a dredging contract within the engineering department, but it found no evidence of serious wrongdoing by Beck. Save for a few petty mistakes in his expense accounts, the commission exonerated him. Settell went to jail for three years. Although another attempt "to get" Sir Adam, in the words of the Toronto *Globe*, had failed, the critics continued the battle of the books against Hydro. Beck thundered back with vigorous refutations in pamphlets that put his fighting spirit on full display. Returning to London one night by train, he gestured in some excitement to his travelling companion and long-time ally Edward Victor Buchanan, head of London's utilities: "Look out there! The lights in the farms. That's what I've been fighting for."

The political struggle and quarrels with his daughter over her determination to marry Strathearn Hay, whom he deemed unsuitable in part because he was related to the Hendrie family, exhausted Beck, whose health and mental outlook deteriorated. It took Howard Ferguson's intervention to persuade him to attend Marion's wedding in January 1925. Ordered to rest by his doctors, who had diagnosed his illness as pernicious anaemia, Beck went to South Carolina for a holiday in February, and then he underwent transfusion treatment at Johns Hopkins Hospital in Baltimore. There he brooded about his beloved Hydro, strategies for the hydroelectric development of the St Lawrence River, and the continuing machinations of the private power interests, and he grumbled that the premier and his colleagues in government were neglecting him. He was a broken man by his own admission.

In May, Beck quietly slipped back to his home in London, where he attempted to conduct Hydro business by telephone from his bedroom. He weakened rapidly over the summer and died on 15 Aug. 1925 in his 69th year. Beck's passing shocked the province; the seriousness of his condition had not been widely understood. The death announcement occasioned a spontaneous outpouring of grief, with eulogies pouring in from every quarter. His obituaries filled pages in the newspapers. "Canada has not produced a greater man than the late Sir Adam Beck," declared *Saturday Night* (Toronto) as it enshrined him in the national pantheon along with Sir John A. Macdonald*, Lord Mount Stephen [STEPHEN], and Sir William Cornelius Van Horne*. Ontario city halls were draped in black, the Hydro shops and offices closed in tribute, and in London business ceased for an hour. Thousands lined the streets for his funeral cortège. The ceremony at St Paul's Anglican Cathedral, attended by all the major political figures of the province, was also broadcast over the radio. As his funeral train mournfully passed from London across Beck's political heartland to Hamilton, where he was to be interred in Greenwood Cemetery under a granite cross beside his wife, farmers and their families paused from their toil and men swept their hats from their heads. The entire Toronto City Council attended his burial. It is a small irony that Beck lies in what he would have considered enemy ground, Hamilton, the last bastion of private power. But for once his wish to be beside his wife overcame his prejudices.

Sir Adam Beck's death marked the end of an unusual period in Ontario politics, one in which the chairman of Hydro had exercised greater power and influence than the premier and commanded a broad-based, populist political following much stronger than any political party. In building Hydro, Beck almost succeeded in creating an institution that was a law unto itself and for a long time it would continue to demonstrate some of the characteristics of independence. He died a wealthy man with an estate valued at more than $627,000, although his manufacturing business had been in decline for some years. His salary from his chairmanship of Hydro over 20 years totalled $197,000. Some of his wealth may have come to him from his wife. After making numerous small bequests to relatives and charities, he left a trust fund of approximately half a million dollars to his daughter and her heirs.

Beck's memory was kept alive by the Ontario Municipal Electric Association, Hydro, and the citizens of London. In 1934 Toronto and the Hydro municipalities raised a splendid monument to him that still commands University Avenue. This brooding statue, by Emanuel Otto Hahn*, and Beck's grave in Hamilton became sites of regular pilgrimages and wreath-laying ceremonies by the heirs and successors to the OMEA as they struggled to perpetuate the notion of Hydro as a municipal cooperative. Hydro publications regularly stressed the vision and legacy of Beck during the era of growth after World War I; eventually the much enlarged power stations at Queenston were renamed Beck No.1 and Beck No.2 in his honour. In London a new collegiate was named after him and a nearby public school was named after Lady Beck. The Women's Sanatorium Aid Society of London built a charming chapel, St Luke's in the Garden, across from the Queen Alexandra Sanatorium in memory of the Becks in 1932. The sanatorium itself became the Beck Memorial Sanatorium in 1948. In print, W. R. Plewman's vivid 1947 biography captured the greatness of Beck and the tempestuous nature of his personality. Merrill Denison*'s commissioned history of Hydro in 1960 established continuity between the transcendent hero figure at the beginning and the transforming, province-girdling corporation Hydro had become in the post-war era.

As the obituaries noted, Hydro itself was Beck's greatest monument. He worried on his deathbed that political partisanship would overcome it and that Hydro as an independent entity would not survive. But in his absence it continued to flourish, firmly rooted in the towns and cities, along the back concessions, and amongst the merchants, workers, farmers, and homemakers of the province. Hydroelectricity generated and delivered by a crown corporation to municipally owned utilities at the lowest cost had become an Ontario institution that would outlive changing governments and passing ideologies. That had largely been Sir Adam Beck's doing.

H. V. NELLES

Sir Adam Beck's publications include *Report of the Hydro-Electric Power Commission of Ontario* (1906) and *The genesis of the power movement* (Report no.ORR–101.–12, 1907), both of which are held at the Hydro One Inc. Corporate Arch. (Toronto). Beck also published *The conservation of the water-powers of Ontario: an address delivered by Honourable Adam Beck before the first annual meeting of the Commission of Conservation* ([Ottawa, 1910?]; repr. from Commission of Conservation, *Annual report* ([Ottawa]), 1910; *Hydro-electric power for the farm: special interview with Sir Adam Beck on uses and development of electricity in rural districts* ([n.p., 1919?]; repr. from *Farm and Dairy* (Peterborough, Ont.), 18 Dec. 1919); *Re "Murray report" on electric utilities: refutation of unjust statements contained in a report published by the National Electric Light Association entitled, "Government owned and controlled compared with privately owned and regulated electric utilities in Canada and the United States" respecting the Hydro-Electric Power Commission of Ontario* (Toronto, 1922); *Re "Sutherland commission" majority report; statement respecting findings and other statements contained in majority report of the commission (known as the "Sutherland commission") appointed to inquire into the subject of hydro-electric railways* (Toronto, 1922); *Errors and misrepresentations made by the hydroelectric inquiry commission (known as the Gregory commission) respecting the publicly owned and operated hydro-electric power undertaking of municipalities in the province of Ontario* (Toronto, 1925); *Misstatements and misrepresentations derogatory to the Hydro-Electric Power Commission of Ontario contained in a report published by the Smithsonian Institution entitled "Niagara Falls: its power possibilities and preservation", under the authorship of Samuel S. Wyer, examined and refuted by Sir Adam Beck* (Toronto, 1925); *A statement by Sir Adam Beck protesting against the exportation of electric power, with special reference to the proposed lease of the Carillon power site* (Toronto, 1925); and *Unjust and harmful proposals published by authority of an organization known as the Canadian Deep Waterways and Power Association under the chairmanship of Mr. O. E. Fleming, examined and exposed by Sir Adam Beck* (Toronto, 1925).

AO, F 5; F 6; F 8; RG 35; RG 55-17-33, 5, 15 May 1885; 1 Jan., 21 May 1888; RG 55-17-57-5, nos.408, 433, 615.

Hydro One Inc. Corporate Arch., Acc. no.90.001 (*Report of the commission appointed to inquire into hydro-electric radials*), 1921; Acc. no.90.007 (*Gregory commission final report*), 1924; Report no.ORR–104.11–11 (E. W. B. Snider, chairman, *Report of the Ontario Power Commission to the mayors and municipal councils of Toronto, London, Brantford, Stratford, Woodstock, Ingersoll, and Guelph*), 28 March 1906. London Public Library, London Room (London, Ont.), London obituaries scrapbook, 1: 7–8. Univ. of Western Ont. Arch., J. J. Talman Regional Coll. (London), B4691–94 (legal papers of John William Godfrey Winnett, London, c. 1900–40); B4919–28, X1936– (Arthur and Edmund Carty papers, 1838–1974 . . .), "Notes for a biography of Sir Adam Beck"; VF116 (corr. between Sir Adam Beck and J. W. G. Winnett, 1915, 1918–19, 1921, 1923–25); Will copybook (Middlesex County Surrogate Court), 1922, 1, p.120, no.15529; 1925, 2, p.423, no.17469. *Evening Telegram* (Toronto), 17 Oct. 1921, 17 Aug. 1925. *Hamilton Spectator*, 8 Sept. 1898, 17 Aug. 1925. *London Advertiser*, 8 Sept. 1898, 17–18 Oct. 1919. *London Free Press*, 8 Sept. 1898, 18–19 Aug. 1925. *Toronto Daily Star*, 17 Oct. 1921, 17 Aug. 1925. F. H. Armstrong, *The Forest City: an illustrated history of London, Canada* ([Northridge, Calif.], 1986). E. B. Biggar, *Hydro-electric development in Ontario: a history of water-power administration under the Hydro-Electric Power Commission of Ontario* (Toronto, [1920]). E. V. Buchanan, *A history of electrical energy in London* ([London, 1966]); *London's water supply: a history* (London, [1968]). *Canadian annual rev.* A. C. Carty, "Sir Adam Beck," Waterloo Hist. Soc., *Annual report* (Kitchener, Ont.), 13 (1925): 159–66. City of London, *Minutes of council*, 1902–4, 1910. J. T. H. Connor, *A heritage of healing: the London Health Association and its hospitals, 1909–1987* (London, 1990). Merrill Denison, *The people's power: the history of Ontario Hydro* ([Toronto], 1960). *Directory*, London, 1894–1923. D. E. Dodd, "Delivering electrical technology to the Ontario housewife, 1920–1939: an alliance of professional women, advertisers and the electrical industry" (PHD thesis, Carleton Univ., Ottawa, 1989). E. C. Drury, *Farmer premier: memoirs of the Honourable E. C. Drury* (Toronto, 1966). K. R. Fleming, *Power at cost: Ontario Hydro and rural electrification, 1911–1958* (Montreal and Kingston, Ont., 1992). N. B. Freeman, *The politics of power: Ontario Hydro and its government, 1906–95* (Toronto and Buffalo, N.Y., 1996). P. W. Graham, *Sir Adam Beck* (London, 1925). C. W. Humphries, *"Honest enough to be bold": the life and times of Sir James Pliny Whitney* (Toronto, 1985). Kitchener Light Commissioners, *The origin of the Ontario hydro-electric power movement* ([Kitchener, 1919]). London Health Assoc., *The story of the Beck Memorial Sanitorium* (London, 1949). *The London Hunt and Country Club: a distinguished tradition*, ed. Brandon Conron (London, 1985). H. V. Nelles, *The politics of development: forests, mines & hydro-electric power in Ontario, 1849–1941* (Toronto, 1974). Ontario Hydro, *The Hydro-Electric Power Commission of Ontario: its origin, administration and achievements* (Toronto, 1928). W. R. Plewman, *Adam Beck and the Ontario Hydro* (Toronto, 1947). Frank Proctor, *Fox hunting in Canada and some men who made it* (Toronto, 1929). Queen Alexandra Sanatorium, *Annual report* (London), 1910–48. B. S. Scott, "The economic and industrial history of the city of London, Canada, from the building of the first railway, 1855, to the present, 1930" (MA thesis, Univ. of Western Ont., 1930).

BECK, NICHOLAS DU BOIS DOMINIC, lawyer and judge; b. 4 May 1857 in Cobourg, Upper Canada, son of John Walton Romeyn Beck and Georgiana Boulton; grandson of George Strange Boulton*; m. first November 1886 Mary Ethel Lloyd (d. 30 April 1904), and they had two daughters and two sons; m. secondly 9 Jan. 1906 Louisa Adelaide Teefy in Richmond Hill, Ont.; m. thirdly 10 April 1928 Jeanne Cecilia Tilley in Vancouver; d. 14 May 1928 in Seattle, Wash.

Nicholas D. Beck grew up in Peterborough, where his American-born father was the Anglican rector. He received his primary education there, followed by attendance at the collegiate institute. After reading in a local law office and gaining admission to the bar in 1879, he extended his professional preparation at Osgoode Hall and the University of Toronto (LLB 1881). He then practised in Peterborough. In 1883 he joined a contingent of lawyers bound for Winnipeg to take advantage of the opportunities resulting from railway building and real-estate speculation. Beck went into partnership with James-Émile-Pierre Prendergast*, a bilingual Roman Catholic who would enter the Manitoba assembly as a Liberal in 1885 and become a defender of separate schools. Another early associate, the Reverend Hippolyte Leduc, was responsible, it is claimed, for Beck's conversion to Catholicism in 1883. He began editing the Catholic *Northwest Review* (Winnipeg) and represented the Collège de Saint-Boniface in the senate of the University of Manitoba [*see* Alexander Morris*].

In 1889 Beck left Winnipeg to join the Calgary firm of James Alexander LOUGHEED. His relocation to Edmonton two years later followed the region's settlement and the completion of a railway from Calgary. He was appointed crown prosecutor and the town's solicitor when it was incorporated in 1892. Among the by-laws he drafted was one that prohibited cycling on the new wooden sidewalks; amusingly, he was the first person prosecuted. In 1893, the year he was named a dominion QC, he formed a partnership with Edward Corrigan Emery. Beck's strength lay in litigation, but as was common in the profession his firm also handled mortgage moneys and worked with real-estate agents, in addition to such clients as the city. Among its prominent boosters, they carried out the legal tasks involved in establishing the Edmonton Club and the Edmonton Industrial Exhibition Association. Professionally, Beck convened the first meeting, in Calgary in 1899, of the benchers of the Law Society of the North-West Territories, served as its first vice-president and was elected president (1901–7), and provided leadership as the principal editor of the *Territories Law Reports* (Toronto) from 1900 to 1910.

By 1900 Beck, initially a Conservative, had become a strong supporter of the Liberal party in its move to recognize the special status of Catholic separate schools. In 1892 the territorial assembly had passed, without federal consent, an ordinance that reduced the minority's privileges by regularizing inspections, requiring the certification of teachers, and providing for government control of the selection of textbooks. A test case involving a teaching sister at St Joachim's Mission school in Edmonton led Beck, who was chairman of the separate school board, to prepare in October 1893 a petition asking for federal disallowance of the controversial ordinance. In February, he and other petitioners were disappointed when the government of Sir John Sparrow David Thompson* declined to act. As events surrounding the school question in Manitoba unfolded, the Catholic hierarchy and laity, including Beck, remained concerned about the further erosion of rights in the northwest. At the consecration in 1895 of the Edmonton General Hospital, run by the Grey Nuns, Beck's remarks on behalf of St Joachim's trustees left little doubt that he saw the success of remedial legislation for Manitoba as a means of overcoming the territorial ordinance. After the federal election of 1896, when Edmonton's Catholic laity petitioned the new Liberal government of Wilfrid Laurier* to express their fears, Liberal MPs thought that Beck was behind the action.

Agitation for provincial autonomy brought educational matters forward again. In 1904 Archbishop Adélard Langevin* of St Boniface asked Beck to prepare an open letter on the "vested rights" of Catholics to have separate-school districts. Beck was reticent, however – he feared reaction in the press. His approach reflected more the wishes of Bishop Émile-Joseph Legal* of St Albert, who had been invited by Donato Sbarretti y Tazza, the apostolic delegate in Ottawa, to draft a clause defending denominational schools for inclusion in the Autonomy Bills creating Alberta and Saskatchewan. But Beck was still concerned. No rights to such schools had been legally guaranteed when the territories had entered confederation in 1870. As a result, he proposed a clause that would guard de facto rights and call for a clearer definition of the revenues that Catholic schools could expect to receive.

Controversy erupted in 1905 around the resignation of interior minister Clifford SIFTON over the Laurier government's proposed clause to protect the existing separate system. Beck was content with this proposal, but he was adamant that defence should not be left to provincial legislatures without the safeguard afforded by section 93 of the British North America Act. By March 1905 he was in Ottawa advising Sbarretti, who he thought might cede too much. In the end the clause negotiated between the delegate and the prime minister seemed to satisfy Beck as the best that could be expected. His pleasure was sustained by the triumph of the Liberals under Alexander Cameron

Rutherford* in Alberta's first election, which gave promise of additional protection.

When the provincial courts were organized in 1907, Beck was appointed a puisne judge of the Supreme Court by Laurier, on Rutherford's suggestion. Although his notebooks reveal work on many aspects of jurisprudence, his major judgements involved financial law and liability. His expertise in these areas served him well in the wake of the Alberta and Great Waterways Railway crisis [see Charles Wilson CROSS]. Facing allegations of impropriety and party opposition, Rutherford gave notice in March 1910 that three justices, David Lynch SCOTT, Horace Harvey*, and Beck (as chair), would form a royal commission to examine the fiduciary dealings between members of the government and the railway, especially with respect to bond guarantees. Their reports became public in November. Scott and Harvey's was inconclusive but Beck was of the opinion that any wrongdoing was "disproved," a finding the Calgary *Albertan* believed was simply a whitewash of an inept government.

Beck was regarded by his peers as a meticulous and serious jurist, confident in dissent yet convincing enough over time, including his years with the appellate division after 1921, to have his judgements cited frequently. His seemingly humourless resolution in legal matters, however, drew merciless criticism from Robert Chambers EDWARDS of the Calgary *Eye Opener*. During his career on the bench his interest in education and religious matters had continued. A member of Alberta's Educational Council since 1906, he was named a senator and first vice-chancellor in 1908 of the new University of Alberta, which awarded him a LLD that year, and in 1913–14 he was among the original honorary lecturers for its faculty of law. Within his church he became a governor of the Catholic Church Extension Society and in 1926 a vice-president of the Catholic Truth Society. Nicholas Beck died of angina at age 71 while on vacation in Seattle; he was buried in Edmonton.

RICHARD A. WILLIE

AO, RG 80-5-0-355, no.21632. City of Edmonton Arch., Newspaper clipping files, biog. file, Nicholas D. Beck. Legal Arch. Soc. of Alta (Calgary), 09-00-00 (Calgary Bar Assoc. fonds), 1973–84, vols.1–16; 12-00-01 (Nicholas DuBois Dominic Beck fonds), judge's notebooks ser., 1907–28; 60-00-00 (Law Soc. of the North-West Territories fonds), roll of advocates and minutes, vol.1, 1886–1907; Reference library files, Nicholas DuBois Dominic Beck file, including "Articles of partnership dated October 1st. 1893, Nicholas D. Beck and Edward C. Emery" (copy) and Univ. of Alta, faculty of law file, W. H. Johns, "History of the faculty of law, the University of Alberta." *Calgary Herald*, 15 May 1928. *Liberal* (Richmond Hill, Ont.), 11 Jan. 1906. *Vancouver Sun*, 10 April 1928. D. R. Babcock, *Alexander Cameron Ruther-*

ford: a gentleman of Strathcona (Calgary, 1989). Emery Jamieson, *The Emery Jamieson story* (Edmonton, 1993). F. C. Jamieson, "Edmonton courts and lawyers in territorial times," *Alberta Hist. Rev.* (Edmonton), 4 (1956), no.1: 3–9. L. [A.] Knafla and Richard Klumpenhouwer, *Lords of the western bench: a biographical history of the supreme and district courts of Alberta, 1876–1990* (Calgary, 1997). M. R. Lupul, *The Roman Catholic Church and the North-West school question: a study in church-state relations in western Canada, 1875–1905* (Toronto, 1974). L. G. Thomas, *The Liberal party in Alberta: a history of politics in the province of Alberta, 1905–1921* (Toronto, 1959).

BÉGIN, LOUIS-NAZAIRE, Roman Catholic priest, professor, author, archbishop, and cardinal; b. 10 Jan. 1840 in Lévis, Lower Canada, son of Charles Bégin, a farmer, and Luce Paradis, a cousin of Bishop Ignace Bourget*; d. 18 July 1925 at Quebec.

The sixth of ten children, Louis-Nazaire Bégin attended the model school in Lévis in 1855 and the Collège Industriel de Saint-Michel (in Saint-Michel-de-Bellechasse) in 1856. In 1862 he received the degree of *baccalauréat ès arts* from the Petit Séminaire de Québec, where he had been a student since 1857, and he was the first to be awarded the Prince of Wales Prize, instituted by the future monarch during his visit to North America two years earlier.

Bégin enrolled in the Grand Séminaire de Québec in 1862, but after a year there, the superior, Elzéar-Alexandre Taschereau*, who was also rector of the Université Laval, sent him to Rome to study at the Roman College (Pontifical Gregorian University), along with the brothers Louis-Honoré and Benjamin* Pâquet. Taschereau, who had earned his doctorate there in 1856, designed a study program for them, in the expectation that they would form the core of the faculty of theology at Laval, which was to be fully organized in 1866. The three students took advantage of their stay to forge strong ties with, among others, Henri Brichet, Zefferino Zitelli, and Giovanni Pierantozzi. These men would all later hold office in the Sacred Congregation of Propaganda, the body within the Holy See that was responsible for Canada, and their assistance would be invaluable in future struggles. The long summer holidays gave the young cleric an exceptional opportunity to visit other countries in western Europe. On 10 June 1865 he was ordained to the priesthood by Costantino Cardinal Patrizi in the basilica of St John Lateran.

After obtaining his doctorate in canon law in 1866, Bégin spent another two years abroad. To further his historical and linguistic knowledge, he enrolled first in the University of Innsbruck in Austria. While there, he placed orders on behalf of the Séminaire de Québec for reproductions of famous works of art by Tyrolean artists. He then spent four months in Palestine and also visited Egypt, where he collected archaeological objects for one of the museums in the Université Laval. Although he was far away, he kept abreast of developments at home and approved of Taschereau's decision to dismiss professors who supported the ideas of Mgr Jean-Joseph Gaume on the replacement of pagan authors by Christian ones in the college curriculum.

During his teaching career at the Université Laval, which began upon his return home in July 1868, Bégin gave courses in dogmatic theology, Holy Scripture, and church history. From 1871 to 1884 he was closely associated with the university administration through the various offices he held, including those of member of the university council, prefect of studies at the Petit Séminaire, and director of both the Petit Séminaire and the Grand Séminaire. During this eventful period of his life he delivered many public lectures of a historical or literary nature, and published a series of works on apologetics and popular theology. His delicate health was severely taxed by these endeavours and he was obliged to take occasional periods of rest.

Bégin's scholarly work achieved recognition, nonetheless. In 1882 the governor general, the Marquess of Lorne [Campbell*], invited him to be a charter member of the Royal Society of Canada [*see* Sir John William Dawson*]. Bégin belonged to section I, which was devoted to history, archaeology, and French literature and he would serve as its president in 1908. Lorne also wanted this section to safeguard the purity of the French language, an objective Bégin took seriously. His increasingly heavy administrative and pastoral duties led him on several occasions to submit his resignation to the society, which invariably refused to accept it, being only too glad to count among its members a prelate who was clearly destined to become a prince of the church. In 1915 the society would publish in its *Proceedings and Transactions* (Ottawa) the lecture he delivered that year on church-state relations. Around 1882 Bégin also entered the Academy of Arcadia in Rome, a literary society founded in 1690. The academy, which had lost some of its lustre during the 19th century, was made up mainly of Roman nobles and people from outside Italy.

During the crisis that rocked the church in the province of Quebec towards the end of the 19th century, Bégin enjoyed the ever-increasing confidence of Taschereau, who had been named archbishop of Quebec on 24 Dec. 1870. He gave the archbishop his unqualified support in a series of disputes with Bishop Ignace Bourget of Montreal and Bishop Louis-François Laflèche* of Trois-Rivières. Nevertheless, observers with as widely divergent points of view as Bishop George Conroy* and Abbé Joseph-Gauthier-Henri Smeulders, two special envoys from the Holy See, concurred that the lower clergy largely shared the views of the Montreal–Trois-Rivières group. The ideological tension that marked Pius IX's pontificate and contemporary Catholicism transformed what was essentially a conflict of interest into political and doctrinal confrontation. There was, however, one basic principle on which the protagonists were divided: the degree of autonomy that should be enjoyed by the Canadian church, its leaders, and its members, in relation to state structures dominated since 1867 by English-speaking Protestants. This question took on an important nationalist dimension. In any event, the Montreal–Trois-Rivières group was accused by their ecclesiastical and lay opponents of political interference because they publicly attacked the Catholic political elite for its perceived inability to defend the interests it represented.

One of the main disputes concerned the founding of a French-language university in Montreal, and, specifically, the control of faculty appointments. Bourget wanted to name candidates who shared his views, whereas the Séminaire de Québec would not countenance the existence of a rival seat of Catholic learning. In 1876 Rome issued a decree recommending that a branch of the Université Laval be established in Montreal, rather than an independent university. Bourget resigned soon afterwards. The following year Rome sent Conroy as an apostolic delegate and his mission in part was to set up the branch on terms largely acceptable to the Université Laval. He failed to reconcile the widely divergent interests and the arrangement he in the end reached displeased people in Montreal. After Bourget's departure, it fell to Laflèche to uphold the interests of those whom the apostolic delegate had excluded from the branch of the university. Tempers flared. Bégin denounced the narrow-mindedness, ignorance, and bad faith of Laflèche, whom he perceived as the source of all the trouble. "This would be a good time to *squash him*," he confided to a friend on 25 Jan. 1883. As director of the Grand Séminaire, Bégin wanted to close the branch in order to teach the disaffected Montrealers a well-deserved lesson. Taschereau, for his part, embraced a proposal (formulated in 1870 by some priests from Nicolet) to divide the diocese of Trois-Rivières [see Calixte Marquis*] and thus put an end to Laflèche's obstructionism. This request gained the support of a majority of bishops in the ecclesiastical province of Quebec, who in 1883 submitted, at Rome's request, the names of three priests as candidates to head the future diocese of Nicolet, with Bégin at the top of the list. Taschereau threw all his weight behind Bégin's candidacy, but failed to achieve his objective.

In October 1883, with Taschereau threatening to excommunicate those who opposed Conroy's arrangement, the Holy See sent a second representative, Smeulders, to promote an agreement that would still be favourable to the Séminaire de Québec. Taschereau decided, however, to short-circuit the apostolic commissioner, fearing that the opposition might succeed

in winning him over. In 1884 he and Bégin left for Rome, where together they spent eight months making the most of the connections they had built up over the years with Father Brichet, Monsignor Zitelli, Bishop Ignazio Persico, and Edward Henry Cardinal Howard of England. At first, they were successful, but with the erection in 1886 of the ecclesiastical province of Montreal, and the publication in 1889 of the papal bull *Jamdudum* conferring greater autonomy on the Montreal branch of the Université Laval [see Édouard-Charles Fabre*], a balance that had been temporarily disturbed was restored.

Shortly after returning from the Eternal City, Taschereau had submitted Bégin's name for the position of principal of the École Normale Laval at Quebec, made vacant by the death of Abbé Pierre Lagacé. The province's Council of Public Instruction ratified the proposal in January 1885, despite the strong opposition of Bishop Laflèche and Bishop Jean Langevin* of Rimouski, who falsely accused Bégin of sympathizing with secularists because of his friendship with Liberals such as François Langelier*. Bégin's new position made it necessary for him to end his association with the Séminaire de Québec.

His initial priority was the survival of the École Normale, since the provincial government wanted to put teacher training in the hands of the classical colleges, a move Laflèche enthusiastically supported. But Bégin succeeded in winning over a majority of bishops on the Council of Public Instruction. During his term as principal, he found time to publish a textbook on the teaching of Canadian history, which would go through several editions. At Taschereau's request, he also wrote a new catechism, which was approved by the bishops in 1888. This manual would not be replaced until 1951.

The sudden death of Bishop Dominique Racine* of Chicoutimi in January 1888 opened the way to the episcopacy for Bégin. The clergy of Chicoutimi opposed the appointment of an outsider, however, and they won the support of Laflèche. On four occasions Taschereau urged Rome to appoint his candidate, and Bégin was finally consecrated bishop of Chicoutimi on 28 October in the basilica of Notre-Dame at Quebec. At the time of his consecration, the diocese, which had been erected ten years earlier, had 71,000 members, almost all of whom engaged in farming or forestry. The homogeneous character of the population was a source of pride for Bégin. In his report on the state of the diocese, dated 22 Feb. 1890, he informed the Holy See that in Chicoutimi "there are no unbelievers, no ungodly [or] indifferent persons, no supporters of freemasonry ... everyone practises the Catholic religion." He also boasted of the fact that his clergy stood aloof from the politico-religious struggles then threatening to unleash "a racial and religious war" in Canada.

The bishop pursued three main objectives in Chicoutimi. First, he strengthened clerical education. He himself took over the direction of the diocesan seminary, taught courses there, and, in order to create a competent professoriate, assumed the expenses of the most talented students who went to study in Rome. Thanks to these efforts, the Grand Séminaire de Chicoutimi gained affiliation to the Université Laval in 1890. Secondly, the bishop's residence, the seminary, and the cathedral underwent substantial renovations. Finally, in order to further his people's spiritual well-being, he erected seven new parishes, supported the cause of temperance, and oversaw the development of three devotional societies: the Association des Familles, the Garde d'Honneur du Sacré-Cœur de Jésus, and the Congrégation des Dames de Sainte-Anne. In 1891 Bégin gave his approval for the establishment in Baie-Saint-Paul of a teaching community, which would be called the Little Franciscans of Mary [see Marie BIBEAU]. He encouraged the establishment of the Trappists in Mistassini [see Pierre Oger*] the following year.

Chicoutimi was, however, only a brief phase in Bégin's career. In May 1891 Taschereau was already urging the Sacred Congregation of Propaganda to make him his coadjutor, a request supported by the clergy of the archdiocese. Named archbishop of Cyrene and coadjutor of Quebec in December, Bégin would also serve as administrator *sede vacante* of the diocese of Chicoutimi until May 1892. On 12 Jan. 1892 he unburdened his soul to a friend: "Quebec terrifies me . . . I dread . . . the many and difficult matters [to be dealt with]. There is neither rest nor respite." Indeed, the archdiocese contained at that time twice as many parishes and five times as many parishioners as the diocese he had reluctantly left. In 1891 the provincial capital had a population of 63,000 (as opposed to 2,300 in the town of Chicoutimi), and it would double over the next 40 years. Industry, especially the manufacture of footwear, as well as rail transport and shipping, formed the core of working-class life. Despite a constant decline in the number of its English-speaking and Protestant inhabitants, the city of Quebec was still subject to external influences, a result of its activity as a port and the large number of immigrants it took in.

Bégin was granted right of succession to the see of Quebec on 22 March 1892. With Taschereau's mental and physical health rapidly deteriorating, the coadjutor took over complete control of the archdiocese more than a year before Rome formally conferred it on him on 3 Sept. 1894. On Cardinal Taschereau's death on 12 April 1898, Bégin would automatically succeed him.

The new archbishop of Quebec would be a more skilful ecclesiastical leader than his predecessor. Although the two prelates shared a taste for things of the spirit, and their advanced studies set them apart from the other bishops in the province, their personalities were very different. Taschereau had the reputation of being cold, reserved, and taciturn; Bégin was known for his warmth, sociability, and spontaneity. Contemporary observers agree that Cardinal Taschereau was tormented by indecision and readily let himself be influenced by his entourage. Bégin's actions, on the other hand, would be marked by good judgement and firmness.

The French Canadian church had great need of Bégin's talents, for it was being called to play an important role in the tensions troubling Canada, which had been mounting since the execution of Louis Riel* in 1885. What was at issue in these conflicts was the place French Canadians would occupy in confederation. One of the major questions had to do with the religious and linguistic status of Catholic and French-speaking minorities. The Anglo-Protestant majority wanted to build an essentially British country by means of English-language common schools.

With the Holy See's division of the ecclesiastical province of Quebec in 1886 and the renewal of the episcopate at the end of the 19th century, the French Canadian church was slowly regaining its unity. It was, nonetheless, weak and isolated, seriously damaged by accusations of political interference that had long been levelled against it both in Canada and abroad. These accusations would be skilfully exploited by a Liberal party that, in its rapid rise to power, was endeavouring to accommodate the demands of the country's Anglo-Protestant majority, without having to deal with a church deemed difficult and intransigent. The heightened tension caused an ethnic polarization that increasingly induced Irish Catholics to identify with Anglo-Protestants rather than with their co-religionists. For its part, the Holy See blamed the French Canadian church for mixing religion, politics, and ethnic interests, and for hindering the conversion of North America, a goal it considered at last achievable because of the large numbers of Catholic immigrants.

It was in these circumstances that a prolonged drama began to unfold in 1896, on the eve of a federal election. Bégin wrote a collective pastoral letter from the bishops of the province of Quebec requiring voters, as a matter of conscience, to cast their ballots for candidates who formally undertook to support a federal law reinstating the confessional school system that had been abolished in Manitoba in 1890 [see Thomas Greenway*]. This move did not have the expected effect, since Wilfrid Laurier*, the Liberal leader, who favoured an amicable accord with the government of Manitoba, came to power on 23 June 1896. A few months later, Bégin described the Laurier–Greenway agreement reached between the new prime minister and his Manitoban counterpart as a "shameful treaty" and "an absolutely immoral act."

Bégin

"There was no need to spend so much time pretending to negotiate in Winnipeg in order to arrive at this minuscule compromise," he declared on 3 Jan. 1897 in a letter to Miecislaus Cardinal Ledóchowsky. The coadjutor now considered that the church should try a new approach to get the debate on the right track – constitutional protection for minority rights.

Meanwhile, the Liberals, believing themselves victims of undue clerical interference, persuaded the Holy See to send Rafael Merry del Val on a special mission to Canada in March 1897. Like Taschereau in the time of Smeulders, Bégin sought to limit the apostolic delegate's efforts by going to Rome to plead his case directly. He returned empty-handed, however. Before leaving the Eternal City, he appointed Dominique-Ceslas Gonthier*, a Dominican, as his agent in Rome and thus managed to obtain an advance copy of the report that Merry del Val submitted to the Holy See in September. In a document setting out his observations, the archbishop rejected the report's claims that the actions of the clergy were dictated by a partisan spirit and ethnocentrism. He even went so far as to defend Laflèche, his erstwhile sworn enemy, who had denounced Laurier's "sunny ways" from the pulpit during the election campaign. Bégin accused the delegate of letting himself be manipulated by the "active and leading part" of the Liberal party, which was capable of "every kind of deceit and all the treachery," and of brushing aside the French Canadian episcopacy, though it constituted at least two-thirds of the Catholic hierarchy in Canada.

Despite this harsh criticism, the encyclical *Affari vos*, which was published by Leo XIII at the end of 1897 to deal with the school crisis, reflected the influence of the delegate rather than that of the archbishop, even though Bégin had written a first draft of it. While declaring that the Laurier–Greenway agreement was "defective, imperfect, inadequate," the pope called on Catholics to work for its improvement. After consulting Archbishop Paul Bruchési* of Montreal, Bégin issued a pastoral letter longer than the encyclical which recapitulated the ideas in his draft that were not included in the papal text. He emphasized the need for Catholics to remain united around their religious leaders so that the confessional school system would be fully restored in Manitoba. Privately, the archbishop of Quebec opined that the prospect held out in the encyclical of a gradual improvement in the Laurier–Greenway agreement was an idle fantasy, given the fierce opposition of the political forces in Manitoba. He confided to Adélard Langevin* on 6 Dec. 1898 that the agreement was nothing but a "house of cards that the slightest breath of Protestant fanaticism would soon be enough to topple." The Holy See, for its part, fearing that the bishops might hinder the much sought-after reform of the accord, forbade them to speak out.

Bégin's scepticism deepened in August 1899 when Rome, at the intense urging of Laurier, established a permanent apostolic delegation in Canada, with Diomede Falconio as the first incumbent. The archbishop of Quebec wrote to Cardinal Ledóchowsky on 19 Jan. 1898 that he suspected the prime minister of wanting to "cast discredit on the episcopate and convince the faithful that a Delegate has become necessary to keep it under control." Although in favour of the delegation in principle, Bégin thought it should have been the culmination of a process through which the bishops of Canada worked together to establish a plenary council of the Canadian church as a first step.

The second apostolic delegate, Donato Sbarretti y Tazza, who was appointed in December 1902, ardently supported the convening of a council, but the idea now left Bégin rather cold. This body would, in Bégin's view, simply legitimize the delegation's excessively conciliatory positions in regard to federal policies on minorities and Sbarretti's ambition to replace the French Canadian episcopacy as the effective head of the Canadian church. The two men were thus at daggers drawn. Bégin would succeed in having his candidate, Paul-Eugène Roy, named auxiliary bishop of Quebec in 1908 despite the opposition of Sbarretti, who considered him hostile towards the delegation. Sbarretti would, however, get the better of Bégin on the matter of the council, which was held at Quebec under the delegate's chairmanship in 1909.

While the archbishop of Quebec seemed to have the ear of the Sacred Congregation of Propaganda, Sbarretti had contacts at the secretariat of state, which since 1903 had been headed by Cardinal Merry del Val, who was still keenly interested in Canadian affairs. When, as a result of administrative reforms adopted by Rome, the Canadian dioceses were removed from Propaganda's area of responsibility in 1908, Bégin lost a valuable source of support. This change did not, however, prevent him from receiving his cardinal's hat on 25 May 1914, at the same time as his former classmate the future Pope Benedict XV.

Apart from the activities of the apostolic delegates, it was Rome's policy in episcopal nominations that Bégin called into question. He suspected the Holy See of favouring English-speaking candidates for the dioceses on the prairies, formerly held by francophones, as well as some in Ontario where French Canadians made up a large proportion, or even a majority, of the faithful. In Bégin's view, bishops of Irish extraction seemed already to be working tirelessly to assimilate the francophone minority and European immigrants. In a letter to Girolamo Maria Cardinal Gotti, dated 2 June 1907, the archbishop was quick to emphasize all the harm Vatican policies had caused among the faithful. "Hearts are now being pierced by doubt, many people are wondering whether the church really loves us . . . and the traditional veneration for the apostolic Holy See is rapidly growing weaker."

Ethnic hostilities intensified within the Canadian church, as was shown in the address given by Archbishop Francis Alphonsus Bourne of Westminster to the 1910 International Eucharistic Congress in Montreal. That year, Bégin resigned from the board of governors of the Catholic Church Extension Society, much to the displeasure of Archbishop Fergus Patrick McEvay* of Toronto, who was its chancellor. The organization, which was dedicated to helping aboriginal people and immigrants, was headed by Alfred Edward BURKE, who staunchly supported British imperialism and assimilation. The following year, Bégin set up a parallel body at Quebec, the Œuvre Protectrice des Immigrants Catholiques, putting Abbé Philippe Casgrain in charge. Furthermore, when the newly chosen bishop of London, Michael Francis Fallon*, took up arms against members of his clergy and flock whom he described as nationalists because they supported the regular use of French, Bégin encouraged them to complain to Rome. In subsequent years, he argued vainly in favour of dividing the diocese of London so that a French-speaking one could be erected in Windsor and Fallon could be assigned to an English-speaking one.

The Canadian church went through the worst crisis of its history, when the Ontario government passed Regulation 17 in 1912 [see Sir James Pliny Whitney*]. Although the Catholic bishops of Ontario supported Fallon's initiatives – calling for an end to bilingual schools – the French Canadian episcopate stood behind Bégin and sought the intervention of Benedict XV and the federal government in this matter. Bégin publicly encouraged Franco-Ontarian pupils to defy the law, which he considered was unjust, and he legitimized the involvement of the Quebec provincial government in the dispute.

The Holy See adopted a position reminiscent of the one it had taken some 20 years earlier with regard to Manitoba. The pontifical letters *Commissio divinitus* (1916) and *E litteris apostolicis* (1918) reflected the influence of the apostolic delegate Pellegrino Francesco Stagni, who rejected the idea that language was the guardian of the faith, a claim endorsed by the Quebec episcopate. While supporting the right of Franco-Ontarians to have their language taught at school, the Holy See insisted that pupils acquire an adequate knowledge of English. The second letter, however, confirmed that French Canadians should "desire and seek to obtain some broader concessions." Although Bégin was satisfied with this position, the fact remains that Rome's judgement on the French Canadian episcopate, its positions, and its actions was severe and all-encompassing. The apostolic delegate, for his part, felt fully justified when the highest tribunal in the British empire, the Judicial Committee of the

Privy Council, on 2 Nov. 1916 upheld the constitutionality of Regulation 17. In the more relaxed climate that followed the interventions from Rome and the ruling from London, the Canadian archbishops agreed on a proposal that would create in Ontario a Roman Catholic school system in which Franco-Ontarian pupils would have access to a bilingual education.

Throughout these years of sharp ethnic confrontation, the archbishop of Quebec may have overestimated the rights granted to minorities by the constitution. Like Bishop Bourget before him, he was, however, guided by a clear and simple idea of the place of French Canadians in confederation. "Far from being considered a conquered people," he told Cardinal Gotti on 2 June 1907, "we possess all the prerogatives of sovereignty." While Bégin was not in a position to appreciate the long-term factors that led to the erosion of a minority ethnic group's language, he knew perfectly well that the French Canadian bishops were better able than their English-speaking counterparts to foster short-term cultural retention among French Canadian minorities and European immigrants.

As a prominent participant in the protest movement in favour of minority rights, Bégin probably saw the war as a good opportunity to display the church's unshakeable loyalty to the British cause. The collective pastoral letter issued by the bishops of the ecclesiastical provinces of Quebec, Montreal, and Ottawa in September 1914 included moral support for Canadian participation in the conflict, and the circular Bégin sent out to the clergy in January 1917 "on the subject of the National Service questionnaire" ordered them to advise their "parishioners to reply conscientiously to the questions asked, so as to comply with the wishes of the civil authority." On the other hand, Bégin considered that the Military Service Act, which was passed in July, went beyond Canada's obligations to Great Britain and reneged on the government's promise to the Quebec bishops not to resort to conscription. When a riot broke out at Quebec on Easter Monday 1918, after compulsory service was put into effect [see François-Louis LESSARD; Georges Demeule*], Bégin flatly condemned the violence. At the same time, he found himself compelled to put pressure on the federal government to grant exemption to young ecclesiastics not yet ordained.

After the struggle for minority rights, the social question was the other major theme of Bégin's episcopate. He was not opposed in principle to industrialization and urbanization, but he believed that the mass culture they had engendered elsewhere, especially in the United States, threatened French Canadian culture and the Catholic faith. In the face of this mass culture promoted by the press, theatre, novels, and department store catalogues, the church had to provide leadership in order to ensure the cohesion of society. To this end, Bégin erected more than 60 new parishes in his archdiocese and established about 30 religious communities at Quebec. Some of these were contemplative orders, others were active in pastoral work, teaching, missions, and social and devotional causes. He often issued instructions to the people of his diocese, banning reading material and theatrical performances that he considered contrary to Catholic morality. He also exploited the popularity of temperance campaigns at the beginning of the 20th century to promote the role of the clergy as leaders. He brought pressure to bear on the various levels of government to prohibit the excessive use of alcohol. In the 1910s, under the sway of his auxiliary, Bishop Roy, who was leading a veritable crusade in favour of temperance, he even went so far as to advocate total abstinence.

In the archbishop's eyes, however, it was not enough simply to instil Christian values. The church had to create temporal institutions as well. Bégin encouraged his clergy to take an active part in setting up producers' cooperatives, consumers' cooperatives, and credit unions, thereby creating bonds of social and national solidarity under the sponsorship of the church. He was also a precursor of Catholic trade unionism. He earned this reputation thanks to the success of his efforts as a mediator in the dispute between employers and footwear workers at Quebec late in 1900 [see Gaudiose HÉBERT]. In the ruling he handed down as arbitrator in January 1901, the archbishop urged the unions to delete from their constitutions certain sections he considered too hostile to employers, and to agree to have a chaplain with voting rights at their meetings. Although some union leaders later denounced the paternalism of the agreement and the church's willingness to involve itself in purely secular matters, the gains achieved should not be underestimated: union recognition in an industry marked by discord and opposition to any form of labour organization, as well as the establishment of a mechanism for settling industrial disputes.

Through a pastoral letter dated 31 March 1907, Bégin reorganized the religious, national, social, and intellectual associations of the archdiocese into a central body known as the Action Sociale Catholique, of which Roy became the director. At the same time he created the Œuvre de la Presse Catholique, which led to the launching on 21 December at Quebec of *L'Action sociale* (which would become *L'Action catholique*), a daily newspaper founded jointly by Bégin, Roy, Abbé Stanislas-Alfred Lortie*, and Adjutor Rivard*, a lawyer. At a time when newspapers were either the official organs of the two major political parties or the pre-eminent dispensers of mass culture, *L'Action sociale* stood out as a vehicle of a Catholic urban-industrial counter-culture based on the teachings of the church.

The cardinal's advancing years forced him increasingly to surrender diocesan administration to Roy, who had become his coadjutor with right of succession in 1920. In 1924, because of Roy's poor health, Rome gave him a second auxiliary, Joseph-Alfred Langlois. The following year, a few weeks after celebrating the 60th anniversary of his ordination, Bégin suffered an attack of paralysis and died. An impressive funeral was held on 25 July in the basilica of Notre-Dame.

A tall man with an air of distinction, Bégin retained the modest ways of his humble beginnings. Despite the honours he accumulated in the course of his life, he was always a man of good sense and moderation. For this reason, he found it difficult to endure the haughtiness of someone like Merry del Val. While he recognized that the French Canadian hierarchy was not without its faults, he knew that "many European eagles become quite ordinary birds when we get a closer look at them," as he stated in his memorandum on Merry del Val's report. His ready smile, his gentle and lively eyes, his ease in speaking, and his courtesy drew people to him. He had no difficulty, therefore, in recruiting experienced helpers for the many charitable endeavours he sponsored. Despite his advanced studies, published works, and membership in prestigious cultural organizations, Bégin did little or no reading because he was overburdened with his administrative responsibilities.

Louis-Nazaire Bégin was first and foremost Rome's man. At the age of 82 he made the last of more than 30 journeys to the Eternal City. It was there that he found his inspiration, his religiosity, his doctrine, his social and intellectual models. The most rigid positions taken by Rome, such as the one against modernism in 1907, did not shake this churchman's orthodox beliefs. He took pride also in the doctrinal conformity of his clergy. In 1915, in order to get closer to canonical ideals, he revived the metropolitan chapter of Quebec, which had gradually faded away soon after the conquest. Although he never took part in a conclave, arriving in Rome too late in 1914 and 1922, he was truly loyal to the papacy. Yet he had to face the bitter reality that the Holy See did not share his vision of the place of French Canadians in confederation and in the Canadian church. Nevertheless, by tirelessly defending the rights of minorities and by helping build a public Catholic culture in the province of Quebec (the only one north of the Rio Grande), Bégin proved a leading figure in French Canada.

ROBERTO PERIN

The most complete bibliography of the writings of Louis-Nazaire Bégin can be found in Simon Héroux, "Les relations entre l'Église et l'État d'après le cardinal Louis-

Nazaire Bégin, 1840–1925" (thèse de PHD, univ. d'Ottawa, 1973). Several of Bégin's publications have been preserved on microfiche and are listed in CIHM, *Reg.*

ANQ-Q, CE301-S19, 11 janv. 1840. Arch. de l'Archidio-cèse de Québec, 31-17A (papiers cardinal L.-N. Bégin). Arch. de l'Évêché de Chicoutimi (Chicoutimi, Qué.), Reg., sér.B, actes, vol.I (1878–1900): 377–79. Archivio della Propaganda Fide (Rome), Acta, vols.247, 253; Nuova serie, vols.120, 240–42, 462; Scritture originali riferite nelle Congregazioni generali, vols.1030, 1040; Scritture riferite nei Congressi, America settentrionale, vols.14, 26, 28. Archivio Segreto Vaticano (Rome), Delegazione apostolica degli Stati Uniti, VI. MCQ-FSQ, Séminaire 71, no.127; Séminaire 88, no.19A; SME, 10 févr. 1879; SME 1/MS-34.2, 24 nov. 1875, 28, 31 janv. 1878; MS-34.3, 16 janv., 8 févr. 1879, 23 nov. 1880; SME 9/72/100; 9/105/47; 13/33; 13/674: 43; 13/678. *L'Action catholique* (Québec), 20 juill. 1925, 7 janv. 1940, suppl. *L'Événement*, 23 avril 1898. "Mgr Bégin, second évêque de Chicoutimi," *La Semaine religieuse de Québec*, 25 oct. 1888. André Pillet, "Son Éminence le cardinal L.-N. Bégin, archevêque de Québec," *La Semaine religieuse de Québec*, 17 sept. 1925. *Almanach de l'Action sociale catholique* (Québec), 10 (1926): 12–15. "Le cardinal Bégin," RSC, *Trans.*, 3rd ser., 20 (1926), proc.: v–x. Robert Choquette, *Language and religion: a history of English-French conflict in Ontario* (Ottawa, 1975). P. [E.] Crunican, *Priests and politicians: Manitoba schools and the election of 1896* (Toronto and Buffalo, N.Y., 1974). *Histoire du catholicisme québécois*, sous la dir. de Nive Voisine (2 tomes en 4v. parus, Montréal, 1984–), tome 2, vol.2 (Philippe Sylvain et Nive Voisine, *Les XVIIIᵉ et XIXᵉ siècles: réveil et consolidation (1840–1898)*, 1991); tome 3, vol.1 (Jean Hamelin et Nicole Gagnon, *Le XXᵉ siècle: 1898–1940*, 1984). André Lavallée, *Québec contre Montréal; la querelle universitaire, 1876–1891* (Montréal, 1974). M. G. McGowan, "'Religious duties and patriotic endeavours': the Catholic Church Extension Society, French Canada and the prairie west, 1908–1916," CCHA, *Hist. studies*, 51 (1984): 107–19. Martin Pâquet, "Marquage identitaire et pastorale catholique: l'Œuvre protectrice des immigrants catholiques, 1912–1930," in *Constructions identitaires et pratiques sociales*, ed. J.-P. Wallot *et al.* (Ottawa, 2002). Marius Paré, *L'Église au diocèse de Chicoutimi* (3v. parus, Chicoutimi, 1983–), 2 (*1888–1892*, 1987). Roberto Perin, "French-speaking Canada from 1840," in *A concise history of Christianity in Canada*, ed. Terrence Murphy (Toronto, 1996), 190–260; *Rome in Canada: the Vatican and Canadian affairs in the late Victorian age* (Toronto, 1990). Giovanni Pizzorusso, "Donato Sbarretti, delegato apostolico a Ottawa, e la difficile organizzazione del Concilio plenario canadese (1909)," *Annali accademici canadesi* (Ottawa), 6 (1990): 77–88; "Un diplomate du Vatican en Amérique: Donato Sbarretti à Washington, La Havane et Ottawa (1893–1910)," *Annali accademici canadesi*, 9 (1993): 5–18. Jacques Rouillard, *Les syndicats nationaux au Québec, de 1900 à 1930* (Québec, 1979). Robert Rumilly, *Mgr Laflèche et son temps* (Montréal, [1938]). Matteo Sanfilippo, "Diomede Falconio e l'Église catholique en Amérique du Nord," *Canadian Studies Rev.* (Fasano, Italy), 5 (1992): 43–47; "Roman archives as a source for the history of Canadian ethnic groups," CCHA, *Hist. studies*, 60 (1993–94): 83–101. Pierre Savard, "L'Italia nella cultura franco-canadese dell'Ottocento," in *Canadiana: problemi di storia canadese*, ed. Luca Codignola (Venice, 1983), 91–106;

"Le journal de l'abbé Benjamin Pâquet, étudiant à Rome, 1863–1866," *Culture* (Québec), 26 (1965): 64–83. André Simard, *Les évêques et les prêtres séculiers au diocèse de Chicoutimi, 1878–1968; notices biographiques* (Chicoutimi, 1969). Donald Tremblay, "Mgr Pellegrino Francesco Stagni, O.S.M., et l'Église canadienne, 1910–1918" (thèse de PHD, univ. Laval, Québec, 1995).

BÉLANGER, DINA (baptized **Marie-Marguerite-Dina-Adélaïde**), named **Marie Sainte-Cécile-de-Rome**, Religious of Jesus and Mary, musician, author, and mystic; b. 30 April 1897 at Quebec, only daughter of Octave Bélanger, a bookkeeper, and Séraphia Matte; d. 4 Sept. 1929 at the Couvent Jésus-Marie in Sillery, Que.; since May 1990 her tomb has been in the chapel of the provincial house of the Religious of Jesus and Mary in Sillery.

Dina Bélanger grew up in the parish of Notre-Dame-de-Jacques-Cartier, in Saint-Roch ward in the city of Quebec. She received her elementary and secondary schooling at the convents of Saint-Roch and Jacques-Cartier and at the Pensionnat Bellevue, all of which were run by the Congregation of Notre-Dame. At the age of eight she began music lessons with the nuns, who until 1914 remained her teachers. That year she began studying with Joseph-Arthur Bernier, the organist for the parish of Notre-Dame-de-Jacques-Cartier. Finding that Dina was very gifted musically, he spoke to Abbé Omer Cloutier, the parish priest, who advised her parents to enrol her at the Institute of Musical Art in New York. Thus she attended this conservatory from 1916 to 1918, living at Our Lady of Peace residence with the Religious of Jesus and Mary. She achieved remarkable success in music, particularly with harmony, which requires the kind of mathematical mind she had inherited from her father.

On her return to Quebec, Dina lived with her parents, gave brilliant concerts in support of charitable causes at Quebec, and helped her mother as a volunteer in their parish. But the call of Christ, which she had heard from youth, led her to abandon everything and enter the Couvent Jésus-Marie in Sillery on 11 Aug. 1921. She was 24 years old. Assuming the name of Marie Sainte-Cécile-de-Rome, she took her religious vows on 15 Aug. 1923 and went to the Couvent Jésus-Marie in Saint-Michel (Saint-Michel-de-Bellechasse), near Quebec City, where she taught music. She stayed there only five weeks, however. After caring for a sick pupil, she contracted scarlet fever; she had to return to Sillery, where, because she did not have a strong constitution, the disease developed into tuberculosis.

From then on, Dina's life was spent in love and suffering, interspersed with periods of teaching music to young people, who found in her a favoured friend of the Lord. She died on 4 Sept. 1929 at the age of 32, having spent eight years in religious life.

It was through her autobiography, written at the request of the superiors of her community and published in 1934 as *Une vie dans le Christ*, that Dina became known after her death. The account of her human experience and spiritual development revealed her as a mystic, a person who to an unusual degree perceived the presence of God in herself and in the world. According to Pope John Paul II, "She had musical gifts that no doubt prepared her for the acceptance of the divine presence and for praise that transcends words." From a theological perspective, the mystical life of Dina Bélanger, lived out in the company of the Virgin Mary, was centred on the mystery of love, and the symbolism of the heart serves as a guiding theme to convey this experience. In an original way, she entered into the mystery of the heart of Jesus: the tender or Sacred Heart, in which she at first "hid." Then, after much inner torment, she was introduced into the Heart of the Trinity, and experienced an intimate union with the Trinity. In a third stage she perceived the mystery of the eucharistic heart of Jesus and his heart in the throes of death, at which time a mission to priests and consecrated persons was entrusted to her by the Holy Spirit. In the fourth and final stage, her life was spent in "the Essence of the Heart of God." Thus she experienced Christ-centred spirituality: Dina was identified with Christ, her "divine Substitute," whom she offered unceasingly to the Father in order to bring the redeeming mystery into being on earth. She enriched the church with a broader understanding of the mystery of love, from the doctrinal standpoint of the mystical body and the union of the baptized with the most Holy Trinity. By her prophetic testimony, written at the request of her superiors, she touched young people, parents, priests, consecrated persons, artists, the sick, in short, all those who, looking upon her, opened their hearts to love.

From 1934 to 1953, 43,000 copies of *Une vie dans le Christ*, published in French and English, would be sold, as well as half a million excerpts from it. During the same period the work would be translated in full into German, Italian, Spanish, and Tamil, and in part into other languages including Dutch and Chinese. The period of the second Vatican Council would bring the book's popularity to a temporary halt, but since 1970 there has been steady interest in it. And so, the promise Christ made to Dina shortly before she entered the convent was fulfilled: "You will do good above all by your writing."

After her death, many favours were obtained through her intercessions, and diocesan proceedings for her beatification began at Quebec in 1939. She was beatified in Rome on 20 March 1993. The first prospective saint to be born in Quebec, the cradle of French Christian civilization in North America, Dina Bélanger followed in a long line of spiritual souls and mystics, most of them from France, who for 350 years had brought glory to the country. Though her whole life was inward and hidden, she deserves a place alongside the great mystics of its early days, including Marie de l'Incarnation [Guyart*], Marie-Catherine de Saint-Augustin [Simon*], and Marguerite Bourgeoys*. In her, the "spiritual springtime" of the country is reborn.

GHISLAINE BOUCHER

The archival records concerning Dina Bélanger were unfortunately destroyed in a fire at the Couvent Jésus-Marie at Sillery, Que., in 1983. After Bélanger's death, the authorities of her community had had her manuscript journals transcribed and had turned them over to Dom Léonce Crenier for publication. The resulting text appeared as *Une vie dans le Christ: Marie Sainte-Cécile de Rome (Dina Bélanger), religieuse de Jésus-Marie (1897–1929); autobiographie et témoignages* (2v., Sillery, 1934). This work has since gone through five French editions and as many in English, and has also been translated into several other languages.

Among the many books and articles devoted to Dina Bélanger, a partial listing of which appears in Congregatio Pro Causis Sanctorum, *Beatificationis et canonizationis servae Dei Mariae a S. Caecilia Romana (in saec. Dinae Bélanger), sororis professae e Congregatione religiosarum Iesu et Mariae (1897–1929); relatio e voti del congresso speciale, 25 ottobre 1988* (Rome, 1988), the following are of particular note: Ghislaine Boucher, *Dina Bélanger, Marie Sainte-Cécile-de-Rome, 1897–1929; itinéraire spirituel* (Montréal, 1983); H.-M. Guindon, *Toute à toi; Marie dans la vie spirituelle de la vénérable Dina Bélanger* (Montréal, 1989); Irène Léger, *Courage d'aimer: Dina Bélanger, religieuse de Jésus-Marie (en religion Marie Ste-Cécile de Rome), 1897–1929* (Montréal, 1986); Fernand Ouellette, *Dina Bélanger* (Saint-Laurent, Qué., 1998).

BELL, ALEXANDER GRAHAM, teacher of the deaf, inventor, and scientist; b. 3 March 1847 in Edinburgh, Scotland, second son of Alexander Melville Bell and Eliza Grace Symonds; m. 11 July 1877 Mabel Gardiner HUBBARD in Cambridge, Mass., and they had two sons and two daughters; d. 2 Aug. 1922 near Baddeck, N.S.

Alexander Bell owed much to his paternal grandfather, Alexander, who had moved away from Fifeshire, where several generations of the family had toiled as shoemakers, to blaze a career in the emerging art and science of elocution. The grandfather's love of acting led him to develop his skills in speech, which resulted in his move to Dundee in 1826 to teach elocution full-time. He soon turned his interest to speech impediments, particularly stammering, and began work on a textbook. It was during a journey to Edinburgh by his wife, to deliver the manuscript, that an acquaintance discovered her affair, which culminated in divorce. These events prompted him in 1834 to move with his youngest son, Melville, to London, where a year later he published *The practical elocu-tionist*. It used comma-like symbols to indicate word groupings and emphasis, forming the basis of a system to visualize speech and the underpinning of a vocation that would concern three generations of Bells.

Not long after his father remarried, Melville, who had worked long hours as a draper's assistant in London, was sent to Newfoundland in 1838 to improve his health. He lived with a family friend in St John's and found work as a clerk in a shipping house. In addition to helping other clerks and shopmen get shorter work hours and organizing acting classes and plays, he began treating stammerers, using his father's methods. His success won him public accolades before his departure for England in 1842. He joined his father and embarked on original investigations into the physiology of the vocal organs. During a visit to Edinburgh the following year, he was introduced to Eliza Symonds, an English miniature painter ten years his senior. In a memoir written for his grandchildren he recalled that "it was not exactly a case of love at first sight, but it was a case of *struck* at first sight." Melville was drawn to her, largely for her cultivated mind but in part, he admitted, out of sympathy, which was heightened by her partial deafness. Their long and loving relationship would be a force in Aleck Bell's life.

Married in 1844, they moved to Edinburgh. Melville's first published work, *The art of reading*, appeared there in 1845 and he used it in his lectures on elocution. He also read publicly from the "ungodly" works of Charles Dickens, a practice that led to a request from his church to cease. Bell changed his church instead. His prosperity, from the growing interest in his lectures, enabled the couple to move to a spacious flat on South Charlotte Street, where Aleck was born. Early instruction was provided by both parents. His interest in biology came from his father, who encouraged his passion for collecting natural specimens; his mother passed on her love of music. He apparently possessed a keen faculty to play by ear, which he claimed he lost when he learned to read music. Lessons from the distinguished pianist Benoît-Auguste Bertini inspired him to want to become a professional musician. Although he later lost this desire, the experience was not wasted: "I am inclined to think . . . that my early passion for music had a good deal to do in preparing me for the scientific study of sound," he would later write in his autobiography.

Eliza Bell imbued her three sons with her deep piety, which influenced Aleck "at least until I reached years of discretion," he recalled. The family was also steeped in liberalism. Aleck's grandfather despised dogma, disdained inherited titles, and believed passionately in merit and the ability of education to raise the worth of an individual. Aleck began more formal schooling in 1857 when he was sent to Hamilton

Place Academy; by his own admission, he was a poor student and lacked ambition. A brooding loner, he confessed to a propensity to dream, no doubt stimulated by the love of reading instilled in him by his father and grandfather. He found many idyllic spots for reverie after his parents bought Milton Cottage, near Edinburgh, in 1858. On his birthday that year he took his middle name, inspired by the surname of Alexander Graham, a former student of Melville's in Newfoundland who visited the family and impressed young Aleck.

Dreaming, rambles at Milton Cottage, and botanical collecting fuelled Aleck's curiosity, and his desire to invent. He devised his first practical contrivance later in 1858. He and a friend, Benjamin Herdman, had been playing around the Herdman flour mill when Ben's father admonished them to do something useful. When Aleck asked what they could do, John Herdman held out some grain and told them they would be a big help if they could remove the husks. Aleck surprised him when he produced a process to do just that, based on wire brushes on a set of rotating paddles in an existing machine. At Milton Cottage the darkroom installed by Melville Bell sparked in Aleck a keen interest in the new art form of photography, which he would use to document his work later in life.

A pivotal event in Bell's life came at age 15, when he was sent to London to spend a year with his recently widowed grandfather. Bell credits him with sparking the zeal that would drive his life's work. Grandfather Bell made Aleck ashamed of his gross ignorance of ordinary subjects of study and aroused in him, Bell recalled, "the ambition to remedy my defects of education by personal study." The elder Bell also impressed upon him the singular importance of speech, which the grandfather viewed as the paramount characteristic of humankind: "Perhaps, in no higher respect has man been created in the image of his Maker." Before Aleck left London, he and his father called on Charles Wheatstone, a leading scientist and telegraph researcher, to see his model of Wolfgang von Kempelen's 18th-century "speaking machine." The device inspired Aleck and his brother Melville James (Melly) to build their own version of a talking larynx.

Edinburgh in Bell's youth was dubbed the Athens of the North in recognition of its scientific, medical, and literary achievements, which had eclipsed those of London. The iron steamship, the breech-loading rifle, the pedal bicycle, and Joseph Lister's techniques of antiseptic surgery were invented there, and its academies made it a Mecca for European scientists. The Bell house attracted many of the greats of the era, and Aleck met men such as Wheatstone, again, and noted phonetician Alexander John Ellis of London. At 16, however, Aleck longed to be on his own. He secured a position as a pupil-teacher of elocution and music at an academy in Elgin. After a year at the University of Edinburgh in 1864–65, he returned to Elgin and in 1866–67 he taught in Bath. During these years he continued his experiments in speech physiology to study, using dogs and cats, the pitch and formation of vowel sounds, which his father encouraged him to write up. Impressed with his report of March 1866, Alexander Ellis invited him to join the Philological Society in London though he was still a teenager.

In 1867 tragedy struck the family, now in London, when Aleck's younger brother, Edward Charles, died of tuberculosis. That same year his father published his landmark treatise, *Visible speech: the science . . . of universal alphabetics*, and made Aleck his assistant, placing him in charge of his practice of teaching the deaf during his absences to promote his "visible speech," universal alphabet, and system of phonetics. From 1868 to 1870 Aleck took courses in anatomy and physiology at University College in London, but he never completed his degree. In May 1868 his father had asked him to adapt the visible speech method to teach deaf children at a school in Kensington (London) while he and his brother made a lecture tour of North America. That August, en route to Chicago, they visited a Scottish friend, the Reverend Thomas Henderson, in Paris, Ont., where Melville fell in love with the countryside. His lecture in Boston, at the Lowell Institute, led the city's school board to open a special day school for the deaf the following year, with Sarah Fuller as principal, to experiment with the new oral techniques of speech instruction.

In the summer of 1869, with Melville Bell considering a return engagement in Boston, Henderson encouraged him to emigrate to Canada. The Bells considered the idea because of Melly's illness, but put it off; Melly died of tuberculosis in May 1870. The family then took up Henderson's invitation. At what would be one of their last dinners at home in London that summer, Ellis urged Aleck to examine a recent work by German physicist Hermann Ludwig Ferdinand von Helmholtz. After reading a French translation of *On the sensations of tone*, Bell exclaimed that it would soon be possible to "talk by telegraph." The book also inspired him to learn more about electromagnetism and electricity – critical ingredients in his subsequent work on a speaking telegraph – but he would have to do so in the New World.

Bell, his parents, and his widowed sister-in-law arrived in Quebec City on 1 August and then journeyed to Paris. They learned of a country cottage for sale outside nearby Brantford and, before the week was out, Melville Bell had bought the property, named Tutelo Heights, which overlooked the Grand River. Aleck quickly found a favourite spot: "It was my custom in the summer time to take a rug, a pillow, and an interesting book to this cozy little nook," he later wrote, "and dream away the afternoon in luxurious idleness."

In April 1871 Bell left his parents to teach at Fuller's school in Boston. The idea that deaf children could be taught to speak was a novel concept in North America. The prevailing views were that the deaf had no place in normal society and that a person who was deaf was *ipso facto* dumb. The Bells rejected these notions, and Aleck's demonstration of how the techniques of visible speech could be used to instruct teachers met with success in Boston. Within a few weeks he was able to teach children to use more than 400 syllables. This progress led to demonstrations at the Clarke Institution for Deaf-Mutes in Northampton and the American Asylum for the Education and Instruction of the Deaf and Dumb in Hartford, Conn. Demand for his services became so great that he opened his own school in Boston in October 1872. The requirements for teachers were "a good English education . . . , a correct ear, a practical knowledge of teaching, and a pleasant and attractive bearing toward children."

Until his death Bell saw himself above all else as a teacher of the deaf. He regarded this work to be his greatest contribution to humanity, yet seldom got public recognition or sympathy for it. He was a leading proponent of the so-called oralist school, which held that the deaf could be taught to speak without the use of manual sign language, then the more widely used method. But his embrace of oral methods overshadowed his solid scientific understanding of deafness and propelled him to the centre of a controversy that would rage for much of the next half century. More zealous advocates of oralism embarked on a fanatical campaign to banish sign language. Although Bell disagreed with many of their professed reforms, including the formation of segregated boarding schools, his name remained associated with the oralist camp.

From experiments at schools like Bell's, the use of oral techniques progressed to the point where 40 per cent of deaf students were being taught without sign language by the turn of the century. Within two more decades the proportion doubled to 80 per cent. The concerns of representatives of the deaf, who were opposed to the exclusive use of the oral method, went unheard by educators. Oralism, however, met with reduced success as science conquered many of the infectious diseases that robbed children of their hearing after their language skills had developed and as the proportion of congenitally deaf students increased. One must remember that Bell's enthusiasm for it was shaped in part by the positive role that oral techniques had with two close family members: his mother, who had made dramatic progress using her husband's techniques, and later his wife.

Bell had first met his future father-in-law on 8 April 1872. A prominent patent attorney, Gardiner

Greene Hubbard was president of the Clarke Institution. His daughter Mabel had lost her hearing to scarlet fever in 1863 at the age of five. It was a fortunate contact for Bell on two counts. Hubbard asked Bell to tutor her and he had a fascination for electrical inventions, particularly anything related to the telegraph. At the same time Bell maintained his close relationship with his father in Brantford, whose diary of their correspondence and talks would become a crucial document in the defence of Aleck's patents. It was, in fact, in a letter to his father of 11 Nov. 1872 that Aleck, never one to be intimidated by untested possibility, explored the extraordinary idea of a telegraph that would send numerous messages simultaneously along a single wire. Bell was inspired that fall by public lectures at the Massachusetts Institute of Technology, which set him first on a path to duplicate some of Helmholtz's experiments with electrical current, and then in the direction of the telephone. As biographer Robert V. Bruce states, he had the talents, temperament, and background that prepared him for the task. He had thus arrived at the right time in the right place. Not only was Boston a burgeoning intellectual hub of engineering and science, but it was home to enterprising capitalists as well.

Bell's appointment as professor of vocal physiology and elocution at Boston University in early 1873 meant that he had to relegate his experimental work on the multiple telegraph to the night-time. That November he began tutoring Mabel Hubbard. The 26-year-old teacher was instantly smitten with the 15-year-old girl. Her father was taken by Bell's telegraph idea. He recognized its potential and saw it as a means to unseat the much-loathed Western Union Telegraph Company from its monopoly position. In the spring of 1874, however, experiments with two new scientific devices turned Bell's attention from telegraphy to acoustics. Both instruments could make speech visible. The phonautograph, invented in France by Leon Scott, could trace a sound from a vibrating membrane onto a piece of smoked glass drawn past its bristle. The other device was Karl Rudolf Kœnig's manometric capsule, which analysed sound by means of the alterations produced in the shape of a flame by aerial vibrations. To provide a realistic membrane for his own experiments with the phonautograph, Bell obtained a dead man's ear from an otologist. Before returning to Brantford for a visit, on 13 June he attended the second convention of articulation teachers of the deaf and dumb, in Worcester, Mass., and was elected president.

Bell was neither the first nor the only one to conceive of the telephone, contrary to the myth perpetuated by the companies of the Bell system. None of the work that led to it could have progressed without Michael Faraday's pioneering experiments on electromagnetism and induction of currents. Numerous scientists had suggested electrically induced speech.

Charles Wheatstone experimented with sounding boards; Charles Grafton Page of Salem described a phenomenon he named galvanized music – the sound made when an electric circuit connected to a magnet was broken. Joseph Henry, a physicist at the College of New Jersey, wrote in 1846 of the possibility of contriving a keyboard-like device with a rubber glottis that would use electromagnets to utter words spoken at the end of a telegraph line. In France, Charles Bourseul reported in 1854 that flexible plates would vibrate in sympathy with varying air pressures, which could be used to make the plates open or close an electric circuit. Antonio Meucci of Italy worked with primitive variants of the telephone in the 1850s and Philipp Reis, a German schoolteacher who invented a transmitter that sent audible sounds along a telegraph wire, coined the term telephony in a lecture in 1861. And then there was Elisha Gray, Bell's most famous rival, who, allied with Western Union, began experimenting with the telegraphing of tones in 1866.

It was Bell, however, who first satisfactorily solved the problem of turning sound into an electrical impulse at a transmitter and then converting the signal back to audible speech through a receiver. He wrote that the inspiration for his breakthrough came to him at his "dreaming place" behind his parent's house at Tutelo Heights on 26 July 1874. He had just completed his phonautograph when, dramatically, the action of the eardrum membrane fused in his mind with his experiments on electrical induction, his memories of sound-activated piano wires, and his reading of Reis's work on currents and of Bourseul's on vibrating plates (in the 1872 translation of Jean-Baptiste-Alexandre Baille's book on electricity). "It would be possible to transmit sounds of any sort if we could only occasion a variation in the intensity of the current exactly like that occurring in the density of air while a given sound is made," he would later recall. He theorized that sound-vibrated, magnetized reeds could induce an undulating current which could be transmitted through a wire to an electromagnet that would convert the current into pulses which in turn would vibrate a diaphragm, thus reproducing the original sound. One difficulty was the weakness of the induced current, on account of the limited power of the vocal source. His full description of these ideas, in a letter to his father that November, would guarantee Bell the primacy of conception.

After returning to Boston in September, Bell continued his teaching. While in Ontario he had attended the convention in Belleville of the American Instructors of the Deaf and Dumb, where he spoke on the difficulty lip-readers had in differentiating between such consonants as P and B. To carry on with his experiments during the evenings and nights, he rented space for a laboratory in the attic of his electric equipment supplier, Charles Williams, whose shop at

109 Court Street in Boston was a haven for inventors. Williams also hired out assistants and Thomas Augustus Watson was assigned to Bell in January 1875. Watson recalled the 27-year-old Bell as "a tall, slender, quick-motioned young man with a pale face, black side-whiskers and drooping mustache, big nose and high, sloping forehead crowned with bushy jet-black hair."

Bell's progress on the telephone was swift. On 1 March he reported his findings to Joseph Henry, then head of the Smithsonian Institution in Washington. "You have the germ of a great invention," Henry replied when Bell outlined his vision for a working telephone. He advised Bell to refrain from publishing any details until he had worked out the problems. When Bell protested that he lacked the requisite knowledge of electricity, Henry retorted: "Get it!"

Gardiner Hubbard was not so thrilled and felt that talking by wire could wait. A few days earlier he and Thomas Sanders, a leather merchant and father of one of Bell's students, had signed an agreement with Bell to share equally in the profits from any of his telegraphic inventions in return for their financial support. Frustrated at the delay in getting a multiple telegraph, Hubbard delivered Bell a stark ultimatum that spring: Bell had to choose between Mabel and his work on the electrical transmission of speech. Bell's determination on both counts, Western Union's rejection of his multiple telegraph (because of Hubbard's involvement), and important discoveries in telephony all contributed to winning Hubbard over. On 4 May Bell wrote to him about his idea for overcoming the weakness of induced currents by using a different principle of transmission: "I have read somewhere that the resistance offered by a wire . . . is affected by the *tension of the wire*. If this is so, a *continuous current of electricity* passed through a vibrating wire should meet with a varying resistance, and hence a pulsatory action should be induced in the current. . . . [Thus] the *timbre* of a sound could be transmitted . . . [and] the strength of the current can be increased . . . without destroying the *relative intensities of the vibrations*." This letter established Bell's priority in conceiving variable resistance, the final key to the telephone. Bell, however, had yet to bring the principles together.

The first major breakthrough came during the evening of 2 June at Bell's laboratory. He and Watson were in different rooms tuning the reeds of three sets of transmitters and receivers for an experiment with the multiple telegraph. One of Watson's reeds, screwed down too tightly, was stuck to its electromagnet. With the transmitters off, Watson plucked it to free it. Instantaneously, Bell heard the twang of a vibrating reed in his receiver. Inadvertently they had successfully reproduced sound: using residual magnetism, the plucked reed had induced an undulating current, which activated the electromagnets in Bell's room, making the reeds there vibrate audibly in the same way. Recognizing the significance of this phenomenon, an astounded Bell put his ear over one of his reeds. He heard the sound of Watson's reed. Within days Watson had made primitive telephone sets using membrane diaphragms and undulatory currents.

In September, Bell again visited Brantford, where he improved the telephones. At the suggestion of his parents' doctor, he placed a thin iron disc on the parchment membrane and found the telephones became more audible. Back in Boston later that month, he started to develop patent specifications while Watson continued to work on the quality of the devices. Bell had already sold the United States rights to Hubbard and both men were keen to find a buyer for the foreign rights. Because a British patent was key, and could not be granted if a patent was pending in the United States, Bell and Hubbard held off applying for the American patent.

In early October, Bell returned to Brantford with the idea of offering the rights to Sir Hugh Allan*, the powerful financier who ran the Montreal Telegraph Company. But when he explained to his parents' neighbour George Brown*, owner of the Toronto *Globe*, his need for an introduction to Allan, Brown made his own offer for the rights and promised to file for the British patent that February, during a trip to London. They reached an agreement in Toronto shortly after Christmas. Bell delivered his specifications to him in New York City on 25 Jan. 1876, the day before the publisher set sail. Brown and an associate completed their search for any infringing claims and filed Bell's application on 16 February. Brown had, however, little real understanding of Bell's work and, without cabling him, decided "to go no further in the business," apparently doubting the practicality of Bell's invention. Fortunately for Bell, Hubbard, who had grown impatient waiting for Brown's confirmation of the British filing, submitted the United States patent application on 14 February. A rival application was filed by Elisha Gray just hours later. On 7 March Bell won his telephone patent, the second of the 30 issued to him between 1875 and 1922. Titled "Improvements in Telegraphy," it was destined to become the single most lucrative patent ever awarded in the history of invention, and one of the most contested.

Bell's telephone had not transmitted a complete, audible sentence, though, significantly, he had revised his specifications early in January to incorporate a variable-resistance transmitter. On 8 March he and Watson began three days of further experiments on the telephone, which soon acquired a speaking-tube mouthpiece. On the 10th Bell transmitted the first intelligible sentence: "Mr. Watson – Come here – I want to see you." The summons was not as elegant as Samuel Finley Breese Morse's first telegraph message – "What hath God wrought?" – but it has become more widely known. It is commonly cited with the words "to see" missing. Bell recorded them in his notebook, but Watson left them out in his notes, which he later relied on in his widely quoted memoirs. Greater controversy has raged over which city may lay claim to the telephone: Boston or Brantford. The prevailing view is typified by its description as "the great Yankee invention" in a major book on telephone history in 1985. Bell believed that both cities could rightly claim a critical share in its development, and he addressed the question on numerous occasions. At a board of trade banquet in his honour in Brantford in 1906 he carefully claimed, it was reported, that the city was "the birthplace of the first idea and the first experiments, the home of the solution of the problem." In a letter to the local *Daily Expositor* in March 1916 he stated that "Brantford is justified in calling herself 'The Telephone City.'" The following year, at the dedication of a monument to him there, he recalled that "the telephone was conceived in Brantford in 1874 and born in Boston in 1875."

The development of the telephone had coincided with the United States centennial. Bell took a booth at the Philadelphia Centennial International Exhibition, at the urging of Mabel, now his fiancée, and on 25 June 1876 he demonstrated a working version of his telephone. The new inventions and machines on display at the fair, which was billed as a monument to the "Progress of the Age," were already remaking society. In addition to the telephone there were the typewriter, the electric light, packaged yeast, the internal combustion engine, and the mighty 700-ton Corliss steam engine. Yet the North American economy, in the midst of depression, gave little cause for celebration, and in both Canada and the United States, telecommunications remained dominated by the large telegraph companies.

Bell returned to Canada later that summer and made the world's first long-distance telephone call on 3 August, from Wallace Ellis's general store in Mount Pleasant to Tutelo Heights, four miles away. He used the line of the Dominion Telegraph Company, which he connected to his father's house with stove-pipe wire. His tests culminated in an eight-mile-long trial between Brantford and Paris on the 10th, when listeners in Robert White's boot and shoe store heard voices, music, and singing come in over the wire from the Bell home. The test, which "afforded much pleasure and information to those present," according to the *Daily Expositor*, attracted more attention to the inventor, including a report in *Scientific American* (New York).

Aleck Bell married Mabel Hubbard on 11 July 1877 at her home in Cambridge. Throughout their lives she would remain, in the words of her biographer, Bell's "silent partner." After their honeymoon, including some time in Brantford, they went to England for an extended trip, during which Bell demonstrated his telephone to Queen Victoria and sought to interest British capitalists. Two days before his wedding, the Bell Telephone Company of Boston had been incorporated as a trusteeship by Bell, Watson, Gardiner Hubbard, and Thomas Sanders. The next day Bell assigned 75 per cent of his Canadian rights to his father and the remainder to Charles Williams, his equipment maker. Melville Bell appointed his friend Thomas Henderson as his son's agent in Ontario. They licensed Hugh Cossart Baker Jr, a Hamilton street railway promoter, to lease telephones in Ontario. He organized the first public demonstration of a telephone in Canada on 29 August; the first telephone lease in Canada, signed on 18 October, connected Baker's home to those of two colleagues. The following month he installed a pair of telephones in Ottawa, linking the office of Prime Minister Alexander Mackenzie* with Rideau Hall, the governor general's residence. For the next two years Bell's father promoted the business in Canada and solicited agents for other provinces.

Bell not only invented the telephone, he had also conceived of a system to make a business out of it. He outlined his plan in a letter to his father on the same day that he uttered the first sentence to Watson: "I feel that I have at last struck the solution of a great problem – and the day is coming when telegraph wires will be laid on to houses just like water or gas – and friends converse with each other without leaving home." He elaborated on his vision in a remarkable prospectus for British financiers on 5 March 1878: "It is conceivable that cables of Telephonic wires could be laid under-ground or suspended overhead communicating by branch wires with private dwellings, counting houses, shops, manufactories, etc. . . . establishing direct communication between any two places in the City. . . . I believe that in the future wires will unite the head offices of Telephone Companies in different cities and a man in one part of the Country may communicate by word of mouth with another in a distant place."

In practice, developing the business in Canada proved "very up-hill work" for Melville Bell. After Dominion Telegraph had rejected his offer to sell his stake for $100,000 in the fall of 1879, it was acquired by the National Bell Telephone Company, the product of a merger that spring of Bell Telephone of Boston and the New England Telephone Company. In 1880 National Bell would hire Charles Fleetford Sise* to incorporate and run the Bell Telephone Company of Canada. Bell's parents sold their Brantford home in April 1881 – its name was later changed to Tutela Heights – and moved to Georgetown (Washington) to be closer to Aleck, Mabel, and their first daughter, Elsie May, who had begun wintering in Washington in 1879 and took up permanent residence there in 1882.

Although Bell's research in communications ended in 1880, he faced a legal struggle for the next 12 years as National Bell successfully defended more than 600 patent cases, producing a nine-foot-high stack of testimony. During the six years that he spent in this field he had unleashed his boundless energy and curiosity on a range of other pursuits, driven by a quest for discovery. His audiometer, devised in 1879 to measure hearing ability, led to his name being adopted for a unit of measuring sound and electric signals – the decibel. His last invention in telecommunications came early in 1880, while he was working with Charles Sumner Tainter, an optical-instrument maker. To power a telephone circuit, they had developed a battery cell from selenium, a light-sensitive chemical. A beam of sunlight was reflected onto the cell from a voice-vibrated mirror; the vibrations varied the beam's intensity and the cell's resistance and made its current undulating. The current was then transformed into audible sound through a receiver. "I have heard a ray of the sun," Bell wrote his father on 26 February. His photophone accomplished a wireless transmission 16 years ahead of Guglielmo Marconi's radio transmission and presaged modern fibre optics. Bell would explain the restless motivations he experienced in arriving at such inventions in a speech to a patent congress in Washington in 1891: "The inventor is a man who looks around upon the world and is not contented with things as they are. He wants to improve whatever he sees, he wants to benefit the world; he is haunted by an idea. The spirit of invention possesses him, seeking materialization." Bell's vast papers and notebooks have allowed biographers to isolate other factors: his pride, a reliance on analogy, constructive doubt, steely self-confidence, tenacity of application, meticulous records, and the satisfaction of fulfilled ambition.

The riches from the telephone, which were ably tended by Mabel, allowed Bell to let his inventive genius run free. Their homes in Washington were elegant and costly affairs. Bell used the 50,000 francs that came with the Prix Volta, awarded to him by the French government in 1880, for the phone, to finance a laboratory in Washington to promote research and invention to benefit the deaf. After the death of a newborn son the following year from respiratory failure – the Bells' second son would die at birth in 1883 – he focused on medical research. He developed a vacuum jacket (a precursor to the iron lung) and made headlines when he invented a metal detector (a forerunner to ultrasound), which used sound waves to detect a bullet in a body, in a bid to save President James Abram Garfield. Later he married this instrument to a needle probe connected to a telephone receiver, which sounded when the needle touched a

bullet. Though he let an outside firm commercialize this telephonic probe, it won him a rare honorary doctorate of medicine in 1886 from Germany's prestigious Rupert Charles University of Heidelberg – one of the many degrees and prizes eventually bestowed on him.

Bell wished he had been more aggressive in pursuing phonographic devices. One, the graphophone, developed with his cousin Chichester A. Bell and Sumner Tainter at the Volta Laboratory in 1882, had a floating stylus that recorded on, and played from, a reusable wax cylinder. Thomas Alva Edison had beaten him to market with a practical phonograph years earlier, causing Bell to regret that he had "let this invention slip through my fingers," but his patents from his phonographic inventions were still his most lucrative after the telephone. He was no accumulator of wealth. When he sold his share of stock in the graphophone holding company, for $100,000, he turned it over to his father as a trust fund for deaf research. His funding also helped keep *Science* (New York) afloat until it became the official journal of the Washington-based American Association for the Advancement of Science in 1900.

Although Bell had become a naturalized American citizen in 1882, his ties to Canada were strengthened in the summer of 1885 when he and Mabel visited Baddeck, on the Bras d'Or lakes of Cape Breton Island, N.S. They were drawn by the book on Baddeck by travel writer Charles Dudley Warner and perhaps by the temperate climate – Bell hated hot summer weather. The area and its people reminded him of Scotland. The following summer they rented a cottage, which they later bought, and began buying up land on Red Head, a large point on Baddeck Bay. For the next 36 years, until he died, Bell would divide his time between Washington and Nova Scotia. In November 1893 he completed a 13-bedroom mansion on Red Head which he named Beinn Bhreagh (pronounced Ben Vreeah), Gaelic for beautiful mountain. It was designed by a Boston firm and constructed by the company of Nelson Admiral Rhodes*; the Halifax *Morning Chronicle* termed it the "Bell Palace." His time there increased his fondness for the northern dominion. "Though I cannot claim to be a Canadian . . . ," he later stated, "I have a warm spot in my heart for Canada." Beinn Bhreagh, as well as Washington, became a centre for Bell's scientific studies, which turned time and again to deafness.

In 1882 he had opened a private day school for the deaf in Washington, but distracted by patent fights, he was forced to close it in 1885. His interest in the inheritance of deafness drove his venture into genetics. In the title of a paper in 1884 he had used the poorly chosen phrase "a deaf variety of the human race." His discussion was taken out of context by press reports, which further inflamed deaf groups. He used a lecture before the National Deaf-Mute College in 1887 to set the record straight. This paper, along with a follow-up study by Edward Allen Fay, financed by Bell and published in the *American Annals of the Deaf* (Washington), is considered the most useful study of human heredity produced by 19th-century researchers. Biographer Robert Bruce states that it may be counted as Bell's "most notable contribution to basic science, as distinct from invention." Bell's interest in heredity also drew him into eugenics – his sheep-breeding project at Beinn Bhreagh became his longest, continuously running experiment – though his inherent scepticism led to uneasiness about "eugenic cranks."

Bell met his most famous deaf student in 1887. Helen Keller, whose blindness made her solitude complete, was six years old when her father brought her to Bell in Washington. She loved him at once: "I did not dream that that interview would be the door through which I should pass from darkness into light." Bell maintained his relationship with the Kellers for over 30 years. In addition to teaching Helen, he established a trust fund for her education at Radcliffe College and often welcomed her at Beinn Bhreagh. Her main teacher, Anne Mansfield Sullivan, was struck by Bell's courtesy and ability to put people at ease. "He answered every question in the cool, clear light of reason." Bell also made a strong impression when he gave evidence in England in 1888 to the royal commission on the blind and the deaf and dumb. He fully confronted the rival theories and claims of Edward Miner Gallaudet and fielded more than 600 questions; the printed evidence is regarded as the most comprehensive statement of Bell's philosophy and aims regarding the education of the deaf.

Bell and Gallaudet held equally fervent, but irreconcilable, views on the value of their preferred techniques – oralism and manualism respectively. Each held that his preference came naturally to the deaf. Gallaudet, like his father Thomas Hopkins, maintained that gesturing was the ultimate form of human communication, a gift from God that could remedy deafness. He told the British commission that the deaf were taught best by deaf teachers using sign language. Bell, like his father and grandfather, felt speech was what defined being human. He had told Edward Gallaudet in a letter, which he shared with the commission, that, no matter how imperfectly uttered, speech was critically important to a deaf person. He rejected the idea of deaf teachers because, he believed, they could not teach articulation and would thus perpetuate deafness.

Exploration interested Bell and his father-in-law. When Hubbard cofounded the National Geographic Society in 1888, Bell was named its first president; he would hold the post until 1903. Bell the lover of photography is credited with launching the society's illustrated mass-market journal, the *National Geographic Magazine* (Washington). He defined its broad role, which mirrored his own wide range of interests, when he admonished Gilbert Hovey Grosvenor, the magazine's first editor and his son-in-law, to cover "the world and all that is in it."

Less well known was Bell's pioneering work with a novel form of medical photography, the X-ray. One of his daydreams was "seeing with electricity." Just four months after the discovery of X-rays by Wilhelm Conrad Röntgen in November 1895, Bell bought a Crookes' tube and produced his own X-ray apparatus at Beinn Bhreagh. His earliest radiograph, of coins inside a purse, was taken with the assistance of William H. D. Ellis on 10 June 1896, four months after the first diagnostic radiograph was made in Canada, at McGill University. Bell took a number of clinical X-rays over the next several years; he envisaged stereoscopic radiographs to produce three-dimensional X-rays of the skeleton, presaging the modern CAT scan, and wondered whether X-rays could produce sounds in a telephone. Bell is believed to be the first to suggest the use of a radioactive substance *in vivo* to treat deep-seated cancerous masses. In a letter to his physician, published in *Science* in July 1903, he described an apparatus to seal a small radium source inside a glass tube.

With his large frame, flowing white beard, and ever-present tweed suit, Bell appeared larger than life. This patron of science and the deaf carried himself, Bruce states, "with the majesty of a Moses and the benevolence of a Santa Claus." Yet he never claimed perfection and could be temperamental and obstinate. David Grandison Fairchild, husband of his second daughter, Marian Hubbard (Daisy), described him as a loner. His isolation was frequent at Beinn Bhreagh, where he spent long hours every weekend thinking in his beached houseboat, the *Mabel of Beinn Bhreagh*. Although proud of her husband's work, Mabel stated that she was jealous of his time away from her, just as their daughters felt some jealousy at his time with Helen Keller. Mabel's unstinting support was nonetheless revealed in a letter she wrote to her husband, in which she expressed her admiration of the "quiet, persistent courage with which you have gone on after one failure after another." Yet Bell valued learning from failures as much as from successes. "In scientific researches, there are no unsuccessful experiments; every experiment contains a lesson," he wrote. "If we don't get the results anticipated and stop right there, it is the man that is unsuccessful, not the experiment."

Bell tasted failure more often with flight than with any other pursuit. On 23 Sept. 1877, while walking along a beach in Scotland, Bell, inspired by a seagull in flight, had drawn a flying machine, complete with ailerons. This sketch bears a striking similarity to drawings made by the Renaissance artist and inventor Leonardo da Vinci. (Scholars who have examined Bell's notebooks are often struck by the parallel between these two great generalists.) Bell began to build on his sketch in 1891 when he financed the experiments of Samuel Pierpont Langley, an American physicist and secretary of the Smithsonian. Langley became a close friend and, in 1898, was instrumental in obtaining Bell's congressional appointment as a regent of his institution, an honorific post Bell held until his death.

Bell's vision of flight was as sweeping as his grand concept of the telephone. He predicted in 1907 that it would not be long until "a man can take dinner in New York and breakfast the next morning in Liverpool." He foresaw too the strategic importance of military air power and wrote, in a magazine in 1908, "The nation that secures control of the air will ultimately rule the world." Over a 31-year period that began with his sponsorship of Langley's work, Bell and his associates would conduct more than 1,200 flight-related experiments, most of them at Baddeck. His initial dream was to prove simply that tetrahedral designs, which he patented in 1903, could be used to make light but strong structures for flying machines. He conducted hundreds of repetitive experiments on the sloping meadow of Red Head that he named the kite field. To the residents of Baddeck who watched, they had a fanciful air. A boatman who observed one flight stopped short, in an account cited by John Hamilton Parkin, of describing Bell as a lunatic: "He goes up there on the side of the hill on sunny afternoons and with a lot of thing-ma-jigs fools away the whole blessed day, flying kites, mind you. He sets up a blackboard and puts down figures about these kites and queer machines he keeps bobbing around in the sky. Dozens of them he has. . . . It's the greatest foolishness I ever did see." The kites had equally fanciful names, like the *Codger* and the *Frost King*. The latter, made of 1,300 red-silk cells, lifted an assistant 30 feet in the air on 28 Dec. 1905. Bell's tetrahedral experiments also spawned a cottage industry in Cape Breton as hundreds of farm homes helped make cell frames of spruce, bamboo, and metal.

The immense size of the kites soon dwarfed the design expertise of Bell and his staff at Beinn Bhreagh, so in the summer of 1906 Bell and Mabel set out to recruit some young talent. They first approached John Alexander Douglas McCurdy*, a fearless native of Baddeck and son of Arthur Williams McCurdy, Bell's chief assistant at Beinn Bhreagh. Best of all, he was studying engineering at the University of Toronto. He agreed to be hired, and put the Bells on to a friend and recent engineering graduate, the athletic Frederick Walker (Casey) Baldwin*. Baldwin's first task was to erect a huge tower to prove that

tetrahedrals could also be used in building construction. The following year Bell drew in two other men whose expertise was crucial in moving the group toward powered flight. Glenn Hammond Curtiss, whom Bell met at an air-club show, came to Beinn Bhreagh as the group's expert on engines. Thomas Etholen Selfridge, a 25-year-old lieutenant in the United States army and the military's authority on aviation, contacted Bell to find out more about his experiments. Bell asked President Theodore Roosevelt if he could borrow Selfridge, who arrived at Beinn Bhreagh in September. One of their first projects was the *Ugly Duckling*, a catamaran-style boat designed to test aerial propellers. It spawned 13 years of research with powered watercraft, or hydrodromes, as Bell termed them.

Mabel Bell is credited with proposing that the five men create a formal organization, the Aerial Experiment Association, to finance their work and share in any patent profits. With Bell assuming the roles of coordinator and promoter, in addition to his work as an airplane designer and inventor, and Mabel providing the initial capitalization, the AEA was formed in Halifax on 1 Oct. 1907. Its simple goal, Selfridge stated, was "to get into the air." But the group had been preceded some years before by the Wright brothers: in a secret flight in December 1903 Orville Wright had ascended in a powered craft at Kill Devil Hills, N.C. The AEA would first go aloft with a kite. Their task was to complete the *Cygnet*, a behemoth made of more than 3,300 red-silk tetrahedral cells on pontoons and Bell's largest kite ever. Selfridge rose 104 feet over Great Bras d'Or Lake on 6 Dec. 1907 but he had to be rescued from the freezing water when the tow rope failed to be cut after the delicate craft landed (it was torn to pieces). Bell then agreed to expand their experimentation to include biplane designs.

The group moved to Hammondsport, N.Y., for the winter and took with them a silk glider named the *Red Wing*, in which they later installed a Curtiss engine. Baldwin believed he was the first British subject to pilot a heavier-than-air craft when he took it up on 12 March 1908. It crashed on the 17th. Three days later, in a letter to Baldwin, Bell came up with the idea of "moveable wing tips," to achieve what the Wrights had pioneered with wing warping, and he suggested they be controlled by cross wires worked by the pilot. He patented the device, calling it the aileron. (Baldwin's family later maintained that Casey had come up with the idea.) The *White Wing*, the AEA's next aerodrome, as Bell preferred to call them, was flown by Baldwin on 18 May. In addition to ailerons, it had a three-wheel undercarriage to aid take-off and landing. It too crashed. The AEA entered its third craft, the *June Bug*, in a competition on 4 July sponsored by *Scientific American* for the first public flight over a kilometre-long course. The craft won and it flew 150 more times without crashing.

The *Silver Dart* entered the Canadian record books as the first powered, heavier-than-air machine to fly in Canada. McCurdy was its chief designer. After tests in Hammondsport the frail-looking craft was taken to the ice of Baddeck Bay. McCurdy's flight of 23 Feb. 1909 – half a mile at 45 miles per hour – was the first by a British subject in the empire. Several longer flights followed. On 27 March Bell spoke to the Canadian Club in Ottawa about his group's successes in aviation. In response, and flushed with imperial pride, Governor General Lord Grey*, who would visit Beinn Bhreagh in December, praised their efforts and finance minister William Stevens FIELDING held out the prospect of government support.

The AEA was dissolved at the end of March but, buoyed by its feats, Bell, Baldwin, and McCurdy soon founded the Canadian Aerodrome Company at Baddeck to make airplanes for the military. Although the government of Prime Minister Sir Wilfrid Laurier* refused to provide funding, the Canadian army supported test flights at Petawawa, Ont., where the *Silver Dart* was damaged beyond repair in August 1909. The dogged efforts of the group over the next five years to interest the military in Canadian-built aircraft were, states Parkin, frustrated by "pettiness, ignorance, and futility in high places." In December 1914 the minister of militia and defence, Major-General Samuel HUGHES, rejected any funding or plans for aviation, despite the outbreak of World War I.

Bell and Baldwin got out of the sky. By 1912 they were focusing their efforts on the development of full-sized hydrofoils that would travel over the water. Their first craft, *HD-1*, attained a speed of 45 miles per hour in July 1912. Bell's last major achievement was *HD-4*, which, with support from the Canadian and American navies, set a world marine speed record on 9 Sept. 1919 of 70.86 miles per hour, which would stand for ten years. By 1919 Bell was suffering from advanced diabetes, a dangerous condition that perhaps influenced his decision not to fly or ride in hydrofoils. Two photographs of the *HD-4*'s speed trial suggest how he may have felt: the first shows him standing on a wharf at Beinn Bhreagh looking out while the craft roars across the bay with Mabel at the helm; the second, taken moments after her return, captures their fond embrace.

To the end Bell remained a gentle, loving humanist. Long an advocate of women's rights, by 1910 he had brought Mabel round to his way of thinking; on his 66th birthday they both cheered a suffrage parade in Washington. He loved music, abhorred racial intolerance, and during the Great War forced himself on occasion to shelve his disdain for conflict in order to support the war effort. Following the Halifax explosion of 6 Dec. 1917 the Bells sent blankets and clothing. When they were in residence in Nova Scotia, from spring to fall, they were active members of Baddeck society. The Bells loved America but they rejoiced too in Beinn Bhreagh – it seemed always to vibrate with family and guests – and they came to know Cape Breton intimately.

A single invention, the telephone, would have been enough to guarantee Bell's place in history. But the scope of his interests and the significance of his visionary insights continue to impress, and enlighten. In a paper in 1917, on the depletion of natural resources, he stated that the unchecked burning of fossil fuels would lead to a "sort of greenhouse effect" and global warming. A practical dreamer, he offered timeless advice in a discussion of his thought processes in an article in 1918: "We are all too much inclined, I think, to walk through life with our eyes closed. . . . We should not keep forever on the public road, going only where others have gone; we should leave the beaten track occasionally and enter the woods. Every time you do that you will be certain to find something that you have never seen before. . . . Follow it up, explore all around it; one discovery will lead to another, and before you know it you will have something worth thinking about to occupy your mind, for all really big discoveries are the results of thought." Bell kept his mind so occupied until his own journey of discovery ended on 2 Aug. 1922, when, with Mabel at his side at Beinn Bhreagh, he died of complications from his diabetes. He was buried on the hilltop there, overlooking Baddeck Bay; Mabel was interred beside her husband following her death on 3 Jan. 1923. Their gravestone refers to Alexander Graham Bell's three homes: "Born Edinburgh . . . Died A Citizen of the U.S.A. . . . Here Rest [Aleck and Mabel]."

He would have appreciated the tribute from the Bell system, which briefly silenced every telephone in North America during his funeral. This was a man, after all, who relished silence and despised the intrusion of his infernal invention, once ripping a phone off his own wall. Yet few have done as much to conquer silence, distance, and physical obstacles to travel. Arguably no single person may do so again. With him died the era of the lone inventor, the work of Bell, Edison, George Eastman, the Wrights, and Henry Ford being taken up by vast corporate enterprises.

As to the legacy for which the world chiefly remembers him, the telephone, Bell would no doubt recognize a lingering paradox. While modern society's dependence on the telephone has grown so great that entire economies can be reduced by a failure of digital networks, nine-tenths of the world's population remains without a telephone. Although pundits predict the true death of distance and the transformation of the human race into one gossiping family, the

Bell

realization of Bell's grand system is still a long way off.

LAWRENCE SURTEES

[The bulk of Bell's personal papers are preserved in the Library of Congress, Manuscript Div., Washington, in the immense Alexander Graham Bell family papers (0330M). The collection contains 147,000 items, including Bell's voluminous correspondence, books and papers, laboratory notebooks recording his daily work from 1865 to 1922, journals and diaries, legal transcripts, clippings, and photographs. A selection of some 4,700 items has been made available online as part of the Library of Congress's "American Memory" program and can be consulted at *memory.loc.gov/ammem/bellhtml*.

The Manuscript Div. also holds the Grosvenor family papers (0622D), which include 180 volumes of letters and biographical material collected by Bell's son-in-law Gilbert H. Grosvenor, and the Hubbard family papers (0183D). An extensive collection of Bell's professional and private photographs is available in the Gilbert H. Grosvenor coll. in the Library of Congress's Prints and Photographs Div. Significant manuscript materials related to Bell's work with the deaf are found at the Volta Bureau Library of the Alexander Graham Bell Assoc. for the Deaf and Hard of Hearing in Washington.

The Bell Museum at the Alexander Graham Bell National Hist. Site of Canada in Baddeck, N.S., houses the pre-eminent collection of Bell papers and records in Canada. Its holdings include a full set of the journals known as the "Home Notes" (135v.) and Bell's mimeographed newsletters, the "A.E.A. Bull." (41v., 1907–9) and the "Beinn Bhreagh Recorder" (25v., 1909–23). Several volumes of the "Recorder" are also available on microfilm at LAC, MG 30, B78. A comprehensive index to Bell's papers has been compiled by the Alexander Graham Bell Institute at the Univ. College of Cape Breton, Sydney, N.S. The Bell Institute has also developed an online version of portions of the Bell family collection, which can be viewed at its website, *bell.uccb.ns.ca*.

Useful collections at the LAC include the George Brown papers (MG 24, B40, 10: 2398, 2416), for Brown's letters to his wife concerning the telephone patent rights, and the Charles Fleetford Sise papers (MG 30, D187), for a copy of the first telephone lease in Canada. A number of photographs are available in the Notman Photographic Arch. at the McCord Museum of Canadian Hist., Montreal.

A key work in Bell's early career is the book published by his father on *Visible speech: the science . . . of universal alphabetics . . .* (London, 1867). Bell published a brief autobiography under the title "Prehistoric telephone days" in the *National Geographic Magazine* (Washington), 41 (January–June 1922): 223–41. His final deposition of 1892 in the telephone patent litigation is available as *The Bell telephone: deposition of Alexander Graham Bell in the suit brought by the United States to annul the Bell patents* (Boston, 1908; repr. New York, 1974). A full account of the photophone appears in Bell's paper "On the production and reproduction of sound by light," *American Journal of Science* (New Haven, Conn.), 3rd ser., 20 (July–December 1880): 305–24. He suggested using radium implants to treat cancer in "Radium and cancer," *Science* (New York), new ser., 18

(July–December 1903): 155–56. A complete bibliography of Bell's published writings and addresses, as well as a list of his patents, is provided in H. S. Osborne, "Biographical memoir of Alexander Graham Bell, 1847–1922," National Academy of Sciences, *Biog. memoirs* (Washington), 23 (1943), 1st memoir, 1–29.

The most authoritative biography is R. V. Bruce, *Bell: Alexander Graham Bell and the conquest of solitude* (Boston, 1973). Other biographical accounts include: E. S. Grosvenor, "A man for all times," *AT&T Focus* (n.p.), October 1991; E. S. Grosvenor and Morgan Wesson, *Alexander Graham Bell: the life and times of the man who invented the telephone* (New York, 1997); Lilian Grosvenor, "My grandfather Bell," *New Yorker*, 11 Nov. 1950: 44–48; Dorothy Harley Eber, *Genius at work: images of Alexander Graham Bell* (New York, 1982); George Kennan, "A few recollections of Alexander Graham Bell," *Outlook* (Middleton, N.S.), 27 Sept. 1922; J. [A.] Mackay, *Sounds out of silence: a life of Alexander Graham Bell* (Edinburgh, 1997); and C. D. MacKenzie, *Alexander Graham Bell, the man who contracted space* (Boston, 1928). L.S.]

Daily Expositor (Brantford, Ont.), 1916. *Daily Mail and Empire*, 4, 19 March 1930. *Globe*, 11 Aug. 1875. *Morning Chronicle* (Halifax), 1 Dec. 1893. J. [E.] Aldrich, "Alexander Graham Bell," in *A new kind of ray: the radiological sciences in Canada, 1895–1995*, ed. J. E. Aldrich and B. C. Lentle (Vancouver, 1995), 20–23. D. C. Baynton, *Forbidden signs: American culture and the campaign against sign language* (Chicago, 1996). B. W. Brannan with P. T. Thompson, "Alexander Graham Bell: a photograph album," U.S., Library of Congress, *Quarterly Journal* (Washington), 34 (1977): 73–96. J. M. S. Careless, *Brown of "The Globe"* (2v., Toronto, 1959–63), 2. Lewis Coe, *The telephone and its several inventors: a history* (Jefferson, N.C., 1995). C. S. Fischer, *America calling: a social history of the telephone to 1940* (Berkeley, Calif., 1992). R. W. Garnet, *The telephone enterprise: the evolution of the Bell System's horizontal structure, 1876–1909* (Baltimore, Md, 1985). *A history of engineering and science in the Bell system*, ed. M. D. Fagen et al. (7v., [New York], 1975–85), 1. J. H. Parkin, *Bell and Baldwin: their development of aerodromes and hydrodromes at Baddeck, Nova Scotia* (Toronto, 1964). William Patten, *Pioneering the telephone in Canada* (Montreal, 1926). L. M. Toward, *Mabel Bell: Alexander's silent partner* (Toronto, 1984).

BELL, GORDON, physician, professor, bacteriologist, and sportsman; b. 22 May 1863 in Pembroke, Upper Canada, son of John Bell and Mary Ann Wight; m. 19 Aug. 1897 Grace Campbell McEwan in Elton, Man., and they had a son and a daughter; d. 8 Aug. 1923 in Winnipeg and was buried there in Elmwood Cemetery.

Gordon Bell's father, a great lover of nature and classical literature, emigrated from Scotland and established a lumber business in Pembroke. His mother was active in their community and the couple kept a large library in their home. In his early years Gordon attended the private school of Mrs Margaret McDougall, an author and poet. He then studied at local public and high schools, where he gained a broad knowledge of mathematics, the sciences, and the classics. He had a shy and reserved disposition, possessed a keen sense of humour, and was sympathetic and generous towards others.

Bell attended the University of Toronto and obtained a BA with distinction in 1886. Hearing of the excellence of the newly formed Manitoba Medical College in Winnipeg, he enrolled in 1887; he would graduate three years later. During his second year at the college, he contacted typhoid fever which caused a severe infection and necessitated the amputation of his right leg in 1889. He was fitted with a wooden leg and limped, but this misfortune did not diminish his spirit or his will to continue his studies. Bell registered with the College of Physicians and Surgeons of Manitoba on 17 June 1891; at the time the annual dues were $2. He would also register with the College of Physicians and Surgeons of the North-West Territories on 3 July 1905 and with the College of Physicians and Surgeons of the Province of Alberta in 1906.

After graduation, Bell had been appointed superintendent and medical officer of the Brandon asylum, a position he held for three years. He resigned to take up graduate studies in Vienna in ophthalmology, pathology, histology, and the new science of bacteriology. After returning to Winnipeg, he practised as a partner with James Wilford GOOD, the first eye specialist in western Canada, from about 1893 to 1897. During that time he acted as lecturer in histology and pathology at the Manitoba Medical College in 1894 and demonstrator in anatomy there in 1895. He would continue as professor of bacteriology, pathology, and histology from 1896 to 1905, professor of pathology from 1905 to 1916, and professor of bacteriology from 1916 to 1923. A laboratory for his work was built in 1897 at Kate Street and McDermot Avenue, adjacent to the medical college. There he often had practitioners and students meet for discussions and consultations on medical problems. He demonstrated the use of his microscope, using diseased tissue and bacteria from sick patients.

On 1 April 1897 Bell was appointed provincial bacteriologist by the government of Thomas Greenway*. His energy went into recommendations for solving major public health problems such as tuberculosis, typhoid fever, diphtheria, and venereal disease, setting standards for milk suppliers and food distributors, controlling sewage disposal, and providing clean drinking water. Legislation was passed to ensure that the standards he helped to establish were met and enforced. Bell was at the forefront of a movement to have a clean and plentiful source of water for Winnipeg; finally, in 1913, construction began on an aqueduct from Shoal Lake to Winnipeg [see Henry Norlande RUTTAN].

In 1904 Bell was a delegate to the annual convention of the Canadian Association for the Prevention of Tuberculosis in Ottawa and asked Prime Minister Sir Wilfrid Laurier* for federal government aid to erect sanatoriums in the provinces. Four years later the Winnipeg Anti-Tuberculosis Society was formed and Bell was working to establish a sanatorium for the province. The Manitoba Sanatorium was erected at Ninette in 1909. Bell served as a member of its executive and its board of directors to 1923.

In 1916 the provincial bacteriologist was made ex officio a member of the Provincial Board of Health; Bell served as the board's chairman and as chief health officer of the province from then until his death. He was instrumental in having amendments to the Public Health Act passed in 1916 [see James William ARMSTRONG] that introduced public nursing to Manitoba. Initially, five public health nurses were employed; by 1922 there were 53. During the influenza epidemic that followed World War I, Bell tried unsuccessfully to develop a vaccine. He concluded that the fatalities were due to a superadded infection of streptococcus. He was the first in the west to use an anti-serum to treat glanders, an infection of horses which at times spreads to humans, causing respiratory disease and death.

With his sense of humour Bell was in demand as an after-dinner speaker and he often addressed the annual dinner of the Manitoba Medical College. In spite of his physical handicap, he fished and canoed. Along with several other physicians, he built a hunting lodge on Lake Manitoba near Delta Marsh. He was a keen duck hunter, president of the Fort Garry Gun Club, and a Manitoba trap-shooting champion. The clear water of Fox Lake, near Minaki, Ont., was brought to the attention of Dr Bell by several medical students. In 1912, with a number of friends, he formed the Namaycush Fishing Club and built a lodge at the lake. At the summer home he erected near the lodge, he cleared a ½-acre garden with his own hands and grew numerous flowers and plants, including blueberries. With his friends he built a boat, a windmill, a dam, and a waterwheel.

In early August 1923 Bell was investigating streptococcal throat infections in Brandon, Man., with pathologist Sidney J. S. Pierce. He gathered specimens, consulted with a colleague in Winnipeg, and then took a trip to Fox Lake, where he was seized with chills, fever, and sore throat; he died within 48 hours from streptococcal septicaemia.

Bell's memory was honoured in a variety of ways. An annual lecture was established by the Winnipeg Medical Society; the first was delivered on 11 April 1924 by James Bertram Collip*, a co-discoverer of insulin. A high school in Winnipeg was named for Bell. At the official opening on 12 Nov. 1926 a plaque was unveiled and an address was given by Dr Edward William Montgomery*, a close friend. A new Gordon Bell High School was built in 1960. At Fox Lake his friends placed a plaque on the fishing lodge. A Gordon Bell Memorial Fund was established for research and clinical investigation at the Manitoba Medical College and the Winnipeg General Hospital. In 1997 a plaster bust of Bell, executed by Winnipeg artist Marguerite Taylor [Judd*] during the 1920s, was located and presented to the University of Manitoba's faculty of medicine. Two years later it was bronzed and mounted on a pedestal.

I. I. MAYBA

College of Physicians and Surgeons of Manitoba (Winnipeg), Record of registration, 1891. Elmwood Cemetery Company (Winnipeg), Burial records, sect.14, lot 296. Man., Dept. of Finance, Consumer and Corporate Affairs, Vital statistics (Winnipeg), no.1897-001455. Univ. of Manitoba, Faculty of Medicine Arch. (Winnipeg), 21.9, Gordon Bell file. Univ. of Manitoba Libraries, Neil John Maclean Health Sciences Library (Winnipeg), L. G. Bell, "Fox Lake: an informal history" (typescript, Winnipeg, n.d.). *Winnipeg Free Press*, 20 Aug. 1960. L. G. Bell, "My father – Gordon Bell," *Winnipeg Clinic Quarterly*, 23 (1970): 77–93. F. T. Cadham, "Memorable personalities – II: Gordon Bell – a friend of all the world," *Univ. of Manitoba Medical Journal* (Winnipeg), 21 (1949–50): 61–67. Canadian Medical Assoc., *Journal* (Toronto), 13 (1923): 772–73. Ian Carr and R. E. Beamish, *Manitoba medicine: a brief history* (Winnipeg, 1999). Ross Mitchell, "Medical history: Dr. Gordon Bell, 1863–1923," *Manitoba Medical Rev.* (Winnipeg), 39 (August–September 1959): 521–23; *Medicine in Manitoba; the story of its beginnings* ([Winnipeg, 1955?]). E. W. Montgomery, *Address delivered at the unveiling of a memorial tablet at the Gordon Bell School, Winnipeg, November 12, 1926* (n.p., 1926?); *Gordon Bell, physician and naturalist* ([Winnipeg, 1931?]). *Standard dict. of Canadian biog.* (Roberts and Tunnell). Univ. of Manitoba, *The centennial program, 1883–1983, the Manitoba Medical College, 1883–1919, becoming the faculty of medicine, the University of Manitoba, 1919–1983* ([Winnipeg], 1983).

BELL, JOHN HOWATT, lawyer, politician, and newspaper editor; b., probably on 13 Dec. 1845, in Cape Traverse, P.E.I., son of Walter Bell and Elizabeth Howatt; m. 7 July 1882 Helen Howatt in Sarnia, Ont.; they had no children; d. 29 Jan. 1929 in Los Angeles, Calif.

John H. Bell's father emigrated from Scotland in 1820 and began farming in the Cape Traverse area of Prince Edward Island. John attended local schools, Prince of Wales College in Charlottetown, and Albert College in Belleville, Ont., where he received a BA in 1868 and an MA a year later. He pursued the study of law in Toronto and Ingersoll and was called to the bar of Ontario in 1874. He practised in Ottawa until early 1882 when he moved to Manitoba. After being admitted to the bar there, he opened a practice in Emerson. He did not long remain in Manitoba. In July 1882 he married his first cousin Helen Howatt of

St Eleanors, P.E.I., daughter of the former anti-confederate MHA Cornelius Howatt*. Two years later Bell returned to his native province and was called to its bar. He practised law in Summerside, first on his own and later in partnership with Alexander Bannerman Tanton. He would be made a KC in 1910.

Bell's political career began in 1886 when he was elected as a Liberal to the House of Assembly for Prince County, 4th District. He was re-elected in 1890, and after the legislature was reorganized in 1893 to eliminate the upper chamber he became one of the district's two representatives in the Legislative Assembly. By 1896 he was quarrelling with his premier, Frederick Peters, and when the death of Alexander Laird*, Bell's running mate in 4th Prince, brought about a by-election, he gave his support to the candidate from the Patrons of Industry, an offshoot of the Ontario populist agrarian movement [*see* George Weston Wrigley*] that had been brought to Prince Edward Island by Duncan McLean Marshall*. Bell was at the time editor of the Summerside *Pioneer* and even before the election call had given favourable coverage to the Patron platform. Faced with a withdrawal of government advertising, the paper's owners dismissed him as editor in August 1896. Support for the Patrons split the electorate in the September vote and allowed the Conservatives to take the seat. Bell evidently patched up his differences with the Liberals. Re-elected in the provincial general election of 1897, he resigned at the end of the 1898 session and successfully contested the House of Commons by-election for the district of Prince East, succeeding John Yeo, who had been appointed to the Senate. Bell was defeated in the federal election of 1900 and returned to his law practice.

He re-entered provincial politics in September 1915, when he was elected in his old seat of 4th Prince. The Liberal party was then confronted with a leadership crisis. Benjamin Rogers, whose term as lieutenant governor had come to an end, had been chosen as leader, but at age 78 found himself without a seat following the election, even though the party had increased its numbers from 2 to 13. Soon faced with a by-election without a leader, the party passed over a number of its young and dynamic backbenchers (including future premiers Walter Maxfield Lea* and Albert Charles Saunders*) and turned to Bell. He became leader of the opposition in December 1915 at 70 years of age. An avid debater, Bell was named in the house in 1916 for stating that the government of John Alexander Mathieson* had falsified several accounts. In the general election of 1919 he led the party to success, with the Liberals taking 24 of the 30 seats. Wayne E. MacKinnon, the historian of the Liberal party in Prince Edward Island, states that, as premier, Bell was a poor leader with little control of his cabinet. In 1922, to the great delight of the opposition, Bell and his attorney general, James John

Johnston, would clash on the floor of the house over a measure which Johnston introduced as a government bill but which Bell attacked as "exceedingly dangerous legislation."

The fight for open access to Island roads having been resolved during the administration of Conservative premier Aubin-Edmond Arsenault*, the Liberals, once in power, took up the cause of improved highways. Before 1917 there had been restrictions on running automobiles on the province's roads, many of which were in very poor condition. In 1920, taking advantage of a dominion government program to pay 40 per cent of the cost, the province embarked on an ambitious plan of highway improvement. By 1923 the Liberals were boasting that with over 5,000 miles the Island had more roads per capita than any province in Canada. In order to finance the provincial share of the cost the government had floated a major bond issue, which substantially increased the provincial debt. The interest charges were supposed to be paid out of revenues from automobile registration, but as this source fell short, general revenues were used. This situation compounded a financial problem for the Bell administration, which had already introduced a number of additional taxes, including a controversial poll tax of $3.00.

Although Prince Edward Island was never the lead province in the Maritime rights movement, in 1920 Bell had moved a resolution and spoken at length in the legislature on the necessity of joint action to press claims against the dominion. That year his government faced another issue involving the federal government: the fate of the Charles Dalton Sanatorium. This institution had been built and presented to the province by fox rancher and philanthropist Charles Dalton* in 1913 as a tuberculosis hospital and had been taken over by the dominion government for use as a military hospital between 1917 and 1919. Faced with high operating expenses as a result of "vast enlargements" made by Ottawa, Bell refused to accept the return of the institution to the province. Its subsequent closure and abandonment was seen by some as a snub to Dalton's allegiance to the Conservative party and by others as a waste of a much needed gift to the province.

Bell confronted a far different electorate in 1923 than he had encountered in 1919. In his campaign in 1919 he had promised votes for women, and with support from both sides of the house the government had extended the franchise to them in 1922. However, it was not the change in the voters that was the primary issue in the election but rather the imposition of a wide range of new taxes to address the growing costs of government. The Conservatives under James David Stewart* appealed to the fiscal interests of the voters and the Bell government was soon in difficulties. With the personal loss of his seat and the party going into opposition with only five seats, the 77-year-old Bell resigned as leader and retired from public life. He had been the first premier to lead his party from opposition to government and remain as leader until defeat.

In his later years Bell travelled a good deal and gave local lectures on his trips to the Middle East. The *Charlottetown Guardian* subsequently stated that "it was indeed as a lecturer and as a versatile impersonator rather than in politics that Mr. Bell excelled." In 1929 he was spending the winter in California when he died in Los Angeles three days after being struck by an automobile. He was buried in Summerside. Obituaries followed partisan lines. The Conservative *Guardian* noted that owing to his advanced years he had been "naturally disinclined to adopt new ideas or accept financial obligations, however urgent"; the Liberal *Evening Patriot* (Charlottetown) referred to him as the "Gladstone of Prince Edward Island," alluding to his age and statesmanship. The papers were united in recognizing his debating skill and for many years Prince of Wales College awarded the John H. Bell prizes in debate.

HARRY TINSON HOLMAN

No collection of John Howatt Bell's private papers has survived. The PARO holds correspondence files consisting primarily of outgoing correspondence while Bell was premier (RG 25, ser.25).

AO, RG 80-5-0-117, no.5537. PARO, Acc. 2323: 2109–71 (Bell family); P.E.I. Geneal. Soc. coll., family files, Bell and Howatt family files; RG 6.1, ser.19, subser.2, file 90. People's Cemetery (Summerside, P.E.I.), Tombstone inscription. *Charlottetown Herald*, 16, 23 Sept. 1896. *Morning Guardian* (Charlottetown), 31 Aug. 1896; continued as the *Charlottetown Guardian*, 21 Dec. 1915, 30–31 Jan. 1929. *Patriot* (Charlottetown), 20 Dec. 1915, 17 April 1920, 26 April 1922, 30 Jan. 1929. *Pioneer* (Summerside), 9, 16, 23 March 1896; 2 Feb. 1929. *Summerside Journal*, 3 Aug. 1882. *Canadian annual rev.*, 1915–23. *Canadian directory of parl.* (Johnson). *CPG*, 1886–1900, 1915–23. *Cyclopaedia of Canadian biog.* (Rose and Charlesworth), vol.3. Katherine Dewar, "John A. Dewar: the principled maverick," *Island Magazine* (Charlottetown), no.43 (spring/summer 1998): 3–7. Edward MacDonald, *If you're stronghearted: Prince Edward Island in the twentieth century* (Charlottetown, 2000). Frank MacKinnon, *The government of Prince Edward Island* (Toronto, 1951). W. E. MacKinnon, *The life of the party: a history of the Liberal party in Prince Edward Island* ([Charlottetown], 1973). *Maple Leaf* (Oakland, Calif.), 22 (February 1929): 51. P.E.I., Legislative Assembly, *Journal*, 2 May 1916; 1920: 41–42.

BELL, MABEL GARDINER. *See* HUBBARD

BELLIVEAU, ALPHÉE, teacher and school administrator; b. 9 July 1851, probably in Belliveau Village, N.B., where he was baptized the following month, son of François Belliveau and Madeleine Landry; m. 4 Aug. 1885 Marie Babineau in Saint-Louis de Kent,

N.B., and they had five sons and two daughters; d. 1 June 1927 in Sainte-Anne-de-Kent, N.B.

Alphée Belliveau likely attended the elementary schools in his region before enrolling in the Séminaire Saint-Thomas. This institution, which had been founded in Memramcook in 1854 by Abbé François-Xavier-Stanislas Lafrance*, closed in 1862. It was replaced by the College of Saint Joseph, which Camille Lefebvre*, of the Holy Cross Fathers, established in 1864. Belliveau was one of the first Acadian students at this college, which his father had decided he and his brothers should attend. A fairly prosperous farmer, the elder Belliveau would be described by Father Lefebvre, in an article in the Moncton newspaper *L'Évangéline* on 17 Aug. 1933, as "the champion of education in [the] parish of Memramcook." Alphée began his secondary studies in the commercial course, and then transferred to the classical program. Among his classmates were Pascal Poirier*, who would later be an author and senator, Pierre-Amand Landry*, who would become a politician and judge, and his cousin Placide GAUDET, who would be the author of important works on Acadian genealogy.

Around 1870 Belliveau left the College of Saint Joseph and became a teacher at Memramcook. He taught there until 1874, when he left to practise his profession in Grosses Coques and Saulnierville, in Nova Scotia. Although he did not have a teaching certificate, he was allowed to teach in elementary schools, but at a lower salary than a certified teacher. His return to New Brunswick in 1879, when the great school crisis of the 1870s [see John Costigan*] was nearing its end, was a turning point in his career. On the initiative of the superintendent of education, Theodore Harding Rand*, a preparatory department for francophones had been created in 1878 at the Normal School in Fredericton in order to attract a greater number of them to this institution, where the only language of instruction was English. After a period of three to five months in this class, students received a "local licence," valid for two years. Valentin Landry* was the first professor in charge of this program, but he did not stay long since he accepted a position as inspector of schools in 1879. The 28-year-old Belliveau was invited to take his place.

Like others in the new Acadian elite, such as Pierre-Amand Landry, Belliveau was a man of compromise and an advocate of good relations between Acadians and the anglophone community. The preparatory department, where he taught after 1879, did not enjoy unanimous support. On 9 Dec. 1880, for instance, in the Shediac newspaper *Le Moniteur acadien*, the Acadian nationalist leader Abbé Marcel-François Richard* asserted, "This department is French [only in having a] French professor and [some] French students." In 1883 this section of the Normal School became the French department and Belliveau became its head.

Despite conditions that were often difficult, Belliveau spent some 40 years as the only French-speaking professor at the Normal School in Fredericton. He was not able to buy a house on his salary of $1,400 a year and he often had to borrow money. Altogether he taught more than 2,000 students. Although enrolment was low in 1879, it increased considerably over the years. At the beginning of the 20th century, the French department had several dozen students, from every Acadian region in New Brunswick. These future teachers took courses in both French and English. On the successful completion of an initial five-month session, they received a third-class teaching certificate entitling them to teach in the public schools of the province. In order to obtain a higher grade of teaching certificate (and thereby access to better working conditions), they could either return to the French department for another session or enrol in the Normal School. J.-Théodule Lejeune, who would succeed Belliveau in 1920, opted for the latter.

The courses dealt mainly with subjects then being taught in the schools, such as commercial arithmetic and science. Belliveau, who was both department head and professor, took responsibility, in particular, for giving instruction on teaching methods for spelling and grammar. Very few French-language textbooks were available in New Brunswick, a situation that was regularly denounced in the Acadian press. Belliveau's timid attempts in this regard met with little success.

Belliveau is remembered as being authoritarian, but intelligent and studious, and well liked by his students. A polyglot, he spoke seven languages, including Volapük, a language created in 1879 by a German, Johann Martin Schleyer, that was later displaced by Esperanto. He was also one of the early members of the French-speaking community in Fredericton. The Acadian MLAs were in the habit of getting together at his home. His wife, Marie Babineau, who had been one of his first students at the Normal School, shared his interest in promoting the French and Acadian presence. Indeed, all their children studied in French in Fredericton, despite the fact that the city was a stronghold of the Anglo-loyalist tradition, and they enjoyed the benefits of a higher education. While she was still single and teaching in Saint-Louis de Kent, Marie had designed and made the first Acadian flag, at the request of her curé, Abbé Richard. This flag was adopted at the second Convention Nationale des Acadiens, which was held in 1884 in Miscouche, P.E.I.

Alphée Belliveau and his family manifestly were closely attached to the Roman Catholic Church, like many Acadian families of that time. One of his sisters was a nun and two of his brothers became priests, the best known being Mgr Philippe Belliveau. Two of Alphée and Marie's children chose the religious life: Alice entered the Congregation of Notre-Dame, and Hector, who brought his parents to live with him in 1923, was ordained to the priesthood in 1914.

MAURICE BASQUE

The original Acadian flag created by Alphée Belliveau's wife, Marie Babineau, is preserved at the Musée Acadien at the Univ. de Moncton, N.-B. Hector Belliveau is the author of a biography of his father entitled "Alphée Belliveau: 40 ans de vie française à Fredericton, 1880–1920; un témoignage," Soc. Hist. Acadienne, *Cahiers* (Moncton), 7 (1976): 27–33.
Centre d'Études Acadiennes, Univ. de Moncton, Fonds Hector-Belliveau. LAC, RG 31, C1, 1901, Fredericton, St Anne's Ward: 22. *L'Évangéline* (Moncton), 9 juin 1927. S. M. Andrew, *The development of élites in Acadian New Brunswick, 1861–1881* (Montreal and Kingston, Ont., 1997). Fernand Arsenault et Edmour Babineau, *Philippe Belliveau* (Moncton, 1988). Maurice Basque, *De Marc Lescarbot à l'AEFNB: histoire de la profession enseignante acadienne au Nouveau-Brunswick* (Edmundston, N.-B., 1994). J.-H. Béliveau, *Genealogical dictionary of Belliveau–Béliveau families in North America* (Trois-Rivières, Que., 1986). Gilberte Couturier LeBlanc *et al.*, "French education in the Maritimes, 1604–1992," in *Acadia of the Maritimes: thematic studies from the beginning to the present*, ed. Jean Daigle (Moncton, 1995), 523–62. J.-E. Picot, *Les écoles normales du Nouveau-Brunswick, 1848–1973* (Fredericton, 1974). A.-J. Savoie, *Un siècle de revendications scolaires au Nouveau-Brunswick, 1871–1971* (2v., [Edmundston], 1978–80).

BELL-SMITH, FREDERIC MARLETT, painter and educator; b. 26 Sept. 1846 in London, England, eldest son of John Bell-Smith and Georgianna Maria Boddy; m. 4 July 1871 Annie Myra Dyde in Montreal, and they had three sons; d. 23 June 1923 in Toronto.

Although recognized primarily as an artist, Frederic Marlett Bell-Smith was a person of wide-ranging interests, equally accomplished as a teacher, photographer, actor, raconteur, and writer. In 1866 his parents emigrated to Canada and settled in Montreal, where Frederic joined them a year later. He was by this time a practising artist, having studied at the South Kensington Art School and with his father, a portrait miniaturist who in London had been secretary-treasurer of the National Institution, a society of painters. In Montreal, where he lived until 1871, the future pattern of Frederic's career emerged. Showing his characteristic resourcefulness and motivation, he worked for a photographic studio and was a founding member of the Society of Canadian Artists, with his father as president. His first exhibition, at the Art Association of Montreal in 1868, featured urban sports and leisure activities. He also saw action against the Fenians when he served with the Victoria Rifles of Canada in 1870. The following year Bell-Smith, born into the Church of England, married Annie Myra Dyde at the Mountain Street Methodist Church in Montreal, and it may have been around this time that he changed his religious affiliation. The couple then moved to Hamilton, Ont.

For the next ten years the Bell-Smiths lived in Hamilton and Toronto while Frederic expanded his endeavours to include teaching at the Ontario School of Art and freelance illustration for such publications as the *Canadian Illustrated News* (Montreal) and for what would become *Picturesque Canada* ... (Toronto) [*see* Lucius Richard O'Brien*]. In the meantime he continued his employment in photography and exhibited his work almost yearly; he joined the Royal Canadian Academy of Arts at its founding in 1880 and was appointed academician six years later. This decade was marked by the death in 1881 of Charles Robert, one of the Bell-Smiths' three sons, and that year the family moved to London, Ont. At Alma Ladies' College in nearby St Thomas, Bell-Smith was appointed art director and professor of elocution and was soon taken on as drawing master at London's Central School. He founded the Western Art League, and travelled through Europe and North America on sketching trips. On a subsequent visit to Paris he would study at the Académie Colarossi, and with such artists as Benjamin-Constant, Gustave Courtois, Joseph Blanc, and Edmond-Louis Dupain.

In 1887, thanks to the free Canadian Pacific Railway passes given to artists by William Cornelius Van Horne*, Bell-Smith had the opportunity to fulfil one of his early dreams and see the Rockies. This was a defining moment: for him, reportedly, the mountains forever after "beckoned the enraptured pilgrim to explore their mysteries and their shrines." Over the next three decades he would visit the Rockies at least eleven times, and such mountain landscapes as *The silent sentinel of the north*, *Heart of the Selkirks*, and *An ice-crowned monarch of the Rockies* became a staple of his output. As an artist, Bell-Smith represented the late-19th-century manner of presenting a subject so as to arouse in the viewer the kinds of emotions evoked by narrative fiction. Working mostly in watercolours and oils, he was popular and prolific, usually producing small, easily marketable pictures meant to grace middle-class homes.

In 1888 Bell-Smith returned to live permanently in Toronto. Until 1890 he served as principal of the Parkdale Art School and then of the Toronto Art School (west end branch). In 1891 he and his wife endured the death of another son, Claude Pelham. Notwithstanding this personal tragedy, Bell-Smith became increasingly successful and was able to make a living wholly from painting. He also started to produce larger compositions, the most celebrated being *Lights of a city street*, painted in 1894. This crisp, detailed depiction of the corner of King and Yonge in Toronto after the rain captured a moment of urban life, with its streetcars, newsboys, policemen, and

93

well-dressed crowds. In its highly contrasted lights and shadows and deep perspective, the painting shows the artist's love of photography, both for its ability to arrest time, as well as for its value as a means of documentation. In 1895 the preparatory work for three large history paintings based on the events surrounding the sudden death in England of Sir John Sparrow David Thompson* led to an unprecedented privilege for a North American artist: Bell-Smith was granted a private sitting from Queen Victoria so that he could accurately portray her in one of these works. Ever dramatic, Bell-Smith capitalized on this occasion, writing an article entitled "How I painted Queen Victoria," where he recalled "a little old lady, very short, and very stout," with whom he conversed mainly in German.

The early years of the new century were Bell-Smith's heyday – he retained an administrative association with Alma Ladies' College from 1897 to 1910 and served as president of Toronto's New Water Color Society, as well as the Ontario Society of Artists. He also participated in exhibitions in Buffalo, N.Y., Liverpool, and Montreal. As an article in *Maclean's* (Toronto) for 1912 observed, his increasingly masterful technique and the aesthetic appeal of his paintings ensured that "'a Bell-Smith' has become a necessary adjunct in every collection of importance in the Dominion."

During the Great War, Bell-Smith painted the activities of the Canadian Expeditionary Force in training at Camp Borden, Ont., and executed a relief map model of the Rockies for the Grand Trunk Pacific Railway. He indulged his abiding passion for acting and dramatic recitations in performances of "habitant" poems, such as those by William Henry Drummond*, and scenes from the novels of Charles Dickens. It was said that he even looked like a Dickens character, and his friends in the Toronto Dickens Fellowship, where he served as president from 1910 to 1920, often debated whether "old Bell" was more gifted as an actor or a painter.

In 1918 Bell-Smith made his last journey to his beloved Rocky Mountains, whose mystic qualities had long captured his imagination. He spent the next summer painting at the Bon Echo Inn, the country home on Mazinaw Lake, Ont., of the theosophist and spiritualist Flora MacDonald Denison [MERRILL]. He was probably still painting when he fell in the basement of his Toronto home in May 1923. He died the next month. A memorial exhibition of his work was held in Toronto and in 1928 Bell-Smith's painting of Mount Hurd, B.C., was reproduced on a Canadian 10-cent stamp. Bell-Smith combined energy, creativity, and salesmanship with an awe for nature as an example of God's legacy to human resourcefulness.

MOLLY PULVER UNGAR and VICKY BACH

F. M. Bell-Smith is the author of *Little Nell: adapted from "The old curiosity shop" of Charles Dickens* (Toronto, [1909?]).

Roger Boulet's biography, *Frederic Marlett Bell-Smith, 1846–1923* (Victoria, 1977), is the most comprehensive account available about Bell-Smith. Well-researched and abundantly illustrated with reproductions of paintings as well as family photographs, it contains a lengthy bibliography, a list of Bell-Smith's principal exhibitions during his lifetime, and a chronology. A collection of catalogues and newspaper and magazine clippings, some, but not all, of which are cited individually in Boulet, can be found in the National Gallery of Canada Library (Ottawa), Artist file, Bell-Smith, F. M.

ANQ-M, CE 601-S105. AO, F 1140. Paul Gessell, "A treasure is rediscovered: historic painting depicts former PM's state funeral," *Ottawa Citizen*, 26 Oct. 1998. *Canadian men and women of the time* (Morgan; 1898 and 1912). *A dictionary of Canadian artists*, comp. C. S. MacDonald (7v. to date, Ottawa, 1967–). *Standard dict. of Canadian biog.* (Roberts and Tunnell), vol.2. Winnipeg Art Gallery, *150 years of art in Manitoba: a struggle towards a visual civilization; a Winnipeg Art Gallery exhibition commemorating Manitoba's centennial, May 1–Aug. 31, 1970*, comp. B. L. Pitman and Hanspaul Hager ([Winnipeg, 1970]).

BENGOUGH, JOHN WILSON, cartoonist, editor, publisher, author, entertainer, and politician; b. 7 April 1851 in Toronto, son of John Bengough and Margaret Wilson; m. there first 30 June 1880 Helena (Nellie) Siddall (d. 1902); m. secondly 18 June 1908 Mrs Annie Robertson Matteson in Chicago; there were no children of either marriage; d. 2 Oct. 1923 in Toronto.

On 24 May 1873, at the age of 22, John Wilson Bengough published the first issue of *Grip*. For the next two decades this Toronto weekly would carry puns, jokes, satire, and especially cartoons about virtually every topic of the day in late-19th-century Canada. The name *Grip* was borrowed from the raven who regularly accompanied the feeble-minded central character of Charles Dickens's 1841 novel *Barnaby Rudge*, while the magazine itself was probably modelled on *Punch* (London), whose cartoonist, John Tenniel, Bengough greatly admired. Bengough edited and published this little magazine; his voice dominated its pages through reams of poetry, outrageous puns, satirical paragraphs, and "Croaks and Pecks" of the raven. His humour was often broad: "To cultivate a Canadian National Spirit. – Grow barley," or "A Fenian Scare – threatened lack of whiskey." Above all, however, *Grip* featured Bengough's cartoons and caricatures. Some were large enough to fill an entire page and many revealed the influence of Thomas Nast, the great Republican cartoonist of *Harper's Weekly* (New York); Bengough turned Nast's Republican elephant into a symbol for Sir John A. Macdonald*'s National Policy, for instance. Others, which appeared in odd corners almost as fillers, were little gems of social and personal commentary.

"The Pun," *Grip* proclaimed, "is mightier than the Sword," for Bengough's humour was purposeful. In 1888 he explained "that the legitimate forces of humor and caricature can and ought to serve the state in its highest interests, and that the comic journal which has no other aim than to amuse its readers for the moment, falls short of its highest mission." The humorist was also a moralist intent upon both amusing and instructing his readers. Given his background and beliefs, this penchant is not surprising.

Bengough's family circumstances were modest and so was his education. His immigrant parents, a Scottish cabinetmaker and his Irish wife, sent him to the common and grammar schools of Whitby, where the family lived for a time; he was then briefly articled to a local lawyer. After learning something of the printing trade at the Whitby *Gazette*, he moved on to Toronto where he became a junior reporter with George Brown*'s *Globe* in 1871 or 1872. This early association with Liberal party journalism was natural enough since his father was a known party worker. Though Bengough would loudly declare *Grip*'s political disinterestedness and sometimes throw his support behind independent candidates or representatives of Alexander Sutherland*'s "Third Party," he always came back to the Liberal party, especially in the years after *Grip*'s demise. His cartoons would appear in a great variety of publications at home and abroad, but Liberal newspapers and party publications provided him with much of his income. His ambition to become a Liberal member of the Senate was gently rebuffed by Sir Wilfrid Laurier*; he nevertheless remained loyal.

Grip's politics, during its earliest years, remained undefined. Frequent gibes at George Brown allowed it to claim independence. On the other hand, the weekly showed no sympathy for the Conservatives, particularly after the Pacific Scandal of 1873 offered Bengough an opportunity to express unlimited moral outrage – especially pictorially. Indeed, it was that controversy which provided *Grip* with an opportunity to win a wide audience. Bengough's often reprinted cartoons from this period captured the essence of John A.'s physiognomy: his prominent nose, sly eyes, fashionable coiffure, and nonchalant attitude contrasted, for example, with Alexander Mackenzie*'s upright Scottish Presbyterian mien. "I admit I took the money and bribed the electors with it," Bengough's Macdonald remarks. "Is there anything wrong about *that*?" The question was certainly rhetorical.

Though Bengough continued to direct his verbal and pictorial gibes at the Conservatives – Macdonald would remain his favourite target until his death in 1891 when Bengough published a poetic tribute – the 1880s saw the flowering of *Grip*'s own reformist platform. It was founded upon Bengough's religious outlook and drew on a variety of ideas that were common to late-19th-century social critics in the English-speaking world. These reform nostrums, which Bengough propagated but did not originate, advocated social regeneration through the adoption of attitudes and policies sometimes described as applied Christianity or the Social Gospel.

Bengough's own religious upbringing was Presbyterian but he apparently imbibed few of the distinctive doctrines of that denomination. Instead, at least in his mature years, his religion eschewed doctrine in favour of ethics. Like many other social reformers he believed that theologically informed preaching reflected conservative other-worldliness while moralistic preaching concerned the here and now. He made his position plain in an 1875 poem criticizing churches, "Whose preachers preach theology a deal more than they should, / And try to make men wise when they should try to make them good."

This moralistic religion was not based on any sophisticated understanding of the intellectual currents which challenged religious orthodoxy in the late 19th century. Bengough rejected the claims of the "higher critics" who questioned literal readings of the Bible, and of Darwinians whose scientific materialism raised even more radical doubts about religion. In a satirical poem entitled "The higher criticism" Bengough professed his continuing adherence to the simple religious truths he had learned from his mother. Creations such as Professor Spencer E. Volushin and the Very Reverend Archdeacon Diaphanous Dixie, DD, were used by *Grip* to expound the simple moral claim that right conduct, not doctrinal purity, was the true test of religious convictions. It is not difficult to understand why writers like Charles Dickens would appeal to the Toronto cartoonist.

Bengough's platform contained a number of planks familiar to contemporary moral reformers. He ardently advocated the prohibition of alcoholic beverages, believing that they took a particularly heavy toll among working people. It was also in the interest of this class that he opposed Sunday streetcars, which he thought would destroy the sabbath as a day of rest. So, too, in the 1880s he took up the cause of women's suffrage and the admission of women to such professions as the law, reversing his earlier opposition to "The Female Righter." But Bengough went beyond these modest demands for change, perhaps because he increasingly realized that such social sins as alcohol consumption had their roots in more fundamental problems. By the 1880s Bengough had discovered, and accepted, the analysis of the ills of emerging industrial capitalism presented by the American social critic Henry George. In *Progress and poverty* (1879) George, whose moralistic language appealed to Bengough, explained that the existence of poverty in the midst of the plenty created by science and technology was the result of an inequitable fiscal system. This system failed to tax the unearned increment on land whose value increased not through the owner's labours, but rather as a consequence of increased demand arising from population growth. At the same time the protective tariff promoted monopoly and increased prices unnaturally. George's alternative, what Bengough would call "The Whole Hog Solution," was obvious: a single tax on unimproved land values and free trade. Once he had discovered George's teachings Bengough became a lifelong missionary in the single-tax cause, cartooning, writing, and speaking across Canada and as far away as Australia in the hope that its adoption would regenerate industrial society, "this travesty of Christianity." Advancing his single-tax beliefs Bengough attacked Macdonald's National Policy, thundered against monopolists, took up the cause of farmers and workers, and excoriated all those – including his friend Principal George Monro Grant* of Queen's College in Kingston and his enemy Goldwin Smith* – who were blind to the Georgite light. In this crusade he was joined by a sprightly band of regenerators which included Thomas Phillips Thompson*, a Bellamyite socialist, Samuel Thomas Wood*, an economics and nature writer for the *Globe*, and other members of the Toronto Anti-Poverty Society, the Knights of Labor, and the Patrons of Industry.

Grip's "Solid Platform" included several other items that revealed a harsher side to Protestant reformism, and Bengough's support for "Anglo-Saxon" nationalism. He promoted independence under a republican form of government and the alliance of all Anglo-Saxon nations, rejecting both Lieutenant-Colonel George Taylor DENISON's "Imperial Federation" and Goldwin Smith's annexationism while accepting their common belief in Anglo-Saxon solidarity. His advocacy of the complete separation of church and state and of English as the one official language, obviously directed at Roman Catholics and French Canadians, was a stark manifestation of his ethnic nationalism. He looked forward to the day "when the monstrosity of a double official language and dual schools will be done away with throughout the whole country. Our real national life will date from that day." While Bengough deplored the social and economic deprivations suffered by Canada's native peoples, he had only scorn for Louis Riel*'s effort to unite Métis and native people in the 1885 rebellion. His special *Canadian Pictorial and Illustrated War News* was bombastically nationalistic, as was his poem celebrating Major-General Frederick Dobson Middleton*'s victory at Batoche (Sask.):

Who says that British blood grows tame,
  Or that the olden fire is gone,
Must first forget Batoche's name,
  And how that day was fought and won!

Grip strongly supported Riel's death sentence, adding, however, that the real authors of the rebellion should be "exposed and punished whether they turn out to be plotting speculators at Prince Albert or drowsy Ministers at Ottawa."

Assessing *Grip*'s public impact or financial condition is extremely difficult since accurate records are lacking. In the mid 1880s, at its peak, it claimed a paid circulation of 7,000 to 10,000 and 50,000 readers, and there is evidence that the country's leaders paid it some attention. Then published by Grip Printing and Publishing Company, of which Bengough was a director, it had been through a series of partnerships in which Bengough was associated first with Andrew Scott Irving*, then with his brother George, and finally with his brother Thomas and Samuel John Moore*. But its existence was always precarious and the depression of the early 1890s spelled its death. Bengough gave up the editorship in 1892 when new management appointed T. Phillips Thompson to the post. A year later Bengough returned but he failed to revive his creation.

During the next quarter-century Bengough maintained a public profile through his cartoons in a wide variety of publications: the Toronto *Globe*, the *Toronto Daily Star*, the *Montreal Daily Star*, and *Saturday Night* (Toronto). His work also appeared in such single-tax publications as the *Public* in Chicago and the *Square Deal* in Toronto. He attracted large audiences to his "chalk talks," which he had begun in 1874 and which took the main elements of *Grip* – cartoon, puns, satire, and advocacy of social reform – and put them on stage in numerous large and small Canadian communities as well as in the United States, Great Britain, Australia, and New Zealand. Then there were his numerous publications. The two-volume *Caricature history of Canadian politics* (1886) reproduced many of *Grip*'s finest political cartoons. *The gin mill primer* (1898) presented the Prohibition case, and *The up-to-date primer* (1896) and *The whole hog book* (1908) were single-tax tracts. *Chalk talks* (1922) brought together many of his most popular illustrated lectures and set out his reform philosophy. Finally there were the poetry collections, *Motley: verses grave and gay* (1895) and *In many keys: a book of verse* (1902), which brought together largely unmemorable verse of humour, political satire, pathos, religious sentimentalism, and patriotism.

Since Bengough the journalist had always focused on politics, it was natural that he should be drawn directly into public life. In the 1890s he served as president of the Toronto Single Tax Association and was active in the People's Forum; later he joined the Canadian Peace and Arbitration Society and became a director of the Toronto Industrial Exhibition. In 1907 he won election as an alderman for Toronto's Ward 3, and he was re-elected in 1908 and 1909. This new pulpit provided him with an opportunity to preach and promote causes with which he had long been identified: tax reform, tenant's rights, sanitary improvement, public ownership of hydroelectricity, and the restriction of liquor licences. Perhaps frustrated by his failure to win much support for some of these reforms, he left council before the completion of his third term in order to return to the lecture circuit.

Though Bengough's career as a public figure had passed its peak when Canada entered the war in 1914, he had by no means fallen silent. He now turned his talents to promoting the war effort, including support for conscription as the clearest expression of patriotism, a position taken by many English-speaking reformers. Nevertheless, he remained faithful to the Liberal party and especially to William Lyon Mackenzie King*, whose *Industry and humanity* . . . (Toronto, 1918) Bengough enthusiastically praised. In the 1921 election he applied his cartooning skills to support the new Liberal leader. He then returned to the lecture platform. In 1922, following a strenuous western tour, he travelled to the Maritimes where he collapsed during a performance in Moncton, N.B. He died suddenly the following year at his home at 58 St Mary Street while working on a cartoon supporting an anti-smoking campaign. He had never deserted the good old cause of moral reform.

Bengough's reputation rests mainly on his greatest achievement, *Grip,* and the cartoons he sketched for the witty little reformist magazine that flourished in dour late-Victorian Toronto. He was not a great artist; his cartoons, though often well drawn, were too crowded and he rarely resisted the temptation to explain and preach. A few of his most striking images he borrowed from others, but the cartoons he published under the pseudonym L. Côté demonstrated that he could draw in contrasting styles. He had a talent that fixed, probably forever, the historical image of numerous public figures of his time, most notably Sir John A. Macdonald. He also had a passionately held viewpoint which gave his cartoons an edge that both simplified issues and ensured that his readers were drawn into his vision of moral conflict. Principal Grant came close to the mark when he said of Bengough, "You may think him at times Utopian. . . . In the best sense of the word, he is religious." A punster with a vision of "thingsastheyoughttobe."

RAMSAY COOK

[The J. W. Bengough papers, largely composed of drafts of articles and speeches and clippings from various sources, are held at the McMaster Univ. Library, Div. of Arch. & Research Coll., Hamilton, Ont.

Bengough's major publications, other than *Grip* (1873–94), include: *The Grip cartoons, vols. I and II, May 1873 to May 1874* (Toronto, 1875); *The decline and fall of Keewa-*

tin: or, the free-trade redskins; a satire (Toronto, 1876); *Bengough's popular readings: original and select* (Toronto, 1882); *A caricature history of Canadian politics* . . . (2v., Toronto, 1886; an abridged one-volume edition, selected and introduced by Douglas Fetherling, was published in 1974); *The Prohibition Aesop: a book of fables,* published in Hamilton some time between 1889 and 1897; *The up-to-date primer* . . . (New York and Toronto, 1896; reprinted with an introduction by Douglas Fetherling, 1975); *The whole hog book: being George's thoro' going work "Protection or free-trade?" rendered into words of one syllable, and illustrated with pictures; or, a dry subject made juicy* (Boston, 1908); and *Bengough's chalk talks: a series of platform addresses on various topics, with reproductions of the impromptu drawings with which they were illustrated* (Toronto, 1922).

Among secondary sources, Stanley Paul Kutcher's dissertation "John Wilson Bengough: artist of righteousness" (MA thesis, McMaster Univ., 1975), is the most complete. Carman Cumming, *Sketches from a young country: the images of "Grip" magazine* (Toronto, 1997), is a critical examination of *Grip*'s journalism, while Ramsay Cook, *The regenerators: social criticism in late Victorian English Canada* (Toronto, 1985), places Bengough in context with his contemporaries. R.C.]

AO, RG 22-305, nos.15572, 48698; RG 80-5-0-95, no.13355; RG 80-8-0-262, no.3212; RG 80-8-0-912, no.6264. *Daily Mail and Empire*, 3 Oct. 1923. *Globe*, 2 July 1880. *World* (Toronto), 19 June 1908.

BENNETT, PHILIP, machinist and labour organizer; b. *c.* 1876 in Cupids, Nfld; twice married, with three children; d. 10 Aug. 1922 in St John's.

Philip Bennett's life traced several important patterns. He was one of many young Newfoundlanders compelled to emigrate to Canada in search of work and, like others, he did so with the intention of returning home. His job experiences off the Island brought him into contact with labour leaders and helped shape his working-class consciousness. Upon completion of his training as a machinist in Nova Scotia, Bennett found employment in St John's in the railway shops of the Reid Newfoundland Company [see Sir Robert Gillespie Reid*; Sir William Duff REID], the largest employer on the Island. The company's high profile and tough-minded management style made it a target of labour activism, especially in St John's where it engaged nearly 25 per cent of the male labour force.

Bennett's activism fitted a discernible trend among skilled craftsmen. Across North America machinists assumed leadership roles in the fight for union recognition and workers' control on the shop floor as part of a larger project for social justice. The Reid railway sheds were perhaps the one location in Newfoundland where working men of different trades and skills could share their opinions, vent their frustrations, and express their hopes for the future. The coming of World War I, and the harsh realities of profiteering merchants, rampant inflation, and poor housing conditions, rallied workers to the cause of forming one big industrial union to unite the island. In April 1917 Bennett and several other Reid employees founded what shortly became known as the Newfoundland Industrial Workers' Association. As its first president, Bennett brought a determined social activism and a measure of pragmatism to his duties. Lacking the charisma of William Ford Coaker*, the leader of the Fishermen's Protective Union, he appealed to his followers as a humble yet resolute man who shared their vision for social reform.

Having started with 35 members, the NIWA claimed over 3,500 by the following year. Unlike earlier attempts at unionization, which had been split by religious sectarianism and the ever-present conflict between urban dwellers and baymen, the association parlayed initial enthusiasm into concrete membership gains. Inquiries came from communities throughout the island. The union soon began to push for progressive legislation that included limits on child labour, workers' compensation, factory acts, worker-owned housing, and cooperative retail ventures. Bennett was active in the NIWA Co-operative Stores, established early in 1918. Sensitive to issues of gender, the association organized a "ladies' branch" under Julia Salter* Earle that August in the hope attracting working women into its ranks. Bennett was particularly moved to act in the interests of children and "girl workers," who he felt were exploited by local merchants. The previous May the NIWA had started its own biweekly newspaper, the *Industrial Worker*, and in 1919, in an effort to rise above traditional party politics, it formed an independent Workingmen's party.

Wartime circumstances had pushed the NIWA into its most dramatic event, a strike against the Reid Newfoundland Company, early in 1918. On 27 March the machinists, electricians, blacksmiths, and general labourers of the railway shops in St John's downed tools and left the premises. These workers were joined by many others in what soon assumed the shape of a general strike. The walkout was timed to coincide with the end of the annual seal hunt. This move pressured Reid since delays in servicing returning sealers would have considerable consequences on the local economy. Although the central issue was low wages, more complex matters of job classifications and workplace rights also played a part. Bennett himself opposed strikes on principle, but his efforts to obtain a negotiated settlement met with the steely resistance of Reid managers, who doubted the association's ability to sustain the walkout. Yet the strike held: telegrams of support proclaiming "all solid along the line" were transmitted by NIWA branches along the length of Reid's Newfoundland Railway.

Even with the impressive solidarity of the strikers the NIWA needed the help of the government of William Frederick Lloyd* to broker an agreement. It was in these discussions that Bennett's diplomacy and tact proved invaluable. A formula to settle the dispute was reached with the company on 12 April; modest wage increases and guarantees of fair job classifications were negotiated later. More important, perhaps, was that the men and women of the union had taken on Newfoundland's largest employer and forced it to allow its workers to organize and to bargain collectively.

Following the strike, Bennett's deteriorating health due to tuberculosis led to reduced activity on behalf of the NIWA. In 1919 he stepped down as president to serve instead as vice-president. Declining his organization's offer of an expenses-paid trip to a Canadian sanatorium, he continued to travel and organize for the NIWA until obliged, eventually, to retire. The association itself would endure, despite severe postwar depression, until 1943. By that time Islanders could turn to other national and international union organizations. When he died in St John's at the age of 46, Bennett left a legacy of working-class militancy which has remained vibrant in Newfoundland and Labrador to this day.

PETER S. McINNIS

Memorial Univ. of Nfld, Folklore and Language Arch. (St John's), Tape C-7232 (R. Hattenhauer, interview with T. C. Noel, 26 May 1967). PANL, GN 2/5, file 344; MG 17, files 365–410; MG 73, 1916–25. *Daily News* (St John's), 1916–22. *Evening Advocate* (St John's), 1922. *Evening Telegram* (St John's), 1916–22. *Industrial Worker* (St John's), 18 May 1918. *St. John's Daily Star*, 1916–21. *The book of Newfoundland*, ed. J. R. Smallwood *et al.* (6v., St John's, 1937–75; vols.1–2 repr. [1968] and 1979). Ron Crawley, "Off to Sydney: Newfoundlanders emigrate to industrial Cape Breton, 1890–1914," *Acadiensis* (Fredericton), 17 (1987–88), no.2: 27–51. *DNLB* (Cuff *et al.*). P. [S.] McInnis, "All solid along the line: the Reid Newfoundland strike of 1918," *Labour* (St John's), 26 (1990): 61–84. A. B. Morine, *The railway contract, 1898, and afterwards: 1883–1933* (St John's, 1933). P. [F.] Neary, "Canadian immigration policy and the Newfoundlanders, 1912–1939," *Acadiensis*, 11 (1981–82), no.2: 69–83.

BENOIT, ZÉPHIRIN, firefighter and chief of the fire brigade; b. 5 March 1850 in Saint-Jean-Chrysostome (Saint-Chrysostome), near Châteauguay, Lower Canada, son of François Benoit, a farmer, and Julienne Sainte-Marie; m. 4 Nov. 1871 Rose de Lima (Délima) Dussault in the parish of Notre Dame in Montreal, and they had three sons and three daughters, two of whom survived them; d. 29 Sept. 1930 in Montreal.

Zéphirin Benoit attended Saint-Rémi school in Napierville and then at the age of 14 went to live in the United States, where he continued his studies. On his return to Quebec four years later, he worked as a clerk in a grocery store. His career as a firefighter began in 1871 with the Montreal fire department. On

9 Aug. 1875 he was appointed chief of the fire department and the police in Saint-Henri, a newly incorporated town. His task was to organize the fire-fighting service in this municipality of about 6,000 people. For 13 years, with only four men under his command, he managed the service efficiently and never had to report a fatality among the firefighters. He himself was seriously injured, however, during a tannery fire in 1885, when he fell from the fifth floor into the ruins of the building.

On 29 Oct. 1888 the city of Montreal appointed him to replace William Patton as chief of the fire brigade, which was under the jurisdiction of the fire department. While he was in command of the brigade, it averaged 170 men on its roster. Benoit introduced many improvements. In 1889, for example, he instituted a night patrol to locate fires quickly and reduce the number of conflagrations. The following year he made a proposal to the fire committee, the body having authority over the fire department, that it hire physicians to treat injured or sick firefighters. As a result, it appointed two physicians who took up their duties in May 1891. Chief Benoit also added to the fire brigade's equipment by purchasing a single-tank chemical pump as well as a water tower for fighting fires in tall buildings. In 1891 he divided the territory of Montreal into three districts (east, centre, and west) to ensure a better allocation of the brigade's personnel and more effective fire-fighting. Realizing also that having electrical power lines in the city streets interfered with the activities of fire-fighters, he suggested that the wires be buried in conduits (the first underground cables would not be laid until 1913). In 1892 he inspected the city's public buildings and drafted recommendations for eliminating potential fire hazards, planning emergency measures, providing public buildings with appropriate safety equipment, and reducing the loss of human life. Since Montreal had grown with the annexation of the villages of Hochelaga (1883), Saint-Jean-Baptiste (1886), and Saint-Gabriel (1887), a fourth district (northeast) was added in 1893. In 1894 Benoit patented a dual-action reel he had invented, which could hold 1,000 feet of hose. In the same year he proposed that a fund be set up in aid of injured or sick firefighters. The provincial government would act on this suggestion in 1898 by amending the regulations of the Montreal Firemen's Benefit Association to allow the establishment of a retirement or pension fund. In 1894 he also succeeded in getting the municipal building code changed, to ban the use of sawdust as filler for floors, walls, and roofs. Two years later he purchased an attachment for the nozzle of a fire hose, called a Décarie, which allows the stream of water to be varied from a quarter inch to one inch in diameter.

During Benoit's term as fire chief, Montreal underwent unprecedented urban development. Population growth, urban expansion, and increased building activity multiplied the problems connected with fire-fighting. The brigade had to combat on average 680 fires a year, including major ones at the Asile de Longue-Pointe (1890), the Pensionnat Villa-Maria (1893), the Eastern Abattoir (1897), the Montreal Board of Trade (1901), and the Windsor Hotel (1903). Twelve firefighters were killed in the line of duty during this period. Chief Benoit regularly recommended the construction of new fire stations as needed. After more than 20 years in service, he retired on 1 Jan. 1909. In the course of his career he had received various decorations: gold and silver medals for acts of devotion to duty, a gold medal at the international fire-fighters' tournament in London, England (1896), and from France a rescuer's rosette (1900) and a service medal for courage and dedication.

A few months after his retirement, however, Benoit's integrity was called into question during the hearings of the royal commission to make a general and complete inquiry into the administration of the affairs of the city of Montreal. Set up on 7 April 1909, this inquiry was conducted by Lawrence John CANNON. In the report Cannon submitted on 13 December, the judge accused Benoit of embezzlement and of maladministration in the appointments and promotions to the fire brigade, and recommended that he be forced to repay one-half the costs of the inquiry, a sum of $571.20. This recommendation would not be accepted, however, by the new city council elected in February 1910.

Although the conclusions of the Cannon inquiry tarnished Zéphirin Benoit's reputation, they should not cause his substantial improvements to the Montreal fire-fighting system or his ingenuity to be forgotten.

HÉLÈNE CHARBONNEAU

ANQ-M, CE601-S51, 4 nov. 1871; CE607-S6, 10 mars 1850. VM-DGDA, P23, Procès-verbaux du conseil, 9 août 1875; VM1, Dossiers d'employés, Zéphirin Benoit; Procès-verbaux, 29 oct. 1888; VM6, Dossiers de coupures de presse, D1031.8 (chefs du Service d'incendie); VM50, Rapports, 19 oct. 1908. *Le Devoir*, 30 sept. 1930. *La Presse*, 31 oct. 1908. *Canadian Patent Office Record* (Montreal), 22 (1894). L. J. Cannon, *Rapport sur l'administration de la ville de Montréal, décembre 1909* (s.l., n.d.). Huguette Charron et Françoise Lewis, *Les débuts d'un chef, Zéphirin Benoit; la naissance d'une ville, Saint-Henri, 1875–1888* (Montréal, 1999). J.-C. Lamothe, *Histoire de la corporation de la cité de Montréal depuis son origine jusqu'à nos jours* . . . (Montréal, 1903), 537. Ville de Montréal, Dép. des incendies, *Rapport annuel du chef du département des incendies*, 1889–1909.

BERNIER, ARTHUR (baptized **Louis-Arthur**), bacteriologist, pathologist, and professor; b. 1 Oct.

Bernier

1873 in Montreal, son of Charles-Télesphore Bernier, a merchant, and Aurélie-Julienne Rivard-Bellefeuille; d. unmarried 29 April 1928 at Notre-Dame Hospital in Montreal.

After completing his elementary schooling at the École Olier in Montreal, Arthur Bernier entered the Collège Sainte-Marie for his classical studies. In 1893 he began his medical course at the Montreal branch of the Université Laval. He received his MD with distinction in 1897, and became an intern at Notre-Dame Hospital. On 7 July of that year he was licensed to practise by the College of Physicians and Surgeons of the Province of Quebec. Interested in bacteriology, a new specialty whose importance he fully understood, and probably influenced by Dr Michel-Thomas Brennan of Notre-Dame Hospital, who had set up a small bacteriology laboratory there, he decided in 1898 to spend a year studying at the Institut Pasteur in Paris. He took a course in "microbial technique" [see Oscar-Félix MERCIER] that had been started on 15 March 1889 by Dr Émile Roux, a close associate of Louis Pasteur. Roux also won renown for his research on diphtheria vaccine. He had an assistant, Alexandre Yersin, who would discover the plague bacillus in 1894. At the time Bernier enrolled in the course, which was based essentially on medical bacteriology, it was taught jointly by Dr Roux and Dr Élie Metchnikoff. The latter would become one of the founders of immunology, mainly as a result of his work on phagocytosis. To this team of pioneers were added Louis Martin and Gaston Ramon, who would carry out experiments on diphtheria immunization under Roux's direction. It was as part of this team that Bernier began to learn about research on diphtheria immunization and studies of the immune system. Some of his published work would deal with these subjects.

On returning to Canada in 1899, Bernier was appointed demonstrator (or research assistant) in bacteriology and general pathology in the Montreal School of Medicine and Surgery, which was the faculty of medicine at the Université Laval in Montreal. He was thus able to put into practice the techniques of bacteriological analysis he had recently learned. The following year he became physician at the general dispensary of Notre-Dame Hospital, then pathologist, and later head of the hospital's laboratory. His competence in the fields of pathology and medical bacteriology was soon recognized. In 1902 he was promoted to associate professor of bacteriology, and from 1908 he held the chair of general pathology. Two years later he became the first person appointed to the chair of bacteriology in the Montreal School of Medicine and Surgery. He would retain this office for the rest of his life. Soon after assuming his duties, he increased the time that medical students would have to devote to the study of bacteriology and to labora-

tory work from 60 to 120 hours. Throughout his academic career, he would introduce new theoretical elements (such as the role of antibodies, the effects of immunization, and the discovery of new bacteria) into his explanation of the mechanisms of infection. He would also strive to incorporate recent techniques in medical bacteriology that made it possible to detect and prevent infectious diseases. Thus the quality of instruction given to medical students was constantly enhanced. Concern about improving public health led Bernier to accept appointment in 1908 as chief bacteriologist for the Board of Health of the Province of Quebec, an office he would retain on a part-time basis until the end of his life.

An indefatigable worker who missed no opportunity to promote the establishment of medical bacteriology in the province of Quebec, Bernier agreed in 1911 to help Dr Hector Baril and Dr Amédée Marien organize the laboratory at the Hôtel-Dieu in Montreal. His assistance was valuable: he obtained $1,000 from the faculty where he worked for the purchase of laboratory equipment (microscopes, glass utensils, and Bunsen burners). He was also involved in planning the layout of the laboratory and in designing the course of studies that would be provided there. In recognition of his efforts, the management of the Hôtel-Dieu appointed him head of the laboratory two years later. In addition, he taught the course on public health there. His term of office was brief, however; in 1914 he left his position to devote himself almost exclusively to teaching bacteriology and general pathology at the Montreal School of Medicine and Surgery, where he became one of the few full-time professors. In 1918 he was elected a member of its council, where he joined such other leading practitioners as Louis de Lotbinière Harwood*, Amédée Marien, Oscar-Félix Mercier, Télesphore Parizeau, and René de Cotret, who would be instrumental in shaping the scientific basis of the faculty. Bernier would hold two other teaching positions at the Université de Montréal, one in bacteriology in the faculty of dental surgery, and another, from 1925, in practical hygiene at the École d'Hygiène Sociale Appliquée.

Bernier was also a member of the Society of American Bacteriologists. In 1922 he became a founding member and first president of the Société de Biologie de Montréal, which was still active at the beginning of the 21st century. This initiative by a group of professors from the faculties of science and medicine at the Université de Montréal sought to disseminate scientific and medical knowledge, develop research projects, and increase cooperation with researchers in the rest of Canada. In 1923 Bernier was also one of the founding members of the Association Canadienne-Française pour l'Avancement des Sciences.

Throughout his career, Bernier strove to keep up with the most recent advances in bacteriology, picking out key contributions from European and American schools. At the laboratory of the Board of Health of the Province of Quebec, for example, he ushered in a new era by reorganizing the bacteriological examination service. He was always looking for better ways of identifying gaps in prophylactic methods (preventive techniques), in order to improve the work done by this board in the field. He also refined health statistics to make them more complete and detailed. Shortly after the end of World War I, he set up a serology laboratory for the detection of syphilis (in particular, through the new Wassermann reaction test) and its treatment. In 1927 alone, more than 26,000 tests were carried out in the board's laboratories, demonstrating the important contribution made by this agency to the fight against venereal disease.

A year before he died, Bernier collaborated with Dr Joseph-Albert Baudoin in manufacturing and distributing the tuberculosis vaccine known as BCG. Intended for newborn infants, this vaccine had been developed a few years earlier by French researchers Albert Calmette and Camille Guérin. Bernier hoped at the time to have this prophylactic measure used throughout the province and wanted to expand immunization against diphtheria.

Arthur Bernier was a meticulous and competent teacher who was always eager to introduce his students to the latest technical and theoretical developments in medical bacteriology. He also helped broaden the scope of pathology by adding to histology a new method of investigating the causes of disease. His efforts to make a noticeable improvement in diagnosis and prevention were especially laudable, given that he had had to overcome the reluctance of many colleagues, who preferred traditional methods. Because of his notable contribution to the teaching of medical bacteriology and to the development of laboratories, Bernier ranks among the most important pioneers not only in bacteriology but also in scientific medicine itself in Canada.

DENIS GOULET and PHILIPPE HUDON

Arthur Bernier wrote many reports for the Board of Health of the Prov. of Quebec and several articles in *L'Union médicale du Canada* (Montréal), among which are "Les anticorps," 36 (1907): 96–101; "À propos de génération spontanée," 36: 354–59; and "Le spirochète de la syphilis," 35 (1906): 264–67.

ANQ-M, CE601-S51, 5 oct. 1873. Arch. de l'Hôpital Notre-Dame (Montréal), Procès-verbaux du bureau médical, 1892–1928; Rapports annuels, 1892–1928. Arch. de l'Institut Pasteur (Paris), Cours de microbie technique, MP 29048 (liste des personnes ayant suivi les cours, 1889–1970). *Le Devoir*, 30 avril 1928. *La Patrie*, 30 avril, 2 mai 1928. *La Presse*, 30 avril 1928. J.-A. Breton, "Nécrologie: le professeur Louis-Arthur Bernier, 1873–1928," *L'Union médicale du Canada*, 57 (1928): 376–78. College of Physicians and Surgeons of the Prov. of Quebec, *Medical reg.* (Montreal),

1897; 1911. École de Médecine et de Chirurgie de Montréal, *Annuaire*, 1890–1919. Denis Goulet, *Histoire de la faculté de médecine de l'université de Montréal, 1843–1993* (Montréal, 1993). Denis Goulet *et al., Histoire de l'hôpital Notre-Dame de Montréal, 1880–1980* (Montréal, 1993). Denis Goulet et Othmar Keel, "Les hommes-relais de la bactériologie en territoire québécois et l'introduction de nouvelles pratiques diagnostiques et thérapeutiques (1890–1920)," *RHAF*, 46 (1992–93): 417–42. Univ. de Montréal, Faculté de médecine, *Annuaire*, 1920–28.

BERTRAND, JULIE (Julienne), named **Marie de Saint-Basile**, first Canadian superior general of the Sisters of the Holy Cross and the Seven Dolours; b. 1 Dec. 1844 in Sainte-Scholastique (Mirabel), Lower Canada, daughter of Olivier Bertrand, a carpentry contractor and farmer, and Julia Welch, who was probably of Irish descent; d. 2 April 1923 in Saint-Laurent, Que.

In 1851 Julie Bertrand began her studies at the local boarding school, which had been opened the previous year by the Marianite Sisters of Holy Cross. This French congregation had come to Saint-Laurent, near Montreal, in 1847, with the priests and brothers of the Congregation of Holy Cross, at the invitation of Bishop Ignace Bourget* [*see* Léocadie Gascoin*]. Accepted as a postulant in Saint-Laurent on 24 Aug. 1859, Julie entered the noviciate on 28 December; she was then given the name Sister Marie de Saint-Basile, in honour of Basile Moreau, the founder of the Congregation of Holy Cross.

As she had been a gifted student at the convent and had attracted attention as a novice, Sister Marie de Saint-Basile was assigned responsibilities in this teaching community, despite her youth: monitor, teacher, person in charge of the final academic year, academy director, and prefect of discipline. She worked in most of the houses in the province of Canada: Saint-Martin (Laval) from 1862, Saint-Laurent from 1865, Académie Saint-Ignace (Montreal) in 1873, Varennes in 1874, and Saint-Alphonse-de-Liguori (Saint-Liguori) from 1875.

While she was in Saint-Laurent and responsible for the final academic year, the young community was experiencing a major crisis. The Congregation of Holy Cross had branched out into the United States, and the French superiors were having difficulty managing the huge expansion of their establishment in Indiana, brought about through the efforts of Father Édouard Sorin. Léocadie Gascoin, named Marie des Sept-Douleurs, the founder of the Marianite Sisters of Holy Cross in Le Mans, France, and the second superior in Saint-Laurent in 1849, had become provincial in 1857 and superior general in 1858, but she had returned to France in 1863. From there she kept a tight rein on the administration of the Canadian province, in accordance with the constitutions. The three North American provinces (Indiana, Louisiana, and

Canada) merged in 1865 and as a result the noviciate for all the North American houses of the Marianite Sisters was transferred to Indiana, despite the protests of the Canadian nuns. Then the American branch of the Marianite Sisters seceded from the mother house in 1869. The superior general now found that she had to curb the expansion of her Canadian branch, in order to remain faithful to the spirit of Moreau and avoid another split.

In 1876 Sister Marie de Saint-Basile was chosen for the difficult mission of setting up a boarding school in Sainte-Rose, a parish on Île Jésus that had been hoping for the arrival of another teaching congregation. To her success among the parishioners was added a further achievement: 24 of the 28 pupils in the final year of studies chose to enter the Saint-Laurent noviciate. It was as superior of this school that Marie de Saint-Basile became involved three years later in the steps taken by the nuns in Saint-Laurent to obtain their independence from the French congregation. Elected by the sisters as an official delegate to the meeting of the general chapter in 1879, she accompanied the provincial superior, Mother Marie de Saint-Alphonse-de-Rodriguez, to Le Mans. She found herself caught up in a conflict between the Canadian sisters and Marie des Sept-Douleurs, who, according to Bishop Édouard-Charles Fabre* of Montreal, "puts obstacles that hinder the development and prosperity of the establishments in the province." After their delegates returned, the Canadian nuns, whose requests had been denied any consideration, sent a petition to Rome on 23 Aug. 1880 to sever all canonical ties with the French congregation. This move, which was seen by the founder as an unpardonable act of insubordination, was severely dealt with by exemplary punishments and changes of obedience, much to the confusion of the Canadian nuns. They held their ground, however, because having to refer all decisions to the general administration was causing major inconveniences. They had the support of Bishop Fabre, of Abbé Gédéon Huberdeau, a representative in Rome, and of their spiritual director in Varennes, Abbé François-Xavier Bourbonnais, who judged that the request of the Canadian nuns "was not an illegitimate revolt."

After Rome had put an end, "for a time," to all dependence of the congregation with regard to the mother house in December 1882, Bishop Fabre assumed oversight of it. He consulted with the nuns who had held positions of authority, chose the members of the council, and appointed Marie de Saint-Basile (who was only 38 years old) vicar superior of the Sisters of the Holy Cross and the Seven Dolours, as the "new" congregation was called. It may be surmised, then, that she was seen by her colleagues as a key figure in the separation and the logical person to accept the consequences of it. The situation was complicated by the fact that the former constitutions were still in effect. Mother Marie de Saint-Basile wrote to the bishop in 1885: "To reach an agreement with France is absolutely impossible. Our situation would be untenable." Provisional constitutions were adopted in 1889 and the first chapter meeting, held in 1890, enabled Mother Marie de Saint-Basile to be elected the first superior general, an office to which she would be re-elected at the 1896 chapter meeting.

In 1882 the congregation consisted of 90 professed sisters and 22 novices. It had eight establishments in Montreal and the surrounding region, one in Ontario, and one in Connecticut. The new superior now began opening a string of houses, almost all located in the "Canadian" parishes of New England. Like many other religious orders in the province of Quebec, the Sisters of the Holy Cross found that region to be one where their expansion was unhindered by the presence of the older congregations and was facilitated by the development of the railway system. Marie de Saint-Basile directed this growth personally by making regular visits to the Franco-American houses. By 1902, when the superior general gave up her responsibilities, the congregation had undergone an unstoppable expansion: 428 professed sisters, 47 novices, and 28 postulants, in 33 different houses. It had been divided into three provinces – Notre-Dame-des-Sept-Douleurs (Quebec), Sacré-Cœur (New England), and Saint-Joseph (two houses in Ontario, four in the United States, and two in Quebec) – and the mother house had been enlarged by extensive building projects. Rome had issued a decree approving its constitutions in 1897, "after a wait of three years, rather than seven or ten years, because [they were] well drafted," according to Marie de Saint-Basile. For her, these were "sweet consolations and powerful encouragements," for she had often referred to "the heavy burden" of her responsibility.

Mother Marie de Saint-Basile, who had been in the front line of the struggle leading to the autonomy of the Canadian province, had exercised authority on the basis of prudence, respect for rules, and administrative skill. Her circular letters were short and effective, and seemed austere and repetitive: bans on travel and visits, restrictions on purchases, a search for the religious spirit in small things. Despite the difficult circumstances surrounding the foundation of the Canadian province, she maintained spiritual ties with the founders and with the other branches of Holy Cross. She recommended that "vocations be cultivated with good sense and discernment." She also looked after the religious and pedagogical training of the young nuns, whom she brought together every summer at the mother house. Her correspondence was focused primarily on the material security of the congregation's houses. Unfortunately she destroyed her personal papers a few months before she died, so that less official and more intimate insights are not available.

Following her term as superior general, Marie de Saint-Basile was provincial superior of the province of Notre-Dame-des-Sept-Douleurs until August 1905. She then took on less onerous responsibilities as local superior in Saint-Martin (1905–11) and in the parishes of Notre-Dame-du-Rosaire (1911–14) and Saint-Alphonse-d'Youville in Montreal (1914–20). In 1920 she returned to the mother house with the nuns who were sick, and she carried out simple administrative duties despite a chronic illness. She died on Easter Monday, 2 April 1923.

Mother Marie de Saint-Basile was remembered for the high regard in which she was held in her congregation and in the province of Quebec, doubtless because of the firmness and skill with which she led the Sisters of the Holy Cross under difficult circumstances. In the field of girls' education, she offered skilful assistance to the prefects general of studies, who maintained the educational reputation of this congregation in the eyes of the public.

MICHELINE DUMONT

ANQ-M, CE606-S22, 1er déc. 1844. Arch. des Sœurs de Sainte-Croix (Saint-Laurent, Qué.), Annales de la congrégation des Sœurs de Sainte-Croix et des Sept-Douleurs, 2, 3; Circulaires de sœur Marie de Saint-Basile; Circulaires de sœur Marie des Sept-Douleurs; Corr., lettres de sœur Marie de Saint-Basile; Mgr Fabre avec la Sacrée Congrégation de Rome; sœurs de Saint-Laurent avec Mgr Bourget; sœurs de Saint-Laurent avec Mgr Fabre; Dossier concernant la pétition de 1882. Étienne et Tony Catta, *La très révérende mère Marie des Sept-Douleurs, 1818–1900, et les origines des Marianites de Sainte-Croix* (Le Mans, France, [1958]). Guy Laperrière, *Les congrégations religieuses: de la France au Québec, 1880–1914* (2v. parus, Sainte-Foy, Qué., 1996–), 1. *Sainte-Croix au Canada, 1847–1947* (Montréal, 1947).

BESSETTE, ARSÈNE (baptized **Moïse-Arsène**), journalist and writer; b. 20 Dec. 1873 in Saint-Hilaire (Mont-Saint-Hilaire), Que., son of Moïse Bessette, a farmer and politician, and Valérie Lapalme; m. 16 Nov. 1907 Albina Lareau in Saint-Jean (Saint-Jean-sur-Richelieu), Que.; they had no children; d. 21 June 1921 in Montreal.

Arsène Bessette was the eldest in a family of eight. After attending the primary school in his native village, he obtained his classical education (1888–95) at the Collège Sainte-Marie-de-Monnoir, in particular through the generous support of Louis-Philippe BRODEUR, the MP for the riding of Rouville from 1891. In 1898, as he was in no position to enrol in university – doubtless because of lack of funds – he embarked on a career in journalism, with a brief spell apprenticing at *La Patrie*. On 3 November of the following year, under the pseudonym Jean Rémuna, he published a story

entitled "Michel Carabin" in *Le Canada français/Le Franco-Canadien*, a Saint-Jean weekly; its editor at the time was his friend Gabriel Marchand, the son of Félix-Gabriel Marchand*, one of the newspaper's founders. The story relates how the eponymous hero, a staunch supporter of the Liberal party, prevents the tight-fisted Father Crétin, whose vote had been bought by the Conservatives, from getting to the polling station. On 28 June 1901 Bessette announced in *Le Canada français* that he was giving up Jean Rémuna, the pseudonym he had hitherto used, explaining: "[He] was neither big nor little, neither witty nor stupid, neither good nor evil; he was not a man, far less a woman, he was my pseudonym." From then on he published articles under his own name on a variety of topics (including happiness, influenza, patriotism, and current affairs), as well as a small number of stories, anecdotes, and novellas. He remained a regular contributor to this paper until the end of 1917, apart from a brief interruption between 1903 and 1905 that can only be partly explained by his collaboration with the short-lived Montreal periodicals *L'Étincelle* and *La Vie artistique*.

Through the good offices of his friend Idola Saint-Jean*, he began in 1903 to correspond with a Breton teacher and, later, writer, Marie Le Franc, whom he invited to Canada in 1906 with decided intentions. No sooner had the young woman arrived in Montreal, however, than the idyll came to an end. On 16 Nov. 1907 Bessette married one of his colleagues at *Le Canada français*, Albina Lareau, who was known as Pimprenette.

Bessette, who had put on a one-act comedy in 1904 entitled "Les pantins," which remains unpublished, wrote an article three years later in *Le Canada français* attacking censorship in the theatre. The nature of this piece was such that the chancellor of the archdiocese of Montreal, Émile Roy, was compelled to write a letter of protest to Gabriel Marchand on 7 Nov. 1907: "*Monseigneur* [the archbishop of Montreal], knowing the fine traditions of your family, is convinced that you do not share such opinions, and that they will no longer find expression in your newspaper." Reprimanded at that time by his employer, Bessette stepped out of line again in 1909, when he pronounced himself in favour of the creation of a French theatre company in Montreal. This time he aroused the wrath of the Quebec ultramontane weekly *La Vérité*.

In 1914 Arsène Bessette had his only novel, *Le débutant*, published in Saint-Jean by La Compagnie de Publication Le Canada Français. It is not known if he had shown it to his friends, if the publisher of *Le Canada Français* had read the manuscript, or if Bessette himself sent the press release to *La Presse*, in which his work was described as a novel of the soil and an interesting portrait of social customs with most of the action taking place in the countryside.

What is known is that the book was dedicated to "fellow journalists, to the sincere and upright men in public life, [and] to all those who have lost their illusions, before or at the same time as their hair." The dedication was a premonition, for the author would quickly lose his own illusions when the critics ignored his novel. Since Bessette was on the members list of the masonic lodge L'Émancipation [see Adelstan de Martigny*] published in *Le Devoir* in 1910, not everyone would have been well disposed towards him, which doubtless explains why the publication of his novel – "the only work of fiction in Quebec literature inspired by masonic ideas," according to Roger Le Moine – met with a conspiracy of silence. The fact that the book did not come out in one of the major urban centres is not enough to account for the critics' indifference; on the other hand, their lack of interest may have discouraged Bessette from publishing the two further volumes that were announced when *Le débutant* appeared.

What is the novel about? Paul Mirot, the hero of the story, and his introduction to journalism, to the world of letters, and to love, was probably a projection of the author. Indeed, Paul has much in common with his creator, for, like Bessette, he is determined, courageous, witty, and intelligent. These qualities led the owner of *Le Populiste* to hire Paul as a journalist. Soon appreciated by both his employers and his readers, he also wins the heart of Simone Laperle, the beautiful and wealthy cousin of his best friend, Jacques Vaillant. Having become his mistress, the young woman introduces him to society. In partnership with Vaillant, Mirot founds a newspaper, in which he denounces the rigidity of society. He is also engaged in writing a novel that deals with the dangers of nationalistic ideology in literature. The newspaper is censured for its supposedly revolutionary ideas and ceases publication. Mirot's novel is banned and he loses his job at the newspaper where he is then working. In addition, the death of Simone closes his love life. The novel ends in complete failure, yet the hero remains confident about the future, while attaching no importance to the past.

Contrary to what literary critics would assert for many years, Bessette himself did not lose his job at *Le Canada français* when *Le débutant* was published, nor was the novel condemned by the archbishop. The writer remained on the staff of *Le Canada français* until the end of 1917, when he moved to Montreal to work for *Le Pays* and *La Presse*. In 1920 he became an inspector for the Montreal Tramways Commission.

Arsène Bessette died suddenly on 21 June 1921 while visiting a friend. Notices of his death appeared in several newspapers, but *Le Canada français*, where he had worked for more than 15 years, had only a short article on the life of this writer who had dreamt of becoming famous but whose passing went unremarked. Yet Bessette's only book, which was well written and carefully researched with regard to the political situation in the province, was distinctly superior to the other Québécois novels written by his generation. As well, by exploring the theme of free love, it anticipated Jean-Charles Harvey*'s *Les demi-civilisés*, which would cause a scandal when it came out in 1934.

AURÉLIEN BOIVIN

[Arsène Bessette's novel, *Le débutant*, was reprinted in Montreal in 1977, thanks to Madeleine Ducrocq-Poirier, and again in Saint-Laurent, Que., in 2002. The author is grateful to Marie-Frédérique Desbiens, a third-year literature student at the Université Laval, Quebec, for her assistance with the research for this biography. A.B.]

ANQ-M, CE602-S16, 21 déc. 1873. Centre de Recherche Interuniversitaire sur la Littérature et la Culture Québécoises, Univ. Laval, Arch. du projet DOLQ; Arch. du projet Histoire de la vie littéraire au Québec. LAC, MG 30, D135. Réjean Beaudoin, "La quasi-dissidence d'un débutant de 1914," *Le Jour* (Saint-Laurent), 1ᵉʳ juill. 1977. "Il publiera un roman du terroir," *La Presse*, 28 févr. 1914. *La Presse*, 23 juin 1921. René Dionne, "Un maillon de la chaîne: *Le débutant* d'Arsène Bessette," *Les Lettres québécoises* (Montréal), no.6 (avril–mai 1977): 24–25, 31. *DOLQ*, vol.2. Madeleine Ducrocq-Poirier, *Le roman canadien de langue française de 1860 à 1958: recherche d'un esprit romanesque* (Paris, 1978). Hamel *et al.*, *DALFAN*, 133–34. Pierre Hébert et Patrick Nicol, *Censure et littérature au Québec* (Saint-Laurent, 1997). *Histoire de l'édition littéraire au Québec au XXᵉ siècle*, sous la dir. de Jacques Michon (1v. paru, Saint-Laurent, 1999–), 1 (Jacques Michon, *La naissance de l'édition, 1900–1939*, 1999). Albert Laberge, *Journalistes, écrivains et artistes* (Montréal, 1945). Roger Le Moine, *Deux loges montréalaises du Grand Orient de France* (Ottawa, 1991). *Mariages du comté de Saint-Jean (1828–1950)*, comp. Irenée Jetté *et al.* (Sillery, Qué., 1974). *Les relations entre la France et le Canada au XIXᵉ siècle* (Paris, 1974). Normand St-Pierre, "La censure du roman *Le débutant* (1914) de Arsène Bessette: le texte et l'institution" (mémoire de MA, univ. du Québec à Montréal, 1984).

BEST, EDNA MAY WILLISTON (Sexton), feminist, social activist, and war worker; b. 25 June 1880 in Shediac, N.B., daughter of James Edward Best and Maria Porter; m. 25 June 1904 Frederic Henry Sexton, and they had a son and a daughter; d. 14 Dec. 1923 in Halifax.

May Best's father, a merchant and native of Horton, N.S., fell on hard times after the death of his first wife in 1864. He moved to Shediac, where he remarried, taught school, and then took up farming. Both he and his second wife died prematurely; May was subsequently raised by family in Boston. Endowed with "striking intellectual ability," she completed the Girls' High School there, entered the Massachusetts Institute of Technology in 1898, and obtained a bachelor of science degree in 1902 with high honours in chemistry. After working briefly in the research laboratory of the General Electric Company at Schenectady, N.Y., she married colleague Frederic Sexton (MIT, SB 1901), who had just been appointed to Dalhousie University, Halifax.

Sexton embraced the life of faculty wife and young mother, but chafed at the limitations of a backwater community still resistant to the full participation of women in civic and intellectual life. Disinclined to pursue the traditional routes of church and charitable volunteerism, she sought other outlets for her restless energy. She became a board member in 1905 of the Ladies' Musical Club of Halifax, founded that year by Kate MACKINTOSH and others, and used it as an entrée to the Local Council of Women. Within the LCW she established herself as an able committee person, podium speaker, and newspaper columnist, involved in almost every issue the council championed after 1906, including objectionable literature, public health, care of the feeble-minded, the prevention and treatment of tuberculosis, the playground movement [see Mabel Phoebe Peters*], and consumer advocacy. Some of these causes were also central to the Imperial Order Daughters of the Empire, in which Sexton was active after 1909, serving a term as first municipal regent.

Frederic Sexton's appointment in 1907 as founding principal of the Nova Scotia Technical College positioned the young couple to become leaders in progressive education and social reform. During 1908–9, for example, May Sexton campaigned vigorously but unsuccessfully in favour of an industrial school for young women, arguing that such training would equip them to enter the workforce with a competitive advantage as skilled domestics, dressmakers, seamstresses, and milliners. As the issue of female enfranchisement resurfaced provincially during the pre-war years, both husband and wife publicly supported the appointment of women to school boards. This was viewed as a preliminary step in the campaign for voting rights and was a measure endorsed repeatedly by the LCW. In April 1913, as yet another enabling bill proceeded through the legislature, Sexton was one of a trio who represented the LCW before the Legislative Council, "making out their case with admirable clearness and reasonableness"; yet again, however, the initiative was lost.

With the declaration of war on 4 Aug. 1914, Halifax was changed overnight from a sleepy and complacent imperial outpost into a marshalling station for Canada's overseas efforts; the need for timely and effective response from its citizens was unprecedented. From within a generally disorganized private sector, the LCW emerged as a leader in the civilian war effort. Meeting on 5 August, the council established a "Central Red Cross and Relief Committee

for the Women of the Province," endorsed by the military and charged with coordinating the entire provision of hospital supplies from Nova Scotia, for both overseas and home-defence needs. The vision of the committee as a province-wide agency had been Sexton's idea.

Initially the production and packing of supplies was carried out at the LCW's headquarters. From June 1915, however, Principal Sexton made the technical college available; his wife served as chair of the work committee. Bringing her "very strong executive ability" and "outstanding personality" into this charged atmosphere, Sexton organized parties of up to 100 women daily into assembly-line teams, complete with project supervision and product inspection. Each team produced a specific item on a weekly rota – hospital suits, bathrobes, shirts, pyjamas, socks, pneumonia jackets, surgical dressings and bandages, sheets, pillow cases, towels, operating gowns and masks – and, over the duration of the war, together they assembled some 10,635 Christmas stockings filled with treats. The Red Cross was especially proud of the egalitarian nature of these work parties, which crossed the colour line and included women of all ages from all social classes.

In order to attract the considerable sums needed to sustain these and other Red Cross initiatives, Sexton began fund-raising in 1915 through a series of patriotic lectures delivered around Nova Scotia. Audiences warmed to her "charming and clever manner" as she presented "Principal Sexton's New War Slides," accompanying them with a commentary which "brought the awfulness of war home to us," the minutes of one organization recorded, "in a way that all detailed newspaper accounts never could." On one occasion in Halifax, her presentation to the Rotary Club resulted in commitments from over 500 city businessmen, each undertaking to contribute $2.00 per month indefinitely for hospital supplies. On another occasion, she persuaded miners and steelworkers in New Glasgow, Trenton, and Westville to pledge payroll deductions totalling $5,000 monthly for general war work. Sexton was not the only Red Cross fund-raiser active in Nova Scotia, but her eloquence and determination were significant factors in the province's phenomenal war record: an estimated $1 million was raised for the Canadian and British Red Cross societies alone over a four-year period.

From its establishment in 1914 the Nova Scotia branch of the Red Cross grew rapidly under the presidency of Agnes Dennis [Miller*], attracting the best of Halifax's clubwomen. Its principal strength lay in a large but extremely efficient administrative structure; at its zenith, this consisted of five vice-presidents, Sexton included, with an executive committee of over thirty. Together, these women could respond almost immediately to any emergency. Entirely a woman-led organization, the Red Cross nevertheless worked effectively with various Halifax businessmen, chiefly because of the financial management or philanthropic assistance they could provide. Although there were other civilian organizations active provincially in the war effort, many of them women-based, none ever achieved the prominence or service record of the Red Cross.

As the war progressed, the Nova Scotia branch diversified into new activities focused on troop movements through Halifax. A subcommittee under Sexton provided volunteers to meet all incoming hospital vessels and assist in trans-shipment to outgoing hospital trains. In 1916, responding to the influx of invalided soldiers into the city's overcrowded military facilities, the organization offered to set up and finance a 25-bed convalescent home. The immediate objective was to assist a group of frostbitten Jamaican soldiers left without care as a result of international bureaucratic wrangling. A committee co-chaired by Sexton and Joseph Linton Hetherington negotiated government approval, and then worked closely with the IODE and local benefactor William James Clayton to establish the home, which drew attention as the first wartime convalescent facility in Canada to provide vocational training.

In the aftermath of the Halifax explosion in 1917 Sexton's formidable abilities were called upon yet again. On the day of the disaster the Canadian Red Cross set up a medical supply committee, co-chaired by Sexton and responsible for coordinating 44 volunteers in the purchase and delivery, twice daily, of all the supplies required by each of the 57 temporary hospitals and dressing stations scattered throughout Halifax and Dartmouth. For a time this initiative largely diverted the work of Sexton's hospital supply teams and entirely drained their inventory. The committee, which worked 12- to 15-hour days initially, continued well into 1918.

With the end of the war imminent, the focus of attention shifted to returning soldiers; once more, Sexton was in demand. In 1918 she became replacement convenor of the Red Cross hospital committee. She immediately enlarged it and introduced the most recent British standards regarding convalescent care and volunteer services. Libraries and sun parlours were installed in Camp Hill Military Hospital and a large roster of weekly visitors was organized. Also during 1918 the military canteen in Halifax originally established by the American National Red Cross was briefly under Sexton's "brilliant management"; in one month alone, 3,000 meals were served to transient soldiers.

Like many other Halifax women drawn into the war effort, Sexton participated fully in other community-based groups, chiefly the LCW, the IODE, the Halifax Playgrounds Commission, and, in 1917–18,

the short-lived Nova Scotia Equal Franchise League, of which she was third vice-president and which saw the vote for women finally become a reality in Nova Scotia [see George Henry MURRAY]. Apart from public advocacy, Sexton excelled at coordination, bringing structure to various initiatives and liaising effectively with other women leaders such as Edith Jessie Archibald*, Charlotte McInnes, and Eliza Ritchie*. She was arguably Nova Scotia's most visible war worker and, among her generation, the Nova Scotian woman most committed to broad social action and best equipped to articulate the necessary strategies.

All this did not come without cost. Late in 1918 Sexton's health broke completely. She retired from public life and although she subsequently travelled extensively with her husband, she did not recover. Rarely seen in public, she was nevertheless consulted continuously by those who shared her deep commitments. Her death in 1923 from uraemic poisoning was sudden but not unexpected. Eulogized by the *Halifax Herald* as "a born leader, magnetic, full of enthusiasm in all good," she was mourned throughout Nova Scotia.

LOIS K. YORKE

LAC, RG 31, C1, 1881, Shediac, N.B., div.3: 39 (mfm. at PANB). NSARM, MG 20, 160; 183, no.1; 204; 321; 535; 567, no.1 (mfm.); RG 32, M, Kings County, no.64/1852. St Andrew's Anglican Church (Shediac), RBMB, 17[?] Nov. 1868, 29 Aug. 1880 (mfm. at PANB). *Christian Messenger* (Halifax), 28 Sept. 1864. *Halifax Herald*, 15 Dec. 1923. *Morning Chronicle* (Halifax), 15, 17 Dec. 1923. *Presbyterian Witness* (Halifax), 17 July 1852. Canadian Red Cross Soc., Nova Scotia Div., *Annual report* ([Halifax]), 1918–19; *Nova Scotia Red Cross during the Great War, nineteen fourteen–eighteen* (Halifax?, 1919?). C. L. Cleverdon, *The woman suffrage movement in Canada*, intro. Ramsay Cook (2nd ed., Toronto, 1974). *Directory*, Can., 1871. Mass. Institute of Technology, Class of 1901, *Decennial record, 1901–1911* (Boston, [1911]); Class of 1902, *First record book . . .* (Brookline, Mass., 1904). N.S., House of Assembly, *Journal and proc.* (Halifax), 1913. *Nova Scotia's part in the Great War*, comp. and ed. M. S. Hunt (Halifax, 1920).

BEST, THOMAS HENRY, businessman; b. 17 April 1850 in Perrytown, Upper Canada, son of John Best and Ellen (Elonor) Cory; m. 22 Aug. 1876 Clara Melissa Wiggins in Collingwood, Ont., and they had three sons and six daughters; d. 1 Aug. 1928 in Toronto.

Thomas H. Best's parents immigrated from Newry (Northern Ireland) and settled on a farm in the Port Hope area of Upper Canada. In the 1850s the family moved to a farm near Dunedin, south of Collingwood. At 18 Thomas travelled to Chicago and Buffalo, N.Y., where, as a department store employee, he gained experience in retailing, marketing, and advertising. By 1871 he had returned to the family farm and was working as a store clerk, likely in Collingwood. Eventually he became manager there of the region's largest store, the Melville Fair Company. In 1876 he married the daughter of a local dry goods merchant; by 1891 he had his own merchant tailoring business. An active participant in the civic and religious life of Collingwood, he served on the town council, the public school board, and the board of managers of the Presbyterian church. He also held the positions of secretary of the Collingwood Reform Association and superintendent of the Mechanics' Institute library. "Ever of a literary turn, a persistent reader and a lover of books," according to a local history, he devoted a good deal of time to the library.

In 1891, for reasons that are not clear, Best moved to Toronto, where he established a tailoring business with John Stone on Yonge Street. By this time he had become interested in making Canadians more aware of public affairs and the literary contributions of their compatriots. In March 1893 he helped launch the monthly *Canadian Magazine of Politics, Science, Art and Literature* under the editorship of James Gordon Mowat. It was published by the Ontario Publishing Company Limited, an enterprise organized expressly for this purpose, with Best as managing director, and formally incorporated in May. Notwithstanding the fact that at the beginning its president, James Colebrooke Patterson, was the minister of militia and defence, and one of its vice-presidents, Thomas Ballantyne*, was the speaker of the Ontario legislature, the key to the magazine's solvency and longevity would be advertising support and effective business practice, areas in which Best excelled. For the next 35 years the world of publishing and printing would be his focus.

The late 19th century was an inauspicious time for publishing a magazine in Canada. As Best undoubtedly knew, home grown magazines were unable to compete with American journals in Canada, they had limited access to markets in the United States, and increasing customs duties made production expenses prohibitively high. The *Canadian Magazine* cost 25 cents an issue, a comparatively high price but the same as that of such American models as *Scribner's* (New York) and *Harper's* (New York). The *Canadian Magazine*'s founders promised at the outset that "timely articles on political and other public questions of interest to the Canadian people will appear every month from the pens of leading statesmen and writers of various shades of political opinion." Furthermore, the magazine intended to follow the policy of "cultivating Canadian patriotism and Canadian interests."

The subsequent mixture of plentiful advertisements, line drawings, quality reproductions of photographs and paintings, articles on politics, travel, science, and art, and selections of poetry and fiction contributed to the survival of the *Canadian Magazine*, which developed what literary historian Carl Klinck terms a "reliable formula." Its first volume offered readers the broad range of topics that would become characteristic of the magazine, including pieces by Ontario Publishing director James Wilberforce LONGLEY on coal and fruit-growing in Nova Scotia, John Joseph MACKENZIE on bacteria, William Hamilton Merritt* on domestic steel production, George Monro Grant* on the National Policy, the Reverend William Schenck Blackstock on criminology and regeneration, and James Laughlin Hughes* on humour in the classroom.

In 1897, during the editorship of John Alexander Cooper* and after some hard bargaining, likely by Best, Ontario Publishing took over *Massey's Magazine* (Toronto) [*see* Walter Edward Hart Massey*] to encourage "one strong and purely Canadian magazine." Following this buyout, which doubled the circulation of the *Canadian Magazine*, Best ("in view of this increase in power") announced a 50 per cent increase in advertising rates on 1 June 1897. In return, he believed, the takeover would make the *Canadian Magazine* the dominion's "best advertising medium," which could boast more artistry and foreign advertising "than any other two publications in Canada." In addition, small promotional booklets would be issued to solicit "judicious advertising" and to highlight the authors and topics in upcoming volumes. Subsequent issues would feature advertising from a wide range of clients, including banks, insurance companies, schools and colleges, brand-name producers, and railways.

With the *Canadian Magazine* running smoothly, Best began to consider other efficiencies. In 1901 Ontario Publishing took on the publication of the *Canada Lancet* (Toronto), the country's most prestigious medical journal. As well, an office was opened in London, England. Best also examined the savings to be gained from in-house printing. In 1911, by which time his son Thomas Wilbur had joined the business as a traveller, Ontario Publishing bought the printing firm of Newton and Treloar and renamed it the T. H. Best Printing Company. Guided by Best's decision to run the two companies as separate entities, Best Printing branched out into business apart from the journals, a move that brought the company into conflict with what Best saw as the printing cartel run by Hugh Cameron MacLean* and William Southam*. Best's venture was saved by the Macmillan Company of Canada Limited when it contracted with Best Printing to produce all of its textbooks.

In 1913 Best purchased bookbinding equipment, and book production became an increasingly lucrative part of his activities. Eight years later Ontario Publishing was formally taken over by Best Printing, with Thomas becoming president and Wilbur vice-president. Despite his age, Best Sr devoted himself to overseeing the growth of his new printing establishment. In 1922 he sold his interest in the *Canadian Magazine*, which then had a circulation of 30,000. Six years later he died at his home on Dunvegan Road in Toronto.

Thomas H. Best's sense of business and his appreciation for culture had enabled him to become the driving force behind one of the few successful popular magazines in Canada, as well as the owner of one of Ontario's largest printing houses, which would be handed down through two generations. An innovator in methods of business and salesmanship, Best represented that sector of the business class to whom financial gain was the reward for the virtues of efficacy, thrift, public benefit, and progress.

MOLLY PULVER UNGAR and VICKY BACH

Family information was kindly given to the authors by J. Kirby Best of East Lyme, Conn., a great-great-grandson of the subject, in a March 2000 interview.

AO, RG 22-305, no.60383; RG 80-5-0-60, no.9889. LAC, RG 31, C1, 1871, Nottawasaga Township, Ont., div.1: 30; 1891, Collingwood, Ont., div.2: 28. North York Central Library, Canadiana coll., John Alexander Cooper papers. *Daily Mail and Empire* (Toronto), 2 Aug. 1928. *Globe* (Toronto), 2 Aug. 1928. *Canadian Magazine*, March 1893–September 1924. *Canadian men and women of the time* (Morgan; 1912). *Canadian Printer and Publisher* (Toronto), December 1895: 1; May 1958: 75. *Dict. of Toronto printers* (Hulse). *Directory*, Toronto, 1892–1928. Huron Institute, *Papers and records* (3v., Collingwood, Ont., 1909–39), 2: 18. *Ontario Gazette* (Toronto), 1893: 626. G. L. Parker, *The beginnings of the book trade in Canada* (Toronto, 1985). "Profile," *Quill & Quire* (Toronto), 25 July 1969: 4–5. *Standard dict. of Canadian biog.* (Roberts and Tunnell), vol.2. H. E. Stephenson and Carlton McNaught, *The story of advertising in Canada; a chronicle of fifty years* (Toronto, [1940]). Fraser Sutherland, *The monthly epic: a history of Canadian magazines, 1789–1989* (Markham, Ont., 1989).

BIBEAU (Bibeault), MARIE (Mary), named **Marie-Anne-de-Jésus**, first superior general of the Little Franciscans of Mary; b. 9 Oct. 1865 in Sorel, Lower Canada, daughter of Pierre Bibeault, a farmer, and Catherine Latraverse; d. 30 April 1924 in Baie-Saint-Paul, Que.

Marie Bibeau attended the elementary school in her village, where she obtained a basic education, and subsequently worked as a dressmaker. Around 1887 she emigrated to Massachusetts with her family and settled in Manchaug, south of Worcester, where there was a large Franco-American community. The parish priest of Notre-Dame-des-Canadiens in Worcester, Joseph Brouillet, was then making arrangements to open an orphanage in a house he had bought. His intention was to found a religious community that

would take charge of this charitable work and he persuaded two women teachers, both Third Order Franciscans, and Marie-Louise Rondeau, a student at the convent of the Sisters of the Presentation of Mary in Saint-Hyacinthe, Que., to form its nucleus. The orphanage opened on 13 Aug. 1889. Drawn to the religious life, Marie Bibeau decided to join the group and she was received as a postulant on 7 Oct. 1889. On 24 November she donned the habit and was given the name Marie-Anne-de-Jésus. The community, which was in the Franciscan spiritual tradition, had three novices and two postulants to take care of some 40 children. They had a great deal of work, and daily appeals for funds, making and mending the children's clothing, and teaching left little time for the religious life.

In the summer of 1890 the sisters had to face the fact that their community was at risk because of decisions made by its founder, who had, moreover, acted without episcopal authorization. Brouillet had accepted too many candidates, they had taken the habit hastily after only rudimentary religious instruction, and the workload had increased substantially following too rapid expansion. In addition, his disagreement with the community's chaplain, the Oblate Zotique Durocher, about the training of novices, as well as his imprudent financial management, had created serious instability. The "nuns," who had "no security, either spiritual or temporal," according to their legal adviser, Ambroise Choquet, took the advice of friends and benefactors and applied for civil recognition under the name of Sœurs Oblates de Saint-François d'Assise on 10 Sept. 1890. They obtained the protection of Bishop Patrick Thomas O'Reilly of Springfield, Mass., who informed them, however, that they were not nuns. A lengthy dispute began between the Oblate sisters and Brouillet, who spread a rumour that they had been excommunicated and who refused them the sacraments. He even called in a sheriff to evict them from their house in January 1891.

After taking refuge in an abandoned dwelling in Worcester ("the house of misery," as they called it), the 15 "nuns" opened a new orphanage and tried to resolve their problems. They were put in touch with the parish priest of Baie-Saint-Paul in Quebec, Ambroise Fafard, who had founded a hospice in his parish in 1889 and was looking for a community to manage it. Sister Marie-Anne-de-Jésus and Sister Marie-Joseph (Marie-Louise Rondeau) went to Baie-Saint-Paul to discuss the project and to meet Bishop Louis-Nazaire BÉGIN of Chicoutimi. They decided to set a new course for their "community" on 13 Nov. 1891, while retaining their orphanage in Worcester. The "Brown Nuns" had now arrived in Baie-Saint-Paul, but they would have to do their noviciate again, since they were not really nuns. Sister Marie-Anne-de-Jésus was closely involved in the many negotiations connected with this difficult beginning, in her capacity as first superior general, an office to which she was elected in January 1892. She described in a letter "the days strewn with thorns on which [the sisters had been] wounded many times."

The Hospice Sainte-Anne in Baie-Saint-Paul did, however, force the "Brown Nuns" to rethink their original mission. Fafard had signed an agreement with the Quebec government to accept 50 insane patients in addition to the 20 or so elderly people already in its care. The superior wrote: "Our idiots are giving us a great deal of trouble." She worked alongside her sisters, and, in her outspoken way, referred to herself as a "stopgap." She organized appeals in the countryside. "We pick up everything: hens, geese, turkeys, sheep, all in the same wagon," she explained. Every year she returned to her home parish to raise funds, an activity at which she was reputed to be effective. As well, she welcomed the Franciscan Missionaries of Mary, who came from France in May 1892, seeking to integrate the 11 "founding women" into their congregation. When this merger failed (the constitutions of the French community were not consistent with the charitable work being undertaken), Mother Marie-Anne-de-Jésus had the satisfaction of obtaining, on 7 June 1892, authorization from the diocese to establish the Little Franciscans of Mary and open a noviciate. In 1902 she would ask Franciscan Berchmans-Marie Mangin to help draw up the fledgling congregation's constitutions and provide a Franciscan education for the nuns.

It proved difficult, however, to carry on the charitable work in Worcester. The superior general met with Bishop Bégin of Chicoutimi and his successor, Michel-Thomas Labrecque*, as well as with Bishop Thomas Daniel Beaven of Springfield and the apostolic delegate to Washington, Mgr Sebastianni Martinelli, to settle the matter. Abbé Brouillet, "who likes to create a brouhaha," as Labrecque put it, continued to make slanderous comments and tried in every way to prevent the young community from keeping its orphanage in Worcester. The nuns could, however, count on the support of their first chaplain, Father Durocher, of their confessor, the Jesuit Darveni-Hugues Langlois, and of Abbé Fafard. The issue dragged on and was not settled until 7 Dec. 1897. Bishop Beaven accepted the nuns into his diocese, but they would have to turn their orphanage into a home for the elderly, since the Sisters of Charity of the Hôpital Général of Montreal were already taking care of orphans in Worcester.

After the death of Fafard on 12 Aug. 1899, Mother Marie-Anne-de-Jésus showed the strength of her personality. It was she who completed the extensive projects begun by the founder of the hospice. Taking charge of the construction required by the expansion of the work with the insane, she also undertook the building of the mother house in Baie-Saint-Paul, and negotiated a series of contracts with the government. She managed the community's farm and the electrical company that serviced the hospice, its outbuildings, and the village. As well, she directed the organization of fund-raising appeals and celebrations and the improvement in services to the mentally ill, and she planned the expansion of the community, including the opening of five schools in New England. Her keen intelligence, administrative skill, and bold faith won her the admiration of religious and lay leaders alike. In 1908 the Hospice Sainte-Anne was home to 105 patients (epileptics, idiots, and those "lacking human feelings"), 39 elderly persons, 20 private boarders, and 79 nuns. Of the more than 100 people in the community, only six were laity, and the nuns were regularly called on for such heavy labour as piling bricks, repairing mortar, painting walls and porches, digging potatoes, and crushing flax.

In 1908 Mother Marie-Anne-de-Jésus asked to be relieved of her responsibilities as superior general because of failing health. From then on she played a much less visible role. Her talents as a healer, her marvellous recipes for sweets, and her compassion for her parishioners were highly praised. In 1920 she accepted the office of procurator general (or bursar), which she relinquished in 1923 for reasons of health. She died on 30 April 1924; her last words, according to the superior general, Marie-Claire-d'Assise, were: "I see absolutely nothing in my life that can be considered a work of charity."

For nearly 20 years, however, Mother Marie-Anne-de-Jésus had found her life taken up by the difficult task of managing a Franciscan community. Working with the American founder, Mother Marie-Joseph, as her chief associate in this venture, she was the Canadian founder and carried out the most difficult negotiations.

MICHELINE DUMONT

ANQ-M, CE603-S7, 10 oct. 1865. Arch. des Petites Franciscaines de Marie (Baie-Saint-Paul, Qué.), Album-souvenir des noces d'argent de l'hospice Sainte-Anne; Annales de la fondation de la communauté; Dossier personnel de mère Marie-Anne-de-Jésus. Michelle Garceau, *Par ce signe tu vivras: histoire de la congrégation des Petites Franciscaines de Marie (1889–1955)* (4ᵉ éd., Baie-Saint-Paul, 1989). Marguerite Jean, *Évolution des communautés religieuses de femmes au Canada de 1639 à nos jours* (Montréal, 1977), 121–24. Petites Franciscaines de Marie, *Notice sur l'Institut des Petites Franciscaines de Marie* (Baie-Saint-Paul, 1916; 2ᵉ éd., 1927). Margaret Porter, *Mille en moins: histoire du centre hospitalier de Charlevoix (1889–1980)* (Baie-Saint-Paul, 1984).

BICKERDIKE, ROBERT, businessman, politician, and social reformer; b. 17 Aug. 1843 in Kingston, Upper Canada, son of Thomas Bickerdike, a farmer,

Bickerdike

and Agnes Forster Cowan; m. 4 Dec. 1866 Helen Thomson Reid (d. 1907) in Montreal, and they had at least three sons and six daughters; d. 28 Dec. 1928 in Lachine, Que.

Robert Bickerdike's ancestors, of Norman descent, hailed from one of the oldest families in England, the de Bickers, who had settled in Yorkshire late in the 11th century. In memory of Robert Bickerdike, who was executed for his Roman Catholic faith in 1585, the eldest son of every branch of the Bickerdike family was named Robert.

Born in Berkshire, Thomas Bickerdike, the youngest son of a Protestant branch of the family, had arrived in the Canadas by 1820. He left Upper Canada in the late 1840s and moved to Saint-Louis-de-Gonzague, in Beauharnois county, Lower Canada, where he purchased a small farm. His son Robert was educated in the village of Beauharnois and probably became fluent in French at that time. He worked on the family farm until age 17 and then moved to Montreal, where he became a butcher. Sometime in the mid 1860s he started a pork-packing business. In June 1875 he formed a partnership with Duncan McCormick as the Robert Bickerdike Company, pork butchers and packers in Saint-Henri (Montreal) and shortly afterwards he moved to that town. The following year he entered the livestock export trade, which was just getting under way; he would eventually become one of the most successful cattle exporters in Canada.

In 1881 Bickerdike organized the Dominion Abattoir and Stock Yards Company Limited in Saint-Henri with butchers Edward Charters, William Morgan, and Robert Nicholson, leather manufacturer Pierre Claude, soap and oil maker William Strachan, and cattle dealer Robert J. Hopper. The firm had an authorized capital of $200,000. Bickerdike was its managing director. To protect his growing investments, he branched out into insurance, founding the Live Stock Insurance Company in 1884; he would act as its president in 1898. By the mid 1880s, in addition to running his abattoir and cattle export business, he was acting as an insurance and shipping agent. During this decade he also served as a cattle inspector for various insurance companies. In 1887 he was secretary of the Dominion Livestock Association.

In 1892 the cattle export trade was severely disrupted by a British embargo on Canadian livestock which originated with the discovery of diseased cattle. Bickerdike vigorously objected to the embargo and on several occasions asked the British Board of Agriculture to lift it. He insisted that the Canadian cattle were not diseased and that the British were using the embargo as a pretext to protect their domestic trade from competition. Concerned that the dispute would threaten the broader trade relationship between Canada and Great Britain, he cautioned the British against looking to France and the United States as alternative trading partners. The embargo would still be in effect in 1912.

In 1893 Dominion Abattoir was reorganized. With the exception of Bickerdike, the original partners left and were replaced by cattle exporter Louis Delorme and accountant Wellington E. Bell. The firm's capital, now $250,000, could be expanded to $1,000,000 and the company obtained the right to issue bonds, acquire other firms, and construct waterworks. Seven years later it was renamed Robert Bickerdike and Company Limited. Meanwhile, Bickerdike's involvement in insurance became an increasingly important part of his business activities. He was appointed branch manager of the Western Assurance Company, a general insurance company, in 1900 and he would continue with this firm until 1924. In addition he acted as branch manager for the Quebec Fire Assurance Company in 1900 and 1901, and would serve in the same capacity for the Union Marine Insurance Company of Halifax, Nova Scotia from 1901 to 1912. In 1910 he began to appear on the boards of various insurance companies; he served as a director of several well-known firms, including the Canada Life Assurance Company from at least 1912 to 1917.

Bickerdike had left the cattle export trade in 1911. He would continue alone in Robert Bickerdike and Company in insurance and finance until 1919. His knowledge of finance had led him to serve from 1891 to 1911 as vice-president of the Banque d'Hochelaga. In 1911, with Conservative MP Rodolphe Forget*, he founded the Banque Internationale du Canada, an institution which focused on attracting investment from France. Over a year later tension between French and Canadian investors brought the institution to bankruptcy.

Active in a wide range of businesses, Bickerdike had been a founder in 1892 of the St Henri Light and Power Company (renamed the Standard Light and Power Company the following year) and he served as its president from at least 1898 to 1905. He presided over the Montreal and Great Lakes Steamship Company from about 1909 to 1912 and the Canada Securities Corporation from 1910 to 1914. He was a director of numerous firms, including the Marconi Wireless Telegraph Company of Canada Limited from about 1909 to 1917.

An important contributor to Montreal's rise as the dominant Canadian urban centre in the early 20th century, Bickerdike had been president of the Montreal Board of Trade in 1896. A member of the Montreal Harbour Commission from 1896 to 1906, he served for a time as acting chairman. He invested much time and energy in building up the harbour and as an MP he defended its interests in the House of Commons. Bickerdike pier remains a lasting monument to his important contributions.

While a resident of Saint-Henri, Bickerdike had sat

for a few months in 1875 on its town council. His principal foray into municipal politics, as pro-mayor of Summerlea (Lachine), took place in 1895–96, soon after he moved there. He departed from his family's long-standing affiliation with the Conservatives and entered provincial politics in 1897 as a Liberal, winning in Montreal, Division No.5. In 1900 he began a 17-year stint in federal politics. He was easily elected under the Liberal banner for St Lawrence, a Montreal riding with a large French Roman Catholic population and a smaller Jewish one. As a politician, he was best known for his stand on important social issues, but his parliamentary record also includes several short speeches aimed at furthering economic interests closely related to his business endeavours, including the cattle export trade. A man the *Ottawa Citizen* once described as a "pillar" of the Liberal party, he sat in the house through much of Sir Wilfrid Laurier*'s tenure as prime minister. Although he was a lifelong friend of Laurier, he broke with his leader during World War I over Laurier's position against conscription. His letter of resignation in 1917 mentioned the military service of his sons and grandsons.

Most noteworthy were the positions Bickerdike took as a politician on some of the dominant social and cultural issues of the early 20th century. A champion of the linguistic and confessional rights of minorities, he once referred to Quebec as a model with regard to its treatment of the English Protestant minority. A member of the Protestant committee of the Council of Public Instruction from 1911 to 1923, he felt that Quebec's record vis-à-vis its minorities was particularly strong with regard to schooling. In 1905, on the controversial question of linguistic and confessional school rights for the French Catholic communities in the newly created provinces of Alberta and Saskatchewan [*see* Laurier], he had pleaded in favour of the minorities. He warned against those who sought to promote conflict in order to gain political advantage.

A Presbyterian of unquestionable faith, Bickerdike represented a federal riding with an important Jewish electorate and he enjoyed referring to himself as the Jewish representative in the house. In 1906 he challenged the prevalent thought that only Sunday, the Christian day of rest, should be respected. While other MPs contended that Jews were merely guests in a Christian society and therefore subordinate to the religion of the majority, Bickerdike defended their liberty to observe a different sabbath. Jews, he told his peers, deserved equal respect in practising their religion and should therefore be allowed to close their businesses on Saturday and open them on Sunday.

Throughout his political career Bickerdike demanded equal rights for all citizens regardless of denomination. In 1910 he moved that the protection provided to young Protestants and Catholics under the Juvenile Delinquents Act of 1908 be extended to include all others, especially Jews. On another occasion, he expressed concern that denominational quotas might be used in educational institutions in Canada. In 1912 he proposed to have removed from Queen's University's charter the reference to its "distinctively Christian" character and the requirement of "the profession of Christianity" for hiring purposes. In 1917 he urged that the vote be extended to "the loyal women of Canada" and that they receive the same political rights and privileges enjoyed by men. Over the course of his political career, Bickerdike was an outspoken supporter of the poor and the disenfranchised and a standard-bearer for liberal ideals. Many of his spirited speeches evinced righteous indignation at the prevailing attitudes and laws of the day. Whether pushing for prison reform, lobbying on behalf of religious minorities, or advocating the prohibition of cigarette sales to minors, he worked tirelessly.

For Bickerdike, the abolition of capital punishment was an imperative and to some extent his life's mission. Few spoke as loudly or as eloquently as he did for this reform. In 1914 and again in 1916 he introduced a bill to replace the death penalty with a life sentence. He opposed capital punishment on many grounds, considering it an insult to Christianity and religion in general and a blot on any civilized nation. "There is nothing," he stated in the house, "more degrading to society at large . . . than the death penalty." He also spoke of class disparities, pointing out that the punishment was administered to the poor far more often than to the wealthy. He refuted the notion that state-sponsored killing acted as a deterrent to murder and cautioned against the possibility of mistake. Though he never stopped fighting for this cause, he did not live to see it realized; capital punishment would not be abolished in Canada until 1976.

In private life Bickerdike was a founder and president of the National Prison Reform Association, established in 1916. Three years later it merged with the Honour League of Canada to become the Canadian Prisoners' Welfare Association. This body lobbied against capital punishment, helped care for prisoners' families, and sought employment for offenders following their release. Bickerdike would serve as honorary president until his death. In the commons he called attention to the awful conditions in Canadian penitentiaries. His strong Christian faith underpinned his demands for prison reform. In 1917, in the midst of World War I, he moved a resolution in the house to grant all prisoners the opportunity to enlist for active service, and thereby give them the opportunity to redeem themselves while aiding the cause of their country.

Bickerdike was a leader in community works. His contributions to hospital activities included service as governor of the Royal Victoria Hospital starting in 1896, as life governor of the Montreal General Hospital from 1898, and as both governor and president for a time of the Western Hospital of Montreal. He was president of the St George's Society in 1912. His interest in recording Canada's heritage led to his involvement in the Numismatic and Antiquarian Society of Montreal. Known for his personal generosity, he had established, according to an obituary, an "understanding with the minister of his church [in Lachine] that no one was to go hungry."

An invalid for the last three years of his life, Robert Bickerdike died on 28 Dec. 1928 at his home, Elmcroft, in Lachine. Although he never sought recognition, he was offered a knighthood for his support of the war effort. Before the honours list could appear, however, the House of Commons adopted a resolution in 1919 which temporarily ended the granting of titles to Canadians. He was remembered as someone with a great appetite for life and was universally admired for his unyielding integrity, generosity, and charity.

JACK JEDWAB

ANQ-M, CE601-S120, 4 déc. 1866; TP11, S2, SS20, SSS48, vol.6-o, 31 juill. 1875, no.450; vol.11-o, 15 juill. 1911, no.64; vol.17-o, 6 janv. 1919, no.1265; vol.21-o, 14 mai 1900, no.1087. LAC, MG 26, G. Gazette (Montreal), 29 Dec. 1928. R. C. Brown and Ramsay Cook, Canada, 1896–1921: a nation transformed (Toronto, 1974). Can., House of Commons, Debates, 1900–17; Parl., Sessional papers, 1891, no.7b. Canada Gazette, 26 Feb. 1881. Canadian men and women of the time (Morgan; 1898 and 1912). CPG, 1897–1917. Directory, Montreal, 1875–1917. DPQ. H. B. Neatby, Laurier and a Liberal Quebec; a study in political management, ed. R. T. Clippingdale (Toronto, 1973). Que., Statutes, 1893, c.79; 1900, c.80. Rumilly, Hist. de la prov. de Québec. The storied province of Quebec; past and present, ed. W. [C. H.] Wood et al. (5v., Toronto, 1931–32).

BIENVILLE, LOUYSE DE. See MARMETTE, MARIE-LOUISE

BILSKY, MOSES, merchant and communal leader; b. 10 Dec. 1829 in Kovno (Kaunas, Lithuania), son of Ely Bilsky; m. 1874 Pauline Reich in Brooklyn (New York City), and they had six sons and six daughters; d. 4 Jan. 1923 in Ottawa.

After Moses Bilsky arrived in the Canadas in 1843, he lived with his father in Montreal and then in Kemptville, Upper Canada. When Ely Bilsky went to Palestine – some accounts say he returned to Russia – Moses stayed with relatives in New York State. He moved to Ottawa in 1856 or 1857, the first Jew to locate there.

In 1862 he was in the Cariboo goldfields of British Columbia. Finding the lawlessness and cost of living there distasteful, and recognizing the small likelihood of success, he went to San Francisco, where, in the midst of the Civil War, he joined the Union forces. He

was wounded while attempting to quell rioting in that city following the assassination of Abraham Lincoln. After the war he was offered a mining job in South America, but once he landed in Panama he discovered that he had been hired to participate in gun-running to Mexico, in an attempt to overthrow Emperor Maximilian. Without funds for passage, he stowed away on a ship back to San Francisco.

By 1874 Bilsky was on the east coast, where he married Pauline Reich, a native of Berlin. They then resided in New York; their first child, Alexander, was born in the United States in 1876. The family soon moved to Ontario and lived in Kemptville, Mattawa, and then Ottawa, where in 1877 Bilsky opened a pawnshop. About 1901 he took Alexander into his second business, a watchmaking, jewellery, and optician's shop, forming M. Bilsky and Son Limited. During the interval the family spent some time away from Ottawa: they were in Mattawa from about 1882 to 1885 and in Montreal from 1885 to 1891.

The Bilsky residence on Nicholas Street became the centre of Jewish life in Ottawa. Immigrants found a ready welcome and Pauline would rise early to wash and mend their clothes, hoping to diminish their embarrassment over their limited belongings. On holy days, services were conducted, usually by Moses (who may have been illiterate in English). He acquired the city's first Torah, from New York, and in 1892 was instrumental in founding the first synagogue, Adath Jeshurun, beside his pawnshop. He also organized a chevra kadisha (burial society) and, in 1899, a Zionist society. In the larger community, he belonged to the masonic lodge in Kemptville and the Foresters in Montreal.

According to the Ottawa Evening Journal, Bilsky retired from business in 1915, at which point M. Bilsky and Son was reorganized as Bilsky Limited. Some members of his large family became prominent. His daughter Lillian* was active in national and international philanthropy; her husband, Archibald Jacob Freiman, established a department store in Ottawa and would serve as president of the Zionist Organization of Canada. Another son-in-law, Allan Bronfman* of Winnipeg and Montreal, was a lawyer, industrialist, and community activist.

Ottawa's regard for Moses Bilsky was demonstrated following his death in January 1923 at his home, then on Daly Avenue. The Ottawa Citizen, which announced his passing on its front page, described him as a man of "sterling worth and honesty" in business. Despite the extreme cold, his funeral was attended by a large crowd of all faiths, including Mayor Frank H. Plant and members of the city council, the provincial legislature, and the dominion parliament. After the King Edward Avenue Synagogue was filled, hundreds stood in the street. Bilsky's remains were taken into the sanctuary during the service, a rarity in Jewish practice and the first time such an honour had been granted in Ottawa.

STEPHEN A. SPEISMAN

AO, RG 80-2; 80-8-0-915, no.9448. BCA, GR-0216, vols.34–35. LAC, RG 31, C1, 1901, Ottawa, St Nicholas Ward, div.3: 22 (mfm. at AO). *Ottawa Citizen*, 6 Jan. 1923. *Ottawa Evening Journal*, 5 Jan. 1923. *Yiddisher Zhurnal/ Daily Hebrew Journal* (Toronto), 8 Jan. 1923. *Canadian Jewry, prominent Jews of Canada . . .* , ed. Zvi Cohen (Toronto, [1933]). *Directory*, Ottawa, 1878–1901. Bernard Figler, *Lillian and Archie Freiman: biographies* (Montreal, 1962). *The Jew in Canada: a complete record of Canadian Jewry from the days of the French régime to the present time*, ed. A. D. Hart (Toronto and Montreal, 1926). Ontario Geneal. Soc., Ottawa branch, *The United Jewish Community Cemetery, concession IV, lot 7, Gloucester Township, Carleton County, Bank Street, Highway 31, Ottawa, Ontario* (Ottawa, 1997), sect.1: 1–2.

BIRGE, CYRUS ALBERT, merchant, accountant, and industrialist; b. 7 Nov. 1847 in Trafalgar Township, Upper Canada, son of Herman P. Birge and Helen M. Ainslie, farmers; m. first 30 Aug. 1870 Rebecca Jane Coote (d. 1898) in Oakville, Ont., and they had a son and a daughter; m. secondly 19 Feb. 1902 Margaret Vanstone (d. 1904) in Wingham, Ont., and they had a son; m. thirdly 1908 Mabel I. Sturt of Brooklyn (New York City); d. 14 Dec. 1929 in Hamilton, Ont.

Cyrus Birge's father came from Hartford, Conn., about 1840 and settled in the Oakville area; in 1842 he married Helen Ainslie of nearby Nelson Township. Despite his father's death in 1855, Cyrus was able to spend several years at local schools, including the Oakville Grammar School. At age 18 he started to learn the dry-goods business but three years later he decided to enrol in medicine at Victoria College in Cobourg. After only a year, ill health prompted him to return to Oakville, where he worked for a dry-goods merchant. He opened his own grocery store in Stratford in 1870, and then one in Chatham. Two years later he joined the Great Western Railway as an accountant in its engineering department. Initially he worked in Hamilton but he also spent some time in London. In 1882 he left to become manager of the Canada Screw Company, a financially troubled firm in Dundas that had been purchased in 1876 by the American Screw Company of Providence, R.I. Birge put the firm back on its feet. As part of the trend to use female labour in factories, it hired young women to run new American screw-making machinery. In 1883 Birge formed a partnership with American industrialist Charles Alexander to operate the factory, which was coaxed with tax incentives to move to Hamilton in 1887. Birge was vice-president and managing director from 1883 to 1898, when he bought out the American investors and became president. In 1907 his company merged with another large Hamilton operation, the Ontario Tack Company, which had also been started by American investors. The new company, which kept the name Canada Screw and Birge as president, moved to a large, technologically sophisticated plant in Hamilton's growing industrial east end.

Birge's interest in the iron industry had already brought him into another important project. In 1895 he and a group of other local businessmen, including Andrew Trew Wood*, William Southam*, John Henry Tilden, and John MILNE, established the Hamilton Blast Furnace Company Limited to take over the smelting operations of the Hamilton Iron and Steel Company Limited, which had been incorporated in 1893 but had been hit by extreme depression in the iron trade. Birge served on the board of Hamilton Blast Furnace until a union in 1899 with the Ontario Rolling Mills Company, also of Hamilton, created the Hamilton Steel and Iron Company Limited. In 1910 a much larger merger brought together iron and steel plants across central Canada (Birge's Canada Screw, Hamilton Steel and Iron, Montreal Rolling Mills, Canada Bolt and Nut of Toronto) to create the Canadian Steel Corporation Limited. Immediately renamed the Steel Company of Canada Limited [*see* Wilmot Deloui Matthews*], it would eventually include Dominion Wire Manufacturing of Montreal as well. Though Birge was close to retirement, he had participated in the negotiations and his substantial capital in the new venture brought him the position of vice-president. However, he took no active part in the new firm's operations, which were left largely in the hands of Robert HOBSON.

By this point Birge had become a respected member of the Hamilton business community. The Bank of Hamilton made him a director in 1904, vice-president in 1914, and president in 1923, the year it merged with the Canadian Bank of Commerce. He was then added to its board of directors. As president of the local Mercantile Trust Company, he presided over its merger with National Trust a year later. In the tight network of overlapping directorships in Hamilton industries, Birge had also joined the boards of several other firms, including Sawyer-Massey in 1910, Hamilton Stove and Heater (as vice-president) in 1913, and Dominion Power and Transmission (as vice-president) in 1916. Like several other local businessmen, he had connections and investments that extended beyond Hamilton. He was president of Sovereign Fire Insurance, vice-president of Turbine Steamship, and a director of British American Oil, Chinook Coal, and Lake of the Woods Milling. As befitted such involvement, he was a member of the boards of trade of both Hamilton and Toronto, and in 1903 he was a Canadian delegate to the Fifth Congress of Chambers of Commerce of the Empire in Montreal.

Brusque and opinionated, Birge had also taken a leadership role in the broader business community. He had been a member of the Canadian Manufacturers' Association for some 20 years and an executive member before the association undertook a complete reorganization in 1900 to make it a more effective lobbying force. Birge must have played a prominent role in this reconstruction since he was chosen as vice-president for Ontario in 1900, national vice-president in 1901, and president in 1902. In these capacities he was expected to promote the interests of manufacturers in the all-important areas of tariff, transportation policy, and industrial relations. During his term as president the CMA followed the recommendation of a special committee and struck a vigorous anti-union stance, specifically directed against any pro-labour legislation. In his presidential address of 1903 Birge proclaimed that the employer "must be free to purchase without interference such labor as he requires" and attacked the growing links between Canadian unions and their American counterparts. In subsequent years, he served on the CMA's important tariff committee. When a branch of the CMA was organized in Hamilton in 1909, he joined its executive, and in 1912–13 he served as chair.

Birge was a staunch Methodist who believed that a business leader should take an active role in the organizational life of his church. At Hamilton's Wesley Methodist Church, he was Sunday school superintendent for 17 years and a steward and trustee for 28. He also attended the General Conference of the Methodist Church of Canada and served on its church union committee. Yet he became uncomfortable with the progressive Social Gospel movement that was percolating through this church early in the 20th century. At the General Conference of October 1918, in Hamilton, he was one of only four delegates to oppose a report calling for the shift of economic life "from a basis of competition and profits to one of co-operation and service." He was more comfortable with paternalistic charity. In 1907 he had donated $50,000 to Victoria University in Toronto to match the sum American industrialist Andrew Carnegie had provided to endow its library. In 1915 he became chair of Hamilton's branch of the Canadian Patriotic Fund, set up to provide for wives and children of men serving in the armed forces, and he later sat on the organization's national executive.

Birge belonged to two mass-membership fraternal societies, the Oddfellows and the Ancient Order United Workmen, but his wealth and powerful connections gave him access to a more exclusive world of private recreation. With other upper-class men, he retired to the Hamilton, National, and Toronto clubs; for outdoor sports, he frequented the Caledon Mountain Trout, the Tamahaac, and the Hamilton Golf and Country clubs. He died suddenly on 14 Dec. 1929.

Cyrus Birge had risen from relatively modest rural roots to prominence in southern Ontario business circles. His success no doubt rested on managerial skills learned inside a large railway corporation, entrepreneurial abilities acquired in the late-19th-century wave of industrialization, and participation in the collaborative projects of fellow capitalists in Hamilton who marshalled the resources needed to create mass production. In this new era, Birge became a more passive, but still respected investor, whose great wealth brought him onto many corporate boards and whose Methodist faith propelled him toward a life of public service.

CRAIG HERON

AO, RG 80-5-0-7, liber 6, f.108; RG 80-5-0-302, no.9193. LAC, MG 28, I 230, 16: 1909–10, 1912–13. *Hamilton Spectator* (Hamilton, Ont.), 14 Nov., 14 Dec. 1895; 14 Dec. 1929. Richard Allen, *The social passion: religion and social reform in Canada, 1914–28* (Toronto, 1971; repr. 1990). *Annual financial rev.* (Toronto and Montreal), 1904: 54; 1908: 60; 1910: 26; 1914: 98; 1916: 404; 1923: 114. Can., *Statutes*, 1896, c.48. *Canada Gazette*, 11 June 1910: 3900; 25 June 1910: 4129. *Canadian annual rev.*, 1902–28/29. *Canadian Engineer* (Toronto and Montreal), 7 (1899–1900): 141. *Canadian history makers . . .* (Montreal, 1913). *Canadian Machinery and Manufacturing News* (Toronto), 11 (January–June 1914): 92. *Canadian men and women of the time* (Morgan; 1912). *Canadian Mining Rev.* (Ottawa), 14 (1895): 82. Canadian Patriotic Fund, Hamilton and Wentworth Branch, *Five years of service, 1914–1918* ([Hamilton?, 1920?]). S. D. Clark, *The Canadian Manufacturers' Association: a study in collective bargaining and political pressure* (Toronto, 1939). *Directory of directors* (London, Eng.), 1912, pt.I, 25. *Encyclopaedia of Canadian biography . . .*, vol.2. *Industrial Canada* (Toronto), 4 (1903–4): 111; 5 (1904–5): 328; 6 (1905–6): 204–6; 7 (1906–7): 266–68. *Iron Age* (New York), 61 (January–June 1898): 12. William Kilbourn, *The elements combined: a history of the Steel Company of Canada* (Toronto and Vancouver, 1960), 42–43, 59, 71–73, 75. *Newspaper reference book*. Ont., *Statutes*, 1895, c.67; 1896, c.80. Victor Ross and A. St L. Trigge, *A history of the Canadian Bank of Commerce, with an account of the other banks which now form part of its organization* (3v., Toronto, 1920–34), 3. *Who's who and why*, 1921.

BIRKS, HENRY, businessman specializing in the sale of gold and silver articles, and philanthropist; b. 30 Nov. 1840 in Montreal, son of John Birks, a pharmacist, and Ann Massie; m. 16 Jan. 1868 Harriet Phillips Walker in Toronto, and they had three sons; d. 16 April 1928 in Montreal.

Henry Birks's parents were from Barnsley, in Yorkshire, England, and they immigrated to Canada in 1832. Before leaving, John Birks had signed a contract to work for a firm in Montreal, where he soon opened a pharmacy.

Henry took commercial studies at the High School of Montreal, which he completed in 1856. He then spent a winter in Rivière-du-Loup (Louiseville) with notary Jean-Baptiste-Arthur Chamberland in order to learn French. On 22 April 1857 he began working as a clerk for Joseph Savage and Theodore Lyman, whose jewellery store on Rue Notre-Dame in Montreal was considered the finest of its kind in Canada. Birks is believed to have met Lyman earlier, when he attended Sunday school at the Congregational Church and was taught by him. A founding member of the Young Men's Christian Association in Montreal [see Alfred Sandham*], Lyman must surely have interested the young man in this cause, since Birks would contribute $25,000 to the YMCA in 1909. Birks became a partner in Savage and Lyman's company in 1868. Unfortunately, the depression of 1873 hit the firm head on, and it was forced into bankruptcy in 1878, a year after Birks had left it. The assignee put him in charge of liquidating the assets.

Around 27 Feb. 1879, with a capital of $3,000, Birks opened a small shop of the same kind at 222 Rue Saint-Jacques, in the heart of the city's business section. His enterprise was called Henry Birks and Company and he immediately instituted new business practices for customers: cash sales only and the same price for everyone. During its first year the store had a turnover of $30,000. This figure increased by 25 per cent over the next four years and in 1885 Birks moved to larger quarters at 232 Rue Saint-Jacques. In 1893, with annual sales 500 per cent higher than those of his first year, he went into partnership with his three sons, William Massey, John Henry, and Gerald Walker as Henry Birks and Sons. The first notable result of this partnership came the following year, when the store was installed in new premises on Phillips square, at the corner of Rue Sainte-Catherine and Avenue Union [see Edward MAXWELL]. In moving, the business was following the development of the city, since at that time Rue Sainte-Catherine was becoming its main commercial artery. A little later a period of expansion outside Montreal would begin.

The Birks firm started as a gift shop that specialized in retail sales of jewellery, gold and silver pieces, and clocks, advertising articles in silver plate as well as sterling silver. A workshop to make jewellery was opened over the store in 1887. The following year an "artistic department" sold articles made in European workshops but purchased from American suppliers. The company also bought supplies on the local market. On 17 Feb. 1896, for instance, John Leslie, the administrator of the large silverware manufacturer Hendery and Leslie, signed an agreement with the Birks company making it the exclusive distributor for the city of Montreal of its non-religious gold and silver articles, with the exception of commemorative spoons. Henry Birks and Sons also published its first

annual catalogue in 1896. The next year the company purchased Hendery and Leslie, along with its designs, equipment, and labour force. Thereafter the company founded by Birks produced its own merchandise and hence exercised stricter control over what it sold. At the same time, it also stated its intention to specialize in gold and silver. From then on the volume of business increased and the sales network expanded. Noticing that a large number of mail orders came from Ottawa, in 1901 the company opened a store there, its first outside Montreal. This move would be repeated many times, and before World War II the company would in effect enjoy a monopoly over the market for gold and silver articles in Canada. It secured this control by purchasing numerous stores and companies across the country (in Ottawa in 1902 and 1911, Winnipeg in 1903 and 1913, Toronto in 1905, Vancouver in 1906, Montreal in 1907, Halifax in 1919, and Calgary in 1920) and opening branches in Canada and abroad (in London in 1925 and Antwerp in 1929).

Henry Birks belonged to a particular group of Canadians in the second half of the 19th century, and in a sense he was their prototype. The son of immigrants, he acquired an education focused mainly on commerce, and then proceeded to put it into practice by working in a large firm. As soon as circumstances permitted, he started his own company, which continued to prosper until it became a Canada-wide empire. The story of the founding and evolution of the Birks company shows the radical change that took place in the gold and silver trade at the time. Obviously, Birks did not work with hammer and anvil. He started out in business by obtaining supplies from various manufacturers and went on to integrate production into his own firm by buying out his main supplier. He and his sons gave the Canadian gold and silver business a specifically industrial base. The artist had made way for the entrepreneur.

RENÉ VILLENEUVE

Between 1936 and 1979 Henry Birks's grandson Henry Gifford Birks amassed a vast collection of Canadian silverware. This collection, which was donated to the National Gallery of Canada on 1 Dec. 1979, is the principal record of the output of Henry Birks and Company, Henry Birks and Sons, and Henry Birks and Sons Limited, and of its predecessors and suppliers.

ANQ-M, CE601-S95, 20 juin 1841. AO, RG 80-27-2, 67: 55. Musée National des Beaux-Arts du Québec (Québec), Fonds Gérard-Morisset, dossier Birks, Henry and Sons. *Gazette* (Montreal), 17 April 1928. *La Minerve*, 28 févr., 5 août, 10 sept., 11 déc. 1879; 4 déc. 1888. Henry Birks and Sons, *Catalogue* ([Montreal?, 1913?]); *Catalogue, 1906: the gold and silversmiths, diamond merchants* (Toronto, 1906). R. [A. C.] Fox, *Presentation pieces and trophies from the Henry Birks Collection of Canadian Silver* (exhibition catalogue, National Gallery of Canada, Ottawa, 1985). A. R.

Blackburn

George, *The house of Birks* ([Montreal?], 1946). J. E. Langdon, *Canadian silversmiths, 1700–1900* (Toronto, 1966). K. O. MacLeod, *The first century: the story of a Canadian company* (Montreal, 1979). T. D. Nanavati, "Nineteenth century Canadian presentation silver" (MA thesis, Univ. of Toronto, 1977). Ryrie-Birks Limited, *The romance of the silver craft* (Toronto, 1925). Ryrie Bros, *Diamond merchants, jewellers and silversmiths, 1917* (Toronto, 1917). Ramsay Traquair, *The old silver of Quebec* (Toronto, 1940). René Villeneuve, *Quebec silver from the collection of the National Gallery of Canada* (exhibition catalogue, Ottawa, 1998).

BLACKBURN, VICTORIA GRACE, journalist and author; b. 17 April 1865 at Quebec, fifth daughter of Josiah Blackburn* and Emma Jane Delamere; d. unmarried 4 March 1928 in London, Ont.

Grace Blackburn was born in Quebec City, possibly when her father, the publisher of the *London Free Press*, was there on political or newspaper business. After schooling in Hellmuth Ladies' College in London, she taught in the United States in the 1890s. She had begun writing in 1894 for the *Free Press*, then under the direction of her brother Walter Josiah, and in 1900 she became its literary and drama critic. She spent some time in New York studying criticism and in 1906–10 was in Europe with her sisters, immersing herself in cultural affairs. In 1918 she assumed the position of assistant managing editor, which she would hold until 1928. For three decades she was a leading figure in the cultural life of London. Her manner of commentary ranged from imperiousness, which she could turn on London (a city that "has not believed sufficiently in herself"), to firm appreciation, of such masterworks as Romney's paintings of Emma Hart, Wordsworth's poetry, and Venice's ducal palace.

Although nepotism can be reasonably inferred from Blackburn's career at the *Free Press* – her sister Susan May was also a staffer and a shareholder – a fair assessment of her output (often under the name Fanfan) would have to acknowledge her productivity and intellectualism. In addition to her criticism, she contributed essays, travelogues, editorials, and poems. The demands of daily journalism imposed some limits on her literary effort and gave occasion to such awkward items in the *Free Press* as her approving (but now embarrassing) description of Helen Keller in 1913 as the "High Priestess of the Blind" and her farewell in 1924 to Middlesex County writer Peter Gilchrist McARTHUR as "a son of the soil and a gentleman; such a gentleman as perhaps only a son of the soil can be. The immediate soil of which he was the son, is the soil of Canada." In a later account of Blackburn, Professor James Albert Spenceley of London credits her with stronger literary and lyrical sensibilities.

Blackburn produced, in addition to her work for the *Free Press*, dozens of poems, two known plays, and a novel. From her verse, some of it superficial, certain typical devices and themes emerge: sudden shifts from satire to tragedy, a gift for aphorisms, and a fondness for archaic language, exotic locales (Renaissance France for example), tortured aesthetes, and doomed love. Her two one-act plays, preserved in the University of Western Ontario Archives, are "Seal of confession," a drama set in a priest's home in France, and "The little gray," a farce set in a New York dress shop. The former explores Blackburn's motif of noble self-sacrifice; the latter shows her love of dialect, humour, and satire aimed at her own class; both are full of clumsy staging.

Blackburn's writing about World War I is superior to her other work. In "Christ in Flanders," one of the four poems by her included in John William Garvin*'s *Canadian poems of the Great War* (Toronto, 1918), the wounds of a female survivor resemble those of the crucified Christ. Her most successful endeavour, posthumously published, is *The man child* (Ottawa, 1930), which deserves renewed attention. Written about 1916, it begins in a fictionalized version of London and area during the 1890s and moves to the trenches of France, where the young Canadian hero, Jack Winchester, will be killed. Like many Canadian novels on the war, it explores the "right stuff" among volunteers and, resorting to popular symbolism, likens Canada to David fighting the Teutonic Goliath. The novel gathers force as the trials and triumphs of Jack's widowed mother give way to the imminence of conflict. Blackburn's love of drama is apparent in the way her characters articulate different points of view over the gathering storm. Striking too is the realization that her most intelligent characters appear, at first, appalled at the thought of England fighting its natural ally, Germany, and siding with dissolute France. Once the war begins, Jack and a friend leave medical school, whose dean plays a role in the story, to enlist. When the novel shifts to an epistolary mode, Jack's friend sends a letter home asking, "Do you remember that poem of Walt Whitman's the Dean is so fond of," and quoting from Whitman's "The compost." This may have been unusual content for a letter from the front but not for a novel set in London (where Richard Maurice Bucke*'s enthusiasm for Whitman was well known) and written by Blackburn (who gave a paper in 1916 comparing Whitman to Rodin). Following a scene with the two youths lost and under fire in No Man's Land, the closing line ("What rites! What obsequies!") sounds a Whitmanesque note. One of Blackburn's great friends, fellow Anglican and poet Robert Winkworth Norwood*, appears in the novel thinly disguised as the Reverend Norman Brooks. Like him, Norwood, the rector of Cronyn Memorial Church in London from 1912 to 1917, was a modern thinker and dynamic preacher who saw the war as an opportunity for everlasting peace.

Grace Blackburn's determination to honour Canada's war dead led her to support the proposed erection near London of a monument of perpetual light. Although her backing was not sufficient to raise the $10,000 it would have cost, she was involved in a more modest memorial completed in 1926. Tall, charming, and full of humour, she was active in London's theatre and many clubs and associations; she was a founder in 1910 of the local Women's Canadian Club and its president in 1918–19, and in 1921–23 she served as president of the London Women's Press Club. It is difficult from a modern viewpoint not to feel some scepticism about the grand claims made for Blackburn in her lifetime, but her intellect and commentary were much lauded. In 1916 J. W. Garvin praised her in an anthology as "a writer with a large brain and a big, warm heart: a twentieth century thinker, with the individuality of original thought and expression; a poet just beginning to realize her gift." In 1924 novelist Arthur John Arbuthnott Stringer recognized her sharp critical sense. Such approval continued after her death. In December 1930 the *London Advertiser* (owned by the Blackburns from 1926) quoted the estimate of *Canadian Homes and Gardens* (Toronto) that *The man child* was "a very beautiful contribution to Canadian literature and perhaps to literature generally."

One of the few traces of Blackburn's contributions in London is the historical plaque outside the home at 652 Talbot Street where she lived for 16 years with three of her sisters. As a Canadian woman in the early 20th-century newspaper business who produced one good, interesting novel and had a strong command of vocabulary, Grace Blackburn may find new friends in this century.

JAMES STEWART REANEY

Victoria Grace Blackburn is the author of *Fanfan's poetry (the collected poetical works of Victoria Grace Blackburn)*, ed. E. H. Jones (London, Ont., 1967).

AO, RG 22-321, no.18961. St Paul's Anglican Cathedral (London), RBMB. Univ. of Western Ont. Arch., J. J. Talman Regional Coll. (London), Blackburn fonds, writings of Victoria Grace Blackburn. *London Advertiser*, 20 Dec. 1930. *London Free Press*, 22 Feb. 1913, 29 Oct. 1924, 3 Feb. 2002. *Canadian poets*, ed. J. W. Garvin (Toronto, 1916), 383–88. Nancy Geddes Poole, *The art of London, 1830–1980* (London, 1984). M. L. Lang, *Women who made the news: female journalists in Canada, 1880–1945* (Montreal and Kingston, Ont., 1999). Flora MacDonald [Merrill (Denison)], "Miss Grace Blackburn," *Sunset of Bon Echo* (Toronto), 1 (March 1916–April/May 1920), no.3: 19. Michael Nolan, *Walter J. Blackburn, a man for all media* (Toronto, 1989). *Standard dict. of Canadian biog.* (Roberts and Tunnell). F. B. Ware, *History of Cronyn Memorial Church, London, Ontario, 1873–1949* ([St Thomas, Ont., 1949]). *Who's who in Canada*, 1922.

BLACKSTOCK, GEORGE TATE, lawyer; b. 1 April 1856 in Newcastle, Upper Canada, son of William Schenck Blackstock and Mary Hodge Gibbs; m. 25 Feb. 1880 Emiline (Emma) Moulton Fraser in Bay City, Mich., and they had two sons and a daughter; d. 27 Dec. 1921 in Toronto.

George Tate Blackstock's childhood was marked by hardship and uncertainty. His father was a Wesleyan Methodist minister of Scottish-Irish descent, and for many years the family led a migratory life on the ministerial circuit. Despite frugal domestic management, they often struggled, living on credit and accepting food and other commodities in lieu of salary, which many poorer communities could not afford. Sometimes the children stayed with relatives of their mother, a member of a prominent family in Oshawa, Ont. A knowledge of the Bible, Shakespeare, and classical literature was assiduously cultivated by William Blackstock in his children. Following the Blackstocks' move to Goderich, George briefly attended grammar school there. Largely owing to his mother's inheritance and the assistance of her family, in 1871 he was admitted to Upper Canada College in Toronto, where he studied rhetoric. Intent on a career in law, he entered Osgoode Hall in 1874 and graduated four years later.

Called to the bar in 1879, Blackstock worked initially with the Toronto firm of Rose, Macdonald, and Merritt, and rapidly established a reputation as an accomplished civil lawyer. Said to have possessed a commanding physical presence in the courtroom, he was described as "a dark-haired, good looking fellow, with an easy and friendly gift of conversation and an entire freedom from restraint or nervousness on social occasions." In 1880–81 he lectured at Osgoode Hall on the Statute of Frauds as part of a series organized by the school's Legal and Literary Society. He joined Wells, Gordon, and Sampson in 1882 but soon left to open his own practice, where he would handle both civil and criminal litigation. As counsel for the Canadian Pacific Railway between 1881 and 1894, he participated in the arbitration proceedings between the railway and the dominion government in connection with western development. One of the first trustees of the York County Law Association in 1885, on 2 Dec. 1889 he was appointed a federal QC. In 1890 his skilful, though unsuccessful defence of Reginald Birchall* in a sensational murder trial considerably enhanced his standing as a pre-eminent trial lawyer.

In 1892 Blackstock joined Beatty, Blackstock, Nesbitt, and Chadwick, a firm that was strongly rooted in Toronto's Conservative establishment, and where his brother, Thomas Gibbs Blackstock, and David FASKEN were both successful corporate lawyers. As one of the first partners with a barrister's practice, George helped establish its reputation in litigation. Blackstock was secured for many important actions, both as a defence counsel and as a crown prosecutor. He was involved in two high-profile cases of alleged combines: in 1909 he unsuccessfully prosecuted the Dominion Wholesale Grocers' Guild, which he denounced as "an iron heel on the neck of the people," and in 1913 he found insufficient evidence to prosecute the Stamped Ware Association, which included the firm of John MCCLARY. One of his most notable moments as a crown counsel occurred in Hamilton in 1909 during the inquest into the murder of Ethel Caroline Kinrade, which aroused intense national coverage in the media. The chief witness, the victim's sister, was subjected to a gruelling cross-examination by Blackstock that was dramatically punctuated by her fainting after he had implicated her in the crime. Upon returning from one of his annual trips to England in May 1913, Blackstock and four other lawyers left Beatty Blackstock to form a new firm, Blackstock, Galt, and Gooderham.

A Conservative and passionate advocate of imperial unity, Blackstock had been encouraged to enter politics by his uncles Thomas Nicholson Gibbs* and William Henry Gibbs, both of whom served in the government of Sir John A. Macdonald*. During the 1880s Blackstock and Macdonald corresponded on a variety of issues; on three occasions, for example, Blackstock interceded unsuccessfully on behalf of William Albert Reeve* for a judgeship in Manitoba. He was returned in neither of the constituencies in which he ran: the provincial seat of Lennox (1884, 1885) and the federal riding of Durham West (1887, 1891). Macdonald's death and the decline of the party seem to have put an end to his ambitions, though he remained active on party committees and distinguished himself as a tireless campaigner for the Conservative cause.

Blackstock was renowned for his eloquence and wit as an orator and was frequently invited to banquets, political rallies, and prominent society gatherings in Canada, Britain, and the United States. "I am feted everywhere," he wrote from New York in 1903, "dinners and luncheons all the time. . . . They all say I am the best known private foreigner in the U.S." His speeches and articles in the press, generally on political themes, were widely quoted. Addressing the Canadian Manufacturers' Association in September 1907, he appealed for "a loftier conception of Imperial duty" and criticized Canada's poor contribution to the maintenance of the British armed forces and the burdens of empire. A speech to the Canadian Club in Toronto earlier the same month was hailed by *Saturday Night* as "the wittiest and most entertaining of the year and the one most direct in its appeal, which was for high ideals of Canadian citizenship and statesmanship." In March 1911 he founded, with Alexander Whyte Wright* and MLA Arthur Clarence Pratt, the Canadian branch of the Imperial Mission, an English association, and was elected its first president. The branch decided to promote imperial unity

by fighting against reciprocity, then being championed by the government of Sir Wilfrid Laurier*. Blackstock's reputation in England was prodigious; he had been in great demand as a speaker for the National Conservative Union during the British election of 1910, and he later declined several invitations to run for parliament.

Blackstock suffered illnesses that forced him on occasion to neglect his legal career, and these were complicated by his personal circumstances. In the 1890s he had become increasingly distraught over "domestic worries." He confided to a friend that "when waiting for his turn to address the court the perspiration would drop off his finger-ends." Medical specialists in New York and Toronto, among them Dr Daniel Clark*, diagnosed him as a "chronic, hysterical hypochondriac," and he spent time in several American institutions. His wife divorced him on 1 Oct. 1896 in Newport, R.I., on the grounds of non-support, though it remains unclear, as a history of Beatty Blackstock puts it, "whether his family problems were the source or the result of his personal difficulties." Eventually, failing health and impaired eyesight obliged him to withdraw from active practice altogether.

Prior to the outbreak of World War I, he again fell ill, in England, and he eventually returned to Canada, where he was cared for by two of his sisters. He lived in Buffalo, N.Y., for some time after the war. Following his death at his Toronto home, he was widely eulogized. One friend, a prominent member of the New York bar, eloquently captured the loss felt by many when he said, "It is an example of the utter prodigality of nature to have endowed this man with so many brilliant and engaging qualities and then to have wrecked his physical power and left him so helpless in the prime of life."

S. CRAIG WILSON

George Tate Blackstock is the author of "Canada and the Venezuelan settlement," *Canadian Magazine*, 8 (November 1896–April 1897): 170–75.

AO, RG 22-305, no.44453. *Bay City Daily Tribune* (Bay City, Mich.), 26 Feb. 1880. *Daily Mail and Empire*, 2 Oct. 1896, 28 Dec. 1921. *Evening Telegram* (Toronto), 28, 30 Dec. 1921. *Globe*, 3 Oct. 1896; 30 Oct. 1905; 25 July 1906; 27 Sept. 1907; 9 Jan., 11–13 March, 5 May 1909; 28, 30 Dec. 1921. *Toronto Daily Star*, 28 Dec. 1921. *World* (Toronto), 2 Oct. 1896, 30 Oct. 1905. Frank Arnoldi, "George Tate Blackstock," *Canadian Magazine*, 58 (November 1921–April 1922): 424–35. C. M. Blackstock, *All the journey through* (Toronto, 1997). *Canadian men and women of the time* (Morgan, 1912). C. I. Kyer, "The transformation of an establishment firm: from Beatty Blackstock to Faskens, 1902–1915," in *Essays in the history of Canadian law*, ed. D. H. Flaherty *et al.* (8v. to date, [Toronto], 1981–), vol.7 (*Inside the law: Canadian law firms in historical perspective*, ed. Carol Wilton, 1996): 161–206.

BLAIN, JOSEPH (baptized **Marie-Joseph-Théophile**), Roman Catholic priest, Jesuit, teacher, lecturer, and astronomer; b. 30 Oct. 1859 in Saint-Rémi-de-La Salle (Saint-Rémi), Lower Canada, son of Théophile Blain, a farmer, and Apolline Martin; d. 18 Sept. 1925 in Sault-au-Récollet (Montreal).

After studying at the Collège Sainte-Marie in Montreal from 1870 to 1878, Joseph Blain entered the noviciate of the Society of Jesus in Sault-au-Récollet on 30 July 1878. He pronounced his vows there in 1880 and embarked on the study of arts. He then took three years of philosophy, spending 1882–83 at the Collège Sainte-Marie and the next two years at Stonyhurst College in England. In 1885 he was sent with the first contingent of Jesuits to the Collège de Saint-Boniface in Manitoba, which Archbishop Alexandre-Antonin Taché* had recently entrusted to the Society of Jesus. After teaching various subjects there until 1889, he studied theology for four years (1889–93) at the scholasticate on Jersey, under the direction of Jesuits from Paris, and for another year (1893–94) at the Scolasticat de l'Immaculée-Conception in Montreal. On 3 Sept. 1893 he was ordained to the priesthood in Montreal by Archbishop Édouard-Charles Fabre*. He undertook theological studies in Sault-au-Récollet in 1894–95, and taught philosophy at the Scolasticat de l'Immaculée-Conception from 1895 until 1898.

In 1898 Blain returned to the Collège de Saint-Boniface as prefect of studies and teacher of natural science and mathematics. His competence in these fields was recognized and appreciated by the students, who also enjoyed his fine qualities as a pedagogue and his intelligence. In the years that followed he was responsible for reforming the science curriculum. He also provided the college with an outstanding physics and chemistry laboratory.

Blain was an honest, upright man, and his advice was highly regarded. While he lived in St Boniface (Winnipeg), he contributed to the town's intellectual life by giving lectures on literary, religious, and scientific topics. He also wrote occasional poems in French and Latin. His scientific interests, combined with his nationalistic convictions – "the language guardian of the faith; the faith guardian of the language," he would declare in 1916 in a lecture on the French Canadian parish – led him to take part in expeditions that would result in the discovery of Fort Saint-Charles on Lake of the Woods. The first expedition, undertaken in 1890, was unsuccessful. It was followed in 1902 by a second, headed by Archbishop Adélard Langevin*, during the course of which the Société Historique de Saint-Boniface was founded, with Blain as one of its charter members, for the purpose of highlighting the contribution of francophones in the Canadian west. It was necessary to wait for the expeditions that took place in the summer of 1908 before the anticipated results were achieved; excavations then made it possible to identify Fort Saint-Charles and the remains of Jean-Baptiste Gaultier* de La Vérendrye and his companions, including the Jesuit priest Jean-Pierre Aulneau*, who were killed in 1736. Father Blain undertook to photograph the bodies and the objects unearthed. He and Father Julien Paquin gave a lecture on these discoveries on the occasion of the blessing of the new cathedral in St Boniface in 1908.

Blain was interested in astronomy and in 1908 he became a member of the Royal Astronomical Society of Canada, before which he read a number of papers. The following year he installed western Canada's first seismograph in the Collège de Saint-Boniface. He was the director of the college's seismographic observatory for more than ten years. This observatory, which formed part of the Jesuit Seismological Service, would unfortunately be destroyed when the college burned down in 1922. In 1909 he helped found the Association des Anciens Élèves du Collège de Saint-Boniface, becoming its first chaplain.

In 1911, after a year's rest in Fort William (Thunder Bay), Ont., Blain was sent to Edmonton, along with Father Gustave Jean, to conduct negotiations for the founding of the Jesuit Collège d'Edmonton, which would enrol its first students in 1913. He then returned to his position as a teacher at the Collège de Saint-Boniface and he remained there until 1920, when he left to teach philosophy at the Collège d'Edmonton until 1925.

Throughout his time at the Collège de Saint-Boniface, Blain took a keen interest in its development. With regard to the college's difficult financial situation in the second decade of the century, he deplored the fact that there were four colleges in St Boniface. In 1914, when the question arose of requesting that the college become independent from the University of Manitoba (to which it had been attached since the establishment of the latter in 1877), Blain, as his institution's representative on the university's commission on studies, recommended that the college have some degree of autonomy within the university. When the government of Tobias Crawford Norris* amended the Public Schools Act in 1916, abolishing bilingual schools in Manitoba, he came to the defence of the classical colleges. The University of Manitoba granted him an honorary LLD in 1922.

Joseph Blain died on 18 Sept. 1925 at the noviciate of the Society of Jesus in Sault-au-Récollet, to which he had recently returned. A cultured man, he was an outstanding scientist and an exceptional pedagogue. In the field of education he took a particular interest in the development of science, which he had tried in many ways to make more widely known.

GILLES LESAGE

119

Blaylock

Joseph Blain is the author of three articles: "Au fort Saint-Charles," *Les Cloches de Saint-Boniface* (Saint-Boniface [Winnipeg]), 13 (1914): 177–79; "Centenaire de l'église de Saint-Boniface; sonnet à S.G. Mgr Arthur Béliveau, archevêque de Saint-Boniface: *in veritate et charitate*," *Les Cloches de Saint-Boniface*, 17 (1918): 173; and "Le givre," *Le Manitoba* (Saint-Boniface), 11 févr. 1914. He may also have written "Au lac des Bois: découverte du site de l'ancien fort Saint-Charles," *La Presse*, 27 déc. 1902.

ANQ-M, CE604-S14, 30 oct. 1859. Arch. de la Compagnie de Jésus, Prov. du Canada Français (Saint-Jérôme, Qué.), BO-17 (Joseph Blain). *Le Devoir*, 19 sept. 1925. *La Liberté* (Saint-Boniface), 8 févr., 28 mars 1916; 23, 30 sept. 1925. *Le Manitoba*, 9 août 1908, 2 nov. 1910, 10 févr. 1915, 24 mai 1922. *Manitoba Free Press*, 22 Oct. 1910, 13 May 1911. *La Semaine religieuse de Québec*, 1er juin 1922. "À la mémoire du R.P. Blain, S.J.," *Les Cloches de Saint-Boniface*, 24 (1925): 214. J.-B.-A. Allaire, *Dictionnaire biographique du clergé canadien-français* (6v., Montréal et Saint-Hyacinthe, Qué., 1908–34), 2: 61. T. J. Campbell, "Out of the grave: the discovery of Fort St. Charles in 1908," Soc. Hist. de Saint-Boniface, *Bull.*, 5 (1915). *Canada ecclésiastique*, 1899–1911. "Découverte historique – 1908," *Les Cloches de Saint-Boniface*, 78 (1979): 34. "Ding! Dang! Dong!," *Les Cloches de Saint-Boniface*, [9] (1910): 128; 17 (1918): 212. "Feu le R.P. Joseph Blain, S.J.," *Les Cloches de Saint-Boniface*, 24: 185–87. "Former college teacher honored," *Pennant* (St Boniface), 1 (1922): 19. Gérard Jolicœur, *Les jésuites dans la vie manitobaine* (1v. paru, Saint-Boniface, 1985–). L.-A. Prud'homme, "Découverte historique: le fort Saint-Charles retrouvé," *Les Cloches de Saint-Boniface*, 7 (1908): 205–34; "La littérature française au Nord-Ouest," RSC, *Trans.*, 3rd ser., 9 (1915), sect.I: 247–64. "Le R.P. Joseph Blain, S.J.," *Les Cloches de Saint-Boniface*, [9]: 281–82. "Le R.P. Joseph Blain, S.J., LL.D.," *Les Cloches de Saint-Boniface*, 21 (1922): 115–16. Soc. Hist. de Saint-Boniface, *Bull.*, 1 (1911).

BLAYLOCK, HARRY WOODBURN, lawyer, businessman, and chief commissioner of the Canadian Red Cross; b. 6 Jan. 1878 in Paspébiac, Que., son of the Reverend Thomas Blaylock and Eleanor Mariane Lowndes; m. 30 Sept. 1905 Agnes Georgina Mills in Calgary, and they had one son; d. 25 Jan. 1928 in Montreal.

Harry Woodburn Blaylock was born into the family of a priest of the Anglican diocese of Quebec. He was only 10 when they moved to Danville in the Eastern Townships, where his father had been called to carry on his ministry. He studied at Bishop's College School and Bishop's College in Lennoxville, graduating with a BA in 1897. Like many young men of social standing, Blaylock served in the non-permanent militia. He spent the year 1898 with the 54th (Richmond) Battalion of Infantry, whose first company was based in Danville. Military life apparently held little attraction for him, however, and he remained an acting lieutenant for less than a year. In 1900 he enrolled in the faculty of law at McGill University and he completed his BCL with distinction in 1903. During this period he also worked for George Alexander Drummond*, an industrialist in the sugar trade and leading figure in the Bank of Montreal who in addition was an influential senator. Drummond entrusted him with the preparation of legal documents related to his real estate transactions. On receiving a Macdonald scholarship from McGill, Blaylock decided to spend a year studying international law in Paris, in 1903–4. On his return he settled in Montreal, where he embarked on a law career that would prove undistinguished.

It was at this time that Blaylock first met Agnes Georgina Mills, daughter of James MILLS, an educator and member of the federal Board of Railway Commissioners. After they were married in 1905, he decided to practise law in Calgary, and he became a founding partner there in the legal firm of Bergeron and Blaylock. In 1907 he suddenly gave up law and moved to London, England, where he involved himself in major construction projects connected with the interests of Sir George Alexander Drummond.

Up to this point, Blaylock's career had not risen to the heights that a brilliant education and excellent family and political connections might have suggested. It was through an accident of history that his predisposition to action was fully revealed. For some years Blaylock had been acquainted with Lady Drummond [Grace Julia Parker*], Sir George Alexander's second wife, who was one of the most active women in the Canadian Red Cross Society. When World War I broke out, he offered his services to this organization and served for a few months in its London office along with Lady Drummond. The untimely death of its chief commissioner, Lieutenant-Colonel Jeffrey Hale Burland*, in October 1914, and his replacement by his deputy, Lieutenant-Colonel Charles Alfred Hodgetts, opened the way for Blaylock to become deputy commissioner.

In this capacity Blaylock was put in charge of the society's operations in France. His duties included supervising the transport of humanitarian aid and providing services for Canadian soldiers (and occasionally for French civilians). The Red Cross made a wide range of services available and distributed all sorts of goods, from cigarettes, clothing, and food to medical instruments and supplies, and complete equipment for dressing stations. It even set up ambulance convoys, an especially important initiative since evacuation of the wounded, which had previously been neglected, changed considerably during World War I, thanks largely to the Red Cross. The rapid and comfortable transfer of wounded men from the front line to the rear would be one of the decisive factors in significantly reducing the mortality rate.

Blaylock based his task of logistical supervision on a simple maxim: "When help [is] needed it must be given and given speedily." During the first months of the war, he administered aid from the Canadian public through his charitable agency as did others at the time, though on a much larger scale. The work of the Red Cross took a more dramatic direction, however, when the second battle of Ypres began in April 1915. In this first large-scale engagement, Canadians were shelled and gassed, and they suffered heavy losses. The medical posts behind the front lines had no morphine, and it was Blaylock's organization that would bring 10,000 injectable units up to the front. It was shortly after this experience that the horror of trench warfare was first revealed to him. Victims of gas attacks, men who had lost limbs, and others who were seriously wounded arrived by the hundreds and soon were occupying every available bed in Boulogne, France. Operations during the next 18 months would bring new contingents of suffering humanity. Blaylock was deeply affected by what he saw, but at great personal sacrifice he continued his efforts to ease the suffering of modern war, to the point that he was overcome by fatigue and psychological shock. As a result, he had to stay at Hospital No.14 in Boulogne for three weeks, and then to take three more weeks of rest cure at the end of 1916 and the beginning of 1917 for his nervous prostration.

Once he had recovered, Blaylock resumed his work with vigour and dedication and with a zeal that took him closer to the front than was strictly necessary from any administrative need. When the Red Cross was advised that a large-scale attack was imminent early in April 1917 (it was to take Vimy Ridge), he headed for the main clearing station, where thousands of wounded men soon began to arrive. He was profoundly moved. "Words fail one in trying to describe the horror of it all, but one noticed with wonder and admiration the cheerfulness and self-sacrifice of the wounded. No one seemed so badly hurt but that, in his opinion, the chap next to him was worse, and needed attention first. Men with arms hanging limp were struggling to help men whose legs were wounded; everyone seemed to be thinking of his neighbour."

When Blaylock was asked to replace Hodgetts as chief commissioner of the Canadian Red Cross overseas in April 1918, his experience made him ready to take on this office. He went back to London, where a much wider range of services was offered than in France. There were, for instance, five hospitals administered by the Canadian Red Cross, a convalescent home for officers, and a rest home for nurses in and around London. Blaylock remained in England after the armistice to put the affairs of the Red Cross in order and wind up the society's wartime activities. In June 1919, however, this man of average build (at five feet ten and one-half inches and 155 pounds) found his health threatened again, this time by an attack of pleurisy that confined him to bed.

Blaylock received many British and foreign decorations for his wartime services: mention in dispatches (13 Nov. 1916), commander of the Order of the British Empire (7 July 1918), Legion of Honour (knight, 2 May 1917, and officer, 24 Oct. 1919), commander of the Order of the Crown of Italy (8 March 1920), Order of St Sava, 4th class (Serbia, 7 June 1919), and knight by grace and devotion of the Order of Malta (7 Jan. 1920). On 7 Oct. 1918 he had also been made an honorary colonel in the Canadian militia.

Back in Montreal in 1922, Blaylock resumed his place in the business world, as counsel or administrator for the Montreal Development and Land Company Limited and the Westmount Development Company, among others. During the last six years of his life he was involved in the construction and management of commercial and residential buildings in downtown Montreal, Westmount, and Notre-Dame-de-Grâce ward (including Richelieu Place, Chelsea Place, and Trinity Apartments).

Blaylock's brother, Selwyn Gwillym, was a metallurgist, and this fact may have influenced the choice of career made by his son, Peter Woodburn; like his father and uncle, Peter would study at Bishop's College and McGill University, where he obtained a BSc. He went on to become one of the vice-presidents of Shawinigan Chemicals. Harry Blaylock died in Montreal at the age of 50, leaving his wife, son, and brother. Like many of his English Canadian compatriots, he could have used his connections to take command of a unit at the front in World War I. He chose instead to follow Lady Drummond and take up her favourite charity, the Red Cross. In retrospect, this was the right choice, for Blaylock made outstanding efforts to alleviate the suffering of his fellowmen.

YVES TREMBLAY

AC, Bonaventure (New Carlisle), État civil, Anglicans, New Carlisle and Paspébiac Anglican Church, 7 févr. 1878. LAC, RG 150, Acc. 1992–93/166, box 817-1. Alberta Geneal. Soc., Edmonton branch, *Alberta: index to registration of births, marriages and deaths . . .* (1v. to date, Edmonton, 1995–), 1 (*1870 to 1905*). Kenneth Cameron, *History of No.1 General Hospital, Canadian Expeditionary Force . . . 1914–1919* (Sackville, N.B., 1938). Can., Dept. of Militia and Defence, *Militia list* (Ottawa), January 1899, January 1919, December 1922. *Canadian Almanac . . .* (Toronto), 1875–1912. *Canadian annual rev.*, 1918–19. *Canadian men and women of the time* (Morgan; 1912). *Canadian who's who*, 1910. Andrew Macphail, *Official history of the Canadian forces in the Great War, 1914–19: the medical services* (Ottawa, 1925). Mary Macleod Moore, *The Maple Leaf's Red Cross: the war story of the Canadian Red Cross overseas* (London, [1919]). Nicholson, *CEF*. Geoffrey Noon, "The treatment of casualties in the Great War," in *British fighting methods in the Great War*, ed. Paddy Griffith (London, 1996), 87–112. *Standard dict. of Canadian biog.* (Roberts and Tunnell), 2.

Bond

BOND, Sir ROBERT, politician and country gentleman; b. 25 Feb. 1857 in St John's, son of John Bond of Kingskerswell, England, and Elizabeth Parsons; d. unmarried 16 March 1927 in Whitbourne, Nfld.

John Bond first worked in Newfoundland for Samuel Codner* of Kingskerswell, and eventually owned his own business in St John's. He and Elizabeth Parsons married in 1847 and had seven children, of whom Robert Bond was the sixth. Robert spent five years at St Andrew's School in St John's and then a year at the General Protestant Academy. In April 1872 he was enrolled at the Taunton Wesleyan Collegiate Institution in Somerset, England. Two months later his father was seized with paralysis and died. In 1925 Robert would remember "the debacle of 1872–3." Nevertheless, he persevered in his studies, and won a prize for solo singing. At some stage he learned to play the piano.

John Bond had willed that his real and personal property in Newfoundland should be liquidated following his death and the proceeds invested in interest-bearing securities. The interest was to be paid first to Elizabeth but bequests were made to surviving children as well. Robert and his brothers George John and Henry benefited from these, and George and Robert were also beneficiaries under the wills of Henry and of their cousin John Bussell Bond of Montreal, who helped manage the family affairs. When Elizabeth died in 1900, her life interest in the residue of her husband's estate passed in equal shares to George and Robert.

On 10 April 1874 John Bond's estate had been valued at $54,932.66. As of 14 June 1886 it held to the credit of Elizabeth and Robert (half each) 200 shares in the Canadian Bank of Commerce, 100 shares in the Banque du Peuple, and 19 shares in the Ontario Bank. From John B. Bond, Robert ultimately received 24 shares in the Bank of Montreal. In 1896 Elizabeth and Robert lost $7,062.50 through the failure of the Banque du Peuple [see Jacques Grenier*] and $2,974.68 through the sale of their shares in the Ontario Bank. Despite these reverses, Robert was a wealthy man through the whole of his adult life. Money allowed him to be that *rara avis* in Newfoundland public life – the politician who could pay his own way.

On 11 Dec. 1874 Robert and Elizabeth (as guarantor) entered into an agreement with the prominent St John's lawyer William Vallance Whiteway* whereby Robert became a law clerk for a term of five years. Bond was not, however, called to the bar, apparently for medical reasons. After travelling to Europe in 1880 and spending some ten weeks camping on the west coast of Newfoundland the following year, he entered politics. Whiteway had become premier in 1878, and in 1881, as part of his policy of progress, construction was started on a railway from St John's

to Halls Bay. In the general election of 6 Nov. 1882, which Whiteway won handily, Bond was returned for the government in Trinity Bay. Whiteway's Conservative party was Protestant in nature but had formed an alliance in the House of Assembly with Roman Catholic Liberals. The government's main opponents at this time were St John's merchants opposed to the railway scheme.

In 1884 the syndicate contracted to build the railway went bankrupt, and the next year, taking advantage of a Protestant-Catholic blow-up at Harbour Grace in 1883, the merchants were able to separate Whiteway from his Roman Catholic supporters. As a consequence of this realignment, Bond succeeded Robert John Kent*, a leading Liberal, as speaker of the house on 27 Feb. 1885, two days after he had turned 28. Whiteway was eased out of office in October and was replaced as premier by Robert Thorburn*, who made an outright sectarian appeal. A general election, which Thorburn won, followed on 31 October, and Bond was elected as an independent in Fortune Bay. Thorburn offered him the speakership of the new house but he declined because he "could not conscientiously unite with a sectarian government."

In February 1888, at the urging of Bond and the Canadian-born Alfred Bishop Morine*, Whiteway agreed to head a new political party. Bond became its secretary, but Morine soon bolted when he was resisted in his scheming for confederation. The previous year Bond had introduced a bill, passed by the legislature, that provided for the secret ballot, and the election of 6 Nov. 1889 would be the first held under the new dispensation. Bond wrote the manifesto of the Whiteway (or Liberal) party. Dated 22 June 1889, it promised railway construction and resource development, but rejected confederation. Whiteway won the election and Bond was returned for Trinity. On 17 Dec. 1889 he was appointed colonial secretary in the new government.

Bond's business interests had also developed apace in the 1880s. On 18 Feb. 1884 he and Alexander McLellan Mackay* bought a property of eight square miles in the interior of the Avalon peninsula. Near its centre was Harbour Grace Junction, which the railway from St John's had reached the year before. In 1887 the property was transferred to the Townships Timber and Land Company, which had Bond and Mackay as principal shareholders. Bond was elected president of the company, which sought "to establish a Township, carry on a lumber business, and dispose of the lands by sale to bona fide settlers." In 1887 a plan was devised for the proposed town, and in May 1889, on Bond's initiative, the legislature passed a bill changing the name of Harbour Grace Junction to Whitbourne, in honour of Sir Richard Whitbourne*, an early English promoter of Newfoundland.

Bond set out to make Whitbourne, Newfoundland's first inland town, a model community. The company ran a sawmill at Junction Lake, and Bond built a house near Whitbourne which he first used "as a hunting box" and then enlarged into a permanent home known as The Grange. In 1903, after the company had decided to wind up its business, he bought the entire Whitbourne property at public auction. By this time he had left his lovely Victorian neo-Gothic residence in St John's and was living at The Grange (his mother had died there). Over the years he devoted considerable time, energy, and money to the beautification and development of his estate. His house stood on a hill, was situated near a lake, and had a commanding view. At The Grange, Bond was the master of all he surveyed.

He had also been involved from the late 1870s onwards in mining speculation. He had an interest in the Colchester mining property situated on the Southwest Arm of Green Bay, and on 15 Dec. 1892 he obtained a grant for another mining property, northwest of Georges Lake and inland south of Bay of Islands. Over the years he spent twenty thousand dollars developing this property, which had an asbestos deposit, but he never realized a return from his investment and was never able to sell the mine.

As colonial secretary, Bond was deeply involved in the continuing struggle over the French Shore, the ribbon of territory along the northern and western coasts of the island where French fishermen enjoyed fishing and landing rights. In July 1890 Bond and Liberal MHA George Henry Emerson (speaker of the House of Assembly) visited the area. They then went to England, where they joined Whiteway and Augustus William Harvey* as an official delegation to press Newfoundland's claim for full control of its territory. They did not get very far in their lobbying vis-à-vis the French, but Whiteway was able to persuade the British to allow Newfoundland to seek a reciprocity agreement with the United States.

The background to this initiative was tangled and involved American fishing rights under the Anglo-American Convention of 1818. A number of disputes had flared up over the meaning of the fisheries clauses, but these had been smoothed over by provisions first in the Reciprocity Treaty of 1854 and then in the Treaty of Washington in 1871. Until the United States served notice that it intended to abrogate the latter treaty on 1 July 1885, Newfoundland had not challenged the principle of British North American solidarity in negotiations with the Americans. But the American action and its diplomatic aftermath encouraged experimentation. By permitting Newfoundland to explore prospects in Washington, the British seemingly accommodated this.

Bond was chosen to represent Newfoundland in the proposed negotiations. On 7 Oct. 1890 he met with Secretary of State James Gillespie Blaine in Washing-

ton and he subsequently went to New York and to Boston and Gloucester, Mass., to explain Newfoundland's position to various business groups. On 18 October the British envoy to the United States, Sir Julian Pauncefote, submitted a draft convention for Blaine's consideration, whereupon Bond returned to Newfoundland. He was summoned back in November for further discussion. Having learned to his chagrin that Pauncefote was not authorized to sign the proposed convention, Bond seized the initiative and met privately with Blaine in mid December. These talks produced an agreement that Bond later claimed in the House of Assembly "could not but be acceptable" to his "bitterest opponent . . . in the island." He returned home flushed with triumph, but disappointment followed when the imperial authorities decided to hold the Bond-Blaine Convention in abeyance, on the grounds that the talks in Washington had been unofficial and that Canada had not been properly consulted. In effect, Canada was allowed to veto a deal that Newfoundland valued highly.

Needless to say, this outcome soured relations between St John's and Ottawa. In the spring of 1891 Newfoundland denied Canadian fishermen licences to purchase bait and a bitter round of mutual reprisals followed. On 25 June, while this sparring was in progress, Bond mused to Whiteway about Newfoundland's long-term prospects given the realities of falling public revenue and continuing migration from the colony. His preferred option was reciprocity with the United States "apart from the Canadians." If this could not be achieved, the colony should seek a financial guarantee from the imperial government "but not subject to us handing over the control of our affairs to them." Otherwise, the only recourse was confederation. Present circumstances might be propitious for obtaining favourable conditions. The threat of reciprocity could be "used as a lever," as could the disruption of the bait supply, which was already causing Canada "a considerable loss." As Bond imagined events unfolding, the negotiation of terms of union by Whiteway would be followed by a plebiscite in Newfoundland.

Confederation would indeed become a live issue, but in circumstances quite unlike those imagined by Bond. In the interim, from 9 to 15 Nov. 1892, the two countries held a conference at Halifax to try to resolve their differences. Newfoundland was represented by Whiteway, Bond, and Harvey and Canada by Mackenzie Bowell*, Joseph-Adolphe Chapleau*, and Sir John Sparrow David Thompson*. Various proposals were examined, but in the end nothing concrete was achieved and Newfoundland continued to lobby the imperial government to complete the Bond-Blaine Convention.

On 29 July 1893, following several months of reflection, ill health, and growing disillusionment with

Whiteway's performance (especially in relation to French Shore matters, where he objected to the premier's propensity to compromise), Bond submitted a letter of resignation from the government, but he did not in fact leave. In the election of 6 Nov. 1893 he was returned in Trinity and the government won a seemingly comfortable majority of 13 seats. But on 6 Jan. 1894, with Morine to the fore, the Tories petitioned the Supreme Court under the Controverted Election Act of 1887 alleging wrongdoing by Whiteway, Bond, and 15 other Liberals. In the first case to be heard, the judge, Sir James Spearman Winter*, found that public funds had been spent without proper authority and the two members involved were unseated and disqualified. Faced with the prospect of losing his majority by judicial attrition, Whiteway told Governor Sir John Terence Nicholls O'Brien* that he intended to act on behalf of those adversely affected by the litigation. When the governor proved uncooperative, Whiteway resigned, and on 14 April Augustus Frederick Goodridge formed a minority Tory government. Court proceedings continued and on 25 July 1894 Whiteway and Bond were themselves unseated and disqualified.

This upheaval was followed in December 1894 by the failure of the colony's two main banks, the Commercial Bank of Newfoundland and the Union Bank of Newfoundland, as foreign investors and financiers lost confidence in the local economy and maladministration caught up with the banks' directors [see James Goodfellow*]. Since the Newfoundland Savings Bank, the only other financial institution in St John's, had its assets tied up in unsaleable colonial debentures and notes of the failed banks, its position was also threatened.

With the government itself facing bankruptcy, Goodridge sought financial assistance from the imperial government. When this was not forthcoming, he resigned, and on 13 Dec. 1894 a Liberal administration led by Daniel Joseph Greene was formed. Greene immediately had legislation passed removing the disqualifications from the unseated members, and then he too resigned. These moves cleared the way for Whiteway to become premier again on 8 Feb. 1895. Bond was reappointed colonial secretary the same day and from 25 April 1895 he sat in the Legislative Council. He would return to the House of Assembly when he was acclaimed in Twillingate in a by-election scheduled for 26 Sept. 1895. He was to represent this district for the remainder of his political career.

Back in office, Whiteway and Bond faced a bleak situation but they nonetheless refused to accept an imperial demand for an inquiry by royal commission in return for assistance. Instead, they approached Canada to ascertain what terms would be available for confederation. Since Whiteway was in poor health, Bond led the delegation to Ottawa in March 1895. Negotiations commenced on 4 April but the Canadians offered less than the Newfoundlanders were prepared to accept, and the British were unwilling to bridge the difference.

Bond had better luck with the bankers. With the help of the railway promoter Robert Gillespie Reid*, who had burst on the Newfoundland scene in 1890, he was able – through intelligent and tough-minded negotiation – to rescue the colony's finances with timely loans in Montreal and London. As part of a complex deal, Bond backed a short-term loan for the savings bank with a personal guarantee of $100,000. On 23 July 1895 he arrived back in St John's a conquering hero. Thereafter he had a golden reputation as the man who had been willing to risk his fortune to save his country. In fact, the personal guarantee he made cost Bond and his mother the reverse they suffered in the failure of the Banque du Peuple. Because of it, his broker "was not in a position to sell out" and the result was a "total loss."

Despite Bond's success, the Liberals lost the election of 28 Oct. 1897 to a revived Tory party led by Winter, who had abandoned his judgeship. Whiteway was personally defeated and left it to his caucus to decide who should lead them in the assembly. Bond was duly selected, but Whiteway, who nominally remained leader of the party, eventually became embittered and turned against him.

On 3 March 1898 the Winter government entered into a contract with Robert G. Reid for the operation of the trans-island railway, which Reid had finished building to Port aux Basques (Channel–Port aux Basques) under agreements, involving financial payments and land grants, made in 1890 and 1893. Winter's 1898 contract, the details of which had been known since 22 February, gave Reid the right to operate the railway for a 50-year period and additional land grants in return for an immediate payment of $1 million. At the end of this period Reid's heirs would own the railway. Reid also undertook to establish a coastal steamer service, take over the government telegraph lines, purchase the dry dock in St John's, and provide the capital with electricity and a streetcar service. Bond condemned the contract, which required legislative approval, on the grounds that it would transfer public assets for much less than their worth and establish a monopoly. By contrast, Edward Patrick Morris*, the Liberal member for St John's West, endorsed the deal because it would relieve the financial crisis and provide badly needed employment, particularly in the capital. At a caucus meeting on 23 February he had broken with Bond on the issue. When Bond lost the fight in the assembly, he called upon the Colonial Office to disallow the legislation embodying the Reid contract, but the imperial authorities refused to interfere.

In November 1898, while the battle over the contract was still raging, it became known that Alfred

Morine, a member of the cabinet, had acted as Reid's solicitor during the drafting of the railway bill and was still representing him. Morine was forced to resign by Governor Sir Herbert Harley Murray* and this move split the government party. Four leaders – Winter, Morine, Bond, and Morris – now bargained for support, but Bond was able to turn this situation to his advantage. At a public meeting in St John's on 20 Oct. 1899 he was unanimously chosen as leader of the Liberal party after a letter of resignation had been read out from Whiteway. Having thus far played a secondary and supportive role to Whiteway, Bond had finally found a cause – the railway contract – that allowed him to outflank his old mentor.

On 19 Feb. 1900, with Morine in England, the Winter government lost a no-confidence vote in which several of Morine's supporters broke ranks to join Morris, who in turn linked up with Bond. This defeat led to the resignation of the government and to the swearing in of Bond as premier on 15 March (he would also serve as colonial secretary). Having reached the top of the greasy pole of Newfoundland politics, Bond sought an immediate dissolution, but this was refused by Governor Sir Henry Edward McCallum, who favoured a fall election. Morris entered the Bond cabinet with a promise from the new premier, reluctantly given, that the Reid contract would be modified rather than cancelled. When the government, which had a majority of only two, entered into negotiations with Reid's son WILLIAM DUFF over revising the contract, no agreement could be reached. But politically this outcome was an asset rather than a liability, for in the general election of 8 Nov. 1900 Bond won an overwhelming victory, taking 32 of 36 seats against a Morine-led opposition financed by the Reids.

His first priority after the election was to renegotiate the railway contract. This effort succeeded, and on 2 Aug. 1901 a new act became law whereby R. G. Reid gave up his reversionary interest in the railway, as well as control of the public telegraph system, and the government returned his $1 million with interest. For a payment of $850,000 Reid handed back 1.5 million acres in land grants and was permitted to form the Reid Newfoundland Company, which managed his landholdings and operated the railway, the coastal steamers, the St John's street railway and electrical services, and the dry dock. With this legislation, an uneasy peace between Bond and the Reids was achieved.

During his premiership both Bond and Newfoundland attracted recognition in a number of ways. On 24 Oct. 1901 Bond was invested a knight during the visit to St John's of the Duke and Duchess of Cornwall, and in 1902 he was sworn to the imperial Privy Council. He was also given the freedom of the city of Edinburgh in 1902 and of the City of London, Manchester, and Bristol in 1907. On 26 July 1902 he was awarded an honorary LLD by the University of Edinburgh. In 1901 international attention had been drawn favourably to Newfoundland when, on 12 December, Guglielmo Marconi, who was welcomed to the colony and assisted by Bond, received the world's first wireless message on Signal Hill, St John's. Bond's keen interest in this project was in keeping with his longstanding advocacy of a rapid transatlantic ship and train transportation route via Newfoundland.

Bond represented Newfoundland at the 1902 and 1907 colonial conferences in London and was photographed on both occasions with the other leaders of the British empire. At the 1902 conference he urged the enlargement of the force for which recruitment had started in Newfoundland in 1900 under the United Kingdom's Royal Naval Reserve Volunteer Act of 1896. In the 1914–18 war the first Newfoundlanders to go overseas would be members of this reserve. In a further gesture of imperial solidarity, he introduced a bill, which received unanimous consent in the House of Assembly on 24 April 1903, to establish Empire Day [see Clementina Trenholme*] as a public holiday in the colony.

Economically, Bond benefited from large catches and good prices in the fishing industry and the revenue available from new timber and mining operations, especially the iron-ore mines on Bell Island, which had opened in 1895 under Canadian auspices to meet the needs of the blast furnaces at Sydney, N.S. Rising revenues enabled the government to be fiscally prudent while increasing expenditure on education, marine works, agriculture, and the colony's communication system. In small communities it encouraged the unification of denominational schools into "amalgamated" ones, and in 1904 it began a coastal steamship service with Bowring Brothers to supplement that offered by the Reids. In labour relations, the Bond government weathered strikes of miners on Bell Island in 1900, of sealers in St John's in 1902 [see Simeon Kelloway*], of longshoremen in St John's in 1903, and of railway workers (against Reid Newfoundland) at Placentia in 1904.

As premier, Bond renewed his quest for reciprocity with the United States. Canada still strongly opposed a separate Newfoundland–United States deal but Ottawa's arguments could no longer be sustained in London. Years had passed since the Bond-Blaine Convention had been negotiated, and Newfoundland could now scarcely be held accountable for undermining Canada's bargaining position. In August 1902, with British approval, Bond went to Washington and began talks with Secretary of State John Milton Hay. Their agreement, signed in November, provided, *inter alia*, for duty-free entry into the United States for a sizeable list of Newfoundland exports and for privileged treatment of American fishing vessels in relation to a wide range of activities in Newfoundland. The proposed

125

arrangement was a tribute to Bond's persistence and skill but Massachusetts senator Henry Cabot Lodge, champion of the New England fishing industry and a key member of the Senate foreign relations committee, scuttled it. The agreement was not reported out of the committee until January 1905 and then only in an amended form that Newfoundland could not accept. Bond had lost another round in an old battle, and in the process had acquired a formidable new adversary.

Unquestionably, his greatest triumph as premier was in relation to French rights in Newfoundland. He had failed to get the French Shore question on the agenda of the 1902 Colonial Conference, but in 1904 he became the unintended beneficiary of France's decision to seek a rapprochement with Great Britain. Suddenly, the way was clear for London to trade off concessions elsewhere in the world for a satisfactory resolution of the French Shore issue. Under the terms of the deal eventually embodied in the Entente Cordiale of 8 April 1904, France renounced her rights in Newfoundland under the Treaty of Utrecht (1713), but retained summer fishing, though not landing, rights along the former Treaty Shore. A note accompanying the agreement guaranteed that Newfoundland would not be allowed to cut off bait supplies to French fishermen working legitimately on the coast by denying them purchasing licences.

Bond approached the agreement cautiously but soon embraced it enthusiastically and fought back a motion of censure against the imperial government brought in the legislature on 27 April 1904 by the diehard Morine. At a stroke, a burden that Newfoundland had carried for almost 200 years had been lifted. Although Bond was fortunate to be in charge at the time, he was given full credit for the outcome. He was in consequence a national hero twice over. "The heritage is won at last," the St John's *Evening Telegram* trumpeted, "and to our children we can transmit unsullied and unstained by alien rights the rough and rugged shore of old Newfoundland." The settlement highlighted Newfoundland's general progress in this period and its status as an emerging North Atlantic dominion of the British empire.

It also set the stage for the general election held on 31 Oct. 1904. In this contest Bond's Liberals faced a United Opposition party that had five leaders – Donald Morison, Winter, Goodridge, Morine, and the now disaffected Whiteway – and no real policy other than to oust the government. Bond characterized the opposition as Reid-backed confederates and ran on the government's "record of public service." He won 30 of 36 seats, and of his five main opponents only Morine was elected.

On 12 Jan. 1905 the government added to its laurels by signing an agreement with the Anglo-Newfoundland Development Company Limited that led to the opening of a pulp and paper mill at Grand Falls.

The same year, however, Bond again crossed the Reids by refusing to buy their railway and steamship operations. Not surprisingly, this episode increased their determination to drive him from office. They did not have to wait long to get their chance, for in 1905 Bond also embarked on a crusade that ruined his political career. What he now attempted was to pressure his New England opponents into accepting the Bond-Hay agreement by disrupting their fishing operations in Newfoundland.

The Foreign Fishing Vessels Act of 1893 was amended so as to cut the Americans off from engaging local crews, buying fish, or obtaining necessary supplies. When the Americans countered by carrying on these activities outside the three-mile limit, Bond sought to close the loophole by a further amendment to the act, but this was vehemently opposed by Washington and blocked by London. The British saw no reason to jeopardize their developing friendship with the United States, a high policy objective, over the upstart behaviour of a minor colony. Bond had badly overstepped himself and soon paid the price for his miscalculation.

For the 1906–7 fishing season Bond's machinations were circumvented by an Anglo-American *modus vivendi* that was imposed on Newfoundland. Another such agreement followed for 1907–8. In the meantime, the British had concluded that the only way out of a tricky situation in Newfoundland was to refer all outstanding issues under the Convention of 1818 to the Permanent Court of Arbitration at The Hague. Bond at first stubbornly refused this fig leaf, but while attending the Colonial Conference of 1907 gave way on the issue. His capitulation left the British to secure Canadian agreement for the proposed arbitration, something that Prime Minister Sir Wilfrid Laurier*, still smarting from the Alaska boundary decision of 1903, only reluctantly gave.

Bond's last act in a long fisheries struggle was to agree, after more *Sturm und Drang*, to the terms of the reference to the Hague court, but this accommodation could not save him politically. As a result of his systematic defiance over many years of Ottawa, Washington, and London, he had accumulated many enemies abroad. Moreover, Newfoundlanders themselves were far from united in the struggle he had unleashed. On the west coast, the centre of the American fishery, Bond faced strong opposition from fishermen who enjoyed a profitable trading relationship with the New Englanders, and their cause found a sympathetic ear in Governor Sir William MacGregor, who sought to counter his first minister at every turn. Lord Grey*, the Canadian governor general, hoped that Bond's discomfiture would provide an opening to bring Newfoundland into Canada. He and others, such as businessman Harry Judson CROWE, plotted to this end but ultimately nothing came of their efforts.

A more ominous development for Bond was the resignation from his cabinet on 26 July 1907 of Edward Morris (now Sir Edward), who had a fine political touch. Ostensibly, Morris broke with Bond over the wages being paid to road labourers in his constituency, but his departure was obviously timed to take advantage of Bond's increasing adversity. In March 1908 Morris launched the People's party, which brought together various interest groups and had close ties to the Reid Newfoundland Company. When an election was held on 2 Nov. 1908, the Bond and Morris parties each elected 18 members.

The deadlock produced a prolonged constitutional crisis. On 18 Feb. 1909 Bond advised the governor to dissolve the new house on the 25th, the day it was scheduled to open. When MacGregor refused, Bond submitted his resignation, which took effect on 3 March. Morris then became premier and a dissolution followed on 10 April. In the election held on 8 May, the People's party won 26 seats and the Liberals 10. Bond's loss was the more galling because of an incident that had occurred at Western Bay during the campaign. While landing there from a small boat on 30 April, he had been kicked back into the sea. Alfred W. Bishop, a fisherman, had been convicted in connection with this assault, but Bond's accusations against John Chalker Crosbie*, the local People's party candidate, who had been present on the wharf at the time, were to no avail. In 1905 Bond had gambled his political future on his ability to deliver for Newfoundland internationally, but he had misread diplomatic realities and underestimated the domestic political consequences of a punishing external fight. For his miscalculation, he paid a price that would haunt him for the rest of his life.

After the election Bond was a reluctant leader facing an entirely new situation in Newfoundland politics brought on by the formation of the Fishermen's Protective Union (FPU). This organization, which flourished in the old Liberal territory of the northeast coast, had been established in 1908 by William Ford Coaker*, a former canvasser for the Liberals whom Bond had rewarded in 1902 with a minor appointment but who had annoyed the government by his union activities. Tired and dejected after fighting two bruising elections in just over six months, Bond was slow to recognize the potential of the FPU and of the challenge it posed for the Liberal party.

The FPU tapped into a deep and profound disillusionment among fishermen with Newfoundland's economic system and grew rapidly in the northern bays. In 1910 it decided upon political action, with the object of holding the balance of power after the next election and thereby advancing its agenda of cooperation and fairness to the country's small producers. Coaker's emergence at the head of the FPU eventually forced Bond, a proud man, to deal as an equal with a former recipient of his patronage.

Coaker initially wanted an alliance with Bond, and on 16 Nov. 1911 he wrote to the Liberal leader in this regard. Bond replied that he believed in "union as a principle" and had advised Liberal supporters to join the FPU. Unions, he wrote, had often been of "real value by promoting intelligent communication between workpeople separated by wide areas and in ascertaining the due recompense of labour." But Bond rejected the idea of a union party, telling Coaker that if he had known the FPU intended to run its own candidates, he would not have endorsed membership in the organization. The FPU should support "whatever political party" came "nearest to its ideals," realizing that if it fought both parties, it could "hardly expect after the contest to exercise influence upon either." "It has to be remembered that the two existing political parties, be they good or bad, stand for the whole people of the Colony, and that they ought to take into consideration the interests of the whole people."

Coaker rejected this advice, and at the annual convention of the FPU on 27–30 Nov. 1911 won approval for the drafting of a political platform. To Bond's chagrin, several senior Liberals were present as guests. An effort by William Frederick Lloyd*, editor of the *Evening Telegram*, a Liberal paper, to broker a deal between Bond and Coaker failed to overcome the deep division between them. As a result, when the FPU met in convention at Bonavista on 12–16 Dec. 1912 it proceeded to adopt its own election platform, which promised sweeping changes in the way Newfoundland was organized economically and socially.

With retirement very much on his mind and with his health failing, Bond went to England in February 1913 for medical examination. He thereby missed the pre-election session of the House of Assembly, leaving his members, who feared the consequences of a separate FPU campaign, demoralized and disorganized. On his return in April, Lloyd, James Mary Kent, and other senior Liberals pressed him to open negotiations with Coaker for an electoral pact. On 15 August, Bond invited the FPU leader to The Grange "to go fully into the matter undisturbed." They met on 18 August, and on the 26th Bond followed up with a letter proposing a joint electoral effort whereby six nominations, one-sixth of the total needed for a full slate, would be reserved for the FPU. This offer, Bond maintained, was "very liberal recognition, for it must be remembered that the great majority of the fishermen are not Union men, and their views and interests may be at variance. If the Union has a claim to special representation, so has every trade, profession and business." In return, Coaker pledged support for Bond's leadership and for a "United Opposition," but the alliance was less than solid. In his manifesto, published on 3 October, Bond played down his connection to the Bonavista Platform. On the other hand, Coaker nominated nine candidates instead of six, including seven in the eleven northern districts.

When the election of 30 Oct. 1913 was held, it was Morris who prevailed; the People's party won 21 seats, the Union party 8, and the Liberals 7. With the exception of Port de Grave, where George Frederick Arthur GRIMES was successful, all the Union party seats were in the north; the FPU had enjoined the voters to "sink or swim with Coaker." The election put Bond in a most invidious position, "almost beyond the conditions of dignity and self-respect," he complained. The Unionist members owed their first loyalty to Coaker, who had worked with the Liberals only as a "mere matter of expediency." Coaker's purpose would now be to lead the Union party to power in its own right. On 2 Jan. 1914 Bond resigned both the leadership of the Liberal party and his seat. James M. Kent then became leader of the party and, with Coaker's approbation, leader of the opposition. Bond's humiliation was made complete when Coaker was elected by acclamation in the by-election called to fill the vacant Twillingate seat.

From the quiet of The Grange, Bond followed political developments in Newfoundland through the Great War with a mixture of anger and disgust. Various appeals were made to him to re-enter public life, but he never sallied forth again. "I have had a surfeit of Newfoundland politics lately," he acidly observed in November 1918, "and I turn from the dirty business with contempt and loathing."

Bond's denouement in the 1920s mixed a measure of contentment with considerable anguish. He never married but had living with him at the big house his cousin, the widowed Sarah Roberts, more than 19 years older than himself, and his housekeeper Mary Ford, "the good and faithful Mary." Visitors were few. "I am not," he would later write, "what the Americans designate 'a good mixer.' I am a very conservative Englishman." His great delight was the daily round of The Grange and its farming operation. Bond enjoyed working with his hands and liked being out and about in his "Irish tweed jacket and riding breeches." Nevertheless, on 28 Aug. 1922 he listed the Whitbourne estate for sale (though not for press advertisement) with Dowden and Edwards of St John's. Nothing came of this initiative and in August 1924 he tried, again unsuccessfully, to sell the property to the government. In the end, he never moved. Instead he continued to indulge his love of country pursuits, which he believed had enabled him "to escape a tragedy and to convert my retirement from active politics into a pleasure." He lived graciously, read widely, enjoyed bird-watching, loved music, and was an early radio enthusiast. Although he claimed to hate letter writing, he kept up a lively correspondence with his brother George and the latter's son and daughter, Frank Fraser and Roberta.

Bond disliked St John's and in the 1920s only infrequently visited the capital. Undoubtedly, his attitude was mixed up in his last years with his profound despair over "the deplorable condition of our public affairs." With his ouster in 1909, he believed, Newfoundland had forsaken the "high-road of financial honesty" and was headed for a cataclysm that could only be avoided by "a radical change" in administration. His disillusionment extended even to the value of his own knighthood, which he described in 1920 as a "worthless appendage" given that "creatures of all kinds are dubbed knights and lords." No doubt this vitriol was directed against his old nemesis Sir Edward Morris, who in 1918 had received a barony. When Sir Richard Anderson Squires*, who had become premier in 1919 with Coaker's support, called a general election for 3 May 1923, Bond forecast the worst: "My poor country! 'The last phase.'" Squires was re-elected, but his government soon became embroiled in financial scandal and fell from power. Bond felt vindicated. "The community is rotten to the core. One is ashamed of this condition of things, heartily ashamed and sorry. But I will admit some satisfaction in looking down from this height, – it is the highest land in Avalon, – and saying to the dupes, – 'I told you so.'" Even at this late date, he probably still imagined himself the political saviour of Newfoundland, but he was always content to indulge his hurt rather than seize an opportunity. When a public movement was started in 1926 to have him named governor, Bond growled that he "would much prefer to snare rabbits for a livelihood than to entertain the aristocracy that now finds its way into Government House." In his despair over his country's politics in the 1920s he helped foster the climate of opinion that in 1934 made possible the suspension of self-government in Newfoundland in favour of a commission of government [*see* Frederick Charles Alderdice*].

As the 1920s wore on, Bond was gradually overtaken by the problems of sickness and old age. He had a history of worrying about his health, and in 1921 had experienced an "explosion" that had left him "shattered in mind and body." Cousin Sarah's death from cancer in April 1924 rendered him broken and disconsolate. "I have passed through an experience," he told Fraser, "that I hope you will never have, and I have passed through it alone. Alone! I now know all that word means, the misery, the despair, the horror it connotes." As his physical condition deteriorated, he looked to family members, principally his niece, for emotional support. He was proud of Roberta's academic achievements and her dedication to the sick (she would graduate in medicine from Dalhousie University in 1925), but he was not above bringing to her attention – teasingly perhaps but revealingly all the same – that the medical profession was "too indelicate for the female sex to dabble in." He very much wanted Roberta to be the third woman in his life, after his mother and Sarah. Sadly for him, her understandable aspirations for a life of her own did not always mesh with his unquenchable personal needs.

In April 1924, having detected that something was bothering the 21-year-old Roberta, Bond invited her confidence: "Come out with it and I will see if I can prescribe a cure for your disease. I hope it is not a love affair for in that disease I unfortunately have no experience." When, however, she told him that she was contemplating marriage to Edward Wilber Nichols, a classicist at Dalhousie who was 20 years her senior, he did not hesitate to interfere in the bluntest terms. Indeed, he attempted, unsuccessfully, to "veto" the marriage, telling her, in effect, that Nichols was not good enough for her. He also blamed her for an injury he had suffered soon after she visited The Grange in 1924. "It might have been all avoided," he scolded, "if you had not so precipitately left me to the fates." Roberta's relationship with her devoted but irascible and possessive uncle survived his harsh words, though it must have been sorely tested. After obtaining her degree, she went to stay with him and to practise in the Whitbourne area. Her presence buoyed him up but his physical decline continued inexorably. When she left Newfoundland in June 1926, he followed her with a blameful letter.

Christmas that year was "a quiet one." Although Bond enjoyed the rituals of the season, and liked to decorate his house "with evergreens and ferns and flowers," he sat alone at the table for Christmas dinner. No doubt Mary Ford came in afterwards for "her annual glass of old port wine," but there was no mistaking the melancholy of the occasion, the more so because Bond was convinced that "the dear ones" who had once dined with him "were not far away." On 1 Feb. 1927, alarmed by the irregularity of his heartbeat, Bond went to St John's to see his physician, James Sinclair TAIT, who was surprised at the change for worse in his condition. He could hardly make it back to Whitbourne. On 28 February, three days after his 70th birthday, he told his brother that he was "failing rapidly." George Bond arrived in St John's on 10 March and the same day he and Dr Tait travelled to Whitbourne, where they found Robert at death's door. Though now himself 76, George set about giving his brother "poor rough, ignorant nursing." The end came "very quietly" at about 8:30 P.M. on 16 March.

George took charge of laying out the corpse and waked the remains in the house until 21 March, in deference to Robert's request that he not be buried until George was "sure that he was dead." Robert had made it known that he "wanted no fuss or parade." Accordingly, the ceremony on 21 March was a simple one. The remains were carried to St John the Baptist Anglican Church in the estate's express wagon, which George had painted black for the occasion. To accommodate the many friends and public figures who came out from St John's, the Newfoundland Railway laid on a special train (at, George noted, its usual tariff). When all was done, Bond was buried in the rocky soil of the Avalon peninsula, a region he had explored as a youth and celebrated as a man. A sheaf of carnations sent by Roberta had been placed "across his heart inside the casket."

Bond left behind him a tangled will, made on 28 Dec. 1914, in which he named George as executor. The inventory attached to the petition for probate valued the estate at $92,750 (in a 1924 accounting Bond had estimated his worth at $141,251.86). He left his Whitbourne holding, described as "an ideal property," to the governor and Executive Council "to be held in trust by them for the people of Newfoundland as a Model Farm forever." Most of the rest of his estate passed to Fraser but there were specific bequests to George, Roberta, Sarah (had she been living), and Mary Ford. After due consideration, the government declined the gift of the property on the grounds that the proposed model farm would be costly, of limited educational benefit, impractical to operate "free from political control," and an unfair source of competition for private farmers. It accepted various bequests to the museum in St John's, however, and these were presented to the governor at a ceremony held in Government House on 7 Oct. 1927.

Since the will was silent on what should be done if the government declined the Whitbourne property, George Bond sought the direction of the Supreme Court. The decision in 1928 awarded the property to Fraser, who coveted it. In 1949 Fraser sold the residence and four square miles of the estate to the new province of Newfoundland, which planned to establish a reform school there. Three years later authority was given for The Grange, the house of Bond's dreams and the monument to all he held dear, to be removed. In this act of blind cultural vandalism the people of Newfoundland and Labrador lost one of their most unusual and important legacies.

In his public life Bond had been a Newfoundland nationalist, an ardent imperialist, and an advocate of reciprocity with the United States. This impossible combination produced much torment and disappointment. In his private life, especially in his project of The Grange, he sought to create a world within a world, but this goal too proved elusive. Though his vocation was politics, it was the visionary project at Whitbourne that defined the man. Bond was a complex historical figure whose career was emblematic both of Newfoundland's ambitions and of its limitations. He is remembered variously, most intimately in a memorial window, depicting William Holman Hunt's *The Light of the World*, at St John the Baptist, Whitbourne. This window was donated by Fraser

Boomer

Bond and Roberta Nichols and was dedicated on 7 Sept. 1927.

MELVIN BAKER and PETER NEARY

Centre for Newfoundland Studies, Memorial Univ. of Nfld, Arch. (St John's), COLL-236 (George J. Bond papers); COLL-237 (Robert Bond papers). Memorial Univ. of Nfld, Dept. of Geography, Gordon Handcock coll. PANL, GN 2/39/A, 1921, Whitbourne. Private arch., Randall Nelson (Ottawa), Bond family research collection; J. R. Nichols (Digby, N.S.), Bond family research collection. Queen's College, Taunton (Somerset, Eng.) [formerly Taunton Wesleyan Collegiate Institution], Admissions reg. Univ. of Edinburgh Library, Special Coll. Dept. *Daily News* (St John's), 1909. *Evening Herald* (St John's), 1898. *Evening Mercury* (St John's), 1889. *Evening Telegram* (St John's), 1889–90, 1894–95, 1898–1901, 1904, 1909, 1914, 1923, 1927, 1949. *Royal Gazette and Newfoundland Advertiser* (St John's), 1889, 1894–95, 1900, 1909. *Times* (London), 1907. Melvin Baker, "The government of St John's, Newfoundland, 1800–1921" (PHD thesis, Univ. of Western Ont., London, 1980). Melvin Baker and P. [F.] Neary, "Sir Robert Bond (1857–1927): a biographical sketch," *Newfoundland Studies* (St John's), 15 (1999): 1–54. A. K. Bond, *The story of the Bonds of earth* (Baltimore, Md, 1930). *Burke's genealogical and heraldic history of the peerage, baronetage and knightage*, ed. Peter Townend (104th ed., London, 1967). B. C. Busch, "The Newfoundland sealers' strike of 1902," *Labour* (St John's), 14 (1984): 73–101; *The war against the seals: a history of the North American seal fishery* (Kingston, Ont., and Montreal, 1985). St John Chadwick, *Newfoundland: island into province* (Cambridge, Eng., 1967). Jessie Chisholm, "Organizing on the waterfront: the St John's Longshoremen's Protective Union (LSPU), 1890–1914," *Labour*, 26 (1990): 37–59. D. J. Davis, "The Bond-Blaine negotiations: 1890–1891" (MA thesis, Memorial Univ. of Nfld, 1970). *Decisions of the Supreme Court of Newfoundland, 1927–31*, ed. E. P. Morris *et al.* (St John's, 1948), 12. *Directory*, St John's, Harbour Grace, and Carbonear, 1885/86. *DNLB* (Cuff *et al.*). W. J. S. Donnelly, *A general statement of the public debt of the colony of Newfoundland from its commencement in 1834 down to 31st December 1900, and a yearly analysis of the same* (St John's, 1901). *Encyclopedia of Nfld* (Smallwood *et al.*), 4. F. W. Graham, *"We love thee, Newfoundland": biography of Sir Cavendish Boyle, K.C.M.G., governor of Newfoundland, 1901–1904* (St John's, 1979). J. [K.] Hiller, "A history of Newfoundland, 1874–1901" (PHD thesis, Univ. of Cambridge, 1971); "The Newfoundland fisheries issue in Anglo-French treaties, 1713–1904," *Journal of Imperial and Commonwealth Hist.* (London), 24 (1996): 1–23; *The Newfoundland railway, 1881–1949* (St John's, 1981); "The origins of the pulp and paper industry in Newfoundland," *Acadiensis* (Fredericton), 11 (1981–82), no.2: 42–68; "The political career of Robert Bond," in *Twentieth-century Newfoundland: explorations*, ed. J. [K.] Hiller and P. [F.] Neary (St John's, 1994), 11–45. R. B. Joyce, *Sir William MacGregor* (Melbourne, Australia, 1971). Margaret McBurney and Mary Byers, *True Newfoundlanders: early homes and families of Newfoundland and Labrador* (Toronto, 1997). I. D. H. McDonald, *"To each his own": William Coaker and the Fishermen's Protective Union in Newfoundland politics, 1908–1925*, ed. J. [K.] Hiller (St John's, 1987). Harvey Mitchell, "Canada's negoti-ations with Newfoundland, 1887–1895," *CHR*, 40 (1959): 277–93; "The constitutional crisis of 1889 in Newfoundland," *Canadian Journal of Economics and Political Science* (Toronto), 24 (1958): 323–31. P. [F.] Neary, "The embassy of James Bryce in the United States, 1907–13" (PHD thesis, Univ. of London, 1965); "Grey, Bryce, and the settlement of Canadian-American differences, 1905–1911," *CHR*, 49 (1968): 357–80; *Newfoundland in the North Atlantic world, 1929–1949* (Montreal and Kingston, 1988). P. [F.] Neary and S. J. R. Noel, "Newfoundland's quest for reciprocity, 1890–1910," in *Regionalism in the Canadian community, 1867–1967*, ed. Mason Wade (Toronto, 1969), 210–26. *Newfoundland: economic, diplomatic, and strategic studies*, ed. R. A. MacKay (Toronto, 1946). *Newfoundland in the nineteenth and twentieth centuries: essays in interpretation*, ed. J. [K.] Hiller and P. [F.] Neary (Toronto, 1980). Nfld, General Assembly, *Proc.*, 1911, 1927; House of Assembly, *Journal*, 1885, 1887. S. J. R. Noel, "Politics and the crown: the case of the 1908 tie election in Newfoundland," *Canadian Journal of Economics and Political Science*, 33 (1967): 285–91; *Politics in Newfoundland* (Toronto, 1971). W. G. Reeves, "The Fortune Bay dispute: Newfoundland's place in imperial treaty relations under the Washington treaty, 1871–1885" (MA thesis, Memorial Univ. of Nfld, 1971). J. R. Smallwood, *Coaker of Newfoundland: the man who led the deep-sea fishermen to political power*, ed. Melvin Baker (Port Union, Nfld, 1998). G. F. G. Stanley, "Further documents relating to the union of Newfoundland and Canada, 1886–1895," *CHR*, 29 (1948): 370–86. F. F. Thompson, *The French Shore problem in Newfoundland: an imperial study* (Toronto, 1961). *Twentieth-century Newfoundland: explorations*, ed. J. [K.] Hiller and P. [F.] Neary (St John's, 1994). Fred Vallis, "Sectarianism as a factor in the 1908 election," *Newfoundland Quarterly* (St John's), 70 (1974), no.3: 17–28. *Whitbourne, Newfoundland's first inland town: journey back in time – 1884–1984*, comp. J. S. R. Gosse (Whitbourne, Nfld, 1985). W. V. Whiteway, *Duty's call: Sir W. V. Whiteway states his position* (St John's, [1904]).

BOOMER, HARRIET ANN. *See* MILLS

BOOTH, JOHN RUDOLPHUS, industrialist; b. 5 April 1827 near Waterloo, Lower Canada, son of John Booth and Eleanor Rooney (Rowley); m. 7 Jan. 1853 Rosalinda Cooke (d. 1886) in Kingsey township, Lower Canada, and they had five daughters and three sons; d. 8 Dec. 1925 in Ottawa.

The second eldest of the five children of an Ulster-man and his wife, John R. Booth was born in the Eastern Townships. Historian William E. Greening reports that as a child he "spent his spare time building miniature mills and bridges along the tiny rivulet that flowed through his father's farm." Whatever his early interests, it was with a modest elementary education that he left home as a youth. He contemplated joining the California gold rush before finding employment with the Central Vermont Railroad, chiefly as a carpenter on bridge projects. He also had some involvement in the construction of a paper mill in Sherbrooke, Lower Canada, and a sawmill near Hull. Upon completion of the latter, its owner, Andrew Leamy, engaged him to manage the operation for a year. He then ran a shingle mill in premises in Hull rented from Alonzo Wright*, but within months it was destroyed by fire.

Around 1854 Booth and his wife had moved across the river to Ottawa, where J. R., as he became known, furthered his understanding of the lumber trade and water-power. Having leased Philip Thompson's large sawmill on Chaudière Island, between Hull and Ottawa, which was selected in 1857 as Canada's capital, he tendered successfully in 1859 for a contract to supply lumber and timber for the new Parliament Buildings [see Thomas McGreevy*]. In harvesting timber for this project, he is credited with introducing horses to replace oxen in skidding logs to water. (The acreage he acquired southwest of Ottawa for pasturing his horses would later become the Dominion Experimental Farm.)

The financial success of the contract, and of a short-lived partnership with American lumberman Albert W. Soper, allowed Booth in 1864 to purchase the Thompson mill and the adjoining mill-lots of Lyman Perkins. More significant, his reputation for reliable performance facilitated his access to additional capital. In 1867, with the backing of the Bank of British North America and on the advice of his cousin Robert R. Booth of Pembroke, he bought the valuable pineries on the Madawaska River previously owned by John Egan*. Following this acquisition, which he later described as the basis of his fortune, he joined the effort to construct works to facilitate timber drives, as a founder of the Upper Ottawa Improvement Company, formed in 1868 to build dams, slides, and piers; in 1888 he would become the founding president of the Madawaska Improvement Company Limited. In addition to steadily expanding his milling and driving operations, he had established docks and a lumber storage and distribution centre in 1868 at Rouses Point, N.Y., a planing mill and box factory in 1875 in Burlington, Vt, and a sales office in 1877 in Boston. With these facilities he was said to be "the only Canadian lumberman at the time who manufactured his own lumber in his own American mill."

During the economic downturn of 1874–76 Booth had continued to accumulate timber limits at low prices, thus eliminating his dependence on other suppliers. Eventually covering 640,000 acres, his limits extended throughout the Ottawa watershed, encompassing parts of the Madawaska, Bonnechere, Petawawa, Mattawa, and Montreal rivers in Ontario and the Coulonge, Black (Noire), Dumoine, and Kipawa rivers in Quebec. Montreal lumber merchant and biographer George Arthur Grier has claimed that Booth, an incessant traveller throughout his domain, "knew the forest as a sailor knows the sea, and his success was largely due to the fact that he never overestimated its potentialities." Between 1872 and 1892 his

manufacture of lumber increased from approximately 30 million board feet to 140 million, an expansion that made his operations the largest in the world. Booth's output of 115 million feet in 1896 was more than double that of any other major Ottawa valley firm, including McLachlin Brothers of Arnprior [see Daniel McLachlin*] and Bronsons and Weston of Ottawa [see Henry Franklin Bronson*]; by 1900 all of the coastal mills in British Columbia [see John Hendry*] were producing only 100 million feet annually.

As a natural extension of milling, Booth's operations had grown to include a far-reaching transportation network. His involvement with forming and financing the Canada Atlantic Railway in 1879 [see Donald Alexander Macdonald* (Sandfield); William Goodhue Perley*] had drawn him into construction when the original proponents were unable to complete the project. He embraced this new phase of his career with enthusiasm. Railways offered his lumber business three major advantages: reduced labour costs on timber drives, freedom from the seasonal constraints on shipping, and speed. In 1882 Booth completed the 136-mile linkage of the CAR between Ottawa and Coteau-Landing (Les Coteaux) on the St Lawrence, from which point the line eventually secured access to the Central Vermont; initially, the crossing had to be done by barge, but in 1890 this interruption was eliminated by the opening of a railway bridge across the river. To link the pinelands of Georgian Bay, his own upper limits, and the Ottawa River, Booth had started in 1884–86 with a small railway connecting lakes Nipissing and Nosbonsing. Next, the Ottawa, Arnprior and Renfrew and Ottawa and Parry Sound railways were chartered in 1888 and amalgamated in 1891 as the Ottawa, Arnprior and Parry Sound Railway, which was built in 1892–96. During construction, in 1893 Booth successfully disputed the rights to a strategically important pass near Wilno, which the rival Canadian Pacific had also claimed, and he sought to influence the southern boundary of the newly created Algonquin Park [see Aubrey White*] to avoid conflict with his line. (In the end, it ran through the park and Booth secured limits there.) Apart from the advantage the OAPS offered Booth in the lumber trade, for others the route cut 800 miles off the journey from Chicago to Montreal, with mile-a-minute service along the Ottawa–Montreal segment. To secure even more traffic, especially grain, Booth established elevators at Depot Harbour near Parry Sound, as well as at Duluth, Milwaukee, and Coteau-Landing. He eventually added a small fleet of ships to what was recognized as the largest privately owned railway in the world. The OAPS was merged in 1899 into the Canada Atlantic, and in 1904 Booth sold it for $14 million to the Grand Trunk, which he served as a director until it became part of the Canadian National system.

Booth

The empire of J. R. Booth was constantly susceptible to devastation by fire, in the bush, on his railways, and at the Chaudière. His mills were severely damaged in 1893 and again in 1894, when, not surprisingly, he needed 20 British, 5 American, and 3 Canadian firms to underwrite his insurance. In 1895 his Burlington facility was gutted. The disastrous fire of 1900 that cut through Hull and Ottawa caused Booth losses estimated at between one and one and a half million dollars. A major fire in 1903 consumed 10 million feet of lumber, 8 railway cars, and numerous buildings and nearby homes. On the occasion of a conflagration at his mill in September 1913, the second in a week, his son and superintendent, Charles Jackson, discounted the likelihood of arson: the fire, he told the *Ottawa Evening Journal*, appeared "to be just one of those things which visit such plants periodically." The risk had become such a concern to Ottawa's residents and city council, however, that there was considerable resistance in 1917 to J. R. Booth's use of a river-lot at the end of Bronson Avenue for storage. It was the government's need for the property to house a new heating plant for the Parliament Buildings that pushed Booth's mountains of lumber out of Ottawa.

With vast timber resources at his disposal, Booth's concepts of conservation were largely defined in terms of controlling bush fires, which he usually blamed on settlers and prospectors. At the same time his mills attracted attention as concern mounted over the effect of sawdust, trimmings, and other waste on navigation and fisheries. Following the passage of federal legislation in 1873 that prohibited dumping in water, Booth was convicted and fined. Despite a vigorous legal campaign begun against him and other owners in 1885 by Antoine Ratté, an Ottawa wharfinger and boatbuilder whose business suffered from mill refuse, Booth declined to alter his practices until early in the 20th century. He complied, it appears, only because a fire that destroyed much of his plant provided an opportunity to introduce new procedures to eliminate dumping directly into the water.

Beginning in the 1850s, the periodic public examinations of the crown's water rights and works at the Chaudière, including Albert and Victoria islands, had become matters of consequence to the industrial complexes concentrated there. Crown reviews led to legal adjustments to Booth's ownership in 1889 and 1901. His interests stood to be affected too by Quebec's grant to private hands of 31 acres of river-bed, which figured prominently in the complex legal preparations begun in 1900 by Æmilius Irving* and others for a reference to the Supreme Court of Canada over jurisdiction and the exact location of the Ontario–Quebec boundary. In February 1903 a perplexed *Ottawa Citizen* asked "Who owns the river?" The matter was no clearer in 1905 when Ezra Butler Eddy* of Hull took Booth to court over water diversion.

As the traditional lumber trade approached its zenith – the final raft of squared timber would be taken down the Ottawa by Booth's men in 1908 – Booth embarked upon a number of new ventures. Following a fire at McKay Milling at the Chaudière, he purchased the site for pulp production, a sector pioneered by Eddy. Constructed in 1905, the new plant let him make more effective use of the large quantities of softwood he had previously been forced to sell. Also in 1905, his winning bid for the 1,700-square-mile concession of the Montreal River Pulp Company allowed him the convenience of cutting both pulpwood and pine in the same limits. With 26 grinders, the ground-wood section of Booth's mill was capable of a daily production of 182 tons; four digesters provided 30 more of sulphite pulp. Upon encountering difficulties in disposing of his pulp, Booth entered the papermaking business with a mill that put out some 150 tons of newsprint daily. Other new undertakings were purely speculative. In association with Michael John O'Brien*, for instance, Booth used the Dominion Nickel-Copper Company to consolidate mineral properties in the Sudbury area. These holdings, which the principals never intended to develop, would be sold in 1915 to the British America Nickel Corporation, a syndicate organized by Frederick Stark Pearson*. Booth's ventureship was also evident in his board positions, including directorships in Foster-Cobalt Mining (1907) and Canada Cement (1909).

By all accounts Booth, a short man with a white beard and unfading physical vitality, was a picturesque figure, though his rough language, disdain for publicity, and plain dress put him, according to Sandra Gwyn, "decidedly beyond the pale" in Ottawa society. Still, his commercial stature commanded attention. Even late in life, he was renowned for his memory, his detailed knowledge of plant operations, and his direct participation in virtually every aspect of his firm, an involvement that periodically led to injury. There are any number of stories about visitors who eventually located him in his lumber yards or at building sites. One typical legend credits him with identifying a new horse on the day of its arrival at his mill, despite the fact that about 500 horses worked in his yards and woods. Not until 1921, during a trade slump and when Booth was 93, did he convert his operation from a sole proprietorship to John R. Booth Limited.

His managerial style was captured by Charles Christopher Jenkins in *Maclean's* (Toronto) in 1922: "So far as one can learn, John R. Booth has never encouraged initiative or originality in those he has hired as executives, a failing which seemingly has not debarred him from becoming one of the wealthiest and mightiest masters of industry in Canada." More recently, archivist Neil Forsyth has portrayed Booth as "autocratic in the extreme; employees did what they were told or departed." In testimony to the royal commission on the relations of labour and capital in 1889, Booth frankly professed no knowledge of regulations under the Ontario Factories' Act. Writer Doris French has characterized his association with labour as "old-fashioned and feudal"; no model employer, J. R. knew that his workforce was transient, seasonal, and traditionally resistant to organization. He was a leading figure in opposing a general strike that affected his Burlington mill. In 1891 Booth and eight other owners were hit with a massive, prolonged strike by Chaudière millworkers over subsistence wages and 11- or 12-hour days, an action eventually led by the Knights of Labor. The call-up of police and the militia probably had Booth's approval if not his active encouragement. In a strike in 1918 unionized paper-mill workers in Ottawa demanded increased wages from Booth or a public investigation, but he flatly refused any concession; they struck again in 1921.

There were, of course, paternalistic exceptions in Booth's treatment of labour. During a strike at the Grand Trunk that shut down his mills in July 1910 and put 2,000 men out of work, he paid his employees full wages for their lost time. In the somewhat misleading words of the *Citizen*, "By one of the most generous acts in a long career of charitable deeds and looking after the best interests of his many employees, Mr. Booth had again shown the men that he was one of them." He has also been credited with introducing the eight-hour day to the forest industries of the Ottawa valley in 1911 on his own initiative.

Although there is some indication that Prime Minister Sir Charles Tupper* may have attempted to recruit him as a Conservative candidate in May 1896, Booth was by no means prominent politically. He usually devoted such time as he cared to allocate to public affairs to matters directly related to his industrial concerns. As a papermaker, for example, he joined ranks with Charles Christopher (Carl) Riordon, E. B. Eddy, and others to campaign for prohibitions on the export of unmanufactured pulpwood to the United States, and he successfully lobbied for cutting rights to birch in Algonquin Park. Only in opposition to Sir Wilfrid Laurier*'s advocacy of reciprocity in the federal contest of 1911 did he appear to take an active role in the electoral process.

In Ottawa, Booth, a Presbyterian, quietly made substantial financial contributions to community projects, including the Young Men's Christian Association building and St Luke's Hospital [*see* Annie Amelia Chesley*], which he helped found in 1897 and endowed in 1914 with a new wing. Described as "a believer in and a generous patron of clean, manly

sport," he was a member of the Ottawa Amateur Athletic Club and the Ottawa Rowing Club. In 1903 he was named honorary president of the Canadian Reading Camps Association, which distributed literature to and promoted night schools in lumber and mining camps. At the time of World War I, he made the largest donation to purchase equipment for the No.1 Automobile Machine-Gun Brigade.

By the time he was in his nineties, Booth had achieved a reputation of legendary proportions tinged with the romance of the northern woods, even though by 1919 his production was being eclipsed by that of W. C. Edwards and Company Limited and others. On 27 March 1920, in a rare public appearance and to a "rousing ovation," Booth dropped the puck for a Stanley Cup match between the Ottawa Senators and the Seattle Metropolitans. Within the timber industry he received plaudits as honorary president of the Canadian Lumbermen's Association. Booth's achievements inspired C. C. Jenkins to describe him in 1922 as one of those "men who have transformed the dreamy melody of the living waters into a roaring chant of commercial conquest." In the words of Michael Grattan O'Leary* in the *Ottawa Evening Journal* in 1925, the Booth to remember was "not the great magnate whose wealth is the envy of many and the wonder of more; but the great pioneer, the man whose genius and imagination tamed the wilderness . . . and, above all, did more than any man of his time to build up this Ottawa Valley." On the occasion of his death in December 1925, following two months of confinement at his Ottawa residence, Prime Minister William Lyon Mackenzie King* generously referred to him as "one of the fathers of Canada." Buried beside his wife in Beechwood Cemetery in Ottawa, Booth was survived by his sons Jackson and John Frederick and his daughter Helen Gertrude Fleck.

Booth's fortune was a subject of much speculative commentary during the latter years of his life, with estimates ranging up to $100 million. At the time of the marriage in 1924 of his granddaughter Lois Frances Booth to Prince Erik Christian Frederik Alexander of Denmark, it was rumoured that Booth contributed half of her $4-million dowry. J. R. issued a formal denial. At his death his estate was officially valued at almost $7.7 million; the property was later re-evaluated upwards. Although succession duties exceeding $4 million were paid in 1927, Ontario premier Mitchell Frederick Hepburn* subsequently claimed more and invoked the legislature to overcome the legal obstacles. The heirs eventually paid another $3 million.

Contemporaries often referred to J. R. Booth as a lumber king, the equivalent perhaps of today's media moguls. Booth understood the regional economy of the Ottawa valley and its relationship to international trade as well as or better than any of his peers.

Borland

Through hard work, resolute determination, and longevity he contributed greatly to the private economy of the government town that Ottawa had become.

JAMIE BENIDICKSON

Virtually no papers have survived for J. R. Booth personally or for the Booth company.

ANQ-E, CE502-S42, 7 janv. 1853. AO, F 137; F 1027, package 50; RG 22-354, no.12659; RG 80-8-0-108, no.2379; RG 80-8-0-988, no.10201. LAC, RG 31, C1, 1871, Ottawa, Victoria Ward, div.2: 119. Ottawa Land Registry Office, Abstract index to deeds, Chaudière lots (mfm. at AO). *Globe*, 9 Dec. 1925. *Ottawa Citizen*, 27 June 1894, 27 April 1900, 14 Feb. 1903, 19–28 July 1910, 29 March 1920. *Ottawa Evening Journal*, 21 April 1893, 4 Aug. 1910, 8 Sept. 1913, 17 Aug. 1917, 13 June 1925. *Ottawa Free Press*, 27 May 1886. *Canada Lumberman* (Toronto), 41 (1921). *Canadian annual rev.*, 1907–20. C. F. Coons, "The John R. Booth story," *Your Forests* (Toronto), 11 (1978), no.2: 8–26. *Encyclopaedia of Canadian biography . . .*, vol.2: 2. Neil Forsyth, "J. R. Booth: career of a lumber baron," *Archivist* (Ottawa), 14 (1987), no.5: 10–11. Doris French, "The Booths of Ottawa," *Chatelaine* (Toronto), 36 (1963), no.12: 22–23, 65–68, 71–75. Peter Gillis, "Rivers of sawdust: the battle over industrial pollution in Canada, 1865–1903," *Journal of Canadian Studies* (Peterborough, Ont.), 21 (1986–87), no.1: 84–103. W. E. Greening, *The Ottawa* ([Toronto], 1961). B. W. Hodgins and Jamie Benidickson, *The Temagami experience: recreation, resources, and aboriginal rights in the northern Ontario wilderness* (Toronto, 1989). J. W. Hughson and C. C. J. Bond, *Hurling down the pine; the story of the Wright, Gilmour and Hughson families, timber and lumber manufacturers for the Hull and Ottawa region and on the Gatineau River, 1800–1920* (2nd ed., Old Chelsea, Que., 1965). C. C. Jenkins, "J. R. Booth – on the job at 95," *Maclean's* (Toronto), 35 (1922), no.10: 15–16, 61–62. G. S. Kealey and B. D. Palmer, *Dreaming of what might be: the Knights of Labor in Ontario, 1880–1900* (Toronto, 1987). *Labour Gazette* (Ottawa), 18 (1918): 917. R. S. Lambert with Paul Pross, *Renewing nature's wealth: a centennial history of the public management of lands, forests & wildlife in Ontario, 1763–1967* ([Toronto], 1967). A. R. M. Lower, *Great Britain's woodyard: British America and the timber trade, 1763–1867* (Montreal and London, 1973). J. S. P. McLaren, "The tribulations of Antoine Ratté: a case study of the environmental regulation of the Canadian lumbering industry in the nineteenth century," *Univ. of New Brunswick Law Journal* (Fredericton), 33 (1984): 203–59. H. V. Nelles, *The politics of development: forests, mines & hydro-electric power in Ontario, 1849–1941* (Toronto, 1974). *Standard dict. of Canadian biog.* (Roberts and Tunnell), vol.1. J. R. Trinnell, *J. R. Booth: the life and times of an Ottawa lumberking* (Ottawa, 1998).

BORLAND, ROBERT, businessman and miner; b. 28 Aug. 1839 near Bowmanville, Upper Canada, son of Hiram Borland and Ann Frank; m. 23 Feb. 1898 Christina Glassey in Clinton, B.C.; they had no children; d. 22 Jan. 1923 in Quesnel, B.C.

William Borland, Robert Borland's ancestor, came to Upper Canada from New Hampshire with his wife and family in 1799, settled in Durham County, and served with the 1st Durham Militia during the War of 1812. Nothing is known of Robert's early life except that he did not stay long on the family farm in Durham, near Bowmanville. He arrived in British Columbia about 1862 and took part in the Cariboo gold rush and in 1867 in the short-lived rush on Cedar Creek at Quesnel Lake.

In 1869 Borland formed a partnership with George Adolphus Vieth, a Halifax native, and together they purchased Willow Ranch, on the Keithley Creek delta at Cariboo Lake. Located on the pack-trail linking the Cariboo wagon road and Barkerville [see William Barker*], the ranch had been an important stopping place during the gold rush. It produced grain for pack-train animals and large quantities of vegetables, and, under Vieth and Borland's management, it became the social and commercial centre of the east Cariboo region. The post office, saloon, store, and hotel established at Keithley Creek served a population of 100 to 200 miners. With a third partner, Robert McNab, Vieth and Borland opened a second store, at the junction of Little Snowshoe and Keithley creeks on the trail to Barkerville. At both stores miners paid with gold dust or with furs in winter. To help some of them over rough times, Vieth and Borland often held mortgages on their claims. In this way the two merchants, who also worked the Grotto and Onward mines on Keithley Creek, acquired a number of lucrative claims on Little Snowshoe.

About 1884 Vieth and Borland purchased the 150 Mile stopping-house on the Cariboo Road from Gavin Hamilton, a former Hudson's Bay Company factor. Here they raised cattle, harvested grain, and operated a post office, saloon, and hotel. Known for their social involvement, they took their turn in the round of winter festivities by hosting "Batchelor Balls." As well, they cared for a number of gold-rush old-timers at both Keithley Creek and 150 Mile House, keeping them employed chopping wood and carrying out other chores. Another pioneer, Martha Hutch, a native woman who supervised the laundry at Keithley Creek, was looked after until her death.

In 1888 Vieth and Borland contracted with the HBC to pack freight from Hazelton to Babine Lake at two cents per pound for 200,000 pounds. That same year Borland, who occasionally went along on trips, accompanied the train from Quesnel to Hazelton on the Skeena River. Arriving at the time of the affair sparked by the shooting of a Gitksan Indian, he was considered neutral and given passage down the Skeena to Port Essington, where he caught a boat to Victoria. Striding into a sitting of the provincial legislature, he startled the members with the announcement, "Gentlemen, do you know there is a war on?"

As a result of the completion of the Canadian Pacific Railway, a hydraulic-mining boom took place in east Cariboo between 1890 and 1910. Vieth and Borland held shares in the South Fork Hydraulic Mining Company, which worked a site two miles above Quesnel Forks on the South Fork (Quesnel) River. Privately acquired in 1894 by a group of CPR directors and renamed the Cariboo Hydraulic Mining Company (later Consolidated Cariboo Hydraulic Mining), it employed over 200 men at the Bullion Pit mine. Vieth and Borland drove in cattle from their 150 Mile ranch to supply this camp. The partners, in fact, advertised 150 Mile House in the *Ashcroft Journal* as "the distributing point for all the hydraulic mines at Horse Fly, North and South Forks and main Quesnelle River, also the stock ranges of Chilcoten and Beaver Lake Valley." The mining boom led as well to the survey of Quesnel Forks into town lots in 1892. Vieth and Borland purchased two and opened another hotel, store, and saloon.

It appears from their correspondence and ledgers that Vieth was the accountant during their long partnership, which would last until Vieth's death in 1906. But Borland was also astute, especially in land purchases. By signing countless petitions and visiting government representatives in Victoria, the two men gained improvements to trails and wagon roads. On one occasion they took matters into their own hands by clearing a pack-trail near the Frypan Mountains in the Omineca region and then requesting reimbursement. Their only competition was Peter Curran Dunlevy, a native of Pittsburgh who owned a hotel at Soda Creek, invested in mines at Barkerville, real estate in Vancouver, and a railway and quarry on Vancouver Island, and transported supplies into the Cassiar region. Vieth and Borland were more localized than Dunlevy: except for their wide-ranging packing business, they concentrated on east Cariboo and the Cariboo Road.

In 1898 Vieth and Borland sold their pack-train business, once valued at $4,800 and consisting of 60 pack-mules, 5 riding mules, 8 four-year-old mules (halter-broken), and 1 bell-mare. Borland personally delivered the train to Glenora, in northwestern British Columbia. Following the sale of 150 Mile House in 1899, he acquired the William Pinchbeck ranch on nearby Williams Lake on his own. Under his management, this ranch, which he named Kinlochaline, was known as "one of the best fodder producing farms in the district." He sold the land to the provincial government about 1913; it became the Pacific Great Eastern Railway terminus in 1919 and the town-site of Williams Lake.

Following George Vieth's death, Borland had taken on responsibility for managing Willow Ranch as well as Kinlochaline. After the latter's sale, he spent his remaining years at Willow Ranch. Despite his apparent good fortune, his personal life may not have been altogether happy. His marriage in 1898 to 21-year-old Chryssie Glassey ended in divorce after she spent a lot of his money and then left him. Robert Borland was described in the *Vancouver Daily Province* in 1923 as "powerfully built, very strong, resourceful and dependable and generally well liked by all those whom he served." Few could match his kindness and generosity. He had provided eight double teams for the funeral of Beaver valley pioneer Frank Guy, for example, and had deferred the grocery charges of ailing miner John (Aurora Jack) Edwards. In contrast to the boom-and-bust nature of so much mining activity, Vieth and Borland's investment in the Cariboo demonstrates their long-term commitment to the region. Borland died in January 1923 in Quesnel and was buried at Keithley Creek; he left his estate to a niece, Mabel Borland. Borland Creek at 150 Mile House, Borland Street in Williams Lake, and Mount Borland near Cariboo Lake are named for this popular merchant and miner.

MARIE ELLIOTT

Information on Robert Borland was obtained by the author from Gary O. Borland, a second cousin of the subject, in February 1999. The Jack Lynn Memorial Museum (Horsefly, B.C.) has an invitation to one of the Batchelor Balls given by Vieth and Borland on display in its collection.

AM, HBCA, B.290/e/1–3. AO, RG 22-191, no.1237. BCA, GR-0216, vol.33; GR-1052; GR-1440, 1815/89, 4649/92, 2234/95; GR-1676, vol.1/72a; MS-2561. LAC, RG 1, L3, 48: B14/230; 85: B leases, 1802–18/148; 86: B leases, 1816–37/152; RG 31, C1, 1871, Darlington Township, Ont., div.1: 10. *Ashcroft Journal* (Ashcroft, B.C.), 1896, 5 Feb. 1898, 26 July 1902. *Daily Colonist* (Victoria), 15 Oct. 1890. *Vancouver Daily Province*, 23 Jan. 1923. J. A. Roberts, *Cariboo chronicles: Williams Lake golden jubilee, 1929–1979* ([n.p., 1979]).

BOSTOCK, HEWITT, rancher, businessman, and politician; b. 31 May 1864 in Walton on the Hill, Surrey, England, eldest son of Samuel Bostock and Marian Iliff; m. 12 June 1890 Lizzie Jean McCombie Cowie in Surbiton, England, and they had four daughters and three sons; d. 28 April 1930 in Monte Creek, B.C.

Hewitt Bostock's father, Samuel, profited handsomely from investments on the London Stock Exchange during the mid-Victorian boom. His success allowed him to move his family to The Hermitage, in the parish of Walton on the Hill near Epsom, where he cultivated the style of a country squire and where Hewitt was born. Although Samuel died when his eldest son was only four, the family's substantial fortune did not fail. At the age of 10 Hewitt was enrolled at a boarding school in Brighton and he subsequently studied in Guildford. His early education was followed by a mathematics degree at Trinity College, Cambridge, which he attended from 1882 to 1885 and where he would obtain an MA in 1890. Despite a bout with pneumonia, contracted whilst on a climbing expedition in Switzerland in 1881, he demonstrated ability as a rower at Cambridge in 1883. Bostock accumulated diplomas, but gives the impression of an intellectual dilettante: he obtained only a third in his BA, and although he would be called to the bar in 1888 by Lincoln's Inn in London, he never practised law.

In 1886 Bostock made his first foray to Canada, travelling with his sister Marian Iliff (May) and some friends. Touring Ottawa, Bostock inspected the Parliament Buildings and saw the Conservative prime minister, Sir John A. Macdonald* (whom he described as "a fine-looking man"). An Anglican, he also made connections with Canon William Henry Cooper, who the next year took over the Church of England mission in Kamloops, B.C. It appears to have been this meeting that led Bostock to visit the Thompson valley in 1888, part-way through a tour of North America, the Antipodes, China, and Japan. During this visit he purchased the ranch of Jacob Duck, an English settler, for $45,000. Possibly he viewed the property at Ducks, as the area was known, as little more than another investment in an already bulging portfolio, an exotic revenue-generating retreat on which he would vacation from time to time. In 1890 Bostock and his new bride, Lizzie, spent part of their honeymoon at the ranch, and they repeated the visit in 1891. Two years later the Bostocks moved from England to British Columbia, where they erected a fine home in an exclusive Victoria neighbourhood, leaving the ranch in the hands of a manager.

Although a Conservative in England, Bostock found in Canada that he preferred the Liberal policy of freer trade to the tariff that Macdonald's government had introduced. In April 1894 he established the *Province* newspaper in Victoria, which ran as a weekly and was critical of the National Policy. That September Liberal leader Wilfrid Laurier* visited British Columbia and persuaded Bostock to run for parliament in the Yale-Cariboo constituency. The decision to do so led him to spend more time at Monte Creek, as Ducks was now called, where he built a generously proportioned ranch house for his growing family. Around the same time he established the Kootenay Lumber Company. By 1895 he had made a sufficiently good impression on the locals that he was elected first president of the Kamloops Agricultural Association.

The 1896 federal election saw Bostock take up his career in politics. He quietly purchased the Kamloops *Inland Sentinel*, setting up Francis John Deane, a Liberal, as his editor. With Bostock in the shadows, Deane ran an effective and expensive campaign against the powerful Conservative incumbent, John Andrew Mara, while Bostock visited one hamlet after another. Having spent $1,350 to Mara's $500, Bostock won the election with a comfortable majority and served a single term under Laurier, acting as one of the caucus whips. Otherwise, his principal claim to fame as an MP was the introduction of a bill that, had it passed, would have formalized the practice of railway companies carrying parliamentarians free of charge. Like many of his contemporaries, Bostock was vocal in his opposition to further Chinese immigration to Canada, which he viewed as a racial, social, and economic threat. He also regarded southern Europeans with contempt, claiming in 1897 that "the Italians were nearly as great a menace as the Chinamen." Bostock did not seek re-election in 1900.

At the turn of the century Bostock made two important moves. First, in 1898, responding to entreaties from the business community in Vancouver, he established a daily edition of the *Province* on the mainland, running it in partnership with Walter Cameron NICHOL (to whom he subsequently sold his interest). Second, he disposed of his house in Victoria, and moved with his family to the Monte Creek ranch. Bostock found further opportunities to invest locally, becoming president of the Tranquille Creek Hydraulic and Quartz Mining Company Limited and building two business blocks on Kamloops's Main Street.

In 1904 Bostock was appointed to the Senate. Ten years later he became leader of the Liberals in the upper house. Along with most of his party, he opposed the Naval Aid Bill of 1913 and the War-time Elections Act of 1917, both introduced by the Conservative government of Robert Laird Borden*. In contrast to his earlier nativism, he objected to the cynicism of the latter bill in so far as it disenfranchised loyal immigrant Canadians. Nonetheless, he threw in his lot with the pro-conscription forces and travelled the west in 1917 advocating a union government. (The previous year his son Alexander Hewitt had been killed in action in France.) Bostock entered William Lyon Mackenzie King*'s first cabinet as minister of public works in late December 1921, a position he relinquished a little over a month later when he became speaker of the Senate. By that time Bostock had achieved some notoriety as an opponent of railway nationalization. In 1925 Bostock was one of Canada's delegates at the sixth assembly of the League of Nations at Geneva. A young man when he had entered politics, by the time of his death in 1930 he had outlived all but a handful of his contemporaries from the Laurier government and was one of the most senior members of the Senate.

Described in his obituaries and memorials as "courtly," a "country gentlemen," and "a man of culture, ability, genial disposition and fine presence," Bostock appears to have made a career out of being stately. His associations included the Canadian branch of the British Empire League, the Canadian Forestry Association, the Interior Stock Raisers' Association of British Columbia, the Rideau Club in Ottawa, the first golf and badminton clubs in Victoria, the masonic lodge, the Alpine Club of Canada, and the St John Ambulance Association, of which he was national president at the time of his death. In addition, he was a fellow of the Royal Colonial Institute and Royal Agricultural Society of England. As patriarch of a family that included three sons and four daughters, he emphasized the advantages of further education: two sons obtained engineering degrees (and one of them a PHD in geology) and his eldest daughter trained at the University of London and practised as an MD in London and India.

Hewitt Bostock died of uraemia and was buried on his Monte Creek property, in the family cemetery near the small wooden church he had built in 1926 in memory of his son Alec. In 1932 a mountain about 100 miles to the southwest was given the name Mount Hewitt Bostock.

JOHN DOUGLAS BELSHAW and
ELISABETH DUCKWORTH

Kamloops Museum and Arch. (Kamloops, B.C.), Vertical files, Bostock family. *Inland Sentinel* (Kamloops), 4 Sept. 1896; 12 Feb., 30 April 1897. *Times* (London), 14 June 1890, 30 April 1930. Mary Balf, *Kamloops: a history of the district up to 1914* (3rd ed., Kamloops, 1989). A. L. Earl, "Monte Creek: the western frontier: politics, murder and robbery," in *Reflections: Thompson valley histories*, ed. Wayne Norton and Wilf Schmidt (Kamloops, 1994), 131–34. *Standard dict. of Canadian biog.* (Roberts and Tunnell).

BOURGEOIS, NATHALIE. *See* MELANSON

BOURQUE, EDMOND-JOSEPH, physician and professor; b. 22 Jan. 1843 in L'Assomption, Lower Canada, son of Édouard Bourque, a farmer, and Olive Jeannot, *dit* Lachapelle; m. first 27 May 1867 in Sainte-Scholastique (Mirabel), Lower Canada, Iphigénie Desjardins, sister of Alphonse*, a lawyer and future MP, and of Louis-Édouard* and Henri, who would both make a name as ophthalmologists, and they had eight children, including Henri, a rector of the Collège de Saint-Boniface in Manitoba, and Edmond, a physician in Ottawa; m. secondly 31 July 1911 Georgine Gagnon in Montreal; they had no children; d. 12 Dec. 1921 at the convent of the Sisters of Charity of Providence in L'Assomption.

In 1854 Edmond-Joseph Bourque entered the Collège de L'Assomption, where he was a classmate of Wilfrid Laurier*. He turned next to medicine, enrolling in the Montreal School of Medicine and Surgery in 1862. After graduating in 1865, he was in general practice for 20 years, first in Saint-Valentin, near the Richelieu River, for seven years, and then in Montreal.

In 1885 the government of John Jones Ross*, determined to exercise greater control over the asylums it funded in the province, set up medical boards for the Asile de Beauport and the Asile de Longue-Pointe (also known as the Hôpital Saint-Jean-de-Dieu). Comprised of three government-appointed physicians, these boards were responsible for the admission, treatment, and discharge of mentally ill patients. The legislation, which was known as the Ross Act, was passed at the request of the Montreal Medico-Chirurgical Society, which had embraced the criticisms of the English alienist Daniel Hack Tuke about the deplorable state of the province's asylums. Taking the position that this statute violated the contract they had signed with the government, the Sisters of Charity of Providence, who administered the Asile de Longue-Pointe, decided not to obey the directives of the medical board, whose superintendent was Henry Howard*, and they hired three attending physicians. The asylum's medical staff now included two categories of physicians: those appointed by the government and those employed by the sisters. Bourque was one of the latter. He was immediately sent to Europe at the sisters' expense to specialize in psychiatry. He undertook a six-month training period, during which he visited many asylums in England, Belgium, and France, and attended clinical classes on mental illness in London and especially in Paris. On his return to Canada in 1886, he was appointed head of the medical staff for the Asile de Longue-Pointe, a position he held until 1909.

When he took up his duties, Bourque found himself responsible for the daily treatment of the asylum's 950 patients. He lost no time in introducing substantial changes. For example, about 40 cells were demolished and replaced by public wards. Bourque also did away with metal restraints, whose use had been sharply criticized by Tuke; instead he introduced the straitjacket, a more flexible device he had seen utilized in Europe. Unfortunately, these reforms came to an abrupt halt in May 1890 when the asylum burned down. Bourque himself almost lost his life during the blaze, which left some 80 people dead. Temporary wards were built to house patients and it was not until 1901 that a new hospital, with a capacity of 2,000 beds, was opened.

Relations between Bourque and the Sisters of Providence seem always to have been extremely cordial. Testifying in 1888 before the royal commission on lunatic asylums, which had been set up the previous year by the government of Honoré Mercier* with a view to resolving the crisis surrounding institutions for the care of the mentally ill, Bourque indicated that the sisters had never put any restrictions on the treatments he proposed. In 1889 he and his assistant, Dr Adélard Barolet, accompanied the director of the asylum, Cléophée Têtu*, named Thérèse de Jésus, and Sister Madeleine du Sacré-Cœur to Europe, where they visited some 40 asylums. However, Bourque's relations with the hospital's medical board were rather strained during the early years. For example, he noted in 1888 that it did not consult him before deciding to discharge some patients. The following year, at an international congress on mental medicine in Paris, he defended the system of private asylums in existence in Quebec, taking a view opposite to that of the medical superintendent of the Asile de Longue-Pointe, Dr Emmanuel-Évariste Duquet (Duquette), who favoured public asylums. Bourque's participation in this congress gained him membership in the Société Médico-Psychologique of Paris.

The crisis of the 1880s was finally resolved by a compromise. Although there remained two categories of physicians at the Asile de Longue-Pointe, some degree of understanding was reached, especially after the appointment of Georges Villeneuve as medical superintendent in 1894, with the two groups arriving at a consensus on the etiology and the classification of mental illness. A similar understanding at the provincial level paved the way for the formation in 1898 of the Société Médico-Psychologique de Québec, whose first president was Arthur Vallée*, the medical superintendent of the Asile de Beauport; Bourque and the other physicians hired by the nuns collaborated with the society.

However, Bourque was to make his most important contribution at the theoretical level. On his return from Europe he had disseminated in L'Union médicale du Canada the teachings of Valentin Magnan, a French psychiatrist whose theory of degeneration, emphasizing an acquired or hereditary predisposition to mental illness, would be the dominant paradigm of Quebec psychiatrists until early in the 1920s. In addition, Bourque's clinical teaching on mental illness, which he had begun upon his return, had been recognized in 1888 by the Montreal School of Medicine and Surgery.

By both his practice and his teaching, Edmond-Joseph Bourque helped to advance French neuropsychiatry in Quebec.

GUY GRENIER

Edmond-Joseph Bourque is the author of "Le délire chronique," L'Union médicale du Canada (Montréal), 15 (1886): 193–98; "De la céphalée des adolescents," La Gazette médicale de Montréal, 1 (1887): 59–63; "Clinique des maladies mentales," La Gazette médicale de Montréal, 2 (1888): 388–90; and "Paralysie générale des aliénés," La Gazette médicale de Montréal, 3 (1889): 149–55.

ANQ-M, CE605-S14, 22 janv. 1843; CE606-S22, 27 mai 1867. ANQ-Q, E104. Le Devoir, 13 déc. 1921. La Presse, 13 déc. 1921. Adélard Barolet, "Rapport du Congrès international de médecine mentale," La Gazette médicale de Montréal, 3: 433–37. Denis Goulet, Histoire de la faculté de médecine de l'université de Montréal, 1843–1993 (Montréal, 1993). Guy Grenier, "L'implantation et les applications de la doctrine de la dégénérescence dans le champ de la médecine et de l'hygiène mentales au Québec entre 1885 et 1930" (mémoire de MA, univ. de Montréal, 1990). Peter Keating, La science du mal: l'institution de la psychiatrie au Québec, 1800–1914 ([Montréal, 1993]). Montreal School of Medicine and Surgery, Annuaire, 1862–65. Sœur Thérèse de Jésus [Cléophée Têtu] et sœur Madeleine du Sacré-Cœur [Madeleine Desjardins], Récit de voyage d'Europe . . . 1889 (s.l., n.d.). D. H. Tuke, The insane in the United States and Canada (London, 1885).

BOWER, JAMES, farmer, businessman, and agrarian leader; b. 26 Jan. 1860 in Mono Township, Upper Canada, son of James Bower and Dorothea Laverty; m. 21 Feb. 1883 Catherine Elizabeth McLean (d. 1931) in Mono Township, Ont., and they had seven sons and two daughters; d. 16 May 1921 near Red Deer, Alta.

James Bower's mother and father were born in Ireland and became part of the surging wave of British immigration that began washing over Upper Canada after the Napoleonic Wars. His father carried on his trade of blacksmith north of Toronto and farmed, first near Georgian Bay and then in Mono Township, not far from Orangeville. Both Anglicans, his parents had been married by Bishop John Strachan* – that rigid and powerful patriarch of the colonial political elite – but the less formal and democratic James Bower became a Methodist. The youngest of seven children, Bower proved energetic and ambitious: he operated a farm, a planing mill, a sash and door factory, and an electric light utility, and he acted as a building contractor in the Orangeville area.

After two accidents struck his businesses, Bower, like growing numbers of restless fellow Ontarians, sought a new frontier of opportunity in "the last, best west." The bushy-moustached pioneer intended to look for land north of Red Deer, but during a stop at the village in 1899 he missed his train and bought property nearby. He soon accumulated more land and produced the brick for a district school and his commodious house, which he built in 1905. A prosperous and progressive farmer, Bower raised Percheron horses, imported from France, and registered Shorthorn cattle, and in 1907 he purchased the first International Harvester gasoline tractor in western Canada.

Like many successful agriculturalists, Bower became a leading light in the farm movement. In 1908 he was active in the Central Alberta Stock Growers' Association and the Alberta Farmers' Association. In the same year he was appointed to a government commission that heard evidence about the pork industry. The commission recommended in 1909 that the province construct and operate a processing plant once producers had signed contracts to supply 50,000 hogs per year. To Bower's chagrin, farmers failed to pledge enough animals, and the plant was never built.

In 1909 the AFA amalgamated with the Canadian Society of Equity, a rival farm organization, to form the United Farmers of Alberta. Bower's stature was such that he was elected the first president of the UFA and continued to be elected until he stepped down in 1912. Shortly after becoming president, he sought to gain access to British Columbia markets for Alberta farm products, and to this end he proposed municipally owned abattoirs, which would compete with the meat-trade monopoly, and lower railway rates. A conference of Alberta and British Columbia business interests held in Vancouver in 1910, which Bower organized and chaired, endorsed these suggestions, and in 1910–11 he worked with the Vancouver Board of Trade in a vain attempt to end freight-rate discrimination against the west. In 1909 Bower had helped to found and was president of the Red Deer Co-operative Association, the first UFA cooperative. It did an impressive business in its initial year, selling livestock, hay, and grain, and served as a model for other UFA cooperatives. Bower worked tirelessly for national cooperative legislation.

Like most prairie farmers, Bower was an ardent believer in freer trade. When Prime Minister Sir Wilfrid Laurier* toured the Canadian west in 1910, Bower greeted him at Red Deer on 10 August and at Lethbridge on 1 September, and along with other UFA leaders he made an impassioned plea for lower tariffs and other measures. As vice-president of the Canadian Council of Agriculture and president of the UFA, Bower was one of some 800 farmers' representatives who on 16 Dec. 1910 descended upon the nation's capital in the great "siege of Ottawa" in order to address the government [see James Speakman*]. Following up a paper that he had left with Laurier in Alberta, Bower requested that railway companies be held liable for livestock killed by trains, a campaign that he had spearheaded and would fight without ceasing.

To the delight of Bower and farmers across the country, in early 1911 the Laurier government struck a reciprocity agreement with the United States, which promised to open the American market for Canadian natural products. By this time Bower had become a figure of national importance. Elected president of the CCA for 1911–12, he lobbied federal politicians to support reciprocity, a federal export system for chilled meat, a bill that would reform the grain industry, and federally owned and operated grain terminals. In the run-up to the federal election in September he exhorted UFA members to vote for pro-reciprocity candidates, which effectively meant Liberal candidates. He suggested that the agreement would not only increase prices of agricultural products, but by expanding north-south trade would force the railway companies to lower freight charges. To his bitter disappointment and that of most Canadian farmers, Robert Laird Borden*'s Conservatives won the election and scrapped the reciprocity deal. Bower was, however, able to take some satisfaction in the new govern-

ment's construction of terminal elevators in 1913–16. His efforts to improve the provincial country elevator system also bore fruit. Although he had originally echoed most farmers' wish for a government-owned line of elevators, he and the rest of the UFA elevator committee were unimpressed with Manitoba's experiment with public elevators, and in 1912 they steered the UFA to agitate for a government-financed, farmer-controlled cooperative scheme. As a result, in 1913 the Alberta Farmers Co-operative Elevator Company Limited was created [see Edwin Carswell*]. In 1917 it would merge with the Grain Growers' Grain Company to become United Grain Growers Limited.

Unable to carry on for health reasons, in early 1912 Bower had retired as UFA president and had been succeeded by William John Tregillus*. The following year he, his wife, and his youngest children moved to Vancouver, while his older sons remained in Red Deer. Always interested in politics, in the Alberta provincial election campaign of 1913 Bower publicly endorsed the Liberal government of Arthur Lewis Watkins Sifton, approving of its hail-insurance program, its provision for direct legislation, and its support for the Alberta Farmers Co-operative Elevator Company. In 1916 Bower and his family returned to the Red Deer farm, where he remained until his death in 1921 at age 61. Having faithfully shepherded the UFA in its first three years, Bower died only two months before the UFA under President Henry Wise Wood* won the 1921 provincial election and formed a majority government with Herbert Greenfield* as premier.

BRADFORD J. RENNIE

The author would like to thank Ted Bower of Calgary (subject's grandson) and Dorothy and Ruth Bower of Red Deer, Alta (subject's granddaughters) for consenting to interviews and for allowing him access to documents and letters in their possession.

GA, BR UFA, minutes and reports of annual conventions, 1910–12. Grain Growers' Guide (Winnipeg), March 1909; 9 March, 6 April, 1, 22 June, 24, 31 Aug., 21 Sept., 21, 28 Dec. 1910; 15 Feb., 1, 15, 29 March, 12 July, 16 Aug., 20 Sept., 4 Oct. 1911; 25 May 1921. Red Deer Advocate, 20 May 1921. Canadian annual rev., 1910, 1913. D. G. Embree, "The rise of the United Farmers of Alberta" (MA thesis, Univ. of Alta, Edmonton, 1956). Farm and Ranch Rev. ([Calgary]), 4 (1908), no.1. Red Deer East Hist. Soc., Mingling memories (Red Deer, 1979). B. J. Rennie, The rise of agrarian democracy: the United Farmers and Farm Women of Alberta, 1909–1921 (Toronto, 2000).

BOYLE, JOSEPH WHITESIDE, sailor, entrepreneur, prizefighter, sourdough, intelligence agent, and royal confidant; b. 6 Nov. 1867 in Toronto, youngest of the four children of Charles Boyle and Martha Bain; m. first 6 June 1889 Emilie Josephine Raynor in New York City; m. secondly c. 1908 Elma Louise

Boyle

Humphries in or near Detroit; d. 14 April 1923 in London, England.

Despite a plethora of unsubstantiated claims about his achievements, Joseph Boyle is one of Canada's genuine but little known heroes. Of Irish and Scottish parentage, he moved with his family to Woodstock, Ont., when he was very young. There his father, a racehorse trainer, continued his business and became a successful cattle breeder. Thoroughbreds trained by him won the Queen's Plate in 1862, 1883, 1897, and 1898. Educated in 1883–84 at Woodstock College, a school with a strong Baptist tradition, Boyle often accompanied his father to racing meets, and it was during a trip to New York in 1885 that he ran off to sea. Three years later he returned to the city a mature, hardened young man.

Almost immediately he married a young Belgian divorcee, Emilie Raynor. Profiting from his father's turf connections, he then started a successful feed and freighting business. By 1896, in addition to Emilie's son by her previous marriage, there were three children, a son and two daughters, and a third daughter on the way. The union was never a success, and it failed the following year. Around this time Boyle, a strong, powerful, heavy-limbed, and rugged-looking six-footer who had become involved in sports, undertook to manage and spar with an Australian heavyweight, Francis (Frank) Patrick Slavin. Hoping to capitalize upon Slavin's reputation – he had fought notable bouts in England and was once considered to be a contender for the world championship – the two embarked on an exhibition tour that eventually took them to Juneau, Alaska. Arriving at the height of excitement over the Klondike gold strikes they headed for the diggings in July 1897, joining the first party to reach Dawson via the White Pass. By then, however, most of the choice gumboot mining sites had been staked and Boyle, realizing that fortunes could still be made by using hydraulic methods on ground unsuitable for pick-and-shovel mining, left Dawson for Ottawa in September, intent upon obtaining a concession from the federal government. On 1 December Slavin, who remained behind, applied on their behalf for a lease of ground on the Klondike River.

Through persistent lobbying of Clifford SIFTON, the minister of the interior, Boyle, who bought out Slavin's interest in the partnership in 1899, was on 5 Nov. 1900 finally granted a lease on approximately 40 square miles fronting the river between the mouths of Bonanza and Hunker creeks. In spite of local opposition and numerous law suits Boyle gained control of the Canadian Klondyke Mining Company Limited in 1909. With subsequent financial backing from English interests, notably Granville Mining (of which Arthur Newton Christie Treadgold* was managing director), he consolidated his control in 1911–12. He then parlayed his concession into a placer empire which at its zenith consisted of four dredges (three of them the world's largest) and a power plant to operate them (a plant which also enabled him to become the sole supplier of electricity to Dawson). Civic- and sports-minded, Boyle spearheaded efforts for community improvements, promoted boxing events, and in 1904–5 financed a hockey team, variously known as the Klondikers, the Nuggets, and the Wanderers, which unsuccessfully challenged the Ottawa Silver Seven, the Stanley Cup holders [see Francis Clarence McGee*].

With the outbreak of World War I, Boyle, too old to enlist, volunteered to recruit and finance a 50-man machine-gun company, a contribution for which he would be awarded the honorary rank of lieutenant-colonel by the minister of militia and defence, Samuel HUGHES. As the conflict continued his mining company began to experience money problems and operational difficulties, forcing him to travel to England in 1916 to meet shareholders. There, to the detriment of his business affairs, he undertook a mission to Russia on behalf of the American Committee of Engineers in London to help reorganize the country's railway system.

Boyle reached Russia in July 1917, and despite grudging support from the British Foreign and War offices, and difficulties caused by Bolshevik revolutionaries, he was instrumental in rationalizing rail traffic within the military zone extending from Petrograd (St Petersburg) to Odessa (Odesa, Ukraine). In November his leadership proved to be decisive in clearing the Moscow knot, a bottleneck of abandoned, damaged, and destroyed rolling stock paralysing the city's marshalling yards. His part the following month in returning the Rumanian archives and paper currency – not, as claimed, bullion and the crown jewels – from Moscow, where they had been sent for safekeeping, and his efforts in February 1918 as the principal intermediary on behalf of the Rumanian government in effecting a ceasefire with revolutionary forces in Bessarabia were notable exploits. They, together with his rescue in March–April of some 50 high-ranking Rumanians held in Odessa by revolutionaries, made Boyle a national hero in Rumania and a powerful influence within its royal court. At the Paris Peace Conference in 1919 he was instrumental in helping the country to obtain a $25-million credit from the Canadian government. He was rumoured to be Queen Marie's lover, but there is no incontrovertible evidence to substantiate this claim.

Throughout his service in Russia and Rumania, Boyle, in cooperation with Captain George Alexander Hill, a Russian-speaking member of the British secret service, and the extant intelligence network, carried out clandestine operations against German and Bolshevik forces in Bessarabia and southwestern Russia. Unilingual, disdaining disguise, and insistent upon wearing his Canadian uniform (to the exasperation of British and Canadian authorities), he received altogether eight decorations from Great Britain, France, Rumania, and Russia.

By the time Boyle returned to England in 1919 his Klondike holdings were in receivership. To recoup himself he attempted on behalf of the Royal Dutch Shell petroleum company to secure an oil concession in the Caucasus from the Soviet government. The venture failed, and Boyle, who had never fully recovered from a stroke suffered in 1918, died of heart failure in Hampton Hill, London, on 14 April 1923. The *Times* noted the passing of "a man of iron build, square-shouldered, blue-eyed, level-browed, with an indomitable will and somewhat turbulent disposition." Boyle's remains were returned to Canada in 1983 and reinterred in Woodstock.

WILLIAM RODNEY

[Material covering Boyle's northern period is noted in newspapers published in Dawson City, Y.T., during and after the gold rush. The background to the Yukon's economic and political development is covered in Canadian government reports issued by the Dept. of the Interior and in the department's annual reports in Can., Parl., *Sessional papers*, as well as in various monographs. Boyle's service in Rumania and Russia is reported upon in items scattered throughout the North American and European public press. The most extensive and reliable information about his wartime actions is contained in official unpublished files, including his surviving papers. These records are held by the LAC (including Boyle's papers at MG 30, E428); the National Arch. (G.B.); the Public Record Office of Northern Ireland, Belfast; the French Ministère des Affaires Étrangères, Paris; and the Directa Generala a Arhivelor Statuli, Bucharest. Detailed references are available in the author's full-length biography, *Joe Boyle, king of the Klondike* (Toronto, 1974). Articles tracing Boyle's career, in whole or in part, are relatively few in number, and are largely inaccurate and of a sensational nature. Principal biographical studies of Boyle's life and times, including works that touch variously upon his career, are listed below. W.R.]

Circuit Court of Cook County Arch. (Chicago), divorce file no.S-263982. Kim Beattie, *Brother, here's a man! The saga of Klondike Boyle* (New York, 1940). Lewis Green, *The gold hustlers* (Anchorage, Alaska, 1977). G. A. Hill, *Go spy the land, being the adventures of I.K.8 of the British secret service* (London, 1932). Marie, Queen Consort of Ferdinand I, King of Rumania, *Ordeal; the story of my life* (New York, 1935). Hannah Pakula, *The last romantic: a biography of Queen Marie of Roumania* (New York, 1984). E. G. Pantazzi, *Roumania in light and shadow* (London, 1921). L. W. Taylor, *The sourdough and the queen: the many lives of Klondike Joe Boyle* (Toronto, 1983).

BRAITHWAITE, HENRY A., woodsman and guide; b. 12 Jan. 1841 (some sources give 12 Jan. 1840) near Fredericton, son of Alfred Braithwaite, a native of England; m. Sarah Flinn of New Brunswick,

and they had at least three daughters; d. 2 Jan. 1927 in Fredericton.

The several biographical articles on Henry Braithwaite, the first sportsman's guide of European ancestry in New Brunswick, are largely uninformative on his origins and childhood. It has been stated by author Bruce Stanley Wright* that he first lived in the Fredericton area for seven years and then at Penniac, in St Marys Parish; it is not known with whom he resided or if he used the Braithwaite surname. The name is not found in the 1851 or 1861 census, but it does occur in the 1871 return for St Marys Parish in a household consisting of Henry "Brethright" (aged 30), his wife, Sarah (35), three daughters, and a lodger. The family's religion is given as Methodist.

From his boyhood, Braithwaite followed the life of a woodsman, his mentor being the legendary Maliseet guide Gabriel Acquin*, a frequent visitor at the home in which he was living. "I stormed him with questions about game and hunting," Braithwaite said, "and finally got in his favor enough to get trips to the woods with him." His first assignment, at age 13, was as Acquin's assistant on a hunting trip up the Nashwaak River by Lieutenant-Governor John Henry Thomas Manners-Sutton* and two companions. After a day they discovered they had forgotten their keg of rum. Braithwaite was sent to fetch it on his toboggan. "I tell you I was a proud boy when I heard the party cheering," he recalled of his return. "I thought they were cheering me then. Afterwards I thought maybe it was the keg!" At 14 he took a job cooking in a lumber camp. His later pattern of employment was to trap and hunt in the fall and spring, take labouring jobs in the summer, and work in lumber camps in the winter, but the combined proceeds were insufficient to support his family. In 1882 land surveyor Edward Jack trained him in surveying and the techniques of lumber cruising, and for several years Braithwaite offered his services to lumber firms. It was not until 1889 that he was able to pursue his favourite activities of guiding, hunting, and trapping full-time.

In the early 1870s he had blazed a trail north from the Southwest Miramichi River in York County through dense woods to the lakes at the head of the Little Southwest Miramichi. In this largely unexploited hinterland, he started a hunting and trapping business in 1874 and was soon employing several assistants. They hunted in the fall, trapped in the winter, and bagged black bears in the spring. In the 1880s bears were the most profitable part of the business, as furriers in England strove to meet the demand for the bearskin busbies that were being adopted for regimental uniforms.

In his account of his expedition to the Little Southwest lakes in 1883, Jack referred to Braithwaite's "old hunting camp" near a stream named the Crooked Deadwater. This was the base of his trapping operation. Along his traplines, which reached out towards the Rocky, Clearwater, and Burnthill brooks and the headwaters of the Dungarvon and Renous rivers, he had erected windproof lean-tos with fireplaces for overnight lodging or use in stormy weather. In Jack's opinion, Braithwaite was not only a successful trapper but "without doubt ... the best hunter in New Brunswick." Later observers concurred, remarking on his ability (like that of the great aboriginal hunters) to follow animal tracks over hard, dry ground, his masterly use of the birchbark horn to call moose, his survival and travel practices, his regimens for preserving food and preparing meals, and his commitment to conservation at a time of widespread indifference to animal welfare and the environment. In several reports, his strengths of character and personality are also noted. "He is not only the most expert of woodsmen and hunters," stated Professor William Francis Ganong*, "but a courteous gentleman as well."

In the 1890s the hunting and sport-fishing industry in New Brunswick came of age. Because of his expertise and unparalleled knowledge of a vast region rich in fish and game, Uncle Henry, as he came to be known, was in the forefront of its development. The "doyen of New Brunswick guides" led a party of colleagues to an early sportsmen's show in Chicago. In 1899, when the New Brunswick Guides' Association was formed, he was elected president. Word of his "magical sporting kingdom" spread rapidly thanks in no small degree to the many writers among his clients. Frank H. Risteen of Fredericton, a frequent hunting guest, mythologized him in the popular press of Canada and the United States. American journalist Frederic Irland, who first visited in 1894, recounted his experiences in *Scribner's Magazine* (New York). In 1902 Emerson Hough of Chicago used a stopover at the Crooked Deadwater as subject matter for an article in *Forest and Stream* (New York). Five years later Ralph Pulitzer of the New York *World*, his wife, and a servant arrived with much ado to spend five weeks with "the great white hunter." When he attempted to arrange a visit, Thomas Martindale, the author of *With gun and guide* (Philadelphia, 1910), was astonished to learn that his services were booked three years ahead. One of Braithwaite's closest literary friends was York County native Charles George Douglas Roberts*, who, in preparation for his well-known nature stories, had turned to him for advice on animals. Roberts acknowledged his debt by dedicating *Red Fox* (Toronto, 1905) "To Henry Braithwaite, Master of Woodcraft." Setting aside his disdain for absurdity, Braithwaite stated that "if Charlie Roberts put an elephant in the New Brunswick woods, I would enjoy reading his story about it." Braithwaite's own literary talents were modest in comparison with those of such guests, but he penned some short pieces

on forest life that played a part in popularizing his name and promoting his business.

His hospitality was extended as well to many non-literary figures, including Lord Hawke and other trophy hunters from Britain. Among the American businessmen introduced to the lakes at the head of the Little Southwest was George Dupont Pratt of New York, who in 1909 erected one of the most elaborate summer retreats in the province on the shores of Holmes Lake. "I've had 'em," Braithwaite stated, "lords and dukes from England and millionaires from the United States, more than I can ever remember. Some of them were the best of sports; some were not." One who was not was a finicky Englishman who insisted that his bathtub accompany him into the woods, and whom Braithwaite allegedly dubbed His Royal Queerness.

Although Braithwaite's business was based at the Little Southwest lakes, his hunting grounds later stretched northward some 200 kilometres to the Nepisiguit and Restigouche river systems and beyond. "Henry has more houses than many a millionaire can boast," claimed Frederic Irland in 1900. "Almost anywhere from the Dungarvon to the Matapedia, and from the mouth of the Miramichi to the head of the Temiscouata, you are within a day's journey of one of his snug camps." During his most vigorous time as a guide, Braithwaite said he had 22 camps in New Brunswick and several in Quebec.

For many years his activities were viewed with favour by provincial authorities, who saw that he was generating revenue and employment. After competitors started to jostle for a share of his business, however, legal challenges began to be exchanged. In 1907 Braithwaite touched off an unfortunate chain of events by having Arthur Robinson, a New York sportsman with a lodge on Holmes Lake, charged with killing game out of season. When the charge was not sustained at trial, Robinson had the same accusation brought against Braithwaite. His culpability was not proved, but he admitted that an American hunter he had guided had shot a caribou out of season. For failing to prevent or report this infraction, he was fined in 1908. The conviction was overturned the next year, but provincial officials nonetheless suspended his guide's licence as "punishment" for having preferred the charge against Robinson. Intense jealousies had been aroused and large egos bruised, making the rights and wrongs of the dispute difficult to ascertain.

In the fall of 1913 Braithwaite had as his guest the Earl of Kingston, a big-game hunter. When they came out of the woods for Christmas, friends gathered to celebrate the 60th anniversary of Braithwaite's shooting his first caribou. Kingston presented him with a purse contributed by Canadian, American, and British sportsmen, and congratulatory telegrams were read, including one from Irland addressed to "Henry, King of Guides and Prince of Men." He was now in his seventies and his reign was drawing to a close. In subsequent years he often trapped and hunted alone. Once, in 1920, he was away for so long that a search party was sent to find him, which it did, alive and well in a camp 43 kilometres from the nearest settlement.

Among the last articles published about Braithwaite during his lifetime was one based on an interview he gave at his daughter's home in 1924 to Kate Haws Miles for the Halifax *Sunday Leader.* "There is nothing about his personal or physical appearance," she wrote, "except the eyes which are so alive and so bright, to proclaim seventy years spent in the open. He seems no more ill at ease in the quartered oak and plush upholstery of his daughter's parlour than would any man who has his own pet arm chair or rocker in some snug corner. But when one searches deeper and listens to the quiet philosophy of the man, then one realizes that he is different. There is more than a touch of Thoreau about him. . . . A simple directness, a scorn of subterfuge, a penchant for accuracy that is almost an obsession reflects the natural environment and the companionship of the dwellers in the silent places."

More than 75 years after his death in 1927, the legend of Henry Braithwaite is still robust, and there are several tangible reminders to be found of his legacy. One of the last woods cabins he occupied is on exhibit at the Central New Brunswick Woodmen's Museum near Boiestown. Many of the names of natural features within his former domain were assigned by him in memory of guests and employees. His own name is perpetuated by Braithwaite Lake in Stanley Parish and Braithwaite Mountain on the boundary between York and Northumberland counties.

W. D. HAMILTON

One of Henry A. Braithwaite's reminiscences was published as "Characteristics of bears," *Family Herald and Weekly Star* (Montreal), 13 April 1924.

LAC, RG 31, C1, 1871, York County, N.B., St Mary's parish, div.1: 39. N.B. Museum, (Saint John), W. F. Ganong fonds, folder 4, Braithwaite to Ganong, 27 Dec. 1904; 11 Jan. 1905; 25 Jan., 15 Oct. 1907. PANB, RS141C5, F18910, no.7102. Saint John Free Public Library, Biog. file. *Daily Gleaner* (Fredericton), 26 Dec. 1913. *North Shore Leader* (Newcastle, N.B.), 5 March 1909. *Saint John Globe*, 3 Jan. 1927. "Seventy years in woods with New Brunswick's oldest guide," *Family Herald and Weekly Star* (Montreal), 19 March 1924. *Union Advocate* (Newcastle), 21 Aug. 1907; 6 Jan. 1915; 9, 16 March 1920; 4 Jan. 1927. *World* (Chatham, N.B.), 18 Nov. 1908; 24, 27 Feb. 1909. P. D. Clark, *Woods, places, bears n' faces* (Fredericton, 1995). W. F. Ganong, "On the physiographic characteristics of the southwest (Tuadook, or Crooked Deadwater) branch of the Little Southwest Miramichi River," N.B., Natural Hist. Soc., *Bull.* (Saint John), no.23 (1905): 320–28. W. T. Griffin, *You're on the Miramichi* (Fredericton, 1981). Harry Hagerman, "Henry Braithwaite" (typescript, n.d.; copy in possession of W. D. Hamilton, Saint John). W. D. Hamilton, *Dictionary of Miramichi biography; biographical sketches of men and women born before 1900 who played a part in public life on the Miramichi: Northumberland County, New Brunswick, Canada* (Saint John, 1997). Frederic Irland, "Sport in an untouched American wilderness," "The coming of the snow," and "The beguiling of the bears," *Scribner's Magazine* (New York), 20 (July–December 1896): 350–62; 27 (January–June 1900): 87–91; 30 (July–December 1901): 313–27. Edward Jack, "An expedition to the headwaters of the Little South-West Miramichi," ed. W. F. Ganong, *Acadiensis* (Saint John), 5 (1905): 116–51. K. [H.] Miles, "'Uncle Henry,' one of New Brunswick's popular characters," *Busy East of Canada* (Sackville, N.B.), 14 (1923–24), no.10: 21–23; reprinted from the Halifax *Sunday Leader. Prominent people of New Brunswick . . .*, comp. C. H. McLean ([Saint John], 1937). "Salmon angling, a never-failing fountain of youth," comp. R. P. Allen, *Maritime Advocate and Busy East* (Sackville), 33 (1942–43), no.7: 5–7, 28–29. Ruth Scott, *Nashwaaksis, 1765–1973: a history* (Nashwaaksis, N.B., 1986). C. S. Stewart, *Recollections* (Fredericton, 1990). B. S. Wright, "New Brunswick's first white hunter: the story of Henry Braithwaite," *Atlantic Advocate* (Fredericton), 60 (1969–70), no.10: 34–37. D. M. Young, "Introduction," in Nashwaak Bicentennial Assoc., *And the river rolled on: two hundred years on the Nashwaak* (Fredericton, 1984).

BREEN, WILLIAM WRIGHT, athlete and businessman; b. 6 Dec. 1882 in Winnipeg, son of Richard Breen, caretaker of the Dominion Lands Office, and Sarah Ann Wright; m. 7 Jan. 1911 Mabel Campbell Rankin in Moose Jaw, Sask., and they had one son; d. 3 Sept. 1927 in Rochester, Minn., and was buried three days later in Winnipeg.

William Breen, usually known as Billy, was one of Winnipeg's best athletes in the early 20th century. He was a skilful bowler and golfer. As a young man he excelled in soccer. The sport in which he achieved a national reputation, however, was hockey and his career illustrates both the problems confronted and the possibilities enjoyed by the foremost hockey players of his era.

Breen was a member of a respected Winnipeg family. His parents had come to the city directly from Ireland early in the 1880s and had helped found Young Methodist Church. His athletic abilities were evident during his years at Mulvey School and Central Collegiate. From 1899 until 1907 he was a member of either the Winnipeg Hockey Club or the Winnipeg Rowing Club's hockey club. The organizations he belonged to were always part of the best senior amateur league in Manitoba, and in those years the best senior amateur league in Manitoba was always one of the best in Canada. Breen led the league in goals during five of his eight seasons. In 1903–4 he was a star on the Rowing Club team that challenged the Ottawa Silver Seven [*see* Francis Clarence McGee*] for the

Stanley Cup. The Winnipeg team lost two of the three games in the strongly contested series; seven of its nine players were hurt. Included in the *Manitoba Free Press*'s list of injured players was Breen, "bruised and broken-up."

During 1907–8 and 1908–9 Breen played in a professional hockey league in Manitoba. The league was not successful, and it ceased to operate early in 1909. It experienced difficulties that were common in early professional leagues in many sports: extremely violent games, "fixed" matches or at least allegations of "fixing," players and owners who broke contracts or agreements, and teams which folded part way through a season.

After his professional experience, Breen never again played high-quality hockey. He did not join other Manitobans who by this time were accepting offers to play for professional clubs in eastern Canada, in the United States, or, after 1911, on the Pacific Coast. Just why he stayed home is not known. Perhaps he considered himself a bit small (he was approximately five feet six inches tall and weighed 140 pounds) for the professional game; his age may have been a factor; perhaps also he wanted to keep his position as a bookkeeper with Codville Company, wholesale grocers in Winnipeg.

Breen would have played senior amateur hockey in Winnipeg if he had been able to regain his amateur status. In the years from about 1910 to 1914 Winnipeg had the best senior league in Canada and Breen wanted to play in it. The officers of the Manitoba branch of the Amateur Athletic Union of Canada were opposed to professional sport and wanted to punish those who had fostered it. Winnipeg lawyer Robert Allison Coyne Manning argued that Breen and others who had played professional hockey in 1907–9 had done so only because during those specific years the calibre of amateur hockey was so weak. Breen became a referee and a coach and it was for his dedicated work in these roles that he finally reinstated as an amateur in 1913. By this time, however, he had not played for four seasons and he did not attempt a comeback.

In 1914 Billy Breen joined his two brothers, Nixon John and Thomas George, in forming Breen Motor Company Limited, a successful automobile dealership. He was secretary-treasurer of the company when he died of lymphosarcoma in 1927. He was also a member of several prestigious organizations, including the Carleton Club and the St Charles Country Club.

MORRIS MOTT

AM, MG 10, D17; D26. Minn., Dept. of Health, Registry of vital statistics (Minneapolis), Death records, 3 Sept. 1927. Private arch., Morris Mott (Brandon, Man.), Amateur Athletic Union of Canada, Manitoba sect., minutes, 1912–20; Ed Sweeney (Winnipeg), Information on W. W. Breen. St John's Anglican Cathedral (Winnipeg), Reg. of burials, 6 Sept. 1927. *Manitoba Free Press*, 1899–1913, 5 Sept. 1927. *Winnipeg Telegram*, 1907–8. *Winnipeg Tribune*, 1907–10, 6 Sept. 1927. F. S. Cosentino, "A history of the concept of professionalism in Canadian sport" (MA thesis, Univ. of Alta, Edmonton, 1973). R. S. Gruneau and David Whitson, *Hockey night in Canada: sport, identities and cultural politics* (Toronto, 1993). Bruce Kidd, *The struggle for Canadian sport* (Toronto, 1996). K. L. Langsley, "The Amateur Athletic Union of Canada and changing concepts of amateurism" (PHD thesis, Univ. of Alta, 1971). Alan Metcalfe, *Canada learns to play: the emergence of organized sport, 1807–1914* (Toronto, 1987); "The meaning of amateurism: a case study of Canadian sport, 1884–1970," *Canadian Journal of Hist. of Sport* (Windsor, Ont.), 26 (1995), no.2: 33–48. Don Morrow, "A case study in amateur conflict: the athletic war in Canada, 1906–08," *British Journal of Sports Hist.* (London), 3 (1986): 173–90. Morris Mott, "The problems of professionalism: the Manitoba Amateur Athletic Association and the fight against pro hockey, 1904–1911," in *Winter sports in the west*, ed. E. A. Corbet and A. W. Rasporich (Calgary, 1990), 132–42; "'Tough to make it': the history of professional team sports in Manitoba," in *The geography of Manitoba: its land and its people*, ed. John Welsted *et al.* (Winnipeg, 1996), 302–14.

BRETT, ROBERT GEORGE, physician and surgeon, businessman, politician, and lieutenant governor; b. 16 Nov. 1851 near Strathroy, Upper Canada, son of James Brett and Catherine Mallon; m. 26 June 1878 Louise Theodora Hungerford (d. 1935) of Watford, Ont.; d. 16 Sept. 1929 in Calgary.

Robert George Brett's Irish parents immigrated to Upper Canada in 1846, settling first in London and then on a farm near Strathroy, where Brett was born. They moved into town when Brett was ten years of age so that he could attend the Strathroy Grammar School. The lad greatly admired the family physician, Dr Friend Richard Eccles, and was apprenticed to him. He attended Victoria College medical school in Toronto, graduated MD in 1874, and briefly practised with Eccles. Later in 1874 he established a practice at Arkona in Lambton County, where he would serve a term as reeve. In 1876 he took postgraduate training in New York and Philadelphia, demonstrating an interest in upgrading his skills that he would repeat in 1894 when he studied surgery and gynaecology in Vienna. In 1878 he married Louise T. Hungerford. All four of their children predeceased them: Genevieve died in infancy in 1881, Blanche Guinevere at the age of two in 1886, Robert Earle in 1912, and Reginald Harry in 1925.

In 1880 Brett had moved to Winnipeg, perhaps to seek larger professional opportunities in the rapidly developing west or to participate in the real estate boom of the period. He did open a practice there, and in 1883 was one of the founders of the Manitoba Medical College, in which he held the chair of materia medica and therapeutics and later was professor of gynaecology and obstetrics. He served for some years as a councillor and member of the board of studies at the University of Manitoba. He had apparently lost his investments in real estate with the collapse of the boom in 1881 and had to use his practice to pay off his debts. He was appointed assistant surgeon for the 90th (Winnipeg) Battalion of Rifles. A Conservative in federal politics and an Anglican in religion, he was also a freemason and a founding member (1880) of the Winnipeg Lodge of Perfection, with which he long remained affiliated.

In 1883 Brett was appointed a company physician for the Canadian Pacific Railway, then still under construction; ultimately he became chief surgeon for the CPR in the Banff region, including the collieries at Canmore, Anthracite, and Bankhead (Alta). In August 1883 he arrived at the end of steel in Calgary, on the first passenger coach to cross the Bow River there. Near the Continental Divide was a temporary construction community called Holt City (Lake Louise), where he established a small hospital. During his travels along the line of construction in the mountains he became interested in the sulphur hot springs at Banff and at Halcyon Hot Springs on the Arrow Lakes, B.C., and thought that they might be developed as great spas, rather like those in Europe and the United States. In 1886 he settled in Banff and built the Banff Sanitarium on the south side of the Bow River. Developed as a combined hotel and hospital specializing in the treatment of ailments such as arthritis and certain skin problems which benefited from the hot mineral waters, the sanatorium averaged about 2,200 registered guests per annum before 1900. It was described on its letterhead as "an elegantly equipped Private Hospital, with a staff of trained nurses in attendance," and as "the most complete Bathing establishment in the Dominion, where Turkish, Russian, tub, plunge, shower, and douche baths are given, with water from the Hot Sulphur Springs, under medical supervision." In 1909 Brett built nearby the Brett Hospital, at which he was chief surgeon. The sanatorium continued mainly as a hotel and was renamed Bretton Hall in 1915.

Brett was a genial and popular personality with some political ambitions. He was elected in 1888 to the Legislative Assembly of the North-West Territories for the constituency of Red Deer, which then included Banff. Almost immediately the assembly was embroiled in a controversy over the extent of its powers. Federal legislation passed in May had allowed it to deal only with the small income derived from territorial taxation. The far larger annual federal grant remained under dominion control and was to be expended under the authority of the lieutenant governor. Furthermore, the lieutenant governor was empowered to select an advisory council which would be severally responsible to him, not collectively responsible to the elected assembly. The first council, appointed in November by Lieutenant Governor Joseph Royal*, included the able and determined young Frederick William Gordon Haultain*, who was prepared to take confrontational measures to force the federal government to concede both local control of the federal grant and a council responsible to the assembly. Royal at first seemed willing to allow the substance of Haultain's demands with respect to federal funds, but in 1889 he made it clear that he must govern according to the limitations imposed by the federal statute. On 29 Oct. 1889 Haultain and his colleagues resigned. Royal consulted with Haultain about a successor, and, he told Prime Minister Sir John A. Macdonald*, "we both agreed that Dr. Brett, of Banff, seemed to possess the qualifications required."

The new council under Brett announced that it would act as an executive only with respect to locally raised finances and such duties as were assigned by the territorial ordinances to the lieutenant governor in council. Brett and his three colleagues actually agreed that ultimately responsible government must be granted, but they believed in working for it gradually and within existing law. Moreover, they thought that full responsible government would be premature. The assembly promptly voted, 13-8, a motion of no-confidence, thus raising explicitly a question previously only implicit: was the council responsible to the assembly or to the lieutenant governor? On 11 November Brett sent Royal a letter of resignation; Royal the next day declined to accept it, on the grounds that the council had not had time to carry out any acts of administration that would merit a vote of no-confidence and that to accept the resignation would undermine his prerogatives. On 16 November Royal told Macdonald that "Dr. Brett is holding his own with firmness and much ability" and claimed that "in Regina public opinion is in favor of Dr. Brett's attitude, and from all I can hear this is also the opinion generally in the country." Nevertheless, the assembly refused to pass the territorial estimates until it had a full accounting of the supply vote of the previous year, which Royal had refused to provide. The Brett council tendered its resignation a second time, and it was accepted on 16 November.

No member of the assembly now could be found to form a council unless Royal would agree to account for the expenditures of 1888–89 and allow the assembly control of the preparation of all estimates and expenditures. The assembly also passed an ordinance requiring a council of two, to be selected by the assembly (which then named Thomas Tweed and John Ryerson Neff); this measure was disallowed by the federal government. In discussion with Royal, Tweed "earnestly advised that I should send for Dr.

Brett whom he highly praised for his ability, moderation and popularity." Once more, Brett agreed to form a council, which he had done by early February 1890. "They are good men," Royal told Macdonald, "and are in perfect accord with me as to the law being strictly adhered to." Since the assembly was not in session, this council was able to govern with few problems through most of 1890. When the house again met, at the end of October, opposition to the council was uncompromising: its members and supporters were not allowed to serve on committees, its motions and legislative proposals were refused. Brett responded that he and his colleagues knew themselves to be within the law and would carry on in spite of the abuse to which they were subjected. It was a mistake for the assembly to have attempted to choose the Advisory Council, he argued, because under the act it was clear that the lieutenant governor had this right. He affirmed that if the assembly was willing to be governed by the law as it was, he and the other members of the council would willingly resign; otherwise, they would continue as long as the country needed them. The session closed at the end of November.

Clearly the territories were becoming ungovernable, and some change was essential. In May 1891 Brett and fellow councillor John Felton Betts travelled to Ottawa to try to induce the government to permit responsible government. They requested that the assembly be able to control moneys voted for schools, roads, bridges, and other local expenditures, that the lieutenant governor be empowered to dissolve the assembly, and that the Advisory Council be made responsible to the house. In addition, they asked for a hospital grant, a grant of land for a university, and a generous three-year subsidy for the purposes of government in the territories. Amendments to the North-West Territories Act in September only partially met these requests: the lieutenant governor now could dissolve the assembly; the federally appointed legal experts who had sat with the assembly since 1888 were removed; and a significant portion of the federal grant was placed under control of the house. However, the lieutenant governor retained authority over part of the dominion grant. New elections were held on 31 October, and, in the words of historian Edmund Henry Oliver, "the old Advisory Council simply dropped out of existence when the old Assembly itself ceased to exist." Late in December Royal called on Haultain to form what was now called the Executive Committee, and Brett's brief and difficult career in government ended.

Brett continued in the assembly until 1899: he was re-elected for the new Banff constituency in 1891 and 1894, and narrowly defeated Arthur Lewis Watkins SIFTON in 1898. However, Sifton contested the election on the basis of corrupt practices and prevailed over Brett in the by-election held on 27 June 1899. Brett had remained a strong advocate of responsible government for the territories, which had finally been granted in 1897, but particularly favoured separate provincial status for the District of Alberta. He was for several years the leader of the opposition in the assembly, but he also was responsible for the shaping of public health legislation.

Brett's interest in politics continued after his defeat. Only ill health prevented him from contesting the by-election occasioned by Sifton's appointment to the territorial government in 1901. When the status of the North-West Territories was being considered in 1905 and it was rumoured that two new provinces would be created, he went to Ottawa to lobby for Banff as the provincial capital of Alberta. After the passage of the Autonomy Acts later that year he was a candidate in Banff for election to the Legislative Assembly of Alberta but was defeated. In 1909 he was chosen president of the Alberta Conservative Association and ran unsuccessfully for the Cochrane riding in the provincial election.

In 1908 and again in 1912 Brett was appointed to the senate of the University of Alberta, which in 1915 conferred an honorary LLD upon him. He had been instrumental in 1889 in founding the North West Territories Medical Association, of which he was first vice-president and president in 1891 and 1897. He served as the first president of the College of Physicians and Surgeons of the Province of Alberta in 1906–7, and held the office again in 1919–20. He also was president of the Alberta Medical Association, 1906–7 and 1914–15. In 1905 he had been licensed as a pharmacist, undoubtedly to facilitate the development of a drugstore in connection with his hospital. In July 1913 he was named a licentiate of the Medical Council of Canada, and in 1921 he became its president. He was active as well in the Canadian Medical Association.

On 6 Oct. 1915 Brett succeeded George Hedley Vicars BULYEA as lieutenant governor of Alberta, a position he would hold until 20 Oct. 1925. In 1918 he leased his medical properties, including the Brett Hospital, two drugstores, and the Canmore Hospital, to his former professional associates: his surviving son, Dr Reginald Harry Brett, and Dr Gilbert McIntosh Atkin. In 1914 he had become president of the Alberta branch of the Canadian Red Cross Society, and he actively used his position as lieutenant governor to raise money and supplies for the charity's war effort. He also became chief scout of the Boy Scouts in Alberta, an organization in which he took considerable interest. On 19 April 1916 he was made an honorary colonel of the 82nd Infantry Battalion of the Canadian Expeditionary Force. Interested in redeveloping the flow of immigrants to the land in western Canada, he became in June 1923 a founding director of the Canada Colonization Association, under the presidency of Sir Augustus Meredith NANTON. One of his last activities as lieutenant governor was to participate in October 1925 in the inauguration of long-distance telephone links between Edmonton and the northern United States. In 1927 the federal government conferred on him the title of "Honourable" as a gesture, in Canada's diamond jubilee year, marking "the important place held by the Provinces in the Federal system of Canada."

Even before the end of his term Brett had been under medical care for heart problems. For two or three years after his retirement he lived in California, but he returned to reside in Banff. He died in hospital in Calgary on 16 Sept. 1929 and was buried in the family mausoleum in Banff. By the time of his death his active political career seemed remote; he was remembered both for his identification with the development of Banff and, by an affectionate public, as a man who was amiable, kind, approachable, and "the most democratic" of lieutenant governors of his time. Mount Brett, west of the town of Banff, was named in his honour. A painting of Brett by Victor Albert Long hangs in the Legislature Building in Edmonton.

DAVID J. HALL

[The two most useful collections of Brett's papers are the Brett family fonds at the Whyte Museum of the Canadian Rockies, Arch. and Library, Banff, Alta (M1/V83) and the Brett fonds at the GA (M 131, M 132); the Brett file in the PAA (PR1969.282) is negligible. Yet these collections are frustratingly incomplete, including virtually nothing on Brett's political career. There are extensive family photograph albums in the Banff collection, but a large number of the pictures are unidentified. The small collection of Mrs Brett's papers there are of some limited use. Newspaper accounts in the Banff *Crag and Canyon* (1900–5) and the weekly *Calgary Herald* (1886–1925) proved more helpful in piecing together certain aspects of Brett's career.

Among secondary sources, Brett's brief period of prominence in the North-West Territories between 1888 and 1891 is covered in E. H. Oliver, "The contest between Lieutenant-Governor Royal and the Legislative Assembly of the North-West Territories, 1888–1893," RSC, *Trans.*, 3rd ser., 17 (1923), sect.II: 81–118. Also useful is L. H. Thomas, *The struggle for responsible government in the North-West Territories, 1870–97* (Toronto, 1956). The most thorough article on Brett's enterprises in Banff is F. C. Harris and G. M. McDougall, "The Banff Sanitarium Hotel," in G. M. McDougall *et al.*, *Medical clinics and physicians of southern Alberta* (Calgary, 1992), 181–204. H. C. Jamieson, *Early medicine in Alberta: the first seventy-five years* ([Edmonton, 1947]), is essential for understanding the context in which Brett practised medicine. There is no serious study of Brett's term as lieutenant governor. D.J.H.]

LAC, MG 26, A; H; J; MG 27, II, D15. Univ. of Alta Arch. (Edmonton), 509.1 (R. G. Brett file); file 2315-5 (honorary degree recipients). UTA, Reg. of students. Whyte

Museum of the Canadian Rockies, Arch. and Library, Maps of Banff, 1922, detailing Bretton Hall and Brett Hospital. *Calgary Albertan*, 17–20 Sept. 1929. *Calgary Herald*, 17 Sept. 1929, 16 Nov. 1935. John Blue, *Alberta, past and present, historical and biographical* (3v., Chicago, 1924). Can., Parl., *Sessional papers*, reports of the Dept. of the Interior, 1886–1900. *Canadian annual rev.*, 1901–29. CPG, 1888–99, 1915–25. *Directory of the Council and Legislative Assembly of the North-West Territories, 1876–1905* (Regina, 1970). *Dominion Illustrated* (Montreal), 21 Sept. 1889. G. S. Fahrni, *Prairie surgeon* (Winnipeg, 1976). F. W. Gershaw, "An early convention," *Alberta Medical Bull.* (Edmonton), 19 (1954), no.1: 38. J. M. Gibbon with M. S. Mathewson, *Three centuries of Canadian nursing* (Toronto, 1947). Ernest Ingersoll, *The Canadian guide-book, part II: western Canada . . .* (New York, 1892). G. R. Johnson, "Place names up to 1930 commemorating medical men who have practised their profession in Alberta," *Alberta Medical Bull.*, 18 (1953), no.2: 53–54. R. C. Johnson, "Resort development at Banff," *Alberta Hist.* (Calgary), 23 (1975), no.1: 18–24. Robert Lampard, "Robert George Brett: 'We shall not look upon his like again'," *Alberta Hist.*, 51 (2003), no.2: 13–22. G. E. Learmonth, "The fiftieth anniversary of the Alberta Medical Association," *Alberta Medical Bull.*, 20 (1955), no.3: 51–57. C. C. Lingard, *Territorial government in Canada: the autonomy question in the old North-West Territories* (Toronto, 1946). E. G. Luxton, *Banff: Canada's first national park; a history and a memory of Rocky Mountains Park* (Banff, 1975). A. O. MacRae, *History of the province of Alberta* (2v., [Calgary], 1912), 1. Jim McDonald *et al.*, *Hotsprings of western Canada: a complete guide* (Vancouver, 1978). H. [M.] Neatby, "The medical profession in the North-West Territories," in *Medicine in Canadian society: historical perspectives*, ed. S. E. D. Shortt (Montreal, 1981), 165–88. G. H. W. Richardson, "The Conservative party in the provisional district of Alberta, 1887–1905" (MA thesis, Univ. of Alta, 1976). Dean Robinson, "Early 'C.P.R.' doctors of Alberta and the west," *Alberta Medical Bull.*, 18, no.3: 24–27. Patricia Roome, "A report on Dr. Robert George Brett (1851–1929) and the Sanitarium Hotel" (typescript, 1970; copy in the Brett family fonds in Banff). Edward Roper, *By track and trail: a journey through Canada* (London, 1891). *Saturday Night*, 9 Aug. 1924: 3. Douglas Sladen, "The hot springs of the Canadian northwest," *Dominion Illustrated*, 19 Sept. 1891: 276–78; *On the cars and off: being the journal of a pilgrimage along the queen's highway to the east, from Halifax in Nova Scotia to Victoria in Vancouver's Island* (London and New York, 1895). G. D. S[tanley], "Medical pioneering in Alberta: Dr. Robert George Brett (1851–1929)," Calgary Associate Clinic, *Hist. Bull.*, 4 (1939–40), no.1: 5–12. [H. C. Stovel], *50 Switzerlands in one: Banff the beautiful, Canada's national park . . .* (Banff, [1914?]). H. H. Thomas, *From barnacle to Banff* (2nd ed., [Calgary?], 1945). Univ. of Alta, *Calendar*, 1908/9, 1912/13.

BRIGGS, WILLIAM, Methodist minister and publisher; b. 9 Sept. 1836 in Banbridge (Northern Ireland), son of Thomas Briggs and Mary ——; m. 27 Aug. 1868 Rosalie Marian Clarke (d. 1919) in Montreal, and they had a son; d. 5 Nov. 1922 in Port Credit, Ont.

Briggs

William Briggs was born into a Scottish-Irish family. His mother died when he was six. Around this time the family moved to Liverpool, England, where Briggs was educated at Mount Street Grammar School and Liverpool Collegiate Institute. He subsequently acquired some commercial training, but soon rejected the idea of a business career. According to the Reverend John Saltkill Carroll*, Briggs experienced "an undeniable conversion" in boyhood, and he was soon preaching in and around Liverpool. He immigrated to the Canadas in his early twenties and was introduced into the Canada Conference of the Methodist Church. Received on trial as a lay preacher at Durham (Ormstown), Lower Canada, in 1859, he was ordained into the ministry in 1863. During the next 15 years he served at churches in Toronto, Hamilton, Montreal, London, Cobourg, and Belleville.

By the late 1870s Briggs was at the height of a successful ministerial career. In 1876 he had become pastor at the centre of Canadian Methodism: Metropolitan Church in Toronto. Though little is known of his religious or social views, he was a popular preacher, by all accounts one who combined theology with humour and pragmatism. "While others have been best at first, and have gradually degenerated into mere dawdling, goody-goody talkers," one newspaper reported, "Mr. Briggs has gone steadily forward in pulpit power, in broad mental culture, and in general excellence and influence." His administrative abilities had been recognized with appointments as financial secretary (1874) and secretary (1876–77) of the Toronto Conference and chairman of the district (1875).

In February 1879, as part of a reorganization of the church's publishing wing in Toronto, the Methodist Book and Publishing House, Briggs was elected book steward, or business manager. The house was then a small bookstore and plant that sold bibles, hymn books, catechisms, commentaries, biographies, and Sunday school books, printed such publications as the *Christian Guardian*, and did a small amount – two or three titles a year – of original publishing. Under Briggs's leadership, it was to become one of the most important Canadian publishing houses by the end of the century.

As book steward, Briggs continued to concentrate on church-related material; the output of Sunday school publications, in particular, expanded greatly. However, with the house firmly established as a profitable business and ensconced in new quarters in 1889, his energies turned to the development of a secular list. The number of British and American works that it reprinted rose dramatically; non-religious works appeared under the imprint "William Briggs." The firm also entered the school-textbook market and was active in commercial job printing.

Perhaps most important, Briggs oversaw a significant increase in the number of Canadian publications.

By the 1890s his house was publishing about 20 original works each year. Some were about religion or were written by Methodist scholars, among them George John Blewett*, but new subject areas were also developed, especially history, fiction, and poetry. Most of the titles in these areas dealt with Canadian subjects. Indeed, the Methodist Book and Publishing House consciously presented itself as a publisher of Canadian works, frequently emphasizing the patriotic and nation-building aspects of its activities. Briggs was aware that a market was developing for books by Canadian authors and dealing with Canadian themes, and his success lay in his ability to respond to this cultural nationalism. Possessed of sharp critical and commercial faculties and capable of gauging public tastes, Briggs provided opportunities for Canadian authors, offering them encouraging editors such as Edward Samuel Caswell*, and he trained a new generation of publishers. Among the bestsellers to emanate from his house were *Songs of a sourdough* (1907) by Robert William Service* and *Sowing seeds in Danny* (1908) by Helen Letitia McClung [Mooney*].

Briggs's involvement with books did not curtail his participation in other areas of the church. He continued to preach and was a delegate to every General Conference between 1874 and 1918. As well, he was a delegate to the General Conference of the Methodist Episcopal Church in the United States (Washington, 1882) and to ecumenical conferences in Washington (1891) and London (1901). Awarded an honorary DD in 1886 by Victoria University in Cobourg, he was a member of its board of regents in 1906–7. He also held positions outside the church: he became a member of Toronto's Board of Trade in 1898 and served terms as president of the Master Printers' and Bookbinders' Association of Toronto.

Accounts of Briggs often mentioned his blend of personal sincerity, geniality, and commercial aggressiveness. In 1880 John Carroll described him physically: medium in height and weight, "oval yet full-faced, with a noticeably well-developed head, beyond the average size." "As a man," Carroll continued, "he is modest without bashfulness; as a Christian, religious without cant; as a preacher, fervent and eloquent without rant; as a platform speaker, ready, pointed, and pertinent; and as a Connexional business man, capable and successful without being fussy and pretentious."

In the last decade of Briggs's stewardship, original publishing declined. He seemed more concerned with the erection of a substantial new building in 1913–15 and the sale of foreign books (agency publishing), a valuable part of the business. The General Conference named him book steward emeritus in 1918, when he was succeeded by the Reverend Samuel Wesley Fallis, and he stepped down altogether in 1919. On 1 July of that year the Methodist Book and Publishing House was renamed Ryerson Press after its founder, Egerton

Ryerson*, and in 1920 it began a fresh phase under its new editor, Lorne Albert Pierce*. At a time when religious impulses were expressing themselves more and more in secular form, Briggs had steered the house away from its earlier focus on creed and narrow denominationalism and had been instrumental in its major expansion. As the *Bookseller and Stationer* (Toronto) commented, during his career as steward the name of William Briggs "became a household word wherever books were read in Canada."

Briggs died in 1922 at his son's home in Port Credit and was buried in Mount Pleasant Cemetery in Toronto. He left an estate worth more than $80,524, a personal testament to the sound business sense of a popular Methodist preacher.

DANIELLE HAMELIN

ANQ-M, CE601-S109, 27 août 1868. AO, RG 22-359, no.4066. UCC-C, Fonds 513/1, 83.061C. *Christian Guardian*, 16 April 1919. *Daily Mail and Empire*, 6 Nov. 1922. *Bookseller and Stationer* (Toronto), 38 (1922): 62. Christina Burr, "The business development of the Methodist Book and Publishing House, 1870–1914," *OH*, 85 (1993): 251–71. *Canadian men and women of the time* (Morgan; 1898 and 1912). J. [S.] Carroll, "The Rev. William Briggs," *Canadian Methodist Magazine* (Toronto and Halifax), 12 (July–December 1880): 97–99. *The chronicle of a century, 1829–1929: the record of one hundred years of progress in the publishing concerns of the Methodist, Presbyterian and Congregational churches in Canada*, ed. L. A. Pierce (Toronto, 1929). Dana Garrick, "The United Church of Canada Board of Publication collection: a major resource for the history of the book in Canada," Biblio. Soc. of Canada, *Papers* (Toronto), 32 (1994): 11–30. G. L. Parker, *The beginnings of the book trade in Canada* (Toronto, 1985). L. A. Pierce, *The house of Ryerson, 1829–1954* (Toronto, 1954). *The Ryerson imprint: a check-list of the books and pamphlets published by the Ryerson Press since the foundation of the house in 1829*, comp. W. S. Wallace (Toronto, 1954). Judith St John, *Firm foundations: a chronicle of Toronto's Metropolitan United Church and her Methodist origins, 1795–1984* (Toronto, 1988). *Standard dict. of Canadian biog.* (Roberts and Tunnell), vol.2.

BRISTOL, EDMUND JAMES, lawyer, businessman, and politician; b. 4 Sept. 1861 in Napanee, Upper Canada, son of Amos Samuel Bristol, a physician, and Sarah Minerva Everitt (Everett); m. 21 Sept. 1899 Mary Dorothy Armour; they had no children; d. 14 July 1927 in Toronto.

Edmund Bristol inherited a family tradition of patriotic service to the crown. The Bristols were of English descent, but their claim to prominence rested in their status as loyalists. Edmund's great-grandfather had fought in the American revolution, his grandfathers in the War of 1812, and his father against the Fenians.

After studying at Napanee's public schools and Upper Canada College in Toronto, Bristol attended the University of Toronto to prepare for a career in law. As an undergraduate, he was elected president of University College's Literary and Scientific Society. He received his BA in 1883 and proceeded to study at Osgoode Hall. Called to the bar on 17 May 1886, he remained in Toronto, becoming a partner in Howland, Arnoldi, and Bristol, and he began to dabble in Conservative politics. He was named a federal QC in 1896 and an Ontario KC in 1908. His marriage to Dorothy Armour in 1899 produced a connection that would significantly aid his career. His father-in-law, John Douglas Armour, was chief justice of Ontario, and his brother-in-law Eric Norman Armour became a law partner in 1902.

A recognized authority on corporate and international law, Bristol devoted most of his time to his practice and other business pursuits, in which he was quite successful. With offices on Victoria Street, in the heart of Toronto's financial district, he facilitated many corporate mergers, acquisitions, and capitalizations. For example, he negotiated the merger of two dry-goods retailers to form Murray-Kay Limited in 1910. As well, he used his political connections to secure investments, licences, and incorporations for the newly formed Canada Securities Corporation, an upstart rival to such trading firms as the Dominion Securities Corporation, established by George Albertus Cox*. However, most of his efforts were directed towards transportation: he was a director of Northern Navigation, Canada Steamship Lines, and Richelieu and Ontario Navigation, which was undergoing major growth through amalgamation. His personal portfolio was such that he could routinely make $1,000 stock trades. Bristol's interests took him regularly to London, Paris, and New York, and on occasion he would combine business and politics. During one trip to London, in 1917, he represented the Department of Marine and Fisheries during negotiations on shipping matters with the imperial government.

Bristol's political influence had been shaped during terms as vice-president and president of both the Toronto Conservative Association and the Ontario Conservative Association. In a by-election in Toronto Centre in 1905, he was returned by acclamation to the House of Commons. He would hold this riding, which became Toronto East Centre in 1925, until 1926. E. N. Armour, himself a one-time parliamentary candidate, handled his campaigns as well as his business and political correspondence during his trips.

Bristol was a rare parliamentarian. His administrative skills made him far more useful than did his lacklustre oratorical ability. During World War I he ably served Albert Edward KEMP, the MP for Toronto East, chair of the War Purchasing Commission, and then minister of militia and defence and later of overseas military forces. Bristol's job really seems to have been to deal with Kemp's mail, especially during his two years in purchasing. Kemp once protested Bristol's frequent absences, claiming he needed his aid "day and night." Following the war, Bristol served as a minister without portfolio for three months in 1921 in the cabinet of Arthur Meighen*. During his two decades as an MP, he spent little time in the house. When he appeared during debate in 1915, George Perry Graham* had paused to "welcome this stranger." To win support, Bristol relied on back-room organizing rather than rhetoric. In 1911 he had attended campaign strategy meetings with federal leader Robert Laird Borden* and Ontario premier Sir James Pliny Whitney*. As president of the Ontario Conservative Association, he managed provincial campaigns through the 1920s.

Much of Bristol's surviving political correspondence deals with patronage, and it is here that he becomes particularly interesting. Since Jewish and Italian constituents were proportionately over-represented in his riding, this material provides an excellent snapshot of the accommodations negotiated between them and the Anglo-Protestant bourgeoisie who controlled the political apparatus. Bristol seems remarkable for his lack of ethnic prejudice, though his tolerance may simply have been the sign of an astute politician. His tireless efforts on behalf of his Jewish, and to a lesser extent Italian, supporters played a crucial role in creating space for these groups within the Canadian polity.

This patronage system shone brightest in the years of fat government spending at the beginning of the Great War. Demands for military uniforms soared and much of the supply came from the Jewish garment manufacturers in Toronto Centre. Although Bristol repeatedly complained to cabinet that the Toronto faithful were not receiving their fair share of contracts, he personally negotiated the allotment of numerous orders. In January 1915 he defended his record on this score to Mayor Thomas Langton Church*. But as Bristol quickly discovered, even his patronage network was unable to meet the government's demand for supplies. Moreover, the inefficiency of the process greatly elevated both contractors' expectations and voters' antagonism to the system. When Borden's Union coalition fought the election of 1917, it placed the elimination of patronage just below winning the war in its platform. The resulting reforms to government purchasing deprived Bristol of his most useful tool in political management, and his interest in the welfare of individual constituents declined sharply. Nonetheless, his organizational abilities remained unimpaired. The federal caucus appointed him to run the 1921 campaign in central Ontario and he was a key organizer for the national, as well as the provincial, party throughout the 1920s.

Bristol's status in his professional and political affairs was reflected in his social life. An Anglican, he belonged to prestigious clubs in Toronto, Ottawa, Montreal, and London; in 1895 he won the Royal Canadian Yacht Club's Prince of Wales Cup. As members of the Toronto Hunt Club, both he and his wife were keen golfers who also enjoyed riding and hunting. Struck down by a brain haemorrhage in February 1927, Bristol suffered a second one on 13 July and died a day later. For a man who had handled so much wealth, he left an estate worth only $23,000.

ALAN GORDON

AO, F 68; RG 22-305, no.57455; RG 80-8-0-1052, no.4650. LAC, MG 27, II, D9, 28, 54, 83; MG 30, A16, 25. Alan Gordon, "Patronage, etiquette, and the science of connection: Edmund Bristol and political management, 1911–21," *CHR*, 80 (1999): 1–31; "Taking root in the patronage garden: Jewish businessmen in Toronto's Conservative party, 1891–1921," *OH*, 88 (1996): 31–46. Norman Ward, "The Bristol papers: a note on patronage," *Canadian Journal of Economics and Political Science* (Toronto), 12 (1946): 78–87.

BRODEUR, LOUIS-PHILIPPE (baptized **Louis-Joseph-Alexandre**; no explanation has been found for the change of name; he is listed in the 1871 census simply as **Philippe**), lawyer, politician, and judge; b. 21 Aug. 1862 in Belœil, Lower Canada, son of Toussaint Brodeur, a farmer, and Justine Lambert; m. there 27 June 1887 Emma Brillon, and they had four sons and one daughter; d. 2 Jan. 1924 at Spencer Wood, Sillery, Que., and was buried 5 January in Belœil.

Louis-Philippe Brodeur grew up in a Liberal family. His father and his maternal grandfather, Pierre Hébert-Lambert, supported the Patriotes and on 25 Nov. 1837 fought in the battle of Saint-Charles-sur-Richelieu, where the latter was killed. As a result, Brodeur's childhood was imbued with the memory of these events and it was inevitable that he would throw in his lot with the Liberals.

From 1875 to 1881 Brodeur studied at the Séminaire de Saint-Hyacinthe, where his marks ranked him as one of the best students of his year. He then enrolled in the faculty of law at the Université Laval in Montreal and reportedly articled in that city in the law firm of Honoré Mercier*, the rising star in the Quebec Liberal party at the time. Graduating in 1884, Brodeur was called to the bar in July of that year. He would be made a QC in 1899. The young lawyer first opened an office in Montreal with Edmond Lareau*. He is believed to have also worked with François-Xavier Dupuis, among others. He subsequently made the acquaintance of Raoul Dandurand*, another young Liberal, with whom he would go into partnership around the middle of 1891. Brodeur and Dandurand began to engage seriously in politics and they soon attracted attention. Brodeur was invited to be the federal Liberal candidate for Rouville.

The election of 5 March 1891, which made Brodeur the Liberal MP, marked a turning point in his career.

Like many others, he sought to rise through the ranks of the party. While waiting to be offered important political assignments, he wrote the occasional article for *L'Électeur* (Québec) and *La Presse* and *La Patrie* (Montréal). For *La Patrie* his contributions would include a series about the Manitoba schools question, praising the settlement reached by Wilfrid Laurier* and Thomas Greenway*. In 1896, with Philippe-Auguste Choquette* and Frédéric-Ligori Béïque*, he founded *Le Soir*. This newspaper was intended to be the organ of the federal Liberal leader, Laurier, in opposition to *La Patrie*, the radical Liberal paper of Honoré Beaugrand*. Brodeur was, with Choquette, the owner and publisher of *Le Soir*, and he sat on its editorial board along with Horace Archambeault* and Christophe-Alphonse Geoffrion*. Founded to spread the message of moderate Liberals during the 1896 election campaign, it proved ephemeral, the last issue appearing on 31 August, after only four months of publication.

Brodeur was returned in Rouville in the federal election of 23 June 1896, which brought Laurier's Liberals to power. Hoping to make his leader's task easier, he offered to resign his seat to make way for a potential cabinet minister who had been defeated. Laurier would not forget this offer, and when he was selecting his cabinet, he summoned Brodeur to Ottawa. The young MP thought he would have to give up his seat, but during their meeting Laurier offered him the post of deputy speaker of the House of Commons. Brodeur's increasingly important party responsibilities – writing for the party newspapers and organizing meetings in the province – revealed his abilities. Laurier had him elected speaker of the house on 29 Nov. 1900, and he took up his duties on 6 Feb. 1901. His loyalty to his leader, whose moderate liberalism and respect for institutions he shared, enabled him to rise through the ranks.

Late in 1902, after forcing Joseph-Israël Tarte* to resign, Laurier embarked on a thorough reorganization of his party, which he used to reward his most faithful supporters. Thus, on 19 Jan. 1904 Brodeur became minister of inland revenue. He held this portfolio only a short time, for on 6 Feb. 1906, following the sudden death of Raymond Préfontaine*, he was appointed minister of marine and fisheries and given responsibility for the political district of Montreal.

At first, Brodeur was Laurier's man in charge of patronage in the province of Quebec. The lists for handing out favours were among the things he controlled. Then he became an important adviser to the prime minister, as the tasks he would be called to carry out show. In a political system where loyalty to the leader ensured advancement, Brodeur's devotion to Laurier, combined with his leadership qualities, guaranteed him a choice spot. It was probably at this time that Brodeur began to figure as one of the most prominent Liberals in the province. In 1908 he was responsible for the election campaign for all of Quebec. Early in his ministry he proposed a major reform in the Montreal Harbour Commission and he improved navigation on the St Lawrence by having buoys put in place and getting the shipping lane deepened.

Brodeur came to play an important role in strengthening Canada's stature in international affairs. After the settlement of the Alaska boundary dispute in 1903, an issue in which Great Britain abandoned the colony, Laurier became increasingly convinced that Canada should take charge of its own affairs. An occasion arose in 1907, when the Liberal government decided to negotiate trade agreements with France and Italy. Laurier, who was highly regarded in Great Britain, received the authority to send two ministers – William Stevens FIELDING, minister of finance, and Brodeur were chosen – to hold discussions with the two countries, on condition that the final agreement be countersigned by the British ambassador. The negotiations began in France, where Brodeur acted on his own since Fielding spoke no French and the French negotiators spoke no English. This mission was successful; it marked a decisive step forward in trade relations between Canada and foreign countries. In August 1907 the representatives of France and Canada concluded an agreement providing for lower import duties on some products. However, given the duration of the negotiations in Paris and the imminent opening of parliament, Brodeur and Fielding returned to Canada without going to Italy. In recognition of his participation, Brodeur was made an officer of the Legion of Honour in 1908.

As minister of marine and fisheries, Brodeur also dealt with the creation of a Canadian navy, which had become a crucial issue given German military threats in Europe. Although the idea had been advanced during the administration of his predecessor, Préfontaine, following the 1902 colonial conference, it was during Brodeur's term in office that the navy was established. Laurier, Brodeur, and Sir Frederick William Borden*, minister of militia and defence, represented Canada at the 1907 imperial conference, at which a plan for centralizing the naval defence of the British empire was discussed. Like Laurier, Brodeur rejected this plan, maintaining that Canada, which had been responsible since 1885 for its fishing grounds and the Great Lakes, was quite capable of taking charge of the defence of its coasts. In the same spirit, Brodeur wrote to Laurier late in 1908 that the time had come for Canada to pass its own legislation on naval matters. On 29 March 1909, on a motion by George Eulas Foster*, the House of Commons agreed in principle to the creation of a Canadian navy. In August 1909 Brodeur and Borden represented Laurier at another imperial conference. After strong opposition from the Canadian delegates, Great Brit-

151

ain's first lord of the Admiralty, Reginald McKenna, abandoned the idea of including Canada in his imperial navy. He agreed that Britain should lend two warships and that Canada would organize its own naval defence. In his capacity as minister of marine and fisheries, Brodeur now set to work.

The bill to create a Canadian navy was introduced in the House of Commons on 12 Jan. 1910. It provided for Canada to assume responsibility for the defence of its eastern and western coasts, freeing Great Britain from this burden and thereby enabling it to concentrate on organizing its own defence. The bill was attacked on all sides; it suited neither the French Canadian nationalists led by Henri Bourassa*, who had not held a seat in the house since October 1907, nor the English Canadian Conservatives led by Robert Laird Borden*. The former considered the bill too generous towards the British navy, which would be able to make use of the Canadian navy in the event of an emergency; the latter accused it of underestimating Great Britain's needs. Brodeur was ill and unable to take part in the debate. He was absent on the day the bill was introduced and had to count on Laurier and Rodolphe Lemieux* to defend it. On 4 May approval was given to the act creating the Department of the Naval Service.

In all likelihood suffering from serious intestinal ailments, Brodeur stayed out of politics for a good part of 1910, and it seemed his career would soon come to an end. Ill health did not, however, prevent him from accepting responsibility for the new department, in addition to his existing ministerial duties. Moreover, he led the Liberal forces in the federal by-election of 3 Nov. 1910 in Drummond and Arthabaska, where he had to face the Conservatives and Nationalistes led by Bourassa, Armand La Vergne*, and Frederick Debartzch Monk*. Henri-Sévérin Béland*, the Liberal MP for Beauce, assisted him in this task. The election resulted in a surprise victory of the Nationalistes and a bitter defeat for the Liberals. In mid 1911, Brodeur accompanied Laurier to London for the coronation of George V and the imperial conference. The minister was then in the process of organizing the navy. Meanwhile, in Canada, the Liberals were preparing for the expected election following negative reaction to the reciprocity agreement with the United States [see Laurier].

Brodeur took no part in this election, which proved a disastrous one for the Liberals. Because of his illness, he was physically less and less able to perform all his political tasks. He was also beset by insinuations of corruption, the most insistent coming from Godfroy LANGLOIS, who in Le Canada and Le Pays attacked him for patronage. Brodeur had to resign. On 11 Aug. 1911, the day after he retired from political life and shortly before his 49th birthday, he was named to the Supreme Court of Canada. His was a purely political appointment (the last, apparently, in the court's history). Despite an honorary doctorate conferred on him by the Université Laval in 1904, Brodeur had few accomplishments to his credit in his legal career.

At the Supreme Court, Brodeur became the champion of the principles and distinctive features of the Quebec Civil Code. English Canadian judges seemed inclined to read the Civil Code in light of the common law. In a number of judgements, Brodeur reiterated that any analogy of this kind can only lead to serious errors of interpretation. Clearly, he looked at some of his colleagues with a critical eye. On 19 July 1918 Brodeur and one other judge, John IDINGTON, dissented from a Supreme Court decision which validated an order in council authorizing the cabinet to cancel exemptions that the Conservatives had initially granted under the Military Service Act of 1917. Even though the cancellations were upheld, he registered his dissent once again, an event that stood out in a judicial career that was, on the whole, rather uneventful.

Illness continued to plague Brodeur and made his life increasingly difficult. In 1923 he expressed a wish to retire because of his deteriorating health and the gnawing arthritis that made it painful for him to write his decisions. When his mind was made up, his Liberal friends did not forget him. First among them was Prime Minister William Lyon Mackenzie King*, to whom Brodeur had been very helpful during the transfer of power after Laurier's death in 1919. On 19 Sept. 1923, in the company of Fielding and Charles Murphy*, King reached the decision to offer Brodeur the post of lieutenant governor of Quebec, and he went to his home to put the proposal to him. Surprised but grateful, Brodeur accepted. For him, this appointment was a confirmation of the esteem in which he was held by his Liberal friends and former colleagues. He resigned from the Supreme Court on 10 October and was sworn in as lieutenant governor on the 31st.

Brodeur barely had time to take up his new duties. On 23 December the symptoms of his illness became persistent and on the 30th he suffered an intestinal haemorrhage. He died on the morning of 2 Jan. 1924, succumbing to a disease that had dogged him all his life. On that day King wrote in his diary: "In this [death] I lost a devoted and true friend, and the party as well. His kindness of heart it would be difficult to surpass. In all that pertained to my coming into 'Laurier House' he was like a brother or a father."

From about 1906 until his enforced retirement from public life in August 1911, Louis-Philippe Brodeur had been, next to Laurier, the most important Liberal in Quebec. He had successfully managed the provincial Liberal machine, which had played a decisive role in the survival of Laurier's various governments, and he had done so always in harmony with the leader's thinking. A front-line fighter in the quest for Canada's diplomatic independence, he had been responsible for the first purely Canadian international trade negotiations. As the man responsible for the creation of the navy, the forerunner of the Royal Canadian Navy and the Naval Reserve Force, he had linked his name with a great national institution. Illness abruptly brought to an end the accomplished career of one of Laurier's most trustworthy lieutenants.

RENÉ CASTONGUAY

[Material concerning Louis-Philippe Brodeur is held in various repositories. Collections at the LAC include Brodeur's own papers (MG 27, II, C4) as well as those of Victor-Gabriel Brodeur (MG 30, E312), William Lyon Mackenzie King (MG 26, J), and Wilfrid Laurier (MG 26, G). At the ANQ-Q, information on the final weeks of Brodeur's life is provided in the diary of Denis-Benjamin Papineau (P569), the lieutenant-governor's aide-de-camp. Brodeur's papers at the ANQ-M (P64) include letters, photographs, and five scrapbooks of newspaper clippings; in addition, this repository holds his baptismal and marriage records (CE601-S49, 23 août 1862, 27 juin 1887). Interesting details are also found in the memoirs of Brodeur's friends and contemporaries: L.-O. David, *Souvenirs et biographies, 1870–1910* (Montréal, 1911), and Raoul Dandurand, *Les mémoires du sénateur Raoul Dandurand (1861–1942)*, Marcel Hamelin, édit. (Québec, 1967).

Little has been written on Brodeur's career, but information on him can be found in biographies of his major contemporaries and works on the cases which he defended: Réal Bélanger, *Wilfrid Laurier; quand la politique devient passion* (Québec et Montréal, 1986); R. MacG. Dawson and H. B. Neatby, *William Lyon Mackenzie King: a political biography* (3v., Toronto, 1958–76); B. L. Vigod, *Quebec before Duplessis: the political career of Louis-Alexandre Taschereau* (Kingston, Ont., and Montreal, 1986); Robert Rumilly, *Honoré Mercier et son temps* (2v., Montréal, 1975); John Hilliker and Donald Barry, *Canada's Department of External Affairs* (2v., Montreal and Kingston, 1990–95), 1; and M. L. Hadley and Roger Sarty, *Tin-pots and pirate ships: Canadian naval forces and German sea raiders, 1880–1918* (Montreal and Kingston, 1991). For his Supreme Court career, see Ian Bushnell, *The captive court: a study of the Supreme Court of Canada* (Montreal and Kingston, 1992); J. G. Snell and Frederick Vaughan, *The Supreme Court of Canada: history of the institution* ([Toronto], 1985); and J.-L. Baudouin, "L'interprétation du Code civil québécois par la Cour suprême du Canada," *La Rev. du barreau canadien* (Ottawa), 53 (1975): 715–37. Mention should also be made of an article on Brodeur by his grandson N. D. Brodeur, "L. P. Brodeur and the origins of the Royal Canadian Navy," in *The RCN in retrospect, 1910–1968*, ed. J. A. Boutilier (Vancouver and London, 1982), 13–32, and of the Brodeur family history, Clément et Grégoire Brodeur, *Brodeur: essai sur l'histoire et la généalogie de la famille Brodeur en Amérique* (Saint-Hyacinthe, Qué., 1981). R.C.]

BRODEUR, MARIE-LOUISE. *See* MARMETTE

BRONSON, ELLA HOBDAY. *See* WEBSTER

BROOKFIELD, SAMUEL MANNERS, building contractor and entrepreneur; b. 29 Nov. 1847 in Ecclesfield, England, fourth of the six children of John Brookfield, an engineer and contractor, and Mary Storrs; m. 28 Feb. 1877 Annie Waites in Ashton upon Mersey, England, and they had one son and a daughter who died in infancy; d. 22 Aug. 1924 in Halifax.

Samuel M. Brookfield's family immigrated to Nova Scotia in 1852, removed to New Brunswick, and returned to Nova Scotia in 1860. Samuel attended the Saint John Grammar School and later King's Collegiate School in Windsor, N.S., before going to work as his father's purchasing agent. Between 1862 and 1870 John Brookfield undertook much of the extensive rebuilding of the defences of Halifax initiated by the imperial government. He moved into civilian construction in 1866, taking over (from George Lang*) and completing the construction of the Provincial Building, designed by David Stirling*. Upon his death in 1870, Samuel assumed direction of the business. Throughout his career he would remain the most important building contractor in Nova Scotia. He also engaged in building projects in New Brunswick and Newfoundland.

Brookfield's involvement in the burst of industrial growth in Halifax that followed the opening of the Intercolonial Railway in 1876 extended beyond his role as a builder. He served as a director of the Nova Scotia Sugar Refinery and of the Nova Scotia Cotton Manufacturing Company; the refinery had been constructed by his firm in 1880–81 and the factory in 1882–83. He also built the Halifax Sugar Refinery (1883–84). In 1887 he and five others from Halifax founded the Eastern Canada Savings and Loan Company. Brookfield became the first president, a position he was to hold for the rest of his life. The success of this conservatively managed firm was attributed by vice-president William Chamberlain Silver* to "the safety of its securities – all the investments being mortgages on real estate with ample margin."

Brookfield's most ambitious project was the construction and management of the Halifax graving dock. Technological change had undermined the Nova Scotian mercantile economy dependent upon wooden sailing vessels, and existing facilities were inadequate not only for the Royal Navy but for the steel-hulled steamships that were coming to dominate maritime commerce. Incorporated in London in 1885 with Brookfield as chairman, the Halifax Graving Dock Company was financed primarily by English capital, assisted by subsidies of $10,000 each for 20 years from the British Admiralty, the dominion government, and the City of Halifax. The dry dock opened in 1889, but demand proved disappointing and interest payments fell into arrears. The company restructured its debt in 1897, and Brookfield personally took over its operation, remaining managing director when his son John Waites Brookfield became manager in 1904. Increasingly he delegated the running of his construction business to Henry Roper, who was made manager in 1906 when the firm was incorporated as S. M. Brookfield Limited.

By 1918 the graving dock had become sufficiently profitable to redeem all the company's debt, although dividends were never paid to the shareholders. It had been damaged in the Halifax explosion of December 1917, but Brookfield had succeeded in getting it back in operation within two months. In June 1918, in order to create an integrated building and repair facility for steel ships on the east coast, the Canadian government proceeded with a controversial expropriation of the properties of the Halifax Graving Dock Company for $1,250,000; these assets were first leased and then sold to the newly formed Halifax Shipyards Limited. Brookfield and the other shareholders unsuccessfully contested the expropriation before the Exchequer Court of Canada, obtaining only a slight increase in compensation when the judgement came down in 1920.

Brookfield's drive to generate business for the graving dock involved him in both salvaging and shipping. The purchase and repair of the *Ulunda*, which had been stranded in the Bay of Fundy, led to the creation in 1892 of the Halifax, Liverpool and London Steamship Company, transformed the following year into the Canada and Newfoundland Steamship Company upon receipt of a Newfoundland mail contract. The company operated the *Ulunda* and two other vessels between Halifax, St John's, and Liverpool on a year-round basis until sold in 1898 to Furness, Withy and Company. Brookfield was also instrumental in 1908 in the formation of the Halifax Salvage Association, noted for its success in retrieving the 10,000-ton Canadian Pacific Railway steamship *Mount Temple* that year.

In 1910 Brookfield became the first president of the Maritime Telegraph and Telephone Company, which rapidly achieved a dominant position in the industry; he would hold the presidency until his death. Five years later he founded the Halifax Power Company, but his vision of exploiting the hydroelectric potential of the Northeast River near Halifax failed because of the difficulty of raising capital in wartime. Brookfield was also a key figure in the North West Arm Land Company, a firm headed by his son that engaged, unsuccessfully, in the development of a subdivision. Unlike contemporaries such as Benjamin Franklin Pearson*, John Fitzwilliam Stairs*, and William Maxwell Aitken*, Brookfield did not make significant investments in offshore enterprises. Instead he concentrated his energies at home, holding directorships in firms as diverse as the Nova Scotia Car Works and the Halifax Academy of Music, as well as dabbling in mining properties. He did, however, become a director of the Mexican Northern Power Company, incorporated in 1909.

While opposing the closed shop, Brookfield accepted craft unionism and had the reputation of being a benevolent employer. A Methodist known for his generosity and a leading freemason, he served as a trustee and choir member of the Grafton Street Methodist Church and as a regent of Mount Allison College in Sackville, N.B., which awarded him an honorary DCL in 1917. He was the mainstay of the Protestant Industrial School for boys in Halifax, served as a director of the Protestant Orphans' Home and the Young Men's Christian Association, and was honorary president of the Boy Scouts, the Sailors' Home, and the Navy League. Although a declared Conservative, he had little to do with politics except for a brief period (1876–77) as an alderman.

Travelling to work by tram, by legend the earliest to arrive in the morning and the last to leave at night, Brookfield, an obituary noted, "was always to be seen at the motorman's shoulder, waiting for the car to come to a standstill, and was the first, never the last, to alight." His wife predeceased him on 23 Feb. 1909. Brookfield bequeathed his entire estate of $248,238.98 to his son, who also succeeded him as president of S. M. Brookfield Limited, renamed the Brookfield Construction Company Limited.

HENRY ROPER

Halifax County Court of Probate (Halifax), Estate papers, no.10787. NSARM, 1990-215/014, no.1; MG 1, vol.150c, nos.1–2; MG 100 vol.88, no.3.1. P. R. Blakeley, *Glimpses of Halifax, 1867–1900* (Halifax, 1949; repr. Belleville, Ont., 1973). Harry Bruce, *A century at Central Trust: the story of its growth* (Halifax, 1987). Susan Buggey, "Building Halifax, 1841–1871," *Acadiensis* (Fredericton), 10 (1980–81), no.1: 90–112. J. E. Chute, "Halifax's new south end: the North West Arm Land Company and a parkland legacy," Royal N.S. Hist. Soc., *Journal* (Halifax), 3 (2000): 33–53. *The city of Halifax, the capital of Nova Scotia, Canada: its advantages and facilities . . .* , comp. J. Isaacs (Halifax, 1909). *In memoriam, Samuel M. Brookfield, D.C.L.* (Halifax, n.d.). Ian McKay, *The craft transformed: an essay on the carpenters of Halifax, 1885–1985* (Halifax, 1985). Henry Roper, "The Halifax Board of Control: the failure of municipal reform, 1906–1919," *Acadiensis*, 14 (1984–85), no.2: 46–65. J. S. Scott, "The foundation and structure of a building business," *Port and Province* (Halifax), September 1937. V. L. Settle, "Halifax Shipyards, 1918–1978: an historical perspective" (MA thesis, St Mary's Univ., Halifax, 1994).

BROWN. *See also* CRAWFORD BROWN

BROWN, ADA MARY (Courtice), educator, social reformer, and office holder; b. 4 Nov. 1860 near Bloomfield, Upper Canada, daughter of Stephen Keyes Brown, a farmer, and Eliza Jane White; m. 24 Oct. 1888 Andrew Cory Courtice in Toronto, and they had a son and a daughter; d. there 24 Aug. 1923 and was buried in Prince Albert, Ont.

The only daughter of devout, humanitarian Quakers, Ada Brown was born on her maternal grandfather's farm, raised near Pickering, Ont., and educated at Pickering College and the Ontario Ladies' College in Whitby. She then taught music. In 1886 or 1887 the family moved to Toronto after a split in the Quaker community in Pickering. Although she and her parents later left the Quakers, her Christian faith, characterized by devotion to philanthropic and moral reform, would play a significant role in defining her life's work.

In 1888 Ada married Andrew C. Courtice, the minister of Parliament Street Methodist Church, where she was a soloist. Subsequent postings took them to London, Montreal, and Kingston. A strong Christian socialist, temperance advocate, and later a pacifist, Andrew was named editor of the Methodist *Christian Guardian* in 1894 and he, Ada, and their children moved back to Toronto.

From an early date Ada and Andrew, who was removed from his editorship in 1902, were intent on setting up their own school. In preparation, Ada met frequently with kindergarten specialist Adaline Augusta Hughes and her husband, school inspector James Laughlin Hughes*, who together exposed her to progressive educational theories. In 1907 the Courtices opened a school on Howard Avenue with the aim of developing each pupil "physically, mentally and morally" and promoting "self-knowledge, self-control and healthy life." A year later they founded the Balmy Beach College and School of Music and Art on Beech Avenue, which Ada would operate for ten years after her husband's death on 10 Nov. 1908.

Strong-willed and resourceful, Ada Courtice had a diverse range of interests. She was an advocate of peace and women's suffrage and advancement, and was involved with a number of reform organizations, including the National Council of Women of Canada and the Local Council in Toronto. From 1905 to 1913 she convened the National Council's standing committee on peace and arbitration. Although her attempts to establish subcommittees within local councils across Canada proved disappointing, she held tightly to her pacifist convictions; during World War I she would oppose conscription.

Most of Courtice's efforts had focused on bettering society by aiding children through improvements in education and family life. She most certainly knew of the movement to form home and school clubs, which, in Ontario, were associated with kindergartens or were organized as art leagues and mothers' clubs. They tended to favour social events, sports, and fundraising. At her Balmy Beach school Courtice established a mothers' club. In 1914 she joined the education committee of the Toronto Local Council and,

with its support, ran unsuccessfully for election to the Toronto Public School Board (the highest civic office a woman could hold). Her platform included the use of schools as social centres, improved playgrounds and physical education, more emphasis on vocational education, and better ways to prevent smoking and drinking among boys.

At a meeting of the Local Council on 12 Feb. 1916, on a motion by Courtice, the Toronto Home and School Council was formed. She was elected president, and Ada Hughes honorary president. This council, which included teachers and school officials as well as parents, was distinguished by its early focus on political action and educational reform. Its objectives were to provide a centre for the city's existing home and school clubs, to study educational issues, and to form "a committee to work in the interests of the municipal elections." The council was not afraid to criticize schools and lobby for change. It promoted women as candidates in board elections, backed female teachers, supported the expansion of kindergarten, domestic science, and school health programs, and endorsed welfare measures for the poor. In one address to the council, Courtice spoke of its ability "to create interest in standards of home and school life, in a way that few organized efforts can do. It is because the home and school are the rock bottom foundations of individual and national character, that we have faith in our movement."

In January 1917, with the council's support, Courtice and Dr Caroline Sophia Brown* secured seats on the school board. For four years Courtice worked to alter curriculum through the addition of French, agriculture, household science, and manual training, and through changes in the physical environment of schools, with an emphasis on more play and athletics. As well, she pushed for special educational facilities for slow learners and the handicapped. Her tenacity is illustrated by her challenge in 1917 of the board chairman's defence of a principal who had allegedly kissed a female student and by her unflinching support the following year of Freda Held, a teacher whose German parentage attracted vicious wartime abuse.

In May 1919 Courtice called a meeting, under the auspices of the Toronto Home and School Council, to discuss the advisability of forming a provincial body. A loosely organized coalition – of home and school associations, mothers' clubs, and school and art leagues – soon emerged, known as the Ontario Federation of Home and School Associations. By 1920 it had expanded to include representatives from teachers, inspectors, and women's institutes. It received a grant from the provincial Department of Education and gained status as a section within the Ontario Educational Association.

Courtice resigned her presidency of the Toronto council in 1920 and assumed the position of organizing secretary for the Ontario Federation. In her annual report for 1921–22 she stressed the importance of homes and schools working together and the democratic underpinning of such joint effort: "We are expressing a type of education not undertaken heretofore in a movement of the people, for and by people themselves, . . . the people of the neighbourhood must find and study their own problems and be able to create public opinion for advancement." After Courtice was defeated in the school board elections of January 1921, in a wave of reaction, she devoted her attention to the expansion of local home and school clubs. In February the Toronto council established a home education committee, and Courtice agreed to serve as its convenor. It circulated lists of useful books, produced pamphlets for mothers, and distributed material on such topics as scientific budgeting for families and the proper balance of work, rest, and recreation.

By the time of Courtice's death from intestinal cancer in 1923, some 270 individual home and school associations had been formed throughout Ontario. Within a decade, however, what had started as a reform organization of middle-class women, with lofty ideals to change society through improved childhood education, had become less a challenge to the school system than a vehicle for accommodating accepted practices.

NANCY KIEFER

AO, RG 80-5-0-165, no.14443; RG 80-8-0-911, no.4675. LAC, RG 31, C1, 1901, Toronto, Ward 4, div.4: 9 (mfm. at AO). *Globe*, 11 Nov. 1908. L. M. Burgoyne, *A history of the home and school movement in Ontario* ([Toronto, 1934?]). *Canadian annual rev.*, 1916: 425. *Canadian men and women of the time* (Morgan; 1898). T. [A.] Crowley, "Ada Mary Brown Courtice: pacifist, feminist and educational reformer in early twentieth-century Canada," *Studies in Hist. and Politics* ([Lennoxville, Que.]), 1 (1980): 76–114; "Parents in a hurry: the early home and school movement in Ontario," *Social Hist.* (Ottawa), 19 (1986): 323–42. Kari Delhi, "For intelligent motherhood and national efficiency: the Toronto Home and School Council, 1916–1930," in *Gender and education in Ontario: an historical reader*, ed. Ruby Heap and Alison Prentice (Toronto, 1991), 147–63. Alison Prentice et al., *Canadian women: a history* (Toronto, 1988), 183. T. P. Socknat, *Witness against war: pacifism in Canada, 1900–1945* (Toronto, 1987). Veronica Strong-Boag, "Peace-making women: Canada, 1919–1939," in *Women and peace: theoretical, historical and practical perspectives*, ed. Ruth Roach Pierson (London, 1987), 170–91. Toronto Home and School Council, *Year-book*, 1927/28.

BROWN, ANNIE GARDNER. *See* BARR

BROWN, CATHERINE. *See* TRASK

BRUNET, FRANÇOIS-XAVIER, priest and bishop; b. 27 Nov. 1868 and baptized two days later in the parish of Saint-André-d'Argenteuil, Que., son of François Brunet and Léocadie Joly; d. 7 Jan. 1922 in Montreal.

In 1873 François-Xavier Brunet's parents settled in Ottawa, where his father worked as a carter. François-Xavier received his elementary education from the Brothers of the Christian Schools and did his commercial and classical studies at the College of Ottawa, graduating with a BA in 1890. He then decided to enter the priesthood and studied theology at the Grand Séminaire d'Ottawa. On 23 Sept. 1893, at the age of 24, he was ordained by Archbishop Joseph-Thomas Duhamel* of Ottawa. After serving as curate in Ottawa, as well as in Masson (Masson-Angers), Thurso, and Aylmer in Quebec, Brunet became curé in Mayo, near Buckingham, Que., in 1895. There he built the parish church for the Irish families and had a chapel erected for the German families. Appointed parish priest of Bourget, Ont., in 1900, he was called four years later to serve as secretary to Archbishop Duhamel, and then to his successor, Charles Hugh GAUTHIER.

On 6 Aug. 1913 Brunet was chosen bishop of the new diocese of Mont-Laurier, created through the subdivision of the diocese of Ottawa that April. In 1879, after a decade of expeditions to the northern part of his parish, the curé François-Xavier-Antoine Labelle* of Saint-Jérôme had put forward the idea of subdividing the dioceses of Montreal and Ottawa to create a new one in the north. He saw his work of agricultural colonization as the essential bulwark against the Protestants in the county of Argenteuil, who wanted to occupy the same territory. After the bishop of Montreal had refused to split his diocese, Labelle had left it to the religious authorities in Ottawa, who had piloted the project until 1913, changing the location of the proposed bishop's palace, however, from Nominingue to Mont-Laurier. Brunet was thoroughly familiar with the strengths and weaknesses of the territory being entrusted to him, with its farmland and forests. As secretary to the bishops of Ottawa, he had accompanied them on their pastoral visits to every parish in the vast diocese and had been put in charge in 1912 of an inquiry into the advantages and disadvantages of erecting a diocese with a seat in Mont-Laurier. Known for his "passion for work," he accepted the appointment with humility, for he knew what it would cost him to set up the new diocese. He was consecrated bishop on 28 October by his metropolitan, Archbishop Gauthier, in the presence of many bishops and priests representing Quebec, Ontario, western Canada, and the Maritime provinces. He then left by train for the upper reaches of the Laurentians. His reception at Mont-Laurier was magnificent. The procession headed towards the little wooden church along a route lined with flags, streamers, arches of fir boughs, foliage-draped poles, and lights. The event gave the new bishop an opportunity to praise the work of Labelle and Archbishop Duhamel, the late chief architects of the spiritual and temporal development of the northern townships that would be his new field of missionary endeavour.

At that time, Bishop Brunet could count on the dedication of 48 fairly young priests, and his priority was to organize the diocese. He surrounded himself with men whose experience and energy would assist him in his plans. To the post of vicar general he appointed a curé known for his diplomacy and skill in his work as a colonizer and mediator, Samuel Ouimet of Saint-Jovite, who had been one of the closest colleagues of Labelle. Alphonse Génier, the energetic curé from Mont-Laurier, became his diocesan bursar, assigned to take charge of the construction of a true bishop's palace. To the cathedral parish, he named one of the strong personalities among his clergy, the curé Joseph-Eugène Limoges, who would succeed him in 1922.

There was no lack of work, for everything remained to be done. In 1913 the diocese had 30,400 Roman Catholics – 4,240 French-speaking families, 200 English-speaking, and 66 aboriginal – located in 28 parishes and seven missions. There were fewer than 2,000 Protestants. Besides setting up the spiritual and temporal structures, Brunet had to erect the various buildings in the fledgling diocese. In the spring of 1914 he asked his people for financial help in building his episcopal residence, which would be inaugurated on 28 October, the first anniversary of his consecration. Even before beginning the construction of his cathedral, he turned his attention to building a diocesan seminary. It was erected near the new bishop's residence and on 6 Sept. 1915 Brunet and the young superior, Abbé Rodolphe Mercure, welcomed the first 110 pupils to the Séminaire Saint-Joseph, which was affiliated to the Université Laval at Quebec. Brunet himself taught the courses in theology to the older seminarians. He wanted to create an atmosphere and instil a spirit of brotherhood and solidarity, rather than simply provide a course of studies. On 16 June 1918 he blessed the cornerstone of his cathedral, a handsome stone building overlooking the Rivière du Lièvre.

During his eight-year episcopate, Bishop Brunet presided over the ordination of 29 new priests, who became his colleagues in the diocese. He ordered the erection of 12 new parishes and travelled four times through all the townships in the valleys of the Gatineau, the Lièvre, the Rouge, the Maskinongé, and the Diable in order to learn about the spiritual and temporal problems of the people in his diocese. In the spring of 1920 he made his sole journey *ad limina* to Rome, to meet Pope Benedict XV.

In January 1921 Rome authorized Bishop Brunet to set up the community of Sœurs de Notre-Dame de Mont-Laurier, so that the need for teachers in the parish schools of his diocese could be met. A month later he was one of the bishops who pressed for the founding of the Séminaire des Missions Étrangères, which was erected in Pont-Viau in 1924. Priests would go out from this seminary to work in many parts of the world. On returning in December 1921 from a journey to St Boniface (Winnipeg), Man., to attend the consecration of Bishop Joseph-Henri Prud'homme, Brunet had to take to his bed. A few days later he was transported to the Hôtel-Dieu in Montreal, where he died on 7 Jan. 1922 at the age of 53. After the funeral service, his remains were placed in the crypt of his cathedral in Mont-Laurier.

During his short, eight-year episcopate, François-Xavier Brunet was able to set his diocese on a firm foundation. He was a builder who erected 12 new parishes, founded the Séminaire Saint-Joseph, and constructed the episcopal residence and the cathedral. He had a keen sense of observation, sound judgement, and great facility with words. Through his knowledge of the human condition, he was able to choose remarkable colleagues to lay the cornerstones of his diocese.

LUC COURSOL

The fundamental sources for the episcopate of François-Xavier Brunet are held at the Arch. du Diocèse de Mont-Laurier, Qué.

ANQ-M, CE606-S7, 29 nov. 1868. A.-M. Cadieux et Louise Paradis, "Le programme de colonisation du curé Labelle," *Les Cahiers d'hist. de la rivière du Nord* (Saint-Jérôme, Qué.), 1 (1983), no.1: 3–15. Luc Coursol, *Histoire de Mont-Laurier* (1v. paru, Mont-Laurier, [1985]–); *Mont-Laurier, 1901–1922: capitale des cantons du Nord* ([Mont-Laurier, 1983]); *Un diocèse dans les cantons du Nord: histoire du diocèse de Mont-Laurier* (Mont-Laurier, 1988). Richard La Grange, *Le Nord, mon père, voilà notre avenir . . . : une histoire de L'Annonciation et de canton Marchand* (L'Annonciation, Qué., [1986]). Maurice Lalonde, *Notes historiques sur Mont-Laurier, Nominingue et Kiamika* ([Beauceville, Qué., 1937]). Albiny Paquette, *Hon. Albiny Paquette, soldat, médecin, maire, député, ministre; 33 années à la législature de Québec: souvenirs d'une vie de travail et de bonheur* (s.l., [1977?]). J.-P. Poulin, "Petite histoire du diocèse," *L'Élan* (Mont-Laurier) (a narrative that appeared from 1962 to 1965). Séminaire Saint-Joseph, *Annuaire* (Mont-Laurier), 1915–65.

BRYMNER, WILLIAM, artist and educator; b. 14 Dec. 1855 in Greenock, Scotland, son of Douglas Brymner* and Jean Thomson; m. 12 Sept. 1917 Mary Caroline Larkin, née Massey, in Montreal; they had no children; d. 18 June 1925 in Wallasey, England, and was buried there.

William Brymner was an influential art teacher and a distinguished Canadian figure and landscape painter. Born in Scotland, he moved with his family to Melbourne, Lower Canada, in 1857. He first attended St

Francis College in neighbouring Richmond. In 1864 his family relocated to Montreal. Brymner completed his studies at a private school and at the Petit Séminaire de Sainte-Thérèse in Sainte-Thérèse-de-Blainville (Sainte-Thérèse). In 1870 he was briefly apprenticed to Montreal architect Richard Cunningham Windeyer. He also attended night classes at the National Institute of Fine Arts, Sciences, Arts, Trades and Industries, founded in 1871 by Joseph Chabert*. His father's appointment in May 1872 to the federal Department of Agriculture as clerk in charge of archives (he would become head of the Canadian archives) took the family to Ottawa. William found work as a clerk in the same department and by 1874 as a draftsman in the Department of Public Works, attached to the office of the chief architect, Thomas Seaton Scott*. In September 1876 he executed a set of pen-and-ink drawings of Quebec City commissioned by Governor General Lord Dufferin [Blackwood*] through Scott.

With financial support from his father, Brymner sailed for Europe in February 1878 to study architecture. He settled in Paris, where initially he worked as an exhibition designer for the Canadian commissioner to the universal exposition held there that year. The following summer he took drawing lessons with Charles-François Pinot. In October he enrolled at the Académie Julian, studying with Jules-Joseph Lefebvre and Gustave Boulanger. Newly committed to painting, he continued at Julian's until 1880 with Tony Robert-Fleury and Adolphe-William Bouguereau. In April 1879 he had begun independent studies with Charles Durand, known as Carolus-Duran, and he supplemented this instruction with anatomy courses at the École des Beaux-Arts. Brymner embraced French academic tenets of good draftsmanship, formal harmony, and technical excellence, but reacted against the artificiality of much studio-produced academic painting on grand themes. He early affiliated himself with a group of contemporary naturalist painters inspired by the Barbizon School, and led by Jean-François Millet, adopting their practice of sketching in rural settings in a quest for picturesque subjects and natural effects. During the summer of 1879 he painted in the French and Belgian countryside.

Brymner returned to Ottawa in the summer of 1880 and accepted the position of headmaster at the new Ottawa Art School. That winter he tried his hand at etching, producing his only known print, *Old man painting at the Louvre, Paris*. Teaching helped fund a second trip to France in May 1881, but rheumatic fever forced his return in October to Ottawa, where he spent the winter recovering. In April 1882 he sent his first works to the annual exhibitions of the Art Association of Montreal (AAM) and the Royal Canadian Academy of Arts (RCA), held jointly that year in Montreal. He returned to the Ottawa Art School in the fall of 1882.

In May 1883 Brymner was made an associate of the RCA. The summer found him back in France, sketching at Pontaubert with British painter Frederick Brown. He also visited Yorkshire, England, where he returned the following May for seven months. Here he painted with British artist Frederick William Jackson and Canadian-born James Kerr Lawson. At Runswick Bay he painted his first major canvas, *A wreath of flowers*, which he would send to the exhibition of the RCA in 1885. Based on outdoor life studies, this picture typifies Brymner's youthful style, showing his early narrative interests and demonstrating his mastery of the human figure and landscape and his refined tonal naturalism. In January 1885 he concluded his studies at the Académie Julian and went sketching at Brolles, in the forest of Fontainebleau. The acceptance of *Border of the Forest Fontainebleau* to the annual Paris Salon in May firmly established his professional credentials.

Brymner spent the summer of 1885 in Canada, travelling in the Baie-Saint-Paul region of Quebec. Applying French methods to Canadian subjects, he produced some of his best work around this time, including *Sad memories* and *The weaver*, painted at Baie-Saint-Paul, and *Crazy patchwork* (1886), portraying his younger sister. He quickly built a reputation as one of the outstanding Canadian figure and landscape painters of his generation. In February 1886 he was elected a full member of the RCA. His diploma piece, *A wreath of flowers*, was one of four of his paintings featured in the Canadian section of the Colonial and Indian Exhibition held that summer in London, England. The same year he became a member of the Ontario Society of Artists. After a trip by train through western Canada, during which he painted at the Blackfoot Indian Reserve in Gleichen (Alta) and in the Selkirk Mountains, he accepted an appointment as director of the AAM's school of art. He would hold the post from 1886 to his retirement in 1921.

A respected and benevolent teacher, Brymner was reportedly "universally beloved by students and confreres, not only for his craftsmanship, but also for his kindly disposition." He helped introduce French methods and aesthetic concepts to a new generation of Canadian artists, among them Clarence Gagnon*, Alexander Young Jackson*, and members of the Beaver Hall Hill Group, such as Lilias Torrance* (Newton). He emphasized drawing as "the foundation of all the graphic and plastic arts," and the importance of direct observation of nature. While faithful to his own academic training, he championed freedom of artistic expression for others. As Jackson recalled, Brymner "was no radical, but he encouraged his students to be independent. . . . Among his fellow academicians he would stand for no intolerance or injustice toward the younger artists." Based in Montreal, Brymner divided his time between winter teaching duties and holidays spent painting in Europe and Canada. In the summer of 1889 he returned to France; in 1891 he painted in Killarney (Republic of Ireland) with Canadian James Macdonald Barnsley. He travelled to the Canadian Rockies in the summer of 1892 on a major commission for the Canadian Pacific Railway to produce scenic views for public display, some of which were exhibited at the World's Columbian exposition in Chicago in 1893. He returned west the next year to work in Field and Glacier, B.C., and in Gleichen.

By the 1890s Brymner had developed a distinct personal style. Landscape painting was a primary interest, but he also produced some notable genre and portrait paintings. As exemplified by *Early moonrise in September* (1899), his interpretation of the Canadian landscape grew more painterly and concerned with atmospheric effects. A similar trend towards intimate, evocative portrayals occurs in his figure paintings, many executed in watercolour, his preferred medium in these years. *The grey girl* (1897) and *The picture book (Two girls reading)* (1898), both watercolour on linen, bear comparison with the tonal compositions of James Abbott McNeill Whistler. Trips to Venice in 1901 and 1902, where he painted with James Wilson MORRICE and Maurice Galbraith Cullen*, and to sunny Martigues, France, in 1908 further directed Brymner towards a more impressionistic style. Excursions to the coast of Nova Scotia, including Louisbourg (1909, 1910, and 1914) and Pictou (1912), produced a number of luminous studies of land and sea. One such painting, *Incoming tide, Louisbourg*, won the AAM's Jessie Dow prize in 1915.

A commission for a decorative mural cycle for the summer home of Charles E. L. Porteous on the Île d'Orléans, Que., had brought Brymner in 1899 to the Cote-de-Beaupré, where he produced many sketches of the terrain and people of the St Lawrence River valley, serving both for the murals and for new pictures. His skills as a muralist brought other commissions, notably in 1907 for three decorative paintings for Edward Seaborne Clouston* and his daughter Mrs John L. Todd at their summer homes in Senneville. A favourite sketching ground in later years was Saint-Eustache, which Brymner had first discovered in 1896 with Cullen and where in 1905 the artists had built a shared studio.

Brymner regularly exhibited in the major annual arts exhibitions in Canada, including the Canadian National Exhibition in Toronto, as well as in many international shows. He was a gold and silver medallist respectively at the 1901 Pan-American Exhibition in Buffalo and the 1904 Louisiana Purchase exposition in St Louis. A founding member of the Montreal Water Colour Society (1889) and the Pen and Pencil Club of Montreal (1890, president in 1893), he was active as well in the Toronto-based Canadian Art

Club (1908–15) and from 1912 in the Arts Club of Montreal, serving as its president in 1916–17. In 1907 he was elected vice-president of the RCA and in May 1909 he became president. In 1916 he was named a CMG and had a solo exhibition at the Arts Club of Montreal. A stroke in 1917 effectively ended his painting career, however, and forced his resignation as president of the RCA that December. In early 1921, after a second solo exhibition at the Arts Club, he retired from teaching and spent his remaining years travelling, mainly in France and Italy, with his wife. He died while visiting her family in Wallasey, England. The quality and diversity of his art work as well as his many contributions as an art teacher earned Brymner a reputation as one of the major Canadian artists of his generation.

VICTORIA BAKER

Works by William Brymner are held in public and private collections across Canada, including the Agnes Etherington Art Centre, Queen's Univ., Kingston, Ont.; the Art Gallery of Hamilton, Ont.; the Beaverbrook Art Gallery, Fredericton; the Art Gallery of Ontario, Toronto; the McCord Museum of Canadian Hist., Montreal, and the Montreal Museum of Fine Arts; the LAC and the National Gallery of Canada in Ottawa; and the Musée National des Beaux-Arts du Québec in Quebec City. His murals for the former Charles E. L. Porteous home remain *in situ*. Original illustrations by Brymner were published in [Joshua Fraser], *Shanty, forest and river life in the backwoods of Canada* (Montreal, 1883) and in H. C. Walsh, *Bonhomme: French-Canadian stories and sketches* (Toronto, 1899). Brymner's publications include "'Progress in art'" and "Village life in three countries," *Univ. Magazine* (Montreal), 6 (1907): 239–46 and 11 (1912): 309–26.

McCord Museum of Canadian Hist., William Brymner papers. National Gallery of Canada, Library, William Brymner file; William Brymner papers. Fern Bayer, *The Ontario collection* (Markham, Ont., 1984). Janet Braide, "Les murales de Brymner à l'île d'Orléans," *Vie des Arts* (Montréal), no.97 (hiver 1979–80): 62–65; "A visit to Martiques, summer 1908: impressions by William Brymner," *Journal of Canadian Art Hist.* (Montreal), 1 (1974), no.1: 28–32; *William Brymner, 1855–1925: a retrospective* (exhibition catalogue, Agnes Etherington Art Centre, 1979); "Wreath of flowers," *Journal of Canadian Art Hist.*, 2 (1975), no.1: 83–84. *Canadian encyclopedia*. *Canadian men and women of the time* (Morgan; 1898 and 1912). W. [G.] Colgate, *Canadian art, its origin & development* (Toronto, 1943; repr. 1967). *A dictionary of Canadian artists*, comp. C. S. MacDonald (7v. to date, Ottawa, 1967–), 1. Dale Ethier, "Quebec City and William Brymner," *Archivist* (Ottawa), 17 (1990), no.2: 10–11. J. R. Harper, *Early painters and engravers in Canada* (Toronto, 1970); *Painting in Canada, a history* ([Toronto], 1966). R. J. Lamb, *The Canadian Art Club, 1907–1915* (exhibition catalogue, Edmonton Art Gallery, 1988). David McTavish, *Canadian artists in Venice* (exhibition catalogue, Agnes Etherington Art Centre, 1979). N. [McF.] MacTavish, *The fine arts in Canada* (Toronto, 1925; repr., [intro. Robert McMichael], 1973). *Montreal*

Bulyea

Museum of Fine Arts, formerly Art Association of Montreal:
spring exhibitions, 1880–1970, comp. E. de R. McMann
(Toronto, 1988). National Gallery of Canada, *Canadian art*
(2v., Ottawa, 1988). D. [R.] Reid, *A concise history of*
Canadian painting (Toronto, 1973). A. H. Robson, *Cana-*
dian landscape painters (Toronto, 1932). *Royal Canadian*
Academy of Arts; exhibitions and members, 1880–1979,
comp. E. de R. McMann (Toronto, 1981). Rebecca Sisler,
Passionate spirits; a history of the Royal Canadian Acad-
emy of Arts, 1880–1980 (Toronto, 1980). *Standard dict. of*
Canadian biog. (Roberts and Tunnell). W. R. Watson, *Ret-*
rospective: recollections of a Montreal art dealer (Toronto
and Buffalo, N.Y., 1974).

BULYEA, GEORGE HEDLEY VICARS, busi-
nessman, politician, and lieutenant governor; b. 17
Feb. 1859 in Gagetown, N.B., son of James Albert
Bulyea and Jane Blizzard, farmers; m. there 29 Jan.
1885 Annie Blanche Babbit; d. 22 July 1928 near
Peachland, B.C.

G. H. V. Bulyea's parents were both of loyalist
descent. He was educated at the grammar school in
Gagetown and at the University of New Brunswick,
graduating in 1878 with a specialization in mathematics and French. He taught at the Sheffield Academy
from 1878 to 1882, after which he went west to Winnipeg and then in 1883 to Qu'Appelle (Sask.). There
he engaged in varied business enterprises, including
selling furniture and insurance and dealing in grain,
flour, and feed. By 1886 he was a school trustee, a
founding member of the South Qu'Appelle Agricultural Association, and treasurer of the local council of
the Royal Templars of Temperance; in 1888 he was
president of the Northwest Prohibitory Alliance. In
religion he was a Baptist. His wife, Annie, would later
be heavily involved in the Woman's Christian Temperance Union and Baptist Ladies' Aid of Regina, and she
served as president of the Local Council of Women
there from 1901 to 1905. Their only child, Percy
McFarlane Bulyea, died aged 15 in 1901.

Bulyea ran for the South Qu'Appelle seat in the
Legislative Assembly of the North-West Territories
in 1891, but lost; he was, however, successful in
1894, and was re-elected in 1898 and 1902. He
served in the government of Premier Frederick William Gordon Haultain* from 7 Oct. 1897, first as a
non-resident member (essentially a minister without
portfolio) and then, from January 1898, as Yukon
commissioner. He was appointed commissioner of
agriculture and territorial secretary on 12 Jan. 1899,
and on 4 Feb. 1903 he became commissioner of public works, a position he held, while remaining territorial secretary, until 1905. He was a partisan Liberal in
federal politics and a strong advocate of territorial
rights: as early as 1890 he had argued that a council
responsible to the assembly should control spending
both of the territorial revenues and of the annual federal grant. By 1897 responsible government had been

achieved, but the territorial government faced rapidly
growing demands for services as a result of national
policies to settle the west. The size of the federal
grant never kept pace with the pressures on the local
government, and the resulting tension fuelled a popular demand for full provincial status.

Bulyea himself was in a stressful situation. On the
one hand, he was loyal to the federal Liberals, was
one of their principal organizers in the District of
Assiniboia, and was anxious that the local government, officially non-partisan, not be in conflict with
Ottawa. On the other hand, as a member of the territorial government he was acutely aware of the difficulties resulting from federal underfunding of the
region, and he knew how popular the provincial
rights cry of Premier Haultain was. Haultain identified himself more and more publicly with the federal
Conservative party, particularly after opposition
leader Robert Laird Borden* took up the territories'
cause in 1902. Bulyea accompanied Haultain to
Ottawa early in 1903 to push the autonomy issue, but
later that year and in 1904 he appeared to fall out
with his leader when he suggested that additional
funds and the authority to charter railways would satisfy much of the demand for provincial rights.

Haultain and Bulyea represented the territorial government during negotiations in Ottawa on provincehood in January and February 1905. Bulyea supported,
in particular, the revised education clause of the
Autonomy Bills as it emerged following the resignation of Clifford SIFTON from Sir Wilfrid Laurier*'s
cabinet, believing that it could be defended among
western Liberals. On 25 July the prime minister, having concluded that Haultain's public antagonism to
aspects of the settlement precluded his being given a
position, offered the lieutenant governorship of the
new province of Alberta to Bulyea (the Saskatchewan
office went to Amédée-Emmanuel FORGET). "Your
long and faithful services to the party," wrote Laurier,
"entitle you to the best that may be in the gift of the
party." Bulyea accepted, and was sworn into office
when the province came into being on 1 Sept. 1905; he
was reappointed to a second five-year term on 5 Oct.
1910.

The duties of a lieutenant governor normally were
largely ceremonial. On 24 Nov. 1905 Bulyea drove
the last spike on the Canadian Northern railway to
Edmonton; on 15 March 1906 he opened the first session of the first Alberta legislature in the Thistle Rink
in Edmonton. He was granted the LLD degree in 1908
by both the University of Alberta and his alma mater.
Two years later he was drawn into activities of a different kind when the Liberal government of Alberta's
first premier, Alexander Cameron Rutherford*, began
to unravel in light of the scandal surrounding an
ineptly drawn contract to build the Alberta and Great
Waterways Railway [*see* Charles Wilson CROSS].

Bulyea told Laurier in February that "a scapegoat or scapegoats" would have to be found, and hoped that "no serious effects or rather injury will accrue to the Liberal party." It soon was clear that the scandal would claim the premier, and Bulyea, Laurier, and Senator Peter Talbot, president of the Alberta Liberal Association, engaged in a search for a replacement who could unite the badly divided government caucus. Finally, they agreed upon Chief Justice Arthur Lewis Watkins SIFTON. Bulyea informed the legislature on 26 May 1910 that he had accepted Rutherford's resignation and had called on Sifton to form a government; he prorogued the legislature to allow Sifton time to get elected and to consolidate his government. The opposition howled in rage at this "unconstitutional" procedure; even Bulyea told Laurier, "I am afraid that I had to do a few things that a L.G. is not supposed to do but I think I was justified by results and in proroguing the house I had the support both of the outgoing and incoming premiers and needless to say practically all of the members of the House." His remaining years in office were relatively uneventful.

After his retirement as lieutenant governor in 1915, when he was succeeded by Robert George BRETT, Bulyea was appointed on 20 October chairman of the Board of Public Utility Commissioners in Alberta, a position he occupied until 1 May 1923. He died at his ranch near Peachland, B.C., on 22 July 1928 and was buried at Qu'Appelle five days later. A portrait by Victor Albert Long hangs in the Legislature Building in Edmonton.

DAVID J. HALL

[There is no significant collection of Bulyea papers. The most useful primary sources for his correspondence are the Laurier and Sifton papers in LAC, MG 26, G, and MG 27, II, D15, respectively. Much valuable material is also available in *The formation of Alberta: a documentary history*, ed. D. R. Owram (Calgary, 1979). By far the most important secondary source is L. G. Thomas, *The Liberal party in Alberta: a history of politics in the province of Alberta, 1905–1921* (Toronto, 1959). D.J.H.]

LAC, MG 26, A; H. PAA, PR1966.93/8; PR1969.42. Univ. of Alta Arch. (Edmonton), file 2315-5 (honorary degree recipients); A. C. Rutherford fonds. *Calgary Herald*, 23 July 1928. *Edmonton Journal*, 23 July 1928. *Qu'Appelle Progress* (Qu'Appelle, later called Qu'Appelle Station [Qu'Appelle, Sask.]), 1885–86, 1889; continued as *Progress*, 1899. Alta, Board of Public Utilities Commissioners, *Annual report* (Edmonton), 1915/16–23. *Alberta in the 20th century: a journalistic history of the province*, [ed. Ted Byfield *et al.*] (12v. to date, Edmonton, 1991–), 2–3. F.-J. Audet, *Dictionnaire biographique des gouverneurs, lieutenants-gouverneurs et administrateurs du Canada et de ses provinces, 1604–1921* (2v., s.l., s.d.). D. R. Babcock, *Alexander Cameron Rutherford: a gentleman of Strathcona* (Calgary, 1989); "Autonomy and alienation in Alberta: Premier A. C. Rutherford," *Prairie Forum* (Regina), 6 (1981): 117–28. John Blue, *Alberta, past and present, historical and biographical* (3v., Chicago, 1924), 1. *Canadian annual rev.*, 1901–28. *Canadian men and women of the time* (Morgan; 1912). *CPG*, 1901–15. *Cyclopædia of Canadian biog.* (Rose and Charlesworth), vol.3. *Directory of the Council and Legislative Assembly of the North-West Territories, 1876–1905* (Regina, 1970). D. J. Hall, *Clifford Sifton* (2v., Vancouver and London, 1981–85). J. S. Heard, "The Alberta and Great Waterways Railway dispute, 1909–1913" (MA thesis, Univ. of Alta, 1990). C. C. Lingard, *Territorial government in Canada: the autonomy question in the old North-West Territories* (Toronto, 1946). J. G. MacGregor, *A history of Alberta* (Edmonton, 1972). A. O. MacRae, *History of the province of Alberta* (2v., [Calgary], 1912), 1. Howard Palmer with Tamara Palmer, *Alberta: a new history* (Edmonton, 1990). *The parliamentary guide and work of general reference for 1898–9 . . .*, ed. A. J. Magurn (Winnipeg and Ottawa, 1898). J. T. Saywell, *The office of lieutenant-governor: a study in Canadian government and politics* (Toronto, 1957; repr. 1986). Univ. of Alta, *Calendar* (Edmonton), 1908/9–1910/11.

BUOTE, FRANÇOIS-JOSEPH, teacher, printer, and newspaperman; b. 1 Nov. 1861 in Tignish, P.E.I., only child of Gilbert Buote* and Madeleine Gallant; m. 6 Jan. 1886 Marie-A. Goguen in Cap-Pelé, N.B., and they had one son, who died in infancy, and one daughter; d. 20 Oct. 1922 in Tignish.

François-Joseph Buote received his elementary education in the Tignish area, where his father was a teacher, and in St Marys Bay, N.S., where Gilbert taught from 1873 to 1877. After a year at St Dunstan's College in Charlottetown, he spent three years at the Collège Saint-Louis in Saint-Louis de Kent, N.B., founded by Marcel-François Richard*. This experience gave him a much better academic background than that acquired by most young Acadians of his time. When the Buote family moved to Maine in 1882, François-Joseph learned the trade of a printer there. Following his return to New Brunswick with his parents in 1885, he taught school in the district of Cap-Pelé and studied at the Normal School in Fredericton in the summers [see Alphée BELLIVEAU]. At some point in the late 1880s he worked as a printer for the *Courrier des provinces Maritimes* in Bathurst. In 1891 he started in Cap-Pelé his first periodical, *Buote's Monthly and Commercial Advertiser*. No copy of this magazine is extant, however, nor is there any information as to its contents.

In 1893 François-Joseph returned to Tignish, one of the principal Acadian centres in the Maritime provinces; his parents had already been there for two years. Gilbert had become principal of the local school, and François-Joseph set up as a jobbing printer. Together in 1893 they founded the province's first French-language newspaper, *L'Impartial*, Gilbert being the editor and his son the first printer and publisher. This weekly, which began with four pages, mainly covered issues of interest to Island Acadians.

It promoted the French language and pride in Acadian heritage while stressing friendly cooperation with anglophones. Gilbert contributed long articles on local history and genealogy, which remain a valuable source of information, and often the only one. In addition, the paper advocated such projects as an association for Acadian teachers, cooperative cheese factories, and mutual insurance societies. *L'Impartial* also printed some world news and covered political matters, more or less living up to its name. For the centennial celebration at Tignish in 1899, which the Buotes organized, a special illustrated number of the paper was issued; it, too, is a primary source for local history and genealogy.

The newspaper never seems to have been a money-maker; it suspended publication at least once during its 22-year history, apparently for several years. After Gilbert's death in 1904, François-Joseph's wife, a former teacher, assisted with its production. The paper's demise in 1915 may have been due as much to financial difficulties as to the shortage of newsprint occasioned by World War I. Buote, however, had apparently never been at a loss for ways to augment his income. He sold books and stationery, acted as an agent for a bicycle company and an insurance company, and continued his job printing. In August 1918 he began publishing an English-language monthly, *Buote's Magazine*. Only two or three numbers of this magazine exist, and it seems probable that these were the only ones printed. Buote apparently considered the journal a continuation of *L'Impartial*, since the title page says it was a "new series" of a publication "established in 1893."

Buote was considered to be "a speaker of the first order" in both French and English. He was invited to address Acadian groups living as far away as Lawrence, Mass. In 1908 he was named president of the Société Nationale de l'Assomption. Five years later he organized the Convention Nationale des Acadiens held in Tignish and at that time relinquished the office of president to Pascal Poirier*. He was severely criticized in some quarters for his delay in holding this meeting, originally scheduled to take place in 1911, and for his failure to make sufficient preparations for it. The conference was largely unproductive, derided by J.-O. Gallant, editor of *L'Évangéline* (Moncton, N.-B.), as "some sort of picnic" rather than "a working assembly."

Locally, Buote was involved in many organizations, usually as secretary. He not only promoted the mutual benefit societies that proliferated in the late 19th and early 20th centuries but helped introduce no fewer than three of them to the district, including a branch of the Société l'Assomption [see Rémi Benoît*], of which he was president for a time. Among other projects in which he participated were the local Farmers' Institute, the cooperative cheese factory, and the committee for the beautification of Tignish. Provincially, he sat on the Commission on Education, appointed in 1908.

In 1900 Buote had run unsuccessfully in the provincial election as a Conservative candidate in Prince County, 1st District. Later, however, he and his father shifted their allegiance to the Liberals. By 1914 the front page of *L'Impartial* bore the inscription "Organ, in the French language, of the Liberal party of the Maritime provinces." In 1919 François-Joseph successfully proposed William Lyon Mackenzie King* as the Liberal candidate in a federal by-election in Prince that year (he was elected by acclamation), and a friendship developed between the two men.

Sometime after the demise of his newspaper, Buote who had long been interested in fox ranching, then at the height of its development [see Robert Trenholm Oulton*], moved with his family to Trois-Rivières, Que., to manage a ranch there. However, a historian who knew the Buotes claims that he was on the point of reviving *L'Impartial*, and had even bought new printing equipment, when he died suddenly in 1922.

François-Joseph Buote seems to have had an intense desire to be involved in everything that was going on. His promotion of many causes was partly an expression of this trait. Like his father, he was "sometimes impatient, demanding, and seldom conciliatory," characteristics that made him difficult to work with and an implacable enemy. Nevertheless, he contributed much to Acadian life on Prince Edward Island and is one of the most important figures of its "renaissance" in the latter part of the 19th century.

EMILY ELIZABETH CRAN

The fullest run available for *L'Impartial* (Tignish, Î.-P.-É.), 22 juin 1893–11 juill. 1915, is in the Centre d'Études Acadiennes, Moncton, N.-B.; a less complete file is available on microfilm. The best copy of *L'Impartial illustré*, the souvenir issue produced for the Tignish centennial in 1899, is in the possession of Mr J.-Henri Gaudet of Tignish; two incomplete copies are held by Mr Reg Porter of Charlottetown, who also holds the surviving issues of *Buote's Magazine* (Tignish).

A scrapbook of material relating to the family assembled around 1921 by Alma Buote is also in the possession of Mr Gaudet.

Le Moniteur acadien (Shédiac, N.-B.), 1886, 1891, 1898. Georges Arsenault, *Les Acadiens de l'Île, 1720-1980* (Moncton, 1987). D. B. Baker, "La Convention nationale des Acadiens – Tignish, Île-du-Prince-Édouard, août, 1913," Soc. Hist. Acadienne, *Cahiers* (Moncton), 15 (1984): 21–31. J.-H. Blanchard, *Acadiens de l'Île-du-Prince-Édouard* ([Charlottetown], 1956). Yvon Léger, "Les Buote de l'Île-du-Prince-Édouard," Soc. Hist. Acadienne, *Cahiers*, 24 (1993): 151–82. *Souvenir program of the centennial celebration of the Church of St. Simon and St. Jude, Tignish, Prince Edward Island*, comp. Alma Buote (Sackville, N.B., 1960).

BURCHILL, JOHN PERCIVAL, lumberman, businessman, and politician; b. 6 Feb. 1855 on Beaubears Island, N.B., son of George Burchill* and Bridget Percival; m. 4 Jan. 1882 Eliza Bacon Wilkinson (d. 4 Jan. 1921) in Bushville, N.B., and they had two daughters and one son; d. 18 Dec. 1923 in Newcastle, N.B.

John Percival Burchill, or J. P. as he was known to all, was educated at the parish school and the Chatham grammar school as well as through the Maritime equivalent of the grand tour. For J. P. this was a two-year trip to visit relatives in New Brunswick, New England, and as far west as St Louis, Mo. When he returned home in 1873, he joined his father in the lumber business at Nelson (Nelson-Miramichi) and continued his practical education with small business ventures outside the family firm.

In 1875 his father purchased a sawmill, and J. P. gradually took over the management of the company's outside operations. He and his younger brother, George, joined their father in 1881 as partners in the new firm of Geo. Burchill and Sons. George Jr began to assume the management of the inside operations. With timber leases on over 100 square miles of crown land and their own sawmill, they constituted a mid-sized lumbering firm in New Brunswick.

J. P. first ventured into politics in 1878 and was elected to the Northumberland County Council. He was selected warden in 1882, his last year on the council. In the provincial general election that year he was returned to the House of Assembly in the four-member riding of Northumberland. Although Burchill was a Liberal, the party system in New Brunswick had not yet stabilized and members were often referred to as government or anti-government forces. Many were called "loose fish"; they frequently crossed the floor in the assembly to achieve their political ends. Burchill was not one of them, but he was independent in his Liberal affiliation and the needs of the lumber trade commonly guided his decisions. Lumber was not only his business, it was also the economic base for the province.

In Fredericton, Burchill sat on the opposition side of the assembly. But the election had left the house almost evenly divided, and after an attempt to govern Premier Daniel Lionel Hanington resigned and Andrew George Blair* became premier in 1883. Burchill was now a member of the government and, being inexperienced, he supported Blair's changes to the crown land regulations. These adjustments were contrary to the wishes and needs of the lumber industry. As a consequence, he was defeated in the election of 1886.

He did not have to wait long to try again; a by-election was needed in 1887, and during the campaign Burchill admitted in a letter published in the *Daily Sun* (Saint John) that he had been wrong in supporting the changes to the timber regulations. He won this election. The late 1880s were a period of an extended depression, and although he championed the cause of the lumbermen, both in public and directly to the premier, he was unable to bring about regulatory change. Because of the opposition in the assembly and the prolonged slump, it was obvious that control of the crown lands was going to be an issue in the election of 1890. Premier Blair called it for January, and was accused of disenfranchising a large portion of the population. The lumberers were in the woods for the winter and would not be able to vote. Although nominally Liberals, Burchill and the other members from Northumberland were elected in opposition to the government on the matter of the timber regulations.

The election left the assembly evenly split between the government and anti-government members, with seven or eight independents, including the four Northumberland members, holding the balance of power. The four struck a deal with the government to have the timber regulations changed. Blair thus had his majority. One of the four Northumberland members, Lemuel John Tweedie*, became the surveyor general, two reaped a public works reward, but Burchill was content with a reduction in stumpage fees. The press and the opposition were vicious in their condemnations. Burchill was re-elected in 1892, 1895, and 1899. In the assembly the animosity and name-calling following "the Northumberland deal" were soon forgotten, and in 1893 Burchill was unanimously chosen speaker, a position he held until 1899. He was defeated in the general election of 1903.

Following J. P.'s defeat, George Sr retired from the firm, leaving J. P. and George Jr as the active partners. George Jr died in 1906 and George Sr a year later, however, and J. P. was left to operate the business alone. He was not a candidate in March 1908, when the Liberals lost to the Conservatives under John Douglas Hazen*, but he came out of retirement to win a by-election in December 1908 and served as an MLA until 1912. He did not stand in the election that year.

In 1913 the Conservative administration of James Kidd FLEMMING changed the crown land regulations to give the government the power to renew leases without going through the normal process of a public offering. With the premier's knowledge, or so a subsequent royal commission would conclude, an employee of the Crown Lands Department then demanded money from the lumbermen and in return assured them that their leases would be renewed without public auction. The plan, which was intended to raise $100,000 for the Conservative party, largely worked; $71,665 was contributed, of which Burchill paid his share. But the scheme was exposed in 1914, Flemming resigned, and the government was defeated at the next election in 1917. Perhaps prompted to come out of retirement to fight the administration because of this and other scandals, Burchill was successful in that contest. He served one term on the government side under Premier Walter Edward Foster* but lost in 1920 and left politics.

It was not only in the political arena that Burchill contributed to the lumber industry. In the 1880s, after he had assumed control of the outside operations of the family business, the firm had begun improving the lot of the workers in their establishments. Their camps were among the best equipped in the New Brunswick woods and they were known as fair and benevolent employers. Burchill was also president of the North West Boom Company and a director of the South West Boom Company. These were cooperative ventures for the benefit of lumber operations of all sizes which drove their logs down the Miramichi every spring. The participants paid according to the number of logs they had in the drive. He became the first president of the Lumbermen and Limit Holders' Association of New Brunswick when it was formed in 1913.

Burchill served as president of the Miramichi Steam Navigation Company for at least 15 years before its business was wound up in January 1920, and he was a founder of its successor, the Miramichi River Service Limited, the following June. He also sat on the Miramichi Pilotage Commission. A founding director of the Miramichi Agricultural Exhibition Association Limited, he was its president from 1915 to 1917. He belonged to the freemasons and served two terms as worshipful master of Northumberland Lodge No.17. He was also a past master of the Sons of Temperance. A vestryman of St Paul's Anglican Church in Bushville, he was buried in the church cemetery.

BURTON GLENDENNING

PANB, MC 1156; MC 1246; RS68, 1906. J. G. Burchill, *A Miramichi saga* ([Miramichi?, 2000?]). *CPG*, 1880–1920. A. T. Doyle, *Front benches & back rooms: a story of corruption, muckraking, raw partisanship and intrigue in New Brunswick* (Toronto, 1976). *Elections in New Brunswick, 1784–1984* (Fredericton, 1984). Burton Glendenning, "The Burchill lumbering firm, 1850–1906; an example of nineteenth century New Brunswick entrepreneurship" (MA thesis, Concordia Univ., Montreal, 1978). W. D. Hamilton, *Dictionary of Miramichi biography; biographical sketches of men and women born before 1900 who played a part in public life on the Miramichi: Northumberland County, New Brunswick, Canada* (Saint John, 1997). Diane Myles, *Speakers of the Legislative Assembly, province of New Brunswick, 1786–1985* (Fredericton, 1986). Jane Percival Dollahan, *The ancestors and descendants of John Percival of the Miramichi* (Tucson, Ariz., 1972). *Prominent people of New Brunswick . . .* , comp. C. H. McLean ([Saint John], 1937). *Prominent people of the Maritime provinces* (Montreal, 1922).

BURGESS, THOMAS JOSEPH WORKMAN, physician, botanist, asylum superintendent, professor, and author; b. 11 March 1849 in Toronto, son of Thomas Burgess, a merchant tailor, and Jane Rigg, both from Carlisle, England; m. 15 April 1875 Jessie McPherson in Toronto, and they had four daughters; d. 18 Jan. 1926 in Montreal and was buried 20 January in Toronto.

Thomas Joseph Workman Burgess attended Upper Canada College in Toronto from 1862 to 1866 and then completed his medical studies at the University of Toronto. Awarded the Starr gold medal by the faculty of medicine, and the first silver medal by the university, he graduated in 1870. He immediately joined the medical staff of the Asylum for the Insane in Toronto, which was under the direction of his godfather and mentor, the renowned Joseph Workman*. In 1872 he accepted a position as surgeon for the international commission responsible for determining the Canadian-American boundary from Lake of the Woods to the Rocky Mountains [see Samuel Anderson*]. Travelling widely throughout Canada in this capacity, he developed an interest in botany, a subject to which he would devote many articles and lectures.

From 1875 to 1887 Burgess worked at the Asylum for the Insane in London, Ont., initially as assistant physician and then as assistant superintendent. Following a dispute with superintendent Richard Maurice Bucke*, he was transferred in 1887 to the Asylum for the Insane in Hamilton, where he was assistant superintendent until 1890. While in Hamilton he participated as a botanist in the activities of the Hamilton Association, serving as vice-president from 1888 to 1890. In May 1890 he became the first medical superintendent of the Protestant Hospital for the Insane in Verdun, Que. During his 33 years in this post, the number of patients in the hospital increased from 139 to 800.

From the very beginning Burgess saw to it that patients in this new institution were treated in the most humane manner, as the annual reports he wrote from 1891 to 1923 show. Although he considered insanity a somatic disease, he had doubts about the effectiveness of medication alone and therefore concentrated his efforts on mental treatment. Opposed to all forms of physical restraint for mental patients, he instead set up an extensive program to keep them occupied (work, physical activity, and leisure pursuits), a practice he had had an opportunity to observe at the London asylum under Bucke's leadership. In his 1896 annual report Burgess noted that 66 per cent of the patients were engaged in some occupation. From 1901 he also encouraged the admission of private patients (who paid to enter the asylum and who were not subject to the same administrative constraints as public patients in the matter of being discharged) and he declared himself in favour of trial releases for patients who were not fully cured but whose mental health had improved. In 1903 he began implementing an "open-door policy," leaving the patients' dormitories unlocked and letting those whose condition allowed it to move about freely and unsupervised within the asylum. In addition, he organized many outings for them and encouraged the public to attend the social evenings held at the asylum. From time to time there were patients who took advantage of such opportunities to run away, but experience showed that they usually came back to the asylum of their own accord after a few days.

Although such reforms were being promoted at the same time by the superintendents of the Asile de Beauport and the Hôpital Saint-Jean-de-Dieu, Burgess had enjoyed much more favourable circumstances for putting them into practice. Unlike the French-speaking asylums, the one in Verdun benefited from the financial support of the wealthy families in Montreal's English-speaking community. In 1892, for example, a gift from John Henry Robinson Molson made possible the construction of a gymnasium, bowling alley, and curling rink. Through the generosity of George Bull Burland, in 1898 a pathology laboratory was built which Andrew Macphail* directed. In 1900 and 1910 the many donations of Dr James Douglas of New York, whose father had founded the Asile de Beauport [see James Douglas*], made possible the purchase of the land on which the nurses' residence and the recreational centre known as Douglas Hall were erected.

In return for their gifts, donors were permitted to sit on the institution's board of directors. This *modus operandi* had been conceived initially by Alfred Perry, who had collaborated with Cléophée Têtu*, named Thérèse de Jésus, in founding the Asile de Longue-Pointe. The board of directors gave Burgess full authority in the treatment of patients and the hiring of staff. He nonetheless experienced disappointments. He always found it very difficult to retain his most competent assistants and employees because of their heavy workloads and modest salaries. He was also faced with the problem of overpopulation in his hospital. During the first decade of the century, like many alienists of the time, Burgess identified heredity as the principal cause of the increased incidence of mental illness and he was drawn to eugenics. In his 1907 report, for instance, he suggested that the Quebec provincial government, like some American states, should forbid the marriage of carriers of defects considered hereditary, or should introduce compulsory sterilization of alcoholics and other "degenerates." After noticing in 1905 that nearly 40 per cent of the patients admitted to the Protestant Hospital for the Insane in Verdun had not been born in Canada, he took a clear stand in favour of greater control over immigration. Following the enactment of more restrictive immigration laws in 1906 and 1910, Burgess annually listed numerous mental patients whom he considered candidates for deportation.

Burgess also devoted a great deal of time to promoting psychiatry as a medical specialty. In 1893 he gave a series of lectures on mental illnesses at McGill University (where he would become a full professor in 1899). He also undertook some research into mental diseases, with the help of Dr Macphail and his assistants, including an experimental study in 1895 on the treatment of mental deficiency by the use of thyroid extracts. In 1901 he would try to establish a link between epilepsy and glycosuria. These studies did not lead to conclusive results, however. In 1896 he set up a training school for nurses at the Verdun asylum, where he also taught, as did the rest of the institution's medical staff. That year he was honorary secretary of a section on nervous and mental illnesses and medical case-law at a pan-American medical congress held in Mexico City. In 1898, to advance their specialty, some 20 alienists from the province of Quebec came together to form the Société Médico-Psychologique de Québec. Burgess was its first vice-president and became its president in 1899. Completely at ease with his French-speaking colleagues and fluent in their language, he encouraged them to establish ties with other North American alienists. He undertook in June 1902 the task of organizing the meeting of the American Medico-Psychological Association, which was held in Montreal. In 1904–5 he became the third Canadian – after Daniel Clark* in 1891–92 (when the association was called the Association of Medical Superintendents of American Institutions for the Insane) and Bucke in 1897–98 – to serve as president of this organization, which was the forerunner of the current American Psychiatric Association. In 1918 he was a member of the Canadian National Committee for Mental Hygiene, whose objectives were to identify the various segments of the population that showed a high risk of mental illness, to organize research on the functioning of the brain and nervous system, and to conduct public information campaigns about insanity and ways of avoiding it.

Credited with being the first to devote himself to the history of psychiatric institutions in Canada, Burgess gave a lecture on this subject to the Royal Society of Canada in 1898. In 1913 the American Medico-Psychological Association delegated him to write the Canadian section of a book entitled *The institutional care of the insane in the United States and Canada*, which was published in Baltimore, Md, in 1916 and 1917.

Burgess was active in many learned societies, both in Canada and in other countries. He became a member in 1885 of the Royal Society of Canada and in 1886 of the American Association for the Advancement of Science, and he took advantage of these forums to publicize his work on Canadian flora. By the beginning of the 1880s Burgess was a regular contributor to the American journal *Botanical Gazette*, whose pages described the rare plants he had discovered in the course of his travels with botanist John Macoun* in southern Ontario and Nova Scotia. In the fifth volume of Macoun's *Catalogue of Canadian plants*, Burgess wrote the sections on ferns. He also took part in meetings of the Canadian Medical Association and the British Association for the Advancement of Science.

By establishing ties with the academic world and serving as an intermediary between the French-speaking alienists of Quebec and their English-speaking colleagues in the rest of North America, Thomas Joseph Workman Burgess made an important contribution to the institutionalization of psychiatry at the beginning of the 20th century. As superintendent of the Protestant Hospital for the Insane, he tried to break down the barriers around the asylum by creating interaction between it and the outside world. Such opening up was quite typical of the life and work of this prolific author, a man active in numerous organizations and interested in many different fields of endeavour.

GUY GRENIER

Thomas Joseph Workman Burgess assisted in the preparation of H. M. Hurd et al., *The institutional care of the insane in the United States and Canada*, ed. H. M. Hurd (4v., Baltimore, Md, 1916–17; repr. New York, 1973). He also prepared several entries for John Macoun, *Catalogue of Canadian plants* (7v., Montreal, 1883–1902), 5 (*Acrogens*, 1890): 253–87. He published a large number of articles in scientific journals and newspapers. For the Hamilton Assoc., *Journal and Proc.* ([Hamilton, Ont.]), he contributed: "How to study botany" (no.4 (1886–88): 27–53); "Orchids" (pp.113–16); "Notes on the history of botany" (pp.116–17); "Notes on the flora of the forty ninth parallel, from the Lake of the Woods to the Rocky Mountains" (pp.117–20); "The Lake Erie shore as a botanizing ground" (no.5 (1888–89): 41–59); and "Notes on the genus Rhus" (no.8 (1891–92): 119–30). In the *Montreal Medical Journal* he published "Thyroid feeding and its application to the treatment of insanity" (24 (1895–96): 842–52); "A compendium of insanity" (27 (1898): 549–50); "Two cases of ephemeral mania, uncomplicated with epilepsy, intemperance or parturition" (28 (1899): 938–41; also published in French in *L'Union médicale du Canada* (Montréal), 28 (1899): 715–20); "The insane in Canada; presidential address: American Medico-Psychological Association, San Antonio, Texas, April 18th, 1905" (34 (1905): 399–430; also published in the *American Journal of Insanity* (Baltimore), 62 (1905–6): 1–36); and "The family physician and the insane" (36 (1907): 100–17). His articles in the *Botanical Gazette* (Crawfordsville and Logansport, Ind.) include: "Notes from Canada" (7 (1882): 95–96); "Trifolium hybridum, L." (p.135); "A botanical holiday in Nova Scotia" (9 (1884): 1–6, 19–23, 40–45, 56–59); and "Aspidium Oreopt-

eris Swz." (11 (1886): 63). Burgess also published: "Art in the sick room," *Times* (Hamilton), 5 Jan. 1889; "Canadian Filicineæ," RSC, *Trans.*, 1st ser., 2 (1884), sect.IV: 163–226 (with John Macoun); "A historical sketch of our Canadian institutions for the insane," RSC, *Trans.*, 2nd ser., 4 (1898), sect.IV: 3–122; "On the beneficient and toxical effects of the various species of Rhus," *Canadian Journal of Medical Science* (Toronto), 5 (1880): 327–34; "Polypus of the heart," *Canadian Journal of Medical Science*, 4 (1879): 139–40; and "Recent additions to Canadian Filicineæ, with new stations for some of the species previously recorded," RSC, *Trans.*, 1st ser., 4 (1886), sect.IV: 9–18.

AO, RG 80-5-0-54, no.11075. LAC, RG 31, C1, 1871, Toronto, St David's Ward, div.4: 8; 1891, Verdun, Que. *Gazette* (Montreal), 19 Jan. 1926. *Montreal Daily Star*, 19 Jan. 1926. *La Presse*, 20 janv. 1926. C. H. Cahn, *Douglas Hospital: 100 years of history and progress* (Verdun, 1981). *Canadian men and women of the time* (Morgan; 1912). *Canadian who's who*, 1910. *Directory*, Montreal, 1908–10. Denis Goulet et André Paradis, *Trois siècles d'histoire médicale au Québec; chronologie des institutions et des pratiques (1639–1939)* (Montréal, 1992). Guy Grenier, "L'implantation et les applications de la doctrine de la dégénérescence dans le champ de la médecine et de l'hygiène mentales au Québec entre 1885 et 1930" (mémoire de MA, univ. de Montréal, 1990). John Macoun, *Autobiography of John Macoun, M.A. . . .*, intro. E. T. Seton ([Ottawa], 1922). André Paradis, "Thomas J. W. Burgess et l'administration du Verdun Protestant Hospital for the Insane (1890–1916)," *Canadian Bull. of Medical Hist.* (Waterloo, Ont.), 14 (1997): 5–35. Protestant Hospital for the Insane, *Annual report* (Verdun), 1891–1923. *The roll of pupils of Upper Canada College, Toronto, January, 1830, to June, 1916*, ed. A. H. Young (Kingston, Ont., 1917), 145. S. E. D. Shortt, *Victorian lunacy: Richard M. Bucke and the practice of late nineteenth-century psychiatry* (Cambridge, Eng., 1986).

BURKE, ALFRED EDWARD, Roman Catholic priest, church society administrator, editor, and army chaplain; b. 8 Sept. 1862 in Georgetown, P.E.I., son of James Burke and Mary Moar; d. 15 Dec. 1926 in Rome.

Descended from Irish immigrants, James Burke operated a shipping business in Georgetown; his wife's family had come from the Orkney Islands in Scotland. After completing his public school education in Georgetown in 1877, Alfred Edward Burke, the fourth of seven children, enrolled at St Dunstan's College in Charlottetown, where he excelled in literature. In 1880 he began studies at the Séminaire de Québec; he graduated with the highest honours and was ordained priest on 30 May 1885. He then became an assistant at St Dunstan's Cathedral in Charlottetown and secretary to Bishop Peter McIntyre*. While a curate there he prepared an extensive report on all Island parishes and convents, and assumed temporary duties as an assistant pastor at Rustico and administrator of St Joachim's parish at Vernon River.

On 22 Sept. 1887 McIntyre appointed Burke pastor of Sacred Heart parish at Alberton, in Prince

County. It was there, and in the adjoining parish of St Mark, Lot 7, that he would win accolades as a zealous priest who was interested in practically every detail of parish life. Upon his arrival he was shocked by the low state of religion. He initiated remedies that included religious instruction for adults, the training of an organist, and the formation of a temperance association. On one occasion his breaking into a grog-shop and destruction of its wares led to criminal charges, which on appeal were dropped. (His interest in temperance continued, and in 1908 he would serve as president of the Island branch of the Dominion Alliance for the Total Suppression of the Liquor Traffic.) In 1893 Burke's belief that young men required life insurance, to protect their families, prompted him to set up a branch of the Catholic Mutual Benefit Association. From this pioneering establishment he founded branches across the Island, and in 1904 he was elected a grand trustee on the CMBA's national executive.

To familiarize himself with the rural character and work of his parishioners, Burke, who had no farming experience, undertook a rigorous study of agriculture and acquired considerable expertise. He organized the Alberton agricultural exhibition in 1892, was a charter member (1898) and president (1903–7) of the Fruit Growers' Association of Prince Edward Island, was a member of dairy and stockbreeders' associations, served as a vice-president of the Maritime Bee Keepers' Association and of the Prince Edward Island Poultry Association (1908), and became an expert on reforestation and a provincial vice-president of the Canadian Forestry Association. In addition, he helped establish the West Prince Board of Trade (1903). Such activism won him recognition. In 1904 his lecture in Ottawa on reforestation on the Island had been attended by Prime Minister Sir Wilfrid Laurier* and Governor General Lord Grey*. Two years later the University of North Carolina presented him with an honorary doctorate in forestry.

Burke's energy – his recreations were swimming and boating – infused his promotion of public works and his imperial and political partisanship. In 1905 he had advocated a tunnel under the Northumberland Strait, a link that he saw as the surest means of securing the Island's economic vitality. He strongly believed too that the health of his province, and of the dominion, was tied to the fortunes of the British empire. He and other anglophone Catholics, among whom he had a large following, were smitten with a vision of a Canada in which the values of Catholicism would be transmitted through the English language. In a speech in Toronto to the Empire Club of Canada in 1910, he attributed his unabashed patriotism and imperialism to the late Cornelius O'Brien*, the Island-born archbishop of Halifax who had been a prominent member of the Imperial Federation League.

Burke's unbridled energy was also evident on the hustings, where he openly supported the Conservative party. He was a friend of federal opposition leader Robert Laird Borden* and an admirer of former senator and lieutenant governor George William Howlan*. In 1901 his political writings in the local press had incurred the wrath of McIntyre's successor, James Charles McDonald*, who ordered Burke to write only with his clearance, except on historical and scientific matters. When Burke appealed to his bishop's superior, O'Brien, McDonald claimed that Burke's polemics had been detrimental to religion on the Island. As a result of O'Brien's intervention, the ban on Burke was limited to matters of religion.

It must have been a relief to McDonald when Burke agreed in 1908 to direct the new Catholic Church Extension Society of Canada. While in Quebec City that year for its tercentenary and to receive a DD from the Université Laval, he had been approached by Archbishop Fergus Patrick McEvay* of Toronto and others to take charge of a home-mission organization roughly patterned on the American Catholic Church Extension Society, established in 1905. It was the founder of this society, the Reverend Francis Clement Kelley, an Islander and one-time altar boy of Burke's, who had recommended him. Under Burke, the Toronto-based CCES, which would receive a pontifical constitution in 1910, was responsible for establishing missions to native peoples and immigrants in the west: raising funds, building churches, recruiting priests, supplying vestments and plate, and providing literature.

Burke threw himself into the work of the CCES. Not only did he assume its presidency, he also made himself editor of the *Catholic Register*, which the society had purchased in November 1908 and renamed the *Catholic Register and Church Extension*. Both within its pages and without, he took up the cause of southern and eastern European Catholic immigrants, who lacked clergy and religious materials. In an address to the first American Catholic Missionary Congress, in Chicago in 1908, he advocated the recruitment of missionary priests. A year later he spoke to the first Plenary Council of prelates in Canada and secured a commitment of $5,000 a year from each diocese. As well, he used the *Register* to publicize the threat posed to the Ukrainians by Protestant proselytizers, whom he likened to wolves ravaging the sheepfold [*see* Joseph Czerniawski*]. Within three years he could claim modest success: society revenues averaged over $16,000 per year, the paid circulation of the *Register* increased from 3,000 to more than 17,000, and aid to the Ukrainian Catholics was substantial. The CCES nonetheless had difficulty recreating a viable church structure within that community: the liturgical and cultural differences between CCES supporters and the Byzantine-rite Ukrainians posed a constant problem.

In addition to nurturing faith on the frontier, Burke and his colleagues used the CCES to acculturate Catholic immigrants. To Burke's supporters it was essential for their survival that new Canadians learn the English language and embrace British laws and political customs. When southern and eastern European priests could not be recruited, Burke and McEvay, the society's chancellor, called for English-speaking clergy with ability in Italian, Ukrainian, Hungarian, and Polish.

The dual purpose of Catholicizing and Canadianizing, combined with Burke's imperialism, confirmed the fears of Catholic leaders in French-speaking Canada that the CCES was merely an agent of Anglicization. Archbishops Joseph-Thomas Duhamel* of Ottawa and Paul Bruchési* of Montreal had refused Burke's early requests to locate his society's headquarters in their dioceses. Adélard Langevin* of St Boniface, Man., bitter that he had not been consulted about a society that was to operate primarily in his archdiocese, was infuriated when Burke sent two priests to investigate the immigrant "situation" there without his permission. The CCES, Langevin confided to one of his priests, was a central Canadian plot to discredit his work and institute Irish Catholic control in the west. Suspicions of Burke's opposition to French Canadian Catholic aspirations were strengthened in 1910 when he supported Bishop Michael Francis Fallon*'s criticism of bilingual schools in Ontario. Because of this seeming alliance, Archbishop Louis-Nazaire BÉGIN of Quebec and Bishop Joseph-Alfred Archambeault* of Joliette resigned from the CCES's board, leaving Bishop Émile-Joseph Legal* as its only French-speaking governor. Undaunted, neither Burke nor McEvay backed down. Burke would use the *Register* to bludgeon the editors of *L'Action sociale* (Québec) and *Le Droit* (Ottawa), who had criticized English Catholic aggression in the west. By 1913, having recognized the embarrassment caused by such infighting, apostolic delegate Pellegrino Francesco Stagni insisted that the new archbishop of Toronto, Neil McNeil*, silence Burke on issues relating to French Canadian nationalism.

McNeil had discovered from surveying the work of the CCES that many French Canadian prelates loathed Burke, and that some English-speaking Catholics felt he was keeping the society from reaching its full potential (revenues were a fraction of what they could have been). McNeil, however, had little room to manoeuvre. A papal appointment, Burke could not be removed by his archbishop or the society's board, which still supported him. McNeil even failed to secure his episcopal appointment to British Columbia or the Yukon, a move he thought would obviate the need to petition Rome for his removal. Acrimony persisted until 12 Aug. 1915, when Burke resigned as president and editor. Upon his departure, Pope Benedict XV raised him to protonotary apostolic, the highest rank of monsignor.

Burke was an unwavering supporter of Canada's participation in World War I. The *Register* had devoted much space to reporting Allied advances and German atrocities, and encouraging Canadian backing of Britain. Three days before his resignation Burke secured an informal appointment as "a sort of inspecting Chaplain for his Church" in the Canadian chaplaincy service. Within a month he had proceeded to England, where, on 15 October, he accepted officially a commission as an honorary major and chaplain. Through his Conservative connections and loyalty to militia minister Sir Samuel HUGHES and the Reverend Richard Henry Steacy, the senior chaplain and an Anglican, he then secured promotion to lieutenant-colonel and presumed himself to be the senior Catholic chaplain. His boldness outraged the other Catholic chaplains, many of whom had served longer (most at the rank of captain) and who resented the fact that Burke had no fixed duties with a brigade or hospital. He had set up headquarters at the Regent Palace Hotel in London, and spent his time touring from post to post with his own staff car and driver. He insisted that his position was endorsed by the apostolic delegate and the Canadian bishops. Stagni, however, though he had commended his enlistment, was clear that Burke had not been commissioned "supervising chaplain."

What enraged Burke's colleagues most was his open assurance that Catholic troops were being well served and that there was no urgency to increase the number of priests. Prior to his arrival, the chaplains had, in fact, been desperate for assistance; many wounded and dying soldiers, they claimed, were going without the sacraments. By July 1916 Burke had prompted a revolt led by Captain Wolstan Thomas Workman, a Franciscan chaplain, and Captain John Joseph O'Gorman, a priest from the archdiocese of Ottawa. Well connected to the episcopacy and military bureaucrats in Canada, O'Gorman set in motion actions that led to the reform of the service, Workman's appointment as senior Catholic chaplain, and Burke's resignation on 21 Sept. 1917.

Burke returned not to Toronto but to Wilmette, Ill., to stay with his friend, now monsignor, Francis Kelley. Burke's name surfaced briefly in Toronto early in 1919 in connection with a national educational committee formed by the Navy League of Canada. Later that year Kelley decided to send him on a fact-finding mission to Mexico, where the anti-clerical measures of president Venustiano Carranza had forced its bishops into exile in the United States. With the approval of the Department of State, Burke travelled to Mexico on behalf of the bishops and the American CCES. Again he stirred up controversy: he claimed to represent the American hierarchy and exhibited an unanticipated level of faith in Carranza, who he thought, given Mexico's revolutionary politics, was the "most conservative ruler" it had ever had. He added fuel to the fire when, in the Jesuit journal *America* (New York), he criticized Mexico's religious orders and clergy for being too distant "from the life of the people." His outlook enraged the exiled bishops and Kelley demanded his recall.

Burke went to Toronto, but given the lack of work and McNeil's ill will, he proceeded to Rome, where he reported on Mexico to Pope Benedict. Burke returned in 1921 to North America and served briefly on the Pacific coast with the American CCES. Back in Rome, he took up freelance writing, working out of the Knights of Columbus Bureau, and continued his squabble with McNeil over his stipend from the Toronto archdiocese. He visited North America just one more time, in June 1926 for the International Eucharistic Congress in Chicago. Burke suffered a stroke that autumn; he died in December and was buried in Campo Santo cemetery near St Paul's Outside the Walls church in Rome. It was a peaceful end for a controversial priest. In his memoirs, Kelley wrote of Burke: "His opinions were like dogmas of Faith. No wonder Canada split over him. Half of his world swore by him and the other half at him."

MARK G. MCGOWAN

[There is some question about Alfred Edward Burke's date of birth. *Canadian men and women of the time* (Morgan; 1912) and Art O'Shea, *A. E. Burke* (Charlottetown, 1993) both cite 8 Sept. 1862, although in the biographies and parish reports compiled by Burke for Bishop Peter McIntyre (Arch. of the Diocese of Charlottetown, Peter McIntyre papers, case 4/file 10), Burke gives his birth date as 8 Sept. 1860. His attestation paper for the Canadian Expeditionary Force (LAC, RG 150, Acc. 1992–93/166) confirms 1862. M.G.McG.]

Burke delivered "The Irishman's place in the empire" to the Empire Club of Canada, a talk that appears in its *Speeches* (Toronto), 1909–10: 225–32. He also spoke on "The need of a missionary college" before the Catholic Church Extension Soc. of the United States of America; this speech was published in *The first American Catholic Missionary Congress* (Chicago, 1909), 77–84. He wrote *The tunnel between Prince Edward Island and the mainland* ([n.p.], 1905?]), a copy of which can be found in the Borden papers at LAC, MG 26, H, 318: 188794–807.

Arch. de la Soc. Hist. de Saint-Boniface (Winnipeg), Fonds de la Corporation archiépiscopale catholique romaine de Saint-Boniface, sér. Langevin. Arch. of the Diocese of Charlottetown, J. C. McDonald papers; Sacred Heart (Alberton), annual parish report, 1888. Arch. of the Roman Catholic Archdiocese of Toronto, Burke clergy personnel file; First World War coll.; MN DS15 (McNeil Roman corr.); Neil McNeil papers; OC07 (Catholic Church Extension Soc. papers); OC20 RR01 (Ruthenian and Ukrainian papers, memorial to the first plenary council, 1 Oct. 1909). Archivio Segreto Vaticano (Rome), Delegazione apostolica del Canadà, 130.1, 184.18. LAC, MG 27, II, C1; III, B8; RG 9, III, 393, 4618. PARO, P.E.I. Geneal. Soc. coll., family files, subject's file. *Catholic Register* (Toronto), 1908–16. *Daily Mail and Empire*, 11 May 1905. *Le Droit* (Ottawa), 9 sept. 1913. *Canadian* (London, Ont.), 10 (1904), no.12: 5. *Canadian album* (Cochrane and Hopkins), 3: 435. *Canadian annual rev.*, 1908–19. *Canadian who's who*, 1910. *The Catholic Church in Prince Edward Island, 1720–1979*, ed. M. F. Hennessey (Charlottetown, 1979). D. W. Crerar, "Bellicose priests: the wars of the Canadian Catholic chaplains, 1914–1919," CCHA, *Hist. Studies*, 58 (1991): 21–39. J. P. Gaffey, *Francis Clement Kelley and the American Catholic dream* (2v., Bensenville, Ill., 1980). F. C. Kelley, *The bishop jots it down: an autobiographical strain on memories* (New York and London, 1939). J. C. Macmillan, *The history of the Catholic Church in Prince Edward Island from 1835 till 1891* (Quebec, 1913). M. G. McGowan, "'Religious duties and patriotic endeavours': the Catholic Church Extension Society, French Canada and the prairie west, 1908–1916," CCHA, *Hist. Studies*, 51 (1984): 107–19; "Toronto's English-speaking Catholics, immigration, and the making of a Canadian Catholic identity, 1900–30," in *Creed and culture: the place of English-speaking Catholics in Canadian society, 1750–1930*, ed. Terrence Murphy and G. [J.] Stortz (Montreal and Kingston, Ont., 1993), 204–45; "A watchful eye: the Catholic Church Extension Society and Ukrainian Catholic immigrants, 1908–1930," in *Canadian Protestant and Catholic missions, 1820s–1960s; historical essays in honour of John Webster Grant*, ed. J. S. Moir and C. T. McIntire (New York, 1988), 221–43. *Past and present of Prince Edward Island . . .*, ed. D. A. MacKinnon and A. B. Warburton (Charlottetown, [1906]).

BURKE, JOHN, poet, printer, and impresario; b. 1851 in St John's, son of Captain John Burke and Sarah Theresa Rutledge; d. there 9 Aug. 1930.

The most famous of Newfoundland's song makers, John Burke has come to be known as the "Bard of Prescott Street" after the street in downtown St John's on which he lived almost his entire life. His father, a successful sealing captain, died at sea in 1865 and young John, who had likely been educated at St Bonaventure's College, began work in the grocery store his mother opened in their home. He, his brother, and his sister, all unmarried, lived together till their deaths. A grocer, auctioneer, printer, actor, singer, poet, theatre manager, and producer of stage shows, he shifted among sources of income for years, but never strayed far from being an entertainer. Not known to take part in sports, Burke was a lifelong fan who was especially fond of boxing; he served at least one year (1903) on the prestigious St John's Regatta committee.

He was known as a humorous man and a quick rhymer, able to transform the tragic into the comic. From the mid 1880s until the late 1920s, Burke published "slips" – broadside ballads of his own composition. Out of newsworthy events and local tales would come a ditty or commemorative song. Printing them himself, he sold the ballads from his door, and young boys hawked them throughout the city. He used his own press but later he also employed other local printers, especially for large jobs.

His turning to alternative sources of income may have been spurred by the 1892 conflagration that destroyed most of downtown St John's, including his mother's grocery. One of his earliest known songs is "The July fire," which makes witty jokes of the hardships, losses, and insurance claims that followed the disaster. Around this time he began putting on entertainments. From the 1890s to World War I he was a popular impresario in the city, producing public concerts, skits, and parodic operas. Well received by all classes, his stage shows generated the local saying "as funny as a Burke play." At his peak at least one of his shows was expected every season. Each was a collection of his songs, new and old, often with a longer centrepiece. After his high-cultured cousin Charles Hutton* produced *The geisha: a story of a tea house* (an 1896, Gilbert-and-Sullivan-like operetta by Owen Hall, Harry Greenbank, and Sidney Jones), Burke wrote and produced *The Topsail geisha: a story of the wash house*.

He compiled his songs in a dozen or more small books, 50–90 pages, scattered with jokes and advertisements. Some of his earliest songsters were collaborations with James Murphy (another popular poet) and George T. Oliver. Burke's advertising copy was as entertaining as his songs. Custom-made poems for advertisers sat next to rhymed curses on merchants who bought no space:

May his pipe never smoke, may his teapot be
    broke,
And to add to the joke may his kettle not boil,
May two dogs and a crackie munge up his tobaccy,
The narrow-faced miser who never could smile.

Burke's satirical songs, about every conceivable topic, have a cutting, absurdist edge of black humour. His weddings and parties are tumultuous. His dinners are unimaginably huge or inedible. His genteel citizenry is laughably assuming. His self-deprecation is endearing.

When complaints arose about burning garbage, Burke wrote "Don't you remember the dump, Maggie . . ." (based on "When you and I were young, Maggie" by George Washington Johnson and James Austin Butterfield). After fire damaged a china warehouse and passers-by helped themselves to the goods, Burke's "Scramble for the teapots at the fire" made fun of the people whose kitchens sported new crockery. His "Trinity cake" is pure surrealist humour – a cake so filled with strange ingredients that it is inedible, even uncuttable:

Ellen Reardigan wanted to taste it,

And she struggled near ready to bust,
When the sealers attacked it with hand-spikes,
    To try to remove the top crust.
Then McCarthy went out for a hatchet,
    And Flannigan grabbed an old saw[.]
That cake was enough, be the powers,
    To paralyze every man's jaw.

In 1927 the city council threatened to cut off the water to citizens who had not paid their taxes. Burke's burlesque song "Stoppage of water" had broad double meanings throughout.

His most famous song is "The Kelligrews soiree," taking off the townspeople who regularly made the short train ride to Conception Bay for elegant get-togethers. Burke's soirée is anything but elegant. In an effort to extend his popularity, Burke registered it (and two other songs) at the United States Copyright Office. "The Kelligrews soiree" was distributed by an American sheet-music press, but international commercial success eluded him.

Not all Burke songs are humorous. "Lines on the sad death of . . ." starts the title of more than a few of them. Drownings, murder, riot, natural deaths, and shipwrecks were all grist for his mill. Local and foreign sporting events, too, were honoured in his poems. Though St John's had several newspapers, Burke's slips, printed on the spur of the moment, may have provided the first news that people had of such events.

More of John Burke's songs have survived than those of any other Newfoundland song maker. No doubt their durability is partly due to his easy access to a press. But it is just as true that his ballads have been reprinted more frequently than others. His songs have remained popular and fresh for a century in both the oral tradition and the commercial repertoire. Ron Hynes's casting of Burke's "Old Brown's daughter," the original air of which was lost, and Great Big Sea's "Excursion around the bay" (a rendition of "The Harbour Grace excursion") are excellent modern versions of his songs. In 1983 a music award was inaugurated in Burke's name by Esso Petroleum Canada and the Newfoundland and Labrador Arts Council.

John Burke died in poverty almost a decade after his last successful show, *Cotton's patch*, a satire on the use of airplanes to spot seal herds. Cinemas, gramophones, and radio had already made his skills obsolete. His slips were no longer being hawked and his attempts to widen his audience had failed. Burke's better-off cousin Charles Hutton paid for his funeral.

PHILIP HISCOCK

Two recent collections of John Burke's songs and ballads are available: *The ballads of Johnny Burke: a short anthology*, ed. Paul Mercer ([St John's], 1974), and *John White's collection of the songs of Johnny Burke*, ed. W. J. Kirwin (St John's, 1982).

Memorial Univ. of Nfld, Folklore and Language Arch. (St John's), Tapes, 78-237 (Paul Mercer, interviews with Ken Hall, Mary-Ann Duggan, James Higgins, and Hugh O'Neill, 1973–74). *Evening Telegram* (St John's), 11 Aug. 1930. M. P. Murphy, "The balladeers of Newfoundland," *Daily News* (St John's), 27 July, 18 Oct., 16 Nov. 1966. *Encyclopedia of Nfld* (Smallwood *et al.*). J. D. Higgins, "The Bard of Prescott Street" (lecture delivered to the Nfld Hist. Soc.; typescript, St John's, 1970; copy in the Centre for Newfoundland Studies, Memorial Univ. of Nfld). Paul Mercer, "A bio-bibliography of Newfoundland songs in printed sources" (MA thesis, Memorial Univ. of Nfld, 1979), 73–81. M. P. Murphy, *Pathways through yesterday*, ed. G. S. Moore (St John's, 1976), 148–65. *Newfoundland songs and ballads in print, 1842–1974: a title and first-line index*, comp. Paul Mercer (St John's, 1979). Michael Taft, "The Bard of Prescott Street meets Tin Pan Alley: the vanity press sheet music publications of John Burke," *Newfoundland Studies* (St John's), 6 (1990): 56–73.

BURRISS, RUFUS ALLEN, Disciples of Christ minister, office holder, promoter of colonization, and politician; b. 30 July 1859 in Lewis County, Ky, son of Marcus L. Burriss and Sarah R. Hamlin; m. 16 Jan. 1884 Hester Ann Watts in Fort Erie, Ont., and they had four daughters and two sons; d. 31 Jan. 1930 in Ashville, Chautauqua County, N.Y.

Raised a "poor farmer boy" in Illinois, Rufus A. Burriss moved to Ontario about 1893 as pastor of the Disciples of Christ church at Bowmanville. He came under the influence of Daniel Francis Burk*, pre-eminent boomer of northwestern Ontario, who was a native of that town. Determined to help the "tenant farmer and others who are being oppressed" to escape from "landlordism" and become freeholders, Burriss conceived a Christian colonization scheme in this region for "poor renting families" from the United States. "We will plant the cause of Christ upon the banks of Rainy River," he proclaimed in December 1897 in the Disciples publication *Christian Standard* (Cincinnati, Ohio). This promotion attracted a large correspondence. Robert Beith, MP for Durham West, lobbied Clifford SIFTON, the Liberal minister of the interior, to assist Burriss. Despite scepticism on the part of the bureaucracy, he was hired on commission as dominion immigration agent for "New Ontario" on 1 Feb. 1898 and that summer he moved his family from Bowmanville to Port Arthur (Thunder Bay).

Burriss's job was to promote agricultural settlement in cooperation with the Ontario government and its crown-lands agents, on whom he would depend for surveys and colonization roads. The attraction for each settler was 160 acres of free-grant land. Using the slogan "Manless Land for Landless Men," Burriss lectured with missionary zeal, gave lantern shows in the American Midwest, wrote for the press, and distributed pamphlets, circulars, notebooks, maple-leaf brooches, and souvenir postcards. His aggressive, evangelical promotion, which targeted the poor, suited Sifton's belief that "just as soon as you stop advertising . . . the movement is going to stop" and his preference for settlers of humble origin. After a joint arrangement had been made with Ontario's Bureau of Colonization, Burriss was taken on by the Department of the Interior in May 1901 at a salary of $1,000 per annum. The opening in 1902 of the Canadian Northern Railway through the Rainy River valley aided his efforts as did his role as secretary-treasurer of the West Algoma Agricultural Society and the New Ontario Industrial Exhibition.

Following Sifton's resignation in February 1905, Burriss's situation became uncertain. His fellow agent at Port Arthur, Conservative appointee James Michael McGovern, resented him, and the commissioner of immigration at Winnipeg, John Obed Smith, had no use for the Port Arthur agency. Because the dominion was focusing on western Canada, Burriss's work was an anomaly: it could be done by Canadian agents resident in the United States and the Ontario Bureau of Colonization. The first attempt to close his office came in January 1906 but failed because of the intervention of Liberal friends. The second try, made after the Conservatives had come to power in October 1911, was successful and he was dismissed as of 31 December. The cost to Canada for his salary and expenses from 1898 to 1911 totalled $26,929.56.

Burriss subsequently turned to real estate, in which he had been speculating since at least 1901. Also, he served on the Port Arthur City Council in 1913–15. As late as March 1919 this council and the Board of Trade of Fort William (Thunder Bay) were both urging the government to reinstate him. He moved to the United States in 1919 to accept temporary work for the Disciples of Christ in various parts of New York State. His last pastorate comprised the churches at Bridgeburg (Fort Erie), Ont., and nearby Windmill Point. Following hospitalization in Buffalo, N.Y., he died at his home in Ashville and was buried in Greenwood Cemetery in Bridgeburg.

According to Mae Nugent Burriss, a daughter, Rufus A. Burriss may have attracted as many as 3,000 families to northwestern Ontario. Not all of them took free land, however – many settlers were able to purchase established farms or better land – and fewer were American than he had desired; for every American family, he claimed in 1901, about three came from eastern Ontario. The settlers located in Dorion Township, the Slate River valley townships of Paipoonge and Neebing, the Whitefish River valley townships of O'Connor, Gillies, and Conmee, and the 37 tiered townships along the Rainy River. They supplemented their income from farming by lumbering and working for the railway. A township and settlement west of Fort Frances were named for Burriss.

Burrows

Although the Christian aspect of his settlement scheme there, including the town-site of Christiana, did not prosper, he did attract American evangelicals such as preacher Clara Babcock of Illinois, said to be the first ordained woman amongst the Disciples. Burriss and his mentors D. F. Burk and James Conmee* of Port Arthur can take credit for promoting agricultural settlement in northwestern Ontario, land which most colonization bureaucrats dismissed as "rocky wilderness."

F. BRENT SCOLLIE

Rufus Allen Burriss's article "My first moose," *Canadian Courier* (Toronto), 11 Nov. 1911: 9–11, contains some useful biographical information. The online catalogue of the LAC lists other publications by Burriss, all of which pertain to "New Ontario" and the Rainy River district.

AO, RG 80-2-0-422, no.21634; RG 80-3-2-75, no.901112. Church of Jesus Christ of Latter-day Saints, Geneal. Soc., International geneal. index. DCB, Biog. data file, Burris/Burriss family, notes by M. N. Burriss, the subject's daughter. LAC, RG 31, C1, 1901, Port Arthur [Thunder Bay], Ont., Ward 2: 19; RG 76, 165, file 47195. *Bridgeburg Review* (Bridgeburg [Fort Erie], Ont.), 6 Feb. 1930. *Daily Times-Journal* (Fort William [Thunder Bay], Ont.), 9 Nov. 1901, 22 Sept. 1904, 18 March 1919. *Weekly Herald and Algoma Miner* (Port Arthur), 26 Aug. 1898, 2 Sept. 1899. Reuben Butchart, *The Disciples of Christ in Canada since 1830 . . .* (Toronto, 1949). Can., Parl., *Sessional papers*, reports of the Dept. of the Interior, part II, immigration, 1898–1903. W. R. and N. M. Wightman, *The land between: northwestern Ontario resource development, 1800 to the 1990s* (Toronto, 1997).

BURROWS, THEODORE ARTHUR, sawmill owner, railway land commissioner, lumber merchant, politician, and lieutenant governor; b. 15 Aug. 1857 in Ottawa, son of Henry John Burrows and Sarah Sparks; grandson of John Burrows*; m. 25 Oct. 1899 Georgina Kathleen Creasor in Owen Sound, Ont., and they had a son and a daughter; d. 18 Jan. 1929 in Winnipeg.

Orphaned at an early age, Theodore Arthur Burrows attended public schools in Ottawa and arrived in Winnipeg in 1875. He worked briefly for his uncle William Ogilvie at the Dominion Lands Survey. A restless young man, Burrows tried and abandoned both legal studies and a career in real estate before he found his niche. In 1878 he formed a partnership to purchase a small sawmill at Fort Alexander. In 1883 he dissolved this partnership and established the Selkirk Lumber Company. Lumber was in great demand at the time. Within three years the firm became one of the largest in the province, producing 4,000,000 board feet per year.

Business and politics were often the foundation of lucrative careers in 19th-century Canada. In 1890, during a slump in the lumber industry, Burrows built a colonization road into the Dauphin area. He thought that connections to prominent politicians would help him to develop the lumber resources of this newly opened settlement frontier, so in 1892 he stood in Dauphin for election to the Legislative Assembly as a Liberal Conservative (the label was consciously ambiguous). He successfully promoted a railway link to his constituency. Burrows was appointed land commissioner for the Lake Manitoba Railway by its contractors, William MACKENZIE and Donald Mann*, in 1896. The position gave him access to information about future routes and allowed him to acquire valuable timber berths along the railway pushing up into northwestern Manitoba. Moreover, Burrows's sister Elizabeth Armanella (Arma) had married Liberal politician Clifford SIFTON in 1884. When Sifton became federal minister of the interior in 1896, and thus responsible for the disposition of western resources, Burrows's prospects continued to improve.

Burrows's success in acquiring timber berths was quite evident during the period when Sifton had discretionary authority to allot them and, in addition, was willing to influence the tendering system. Sifton's actions brought howls from the Conservative opposition who hounded him on the subject in the House of Commons from 1899 to 1906 – to little avail as it turned out. Until Sifton resigned his portfolio in 1905, Burrows used their relationship to advance his business interests. By 1908 Burrows held more timberlands in western Canada than any other person.

Burrows's prominence as a businessman had launched his political career and in the end it was also his undoing. Although he was a major employer in the Dauphin district, his hold on his seat in the assembly was chancy. He had won by only nine votes in 1892 and when he sought re-election in January 1896 he increased his margin by just three votes; he defeated Archibald Glenlyon Campbell* on both occasions. He continued to identify himself as a Liberal Conservative, but supported Liberal premier Thomas Greenway*. Not an active member, he depended a good deal on his railway connections and on Sifton's access to local patronage. Although only issues of economic development affecting his own district (and thus himself) drew his interest, his performance was enough to win him another term in 1899; during this term he sat as a Liberal. He declined to stand in 1903. But he was not finished with politics.

The following year, as one of Sifton's Manitoba lieutenants, Burrows was well placed to win the nomination in the new federal constituency of Dauphin. Election notices were delayed, however, and the vote postponed until after the national election on 3 November. When it was evident that Sir Wilfrid Laurier*'s Liberal party had won a comfortable majority, Burrows's Conservative opponent withdrew, allowing him to win by acclamation. In the House of Commons,

Burrows devoted himself to western development, especially to the Hudson Bay Railway and the extension of Manitoba's boundaries. He was continually badgered by the opposition over his timber business. From 1906 to 1908 the Conservatives under Robert Laird Borden* waged a campaign to discredit the government on charges of corruption and Burrows was an inviting target. They failed to overturn Laurier in the general election of 1908 but the attacks proved politically fatal to Burrows. He was beaten rather badly.

Burrows then confined himself to the consolidation and expansion of his lumber business. In Manitoba he had two major sawmills, in Grandview and Bowsman, and other lesser operations under various company names, making him the largest producer of lumber in the province. In north-central Alberta he and Sir Daniel Hunter McMillan* were the principal shareholders of the small Imperial Pulp Company. In 1911 he formed the larger Phoenix Lumber Company to carry on operations there. The following year he began to expand his retail operations. His prosperous Northern Lumber Company eventually had some 30 retail outlets across the prairies. Burrows had been a founding member of the Western Retail Lumbermen's Association, established in 1890 to serve its members by limiting entry to the business and holding the line on prices.

Although Burrows never stood for office again, he maintained a keen interest in the fortunes of the Liberal party. After World War I, he deplored the emergence of the Progressive party and only reluctantly cooperated with it to avoid three-party elections. He was gratified to see the Liberals win a majority in the election of 1926. Later that year, when Sir James Albert Manning AIKINS relinquished the lieutenant governorship of Manitoba, Burrows was a candidate to succeed him both because of his Liberal credentials and his financial ability to bear the social expenditures of the office. Pressure on Prime Minister William Lyon Mackenzie King* from Sifton and John Wesley Dafoe* of the *Manitoba Free Press* (Winnipeg) combined to secure him the position in October. It was now largely a ceremonial office and, by all accounts, Burrows was a social success – but not for long. He died of complications from appendicitis in January 1929.

Burrows was typical of many frontier entrepreneurs. Political and social connections were at the service of personal ambition and business. He used his connections, as well as his ability, to win a prominent place in the developing prairie west.

J. E. REA

AM, MG 12, J. Man. Culture, Heritage and Recreation, Hist. resources branch (Winnipeg), Lyle Dick, "T. A. Burrows, timber baron of the northwest" (unpublished research paper, 1976). LAC, MG 26, J; MG 27, II, D15; RG 15. QUA, Thomas Alexander Crerar fonds. Univ. of Man. Libraries, Dept. of Arch. and Special Coll. (Winnipeg), J. W. Dafoe fonds. A. F. J. Artibise, *Winnipeg: a social history of urban growth, 1874–1914* (Montreal and London, 1975). R. C. Brown, "The politics of Billingsgate," in *The west and the nation; essays in honour of W. L. Morton*, ed. Carl Berger and Ramsay Cook (Toronto, 1976): 161–73. J. M. S. Careless, "The development of the Winnipeg business community, 1870–1890," RSC, *Trans.*, 4th ser., 8 (1970): 239–54. CPG, 1892–1908. D. J. Hall, *Clifford Sifton* (2v., Vancouver and London, 1981–85). D. F. Parrot, "Grandview and Theodore A. Burrows," *Manitoba Hist.* (Winnipeg), no.21 (spring 1991): 22–23. T. D. Regehr, *The Canadian Northern Railway, pioneer road of the northern prairies, 1895–1918* (Toronto, 1976). Theodore Sparks, "The early lumber industry of Winnipeg," in *"Northwest Review," 45th anniversary* (Winnipeg, 1930). *Standard dict. of Canadian biog.* (Roberts and Tunnell). Deborah Welch, "T. A. Burrows, 1857–1929: case study of a Manitoba businessman and politician" (MA thesis, Univ. of Man., 1983).

C

CAIRNS, JAMES FREDERICK, teacher, editor, businessman, and office holder; b. 23 March 1870 in Lawrenceville, Que., son of Hugh Cairns, a Methodist minister, and Maria Mountain; m. 1900 Edith Beatrice Moore of Chatham, Ont., and they had a son; d. 18 March 1928 in Saskatoon, Sask.

Born to parents of Irish descent, James Frederick Cairns was educated at the academy in Knowlton, Que., Albert College in Belleville, Ont., and Victoria University in Cobourg, from which he graduated in 1890. After teaching for nine years at the Chatham Collegiate Institute, he edited the *Canadian Wheelman: a Journal of Cycling* (London, Ont.) and managed opera houses in Chatham and London. Nothing in his early life suggested he would own one of the premier department stores in western Canada.

Cairns and his wife went west in 1902, arriving in Saskatoon, then a small village. Mill owner James Robert Wilson recounted meeting him: "On one cold afternoon I noticed a man walking across the prairie toward the mill. He asked what I thought of Borden village [to the northwest] and mentioned that he thought of starting a bakery and grocery store there." Persuaded by Wilson to stay in Saskatoon, he opened a bakery in December. When the trainloads of colonists led by Isaac Montgomery Barr* arrived in the spring of 1903, he worked 24 hours a day, one of a handful of merchants who did not gouge them. Later that year he moved to a large store with a theatre on its second floor; among the performers were poet Emily Pauline Johnson*, actor Walter Jackson McCrea*, and the touring company of Thomas Henry Marks*. His third store opened in 1906 at the centre of the growing city and soon employed 75 people. It was replaced six years later by a splendid five-storey building at 2nd Avenue and 23rd Street. Financed in part by the Canadian Agency (an English investment firm) and executed in the Chicago School style by the Montreal firm of David Robertson Brown and Hugh A. Vallance, who had designed the University of Saskatchewan, the store welcomed 12,000 people on opening day (17 March 1913) and had 250 employees in 25 departments. Because of Cairns, property prices at this location jumped during Saskatoon's boom years to almost $2,000 a front foot on land that had cost $20 an acre 20 years earlier. In 1917 the J. F. Cairns Company Limited was incorporated.

Though best known as a merchant, Cairns played other important roles in the young community. He was the secretary of the Board of Trade at its founding in January 1903 and president the following year. In 1904 and 1905 he took part in delegations to attract more railways. He served as first chair (1908–14) of the Collegiate Institute Board and remained a member until 1923. "Not only was Mr. Cairns the prime mover of creating the school board," recalled secretary W. P. Bate, "he nursed it through its adolescence, and started it on the high road to success." He served as well with the parks commission and the industrial fair, and was first president in 1911 of the Saskatoon Auto Club, which opened a resort at nearby Pike Lake. (It was there, on 15 June 1917, the darkest day of Cairns's life, that his son, Hugh Charles John (Jack), drowned.) In 1914 and 1915 he was a board member of the Young Men's Christian Association. Eminent too in sports, he built a baseball stadium, Cairns Field, which sat 1,700 and drew an opening-day crowd of 6,422 on 14 May 1914. Playing professionally in the Western Canada League and sponsored by Quaker Oats, the Saskatoon Quakers won titles that year and in 1919; a number of Quakers made it to the major leagues. In 1921 Cairns was president of the Saskatoon Baseball Club. As was consistent with his public prominence, he was a freemason, a Shriner, a Rotarian, and an Oddfellow and he belonged to clubs in Saskatoon, Winnipeg, and Los Angeles.

Cairns was deeply involved in early industrial projects, most of them failures. A founder in 1904 of the Saskatoon Cement Works, which flourished, he had a stake too in the Saskatchewan Power Company, established in 1908 to dam the South Saskatchewan River, but it failed for lack of capital in 1912. He then joined the Canadian Agency in an attempt to acquire the company's charter and the rights to construct a street railway. Cairns worked behind the scenes to secure city council's backing and discourage public debate; he was thus not the faultless figure lionized by American writer Elbert Hubbard. When the scheme ground to a halt, Cairns and Canadian Agency representatives concentrated on developing subdivisions. He had an interest as well in Saskatoon Gas and Oil in 1911 and Saska-Alta Petroleum Products in 1914, and was a prime mover and first president in 1914 of the Industrial League, formed to bring industry to Saskatoon, though by then its real-estate boom had ended and credit had dried up.

In politics Cairns was an active Liberal. Within three weeks of his arrival in 1902, he was at a party meeting. "Every Liberal in town was there," he remembered. "There were seven of us." Nominated as an electoral candidate in 1906 and 1908, he stepped aside each time; selected again in 1915, he withdrew in 1917 in favour of a Unionist candidate.

In 1924 Cairns sold his store to the Hudson's Bay Company. The following year he became manager of one of Saskatchewan's new liquor stores, a sign of the end of Prohibition. He died in 1928, just short of 58 years and much mourned. Cairns left two monuments to his industry, his store and Cairns Field, both now demolished.

DONALD CAMERON KERR

Daily Phoenix (Saskatoon), 30 Oct. 1907; 28 July, 24 Dec. 1908; 5 March 1910; 2, 15, 18 April 1912; 4 Feb., 17 March 1913; 13, 15–16 May, 15 Oct. 1914; 28 May 1915; 30 Oct. 1917; 8 March, 23 Aug. 1919; 19 March 1928. *Daily Star* (Saskatoon), 16 Jan. 1916. *Saskatoon Phoenix*, 9 Dec. 1902; 26 Jan., 20 March, 3 Aug. 1903; 29 Jan., 5 Feb., 11, 19–20 May 1904; 26 Jan., 17 Feb. 1905; 11 Jan. 1906. N. F. Black, *History of Saskatchewan and the North-West Territories* (2v., Regina, 1913). Lorraine Blashill, *From a little stone school: the story of the development of the Saskatoon public school system over the past one hundred years* (Saskatoon, 1982). John Gilpin, "The dark side of the 'Saskatoon Spirit'; James F. Cairns and power, street railway and land development in Saskatoon, 1908–1914," *Saskatchewan Hist.* (Saskatoon), 45 (1993), no.2: 15–23. Hist. Assoc. of Saskatoon, *Narratives of Saskatoon, 1882–1912, by men of the city* ([Saskatoon, 1927]). Elbert Hubbard, *Cairns of Saskatoon* (East Aurora, N.Y., 1913). Don Kerr and S. [D.] Hanson, *Saskatoon: the first half-century* (Edmonton, 1982). *Who's who and why*, 1921.

CAMPBELL, ARCHIBALD WILLIAM, surveyor, civil engineer, editor, and civil servant; b. 14 May 1863 in Wardsville, Upper Canada, son of Cameron John Campbell and Elizabeth McLachlan; d. unmarried 9 May 1927 in Ottawa.

Archibald Campbell's father had immigrated to western Upper Canada from Caithness, Scotland. His mother, also of Scottish background, had been brought up on the family farm in Ekfrid Township; the Campbells moved there from Wardsville in 1864. Archibald received his early education in local schools and graduated from St Thomas High School. He was apprenticed in engineering and surveying for three years to the county engineer for Middlesex and Elgin and under James Anthony Bell, the city engineer in St Thomas. Commissioned a provincial land surveyor in April 1885, he began practice there. In 1888, the year he joined the Canadian Society of Civil Engineers, he formed a private partnership with Bell, specializing in waterworks, drainage systems, and bridges.

In 1891 Campbell succeeded Bell as city engineer and was a founding editor of the monthly *Municipal World* (St Thomas). He compiled its "Engineering Department" section, which ranged over the responsibilities of municipal engineers, from water and sewer systems to the placement of electricity lines. He was particularly interested in improved roadways and soon became recognized as a progressive advocate. Every aspect of building and managing rural and urban roads was covered in detail. "A good road-bed pays," he wrote in May 1892. "It saves power, shortens distance and time, increases speed, insures comfort and safety, and is, in whatever way you state it, a good investment." Public attention to roads had been eclipsed by enthusiasm for railways, but in the 1890s the bicycle craze and the formation of the Ontario Good Roads Association spurred renewed interest. Campbell's concern was practical: the construction and maintenance of good roads, from the farm gate to the markets and the grain elevators, meant that horses could easily pull greater loads and that transportation costs could be lightened and consumers' prices lowered. A second factor in his interest was improving the professional status of engineering. Roadwork was the responsibility of municipalities, which usually farmed the tasks out to influential citizens who then employed statute labour. The system was haphazard and standards were shoddy. Campbell used the *Municipal World* to champion the use of trained engineers. "Good engineering . . . becomes a source of economy instead of an expense to municipal government," he argued in April 1892. "It is therefore real economy to employ a man thoroughly qualified, and to pay him a liberal salary."

Campbell's advocacy, and the convenient fact that he was a Liberal, led to his appointment in April 1896 as provincial instructor in roadmaking, under Minister of Agriculture John Dryden*. In 1900 his position, then styled commissioner of highways, was transferred to Public Works, where he effectively became deputy minister. Through his influence, public dependence on statute labour and toll roads was

reduced. In 1902 the beleaguered Liberal government of George William Ross*, seeking re-election, set aside a million dollars to assist counties in highway construction. Campbell stayed in his post when the Conservatives replaced the Liberals at Queen's Park in 1905. The promotion of high-grade roads was a growing concern for provincial authorities, particularly after motor vehicles began appearing; 178 automobiles were registered in Ontario in 1903 but in 1910 there were 4,230.

By then Campbell's administrative skills had attracted the attention of the federal minister of railways and canals, George Perry Graham*, who had him appointed as his deputy minister in February 1910. In addition, Campbell assumed the chair of the Canadian Government Railways' managing board. He thus became the executive officer of one of the largest federal departments, with more than 4,000 employees, including a large, professional engineering corps, among them Ernest Marceau* and Collingwood Schreiber*. Campbell's annual report for 1912–13 recorded that 8,591 miles of public and private railways were under construction (down some 300 miles from the previous year) and 29,303 were in operation; the aggregate tonnage passing through the canals had risen from 47,587,245 to 52,053,913. The most notable projects underway at this time were the National Transcontinental Railway [*see* Francis Cochrane*] and the new Welland ship canal. After 1914 Campbell ushered his department through the demands of wartime transportation and nationalizing the Canadian Northern Railway [*see* Sir William MACKENZIE]. In June 1918 he took a leave of absence at full pay to investigate highway improvements for the reconstruction committee of the Union government of Sir Robert Laird Borden*. He resigned as deputy minister in June 1919 and was appointed dominion commissioner of highways.

During his years in Railways and Canals, Campbell had continued his promotion of roads. He attended conferences, gave papers, and was active in both the Canadian Cement and Concrete Association and the good roads committee of the Canadian Society of Civil Engineers. His appointment in 1919 was linked to the passage that year of the Canada Highways Act, which allocated 20 million dollars over 5 years to provide 40 per cent of the cost of constructing or improving roads for a national highway system. The provinces would contribute 60 per cent. All projects had to be approved by both levels of government and had to meet current engineering standards for the type of road (paved or gravel) being built. Campbell and his small staff reviewed all the proposals. The submission and approval of plans took longer than anticipated, so allocation was extended to 1928. This shared-cost program was an important stimulus to highway construction in the 1920s – in 1921 Camp-

Campbell

bell's office planned 17,951 miles – but the combined funding was only a tiny portion of what was needed to build a first-class system. In 1922 there were a mere 1,000 miles of paved highways in Canada. Campbell nonetheless travelled extensively to examine roadways, prepared specifications, and worked closely with the provincial departments of highways. In addition, he was a regular delegate at the conventions of the Canadian Good Roads Association, the Ontario Motor League, and the Canadian Automobile Association, where, among other measures, he advocated the abolition of speed limits.

In May 1927 Campbell, who had just returned from a motor tour of the roads between Ottawa, Montreal, and Quebec City, died suddenly in his rooms at the Victoria Chambers on Wellington Street, across from his west block office. The cause was stomach haemorrhaging and cardiac failure. A bachelor, he had devoted his life to his work and his causes – good roads and the professionalization of engineering. During his Ottawa years he developed an international reputation as an expert on highway construction and maintenance and was known throughout North America and Europe as "Good Roads" Campbell. After a memorial service at his Ottawa church, St Andrew's Presbyterian, Senator George Graham, his former minister, accompanied his body by train to Appin, Ont., for burial in the family plot in Longwoods Cemetery near Melbourne. His small estate, including his shares in Municipal World Limited, went to a brother, a sister, and a niece. Archie Campbell, the St Thomas *Times-Journal* noted, "was a maker of Canada and his work is the best and most permanent monument to his memory that could be devised."

ROBERT CRAIG BROWN

Archibald William Campbell's publications include *Road bulletin no.1* ([Toronto, 1896?]), *Road bulletin no.2* (Toronto, 1896), and *The streets of Saint John: report* (Saint John, [1897?]). A summary of his report on Winnipeg streets appears in *Reports on Winnipeg pavements*, comp. H. N. Ruttan (Winnipeg, 1900). His articles are listed in *Science and technology biblio.* (Richardson and MacDonald).

AO, F 977-6, Longwoods Cemetery, Caradoc Township, Ont.; RG 22-354, no.13218; RG 80-8-0-1056, no.10042. LAC, RG 32, 425, P.C. 1528, 22 June 1918; P.C. 1021, 15 May 1919. *Ottawa Evening Journal*, 10 May 1927. *Times-Journal* (St Thomas, Ont.), 10 May 1927. Assoc. of Ontario Land Surveyors, *Annual report* (Toronto), 1928: 114–16. Can., House of Commons, *Debates*, 1919; Parl., *Sessional papers*, 1918, no.30: 427; 1921, no.20: 83–84. *Canada Gazette*, 5 Feb. 1910: 2301. *Canadian annual rev.*, 1905–1925/26. *Canadian men and women of the time* (Morgan; 1898 and 1912). E. C. Guillet, *The story of Canadian roads* (Toronto, 1966). *Municipal World* (St Thomas), April 1892: 41; May 1892: 53. Ont., Legislature, *Sessional papers*, 1897, no.24; 1901, no.27; 1906, no.27. Statistics Canada, *Historical statistics of Canada*, ed. F. H. Leacy (2nd ed.,

Ottawa, 1983; also available online at Statistics Canada's website, *www.statcan.ca*), ser.T147, T171. *Who's who in Canada*, 1925/26.

CAMPBELL, CATHERINE ANNE, named **Mother Ignatia**, member of the Congregation of the Sisters of St Joseph and educator; b. 17 Nov. 1840 in Thorah Township, Upper Canada, daughter of Kenneth Campbell, a farmer, and Ann McEwen; d. 3 Jan. 1929 in London, Ont.

A native of Glengarry County, Kenneth Campbell settled in Thorah in the 1820s; his wife was from Scotland. Strongly Roman Catholic, the family encouraged church vocations: Catherine Anne Campbell's brother Kenneth A. entered the priesthood and four of their nieces would become religious. After her early education in a township school and the requisite postulancy, Catherine Anne assumed the habit of the Sisters of St Joseph of Toronto on 3 May 1856. She was received into the community by its founder, Mother Delphine [Marie-Antoinette Fontbonne*], and given the name Sister Ignatius. Over the next 11 years she taught in various schools which were under the sisters' direction in the diocese of Toronto. The order was expanding rapidly [*see* Ellen Dinan*] and in 1867, under the name Sister Ignatia, she was appointed superior of the community's mission in Thorold, Ont.

Her experience as a teacher and administrator well qualified her to go to London with four other sisters in December 1868 to establish a branch of the congregation. Under the direction of Sister Teresa [Margaret Brennan*], they were to teach in parish schools and visit the sick and infirm, the poor, and the jailed. They opened an orphanage, Mount Hope, on 2 Oct. 1869; that same year Sister Ignatia was appointed assistant superior. On 18 Dec. 1870, eight days after the branch had become independent of Toronto, Bishop John Walsh* named her general superior of the Sisters of St Joseph of the Diocese of London, who were formally incorporated in February 1871.

As superior, she oversaw the growth of the sisterhood in London. Mount Hope, which served as a home for the infirm and the elderly as well as an orphanage, mother house, and noviciate, was extended, with the new building being dedicated on 7 Oct. 1877. In 1889 she negotiated the purchase of the former Hellmuth Ladies' College, which after extensive renovation was dedicated and named Mount St Joseph Motherhouse, Noviciate, and Orphanage on 26 April 1900. Renamed the House of Providence, Mount Hope became a facility for the elderly. Beyond London, the sisters established convents and staffed schools throughout southwestern Ontario, including Goderich (1873), St Thomas (1879), Ingersoll (1879), Belle River (1889), and Walkerville (Windsor) (1894). Mother Ignatia made the arrangements under which the community provided domestic service for the Congregation of St

Basil at Assumption College in Sandwich (Windsor) from 1884 to 1904. As well, she oversaw the establishment of St Joseph's Hospital in London (1888) and St Joseph's Hospital in Chatham (1890).

The service performed by the sisters in these centres is inestimable. Their response to a major disaster in London may well have been typical. Following the loss of nearly 200 lives in the capsize of the excursion steamer *Victoria* on 24 May 1881, Mother Ignatia sent ten sisters out through the city to help bereaved families and orphans.

Mother Ignatia served as general superior until 1902, when changes in canon law required that she relinquish her office. Immediately elected to the community's general council, she subsequently served as first councillor, mother assistant, and superior of the convent in St Thomas (1902–10), fourth councillor (1911–14), and chair of the committee to revise the community's constitutions. During her terms on general council, the community established foundations in Sarnia (1906) and in Seaforth and Woodstock (1913). In 1914 it acquired, as its new mother house, Sacred Heart Convent in London, formerly the residence of the Religious of the Sacred Heart.

Between 1870 and her death in 1929 at Sacred Heart Convent, the Sisters of St Joseph of London had grown exponentially: 365 were received into the community, only 49 of whom died before her. Mother Ignatia is one of 50 prominent citizens memorialized in a bronze sculpture, *People and the City: a Monument for the City of London*, unveiled in 1991 at the corner of Queens Avenue and Wellington Street.

ELIZABETH M. SMYTH

[The author wishes to thank the Congregation of the Sisters of St Joseph of London, Ont., who made available the material on which this biography is based. E.M.S.]

Sisters of St Joseph of Toronto Arch., Acts of profession, 15 Oct. 1858; Community annals. Esther Bardawill, *Mother Ignatia Campbell* (London, 1993).

CAMPBELL, ROBERT, Presbyterian minister, botanist, educator, and author; b. 21 June 1835 near Perth, Upper Canada, seventh son of Peter Campbell, a farmer and elder of the Presbyterian Church, and Margaret Campbell; m. 29 Dec. 1863 Margaret Macdonnell, sister of Daniel James Macdonnell*, in Fergus, Upper Canada, and they had seven sons, three of whom died before reaching adulthood, and three daughters, one of whom died at age 24; d. 15 March 1921 in Montreal.

Peter Campbell's parents immigrated to Canada from Scotland in 1817 and settled near Perth that same year. An able student, Robert was able to obtain a classical education from a well-educated Irish schoolmaster at the local common school. After a conversion

experience in 1852, he began to prepare for the ministry. He graduated in 1856 from Queen's College, Kingston, with a BA (honours in all subjects) and later that year he became headmaster of Queen's College School. He continued to study, receiving an MA from Queen's in 1858. Although licensed to preach by the presbytery of Bathurst in 1860, he went abroad, visiting the British Isles and the Continent. He seems to have already had a reputation as a preacher, because on his return he received invitations from several congregations. He chose St Andrew's Church in Galt (Cambridge); on 10 April 1862 he was ordained and inducted into that congregation. After four years there, he accepted a call from the famous St Gabriel Street Church in Montreal. Campbell would retain this charge until his retirement in 1909, a ministry of 43 years. He held the title of minister emeritus from 1909 until his death.

Though his doctrine was Calvinist, Campbell nevertheless adhered to the Church of Scotland rather than its Free Church counterpart. Both of his congregations, in Galt and Montreal, were part of the Synod of the Presbyterian Church of Canada in connection with the Church of Scotland. His call to the St Gabriel Street Church represented a daunting task. The Reverend Henry Esson* had led St Gabriel Street into the Free Church after the disruption of 1843 [*see* Robert Burns*], but not without substantial dissent. The church and the manse were given back to the Synod of the Church of Scotland in 1864. Thus Campbell inherited not just a previously prestigious pulpit but also a history of dispute and a vastly shrunken congregation. He worked with confidence and enthusiasm. He began with between 40 and 80 families; by 1875–76 the church had 196 families and 358 communicants, making it the fourth largest Presbyterian congregation in Montreal.

Proud of his Scottish heritage, Campbell was a founding member of the Celtic Society of Montreal, established in 1883. Philosophically he was trained in the Scottish common sense tradition and espoused its realism; he remained unimpressed with the philosophical idealism sweeping through the church's institutions of higher learning and had little time for the theological liberalism that accompanied it. Although conservative in his socio-political outlook as well, he did not completely trust the bullish capitalism of his age. Campbell was doctrinally conservative but not reactionary. In spite of his high praise for the Westminster Confession, he sometimes qualified his acceptance of it. He agreed with some of the results of higher criticism of Christian Scriptures. No exponent of cultural Christianity, he remained evangelical in outlook. He averred that "every baptized child of the Church needs spiritual regeneration as much as any Hindu or Hottentot." To a certain degree, he fell between the cracks, not nearly up-to-date enough for the theological liberals of his day, but not sufficiently conservative to satisfy strict Calvinist orthodoxy.

Campbell was both an ecumenist and a fervent Scottish Presbyterian. As an ecumenist, he freely recognized a valuable Christian witness in the other Canadian denominations he termed "evangelical": Anglican, Baptist, Congregationalist, and Methodist. He also found a place in Christendom for the Roman Catholic Church; he even had nice things to say about the Unitarians. Of the Jews, Campbell comments: "Over against [the crucifixion of Christ] is to be placed the fact that our great redeemer was a Jew, and that Christians owe the large sources of their religion to that remarkable people." As an unapologetic Scottish Presbyterian, he aggressively supported a union of the various branches of Presbyterianism in 1875, but later strongly opposed the union of Scottish and English denominations in Canada, finally consolidated in the establishment of the United Church of Canada in 1925. He tested severely his rugged constitution in his all-out fight to get the Presbyterian union through the Quebec legislature in 1875 and he would similarly ignore the limitations of old age as a leader in the struggle against interdenominational union.

In addition to his pastoral work, Campbell was a trustee of Queen's College for many years and for two academic years (1880–82) he was a lecturer in church history there. His writings give evidence of his acquaintance with current topics such as socialism, evolution, and higher criticism of the Bible. Queen's conferred on him an honorary DD IN 1887. As soon as the union of 1875 had made it possible, he served the erstwhile Free Church theological college, Presbyterian College of Montreal, as a member of its board of managers from 1875 to 1883. He taught church history there as well, in 1904–5 and in 1916. Except for a brief hiatus (1894–95), he was a senator of the college from 1883 until his death, a tenure that made him one of its longest serving, most influential senators.

From 1892 until his death Campbell was senior clerk (secretary) of the General Assembly, the most important post in Presbyterian churches within the Scottish tradition. The clerk's word is authoritative in the intricacies of Presbyterian practice. Certainly Campbell's consummate skill in the position was freely acknowledged by friend and foe alike. The other high post in Presbyterianism is that of moderator of the General Assembly. Campbell had this honour in 1907.

Campbell had a considerable public role, especially in Montreal. He was a founding member and chaplain of the St Lawrence Curling Club. He was also active in such charitable organizations as the Prisoners' Aid Society. No stranger to legislators, he acted as lobbyist or publicist on numerous issues involving the church.

An avid botanist, Campbell collected flowers both at home and abroad, and his hiking undoubtedly contributed to his near-legendary vitality. Active in the Natural History Society of Montreal, he contributed 17 articles on botany to its *Canadian Record of Science*, of which he was editor for a number of years. In 1895 he became president of the society.

His literary output, while not extraordinary, was respectable for a conscientious parish minister. He is best remembered for his minutely detailed *History of the Scotch Presbyterian Church . . .* (Montreal, 1887). Over 800 pages long, it contains many small biographies of founders of Presbyterianism in Montreal and is still consulted today. His *Relations of the Christian churches to one another . . .* (Toronto, 1913) is a polemical but charitable refutation of church union. The best known of his shorter works are *On the union of Presbyterians in Canada* (Montreal, 1871) and *The pretensions exposed . . .* (Montreal, 1878), a vitriolic tract against ministers claiming to represent the true Church of Scotland. Less acerbic was his *Union or co-operation . . .* (Montreal, [1906?]). He wrote numerous articles for church magazines; the prestigious *Catholic Presbyterian* (London and New York) published his "Rise and progress of the Presbyterian Church in Canada" in 1879.

All the sources converge on two of Campbell's traits: his optimism and his vigour. He evidently had an irrepressible enthusiasm and an almost irritating ability to see hope in the most thorough defeats. He evangelized confidently in his east-end Montreal parish even when it seemed that once established as church members many of his flock moved to the more prosperous west end of the city. He retired from the pastorate at age 74 and kept up a punishing schedule of engagements. The last active day of his life – 28 Feb. 1921 – he participated in a meeting of the presbytery of Montreal, as had been his wont for 53 years; that evening he planned to attend a meeting of the Natural History Society of Montreal (of which he was honorary president). He was en route when the streetcar in which he was riding lurched forward and left him with injuries which would prove fatal two weeks later. His death robbed the Presbyterian Church in Canada of one of its most distinguished elder statesmen, the Quebec Christian community of a renowned ecumenist, and the Canadian scientific community of an acute observer of nature.

DAN SHUTE

Science and technology biblio. (Richardson and MacDonald) lists numerous articles on botany which Robert Campbell published in the *Canadian Record of Science* (Montreal) and the *Canadian Horticultural Magazine* (Montreal). Some of these articles, as well as the works mentioned in the biography and other writings by Campbell, are listed in CIHM, *Reg.*
AO, RG 80-27-2, 79: 112. *Canadian men and women of*

the time (Morgan; 1898 and 1912). N. K. Clifford, *The resistance to church union in Canada, 1904–1939* (Vancouver, 1985); "Robert Campbell, the defender of Presbyterianism," in *Called to witness: profiles of Canadian Presbyterians . . . ,* ed. W. S. Reid and J. S. Moir (4v. to date, [Toronto; Hamilton, Ont.], 1975–), 1: 53–66. [James Croil], *A historical and statistical report of the Presbyterian Church of Canada, in connection with the Church of Scotland, for the year 1866* (Montreal, 1867). G. C. Heine, *A brief sketch of the life and work of the Rev. Robert Campbell, D.D., minister of St. Gabriel Church, Montreal* (Montreal, 1922). Presbyterian Church in Canada, General Assembly, *Acts and proc.* (Toronto), 1921–22. Ephraim Scott, "The late Rev. Robert Campbell, D.D.," *Presbyterian Record* (Montreal) 46 (1921): 104–6. Hew Scott *et al.*, *Fasti ecclesiæ scoticanæ: the succession of ministers in the Church of Scotland from the Reformation* (new ed., 11v. to date, Edinburgh, 1915–): 7. *Standard dict. of Canadian biog.* (Roberts and Tunnell).

CANNON, LAWRENCE JOHN, lawyer, office holder, and judge; b. 18 Nov. 1852 at Quebec, son of Lawrence Ambrose Cannon, a lawyer and city clerk at Quebec, and Mary Jane Cary; m. 2 Aug. 1876 Marie-Hermine-Aurélie-Alida Dumoulin, daughter of Jean-Gaspard Dumoulin* and Alida Pacaud, in Saint-Christophe-d'Arthabaska, Que., and they had eight children; d. 30 Jan. 1921 at Quebec.

The great-grandson of Edward Cannon*, an Irishman who settled at Quebec in 1795 and worked there as a master mason with his son John*, Lawrence John Cannon belonged to one of the city's prominent families. At his baptism, his godfather was Augustin-Norbert Morin*, who was then co-premier of the Province of Canada with Francis Hincks*. Lawrence John did his classical studies at the Séminaire de Québec (1862–70) and the Séminaire de Nicolet (1870–71), and then enrolled at the Université Laval, where he obtained a degree in law in June 1874. Called to the bar in July, he practised for a few months at Quebec before moving in 1875 to Arthabaskaville (Victoriaville), where he went into partnership with Édouard-Louis Pacaud*. He soon became part of the little circle of friends which included the Pacaud brothers, Wilfrid Laurier*, Marc-Aurèle Plamondon*, and Joseph Lavergne. As the Liberal candidate for the riding of Drummond and Arthabaska in the federal election of 20 June 1882, Cannon was defeated by the Conservative incumbent, Désiré-Olivier Bourbeau. When the Temperance League of the County of Arthabaska was founded in 1885, he was a member of the first board of directors, along with Laurier and others. On 2 Feb. 1891 the government of Honoré Mercier* appointed him deputy attorney general and law clerk for the province of Quebec, an office he retained under successive Conservative and Liberal administrations until 1905. On 29 July of that year he became a judge of the Superior Court for the district of Trois-Rivières.

The most important event in Cannon's judicial career was his appointment on 7 April 1909 by the government of Sir Lomer GOUIN as a one-man royal commission to make a general and complete inquiry into the administration of the affairs of the city of Montreal. This commission, which would also be known as the Cannon inquiry, was set up in response to pressure from a committee of citizens which, among others, included former mayor Hormisdas Laporte*, notary Victor Morin, and Senator Raoul Dandurand*. In view of the inefficient management by the committees of the city council, these citizens called for reforms in the municipal administration and especially for the creation of a board of control having the executive power. With the assistance of a secretary, lawyer Arthur Gagné, Cannon commenced his work on 19 April but adjourned it until 27 April, the date on which the inquiry really began. He held 115 sessions and heard 914 depositions, in the course of which 548 pieces of evidence were produced. His mandate required him to submit a report before 15 July, but the hearings, at which the lawyers for the citizens' committee, Joseph-Léonide PERRON and Napoléon-Kemner Laflamme, acted as prosecutors, did not conclude until 14 September.

Reported in detail by the Montreal press, the hearings showed that there had been corruption and patronage in the innermost reaches of the city's administration. On 20 September, before Cannon had submitted his report, the provincial government held a referendum on the amendments it had made to the city's charter under a statute enacted in May 1909. These amendments reduced the number of aldermen per ward and created the board of commissioners, a board of control consisting of the mayor and four members elected for four years. A third of the citizens of Montreal took part in the referendum; 88 per cent voted in favour of creating a board and 92 per cent for reducing the number of aldermen from two to one per ward.

On 13 Dec. 1909 Cannon finished writing his report. He made it clear from the outset that the evidence presented to him enabled him to "form an accurate idea of the existing abuses and irregularities in the civic administration of Montreal." Following the course of the inquiry, he dealt first with the organization and operation of the police. He concluded that there was systemic tolerance with regard to houses of prostitution, gaming houses, and the sale of alcohol on Sunday, that appointments and promotions required payments, and that the chief of police was sometimes "a too subservient instrument in the hands of certain aldermen." He recommended that the police commission, composed of aldermen who supervised the police department, be abolished, and that the number of police officers be increased. Turning to the fire department, the judge again attacked a jobs-for-sale system controlled by go-betweens, aldermen, and officers of the fire brigade [*see* Zéphirin BENOIT]. His

Carey

comment on the situation was unequivocal: "It is hard to imagine a more wretched occupation." The evidence concerning the roads department led him to the conclusion that it had to be entirely reorganized if it was to become economical, efficient, and honest. He recommended the abolition of the roads commission which supervised the department.

When he made these recommendations, Cannon knew that the voters had approved the board of commissioners, which marked the end of commissions made up of aldermen. He noted that this new authority "will have to find a solution to current abuses." Evidence of corruption and patronage involving other authorities was mentioned by the judge. For example, he was led to describe the city's decision to drop charges against dairymen who supplied products of inferior quality as "quasi-criminal interference from the aldermen," because, in his view, it endangered the health of the population. On the completion of his general inquiry, Cannon concluded that "the administration of the affairs of the City of Montreal by its Council since 1902 has been saturated with corruption arising mainly from the scourge of patronage" and that reduction of the number of aldermen and creation of a board of control would improve municipal administration. His recommendations concerning the creation of a "council composed of aldermen, representing the whole city," as well as prosecution and fines for the individuals named by the inquiry, would not be acted on. In February 1910 the candidates backed by the citizens' committee took control of the city council. All the aldermen incriminated by the report either were defeated or did not stand for re-election. The board of commissioners would be retained until 1918.

On 6 July 1910 judge Lawrence John Cannon was transferred to the Quebec district, where he served until his death in 1921. The daily *Le Soleil* referred to him at this time as "that brilliant magistrate whose worthy and honourable career had won him the esteem and respect of all," and it mentioned that his report on the administration of Montreal "is still famous both for the facts brought to light and for the conclusions of the learned judge." Two of Cannon's sons would also be appointed to the bench: Lawrence Arthur Dumoulin*, judge of the Court of King's Bench and of the Supreme Court of Canada, and Lucien, judge of the Superior Court for the district of Quebec.

MARIO ROBERT

Lawrence John Cannon is the author of *Rapport sur l'administration de la ville de Montréal, décembre 1909* (s.l., n.d.) and, with François Laroche, of *Tariffs of officers of justice and registrars in the province of Quebec, with supplement and index* (Quebec, 1902), also published in French.

ANQ-MBF, CE402-S2, 2 août 1876. ANQ-Q, CE301-S1, 18 nov. 1852. VM-DGDA, P39; VM6, Dossiers de coupures de presse, D010.9: enquête-commission Cannon-année 1909.

Le Soleil, 31 janv., 1er févr. 1921. J.-P. Brodeur, *La délinquance de l'ordre: recherches sur les commissions d'enquête* (1v. paru, La Salle, Qué., 1984–), 55–71. *Canadian men and women of the time* (Morgan; 1898). I.-J. Deslauriers, *La Cour supérieure du Québec et ses juges, 1849–1er janvier 1980* (Québec, 1980), 166. "Les disparus," *BRH*, 33 (1927): 210. Michel Gauvin, "The reformer and the machine: Montreal civic politics from Raymond Préfontaine to Médéric Martin," *Journal of Canadian Studies* (Peterborough, Ont.), 13 (1978–79), no.2: 20–21. Linteau, *Hist. de Montréal*, 258–60. C.-V. Marsolais *et al.*, *Histoire des maires de Montréal* (Montréal, 1993), 198–204. Que., *Statutes*, 1885, c.54. P.-G. Roy, *Les juges de la prov. de Québec*, 90–91. Rumilly, *Hist. de Montréal*, 3: 397–412.

CAREY, DAVID ARTHUR, machinist, newspaper reporter, trade-union leader, and office holder; b. 2 Jan. 1859 in Dublin, son of John Carey and Elizabeth Carter; m. first 31 July 1878 Agnes Theresa Monaghan in Toronto; m. there secondly 19 Oct. 1886 Annie Glynn, and they had a daughter and two sons; d. there 26 March 1927.

David A. Carey immigrated to Canada with his family in 1861 or 1862. They lived in Quebec and Montreal, where David was educated in separate schools. After apprenticing as a machinist, he moved to Toronto and found work as a stove mounter and then in the agricultural implements factory of Hart Almerrin Massey*. In 1878 Carey married Agnes Monaghan, but the union ended tragically: she died at age 19 on 2 Feb. 1879, a day after giving birth to twin girls – one was stillborn, the other lived only six months. David remarried in 1886; for several years the Careys lived on Markham Street and, like many families, they supplemented their income by taking in a boarder.

During the 1880s Carey played an important role in the Toronto labour movement. In 1882 he had joined the Knights of Labor Maple Leaf Local Assembly 2622, which consisted primarily of Massey employees, and he served as district master workman for five years. Along with other experienced labour figures, notably printer Daniel John O'Donoghue*, tailor Alfred Fredman Jury*, painters Charles March* and John W. Carter, and journalist Thomas Phillips Thompson*, Carey outlined strategies that would shape the course of the movement for the next decade. Observing that labour's interest had been damaged by the public, partisan activity of various Knights leaders, particularly Alexander Whyte Wright*, Carey resolved in 1891 that the order's District Assembly should cancel the credentials of any delegate who worked for the Conservatives or the Reformers. His denunciation of political involvement resulted in a shift in labour lobbying from the Knights' legislative committee to the Trades and Labor Congress of Canada, a move that would weaken the Knights' position.

Carey also belonged, in these years of turmoil, to the Toronto Trades and Labor Council, which had been pivotal in the organization of the Trades and Labor Congress in 1883. He represented the TTLC at the TLC's annual meetings in 1894, 1895, 1896, 1900, and 1901, and was president of the TLC in 1896–98. At its convention in 1897 he called for concrete reforms, such as public employment bureaus, and broad social and political action, to eradicate the defective "social customs" that were holding back Canada's toilers. "The educating and new power of the press, properly described as the library of the workingman and the reception of political power, have infused new ideas, new principles and new aspirations into the heads and hearts of the workers," he maintained. This interest in the press may have been prompted too by Carey's shift of careers: about 1892 he had become a reporter with the Toronto *Evening Telegram*.

During this era the TLC struggled to define the position of Canadian labour more exactly with reference to the American Federation of Labor. Canadian locals demanded a greater share of its income, and some trade unions even wanted separation from the giant international. The movement for autonomy had begun at the 1894 meeting of the TLC, where a committee composed of Carey, Quebec machinist Patrick Joseph Jobin*, and Ottawa market gardener James W. Patterson proposed that the congress reconstitute itself as a Canadian labour federation with the power to issue charters and perform all the other duties of a national labour organization. At the convention the following year, however, the congress's leaders showed a reluctance to work towards autonomy. Two years later a motion to establish a Canadian federation was defeated.

Although the question of international as opposed to national unionism had been settled, the problem of having large numbers of organized workers in Canada paying dues to essentially American organizations remained. In 1898 Carey and TLC secretary George W. Dower (a Toronto typographer) met with Thomas Kidd, who had recently been selected as the AFL's first fraternal delegate to the TLC. They discussed a proposal by the AFL to make a $100 grant to the TLC to aid its legislative committee and curb dissatisfaction among its members. The TLC accepted the proposal and elected Carey as its first fraternal delegate to the AFL. The TLC was apparently unaware that the AFL was acting in its own interest. By 1901 Carey was clearly pitching the AFL line: more pure labour legislation and less direct political involvement. A Canadian federation was set up by unions expelled from the TLC in 1902, but it remained weak. This failure to organize an effective national body ultimately paved the way for the dominance of the AFL style of international unionism.

Carey remained active in the local labour movement. He served on the board of directors of the Tor-

onto Labor Temple Company Limited from its formation in 1904, was its president for many years, and worked on numerous arbitrations. He was a familiar figure among Toronto workers, particularly those on the waterfront and at Union Station, where his duties as a reporter often took him. A bandsman in his youth, Carey was active as a representative and district officer of the American Federation of Musicians, which had been formed in 1896 and had expanded into Canada in 1901. According to the *Labor Leader* (Toronto), he was responsible for "many conciliations between irate theatre proprietors and orchestras."

In October 1917 Newton Wesley Rowell*, a member of the newly formed federal Union government, pushed Carey's name for the post of undersecretary of labour. Carey had, helpfully, dampened resistance against conscription within the TLC and, Rowell believed, he could speak for Ontario's Irish Catholics, who felt under-represented in Ottawa. In the general election in December, Carey ran in Toronto South under the Independent Labor banner, but his candidacy was tainted by questions about his motives for going to Ottawa, and he lost to Charles SHEARD. About 1925 he left the *Telegram* to become manager of the Labor Temple, situated on Church Street.

A devout Roman Catholic, Carey served on Toronto's Separate School Board for 35 years. He worshipped at St Mary's Church on Bathurst Street, was a founder there of St Mary's Athletic Association, and belonged to the Third Order of St Francis and the Knights of Columbus. He later attended St Francis' Church on Mansfield Avenue, where his son Harold became the curate; his daughter entered the Sisters of St Joseph.

While attending the convention in May 1926 of the American Federation of Musicians in Salt Lake City, Utah, Carey experienced heart trouble, which would continue to plague him. He died at his home on Montrose Avenue in Toronto in March 1927 and was buried in Mount Hope Cemetery.

CHRISTINA BURR

AO, RG 80-2-0-138, no.37217; RG 80-5-0-78, no.12930; RG 80-5-0-147, no.14775; RG 80-8-0-59, no.17075; RG 80-8-0-1050, no.2675. Mount Hope Cemetery (Toronto), Gravestone and burial records. LAC, RG 31, C1, 1901, Toronto, Ward 5, div.11: 3 (mfm. at AO). St Michael's Cemetery (Toronto), Burial records. *Globe*, 28 March 1927. *Labor Leader* (Toronto), 1 April 1927. R. H. Babcock, *Gompers in Canada: a study in American continentalism before the First World War* (Toronto and Buffalo, N.Y., 1974). *Canadian annual rev.*, 1903–4, 1917, 1921, 1923. *Canadian men and women of the time* (Morgan; 1912). *CPG*, 1918. *Directory*, Toronto, 1883–1927. Eugene Forsey, *Trade unions in Canada, 1812–1902* (Toronto, 1982). G. S. Kealey, *Toronto workers respond to industrial capitalism, 1867–1892* (Toronto and Buffalo, 1980). G. S. Kealey and B. D. Palmer, *Dreaming of what might be: the Knights of Labor in Ontario, 1880–1900* (Toronto, 1987). H. A. Logan, *Trade unions in Canada: their development and functioning* (Toronto, 1948). Middleton, *Municipality of Toronto*. James Naylor, *The new democracy: challenging the social order in industrial Ontario, 1914–25* (Toronto, 1991). Margaret Prang, *N. W. Rowell, Ontario nationalist* (Toronto and Buffalo, 1975).

CARMAN, WILLIAM BLISS (he chose Bliss Carman as his authorial name in 1884), poet, essayist, journalist, and editor; b. 15 April 1861 in Fredericton, son of William Carman, a barrister and court official, and Sophia Mary Bliss; d. unmarried 8 June 1929 in New Canaan, Conn.

Bliss Carman, whose ancestors were loyalists, was educated at the Collegiate School in Fredericton, where George Robert PARKIN was headmaster, and at the University of New Brunswick (BA 1881, MA 1884); he subsequently attended the University of Edinburgh (1882–83) and Harvard University (1886–87). After returning to Fredericton from Scotland in 1883, he had tried his hand at teaching, surveying, and the law, and had written reviews for the *University Monthly*, activities that reflected his restlessness and his journalistic bent. At Harvard, he was heavily influenced by Josiah Royce, whose spiritualistic idealism, combined with the transcendentalism of Ralph Waldo Emerson, lies centrally in the background of his first major poem, "Low tide on Grand Pré," written in the summer and winter of 1886. After again returning briefly to the Maritimes in the late 1880s, he moved permanently to the United States, where he worked for two years (1890–92) as literary editor of the *Independent* (New York), the first of many similar positions on various American magazines. In 1894 he helped to found the *Chap-Book* (Boston), between 1895 and 1900 he wrote a weekly column for the *Boston Evening Transcript*, and in 1904 he published the ten volumes of *The world's best poetry* (Philadelphia), of which he was editor-in-chief.

Even before his permanent removal to the United States in February 1890, Carman had begun, with the help of his cousin Charles George Douglas Roberts*, to establish a reputation for himself as an accomplished and promising poet. In 1893 he published his first collection of poems, *Low tide on Grand Pré: a book of lyrics*, and in ensuing years his gift for lyricism resulted in over twenty more books of poetry, including the three volumes of the *Vagabondia* series (1894–1900) that he co-authored with the American poet and essayist Richard Hovey. Under the tutelage, first of Hovey's companion, Henrietta Russell, and then of the woman who became a major love of his life, Mary Perry King, he drew on the theories of François-Alexandre-Nicolas-Chéri Delsarte to develop a strategy of mind-body-spirit harmonization aimed at undoing the physical, psychological, and spiritual damage caused

by urban modernity. By terms charmingly, orotundly, and fancifully expounded in such prose works as *The kinship of nature* (1903) and, with Mrs King, *The making of personality* (1908), his therapeutic ideas resulted in the five volumes of verse assembled in *Pipes of Pan* (1906), a collection that contains many superb lyrics but, overall, evinces the dangers of a soporific aesthetic. It was a combination of these concerns and the discipline of the Sapphic fragments that produced his finest volume of poetry, *Sappho: one hundred lyrics* (1903).

Like other members of the "confederation" group of Canadian poets (Roberts, Archibald Lampman*, William Wilfred Campbell*, Duncan Campbell Scott*, and Frederick George Scott*), Carman was lifted to fame in Canada by the wave of post-confederation nationalism and its accompanying call for a distinctive and distinguished Canadian literature. Outside the country, however, he was widely regarded not merely as a typical Canadian poet, but also as one of the most prominent American poets of the generation that was coming to maturity in the 1880s and 1890s. "I passed everywhere for a 'young American writer,'" he told a correspondent after a trip to Paris in 1896; "I wept inwardly, but could not refuse the compliment." His impact on American letters is suggested by the fact that in 1909 Wallace Stevens composed poems "to the accompaniment" of a line from Carman's "May and June" and by his appointment as editor of *The Oxford book of American verse* (1927). Nor was Carman's influence and reputation confined to North America: during the 1890s his work was well received by Arthur William Symons and other discerning British readers, and in 1904 Francis Thompson described him as "a Canadian poet of deserved repute this side the water, with a lusty and individualised joy in nature."

Much of Carman's writing in poetry and prose during the decade preceding World War I is as repetitive as the title of *Echoes from Vagabondia* (1912) intimates, but after the war (and after a battle with tuberculosis in 1919–20) he resumed his spiritual adventurousness under the influence of theosophy and other esoteric philosophical systems. During the war Carman had worked with a group of American writers to bring the United States into the conflict and in the years that followed he renewed his ties with Canada, which rewarded his loyalty in several highly successful reading and lecturing tours (1920–29) and in various honours, including corresponding membership in the Royal Society of Canada (1925) and the society's Lorne Pierce Medal for distinguished service to Canadian literature (1928). It was during the first of his Canadian tours that he was unofficially dubbed the poet laureate of Canada. Four volumes of poems published in the 1920s, most notably *Later poems* (1921) and *Far horizons* (1925), reflect his spiritual and patriotic awakenings, as do *Talks on poetry and life . . .* (1926), a collection of lectures and readings delivered at the University of Toronto, and *Our Canadian literature: representative verse, English and French* (1935), an anthology completed after his death by Lorne Albert Pierce*. With another book of poetry (*Wild garden*) recently published and another (*Sanctuary: Sunshine House sonnets*) in preparation, Carman died of a brain haemorrhage on 8 June 1929 at New Canaan, where he had spent at least part of every year since 1897 in order to be near Mrs King. His ashes were buried in Forest Hill Cemetery, Fredericton, and a national memorial service was held at the Anglican cathedral there. Not until 13 May 1954 was he granted the wish that he had expressed in 1892 in "The grave-tree": "Let me have a scarlet maple / For the grave-tree at my head, / With the quiet sun behind it, / In the years when I am dead."

A major reason for the long delay in granting Carman's wish was the shift in poetic taste that began with the triumph of modernism in Canada between the wars and led to the dismissal of such phrases as "scarlet maple" and "quiet sun" as sentimental and vague. The continuing underestimation of Carman is to be regretted, for at his best he is one of the finest lyricists that Canada has produced and several aspects of his thought, not least his belief in personal harmony and his reverence for external nature, will always have much to recommend them. "I have known few poets anywhere . . . who . . . so dedicated himself to the service of poetry as Bliss Carman," wrote Padraic Colum in the prefatory note to *Sanctuary*. "His life had a frugal dignity which was in itself a rare and a fine achievement. The tweeds that he wore had given him long service; they were always carefully pressed and spotless; that wide-brimmed hat he had worn for many seasons. Yet there was always something in his attire that corresponded to the gaiety and color of his mind – a bright neck-tie, a silver chain, a turquoise ornament that some Indian friend had bestowed upon him. He was a tall man. But that exceptional build was contained in a thin integument. He bled easily; he was sensitive over every part of his great frame. However, that irritability that usually goes with the thin skin was no part of his nature. Bliss Carman was above everything else a sweet-natured man. I am sure that no one ever parted from him without thinking, 'I hope I shall see dear Bliss Carman again.'" "He was like an old king from a fairy story," added Margaret Lawrence, one of several women who had been devoted to him. "He spoke his words distinctly, giving them their due, as one who loved them dearly."

D. M. R. BENTLEY

Listings of the collections in which Bliss Carman's letters are preserved are provided in Muriel Miller, *Bliss Carman: quest and revolt* (St John's, 1985), and *Letters of Bliss Carman*, ed. H. P. Gundy (Kingston, Ont., and Montreal, 1981). Gundy's edition also contains notes on the major Carman collections, which include the Bliss Carman fonds at QUA; the Bliss Carman papers at Neilson Library, Smith College (Northampton, Mass.); the Odell Shepard coll. and W. I. Morse Canadiana coll. in Harvard College Library, Houghton Library, Dept. of MSS (Cambridge, Mass.); and material in the Baker/Berry Library, Dartmouth College (Hanover, N.J.) and in several collections in the Univ. of N.B. Library, Arch. and Special Coll. Dept. (Fredericton), among them MG L10 (C. G. D. Roberts fonds) and MG L32 (I. St. J. Bliss coll.). *Bliss Carman's letters to Margaret Lawrence, 1927–1929*, ed. D. M. R. Bentley, assisted by Margaret Maciejewski (London, Ont., 1995), contains a particularly illuminating correspondence. "A primary and secondary bibliography of Bliss Carman's work," comp. J. R. Sorfleet, is available in *Bliss Carman: a reappraisal*, ed. and intro. Gerald Lynch (Ottawa, 1990), 193–204. Since the appearance of Sorfleet's bibliography, the journal *Canadian Poetry* (London, Ont.) has published several articles on Carman's poetry and impact.

CARNOCHAN, JANET, educator and historian; b. 14 Nov. 1839 in Stamford (Niagara Falls), Upper Canada, second daughter of James Carnochan and Mary Milroy; d. unmarried 31 March 1926 in Niagara-on-the-Lake, Ont.

Janet Carnochan's parents emigrated from Ayrshire, Scotland, to Stamford around 1830. Her father was a cabinetmaker and carpenter, an occupation that he continued to follow, first in Stamford and then, after the family's move in 1841, in Niagara (Niagara-on-the-Lake). With her four siblings, Carnochan spent her childhood and adolescence in Niagara, where she attended the local schools and St Andrew's Presbyterian Church. Like many young, single women in Upper Canada in the mid-19th century, she became a teacher by applying for a certificate of qualification in 1856. The following year, at age 17, she began teaching at the Niagara public school.

Carnochan pursued further qualifications in 1859 by attending the Toronto Normal School. She received a first-class provincial normal school certificate and went on to teach at Brantford Union School and then at Kingston's Wellington Street public school. She remained at this school for five years, until her mother's illness necessitated her return home to manage her parents' household. After her mother recovered, Carnochan taught for a year in a rural school near Peterborough. But when the principal's position at the Niagara public school became vacant, she applied for the job and, upon being accepted, returned home in 1872. Few sources document her years as a public school principal, but tributes later stressed her dedication to teaching and the esteem in which she was held. Two years after a new high school building in Niagara was completed in 1876, Carnochan joined its staff, and she remained there until her retirement in December 1900.

Carnochan

While teaching school, Janet Carnochan also channelled considerable energy into travel and voluntary work. She turned her experience of being shipwrecked off Sable Island, N.S., while en route to Britain in 1879 into a narrative that appeared in the *Canadian Methodist Magazine* (Toronto and Halifax) three years later. After her return to Niagara in 1872, she had become active in St Andrew's Church, teaching in its Sunday school and helping to raise funds for the church. She also sat on the board of managers from 1892 to 1895 and was secretary of the women's missionary society from 1887 until her death in 1926. In addition to her church work, Carnochan served on the board of the Niagara Public Library as secretary and treasurer and from time to time as temporary librarian. In 1893 she was chosen as one of 20 Canadian women to attend the World's Congress of Representative Women in Chicago.

Though schoolteaching occupied more than 40 years of Janet Carnochan's life, it is her informal educational work as a local and regional historian, historical preservationist, and museum director that is remembered today. She began making forays into historical writing in the 1890s with accounts of Niagara's Anglican and Presbyterian churches, and throughout the rest of her life she continued to contribute articles and deliver papers on historical subjects. She even wrote poetry on such patriotic themes as "Has Canada a history?" In 1895 Carnochan became the president of the newly established Niagara Historical Society, which she had helped to found (an earlier endeavour by Niagara resident and historian William Kirby* had been short-lived). She would be a leading figure in the society until 1925, serving as president, corresponding secretary, and editor of its reports and publications.

After her retirement from teaching in 1900, Carnochan was even more involved in historical activities. She became curator of the NHS's collections in 1901 and spearheaded its drive for the construction of Memorial Hall. Opened in 1907, it was the first building erected as a museum in Ontario. She also represented the society at the annual meetings of the Ontario Historical Society. From 1901 to 1911 she sat on the monuments committee of the OHS, and from 1914 to 1919 she was that society's vice-president. In addition to her activities with these organizations, Carnochan wrote a historical column in the local paper, the *Niagara Times*. Her *History of Niagara . . .*, printed by William BRIGGS in Toronto, appeared in 1914, with a foreword by Arthur Hugh Urquhart Colquhoun, deputy minister of education for Ontario, who praised it as "an example of elaborate and untiring investigation." Carnochan also expended much energy in attempts to preserve historical landmarks in Niagara, such as Butler's Burying Ground, forts George and Mississauga, and the military reserve, or commons.

Janet Carnochan was certainly not unusual in her historical activities; her work must be placed within the larger context of provincial, national, and international movements to preserve and commemorate the past. She was a frequent correspondent with other like-minded individuals and organizations, such as the OHS's secretary and provincial archaeologist David Boyle* and the Women's Canadian Historical Society of Toronto [*see* Sara MICKLE]. Like them, she was steadfast in her support of English-Canadian nationalism and believed in the importance of the country's ties to Britain and its membership in the empire. But unlike other imperialists active in the historical movement, such as Clementina Fessenden [Trenholme*], Carnochan was fairly liberal in her political outlook. She wrote sympathetically about the travails of transported reformer Benjamin Wait* following the rebellion of 1837–38 and portrayed his wife, Maria Smith, as a heroine for her attempts to win his pardon. She depicted the Niagara area as a refuge for fugitive slaves, partly in order to remind her contemporaries of the historical and ongoing significance of such British values as anti-slavery. There is no record of her public support for women's suffrage, but she was enthusiastic about attempts to memorialize Canadian women such as Laura Secord [Ingersoll*] and maintained that women's work in building the Canadian nation must be recognized by historians.

Carnochan believed that historical narratives played a critically important role in creating national identity, but she also was genuinely fascinated by the past and was passionately devoted to historical investigation. Unlike that of some of her contemporaries, her work was based on extensive research in written and material sources. Both during and after her lifetime, Janet Carnochan received a number of local, provincial, and national tributes to her endeavours, including having a Toronto teachers' chapter of the Imperial Order Daughters of the Empire named in her honour.

CECILIA MORGAN

In addition to the works mentioned in the text, Janet Carnochan is the author of *Shipwrecked on Sable Island*, ed. J. L. Field (St Catharines, Ont., 1986).

AO, F 1138, ser.F-I, minutes, 1895–1952; F 1139-3, MU 5422–29; F 1139-4, 1898–1925, MU 5440. Brock Univ. Library, Special Coll. and Arch. (St Catharines), RG 9 (Joseph Edward Masters fonds), Janet Carnochan. Niagara Hist. Soc. Museum (Niagara-on-the-Lake, Ont.), Carnochan coll. *Canadian men and women of the time* (Morgan; 1898 and 1912). C. M. Coates and Cecilia Morgan, *Heroines and history: representations of Madeleine de Verchères and Laura Secord* (Toronto, 2002). J. L. Field, *Janet Carnochan* (Markham, Ont., 1985). Gerald Killan, *Preserving Ontario's heritage: a history of the Ontario Historical Society* (Ottawa, 1976). Cecilia Morgan, "History, nation, and empire: gender and southern Ontario historical societies, 1890–1920s," *CHR*, 82 (2001): 491–528. F. D. Smith, "Miss Janet Carnochan: a sketch and an appreciation," *Canadian Magazine*, 38 (1912): 293–97.

CARON, JOSEPH-ÉDOUARD, farmer, office holder, and politician; b. 10 Jan. 1866 in Saint-Roch-des-Aulnaies, Lower Canada, son of Édouard Caron, a farmer, and Marie des Anges Cloutier; m. there first 3 July 1888 Léopoldine Gastonguay (d. 1894); m. secondly 2 Aug. 1897 Mathilda Destroismaisons in the neighbouring village of Sainte-Louise, Que., and they had three children; d. 16 July 1930 at Quebec and was buried 19 July in Sainte-Louise.

Joseph-Édouard Caron grew up on a farm on the third row of concessions at Sainte-Louise. After three years of a commercial course and a year of classical studies at the Collège de Sainte-Anne-de-la-Pocatière, he returned to his father's farm at the age of 14. There he witnessed the beginnings of the dairy industry in the region, with a growing number of butter and cheese factories, which left him with the abiding conviction that agriculture could be profitable provided farmers used more efficient farming methods. By installing a silo to store fodder, he himself would set an example of the reforms to be carried out.

Caron began his long public career in 1893, becoming secretary-treasurer of the municipal council of Sainte-Louise. He would hold this office, as well as that of secretary-treasurer of the school board from 1899, until 1910. He was also secretary-treasurer of the county council from 1895 to 1913, and of the Société d'Agriculture du Comté de L'Islet.

Brought up in a Liberal family, Caron had become active in the political arena at age 17. A member of the electoral machine of François-Gilbert Miville Dechêne, who represented L'Islet riding in the Quebec legislature from 1886 to 1902, Caron distanced himself from the Liberal party in 1899, when Prime Minister Sir Wilfrid Laurier* agreed to send a contingent of Canadian troops to South Africa to aid Great Britain in her war with the Boers. At the urging of a coalition of Liberal supporters and Conservatives in the constituency, he ran against the sitting member, Liberal Arthur Miville Dechêne, in the federal election of 7 Nov. 1900. Despite divisions within the local Liberal organization, Dechêne retained his seat. Caron would be accused of having betrayed his party on this occasion, but he defended himself by declaring that he had acted from anti-imperialist convictions. He would, indeed, be a fierce opponent of conscription, attacking it in speeches and in articles in *Le Soleil*. He would even head the Quebec provincial delegation that marched on Ottawa in May 1918 to protest the mobilization of farmers' sons.

On 15 Jan. 1902 Caron was again a candidate in L'Islet in the by-election made necessary by Arthur Miville Dechêne's resignation upon his appointment to the Senate. He ran as a Conservative, but without renouncing his allegiance to the Liberal party. This second attempt also failed. The untimely death in May 1902 of François-Gilbert Miville Dechêne would allow him to realize his political ambitions, however. On 26 Sept. 1902, at the age of 36, he was acclaimed as a Liberal in the provincial riding of L'Islet. He would be re-elected by acclamation in 1904 and by a majority of 470 in 1908.

As a backbencher, Caron took part in various debates concerning the interests of rural voters. Lumbering, colonization, roads, and especially agricultural issues held his attention. In May 1905, for instance, soon after Lomer GOUIN had formed his first cabinet, Caron made judicious suggestions to the new minister of agriculture, Auguste Tessier. In particular, he proposed that a system of compulsory inspection and categorization of dairy products be instituted to improve quality control. He also made a fervent plea for the promotion, among the province's schoolchildren, of agriculture as an occupation. On 21 Jan. 1909 he was appointed minister without portfolio.

At the end of that year, Gouin shuffled his cabinet and Caron became minister of agriculture. His predecessors, who were mostly lawyers, had not always had a practical knowledge of the problems. When the premier, who was much more at home with financial and industrial matters, decided to offer the agriculture portfolio to Caron, a farmer, he made a strategic choice. Caron was sworn in on 18 Nov. 1909 and would retain this office continuously until April 1929. Defeated in his constituency in the election of 15 May 1912, he would immediately be re-elected in Îles-de-la-Madeleine, by a majority of 191, and he would hold this seat without opposition until 1927. In addition to agriculture, his responsibilities would include highways from 1912 to 1914.

Caron was imbued with an agriculturalist ideology. He liked to repeat, from any and every available platform, that work on the land constituted the true foundation of the prosperity of nations. He also warned rural people against the illusory charms of city life. Unlike the most conservative representatives of this school of thought, however, he did not preach a simple return to the traditional way of life and its values. Indeed, the minister saw modernization of farming methods and increased activity in the marketplace as the ways of procuring a decent income for farmers and thereby stemming the rural exodus that the province of Quebec was experiencing at the outset of the century.

When he came to the ministry of agriculture, which then had about 40 employees, Caron was able to rely on a competent deputy minister, George-Auguste Gigault*, who held this office until his death in 1915. The successor to curé François-Xavier-Antoine

Caron

Labelle*, Gigault had reoriented the ministry's policy by supporting local farm clubs and adopting various measures to improve the quality of dairy products. There was still much to do, but financial resources were limited. Things would change, however, during Caron's term of office.

From 1912 to 1924, under the act passed in April 1912 to promote agriculture, a federal subsidy was paid to the provinces. Until 1919 it represented more than a quarter of Caron's budget, and ensured that Quebec, like Ontario, equipped itself with a team of county agronomists. The agricultural schools in Oka and Sainte-Anne-de-la-Pocatière, as well as Macdonald College in Sainte-Anne-de-Bellevue, received a substantial part of the federal assistance. From 1916 all the able graduates of these three institutions were hired by the ministry. By the end of 1929 the province's agronomical service, which had been set up in November 1913, would have a staff of 77 agronomists and 13 assistant agronomists. Although these experts were not at first always well received in the countryside, they provided valuable services to farmers. Through lectures, demonstrations, exhibitions, and contests, they persuaded farmers to make gradual changes in their methods. For instance, the use of good breeding stock, along with improved feed for the herds, led to an increase in milk production, despite a decrease in the number of cows. The agronomists' work would show even greater results, however, after World War II.

When the federal subsidy was frozen after 1919, and withdrawn five years later, the ministry had to draw more heavily on the provincial treasury. The amount voted for agriculture by the Legislative Assembly almost doubled between 1919 and 1923 and continued to rise after that. Although the Service Agronomique was an important item in the budget, the various programs to stimulate agriculture accounted for most of it. In 1927–28 the ministry's budgetary appropriation exceeded $2 million, whereas 20 years earlier it had been only $228,000.

Among the noteworthy measures adopted during Caron's term of office were the act passed in 1915 providing for the compulsory inspection of butter and cheese factories, the organization of short courses in agriculture for farmers, the establishment of demonstration farms in various places across the province, and the opening in Rimouski in 1926 of the first agricultural middle school to train model farmers. He also encouraged poultry farming and fruit growing, but his greatest source of pride was the agricultural cooperatives which proliferated from 1910. The earliest ones had been the work of Gigault, as Caron's opponents never failed to remind him, but he soon embraced the system and consistently supported the movement throughout his career. In particular, he gave it greater cohesion by forcing the three central

cooperatives to amalgamate. The Coopérative Centrale des Agriculteurs de Québec, formed in 1910 as the Société Coopérative Agricole des Fromagers de Québec, had enabled producers to obtain a fair price for the province's cheese, which had fallen out of favour on the British market. The Comptoir Coopératif de Montréal, founded in 1913, had specialized in selling merchandise to farmers for use in their farming operations. The Société Coopérative Agricole des Producteurs de Semences de Québec had been set up in 1914 and was based in Sainte-Rosalie. These three bodies merged to form a large provincial organization, the Société Coopérative Fédérée des Agriculteurs de la Province de Québec, better known as the Coopérative Fédérée de Québec or Quebec Federated Co-operative.

The three central cooperatives had provided good service to farmers, but as time went on competition between the first two was putting the movement's very existence at risk. Many people were hoping for a merger. Caron speeded matters up following the sale on 19 Oct. 1921 of Le Bulletin des agriculteurs (Montréal), the official organ of the Coopérative Centrale des Agriculteurs, to a group led by agronomists Firmin Létourneau and Joseph-Noé PONTON which supported the United Farmers. A movement that had developed first in the western provinces [see James Speakman*], the United Farmers had gained considerable ground in Quebec beginning in 1918, and the minister feared it would come to control the province's cooperatives. He manoeuvred in such a way as to have the directors of the Coopérative Centrale who had agreed to the sale replaced by men who were utterly loyal to him. He then had his proposal for a merger ratified by the directors of the three cooperatives and submitted it for approval by the shareholders at a hastily called meeting on 31 Oct. 1922. The statute incorporating the Société Coopérative Fédérée des Agriculteurs de la Province de Québec was enacted on 29 December. The cooperative's first charter granted the minister substantial powers, tantamount to putting it under his supervision. Caron also appointed the ministry's accountant to be the manager of the cooperative. These decisions were widely criticized in newspapers not of the Liberal persuasion.

Caron did not show the same broadmindedness in party politics as he did in the administration of his ministry. Responsible for ensuring support for the Liberal party in rural constituencies, he had every reason to fear the rise of the United Farmers at the beginning of the 1920s. Even after its leaders had been defeated at the polls and had redirected their energies towards organizing farmers' unions, he continued to fight them relentlessly, a more questionable stance on his part. This ideological battle turned into a personality conflict between Caron and Ponton.

These events cast a cloud over the last part of

Caron's career as a minister. To make matters worse, he suffered from serious stomach ailments, something not calculated to improve his disposition. Agronomist Jean-Charles Magnan, who was present in 1929 when Caron bade farewell to the staff of the ministry he had run for nearly 20 years, noted: "That day, he showed himself as fatherly, humble, and human. His heartfelt and friendly words moved us deeply. He was revealing himself in a new light, exhibiting genuine qualities of kindness, generosity, and sympathy. ... When he left, we were almost beginning to miss him."

A man of great integrity in cabinets that were not always above reproach, Caron was a loyal colleague of Sir Lomer Gouin and his successor, Louis-Alexandre Taschereau*. He referred to himself as Gouin's "political pupil," and kept up his friendship with him until the end of his life. Taschereau recognized his services by appointing him to the Legislative Council on 23 Dec. 1927, so that he could continue as minister of agriculture despite his health problems. Late in 1929, irritated by statements made by his ambitious successor, Joseph-Léonide PERRON, implying that nothing had been done for agriculture in Quebec until then, Caron obtained Taschereau's assurance that these remarks had in no way lessened the confidence he had always shown in him.

Possessed of keen intelligence and biting wit, Caron was a fine orator and also a glutton for work – he is said to have typed most of his own correspondence. He was an effective minister and a formidable debater. On the other hand, he was ill served by his stubbornness, which ruled out any compromise with his opponents. He had, however, a clear understanding of the problems of rural life. More than any previous minister he helped to popularize agricultural knowledge. Although the cooperatives did not owe their origins to him, he made them a key instrument in the province's agricultural policy during his term of office. Even after he was appointed minister of agriculture, he continued to go to Sainte-Louise, where his land was being worked by a farmer. According to a friend of the family, he liked to chat with his fellow parishioners, who had no hesitation in coming to him with their problems after mass or at his home. He took great pride in his rural roots, and debaters on both sides of the Legislative Assembly had to acknowledge his competence in agricultural matters.

Forced to leave politics in April 1929 for reasons of health, Joseph-Édouard Caron accepted the office of vice-president of the Quebec Liquor Commission. He died in July of the following year at the age of 64, leaving his heirs an estate valued at nearly $180,000, including a portfolio of some $50,000, consisting mainly of shares in mining companies. In 1918 the Université Laval had recognized Caron by conferring on him an honorary doctorate in agricultural science.

In 1928 his son Amédée had succeeded him as the MLA for Îles-de-la-Madeleine.

JACQUES SAINT-PIERRE

ANQ-Q, CE302-S20, 2 août 1897; S25, 10 janv. 1866, 3 juill. 1888; E9, S100, SS1, SSS1, 1982-10-004/7, dossier 3233/12; /8, dossier 3163/13; /10, dossier 3280/23; P350/1, 29 nov., 7 déc. 1929. Arch. de la Côte-du-Sud et du Collège de Sainte-Anne Enr. (La Pocatière, Qué.), F129 (famille Destroismaisons), 512/2, 512/13, 512/74. LAC, MG 27, III, B4, 27: 13508–35 (mfm. at ANQ-Q). *L'Action catholique* (Québec), 17 juill. 1930. *Le Soleil*, 18 janv. 1921, 17 juill. 1930. Claude Beauchamp, "Les débuts de la coopération et du syndicalisme agricoles, 1900–1930: quelques éléments de la pratique," *Recherches sociographiques* (Québec), 20 (1979): 337–81. *BCF*, 1929: 104. *DPQ*. Nicole Lacelle, *"Le Bulletin des agriculteurs," 1921–1929: les visages d'un journal* (Montréal, [1981?]). A[rmand] L[étourneau], "Joseph Édouard Caron, 1866–1930," *Le Journal d'agriculture* (Montréal), 34 (1930–31): 17. J.-C. Magnan, *Confidences* (Montréal, [1960]), 133–36; *Le monde agricole* (Montréal, 1972), 79–81. Qué., Assemblée Législative, *Débats*, 1902–12, 1924; Assemblée Nationale, *Les grands débats parlementaires, 1792–1992*, Réal Bélanger *et al.*, compil. (Sainte-Foy, Qué., 1994), 209–11; Parl., *Doc. de la session*, rapport du ministre de l'agriculture, 1910–30. Rumilly, *Hist. de la prov. de Québec*, vols.14–31. *Ste-Louise-des-Aulnaies, 1859–1984: album-souvenir* (Sainte-Louise, Qué., 1984), 115, 118–19. Jacques Saint-Pierre, *Histoire de la Coopérative fédérée: l'industrie de la terre* (Québec, 1997).

CARRUTHERS, JAMES, grain merchant and financier; b. 13 Aug. 1853 in Toronto, son of Andrew and Janet Carruthers; m. there 9 Feb. 1875 Louisa Coleman, and they had three sons; d. 19 Sept. 1924 in Montreal.

James Carruthers was born into a family of Scottish immigrants from the Dumfries region who came to Toronto towards the end of the 1840s. His father worked for a long time for the mail service of the Grand Trunk Railway Company, earning enough to buy a house. Despite his modest origins and apparently only a few years of education, Carruthers was to have a brilliant career as a businessman, skilfully turning his varied professional experiences to good advantage.

Carruthers probably had his first contact with the grain business at the beginning of the 1870s, when he went to work for the Toronto firm of T. C. Chisholm. Around 1875 he was hired by the Montreal and Toronto grain merchants Crane and Baird, and he was in charge of the company's Toronto office. At the time, barley was moving through this port in large quantities, and wheat was just starting to be produced in western Canada. He became a partner in the firm in 1879 but left it in 1885 to join with James Sylvester Norris in founding a grain trading company, Norris and Carruthers. Norris lived in Montreal, where the company owned an office and a warehouse, while

Carruthers

Carruthers lived in Toronto, where it rented premises in the Board of Trade building. At almost the same time, the first shipments of western grain reached Montreal, thanks to the link between Winnipeg and Port Arthur (Thunder Bay), Ont., established by the Canadian Pacific Railway Company in 1883. Norris and Carruthers dissolved their partnership towards the end of 1893, and the latter immediately founded the company that would become the largest grain exporting firm in Canada, James Carruthers and Company.

By the mid 1890s Carruthers was a prosperous merchant, living in an elegant neo-Romanesque residence on Toronto's prestigious Jarvis Street. His firm had offices in Montreal, Toronto, and Winnipeg, and would soon open one in New York. In 1898 he also became a shareholder in a large grain elevator company in Manitoba. In addition Carruthers was very active in the chambers of commerce and grain exchanges in Canada and the northern United States, and he made numerous business trips to Great Britain. This extensive network was very useful to him from 1900 to 1920, when exports of Canadian wheat became the engine of Canada's economic growth. He carved out the lion's share of this trade for himself, and by the early 1910s he became known as "Canada's Wheat King."

The grain export business naturally led Carruthers to collaborate with various maritime shipping companies. This sector was completely reorganized in 1913, when Canadian and British businessmen formed Canada Steamship Lines by purchasing and merging a number of shipping companies, including the Richelieu and Ontario Navigation Company. The new investors, who had a big stake in the grain business, chose as their president its most eminent representative, James Carruthers. In 1913 he had to answer critics anxious about the creation of this quasi-monopoly. Then in November the brand new, ultra-modern freighter *James Carruthers* sank on the Great Lakes, with its cargo of grain, during a violent storm. He resigned in 1919 after opposing the boards of directors in Montreal and London, England, which were recommending the payment of generous dividends at a time when he wanted to build up a large reserve as a hedge against the volatility of the Canadian wheat market. As it turned out, the price of wheat collapsed at the beginning of the 1920s.

Carruthers was famous also for his activity in the financial and industrial sectors. He had been first vice-president of the Sovereign Bank of Canada in 1902 and was a director of the Dominion Bank from 1907 to 1923. He also had interests in insurance and trust companies. At the same time, he had investments in, among other things, the mining industry – including a coalmine on Vancouver Island – and the largest fish refrigerating company in Prince Rupert, B.C.

As a grain merchant, Carruthers expressed his opinion on several important political issues, generally through the press. He supported protective tariffs, a system favouring the Canadian bourgeoisie to which he belonged. Conversely, in 1911 he firmly opposed the plans for commercial reciprocity put forward by the government of Sir Wilfrid Laurier*, predicting, among other things, that the Montreal malt industry would begin processing Russian barley instead of Canadian. The western farmers, however, did not fear competition and even called for free trade with the United States. In the face of the determination they showed, in 1913 Carruthers had to change his views. During World War I he took part in all the political discussions to ensure that the Allies would have the supplies they needed – to the considerable benefit of James Carruthers and Company Limited.

James and Louisa Carruthers had three sons, all of whom worked in his businesses. The eldest, George Andrew, was in charge of the company's Winnipeg office and later enlisted in the army. The other two died very young, Edgar around 1907 and William in 1915. Shortly after Edgar's death, James Carruthers left Toronto and settled permanently in Montreal, which by then had become the country's principal grain port. He and his wife lived in new apartments and stylish hotels, including the Ritz-Carlton. He remained active in the business world, made substantial donations to hospitals, and purchased military *matériel* for the Canadian army during World War I. He was a keen sportsman and between 1906 and 1908 he and Sir Hugh Montagu Allan* bought large parcels of land on which the Montreal Jockey Club's racetrack was built. Many of the Montreal bourgeoisie, as well as an impressive number of dignitaries, attended his funeral in September 1924.

The enormous success enjoyed by James Carruthers stemmed largely from his ability to take advantage of a favourable combination of circumstances. At the time of his death, the grain business was still a commercial sector that could attract his grandson, George Andrew Carruthers, and he entered James Carruthers and Company Limited in Winnipeg in 1923.

GUY MONGRAIN

ANQ-M, CN601-S480, 26 avril 1906; TP11, S2, SS20, SSS48, vol.8-o, 18 sept. 1879, no.806; vol.12-o, 12 mars 1885, no.30; vol.13-o, 13 déc. 1886, nos.134–35; vol.23-o, 25 juin 1902, no.127. AO, RG 22-305, no.2557; RG 80-5-0-54, no.10984. LAC, RG 31, C1, 1871, 1881, 1901, Toronto, St James' ward, div.6. Palais de Justice, Montréal, Cour supérieure, Greffes, R. H. Barron, 30 mars, 26 juill. 1906; 27 août 1908; H. M. Marler, 17 nov. 1908. *Gazette* (Montreal), 5 June 1897; 12 Feb. 1919; 20, 23 Sept. 1924. *Globe* (Toronto), 20 Sept. 1924. *Manitoba Free Press*, 20 Sept. 1924. *Montreal Daily Star*, 12 Feb. 1919, 20 Sept. 1924. *La Presse*, 12 févr. 1919, 20 sept. 1924. G. M. Adam, *Toronto, old and new: a memorial volume* ... (Toronto, 1891; repr. 1972). C. W. Anderson, *Grain: the entrepreneurs* (Winnipeg, 1991). *Annual financial rev.* (Toronto and Montreal), 1901–24. *Canadian annual rev.*, 1902–24. *Canadian history makers* ... (Montreal, 1913). T. E. Champion, *The Methodist churches of Toronto* (Toronto, 1899). E. A. Collard, *Passage to the sea: the story of Canada Steamship Lines* (Toronto, 1991). *Directories*, Montreal, 1880–1924; Toronto, 1846–1909. *Encyclopaedia of Canadian biography* ... , vol.2. V. C. Fowke, *The National Policy and the wheat economy* (Toronto, 1957). Thomas Galbraith, *General financial and trade review of the city of Toronto for 1880* ([Toronto], 1881). Ross Hamilton, *Prominent men of Canada, 1931–32* (Montreal, [1932?]). D. C. Masters, *The rise of Toronto, 1850–1890* (Toronto, 1947). *Montreal, old [and] new: entertaining, convincing, fascinating; a unique guide for the managing editor*, ed. Lorenzo Prince *et al.* (Montreal, n.d.). *Prominent people of the province of Quebec, 1923–24* (Montreal, n.d.). Benjamin Sulte *et al.*, *A history of Quebec, its resources and its people* (2v., Montreal, 1908), 2. A. S. Thompson, *Jarvis Street: a story of triumph and tragedy* (Toronto, 1980). C. F. Wilson, *A century of Canadian grain: government policy to 1951* (Saskatoon, 1978).

CARSON, WILLIAM OLIVER, librarian and civil servant; b. 8 March 1874 in London, Ont., son of William John Carson, a teacher, and Flora McDonald; m. there 31 Oct. 1900 Elma Pearl Ashwell (d. 16 Feb. 1965), and they had two daughters; d. 27 Sept. 1929 in Toronto and was buried in Mount Pleasant Cemetery, London.

William Oliver Carson attended schools in London, where his father became a principal and, in 1891, inspector of public schools. In his youth Carson worked as a photographer and successfully ran for alderman on city council. His appointment in December 1906 as librarian of the London Public Library was attributed by some to Conservative influence at the municipal level; however, Carson quickly demonstrated the requisite administrative talent. In 1908 he established open access to book stacks, including fiction, and two years later he reorganized the reference and reading rooms. He advocated in-service training for promising assistants and promoted the library by speaking to such groups as the London and Middlesex Historical Society. The addition of a children's room in 1913 was followed in 1915 by the appointment of a full-time children's librarian and the introduction of a story hour. On 23 Dec. 1915 a branch was opened in the east end of the city at Dundas and Rectory streets; moved in 1926 to the corner of Dufferin and Quebec, it would be renamed the W. O. Carson Branch Library in 1961 to commemorate his tenure as chief librarian.

Carson became an important figure in the Ontario Library Association. He joined the executive in 1911 as a councillor, served as president in 1914–15, and spoke regularly at its annual meetings. In 1912 he delivered a thoughtful paper on the benefits of librari-

ans' education and professional training. His presidential address in 1915 outlined his basic philosophy that strong local financing, capable leadership, efficient services, and good community relations would ensure the progress of public libraries and make them an effective national force.

The impression he made at the provincial level stood Carson in good stead when he applied for the post of inspector of public libraries in the Ontario Department of Education. Successful, he assumed his duties in April 1916. His office was responsible for public library development and worked with related institutions such as the Canadian Free Library for the Blind. It also dispensed grants to more than 30 historical, literary, and scientific societies. Despite the austerity of wartime Carson displayed vigour from the outset. His first reform was publication of the *Ontario Library Review and Book-Selection Guide*. Established in June 1916, funded by the provincial government, and distributed to all libraries, the *OLR* kept readers abreast of important issues bearing on libraries and served as an aid in the selection of books. The journal, to which Carson contributed numerous editorials and articles, was immediately popular. Carson also oversaw the extension of the department's existing training-school program to two months in 1917, with the aim of improving standards in librarianship.

The inspector undertook a reconsideration of all aspects of public library legislation, especially provincial and municipal financing (which had remained mostly unchanged since 1882). By early 1920 Carson had prepared a series of revisions to the Public Libraries Act. These provided for an enhanced municipal library rate set at a minimum of 50 cents per capita; better regulations governing qualifications for librarians; and more powers to the minister of education to improve travelling libraries, library training, and administrative standards. The new act was well received and the minimum per capita rate was an innovation emulated in other North American jurisdictions in subsequent decades.

Because he believed that the success of libraries depended upon qualified personnel, Carson had persuaded the department to extend library training to three months in 1919. The Toronto Public Library served as the home for the Training School for Librarianship (renamed the Ontario Library School in 1923) until 1927; Dorothy A. Thompson, hired by Carson to assist in the public libraries branch, was the instructor in charge from 1920 to 1927. To encourage candidates, no fees were charged, texts and supplies were provided, and a large portion of students' travelling expenses was reimbursed.

Although this short course in training satisfied most needs during the 1920s, Carson personally considered that a professional one-year course, following the example of library-school education at various American universities, was ideal. It was not, however, until September 1928 that a one-year academic program, under the directorship of Winifred Glen Barnstead*, began at the Ontario College of Education in arrangement with the University of Toronto. The Department of Education continued to assist with financing the school's operations; thus, the university granted diplomas to graduates and the department issued certificates.

Carson strengthened the role of the public libraries branch and expanded quarters for his staff. Much of their work consisted of assigning travelling libraries to rural areas and checking more than 500 annual library reports. The branch also issued *Reference work and reference works: containing hints on reference library service* ... in 1920, a pioneering Canadian library publication. At times, the inspector's role was not free from controversy. When the minister of education, Robert Henry GRANT, ordered Carson to conduct a special report on Hamilton Public Library in the early part of 1921, he reluctantly dissected the library's operations. His proposals for remedial action roused some disagreement but ultimately improved services.

In the 1920s Carson was active in the American Library Association, serving two terms on its council. He contributed a separate chapter on Canadian activities as one of seven commissioners in the ALA's 1924–26 landmark study of adult education. Although there was a growing interest in forming a Canadian library organization in affiliation with the ALA at the association's annual conference in Seattle in July 1925, where Carson presided over three gatherings of the Canadian members, and at the ALA's Toronto meeting of June 1927, he was unwilling to support this cause. The inspector, following the premier and minister of education, George Howard Ferguson*, was reluctant to endorse actions that were too closely connected with American-based organizations. Moreover, Carson did not believe that a national body could be successfully launched at the time. He favoured the step-by-step building up of provincial associations or councils from coast to coast to provide the basis for a national organization, taking as his model Ontario's example of cooperation between the OLA and the Department of Education. Carson's colleague George Herbert Locke*, chief librarian at the Toronto Public Library and ALA president in 1926–27, was much more active in promoting a Canadian body and a better representative of Ontario's library interests on the national stage.

Physically slight and rather frail, Carson was a determined, persuasive man whose sense of duty, integrity, and pragmatism could carry the day to the detriment of his own popularity. In religion he was a member of the Bloor Street Presbyterian (United) Church. His schooling, managerial concerns, tendency to move slowly, and local and provincial roles did not suit him for national undertakings, such as the formation of a Canadian library association. However, the London Public Library and the free libraries of Ontario benefited greatly from his ideas and efforts for almost a quarter century. His most lasting contributions were the *OLR*, which continued in print until 1982; the Public Libraries Act of 1920, which served as a framework for legislation until 1966; professional training and certification of librarians; and an expanded public libraries branch.

LORNE D. BRUCE

William Oliver Carson authored numerous articles, including "Reference work in the library," "The status and training of the public librarian," "The Canadian public library as a social force," and "Libraries in war-time and some factors that require consideration," Ontario Library Assoc., *Proc.* (Toronto), 1909: 22–35; 1912: 106–14; 1915: 36–42; 1917: 59–62; "The Ontario public library rate," American Library Assoc., *Bull.* (Chicago), 15 (1921): 126–28; "Canadian considerations," in *Libraries and adult education; report of a study made by the American Library Association* (Chicago, 1926), 93–102; and "Public libraries of Ontario," *Library Journal* (New York), 52 (1927): 451–56. His "Report of special inspection of the Hamilton Public Library" (typescript, 1921) and some related material is preserved in Hamilton Public Library, Special Coll. Dept. (Hamilton, Ont.), Arch. of the Hamilton Public Library, I-A-3. Material at the London Public Library (London, Ont.) includes annual reports and library board minutes, 1905–30, as well as a library and art museum scrapbook index, vol.1, 1914–64, and a photograph of Carson (reproduced in the author's *Free books for all* ... , *infra*).

AO, F 1195; RG 2-43, library inspectors' records, 1911–37; RG 2-146; RG 2-226; RG 2-227; RG 2-228; RG 2-232; RG 2-373; RG 80-5-0-281, no.10868; RG 80-8-0-1120, no.7043. L. [D.] Bruce, *Free books for all: the public library movement in Ontario, 1850–1930* (Toronto, 1994). G. H. Locke et al., "Mr. W. O. Carson," *Ontario Library Rev.* (Toronto), 14 (1929–30), no.2: 40–41. Ont., Legislature, *Sessional papers*, reports of the inspector of public libraries, in reports of the minister of education, 1916–28. *Standard dict. of Canadian biog.* (Roberts and Tunnell), 1. Basil Stuart-Stubbs, "1925: CLA launched ... in Seattle?" "1925: CLA launched ... in Seattle? part 2," "1927: CLA born again ... in Toronto?" and "1927–30: the muddle years [CLA]," *Feliciter* (Ottawa), 44 (1998), no.5: 20–25; no.6: 26–31; 45 (1999): 98–105, 122; 46 (2000): 148–49.

CARVELL, FRANK BROADSTREET, lawyer, businessman, and politician; b. 14 Aug. 1862 in Bloomfield, N.B., son of A. Bishop Carvell and Margaret Lindsay; m. 28 July 1887 Caroline B. Parks in Lakeville, N.B., and they had a daughter; d. 9 Aug. 1924 in Woodstock, N.B.

Frank Carvell was born in the village of Bloomfield, about a mile from the Maine border and twenty miles from Woodstock. His father was a farmer descended from loyalist stock; his mother was of Ulster Irish background. The family, which included altogether four boys and two girls, were devout Wesleyan Methodists and Frank attended church regularly throughout his life.

Carvell was educated in the public schools of Bloomfield and Woodstock and then taught school for a time, obtaining a first-class teacher's licence in December 1884. Two years after his marriage to Carrie Parks in 1887, he enrolled in Boston University. He was awarded the LLB degree with honours in 1890 and returned to Woodstock to practise law with Lewis Peter Fisher. Quickly successful, he earned a reputation as a powerful advocate and formidable prosecutor. He was elected to the Carleton County Council and became a well-known businessman who held considerable stock in the Woodstock Power Company and the Carleton Electric Company. He was also a director of the New Brunswick Telephone Company Limited. In due course he purchased the *Carleton Sentinel*, a vigorous voice for Liberalism in the province, and he was for a time a principal shareholder in the *Carleton Observer* as well. For several years he served in the 10th (Woodstock) Field Battery of the Canadian militia, retiring as a major in 1906. The following year he was gazetted a KC.

In 1899 Carvell had successfully contested the Carleton seat in the provincial election as a Liberal candidate. He resigned in the fall of 1900 to run for Carleton in the Canadian House of Commons and lost by 255 votes to the incumbent Conservative lumber merchant from Woodstock, Frederick Harding Hale. Carleton County had a population of just over 21,000 in 1901, and Woodstock, Carvell's home base, 3,644. A great majority in the county earned their livelihood from the land. Sturdy, hard-working rural people, practically all of whom had been born within the province, they were English-speaking and Protestant and many harboured a strong anti–Roman Catholic bias. Both locally and federally Carleton was long regarded as a Conservative stronghold. Carvell challenged the dominant religious and political sentiments of the county. In New Brunswick politics, where he was deeply engaged during his Ottawa years, he strongly championed a tight alliance between Roman Catholic Liberals, who dominated the northern half of the province, and Protestant Liberals in the south. In national politics he took the seat as a Liberal in 1904, when he had a majority of 274, and again in 1908 and 1911. In 1917, in the conscription election, Carvell would win the Victoria and Carleton seat as a Unionist (conscriptionist Liberal) by acclamation.

Until the government of Sir Wilfrid Laurier* was defeated in 1911, Carvell was a minor figure in Liberal affairs in Ottawa. Henry Robert Emmerson*, minister of railways and canals, was New Brunswick's spokesman in the party until he was forced to resign over a personal scandal in 1907. Carvell's friends then launched a campaign urging his appointment as New Brunswick's member in the cabinet. But Laurier had other petitioners too. "Every mail brings me a batch of letters, divided into two sets of opinion; one set for [William PUGSLEY] and the other for Carvell. The longer this is allowed to remain the worse it must be." Pugsley, who had been a senior member in the Liberal New Brunswick government since 1900 and was briefly premier in 1907, won out. Laurier appointed him minister of public works at the end of August. Two years later, in May, Pugsley was promoting Carvell to Laurier for an appointment to the Supreme Court of New Brunswick. Laurier was not enthusiastic and himself asked Carvell to stay in the House of Commons. Against his wife Carrie's wishes, Carvell agreed, telling Laurier that he had "decided to remain as requested."

After 1911, in opposition, Carvell acquired the prominence that had so long eluded him as a government backbencher. His sharp tongue and belligerent speaking style made him one of the most persistent and damning critics of Robert Laird Borden*'s government. A favourite target was the minister of militia and defence, Samuel HUGHES. Carvell was convinced that Hughes was extravagantly wasting the public's money. In the committee on supply in March 1912 he went after Hughes at every turn. The minister, he said, "talks about defending our homes, our wives, sisters and sweethearts, and all that tommyrot. He knows there is no danger of invasion. . . . The great trouble with my hon. friend and with his general staff is that they spend too much money on fuss and feathers and gold lace and not enough to teach young men how to shoot." Just days later Carvell turned his attention to Alfred Bishop Morine*, a former minister of finance and receiver of customs in Newfoundland. Borden had recently appointed him head of a commission to make recommendations on improving and reforming the public service. Carvell charged that Morine, while Newfoundland's finance minister, had also been on retainer as solicitor for Robert Gillespie Reid*, a railway contractor who had extensive dealings with the Newfoundland government. Morine quickly replied in the press that he had indeed been a legal adviser to Reid and "openly acted in that capacity," adding that other counsel for Reid had sat in a previous Newfoundland government. Borden, taken completely by surprise, announced that Carvell's allegations were of an "exceedingly grave character." Morine dispatched long memoranda to the prime minister, each more desperate than the last, seeking to refute Carvell's allegations. But within days he was gone, resigned, leaving Borden's prized Public Service Commission besmirched and Carvell with a new nickname: "Lord High Executioner."

Using the same combative tactics, Carvell joined

Carvell

New Brunswick Liberal organizers Edward S. Carter and Peter John Veniot* in forming the "Dark Lantern Brigade" to crusade against James Kidd FLEMMING's Conservative government. Flemming, who represented Carleton in the provincial house, was Carvell's "personal adversary." In March 1914 Carvell, in Ottawa, charged that a member of Flemming's caucus and promoter of the tiny Southhampton Railway in New Brunswick, James K. Pinder, had illegally received federal subsidies for building the road. A commission in July confirmed the charges. Meanwhile, backed by Carvell, Louis-Auguste Dugal, one of two Liberal members in the New Brunswick house, in April charged that Premier Flemming was involved in kickbacks to his party in the renewal of timber licences and in similar kickbacks from the contractors for the Saint John and Quebec Railway. Two provincial royal commissions, both chaired by judge Harrison Andrew McKeown*, were appointed to investigate the charges and Carvell served as lead counsel for Dugal. Made public in November, the commissions' reports exonerated Flemming on the charge that he had directed the kickback scheme for timber licence renewals but found that he had compelled a railway contractor to make a contribution to the party. The following month Flemming resigned from office and his seat in the legislature.

In parliament Carvell continued to snipe at the perceived follies and misdeeds of the Borden government. In 1915 John Dowsley REID, the minister of customs, "my sanctimonious friend," "a gentleman who could not do a political wrong if he wished, a gentleman who never employed an official excepting under the greatest of necessity," was accused of wasting precious public funds in wartime. William Thomas White*, the respected minister of finance who had raised tariffs to meet the increased expenditures of the war, was another target. Carvell was suspicious. The tariff increases, he insinuated, had less to do with war necessities than with paying for the spendthrift habits of Reid, Hughes, and their cronies on the government benches. "This country is at war," he lectured, and "the Government . . . have no right to tax the people white in order to satisfy and placate their political friends over the country." The following year Carvell was at the front of the opposition attack on corruption in the Shell Committee scandal. He accused the government of trying to "cover up their tracks and whitewash and cleanse the character of the Minister of Militia and Defence" while they "refused investigations of things which any reasonable intelligent man knows are so dishonest that they would stink in the nostrils of every man in Canada."

Now, when he had become a prominent party figure, the New Brunswick Liberals desperately wanted Carvell to come home and lead the listless and ineffective provincial party. Laurier would have none of it. "Carvell is too good a man to let go," he wrote. "I know he would be a tower of strength to our friends in New Brunswick, but we have the tower in Ottawa and must keep him."

In 1917, in the darkest days of the war, Carvell reached a decisive turning point in his political career. A long-time foe of the "curse of public ownership," he was adamantly opposed to the government takeover of the Canadian Northern Railway [see Sir William MACKENZIE]. And he was disgusted by the blatant political jobbery inherent in the War-time Elections Bill. As he told Laurier, "The Government are disfranchising Austrians, Germans, British subjects; they are disfranchising women; in fact, it seems to me that they are disfranchising anyone who they think will vote Liberal." Conscription was another matter and here Carvell dramatically broke with his leader and his party. "I look upon it as our duty to send all the men that we possibly can, in order to make this war the success that the whole civilized world is praying that it will be." He categorically dismissed any notion that, as the Liberal party proposed, a referendum be held before conscription was implemented. "There is not a stronger democrat in Canada than I am; there is no man who, under ordinary conditions, has greater faith in the people than I have. But I am constrained to come to the conclusion that we are at war, and this is not an ordinary political matter; it is a question of life or death for civilization."

As the Liberal party quarrelled and split over the issue, Borden approached Carvell about crossing the floor. Carvell refused. In late September 1917 he helped Laurier with a plan for what Laurier would do about conscription if he won the forthcoming election. Then, suddenly, Conservatives were awash in rumours that Laurier was going to resign and that Carvell would become the new leader of the Liberal party and join the Union government. New Brunswick Tories were appalled. They told Borden that Carvell would join the Union government only to "wreck it," that he could not command the support of Conservatives in his own constituency, and that the move would be "suicidal" for the party in the province. For his part, Laurier did not resign, but Carvell did join the Union government as minister of public works on 13 October. Borden told a New Brunswick Tory that "Carvell has been altogether too bitter in his political warfare" but "now that he has come in he comes in whole-heartedly." Laurier confessed that "Carvell is more and more an enigma for me."

Carvell had joined for the duration of the war. It was a difficult role for him and for his colleagues. His talent as a destructive critic had to be reined in for the responsibilities of governing. Several victims of his slashing attacks now sat with him in cabinet. He did not like them and they did not like him. Still, there was a job to do. He was chairman of the committee overseeing the construction of the new centre block of the Parliament Buildings following the disastrous fire of 1916. Just before the conscription election in December 1917, he and his old foe J. D. Reid were dispatched to Halifax to organize and supervise relief efforts after the Halifax explosion. Though in office, he remained an adamant opponent of government ownership and operation of railways, telling a Montreal audience in February 1918 that "Government operation of railways has been one of the most tragic failures this country has ever seen." As soon as the war was over he announced his opposition to the business profits tax, initiated in 1916 but an "improper" measure in peacetime. Yet he firmly believed in extending the scope of the income tax, arguing that the tax on higher incomes should be increased and that every person earning one thousand dollars should pay "not a very big tax, but enough to cause him to realize that he is helping to pay the taxes of this country." In his own department he took pride in cutting expenditures by 2 million dollars in fiscal 1917–18 and another 1.5 million in 1918–19. In the spring of 1919, however, with the war over and rising unrest in Canada, he defended increased expenditure on public works in major cities to keep people employed. This, he told the commons during the debate on the speech from the throne, would ensure that "we shall have no Bolshevism or anarchism and many of our difficulties will be solved." Then, almost as suddenly as he had entered the government, Carvell, in August 1919, announced his resignation.

Carvell was willing to rejoin the Liberals but they would not have him. As the Saint John *Telegraph Journal* later remarked, he had "burned his bridges behind him" in 1917. Instead, Borden offered and he accepted the chairmanship of the Board of Railway Commissioners. There, in a quasi-judicial position, regulating the railways, telegraphs, and telephones, Carvell and his fellow commissioners were responsible for the investigation of railway accidents (there were 2,093 in 1920 with 254 persons killed and 2,330 injured), authorizing the placement of railway stations and the level of service they would provide, and approving freight tariffs and telephone and telegraph rates. Most of the nearly 4,000 applications the board received annually were routine and handled by the staff. But the commissioners conducted investigations and public hearings and rendered written judgements in major cases. Here Carvell's legal training in Boston decades before came to the forefront in his carefully crafted decisions on complex issues.

It was a long way from the excitement and challenge of blistering attacks in opposition, even from the brief flirtation with power in the cabinet. Nevertheless, the appointment kept Carvell involved in public life while allowing him ample opportunity to return home to Woodstock on weekends to his family and his beloved farm on the outskirts of town, where he had four hundred head of purebred cattle. That was Carvell's routine in the early 1920s. Then, on a hot and humid Saturday, 9 Aug. 1924, just before dusk, he died. He had arrived from Ottawa in mid afternoon, gone to the farm, and walked to the far end of the property where his farmhands found him, dead of a stroke. Predeceased by his daughter, he was survived by his wife, one brother, and his two sisters.

Carvell had been a stern, combative man in public life, a man who took pleasure in punishing, withering criticism of his enemies. For all but a few he was aloof from supporters and colleagues and feared by his opponents. In his family life he was a sympathetic, loving, and generous husband and father, and he was passionately interested in his farm and cattle. Neither in public nor in private did he lose his serious demeanour. He seemed, even to friends, devoid of a strong sense of humour and the enjoyment of life. As his own newspaper, the *Carleton Sentinel*, observed, Frank Carvell "did not know how to play."

ROBERT CRAIG BROWN

The main collections of manuscripts documenting Carvell's career are held at the LAC: Sir Robert Laird Borden papers (MG 26, H), Sir George Eulas Foster papers (MG 27, II, D7), Sir Edward Kemp papers (MG 27, II, D9), Sir Wilfrid Laurier papers (MG 26, G), and Arthur Meighen papers (MG 26, I). Useful newspapers are the *Carleton Sentinel* (Woodstock, N.B.), *Gazette* (Montreal), *Globe* (Toronto), *Halifax Herald*, *Morning Chronicle* (Halifax), *Ottawa Citizen*, *Ottawa Evening Journal*, *Telegraph-Journal* (Saint John), and *Woodstock Press*. R. C. Brown, *Robert Laird Borden: a biography* (2v., Toronto, 1975–80). R. C. Brown and Ramsay Cook, *Canada, 1896–1921: a nation transformed* (Toronto, 1974). Can., Census and Statistics Office, *Canada year book* (Ottawa), 1913; Dominion Bureau of Statistics, *Canada year book* (Ottawa), 1922/23; House of Commons, *Debates*, 1904–19; Parl., *Sessional papers*, report of the Board of Railway Commissioners, 1920–24; report of the minister of public works, 1918–19. *Canadian annual rev.*, 1901–24/25. A. T. Doyle, *Front benches & back rooms: a story of corruption, muckraking, raw partisanship and intrigue in New Brunswick* (Toronto, 1976). H. G. Thorburn, *Politics in New Brunswick* (Toronto, 1961).

CASHIN, Sir MICHAEL PATRICK, businessman, office holder, and politician; b. 29 Sept. 1864 in Cape Broyle, Nfld, son of Richard Cashin and Catherine Coady; m. 23 Oct. 1888 Gertrude Clare Mullowney in Witless Bay, Nfld, and they had four sons and one daughter; d. 30 Aug. 1926 in St John's.

Michael Cashin received his early schooling in Cape Broyle and during the summers crewed for his father, an inshore fisherman. After completing his education at St Patrick's Hall School and St Bonaventure's College in St John's, he worked there briefly as a clerk. In 1886 his brother John died. With a loan from St John's merchant Edgar Rennie Bowring,

Cashin

Michael took over, revitalized, and expanded his brother's fishing business at Cape Broyle. The business prospered, and Cashin's wife, Gertrude, played a significant role in it. Their activities included the provision of bait, ice, and other supplies to American and Nova Scotian banking vessels and the purchase of cod oil from them. In the early 1900s the Cashins and Bowring Brothers invested briefly in a developing whaling industry in Newfoundland and established a whaling factory at Cape Broyle. Bowrings had the controlling interest with the Cashins being responsible for the plant and workers.

Cashin was also the "King of the Wrecks." The eastern coast of the Avalon peninsula, and especially the area near Cape Race, has historically earned a reputation as a graveyard for ships. Salvaging material from shipwrecks was the responsibility of government officials known as wreck commissioners, who entered into agreements with local fishermen to save the cargoes. The spoils were split among the fishermen, the owners and underwriters, and the wreck commissioner. Cashin's association with Bowring Brothers, the exclusive agents for Lloyd's of London in Newfoundland, gave him the opportunity in the late 1890s and early 1900s to gain financially by salvaging wrecks. Through both personality and physical strength, he established his authority over the fishermen, who looked to the wrecks as a means of supplementing their incomes.

His wife's astute management of their business allowed Cashin to concentrate on a public career. He had entered politics in 1893 and won election as an independent to the House of Assembly for Ferryland, a district that would continue to return him by substantial majorities. Soon after taking his seat he joined the Liberal party of Prime Minister Sir William Vallance Whiteway*. Whiteway lost the 1897 election to Conservative leader Sir James Spearman Winter*, and Robert BOND assumed the leadership of the defeated Liberals in the assembly. The following year the Winter government signed a controversial contract with railway builder Robert Gillespie Reid*, and the Liberals split on the matter. Several, including Cashin, joined Bond's rival, St John's West MHA Edward Patrick Morris*, in supporting the contract. In 1900, however, Morris and Cashin returned to Bond's Liberal party, which in that year won a resounding electoral victory.

In March 1905 Cashin broke with Bond and sat as an independent Liberal. He disagreed with the government's Foreign Fishing Vessels Act of that year, which prohibited American vessels from purchasing bait or supplies, or engaging Newfoundland crews, within Newfoundland's territorial waters, a measure that threatened the livelihood of many of his constituents. He became a vocal critic of the government, the small group of Conservative representatives provid-

ing little opposition. In 1907, after Morris had also left the government, he and Cashin cooperated closely with the Conservatives, with Morris being the acknowledged alternative to Bond.

When Morris's newly formed People's party won election in 1909, Cashin became minister of finance and customs, a position he would hold until 1919. All his budget speeches would be written by Patrick Thomas MCGRATH, his closest political adviser. Cashin oversaw a period of great prosperity between 1909 and 1913, but it was a prosperity built in part on trade deficits. Government revenues depended generally on a customs tariff and Newfoundland imported more than it exported. The administration spent liberally on branch railways, including a line through Cashin's district from St John's to Trepassey. In 1913–14 and 1914–15 the government experienced budgetary shortfalls. After the outbreak of World War I, however, Newfoundland prospered from increased demands for its fishery products and there were substantial surpluses between 1915 and 1919. During the war Cashin served as vice-chairman of the Newfoundland Patriotic Fund and of the finance committee of the Patriotic Association of Newfoundland. He also supported the decision of the government of William Frederick Lloyd* to enact conscription in April 1918.

Lloyd had been brought into the government in 1917 when Morris formed a coalition with the opposition, which consisted of Lloyd's Liberals and seven representatives of the Fishermen's Protective Union under William Ford Coaker*. Following Morris's resignation on 31 Dec. 1917 to accept a peerage in Britain, Lloyd became prime minister in January. After the armistice in November 1918, there was no further rationale for the coalition. Anticipating a general election, which the assembly in April 1919 scheduled for November, and wishing to distance himself from the FPU's influence, Cashin moved to claim the leadership of the remnants of the People's party, whose members still constituted a majority in the assembly. On 20 May he moved a vote of no-confidence in his own government and the motion was seconded by the prime minister. The vote carried that day and on 22 May Cashin formed a new administration.

In the election on 3 November Cashin's newly named Liberal-Progressive party was soundly defeated by a coalition alliance headed by Coaker and Liberal leader Richard Anderson Squires*. Cashin presented a vigorous opposition in the assembly to Prime Minister Squires and his government. He was especially critical of Coaker, now minister of marine and fisheries, and his efforts to regulate the price of fish and the marketing of fish overseas.

In 1923 a combination of ill health and the need to broaden his party's appeal among Protestant voters brought Cashin's resignation as leader in favour of John Robert Bennett*. He nevertheless left his safe

Ferryland seat that year to run in the three-member district of St John's West, where Squires was a candidate. He placed second, just 11 votes ahead of Squires. The Squires government won re-election, but a series of scandals later in the year led it to resign. There then followed several brief administrations as political factions changed allegiance. Another election took place in 1924, but Cashin did not stand. He retired from public life because of continuing ill health, due evidently to diabetes. His son Peter John* was successful in his old district of Ferryland.

For his services during the war, Cashin had been created a KBE in 1918. In 1925 he received a honorary degree from Niagara University in Niagara Falls, N.Y., for his public career. "From the fishing boat to Prime Minister's chair he went," journalist Joseph Roberts Smallwood* wrote of him in 1926. "He started in common with every fisherman and he never forgot that such was his beginning. . . . With him down through his forty years of public endeavor he carried the wholesome tang of the sea."

MELVIN BAKER

Fishermen's Advocate (Port Union, Nfld), 3 Sept. 1926. Peter Cashin, *My life and times, 1890–1919* (Portugal Cove, Nfld, 1976); "Sir Patrick McGrath: a biography"(Canadian Broadcasting Corporation radio broadcast, St John's, 1967; transcript in Memorial Univ. of Nfld, Centre for Newfoundland Studies, St John's). *Encyclopedia of Nfld* (Smallwood et al.), 5: 636–37. I. D. H. McDonald, *"To each his own": William Coaker and the Fishermen's Protective Union in Newfoundland politics, 1908–1925*, ed. J. K. Hiller (St John's, 1987). *Newfoundland Quarterly* (St John's), 26 (1926–27), no.2: 24. S. J. R. Noel, *Politics in Newfoundland* (Toronto, 1971).

CASHMAN, ELLEN (also known as **Nellie Pioche** and **Irish Nellie**), miner, prospector, philanthropist, and businesswoman; b. *c.* 1845 near Queenstown (Cobh, Republic of Ireland), daughter of Fanny Cashman; d. unmarried 4 Jan. 1925 in Victoria.

With thousands of other desperate Irish Catholic immigrants, Nellie Cashman came to Boston with her mother and sister about 1860. They then moved west, making their home in San Francisco in 1869. It was there that Nellie and her mother contracted mining fever and they soon left for the silver camps of Nevada, stopping in Virginia City, the Comstock, and Pioche. In 1872 the Cashmans opened the Miner's Boarding House in Pioche, a venture that marked the beginning of Nellie's lifelong pattern of operating a small business to support her mining ventures. After only a year in Pioche, Nellie, with an otherwise all-male party of 200 Nevada prospectors, headed for the remote Cassiar gold-mining district of northern British Columbia. There, she later told reporters, she "alternately mined and kept a boarding house for miners," which she ran through the summer of 1873. In the

fall she relocated in Victoria, where she intended to winter in the milder climate of the coast.

While Cashman was sitting out the winter, news of a shortage of supplies and an outbreak of scurvy at a camp in the Cassiar incited her to action. After persuading six men to accompany her, she set out on a relief run against all odds. For 77 days they trudged through deep snow, surviving avalanches, extreme temperatures, and all manner of storms. Upon her arrival, Cashman nursed the scurvy victims and distributed food and supplies. She spent two years in the Cassiar, during which time she helped the Sisters of St Ann raise funds to build St Joseph's Hospital in Victoria [*see* Salomée Valois*]. Her heroic winter journey and her philanthropic commitment earned her the nicknames Miner's Angel and Angel of the Cassiar. Moreover, her colourful personality and quick wit established her as a favourite with journalists, who would follow her activities for many years. (Much of the information about her is difficult to verify because various newspapers reported wildly different stories.)

Cashman left the Cassiar in 1876 and toured the mining camps of the American west before arriving in 1879 in Tucson, in the Arizona Territory, to prospect and establish the Delmonico Restaurant. Tucson's boom was waning, however, and within a few months she pushed on to the new silver camp of Tombstone. Here Irish Nellie funded her mining ventures with a series of businesses that included a boot and shoe store, a grocery, a restaurant, a boarding house, and a hotel.

As she had done in British Columbia, she balanced her businesses and prospecting with charitable work. She raised money to establish St Mary's Hospital in Tucson in 1880 and a Roman Catholic church, a hospital, and the first public school in Tombstone between 1880 and 1885. In Tombstone she was also an active member of the Irish National Land League, which supported the needy families of Irish miners. After the death in 1884 of her sister, Frances, she acted briefly as foster mother to her five nieces and nephews. Her reputation for warm-heartedness would follow her for the rest of her life. Unlucky miners could almost always find a room and a meal at her establishments even if they could not pay, and miners without money for a new prospect could often negotiate a grubstake with her. She might have lived out her life in ease, but Tombstone's boom went bust in 1886 and her businesses collapsed. The following year she headed out for new eldorados, a prospecting tour that included New Mexico, Idaho, Wyoming, Mexico, South Africa, and new camps in Arizona.

In 1897, at her hotel in Yuma (Ariz.), Cashman heard of the great gold discoveries in Canada's Yukon territory [*see* Shaaw Tláa*]. She could not resist the call of the Klondike. As she told the *Arizona Daily Citizen* (Tucson) in September, she intended to leave as soon as she could organize a party of prospectors and raise

Cassé

$5,000. By February 1898 she and two male companions were in Victoria assembling supplies and planning their route northward. When asked by the Victoria *Daily Colonist* what a lady prospector might wear for such a journey, she shocked the journalist by replying, "I dress . . . in many respects as a man does, with long heavy trousers and rubber boots. Of course, when associating with strangers, I wear a long rubber coat. Skirts are out of the question up north as many women will find out before they reach the gold fields." Interestingly, all of the surviving pictures of Cashman show her wearing respectable full-length skirts and shirt-waists, characteristic of female attire of the period.

Cashman was among the 30,000 or more stampeders who descended on Dawson in the early summer of 1898. Like many others, she had arrived too late to stake a claim on the richest ground, though the one she purchased on Bonanza Creek yielded over $100,000. But wealth was fleeting for Nellie Cashman: "I spent every red cent of it buying other claims and prospecting the country. I went out with my dog team or on snow shoes all over that district looking for rich claims." As a female miner, Cashman was exceptional – in 1901 only one per cent of the miners in the Yukon were women. The largest group of mining women appear to have established claims only to increase family holdings. To support her mining habit during her residence in Dawson, Cashman operated a restaurant and later a grocery store in the Donovan Hotel, one of two run by female proprietors in Dawson in 1901 (the other 27 shops were owned by men, often as family enterprises).

From Dawson, Cashman followed the lure of gold to Alaska, first to Fairbanks in 1905 and then in 1907 to the Koyukuk region, where she mined and prospected into her late seventies. In the spring of 1924 she contracted double pneumonia and was hospitalized in Fairbanks; determined to come "home to die," she moved to St Joseph's Hospital in Victoria in October. She passed away there in January 1925 and was buried in Ross Bay Cemetery.

CHARLENE PORSILD

Arizona Hist. Soc., Southern Arizona Div. (Tucson), Photographs of Ellen Cashman, including negative no.1847. LAC, RG 31, C1, 1901, Dawson City, Yukon. Sisters of St Ann Arch. (Victoria), Photograph of Ellen Cashman. *Arizona Daily Citizen* (Tucson), 15 Sept. 1897. *Daily Arizona Citizen* (Tucson), 29 July 1879. *Daily Colonist* (Victoria), 15 Feb. 1898, 11 Jan. 1925. *Ely Record* (Pioche, Nev.), 4 Sept. 1872. Don Chaput, *Nellie Cashman and the North American mining frontier* (Tucson, 1995). *Directory*, San Francisco, 1869. Suzann Ledbetter, *Nellie Cashman: prospector and trailblazer* (El Paso, Tex., 1993). M. J. Mayer, *Klondike women: true tales of the 1897–98 gold rush* ([Athens, Ohio], 1989). C. [L.] Porsild, *Gamblers and dreamers: women, men, and community in the Klondike* (Vancouver, 1998). Sally Zanjani, *A mine of her own: women prospectors in the American west, 1850–1950* (Lincoln, Nebr., 1997).

CASSÉ, PIERRE-ZACHARIE. *See* LACASSE, ZACHARIE

CAUX, JEAN, known as **Cataline**, miner and packer; b. in France; d. 22 Oct. 1922 in Hazelton, B.C.

As Cataline, he is a larger-than-life, almost mythic figure in the history of British Columbia, commemorated by a statue at Williams Lake. As Jean Caux or John Cox (as his name was usually pronounced), he was a prominent, and the longest lasting, pack-train operator during the era of packing transportation (1858–1914) in the province. Despite the legends that envelope him, and the paucity of reliable sources, his career can be reconstructed with reasonable certainty.

A native of France, born about 1829 in the Pyrenees region (possibly at Oloron), Caux appeared in British Columbia as a miner on the Fraser River in 1858. He had probably come there, as did so many others, from the gold fields of California. By 1862 Cataline – the origin of the name is not clear though some sources link it to the Spanish region of Catalonia – had switched to running a pack-train of mules and horses, the indispensable means of supplying the gold mines of the Cariboo and later those of the Omineca and Cassiar districts. Beginning with three or four animals, he slowly built up the size of his train until, by 1869, he was a principal packer. The maximum size of his train was around 40 animals, though the number fluctuated from season to season. In the 1870s and 1880s he wintered his animals in the valleys west of Ashcroft and in the spring he moved them north to the terminus of the Cariboo wagon road at Quesnel. It served as the loading point for the cargoes that his pack-train carried, in perhaps two or three journeys each summer, into the northern parts of British Columbia. By the start of the 20th century Cataline had shifted his base north to Hazelton, at the junction of the Skeena and Bulkley rivers. From there he supplied the nine repeating stations between Hazelton and the Nass River on the Yukon telegraph line (after its completion in 1901) and the hard-rock mines in the far north.

By 1900 Cataline had become a legendary figure. Tall and broad set, he sported a flowing moustache and shoulder-length hair. His toughness, his resistance to cold, and his skill with a throwing knife were unequalled. When he took a drink of liquor, which he consumed in vast quantities, he would often massage the last drops into his hair. On the trail he always wore a sombrero, a frock coat, a stiff white shirt, and high leather boots in which he kept his knife. He would not take off his shirt until he reached his train's destination, where he would purchase a new one and discard the old. He had children with at least two indigenous women. Reputedly made a naturalized citizen by judge Matthew Baillie Begbie* at a chance meeting on the Cariboo road, Cataline could sign his name (as Jean Caux) but could not read or write; he depended upon others to compose his letters and telegrams. His speech was a mélange of languages. His pack-train crews were made up of men of indigenous, Chinese, European, and mixed descent. His feats as a packer, including carrying huge pieces of mining equipment over long distances in the late 1890s, were widely reported and admired. He was known for his reliability – no mine or station was too remote.

Cataline's qualities made him a legendary figure, and a poor businessman. He relied on loans from banks, but it was almost impossible to cost some shipments because of the vagaries of the weather and the condition of the trails. He accumulated no savings and about 1912 he was forced to sell his pack-train in order to meet his debts. He spent his last years at Hazelton, dependent on the charity of others, and died there in 1922. If Jean Caux was not, as sentiment would have it, "the last packer of British Columbia," he did embody the qualities of the pack-train crews – men and women on the margin of settled society – and his withdrawal from the transportation business coincided with the close of the packing era.

RODERICK J. BARMAN

BCA, E/C/B81.3; E/C/B172.2; E/E/C61; E/E/H85; E/E/M311; E/E/M963; GR-1372, F 1369, J. T. Pidwell, tolls collected at Clinton, 1869; GR-2025, 8: ff.231, 237; GR-3049, vol.1, mining licence, 19 Feb. 1859; MS-0676, 4, file 12; 9, file 19; MS-2018; VF42, frames 1197–99. LAC, RG 3, D-3, ser.6, vol.5 (mfm.). *Victoria Daily Times*, 27 Oct. 1922. R. J. Barman, "Packing in British Columbia: transport on a resource frontier," *Journal of Transport Hist.* (Manchester, Eng.), 21 (2000): 140–67. Sperry (Dutch) Cline, "Cataline," in *Pioneer days in British Columbia: a selection of historical articles from "BC Outdoors" magazine*, ed. Art Downs (4v., Surrey, B.C., 1973), 1: 98–103. *Directory*, Victoria, 1874: 89. Hilda Glynn-Ward [Hilda Glynn (Howard)], *The glamour of British Columbia* (Toronto, 1932), 116–17.

CAZENEUVE (Cazenuve), PAUL. *See* ALBA, GEORGES

CHADWICK, EDWARD MARION, lawyer, heraldist, and genealogist; b. 22 Sept. 1840 near Jerseyville in Ancaster Township, Upper Canada, third son of John Craven Chadwick and Louisa Bell; m. first 28 June 1864 Ellen Byrne Beatty in Toronto; m. there secondly 20 Feb. 1868 Maria Martha Fisher, and they had five sons and two daughters; d. there 15 Dec. 1921.

Marion Chadwick's father came to Upper Canada from Northern Ireland about 1837 and settled in Ancaster. Around 1850 the family moved to Guelph, where John Craven Chadwick served as a justice of the peace and was active in the Church of England. The extended Chadwick family were large landholders and very prominent in the Guelph area.

Marion could not have been much older than the minimum age of 16 when he began to study law in Toronto. At the time legal education was primarily a matter of apprenticeship to an established practitioner. Students were, however, given a list of readings on which they were examined by the Law Society of Upper Canada. Chadwick and a fellow student, Calvin Browne, compiled an impressive book, published in Toronto in 1862, to assist others in preparing for the society's questions. The authors pointed out that their work was to be used by the student "as an *aid* to the study of the books upon which he will be examined, but never to be read in *lieu* of them." This was the first of many books and pamphlets that Chadwick would write, although it was to be his only "law book."

Admitted as a solicitor in 1862, Chadwick was called to the bar the following year. In February 1863 he entered into partnership with William Henry Beatty*, who by the turn of the century would use his marital connection to the Gooderham and Worts families to make their firm the largest law firm in the country. They would be partners for almost 50 years. In 1864 Chadwick married Beatty's sister, Ellen Byrne. Regrettably, she died the following February at the age of 21, likely in childbirth.

Chadwick's legal practice focused on conveyancing and estates. Although he never applied to be made a KC, the honour eventually came to him in 1910. According to John Beverley Robinson, who joined the firm in 1918, Chadwick designed most of the forms used – deeds, powers of attorney, mortgages, and the like. He was also known for avoiding excess verbiage and ignoring punctuation, "claiming that if the words did not speak for themselves the deed was not properly drawn."

Chadwick was heavily involved in the affairs of the Church of England in Toronto, favouring the high church rather than the low, evangelical branch. He was a representative to diocesan and provincial synods, and beginning in 1883 he was a key player in a significant, albeit much troubled, project – the building of the Cathedral of St Alban the Martyr just north of the then city boundaries in the area which came to be known as the Annex. Sir William Pearce Howland*, who had previously owned the land, had sold it to a syndicate headed by W. H. Beatty and his own son Oliver Aiken; the syndicate in turn sold four and a half acres to the diocese and offered Bishop Arthur Sweatman* financial encouragement to begin his cathedral, intending that it should be the centrepiece of a new residential development. When the building had progressed enough, the partially completed structure began to be used for services. Chadwick moved into a house on Howland Avenue across from St Alban's, where he acted as lay canon and treasurer. After the project ran into financial difficulty, he was criticized for his multi-faceted role in it. Not only had he done the real estate and conveyancing work for the syndicate but he had served on the building committee of the cathedral and had pushed for his son William Craven Vaux to assume the role of architect. His response was a privately published pamphlet setting out the history of the project and naively, but sincerely, explaining his selfless motives.

Perhaps it is not surprising that, as a founder of a firm in which family connections were so important, Chadwick was a noted genealogist. As time went on and he began to lose his hearing, genealogical research consumed more and more of his energy. In part inspired by the centenary of the founding of the province, he wrote a work entitled *Ontarian families*. This extensive, two-volume study of United Empire Loyalist and other early families was published in Toronto in 1894–98. From 1898 to 1901 he continued his work in the *Ontarian Genealogist and Family Historian*, a quarterly journal. He also wrote a genealogical study of his own family, *The Chadwicks of Guelph and Toronto* . . . , which he privately published in 1914.

Chadwick was one of Canada's leading heraldists, and *Ontarian families* includes many coats of arms which he had researched and drawn. He was an active participant in debates about such subjects as whether there were laws that controlled the acquisition and regulation of coats of arms (he thought not). In 1901 he published *Ye armiger*, the first heraldic study from a Canadian perspective. He encouraged the use of Canadian flora and fauna in heraldry and was instrumental in securing the maple leaf as a Canadian national symbol. He also designed the shield for Saskatchewan (1905), the coat of arms of the General Synod of the Church of England in Canada (1908), and a new augmentation of the Ontario shield (1909).

Having grown up near the Six Nations Reserve, Chadwick had developed an interest in and sympathy for Canada's aboriginal peoples and had come to have many native friends. He was made an honorary chief of the Turtle clan of the Mohawk. The name Shagotyohgwisaks, meaning "one who seeks a gathering of the people," was given him for his advocacy of the formation of a Six Nations militia regiment. (He himself served as an officer in the Queen's Own Rifles from 1866 to 1882, retiring with the rank of major.) He collected native regalia, now housed in the Royal Ontario Museum, and wrote *The people of the longhouse* (Toronto, 1897) about the Iroquois and their genealogy, symbols, and customs.

Chadwick died at his home in Toronto on 15 Dec. 1921. It was only fitting that his funeral service, presided over by Bishop James Fielding Sweeney*, was held in St Alban's, the church he had worked to build. He was buried in St James' Cemetery.

C. IAN KYER

The guide for law students that Chadwick wrote with Calvin Browne was published under the title *Osgoode Hall examination questions; given at the examinations for call with and without honours, and for certificates of fitness, with concise answers* . . . (Toronto, 1862). His defence of the failed cathedral project was issued privately as *Monograph of the Cathedral of St. Alban the Martyr, 1920–21* (Toronto, 1921; copy in Anglican Church of Canada, Diocese of Toronto). Chadwick's *Ontarian families: genealogies of United-Empire-Loyalist and other pioneer families of Upper Canada* (2v., Toronto, 1894–98), has been reprinted a number of times, most recently in 1972. For further details concerning the items mentioned in the text and other writings by Chadwick, see CIHM, *Reg.*, and R. M. Black, *infra*.

On 22 May 1908 Chadwick donated to the government of Ontario a three-volume manuscript entitled "An ordinary of arms borne in the province of Ontario." The original, as well as a microfiche copy, is preserved in the Ontario Legislative Library, Toronto.

Anglican Church of Canada, Diocese of Toronto Arch., St Alban-the-Martyr (Toronto), records. Fasken Martineau DuMoulin Arch. (Toronto), J. B. Robinson, memoirs; uncredited newspaper clipping pasted into the firm's copy of E. M. Chadwick, *Ontarian families*, on the funeral service for Chadwick: "Honored in death: Bishop Sweeney pays high tribute at service in St. Alban's." Irish Law Soc. Arch. (Dublin), E. M. Chadwick to Violet Baker, 23 Sept. 1921 (copy in Fasken Martineau DuMoulin Arch.). Law Soc. of Upper Canada Arch. (Toronto), 1–5 (Convocation, rolls), barristers' roll, 1863, 1880. *Globe*, 16 Dec. 1921. *Toronto Daily Star*, 17 Dec. 1921. R. M. Black, "Shagotyohgwisaks: E. M. Chadwick and Canadian heraldry," *Heraldry in Canada* (Ottawa), 24 (1990), no.3: 2–17.

CHAMBERLAIN, THEODORE F., doctor, politician, businessman, and civil servant; b. 6 July 1838 in Smith's Mills (Harlem), Upper Canada, son of Dr Asher (Ashern) Augustus (Augustine) Chamberlain and Eliza Ann Toffy; m. 3 July 1862 Annetta Jane Parish in Farmersville (Athens), Upper Canada, and they had five children, of whom a son and a daughter survived infancy; d. 5 March 1927 in Chaffey's Lock, Ont.

The son of American parents who had settled as children in Leeds County, Upper Canada, Theodore Chamberlain received his early education at the local school in Bastard Township, supplemented by sabbath schools and lessons in Latin at home. In 1853, after two years as a merchant's clerk in nearby Elgin, he studied dentistry in Ottawa. He then practised in the Leeds area, Pawling, N.Y. (his mother's birthplace), and New York City, but returned to Canada in 1858 at his father's behest to pursue a medical degree at Queen's College in Kingston. He graduated in 1862 and hung his shingle in Morrisburg, on the St Lawrence River. Although he styled himself a "physician, surgeon and accouchear," he was, like many 19th-century doctors, a medical jack of all trades, running a drugstore (1866–73), teaching medical students, and acting as Morrisburg's officer of health, coroner for the United Counties of Stormont, Dundas and Glengarry (1868–79), and a consulting physician for life insurance companies.

As Chamberlain's practice prospered, he threw himself into municipal politics, becoming village councillor (1873–77, 1884–86), reeve (1877–81), and counties warden (1879–80). Additional to this activity was his superintendence of the local school board, a commission in the Leeds militia, a directorship in the Dundas Agricultural Association, and membership in the Methodist Church, masonic lodges, and temperance organizations. In provincial politics, he followed in the footsteps of his father, a Baldwinite reformer "of the old school." In 1879 he accepted the nomination of the Reform convention of Dundas as its candidate for the Legislative Assembly. Defeated by 81 votes, he ran federally in 1882 but again lost by a narrow margin.

These rejections, though disappointing, allowed Chamberlain to devote time to his expanding business interests, where family connections proved important. In 1873 he sold his drugstore and established the first of three cheese factories in partnership with his brother-in-law W. G. Parish. In the 1870s and 1880s he travelled a great deal, with frequent trips to the United States, but it was northern Ontario that captured his enduring interest. Many summers were spent hunting, prospecting, and surveying around Lake Superior, Georgian Bay, and Lake Nipissing. The Parry Sound and Muskoka districts, which Chamberlain visited as a tourist in search of the sublime and the untamed, also provided economic opportunities. He received "a handsome competence" from the sale of timber rights in 1872 and in 1877 he became a director of the Parry Sound Lumber Company, owned by another brother-in-law, Liberal MLA John Classon Miller*. In 1888 Chamberlain Township in the northerly Timiskaming district would be named in his honour.

The provincial contest of December 1886 proved a turning point in Chamberlain's political fortunes. Elected for Dundas, he kept a low profile as a new member of the government of Oliver Mowat*, voting with the majority, serving on the standing committees for railways and municipalities, and introducing a housekeeping amendment of the Municipal Act. His legislative career was cut short after only one session, when his return was contested and the ensuing by-election, in January 1888, was carried by James Pliny Whitney*. He was not forgotten by the Liberals, however. In 1890 he was named to fill the vacancy in the provincial inspectorate of asylums, prisons, and public charities (hospitals, refuges, and orphanages) caused by the death of Dr William T. O'Reilly. Chamberlain, who turned over his medical practice in Morrisburg to his son, Watson Parish, and began work as inspector of prisons and charities in October,

inherited a system created largely by John Woodburn Langmuir*. His 14-year tenure was characterized less by innovation than by the growth of the system. For instance, the number of hospitals receiving grants for the care of indigent patients under the Charity Aid Act ballooned from 16 to 61. Chamberlain's glowing, often platitudinous, reports satisfied his political masters, and helped the province sustain its boast that its system was second to none. Behind the reports, as his correspondence reveals, was an inspector who, committed to centralization, involved himself in the affairs of individual patients, oversaw every institutional expenditure (no matter how trivial), and held to a punishing schedule of inspectorial trips. In 1893 he displayed his detailed knowledge in a pamphlet aimed at resolving sectarian misunderstandings about the funding of Roman Catholic and Protestant charities.

Official satisfaction with the hospitals was not unexpected – most were new and Chamberlain's relationships with their administrators were cordial. As for the provincially funded prisons, concerns were occasionally raised about classification, recidivism, and rehabilitation, but few hard questions were asked so long as they continued to generate profits through work programs. The 51 county jails and lock-ups were of a different order. Most had been constructed in the Upper Canadian period, and Chamberlain was highly critical of their condition. Twice-annual inspections – usually by Chamberlain, often unannounced – were invariably followed by demands to county councils that rotting cells be repaired, kerosene lighting replaced with electricity, and connections made to municipal sewage systems. In 1892 he even ordered the jailer at Mattawa to mow the lawn. Changes were slow in coming, but, overall, material conditions in the jails improved significantly on Chamberlain's watch. Of greater concern was the use to which they were put. Throughout the 1890s over a quarter of all inmates were lunatics, paupers, and others committed under the Vagrants Act. A dismayed Chamberlain pointed in 1891 to the impossibility of properly classifying prisoners in such an environment, which he characterized as "inhuman, unchristian and unpatriotic." Although grants were available for erecting poorhouses, parsimonious local officials preferred the cheaper, more expedient solution of housing the destitute in the jails. Chamberlain eroded these savings by instructing that paupers be supplied with civilian clothing and improved diets. It was not long before he was threatening to use the courts to force county councils to construct proper accommodations. His greatest triumph came in 1903 when legislation required each county to erect a poorhouse by 1906.

Chamberlain did not remain in office to see the full fruition of his crusade. Leaving in 1904 to contest the federal election in Dundas, he was defeated after a "hot fight," but in 1906, at age 67, he secured another patronage plum: federal health inspector of public works. Between June 1906 and his resignation in March 1908, he monitored conditions in railway construction camps in the four western provinces, sleeping in tents and frequently travelling on foot as he enforced compliance with the Public Works Health Act. In 1909 he was hired by the Department of Indian Affairs to value the timber on the Dokis Indian Reserve near Lake Nipissing [see Migisi*]. When rights were auctioned in June 1909 – to benefit the band – Chamberlain himself paid $182,000 for a berth, which he logged to great profit.

His government service at an end, the indefatigable Chamberlain returned to Morrisburg, where he again worked as a physician, dispensed veterinary medicine, and, until 1919, ran a sanatorium out of his large residence. Widowed in July 1924, he died of pneumonia at his retirement cottage at Chaffey's Lock in 1927 and was buried in the family plot in Athens.

PATRICK J. CONNOR

Theodore F. Chamberlain is the author of *Aid to Protestant and Catholic hospitals: official statement by the inspector of hospitals and charities for Ontario; falsehoods exploded; the truth regarding the matter* ([Toronto, 1893]).

AO, F 1023; F 1941-18, vol.2; RG 22-179, no.8234; RG 55-1, liber 7: f.6; RG 63-A-10; RG 80-8-0-950, no.4383; RG 80-8-0-1066, no.19808; RG 80-27-2, 28: 63. LAC, RG 38, A-2, 418: 1127–30. *Athens Reporter and County of Leeds Advertiser* (Athens, Ont.), 10 March 1927. *Canadian Illustrated News* (Montreal), 2 March 1878. *Dundas County Herald* (Morrisburg, Ont.), 27 March 1879, 1 Jan. 1880. *Dundas Courier* (Morrisburg), 11 Jan. 1867. *Evening Recorder* (Brockville, Ont.), 14 Oct. 1904. *Morrisburg Courier*, 18 Dec. 1867, 29 April 1870. *Ottawa Citizen*, 23 July 1909. *Recorder and Times* (Brockville), 11 July 1924, 9 March 1927. Can., Parl., *Sessional papers*, reports of the Dept. of Agriculture, 1906/7–10. J. S. Carter, *The story of Dundas, being a history of the county of Dundas from 1784 to 1904* (Iroquois, Ont., 1905). *Cyclopædia of Canadian biog.* (Rose and Charlesworth), vols.1 and 3. J. G. Harkness, *Stormont, Dundas and Glengarry; a history, 1784–1945* (Oshawa, Ont., 1946). T. W. H. Leavitt, *History of Leeds and Grenville, Ontario, from 1749 to 1879 . . .* (Brockville, 1879; repr. Belleville, Ont., 1972). Ont., Legislature, *Journals*, 1887: 20; *Sessional papers*, 1873, no.11; 1874, no.39; reports of the inspector of asylums, prisons, and public charities, 1890–1905.

CHAMBERLIN, EDSON JOSEPH, railway official; b. 25 Aug. 1852 in Lancaster, N.H., son of Joseph Mark Chamberlin and Rae Ann ——; m. 1876 Sara Griffin Place in St Albans, Vt.; they had no children; d. 27 Aug. 1924 in Pasadena, Calif.

Edson J. Chamberlin was educated at local elementary schools and at the Montpelier Methodist Seminary in Montpelier, Vt. He entered the service of the Central Vermont Railroad in 1871, and worked in several junior positions before being appointed secretary to the president and the general manager. In 1884 he became superintendent of the Ogdensburg and Lake Champlain Railroad, which provided the Central Vermont with connections to the St Lawrence and the Great Lakes. He was also responsible for the ships of the Central Vermont that plied between Chicago and Ogdensburg, N.Y.

After two years with the Ogdensburg and Lake Champlain system – he would return to the Central Vermont as president in January 1913 – Chamberlin moved to Ottawa to become general manager on 1 Sept. 1886 of the much larger Canada Atlantic Railway, controlled by timber magnate John Rudolphus BOOTH. This railway, which enjoyed traffic exchanges with the Grand Trunk, the Northern, and the Central Vermont systems, served as a vital transportation link between the upper lakes and Lake Champlain. As general manager, Chamberlin also took an interest in timber operations in the Ottawa valley, which provided most of the railway's local freight; for 17 years he was president of the Colonial Lumber Company Limited, based in Pembroke, Ont.

Chamberlin developed a modest presence in Ottawa society. By the late 1890s he and his wife, an American, were living at 333 Metcalfe Street, and in 1897 Mrs Chamberlin was president of the Ottawa Decorative Art Society. A clubman and golfer, Edson was still mostly interested in railways; he was a director of the Montreal, Portland and Boston, but his primary focus was the CAR.

The strategic location of the CAR would make it a takeover target for all three of Canada's transcontinental systems: the long-established Canadian Pacific, the Canadian Northern, and the Grand Trunk Pacific/National Transcontinental. In mid 1904 negotiations were sufficiently advanced that an announcement of purchase by the Canadian Northern was widely anticipated. At the last minute, however, the federal government intervened and the CAR was acquired by the Grand Trunk Railway, effective 1 Jan. 1905. The sale was disappointing to many of those involved in the earlier negotiations, and resulted in Chamberlin's immediate resignation, though he would retain his position with Colonial Lumber and continue to maintain a residence in Ottawa. Following his abrupt departure from the CAR, he engaged in railway contracting in Canada, South America, and Mexico. He formed, for instance, the Standard Construction Company, which obtained contracts for sections of the Morelia and Tacambaro Railway through the state of Michoacán in Mexico. He was also the railway's president.

In 1909 the elevation of Charles Melville Hays* to the presidency of the Grand Trunk resulted in Chamberlin's appointment that year as vice-president and general manager of the Grand Trunk Pacific, an affiliated company whose main line was to extend from Winnipeg to Prince Rupert, B.C. The government-built National Transcontinental Railway, which the GTP in 1904 had agreed to lease once construction was completed, was to link the GTP and the Grand Trunk's eastern system. In 1909 both the GTP and the NTR were still being built, but the former had already become embroiled in several local disputes that tarnished its image in western Canada. Construction of its main line was being financially assisted by the federal and provincial governments. GTR officials, however, were disappointed when, mainly because of western demands, Ottawa also granted assistance to the rival Canadian Northern. There was insufficient western traffic to justify two new transcontinental systems. The GTP was particularly vulnerable: it was being squeezed in the south by the CPR and in the north by Canadian Northern branch lines. As a result, it never developed an adequate traffic base; its prospects were further undermined when construction costs on its lines and on the NTR significantly exceeded original estimates. The GTP could become profitable only if there were many years of sustained immigration and settlement.

A month after the unexpected death of C. M. Hays, when the *Titanic* sank in April 1912, the GTR's directors chose Chamberlin as his successor. (By this time he was evidently living in Winnipeg.) It was his misfortune to take over the presidency just when the affairs of the GTP and the NTR threatened to draw them, and the affiliated GTR, into a financial morass. Fear of a possible European war made it difficult and much more expensive to borrow money at a time when the GTP and the NTR were facing heavy construction costs. Restrictions on emigration by various European governments were reducing the flow of settlers to the west, and with the outbreak of war in 1914 the cost and availability of labour, rolling stock, and supplies would become extremely problematic. Chamberlin's skills fell short of the leadership needed to contend with these difficulties, which may well have been insurmountable. Cast by railway historian G. R. Stevens as a muddler of "mediocre" ability, in August 1913 Chamberlin unwisely, and publicly, confirmed the GTP's obligation to take over the NTR at its completion. (The last spike would be driven on 17 Nov. 1913.) He had a knack, moreover, for irritating key members of the federal cabinet, including finance minister William Thomas White*.

Chamberlin and other Grand Trunk officials responded to the crisis facing them in several ways. They attempted to reduce costs but felt they had to complete the main line and open it to traffic as quickly as possible. More troublesome were the terms under which the GTP was to lease the NTR, from Winnipeg to Moncton. In light of its huge cost overruns, this line could not be operated profitably,

and Chamberlin tried hard to alter or escape the terms of the lease, or at least delay the takeover by finding fault with work the government believed was satisfactory. The government did not back off. In January 1915 the minister of railways and canals, Francis Cochrane*, called on the GTP to assume responsibility for the eastern division without delay. Again Chamberlin prevaricated, and owing in part to his efforts the GTP never would take over the NTR.

Grand Trunk officials hoped the government would either take control of the western lines or allow the GTP to go into receivership without dragging the parent company into bankruptcy. Instead, in June 1916 the government appointed a royal commission to recommend solutions to the problems of the GTR/GTP/NTR and the Canadian Northern, which too had become heavily obligated to the government [*see* Sir William MACKENZIE]. That fall the commission gave Chamberlin a golden opportunity to state how his company "might have suffered hindrance in carrying out its programme." His written report, in G. R. Stevens's estimate, constituted an "appalling *gaffe*." Chamberlin's harsh criticism of the assistance given the Canadian Northern, his inflammatory rhetoric, and his vehement defence of GTR policies based on excessively optimistic projections of western development antagonized the commissioners, and key politicians and government officials as well. When Chamberlin later testified in person, he only managed to confirm the GTR's dire situation.

The commission reported in April 1917 but was divided over what course to take. The government decided in June to nationalize the Canadian Northern and to give $7.5 million to the GTP, a move that was tantamount to taking over the Grand Trunk system. Complicated and messy, this transfer would take another two years to accomplish, but it was clear that the GTR and its president had lost the battle. Elderly, angry, and in poor health, Chamberlin resigned on 29 Aug. 1917. It was left to his successor, Howard George Kelley, to obtain what shareholders thought was fair compensation.

Chamberlin spent the last years of his life in declining health in Pasadena, where he died in 1924. A Canadian Press dispatch announcing his death described him as "one of the most competent and successful railwaymen in the Dominion." Historians have rendered a much harsher judgement on his career.

THEODORE D. REGEHR

LAC, RG 31, C1, 1901, Ottawa, Central Ward, div.8: 25. *Globe*, 28 Aug. 1924. *New York Times*, 28 Aug. 1924. *Canadian men and women of the time* (Morgan; 1898 and 1912). A. W. Currie, *The Grand Trunk Railway of Canada* (Toronto, 1957). Frank Leonard, *A thousand blunders: the Grand Trunk Pacific Railway and northern British Columbia* (Vancouver, 1996). H. A. Lovett, *Canada and the Grand Trunk, 1829–1924* . . . ([Toronto, 1924]; repr. New York, 1981). J. N. Lowe, "Canada's third transcontinental railway: the Grand Trunk Pacific/National Transcontinental railways," *Journal of the West* (Los Angeles), 17 (1978), no.4: 52–61. *Poor's manual of railroads* (New York), 1909. G. R. Stevens, *Canadian National Railways* (2v., Toronto and Vancouver, 1960–62), 2. F. A. [A.] Talbot, *The making of a great Canadian railway . . . the construction of the nearly completed Grand Trunk Pacific Railway from the Atlantic to the Pacific* . . . (London, 1912). *Who's who and why*, 1919/20.

CHAMBERS, ERNEST JOHN, militia officer, journalist, author, and civil servant; b. 16 April 1862 in Penkridge, England, youngest son of Edward Thomas Chambers and Louisa Percy Davies; m. 31 Aug. 1898 Bertha Macmillan of Kingston, Ont., and they had a son and a daughter; d. 11 May 1925 in Vaudreuil, Que.

Ernest J. Chambers attended grammar school in Penkridge, and in 1870 the family immigrated to Canada, where his father would become headmaster of the British and Canadian School in Montreal. Chambers continued his education at the Prince Albert School in Saint-Henri-des-Tanneries (Montreal) and then at the High School of Montreal. During his youth he displayed an affinity for the militia: he progressed quickly to a captaincy in the Montreal High School Cadet Rifles and during the 1880s he was an officer in the 6th Battalion of Infantry (Fusiliers).

Like his brother Edward Thomas Davies*, Chambers became a journalist. As a field correspondent for the *Montreal Daily Star*, he journeyed west in 1885 to cover Major-General Frederick Dobson Middleton*'s drive to suppress the Métis uprising. He was a volunteer galloper at the battles of Fish Creek and Batoche (Sask.), and contributed to the operations against Big Bear [Mistahimaskwa*], for which efforts he was decorated. In 1888–89 he was managing editor and publisher of the *Calgary Herald*.

He subsequently returned to Montreal, where in 1893–96 he was joint proprietor and editor of the *Canadian Military Gazette*. The degree to which militarist and imperialist interests guided Chambers, who had resumed service with the 6th Battalion, is evident from the regimental histories he began producing in 1897. In *Origin and services of the 3rd (Montreal) Field Battery of Artillery* (Montreal, 1898), for example, he portrayed a unit that was proud to display its "determination to keep the Union Jack flying for all time over this broad Dominion." On the militia's formation in April 1903 of an intelligence corps, the Corps of Guides, Chambers became a captain and intelligence officer for Military District No.5 (Montreal and southwest Quebec). Chambers was also prominent in Montreal's musical circles. Associated with the Montreal Amateur Operatic Club and the choir of Christ Church Cathedral, in 1901 he had been appointed honorary secretary in Canada of two British bodies, the Royal Academy of Music and the Royal College of Music.

Chambers left Montreal for Ottawa as a result of his prestigious appointment on 1 March 1904 as gentleman usher of the Black Rod, a functionary in the Senate. His official presence increased four years later when he took on the editorship of the *Canadian parliamentary guide*. As well, in 1912 he became secretary of the Canadian branch of the Empire Parliamentary Association. On moving to Ottawa, Chambers had brought with him his attachment to the Corps of Guides, in which he was promoted major (1911), lieutenant-colonel (1915), and colonel (1917).

Following the eruption of World War I in 1914, the government had initiated the surveillance of international cable and wireless transmissions. In addition to his parliamentary duties, Chambers worked as a censor at military headquarters. Given his journalistic experience, he was occasionally called upon to speak to the press. Within a year, leakages of sensitive information forced the cabinet to tighten control: on 10 June 1915 the office of chief press censor was created by an order in council under the War Measures Act. Possessed of superb interpersonal skills, extensive contacts in the news world, and solid militia and imperial credentials, Chambers was named to the post, with authority to block any source criticizing military policy, promoting disaffection, aiding the enemy, or otherwise "hindering the successful prosecution of the war." To encourage cooperation he initially had instructions distributed widely to publishers, police services, government officials across Canada, and any party likely to handle information on the war.

Chambers proved untiring and unyielding in his efforts to shelter citizens from printed material that might compromise their commitment to the war, including accurate news of the gruesome realities of trench warfare. If newspapers wanted to print soldiers' correspondence, he insisted that unsullied images be conveyed. Some editors, such as Frederick William Field of the *Monetary Times* (Toronto), took the precaution of having Chambers screen letters. Heartily endorsed by the chief censor were innocuous selections such as "the trenches were not so bad," but when it came to one private's claim that "the man who said war was hell did not know anything about it, for it [was] far worse," he insisted that the scissors be applied. Regulations introduced between 1915 and 1918 gave him considerable discretion too in shaping the content of publicly viewed photographs and movies, theatrical productions, gramophone recordings, and even sheet music.

During his tenure, working usually with great tact, sometimes with heavy-handedness, Chambers banned 253 tracts; of these 222 came from the United States, 164 appeared in a language other than French or

English, and 93 espoused leftist philosophy. In his bans and surveillance, he reflected and reinforced intolerance of pacifism, official antipathy towards socialism, and strong nativist tendencies. At the outset of the war, Chambers had wanted to move forcefully against the foreign-language press, but his powers then were limited and his political masters were cautious. He did try several times to restrain criticism of the war by Henri Bourassa*'s *Le Devoir* (Montréal) but Prime Minister Sir Robert Laird Borden* intervened each time, fearing backlash. Chambers's powers nevertheless mounted steadily. An order in council in September 1918 allowed him to close down all publications in an "enemy language." Subsequent amendments extended his mandate to targets that had nothing to do with war. In the aftermath of the Winnipeg General Strike in 1919, for instance, the Yiddish *Volkstimme*, which had supported the strikers, was banned.

The position of chief press censor was dissolved at the end of 1919. Chambers, who transferred to the Guides' reserve list in April 1920, nonetheless continued to wage battle against those he perceived as enemies. He served, for instance, as an informal adviser to the Royal Canadian Mounted Police on "dangerous" left-wing tendencies in such publications as the *British Columbia Federationist* (Vancouver) and the *Searchlight* (Calgary).

When not tied to parliamentary duties, Chambers spent much of his time enjoying his favourite recreations in the Ottawa area and in Quebec: golf, yachting, shooting, and fishing. He edited the *Canadian parliamentary guide* and served as Black Rod until his death at his summer home in Vaudreuil, after a short pulmonary illness. An Anglican, he was buried in Mount Royal Cemetery in Montreal. Eulogies and obituaries focused less on his draconian achievements as a wartime censor and more on his literary output and service on Parliament Hill. As the *Ottawa Evening Journal* noted, "He fitted into Parliamentary ritual and symbolism with an appropriateness that none could excel."

JEFFREY A. KESHEN

Publications by Ernest John Chambers include *The Montreal Highland Cadets; being a record of the organization and development of a useful and interesting corps, with some notes on the cadet movements in Britain and Canada* (Montreal, 1901); *The Queen's Own Rifles of Canada; a history of a splendid regiment's origin, development and services . . .* (Toronto, 1901); *The Governor-General's Body Guard, a history of the origin, development and services of the senior cavalry regiment in the militia service of the Dominion of Canada . . .* (Toronto, 1902); *"The Duke of Cornwall's Own Rifles"; a regimental history of the Forty-Third Regiment, active militia of Canada* (Ottawa, 1903); *The 5th Regiment, Royal Scots of Canada Highlanders; a* *regimental history* (Montreal, 1904); *The book of Canada; illustrating the great dominion . . .* (Montreal, [1905]); *The Royal North-West Mounted Police: a corps history* (Montreal, 1906); and *The Canadian militia; a history of the origin and development of the force* (Montreal, [1907]).

LAC, MG 26, H; RG 6, E1. *Ottawa Evening Journal*, 12–13, 15 May 1925. W. A. Bausenhart, "The Ontario German language press and its suppression by order-in-council in 1918," *Canadian Ethnic Studies* (Calgary), 4 (1972), no.1/2: 35–48. Can., Dept. of Militia and Defence, *Militia list* (Ottawa), 1903–20. *Canadian annual rev.*, 1903: 412. *Canadian men and women of the time* (Morgan; 1912). *CPG*, 1905: 39; 1918: 87. *Canadian who's who*, 1910. *Cyclopædia of Canadian biog.* (Rose and Charlesworth), vol.3. W. Entz, "The suppression of the German language press in September 1918 (with special reference to the secular German language papers in western Canada)," *Canadian Ethnic Studies*, 8 (1976), no.2: 56–70. G. S. Kealey, "The early years of state surveillance of labour and the left in Canada: the institutional framework of the Royal Canadian Mounted Police security and intelligence apparatus, 1918–26," in *Espionage: past, present and future?* ed. W. K. Wark (London, 1994), 129–48; "State repression of labour and the left in Canada, 1914–20: the impact of the First World War," *CHR*, 73 (1992): 281–314. J. A. Keshen, *Propaganda and censorship during Canada's Great War* (Edmonton, 1996). Arja Pilli, *The Finnish-language press in Canada, 1901–1939: a study in the history of ethnic journalism* (Helsinki, 1982). *Who's who and why*, 1919/20. *Who's who in Canada*, 1922.

CHANG TOY ((**Chen Cai** in Mandarin), known also as **Chan Doe Gee (Chen Daozhi)** and **Chan Chang-Jin**, but generally as **Sam Kee (San Ji)**), labourer and businessman; b. 16 May 1857 in Cheong Pan village, Panyu county, Guangdong province (People's Republic of China); m. twice, and had at least six sons and two daughters; d. 1921.

Chang Toy was of Hakka origin, a member of an ethnic and linguistic minority in Guangdong province. Although family tradition claims that his parents were farmers, several factors suggest that they were members of the local elite, even if they did not have gentry status. When Chang was three years old, his father died. Normally such a death would be a severe economic setback for a peasant family, but the fact that Chang was still able to receive three years of schooling indicates that his family did not need his labour to survive and hence was relatively well off. The circumstances of his first marriage, arranged when he was a child so that his mother could keep his child bride as a servant, also imply a certain prosperity. High status is further suggested by an incident involving his elder brother Boon Bak. Accused of counterfeiting, Boon Bak successfully intervened with a district magistrate to have the officials who had come to arrest him reprimanded, and apparently the charges were dropped as well. Boon Bak, whatever his activities, must have been sufficiently wealthy or well connected to gain the favour of the magistrate. Along with Yee Bak, Chang's second eldest brother and eventual business associate, Boon Bak played an important role in Chang's upbringing, teaching him martial arts. This training appears to have instilled in him considerable self-confidence, which stood him in good stead, both in China and in Canada.

Leaving his wife in China, Chang came to British Columbia in 1874 as a contract labourer. Like many other migrants from Guangdong, he had agreed to work in a fish cannery for a season in exchange for his passage money. Unfavourable winds delayed his ship's arrival, so he had to work only for a month and a half to fulfil his contract. He then moved to Victoria, where he stayed for a short time at the Wing Chong Company. There he came to the attention of the proprietor, Chu* Lai, a Hakka from the same village. Chang declined an offer to join Chu's business, but the two became close friends. Chu would even arrange Chang's second marriage in 1892. Around 1876 he worked at a sawmill in New Westminster. While there, at the urging of the foreman, he used his martial arts training to knock down a white co-worker who had been harassing him and he thus earned the respect of his fellow workers. After a year at the sawmill Chang moved to Granville (Vancouver), where he bought an interest in a Chinese laundry, probably the Wah Chong laundry, which also sold a few Chinese groceries. Shortly after his arrival, Chang's partner sold him his interest in the store. Chang then arranged for the Wing Chong Company to be his wholesale supplier. His store quickly became a contact point for other Hakka and natives of Panyu in search of work. He started contracting their labour for land clearing, salmon canning, and sugar refining. Within a few years he was also carrying on a trade in charcoal, operating three charcoal burners. The charcoal was a by-product of the land-clearing operations and was readily marketed to the Canadian Pacific Railway as well as to local consumers. After the great fire of 1886 in Vancouver, Chang moved to Steveston, where he opened a store and continued labour contracting.

The Sam Kee Company, for which Chang is best known, was operating in Vancouver by the early 1890s. Chang was the principal partner in the firm, which became an extensive import and export business. It acted as a wholesaler of rice and of merchandise from China for businesses owned by natives of Guangdong and Anglo-Europeans alike, while at the same time exporting commodities such as salmon and salt herring from British Columbia to China and Japan. Chang was the main supplier of capital for some of the fish packers with whom he dealt. For others he acted as a purchaser of supplies. Still others rented land, buildings, or equipment from him. In 1907 the company's annual revenues were between $150,000 and $180,000 and it was one of the four most important firms in Vancouver's Chinatown. The firm's real estate holdings were also extensive. They included ten lots in Chinatown itself as well as lots in other parts of Vancouver and waterfront property and buildings in Nanaimo. In Vancouver it also owned five residential hotels in 1910 and operated another two for a German investor. These businesses were often fronted by Anglo-European factotums.

Chang's business activities brought him into considerable contact with whites, even though he spoke little or no English. The closeness of these relations was demonstrated after the anti-Asian riot of 1907 in Vancouver. During the night of 6–7 September, following a rally organized by the Asiatic Exclusion League, a mob rampaged through Chinatown. Chang responded by sending his two younger sons to stay in the homes of prominent Vancouver citizens Ewan Wainwright McLean and John Joseph Banfield. In another instance, after the Chinese revolution of 1911, Chang was able to pressure the British authorities in Hong Kong to intercede with the Chinese government in Canton to get a shipment of lumber which had been waylaid delivered to its proper destination. His close connections to the Anglo-European business establishment did not delude Chang as to the extent of anti-Chinese racism. He had also responded to the riot of 1907 by proceeding with his partner, Shum Moon, who was president of the Vancouver Chinese Benevolent Association, to local hardware merchants McLennan and McFeely [see Robert Purves MCLENNAN], where they purchased the firm's stock of revolvers to distribute to their fellow merchants. This activity occasioned considerable apprehension in the English-language community. At the same time Chang was not above profiting from the system of racial discrimination. By 1905 his company had become the Chinese agents for the Blue Funnel Line, which rivalled the CPR's ships on the trans-Pacific route. Chang's advertisements in Chinese specified that since the line had only one class of accommodation (unlike the Canadian Pacific) Chinese would face no discrimination on board.

Chang was also active within the Chinese community. He was one of a group of Chinese merchants who petitioned Vancouver's city hall in 1899 protesting against indiscriminate police raids in Chinatown. A founder of the Chinese Empire Reform Association [see YIP Sang] in 1900, he served as president of its Vancouver chapter. In 1905 he established the association's school and a suite for travelling scholars on the third floor of the Sam Kee Company building, sending his own children there. He was invited to be the first Chinese consul in 1908, but he refused on the grounds that his English was not good enough. Chang carried on business until 1920. He passed away the following year at an undetermined location.

Chang Toy was among the handful of migrants from

China to Canada during the 19th century who were able to parlay business acumen, hard work, and family and ethnic connections into a sizeable fortune. By the early 20th century he was one of the leading merchants of British Columbia. His business interests spanned both sides of the Pacific and extended beyond the Guangdong ethnic sector into the mainstream of the British Columbian economy.

TIMOTHY J. STANLEY

City of Vancouver Arch., Add. MSS 571 (Sam Kee Company papers). Private arch., Theodore Chang (Vancouver), [Bob Chan], "Sanji huo Chen Cai (1857–1921)" (MS, n.d.); translated into English as "Chang Toy or Sam Kee (1857–1921)" (MS, n.d.). *Vancouver Daily Province*, 9 Sept. 1907. Harry Con *et al.*, *From China to Canada: a history of the Chinese communities in Canada*, ed. Edgar Wickberg (Toronto, 1982; repr. 1988). *Directory*, B.C., 1882–85. Paul Yee, "Chinese business in Vancouver, 1886–1914" (MA thesis, Univ. of B.C., Vancouver, 1983); *Saltwater city: an illustrated history of the Chinese in Vancouver* (Vancouver, 1988); "Sam Kee: a Chinese business in early Vancouver," *BC Studies* (Vancouver), nos.69/70 (spring–summer 1986): 70–96.

CHAPUT, CHARLES (baptized **Charles-Benjamin-Léandre**), businessman; b. 14 Nov. 1841 in Montreal, son of Léandre Chaput and Hélène Saint-Denis; m. there first 23 Aug. 1865 Roseanne (Rose Anne) Smith (d. 1883), and they had five children; m. there secondly 21 Jan. 1885 Clara Turgeon, née Chevallier (d. 1893); m. there thirdly 26 Sept. 1894 Léda Patoine, widow of Adolphe Hamel, a merchant; d. 1 Feb. 1926 in Montreal.

Charles Chaput's father was originally from L'Assomption in Lower Canada; he settled in Montreal around 1832. In 1841 or 1842 he opened a retail grocery that initially also housed a tavern. The store was then situated in the West Ward on Rue des Commissaires, opposite the Sainte-Anne market. The tavern closed around 1850. About the same time, Léandre went into partnership with his brother-in-law Édouard Saint-Denis.

Charles did commercial studies in Montreal and received further instruction from a tutor in French, Pierre Garnot. In 1857, at the age of 16, he joined his father's firm as a clerk. He became a partner in 1862 and the business was renamed L. Chaput, Fils et Compagnie. When Léandre retired in 1876, Charles became head of it, with Édouard Saint-Denis. By 1896 he was in sole charge. Over the years the company had moved into wholesale business and from the 1890s this would be its only sphere of activity. At that time, food merchandising in Montreal was being spurred by improvements in rail transport, expansion in the food industry, and the rapid growth of the city's population. Several other food wholesalers set up in Montreal in the same period but L. Chaput, Fils et

Compagnie Limitée (the name under which the firm was incorporated in 1912) would remain one of the leading enterprises of this kind in the city until the mid 1920s.

For many years the sale of wine and spirits constituted a substantial part of the company's business and revenues, as it also was for its major competitors. When the Quebec Liquor Commission was set up in 1921, this source of income disappeared. Despite the loss, the firm's annual turnover amounted to $5 million in 1924, and its inventory was estimated at $1 million. Specializing in the importation of tea and coffee, as well as in the sale of popular pharmaceutical products, it had some 200 employees at this time, including 35 sales representatives who travelled all over Quebec and Ontario. Its products were also marketed in the Maritimes. According to *Le Devoir*, the firm had a fleet of 15 trucks that delivered goods within a 50-mile radius of Montreal. It also had a large warehouse in the north of the city on Rue Atlantic, and from 1889 a store with five storeys on Rue de Brésoles. Some of the products were packaged at the latter, a number of its own brands having been launched. It appears that it was one of the first wholesalers in the province of Quebec to adopt this practice, as well as one of the first companies to use bilingual labels.

In addition to losing the revenue from the sale of wine and spirits, the firm had to contend with the economic downturn that followed World War I. Canadian food wholesalers had trouble retaining their share of the market: business practices were changing and in the marketing of products they increasingly found that they were vying with the manufacturers themselves. Competition became fierce, and, as a result, many firms went under and there was a series of important mergers. Thus in 1926, a few weeks before the death of Charles Chaput, L. Chaput, Fils et Compagnie Limitée merged with one of its major competitors, Hudon, Hébert et Compagnie Limitée whose president was Zéphirin Hébert, the son of Charles-Polycarpe Hébert*, to form Hudon, Hébert et Chaput Limitée.

Up to this point Chaput's company had always been run by members of the family, along with several partners chosen from among former employees. The latter included Louis-Élie GEOFFRION, an important member of the firm from 1884 to 1912, and Ferdinand Prud'homme, a partner from 1896 and for many years the company's secretary-treasurer, a post he continued to hold in 1926. At the time of the merger, Charles Chaput was still president; his son Armand, who had been a partner since 1899, was vice-president and general manager; another son, Émile, a partner since 1909, was one of the directors. The share capital, estimated at $1 million in 1924, was also held by the Chaput family and its employees.

Success in the grocery business enabled Léandre Chaput and his son Charles to ascend the social ladder. The marriages contracted by some of the latter's children show that the family belonged to the elite in Montreal and indeed in Canada. Charles's eldest daughter, Rose-Anna, became the wife of Gabriel Marchand, a lawyer and son of Félix-Gabriel Marchand*, the premier of Quebec from 1897 to 1900; his son Émile married Rosalie Loranger, the daughter of a judge, Louis-Onésime Loranger*. Furthermore, the dignitaries present at Charles Chaput's funeral included Charles Duquette, the mayor of Montreal, senators Charles-Philippe Beaubien*, Frédéric-Ligori Béïque*, and Raoul Dandurand*, as well as Janvier-Arthur Vaillancourt, the president of the Banque Canadienne Nationale.

Although he never stood for election as the candidate of a political party, Charles Chaput nevertheless took an active part in municipal politics. He was one of the leaders of the Committee of Citizens in Montreal, which was formed in 1908 and was associated with the reform movement. Moreover, his business career was not confined to running the family firm. He was president of the Montreal Wholesale Grocers' Association, a member of the board of the Chambre de Commerce du District de Montréal (around 1894–96), a director and vice-president of the Montreal Board of Trade, and a director of the International Mercantile Agency. He served on the board of Ogilvie Flour Mills Company Limited from 1911 until his death, as well as on that of the Canada Life Assurance Company. He also took an interest in the financial sector, and was a director of the Banque d'Hochelaga from 1890 until 1900. Within these circles, Chaput became known as a person of integrity, "a man who spoke little and preferred to reflect," according to the newspaper *La Presse*. On his death, *Le Canada* (Montréal) referred to him as "one of the leading figures in the business world of the city."

SYLVIE TASCHEREAU

ANQ-M, CE601-S1, 23 août 1865, 21 janv. 1885; CE601-S6, 26 sept. 1894; CE601-S51, 15 avril 1839, 14 nov. 1841; TP11, S2, SS20, SSS48, vol.2 et 3-o, 19 févr. 1867, no.3880; vol.6-o, 11 mars 1876, nos.831–32; vol.11-o, 1er févr. 1884, no.227; vol.19-o, 1er févr. 1896, nos.11–12; vol.21-o, 1er févr. 1899, no.17, 23 août 1899, no.506; vol.29-o, 1er févr. 1909, no.237; vol.33-o, 1er févr. 1912, nos.119–20. *Le Canada* (Montréal), 2, 4 févr. 1926. *Le Devoir*, 23 août 1924; 2, 4 févr. 1926. *La Presse*, 1er févr. 1926. W. H. Atherton, *Montreal, 1534–1914* (3v., Montreal, 1914), 3: 656–60. Gilles Couvrette, "L'épiciers en gros de Montréal," *L'Actualité économique* ([Montréal]), 16 (1940–41): 118–37. *Directory, Montreal, 1842–1926*. Linteau, *Hist. de Montréal*. David Monod, *Store wars: shopkeepers and the culture of mass marketing, 1890–1939* (Toronto, 1996).

CHAREST, ELZÉAR (baptized **Tiburce-Elzéar**), architect and office holder; b. 4 June 1850 in Châ-

teau-Richer, Lower Canada, son of Tiburce Charest, a doctor, and Rose (Rosalie) Paquet; m. 3 July 1876 Elmire Bazin at Quebec, and they had 16 children; d. there 6 April 1927.

Elzéar Charest is listed as an architect in the Quebec City directories from 1875. In 1880, while still apprenticed to architect Joseph-Ferdinand Peachy*, he collaborated with sculptor Louis JOBIN in creating the allegorical float for the town of Beauport in the Saint-Jean-Baptiste parade. His early work as an architect on his own, which included several houses built between 1880 and 1885 in Saint-Jean ward and at Saint-Sauveur (Quebec), suggested he was destined to embrace the eclectic style prevalent towards the end of the 19th century. His first important public building, the Saint-Pierre market in Saint-Sauveur (1888), deviated little from the standard mansard-roof design established a few years earlier by architect Paul Cousin in the Montcalm market. On the other hand, Charest's plan for Zéphirin Paquet*'s department store on Rue Saint-Joseph in Quebec City (1890) is remarkable in several respects, with features that were surprisingly modern for the time; for example, this six-storey granite building was equipped with an elevator and electric lighting. However, the lack of discernible dominant elements in the façade shows how difficult it was to reconcile ornamental expression with the new rational values called for in a department store building. As well, when Charest was chosen in the competition for the construction of the new city hall at Quebec in 1890 (the jury was chaired by Eugène-Étienne Taché*) his plan, which was too reminiscent of the Second Empire decorative tradition, was soon dropped by the city council; after a long delay, it was replaced by a proposal from Georges-Émile TANGUAY (1894) that enjoyed the support of the city engineer, Charles Baillairgé*.

Following this repudiation, Charest was offered the post of director of the provincial Department of Public Works in 1891, probably as a form of compensation thought up by Taché, who was then deputy minister for crown lands. Charest succeeded engineer Jean-Baptiste Derome and would remain in charge of the department until 1915, serving under eight different ministers and several administrations. Principally responsible for the construction and maintenance of public buildings throughout the province, Charest took advantage of a situation he judged propitious for the invention of symbols expressing the identity of provincial institutions. To this end, he turned to the kind of heraldic and architectonic idiom introduced by the work of Taché and, to a lesser extent, by the beautification plans of Governor General Lord Dufferin [Blackwood*]. At the same time he devised a personal interpretation of the "fortress style" inspired by medieval castles that was characterized by the concentration of embellishment in the roofs and by the almost exclusive use of sheet metal. The courthouse in Hull, built between 1891 and 1894 and now no longer standing, was an excellent example of the fortress style. The ornamentation consisted solely, however, of sheet metal; the humble materials used were in sharp contrast to Charest's original ambition to impose a distinctive provincial style of architecture through a network of public buildings in small towns.

By choosing to focus on decorative details rather than develop a cohesive architectural style and, above all, by confining himself to a traditionalism out of touch with the political expectations of the day, Charest failed to entrench his proposals and as a result, by around 1910, he found himself to a certain extent professionally marginalized. In fact, for the construction of the courthouse at Sherbrooke (1904–6), he recycled the principal features of the design he had submitted 13 years earlier in the competition for the city hall at Quebec. In the Sherbrooke design, the fortress style was enhanced by reference to the symmetry and hierarchy of plans typical of the Second Empire. In the case of the École Normale of the Sisters of the Good Shepherd in Chicoutimi (1907), Charest opted for a building heavily marked by classical rhetoric, thereby acknowledging that the fortress style had failed to become a representative form of public building within the province of Quebec. The house he built for himself in Saint-Jean ward (804–10 Rue Richelieu, 1907), complete with its corner turret, would be the final expression of Charest's adventure in this type of ornamentation, an adventure that nevertheless remains a conspicuous contribution to the architectural originality of Quebec City.

PATRICK DIEUDONNÉ

ANQ-Q, CE301-S6, 4 juin 1850; S97, 3 juill. 1876. *L'Action catholique* (Québec), 6 avril 1927. *L'Événement*, 7 avril 1927. *Le Journal de Québec*, 30 nov. 1877; 27 mars, 5 juill. 1880; 5 mai 1881; 22 févr. 1883; 25 janv. 1884; 27 févr. 1886. *La Minerve*, 27 févr. 1886. *La Semaine commerciale* (Québec), 5 juill. 1907. *Le Soleil*, 7 avril 1927. Claude Bergeron, *Architectures du XXᵉ siècle au Québec* (Québec, 1989), 95. Robert Caron, *Inventaire des permis de construction des Archives de la ville de Québec, 1913–1930* (3v., Ottawa, 1980). Guy Coutu, *Chicoutimi: 150 ans d'images* ([Chicoutimi, Qué.], 1992), 222–23. Patrick Dieudonné, "Le style forteresse ou l'apport d'Elzéar Charest à l'éclectisme québécois," *Continuité* (Québec), 45 (automne 1989): 12–16. *Early Canadian court houses*, comp. Margaret Carter (Ottawa, 1983). Luc Noppen et al., *Québec monumental, 1890–1990* (Sillery, Qué., 1990), 78. Luc Noppen et Lucie K[oenig] Morisset, *Québec, de roc et de pierres: la capitale en architecture* (Sainte-Foy, Qué., [1998]), 85–88. J. R. Porter et Jean Bélisle, *La sculpture ancienne au Québec; trois siècles d'art religieux et profane* (Montréal, 1986), 237. Que., Parl., *Sessional papers*, report of the commissioner of public works and colonization, later the commissioner of colonization and public works, 1900–2.

CHASSÉ, HENRI (baptized **Marie-Joseph-Émilien-Henri**), journalist and officer; b. 30 Dec. 1885 at Quebec, son of Honoré Chassé, a lawyer, and Émilienne La Roque; m. there 11 Oct. 1920 Raymonde Tanguay, daughter of Georges Tanguay, a Quebec businessman, and they had three sons; d. 9 July 1928 at the Royal Victoria Hospital in Montreal.

Henri Chassé showed an interest in military life at an early age. By 15 March 1902 he was already a captain in the militia. The death of his father in 1903 forced him to interrupt his studies at the Petit Séminaire de Québec, where he had been enrolled since 1898. He presumably then went to work at the Imprimerie Chassé, which had been founded by his father and now was being run by his mother, who had become the head of a family of nine children. From 1 Feb. 1905 to July 1914 he would serve successively in the Signalling Corps, the 89th (Temiscouata and Rimouski) Regiment, and the 5th Field Artillery Brigade. In 1909 the Conservative owners of the printing house that produced the newspaper *L'Événement* suggested to Émilienne La Roque that they merge their company with hers. At the same time, they put her in charge of the newspaper, for which her husband had worked before founding *L'Avant-Garde* at Quebec in 1896; he had also written for the Quebec newspaper *Courrier du Canada*. In all likelihood Henri began his journalistic career at *L'Événement* shortly after the merger. He stayed at this job and had become the paper's news editor by the time World War I broke out. He was 28 years old. Within a few weeks he volunteered for overseas service.

In October 1914 Chassé was recruiting for the 22nd Infantry Battalion, which he joined officially on 6 November in Saint-Jean (Saint-Jean-sur-Richelieu), with the rank of lieutenant. This battalion would be the only French Canadian infantry unit to see action during World War I. Chassé was already so proud to be serving in the 22nd Battalion that the physician who examined him on 5 November noticed he had a tattoo of its crest: a beaver and the motto *Je me souviens*.

After months of training in Saint-Jean and then Amherst, N.S., Chassé embarked with his unit on the *Saxonia* on 15 March 1915. He was promoted captain during the battalion's stay in England that summer, and went to France with it on 15 September; he attained the rank of major and became second in command on 6 Oct. 1916. He returned to England on 4 April 1917 to take a third-level course for officers. On 15 August, during the battle for Hill 70 in France, he was in command of Company A. For the gallantry and courage he displayed on that occasion, he was awarded the Military Cross on 18 Oct. 1917. Chassé was reappointed second in command of the battalion on 6 Sept. 1918, and he led it during the occupation of the Faubourg Saint-Roch, on the outskirts of Cambrai, on 10 October. On 8 March 1919 he would receive the Distinguished Service Order for his leadership. Chassé had the honour of being in command of the battalion when it passed through the city of Bonn, Germany, in December 1918. After returning to Canada on 16 May 1919, he was demobilized on 30 September and settled at Quebec. He had been wounded in action twice.

Chassé was promoted to the rank of lieutenant-colonel on 25 July 1919 and became the first commanding officer of the 22nd Regiment of Canada's Permanent Force on 1 April 1920. It became the Royal 22nd Regiment on 1 June 1921, in recognition of the 22nd Battalion's valour under fire. Chassé received this honour when in command, and it had been preceded by another one on 25 March 1921, when Marshal Ferdinand Foch, commander-in-chief of the Allied armies from the end of March 1918 until the armistice on 11 November, had gladly accepted his invitation to become the regiment's honorary colonel.

Chassé relinquished command of the 22nd on 15 Sept. 1924 to become deputy adjutant and quartermaster general of Military District No.4; he probably moved to Montreal. He held this post until his death four years later from an attack of inflammatory rheumatism, which he is believed to have contracted in the trenches in Flanders. He was 42 years old.

A soldier and a man of action, Henri Chassé preferred life in the trenches to the monotony of the barracks. Motivated by a sense of duty, he chose to stay at the front in the spring of 1916, rather than return to Canada as second in command of the 178th Infantry Battalion. He distinguished himself by his zeal for work, good humour, and attachment to his unit and his men. He remains closely linked to the first ten years of the history of the French Canadian infantry regiment. He had the particular honour of overseeing the transition from the 22nd Battalion to the Royal 22nd Regiment. He and the other members of the battalion who accompanied him into the new regiment had succeeded in their aim: to make the second a worthy successor to the first. Two of Chassé's sons, Pierre and Henri, would later command the regiment's 1st Battalion.

JEAN-PIERRE GAGNON

Henri Chassé is the author of *Souvenirs de guerre* (Québec, 1920).

ANQ-Q, CE301-S97, 31 déc. 1885; Index BMS, dist. judiciaire de Québec, Notre-Dame de Québec, 11 oct. 1920. LAC, RG 150, Acc. 1992–93/166, box 1655-38. Private arch., Estelle Lafleur (Chassé) (Hull, Que.), Henri Chassé fils, "50 ans au service du Canada; portraits, souvenirs et anecdotes" (MS, 1997); papers concerning Henri Chassé. Royal 22ᵉ Régiment Museum (Quebec), AV5/172/2 ("Journal du Royal 22ᵉ Régiment, 1920–1939"); D-6/172 (J.-P. Gagnon fonds); Military personnel files. *Le Devoir*, 10 juill. 1928. Joseph Chaballe, *Histoire du 22ᵉ bataillon canadien-français . . .* (Montréal, 1952). J.-P. Gagnon, *Le 22ᵉ bataillon (canadien-*

français), 1914–1919; étude socio-militaire (Québec et Ottawa, 1986).

CHEN CAI (Chen Daozhi). *See* CHANG TOY

CHIPMAN, CLARENCE CAMPBELL, office holder and HBC officer; b. 24 May 1856 in Amherst, N.S., son of John Allen Chipman, a postmaster, and Abbie Whidden Brown; m. 25 April 1882 Ada Jane Borradaile (d. 1913) in Ottawa, and they had at least one son and three daughters; d. 11 Feb. 1924 in Royal Leamington Spa, England.

Educated in Amherst, Clarence Campbell Chipman is said to have worked in the federal departments of Agriculture, Public Works, and Finance before 1882. In 1880 he was with the Department of Finance in Ottawa, but he most likely did not join the civil service in 1867, as some sources have claimed. On 27 Jan. 1882 he became private secretary to Sir Charles Tupper*, minister of railways and canals. When Tupper was officially appointed Canadian high commissioner in London in May 1884, Chipman accompanied him there as assistant secretary and accountant. In this position Chipman organized Canada's contribution to the universal exposition held in Antwerp the following year and in 1886 he served as accountant for Canada's participation in the Colonial and Indian Exhibition in London. After acting as Tupper's assistant in the Atlantic fisheries negotiations in Washington in 1887–88, he was promoted chief clerk in the Department of Marine and Fisheries and private secretary to the minister, Tupper's son CHARLES HIBBERT, on 1 July 1888. He participated in the negotiations over the seal fishery in the Bering Sea in 1889 [*see* Sir Charles Tupper] and was later said to have written a treatise on the fisheries of Canada in 1891.

On 12 May 1891 Chipman was appointed trade commissioner of the Hudson's Bay Company, a senior Canadian position within the firm. He was one of a series of professional administrators who were hired from outside the HBC by its London committee in the late 19th and early 20th centuries to shake up the managerial staff. The HBC, and particularly its governor, Sir Donald Alexander Smith*, had been attracted by Chipman's administrative abilities. As well, Smith had sought someone who would adhere to his policy of fiscal restraint. As commissioner, Chipman supervised over 100 posts, shops, and depots stretching from Quebec to the Yukon; he hired managers, checked accounts, and developed strategies to comply with the wishes of the London committee. He served in his new post until October, when the committee decided to separate the fur trade into two departments, fur trade and saleshop (retail trade), but to combine their administration with that of the land department under a single person, Chipman, who was named chief commissioner.

Faced with falling profits from furs and competition from companies with smaller infrastructures, the London committee issued Chipman a mandate in 1892 to reduce costs. Chipman followed this course of action rigorously, generating the greatest amount of profit while effecting strict economy and promoting efficiency. He expanded the firm's network of steamships in order to move more goods at lower costs and he promoted the use of the telegraph to bring news of international fur prices to traders. The firm's administrative operations were centralized in Winnipeg, eliminating haphazard accounting and overlap of personnel. The HBC adopted a conservative approach to land sales, selling only when market conditions were favourable, and it expanded its retail department. Chipman introduced cost accounting, price standardization, and regular inspections. He also suggested that cash replace barter in trading for furs. In 1910 the company embarked on a thorough inspection of the retail business and afterwards decided to divide it into departments by "placing at the head of each a man especially conversant with these respective interests."

In May 1911 Chipman was demoted to the position of commissioner of the land department. On 12 September the London committee, which had new members who wanted to change the firm's methods, resolved that he be given notice. He was to be paid at the rate of £1,500 a year to 31 May 1912, after which time he would receive his pension. Following his departure, the HBC reverted to the structure it had abandoned on his appointment in 1891 and enhanced the role of middle managers. Thus, the company's operation in Canada became more specialized as its bureaucratic structure was enlarged. This development would not have been possible without the measures Chipman had brought in to make its management more effective.

Clarence Campbell Chipman moved to England in 1911 with his wife and two of his daughters. He purchased Woodlands, a home in Roehampton (London). In 1923 he moved to Arnathwaite House in Royal Leamington Spa, where he stayed until his death the following year.

PAUL NIGOL

The correspondence of Clarence Campbell Chipman while he served as trade commissioner and then chief commissioner of the Hudson's Bay Company can be found in the following series at the AM, HBCA: D.13–D.14, D.17–D.22, D.24–D.27, D.44.

AM, HBCA, A.1/160, ff.106–7. AO, RG 80-5-0-105, no.1911. Church of Jesus Christ of Latter-day Saints, Geneal. Soc., International geneal. index. *Ottawa Free Press*, 25 April 1882. *Times* (London), 13 Feb. 1924. C. J. Brydges, *The letters of Charles John Brydges, 1883–1889; Hudson's Bay Company land commissioner*, ed. Hartwell Bowsfield, intro. J. E. Rea (Winnipeg, 1981), xi–lxxxii. Can., Dept. of the Secretary of State, *The civil service list of Canada . . .* (Ottawa), 1883–91. *Canadian men and women of the time* (Morgan; 1898 and 1912). "C. C. Chipman, commissioner Hudson's Bay Co., 1891–1911," *Beaver* (Winnipeg), 4 (1923–24): 218–19. *Directory*, Ottawa, 1880–83. J. S. Galbraith, "Land policies of the Hudson's Bay Company, 1870–1913," *CHR*, 32 (1951): 1–21. P. C. Nigol, "Efficiency and economy: commissioner C. C. Chipman and the Hudson's Bay Company, 1891–1911" (MA thesis, Univ. of Man., Winnipeg, 1994). E. J. Stardom, "Adapting to altered circumstances: trade commissioner Joseph Wrigley and the Hudson's Bay Company, 1884–1891" (MA thesis, Univ. of Man., 1987).

CHIROUSE, EUGÈNE-CASIMIR (named at birth **Eugène**), Roman Catholic priest, Oblate of Mary Immaculate, and missionary; b. 15 June 1854 in Hostun, Bourg-de-Péage, France, son of Félicien Chirouse, a hatter, and Pauline Vallon; d. 3 Feb. 1927 in Vancouver.

After attending the Oblate juniorate at Notre-Dame de Lumières in France, on 28 July 1873 Eugène-Casimir Chirouse entered the Oblate noviciate at Notre-Dame-de-l'Osier, where he made his religious profession on 29 July 1874. He took his perpetual vows at the Autun scholasticate on 15 Aug. 1875 and was ordained there on 7 June 1879. Sent to British Columbia, where his uncle Eugène-Casimir Chirouse was serving as an Oblate missionary, he arrived in New Westminster in October 1879 with fellow Oblate Jean-Marie-Raphaël LE JEUNE.

Chirouse spent the winter at St Charles's mission in New Westminster and then was assigned to St Mary's mission, where he would serve until 1927. While stationed at St Mary's, he was active in ministering to native groups further afield; he made three visits each year to native camps on the coast as far north as Bute Inlet and in the interior up to Lillooet. He also participated in the large religious gatherings the Oblates organized for natives. Perhaps the most significant of these for him was his uncle's funeral, held at St Mary's in June 1892 and attended by 1,200 natives.

Earlier in 1892 Chirouse had been arrested in an incident at LaFontaine (Fountain) that redounded not only on him, but also on Oblate practices in British Columbia. On 18 March 1892 the council of the Fountain band had asked Chirouse, who had just ended a mission there, for advice on the punishment of Lucy Curry and a young man who had been "detected in improper intimacy." Chirouse recommended 15 lashes and left the council to carry out the sentence. The next morning he continued on his course and was thus unaware of Lucy's repeat offence, and identical punishment, on 19 March. On 29 March, Chirouse, Chief Kilapoutkue, and two other men of the Fountain band were charged with assault. All four were arrested and, after a preliminary inquiry before Lillooet justice of the peace John Martley, were remanded to a higher court for trial. Under the Speedy Trials Act, Chirouse was tried by county court judge Clement Francis Cornwall on 3 May 1892. Acting without a jury, Cornwall found Chirouse guilty of causing grievous bodily harm and sentenced him to one year in jail. Kilapoutkue and the two other native men were also found guilty and were sentenced to six months and two months respectively. A public outcry supporting Chirouse ensued and several editorials and open letters appeared in provincial newspapers. In May, Bishop Paul Durieu* personally appealed to Governor General Lord Stanley*, who revoked the sentences of all four men.

For the Oblates and most interested British Columbians, the primary issue was the natives' use of physical coercion and the Oblates' sanction and encouragement of it. A commonly repeated defence of Chirouse was that native chiefs had a traditional right to use corporal punishment to control members of their bands. In a notice of 10 Oct. 1873 Chief Justice Matthew Baillie Begbie* had recognized the right of native chiefs to use such measures to ensure social peace; justices of the peace were not to interfere except in cases of excessive severity. In issuing similar notices to individual Oblates, however, he also seems to have sanctioned their right to promote physical punishment, which they did. By 1876 Begbie had decided that such punishment could be meted out only for legal infractions, not for sins. Contemporary historians have come to see "force and coercion" as underpinning what has been called the "Durieu system," a two-pronged method of proselytization which aimed at repressing vice and sin and forming true Christian spirituality in native communities. Chirouse's conviction, it has been argued, heralded the end of the Durieu system in British Columbia: the Oblate use of force would no longer be sanctioned by the government or countenanced by the populace. A close examination of Durieu's instructions to his missionaries, however, suggests that in seeking to achieve both goals of the two-pronged system, he did not rely solely on physical coercion.

Despite his long service as a dedicated missionary and educator in British Columbia, Eugène-Casimir Chirouse is best remembered for the events of 1892. After his sentence was revoked he returned to St Mary's, where he served as director of the school and at various times as superior of the mission. In the 1880s the mission school had had an average of 25 students. It became a government-funded industrial school in 1893, after which the average attendance rose to 62 pupils. Concentrating on agricultural instruction for boys and domestic training for girls, it drew its students from the Fraser Canyon region. Chirouse continued to work there until mid January 1927, when he was admitted to St Paul's Hospital in

Vancouver, suffering from carcinoma of the stomach. He died three weeks later and was buried in the Oblate cemetery in Mission.

LYNN BLAKE

Arch. Départementales, Drôme (Valence, France), État civil, Bourg-de-Péage, 16 juin 1854. Arch. Deschâtelets, Oblats de Marie-Immaculée (Ottawa), HE 1791.D96C 17 (copie de lettres au père J.-M.[-J.] Le Jacq, 27 nov. 1883–25 févr. 1884, sur la "Direction des sauvages"); P 1-7296 (fonds de la province oblate St Peter, 1850–90); P 1091-1104 (cas de Lucie). BCA, GR-2951. Roman Catholic Archdiocese of Vancouver Arch., Early bishops' corr. Gaston Carrière, *Dictionnaire biographique des oblats de Marie-Immaculée au Canada* (4v., Ottawa, 1976–89), 1: 201. E. McC. Lemert, "The life and death of an Indian state," *Human Organization* (New York), 13 (1954–55), no.3: 23–27. *Month* (London), June 1892. Paul Tennant, *Aboriginal peoples and politics: the Indian land question in British Columbia, 1849–1989* (Vancouver, 1990). Margaret Whitehead, *The Cariboo mission: a history of the Oblates* (Victoria, 1981).

CHOQUET, FRANÇOIS-XAVIER, lawyer, judge, and social reformer; b. 8 Jan. 1851 in Varennes, Lower Canada, son of Jean-Baptiste Choquet, a farmer, and Adéline Provost; m. 10 June 1884 Marie-Caroline Barry in Trois-Pistoles, Que.; they had no children; d. 31 Dec. 1926 in Montreal.

François-Xavier Choquet was born to a farming family in Varennes which placed a high value on education and permitted him to attend the Collège de L'Assomption from 1863 to 1869 and the Petit Séminaire de Montréal from 1869 to 1871. Following his classical education, he pursued legal training in the Montreal office of Louis-Amable Jetté* and at McGill College. He received a BCL in 1874 and was called to the bar the following year. He practised with Jetté and Frédéric-Ligori Béïque*, both prominent Liberals, until 1878 when Jetté was named to the Superior Court. For years he had his own firm and then in 1886 he joined another prestigious partnership, also headed by Rouges, that of Honoré Mercier*, Cléophas Beausoleil*, and Paul-Gédéon Martineau. After Mercier departed in 1891 the firm was renamed Beausoleil et Choquet and the following year it became Beausoleil, Choquet et Girard. Choquet's Liberal connections are evident in his choice of associates and are confirmed in his work; it was his firm that was charged with handling all electoral disputes for the Liberal party.

During the 1890s Choquet's fine legal reputation was rewarded: on 7 March 1893 he obtained a federal nomination as QC and from 1894 to 1897 he served as a member of the council of the Montreal bar. His political commitment was an additional factor in his appointments as a commissioner to revise the charter of Montreal (September 1897), as a judge of sessions of the peace, police magistrate, and licence commissioner (24 Dec. 1898), and as a federal extradition commissioner (20 July 1901). He would remain active as judge and extradition commissioner for more than 20 years.

In the first decade of the 20th century Choquet became a social reformer, advocating child welfare. In this activity he was joined by his wife, Marie-Caroline Barry. The couple worked to establish the Children's Aid Society of Montreal and in 1908 Choquet became its first president. Marie-Caroline was one of the three vice-presidents. The Choquets vigorously supported the federal Juvenile Delinquents Act, passed in 1908. The act provided for the establishment of provincial and municipal juvenile courts with wide powers of investigation and sentencing and it forbade the incarceration of young offenders with adults. In 1910 the Quebec government proclaimed the act and took steps to create a juvenile court in Montreal. The Montreal Juvenile Delinquents' Court officially opened in March 1912 with Choquet as its first judge.

At the court's opening, Choquet shared his understanding of the legislation's aims, that each young delinquent "be treated, not as a criminal, but as a misdirected and misguided child, and one needing aid, encouragement, help, and assistance." For more than a decade Choquet served as judge of the juvenile court, embracing child-saving ideas prominent in English-speaking Canada and in the United States. The press, with affection and deference, named him the Children's Judge and his recasting of a law court into a "home of mercy" was lauded as a sign of progress. He was a strong supporter of probation in lieu of confinement but did support the Borstal system for youthful offenders (a system developed at Borstal prison, in Kent, England, which included education, work, vocational training, and group counselling). Working with him in the court were probation officers Rose Henderson* and Marie Clément and clerk Owen Dawson. He stepped down as judge in April 1922. The Montreal juvenile court had been shaped by the presence of this fatherly figure whose progressive ideals irreversibly altered the treatment of youthful offenders in the city.

During his long and distinguished career François-Xavier Choquet had earned a reputation as a compassionate friend of youth and a tireless servant of the state. He died in 1926 after a brief illness; his funeral cortège included senators Béïque and Donat Raymond and several ministers and judges.

TAMARA MYERS

François-Xavier Choquet is the author of "The juvenile court," an article published in the *Canadian Municipal Journal* (Montreal), 10 (1914): 232–33.

LAC, MG 30, C27, 7: 25A.35.4 (letter from K. Weller to W. L. Scott). *Le Devoir*, 23 mars 1912. *Gazette* (Montreal), 24 Oct. 1907, 1 Jan. 1927. *Montreal Daily Star*, 4 Jan. 1927. *Montreal Herald*, 3 Jan., 8 June 1912; 3 March 1914; 11, 20 April 1922. *La Presse*, 13 janv., 8 juin 1923; 3 janv. 1927. W. H. Atherton, *Montreal, 1534–1914* (3v., Montreal, 1914). I.-J. Deslauriers, *Les tribunaux du Québec et leurs juges: Cour provinciale, Cour des sessions de la paix, Tribunal de la jeunesse, Cour municipale* (Cowansville, Qué., 1987). L. E. Mendelsohn, "History of the Montreal juvenile court: an historical-descriptive study of the Montreal juvenile court, later known as the Social Welfare Court" (MSW research report, McGill Univ., Montreal, 1969). Tamara Myers, "The voluntary delinquent: parents, daughters, and the Montreal Juvenile Delinquents' Court, 1918," *CHR*, 80 (1999): 242–68. Jean Trépanier et Françoise Tulkens, *Délinquance & protection de la jeunesse: aux sources des lois belge et canadienne sur l'enfance* (Montréal, 1995).

CHURCHILL, MATILDA MOORE. *See* FAULKNER

CLARK, MICHAEL, physician, rancher, and politician; b. 12 May 1861 in Belford, England, son of Michael Clark, a grocer, and Jane Hall; m. 3 Aug. 1882 Elizabeth Smith in Hamilton, Ont., and they had four sons; d. 29 July 1926 near Olds, Alta.

Michael Clark was educated at Elmfield College in York, England, where he earned a gold medal in languages, and the University of Edinburgh (MB, CM). In 1882, while a medical student, he visited Canada to marry the eldest daughter of George Smith of Cherrybank Farm near Hamilton, whom he had known before the family emigrated. After graduation he practised in northern England; at Newcastle upon Tyne he also sat on the local school board. In 1902, for reasons of health and apparently also to establish careers for his sons, he moved to Alberta and began farming northwest of Olds. He soon got into politics. A Liberal, he ran unsuccessfully for the seat of Rosebud in 1905 in the province's first election. Three years later he was returned to the House of Commons for Red Deer, which he would represent until 1921. Little is known of his medical practice. A Methodist in his youth, he enjoyed walking and swimming, supported women's suffrage, and in 1911–12 served on the board of the University of Alberta.

Politically Clark established a reputation for his idealism, the strength of his convictions, and his representation of western and agrarian interests. Considered in the commons "a party of one" for his "old-time" doctrines of free trade, he took some swings at protection and was prepared to exceed the measures proposed by the government of Sir Wilfrid Laurier* in January 1911 for reciprocity with the United States. In a verbose supportive speech on 23 February, he proudly linked his beliefs to the early free-trade principles of Sir Robert Peel and Richard Cobden in Britain. The Conservative response came from Ontario MP Richard Blain, who dismissed Clark as a foreign anachronism and asked why he had never voted against any of the tariffs sustained by the Liberals. Following their defeat that year, Clark became a vigorous critic of Robert Laird Borden*'s government. In 1913 he saw its Naval Aid Bill as a stimulus to the "mad war of armament." According to one summary, with "canny humour and clear directness" he attacked the "German 'scare' as being an attenuated thing resting in disordered minds, assumed the extreme and well-known English Radical view as to . . . preparations for war, [and] deprecated any form of Imperial Federation." After the outbreak of conflict in August 1914, however, his politics shifted dramatically as he placed his loyalty to Britain first, a sentiment reinforced by the enlistment of his son Michael. At a Liberal convention in Calgary that month, he sponsored a resolution to terminate partisanship while the crisis threatened the British empire.

In 1917 Clark parted with Laurier to support conscription, one of the earliest western Liberals to do so. He backed the Union government formed by Borden in October 1917 but, perhaps because of illness, refused a place in cabinet. During the campaign for the general election in December, he angered many Liberals, including his own riding organization, which rejected his candidacy, by insisting on the need for a coalition to coordinate the war effort. A party led by Quebec, he claimed in a shot at Laurier, was not up to the task. He won Red Deer as a Liberal-Unionist, but did not always embrace the government's reformist initiatives after the war. In 1919 in the committee on hereditary titles for Canadians, headed by William Folger Nickle*, who wanted them abolished, Clark defended tradition and the "splendid place" of the British nobility in the war.

During the parliamentary session of 1920 Clark joined the rural-oriented Progressive party under Thomas Alexander Crerar*. The association did not last long: in September 1921, in a widely publicized break, Clark told Crerar he would not be running as a Progressive in Alberta because of his distaste for the "class" politics of the United Farmers there. In December he stood as a Liberal in the Saskatchewan riding of Mackenzie, but was defeated by a Progressive. He subsequently retired from politics. Predeceased by his wife and two sons, he died at his Belford Glen Ranch in 1926 and was buried in Olds.

Throughout his public career, Clark had been acclaimed as the "finest speaker in western Canada." Though rarely on his feet in parliament "for any length of time," he commanded the attention of every MP, one reporter said, expressing an estimate found repeatedly in the press.

WARREN M. ELOFSON

AO, RG 80-5-0-112, no.12562. GRO, Reg. of births, Belford, 12 May 1861. *Calgary News Telegram*, 30 April 1912. *Farmer's Telegram and Family Magazine* (Winnipeg), 3 Oct. 1917. *Morning Albertan* (Calgary), 29 April 1912, 6 Dec. 1917. *Olds Gazette* (Olds, Alta), 6 Aug. 1926. *Strathmore and Bow Valley Standard* (Strathmore, Alta), 4 Aug. 1926. John Blue, *Alberta, past and present, historical and biographical* (3v., Chicago, 1924), 1: 136. Can., House of Commons, *Debates*, 23 Feb. 1911: 4143–69. *Canadian annual rev.*, 1910, 1913, 1916, 1919, 1921. *CPG*, 1918. *Olds: a history of Olds and area* (Olds, 1980). *See Olds first: a history of Olds and surrounding district* ([Olds], 1968). L. G. Thomas, *The Liberal party in Alberta: a history of politics in the province of Alberta, 1905–1921* (Toronto, 1959). Univ. of Alta Arch., *Who's who at the University of Alberta, 1908–1919* ([Edmonton], 1991). *Who's who* (London), 1910. *Who's who in Canada*, 1925/26.

CLARKE, CHARLES KIRK, psychiatrist, asylum superintendent, educator, and hospital administrator; b. 16 Feb. 1857 in Elora, Upper Canada, son of Charles Clarke* and Emma Kent; m. first 20 Oct. 1880 Margaret DeVeber Andrews (d. 1902) in Parkdale (Toronto), and they had four sons and two daughters; m. secondly 20 July 1904 Theresa Gallagher in Kingston, Ont.; d. 20 Jan. 1924 in Toronto.

After graduating from high school in Elora, Charles K. Clarke began work in 1874 as a clinical assistant at the provincially run Asylum for the Insane in Toronto. His hiring was largely due to the fact that two of his sisters had married psychiatrists, one a son of the asylum's superintendent, Joseph Workman*. Clarke received his medical degrees from the University of Toronto (MB 1878, MD 1879), and in 1880 he was appointed assistant medical superintendent of the Hamilton asylum, where he found the staff an "uncontrollable rabble." In 1882–85 he occupied the same position at the Rockwood Asylum in Portsmouth (Kingston). Upset by asylum politics, he decided to resign but when Rockwood's medical superintendent, Clarke's brother-in-law William George Metcalf*, was killed by a patient in 1885, Clarke was promoted superintendent. He accepted, he later said, "to protect several hundred defenseless creatures from a political hireling who might be pitchforked into the position."

At Rockwood, Clarke introduced an infirmary for acute cases, occupational therapy, and a psychiatric training program for nurses, the first in Canada. In 1895 he was named professor of mental diseases at nearby Queen's College, which would confer an LLD on him in 1906. In 1904 he became co-editor of the *American Journal of Insanity* (Baltimore). The next year he succeeded Daniel Clark* as head of the Toronto asylum, a position he would hold until 1911, when he became medical superintendent of the Toronto General Hospital. A founder and vice-president in 1907 of the Canadian Hospital Association, a year later he assumed the posts of psychiatrist at the TGH and, at the university, professor of psychiatry and dean of the faculty of medicine. He stepped down from the superintendence of the hospital in 1917, becoming its medical director, and left it altogether the following year when he was made medical director of the Canadian National Committee for Mental Hygiene. Two years later he resigned as dean to devote his full energy to this committee.

Despite Clarke's dedication to psychiatry, his personal interests were diverse. At age 15 he had lost two middle fingers in a hunting accident, but he still became quite adept with his hands, building boats, a house, and a pipe organ, among other projects. He was an avid tennis player – in 1890 he and Dr William Gage won the Canadian doubles championship. In later years he took up golf and played the violin in the Toronto Symphony Orchestra. Associates remembered him as a "mirthful conversationalist." A serious naturalist and ornithologist, he had a summer home in eastern Ontario.

Clarke's professional career can be broken into two stages. The first, until 1911, was accented by his service in the asylum system, where, for most of the 19th century, psychiatry was based. The physicians of Workman's generation believed there was little they could do for patients other than shelter them, hoping their symptoms would remit. But by the turn of the century, more and more psychiatrists, dissatisfied with practice in asylums, began looking outside for ways of preventing and treating mental illness. The upshot was a growing interest in outpatient psychiatry, child-guidance clinics, Freudian psychoanalysis, scientific research into the biological conditions of mental disease, and such eugenic policies as sterilization and restrictions on marriage and immigration. Essentially conservative, Clarke did not subscribe to some of these new directions – including Freudianism and "sex problems *ad nauseam*" – but quite often he was in the forefront of innovative thinking.

During the asylum phase of his career Clarke worked constantly to improve the conditions of patients. Possessed of an authentic fondness for the mentally ill, he abhorred the stigma they traditionally bore. Following the lead of Metcalf, Richard Maurice Bucke*, and others, at Rockwood he had rebelled against traditional techniques, easing restraints on patients and attempting to treat them humanely. He tried assiduously to destroy any resemblance between an asylum and a prison, and would eventually succeed in reducing the stigmatic designation by having Ontario's asylums renamed hospitals for the insane. But while he rejected many past policies he did not strictly oppose gynaecological surgery on patients to cure disorders; he did, however, object to the appeal made by R. M. Bucke and Alfred Thomas Hobbs of the London asylum to the National Council of Women of Canada to gain wider support for this type of treatment. A frequent expert witness at trials, he argued that some criminals were actually insane and not responsible for their actions. For instance, though he had not examined Métis leader Louis Riel*, he later diagnosed him as an "insane paranoiac" who should not have been hanged.

By the 1890s Clarke's enthusiasms had begun to wane. His persistent requests of the government, for more resources and policies for better care, had fallen on deaf ears. Physically strong, he had survived a number of attacks by patients, but too many incurable and violent cases appeared to be entering his wards. His interests, in fact, were shifting to preventive psychiatry or, as it was called, mental hygiene. A steady source of professional articles in journals, he longed to found an institute where, unlike in an asylum with its never-ending administrative demands, he would have time to examine patients thoroughly and oversee the scientific study of mental diseases. Undoubtedly Clarke would have excelled in such an environment – few physicians had a keener clinical eye when it came to distinguishing one psychiatric condition from another. His model was the clinic in Munich of pioneering German psychiatrist Emil Kraepelin.

When Clarke accepted the Toronto job in 1905 he hoped his dream could be realized. Working closely with provincial secretary William John Hanna*, he researched the project and travelled to Europe with others in 1907 to inspect psychiatric facilities there. Ultimately his plan fell through, though in 1909 he would introduce Kraepelin's classification of mental diseases. Clarke put some blame for this failure on politicians and professional rivals among hospital neurologists, but he mainly held his colleagues in asylum psychiatry responsible. If his charge is true, it is hard to fault them for complaining: Clarke wanted to monopolize the most interesting and treatable patients, and dispatch the rest to the public asylums.

Clarke's resignation from the Toronto asylum in 1911 highlighted his transition to the second stage of his career. He now devoted himself to prevention and the treatment of psychiatric outpatients. He had already opened an outpatients' clinic at the TGH in 1909 under the direction of the brilliant Dr Ernest Jones; it was discontinued in 1913, when Jones left and pending completion of a new hospital complex, but a new Social Service Clinic was opened in the spring of 1914. There Clarke, Clarence Meredith Hincks*, and other psychiatrists diagnosed troubled young men and women sent by Toronto's schools, courts, and social agencies. Still interested in provincial policy regarding the mentally handicapped, in 1912 Clarke had helped form the Provincial Association for the Care of the Feeble-Minded. At the same time that it argued for better care, he and others castigated the government for its reluctance to segregate "imbeciles" from their families.

During the early years of World War I, much of Clarke's attention shifted to that conflict. Military service depleted the staff of the TGH, which gradually began filling up with returning servicemen. In 1915, the same year that Clarke established a groundbreaking clinic for venereal diseases, he helped in the organization of No.4 Canadian General Hospital unit, which went overseas, and in 1918 he became consultant in psychiatry to Military District No.2 (Toronto and central Ontario). The following year the federal Department of Soldiers' Civil Re-establishment selected Clarke and one of its own psychiatrists, Captain Clarence B. Farrar*, to conduct a country-wide examination of asylums, in part to push for greater provincial aid for mentally disturbed veterans. In Ontario the two doctors encountered resistance from the office of provincial secretary William David McPherson, which, mindful of Clarke's record of criticism, insisted that only provincial inspectors could visit hospitals there. According to Farrar, Ontario held Clarke to be a *persona non grata*.

During the war years Clarke returned to an issue that had preoccupied him for some time. After 1900, in an extreme demonstration of preventive medicine, he had emerged as one of the most vocal and most publicity-seeking critics of Canadian immigration. The years between the end of the century and the war witnessed an enormous boom of newcomers, from 21,716 in 1897 to 400,870 in 1913. As a result, a growing number of foreign-born patients began appearing in Ontario's asylums – Clarke saw many more in Toronto than he had at Rockwood. The composition of this influx concerned him. Of the 1,244,597 immigrants who came between 1900 and 1909, 315,151 were from central and eastern Europe. Mostly anecdotal information conveyed the impression that a large percentage suffered from hereditary mental disability. Such impressions drew attention to Canada's immigration law. Before 1902 virtually no medical inspections were made at the points of entry, and the laws governing deportation were inadequate. Even when inspection was begun there were too few physicians and facilities to handle the flow at the busiest ports. Later amendments to the Immigration Act helped, but the testimony of medical inspectors and public-health officials stressed that too many mentally and physically handicapped immigrants were still entering the country. Clarke agreed, and his inspection in 1901 of the hospital for the insane at New Westminster, B.C., which housed considerable numbers of Chinese-born patients, reinforced his view. In 1905 he stepped up his lobbying for more and better-trained psychiatrists as medical inspectors. In addition, he began publishing articles on the "defective and insane" immigrant. However, in 1907–8, he later recalled, he found himself "in the centre of an unpleasant controversy, as the facts and figures presented did not appeal to practical politicians who were anxious to cultivate the vote of the new immigrant who had recently arrived." He therefore toned down his campaign, concluding that the time was not ripe for aggressive activism.

In 1916, sensing that changing circumstances had revitalized public opinion, Clarke rejoined the immigration debate. Many Canadians now felt that the best and healthiest young men of Canada were being sacrificed on the battlefields while the unfittest stayed home and begat their own kind. Such concern would lead to heightened fear about the immigration of unfit aliens once the war was over. The Provincial Association for the Care of the Feeble-Minded folded in 1918 when Clarke, Hincks, Helen MacMurchy*, and others founded the Canadian National Committee for Mental Hygiene, initially to attend to the psychiatric care of soldiers. It favoured prevention, including the screening of immigrants, whom it viewed as a primary source of mental degenerates (and therefore also of vice, disease, and unemployment). The growing interest in mental health, thus perceived, persuaded Clarke that the time was right to renew pressure on Ottawa. He drew on the enormous literature in the United States about immigration, much of which was part of the eugenic movement then sweeping North America. (Coined in 1883 in Britain, the term eugenics meant the study of heredity and the production of healthy offspring through the prevention of inherited disease.) A convert like most physicians of his day, Clarke believed that many European nations were trying to get rid of their insane and otherwise "defective" citizens by sending them to Canada or the United States, where, by reproducing their own kind, they posed a national menace.

Clarke used various means to alert public and official opinion to the eugenic dimensions of immigration. The receptive *Public Health Journal* (Toronto) published his denunciation in 1916 of the "defective immigrant" and in 1918 his theory on feeble-mindedness as the foundation of criminality. Among MPs he circulated copies of his unpublished novel, "The amiable morons," a thinly disguised account of Valentine Shortis*, the Irish immigrant who in 1895 had killed two men and wounded a third with no apparent emotion or motive. Clarke had testified at Shortis's trial that he was a hereditary degenerate who had been insane at the time of the murders. Avoided by publishers, the manuscript emphasized the link between immigration and hereditary illness.

As a result of the efforts of Clarke and the CNCMH, in 1919 parliament approved amendments to the Immigration Act, but Clarke remained dissatisfied. Medical inspectors continued to serve merely in advisory roles, filling out forms and relying on civil officials to decide on admissions. Frequently these officials overlooked entry regulations when ordered to do so by government authorities. For Clarke and many other psychiatrists, the system would remain inefficient until inspectors were posted abroad, at the ports of embarkation, a reform that would not materialize until 1928.

After 1919 Clarke continued to find an audience. From his Toronto clinic he drew statistical findings about immigrants that are now seen as dubious and unrepresentative, but which were then readily received in many quarters. His often sensationalized linkage of feeble-mindedness, immigration, and national degeneration fed into the premises of such moral reformers as Charlotte Elizabeth Hazeltyne Whitton*, who were glad to have "scientific" endorsement of extreme, even nativist, immigration policies. In 1920 a meeting of the Presbyterian Church's Canadian Council for the Immigration of Women proved very receptive to Clarke's constructs and his proposals to weed out Jewish children fleeing famine in Ukraine. On another occasion that year, the arrival at Saint John of the first contingent of Barnardo orphans to come to Canada since the war, Clarke staged a public demonstration to reinforce his preferences and arguments. Though the children had been carefully examined in England, Clarke and "an array of medical experts" nonetheless put them through "thorough tests – followed by congratulations on the high-grade type of children."

Clarke's crusade helps explain how, in delivering the prestigious Maudsley Lecture before the Royal Medico-Psychological Association in England on 24 May 1923, he could announce that immigration had pushed Canada to the brink of crisis. It was being "bled white" by emigration to the United States and pumped full of defectives, many of them British. The lecture underscored the fact that the issue exerted a powerful, almost mesmeric attraction on his mind. He campaigned so relentlessly that he alienated numerous provincial and federal authorities. On occasion acerbic, combative, and stubborn, he was rarely diplomatic when it came to immigration and other concerns that he felt strongly about. Such force was necessary to sway minds on what, in his opinion, were vital public-health questions. By the late 1920s, however, the psychiatric profession was beginning to move away from the crude eugenics advocated by Clarke and the CNCMH.

Though Clarke's professional life was largely taken up with CNCMH activities after 1918, other involvements contributed to his high profile. His controversial campaign for a true psychiatric clinic bore fruit in 1921, when a site was secured on Surrey Place near the TGH and the university; in 1923 Clarke was present at the laying of the cornerstone for the Toronto Psychiatric Hospital. Commissioned that year to assess Homewood Retreat, a private asylum near Guelph, he scored the sharp decline in its facilities for the acutely insane and the human costs of a greater resort to chemical and mechanical restraint. During the 1920s two of his children were also active in the field: Eric Kent was a psychiatrist in Toronto's health department, while Emma DeVeber, who had served overseas as a nurse and at the TGH clinic, was supervisor of mental hygiene nursing with the city. An Anglican – his second wife was a lifelong Roman Catholic – C. K. Clarke died of cardiovascular disease in 1924 and was buried in Mount Pleasant Cemetery. The Clarke Institute of Psychiatry in Toronto, which was named in his honour in 1966, merged into the Centre for Addiction and Mental Health in 1998.

If Clarke's commitment to public-health reform went as far as punitive eugenic policies, it was less a comment on him than it was a reflection of the times. His bending of clinical findings for eugenic purposes had resulted in part from the inexactitude of diagnosing feeble-mindedness. But in clinical situations where the symptom-pictures were more precisely defined, as in the diagnosis of dementia praecox (schizophrenia), he was on surer ground. That he possessed much purer psychiatric knowledge and ability is affirmed by his scientific publications and professionally significant advancement of Kraepelin's classification. He had played a seminal role too in many of the momentous changes that had occurred in the field, especially in the break from asylums. Clarke served as mentor for some of the luminaries of the next generation of Canadian psychiatrists, including the internationally renowned Hincks and Farrar, who regarded Clarke as "the father of Canadian psychiatry."

IAN DOWBIGGIN

[Manuscript sources for a study of Clarke's life can be found in a number of locations. Many of his published and unpublished papers are available in the C. K. Clarke fonds in the Centre for Addiction and Mental Health Arch., located at the Centre's Queen Street site in Toronto. Clarke's involvement in the debate over immigration is documented in LAC, RG 76 and AO, RG 63. His correspondence with other North American psychiatrists is scattered among various collections, among them the G. A. Blumer papers in the Isaac Ray Medical Library, Butler Hospital, Providence, R.I., and the Adolf Meyer papers at the Alan Mason Chesney Medical Arch. of the Johns Hopkins Medical Institutions, Baltimore, Md.

Clarke published one book, *A history of the Toronto General Hospital* . . . (Toronto, 1913), and numerous articles, some of which are catalogued in Cyril Greenland, *Charles Kirk Clarke: a pioneer of Canadian psychiatry* (Toronto, 1966). Among the medical journals to which he contributed were the *American Journal of Insanity* (Baltimore), the *Canadian Journal of Mental Hygiene* (Toronto), the *Journal of Mental Science* (London), the *Public Health Journal* (Toronto), and the *Bull.* of the Ontario Hospitals for the Insane (Toronto). Clarke also wrote the foreword to William George Smith's book *A study in Canadian immigration* (Toronto, 1920). I.D.]

AO, RG 80-5-0-95, no.12772; 80-5-0-322, no.8081. *Daily British Whig* (Kingston, Ont.), 21 Jan. 1924. Rainer Baehre, "The ill-regulated mind: a study in the making of psychiatry in Ontario, 1830–1921" (PHD thesis, York Univ.,

Toronto, 1985). T. E. Brown, "'Living with God's afflicted': a history of the Provincial Lunatic Asylum at Toronto, 1830–1911" (PHD thesis, Queen's Univ., Kingston, 1981). *Canadian annual rev.*, 1920. Jay Cassel, *The secret plague: venereal disease in Canada, 1838–1939* (Toronto, 1987). Ian Dowbiggin, *Keeping America sane: psychiatry and eugenics in the United States and Canada, 1880–1940* (Ithaca, N.Y., 1997); "'Keeping this young country sane': C. K. Clarke, immigration restriction, and Canadian psychiatry, 1890–1925," *CHR*, 76 (1995): 598–627. C. B. F[arrar], "I remember C. K. Clarke," *American Journal of Psychiatry*, 114 (1957–58): 368–70. Cheryl Krasnick Warsh, *Moments of unreason: the practice of Canadian psychiatry and the Homewood Retreat, 1883–1923* (Montreal and Kingston, 1989). K. J. McConnachie, "Science and ideology: the mental hygiene and eugenics movement in the inter-war years, 1919–1939" (PHD thesis, Univ. of Toronto, 1987). Angus McLaren, *Our own master race: eugenics in Canada, 1885–1945* (Toronto, 1990). Wendy Mitchinson, *The nature of their bodies: women and their doctors in Victorian Canada* (Toronto, 1991). Desmond Morton and Glenn Wright, *Winning the second battle: Canadian veterans and the return to civilian life, 1915–1930* (Toronto, 1987). Geoffrey Reaume, *Remembrance of patients past: patient life at the Toronto Hospital for the Insane, 1870–1940* (Toronto, 2000). *TPH: history and memories of the Toronto Psychiatric Hospital, 1925–1966*, ed. Edward Shorter (Toronto, 1996). Mariana Valverde, *The age of light, soap, and water: moral reform in English Canada, 1885–1925* (Toronto, 1991). *Vital statistics from N.B. newspapers* (Johnson), 53, nos.137, 2530.

CLARKE, LIONEL HERBERT, grain merchant and office holder, b. 20 July 1859 in Guelph, Upper Canada, son of William Clarke and Clara Piggott Strange, widow of William Dummer Powell; m. there 10 Feb. 1891 Anne Clara Gertrude Small, and they had three sons and a daughter; d. 29 Aug. 1921 in Toronto.

The son of an Irish-born physician turned magistrate and businessman, Lionel H. Clarke was educated at Trinity College School in Port Hope. Around 1878 he moved to Palmerston, northwest of Guelph, to pursue the grain business. About 1889 he expanded to Toronto, where by 1893 he had established L. H. Clarke and Company in partnership with Wilmot Deloui Matthews*. Operating out of offices in the new Board of Trade Building, in 1900 they founded a second firm, Canada Malting Company Limited. Despite tariffs that made Canadian malt uneconomical for brewers in the United States and western Canada and fires that destroyed the partners' Palmerston works and in 1913 badly damaged Canada Malting's Winnipeg plant, Clarke would focus on this trade for the remainder of his life. He achieved a respectable prosperity, which included appointments to the boards of other companies.

As he found economic security, he turned his attention to public life. Nominated by the Conservatives to contest Wellington North in the federal elections of 1891 and 1896, he lost each time. Business prevented him from running in 1900, but he helped secure the return of Edwin Tolton, a farmer and grain dealer, and remained involved in Conservative circles. His friendship with provincial leader James Pliny Whitney*, who became premier in 1905, led to his appointment in November 1908 to the Queen Victoria Niagara Falls Parks Commission. His passion for flowers resulted in gardens throughout the park, he protected its interests in negotiations with the hydroelectric companies at the falls, and he was a driving force behind the development of the riverside drive from Queenston. Federally, Clarke was a frequent adviser to Sir Robert Laird Borden*, whose government appointed him in 1917 to the Board of Grain Supervisors of Canada. Headed by Robert MAGILL, the board determined market needs, set prices and took orders, and regulated distribution within Canada until its replacement by the Canadian Wheat Board in 1919.

Despite his provincial and national interests, Clarke's local contributions were his most significant legacy. In 1888 he had joined Toronto's Board of Trade, which, within the year, became concerned about attempts by the Canadian Pacific and Grand Trunk railways to solidify their domination of Toronto's waterfront. The city's port and commercial districts were separated by a wide band of level crossings, where trains took several lives each year and frequently blocked the movement of goods to and from the wharves. The port had gone into decline, unable to compete with railways whose policies and rates, it seemed to board members, favoured Montreal over Toronto. The fire that destroyed 14 acres of the city's core in 1904 provided an opportunity to deal with the crossings. The railways favoured bridges over their tracks. The board proposed a viaduct to raise the trackage, a plan for which was ready in June 1907, when Clarke was vice-president of the board and a member of its railway and transportation committee. Approved by city council in September, the plan was handed back to Clarke to take to the federal Board of Railway Commissioners, which ordered the railways to construct a viaduct. Much of the credit for this accomplishment went to Clarke during his presidency in 1908, though it would take another five years to forge an agreement.

The fire of 1904 had also forced the city to deal with the issues of water supply and sewage disposal, and thereby clear the way for federal support of harbour improvements. Silt and sewage blocked the wharves at a time when plans to expand the Welland Canal and build a deep waterway along the St Lawrence offered hope for Toronto's development as a major distribution centre. The problem was driven home to Clarke when the master of a Scottish steamer appeared at his door in 1908 to complain that insufficient water at the wharves hindered the discharge of

216

his cargo and about the lack of public docks and high handling charges. Along with such Board of Trade members as William James GAGE, Clarke was instrumental in persuading federal and municipal officials to replace the existing harbour trust with a commission capable of building the needed public wharves, dredging a deeper harbour, and creating by means of infill industrial sites in Ashbridges Bay [see Sir John Alexander Boyd*; John Irvine Davidson*].

When Ottawa formed the Toronto Harbour Commissioners in May 1911, Clarke became its chairman, a position he would hold until his death. In 1912, expanding upon earlier proposals put forward by the railway companies, the Toronto Guild of Civic Art, and the Board of Trade, he directed the preparation of a plan for waterways, parks, and roads that would serve as a blueprint for development until the 1950s. Its details and implementation were left to a staff headed by engineer Edward Lancelot Cousins*, but Clarke brought vision to the project and played an important role in the meetings, inspections, and presentations that won financial support for a scheme estimated to cost more than $24 million. As industrial sites emerged, he advised the staff on leases. In 1913, as an alternative to the city's purchase of the utility and street railway interests of Sir William MACKENZIE, he surprised city council with proposals for a bold system of underground and surface lines emanating from the lakefront. Although the harbour commissioners and the railways reached an agreement that year on the viaduct and a new Union Station, Clarke would die before the completion of the viaduct and waterfront plans.

In addition to his parks and harbour work, Clarke served on the Toronto and York County highway commission from 1911 to 1913. With his wife he ran summer camps at Vineland, on the Niagara peninsula, for residents of the Toronto Boys' Home. Clarke's public and charitable involvement likely provided some distraction from the loss of his eldest son, Lieutenant Lionel Esmonde Clarke, in June 1916 in Belgium. His serious demeanour and forcefulness hid his warmth and sense of humour; known to shun publicity, he preferred to spend time with his family and pursue his hobbies of riding, hunting, angling, and reading. It surprised many when he was appointed lieutenant governor of Ontario on 27 Nov. 1919, though his populist approach suited the reform spirit of the recently elected United Farmers government of Ernest Charles Drury*. There was less formal ceremony at Clarke's official residence in Chorley Park, which became a rallying point for interest groups who sought his recognition. As the Clarkes embraced a heavy schedule of public and social duties, their sense of humanity changed Ontarians' perception of the role of lieutenant governor. The premier and Clarke disagreed publicly in 1920 over the government's proposal to close

Government House as a cost-saving measure, but Drury would remember him as "a gentleman and a man of taste."

By the summer of 1921 stomach cancer had confined Clarke to his summer residence on Copperhead Island in Georgian Bay. He died at Government House in August and received a state funeral at St Paul's Anglican Church. Few would have argued with the assessment by Senator Angus Claude Macdonell in 1918 that there was no more disinterested man in the service of his country than Lionel H. Clarke.

MICHAEL B. MOIR

Lionel Herbert Clarke published an illustrated article on the Toronto waterfront development, "Putting a new front on Toronto," in *Canadian Magazine*, 42 (November 1913–April 1914): 205–15.

AO, F 775, MU 2131, 1920, no.6; RG 3-4-0-11; RG 24-12; RG 80-8-0-803, no.5484. Toronto Port Authority Arch., RG 1 (records of the board of commissioners)/5, box 2, folder 9, A. C. Macdonell to L. H. Clarke; RG 3 (central registry files), box 148, folder 15, financial report by R. G. Dun and Co., 26 Jan. 1933; box 230, folders 22–23. *Daily Mail and Empire*, 28 Nov. 1919; 16 July, 30 Aug. 1921. *Evening Telegram* (Toronto), 26 Nov. 1913, 30 Aug. 1921. *Globe*, 29 Nov. 1919. *Star Weekly* (Toronto), 29 Nov., 6 Dec. 1919; 9 July 1921. *Toronto Daily Star*, 29–31 Aug., 30 Sept. 1921. *Toronto Sunday World*, 19 Aug. 1921. *World* (Toronto), 11 Feb. 1891. *Canadian annual rev.*, 1913. *Directory*, Toronto, 1893–1921. E. C. Drury, *Farmer premier: memoirs of the Honourable E. C. Drury* (Toronto, 1966), 104. G. W. Englehardt, *Toronto, Canada: the book of its Board of Trade ...* ([Toronto, 1897]). W.J. Gage, *Address of Mr. W. J. Gage, president of the Board of Trade of the City of Toronto, delivered at annual meeting, January 19, 1911* ([Toronto, 1911]). C. M. Johnston, *E. C. Drury: agrarian idealist* (Toronto, 1986). Roy Merrens, "Port authorities as urban land developers: the case of the Toronto Harbour Commissioners and their outer harbour project, 1912–68," *Urban Hist. Rev.* (Toronto), 17 (1988): 92–105. Ont., Legislature, *Sessional papers*, 1909, no.5: 5. *Ontario Gazette* (Toronto), 1900: 738, 1017. W. R. Plewman, *Adam Beck and the Ontario Hydro* (Toronto, 1947). G. H. Stanford, *To serve the community: the story of Toronto's Board of Trade* (Toronto, 1974). Jeffrey Stinson and Michael Moir, *Built heritage of the east bayfront* (Can., Royal commission on the future of the Toronto waterfront, *Technical paper*, no.7, Toronto, October 1991). Toronto, Board of Trade, *Annual report*, 1895–1921 (mfm. at TRL); *Board of Trade News*, December 1919, September/October 1921 (copies at TRL). *The Torontonian society blue book and club list* (Toronto), 1921. *Who's who and why*, 1921.

COCHRANE, WILLIAM EDWARD, rancher; b. 8 Sept. 1858 in Packington, near Lichfield, England, son of Basil Edward Arthur Cochrane and Sally Caroline Fitzgerald; m. 19 Feb. 1887 Evelyn Constance Clementina Lamb (d. 28 May 1908) in London, and they had one son; d. 7 March 1929 in Ballycarney (Republic of Ireland).

Cochrane

William E. Cochrane, known as Billy, was a grand-nephew of the famous seaman Thomas Cochrane, 10th Earl of Dundonald. Among his other relatives were Sir Thomas John Cochrane*, an early governor of Newfoundland, and Douglas Mackinnon Baillie Hamilton Cochrane*, who as the 12th Earl of Dundonald would become commander of the Canadian militia. Billy was one of a number of well-to-do young Britons who came to the Alberta foothills in the 1880s in search of adventure. He stayed to play an important part in the economic and social development of the region. Although the historiography of the Canadian range has tended to emphasize the role of four or five large corporate ranch companies [*see* Matthew Henry Cochrane*; Frederick Smith Stimson*], more recently it has been argued that numerous smaller family ranches buttressed the cattle industry with capital and contributed enormously to innovation and adaptation in ranching. Cochrane's life in Alberta epitomized the achievements of this group.

The Little Bow Cattle Company, known as the CC Ranch because of its brand, was organized in 1884 by Cochrane, his cousin Thomas Belhaven Henry Cochrane, Hugh Graham, and brothers Ted and Frank Jenkins. A foundation herd of 359 head of cattle and 12 saddle-horses was imported from Montana in September 1884. A snugly sited ranch house was built on Mosquito Creek, a few miles west of Cayley. Early setbacks encouraged Billy's partners to pursue other options and Cochrane was left the sole boss of the CC. His pride and joy was a small herd of purebred Galloway cattle. From it he raised young bulls to sell to neighbouring ranchers. They were prized for their hardihood and foraging abilities. In addition, Cochrane ran a regular range herd of about 400 cows, which yielded 220–75 calves each year. The ranch reported a total of 800 head of cattle and 40 horses in 1890.

Cochrane matured to become a conscientious and responsible rancher, always looking for ways to improve his stock and streamline production. Not only did he nurture a purebred herd on enclosed pastures, but he put up hay for calves and weak cattle from an early date. Later he pushed the stock association to keep the bulls separate from the cows until midway through the summer so that winter calving would be eliminated. Cochrane had thus brought with him attitudes towards stock rearing drawn from the British pastoral tradition. The geographer Terry G. Jordan has shown how these ideas fused with methods from the midwestern United States to ensure that ranching in the Canadian foothills differed markedly from the extensive open range methods of "the Anglo-Texan ranching complex." Cochrane's leadership was felt far beyond the boundaries of his ranch. For several years he organized the cowboys who rode for the Mosquito Creek Wagon at the roundup, and when his neighbour Alfred Ernest Cross* was laid up

after an accident Cochrane managed the A7 Ranche for him. He was a leading figure in the fight against predators, and, in 1904, it was he who built the huge dipping vat in which all the district's cattle were treated for mange.

Cochrane was one of a group of friends who provided capital for Cross's Calgary Brewing and Malting Company; he purchased $1,000 of stock in 1892 and later added another $500. Perhaps more important than his financial backing was his wholehearted personal support for his friend. When Cross was sick and beset with problems in the late 1890s, Billy wrote: "It seems hard that you should chuck up now, after bearing all the expense and trouble and considerable wear and tear. . . . I am quite willing to stay with the brewery as long as you do and as long as you control the management." The company would continue to provide Cochrane with a modest income until his death.

There was, however, another side to Billy Cochrane. One of his friends described him as having "a kiss from the devil on his cheek." He enjoyed the physical demands of working an isolated ranch and earned the respect of his men by his willingness to turn his hand to any chore, but he expected to play as hard as he worked. During his first years in Alberta he was a leading member of the Wolves' Den, an extremely ungentlemanly "gentlemen's club," which met in an old boxcar by the rail tracks in Calgary. Cochrane knew the Grant family, who produced Glen Grant Scotch whisky, and was able to ensure that there was always a barrel of ten-year-old whisky on hand to nourish their storytelling and poker games. While at their ranch, Billy and his wife, Evelyn, hunted coyotes on horseback, played and supported polo, shot and fished, and entertained frequently. Once Cochrane could rely on a trusted foreman, he adopted the habit of spending the winter in Britain, where he enjoyed fox-hunting from his family home in Leicestershire and shooting grouse in Scotland and pheasants in Dorset. The couple would also spend time in London, staying at the British Hotel, dining at the Café Royal, and catching up with the latest plays. In 1909, after Evelyn's death, Cochrane sold his ranch and retired to Scotland. He continued to hunt and fish, and travelled widely, making frequent visits to Alberta. During World War I he falsified his age to join the 1st Sportsman's Battalion of the Royal Fusiliers (City of London Regiment), but he did not see action. At his death his principal residence was Ravenstone Castle, near Whithorn, Scotland. He left an estate worth $1,250,000, which took some years to wind up.

Billy Cochrane displayed many of the characteristics of the reviled "remittance man." He had a wild streak which he made no attempt to control even when he was a middle-aged family man. He expressed his support for Calgary Brewing and Malting by sampling beer copiously wherever he happened to be and then sending reports to Cross. He also made every effort to lure the overly conscientious Cross into a night or two on the town. Cochrane was a creature of his times during which money insulated the landowning class from many of the realities of life. His story is important because it demonstrates that the cultural baggage that well-off Britons brought to Alberta – customs which seemed bizarre and risible to others – in no way precluded these privileged immigrants from making substantial contributions to the settlement of what Billy often referred to as "the bald headed" prairie.

SIMON M. EVANS

GA, M 289; M 6552. GRO, Reg. of births, Lichfield, 8 Sept. 1858; Newcastle upon Tyne, 8 Jan. 1858; Reg. of marriages, St George Hanover Square (Middlesex), 19 Feb. 1887. D. H. Breen, *The Canadian prairie west and the ranching frontier, 1874–1924* (Toronto, 1983). *Burke's genealogical and heraldic history of the peerage, baronetage and knightage*, ed. Peter Townend (105th ed., London, 1970). Cayley Women's Institute, *Under the chinook arch: a history of Cayley and surrounding areas* ([Cayley, Alta], [1967?]). S. M. Evans et al., *Cowboys, ranchers and the cattle business: cross-border perspectives on ranching history* (Calgary, 2000). High River Pioneers' and Old Timers' Assoc., *Leaves from the Medicine Tree . . .* ([Lethbridge, Alta], 1960). T. G. Jordan, *North American cattle ranching frontiers: origins, diffusion, and differentiation* (Albuquerque, N.Mex., 1993). Sherrill MacLaren, *Braehead: three founding families in nineteenth century Canada* (Toronto, 1986). Nanton and District Hist. Soc., *Mosquito Creek roundup: Nanton-Parkland* (Nanton, Alta, 1975).

COLDWELL, GEORGE ROBSON, lawyer and politician; b. 4 July 1858 in Darlington Township, Upper Canada, son of William Edward Coldwell and Mary Robson, both originally from Yorkshire, England; m. Annie Anderson of Brampton, Ont.; d. 24 Jan. 1924 in Brandon, Man.

George Coldwell attended grammar school in Clinton, Ont., and then went to Trinity College School in Port Hope. From there he entered Trinity College, Toronto, where he earned a BA in 1880. He subsequently studied law, in Seaforth, in Toronto, and, after moving to Manitoba in February 1882, in Winnipeg. He was called to the Manitoba bar in November 1882.

Early in 1883 Coldwell settled in Brandon and began to practise there. He was joined by Thomas Mayne Daly*, who was called to the bar the following year. Their successful general partnership lasted until 1892, when Daly moved to Winnipeg. Coldwell afterwards established other partnerships. He would be named a KC in 1903. From about 1887 to 1907 he served on the Brandon City Council, during which time he became widely known and admired. After the

death on 4 Nov. 1907 of Brandon's representative in the Legislative Assembly, Stanley William McInnis*, Conservative premier Rodmond Palen Roblin* invited Coldwell to enter his cabinet as provincial secretary and municipal commissioner. Coldwell was sworn in on 14 November and four days later he was elected by acclamation at a by-election in Brandon.

On 5 March 1908 Coldwell was appointed Manitoba's first minister of education, the post for which he would be remembered (eight months later he resigned as provincial secretary). He was re-elected easily in the general election of 11 July 1910. In the spring of 1912 he introduced and guided through the assembly a series of changes to the Manitoba Public Schools Act of 1897 which became known as the Coldwell amendments. The story behind them is tortuous, if instructive.

For many years, and particularly after the creation of Saskatchewan and Alberta in 1905, Manitoba had been clamouring for extension of its boundaries northward. In 1911 the time seemed propitious. Roblin's government had given important and dependable support to the federal Conservative party in the first decade of the 20th century. Now there appeared to be a real chance of victory in the federal election. The Manitoba Conservative party and its electoral machine took full part in the federal campaign and, despite the popularity of reciprocity on the prairies, Roblin delivered eight of the province's ten seats to Conservative leader Robert Laird Borden*, who became prime minister on 10 Oct. 1911. Among Borden's promises was a commitment to extend Manitoba's boundaries to Hudson Bay. The territory that would be included in the enlarged province, much of the District of Keewatin, would be subject to Manitoba's school legislation, however, and therein lay the rub.

Catholics, especially those in Winnipeg and Brandon, were not likely to applaud the extension of school legislation that taxed them to support public schools and denied any public funds to Catholic parochial schools. In much of the rest of the province there was local religious and linguistic homogeneity, so the Roblin government practised an easy political tolerance. In the French-speaking communities up the Red River from Winnipeg, for example, the local public schools were, in practice, Catholic schools. There were no such arrangements in the urban areas, however, where Catholics were very much a minority.

In addition to the unhappy Manitoba Catholics there were other obstacles to the extension of the province's boundaries. A group of French Canadian Conservative Nationalistes allied with Borden's government and led by backbencher Paul-Émile Lamarche strongly opposed the federal bill to extend the boundaries because it provided no guarantees for Catholic schools in the district to be annexed. Despite verbal assurances by Robert Rogers*, the federal minister of the interior and a close friend of Roblin's, that the Manitoba premier would deal fairly with the district's Catholics, Lamarche and six of his colleagues voted against the legislation, which passed on 12 March. Other Conservative Nationalistes, such as Frederick Debartzch Monk*, remained loyal to Borden's government. The federal Conservatives' cohesion was badly damaged. The Coldwell amendments, it was hoped, would help to heal the breach.

In mid March Archbishop Adélard Langevin* of St Boniface was asked by a Conservative friend to open negotiations with Rogers and the Roblin government over changes to the Public Schools Act. Langevin accepted and thought he had obtained major improvements. The measures introduced into the Manitoba assembly by Coldwell on 1 April were declaratory rather than substantive. The Laurier–Greenway compromise of 1896 [see Thomas Greenway*] had provided that in rural schools with 25 Catholic pupils, or urban schools with 40, a qualified teacher of that faith would be provided if their parents requested one. This provision also applied to Protestants in heavily Catholic areas. Coldwell's amendments proposed that any reference to school be interpreted to mean "any and every school building [and] school room." If applied to individual classrooms, the legislation could have the effect of allowing public aid to parochial schools in the cities.

To the extent that they mollified the Nationalistes in Borden's government, the Coldwell amendments may have been successful. The Catholics of Winnipeg and Brandon, however, won no benefit from them. The Roblin government neglected or chose not to take the necessary step to make the amendments effective. They did not repeal another section of the Public Schools Act which levied heavy penalties on any school trustee who permitted the segregation of children by religion during the school day. Urban Catholics were dismayed, and the *Manitoba Free Press* could say smugly a year later that the Coldwell amendments "have not to date changed by a hair's breadth the status of the Public School in Manitoba."

Although Coldwell's entry into provincial politics had been auspicious, his departure was inglorious. In 1915 he was linked to the scandal over construction of the new parliament building that caused Roblin's government to resign in May. Both the contractor and the Conservative party were the financial beneficiaries of massive overpayment by the government. A royal commission chaired by Chief Justice Thomas Graham Mathers reported on 24 Aug. 1915 that Roblin, Coldwell, and two other cabinet ministers, Walter Humphries Montague and James Henry Howden, had entered into a fraudulent conspiracy. The four men were brought to trial on 24 July 1916; it resulted in a hung jury on 28 August and a new trial was ordered. The following year the crown stayed proceedings.

The ostensible reason was the ill health of Roblin and Howden (Montague had since died), but this hardly explains why the charges against Coldwell were dropped. By then Coldwell had returned to his law practice; he continued to work until his death in 1924.

J. E. REA

AM, MG 13, G1; MG 14, B36; RG 18, A4, boxes 10–11. LAC, RG 31, C1, 1871, Hullett Township, Ont., div.1: 2. Univ. of Man. Libraries, Dept. of Arch. and Special Coll. (Winnipeg), J. W. Dafoe fonds. *Manitoba Free Press*, 25 Jan. 1924. Réal Bélanger, *Paul-Émile Lamarche: le pays avant le parti (1904–1918)* (Sainte-Foy, Qué., 1984). *Canadian annual rev.*, 1912. *Canadian men and women of the time* (Morgan; 1912). G. R. Cook, "Church, schools, and politics in Manitoba, 1903–12," *CHR*, 39 (1958): 1–23. *CPG*, 1908–15. "Documents inédits: correspondance Langevin–Audet," *RHAF*, 1 (1947–48): 271–77. A. I. Inglis, "Some political factors in the demise of the Roblin government: 1915" (MA thesis, Univ. of Man., 1968). J. A. Jackson, *The centennial history of Manitoba* ([Toronto], 1970). W. L. Morton, *Manitoba: a history* (Toronto, 1957).

COLLISON, WILLIAM HENRY, Church of England missionary and clergyman; b. 12 Nov. 1847 in County Armagh (Northern Ireland), son of John J. Collison and Mary Emily Maxwell; m. 19 Aug. 1873 Marion M. Goodwin (d. 1919), and they had five sons and three daughters; d. 21 Jan. 1922 in Kincolith (Gingolx), B.C.

Educated at the Church of Ireland Training College in Dublin, William Henry Collison began his career as a schoolmaster in charge of an industrial school at Cork. In November 1872 he read of the Church Missionary Society's need for recruits, and determined to apply. The following April he entered the Church Missionary College in Islington (London) for a brief period of training. The CMS decided that his qualifications made him a suitable assistant for William Duncan*, the lay missionary in charge of the North Pacific mission, centred at Metlakatla, B.C. The society, which had difficulty in placing ordained missionaries there, opted to send Collison out as a layman with a view to his later ordination, and gave him permission to marry before leaving. His wife, Marion Goodwin, was well prepared for the mission field: she was a deaconess and a trained nurse who had served in the Franco-German War and during a smallpox epidemic in Cork.

The Collisons arrived in Victoria on 25 Oct. 1873. They were met by Edward Cridge, the dean of Christ Church Cathedral, with whom they resided before leaving for Metlakatla in early November. Cridge was engaged in a bitter dispute with George Hills*, the bishop of British Columbia. By staying with Cridge and failing to present his credentials to Hills, Collison became embroiled in the factional politics of the diocese.

At Metlakatla, his first task was to learn the Tsimshian language. By the following summer he could conduct the greater part of church services without an interpreter. As well as preaching, his duties included visiting and teaching, and initially he was confident of success. However, the mission was in a state of tension. Duncan and Cridge, who shared a commitment to low-church evangelicalism, were friends, and consequently the Hills–Cridge dispute disordered relations between Duncan and Hills. Given Duncan's increasing hostility to ecclesiastical authority, Collison's ordination was put off. Earnest and not particularly anxious for promotion, he persevered in his missionary duties, while managing to retain Duncan's confidence. He became interested in the Haida when a group from Masset, on the Queen Charlotte Islands, visited Fort Simpson (Lax Kw'alaams) in 1874 and 1875. During these visits he began to evangelize Chief Seegay, whose half-Tsimshian wife acted as translator. In June 1876 Collison was begged to minister to Seegay since he was dying of tuberculosis. Collison made the voyage to Masset, and on his return obtained permission to open a mission there. After the Collisons' move in November, William expanded his knowledge of Haida, eventually translating portions of the Bible and the Book of Common Prayer and composing hymns in this language.

While the Collisons were at Masset, Duncan and Hills's relationship deteriorated, and Hills asked the CMS to send Bishop William Carpenter Bompas* of Athabasca to intervene. He arrived at Metlakatla in November 1877 and spent the winter. The following March at Kincolith, a CMS mission among the Niska (Nisga'a) at the mouth of the Nass River, Collison was ordained deacon and priest by Bompas, who also negotiated a redistribution of duties, assigning Duncan the secular affairs of Metlakatla and Collison the "spiritual charge" of Metlakatla, Kincolith, and the Queen Charlottes. Reluctantly, Collison left the Haida mission in 1879 and returned to Metlakatla, where he soon encountered more conflict. William Ridley, who had arrived with the support of the CMS to take up duties as bishop of the newly formed diocese of Caledonia, had quickly run foul of Duncan, who prohibited Communion and confirmation and resisted translation work. From London the society wrote Collison letters of encouragement that acknowledged his difficult position, and urged him to maintain calm in the face of factionalism and sporadic violence. In 1882, after Ridley had formally removed Duncan from connection with the CMS, the situation became so tense that Collison was compelled to leave Metlakatla for a time. Collison asked to be sent to another mission, and in May 1884 he and his family moved to Kincolith. He learned more Niska, and soon translated the services of Morning and Evening prayer. Marion Collison's role was equally significant. Like other missionary wives, she was responsible for teaching European domestic skills to the native women, and for modelling appropriate female behaviour. As a nurse, she helped avert a smallpox epidemic. Collison regarded her medical contributions as central to his work: "Her skill in ministering to the sick, and in dressing the wounds of those injured, tended in no small degree to bring them under the influence of the teaching of the Gospel of Salvation."

In 1891 Collison, whose support of Ridley and the CMS was unwavering, was unanimously selected as the diocese's first archdeacon. A serious blow came in September 1893 when the church at Kincolith and three-quarters of the village were destroyed by fire. Shortly after rebuilding had begun, a fervent spiritual revival threatened to undermine the stability of the community. In response, Collison introduced a native branch of the Church Army, a strongly evangelical Anglican organization that emphasized enthusiastic worship, and promoted native leadership within the church-sponsored society.

When Ridley resigned as bishop in 1904, Collison declined to be nominated to the episcopacy, choosing to remain at Kincolith. At his death there in 1922 he was the longest serving CMS missionary in the North British Columbia mission (as North Pacific had been renamed) and he was the only remaining missionary funded directly by the CMS. His letters to the society and his autobiography, *In the wake of the war canoe*, reveal a moderate and conscientious man who strove to maintain "the best interests of the mission" in the face of schism. Despite Duncan's blatant failure at times to recognize his contributions, Collison was remarkably reticent in his autobiography about the difficulties at Metlakatla. He was noted for his warmth, generosity, and hospitality, and for his commitment to his work.

Collison's interaction with the native peoples was complex. He respected the converts, became fluent in Tsimshian, Haida, and Niska, and was sensitive to the importance of the clan system. (According to his son William Edwin, also an ordained missionary, he had been adopted into the Eagle clan of the Haida.) On the other hand, he fiercely opposed potlatching and traditional native medicine, and encouraged the Niska at Kincolith to accept the Indian Advancement Act of 1884, which replaced traditional hierarchies of power with a system of elected chiefs and band councils supervised by an Indian agent. Perhaps these contradictions can best be explained by Collison's own theory of missions, with its implication that the missionary was the best judge of what was appropriate for his converts: "It is incumbent on the missionary to welcome and foster whatever tends to the uplifting and improvement of the people amongst whom he labours, whilst carefully guarding against whatever tends to degrade or defeat his mission."

GAIL EDWARDS

[William Henry Collison's autobiography, *In the wake of the war canoe* . . . (London, 1915), appeared in an identical edition in Toronto the following year. An abridged version, edited and annotated by Charles Lillard, was published in Victoria in 1981, but it omits many of the details of Collison's missionary activities. None of Collison's Haida translations seem to have been printed, although they may have formed the basis of the later translation work by the Reverend Charles Harrison, CMS missionary at Masset in 1882–90, published by the Society for Promoting Christian Knowledge and the British and Foreign Bible Society. G.E.]

Two letters by Collison appear in the *Church Missionary Intelligencer and Record* (London): "First letter from Queen Charlotte's Islands," [3rd] ser., 2 (1877): 374–77, and "News from Queen Charlotte's Islands," [3rd] ser., 3 (1878): 516–18. Reports by Collison, Duncan, and other British Columbia missionaries were published there as "North Pacific Mission," [3rd] ser., 4 (1879): 557–66.

LAC, MG 17, B2, C, C.1/M.9–M.10; C.2/O; G, C.1/P.3; C.2/L; C.2/O (mfm.). *Daily Colonist* (Victoria), 24 Jan. 1922. Alexander Anderson, "An official view of Metlakahtla," *Church Missionary Intelligencer and Record*, [3rd] ser., 6 (1881): 50–52. "Bishop Ridley and the North Pacific Mission," *Church Missionary Intelligencer and Record*, [3rd] ser., 9 (1884): 165–67. Church Missionary Soc., *Report of the deputation to Metlakatla: (General Touch and the Rev. W. R. Blackett)* ([London, 1886]). [Edward Cridge and W. J. Macdonald], *The Church and the Indians: the trouble at Metlakahtla* ([Victoria, 1882]). F. [H.] DuVernet, "Hagwilyaen, Shimoigit," *Across the Rockies* (London), 13 (1922), no.2: 23–24. "The government commission at Metlakahtla," *Church Missionary Intelligencer and Record*, [3rd] ser., 10 (1885): 340–54. Hugh McCullum and Karmel Taylor McCullum, *Caledonia 100 years ahead* (Toronto, 1979). Peter Murray, *The devil and Mr. Duncan* (Victoria, 1985). E. P. Patterson, *Mission on the Nass: the evangelization of the Nishga (1860–1890)* (Waterloo, Ont., 1982). F. A. Peake, *The Anglican Church in British Columbia* (Vancouver, 1959). [William Ridley], *Senator Macdonald's misleading account of his visit to Metlakatla exposed* ([Victoria], 1882). E. O. S. Scholefield and F. W. Howay, *British Columbia from the earliest times to the present* (4v., Vancouver, 1914), 4: 1369–70. Eugene Stock, *The history of the Church Missionary Society, its environment, its men and its work* (4v., London, 1899–1916). Jean Usher [Friesen], *William Duncan of Metlakatla: a Victorian missionary in British Columbia* (Ottawa, 1974).

COMEAU, NAPOLÉON-ALEXANDRE (baptized **Alexandre-Napoléon**), hunter, fishery warden, office holder, naturalist, and author; b. 11 May 1848 at the trading post of Îlets-Jérémie (Colombier), Lower Canada, son of Antoine-Alexandre Comeau, an HBC agent, and Luce Hall, known as Mary Bédard; m. first 14 June 1871 Marie-Antoinette Labrie (d. 1889), probably in Godbout, Que. (the marriage is recorded in the register in Betsiamites, Que.); m. secondly 23 Nov. 1889 Victoria Labrie in Saint-Patrice-de-la-Rivière-Pentecôte (Rivière-Pentecôte), Que., and they had nine boys and three girls; d. 17 Nov. 1923 in Godbout.

Raised haphazardly in the various trading posts in Îlets-Jérémie, Mingan, and Sept-Îles where his father was in charge, Napoléon-Alexandre Comeau soon became multilingual; as a child he learned to speak fluent French, English, Montagnais, Naskapi, and Inuktitut. In 1859–60 he attended G. W. Lawler's French and English academy in Trois-Rivières. After this sole year of schooling he returned to the north shore of the St Lawrence. There he became an accredited fishery warden on the Rivière Godbout, which was an excellent salmon river and a favourite fishing spot for Canadian and American businessmen and politicians. He worked in this capacity for more than 60 fishing seasons. In the winter of 1862, with the help of the Montagnais hunter Plutée Ashini, he also began to learn how to carry on trapping, the main economic activity of the region. The furs, which in some cases fetched high prices, were sold at the trading posts of the several companies operating in the Betsiamites reserve and the surrounding area. Comeau also acted as a middleman between the Montagnais hunters and the Hudson's Bay Company.

Towards the end of the 1870s Comeau gave up trapping for various administrative activities, which he would engage in for many years. He was simultaneously postmaster (from 1877), fisheries agent (around 1879), and telegraph agent (around 1884) for the settlements in his region (Manicouagan, Godbout, Baie-des-Cèdres, Pointe-des-Monts, Îlets Caribou, Îles de Mai, and Rivière-Pentecôte). In addition, thanks to a knowledge of anatomy acquired in the course of his work by experience and reading, and his generosity, as well as a rudimentary training given to him by two physicians from the Jeffery Hale's Hospital at Quebec, he provided basic medical care to dozens of aboriginal and pioneering European families. During his productive career as an acknowledged "male midwife," he assisted in some 200 deliveries.

In January 1886 Comeau attained fame by rescuing two relatives who had become lost on the St Lawrence River during a severe storm. After wandering about on the ice for a great many hours, he succeeded in guiding them to the south shore. This adventure caught the attention of the press and brought him a number of awards. The name and coat of arms of the town of Baie-Comeau, which was incorporated in 1937, would commemorate this exploit.

Inquisitive, self-taught, and thoroughly familiar with the mysteries of outdoor life in the Labrador region, Comeau proved a well-informed naturalist. His meetings and correspondence with Canadian and American scientists enabled him to make good use of his vast expertise and his knowledge of the fauna of the north shore region and in particular of its salmon. He collaborated with researchers from the Université

Laval at Quebec and the Smithsonian Institution in Washington, especially through his inventory of the birds from around Pointe-des-Monts, which was published in 1882 in the *Bulletin* of the Nuttall Ornithological Club in Cambridge, Mass.

Comeau's skills, his hunting and fishing exploits, and his knowledge of aboriginal culture formed the basis of the articles he published in the *National Geographic Magazine* (Washington) and in *Forest and Stream* (New York). In 1909 he brought out at Quebec an autobiography full of anecdotes and observations which also included his inventory of birds; entitled *Life and sport on the north shore of the lower St. Lawrence and gulf*, it would be reissued in 1923 and 1954. A French translation by Nazaire LE VASSEUR was published at Quebec in 1945 and reprinted in 1983 under the title *La vie et le sport sur la Côte Nord du bas Saint-Laurent et du golfe*.

The federal government confirmed the importance of Comeau's experience by appointing him co-chair of an inquiry, held in 1914, into the fisheries of the Hudson Bay region. During the following years he played an active part in drafting the Canadian-American agreement on migratory birds. He was an energetic member of and lecturer before the Provancher Society of Natural History of Canada, which he had helped found, and of the American Ornithologists' Union.

The Provancher Society erected a monument in Godbout to honour Napoléon-Alexandre Comeau soon after his death. A replica was installed in the Jardin Zoologique de Québec in 1933. A number of Quebec writers have taken an interest in him; Yves Thériault* wrote a biography entitled *Roi de la Côte Nord*, which was published at Montreal in 1960.

PIERRE FRENETTE

ANQ-CN, CE901-S9, 23 nov. 1889; S10, 30 juill. 1848. ANQ-Q, ZQ6-S315, 14 juin 1871. *L'Événement*, 19 nov. 1923. Pierre Frenette, *Napoléon-Alexandre Comeau* (Montréal, 1981). Pauline L[e Vallée] Boileau, *La Côte-Nord contre vents et marées: biographie romancée de Napoléon-Alexandre Comeau (1848–1923)* (Sillery, Qué., 1998). C. D. Melvill *et al.*, *Reports on fisheries investigations in Hudson and James bays and tributary waters in 1914* (Ottawa, 1915). Robert Parisé, *Géants de la Côte-Nord* (Québec, 1974).

CONAN, LAURE. *See* ANGERS, FÉLICITÉ

CONNOLLY (Connelly), MARY, named **Sister Mary Clare**, member of the Sisters of Charity of Halifax and teacher; baptized 6 June 1840, aged two days, in Halifax, daughter of Patrick Connolly and Mary Broderick (Brauderick, Brawdorick); d. 10 April 1922 in Wellesley, Mass.

Mary Connolly's parents were part of a wave of Irish Catholic immigration to Canada in the 19th century. They married in Halifax on 28 Aug. 1839, and

Mary, their first child, was born the following year. The family included two other children who would become religious: Catherine also entered the Sisters of Charity of Halifax and John J. became a Jesuit. The Connolly family belonged to St Mary's Cathedral parish and the children attended the parochial school. In 1849, at the request of Bishop William Walsh*, the Sisters of Charity of New York took on the instruction of the girls in the parish, and they continued this work until 1855 when the newly established Sisters of Charity of Halifax, an outgrowth of the New York group, replaced them [*see* Rosanna McCann*].

Mary Connolly was among the first young women to join the Sisters of Charity of Halifax, on 1 May 1856 at the age of 15 years. After a postulancy of three months, she entered the noviciate as Sister Mary Clare and she was professed in 1858. Once the congregation was permitted to pronounce perpetual vows, she would be the first member to do so, on 28 July 1908, and thus her community number is One. Immediately upon entering the congregation, she was appointed to teach at St Mary's Girls' School. She remained there until May 1858 when she became local superior of St Peter's Convent in Dartmouth and teacher at its school. The school, which had opened its doors some months before, began with about 40 female pupils but, unlike the schools the sisters ran in Halifax, it did not experience any significant increase in enrolment. Sister Mary Clare blamed the lack of growth on the nature of Dartmouth, "the majority of the people being protestant and very bigoted."

In 1862 Sister Mary Clare was one of two sisters appointed, at the request of Archbishop Thomas Louis Connolly*, to a house of refuge in Dutch Village (Halifax) for "fallen women" committed to the congregation's care by the courts. She recorded in her diary that "the first arrivals . . . were of the most degraded type . . . discontented, idle, and quarrelsome; they would dispute and come to blows for the merest trifle." All four ran away at different times but three were returned by police and were soon joined by five more residents. Though the archbishop was disappointed, after a year's trial the sisters withdrew from this work because they could see no improvement in the women, and because it had been very difficult to bring basic supplies from Halifax, then some three miles away, especially during the winter.

Sister Mary Clare was one of three sisters who volunteered and were chosen for a perilous assignment in 1866. On 8 April that year the *England* arrived in Halifax with cholera raging on board. The ship was ordered to drop anchor off McNabs Island and the passengers, the majority of them Irish Catholics, were quarantined there. After visiting McNabs and grasping the gravity of the situation, Archbishop Connolly went directly to St Mary's Convent on Barrington Street and summoned all the sisters to the

Conybeare

parlour. According to Sister Mary Clare's journal, "His Grace told of his visit to the cholera station, and the suffering and distress of the poor people. All of them in such a state of fear and excitement, and many poor children, whose parents had been carried off by the pestilence, having no one to care for them. His Grace then wanted to know how many Sisters would volunteer to go and take care of those children." When every sister volunteered, the archbishop initially picked two, Sister Mary Clare and a novice, Sister Mary Vincent. The archbishop used the opportunity of their departure to display publicly the "charity of the Catholic faith" and accordingly, at 8:30 the next morning, 16 April, the two chosen sisters along with the archbishop, the mother superior, and another member of the congregation walked to the Market Wharf where they and the archbishop boarded a rowboat to go to McNabs. A third sister, Mary Alphonsus, soon joined them on the island.

For approximately one week the sisters worked among the immigrants, caring especially for the many children left orphaned. The city sent convicts, who were provided with a barrel of rum daily, to dig graves. Unfortunately, the sisters could hear the often drunken and profane gravediggers doing their work and, as Sister Mary Clare remarked, "it was easy to meditate on hell in those days." After the sisters left the island they were required to spend two weeks in quarantine before returning to the congregation.

In 1864 Sister Mary Clare had resumed teaching at St Mary's School in Halifax. She remained there until 1878, when she went to Church Point for two years. Subsequently, she taught at a number of institutions in Halifax. At various times she held office within her congregation, as assistant superior, treasurer, and mistress of novices. The last was an important position that had as its main task the development of young women who aspired to be Sisters of Charity. While teaching at Mount St Vincent Academy in Rockingham (Halifax) from 1892 to 1902, she served a final term (1892–98) as mistress of novices, during the course of which 82 young women entered the congregation. In 1902 she was sent to Wellesley, Mass., where in addition to teaching at the Academy of the Assumption she acted as vicar, second in command to the local superior, until her retirement in 1919. "Gentle, spiritual, and austere in character," according to one of the congregation's historians, she died of bronchopneumonia and endocarditis in 1922, and was buried in St Mary's Cemetery in Needham, Mass. At the time of her death the Sisters of Charity of Halifax numbered 400 members in 35 houses in Nova Scotia, New Brunswick, Massachusetts, and Bermuda, serving schools, orphanages, hospitals, and a home for single expectant mothers.

HEIDI MACDONALD

Arch. of the Archdiocese of Halifax, St Mary's Cathedral (Halifax), RBMB. Arch. of the Sisters of Charity (New York), Sister Elizabeth A. Vermaelen, "Elizabeth Seton – educator" (paper presented at secondary school forum, April 1974, New York). Sisters of Charity of St Vincent de Paul Arch. (Halifax), Biog. records of professed sisters, 1859–1951: Sister Mary Ann Connolly; Sister Mary Clare Connolly. *Halifax Citizen*, April 1866. *Morning Chronicle* (Halifax), April 1866. *Dictionary of Jesuit biography: ministry to English Canada, 1842–1987* (Toronto, 1991). Judith Fingard et al., *Halifax: the first 250 years* (Halifax, 1999). J. B. Hanington, *Every popish person: the story of Roman Catholicism in Nova Scotia and the church of Halifax, 1604–1984* (Halifax, 1984). *Historical statistics of Canada*, ed. M. C. Urquhart and K. A. H. Buckley (Toronto, 1965). [M. A. McCarthy, named] Sister Francis d'Assisi, *A forgotten mother, Mother Rose McAleer, 1827–1870; our first Canadian mother, Mother Mary Josephine Carroll, 1815–1877; a gentle mother, Mother Elizabeth O'Neill, 1832–1908* (Halifax, 1968); *Mother Mary Basilia McCann, first mother superior of the Halifax daughters of Blessed Elizabeth Seton, 1811–1870* (Halifax, 1968). [Mary Power, named] Sister Maura, *The Sisters of Charity, Halifax* (Toronto, 1956).

CONYBEARE, CHARLES FREDERICK PRINGLE, lawyer, office holder, businessman, and author; b. 19 May 1860 at Little Sutton House, Chiswick (London), England, son of Henry Conybeare and Anne Newport Moore; m. 24 June 1890 Ida Attwood in St Paul, Minn., and they had a son and two daughters; d. 30 July 1927 in Lethbridge, Alta.

Charles F. P. Conybeare came from a well-educated family; his grandfather William Daniel Conybeare was a noted geologist and cleric and his father was a civil engineer. After attending Westminster School in London in 1868–69 and 1873–74 and Christ Church, Oxford, he joined the British merchant marine in 1875. Discharged for near-sightedness, he came to Canada, where he tried to farm, without success. He landed in Winnipeg in June 1880 and was articled to a law firm. In December 1885 he founded his own practice in the fast-growing settlement of Lethbridge; he was admitted to the bar of the North-West Territories that year and appointed a notary in 1886. He served as a crown prosecutor from 1888 to 1897. Appointed QC in 1894, he was elected a bencher of the Law Society of the North-West Territories in 1899 and founding vice-president of the Law Society of Alberta in 1907.

Conybeare's many partners included William Alfred Galliher (1888–97) and William Carlos Ives (1901–6), who both became judges. According to local lore, he had difficulty retaining apprentices and partners until his later years because he kept three or four of his chow dogs, some of which smelled, in his office. He was the solicitor for the municipality of Lethbridge, the Bank of Montreal, the Canadian Pacific Railway, Alberta Railway and Coal, North-Western Coal and Navigation, and Canadian North-

West Irrigation; other clients numbered the cattle companies of William G. Conrad. Interested in irrigation [*see* William PEARCE], he was a member of the South Western Territorial Irrigation League in 1894. As Lethbridge's major lawyer, he handled a wide range of civil and criminal matters, including a steady flow of wills and inheritances. Assiduous in his work, he enjoyed the courtroom, where he maintained a gentlemanly presence. He was particularly adept in thorny questions involving the law of contract across jurisdictions. Among his more controversial interventions was one to support the readmission of a local solicitor disbarred for retaining clients' money. At sittings of the Supreme Court of Alberta in Lethbridge, he often acted for the CPR in cases of negligence. In the 1920s he returned to crown prosecutions. In one notable case of carnal knowledge before the Supreme Court in 1925 (*The King* v. *Arnold Baines*), he persuaded it to hear the testimonies of seven- and eight-year-old girls, which generally were non-admissible.

Conybeare was a major figure in the social, cultural, and economic life of Lethbridge. A member of the Sons of England, the Overseas Club, and the Cricket Club and the Turf Association in Lethbridge, he was a founder there of the Chinook Club and, in 1894, of the Pemmican Club, an association of territorial old-timers initiated by Dr Frank Hamilton MEWBURN. In 1890 he had served on the committee that pioneered the Great Falls and Canada Railway, and he participated in the early years of the Alberta Railway and Coal and the Canadian North-West Irrigation companies. A promoter of the Bank of Winnipeg, he was involved in starting Lethbridge Brewing and Malting, British Canadian Trust in 1901, and Lethbridge Brick and Terra Cotta in 1903. He chaired the public school board in 1890–93 and served as president of the Lethbridge Board of Trade and Civic Committee in 1893 and 1907–8 as well as founding president of the Southern Alberta Boards of Trade in 1907. His wife would join him in his public endeavours in 1911, as treasurer of the newly formed Women's Civic Club of the Board of Trade. Despite his prominence, his only foray into politics was a bid for the Council of the North-West Territories in 1887, which he lost to Frederick William Gordon Haultain*.

His marriage in St Paul in 1890 had been a curious event: his fiancée, Letitia Attwood, died just before his arrival so he asked her sister, who, it was said, agreed because she "was so acutely overcome by his anguish." Their home, Riverview (originally built by Charles Alexander Magrath*), featured stained-glass windows overlooking a courtyard and a large and famous library. The Conybeares also developed a seven-acre garden; its lawns and English-style maze were considered exceptional. Charles started all the trees, hedges, and shrubs from seeds and slips obtained from England.

An avid patron of the arts, Conybeare belonged to the Knights of Pythias – he was its chancellor as well – and the Dramatic Order of the Knights of Khorassan. In addition to producing libretti for unidentified musical comedies performed in Lethbridge and throughout the west, he wrote two books of poetry: *Vahnfried* (London, 1903) and *Lyrics from the west* (Toronto, 1907). The latter reveals his staunch attachment to both Canada and the British empire. "Canada's flag," for example, asks

> What spell from the storm-lashed Atlantic extending
> To where the Pacific its blue water rolls;
> Each province in concord and unity blending,
> Can make for each other such love in their souls?

In "Britons all to-day" he was equally prosaic about Canadian support for the empire in the South African War: "Unfurl the Union banner, – let it wave across the seas; . . . Britons all to-day – linked across the sea, / Pealing out with joyous shout the chorus of the free." His romantic side is revealed in "For my wife," which ends "My heart-strings throb with a joy that reveals / The songs that can never be sung." He would receive honorary DCLs from Bishop's College in Lennoxville, Que., in 1907 and the University of Alberta in 1908 (*ad eundem gradum*). A stalwart of the Church of England, he had paid half the cost of building St Augustine's Church in Lethbridge in 1886–87. Archdeacon Cecil Swanson later considered him the rock of the parish. Appointed solicitor of the diocese of Calgary in 1900, he became its first chancellor in 1904, a position he would maintain until 1916. As a member of synod, he never missed a meeting, and he sat on the committee that edited a new hymnal in 1908. In matters of temperance, he did not take a hard line. Elected president of the Moderation League of Alberta in 1919 and 1923, he headed efforts to urge the province to repeal its Prohibition legislation and assume full control of liquor sales.

Charles F. P. Conybeare died on 30 July 1927. A mild and unassuming person who enjoyed swimming and boating, he had spent his last years in isolation since his wife had died. His funeral was held on the lawn of his home, his casket under an elm he had planted from seed. The service, at which Bishop Louis Ralph Sherman officiated, was accompanied by a choir and a portable organ.

LOUIS A. KNAFLA

Charles Frederick Pringle Conybeare's major reported cases appear in *Alberta Law Reports* (Toronto), 1908–20. Photographs of him in his law office (with one of his chows) (P19694784000) and of his home (Riverview) (P19841005002) are in the Sir Alexander Galt Museum and

Arch. (Lethbridge, Alta). The GA holds a headshot of Conybeare (NA-4082-3).

GA, M 1931. GRO, Reg. of births, Chiswick (London), 19 May 1860. Legal Arch. Soc. of Alta (Calgary), fonds 5, vol.60, file 923–vol.68, file 946 (Law Soc. of Alta, minutes of convocation, 1907–27); fonds 30 (Conybeare, Church, McArthur, and Davidson coll.). PAA, GR1978.235. *Lethbridge Herald*, 31 July 1927, 18 June 1985. *Lethbridge News*, 11 Dec. 1885; 8, 29 Dec. 1886; 30 March, 5, 13 April, 24 Aug., 19 Oct. 1887; 18 June, 2, 16 July 1890; 5 April, 12 Dec. 1894; 17 March 1897; 26 Jan. 1899. *Canadian annual rev.*, 1921: 830. *Canadian men and women of the time* (Morgan; 1898 and 1912). Alex Johnston, *Lethbridge, from coal town to commercial centre: a business history*, ed. Irma Dogterom and L. G. Ellis (Lethbridge, 1997). L. A. Knafla, "From oral to written memory: the common law tradition in western Canada," in *Law & justice in a new land: essays in western Canadian legal history*, ed. L. A. Knafla (Toronto, 1986), 31–77; "Report on the legal careers of Conybeare, Macleod and Scott" (paper prepared for Alta Culture, Historic Sites Service, Edmonton, 1985). M.-L. Loescher, "Dr. C. F. P. Conybeare, Lethbridge's pioneer lawyer," Whoop-Up Country Chapter, Hist. Soc. of Alta, *Newsletter* (Lethbridge), no.1 (January 1990): [3–4]; "Dr. Conybeare 'was the church'" (1966) (copy in the Sir Alexander Galt Museum and Arch.). A. O. MacRae, *History of the province of Alberta* (2v., [Calgary], 1912). *The record of old Westminsters: a biographical list . . .*, comp. G. F. R. Barker and A. H. Stenning (London, 1928). *Who's who and why*, 1919/20. *Who was who . . . : a companion to "Who's who," containing the biographies of those who died during the period* [1897–2000] (10v. and an index to date, London, 1920–), 2 (*1916–28*).

COOME, SARAH HANNAH ROBERTA. *See* GRIER

CORDASCO, ANTONIO, labourer, employment agent, banker, and newspaper owner; b. 5 June 1863 in Italy, son of Carlo Cordasco and Tomassina (Tommasina) Gagliardi (Galiardi); m. 16 April 1891 Maria Concetta La Pietra in Montreal, and they had four sons and two daughters; d. there 19 April 1921.

Born most likely in the region of Calabria, Antonio Cordasco arrived in Canada in 1886, when the first contingents of seasonal Italian labourers appeared in the industrial landscape. His early association with railway construction, and no doubt his ambition, allowed him to move up the ranks of the Canadian Pacific Railway's work crews from labourer to foreman. It was probably as a foreman that he became active in recruiting labourers. In 1901, faced with a major labour conflict, the CPR turned to him for help, offering to pay him a dollar for each strike-breaker he delivered. He was able to meet the challenge by availing himself of contacts with labour-recruiting agencies in a number of northeastern American cities and supplied the CPR with about 2,000 men. As a result, that year he became the CPR's exclusive recruiter of Italian workers.

During the early 1900s, when the CPR undertook a major expansion of its rail system and developed natural-resource industries along its lines, it was Canada's leading employer of migrant labourers – most of them unskilled seasonal workers needed for the construction and the maintenance of rail lines. In a typical year several thousand Italian labourers were in its employ, along with several thousand belonging to a variety of other nationalities. The system of recruiting migrant labour had become known throughout North America as the *padrone* system. Though severely restrained in the United States by federal legislation starting in 1885, the system had been allowed to persist in Canada. Labour recruitment would become subject to strict government regulation only after 1905. During the brief period – in the late 19th and early 20th centuries – when the *padrone* system was most in vogue in Canada, Cordasco emerged as its leading entrepreneur, largely because of the privileged relations he had established with the CPR.

From the office he set up on Rue Saint-Jacques in Montreal about 1901, Cordasco directed an elaborate network, ranging from recruiters in Italian villages to arrangements with steamship companies which allowed workers to travel on prepaid tickets. Once the workers had arrived in Canada and had paid the one dollar commission Cordasco exacted, they were organized into work gangs and entrusted to gang leaders – associates of Cordasco who were often also foremen for the CPR. Even in remote camps stretching from northern Ontario to British Columbia, labourers afforded Cordasco a source of revenue, since he acted as the exclusive supplier of food commodities, charging from 60 to 120 per cent above cost.

Besides satisfying the workers' need for jobs, Cordasco provided them with other services. By 1903 he had gone into banking. As a *banchista* (the term employed at the time for a private banker), he arranged for the transfer of earnings to families in Italy. The *Corriere del Canada*, a Montreal-based newspaper controlled by Cordasco early in the decade, served more as a tool for his recruiting than as a bona fide community paper. Cordasco, in fact, proved capable of launching particularly aggressive publicity campaigns in order to stave off competition from other Montreal *padroni* and employment agencies. In one case, on 27 Jan. 1904, he mounted a public event in which some 60 foremen and 2,000 workers marched through Montreal. At the height of the ceremony, his faithful assistants solemnly placed on his head a crown that was a replica of the one worn by the king of Italy, calling him "The King of Italian Labourers."

In the spring of 1904 thousands of Italian labourers flocked to Montreal in response to advertisements by Cordasco and other *padroni*. When a late thaw delayed the beginning of the work season, the unemployed men were forced to rely on public charity. At the request of civic authorities, a federal royal commission was appointed to inquire into the immigration of Italian labourers to Montreal and the alleged fraudulent practices of employment agencies. Although several agents in the city testified, Cordasco was a prime target. The proceedings of the inquiry, headed by judge John Winchester, constitute probably the richest documentation on the workings of the *padrone* system. As a result of the investigation, Cordasco's reputation suffered significantly. He was drawn into a number of court battles over fees he had exacted and wages he had not paid. The inquiry also led to the termination of his relations with the CPR. Despite the collapse of his recruiting empire, he managed to pursue his activities as a *banchista* and he acted as a steamship agent. He had become a naturalized British subject in 1902. At his death in 1921, his private banking business was still operating; it was taken over by his son Thomas Antonio (Anthony). Another son, Charles M., had served as a lieutenant in the Royal Flying Corps during World War I and was a prominent foreign exchange broker in Montreal.

BRUNO RAMIREZ

One of the most important sources of information on Antonio Cordasco's activities is Can., Royal commission to inquire into the immigration of Italian labourers to Montreal and the alleged fraudulent practices of employment agencies, *Report of commissioner and evidence* (Ottawa, 1905), which was published both separately and in Can., Parl., *Sessional papers*, 1905, no.36b. The French report has been republished as "Document: Rapport de la Commission royale sur l'immigration des journaliers italiens et des procédés fraduleux des bureaux de placement," introd. Bernard Dansereau, RCHTQ [Regroupement des Chercheurs-Chercheuses en Hist. des Travailleurs et Travailleuses du Québec], *Bull.* (Montréal), 22 (1996), no.1: 3–39.

BCM-G, RBMS, Notre-Dame de Montréal, 16 avril 1891; Saint-Jacques-le-Majeur (Montréal), 21 avril 1921 (mfm.). LAC, RG 31, C1, 1901, Montreal, Saint-Antoine Ward, subdist. A-3: 11. *Directory*, Montreal, 1906–21. R. F. Harney, "Montreal's king of Italian labour: a case of padronism," *Labour* (Halifax), 4 (1979): 57–84. Gunther Peck, "Reinventing free labor: immigrant padrones and contract laborers in North America, 1885–1925," *Journal of American Hist.* (Bloomington, Ind.), 83 (1996–97): 848–71. Bruno Ramirez, *Les premiers Italiens de Montréal: l'origine de la Petite Italie du Québec* (Montréal, 1984). Paul Tana, *Caffè Italia* (video recording in French and in Italian with French subtitles, Montreal, 1985).

COSTANZO, FILUMENA (Florence) (Sanfidele (Lassandro)), bootlegger's accomplice and convicted murderer; b. 1900 in Cosenza, Italy, daughter of Vincenzo Costanzo and Angela ——; m. 16 Oct. 1915 Carlo (Charles) Sanfidele in Fernie, B.C.; they had no children; d. 2 May 1923 in Fort Saskatchewan, Alta.

Filumena Costanzo immigrated to Canada with her mother and father, sister and brother, in 1909. The family settled in Fernie, where Costanzo's father was employed as a coalminer, the primary occupation in the Crowsnest Pass [*see* Frank Henry Sherman*]. In 1915, at the age of 14, Florence (who had changed her name on the advice of a teacher) married 23-year-old Carlo Sanfidele. As was the custom among Italians at the time, the marriage had been arranged by her father. Shortly after it took place, she and her husband moved to Pennsylvania in search of employment, but within only a few months they had returned to Canada, settling in Blairmore, Alta. It appears that Carlo adopted the surname Lassandro because he had entered the United States illegally and hoped he could avoid prosecution under the assumed name. By 1916 he was employed in Blairmore as a chauffeur to local businessman Emilio Picariello.

On 1 July 1916 Prohibition came into force in Alberta, making the sale of alcohol illegal. Soon after introduction of the legislation, a brisk bootlegging trade developed which involved the transportation of alcohol from neighbouring wet jurisdictions, including British Columbia and Montana, to southern Alberta and the clandestine sale of the illicit product to slake the thirst of the local mining community. By this time Carlo was working for Picariello as manager of the Alberta Hotel in Blairmore in addition to serving as a chauffeur. As part of his duties he took his employer's powerful McLaughlin Six motor car on bootlegging runs. Picariello's operation was extensive, stretching from Nelson, B.C., to Regina. His son Stefano (Steve) also was a driver. Picariello was able to continue his runs into British Columbia even after the sale of alcohol was prohibited there in 1917 and its manufacture was banned the following year. Florence Lassandro and the young Picariello were close in age and Picariello Sr believed the appearance of a young couple crossing the border seemingly out for an afternoon picnic was the perfect cover. As a result, the two rode together on numerous runs. On occasion, Florence drove alone. But whether alone or with Stefano Picariello, she participated in this illegal activity over several years.

On 21 Sept. 1922 officers of the Alberta Provincial Police pursued and attempted to intercept an automobile believed to contain illegal liquor and driven by Picariello's son. As the car entered the main street in Coleman, Alta, the local police signalled it to stop, but when no attempt was made to comply, Constable Stephen Oldacres Lawson fired at the vehicle, striking Stefano in the hand. The police gave chase, but Picariello's vehicle soon outdistanced them and they abandoned their pursuit. News of the incident reached Emilio Picariello that evening. Believing that his son might have been seriously injured or even killed, he armed himself and, together with Florence Lassandro, drove to the Coleman police barracks. Constable Lawson emerged and heated words were exchanged. As the confrontation escalated to physical grappling, two shots were fired apparently from P(c)ariello's vehicle, both of which missed Lawson. The constable turned away from the car, perhaps to retrieve his own firearm, and a third, fatal shot struck him in the back. His wife and one of his daughters witnessed the incident from the doorway of the barracks. Picariello and Lassandro immediately fled in their vehicle and eluded the police during the night of 21–22 September. They were finally apprehended in Blairmore late in the day on the 22nd.

Both Picariello and Lassandro were charged with murder. After a preliminary hearing in Coleman, the pair were remanded for trial in Calgary before Mr Justice William Legh Walsh*. With the financial means to retain top-flight counsel, Picariello hired prominent Calgary defence lawyer John McKinley Cameron* to act for both accused. The trial attracted much local and national attention. Prohibition itself was extremely controversial and Picariello's reputation as a rum-runner was well known. Also, the shooting of a policeman, then as now, was regarded as a particularly contemptible act. At the same time, Picariello was conspicuous in the Blairmore area as a local politician and a philanthropist and was widely called the "Emperor."

Cameron believed that a mysterious bystander had been responsible for the fatal shot but no supporting evidence could be found and the argument presented in court, also reasonably consistent with the facts, was that of self-defence. The jury, however, was unconvinced and the six-day trial resulted in convictions. In passing the obligatory sentence of death, Walsh acknowledged that some leniency might be extended to Lassandro because she was a woman, but that she should nevertheless prepare to meet her end. On Picariello's instructions, Cameron appealed to the Supreme Court of Alberta and, upon dismissal of the case there, to the Supreme Court of Canada. The original convictions were upheld.

Jailed in Fort Saskatchewan, with no reprieve or commutation despite further efforts by her lawyer, Lassandro spent the night before her execution in prayer with a Franciscan priest. Then in the early dawn of 2 May 1923, minutes after Picariello had met his end, she in turn ascended the scaffold steps. Protesting her innocence to the last and maintaining that she forgave "everyone," Florence Lassandro was hanged.

Reaction to the conviction and execution of Lassandro and her co-accused was mixed. The Italian community in the Crowsnest Pass was appalled but there is evidence of a general view in Calgary that their treatment was entirely appropriate. An appeal by Lassandro's family to have her remains returned to Blairmore was refused by the provincial government and both Lassandro and Picariello were interred in an unmarked grave in a north Edmonton cemetery.

With its ingredients of murder, courtroom drama, and ultimate tragedy, the story of Florence Lassandro's brief life has received considerable attention, both literary and theatrical, including a full dramatic opera. Sometimes portrayed as an innocent victim caught up in events or controlled by the Svengali-like Picariello, she remains something of an enigma. What is clear, however, is that her death on the Fort Saskatchewan gallows provided fuel and focus for the public debate on both Prohibition and capital punishment.

NEIL B. WATSON

GA, M 4843/30–31; M 6242; M 6840. *Blairmore Enterprise* (Blairmore, Alta), 1922–23. *Calgary Herald*, 1922–23. F. W. Anderson, *A dance with death: Canadian women on the gallows, 1754–1954* (Saskatoon and Calgary, 1997). Brian Brennan, *Scoundrels and scallywags: characters from Alberta's past* (Calgary, 2002). Jock Carpenter, *Bootlegger's bride* ([Calgary], 1993). Ann Chandler, "The lady & the bootlegger," *Beaver* (Winnipeg), 84 (2003–4), no.3: 40–44. *Citymakers: Calgarians after the frontier*, ed. Max Foran and S. S. Jameson (Calgary, 1987). R. E. Spence, *Prohibition in Canada: a memorial to Francis Stephens Spence* (Toronto, 1919).

COTES, SARA JEANNETTE. *See* DUNCAN

COTTON, WILLIAM LAWSON, newspaperman; b. 23 July 1848 in New London, P.E.I., eldest son of Richard Cotton, a Bible Christian preacher, and Maria Lawson; m. 17 June 1874 Margaret Ellin Harris in Charlottetown, and they had four daughters, one of whom died in infancy, and four sons; d. there 31 March 1928.

William L. Cotton left school in New London at 16 to learn the printing and newspaper business in Charlottetown under the direction of John Ings, editor of the *Islander*. After two years in Halifax as a reporter for Edmund Mortimer McDonald*'s *Halifax Citizen* in the early 1870s, he returned to Charlottetown, where in June 1873 he became editor and manager of the *Examiner*, owned by Jedediah Slason Carvell*. Two years later he bought the paper and in 1877 he turned it into a daily, the first in Prince Edward Island. The move was a bold one, but a spirit of optimism was abroad in Charlottetown, and large homes and new public buildings were under construction. The boom did not last, but the *Examiner* did, and its main competitor, the *Patriot*, followed suit in becoming a daily in 1881. At least until 1901 Cotton continued to publish a weekly edition as well. In 1922 the *Examiner* was absorbed by the *Charlottetown Guardian*, with which it had been merged in 1915, and Will Cotton retired after having edited it for 49 years. However, he sat on the *Guardian*'s editorial board, and wrote a column for the paper, mostly essays in Island history that were brought together and republished in 1927 under the title *Chapters in our Island story*.

He had continued the *Examiner*'s tradition of support for confederation established by its founder, Edward Whelan*, and just a month after he became editor the Island entered the Canadian union. For four decades the *Examiner* was the only Conservative paper in Charlottetown, and Cotton himself was a lifelong Conservative, although the *Guardian* noted when he died that he maintained "a spirit of independence which at times made him restless under party discipline." He was no reactionary, however, and he wrote early editorials urging free education, land reform, construction of the Prince Edward Island Railway "from Georgetown to Cascumpec," and installation of an up-to-date water and sewage system in Charlottetown. Around 1880 the standard of coverage and commentary in the paper began to decline, but Cotton continued to take stands from time to time. For example, when it was still an issue of controversy, he urged on his fellow Islanders acceptance of the automobile, which the provincial legislature had banned from the public roads in 1908 in an act that remained in force until 1913, when motor vehicles were allowed to operate on Mondays, Wednesdays, and Thursdays. He also wrote knowledgeably on agricultural matters – a necessity for a newspaper editor in the Garden Province – and his readers were treated to complete descriptions of the people and places he encountered on several trips he made, to the west and to Britain with Margaret Ellin in 1922.

Cotton served for many years as chairman of the trustees of St Peter's Anglican Cathedral in Charlottetown. These trustees constituted an unusual form of church government that had been designed to protect St Peter's Anglo-Catholic character when it was made the Anglican cathedral for Prince Edward Island in 1879 by Hibbert Binney*, the bishop of Nova Scotia, who had episcopal jurisdiction over the Island. Cotton's marriage had been only the second solemnized in St Peter's after its erection as a chapel of ease for the parish church of St Paul's in 1869. Cotton also served for many years as secretary and treasurer of the Island's Children's Aid Society.

He was an even-tempered, dark-haired man with a bushy beard, married to a wife who set exacting standards of respectability and decorum for her husband and their large family. There was, however, one room in their home that was his sole domain, where Margaret Ellin's writ did not run. The fact that there was no source of heat in the room made no difference to Cotton, and he used it in winter as well as summer, well bundled up.

Cotton died in 1928 and his wife in 1944. A stained glass window in their memory was subsequently installed in All Souls' Chapel at St Peter's Cathedral, the masterpiece created by two of her brothers, architect William Critchlow Harris* and painter Robert Harris*. One of the finest such windows in Prince

Edward Island, it was designed by Frederick W. Cole and made by the English firm of William Morris of Westminster (London). Its subject is Christ, who is shown robed and crowned as King, reigning from the cross. Important portraits of the couple by Robert Harris form part of the permanent collection of the Confederation Centre Art Gallery and Museum in Charlottetown, and are often included in the gallery's exhibitions.

ROBERT CRITCHLOW TUCK

[Family information was graciously supplied to the author by Frederick E. Hyndman of Charlottetown, a great-grandson of Will and Margaret Ellin. R.C.T.]

PARO, P.E.I. Geneal. Soc. coll., family files, Cotton family, contemporary obit. notices and tributes. *Charlottetown Guardian*, 1922–28. *Examiner* (Charlottetown), 1875–1922. *Canadian annual rev.*, 1913. *The Island family Harris: letters of an immigrant family in British North America, 1856–1866*, ed. R. C. Tuck (Charlottetown, 1983). PARO, "Checklist and historical directory of Prince Edward Island newspapers, 1787–1986," comp. Heather Boylan (Charlottetown, 1987). Deborah Stewart, "The Island meets the auto," *Island Magazine* (Charlottetown), no.5 (fall/winter 1978): 9–14.

COUTICE, ADA MARY. *See* BROWN

COUTURE, JOSEPH-ALPHONSE, veterinarian, professor, school administrator, office holder, lecturer, and author; b. 15 Dec. 1850 in Sainte-Claire, Lower Canada, son of Joseph Couture, a shoemaker, and Delphine Roy; m. 12 Aug. 1873 Agnès Ledoux in Montreal, and they had three sons and three daughters; d. 12 March 1922 at Quebec.

After studying at the Petit Séminaire de Sainte-Thérèse, Joseph-Alphonse Couture enrolled in the School of Military Instruction of Montreal. He joined the Canadian militia in 1866 and took part in the campaign to drive back the Fenians. Encouraged by the ultramontane zeal of Bishop Ignace Bourget*, he left Canada in February 1868 with the first detachment of Papal Zouaves to lend support to Pope Pius IX.

On his return in 1870, Couture began studying veterinary medicine at the Montreal Veterinary College, where he took courses conducted in English by Duncan McNab MCEACHRAN, a Scottish professor trained at Edinburgh Veterinary College. The rigorous three-year program of studies, taught jointly by the faculty of medicine of McGill College and the Montreal Veterinary College, compared favourably with that of the best veterinary schools in North America. The curriculum included anatomy, dissection, therapeutics, medicine, surgery, and veterinary obstetrics. Visits were organized to large stables and butcher shops in the city, as were shifts on duty at the college dispensary. Pathologic and microscopic demonstrations by Dr William Osler* rounded out a sound theoretical and practical training. In 1873 Couture received his diploma in veterinary medicine, which was raised to a doctorate in 1890, after the college became the faculty of comparative medicine and veterinary science of McGill University.

In 1877, through a grant from the provincial government, McEachran created a French-language teaching section within the Montreal Veterinary College. He reached an agreement with the Montreal School of Medicine and Surgery – then affiliated with Victoria College in Cobourg, Ont. – by which the school assumed responsibility for the teaching of medicine, and he hired the first Canadian francophone veterinarians, Orphir Bruneau, Couture, and later Victor-Théodule Daubigny*, to teach part of the course in veterinary medicine. In addition to helping McEachran and Osler with their research into different types of animal pathology (actinomycosis, bovine pleuropneumonia), Couture taught materia medica, ran the anatomy demonstrations, and maintained his own veterinary office. He would serve on the board of examiners of the college for more than 20 years. Courses in the francophone section would continue until 1885, but Couture stopped teaching there in 1880, having accepted the year before a position as inspector at the animal quarantine station in Lévis, which was the largest animal transfer station in Canada.

In 1875, at a request of the federal government made in response to increased transatlantic commercial traffic with the British Isles, McEachran had helped organize the first system in Canada for the quarantine and isolation of livestock. The object was to prevent animals infected with contagious diseases from entering the country. In his capacity as a full-time inspector (a position he would retain for the rest of his life), Couture annually saw 600 to 1,200 of the finest specimens of improved breeds (cattle, horses, swine, and sheep), new successes from European breeders achieved by cross-breeding and selection. Thousands of animals purchased by wealthy livestock importers from Quebec, Ontario, and the new western territories (John Henry Pope* and Matthew Henry Cochrane*, among others) were examined by Couture, who thus had an opportunity to compare their respective qualities. In the light of this experience, he would become a promoter of livestock farming based on the purity of animal breeds; in other words, he would favour selection, as opposed to cross-breeding.

Taking advantage of the demand for practising veterinarians, Couture found the support necessary to establish the first francophone school of veterinary medicine in Canada, the École Vétérinaire de Québec, in 1885. The provincial Department of Agriculture and Public Works gave financial assistance (an annual grant of $2,000), and affiliation with the Université Laval at Quebec provided for medical training, insti-

tutional recognition, and the conferring of diplomas. Located on Rue des Jardins, the school took as its model the Montreal Veterinary College: high admission standards ("the equivalent of a good and complete commercial or industrial course," according to the university's calendar), a three-year course of studies, and full medical and veterinary training split between a specialized school and a school of advanced studies. The program included general pathology, veterinary medical and surgical pathology, veterinary materia medica, chemistry, histology, botany, practical anatomy, comparative anatomy of domestic animals, rudiments of entozoology, physiology, and veterinary clinical practice. In addition, a small hospital for horses, which was in an annex to the school, served both as a clinic for the students and as a horse treatment centre for the Upper Town. In 1887 Ernest F. J. MacKay, who had earlier completed a year of studies at the francophone section of the Montreal Veterinary College, received the first diploma granted by the École Vétérinaire de Québec.

For nine years Couture would keep the institution at arm's length. As early as 1889 financial misunderstandings with the administration of the Université Laval occasioned friction. The small enrolment (only 13 graduates from its founding to 1894) touched off a debate between Couture and his associates (the provincial department and the university). Unfortunately these discussions made no mention of the high quality of instruction provided by Couture and his assistants, Dr Peter H. Cummins and Dr John Duncan DuChene; for example, they boldly included courses in hygiene, the inspection of milk and meat, and even microbiology in a regular curriculum in itself marked by the use of the anatomical and clinical method. The government withdrew its grant in 1893 and chose instead to concentrate its financial assistance on the new École de Médecine Comparée et de Science Vétérinaire de Montréal. This institution had resulted from the merger of the École de Médecine Vétérinaire Française de Montréal (founded in 1885 by Daubigny and Bruneau and affiliated with the Montreal School of Medicine and Surgery) and the École Vétérinaire Française de Montréal (founded in 1886 by Daubigny and others and affiliated with the Université Laval). The new school would move to the Institut Agricole d'Oka in 1928 and to Saint-Hyacinthe in 1947; in 1969 it would become the faculty of veterinary medicine of the Université de Montréal. Couture assumed the operating costs for a year before closing his school in 1894.

Along with his duties as inspector and professor, Couture served as the first official government veterinarian of the province of Quebec from 1884 to 1895. As part of his responsibility, he had to arrange for the sanitary inspection of the Dominion Vaccine Establishment at Sainte-Foy, which was financed by the

Department of Agriculture and Public Works and run by Edmond Gauvreau, a professor of hygiene at the Université Laval and the École Vétérinaire de Québec. This establishment was in fact a farm created for the express purpose of providing smallpox vaccine of a high quality to doctors who requested it. A mild form of the virus, also called vaccine or cowpox, was taken from the pustules that formed on a previously inoculated cow. Couture was responsible for examining these virus-producing animals, which had to be completely free of infectious diseases such as the tuberculosis that was then prevalent.

As the official veterinarian, Couture also emphasized the importance of actively combating contagious animal diseases. He advocated sanitary policing measures to prevent the spread of infections and tried to persuade the public authorities to support these measures financially. In 1889, after assessing various epidemics, he called for the adoption of "laws ordering the destruction of animals found [to be] contaminated and contagious," but without success. In one of his reports to the government, published that year, he wrote of having examined a horse with glanders owned by a dairy farmer who "travelled daily through the busiest parts of Quebec and Lévis and spread contagion." In 1890, inspired by Pasteur's work on anthrax, Couture proposed that animals be vaccinated with samples of a mild anthrax virus, which he himself ordered from the Institut Pasteur in Paris and experimented with at the clinic of the École Vétérinaire de Québec. In 1893 he suggested setting up a "laboratory-warehouse" where various preventive inoculations would be made available to veterinarians. Unfortunately no systematic inoculation program would be in effect until the 1920s.

From 1888 Couture regularly recommended government participation in the fight against infectious diseases that could be transmitted from animals to humans. He and McEachran made known that milk for human consumption could act as a vector for transmitting bovine tuberculosis to humans. A lengthy scientific, social, and economic debate ensued in the province. In 1893, only three years after the discovery of tuberculin by the team working with German scientist Robert Koch, Couture recommended tuberculin testing of all cattle. The skin test made it possible to detect tuberculosis in dairy herds whose milk was endangering the lives of consumers with fragile immune systems, such as children and the indigent. Once Couture had raised the question, it would be debated for a long time. Pasteurization of milk would not be carried out systematically in Quebec until the 1930s.

In 1885 Couture served as secretary to a commission (which also included Édouard-André Barnard*, an agronomist, and Siméon Le Sage*, a civil servant) that was appointed at the request of the Council of Agriculture of the Province of Quebec to study the "Canadian cow." At a time when the dairy industry was becoming the focus of agriculture, much consideration was devoted to this topic. While recognizing the morphological weaknesses of this breed of cattle, including its small size, Couture took a stand, as the official government veterinarian, against the members of the Council of Agriculture, who were powerful promoters of imported dairy breeds from England and Holland, such as Ayrshires and Holsteins. He spelled out the main physical characteristics of the breed, which had probably come from France in the 17th century. It was hardy, black and tawny in colour, and easy to feed. It required little care and came from the same stock as the Jersey and Guernsey breeds. In 1886 the commission opened a genealogical book (the herd-book or register of the best animals available for breeding). Couture also conducted studies on milk productivity which showed that the very low cost of production and the high fat and protein content of milk from the Canadian cow might prove beneficial to the rapidly growing butter industry. In this debate Couture took the position that it was better to improve an existing breed (through reproduction, selection, appropriate maintenance and care, and sometimes even cross-breeding) than to advance risk capital for the purchase of a new herd. In spite of opposition, Couture and his allies succeeded in putting across their point of view: "Noireaude," the Canadian cow, would graze in a large proportion of Quebec meadows until the mid 20th century, and it was still found at the beginning of the 21st century in some parts of the province.

In 1884 Couture began the same kind of crusade in favour of the "Canadian horse." After discovering, in his capacity as official government veterinarian, that the breed was nearly extinct – through cross-breeding and sales to the United States after the Civil War of the 1860s – he obtained backing from promoters interested in ensuring its survival. Once again, he spelled out the specific characteristics, collected some animals suitable for breeding, and obtained government recognition of the genealogical book (the stud-book). In 1895 he was one of the principal founders of the Société Générale des Éleveurs d'Animaux de Race Pure de la Province de Québec, and he would serve as its secretary for the rest of his life. An affiliated society, the Société des Éleveurs de Chevaux Canadiens, ensured into the 21st century the survival of this small, sturdy, multi-purpose horse, which is well adapted to cold climates.

Couture also contributed to the literature on animal husbandry and animal pathology. In 1882 he published at Quebec *Traité sur l'élevage et les maladies des bestiaux*. Reissued two years later, this volume seems to have been the first work in French Canada directly related to these topics. Between 1890 and

Cowperthwaite

1895 Couture wrote several popular scientific articles useful to farmers for *Le Journal d'agriculture illustré*, a periodical published in Montreal; these writings, which were sometimes awkward in style, dealt with the health of animals. From 1882 to 1900 Couture was also agriculture editor of *Le Progrès du Saguenay* (Chicoutimi). For the members of the Industrial Dairy Society of the Province of Quebec, he provided some ten scientific papers on ways of raising dairy cattle. During the 1890s he regularly participated in lecture tours organized by agronomists in the Department of Agriculture and Public Works for parish farm clubs. At the end of the 19th century Couture belonged to a new group, consisting of specialists on agrarian questions whose views were moderately nationalistic, progressive, and open to the world, and who wanted to modernize the way farming practices were shaped. Their method of disseminating information, which was intended for large producers as well as small farmers, was both elitist and popular.

Couture had quickly become one of the prominent citizens of Quebec and he took an active part in the city's social life. A friend and colleague of Édouard-André Barnard and Jules-Paul Tardivel*, he wrote several columns, under the pseudonym Jérôme Aubry, for the newspaper *La Vérité*, in which, in particular, he supported the anti-imperialist campaign then being conducted. He also participated in discussions organized by the Institut Canadien de Québec. In 1892 he was one of the founders, along with Abbé Théophile Montminy*, Jean-Charles Chapais, and Barnard, of the Syndicat des Cultivateurs, and he served as its first secretary. This was the first attempt to bring together the farmers who belonged to the province's farm clubs. He was also a shareholder (1897–1914) and director (1900–14) of the Chicoutimi Pulp Company [*see* Joseph-Dominique GUAY].

Couture left his mark on the history of veterinary medicine in the province of Quebec by founding a veterinary school and by his involvement in the system of animal quarantine. Clearly, however, his contribution goes well beyond these two aspects. He was one of the first formally trained veterinarians, the men who, by taking an interest in animal pathology, contributed to the revival of agriculture in the areas of dairy farming and livestock breeding. He was a founder of the Montreal Veterinary Surgeons Association in 1875, and the first vice-president of the Association Médicale Vétérinaire Française, which began in 1886, but his high profile in public life was his chief contribution to advancing the rights and professional interests of veterinarians. Although he was a frequent critic of charlatanism, his complaints did not strike a chord in a society where quack and blacksmith were important figures.

Joseph-Alphonse Couture was very active for the last 20 years of the 19th century and he influenced not only the veterinary profession but the entire field of agriculture in the province of Quebec. He helped modernize farming practices by encouraging the adoption of new methods of livestock breeding focused on reproduction and on the special care to be given the animals. He favoured zootechnical development adapted to the available resources. He also worked to ensure constant improvement in the quality of herds by disseminating scientific research that showed the way in his time and he carried on the fight against animal diseases that can be transmitted to humans.

DENIS GOULET and FRÉDÉRIC JEAN

Joseph-Alphonse Couture is also the author of *Choix des vaches laitières d'après le système Guenon* (Québec, 1884), *Précis de médecine vétérinaire à l'usage des cultivateurs* (Québec, 1895), and *Le bétail canadien* (Québec, [1900?]). In addition to contributing to several periodicals, as mentioned in the text, Couture gave three lectures: "Physiologie de la digestion," "Physiologie de la lactation et production du lait," and "La race bovine canadienne." These were published in the reports of the Industrial Dairy Society of the Province of Quebec, respectively in 1888, 1890, and 1893.

The following sources provide the most information: *Le Soleil*, 22 juin 1901, 13 mars 1922; Can., Parl., *Sessional papers*, reports of the minister of agriculture, 1874–1910; Que., Parl., *Sessional papers*, reports of the commissioner of agriculture and public works (commissioner of agriculture and colonization; commissioner of agriculture), 1872–1904; Soc. d'Industrie Laitière de la Prov. de Québec, *Rapport* (Québec), 1882–1906.

ANQ-M, CE601-S1, 12 août 1873. ANQ-Q, CE306-S6, 15 déc. 1850. *L'Action catholique* (Québec), 14 mars 1922. *Le Devoir*, 14, 16, 27 mars 1922. Denis Goulet et André Paradis, *Trois siècles d'histoire médicale au Québec; chronologie des institutions et des pratiques (1639–1939)* (Montréal, 1992). René Hardy, *Les Zouaves: une stratégie du clergé québécois au XIXᵉ siècle* (Montréal, 1980). Bruno Jean, *Les idéologies éducatives agricoles (1860–1890) et l'origine de l'agronomie québécoise* (Québec, 1977). Firmin Létourneau, *Histoire de l'agriculture (Canada français)* ([Montréal], 1950). Michel Pepin, *Histoire et petites histoires des vétérinaires du Québec* ([Montréal], 1986). M.-A. Perron, *Un grand éducateur agricole: Édouard-A. Barnard, 1835–1898; étude historique sur l'agriculture de 1760 à 1900* ([Montréal], 1955). J. F. Smithcors, *The veterinarian in America, 1625–1975* (Santa Barbara, Calif., 1975). P. M. Teigen, "The establishment of the Montreal Veterinary College, 1866/67–1874/75," *Canadian Veterinary Journal* (Ottawa), 29 (1988): 185–89.

COWPERTHWAITE, HUMPHREY PICKARD, Methodist clergyman and administrator; b. 30 Nov. 1838 near Sheffield, N.B., son of Hugh Cowperthwaite, a farmer, and Elizabeth Ann Hunter; m. 19 July 1867 Annie A. S. Buchanan in Jacksontown, N.B., and they had at least three sons and two daughters; d. 26 Dec. 1924 in St John's.

Educated in the parish school of Sheffield, Humphrey Pickard Cowperthwaite was reared by his pious mother, who like his father was converted under the Methodist ministry of George Seaton Milligan*. It was not until his 18th year, however, that he himself experienced a life-changing conversion under the preaching of John Prince on the Woodstock circuit. His call to ministry ripened slowly, after serious doubts about his vocation. In 1861 he was received on trial in the Eastern British America Conference and stationed at Sussex Vale (Sussex Corner), N.B. Probationary appointments in Nova Scotia, at Pugwash (1862) and Windsor and Falmouth (1863), were followed by studies in 1864–67 at Mount Allison Wesleyan College in Sackville, N.B. After receiving his AB in 1867, he was ordained in Halifax. That same year he married Annie Buchanan, a fellow graduate and daughter of William M. Buchanan, a former lecturer in geology and chemistry at the University of Glasgow.

From 1867 until 1889 Cowperthwaite served churches in Nova Scotia (Horton, 1867–70), New Brunswick (Fairville, 1870–73; Saint John, 1885–87), and Prince Edward Island (Tryon, 1873–76, 1888–89; Cornwall, 1876–79, 1882–84; Charlottetown, 1879–81). During this period, he not only earned an MA from his alma mater in 1870, but he also developed into a respected and capable churchman. He held several posts, among them financial secretary (1874–78, 1883), journal secretary (1878–79), and president (1889) of the New Brunswick and Prince Edward Island Conference and district chairman of the Island (1879–80, 1882, 1888–89). As well, in 1882 and 1883 he was a delegate to the General Conference.

Cowperthwaite began work in Newfoundland in August 1890 and would continue there for three decades until severe debilitation ended his labours. During this period he served on circuits in St John's (Gower Street, 1890–93, 1899–1903; George Street, 1893–96; Cochrane Street, 1903–7) and at churches in Carbonear (1896–99) and Harbour Grace (1907–8). The historian of Gower Street offers the following portrait of Cowperthwaite: "A man of striking appearance, somewhat on the portly side, adorned with a trim Prince of Wales ... beard, and possessed of a strong yet affable personality, he was also a man of considerable scholarship, widely read and highly articulate, an accomplished orator, in fact." His appeal in urban Newfoundland rested on his combination of patriotic values and a progressive version of Methodist spirituality rooted in revivalism and personal holiness. During the South African War and World War I this loyalist descendant rallied Methodists around the flag and the empire. (His paternal grandfather had left New Jersey in 1783 for pioneer life in New Brunswick.) Theologically, he felt that the proclamation of the kingdom was a spiritual leaven capable of changing society by individual

example and collective action. Such stimulation, he thought, would produce a moral revolution with tangible, ameliorative effects, including the removal of dishonesty in business, the prohibition of alcohol, and the elimination of gambling and other social vices. In deciding moral issues he was guided by biblical precept and personal experience, as is evident in his rejection of bazaars as an unscriptural means of fund-raising.

In his ministry in St John's, Cowperthwaite had confronted two crises: the fire of 1892 [see Moses Monroe*] and the bank crash of 1894 [see James Goodfellow*]. The former destroyed the Gower Street Church; the latter nearly bankrupted the country. Cowperthwaite rebuilt the church within months as a temporary structure called the "Tabernacle" at the intersection of Parade Street and Harvey Road. The victims of the bank crash he treated pastorally and through benevolence where needed. Recognized for his administrative skills, he was chosen as president of the Newfoundland Conference in 1896 and as chairman of the St John's and Carbonear districts. Granted a DD by Mount Allison in 1903, he retired on 15 Nov. 1908, the year his wife died. He was called out, however, to supply at Gower Street for two more terms, 1910–11 and 1913–14. Such supernumerary work, which was considerable, ended only when he became paralysed and housebound in 1921, at age 83. The "grand old man" of Newfoundland Methodism, as he is occasionally depicted, died three years later and was buried in the General Protestant Cemetery; he was survived by a daughter and two sons.

Today, a street in St John's reminds people of his existence, but hardly anyone remembers the man for whom it is named.

HANS ROLLMANN

The UCC, Newfoundland Conference Arch. (St John's), holds a typescript copy of Humphrey Pickard Cowperthwaite's "Gower Street Methodist Church" (n.d.). He also wrote "Bazaars or straight giving, which?" *Methodist Monthly Greeting* (St John's), October 1894: 157–58; November 1894: 174–75; December 1894: 178–79, and "Cochrane Street Methodist Church," *Newfoundland Quarterly* (St John's), 5 (1905–6), no.1: 6–7. The *Methodist Monthly Greeting*, the official publication of the Methodist Church in Newfoundland, contains numerous entries on Cowperthwaite's life and work from 1890 until his death in 1924, and has been a major source in the preparation of this article. Of particular interest are Mark Fenwick, "The late Rev. H. P. Coperthwaite, M.A., D.D.," January 1925: 3; "Mrs. (Dr.) Cowperthwaite passes away," September 1908: 9; and "Rev. Dr. Cowperthwaite," December 1923: 8–9.

Daily Globe (St John's), 27, 29 Dec. 1924. *Daily News* (St John's), 27 Dec. 1924. *Evening Advocate* (St John's), 30 Nov. 1918. *Evening Telegram* (St John's), 28 July 1890; 27, 29 Dec. 1924. "Mrs. A. B. Cowperthwaite," *Free Press* (St John's), 25 Aug. 1908. *Provincial Wesleyan* (Halifax), 10

Crawford Brown

July 1867. *A century of Methodism in St. John's, Newfoundland, 1815–1915*, ed. J. W. Nichols (St John's, [1915]), 27–28, 30. G. H. Cornish, *Cyclopædia of Methodism in Canada* ... (2v., Toronto and Halifax, 1881–1903), 1: 382, 777; 2: 50, 71. *Encyclopedia of Nfld* (Smallwood *et al.*), 1: 553. D. G. Pitt, *Windows of agates; the life and times of Gower Street United (formerly Methodist) Church in St John's, Newfoundland: 1815–1990* (2nd ed., St John's, 1990). *Vital statistics from N.B. newspapers* (Johnson), 25, no.1229; 44, no.44; 54, no.2028; 64, no.3069. *When was that?* (Mosdell), 26–27.

CRAWFORD BROWN, THOMAS, Presbyterian minister and military chaplain; b. 18 Jan. 1874 in Richmond, Carleton County, Ont., son of Thomas Brown, a Scots pioneer farmer, and Sarah Crawford; m. 16 June 1909, in Toronto, Eallien Necora Melvin-Jones (d. 1933), only daughter of Lyman Melvin Jones*, and they had a son and a daughter; d. there 9 July 1929.

Thomas Crawford Brown was one of the most renowned churchmen of his day in Toronto. From a humble birth he achieved an education which exceeded that of most of his peers. After attending the public school in Richmond and the collegiate school in Almonte, he enrolled in arts at Queen's College in Kingston, where he also completed the course in theology; he obtained a BA in 1903 and an MA in 1904. An outstanding scholastic record at Queen's was highlighted by his winning the double gold medal in philosophy, the gold medal in political science, and the Sir John A. Macdonald prize. These awards, and the recommendation of Principal Daniel Miner GORDON, led to postgraduate work in arts and theology at the University of Edinburgh (1904–5). In Edinburgh, Crawford Brown was ordained a deacon and served as first assistant minister at St Giles' Cathedral.

Crawford Brown's desire for the ministry drew him back to Canada, where he received a call to St Andrew's Presbyterian Church, Toronto. He was ordained and inducted as minister on 16 Nov. 1905. It was virtually unprecedented for a new graduate to be called to a large metropolitan congregation, but at first glance there was much to commend him as a clergyman. With strong features, exceptional good looks, and a frame over six feet in height, he brought a commanding presence to the pulpit. Initially, however, the position at St Andrew's seemed more than he could handle. Lacking self-confidence, he failed to provide leadership and dreaded the pressures of weekly preaching. Dr Thomas Eakin came to his rescue and acted as his mentor and pulpit assistant. Crawford Brown also rallied within himself, drawing upon his education and experiences at St Giles', to confront the personal and ministerial battles that awaited him.

Believing that worship at St Andrew's lacked proper decorum and reverence, Crawford Brown changed the order of service to reflect the liturgy of St Giles'; he also had the interior remodelled to provide for a chancel and a central aisle. He championed the drive for a new organ at St Andrew's, and by 1908 the church had a second instrument, completely constructed by Casavant Frères within its confines. Crawford Brown fought tirelessly against church union, and his efforts were not in vain. In 1912 the first congregational vote on the matter showed 47 members for union and 182 against. A similar poll on 22 Dec. 1924 recorded 19 votes in favour and 733 opposed. St Andrew's stayed out of the United Church of Canada and continued with the ongoing Presbyterian Church in Canada.

In August 1908, at age 34, Crawford Brown had become sick with an unknown illness that required a seven-month leave of absence. Poor health would continue to plague his ministry and force him to resign from St Andrew's in May 1915. The minutes of the kirk session record the elders' dismay at losing him and their appreciation for "his high standard of personal character, his loyalty to the forms and service of the Church, his declaration of a free Gospel, and the consoling power of his ministrations in the house of mourning." Crawford Brown had been determined that illness would not deprive him of personal happiness and charitable endeavour. On 16 June 1909, at St Andrew's, he had married Eallien Necora Melvin-Jones, a union that produced two children. Despite a young family and an active ministry he found time to participate in many organizations: the House of Industry, the provincial council of the Victorian Order of Nurses, the dominion council of the British and Foreign Sailors' Society, the Navy League of Canada, the masonic order, the St Andrew's Society, the Canadian Club, the Empire Club of Canada, the Victoria Club, the Toronto Skating Club, the Canadian Military Institute, and the Canadian Institute.

When World War I broke out Crawford Brown fully expected to proceed overseas with the 48th Highlanders, the regiment which had appointed him chaplain in 1907, but on 23 Aug. 1914 he was informed that because of continuing bad health he would not accompany his unit to England. His chaplaincy work continued at the military barracks in Exhibition Park, Toronto. In 1917 he became, in addition, a chaplain at the Royal Flying Corps' No.4 School of Military Aeronautics, University of Toronto, and at other RFC stations in the Toronto area. The following year, his health evidently improved, he would be seconded to the chaplain service of the Canadian Expeditionary Force, but he did not go overseas. An honorary major, he was demobilized in 1919. Crawford Brown had been an ardent supporter of voluntary enlistment and later conscription; he served as the president and chairman of the Ministerial Patriotic League of Canada and honorary secretary of the Speakers' Patriotic League.

In November 1918 Crawford Brown's health was again compromised by a severe attack of influenza leading to broncopneumonia. Unable to resume full-time ministry, he became a popular supply minister, preaching in hundreds of churches over the next 11 years. He also continued his duties as padre to the 48th Highlanders, officiating at the presentation of the regiment's second stand of colours on 24 May 1925 and participating in its celebration of the tenth anniversary of peace on 11 Nov. 1928. He worked tirelessly in favour of his most cherished causes, especially as Canadian representative of the British Settlement Society. Returning in 1929 from a voyage to England in connection with this organization he became seriously ill with an embolism on board ship. After his arrival home the family believed that his recovery was certain; however, the blood clot intensified and he died on 9 July. Even though his ministry at St Andrew's had ended 14 years before, he was deeply mourned by the people there. "St. Andrew's felt," the congregation's historian remarked, "that it had suffered infinite loss. . . . rich and poor, gathering about his grave, felt that a gracious personality had passed out of their lives, leaving only a memory behind, but an inspiring memory."

THOMAS HAMILTON

AO, RG 22-305, no.63082; RG 80-5-0-388, no.2932. 48th Highlanders Museum (Toronto), Regimental records, 1907, 1914, 1925, 1928. LAC, RG 150, Acc. 1992–93/166, box 1180-16. QUA, Queen's Hist. coll., Deceased alumni ser., locator no.3599. St Andrew's Presbyterian Church (Toronto), Minutes of the kirk session, 1905–29. *Globe*, 3 March 1915: 11; 10 July 1929: 13. *Mail and Empire* (Toronto), 3 March 1915, 10 July 1929. Kim Beattie, *Dileas: history of the 48th Highlanders of Canada, 1929–1956* ([Toronto], 1957]). Can., Dept. of Militia and Defence, *Militia list* (Ottawa), 1907–22. Duff Crerar, *Padres in no man's land: Canadian chaplains and the Great War* (Montreal and Kingston, 1995). Middleton, *Municipality of Toronto. National encyclopedia of Canadian biography*, ed. J. E. Middleton and W. S. Downs (2v., Toronto, 1935–37), 1: 24–25. S. C. Parker, *The book of St. Andrew's: a short history of St. Andrew's Presbyterian Church, Toronto* (Toronto, 1930). *Presbyterian Record* (Toronto), 54 (1929). Queen's College and Univ., *Calendar* (Kingston), 1897/98–1905/6. "Rev. T. Crawford Brown, MA," Presbyterian Church in Canada, General Assembly, *Acts and proc.* (Toronto), 1930, app.: 303. *Standard dict. of Canadian biog.* (Roberts and Tunnell), vol.1: 128–29.

CREASE, SARAH, Lady CREASE. *See* LINDLEY

CREELMAN, GEORGE CHRISTIE, educator and office holder; b. 9 May 1869 in Collingwood, Ont., son of James Rutherford Creelman and Isabella Christina Patterson; m. 8 Sept. 1892 Ada Ross Mills, daughter of James MILLS, in Guelph, Ont., and they had two daughters and three sons; d. 18 April 1929 near Beamsville, Ont.

Descendants of northern Irish settlers in Nova Scotia, George Creelman's parents moved to New Brunswick and then, in the 1860s, to Ontario. Creelman would spend most of his life in the service of agricultural education, but he was not born on a farm – his father was a music teacher in Collingwood. By the time he was nine, however, the family had moved to a fruit farm in nearby Grey County. Educated at Collingwood's collegiate institute, from 1885 to 1888 George attended the Ontario Agricultural College and Experimental Farm in Guelph, through which he earned a bachelor of agricultural science degree.

Like many early graduates, Creelman found better job opportunities in the United States. He became an assistant professor of biology at the Mississippi Agricultural and Mechanical College in 1889 and a full professor in 1892, a position he would hold until 1899. During these years he continued his own education, obtaining an MSC from his Mississippi college and doing summer studies at Cornell and Wisconsin universities and the Michigan State Agricultural College. He served as vice-president of the teachers' association in Mississippi in 1892–93, and was largely responsible for botany being taught in its public schools.

By the late 1890s the job situation in Canada for OAC graduates had changed, as new positions were created. When Ontario's superintendent of Farmers' Institutes, Frederick W. Hodson, became the first federal livestock commissioner in 1899, Creelman returned to Ontario and took over the superintendency, which led to other connections. His association with the Women's Institutes, for which he compiled a handbook in 1902, would involve him in the drive for female education. He served as well as superintendent of the province's agricultural societies branch from 1902 and as secretary of the Fruit Growers' Association of Ontario. When James Mills retired in early 1904 from the presidency of the OAC, the Liberal minister of agriculture, John Dryden*, chose Creelman as his successor.

Creelman inherited a strong staff, a structure for education by extension, and some respect from farmers for the college. According to the *O.A.C. Review*, he "had the strength of youth and the fire of enthusiasm on his side, as well as known ability for organisation and management." As president, he built on Mills's policies that the college had to be taken to the farmer and that agricultural education should be fundamentally practical in nature. Creelman's past work with the Farmers' Institutes and his teaching experience facilitated his enlargement of the college's extension program. With the aid of the deputy minister, Charles Canniff James, he helped establish the agricultural representatives system, which placed OAC graduates in various counties to coordinate year-round educational services to farmers, in ways that the simpler Farmers' Institutes could not. Creelman also promoted extension by trying to attract farmers and their sons to the OAC for short courses, if not for its full program, and by showing how the work of the Women's Institutes blended with that of the Macdonald Institute of Home Economics at the college. "Our farm girls must be taught systematically, either in their own homes or somewhere else, the science and practice of homemaking," he said in the *Farming World and Canadian Farm and Home* (Toronto). By 1919 he was working with the federal Soldiers Settlement Board and the Department of Soldiers' Civil Re-establishment, which sponsored short courses at the OAC for veterans interested in farming.

During his 16 years in Guelph, Creelman's contributions were not restricted to the OAC. He gave speeches in the United States and travelled extensively. One trip to Australia and the Far East took five months and in 1908 he was a delegate to investigate agricultural methods in Europe. For some time he was a secretary of the American Association of Farmers' Institutes and in 1905 he became its president. A senator of the University of Toronto, he was awarded an LLD in 1910 by McMaster University, then in Toronto. During his tenure (1917–19) as Ontario's commissioner of agriculture, an advisory position created primarily to counter food shortages, he supported the wartime initiatives of acting minister of agriculture and Conservative premier Sir William Howard Hearst*, and in 1918 he went to England and France to assess shortages there.

Despite its progress, the OAC had not outgrown the problem of being plagued by partisan politics. Creelman's Liberal affiliations, and his appointment by the Conservatives in 1917, may have caused concern in some quarters, especially after the election two years later of a United Farmers government. In 1920 its man, Joseph Benson Reynolds, replaced Creelman, who was shunted to England as Ontario's agent general. He lasted for only a year because of ill health.

Back in Canada, Creelman took up the job of general manager of the Niagara Peninsula Fruit Growers' Association – he had farms in the region, near Beamsville and Vineland – but by May 1921 his health had forced him to resign. After some months' rest he found the energy to become active again in veterans' rehabilitation and agrarian promotion. Elected president of the Canadian Society of Technical Agriculturists in 1926, he undertook a study of agriculture for the Province of New Brunswick the following year. A Presbyterian and ardent lawn-bowler, this ever-optimistic champion of the land found innumerable ways to demonstrate his simple philosophy of life: to be happy and make others happy. He died suddenly in 1929 at his Beamsville farm and was buried in Woodlawn Cemetery in

Guelph. In his funeral tribute the Reverend Henry John Cody*, a former minister of education who knew Creelman well as a "constructive pilgrim," said that he had always been influenced by the conviction that "agriculture was the great basis industry of this country. He believed in the dignity of the farmer's career, and he knew his difficulties and his problems. No man better understood the points of contact between the town and the country."

MARGARET DERRY

Creelman's reports as president of the Ontario Agricultural College and Experimental Farm from 1905 to 1920 appear in Ont., Legislature, *Sessional papers*. Other addresses and papers by Creelman published there include the following: 1902, no.22: 137–38; 1905, no.22: 205–7; 1906, no.21: 18–20; no.22: 33–37; 1907, no.21: 35–38; 1908, no.21: 174–76; 1912, no.38: 159–65; and 1917, no.37: 70–76.

AO, RG 22-235, no.6161; RG 80-5-0-200, no.12780. LAC, RG 31, C1, 1871, Collingwood, Ont.: 50. Univ. of Guelph Library, Arch. and Special Coll. (Guelph, Ont.), G. C. Creelman papers; RE1, OAC A0679 (Creelman scrapbook materials). *Beamsville Express* (Beamsville, Ont.), 24 April 1929. *Canadian annual rev.*, 1920: 520; 1921: 564. *Canadian men and women of the time* (Morgan; 1898 and 1912). *Farming World and Canadian Farm and Home* (Toronto), 1 Feb. 1904: 94–95; 1 Sept. 1904: 610; 15 Nov. 1905: 818; 15 Oct. 1907: 979. D. A. Lawr, "Development of agricultural education in Ontario, 1870–1910" (PHD thesis, Univ. of Toronto, 1972). *O.A.C. Rev.* (Guelph), April 1897; January 1903; February, October, December 1904; December 1906; January, April 1908; November 1909; June 1910; June 1912; January, December 1913; January, December 1915; December 1916; January 1918; July 1924; June, September 1928. A. M. Ross, *The college on the hill: a history of the Ontario Agricultural College, 1874–1974* (Vancouver [and Guelph], 1974). A. M. Ross and T. [A.] Crowley, *The college on the hill: a new history of the Ontario Agricultural College, 1874–1999* (2nd ed., Toronto, 1999).

CREIGHTON, ELIZA JANE (Harvie), homemaker and social reformer; b. 11 March 1840 near Peterborough, Upper Canada, daughter of Kennedy Creighton and Laura Hart; m. 1 May 1861 John Harvie* in Aurora, Upper Canada, and they had a son and three daughters; d. 22 June 1929 in Toronto.

Lizzie J. Creighton, as she was known publicly and to her family, was the second of the five surviving children of an Irish-born Methodist minister and his wife, a native of Pennsylvania. She had a childhood of change: by the time she was ready for formal schooling, in Bytown (Ottawa), she had been in ten parsonages. She finished her education at the Wesleyan Ladies' College in Dundas. When she was at home, she and her brother John R. ran their father's Sunday school, a vocation she would follow throughout her life. A slight woman, perhaps five and a half feet in height, she had a strong face (to judge from her pictures) and was precise in her habits.

In 1860, when her father was chair of the church's Barrie district, she attracted the attention of John Harvie, the senior conductor on the Northern Railway. Family tradition says she picked him out as he was dancing in a hotel in Aurora. Following their marriage by her father, they settled in Toronto, near the Northern's yards. John was a staunch Presbyterian, and Lizzie converted. In 1865 they were living in Collingwood, where John was the station agent, but the next year they were back in Toronto. On John's appointment as train and traffic manager of the Northern, the family moved into a house supplied by the railway. Lizzie must have been busy. By the time she was 29, she had four children, a large house, and her work in West Presbyterian Church. In July 1874 tragedy struck when her daughter Mary died. Her reaction was a wonderful example of her approach to life: health care for children must be improved. That winter she participated in meetings with Elizabeth Jennet McMaster [Wyllie*], Lady Macdonald [Bernard*], and others which led to the opening of the Hospital for Sick Children in March 1875.

Other philanthropic work soon followed. In 1876 a group of laywomen formed the Woman's Foreign Missionary Society of the Presbyterian Church in Canada (Western Division). Harvie became its foreign secretary, a post she would hold until 1896, with one interruption due to ill health in 1888–90. The society focused on missions abroad [see Agnes Maria Turnbull*] and native schools and missions in the Canadian west. Not only did it raise money for these operations, in the case of the western missions it helped collect clothing and blankets. In addition to handling correspondence, Harvie toured Ontario, setting up auxiliaries and mission bands, visiting branches, and making speeches. The society's *Monthly Letter Leaflet* gives many glimpses of her activities. By 1876 she had also joined the board of the Women's Christian Association, which ran a boarding house for single, young working women, principally from outside Toronto. Volunteer members also visited females in the city jail. Harvie sat on the jail committee (and on the hospital and house of industry committees) and she soon realized that a discharged inmate had no support if she wanted to change upon re-entering society. In early 1878 she persuaded the WCA to open the Haven, a lodging house for former prisoners. To fund this operation (named the Toronto Prison Gate Mission), she employed the technique that had worked for the children's hospital: start the project and have the city's philanthropically inclined provide the necessary resources. By 1878 she had become, as well, corresponding secretary of the Toronto branch of the Woman's Christian Temperance Union, which had been brought to Ontario by Letitia Youmans [Creighton*], possibly a distant cousin. Harvie assisted in the formation of the provincial WCTU. She must have found it easy to join the temperance movement: her father and husband had both lived in communities degraded by alcohol and were proponents of prohibition.

Harvie's volunteer work was interspersed with domestic crises. In 1878 the Northern made her husband stationmaster of Toronto's new Union Station, a move he resented. It meant the loss of the company residence, but through his dabbling in real estate another house was found. His poor health forced a long leave of absence and a recuperative trip to Scotland – Harvie remained in Toronto, anxious about the future – and he finally retired from the Northern in 1881. Her other concern was their rebellious elder daughter, Jean Ferguson. Harvie managed to find occupation for her on the WCA's board and the ladies' committee of the Hospital for Sick Children, of which Harvie was a president. Jean married in 1885. The same year John became permanent secretary of the Upper Canada Bible Society and Lizzie's father had a violent stroke. (The Creightons subsequently moved in with the Harvies.)

From her work for the hospital, Harvie knew Emily Howard Stowe [Jennings*] and Jenny Kidd Trout [GOWANLOCK], two doctors who also sat on the WCA's board. Originally forced to go to the United States for training, they were determined to provide medical education for women in Ontario. In 1883, with Harvie as treasurer, Woman's Medical College opened in Toronto. It was likely through Harvie that Stowe's daughter, Ann Augusta*, became acting physician to the Prison Gate Mission. The Haven created some tension within the WCA. Most of its directors preferred the more genteel parts of the operation, such as Christian instruction, but as its corresponding secretary and its president from 1887, Harvie was devoted to its practical success. Under her direction the Haven was opened to "every lost woman" (not just former inmates), the city was divided into districts for systematic fund-raising, and a new building was erected. Her continuing commitment to working women was illustrated in May 1887 when she became the founding president of the Toronto Young Women's Christian Guild (the highly successful predecessor to the city's Young Women's Christian Association). Its relations with the WCA were soured at one point by a legacy from William Gooderham*, which was directed to an organization that could have been either the guild or the association. The case went to court, but a settlement was arranged before judgement.

In 1894, a year after Harvie had attended the Woman's Congress staged in Chicago by the National American Woman Suffrage Association, the WFMS decided to send two executive members to the west to get information regarding its work there, especially to see if its collection of clothing and blankets was justified. On 1 Aug. 1894 Harvie, secretary of supplies Cecilia Mary Jeffrey, and their husbands set out, following an itinerary prepared by the Reverend Andrew Browning Baird of Manitoba College. Harvie was back on 18 September, having covered some 4,300 miles by rail and steamboat and over 600 miles of trails. The ladies had visited every Presbyterian mission and reserve school, as well as all of the society's auxiliaries in Manitoba and the northwest. Their report reflects contemporary views of aid and assimilation. The schools were well run, the mission personnel and teachers were dedicated, and the natives who had converted and lived nearby were better off than the non-Christians. Harvie and Jeffrey found that more money was needed and that clothing and blankets were vitally important.

Major changes occurred in Harvie's life in the 1890s. After a protracted battle, the all-male trustees of the Hospital for Sick Children, led by John Ross Robertson*, wrested total financial control from the ladies' committee in 1891. The real estate investments of her husband were hit by recession, her daughter Laura left home on her marriage to her cousin the Reverend William Black Creighton (for whom Harvie would find a job at the *Christian Guardian*), her unambitious son finally married, and her father died in February 1892 and her mother in December 1895. The Harvies then moved to a boarding house. Lizzie's new-found liberty, including her resignation from her positions in the WFMS and the Prison Gate Mission, had allowed her in April 1896 to accept a paying job in social work, as the first assistant of John Joseph Kelso*, Ontario's newly appointed superintendent of neglected and dependent children. Hired to visit and report on foster children across the province, she was well suited for this daunting task, which she entered upon with all the enthusiasm she had displayed at the WFMS and the WCA. In 1905 alone she made 830 visits. She would retire only in 1911 at the age of 71, four years after John's retirement from the Bible society.

After living in a series of boarding houses, the Harvies ended their rootless existence by moving into a flat in the residence of their daughter Jean. Following John's demise in a sanatorium in 1917, Harvie stayed with Jean until the latter's death in 1923. She spent her last years in Laura's home. To the end she remained willing to correct and improve family and visitors.

PHILIP CREIGHTON

Lizzie J. Harvie's contributions to the Women's Christian Assoc., the Prison Gate Mission and Haven, the Toronto Young Women's Christian Guild, and the Hospital for Sick Children are noted in the annual reports for these organizations reproduced on microfiche in CIHM. Her reports as a visitor in the neglected children's branch of the Department of the Provincial Secretary are found in Ont., Legislature, *Sessional papers.*

AO, RG 80-8-0-1119, no.5256. *Globe*, 24 June 1929. *Canadian men and women of the time* (Morgan; 1912). Philip Creighton, "John Harvie," *York Pioneer* (Toronto), 81 (1986): 1–15. *Directory*, Toronto, 1880–85. Presbyterian Church in Canada, Woman's Foreign Missionary Soc. (Western Div.), *Monthly Letter Leaflet* (Toronto), 1884–96 (available on microfiche in CIHM).

CREIGHTON, JAMES GEORGE AYLWIN, engineer, journalist, lawyer, and athlete; b. 12 June 1850 in Halifax, eldest son of William Hudson Creighton and Anna Fairbanks; cousin of folklorist Mary Helen Creighton*; m. 25 June 1878 Eleanor Platt in Montreal; they had no children; d. 27 June 1930 in Ottawa.

Educated at Halifax Grammar School, where he graduated at age 14, James George Aylwin Creighton went on to earn a BA with honours at Dalhousie College in 1868. He then studied under Sandford Fleming*, who as engineer-in-chief for the Intercolonial Railway hired him to work on surveys in Nova Scotia. Creighton moved to Montreal in 1872 and was employed as an engineer on the Lachine Canal, Montreal Harbour, and other public works. He was elected an associate of the Institution of Civil Engineers of Great Britain in 1876.

The following year Creighton entered McGill College and began legal studies with barrister Donald Macmaster; he obtained a BCL degree in 1880. On 9 July that year he was called to the Quebec bar, and two years later he became a partner in the firm of Barnard, Beauchamp, Creighton, and Doucet of Montreal. As a young advocate in 1881, he had to testify at the inquest into the death of his younger brother Harry Montgomery, who was the victim of a stabbing. During his law studies Creighton was also active as a journalist and served as correspondent for the Montreal *Gazette* in the press gallery of the House of Commons.

This experience and legal training led to his appointment on 3 March 1882 as law clerk to the Senate, a position he would hold for 48 years. The *Ottawa Citizen* hailed the choice, saying, "Mr. Creighton will fill the position with credit," a prediction he fulfilled from the beginning. On 27 June the same year he added the title of master in chancery, and in 1909 he became parliamentary counsel to the Senate. Between 1885 and 1886 he was employed in the consolidation and revision of the statutes of Canada [*see* George Wheelock Burbidge*]. He was also instrumental in drafting important legislation, including the Gold and Silver Marking Act (1906), which was almost entirely the product of his legal skills. Creighton supplemented his $2,500 annual salary from the Senate by writing articles for *Scribner's* (New York) and other magazines. He was made a CMG in 1913; he was also appointed a KC.

Throughout his engineering and legal career, Creighton pursued his love of sports, which he had first developed during his boyhood in Halifax, where a freewheeling, stick-ball game called "ricket" or occasionally "hockey" was played on ice. In Montreal, Henry Joseph, a teammate, later credited him with organizing the first public exhibition of ice hockey at the Victoria Skating Rink on 3 March 1875, played by two teams drawn from the club, where Creighton also served as a judge of figure skating. His nine-man team won two "games" (goals) to one over the opposition led by Charles Torrance. "It was this exhibition which aroused city-wide interest and gave rise to the formation of other ice hockey teams and to the rapid development of the game," McGill's physical education director Emanuel M. Orlick would write in the *Gazette* in 1943.

On the hockey rink, Creighton was praised for his ability to pass the flat, circular piece of wood in use at the time as a puck and for his attempts to initiate combination play. In 1876, while he was captain of a team from the Montreal rugby football club, of which he was vice-president, it was noted that he played "offside," or ahead of the puck carrier, evidence that early Montreal games were played under the newly formed (field) Hockey Association and rugby rules, rather than the so-called Halifax rules, which permitted forward passing. In February 1877 he captained a team from the Metropolitan Club against members of the St James' Club. On this occasion the *Gazette* published "the rules of the game"; only the word "ice" distinguished them from field hockey regulations in use at the time. As vice-president of the football club, Creighton led a Montreal delegation to a meeting in Toronto in October 1875 to organize an interprovincial association and moved a successful motion to adopt "rugby union rules," with their vital "onside" stipulation.

Barrister and businessman Byron Arthur Weston of Dartmouth, N.S., described Creighton as "tall and spare." He weighed only 144 pounds at age 25, when he played rugby for Canada against Harvard University. Though he was "quiet and retiring," according to Senator Charles Elliott Tanner of Pictou, N.S., Creighton's name appeared in a magistrate's court docket in an unresolved case in 1883 that involved the burning of cayenne pepper and removal of furniture from an apartment. One of the few members of his family not to enter the Creighton business in Halifax (his grandfather had operated James G. A. Creighton and Son, a ship chandler and wholesale food business), he seldom returned to the city of his birth. He maintained connections with his home province, however, and in 1874 wrote a testimonial for spring skates – the "first in the world adjustable with a lever" – made by the Starr Manufacturing Company of Dartmouth.

After moving to Ottawa, where he preferred to be known under the old family name of Aylwin rather than James, Creighton continued his interest in sports. He was a key member of the Rideau Rebels hockey club, formed in 1889 and made up of two sons of Governor General Lord Stanley*, viceregal aides-de-camp, members of parliament, and senators. The team occasionally travelled in the governor general's private railway car and helped to promote the sport across southern Ontario with exhibition games in such centres as Kingston, Lindsay, and Toronto. Creighton was in his 40th year when he played his last game with a parliamentary team against Government House.

Credited by some modern-day writers with being the "inventor of hockey," the modest law clerk never claimed that honour or participated in early debates over the birthplace of the game. A few years before his death, he wrote to Rebel teammate and former MP Henry Alfred Ward to stake his only sporting claim: that he had had the honour to be captain of the first regular hockey club to be formed in Canada, which was at Montreal in 1877. Before the Montreal winter carnival popularized the game, Creighton described the city's interest in outdoor sports in an article, "French-Canadian life and character," for *Picturesque Canada* (1882–84), edited by George Monro Grant*. He cited "the brilliant fancy dress entertainments" that attracted royalty to the Victoria Skating Rink, listed curling, golf, bicycle, and football clubs, and saluted lacrosse – "the national game of Canada" – but ignored the ice game he had helped to foster.

A long-time member of the Rideau Club of Ottawa, Aylwin Creighton died there of a heart attack in 1930. At his funeral former prime minister Sir Robert Laird Borden* was among the mourners. Obituaries listed his recreations of angling, exploration, book collecting, and skating but made no mention of his part in helping to found Canada's national winter sport. More recently hockey historian Michael McKinley has observed that "Creighton's genius in putting hockey under a roof was to allow it to grow in a kind of sporting hothouse, protected from the harsher elements." Authors Sydney Francis Wise and Douglas Mason Fisher have classed him with the founders of organized lacrosse and basketball, William George Beers* and James Naismith*, as among "the rare few who originate or crystallize games or competitions." In 1993 Creighton was inducted into the Nova Scotia Sport Hall of Fame as the "father of organized hockey." At the Hockey Hall of Fame in Toronto, this trailblazer has been nominated but not yet inducted as a builder.

J. W. FITSELL

ANQ-M, CE601-S68, 25 juin 1878. MUA, RG 46, J. W. Regan to Henry Joseph, 29 March 1944. Private arch., J. W.

Fitsell (Kingston, Ont.), Team photograph of the Ottawa Rideau Rebels, 1889; M. J. Pothier (Dartmouth, N.S.), Creighton family tree. *Gazette* (Montreal), 3–4, 17 March 1875; 27 Feb. 1877; 27 Nov. 1943. *Ottawa Citizen*, 4 March 1882, 28–30 June 1930. *Ottawa Evening Journal*, 28–30 June 1930. *Canadian men and women of the time* (Morgan; 1912). *CPG*, 1927. J. W. Fitsell, *Hockey's captains, colonels and kings* (Erin, Ont., 1987), 30–39. Michael McKinley, *Putting a roof on winter: hockey's rise from sport to spectacle* (Vancouver and New York, 2000). Nevill Miroy, *The history of hockey* (Laleham-on-Thames, Eng., 1986). B. M. Patton, *Ice-hockey* (London, 1936). *Who's who in Canada*, 1929. S. F. Wise and Douglas Fisher, *Canada's sporting heroes* (Don Mills [Toronto], Ont., 1974).

CRESTOHL, HYMAN MEYER, rabbi; b. 15 Sept. 1864 in Poland; m. Rose Weitzman, and they had three sons; d. 5 May 1928 in Montreal.

Hyman Meyer Crestohl received an extensive education in the literary sources of Orthodox Judaism in his native Poland and obtained his rabbinical ordination from eminent authorities there. He also was exposed in his youth to an informal education in contemporary European literature and thought, in a manner which was not uncommon among rabbinical students at the time. After his ordination he served as rabbi in Siedlce. He was a Zionist by conviction and became an early member of Mizrachi, the religious faction of the Zionist movement. An activist and a propagandist for Zionism, he was in contact with many of the movement's political leaders in Europe, such as Chaim Weizmann, Nahum Sokolow, and rabbis Samuel Mohilewer and Isaac Jacob Reines.

In 1904 Crestohl went to New York as an emissary of Mizrachi and he stayed there until 1911. During this period he probably visited Canada in connection with his promotion of the Mizrachi movement. It is likely that the contacts he made led to his immigration to Canada in 1911 and to his nomination as rabbi of Ohev Sholom synagogue in Quebec City that year. He found in Quebec City a small Jewish community of approximately 400 persons. Most had come from eastern Europe in the 1890s and were engaged in commerce. The congregation was the city's second and it had been founded only a year before his arrival. Crestohl's activities were hardly limited to his congregation. During his eight years as rabbi, he maintained ties with the Zionist movement in Canada, founding and acting as first president of the Dorshei Zion Society of Quebec City and serving on the council of the Federation of Zionist Societies of Canada [*see* Clarence Isaac de Sola*]. During World War I he was also active in ministering to the religious needs of Jewish soldiers training at Valcartier.

In 1919 Crestohl moved to Montreal, where he served from 1920 to 1928 as rabbi of the Hadrath Kodesh congregation, founded by immigrants from Russian Poland. His own Polish origins had no doubt helped him obtain the post. Almost all synagogues founded by eastern European immigrants were unable to furnish rabbis with an adequate income, so Crestohl also functioned as a *shohet* (ritual slaughterer) in Montreal's kosher meat industry. In 1920 he became first president of the Mizrachi Organization of Canada.

Crestohl was well known as a scholar of rabbinic literature and he wrote many works on this subject. The fact that his works remained in manuscript, however, most likely because he was unable or unwilling to raise money for their publication, served to limit his influence to the Jewish community in Montreal. Only one of his treatises was published, posthumously by his children.

IRA ROBINSON

Hyman Meyer Crestohl is the author of *Sefer heker davar* [Investigation of the subject] (Montreal, 1960).

Canadian Jewish Congress National Arch. (Montreal), H. M. Crestohl file. LAC, MG 30 D216. "Ha-rov Hayyim Meyer Crestohl shtarbt plutzling" [Rabbi Hayyim Meyer Crestohl dies suddenly], *Keneder Odler* [Eagle] (New York), 6 May 1928. "Revered scholar passes," *Canadian Jewish Chronicle* (Montreal), 11 May 1928. *Archival sources for the study of Canadian Jewry*, comp. L. F. Tapper (2nd ed., Ottawa, 1978).

CROCKET, JAMES HARVIE, journalist and newspaper publisher; b. 20 April 1859 in Campbellton, N.B., son of William Crocket, a noted educator, and Marion Caldwell; m. 11 Aug. 1885 Annie Maud Vradenburgh (d. 1927) in Fredericton, and they had two sons and two daughters; d. 17 April 1930 in Salamanca (Fredericton).

Of Scottish descent, James H. Crocket obtained his early education at the Presbyterian Academy in Chatham, N.B., where his father was principal. In 1870 his father was appointed head of the Normal School in Fredericton and James subsequently attended the Model and Collegiate schools there. In 1875, at age 16, he began his career in the newspaper business as a correspondent for the *Saint John Daily News*. Two years later he moved to Saint John to work on the staff of the paper. He joined A. W. Patterson as co-publisher of the *Gleaner* (Chatham) in 1879, but the weekly lasted only until about April of the following year. In 1881, in partnership with Herman Henry Pitts, he started the *York Gleaner* (Fredericton), a single-sheet weekly, well named in that it consisted of gleanings from other papers. Later that year he acquired Pitts's shares and became the sole owner. The paper continued until December 1884, but meanwhile, in May, Crocket had started a tri-weekly edition, the *Gleaner* (a semi-weekly edition may have existed earlier in the decade). On 25 Nov. 1889 it became the *Daily Gleaner*, reflecting the change in frequency of publication. Crocket would remain as president and managing editor until his death in 1930. During a brief period in 1909 he took on the additional task of directing the *Standard* (Saint John).

Crocket managed his paper efficiently. At the printing plant, he adopted the latest innovations in equipment. Initially the *Gleaner* had been produced with a hand-turned press. This was replaced by a steam-driven, flat-bed press, followed in 1908 by a rotary press. In 1907 he had a Linotype installed and the next year he added the first stereotype equipment in Fredericton. In 1907 as well he had brought the first "news wire" service to the city. His improvements paid off. From a circulation of 500 in 1893, the daily grew steadily, reaching almost 2,000 in 1903 and 6,000 in 1922, the largest circulation of a daily in the province. His brother Charles Stewart (Stuart) Ogg Crocket was also in the newspaper business. From 1897 to about 1904 he was publisher of the *Weekly Globe* (St Stephen (St Stephen–Milltown)). As publisher-editor of the *Tribune* (later the *Campbellton Tribune*) from 1905 to 1939, Charles would be described by historian John Russell Harper as an "outstanding spokesman for the interests of northern New Brunswick."

James Crocket had a reputation as a vigorous and hard-hitting editorial writer, basing his arguments on sound research. A partisan of the Conservatives at the turn of the century, he played an important role in party leader John Douglas Hazen*'s election to the Legislative Assembly in 1903. During the debate in the assembly in 1906 on the financial state of the province, the opposition claimed that the government of Lemuel John Tweedie* had overdrawn its account. The *Gleaner* enjoined the administration to "come clean" with its constituents. According to the paper, the banks had refused the government an advance of $38,000.

Crocket's aggressive style was evident in the *Gleaner*'s editorial on what would become known as the Emmerson affair. In the House of Commons on 19 Feb. 1907 a Conservative MP from New Brunswick, George William Fowler, accused ministers or members of Sir Wilfrid Laurier*'s government of connections "with women, wine and graft." An editorial in the *Gleaner* on 27 March identified New Brunswick MP Henry Robert Emmerson*, minister of railways and canals, as one of the individuals in question and went on to claim that Emmerson had been ejected from a Montreal hotel because of his immoral associations. Emmerson denied the *Gleaner*'s reports but resigned his portfolio. He then took steps against the *Gleaner* and the papers that had reprinted the editorial. On 21 May, Crocket was arrested on a charge of defamatory libel. At trial he was defended by Hazen; Emmerson's counsel was William PUGSLEY,

who would soon replace him as New Brunswick's representative in Laurier's cabinet. As a result of justice Pierre-Amand Landry*'s declaration in June 1907 that the *Gleaner*'s statements, regardless of their accuracy, were in the public interest, Emmerson explained to the press that it was a "waste of time to proceed with the case." In January 1908 the Supreme Court of New Brunswick heard an application on behalf of Crocket to dismiss the action. No one appeared for Emmerson and the case was dropped.

In close contact with federal and provincial Conservatives, Crocket worked behind the scenes in 1914 to obtain the resignation of Conservative premier James Kidd FLEMMING following charges of corruption. According to the *Canadian annual review* for 1919, after a second major scandal rocked the party, Crocket "urged a change of leadership at once" and he would continue to press the issue for some time. There was discontent within the party in Fredericton for other reasons. It was felt by some, including the Crocket family, that a prominent Conservative lawyer, Richard Burpee Hanson*, had not sufficiently supported Crocket's brother Oswald Smith in his pursuit of a nomination to the Court of King's Bench in 1913. Hanson had, moreover, opposed James's desire to be appointed to the Senate. Hanson, who had a financial interest in the *Gleaner*, was concerned about what he felt was Crocket's less than enthusiastic support for some of his projects as Crocket gradually shifted his support to the Liberals in the early 1920s. The conflict climaxed on 14 Feb. 1924 with an editorial in the *Gleaner* that made five accusations against Hanson. Included were charges that he had altered a court decree, that he had advised both parties in a case in 1922, and that in another lawsuit he had "supposedly" fabricated evidence which was found to be missing. Hanson demanded a retraction. The *Gleaner* refused and the case went to court. Hanson was awarded $100. An appeal by the *Gleaner* was unsuccessful. By 1923 Crocket was firmly in the Liberal camp and he would remain there for the rest of his life.

Following Crocket's death in 1930, the management and ownership of the *Gleaner* passed to his sons, James Alexander and William Wallace. In addition to having been a successful businessman and a noteworthy newspaper editor and publisher, James Harvie Crocket had played a role in the province's political dramas.

ERIC L. SWANICK

Daily Gleaner (Fredericton), 19 April 1930. *Union Advocate* (Newcastle, N.B.), 23 April 1930. *Canadian annual rev.*, 1903, 1907–8, 1916–17, 1919. W. W. Crocket, "The press in Fredericton," in *Fredericton's 100 years; then and now*, ed. Frank Baird (Fredericton, [1948]), 226–33. A. T. Doyle, *Front benches & back rooms: a story of corruption, muckraking, raw partisanship and intrigue in New Brunswick*

(Toronto, 1976). Charles M. McK. Ferris, "The New Brunswick elections of 1917" (MA thesis, Univ. of N.B., Fredericton, 1974). R. E. Garland and L. G. Machum, *Promises, promises . . . an almanac of New Brunswick elections, 1870–1980* (Saint John, 1979). *Hanson v. The Gleaner, Limited* (1925), *New Brunswick Reports* (Toronto), 52: 195–214. J. R. Harper, *Historical directory of New Brunswick newspapers and periodicals* (Fredericton, 1961). Louise Manny, "From Miramichi to Fredericton: a *Gleaner* story," *Atlantic Advocate* (Fredericton), 58 (1967–68), no.1: 22–24, 27. [J. A. Neville], *Fredericton newspapers and their times* (n.p., [1933?]). *N. W. Ayer & Son's American newspaper annual and directory . . .* (Philadelphia), 1884, 1893, 1903, 1922. *New Brunswick newspaper directory, 1783–1988*, comp. H. [C.] Craig (Fredericton, 1989). *Prominent people of New Brunswick . . .* , comp. C. H. McLean ([Saint John], 1937). W. W. Thorpe, "Richard Burpee Hanson: a study of his relations with the constituency of York-Sunbury" (MA thesis, Univ. of N.B., 1973). *Vital statistics from N.B. newspapers* (Johnson), vol.64, no.663.

CROSS, CHARLES WILSON, lawyer and politician; b. 30 Nov. 1872 in Madoc, Ont., son of Thomas Cross, a merchant, and Marie Mouncey; m. 1 Jan. 1900 Annie Louisa Lynde in Edmonton, and they had one son and two daughters; d. 2 June 1928 in Calgary.

Charles W. Cross was educated in Toronto at Upper Canada College, the University of Toronto, and Osgoode Hall. Lured by a western economy beginning to boom, he moved to Edmonton in 1897 and opened a law firm. Active in the Liberal party, by 1905 he was generally viewed as Edmonton's second most influential Liberal after Frank Oliver*. He was chosen by city council in February that year as one of a three-man deputation being sent to Ottawa "to look after Edmonton's interest" in the negotiation of the terms by which the North-West Territories would become one or more provinces.

Though he was only 32, Cross was named attorney general when Alberta's first cabinet was announced by Premier Alexander Cameron Rutherford* on 6 Sept. 1905. Second in command to the premier, he had never faced the voters, but in the provincial election on 9 November he was returned handily as the MLA for Edmonton. He would be re-elected to the Legislative Assembly four times and would be a central figure in the two major controversies of the Liberals' 16-year tenure.

In his initial term Cross could take pleasure in the assembly's selection of Edmonton to be the provincial capital. Although much of the legislation he introduced as attorney general was conservative, he was responsible for the first workmen's compensation bill in 1908, which addressed some of labour's concerns.

The government was rather more generous in its guarantees to railway companies than it was to workers. The Alberta and Great Waterways Railway received the most favourable terms of all for its planned line linking Edmonton and Fort McMurray. Boosters argued that the connection was essential if the oil-sands and other resources were to be developed. The election of 1909 returned a large Liberal majority, with Cross winning easily, but the size of the guarantee to the A&GW and the creditworthiness of the company became the dominant issue in the legislature. It divided the Liberals, with critics both among dissident party members and in the opposition suggesting that some cabinet ministers had a financial interest in the company. Premier Rutherford tried to fend off censure by appointing a royal commission, made up of David Lynch SCOTT, Horace Harvey*, and Nicholas Du Bois Dominic BECK of the Alberta Supreme Court, to investigate whether any members of the government had a personal stake in the A&GW, but the split in Liberal ranks and the public outrage were so great that he stepped down before it could report. His successor was chosen by the party leaders in Ottawa and Lieutenant Governor George Hedley Vicars BULYEA, and their goal was to pick someone who could pull the Liberal factions together. On 1 June 1910 the new premier, Arthur Lewis Watkins SIFTON, named a cabinet that included only one minister from the previous administration. Charles Cross, so recently the heir apparent to Rutherford, was left an ordinary MLA.

The majority report of the commission, signed by Harvey and Scott and filed later in 1910, was critical of both Rutherford and Cross, claiming that they had risked millions of public dollars. Promoters of the A&GW had provided them with "misleading, unreliable, and in many respects absolutely false" information, which they had failed to verify. It concluded, however, that "the evidence does not warrant the finding that there was or is any personal interest on the part of Dr. Rutherford or Mr. Cross."

Cross remained unrepentant, defending the former government's aid to railways, including the guarantee to the A&GW, as necessary if the mineral resources of northern Alberta were to be developed. His stance had the support of the Edmonton Board of Trade but not of Frank Oliver, who became his bitter political enemy. Cross led an important faction within the Liberal legislative caucus, and Premier Sifton attempted to fashion a railway policy that would placate both it and the opponents of lavish government aid to privately owned lines. On 4 May 1912 Cross once again became attorney general. He announced that he was re-entering the cabinet because "Premier Sifton's adoption of the great railway program of 1912, which requires construction of about 1450 miles of new lines in the next three years, made it proper for me to support and join his government."

He remained a powerful minister until the Alberta party, like Liberals throughout English Canada, divided in 1917 on another issue: conscription. He stayed loyal to Sir Wilfrid Laurier* even as Sifton left for Ottawa to join a conscriptionist cabinet and Charles Stewart* succeeded to the premiership. Cross joined with his former enemy Frank Oliver to oppose the Union government. Though Stewart left him in his portfolio at first, he tried to get him to resign and become the province's agent general in London. Cross refused the offer, so the premier fired him on 23 Aug. 1918.

Cross's expulsion left Alberta Liberals more divided than ever, just as the United Farmers of Alberta [see Percival BAKER; Henry Wise Wood*] were beginning to consider nominating their own candidates rather than simply trying to influence those of the old parties. In the election on 18 July 1921 they reduced the Liberals to only 15 of 61 seats. Cross was one of the survivors, but his days as a key figure were over. He had been virtually silent in the debates after his ouster from cabinet and during the UFA period was more concerned with his law practice than the legislature. Moving to federal politics in the general election of 1925, he was returned to the House of Commons in the riding of Athabaska. He lost the seat to a UFA member in the 1926 election and died of a heart attack two years after.

Cross had been a notable lacrosse player in his youth, and in later years he was on the executive of the Canadian Amateur Athletic Union. Of Scottish ancestry, he was a member of First Presbyterian Church in Edmonton. The main focus of his life, however, appears to have been politics, and in particular the arrangement of government assistance to railways. His legacy was a controversial one: he could claim a good portion of the credit for the many miles of line in Alberta, but his critics could argue that too many miles had been built and that the taxpayers had been left responsible for huge debts from the socialization of risk for private endeavours.

ALVIN FINKEL

Calgary Herald, 4 June 1928. *Edmonton Bulletin*, 6 May 1912, 24 Aug. 1918. John Blue, *Alberta, past and present, historical and biographical* (3v., Chicago, 1924). *Edmonton: the life of a city*, ed. Bob Hesketh and Frances Swyripa (Edmonton, 1995). *The formation of Alberta: a documentary history*, ed. D. R. Owram (Calgary, 1979). Howard Palmer with Tamara [Jeppson] Palmer, *Alberta: a new history* (Edmonton, 1990). L. G. Thomas, *The Liberal party in Alberta: a history of politics in the province of Alberta, 1905–1921* (Toronto, 1959).

CROW, NORTON HERVEY, civil servant and amateur sports leader; b. 6 July 1878 in Pelham Township, Ont., eldest son of Judson Comfort Crow, a schoolteacher, and Casandria Marie Pettee; m. Ella McKinley Harriman, and they had a daughter; d. 14 Sept. 1929 in Toronto.

Of Presbyterian, loyalist background on the Niagara peninsula, Norton Crow went to Toronto about 1898 to become a clerk in the provincial treasurer's office. After building an outstanding reputation in baseball and speed skating with the Central Young Men's Christian Association – a bastion of "muscular Christianity" – he was drawn into volunteer sports leadership during the "amateur wars" of 1906–9. Sportsmen were bitterly divided over whether athletes should be paid for their efforts. The idea of non-payment (amateurism), which had emerged from the aristocratic Victorian prejudice against wage labourers, reinforced the ideal of heroic, selfless play that attracted the middle class to sports, and it kept costs down. The practice of paying athletes (professionalism) grew out of carnival contests, stakes races (the structure of the championships won by Jacob Gill Gaudaur*, Edward Hanlan*, and William Joseph O'Connor*), and team sports such as baseball where recruiting better players with cash gave a ready advantage.

These differences made the Toronto-based Canadian Amateur Athletic Union, the association of clubs which attempted to regulate the main sports, ungovernable. In 1906 the liberal faction, led by the Montreal Amateur Athletic Association, stormed out of the Union to form the Amateur Athletic Federation of Canada, which would allow a measure of professional-amateur cooperation along the lines of that found in American baseball and British soccer. During the next few years, while athletes, sportswriters, and fans argued on, Union and Federation leaders stumped the country to win adherents.

Norton Crow was an ardent, bedrock amateur. As secretary of the CAAU, he had quickly become a leader of the amateurs' campaign, along with newspaperman John Ross Robertson*, sportswriters Francis Nelson* and William Abraham Hewitt*, police chief William Stark, and lawyer James George Bowes Merrick, all of Toronto. Though they out-organized their rivals, making strict amateurism the ruling orthodoxy, a truce was arranged in September 1909. Crow became the secretary of the amalgamated body formally created in November, the Amateur Athletic Union of Canada, and soon emerged as its driving force.

Crow was convinced that amateur sport could instil in participants a disciplined sense of citizenship and a love of Canadian institutions. He set out to take this vision into the Maritimes, Ontario's hinterland, and the western provinces, where the CAAU had had little influence, and bring the most popular sports under the control of the AAUC. In addition to stepping up its efforts to send strong teams to Olympic and other international competitions, he would help it restore sports activity throughout Canada after World War I. When, as a result of a western lobby, the Canadian Amateur Hockey Association was formed in 1914 to confront professionalism, Crow, the disciple of amateurism, was chosen as its first secretary.

Crow's plan for realizing his goals, set out in public statements and voluminous annual reports, called for new facilities, the expansion of physical education in schools, the training of coaches and other leaders, and the staging of "Canadian Olympics," in which amateur championships would be held every four years. First envisaged by Crow in 1910, these games would, he believed, kindle at home the enthusiasm that the Olympics had created throughout the world since their launch in 1896. After observing the value of sports to the war effort, he and his colleagues began a concerted effort to bring about federal and provincial ministries of sports. Despite his enthusiasms, Crow was never a keen promoter of women in sport, though by 1924 he was forced to recognize that female competition, especially in track and field, had to be reckoned with [see Velma Agnes SPRINGSTEAD]. In 1924 Crow, who had managed Canada's team at the Festival of Empire Games in London in 1911, proposed "an All-British Empire Games, to be held between the Olympic Games," to provide another incentive for Canadian athletes, stimulate opportunities within the dominion, and foster national pride.

In 1920, in his position as a treasury clerk, Crow had been asked to draft provincial legislation for the regulation of boxing (previously prohibited but much liked by war veterans) and the promotion of amateur sport. The Ontario Athletic Commission Act provided for the implementation of many of Crow's ideas, including the development of coaches, the creation of a provincial training centre near Orillia, more physical education in schools, and the subsidization of amateur organizations. This act would be an important precedent for the federal Fitness and Amateur Sport Act of 1961.

Unfortunately, Norton Crow saw few of these projects come to fruition. In 1925, pressed by his new duties as principal clerk of the treasury, enervated by his father's sudden death during the inaugural service of the United Church of Canada, and in failing cardiovascular health, he suddenly retired from the AAUC. He died four years later, just 51. In 1932 the AAUC created the Norton Crow Memorial Award for the amateur athlete of the year; it continues to be given, to the outstanding male athlete, at the Canadian Sports Awards. Crow's initiatives and thinking can be readily recognized in the Commonwealth Games (begun in 1930) and the Canada Games (1967), and in today's sports sciences and the national coaching certification program.

BRUCE KIDD

AO, RG 80-2-0-120, no.33209; RG 80-5-0-66, no.6130. Canada's Sports Hall of Fame (Toronto), Letter from Ella Crow to Douglas Fisher, 1966. *Toronto Daily Star*, 16 Sept. 1929. *Canadian annual rev.*, 1909: 313–15. *Directory*, Toronto, 1898–1925. Bruce Kidd, "'Making the pros pay' for amateur sports: the Ontario Athletic Commission, 1920–1947," *OH*, 87 (1995): 105–28; *The struggle for Canadian sport* (Toronto, 1996).

CROWE, GEORGE READING, businessman and politician; b. 22 Oct. 1852 in Old Barns, N.S., son of James Crowe, a shipbuilder, and Harriet Archibald; m. 29 Dec. 1875 Mary Elizabeth Alexander (d. 1918) in Clifton, N.S., and they had two daughters and one son; d. 7 Sept. 1924 in Winnipeg.

After receiving a public school education in Nova Scotia, George Crowe worked for his father in shipbuilding. He received some instruction in business in Halifax and was employed for a brief period in Saint John. His attention turned to railway construction, a burgeoning industry during the 1870s. Crowe found a job with the Intercolonial Railway, but the northwest beckoned and he moved to Manitoba in 1879. The province was rapidly expanding its rail system and Winnipeg was proving to be the gateway to the west.

Crowe's career would see him active in almost all the significant industries of western Canada. He acted as a subcontractor for construction on the Canadian Pacific Railway east and west of Rat Portage (Kenora, Ont.). In 1883 he entered the lumber business in the Point Douglas (Winnipeg) area, founding Boyd and Crowe with Nathaniel Boyd. By 1890 the firm no longer existed and Crowe had established H. Crowe and Company, lumber and grain merchants, with his brother Herbert. Soon the firm concentrated exclusively on the growing grain trade. As Manitoba, and Winnipeg in particular, developed into the centre of the trade on the prairies, Crowe became increasingly influential in the business. In 1893 the Crowes and four other Winnipeg grain firms, including that of Nicholas Bawlf*, merged and established the Northern Elevator Company Limited to compete with eastern-based firms. George was vice-president of the company for several years and as its representative he served as president of the Winnipeg Grain and Produce Exchange in 1895. By 1905 the highly successful firm would own and operate over 134 elevators in the northwest, each with an average capacity of 30,000 bushels. Crowe, who would be called "the dean of the export grain trade of western Canada" by the *Manitoba Free Press*, would remain active in the trade until 1920.

In 1903 Crowe served as president of the Winnipeg Board of Trade. That year, with broker Augustus Meredith NANTON and several other prominent men, he successfully petitioned the Legislative Assembly of Manitoba for incorporation of the Winnipeg Stock Exchange and the Northern Bank. A founder of the Canadian Fire Insurance Company (1887), the Great-

West Life Assurance Company (1891), the British Empire Grain Company Limited, and the Missisquoi Marble Company, he also served as a director of these firms. He was a vice-president of the Northern Trusts Company by 1905 and he became a director of the Royal Bank of Canada in 1907.

A Conservative, Crowe served as president of the Liberal-Conservative Association of Winnipeg. He had been elected to the Winnipeg City Council for 1885 and he held office again from 1912 to 1914. An active Presbyterian, he was a commissioner of the General Assembly of the Presbyterian Church in Canada and vice-president of the Canadian council of the Laymen's Missionary Movement for Saskatchewan and Alberta. He had been appointed to the board of management of Manitoba College in 1886; he would serve until his death and from 1914 to 1918 he was its chairman. In 1904 he had joined the Citizens' Committee that fought against segregated prostitution in Winnipeg [see Frederic Beal Du Val]. A member of the elite Manitoba Club, he was president of the Winnipeg branch of the Canadian Club in 1907 and 1908. He contributed generously to the Young Men's Christian Association of Winnipeg.

George Crowe was typical of the Anglo-Protestant elite that had come to dominate Manitoba in the years following the Red River resistance of 1870. He had arrived in Winnipeg during the turbulent early years and he benefited from its spectacular growth. He reflected the boosterism that the city exuded in abundance. He died in September 1924 and was buried in Winnipeg's Elmwood Cemetery.

ROBERT A. WARDHAUGH

Church of Jesus Christ of Latter-day Saints, Geneal. Soc., International geneal. index. *Manitoba Free Press*, 9 Jan. 1904, 27 May 1911. *Winnipeg Tribune*, 8 Sept. 1924. A. G. Bedford, *The University of Winnipeg: a history of the founding colleges* (Toronto and Buffalo, N.Y., 1976). George Bryce, *A history of Manitoba; its resources and people* (Toronto and Montreal, 1906). *Canadian men and women of the time* (Morgan; 1912). *Directory*, Winnipeg, 1884–90. A. [G.] Levine, *The exchange: 100 years of trading grain in Winnipeg* (Winnipeg, 1987).

CROWE, HARRY JUDSON, businessman and philanthropist; b. 28 Nov. 1868 in Halifax, son of John F. Crowe and Mary Doyle; m. 10 July 1895 Helen Rose Quirk in Bridgetown, N.S., and they had two sons; d. 25 May 1928 in Toronto.

Harry J. Crowe was educated in public schools in Halifax, the preparatory school at Horton Academy in Wolfville, and the Halifax Business College and Writing Academy. After graduation he worked for a year with a Halifax grocery firm, taking responsibility for its banking affairs, and in 1884 or 1885 he joined his father's wholesale grocery firm. Crowe

purchased his father's interest around 1890 and managed the company with one of his brothers. A joint venture with a Boston adventurer to develop mining properties in the western United States failed, and he was forced to sell the Halifax firm to cover his losses. After acquiring a half-share in a grocery store and lumbering business in Bridgetown, Crowe developed a strong interest in lumbering and established sawmills in different parts of the province.

He went to Newfoundland about 1902 to enter the timber trade there and became enthralled with the industrial potential of the island. Shortly afterwards he divested himself of his Nova Scotia operations. He befriended Robert Gillespie Reid* and his sons WILLIAM DUFF and Henry Duff, who owned Newfoundland's railway system and held extensive timber, land, and mineral assets. In 1903 he established the Newfoundland Timber Estates Company Limited with W. D. Reid, Henry Melville WHITNEY of Boston, and Benjamin Franklin Pearson* of Halifax. This firm conducted lumbering operations at Glenwood and Millertown, on properties purchased from Lewis H. Miller*, and at Gander Bay. Crowe realized that Newfoundland wood was better suited to papermaking than to lumbering and proceeded to purchase most of the available timber operations in central Newfoundland. Working with the Reids, he helped to bring the Harmsworth newspaper interests of England to Newfoundland; as the Anglo-Newfoundland Development Company Limited, this group purchased many of the holdings of Newfoundland Timber Estates and established a pulp and paper mill at Grand Falls, which commenced operations in 1909. Crowe also helped to persuade A. E. Reed and Company Limited, another English firm, to establish a pulp mill at nearby Bishop's Falls; it got underway in 1911.

Crowe's method of conducting business was to purchase existing timber grants instead of acquiring the rights directly from the crown. The properties were then grouped together under one or other of his holding companies. Before 1914 he conducted extensive logging operations in the Botwood and Point Leamington areas. By that time his various concerns were providing the Grand Falls and Bishop's Falls mills with over one hundred thousand cords of pulpwood annually. He seems to have continued his operations at Botwood, at least, throughout the war years.

In 1911 Crowe had met with William Ford Coaker*, the leader of the Fishermen's Protective Union, which included loggers within its ranks. Crowe agreed to improve conditions in his 12 camps by upgrading sleeping and eating accommodations, installing baths, and providing a medical doctor to look after the loggers' needs. He also undertook to employ union men and guaranteed a monthly wage for each logger. Botwood, Crowe's main centre of operations, was the site of further interventions by him. Since he deplored

Crowe

Newfoundland's denominational school system, which he told a public audience at Botwood in 1910 "caused the lack of development in the people, as well as the resources of this Island," he funded a non-denominational kindergarten there in 1915. Consisting of approximately 45 students, aged four to seven years, it was conducted by a teacher, Edna Alexander, he brought in for a year from Toronto, where he had taken up residence around 1910. He also arranged for domestic science classes to be taught in the community. In 1916 he secured the loan for a year of two teachers from the Toronto Board of Education to continue the kindergarten school in Botwood and establish another in Twillingate.

During 1915 Crowe was also active in the successful campaign to have Prohibition adopted in Newfoundland. He arranged for Dr Carolyn E. Geisel, an American surgeon and public health advocate, to tour Newfoundland communities giving lectures on the virtues of both Prohibition and public health. Crowe accompanied her on this tour. Her visit resulted in the formation of short-lived health clubs in a number of communities. On the recommendation of Dr John Harvey Kellogg, superintendent of the Battle Creek Sanitarium in Michigan, Crowe in November 1915 secured the services of an American dietitian and domestic science expert, public health nurse Margaret Craig, who came to Botwood and nearby communities to advise the health clubs.

From his first entry into Newfoundland's business life, Crowe had befriended most of the island's leaders and he remained on good terms with whatever government was in power. An avid confederate, he worked actively to promote Newfoundland's union with Canada and, in both 1909 and 1915–16, he served as an intermediary in failed discussions between Canadian and Newfoundland politicians and the Reid Newfoundland Company on the matter. His confederate views were part of his wider belief that all Anglo-Saxon countries should have close relations. Since 1902 he had advocated a union of the English-speaking countries, including the United States, through a commercial preference. In a 1910 interview in the Montreal *Gazette*, for example, he called for a reciprocity agreement between Canada, Newfoundland, Great Britain, and the United States. In 1915 Crowe first visited the British West Indies and he quickly became an advocate of their political union with Canada, and with Newfoundland, an idea that received the endorsement of the London *Times*. He promoted his views through frequent public speeches and contributions to the press. His ambitions were partially realized in 1921, when Canada ratified an agreement with the British West Indies that extended mutual trade preferences and provided for the subsidization of steamship service between the region and Canada.

In the last years of his life Crowe sold the timber properties in the White Bay area that he had acquired in 1923 to the International Paper Company, which was pursuing an aggressive policy of expansion and had been urged by Crowe to look at the Newfoundland market. He also sold to this American firm his properties in the Bay d'Espoir region on the south coast of the island. From 1912 he had unsuccessfully promoted the construction of a railway from Bishop's Falls to Bay d'Espoir to allow for the development there of a pulp and paper mill based on the substantial hydroelectric power in the region. In 1922 he had failed as well in his attempts with British and American interests to acquire the bankrupt Newfoundland Railway from the Reid Newfoundland Company.

The sale of his properties apparently made Crowe a much wealthier man, but his ability to enjoy his good fortune was hampered by long-standing ill health. In 1927 he suffered a paralytic stroke and sought help at the Battle Creek Sanitarium only to undergo a second attack there. He died the following year at his home in Toronto. The value of his estate's assets, after his debts were discharged, was $676,000, of which $168,000 represented his timber holdings in Newfoundland. In his will he left a fund to the Salvation Army to train men and women for service in India and another to be used to establish scholarships for graduate nurses in Canada and Newfoundland. Before his death Crowe had often provided financial assistance to Memorial University College in St John's to help support summer school at the college for schoolteachers. His widow established a scholarship in his honour at Memorial, with preference to be given to high school graduates from the White Bay area.

William Coaker wrote a warm tribute to Crowe in the *Fishermen's Advocate* (Port Union, Nfld), considering him to be "one of the few men in his time who worked sincerely and incessantly through good and ill repute, without faltering, for the benefit of Newfoundland." A spiritual man himself, Coaker noted that Crowe was "seriously inclined religiously and spent many hours in discussing the mysteries beyond the vale with the writer. He was steadfast in the belief that life here was the beginning of an existence that never ended." Another observer wrote that Crowe was "the interesting and unusual combination of capitalist, man of affairs and the dreamer. He could, in the twinkling of an eye, turn his attention from weighty business problems, having to do with material progress, to the most idealistic plans for the betterment of any class of people."

MELVIN BAKER

AO, RG 22-305, no.59468. Centre for Newfoundland Studies, Memorial Univ. of Nfld (St John's), Arch., COLL-237 (Robert Bond papers), file 10.01.079, Crowe to Bond, 23

June 1922. PANL, GN 2/5, file 196A, Crowe to William Halfyard, 16 Nov. 1917; W. B. Grieve to Halfyard, 23 Nov. 1917. *Daily News* (St John's), 26 May 1928. *Fishermen's Advocate* (St John's), August 1911; (Port Union, Nfld), 1 June, 6 July 1928. *Globe*, 26 May 1928. *Halifax Herald*, 13 July 1895. *Mail and Advocate* (St John's), 11 Oct., 24, 30 Nov. 1915. *Twillingate Sun* (Twillingate, Nfld), 26 Nov. 1910; 3 Dec. 1910 (quoting the Montreal *Gazette*); 2 May 1911. J. [K.] Hiller, "The origins of the pulp and paper industry in Newfoundland," *Acadiensis* (Fredericton), 11 (1981–82), no.2: 42–68; "The politics of newsprint: the Newfoundland pulp and paper industry, 1915–1939," *Acadiensis*, 19 (1989–90), no.2: 3–39. *Re Harry J. Crowe, deceased* (1933), *Newfoundland Law Reports* (St John's), 13: 105–9. *National encyclopedia of Canadian biography*, ed. J. E. Middleton and W. S. Downs (2v., Toronto, 1935–37), 1: 118–20. Nfld, Royal commission on forestry, *Report* (St John's, 1955), 197–204. W. G. Reeves, "'Our Yankee cousins': modernization and the Newfoundland–American relationship, 1898–1910" (PHD thesis, Univ. of Maine at Orono, 1987). *Standard dict. of Canadian biog.* (Roberts and Tunnell), vol.1. *Who's who in Canada*, 1927.

CUMMINGS, EMILY ANN McCAUSLAND. *See* SHORTT

CURRAN, WILLIAM HENRY, logger and farmer; b. 1 April 1843 in Providence, R.I., son of James Curran and Mary George; d. 4 April 1930 in New Westminster, B.C.

William Henry Curran typifies the resourceful 19th-century wanderer who did nothing outstanding, yet persevered and left an imprint in the form of numerous descendants. He exemplifies the generation of men who arrived in British Columbia during the gold rush of 1858–65 and who, responding to the gender imbalance among newcomers (by 1871 there were roughly three adult males for every adult female), cohabited with aboriginal women. Curran was a survivor committed to his family at a time when it would have been far easier to walk away, as did so many men, from such responsibilities.

The son of a father born in Ireland and a mother who came from Newfoundland, Curran left home at the age of 14 to become a drummer boy in the army sent by the United States government to quell the Mormons in Utah. According to the story he recounted in old age, he reached the Pacific northwest by 1861 and for the next couple of years moved back and forth between Victoria and Washington Territory. Curran's parents had a cloth-dye business that was being superseded by new technology, so they and their younger son Frederick Johnson soon joined Curran in British Columbia.

By 1866 Curran was living with Mary Sitkwa Whilemot, a Cowichan woman born sometime in the 1840s who already had two children, Mary Ann Walker and James Walker, by earlier relationships with newcomer men. William and Mary had their first child together in 1867, the same year that he pre-empted 100 acres on the west coast of Salt Spring Island. Elizabeth (Eliza) Jane was followed by Ellen in 1870, Alice in 1872, William Jr in 1874, Julia in 1876, Margaret in 1878, and Edith Rose in 1883.

Curran worked hard to support his growing family. He later stated that he had once run for the provincial legislature but, if so, it must have been before British Columbia entered the Canadian confederation in 1871 since he does not appear on the lists of candidates in that year or later. By 1874 he had abandoned his Salt Spring property for land on the southern end of Thetis Island further north. The shift may have been at Mary's initiative, for her mother and brother Jacob lived there or on Kuper Island, joined to Thetis at low tide. Curran logged with oxen and farmed over the next two decades. He acquired six quarter-section lots between 1874 and 1887 and built three log houses in different parts of the island. At some point his brother Fred and wife Rose moved nearby.

Curran took considerable care that his children were educated. He sent at least some of his daughters to the convent school established in the Cowichan valley by the Sisters of St Ann [*see* Salomée Valois*]. In 1870 Curran's stepdaughter Mary Ann was enrolled; Eliza and Ellen followed in 1874. As for the two boys, no comparable private or public school existed and their level of literacy remained below that of their sisters. Despite his daughters being schooled as Catholics, Curran was an Anglican. When on 25 Dec. 1883 he married the mother of his children, it was in a Church of England ceremony at the Indian mission established in 1880 on Kuper Island.

Mary Sitkwa Whilemot Curran died in 1894. By then their children were mostly married. At loose ends, Curran went homesteading around Shuswap Lake in the southern interior. By now in his late fifties, he found a new wife, Elizabeth Toma, born in 1876 and so over 30 years his junior. Also an aboriginal woman, Elizabeth was (unlike Mary) literate, said to have been educated by Oblate missionaries. Curran soon had another family, which eventually would include seven children: Edith Rose, Louise Ellen, James, Victor, Agnes, George, and Thomas.

In 1901 Curran was still in the southern interior, farming in a modest fashion, but the family was living at Chemainus on Vancouver Island in 1911 when Curran pre-empted land on remote Lasqueti Island. He and Elizabeth built a small house and barn there, cleared land, and planted a vegetable garden and orchard. According to one of their sons, Curran also raised hay and, when it was very cold in the winter, sold it in the interior at a good price.

At a time when persons of mixed race were easy targets in a racially charged Canada, Lasqueti's isolation gave a refuge. Family recollections speak to a strong sense of community. A long-time islander remembered that "the Curran home was always open to their neighbours." Descendants have stressed how "everyone lived together – a version of utopia – there was great hospitality along the coast in those days – everyone looked after you – we all piled in together, lived together, ate together."

According to a local historian who got her information from a descendant, "Schooling was intermittent for the young Currans." "In their home they had but a few books and these were read over and over again." The children attended the first school opened on Lasqueti in 1913 but it closed in 1917 after a second school began, too far away for them to attend. In part for that reason Curran's second family led, as had their predecessors, mostly modest lives.

Age eventually caught up with William Henry Curran. Soon after moving to Lasqueti, he severely injured his back and thereafter he walked with a serious limp. However, as he wrote proudly in 1924, "the hair on my head has never turned gray; my hair is light-coloured, and the same as in my boyhood days." Curran died in 1930, aged 87. Elizabeth had moved back to her girlhood home near Kamloops shortly before her death in about 1929. Today hundreds of Curran descendants contribute to every aspect of British Columbia's society and economy.

JEAN BARMAN

[Details concerning William Henry Curran and his family were obtained in conversations with descendants Victor Edward Curran, Lewella Duncan, and Ed Philips at Victor Curran's 90th birthday celebration in Vancouver on 15 Jan. 1994, as well as from family information given out at the party. Additional information was drawn from the author's conversation with Georgina Curran Surgenor, a granddaughter of Fred Curran, on 24 Oct. 1998, from a manuscript family history supplied by Joe Warnock, a great-grandson of the subject, and from an e-mail message dated 2 June 2002 from Everette Surgenor, a great-granddaughter of Fred Curran. J.B.]

Anglican Church of Canada, Diocese of British Columbia Arch. (Victoria), Kuper Island Mission fonds, RBMB. BCA, A/E/R54/R54; /R54A; /R54.3; GR-0766, boxes 7, 13; GR-2951, nos.1894-09-045654, 1930-09-442438 (mfm.); VF36, frames 0941–43. LAC, RG 31, C1, 1881, Cowichan, B.C., dist.191, household 199; 1891, Salt Spring Island, B.C., dist.3, household 41; 1901, Vancouver, household 154; Yale East, household 16. St Edward's Church (Duncan, B.C.), St Ann's Church, reg. of baptisms and marriages, 1859–85. Sisters of St Ann Arch. (Victoria), RG II, S36, box 1 (pupils's reg., St Ann's Convent, Cowichan, Vancouver Island, 1864–April 1929). B.C., Legislative Assembly, *Sessional papers*, voters' lists, 1874–94. Elda Copley Mason, *Lasqueti Island: history & memory* (Lantzville, B.C., [1991]). *Electoral hist. of B.C. Memories of the Chemainus valley: a history of people …* , comp. Lillian Gustafson and Gordon Elliott ([Chemainus, B.C.], 1978).

CYCENO, ROSE. *See* STARKMAN, BESHA

D

DAINES, SARAH. *See* HYMAS

DALE, WILLIAM, educator and farmer; b. 1 Oct. 1848 in Kearby, near Wetherby, England, son of William Dale and Frances Stephenson (Stevenson); m. 10 April 1901 Florence Frederika Ryckman in Brockville, Ont., and they had three daughters and one son; d. 16 Feb. 1921 in St Marys, Ont.

William Dale was educated at St Marys Grammar School, near the family farm in Perth County, Upper Canada. At Upper Canada College in Toronto in 1866–67, he was head boy for a time. He attended the University of Toronto, where he received a BA with first-class honours in classics, mathematics, and general proficiency in 1871 and an MA in 1873. In these years Dale began writing a journal. He was not impressed with his education. Sounding a nationalist note, he thought that many professors were "second or third rate men from the Universities of Britain [who] … do as little as possible to point the way to the higher paths of knowledge." Dale began teaching in 1871 as headmaster of Uxbridge High School and

in 1875–76 he was principal at St Marys High School. There, one of his pupils was the future novelist Charles William Gordon*, who remembered him as a "clumsily dressed, farmerlike man." Gordon credited Dale with instilling an appreciation of the classics and a sense of the "beauty of human speech."

In 1876 Dale was appointed rector of Quebec High School. He never developed close ties with French Canada, where he felt his isolation keenly; he was convinced that English-speaking Canadians were destined to "complete ostracism" there. He publicly criticized the power of the Roman Catholic hierarchy and, according to his journal, his comments on Canadian history raised "a nest of hornets." Critical of French Canadian nationalism, which stressed "the oppression suffered at the hands of the English," Dale argued that everything progressive in French Canada, such as good government, freedom of education, and prosperity, "resulted entirely from the Conquest."

Dale returned to Ontario in 1879. He subsequently served for some time as an examiner for the provincial Department of Education and for the University of

Toronto and Trinity College. In 1884 he was appointed tutor in classical literature at University College, where he was also registrar from 1885 to 1887. He did not publish, preferring the classroom and public-lecture forum. His addresses to the university community displayed his catholicity of interests. Echoing the English educator Thomas Arnold, he thought that there were discernible and fixed standards of virtue and truth and that the purpose of teaching was to bring them to light. But he feared that "mankind is in a sort of hopeless despair" because "religion appears to have lost something of its old influence" and science had failed to provide any consoling answers. It was necessary, he argued, to look to the achievements of past civilizations, such as Rome, and especially its poets, for moral and civic guidance.

Dale became lecturer in Latin and Roman history in 1887; in 1892 he would be appointed associate professor of Latin, while retaining his lectureship in history. He became a severe critic of the university federation act of 1887. Vice-Chancellor William Mulock*'s design to build an institution that emphasized science and particularly medicine was a special concern. "It is clearly the intention of the Mulock gang to destroy the Arts Faculty," he confided in his journal. He was alarmed by the increasing amount of funds being steered to the newly reconstituted faculty of medicine and by the generous financial deals that had been struck for the affiliating theological colleges, Victoria and Wycliffe. These resources, Dale thought, should have gone to University College for the purposes of providing students with a general education. A traditionalist, Dale believed that the purpose of university was the cultivation of virtuous citizenship and he was concerned about the growing stress on research and training professionals. He was also critical of the continuing reliance on non-Canadian faculty. In 1890 he wrote a stern letter to the minister of education, George William Ross*, arguing that Canadians should be promoted to the most prestigious chairs at the university. He pointed out that the faculty members professing the core subjects, such as classics, mathematics, and modern languages, were mostly Canadian, had the largest teaching loads, yet were paid significantly less and held less important positions than foreign-born and -trained professors.

Dale's dismissal from the University of Toronto in 1895 was precipitated by the controversies over faculty appointments and free speech that had erupted on campus. Under the university act the hiring of faculty was controlled by the government of Ontario. Suspicions of nepotism arose in the *Varsity*, the student newspaper, when George MacKinnon Wrong*, son-in-law of Chancellor Edward Blake*, was appointed lecturer in history and then quickly promoted professor. Dale presented the editor of the *Globe*, John Stephen WILLISON, with an explosive letter which was printed on the

first page of the 9 Feb. 1895 edition. The letter was contemptuous of Wrong's scholarly abilities and suggested that, if current hiring practices endured, "the professoriate of the University will have lost the respect both of students and public, and the results to learning will be most disastrous." Dale recommended that the appointment of professors be made independently of the government. He was promptly dismissed on 14 February. For the students, Dale was a champion of free speech and, led by William Lyon Mackenzie King* and others, they boycotted classes, demanding his reinstatement. But for the university, his letter had been a serious breach of collegiality.

During this controversy James Loudon*, the beleaguered president of the university, argued that Dale's attack had been motivated by jealousy of his more research-oriented and productive colleagues. Dale's bold but naive actions were probably rooted in more complex considerations. He was troubled by the growing specialization of university life and the more intense critical spirit in modern scholarship. He saw little value in the stress on archival research by more empirically oriented historians. "They bury themselves in the mines of original research and . . . the result of their labour is for the most part a mere bibliography, which is worse than useless for real knowledge." The new scholarship had failed, in his view, to produce "readable" essays of "lasting effect."

Dale secured a position as professor of Latin at Queen's College in Kingston from 1895 to 1900 and from 1900 to 1904 he was a special lecturer at McMaster University, then in Toronto. By the time of his marriage in 1901 he had returned to St Marys to operate his family's cattle farm. He served on the town council there and was mayor in 1918 and 1919. At his death in 1921 he was still a member of the senate of the University of Toronto, having been elected continuously since 1893.

DAVID B. MARSHALL

Dale's departure from the University of Toronto is the subject of James Crerar Reaney's play *The dismissal; or, twisted beards & tangled whiskers* ([Erin, Ont.], 1978).

AO, RG 2-29-1-35, Dale to George Ross, 9 Dec. 1890; RG 22-267, no.8018; RG 80-5-0-292, no.10403. GRO, Reg. of births, Knaresborough, 1 Oct. 1848. UTA, A1973-0026/ 077(29); B1975-0013/001–2. *Globe*, 5–17 Feb. 1895. *St. Marys Journal-Argus* (St Marys, Ont.), 24 Feb. 1921. Allan Bowker, "Truly useful men: Maurice Hutton, George Wrong, James Mavor and the University of Toronto, 1880– 1927" (PHD thesis, Univ. of Toronto, 1975). H. W. Charlesworth, *More candid chronicles: further leaves from the note book of a Canadian journalist* (Toronto, 1928). Ralph Connor [C. W. Gordon], *Postscript to adventure: the autobiography of Ralph Connor* (New York, 1938). W. J. Loudon, *Sir William Mulock: a short biography* (Toronto, 1932); *Studies of student life* (8v., Toronto, 1923–[4–?]), 5. A. B. McKillop, *Matters of mind: the university in Ontario, 1791–1951* (Toronto, 1994). Ont., Royal commission on the discipline in the University of Toronto, *Report of the commissioners* (Toronto, 1895). *The University of Toronto and its colleges, 1827–1906*, ed. W. J. A[lexander] (Toronto, 1906).

DANDURAND, DAMASE, first Canadian-born Oblate of Mary Immaculate, architect, and vicar general; b. 23 March 1819 in La Prairie, Lower Canada, son of Roger-François Dandurand, a notary, and Marie-Jovite Descombes-Porcheron; d. 13 April 1921 in St Boniface (Winnipeg).

The father of Damase Dandurand died on 14 Dec. 1821, and on 15 June 1825 his mother married Pierre-Paul Démaray*, a notary. Damase first attended an English school in Montreal, boarding with his uncle Gordon Forbes, who inspired in him a taste for construction and architecture. He thus acquired a good knowledge of English, which would prove indispensable in his future responsibilities. He then moved to Saint-Jean (Saint-Jean-sur-Richelieu), where his mother now lived. Because of his delicate health, he continued his schooling with private tutors up to the fifth year (Belles-Lettres) of the classical program. From 1832 to 1835 he finished his classical studies at the Collège de Chambly.

At 16, Dandurand chose to become a priest. He began teaching at the Collège de Chambly while studying theology there. His remarkable precocity is evidence of his above-average talent. Summoned to Montreal in 1840, he spent some time at the Grand Séminaire and is believed to have been in the service of Bishop Charles-Auguste-Marie-Joseph de Forbin-Janson*, who was then in Canada. By special permission because of his age, he was ordained a priest on 12 Sept. 1841 by Bishop Rémi Gaulin* of Kingston. On 2 December six Oblates of Mary Immaculate arrived from France at the request of Bishop Ignace Bourget* of Montreal to their founder, Bishop Charles-Joseph-Eugène de Mazenod of Marseilles [see Jean-Baptiste Honorat*].

Dandurand immediately thought of joining their order. He began his noviciate on 24 December and pronounced his vows at Christmas the following year. From then on he took part in many missions and retreats in the diocese of Montreal and even across the American border. He was particularly in demand in areas where English-speaking Catholics were present. In early 1844 he made two extensive tours through the Eastern Townships, including Stanbridge, Dunham, Granby, and Stanstead. In May, shortly after the Oblates had been put in charge of the Catholic mission in Bytown (Ottawa), he was called to serve the Irish community there, but when Father Michael Molloy, a true son of Ireland, arrived the following year, he resumed preaching in the diocese of Montreal.

Recalled to Bytown in 1847 because of the typhus epidemic raging there, Dandurand contracted the disease after a few weeks, and he would always remember this episode with horror. Soon after his recovery, Joseph-Bruno Guigues*, an Oblate who was now bishop of the diocese of Bytown, appointed him curé of the parish of Notre-Dame, where he was in charge from 1848 to 1874. Over the years he contributed to the construction of the cathedral, begun in 1841, by correcting the arrangement of the windows on the side walls. (He replaced a row of superposed windows with one of large windows.) He also erected the two towers and added a deep apse to the nave, all in Gothic style from his own plans. A generous and enterprising priest, he participated in the developments that enabled the ill-reputed village of Bytown to achieve the status of capital city. In particular, he supported the teaching and charitable work of the women who became the Sisters of Charity of Ottawa [see Élisabeth Bruyère*] by directing to them some of the parishioners' charitable donations and by guiding towards them young women in search of their future. He reportedly also obtained the assistance of the Brothers of the Christian Schools. On various occasions Dandurand was appointed administrator of the diocese in the absence of the bishop, and he became his vicar general in 1862.

Some of Dandurand's religious superiors, including Father Florent Vandenberghe, suspected that Bishop Guigues did not always respect the interests of his own congregation. Worried also about the legal implications of the vicar general's administration, they decided in 1870 to put an end to the agreement of 1856 which had defined the role of the Oblates in Ottawa, but they let Dandurand remain in the service of the diocese. Although he had experienced conflictual situations, he was by no means an ideologue. He had rather kept in step with the thinking of his bishop, whose pastoral letters (very likely written by others) showed strong ultramontane overtones, but whose administration was marked by realism and compromise.

When Guigues died on 8 Feb. 1874 Dandurand became administrator of the diocese, according to the wishes of the former bishop, who had also mentioned him as his most appropriate successor. "He has been my right hand, my support, my consolation, my other self," he had written a few months earlier. But the Oblates objected to the appointment of one of their number, and furthermore, there were differences of opinion with regard to Dandurand. After a painful waiting period, the controversial choice of Bishop Joseph-Thomas Duhamel* added to his distress. For a while he even considered transferring to the secular clergy.

Dandurand was clearly in the throes of a severe depression. He agreed to a trip to France as a diversion from his troubles, but refused to serve in the parish he was offered in England. It was at this point that Archbishop Alexandre-Antonin Taché* of St Boniface invited him to Manitoba. The adjustment was painful, and Dandurand had the impression of living past his time. He would remain absent from the enormous transformations that the west would undergo in this period. After a brief stay in 1875–76 in the emerging city of Winnipeg, he was appointed curé of the neighbouring parish of St Charles, which was largely Métis. He served there from 1876 until 1900.

Dandurand was in his eighties when Adélard Langevin*, archbishop of St Boniface since 1895, offered him the hospitality of his residence. He did not remain idle, but with energy and compassion took care of the old people and orphan girls at the Hospice Taché and the Hospice d'Youville in St Boniface; in 1915 he retired to the Juniorat de la Sainte-Famille, among his Oblate brothers.

On the celebration of his 100th birthday, Damase Dandurand, who was still mentally and physically alert, celebrated mass and spoke several times. Completely lucid to the end, he died surrounded by respect and affection. He was buried on 16 April 1921 in the cemetery of the juniorate, following a funeral in the cathedral at St Boniface. He was remembered as a serene, compassionate, and considerate old man. Avoiding involvement in linguistic and nationalistic conflicts, in the first half of his life he had helped his European colleagues adapt to the realities of Canadian life, and had played a part in defining a prominent role for the Oblates of Mary Immaculate in Ottawa.

ÉMILIEN LAMIRANDE

Information on Father Damase Dandurand is available in several archival repositories, among them the parish archives of Notre-Dame (Ottawa) for the years 1844–45 and 1848–75; St Mary's (Winnipeg), 1875–76; St Charles, Man., 1876–1900; and St Boniface cathedral (Winnipeg); and the Arch. of the Archdiocese of Ottawa, in the Notre-Dame parish file. A document entitled "Archives of the Catholic Church of Bytown," written in part by Father Dandurand, is also in the archdiocesan archives. Additional information is found in the Arch. de la Chancellerie de l'Archevêché de Montréal, RC 4: ff.54, 65r; the Arch. de l'Archidiocèse de Québec, 321 CN (diocèse d'Ottawa); and the St Charles parish file at the Arch. de l'Archevêché de Saint-Boniface. The following materials are also useful: Arch. Deschâtelets, Oblats de Marie-Immaculée (Ottawa), HEB 3178.D15 (dossier Damase Dandurand); Arch. Provinciales O.M.I. (Montréal), Codex historicus, Longueuil, and Dossier Dandurand; Arch. Générales des Oblats de Marie-Immaculée (Rome), Dossier Damase Dandurand, Dandurand à Mazenod, 3 déc. 1845; Archivio della Propaganda Fide (Rome), Scritture originali riferite nelle Congregazioni generali, vol.1003; and Arch. des Sœurs Grises (Winnipeg), Chroniques de la maison vicariale de Saint-Boniface, VII–VIII.

ANQ-M, CE601-S3, 24 mars 1819. Le Devoir, 14 avril 1921. La Presse, 22 mars 1919. Gaston Carrière, Dictionnaire biographique des oblats de Marie-Immaculée au Canada (4v., Ottawa, 1976–89), 1: 248–49; Histoire documentaire de la Congrégation des missionnaires oblats de Marie-Immaculée dans l'est du Canada (12v., Ottawa, 1957–75), 1; "La vocation oblate du père Damase Dandurand," Études oblates (Ottawa), 15 (1956): 159–63. Le centenaire du R.P. Damase Dandurand, O.M.I. (Saint-Boniface [Winnipeg], 1919). Robert Choquette, L'Église catholique dans l'Ontario français du dix-neuvième siècle (Ottawa, 1984). [Georges Derouzier, dit] père Alexis de Barbezieux, Histoire de la province ecclésiastique d'Ottawa et de la colonisation dans la vallée de l'Ottawa (2v., Ottawa, 1897). "Feu le R.P. Damase Dandurand, O.M.I.," Les Cloches de Saint-Boniface (Saint-Boniface), 20 (1921): 63–68. Émilien Lamirande, Une figure méconnue, Damase Dandurand (1819–1921): le premier oblat canadien (Ottawa, 1996). Normand Pagé, La cathédrale Notre-Dame d'Ottawa; histoire, architecture, iconographie (Ottawa, 1988).

DANDURAND, JOSÉPHINE. See MARCHAND

DARLING, FRANK, architect; b. 17 Feb. 1850 in Scarborough Township, Upper Canada, son of William Stewart Darling, a Church of England clergyman, and Jane Parsons; d. unmarried 19 May 1923 in Toronto.

The eldest son of the rector of Scarborough and later of the Church of the Holy Trinity in Toronto, Frank Darling was educated at Upper Canada College in Toronto and Trinity College School in Weston (Toronto). In 1866, after a short time as a bank teller, he joined the architectural office of Thomas Gundry and Henry Langley* as an apprentice. In late 1869 or early 1870 he left Toronto to train in London with one of the greatest architects of the age, George Edmund Street. Before returning in 1873, he also worked briefly with Arthur William Blomfield. This British experience had a profound effect on Darling. From Street he learned that the principles of Gothic architecture could form the basis of modern design. From Street's students Richard Norman Shaw, William Eden Nesfield, and Philip Speakman Webb he saw how historical forms could be skilfully adapted to meet the needs of contemporary life.

Darling began private practice in Toronto in 1873, when he entered into partnership with Henry Macdougall. His first commissions came from the city's Anglicans, and included the churches of St Matthias (1873–74), St Thomas (1874), and St Luke (1881) as well as the convocation hall (1877) and chapel (1884) of Trinity College. This early work was mostly executed in brick in a manner reminiscent of Street, Shaw, and Nesfield. Other projects show Darling in a continuing state of artistic experimentation: the Home for Incurables (1879–81) is an exercise in Shaw's eclecticism and the Victoria Hospital for Sick Children (1889) reveals the influence of American Henry Hobson Richardson.

In 1880 Darling, who was then in partnership with Samuel George Curry (a Port Hope native), had submitted a design modelled on Street's plan for the Law Courts in London to the competition for Ontario's new parliament buildings. Although Darling placed first, delays and back-room deals meant that his plan would never be built [see Kivas Tully*]. The competition nonetheless brought him recognition and, in 1885, the chance to do something new: a branch in Toronto for the Bank of Montreal. Its obtusely angled site at the corner of Front and Yonge was difficult, but he responded with a masterful essay in the newly fashionable classical mode, in which a carefully ornamented stone façade introduced a stunning glass-domed hall [see Joseph McCausland*]. Functional and stylish, the bank was a success for Darling. In it he anticipated the taste for monumental public architecture that would sweep North America in the first decades of the 20th century.

After 1885, Darling's commissions, besides the hospital, included the Toronto Club (1888) and additions to Trinity College. In 1892 he took into partnership an associate from the hospital project, the British-trained John Andrew Pearson*, who would work with him for the rest of his career. The years of Darling's greatest achievement began in 1898, when he was retained by the Canadian Bank of Commerce to design branches in Winnipeg and Toronto. Like its competitors, the Commerce found architecture an effective vehicle for self-promotion. Darling subsequently designed dozens of branches for the Commerce, as well as for the Metropolitan, Sterling, Dominion, Union, and Nova Scotia banks. Most of the Commerce buildings featured façades of stone and brick and were grandly classical in the manner of the English baroque or the French École des Beaux-Arts. They ranged from impressive structures with giant columns and massive stone entablatures, as in Montreal (1903–8), Vancouver (1906–8), and Winnipeg (1910–12), to handsome pavilions scaled to the needs of small towns and city neighbourhoods. Particularly charming were a series of prefabricated frame branches in frontier towns across the west that had been produced, shipped, and erected by the British Columbia Mills, Timber and Trading Company [see John Hendry*]. Darling's work for the Commerce brought social and financial success and offers of patronage, especially from a small circle of powerful Toronto businessmen. Besides George Albertus Cox* and Byron Edmund WALKER, both presidents of the Commerce, this group included a childhood friend, Dominion president Edmund Boyd OSLER, as well as meat packer Joseph Wesley Flavelle*, for whom he designed a house at Queen's Park (1901–2). Among his other important projects from this period were Convocation Hall at the University of Toronto (1904–7), the Royal Ontario Museum (1909–14), the Toronto General Hospital (1909–13), the Winnipeg Grain and Produce Exchange (1909–10), new buildings for Dalhousie University in Halifax (1912–15), and the headquarters of Sun Life Assurance in Montreal (1916–18).

The scale of this production had an enormous impact on the look of Canada's towns and cities. At a time when many businessmen preferred to hire American architects for high-profile commissions, Darling's bank architecture became recognizable for its balance of English and North American trends. For many buildings he modulated his characteristically classical language to suit specific conditions, as in his frequent use of Romanesque motifs on the campus of the University of Toronto. His accomplished, thoughtful approach to design, artistic confidence, and high standard of execution won him the admiration of his peers. He was made a member of the Royal Canadian Academy of Arts in 1886, president of the Ontario Association of Architects in 1895, and a director of the Toronto Guild of Civic Art in 1907. Darling claimed to abhor professional infighting, but, as president of the OAA, he became enmeshed in the association's unsuccessful efforts to secure compulsory registration, a step not all architects supported. He nevertheless remained a popular figure, known increasingly for his bold projects. Named to the federal planning commission for Ottawa and Hull in 1913, he was awarded the gold medal of the Royal Institute of British Architects two years later (the only Canadian architect so recognized) and honorary doctorates from the University of Toronto (1916) and Dalhousie (1922). Darling's professionalism generated equal respect among his clients. In his ongoing work for Dalhousie, which included Shirreff Hall (1920–21) [see Jennie Grahl Hunter SHIRREFF], Darling, in the estimate of university historian P. B. Waite, was "ingenious, flexible, sensitive to local conditions, and best of all, willing to listen to suggestions." A close friend, architect C. Barry Cleveland, maintained that he stood "for absolutely straight and upright dealing."

Darling combined a quiet charm with refined tastes. According to one biographer, "He had a good-natured tolerance, and on occasion he was master of the mordant phrase. A poor story-teller, but a good listener, geniality and wit went hand in hand with him, more especially when he could be provoked into exercising his ability as an architectural critic." His collection of etchings and prints was strong in 17th-century French portraiture; his architectural library represented 20th-century modernists and landscapists as well as earlier revivalists. He was an enthusiastic golfer and clubman, and a conservative in politics. A lifelong bachelor, he was decidedly loyal to his family and friends; his widowed mother lived with him for several years before her death in 1909, and he took a particular interest in his nieces and nephews. In his will, Darling, who deeply regretted his inability to speak French and German, left a sum for a great-nephew's education, especially in the "modern languages." Valued at more than $183,000, his estate would be distributed largely among his relatives, his servants and chauffeur, and J. A. Pearson. Provision was also made for the continued residential and financial needs of an old Scarborough acquaintance and her separated daughter. After eight months of poor health due to heart trouble, Darling died in May 1923 at his home at 11 Walmer Road. He was buried in the family plot at St John's, Norway (Toronto).

Darling had avoided controversy and written little. Others championed his architecture. Critic and professor Percy Erskine Nobbs* saw in his work support for his own belief that Canadian architecture could develop a distinctive voice only by charting a middle ground between the architectural cultures of Britain and the United States, with careful attention to local needs. This approach had been Darling's modus operandi. At a time of rapid architectural change, his ability to combine ideas, materials, and techniques from London, New York, and Chicago into a unified whole (without copying) was exceptional. Buildings such as his Bank of Nova Scotia in Winnipeg (1907–8) display a hybrid quality that was expressive of the complex patterns of Canadian intellectual and cultural life in the years leading up to World War I. The new houses of parliament in Ottawa (1916–27), designed by Pearson and Jean-Omer Marchand*, reflect in their spirit of progressive traditionalism, blend of references, and balance of old and new the substantial impact of Darling and his office. By adapting the fashions of the day to the wishes of his clients, he had helped shape an independent voice for Canadian architecture and lay the foundation for the creative exploration of Canadian themes by such architects as John MacIntosh Lyle* in the 1920s.

KELLY CROSSMAN

Frank Darling's address as president of the Ontario Assoc. of Architects appears in *Canadian Architect and Builder* (Toronto), 9 (1896), no.2: 17–19.

AO, RG 22-305, no.47775; RG 80-8-0-910, no.4200. LAC, RG 31, C1, 1901, Toronto, Ward 4, div.2: 7 (mfm. at AO). Univ. of Waterloo Library, Doris Lewis Rare Book Room (Waterloo, Ont.), William Dendy, "Frank Darling, 1880–1923, Canadian architect" (typescript with plates, 1979). *Globe*, 21–22 May 1923. E. [R.] Arthur, *Toronto, no mean city* ([Toronto], 1964; 3rd ed., rev. S. A. Otto, 1986). James Borcoman *et al.*, *Money matters: a critical look at bank architecture* (exhibition catalogue, Canadian Centre for Architecture, Montreal, 1990). *Canadian annual rev.*, 1913: 333; 1916: 797; 1921: 241. Kelly Crossman, *Architecture in transition: from art to practice, 1885–1906* (Kingston, Ont., and Montreal, 1987). William Dendy, *Lost Toronto* (Toronto, 1978). William Dendy *et al.*, *Toronto observed: its architecture, patrons, and history* (Toronto, 1986). M. E. and Merilyn McKelvey, *Toronto, carved in stone* (Toronto, 1984). G. E. Mills and D. W. Holdsworth, "The B.C. Mills prefabricated system: the emergence of ready-made buildings in western Canada," *Canadian Historic Sites: Occasional Papers in Archaeology and Hist.* (Ottawa), no.14 (1975): 127–69. National Gallery of Canada, *Canadian art*, ed. C. C. Hill *et al.* (2v., Ottawa, 1988–94), 1: 254. Geoffrey Simmins, *Ontario Association of Architects: a centennial history, 1889–1989* (Toronto, 1989). David Spector, "The buildings of the Winnipeg-based Union and Northern Crown banks: a glimpse into early twentieth century corporate architecture," *Manitoba Hist.* (Winnipeg), no.21 (spring 1991): 25–31. *Standard dict. of Canadian biog.* (Roberts and Tunnell). Toronto Region Architectural Conservancy, *Terra cotta – artful deceivers* (Toronto, 1990). P. B. Waite, *The lives of Dalhousie University* (2v., Montreal and Kingston, 1994–98), 1.

DAVID, LAURENT-OLIVIER, journalist, newspaper owner, author, lawyer, office holder, and politician; b. 24 March 1840 in Sault-au-Récollet (Montreal), son of Stanislas David, a farmer and militia captain, and Élisabeth Tremblay; m. first 1 July 1869 Albina Chenet at Quebec, and they had one son and ten daughters; m. secondly 18 Oct. 1892 Ludivine Garceau in Boston; they had no children; d. 24 Aug. 1926 in Outremont, Que.

Laurent-Olivier David achieved high standing in his classical studies at the Petit Séminaire de Sainte-Thérèse, where, as he later noted in *Les gerbes canadiennes*, he "worked hard, studied, laughed often, and sometimes wept." He then enrolled in the law school of François-Maximilien Bibaud* at the Collège Sainte-Marie in Montreal. Called to the Montreal bar in April 1864, he practised until September 1872 with Joseph-Alfred Mousseau*, a future Conservative premier of Quebec. His life would not be confined to the law, however. Patriotic fervour had already welled up within David, and he would never lose it.

As a law student, he was a member of the Cercle Littéraire, a group organized by the founders of the Cabinet de Lecture Paroissial that had been created in opposition to the Institut Canadien in Montreal and hoped to attract students in law and medicine. At the meeting it held on 1 Oct. 1861, he delivered a lecture entitled "Essai sur la littérature nationale," which was published on 12 October in *L'Écho du Cabinet de Lecture Paroissial* in Montreal; in it he expressed the wish that literature might become "the faithful expression of the natural beauties of our country."

In January 1862, with a group including Mousseau, Ludger Labelle*, Louis-Wilfrid Sicotte*, and Joseph-Adophe Chapleau* (another future Conservative premier of the province), David became a co-owner of the Conservative *Le Colonisateur*. He and André-Napoléon Montpetit were its sole editors when this Montreal newspaper ceased publication in June 1863. David then became an editor with *L'Union nationale*, which had been founded in Montreal in 1864 by Médéric Lanctot*, C.-E.-E. Bouthillier, Toussaint Thompson, and Labelle to oppose confederation. On 3 September its prospectus mentioned that the founders "had often fought under other colours. Today, they understand that the reconciliation of parties is the country's salvation." According to its editors, Canadian confederation was in no way necessary and indeed threatened to cause conflicts in Lower Canada. It was while working at this paper (which would cease publication in November 1867, shortly after confederation) that David met Wilfrid Laurier*. Their friendship would last until the end of Laurier's life.

In *L'Union nationale*, David wrote a scathing criticism of a lecture entitled "Le principe des nationalités," which had been delivered by Gonzalve Doutre* on 1 Dec. 1864 at the Institut Canadien in Montreal and had appeared shortly afterwards in *Le Pays*, a Liberal newspaper in that city. On this occasion David revealed himself a conservative far removed from the liberal ideas of Doutre. That this was a period of transition for liberalism should be noted. On the one hand, French liberal ideas, British liberalism, and a degree of religious liberalism were beginning to undermine traditional thinking. On the other hand, the Institut Canadien, the centre for the Rouge movement in Montreal whose objectives David supported (though he was not a member), was heading into decline.

With the coming of confederation, David shifted his political allegiance. He moved from the Conservatives to the Liberals and became active in politics. He was defeated in the constituency of Hochelaga by Louis Beaubien* in the provincial election of 1867. As David would note in *La jeunesse et l'avenir . . .* (which came out in Montreal in 1926), Beaubien was an "educated farmer [and] forceful speaker who naturally had the support of the agricultural class" in a vote where the pastoral letters of bishops and the sermons of curés were highly influential. He continued practising law until 1870, when along with Mousseau and George-Édouard Desbarats* he founded the Montreal weekly *L'Opinion publique*. He would be its editor-in-chief from 1 Jan. 1870 until he resigned in 1873.

In this first-rate publication, David got into his stride and conveyed the essence of the intellectual constants and ambiguities that would stay with him all his life. The weekly's political allegiance is hard to define. Nationalist with a liberal bent that was sometimes tenuous, the periodical seemed made in the image of its editor-in-chief. David's pen turned out reflections on politics, business, the economy, colonization, industrialization, and relations with the United States. On the subject of the province's educational system, David believed that it produced too many priests and members of the liberal professions, and that it was not well adapted to the country's needs. On 5 Feb. 1870 he asked: "What use will it be for French Canadians to speak Greek and Latin, if they are found incapable of filling all the lucrative jobs, if the best positions are denied them, if the doors are closed to them at all those business establishments where thousands of our English compatriots find a decent living?" Nonetheless, in a collection of essays, entitled *Au soir de la vie*, which was published in Montreal in 1924, David would write with pleasure about Cicero, Pliny the Younger, Socrates, Plato, and Aristotle. His articles on religion demonstrate his faithfulness to the church.

It was in *L'Opinion publique* that David began his "Galerie nationale," a series of portraits of personalities such as Bishop Ignace Bourget*, Joseph-Rémi Vallières* de Saint-Réal, and Emma Albani [LAJEUNESSE]; these articles would be picked up again and printed as volumes (some quite slim). He also published in the paper a collection of texts entitled "Les hommes de 37–38" that would serve as the background for *Les Patriotes de 1837–1838*, a work brought out in Montreal in 1884. Jean-Olivier Chénier*, Ludger Duvernay*, and Bonaventure Viger* are among those who figure in it. In his essays on the Patriotes, David portrays them as heroes who, by defying authority, caused Bishop Jean-Jacques Lartigue* to issue his famous pastoral letter of 24 Oct. 1837. To the bishop who had described them at that time as brigands, rebels, and bandits, he would reply in *Le clergé canadien: sa mission, son œuvre*, a pamphlet published in Montreal in 1896, "Let us say in passing that a few of these bandits later became the leaders of the Conservative party and the idols of the clergy before whom the people were duty bound to bow down." Such musings on the Patriotes occur regularly in David's writing, which suggests that he encouraged rebellion and rejection of authority. Indeed in 1892 curé Louis-Eugène Duguay would complain to Bishop Louis-François Laflèche* that *Les Patriotes de 1837–1838*, a seditious book, was being given as a prize in the schools in his diocese. Towards the end of 1873 David left the newspaper in which he had expressed most of his ideas. He resigned because, unlike his colleagues, he did not want to defend a government mired in the Canadian Pacific Railway scandal. "What a lot of disappointments and problems this exaggerated concept of honour in this affair brought me," he would admit in *Souvenirs et biographies, 1870–1910*.

In Montreal in April 1874, David became cofounder and co-owner, with Cléophas Beausoleil*, of *Le Bien public*. It was the official organ of the Parti National, formed in 1871 by Laurier, Louis-Amable Jetté*, Frédéric-Ligori Béïque*, and Honoré Mercier*, among others. David would declare in *Mes contemporains* that the party had been "only a decoy, a strategic ploy invented to bring the Liberal party to power." In *Le Bien public*, David and Beausoleil proved a bit too liberal on the subject of relations between church and state. Always on guard, the ultramontanes were not slow to reply. The newspaper, which was condemned from the pulpit, ceased publication on 20 May 1876, out of loyalty "to its program in favour of a protective tariff," as David would note in his *Mélanges historiques et littéraires*. But according to Mason Wade in *The French Canadians, 1760–1945*, which was published in Toronto in 1955, the journalist "took refuge from the ultramontane storm as a translator at Ottawa," a position he obtained in May 1876, thanks to Laurier, and held for two years. Six months after the disappearance of *Le Bien public*, Bishop Laflèche – who had officially encouraged François-Xavier-Anselme Trudel* to promote the *Programme catholique*, which had been drawn up in 1871 to counteract liberalism – denounced from Rome the newspaper that had preached "the quintessentially liberal theory of the separation of church and state."

Meanwhile David and Beausoleil had founded *Le Courrier de Montréal*, which lasted from October 1874 to October 1876. David had also run as a Liberal candidate in Hochelaga in the 1875 provincial election and had been defeated again by Louis Beaubien. *Biographies et portraits* was published in 1876 in order to "encourage young people to follow the examples of virtue and patriotism" displayed by such men as Bishop Joseph-Octave Plessis*, Évariste Gélinas*, and Joseph Papin*. The book included 21 articles that had first appeared in various newspapers or in pamphlet form between 1870 and 1876. In the same vein, David would bring out in 1894 *Mes contemporains*, a collection of laudatory biographies, most of which had already appeared in *Le Bien public*. *Souvenirs et biographies, 1870–1910*, published in 1911, would add other important characters, among them Médéric Lanctot, Wilfrid Laurier, and Louis-Rodrigue Masson*, to his previous volume, *Mes contemporains*. Through all these portraits, David developed some of his favourite themes: talent, health, work, perseverance, the need for commercial schools to enable French Canadians to compete with English Canadians, the pitfalls of politics, the difficulties of journalism, material success. All three books came out in Montreal.

In September 1878 David made another attempt to win a seat in Hochelaga, this time in a federal election, but he was defeated by Alphonse Desjardins*. He went back to work as a journalist at *La Tribune*, of which he was owner and editor from October 1880 to May 1884. In this Liberal Montreal newspaper, he continued the struggle to unite Liberals and Conservatives at the provincial level.

In 1885 David became involved in the Riel affair [*see* Louis Riel*]. One of the ways he did so was by becoming the leader, with Georges Duhamel*, of the Comité des Amis de Riel in Montreal. In the provincial election held the following year, he became the Liberal MLA for Montreal East, defeating the Conservative Louis-Olivier TAILLON and Adélard Gravel of the Parti National. In *Au soir de la vie* he would describe this electoral victory as compensation for his efforts in the Riel affair. During his term, he and Narcisse-Henri-Édouard Faucher* de Saint-Maurice represented the province of Quebec at the 17th congress of French Canadians, held in Nashua, N.H., in 1888. He did not run in the 1890 provincial election, but was a candidate in the federal one held the following year, when he lost to Alphonse-Télesphore Lépine in Montreal East, and in the 1892 provincial one in the constituency of Napierville, where Louis Sainte-Marie was elected.

These electoral defeats put an end to David's political career. From now on he relied entirely on his law practice and his literary talent to support his family. From 1888 to 1893 he was president of the Association Saint-Jean-Baptiste de Montréal. With the support of Béïque and Joseph-Xavier Perrault*, he survived the financial saga of the Monument National, which was opened in Montreal in 1893. David's play *Le drapeau de Carillon: drame historique en trois actes et deux tableaux* would be performed there in 1901. Published the following year in Montreal, this play spoke out for harmony between French-speaking and English-speaking Canadians.

In 1890 David became a member of the Royal Society of Canada. Two years later he began working as a clerk for the Montreal city council, an office he would hold until April 1918. Late in the summer of 1896, shortly after Laurier came to power, he published *Le clergé canadien: sa mission, son œuvre*, with the approval and financial assistance of the new prime minister. The content of this inflammatory pamphlet, which attacked the actions of the Roman Catholic clergy over the previous 50 years and denounced its undue influence in elections and its stand on the Manitoba schools question [*see* Adélard Langevin*], seemed to be the long-considered answer of Laurier's Liberals to the ultramontane clergy and in particular to Bishop Laflèche. The rebuttal from P. Bernard (the pseudonym of the Dominican Dominique-Ceslas Gonthier*), which promptly appeared in two volumes at Quebec under the title *Un manifeste libéral: M. L.-O. David et le clergé canadien*, was scorching. The affair was soon over. At the end of December, after listening to delegations from both sides, Rome put the pamphlet on the Index. *L'Électeur*, a Quebec paper that had begun publishing excerpts from the work, had to change its name (it became *Le Soleil*) to escape the wrath of the clergy. David quickly obeyed by withdrawing his pamphlet, but in 1899 he would write a letter to Archbishop Paul Bruchési* of Montreal saying he would go to his grave "convinced" that the church had committed a "serious error" in condemning what he had written in this piece. According to his explanation in *Mélanges historiques et litté-*

raires, he had only meant to put the clergy on guard against themselves, because "there is nothing finer or better on earth than the Catholic priesthood." In *L'Union des deux Canadas, 1841–1867*, which came out in Montreal in 1898, David took up the same themes. After denouncing the undue political influence of the clergy, as well as Lord Durham [Lambton*] and his wish to assimilate French Canadians, he attempted to prove that the latter were not "a people with no history, and no literature." Five years later, his friend Laurier made him a senator for the division of Mille-Isles. In 1905 David devoted a book to him, which was published in Montreal under the title *Laurier et son temps*; in 1919, soon after the politician's death, he would bring out a new edition of it in Beauceville as *Laurier: (sa vie, ses œuvres)*. In this work he described what he considered the great moments in the life of the man whom he had "so greatly loved and admired."

After the publication of three other volumes in Montreal, *Histoire du Canada depuis la Confédération, 1867–1887* in 1909, *Mélanges historiques et littéraires* in 1917, and *Les gerbes canadiennes* in 1921, David revealed his innermost thoughts in *Au soir de la vie*. A calm, traditional octogenarian, who was conservative in his thinking, he expressed his views in particular on modern questions – the constitutional status of Quebec in Canada, strikes, women's suffrage. Two years earlier, his only son, Athanase*, who was destined to have a notable political career, had founded the Prix David for literature in his father's honour.

When he died on 24 Aug. 1926, Laurent-Olivier David was given a splendid funeral. In a letter to poet Jean Charbonneau, dated 12 Feb. 1917, he had summed up his goals, stating that he wrote "not only for political purposes, but also to demonstrate the need to promote colonization, the establishment of technical, industrial, and commercial schools, and the overall improvement [of the] educational system, [as well as] to call for freedom in the political arena, and to fight against religious excesses." With varying degrees of skill, he had taken part in every struggle and had remained faithful all his life to the ideas that he had first championed in his youth: his religion and his country.

JEAN LANDRY

The major writings of Laurent-Olivier David have been mentioned in the biography. For a complete list of his works, consult the following: Hamel *et al.*, *DALFAN*, 377–79; *DOLQ*, vols. 1, 2.

ANQ-M, CE601-S4, 24 mars 1840. ANQ-Q, CE301-S97, 1er juill. 1869. Arch. du Séminaire de Trois-Rivières, Qué., 0016 (fonds Louis-François Richer-Laflèche). Centre for Research on French Canadian Culture (Ottawa), P2 (fonds Jean-Charbonneau). Mass., State Dept. of Public Health, Registry of vital records and statistics (Boston), Marriage records, Lowell, Mass., 18 Oct. 1892. *Le Bien public* (Montréal), 20 mai 1876. *Le Canada* (Montréal), 25 nov. 1911. *Le Courrier du Canada* (Québec), 18 oct. 1861. *Le Devoir*, 24–25 août 1926. *Le Monde illustré* (Montréal), 4 déc. 1886. *L'Opinion publique* (Montréal), 5 févr. 1870. *La Presse*, 29 déc. 1896. *L'Union nationale* (Montréal), 8 sept. 1864. *DPQ*. Thérèse Dufresne, "Bibliographie de M. L.-O. David" (école de bibliothécaires, univ. de Montréal, 1944). J. Hamelin *et al.*, *La presse québécoise*, vols. 2, 3. Pierre Hébert et Patrick Nicol, *Censure et littérature au Québec* (Saint-Laurent, Qué., 1997). Jacques Lacoursière, *Histoire populaire du Québec* (4v. parus, Sillery, Qué., 1995–), 3. Marcel Lajeunesse, *Les sulpiciens et la vie culturelle à Montréal au XIXe siècle* (Montréal, 1982). Yvan Lamonde, *Gens de parole: conférences publiques, essais et débats à l'Institut canadien de Montréal (1845–1871)* (Montréal, 1990). L. L. LaPierre, *Sir Wilfrid Laurier and the romance of Canada* ([Toronto], 1996). Edmond Lareau, *Histoire de la littérature canadienne* (Montréal, 1874). Jean-Marc Larrue, *Le monument inattendu: le Monument-National de Montréal, 1893–1993* (LaSalle, Qué., 1993). Le Jeune, *Dictionnaire*. Dorylas Moreau, "Le débat L.-O. David–P. Bernard (1897–1898) à propos du libéralisme" (mémoire de MA, univ. Laval, Québec, 1972). [Alexis Pelletier], *Coup d'œil sur le libéralisme européen et sur le libéralisme canadien: démonstration de leur parfaite identité* (Montréal, 1876). Jacques Rouillard, *Histoire du syndicalisme au Québec: des origines à nos jours* (Montréal, 1989). Robert Rumilly, *Hist. de Montréal*; *Histoire des Franco-Américains* (Montréal, 1958). Arthur Savaète, *Voix canadiennes: vers l'abîme* (12v., Paris, [1905–22]), 3; 7. Un catholique [Alexis Pelletier], *La source du mal de l'époque au Canada* ([Montréal], 1881).

DAVIDSON, GORDON CHARLES, historian, army officer, university professor, and author; b. 8 Aug. 1884 in Union, Elgin County, Ont., one of the eight children of James Davidson, a farmer and blacksmith, and Jane Grant; d. unmarried, by suicide, 30 May 1922 in Vancouver.

Gordon Davidson moved to British Columbia at a young age and in 1906 he acquired his undergraduate degree extramurally from the University of Toronto through New Westminster's Columbian Methodist College, where two of his brothers had taught. He remained in the west for his graduate training; in 1908 he completed a master's degree in history at the University of California in Berkeley, writing a thesis entitled "Report on the manuscripts on British Columbia in the Bancroft collection." After teaching high school in California for three years, he returned to Berkeley for doctoral studies. He spent 1914–15 in England on a travelling scholarship and completed his PHD in 1916. His thesis on the fur trade in the Canadian west was based upon exhaustive research in Canadian, British, and Californian archives and was published two years later in Berkeley as *The North West Company*.

The major academic contribution of Davidson's

brief career, *The North West Company* provides a detailed narrative of this fur-trading company from its formation late in the 18th century [*see* Simon McTavish*] to its union with the Hudson's Bay Company in 1821 [*see* Simon McGillivray*]. The first academic study devoted to the company itself, it was described by historian and author Lawrence Johnson Burpee* as "an excellent piece of work, scholarly, painstaking, accurate and at the same time readable." Burpee noted that perhaps its greatest contribution lay in the vast primary material Davidson had consulted and made available for the first time in published form.

In his focus on research in primary sources, Davidson represented the ideals of an emerging generation of university-trained, professional historians in Canada. Indeed, he was himself the product of an American graduate program, where the research ideal – the premise of the nascent historical profession – was stronger than in either Canada or Britain. Davidson's approach in *The North West Company* also reflected American influences. At Berkeley he had studied under Herbert Eugene Bolton and had been attracted by his hemispheric approach and his focus on material forces and the "westward movement" of history across the continent. Thus, Davidson's work was unfettered by the political-constitutional focus and the emphasis upon central Canada which dominated the historical writing of his own country.

Davidson's promising career would be cut short, a legacy of World War I. In June 1916 he had enlisted in the 196th (Western Universities) Battalion in Vancouver, and while overseas he was commissioned a first lieutenant in the 1st Canadian Mounted Rifles Regiment. He soon distinguished himself in action on the Western Front, winning the Military Cross at the battle of Passchendaele in October 1917. He also received a serious head wound (shrapnel fractured his right jawbone) and spent six months recuperating in hospital. Demobilized on 31 March 1919 Davidson eventually resumed his academic career, securing a temporary position in 1921 at the University of British Columbia (where his brother James Grant Davidson was associate professor of physics). Davidson was unable to escape the shadow of the war, which already had claimed the lives of two of his brothers. After he had been only a few months at UBC, the pressures of teaching weighed heavily on a psyche made fragile by combat and injury in France and Belgium, and Davidson was informed that his appointment would not be renewed. On 30 May 1922, while packing for a scheduled trip back to his father's farm in Union, he used his service revolver to end his own life.

Had he lived, Davidson would no doubt have made significant contributions to Canadian – and most particularly British Columbian – historical writing. Well versed in the primary holdings and exposed to the research ideal and latest historiographical trends of the American west, Davidson was one of the first academic historians to undertake a scholarly and analytical study of Canada's far west.

CHAD REIMER

Gordon Charles Davidson is the author of *The North West Company* (Berkeley, Calif., 1918; repr. New York, 1967), based on his doctoral thesis of the same title, completed in 1916 at the Univ. of California, Berkeley. The notes he made for his thesis and a copy of his "Report on the manuscripts on British Columbia in the Bancroft collection . . ." (M.LITT. thesis, Univ. of Calif., 1908) are at the Bancroft Library, Univ. of California.

AO, RG 80-2-0-211, no.6046. LAC, RG 31, C1, 1891, Yarmouth, Ont.; RG 150, Acc.1992–93/166, box 2319-49. Univ. of B.C. Library, Univ. Arch. (Vancouver), President's office, corr.; W. N. Sage, boxes 32–39 (misc. corr.). *Vancouver Daily Province*, 3 June 1922. *Vancouver Sun*, 31 May, 1 June 1922. *World* (Vancouver), 31 May 1922. L. J. Burpee, "The North West Company . . . ," *CHR*, 1 (1920): 71–74.

DAVIES, Sir LOUIS HENRY, lawyer, politician, and judge; b. 4 May 1845 in Charlottetown, son of Benjamin Davies and Kezia Attwood Watts; m. 23 July 1872 Susan Wiggins in St Eleanors, P.E.I., and they had two sons and three daughters; d. 1 May 1924 in Ottawa.

Of Huguenot background, Louis Davies's paternal grandfather was born in Wales and came to the Island about 1812. Louis was educated at Charlottetown's Central Academy and Prince of Wales College, and he subsequently read law at the Inner Temple in London. He was called to the bar in England in 1866 and, after a stint in the London law office of Thomas Chitty, on the Island a year later. Handsome and articulate, he quickly established a reputation as an orator and a first-rate cricket player. It was rumoured that his father, as the Island's colonial secretary in 1869, invited his son to become solicitor general. In any event, young Davies did serve in that capacity in 1870 and 1872.

Throughout his early career he followed the lead of his father in opposing confederation with Canada. On 4 Feb. 1870 Louis introduced a motion at the Charlottetown Debating Club that the terms of union lately proposed [*see* Robert Poore Haythorne*] "are not just and equitable to PEI, and should not be accepted." Benjamin saw the transinsular railway advocated by the government of James Colledge Pope* in 1871 as nothing but a ploy designed to put the Island in debt from which it could escape only with Canadian assistance. Louis joined him at many public meetings in opposition to Pope's policy. In 1872 he successfully ran for the House of Assembly in 4th Kings, a constituency that was liberal and opposed the railway and the prevailing system of proprietorial land tenure. As soon as he was seated in the house, he challenged Pope, but he managed to avoid the sort of physical confrontations that had led to the convictions of assemblyman David Laird* in police court. By 1873, despite their anti-confederation stances, the Davieses were willing to consider further negotiations with Canada, given the debt that the railway had in fact imposed on the colony. "Wise men changed their opinions when necessary," Louis later argued in the assembly, "fools never did so."

The entrance of the Island into the Canadian union on 1 July 1873 brought rapid political change. Several Liberals, headed by Laird, were elected to the federal House of Commons. The provincial party, its ranks thinned, chose Davies as its leader early in 1874. With confederation resolved, the assembly considered several issues that had been set aside in the interim. Like his father, Davies firmly supported legislative action to eliminate the Island's landed proprietors. He opposed the Land Purchase Bill of 1874, introduced by the government of Lemuel Cambridge Owen*, because it was too generous to the proprietors, and was not unhappy when it was reserved. A revised bill was proposed later in 1874, the same year that Davies began construction of Riverside, a large house in Charlottetown that he would occupy for part of every year until he died. The Land Purchase Act of 1875 was seen by contemporaries as a triumph for Davies, particularly in its provision for a land commission to set the purchase price of proprietorial land. As a lawyer, Davies initially declined to act for the tenantry before the new commission, but he relented and appeared along with Samuel Robert Thomson*; Edward Jarvis Hodgson appeared for the owners. Davies totally dominated the proceedings. His strategy was to build a case by looking for weaknesses in titles and diminishing the quality of the lands and the proprietorial improvements. Most observers thought he got a better deal for the tenants than anyone expected, with awards to the proprietors running at a fraction of what had been demanded.

The proprietors, however, did not accept without a fight. In November 1875 Hodgson appealed to the Island's Supreme Court on behalf of Charlotte Antonia Sulivan, whose agent was George Wastie DeBlois*. Hodgson argued that the awards did not describe the lands in sufficient detail, that proper legal procedures had not been followed, and that the British North America Act did not permit such legislation as the Land Purchase Act. In January the court decided for Sulivan. Davies persuaded his government colleagues to appeal to the newly created Supreme Court of Canada in the name of the Island's commissioner of crown lands, Francis Kelly*. *Kelly v. Sulivan* thus became the court's first case. Hodgson insisted that it could not hear the appeal because the appellant had not exhausted all the courts on the Island, specifically

the little known Court of Error and Appeal, composed of the lieutenant governor in council. This local court was mentioned in statutes (and is now known to have functioned), but no record of its ever having met could be found in 1876, a point emphasized by Davies and his associates. In January 1877 the chief justice of the dominion court, William Buell Richards*, rejected the argument on jurisdiction since the Island court, if indeed it existed, had been abandoned. The remainder of the appeal went in favour of the province: the legislature had the right to pass the Land Purchase Act and the Island's Supreme Court had authority only to see that matters were properly before the land commissioners and that no fraud was committed.

As the land case was unfolding, political attention also turned to the school question, which too had been put on hold during the uncertainties of confederation, but had earlier agitated the electorate. In the assembly in 1876 Davies had proposed and chaired a legislative committee, which reported that the Island's Protestant and Catholic schools were in much need of reform and that there had been a substantial increase in sectarian teaching in recent years. A member of St Paul's Anglican Church in Charlottetown, Davies made it clear that he favoured a single, non-sectarian system. Disagreements on educational policy were sufficiently strong to force the realignment of the traditional parties for the election of August 1876. J. C. Pope led the "Sectarian School" party against the "Free School" party headed by Davies, who decided to run in Charlottetown along with former adversary George DeBlois against Pope and Frederick de St Croix Brecken*. Davies spoke at meetings across the province and the Free Schoolers swept to victory. In Charlottetown he and DeBlois were easy winners. His party paid a price, when William Wilfred Sullivan* led the defection of four Liberals, but as a coalition of Protestant MHAs, the Free Schoolers still had a majority. When John Yeo refused to become premier, Davies accepted the post, and that of attorney general, and appointed DeBlois as provincial secretary and treasurer. The alliance was an uneasy one, since Deblois became concerned over Davies's involvement on behalf of the federal Liberals in a by-election late in 1876. To add to the strain, before Davies faced the assembly he fought off a bout of scarlet fever, which killed one of his sons. The new government met the house early in 1877, and moved quickly on schools. Adapted from New Brunswick legislation [*see* George Edwin King*], Davies's Public Schools Bill, which passed in April, provided for a provincial board of education and non-sectarian schools. Catholic bishop Peter McIntyre* protested bitterly against the legislation and lobbied in Ottawa for its disallowance, but he was forced to come to terms with the province.

Davies's administration had other difficult questions to face. Before confederation, Island governments had run deficits; a system of indirect taxation based on import duties proved inadequate. The financial settlement reached with Canada in 1873 masked the shortcomings, but by 1876 it was clear that taxation reform was necessary. It was equally clear that such change would be contentious, as was demonstrated in Charlottetown that year when the city council petitioned the assembly for authorization to borrow money and tax personal property as well as rentals. Within days a petition signed by 600 citizens, including most of the city's leading Tories, opposed the request; in the assembly Davies supported the proposed tax on property. In March 1877 he introduced a provincial taxation bill that authorized a revised land tax based on public assessment. The bill drew fire. Charlottetown and Summerside, which had municipal assessment, were exempted, and there was no mechanism for appeal. In meetings across the province, farmers complained about these inequities and the invasion of privacy.

With the countryside well agitated, Davies left to attend the Halifax Fisheries Commission [see S. R. Thomson], which was to settle Canadian-American differences left over from the Treaty of Washington (1871). It met every weekday from August to November. Faced with a well-appointed sideboard, short hours, and good pay, Davies preferred to remain until the end of the hearings, which decided in favour of a large award to Canada. While he was absent, criticism of his Assessment Act grew to fever pitch. The proprietors also roused themselves for a final contest with the land commission. Two of them, both Catholic McDonalds, appealed their awards to the Island's Supreme Court, which granted nullification in August. Davies refused to negotiate new awards, however, and the court decided against the proprietors in 1878.

In the assembly that year, W. W. Sullivan continued to hammer at the coalition. Davies tried to mollify the critics of assessment by amending the legislation to provide for a court of appeal, but it was probably too late. The government was also stung by criticism of the financing of a new lunatic asylum. The coalition officially came unglued over Davies's intense campaigning for the federal Liberals. On 29 Aug. 1878 George DeBlois and three Conservative colleagues resigned from the Executive Council, leaving Davies and a rump of Protestant Liberals to face the assembly. Davies made some attempt to attract Catholic support, but was told by assemblyman Nicholas Conroy* that Catholic voters found the acts of 1877 so offensive "that they will not readily forgive the gentleman under whose guidance those obnoxious laws had been enacted." Following a motion of no-confidence on 6 March 1879, Davies resigned. In the ensuing election he and the Liberals went down to defeat; he returned to private practice and in 1880 was named a QC.

Although he was not to know it, the defeat marked the conclusion of his most fecund period of public service. He had settled the land and school questions – the most contentious issues on 19th-century Prince Edward Island – but in local political terms he had nowhere to go. Not surprisingly, he moved on to Ottawa, though he would always remain visible on the Island and be active in its fraternal, financial, and charitable organizations. He served for many years as president of the Merchants' Bank of Prince Edward Island and of the Charlottetown Club, and in 1898 he was appointed an honorary lieutenant-colonel of the 4th (Prince Edward Island) Garrison Artillery Regiment.

In 1882, when public hostility to him had receded, Davies was elected to the House of Commons for Queens, which he would represent until 1896, when he was returned for Queens West. Beginning with his maiden speech in the house, delivered almost before he had unpacked, he established a reputation for his willingness to take on any of the Conservative government's front-benchers. He also advanced in the inner circles of his party. He faithfully supported Edward Blake*, and after Wilfrid Laurier* became leader in 1887, he emerged as Laurier's Maritimes lieutenant and a trusted strategy adviser, particularly on the Manitoba school question, where he felt his Island experience gave him special competence. Elected president of the Maritime Provinces Liberal Association in 1893, he was responsible for organizing the region for the 1896 election, which brought the Liberals to power.

Laurier made him minister of marine and fisheries, an area of considerable importance to the Maritimes. During Davies's five years in this portfolio, a commission established fishing seasons and size limits for lobsters, a marine biological station was set up [see Moses Harvey*], and Canadian sovereignty was confirmed by an expedition to Baffin Island [see William Wakeham*]. Davies was also involved in a number of diplomatic missions. He went to Washington in 1896 to discuss reciprocal trade. A year later he accompanied his chief to the Imperial Conference in London; knighted there on 22 June, in July he was involved in legal presentations over Belgian and German trade treaties and, before the Judicial Committee of the Privy Council, over the division of federal and provincial jurisdictions in Canada's fisheries. In 1897 he also accompanied Laurier (both acting as observers) to a meeting in Washington concerning the Bering Sea seal fishery. He met with the Americans again in 1898 in a series of gatherings that agreed to resolve pressing Canadian-American questions through a joint high commission. He was named to this commission, which broke off discussions in 1899 because of differences over the Alaska boundary. Later that year, when he attended the boundary talks in London, he was authorized to discuss with the Admiralty the possibility of a Canadian naval reserve. Nothing came of this initiative, although on his return Davies began upgrading his ministry's fisheries protection service. In his entry in Henry James Morgan*'s *Canadian men and women of the time* (1912) it is claimed that he was the "father" of the imperial preferential tariff [*see* William Stevens FIELDING] and of the dominion's naval contingent. Neither claim has survived in Canadian historical writing.

In September 1901 Laurier named Davies to the Supreme Court of Canada, doubtless to reward his service to Canada and the party. The *Canada Law Journal* (Toronto) complained; other observers thought Davies lacked legal experience and was too political. The charge of inexperience was somewhat unfair. Davies had been a solicitor general of Prince Edward Island and an eminently successful lawyer in the land question. He would have over 20 years on the bench to prove his critics wrong. Instead, he remained intimately involved in Liberal politics. He became known for his lack of judicial independence and as a formalistic conservative and minimalist whose decisions challenged neither the status quo nor the lower courts. Few if any of his judgements have been cited for their cogency. To some extent his unwavering support of the powers of legislatures (as in *Quong-Wing v. the King* in 1914 or *Re George Edwin Gray* in 1918 [*see* John IDINGTON]) may have reflected his encounters with Island proprietors who had used the courts to thwart the assembly. Honours did come to him – a portrait by fellow Islander Robert Harris* in 1902, a knighthood in the Order of St John of Jerusalem in England in 1913, and appointment to the imperial Privy Council in 1919 – but they were as much for the office as the man. Among his many affiliations, he was a president of the St John Ambulance Association, the Canadian Society of Charities and Correction, the Ottawa Anti-tuberculosis Association, and the Ottawa Archaeological Society. Lady Davies was equally active, as a founder of the local branch of the Women's Canadian Historical Society and a vice-president of both the Ottawa Humane Society and the National Council of Women of Canada.

In 1918, following the resignation of Sir Charles Fitzpatrick* as chief justice of Canada, Davies campaigned vigorously to become his successor. Part of his appeal was that he would supposedly resign in 1921, when his pension rights reached their maximum. Prime Minister Sir Robert Laird Borden* carried the appointment in cabinet with difficulty, effective 23 October. Davies was ill, old, and undistinguished. Although virtually inactive by 1923, he remained in office until his death in 1924, chiefly because of pension problems.

At his passing, Island newspapers described Davies as the province's most brilliant son. Since that time he has been largely forgotten, commemorated only by the naming of the Island's Supreme Court

buildings after him. He has been neglected partly because fashions in historical reputations change – male lawyers, legislators, and judges are legion – and in part because he left no private papers and few published records, except in Island newspapers, *Hansard*, and the *Reports* of the Supreme Court of Canada. Moreover, no important off-Island achievements can be directly associated with him, and the on-Island ones date to a period with which few are familiar. Despite his elevation to the highest judicial office in the land, Davies's Island career is probably more significant than his federal one.

J. M. BUMSTED

AO, F 2; RG 22-354, no.11654. LAC, MG 26, G: 188648. *Charlottetown Guardian*, 2 May 1924. *Examiner* (Charlottetown), 29 March 1879. *Herald* (Charlottetown), 25 Oct. 1871. *Islander* (Charlottetown), 23 July 1869. *Patriot* (Charlottetown), 22 Feb. 1873, 1 July 1875. D. [O.] Baldwin, "The Charlottetown political elite: control from elsewhere," in *Gaslights, epidemics and vagabond cows: Charlottetown in the Victorian era*, ed. D. [O.] Baldwin and Thomas Spira (Charlottetown, 1988), 32–50. J. M. Bumsted, "Sic transit gloria ...," *Island Magazine* (Charlottetown), no.47 (spring/summer 2000): 13–14. J. S. Cairns, "Louis Davies and Prince Edward Island politics, 1869–1879" (MA thesis, Dalhousie Univ., Halifax, 1982). *Canada Law Journal* (Toronto), 37 (1901): 677. *Canadian men and women of the time* (Morgan; 1898 and 1912). *CPG*, 1874, 1877, 1898–99. J. T. Gay, *American fur seal diplomacy: the Alaskan fur seal controversy* (New York, 1987). *Kelly v. Sulivan* (1876), *Canada Supreme Court Reports* (Ottawa), 1: 3–64. Frank MacKinnon, "The Island knight: a sketch of the Rt. Hon. Sir Louis Davies," *Island Magazine*, no.47: 3–12. W. E. MacKinnon, *The life of the party: a history of the Liberal party in Prince Edward Island* ([Charlottetown], 1973). *A nation's navy: in quest of Canadian naval identity*, ed. M. L. Hadley *et al.* (Montreal and Kingston, Ont., 1996). P.E.I., House of Assembly, *Debates and proc.* (Charlottetown), 12 March 1874: 91–92. *Report of proceedings before the commissioners appointed under the provisions of "The Land Purchase Act, 1875"*, reporter P. S. MacGowan (Charlottetown, 1875). I. R. Robertson, "Religion, politics, and education in Prince Edward Island from 1856 to 1877" (MA thesis, McGill Univ., Montreal, 1968). I. L. Rogers, *Charlottetown: the life in its buildings* (Charlottetown, 1983). J. G. Snell and Frederick Vaughan, *The Supreme Court of Canada: history of the institution* ([Toronto], 1985). *Standard dict. of Canadian biog.* (Roberts and Tunnell). *Vital statistics from N.B. newspapers* (Johnson), 10, no.786; 14, nos.410, 443; 32, no.926. *Who's who and why*, 1919/20.

DAVIES, WILLIAM, meat packer and breeder; b. 23 June 1831 in Wallingford, England, son of Charles Davies and Rachel Smallbone; m. first 21 April 1853 Emma Holtby (d. 1906) in Reading, England, and they had 12 children; m. secondly 9 Feb. 1907 Rosa Bessie Talbot in Hamilton, Ont.; d. 21 March 1921 in Toronto.

A son of Baptist parents of Welsh descent on his father's side, William Davies left school at 12 to serve an apprenticeship in trade. By his early twenties he had his own business in Reading, retailing groceries and curing meats. In 1854 he emigrated to Canada with his wife and first child, and entered the provision business in Toronto. He overcame various false starts and reverses, expanded from retail to wholesale, formed William Davies and Company in 1857, and developed an extensive trade, exporting cheese, butter, and eggs to Britain. His products, often of American origin, reflected opportunities generated by the Reciprocity Treaty of 1854.

In 1860 Davies copied several other Toronto provision merchants in beginning to ship cured sides of hogs (bacon) to England. Relatives in the south of England retailed them and begged for more. About 1861 Davies established what is said to have been the first building in Canada wholly devoted to the cutting and smoking of meats. Struggling to improve and standardize his product, he began buying hogs live rather than slaughtered, and in 1874 erected a large packing and slaughterhouse on Front Street near the mouth of the Don River.

Davies was a classic rugged individualist in business. By dint of hard work and personal austerity, constant attention to quality, reinvestment of profits, and determined innovation, he outpaced the many other Ontario packers and provision men trying to exploit British demand for North American meat. He came to specialize in exporting sides of leaner, lighter hogs, often fed on a peameal mash, and was very energetic in encouraging Ontario farmers to improve their breeds so as to differentiate their hogs from fat, heavy American porkers. Like other early meat packers, he found there was revenue in by-products such as lard; he also opened several retail outlets in Toronto. Experimental shipments of chilled beef to England in 1876, however, did not prove profitable. Davies's volume of hogs grew from about 30,000 a year in the mid 1870s to upwards of 80,000 by 1888, more than that of all other Ontario exporters combined. Net profits averaged about $30,000 a year in the mid 1880s. Davies also pioneered in establishing a small profit-sharing scheme for his workers.

Suffering from deafness and with his two eldest sons (James and William) ill with tuberculosis in the early 1890s, Davies decided to bring in an outsider to manage the business. In 1892 he sold a 44 per cent interest in the operation to Joseph Wesley Flavelle*, an experienced provision merchant with a reputation for an earnest, church-flavoured approach to life and business, not dissimilar to Davies's own outlook. A new firm, William Davies Company Limited, was created to take over the assets of Davies's partnership with his sons, and Flavelle became its managing director, with Davies continuing in the business as president.

Under Flavelle's brilliant management, and with cheap raw material available in Canada and a rising demand for lean, premium bacon in Britain, business soared. By 1900 almost half a million hogs a year were being shipped to the Davies factory for slaughter and export, shareholders were receiving in dividends close to a 100 per cent annual return on their capital, and both Flavelle and Davies had become millionaires. The Davies company was said to have been the largest pork-packing operation in the British empire, and it seems that Toronto's nickname, Hogtown, dates from the early 1900s.

Despite this growth, Davies was a conservative force in his company's expansion. He resisted many of Flavelle's projects, but in the end admitted that his judgement in these matters had been wrong. In 1909 Flavelle triggered provisions in their 1892 agreement that led to Davies's retirement from the business, although he retained a substantial minority interest. In 1919 a grandson, Edward Carey Fox, bought control of the company from Flavelle, but it faltered; in 1927 the enterprise was folded into Canada Packers Limited.

William Davies was a lifelong and ardent Baptist, and he gave generously to church causes, including McMaster University in Toronto and Brandon College in Manitoba. He also supported hospitals and sanatoria for victims of tuberculosis. An avid gentleman-farmer whose fortune had been made from the bounty of the land – he himself owned a farm near Markham and then one on Kingston Road in Scarborough Township – he was an expert in the breeding of both hogs and horses. Following his retirement in 1909, he maintained his private interests and travelled. The most important pioneer in the Canadian meat-packing industry, he died in 1921, never having recovered from injuries caused some months earlier by a goat that had butted him while he was relieving himself on a roadside in the American south.

MICHAEL BLISS

[A small collection of William Davies papers is held at the Univ. of Western Ont. Arch., J. J. Talman Regional Coll., London. Most of its contents were published as *Letters of William Davies, Toronto, 1854–1861* (Toronto, 1945), edited with an introduction by William Sherwood Fox, a grandson of the subject. The collection includes various letters Davies published in agricultural journals on the need for improvements in hog breeding and the industry generally, but does not contain his important personal memoir, "The early history and development of Canada's export bacon trade," *Farming World* (Toronto), 2 Sept. 1901: 217–18. According to *Canadian men and women of the time* (Morgan; 1912), Davies was also the author of a memoir entitled "Reminiscences of a pioneer" (1904), but this item has not been found.

The post-1892 history of the William Davies Company, and Davies's role in it, is chronicled in the author's book *A Canadian millionaire: the life and business times of Sir Joseph Flavelle, bart., 1858–1939* (Toronto, 1978). Many of

261

the details of the company's later history are derived from documents in the Joseph Flavelle fonds at QUA and in the McLean family papers at the AO (F 277, MU 1127). Davies's philanthropic activities are recorded in Middleton, *Municipality of Toronto*, vol.3: 84. M.B.]

AO, RG 22-305, no.43081; RG 80-5-0-370, no.21885; RG 80-8-0-314, no.2498; RG 80-8-0-802, no.2663. Berkshire Record Office (Reading, Eng.), Wallingford Baptist Chapel (Wallingford), Reg. of births, 23 June 1831 (mfm.). DCB, Biog. data file, William Davies, typescript biog. by W. S. Fox (1961). GRO, Reg. of marriages, Baptist Meeting House, Kings Road (Reading), 21 April 1853. *Commemorative biographical record of the county of York . . .* (Toronto, 1907), 348–49. *Illustrated Toronto, past and present, being an historical and descriptive guide-book . . .*, comp. J. Timperlake (Toronto, 1877), 284–86.

DAVIS, AGNES MARY. *See* SCOTT

DAVIS, Sir MORTIMER BARNETT, manufacturer, financier, and philanthropist; b. 6 Feb. 1866 in Montreal, third son of Samuel Davis* and Minnie Falk; m. 12 June 1898, in San Francisco, Henriette Marie Meyer, daughter of Charles Meyer, a banker and philanthropist of that city, and they had one child who survived infancy; divorced in 1924 and m. in the same year Eleanor Curran, Countess Moroni (d. 1963); d. 22 March 1928 in Cannes, France.

Mortimer Barnett Davis was born into a family of Jewish immigrants in Montreal. His father had settled there around 1861 and had soon made his mark as one of the largest cigar manufacturers in the metropolis. Mortimer Barnett grew up, then, in increasingly affluent surroundings. His bar mitzvah in 1879 was held at the Spanish and Portuguese congregation of Montreal, Shearith Israel. After studying at the High School of Montreal, around 1880 he followed his elder brothers Eugene Harmon and Maurice Edward into the family firm, S. Davis and Sons, to learn the various aspects of the cigar industry. On finishing his apprenticeship, he seems to have set out as a travelling salesman.

In 1888 S. Davis and Sons purchased another Montreal firm, D. Ritchie and Company. This acquisition enabled it to increase its production capacity, thanks to a factory located on Rue Dalhousie near the Lachine Canal, and to diversify its products by adding pipe tobacco and snuff, as well as cigarettes, which were beginning to be made in Montreal. Cigarette manufacturing was experiencing rapid changes as a result of technological progress, including the introduction of the Bonsack machine which made it possible to roll cigarettes mechanically; D. Ritchie and Company began using this device in 1888, just a few years after its invention. A partner and part owner of this firm, Mortimer Barnett also became its manager in 1894, according to *Montreal illustrated*.

At that time, the North American cigarette industry was also going through extensive restructuring, which

had a major effect on Canadian firms. In 1895 the American Tobacco Company, an enterprise founded by James Buchanan Duke that controlled about 90 per cent of the American market and held the rights to the Bonsack machine, purchased D. Ritchie and Company and the American Cigarette Company, another Montreal cigarette manufacturer. Its Canadian interests were transferred to the American Tobacco Company of Canada, which was formed on 1 September. The Davis family became a minor partner of the Duke family, with 25 of the 10,000 shares issued by the new corporation. Samuel Davis retired from S. Davis and Sons the following month and Mortimer Barnett also left the family firm, which remained in the hands of two of his brothers. Shortly afterwards, Mortimer Barnett was named president of the American Tobacco Company of Canada.

Under Davis's direction, this company established a virtual monopoly of tobacco, buying up firms that made a wide range of tobacco products and extending its geographical base beyond the confines of Montreal. In 1898, for instance, it purchased the Empire Tobacco Company in Granby, and in 1903 the B. Houde Company Limited at Quebec. At that time, with its subsidiaries, it controlled 80 per cent of the Canadian cigarette market and 60 per cent of the market in chewing tobacco, pipe tobacco, and snuff. Its imposing factory in the Saint-Henri district of Montreal, which was also the head office, was built in 1907.

During these years, conflicts between the two great tobacco corporations, the American Tobacco Company, based in the United States, and the Imperial Tobacco Company in Great Britain, led to their sharing the international market. The British-American Tobacco Company Limited, which was jointly owned by the two corporations, was formed in 1902. Six years later it purchased the American Tobacco Company of Canada, which became the Imperial Tobacco Company of Canada Limited. Davis was its first president.

Inspired by the practices of the American Tobacco Company and the cigar company founded by his father, Davis combined consolidation of production with a marketing strategy that was both skilful and ruthless. He attempted to control the distribution networks for tobacco products by requiring wholesalers to sign exclusive contracts. Imperial Tobacco even set up its own network of tobacco retailers at the beginning of the 1920s. The firm counted on advertising and promotional campaigns to boost its brand names and win customer loyalty. The financial power of the industrial empire presided over by Davis earned him the title of "Tobacco King," but he had to share it with his great rival, Montreal businessman Sir William Christopher Macdonald*.

Davis was also the driving force behind the consolidation of the Canadian cigar industry, which was severely shaken by World War I and by increasing competition from cigarettes. In 1916 he had bought out the family firm (then in the hands of his brothers Maurice Edward and Melvin Henry and being liquidated), and he had become the principal shareholder and president of the reorganized company, known since 1908 as S. Davis and Sons Limited. To restore its finances and reduce the costs of cigar production, Davis turned to subcontracting, signing numerous contracts in 1919 with small cigar manufacturers in Montreal. He also moved part of his production to Port Hope, in Ontario. Such a strategy was clearly designed to reduce fixed costs, but also undoubtedly to bypass the powerful trade union of cigar makers. In 1920 Davis coordinated the formation of the General Cigar Company, which would merge his company and his major rivals into a large cigar trust. In addition to acquiring S. Davis and Sons Limited in July 1920, General Cigar had absorbed the Brener Company Limited of Farnham on 30 June, and would take over Vallens and Company Limited of London, Ont., on 4 October. Davis was chairman of the corporation's board of directors and its majority owner. In keeping with his policy of concentration, he persuaded the shareholders of Imperial Tobacco to buy up a majority of the shares of General Cigar in July 1921. Davis remained at the head of Imperial Tobacco until 1926, when he was succeeded by a long-time business associate, David Patterson.

While the tobacco industry in all its forms remained Davis's main sphere of activity, his interests extended to other fields that promised substantial profits. In 1905 he had invested in spirits and incorporated, with some other businessmen, the H. Corby Distillery Company Limited in order to purchase the Corby distillery, a firm near Belleville, Ont., that had been founded by Henry Corby*. He served as president from 1907 to 1922. He seems to have been involved also in organizing the Canadian Industrial Alcohol Company Limited, which was incorporated in 1918 to produce industrial alcohol; he was its president and then chairman between 1918 and 1924. He also had interests in mining, being part of the senior management of the Nova Scotia Silver Cobalt Mining Company and the Consolidated Asbestos Mining Company, and he owned shares in mines in the gold-rich region near Porcupine, Ont.

Well known for his administrative and financial skills, Davis was also invited to sit on the board of directors of the Union Bank of Canada from 1906 to 1910 and the Royal Bank of Canada from 1916 to 1928. Around 1917 he was a director of the National Car Company in Hamilton and, in 1928, a director of the Crown Trust Company, the United States Rubber Company, and its Canadian subsidiary, the Canadian Consolidated Rubber Company. He was also a member of the Montreal Board of Trade and the Montreal Stock Exchange.

Like most of the upper class of his generation, Davis adopted a way of life in keeping with his great personal wealth. He took up residence in the Square Mile in Montreal, as his father had done, and he built an immense and luxurious residence on Avenue des Pins in the neoclassical style, which was finished in 1907. There Davis and his wife hosted fashionable receptions and numerous balls. He associated with the Duke of Connaught, the governor general of Canada, and he belonged to the most exclusive private clubs. Horticulture was one of his great passions and he took part in the activities and exhibitions of the Montreal Horticultural Society and Fruit Growers' Association of the Province of Quebec. While his wife collected works of art, Davis acquired a full stable of racehorses. He also owned an imposing country home, Belvoir, in Sainte-Agathe-des-Monts, and during the last years of his life spent more and more time at Les Glaïeuls, his villa in Cannes.

In November 1919 Davis summed up in the *Canadian Jewish Chronicle* the principles guiding his philanthropic activities: "Every man of means owes a duty to his fellow-men. Every Jew owes a duty to his fellow-Jew." His generosity extended to a variety of causes and institutions in the province of Quebec and the rest of Canada. Especially affected by the fate of his co-religionists, he was one of the most important philanthropists in the history of the Canadian Jewish community. He held leadership positions in a number of associations and chaired fund-raising campaigns. He was interested mainly in charities promoting public welfare and health in Montreal: the Baron de Hirsch Institute and Hebrew Benevolent Society of Montreal, of which he was a benefactor and the president in 1908 and 1910; the Mount Sinai Sanatorium in Sainte-Agathe-de-Monts, of which he was a principal sponsor; and the Young Men's Hebrew Association, to which he donated $400,000 in 1926 for the construction of a community and sports centre. He gave particular support to efforts at rationalizing social services and their financing. When the Federation of Jewish Philanthropies of Montreal was established in 1916, he was named honorary president.

Davis also supported Canada-wide and international charities and these activities brought him into contact with the leaders of the Jewish communities in France and Great Britain. From 1907 to 1913 he was president of the Canadian committee of the Jewish Colonization Association. In 1915 he helped organize the Canadian Jewish Committee for the Relief of War Sufferers, which sought to help the Jews of Russia. He served as honorary chairman of the campaign and contributed $19,000 to it.

His activities in the political and cultural fields were more modest and less frequent. For a few years he was vice-president of Temple Emanu-El, which his father had helped found. He made a donation to

Davis

McGill University to finance a course in Hebraic religious and literary studies in the faculty of arts, and he supported the Montreal Jewish press and Jewish education. For a short time he was honorary president of the Federation of Zionist Societies of Canada, which was formed in 1899 [see Clarence Isaac de Sola*].

In a letter to William Lyon Mackenzie King* in 1916, Montreal lawyer Samuel William Jacobs* described Davis as "the leading Jew in Canada." In recognition of his success in business, his philanthropic activities, and his status in the Canadian Jewish community, he was knighted by King George V that year, becoming the first Canadian-born Jew to receive such an honour.

The lack of family archives makes it impossible to do a thorough analysis of Davis's private life. In 1898 he married Henriette Marie Meyer, a young woman from a well-to-do San Francisco family. They had a son, Mortimer Davis, who was born in 1901. A second child apparently died at birth. In the years that followed, they adopted her nephew Philip, who took the name Philip Meyer Davis. At the beginning of the 1920s, when he was in his fifties, Davis is believed to have fallen in love with a beautiful young woman of very modest background, Eleanor Curran. He decided to seek a divorce, which led to lengthy negotiations and a settlement requiring him to pay his wife more than $1 million. According to some sources, in order to enhance the social standing of his beloved, he arranged for a brief marriage between her and an Italian count. After they were both divorced, Davis was then able to marry the Countess Moroni in 1924. Thereafter he seems to have devoted himself to worldly pleasures on the French Riviera, but not for long, since he died suddenly, of a heart attack, at the age of 62. On 12 April 1928, thousands of people came out to watch the funeral procession from his residence on Avenue des Pins to the Temple Emanu-El in Westmount.

Sir Mortimer Barnett Davis is remembered as a competent and determined man who was bold and energetic, but also as a fighter who brooked no opposition. At the time of his death, his personal fortune was estimated to be at least $50 million. His will provided for numerous bequests to relatives and friends, as well as a sum of $400,000 to be divided among four Montreal institutions: the Montreal General Hospital, the Notre-Dame Hospital, the Federation of Jewish Philanthropies, and the Young Men's Hebrew Association. His principal heirs, however, were his son and his widow, who shared the income from his estate. The will stipulated that at the end of 50 years the capital should be paid to Davis's children and their offspring. By 1978 his few descendants had long since died, his son in 1940 and his adopted son during World War II. Davis had, however, anticipated such an eventuality: the will provided that his fortune should then be used for philanthropic purposes and

that three-quarters of it should go to finance a hospital in Montreal. He wanted the hospital to bear his name and serve the needs of all the people in the city, but be run by a board of directors on which the majority would be Jewish. In 1978 it was decided to give $10 million to the Jewish General Hospital in Montreal, which had opened in 1934. Thereafter, this institution would be known as the Sir Mortimer B. Davis Jewish General Hospital.

JOANNE BURGESS

The Allan Raymond Coll. at the Jewish Public Library Arch. (Montreal) and the Sir Mortimer B. Davis fonds (P0045) at the Canadian Jewish Congress, National Arch. and Reference Centre (Montreal), hold numerous documents and press clippings relating to Davis and his successors. Information about the evolution of S. Davis and Sons, S. Davis and Sons Limited, and General Cigar can be found in the Imperial Tobacco Canada Limited Arch. (Montreal). Of particular interest are minute-book no.1 and a letter dated 14 June 1921 in file 12499.

ANQ-M, CE601-S97, 14 févr. 1866; TP11, S2, SS20, SSS48, vol.13-o, 11 mai 1888, no.1158. LAC, MG 26, G: 116039–40; H, 327: 193229–32; J1, 32: 28228–808; RG 95, ser.1, 1356. Janice Arnold, "Historian collects memorabilia on businessman," Canadian Jewish News (Montreal), 30 April 1998. Le Devoir, 18 avril 1928. Gazette (Montreal), 2 Dec. 1895, 27 March 1930. Jewish Times (Montreal), 20 Dec. 1897; continued as Canadian Jewish Chronicle, 22 Oct. 1915; 1 Sept. 1916; 20 April, 18 May 1917; 7 Nov. 1919; 4 March, April 1921. Montreal Daily Star, 10 April 1928. "Noted humanitarian Lady Davis, CBE, dies," Montreal Star, 23 Dec. 1963. Noel Wright, "Jewish General gets windfall," Montreal Star, 6 May 1978. W. H. Atherton, Montreal, 1534–1914 (3v., Montreal, 1914), 3: 375. S. [I.] Belkin, Through narrow gates; a review of Jewish immigration, colonization and immigrant aid work in Canada (1840–1940) ([Montreal, 1966]), 49. Canadian men and women of the time (Morgan; 1912). Canadian who's who (1910). Directory, Montreal, 1869–71, 1874–78, 1884–95. Encyclopedia Canadiana, ed. K. H. Pearson et al. ([rev. ed.], 10v., Toronto, 1975). The Jew in Canada: a complete record of Canadian Jewry from the days of the French régime to the present time, ed. A. D. Hart (Toronto and Montreal, 1926), 305, 309, 337. J.-L.-K. Laflamme, Le centenaire Cartier, 1814–1914; compte rendu des assemblées, manifestations, articles de journaux, conférences, etc., qui ont marqué la célébration du centenaire de la naissance de sir George-Étienne Cartier et l'érection de monuments à la mémoire de ce grand homme d'État canadien (Montréal, 1927), 48–50. R. D. Lewis, "Productive and spatial strategies in the Montreal tobacco industry, 1850–1918," Economic Geography (Worcester, Mass.), 70 (1994): 370–89. Montreal illustrated, 1894 . . . (Montreal, [1894]), 324. P. C. Newman, The Canadian establishment (2v., Toronto, 1975), 1: 262. Prominent people of the province of Quebec, 1923–1924 (Montreal, n.d.). S. A. Thomas, "Three Montreal residences by the architect Robert Findlay" (MA student paper, McGill Univ., Montreal, 1976). Gladys Wilson, Memoirs of a Canadian duchess (Montreal, [1986]), 25–26. H[irsch] Wolofsky, Journey of my life: a book of memories, trans. A. M. Klein (Montreal, 1945), 54, 68–71.

DAVIS, WILLIAM, coalminer; b. 3 June 1887 in Gloucestershire, England, son of Thomas Davis and Annises Dufly; m. 30 Oct. 1907 Myrtle MacPherson (d. 1955) at Dominion No.6 (Donkin), N.S., and they had five daughters and five sons; d. 11 June 1925 at Waterford Lake, N.S.

William Davis's father was a miner and a 14-year old brother had died in the Springhill explosion of 1891 [*see* Henry Swift*]. Davis himself worked at Nos.1, 6, 12, and 16 collieries of the Dominion Coal Company Limited in Cape Breton, beginning in 1905. He was a pumpman at No.12 colliery in New Waterford in November 1920 and a year later started as a roadmaker there. By 1925 he and his wife Myrtle, who was also from a mining family, were raising a family of nine. The intense conflict between Nova Scotia miners, organized as District 26 of the United Mine Workers of America, and the British Empire Steel Corporation (Besco), which had resulted in 58 strikes on the Sydney coalfield in 1920–25, culminated that year. The clash was the most costly, bitter, and determined one of the decade.

The miners' latest contract had expired on 15 Jan. 1925 and Besco, under its stubborn president, Roy Mitchell Wolvin*, was serious about breaking the union. On 2 March credit at company stores located in areas of strong union militancy was cut off. Four days later almost 12,000 miners went on strike. At this point Besco vice-president John Ernest McLurg summarily dismissed a reporter's analogy: "Poker game, nothing, we have all the cards. . . . Let them stay out two months or six months, it matters not; eventually they will have to come to us. . . . They can't stand the gaff." That attitude and the latter phrase steeled the workers' resolve, though thousands of Cape Bretoners were reported to be "on the verge of starvation" over the next three months. The company refused arbitration and on 4 June District 26 began 100 per cent picketing. The miners quickly expelled company men who had taken over a power and pumping station located at Waterford Lake. More than 30 union men were arrested during the next few days.

Besco gathered all its available police and late on the 10th this force escorted 30 company men to restart the plant and the mine pumps. The next morning the company police sent a provocative patrol through New Waterford, an action that led to a small clash with a group of miners. It was followed by an open-air meeting and a decision by the miners to approach the plant workers and ask them to quit. The crowd (estimates ranged from 700 to 3,000) arrived at the site around 11:00 A.M. Before the spokesman could state his request the company police charged. Or perhaps the horses bolted – neither the animals nor the police were trained. The police fired over 300 shots. A policeman bore down on the 5 foot 3 inch, 150-pound Davis; as he struggled to turn the horse away another policeman

shot him in the heart. He was dead within five minutes. Within ten minutes the police were in full retreat, leaving behind many wounded.

Maybe Davis had been looking for a son who had skipped school, or getting water for his family or milk for his youngest child, as local sources mention, but it is just as likely that he was supporting his fellow unionists. Later reports suggest he was on picket duty. On Sunday, 14 June, an estimated 5,000 mourners attended his funeral; it was the largest ever seen in New Waterford. After his interment in the Union Grove Cemetery at Scotchtown they quietly dispersed. But their anger and frustration fuelled raids on company stores and other property throughout the month, in spite of the presence of a provincial police force and an estimated 2,000 Canadian troops. Only the North-West rebellion of 1885 had brought more military forces into an internal conflict.

A few weeks after William Davis Jr was born on 23 Sept. 1925, and two months after the strike was settled, Besco policeman Joseph MacLeod appeared at a preliminary hearing in Sydney on a charge of murder. There was a problem with positive identification, not surprisingly, given the brief and intense mêlée at Waterford Lake. Also, the crown prosecutor agreed with the defence that MacLeod should not be singled out of the many policemen who had "charged the mob." Davis's death was due to a stray shot; the case was closed.

Two District 26 conventions strongly supported the idea of a fund for the Davis family, and a second resolution endorsed 11 June as an "idle day." On Friday, 11 June 1926, many Cape Breton miners did not go to work; they assembled at the union hall in New Waterford and paraded to Calvin United Church. The practice of not working on Davis Day spread throughout District 26, although it did not become a day with pay for 43 years. Davis's widow would eventually receive a monthly sum from the miners and in time she managed to purchase a headstone. Robert, a son, was soon working underground and the family stayed together.

Davis Day was renamed District Memorial Day in 1938, and in 1970 the date was changed to the second Monday in June. Four years later the original name and date were restored. New Waterford, since 1985, has had Davis Square, and the Davis Wilderness Trail, started in 1996, follows the route taken by the miners to Waterford Lake in 1925. Davis Day continues.

DON MACGILLIVRAY

Cape Breton Development Corporation, Dominion Coal Company (Glace Bay, N.S.), Human resources dept., employment records. LAC, RG 31, C1, 1901, Springhill, N.S., dist.2: 14 (mfm. at NSARM). NSARM, Churches, All Saints' Anglican (Springhill), reg. of baptisms, 6 June 1894 (mfm.); RG 32, M, Cape Breton County, no.348/1907. Private arch., Don MacGillivray (Sydney, N.S.), David Frank, interview with Robert Davis, 24 July 1975. *Sydney Post*, 10 March, 4–10, 12–13, 19 June 1925. *Sydney Record*, 11 June, 9 Oct. 1925. Edith [Davis] Pelley, "Edith Pelley, William Davis's daughter; an interview, with photographs, by Norman MacKinnon," *Cape Breton's Magazine* (Wreck Cove, N.S.), no.60 ([1992]): 45–54. C. M. Lamey, "Davis Day through the years: a Cape Breton coalmining tradition," *Nova Scotia Hist. Rev.* (Halifax), 16 (1996), no.2: 23–33. M. W. Littler, "Mary Willa Littler and 'The Strangers' Grave,'" *Cape Breton's Magazine*, no.71 ([1997]): 33. Don MacGillivray, "Military aid to the civil power: the Cape Breton experience in the 1920's," *Acadiensis* (Fredericton), 3 (1973–74), no.2: 45–64.

DAYODEKANE. *See* NEWHOUSE, SETH

DEANE, RICHARD BURTON, (R)NWMP officer and author; b. 30 April 1848 in Ootacamund, India, son of Henry Deane, a Church of England clergyman, and Aurora Cavendish Lewis; m. first 7 Nov. 1870 Martha Critchell Ridout on the Isle of Portland, England, and they had three sons and two daughters; m. secondly 22 April 1908 Mary Dennehy in Calgary; m. thirdly 19 Feb. 1917 May Thyne in London, England; d. 13 Dec. 1930 in Diano Marina, Italy.

With his drooping moustache, tall and lean frame, pale complexion, cold eyes, and acerbic tongue, R. Burton Deane was a strong, vaguely threatening presence. As a mounted policeman for 31 years, he participated in the transformation of the southern Canadian prairies from the open plains of 1883 to the populated farming country of 1914.

In many respects Deane was a typical officer. He came from a respectable but not wealthy family, had a military background, was Anglican, knew about military and criminal law, and held the values of the Anglo-Canadian elite. The core of his life's work was in Canada, but he was not wholly Canadian, either by birth or by inclination. In a sense, his career here was that of an imperial officer, and he no doubt cherished being awarded the Imperial Service Order in 1915. For him the British empire was a living reality, not a detached abstraction. Yet even after his retirement to England his thoughts remained on his Canadian experiences, as is evidenced by his extensive writing. Indeed, next to his skin for the rest of his life he wore the scratchy standard-issue underwear of the Royal North-West Mounted Police.

At the time of Deane's birth, his father was a chaplain for the East India Company. Although the family moved to England about 1851, the spell of India and empire on them remained strong. At the grammar school in Ipswich and within the fold of the Church of England, Deane was taught the perceptions of the gentry. He was an adequate student in academic subjects but excelled in sports, especially cricket.

In 1866, at age 18, he joined the Royal Marines as a second lieutenant, and he was promoted first lieu-

tenant a year later. Further advance was halted by a huge reduction of manpower in the unit. Still, he served on various cruises and saw action in the 1873–74 campaign against Ashanti warriors in present-day Ghana. In 1876 the marines recognized Deane's organizational skills by naming him adjutant of the 3,500-strong Chatham division, but promotion to captain was unavailable until 1881. By then he had a wife and five children and, if he remained merely a captain, he faced mandatory retirement in less than a decade on what he considered an inadequate pension. He therefore arranged early retirement and moved his family to Canada in 1882. Using the influence of his cousin Thomas Charles Patteson, a prominent Canadian Conservative, he secured a position as aide to Governor General Lord Lorne [Campbell*] for a few months and eventually persuaded Prime Minister Sir John A. Macdonald* to appoint him an inspector in the North-West Mounted Police as of 1 July 1883.

At the new police headquarters in Regina, Deane's initial responsibility was to train recruits and to prepare standing orders for the force. In less than a year he was made the adjutant and was promoted to the senior rank of superintendent at the substantial yearly salary of $1,400. During the North-West rebellion of 1885, Deane was left in charge at Regina during the absence of Commissioner Acheson Gosford Irvine. After hostilities ceased, he became responsible for the prisoners, including Louis Riel*. Evidently Riel appreciated Deane's permission to write in the commissioner's office and even dedicated a poem to his jailer.

When Irvine was removed in 1886, Deane thought he was a candidate for the position, but Lawrence William Herchmer*, with better connections and longer service in western Canada, was named. Deane and Herchmer were able bureaucrats but abrasive and strong-willed individuals. Consequently, they clashed at every turn, and keeping both of them in Regina was impossible. Deane was replaced as adjutant, and then sent east on a recruiting trip before finally being given command of the relatively new Lethbridge (Alta) division in 1888.

Deane arrived at his new post on his 40th birthday and for the next 26 years he was the commanding officer of one of the mounted police divisions on the southern Canadian plains. For the first decade it was the Lethbridge one; from 1898 to 1902 he was the de facto supervisory superintendent for both Lethbridge and Fort Macleod; from 1902 to 1906, after falling foul of Clifford SIFTON, the minister of the interior, for bringing to justice some of Sifton's friends, he was relegated to the Maple Creek (Sask.) division; and from 1906 to 1914, following a change of minister in Ottawa, he held the choice posting of Calgary, where the house that was built for him was the best at any mounted police barracks and, as Deane House, is now a provincial historic site.

As a divisional commanding officer, Deane demonstrated a high degree of competence at the numerous tasks required. He demanded much of his men and with his sharp tongue did not hesitate to cut down anyone who failed in his duty. Yet he gave credit where due and was realistic in his expectations. Although he was frequently judgemental with regard to those who attracted the attention of the police, he was sometimes bemused and even capable of genuine sympathy for unfortunates who were simply victims of a world that overwhelmed them. He had no belief in the perfectibility of society. But while Deane was an efficient and not inconsiderate superintendent, his superiors often found him difficult to discipline, for he was supremely confident and hotly and skilfully opposed criticism.

Deane's official reports paint a vivid picture of the pioneer prairies. Of course, the positive side of development is represented but all types of humanity appear, from incompetent judges to murdered prostitutes, from drunken brawlers to cattle rustlers, from battered women to starving aboriginals, from fanatical ministers of religion to insane destitutes. He relates everything from the most serious crimes to petty internal police squabbles including an incident in which some constables threw the bedding of an unpopular non-commissioned officer down the latrine. His accounts are more intriguing than those of other commanding officers since they are full of personal opinion, humour, sarcasm, Latin and French phrases, and irony. On one occasion, for example, his report began, "The new criminal year . . . opened gaily with an indecent assault, a robbery and a culpable homicide."

The range of Deane's competence and interest extended well beyond policing. He was an accomplished magician, whose performances had made him a skilled actor, director, and producer by the time he landed in Canada. He became a founding father of theatre in both Regina and Lethbridge. A fine cricketer who had played on high calibre teams in England, even against touring professionals, he continued to play, when possible, until 1897. He held senior posts in the masonic order and served as a warden and occasional lay reader for the Church of England. In addition, he was an avid gardener, a collector of recipes, and a dabbler in business schemes.

Deane had five children, two of whom predeceased his first wife, who died in 1906. He remarried in 1908, just days before his 60th birthday so that his bride would be eligible for a widow's pension. It was not to be, for she fell ill and, although attended by Deane's son Reginald Burton, a physician, she died in 1914.

Deane buried her, left Calgary on 30 September that year, and retired to England. In 1916 his book *Mounted police life in Canada: a record of thirty-one years' service*, was published. Although flawed in organization, it remains a valuable source on the history of the force. Certainly it was no whitewash for Deane was quick to criticize personalities both outside and inside the organization. He continued his writings but in 1917 married for a third time and thereafter evidently slipped into a tranquil retirement in Somerset, living on his pension and tending his beloved roses. He died in 1930 in Italy, where he had apparently gone for his health.

WILLIAM M. BAKER

Details of Richard Burton Deane's personal and family life have been gleaned from researches in the India Office Records in the Oriental and India Office Collections of the British Library (London), the GRO, the Royal Marine records in National Arch. (G.B.), ADM, and the Suffolk Record Office, Ipswich, Eng. Materials relating to Deane in Canada include his papers in the GA (M 311, M 313, M 3933, M 6017), and at the LAC (MG 29, E48). The records of the Royal Canadian Mounted Police in LAC, RG 18 contain thousands of reports, records, and letters written by, to, or about Deane, or on matters in which he was involved. Deane's own reports may also be found in the annual reports of the North-West Mounted Police, 1883–1903, and of the Royal North-West Mounted Police, 1904–14, printed in Can., Parl., *Sessional papers*.

Deane's book, *Mounted police life in Canada: a record of thirty-one years' service* (London, 1916), has been reprinted (Toronto, 1973), and one of his shorter pieces, "The story of Joe Bush," has been edited by W. M. Baker and published in *Alberta Hist.* (Calgary), 40 (1992), no.4: 3–15.

W. M. Baker, "Captain R. Burton Deane and theatre on the prairies, 1883–1901," *Theatre Research in Canada* (Toronto), 14 (1993): 31–59; "Superintendent Deane of the mounted police," *Alberta Hist.*, 41 (1993), no.4: 20–26. William Beahen, "For the sake of discipline: the strange case of Cst. Basil Nettleship – deserter," *RCMP Quarterly* (Ottawa), 49 (1984), no.3: 41–45. William Beahen and S. [W.] Horrall, *Red coats on the prairies: the North-West Mounted Police, 1886–1900* (Regina, 1998). S. W. Horrall, "The (Royal) North-West Mounted Police and prostitution on the Canadian prairies," *Prairie Forum* (Regina), 18 (1985): 105–27. R. C. Macleod, *The NWMP and law enforcement, 1873–1905* (Toronto, 1976). A.-M. Mavromichalis, "Tar and feathers: the mounted police and frontier justice," *Alberta Hist.*, 43 (1995), no.2: 16–24. *Pioneer policing in southern Alberta: Deane of the Mounties*, ed. W. M. Baker (Calgary, 1993).

DE CELLES. *See* DUCLOS

DÉGRÈS, IRÈNE-MATHILDE, named **Saint-Paul**, provincial superior of the Servants of the Holy Heart of Mary; b. 13 Oct. 1854 in Cernay-en-Dormois, France, daughter of Jean Dégrès, an army bootmaker, and Bélissante Gérard; d. 27 Sept. 1921 in Limoilou ward, Quebec City.

Despite opposition from her mother and stepfather, Irène-Mathilde Dégrès decided to become a teacher, but she failed the required examinations. She was then driven from home by her stepfather, worked for a few years in Reims, and experimented with the contemplative life. Eventually she made her way, in 1877, to the Institut des Servantes du Saint-Cœur de Marie, which had been founded in Paris in 1860 by Jeanne-Marie Moisan and Father François-Jean-Baptiste Delaplace. This congregation devoted itself to protecting orphaned boys and girls and to teaching. Irène-Mathilde Dégrès, now known as Sister Saint-Paul, took her vows in October 1878, and in May 1880 she was appointed mistress of novices. As secretary to Delaplace, she also was involved in drafting the congregation's constitutions. In 1895 she was sent to North America to visit the houses that had been founded in Illinois in 1889 and in Canada in 1892. This mission earned her an appointment as assistant general in 1896. When the first laws restricting the activities of religious congregations were passed in France, she was sent out to direct the Canadian province; she arrived at Quebec in 1903 with a group of 21 nuns.

The Canadian province had been started in 1892 in Saint-Éphrem-de-Tring, in the Beauce region of Quebec, at the request of the curé, Léon-Maxime Morisset, who wanted a congregation that could teach both boys and girls. The new provincial decided, however, to establish the provincialate in the congregation's house in Limoilou, in the environs of Quebec City, which was a better location. When Mother Saint-Paul arrived, the congregation had three boarding schools that were unusual in including both boys and girls, and five mixed day schools. The instruction they provided was, for the most part, at the elementary level. The arrival of the new contingent in 1903 made it possible to open five more schools. Although the provincial regretted the misfortunes that "afflict poor France," she added, in a letter to the superior general, "Providence is giving us . . . the opportunity to establish ourselves in Canada, to make us take our place among the best congregations in the country." Indeed, Mother Saint-Paul was approached in 1904 to take on responsibility for a school of home economics in Saint-Pascal, in the Kamouraska region, where the congregation was operating a school. However, because she lacked qualified staff, and recognized the competencies of the Congregation of Notre-Dame, she had to decline the responsibility.

In 1905 Mother Saint-Paul decided to open a noviciate in Limoilou. This move would involve a difficult negotiation to close the existing one in Saint-Éphrem-de-Tring, "where the novices," in her view, "have no religious guidance whatsoever." It would require a visit from the mother general in 1912 to close it. In 1907 Mother Saint-Paul had managed to have the transfer of the corporate seat of her congregation's Canadian province to Limoilou legally recognized. Her correspondence shows what a hard task

that was. The mixed classes were overcrowded, some having as many as 78 to 84 children. Accommodating both boys and girls necessitated doubling the number of staff in the three boarding schools. The integration of the French nuns posed a problem. "It takes at least a year to get used to the ways of the country," she commented. "There are teachers who are far from strong in their educational background and teaching methods. Eventually this [weakness] is noticed and it is not helpful for us." "There are so many things to settle in order that our French and Canadian sisters can blend together as perfectly as possible." It should be noted that a third of the French nuns would eventually return to France. Many Canadian women felt called to the congregation – more than 150 in 20 years. To justify to the French authorities the fact that most of these women were admitted without a dowry, the provincial told them, "This is the way it is in all communities in Quebec." However, after appointing a Canadian superior, Mother Saint-Paul began to "regret" this move, and saw it as "a lesson not to put a Canadian at the head of any charitable organization for a long time!"

In 1914, because of the war, Mother Saint-Paul had to take over the development of her province almost single-handedly. She managed it prudently and with a firm hand. One of her schools was requisitioned in October 1918 for the care of victims of the Spanish influenza. When illness forced her to give up her position in 1920, after six successive terms of office, the Canadian province of the Servants of the Holy Heart of Mary had 20 houses and 178 nuns. She died on 27 Sept. 1921. Mother Saint-Paul had left a distinct mark on her congregation by maintaining very strong ties with France. And yet it developed mainly in Canada. Not until 1938 would a Canadian, Marie-Thérèse Dionne, named Sainte-Eugénie, lead the province; she would become superior general nine years later.

MICHELINE DUMONT

Arch. Départementales, Marne (Châlons-en-Champagne, France), État civil, Cernay-en-Dormois, 13 oct. 1854. Arch. des Servantes du Saint-Cœur de Marie (Beauport, Qué.), Corr. externe de mère Saint-Paul, 1903–20; Corr. interne de mère Saint-Paul, 1904–19; Lettres circulaires de mère Saint-Paul; Lettres du fondateur, F.-J.-B. Delaplace, aux religieuses; Listes des Servantes du Saint-Cœur de Marie depuis la fondation au Canada; Procès-verbaux du conseil général, 1882–1960 (copies); Procès-verbaux du conseil provincial, 1903–46; "Racines SSCM" (bulletins dactylographiés, no.18 (octobre 1992) et no.20 (novembre 1993)). Rapport fait au jubilé de diamant du père fondateur. Guy Laperrière, *Les congrégations religieuses: de la France au Québec, 1880–1914* (2v. parus, Sainte-Foy, Qué., 1996–), 2. R[ené] Piacentini, *Un esclave de la Divine Majesté: F. J.-B. Delaplace, de la Congrégation du Saint-Esprit, fondateur de la Congrégation des Sœurs Servantes du Saint-Cœur de*

Marie, 1825–1911 (Beauport et Montgeron, France, 1952). *La révérende mère Saint-Paul de la Congrégation des Sœurs Servantes du Saint-Cœur de Marie, 1854–1921* (Paris, 1922). Servantes du Saint-Cœur de Marie, *Cinquante ans de vie canadienne: 1892–1942; l'Institut des Sœurs Servantes du Saint-Cœur de Marie effeuille ses souvenirs aux rayons d'un jubilé d'or* ([Beauport, 1944]).

DE LAMARRE, ELZÉAR, Roman Catholic priest, professor, author, magazine editor, and founder of religious works; b. 8 Sept. 1854 in Sainte-Brigitte-de-Laval, Lower Canada, son of Charles De Lamarre, a sailor and then a farmer, and Luce Laroche; d. 21 April 1925 in Chicoutimi, Que.

The seventh of ten children, Elzéar De Lamarre grew up at Hébertville in the Lac-Saint-Jean region, where his parents had settled around 1858 to work a piece of land. Through the generosity of the local curé, who had noticed his intelligence, at the age of 16 he entered the Petit Séminaire de Québec, where he did his classical studies. As was often the case at the time, he went on in 1878 to the Grand Séminaire, choosing the one in Chicoutimi. There he began to study theology; he also acted as study master for the youngest pupils and taught versification and belles-lettres (the fourth and fifth forms), an indication of his intellectual ability. Ordained to the priesthood on 29 June 1883, he served for a number of years in parishes, including those of La Malbaie and Les Éboulements. In 1889 the new bishop of Chicoutimi, Louis-Nazaire BÉGIN, who wanted to staff the Séminaire de Chicoutimi with well-educated priests, sent him for further studies at the college of the Sacred Congregation of Propaganda in Rome, where he obtained a doctorate in theology in 1891. The Université Laval would also confer a similar degree on him in 1902.

On his return from Rome in 1891, Abbé De Lamarre took on assignments in teaching, staff training, group leadership, and administration at the Séminaire de Chicoutimi (both junior and senior levels). He was superior of the seminary from 1899 to 1905 and bursar from 1905 to 1908. Nonetheless, his name is mainly associated with the founding and development of pious and charitable works, some of which achieved notable success. Their guiding principle was devotion to St Anthony of Padua, which was doubtless the result of a pilgrimage that De Lamarre made to Padua, Italy, in 1891; its practice was strengthened by an active correspondence between the priest and the Italian proponent of that devotion, Canon Antonio Locatelli, with whom he had struck up a friendship during his stay in Rome. The Recollets had begun to arouse interest in the holy man of Padua among the Catholics of New France in the 18th century. Orders and congregations of the Franciscan family had kept it alive until there was a new surge in the popularity of the devotion at the time of the Catholic religious reawakening in Quebec in the second half of the 19th century. The promotion of ultramontane piety and the expansion of popular devotions infused with intense emotionalism were part of the wider context within which De Lamarre carried on his work.

Thanks to De Lamarre's energetic efforts, the promotion of the veneration of St Anthony grew spectacularly in the 1880s and 1890s. In 1894 he founded an orphanage for girls which was known as the Orphelinat Saint-Antoine. The Augustines de la Miséricorde de Jésus (Augustinian nuns) agreed to take charge of it at the Hôtel-Dieu Saint-Vallier in Chicoutimi. He immediately linked it with the Œuvre du Pain de Saint Antoine, whose purpose was to ensure financial support for the orphanage. In the same year he brought out in Chicoutimi *La dévotion à saint Antoine de Padoue*, which went through several editions including an English one by 1895. In June 1895 he and Abbé Victor-Alphonse HUARD launched *Le Messager de Saint-Antoine*, of which he would be the guiding spirit for 30 years. In a general way, the magazine sought to educate readers in prayer and reliance on God in daily life, as well as to develop the practice of Christian virtues. More specifically, its aim was to promote the devotion to St Anthony and to support De Lamarre's charitable works. Each monthly issue contained an editorial that for the most part dealt with religious matters, articles reprinted from other magazines, an episode from the life of St Anthony, news about the church, personal witnessing, lists of favours sought and obtained, accounts of miracles, and announcements. It also progressively became an instrument for promoting devotion to the Virgin Mary. With more than 10,000 copies printed for each issue during the first decade of the 20th century, there were readers in Canada and the eastern United States. In January 1896 De Lamarre launched *St Anthony's Canadian Messenger*, an English version of *Le Messager*, which was published until December 1903. While he was superior, De Lamarre in 1904 founded a religious community for women, the Sœurs de Saint-Antoine de Padoue, which was made responsible for the maintenance of the Séminaire de Chicoutimi. He also drafted the first constitution and rules for this congregation, which would adopt the name of Sœurs Antoniennes de Marie, Reine du Clergé, in 1929.

In 1907 De Lamarre bought a property on Lac Bouchette, south of Lac Saint-Jean, and had a house and chapel built there, where he could relax. (The chapel would be decorated by his cousin, the painter Charles HUOT.) The Ermitage San'Tonio, as he called it, soon became a regional centre for pilgrimages to Notre-Dame de Lourdes. One day while out walking, De Lamarre had discovered a cave similar to the one at Lourdes, in France, and he had a statue of the Virgin Mary set up in it. People from the surrounding area went there to pray; after testimonies were given about favours received as a result of visiting the site, the number of visitors continued to increase. In 1922 a 50-room inn was built to accommodate the pilgrims.

De Lamarre also helped make the place popular through his commitment to spreading the devotion to St Anthony. For instance, he was North American director of the Universal Association of St Anthony of Padua from 1895 to 1925, a period during which he paid particular attention to dedicating children to the saint. In 1920 he published in Montreal the *Manuel du pèlerin*. Meanwhile, thanks to *Le Messager*, various religious and votive forms (miraculous responses, novenas, the month of St Anthony) were being introduced among the faithful, who came in ever-increasing numbers to the hermitage.

Like many priests of his day, De Lamarre took great pleasure in writing, a pleasure manifest in his religious writings, of course, but also in other forms. In 1892, for instance, he was one of the founders of *L'Oiseau-mouche*, the college newspaper of the Petit Séminaire de Chicoutimi, for which he wrote under the pseudonym of Livius. In 1924, under the name of C. de La Roche, he brought out at Quebec a work about his nephew Victor De Lamarre*, *Victor De Lamarre, le roi de l'haltère*. He was also the author of *Ad limina apostolorum*, a symphonic ode composed in 1883 to welcome Bishop Dominique Racine* of Chicoutimi on his return from Rome. It was set to music by Abbé David-Odilon Dufresne.

A man of many talents, Abbé Elzéar De Lamarre seems to have been rather unassuming and conciliatory by nature. The records show only one case where he was at odds with the diocesan authorities. The difference of opinion occurred near the end of his life, with Bishop Michel-Thomas Labrecque*, on the question of transferring the sanctuary at Lac Bouchette to the Capuchins rather than to the diocesan church in Chicoutimi. The priest had had difficulty finding a religious congregation willing to carry on his work, probably because of the sanctuary's burden of debt. The bishop of Chicoutimi finally gave in to De Lamarre's last wishes, and on 21 Oct. 1925 the Capuchins became the owners of the sanctuary and of *Le Messager de Saint-Antoine*. Both of these endeavours are thriving today, as are the Œuvre du Pain and the Sœurs Antoniennes de Marie; all of them keep alive the memory of a priest considered a "holy man."

CLAUDE GILBERT

Much information concerning Father De Lamarre and his works is available at the Arch. du Diocèse de Chicoutimi, Qué., and the Arch. des Sœurs Antoniennes de Marie, Chicoutimi.

ANQ-Q, CE301-S27, 10 sept. 1854. *Le Progrès du Saguenay* (Chicoutimi), 23 avril 1925. Antonio Dragon, *L'abbé Delamarre, fondateur des Sœurs antoniennes de Marie et des pèlerinages du Lac Bouchette* ([Chicoutimi], 1974). *Évoca-*

tions et témoignages: centenaire du diocèse de Chicoutimi, 1878–1978 (Chicoutimi, 1978). Louise Gagnon-Arguin, "La dévotion à Saint-Antoine à travers *le Messager de Saint-Antoine*; essai d'analyse d'une dévotion populaire" (mémoire de MA, univ. Laval, Québec, 1978). André Simard, *Les évêques et les prêtres séculiers au diocèse de Chicoutimi, 1878–1968; notices biographiques* (Chicoutimi, 1969), 93–95. Laurent Tremblay, *Au service du royaume; spiritualité de l'abbé De Lamarre* (Chicoutimi, 1979).

DENISON, FLORA MacDONALD. *See* MERRILL

DENISON, GEORGE TAYLOR, lawyer, militia officer, author, politician, police magistrate, and imperialist; b. 31 Aug. 1839 in Toronto, eldest child of George Taylor Denison* and Mary Anne Dewson; m. first 20 Jan. 1863 Caroline Macklem (d. 1885) in Chippawa, Upper Canada, and they had three sons and three daughters; m. secondly 1 Dec. 1887 Helen Amanda Mair in Perth, Ont., and they had two daughters; d. 6 June 1925 in Toronto.

Known by contemporaries as the "watchdog" of the British empire, George Taylor Denison inherited a family legacy of antipathy to the United States, loyalty to the crown, conservative political values, and military service. His great-grandfather, a brewer and farmer from Yorkshire, was induced to immigrate to Upper Canada in 1792 by the province's receiver and auditor general, Peter Russell*. For managing Russell's estate at York (Toronto), he received a 1,000-acre grant. His grandfather George Taylor Denison I, who married the daughter of a prominent landowner and United Empire Loyalist, added to the family tradition of imperial service by enlisting with the 3rd York Militia during the War of 1812. The tradition continued with his father, George Taylor Denison II, who served during the rebellion of 1837–38, played an important role in the reorganization of the Canadian militia in 1855, and commanded the 1st Volunteer Militia Troop of Cavalry of York County (designated the Governor General's Body Guard in 1866). As well, he was an alderman for St Patrick's Ward in Toronto. The burden of tradition and expectation thus weighed heavily upon George Taylor Denison III.

As befitted his family's social status, Denison was educated at Upper Canada College, where his performance was unspectacular. Expelled from Trinity College by provost George Whitaker* for insubordinate behaviour, he transferred to the University of Toronto and earned a degree in law. Called to the bar in 1861, he would later go into practice with his brother Frederick Charles*. The law, however, held no interest for him. His heart was with the militia. Gazetted cornet in his father's troop in the fall of 1854, he rapidly rose through the ranks, from captain in 1857 to lieutenant-colonel and commander in 1866.

Denison's passion for military matters and gift for polemics first became evident in 1861 when, in the wake of the *Trent* affair [*see* Sir Charles Hastings Doyle*], he anonymously published *Canada, is she prepared for war?* (Toronto). This pamphlet, which urged British North Americans to uphold their forefathers' martial valour and to ready themselves against a possible attack from the United States, ignited a lively newspaper debate and soon resulted in another tract, *The national defences . . .* (Toronto, 1861), in which Denison argued for a properly trained and equipped mounted infantry. In *A review of the militia policy of the present administration* (Hamilton, 1863) he responded (under the pseudonym Junius) to the defeat of John A. Macdonald*'s Militia Bill of 1862 with a scathing attack on the government's neglect and ignorance of military matters.

Denison aspired to a career as a professional soldier, but his sympathy for the South during the American Civil War ultimately cost him his ambition. His identification with the South came naturally: it represented an idyllic society that embodied the social order, conservative values, and chivalric traditions he wished to see maintained in British North America. He drew parallels between his loyalist ancestors, who had fought to uphold their principles against the demagoguery of American patriots, and the southerners, who were struggling to preserve their identity and way of life. Fearing the consequences of a northern victory for the future of British North America, Denison actively backed the Confederate cause despite Britain's official neutrality. In September 1864 he received a visit from his uncle George Dewson of Florida, who had been commissioned to assess support for the Confederacy in British North America. Denison's farm home, Heydon Villa, on his father's estate in west Toronto, became a haven for Confederate agents, exiles, and sympathizers and a clearing house for smuggled documents. He also became involved in efforts to purchase the steamer *Georgian*, which was to be used as a raider on the Great Lakes. The diplomatic crisis and lawsuits that followed the discovery of this plan effectively ended his prospects for a full-time military career, a disappointment that repeated promises from politicians and his own tireless efforts could not reverse. A frustrated Denison entered local politics and served as a councilman for St Patrick's Ward from 1865 to 1867. He commanded the Governor General's Body Guard during the Fenian raids of 1866 and wrote *Modern cavalry: its organisation, armament, and employment in war . . .* (London, 1868), an impassioned case for mounted infantry based on his own experience and close study of the Civil War. He suffered another blow to his ego when British critics dismissed the book as the work of a mere colonial.

Appalled by the lack of national spirit following confederation, disillusioned by the state of Canadian politics, and fearful of the United States, Denison joined with Charles MAIR, William Alexander Foster*, and others to found the Canada First movement in 1868. Inspired by Thomas D'Arcy McGee*'s vision of a northern nation, Canada First celebrated the new dominion's rugged landscape and climate and its Anglo-Saxon/Protestant heritage. This small social group was hurled into national prominence by the Red River uprising of 1869–70. Seeing the actions of Louis Riel* and his followers as an affront to Canada's territorial ambition, the group launched a vigorous assault upon the "traitors." Denison led the charge, writing bellicose letters to the newspapers, organizing demonstrations, and appealing to all loyal English-speaking Canadians to defend their birthright. Special venom was reserved for Sir George-Étienne Cartier*, the militia minister who had blocked Denison's advancement to the post of adjutant general of cavalry and who, in Denison's eyes, represented French Canadian opposition to the force sent to Red River.

The success of these tactics had a lasting effect on Denison. The same belligerent rhetoric and fearmongering would characterize his later campaigns against closer economic relations with the United States and on behalf of imperial unity. His immediate priority, however, was ensuring the Anglo-Saxon character of the northwest. He and his Canada First associates created the North West Emigration Aid Society in 1870 to assist in the recruitment of desirable settlers. Denison outlined his national vision in an address he first delivered in Weston (Toronto) in early 1871, "The duty of Canadians to Canada," in which he attacked British indifference and warned of the dominion's vulnerability. Canada's destiny, he insisted, depended on the cultivation of pride and patriotism, the development of its resources, and the creation of politics freed of faction and dedicated to the national good. Such a course would allow Canada to assume its rightful place as a full partner in the empire. Disillusioned with the governing Conservative party, he sought election to the House of Commons for Algoma as a Liberal in 1872. Defeated by John Beverley Robinson*, he was rewarded for his efforts by friends in the provincial Liberal government of Oliver Mowat* and made Ontario's emigration commissioner in London. His exposure there to reviving imperialist feeling reinforced his Canada First sentiments. The position was temporary, however, and he returned to Canada in early 1874, with no immediate prospects before him.

As Denison approached middle age, he was haunted by his lack of personal accomplishment. "If a man does not make his mark in the world or be in a fair way of doing it before he is forty he will never do anything afterwards," his father had once warned him. When he learned of the substantial cash prizes offered by the Russian government for the best history of cavalry, he decided to return to his first love, the military, and resolved to make his reputation as a military historian. He threw himself into the work, rising early to read and write, acquiring a large library on military history at great expense, and travelling to London and St Petersburg to do research. Denison completed his magnum opus in December 1876 and presented the manuscript to the prize committee in person, but it refused to consider his work on the grounds that the translation, done by a Russian woman in New York, was sub-standard. Only after the book appeared in English was he awarded the 5,000-rouble first prize. Although *A history of cavalry from the earliest times, with lessons for the future* (London, 1877) received mixed reviews at the time, it has since been hailed as the definitive work in the field.

On his return to Canada in 1877, Denison assumed the post of police magistrate for the City of Toronto, a position he would retain until the summer of 1921. He owed the appointment to Oliver Mowat. Denison's contemporary seat on the Board of Police Commissioners was not seen as a conflict of interest. He ran his court like a well-oiled machine. Much to the annoyance of the city officials who paid his salary, he routinely cleared his docket in a couple of hours before lunch. Usually faced with an enormous caseload, and with little interest in the causes or prevention of crime, he had no use for legal technicalities or procedural niceties. His was "a court of justice, not a court of law," he proudly asserted. By his own admission, he relied more on intuition than on evidence. Although he liked to boast that he judged impartially, some groups fared better than others: retired soldiers and members of Toronto's respectable classes could expect leniency but striking workers, parvenus, Irishmen, and blacks invariably received harsh treatment. Denison nonetheless took a paternal interest in the unfortunate members of the lower classes who filed through his court. He championed legal aid, chastised the legal profession for profiting from people's misfortunes and prolonging cases, and denounced moral reform groups that tried to impose their standards upon criminal elements "who offended their tender susceptibilities." His unorthodox methods were notorious – his court even became something of a tourist attraction. By the time of his retirement, there were calls for a full overhaul of the then outmoded Police Court, which consisted of four magistrates, including Rupert Etherege Kingsford*, women's and children's divisions, and seven clerks.

Denison's swift administration of justice freed him to pursue other interests. An Anglican of evangelical inclination, he helped found and served on the first board of management of the Protestant Episcopal Divinity School [*see* James Paterson Sheraton*]. He became one of the principal forces behind the revival of the loyalist tradition, as an organizer of the loyalist centennial celebrations in 1884 and a founding member in 1896 of the United Empire Loyalist Association of Ontario. He broadcast the tradition long and often. In his presidential address to the Royal Society of Canada in 1904, for instance, he spoke on the loyalist influence in Canadian history. He found in the tradition not only the reflected glory of his ancestors' accomplishments but also a usable past, which could be called upon to justify closer ties to Britain and the empire and to attack opponents who advocated greater independence or closer economic and political relations with the United States. As constructed by Denison and others, the tradition served too to defend a social order threatened by industrialization, urbanization, and immigration. Denison's rabid anti-Americanism, in fact, owed much to his fear that the social ailments afflicting the United States would soon infect Canada.

Denison's patriotism had been tested in the spring of 1885, when he and the Governor General's Body Guard saw service during the North-West rebellion. Because of his lingering hostility to the federal government, he had little enthusiasm for the conflict and had initially refused to volunteer his troop. He objected, he told Charles Mair in March, to the use of the militia "to defend a Government of land sharks who have villainously wronged the poor native and the actual settler." Moreover, he had been deeply shaken by the death of his wife on 26 February. His fighting spirit returned with the formation in May of the Canadian branch of the Imperial Federation League; he was named chair of the branch's organizing committee, and would later be vice-president and president. Although Denison and the league succeeded in whipping up nationalistic fervour, especially after the appearance in 1887 of the movement for commercial union with the United States [*see* Erastus Wiman*], they failed to convince the league's British members of the virtue of imperial trade preferences. When internal divisions caused the league to collapse, Denison played an important role in 1895 in creating a new organization, the British Empire League, and he would serve as president of its Canadian branch for many years. Although military considerations dominated Denison's imperial outlook, he frequently used the rhetoric of religious crusade in his speeches and writings, and his evangelical Anglicanism certainly helped shape his view of events. In this religious sense, his imperialism was comparable to that of George Monro Grant* and George Robert PARKIN.

Colonel Denison remained in the vanguard of the imperialist cause throughout the remainder of his life. He championed Canadian participation in the South African War and contributions to the Royal Navy, he surpassed most imperialists by campaigning in 1902 for an imperial defence fund derived from duties on foreign imports into Britain and the colonies, and he vigorously opposed the efforts of Sir Wilfrid Laurier*'s government to negotiate reciprocity with the United States in 1911. A frequent speaker and newspaper commentator, he brought to the cause an unrelenting drive and a steely resistance to criticism. Passed over several times for imperial honours, he eventually claimed he had not wanted any. "His self-laudation has long been a standing joke in Canada," Governor General Lord Minto [Elliot*] confided to Colonial Secretary Joseph Chamberlain in 1900. As well, some British career soldiers regarded his Body Guard as a showy, lightweight outfit, top-heavy with officers and NCOs. Unswayed, he chronicled his efforts on behalf of the empire, and his arguments for federation and against free trade, in *The struggle for imperial unity* . . . (Toronto, 1909). With the approach of war in Europe, he found a new demon, Germany. Although his combination of anti-Americanism, imperialism, and nationalism lost much of its force in the years following World War I, Denison remained unmoved in his convictions.

Despite his celebrity, relatively little is known about his private and family life. He kept a daily diary from 1864 until his death, but rarely recorded his deepest personal thoughts. In 1863 he had married the niece of the Reverend Thomas Brock Fuller*; in 1887 he married Charles Mair's 22-year-old niece. He appears to have been a demanding but loving father who impressed on his sons the same spirit of loyalty, duty, and family pride that had been implanted in him during his own childhood. Extremely class-conscious, he raised his daughters to assume their rightful place at the top of respectable society.

His stern and headstrong manner notwithstanding, Denison had a great sense of humour and relished the caricatures drawn of him in the press. He was almost always portrayed in military uniform striking the pose of the stereotypical British officer and gentleman. He loved to entertain and Heydon Villa, which he rebuilt in 1880, became a regular stop for notables visiting Toronto. A man of boundless energy and ambition, he kept up an exhaustive correspondence with the public men of his day. He thoroughly enjoyed the cut and thrust of vigorous debate but his absolute faith in the correctness of his beliefs cost him several friendships, including that of Goldwin Smith*, whom he almost single-handedly had ostracized from polite Toronto society. By 1922 Denison's health was failing and he died at Heydon Villa in 1925 at the age of 85.

George Taylor Denison had been raised to be a public man. Although few could match his contribution to the discussions of the great political issues of the day, his life was full of disappointments. Unable to achieve a military career or high elected office, he settled into a series of patronage appointments and crusades. His impact on Canadian opinion lay as much in the opposition he provoked as in the causes he advocated. In many respects, his life reflects the ideas and standards, the frustrations and anxieties, of a class and a generation whose values were fading before the forces that were transforming Canada into a North American nation.

NORMAN KNOWLES

George Taylor Denison's 1861 pamphlet *Canada, is she prepared for war? or, a few remarks on the state of her defences* was issued anonymously "*by a native Canadian.*" In addition to the works mentioned in the text, his publications include *The petition of George Taylor Denison, Jr.: to the Honorable the House of Assembly, praying redress in the matter of the seizure of the steamer "Georgian"* . . . (Toronto, 1865); *History of the Fenian raid on Fort Erie; with an account of the battle of Ridgeway* (Toronto, 1866); "A visit to General Robert E. Lee," *Canadian Monthly* (Toronto), 1 (January–June 1872): 231–37; *Reminiscences of the Red River rebellion of 1869* ([Toronto?], 1873); *Canada and her relations to the empire* (Toronto, 1895); "Sir John Schultz and the 'Canada First' party," *Canadian Magazine*, 8 (November 1896–April 1897): 16–23; *The British Empire League in Canada* . . . (Toronto, 1899); *Soldiering in Canada: recollections and experiences* (Toronto, 1900); "Canada and the Imperial Conference," *Nineteenth Century and After* (London), 51 (January–June 1902): 900–7; "The United Empire Loyalists and their influence upon the history of the continent," RSC, *Trans.*, 2nd ser., 10 (1905), proc.: xxv–xxxix; and *Recollections of a police magistrate* (Toronto, 1920).

AO, F 10009; F 1076-A-11; RG 80-8-0-151, no.6419. LAC, MG 29, D61; E29. QUA, Charles Mair fonds. TRL, SC, Denison family papers. United Empire Loyalists' Assoc. of Canada, Toronto Branch Arch., Corr.; Minutes. *Leader* (Toronto), 23 Jan. 1863. Carl Berger, *The sense of power; studies in the ideas of Canadian imperialism, 1867–1914* (Toronto and Buffalo, N.Y., 1970). *Canada Law Journal* (Toronto), 36 (1900): 517–20. *Canadian annual rev.*, 1902–17. *Canadian Journal of Commerce* (Montreal), September 1890: 570. *Canadian men and women of the time* (Morgan; 1898 and 1912). *The centennial of the settlement of Upper Canada by the United Empire Loyalists, 1784–1884* . . . (Toronto, 1885). E. M. Chadwick, *Ontario families: genealogies of United-Empire-Loyalist and other pioneer families of Upper Canada* (2v., Toronto, 1894–98; repr., 2v. in 1, Lambertville, N.J., [1970]; repr., vol.1, intro. W. F. E. Morley, Belleville, Ont., 1972). J. F. Fraser, *Canada as it is* (London, 1905). D. [P.] Gagan, *The Denison family of Toronto, 1792–1925* (Toronto, 1973). G. H. Homel, "Denison's law: criminal justice and the Police Court in Toronto, 1877–1921," *OH*, 73 (1981): 171–86. Norman Knowles, *Inventing the loyalists: the Ontario loyalist tradition and the creation of usable pasts* (Toronto, 1997). *Lord Minto's Canadian papers: a selection of the public and private papers of the fourth Earl of Minto, 1898–1904*, ed. and intro. Paul Stevens and J. T. Saywell (2v., Toronto, 1981–83). Desmond Morton, *Ministers and generals: politics and the Canadian militia, 1868–1904* (Toronto and Buffalo, 1970). *Trinity College conducted as a mere boys' school, not as a college* (Toronto, 1858). H. M. Wodson, *The whirlpool: scenes from Toronto Police Court* (Toronto, 1917).

Denny

DENNY, Sir CECIL EDWARD, NWMP officer, Indian agent, author, and archivist; b. 14 Dec. 1850 in Shedfield, England, elder son of the Reverend Robert Day Denny and his second wife, Frances Johnson Kerton Waller; d. unmarried 25 July 1928 in Edmonton.

Cecil Edward Denny was educated at Cheltenham College in England in 1862–63 and in France and Germany. At 19 he emigrated to the United States, where he farmed south of Chicago. In April 1874 he joined Canada's North-West Mounted Police as a constable but, trading on a recommendation by Sir Stafford Henry Northcote, he secured appointment as a sub-inspector on 11 May, before his contingent left Toronto for Manitoba under the command of Commissioner George Arthur FRENCH. Denny took part in the Long March west and he remained at Fort Macleod (Alta) during the winter of 1874–75. In March 1875 he accompanied Assistant Commissioner James Farquharson Macleod*, guide Jerry Potts*, and two constables on a trip to Helena (Mont.) that has become part of the Mounties' legend. Caught by a storm, the men were nearly frozen to death and were only saved by Potts's skill.

That summer F Division, under Éphrem-A. Brisebois*, with Denny second in command, marched north to build a new post, Fort Brisebois, subsequently Fort Calgary (Calgary). Brisebois was an uninspiring leader and Denny, who got on well with his troops, was away for much of the winter. By spring the men were mutinous. Brisebois resigned in August 1876 and Denny was left in command until Lief Newry Fitzroy Crozier* arrived to take charge. Crozier remained at Fort Calgary until late 1877 or early 1878, after which Denny was the senior officer. In 1880 Calgary was reduced to an outpost and Denny was transferred to Fort Macleod.

Fort Calgary was in the northern territory of the Blackfoot and Denny had come to like and respect them. Although he recognized that they would have to adapt to changing circumstances, he was usually as generous and flexible as his official position allowed. Apparently the Blackfoot liked and trusted him. In August 1876 Blackfoot chief Crowfoot [Isapo-muxika*] told him that the Sioux had proposed a joint attack on the Cree and the whites. The Blackfoot rejected the alliance and Crowfoot sought, and received, assurance from Denny that if the Sioux attacked the Blackfoot, the police would come to their assistance.

Denny attended the negotiation of Treaty No.7 in 1877 as a member of the police escort, signed the treaty as a witness, and assisted in the initial payments. Although the leading figures, both native and white, were enthusiastic about the treaty, Denny recalled that "many of the Indians . . . were dissatisfied that any treaty had been made at all." He believed that the sham battle staged after the signing was only

half in jest. During the negotiations Crowfoot had suggested that the Blackfoot, the Blood, and the Sarcee should share a common reserve along the Bow River. The concentration strengthened the Blackfoot's bargaining position and increased Crowfoot's prestige. Within a year, however, the Blood had opted for a separate reserve near Fort Macleod. Crowfoot was not consulted on the change and it fell to Denny to tell him. Not surprisingly, Crowfoot was annoyed and Denny considered the meeting the most difficult he had had as a policeman.

By the spring of 1879 the buffalo had been exterminated on the Canadian plains. The Blackfoot were starving and they appealed to Denny at Fort Calgary for aid. By July he was distributing 2,000 pounds of beef per day. This issue, which was made on his own authority and contrary to his instructions, was a humanitarian reaction, but it was also a recognition of reality. Denny reported that if he did not feed the Indians "they will take the matter into their own hands and help themselves."

When necessary, then, Denny bowed to the inevitable. In other cases he mediated. In the summer of 1880 he intervened in a dispute between large Cree and Blackfoot camps near Blackfoot Crossing (Alta). The Cree were preparing to avenge the killing of one of their number by the Blackfoot. Denny, with only six policemen to back him, induced the Blackfoot to offer compensation and then persuaded the Cree to accept the offer. Negotiation did not always work. The Sarcee, like the Blood, were unhappy sharing a reserve with the Blackfoot. In November 1880 they moved to Fort Calgary and demanded that they receive their rations there. The lone sergeant at the post had little choice but to issue supplies and to send for help. Denny led the relief force, eight men and a sergeant. After three days of tense negotiations, the Sarcee agreed to go to Macleod for rations. The next morning, when the camp showed no signs of moving, Denny lined his men up with loaded rifles and he and his sergeant began to pull down the tents. Although a shot was fired over the sergeant's head, they continued, and the Sarcee decided to move rather than fight.

Denny was forced to resign from the NWMP on 6 June 1881 after Percy Robinson, a clerk in the Indian department at Fort Macleod, sued him for having induced his wife to desert him, and "for having criminal connection with her." Although Denny was found not liable, he was subsequently judged guilty of having broken into Robinson's house and having threatened to beat him. His relationship with Victoria Robinson did not end at this time – it seems probable that he had at least one child with her.

Denny had been an able officer and some officials accepted his explanation that the Robinson affair was an attempt to blackmail him. In October 1881 Indian commissioner Edgar Dewdney* appointed him as

Indian agent at Fort Walsh (Sask.). The following January he was transferred to Blackfoot Crossing, where a dispute over rations threatened to erupt in violence. The trouble was settled before he arrived, but only after a substantial display of force. Crowfoot, usually a supporter of the police, had played a role in defying them and Dewdney hoped that Denny, as an "old friend," could influence the chief. Initially Denny was given charge of the northern part of Treaty No.7 but within a few months he was made agent for the whole treaty area, which covered most of modern Alberta south of the Red Deer River.

Denny blamed the trouble at Blackfoot Crossing on an inequitable system of distributing rations and on the men in charge. He described them as a "rough class of Americans . . . who dislike Indians and are not very choice in the language they use towards them." He reformed the issue of rations, replaced some employees, and distributed the tools the Indians at Blackfoot Crossing needed to begin farming. He "found the Blackfoot willing to work had they received assistance but they had been badly neglected."

As an agent, Denny encouraged the Indians to take up agriculture and abandon their traditional ways. Sometimes he had to temporize. When the Blood wished to retaliate against horse-stealing raids by Cree from the Cypress Hills, Denny provided the leader, White Calf [Onista'poka*], with a letter to Commissioner Acheson Gosford Irvine at Fort Walsh, asking for his help in recovering the horses. White Calf took about 200 warriors with him, far more than Denny had expected. Denny was criticized for condoning a war party but he argued that, by directing what could not be prevented, he had avoided a larger clash. Denny tried to reduce the incidence of horse stealing and raids by enrolling some members of the Blood warrior society in an informal police force. The force occupied the more restless spirits in the camp, brought them under Denny's influence, and provided a counterbalance to Red Crow [Mékaisto*], the head chief. Denny also tried to dilute Red Crow's authority by promoting the election of an ineffectual leader, Calf Tail, as a second head chief.

Within months of his arrival in Treaty No.7, Denny had become embroiled in a dispute with the inspector of Indian agencies, Thomas Page Wadsworth. The pretext for the dispute was Denny's lax, perhaps corrupt, administrative style, but it was exacerbated by jurisdictional disputes and personality differences. At a more fundamental level, Wadsworth represented the government's drive to reduce expenses. Denny favoured a more generous policy of gradual reduction. On his arrival at Macleod he had dismissed an employee who had been issuing rations, in part because he had found a surplus of 60 sacks of flour on hand. Such a surplus, he reasoned, "cannot be got if the Indians have been getting their full rations; for

my part I would rather see the flour short than over." Although he was often accused of currying favour with the Indians through his liberal issue of supplies, he actually reduced government commitments by striking many individuals off the band membership lists. On the Blood Reserve, for instance, he reduced the number from 3,542 to 2,589. During the summer of 1883 there was an unusual amount of sickness and death among the Indians of Treaty No.7. The doctor who investigated the outbreak attributed it to the poor quality of the flour issued as rations. Although Denny had certified the flour, tests revealed it to be several grades lower than the standard contracted for, and some of it was tainted with weed seeds. It was not clear whether Denny had been careless in his certification or whether he had been in collusion with the contractors. The matter would probably have resulted in his dismissal had not another development intervened. When the Department of Indian Affairs ordered Denny to lay off many of his staff, he protested to Dewdney on 14 Jan. 1884 that he could not manage the agency properly and then he resigned. On 15 Mar. 1884 he wrote a bitter letter to the minister, complaining of his treatment, condemning Ottawa's management of Indian affairs in Treaty No.7, and predicting trouble "costly to the government."

Trouble came in Treaty No.6, not in No.7. When Denny heard of the clash at Duck Lake in late March 1885 between the Métis and the NWMP [*see* Gabriel Dumont*], he offered his services to Dewdney. He was temporarily placed in charge of Treaty No.7 and his first act was to increase rations to the Blood. At Blackfoot Crossing he found that the Blackfoot had received messages urging them to join the rising. Crowfoot may have been sympathetic but he was pessimistic about the chance of success. When the Blood and the Peigan made it clear that they would not join, Crowfoot declared his loyalty to the crown. A confident Denny told Dewdney in April that "if any trouble is caused it will be the fault of the whites and not the Indians."

The most likely source of trouble was Thomas Bland STRANGE, a retired British officer, a rancher, and the commander of the Alberta Field Force. He had a strained relationship with the Blackfoot, whom he suspected of killing his cattle. He issued orders to his ranch hands and to members of his field force to fire on anyone found running off horses or killing stock. Denny objected that the Blackfoot were loyal and he tried to ensure that no militia would enter their reserve without his permission. With Dewdney's support, he threatened to withdraw Indian agents if Strange did not quit interfering. On Denny's advice, Dewdney countermanded Strange's orders that Indians were to be confined to their reserves. Denny also intercepted insulting and threatening messages from Strange to Crowfoot. The situation was resolved only when Strange left Calgary for Edmonton during the rebellion.

Dewdney was pleased with Denny's work and used him to sound out opinion in Treaty No.7 during the winter of 1885–86, but he did not give Denny the permanent reappointment he expected. Possibly the Indian department had decided that Denny's conciliatory, but expensive approach to managing the Indians was no longer necessary. As well, Denny's personal life had made him enemies. Father Albert Lacombe* described him as "a notoriously dissolute character, a libertine and addicted to the excessive use of alcohol," one who should never be employed by the Indian department. In Ottawa its deputy superintendent general, Lawrence Vankoughnet, regarded him as a "morally bad man" and "thoroughly unprincipled."

While he was still a police officer, Denny had started ranching on a small scale. In 1878–79 he imported a small herd of cattle and claimed land near Fort Calgary. He sold this claim to his partner, John Stewart, in 1882–83, and established a second ranch north of Fort Macleod. It was not a success and he abandoned it about 1890.

Denny's life, in fact, was coming unravelled and his name appeared in court reports several times between 1885 and 1894, mainly for charges involving liquor. The most serious incidents were two charges of "shooting with intent" brought by Victoria Robinson and Corporal George Greenacre of Macleod in 1892. By their account someone had broken into her house and set fire to some bedding. She and Greenacre had surprised the intruder and given chase in the dark. The fugitive fired on them and fled but was caught. It was Denny. His defence was that he was the victim of a series of coincidences, possibly contrived to discredit him. A jury acquitted him.

During the years 1890–1922 Denny supported himself by a series of short-term jobs. He was a police scout, a herder at the Milk River quarantine station, and a night-clerk in a Lethbridge hotel. In 1897–99 he was in the area of Fort Steele, B.C., as a prospector, jailer, newsagent, and justice of the peace. By 1900 he was in Montana working as a miner/prospector and fire-ranger. He was employed as a packer on the Peace River–Yukon trail from 1904 to 1906, on railway construction, and around 1913–17 as a fire-ranger in the Lac la Biche area of Alberta. In October 1916 he homesteaded near Colinton. Although sometimes on the verge of destitution, he was able to write a memoir, *The riders of the plains: a reminiscence of the early and exciting days in the north west* (Calgary, 1905). This first-hand account of the NWMP helped to establish the view of the force as the key element in bringing about the peaceful settlement of the Canadian west. It reveals Denny's sympathy for the Indians as they struggled to adjust. A proponent of gradual change, he still believed that assimilation was necessary and supported drastic means, such as residential schools, to achieve it.

On 24 Nov. 1921 Denny succeeded his half-brother as baronet of Tralee Castle in County Kerry (Republic of Ireland). The succession made him Sir Cecil but brought no material reward. The following May he was appointed assistant archivist of Alberta. While in this position he researched and drafted his second historical account, later published as *The law marches west* (Toronto, 1939). An expanded version of *Riders*, it focuses on the same themes. Denny's services were "dispensed with" on 24 Aug. 1927, probably because of his drinking. In poor health, he died in July 1928 at the University of Alberta Hospital.

As a policeman and an Indian agent, C. E. Denny had worked mainly with the Indians of Treaty No.7. His approach was to make changes slowly, to use rations to persuade when necessary, and to co-opt Indian practices and individuals where possible. This method of proceeding, which reflected his sympathy for the Blackfoot, did not serve him well when the government became impatient with slow, expensive progress. Today he is remembered for *The riders of the plains* and *The law marches west*, both valuable accounts of the early years of the NWMP and of the attitudes of one of its officers. Denny's view of the police as responsible for the peaceful settlement of the Canadian west is in accord with, and indeed helped shape, the traditional heroic view of the NWMP.

ALAN B. McCULLOUGH

The major sources for Denny's life are his published memoirs, *The riders of the plains* . . . (Calgary, 1905) and *The law marches west*, ed. W. B. Cameron (Toronto, 1939; 2nd ed., 1972), and official correspondence by or concerning him in LAC, RG 10 and RG 18; MG 27, I, C4, 2; MG 29, E40, file 2; and in GA, M 320. An account by Denny of his experiences on the Peace River–Yukon trail has been published as "Trail to the Yukon," in *Alberta Hist. Rev.* (Calgary), 15 (1967), no.3: 24–28.

PAA, GR1970.313, Denny file; GR1978.235/72; OC 845/22. Can., Dept. of Indian Affairs, *Annual report* (Ottawa), 1879–85; North-West Mounted Police, *Annual report* (Ottawa), 1874–98.

DE SÈVE, ALFRED (baptized **Joseph-Alfred-Marie Desèves**), violinist, music teacher, and composer; b. 26 Jan. 1858 in Montreal, son of Alexandre Desèves, a lawyer, and Marie-Marguerite Lenoir-Rolland; m. 1880 Joséphine Bruneau, a pianist; they had no children; d. 25 Nov. 1927 in Montreal.

Growing up with two brothers and several sisters who almost all practised music, Alfred De Sève early showed an aptitude for the violin. After a few lessons with a Mr Doré, at the age of seven he began taking classes with Oscar Martel, a teacher at the Petit Séminaire de Montréal; De Sève gave his first recital there after only six months of study. In 1869, Martel having left Montreal for a year, De Sève found a fine teacher in Frantz Jehin-Prume*. His training must have been irregular for the next seven years, since both his teachers divided their time between Canada and Europe.

In 1873 De Sève completed his classical studies at the Petit Séminaire de Montréal, which he had attended since 1869. Three years later, with the encouragement of Jehin-Prume, he set out for Paris. He registered first with the Spanish violinist and composer Pablo de Sarasate, who wanted to get him into the Conservatoire de Paris. Instead, De Sève went to virtuoso Henri Vieuxtemps, who, despite his considerable age and poor health, agreed to take him under his wing. The young Canadian soon moved on to Hubert Léonard, with whom he studied for 18 months. Between February and June 1878 he caused a stir in Parisian high society. Buoyed by his successes, having even acquired the honorary title of court violinist to Isabella II, queen of Spain, he arrived back in Canada toward the end of the summer of 1878.

Upon his return De Sève gave many concerts in the principal cities of the dominion, where he was warmly received. At a party given in Ottawa at the residence of the governor general, the Marquess of Lorne [Campbell*], his wife, Princess Louise, appointed him "violinist to Her Royal Highness." In 1880 he married pianist Joséphine Bruneau; her mother had taken as her second husband Louis-Olivier TAILLON, who would become premier of the province of Quebec. Joséphine served as her husband's accompanist until a nervous disease gradually caused her to slip into a catatonic state.

Despite the promise of an excellent career in Canada, De Sève exiled himself to Boston in 1881. Here, in a city with broader and more prestigious opportunities, the most active period of his artistic career began. From 1881 to 1889 he taught violin at the New England Conservatory of Music, where its 1888–89 yearbook says he became "one of our most popular teachers." He joined the Boston Symphony Orchestra at its foundation and took part in the 1881–82, 1883–84, and 1884–85 seasons, performing as soloist in Mendelssohn's Concerto in E minor, op.64, and Saint-Saëns's Introduction and rondo capriccioso op.28. He also held important positions in various Boston ensembles that took him to many parts of the United States to perform. In 1891 he succeeded Calixa Lavallée* as choir master at the Cathedral of the Holy Cross in Boston; the two men had maintained cordial ties from at least the time of the violinist's stay in Paris. De Sève seems to have amassed a sizeable fortune from these activities and he reinvested it in Montreal in properties and the stock market. It was, in fact, the management of his affairs (and

probably also the state of his health) that led him to return there in 1899.

De Sève took part in a few concerts at Montreal's Her Majesty's Theatre in the company of his wife in 1900, and then played in several string quartets until 1906, with such musicians as Émile Taranto, Joseph-Jean Goulet*, and Jean-Baptiste Dubois*. But it was above all to teaching that he devoted the rest of his life. He taught at the McGill Conservatorium of Music from 1904 to 1906, and he subsequently had a private studio on Avenue Esplanade. A number of his students enjoyed active careers, among them Alexander Brott, Albert Chamberland, Eugène Chartier, Marcel Saucier, Lucien Sicotte, and Noël Brunet. De Sève died on 25 Nov. 1927 of a heart condition from which he had been suffering since his years in the United States. He left several compositions, mainly for violin and piano, which were published in Boston. In 1931 a Montreal street in Saint-Henri ward, where he was born, was named after him.

A robust, obstinate man, Alfred De Sève was a soloist who played with solid technique and sometimes excessive intensity, but his artistic sincerity was praised. His personal magnetism had a profound effect on his many students. In an article published in *Le Devoir* several days after the musician's death, Arthur Letondal celebrated him "for his enormous talent, for his glorious career, and for the lustre he imparted to the art of music in Canada."

JACQUES-ANDRÉ HOULE

Two compositions by Alfred De Sève are preserved in the Bibliothèque Nationale du Québec (Montréal): *Angels lullaby, op. 7* (Boston, 1918) and *Slumber song* (Boston and New York, 1890). Despite extensive research, it has proven impossible to locate De Sève's marriage record.
ANQ-M, CE601-S6, 26 janv. 1858. Boston Public Library, Boston Symphony Orchestra scrapbooks, comp. A. A. and M. A. Brown *et al.* (mfm.), 1881–82. MUA, RG 39, c.68. "Au conservatoire du McGill: les professeurs canadiens-français," *La Patrie*, 16 mai 1904. L.-O. David, "Alfred Desève," *L'Opinion publique* (Montréal), 10 oct. 1878; "Concert Desève," *L'Opinion publique*, 17 oct. 1878. *Le Devoir*, 25 nov. 1927. Arthur Letondal, "Alfred De Sève," *Le Devoir*, 28 nov. 1927. "Mr Desève's concert," *Canadian Spectator* (Montreal), 21 Dec. 1878. *Le Monde illustré* (Montréal), 13 oct. 1894. "Notre violoniste canadien à Paris," *L'Opinion publique*, 30 mai 1878. Léon Trépanier, "Petite histoire locale," *La Voix populaire* (Montréal), 3, 17, 24, 31 oct., 7 nov. 1951. "Alfred De Sève," *Le Canada artistique* (Montréal), 1, no.1 (prospectus, décembre 1889): 1. *Encyclopedia of music in Canada* (Kallmann *et al.*). J.-A. Houle, "Frantz Jehin-Prume (1839–1899): son apport culturel au milieu québécois" (thesis, Music Conservatory of Quebec, Montreal, 1989). M. A. De W. Howe, *The Boston Symphony Orchestra, 1881–1931* (New York, 1931). Arthur Laurendeau, "Musiciens d'autrefois: Alfred Desève," *L'Action nationale* (Montréal) 35 (1950): 186–96. *The musical red book of Montreal . . .* , ed. B. K. Sandwell (Montreal, 1907).

Deskaheh

New England Conservatory of Music, *Calendar* (Boston), 1888–89. *Les rues de Montréal* (Montréal, 1995).

DESKAHEH (Levi General), farmer, Cayuga chief, and activist; b. 15 March 1873 in Tuscarora Township, Ont., son of William General and Lydia Burnham; m. before 1898 Mary Bergen, and they had four daughters and five sons; d. 27 June 1925 on the Tuscarora Reservation, N.Y.

A descendant of Iroquois with some Scottish-Irish ancestry, Levi General was born on the Six Nations Reserve on the Grand River. His Oneida mother and Cayuga father, who ran their own farm but worked out during harvest season, had a family of eight, Levi being one of the older children. At primary school he had Christian teachers, but he remained an adherent of the traditional Longhouse religion.

The Six Nations community contained two distinct religious worlds: that of the Mohawk, Oneida, Tuscarora, and Iroquois allies such as the Delaware, who accepted Protestant Christianity, and that of the Seneca and Onondaga, who adhered to the teachings of Skanyátaí.yo⁹ (Handsome Lake), who had reformed the Iroquois religion in the early 19th century. The Cayuga included both Christian and Longhouse adherents. Generally the Christian Iroquois promoted social adjustment through the adoption of commercial agriculture and education in English; the Longhouse people championed the old ways, including hereditary chiefs, autonomy, and resistance to the Indian Act. Roughly a quarter of the reserve in 1890 identified with the Longhouse faith [*see* John Arthur Gibson*]. The Confederacy Council of some 75 chiefs became the only institution where members of the two traditions met regularly. By the turn of the century the chiefs had bridged their differences and were administering the Grand River territory effectively. Since council enjoyed widespread support, the Department of Indian Affairs did not interfere.

After leaving school, General had worked as a lumberjack in the Allegheny Mountains in western New York and Pennsylvania. An accident forced him to return and he began to farm near Millpond, in the vicinity of Ohsweken on the Six Nations Reserve. Enos T. Montour, a Delaware, recalled that "he had a good home and family, stockyard animals, and a sprinkling of cats and dogs." He married the daughter of a Cayuga mother and a non-Indian father. His first language was Cayuga, and he participated actively in Longhouse ceremonies.

By World War I divisions were evident within council. The moderate, largely Christian element favoured continued cooperation with the Indian department and a degree of local autonomy, while the traditionalist group held to the system of hereditary chiefs and wanted more autonomy, based on the Six Nations' historical claim to a special political status under a proc-lamation of Frederick Haldimand*, governor of Quebec, in 1784. A third faction, outside council and composed mainly of Iroquois soldiers in France, petitioned Ottawa in 1917 for an elected council.

That same year Louise Miller, the matron of the Young Bear clan of the Cayuga, installed General as its new hereditary chief, or deskaheh, on the Confederacy Council. A powerful orator, he would advance quickly: deputy speaker of council in 1918 and speaker in 1922. During the war the federal government had introduced military registration and conscription and after the armistice it had set land aside on the reserve for Iroquois veterans and granted them mortgages. Deskaheh and the majority of chiefs challenged both conscription and the suppression of council's right to control land as intrusions on Iroquois sovereignty. Then, in 1920, the government amended the Indian Act to allow for compulsory enfranchisement and the removal (without consent) of an individual's Indian status. This perceived infringement of civil liberty generated resentment and drew support to Deskaheh's increasingly radical position.

Deskaheh pressured the government to review the Six Nations' historical status, specifically their right to recognition as allies, not subjects, of the British crown, and hence to immunity from federal control. When council's Canadian lawyers failed to obtain Ottawa's agreement to such an investigation, in 1921 council hired George Palmer Decker, an American lawyer who had worked on legal issues for the Oneida in New York State. With funds raised by a finance committee of council, Deskaheh and Decker made a special trip to England that year. Deskaheh had come only a distant third in the popular vote held by council to select an Iroquois delegate to accompany the lawyer: he obtained 107 votes compared to 293 for Iroquois medical doctor J. A. Miller and 252 for David S. Hill, secretary of the Six Nation Agricultural Society. Yet, as Hill explained to Decker, council chose Deskaheh since the Longhouse people "are so suspicious of any person not of their faith, we thought it better to give way to one of them." In England, Deskaheh and Decker learned that the Colonial Office considered the Six Nations to be British subjects, a decision later reinforced by Ontario's courts. Hope for a federal investigation, however, was renewed following the election in December 1921 of William Lyon Mackenzie King* and the Liberals.

Deskaheh moved to strengthen his position. The upheaval on the Six Nations Reserve was reflected in the "small riot" that broke out there in April 1922. Although the King government reversed several policies of the previous, Conservative administration, including compulsory enfranchisement, the measures it introduced were no more palatable. In response to grievances voiced by both moderates and radicals at

278

Six Nations – the government's reduction of a native trust fund, introduction of laws "with a view to the dissolution of the Six Nations," ignorance of council's wishes to "improve education," and mortgaging of reserve land – Charles Stewart*, the superintendent general of Indian affairs, offered in June to form a royal commission. After much difficult negotiation, including Iroquois threats to take the status issue to the newly formed League of Nations in Switzerland, the proposal was accepted, but the Department of Indian Affairs and council, now dominated by the radicals, both continued to press. In September, Deskaheh brought together the Longhouse chiefs, the pro-sovereignty Christian chiefs, and the Mohawk Workers Association, which sought total sovereignty. In December, without requesting council approval, the Royal Canadian Mounted Police raided the Six Nations territory to investigate reports of liquor manufacturing.

Not everyone in the Six Nations community supported Deskaheh and the radicals. Some resented the anti-British nature of their campaign. In July 1922 council secretary Asa R. Hill described the Cayuga chief as "an agitator of the worst type with no desire to come to any understanding. I am afraid that his actions will mean the breaking up of the confederacy." Frederick Ogilvie Loft* of Toronto, a Mohawk chief and founder of the League of Indians of Canada, the country's first pan-Indian political organization, also had doubts about Deskaheh's confrontational approach. In a letter to Prime Minister King in December, he claimed that General, as council's speaker, had been acting as a "dictator," one who "occupies no position superior to any other Chief of the Six Nations. . . . He holds no mandate from the people of the Six nations to warrant his actions; indeed, contrary to the spirit of our Confederacy." But by 1923 Deskaheh and his supporters had control of council; some moderates, irritated by the government's actions, had joined them and others – like Hill, who was deposed as secretary – had been replaced.

After the RCMP raid, Deskaheh, convinced that the government was insincere, resolved to take the Six Nations' case to the League of Nations. When deputy superintendent general Duncan Campbell Scott* learned of this move, he persuaded Stewart to locate a permanent RCMP detachment at Ohsweken. Negotiations then broke down, and Stewart set up a one-man inquiry instead. Andrew Thorburn Thompson, a lawyer and former officer who had commanded Iroquois soldiers, was selected in March 1923 to head it.

Deskaheh and G. P. Decker arrived in London in August en route to Geneva. They lobbied for international recognition of the Six Nations as an independent state, under article 17 of the League's covenant. Ties with Ottawa would be cut, the Indian Act would no longer control local government, the Six Nations would have their own laws, the chiefs would be in charge of funds, and council would hire its own employees and police. Decker remained only briefly in Geneva, where it proved difficult to obtain access to the League, but Deskaheh stayed for over a year, financially supported by a Swiss group, the Bureau International pour la Défense des Indigènes. One of Deskaheh's great allies was René Claparède, a Swiss writer who championed the rights of indigenous peoples around the globe. Deskaheh's efforts at the League proved fruitless. Although some countries appeared willing to discuss the issue, British objections to a review of what it regarded as a domestic Canadian matter were decisive.

During Deskaheh's absence, his supporters at home boycotted Thompson's hearings. Ready in November 1923 but not released for another nine months, Thompson's report recommended the establishment of an elected council. Without consultation, the government deposed the hereditary council and, though voter participation was slight, a new council was elected in October 1924. Its existence deprived Deskaheh of his right to speak for the Six Nations.

Disillusioned and in poor health, he returned to North America in early 1925. At Six Nations, he had told George Decker, he expected to receive the same treatment as Gandhi in India, who was jailed but was eventually released "because his people had the power stronger then the British colonies, so they had to discharged him." Deskaheh remained briefly with Decker in Rochester, and then moved to stay with his friend Chief Clinton Rickard on the Tuscarora Reservation in western New York, where he died. He was buried in the Upper Cayuga Longhouse cemetery at Six Nations. The speeches given on that occasion, in Iroquoian languages, urged those in attendance to continue Deskaheh's work. The RCMP report of the event noted that, unless new leaders came forward, the agitation he had started would wither. The status issue resurfaced again at the League of Nations in 1929–30 but without effect. Deskaheh's trip to the League of Nations in 1923–24 nonetheless marks the first attempt by North American First Nations to take their claims for sovereignty to an international forum.

DONALD B. SMITH

The author wishes to thank Germaine General-Myke for genealogical information on the family of Levi General. As Deskaheh, General is the author of *The redman's appeal for justice, August 6, 1923* (London, 1923).

Canadian Museum of Civilization, Information management services (Hull, Que.), Acc. 89/55 (Sally M. Weaver coll.), box 468, file 30 ("Iroquois politics, 1847–1940," 1975). LAC, RG 10, 2285, file 57169-1B, pt.3; RG 31, C1, 1871, 1881, 1901, Tuscarora Township, Ont. St John Fisher College, Lavery Library (Rochester, N.Y.), G. P. Decker papers. Ville de Genève, Suisse, Dép. municipal des affaires culturelles, Bibliothèque publique et universitaire, ms. fr. 3993 (Affaire "Six Nations"); ms. var. 1/15 (Les Six Nations iroquoises). *Canadian annual rev.*, 1922: 267–68. Carl Carmer, *Dark trees to the wind: a cycle of York State years* (New York, 1949), 105–17. *Deskaheh: Iroquois statesman and patriot* ([Rooseveltown, N.Y., 1978?]). "Documents: introduction to documents one through five; nationalism, the League of Nations and the Six Nations of Grand River," ed. Laurie Meijer Drees, *Native Studies Rev.* ([Saskatoon]), 10 (1995): 75–88. D. M. Johnston, "The quest of the Six Nations Confederacy for self-determination," Univ. of Toronto, Faculty of law, *Rev.*, 44 (1986): 1–32. Nellie Ketchukian, "Chief Deskaheh, George Decker and the Six Nations vs. the Government of Canada," *Iroquoian* (Rochester), no.11 (fall 1985): 12–18; "The Decker papers II: Decker and Chief Deskaheh in Geneva, 1923," *Iroquoian*, no.12 (spring 1986): 79–83. E. T. Montour, *The feathered U.E.L.'s: an account of the life and times of certain Canadian native people* (Toronto, 1973), 125–29. René Naville, *Amérindiens et anciennes cultures précolombiennes* (Genève, 1973), 144–49. Clinton Rickard, *Fighting Tuscarora: the autobiography of Chief Clinton Rickard*, ed. Barbara Graymont (Syracuse, N.Y., 1973), 58–68. Joëlle Rostkowski, "Deskaheh's shadow: Indians on the international scene," *European Rev. of Native American Studies* (Budapest), 9 (1995), no.2: 1–4; "The redman's appeal for justice: Deskaheh and the League of Nations," in *Indians and Europe: an interdisciplinary collection of essays*, ed. C. F. Feest (Aachen, Netherlands, 1987), 435–53. Annemarie Shimony, "Alexander General, 'Deskahe,' Cayuga-Oneida, 1889–1965," in *American Indian intellectuals; 1976 proceedings of the American Ethnological Society*, ed. Margot Liberty (St Paul, Minn., 1978), 158–75. E. B. Titley, *A narrow vision: Duncan Campbell Scott and the administration of Indian affairs in Canada* (Vancouver, 1986). S. R. Trevithick, "Conflicting outlooks: the background to the 1924 deposing of the Six Nations Hereditary Council" (MA thesis, Univ. of Calgary, 1998). Richard Veatch, *Canadian foreign policy and the League of Nations, 1919–1939* (Toronto, 1975), 91–100, 201–2. Sally Weaver, "The Iroquois: the Grand River reserve in the late nineteenth and early twentieth centuries, 1875–1945," in *Aboriginal Ontario: historical perspectives on the First Nations*, ed. E. S. Rogers and D. B. Smith (Toronto, 1994), 182–212.

DESROSIERS, AUGUSTIN (he also signed **Auguste**), industrialist, contractor, architect, and politician; b. 31 Jan. 1847 in Rivière-du-Loup (Louiseville) Lower Canada, son of David Desrosiers, a tanner, and Marguerite Godin; m. first around 1872, in the United States, Agnès Méthot of Rivière-du-Loup, and they had one son and two daughters; m. secondly 23 Feb. 1881 Caroline Coulombe in Louiseville, and they had one son; d. there 13 May 1927.

Augustin Desrosiers started out as an apprentice joiner with Pierre Hamel, who owned the shop next door to that of Augustin's father in the village of Rivière-du-Loup. At the beginning of the 1870s Desrosiers left his birthplace and joined Hamel in Syracuse, N.Y. Then he went with his elder brother David

to Westfield, Mass., where he worked for an organ builder. Returning to his native village in 1873, he was able to make immediate use of the knowledge he had acquired in the United States when the *fabrique* hired him to renovate the organ in the parish church, enlarge the rood-loft, and construct another above it. In 1874 he was called on to construct the Rivière-du-Loup convent of the Sisters of the Assumption of the Blessed Virgin Mary [*see* Edwige Buisson*], for which he drew up the plans. In the same year, in preparation for carrying out this large contract, Desrosiers opened a door and window factory in Rivière-du-Loup with his brother David, under the name A. Desrosiers et Frère.

Desrosiers was commissioned in 1878 to do other projects: erecting a building for the Rivière-du-Loup market and a house for a doctor's widow, and drawing up the plans for a hotel. He now decided to expand and diversify his activities. That year he and his brother had a sawmill built, with a door and window factory and a planing mill attached. A steam engine provided the power to run the various parts of this industrial complex, which was located on the river to the south of the village. It appeared certain that A. Desrosiers et Frère would be a profitable enterprise, since the Hunterstown Lumber Company's sawmill, the largest production facility in the parish, had recently shut down as a result of the negative effects the current economic crisis was having on forestry-related activities. As entrepreneurs, the Desrosiers brothers hoped to capture the local market for wood products which the American firm had previously controlled.

A succession of events cast a shadow over Desrosiers's plans, however. In 1878 his son and elder daughter died, as did his wife on 26 July 1879. Less than a month later, he was forced to declare bankruptcy, despite the financial support he had received from his father and his cousins Odilon and Agapit Desrosiers during the summer of 1879. Determined to carry on, Augustin and his brother reached an agreement with their creditors at the end of 1879. Once again David Desrosiers came to his sons' assistance by acting as guarantor for the repayment of their debts. In the event, on 2 Jan. 1880 the receiver ceded their property back to them. But Augustin's troubles were not over. Between 1880 and 1883 three people sued him for money owed. In July 1881 the Desrosiers brothers' industrial complex was auctioned off at the church door as a result of legal action taken by Léon Thérien, a Louiseville farmer who had sold them the land on which it had been built. However, the two brothers kept the door and window factory they had erected in 1874.

A few years later Desrosiers embarked on other projects, not all of which materialized. In 1887 he took out two loans totalling $3,000 from the corporation of the town of Louiseville and borrowed $800 from his father in order to build a new door and window factory. It also made organs for churches in Quebec, Ontario, and the United States. This factory, which had six employees in 1891, would remain in operation until after the death of its founder. In 1892 Desrosiers and four other entrepreneurs set up the Montreal Match Company, a match factory in Louiseville. Friction within the management brought about the company's liquidation even before it had begun production. Along with his industrial activities, Desrosiers continued to take on building contracts; from 1890 to 1896 he erected another match factory, a hotel, a school in Louiseville, an Anglican church in Sainte-Ursule, and two presbyteries, one in Louiseville and the other in Saint-Jérôme. Between 1900 and 1912 he entered into partnerships to open two insurance agencies in Louiseville. Desrosiers was well regarded by his fellow citizens, and served as mayor of Louiseville during the year 1902–3. While in office he continued his predecessors' policy of promoting industry.

Augustin Desrosiers is an excellent example of the dynamism of French Canadian businessmen. Armed with the experience he had gained in a family environment that included a number of artisans, he set up some of the largest industrial units in Louiseville in the last quarter of the 19th century. But his enthusiasm and energy ran up against a difficult economic situation and problems of financing. Unable to get help from the banks, Desrosiers, like many other French-speaking industrialists in the province, had to obtain loans from individuals by mortgaging property. This method of financing greatly reduces an entrepreneur's flexibility and makes long-term planning impossible. His career also shows the central role of the family within business. When setting up a company or looking for capital, Desrosiers turned first to his relatives.

JOCELYN MORNEAU

ANQ-MBF, CE401-S15, 31 janv. 1847, 23 févr. 1881; CN401-S106, 11 mai 1878; TP11, S3, SS2, SSS1, dossiers 67 (1879), 10 (1880), 566 (1893); SS20, SSS48. Arch. paroissiales, Saint-Antoine-de-Padoue (Louiseville, Qué.), RBMS, 1927. LAC, RG 31, C1, 1851, 1861, 1871, Rivière-du-Loup (Louiseville). *Le Courrier de Maskinongé* (Louiseville), 1878–79. *L'Écho de Louiseville* (Louiseville), 1895–96. *Le Journal des Trois-Rivières* (Trois-Rivières, Qué.), 1874. Germain Lesage, *Histoire de Louiseville, 1665–1960* (Louiseville, 1961). Jocelyn Morneau, "Louiseville en Mauricie au XIXᵉ siècle: la croissance d'une aire villageoise," *RHAF*, 44 (1990–91): 223–41; *Petits pays et grands ensembles; les articulations du monde rural au XIXᵉ siècle: l'exemple du lac Saint-Pierre* (Sainte-Foy, Qué., 2000). Que., Parl., *Sessional papers*, report of the secretary and registrar of the province of Quebec, 1892.

DEVILLE, ÉDOUARD (named at birth **Daniel-Édouard-Gaston**), surveyor, civil servant, and author; b. 21 Feb. 1849 in La Charité-sur-Loire, France, son of Charles Deville, a physician, and Estelle Tallard; m. 21 Feb. 1881 in Quebec Joséphine Ouimet, daughter of Gédéon Ouimet*, superintendent of public instruction, and they had one son; d. 21 Sept. 1924 in Ottawa.

Édouard Deville studied at the naval school in Brest and upon graduation in 1868 entered the French navy as a hydrographer. After spending several years, mostly in the South Pacific and Peru, on hydrographic surveys, he retired with the rank of captain in 1874. He immigrated to Quebec with his widowed mother and his sister that same year. Acting as astronomical assistant to Edward David Ashe*, he resurveyed parts of the upper Ottawa valley for the Quebec Crown Lands Department. He obtained his credentials as provincial land surveyor in 1877 and the next year successfully passed examinations for the commission of dominion land surveyor and the more difficult ones for the prestigious qualification of dominion topographical surveyor. These achievements brought him to the attention of Surveyor General Lindsay Alexander Russell, who invited him to join the examining board for dominion surveyors early in 1879. Over the next year he provided Russell with examination questions and astronomical tables, and cooperated in determining the longitude of Ottawa.

Deville left the Quebec Crown Lands Department to join the federal Dominion Lands Survey in 1880. His first year found him working in the Touchwood Hills (Sask.). Such were his abilities that he was promoted inspector of surveys in 1881 and chief inspector the following year. The second position took him out of the field and into the Ottawa office. During Russell's illness in 1884, he served as acting surveyor general, a rank that became permanent on Russell's retirement in 1885.

During Deville's first year in office, his staff began surveying the mountainous Canadian Pacific Railway belt in British Columbia. Open to the potential of photography to aid in the survey of difficult terrain, he supplied one man with a survey camera in 1886 and soon developed what became known as phototopography or photogrammetry. The first person to make this method work (it had been suggested in France in the early 1850s), he issued a guide to the new method in a limited edition in 1889. His interest in photography – he was a keen amateur photographer – also resulted in the use of copy cameras to reproduce maps for field use.

Deville was instrumental in bringing about Canada's adherence to the International Astronomical Union and the International Geodetic and Geophysical Union, established in 1919. Under a reorganization of the Department of the Interior in 1922, the

Geodetic Survey of Canada, which had been under the direction of William Frederick King* until his death in 1916, amalgamated with the international boundary commission and the topographical surveys branch of the department to form the Bureau of Surveys with Deville as director general. He continued to work until April 1924, when illness forced him to remain home. During his tenure he had brought scientific rigour to his branch, had strongly supported astronomical work, had used photography increasingly, and had stimulated cartography.

Deville had been a founding fellow of the Royal Society of Canada in 1882. An active participant in its affairs, he was secretary of section III from 1892 to 1912. His broader scientific interests led to his involvement in the Canadian Engineering Standards Association, the Town Planning Association of Canada, the Air Board, and the Association of Dominion Land Surveyors. A long-time parishioner of Sacré-Cœur in Ottawa, he was also a member of the St Luke's and Civic hospital boards, as well as a governor of the Alliance Française. Highly esteemed by the surveying and scientific communities, he was honoured with an LLD by the University of Toronto in 1905 and the Imperial Service Order in 1916. The Engineering Institute of Canada named him an honorary member in 1922. His colleagues considered Deville an exemplary scientific civil servant and respected him for his mathematical accomplishments. He had skilfully directed a forward-looking organization, one that employed the latest techniques to deal with the significant challenges of Canadian surveying.

RICHARD A. JARRELL

Édouard Deville is the author of *Examples of astronomic and geodetic calculations for the use of land surveyors* (Quebec, 1878) and *Photographic surveying: including the elements of descriptive geometry and perspective* (Ottawa, 1889; rev. ed., 1895). In addition, he contributed to the third edition of Can., Dominion lands branch, *Manual shewing the system of survey of the dominion lands, with instructions to surveyors* (Ottawa, 1871; [3rd ed.], 1883). These and other publications by Deville are listed in CIHM, *Reg.* A list of the papers he delivered before the Royal Society of Canada is available in RSC, *Index to the "Transactions" and other publications, 1882–1982,* comp. R. H. Hubbard (Ottawa, 1987). His reports as acting surveyor general and as surveyor general can be found in Can., Parl., *Sessional papers,* reports of the Dept. of the Interior, 1884–1918.

ANQ-Q, CE301-S1, 21 févr. 1881. Arch. Départementales, Nièvre (Nevers, France), État civil, La Charité-sur-Loire, 23 févr. 1849. LAC, MG 29, E114, file 1; RG 15, 82; 240, file 15882. *Le Droit* (Ottawa), 22 sept. 1924. *Globe,* 22 Sept. 1924. *Ottawa Citizen,* 22 Sept. 1924. *Ottawa Evening Journal,* 22 Sept. 1924. *Toronto Daily Star,* 22 Sept. 1924. *Canadian men and women of the time* (Morgan; 1898 and 1912). J. D. Craig, "Dr. Edouard Gaston Deville, director general of surveys, Department of the Interior, Ottawa," Royal Astronomical Soc. of Canada, *Journal* (Toronto) 18 (1924): 405–11. D. B. Dowling, "Edward Gaston Daniel Deville," RSC, *Trans.,* 3rd ser., 19 (1925), proc.: viii–ix. "E. G. Deville, I.S.O., D.T.S., hon. M.E.I.C.," *Engineering Journal* (Montreal), 7 (1924): 686–87. R. A. Jarrell, *The cold light of dawn: a history of Canadian astronomy* (Toronto, 1988). J. G. MacGregor, *Vision of an ordered land: the story of the Dominion Land Survey* (Saskatoon, 1981). D. W. Thomson, *Men and meridians: the history of surveying and mapping in Canada* (3v., Ottawa, 1966–69), 2–3.

DEVINE, EDWARD JAMES, Roman Catholic priest, Jesuit, editor, and author; b. 3 March 1860 in Bonnechere Point (Castleford), Upper Canada, son of John Devine and Maria McDonnell; d. 5 Nov. 1927 in Toronto.

After a public school education in Ottawa and experience as a printer in New York City, Edward James Devine returned to Canada to enter the Society of Jesus on 4 Sept. 1879 at Sault-au-Récollet (Montreal). During ten years of studies, including a year, 1882–83, near London, England, headaches interrupted his work and made his priestly education difficult for him. His taste for church history began at Trois-Rivières in 1883 when he examined the parish registers which included entries of Jesuit missionaries Paul Le Jeune* and Jacques Buteux* from as early as 1634. In 1885, with other Jesuit students, Devine moved to the newly founded Scolasticat de l'Immaculée-Conception in Montreal. He was able to persuade the rector to buy a Peerless Press to print the college calendar, the Canadian Jesuits' yearly *Catalogus . . . ,* and eventually and most important of all, the *Canadian Messenger of the Sacred Heart.*

Between 1885 and 1889 Devine worked at the Collège Sainte-Marie with Jesuit archivist Arthur Edward Jones, who was classifying Jesuit documents from the 17th and 18th centuries. From material in these archives, Devine estimated the actual value of the Jesuit estates [*see* Antoine-Nicolas Braun*] confiscated in 1800 to be worth $7,000,000. The society in fact received compensation of $160,000 from the provincial government of Honoré Mercier* in January 1889 after the passage of the Jesuits' Estates Act the previous year. In March 1889 a bill prepared by MPs D'Alton McCarthy* and William Edward O'Brien calling for federal disallowance of the act was introduced in the House of Commons. Jones and Devine supplied members of the house, especially the minister of justice, Sir John Sparrow David Thompson*, with facts and documents that helped defeat the motion. Devine was ordained to the priesthood in Montreal on 14 July 1889.

Devine welcomed the opportunity in 1893 to replace the legendary Jesuit Richard Baxter* in the missions along the Canadian Pacific Railway on the north shore of Lake Superior. Like Baxter, he lived modestly, and when in Schreiber, Ont., he stayed in a small shed he constructed up against the church. He completed churches in West Fort William and Murillo. Averaging around 30,000 miles of railway travel a year, he published a number of articles about the CPR in the *Month* (London, England). They came to the attention of Thomas George SHAUGHNESSY, vice-president of the CPR, who extended free passes to Jesuit missionaries in appreciation for their work in inspiring and stabilizing the railway communities.

In 1899 Devine returned to Montreal, where he took up the editorship of the *Canadian Messenger*. Subsequently he gave many retreats across the country and was well known as a spiritual guide and an entertaining speaker. He was preaching at St John's, Nfld, in 1902 when he was assigned to the Alaska mission on the opposite side of the continent. His adventures travelling to the Pacific coast were described in a series of articles, "Alaskan letters," which appeared in the *Canadian Messenger* in 1903–4. They formed the basis of *Across widest America, Newfoundland to Alaska, with the impressions of two years' sojourn on the Bering coast*, which he published when he returned to Montreal in 1905 and reissued in New York City the following year. At this time as well he brought out a novel, *The training of Silas* (Montreal and New York, 1906). Most of the remainder of his works were published in Montreal. To deepen appreciation of Christian life and family values for Catholics, he wrote *Fireside messages: adapted for reading in Catholic homes* in 1911. *Historic Caughnawaga* followed in 1922. After leading a pilgrimage to the major shrines of Europe in the summer of 1922, he published *Our tour through Europe* the next year. Also in 1923 he gathered together a series of pamphlets he had written on Jesuit martyrs, added a preface, and published the manuscript as *The Canadian martyrs*. It would go through another edition two years later as *The Jesuit martyrs of Canada*. To mark the erection of the Martyrs' Shrine Church near Midland, Ont., in 1925–26 he wrote the slim volume *Old Fort Ste. Marie: home of the Jesuit martyrs*. He was a longtime member of the Canadian Authors Association.

Devine had edited the *Canadian Messenger* until his departure for Alaska in 1902 and on his return three years later he again took the helm of this important publication to promote Catholic literature and devotion to the Sacred Heart across Canada. A separate French monthly, *Le Messager canadien du Sacré-Cœur de Jésus* (Montréal), edited by Jean-Baptiste Nolin*, had been founded in 1892. Each month the pope would select a general intention which would be disseminated in the magazines and prayed for by the members and friends of the Apostleship of Prayer [*see* Nolin]. By 1920 members and friends numbered more than 6,000,000 around the world and 180,000 in Canada. The articles on monthly intentions, many of which Devine wrote, gave the *Canadian Messenger* an ultramontane ring, since they emphasized missionary zeal, love of Roman devotions, and papal loyalty. Under his leadership the magazine discussed other topics of concern to Catholics, such as family spirituality, personal holiness, and community devotions, but prudently tempered them with a consideration of Catholic social thought, workers' rights, and higher education for Catholics.

After his return to Montreal, Devine also became a principal organizer of the Catholic Sailors' Club, the Catholic Women's League, and the Montreal Convalescent Home. The most celebrated service he rendered to the Canadian Catholic Church was his appearance before the apostolic commission on the holiness of the Jesuit martyrs held in Quebec City in 1922. Presented with great clarity, his lengthy testimony advanced the process of their beatification. This work came to fruition in Rome in 1925, two years before his own death, when the Catholic Church beatified the eight Jesuit martyrs, Jean de Brébeuf*, Gabriel Lalemant*, Isaac Jogues*, Antoine Daniel*, Charles Garnier*, Noël Chabanel*, René Goupil*, and Jean de La Lande*.

Devine's brief work in the missions maintained the Jesuit tradition of service for navvies, miners, and native peoples. His research on Jesuit history publicized the importance of religion in early Canada. His editorial and organizational skills helped to establish the *Canadian Messenger*, which was to become the longest-running Canadian Catholic monthly in English, a magazine published continually from 1891 to this day. Probably the best known Canadian Jesuit at the time of his death, Devine was the youngest of a group of conspicuous Jesuits who were recognized as skilled writers and preachers (among the others were George B. Kenny, William J. Doherty, Arthur Edward Jones, and Gregory O'Bryan*). While not a trained historian, Devine was an energetic author who provided information and inspiration to many. His memoirs reveal a sensitive person who enjoyed a humorous story well told.

TERENCE J. FAY

In addition to the publications mentioned above, and numerous articles in the *Canadian Messenger of the Sacred Heart*, Edward James Devine's writings include: "An ancient Jesuit shrine restored," *Woodstock Letters* (Woodstock, Md), 55 (1926): 397–404; "The end of the Jesuit estate affair," *Woodstock Letters*, 19 (1890): 85–91; *Irish soldiers in Canada, 1755–60: contribution to a disputed chapter in Canadian history* (Montreal, 1912); "Les Jésuites et les Iroquois," *Le Canada français* (Québec), 2ᵉ sér., 12 (1924–25): 763–72; "Jesuits versus Orangemen," *Woodstock Letters*, 18 (1889): 233–44, 285–304; "Masters and workmen," *Catholic Record* (London, Ont.), 6 July 1918.

Dewart

Arch. de la Compagnie de Jésus, Prov. du Canada Français (Saint-Jérôme, Qué.), D-7 (E. J. Devine), E. J. Devine, lettres d'Alaska. Soc. of Jesus, Upper Canada Prov. Arch., Regis College (Toronto), A-126, A-217a (E. J. Devine file). *Catholic Record*, 19 Nov. 1927. *Montreal Daily Star*, 7 Nov. 1927. *Les Nouvelles* (Montréal), novembre 1927. *True Witness and Catholic Chronicle* (Montreal), 18 Nov. 1896. *Dictionary of Jesuit biography: ministry to English Canada, 1842–1987* (Toronto, 1991). T. J. Fay, "The *Canadian Messenger of the Sacred Heart*, 1905–1927: window on ultramontane spirituality," CCHA, *Hist. studies*, 64 (1998): 9–26. P. J. Mulrooney, "A modern apostle of the Jesuit martyrs: Father Devine, s.J., 1860–1927," *Martyrs' Shrine Message* (Midland, Ont.), 5 (1941), no.1: 18–19. T. P. Slattery, *Loyola and Montreal* (Montreal, 1962). *Woodstock Letters*, 57 (1928): 260–64.

DEWART, HERBERT HARTLEY, lawyer and politican; b. 9 Nov. 1861 in St Johns (Saint-Jean-sur-Richelieu), Lower Canada, son of Edward Hartley Dewart* and Dorothy Matilda Hunt; m. 5 Feb. 1891 Emma J. Smith in Sparta, Ont.; d. 7 July 1924 near Uxbridge, Ont.

Hartley Dewart was born in St Johns during E. H. Dewart's time there as a Wesleyan Methodist preacher. In 1865 the family moved to Toronto, where his Irish-born father would rise to prominence as editor of the *Christian Guardian* and as a regent of Victoria University. Groomed for success in public life, Hartley attended Toronto's model school and collegiate institute; his oratorical gifts were undoubtedly encouraged by Dewart Sr, whose tracts included *The Canadian speaker and elocutionary reader* (Toronto, 1868). As a youth, Hartley was introduced to two of E. H. Dewart's most cherished causes: Liberal politics, where he would follow his father's convictions, and temperance, on which they would part ways.

In 1883 Dewart graduated from the University of Toronto with a BA. Recognizing law as a stepping stone to political life, he attended Osgoode Hall and was called to the bar in 1887. While studying law he had helped form the Young Men's Liberal Club, which he would serve as president in 1887–88. He practised in Toronto with various partners, among them William Edgar Raney*, a future political opponent, and in 1891 he was appointed a crown attorney for York County.

In 1895 Dewart was thrust into the limelight when, during the headline-grabbing trial of seamstress Clara Ford for murder, Britton Bath Osler* withdrew from the prosecution on account of his wife's death. The case seemed open-and-shut – Ford had confessed – but Dewart was unequal to the wily, seasoned defence lawyer, Ebenezer Forsyth Blackie Johnston*, and the jury made the extraordinary decision to acquit. Dewart's silver (and frequently sharp) tongue had nonetheless attracted admiration from the press and fellow members of the bar. In 1899 he was made a QC, and

his reputation grew as he helped prosecute some of the most colourful criminal cases at the turn of the century. Despite his later rise in politics, many contemporaries would hold him in greater esteem as a lawyer. After resigning as crown attorney in 1904, he continued in private practice, taking on civil work as well as criminal defences and acting as a solicitor for several prominent corporations, including the Canadian Pacific Railway. A leading member of the bar, he would be elected a bencher of the Law Society of Upper Canada in 1911. Following his father's example, he also found time to become involved in higher education (in 1906 he was elected to the senate of the University of Toronto, where he was an examiner in English), to write (on Irish-Canadian poetry among other topics), and to lecture. In January 1906, for instance, he addressed the Young Men's Liberal Club on the "popular character of the policy of the Liberal government in dealing with corporate power."

While in practice, the ambitious Dewart, an ardent admirer of Sir Wilfrid Laurier*, carefully cultivated ties to both the federal and the provincial Liberal organizations. His occasional participation as an opposing counsel in public investigations strengthened his understanding of electoral and governmental machinations. He ran unsuccessfully in two federal elections: 1904 (Toronto South) and 1911 (York Centre). His public profile changed in August 1916 with his entry into the Ontario legislature following a by-election in Toronto Southwest, the first time the Liberals had taken a Toronto seat since 1890. Though Dewart was a parliamentary neophyte, his aggressive debating skills, eloquence, and sterling legal talents soon shone.

Propelled and sometimes hampered by a streak of independence, he did not hesitate to take controversial stands on such sensitive issues as Prohibition and wartime conscription, both of which he opposed on constitutional grounds. From the time of his election he openly disavowed Liberal temperance policy, a stand that started a bitter feud with party leader Newton Wesley Rowell*. The split was exacerbated by Rowell's move in 1917 to the federal Union government, which Dewart and other so-called Laurier Liberals vigorously disliked. In June 1919 Dewart managed to take the Liberal leadership in Ontario, only to be denounced by Rowell and the Liberal press. The *Christian Guardian* dismissed him as the "chief representative of the liquor interests in the legislature."

Shortly after assuming the helm, Dewart faced his first test, the election of October 1919. Although it had been 14 years since the Liberals were in power, he set his sights on the premiership, but he misjudged the target. Party divisions undermined Liberal chances. Moreover, by focusing on his long-time rival, Conservative campaign manager (and future leader) George Howard Ferguson*, he miscalculated; like many urban politicians, he underestimated the simmering discontent among rural Ontarians. Voters found a protest voice in the upstart United Farmers of Ontario. During their turbulent four-year term, the irascible Dewart censured them relentlessly, especially Premier Ernest Charles Drury* and Attorney General W. E. Raney, but, with the Liberals plagued by internal discontent, he was unable to steer the party effectively in opposition. In 1921, suffering from ill health and bitter over the infighting, he relinquished his leadership to Liberal whip Francis Wellington Hay*. In the house, however, his combativeness continued unchecked. In May 1922, as Raney's bill authorizing a tax on racetrack betting was about to receive royal assent, Dewart, in "unprecedented" and "sensational" fashion, stood up and asked Lieutenant Governor Henry Cockshutt* if he had been advised of the bill's constitutionality. His final hour in electoral politics closed in June 1923 when he was soundly defeated by an undistinguished Conservative.

Dewart did not sink into a life of contemplation. He continued in private practice and later in 1923 he was appointed to the commission charged with producing a new consolidation of the statutes of Canada. That same year rumours circulated about his appointment to the Supreme Court of Canada, a post for which he likely yearned. Aged 62, he died at Brookdale, his country home near Uxbridge – obituaries assigned overwork as a cause – and was buried in Toronto's Necropolis. He was survived by his wife, mother, and brother. At his funeral, the roster of honorary pallbearers, among them Prime Minister William Lyon Mackenzie King*, and the messages of condolence from the likes of Ernest Lapointe*, Mackenzie's minister of justice, suggest that Dewart, had he lived, might well have received further rewards for his decades of public service and party loyalty.

CAROLYN STRANGE

ANQ-M, CE604-S32, 12 févr. 1862. AO, RG 80-5-0-185, no.2567. LAC, MG 27, II, F1. *Globe*, 8–10 July 1924. *Canadian annual rev.*, 1915–23. *Canadian men and women of the time* (Morgan; 1898 and 1912). H. [W.] Charlesworth, *Candid chronicles: leaves from the note book of a Canadian journalist* (Toronto, 1925). *Cyclopædia of Canadian biog.* (Rose and Charlesworth), vol.3. *Directory*, Toronto, 1887–1923. Peter Oliver, *G. Howard Ferguson: Ontario Tory* (Toronto, 1977). Margaret Prang, *N. W. Rowell, Ontario nationalist* (Toronto and Buffalo, N.Y., 1975). Carolyn Strange, "Wounded womanhood and dead men: chivalry and the trials of Clara Ford and Carrie Davies," in *Gender conflicts: new essays in women's history*, ed. Franca Iacovetta and Mariana Valverde (Toronto, 1992), 149–88.

DICKIE, ALFRED, lumberman, politician, and office holder; b. 28 March 1860 in Upper Stewiacke, N.S., son of James Edward Dickie, a merchant, and Harriet Tupper; m. 1886 Alice Amelia Dickie of Cornwallis, N.S., and they had three sons and two daughters; d. 6 Sept. 1929 in Halifax.

Alfred Dickie was educated in the public schools of Upper Stewiacke and at Dalhousie University in Halifax (BA 1879, MA 1883). He started his lumbering career in Stewiacke in 1890 in partnership with Avard Black, whom he bought out after six months, forming the Alfred Dickie Lumber Company. In 1896 he acquired a property and sawmill at Tusket in Yarmouth County, where T. N. McGrath, his assistant at Stewiacke, moved as manager and half owner. The following year he purchased properties at Ship Harbour and Liscomb, and in 1904 an area on the Sherbrooke River. By 1897 his firms constituted the leading lumber exporter in Nova Scotia next to the operations of Thomas Gotobed McMullen of Truro; Dickie and McGrath held 18,000 acres in the western part of the province and Alfred Dickie Lumber had 65,000 in Colchester, Pictou, Halifax, and Guysborough counties. The produce of Dickie's Stewiacke mill was transported on the Intercolonial Railway to Halifax; lumber from the Tusket mill was sent by steamship – he owned several – and later by the Halifax and South Western Railway. In 1900 Dickie formed, and became president of, the Grand River Pulp and Lumber Company, which cut pulpwood in Labrador and held 500 square miles of timber limits around Hamilton Inlet. It was these lands that sparked the ownership dispute over Labrador between Quebec and Newfoundland, with Quebec officials intervening by stamping Dickie's pulpwood as crown wood belonging to their province.

Beneath the veneer of prosperity, however, Dickie's business ventures suffered from the natural calamities that often struck forest and sawmilling operations and from the uncertain and volatile business cycles that plagued the lumber industry. His steam mills were seriously affected by fires; by 1897 Dickie had endured at least four that destroyed or damaged his facilities. Forest operations were heavily dependent on manpower, horses, and water and snow conditions. A dearth of water or an over-abundance or lack of snow could prove disastrous. With the rapid expansion of his business, these problems clearly contributed to Dickie overextending himself. By 1904 the manager of the Royal Bank of Canada in Nova Scotia, who financed his operations, was "taken severely to task" by his superior in Montreal for allowing Dickie's loans to reach the "enormous" figure of $634,040.39 without security. Dickie himself was criticized for not having incorporated his business and for carrying too little insurance on his stationary mills and none on his lumber shipments. Two years later all Dickie's assets were transferred to the Royal Bank, though he did retain one share to qualify as a director. He was appointed manager at a salary of $833 per month.

From 1904 Dickie continued to act as a prominent

Nova Scotian lumber baron. He posed as an owner, continued to manage his old properties, and was the frontman in seeking to sell them. In the prospectus of sale, it was stated that, according to conservative estimates, his properties were capable of producing and exporting 50–60 million board feet per year, and that the extent of his forest lands in Nova Scotia was between 350,000 and 400,000 acres. In 1904 Dickie was instrumental, with other Nova Scotian lumbermen and the provincial government, in sponsoring a report on Nova Scotia's pulpwood lands by Robert Mason of New York and Joseph Bureau of Quebec. Two years later his Nova Scotia and Labrador properties were offered for sale by the Forest Exploration and Lumber Company of Montreal, the latter at the price of $1,000,000. On 30–31 May 1907 Dickie and McGrath played a leading role in the annual meeting in Yarmouth of the Lumbermen's Association of Western Nova Scotia; the whole group was photographed during a visit to their mill in Tusket. In 1908 there were prospects of selling the Nova Scotia properties to the Traubridge Syndicate of London, England, and Dickie requested that the Royal Bank underwrite the bonds or stocks of the syndicate to the extent of $100,000. In the end, however, the effort failed.

In October 1911 Dickie and McGrath Limited had to cancel orders because their logs had been stranded all summer as a result of drought and the cold season was about to set in. The following year Dickie lost an entire winter's output of logs in Labrador. Then, in 1913, he and the Royal Bank finally managed to dispose of most of his forest lands. An American firm, the S. D. Warren Company, purchased the Tusket lands. Archibald Fraser*, of the Fraser Pulp and Lumber Company Limited in Plaster Rock, N.B., bought 247,815 acres of Dickie's remaining lands.

Dickie nonetheless managed to reconstitute Dickie Lumber as the Canadian Lumber Company Limited in Stewiacke. Although he retired and moved to Halifax in 1912, he continued to serve as president of this company and have an interest in it until his death. His son Rufus Edward, a one-time president of the Canadian Lumbermen's Association, was its general manager. Despite his crash, Alfred Dickie succeeded in building up his holdings once more. He certainly thought highly of his part in Nova Scotia's lumber industry. In testimony in Halifax before the federal royal commission on pulpwood in 1923, he confidently stated that "my operations and experience, I think, are larger . . . than any other individual ever has had in Canada." At the time, he held 25,000 acres of forest lands in Nova Scotia and considerable lands in Labrador, and both tracts were for sale. In 1914 he negotiated with Walker Brothers in Boston and William Whitmer and Sons in Philadelphia for the sale of his Nova Scotia holdings but the deliberations came to naught. In the 1920s he continued to pay $160 to Newfoundland's minister of agriculture and mines for the lease of 80 square miles of timber limits in Labrador.

Throughout his career Dickie was heavily involved in public affairs. In the provincial elections of 1894 and 1897 he unsuccessfully contested the riding of Colchester, in which Stewiacke was located. He was a school commissioner for Colchester, the first mayor of the town of Stewiacke from 1906 to 1911, the president of the local branch of the Canadian Manufacturers' Association, and an elder in his Presbyterian church. In Halifax he served as school commissioner in 1921–23, and president of the North British Society. He was involved there as well in the Halifax Association for Improving the Condition of the Poor, and was an elder of Fort Massey Presbyterian (United) Church.

After being confined by ill health to his home on South Park Street for two months, he passed away on 6 Sept. 1929 and was buried in the family plot at Stewiacke. Despite the ups and downs of his ventures, he died a wealthy man, with an estate valued at $315,000 plus life insurance.

L. ANDERS SANDBERG

Dalhousie Univ. Arch. (Halifax), MS 4-64 (Alfred Dickie fonds, 1860–1929); MS 4-123 (Forest Exploration Lumber Company). LAC, RG 39, 593. *Halifax Herald*, 7, 9 Sept. 1929. "Alfred Dickie joins great majority," *Canada Lumberman* (Toronto), 49 (1929), no.19: 40. *Canadian men and women of the time* (Morgan; 1912). A. W. H. Eaton, *History of King's County* . . . (Salem, Mass., 1910; repr. Belleville, Ont., 1972). R. S. Johnson, *Forests of Nova Scotia: a history* (Halifax, 1986). Mike Parker, *Woodchips and beans: life in the early lumber woods of Nova Scotia* (Halifax, 1992). B. R. Robertson, *Sawpower: making lumber in the sawmills of Nova Scotia* (Halifax, 1986). *Trouble in the woods: forest policy and social conflict in Nova Scotia and New Brunswick*, ed. L. A. Sandberg (Fredericton, 1992).

DICKSON, EMMA LUCY. *See* WELLS

DIONNE, CHARLES-EUSÈBE, taxidermist, museum curator, ornithologist, naturalist, and author; b. 20 July 1846 in Saint-Denis, near Kamouraska, Lower Canada, son of Eusèbe Dionne and Amélie (Émilie) Lavoie; m. 6 May 1879 Marie-Émélie Pelletier at Quebec; they had no children; d. there 25 Jan. 1925 and was buried 28 January in the Saint-Charles cemetery.

Charles-Eusèbe Dionne was the eldest in a hardworking family of 11 children: six boys and five girls. Despite their modest means (Eusèbe was a cobbler and farmer), both parents attached considerable importance to education. As a child, Charles-Eusèbe showed a predilection for nature, especially birds. He did his share of the farm work from an early age, attended local rural schools, and completed elementary schooling at about 14. Eager to learn and endowed with a keen intelligence, he used his free time to increase the knowledge he had acquired at school by reading the few books he could find. He also attended private classes given by a teacher in the village.

In 1865 Dionne went to Quebec; obtaining a routine job (as a handyman) at the Séminaire de Québec, he immediately came to the attention of his employers and in 1866 he was promoted to the position of attendant in the faculty of law at the Université Laval. This post gave him access to the university library and to books on natural history not previously available to him. He was now able to continue his personal education through reading and attending evening classes, with the encouragement of the priests at the seminary. Strongly motivated and possessed of an astonishing capacity for work, Dionne acquired a good knowledge of natural science, English, and Latin. He began studying taxidermy, which he would master within a few years; it would lead him to assemble collections of natural history specimens. From 1867 he took a keen interest in entomology (Abbé Léon Provancher* would recognize Dionne's competence in 1879 by naming a new species in his honour – *tryphon dionnei*). By 1887 his entomological collection contained some 1,525 species. Always meticulous, Dionne noted his findings about the anatomy, diet, and economic importance of the animals he mounted or observed, and about plant life. He would later use this material in his publications.

After his humble beginnings at the Séminaire de Québec and several years as assistant librarian, Dionne's personal and intellectual merits, as well as his store of knowledge, which he kept up to date, were acknowledged by his superiors there. In 1882, on the death of François-Xavier Bélanger*, he was appointed curator of the Musée Zoologique at the Université Laval with an annual salary of $350. As curator, he was instrumental in developing the university's natural history collections and in displaying the fauna of Quebec to the students and the public by means of mounted specimens. The university would recognize the value of his work by granting him an MA in September 1902 and an honorary doctorate in science a few days before his death.

In 1893 Dionne was made an elective member of the American Ornithologists' Union, in recognition of his competence as a North American ornithologist. It was mainly through his publications that he had become known to the public and to naturalists in Quebec, the rest of Canada, and the United States. In 1883 he had published at Quebec *Les oiseaux du Canada*, which had been favourably received in French-speaking circles, although the English-speaking critics had been harsher in their assessment of its worth. His *Catalogue des oiseaux de la province de Québec, avec des notes sur leur distribution géographique* was brought out at Quebec in 1889. It was

a new edition of his first work, with information not relating to Quebec deleted and appropriate data added from the *Check-list of North American birds*, which had been published in New York by the American Ornithologists' Union in 1886. *Les mammifères de la province de Québec* came out at Quebec in 1902 and met with immediate success throughout the province. Here, for the first time, information was available in French about the mammals of Quebec. His major work, *Les oiseaux de la province de Québec*, was published at Quebec in 1906. This volume of more than 400 pages presented every species of bird that had been recorded in Quebec. One of its great virtues was that, for the first time in Canada, French terminology for the anatomy of birds was given, as well as consistent French names for all the species included. The information it contained combined various observations that Dionne had made with a synthesis of ornithological knowledge either provided by the best writers of the time, among them Elliott Coues and Robert Ridgway, or taken from sources such as the 1895 *Check-list of North American birds*. The details about the geographical distribution of species in Quebec were based on notes that Dionne had accumulated throughout his career, especially in the Quebec and Saint-Denis regions. He also relied on the works of Napoléon-Alexandre COMEAU for the Godbout and Côte-Nord region and of Ernest Douglas Wintle for the Montreal region (*The birds of Montreal*, published in Montreal in 1896). For a long time *Les oiseaux de la province de Québec* was the only book dealing exclusively with the birds of the province, and it helped make them better known to the French-speaking community. Dionne also had a number of articles dealing with the distribution of birds in Quebec in prominent scientific journals such as the *Auk* (the American Ornithologists' Union) and *Le Naturaliste canadien*. It was in the latter journal also that his long article on spiders, "Nos araignées: mœurs et description," appeared in 1910; the result of meticulous observations, it was brought out in pamphlet form at Quebec that same year.

Apart from local excursions, a few visits to Saint-Denis, and an expedition to collect fish in the estuary and Gulf of St Lawrence and the Baie des Chaleurs in 1882, a trip to Trois-Rivières, Montreal, and Ottawa in 1907, a cruise on the Saguenay in 1914, and another trip to Montreal in 1916–17, Dionne travelled little, especially outside the province of Quebec. He did, however, visit the Field Museum of Natural History and the Columbian exposition in Chicago in 1893, as well as the American Museum of Natural History and the zoos at New York in 1911. He spent some weeks in Europe in 1912, travelling around several regions of Italy, Switzerland, France, and England. Among the places he visited in Paris were the Muséum National d'Histoire Naturelle and the

Dixon

Jardin des Plantes. In London he went to the British Museum.

An exceptional self-educated man, Charles-Eusèbe Dionne in a noteworthy way helped make nature, and especially birds, known and appreciated at a time when the daily necessities of life took precedence. Although his immediate influence was mainly confined to the Quebec City region, his works circulated more widely in French-speaking parts of the country for many years.

HENRI OUELLET

ANQ-BSLGIM, CE104-S15, 21 juill. 1846. ANQ-Q, CE301-S22, 6 mai 1879. MCQ-FSQ, SME 1/MS-34.6, 16 sept. 1902; MS-34.10, 13 mai 1918; MS-34.11, 25 janv. 1925; Séminaire, 561, no.18; SME, 1er juill. 1873, 19 juin 1877, 7 oct. 1907, 19 janv. 1925. La Presse, 8 sept. 1937. D. A. D. [D.-A. Déry], "In memoriam: Charles Eusebe Dionne, born July 11, 1845, died January 25, 1925," Canadian Field-Naturalist (Ottawa), 39 (1925): 61–63. "Feu C.-E. Dionne," Le Naturaliste canadien (Québec), 52 (1925): 171–75. Victor Gaboriault, Charles-Eusèbe Dionne, naturaliste, né à Saint-Denis-de-la-Bouteillerie (La Pocatière, Qué., 1974). H. F. L[ewis], "Dr. Charles Eusebe Dionne," Auk: a Quarterly Journal of Ornithology (Lancaster, Pa), 42 (1925): 308–9.

DIXON, JOHN, businessman and rancher; b. 4 May 1850 in Smith Township, Upper Canada, son of Joseph Dixon and Margaret Brown; m. 20 June 1877 Agnes Christie (Addie) Dawson in South Monaghan Township, Ont., and they had two daughters and two sons; d. 3 Jan. 1922 in Maple Creek, Sask.

Few men of the early west can rival John Dixon in vision and accomplishment. Descended from one of the oldest families in Peterborough County, Upper Canada, his grandparents having arrived from Alston, Cumberland, England, in 1818, Dixon received his education there and later at the School of Military Instruction in Kingston. He then entered into a general mercantile business with his younger brother Isaac Chester in Oshawa.

In 1882 John, who was interested in business opportunities in the west, made an exploratory trip as far as Brandon, Man. Favourably impressed, the brothers decided to relocate. The following year they sold their property, saw to the temporary welfare of their wives (who were sisters and both pregnant at the time), secured a train car for their merchandise, and headed west with Calgary as their intended destination. By April 1883 they had reached the end of the rails at Maple Creek and, aware that the Canadian Pacific Railway would not get to Calgary until the fall, they set up business in a tent amidst the bustling community. Recognizing the potential of the area, the Dixons decided to remain and secured temporary quarters from the CPR until their new frame store was completed in 1884.

From this small store Dixon Brothers expanded over the next two decades to become one of the largest and most reputable firms between Moose Jaw (Sask.) and Calgary. The partnership operated smoothly with John managing its various enterprises and Chester concerning himself with day-to-day operations. During the store's formative years John Dixon was particularly astute in establishing business relationships with the CPR, the North-Western Coal and Navigation Company Limited of Lethbridge (Alta) [see Elliott Torrance GALT], the local "76" ranches of the Canadian Agricultural, Coal and Colonization Company, and A Division headquarters of the North-West Mounted Police at Maple Creek.

John Dixon was quick to capitalize upon other business opportunities that arose with the opening of the frontier. In 1884 he secured the government contract for the post office and located it in the company's store. The firm also offered banking services to the community until a branch of the Merchants' Bank of Canada was inaugurated in 1901. From 1888 to 1894 Dixon Brothers engaged in the buffalo bone trade as well, shipping carloads of bones to dealers and fertilizer firms in Minnesota and Illinois. The trade was so successful in 1890 that, in addition to the 31 cars already sent, John Dixon petitioned the CPR for others to accommodate the inundation of bones they had stockpiled at various railway sidings.

Shortly after their arrival in 1883, the Dixons had established one of the largest ranches in the northwest. They ran hundreds and at times thousands of cattle, horses, and sheep on the vast open-range grasslands north of Maple Creek. Following the devastating winter of 1906–7 and the succeeding influx of homesteaders, they were forced to consolidate their operations. However, at the time of John Dixon's death, the DB Ranch, as it was known, still had over 24,000 acres of deeded and leased lands.

The success of the Dixons' various enterprises was the result of shrewd management, efficient operations, and a compatible business relationship. Although John was the predominant partner and manager, Chester brought invaluable skills that complemented his brother's. Also of significance was their close personal relationship, strengthened by their ties through marriage. Their wives and young children had joined them in Maple Creek in the fall of 1883 and the two families shared a commodious home on the west side of the town site, a congenial arrangement that continued for over 30 years.

The more entrepreneurial of the two brothers, John was also opportunistic and he managed to secure a number of important government appointments that were advantageous to both the firm and his own ambitions. Not only was he chosen as the second postmaster for Maple Creek in 1884, but he became a notary public in 1889 and a licence commissioner and justice of the peace in 1892. He was also the more civic-minded. During the North-West rebellion [see Louis Riel*] he was a member of the Home Guard and allowed the store to be used as a small armoury, from which weapons were distributed to the settlers. He was the principal influence behind the development of Maple Creek, which fast became one of the major shipping points for western beef. Instrumental in forming almost all of its early institutions and organizations, he at one time or another held executive positions with most. Among his numerous offices, he was president of the first board of trade in 1889, first mayor of Maple Creek in 1903–4, and first president of the Saskatchewan Range Growers' Association in 1906. He was active in the masonic order, as a charter member of Maple Leaf Lodge No.56 in Maple Creek (1893) and as district deputy grand master of the Grand Lodge of Manitoba (1903–4) and the Grand Lodge of Saskatchewan (1907–8). He also held executive positions with the local branches of the Ancient Order United Workmen and the Independent Order of Foresters.

A devoted Methodist, Dixon had been active in securing the services of an itinerant minister in 1884 and in establishing a church two years later. His interest in church and education led to his support of the founding of Alberta College in Edmonton in 1903 and his appointment to its first board of governors, a position he held until 1912.

Dixon, a staunch Liberal and confidant of Thomas Walter Scott*, the Liberal leader in Assiniboia West who would become first premier of Saskatchewan, was not without political aspirations of his own. During the discussions leading to provincial autonomy in 1905, and on other occasions over the ensuing years, he lobbied for a seat in the Canadian Senate. Although he had the support of Scott, who told him in 1905 that he knew no one in the North-West Territories "better fitted generally to occupy a seat in the Senate with credit to himself and advantage to the country," the appointment did not materialize. Following consultation with Scott, Dixon resigned from his government positions that year and ran as the Liberal candidate for Maple Creek in the first provincial election. In a surprising but well-contested race he lost to the Provincial Rights candidate, David James Wylie, a prominent rancher who nevertheless did not have Dixon's public profile. Although Dixon never again ran for office, he continued to advise the government, especially in matters related to southwest Saskatchewan. In 1906 he was reappointed a notary public. He was also named to the board of governors of the new University of Saskatchewan in 1908 and of Regina College in 1912; he held both positions until 1921.

Dixon had continued to explore business opportunities, invest in real estate, and purchase shares in numerous companies throughout the prairies, for both the firm and on occasion himself. In 1909 he became a major shareholder in the Alberta Clay Products Company Limited of Medicine Hat, Alta; he was its vice-president from 1911 to 1920 and president in 1921. Dixon also sat on the board of directors for the Saskatchewan Loan and Investment Company Limited of Moose Jaw (1912–21) and was vice-president of the Canadian Hunt Manufacturing Company Limited of Maple Creek (1920–21).

The death of Chester Dixon in 1918 was a blow to John and to the firm. Fortunately, Chester's sons Alfred Lyman and Dawson Chester were able to fill the void and operations continued. Although John had relied heavily on Chester, he also consulted frequently with his elder brother Jonathan B., a lawyer in Reno, Nev. Dixon's astute business sense, awareness of stock market trends, and shrewd leadership are evident in his correspondence with Jonathan, especially in regard to his role with Alberta Clay Products, one of Medicine Hat's leading industries. Their correspondence in late 1920 reveals that the federal government had considered Dixon as successor to Sir Richard Stuart Lake, the lieutenant governor of Saskatchewan. In one letter Dixon cites a number of personal reasons for not accepting the position; however, he intimates that he is still desirous of a seat in the Senate. Had he won the election of 1905, and had his friend Premier Scott not been forced by ill health to resign in 1916, he might eventually have realized his dream.

John Dixon died suddenly on 3 Jan. 1922 at his home in Maple Creek. His death was a shock to his family, his community, and his province, all of which he had helped shape. He had come west with a vision, spent a lifetime pursuing it, and left an indelible impression. John and Chester's two original investments, the store and ranch, continued to operate under John's nephews; the ranch would be sold in the mid 1940s and the store in December 1958.

DONNY WHITE

AO, RG 80-5-0-74, no.7372. GA, M 1462. Medicine Hat Museum and Art Gallery Arch. (Medicine Hat, Alta.), M94.1 (Maple Creek vital statistics), files 1–92; M2002.1 (John Bennett coll.), files 2390–98; Library, Biog. community information, clippings and biog. files, Dixon, John. Saskatchewan Arch. Board (Regina), R-31 (Dixon Brothers coll.), letter-books and files. Southwestern Saskatchewan Old Timers' Museum (Maple Creek, Sask.), Dixon Brothers coll. *Maple Creek News* (Maple Creek), 1922. *Medicine Hat News* (Medicine Hat), 1922. *Peterborough Examiner* (Peterborough, Ont.), 28 June 1877. Alberta College, *Calendar* (Edmonton), 1907–8, 1910–12; *Yearbook*, 1904 (copies at City of Edmonton Arch., MS 254). Lawrence Binkley *et al.*, *Maple Leaf Lodge #9 A.F. & A.M.–G.R.S., 1893–1993* (Maple Creek, 1993), 2. N. F. Black, *History of Saskatchewan and the North-West Territories* (2v., Regina, 1913), 1. *Canadian encyclopedia*, 3: 1663. Eileen and Glen French, *Dawson:*

Dixon

Dawson family history, 1653–1997, from Yorkshire, England, to Ontario, Canada (n.p., 1998). *Maple Creek & area: where past is present* (2v., Maple Creek, 2000), 1. A. L. O'Farrell, "Maple Creek's first bank," *Canadian Cattlemen* (Calgary), 13 (1950), no.2: 35. *Our pioneers*, [comp. Gwen Pollock] ([Maple Creek, 1979?]). Univ. of Regina, [*Calendar*], 1912–21 (copies at Univ. of Regina Arch. and Special Coll.). Univ. of Sask., *Calendar* (Saskatoon), 1908–21 (copies at Univ. of Sask. Arch.). Ruth Dixon Yuill, *From England to Canada* ([Medicine Hat, 1980?]; copy in Medicine Hat Museum and Art Gallery Arch., M2002.1, file 2397).

DIXON, WINONA MARGARET. *See* FLETT

DMYTRIW, NESTOR, Greek (Eastern rite) Catholic priest, interpreter, and author; b. 1863 in Utishkiv (Ukraine); d. 27 May 1925 in Elizabeth, N.J.

Nestor Dmytriw was born into a peasant family in Galicia (Ukraine). While a theology student at the Greek Catholic Theological Seminary in Lemberg (Lviv, Ukraine), he belonged to a group of students who emphasized the importance of community service. In the early 1890s, with the beginning of massive emigration to North America from the Ukrainian regions of the Austro-Hungarian empire (Galicia, Bukovyna, and, to a lesser extent, Transcarpathia), the need for spiritual leaders of the Greek Catholic and Orthodox churches in the New World moved Dmytriw and his friends to urge young priests to follow the immigrants.

In 1895, after his ordination, Dmytriw himself arrived in the United States, where he combined missionary work among the Ukrainian industrial labourers of Pennsylvania with journalism. He became associated with the first Ukrainian-language newspaper in North America, *Svoboda* [Liberty], which originated in Jersey City, N.J. The paper, which featured stories about the immigrant experience in the United States and Canada, was widely read in Galicia and thus became the first major link between North America and Austrian Ukraine.

After *Svoboda* received letters from early Ukrainian settlers in the Canadian west desperately requesting the services of a priest, the newly formed Ruthenian National Association (renamed in 1914 the Ukrainian National Association), a mutual aid society in the United States, sent Dmytriw to Canada. With assistance from Jósef Olesków*, later known as the father of Ukrainian immigration to Canada, Dmytriw, who spoke Ukrainian, German, and English, was appointed an interpreter for the Canadian immigration branch. There he joined the first Ukrainian immigration officer, Cyril GENYK. His position enabled him to become a keen observer of the settlement process.

Although Dmytriw was in Canada for only a short time, April 1897 to August 1898, he left a lasting legacy. As the first Ukrainian priest in Canada, he organized the earliest Ukrainian parishes: at Terebowla (Valley River) and Stuartburn in Manitoba and at Edna (Star) in Alberta. He provided spiritual care when the settlers needed it the most. His advocacy of a separate Greek Catholic church in Canada was initially strongly opposed by the Roman Catholic hierarchy [*see* Adélard Langevin*], but it would finally be realized in 1912 with the appointment of Nykyta Budka* as apostolic exarch for Ukrainian Catholics in Canada. Catholics formed the vast majority of the nearly 150,000 Ukrainians who had immigrated to Canada by that date.

Dmytriw's most important contribution to Canadian history lies in his writings. His best known and probably his most influential work initially appeared as articles in *Svoboda* in 1897 and was published that year as a booklet entitled *Kanadiis'ka Rus'/Canadian Ruthenia*. Other notable articles in *Svoboda* based on his experiences and astute observations included "Z Halifaksu do Winnipegu" [From Halifax to Winnipeg], "Vona vyishala za menonita" [She married a Mennonite], "Obrazky z Kanady" [Images of Canada], "Tymko Hawryliuk," "Assimilation," and "Rus'ka paskha a frantsuz'kyi ks'ondz" [Ruthenian Easter and the French priest]. These writings, often sprinkled with satire and sarcasm, emphasized the shock of cultural and physical adjustment to Canada. A devoted and trusted pastor, Dmytriw saw himself as guardian of and teacher to the disoriented Ukrainian pioneers. Most of his vivid stories dwell on their difficulties and failures, which he attributed largely to their unpreparedness. Ignorant of Canada and unable to speak English, they received little guidance from immigration authorities; in fact, many fell victim to unscrupulous land speculators. Dmytriw agreed with Olesków that Canada was not for everyone. Since successful homesteading required capital and intelligence in addition to hard work, only those peasants with means and literacy should contemplate it. Furthermore, he recognized the psychological difficulties of adjustment on the harsh and remote Canadian prairies. Still, to those determined to come, he offered much practical advice.

From his travels across Canada, Dmytriw realized that Ukrainians were held in contempt by earlier settlers. Instances of drunkenness and boorish behaviour, which he blamed on the legacy of serfdom, caused them to be viewed as undesirable. He severely criticized the Ukrainian intelligentsia and clergy for failing to educate the peasantry. He held up as role models those Ukrainian immigrants who strove to learn English, Canadian farming methods, and the perceived higher culture of their new homeland. Despite his seeming pessimism, he believed that the children of the immigrants would succeed in Canada.

Physical exhaustion and financial difficulties obliged Dmytriw to return to the United States in 1899 for a well deserved rest. There he continued to contribute to *Svoboda*, writing on social and church topics. The popularity of his Canadian stories prompted him to publish his observations of Ukrainian life in Pennsylvania. On occasion, he even encouraged unemployed miners and industrial workers to take up farming in western Canada. He served several Ukrainian Catholic parishes in Pennsylvania and New Jersey. A liberal thinker and a social activist, he was often at odds with the conservative elements in the Ukrainian church. Little is known about his final years.

OLEH W. GERUS

Nestor Dmytriw is the author of *Kanadiis'ka Rus'; podorozhni spomyny/Canadian Ruthenia* [; travel reminiscences] (Jersey City, N.J., 1897; repr. Winnipeg, 1972) [text in Ukrainian].

Encyclopedia of Ukraine, ed. Volodymyr Kubijovyc (5v. in 6, Toronto, 1984–93). *Jubilee book of the Ukrainian National Association: in commemoration of the fortieth anniversary of its existence*, ed. Luka Myshuha (Jersey City, 1936) [text in Ukrainian]. V. J. Kaye, *Early Ukrainian settlements in Canada, 1895–1900; Dr. Josef Oleskow's role in the settlement of the Canadian northwest* (Toronto, 1964). M. H. Marunchak, *Biographical dictionary to the history of Ukrainian Canadians* (Winnipeg, 1986) [text in Ukrainian]. Jaroslav Petryshyn, *Peasants in the promised land: Canada and the Ukrainians, 1891–1914* (Toronto, 1985). Julian Stechishin, *History of Ukrainian settlements in Canada* (Edmonton, 1975) [text in Ukrainian], translated by Isidore Goresky as *A history of Ukrainian settlement in Canada*, ed. David Lupul (Saskatoon, 1992).

DOMINO NOIR. *See* MARMETTE, MARIE-LOUISE

DOMVILLE, JAMES, businessman, politician, and militia officer; b. 29 Nov. 1842 in Belize, British Honduras (Belize), only son of James William Domville and Frances Usher; m. 25 April 1867 Anne Isabella Scovil in Portland (Saint John), N.B., and they had three sons and five daughters; d. 30 July 1921 in Rothesay, N.B.

James Domville was reputedly a descendant through his mother of an early archbishop of Armagh (Northern Ireland). His father, who would move to New Brunswick in 1875, attained the rank of major-general in the Royal Artillery in 1868, having served in India, British Honduras, and Barbados. The younger Domville was groomed for active service. He attended the Royal Military Academy in Woolwich (London), a school in Bonn (Germany), and the École Spéciale Militaire de Saint-Cyr in France, but in 1858 he joined Michael Cavan and Company in Barbados. A division of Cavan, Lubbock and Company of Great Britain, the firm engaged in a general goods trade that served as Domville's introduction to mercantile affairs. Henceforth his military career would be limited to the militia of New Brunswick, where he moved in 1866. Settling in the port of Saint

John, he served in the militia during the Fenian raid that year and, in business, established a direct trade with the British West Indies that undoubtedly owed much to the contacts he had developed under Cavan.

As James Domville and Company, he dealt in teas and other goods from offices on the North Wharf in Saint John. Soon after his arrival he formed a partnership with merchant William Henry Scovil, whose daughter he married in 1867. Under the name Domville, Scovil and Company, the two men operated a variety of manufacturing businesses, including a merchant-bar and iron-rolling mill at Moosepath station, on the Intercolonial Railway northeast of Saint John, and a nail factory at nearby Coldbrook. Following his father-in-law's death on 8 July 1869, Domville assumed full ownership of the company. Its several operations subsequently came to be known as the Coldbrook Rolling Mills Company, which, under Domville's management, did quite well during the 1870s; federally incorporated in 1873, it paid a dividend of 12 per cent the following year. His interests eventually embraced resources and financial services. Through the General Oil Shales Company he urged the development of oil reserves in Albert County in southeast New Brunswick. In 1872 he helped establish the Maritime Bank of the Dominion of Canada in Saint John. He served as a director and a president, as did his father, but his reputation was tarnished by revelations in 1880 of his heavy indebtedness to the bank, which failed in 1887. Domville also served on the boards of two Montreal-based companies, Globe Mutual Life Assurance and Stadacona Fire and Life Insurance. His businesses were primarily located between the Bay of Fundy and the Ottawa valley, but as early as the late 1870s he was looking at opportunities in western Canada.

The expansion of his business enterprises led Domville into politics. Returned to the House of Commons in 1872 as the Conservative member for Kings – he established a home there (in Rothesay) in the early 1870s – he was defeated by George Eulas Foster* in 1882. An article in the Saint John *Telegraph-Journal* in 1929 would note that Domville had introduced a new style of electioneering that "did not appeal to the quiet thinkers" or "the rigid Baptists ... [who] were seeing a new apostle in the suave, eloquent and persuasive Foster." An Anglican, Domville may well have been less to the liking of local Baptists than Foster, who was one of their own. Moreover, as Foster put it, "his habits did not commend themselves to the Temperance wing of the electorate" in 1882. Domville, in fact, had been an open-fly participant in the famous drinking spree in the commons in April 1878, prior to the passage of the Canada Temperance Bill. But a deeper cause of displeasure lay in the National Policy of the Conservative government of Sir John A. Macdonald*. During a debate on its trade and industrial policies in 1879, Domville had nearly come to blows with fellow New Brunswicker Arthur Hill Gillmor*, the Liberal MP for Charlotte. Domville's network of business associates in central Canada led him to support the government's protectionist policies, yet voters in Kings came to realize that they were not fostering the development of local manufacturing. Domville's defeat in 1882, then, was as much a result of trade issues as personalities. Thus began a 14-year absence from the commons in which he rethought his position and his allegiance to the Conservative party.

Domville's time in Ottawa overshadowed his short career as a municipal politician between 1877 and 1880. During his term as an alderman on Saint John's Common Council, he chaired its finance committee, but he gave local matters short shrift. Saint John newspapers did not lament his failure to be re-elected in 1880. The *Daily Telegraph*, for instance, remarked on 7 April 1880 that Domville had appeared more promising as a candidate than he was in office: "The intermittent attention that gentleman was able to give the business did not do much good to the city and scarcely added anything to his reputation. His mind is not adapted to a small business of a city like ours and since he began to be troubled with the Western fever he wisely resolved to leave the field to others."

Yet it was also during this period that Domville launched his most enduring public work. The great fire of 1877 in Saint John, which had destroyed many private libraries as well as his commercial premises, prompted him to adopt the idea of a public library. Common Council had discussed such a project prior to the fire, and the disaster gave it impetus. Through Domville's efforts, circulars were distributed requesting donations. The initiative brought in almost 3,000 books, which were committed to a city-administered trust in 1880. To a degree the books reflected Domville's professional and personal interests. William Elder*, an MHA for Saint John County and City, estimated that not more than half were worth including, "the others consisting mostly of statistical works, containing materials for the speeches of politicians." At a meeting on 14 Sept. 1880 Domville described the collection as "nearly all works of reference" and noted that there were "a number of valuable books . . . which could not be procured in America." Some were culled, but even so, when the library opened on 18 May 1883, it could offer 2,285 volumes.

A member of masonic bodies in Saint John and a president of the Kings County Board of Trade, Domville also maintained a local profile through the militia. He joined New Brunswick's 8th Regiment of Cavalry in 1878, and was promoted lieutenant-colonel and its provisional commanding officer on 23 April 1880; he was confirmed as commander on 2 July 1881. The unit was designated the 8th (Princess Louise's New Brunswick) Regiment of Cavalry in

1884. Domville offered it for imperial service in the Sudan that year, and again in 1896. Though the offer was refused both times, the profusive thanks of Colonial Secretary Joseph Chamberlain in 1896 gave the regiment and Domville much publicity.

Sustained perhaps by his continuing local prominence, Domville remained determined to return to federal politics. For the elections of 1885 (a by-election), 1887, and 1891, he placed himself among the strange assortment of candidates billed as independents. In New Brunswick this group of adamant individualists were disappointed with the results of the National Policy and felt betrayed by the Macdonald government's preference for Halifax as the leading transatlantic port over Saint John. At each election, however, Domville was defeated by Foster. His dissatisfaction finally led him into the Liberal camp, and in 1896, with Foster running in York, he re-entered the commons for Kings. Though denied his request to be made minister of militia and defence, he enjoyed a good relationship with Liberal leader Wilfrid Laurier*. He travelled to England with the prime minister for the diamond jubilee of Queen Victoria in 1897, and his professional experience made him an ideal choice as chair of the commons' standing committee on banking and commerce. Some historians see Domville, certainly after his return to parliament, as a shameless self-promoter. Desmond Morton, for one, views him as "one of the most troublesome of the political colonels in the Jubilee contingent."

In Ottawa, Domville found time to pursue commercial projects in Ontario, as well as the west. He was a vice-president of the Ottawa River Railway Company, incorporated in 1903, and a president of its successor, the Central Railway Company of Canada. (Neither line was built.) In 1897, with the support of a consortium in England, he had commissioned a firm in North Vancouver to build two steamers and he planned a rail line, later named the Edmonton, Yukon and Pacific, to service the newly discovered Klondike goldfields. These projects were ill-starred. The railway was surveyed but never laid, and the *Lightning* and the *James Domville* would meet untimely ends. The latter vessel, however, became the first steamer flying the British flag to reach the Klondike via the Yukon River, in October 1898. Although the North-West Mounted Police force there had been strengthened in February [see Sir Samuel Benfield Steele*], this additional demonstration of sovereignty helped quell American ambitions to claim the territory. The previous month Domville had arrived in Dawson overland from Skagway, Alaska, where he had been visiting the survey party tracing a route for the railway. He was no sooner in Dawson than his feisty character, which had led neighbours in New Brunswick to describe him as "cranky," manifested itself. Asked by a reporter for his thoughts on the royalty that former commissioner James Morrow Walsh* had imposed on all gold mined in the Yukon, Domville remarked, "I don't care a ——— for him. I am James Domville, member of Parliament for Kings County, New Brunswick. Why should I care for such fellows as Walsh?" Boasting that the *James Domville* had 20 guns on board, he declared he would unload and set up a power plant, regardless of the royalty. Though he departed before the steamer arrived, he left no doubt about his disdain for territorial authorities.

Domville gained even greater notoriety during the tensions and politics that complicated the reforms being undertaken by Laurier's minister of militia and defence, Frederick William Borden*. Scheduled to retire from his command of the 8th in July 1898, Domville refused, in part because of his dislike of both Borden and his regimental second, Saint John newspaperman Alfred Markham, who had opposed his election two years before. District commander George Joseph Maunsell* held Domville to be a competent officer who deserved to have his command extended. Nonetheless, intense pressure was put on Domville by G. E. Foster, who charged him in the commons with a misappropriation of militia funds, and by the new general officer commanding, Major-General Edward Thomas Henry HUTTON, who was appalled by Domville's intransigence and by reports of his drinking and his "irregular" conduct in the Yukon. Only in August 1899, after being cleared of the charges, did Domville resign. Even then, he tried to keep his military ambitions alive by offering, later in the year, to raise a regiment for the South African War.

Defeated in the election of 1900, he still carried enough weight to be named to the Senate in 1903, in place of A. H. Gillmor, and to be made honorary colonel of the 8th Regiment in 1904, a recognition that had been refused by Governor General Lord Minto [Elliot*] in 1900. During the naval debate of 1909, with the Liberals favouring a Canadian naval service, he displayed strong conservative and imperialist sensibilities by supporting a direct contribution to the British navy. Near the end of his senatorial career, in a move that reflected his commercial knowledge of natural resources, he was named in 1920 to a special committee on the development of oil shales, iron ores, and coal deposits.

In February 1921 Domville's residence outside Saint John in Rothesay burned to the ground. What was not destroyed fell victim to students from nearby Rothesay Collegiate, who, realizing they could not extinguish the blaze, started rescuing what they could. Unfortunately, possessions from the first floor, stacked on the grass, were stolen or crushed by items tossed from the upper storeys. A mattress landed on the Domvilles' crystal and china, and a book knocked their son unconscious. Domville and his wife spent the remainder of their lives at the Kennedy Hotel in

Rothesay. James Domville died on 30 July 1921 and, following religious services in Rothesay, his body was taken to Fernhill Cemetery in Saint John, where John G. Leonard, the worthy master of Albion masonic lodge, presided over the interment.

PETER J. MITHAM

PANB, MC 1156. *Daily Gleaner* (Fredericton), 13 Aug. 1898. *Daily Sun* (Saint John), 20 Nov. 1883. *Daily Telegraph* (Saint John), 7 April, 15 Sept., 24 Nov. 1880. *Kings County Record* (Sussex, N.B.), 15 July 1997. *Morning News* (Saint John), 9 July 1869. *Saint John Globe*, 1 Aug. 1921. *Telegraph-Journal* (Saint John), 25 Nov. 1929. *Atlas of Saint John, city and county, New Brunswick*, comp. F. B. Roe and N. G. Colby (Saint John, 1875; repr. in *Historical atlas of York County, N.B., and St. John, N.B.*, Belleville, Ont., 1973). Can., Dept. of Militia and Defence, *Militia list* (Ottawa), 1905; Parl., *Sessional papers*, 1885, no.7: 41; *Statutes*, 1873, c.121. *Canadian annual rev.*, 1909. *Canadian men and women of the time* (Morgan; 1898 and 1912). *Canadian who's who*, 1910. *CPG*, 1873, 1897, 1918. *Directory*, N.B., 1871. Free Public Library, *Saint John Free Public Library: 50th anniversary of the Carnegie Building, 24 June 1904 to 24 June 1954* (Saint John, 1954). Robert Hook et al., *Rothesay: an illustrated history, 1784–1920* ([Rothesay, N.B.], 1984). Douglas How, *The 8th Hussars: a history of the regiment* (Sussex, 1964). *Lord Minto's Canadian papers: a selection of the public and private papers of the fourth Earl of Minto, 1898–1904*, ed. and intro. Paul Stevens and J. T. Saywell (2v., Toronto, 1981–83). Carman Miller, *The Canadian career of the fourth Earl of Minto: the education of a viceroy* (Waterloo, Ont., 1980). Desmond Morton, *Ministers and generals: politics and the Canadian militia, 1868–1904* (Toronto and Buffalo, N.Y., 1970). R. T. Naylor, *The history of Canadian business, 1867–1914* (2v., Toronto, 1975). Norman Penlington, *Canada and imperialism, 1896–1899* (Toronto, [1965]). *St. John and its business: a history of St. John . . .* (Saint John, 1875). *Standard dict. of Canadian biog.* (Roberts and Tunnell). *Vital statistics from N.B. newspapers* (Johnson). P. B. Waite, *Canada, 1874–1896: arduous destiny* (Toronto and Montreal, 1971). W. S. Wallace, *The memoirs of the Rt. Hon. Sir George Foster, P.C., G.C.M.G.* (Toronto, 1933). *Who's who and why*, 1919–20. J. R. H. Wilbur, "The stormy history of the Maritime Bank, (1872) to 1886," N.B. Hist. Soc., *Coll.* (Saint John), no.19 (1966): 69–76.

DOUCET, STANISLAS-JOSEPH, priest, Acadian patriot, homeopath, inventor, and author; b. 8 July 1847 in Bathurst, N.B., only son of François-Xavier Doucet, a farmer, and Rachel Boudrot (Boudreau); d. 1 Dec. 1925 in Grande-Anse, N.B.

After his elementary schooling in Bathurst, Stanislas-Joseph Doucet studied at St Michael's Academy in Chatham, and in September 1868 enrolled in the Grand Séminaire in Montreal. He was ordained to the priesthood for the diocese of Chatham on 31 July 1870 in Charlottetown. Since Bishop James Rogers* of Chatham was attending the first Vatican Council, which proclaimed papal infallibility, the ordination

Doucet

was conferred by the bishop of Charlottetown, Peter McIntyre*. Doucet was immediately appointed curate in Tracadie, N.B. In 1871 he became a curé, and he held this status for the rest of his life. He served at the following places: Shippagan, with responsibility for the islands of Lamèque and Miscou, in 1871–72; Saint-Charles, in Kent County, with responsibility for Richibucto, from 1872 to 1877; Pokemouche from 1877 to 1887; Shippagan from 1888 to 1898; and Grande-Anse from 1898 to 1925. In 1900 Rogers appointed him vicar general, a post he held until the bishop's death in 1902. When Bishop Thomas Francis Barry of Chatham got him an appointment from Rome as domestic prelate in November 1916, Abbé Doucet assumed the title of monsignor. In 1920 Patrice-Alexandre Chiasson became the first Acadian bishop of Chatham and he also made Doucet vicar general.

Considered a great patriot by his contemporaries, Doucet was one of the moving spirits behind the "Acadian renaissance." He played a prominent role at five of the Conventions Nationales des Acadiens held between 1881 and 1921, putting forward his ideas on the major topics of Acadian nationalism, including the choice of a date for a national holiday (1881) and of a flag (1884) [see Marcel-François Richard*]. At the meetings in 1905 he took stock of Acadian achievements in various fields. Three years later he was a member of the commission on relations between the Acadians of the Maritime provinces and those of the United States. In the 1921 convention he declared himself in favour of protecting historic sites (the fortress of Louisbourg and Fort Beauséjour).

Abbé Doucet had played an active role in founding the *Courrier des provinces Maritimes* in Bathurst in 1885. Subsequently, between 1890 and 1915, he used the press on many occasions to make known his views on important matters, such as the language question. He gave a lecture on this subject at the University of New Brunswick in Fredericton in 1896, and he published the text that year in Saint John under the title *Dual language in Canada: its advantages and disadvantages*. . . . With his friend and colleague Abbé Marcel-François Richard, he also waged a campaign for the appointment of the first Acadian bishop in the Maritimes. At the time the Acadians formed a majority in the Catholic community, but all the positions of authority in the church were held by Irish Catholics. When Édouard-Alfred Le Blanc* was named bishop of Saint John in 1912, Abbé Doucet described the happy event as a "grand arrangement," undoubtedly an allusion to "grand dérangement," a term used to describe the expulsion of 1755 [see Charles Lawrence*]. That year he took part in the Congrès de la Langue Française at Quebec.

With regard to political activity, Doucet did his utmost – by writing newspaper articles, taking part in meetings, and signing petitions – to support both provincial and federal Acadian candidates who were trying to get elected in New Brunswick. From 1904 until the end of his life he took an interest in the appointment of a second Acadian senator (he wanted there always to be two Acadians in the Senate, where Pascal Poirier* had sat since 1885). He even wrote to a number of prime ministers about this matter.

Mgr Doucet played an important role in the founding of the Collège du Sacré-Cœur in Bathurst, which the Eudists had opened first in Caraquet in 1899 [see Joseph-Théophile Allard*; Prosper Lebastard*]. On 30 Dec. 1915 the college burned down, and the Eudists then set another up temporarily in the noviciate-scholasticate they had built in Bathurst. It too fell victim to flames on 6 March 1917. Meanwhile, a lengthy debate was going on about where to rebuild the school. Mgr Doucet put pressure on the bishop of the diocese, in particular by circulating petitions, to have it permanently established in Bathurst, and it was eventually there that the building designated for the noviciate welcomed its first students in 1921.

In order to broaden his knowledge, Doucet made three trips to Europe and the Holy Land (in 1886, 1900, and 1922) and one to the Columbian exposition in Chicago in 1893. He also read widely. It was as a homeopath that he showed the greatest skill and was most highly regarded. During his time as curé in Pokemouche, the lack of a doctor in the region had prompted him to take an interest in this approach to therapy, which he would practise for the rest of his life. His medical library contained some 60 recent books, and he subscribed to a journal that specialized in homeopathy. He sent to Philadelphia for the medicines he needed to treat his patients, who lived up to 40 miles away. Others obtained by mail the little white pills for which he was famous. To simplify his consultations, he numbered his medicines, thereby enabling patients to renew their prescriptions without having to memorize the scientific names. Nicknamed the "miracle man" by some of them, in the end he irritated the physicians who were slowly coming to set up practice in the region, by taking away their clientele. In 1916 Dr L.-G. Pinault of Campbellton complained to the bishop that the homeopath had made a wrong diagnosis for two of his patients.

An inquiring and scholarly man, Abbé Doucet also carried out experiments with electricity. In 1891 he had obtained a patent in the United States and Canada for an electric signal system for railways, to prevent collisions on tracks. The invention appears to have been used by a company in Philadelphia. In 1895 he proposed that "a tunnel for electric vehicles" be built between New Brunswick and Prince Edward Island. A self-educated man, Doucet also gave a number of lectures as an amateur astronomer. He made a small-scale model of the solar system and displayed it in his presbytery. In order to explain the rotation of the earth, he installed a pendulum in the bell tower of the church in Grande-Anse. He was, incidentally, the prime mover of this church, for which he drew up the plans and built the model. He also raised some of the money for its erection through monthly collections, various activities on the work site (demonstrations using electrical apparatus of his own design, for example), and picnics. Construction of the building went on from 1902 to 1912.

In 1905 the Shediac newspaper *Le Moniteur acadien* published the only poem that Abbé Doucet ever wrote in French, "Les anges de la terre." He published two poems in English, as pamphlets, in Saint John: *The soul: a philosophic poem* in 1917 (of which a second edition, brought out in 1923, contained about 100 additional lines) and *Emmanuel, the living bread* in 1922. In 1912 he had composed, to the tune of *La Marseillaise,* the words of a patriotic song, *En avant!*, which was very popular with Acadians at the beginning of the 20th century. He also played the violin, piano, and organ.

Acadia lost a remarkable man when Mgr Stanislas-Joseph Doucet died. His friends and fellow workers had a high regard for the "thoughtful diplomacy" he displayed in everything he undertook. His contemporaries were impressed with his learning and his various skills.

ÉLOI DEGRÂCE

[A detailed list of the works used to study the life of Stanislas-Joseph Doucet may be found in the author's *Mgr Stanislas-J. Doucet* (Shippagan, N.-B., 1977). Several archives hold documents that were consulted during the preparation of this book: the Arch. des Pères Eudistes (Charlesbourg, Qué.), the Arch. du Diocèse de Bathurst, N.-B., the archives of the parishes where Mgr Doucet was priest, and the Centre d'Études Acadiennes, Univ. de Moncton, N.-B., which holds the Fonds S.-J. Doucet, as well as archival collections for many of Doucet's contemporaries. The PANB has a microfilm copy of the subject's baptismal certificate (MC290, F1456, 8 juill. 1847).

The three Acadian newspapers of the time are useful for studying the subject's career: *Courrier des provinces Maritimes* (Bathurst), *L'Évangéline* (Moncton), especially 25 oct. 1923, and *Le Moniteur acadien* (Shédiac, N.-B.), especially 10 déc. 1925. É.DEG.]

DOUGALL, LILY, author; b. 16 April 1858 in Montreal, youngest of the nine children of John Dougall* and Elizabeth Redpath; granddaughter of John Redpath*; d. unmarried 9 Oct. 1923 in Cumnor, England.

The daughter of a prosperous merchant and founder of religious newspapers, including the *Montreal Witness*, Lily Dougall received her early education in private schools; afterwards, while living briefly as companion to an aunt in Edinburgh in 1881, she began taking courses at the Edinburgh Association for the University Education of Women in preparation for a writing career. About 1885 she enrolled in the University of St Andrews in Scotland and in 1887 she obtained an LLA (lady literate in arts), the equivalent to the MA awarded to men. From 1885 to 1900 she divided her time between Great Britain and Canada. After 1900 she decided to make her home in England, largely for health reasons (she suffered from asthma), but she continued to spend extended periods in Canada, for the most part at the Montreal home of her brother John Redpath*.

Dougall published her first short story in 1889. Her short fiction would appear in journals such as *Temple Bar* (London), *Atlantic Monthly* (Boston), *Longman's Magazine* (London), and *Chambers's Journal* (London and Edinburgh). Her first novel, *Beggars all* (London, 1891), was hailed by critics and public alike. Set in England, it entertains with a suspenseful and unusual plot and intriguing characters, while challenging current moral and ethical assumptions, a combination which would continue to characterize her fiction. In the intellectual quality of her writing and her concern with everyday actions she recalls George Eliot. Her second novel, *What necessity knows* (London, 1893), set in Canada, also received high praise. In its broad scope it resembles Eliot's *Middlemarch . . .* (London, 1871–72), but it also has parallels with Jane Austen's novels, notably *Pride and prejudice* (London, 1813). A complex novel, written in a style that is witty, richly symbolic, and lyrically descriptive of the Canadian landscape, *What necessity knows* is multi-layered. It may be read for its love triangles, its portrayal of the social and psychological diversity of British immigrants in the Eastern Townships, its exploration of spiritual regeneration, and its demonstration of the effectiveness of strong, independent-minded women.

Ever the scholar, Dougall made a point of consulting experts. She sent her early stories and novels to Henry Sidgwick, professor of moral philosophy at Cambridge and a founder and first president of the Society for Psychical Research. From her early years Dougall had been intrigued by mental telepathy, spiritualism, faith healing, and the relationship of the spiritual, psychological, and physical worlds and in 1895 she joined the society; she would remain a member for many years.

Dougall's next three novels are also set in Canada. The most overtly didactic is *The Zeit-geist* (London, 1895), the story of the conversion of the protagonist from a dissolute life to a deeply spiritual and philanthropic one in which he becomes a freethinker and essentially a pantheist. For this novel, Dougall sought the advice of Oxford philosophers William Wallace and Edward Caird.

In 1899 Dougall published *The Mormon prophet* (London), a novel about the rise of Mormonism based on research in the archives of the Church of Jesus Christ of Latter-day Saints and interviews with those who had known the church's founder, Joseph Smith; it was primarily concerned with the complex character of Smith. Dougall met with philosopher and psychologist William James to discuss Smith's visions, supposed revelations to him, and, in a more general way, mysticism.

Dougall's first theological work, *Pro Christo et ecclesia* (London, 1900), published anonymously because of its controversial nature, was greeted by critics as a "work of great power" and its author was thought to be an eminent clergyman. Here Dougall develops the ideas she dramatized in her fiction, urging a renewal of Christianity based on love and joy, criticizing sectarianism, and stressing the necessity that Christianity adapt to new knowledge. Although she published three more novels within the next eight years, she turned to writing religious and philosophical works anonymously. As her identity gradually became known, she was increasingly consulted by other scholars.

After having lived in several places in England, Dougall moved in 1911 to Cumnor, near Oxford, where her home became a centre for philosophical discussion. Contributors to the four collections of essays which came out of these discussions included scholars from a broad array of disciplines. In her own works she explored such issues as the psychological aspects of religious experience, the relationship between religion and science and between religion and art, and the responsibility of churches to be concerned with social issues. She was ecumenical in her attitude to Christianity: she participated in meetings of Christian Scientists and was asked to write for their publication; she was invited to publish in the Unitarian *Hibbert Journal* (London); she attended the summer school of the Society of Friends and wrote for their monthly journal; and she held a conference on faith healing in her home. The relationship between physical, psychological, and spiritual health developed into one of her main interests. She became an active member of the Guild of Health and wrote a book for its study groups. Increasingly concerned with social and political issues, she attended conferences and meetings on a broad range of issues, including Fabian socialism.

In his text *In defence of the faith* (Oxford, 1927), an overview of the development of modernism in the Anglican church in the early 20th century, Charles Gardner includes Dougall in his chapter "Some women rebels," praising *Pro Christo et ecclesia*. "To those brought up in the old puritan Evangelicalism it was a new gospel. Pharisaism is tracked down and laid relentlessly bare, and a soft light is turned onto the exquisitely human Figure of the gospels." Commenting on Dougall's collaboration with the "bril-

liant" Cyril William Emmet in *The Lord of thought . . .* (London, 1922), he observes, "Miss Dougall has much to say that is illuminating and stimulating on the apocalyptic problem." Gardner is intrigued by the remarkable influence Dougall had on contemporary scholars and philosophers, such as Burnett Hillman Streeter, Percy Dearmer, Harold Anson, and on literary critic Arthur Clutton-Brock.

Dougall's novels were published in both Great Britain and the United States and widely and favourably reviewed, as were her philosophical and religious works. She was an intellectual writer with an enquiring mind who used her skills to challenge the status quo in society and in religion and she was admired by many of the foremost scholars of her day. She died suddenly of heart failure at her home in Cumnor.

LORRAINE MCMULLEN

Lily Dougall is the author of numerous novels and religious works. A partial list is available in CIHM, *Reg*. Other works are cited in the catalogue of the LAC. Some of her correspondence, biographical notes about her, and financial records can be found in the John Dougall and family fonds (LAC, MG 29, C34). The Bodleian Library, Univ. of Oxford, Dept. of Special Coll. and Western MSS, holds additional correspondence, newspaper articles, unpublished manuscripts, business papers, and various biographical materials. Biographical information is also provided in Victoria Walker's introduction to Dougall's book *What necessity knows* (Ottawa, 1992), 7–23.

ANQ-M, CE601-S95, 18 juill. 1858. Mount Royal Cemetery Company (Outremont, Que.), Dougall family memorial marker. *Gazette* (Montreal), 11 Oct. 1923. *Manchester Guardian* (Manchester, Eng.), 16 Oct. 1923. *Times* (London), 11 Oct. 1923. Joanna Dean, "Mysticism and religious modernism: Lily Dougall (1858–1923)," Canadian Soc. of Church Hist., *Hist. papers* (n.p.), 1996: 57–84. Edinburgh Assoc. for the Univ. Education of Women, *Calendar*, 1879–82. Charles Gardner, *In defence of the faith* (Oxford, 1927). Lorraine McMullen, "Lily Dougall: the religious vision of a Canadian novelist," *Studies in Religion* (Waterloo, Ont.), 16 (1987): 79–90; "Lily Dougall's vision of Canada," in *A mazing space: writing Canadian women writing*, ed. Shirley Neuman and Smaro Kamboureli (Edmonton, 1986), 137–47. *The Oxford companion to Canadian literature*, ed. William Toye (Toronto, 1983). R. N. Smart, "Literate ladies – a fifty year experiment," Alumnus Assoc. of the Univ. of St Andrews, *Alumnus Chronicle* (St Andrews, Scot.), 59 (June 1968): 21–31. *Standard dict. of Canadian biog.* (Roberts and Tunnell). B. H. Streeter, *In memoriam, Lily Dougall; a sermon preached at Cumnor Church on Sunday evening, October 21, 1923* (Oxford, n.d.).

DOW, JEAN ISABELLE (baptized **Jane Isabella**), medical missionary; b. 25 June 1870 near Fergus, Ont., fifth of the eight children of Peter Dow and Agnes Wilson; d. unmarried 16 Jan. 1927 in Peking (Beijing, People's Republic of China), and was buried in Changte (Anyang).

Jean Dow is representative of the first generation of Canadian women doctors who chose a missionary career. A granddaughter of Scottish immigrants, she grew up in a progressive "farm home of the best type" with a large library. The Dows were members of the very mission-minded Melville Presbyterian Church in Fergus and it was in this atmosphere that Jeannie, as she was known, felt called to foreign-mission work. A winsome, beautiful girl, she was inordinately shy and quite brilliant. She graduated from primary school at age 10 and high school at 13, and was a teacher by 15. After attending model school in Mount Forest, in 1891 she applied to the Presbyterian Woman's Foreign Missionary Society, intending to enter Woman's Medical College in Toronto. She received her MB from Trinity College in 1895 and on 30 September of that year was appointed to succeed the late Dr Lucinda Graham in North Honan (Henan), China.

The Presbyterian mission there had been founded in 1888 by Jonathan and Rosalind Goforth and others, but they had been unable to gain a foothold in the province because of anti-foreign attitudes. Eventually, in 1894, they managed to lease a house in Chuwang, a "wretched" town inside the border. By the time Dow arrived, they had been forced out, but the station was soon re-established.

Studying Chinese gave Dow new freedom – "loosening my English tongue" she called the experience. She learned the colloquialisms of illiterate women and the Chinese equivalents of medical terminology. "Medicine was her profession," in the words of one biographer, "Evangelism was her passion." She was always surrounded by women, "gossiping the gospel" as she asked about their families. "Day by day they come in ceaseless procession to the dispensary," she wrote. In 1897 she opened the first women's hospital in Honan – a mud-brick ward and chapel-dispensary, which treated 400 patients in its first month. The Boxer rebellion of 1900 forced a harrowing evacuation to the coast, with the missionaries being mobbed and beaten. Dow then went on furlough, during which she studied tropical medicine in New York City, "to get rid of the rust" according to mission historian Margaret H. Brown.

Jean Dow returned in April 1902 and "dwelt among the ruins" in Chuwang while making extensive evangelistic tours. When the Chuwang station was closed she moved to Changte, a major city, where she opened a women's hospital. As the only practising female physician in North Honan for 20 years – other, married women doctors did not practise – she was at the centre of a controversy over separate facilities for women. Governed by an all-male presbytery, the North Honan mission considered separate wards "useless and unnecessary." Dow got around the opposition unobtrusively; in 1904 and again in 1913, when a new men's hospital was constructed, she adapted the old buildings as women's wards.

Dow's practice had grown from simple surgery for such problems as cataracts and wolf bites to complicated obstetric treatments and X-rays. Her foremost achievement, with Dr William McClure, was her work on the microbe causing kala-azar, the sandfly-transmitted disease that decimated the children of north China. During the famine of 1920–21 she was credited with saving 400 expectant mothers and children. For her heroic services the Chinese government gave her a medal. She was held in the "highest esteem" too by her mission, as much for her physical and spiritual beauty and strong "womanhood" as for her medical skill.

Despite her fluency in Chinese, her natural reticence hindered her relations with colleagues. Here she was helped over a 30-year period by her "beautiful friendship, based on mutual love," with another Scots missionary from Wellington County, a nurse named Margaret I. McIntosh. Because Dow was "never articulate in public" (so Margaret Brown recalled), in discussions of her work she would whisper responses to Margaret, who would repeat them aloud. When women were admitted to the mission's executive committee, Dow was one of the two female members, a role she filled with common sense for several years. In the 1920s her drive for facilities for women was challenged by a new generation of professionals, men and women, who argued for integration on the ground that separate realms led to substandard facilities. The mission, however, deferred to Dow and Dr Isabelle MacTavish, allowing them to build the only women's hospital in North Honan.

Jean Dow went on furlough at the beginning of civil unrest in 1925. A few months earlier the mission had voted unanimously to join the United Church of Canada. She returned to China in October 1926 in time to open the hospital she had worked for. She was there only two months before she succumbed to an internal complaint and was taken to the Peking Union Medical Hospital, where she died, worn out at 56. Her body was buried in the mission cemetery at Changte.

If Dow had stayed in Canada, she might never have "loosened" her tongue or built a hospital. As one colleague said at her memorial service, being a pioneer worker "she was at liberty to set up her own ideals of personal worth and work, and did set these very high. ... She touched multitudes of lives for good." According to recollections compiled in the 1980s, the women of Honan who remembered her agreed.

ALVYN J. AUSTIN

AO, RG 80-2-0-12, no.19270. LAC, RG 31, C1, Nichol Township, Ont., 1871, div.1: 58; 1881: 13 (mfm. at AO).

Dowling

UCC-C, Biog. file; Fonds 127, 79.205C, boxes 5–9; Photographs. UTA, A1973-0026/87, files for J. I. Dow (53), her brother the Reverend James A. Dow (52), her cousin Dr James Dow (51), and other relatives. *Daily Mail and Empire,* 18 Jan. 1927. *Evening Telegram* (Toronto), 18 Jan. 1927. *Globe,* 18, 22 Jan., 8 Feb. 1927. *New Outlook* (Toronto), 9 March, 27 April 1927. A. J. Austin, *Saving China: Canadian missionaries in the Middle Kingdom, 1888–1959* (Toronto, 1986). D. McD. Beattie, *Pillars and patches along the highway: a history of Nichol Township* ([Elora, Ont., 1984]). M. H. Brown, "History of the Honan (North China) missions of the United Church of Canada, originally a mission of the Presbyterian Church in Canada, 1887–1951" (4v., typescript, n.p., [1970]; copy in UCC-C). Ruth Compton Brouwer, *New women for God: Canadian Presbyterian women and India missions, 1876–1914* (Toronto, 1990). [M. R. Griffith], *Jean Dow, M.D.: a beloved physician* (Toronto, [193-?]). Carlotta Hacker, *The indomitable lady doctors* (Toronto, 1974). *Presbyterian Record* (Montreal), 1895–1926. Hugh Templin and J. M. Imlah, *Melville Church, Fergus: a history of the congregation from 1845 to 1945* (Fergus, Ont., 1945).

DOWLING, THOMAS JOSEPH, Roman Catholic priest and bishop; b. 28 Feb. 1840 in Shanagolden (Republic of Ireland), son of Martin Dowling; d. 6 Aug. 1924 in Hamilton, Ont.

Thomas J. Dowling immigrated from Ireland to Hamilton with his family in 1851. He attended a "select school" there and then went to St Michael's College in Toronto, where he studied under famed Basilian orator Michael Joseph Ferguson and excelled in public speaking and literature. After further study at the Grand Séminaire de Montréal, he was ordained at St Mary's Cathedral in Hamilton on 7 Aug. 1864 by Bishop John Farrell*. Dowling's initial posting within the Hamilton diocese, in October, was to a large mission area based in Paris, where he quickly displayed talents as a builder priest and orator of note. To retire the debt on the uncompleted church in Paris, he went on a successful lecture and fund-raising tour that included Chicago and Pennsylvania.

In 1881 he became the diocese's vicar general. As such, he acted as interregnal administrator between the death in 1882 of Farrell's successor, Peter Francis Crinnon, and the appointment in 1883 of James Joseph Carbery. On 29 Jan. 1884 Dowling was honoured as diocesan administrator at a banquet given in Paris by his fellow clergymen, whose gift, a purse of $500, he put into the building fund of his church.

In December 1886 Dowling was elected to succeed Jean-François Jamot* as bishop of Peterborough. Consecrated in Hamilton on 1 May 1887, he proceeded to develop the policies that would define his episcopal career: a commitment to the physical development of the church, a willingness to travel, and a recognition of the needs of non-English-speaking Catholics. Despite the vastness of his diocese, which stretched to the Manitoba border, Dowling in a very short episcopate managed to visit Sudbury, Sault Ste Marie, and the Lakehead. He provided full-time priests for his diocese's many French-speaking communities and ensured that, at Christmas and Easter, priests fluent in Dutch, German, and Italian were made available to parishes where these were the first languages of significant numbers.

Following the death of Carbery in December 1887, rumours circulated that Dowling's Hamilton upbringing made him the logical successor. As was customary, he denied any interest. However, when the Vatican announced that he would indeed be Hamilton's fourth bishop, he admitted, "It is a consolation for me to know that I am not a stranger to the diocese, that I am returning, as it were, to the home of my childhood, amongst kind and esteemed friends of the clergy and laity." He was transferred to Hamilton on 11 Jan. 1889 and installed on 2 May.

During his episcopate in Hamilton, Dowling continued his attention to the physical expansion of the church. Within two years he had arranged for the building of six churches, three convents, and nine schools and for the enlargement of an orphanage. In addition, he exhibited characteristics which differentiated him from his fellow bishops, several of whom remained aloof from both their clergy and their flock. At the time of his appointment one correspondent spoke of "his truly brotherly regard for his fellow priests . . . and thoroughly conscientious fulfillment of his pastoral duties." It was especially his relationship with the laity that set Dowling apart. Highly sociable – photographs reveal an open, round face, a high forehead, and tousled hair – he was a poet and a singer. His verse, original if not always distinguished, was readily offered, often in congratulatory form at farewells, priestly anniversaries, baptisms, and weddings. At funerals for priests and nuns there would be lamentations, eulogies, or both. As a singer, Dowling regularly performed at concerts in schools and St Joseph's Orphanage in Hamilton, and without fail at St Patrick's Day festivities. Newspaper accounts indicate that he expected to be called upon on such occasions; when he was not, he openly expressed disappointment.

Dowling's reaction to the massive influx of immigrants that had begun in the 1890s paralleled episcopal response in some other large urban centres. Much like Fergus Patrick McEvay* in Toronto, he argued it was the responsibility of the church to provide services in the language of the foreigners. He consequently arranged such services for Germans, Italians, and Poles. The Germans in Waterloo County and the Walkerton-Hanover area were the easiest to satisfy. His initial action was to issue a blanket *celebret* to Father Louis G. F. H. Funcken, superior of the Congregation of the Resurrection in Berlin (Kitchener), who was sent to Europe to recruit German-speaking priests. The long-term solution was closer to home: St Jerome's College, run by the Congregation, became a source of native-born, German-speaking clergy. Hamilton's growing Italian community was similarly well served: in 1908 St Anthony of Padua parish was established in the city's east end. Five years later Dowling called on the Italians of Guelph, going so far as to visit the homes of prominent members of the community and converse through a translator. By 1922 the Italian population there was sufficiently large that a separate parish had been created.

The Poles were more problematic, though the Resurrectionists, who had been founded to minister to Polish émigrés in France, had laid some groundwork. The problems included rivalries within the Congregation, fears that a schism among Polish American Catholics might be repeated in Canada, traditional linkages between Polish nationalism and Catholicism, and the opposition of some priests to ethnically based Polish parishes. Despite such pressures, Dowling acceded to requests from Polish communities. In 1911 a lot was allocated at Barton and St Ann streets in Hamilton for St Stanislaus Church. A year later Sacred Heart parish in Berlin was opened. Less successful were Dowling's efforts to service the non-Latin-rite faithful in Berlin and Owen Sound. There was difficulty finding priests for them and those who arrived left, complaining of the antagonism of the local Latin-rite pastors.

Given his background, Dowling had always been drawn to Irish politics and Irish perspectives in Canada. He fully embraced the idea of a distinctive Canadian identity expressed by Thomas D'Arcy McGee*. As a parish priest in Paris in 1866, Dowling made his opinions of the Fenians abundantly clear by acting as a chaplain for the local militia. A firm believer in the work of Daniel O'Connell, the Irish leader who had favoured constitutional solutions, he spoke frequently on Irish affairs and contributed to the *Irish Canadian* (Toronto). Though he recognized that the Irish in Canada were better off than those at home, he joined Archbishop John Joseph Lynch* of Toronto and other prelates in discouraging "improvident emigration" to urban areas. Hamilton's Irish ghetto, which existed literally in the shadow of St Mary's Cathedral, was a constant reminder of what could go wrong.

In an attempt to separate partisan and religious affairs, Dowling made the necessary disclaimer in 1889 that he was "above and beyond the sphere of politics." Still, though he may have been less obvious than some of his more flamboyant episcopal colleagues, he quietly wielded considerable power. In 1888 he had approached Lynch with a request that Prime Minister Sir John A. Macdonald* be asked to ensure that the "right" candidate received a judicial appointment. He advised Lynch to inform Macdonald that here was an "opportunity . . . of conciliating a

young bishop whose people form his balance of power in several doubtful constituencies." Dowling himself intervened for the Tories in Northumberland County in 1887 and in Haldimand County in 1895. In addition, his advice was sought over the Jesuits' Estates Act and the Manitoba school question. When these controversial issues caused influential Conservative spokesman D'Alton McCarthy* to go his own way and divide the party, Macdonald asked Dowling to explain to Catholics that the renegade's views were not sanctioned by the Tory hierarchy. In February 1891 the prime minister encouraged Dowling to urge his parish priests to sermonize on the evils of unrestricted reciprocity, which could lead to annexation by the United States and reduced rights for Canadian Catholics.

After Macdonald's death in June, Dowling sustained his affiliation with the Conservatives. He was especially pleased at their choice as leader in 1892 of John Sparrow David Thompson*, a Catholic and an ally of Bishop John Cameron* of Antigonish, N.S. Dowling even found it possible to forge an alliance with Mackenzie Bowell*, Thompson's successor and a former grand master of the Orange order, but there is no evidence that the affiliation continued through the short-lived prime ministership of Sir Charles Tupper*. At the same time it does not appear that Dowling's support shifted to the Liberal government of fellow-Catholic Wilfrid Laurier*. Their relationship was somewhat limited and formal. It was not until Laurier's defeat 15 years later by Conservative Robert Laird Borden* that Dowling renewed his requests for federal placements for Catholics.

Provincially Dowling's political involvement was less predictable. In the 1880s he had readily joined Lynch and Bishop James Vincent Cleary* of Kingston in supporting the Liberals of Oliver Mowat* and opposing the "no popery" policies of the Conservatives under William Ralph MEREDITH. Relations between the episcopal hierarchy and Mowat's successors declined, however, after his departure for federal politics in 1896. Arthur Sturgis Hardy* was thought by Dowling to have snubbed him by not paying a call during a visit to Hamilton. Under George William Ross* the relationship deteriorated further: in 1900 Dowling complained that patronage positions in the Hamilton area originally designed as "Catholic" were being given to Protestants. By 1905, largely in response to scandals surrounding the Ross government, he had joined with other members of the hierarchy in support of James Pliny Whitney*'s Conservatives.

Like his episcopal counterparts, Dowling was a strong champion of separate schools, though somewhat more modernistic in his approach. A supporter in 1888 of Lynch's opposition to the introduction of the secret ballot in school board elections, by 1894, despite continuing episcopal resistance, he recognized the inevitability of such change. Similarly, while others resisted expansion of separate secondary schools beyond fifth form, in 1916 Dowling thought it necessary that Catholic students should have the same opportunities as their peers in the public system and that the extra education was necessary to train Catholic teachers. He was also supportive of the general education offered by the Toronto-based Catholic Church Extension Society [see Alfred Edward BURKE]. When other bishops questioned the society's effectiveness, Dowling helped ensure its survival by encouraging Toronto archbishop Neil McNeil* and possibly donating money.

The bishop of Hamilton had displayed some tolerance in the controversy over French schools in Manitoba; he believed that a compromise solution would enhance the position of separate schools in Ontario. He would go no further, however, refusing in 1896 to join his Quebec colleagues in protest over Laurier's compromise with Manitoba premier Thomas Greenway*. On the other hand, in the dispute surrounding Ontario's Regulation 17 of 1912, which restricted the use of French in schools and divided the hierarchy, Dowling attempted to preserve the links with the French-speaking bishops and thus reduce the division, but he was overridden by Michael Francis Fallon*, the bishop of London, and others.

Dowling presided as prelate until his death in 1924. It was reported then that he had turned down the archbishopric of Toronto three times; certainly in 1898 he had rejected the chance to succeed John Walsh*. In 1914, after 50 years as a priest and 25 as a bishop, he was honoured with appointment as assistant bishop at the pontifical throne and domestic prelate.

After 1914 Dowling's pace slowed considerably. By 1920 his ill health was acknowledged: the diocese was being run by an administrator and episcopal functions such as confirmation were being performed by missionary bishops. When Dowling died, on the eve of the 60th anniversary of his ordination, he was North America's oldest active bishop. Although his work had been less public than that of some colleagues, it is clear that he was both a builder priest and, until his health failed, an excellent administrator. His greatest legacy was his recognition that, with the influx of non-anglophone immigrants after the turn of the century, the church in English-speaking Canada, so long Hibernian in nature, had to change to survive.

GERALD J. STORTZ

Arch. of the Roman Catholic Archdiocese of Toronto, L (Lynch papers); MN (McNeil papers). Arch. of the Roman Catholic Diocese of Hamilton, Ont., T. J. Dowling papers; Dowling scrapbook. Arch. of the Roman Catholic Diocese of Peterborough, Ont., T. J. Dowling papers. LAC, MG 26, A, Macdonald to Dowling, 16 Dec. 1887; Dowling to Macdonald, 28 March 1889. Catholic Record (London, Ont.), 1884–1924, esp. 16 Aug. 1924. Catholic Weekly Review (Toronto), 5 May 1887. Hamilton Spectator, 7 Aug. 1924. Paris Star (Paris, [Ont.]), 19 July 1866. Edgar Boland, From the pioneers to the seventies: a history of the diocese of Peterborough, 1882–1975 (Peterborough, 1976). Alex Bros, "Polish immigrant relations with the Roman Catholic Church in urban Ontario, 1896–1923" (MA thesis, Wilfrid Laurier Univ., Waterloo, Ont., 1986). Canadian album (Cochrane and Hopkins), 1: 310. Canadian men and women of the time (Morgan; 1898). Cyclopædia of Canadian biog. (Rose and Charlesworth), vol.1. DHB, vol.2. Ken Foyster, Anniversary reflections: 1856–1981; a history of Hamilton diocese (Hamilton, [1982]). Marjorie Freeman Campbell, A mountain and a city: the story of Hamilton (Toronto and Montreal, 1966). Theobald Spetz, The Catholic Church in Waterloo County . . . ([Toronto], 1916). G. J. Stortz, "Thomas Joseph Dowling, the first 'Canadian' bishop of Hamilton, 1889–1924," CCHA, Hist. studies, 54 (1987): 93–107.

DOYON, CONSTANT (baptized **Paul-Victor-Emmanuel**), Dominican, missionary, and military chaplain; b. 27 Jan. 1875 in Saint-Guillaume, Que., son of Charles Doyon, a farmer, and Odile Chaussé; d. 18 Oct. 1927 in Saint-Michel-des-Saints, Que.

After classical studies at the Séminaire de Saint-Hyacinthe (1887–93) and the Séminaire de Nicolet (1893–96), Paul-Victor-Emmanuel Doyon entered the Dominican order in 1896 under the name of Constant. He did his noviciate in Saint-Hyacinthe and his studies at the Dominican monastery in Ottawa, where he was ordained priest on 31 May 1901. He was in France in 1902 and 1903, and subsequently was given administrative responsibility until 1907 for Le Rosaire, Le Rosaire pour tous, and the Rosary for Everyone, three Dominican magazines published in Saint-Hyacinthe. He then became a preaching missionary and put a great deal of energy into the cause of temperance. During World War I he served in the Canadian Expeditionary Force from 1915 to 1918 and afterwards resumed his work as a missionary.

Doyon joined the ranks of the 22nd Infantry Battalion [see Henri CHASSÉ] as a chaplain on 17 Feb. 1915, with the rank of honorary captain. It would be the only French Canadian infantry unit to see action during World War I. Doyon signed up at the age of 40 and succeeded Major Philippe-Henri-Duperron Casgrain. During the battalion's stay in Nova Scotia in the spring of 1915, he helped it win the affection and esteem of the people of Amherst by creating a conference of the St Vincent de Paul Society among the members of the regiment. Colonel Frédéric-Mondelet Gaudet*, the battalion's first commander, congratulated him "for this valuable work of simple and kindly charity." Doyon left Canada on 20 May 1915 to go overseas with his unit. In England he was attached to the headquarters of the 5th Brigade of the 2nd Canadian Division on 8 Sept. 1915, and he went to France a week later. He took on an immense task at the front because for many months he was the only

Roman Catholic priest serving with the 5th Brigade, and it had a much higher than average number of Roman Catholics in its ranks since it included the French Canadian 22nd Battalion. He distinguished himself by his zeal, his dedication, and his conscientious devotion to duty. On 13 Feb. 1917 he was transferred to the headquarters of the Canadian Training Division in Shorncliffe, England. Except for a four-month stay in Canada in 1917, he worked until the end of the war with French Canadians in England in the 10th Reserve Battalion, the 150th Infantry Battalion, and the quarantine camp at Frensham Pond. He returned to Canada permanently on 18 Dec. 1918, having served overseas for more than three years. On 29 March 1920 he was appointed honorary chaplain of the Saint-Hyacinthe regiment.

Doyon was a tireless worker; when he was recalled to England in February 1917, he dreamed of returning to the front. On 1 March 1918 he asked to be appointed chaplain to the French Canadian soldiers serving in "Anglo-Protestant units" at the front. He felt a close attachment to French Canada and in a letter referred to the "sorrows of the days we French Canadians [overseas] are living through." The French Canadian soldiers were the only ones who spoke French in the British armed forces, into which the Canadian Expeditionary Force had been integrated. They also formed a Roman Catholic entity within a primarily Protestant body. Contrary to the custom of the time, Doyon wrote much of his correspondence as a military chaplain in French. He was proud to be the chaplain of the 22nd Battalion. A few months after the battle of Courcelette, France, which was fought in September 1916, he noted that, "French Canada has played a grand and glorious role in the war."

Constant Doyon died on 18 Oct. 1927 at the age of 52. He was granted a military funeral, which was conducted in Saint-Hyacinthe. He remained self-sacrificing until the end, despite his precarious state of health following a severe attack of paralysis that affected him for the last three years of his life. In the eyes of his provincial superior, Pie-Marie Béliveau, he was a "fiery soul." "For twenty years," Béliveau observed after his death, "he devoted himself to his high calling [as a missionary] with such ardour that [even] the most courageous could not always follow him."

JEAN-PIERRE GAGNON

Constant Doyon is the author of *Au régime de l'eau* (Québec, 1919) and *La lutte antialcoolique: simples articles* (Québec, 1911; 2ᵉ éd., 1913).

ANQ-MBF, CE403-S11, 27 janv. 1875. LAC, RG 9, III, C15, 4621; RG 150, Acc. 1992–93/166. Royal 22nd Regiment Museum (Quebec), D-6/172 (J.-P. Gagnon fonds). *Le Devoir*, 18 oct. 1927. J.-B.-A. Allaire, *Dictionnaire biographique du clergé canadien-français* (6v., Montréal et Saint-Hyacinthe, Qué., 1908–34), 6: 259–60. P.-M. Béliveau, "Décès du R.P. Doyon," *La Rev. dominicaine* (Saint-Hyacinthe), 33 (1927): 687–90. D. W. Crerar, *Padres in no man's land: Canadian chaplains and the Great War* (Montreal, 1995).

DROLET, FRANÇOIS-XAVIER, mechanic and industrialist; b. 9 May 1849 at Quebec, son of Alexandre Drolet, a carpenter, and Rosalie Fréchette; m. there first 24 Jan. 1871 Émilie Lainez (d. 10 Oct. 1907), and they had 12 children, of whom five sons and two daughters reached adulthood; m. there secondly 27 April 1908 Georgianna Leteau, widow of Gaudiose Simard; they had no children; d. 21 Feb. 1924 at Quebec.

Born into a family of craftsmen, François-Xavier Drolet was educated by the Brothers of the Christian Schools for a short time and then worked in various industries, where he learned to be a mechanic. He was employed in the carpenter's workshop of Joseph Archer Sr from 1862 to 1864, George Benson Hall*'s sawmill at Montmorency Falls from 1864 to 1871, the construction business of Simon Peters at Quebec, the foundry and machine shop of Carrier, Laîné et Compagnie in Lévis from 1872 to 1874 [see Charles William Carrier*], and the smaller firm of Tweddell and Campbell (mechanics and founders) in Saint-Roch ward in Quebec City.

On the strength of this experience, Drolet went into partnership in December 1875 with a fellow mechanic, Pierre Audard, under the name of Drolet et Audard. They rented a shed on Rue Saint-Joseph in Saint-Roch and advertised that they were in the business of making and repairing steam engines of all kinds. Their tools and experience were their only capital. The partnership agreement, which was valid for ten years, stipulated that each partner was to receive an income of $12 a week. Early in 1878, in an effort to become firmly established, the small business signed an eight-year lease on the property on Rue Saint-Joseph, with an option to purchase. That year they joined Pierre Guérard, a founder, to set up the firm of Drolet, Audard, et Guérard. In the spring of 1879 it purchased a parcel of land adjacent to Drolet et Audard. The two companies got off to a difficult start. This was borne out by the dissolution of the second partnership, and the division of its sole assets ($600 worth of tools), in August and of Drolet et Audard in January 1881. Drolet gave Audard $1,275 (to be paid on 1 May) in return for all the assets of the firm: the lease, the tools, and his share of the property. He was consequently in complete control of the enterprise. Things improved rapidly. The Bradstreet credit agency raised its rating from F (no credit) in January 1881 to D (net assets of $1,000 to $2,000) in July 1882. In December 1882 the firm, of which Drolet was now the sole owner, had about 15 employees.

At the beginning of the 1890s, the firm of F.-X.

Drolet

Drolet became one of the largest machine shops in the city, capable of designing, constructing, and repairing steam engines and motors, pumps of all kinds, as well as various machines used in industrial manufacturing and public works. The many tanneries and shoe factories in Saint-Roch were important clients [see Cléophas Rochette*]. Innovation was a key factor in the company's success. In 1899, for example, it obtained a patent in the United States for a "valve gear for engine."

Between 1881 and 1906, Drolet managed to enlarge the machine shops, the shops for building models, and those for casting metal, partly as a result of his purchase in 1892–93, 1901, and 1905 of land on Rue Saint-Joseph and Rue Octave. The workforce grew quickly from about 25 at the end of the 1880s to 50 in 1901 and 60 in 1906. This rapid expansion resulted in increased capital, as witness the improved credit rating, which rose from D to B between 1900 and 1907, while the net assets, which were $5,000 to $10,000 in 1900, reached $35,000 to $50,000. This success enabled Drolet to leave his overcrowded premises and to build a large foundry and an immense machine shop between 1907 and 1909 without going into debt. The new plant was constructed on the site of the former shipyard of Thomas Hamilton Oliver on the south shore of the estuary of the Rivière Saint-Charles, near the Dorchester Bridge. The total cost (including $45,000 for the land) was $91,500 and the location, which had railway access, made it possible for a ramp to be built for the refitting of ships, as well as for installing and repairing their steam engines. In this operation, Drolet realized a substantial capital gain by selling his properties on Rue Octave and Rue Saint-Joseph, which had become a highly desirable commercial thoroughfare, for $80,000 in 1911. Moreover, the city of Quebec exempted him from property taxes for ten years.

Between 1872 and 1892 Émilie Drolet bore 12 children (one of whom was still-born). Until 1889, when Drolet purchased a modest property on Rue Richardson (De La Salle) for $1,000, the family had to move frequently. Ten years later it chose to take up residence in an opulent home on Rue Saint-Vallier. Drolet bought the lots adjoining his new property at a good price and two of his sons settled there. In 1900 he sold his house on Rue Richardson to his eldest daughter, Émilie.

Drolet married Georgianna Leteau in April 1908, not long after the death of his first wife on 10 Oct. 1907. The couple opted for a marriage settlement based on the separation of property. During these years Drolet began getting his sons established. The eldest, Joseph-François-Xavier, became a farmer at Pointe-aux-Trembles (Neuville), while the next three, Gaudiose, Émile, and Arthur, went into the family business once they were past adolescence. The youngest, Camille, entered the Jesuit order. By then about 60 years old, Drolet was thinking of passing on the family industrial heritage. He began the process in May 1913 by organizing a joint-stock enterprise, Compagnie F.-X. Drolet, with a capital of $199,000; he retained 97 per cent of the stock and sons Gaudiose and Émile, along with a few loyal employees, held the rest. In 1920 he sold the factory to the company for $142,000, payable in annual instalments of $5,000. Gaudiose, the eldest of the sons involved in the business, now became president and general manager, with Émile and Arthur as vice-president and treasurer respectively. When François-Xavier Drolet died in 1924, the company's shares were divided equally among his seven children, each of whom received $60,000. (Since Émilie had died before him, but after he had made his will in 1921, her share went to her three children.)

Drolet's business reached its peak during World War I, when it had about 100 employees. In 1918 its sales exceeded $250,000, thanks mainly to its production of shells and bombs. It suffered, however, when industrial activity at Quebec levelled off. At the beginning of the 1920s, new contracts for elevators, fire hydrants, and automobile parts helped keep the business alive, but its profitability, which had enabled it to pay good dividends until 1918, subsequently began to fall off. In spite of significant growth in sales at the end of the 1920s, it had suffered continual losses since 1921. François-Xavier Drolet's career illustrates the rise of a craftsman of inventive mind who built a sizeable family business, but did not extend his economic and social connections outside his enterprise and his family.

MARC VALLIÈRES

ANQ-Q, CE301-S1, 10 mai 1849, 24 janv. 1871; CN301-S305, 1875–81; CN301-S336, 1878–79; Index BMS, dist. judiciaire de Québec, Saint-Roch, 27 avril 1908; P678; TP11, S1, SS20, SSS1, 5 mai 1876, no.1812; 9 sept. 1878, no.2231; 6 avril 1880, no.2484; 18 janv. 1881, no.2607; 9 juill. 1913, no.204. Bureau de la Publicité des Droits (Québec), vol.B-120, no.54798; vol.B-124, no.57496; vol.B-158, no.79938; vol.B-169, no.87282; vol.B-174, nos.90750, 90892; vol.B-196, no.114788; vol.B-197, nos.102417, 102495; vol.B-200, no.106668; vol.B-203, no.106667; vol.B-205, no.108863; vol.B-217, no.117413; vol.B-224, nos.122954, 122956; vol.B-226, no.123988; vol.B-227, no.123989; vol.B-229, no.125161; vol.B-246, nos.133518, 133544; vol.B-250, no.135936; vol.B-347, no.193715; vol.B-353, no.193719; vol.B-360, nos.193714, 193716. L'Action catholique (Québec), 22 févr. 1924. Daily Telegraph (Quebec), "20th century number," January 1900. L'Événement, 22 févr. 1924. Le Soleil, 23 nov. 1907, 22 févr. 1924. Bradstreet Commercial Report (New York), 1878–1925. Directory, Quebec, 1871–1925. Une page d'histoire de Québec; magnifique essor industriel ([Montréal, 1955]), 273–76. Who's who and why, 1914.

DRUMMOND, JOHN DOUGLAS FRASER, farmer, politician, and office holder; b. 23 April 1860 in McGillivray Township, Upper Canada, son of Duncan Drummond and Margaret Fraser; m. 1891 or 8 Dec. 1892 Catherine McEwen, and they had three sons; d. 24 May 1925 in Ottawa and was buried near Nairn in Middlesex County, Ont.

A son of Scottish immigrants, John Drummond began farming after his public school education. Upon his father's death in 1883, he took over the family farm in McGillivray, north of Ailsa Craig; he would attain moderate success in mixed farming and raising Durham cattle. A freemason and member of the Ailsa Craig Presbyterian Church, in public affairs he served McGillivray as a councillor (1891–94), deputy reeve (1895), reeve (1896–98, 1902), and township clerk (1906–21). In addition, he was auditor of the Ailsa Craig Farmers' Co-operative Association, held stock in the United Farmers' Co-operative Company, and sat on the local executive of the United Farmers of Ontario, who had come to power in 1919 under Ernest Charles Drury*.

Despite his experience in local politics, Drummond was not anxious to seek higher office. At a United Farmers meeting at Strathroy in 1921, however, out of a sense of duty and in response to "strenuous urging," he accepted nomination as the Progressive party's candidate for Middlesex West in the upcoming federal election. At the time, farmers in Ontario and the west were publicly rethinking political, economic, and social issues. Challenging what they saw as autocratic domination by the "big interests," they fielded candidates federally as well as provincially. Established in 1920 as the federal wing of the agrarian movement and led by Thomas Alexander Crerar*, the Progressives entered the 1921 contest calling for tariff reform, public ownership of natural resources, utilities, and financial institutions, and the adoption of such popular democratic panaceas as the initiative, referendum, and recall.

At age 61, Drummond ran an effective campaign, pointing to his municipal experience and attacking the pro-tariff government of Arthur Meighen*. He charged that the tariff "had allowed the big interests to get the farmers by the throat." As well, he called for the greater involvement of women in politics and the eradication of blind party loyalty. He won easily, one of 64 Progressives elected, but overall the Liberals were victorious and formed a government under William Lyon Mackenzie King*.

Though quietly attentive to constituency business and of dry humour, Drummond – reputedly the tallest member of the House of Commons at the time – was not known for making speeches. Concerned, however, about the effect of Liberal tariff and tax policies on farmers and consumers, he did deliver insightful critiques of William Stevens FIELDING's budgets of 1922 and 1923. In his charge of 21 May 1923 the somewhat idealistic MP deplored the broken electoral promises of King and Meighen. He was irked too by Meighen's casting of the Progressives, and agrarian politicians in general, as a "menacing enemy." It was those in agriculture, he proudly responded, who filled the "precious railways and precious merchant marine which are standing monuments of the want of foresight of both the old political parties." In a rare display of eloquence, he concluded "strong in the hope that there is somewhere in the distance . . . a hill top radiant with the sunshine of something for the agricultural people, a hill top radiant with the glory of equal opportunity to all and special privileges to none."

Although the Progressives held the balance of power in parliament, they proved unsuccessful in having their platform implemented by the Liberals. Their belief in constituency autonomy, for instance, meant that they did not always act in unison in the house, and their apparent impotence there alienated many adherents.

In the spring of 1925 Drummond underwent minor surgery, but pneumonia set in and he died. Tributes in the commons uniformly expressed respect for his principled behaviour and concern for his riding. Representative of agrarian activism during the 1910s and 1920s, he had joined a movement that proved unable to advance its agenda for change. If he could not help usher in the Progressive platform, Drummond was determined at least to represent his constituents to the best of his ability, and in that he was successful.

KERRY BADGLEY

AO, RG 22-321, no.17048; RG 80-8-0-988, no.9386. *Farmers' Sun* (Toronto), 28 May 1925. *London Advertiser* (London, Ont.), 18, 23–24 Nov. 1921; 25–26 May 1925. *London Free Press*, 7 Dec. 1921, 25 May 1925. *Ottawa Evening Journal*, 25 May 1925. *Parkhill Gazette* (Parkhill, Ont.), 28 May 1925. Kerry Badgley, "Ringing out the narrowing lust of gold, ringing in a common love of good: the United Farmers of Ontario in Lambton, Simcoe and Lanark counties, 1914–1926" (PHD thesis, Carleton Univ., Ottawa, 1996). Can., House of Commons, *Debates*, 1922: 2272–74; 1923: 2973–76; 1925: 3475–76. *CPG*, 1922. *McGillivray Township remembers, 1842–1992* (Ailsa Craig, Ont., 1992). W. L. Morton, *The Progressive party in Canada* (Toronto, 1950). L. A. Wood, *A history of farmers' movements in Canada* (Toronto, 1924; repr., intro. F. J. K. Griezic, Toronto and Buffalo, N.Y., 1975).

DRUMMOND, LEWIS HENRY (baptized **Louis-Henri-Alphonse**, he signed **Louis** when writing to his French-speaking superiors), Roman Catholic priest, Jesuit, educator, editor, public speaker, author, and translator; b. 19 Oct. 1848 in Montreal, fourth child of Lewis Thomas Drummond*, solicitor general of Lower Canada, and Elmire Debartzch, daugh-

Drummond

ter of Pierre-Dominique Debartzch*; d. 28 July 1929 in Guelph, Ont.

Lewis Henry Drummond claimed Irish and Scots ancestors on his father's side and French and German on his mother's, although the Debartzchs came from Danzig (Gdańsk, Poland). Fluent in English and French, he gained an appreciation of both linguistic groups in an era marked by quarrels over language and religion. At the Collège Sainte-Marie in Montreal, which he attended from 1857 to 1865, he completed the classical course with outstanding success in debating and dramatics, interests which would continue for the rest of his life. He then studied geology and surveying with Sir William Edmond Logan* for about two and a half years.

Drummond entered the Jesuit noviciate at Sault-au-Récollet (Montreal) on 29 Jan. 1868. From 1870 to 1872 he taught fourth- and fifth-year classes in the classical program at the Collège Sainte-Marie. Exhausted after composing and giving several performances of a drama in five acts prepared for the golden anniversary of the ordination of Bishop Ignace Bourget*, which was celebrated from 27 to 30 Oct. 1872, he developed symptoms of tuberculosis and was sent to the Jesuits in Laval, France, to rest during 1872–73. He studied philosophy from 1873 to 1876 at Woodstock College in Woodstock, Md, and then taught at St Francis Xavier College in New York City, 1876–77 and 1879–80, and at St John's College in Fordham (New York City), 1877–79. He did his theology at St Beuno's College in Wales from 1880 to 1884 and while there was ordained priest on 23 Sept. 1883. During these years he also served on the editorial staff of the *Month* (London, Eng.).

After a year of spiritual training in Roehampton (London), Drummond returned to Canada. On 7 Aug. 1885 he arrived in St Boniface, Man., to teach at the Collège de Saint-Boniface, just taken over by the Jesuits. He would take the final vows of his order on 15 August the following year. The trial of Métis leader Louis Riel*, which had finished the week before Drummond's arrival, and Riel's hanging on 16 November divided the country and led to Drummond's rapid engagement in the political questions of the west. He began speaking and writing on behalf of French Canadians and of Roman Catholics in general. His training in rhetoric, added to his natural theatrical aptitudes, enabled him to become a public speaker of considerable renown. He gave retreats across the west and preached well-attended sermons in Winnipeg and other parishes in the archdiocese of St Boniface. He was often the guest speaker at religious and secular events. A devoted follower of Archbishop Alexandre-Antonin Taché*, he defended the ultramontane view in disputes over the Jesuits' Estates Act in 1889 [see Honoré Mercier*]. When he spoke in Brandon against D'Alton McCarthy*, who

had criticized the act and Catholics in a speech in Manitoba on 5 August, troops had to be called in to prevent a riot.

In 1890 Drummond became rector of the Collège Sainte-Marie. He was the only anglophone ever to hold that position. Two of his plays, "The conversion of Ireland" and "Moïse en Egypte," were produced while he was at the college and he drew crowds to his sermons for the English congregation at Le Gesù. He also served as president of the administrative council of the Catholic and Protestant night schools of Montreal in 1891.

During 1886–87 Drummond had been one of two representatives of the Collège de Saint-Boniface on the University of Manitoba's board of studies. This experience, together with his rectorship in Montreal, contributed to his new position on the University of Manitoba's council when he returned to the Collège de Saint-Boniface in 1892 as prefect of studies. In addition, he was reappointed to the university's board of studies. He became an editor (though not listed as such) of the archdiocese's English-language newspaper, the *Northwest Review*. In 1895 he published *Acadia, missing links of a lost chapter in American history* (2v., Montreal and New York), his translation of a manuscript by Édouard Richard*. He continued his polemical activities, speaking on school questions, French-English relations, temperance, and even health care. By 1904, however, a bronchial infection forced him to slow down, and his teaching load was reduced from five lectures a day to two. That same year, he was elected a director of the Dominion Educational Association.

Drummond had been more ready than Taché's successor, Archbishop Adélard Langevin*, to accept the compromise offered by the government of Wilfrid Laurier* to settle the Manitoba school question in 1896 and relations between Drummond and his superior had soured. Drummond criticized a statement made by Langevin in 1900 for its biased presentation of the question, one that ascribed all virtues to the French and all vices to the English. He grew closer to the English-speaking Catholics of Winnipeg, who petitioned Langevin in 1906 to establish a parish for them in Fort Rouge, in the southern part of the city. Langevin blamed their actions on Drummond. The petitioners were eventually successful and Drummond became the first pastor of St Ignatius parish in February 1908, a position he held until the fall of that year.

After a few months in Guelph, Drummond moved to New York City to become assistant editor of the new Jesuit journal, *America*. In 1910 he returned to Montreal as assistant to Edward James DEVINE, editor of the *Canadian Messenger of the Sacred Heart*, and he again preached at Le Gesù. Two years later he went to Guelph as assistant pastor. In 1913 Drummond headed west to the Collège Saint-François-Xavier, newly established by the Jesuits in Edmonton. There he lectured in theology to lay teachers and was spiritual director until ill health forced him to return in 1919, to Montreal, where he served as spiritual director at Loyola College and edited the *Loyola College Review*.

With the division of the Jesuits into English- and French-speaking provinces in 1924, it was natural for Drummond to join the province of Upper Canada. Symptoms of Alzheimer's disease forced his move in 1925 to the St Stanislaus noviciate in Guelph, where the novices took turns caring for him. Though he was not confined to bed, he needed constant assistance in the ordinary tasks of life. Yet he never lost his editorial interests and, until the day he died, he wrote comments on magazine articles supplied to him by the novices.

Drummond's lively and eloquent teaching inspired the young men who became the lawyers, judges, and businessmen of St Boniface in the early 20th century, his prestige as an English-speaking priest, public speaker, and professor helped to safeguard the interests of the Collège de Saint-Boniface at the University of Manitoba, and his editorials and willingness to engage in public disputes shaped English-speaking discourse across western Canada. In 1961 the new science complex at Loyola College, Montreal, was named the Drummond Science Building in honour of him and his family.

MARTHA MCCARTHY

Lewis Henry Drummond is the author of "Manitoba: a letter from St Boniface College," *Woodstock Letters* (Woodstock, Md), 16 (1887): 10–20, *The French element in the Canadian northwest* (Winnipeg, 1887), "The Church and the colony," in *Canada and its provinces: a history of the Canadian people and their institutions . . .* , ed. Adam Shortt and A. G. Doughty (23v., Toronto, 1913–17), 2: 379–444, and numerous articles and editorials in the *Northwest Rev.* (Winnipeg), 1885–1913. In addition, a series of exchanges between Drummond and the Reverend Jesse J. Roy was published as *The Jesuit order, or, an infallible pope . . .* ([Winnipeg?], 1889) and *The Jesuits: a reply to the Rev. J. J. Roy . . .* ([Ottawa?, 1889?]). A debate in which he became involved with the Reverend Richard Frederick Littledale resulted in the publication of *Controversy on the constitutions of the Jesuits . . .* (Winnipeg, 1889).

Arch. de la Compagnie de Jésus, Prov. du Canada Français (Saint-Jérôme, Qué.), BO-78-9-13-73 (lettres de Drummond à Désy). Arch. de la Soc. Hist. de Saint-Boniface (Winnipeg), Fonds de la Corporation archiépiscopale catholique romaine, sér. Langevin; sér. Taché. Soc. of Jesus, Upper Canada Prov. Arch., Regis College (Toronto), A-128 (L. H. Drummond files). *Northwest Rev.*, 23 Jan., 19 Nov., 3 Dec. 1904; 2 Feb. 1918. *Dictionary of Jesuit biography: ministry to English Canada, 1842–1987* (Toronto, 1991). Gérard Jolicœur, *Les jésuites dans la vie manitobaine* (1v. paru, Saint-Boniface [Winnipeg], 1985). Martha McCarthy,

"St Ignatius parish, 1908–1929," in *St Ignatius, a growing community* (Winnipeg, 1983).

DRUMMOND, ROBERT, coalminer, trade union leader, journalist, and politician; b. 29 Oct. 1840 in Greenock, Scotland, son of Robert Drummond and Elizabeth McAllister; m. 1871 Mary (May) Douglas Alexander, and they had one daughter who died in childhood; d. 26 Dec. 1925 in Stellarton, N.S., and was buried in Springhill, N.S.

Robert Drummond was one of the most significant figures of 19th-century Canadian labour history. As grand secretary and pre-eminent spokesperson for the Provincial Workmen's Association of Nova Scotia, a union whose membership was mainly comprised of coalminers, and later as the mining industry's voice in the Legislative Council and in his own newspaper, Drummond played an important role in redefining industrial relations and entrenching liberalism in the eastern coalfields.

The son of a grocer, Drummond emigrated from Scotland about 1865. He found employment in the coalmine at Lingan, Cape Breton Island. On his initial visit to the mine he was taken into one of the rooms where the coal was hewn; there he encountered a worker whose misplaced lamp set off a miniature explosion. "This," Drummond would later remember, "was the stranger's first acquaintance with an explosive mine gas mixture."

Nova Scotia coalmining was volatile in every sense from the 1860s to the 1890s. Alongside the venerable General Mining Association, which until 1858 had held monopoly rights on coal, could be found many new American- or central-Canadian-owned mining companies, trying to survive in a newly competitive realm, one that was also influenced by drastic shifts in international market conditions and the policies of a revenue-seeking, increasingly regulatory liberal state. In the absence of adequate safety inspection, and having no union, miners confronted physical danger, irregular work, low wages, and often high-handed bosses. Drummond, like many miners, adapted to these conditions by moving from pit to pit in search of steady work; he also unsuccessfully tried to set up a small shop on his own account. About 1872 he left Cape Breton for the coalfield in mainland Pictou County, where he found employment at the Drummond colliery in Westville; in 1873 it was to be the scene of one of North America's most deadly mine explosions. After a brief stint as a timekeeper at another Pictou mine, he was offered a position around 1874 as the bank boss, or surface supervisor, at the rapidly expanding mine at Springhill, a flourishing new Cumberland County community whose prosperity was built on selling coal to local industrial consumers and, above all, to the Intercolonial Railway.

Born into the lower middle class, well disciplined

Drummond

in the habits of thought and practice of Scottish Presbyterianism, profoundly impressed by and almost monotonously eloquent about such values as thrift, self-help, and independence, Drummond was, many contemporaries would remark, a bright-eyed and materialistic Scot-on-the-make. All his adult life he spoke with a Scottish accent, peppered his talk with quotes from Burns as well as from Shakespeare and the Bible, ardently defended the values of Presbyterianism, and celebrated the triumph of science and material progress with an enthusiasm worthy of Adam Smith or Horatio Alger. In another context and, perhaps, with a less developed rebellious streak, Drummond would have been remembered, if at all, as one of a vast legion of colonials for whom liberal praxis and identification with the British homeland were two sides of the same coin, inseparable aspects of a Victorian ideology of social improvement and individual self-betterment that had all the force of a secular religion. Yet in the two overlapping phases of his public life – 1879–98 in trade unionism and 1891–1925 in the Legislative Council and in mining journalism – Drummond, operating in an unusual context and with unusual qualities of eloquence and self-confidence, challenged and transformed elements of the transatlantic liberal culture that had so deeply shaped him.

Drummond's career as a trade unionist began in early 1879, when the Spring Hill Mining Company, after declaring large dividends in the mid 1870s and having invested £60,000 to take over territories controlled by the General Mining Association, imposed a wage reduction of three cents per box of coal cut. There followed a further three-cent reduction in August, which brought the miners out on strike. Neither wage reductions nor strikes were novelties to the industry, which had been shaken by violent clashes earlier in the decade, but the company's tactic was singularly ill-judged in 1879, when business and coal prices were reviving and the company was conspicuously prosperous. As bank boss, Drummond was in a good position to investigate the merits of the company's case, and he publicized the unflattering results of his inquiries under the nom de plume "A Traveller" in a Halifax newspaper. He lost his job, but gained a career in the labour movement: when he attended a clandestine miners' meeting in Springhill, he was hailed as a hero and, on 29 Aug. 1879, he was placed on a committee to draft a constitution and by-laws for the Provincial Miners' Association. On 1 September he became the salaried grand secretary of the new body. The union's ensuing victory in Springhill enhanced its reputation: by the end of 1879 lodges had been organized in Stellarton, Westville, and Thorburn in Pictou County. The *Trades Journal*, edited by Drummond, was established in January 1880 to bring the association's viewpoint to an even wider audience. That same year the union rebaptized itself as the Provincial Workmen's Association, to welcome workers other than coalminers, and began to organize in Cape Breton, where it encountered fierce opposition from mine managers but ultimate acceptance as the voice of the miners.

Down to 1898 Drummond would be the storm petrel and main lobbyist of the PWA, but he was not its chief bureaucrat or leader in a 20th-century sense. He was fearless in his irreverent denunciations of managers who would not negotiate, and particularly inventive in conscripting the language of a Presbyterian and Scottish "common sense" in the struggle to show that the new union was not a criminal conspiracy but a moderate force for change within the terms of the liberal order. The association's ritual, strongly influenced by freemasonry, probably reflected Drummond's ingrained pragmatism and belief in self-help: prospective members were required to swear, among other things, "not to indulge in visionary theories" or to imagine that there was "a good time coming" when plenty would be easily obtained. They were also counselled that, "in taking a stand against what we consider misdirected impositions of employers, we must not ourselves be unreasonable." "Our object is not to wage a war of labour against capital, nor to drive trade, by oppressive measures, from the locality; on the contrary, by mutual concessions between master and man, we seek to have it carried on with advantage to both." Drummond upheld the values of a classical liberal individualism, and "None cease to rise but those who cease to climb" was both the association's motto and his own cherished belief. They were words of improvement – the PWA would call consistently for mining schools, better training for managers, and more effective mine inspection – but they could also be, when applied to workers, and mine workers particularly, words of resistance, justifying the approximately 70 strikes mounted by the union while Drummond was its grand secretary, one of which – the 1886–87 general colliery strike in Pictou County [*see* Henry Skeffington Poole*] – was among the largest industrial disputes known in Victorian Canada.

However moderate and soothing its documents, the union had a more radical side: the PWA's local records reveal hundreds of day-to-day acts of negotiation and resistance in the pits, as managers were forced to bargain with their employees. Drummond's PWA was not a vast inclusive movement like its contemporary the Knights of Labor, but (excepting a few non-mining lodges) a small, often embattled confederation of coal workers, generally under the leadership of the colliers, the skilled workers who actually cut the coal. The union's Grand Council, frequently a voice of moderation, was regularly contradicted by the local lodges and (until a constitutional change in

1891) by the autonomous Cape Breton subcouncil. Drummond, ever concerned to present the public with a portrait of a union that was decorous and realistic, capable of seeing both sides of demands for wage reductions and of acknowledging the principle of the managers' authority, nonetheless did little to interfere with local lodges who fought for their members' interests. One can often hear him, in the *Trades Journal*, chastising managers, bureaucrats, and politicians for failing to live up to the liberal ideal of the rational, self-contained individualism he championed. Contrary to the image subsequently painted by his critics, and by himself, Drummond was frequently the defender of strikes, even ones which involved a measure of violence against management, as the only way workers could fight for their rights under difficult local circumstances.

In a sense Drummond sanctioned, and even encouraged, the consistent application of a doctrine of liberal individualism to the coal industry – a doctrine which, because it unequivocally defended the right of independent colliers to a large degree of control over their working lives, not to mention better wages, also entailed recognition by management of the workers' right not just to organize a union but also to prescribe a good deal of the mines' day-to-day operations. The PWA's more famous struggles for mine-safety legislation were linked to this conception of working-class independence: those who inspected the mines should be, in part, answerable to the miners, whose lives were at stake in the pits. Drummond was a brilliant propagandist, a master of Victorian rhetoric and fond of a broad Scottish humour; in the *Trades Journal*, widely read in the coal communities, including those in which it had been banned by management, he succeeded in making mine managers and servile workers look unmanly and irrational. In these diverse struggles Drummond was consistently and adamantly a radical liberal who believed that in industrial life, no less than in politics, individuals should be treated with respect and accorded power over the most important aspects of their lives. For him, it was a matter of democratic common sense that managers of coalmines, working the "people's coal," were public officials subject to public scrutiny. Drummond chastised them with all the subtlety of a Presbyterian elder admonishing errant members of his congregation, or (to use an epithet that was once attached to him) a furiously indignant Scottish terrier. That such a defence of workers' collective (and at times violent) activism could coexist in a journal that routinely celebrated the mid-Victorian pieties of temperance, respectability, religion, and decorum can only be explained with reference to the radical liberalism which sustained its editor. Drummond saw no contradiction.

Three additional historical developments of great significance can be associated with Drummond as a trade unionist. First, through the PWA he contributed to the democratization of public life in Nova Scotia. Although demands for universal manhood suffrage had been made before the emergence of the PWA, the association did much to push the issue by entering provincial politics and running candidates in 1886, by petitioning the federal and provincial governments, and by pursuing the matter steadily in the *Trades Journal*. The extension of the franchise in 1889 to the majority of working men was in large measure Drummond's and the PWA's achievement. In the 1890s he would be among the most eloquent Liberal voices raised on behalf of full female enfranchisement, including women's rights to hold public office. Second, with the support of Edwin Gilpin*, inspector of mines from 1879 and deputy commissioner of public works and mines from 1886, Drummond and the PWA pushed hard and successfully for tougher mine laws. Some concerned safety; the abolition in 1891, after a tragic explosion at Springhill [*see* Henry Swift*], of the use of gunpowder in gaseous mines, perhaps the PWA's single greatest achievement, undoubtedly saved many lives. Others involved technical education for miners, the appointment of checkweighmen (officials who recorded daily coal production), the setting of a minimum age at which boys (a vital part of the 19th-century workforce) could enter the pit, and the criteria for determining when one was qualified to become a collier (in 1891 these included one year's experience in the mine). Third, Drummond and the PWA brought about a new recognition of trade unionism as a legitimate force in social and economic life. Written collective agreements, the first signed in 1885 in Springhill, represented an important new approach to industrial relations in Canada. The country's first compulsory arbitration legislation, passed in 1888, although it never tamed the autocracy of managers to the extent the association had hoped, made a tangible difference in Springhill, where the lodge was able to defeat a stubbornly anti-union employer by drawing not only on the arbitration law but also on the personal mediation of Premier William Stevens FIELDING. The coalminers of Nova Scotia were historically among the most creative and radical workers in 20th-century Canada; it is not unrealistic to look for intimations of their dynamism and solidarity in the radical liberal era of the PWA.

In the 1890s Drummond would find himself less and less at home in the PWA, which gradually became more of an industrial union than a craft union implicitly centred on the colliers. Many in the PWA, now increasingly concentrated in a fast-developing Cape Breton, argued for legislation to end company stores and establish an eight-hour day. Drummond, however, opposed any law that prohibited workers from giving orders for supplies in company offices. It

Drummond

was this issue that led him to abandon the leadership of the PWA in 1898, though there had been indications of his frustration earlier in the decade, as he came to realize that he had less influence with the Fielding government than he had hoped.

Drummond's second career, which can be dated from his appointment to the Legislative Council in 1891, distanced him from the workers whose activism he had once justified. After his removal to Stellarton in the early 1880s, he had begun to acquire middle-class respectability. A pillar of St John's Presbyterian Church, he became prominent in local politics (he was a councillor and then mayor in 1899–1900) and the proprietor of his own paper, the business-oriented *Maritime Mining Record* (1898–1924). His appointment to the council had come after he had twice unsuccessfully run for a seat in the House of Assembly, first in 1886 as an independent and then in 1890 as a straightforward Liberal.

It is conventional to write of his second career in terms of unprincipled ambition and opportunism, and it is fair to suggest that by the end of his life Drummond – whose will allocated $19,000 to his kinfolk, church, and favoured charities – had prospered as a result of mining investments, business journalism, and membership in the council. Much of what Drummond said and wrote in this period predictably celebrates the achievements of far-sighted capitalists and the provincial government (although he would become progressively more critical of the latter for its timid approach to mine promotion and development). It was only in his second and last book, his memoirs as a trade union leader written shortly before his death, that he returned to his older radical liberal critique of mine managers, but even here Drummond was concerned to make his union record appear much less combative than in fact it had been.

Drummond in his later years was primarily an apologist for the coal companies. He championed the government's 1893 deal with Henry Melville WHITNEY, through which the Dominion Coal Company Limited swallowed up most of industrial Cape Breton, and he would later write glowingly of the British Empire Steel Corporation (Besco), the giant merger which had taken over much of the industry. Speaking in the Legislative Council in 1910, Drummond defended local capitalists: "Now-a-days so much is said against the capitalist that one might suppose him to be a monster, in human form, whose one object in life was to keep the noses of the workmen to the grindstone. . . . The freest, most independent men in the world to-day are the men of our Nova Scotia coal mines." Far from robber barons, the province's coal operators were, he maintained in a detailed if somewhat indiscreet speech the following year, mainly involved in unprofitable competitive concerns struggling to deliver dividends to their shareholders. After

1918, when the industry entered into a dramatic crisis, he argued on behalf of further mergers of the coal companies, which were justified according to the laws of industrial efficiency, social utility, and the liberal political order. Non–Nova Scotians who believed that the coal communities were impoverished were victims of labour and left-wing propaganda; even the infant mortality statistics cited by some as an indictment of capitalist oppression were interpreted differently by Drummond. Company stores were a boon to the working-class men and women who used them, and if there were any problems with company housing, Drummond wrote in 1922, they were most likely the fault of the occupiers of the houses themselves, who failed to keep them clean and tidy.

Drummond despised District 26 of the United Mine Workers of America, which had replaced the PWA as the union of the miners in 1917–18. Of all the UMWA's critics during its long struggle for acceptance in Nova Scotia, he was the fiercest and best informed. He viewed District 26 as a fifth column of American capitalists keen to damage the local industry, or of misguided and perhaps even insane radicals conspiring with the Soviets in a strange and terrible experiment in collectivism. "What a contrast the U.M.W. is to the old P.W.A., whose executive gave no place in their proceedings to mutual recriminations," he lamented in 1920. A "riot of extravagance" in wage settlements threatened to destabilize the entire industry; workers in pursuit of $80 overcoats and $100 suits were running away from honest labour. "Notoriety is meat and drink to a certain stamp of labour leaders," Drummond remarked, as he ruthlessly satirized the rhetoric of the leaders of District 26. In the depths of the crisis of the 1920s [*see* William DAVIS] Drummond would dismiss "cries of poverty" with arguments that workers had forgotten the habits of "industry, sobriety and thrift" once championed by the PWA. Such vituperative polemics, and they were many, written in the last decade of his life did much to damage his long-term reputation among labour historians and in the coalmining communities of Cape Breton, and made Drummond's very name an object of contempt for leftists. It seemed that the fearless radical liberal terrier had become a reactionary curmudgeon for whom almost anything designed by Besco was blessed.

Yet this impression, valid in some respects, misses aspects of Drummond's second career that went beyond a simple acquiescence in the imperatives of capital. Drummond became, especially in the years before 1914, the ranking authority on the development of mines and mining in Nova Scotia. His long speeches in the Legislative Council were studded with facts and figures; his editorials and articles in the *Maritime Mining Record* were extensively cited, in other newspapers and by politicians on both sides of the House of Assembly. Drummond was highly knowledgeable, and his journal is an indispensable source of insider information. In 1911, defending the interests of the PWA against those of the UMWA, he was able to describe the financial health and future prospects of every coal company listed in the *Report* of the provincial Department of Mines. More generally, Drummond always argued that such companies were exploiting the people's coal, not their own. Along with many "new liberal" intellectuals of his generation, who believed the state had a vital role to play in bringing order to an otherwise unstable capitalist system, Drummond defended a greatly expanded role for government in exploration for minerals and in the supervision of mines. He believed that mining fatalities would be understood only if the government undertook a much more scientific and systematic inspection of mine roofs, sides, and faces. As the foremost intellectual defender of the system evolved by Fielding and carried forward by premiers George Henry MURRAY and Ernest Howard Armstrong*, in which the interests of the provincial state and the mining industry were closely correlated and which saw the coal and steel industries as the vital nuclei of provincial development, Drummond exercised a very real cultural power, down to the crisis of the system in the 1920s. When the province considered limiting hours of labour in the mines, and when the UMWA later demanded an eight-hour day inclusive of the time taken to walk to the working face, Drummond's replies would draw extensively on the practical difficulties of any regulation of hours in a province which had far-running submarine coal deposits and which confronted not only seasonal and other fluctuations in shipping but also the competition of American and British coal in the vital St Lawrence River market.

Drummond spoke with passion and authority, whether on the need for more efficiently managed and supervised "humane institutions" (he served on and chaired this committee in the Legislative Council), against imprisonment for debt, or on behalf of temperance. He was in fact one of the most eloquent new liberals of his day, who sensed acutely the need for an expansive state to rationalize the classical liberal order. Undoubtedly the core passion of his later life was the development of the province's coalfields. His *Minerals and mining, Nova Scotia* (1918) is a hymn of praise to the progress of the mining industries, a work whose boosterism is so extreme that even the events of World War I are seen as illustrations of the marvels of industrial progress. When Drummond died in 1925, the *Halifax Herald* was not alone in saluting an almost stereotypical industrious Scot, burning with "the unquenchable ambition of his race"; many of his radical contemporaries and successors would argue that his stubborn individualism

and his entrepreneurialism were precisely what had ultimately unfitted him as a 20th-century trade-union leader. He nonetheless commanded a great deal of credibility within the state and in society generally.

Nothing was "so repulsive, so offensive, so nauseating to the workingman as to be patronized and patted on the back with the saying 'Oh poor fellow,'" Drummond had remarked concerning a local assessment law in 1892. "What are we," he asked in arguing against the abolition of company stores four years later, "free men, or are we cowards? Are we men, or are we weaklings?" To the end of his days Drummond would defend a radical liberal vision of working-class independence, even as its logical and social preconditions eroded around him – mainly as a result of the state-stimulated monopsonies he himself had welcomed and later praised. Since the 1920s historians of Cape Breton and of Canadian labour have routinely denounced Drummond as the opportunistic antithesis of the socialist trade unionist they admire. It could be argued that they have tended to underestimate the staying power of the profoundly liberal approach to industrial life that Drummond exemplified and which, for better or worse, many Canadian workers have historically preferred. For all his contradictions, inconsistencies, and reversals, and perhaps partly because of them, Drummond, one of Nova Scotia's more interesting new liberal politicians, should also be remembered as a representative and revealing figure in Canadian working-class history. In 1924, when he reminisced about his trade-union career to the Mining Society of Nova Scotia, of which he had been a member – and often an executive member – since 1902, Drummond delighted in reminding his audience about the PWA's first big strike at the Drummond colliery in 1879. The manager, in Drummond's fond memory, was completely humbled by the association's valiant forces. Forced to recognize the union and its representatives, he drew the line at "recognizing" the irritating, offensive figure of its grand secretary, for whom he reserved the Scottish epithet "the clatty little bugger." It was obviously a memory, and an epithet, that 45 years later Drummond, unrevised and unrepentant, still cherished.

IAN MCKAY

Robert Drummond's publications include: *To the officers and members of Keystone Lodge* (Stellarton, N.S., 1896); "The mine and the farm," Mining Soc. of Nova Scotia, *Journal* (Halifax), 14 (1909–10): 15–29; *The sixties and subsequently; paper read August 31st, 1912* (n.p., [1912]); "Mining fatalities," Mining Soc. of Nova Scotia, *Journal*, 19 (1914–15): 49–58; *Minerals and mining, Nova Scotia* (Stellarton, 1918); "The beginnings of trade unionism in New Glasgow," *Evening News* (New Glasgow, N.S.), 7 July 1924 (reissued in Canadian Institute of Mining and Metallurgy, *Trans.* (Montreal), 20 (1924): 914–32); and *Recollec-*

Ducharme

tions and reflections of a former trades union leader ([Stellarton, 1926]).

Dalhousie Univ. Arch. (Halifax), MS-9 (Labour union papers), Provincial Workmen's Assoc., no.27, Holdfast Lodge, Joggins, N.S., minutes. General Register Office for Scotland (Edinburgh), Reg. of births, Greenock (West), 29 Oct. 1840 (mfm. at Scottish Record Office, Edinburgh). Human Resources Development Canada Library (Hull, Que.), Provincial Workmen's Assoc. of Nova Scotia and New Brunswick, Constitution, by-laws, and minutes of proc. of the grand council, 1879–1917 (typescript). NSARM, RG 21. Pictou County Court of Probate (Pictou, N.S.), Estate papers, will of Robert Drummond (mfm. at NSARM). *Eastern Chronicle* (New Glasgow), 29 Dec. 1925. *Evening News*, 28 Dec. 1925. *Halifax Herald*, 21 Feb., 7 March 1895; 28 Dec. 1925. *Trades Journal* (Springhill, N.S.), 1880–82; continued at Stellarton, 1882–91. Canadian Mining Institute, *Monthly Bull.* (Montreal), no.[81] (January 1919)–no.98 (June 1920); continued by the Canadian Institute of Mining and Metallurgy, no.99 (July 1920)–no.124 (December 1924). Eugene Forsey, *Economic and social aspects of the Nova Scotia coal industry* (Montreal, 1926); *Trade unions in Canada, 1812–1902* (Toronto, 1982). Dawn Fraser, *Echoes from labor's wars*, intro. David Frank and Donald MacGillivray (expanded ed., Wreck Cove, N.S., 1992). M. S. Kirincich, *A centennial history of Stellarton* (Antigonish, N.S., 1990). H. A. Logan, *The history of trade-union organization in Canada* (Chicago, 1928). Ian McKay, "'By wisdom, wile or war': the Provincial Workmen's Association and the struggle for working-class independence in Nova Scotia, 1879–97," *Labour* (St John's), 18 (1986): 13–62. *Maritime Mining Record* (Stellarton), 1900–24. Mining Soc. of Nova Scotia, *Journal* 7 (1902–3); minutes for 1902. John Moffatt, *P.W.A. Grand Secretary Moffatt's valedictory report* (n.p., [1917]). N.S., House of Assembly, *Debates and proc.*, 1906, 1910–11; Legislative Council, *Debates and proc.*, 1891–1922. B. D. Palmer, *Working-class experience: rethinking the history of Canadian labour, 1800–1991* (Toronto, 1992). David Pigot, *The Mining Society of Nova Scotia, 1887–1987; a history of the society . . .* (Glace Bay, N.S., 1987). *Post office Greenock directory . . .* (Greenock, Scot.), 1864/65. S. M. Reilly, "The Provincial Workmen's Association of Nova Scotia, 1879–1898" (MA thesis, Dalhousie Univ., 1979). Daniel Samson, "Dependency and rural industry: Inverness, Nova Scotia, 1899–1910," in *Contested countryside: rural workers and modern society in Atlantic Canada, 1800–1950*, ed. Daniel Samson (Fredericton, 1994).

DUCHARME, GUILLAUME-NARCISSE (baptized **Vincent-Guillaume-Narcisse**), office holder, businessman, politician, and philanthropist; b. 3 Jan. 1851 in Châteauguay, Lower Canada, son of Vincent-Valéry Ducharme and Marie Denis; m. 6 July 1880 Marie-Mathilde-Adélia Rivet (d. December 1925) in Sainte-Cunégonde (Montreal), and they had 14 children, five of whom outlived their mother; d. 30 April 1929 in Montreal and was buried in Chambly, Que.

Guillaume-Narcisse Ducharme began his classical studies at the Petit Séminaire de Sainte-Thérèse, which had been founded by his uncle, Abbé Charles-Joseph Ducharme*, and he pursued them at the Petit Séminaire de Montréal from 1863 to 1865. He then left school to work as a clerk in the general store of a cousin in Danville, where he lived for four years before moving back to Montreal. After various jobs in fancy goods shops, he opened a dry goods store in 1881, but he gave it up soon afterwards to devote himself to public affairs.

Since 1878 Ducharme had been secretary-treasurer of the Sainte-Cunégonde school board, a position he would hold until 1903. Appointed postmaster in 1882, he would retain this office for 15 years. In 1884 he took on the job of secretary-treasurer and clerk of the village. As an office holder, Ducharme had a good deal of influence on the municipal council, according to Édouard-Zotique Massicotte*. He participated actively in the development of this Montreal suburban municipality, whose population of about 5,000 in 1881 doubled over the next decade. The village underwent many changes during this period: streets were paved, water mains and sewers were put in, and electric street lights were installed. There was also a Grand Trunk station and a branch of the Banque Jacques-Cartier, where Ducharme was the manager. He probably acquired his wealth through real estate – by 1902 he owned a lot of property.

Although his ideas were not universally shared, as an enterprising man he overcame every obstacle. Favouring the annexation of all the suburban municipalities by Montreal, Ducharme resigned as an office holder in 1891 and ran for a seat on the municipal council. He was defeated, however, and returned to his previous employment. Two years later, he was successful in his second attempt. At that time he was also president of the local section of the Association Saint-Jean-Baptiste de Montréal. His influence extended beyond Sainte-Cunégonde. A member of the Chambre de Commerce du District de Montréal and the Montreal Board of Trade, he was also a director of numerous companies, including Auer Incandescent Light Company Limited, Standard Light and Power Company, and Citizens Light and Power Company. In 1896 Ducharme scaled back his activities for reasons of health. He gave up his offices as councillor and postmaster and spent some time in Europe. Having returned to Canada, he was elected mayor of Sainte-Cunégonde in 1899. He carried out the first stage of his plan for annexation by integrating the municipality into the Montreal streetcar system. After resigning in 1902 to attend to his personal affairs, he moved the following year to Chambly, and would watch the annexation of Sainte-Cunégonde to Montreal in 1905 from a distance. Elected to the municipal council of Chambly in 1914, he was to serve as its mayor from 1915 to 1918.

Despite his important role in municipal affairs, Ducharme's name is mainly associated with the financial sector. He was named to the management of the Banque Jacques-Cartier in 1899, at a time when it was in serious difficulty [see Alphonse Desjardins*], and he succeeded in persuading customers to leave their savings in this French Canadian enterprise, which he revived under the name of Banque Provinciale du Canada. He would serve as its president from 1900 to 1907.

Ducharme also was president of the mutual benefit company La Sauvegarde from its beginnings in 1901. It too was suffering from French Canadians' lack of confidence in their financial institutions. In order to give better guarantees to the policy holders, its founder, Philorum Bonhomme, developed a plan to transform it into a share capital company. Ducharme agreed to invest in the new entity and he would remain its president for the rest of his life. Bonhomme was also supported by leading French Canadian businessmen in Montreal, including millionaire Frédéric-Ligori Béïque*, and politicians such as Henri Bourassa* and Napoléon-Antoine Belcourt*. According to data from 1910, the principal shareholder of the Life Insurance Company La Sauvegarde (the name it had adopted in 1903) was a prosperous merchant from Saint-Timothée, Narcisse Papineau, who bought $50,000 worth of shares. Ducharme owned $20,000 worth.

La Sauvegarde counted mainly on patriotism, as Bonhomme advised its agents. Its sales grew quite steadily from 1903 to 1912, but more slowly for the rest of that decade. Some shareholders were dissatisfied with these results. Dividends were slow in coming, while profits were lower than the Canadian average. Moreover, the construction of a new ten-storey head office in the heart of Vieux-Montréal in 1912 and 1913, which consumed most of the paid-up capital, was not well regarded by the federal superintendent of insurance, who had been overseeing the company since it obtained its federal charter in 1911. As a result, some 15 years after the company had been founded, a group of shareholders were considering selling it to anglophone interests. Ducharme and J.-N. Cabana, who was then the manager, addressed the problem and reviewed the operation of the agencies as well as the internal administration and investment strategy. This reform proved fruitful. From 1920 to 1924, the revenues and the number of policies in force more than doubled and growth continued until 1929 at an average annual rate of nearly 13 per cent.

A Conservative in politics, Ducharme was approached several times to be a candidate for that party. He nonetheless used his own money to finance the Montreal Le Devoir, a nationalist daily founded by Bourassa. The principal shareholder of the publishing company Imprimerie Populaire Limitée, Ducharme helped on two occasions to revive the newspaper. He also supported mutual aid societies, schools, and hospitals.

Guillaume-Narcisse Ducharme was a superb example of a self-made man. From humble beginnings, he became wealthy by investing in the residential development of the Montreal suburbs and increasing his capital by diversifying his interests. As Bourassa wrote a few days after Ducharme's death, he also had "a highly developed sense of social responsibility." His major achievement was the Life Insurance Company La Sauvegarde. In 1929 it ranked third among personal insurance companies founded by French Canadians in the province of Quebec, after the two large mutual aid societies, the Société des Artisans Canadiens-Français and the Alliance Nationale [see Sir Hormisdas Laporte*]. It ranked first, however, among share capital companies. La Sauvegarde would continue to be controlled by the Ducharme family until 1962, when it was purchased by a management company acting on behalf of the Desjardins movement.

JACQUES SAINT-PIERRE

ANQ-M, CE601-S19, 6 juill. 1880; CE607-S7, 20 juill. 1848, 4 janv. 1851. Desjardins Sécurité Financière, Centre de Documentation (Lévis, Qué.), Doc. de La Sauvegarde. Le Devoir, 22 mai 1926; 30 avril, 3 mai 1929. La Patrie, 18 sept. 1902. BCF, 1929: 448–49. Canadian men and women of the time (Morgan; 1912). Compagnie d'Assurance sur la Vie La Sauvegarde, Rapport annuel (Montréal), 1909–30. Encyclopaedia of Canadian biography . . . , vol.2. É.-Z. Massicotte, La cité de Sainte-Cunégonde de Montréal: notes et souvenirs (Montréal, 1893). Newspaper reference book. "Numéro-souvenir," La Vie (Montréal), 41 (1962), no.8. Prominent people of the province of Quebec, 1923–24 (Montreal, n.d.). [Télesphore Saint-Pierre], Histoire du commerce canadien-français de Montréal, 1535–1893 (Montréal, 1894). Benjamin Sulte et al., A history of Quebec, its resources and its people (2v., Montreal, 1908), 2: 667–68. Léon Trépanier, On veut savoir (4v., Montréal, 1960–62), 4: 55–57.

DUCLOS DE CELLES, ALFRED (baptized **Jean-Baptiste-Alfred**), journalist, librarian, and historian; b. 8 Aug. 1843 in the parish of Saint-Laurent, Lower Canada, son of Augustin-Candide Duclos De Celles, a notary, and Marie-Sarah-Anne Holmes; m. 25 Oct. 1876 in Saint-Ours, Que., Eugénie Panet-Dorion, daughter of Eugène-Philippe Dorion*, a lawyer, translator, and man of letters, and Marie Panet; they had one son; d. 5 Oct. 1925 in Ottawa.

After attending the primary school in his native village, Alfred Duclos De Celles enrolled belatedly in 1859 in the Petit Séminaire de Québec, where one of his uncles, Abbé John Holmes*, had taught. While doing his classical studies there, he took care of the library and wrote for the seminary's newspaper, L'Abeille. He was awarded prizes for excellence in history, geography, French, and English (which he had learned as a child), and graduated in 1867.

On 18 Feb. 1867 De Celles was taken on staff at Le

Journal de Québec, standing in for Joseph-Édouard Cauchon* for a few months before becoming his assistant, which he remained until 1872. At the same time, from 1867 to 1871 he studied law at the Université Laval in Quebec City and he would be called to the bar on 12 July 1873. Having acquired this liberal education, De Celles pursued his career as a political journalist in Montreal, where he joined Arthur Dansereau* at *La Minerve*, a Conservative party daily, of which he became editor in 1872. In 1874 he was president of the Club Cartier, which he founded along with other young Montreal Conservatives [*see* Sir Pierre-Évariste Leblanc*] who shared his belief that political commitment was a social and patriotic duty. De Celles had no desire, however, to pursue a career in politics. He was secretary-treasurer and administrator for the party in the Montreal region during the 1878 election, but this active involvement was an exception. It was primarily through his writing, skilled and partisan as it was, that he would serve the Conservatives.

In 1880 De Celles got his reward when he succeeded Antoine Gérin-Lajoie* as assistant librarian of the Library of Parliament in Ottawa. But his love of journalism persisted, and, with a couple of partners, he bought *L'Opinion publique*; he ran this Montreal weekly from Ottawa and wrote regularly for it on a wide variety of subjects from September 1881 to December 1883. Whether in his office in the library or in his letters, De Celles remained passionately interested in party politics; in his role as a go-between, he would ask favours, convey messages, or give advice to his friend Joseph-Adolphe Chapleau*, the premier of Quebec from 31 Oct. 1879 to 29 July 1882. On 3 March 1881 he wrote to Chapleau: "I've seen Dr Dionne [Narcisse-Eutrope Dionne*] of *Le Courrier du Canada*. He's hardly a fan of yours, I presume; he is one of those Quebeckers full of prejudices about Montreal. He wants to be appointed visiting physician of the Marine Hospital. With that [appointment,] you could make him jump at your command."

In January 1884 Alpheus Todd*, the parliamentary librarian, died. Some 40 Conservative MPs urged Sir John A. Macdonald* to appoint a French Canadian – namely, De Celles – to the office. Anglophone MPs, on the other hand, wanted one of their own to have it. A typically Canadian solution was found: the job was split with each position at the same level. Political manoeuvring aside, this decision can be explained by the dual role played by the Library of Parliament at that time, in the absence of a national library. Thus on 6 Aug. 1885 De Celles became the first general librarian, with powers matching those of the new parliamentary librarian, Martin Joseph Griffin, who was appointed on the same day. At that time De Celles's annual salary was $2,400; 12 years later, it would be

$3,200. The reports written by De Celles and Griffin recount their efforts to complete the collection of Canadian works, as well as the purchases made to satisfy the more immediate needs of legislators. Parliamentary sessions set the pace for their work, periods of intense activity and frequent meetings with MPs and ministers alternating with the development of collections and consultation with the educated reading public in the city who used the library. Although an important cultural institution, the Library of Parliament does not appear to have received the support it deserved. De Celles had to use his powers of persuasion to ensure that library staff were paid salaries comparable to those of the other civil servants. The librarians grumbled about the bad behaviour of MPs who disregarded library rules, and they repeatedly complained about lack of space and money. Nevertheless, in the 1890s they were proud to be introducing modern methods of library science, such as the card catalogue.

Wilfrid Laurier* became prime minister of Canada in June 1896. De Celles, whose Conservative zeal had diminished over the years, got on extremely well with him and even published his speeches (in Montreal in 1909 and 1920). In July 1897 De Celles represented Canada as a delegate at the International Library Conference in London. In addition to his other work, he served on the Board of Civil Service Examiners for more than 25 years from 1882 until 1908. He retired from public service in 1920.

Alfred De Celles was involved in many cultural organizations. From the early 1880s he was a member of the Institut Canadien-Français in Ottawa. In 1884 he and others, including Benjamin SULTE and Joseph-Étienne-Eugène Marmette, founded the Cercle des Dix, a body in which literature, history, science, and geography were discussed. In 1885 he became a member of the Royal Society of Canada, doubtless through patronage since at that time he did not meet the criterion for membership of having written at least one book. He would, however, become one of the most active and prestigious members of the society, serving as president of the French section in 1892–93 and 1916–17. From 1901 to 1904 De Celles was also vice-president of the central committee of the Aberdeen Association, whose mission was to provide books for colonists who had recently settled in the Canadian west. He was a member of the Alliance Française in Ottawa and was its president in 1904, 1908, and 1910.

Every summer, in the tranquillity of Les Goinions, his home at Pointe-au-Pic, Que., De Celles devoted himself to his own research. His major work as a historian, *Les États-Unis: origine, institutions, développement*, came out in Ottawa in 1896. Published at his own expense, it received the prize of the Académie des Sciences Morales et Politiques in Paris the following year. He sent a copy to Chapleau on 13 April 1896 suggesting, "I don't ask you to read it, but to have your government buy some copies from me. If you could put a word in with certain ministers. . . ." In later years, having become well known, he had no difficulty publishing and distributing his books throughout French and English Canada. Thus it was he who was invited to write the biographies of Louis-Joseph Papineau* and Sir George-Étienne Cartier*, essays included in a single volume published in Toronto in 1904 for the series *Makers of Canada* [*see* George Nathaniel Morang*]. Ten years later he wrote the introduction to the two volumes about the province of Quebec in the series entitled *Canada and its provinces*; De Celles also contributed to the same volume, an article on colonization, an overview of Quebec's history since confederation, and an account of the province's municipal system. *The "Patriotes" of '37: a chronicle of the Lower Canadian rebellion*, which he brought out at Toronto in 1916, was also part of a prestigious series, the *Chronicles of Canada* [*see* Robert Pollock GLASGOW*].

In his books De Celles took a comprehensive view, without a great deal of emphasis on scholarship or exhaustiveness. He did not hesitate to add personal comments, and it is these commentaries, from an author who had followed the ups and downs of Canadian political life from close quarters and over a long period, that constitute the chief interest of his works. He reserved his praise for Sir Louis-Hippolyte La Fontaine* (whose biography he had written and published in Montreal in 1907), who had achieved responsible government, and for Cartier, who had done his best to protect French Canadian interests after confederation. De Celles wrote the kind of history favoured by Conservatives like himself, men who were moderate in their opinions, Catholic without being ultramontane, nationalist but advocates of mutual accommodation (in the spirit of the Bonne Entente movement [*see* John Milton GODFREY*]), with a belief in material progress through liberal-style economic progress. In his last book, *Laurier et son temps*, which came out at Montreal in 1920, he praised the Liberal leader for these same conciliatory and pragmatic virtues.

Alfred Duclos De Celles never stopped writing. Throughout his life, and even in retirement, he contributed literary and historical essays to a number of journals, including the *Revue canadienne* in Montreal, *Le Canada français* in Quebec City, the *Bulletin des recherches historiques* of Lévis, and the *Transactions* of the Royal Society of Canada, in addition to articles for *La Presse*. His son, who was also named Alfred, followed in his footsteps and became a journalist and writer. Alfred Sr received an honorary doctorate of letters from the Université Laval in 1891 and, in 1896, the title of *officier de l'Instruction publique* of France. In 1901 the University of Ottawa awarded him an hon-orary DCL, in 1903 the French government made him a chevalier of the Legion of Honour, and in 1907 he became a CMG. Among his contemporaries, he was admired for his "lively and sparkling wit," the wide culture of "a true gentleman," and his courtesy, friend-liness, civic sense, and sincerity.

FERNANDE ROY

[The most complete bibliography of the writings of Alfred Duclos De Celles appears in A.-M. Dorion, "Bio-bibliogra-phie d'Alfred Duclos DeCelles" (mémoire, école de biblio-théconomie, univ. de Montréal, 1942). Several archives hold documents pertaining to De Celles. The most important of these fonds is P111 at ANQ-O; it contains letters from Sir Joseph-Adolphe Chapleau, original typescripts, and newspa-per clippings. The Centre for Research on French Canadian Culture (Ottawa) has some letters and news clippings in the Alfred-Duclos-De Celles fonds (P103), important corre-spondence between De Celles and Chapleau in the Joseph-Adolphe-Chapleau fonds (P313), and a number of letters in the Jacques-Gouin fonds (P26). At the LAC, several collec-tions are useful: the Alfred Duclos De Celles collection (MG 30, D271) for news clippings, the Sir Wilfrid Laurier fonds (MG 26, G) for 32 letters from De Celles, the Sir John A. Macdonald fonds (MG 26, A) for 12 letters about the candi-dacy of De Celles for parliamentary librarian, and the Trefflé Berthiaume fonds (MG 29, C117).

The reports of the joint librarians of parliament on the state of the library, which appear in Can., Parl., *Sessional papers* between 1885 and 1911 but were not subsequently printed, contain information about the professional activities of De Celles. The best biographical accounts are Thomas Chapais, "Monsieur Alfred De Celles," *Le Canada français* (Québec), 2ᵉ sér., 13 (1925–26): 153–58; [Auguste Gosse-lin], "Alfred D.-DeCelles," *Le Propagateur* (Montréal), 6 (1909–10), no.4: 1, 24. F.R.]

ANQ-M, CE601-S44, 8 août 1843; CE603-S6, 25 oct. 1876.

DUNCAN, SARA JEANNETTE (Cotes), known as **Garth Grafton**, teacher, journalist, and author; b. 22 Dec. 1861 in Brantford, Upper Canada, daughter of Charles Duncan, a dry-goods merchant, and Jane Bell; m. 6 Dec. 1890 Everard Charles Cotes in Cal-cutta, India; they had no children; d. 22 July 1922 in Ashtead, England.

Sara Jeannette Duncan would have declined the opportunity to begin her own biography with an account of her antecedents. As she wrote in *The imperialist* (London and New York, 1904), she felt that Canadians defined who they were by their merit and choice of occupation, not by their birth. Nonethe-less, her parents were formative influences. Her father, who was born in Cupar, Scotland, immigrated in the 1850s to New Brunswick, where he met his future wife. The two settled in Brantford by 1858 and later became parishioners of the legendary Presbyte-rian minister William Cochrane*. On 18 May 1862 their first daughter was baptized Sara Janet Duncan, the name she would later use for legal purposes (sometimes with the spelling Sarah) and which would appear on her headstone; the Duncans nicknamed her Redney, a name she used only within the family. (She later wrote that she deplored the use of nicknames and diminutives by professional women, which she felt put "an element of incongruity between them and their work, and g[a]ve it a character often undeservedly flippant and frivolous.")

Like many intellectual women of the day, she trained as a teacher, taking her third-class certificate at the Brantford Model School in 1879 and her second-class certificate at the Toronto Normal School in 1882. Her career in teaching, however, was short. Her first poems appeared in print in 1880 and her first article in 1881. These writings suggest that journalism was her goal even while she worked as a supply teacher in Brantford and nearby towns.

In late 1884 Duncan persuaded John Cameron* of the Toronto *Globe* to pay her for articles on the upcoming World's Industrial and Cotton Centennial exposition in New Orleans. She headed south in December. Her articles, published under the pseudonym Garth in both the *Globe* and the *London Advertiser* (London, Ont.) and reprinted in American papers, were so successful that she was offered a regular column in the *Globe* when she returned the following spring. Thus began a remarkable journalistic career. After a summer writing a weekly column for the *Globe*, she moved in the fall of 1885 to Washington, D.C., where by early 1886 she was in charge of the current literature department of the *Washington Post* and was one of its prominent editorial writers. In the summer of 1886 she took over the "Woman's World" section of the *Globe* as a regular member of its editorial staff. She left in November 1887 to work for the *Montreal Star* and in February she became its parliamentary correspondent in Ottawa.

In May 1885 Duncan had begun making regular contributions to the *Globe* under the pen-name Garth Grafton. Her column, "Other People and I," was a precursor to "Woman's World," the section created in 1886 for female readers. These columns, a grab-bag of "delicious scraps," dealt with topics as diverse as life insurance for women, mass-produced interior decor, and the popularity of gilt hairpins. On a more serious note, "Woman's World" also included interviews with prominent women, among them the Mohawk poet Emily Pauline Johnson* and Dr Alice McGillivray (one of Canada's first female physicians), and discussed such issues as the new literary realism and its attraction for women readers. She had defined this attraction in June 1885: "The ordinary detail of humdrum life and circumstance, pen-painted by an artist with sympathies keen enough to detect the mysterious throbbing of the life that is inner and under, fascinates us like our own photographs."

Under her own signature Duncan also wrote a column for the Toronto literary periodical *Week* on the important intellectual issues of the day. These included the effects of Canada's colonial position on the growth of the arts. "We are well-clad, well fed, well read. Why should we not buy our own books!" she lamented in September 1886. "Our enforced political humility is the distinguishing characteristic of every phase of our national life. We are ignored, and we ignore ourselves." She went on to condemn Ontarians as a "camp of Philistines" and cited their newspapers as proof: "Politics and vituperation, temperance and vituperation, religion and vituperation; these three dietetic articles, the vituperative sauce invariably accompanying, form the exclusive journalistic pabulum of three-quarters of the people of Ontario." Well-suited to the *Week*, her strongly defined progressive views on international copyright, women's suffrage, and realist fiction made her work remarkable in such conservative journals as the *Globe* and the *Post*.

Duncan resigned from the *Montreal Star* in 1888 to circle the globe with fellow journalist Lily Lewis. She intended the trip to furnish material for a book. Both journalists described their journeys in the *Star* and, after the pair had arrived in London, England, in May 1889, Duncan revised her notes, with some contributions from Lewis, and submitted the manuscript to the *Lady's Pictorial*. The resulting novel, *A social departure: how Orthodocia and I went around the world by ourselves*, published in London by Chatto and Windus in 1890, relies on the strengths of Duncan's journalism – close observation, description of manners, and wry humour – while transforming the narrator's travelling companion from the sophisticated Lewis into a naive and romantic English girl. *A social departure* provided a pattern for Duncan's early success as a novelist. *An American girl in London* (London and New York, 1891) and *The simple adventures of a memsahib* (London and New York, 1893) rely on the convention of a travelling outsider to create comedic clashes of manners and attitudes. Her first serious novel, *A daughter of to-day* (London and New York, 1894), addresses the theme of the "new woman" in the character of Elfrida Bell, an aspiring artist who champions the French Naturalists and writes a book based on her experiences as a burlesque dancer. Reviewers generally enjoyed the book, but condemned the "bad end" reserved for the heroine, who commits suicide.

A daughter of to-day was the first book to appear under the signature Duncan would use for the rest of her writing life: Mrs Everard Cotes (Sara Jeannette Duncan). She had met Cotes, a British civil servant working at the Indian Museum in Calcutta, early in 1889. He proposed, and the two were married when Duncan returned the following year. Despite plans to move to England in 1894, they remained based in India, where Cotes became a successful journalist, editor of the *Indian Daily News* (Calcutta) from 1894 to 1897, and later managing director of the Eastern News Agency Limited. Duncan never lived in Canada permanently again, though she would continue to visit her family and maintain her connection to Brantford by directing that the royalties on her books be paid into her bank account there. Little is known of her relationship with her husband. In the manner of other grass widows in India, she lived apart from him at times and made frequent trips "home" to England, sometimes accompanied by Cotes but often alone. Although it is tempting to speculate about their association based on her novels, it is unclear whether her strongly individualized and emotionally demanding heroines are conventions of new woman fiction or guides to her personal feelings. Certainly she maintained a harmonious relationship with Cotes, contributing articles and editorials to the papers he edited and accompanying him on working trips to Burma (Myanmar) in 1902 and Canada in 1919. Marriage did not dampen Duncan's ambition or her output. She suggested in an interview in the *Idler* (London) [*see* Robert Barr*] that her move to India had actually facilitated her career: "One's housekeeping is done in a quarter of an hour in the morning. . . . And there is such abundance of material in Anglo-Indian life – it is full of such picturesque incidence, such tragic chance." She maintained a steady schedule of writing and publishing, working every morning until she had completed three or four hundred words. She continued this daily routine even when she was under treatment for tuberculosis in 1900: her autobiographical *On the other side of the latch* (London, 1901) was set in her garden in Simla (the summertime administrative capital of India), where she spent a year recovering. Her chronic lung problems may have been exacerbated by the extreme heat and poor sanitation of Calcutta.

A prolific and popular writer, Duncan published 22 books in all, including two volumes of personal sketches and a collection of short stories. Multi-book contracts negotiated by her literary agents in 1907, 1911, and 1922 suggest that she planned her projects far in advance of publication. Her books usually appeared in serialized versions (in periodicals such as the *Times* and the *Queen* in London and the *News* in Toronto) and then in book form simultaneously in Britain and the United States. She maintained connections with such important figures as George William Ross* (whom she had met in Brantford), Goldwin Smith* of the *Week*, John Stephen WILLISON of the *News*, novelist and editor Jean Newton McIlwraith* of Doubleday in New York, and her agents, Alexander Pollock Watt and his sons Alexander Strahan and Hansard. She played hostess to the

writer Edward Morgan Forster when he visited Simla in 1912 and pursued acquaintances with the American authors William Dean Howells and Henry James, whose work she greatly admired. Forster's letters from Simla offer a glimpse of her life in India. He found her home "quite English," and described her as "clever and odd – nice to talk to alone, but at times the Social Manner descended like a pall." Although her early writings suggest a lively intelligence which never suffered fools gladly, Forster's portrait hints at a thoughtful but exclusive maturity, which perhaps only a few intimates managed to penetrate.

Despite her critical eye and sharp wit, Duncan came to identify herself with the Anglo-Indians of the Raj, possibly because they shared with Canadians a sense of marginality within the empire and similarly lacked any appreciation of their privilege in it. Her Canadian upbringing and adulthood in India made her sympathetic to the problems of representing the perspectives of the colonized. Several of her late works, including *Set in authority* (London and New York, 1906) and *The burnt offering* (London, 1909), deal with Indian nationalism. She saw colonials as more intellectually flexible, less concerned with appearance and more with principles, and more willing to see the world with "the touch of irony and of tolerance" than the British. She loved "the look of wider seas and wider skies" that travel and experiences brought to the British abroad, in contrast to the insular provincialism she deplored.

Duncan's fiction, which illustrates the turn toward local colour realism and description of manners in late-19th-century Canadian fiction, is distinguished by her ironic tone and her interest in creating complex psychological motivation. Like Henry James, she was fundamentally concerned with point of view in fiction. Many of her novels, as their titles indicate, attempt as well to define representative types of characters, often nationally or culturally differentiated. Her work frequently focuses on females, addressing their ethical and personal choices in the context of their dual imperative to develop as individuals and to represent moral ideas. Duncan thus creates a kind of heroine who defines herself through love, travel, and artistic vocation, and whose gender politics is linked to a critique of imperial-colonial relations.

Most of Duncan's novels are set in London or India. The notable exception is *The imperialist*, which depicts a by-election in small-town Elgin, a fictionalized Brantford. The hero, Lorne Murchison, runs for the Liberals on a platform of imperial federation, and his attachment to this cause is represented as a passionate young man's belief in the ideals represented by the monarchy and the history of England. This novel, which demonstrates imperialism as a form of Canadian nationalism, also conforms to the post–Indian Mutiny representation of imperialists as self-sacrificing visionaries misunderstood by those they serve. Duncan had tried to make it her "best book," but contemporary reaction was mixed. The London *Spectator* complained that it hid a medicinal message in a spoonful of jam while the *Globe* asserted that Duncan was disqualified by her gender from writing on political subjects. The *New York Times* praised the work, however, as did *Toronto Saturday Night*: "To the Canadian, to the Ontarian especially, it means more than any other Canadian story, for it gives with truth and with art a depiction of our own community." Duncan wrote two other novels with significant Canadian content, *Cousin Cinderella; or, a Canadian girl in London* (London and New York, 1908) and *His Royal Happiness* (Toronto and New York, 1914), both of which represent the dominion as an approximation of the ideal community. As she had written to Archibald McKellar MacMechan* in 1905, "The Empire is a big place and interesting everywhere, but ours is by far the best part of it, and the most full of the future."

Among modern-day critics, Carol Ann Shields [Warner*] calls *The imperialist* "charming and intelligent" and recommends it as a book that explains "how Canadians think." Carole Gerson argues for Duncan's historical importance as "Canada's most articulate advocate of realism" and "its most accomplished practitioner." Others find her work intriguing in its own right, and surprisingly contemporary in its subject matter and technique. Ajay Heble shows how the "decolonisation of Canada" in *The imperialist* is accomplished through the skilful manipulation of narrative voice. Stephen Scobie also highlights Duncan's technique, praising the subtle and "delicate play around what is said and not said" in her collection of novellas, *The pool in the desert* (New York, 1903).

During World War I, Duncan travelled between India and London, where she worked on original stage plays, which were mainly unsuccessful, and to Toronto, where a stage adaptation of *His Royal Happiness* appeared in January 1915. After Cotes sold the Eastern News Agency in 1919, he joined his wife in her home in Chelsea (London). Duncan came to Canada for the last time later that year with her husband, who was reporting for Reuters on the tour of the Prince of Wales. In 1921 they retired to a house in Ashtead, Surrey, where she died of chronic lung problems (possibly emphysema), exacerbated by her smoking. She was buried in the churchyard of St Giles Anglican Church, in Ashtead, with the inscription "This leaf was blown far." She left an estate worth over $13,000. That all of it was invested in Canada indicates perhaps that she continued to regard her homeland as "full of the future."

MISAO DEAN

A bibliography of Sara Jeannette Duncan's feature articles and uncollected stories, compiled by the author, is available at the DCB/DBC. In addition to the books listed in R. E. Watters, *A checklist of Canadian literature and background materials, 1628–1960* (2nd ed., Toronto and Buffalo, N.Y., 1972), Duncan is the author of *Two girls on a barge*, published in 1891 in both London and New York, written under the pseudonym V. Cecil Cotes, and *Two in a flat* (London, [1908?]), which appeared under the pseudonym Jane Wintergreen. A sampling of her journalism is provided in *Sara Jeannette Duncan: selected journalism*, ed. T. E. Tausky (Ottawa, 1978). Manuscripts of her plays are in the S. J. Duncan coll. of unpublished MSS at the Univ. of Western Ont. Libraries, James Alexander and Ellen Rea Benson Special Coll., London.

AO, RG 22-322, no.5756. Dalhousie Univ. Arch. (Halifax), MS 2-82 (A. McK. MacMechan papers). LAC, MG 30, D29. UCC-C, Fonds 1470, 97.094L, file 1-1. Univ. of North Carolina at Chapel Hill, Wilson Library, Manuscripts Dept., 11036 (A. P. Watt and Company records). *Courier* (Brantford, Ont.), 7 Oct. 1907. *Expositor* (Brantford), 31 Oct. 1877, 13 Jan. 1891. *Times* (London), 24, 27 July 1922. *Canadian men and women of the time* (Morgan; 1898 and 1912). Misao Dean, *A different point of view: Sara Jeannette Duncan* (Montreal and Kingston, Ont., 1991). Florence Donaldson, "Mrs. Everard Cotes (Sara Jeannette Duncan)," *Bookman* (London), 14 (1898): 65–67. E. M. Forster, *Selected letters of E. M. Forster*, ed. Mary Lago and P. N. Furbank (2v., London, 1983–85). Marian Fowler, *Redney: a life of Sara Jeannette Duncan* (Toronto, 1983). Carole Gerson, *A purer taste: the writing and reading of fiction in English in nineteenth-century Canada* (Toronto, 1989). R. E. Goodwin, "The early journalism of Sara Jeannette Duncan, with a chapter of biography" (MA thesis, Univ. of Toronto, 1964). Ajay Heble, "'This little outpost of empire': Sara Jeannette Duncan and the decolonization of Canada," *Journal of Commonwealth Lit.* (London), 26 (1991), no.1: 215–28. Marjory MacMurchy, "Mrs. Everard Cotes (Sara Jeannette Duncan)," *Bookman*, 48 (1915): 39–40. Stephen Scobie, "The deconstruction of writing," in his *Signature event Cantext: essays* (Edmonton, 1989), 25–39. *Standard dict. of Canadian biog.* (Roberts and Tunnell). T. E. Tausky, *Sara Jeannette Duncan: novelist of empire* (Port Credit [Mississauga], Ont., 1980).

DUNLOP, ALEXANDER FRANCIS, architect; b. 4 Aug. 1842 in Montreal, son of Charles John Dunlop, a merchant, and Sophie Fellow; m. there 9 June 1868 Catherine Austin Ekers, and they adopted a daughter; d. there 30 April 1923.

After studying in Montreal in Philips School and Montreal Collegiate School (where Charles Nichols was the principal), Alexander Francis Dunlop got his start in architecture by becoming an apprentice in a firm of practising architects, as was then the custom. He worked in the offices of George Browne* and John James Browne*, but also in that of Joseph Rielle, a surveyor. He noted that this latter experience would prove beneficial to him. He ended his training by spending some time in Detroit, an unusual step for a man of his generation. In 1874 he opened his own practice in Montreal. Except for a short period

(1893–95) when he was in partnership with John Charles Allison Heriot, he managed his firm by himself until he retired around 1913.

Although his work was confined mainly to Montreal and the surrounding region, Dunlop headed one of the largest Canadian operations at this period in the history of architecture, which was in a state of flux as a result of the huge changes brought about by an industrial society. Within this context architects had to redefine their status from a professional standpoint in order to maintain the creative character of their work while accepting the constraints of productivity and economy. The most appropriate way for debating these questions and defending their interests appeared to them at the time to be through associations, and in this regard Dunlop was especially active. In 1883 he was made an associate member of the Royal Canadian Academy of Arts [see John George Edward Henry Douglas Sutherland Campbell*; John William Hurrell Watts*]. He became a fellow in 1890, a councillor in 1892, and vice-president from 1907 to 1913. From 1881 to 1912 he participated regularly in the exhibitions it organized. In 1890 he was also a founding member of the Province of Quebec Association of Architects, one of whose aims was to regulate the right to practise, and he served on its council until 1893. In 1908 the Architectural Institute of Canada was officially created to promote the profession of architect throughout the country. Dunlop became its first president and held this office until 1910.

In an environment that was becoming increasingly protectionist and nationalist, the two professional associations enabled Canadian architects to stand up to an establishment that had long favoured architects from the United States for prestigious commissions. While he acknowledged the need to get his compatriots' abilities recognized, Dunlop nonetheless asserted that good relations must be maintained with the Americans. He also had to overcome his colleagues' fears that the jurisdictions of the two bodies might overlap.

Anxious to improve the quality of Canadian architecture, Dunlop was particularly sensitive to the question of training. Emphasizing the inadequacy of libraries and the lack of a school of architecture, he argued for the introduction of professional training at McGill University and the Université Laval in Montreal. With Edward MAXWELL, he conducted the courses in design offered by the Province of Quebec Association of Architects, and he welcomed into his studio many architects who would be among the best of their generation: Edward Maxwell, David Robertson Brown, John Melville Miller, Robert Findlay, Kenneth Guscotte Rea, Théodore Daoust, and Georges-Alphonse Monette.

Dunlop's production – of which Stephen Robinson has catalogued some 55 examples – followed closely the evolution of architecture in his day. Having begun between 1880 and 1900 with the Victorian splendours of the 19th century, Dunlop's work became gradually more subdued with the rise of academicism, which explains the eclectic nature of his output with respect to construction, materials, colours, styles, and the use to which it was put. In 1890, for instance, he defended the neo-Roman style, claiming that it was appropriate to the climate and the type of stone found locally, and that it could be treated in such a way as to present sculpted decorations. Also according to Dunlop, stone should be preferred to wood or brick. This stylistic vision was manifest in the building he designed with Heriot for Ekers' Brewery (1893–94, now the Musée Juste pour Rire), which was run by his brother-in-law Henry Archer Ekers (who would be elected mayor of Montreal in 1906). With the Temple Building (1889–90) and the Queen's Hotel (1891–93), large commercial buildings now demolished that illustrate the eclectic treatment typical of the late 19th century, Dunlop became one of the first Montreal architects to use steel structures. They also show his interest in new construction methods developed in the United States. In 1909 he erected the Sarah Maxwell Memorial School on the site of Hochelaga School, which had been destroyed in 1907 in a tragic fire that took the lives of a number of the young pupils. From then on, Dunlop had an obligation to revise the fireproofing criteria and safety standards. He would build a number of schools for the Protestant Board of School Commissioners of the City of Montreal.

Two of Dunlop's other creations are even more distinctive and they would be recognized as his most outstanding. The first was St James Methodist Church (1887–89) on Rue Sainte-Catherine, notable for its superior neo-Gothic treatment. In the relationship between its interior and exterior, it is an example of *trompe l'œil*, a device often favoured during the Victorian period. The apsidal end gives the impression that it is a traditional church, built in the form of a Latin cross, where the light coming through the stained-glass windows is meant to flood the whole interior. It is nothing of the sort. Following the dictates of Methodist liturgy, the building is divided in two: the front part corresponds to the church itself and is treated in the form of a theatre, while the rear part includes, among other things, the Sunday school. At the opposite extreme from this exercise, which cheerfully mocks the conventions of openness in art, Dunlop designed with Heriot a building obeying the classical rules to the letter: the home of businessman Hugh Graham* on Rue Sherbrooke, which was later known as Atholstan House because of the title of baron conferred on him in 1917. The severe and elegant treatment of the façades contrasts with the frivolous excesses of the Queen-Anne style that was so widespread at that time. The interior was planned with the same sensitivity. The building was preserved in 1980 by Alcan Aluminium Limited, which set up its management offices there. Built in 1894–95, the house anticipated by several years the fashion of classical renewal and *beaux-arts* academicism.

More than any other project, Atholstan House illustrates the attraction that fashions coming from the south held for Dunlop. A skilled architect and wise adviser, able to surround himself with the best apprentices, he nevertheless avoided excesses of imagination. Moderation and a sense of balance were the hallmarks of the work of this architect who was deeply involved in the advancement of his profession.

JACQUES LACHAPELLE

ANQ-M, CE601-S51, 3 sept. 1842; S63, 9 juin 1868. LAC, MG 28, I 126; I 239. Royal Architectural Institute of Canada (Ottawa), Alcide Chaussé, "History of the inception of the RAIC" (Ottawa, 1939). *Gazette* (Montreal), 1 May 1923. Commission des biens culturels du Québec, *Les chemins de la mémoire* (3v., Montréal, 1990–99), vol.2 (*Monuments et sites historiques du Québec*, 1991). "Organization of the Province of Quebec Association of Architects," *Canadian Architect and Builder* (Toronto), 3 (1890): 112–16. Guy Pinard, *Montréal: son histoire, son architecture* (6v. parus, Montréal, 1986–), 1. Stephen Robinson, "An architect discovered: the work of A. F. Dunlop" (MA thesis, Concordia Univ., Montreal, 1992).

DUQUET, CYRILLE, clockmaker, jeweller, inventor, and politician; b. 31 March 1841 at Quebec, son of Joseph Duquet, a labourer, and Madeleine Therrien (Terrien); m. there 22 Feb. 1865 Adélaïde Saint-Laurent, daughter of Jean-Baptiste Saint-Laurent and Adélaïde Gazzo (Gazeau), and they had 16 children; d. there 1 Dec. 1922.

After studying with the Brothers of the Christian Schools, Cyrille Duquet was apprenticed at the age of 13 to goldsmith Joseph-Prudent Gendron, whose shop was on Rue Saint-Jean in Quebec City. When Gendron decided to move in 1862, Duquet's apprenticeship was coming to an end. He promptly approached the owner of the building with a proposal to go into business for himself at the same address. An agreement was reached, and for a time Duquet shared his premises with Simon Levy, who sold watches and jewellery.

Duquet was undoubtedly reliable and hard-working. He also had a passion for science. Not content just to assemble and install clocks or to make and sell jewellery, he attempted to attract attention by displaying his inventions and creations in his store window. Duquet liked to dazzle, astonish, and fascinate, but he also had a practical mind. With Professor François-Alexandre-Hubert La Rue*, he designed a magnetic sand separator in 1868–69. Around 1870 Duquet invented a device that made it possible to monitor the exact time at which watchmen checking the fire alarm telegraph system reached various points in their rounds. The patent was purchased that year by the New Haven Clock Company in the United States. He also conceived the idea of installing electric clocks in steeples and in the towers of high buildings.

It was Duquet's telephone receiver, however, that brought him fame. He reportedly corresponded with Alexander Graham BELL on the progress of their respective experiments, although none of their letters has thus far been located. What is indeed certain is that Duquet obtained a patent on 1 Feb. 1878 for a number of modifications "giving more facility for the transmission of sound and adding to its acoustic properties," and in particular for the design of a new apparatus combining the speaker and receiver in a single unit. After a few experiments in linking his store on Rue de la Fabrique (where Rue Saint-Jean begins) and a second store – which he and Louis Dalaire owned – in Saint-Roch ward, and in linking Ottawa and Montreal, he began to set up a few regular telephone lines, including one with Spencer Wood, the residence of the lieutenant governor, and another with the Couvent Jésus-Marie in Sillery, where one of his daughters was studying.

Convinced that Duquet was using Bell's invention, Charles Fleetford Sise*, vice-president of the Canadian Telephone Company, ordered him in a letter dated 31 Dec. 1880 to "desist from the manufacture of such telephones." Stung to the quick, Duquet replied on 7 Jan. 1881 that "the patent you are making such a fuss about has expired and is null and void." "Kindly cease your threats of a lawsuit, which do not frighten me in the least," he added, and he concluded, "If you want an unchallengeable patent, I advise you to buy mine ... as soon as possible, because the longer you wait, the more it will cost you." On 11 May 1882 the Quebec Superior Court ruled in favour of the Canadian Telephone Company (which was merged that year into the Bell Telephone Company of Canada). From the $5,000 claimed on 1 April 1881, the company had reduced its "demand for damages to the sum of ten dollars," "being convinced that the Defendant acted in good faith," as judge William Collis Meredith explained.

The real reason the plaintiffs had reduced their claim to such an extent was not Duquet's good faith, but rather the company's interest in his various improvements. On 15 May 1882 Duquet sold his "instruments, patents, patent rights, licence agreements, contracts, plant, apparatus, chattels and good will" for $2,100 and abandoned all projects related to telephones. His fame, however, opened a new world to him: politics. François Langelier*, a prominent Liberal lawyer, had just come onto the municipal scene. As city councillor for Saint-Louis ward, Duquet would be associated with him from 1884 to 1890.

This was a period when the face of the city was changing. Sidewalks were being laid down or repaired, streets were being widened or paved, and the water system was being altered and extended by contractor Horace Jansen Beemer*. Between 1886 and 1889 street lighting was converted from gas to electricity. Duquet loved this kind of challenge. But it was in the realm of electricity that he devoted himself wholeheartedly. He took sweet revenge on Sigismund Mohr*, who had testified against him in 1882. As manager of the Quebec and Levis Electric Light Company, Mohr set up a network of electric lighting whose costs were under constant review by Duquet.

In 1890 Duquet concentrated on his own clock and jewellery business. He sold his house at 153 Grande Allée to John Breakey*, intending to take up residence above the new store being built for him on Rue Saint-Jean, at the foot of Rue de la Fabrique, on the site of his first shop.

Perhaps Duquet had undertaken too much or the economic situation may have been too bleak. In any case, he was on the verge of bankruptcy in July 1896. He had creditors in New York, Boston, Toronto, Hamilton, and, of course, Montreal and Quebec. At the head of the line was Moïse Schwob, with his claim for $9,854.81 of the $19,381.93 owed to non-preferential creditors. To this sum must be added the amount due a preferential creditor, the Quebec Permanent Building Society, for a total debt of $31,825.93. On 5 July Duquet turned over his property, which was valued at $42,448.20, including $19,447.78 for his business and $18,500 for his buildings. At a special meeting of creditors on 28 Sept. 1896, "a resolution was moved by M. Schwob, seconded by Augustin Gaboury, and carried unanimously, that, since Mr Cyrille Duquet had got from his creditors an agreement to accept twenty-five cents on the dollar," he should be authorized to resume "full possession and enjoyment of his property."

In July 1904 Duquet attempted to make a comeback on the municipal scene. He won election as alderman for Palais ward by a narrow majority of ten votes, defeating dentist Henri-Edmond Casgrain*, his neighbour on Rue Saint-Jean and more particularly his rival as a well-known inventor. This time he took his seat along with Simon-Napoléon Parent*, who was both mayor of the city and Liberal premier of the province. The newspaper *L'Événement*, now Conservative again [*see* Louis-Joseph Demers*], listed him as one of Parent's opponents. In its 17 Feb. 1906 issue, it ranked him among the "reform candidates" in the forthcoming election. This time he won a resounding victory, with a majority of 138. Georges Garneau* was also elected to the city council, and he was immediately approached to be the next mayor, replacing Parent, who had left this office in January.

At council meetings Duquet was quite spirited. He was always attracting comment because of his speeches, which were mostly out of order. By joining forces with some 20 MLAs who were bringing suit against *L'Événement*, he eventually turned it against him and he was defeated in the election of February 1908 by Lawrence Arthur Dumoulin Cannon*.

At the age of 67 Duquet could now afford to take stock, to recall the difficulties he had encountered, and the controversies – in particular one in March 1871, when an artisan named P.-E. Poulin had publicly accused him of wrongfully taking credit for creating a chain and cross for the archbishop of Quebec. There was also his venture in the spring of 1887 into the production of natural gas in Louiseville, which had left him, when he went bankrupt, with 400 worthless shares in the Compagnie de Gaz Combustible. But on the other hand, he could walk proudly about his city, remembering how it had changed, admiring the residence built for him on the Grande Allée, the other house where his business was located, and all the clocks on the most beautiful buildings of Quebec, including the city hall, the legislative building, the customs house, and St Matthew's Church. And his name was on the faces of clocks that had movements made in the United States.

From now on Duquet could devote his time to music, his business, and his family. Sixteen children had been born from 1866 to 1887, and eight of them were still alive. His eldest, Eva, had made him a grandfather several times over, much to his delight. His daughter Alice entered the noviciate of the Sœurs Missionnaires de Notre-Dame d'Afrique. His son Georges-Henri chose an artistic career, while Arthur assisted him in his business.

Tireless, curious, tenacious, and at times a dreamer, Duquet was a self-made man of a high order. Among his boundless interests, scientific and technical advances fascinated and stimulated him, and they held few secrets for him. Duquet had achieved the feat of reconciling the arts and business, science and politics. Fiercely independent, he became a legendary figure through his creations and inventions.

DENIS VAUGEOIS

[Jeanne Hardy, the wife of Arthur Duquet, who managed his father's business until 1933, prepared a short biography of Cyrille Duquet which, as she stated, was drawn from family tradition and from contemporary newspaper articles, including pieces by Damase Potvin*, Lorenzo Saint-Mars, and Mgr Victor Tremblay. This unpublished biography of around 10 pages, and several other documents concerning Cyrille Duquet, is held by Denise Duquet (Lamonde) of Sainte-Foy, Qué. A number of useful documents are found in the Bell Canada Information Resource Centre (Montreal), Bell Canada Hist. Coll., 21732, and several articles on Duquet and on the telephone are available in the general collection of the Soc. Hist. du Saguenay (Chicoutimi, Qué.).

A steam-engine Duquet invented in 1865 is at the Collège de Sainte-Anne-de-la-Pocatière (La Pocatière, Qué.); the mace of the Assemblée Nationale du Québec is among the best known of his works as a silversmith. One building bears his name, 1500 Charest Boulevard Ouest in Quebec City, the headquarters of the communications branch of the Ministère de la Culture et des Communications du Québec. Duquet's building on Rue Saint-Jean, which consisted of three storeys, was demolished to make way for a bank, and his residence on the Grande Allée has been replaced by the Loews Le Concorde Hotel. In 1983 the Institut National de la Recherche Scientifique named a new chair of computer and information science in his honour. D.V.]

ANQ-Q, CE301-S1, 31 mars 1841; CE301-S97, 22 févr. 1865; Index BMS, dist. judiciaire de Québec, Notre-Dame de Québec, 2 déc. 1922; P1000, D2396; TP11, S1, SS2, SSS1, dossiers 170 (1891), 730 (1896), 1251 (1885), 1338 (1889), 1411 (1889), 1536 (1873), 1544 (1881), 1955 (1891), 2462 (1890). AVQ, QD4-1A, 1662–63; QD4-1G, 1739-02–05; QP1-4, 40/0004, 62/0005. Monique Duval, "Québec doit le téléphone . . . à Cyrille Duquet," *Le Soleil*, 11 mai 1977. *L'Événement*, 13, 17, 20 févr. 1906; 5 nov. 1907; 10, 18 févr. 1908. *Le Journal de Québec*, 29 nov. 1866; 26 févr. 1868; 27, 31 mars 1871. *Le Soleil*, 16 févr. 1904. "Orfèvrerie: établissement de M. Cyrille Duquet," in *Annuaire du commerce et de l'industrie de Québec . . .* (Québec), 1873: 44–46. René Lagacé, "Cyrille Duquet, inventeur de renom," *Concorde* (Québec), 7 (1956), nos.6–7: 9–11. Alyne Le Bel, "Le magicien de la rue Saint-Jean: l'inventeur Cyrille Duquet," *Cap-aux-Diamants* (Québec), 4 (1988–89), no.4: 45–48. William Patten, *Pioneering the telephone in Canada* (Montreal, 1926).

DU VAL, FREDERIC BEAL, Presbyterian minister, social reformer, and author; b. 21 May 1847 in Prince George's County, Md, son of Edward Willet Du Val, a planter, and Mary Miller; m. 2 Nov. 1876 Corinne L. Kearfott (d. 1909) in Philadelphia, and they had four daughters and four sons; d. 15 May 1928 in Winnipeg.

Of Huguenot and Scottish ancestry, Frederic Du Val was raised in Maryland on a farm known as Floral Hill. As a young man he was sent to Washington, D.C., to work in a mercantile house. Educated at Hightstown Classical Academy in Hightstown, N.J., he went on to receive an MA in 1872 from nearby Princeton College, obtaining gold medals for oratory and debate and a first prize in biblical scholarship. He graduated from the Princeton Theological Seminary in 1875 and served as a Presbyterian minister in Wilmington, Del., and Toledo, Ohio. In 1886 he received a DD from the College of Wooster, in Wooster, Ohio.

Called in 1888 to succeed Daniel Miner GORDON as pastor of Knox Presbyterian Church in Winnipeg, Du Val would hold the post until 1916. His reputation as an outstanding orator, theologian, and moral reformer had preceded him. His sermons had emphasized the idea that the glory of God was best seen in the perfection of human character; this position led him into the Social Gospel movement.

At the time of Du Val's arrival, Winnipeg was a frontier boom town with well-established brothels. Social reformers concentrated their attention on fighting for stricter controls on the liquor traffic and stiffer penalties for violations of the Sunday observance laws. The bordellos had formed a modus vivendi with the police whereby, despite city by-laws, they were allowed to operate with little interference. By 1900, however, as residential construction crept westward toward the red-light district on Thomas (Minto) Street, new residents began to complain. Real estate interests added their voices to the demands for action. This chorus reached a crescendo in 1902, the year in which Du Val was elected chairman of the Winnipeg Ministerial Association.

Described by historian James Henry Gray* as a "pint-sized zealot with a hard glinting eye and luxuriant chin whiskers," Du Val led the campaign against the existence of a segregated district for prostitution. Through his sermons and public-speaking engagements, which had received widespread coverage in the local press, he had already made a name for himself. He had spoken against the Catholic school system from the time of his arrival in Manitoba and his opposition had increased after the Manitoba school question [*see* Thomas Greenway*] reared its head in 1890. He had also been a leader in the struggle for Prohibition. With his forceful personality and powerful oratory, he was "a one-man gang." According to Gray, he soon had his fellow preachers "breathing fire and brimstone from the pulpits." By 1903 they had turned their wrath from booze to brothels.

When his sermons failed to achieve the desired result, Du Val led his fellow ministers in mass action. "Segregation does not segregate and regulation does not regulate," he thundered at one of several special meetings held in November 1903 and attended by hundreds. "It is inevitable that segregated areas become nests of crime." The issue blew up during the mayoralty race of November–December 1903. Du Val and his supporters raised such an outcry that Winnipeg's mayor, John Arbuthnot, withdrew his bid for a fourth term. The candidate Du Val supported, Thomas SHARPE, was elected almost by default and the reformers took over city hall. Raids were carried out on the brothels and segregation was abolished, but when these moves seemed only to scatter the prostitutes throughout the city's downtown and make their elimination more difficult, Du Val began lobbying for increased police control. This also failed to stem the tide, particularly since the city continued to expand rapidly. Du Val persevered in demanding reform. He became a moving force in the Moral and Social Reform Council of Canada, founded in 1907. A federation of religious and social organizations, the league sought to influence municipal legislation, particularly on the question of prostitution.

In April 1909 the Winnipeg Police Commission decided to leave the regulation of brothels to the discretion of its chief of police. Chief John C. McRae favoured segregation, so he re-established a red-light district – on Annabella Street in the isolated Point Douglas (Winnipeg) area – with the cooperation of Winnipeg's most powerful brothel keeper, Minnie Woods. By the following year the burgeoning population of the district had become difficult to contain. Du Val's pamphlet, *The problem of social vice in Winnipeg*, which appeared in 1910, was a strong indictment of segregation. In November of that year the Reverend John George Shearer, one of the founders of the Moral and Social Reform Council of Canada, published a stinging criticism of the district in the Toronto *Globe* after he visited Winnipeg during a tour of western Canada. His denunciation provoked a public outcry in Winnipeg and resulted in the appointment of a royal commission, but municipal authorities managed to deflect much of the responsibility for the problem. In 1912 a series of police raids and arrests shut down numerous brothels, but segregated prostitution would continue in Winnipeg until the 1930s.

An eloquent writer as well as speaker, Du Val authored religious poems, only a few of which have survived. In 1899 he had been appointed to Manitoba College's board of management; he would sit until 1926 and would also serve on the college's senate. In 1901 he became a member of the council of the University of Manitoba. Seven years later he was elected to the joint committee on church union and in 1908–9 he was moderator of the General Assembly of the Presbyterian Church in Canada. He preached in various parts of Canada, including a sermon at the celebrations of the tercentenary of Quebec City in 1908 [*see* Albert Henry George Grey*].

After his retirement from Knox Presbyterian Church in 1916, Frederic Beal Du Val was named pastor emeritus. He remained in Winnipeg until his death in 1928 and was buried in Elmwood Cemetery. He was an important early figure in the Social Gospel tradition that would become associated with Winnipeg.

Robert A. Wardhaugh

Frederic Beal Du Val is the author of *The problem of social vice in Winnipeg* (n.p., [1910]). Examples of his religious poetry are available in H. F. M. Ross, *A brief sketch of the life of the Rev. Frederic B. Duval, D.D. . . .* (Winnipeg, n.d.).

City of Winnipeg, Arch. and records control branch, City Council, minutes, July 1905, January 1906. Private arch., Robert Wardhaugh (Winnipeg), Interview with Frederic Duval, a grandson of the subject, Winnipeg, 16 Feb. 2000. *Manitoba Free Press*, 16–18 Nov. 1903; 9 Jan. 1904; 5 Jan. 1905; 21 Jan. 1907; 16, 19, 24 May 1914; 13 Dec. 1915; 18, 20 March 1916. *Winnipeg Telegram*, 18 Nov. 1903, 21 Jan. 1907. *Winnipeg Tribune*, 14 May 1928. Joy Cooper, "Red lights of Winnipeg," Man., Hist. and Scientific Soc., *Papers* (Winnipeg), ser.3, no.27 (1970–71): 61–74. *Directory*, Winnipeg, 1910–40. J. H. Gray, *Red lights on the prairies* (Toronto, [1971]). W. L. Morton, *Manitoba: a history* (Toronto, 1957). H. A. Robson, *Judge Robson on segregation or toleration of vice . . . the report of the Social Vice Commission, Winnipeg, January 11th, 1911* (Toronto, [1911?]). Margaret [Stovel] McWilliams, *Manitoba milestones* (Toronto and London, [1928]).

DWORKIN, HENRY, businessman, socialist, and community activist; b. 1885 in Ekaterinoslav (Dnepropetrovsk, Ukraine), son of Solomon Dworkin, a merchant, and Anny Rubens; m. 20 Aug. 1911 Dorothy Goldstick in Toronto, and they had a daughter; d. there 14 Jan. 1928.

By some accounts Henry Dworkin came to Toronto in 1905, following his elder brother Edward, who worked in a paper-box factory and reputedly subsisted on bread and tea in order to bring him to Canada. According to Henry's marriage registration, however, he arrived on 1 Jan. 1910. Between 1910 and 1913 directories show the Dworkin brothers – Henry, Edward, Sholem, and Samuel – involved in two enterprises: Dworkin's Jewish Advertising Bureau, opened by Sholem by mid 1909 on Elizabeth Street, in an area heavily populated by immigrants, and a wholesale tobacco business, Independent Cigar Stores, on Elizabeth and Queen.

Within a year or two Henry took over the management of the Advertising Bureau, a stationery shop, foreign-language printery, and agency for Jewish and foreign newspapers. Also known from 1913 as Dworkin Brothers (Henry and Sholem), the bureau, which included a telegraph agency, distributed the *Yiddisher Zhurnal/Daily Hebrew Journal* (Toronto), the *Canadian Jewish Times* (Montreal), and two major Jewish papers from New York, the *Jewish Daily Forward/Vorwärts* and the *Jewish Daily News/Jüdisches Tageblatt*. The bureau had quickly become a Mecca for Jews from eastern Europe and for the unemployed, who hoped to meet others who might help them find work. Henry was remembered for offering his room to those with no place to sleep and for distributing bread. At some point he and Edward tried running a small restaurant on Bay Street but, as journalist Abraham Rhinewine* recalled, it failed because everyone was given food regardless of ability to pay.

By early 1920 Henry and Edward had opened a shop on Dundas Street under the name E. and H. Dworkin, tobacconists, confectioners, and steamship agents. Henry had probably been operating as an agent for a number of years. After World War I, according to one account, when funds he had sent to Poland, to cover the passage for relatives of clients, proved insufficient because of inflation, he travelled to Europe to set things in order, enduring arrest and paying the difference out of his own pocket. He prospered, even though clients frequently did not reimburse him.

Dworkin's agency was driven as much by his philanthropic sympathies as by his need to earn a living. His charitable nature, coupled with his socialist ideology, impelled him to activity within, and outside, the Jewish community. He was joined in his outlook by his wife, whom he had married in 1911 in a ceremony conducted by Maurice Kaplan, cantor at McCaul Street Synagogue. A Torontonian who had received a certificate in midwifery in Ohio in 1909, Dorothy had become on her return the first nurse and a guiding light at the Jewish Dispensary, set up on Elizabeth Street by the Hebrew Ladies' Maternity Aid and Child Welfare Society. On Henry's death she would assume his part in E. and H. Dworkin.

Dworkin's shops always buzzed with socialist conversation and unionist planning as well as philanthropic initiative. In 1915 he was among the proponents of a tag day to assist Jewish war victims in Russia, an activity ultimately forbidden by the city. He was nominated by the socialists as an aldermanic candidate in 1916, but declined in favour of James Simpson*, a gentile labour leader. (He would run in a later election but would be defeated.) Dworkin served on the provisional board of the Federation of the Jewish Philanthropies of Toronto when it was organized later in 1916. In 1919 he was a delegate to the first Canadian Jewish Congress. In a photograph taken that year of him and other volunteer collectors for the Conference for Jewish War Sufferers, he appears as a well-dressed, heavy-set man. His work was matched by that of his wife. Following the Toronto General Hospital's refusal to provide a wing with a kosher kitchen and Yiddish-speaking staff, she and others headed the drive to establish in 1922 the Toronto Jewish Convalescent and Maternity Hospital (renamed Mount Sinai in 1923). When antisemitism became evident at Toronto's Labor Temple in the 1920s, Henry founded the Labour Lyceum on Spadina Avenue to house Jewish unions; he was chairman of its board of directors at the time of his death.

Dworkin was on his way to a meeting there in January 1928 when he was struck by an automobile and fatally injured. His funeral demonstrated his popularity: an overflow of several thousand people, Jews and non-Jews, civic officials and workers, stood in extreme cold in front of the Lyceum, and police reinforcements had to be called in to control the crowd.

STEPHEN A. SPEISMAN

AO, RG 22-305, no.58523; RG 55-17-60-30, no.22983; RG 55-17-60-31, nos.26024–25 CP; RG 55-17-60-46, nos.7971 CPE, 7972 CP; RG 80-5-0-506, no.21763. Ontario Jewish Arch. (Toronto), "Canadian Jewish Congress ballot for Toronto" (1919); MG 6/E1 (Betty Lindgren papers). *Canadian Jewish Times* (Montreal), 21 June 1912. *Evening Telegram* (Toronto), 20 Jan. 1928. *Toronto Daily Star*, 16 Jan. 1928. *Yiddisher Zhurnal/Daily Hebrew Journal* (Toronto), 15 Jan. 1928. *Canadian Jewry, prominent Jews of Canada . . .* , ed. Zvi Cohen (Toronto, [1933]). *Directory*, Toronto, 1906–29. Abraham Rhinewine, *Der Yid in Kanada* [The Jew in Canada] (2v., Toronto, 1925–27), 1. S. A. Speisman, *The Jews of Toronto: a history to 1937* (Toronto, 1979).

E

EATON, Sir JOHN CRAIG, merchant and philanthropist; b. 28 April 1876 in Toronto, third son of Timothy Eaton* and Margaret Wilson Beattie; m. 8 May 1901 Florence (Flora) McCrea in Omemee, Ont., and they had four sons and two daughters (one girl adopted); d. 30 March 1922 in Toronto.

Born in 1876, seven years after the establishment of the Timothy Eaton store on Yonge Street in Toronto, John Craig Eaton became involved in his father's enterprise from an early age. Inheriting his father's business flair, at the age of six he was discovered demonstrating spinning tops in the toy department. Shortly thereafter he appeared at the main entrance encouraging passers-by to come and see the goods available. Educated at the Toronto Model School and Upper Canada College, he joined the Eaton workforce at the age of 16 and fulfilled his apprenticeship by serving in numerous capacities. By 1896 the Eaton store had evolved into a full-line department store whose buyers travelled regularly to the United States, Europe, Great Britain, and Japan. John Craig Eaton, at age 20, furthered his mercantile education by making an extensive trip overseas. In 1898 he became a director of the company.

The death of his brother Edward Young on 3 Oct. 1900 threw greater responsibility to John Craig as the only remaining son active in the firm. The loss resulted in his immediate appointment as vice-president. He thus became, at age 24, right-hand man to his father, to whom he now turned for advice on the management of the family business. When asked whether he could say yes or no, he agreed that he could. Asked further whether he knew which to say at the right time, he acknowledged some difficulty. According to Timothy Eaton, however, that was all he would have to do. Eaton Sr firmly believed that by inculcating a strong sense of cooperation in all workers and involved family members, he could make management by senior staff both quick and effective. On the death of his father in 1907, John Craig would succeed as president.

Perceiving the opportunities for development in the west, John Craig Eaton was largely responsible for the establishment of the company's first branch store, in Winnipeg in 1905, and for its growth over the next decade. In 1916, building upon the catalogue business initiated by his father in the 1880s, he had a mail-order building erected there to facilitate the delivery of goods in western Canada. Additional mail-order outlets were opened in Saskatoon (1917) and Regina (1918). The careful attention paid to western farm statistics recognized that an increase in those figures offered potential growth in retail sales. Promotional efforts were then made to achieve this end. By 1921 Eaton's total sales had increased to $125 million from $22.4 in 1907.

To further expansion of the mail-order business, other offices were opened in Ontario, in Oakville in 1916 and Guelph in 1920. In 1920 as well, to ease distribution problems in the Maritimes, a mail-order building was constructed in Moncton, N.B. Efforts were also made to increase sales by urging local customers to use the burgeoning telephone system. Buying offices were inaugurated in Manchester (1911), Leicester (1913), and Belfast (1913), in New York (1911), in Zurich and Berlin (both 1913), and by 1920 in Tokyo, Yokohama, and Kōbe. With buying offices already established in London and Paris, the company ensured that its stores were constantly supplied with the goods desired by Canadians. Under Eaton's management as well, plans were drawn up for another store in Toronto, at the intersection of Yonge and College streets, but the completion of this project would be delayed until the 1930s.

The Product Research Bureau set up in Toronto in 1916 was motivated by his father's insistence that Eaton customers could depend upon store merchandise. The first incorporated by a Canadian retailer, it undoubtedly evolved from the firm's own expansion into manufacturing. By 1922 the company was producing a wide range of ready-made clothes in factories in Montreal, Toronto, and Hamilton, Ont. This expansion enhanced its ability to provide goods at the volumes and prices so necessary for its markets.

Eaton continued to improve working conditions in his operations: by 1919 he had established Saturday holidays and evening closing at 5:30 P.M. in all stores, factories, and mail-order offices. Furthermore, to avoid any possibility of grievance and to deflect criticism, continuous efforts were made to ensure that wage rates were in line with those paid elsewhere. Since his prime intention was to promote business for

the company on a nation-wide basis, he refused to allow either labour or capital to influence his business decisions.

The Eaton Boys and Girls clubs were but one facet of Eaton's philanthropic interests and these along with scholarships offered at the Young Men's Christian Association and the Ontario College of Art provided educational and recreational facilities for company employees. In addition, he made large contributions to the Toronto General Hospital and the University of Toronto which allowed for the maintenance of a surgical wing and a department of general medicine. Further donations were made to Victoria College, Toronto, and the Winnipeg General Hospital. Eaton received a knighthood for these activities in 1915. Perhaps his most lavish public contribution was the gift, jointly with his mother, of land and funds for a large Methodist church on St Clair Avenue in Toronto. Named after Timothy Eaton, it was constructed in 1912–14, an elaborate monument to a grand sense of family worth.

Throughout World War I Eaton employees on active service continued to draw salaries (either full or half pay, depending on their marital status). As a result, some 3,300 enlisted men received more than $2 million during this time. Because of Germany's involvement in the conflict Eaton ordered a boycott of all German companies, and it was not until 1924 that the company resumed buying operations there.

A long-time supporter of the Liberal party and member of the Reform Club of Toronto, Eaton nevertheless strongly disapproved of the party's 1911 endorsement of reciprocity with the United States. His views led him to combine with 17 other prominent Liberals to publish a manifesto opposing this policy [*see* Sir Byron Edmund WALKER].

With his early death from influenza in March 1922 at the age of 45, the management of the company passed into the hands of close relatives since his sons had not yet reached the age of majority. His will specified that the presidency should eventually go to the son most qualified (John David* would take over in 1942) and that this decision should be left to the discretion of the board of directors. Lady Eaton, active in the arts and in charitable and benevolent societies, survived her husband by 48 years.

JOY L. SANTINK

The main source for this study is the T. Eaton records at AO, F 229.

AO, RG 80-3-2-12, no.901317; RG 80-5-0-296, no.16842. *Golden jubilee, 1869–1919; a book to commemorate the fiftieth anniversary of the T. Eaton Co. Limited, by the Scribe* (Toronto and Winnipeg, 1919). Ross Harkness, *J. E. Atkinson of the "Star"* (Toronto, 1963). J. L. Santink, *Timothy Eaton and the rise of his department store* (Toronto, 1990).

EBY, CHARLES SAMUEL, Methodist missionary, author, and publisher; b. 3 Nov. 1845 in Goderich, Upper Canada, son of Jonas Eby and Hannah Fessant; m. 15 June 1871 Ellie (Nellie) Keppel in Brooklyn (New York City), and they had three daughters and three sons; d. 20 Dec. 1925 in Saskatoon.

Descended from Pennsylvania German stock, Charles Eby was converted when he was 11 at a camp meeting in Elora, Upper Canada, where his family had moved. At about 15 he began a two-year apprenticeship with a saddle and harness maker in Guelph while expanding his education. He then earned a teaching certificate, taught for a year near Guelph, and served as an exhorter in the local Wesleyan church.

At age 19 Eby began preaching, and in 1865 the annual conference of the Wesleyan Methodist Church in Canada permitted him to attend Victoria College in Cobourg as part of his probation for the ministry. After two years he travelled to Europe, where he studied German, French, and theology. He returned to Victoria in 1870 and graduated the following spring (DD 1886). Shortly thereafter he was ordained and married Ellie Keppel.

Eby served the Methodist German missions at Preston (Cambridge) and Paris, Ont., from 1871 to 1874 and those in Hamilton from 1874 to 1876. He visited all the German missions in Ontario, and lectured widely on his European travels in order to raise money for this work. Considered an excellent lecturer and a rousing preacher, he staunchly supported traditional evangelism. He began publishing the biweekly *Der Canadische Evangelist* [Canadian Evangelist] (Preston) in 1872 and personally maintained the journal until 1875 despite financial losses. The magazine was never well received, however, and his financial and propaganda campaigns outside the regular mission channels disturbed many itinerants.

In 1876 Eby was appointed to Japan, where the church had begun work in 1873 [*see* George Cochran*]. The mission authorities believed that his ardent zeal would spark a revival there as well as reawaken the Christian spirit in Canada. After learning basic Japanese, Eby opened a mission in Kōfu in 1878. Although conversions were initially rare, he attracted large crowds through his sermons and his lectures on Western religion and culture. He also helped to train a native Japanese ministry in Tokyo.

Strongly committed to evangelization, Eby considered that the real hindrance to Christian civilization came from the scepticism and secularism inherent in modern Western science and philosophy. For him, the best hope of success lay in attracting the brighter members of the samurai class by presenting Christianity as a logical ethical and moral system as well as a spiritual experience. In 1881–83 he published the *Chrysanthemum* (Yokohama), a monthly aimed at the Japanese intelligentsia but read mostly by the missionary community.

In early 1883 Eby delivered in Tokyo a popular series of lectures on Western theology and philosophy which was published in both English (*Christianity and humanity*) and Japanese. He credited these lectures with increased tolerance of Christianity by the Japanese authorities, and also with helping to promote a spiritual revival and making the Kōfu mission financially self-supporting. Another lecture in early 1884 appeared as *The immediate Christianization of Japan: prospects, plans, results*. On furlough in 1885–86, Eby undertook an exhausting North American tour to promote Methodist missions. In 1886 he presented an important lecture, published in Toronto as *Methodism and the missionary problem*, on the need to devote greater resources to overseas work. Before leaving Canada, he began a campaign for two projects that would dominate his remaining years in Japan.

Eby believed that the best way to convert Japan was to establish a large educational and social-relief mission near the Tokyo Imperial University where special lectures on Christianity could be presented. After modifications to accommodate traditional evangelism, regular church services, and a greater role for native Japanese workers, the Central Tabernacle opened in January 1891. In addition to running it, Eby published *Japan for Christ*, a journal outlining its work. In his second undertaking Eby, recognizing that the Board of Missions in Canada could not afford new recruits, called for "a supplementary force of self-supporting missionaries who, would work in harmony with the mission, and teach to pay expenses." Fifteen men and one women were to work in Japan as part of this "light brigade" of Christian soldiers before it ceased operations in the early 1890s.

Most of Eby's campaigns led to disputes. The Central Tabernacle spent more than one-eighth of the Japan mission budget, yet had little impact on the Japanese intelligentsia. Moreover, Eby proved to be a poor administrator, and his independent financial campaigns embarrassed the Board of Missions. Similarly, the board had no authority over the Self-Support Band, but feared it would have to pay the group's expenses if anything went wrong. Eby had little regard for the wishes of others, and his relations with the Canadian Methodist authorities and the highly nationalistic native Japanese church were often strained. After his return to Canada in 1893 because of exhaustion, the controversies surrounding the Japan mission that he and his supporters had aggravated reached a climax. In late 1895 Eby and others were removed from the work there.

In 1896 Eby accepted an invitation to Homer Street Methodist Church in Vancouver, an institution with an active Japanese and Chinese membership. Three years later he moved to the similarly diverse Agnes Street

Church in Toronto. Subsequently he held a variety of appointments, including Bracebridge (1903–5) and Kingston (1905–7). He then laboured for a year as secretary for eastern Asia of the International Reform Bureau, which opposed prostitution and the use of alcohol and opium. In 1908 he accepted a call from Zion Congregational Church in Toronto, and a year later he opened the People's Institute, a socialist church advocating brotherhood, social action, and peace. After his wife's death in 1912 he lived with a daughter in Saskatoon.

Eby was a man of rare talents, undoubted skills, and restless energy. He had a profound impact on the founding and early progress of the Methodist mission in Japan and did much to encourage Canadian support for mission work. He also strongly promoted ecumenism in church affairs, and strove to have Japan recognized as an equal member of the community of nations. As his obituary noted, he was a refined scholar, an impassioned preacher, and a courageous missionary.

NEIL SEMPLE

Charles Samuel Eby's *Christianity and humanity: a course of lectures delivered in Meiji kuaido, Tokio, Japan* and *The immediate Christianization of Japan: prospects, plans, results* were published in Yokohama in 1883 and 1884 respectively. Among his other works are *How shall we preach Christ?* ([Yokohama, 1885]); *Jikken Shingaku/Experimental theology or, the Methodist standard of preaching*, which he had printed in Japanese (Tokyo, 1888); *The Forward Movement in Japan: an address to the Methodist Church* (Toronto, 1889); and *The world problem and the divine solution* (Toronto, 1914).

UCC-C, Biog. file; Fonds 14/2/2, 78.083C; Fonds 14/2/4, 78.084C, 78.098C; Fonds 14/3/3, 78.092C. *Christian Guardian*, 1871–1908. G. H. Cornish, *Cyclopædia of Methodism in Canada . . .* (2v., Toronto and Halifax, 1881–1903). E. E. Eby and J. B. Snyder, *A biographical history of early settlers and their descendants in Waterloo Township, with Supplement*, ed. E. D. Weber (Kitchener, Ont., 1971). A. H. Ion, "Canadian missionaries in Meiji Japan: the Japan Mission of the Methodist Church of Canada (1873–1889)" (MA thesis, McGill Univ., Montreal, 1972). Methodist Church (Canada, Newfoundland, Bermuda), Missionary Soc., *Annual report* (Toronto), 1884–95; Woman's Missionary Soc., *Annual report* (Hamilton, Ont.; Toronto), 1884–96. Methodist Church of Canada, Missionary Soc., *Annual report* (Toronto), 1874–84. G. R. P. and Howard Norman, *One hundred years in Japan, 1873–1973* (2v., typescript, UCC, Div. of World Outreach, [Toronto], 1981). Neil Semple, *The Lord's dominion: the history of Canadian Methodism* (Montreal and Kingston, Ont., 1996). Wesleyan Methodist Church in Canada, Missionary Soc., *Annual report* (Toronto), 1871–74.

EDDY, JENNIE GRAHL HUNTER. *See* SHIRREFF

EDWARDS, CLARENCE BARTLETT, teacher and office holder; b. 26 Jan. 1862 in Burgessville,

Upper Canada, son of James Edwards, a farmer, and Matilda Bartlett; m. 12 Oct. 1886 Grace Louise Taylor in Birr, Ont., and they had two daughters; d. 1 Nov. 1921 in London, Ont.

Clarence Bartlett Edwards's career as an educator began in Oxford County, where he was born and raised. He attended the Woodstock Grammar School and in 1880 he received a grade-B teaching certificate. He taught for three years near Tavistock before entering the Ottawa Normal School; there he gained a second-class certificate in July 1884. Its principal noted that his manner was "nervous, but energetic" and his "general teaching ability very good."

Edwards rose quickly within his profession. After teaching in London Township, Lucan, and Strathroy, he was principal of St George's School and of Waterloo Street School in London. Noted for his strict discipline and respect for students, in 1894 he was appointed to the London Collegiate Institute, where he taught English and history under the principalship of Francis Walter Merchant*. Six years later he earned a BA from Queen's College in Kingston and an inspector's certificate and a high school principal's and specialist's certificate from the Department of Education. He left teaching to become city clerk of London in December 1902, but in 1904 he returned to education as the city's inspector of public schools.

By the 1900s educators, government officials, businessmen, and social reformers were arguing that, in the wake of increasing industrialization and urbanization, curricula fashioned in the mid 19th century were no longer relevant. The broadened scope of the "New Education" movement embraced household science and industrial training [*see* Adelaide Sophia Hunter*; John Seath*], kindergartens, social studies, hygiene and physical education, and agriculture. As local inspector – the official who, according to education minister Henry John Cody* in 1918, was "the real eye of the educational system" and the key to implementing change – Edwards was instrumental in introducing curricular reform. In 1908 the provincial inspector of technical education, Albert H. Leake, noted that in Ontario there were 13 centres of over 5,000 population, including London, where there was still no manual training or household science. A year later he was able to report that there was a manual-training centre at the London Normal School. By 1920 London had 10 manual and 12 household-science centres.

Edwards was also instrumental in introducing new programs such as health and dental examinations. Indeed, one of his mandates was the physical welfare of staff and students. He was responsible for having many new schools built and for upgrading existing ones. In a report he prepared in June 1909, at which time he oversaw 20 public school buildings and 165 regular and 25 substitute teachers, he noted with satisfaction the "vast improvements" that had been made in heating, ventilation, and sanitary systems. At the same time he deplored the "decided lack" of playgrounds, an issue then being taken up by city council and the school board.

Devoted to the ongoing preparation of teachers – in 1920 he himself would earn a bachelor of pedagogy degree from Queen's – Edwards was actively involved in the Ontario Educational Association and the London Teachers' Association. According to one account, it was his ambition to establish a summer school for teachers at his cottage on Lake Huron. In London this tall, slight school inspector belonged as well to the Canadian Club, the freemasons, the Knights Templar, the Church of England, and the London and Middlesex Historical Society, which he had helped found in 1901.

C. B. Edwards died at the age of 59 of pernicious anaemia at his Windsor Avenue home on 1 Nov. 1921. In his report for that year, John D. Waugh, the province's chief inspector of schools, noted that Edwards had been "in many respects an ideal inspector, helpful, courteous, and systematic," and praised his interest in pedagogy, school architecture, and school management. "The fine Public Schools of the city," Waugh concluded, "will be a lasting monument to his memory."

NANCY KIEFER

Clarence Bartlett Edwards is the author of "Establishment of schools in London, Ontario," in *The establishment of schools and colleges in Ontario, 1792–1910*, comp. J. G. Hodgins (3v., Toronto, 1910), 1: 111–28, and "London public schools, 1848–1871," London and Middlesex Hist. Soc., *Trans.*, 5 (1914): 14–29.

AO, RG 2-301-1-3, nos.6495, 9469/89; RG 2-368, acc. 17857, no.455; RG 2-368-0-1, acc. 10/87; RG 80-5-0-143, no.7262. Marta Danylewycz, "Domestic science education in Ontario, 1900–1940," in *Gender and education in Ontario: an historical reader*, ed. Ruby Heap and Alison Prentice (Toronto, 1991), 127–45. *Directory*, London, 1892–93, 1904. London, Council, "List of the members of council of the town and city of London from the days of its incorporation in the year 1840 to 1908" (photocopy from 1908 London by-laws; copy in the J. J. Talman Regional Coll., Univ. of Western Ont., London). London Collegiate Institute, *Collegiate*, June 1903; copy in the J. J. Talman Regional Coll., Univ. of Western Ont. Ont., Legislature, *Sessional papers*, annual reports of the Dept. of Education, 1901–2, 1905, 1908–9, 1911, 1919–20, 1922. Diana Pedersen, "'The scientific training of mothers': the campaign for domestic science in Ontario schools, 1890–1913," in *Critical issues in the history of Canadian science, technology and medicine*, ed. R. A. Jarrell and A. E. Roos (Thornhill, Ont., and Ottawa, 1982), 178–94. St George's School, *100th anniversary, St. George's School, Waterloo Street, London, Ontario, 1852–1952* (London, 1952), 27, 35. R. M. Stamp, *The schools of Ontario, 1876–1976* (Toronto, 1982). *Standard dict. of Canadian biog.* (Roberts and Tunnell), vol.1. *Who's who and why*, 1921.

EDWARDS, ROBERT CHAMBERS, journalist; b. 17 Sept. 1860 in Edinburgh, son of Alexander Mackenzie Edwards and Mary Chambers; m. 30 June 1917 Katherine Penman in Calgary; they had no children; d. there 14 Nov. 1922.

Bob Edwards's father was a medical doctor in Edinburgh and his mother, according to his own testimony, was a member of the famous Scottish publishing family. Orphaned as a youth, the boy was raised by two maiden aunts. He was apparently educated at a private school in St Andrews and at the Royal High School, Edinburgh. Later he attended the University of Glasgow for three sessions, between 1877 and 1880, but did not graduate.

After he left school Edwards travelled to France where he briefly published an English-language newspaper, the *Traveller* (Boulogne). In 1884 he joined his brother Jack in emigrating to the United States. They first went to Wyoming; there they spent their summers on a ranch at Horseshoe Creek and the winters in Cheyenne. Three years later, Edwards and his brother bought a farm in Iowa but the next ten years of his life are a mystery, revealed only in part through hints in his writings. He mentions being in Chicago, St Paul, Minn., Kansas City, Arkansas, and San Francisco, adding "the only really useful knowledge we possess today has been obtained while knocking about the continent and the United States – broke." In 1897 he arrived at Wetaskiwin (Alta), where he launched the Wetaskiwin *Free Lance*. It was a professional weekly of news, wit, and social comment, produced by a man of considerable journalistic talent and experience. Owning no presses, he had it printed by other newspapers. Within a short time, it was popular far beyond the Wetaskiwin area, but quickly lost its local support after Edwards made humorous comments about local merchants and they cancelled their advertising. Employed briefly by the *Manitoba Free Press* (Winnipeg) in 1899, he soon discovered that he preferred to be his own boss. He returned to Alberta later in the year to publish the *Alberta Sun* at Leduc; he then moved the weekly to Strathcona, across the river from Edmonton. In 1901 he started the *Wetaskiwin Breeze* but the next year, when his friend Jerry Boyce opened a hotel in High River, Edwards decided to join him. On 4 March 1902 he published his first edition of the *Eye Opener*, thus named "because few people will resist taking it."

Although it was the forerunner of the famous Calgary *Eye Opener*, the newspaper was still a small-town weekly which contained a mixture of local news and humour. It was well supported by local advertisers, but Edwards encountered considerable hostility from the clergy because of his excessive drinking and his frequent comments about liquor. During his two years at High River, he invented the character of Peter J. McGonigle, editor of the mythical Midnapore

Gazette who spent much of his time at the bar of Nevermore House. McGonigle was a sage, a gentleman, and a drunk – not unlike Edwards himself. Edwards also invented Albert Buzzard-Cholomondeley, an English remittance man whose "letters" home contained ingenious and hilarious methods of extracting money from his father.

In the summer of 1903 Edwards ran foul of a Presbyterian minister in High River, calling him a "misfit man of God." Shortly thereafter Edwards moved to Calgary, where the *Eye Opener* was soon established as a national newspaper of wit, satire, and political comment. By 1908 it had a circulation of 18,500 copies, with 4,000 being sold in Toronto, 2,600 in Winnipeg, 1,000 in Vancouver, and 1,800 on Canadian Pacific Railway trains.

Politically, Edwards leaned towards the Conservatives, but no party or individual was safe from his vitriolic attacks. When William MACKENZIE and Donald Mann* ("Bill" and "Dan" in the *Eye Opener*) attempted to sell their share in the Winnipeg street railway system for $24 million, Edwards described their holdings as a pile of junk. On learning that Robert J. Stuart was a candidate for Calgary alderman, Edwards ridiculed him with the following comment: "We understand – ha ha! – that – haw haw! – R. J. Stuart – ah-yaw-haw – ha ha ha! – is going to run – oh oh ha ha – for alderman – ha ha ha ha ha ha! – Ha ha ha ha ha ha – ha ha ha ha ha ha ha ha ha!" Edwards considered Sir Wilfrid Laurier*'s government to be corrupt, but at the same time he commented, "A propos Liberal and Conservative parties; of two evils it is best to choose neither."

Because of his outspoken comments, Edwards gained the ill will of a number of politicians and businessmen. In 1905 he fended off a libel suit filed by John Stoughton Dennis and the CPR after he attacked the railway's irrigation project east of Calgary. Richard Bedford Bennett*, as CPR solicitor, acted for the railway. Even though the case was dismissed, Edwards launched a bitter attack on Bennett, Dennis, and the CPR. He concentrated on unsafe railway crossings, particularly the ones at Calgary. In 1906 he began to publish photographs of train crashes, labelling each a CPR wreck. Then, on 7 April 1906, he featured a large portrait of Bennett and captioned it "Another C.P.R. wreck." By 1911, however, Edwards had made a complete about-face and he became a supporter of Bennett, predicting that he might some day become prime minister of Canada. In the meantime, in 1908 the *Eye Opener* had accused Conservative leader Robert Laird Borden* of fathering an illegitimate child. Although no action was taken against Edwards in this instance, a court order was issued to prevent distribution of the newspaper in Borden's home riding of Halifax.

Perhaps the most ludicrous legal case occurred in 1906, when Edwards carried a story about his mythical editor, Peter J. McGonigle, purportedly released from jail after serving time for horse theft. At a banquet tendered for McGonigle in Calgary, a telegram supposedly sent by Lord Strathcona [Donald A. Smith*] was read to the audience. It stated in part, "The name of Peter McGonigle will ever stand high in the roll of eminent confiscators. Once, long ago, I myself came near achieving distinction in this direction when I performed some dexterous financing with the Bank of Montreal's funds. In consequence, however, of CPR stocks going up instead of down, I wound up in the House of Lords instead of Stony Mountain [penitentiary]." Strathcona was reportedly infuriated by the article and instructed his solicitors to take legal action. However, when the nature of the *Eye Opener* was explained by the solicitors' Calgary agents, he was persuaded to abandon the suit.

Another of the *Eye Opener*'s opponents was Clifford SIFTON, whom Edwards accused of having relations with a married woman in 1905, at the time of negotiations for the formation of the provinces of Alberta and Saskatchewan. Three years later, Edwards heard a rumour that Sifton was backing the establishment of a Liberal newspaper in Calgary to counteract the influence of the *Eye Opener*. A short time after, Daniel McGillicuddy launched the Calgary *Daily News* and immediately prior to the election of 1908 he published a stinging personal attack on Edwards, calling him a "miserable wretch of a depraved existence," a libeller, character thief, coward, liar, drunkard, drug addict, and degenerate. Edwards sued for criminal libel and won the case, but McGillicuddy was fined only $100.

Edwards never forgave those involved in the lawsuit. He ridiculed McGillicuddy's lawyer, Edward Pease Davis, to such an extent that the man initiated a successful libel suit and Edwards was forced to publish an apology. Edwards also accused the judge, Nicholas Du Bois Dominic BECK, of political bias, describing him on one occasion as the "narrow, prejudiced, fanatical Beck." As for McGillicuddy, Edwards was bitter even after the man was dead. When Edwards was elected to the Legislative Assembly of Alberta 13 years after the suit, he would write, "Isn't it remarkable, here we are in the legislature and McGillicuddy is in hell?"

Believing that the McGillicuddy case signified a lack of support from Calgarians, Edwards tried to relocate his newspaper in Toronto or Montreal in 1909, but finally moved to Port Arthur (Thunder Bay), Ont., for a year, and then to Winnipeg for 1910 and early 1911. By April 1911, however, he was back in Calgary. During this time, he lost much of his vitriol and began to rely more on humour as a means of political condemnation. He started to sprinkle the pages of the *Eye Opener* with aphorisms such as "Politics is a good game, but a mighty poor business," and with so-called "social notes" which poked fun at the elite. For example, in 1911 he wrote, "We learn that Miss Mary E. Frobisher, of Didsbury, is engaged to be married to the well-known Calgarian, Mr. John T. Billcoe, on Nov. 20. It is apparent that Titania was not the only woman who loved a donkey." Many of his comments related to liquor, for although he tried to stop drinking on several occasions, he never overcame his alcoholism. "Every man has his favorite bird," he wrote. "Ours is the bat." In spite of, or perhaps because of, his drinking problem, he fully supported the introduction of Prohibition to Alberta in 1916. Yet, once the measure was implemented and he saw how drinking had moved from the bar room into the home, he became its outspoken critic.

Bob Edwards remained a bachelor until he was in his late fifties, living in hotel rooms and publishing his newspaper from a tiny office. Occasionally he had secretarial help but he always sent his copy to one of the local daily newspapers to print. In 1913 he met Katherine Penman, a 20-year-old woman just out from Scotland, who initially was in Bennett's law office and then worked in the land titles building. They were married, both unattended, in 1917 but Kate stayed a closed part of her husband's life, her name seldom being mentioned in his newspaper.

Because of Edwards's reputation as a humorist, he was encouraged in 1920 to consolidate his writings in an anthology. Not satisfied with simply reprinting old material, he added new stories and jokes, often embellishing accounts published years before. The result was a 90-page pulp magazine entitled *Bob Edwards' Summer Annual*, which was sold out in a few weeks. An agreement was then made with the Musson Book Company Limited of Toronto to publish the magazine each summer. In total, five annuals were produced, two appearing posthumously.

Over the years, many people had urged Edwards to stand for public office but he had always resisted the temptation; he preferred to take a neutral stand where party politics were concerned. However, in 1921 he finally succumbed, running as an independent and easily winning a seat in the Alberta legislature. Although he had neither advertised nor campaigned, he still polled the second largest vote in Calgary's field of 20 candidates. He sat for one session and made only one speech, in which he condemned the effects of Prohibition. Already ill, he grew worse and passed away on 14 Nov. 1922.

Throughout his life, Bob Edwards used humour and satire to advocate social change. Sympathetic to the poor, he spoke out against political corruption, exposed swindlers and fraudulent real estate salesmen, and favoured law reform, relaxed divorce laws, and Canadian nationalism. In his time he was the best-known journalist in the Canadian west.

HUGH A. DEMPSEY

[The *Calgary Eye Opener* was published and edited by Bob Edwards until 29 July 1922, and was continued by his wife until at least 18 Aug. 1923. The paper was eventually sold to a Minneapolis firm, which continued the *Eye Opener* as a small humour magazine.

The principal sources for information on Edwards's career are [J. W.] G. MacEwan, *Eye Opener Bob: the story of Bob Edwards* (Edmonton, 1957), and the two anthologies of his writings edited by Hugh A. Dempsey, *The best of Bob Edwards* (Edmonton, 1975) and *The wit & wisdom of Bob Edwards* (Edmonton, 1976). A six-part series on his life by Andrew William Snaddon appeared weekly in the *Calgary Herald* between 22 Sept. and 27 Oct. 1956.

There seems to be no body of papers on Edwards or the *Eye Opener*. A small collection, consisting of little more than a few random letters, exists in the GA (M 353, M 354, M 355, M 356, M 2623, M 3826, M 3943). Edwards's birth registration is at the General Register Office for Scotland, and his attendance at the Univ. of Glasgow is documented in the matriculation records in its Arch. and Business Records Centre. Information confirming his father's medical career was obtained from the Royal College of Surgeons, Edinburgh, and the Royal College of Surgeons of England, London.

No complete file of the *Eye Opener* has survived. In 1962 the known extant copies were microfilmed by the Canadian Library Association; some additional issues have subsequently been obtained by the Glenbow Library, Calgary, and the Univ. of Alta Library, Edmonton. The Glenbow Library holds a complete set of *Bob Edwards' Summer Annual* (Toronto). H.A.D.]

G. C. Porter, "Legendary Midnapore character made Calgary laugh; Lord Strathcona was not amused," *Calgary Herald*, 4 Feb. 1939. A. [W.] Snaddon, "Bob Edwards' story a bit of a mystery," *Calgary Herald*, 4 Dec. 1954. *Alberta newspapers, 1880–1982: an historical directory*, comp. G. M. Strathern (Edmonton, 1988). Max Foran, "Bob Edwards & social reform," *Alberta Hist.* (Calgary), 21 (1973), no.3: 13–17. Bertha Hart Segal, "'Bob' Edwards," *Cattlemen* (Winnipeg), June 1950: 18, 35, 42. T. U. Primrose, "Bob Edwards of High River," *Cattlemen*, January 1954: 6, 33.

ÉLIE, Frère. *See* PHANEUF

EMARD, JOSEPH-MÉDARD, Roman Catholic priest, professor, and archbishop; b. 31 March 1853 in Saint-Constant, Lower Canada, son of Médard Emard and Mathilde Baudin; d. 28 March 1927 in Ottawa.

Joseph-Médard Emard grew up in a family that would contribute two priests and three nuns to the Roman Catholic Church. He began his elementary schooling at the age of five under the tutelage of his father, a teacher who had recently become principal of a school in Saint-Hubert. When he was 11, he started his classical studies at the Petit Séminaire de Sainte-Thérèse (1864–67), and he completed them at the Petit Séminaire de Montréal (1867–72). In the fall of 1872 he entered the Grand Séminaire de Montréal. On finishing his theological studies, he was ordained by Bishop Édouard-Charles Fabre* of Montreal on 10 June 1876.

The young man was immediately appointed assistant priest in the parish of Saint-Enfant-Jésus. Emard was eager, however, to go to Rome, a city he associated with the grandeur, power, and triumphant influence of the Roman Catholic Church. His dream came true in the fall of 1877, when he left to study theology and canon law at the Roman Seminary. He made many friends there, both in the curia and at the French Seminary, where he lived. In his accounts of his travels he would describe with complacency the long processions of dignitaries on the occasion of eucharistic congresses and wax enthusiastic about the spiritual power of the church that these events suggested. In a letter to his father written on 9 March 1879, he showed his deep-seated love for Rome and the Roman way of doing things: "When the pope pronounces a blessing from his throne, something in his countenance is no longer of this world; one feels that there is a supernatural influence in all this." He came back to Montreal in 1880 with two doctorates.

On his return, Emard became assistant priest of the parish of Saint-Joseph. He was appointed vice-chancellor of the diocese in 1881, and chancellor eight years later. A tireless worker who never wearied of intellectual endeavours, Emard kept himself informed on various subjects. He subscribed to a few Parisian periodicals, *L'Univers*, *Études*, and *Nouvelle revue théologique*, as well as to some Italian and Irish magazines. In 1883 he began contributing to *La Semaine religieuse de Montréal*, a journal launched the previous year that sought to make known the Roman Catholic point of view on the major issues of the day. He had many articles published in it and would become its editor in 1889. When the faculty of arts of the Université Laval in Montreal was created in 1887, he was invited to teach church history, with the rank of professor. In 1922 he would become a member of the Royal Society of Canada.

On 5 April 1892 Leo XIII appointed Emard titular bishop of the new diocese of Valleyfield. Consecrated on 9 June, he would remain in charge of Valleyfield for 30 years. The new bishop was only 39 and had virtually no experience in parish work. On the other hand, he had a solid theological and canonical education. In addition, the 11 years he had spent in diocesan administration had prepared him well for the episcopate by making him familiar with all aspects of the life of the Canadian church and putting him in touch with its leading figures: Paul Bruchési*, the archbishop of Montreal from 1897; Narcisse-Zéphirin Lorrain, the first bishop of Pembroke, Ont., from 1898; Joseph-Alfred Archambeault*, the head of the newly created diocese of Joliette, Que., from 1904; and Zotique Racicot*, the first auxiliary bishop of Montreal from 1905.

The diocese assigned to Emard was relatively small. Surrounded by the archdioceses of Montreal and Ottawa, and by the dioceses of Alexandria, Ont.,

and Ogdensburg, N.Y., it had some 50,000 Catholics and 35 parishes, organized into five districts: Vaudreuil, Soulanges (Les Cèdres), Châteauguay, Beauharnois, and Huntingdon. A number of religious communities were already at work there: the Sisters of the Holy Names of Jesus and Mary, the Sisters of Charity of Providence, the Sisters of St Ann, the Sisters of Charity of the Hôpital Général de Montréal, the Congregation of Notre-Dame, and the Clerics of St Viator. Emard would complete the embryonic diocesan structure bit by bit. In 1893 he got the property of the parish of Sainte-Cécile transferred to the episcopal corporation. Then, over the years, he enlarged the bishop's palace, built the cemetery chapel, renovated the cathedral (which would be decorated by Toussaint-Xénophon Renaud), and bought a summer house in Port Lewis, near Saint-Anicet, for the seminarians. On the educational side, he soon built a kindergarten and the Collège de Valleyfield, to be followed by a normal school erected in 1908. He had brought the Little Sisters of the Holy Family to the palace and the seminary in 1900. Two years later he welcomed the first Poor Clares, who had come to set up a monastery in Salaberry-de-Valleyfield [*see* Marie-Louise-Thérèse LEMOINE]. In 1904 he put the Sisters of Charity of Providence in charge of the newly opened hospital, housing it in the former Petit Séminaire. He founded six parishes, divided his diocese into three deaneries (vicariates forane), and in 1920 officially installed his canonical chapter. This bustling activity required a sustained effort from everyone. For a long time the diocese carried heavy debts: $80,000 for the bishop's palace, $25,000 for the kindergarten, and $88,000 for the college. But Emard did not win every dispute, and this situation must have been humiliating for a man so conscious of his own authority. The canonical erection in 1913 of the parish of Immaculée-Conception, in the Bellerive district, which was practically forced on him by the militant attitude of the curé and the parishioners, brought this significant admission: "For, remember, I have never wanted a church in Bellerive, and I [still] don't want one!"

According to his contemporaries, Emard showed good judgement, kindness, wisdom, and prudence. A man of medium height, with a majestic and measured gait, he cut an impressive figure. Meticulous in both dress and deportment, serious and calm in his deliberations, prudent and firm in his decisions, he was fond of solemn liturgical entries into his cathedral with the tolling of bells. He celebrated church services with great dignity and always preached from the balustrade, bearing his crozier, and adorned with mitre and pontifical decorations. In conversation he was affable and courteous. This carefully cultivated formality created a distance between him and those with whom he spoke, which could be interpreted as coolness or even duplicity. In his private life, however, he lived simply, and enjoyed being at home and smoking a good cigar in the company of friends. He loved nature, and as often as possible he would get away to Port Lewis, on the shores of Lac Saint-François. There his conversations were lively, cheerful, and endless, but within the bounds of prudent reserve. His sense of duty was always uppermost, and it often overruled his personal inclinations.

Although he attached more importance to content than form in his writings, Emard expressed himself with conviction and precision. His pastoral letters, whether dealing with questions of dogma (the church, the Sacred Heart, the Virgin) or of morals (justice, temperance, family savings), always followed the same plan: a biblical foundation, the development of the question over time, the official doctrine of the church, a detailed description of the actual situation (in which he proved a keen observer of the morals of his flock), and, lastly, an invitation to his hearers to pray and to mend their ways. His eloquence no doubt explains the large number and variety of speaking invitations that came his way from all over, for the consecration of bishops, profession of vows, anniversaries of foundations, consecration of churches, state funerals, commemorative masses, and so on. From 1918 to 1920, in his capacity as ordinary of the Canadian army, he was responsible for the spiritual leadership of the troops.

The church was at the centre of Emard's concerns and thinking. In his view, as he noted in his first pastoral instructions to the people of his diocese, it is a family of believers and the bishop is its pastor; he knows his flock, watches over them, reassures them, and nourishes them with preaching and the sacraments. A priest, he added on the occasion of his sacerdotal meditation at Christmas 1920, "owes . . . to the souls entrusted to him all he is, all he has, and all he does." This image of communion, however, does not imply any idea of equality. His pastoral letter of 9 Feb. 1898 emphasized that the church is "complete in itself, formed of two very distinct classes of members, those responsible for teaching, governing, and sanctifying . . . , [and] the others receiving the full advantage of this triple ministry put in place for their benefit and to which they must submit." This hierarchical structure of the church, consisting of the pope, the bishops, and the priests, does not, in his view, come from human will, or historical development, but from God. It was established by Jesus Christ himself. Consequently, submission is the highest virtue of every Catholic. If Thomas Aquinas, the official teacher of the church, became an eminent example of "intellectual freedom," it was because he made obedience "his constant rule of conduct," Emard declared on 5 March 1918.

In his opinion, the first responsibility of the bishop is not his ministry, but obedience. The first duty of the believer is not discipleship, but compliance. This combination of authority and submission, characteristic of the structure of the church, is also found in the family, where, Emard noted on 24 Dec. 1904, the father is "a lawmaker with no human control, a judge with no appeal in this world, a provider in the image of God himself," and the paternal blessing is the tangible sign of his position. As for the mother of the family, "established by divine right in real subordination with respect to her husband, [she] shares with him, under this hierarchical dependence, the same prerogatives." For Emard, her place is at home, and, in a sermon preached on 13 Oct. 1909 in the church of Saint-Roch at Quebec, he congratulated her for "looking with contempt" at invitations to "compete with men, seeking to invade the courts, enter the lecture halls, force open the doors of parliaments, in short, take over offices and functions which [her] very nature had hitherto reserved for others." In the same way, he told the schoolchildren of his diocese in January 1919, children must develop within themselves, "in their respect for all legitimate authority, a sense of *hierarchical submission*."

The church has a role to play beyond the sphere of religion. Aware of this responsibility, Emard, in his pastoral writings, took an interest in many aspects of the lives of his flock, including agriculture (26 Dec. 1893), the census (14 Feb. 1901), justice (25 Dec. 1901), temperance (25 Dec. 1903), swearing oaths in court (8 Dec. 1905), the war (24 Dec. 1914), and family savings (19 Feb. 1917). In his statements he was usually precise and direct, for example in setting out a detailed program of studies for boys and girls, or in encouraging farmers to adopt new techniques and to organize study groups. On the other hand, he was more vague when he dealt with difficult subjects. While he did not say so openly, he believed that Canada, both for reasons of expedience and on principle, should take part in World War I, and he recognized the legitimacy of conscription.

In *Mes mémoires,* Abbé Lionel Groulx* described Emard as a liberal, not in matters of doctrine, but "by his cast of mind, by his temperament, his leanings," as an admirer of Sir Wilfrid Laurier* and of England, and as a denigrator of the nationalistic aims of French Canadians. What lay behind this comment? At the time, there were four questions, among others, dividing the French Canadian episcopate: the Manitoba schools, language, the idea of patriotism, and loyalty to England [*see* Louis-Nazaire BÉGIN; Charles Hugh GAUTHIER]. On the first of these, Emard took a realistic point of view. It was a serious matter, he wrote in January 1897, for on its solution depended the status of religion in the whole dominion. But while he agreed that the decision of the Manitoba government was unacceptable, he considered there was no need to take up arms, as some bishops had tried.

Emard had the same attitude on the language question. It was true, he told the schoolchildren of his diocese in March 1919, that the French language had saved the national and religious identity of French Canadians, that of "all modern languages it is the most harmonious, the most flexible, the most precise, the clearest, the richest, and . . . the most distinguished," and that they must learn it, write it, and speak it correctly. The English language, however, was spoken on two-thirds of the planet. As a favoured mode of international communication, it was the language of industry, of commerce, of finance, and especially of fellow citizens. French Canadians should therefore make it their duty to learn it if they wanted to play a role in politics.

It was the same story on the subject of patriotism. Although they are bound to France through their initial culture, French Canadians do not live in a province, but in a country where their fellow citizens are Canadians of other origins. According to Emard, Britain had made many legal concessions to French Canadians in favour of their nation and their religion, advantages that Catholics in Britain themselves had not obtained! As British subjects, they must make an effort to acknowledge this fact.

Emard became archbishop of Ottawa on 2 June 1922, following the death of Archbishop Gauthier. Gauthier had been appointed to this office in 1910 despite the fact that he himself had recommended the bishop of Valleyfield for it. Archbishop Emard officially took possession of his seat on 21 September at the age of 69. During his episcopacy, which would last less than five years, he established ten deaneries, created five parishes, and founded the Petit Séminaire d'Ottawa (1925). He died on 28 March 1927 after an illness of several months. He would be succeeded by Bishop Guillaume Forbes*.

In the opinion of Archbishop Joseph-Médard Emard, the only perfect society was the Roman Catholic Church. Therefore, any society, if it was not to fall victim to anarchy and disorder, would be well advised to follow its example, that is, "to demand of its members dependence on superiors and open and devoted submission to authority," as he declared on 22 April 1918. Submission, in his opinion, could even be a substitute for competence. He cited the experience of Canadian soldiers during World War I as proof. They did not have all the strategic training needed, but, as he wrote to the chaplains of the Canadian army in 1918, "the habit of discipline [and] a sense of duty and of obedience to their superiors must have largely compensated" for this lack.

GABRIEL CLÉMENT

Bishop Joseph-Médard Emard is the author of *Le Code de droit canonique: ses canons les plus pratiques pour le ministère avec références à la discipline locale* ([Salaberry-de-]Valleyfield, Qué., 1918); *Le Congrès eucharistique de Montréal* ([Salaberry-de-]Valleyfield, [1910?]); *Œuvres pastorales de Mgr J.-M. Emard, premier évêque de Valleyfield, 1892–1922* (5v., Paris, 1921–24); *Souvenirs d'un voyage en Terre-Sainte* (Montréal, 1884); *Les tendresses du Sacré-Cœur de Jésus: l'enfant, l'ami, le maître, le bienfaiteur, le consolateur; carême prêché à la cathédrale de Valleyfield, 1911* ([Salaberry-de-]Valleyfield, [1911?]; 2e éd., 1914).

ANQ-M, CE601-S18, 1er oct. 1850, 1er avril 1853. Arch. de la Chancellerie de l'Évêché de Valleyfield (Salaberry-de-Valleyfield), Fonds Joseph-Médard Emard, E-6. *Le Devoir*, 28 mars 1927. Yvon Julien, "Visages du Suroît," *Le Journal St-François* (Salaberry-de-Valleyfield), 12 juin 2001. *La Semaine religieuse de Montréal*, 15 juin 1922, 7 avril 1927. *La Semaine religieuse de Québec*, 19 oct. 1922, 31 mars 1927. *BCF*, 1926: 298. L.-A. Belisle, *Références biographiques, Canada-Québec* (5v., Montréal, 1978). *Canada ecclésiastique*, 1928. *Canadian men and women of the time* (Morgan; 1898 and 1912). *Dictionnaire de l'Amérique française; francophonie nord-américaine hors Québec*, Charles Dufresne *et al.*, édit. (Ottawa, 1988), 136. "Les disparus," *BRH*, 36 (1930): 102–3. *DOLQ*, vol.1. *Évêques catholiques du Canada, 1658–1979*, André Chapeau *et al.*, compil. (Ottawa, 1980). Lionel Groulx, *Mes mémoires* (4v., Montréal, 1970–74). *Histoire du catholicisme québécois*, sous la dir. de Nive Voisine (2 tomes en 4v. parus, Montréal, 1984–), tome 2, vol.2 (Philippe Sylvain et Nive Voisine, *Les XVIIIe et XIXe siècles: réveil et consolidation (1840–1898)*, 1991); tome 3, vol.1 (Jean Hamelin et Nicole Gagnon, *Le XXe siècle (1898–1940)*, 1984). LeBlanc, *DBECC*. "Mgr Joseph-Médard Emard," RSC, *Trans.*, 3rd ser., 21 (1927), proc.: xiii–xvii. J.-D. St-Aubin, *Salaberry de Valleyfield, 1842 à 1972: histoire religieuse, municipale, scolaire, commerciale et industrielle* (Salaberry-de-Valleyfield, [1972?]).

ENGLEHART, JACOB LEWIS, businessman, civil servant, and philanthropist; b. 2 Nov. 1847 in Cleveland, Ohio, son of John Joel Englehart, a merchant, and Hannah Rigaret; m. first 11 June 1868 Katy White in New York City; m. secondly 29 Dec. 1891 Charlotte Eleanor (Minnie) Thompson (d. 31 Dec. 1908) in Petrolia, Ont.; he had no children; d. 6 April 1921 in Toronto.

The Englehart family was Jewish and appears to have come to the United States from Germany. Educated in Cleveland, Jacob L. Englehart began his mercantile career in his teens in New York City, where his father had gone into business and his sister Sophie had married a prominent attorney. Between 1866 and about 1883 he was based there as a brewer, a rectifier, and then a merchant specializing in petroleum products. His attention was drawn in the late 1860s to southwest Ontario and the oil resources beneath the farmlands of Lambton and Kent counties between Chatham and Sarnia [*see* James Miller Williams*]. At the centre of the oil boom was the village of Petrolia. In January 1870 Englehart entered the refining business in London, Ont., with partners from that city as well as New York and Mannheim (Germany); six years later, with Isaac Guggenheim, he formed J. L. Englehart and Company and moved his refining operation to Petrolia, where he settled. He modelled his approach on that of men such as John Davison Rockefeller in the oilfields of Pennsylvania; not only did he operate his own field and contract with local farmers for their oil, but he recognized the value of combination. In September 1880 he initiated a merger with other refiners, including his one-time partners Herman and Isaac Waterman (natives of Bavaria), to form the Imperial Oil Company Limited in London. Englehart's role of vice-president and general manager, together with his 20 per cent of the shares, made him the central executive.

After Imperial's works were destroyed by fire in 1883, the firm expanded its refinery in Petrolia and the following year moved its headquarters there. Englehart built a grandiose house. As well, he converted to Anglicanism in the 1880s and became a freemason, and, at some point, a British subject. Photographs portray him as a bald gentleman wearing European-style formal attire, pince-nez, and a Vandyke beard. His marriage in 1891 to the 28-year-old Minnie Thompson, the *Petrolia Advertiser and Canadian Oil Journal* reported, was a grand social event.

Because of the size of its refinery, Imperial held a near-monopoly over the processing of petroleum for sale to the burgeoning market of Canadian railways. To compete with the cheap imports of Standard Oil from the United States, Englehart supported Canada's defensive tariff. When it became clear that the federal government of Wilfrid Laurier* elected in 1896 would not continue this protection, Englehart and the board of Imperial decided in 1898 to sell a majority of its shares to Standard and move its head office and refinery to Sarnia. Englehart sat on the board of the new subsidiary, still called Imperial Oil; he nevertheless remained in Petrolia, in part to run J. L. Englehart and Company, which in 1899 had 233 wells driven by a single power plant over an area of 400 acres. Eventually his wealth spread into other investments. He served as president of the Crown Savings and Loan Company in Petrolia and vice-president of the London and Western Trusts Company. In addition, his influence had begun to take a political turn.

Englehart became a leading financial sponsor of the Conservative party in southwest Ontario. His brother-in-law George Moncrieff was the MP for Lambton East from 1887 to 1896. Provincially, in 1902 he supported the candidacy in Lambton West of his friend William John Hanna*, Imperial's counsel and a member of its board. After Hanna was appointed provincial secretary in the government of James Pliny Whitney* in February 1905, he recommended Englehart as a member of the Temiskaming and Northern Ontario Railway Commission and then in 1906 as its chairman. It

had been launched in 1902 by the Liberal government of George William Ross* to build a line from North Bay to Lake Timiskaming and thereby facilitate settlement in northeast Ontario [*see* August Kruger*]. Traffic, which began in January 1905, was intensified by mining booms at Cobalt, Porcupine, and Kirkland Lake [*see* Benjamin Hollinger*]. For 13 years Englehart would chair the commission and manage the railway, reporting directly to the provincial secretary. He was seen as a slightly eccentric but conscientious public official who was rumoured to give most of his salary to charity.

Although his temperament was too remote and formal for him to become a political figure of any prominence, he took seriously the part he could play as a philanthropist, political backer, and public servant. In 1909, following his wife's death from tuberculosis, he donated X-ray equipment to St Michael's Hospital in Toronto and a year later he honoured her testamentary wish that Glenview, their house in Petrolia, be turned into a hospital. He enjoyed the recognition that came from his contributions to the Conservatives. Though his written English reflected his secondary level of education, he had willingly accepted Whitney's invitation to sit for a term (1906–8) on the board of governors of the University of Toronto.

Englehart's essential place, historically, must rest on his management of the T&NO. In 1905–6 the commission was given responsibility for establishing much-needed town sites at Temagami, Latchford, Cobalt, and Englehart. He presided over the railway's extension in 1908 to Cochrane, where it would meet the National Transcontinental Railway, and in 1911 to the Porcupine gold mines. He negotiated contracts for the running of transcontinental trains to Toronto over the T&NO's tracks. As well, he promoted the railway in terms of community service, especially at times of destructive fires, including those of 1911 at Porcupine and Cochrane and 1916 at Matheson. Within business circles in Toronto, where he became a director of the Bank of Toronto in 1912, he was an effective spokesman for the development of northern Ontario. Sentiment in the north toward Englehart contained a note of resentment at his never having lived in the region. (After leaving Petrolia, he had taken up residence in the Queen's Hotel in Toronto.) There is no question, however, that his direction of the railway, which he travelled over regularly, gave him a clear public image at a time when the T&NO fulfilled a great need in the opening of "New Ontario."

Englehart's health failed in 1919 and he resigned his chairmanship on 28 October, just days after the election of the United Farmers government. At the time he upheld three priorities of the previous Conservative government: building a branch to Kirkland Lake, electrifying the railway, and extending it to

James Bay. Following his death at Wellesley Hospital from a brain haemorrhage, he was buried in Hillsdale Cemetery near Petrolia. His $2-million estate was distributed mostly to relatives and friends.

ALBERT TUCKER

Jacob Lewis Englehart's career with the Temiskaming and Northern Ontario Railway Commission is examined in the author's *Steam into wilderness: Ontario Northland Railway, 1902–1962* (Toronto, 1978).

AO, RG 8-5, boxes 12–13; RG 22-273, nos.4133, 6563; RG 22-305, nos.46014, 46221; RG 55-17-33, nos.111, 185, 403; RG 80-5-0-196, no.5652; RG 80-8-0-343, no.5598; RG 80-8-0-801, no.2946. *Globe*, 7, 11 April 1921. *Petrolia Advertiser and Canadian Oil Journal* (Petrolia, Ont.), 1 Jan. 1892, 6 Jan. 1909. Michael Barnes, *Jake Englehart* (Cobalt, Ont., 1974). *Canadian annual rev.*, 1905–17. *Canadian men and women of the time* (Morgan; 1912). *Cyclopædia of Canadian biog.* (Rose and Charlesworth), vol.3. J. S. Ewing, "The history of Imperial Oil Limited" (MS, Harvard Business Hist. Foundation, Boston, 1951; copy in Imperial Oil Arch., Toronto). *Industrial Canada* (Toronto), 22 (1921–22), no.1: 124, 126. *National cyclopædia of American biography* . . . (63v., New York, [etc.], 1892–1984), 14: 362; 36: 147–48. *Newspaper reference book*. Ont., Legislature, *Sessional papers*, 1900, no.5: 107. *Trow's New York City directory* . . . (New York), 1864/65–82/83. *Who's who and why*, 1919/20: 1143.

ENGLISH, BENJAMIN FRANKLIN, businessman and rancher; b. 19 March 1841 in St Louis, Mo., son of Benjamin Franklin English and Pauline (Paulina, Perlina, Perlena) Durbin (Dunben); m. first Annie Fontaine (having lived together as man and wife from the mid 1860s, they had their union solemnized on 23 Jan. 1883 in the Barkerville district, B.C.), and they had three sons; m. secondly 14 March 1885 Ellen Martin (d. 1927) in Victoria, and they had three daughters and two sons; d. 6 May 1922 in Ashcroft, B.C.

Ben English, also known as Doc English, was one of the countless Americans who, in the late 1850s and early 1860s, were attracted to the possibilities offered by the Fraser and Cariboo gold rushes in the colony of British Columbia. For English the migration north was merely the latest in a series of journeys. In 1846 his family had travelled from Missouri to Polk County, Oregon Territory, where they eventually settled near the Luckiamute River. During this trek, English later recalled, he and his father eluded a number of hostile natives armed with poisoned arrows, one of which struck and killed young Benjamin's horse. The family would stay on the Luckiamute for 17 years before moving to California, where they lived first in Solano County and then in Lake County. In 1856, at the age of 15, English returned to Missouri to lead a pack train of friends and relatives bound for Oregon. It was during his years in Oregon

that he acquired the nickname Doc, which reflected his exceptional ability in handling livestock and what proved to be a lifelong passion for horses, especially racehorses.

Two years after his return to Oregon, English joined a 200-person wagon train that had set out for the Fraser River but was turned back by approximately 800 Indians in the Okanogan valley on the American side of the international boundary. Deterred, the wagoners returned to Oregon, but English retraced his steps in 1860 and eventually arrived in Barkerville. After driving cattle from Oregon to Barkerville for Herman Otto Bowe, English established his own pack train. He then branched out into merchandising and fur trading in a partnership with Orlando Thomas Hance, with whom he established the TH Ranch in the Chilcotin. This association continued until English lost some $3,000 of the ranch's money in a horse race and, in an effort to make good the debt, turned over his portion of the ranch to Hance. English moved on to Deer Park, also in the Chilcotin; in 1873 he pre-empted 320 acres that became the heart of his Deer Park Ranch, which would remain the family home until 1886. After selling this property, the family relocated to the lower Bonaparte River, where they raised cattle and horses. English later moved to the Venables valley. Here the family stayed until 1919, when they resettled in Ashcroft. Throughout his life English repeatedly found success in his numerous ventures and steadfastly refused to retreat in the face of hardship or economic setback.

In April 1864, shortly after he had established himself in Barkerville, British Columbia was thrown into turmoil when 18 road builders and local residents were killed at Bute Inlet by a group of Chilcotin Indians under Chief Klatsassin*. The attack was motivated both by the intrusion of a road being built into the interior by Alfred Penderell Waddington* and by the waves of smallpox that had devastated local aboriginal populations. It is told that English played a central role in the eventual capture of three of the Chilcotin involved but the details of the story reveal it to be an outright fabrication. At best English may have been a member of the 50-man posse led by William George Cox*.

Incidents almost 20 years later reveal the source of the confusion about English's activities. In 1883 he orchestrated the surrender of two Chilcotin men accused of murdering a Chinese miner. Accompanied by a Constable Boswell, English lived amongst the natives where the escapees were believed to be hiding and, after negotiating with aboriginal leaders, managed to capture the accused. Shortly thereafter English was offered $500 by the provincial attorney general's office to organize the capture of two other Chilcotin accused of murder, but he either turned down the offer or was unsuccessful in the attempt.

English's connection with criminal justice continued a few years later when he was involved in the capture of Martin Van Buren Rowlands, the Cariboo bandit. In mid August 1891 a robber held up the British Columbia Express Company stagecoach and made off with $15,000 in gold. Soon afterwards, word of a fabulous gold strike on Scottie Creek began circulating, with Rowlands as the main beneficiary. Suspicions were raised since it was widely accepted that Scottie Creek had been played out, and English and local cattle merchant John Wilson took it upon themselves to investigate. Having followed Rowlands from the creek back into Ashcroft, English and Wilson went to Isaac Lehman, a justice of the peace, and swore out a complaint in support of an arrest warrant. Just as Rowlands was boarding the train to leave, he was arrested by Constable Joseph William Burr and, after further investigation and a trial, was found guilty and sentenced to five years. For their part in the arrest English and Wilson eventually split a $2,000 reward.

Ultimately, English's life symbolizes particular themes of life in late-19th and early-20th-century British Columbia. He is an example of one type of settler who harboured a thinly veiled antipathy towards aboriginal peoples while acquiring a reputation for being adept in dealings with them. Further, he drew upon the tradition of the self-confident and resourceful man of the frontier who engaged in a wide range of activities. Finally, in a number of ways he manifested the pioneer's ability to adjust to the circumstances of a developing society where practical skills provided the means to succeed and prosper.

JONATHAN SWAINGER

BCA, GR-0429, box 1, file 12, 118/83, 141/83, 356/83; box 2, file 5, 1354/92; box 3, file 1, 1478/93; GR-2951, no.1922-09-308037 (mfm.); GR-2962, no.1883-09-172814; no.1885-09-003966 (mfm.). Quesnel Museum and Arch. (Quesnel, B.C.), English Family clipping file. *Ashcroft Journal* (Ashcroft, B.C.), 12 May 1922. *Kamloops Standard-Sentinel* (Kamloops, B.C.), 9 May 1922. *Williams Lake Tribune* (Williams Lake, B.C.), 31 May 1951. Cecil Clark, *B.C. Provincial Police stories* (3v., Surrey, B.C., 1986–93). Pat Foster, "Doc English," *British Columbia Hist. News* (Victoria), 29 (1995–96), no.3: 13–15; "Grandmother and granddaughter: the pioneer spirit," 28 (1994–95), no.2: 2–4. E. S. Hewlett, "The Chilcotin uprising: a study of Indian-white relations in nineteenth century British Columbia" (MA thesis, Univ. of B.C., Vancouver, 1972); "The Chilcotin uprising of 1864," *BC Studies* (Vancouver), no.19 (autumn 1973): 50–72. Mel Rothenburger, *The Chilcotin war* (Langley, B.C., 1978). E. O. S. Scholefield and F. W. Howay, *British Columbia from the earliest times to the present* (4v., Vancouver, 1914), 4: 807–8. M. S. Wade, *The Cariboo Road*, ed. E. A. Eastick (Victoria, 1979). D. R. Williams, ". . . *The man for a new country": Sir Matthew Baillie Begbie* (Sidney, B.C., 1977). R. T. Wright, *Barkerville, Williams Creek, Cariboo: a gold rush experience* (rev. ed., Duncan and Barkerville, B.C., 1993).

EWART, DAVID, civil servant and architect; b. 18 Feb. 1841 in Penicuik, Scotland, third son of John Ewart, a builder, and Jean Cossar; m. first 20 March 1871 Jeanne Marie Doyen (d. 11 Dec. 1885) in York, England, and they had five sons and one daughter; m. secondly 19 May 1887 Annie Sigsworth Simpson (d. 13 June 1938) in Ottawa, and they had four daughters and two sons; d. there 6 June 1921.

David Ewart was born and educated in Penicuik, south of Edinburgh. He apprenticed as a joiner in his father's construction firm, learned architectural drawing from Edinburgh architect Walter Carmichael, and apparently studied architecture at the School of Arts in Edinburgh. By the late 1860s he was employed in Helperby, England, as clerk of works for the Myton Hall estate. In April 1871, at the age of 30 and recently married, he set sail for Canada, armed with testimonials from architects Joseph Taylor, Thomas Dickinson, and James Aitken attesting to his excellent drafting skills and industrious work habits. A friend in Montreal advised him to seek employment with the Department of Public Works in Ottawa. He approached Frederick Preston Rubidge*, the department's assistant engineer and architect, who at that moment happened to be looking for an architectural assistant. On 16 May, only 11 days after arriving in Canada, Ewart was hired on a trial basis at $60 per month.

The engineering and architecture functions of the Department of Public Works were separated in the spring and summer of 1871. Rubidge was superannuated to make room for two new appointees, George-Frédéric-Théophile Baillairgé* as assistant chief engineer and Thomas Seaton Scott* as senior architect (a title that would be changed the following year to chief architect). In October 1871 Scott mapped out a plan for staffing his new office, envisioning a range of positions from "a thoroughly competent head assistant" to a draftsman for tracing. He had Ewart in mind as a "practical draughtsman," one of the mid-level positions. Nevertheless, by January 1875 Ewart had become the highest-paid architectural draftsman in the office, and by 1879 he was de facto assistant chief architect.

In October 1881, ten years after being hired on trial, Ewart gained the office's top position – albeit on an acting basis – when his minister, Sir Hector-Louis Langevin*, orchestrated Scott's resignation-cum-retirement. At the very same moment, however, Thomas Fuller*, one of the original architects of the Parliament Buildings and then living in upstate New York, was corresponding with Samuel Keefer*, a former deputy commissioner of public works in Ottawa, to promote his candidacy as the department's new chief architect. Keefer's strong endorsement of

Fuller was quickly acted on by Prime Minister Sir John A. Macdonald*, and Fuller was in place by December. Ewart reverted to his role as assistant chief architect.

Known for his business capacity, Ewart took care of a considerable amount of Fuller's work, including office supervision and correspondence. In addition, he managed the auditing of accounts for all public buildings controlled by the federal government – the responsibilities of the chief architect's office, unlike those of a private architectural practice, included acquisition, maintenance, and repair. The department's deputy minister, Antoine Gobeil, singled out Ewart in 1892 as "the mainstay of the chief architect's office. I never knew a man to work so much. He works day and night."

Fuller retired in 1896, and approval to appoint Ewart as chief architect was finally given on 2 Nov. 1897. More than 340 new buildings and substantial renovations would be undertaken during his tenure of this office, one of the most productive eras in the history of the chief architect's branch. The office produced a steady string of well-designed public buildings – almost every municipality of any consequence got one – and the standardized plans that emerged in this period resulted in a recognizable federal design vocabulary across the country. Ewart and his staff occasionally equalled the best work being produced in private practice, as in their Edwardian baroque design for the Vancouver Post Office (1905–10). Ewart himself designed in a very controlled, sober manner, favouring Tudor Gothic for his Dominion Archives Building (1904–6), Victoria Memorial Museum (1905–8), Royal Mint (1905–8), and Connaught Building (1913–16), all in Ottawa.

Ewart's otherwise successful tenure as chief architect was not without low points. For example, the department (and therefore the chief architect) was found partly responsible for the collapse of an addition to the west block on Parliament Hill, and 80 feet of the central tower of the Victoria Memorial Museum had to be removed after it began to sink. The edifice Ewart thought one of his best, the Connaught Building, was criticized by his peers in the journal *Construction* (Toronto) as being of "puerile design and questionable construction."

In 1903 Ewart was awarded the Imperial Service Order (one of the first in Canada) in recognition of his career in the civil service. He was also a member of the first executive council (1889) and president (1893) of the Ottawa Institute of Architects, a founding member (1889) and councillor (1891) of the Ontario Association of Architects, and a founding member and councillor (1907) of the Institute of Architects of Canada (later the Royal Architectural Institute of Canada). He retired in 1914 at age 73, but was immediately made dominion consulting architect, a position created specifically for him and one that he held at full salary until his death. A singular devotion to the Canadian civil service came to an end 50 years after it had begun when he died of a stomach malignancy at his home in Ottawa (not, as legend has it, by hurling himself from his truncated museum tower). Four of his sons worked in architecture or engineering. The eldest, John Albert, practised for 65 years, and at his death in 1964 was considered the doyen of Ottawa's architects.

David Ewart had attained the chief architect's office at a time when the position had, by dint of scope and volume of work, evolved from one requiring a master designer – a role so ably played by his predecessor Fuller – to one needing a master administrator. He was ideal for this work, efficiently orchestrating a sizeable office of architectural specialists to produce a high volume of very competent (and occasionally outstanding) construction within a politically demanding context. Professionally, Ewart was a capable architect of buildings; more significantly, he was an accomplished architect of the process of building.

GORDON W. FULTON

The author wishes to thank Helen M. Lyons of Ottawa, and Susan Taylor of Vancouver, the granddaughter and great-granddaughter of the subject, respectively, for providing access to some Ewart family papers.

AO, RG 80-5-0-148, no.2023; RG 80-8-0-809, no.10392. GRO, Reg. of marriages, All Saints North Street, York, 20 March 1871. LAC, RG 11, B1(a), 591; B1(b), 725, 753; B3(a), 2922; RG 31, C1, 1901, Nepean, Ont., dist.52: 11; RG 76, C: 1(a) (mfm.). National Arch. (G.B.), HO 107 1841, Penicuik, Edinburgh County. *Globe*, 27 Aug. 1901. *Ottawa Citizen*, 3 Oct. 1881, 7 June 1921. *Ottawa Evening Journal*, 7 June 1921. *Toronto Daily Star*, 23 June 1906. Margaret Archibald, *By federal design: the chief architect's branch of the Department of Public Works, 1881–1914* (Ottawa, 1983). Can., Dept. of the Secretary of State, *The civil service list of Canada . . .* (Ottawa), 1898–1914; Parl., *Sessional papers*, 1892, no.16C: 487; 1906, no.161: 1–6. *Canadian men and women of the time* (Morgan; 1912). "A competent chief architect and representative government buildings the most pressing need in Canada's advancement," *Construction* (Toronto), 5 (1911–12), no.1: 43–44. "Proposed department building, Ottawa – a gross breach of faith with architectural profession – a beautifully symmetrical and monumental adaptation of Gothic set aside for a design characterized by critic as a 'glorified packing box,'" *Construction*, 3 (1910), no.6: 72–73. *Standard dict. of Canadian biog.* (Roberts and Tunnell), vol.1. *Who's who and why*, 1915/16. Janet Wright, *Crown assets: the architecture of the Department of Public Works, 1867–1967* (Toronto, 1997).

F

FABIEN (Presseault, *dit* Fabien), CLÉOPHAS, carpenter, cabinetmaker, icebox manufacturer, and politician; b. 23 Jan. 1850 in Montreal, son of Paschal Presseault, *dit* Fabien, a carpenter, and Marguerite Labelle; m. there 11 Feb. 1874 Marguerite Cousineau, and they had eight children, five of whom survived him; d. there 9 Jan. 1925.

In his early years Cléophas Fabien attended Joseph-Octave Mauffette's school in Montreal. In the mid 1860s he began working with his father as a carpenter's apprentice. Having learned the rudiments of his trade, in 1866 he became a carpenter's apprentice on the construction of the Canadian parliament buildings in Ottawa [*see* Thomas Fuller*]. It was at this time, as well, that he helped with the repairs to some of the wings of Notre-Dame church in Montreal. During the 1870s and early 1880s Fabien was employed by William Rutherford, a major manufacturer of furniture, doors, and windows in Montreal. In all likelihood, it was there that he acquired a sound training in cabinet-making.

On the strength of his experience, Fabien went into business for himself in 1884. Borrowing $50 from a neighbour, he opened a small plant equipped with a primitive sawmill in the Montreal suburb of Sainte-Cunégonde to make furniture and iceboxes. He apparently produced only six iceboxes during the first year. In October 1888 he went into partnership with Cyrille Paré, a joiner, under the business name of Fabien et Paré. This arrangement enabled him to increase his output of iceboxes to 200 a year, while continuing to manufacture furniture. At the time, Fabien et Paré's iceboxes were simply rectangular cold cupboards, holding 20 to 50 pounds, in which a block of ice was placed. To increase the insulating effect, the inside walls were lined with zinc, while the exterior sheathing was of wood.

During the 1890s the introduction of mechanical processes for making ice in most North American cities increased the demand for zinc and wood iceboxes. Eager to progress beyond the limited scope of cottage-type production, Fabien moved his operation into a three-storey brick building at 3169 Rue Notre-Dame, in Sainte-Cunégonde, in 1891. Equipped with modern, electrically powered machinery, the enterprise had more than 30 employees three years later. In 1910 it began producing electric iceboxes under the Aubin patent. The invention of refrigeration by compressed gas reportedly dates back to 1857, following experiments by the Frenchman Ferdinand Carré. In 1876 the German Carl von Linde invented the first ammonia compressor, which opened the way to significant use of commercial refrigeration for the transportation of perishable foods by ship and train. A method of producing electric iceboxes (the future refrigerators) for the retail trade and home use still had to be found, and Fabien turned his attention to this problem in 1910. He soon had a large clientele of grocers, butchers, restaurateurs, hoteliers, florists, and housewives. In these endeavours Fabien was a pioneer, since in 1923 there were only 20,000 homes in the United States equipped with electric iceboxes, and probably very few in Canada.

To ensure continuity, Fabien incorporated his company in 1919 under the name Compagnie de Glacières C.-P. Fabien Limitée, and brought his four sons and his daughter onto the newly formed board of directors. At the time of his death in 1925 the company was considered the largest of its kind in the province of Quebec, and the second largest in Canada, next to the Eureka Refrigerator Company Limited of Toronto. Its annual output then was some 6,000 iceboxes (with a range of 22 models, priced from $12 to $2,500), of which at least 1,000 were exported to England, South Africa, Latin America, and the West Indies. The company would remain in operation until 1994.

Doubtless attracted by the financial sector, Fabien apparently had close ties to the Alliance Nationale, a French Canadian mutual life insurance company incorporated in 1893 whose president was Hormisdas Laporte*. He was also a member (and later president) of the Union Saint-Joseph de Saint-Henri, a mutual aid society founded in 1887. Elected an alderman in 1901, he served as chair of the municipal finance committee from 1901 to 1902, and as mayor of Sainte-Cunégonde from 1902 to 1905. It was in this latter capacity that he had a new town hall built at a cost of $63,000. The municipality was, however, annexed to Montreal in 1905.

In many respects Cléophas Fabien's career illustrates the rise of French Canadian entrepreneurs in niche markets, outside the realm of industrial mass production, at the end of the 19th century and the beginning of the 20th.

ROBERT TREMBLAY

ANQ-M, CE601-S29, 11 févr. 1874; CE601-S51, 24 janv. 1850; TP11, S2, SS20, SSS48, vol. 14-o, 6 juin 1889, no.668. *Le Devoir*, 25 avril 1925, 5 juin 1928. *La Patrie*, 9–10, 12 janv. 1925. *La Presse*, 9 janv. 1925. *Voix populaire* (Montréal), 26 oct. 1950; 11, 16 juin, 2, 23 juill. 1952. *The book of Montreal; a souvenir of Canada's commercial metropolis*, ed. E. J. Chambers ([Montreal, 1903]), 114. *Canadian trade index* (Toronto), 1901, 1913–15, 1994. *Directory*, Montreal, 1880–1925. J.-H. Fabien, "La famille Presseau-Fabien," Soc. généalogique canadienne-française, *Mémoires* (Montréal), 13 (1962): 123–31. *A history of technology*, ed. C. [J.] Singer *et al.* (8v., Oxford, 1954–94), 5: 45–51. Franz Klingender, "'To lighten the burden of womenkind': the mechanization of domestic equipment, 1890–1960" (hist. assessment, National Museum of Science and Technology, Ottawa, 1994), 15–16. Linteau, *Hist. de Montréal*, 172, 194. Gérald Messadié, *Les grandes inventions du monde moderne* (Paris, 1989), 28–29. *Montreal illustrated, 1894* . . . (Montreal, [1894]). Ronald Rudin, *Banking en français: the French banks of Quebec, 1835–1925* (Toronto, 1985), 116–17.

FAFARD. *See* TOUPIN-FAFARD

FAIRWEATHER, MARION (Stirling), teacher, missionary, and physician; b. 14 Oct. 1846 in Bowmanville, Upper Canada, daughter of David Fairweather, a shopkeeper, and Anna ——; m. 25 Sept. 1888 Charles Stirling in Agra, India; they had no children; d. 28 Feb. 1923 in San Leandro, Calif.

The youngest of the four daughters of Scottish-born parents, Marion Fairweather attended McGill Normal School in Montreal, where she received an elementary-level teaching diploma (1869) and a model-school diploma (1872). She taught in Bowmanville in the interim. In 1872 she wrote to the Foreign Missions Committee of the Canada Presbyterian Church to enquire about appointments for herself and Margaret Rodger, a fellow graduate of McGill Normal School. Because the FMC did not yet have an overseas field, it corresponded with Presbyterian mission boards in Scotland and the United States about a placement for them. It also arranged for them to spend some time at a Presbyterian institution, the Ottawa Ladies' College, perhaps as much to monitor their fitness for service as to prepare them for it. By the autumn of 1873 it had been decided that Fairweather and Rodger should begin work in an American Presbyterian mission in northern India. On Christmas Eve they arrived in the city of Allahabad.

Notwithstanding some peremptory letters from Fairweather to the FMC prior to their departure, she and Rodger seem to have left Canada with its full approval. "As you are our pioneers," FMC secretary Thomas Lowry wrote, "we must be guided very much in our future plans by the information which we may get from you and from other sources respecting the state of affairs in the place to which you have gone." Unlike the taciturn Rodger, Fairweather responded with alacrity to this letter and the opportunity it presented. She urged her American colleagues to advise the FMC on a location for a Canadian mission, and she endorsed their suggestion of Indore, in Central India. Early in 1877, two years after the union that created the Presbyterian Church in Canada, Indore became the site of the church's first mission station in India when Fairweather and Rodger began work there with its official founder, the Reverend James Moffat Douglas*. Arguably the most important figure in the mission's establishment, the supremely confident Fairweather acted first as Douglas's mentor and then as his closest colleague.

After learning of his appointment, she had written to him, to the FMC, and to the church's newly established Woman's Foreign Missionary Society (Western Division) [*see* Marjory Laing*] about the types of work the mission should take up and her "plans" for appointees. She had begun as well to recruit a group of Indian Christian workers to accompany her to Indore. There she worked with Douglas to establish a press and, like him, she attempted to convert high-caste Indian men. She also engaged in the more conventional tasks of a woman missionary in India: school work and visiting zenanas. The latter involved calling on secluded Muslim and high-caste Hindu women, and trying to introduce the gospel through such subterfuges as lessons in reading and needlework. The agency among women about which she became most enthusiastic was medical work. While serving with the Americans, she had come to know their pioneer female medical missionary, Dr Sara Seward. Impressed by the drawing power of her work, especially among elites, Fairweather strongly commended similar practice to FMC convenor William McLaren (MacLaren), in the hope perhaps that the church would finance her training.

By the end of 1879 the mission would have two stations and a Canadian staff of three single women and two ordained men with their wives. At the outset the FMC had not provided formal regulations for the staff, and in this context Fairweather recognized no constraints on her role other than those inherent in being unordained. Her expansive approach aroused resentment among the Canadian workers, while her working relationship with Douglas became a subject of gossip among the Indian staff. In October 1879 the FMC recalled her to Canada without first asking for her version of the conflicting, sometimes bizarre reports about her and Douglas that it had received from the mission. Letters from ordained and secular Europeans in India uniformly testified to her ability and drive, but they could not save her career. Along with the praise, and scorn for the gossip about sexual improprieties, the letters made it clear that she did not fit the conventional image of a submissive Victorian woman, much less that of a lady missionary. An ordained Scottish missionary observed that she was "far indeed from the meekest of women," while a former Church of England chaplain told her "I should have been proud if a sister of mine had had your zeal and ambition, but I should not have let her try to convert native gentlemen." In June 1880, following a meeting with Fairweather (held only at her request), the FMC formalized its decision to remove her from the mission staff. In having to deal with conflicts in a new and distant mission, the FMC was by no means unique, but its arbitrary response was somewhat unusual.

Fasken

Fairweather's efforts to have the FMC reappoint her or help her find another posting came to nothing, as did her vague threat to take legal action. Yet she did not obligingly fade into obscurity. Between 1880 and 1884 she contributed three series of articles on India to the *Canada Presbyterian* (Toronto). For the most part, she forbore using them to present her version of the mission's recent troubles and she kept her tendencies towards self-promotion in check. Collectively, the articles leave the impression of an able, articulate woman whose cultural horizons had been broadened by her residence in India and who had come to hold a more enlightened view of the missionary's task there. In a small way they may also have helped finance the medical studies that preceded Fairweather's return.

Beginning in the autumn of 1880, she spent two years in nurses' training at Charity Hospital, on Blackwell's (Welfare) Island in New York City. She then studied to become a doctor at the Woman's Medical College of Chicago; following her graduation in 1885 she practised briefly to obtain money for supplies. Upon arriving in Agra in January 1887, she worked for the Countess of Dufferin's Fund. Inaugurated in 1885 by the wife of the viceroy, Lord Dufferin [Blackwood*], it financed medical treatment and training for Indian women. A historical account of graduates of the Woman's Medical College claims that Fairweather began providing services soon after her arrival and started a medical school, which quickly had 50 students. Her stay, however, was short. In September 1888 she married Charles Stirling, an Englishman who had graduated earlier in the year from the College of Physicians and Surgeons, Chicago. The couple moved to Delhi, where Fairweather continued working for the Dufferin fund, but Charles's health failed and they returned to the United States.

Details of Fairweather's life thereafter are sketchy. She lived for a time in Chicago, listing electro-therapeutics as her speciality, and she and her husband obtained formal certification to practise medicine. It is not clear whether Allen, Charles's son from a previous marriage, lived with them. By 1914 they both had practices in Oakland, Calif., and they were there when Charles died in 1918. Just two years before her own death Marion moved to San Leandro, where, her obituary reported, she had once owned "considerable property." An initiator to the end, she had opened a sanatorium, which was "doing well" until she succumbed to pneumonia. Like her "beloved husband," she was cremated.

Marion Fairweather's background resembled that of many of the Canadian Protestant women drawn to foreign missionary service, but her subsequent career did not. Like her, many female missionaries challenged the norms of Victorian womanhood, even as they paid lip-service to those norms. Fairweather, however, was remarkable for the degree to which she took unwomanly initiatives and defied the conventions of separate missionary spheres. When her unorthodox conduct in India led to her recall, she redirected her energies and achieved a second, atypical career.

RUTH COMPTON BROUWER

[Materials concerning the lives of Marion Fairweather and Charles Stirling in Oakland, Calif., including local obituaries, California Crematorium records, and the details of their medical qualifications, were supplied to the author by the Oakland Public Library's Oakland Hist. Room. Information on the Fairweather family of Bowmanville, Ont., was drawn from indexes to the *Bowmanville News* and the *Canadian Statesman* (Bowmanville) in the Bowmanville Public Library. R.C.B.]

MUA, RG 30, McGill Normal School records. UCC-C, Fonds 122/1, 79.185C, file 1-1; Fonds 122/8, 79.195C, files 5–9. *Canadian Statesman*, 22 March 1923. *Canada Presbyterian* (Toronto), new ser., 1 (1877–78): 611–12. Ruth Compton Brouwer, "Far indeed from the meekest of women: Marion Fairweather and the Canadian Presbyterian mission in Central India, 1873–1880," in *Canadian Protestant and Catholic missions, 1820s–1960s; historical essays in honour of John Webster Grant*, ed. J. S. Moir and C. T. McIntire (New York, 1988), 121–49; *New women for God: Canadian Presbyterian women and India missions, 1876–1914* (Toronto, 1990). *Presbyterian Record* (Montreal), 2 (1877): 15–26, 155–56.

FASKEN, DAVID, lawyer and businessman; b. 31 Dec. 1860 in Pilkington Township, Upper Canada, son of Robert Fasken and Isabel Milne; m. 1885 Alice Winstanley, and they had a daughter, who died in infancy, and a son; d. 2 Dec. 1929 in Toronto and was buried in Elora, Ont.

In 1837 Robert Fasken emigrated with his family from Scotland; seven years later he took up land near Elora. Born on the family farm, the fifth of ten children, David Fasken attended school in Elora. Upon graduating from the University of Toronto with a BA in 1882, he chose law as a career. He was articled in Toronto first to Beaty, Hamilton, and Cassels and then to the firm of William Henry Beatty*, which did the legal work for the Gooderham and Worts businesses. After his call to the bar in 1885, he practised with this firm.

Beatty was Fasken's mentor but the two differed in several respects. Beatty, a Conservative in politics and an Anglican by religion, was from an upper-middle-class Toronto family. Fasken, a Liberal and a Methodist, was in Beatty's view a raw lad from the farm. Though Fasken shunned publicity, he had drive and ambition, and, according to one biographer, "a capacity for sustained and concentrated effort, close attention to detail, and absolutely unprejudiced weighing of facts" – qualities that endeared him to Beatty. By 1902

Beatty, who had become increasingly involved in business, left the management of Beatty Blackstock, as the firm was known, to Fasken. With 15 lawyers, among them George Gooderham*'s son-in-law Thomas Gibbs Blackstock and his brother George Tate BLACKSTOCK, it was the largest in Canada.

Like Beatty, Fasken combined legal work with a series of successful business ventures. Shortly after the incorporation of the Excelsior Life Insurance Company in 1889, he had bought shares in the struggling company and encouraged the Gooderhams to do so as well. Voted together, these shares gave Fasken control. On 13 Feb. 1900 he was elected president, a position he would hold until his death. Although he directed operations only on a part-time basis, he built the company into a profitable insurer.

Fasken's entrepreneurial spirit also placed him in the front rank of financiers determined to tap the mineral and recreational potential of the Precambrian Shield in "New Ontario." During the construction of the Temiskaming and Northern Ontario Railway in 1903, silver was discovered at Long (Cobalt) Lake. A stampede followed and a town sprang up, but despite the promise, Canadian banks by and large refused finance. The following year Fasken acted quickly with Ellis P. Earle and other New York investors to form the Nipissing Mining Company Limited, which acquired claims covering 846 acres at the centre of the camp. For many years Nipissing's president and a director, Fasken was, as well, a director and substantial shareholder of La Rose Consolidated Mines Limited and Trethewey Silver-Cobalt Mine Limited. In 1909 the *Montreal Daily Star* listed him among the 17 Canadians and 8 Americans whom Cobalt had turned into millionaires. In addition to securing much of the capital needed to mine this rugged locale, Fasken acquired the three powerplants that supplied Cobalt with hydroelectricity. In 1911 he merged them to form the Northern Ontario Light and Power Company Limited, of which he became president; he also organized the Northern Canada Power Company Limited.

Spurred by his initial success at Cobalt, Fasken had grasped other opportunities. Together with his youngest brother and law partner, Alexander, and William George Gooderham, he financed hotels, steamers, and general stores on the TNOR at the new lakeside village of Temagami. In 1910, with Earle, his brother Alex, and others, he formed a syndicate to invest in the newly discovered Porcupine goldfield [*see* Benjamin Hollinger*], northwest of Cobalt and also on the TNOR. Two years later he and a group of other Canadian and American millionaires formed the Canadian Mining Exploration Company Limited; on 31 December its president, Ambrose Monell, stated that in its first eight months 400 properties had been considered for development but most had been rejected. With his brother and Earle, Fasken formed a syndicate to finance the staking of the Flin Flon mine in Manitoba and in 1915 the brothers visited the site, travelling at times by oxen and canoe.

Fasken's firm carried out the legal work for the companies he was involved with, and its growing expertise in mining law attracted new mining clients. He thus reshaped the firm to serve his own business needs. In September 1906, under a revised partnership agreement, he had been formally recognized as Beatty Blackstock's managing partner. He was named a KC in 1910. Five years later the firm's name was changed to Fasken, Cowan, Chadwick, and Rose, and its offices were moved from the Gooderham-related Bank of Toronto building to the new Excelsior Life building on Toronto Street, a move that confirmed Fasken's imprint. Like his own home and other Fasken-financed structures, including an addition to Toronto Western Hospital, the Excelsior building had been designed by his architect friend Edward James Lennox*. Fasken's link to Toronto Western, to which he donated $500,000, was not completely charitable: its doctors provided reviews and opinions for Excelsior, while Fasken's firm was the hospital's solicitor.

In 1914 Fasken had acquired 226,000 acres near Midland, Texas, with the intention of subdividing it for farming. He moved there, likely for health reasons, and by 1918 was spending most of his time at his ranch, returning to Toronto only occasionally. He founded the town of Fasken in 1917, incorporated the Midland Farm Company, and built a railway to the site, but few people moved to the new town, which would die in the 1920s.

When in 1919 Fasken retired from active practice in his law firm because of illness, his brother Alex became managing partner. Despite his activity in Texas, Fasken had continued to maintain a residence in Toronto, as well as large farms near Elora and Clarkson (Mississauga) and a cottage at Temagami. He passed away in Toronto in December 1929, leaving an estate worth $1,792,300, which did not include the valuable oil reserves yet to be discovered on his Texas ranch. The *Toronto Daily Star*, ignoring his other achievements, ran the headline "David Fasken, wealthy mining magnate dies." Today the law firm he managed still bears his name, but little is known of this man with the Midas touch.

C. IAN KYER

AO, RG 22-305, no.63434. Fasken Martineau DuMoulin Arch. (Toronto), W. H. Beatty to C. W. Beatty, 3 Aug. 1892 (copy); Material relating to David Fasken, esp. Fasken family tree (1966); Partnership agreement between W. H. Beatty, E. M. Chadwick, David Fasken *et al.*, 1 Sept. 1906; J. B. Robinson memoirs. LAC, RG 31, C1, 1871, Pilkington Township, Ont., div.2: 7; 1901, Toronto, Ward 4, div.25: 11 (mfm. at AO). Wellington South Land Registry Office

(Guelph, Ont.), Pilkington Township, deeds, vol.2 (1852–62): f.7, no.3528 (mfm. at AO). *Cobalt Daily Nugget* (Cobalt, Ont.), September 1910. *Daily Mail and Empire*, 10 Dec. 1927. *Globe*, 3 Dec. 1929. *Toronto Daily Star*, 4 Dec. 1929. *Canadian annual rev.*, 1909: 348; 1910: 398; 1912: 644. *Canadian men and women of the time* (Morgan; 1912). *Fasken v. Minister of National Revenue*, [1949] *Dominion Law Reports* (Toronto), 1: 810–39. Alexander Fraser, *A history of Ontario: its resources and development* (2v., Toronto and Montreal, 1907), 1: 584–85. *The handbook of Texas* (3v., Austin, Tex., 1952–76), 3: 293. B. W. Hodgins and Jamie Benedickson, *The Temagami experience: recreation, resources, and aboriginal rights in the northern Ontario wilderness* (Toronto, 1989). C. I. Kyer, "The transformation of an establishment firm: from Beatty Blackstock to Faskens, 1902–1915," in *Essays in the history of Canadian law*, ed. D. H. Flaherty et al. (8v. to date, [Toronto], 1981–), vol.7 (*Inside the law: Canadian law firms in historical perspective*, ed. Carol Wilton, 1996), 161–206. Marilyn Litvak, *Edward James Lennox: "Builder of Toronto"* (Toronto, 1995). *Standard dict. of Canadian biog.* (Roberts and Tunnell), vol.2. R. J. Surtees, *The northern connection: Ontario Northland since 1902* (Toronto, 1992).

FAULKNER, MATILDA MOORE (Churchill), schoolteacher, Baptist missionary, and author; b. October or November 1840 in Stewiacke, N.S., daughter of William Faulkner, an engineer, and Nancy Woodworth; m. 16 Sept. 1873 the Reverend George Churchill, a Baptist minister, in Truro, N.S., and they had two sons and two daughters, of whom one daughter survived to adulthood; d. 12 Aug. 1924 in Toronto.

Matilda Faulkner was born and raised in Stewiacke. In her teens her family moved to Truro, where she attended the Model and Normal schools, obtaining a first-class teacher's licence in 1861. At first she taught primary and intermediate classes in Merigomish and at the Model School in Truro; later she moved to the senior department of the Model School, as one of the first Normal School–trained high-school teachers. She also volunteered among the poor, establishing church services and a night school for the black Baptist population of Truro. At the same time she harboured a desire to be an overseas missionary, which she later declared had been instilled in her at the age of 14 after a series of "wonderful meetings" in Stewiacke during which she and members of her family had been baptized.

At first her attempts to serve as a foreign missionary were discouraged since she was a single woman. An opportunity arose in 1871, however, when George Churchill, whom she had met as a student in Truro, asked her to be his wife and accompany him to do missionary work in Asia. After studies at the Woman's Medical College in Philadelphia, she was married and in October 1873 she and her husband joined a group of missionaries – known as the "serving seven" [*see* Mary E. Lamont*] – who had been appointed by the Baptist Foreign Mission Board to go

to Burma (Myanmar), where Hannah Maria Norris* was already labouring, and Siam (Thailand). There were difficulties with the southeast Asian location, however, and at the 1875 meeting of the Baptist Convention of Nova Scotia, New Brunswick and Prince Edward Island a new field was chosen. It was the Telugu country on the western shore of the Bay of Bengal. This decision marked the beginning of Maritime Baptist involvement in India, which has continued to the present.

The Churchills served first at Cocanada (Kakinada) and Bimlipatam, before establishing their own mission station at Bobbili in 1879. Encountering numerous challenges such as the heat, language and cultural barriers, primitive living conditions, and the difficult caste system, Matilda and her husband nonetheless persevered. In 1875 she described villages of mud huts, mainly pariah settlements, where the women she sought to teach were "filthy and ragged, their hair matted, and so forlorn and despairing looking; not pleasant to labour with, nor are their children." Generally the women missionaries worked with women and children, establishing schools and promoting literacy, while the men worked with the men, training some as native preachers. One of Matilda's accomplishments was founding and managing a "Caste Girls' School," in a new building in Bobbili in 1880, which taught mostly Brahman girls. She had previously run a similar establishment in rented premises in Bimlipatam.

Matilda served as a missionary in India from 1875 to 1921, except for brief periods when she returned to Canada or made trips abroad. During her years there she lost three children and, in 1908, her husband. She nevertheless carried on until February 1921, when she went to Toronto to live with her daughter, Elizabeth Maud Stillwell, who had also served as a missionary in India. She died there in 1924 at the age of 83 years 10 months and was buried in Mount Pleasant Cemetery. One obituary observed that she was "a woman of sound judgment, intense spirituality and possessed a most winning personality, which qualities made her an outstanding figure in the missionary personnel of her day." She had been awarded an honorary MA in 1923 by Acadia University in Wolfville, N.S., a recognition that her husband had achieved in 1899.

Matilda's significance lies not only in her pioneering missionary efforts, but also in her literary legacy. In 1916 *Letters from my home in India* was published, a compilation arranged and edited by Grace Dean McLeod Rogers. With rare insights into the methods and mentality of women missionaries, the letters reveal Matilda's steady determination in the face of enormous difficulties and her quiet acceptance of disappointments, personal losses, and, eventually, the infirmities of old age. Her descriptions of her work testify to the special relationships she developed with native women, despite her sharing the patronizing racial attitudes of the British community in India. Her attempts to improve both the spiritual and the physical lot of the natives may be evidence as well of what some historians have called "maternal feminism," the view that women were to be the saviours of society. As Matilda put it, "Give us right-minded, high-souled women, and we will have righteous noble men and children." Like most of her contemporaries, Matilda saw her missionary work as an extension of the accepted womanly roles of home-making, caregiving, and teaching. The feminism of many Nova Scotian women like Churchill, however, was defined by their Christian sensibilities. Summing up her career in 1916, Matilda said, "Often have I failed, sometimes almost faltered, but never have I desired to be aught but a disciple of Christ, privileged indeed to be bearer of His message of light and love to heathen lands."

WENDY L. THORPE

Matilda Faulkner Churchill's *Letters from my home in India: being the correspondence of Mrs. George Churchill (1871–1916)*, ed. G. [D.] McLeod Rogers, was published in both New York and Toronto in 1916 and was reprinted in Toronto in 1924. Selections from the letters for 1871–79 have been reprinted in Margaret Conrad, "Mathilda Faulkner Churchill, 1840–1925," in *No place like home: diaries and letters of Nova Scotia women, 1771–1938*, ed. Margaret Conrad et al. (Halifax, 1988), 122–33. Churchill is also the author of *Reminiscences of Willie Chandler Churchill by his mother* (Saint John, 1882).

AO, RG 80-8-0-950, no.4892. Little White Schoolhouse Museum (Truro, N.S.), Registers for Normal School. NSARM, RG 32, WB, Colchester County, no.142/1873. *Acadian Recorder* (Halifax), 15 Aug. 1924. *Maritime Baptist* (Saint John), 27 Aug. 1924. *Morning Chronicle* (Halifax), 15 Aug. 1924. *Truro Daily News*, 19 Aug. 1924. *Baptist year book of the Maritime provinces of Canada . . .* (Halifax; Saint John, N.B.), 1873–1905, reports of the Foreign Missionary Board. Margaret Conrad, "Recording angels: the private chronicles of women from the Maritime provinces of Canada, 1750–1950," in Canadian Research Institute for the Advancement of Women, *Papers* (Ottawa), no.4 (1982): 12. *Directory*, N.S., 1866/67, 1868/69, 1871. *Index to 1871 census of Colchester County, Nova Scotia* ([n.p.,1998]). M. K. Ingraham, *Seventy-five years: historical sketch of the United Baptist Woman's Missionary Union in the Maritime provinces of Canada* (Kentville, N.S., [1947?]). G. E. Levy, *The Baptists of the Maritime provinces, 1753–1946* (Saint John, 1946). R. K. McCormick, *Faith, freedom & democracy: the Baptists in Atlantic Canada* (Tantallon, N.S., 1993). John March, *A brief history of the foreign missionary enterprise among the Baptists of the Maritime provinces, of the Dominion of Canada* (Saint John, 1892; 2nd ed., rev. J. W. Manning, 1899). Mrs C. H. Martell et al., *Historical sketch of the United Baptist Woman's Missionary Union of the Maritime provinces . . .* (Wolfville, N.S., n.d.). E. C. Merrick, *These impossible women, 100 years: the story of the United Baptist Woman's Missionary Union of the Atlantic provinces* ([Fredericton], 1970). Wendy Mitchinson, "Canadian women and church missionary societies in the nineteenth century: a step towards independence," *Atlantis* (Wolfville), 2 (1976–77), no.2, pt.2: 57–75. N.S., Council of Public Instruction, *Annual report of the superintendent of education* (Halifax), 1864: 40. *N.S. vital statistics, 1835–39* (Holder), no.2135. *Register and circular with brief history and condition of the Normal School of Nova-Scotia, 1862* ([Halifax, 1862?]). H. M. Ross, "'Sisters' in the homeland: vision for mission among Maritime Baptist women, 1867–1920," in *A fragile stability: definition and redefinition of Maritime Baptist identity*, ed. D. T. Priestly (Hantsport, N.S., 1994), 95–112. *United Baptist year book* (Saint John), 1906–24.

FEARMAN, ROBERT CALVER, meat packer; b. 5 June 1858 in Hamilton, Upper Canada, second son of Frederick William Fearman* and Elizabeth Holbrook; m. there 27 May 1885 Frances Sarah French Lister; they had no children; d. there 8 Aug. 1922.

Robert Calver Fearman lived his life according to the examples set by his redoubtable father, founder of the meat-packing firm F. W. Fearman and Company Limited. He was educated in Hamilton's public schools and collegiate and then at the Dundas Wesleyan Boys' Institute. Upon graduation, he set to work in the family business as its secretary-treasurer; in January 1899 he and his brothers Frederick Chester, Henry Holbrook, and Frank Dingwall joined their father in incorporating the company. A cautious beginning in curing hams and bacon and rendering lard had blossomed by that time into a concern that employed approximately 110 workers and generated an output worth over $1 million per year. Its famous Star brand of hams and bacon were shipped across Canada and to France, the West Indies, the United States, and Great Britain, where two-thirds of the company's product was consumed.

F. W. Fearman's demise in 1906 elevated his eldest son, Chester, to the presidency. Unfortunately, times had changed since the firm's peak around the turn of the century and the company now faced circumstances that threatened its fiscal viability. The buyout of the interests of four siblings weakened it, but World War I dealt the most crippling blow. To cope with inflation, it was forced to borrow from the Bank of Hamilton. Revenue from Britain and France shrank, products often spoiled on the way overseas, and renovations made necessary by new government regulations on packing houses were costly.

When Chester died of a stroke in 1918, Robert confronted the unenviable task of trying to put the firm back on its feet. He did not prove equal to the challenge. Post-war inflation and depression made debt reduction impossible without outside finance. Accordingly, in 1920 Fearman called on Ernest Jay Howson of the Toronto accounting and manufacturing specialists Thorne, Mulholland, Howson, and

341

Fernow

McPherson. The "lack of sufficient capital and the extraordinary business conditions" since 1914 compelled him to consider admitting others to the family concern. Such a move, he hoped, would allow reorganization. The public, the *Hamilton Spectator* intoned, would be "pleased to know that Hamilton is not to lose this old-established industry." It continued to struggle, however, and in 1922 the Bank of Hamilton forced it into bankruptcy. (It would nonetheless recover and operate under the controlling interest of the family until 1934.) Robert's efforts had proved unavailing in the wake of the upheavals of the modern era.

In his personal life, as in business, Fearman's desire to emulate and perhaps please his larger-than-life sire was clear. F. W. Fearman had not confined his entrepreneurial activities to the meat-packing industry, and neither did Robert, who served for many years as president of Armstrong Cartage of Hamilton. Like his father, he was a Methodist and was active in Freemasonry, as a member of the Barton and Murton lodges and treasurer of the Tuscan Lodge. Fearman Sr had been a zealous advocate of public education and libraries. Robert loyally adopted these interests, serving on the board of education in 1914–16 and devoting a great deal of time to library boards and committees. In politics, he too supported the Conservatives for their policy of protection for Canadian industries. His wife was a daughter of Joseph Lister, on whose land F. W. Fearman had opened his first shop. For many years the couple lived in Ivey Lodge, the impressive stone house built by Fearman Sr. It was here that Robert's health began to fail. An operation two months before his death failed to restore his vigour, although he continued to take an "active interest in business affairs," and he died in August 1922. He was eulogized as a civic-minded and public-spirited man of sterling character, and the *Spectator* joined in: "A shrewd business man, yet ever kindly to those in need, no one ever appealed to him for help in vain." Fearman went to his grave the epitome of a dutiful, upstanding, and perhaps cowed son of a self-made man, whose success in business was the one aspect of his life that his heir could not emulate.

ANGELA GRAHAM

AO, RG 80-5-0-139, no.12706. Hamilton Public Library, Special Coll. Dept. (Hamilton, Ont.), Scrapbooks, H. F. Gardiner, vol.124; Hamilton Public Library Board, vols.1–2; Herald, vol.L3; Times, vol.L3. UCC-C, Fonds 5/8, 78.004C. Hamilton Herald, 8 Aug. 1922. Hamilton Spectator, 13 April 1920, 8 Aug. 1922. DHB, vol.2. Hamilton Public Library, *Industrial Hamilton: a trail to the future*, "F. W. Fearman Packing Company Limited": *collections.gc.ca/industrial/fearman.htm* (consulted 25 Aug. 2003). *Magazine of industry and daily times, Hamilton, Ont. – reviewing historically the industrial and financial interests* (souvenir ed., Hamilton, 1910; copy in Hamilton Public Library). J. E. Middleton and Fred Landon, *The province of Ontario: a history, 1615–1927* (5v., Toronto, 1927–[28]), 4: 488-89. *Prominent men of Canada: a collection of persons distinguished in professional and political life, and in the commerce and industry of Canada*, ed. G. M. Adam (Toronto, 1892).

FERNOW, BERNHARD EDUARD, forester and educator; b. 7 Jan. 1851 in Inowrazlaw (Inowrocław, Poland), son of Eduard Ernst Leopold Fernow, a lawyer, and his second wife, Clara Nordman; m. 20 June 1879 Olivia Reynolds in Brooklyn (New York City), and they had a daughter, who died young, and four sons; d. 6 Feb. 1923 in Toronto.

From a Prussian family of middling rank, Bernhard Eduard Fernow received his early education at the gymnasium in Bromberg (Bydgoszcz). Subsequent study at the forest academy in Münden (Germany) was interrupted for service as a lieutenant in the Franco-German War and then by a year in law at the University of Königsberg. Upon graduation from Münden with a licence to practise forestry, he went into the Prussian forest service. He became engaged to a New Yorker, Olivia Reynolds, followed her to the United States in 1876, and was made an American citizen in 1883.

Fernow had secured a job in 1878 or 1879 managing the Pennsylvania woodlot and charcoal furnace of Cooper, Hewitt and Company, iron manufacturers. In April 1882 he attended the first American Forestry Congress, in Cincinnati, Ohio. Thanks to the interest of groups such as the Quebec Limitholders' Association and the Fruit Growers' Association of Ontario, the second meeting was held in Montreal the following August [*see* James Little*; George Bryson*]. The congress gave Fernow a valuable platform to advance his views on the need to introduce German ideas about scientific forestry into North America. He quickly gained attention as a rising star; in Quebec he found an ally in politician Henri-Gustave Joly*. Fernow's experience with private woodlands and state forestry in Europe meshed well with Progressive Era ideas about government and forest resources. He had a clear preference for vigorous public policy to ensure their rational development: conservation meant efficient usage and long-term viability, overseen by specially trained personnel. In 1886 he became the first professional forester to head the forestry division of the United States Department of Agriculture.

Awarded an honorary LLD by the University of Wisconsin in 1896, Fernow left the federal service two years later to assume the directorship of the recently established New York State College of Forestry at Cornell University in Ithaca. A popular and stimulating teacher, he enjoyed social gatherings with his students, and he impressed many with his abilities as a dancer, pianist, and horseman. In June 1903, however, the functions of the college were suspended amid controversy over the management of its experimental forest tract. For the next four years Fernow worked as a consulting forest engineer and taught, notably at Yale University in New Haven, Conn., where his lectures became the basis of a book on the history of forestry. He was editor of *Forest Quarterly* (Ithaca) from 1903 to 1916, and then of its successor, the *Journal of Forestry* (Washington), to 1922. In January 1903 he had given a series of impressive lectures in Kingston, Ont., at Queen's College, which granted him an LLD later that year. Both Queen's, with its associated School of Mining and Agriculture, and the University of Toronto had an interest in establishing a forestry program. The provincial royal commission on the University of Toronto, which consulted with Fernow during its work in 1905–6, recommended a school of forestry there.

Fernow had provisionally agreed to establish a program at Pennsylvania State College when, in 1907, he accepted Toronto's offer to become its dean of forestry. Established on 28 March, the faculty became the first such academic unit in Canada. As its head until 1919, Fernow would stamp its curriculum with his ideas about forestry and train a generation of professional foresters. Argumentative and often tactless, he held firm views about the management and conservation of forests that did not always agree with political estimates. He took exception to the extractive, revenue-oriented forest policies of Ontario and its overly optimistic estimates of usable forests and northern lands. Clashes with successive ministers of lands, forests, and mines (Francis Cochrane* and William Howard Hearst*, both northerners), deputy minister Aubrey White*, and commercial lumbermen resulted. A frequent consultant, Fernow was the founding president of the Canadian Society of Forest Engineers in 1908 and he served on the federal Commission of Conservation from 1910 to 1923. His surveys for this commission of the Trent Canal watershed in Ontario and Nova Scotia's timber resources are especially notable pieces of work. He played no role, however, in the creation of the Forest Products Laboratories, established within the Department of the Interior in 1913 and situated at McGill University in Montreal. Though an active teacher, prolific writer, and assiduous administrator, by World War I he was not on the cutting edge of ideas about reforestation, fire prevention, or the exploitation of specific species.

Accused during the war of not encouraging students to volunteer for service and badgered over his German origins, Fernow took pains to address his students about their patriotic duties. Still an American citizen, he avoided getting caught up in 1915 in the "German professors issue," which saw three university members forced out of their positions. Nevertheless, and though his sons had enlisted in the American forces, his wife was forced to stop teaching German to forestry students who needed it for the fourth-year seminar on German silvicultural literature. On 22 June 1918 university president Sir Robert Alexander Falconer* told her husband that German must be only an option.

In increasingly poor health, by 1917 Fernow had begun to think about retirement. He attempted to interest the university in Harvey Reginald MacMillan*, a forestry graduate from Yale, but it was a colleague, Clifton Durant Howe, who succeeded him in 1919. Appointed emeritus professor and given a doctorate by Toronto in 1920, Fernow continued to live on Admiral Road, north of the campus. In 1922 Cornell named its forestry building Fernow Hall in his honour. He died a year later. Following a service in Toronto, his body was cremated and his ashes were taken to his summer home at Point Breeze, N.Y., and strewn on Lake Ontario. His death was widely noted and mourned by the forestry profession in Canada and the United States.

Though certainly not the founder of professional forestry in North America, Fernow, more than any other individual, played a formative role in its development in two countries. Indeed, his career illustrates the important scientific dimension to the North American struggle for the benefits of national forest resources. MacMillan's observation in a letter to Howe, that Fernow "was, and will remain the most outstanding Forester in Canada for many years," has not lost its force.

JAMES P. HULL

The April 1923 issue of the *Journal of Forestry* (Washington) contains a long section devoted to Fernow's death (vol.21, pp.305–48), which also provides a chronology of his life and a bibliography of his writings. Fernow's books include *Economics of forestry: a reference book for students of political economy and professional and lay students of forestry* (New York, 1902; repr. 1972); *A brief history of forestry in Europe, the United States and other countries* (New Haven, Conn., 1907), based on his lectures at Yale (a revised edition was published in Toronto in 1911); and *The care of trees, in lawn, street, and park: with a list of trees and shrubs for decorative use* (New York, 1910). His surveys for the Commission of Conservation appeared as *Forest conditions of Nova Scotia* (Ottawa, 1912) and Committee on Forests, *Trent watershed survey; a reconnaissance* (Toronto, 1913).

AO, RG 22-305, no.50692; RG 80-8-0-909, no.1868. UTA, A1967-0007; A1972-0018; A1972-0025; A1973-0026/101(53); A1976-0006; A1979-0015. *American forests: nature, culture, and politics*, ed. Char Miller (Lawrence, Kans., 1997). *Biographical dictionary of American and Canadian naturalists and environmentalists*, ed. K. B. Sterling *et al.* (Westport, Conn., 1997). *Canadian annual rev.*, 1907–15. *Forest and wildlife science in America: a history*, ed. H. K. Steen ([Durham, N.C.], 1999). R. P. Gillis and T. R. Roach, *Lost initiatives: Canada's forest industries, forest policy and forest conservation* (Westport, 1986). L. H.

Gulick, *American forest policy, a study of government administration and economic control* (New York, 1951). C. D. Howe, "Bernhard Eduard Fernow – an appreciation," *Illustrated Canadian Forestry Magazine* (Ottawa), 19 (1923): 168–69. H. V. Nelles, *The politics of development: forests, mines & hydro-electric power in Ontario, 1849–1941* (Toronto, 1974). Peter Oliver, *G. Howard Ferguson: Ontario Tory* (Toronto, 1977). Ont., Royal commission on the University of Toronto, *Report* (Toronto, 1906). A. D. Rodgers, *Bernhard Eduard Fernow, a story of North American forestry* (Princeton, N.J., 1951; repr., Durham, 1991). J. W. B. Sisam, *Forestry education at Toronto* (Toronto, 1961). H. K. *Steen, The U.S. Forest Service: a history* (Seattle, 1976).

FIDLER, ALFRED DAVIS, railway employee, government official, and sportsman; b. 20 June 1869 in Brantford, Ont., fourth son of James Fidler and Margaret Davis; m. 3 Aug. 1898 Susan M. Spence in Howick Township, Ont., and they had three sons; d. 21 March 1927 in Calgary.

The Fidlers were a railway family who probably located first at Brantford when they arrived in Upper Canada in 1856. Brantford was an important railway town that became integrated into the national transportation system in the 1860s and 1870s when connections were made to the three main trunk lines: the Grand Trunk, the Great Western, and the Canada Southern. In 1871 Alfred Davis Fidler's father, James, was working for the Grand Trunk as a fireman.

The 1881 census finds the Fidlers in St Thomas where the father and two eldest sons were railway workers. Later employment with the Canadian Pacific Railway took all of the family, except for Alfred's sister, Mary, west. William, the second son, settled in Calgary in 1883; he was joined by his father and brothers Charles and Alfred in 1884. In 1888 the family moved to Canmore and in 1889 James, the youngest son, came with his mother. By 1891 John, the eldest, had arrived as well. Canmore was a division point and layover centre for CPR crews and Alfred was engaged in the running trades during the construction of the line; at the time of his marriage in 1898 he was a yardman. He would make an annual salary of $1,000 in 1901. In January 1899 the CPR moved its shops to Calgary and its division point to Lake Louise. Many of the railway's employees relocated in Calgary over the next few years, including Alfred Fidler, now a freight conductor.

Fidler joined the government of Alberta's Department of Public Works as a clerk on 29 March 1909, and in June that year he was appointed an inspector of local improvement districts. His experience with the CPR proved invaluable because of the connections between the railway and the department in bridge building and the shipping of construction materials for local projects. He became an auditor and inspector on 1 Jan. 1912 and then moved to the Department of

Municipal Affairs, created that year, at an annual salary of $1,600. Fidler's pay was increased to $1,800 in 1917 when he became inspector of munitions in the same department during World War I; he was appointed chief inspector in 1918 and made $2,400 annually from 1921 until his death.

One of the department's functions was to administer the organization of municipalities and regulate their planning schemes; the inspector ensured that they followed proper procedures, oversaw the collection of local taxes, and audited the books to make certain they conformed to provincial regulations. It is recorded that Fidler audited the accounts of the municipal district of Cardston in 1922, for example. In July 1925 the secretary-treasurer embezzled funds from the Burlington municipal district, now in Forty Mile County. The municipality and the school districts faced financial ruin and were forced into trusteeship. The council was dissolved on 26 Oct. 1926 and the district was placed in charge of the official administrator, Alfred Fidler. After his untimely death, the deputy minister of the Department of Municipal Affairs, William David Spence, wrote that Fidler had been "employed in the service of the Department since its inception and organization and was engaged in the inspection of municipalities prior to that date as a member of the staff of the Department of Public Works. He was widely known and respected in his work, and had come to be recognized as an authority on municipal matters."

According to his obituary, Alf Fidler was also known to many as "the Father of Baseball in Alberta." This judgement appears to be the exaggeration of an old friend writing a eulogy for a local newspaper. Fidler's family did come from a part of southwestern Ontario that was a hotbed for baseball in the late 19th century. Hamilton, Dundas, Woodstock, Ingersoll, London, and Guelph all had community-rooted professional baseball teams, strengthened by American "ringers" by the 1870s. These towns also hosted touring teams from the United States. Baseball was brought to the prairies by the early settlers from Ontario and the United States (Fidler was said to have been one of the first catchers to come to Alberta). In rural areas the game tended to be associated with activities on holidays, such as Dominion Day, Labour Day, and Victoria Day. The sport helped to build a sense of community in a new settlement and boosted the locality as well.

Fidler's reputation as a ball player was probably the result of the fact that he played one season as a professional at first base for the Fort Worth Panthers in the Texas League, which was D level, in 1892. He was also a catcher, first baseman, and outfielder for teams in Medicine Hat, Canmore, and Calgary; in 1895 the Canmore team, which he had also organized, played only six games. In 1903 box scores in the Calgary *Morning Albertan* show Fidler on first base for the CPR team in the city amateur league. He also played for the Calgary team in a mid-summer tournament against other teams from southern Alberta. In 1906 he was the vice-president of an amateur baseball club in Calgary.

When the Western Canada League was formed in 1907 with professional teams in Edmonton, Calgary, Medicine Hat, and Lethbridge, Fidler was to join the Calgary Bronchos as a player but the scoresheets do not list him in the line-up. He was selected as the manager. The *Albertan* of 28 May 1907 reported that Fidler was to hit the ceremonial first pitch on opening day, but let his son Charles Alfred, known as "young Alf," do it instead. He continued to play competitive amateur baseball in Calgary until he was 40, which earned him the nickname "Old Hoss." For the rest of his life he umpired games throughout the province, including in the WCL.

Alf Fidler represented the tradition of "muscular Christianity," in which manly sport was linked to the religious values – Fidler himself was an Anglican – that shaped the community. He was a gifted and respected athlete, remembered as "one of the squarest shooters in the game." At the time of his death his home was 910 14th Avenue West in Calgary. He died of heart failure at the age of 57 on 21 March 1927, after cutting short a trip to Edmonton by train on government business the night previous. He was buried in Burnsland Cemetery in downtown Calgary, as was his wife after her death in 1954.

DAVID MILLS

AO, RG 80-5-0-257, no.7323. Burnsland Cemetery (Calgary), A block, plot 31. LAC, RG 31, C1, St Thomas, Ont., 1881, dist.163, subdist.C, div.2: 67; dist.175, subdist.A, div.3: 27; 1891, 1901, Canmore, Alta; 1906, Calgary, dist.19, subdist.26: 10. *Calgary Albertan*, 22–23, 25 March 1927. *Calgary Herald*, 22, 25 March 1927; 13 Feb. 1954. *Morning Albertan* (Calgary), 15 May, 24 July 1903. Alta, Dept. of Municipal Affairs, *Annual report* (Edmonton), 1912–27; Treasury Dept., *Public accounts of the province of Alberta* (Edmonton), 1909–11. Alberta Assoc. of Municipal Districts and Counties, *Story of rural municipal government in Alberta: 1909 to 1983* ([Edmonton, 1983?]). Alberta Geneal. Soc., Edmonton branch, *Alberta: index to registration of births, marriages and deaths . . .* (1v. to date, Edmonton, 1995–), 1 (*1870 to 1905*). E. H. Appleby, *Canmore: the story of an era* (Canmore, Alta, 1975). N. B. Bouchier, *For the love of the game: amateur sport in small-town Ontario, 1838–1895* (Montreal and Kingston, Ont., 2003). D. G. Burley, *A particular condition in life: self-employment and social mobility in mid-Victorian Brantford, Ontario* (Montreal and Kingston, 1994). *Directory*, Calgary, 1910–43. B. E. Ducey, *The Rajah of Renfrew: the life and times of John E. Ducey, Edmonton's "Mr. Baseball"* (Edmonton, 1998). E. J. Hanson, *Local government in Alberta* ([Toronto, 1956]). Bill Kirwin, "A colony within a colony: the Western Canada Baseball League of 1912," *Nine: a Journal of Baseball Hist.*

and Social Policy Perspectives (Edmonton), 1995–96: 282–97. Lynne Marks, *Revivals and roller rinks: religion, leisure, and identity in late-nineteenth-century small-town Ontario* (Toronto, 1996). Jack Masson, *Alberta's local governments and their politics* (Edmonton, 1985). Alan Metcalfe, *Canada learns to play: the emergence of organized sport, 1807–1914* (Toronto, 1987). "Mike McCann's minor league baseball page," created by Mike McCann: *www.geocities.com/big_bunko/* (consulted 18 Jan. 2004). Don Morrow, "Baseball," in Don Morrow *et al.*, *A concise history of sport in Canada* (Toronto, 1989), 109–39. M. K. Mott, "Manly sports and Manitobans: settlement days to World War One" (PHD thesis, Queen's Univ., Kingston, 1980). Ontario Geneal. Soc., *Index to the 1871 census of Ontario*, general ed. B. S. Elliott (30v., Toronto, 1986–92). "The southern Alberta pioneers and their descendants," designed by James A. N. Mackie: *www.pioneersalberta.org* (consulted 18 Jan. 2004). L. St. G. Stubbs, *Shoestring glory: a prairie history of semi-pro baseball* (Winnipeg, 1996). Paul Voisey, *Vulcan: the making of a prairie community* (Toronto, 1987). D. G. Wetherell and Irene Kmet, *Useful pleasures: the shaping of leisure in Alberta, 1896–1945* (Regina, 1990).

FIELDING, WILLIAM STEVENS, journalist and politician; b. 24 Nov. 1848 in Halifax, son of Charles Fielding and Sarah Ann Ellis; m. 7 Sept. 1876 Hester Rankine (d. 1928) in Saint John, and they had four daughters and one son; d. 23 June 1929 in Ottawa.

The son of a clerk of the market in Halifax, William Stevens Fielding was scarcely 11 years old when his mother died and he, his three brothers, and their sister were consigned to members of her family. William was placed in the care of his namesake, his uncle William Ellis, a Halifax grocer, with whom he lived until his marriage. Educated at the Royal Acadian School, the Halifax Grammar School, and the National School, William excelled in mathematics. Later he would attend courses at Dalhousie University on rhetoric and Shakespeare. At the age of 16 Fielding obtained employment with the Halifax *Morning Chronicle*, a Liberal journal founded and owned by William Annand*, but edited at this time by Jonathan McCully*. Fielding would remain with the paper for 20 years, working as a reporter, correspondent, and editorial writer and serving as managing editor from 1874 until 1884. For 14 years he was the Nova Scotian correspondent of the Toronto *Globe*, a journal whose editors and editorial policy he admired, an appreciation that the *Globe* reciprocated. On one occasion the *Globe* offered him a staff position but Fielding declined the offer, preferring to remain in Nova Scotia.

Fielding could scarcely have joined the *Morning Chronicle* at a more turbulent time for the journal and the province. McCully's infatuation with confederation following the Charlottetown and Quebec conferences led to his dismissal as editor in early 1865. Both his replacements, Annand and Joseph Howe*, were firmly opposed to the Quebec resolutions. From his

Fielding

privileged vantage, Fielding worked closely with these legendary leaders of the anti-confederation movement and developed a lasting admiration for Howe and his cause. In 1869, after Howe and Archibald Woodbury McLelan* had secured better financial terms for Nova Scotia within confederation, Howe joined Sir John A. Macdonald*'s cabinet in Ottawa, a move that drove a wedge between him and Annand. Fielding skilfully steered a difficult course between his devotion to Howe and his loyalty to Annand, revealing a pragmatism and flexibility that was to mark his public career.

Fielding's employment at the *Morning Chronicle* gave him unusual access to political power and influence. In the confusion that marked the restructuring of post-confederation Nova Scotian politics [*see* Philip Carteret Hill*], the *Morning Chronicle* was the command post for the province's anti-confederation forces, and its editor became its most authoritative voice. As one of the paper's highly partisan, diligent, and articulate journalists, Fielding continued to argue Nova Scotia's cause against confederation and denounce Charles Tupper*'s treachery at the Quebec conference. He was a relentless critic of Macdonald's Conservative government and, after 1878, the provincial Conservative administrations of Simon Hugh Holmes* and John Sparrow David Thompson*. An ardent defender of the old wind, wood, and sail economy, Fielding opposed the National Policy of 1879 [*see* Sir Samuel Leonard Tilley*]. He advocated economy in government, including the abolition of Nova Scotia's Legislative Council. He was especially critical of the accounting practices of successive provincial governments, their calculation of uncollectable debts as assets, and their use of supplementary estimates for routine expenditures. Meanwhile, through his criticism and his continuing association with the Toronto *Globe*, Fielding drew ever closer to the federal Liberal party and its leader, Alexander Mackenzie*.

In this intensely partisan, engaged environment more active political involvement was almost inevitable. In 1879 Fielding helped found the Young Men's Liberal Club in Halifax, and he participated more directly in the organization of the party. Although his lack of personal wealth had prevented him from accepting earlier invitations to run for public office, in June 1882 he contested the provincial constituency of Halifax County. Not only did he win the seat by a small majority, but his party formed the government. His disorganized colleagues (15 of the 24 successful Liberals were neophytes and the other 9 were divided on policy issues) asked Fielding, a novice himself, to assume the positions of premier and provincial secretary. When he declined, William Thomas Pipes*, another newcomer, was chosen premier. Later in 1882 Fielding relented and entered Pipes's cabinet as a minister without portfolio. Organized, energetic, and

meticulous, with a keen business sense, a skilful conciliator, an effective debater, a Halifax resident, and still editor of the *Chronicle*, Fielding soon gained influence, especially within his weak and divided party. Two years later, when party dissension and personal problems forced Pipes to resign, Fielding was the obvious but not unanimous choice to succeed him. Fielding accepted the positions of premier and provincial secretary, the second bringing with it the responsibilities of provincial treasurer.

Fielding's principal obsession as premier was the province's precarious finances, which he attributed to the unfavourable financial terms of its entry into confederation. Since 70 per cent of Nova Scotia's revenue came from the dominion government, he first sought a more advantageous federal settlement. After a petition from the Nova Scotia legislature for better terms, a delegation to Ottawa, and correspondence with Macdonald and the new Liberal leader, an unsympathetic Edward Blake*, had all failed to elicit a favourable response, in 1885 Fielding supported a motion from the legislature calling upon Nova Scotia to consider withdrawing from confederation should the federal government fail to improve the province's financial situation during its current session. Ottawa's subsequent point-by-point rejection of Nova Scotia's claims made an appeal to the people, a repeal election, inevitable.

In May 1886 Fielding moved a resolution asking Ottawa to release the province from confederation that passed the House of Assembly largely along party lines. In the subsequent provincial election Fielding made it clear that the federal government's transportation and tariff policies and its failure to recognize Nova Scotia's claims for better terms had left the province with no other option than secession. While his preference was for Maritime union, in the absence of strong support in New Brunswick and Prince Edward Island, Nova Scotia was prepared to proceed alone. The electorate's response appeared decisive: 29 Liberals, and 1 independent who favoured repeal, were returned as opposed to only 8 Conservative defenders of the union. Fulfilment of the secession mandate, however, was more difficult.

Fielding's own views on secession were conveniently ambiguous. His party's increasingly public divisions on the repeal issue (especially in Pictou and Cumberland counties and in Cape Breton, where the National Policy was promoting industrialization), as well as the British government's opposition, persuaded the cautious premier to temporize, until he could induce the other Maritime provinces to join him or there was a change of government in Ottawa. He tried through both correspondence and personal visits to promote secession and Maritime union in New Brunswick and Prince Edward Island, but leading Liberals there remained timid. The Nova Scotia

Liberals' open split on the repeal issue during the federal election of February 1887, and the party's failure to secure more than 7 of the province's 21 federal seats, proved an irreparable political blow to secession.

Although strong anti-confederation sentiments lingered in Nova Scotia, Fielding's position remained ambiguous. He continued to talk about Maritime union within or without Canada. Yet his active involvement in Honoré Mercier*'s interprovincial conference at Quebec City in October 1887 suggests a pragmatic willingness to seek redress within confederation, despite his initial insistence that his participation was without prejudice to Nova Scotia's political future. Though he mentioned repeal during the provincial election campaign of 1890, in which his party won 28 seats, it was only to reiterate his view that the movement had been stalled by the federal results of 1887. In 1892, however, he refused to attend the Canadian high commissioner's Dominion Day celebrations in London. On the other hand, his active role in Wilfrid Laurier*'s national Liberal convention in Ottawa in 1893 and his subsequent acceptance of an executive position in the Maritime Provinces Liberal Association confirm his willingness to give confederation a chance under Liberal auspices.

Meanwhile, Fielding sought internal means to solve or mask the province's fiscal ills. His creation of a separate capital account that recorded only annual, not accumulated, deficits and his government's voting of insufficient supplies helped to disguise the financial malaise. Securing more favourable interest rates against the province's debt allowance, renegotiating debts, a fortuitous federal refund of provincial moneys that had been spent on certain public works, and the imposition of succession duties all provided some additional relief.

Fielding soon realized, however, that the province's fiscal deficiencies would only be remedied through a more vigorous provincial industrial strategy, one that required a sharp reordering of his party's industrial policy and political philosophy. Since coal royalties accounted for 17 per cent of the province's public revenue, Fielding began his new strategy by extending royalties to slack coal. In 1892, conscious that coal was Nova Scotia's most lucrative resource and aware of the coal industry's capacity for further growth and its implications for public revenue, Fielding, through the mediation of Benjamin Franklin Pearson*, persuaded Henry Melville WHITNEY, a Boston entrepreneur, and his associates to invest in the Cape Breton coalmines. In return for a 99-year lease of the coalfields, the new company agreed to pay royalties of 12.5 cents per ton of coal, an arrangement that was confirmed by legislation early in 1893. By 1896 coal royalties accounted for 32 per cent of the provincial revenue, and they con-

tinued to rise. When reproached by the Conservative leader, Charles Hazlitt Cahan*, for the monopolistic nature and length of the lease, and the province's reliance upon American capital, Fielding made clear that he was firmly committed to the industrialization of Nova Scotia and indifferent to the nationality of the capital and labour required to achieve this objective. The province's and the provincial Liberals' growing dependence upon the coal economy transformed the party's political and ideological agenda, and influenced Fielding's choice of George Henry MURRAY, who represented the industrial heartland of Cape Breton, as his successor in 1896.

Fielding was no less adept at cultivating the political support of labour. Soon after he became premier, he had forged an alliance with the nascent Provincial Workmen's Association and a personal friendship with its influential general secretary, Robert DRUMMOND. When Drummond failed to secure a seat in the House of Assembly in 1886 and again in 1890, Fielding named him to the Legislative Council. Meanwhile Fielding, at Drummond's behest, introduced labour legislation that earned the premier an enviable reputation among miners: fortnightly wages, a minimum working age, mine inspectors, safety regulations, night schools, and compulsory arbitration before authorized lockouts. In Drummond's view Fielding's mining legislation was "the most advanced . . . in the world" and "set the pace even for Britain." Fielding also knew how to placate apprehensive mine owners. When the general manager of the Acadia Coal Company in Stellarton, Henry Skeffington Poole*, objected to the province's legislation requiring mine officials to hold certificates of competence, the premier, somewhat cynically, named Poole chairman of the provincial board of examiners. Fielding would continue to serve Nova Scotia's coal and steel interests as Laurier's minister of finance from 1896 until 1911.

Fielding's transfer to federal politics was not entirely unexpected, since well before 1896 Laurier had identified him as a potential political ally and had worked assiduously to involve him on the national scene. While preparing for the Liberal convention in June 1893 Laurier invited Fielding to a small gathering of friends to plot strategy. He also named the provincial premier first vice-chairman of the convention and chairman of the central resolutions committee, which was responsible, among other things, for initiating a new Liberal policy on trade and tariffs. During the convention the party changed its old program of unrestricted reciprocity with the United States [see Sir James David Edgar*] for a program of tariff reduction and a more modest measure of reciprocity, in an effort to rid itself of the taint of disloyalty and to calm the fears of business. In its new platform it promised to establish a revenue tariff, reduced "to the needs of honest, economical and efficient government," one that would promote freer trade, especially with Britain and the United States. Fielding played a large role in the drafting and adoption of the new policy.

As a founding member and vice-president of the Maritime Provinces Liberal Association, Fielding threw his full support behind Laurier in the election of 1896, though he cautiously refused to contest a seat until the Liberal victory in June assured him a cabinet position. Pressed by Laurier to become minister of finance, in August he won by acclamation the Nova Scotian constituency of Shelburne and Queens and took his place in Laurier's talented first cabinet, among other experienced regional leaders such as Sir Oliver Mowat*, Andrew George Blair*, and Louis Henry DAVIES. Laurier's choice of Fielding for the Department of Finance surprised many observers. And it angered Sir Richard John Cartwright*, the party's long-serving finance critic and a former minister of finance. Free traders were apprehensive: some agreed with John Charlton* that Fielding was "too small a man for his position." While Fielding's appointment may well have been pressed upon Laurier by concerned businessmen such as George Hope Bertram*, anxious to block the access to office of the doctrinaire old free trader Cartwright, they appeared to lean on an open door. The prime minister seemed all too willing to secure a younger man, with less political baggage, and a proven friend of business interests, in the words of the journalist Paul Ernest Bilkey "a Free Trader by profession and a Protectionist in practice," not unlike Laurier himself.

Gradually Fielding assumed the position of elder statesman in the Liberal party, second only to Laurier and increasingly seen as the heir apparent. Several things facilitated his ascendancy. A pragmatic, ambitious, tactful man of flexible political principles, he was a conscientious and able administrator, though inclined to procrastinate. He was also a man of blameless private and public morality, in striking contrast to some of his more high-spirited colleagues, two or three of whom Fielding felt deserved prison terms. Despite his lengthy political service he remained a relatively poor man; money did not stick to his hands. In the view of his political opponents he possessed, as Bilkey commented, "the not uncommon combination of personal rectitude and political dishonesty." He was also a survivor; for quite apart from his personal virtues, by 1905 all the strong provincial leaders, those who had made Laurier's first administration "the ministry of all the talents," had left the cabinet. When Laurier failed to replace them with comparable men, except for Allen Bristol Aylesworth* and the youthful William Lyon Mackenzie King*, Fielding came to be regarded as Laurier's right-hand man, and his logical successor.

Moreover, as minister of finance, Fielding received credit for the rapid economic expansion that characterized the Laurier era, the "indubitable mascot and advance agent of good times," as the Toronto *Globe* described him. During these halcyon days it would have been difficult to be a poor minister. The government derived over 70 per cent of its revenue from excise and custom duties on imports paid for by the vast sums of foreign capital that poured into Canada between the years 1901 and 1921, a situation that owed little to fiscal policy. After 1901 there was not much for a minister to do but watch the revenue increase, gloat over the government's good fortune, and turn the situation to political advantage.

As minister of finance, Fielding endeavoured to develop external trade. In 1897, when efforts by John Charlton and others to negotiate more favourable American tariffs failed, Fielding revised the Canadian tariff in order to facilitate trade with Britain. Although the new tariff provisions applied to all countries that granted Canada similar terms, in essence the minimum tariff became an imperial preference; yet in 1902 Fielding cleverly helped frustrate Joseph Chamberlain's efforts to create an imperial free trade zone. In 1907 Fielding introduced an intermediate tariff, between the general tariff and the preference, designed "as an instrument by which we may conduct negotiations ... with any country which is willing to give Canada favourable conditions." (It was also designed to bridge the gap between Canadian farmers and manufacturers whose diametrically opposed views on commercial policy had been aired before the tariff inquiry commission Fielding had established in 1905.) With this instrument in hand, in 1907 Fielding and Louis-Philippe BRODEUR negotiated a trade treaty with France, and two years later Fielding obtained an agreement to promote trade with the British West Indies.

Although Fielding had made modest tariff adjustments in 1897, and again in 1907, the Conservatives' National Policy remained essentially unchanged under the Liberals. The true father of the Fielding tariff, as his small concessions were named, was probably Joseph-Israël Tarte*, Laurier's minister of public works and a former Bleu, who in 1897 intervened on behalf of Montreal business to prevent Fielding from introducing more substantial changes. While Fielding professed to see the tariff principally as a source of revenue, he appreciated its utility as an instrument of industrial development and was prepared to see it remain for a time. That time ended in 1910 when he and the minister of customs, William Paterson, negotiated a favourable reciprocity agreement with the United States, his most costly political blunder.

During his term of office Fielding took a number of other modest initiatives. He was responsible, for example, for the encouragement of Guglielmo Marconi's experimentation with wireless telegraphy in 1901, the creation of a penny banking system in

1903, and the establishment of a branch of the Royal Mint in Ottawa in 1908. As acting minister of railways and canals in 1903, following the resignation of Andrew George Blair, he helped Laurier negotiate the agreement to construct the National Transcontinental Railway and signed the contract between the government and the Grand Trunk Pacific [see Charles Melville Hays*].

While many political analysts regarded Fielding as Laurier's rightful successor, others felt that he could never become leader owing to his lack of support in Quebec. Until 1905 Fielding's record on provincial rights and moderate tariff policy had won him a favourable reputation in Quebec; however, his support for Clifford SIFTON's opposition to the education guarantees in the Autonomy Bills of 1905 and for the Naval Service Bill of 1910, which provided for the establishment of a small Canadian navy, eroded that reputation. It was the Autonomy Bills, introduced into the house following Laurier's triumphant 1904 re-election, that generated the most bitter feelings against Fielding in Quebec. In these draft bills, designed to provide a constitutional framework for the provinces of Saskatchewan and Alberta, Laurier had guaranteed the two provinces separate schools. Sifton, Laurier's minister of the interior and "the Napoleon of the West," refused to accept this provision and resigned from the cabinet in protest. Fielding supported Sifton, and threatened resignation. In the face of the opposition of his two most powerful colleagues, one from the east and the other from the west, Laurier was obliged to revamp the bills. French Canadian colleagues in the house resented Fielding's strategic intervention in this controversy, partly owing to his reputed sensitivity to religious and linguistic issues in his own province. With Sifton out of the way, Fielding became Laurier's undisputed second in command and his most obvious successor.

In fact, Fielding only narrowly avoided becoming prime minister in November 1908. At that time Laurier, discouraged by the results of the recent election, especially in English Canada, drafted a letter of resignation requesting Governor General Lord Grey* to call upon Fielding to form a government. But Fielding, conscious of continuing French Canadian resentment owing to his role in revising the Autonomy Bills, persuaded Laurier to delay resignation until 1910, after which Fielding would become leader for two sessions and then call an election. The defeat of the Liberal candidate by his Nationaliste opponent in the famous Drummond and Arthabaska by-election of 1910, however, prevented a transfer of power that year and the party's collapse in the general election of 1911 altered the question of succession.

The most prominent issue in this election was the reciprocity agreement with the United States that Fielding had announced so triumphantly in the House of Commons in January 1911. The impetus to improve commercial relations between the two countries had come the previous year from the United States and, for Laurier's government, had coincided with increasing political pressure from farmers for tariff reform [see James Speakman*]. The principal feature of the agreement was the free exchange of natural products and a small number of manufactured goods. The issue, however, backfired. In February, 18 prominent Liberal businessmen in Toronto issued a manifesto protesting the arrangement [see Sir Byron Edmund WALKER]. Confident of the popularity of the reciprocity agreement, Laurier accepted the Conservative party's challenge to call an election for 21 September. Disorganized, ill prepared, and carrying 15 years of political baggage, the ageing Liberal party was defeated. Fielding was among the casualties.

After the election Fielding's chances of replacing Laurier receded. Laurier's own popularity began to rebound, especially in Quebec among disillusioned Nationalistes, notably Henri Bourassa*, the influential proprietor of *Le Devoir*. Sensitive to changing public sentiments, Laurier began to take his distance from his party's rejected trade and naval policy and to focus on the high cost of living. In contrast, Fielding's stubborn commitment to the Liberals' defunct program, made clear in interviews and speeches during his visit to England in 1913, not only offended party members but reinforced the notion that he was chiefly responsible for the party's 1911 electoral defeat. Increasingly, Fielding appeared old and inflexible, and Laurier himself began to consider younger successors, among them W. L. M. King. Although in 1912 Robert BICKERDIKE, the Liberal MP for the Montreal constituency of St Lawrence, had offered to relinquish his seat in favour of Fielding, the party did nothing to redeem Bickerdike's offer, a failure that suggests Fielding's fading political reputation.

This became painfully clear in 1913, soon after Fielding moved to Montreal to resume his career in journalism. His friends planned a large, welcoming banquet, and many speculated that Laurier would use the occasion to announce his own retirement and name Fielding as his successor. Consequently over 200 Liberals, including prominent Liberals from other provinces, gathered to participate in the event. Although the hour was past midnight when Laurier rose to speak, the former prime minister gave a fighting oration that aroused the awe and admiration of his audience, and that contrasted sharply with Fielding's own lacklustre performance. During this speech Laurier announced the new Liberal policy and made it clear that he had no intention of relinquishing the crown. Many party followers were elated. Others were astonished at Fielding's "humiliation." To Henri Bourassa the reason was clear: physically and mentally Fielding was a man of the past, more at home

Fielding

"in the world of the archaeologists and the kingdom of the Seven Sleepers."

Fielding's return to journalism appeared no more successful. He had moved to Montreal in December 1912 to assume the editorship of the *Daily Witness*. The paper was acquired some months later by the Telegraph Publishing Company Limited, of which Fielding was president, and renamed the *Daily Telegraph and Daily Witness*, but it soon encountered financial difficulties. In January 1914 it was purchased by Sir Hugh Graham*, proprietor of the *Montreal Daily Herald*, who merged the two papers. The attempts of Graham, a strong-willed Conservative, to dictate editorial policy led to a "first class blow out." Fielding left the *Montreal Herald and Daily Telegraph* that year and, with James John Harpell and Jack C. Ross, acquired the *Journal of Commerce*, a weekly that he converted into a daily. Fielding served as both editor of the paper and president of the publishing company. This small publication reverted to a weekly in 1915, then became a monthly, and later moved to Sainte-Anne-de-Bellevue. Fielding continued to edit the *Journal of Commerce* until he joined W. L. M. King's cabinet in 1921.

While Fielding's Montreal sojourn may have restored his links with the city's business community, World War I further soured his relationship with French Canada. The problem was his support for conscription and his perceived betrayal of Laurier. Throughout the conscription crisis, Fielding consistently sought a middle way where there was no middle way, perhaps cynically seeking political advantage. In the spring of 1917 he drafted a letter, which he never published, justifying Laurier's refusal to join a coalition government. In it he pleaded with his intended readership for an understanding of French Canada's opposition to compulsory military conscription and called for a referendum to decide the issue. But when western Canadian Liberals began making their peace with Sir Robert Laird Borden*'s Conservatives, Fielding (aware that Laurier was contemplating resignation from the party's leadership) publicly endorsed the formation of a national government, while withholding his approval of Borden's proposed terms for it. In October, when support for Borden's Union government grew among western and Ontario Liberals, Fielding again revised his position and sought to persuade Nova Scotia Liberals to join the Union movement to avoid being isolated. Although he refused a Unionist cabinet post, Fielding endorsed the decision of Alexander Kenneth Maclean*, another Nova Scotian Liberal, to enter Borden's government, gave Borden his full support, and in the election in December was returned unopposed as a Unionist in Shelburne and Queens. He insisted upon sitting on the cross-benches, however, thereby offending many Liberal Unionists.

Fielding might easily have accommodated himself to Laurier's generous criteria for individuals to retain caucus membership: oppose conscription and the Union government; support conscription but oppose the Union government; or run as independent Liberals. But he chose to follow the majority of his party, hoping, perhaps, to play peacemaker and power-broker once the war ended. Whatever popularity his vacillating strategy may have gained him in the rest of Canada, it won him no favour in his native province or in Quebec. In Nova Scotia, despite the efforts of Borden, Fielding, and Premier George H. Murray, Unionist electoral manipulation, and the sobering effects of the great Halifax explosion only 11 days before the election, the Laurier Liberals obtained 45.5 per cent of the popular vote. Moreover, Nova Scotian Liberals, like their Quebec colleagues, would not forgive Fielding his desertion of the old chief, as they made clear during the Liberals' leadership convention in August 1919.

Nevertheless, Fielding made a remarkably strong showing at this gathering. Laurier had called for a national convention immediately after the war, to reunite the party and give it a post-war policy direction. Upon his death in February 1919, the convention became a six-person leadership contest. Although King and Fielding protested their lack of interest in the position, they were the principal contenders and they offered Liberals a stark generational and ideological choice. Fielding's hesitations in seeking the leadership were based on his fear that Laurier loyalists in Nova Scotia and Quebec would spoil his chances, and his strong opposition to the radical platform that had been adopted by the convention in its first two days. When at last he agreed to stand, he threatened, should he be chosen leader, to have his leadership ratified by the parliamentary caucus on the condition that he would not be bound by the program. Opposition to Fielding came from various corners, "quite the fiercest" from his former cabinet colleagues Sydney Arthur FISHER, Sir Allen Aylesworth, Frank Oliver*, and George Perry Graham*, some seeing him as the tool of Montreal's St James Street businessmen. Fielding's greatest support came from the conservative members of his party, such as George H. Murray, Sir Lomer GOUIN, Louis-Alexandre Taschereau*, John OLIVER, William Melville Martin*, and Walter Edward Foster*, from Montreal business interests, and from those who felt his candidacy was essential to the party's unity. With their support he pushed the convention to a third ballot, which King won by only 38 votes. According to Adam Kirk Cameron, a close friend and confidant of Laurier and a Fielding supporter, Fielding obtained a "very heavy vote from Ontario and the West ... and a surprisingly large vote from the province of Quebec, notwithstanding the Autonomy Bills and his attitude toward conscription." But in Cameron's view Fielding "was defeated for leadership of the Liberal party by the people of Nova Scotia," whose delegates had cast over half of the 38 votes separating the two candidates against Fielding. They had also run Daniel Duncan McKenzie, the interim party leader and a Nova Scotian, to prevent Nova Scotia votes going to Fielding. During the course of the ballot Lady Laurier asked Cameron to inform the convention that Fielding was her late husband's choice for leader. Anxious to restore party unity, Laurier, it appears, had concluded that Fielding would be best placed to heal the party's wounds.

Disappointed by the outcome and unhappy with the party's radical program, Fielding threatened to sit as an independent Liberal. Although friends persuaded him to join the front benches, he continued to remind the house that he had never accepted the party's platform. During the 1921 federal election, however, he gave the party his full support, and was re-elected in Shelburne and Queens. By projecting an image of unity, his endorsement of the new leader may well have had "a deciding influence" in Ontario and the Maritime provinces. Fielding's strength at the Liberal convention and his continuing popularity among the more conservative wing of the party prevented King from ignoring him. When the Liberals were returned to power in December 1921, he took up his old post as minister of finance. Although he retained the position until 1925, he remained something of an anachronism, heard but not heeded by the new leader. From late 1923 he was too ill to fulfil his duties, which were assumed by an acting minister, James Alexander ROBB.

The little grey man, who had in the past too frequently chosen the path of silence and compliance, in his old age refused to make concessions to the new era. He disapproved of Canada seeking a separate representation at the Paris Peace Conference, and deplored the country's new obsession with status. He also opposed the idea of Canada obtaining representation in Washington and signing its own treaties. Although he feared that the country was "right at the very verge of independence," he wrote a six-stanza version of "O Canada," and designed a new Canadian flag, since he regarded the Red Ensign inappropriate because it was a sea flag and "more suggestive of the red flag of the communists than of anything Canadian." His world remained the world of pre-war Canada.

A friend of business, despite his free-trade antecedents, Fielding served on the boards of a number of companies, including the Scottish and Dominion Trust Company, of which he was chair. He was vice-president of the Nova Scotia branch of the Canadian Red Cross Society, a governor of Dalhousie University, an engaged member of his Baptist church, and an active clubman in Halifax, Ottawa, and Quebec City. Although he was presented at court on several occasions, he resisted titles for himself. Acadia, McGill, Queen's, Dalhousie, and McMaster universities bestowed honorary degrees and he was made an imperial privy councillor in 1923. His portrait was painted by John Wycliffe Lowes Forster*.

An individual of apparent contradictions, secretive, cautious, and a procrastinator, Fielding was a man of personal probity though, opponents would add, of political deviousness. His friends and supporters saw him as an honest, conscientious, disinterested public servant, a great parliamentarian, tactful, without airs, "one of the brightest intellects Canada has yet produced," and "the greatest Finance Minister Canada has ever possessed." In 1910 his friends "of all shades of political opinion" created a trust fund of $120,000 for him and when he retired in 1925 parliament voted an annuity to its longest serving minister of finance. He died four years later, predeceased by his wife and one of his daughters, and he was buried beside them in Beechwood Cemetery in Ottawa.

CARMAN MILLER

LAC, MG 26, G; MG 30, E70. National Library of Scotland (Edinburgh), MSS 12446–587 (4th Earl of Minto, corr. and papers). NSARM, MG 2, 63–223, 422–541, 784–90(B). Univ. of Toronto Library, Thomas Fisher Rare Book Library, MS coll. 110 (John Charlton papers). P. [E.] Bilkey, *Persons, papers and things: being the casual recollections of a journalist, with some flounderings in philosophy* (Toronto, 1940). Can., House of Commons, *Debates*, 1896–1911; 1922–23. *Canadian men and women of the time* (Morgan; 1898 and 1912). *Cyclopædia of Canadian biog.* (Rose and Charlesworth), vol.3. Robert Drummond, *Minerals and mining, Nova Scotia* (Stellarton, N.S., 1918). [C.] B. Fergusson, *Hon. W. S. Fielding* (2v., Windsor, N.S., 1970–71). D. J. Hall, *Clifford Sifton* (2v., Vancouver and London, 1981–85). D. C. Harvey, "Fielding's call to Ottawa," *Dalhousie Rev.* (Halifax), 28 (1948–49): 369–85. C. D. Howell, "W. S. Fielding and the repeal elections of 1886 and 1887 in Nova Scotia," *Acadiensis* (Fredericton), 8 (1978–79), no.2: 28–46. Donna McDonald, *Lord Strathcona: a biography of Donald Alexander Smith* (Toronto and Oxford, 1996). K. M. McLaughlin, "W. S. Fielding and the Liberal party in Nova Scotia, 1891–1896," *Acadiensis*, 3 (1973–74), no.2: 65–79. N.S., House of Assembly, *Debates and proc.* (Halifax), 1882–96. Benjamin Russell, "Recollections of W. S. Fielding," *Dalhousie Rev.*, 9 (1929–30): 326–40. O. D. Skelton, *Life and letters of Sir Wilfrid Laurier* (2v., Toronto, 1921).

FISHER, SYDNEY ARTHUR, farmer, politician, office holder, and philanthropist; b. 12 June 1850 in Montreal, son of Arthur Fisher and Susan Corse; d. unmarried 10 April 1921 in Ottawa.

Originally from Scotland, Sydney Fisher's paternal great-grandfather, Duncan Fisher*, immigrated to Montreal about 1777 and became a prominent citizen. Sydney's father, who was educated in Montreal and at the Royal College of Surgeons of Edinburgh, became

Montreal's first practitioner of homoeopathy in 1842. Sydney's mother was wealthy and the family travelled in Europe for extended periods. Educated at the High School of Montreal, Fisher graduated the top pupil of his class in 1866 and was awarded the Davidson Medal. He attended McGill College during 1866–68 and obtained a BA in political economy and scientific agriculture from Trinity College, Cambridge, in 1871.

In 1874 and 1875, with capital made available to him from his mother's real estate holdings, Fisher purchased several lots in Brome Township, near the village of Knowlton (Lac-Brome). One of the properties belonged to judge Christopher Dunkin*, a friend of his father and an important farmer in the region. Fisher would develop his holdings, which he named Alva Farm, into a showplace of scientific agriculture. During the 1880s he made many contacts through his involvement in agricultural associations, including the Montreal Ensilage and Stock Feeding Association, the Brome County Agricultural Society, the Dairymen's Association of the Province of Quebec, the Fruit Growers' Association of the Province of Quebec, and the Canadian National Live-Stock Association. In 1884, at a meeting in Montreal of the British Association for the Advancement of Science, he delivered an address entitled "Agriculture in the province of Quebec."

A Liberal, Fisher had failed in his first and only attempt to enter provincial politics, losing a by-election in Brome in November 1879. He was also unsuccessful in his first bid to enter federal politics, at a by-election held in Brome the following October. He obtained a narrow victory in the federal general election of June 1882. A free trader, he spoke in the commons in 1883 against the protectionism of Sir John A. Macdonald*'s government. He viewed increased tariffs on agricultural implements as harmful to farmers and those on materials used for tool manufacture as unhelpful to business. Although his elegant manners and bearing projected the image of a gentleman farmer, he would serve agriculture and politics equally well.

While sitting in the opposition, Fisher developed a close association with Wilfrid Laurier*, the Quebec leader and from 1887 the national leader of the Liberal party. In his extensive correspondence with Laurier, he revealed his belief that English and French Canadians should keep to their separate spheres. He was alarmed at the political climate after the execution of Métis leader Louis Riel* in 1885 and worried by Laurier's suggestion that he be replaced in Brome by a French Canadian candidate in the federal election of 1887. Laurier consequently did some campaigning in the region without Fisher, who nonetheless retained his seat with a majority of 379 votes. During his second term he frequently addressed the commons on matters concerning agriculture, tariffs, or his constituency.

In the federal general election of March 1891 Fisher lost Brome by three votes. He was immediately appointed a justice of the peace. Out of office, he spent his time improving Alva and working for the Liberal party and various agricultural associations. In 1894 he accompanied Laurier during a visit to western Canada. The following year he organized a Liberal rally in Montreal and political meetings elsewhere in Quebec. In the federal election of 1896 he won Brome by over 330 votes.

On 13 July 1896 Fisher was sworn in as minister of agriculture in Laurier's government. A well-educated and experienced politician of independent means, he had excellent qualifications for the post and had demonstrated that he was Laurier's English-Canadian organizer in Quebec. After entering cabinet, he bought a house in Ottawa and was entertained as a sought-after bachelor, in demand at Mme Laurier's dinner parties. During frequent visits to Montreal he stayed with his parents and he wrote to them or his aunt every day he was absent.

An advocate of temperance in a pro-temperance riding, Fisher had become a vice-president of the Dominion Alliance for the Total Suppression of the Liquor Traffic around 1882; he would hold the post for more than 15 years. At the Liberal party's national convention of 1893 he prepared and presented the resolution in favour of a national plebiscite on the prohibition of alcohol. After the Liberals assumed office, Fisher introduced the legislation into the commons in 1898 [see Francis Stephens Spence*]. Although prohibitionists cast the majority of votes, Laurier avoided implementing the measure by pointing to the low overall voter turnout.

As minister for 15 years, Fisher accomplished much for Canadian agriculture. One of his first tasks had been to consult in December 1896 with Julius Sterling Morton, the American secretary of agriculture. Their departments agreed to cooperate in the tracking and reporting of disease in farm animals. The joint system of inspection led to increased livestock trade between the two countries. In the work of his department Fisher relied on the team of experts assembled in Ottawa. Chief among them were William Saunders*, director of the experimental farms system, James Wilson ROBERTSON, dominion commissioner of agriculture and dairying, and James Fletcher*, dominion entomologist. Later, Fletcher's successor, Charles Gordon Hewitt*, botanist Charles Edward Saunders*, and others would distinguish themselves. The work of these specialists led directly to measures such as the control of animal disease, plant disease and pests (the San José Scale Act, 1898, and the Destructive Insect and Pest Act, 1910), and seed purity (the Seed Control Act, 1905), as well as to the school garden movement. Under Fisher, a major expansion of the experimental farms system took place and new branches were created in the department, such as those for seeds, fruits, tobacco, and foreign exhibitions.

During his first term as minister, Fisher had revolutionized the marketing and transportation of Canadian produce, especially dairy products and fruit. Legislation in 1897 and 1898 provided for government subsidies to, and inspection of, cold storage warehouses in major eastern centres and refrigeration facilities on steamships leaving eastern ports for Great Britain and the West Indies. The Canadian Pacific Railway supplied cold storage from 31 points to Montreal. Other improvements followed in order to guarantee the quality of agricultural products. Over 900 cheese factories and creameries were obliged to register with the department and to date accurately their cheese and butter products for export. Fisher later legislated against the sale of oleomargarine, butterine, and spurious or adulterated butter. Under chief veterinary inspector Duncan McNab McEACHRAN and his successor, John Gunion RUTHERFORD, an effort was made to control disease in livestock, especially bovine tuberculosis. One method – the destruction of entire herds – remained controversial; individual farmers or inspectors were often unwilling to implement it because of the costs involved and the non-farming public failed to understand their reluctance. Only wealthy farmers could afford the destruction of an entire herd. Rutherford's solutions, including the testing of imported stock, limited elimination of herds, and prohibitions against the export of infected cattle, gained acceptance. A national meat inspection program introduced in 1907 won the support of the packing industry.

One of the duties Fisher most enjoyed was to serve as an ambassador-at-large for Canada. He had recognized the significance of the Columbian exposition of 1893 for the promotion of trade and cultural exchange and, once in office, he made certain that Canada participated in subsequent events. He attended the universal exposition in Paris (1900), the national industrial exposition in Ōsaka, Japan (1903), the Louisiana Purchase exposition in St Louis, Mo. (1904), and the Alaska-Yukon-Pacific exposition in Seattle (1909). He hired the Canadian staffs, supervised the preparation of exhibits, and ensured that agriculture and emigration to Canada were featured.

As minister, Fisher attended agricultural fairs in England, Scotland, and Wales. He met fellow landowners and consorted with rural regenerators, such as Irish politician Sir Horace Curzon Plunkett. Elitists, these reformers advocated a major investment of human and financial capital in farmland and farming communities – through measures such as the teaching of scientific agriculture, manual training in rural schools, and the protection of water and land resources. Both Fisher and Robertson, who often travelled with him, sought to put Plunkett's idealized concept of rural education into practice in Canada. Robertson was eventually able to persuade Montreal manufacturer Sir William Christopher Macdonald* to provide funding for projects in rural education. Closely connected with Fisher's belief in rural regeneration was his growing pro-imperialist sentiment. He was a supporter of the Navy League of Canada, which wanted to strengthen naval ties between Britain and Canada, but he also envisaged closer economic and cultural ties, which rural regeneration might bolster. Writing to his mother in 1901, he had expressed the hope that in 100 years the Eastern Townships would resemble rural Britain, agriculturally.

Fisher carried his interest in conservation to other areas of activity. He had been a founding member of the Canadian Forestry Association in 1900. In February 1909, along with former cabinet minister Clifford SIFTON and doctor and MP Henri-Sévérin Béland*, he represented Canada at an important North American conference on conservation called by American president Theodore Roosevelt and held in Washington. By April he had drafted and tabled in the commons legislation for the creation of the Commission of Conservation, based on one of the conference's recommendations. Sifton was appointed chairman of the commission, but it was Fisher who defended it and spoke on its behalf in cabinet.

Another responsibility of Fisher's department was the federal archives [see Douglas Brymner*; Sir Arthur George Doughty*] and he played an important role in securing a new building for the repository, opened in 1906; the following year he established the Historical Manuscripts Commission to advise the archives. Also in 1907, as acting minister of public works, he saw to the creation of the Advisory Arts Council. Set up in response to a request from the Royal Canadian Academy of Arts, headed by George Agnew Reid*, it was to counsel the government on matters of art and to purchase works for the National Gallery.

Fisher's department had a branch which administered the registration of copyrights, trade marks, industrial designs, and timber marks. He revised and amended the regulations of the Patent Office in 1904 and insisted on paying patent examiners as scientists. Between 1900 and 1910 he supported the initiatives of publisher George Nathaniel Morang* and economist James MAVOR to protect Canadian authors and publishers from pirating by Canadian, American, and British printers. In 1910 he was a delegate to the Imperial Copyright Conference in London, England, to consider the ratification of international agreements.

By 1907 Laurier's administration faced accusations of patronage and corruption from the opposition. A royal commission on the civil service, appointed that year, revealed negligence, confusion, and inadequacies. The government decided to act, and Fisher piloted important legislation through the house the following year to establish the Civil Service Commission. Michel Gordon La Rochelle and Adam Shortt* were appointed commissioners to oversee the operation of the legislation, supervise admissions and promotions, and administer examinations.

Unmarried and without a family of his own, Fisher had nonetheless demonstrated an early interest in education. He had served for some time in the early 1880s as a member of the district of Bedford's board of examiners for teachers' qualifications. In addition, he attended annual conventions of the Provincial Association of Protestant Teachers and held office as president in 1888. In 1901 he accepted a life membership on the Protestant committee of the Council of Public Instruction. George William Parmelee*, secretary of the committee, and Elson Irving Rexford*, Parmelee's predecessor and confidant, drew Fisher into their campaign to consolidate schools in Protestant municipalities of Quebec. Fisher organized a private meeting in June 1906 at the Windsor Hotel in Montreal of selected school administrators, politicians, journalists, and Protestant committee members. They held a series of political-style meetings throughout the summer in Knowlton, Huntingdon, Richmond, Inverness, Lachute, and Ayer's Cliff to promote their plans. Residents of the Eastern Townships perceived the rallies as designed to justify increased taxes and assert the influence of the McGill Normal School. Fisher continued to support the consolidation of rural schools until about 1919, but his participation may have damaged his reputation as a friend of rural inhabitants.

Fisher had won his riding by substantial majorities in the four general elections from 1896 to 1908. He had found an able organizer in Edward Caldwell and had stayed in touch with successive MLAs in Brome. Newspapers in the Townships – with the exception of the *Waterloo Advertiser* – portrayed him as the head of a substantial spoils system. His power was not absolute, however. Laurier kept a certain amount of patronage to distribute himself. In addition, certain English-speaking Conservatives in the Knowlton area were tenacious in their opposition to him. Fisher's actions in the so-called Dundonald affair illustrate the complexity of his position. In 1904 he temporarily replaced Sir Frederick William Borden* as minister of the militia and defence. In this capacity he refused to approve a militia appointment made by the general officer commanding, Lord Dundonald [Cochrane*], which concerned one of his Conservative opponents. After Dundonald publicly accused Fisher of partisanship, Prime Minister Laurier demanded and obtained the officer's recall.

When the United States approached Canada in the spring of 1910 for a reciprocal trade agreement, Fisher may have been caught off guard. For much of his career he had promoted the lowering or elimination of the tariffs between the two countries. By 1910, however, he was temperamentally and philosophically a pan-Canadian and an Anglophile; he may not have shared the Liberal party's enthusiasm for the American offer. Called on in late February 1911 to speak in the commons after Sifton, who differed with the Liberals over the issue and who spoke approvingly of the preferential tariff introduced in 1897 by William Stevens FIELDING, which had favoured Great Britain, Fisher made do with a history of tariff debates to 1897. Laurier called an election later in 1911. During the campaign, Fisher argued that the Canadian-American agreement would only strengthen Canada's ties to the British empire. He lost his seat to a young Conservative lawyer and militia officer in a wave of pro-imperial and anti-annexation sentiment.

During a fiercely contested by-election in Châteauguay in 1913, Fisher was again defeated. He remained active in the Liberal party, accompanying Laurier on tours and speaking at rallies. He continued to participate in school consolidation campaigns in Quebec, but after 1919 he turned his attention to moral education and compulsory school attendance at the national and provincial levels. Following Laurier's death in 1919, he hosted a meeting at Alva of prominent Liberals to discuss the choice of a new party leader. As one of the country's senior Liberals, he was considered a possible successor to Laurier, but he did not have a broad base of support. At the Liberal party convention held on 7 August, he withdrew early from the leadership race, bringing his vote and that of other prominent Quebec Liberals to William Lyon Mackenzie King*, who was chosen leader.

In failing health, Fisher wrote a will in 1919 setting up a trust fund of $100,000 to promote agriculture and the consolidation of Protestant schools in Brome County. Advised by Rexford that Protestant secondary-school teachers had no interest in teaching scientific agriculture in the way that he, Robertson, and Macdonald had hoped, and discouraged by local resistance to consolidation, he focused instead on strengthening Brome's one-room schools and on prizes for agricultural fairs. He died in 1921 of a heart attack; his eulogy was delivered in Christ Church Cathedral, Montreal. The following year the board of trustees of the Fisher Trust Fund began to create a strong network of one-room schools that would last until 1946.

An elegant and cosmopolitan man, Sydney Arthur Fisher was nonetheless a strong believer in the virtues of rural life. He was an idealist, imbued with contemporary belief in progress and rural regeneration. He was also an able and practical Liberal politician and administrator who, as minister, did much to improve agriculture in Canada.

ANNE DRUMMOND

A list of several of Sydney Arthur Fisher's speeches is in CIHM, *Reg.* One of his lectures, "Agriculture in the province of Quebec," was published in British Assoc. for the Advancement of Science, *Canadian economics: being papers prepared for reading before the economical section, with an introductory report* (Montreal and London, 1885), 85–91.

ANQ-M, CE601-S109, 20 août 1850. LAC, MG 26, G; MG 27, II, D25. Private arch., R. E. Fisher (Montreal), P. S. Fisher, "Some notes on our ancestors" (typescript, n.d.). *Montreal Daily Star*, 22–23 Jan., 23, 25, 27–28 Feb., 8 May 1895. *Montreal Herald*, 10 April 1921. *Observer* (Cowansville, Que.), 2 Jan., 12 March, 21 May, 23 July 1908. *Waterloo Advertiser* (Waterloo, Que.), 4 Oct. 1901; 17 Jan., 11 April, 4, 11 July 1902; 18 March, 4 May 1904. Can., House of Commons, *Debates*, 1882–91, 1896–1911; Parl., *Sessional papers*, report of the Dept. of Agriculture, 1896–1910. *Canadian men and women of the time* (Morgan; 1912). *CPG*, 1881–91, 1897–1911. Raoul Dandurand, *Les mémoires du sénateur Raoul Dandurand (1861–1942)*, Marcel Hamelin, édit. (Québec, 1967). R. MacG. Dawson and H. B. Neatby, *William Lyon Mackenzie King: a political biography* (3v., Toronto, 1958–76). Anne Drummond, "New educationists in Quebec Protestant model and intermediate schools, 1881–1926" (PHD thesis, Univ. of Ottawa, 1994); "Sydney Arthur Fisher and the limits of school consolidation in Brome County, 1901–1921," *Journal of Eastern Townships Studies* (Lennoxville, Que.), no.3 (autumn 1993): 31–47. *Educational Record of the Prov. of Quebec* (Montreal; Quebec), 4 (1884): 294; 8 (1888): 279–80; 16 (1896): 166; 41 (1921): 100. Sandra Gwyn, *The private capital: ambition and love in the age of Macdonald and Laurier* (Toronto, 1984). *History of the federal electoral ridings, 1867–1980* (4v., [Ottawa, 1982?]), 3. *Men of today in the Eastern Townships*, intro. V. E. Morrill, comp. E. G. Pierce (Sherbrooke, Que., 1917). Carman Miller, *The Canadian career of the fourth Earl of Minto: the education of a viceroy* (Waterloo, Ont., 1980). H. B. Neatby, *Laurier and a Liberal Quebec; a study in political management*, ed. R. T. Clippingdale (Toronto, 1973). O. B. Rexford, *The Fisher Trust Fund, 1922–1972* (n.p., 1974). Ronald Rudin, *The forgotten Quebecers: a history of English-speaking Quebec, 1759–1980* (Quebec, 1985). O. D. Skelton, *Life and letters of Sir Wilfrid Laurier* (2v., Toronto, 1921). R. M. Stamp, "Urbanization and education in Ontario and Quebec, 1867–1914," *McGill Journal of Education* ([Montreal]), 3 (1968): 127–35. *Standard dict. of Canadian biog.* (Roberts and Tunnell). *The storied province of Quebec; past and present*, ed. W. [C. H.] Wood et al. (5v., Toronto, 1931–32), 3: 199. E. M. Taylor, *History of Brome County, Quebec, from the date of grants of land therein to the present time; with records of some early families* (2v., Montreal, 1908–37), 1: 179, 181; 2: 228, 231.

FITZGERALD, WILLIAM JAMES, lacrosse player, coach, and carpenter; b. 20 Feb. 1888 in St Catharines, Ont., son of Thomas Fitzgerald, a baker, and Rose Ann Killeen (Kileen); m. there 5 Nov. 1913 Adele (Della) Sheehan, and they had two sons; d. there 30 June 1926.

In St Catharines at the turn of the century, field-lacrosse games were huge summertime attractions. When Billy Fitzgerald, a Roman Catholic, likely of Irish background, took up organized lacrosse in 1904,

the game was played with 12 men per side. Small and agile, he occupied an offensive position called "first home"; he often carried the ball, and was an excellent passer and shooter. In 1907, at age 19, he joined the St Catharines Athletics, a senior amateur team and defending champions of Ontario; during Fitzgerald's two years with this powerful squad they never lost.

In 1909 Fitzgerald turned professional with the Toronto Lacrosse Club. For two seasons he commuted from his parents' home in St Catharines, even though his salary barely exceeded his expenses. Lacrosse was approaching the height of its popularity, however, and his reputation quickly grew. Fitz, as he became known, was a crowd-pleasing standout in a league that included the TLC and six other teams from Toronto, Montreal, Ottawa, and Cornwall, Ont. In July 1909 the Toronto *World* described his performance in scoring a game-winning goal on sodden turf: "Running half the length of the field with the ball, passing several Montreal players on the way, negotiating the defence and finally slashing it past the goal-tender into the net, he carried out a stunt which made him the hero of the day." "The Toronto rooters simply threw a series of fits in their seats and then burst forth in one prolonged spontaneous roar."

Club owner Robert John FLEMING was determined to field a winning team that would attract paying customers. The TLC played its home games in the stadium that had opened in 1909 at the Scarboro Beach Amusement Park. It had a seating capacity of 8,000 and professional lacrosse was a drawing card. Fleming was manager of the Toronto Railway Company, and its Queen Street East line terminated at Scarboro Beach. Fleming allowed anyone carrying a lacrosse stick to ride the line free of charge.

Fitzgerald's fame spread to British Columbia, another hotbed of lacrosse, where an often violent rivalry existed between Vancouver and New Westminster. New Westminster had won the Minto Cup (the senior lacrosse championship of Canada) in 1908, 1909, and 1910. Con Jones, owner of the Vancouver Lacrosse Club, set out to assemble a team that could beat New Westminster, and any other team. He fixed his sights on two players: Édouard (Newsy) Lalonde*, the lacrosse and hockey sensation from Cornwall, and Fitzgerald.

Jones started, and won, a bidding war with Fleming, who also wanted to sign Lalonde. At a time when $1,000 was a good annual salary, Lalonde received $6,500 to play 16 games with the VLC; Fitzgerald got $5,000. (By comparison, the highest-paid athlete in any team sport at the time was Detroit baseball player Ty Cobb, who earned $4,500 for a 154-game season.) A bookmaker in his native Australia, Jones owned a number of cigar shops in Vancouver and a saloon, the Brunswick, which featured billiards and gambling. There, on Saturday nights, Fitzgerald, Lalonde, and other players would join fans around the pool tables or serve customers at the bar. Jones's efforts paid off when the VLC beat New Westminster and the Toronto Tecumsehs to win the Minto Cup in 1911.

Following this victory Fitzgerald moved back to St Catharines. Fleming promised to top Jones's highest offer for 1912 by $500, and Fitzgerald signed with the TLC for $4,000. A skilled carpenter, he also began building houses in St Catharines. In 1913 Jones wanted Fitzgerald back and offered the Toronto club $1,000 for the right to sign him. The demand for houses was so great, however, that Fitzgerald took the year off to concentrate on his business.

He played with the TLC in 1914, but World War I effectively ended lacrosse competition in Canada. Over 2,000 top-level players enlisted, making it nearly impossible for any community to field a team. At the end of the 1914 season, Fitzgerald returned to St Catharines, where, after the birth of his first son that year, he and his family moved into a house he had built. In 1915 he accepted an offer to coach men's lacrosse at Hobart College in Geneva, N.Y.; he was rehired for 1916 but an immigration official in Niagara Falls, N.Y., refused him entry. The college, determined to have the man still widely considered Canada's finest lacrosse player, successfully appealed the decision.

At the conclusion of the war Fitzgerald helped organize a St Catharines team in a new, semi-professional league. In 1919, his last year of competition as a player, he was with Cornwall in a professional league. At 31 he was older than many of his team-mates. It was difficult for him to maintain the pace over an entire game and nagging injuries slowed him down, but he still showed flashes of brilliance. Knowledgeable and respected, he remained in demand in St Catharines as a coach and referee. He also worked with teams at Swarthmore College in Swarthmore, Pa, and the United States Military Academy in West Point, N.Y.

Fitzgerald became ill in December 1925 and the following June he underwent surgery for gallstones. He developed peritonitis and died; he was 38. His death shocked many Canadians. In September former players from Toronto and St Catharines faced off in a memorial game in St Catharines. One-time boxing champion Gentleman Jim Corbett and Canadian sports legend Lionel Pretoria Conacher* were among the thousands in attendance. Conacher was persuaded to don a St Catharines uniform and take part as a tribute to Billy Fitzgerald, one of the greatest lacrosse players of all time. Fitzgerald was inducted into Canada's Sports Hall of Fame (Toronto) in 1961 and the Canadian Lacrosse Hall of Fame (New Westminster) in 1965.

SCOTT CALBECK

[The author would like to thank Margaret Fitzgerald of St Catharines, Ont., the subject's daughter-in-law, for granting access to materials in her possession. S.C.]

AO, RG 22-235, no.5845; RG 80-2-0-291, no.19957; RG 80-5-0-633, no.8717. St Catharines Hist. Museum, Undated clippings from the *Daily Mail and Empire*, *Ottawa Citizen*, *St Catharines Standard*, and Toronto *Evening Telegram*. *Globe*, 23 Feb. 1915. *St Catharines Standard*, 17 April 1916; 30 June, 20 Sept. 1926. *World* (Toronto), 26 July, 9 Aug. 1909. Christina Burr, "The process of evolution of competitive sport: a study of senior lacrosse in Canada, 1844 to 1914" (MA thesis, Univ. of Western Ont., London, 1986). Cleve Dheensaw, *Lacrosse 100: one hundred years of lacrosse in B.C.* (Victoria, 1990). *Directory*, St Catharines, 1898–1926.

FITZMAURICE. *See* PETTY-FITZMAURICE

FLEMING, ROBERT JOHN, businessman, temperance crusader, politician, and civil servant; b. 23 Nov. 1854 in Toronto, son of William Fleming and Jane Cauldwell; m. first 23 Dec. 1879 Margaret Jane Breadon (d. 5 April 1883) in Montreal, and they had a daughter; m. secondly 23 Oct. 1888 Lydia Jane Orford (d. 20 Sept. 1937) in Toronto, and they had four daughters and four sons; d. near there 26 Oct. 1925.

Robert J. Fleming, deemed one of Canada's "greatest executives" at his death, started out in a Horatio Alger style. Born of poor Irish parents on St David Street in Toronto's Cabbagetown district, he dropped out of Park Street School to take a position as a stoker in an office. After attending business school at night, the ambitious youth entered the feed, coal, and wood business in the mid 1870s. By 1885 he had moved into real estate and finance.

Christian principles and social reform were at the centre of Fleming's life. A devout Methodist affiliated with the Liberals, who were more likely to be ardent prohibitionists than most other groups, he became involved with temperance in his twenties. Following his election in 1886 as an alderman for the wet ward of St David's, he pushed for the reduction of liquor licences in Toronto, a position many believed would cost him votes, especially among the Irish, but he was so engaging that he was easily re-elected in 1887, 1888, and 1889. Mayor William Holmes Howland*'s most articulate temperance crusader, in 1887 he succeeded in having a by-law passed to reduce licences. In 1892, with Liberal support, he ran successfully for the mayoralty on a reform platform that included opposition to the operation of the Toronto Railway Company on Sundays. His unpretentious manner and dress, scrappy and entertaining platform style, unwavering support of the working class, and Christian reformist ideals earned him an affectionate nickname – the People's Bob. Riding on his enormous popularity, he was returned in 1893, 1896, and 1897. During the 1897 campaign his shift, to support Sunday cars, brought accusations of bribery. By this time he had moved to the front ranks of the temperance cause, primarily as treasurer of the Ontario branch of the Dominion Alliance for the Total Suppression of the Liquor Traffic and vice-president of the national body. He had served as president of the national prohibition conference in Montreal in 1894 and his Sunday temperance meetings in the Horticultural (Allan) Gardens in Toronto were widely attended. Along with James Laughlin Hughes* and William Houston*, he formed a small band to support female suffrage, largely in hopes of sustaining women's support for temperance.

Hard hit by the real estate collapse of the 1890s, Fleming resigned from the mayoralty on 5 Aug. 1897 to become assessment commissioner for the city. In review, the *Globe* claimed he had accomplished more "good reform in a few years than all the mayors had over the previous ten years." He had fought for a minimum wage for public workers and, in his best known contribution to city management, presided over the creation of a board of control in 1896 [*see* Samuel Morley Wickett*]. After taking on the added job of property commissioner in 1903, he drew on his experience in realty to facilitate the city's acquisition of large pieces of land.

Although Fleming enjoyed public service, he left his job in December 1904 for a much higher salary as general manager of William MACKENZIE's Toronto Railway Company. He would hold this position, which allowed him to pay his creditors, until the company became part of the Toronto Transportation Commission system in 1921. His talent for inspiring confidence did much to shield the TRC's directors, and the associated Toronto Power Company, from the attacks of reformers on the railway's corrupt control of city transit. When, however, he pushed in 1906 for the acquisition of property at old Fort York for a new streetcar line, the project generated concern within the militia department and Toronto's heritage groups [*see* Sara MICKLE]. One major opponent of the TRC, city controller Francis Stephens Spence*, claimed in 1908 that "there is a general bitterness, a hostility, the spirit of Flemingphobia," but the public remained unwilling to attack the agreeable Fleming directly. (At the same time his involvement with Spence in the temperance movement provides an excellent example of the ability of R. J., as he was also known, to work with his critics.) Fleming would eventually manage or serve on the boards of several other Mackenzie firms, including Toronto and Niagara Power, Electrical Development, and the Winnipeg Electric Railway. It was this association that brought him into confrontation by 1917 with Sir Adam BECK in his campaign for public hydro and new radial railways in Ontario. Adding to the security provided by a place in the Mackenzie group, Fleming, a one-time director of the Gold and Silver Mines Development Company and

president of the Rossland Gold Mining, Development and Investment Company, had profitably re-entered the real estate, stock, and mining markets. Public trust led to his appointment to the board of the Toronto Harbour Commissioners in 1921. Drawn by the ongoing issue of radials on Toronto's waterfront, he ran for the mayoralty a final time in 1923, only to lose to Charles Alfred Maguire by 840 votes.

Fleming seems to have led a simple lifestyle. When his Cabbagetown neighbours complained about the cattle at his home on Parliament Street – a vestige of his youth, when his parents had kept livestock – he moved about 1902 to a small estate on St Clair near Bathurst, though his Jerseys would continue to draw criticism. He also owned a farm in the Whitby area. In Toronto, he attended both St Clair Avenue Methodist (St Matthew's United) Church and the more elitist Timothy Eaton Memorial; still committed to temperance, in 1923 he became president of the Dominion Alliance. He moved again, in 1924, to the 955-acre Donlands Farm, between Leaside and the Don River, which he had bought two years before from William Findlay MACLEAN. He died there suddenly of pleurisy in October 1925, leaving an estate worth more than $1 million, and was buried in the city in Mount Pleasant Cemetery.

Robert J. Fleming's career as a public servant had spanned less than two decades, yet thousands of Torontonians and prominent figures from other parts of Canada turned out to mourn his passing. The *Globe*'s lengthy coverage claimed he had been "one of the best-known and most personally popular figures in the city." Mayor Thomas Foster ordered its flag flown at half mast. The source of Fleming's appeal was his knack for combining practical politics, reformist zeal, and an exuberant personality. His unquestionably ethical behaviour and kindly Christian aura won him the respect of many adversaries. Ontario premier George Howard Ferguson*, a staunch opponent of his prohibitionist campaigns, noted sadly that, with Fleming's demise, "a great public figure has been removed."

GAYLE M. COMEAU

ANQ-M, CE601-S109, 23 déc. 1879. AO, RG 22-305, no.53233; RG 80-5-0-165, no.14446; RG 80-8-0-1015, no.37912. *Globe*, 27–28 Oct. 1925. *Toronto Daily Star*, 28–29 Dec. 1906; 17 Feb., 30 Aug., 14 Oct., 25 Nov. 1922; 23 May 1924; 26–27 Oct. 1925. Christopher Armstrong and H. V. Nelles, *The revenge of the Methodist bicycle company: Sunday streetcars and municipal reform in Toronto, 1887–1897* (Toronto, 1977). *Canadian annual rev.*, 1901–24/25. *Canadian men and women of the time* (Morgan; 1898 and 1912). Graeme Decarie, "Something old, something new . . . : aspects of prohibitionism in Ontario in the 1890s," in *Oliver Mowat's Ontario*, ed. Donald Swainson (Toronto, 1972), 154–71. *Directory*, Toronto, 1875–1925. C. A. S. Hall, "Electrical utilities in Ontario under private ownership, 1890–1914" (PHD thesis, Univ. of Toronto, 1968). Middleton,

Municipality of Toronto. H. V. Nelles, *The politics of development: forests, mines & hydro-electric power in Ontario, 1849–1941* (Toronto, 1974). W. R. Plewman, *Adam Beck and the Ontario Hydro* (Toronto, 1947). V. L. Russell, *Mayors of Toronto* (Erin, Ont., 1982). Charles Sauriol, *Remembering the Don: a rare record of earlier times within the Don River valley* (Scarborough, Ont., 1981), 107–12. F. S. Spence, "Some suggestions as to Toronto Street Railway problems," in *Saving the Canadian city: the first phase, 1880–1920 . . .*, ed. Paul Rutherford (Toronto, 1974), 59–63. *Who's who in Canada*, 1922.

FLEMMING, JAMES KIDD, schoolteacher, businessman, and politician; b. 27 April 1868 in Lower Woodstock, N.B., son of Thomas Flemming and Sarah Kerr; m. 24 Dec. 1890 Sarah Helena Flemming (d. 1949) in McKenzie Corner, N.B., and they had three sons, including Hugh John*, and two daughters; d. 10 Feb. 1927 in Woodstock.

After teaching school for two years, James Kidd Flemming became a travelling salesman for a Saint John wholesaling firm, work that made him widely known throughout New Brunswick. He later opened a grocery and farm produce business in Woodstock in partnership with his brother Thomas, but this business was dissolved in 1895. The brothers then bought out the C. A. Harmon general mercantile business in nearby Peel. They also operated a small sawmill in Hartland. When their store went bankrupt, Flemming paid back their creditors a hundred cents on the dollar, though there was no legal requirement for him to do so.

He was defeated in his first two attempts at a seat in the provincial legislature for Carleton in 1895 and 1899, but the following year he won a by-election, and he was re-elected in 1903 and 1908. A tall, strikingly handsome man and a gifted orator, he was at first extremely popular, and many people found his natural charm appealing. After the Conservatives under John Douglas Hazen* came to power in 1908, Flemming was appointed provincial secretary and receiver general. Three years later, on 16 Oct. 1911, he became premier when Hazen entered the federal cabinet of Robert Laird Borden*. He also assumed responsibility for the province's extensive crown lands as surveyor general and for its railways. In June the following year he led the Conservative party to its greatest electoral victory in the history of New Brunswick – 42 of 46 seats in the legislature, in addition to two independent Conservative seats.

Flemming held moderate political views. Although not in favour of government ownership of telephones, he promised to encourage the extension of private lines in rural areas. He supported immigration to repopulate deserted farms and improved roads to enhance the value of farm property. During the 1912 session workmen's compensation was extended to granite workers and stonecutters, and the factories act

strengthened to prevent employment of children under 16. A railway along the west side of the Saint John River valley had long been a dream of the premier's, and it had considerable local support. To assist its construction by the Saint John and Quebec Railway Company, the government introduced legislation guaranteeing $4 million in bonds.

Only two years later the premier faced political ruin. His downfall began in April 1914 when Louis-Auguste Dugal, the Liberal MLA for Madawaska, introduced two motions. The first claimed that in 1913 Flemming, through the agency of William H. Berry, an official in the Crown Land Department and thus under Flemming's direct control, "did unlawfully extort from divers large lessees of Crown Timber Limits within this province, a sum of fifteen dollars per square mile of their said timber limits, over and above the amount of bonus paid by them respectively," as set out in the department's annual report. Dugal charged the premier with acquiring, through Berry, some $100,000 in this way. Before 1913, lumbermen had been able to cut timber on crown-leased limits on the basis of public tendering, paying stumpage for the harvest and eight dollars per square mile. But changes to the legislation introduced that year provided for the fees to be set by the surveyor general, one of the portfolios held by Flemming.

Dugal's second motion contended that the Saint John and Quebec Railway Company contractors had been compelled "to pay and did pay large sums of money to the members of the Government in the year 1912, before they obtained their contracts." Flemming, with responsibility for railways, had personally conducted negotiations with Maine businessman Arthur Robinson Gould, the chief promoter of the railway. Dugal believed he could prove that $10,000 was paid to Flemming and $1,500 to Harry Fulton McLeod, a former provincial secretary. When the MLA addressed the legislature on 9 April regarding these allegations, he requested permission to speak in French. The speaker ruled that he could do so only with the permission of the house. This was readily given, and it marked the first time that French was used in the New Brunswick legislature.

The charges against Flemming had been put together by a powerful group of back-room Liberals known as the "Dark Lantern Brigade" and made up of party organizers Edward S. Carter and Peter John Veniot* and lawyer and MP Frank Broadstreet CARVELL, who had been an MLA for Carleton, the riding represented by Flemming. The trio provided ammunition for the two inexperienced opposition members, both Acadians with only a limited command of English. A "man of ruthless tenacity," Carvell proved to be Flemming's nemesis. As lawyer for the estate of Timothy Lynch, a prominent New Brunswick lumberman, he had discovered that the Lynch company, in renewing a crown lease in 1913, had paid $1,830 to a Conservative political fund.

After Dugal introduced his first motion, Flemming became violently ill, and he did not return to the legislature for the debate, though he was present to introduce legislation that increased the province's guarantee for the railway bonds from $25,000 to $35,000 per mile. George Johnson Clarke became acting premier, and Flemming was given a leave of absence until the charges were disposed of. On 24 April he told the *St. John Standard*, "I have never received one dollar or the equivalent of a dollar directly or indirectly from any limit-holder in the Province of New Brunswick since I have been Minister of Lands and Mines." He was prepared to resign his seat while remaining premier if Carvell would enter the ensuing contest in Carleton, leaving the electors "to judge the case and pronounce their verdict upon it at the ballot box."

The allegations rocked the New Brunswick Conservatives. In an attempt to control the damage, they settled on two royal commissions to inquire into Dugal's charges. The commissions, both chaired by Supreme Court judge Harrison Andrew McKeown*, were established by Lieutenant Governor Josiah WOOD in May. Mariner George Teed led Flemming's defence, and Carvell represented Dugal. Testimony before the timber limits commission was highly damaging to the government. It revealed that Berry had indeed approached crown land lessees to contribute to the Conservative party on the basis of $15 per square mile of timber limits, and a total of $71,000 had been collected from large operators such as John Percival BURCHILL. Berry, a key witness, had fled to the United States before he could be served with a summons, telling friends that he did not intend "to be made a goat" for the Conservatives. Flemming testified before the commission that Berry had told him the lessees "were desirous of making a contribution to the [Conservative] funds" and that he had said any contributions must be "absolutely voluntary." After the "second or third time" they had discussed the matter, he had told Berry that neither of them should have anything to do with the money and that contributions should go directly to the Conservative party treasurer.

On this charge the commission found "That the money was in fact extorted by Berry is fully proved. That the Premier was well aware that moneys were being collected for a purpose unquestionably improper, is also amply shown. It is also manifest that he directed the disposition of such moneys when collected, also that he acquiesced in the collection of such moneys at a time and from a source highly and grievously improper." The inquiry noted that Flemming could not have been ignorant of Berry's activities, but it did not find extortion in his case, stating,

"There is a great deal to support such a view, but, in our opinion, it stops short of such sufficiency of proof as would justify the Commission in declaring the charge of directing the extortion proved."

Far worse for Flemming were revelations concerning the Saint John and Quebec Railway Company. John Kennedy, a railway contractor, testified that in 1912 he had paid Flemming $2,000, after the premier told him that there was an election on, and "you ought to help us along with some money." The premier admitted receiving the money for the Conservative party campaign, but he insisted that no compulsion was involved. Nevertheless, the commission observed that, "while there was no threat or menace in the conversation, we have no hesitation in concluding that compulsion undoubtedly existed . . . we think and find that Hon. Mr. Flemming is guilty of this act of compulsion which has been charged against him."

The commissions' reports were presented to the lieutenant governor in early October but were not made public until 19 November. In the meantime Wood shared their findings with a number of prominent Conservatives, including Hazen and Flemming. On 29 October he sent a letter described as secret to Hazen, saying that he had met with Flemming, who thought he should retain the premiership. Wood wrote, "The report of the Commission, whether right or wrong, I feel we are bound to accept and act upon. It appears to me therefore, my clear duty is not to retain him as Premier . . . he should voluntarily retire." The lieutenant governor added that there could be no objection to Flemming resigning as premier but keeping his seat in the legislature.

Following the release of the commissions' findings, the premier published a lengthy response to the electors of New Brunswick. The inquiries, he argued, had found he had knowledge that a fund was being contributed to, but not that the donations were not entirely voluntary. He did not believe "the extortion was of a very strong character." While he exercised no control over the money, he hoped the party treasurer would return it to the lumbermen. With respect to the railway, Flemming claimed that the allegations were "cruel and unjust." He noted that Kennedy had received a first contract before the money was paid and a second contract not until 15 months after. Once again he challenged Carvell to run against him in Carleton, saying that he had the strongest faith in the justice of the people and he had given them honest and faithful service.

There was widespread public condemnation of the premier. Some of the harshest attacks came from the Protestant clergy. A Congregational minister in Saint John, observing that "God said, thou shall not steal," accused Flemming, a former Sunday school teacher, of "brazen impudence." Even newspapers that normally supported the Conservative party, such as the

Flemming

Ottawa Citizen and the Toronto *World*, were highly critical. Senior Conservatives felt that he must resign both the premiership and his seat. A week after the commission reports were released, newspaperman James Harvie CROCKET, a confidant of Hazen, was sent to Woodstock to meet with local Conservatives. That Lieutenant Governor Wood might dismiss the premier had aroused considerable fear in party circles. The strategy was to get Flemming to step down and for him to challenge Carvell as Conservative candidate in Victoria and Carleton in the next federal election. Initially, Crocket received little support for his plan. "The boys, however, finally agreed with me, that the logical way out of the difficulty was for Flemming to also resign his seat, and Flemming after remarking 'Then I am to become a complete victum [*sic*],' practically consented to do this."

The premier resigned on 6 December and was replaced by Clarke. He expected a federal election to be called within two to three years, but he had to wait eleven years before facing the electorate again. In the 1917 federal election, Sir Robert Borden asked Carvell, now a Liberal Unionist, to help organize support for his Union government in New Brunswick. No Unionist member was to be challenged by a Conservative. There followed one of the most dramatic episodes in New Brunswick politics. Flemming's supporters wanted him to run as a Conservative, but he entered the nomination meeting arm in arm with Carvell, his bitterest enemy, and in the speech of his career, he announced that he was withdrawing as official candidate and urged Conservatives to accept Carvell instead.

Because of ill health, Flemming was unable to run in the 1921 federal election, but four years later he won the seat in Victoria-Carleton in a landslide victory that, in his view, fully vindicated him; he was re-elected in 1926. As a member of the House of Commons, he did not play an active role because of continuing poor health. He called for increased Maritime trade with Cuba and the British West Indies and urged that Canadian grain be shipped through Canadian ports. He also took considerable interest in the affairs of the Canadian National Railways. In private life, he served as president, general manager, and director of Flemming and Gibson, a lumber business in Juniper, N.B.

The railway affair followed Flemming to his deathbed. In 1915 the company had defaulted on its contractual obligations, and the province took over its stock. Gould sought compensation of $500,000, and in 1916 the claim was subjected to arbitration by McKeown. Under questioning by Carvell, Gould admitted that he had paid Flemming $100,000 before the 1912 election. In his report of March 1918, McKeown found that since most of the money had gone to Flemming personally and Gould had "delib-

erately set out by payment of this money, to make his position secure and to evade the consequences of future defaults, should any be made by him, by placing the most trusted public man in the Province under his control," his claim for compensation should be rejected.

When the Liberals, under Walter Edward Foster*, returned to power in New Brunswick in early 1917, they were determined to get to the bottom of the railway controversy. Another commission of inquiry was established, and after commissioner John M. Stevens brought in his report in 1918, the government introduced legislation making the money paid to Flemming and others crown debts. A writ was served on the former premier to recover the $100,000, and technical objections brought by his lawyer were overruled. However, in November 1919 his physician told the court Flemming's health was so poor that he was incapable of appearing or giving evidence, and the case was held over indefinitely. In the end, no action was taken against him.

The railway scandal also pursued Gould into the United States. After he was elected to the Senate from Maine in 1926, his opponents challenged his right to sit because, they claimed, he had bribed the premier of New Brunswick. In a hearing before the committee on privileges and elections, Gould claimed that the railway company, not he, had paid the money. But Flemming was quoted in the *New York Times* as stating, "It is not true I was paid $100,000. . . . For my personal use or benefit, neither Mr. Gould or any of his assistants in the Saint John and Quebec Railway Co. ever paid me a single dollar or any larger amount directly or indirectly while the railway was under construction, nor before nor since." On 25 Jan. 1927 the committee sent Flemming a telegram inviting him to appear before it in Washington, but when the request arrived, he was seriously ill. He died two weeks later.

In 1961 political scientist Hugh G. Thorburn wrote that a common characteristic of all provincial campaigns in New Brunswick was "the attempt by one party to show the other to be either dishonest and corrupt, or irresponsible and wasteful." This was certainly the case in the early years of the 20th century. Despite having won one of the greatest electoral victories in the province's history, James Kidd Flemming was driven from office by alleged and proven scandal dredged up by the opposition. Whether the premier benefited personally from Gould's $100,000 payment, as his enemies alleged, or the money all went to the Conservative party, as he claimed, remains unanswered.

WENDELL E. FULTON

PANB, MC 80/1095; MC 1156. *New York Times*, 25 Jan. 1927. Can., House of Commons, *Debates*, 1927. *Canadian* annual rev., 1912–18. A. T. Doyle, *Front benches & back rooms: a story of corruption, muckraking, raw partisanship and intrigue in New Brunswick* (Toronto, 1976). N.B., Legislative Assembly, *Journal*, 1918, app., Report of the directors and chief engineer of the St. John and Quebec Railway Company for year ending March 15th., 1918: 33–44 (Interim and final report of commissioner J. M. Stevens, K.C., re Saint John and Quebec Railway Co.); 45–77 (Report re Gould arbitration and finding of Hon. H. A. McKeown, chief justice of the King's Bench Division); *Synoptic report of the proc.*, 1900–18; Royal commission concerning St. John and Quebec Railway Company charges, *Report* (Fredericton, 1915); Royal commission concerning timber limit charges, *Report* (Fredericton, 1915) (both royal commission reports also appear in N.B., Legislative Assembly, *Journal*, 1915). *Standard dict. of Canadian biog.* (Roberts and Tunnell). H. G. Thorburn, *Politics in New Brunswick* (Toronto, 1961). U.S., Senate, *Senator from Maine; hearings before a subcommittee of the committee on privileges and elections* (2v. in 1, Washington, 1927).

FLETT, WINONA MARGARET (Dixon), suffragist and social reformer; b. 10 June 1884 in South Dumfries Township, Ont., daughter of Isabella Bowie and James Flett, a farmer; m. 14 Oct. 1914 Frederick John Dixon* in Winnipeg, and they had three children, two of whom survived infancy; d. there 16 May 1922 of pneumonia.

In 1912 Winona Flett left Woodstock, Ont., with her mother and her sister Lynn to live in Winnipeg. On their arrival, Winona and Lynn, "tall handsome businesswomen," joined the newly established Political Equality League (renamed the Manitoba Political Equality League in 1913), which sought to obtain the provincial franchise for women. A stenographer, Winona served as the convener of the league's literature committee. When the league organized a petition for women's suffrage after the victory of the Liberal party under Tobias Crawford Norris* in the general election of August 1915, Flett was in charge of the document bearing the names of 39,584 women. Along with the league's president, Mary Elizabeth Crawford, its secretary, Lillian Kate Beynon* Thomas, and the oldest signatory of the petition, Amelia Burrell, Winona was photographed to record the successful campaign which in January 1916 resulted in Manitoba being the first province in Canada to enfranchise women. Winona was one of eight women to be invited to occupy seats on the floor of the Legislative Assembly, rather than in the public galleries, for the third reading of the bill.

Winona had worked actively in the community for a range of social reforms. She spoke with Beynon Thomas in May 1914 in favour of "a more rigid enforcement of the Factory Act in places where women and children are employed" and stressed the need to appoint a woman factory inspector. She campaigned for a colleague in the MPEL, Fred Dixon, in his successful bid for a seat as an independent Labour candidate in the provincial election of July 1914. At the People's Forum, a series of weekly lectures and discussions organized by James Shaver Woodsworth*, she spoke in 1914 on "Women in industrial and professional life." She would address the Forum again in 1915 and 1918 and she would lecture at the Labour Church [*see* William Ivens*] in 1919.

In October 1914 Flett had married Fred Dixon. Both the bride and the groom were described as having "active interests in various public movements." In 1917, during World War I, Fred opposed the registration of men for military service and conscription; with Winona he became committed to pacifism. Author and pacifist Gertrude Richardson*, who visited the Dixons that year, described them as "people whose ideals are those I call the Ideal of the New Humanity." Winona, she noted, was "a lovely woman, in form, mind and spirit. She shares [her husband's] loftiest ideals. When there was talk of imprisonment for all who resisted registration in the beginning of this year, Mrs. Dixon made all her arrangements to return to the business world, and earn her living, leaving her baby daughter with her mother."

Winona and Fred Dixon and their family were involved in pragmatic progressive politics. Arrested and charged with seditious conspiracy after the Winnipeg General Strike of 1919 [*see* Mike Sokolowiski*], Fred successfully conducted his own trial, arguing that he and other strikers were exercising British freedom of speech and the right to collective bargaining. Campaigning for Fred in the provincial election of June 1920, Winona urged the women of the province to vote Labour, their true champion. Dixon came at the top of the poll and was chosen leader of the Labour MLAs.

At her death, Winona Flett Dixon was described in the *Manitoba Free Press* as "well versed in industrial conditions, especially as they affected women. She was a gifted speaker and was keenly enthusiastic in the support of the principles she advocated." She had been able to combine "motherhood and public service." Attending her funeral were Liberal and Labour politicians, including Norris, the premier of the province, and colleagues from her suffrage and social reform causes. She was 37 years old.

MARY KINNEAR

AM, Events 173/3 (N9905); P 192. AO, RG 80-2-0-209, no.1778. Man., Dept. of Finance, Consumer and Corporate Affairs, Vital statistics (Winnipeg), nos.1914-134063, 1922-018170. *Grain Growers' Guide* (Winnipeg), 29 Dec. 1915, 5 Jan. 1916. *Manitoba Free Press*, 5 May, 2, 7, 9 July, 16 Oct. 1914; 17 May 1922. *Voice* (Winnipeg), 23 Oct. 1914, 22 Jan. 1915. *Western Labor News* (Winnipeg), 17 Jan. 1919; 11, 25 June, 5 Nov. 1920. *Winnipeg Tribune,* 28 Jan. 1916, 19 May 1922. Harry and Mildred Gutkin, *Profiles in dissent: the shaping of radical thought in the Canadian west* (Edmonton,

1997). D. N. Irvine, "Reform, war and industrial crisis in Manitoba: F. J. Dixon and the framework of consensus, 1903–1920" (MA thesis, Univ. of Man., Winnipeg, 1981). B. A. Roberts, *A reconstructed world: a feminist biography of Gertrude Richardson* (Montreal, 1996).

FLYNN, EDMUND JAMES, lawyer, professor, politician, and judge; b. 16 Nov. 1847 in Percé, Lower Canada, son of James Flynn, a fisherman, and Elizabeth Tostevin; m. first 11 May 1875, at Quebec, Augustine Côté (d. 1911), daughter of Augustin Côté*, publisher and owner of *Le Journal de Québec*, and they had 11 children, four of whom survived him; m. secondly 8 Jan. 1912 Marie-Cécile Pouliot, widow of Eugène Globensky, in Montreal; d. 7 June 1927 at Quebec and was buried in Notre-Dame de Belmont cemetery at Sainte-Foy, Que.

The Flynns, who had settled at Percé in the Gaspé region, were of Irish descent. Edmund James Flynn's paternal grandfather, Edmund, was born in Percé, where he managed a large commercial firm and was a customs officer. On his mother's side, his grandfather, John, was from Guernsey and his grandmother from Jersey. His father made his living from business, fishing, and farming. His mother was also born in Percé.

Bilingual and Roman Catholic, Edmund James studied at the Séminaire de Québec from 1860 to 1865. From 1867 to 1869 he had his initiation into administration as assistant registrar, assistant prothonotary, and assistant clerk to the Court of Queen's Bench, registrar of the Circuit Court for the District of Gaspé, and secretary-treasurer of the municipality of Percé. He studied law at the Université Laval in Quebec City from 1871 to 1873, obtaining his degree with distinction. On 16 Sept. 1873 he was called to the bar of the province of Quebec and he took up his profession in the region where he was born. The following year he moved to Quebec, where he was to live from then on. He would practise law there until 1914 in partnership with Édouard Rémillard, François-Xavier Drouin, and Jean Gosselin, and then with his son Francis. He would be *bâtonnier* of the Quebec bar from 1907 to 1909.

From the time he arrived in Quebec, Flynn taught a course in Roman law at the Université Laval, where he was to obtain a doctorate in law in 1878 at the age of 31. He would have a long career there as professor of Roman law until his death, member of the university council from 1891 to 1927, as well as dean of the law faculty and member of the board of governors from 1915 to 1921.

Flynn became interested in politics early in life. In 1874 he was the Liberal candidate for the riding of Gaspé in the federal general election, but because he was appointed at the same time to the faculty of the Université Laval he withdrew from the race. He ran again as a Liberal in Gaspé in 1875, this time in a provincial general election, but he was defeated by Dr Pierre-Étienne Fortin*. The following year Flynn accused him of having benefited from clerical interference. Once exonerated, Fortin bested him again in the by-election that was called for 2 July 1877, after the previous election was declared null and void.

On 1 May 1878 Flynn finally gained a seat, by acclamation, as the Liberal member for Gaspé in the Legislative Assembly. In this general election, his party under Henri-Gustave Joly* came to power, but both Liberals and Conservatives had the same number of seats in the house. The leader of the opposition, Joseph-Adolphe Chapleau*, made offers to some of the Liberal members to persuade them to abandon Joly and shift the balance of the house to the Conservatives. Flynn probably received a specific proposal from Chapleau. On 29 Oct. 1879 he and four of his Liberal colleagues voted for a motion by William Warren Lynch* calling for the establishment of a coalition government. He thereby stood against his party, which was seeking instead to abolish the Legislative Council. By joining the ranks of the Conservative party, these members reduced the Joly government to a minority and it had to resign.

The new premier, Chapleau, paid his debts and gave the renegade from Gaspé the portfolio of crown lands. After a mere year and a half in the Legislative Assembly, Flynn had become a commissioner. Meticulous, honest, and conscientious, he got down to work under the watchful eyes of the Liberals, who tried to embarrass this traitor in the house, especially on the question of the Legislative Council.

When Chapleau resigned as premier in 1882 to move into federal politics, his successor, Joseph-Alfred Mousseau*, did not include Flynn in his cabinet. His time in purgatory did not last long, because Mousseau was replaced in January 1884 by John Jones Ross*, who invited Flynn, a moderate conservative, to become commissioner of railways (1884–86) and then solicitor general (1885–87). In the house in 1886 Flynn had to confront such tough adversaries as Honoré Mercier*, when, in the absence of Ross, he had to defend the provincial government's refusal to censure the federal government's stance in the Riel affair [*see* Louis Riel*].

Early in 1887, Mercier's Parti National came to power on a groundswell of public opinion related to the Riel affair, and Mercier replaced Louis-Olivier TAILLON, who had just succeeded Ross. For the first time Flynn found himself in opposition. Then, in the provincial general election of 1890, in which Mercier was again victorious, he lost the seat he had won as a Conservative in 1879, 1881, 1884, and 1886. He ran in the riding of Quebec in the federal general election of 1891, but was again defeated. During the period when he was out of the house, Flynn devoted himself exclusively to his law practice and university teaching.

Dismissed as premier by Lieutenant Governor Auguste-Réal Angers* following the Baie des Chaleurs Railway scandal, Mercier had to relinquish power on 16 Dec. 1891 to the Conservatives under Charles Boucher* de Boucherville. Within a few days Flynn became commissioner of crown lands again. In the provincial general election of 8 March 1892, taking no chances he ran in two ridings, Gaspé and Matane, as the law allowed. Elected in both, he opted for Gaspé and retained his office as commissioner. At the end of 1892 he was also acting attorney general. An enlightened, efficient man capable of big ideas, in 1895 he revised the mining act, which he had put through in 1880, settled the old question of property titles on the Îles de la Madeleine, and created the Parc National des Laurentides and the Parc de la Montagne Tremblante.

At the beginning of May 1896, Taillon, who had succeeded Boucherville as premier a few years earlier, went to Ottawa to become postmaster general. Since his appointment had been made quickly, Taillon wrote to Lieutenant Governor Chapleau on 4 May that "it is hardly appropriate for me to offer you my opinion on the choice of my successor." Chapleau wanted to offer the office to a member of the moderate wing of the Conservative party, represented by Guillaume-Alphonse Nantel* and Flynn, rather than to a cabinet member connected to its ultramontane or Castor wing. Since Chapleau ruled out the Castors and they ruled out Nantel, Flynn, who was the senior member of the cabinet and against whom no personal objections were raised, was a good compromise. The lieutenant governor made a symbolic offer to Nantel, who refused to form a new cabinet. Thus on 11 May 1896 Flynn became the tenth premier of the province of Quebec. In his cabinet, within which Thomas Chapais* and Louis-Philippe PELLETIER were the strongest members, he kept the portfolio of public works for himself. However, the team would have to function without two party stalwarts, Taillon and Thomas Chase-Casgrain*, who would soon follow Taillon to Ottawa.

Flynn's agenda, which was less austere than Taillon's but more cautious than Mercier's, included conversion of the public debt (through replacement of the bonds in circulation by longer term bonds at a lower rate of interest), higher railway subsidies, reorganization of government departments, more rational development of natural resources, and abolition of the property transfer tax that had been imposed in 1892. The premier, who had in addition been leader of the Conservatives since 13 June, turned his attention to matters related to primary education, in particular financial assistance to poor municipalities and an increase in teachers' salaries. Debt conversion and railway subsidies were the most debated subjects in

the house. Conversely, the legislation known as the Homesteads Act, intended to protect settlers against the seizure of essential property (200 acres of land, house, livestock, farm implements, household equipment), was favourably received.

The Conservatives' term of office was coming to an end, however, and it was time to think about an election. Polling day was set for 11 May 1897. Within only a year of his appointment as premier, Flynn had already accomplished a great deal. During that same period of time, two of his daughters had died of some form of tuberculosis; two others would fall victim to the same disease, one in 1898 and the other in 1906. The Conservative leader was faced with a very unfavourable situation, due, among other things, to the normal wear and tear of being in power, the Liberals' arrival in strength in Ottawa under Wilfrid Laurier*, the strong resentment against the Conservatives because of their decisions on the Manitoba schools question [see Thomas Greenway*] and the Riel affair, as well as the rehabilitation of Mercier, who had died in October 1894. Pelletier, who served as attorney general in Flynn's cabinet, wrote to him on 17 Nov. 1896, "I do not think we can win the election starting as we are at this moment. . . . We have cut costs, we have healed the wounds inflicted on the province: this is good, but it is not enough." Furthermore, the incumbent premier was not well known (especially in Montreal), and with his rather reserved and lacklustre personality he was not an orator who could stir up crowds.

The political agenda Flynn put forward during the campaign was a continuation of his achievements of the previous year. He asked to be judged on his program and its results, and for federal issues to be kept out of the provincial election. The Conservatives mounted a furious attack on the Mercier government, which was still being blamed for all existing ills. As for the Liberal leader, Félix-Gabriel Marchand*, he concentrated mainly on the Conservative government's record and its poor financial management. Laurier's organizers also arrived in strength and the election campaign soon took on the appearance of a confrontation between Flynn and Laurier. On polling day, Marchand's Liberals won an easy victory, taking 52 seats. The Conservative leader, one of the 22 candidates elected for his party, kept his seat in Gaspé, but by a margin of only 11 votes. With the fall of Flynn's cabinet, the last Conservative government in Quebec disappeared and the party was not to regain power in the province. The Union Nationale, which would win the 1936 election, would emerge from a coalition of the Conservative party and the Action Libérale Nationale.

Flynn now became the inconspicuous leader of a demoralized opposition. The country was enjoying a notable period of economic prosperity and both the federal Liberals and their provincial counterparts had everything going in their favour. The latter called an early general election for 7 Dec. 1900 and again swept the province with no difficulty. During the campaign, Flynn made a half-hearted and largely unsuccessful attempt to denounce federal interference in provincial politics. (A few months earlier, Marchand's death had made it necessary for a new premier to be appointed, and it was reportedly Laurier who had decided in favour of Simon-Napoléon Parent*.) Rather than risk running in Gaspé, Flynn chose the riding of Nicolet, where his party had won every election since 1867, with the exception of 1890. He took the seat with a majority of 41 votes.

On 3 Nov. 1904 Laurier was returned to power in the federal election. The next day, while Flynn was still leader of the opposition in Quebec, Parent had the Legislative Assembly dissolved and set 25 November as the day to go to the polls, thereby forcing the voters to make up their minds in record time. Since the Liberals had carried 64 of 74 ridings in 1900, all they had to do was nominate the same members. Flynn was not in the same situation and had little time to get ready. He signed a manifesto denouncing Parent's actions and accusing him of trying to identify his candidature with Laurier's. The opposition would not play that game, he declared. He then ordered his followers to challenge the legitimacy of the election (which he described as a power grab) by abstaining from it. He himself did not run. The directive was not universally followed, and again the Liberals won an easy victory. The following year, having no seat, Flynn resigned as leader of the Conservative party, which by then had only one daily paper, *L'Événement*, and just seven members in the house.

After some 30 years in politics, Flynn now had to resume a professional life with a lower profile – his law practice and university teaching. In 1908 he made a final, unsuccessful bid to return to the political scene by running in Dorchester in the federal general election. He brought his son Francis, recently called to the bar, into partnership with him in 1911. Then came more bereavements. His wife Augustine died that year after a brief illness and in June 1919 Francis died of pulmonary tuberculosis. Flynn had been appointed a judge of the Superior Court for the district of Beauce in June 1914. In June 1920 he became a judge of the Court of King's Bench, an office he held for the rest of his life.

More at home in court or in the classroom than on a political platform, Edmund James Flynn was a conscientious politician known for his attention to detail, his thorough grasp of the issues, and his masterful and careful reasoning. This professor of law carried out some very worthwhile legislative work, especially in the Department of Crown Lands. Eloquent, skilful, and convincing as a speaker, he was especially at ease with constitutional questions. He showed sound judgement; his caution often, indeed, made him hesitate before taking action. But his political instinct, his sensitivity to the moods of the electorate, his vision of the major social issues, as well as his fighting spirit, all came to naught. With his lacklustre, unassuming, and phlegmatic (one might even say austere) personality, this transitional politician, who never learned how to make small talk, became premier of Quebec at the wrong time. Flynn could not compete with such charismatic personalities as Laurier, Joseph-Israël Tarte*, or even Marchand.

MARC DESJARDINS

No biography of Edmund James Flynn exists. The main archival source for his life is a modest collection in ANQ-Q, P734, S1, consisting of correspondence, telegrams, speeches, documents relating to governmental and legislative affairs, and addresses to electors, as well as personal and family information. Additional material is in LAC, MG 27, II, F8. Flynn's speeches are collected in various pamphlets. The *Debates* of the Legislative Assembly of the province of Quebec, 1878–1904, constitute an important source for his political career, particularly those for the sixth session of the eighth legislature (1896–97).

ANQ-BSLGIM, CE102-S19, 18 nov. 1847. ANQ-Q, CE301-S1, 11 mai 1875. BCM-G, RBMS, Saint-Jacques-le-Mineur (Montréal), 8 janv. 1912. *L'Action catholique* (Québec), 7 juin 1927. *Le Devoir*, 7 juin 1927. *L'Événement*, 8 juin 1927. *Le Soleil*, 7 juin 1927. Ken Annett, "To clutch the golden keys: the distinguished career of Edmund James Flynn," *SPEC* (New Carlisle, Que.), 10 (1984), no.42: 14. *Canadian men and women of the time* (Morgan; 1898). Marc Desjardins et al., *Histoire de la Gaspésie* (nouv. éd., Sainte-Foy, Qué., 1999). *DPQ*. Jacques Flynn, *Un bleu du Québec à Ottawa* (Sillery, Qué., 1998). J.-A. Lamarche, *Les 27 premiers ministres* (Montréal, 1997). Laurent Laplante, "Edmund-James Flynn," in "Portraits des premiers ministres du Québec" (Radio-Canada broadcast, Montreal, 1982; copy in BCM-G). *Où sont les cliquards: le groupe Flynn, ce qu'il en coûte à la province* ([Québec?, 1897?]). Rumilly, *Hist. de la prov. de Québec*, vols.8–9, 12. George Stewart, "The premiers of Quebec since 1867," *Canadian Magazine*, 8 (November 1896–April 1897): 289–98.

FORBES, ALEXANDER MacKENZIE TORRANCE, orthopaedic and paediatric surgeon, professor of surgery, and army officer; b. 21 Dec. 1874 in Montreal, son of Alexander MacKenzie Forbes, an insurance agent, and Elizabeth Fisher Torrance; m. there 9 Nov. 1912 Henrietta Muriel Coristine, widow of Dr Howard M. Church, and they had one daughter; d. there 16 May 1929.

MacKenzie Forbes's mother came from a prominent Montreal family that included her grandfather John Torrance* and her cousin David*. After attending the High School of Montreal, Forbes entered McGill University in 1890 at age 15. In 1894 he enrolled in McGill's faculty of medicine, from which he graduated with honours in 1898. Later that year, on 18 September, he obtained his licence to practice. He then worked, probably for a year, as a government physician on the French Shore of Newfoundland and visited Wilfred Thomason Grenfell*'s mission in Labrador, where he saw so many children with bone, foot, and lower limb deformities that he became interested in orthopaedic surgery. He received training in orthopaedics in New York City at the Hospital for the Ruptured and Crippled as a house officer. After returning to Montreal in 1902, he was appointed assistant demonstrator in anatomy at McGill.

Because they had no hospital admitting or operating privileges, Forbes and a group of friends met on 25 Nov. 1902 and decided to open a children's hospital in Montreal where they could treat orthopaedic disease. By November 1903 a building had been rented and converted into a hospital with 10 beds. Francis John Shepherd, Alexander Dougall Blackader*, Harold Beveridge Cushing, Robert Tait McKenzie*, and Forbes formed the medical staff. The Children's Memorial Hospital admitted its first patients in January 1904 and can be considered one of the first institutions in Canada devoted to the treatment of children's orthopaedic diseases.

Forbes was chief of surgery at Children's Memorial and he operated on many types of orthopaedic deformities. Typical operations dealt with club feet, tuberculosis of the spine, scoliosis, the complications of spina bifida, spastic dipligia, defects from osteomyelitis, deformities of spine and limbs from poliomyelitis, torticollis, bowed legs, birth defects of the arms and legs, Volkmann's ischaemic contractures (reflex sympathetic dystrophy), and trauma. He set fractures, reduced dislocations, repaired cleft palates, transplanted tendons, and applied spica plaster splints to the hips, feet, and spine. He was finally given inpatient operating privileges at the Montreal General Hospital in 1906 and was appointed orthopaedic surgeon to the hospital the same year.

After two years, the children's hospital desperately needed to move. Admissions continued to increase and in many cases hospital stay was prolonged because Forbes and the other doctors treated increasingly complex deformities. A new site was chosen on the southwest side of Mount Royal on Cedar Avenue. Money was raised to purchase the land and construct the new hospital in 1907 and the doors opened in 1909. Forbes, who took an interest in every aspect of the hospital's administration, was chief of the hospital and surgical services and Cushing was chief of medicine.

Meanwhile, Forbes had continued to lecture at McGill as demonstrator in anatomy during 1907–9 and as assistant demonstrator in orthopaedic surgery for 1908–10. In 1911 he was appointed the first chief of orthopaedics at the Montreal General. Despite this new appointment, he was named only a lecturer in orthopaedics at McGill the following year; he would hold that post until 1920.

At the outset of World War I Forbes volunteered for military service. In the fall of 1914 he was sent to Valcartier, near Quebec City, to begin training at the newly established No.1 Canadian General Hospital. After eight days at Valcartier he departed with the hospital for Salisbury Plain, England. Although he had no training in psychiatry, Forbes, a captain, had the unpleasant duty of interviewing soldiers who were thought to be unfit for service for psychiatric reasons. He was temporarily commissioned major on 17 April 1915 and the following month his unit went to Boulogne, France. In a tent hospital Forbes and a few other surgeons treated wounds with a quantity of tissue destruction and sepsis never imagined in Montreal. With experience the staff changed its procedures and septic wounds were scrubbed and drained and the majority of the wounded survived. In July 1915 1,065 patients were admitted, 617 of them were wounded, 335 were operated on, and 26 died from wounds. By November 1915, of the 1,993 admissions, 470 were wounded, 321 were operated on, and only 15 died from wounds, a remarkable record. McGill University tried to send its surgeons to the front on rotation, so in December 1915 Forbes was recalled to Canada for military duty; he was discharged on 30 June 1917 and returned to his work in paediatric orthopaedics. After the war he served on the national executive of the Great War Veterans' Association of Canada.

The prolonged hospitalization and rehabilitation of many school-aged patients that Forbes and other surgeons treated created educational problems for the children. The initial solution was to hire a teacher for the children's hospital. Awareness of the problem also led to a greater concern about the education of those crippled children in Montreal who could not attend regular schools and who were not hospitalized. Forbes and his associates thus founded the School for Crippled Children on Cedar Avenue, east of the children's hospital. It opened in 1914 with a few children who were transported to and from the school in hospital ambulances; by the end of the first year almost 100 children were enrolled. Forbes would remain a director until his death.

Forbes's excellent work led to his appointment as clinical professor of orthopaedics at McGill in 1922 and it attracted the attention of the Shriners, a North American fraternity interested in helping crippled children. On Cedar Avenue between the Children's Memorial Hospital and the School for Crippled Children, they established the Shriners Hospital for Crippled Children – Montreal Unit, the 10th in their system of orthopaedic hospitals in North America. It was opened on 18 Feb. 1925. Forbes had been appointed its first chief of orthopaedics on 19 April 1924 and served

Forbes

in this position until he died. Operations by Forbes and other surgeons on indigent crippled children from all over Canada were paid for by the Shriners.

MacKenzie Forbes had been elected to the American Orthopaedic Association in 1908 and became its president in 1928. He was president of the Montreal Medico-Chirurgical Society in 1919. He wrote papers on orthopaedic cases and developed a complicated device for treating scoliosis which was never successful. At the peak of his career he developed myocarditis and died suddenly from this disease in Montreal at age 54. He had made significant contributions to paediatric orthopaedic surgery, to the foundation of two hospitals, and to the organization of educational services for crippled children.

JOSEPH HANAWAY

Alexander MacKenzie Torrance Forbes is the author of "A case of lues venerea with an unusually protracted incubation period," *Montreal Medical Journal*, 28 (1899): 942–43; "Notes on the etiology and pathology of catheter fever: with the results of an investigation as to the prophylactic treatment," *Montreal Medical Journal*, 28: 333–38; *Reconstructive surgery in peace based on orthopaedic surgery in war* (Philadelphia, 1919); *Soldier and the land: vice-president of Great War Veterans' Association points to need of a new national policy for Canada* ([Winnipeg, 1919?]); *Canada in 1920* ([Montreal, 1920?]); and *Essays and lectures on clinical surgery* ([Philadelphia], 1922).

ANQ-M, CE601-S68, 17 mars 1875. BCM-G, RBMB, St George's (Anglican) Church (Montreal), 9 Nov. 1912. LAC, RG 150, Acc. 1992–93/166, box 3178. Shriners Hospitals for Children – Canada (Montreal), Admissions book, 1925–44; Record of operations, 1925–44. W. H. Atherton, *Montreal, 1534–1914* (3v., Montreal, 1914). Kenneth Cameron, *History of No.1 General Hospital, Canadian Expeditionary Force ... 1914–1919* (Sackville, N.B., 1938). Canadian Medical Assoc., *Journal* (Toronto), 21 (1929): 109. L. M. Kruger and S. R. LaForte, *Chiefs of staff, then and now: a history of the chiefs of Shriners Hospitals for Crippled Children, 1922–1994* ([Springfield, Mass., 1994?]). H. E. MacDermot, "Dr. Mackenzie Forbes and his hospital," *McGill News* (Montreal), 27, no.2 (spring 1956): 35, 62. McGill Univ., Faculty of medicine, *Calendar* (Montreal), 1922. Montreal General Hospital, *Annual report*, 1911–12. J. B. Scriver, *The Montreal Children's Hospital: years of growth* (Montreal, 1979). *The storied province of Quebec; past and present*, ed. W. [C. H.] Wood et al. (5v., Toronto, 1931–32).

FORBES, JOHN (baptized **Jean-Paul-Antoine**), priest, White Father, and bishop; b. 10 Jan. 1864 on Île Perrot, Lower Canada, son of John Forbes, a farmer, and Octavie Léger; d. 13 March 1926 in Billère, near Pau, France.

John Forbes came from a family of Scottish descent that had become integrated by language and religion into the French Canadian population through intermarriage. The name John, used by his family and friends from early childhood and by himself all his life, recalled his ancestral roots. His parents moved to Montreal in April 1869. The eldest of 16 children, John received a deeply religious education. In September 1870 he and his younger brother Guillaume* were enrolled in the kindergarten run in the Asile Nazareth by the Sisters of Charity of the Hôpital Général of Montreal. From 1872 to 1878, thanks to their maternal uncle Odilon Léger, a well-to-do merchant who took an interest in their education, John and Guillaume attended the Catholic Commercial Academy of Montreal, which was headed by the famous pedagogue Urgel-Eugène Archambeault*. They were both considered brilliant, well-behaved, and devout students. The Sulpicians, who were the chaplains of their school and the pastors of their parish of Notre-Dame, guided them gently towards the priesthood, making them their altar boys at mass and giving them Latin lessons in the presbytery. In September 1878 they accepted the boys into the third year (Method) at the Petit Séminaire de Montréal. Both brothers donned the cassock on 13 May 1883 while completing their final year (the second of the Philosophy program), and they finished their theological studies in 1886. It was now time for the crucial decisions that would transform their dreams into reality. In the fall of 1881 John had read the story of two martyred Catholic missionaries in Urundi (Burundi), in Africa, and it had kindled in him a desire to devote his life to missionary work among Africans. In 1883 he had met a White Father who had come to Montreal to promote the charitable work of the Society of Missionaries of Africa, a congregation founded in 1868 by Archbishop Charles-Martial Lavigerie of Algiers. This meeting had so fired his enthusiasm that he wanted to leave for Africa at once, but the Sulpicians had counselled him to let his missionary commitment ripen. Time had reinforced his decision and on 12 Aug. 1886, through the financial help of Sulpician Jean-Amable Trémolet, he set sail for Africa. His brother Guillaume would opt for the secular clergy and become bishop of Joliette and later archbishop of Ottawa.

On 3 Sept. 1886 Forbes reached Maison-Carrée, the mother house and noviciate of the White Fathers, which was not far from Algiers. He donned the habit on 22 September and gradually, by making the rules and spirituality of the community his own, he became Father Forbes. In his spare time he studied music and Arabic. In 1887 he did another year of theology at the Séminaire Saint-Louis in Carthage, near Tunis, where he took his vow as a missionary on 25 Sept. 1888 and was ordained on 6 October. His dream was to leave for a mission field, but his superiors assigned him to a teaching position. He was sent to Jerusalem, where he was supervisor of studies at the Séminaire Sainte-Anne, known as the Collège Français, from October 1888 to September 1889, and then professor of

366

French and Greek as well as spiritual director until September 1893. This missionary school trained clergy of the Eastern rite to serve various communities of indigenous Christians who were still in communion with the Roman Catholic Church. Recalled to the mother house, Forbes was assistant director of the noviciate, professor of Arabic and Kiswahili, and spiritual director until the summer of 1900. Two important events occurred during his stay there. In January 1894 he went to London with his superior, Mgr Léon Livinhac, to inform Lord Rosebery, secretary of state for foreign affairs, and Herbert Alfred Cardinal Vaughan about the religious situation in Uganda, where the activities of the Imperial British East Africa Company, which had been charged with developing the territories that were within the British sphere of influence or under the authority of a British protectorate, had poisoned relations between Catholics and Protestants. (In March 1898 the British government would pay £10,000 sterling to the equatorial missions as compensation for damage caused by Protestants.) From September 1895 to September 1896 Forbes toured Canada to solicit donations from Catholics, stir their missionary spirit, and recruit future missionaries. This tour would pave the way for a house to be opened in Canada for the White Fathers.

In the summer of 1900 the time was ripe. The episcopate, the Sulpicians, and many spiritual leaders felt that there was not enough missionary zeal in North America, especially among seminarians. At the urging of Sulpician Charles LECOQ, the White Fathers assigned Forbes the task of setting up an institution for postulants or a missionary school in Canada. Despite his keen desire to work in the African missions, he deferred to the will of his superiors and arrived in Montreal on 2 July 1900, but Archbishop Paul Bruchési*, whose archdiocese was already overburdened with charitable endeavours, expressed reservations. Forbes had more success at Quebec. On 11 March 1901 Archbishop Louis-Nazaire BÉGIN officially authorized him to open a centre there for study and recruitment, adding, however, that he could not give the White Fathers any financial support. That would not stop the project. Since his return from Africa, Forbes had been able to raise enough funds by preaching and lecturing in Canada and the United States, and by other means, to get it set up. On 10 Aug. 1901 he moved into a building he had rented at 41 Rue des Remparts, near the Université Laval, where the students would take courses in theology. He was soon joined by two White Fathers from Africa and on 28 August he welcomed his first six recruits from the province of Quebec. On 8 September, Archbishop Bégin officially blessed the new school for postulants, which moved to a house at 37 Rue des Remparts in May 1902. It was a modest beginning.

During the 13 years that he was its superior, six new postulants on average would enrol annually except for the year 1909–10, when there would be none. After a year of training the postulants went to the mother house in Algiers for their noviciate and to Carthage for their scholasticate. To publicize the cause and the work of the White Fathers, Forbes gave many lectures in parishes and seminaries, often using his projector for illustration. In January 1905 he launched at Quebec the monthly magazine *Les Missions d'Afrique des Pères blancs*, which is still published as *Mission*. In January 1909 he would add an English edition, *African Missions of the White Fathers*.

Father Forbes also helped establish a school for postulants of the Sœurs Missionnaires de Notre-Dame d'Afrique, a community founded in 1869 by Cardinal Lavigerie and Marie-Renée Roudaut, named Mother Marie-Salomé. At her request he sought the approval of Archbishop Bégin, who gave his consent for this new foundation after some hesitation. On 26 Oct. 1903 four White Sisters, including a Canadian, Marie Bourque, named Sister Claire, arrived from Algiers and they opened a school for postulants in the building formerly used by the White Fathers. In 1913, as a result of increasing enrolment, they moved to Lévis.

During all his years as superior, Father Forbes had gone back to Africa only once, for a 30-day retreat at the mother house in 1911. He still dreamed of being a missionary in Africa, and it was with great joy that in May 1914 he learned he had been appointed to teach at the high school in Rubaga (Kampala), Uganda. He left Quebec on 4 July, but the outbreak of World War I changed his itinerary. He was sent to replace the superior of the missionary school run by the White Fathers in Bishop's Waltham, England, where he remained until 15 March 1915. In May he finally reached Rubaga; there he took the official title of superior of St Mary's School, which had opened in February 1908 to prepare young indigenous Catholics through the study of English and other subjects to assume positions with the government, the army, or large landowners. It had an enrolment of some 160 children in 1915–16. Forbes had been superior of this school for nearly three years when he heard on 18 Feb. 1918 that he had been appointed bishop of Vaga and coadjutor to the vicar apostolic of Uganda, Mgr Heinrich Streicher. He was consecrated bishop on 19 May. The vicariate included Uganda, Ankole, Toro, Bunyoro, and part of the Belgian Congo (Democratic Republic of the Congo), a territory Forbes said was "quite as large in area as [the] great province of Quebec." Every year he made his pastoral visit, by bicycle until 1921 and thereafter by motorcycle. He spent about ten days at each post, hearing confessions, conducting confirmations, and offering comfort, ever attentive to the spiritual needs and good government of the indigenous population.

Forget

The education of blacks was a matter of concern for him, and he wanted to have some teaching brothers move in to help the missionaries. For this purpose, as well as to raise money to build a church in Rubaga, which would be his cathedral, he spent the period from March 1922 to December 1923 in Montreal. His efforts would bear fruit. In 1926 four Brothers of Christian Instruction would leave La Prairie for the Uganda missions and, as a result of donations he had collected (more than $100,000, according to his biographer, Abbé Élie-Joseph-Arthur Auclair), the cathedral would be opened for worship that very year.

But Bishop John Forbes would not be present at these happy occasions. Suffering from heart problems, he had to leave Rubaga in February 1925. After spending a few months in Mombasa, Kenya, he went to Paris and then to Billère, where he died of a heart attack on 13 March 1926. He was buried in the cemetery of the White Fathers in Pau. The first Canadian to enter the Society of Missionaries of Africa and the first Canadian bishop from this community, Father Forbes was also one of those heralding the wave of missionary zeal that swept over French Canada beginning in the 1920s.

HUGUETTE FILTEAU and JEAN HAMELIN

The Arch. des Pères Blancs in Montreal holds the most materials on John Forbes, in particular his personal correspondence and his annual reports. Forbes is the subject of a detailed biography by Father É.-J.[-A.] Auclair, titled *Vie de Mgr John Forbes, le premier père blanc canadien, évêque de Vaga et coadjuteur de l'Ouganda, 1864–1926* ([Québec], 1929]).

ANQ-M, CE601-S50, 10 janv. 1864. *Le Devoir*, 15 mars 1926. *Canada ecclésiastique*, 1901–27. J. F., "Mgr John Forbes, des Pères blancs," *La Semaine religieuse de Montréal*, 6 mai 1926. Lionel Groulx, *Le Canada français missionnaire: une autre grande aventure* (Montréal et Paris, 1962). Guy Laperrière, *Les congrégations religieuses: de la France au Québec, 1880–1914* (2v. parus, Sainte-Foy, Qué., 1996–), 2. "Le premier père blanc canadien, son Exc. Mgr John Forbes," *Missions d'Afrique des Pères blancs* (Québec), 47 (1951): 261–71.

FORGET, AMÉDÉE-EMMANUEL (baptized **Emmanuel-Amédée-Marie**), lawyer, office holder, civil servant, and politician; b. 12 Nov. 1847 in Marieville, Lower Canada, son of Jacques-Jérémie Forget and Marie-Flavie Guenette; m. 17 Oct. 1876 Henriette-A. Drolet in Montreal; they had no children; d. 8 June 1923 in Ottawa.

Born to a devoutly Roman Catholic family, Amédée-Emmanuel Forget attended the village school in Marieville, the School of Military Instruction of Quebec, and the Collège de Marieville. His father, a teacher, sent him on occasion to spend time with a family in St Albans, Vt, to master English. Forget considered entering the priesthood but turned it

down for law, which he pursued in the Montreal office of Joseph-Adolphe Chapleau*. Called to the bar in 1871, he continued to work with Chapleau, whom he accompanied to Winnipeg in 1874 for the legal defence of Ambroise-Dydime LÉPINE and his Métis companions. He became intrigued by the west and the possibility of a career there occurred to him. Tall and slim, he projected a dignified bearing. Those who knew Forget described him as charming and considerate, and he was noted for his wit, ingenuity of mind, and diplomatic skills. Legal colleagues were convinced that he was destined for a brilliant career in the courtroom; many were surprised when he looked to public service.

The triumph of the Liberals in the federal election of 1874 made patronage appointments for party stalwarts possible. Forget, an ardent Liberal, was not slow in forwarding his claim. He pressed his contacts in government for a position, reminding them of his fluent bilingualism and work during the election. The canvassing succeeded: on 21 May 1875 he was made a secretary of the commission to enumerate mixed-blood settlers entitled to land grants under the Manitoba Act. Forget arrived in the western province in June and was responsible, with Commissioner Matthew Ryan, for the French-speaking parishes. Following his return to Quebec after the work ended in January 1876, Forget practised law for a while in Saint-Hyacinthe in partnership with Honoré Mercier*, but it was simply an interlude before taking up another appointment he had been soliciting. Ottawa had moved to establish a new governing council for the North-West Territories and on 7 Oct. 1876 David Laird*, then minister of the interior, was made lieutenant governor and Indian superintendent. Forget became his secretary and clerk of council, a posting that required his immediate move west with his new wife and a winter at Fort Livingstone (Livingstone, Sask.), where on 8 March 1877 council held its first session. Forget's role involved preparing the initial ordinances and assisting in the government's move to Battleford (Sask.) that summer.

The Forgets bought a farm and entered into Battleford's lively social life. In addition to the work of council, Forget assisted Laird in his dealings with the native population, which included travelling to make the annual treaty payments. Laird found such tasks tiresome and he resigned as Indian superintendent in February 1879, though he continued as lieutenant governor. That spring the buffalo disappeared and starving Indians began turning up at Battleford. Their presence alarmed the settlers; Henriette Forget, for one, was afraid to leave her house. Difficult negotiations followed and, when provided with food, the visitors returned to their reserves. These experiences with native affairs would serve Forget well in subsequent years. During a summer visit to Edmonton with

Laird, the Forgets met Edgar Dewdney*, who had arrived to take up the new position of Indian commissioner; in late 1881 he became lieutenant governor as well. Although these appointments came from a Conservative government, that of Sir John A. Macdonald*, Forget remained clerk of council.

The decision to build the Canadian Pacific Railway along a southern route across the prairies led to the creation of a new capital, Regina. The Forgets moved there in February 1883. As the number of elected councillors and the volume of legislation grew, Forget's duties expanded; "a capital officer" in Dewdney's estimate, he met the challenge easily. One of council's initiatives was the creation of a system of education. Legislation in 1884 allowed for a board of education divided into Catholic and Protestant sections, each controlling its own teachers, schools, and curriculum [see Charles-Borromée Rouleau*]. Forget, who sat as a Catholic representative from 1886, emerged as a principal defender of the sectarian and bilingual nature of the system, features that came under increasing attack from the Anglo-Protestant element of the population. In 1892 the board was replaced by the Council of Public Instruction, which brought education under a single authority. Forget vehemently opposed this measure and joined the Catholic hierarchy in a futile attempt to have it repealed. Named to the council of instruction without his approval, he nonetheless stayed to fight for Catholic rights, though he was never as intransigent as some clergy. He could find no objection, for instance, to the textbooks prescribed by the council but denounced by Father Hippolyte Leduc and others.

In the summer of 1884 Dewdney had become concerned about reported restlessness among the Métis of the District of Saskatchewan. Their most important grievance was lack of security of land tenure. The arrival of Louis Riel* in July seemed to escalate the agitation and Dewdney decided to investigate. Known to the Métis for his work in Manitoba, Forget was among those dispatched. During his week in September in the area of Batoche and St Laurent (St-Laurent-Grandin), he interviewed Riel and Gabriel Dumont*, among other members of the community, and suggested that Riel be appointed to the territorial council. This proposal, which Riel rejected, had not been endorsed, yet it reflected official thinking on how to neutralize the Métis leader. In his report to Dewdney, Forget noted that the Métis were determined and were expanding their list of demands; appended was a petition outlining Riel's specific requirements on the land question. Forget's major concern was the decline of missionary influence since Riel's arrival. He proposed immediate help with education and agriculture and action on the land issue. The government procrastinated – the commission to settle Métis land claims was not established

until March 1885. Forget was one of the three commissioners authorized to confirm existing holdings and offer scrip in compensation for aboriginal title. The North-West uprising was already under way when they began their determinations in April; the struggle and the scattered nature of settlement presented enormous challenges, and work continued into the following year. Meanwhile, the uprising was crushed and Riel was sentenced to hang. Many French Canadians had a certain sympathy for the Métis cause. Forget, who shared the sentiment, visited Riel in his Regina cell a number of times that fall and made no secret of his opposition to execution. When Riel mounted the scaffold on 16 November, he asked Father Alexis André* to convey his gratitude to Forget and his wife for their kindness. Dewdney noted Forget's subsequent bitterness and felt that he could not be trusted completely.

When Dewdney left office in 1888 to enter the federal cabinet, the position of lieutenant governor and that of Indian commissioner were no longer to be held by the same individual. The former went to Joseph Royal*, a French Canadian MP, while the latter went to assistant commissioner Hayter Reed. There was some opposition to having French Canadians as lieutenant governor and clerk of council at the same time, so Forget was removed and made assistant Indian commissioner, effective 3 Aug. 1888. After Reed left for Ottawa in 1893 to become deputy superintendent general of Indian affairs, Forget was put in charge of the Indian office at Regina. In October 1895 he became Indian commissioner for Manitoba, Keewatin, and the NWT.

Forget never deviated from the Department of Indian Affairs' methods of strict surveillance and coercive tutelage with a view to assimilation. His language betrayed the prevailing prejudices against natives, whom he described as "a people who one generation past were practically unrestrained savages." On reserves he sought out such signs of progress as "the desire to accumulate property" and a decline in paganism and the influence of medicine men. In his report for 1896 he was most optimistic about the potential of industrial schools for "uplifting a savage race and eradicating the nomadic and other inherent tendencies which centuries of a wild and barbarous life have firmly implanted." The skills acquired in these schools were supposed to lead to self-sufficiency, especially through farming. Forget believed that Indians could be good farmers, but his department's agricultural policy lacked coherence. Reed had insisted that Indians tend their crops with hand implements rather than modern machinery – they had to become frugal peasants before evolving into prosperous farmers – and on moving to Ottawa he ordered Forget to persist. Forget was dubious about a policy that was opposed by agents and Indians alike, but he

369

dutifully tried to enforce it. When besieged by requests to permit the use of machinery, he sometimes conceded on the understanding that harvesting by hand had been tried and that the crops were in danger of being lost. He was all too aware from agents' reports that the policy only discouraged Indians from becoming agriculturalists.

Government officials and missionaries were virtually unanimous in recognizing that the continuation of native ceremonies such as the Sun and Thirst dances obstructed cultural and religious transformation. An amendment to the Indian Act in 1895 forbidding the torture and gift-giving segments of these ceremonies gave the authorities some power to combat the practices. Forget urged his agents to invoke the law if "prohibited and revolting" aspects were ever featured and to use the section of the act prohibiting trespass on reserves to keep visitors away and thereby limit the size of gatherings. He ensured that beef tongues issued to the Blackfoot were split to render them useless for the Sun Dance and he approved the withholding of rations from those who danced. Yet he was sufficiently pragmatic to realize that ceremonies could sometimes be condoned under strict conditions. Agreements struck with the Blackfoot were followed by appeals to the "better element" on the reserves to use their influence against future dances. The department approved Forget's use of "wise discretion."

The victory of Wilfrid Laurier* and the Liberals in 1896 brought great satisfaction to Forget, who was a friend of the new prime minister. It also opened the door to higher office, especially important to a Liberal who had laboured long in a bureaucracy dominated by Conservatives, and paved the way for Forget's most enduring contribution to Indian administration: a radical restructuring of western operations. Clifford Sifton, the new interior minister and superintendent general of Indian affairs, was determined to slash the department's operating budget, especially on the prairies, where treaty obligations and security concerns kept costs high. Happy to oblige, Forget provided the blueprint. The Indian commissioner's office was moved to Winnipeg in 1897 and made smaller; its role was reduced to inspecting agencies and schools. The Manitoba superintendency was abolished and agencies were eliminated. Within two years 57 employees had resigned or been dismissed, and the salaries of agents, clerks, and farm instructors had been cut. These measures did produce savings, but it became clear that purging Conservatives was also part of the restructuring. As vacancies opened up, they were filled with Liberals. A willing distributor of the spoils, Forget accepted nominations from prominent western Liberals such as Frank Oliver* and James Hamilton Ross*, and he issued a circular instructing agents to contract for supplies only with government supporters. He was irked when a copy was leaked to the press

by a disgruntled employee, who he suspected was on the termination list.

Forget had been suffering for some years from a chronic infection of the spinal cord, a condition that baffled his doctors and impaired his work. With the Liberals in power, however, a less demanding appointment was conceivable. Royal's successor as lieutenant governor, Charles Herbert Mackintosh*, was to retire in 1898. Forget made his interest in the position known to Laurier and Sifton but he was disappointed when it went to Malcolm Colin Cameron*, an Ontario Liberal. His hopes revived when Cameron died in September 1898. This time he was successful and the appointment was made effective 13 October. The news was generally welcomed in the western press, but there was dissent. Conservative papers were critical of Forget's partisanship in the Indian office and some Catholics felt that his support for the Laurier–Greenway compromise of 1897 on the Manitoba school question had been a "base betrayal."

Most of Forget's work as lieutenant governor was routine and ceremonial. With responsible government entrenched by an amendment to the North-West Territories Act in 1897, political initiative had passed from the office. Along with his easy duties came substantial benefits, including residence in Government House in Regina. One of the finest houses in the west, it became the scene of lavish entertainments. Forget enjoyed his new role immensely. Although ill health occasionally kept him from his functions, he made a point of visiting many of the communities in his domain. His appearances at schools, country fairs, and other events were occasions for grand speeches laced with the boosterism and imperialist jingoism that audiences loved. The man who flaunted his credentials as a true Northwester was never slow to praise the prospects of the region, even to the point of stretching his listeners' credulity. On a visit to Montreal in 1904, for example, he claimed there were no poor people in the NWT.

Forget's friendship with Laurier was of no small importance after 1898. He was a trusted confidant and Laurier sought his advice on party interests and such delicate territorial matters as language, religion, and schools. As his term drew to a close, there was talk of a senatorship, but he preferred reappointment. He explained to Laurier that he had not managed his finances well and would be better able to plan for retirement were a second term offered. The prime minister obliged and Forget was sworn in on 4 April 1904 in Montreal, where he had gone for medical treatment.

In the general election in November, Laurier was returned with a majority. The NWT were now represented by 10 MPs, 7 of them Liberals, a balance that strengthened the prime minister's hand in determining the region's political future. The Autonomy Acts of 1905 granted provincial status to Alberta and

Saskatchewan. Forget learned in July 1905 that Laurier had chosen him as lieutenant governor of the latter, an appointment he had not solicited but gratefully accepted. His inauguration in Regina on 4 September was attended by Laurier and Chief Justice Arthur Lewis Watkins SIFTON. The position allowed Forget to influence the composition of the province's first government. Former territorial premier Frederick William Gordon Haultain* was the logical candidate for the provincial post, but he was a Conservative and opposed the Autonomy Acts' allowance for separate schools and federal control of land and natural resources. Forget feared he would stir up trouble over these issues. With Liberals in most of Saskatchewan's federal seats, he felt justified in calling on provincial Liberal leader Thomas Walter Scott* to become premier. The choice, predictably enough, was not well received in the Tory press; the Toronto *Mail and Empire* denounced Forget as Laurier's "instrument" and cartoons showed Haultain facing a firing squad that included Forget. In the election that December, his decision was vindicated by the defeat of Haultain's Provincial Rights party.

On 29 March 1906 Forget opened the first session of the legislature. Reading speeches from the throne, signing bills, and carrying out other rituals of office were all too familiar to him, and he fulfilled these duties with his customary dignity until the conclusion of his term on 13 Oct. 1910. During these years his health had continued to be a problem and he began to spend summers in Banff, Alta, to avail himself of the sulphur springs. Upon retirement, he and his wife made it their permanent residence. Early in 1911, however, Laurier informed him that a vacant Senate seat for Alberta was his. Forget moved to Ottawa and took his place in the Red Chamber in May 1911, but he made little impact. His only speech of note – a defence of the Laurier–Greenway compromise – was given in 1912, after which illness ate away his strength. He died in 1923 at his home on MacLaren Street and was buried at Notre-Dame-des-Neiges cemetery in Montreal. His wife entered a convent, where she remained until her death in 1928.

Forget was an official of moderate importance who secured a number of noteworthy public positions in Manitoba, the NWT, and Saskatchewan during the pioneer period. His success was due to a combination of competence, charm, and fortuitous configurations in federal politics. He was liked by those he worked with, though his reputation was tarnished by his role of 1896–98 in the spoils system within the Department of Indian Affairs.

E. BRIAN TITLEY

ANQ-M, CE601-S35, 17 oct. 1876; CE602-S21, 12 nov. 1847. LAC, MG 26, A: 42921–33, 42938–40, 90090–92, 90697–703; G: 20121–22, 29946–51, 41516–17, 78710–14, 99633–35, 176042–43, 185782–84; H: 18531; MG 27, II, D15: 12029, 12061–62, 12110, 28483, 128683; MG 29, D27; E106, 18: 463; RG 10, 3802, file 50320; 3825, file 60511-1; 3878, file 91837-23; 3964, file 148285. Saskatchewan Arch. Board (Regina), R-2.77 (A.-E. Forget scrapbook) (mfm.); R-39 (A.-E. Forget papers); SHS 21 (Saskatchewan Hist. Soc. files, corr. and biog. sketch on A.-E. Forget). *Le Devoir*, 11 oct. 1923. *Morning Leader* (Regina), 16 June 1923. Amy Nelson-Mile, "The Forgets had much to offer," *Regina Sun*, 21 March 1999. N. F. Black, *History of Saskatchewan and the North-West Territories* (2v., Regina, 1913), 1. Can., Parl., *Sessional papers*, reports of the Dept. of Indian Affairs, 1895–96; Senate, *Debates*, 1911/12: 602–3, 758–59; 1923: 797–98. *Canadian men and women of the time* (Morgan; 1912). Sarah Carter, *Lost harvests: prairie Indian reserve farmers and government policy* (Montreal and Kingston, Ont., 1990). J. W. Chalmers, *Laird of the west* (Calgary, 1981). T. [E.] Flanagan, *Métis lands in Manitoba* (Calgary, 1991). D. J. Hall, "Clifford Sifton and Canadian Indian administration, 1896–1905," in *As long as the sun shines and water flows: a reader in Canadian native studies*, ed. I. A. L. Getty and A. S. Lussier (Vancouver, 1983), 120–44. John Hawkes, *The story of Saskatchewan and its people* (3v., Regina, 1924), 1. J. K. Howard, *Strange empire: Louis Riel and the Métis people* (New York, 1952; repr. 1974). M. R. Lupul, *The Roman Catholic Church and the North-West school question: a study in church-state relations in western Canada, 1875–1905* (Toronto, 1974). *Pioneers and prominent people of Saskatchewan* (Winnipeg and Toronto, 1924). G. F. G. Stanley, *The birth of western Canada: a history of the Riel rebellions* (Toronto, 1936; repr., intro. T. [E.] Flanagan, 1992). [E.] B. Titley, *The frontier world of Edgar Dewdney* (Vancouver, 1999); *A narrow vision: Duncan Campbell Scott and the administration of Indian Affairs in Canada* (Vancouver, 1986).

FORSTER, ROBERT FRANCIS, Roman Catholic priest, Basilian, educator, and superior general; b. 16 May 1873 near Simcoe, Ont., son of John Forster, a farmer, and Rosanna Harvey; d. 11 Nov. 1929 in Montreal.

Francis Forster attended local schools before transferring in 1890 to the Basilian-run Assumption College in Sandwich (Windsor). "A boy who seemed always enjoying life to the full," he completed his classical studies there in brilliant fashion, winning nearly every prize at graduation. Although small for his age, Forster had a strong personality and fearless self-assurance. He was a natural leader and an accomplished and relentless debater. His determination to win over opponents was a characteristic that would mark his priestly career.

After graduation Forster stayed at Assumption for two more years of philosophy, and then an extra year, studying theology and teaching the junior classes. In 1897 he entered the Basilian novitiate in Toronto and he was ordained a priest on 30 June 1901. He taught belles-lettres at St Michael's College in Toronto from 1901 to 1903, after which he was made superior of St

Basil's College in Waco, Tex. In 1907 he returned to Assumption as superior and he remained there until 1919.

Forster was a thoroughly modern college administrator for whom change was inevitable and healthy. In curriculum, he lifted Assumption out of the 19th century. He immediately added a fourth year to the high school program, which gave the students an opportunity to achieve junior matriculation in conformity to provincial regulations [see John Seath*]. He also welcomed the prospect of affiliating Assumption's college division, or arts department, with the Western University of London, Ontario, and would have achieved this result as early as 1909 if the diocese of London had not been vacant. Instead, he had to let the initiative pass to the new bishop, Michael Francis Fallon*, who for a variety of reasons did not sign articles of affiliation until 1919 and only then on a misunderstanding about the future location of the arts department. Fallon wanted it transferred to Western, where the Ursuline college for women in Chatham would also be moved. Forster was just as adamant that it would stay in Sandwich. Without it, the high school might fail and all the efforts the Basilians had made to build up the Sandwich campus would be in ruins. In spite of the dispute, affiliation was a tremendous leap forward. It offered Assumption graduates proper university degrees for the first time.

At the college itself, Forster was a whirlwind of activity. He eliminated the debt from the chapel, built by his predecessor; he replaced gas lighting with electricity; he refurbished the 1875 and 1884 buildings erected by superior Denis O'Connor*; and he financed the construction of a much-needed gymnasium, dormitory, and central heating plant, in the face of constant interference from Victorin Marijon, who became superior general of the Basilians in 1910. Forster increased the student rolls to capacity and would have expanded them even further had it not been for World War I, the influenza pandemic of 1918, and Bishop Fallon's decision to remove his diocesans from the college. Forster knew each boy by name and home town and monitored his progress. He was especially anxious about those fighting overseas, taking the time to respond to their letters. Also noteworthy is his introduction to the college's front office of a typewriter and the practice of making carbon copies. Typing all his own correspondence, he left a rich archive that reveals a logical mind in control of every detail connected with his religious community and his boarding school.

Forster had entered the Basilians at a time of high tension between the French-speaking members from France and the English-speaking members from Canada and the United States. The French believed, in the words of Father Thomas James Hanrahan, that "religious life consisted precisely in the voluntary and life-long acceptance of obedience to the authority of the Superior." The North Americans looked instead to the community's rules and traditions; in their minds, the superior was but the first among equals in running the community in a democratic fashion. At the general chapter of 1910 a compromise of sorts was reached. The Basilian community divided itself into two provinces, one for France and one for America, each to be governed by a provincial, and the whole to be governed by a superior general. However, this new arrangement simply exacerbated tensions.

In 1911 Forster was made a member of the provincial council for America. He was elected provincial five years later (he continued as superior at Assumption, undoubtedly feeling that the college needed his guidance during the war years) and was re-elected in 1919, when he moved to Toronto. No sooner had he taken his seat on the council than he let it be known that the only solution to "the tyrannical, absolute and unconstitutional administration of Fr. Marijon" was his resignation as superior general and the establishment of an independent government for each province. Rome rebuked him for his harsh opinions, but he was to win the day. In 1914 Rome requested and received Marijon's resignation, and in 1922, in response to a petition from the French province, it issued a decree establishing the Congregation of Priests of St Basil of the Diocese of Viviers, in France, and the Congregation of Priests of St Basil of Toronto. That same year Forster was elected the Toronto congregation's first superior general, and he was re-elected in 1928.

During the years immediately preceding his first election Forster's prime objective was to rewrite the constitutions for the Toronto congregation so that they conformed to the regulations governing every other religious community in the church. His study of the 1917 Code of Canon Law had convinced him in particular that Rome would continue to reject the constitutions, and consequently the Basilians' desire to be a true religious congregation and not just a pious sodality of priests, if they did not include a simple vow of poverty held in common by all members.

Working single-handedly, Forster completed the constitutions by August 1922, when the general chapter met, and he later oversaw the amendments to them. Although Rome gave its approval on 7 May 1923, he had to spend a year contacting each member of the community about the vow of poverty and the desirability of abandoning a largely unregulated community life in favour of unambiguous written rules and an exact observance of them. In the end, most quietly took the new vow. Rome suggested modifications to the constitutions in 1928 and gave final approval ten years later. For the first time since their inception in France in 1822 the Basilians were fully recognized as a religious community.

Forster had continued to accomplish a great deal of good in education. He managed to keep the arts department in Sandwich by winning a decisive Roman judgement against Fallon in 1925; he purchased a building on St Mary Street in Toronto for Basilian scholastics in 1926; he sent Basilians to teach at the Aquinas Institute in Rochester, N.Y., in 1927; he opened the Catholic Central High School in Detroit in 1928; and he supported the changes at St Michael's College that issued in the founding in 1929 of the Institute of Mediaeval Studies under Father Henry Carr*.

Forster died by drowning in Montreal in November 1929. He had been waiting for a ship to dock, lost his footing in the dark, and slipped into the water unnoticed. His body was not recovered until the spring, when he was buried in Mount Hope Cemetery in Toronto. His devotion to Catholic education inspired a generation of Basilian leaders, and his role in transforming the Basilians into a religious community guaranteed their growth and prosperity for many decades and led to his being honoured as the "second founder" of the congregation.

MICHAEL POWER

General Arch. of the Basilian Fathers (Toronto), c. 314 1929.3 (R. F. Forster file), including a typescript copy of an undated item in the Bay City Daily Times (Bay City, Mich.) and a manuscript genealogical chart. Evening Record (Windsor, Ont.), 22 June 1893. Henry Carr, A sketch of the late Very Reverend Father Francis Forster, C.S.B. (address delivered at Father Forster's funeral mass at St Basil's Church, Toronto, 12 May 1930; privately printed; copy in General Arch. of the Basilian Fathers). A documentary history of Assumption College . . . , ed. and intro. Michael Power (4v., [Windsor], 1984–89), vol.3 (Assumption College: the making of a modern school, 1890–1919, 1986). T. J. Hanrahan, The Basilian Fathers (1822–1972): a documentary study of one hundred and fifty years of the history of the Congregation of Priests of St. Basil (Toronto, 1973). W. E. Kelly, "Father Forster: a sketch of the president of Assumption College," Canadian Magazine, 48 (November 1916–April 1917): 289–92. K. J. Kirley, The Congregation of Priests of St. Basil of Viviers, France, 1922–1955 (Toronto, 1981); 1922: before and after ([Toronto], 1992). Michael Power, "Fallon versus Forster: the struggle over Assumption College, 1919–1925," CCHA, Hist. studies, 56 (1989): 49–66. R. J. Scollard, Dictionary of Basilian biography: lives of members of the Congregation of Priests of Saint Basil from its beginnings in 1822 to 1968 (Toronto, 1969), 59. "Very Reverend Francis Forster, C.S.B. (1873–1929)," Basilian Newsletter (Toronto), no.15 (November 1979): 2.

FORTES, JOSEPH SERAPHIM, shoeblack, bartender, porter, swimming instructor, and lifeguard; b. 9 Feb. 1863 in Port of Spain (Republic of Trinidad and Tobago); d. unmarried 4 Feb. 1922 in Vancouver.

Some sources give Joe Fortes's birthplace as Barbados, but an autobiographical article in the Vancouver Daily News-Advertiser states that he was born in Port of Spain. According to another source, his father was a Barbadian "of full African blood" and his mother was "entirely or largely" Spanish or Portuguese; the 1901 census for Vancouver lists him as Trinidadian and Spanish speaking.

At 17 Fortes left Trinidad for England. Residing for five years in Liverpool, he learned to swim at St George's Baths, where he became a swimmer and diver of some note. He won a three-mile race across the Mersey River, received a gold medal for life-saving, and exhibited his talents as part of an 11-person swim team in a tour of English and French seaside resorts.

Fortes came to Granville (Vancouver) on the Robert Kerr, debarking on 30 Sept. 1885. The town was booming because of the lumber industry and its designation as a railway terminus. People moved from Vancouver Island to the mainland in search of jobs, and a number of blacks came as well from eastern Canada, Alberta, the Pacific northwest, the West Indies, and even further afield. Consequently, the centre of British Columbia's African Canadian community changed from Victoria to Vancouver as the century drew to a close. Most members of the black population there, which never numbered more than around 300, lived mainly in what became known as Strathcona or the East End.

For eight months, until the great fire of June 1886, Fortes ran Vancouver's earliest shoeshine stand, in the Sunnyside Hotel on Water Street. Afterwards he worked as a bartender and porter at such local establishments as the Bodega Saloon on Carrall Street in Strathcona and the Alhambra Hotel at the corner of Carrall and Water. Known to be clean, sober, and an expert mixer of cocktails, he was most famous, however, for his volunteer work as a swimming instructor and lifeguard. He was a common sight at English Bay beach, where he taught thousands of children to swim. It was not until around 1897 that the city, in recognition of his services, put him on its payroll as a lifeguard; at some point he was also made a special police constable. He reputedly saved more than 100 people from drowning, including many children and several adults, among them John Hugo Ross, who would die in the sinking of the Titanic. In 1905 his cottage was moved from the foot of Gilford Street to the bank above the beach. Apparently he had no family in the city, but his friend Noel Robinson would state in an obituary that Joe had "a sister in Toronto with whom he corresponded." He certainly earned the respect of countless parents and children.

Fortes died in the Vancouver General Hospital in 1922. It was thought that he had had pneumonia that developed into mumps, but in the end he had a stroke. The city honoured him by arranging the largest public funeral ever held there. Thousands of people, including the mayor, several aldermen, the chief of police, constables, and many ordinary citizens, attended the service at Our Lady of the Holy Rosary Cathedral, and a moment of silence was held in the city's schools. In his memory, $5,000 was raised to erect a water fountain, designed by Vancouver sculptor Charles Marega. Standing in Alexandra Park near the beach he once patrolled, it is simply inscribed "Little children loved him."

SHERRY EDMUNDS-FLETT

BCA, GR-2951, no.1922-09-302410 (mfm.). City of Vancouver Arch., Add. MSS 35 (*Robert Kerr* fonds); Add. MSS 54 (J. S. Matthews coll.), newspaper clippings, Joe Fortes (M3265); topical files, Joe Fortes (01558); Add. MSS 786 (Alan Morley fonds); Vancouver Health Dept. fonds, ser.152 (Mountain View Cemetery reg.), MCR 15-26, vol.19: 33–34 (mfm.). LAC, RG 31, C1, 1901, Vancouver, dist.16: 2. *Daily News-Advertiser* (Vancouver), 19 Jan. 1913. *Vancouver Daily Province*, 16 June 1920. Michael Kluckner, *Vancouver: the way it was* (Vancouver, 1984).

FORTIER, RENÉ (baptized **George-Émile-René**), physician, professor, hospital administrator, and author; b. 4 Aug. 1866 in Sainte-Marie, Lower Canada, son of Joseph-Elzéar Fortier and Marie-Louise-Joséphine Simard; m. 12 Oct. 1896, at Quebec, Alice Boucher de La Bruère, daughter of Pierre Boucher* de La Bruère, a lawyer and superintendent of public instruction, and Victorine Leclère, and they had three daughters and three sons; d. there 8 Aug. 1929.

After classical studies at the Collège de Lévis (1875–84) and the Petit Séminaire de Québec (1884–86), René Fortier took up medicine in the Université Laval at Quebec. During the year 1889–90 he enrolled at the Grand Séminaire de Québec, but he soon abandoned theology to return to his original choice. Coming from a family of physicians (with a father and grandfather in the profession), he graduated as a bachelor of medicine in 1890 and as a doctor of medicine, with honours, the following year. On 30 Sept. 1891 he would be admitted to the College of Physicians and Surgeons of the Province of Quebec. A month before, on 27 August, he had left for Paris, where he would pursue his studies for two years. The varied clinical training he received there included work in obstetrics with Pierre Budin at the Hôpital de la Charité and with Adolphe Pinard at the Baudelocque maternity hospital. He also took courses in gynaecology, hygiene, neurology, and forensic medicine. In his second year he specialized in the treatment of children, under the direction of professors who were pioneers in this field, Jacques-Joseph Grancher and Antonin Marfan. Fortier began his study of paediatrics, paediatric surgery, orthopaedics, and bacteriology at the 800-bed Hôpital des Enfants-Malades in Paris. During his time there he visited several other countries in Europe with his colleague Arthur Simard*.

On his return to Canada in September 1893, Fortier established his residence and consulting office in the Upper Town of Quebec, at the corner of Rue Sainte-Anne and Rue Sainte-Ursule. While physicians in that era limited their careers initially to general practice, Fortier began his by including obstetric care and paediatrics as well. From 1903 his office hours would be devoted exclusively to children. As soon as he arrived back he began working with the rector of the Université Laval, Mgr Joseph-Clovis-Kemner Laflamme*, and the dean of the faculty medicine, Charles-Eusèbe Lemieux, to establish a chair of paediatrics. He began teaching there in January 1894 as an associate professor; he would be appointed a full professor in 1899 and would continue in that position for the rest of his life. In 1894 future physicians were given 15 classes in the theory of paediatrics in each of their third and fourth years, although this instruction was not yet compulsory. (It would become so on 1 Jan. 1910, when the Quebec Medical Act came into force [*see* Albert Laurendeau*].) Paediatric instruction would be increased to about 35 hours a year in 1905, and to 45 hours in 1925. In these courses, Fortier concentrated on information relating to newborn and nursing infants and to early childhood (from birth to the age of 6 to 7 years). Although he was concerned with the general state of the child's health, he went into detail about various ailments and their causes, including digestive complaints related to dietary deficiencies, a subject that gave him an opportunity to explain the benefits of breastfeeding. From 1898 the faculty also charged Fortier with the teaching of hygiene (120 classes a year for first- and second-year students). In 1913, in order to combat epidemics more effectively, especially smallpox, which often broke out in poor urban neighbourhoods, a course in public health would be introduced that would lead to a diploma as an expert in hygiene. Physicians who took this course would then be qualified to work in the civil service. Its 20 classes on paediatric nursing and contagious diseases would be added to Fortier's teaching load.

The institutionalization of abandoned children provided an initial clinical setting for paediatrics, and Fortier worked as the visiting physician at the Hôtel-Dieu du Sacré-Cœur de Jésus from 1898 to 1906. Founded in 1873, this hospital was located in the working-class ward of Saint-Sauveur, in the Lower Town, and served the needs of deserted children and epileptics. Fortier found this work increasing appreciably from 1903. That year, after a number of fruitless requests, he got permission from the hospital to give clinical instruction to the students in the medical faculty. As was the custom then, in return for this permission he looked after, with no salary, the treatment and medical direction in the establishment where the classes were taught. The Dispensaire de Québec, which was in the Hôtel-Dieu, was the first place to benefit from such an agreement with Fortier. In 1907 he would open the "sick children's department," and he would be in charge of it until 1929. In 1905 he also became professor and visiting physician at the Crèche Saint-Vincent-de-Paul, which provided care for illegitimate infants born in the maternity ward of the Hôpital de la Miséricorde and taken in by the Sisters of the Good Shepherd. He would continue to work there for the rest of his life. From 1916 to 1920 Fortier would give practical classes on contagious diseases at the new Hôpital Civique in Quebec. This 58-bed institution on Chemin de la Canardière, founded in 1915 and funded by the city of Quebec, was established for tuberculosis patients and was administered by the Sœurs de la Charité de Québec. Students in the faculty of medicine would also be able to study at the Hôpital du Saint-Sacrement, which opened in 1927 on Chemin Sainte-Foy and would have a paediatric service introduced by Fortier.

The movement to combat infant mortality at Quebec – just as in Montreal [*see* Séverin Lachapelle*], Toronto, and the big American cities – had begun as the work of social reformers, women, physicians, and members of the clergy, only later being taken over by the government. In June 1915 Fortier took part in the opening of a paediatric nursing clinic at the Dispensaire de Québec. A few weeks earlier, a similar facility had opened in Saint-Sauveur ward, under the direction of Albert Jobin. The purpose of these clinics, known as the Gouttes de Lait [*see* Frances-Mathilde Barnard*], was to provide care and clean milk to the children of poor families. Relevant information was made available to their mothers as well. At Quebec, where contagious diseases and diarrhoea were rampant, this service proved indispensable. In 1916, 27 children in 100 died in their first year, not counting stillborn infants. Only Sorel had more dismal figures. In June 1916 Fortier became director of the medical council of the seven Gouttes de Lait at Quebec, but he soon left this post because of a disagreement about his salary with the women comprising the executive committee. The operation would be financed by the provincial government from 1924. In the new organization that resulted from this change of administration, Fortier would be appointed chief physician.

These public experiments with the care of the city's children were pivotal and encouraged other initiatives. In 1923, at the height of his career, Fortier helped found its first hospital for sick children. In January, Irma Le Vasseur*, the first female French-speaking physician in the province, who had co-founded the Hôpital Sainte-Justine in Montreal in 1907, opened a small dispensary on Rue Grande Allée, where Fortier was the first physician and where he admitted the first child as a patient. In May the paediatrician drew up a constitution and by-laws so that the institution could be incorporated under the name of Hôpital de l'Enfant-Jésus and receive government grants. The city's elite gave it their moral support. Three sisters from the Dominicaines de l'Enfant-Jésus, under the medical supervision of Dr Fortier and Dr Édouard Samson, an orthopaedic specialist, were put in charge of its operation. It got off to a precarious start. The hospital moved three times before finding a home in 1927 in a new building on Chemin de la Canardière. The establishment of the hospital, with its 125 beds, reflected the local citizens' interest in child care. Providing clinical instruction to future physicians, it then included two operating rooms, a dental clinic, a laboratory, a radiology room, and a maternity ward. After Fortier's death it would become a general hospital.

An active man who combined the practice of medicine with university teaching, Fortier also championed the interests of his profession. He was secretary of the Société Médicale de Québec from 1897, when it was founded, until 1901. In 1899 the society began publishing the *Bulletin médical de Québec*; Fortier was a member of the editorial committee from 1899 to 1906 and its secretary from 1911 to 1913. He published some 20 articles in it, dealing especially with poliomyelitis, the feeding of infants, and hygiene. In his articles and lectures, Fortier encouraged breastfeeding and the practice of such hygienic measures as the pasteurization of milk and the sterilization of baby's bottles. He sometimes criticized physicians who neglected to send sick children for consultation with specialists. Finally, in the interests of public health, he urged the government to improve the quality of milk for human consumption and to increase its financial support to hospitals.

René Fortier took to his bed in February 1929, suffering from cardio-renal arteriosclerosis, and he died on 8 August. His long-time friend Arthur Simard paid tribute to him, describing him as a shy, emotional, and modest person. With his talent, his fine moral qualities, and his professional dignity, Fortier gained an enviable reputation throughout the province, where he had become "the children's doctor." The career of this pioneer in paediatrics provides a wealth of information about medical practice of the time. The first Quebec City physician to devote himself to paediatrics both privately and in numerous clinics, he taught this discipline at the Université Laval for more than 30 years. He stressed the importance of physicians in general hospitals and encouraged medical specialization, especially through the founding of the Hôpital de l'Enfant-Jésus, where a commemorative plaque in his honour was unveiled in 1937.

FRÉDÉRIC JEAN and ÉRICA BOISVERT

René Fortier wrote several articles, most of which were published in the *Bull. médical de Québec*. He also contributed to *L'Union médicale du Canada* (Montréal), *Journal d'hygiène populaire* (Montréal), and *Bull. sanitaire* (Montréal), and some of his lectures appear in the proceedings of the Association des Médecins de Langue Française de l'Amérique du Nord. Worth mentioning among these texts are: "De l'alimentation artificielle des enfants du premier âge," in *Premier congrès de l'Association des médecins de langue française de l'Amérique du Nord tenu à Québec, les 25, 26 et 27 juin 1902; texte des mémoires* (Québec, 1903), 458–88; "Hygiène des classes ouvrières sous le rapport social et administratif," in *Quatrième congrès de l'Association des médecins de langue française de l'Amérique du Nord tenu à Québec, les 20, 21 et 22 juillet, 1908; texte des mémoires* (Québec, 1910), 176–85; and, in collaboration with Arthur Simard, "Considérations sur l'alimentation des enfants du premier âge en dehors de l'allaitement au sein," *Journal d'hygiène populaire*, 11 (1894–95): 212–29.

At the ANQ-Q, the Fonds René Fortier (P265) includes a medical bag, several surgical instruments, and numerous notes for the courses on paediatrics and hygiene that Fortier gave in the faculty of medicine at the Université Laval in Quebec. His son De La Broquerie Fortier, himself a paediatrician in Quebec and the author of articles on the history of medicine, also gave his name to a collection at the ANQ-Q (P596); it contains, among other things, articles that he wrote about his father. Also useful is Véronique Lépine's "Guide des archives hospitalières de la région de Québec, 1639–1970," which is available on the internet site of the ANQ, in "Instruments de recherche en ligne."

ANQ-Q, CE301-S1, 12 oct. 1896; CE306-S24, 6 août 1866. *Le Soleil*, 8–9 août 1929. Jacques Bernier, *La médecine au Québec: naissance et évolution d'une profession* (Québec, 1989). Rita Desjardins, "L'institutionnalisation de la pédiatrie en milieu franco-montréalais, 1880–1980: les enjeux politiques, sociaux et biologiques" (thèse de PHD, univ. de Montréal, 1998). *Directory*, Quebec, 1893–1930. De La Broquerie Fortier, *Au service de l'enfance: l'Association québécoise de la Goutte de lait, 1915–1965* (Québec, 1966); "Les débuts de la pédiatrie à Québec, 1892 à 1929," *L'Union médicale du Canada*, 112 (1983): 656–63. Denis Goulet and André Paradis, *Trois siècles d'histoire médicale au Québec; chronologie des institutions et des pratiques (1639–1939)* (Montréal, 1992). Univ. Laval, *Annuaire*, 1884–1931.

FOWLER, JAMES, Presbyterian minister, botanist, educator, and curator; b. 16 July 1829 in Bartibog, N.B., eldest child of George Fowlie and Jane McKnight; m. 1 July 1858 Mary Ann McLeod (d. 1890) of Truro, N.S., and they had two daughters; d. 11 Jan. 1923 in Kingston, Ont.

James Fowler's surname was originally Fowlie. It is not known why or precisely when, as a young man, he adopted the name Fowler. His father and his mother's family had emigrated from Scotland to eastern New Brunswick in 1816. George Fowlie eventually established a farm with a grist mill and sawmill at Little Branch on Miramichi Bay, and it was here that Fowler was raised. He might well have been expected, at age 14 and with eight younger siblings, to step into the breach created by the death of his father in 1843. It was evidently a remarkable mother who instead enabled him to attend the county grammar school at Chatham, and from 1850 to 1855 to pursue theological studies at the Free Church College in Halifax, where he took the prize in classics. After teaching for a short period in the academy connected with the college, he returned home and was ordained in 1857.

Fowler began his pastoral career in Black River in his native Northumberland County but shortly removed to Kouchibouguac in neighbouring Kent. In 1861 he took up a charge at Bass River, also in Kent. By this time he had become keenly interested in natural history and revealed a bent for collecting. His scope included geology, conchology, meteorology, and especially systematic botany. Over the next 15 years, while ministering to a far-flung and poor rural congregation, he immersed himself in study of the local and, later, provincial flora. The anchor of this activity, and of all his subsequent work in botany, was his herbarium. He was soon scouting widely for North American and overseas collectors through whom he could expand its taxonomic and geographic scope via exchanges – and relying on his wife to mount the large annual influx of specimens.

Although he corresponded with and twice visited the renowned botanist Asa Gray, of Harvard University, during his years at Bass River, Fowler's chief early mentor in botany was George William Clinton of Buffalo, N.Y. A capable amateur botanist, distinguished judge, and president of the Buffalo Society of Natural Sciences, Clinton reviewed Fowler's early identifications, sent him large collections, and provided moral support during a long-sustained correspondence. Fowler also made important scientific contacts in New Brunswick, especially with the geologists George Frederic MATTHEW and Loring Woart BAILEY, both of whom published notable papers on the climatic and historical contexts of New Brunswick flora.

Late in 1875 Fowler wrote to Clinton that chronic laryngitis might compel him to "cease public speaking for some time, if not for life." He resigned his pastorate in 1876, and spent the next two years in Saint John completing the first catalogue of New Brunswick vascular plants and bryophytes, which would be published by the province in 1879. In 1878 he was appointed instructor in natural science at the Normal School in Fredericton. His comment that the position did "not involve much speaking" is odd, but may reflect his adaptation of the program to his own style. He was nonetheless an influential and popular teacher. Several of his students and others inspired by his example made important local plant collections, and these would enable Fowler to publish a substantially revised catalogue of the provincial flora in 1885.

Fowler was appointed lecturer on natural science, librarian, and curator of the museum at Queen's College in Kingston in 1880, and for the next 12 years he taught its courses in geology, botany, and zoology. He had been warmly recommended for the lectureship by Gray and Bailey, and was promoted to the rank of professor in 1891. With the creation of a professorship in animal biology and physiology in 1892, he gave up his duties in zoology, and after geology was removed to the new School of Mining and Agriculture in 1894, he became the university's first full-time professor of botany. Fowler's most notable achievement at Queen's was the development of a major herbarium, building on the one he had brought with him from New Brunswick. Numbering nearly 50,000 specimens and probably more than 15,000 species by his retirement in 1907, it was at the time second in size and scope among Canadian herbaria only to that established at the Geological Survey of Canada by John Macoun*. He continued to collect intensively while at Queen's, both in eastern Ontario and in the Maritimes, in large part to obtain material for use by his students. In 1900 and 1901, for example, he personally collected a total of more than 12,000 specimens at St Andrews, N.B., and Canso, N.S., using the mobile research station of the Marine Biological Stations of Canada as a base of operations.

While his record of published original research was modest, Fowler was widely respected for his prodigious knowledge of the flora of eastern North America. A maritime knotweed which he had first collected in New Brunswick in 1869 was named *Polygonum fowleri* in his honour by the Harvard botanist Benjamin Lincoln Robinson. Fowler's meticulous and thorough work habits gave his identifications a high degree of reliability, and he was consulted especially on the naming of grasses and sedges. His student and eventual successor at Queen's, William Thomas MacClement, noted that he "did not thrust himself or his work on the attention of the world. A man of greater modesty and less self-assertion could scarcely be found." He was awarded two honorary degrees, MA (1872) and LLD (1900), by the University of New Brunswick, and was elected to the Royal Society of Canada in 1891. That year he was invited to give the inaugural address at the opening of the Queen's theological faculty, an acknowledgement of his stature in the Presbyterian community, and of his exceptional command of classical Hebrew, Greek, and Latin.

About 1904 Fowler began to experience significant memory loss. This progressed rapidly following his retirement at age 77. He remained physically active for many years, but soon recognized no one but his daughter Eliza Annie Law Fowler, who cared for him until his death at age 93. During the next half-century the emphasis in botany at Queen's shifted to physiology, and the herbarium was neglected. It was revived and named the Fowler Herbarium in 1965, and since then has assumed an important role in modern research on plant systematics and conservation.

STEPHEN R. CLAYDEN

James Fowler's reports as curator of the museum were published in the *Queen's Quarterly* (Kingston, Ont.) from 1893–94 to 1905–6. His other publications include: "List of New Brunswick plants," N.B., Secretary for agriculture, *Report* (Saint John), 1878, app.B: 35–63; "Additions to the list of New Brunswick plants [continued from last year's report]," N.B., Secretary for agriculture, *Report*, 1879; "Geology of the Maritime provinces" and "Useful minerals of the Maritime provinces," in F. B. Roe, *Atlas of the Maritime provinces of the Dominion of Canada* . . . (Saint John and Halifax, 1879), 8–13 and 13–14; "Preliminary list of the plants of New Brunswick," N.B., Natural Hist. Soc., *Bull.* (Saint John), no.4 (1885): 8–84; "Arctic plants growing in New Brunswick, with notes on their distribution," RSC, *Trans.*, 1st ser., 5 (1887), sect.IV: 189–205; "Vegetable physiology," *Queen's Quarterly*, 3 (1895–96): 199–208; "How plants use animals: a chapter in ecology," *Queen's Quarterly*, 6 (1898–99): 188–203; "Report on the flora of St. Andrew's, N.B.," *Contributions to Canadian Biology* (Toronto), [1] (1901): 41–48; and "Report on the flora of Canso, Nova Scotia," *Contributions to Canadian Biology*, [2] (1902–5): 59–70.

Buffalo Soc. of Natural Sciences Arch. (Buffalo, N.Y.), Papers of George William Clinton, Fowler to Clinton, 25 July 1865–22 Feb. 1879. Library of the Gray Herbarium Arch., Harvard Univ. (Boston), Historic letter coll., Fowler to Asa Gray, 12 Oct. 1870–22 May 1880. N.B. Museum (Saint John), W. F. Ganong fonds, Fowler to L. W. Bailey, 8 June 1865; 28 Jan., 23 Feb., 27 Sept. 1867; 27 April, 18 May, 8 Dec. 1869; Fowler to G. F. Matthew, 10 Dec. 1866; Fowler to Ganong, 6 June 1904; W. T. MacClement to Ganong, 3 Jan. 1918. Private arch., G. F. MacMillan (Bathurst, N.B.), Geneal. of the Fowlie family. QUA, Office of the University Secretariat fonds, Queen's Letters ser., James Fowler, application and testimonials, 1880, locator no.1244. *Daily Telegraph* (Saint John), 17 Sept. 1880. R. E. Beschel, *A history of the biology department and the Fowler Herbarium of Queen's University, summarized for the opening of Earl Hall on May 19, 1966* ([Kingston, 1966]) (copy at QUA, Dept. of biology fonds); "Presenting: some early history of the biology department," *Queen's Rev.* (Kingston), 40 (1966): 92–99. Bernard Boivin, *Survey of Canadian herbaria* (Quebec, 1980), 86. *Canadian men and women of the time* (Morgan; 1912). A. A. Crowder, "The collection of bryophytes in the Fowler Herbarium, Queen's University, Kingston, Ontario," *Canadian Field-Naturalist* (Ottawa), 88 (1974): 47–55. W. D. Hamilton, *Dictionary of Miramichi biography; biographical sketches of men and women born before 1900 who played a part in public life on the Miramichi: Northumberland County, New Brunswick, Canada* (Saint John, 1997), 130–31. W. T. MacClement, "'The makers of Queen's': James Fowler, M.A., PH.D., F.R.S.C.," *Queen's Rev.*, 2 (1928): 2–4. D. P. Penhallow, "A review of Canadian botany from 1800 to 1895, part II," RSC, *Trans.*, 2nd ser., 3 (1897), sect.IV: 1–56. B. L. Robinson, "The New England Polygonums of the section Aviculare," *Rhodora* (Boston and Providence, R.I.), 4 (1902): 65–73. B. N. Smallman *et al.*, *Queen's biology: an academic history of innocence lost and fame gained, 1858–1965* (Kingston, 1991). *Who's who* (London), 1912.

FOX, MARGARET. *See* TOWNSEND

FRASER, Sir CHARLES FREDERICK, educator, editor, and businessman; b. 4 Jan. 1850 in Windsor, N.S., son of Benjamin DeWolf Fraser and Elizabeth Allison; grandson of James Fraser*; m. first 28 Sept. 1891 Ella Jane Hunter (d. 1909) in Fredericton; m. secondly 15 June 1910 Jane Catherine Roxby Stevens in Brooklyn, Hants County, N.S., and they had one son; d. 5 July 1925 in Halifax.

When Frederick Fraser was seven years old he injured his eye whittling a stick with a pocket knife. Neither his physician father nor the Boston specialist he consulted was able to repair the damage. Although he attended primary school in Windsor, his eyesight deteriorated steadily, and the sight in his other eye also worsened. At the age of 13, when an operation to create an artificial pupil failed, Fraser was enrolled in the Perkins Institution and Massachusetts Asylum for the Blind in Boston, the first and most famous school for the blind in the United States. By the time he left in 1872 he was completely blind.

The following year, abandoning plans to pursue a career in business, Fraser became the superintendent of the new Halifax Asylum for the Blind. The institution then had only half a dozen students and a small building. By the time Fraser retired in 1923 it had expanded significantly. Enrolments in the 1920s averaged about 120 students a year drawn from all three Maritime provinces and Newfoundland.

The program Fraser developed at the school was nearly identical to that followed at the Perkins Institution. It stressed literacy and the skills required for social and economic independence. The youngest children had kindergarten training, followed by four years of grammar school and six years of high school. Fraser strongly advocated physical education and mobility training, and he introduced gymnastics, walking clubs, and ice skating on the school pond; in 1915 the Halifax Local Council of Women would donate playground equipment. Musical training was at the centre of the curriculum, and many students, such as Arthur M. Chisholm*, were prepared for careers as music teachers, piano tuners, and church organists. For years Fraser himself taught music along with academic subjects and chair-caning. The school's industrial program also included broom- and basket-making and similar kinds of craft production. In 1891 typewriting was introduced, and over the next decades massage, shampooing, and bookkeeping were added.

Fraser was an indefatigable lobbyist. He regularly travelled through the Maritimes with a group of teachers and students, lecturing and presenting concerts to promote the school and to raise money. He vigorously pressed the provincial government to provide free education for the blind, which was enacted in 1882. Two years later the name of the institution was changed to Halifax School for the Blind to reflect its educational orientation. Fraser established a provincial circulating library of Braille books in 1881, and in 1898 he was successful in persuading the Canadian Post Office to handle Braille books postage-free.

Fraser's concern for the blind in the Maritimes extended beyond the school. In the 1880s he introduced an extension program, not only to prepare students for attendance at the school, but also to provide instruction to adult blind people in their homes; this work would be formalized in 1893 with the creation of the Home Teaching Society for the Blind of the Maritime Provinces and Newfoundland. By the early 20th century he was advocating prevention of blindness, especially ophthalmia neonatorum which could be successfully treated if identified early enough. In 1911 the Nova Scotia assembly would pass legislation requiring physicians and nurses to report cases of the disease. For many years Fraser promoted the establishment of special workshops for the blind, arguing that the difficulty blind industrial workers had in competing with the sighted made such workshops necessary if they were to lead independent, self-supporting lives. In 1909 he supported the formation of the Maritime Association for the Blind, a self-help group especially concerned with providing employment opportunities. In 1916 he began the Endowment Fund for the Blind to generate additional revenue for the school, the extension movement, the Maritime Association for the Blind, and the Canadian Printing House for the Blind (founded at the school in 1901), and to expand a program of financial assistance, begun in 1883, for graduates embarking on careers or further training. He also supported the Canadian National Institute for the Blind, established in 1918. In that year he served as a consultant to both the Massachusetts Commission for the Blind and the Ontario government, and he presented a number of papers to national and international meetings in his field.

World War I and the Halifax explosion had created an unusual chapter in the history of the school. In 1915 Fraser urged Canada to follow Britain's lead in training blind soldiers. By 1917 the school had a small group of Canadian soldiers, but this work ceased in the months following the explosion that year. Not only had the school building been extensively damaged but many parents withdrew their children, exacerbating the school's financial problems. Moreover, two hundred people were blinded by the explosion, and the school assumed special responsibility for these victims, with help from the Perkins Institution and the American National Red Cross. Training was provided, an eye clinic was established, and extension classes in cooking and sewing were conducted.

Fraser maintained a number of outside interests. He edited a weekly literary and commercial journal called the *Critic* from 1884 to 1894 when it was merged with the *Canadian Colliery Guardian* (Halifax). A long-standing member of the North British Society, he was elected president for 1885. He was the first president of the Halifax Canadian Club and a vice-president of the Halifax Archaeological Institute; in 1908 he was a promoter of the Nova Scotia League for the Care and Protection of Feeble-minded Persons. He worked as well in the Electoral Reform League and the British Empire League. Pursuing his early interest in business, he served as president of Nova Scotia Telephone and Trinidad Consolidated Telephone and as a director of a number of firms including Eastern Trust and Empire Trust.

Fraser's contribution to the welfare of the blind was significant and he received many tributes, including honorary degrees from King's College in Windsor and Dalhousie University in Halifax and special recognition from the provincial legislature in 1913. In 1915 he was knighted on the recommendation of his lifelong friend Sir Robert Laird Borden*. Although more honoured than many, Fraser was in a number of respects typical of those who supervised benevolent institutions in the 19th century. He himself had received specialized training, he worked in a specialized institution supported by philanthropy and the state which emphasized independence and employability, and he was interested in a number of reform causes. However, he was unusual in two ways, first because he shared the disability of his charges, and secondly because, unlike most of his colleagues, who were drawn from the lower middle class, he was a member of the social and economic elite of the province. At the time of his death he left a large estate which included two houses, his home in south-end Halifax and a summer residence in suburban Bedford, and substantial annuities to five of his extended family and friends in addition to the support provided for his widow and son.

JANET GUILDFORD

Halifax County Court of Probate (Halifax), Estate papers, 17: 104 (mfm. at NSARM). *Critic* (Halifax), 7 (1890); 8 (1891). *Evening Echo* (Halifax), 6 July 1925. *Evening Mail* (Halifax), 6 July 1925. *Halifax Herald*, 6 July 1925. *Morning Chronicle* (Halifax), 6 July 1925. *Annals, North British Society, Halifax, Nova Scotia, with portraits and biographical notes, 1768–1903*, comp. J. S. Macdonald ([3rd ed.], Halifax, 1905). M. R. Chandler, *A century of challenge: the history of the Ontario School for the Blind* (Belleville, Ont., 1980). *A genealogical and heraldic history of the peerage and baronetage . . .*, ed. A. P. Burke (80th ed., London, 1921). Halifax Asylum for the Blind, *Report of the board of managers*, 1872–78. Halifax Institution for the Blind, *Report of the board of managers*, 1879–84. Halifax School for the Blind, *Annual report of the board of managers*, 1884–1925. M. A. E. A. McNeil, *The blind knight of Nova Scotia: Sir Frederick Fraser, 1850–1925* (Washington, 1939). *Nova Scotia newspapers: a directory and union list, 1752–1988*, comp. Lynn Murphy et al. (Halifax, 1990). Harold Schwartz, *Samuel Gridley Howe, social reformer, 1801–1876* (Cambridge, Mass., 1956). *A survey and listing of Nova Scotia newspapers, 1752–1957, with particular reference to the period before 1867*, comp. G. E. N. Tratt (Halifax, 1979).

FRÉMONT, ANNETTE. *See* SAINT-AMANT

FRENCH, Sir GEORGE ARTHUR, army, militia, and NWMP officer; b. 19 June 1841 in Roscommon (Republic of Ireland), eldest son of John French and Isabella Hamilton; m. 18 Dec. 1862 Janet Clarke Innes (d. 1917) in Kingston, Upper Canada, and they had two sons and three daughters; d. 7 July 1921 in Kensington (London), England.

George Arthur French was Anglo-Irish, like so many other British army officers of the late 19th century. The fact that he started his military education at Sandhurst, but transferred to the Royal Military Academy in Woolwich (London) and became a gunner, suggests that his family was not well-to-do. Commissions in the Royal Artillery were not purchased as were those in infantry and cavalry regiments.

Appointed a lieutenant on 19 June 1860, French served with the RA in Kingston from 1862 to 1866. In 1869 he was seconded to the Canadian militia as inspector of artillery and warlike stores; though promoted lieutenant-colonel, a rank he would not achieve in the army until 1 Oct. 1887, he probably accepted the move as much for monetary as for career considerations. Conscious of the withdrawal of the imperial forces from Canada, French urged on the Department of Militia and Defence, in his report of 1 Jan. 1870, "the absolute necessity of raising, permanently, a few batteries of garrison artillery." To his recommendation he appended estimates for two batteries. In response the department moved to establish permanent schools of artillery in Kingston and Quebec City for training the militia. While retaining his inspectorship, French was authorized on 20 Oct. 1871 to set up and command Kingston's School of Gunnery (A Battery, Garrison Artillery).

When the government of Sir John A. Macdonald* created the North-West Mounted Police in 1873, the choice of who would be its first commissioner was of the utmost importance. There was no shortage of applicants, among them Thomas Bland STRANGE, commandant of the Quebec artillery school, and several senior militia officers. Macdonald's reasons for choosing French are not on record, but as Kingston's MP, he could hardly have avoided meeting this competent commander. As well, French had served briefly in the Royal Irish Constabulary before entering the army and since it was an important model for the NWMP, his experience may have influenced Macdonald's decision.

Although French took over as commissioner on 16 Oct. 1873, his duties in Kingston did not end until after the end of November. By then the NWMP was already partially in existence. News of the massacre in the Cypress Hills (Alta/Sask.) of Hunkajuka* and some of his followers by a band of Canadian and American traders and hunters had forced the government to advance its timetable; 150 recruits and several officers, among them James Farquharson Macleod*, had been sent to Winnipeg, where they had begun training under William Osborne Smith*. After visiting Winnipeg in January 1874 to assess his command, French returned to Toronto to raise a second contingent.

French, 16 officers (including his brother John*), 201 men, and 244 horses boarded special trains on 6 June and travelled west through Chicago to Fargo (N.Dak.). From there they rode north to Dufferin, Man., where they met the group who had wintered in Winnipeg. French's instructions were to take his force west to what is now southern Alberta and stop the whisky trade being conducted from the Montana Territory. The plan for the journey, which became known as the Long March, was to follow a route just north of the 49th parallel in order to take advantage of the camps and caches established by the international boundary surveyors [see Samuel Anderson*], but reports of fighting near the border between natives and the United States army caused Ottawa to order French to stay well north.

The change created serious difficulties for the NWMP. The only available map of the region, prepared by John Palliser*'s expedition of 1857, turned out to be inaccurate; guides could not be found; and the police were unable to locate feed and water for their horses. At the end of July, nearly a month after the march had begun, French sent a troop and the sickest horses north along the Carlton Trail to the Hudson's Bay Company's Fort Edmonton (Edmonton). The rest moved on across the trackless prairie; by early September it was apparent to most that French had no idea where they were. He did not lose his nerve, however, and kept pushing his weary men westward until they reached recognizable territory. On 18 September they halted and established a camp in the Sweet Grass Hills (Alta/Mont.).

French took a party south to Fort Benton (Mont.) to obtain horses and supplies and to telegraph Ottawa. He also gathered evidence about the Cypress Hills massacre. The government approved his plan to leave most of his force in the Belly River area while he trekked northeast to establish headquarters at Swan River (Livingstone, Sask.). The site, chosen in Ottawa because of its location on the proposed rail line to the Pacific coast, had little else to recommend it, as French discovered when he arrived on 21 Octo-

ber. It was not close to any major concentration of native people, nor was there any settlement in the area. Moreover, the barren locale had been swept by fire and the contractors had not completed the buildings. Convinced that it would not be possible to get all his men and horses through the winter there, French left about 30 men behind and, though he had no jurisdiction in Manitoba, wisely moved his headquarters south to Dufferin.

When French returned to Swan River in the spring of 1875, he loyally tried to make it habitable. In his correspondence with Ottawa, he nonetheless made no secret of his negative opinion of the post and lobbied strenuously to have his headquarters moved to Fort Macleod (Alta), where most of the force's actual policing was centred. Unfortunately for French, the political climate as it affected the NWMP had changed following the formation of a Liberal government in late 1873. The new prime minister, Alexander Mackenzie*, was exceedingly parsimonious and he and his cabinet harboured grave doubts about the wisdom of creating the NWMP in the first place. A Conservative appointee, French was unlikely to receive a sympathetic hearing. Moreover, the fact that he had many suggestions for improving the force, all expensive, confirmed the government's suspicion that he was a profligate.

By early 1876 the situation had become acute. Aware that he no longer had the confidence of the government, French attempted to bring matters to a head. In March he wrote to the minister of justice, Edward Blake*, asking for permission to travel to Ottawa to discuss a host of pressing problems. Permission was refused. In an exchange of telegrams over the next two months, he kept advancing reasons to visit the capital, but his political masters kept denying his requests. When he offered to pay for the trip and still was turned down, he knew his position was untenable. He resigned in July 1876. His officers and men showed a greater appreciation of his work: they gave him a gold watch worth $150 (a large sum for the time) and Mrs French a silver service. The British government also recognized his efforts, with a CMG on 30 May 1877.

French went back to postings with the Royal Artillery in England, interspersed with appointments in Australia and India. He was inspector of warlike stores at Devonport from 1878 until he became commandant of the colonial forces in Queensland in 1883. In 1885 the defence force there was reorganized under legislation drafted by French and based on Canada's system. On his return to England in 1891, he was put in command of the RA at Dover. From June 1892 to October 1893 he served as a chief instructor at the School of Gunnery in Shoeburyness. He then spent two years as a staff colonel commanding the RA in Bombay (Mumbai). His last appointment was as commandant of the colonial forces in New South Wales. Promoted major-general on 25 May 1900, he retired from the army in September 1902 and was made a KCMG that year. He lived in London until his death.

A moderately distinguished army man, French played an important, if brief, role in the history of Canada. He helped facilitate the creation of a permanent defence force. As the first permanent commissioner of the NWMP, he organized it and got it firmly established in the west, but the difficulties involved and the lack of political support from the Mackenzie government led to his early resignation and departure from Canada.

RODERICK C. MACLEOD

AO, RG 80-27-2, 10: 4. LAC, RG 18. *Times* (London), 8, 11, 13 July 1921. *Australian dictionary of biography*, ed. Douglas Pike *et al.* (16v. and index to date, Melbourne, 1966–). Can., Parl., *Sessional papers*, 1871, no.7: 123–31; 1872, no.8: 86–95; 1874, no.7: 37–39, 49–51. *Canada Gazette*, 21 Oct. 1871: 343–46. *Canadian men and women of the time* (Morgan; 1898). *Debrett's peerage, baronetage, knightage, and companionage* . . . (London), 1920. G.B., War Office, *The official army list* (London), 1882, 1910. *Hart's annual army list* . . . (London), 1874, 1893–95, 1901. R. C. Macleod, *The NWMP and law enforcement, 1873–1905* (Toronto, 1976). G. W. L. Nicholson, *The gunners of Canada; the history of the Royal Regiment of Canadian Artillery* (2v., Toronto, 1967–72), 1. H. P. Noble, "The commissioner who almost wasn't," *RCMP Quarterly* (Ottawa), 30 (1964–65), no.2: 9–10. J. P. Turner, *The North-West Mounted Police, 1873–1893* . . . (2v., Ottawa, 1950), 1.

FRIEDLANDER, ELIAS, rabbi; b. probably on 12 July 1846 in Kovno (Kaunas, Lithuania); m. with two sons and two daughters; d. 22 Feb. 1927 in Victoria.

Elias Friedlander received his education in rabbinics at the rabbinical academy of Kovno. Subsequently he immigrated to Germany, where he prepared for the rabbinate at the Jewish Theological Seminary of Breslau (Wrocław, Poland), which taught a blend of traditional Judaism and moderate reform in ritual. At age 21 he accepted his first congregation, in Sunderland, Durham, England, where he served from 1871 to 1878. From 1879 to 1882 he was the spiritual leader of the English and German congregation in Kingston, Jamaica.

In 1884 Friedlander was elected to the position of minister of the Congregation of English, German and Polish Jews of Montreal, one of the largest Jewish congregations in Montreal, which represented a moderate, acculturated traditionalism. Its members had great respect for religious customs and ceremonies within the synagogue, but had largely adopted English Canadian norms in their personal lives. Two years later Friedlander officiated at the consecration of a new synagogue for the congregation, named Shaar Hashomayim. In 1887 he was a founding member of one of the first proto-Zionist societies in Canada, probably the Hovevei Zion Society of Montreal. It never flourished, however. He remained at Shaar Hashomayim until 1896, when he resigned because of differences with the congregation's trustees. From 1896 to 1899 he lived in New York City and Chicago.

In 1899 Friedlander returned to Montreal and he ministered as rabbi to the Reform congregation of Temple Emanu-El until 1901. Reform Judaism had arisen in Germany in the early 19th century when many German Jews sought to transform their religion and their way of life so as to show themselves worthy of equal rights with Christians and to present Judaism as a religion in consonance with western norms. It attempted to renew Judaism through changes in liturgy and the abrogation of numerous Judaic laws which restricted Jews from fully engaging in the life of the Gentile world. In Canada, Reform Judaism had spread much less quickly than in the United States, largely because Jews from England had established a basic pattern of respect for their ancient forms of public worship which neither interfered with their acculturation nor represented a major issue in the debate over their political rights.

Subsequently, from 1905 to 1907, Friedlander served as rabbi of the Shaarey Shomayim Congregation in Winnipeg, which likewise represented acculturated Jews, and as rabbi of a congregation in Vancouver. He spent some time in New York City before being elected rabbi of Temple Emanu-El in Victoria in 1910. He retired from the rabbinate in 1912 and died in Victoria in 1927.

IRA ROBINSON

British Columbia Vital Statistics Agency (Victoria), Death registration records (mfm. at the Victoria Geneal. Soc.). *Victoria Daily Times*, 22 Feb. 1927. *A biographical dictionary of Canadian Jewry, 1909–1914: from "The Canadian Jewish Times"*, comp. L. F. Tapper (Teaneck, N.J., [1992?]). A. A. Chiel, *The Jews in Manitoba: a social history* (Toronto, 1961). C. E. Leonoff, *Pioneers, pedlars, and prayer shawls: the Jewish communities in British Columbia and the Yukon* (Victoria, 1978). B. G. Sack, *History of the Jews in Canada*, trans. Ralph Novek, [ed. Maynard Gertler] ([2nd ed.], Montreal, 1965).

G

GADBOIS, JOSEPH-PIERRE, physician, athlete, sports columnist, promoter of physical education, and office holder; b. 15 Aug. 1868 in Saint-Urbain-Premier, Que., son of Pierre Gadbois, a carpenter, and Aglaé Langlois; m. 31 May 1893 Julia Gauthier in Montreal, and they had three sons and two daughters; d. there 22 Aug. 1930.

When Joseph-Pierre Gadbois was very young, his parents moved to Saint-Jean (Saint-Jean-sur-Richelieu), which he would consider his real home town. He attended the Petit Séminaire de Montréal from 1881 to 1887 and then enrolled in the Montreal School of Medicine and Surgery. The school merged with the medical faculty of the Université Laval's Montreal campus in 1890, and it was from this institution that he received his MD with high honours in 1892. His studies completed, Gadbois took up residence in Montreal, where he specialized in the treatment of alcoholism and drug addiction. Sometime around the month of May in 1893 L. W. Murphy, a Catholic priest, hired him as medical director of a clinical institute he had just opened on Rue Sainte-Catherine, where he treated alcoholics with gold bichloride. Murphy's method, known as the Gold Cure, was questioned by many physicians but was much in vogue in the United States. Late in 1893 Gadbois opened his own hospital on Rue Saint-Laurent, where he used this approach for alcoholics and morphine addicts. In 1895 he announced the publication of two works on the Gold Cure, which he had been studying for three years, but they apparently never came out. Montreal physician Joseph-Edmond Bergeron regarded him at the time as a leading light in the treatment of alcoholism and drug addiction. Gadbois moved his hospital twice, in 1897 and 1899, and around 1900 he put aside the practice of medicine in order to devote his time to promoting sports, hygiene, and physical education.

Gadbois would all his life encourage regular participation in sports and physical exercises. When he was still a child, his father, who was a good wrestler and a powerful arm wrestler, had taught him the rudiments of his art. Young Joseph-Pierre soon excelled at wrestling, boxing, swimming, jumping, canoeing, and handball. In his third year at the Petit Séminaire de Montréal he had won the handball championship, and he retained his title as champion until he finished his studies there.

In October 1900, seeking to rouse his fellow French Canadians' interest in physical exercise, Gadbois opened a gymnasium at his hospital. To spread his ideas, he sometimes gave lectures. From 7 March 1904, the newspaper *La Presse* also provided him with a forum by giving him a column headed "Culture physique." By 1908 it had published more than 500 of his pieces. He also contributed to *La Patrie* (Montréal) and *Le Soleil* (Québec). These columns bore witness to his concerns. Although Gadbois appreciated the advantages of the city, he worried about its effects on the health of his compatriots. He believed that in the country, where they remained in contact with a harsh but abundant nature, they had been able to maintain their strength, sturdiness, and physique. Once they became urbanites, crowded into smoke-filled cities, confined to unhealthy lodgings, and cooped up in poorly ventilated offices, workshops, and stores, they grew sickly and were threatened with degeneration. He thought that physical education, which is not the same thing as exaggerated muscular development, guaranteed health and a balanced and harmonious condition. He advised against overeating and advocated dieting and occasional fasting to cleanse the body. He preached abstinence from alcohol, drugs, tea, and coffee, and recommended drinking plenty of water and eating vegetables, fruit, and nuts. A vegetarian, he gave a lecture at Quebec in 1909 under the auspices of the Vegetarian Society of Canada. It is essential, he noted, to have eight hours sleep every night, keep windows open summer and winter, brave storms, heat, and cold, and get as much sunshine as possible.

Among the sports that could ensure complete development, Gadbois chose wrestling and swimming, but he encouraged participation in many others. The proliferation of hockey leagues prompted him to caution French Canadians against dissipating their efforts and he urged them to work together in all branches of sport. Faced with the popularity of contests of strength in Quebec, he regretted that the lack of uniform rules and methods prevented meaningful comparison between athletes, and he expressed a wish that some feats of strength better suited to the circus than to athletic competition be banned from these tournaments. Gadbois also blamed the educational system for valuing the mind and neglecting the body. In his view, sports and physical education should be compulsory in French-speaking educational institutions. He was delighted when Sergeant-Major Henri-Thomas SCOTT was hired in 1905 to take charge of the teaching of physical education in all the schools of the Montreal Catholic School Commission. In his columns Gadbois also dealt with the health of women, children, and the elderly. He called for medical inspection of schools and recommended that the inspection team include two women physicians – a novel idea in 1907.

Gadbois did not limit himself to writing. He was active in sports as an administrator of associations, promoter of events, judge, and athlete. In 1897 he was elected to the board of the Montreal Swimming Club, of which he would be president from 1904 to 1907. A charter member and vice-president of the Association des Francs-Tireurs de Montréal in 1900, he took part as a marksman in its first organized competition in 1901. He was a life member of one of the most important French Canadian sports organizations, the Association Athlétique d'Amateurs Nationale, which was better known from 1919 by the name of Palestre Nationale. He sat on its board of directors from 1904 to 1907 and in 1922–23, and he served on a number of its commissions from 1918 to 1924. From 1903 to 1909 his name was also frequently associated with the activities of the Club de Raquette le Montagnard. Moreover, he was regularly chosen as a judge by those organizing competitions of strength for women and men. At the famous contest between Louis Cyr* and Otto Ronaldo in 1899, he was not only one of the three judges, but also Cyr's official representative and one of his trainers. In order to demonstrate the physical strength of French Canadians, Gadbois organized, with the support of *La Presse*, a competition with "bags of salt" which aroused exceptional enthusiasm. On 31 Oct. 1907 the 121 competitors were cheered by 300,000 people (an estimate no doubt inflated). One journalist exclaimed that this demonstration surpassed any that Montreal had ever witnessed, even the protest meeting that followed the hanging of Louis Riel*. In 1919 Gadbois became a charter member and secretary of the Fédération Canadienne des Poids et Haltères.

Gadbois was also known at that time as the popularizer of wrestling in Montreal and the leading expert on the subject. Early in the 20th century he organized events and advised and trained wrestlers, thereby contributing to the great popularity of this sport in the period 1904 to 1908. In 1905 one of his protégés, Montreal wrestler Eugène Tremblay, won the world lightweight championship. Montreal began to rival Buffalo and Chicago as a place for championship matches. His extensive knowledge of Graeco-Roman wrestling and all-in wrestling made "the doctor," as he was familiarly called, indispensable. He was chosen as referee for almost all the important matches in Montreal, sometimes at Quebec or elsewhere in the province, and even in Buffalo. To promote his favourite sport more effectively, Gadbois, with his friend George Washington KENDALL, became a leading spirit in the Club Athlétique Canadien, which was incorporated in 1908. The most important of its kind in Canada, this organization sent representatives to the United States, Europe, and as far away as Turkey to seek new stars. The club was also interested in boxing and bowling and it purchased the Canadiens hockey club in 1910. A principal shareholder, Gadbois sat on the board of directors and was elected president in 1908 and 1909.

One of the best handball players in Canada, Gadbois held the title of Montreal champion for some time. Between 1897 and 1904 he made a number of unsuccessful attempts to take the Canadian championship away from Napoléon Lavoie* of Quebec. He was also said to be a champion in amateur and professional wrestling.

Gadbois was interested in politics as well and was active in the Liberal party. In 1909 he was elected secretary-treasurer of the Liberals' Club Saint-Louis, where he rubbed shoulders with MLA Godfroy LANGLOIS and the mayor of Montreal, Louis Payette. From 1 Feb. 1906 to 31 Jan. 1910 he represented Saint-Louis ward on the Montreal city council, where he was elected to eight commissions and sat on 10 committees. Among other things, he appeared before the police commission to request more children's parks and more involvement of officers in gymnastics. His battle against the electricity, water, and gas monopolies placed him in the camp of the "progressives." However, charges of influence peddling, which were brought against him during the royal commission on the municipal administration conducted by judge Lawrence John CANNON in 1909, tarnished his reputation. Almost all the councillors were implicated and eight of them, including Gadbois, were formally charged and sentenced to a fine. Gadbois protested his innocence and claimed to have been unjustly treated. He ran for office again in Saint-Louis ward, but, like most of his former colleagues, he was swept away by the wave that engulfed the council on 1 Feb. 1910.

Thereafter Gadbois disappeared from the sporting scene and began speculating in land. In the fall of 1910 he bought half of a property in Pointe-aux-Trembles, to the east of Montreal, and subdivided it into 1,500 lots. For nearly a year he flooded the newspapers with advertisements, dangling before potential buyers the prospect of fantastic profits, but he met with little success. Early in 1912 he began a new campaign to sell shares in the Three Nations Gold Mine at Porcupine, near Timmins, Ont., but he failed to find enough investors and soon abandoned the endeavour.

On 15 May 1914 Gadbois's career took a new turn. He became a city employee, when he was appointed, jointly with T. C. M. Black, to the new position of superintendent of playgrounds. Mayor Médéric Martin* opposed the hiring of Black and had seen to it that Gadbois would receive a higher salary; Black was an American who, in the mayor's opinion, knew nothing about French Canadian ways, and he did not speak the language of the majority. Black did not accept this arrangement and resigned. On 14 July 1914 the board of commissioners named Gadbois the sole director of the city's playgrounds. For the rest of his life he would work to develop and improve them.

In 1915 he was in charge of eight playgrounds and nine skating rinks. By 1929 he was supervising 24 playgrounds, including one he had had laid out in Sohmer Park, 15 public baths (which had come under his jurisdiction in 1918), and some 100 skating rinks. To learn more about his field, Gadbois visited a number of American cities, including New York. Numerous types of apparatus that he invented were installed in the playgrounds. For more than 15 years he would attend all the major picnics, sports events, and physical education festivals.

In spite of his responsibilities, Gadbois still had a passion for the world of sports. In the early 1920s he was training boxers and guiding their careers. In 1929 he had the pleasure of seeing his daughter Pauline win the provincial tennis championship in the "ladies' doubles" category.

Throughout his career, Joseph-Pierre Gadbois had never been afraid to oppose the ideas of his contemporaries. Just out of university, he had defended controversial methods of therapy. His promotion of vegetarianism is surprising. His campaign to improve the teaching of anatomy and physical education, and to give sports a larger place in the schools, set him apart. Gadbois was one of the small French-speaking elite who burst into the world of sports at the end of the 19th century.

GILLES JANSON

[This biography draws heavily on newspapers, in particular *La Presse*, where Joseph-Pierre Gadbois worked as a sports writer between 1904 and 1908. Many unsigned articles that appeared in the paper from 1907 to 1910 are undoubtedly his, among them "Les tournois athlétiques de *la Presse*," a series of 165 columns published between 14 Oct. 1907 and 9 July 1908. A large number of items concerning Gadbois can also be found in *La Presse* from 1893 to 1930. Other useful newspaper accounts include the following: *L'Autorité nouvelle* (Montréal), 25 janv. 1914; *Le Canada* (Montréal), 24 avril, 3 sept. 1903; 8–9 avril, 24 juin, 3 sept. 1918; 11, 21 févr., 6, 24 mars 1919; 10–11, 17, 22, 24 mai, 4, 8 juin 1926; 23, 25 août 1930; *Le Cultivateur* (Montréal), 13 mai 1893; *Le Devoir*, 15 mai, 21 juill. 1914; 16 nov. 1915; 14 juill. 1916; 20 avril 1918; 23 août 1930; *Le Journal* (Montréal), 14 juin 1902; *La Minerve*, 11, 16 oct., 6 nov. 1897; *Le Nationaliste* (Montréal), 16, 23 janv., 6, 20, 28 nov., 4 déc. 1910; 12, 19, 26 mars, 2 avril, 7 mai, 4, 11, 18 juin, 23 juill., 27 août 1911; 25 févr., 3, 10, 24 mars, 14, 28 avril, 5, 19 mai 1912; 14 juin 1914; *La Patrie*, 16 mars, 24 avril, 9 juin 1903; 30 mars, 1er avril 1929; 23, 25 août 1930; *Le Réveil* (Montréal), 5 janv., 31 août 1915; and *Le Soleil*, 22, 24–25, 29–30 juin, 2–3, 7–8 juill., 24 août, 15 oct. 1908; 26, 28, 30 avril, 6 mai, 16 juin, 9 juill., 21 oct. 1909; 28 mai 1914. G.J.]

ANQ-M, CE601-S51, 31 mai 1893; CE607-S20, 23 août 1868. Arch. de l'Univ. du Québec à Montréal, 1P (fonds de la Palestre nationale), 2/34–38; 13/11. Arch. du Séminaire de Saint-Sulpice (Montréal), Fonds du collège de Montréal, liste des étudiants. VM-DGDA, "Comités et commissions: 1900 à nos jours" (report prepared by the Div. des arch.), 1906–10; P39; VM6, Dossiers de coupures de presse, DO16.293 (J.-P. Gadbois); VM47, procès-verbaux, 20 févr. 1906–17 janv. 1908. "Bulletin," *L'Union médicale du Canada* (Montréal), 21 (1892): 220, 548–51; 22 (1893): 217–19. L. J. Cannon, *Rapport sur l'administration de la ville de Montréal, décembre 1909* (s.l., n.d.). "Correspondance," *L'Union médicale du Canada*, 22: 235–36. *Directory*, Montreal, 1890–1910. P. A. Dutil, "'Adieu, demeure chaste et pure'; Godfroy Langlois et le virage vers le progressisme libéral," in *Combats libéraux au tournant du XXe siècle*, sous la dir. d'Yvan Lamonde (Montréal, 1995), 247–75. Jean de Laplante, *Les parcs de Montréal: des origines à nos jours* (Montréal, 1990), 86–92. É.-Z. Massicotte, *Athlètes canadiens-français; recueil des exploits de force, d'endurance, d'agilité, des athlètes et des sportsmen de notre race depuis le XVIIIe siècle; biographies, portraits, anecdotes, records* (2e éd., Montréal, [1909]), 216–23. "Le sport chez nos Canadiennes," *La Rev. moderne* (Montréal), 10 (1929), no.10: 12.

GAGE, Sir WILLIAM JAMES, teacher, businessman, and philanthropist; b. 16 Sept. 1849 in Toronto Township, Upper Canada, son of Andrew Albert Gage and Mary Jane Grafton; m. 4 May 1880 Ina (Imey) Burnside in Toronto, and they had five daughters, one of whom died in infancy; d. there 14 Jan. 1921.

The youngest of seven children, William J. Gage was born on a farm south of Brampton. His father was originally from Stoney Creek; his mother, a native of South Carolina, had come to Upper Canada in 1812. Educated in Derry West and at the Brampton grammar school, he received his teaching certificate from the Toronto Normal School in 1866 and taught for three years in Broddytown (Brampton) before entering the Toronto School of Medicine. Though he could not tolerate the gruesome aspects of the operating theatre and left the school after a year, he would later channel his time and riches into the field of health.

Gage subsequently focused his passion for efficiency, his energy, and his Methodist ideals on commerce and charity. In 1871 he embarked on his first venture, buying and selling cordwood in Brampton. He then became a bookkeeper with a Toronto publisher, Adam Miller and Company. After Miller's death in 1875, he continued as a partner in the firm, which he took over in 1879 and renamed W. J. Gage and Company. Although the market for textbooks, its most important line, was rife with competition, governmental intrusion, and copyright disputes, Gage achieved considerable success. In 1893 his company was incorporated. A promotional booklet later claimed that "there is . . . not a community throughout the Dominion where the schoolbooks published by this house have not found a place."

After fire destroyed Gage's building on Front Street in 1904, he immediately constructed a five-storey factory on Spadina Avenue, "laid out to handle the business in the most systematic and economic way possible." His integrated operation included a paper plant in St Catharines, sophisticated Miehle presses for colour printing, and the sale of writing paper and envelopes in addition to textbooks. An imposing figure, he presided over a richly decorated office that reflected his thoroughness and attention to detail, qualities also evident in his private life. He was an affectionate but at times controlling husband whose letters to his wife, during his travels on business, frequently reprimanded her for not writing more often.

In 1893, with some wealth at his disposal, Gage had turned his attention to tuberculosis, Canada's most lethal disease. He committed himself to the sanatorium movement – drug treatment would not become available until the 1940s – and investigated sanatoria in Europe and the United States. His offer in 1894 to fund a hospital in Toronto had the backing of the Board of Trade, whose president, Hugh Blain, had encouraged Gage to tackle tuberculosis, but city council hesitated. "No . . . delightful reward awaited the man who tried to start sanatoria, especially in the early years of the movement," Gage would recall. Some critics even sent him threatening letters. Publicly regarded as incurable and contagious, tuberculosis was popularly associated with indigence, squalor, overcrowding, and unhygienic living habits. Gage remained undaunted, however, and in 1895 Hart Almerrin Massey* and other influential citizens threw their weight behind his efforts.

In 1896 Gage helped found the National Sanitarium Association and two years later the Toronto Citizens' Sanatorium Committee, which led to the creation in 1900 of the Toronto Association for the Prevention and Treatment of Consumption and Other Forms of Tuberculosis. Between 1897 and 1913 he established several treatment facilities: the Muskoka Cottage Sanatorium and the Muskoka Free Hospital for Consumptives near Gravenhurst; the Toronto Free Hospital for Consumptives, the King Edward Sanatorium for Consumptives, and the Queen Mary Hospital for Children, all near Weston (Toronto); and a free dispensary in Toronto. In 1912 he initiated the King Edward Memorial Fund for Consumptives. The following year, in recognition of his work, he was made a knight of grace of the Order of St John of Jerusalem in England.

Gage also used his money to promote his political and religious values. In 1893 he had headed a group who purchased the Toronto *Evening Star* to fight the provincial Liberal government, which, by taking control of the copyrights on many textbooks, had undermined Gage's near-monopoly. He also wanted a vehicle for defending the local ban on streetcar service on the sabbath. As chairman of the Citizens' Anti-Sunday Car Association, he challenged Mayor Warring Kennedy to resist mounting pressure for Sunday service, which the *Star* saw as a sign of "degenerate days." Gage's campaigns ended in 1895

when the newspaper was bought by Edmund Ernest SHEPPARD, fronting for Frederic Thomas NICHOLLS and the Toronto Street Railway.

The streetcar commotion, which concluded in 1897 with the authorization of Sunday service, was not the end of Gage's civic involvement. He was active in the Board of Trade, and was a delegate in 1909 to the Congress of Chambers of Commerce of the Empire, where he argued that the colonies should have their own laws on copyright. Elected president of the board the following year, he pushed for the development of the city's waterfront, a board of harbour commissioners, and improved highways between Toronto and York County. "We should plan for a city of a million people," he reasoned in January 1910. In November he took the lead in forming the Ontario Associated Boards of Trade and became its first president.

During the war years Gage's sanatoria interests remained strong. At a cost of more than $100,000, he funded the construction of the National Sanitarium Association's new headquarters and dispensary (the Gage Institute), which opened on 10 Feb. 1915. The following year he helped negotiate the admission of tubercular soldiers to the Muskoka sanatorium, demonstrating in the process his autocratic style and skill in driving hard bargains. In 1917 Gage and his wife set aside $110,000 for the Ina Grafton Homes Corporation, to provide rental accommodation for war widows and orphans. He was granted an honorary LLD that year by Mount Allison College in Sackville, N.B., and in 1918 he was made a knight bachelor.

Gage was much sought after for the boards of other charities and businesses. He chaired the Toronto branch of the Victorian Order of Nurses, and was a director of the Imperial Bank of Canada, the Traders' Bank of Canada, the Ontario Sugar Company, and the Anglo-American Fire Insurance Company. Devastated by the burning of the Muskoka Free Hospital on New Year's Eve 1920, he suffered a stroke and died at his Wychwood Park estate. His church, Trinity Methodist, held two services in his honour. The *Toronto Daily Star* stated that Gage had "combined a kindly and understanding mind with great fixity and tenacity of purpose." He represented a generation of businessmen who put profit-making in the service of humanitarianism to achieve their concept of a better society.

MOLLY PULVER UNGAR and VICKY BACH

AO, F 1193-A-3, box 24, folder 141; RG 22-305, no.42995; RG 80-5-0-95, no.13255. Private arch., Mrs Diana Gage Griffith Tisdall (Toronto), Gage family papers. TRL, SC, Biog. files, vols.2–3, 6. *Toronto Daily Star*, 8 Jan., 8, 11 March, 10, 18 June, 16 July, 2 Oct. 1894; 5, 8, 14–15 Jan. 1921. G. C. Brink, *Across the years: tuberculosis in Ontario* ([Willowdale (Toronto), 1965]). *Canadian annual rev.*, 1901–21. Canadian Assoc. for the Prevention of Tuberculosis, *Annual report* (Ottawa), 1901–21. *Canadian men and women of the time* (Morgan; 1898 and 1912). *Construction* (Toronto), 11 (1918): 168–74. *Dict. of Toronto printers* (Hulse). *Dominion annual reg.*, 1883. G. L. Gale, *The changing years: the story of Toronto Hospital and the fight against tuberculosis* (Toronto, 1979). Ross Harkness, *J. E. Atkinson of the "Star"* (Toronto, 1963). Gerald Killan, *David Boyle: from artisan to archaeologist* (Toronto, 1983). Desmond Morton and Glenn Wright, *Winning the second battle: Canadian veterans and the return to civilian life, 1915–1930* (Toronto, 1987). G. L. Parker, *The beginnings of the book trade in Canada* (Toronto, 1985). *The province of Ontario: a history, 1615–1927*, ed. J. E. Middleton and Fred Landon (5v., Toronto, 1927–[28]), 5: 789–91. Victor Ross and A. St L. Trigge, *A history of the Canadian Bank of Commerce, with an account of the other banks which now form part of its organization* (3v., Toronto, 1920–34), 3. *Standard dict. of Canadian biog.* (Roberts and Tunnell). G. H. Stanford, *To serve the community: the story of Toronto's Board of Trade* (Toronto, 1974). W. J. Gage and Company, *Manufactured stationery, 1909–1910: catalogue no.1* (Toronto, [1909]); *Educational works & school blanks: catalogue no.4, 1911–1912* (Toronto, [1911]); copies in TRL, SC). G. J. Wherrett, *The miracle of the empty beds: a history of tuberculosis in Canada* (Toronto, 1977). *Who's who and why*, 1921.

GAGNON, GUSTAVE (baptized **Gustave-Adolphe-Mathurin**), organist, teacher, university administrator, and composer; b. 6 Nov. 1842 in Rivière-du-Loup (Louiseville), Lower Canada, youngest of the nine children of Charles-Édouard Gagnon, a notary, and Julie-Jeanne Durand; m. 9 July 1873, in Quebec City, Séphora Hamel, daughter of merchant Abraham Hamel and niece of artist Théophile Hamel*, and they had two sons and two daughters; d. there 19 Nov. 1930.

The younger brother of musician and folklorist Ernest Gagnon*, Gustave Gagnon completed the classical studies course at the Collège Joliette and received musical training in Montreal from his brother-in-law Paul Letondal, a blind French émigré who would become a distinguished pianist, cellist, and organist. Gagnon was active over a long period as an organist at Saint-Jean-Baptiste church (1864–70) and at Notre-Dame basilica (1876–1915), both in Quebec City. Like his brother Ernest and others of his generation, he furthered his education in Europe; he was there from 1870 to 1872. In Paris he studied organ with Charles-Alexis Chauvet, piano with Antoine-François Marmontel, and harmony with Auguste Durand. Later in Liège, Belgium, he studied piano with Félix-Étienne Ledent and harmony with Jean-Théodore Radoux. During the summer holidays of 1871 and 1872 he visited the German musical centres of Dresden and Leipzig, where he received organ lessons from Benjamin Robert Papperitz and Louis Plaidy. Highlights of his European sojourn were his meetings with Camille Saint-Saëns and Franz Liszt. He met Liszt first in Rome and later had the opportunity in Leipzig to attend a rehearsal of Liszt's *Legend of St Elizabeth* with the composer conducting.

On his return to Quebec Gagnon began a long, distinguished career as an educator and a few years later he again took up a position as organist. A founder, with Ernest, of the Académie de Musique de Québec in 1868 in order to set province-wide standards and examinations, Gagnon was throughout his career a devoted and high-principled teacher. His students included Joseph-Daniel Dussault, later organist at Notre-Dame church in Montreal, Léo-Pol Morin*, a pianist and influential music critic, and his own son Henri*, who would succeed his father in 1915 as organist at the basilica and hold the post to 1961. Gagnon also taught at the École Normale Laval and the Petit Séminaire de Québec and he helped to establish and taught at the branch of the Dominion College of Music in Quebec City.

Spanning a 60-year period, Gagnon's work as a musician and teacher was highly regarded and recognized. His appointment in 1922 as the first director of the newly formed École de Musique at the Université Laval, where he taught until 1930, is ample testimony of the esteem in which he was held. As the school's first director, he had a major impact on curriculum; importance was attached to church music, such as plainchant and organ music. He was considered a knowledgeable and compassionate teacher and a fine administrator.

As a composer, Gagnon is remembered today for several piano compositions, notably *Reflets du passé* and *Souvenirs de Leipzig*, both in the tradition of the 19th-century descriptive, often virtuosic, character-piece for piano. Also well known is his *Marche pontificale*, composed for either piano or organ and later orchestrated by Joseph VÉZINA. Gagnon's church music includes a harmonized setting of the popular plainchant *Messe royale* by the 17th-century French composer Henry de Thier, *dit* Du Mont. This work was performed in June 1880 on the Plains of Abraham by a 600-voice choir at the same celebrations that included the inaugural performance of Calixa Lavallée*'s *O Canada*.

Often discussed in conjunction with the achievements of his brother Ernest – their lives shared many parallels – Gustave Gagnon's career was marked by unusually long, sustained musical productivity, which contributed to a lasting legacy of high standards in church music and organ performance through the 20th century in French Canada.

GORDON E. SMITH

ANQ-MBF, CE401-S15, 6 nov. 1842. ANQ-Q, CE301-S1, 9 juill. 1873. *Le Devoir*, 19 nov. 1930. *Encyclopedia of music in Canada* (Kallmann *et al.*). Arthur Letondal, "Gustave Gagnon," *La Rev. moderne* (Montréal), 2 (1921), no.8: 13–14. J.-M. Turgeon, *Les vendredis de l'oncle Gaspard* (Québec, 1944), 193–200.

GALLANT, JOSEPH, farmer and businessman, b. 19 March 1839 in Rustico, P.E.I., son of Isidore Gallant, *dit* Bronne, and Sophie Pineau; m. there 18 Nov. 1862 Frances Elizabeth Coffin, and they had five daughters, one of whom died in infancy, and two sons, one adoptive; d. there 23 Sept. 1923.

Joseph Gallant's father was one of the most prosperous Acadian farmers in Rustico. Evidently Joseph attended the local elementary school and worked on the family farm before going to Charlottetown, where he found employment with Carvell Brothers, the largest exporter of merchandise on the Island [*see* Jedediah Slason Carvell*]. By also serving as a stable boy for a well-to-do family who gave him room and board, he was able to save enough money to buy a 50-acre farm when he returned to Rustico.

When he moved onto his farm, Gallant also ventured into the world of business. He opened a small store in his home, where around 1871 he took on the job of postmaster as well. In 1880 he had an impressive house built in Second Empire style in which he kept a store. That year he invested in maritime commerce, having a 77-ton schooner, the *Four Sisters*, built. He bought another one in 1884, the *Acadian*, of 84 tons burden. Gallant was able to export the produce of land and sea, principally to Massachusetts, Newfoundland, Nova Scotia, and New Brunswick, for some 40 years. The ships brought back mainly coal and building lumber. In 1880 *Le Moniteur acadien* sang his praises as a businessman. "Thanks to his skilful management, Mr Gallant sees his business grow and prosper, and success attends him in all his undertakings."

At the end of the 19th century, Gallant was at the height of his career. He owned three stores, two schooners, a farm, and warehouses. Most of his transactions were carried out from his store in Rusticoville, where he had even had a wharf built. He was undeniably the most important businessman in his region and, with Gilbert DesRoches*, one of the most prosperous in the province's Acadian community.

Father George-Antoine Bellecourt*, the dynamic founder in 1861 of the Farmers' Bank of Rustico, had officiated at Gallant's wedding, and the two men were neighbours until 1869. Although Gallant had not been a founding director of the bank, he became its second president in 1878. The bank had experienced quite serious administrative difficulties for several years, and Gallant, along with the cashier (general manager), Adrien Doiron, was responsible for getting it back on a sound footing. He approached the federal government many times in order to get its charter renewed in 1883 and 1891, but it finally expired in 1894. As president, Gallant had to deal with the liquidation of this people's bank, which was a forerunner of the *caisse populaire* [*see* Alphonse Desjardins*] and credit union movements in North America.

When Joseph Gallant, who was nicknamed Dandy Joe, died in 1923, he was quite heavily in debt. It is believed that the man to whom he had entrusted the management of his business in his old age and illness was responsible for this situation. After the death of this pioneer among Acadian businessmen in Prince Edward Island, his lovely home in Rustico, his farm, and his business were sold. Fortunately the residence has been preserved and restored. Known as Barachois Inn, it stands opposite St Augustine's Church and the parish hall that housed the Farmers' Bank of Rustico, now a national historic site.

G<small>EORGES</small> A<small>RSENAULT</small>

Centre de Recherches Acadiennes de l'Île-du-Prince-Édouard (Miscouche, Î.-P.-É.), Fichier généal. LAC, RG 31, C1, 1881, 1891, 1901, Queens County, P.E.I. (mfm. at PARO). PARO, Parish of Saint-Augustin de Rustico, 1890 census. Private arch., Georges Arsenault (Charlottetown), Interview with Théophile Blanchard, 25 April 1986. Supreme Court of Prince Edward Island, Estates div. (Charlottetown), liber 23: f.93; inventory and affidavit, 3 Oct. 1923; order passing the accounts etc., 9 Feb. 1925. *Examiner* (Charlottetown), 15 Feb. 1878; 18 Sept. 1885; 4 May, 6 Nov. 1888; 24 Dec. 1890; 20 Jan. 1892. *L'Impartial* (Tignish, Î.-P.-É.), 26 juill., 11 oct., 29 nov. 1894; 28 févr. 1895; 26 oct. 1899; 26 avril, 25 oct. 1900; 20 nov. 1902; 19 nov. 1903; 31 août 1905; 8 févr. 1910. *Le Moniteur acadien* (Shédiac, N.-B.), 12 août 1880, 24 déc. 1885, 7 déc. 1886, 17 juin 1887, 17 août 1888. Gabriel Bertrand, *Paroisse acadienne de Rustico (Î.-P.-É.) et la Banque des fermiers: recueil de citations épistolaires du père Georges-Antoine Belcourt* (Moncton, N.-B., 1995). *Chappelle's Prince Edward Island almanac and guide book . . .* (Charlottetown), 1885. J. T. Croteau, "The Farmers' Bank of Rustico: an early people's bank," *Dalhousie Rev.* (Halifax), 36 (1956–57): 144–55. *Directories*, Can., 1871; P.E.I., 1889/90. Antoinette Gallant, "Les Bronne: une courte histoire de ma famille," *La Petite Souvenance* (Wellington, Î.-P.-É.), 1 (1979): 9–13. R. J. Graham *et al.*, *The currency and medals of Prince Edward Island* (Willowdale, Ont., 1988). *Harvie's Prince Edward Island almanack . . .* (Charlottetown), 1872. *Ships and seafarers of Atlantic Canada: the Atlantic Canada Shipping Project* (CD-ROM, St John's, 1998).

GALT, ELLIOTT TORRANCE, office holder, businessman, and developer; b. 24 May 1850 in Sherbrooke, Lower Canada, son of Alexander Tilloch Galt* and Elliott Torrance; d. unmarried 15 May 1928 in New York City.

The son of a prominent businessman and politician, Elliott Galt was educated at Bishop's College in Lennoxville, Lower Canada, and then at Harrow, England, and Tours, France. In the late 1860s he visited several European capitals, meeting many of his father's business associates. From 1869 he clerked in the offices of Montreal businessmen, including that of John Rose*. Apparently, Galt did not take life seriously and in 1879 his father asked Prime Minister Sir John A. Macdonald* to post him somewhere away from his friends and "life of self indulgence." Macdonald obliged and made Elliott secretary and clerk to Edgar Dewdney*, newly appointed Indian commissioner in the North-West Territories. Without giving up these positions, Galt became assistant Indian commissioner at Regina in 1881.

Galt adapted well to the northwest. Tall and lean, soft-spoken and scholarly, he loved outdoor sports, and his legendary billiard skills stood him in good stead in western bars and hotels. In his short career with Dewdney, whose main task was to pacify the aboriginal people and settle them on reserves, Galt visited most of the southern territories and experienced, with patience and good humour, all the hardships of sleeping for weeks on end in a tent on the open prairies. He recognized the enormous investment potential of the region and speculated heavily in real estate. He also sent his father coal samples from the southwestern corner of the plains.

In 1883 Galt resigned his posting and became the general manager of the North-Western Coal and Navigation Company Limited, which was intending to open a coalmine on the Belly (Oldman) River at present-day Lethbridge, Alta. Although Alexander Galt had secured the necessary capital in London, it was Elliott who supervised the operation, including the construction of a steamboat, the *Baroness*, designed to haul coal to the main line of the Canadian Pacific Railway at Medicine Hat. The following year he built two more steamers, the *Alberta* and the *Minnow*, but low water levels thwarted the enterprise. In fact, the vessels served their most useful and lucrative role as troop carriers after the defeat in 1885 of Louis Riel* and his followers.

Meanwhile, Alexander Galt persuaded his British associates, principally William Henry Smith and his partner William Lethbridge of bookstall fame, to underwrite the Alberta Railway and Coal Company, which would eventually absorb all the assets of North-Western Coal and Navigation. Under Elliott's supervision, AR&C built a narrow-gauge railway from Lethbridge to the CPR at Dunmore, near Medicine Hat. Galt completed the project in August 1885 and began shipping coal. Since the CPR was the colliery's principal customer, the Galt mines endured a feast-or-famine existence, dependent entirely upon the needs and whims of the railway company. To remain profitable, Elliott Galt expanded the mines and installed the most modern machinery available. On several occasions he defeated striking miners and lowered wages. To break out of the CPR stranglehold, he and some American associates built a rail-

way in 1890 from Lethbridge to the ore-reduction plant of the Anaconda Copper Mining Company at Great Falls, Mont. In 1893, the year his father died, Galt negotiated with Thomas George SHAUGHNESSY the lease to the CPR of both the AR&C's Dunmore–Lethbridge line and the Crowsnest Pass charter it had acquired in 1890; he converted this deal into an outright sale four years later.

The company's collieries continued to expand, becoming one of the largest operations in western Canada, but they remained subject to the vagaries of a peripheral economy. What made the Galt enterprise a success was the relatively large land grants earned for constructing the railways. Totalling over one million acres, these holdings were most suitable for grazing purposes. Since ranch lands were comparatively low in value, in 1893 Galt formed the Alberta Irrigation Company, which proposed to purchase the lands from AR&C, build irrigation canals, and offer the holdings for sale as more profitable agricultural lands. "In our case," Galt later explained, "we had to spend large sums of money to give our land value." In 1896, after years of intense lobbying by Galt and his assistant (and future brother-in-law) Charles Alexander Magrath*, as well as by William PEARCE, the northwest's senior federal civil servant, the government permitted the company to receive its land in a solid block. With Clifford SIFTON, the minister of the interior, signalling government support for the scheme, Galt in 1898 concluded a deal with the Church of Jesus Christ of Latter-day Saints in Utah, by which the Mormons would provide canal-construction crews for a payment to be made half in land and half in cash [see Charles Ora Card*]. Begun that year, the 115-mile canal system was completed in 1900.

Although Galt had no problem disposing of the irrigated lands, he continued to support projects in the region. In 1901 he helped Jesse W. Knight, one of the Mormon settlers, establish a large sugar-beet farm and refinery. The following year he extended the irrigation canal, earning a further 500,000 acres, and in 1903 he completed a branch line, the St Mary's River Railway, from the AR&C line at Stirling to Cardston. Meanwhile, he donated lands near Lethbridge for a model farm; transformed in 1906 into a dominion experimental farm [see William Saunders*], it would become renowned as a research station. He also enlarged the local hospital and gave generously to congregations building their first churches. Although he kept a low profile in Lethbridge, he was influential in local politics. In 1890 he had successfully refused to endorse the town's incorporation unless his companies were exempt from local taxes, except the school levy.

With the completion of the irrigation works, Galt began preparations for his retirement. In 1901 he widened the Canadian section of the Great Falls railway to standard gauge and sold the American portion to James Jerome Hill*'s Great Northern Railroad. Three years later he organized the Alberta Railway and Irrigation Company, which absorbed all the Galt companies. Although named its president, Galt effectively withdrew from the operation because of ill health; in 1905 Augustus Meredith NANTON became managing director, and it was he who spoke for the company during the bitter mineworkers' strike the following year [see Frank Henry Sherman*]. In 1907 Galt tightened the already close relationship between AR&I and the CPR. He negotiated a deal whereby the CPR, already the owner of AR&C's Dunmore-to-Lethbridge line, purchased a controlling interest in the new company. Formalized in 1908, the arrangement was extended in 1912 when the CPR acquired all the assets of AR&I. As for Galt, he had left Lethbridge in 1908 to spend his retirement years in Montreal and Victoria. He died in New York, where he had gone for medical treatment, of complications arising from a heart attack; he was buried in Mount Royal Cemetery in Montreal.

A. A. DEN OTTER

[Elliott Torrance Galt did not leave any personal papers; documentary evidence for his career can be found only in ancillary records. Useful material for tracing the history of the mining and railway companies is contained in the following collections at the LAC: the A. T. Galt papers (MG 27, I, D8); Sir John A. Macdonald papers (MG 26, A); the Van Horne and Shaughnessy letter-books in the Canadian Pacific Railway papers (MG 28, III 20); the C. A. Magrath papers (MG 30, E82); the records of the Department of the Interior (RG 15); and the Sir Clifford Sifton papers (MG 27, II, D15). The GA holds a number of invaluable records in its Alberta Railway and Irrigation Company fonds (M 2431, M 2533, M 3748, M 3749, M 3750, M 7899, M 8532) as well as a microfilmed copy of a company scrapbook. The National Arch. (G.B.) holds the incorporation documents and two lists of shareholders for the North-Western Coal and Navigation Company (BT 31/2974/16713). The invaluable William Pearce fonds in the Univ. of Alta Arch. (Edmonton) is essential for the study of irrigation in Alberta. A complete record of the legislative history of the Galt companies is contained in Can., Statutes.

Five letters written by Galt to his mother while he was Dewdney's assistant have been published as "Letters from Elliott Galt: travelling the prairies, 1879–80," ed. A. A. den Otter, Alberta Hist. (Calgary), 26 (1978), no.3: 21–33. The Manitoba Free Press for 9 Sept. 1904 has a comprehensive story on the Galt enterprises as well as an extensive interview with Elliott Galt, including the quotation cited in the text. The two most recent works which discuss his career are A. A. den Otter, Civilizing the west: the Galts and the development of western Canada (Edmonton, 1982), and H. B. Timothy, The Galts: a Canadian odyssey (2v., Toronto, 1984–87), 2. Marginally useful are C. A. Magrath, The Galts, father and son, pioneers in the development of southern Alberta . . . ([Lethbridge, Alta, 1935]); O. D. Skelton, The life and times of Sir Alexander Tilloch Galt, ed. Guy MacLean (new ed., Toronto, 1966); and E. C. Springett, For my children's children (Montreal, 1937). A.A.DEN O.]

GALT, GEORGE FREDERICK, businessman, athlete, and office holder; b. 1 March 1855 in Toronto, son of Thomas Galt, a lawyer, and Frances Louisa Perkins; grandson of John Galt*; m. first 3 Sept. 1883 Margaret Smith (d. 1915) in Montreal, and they had one son and four daughters; m. secondly 17 Jan. 1917 Muriel Julyan Maunsell, granddaughter of George Joseph Maunsell*, in Winnipeg, and they had one son and one daughter; d. there 15 April 1928.

George F. Galt was born into a powerful family. His father would become chief justice of Ontario in 1887. His uncle Sir Alexander Tilloch Galt*, a prominent Lower Canadian politician and businessman, and his cousin Elliott Torrance GALT would play an influential role in the commercial development of the Canadian northwest. Galt was educated at the grammar school in Galt (Cambridge, Ont.), but at age 15 he left to pursue a career in business. From about 1871 to 1882 he worked for various Toronto firms, including that of Perkins, Ince and Company, wholesale grocers, and held positions as a salesman, commercial traveller, and clerk. According to all reports, he was of almost abnormal physical strength and he quickly made a name for himself in amateur athletics, particularly in rowing. In the 1870s and early 1880s he stroked for the Argonaut Rowing Club of Toronto; in 1880 and in 1881 his team won the Canadian Association of Amateur Oarsmen's competitions.

In 1882, with his cousin John, Galt moved to Winnipeg, where the two men set up the tea-importing and wholesale grocery business of G. F. and J. Galt, later G. F. and J. Galt Limited. The company prospered and would establish branches or agencies in Toronto, Prince Albert (Sask.), Calgary (where Daniel Webster Marsh* was an agent), Edmonton, and Vancouver. By 1897 it was estimated as being worth from $75,000 to $125,000. It went on to develop the highly successful Blue Ribbon Tea Company and followed the lead of the Salada Tea Company Limited [see Peter Charles LARKIN] in offering packaged teas.

The Galts quickly became members of the Anglo-Saxon elite in Winnipeg. A founder of the Winnipeg Grain and Produce Exchange in 1887, George was elected its first vice-president. Before he was 35, he had already served a term as president of the Winnipeg Board of Trade, in 1888–89. His reputation as a sound financial manager soon placed him on the boards of other organizations. He held office as president of the Northern Trusts Company (1904–5), vice-president of the Great-West Life Assurance Company, and director of numerous prominent financial institutions, including in 1910 the Canadian Bank of Commerce. He became a member of the Hudson's Bay Company's

Gastonguay

Canadian committee advisory board [*see* Sir Augustus Meredith NANTON] at its inception in 1911.

Along with another former member of the Argonaut club, Galt had founded the Winnipeg Rowing Club in 1882; he would serve as its captain, president, and coach. Galt stroked the Winnipeg crew to victory at the North American championship in Pullman (Chicago) in 1889. He served as a member of the Central Olympic Committee in 1908. The following year he was elected vice-president of the Canadian Association of Amateur Oarsmen. In July 1910 the Winnipeg crew won the prized Stewards' Challenge Cup at the Henley Royal Regatta, the first time the cup had been taken out of England. The following year Galt retired as president of the Winnipeg club. Later, he would be a founder of several other sporting clubs in Winnipeg and a designer and sailor of yachts. An avid duck hunter, he owned several marshes in Manitoba and entertained governors general Lord Byng* and Lord Willingdon [Freeman-Thomas*] and the Prince of Wales at his lodge on Lake Manitoba.

Galt was an Anglican and a Conservative. During World War I, in an effort to eliminate the existing chaos and profiteering in the acquisition of war materials, Prime Minister Sir Robert Laird Borden* created the War Purchasing Commission. In May 1915 he named Galt to it, along with Hormisdas Laporte* and chairman Albert Edward KEMP. Galt was no doubt chosen because of his business success, his Conservative leanings, and his ties to western Canada. The commission oversaw war appropriations, called for tenders, and awarded contracts for military supplies. Galt served in Ottawa for four years, refused remuneration for this work, and declined a knighthood.

Among his benevolent and philanthropic works Galt was a member of the Order of St John of Jerusalem in England, in which he had been created a knight of grace on 29 July 1913. In 1914 he and John Galt had donated $5,000 each to the Manitoba Patriotic Fund and during World War I he acted as president of the Manitoba section of the Red Cross Society. He had served as treasurer of the Winnipeg General Hospital and was president of its board of directors when he retired in 1921, having contributed 31 years of service to the institution. After a four-month illness Galt died at his home in Winnipeg at age 73 and was buried in St John's cemetery. The Winnipeg Rowing Club presented the George Frederick Galt Trophy to the Canadian Association of Amateur Oarsmen in his memory. It is still a prestigious national award. As an influential businessman and a determined athlete, Galt was one of the builders of Winnipeg during its heyday as an industrial and grain-trading centre.

ROBERT A. WARDHAUGH

ANQ-M, CE601-S1, 3 sept. 1883. *Winnipeg Tribune*, 16 April 1928. A. F. J. Artibise, *Winnipeg: a social history of urban growth, 1874–1914* (Montreal and London, 1975). *Canadian annual rev.*, 1914–18. K. [S.] Coates and Fred McGuinness, *Manitoba: the province & the people* (Edmonton, 1987). *Directory*, Winnipeg, 1885–90. A. [G.] Levine, *The exchange: 100 years of trading grain in Winnipeg* (Winnipeg, 1987). A. A. den Otter, *Civilizing the west: the Galts and the development of western Canada* (Edmonton, 1982). C. S. Riley, *Rowing memories* (Winnipeg, 1934). Victor Ross and A. St L. Trigge, *A history of the Canadian Bank of Commerce, with an account of the other banks which now form part of its organization* (3v., Toronto, 1920–34), 2. *Standard dict. of Canadian biog.* (Roberts and Tunnell). Margaret [Stovel] McWilliams, *Manitoba milestones* (Toronto and London, [1928]). S. F. Wise and Douglas Fisher, *Canada's sporting heroes* (Don Mills [Toronto], 1974).

GASTONGUAY, JOSEPH-NARCISSE, surveyor, civil engineer, office holder, professor, and promoter of colonization; b. 13 Jan. 1849 in Saint-Roch-des-Aulnaies, Lower Canada, son of Jean-Baptiste Gastonguay, a farmer, and Hortense Pelletier (Peltier); m. first 28 April 1879 Marie-Delphine Larivière in Saint-Norbert-d'Arthabaska, Que.; m. secondly 8 June 1901 Hortense-Eugénie Lemieux at Quebec; d. there 28 June 1922.

Joseph-Narcisse Gastonguay was a descendant of Gaston Guay, who arrived at Quebec around 1630 and settled there with his family. During the 18th century the family spread out across the city and on the Beaupré shore. In the 1780s the Gastonguays also established themselves in communities on the south shore, including Saint-Roch-des-Aulnaies, the parish in which Joseph-Narcisse's family were farmers.

Gastonguay attended the classical college de Sainte-Anne-de-la-Pocatière from September 1860 to June 1870. Among its administrators at that time was François Pilote*, an enthusiastic promoter of colonization and agricultural education, and one of the teachers was Alexis Pelletier*, a staunch defender of French Canadian ultramontanism. Gastonguay also spent the year 1871–72 there, studying theology and teaching. He finally opted for secular life.

Gastonguay served his apprenticeship as a surveyor in L'Islet under Pierre-Amable-Eugène Casgrain. On being accepted into the profession on 10 Jan. 1876, he left the south shore and moved to Arthabaskaville (Victoriaville), where he practised until 1895. He soon made a name for himself as a man of practical experience by drawing up the register of property for Arthabaska county and part of the one for Drummond county. Gastonguay was a leading citizen in his community. On 7 July 1884 he was appointed to the village school board and on 9 Dec. 1894 he co-signed with Wilfrid Laurier*, future prime minister of Canada, an application to purchase a bell for the church of Saint-Christophe in the parish of Arthabaskaville, of which he had been a church-warden since 1892.

At the outset of the 20th century Gastonguay was among those who, through the colonization movement, would help change the pattern of settlement of Quebec. At the time, the government considered colonization a temporary solution to the growing exodus of the rural population to the factories of New England. The traditional elites saw it, instead, as the ideal way for French Canadians to protect their religion, language, and nation. In this context, because of his experience as a surveyor Gastonguay was well qualified to identify lands suitable for settlement. In 1895 he was appointed director of colonization operations in the provincial Department of Agriculture and Colonization, an office he would hold until 1914. His work involved visiting the main regions for settlement in order to evaluate the new sites selected. He helped settlers get established, in particular by arranging for roads and bridges to be built and by endeavouring to provide them with a bit of money. In some regions he helped with the purchase of horses, oxen, cows, and sacks of flour for the new arrivals.

Around 1900 Gastonguay moved to the parish of Notre-Dame-du-Chemin at Quebec, where he soon became active in various organizations: the Comité de Québec, which was formed in 1902 to get the symbol of the Sacred Heart included on the French Canadian national flag, the Ligue du Sacré-Cœur, and the Association de l'Adoration Perpétuelle du Très Saint-Sacrement de Québec. He was also a prefect of the Sodality of Our Lady and vice-president of his parish's branch of the Society of St Vincent de Paul. In 1916, along with Monsignor Thomas-Grégoire Rouleau, the principal of the École Normale Laval, he founded the Cercle de Colonisation Notre-Dame-du-Chemin. Affiliated with the Action Sociale Catholique and sponsored by Archbishop Paul-Eugène ROY, this group undertook to attract settlers into the Matapédia valley and provide for their immediate needs. The project began in Albertville and in 1918 the village that had sprung up as a result of logging operations already had 66 families and 450 people. Seven settlements were under the group's guidance; almost all were located in the Matapédia valley (Saint-André-de Restigouche, Sainte-Florence, Causapscal, and Awantjish), but the work also spread into the Gaspé, the lower St Lawrence region, and the south shore. To keep the settlers informed about current laws, lots, and the sale of wood – which brought them additional income – about 20 circles were set up on the south shore.

To unite the efforts of the some 40 groups patterned after the Cercle de Notre-Dame-du-Chemin, in 1917 Gastonguay helped create the Ligue Nationale de Colonisation, of which he was chairman and coordinator. To make its work known, he conducted a major publicity campaign in various newspapers; as well, he had a log cabin built at the provincial exhibition held in Quebec in 1918 to give a practical demonstration of the life awaiting the new settler. In the early 1920s he had the support of Ivanhoë Caron*, a missionary and colonizer who was organizing colonization circles in the Abitibi region. One of Gastonguay's chief accomplishments within the league was the creation in 1921 of an agricultural orphanage at Lac-Sergent, in the Portneuf region, which would be run by the Brothers of Our Lady of Mercy. The idea of setting up such establishments dated from 1883, when one was founded in Montfort. Here poor children and orphans were taught the rudiments of the settler's life in order to encourage a return to the land. Gastonguay was one of the first citizens of Quebec to spend a holiday on the shores of Lac Sergent, and he saw in vacationing a further way to foster the development of the community, on whose council he served in 1921.

Gastonguay's dynamic energy led him to take an interest in another project, outside the province of Quebec. In 1919, in cooperation with Monsignor Joseph-Jean-Baptiste Hallé*, the chaplain of the Ligue Nationale de Colonisation and the first apostolic prefect to Northern Ontario, Gastonguay set up the Comité Dieu et Patrie, with a view to creating new parishes in the region. The following year he wanted to bring the settlement circles, colonization societies, and governmental initiatives into a single organization, but the plan was never carried out. Because of his dedication to the cause of colonization, he was made a knight of the Order of St Gregory the Great by Pope Benedict XV in 1921.

While still working at colonization, Gastonguay made every effort to get his profession recognized. Having served on the board of directors of the Land Surveyors of the Province of Quebec since its inception in 1882, he was elected its president in 1900 and led it for 12 years. It was in this capacity that he campaigned in 1906 for the creation of a polytechnical school at the Université Laval. This large-scale project would require the investment of private funds. Such a prospect did not sit well with some of the priests at the Séminaire de Québec, who saw in it an intrusion by laymen into their realm. Moreover, such a school already existed in Montreal [see Urgel-Eugène Archambeault*] and was connected to the university. Monsignor Olivier-Elzéar Mathieu, the university rector, finally gave his support to a less ambitious undertaking, the École Centrale de Préparation et d'Arpentage. Under the wing of the Land Surveyors of the Province of Quebec, the school opened in September 1907, drawing some 50 students. It was affiliated with the faculty of arts in May 1908. Gastonguay and Alfred Fyen* were its first professors. Gastonguay was a member of the faculty of the university for the rest of his life; he taught courses in topography, geodesy, cartography, survey-ing, and arithmetic, and served as director of studies from 1910 to 1918. At the same time he maintained a private practice and around 1910 he went into part-nership with his son-in-law, Louis Giroux, who had an office on Côte de la Montagne. His son Jules-Paul joined them ten years later.

Joseph-Narcisse Gastonguay died on 28 June 1922 at the age of 73, mourned by his wife, two daughters, and two sons. By his knowledge and savoir-faire, he helped advance the profession of surveying and cre-ate the colonization movement. A lake in northern Quebec was named after him in 1912. In the words of his university colleague Paul Joncas, following his death, he was a "man of heart, principles, and knowl-edge," a professor noted for his enthusiasm, kind-ness, and lucid expression of ideas.

YVES HÉBERT

Joseph-Narcisse Gastonguay produced a number of writ-ings, the most important of which was the beginning of a history of surveying published by the Land Surveyors of the Prov. of Quebec in their *Annual report* (Quebec) between 1891 and 1896. He is also the author of two articles: "La colonisation et les cercles de colonisation," *Almanach de l'Action sociale catholique* (Québec), 3 (1919): 122–23, and "Cercle de colonisation," *La Semaine religieuse de Québec*, 12 avril 1917: 512.

AC, Québec, État civil, Catholiques, Saint-Jean-Baptiste (Québec), 8 juin 1901. ANQ-MBF, CE402-S72, 28 avril 1879. ANQ-Q, CE302-S25, 13 janv. 1849; E9, S100, SS1, SSS1, 1982-10-004/38, dossier 4196/38; /45, dossier 1098/40; /60, dossier 5581/41; P293. *L'Action catholique* (Québec), 28 juin 1922. *Le Devoir*, 28, 30 juin 1922. Assoc. Catholique de la Jeunesse Canadienne-Française, *Le pro-blème de la colonisation au Canada français; rapport officiel du Congrès de colonisation tenu par l'A.C.J.C. à Chicoutimi, du 29 juin au 2 juillet 1919* (Montréal, 1920). *Le centenaire d'Arthabaska* ([Arthabaska, Qué.], 1951). *Directory*, Quebec and Levis, 1908–22. Alcide Fleury, *Arthabaska, capitale des Bois-Francs* (Arthabaska, 1961). Jean Hamelin, *Histoire de l'université Laval: les péripéties d'une idée* (Sainte-Foy, Qué., 1995), 121–25. Yves Hébert, "La colonisation au ser-vice d'une idéologie; l'œuvre colonisatrice de l'abbé Ivan-hoë Caron (1875–1941) en Abitibi (1911–1924)" (mémoire de MA, univ. Laval, Québec, 1986). Paul Joncas, "Monsieur J.-N. Gastonguay, professeur à la faculté des arts de l'univer-sité Laval," in Univ. Laval, *Annuaire*, 1923–24: 252–54. Ligue Nationale de Colonisation, *La Ligue nationale de colonisation, constituée civilement en corporation, sous l'empire des statuts refondus de la province de Québec, 1909–au 1ᵉʳ février 1924; constitution et règlements* (Québec, 1924). Hormisdas Magnan, "Les drapeaux arborés dans la province de Québec," *BRH*, 25 (1919): 141–43. P.-P. Magnan, *Lac-Sergent, comté de Portneuf, P.Q.* (Québec, 1948). J.-R. Pelletier, *Arpenteurs-géomètres, un siècle, 1882–1982* (Québec, 1982). Eugène Robillard, "Une nomen-clature géographique: les nouveaux noms géographiques de l'Abitibi et comté de Pontiac," Soc. de Géographie de

Québec, *Bull.*, 6 (1912): 156–64. É.-G. Talbot, *Généalogie des familles originaires des comtés de Montmagny, L'Islet, Bellechasse* (16v., Château-Richer, Qué., 1971–78), 3. D. W. Thomson, *Men and meridians: the history of surveying and mapping in Canada* (3v., Ottawa, 1966–69), 2. Cyrille et Pierre Tremblay, *50 ans de vie municipale: des faits, des dates, des hommes, des chiffres, 25 février 1921–18 juillet 1971, Lac-Sergent, 1921–1971* (Lac-Sergent, Qué., 1971). Univ. Laval, *Annuaire*, 1908–22.

GAUDET, PLACIDE (he frequently signed **Placide P.** to signify that he was the son of Placide), teacher, journalist, genealogist, historian, and office holder; b. 19 Nov. 1850 in Dupuis Corner (Cap-Pelé), N.B., son of Placide Gaudet and Marie Vienneau, *dit* Michaud; m. 14 Nov. 1890 Marie-Rose Arsenault in Egmont Bay, P.E.I., and they had three daughters, two of whom died before reaching adulthood, and one son; d. 9 Nov. 1930 in Shediac, N.B.

Placide Gaudet's father had died in a fight a few months before he was born, so his mother returned to her father's farm where she, and later her son, worked. Gaudet attended the local school and he developed an interest in Acadian genealogy and his-tory through listening to his grandfather. In January 1862 his mother moved to her father-in-law's farm in Dorchester. When the College of Saint Joseph opened in nearby Memramcook two years later, Gaudet was one of its first students. His mother worked in the kitchen and bakery to pay his fees, and the director, Camille Lefebvre*, took a particular interest in him. After graduating in 1873, Gaudet began to study for the priesthood at the Grand Séminaire de Montréal, but, to the great disappointment of his mother, he was advised to leave by John Sweeny*, the bishop of Saint John, because of ill health. By late November 1874 he had returned to New Brunswick.

On leaving the seminary Gaudet's lifelong struggle with poverty began, as did the first of several desper-ate searches for employment. He wrote to friends from college, seeking work in journalism or the civil service, but was forced into a series of short-term teaching posts. These included about a year, 1875–76, at the Académie de Saint-Louis in Saint-Louis de Kent, a brief period in the public schools of Tracadie and Neguac, and a year with the French department of the grammar school in Shediac. During his spare time he enjoyed researching local history and at about this period he contributed the first of many arti-cles to Acadian newspapers. Since advancement to a higher class of teaching licence would mean an increase in pay, Gaudet enrolled in the regular pro-gram of the Normal School in Fredericton during the autumn of 1881. He received three of the necessary five progress reports, but withdrew before any aver-age or change in professional standing was allotted to him; he returned to teaching. In the Cocagne region he taught during 1882–83 using the "intuitive method of instruction," and some parents complained. He left at the end of the term, but not without publishing a vindication in *Le Moniteur acadien* of Shediac, indicating that Valentin Landry*, then inspector, had found his school in satisfactory condition and had praised his work as "sound and intelligent." Historian and senator Pascal Poirier* would nevertheless write at Gaudet's death that he could think of no one less suited to teach the rudiments of education. Gaudet's plan to have his students collect oral history from the old people of the village was, however, well ahead of its time.

Gaudet's job search began again. In 1882 he had sought work at the Canadian archives [*see* Douglas Brymner*], apparently in competition with Poirier. Narcisse Robidoux, a brother of Ferdinand, the editor of *Le Moniteur acadien,* agreed to support his application if Gaudet could conquer his long-standing difficulty with alcohol. Although Gaudet would continue to struggle with this problem until at least 1901, he obtained a two-year contract (1883–85) with the archives to copy parish registers in Acadian areas. This did not pay the bills, so he took three more short-term teaching jobs and spent an equally short period in Bathurst with the *Courrier des provinces Maritimes* before becoming the editorial secretary of *Le Moniteur acadien* during the fall of 1886. From there he moved to *L'Évangéline* in Weymouth, N.S., where he worked from July 1890 to mid August 1893. In May 1894 he went back to the *Courrier des provinces Maritimes* and stayed until March 1895. His disputes with colleagues and with contributors who ventured to write Acadian history became notorious.

In August 1895 Gaudet moved to Church Point, N.S., to teach at the new Collège Sainte-Anne [*see* Gustave Blanche*]. He also continued to research local history. One student, J. E. Belliveau, would remember his talks there on Acadia with interest. He remained until the college burnt down in January 1899. That year he received a full-time contract from the archives to copy registers in the Acadian parishes of Prince Edward Island and New Brunswick. Brymner, the dominion archivist, was dissatisfied with Gaudet's failure to produce reports of the work he had accomplished. In 1903 only the intervention of friends, including New Brunswick MP John Costigan*, allowed him to keep his job. When Arthur George Doughty* took over the archives in 1904, the two established a good relationship. Gaudet moved to Ottawa to become genealogist at the archives. Under pressure from Doughty, he produced a genealogy of Acadian families over 460 pages long, published in the *Report concerning Canadian archives for the year 1905* (Ottawa, 1906). It was his only lengthy publication.

During his years at the archives, where he would remain until 1924, Gaudet continued to collect material from a variety of sources. Much of his time was occupied by correspondence; he replied, often at great length, to numerous queries for information on Acadian genealogy and history. His remarkable contribution to Acadian genealogy, the transcription of an estimated 50,000 entries from parish registers covering the descendants of almost all Acadian families from the 17th to the early 20th century, made him the unquestioned authority on genealogy and provided a basis for Acadians to begin writing their own history rather than relying on scholars from elsewhere. He was also an important source of information for historians such as Pierre-Marie Dagnaud, William Francis Ganong*, Henri-Raymond Casgrain*, John Clarence Webster*, and Émile Lauvrière, as well as for author Margaret Marshall Saunders*. The stories of Acadian experiences, especially during the deportation of 1755, that he had collected and published were always carefully documented. James de Finney views Gaudet's work as characteristic of a tradition in Acadian literature which attempted to recover scattered fragments of the collective memory. Gaudet's vitriolic criticisms of the works of others were at times justified, though in the case of his 1911 pamphlet *Les données erronées*, which pointed out errors in Joseph-Edmond Roy*'s history of Acadian notaries, personal feelings may have sharpened his pen.

Financial pressures and his reluctance to publish what he considered unfinished work meant that Gaudet's only additional publication was an 84-page booklet entitled *Le grand dérangement*. Written in 1921 in support of the Acadian proposal to construct a commemorative church at Grand Pré, N.S. [*see* David-Vital LANDRY], it was issued the following year by the committee sponsoring the project. Gaudet's thesis, that the evidence convicted only Governor Charles Lawrence* of responsibility for the deportation of the Acadians, and not the British government, was highly controversial.

In spite of frequent disputes with other authors, Gaudet could be a generous friend and ally. He maintained lifelong ties with many correspondents, including most of the Acadian elite. A founder and member of the Ottawa branch of the Société l'Assomption [*see* Rémi Benoît*], he was a hospitable and well-liked member of the capital's Acadian community. He encouraged the establishment of monuments to the Acadian past and gave talks on Acadian history.

In 1924, after he was requested to retire on a monthly pension of $84, he moved to Moncton. The following year, in a letter to his son, he complained of difficulties with his wife, whom he described as suffering from religious mania. At the time of his death, in November 1930, he was living apart from her, in a hospice in Shediac. During his last public appearance a few weeks earlier he had still been eager to share with Acadian children his vast knowledge of the history of their ancestors.

SHEILA ANDREW

The voluminous Placide Gaudet fonds at the LAC consists of typewritten Acadian genealogies (MG 30, C20, 1–19), notes and subject files on Acadian history as well as extracts from parish registers (C20, 20–28), and about 135,000 index cards on Acadian genealogy (C20, 29–118). The Placide Gaudet fonds at the Centre d'Études Acadiennes, Univ. de Moncton, N.-B., just as imposing, contains documentation on Acadian history, including manuscripts (originals, copies, and transcripts), correspondence (originals and copies), notes, and a number of other materials.

In addition to numerous articles published in the local press, Gaudet is the author of "Acadian genealogy and notes," in Public Arch. of Canada, *Report concerning Canadian archives for the year 1905* (3v., Ottawa, 1906), 2; *Les données erronées de monsieur J. Edmond Roy sur les notaires de l'Acadie* (Shédiac, N.-B., 1911); and *Le grand dérangement: sur qui retombe la responsabilité de l'expulsion des Acadiens* (Ottawa, 1922).

Centre d'Études Acadiennes, Fonds du collège Saint-Joseph/univ. de Moncton, 1864–1972, documentation financière, Grand Livre no.1, 1865–78: 33–35; Grand Livre no.1, 1865–84: 1, 9, 22; Fonds Pascal Poirier, 6.1-3; Fonds Valentin Landry, 7.1-2, 7.1-7, 7.1-19. PANB, MC2495, F15653 (mfm.); RS117, A2/2, 1. *L'Évangéline* (Weymouth Bridge, N.-É.), 31 oct.–12 déc. 1895; (Moncton), 30 mars 1916; 4 mai 1922; 28 avril 1927; 13, 20, 30 nov. 1930. *Le Moniteur acadien* (Shédiac), 22 mars 1883. Anselme Chiasson, "Placide Gaudet," Soc. Hist. Acadienne, *Cahiers* (Moncton), 4 (1971–73): 6–23. C.-A. Doucet, *Une étoile s'est levée en Acadie* ([Rogersville, N.-B.], 1973). James de Finney, "Du fait divers au récit commun: le rôle littéraire de l'*Évangéline*," in '*L'Évangéline,' 1887–1982; entre l'élite et le peuple*, sous la dir. de Gérard Beaulieu (Moncton, 1997), 135–53. Pierre et P.-M. Gérin, *Marichette: lettres acadiennes, 1895–1898* (Québec, 1982). "Histoire de la paroisse de Cap Pelé," Soc. Hist. de la Mer Rouge, *Sur l'empremier* (Robichaud, N.-B.), 2 (1986), no.1: 44. René LeBlanc et Micheline Laliberté, *Sainte-Anne, collège et université, 1890–1990* (Pointe-de-l'Église [Church Point], N.-É., 1990). J.-M. Leger, "Placide Gaudet," Soc. Hist. Acadienne, *Cahiers*, [2] (1966–68): 18–22.

GAUTHIER, CHARLES HUGH, Roman Catholic priest, professor, and archbishop; b. 13 Nov. 1843 in Alexandria, Upper Canada, son of Gabriel Gauthier, a farmer, and Mary McKinnon; d. 19 Jan. 1922 in Ottawa.

Of French Canadian and Scottish parentage, Charles Gauthier received his early education from the Brothers of the Christian Schools in Alexandria. Later he attended Regiopolis College in Kingston, from which he graduated with high honours in 1863; he subsequently studied theology at the Grand Séminaire in Montreal. On 24 Aug. 1867, at St John the Baptist Church in Perth, Ont., he was ordained by Bishop Edward John Horan* of Kingston. He served as professor of rhetoric and director of Regiopolis College until 1869, when Horan made him pastor of St John the Evangelist parish in Gananoque, a charge that included missions at Howe Island, Lansdowne, Jones Falls, and Brewers Mills. In 1875 he was transferred to Westport and then, upon the accession of Bishop John O'Brien, to St Mary's parish in Williamstown. He spent 11 years there, during which time he opened a new parish at nearby Glen Nevis (which he also administered), constructed a new rectory in Williamstown, built mission churches in Lancaster (1885) and Martintown (1886), and liquidated the debt of St Mary's. Moved to Brockville in 1886, he acted as regional dean and, after 1891, as vicar general for the archdiocese of Kingston. His fluency in English, French, and Gaelic enabled him to communicate with its principal linguistic groups.

Gauthier's pastoral skills, good humour, and financial acumen were acknowledged by his fellow priests when, in an unprecedented step, 37 of them met and selected him as their choice to succeed Archbishop James Vincent Cleary*, who had died in February 1898. Kingston's clergy were fearful that the Vatican might appoint the bishop of Waterford and Lismore, in Ireland, to succeed the Irish-born Cleary, instead of a Canadian who understood the diocese and its needs. Their petition may have influenced the Canadian bishops' recommendation to Pope Leo XIII, who named Gauthier archbishop on 29 July. He was consecrated in Kingston on 18 October.

Like the priests who supported him, many Kingstonians regarded Gauthier as moderate in both politics and temperament – a striking contrast to his predecessor. "The choice of Msgr. Gauthier has been hailed throughout the country, as a special grace of divine Providence," exclaimed Archbishop Joseph-Thomas Duhamel* of Ottawa. "For me, I consider it a gift of God." The new archbishop continued the energetic pace he had set as a parish priest. Within his diocesan boundaries, which extended west from Dundas County to just beyond the Trent River and from Lake Ontario to Algonquin Park, he administered 41,384 Catholics, who constituted 16 per cent of the diocese's entire population. His frequent travels throughout the diocese and familiarity with its growing towns and villages made it easier for him to approve the construction of new churches and rectories, and renovations of ageing ones, in such centres as Odessa (1898), Ormsby and South Mountain (1899), Lombardy (1900), Frankford (1901), Lansdowne (1901), Merrickville (1902), Lanark (1903), Marmora (1904), Toledo (1907), and Enterprise (1908). His episcopate was also marked by the construction of St Francis' Hospital in Smiths Falls, St John's Convent in Perth, and St Mary's of the Lake Orphanage in Kingston, and renovations to Kingston's Hôtel Dieu hospital.

Gauthier's Kingston years were devoid of the sectarian tension that had earned the city the nickname the Derry of Canada [see John Gaskin*]. His own actions won him respect among its Protestants. When St George's Cathedral was gutted by fire in 1899, for example, he was one of the first to offer sympathy and financial aid to Anglican archbishop John Travers Lewis*. Although he contributed to the atmosphere of toleration and commented on the absence of Protestant proselytizing in his diocese, he still worried that local Catholicism was being endangered by mixed marriages, increased socializing with Protestants, and Catholic attendance at public schools. For Gauthier, the establishment of Catholic schools "wherever possible" was the surest way to strengthen the Catholic minority in a largely Protestant province. In 1901, 4,000 out of 6,000 Catholic children of school age were enrolled in the diocese's separate schools; the remaining 2,000, according to Gauthier, lived in areas with no access to Catholic schools. By the end of his tenure new ones had been created in Belleville, Tweed, and Chesterville.

His interest in separate schools extended beyond his diocese. He quickly became a respected leader among the bishops on the issues of teachers' qualifications, textbooks, and school-tax reform. In 1904 justice Hugh MacMahon ruled that members of Catholic religious orders who were employed as teachers in Ontario must obtain qualifications commensurate with provincial standards. Archbishops Gauthier, Duhamel, and Denis O'Connor* of Toronto, however, were alarmed that many sisters and brothers might leave their teaching posts rather than attend classes in the "Protestant" atmosphere of the provincial normal schools. Believing that the members of orders were already well qualified, through teachers' conventions and experience, Gauthier and his colleagues appealed MacMahon's decision to the Supreme Court of Canada and the Judicial Committee of the Privy Council, but without success. When John Seath*, Ontario's superintendent of education, produced legislation early in 1907 that required the proper certification of teaching sisters and brothers, Gauthier opposed the plan, fearing the closure of at least four convents in his diocese and the demise of Catholic schools that employed religious. Declaring the bill "odious and unjust," he appealed directly to Premier James Pliny Whitney* to allow the teachers to be certified without further qualification. With the passage of the act on 20 April 1907, Gauthier and his colleagues conceded defeat and began working to ensure that the teaching members adapted to the three levels of certification.

Gauthier coordinated efforts by the Ontario bishops to secure better funding for Catholic schools from the government and also to obtain improvements to Copp, Clark's Canadian Catholic readers series. By 1909 he and his long-time friend Archbishop Fergus Patrick McEvay* of Toronto were the instigators and chief negotiators of a quiet diplomacy to procure for the separate schools a larger share of business and corporation taxes and to have public funding extended to the senior grades of Catholic high schools. At one point in the negotiations, in order to win the desired financial concessions, Gauthier and the bishops were prepared to sacrifice their Copp, Clark Catholic textbooks, which would have been very expensive to revise. Doubts about the wisdom of this course of action arose, however. Gauthier asked Whitney to offer Catholic schools more of the taxes in exchange for which the bishops, after removing the "objectionable features," would allow public school readers to be used as supplementary texts in Catholic schools. Negotiations continued but in 1910 the bishops' hopes were dashed when the government shelved plans for Catholic school reforms because of vociferous demands by Franco-Ontarians for the extension of French-language education. Whitney feared that any concessions to the bishops in the midst of these demands would alienate the Orange faction of his government.

The Kingston archbishop's influence in ecclesiastical politics was complemented by the attention shown him by the apostolic delegate to Canada, Monsignor Donato Sbarretti y Tazza. Their close relationship – Sbarretti sought Gauthier's advice and assistance on several occasions – was fortunate for the English-speaking bishops as they moved to exert their influence over the church west of the Ottawa River. Gauthier was known to be vehemently opposed to French Canadian clerical nationalists and, as Bishop Thomas Joseph DOWLING reported Gauthier's position to Rome, their "impertinent interference with the affairs of English speaking provinces." As an integral part of their struggle for control, Gauthier and other English-speaking bishops attempted to secure their own candidate each time a see became vacant. In partnership with McEvay and Archbishop Edward Joseph McCarthy of Halifax, in 1909 Gauthier acquired the services of Father Henry Joseph O'Leary* as the anglophone bishops' agent at the Vatican. With O'Leary's aid and Sbarretti's confidence, Gauthier and his group were successful in several appointments, including that of Michael Francis Fallon* as bishop of London in 1909. Long admired by Gauthier, this controversial cleric was loathed by Franco-Ontarians, particularly in Essex County, for his opposition to bilingual schools.

The "bishop maker" became a victim of his own success. In August 1910 the Vatican named him archbishop of Ottawa, a position left vacant since the death of Duhamel in June 1909. This appointment came in spite of the fact that Gauthier's name did not appear among the original terna (list of candidates) for Ottawa and that Gauthier himself had recommended the "broadminded" Bishop Joseph-Médard

EMARD for the difficult task of administering this explosive archdiocese. Out of 266 priests and brothers there, only 30 were not of French origin. Moreover, for much of the decade, French- and English-speaking Catholics in Ottawa had been bitterly divided over who would control the bilingual University of Ottawa and the Ottawa Separate School Board. Infighting among the board's trustees over teachers' qualifications and spending had prompted the court case that had led to the provincial law on certification. By 1910 demands for the improvement of bilingual schools, spearheaded by the Congrès d'Éducation des Canadiens Français de l'Ontario [see Napoléon-Antoine Belcourt*], had further polarized the church along linguistic lines in eastern Ontario. In Ottawa, Protestants stood on the sidelines and watched with interest as the various Catholic factions waged war in school-council chambers, in the press, and from the pulpits.

Gauthier's colleagues knew full well the trouble that faced him. His fellow bishops in Ontario passed a motion of "confidence and good will" as he embarked on the most difficult task of his career. Bishop Paul LA ROCQUE of Sherbrooke, Que., offered his "condolences" in English. In a similar vein, Prime Minister Sir Wilfrid Laurier* expressed his concern about the "overwhelming" burden placed on his good friend, and his regret that some Catholics had been critical of the Vatican's decision. Francophone Catholics in the archdiocese were distressed by the appointment of Gauthier, whom they considered an anglophone with a French surname. This reaction had been anticipated by Sbarretti, who had received the papal bulls authorizing the appointment in August 1910 but, to avoid too much attention to a controversial selection, withheld the news until after the International Eucharistic Congress in Montreal in September. In speculating about the appointment in Le Devoir on 19 July, Henri Bourassa* had neatly summarized the opinion of French Canadian nationalists when he asserted that Gauthier was "French in name, English in language and education," of advanced age, and appointed only to secure "the definitive nomination of an English-speaking bishop." Contrary to Fergus McEvay's prediction in November that "the crazy opposition" would dissipate, the anger did not subside. When Gauthier was installed at Notre-Dame Basilica on 21 Feb. 1911, both the Société Saint-Jean-Baptiste and the Association Canadienne-Française d'Éducation d'Ontario refused to attend.

The bilingual schools question would dog Gauthier for the rest of his life. In 1912, following the Department of Education's issue of Regulation 17, which prohibited French-language education after the first form, Gauthier was faced with virtual civil war within the Ottawa Separate School Board. Despite his opposition to the francophone demands of 1910,

Gauthier took a more moderate position on bilingual schools in the hope that he might reconcile the factions. In 1912 he appealed to Whitney to allow "a larger measure of French to be taught" in bilingual schools attended exclusively by French Canadian children. The premier refused on the grounds that such a measure would create a "third" school system in Ontario.

By 1914 the situation at the school board had deteriorated. French trustees defied Regulation 17 and, as a result, English-speaking trustees sought an injunction to prohibit the francophones from raising debentures for independent schools and paying salaries to unqualified teachers. In June 1915, after an acrimonious election and bitter confrontations between local priests, the board shut its schools. In September they were reopened by order of the Ontario Supreme Court, and the new premier, William Howard Hearst*, appointed a three-person commission to run the board and ensure its adherence to the provincial regulation. English-speaking clergy and laity lined up in support of the commission, while their French-speaking co-religionists condemned it and francophone bishops appealed to Pope Benedict XV to defend French-language education rights. In 1916 the pope responded with an encyclical, Commisso divinitus, which instructed Gauthier's flock to settle their differences peacefully and not imperil their schools. Neither this intervention nor the mediatory efforts of archbishops Paul Bruchési* of Montreal and Neil McNeil* of Toronto ended the crisis. Later that year, the Judicial Committee of the Privy Council upheld Regulation 17 but ruled the Ottawa School Commission illegal, and attempts were made to reconstitute the original board.

During the crisis Gauthier had become increasingly estranged from the francophone Catholics of his diocese. He was notably absent from the biannual congresses of the ACFEO, despite the presence of other bishops, and his francophone priests expressed their disgust at his inability to rein in actions of the English-speaking Catholics. Gauthier tried to maintain a middle course. He instructed his clergy in unequivocal terms to desist from any public discussion of these "vexed questions." In 1917, in the wake of the papal encyclical and the validation of Regulation 17 by the courts, Gauthier and the Ontario bishops issued a joint pastoral urging Catholics to "obey all the just laws and regulations enacted from time to time by civil authorities" and English-speaking Catholics in particular to consider "sympathetically" the "aspirations and requests" of French Canadian Catholics. The bishops acknowledged the ambiguities of Regulation 17 but endorsed its legality, and echoed the pope by asking that Catholics facilitate "an equitable teaching of the French language together with a thorough acquisition of English." Despite these pleas, the tension in the Ottawa board continued, and local priests continued to complain about the tactics of "the other side."

Although weighed down and sometimes demoralized by the schools issue, Gauthier still managed to conduct his day-to-day administrative affairs in efficient fashion, as he had done in Kingston. He continued to monitor the interactions of Catholics and Protestants, noting the increased numbers of mixed marriages, especially in English-speaking parishes. As the Catholic population of his diocese expanded on both sides of the Ottawa River, he approved the construction of church buildings and erected new parishes, including Saint-Bernardin (1912), Ottawa's Blessed Sacrament (1913) and Saint-Gérard-Majella (1916), Vars (1915), and, in Quebec, Boileau (1915), Fieldville (1915), and Hull's Saint-Joseph (1913) and Notre-Dame-de-Lorette (1916). He also presided over the creation of the diocese of Mont-Laurier in 1913 out of the eastern section of his territory in Quebec and the reorganization of his suffragan dioceses northwest of Ottawa. In 1915 the vicariate of Timiskaming became the diocese of Haileybury and four years later the prefecture of Northern Ontario was carved out of its northwestern section. In addition, he supported special collections for the erection of a diocesan seminary (a project unrealized in his lifetime) and for home missions to Ukrainian Catholic immigrants.

The pressures of episcopal administration and the linguistic crisis took their toll on Gauthier. After 1918 his health declined and his appearances became less frequent. In 1921 he issued his last significant public statement, a lengthy pastoral on the needs of separate schools in Ontario. As he had earlier in his career, he made an eloquent plea to Catholics to continue the fight for a just share of the tax assessment and for the funding of senior grades in high schools. He had never surrendered his hope that funding equity, as promised in the Separate School Act of 1863 [see Sir Richard William Scott*], could be achieved through concerted effort. He would not witness the attainment of full funding.

Shortly before Christmas 1921 Gauthier was rushed to the Ottawa General Hospital, where he died of uraemia at 2:35 A.M. on 19 Jan. 1922. He was buried in Notre-Dame Basilica. His funeral was attended by Prime Minister William Lyon Mackenzie King*, members of his cabinet, numerous bishops, over 500 clergy and religious, a legion of lay leaders, and his brother and two sisters. In eulogies, former adversaries in the bilingual schools controversy now acknowledged him as a "true friend of the separate schools," while non-Catholics paid tribute to him as a loyal citizen who had stirred up "the patriotic spirit of his parishioners" during the Great War. Given the challenges of his life and his enormous pastoral contribution, the most fitting tribute came from the *Ottawa Citizen*, which remarked that he had lived up to his motto, *In fide et lenitate*. Charles Hugh Gauthier had indeed been strong in faith and gentle in administration.

MARK G. McGOWAN

AO, F 5; RG 80-8-0-863, no.9268. Arch. of the Archdiocese of Kingston, Ont., Gauthier papers. Arch. of the Archdiocese of Ottawa, Blessed Sacrament parish papers; Gauthier papers; Toronto corr. Arch. of the Roman Catholic Archdiocese of Toronto, ME (McEvay papers); O (O'Connor papers). Archivio Segreto Vaticano (Rome), Delegazione apostolica del Canadà, 157.37; Secretaria di Stato. LAC, RG 31, C1, 1871, Kenyon Township, Ont., div.2: 31. *L'Action catholique* (Québec), 19 janv. 1922. *Canadian Freeman* (Kingston), 22 June 1898. *Catholic Record* (London, Ont.), 2 April, 16 July, 3 Sept. 1898. *Catholic Register* (Toronto), 26 Oct. 1916, 26 Jan. 1922. *Le Devoir*, 19 juill. 1910, 22 févr. 1911. *Le Droit* (Ottawa), 24 janv. 1922. *Ottawa Citizen*, 19 Jan. 1922. *Ottawa Evening Journal*, 19 Jan. 1922. *La Presse*, 24 janv. 1922. *La Semaine religieuse de Montréal*, 26 janv. 1922. *La Semaine religieuse de Québec*, 2 févr. 1922. *Canadian men and women of the time* (Morgan; 1912). *Canadian R.C. bishops, 1658–1979*, comp. André Chapeau *et al.* (Ottawa, 1980). Robert Choquette, *L'Église catholique dans l'Ontario français du dix-neuvième siècle* (Ottawa, 1984); *La foi: gardienne de la langue en Ontario, 1900–1950* (Montréal, 1987); *Language and religion: a history of English-French conflict in Ontario* (Ottawa, 1975). L. J. Flynn, *Built on a rock: the story of the Roman Catholic Church in Kingston, 1826–1976* (Kingston, 1976). Hector Legros and Sœur Paul-Émile [Louise Guay], *Le diocèse d'Ottawa, 1847–1948* (Ottawa, [1949]). M. G. McGowan, *The waning of the green: Catholics, the Irish, and identity in Toronto, 1887–1922* (Montreal and Kingston, 1999). *Planted by flowing water: the diocese of Ottawa, 1847–1997*, ed. Pierre Hurtubise *et al.* (Ottawa, 1998).

GAUTHIER, LOUIS-ZÉPHIRIN, architect; b. 25 Aug. 1842 in Saint-Barthélémy (Saint-Barthélemy), Lower Canada, son of Amable Gauthier*, a woodcarver, and Euphrosine Gendron; m. first 25 Oct. 1864 Marie-Erménie Bourret in Rivière-du-Loup (Louiseville), Lower Canada; m. secondly 6 Feb. 1890 Marie-Louise Leduc in Sorel, Que.; he was survived by four children; d. 24 Dec. 1922 in Outremont, Que.

Trained by his father, who had been an important artisan in the studio of woodcarver Louis Quévillon* at the beginning of the 19th century, Louis-Zéphirin Gauthier began his career at an early age in the family sculpting and architectural workshop, along with his brothers Édouard, Olivier-Oscar, and Agapit. At the time the Gauthier family was working on the ornamentation for the churches of Sainte-Geneviève (now in Berthierville) and Saint-Barthelémy in the parish which then bore the name Saint-Barthelémi, in partnership with Alexis Milette*, another artisan who had likely come from Quévillon's studio. In this period, when there were no professional schools, sons were taken into their father's studios for their training. Once the apprenticeship was completed, the son could be considered a journeyman in the enterprise.

In keeping with tradition, Gauthier did not take over the studio until his father's death in 1873. His brothers Agapit and Édouard had died by this time and Olivier-Oscar had settled on their father's land. The diocese of Saint-Hyacinthe, which was developing rapidly, called on his services, and Gauthier drew up the plans for many religious buildings in the region, including the Collège du Sacré-Cœur in Sorel, the Saint-Hyacinthe cathedral, and the parish churches of Immaculée-Conception in Saint-Ours and Sainte-Anne and Saint-Joseph in Sorel. He also carried out repairs to many churches, all of them located in the Richelieu valley. The architect, who produced traditional construction plans using only stone and wood, made his home in Sorel until at least 1888. In all likelihood that was the year he went into partnership with Victor Roy, an important Montreal architect who had begun his career in Chicago, where he had learned to use structural metal. Together they built the parish churches of Notre-Dame-de-Grâce in Hull, Saint-Joseph in Ottawa, and Saint-Victor in Alfred, Ont.

After 1890 Gauthier relocated to downtown Montreal on Rue Saint-Jacques. The city was enjoying prosperous times and its population was growing rapidly, circumstances that made it attractive to experienced architects. Gauthier and Roy drew up the plans for other large churches in the diocese of Ottawa, while also keeping busy with residential construction in Montreal. This collaboration produced such large-scale buildings as the churches in Embrun, Vankleek Hill, Hawkesbury, Casselman, and Rockland, in Ontario, and those in Aylmer, Chapeau, and Grenville, in Quebec. But it was in Montreal that the two architects created their most striking religious structure, the parish church of Saint-Louis-de-France, which they began building in 1890 on Rue Roy near Rue Saint-Denis. It is a perfect example of late Victorian architecture and bears witness to the extreme wealth of decoration in which the architects of the period could indulge. Like most of the churches built at that time in large parishes, both urban and rural, the building had a steel framework, which made it possible to create large spaces unobstructed by columns.

After his partner's death in 1902 Gauthier carried on his work in the field of religious architecture with Joseph-Égilde-Césaire Daoust, a young architect trained at the École Polytechnique in Montreal. The firm extended the reach of its expertise by designing institutional buildings. The architects were then concentrating their efforts in the diocese of Saint-Hyacinthe and the archdiocese of Montreal, where the great parish church of Saint-François-d'Assise in Longue-Pointe, built in 1913, remains their major

achievement. At the same time, but especially from 1905 to 1908, they continued to renovate and enlarge existing Roman Catholic churches. Sometimes, as in the case of the church of Sainte-Geneviève (now in Pierrefonds), their mandate was to bring them into line with contemporary taste. They also drew up the plans for a number of residential buildings, including the houses of Joseph-Édouard Laberge and Olivier Gratton, built in Outremont in 1906 and 1912 respectively.

Two other large buildings in Montreal grew out of the collaboration between Gauthier and Daoust: the École des Hautes Études Commerciales de Montréal, a magnificent building begun in 1907 that bears witness to the determination of French Canadians to gain acceptance for themselves in the world of business, and the Male Institution for the Catholic Deaf and Dumb of the Province of Quebec, built in 1916. The church of Saint-Viateur in Outremont, which harked back to Gothic shapes, was the last major work designed by Gauthier. Construction began in 1911, and in 1921 the painter Guido Nincheri, an Italian who had settled in Montreal a few years earlier, began decorating the interior.

Louis-Zéphirin Gauthier, who died in 1922, had carried on the tradition begun by his father Amable, adapting it to the needs of an urban, industrial society. As requested by the dioceses, he provided them with large-scale religious buildings that reflected the triumphalism of the church at the time. His forays into secular construction confirmed his respect for the art of the early 19th century. His son Joseph-Zéphirin, who was born in 1900 and also became an architect, would succeed him. It was in the new city of Outremont, where the family was then living, that he in turn would deploy his talent.

RAYMONDE GAUTHIER

ANQ-M, CE603-S7, 6 févr. 1890. ANQ-MBF, CE401-S12, 28 août 1842; S15, 25 oct. 1864. *Le Devoir*, 26 déc. 1922. *Le Journal de Québec*, 4 juill. 1876. *La Minerve*, 11 août, 29 sept., 29 oct. 1888; 9 sept. 1889; 3 mai 1890; 26 févr. 1895. *La Presse*, 10 mai 1913. *Price Current* (Montreal), 29 Aug. 1890: 15; 2 Dec. 1892: 11; 13 July 1894: 586; 31 Jan. 1895: 864; 6 March 1896: 28; 21 Jan. 1898: 776; [1 April 1905]: 52; [31 March 1906]: 44; [14 July 1906]: 45; [10 Nov. 1906]: 44; [23 Feb. 1907]: 44; [9 Nov. 1907]: 162; [19 Dec. 1908]: 42; 7 July 1916: 32. P.-R. Bisson et Suzel Perrotte, *Inventaire des travaux d'architectes à Outremont de 1904 à 1987* ([Montréal], 1987). Raymonde Gauthier, *Construire une église au Québec: l'architecture religieuse avant 1939* (Montréal, 1993); *La tradition en architecture québécoise; le XXe siècle* (Québec, 1989). J. R. Porter et Jean Bélisle, *La sculpture ancienne au Québec; trois siècles d'art religieux et profane* (Montréal, 1986). Paul Racine, "Louis-Zéphirin Gauthier: un architecte à Sorel à la fin du XIXe siècle," *Le Carignan* (Sorel, Qué.), 5 (1991–92), no.2: 54–62. Émile Vaillancourt, *Une maîtrise d'art en Canada (1800–1823)* (Montréal, 1920).

GENDRON, PHILOMÈNE (baptized Hermine-Philomène), Religious Hospitaller of St Joseph, bursar of the Hôtel-Dieu in Montreal, and founder and director of the Hôtel-Dieu in Campbellton, N.B.; b. 17 July 1840 in Sainte-Rosalie, Lower Canada, daughter of Pierre Gendron, a farmer, and Hermine Hébert; d. 20 Oct. 1921 at the Hôtel-Dieu in Montreal.

Prevented by family obligations from pursuing her studies at the secondary level, Philomène Gendron was taught privately by her uncle Pierre-Samuel Gendron*, a teacher and notary. On 9 Feb. 1863 she entered the noviciate of the Religious Hospitallers of St Joseph at the Hôtel-Dieu in Montreal, where she took her vows on 18 July 1865. She then became assistant to the bursar of the Hôtel-Dieu, and in 1871 bursar of that hospital, a position she held until 1881 (except for an interruption in 1877–78). From 1881 to 1887 she carried out the same duties for the community. In this capacity she was responsible for finances, housekeeping, and the management of property.

Sister Gendron had seen a number of her colleagues leave to found institutions in New Brunswick: at Tracadie in 1868 [see Amanda Viger*], Chatham in 1869, and Saint-Basile in 1873. In 1884 another group set out for Arthabaskaville (Victoriaville), in the province of Quebec. In 1888 the congregation received two new requests to found institutions, one in Windsor, Ont., and one in Campbellton.

Although Sister Gendron sincerely believed she was not cut out to be a founder, she was the one appointed superior of the New Brunswick mission. Abbé John Lawson McDonald, the curé of the parish that had invited the Religious Hospitallers of St Joseph, had asked for some sisters, first to teach, and then, eventually, to run a hospital. The sisters accepted on the understanding that they would be replaced when a teaching congregation could take over from them (the transfer would come in 1922). Two teaching nuns from the Hôtel-Dieu in Chatham would provide this service at first.

On 13 Aug. 1888 Sister Gendron and three fellow nuns boarded the Intercolonial Railway for Campbellton. There, a somewhat dilapidated house served as their residence, school, and hospital. One nun gave music lessons to nine pupils for two dollars each a month. This sum was the sisters' sole income, and during the early years they suffered from cold, cramped quarters, and hunger. It took a great deal of ingenuity and courage on the part of Sister Gendron to get by with such limited means. Fortunately, generous benefactors came to their rescue. By 24 Oct. 1888 a shelter had been erected that could accommodate about 50 pupils, mostly English-speaking. That day, the first patient also arrived, suffering from frostbitten toes. At night he slept on the kitchen table. It was not until the Christmas holidays that a physician per-formed an amputation on him in the classroom, which doubled as the operating room.

Such harsh conditions could not continue, and the construction of a more suitable building became a priority. But construction required the approval of Bishop James Rogers*, who also had to decide on the location and plan of the building. As it happened, his views did not always coincide with those of Sister Gendron. Although the bishop resigned himself to having the building go up at the spot chosen by the superior, he got his way on other issues: postponement of the installation of running water, no more than 11 beds in the hospital area, and stairways without turns. Construction went on from July to December 1890. This three-storey building, 140 by 200 feet, enabled the nuns to accommodate 11 patients, 90 pupils (including boarders), and postulants.

After serving two consecutive three-year terms as superior (the maximum allowed), Sister Gendron acted as mistress of novices until 1897, when she was recalled to the Hôtel-Dieu in Montreal. As chief hospitaller of that hospital, she oversaw the smooth running of the establishment, took care of the admission of patients, and supervised the physician's visits. She returned to Campbellton in 1900 as superior and administrator. During her absence, the number of patients, pupils, and boarders had increased appreciably, and the building opened in December 1890 was no longer adequate. In 1905 Sister Gendron sent two nuns to Montreal to learn about the new methods being used in hospitals and she began making plans for the construction of a real hospital, with a capacity of 50 beds, which would open in 1909. In 1906 she asked to be recalled to Montreal. The mission at Campbellton now had 14 nuns (including novices), 12 of them from the surrounding region. Hard work and extreme poverty had certainly worn the superior down, but the community's records reveal that the local curé's interference had also forced her to carry on an exhausting struggle to maintain a bit of independence. At the age of 66, she resumed the position of bursar at the Hôtel-Dieu in Montreal. In 1910 she began assisting the bursar's office, an activity she continued until 1918 (she was also the community's bursar from 1908 to 1911). While in Montreal, she retained an interest in the Campbellton mission and had to face the sad news that the building constructed in 1890 and the hospital opened in 1909 had both been destroyed by a fire in the town in 1910. Eight years later, the rebuilt hospital was also destroyed by fire. Before her death, however, she learned, to her great joy, that a new Hôtel-Dieu had admitted its first patients on 18 July 1920.

Established under the energetic and patient direction of Sister Philomène Gendron, a woman of intelligence gifted with business acumen, the Campbellton mission was the last of the New Brunswick institutions founded by the Hôtel-Dieu of Montreal. Sister

General

Gendron was aptly described by Bishop Rogers in 1890: "big in body, large in mind, and great in heart."

CORINNE LaPLANTE

ANQ-M, CE602-S25, 18 juill. 1840. Arch. des Religieuses Hospitalières de Saint-Joseph (Montréal), Vie religieuse de la communauté, annales, vols.4–5; nécrologie de sœur Philomène Gendron; procès-verbaux des vêtures et professions, 1858–99; reg. des entrées, 1851–68. Arch. des Religieuses Hospitalières de Saint-Joseph de la Prov. Notre-Dame de l'Assomption (Bathurst, N.-B.), "Petite histoire du premier curé résidant à Campbellton, John Lawson Mac-Donald, 1888–1903" (1953); Sœur Thérèse Plourde, "Fondation à Campbellton en 1888" (texte dactylographié, 1976); "Soixante-dix ans d'évolution, 1888–1958" (texte dactylographié); vie religieuse de la communauté, chroniques des RHSJ de l'Hôtel-Dieu de Campbellton, vols.1–4; offices de l'Hôtel-Dieu de Campbellton, 1869–1921. P.-S. Gendron, *La famille Nicolas Gendron; dictionnaire généalogique* (Saint-Hyacinthe, Qué., 1929).

GENERAL, LEVI. *See* DESKAHEH

GENYK (Genik, Genyk-Berezovsky), CYRIL (Kyrylo), translator, immigration agent, newspaper owner, and community leader; b. 1857 in Bereziv Nyzhnii, Kolomyya county, Austrian crownland of Galicia (Ukraine), son of Ivan Genyk and Ann Pertsovych; m. Pauline Tsurkovsky, and they had three sons and three daughters; d. 12 Feb. 1925 in Winnipeg.

The son of a village mayor, Cyril Genyk prided himself on being descended from a Ukrainian noble family whose privileges had included freedom from serfdom, an important distinction in pre-1848 central Europe. He first studied in Kolomyya and then in Stanyslaviv (Ivano-Frankivs'k), where he graduated from a teacher-training college. After pursuing his education at a gymnasium in Lemberg (Lviv), he passed his baccalaureate. He may have briefly studied law at the Chernivtsi State University, but turned to teaching. His first post, in 1879, was in Kaminne, a town in Nadvirna county. In 1882 he established a school in his native village and taught there.

During his studies Genyk had encountered a group of young activists with populist and socialist ideas, including Ivan Franko, who would become a renowned author and political leader. For purportedly spreading reformist ideas to the peasants of his region, Genyk was arrested in 1880, but he was never brought to trial and was released. In the 1880s he established and ran a milling business and then a producers' cooperative called the Carpathian Store. He served on various regulatory bodies of the cooperative movement in eastern Galicia; he was elected to the Kolomyya county council in 1890.

Among Genyk's contacts was Jósef Olesków*, a professor of agronomy in Lemberg who would be instrumental in the mass emigration of Ukrainians to Canada in the late 19th and early 20th centuries. Olesków asked Genyk to take out the second contingent of settlers he had selected. On 22 June 1896 Genyk and his group of 64 settlers, including his wife and four children, arrived in Quebec City. He led them to Winnipeg and then to Stuartburn in southeastern Manitoba. Since he intended to locate there, he applied for a homestead on 22 August, but within months he changed his mind. In order to be able to send his children to school he moved his family to Winnipeg, where he purchased a house; the homestead application would later be cancelled.

A mature family man, Genyk was well educated, fluent in several languages, and a capable organizer. These qualities led Olesków to recommend him to the Department of the Interior on 27 Aug. 1896 as an immigration agent. On 22 September officials of the department in Winnipeg were authorized to employ him as an interpreter and translator whenever required. The position would soon become a full-time job. Naturalized in 1900, Genyk would serve the department and local government authorities until 1911. For the immigrants he was an able spokesman and a welcome counsellor. In his uniform and peaked cap, he presented an imposing figure when he met them in Quebec City.

In addition to his official duties, Genyk played a significant role in the establishment of the first Ukrainian Canadian institutions, including the Taras Shevchenko Reading Hall, which he founded in his home in 1899 as a cultural society and library. Almost from the outset he had contributed articles to Ukrainian-language newspapers in the United States and he later did so in Canada as well. For example, in *Svoboda* [Liberty] (Mount Carmel, Pa), he urged immigrants to come in the spring, with enough cash to start a household, and to be wary of unscrupulous steamship agents and others who might exploit them. He encouraged his fellow Ukrainians in Canada to give up traditional ways of thinking and ritualistic celebrations, to learn English, and to adjust to the new country. Together with two other Galician activists, Ivan (John) Bodrug and Ivan (John) Negrich, he founded the first Ukrainian-language newspaper in Canada, *Kanadyiskyi farmer/Canadian Farmer* (Winnipeg), in 1903 and established the North West Publishing Company to produce it.

Although he did not profess allegiance to any denomination, Genyk knew of his countrymen's religiosity and favoured the creation of a church for Ukrainians which would be independent of the Greek (Eastern rite) Catholic [see Nestor DMYTRIW] or Russian Orthodox ancestral churches – another break with the past. In 1903–4 he and his associates Bodrug and Negrich worked with Presbyterian ministers in Winnipeg to found a syncretic church, the Independent Greek Church [see Joseph Czerniawski*] and they promoted it in the *Kanadyiskyi farmer.*

400

During his years of service to the Department of the Interior, Genyk was drawn to Liberal politics, especially because the federal Liberal government supported immigration. He was the first Liberal party agent of Ukrainian origin; he recruited workers and campaigned on behalf of Liberal candidates. The *Kanadyiskyi farmer* became the official conveyor of the party's ideas to the Ukrainian community.

Genyk jealously guarded his favoured status with the Liberal party and among the Anglo-Canadians with whom he worked. In addition he greatly enjoyed the prestige associated with his position as a government employee. His sense of his own importance led others to describe him as pretentious and boastful. His fellow activists drew away from him and he appears to have alienated Winnipeg's Ukrainian community generally. His job came to an end with the election of a federal Conservative government under Robert Laird Borden* in 1911. Little is known of him after that date since he dropped out of public life. He moved to the United States to live with two of his children, Eugenia and John, but at some stage he returned to Winnipeg, where he died in 1925.

STELLA HRYNIUK

Dictionary of Ukrainian Canadian biography, pioneer settlers of Manitoba, 1891–1900, ed. and comp. V. J. Kaye (Toronto, 1975). Oleksander Dombrovsky, *Outline of the history of the Ukrainian Evangelical-Reformed movement* (New York and Toronto, 1979) [text in Ukrainian]. *A heritage in transition: essays in the history of Ukrainians in Canada*, ed. M. R. Lupul (Toronto, 1982). J.-P. Himka, *Galician villagers and the Ukrainian national movement in the nineteenth century* (New York, 1988). V. J. Kaye, *Early Ukrainian settlements in Canada, 1895–1900: Dr. Josef Oleskow's role in the settlement of the Canadian northwest* (Toronto, 1964). O. T. Martynowych, *Ukrainians in Canada: the formative period, 1891–1924* (Edmonton, 1991). M. H. Marunchak, *Studies in the history of Ukrainians in Canada* (5v. to date, Winnipeg, 1964–) [text in Ukrainian]. O. I. Sych, *From the "new land": letters of Ukrainian emigrants from Canada* (Edmonton, 1991) [text in Ukrainian].

GEOFFRION, LOUIS-ÉLIE, shop assistant, grocer, and businessman; b. 17 May 1853 in Varennes, Lower Canada, elder son of Élie Geoffrion, a farmer, and Marguerite Beauchamp; m. 4 Feb. 1880 Angélina Lajeunesse in Terrebonne, Que., and they had four daughters and two sons; d. 17 Aug 1923 in Carleton, Que.

Little is known about the childhood of Louis-Élie Geoffrion. He studied at the Collège Industriel de Varennes, and later may have attended a high school in New Haven, Conn. He is thought to have gone to work in 1869 for John Hutchinson, a Montreal grocer. His father died the following year, when Louis-Élie was 17. In May 1876 he joined the firm of L. Chaput, Fils et Compagnie, a leading Montreal grocer [*see* Charles

CHAPUT]. Initially hired as a shop assistant, he learned the trade, was promoted, and eventually, in February 1884, became a partner in the firm which in the course of time had become a wholesaler. Geoffrion was an able and respected businessman who would spend the next 28 years working to make the company thrive. On 31 March 1898 an article in *La Presse* declared that "what especially helped make this company grow was its hiring of L. E. Geoffrion and later taking him on as a partner. M. Geoffrion has outstanding abilities as a businessman; he is a first-rate buyer; he is regarded as one of the leading grocers of the [city's] west end." The same article describes him as a thrifty manager, but one capable of taking risks. For unknown reasons, he left the company in 1912.

Geoffrion was evidently not ready to retire, however, since he remained active in the Montreal business world. Two years after leaving the company, he was running the Merchants Awning Company Limited. During World War I, the Montreal city directories listed him as a "financier." In 1920, at the age of 67, he founded a brokerage house, Geoffrion et Compagnie, in partnership with his son Henri. According to the declaration of partnership, the partners were "to undertake and transact financial operations as members of the Montreal Stock Exchange and also as brokers in stocks and bonds and investment bankers." Henri Geoffrion, who in 1919 had married Juliette Bienvenu, the daughter of Tancrède Bienvenu*, continued to be involved in the company until the early 1930s; his partners included Jacques Fichet (1923) and Horace Pérodeau (1926). At the time of his death, Louis-Élie was still president of Geoffrion et Compagnie; he was also in charge of the Canadian Advertising Agency Limited.

Besides his professional activities, Louis-Élie Geoffrion was very active in various Montreal associations. In 1886 he became a member of the Montreal Board of Trade, a bilingual organization in which he served as a council member in 1906. In the Chambre de Commerce du District de Montréal, which he had joined in 1890, he occupied increasingly important offices as councillor (1892–95, 1897), vice-president (1898–99), and president (1900–1). He headed its delegation to the Congress of Chambers of Commerce of the Empire in London in 1900. He was president from 1904 to 1906 of the Montreal Wholesale Grocers' Association, an organization he had helped found, and in 1907–8 of the Dominion Wholesale Grocers' Guild. He was also a member of the Montreal Harbour Commission in the early 1900s, and belonged to other organizations such as the Association Saint-Jean-Baptiste de Montréal and the Ligue Antialcoolique de Montréal.

Although a supporter of the Liberal party, Geoffrion never stood for election. In the early years of the 20th century he nevertheless was president of the

Georgeson

Montreal Reform Club, the goal of which was, according to its 1904 constitution, "the promotion of the political welfare of the Liberal party of Canada." In 1923 he served on the board of the Montreal Liberal daily newspaper *Le Canada*, which at that time was the organ of the moderate wing of the party.

Louis-Élie Geoffrion was a man highly respected by both the anglophone and the francophone communities in Montreal, or so at least the laudatory obituaries published at the time of his death suggest. Far from confining himself to his strictly professional activities, he had a broad conception of the businessman's role within society and he thus made a contribution to a number of economic, sociocultural, and political associations in the Montreal region.

YVES BÉGIN

ANQ-M, CE601-S10, 17 mai 1853; CE606-S24, 4 févr. 1880; TP11, S2, SS20, SSS48, vol.11-O, 1er févr. 1884, no.227; vol.33-O, 1er févr. 1912, no.119; vol.45-O, 25 juin 1920, no.841. École des Hautes Études Commerciales, Service des arch. (Montréal), P003 (fonds de la Chambre de commerce du Montréal métropolitain), G; P019 (fonds du Bureau de commerce de Montréal), B. LAC, RG 31, C1, 1861, 1871, 1881, Varennes, Que. *Le Canada* (Montréal), 18 août 1923. *Le Devoir*, 18 août 1923. *Gazette* (Montreal), 18 Aug. 1923. *Montreal Daily Star*, 18 Aug. 1923. *La Patrie*, 1er avril 1902, 18 août 1923. *La Presse*, 31 mars 1898, 18 août 1923. *Canadian men and women of the time* (Morgan; 1912). *Constitution and by-laws, Montreal Reform Club, organized June 17th, 1898* (Montreal, 1904). [Télesphore Saint-Pierre], *Histoire du commerce canadien-français de Montréal, 1535–1893* (Montréal, 1894). *Souvenir de Maisonneuve, esquisse historique de la ville de Montréal . . .* (Montréal, [1894?]).

GEORGESON, HENRY (Scotty), stopping-house owner, fisherman, lighthouse-keeper, farmer, and boatbuilder; b. 17 July 1835 in Walls, Scotland; m. 21 Feb. 1881 Elizabeth Sophia (Sophy), a native woman, in Duncan, B.C., and they had four sons and one daughter; d. 2 Feb. 1927 on Galiano Island, B.C.

Born in the Shetland Islands, Henry Georgeson supposedly left home at 14, with limited education, to work on sailing ships. He made voyages to Australia, New Zealand, and China, and "deserted" at San Francisco. With a large number of future Cariboo pioneers, in 1860 he signed a petition for responsible government for the colony of British Columbia, presumably at Hope. He took part in the Cariboo gold rush, and with a partner, George Buchanan, operated a stopping-house at Beaver Pass, on the pack-trail to Barkerville. After selling his half interest for $2,500 in 1863, he settled on a lot on Galiano Island, one of the Gulf Islands. He made formal application to pre-empt the property in 1873. Like many Gulf island residents, he earned seasonal income fishing for the Fraser River canneries. His experience as a mariner gained him a position on the Sand Heads lightship at the mouth of the Fraser from 1868 to 1869.

By the early 1880s increasing traffic, and two shipwrecks off Mayne and Saturna islands, had made it imperative for the federal Department of Marine and Fisheries to install lighthouses on the major channels through the Gulf Islands. To safeguard the heavily used Active Pass, called Plumper Pass on some charts and the shortest route between southern Vancouver Island and the mainland, the first light was planned for Georgina Point on Mayne Island. Georgeson was appointed keeper by an order in council of 21 July 1884. Following the station's completion the next year, he was ordered to light up on 10 June 1885. Other lights would be erected at East Point on Saturna Island in 1887 and Porlier Pass on Galiano Island in 1902. The Georgina Point station was described in a report by deputy minister William Smith* in June 1885: "The building is of wood painted white, and consists of a square tower 42 feet high from the ground to the vane of the lantern, with keeper's dwelling attached." Georgeson held his position here until 31 Dec. 1920, when he retired to his farm on Galiano Island. In 1923 he received the federal Long Service Medal for his 36 years of lighthouse work. He is buried on land that he donated for the Galiano Island cemetery.

The role of lighthouse-keeper in the early years was demanding and hazardous. The clockwork mechanisms for the Georgina Point light and the fog-bell installed about 1887 were wound by hand, as frequently as every two or three hours during the night. Georgeson quickly gained expertise in operating the steam fog-alarm that replaced the bell in 1892. The fixed white coal-oil light, which would not be replaced with an occulting white petroleum-vapour light until 1910, floated in a tub of mercury that produced noxious fumes. The dioptric lenses and reflectors were cleaned daily, with a more thorough cleaning twice weekly. Georgeson was expected to remain alert through the nights, use alcohol in moderation, and maintain accurate records. His carefully kept logs served as evidence on more than one occasion when captains of Canadian Pacific Railway ships complained that the foghorn was not operating. One of the more exciting events in Georgeson's career was the grounding, in dense fog on 13 Oct. 1918, of the CPR's *Princess Adelaide* on the rocks in front of the lighthouse, even though the foghorn was working. There was no loss of life and the ship was refloated. At some point, to assist Georgeson in his duties, a telephone was installed at the Georgina station. For many years it was one of only two telephones on Mayne Island.

Keepers' pay was notoriously meagre. Georgeson's annual salary of $500 increased to $550 in 1888 and, when the fog-alarm was installed, it jumped to $900, from which he paid an assistant, his son George; by his retirement it had risen to $1,680. He augmented his income by building boats for local residents. His wife, Sophia, quite possibly helped him tend the light and, as much as lighthouse duties would permit, they both took part in community activities.

The Georgeson name is synonymous with lighthouse keeping in the southern Gulf Islands. Henry's brother James manned the East Point light from 1889 to 1921 and he too received the Long Service Medal. James's sons Peter and Henry as well as Henry's son George also became keepers.

MARIE ELLIOTT

BCA, GR-0584, vol.23. LAC, RG 12, Acc. H-1988–89/205. National Arch. (G.B.), CO 60/9 (mfm. at BCA). Private arch., Marie Elliott (Mayne Island, B.C.), Copy of Henry Georgeson's diary (original owned by Mary Ellen Harding); Interview with Donald DeRousie of Mayne Island. Private coll. (Mayne Island), Henry Georgeson's logbooks. *Canada Gazette*, 19 (1885–86): 9. Can., Parl., *Sessional papers*, 1885, no.9: xxxii, 130; 1886, no.11: xxviii, 121; 1888, no.5: xxviii; 1892, no.10: 44; 1894, no.11: xxxii; 1912, no.21: 79–80; 1923, no.2: 100. *1881 Canadian census: Vancouver Island*, comp. Peter Baskerville *et al.* (Victoria, 1990), 188–89. Marie Elliott, *Active Pass Lightstation, 1885–1985* (Ottawa, 1985); *East Point Lighthouse, 1887–1987* (Ottawa, 1987); *Mayne Island & the outer Gulf Islands: a history* (Mayne Island, 1984). Janet and G. W. Georgeson, "Henry Georgeson (Galiano Island, 1858–1927)," in British Columbia Hist. Assoc., *A Gulf Islands patchwork: some early events on the islands of Galiano, Mayne, Saturna, North and South Pender* (Sidney, B.C., 1961), 9. Donald Graham, *Keepers of the light: a history of British Columbia's lighthouses and their keepers* (Madeira Park, B.C., 1985).

GIBSON, Sir JOHN MORISON, militia officer, lawyer, office holder, politician, and businessman; b. 1 Jan. 1842 in Toronto Township, Upper Canada, son of William Gibson and Mary Sinclair; m. first 26 Oct. 1869 Emily Annie Birrell (d. 1874) in London, Ont.; m. secondly 26 Sept. 1876 Caroline Hope (d. 1877) in Hamilton, Ont., and they had a daughter who died at birth; m. there thirdly 18 May 1881 Elizabeth Malloch, and they had four sons and two daughters; d. there 3 June 1929.

John Gibson's father immigrated from Scotland in 1826 and found work as a stonemason in the Hamilton area. Following his marriage to the daughter of a farmer in Nelson Township, he purchased a farm in Toronto Township to the east. Not long before he died of consumption in 1845, he wrote to his nephew David Gibson* that this farm was not large enough to support his growing family and that adjacent property was too expensive to purchase. It was left to Mary Gibson to move her family in 1851 to a farm in Oneida Township.

After a year of school there, John was sent to Hamilton, where his sister Jane had located after her marriage, to attend the Hamilton grammar school. In 1854 he transferred to the recently opened Central School, where he flourished academically. In later years he would attribute his success to hard work and perseverance, which he credited principal John Herbert Sangster with teaching him. In June 1859, as the school's head boy, he was selected to test the jets of the Hamilton waterworks during their first public display, in Gore Park. As his career developed, he and his supporters would frequently cite this event as proof of his identification with progressive change in Hamilton.

Gibson wrote the matriculation examination for the University of Toronto in September 1859 and was awarded a scholarship. A member of the inaugural class of University College, he eventually amassed many honours, including the silver medal in classics and modern languages, a prize in oriental languages, and the Prince of Wales medal in his graduating year (BA 1863). In 1861, upon hearing news of the *Trent* affair [see Sir Charles Hastings Doyle*], he had been one of the first to join the university company of the 2nd Battalion Volunteer Militia Rifles (later the Queen's Own Rifles). On his return to Hamilton in 1864, after he had completed his MA, he became an ensign in the 13th Battalion Volunteer Militia Light Infantry. Promoted lieutenant in early 1866, in June he was part of the Hamilton unit that, with other militiamen, confronted the Fenians at Ridgeway [see Alfred Booker*]. Gibson worked his way through the ranks and from 1886 to 1895 he commanded the battalion, spearheading a major recruiting drive and overseeing construction of a new armoury. Following his resignation, on 9 Nov. 1895 he was named honorary lieutenant-colonel.

The focuses of the militia were drill and rifle-shooting. Mastering them required discipline and precision, what Gibson summarized as "faithful and persevering industry," a central tenet in his world-view. Recognized for his marksmanship, he competed as a member of the Canadian team at Wimbledon (London), England, in 1874, 1875, and 1879; he commanded the team in 1881 and the Bisley Cup team in 1907. From 1893 to 1907 he served as president of the Dominion Rifle Association and in 1891–92 and 1897 he was president of the Canadian Military Institute. In 1901 he was appointed honorary colonel of his old battalion and served on the committee that approved the infamous Ross rifle [see Sir Edwin Alfred Hervey ALDERSON], and from 1904 to 1909 he commanded the 15th Infantry Brigade, with headquarters in Hamilton.

In 1866 Gibson had joined the Hamilton law firm of Burton and Bruce as a student. George William Burton, a business specialist, the city's solicitor, and a leading Reformer, became Gibson's mentor, and he provided the young man with an entrée to Hamilton's commercial and political elite. After his call to the bar in Michaelmas term 1867, Gibson continued his legal studies, gaining an LLB from the University of Toronto in 1869. The following year he formed a partnership in Hamilton with Francis Mackelcan, whom he had met through rifle-shooting. Responsibilities were divided, with Gibson concentrating on business law. The firm's reputation was enhanced in 1871 by his nomination as an examiner in law at the University of Toronto and in January 1873 by the appointment of the firm, now Mackelcan, Gibson, and Bell, as solicitor for Hamilton. Gibson would be named a QC in 1890 and elected a bencher of the Law Society of Upper Canada in 1899.

In the 1870s the stage was set for his move into public service. As he would later explain, he was eager "to do all he could for the benefit of those institutions which had helped him as a boy." From 1871 to 1884 he sat on Hamilton's Board of School Trustees, serving as chairman for two years. He championed the upgrading of educational facilities and the hiring of better-educated teachers, and urged the creation of an industrial school and a public library. In addition, he supported the establishment of the Hamilton Art School and was its president for many years. The remarkably active Gibson was, as well, a leading member of Central Presbyterian Church and a supporter of the Hamilton Health Association; he helped organize the Wentworth Historical Society in 1889 and was president of the St Andrew's Society in 1891–92. Beyond Hamilton, he sat in the senate of the University of Toronto from 1873 to 1888. A freemason since 1867, he rose to serve as grand master of the lodge in Canada in 1892–94. In 1896 he collaborated with George Ansel Sterling RYERSON and others in founding the Canadian Red Cross Society, and he was its president until 1914; in recognition he was made a knight of grace of the Order of St John of Jerusalem in England in 1911. Honorary LLDs also came his way, from the University of Toronto (1903) and McMaster University (1909).

Gibson's political career stemmed from the mentorship of George Burton. Largely as a result of his university and Toronto contacts, he also had connections with such leading Reformers as Edward Blake* and George Brown*, and these links made him a valuable asset. He served his apprenticeship as secretary of the Hamilton Reform Association and as a local organizer during the federal election of 1878. He himself ran provincially in Hamilton the following year. During the campaign his allegiance to the city was called into question, with the Tory press portraying him as a "carpetbagger" with ties to Toronto, but he won by a narrow margin.

As a novice MLA, the former chair of the Hamilton board was naturally drawn to educational issues, favouring such causes as the admission of women to the University of Toronto [see Sir Daniel Wilson*], the "Canadianization" of its faculty, and the abolition of special funding for Upper Canada College. Faced by Knights of Labor opponents in February 1883 and December 1886, Gibson was victorious each time. In February 1886 Liberal provincial secretary Arthur Sturgis Hardy* said that Gibson and a few other members had "sailed in under the flag of the workingman" by backing many of the demands of the Knights. Gibson, in fact, like his leader, Oliver Mowat*, was a successful practitioner of co-option, supporting just enough labour-advocated reform to undermine the Knights' call for independent working-class action. During the 1887 federal campaign he used his reputation as a "friend of the workingman" to broker an agreement between labour and the Hamilton Liberals in an unsuccessful attempt to defeat the Tory incumbents.

Although some Reform colleagues grumbled about Gibson's "progressive" tendencies, Mowat and others were sympathetic. From 1884 to 1899 Gibson was chairman of the legislature's private bills committee. Fellow MLA Charles Clarke* remembered him as a "deliberate, if not painfully slow" speaker, though in committee "he seemed intuitively to realize the dubious points of every measure brought before him." A year after Gibson's appointment as provincial secretary in 1889, he suffered an unexpected and disheartening defeat by Thomas Henry Stinson, a popular local businessman and Conservative. Stinson's election was overturned, however, and in the by-election that followed, in 1891, Gibson was again returned. After resuming office as provincial secretary, in 1893 he guided through the legislature the Act for the prevention of cruelty to and better protection of children (the Gibson Act), which, significantly, made child abuse an indictable offence, promoted foster care, strengthened the powers of children's aid societies, and established the office of superintendent of neglected children, to which Gibson appointed John Joseph Kelso*. Elected for the new riding of Hamilton West in 1894, Gibson was made commissioner of crown lands in 1896, in the government of A. S. Hardy. During his tenure (until 1899), he encouraged reforestation in northern Ontario and oversaw new game legislation and the Forest Reserves Act of 1898 [see Aubrey White*]. In March 1898 he again lost his seat, but in a by-election in Wellington East in October he was returned to Queen's Park.

In October 1899 Gibson was appointed attorney general in the government of George William Ross*. A frequent spokesman for an administration that was losing public confidence, his own reputation tainted by scandals that suggested he had participated in or gone along with vote rigging, he found his political position increasingly tenuous. Lost in the bitter partisanship of the Ross years were some of his better pieces of work, including the new municipal assessment and taxation act of 1904. Ross's cabinet shuffle of November 1904, including Gibson's demotion to minister without portfolio, recognized his professions of ill health, and most likely his political liability. Never close to Wellington East, he was a prime candidate for defeat in James Pliny Whitney*'s Conservative sweep of January 1905.

The loss prompted Gibson to shift his full energy to the carefully structured realm of business that overlapped his politics. Capitalizing on his political and social connections, he had first made his mark in 1877, when, with his then father-in-law, Adam Hope*, he helped organize and promote the Landed Banking and Loan Company, which invested in mortgages and municipal debentures and operated a savings bank. Gibson used his connections to attract investors, among them Edward Blake, and he found his own niche as the company's legal adviser. Among the ventures that followed were the Canada Clock Company Limited, chartered by Gibson, Francis Mackelcan, and others in 1881.

It was as a lawyer that Gibson began his profitable association with John Patterson*, a Hamilton businessman who ran an integrated operation that included property management, real estate, mills, a lumber yard, and construction. Their first recorded contact occurred in the fall of 1883 when Gibson and Mackelcan represented the city in a lawsuit brought by Patterson and his brother. Soon, Gibson was their attorney and was offering them mortgage funds to finance their operations; by the late 1880s the Pattersons were Landed Banking's primary customers. From here Gibson took the short step to real-estate investment: by the early 1890s he had assembled a block of almost 200 building lots in eastern Hamilton, some of which he owned outright and in others of which he was a co-owner.

Gibson and Patterson, like other developers there, recognized that new industry could intensify the demand for land and thus boost values. In 1893 Gibson, while city solicitor, acted as legal adviser to the Pattersons in their negotiations to sell east-end land for a smelting works, and he advocated municipal bonuses for the enterprise. Clearly in conflict of interest, he brazenly denied the charge when it was aired in the press. The accusation was not pursued, but the Mackelcan-Gibson law firm was dissolved – Gibson would soon form another, with W. W. Osborne – and he resigned as city solicitor.

Financial interest most certainly underlay his enthusiasm for the establishment of a factory by the Westinghouse Manufacturing Company Limited in the mid 1890s. The proposed site was less than half a mile north of his holdings. When negotiations with the city for municipal bonuses for Westinghouse stalled, Gibson personally renewed the company's option on the site and lobbied council. At the time of the smelting-works controversy, he had argued that, though he opposed municipal bonusing to promote industrial development, there were always exceptions. Westinghouse was one. The *Hamilton Spectator*, never an admirer of Gibson, was forced to admit that credit for the agreement between the city and the company was due "in large measure" to him. For his part in assisting Westinghouse, Gibson was appointed to its board of directors; in 1903 he would transfer this directorship to the newly formed Canadian Westinghouse Company Limited.

Gibson and Patterson's move into transportation was envisaged as yet another way to increase the value of their real estate. In 1894 they began promoting the Hamilton Radial Electric Railway, the route of which was eventually changed to pass over Gibson's land. Together with Liberal businessmen John Dickenson, John Moodie Sr, and John William Sutherland, they also launched a scheme to generate hydroelectricity at DeCew Falls (near St Catharines) and transmit it to Hamilton. Their corporate means, the Cataract Power Company of Hamilton Limited, formed in 1896 with Gibson as president, soon absorbed its local competitors. By 1908, through the purchase of existing local radial and street railways and power companies, Cataract (reorganized in 1907 as Dominion Power and Transmission Company Limited) controlled the electrical supply and radial-railway network of an area stretching from Brantford to Oakville and from Hamilton to Vineland. The company's ambition was to extend its operations to Windsor and Toronto and to meet American transportation systems at Buffalo, N.Y.

The Five Johns, as Gibson's group became known, formed the core of the interlocking directorates that linked the Dominion Power holding company and its subsidiaries. Gibson moved effortlessly from the presidency of Cataract to that of Dominion when it was formally established in March 1907, and he sat on the boards of a number of associated companies, while his law firm provided legal counsel to the conglomerate. In the mid 1910s the Hamilton Hotel Company Limited, which Gibson headed, constructed the Royal Connaught Hotel adjacent to Dominion Power's Terminal Building, thus integrating transit with the potentially profitable service sector. Similarly, the establishment in 1914 of the plant of the National Steel Car Company Limited, of which Gibson was also president, was tied to negotiations between Dominion Power and the city over the Hamilton Street Railway franchise.

Gibson's grand industrial scheme began to founder when he attempted to enter the high-stakes field of nickel refining. As the demand for nickel had grown in the 1890s, Gibson, in concert with Patterson, Moodie, Andrew Trew Wood*, Samuel J. Ritchie* (a disgruntled former member of the Canadian Copper syndicate at Sudbury), and others, devised a plan to establish a electrolytic refining complex in Hamilton, where existing steel operations undoubtedly gave encouragement to the venture. Though Gibson did not directly invest in the nickel syndicate, members of his family, including his wife and brother-in-law, and many close associates did. That the proposed location of the works was near his tract demonstrated once again how industrial promotion and real-estate speculation went hand in hand.

There was another factor that contributed to Gibson's enthusiasm. Industrial demands for electricity offered Cataract the opportunity to expand generation and even out the periods of peak load. The proposed refining process required huge quantities of electricity. In early 1899 Gibson's law firm applied for letters patent for the Hoepfner Refining Company, to mine and refine zinc, lead, silver, and nickel and copper ore. Following his appointment as its president, work began on the plant and a contract was reached with Cataract. Not long after construction had been completed, it was discovered that the process did not work. But, too much had been invested for the project to be abandoned. A number of shareholders banded together to lease the Hoepfner premises and experiments were conducted to discover a new electrical refining process. Gibson believed that, once this process had been found, Hamilton would possess "the largest nickel and copper refining plant in the world." The experiments failed, however, and the refinery never opened.

So critical was the nickel-steel enterprise to Gibson's design that he had reversed his long-standing support for free trade to advocate protective tariffs. As commissioner of crown lands, he had opposed the call of lumbermen for a "manufacturing condition" (export duties on unprocessed material), arguing that it would constitute a breach of faith with timber licensees. The Hardy government, however, reluctantly instituted the condition. For nickel Gibson was willing to abandon free trade. First, he and his partners attempted to use their Liberal connections to persuade the federal government of Wilfrid Laurier* of the need for export duties on nickel ore. When this tactic failed, Gibson pressed his provincial colleagues to extend the manufacturing condition to nickel. Ross initially appeared receptive and brought in an amendment to the Mines Act in 1900, but various factors, including the realization that Gibson's involvement constituted a dangerous conflict of interest, led the government to let the amendment die.

Cataract's electricity nonetheless remained a popular component of Hamilton's identity and Gibson's conglomeration. Public approval began to decline, however, in the early 1900s. As a result of a bitter street-railway strike in 1906, opinion swung to the

side of labour [*see* John Wesley Theaker*]. Moreover, clashes with civic authorities over the quality and cost of transportation and electrical services and the extension of rail lines engendered support for public ownership. In 1914 a municipally run hydroelectric system began operating in direct competition with Dominion Power.

Gibson was unswayed by these trends. He served as his company's principal spokesman during the strike and in the early stages of the battle over municipal ownership. He was still close to the peak of his corporate power – socially prominent and unencumbered by public office, but politically influential nevertheless, and quite prepared to redefine his principles. In 1907 he aggressively pushed for a federal chartering of the Hamilton Radial Electric Railway as a work of general advantage to Canada, which would free it from provincial interference. In so doing he hoped to avoid the justifiable hostility of the Whitney government and overstepped his prior provincialist objection to federal charters for purely local lines. Early in 1908 the Hamilton charter was reluctantly granted by the federal Liberals, with whom Gibson still managed to maintain friendly personal relations.

After his appointment as lieutenant governor of Ontario in September 1908, which brought him to Toronto, Gibson's move from corporate autocracy to viceregal discretion was a rough experience. Initially he planned to carry on as president of Dominion Power. He soon gave it up, but he remained disinclined to accept the notion that he could no longer express his opinions on controversial issues, particularly the ownership of utilities and relations between labour and business. His public criticism of international unions, for example, drew indignant protest from the Trades and Labor Congress of Canada at its gathering in Quebec City in September 1909; that same month, at the opening of a new waterworks system in Guelph, Ont., he blurted out that civic control was not always desirable. Such pronouncements led to calls for him to step down. Only belatedly did he limit himself to ceremonial functions, such as the official opening in June 1913 of the new Toronto General Hospital and of the Grange as the home of the Art Museum of Toronto. Still, he continued to chafe over the restrictions imposed by his office and the unwillingness of the Whitney government to consult him concerning policy. But there were some rewards: on 1 Jan. 1912 he had been made a KCMG.

Following the expiry of his term in September 1914, a month after the outbreak of war in Europe, Gibson returned to Hamilton, where he met great demand to attach his name to a host of charities and projects. He resumed many of his business and legal responsibilities – the descent of National Steel Car into near-bankruptcy proved particularly trying – but mostly his time was spent on war work: colonel-in-chief of the Hamilton Home Guard; a reorganizer of the Hamilton branch of the Red Cross; president of the Soldiers' Aid Commission, set up to raise funds for the families of those serving overseas; vice-president of the Speakers' Patriotic League, which promoted recruitment and the funding of flag-waving associations; and chair of the national committee formed to find ways to get enough steel and nickel for artillery. He was joined in his efforts by Lady Gibson, who, for her part, received the Order of St John of Jerusalem in England in 1916.

Gibson's philosophy of public service had always been voluntarism, so it was with some reluctance that he accepted conscription. Once convinced, he became a leading spokesmen for the Hamilton Recruiting League and embarked on a lengthy correspondence to persuade his old friend Laurier of the necessity of conscription. In the end Gibson's strong feelings caused him temporarily to abandon the Liberals and support the Union government of Sir Robert Laird Borden*. In 1917 he chaired the board of selection formed to establish exemption tribunals under the Military Service Act.

Having experienced great family loss in his early life, Gibson was again afflicted after the turn of the century by the death of three of his sons – John Gordon of tuberculosis in 1908, Francis Malloch in action in France in 1915, and Archibald Hope (a partner in his law firm) of influenza in 1920. Nonetheless, throughout the 1920s he continued to promote philanthropic causes in and outside Hamilton; he was president, for example, of the Canadian National Safety League. One of the oldest members of the active militia, he was promoted major-general in 1921, at the age of 79. His political involvement was largely restricted to offering guidance to such younger Liberals as William Lyon Mackenzie King*. As well, his involvement in Dominion Power, in which he had continued as a director, declined, particularly after its sale to the Power Corporation of Canada in 1925. He then took on a role as the company's corporate memory, offering advice based on his long years of experience.

Sir John Morison Gibson died of a stroke at his home, Ravenscliffe, on 3 June 1929. Buried in Hamilton Cemetery, he left an estate valued at more than $763,000. In eulogies the press made much of his distinguished political, legal, and military careers and his philanthropic involvement. Less attention was paid to his business activities, but it was there that Gibson had truly left his mark by promoting development and providing the infrastructure that helped define Hamilton as a major industrial centre. At the same time his embracement of industrial capitalism had led to a sharp break from the reform tendencies of his early political career and contributed to the disintegration of the increasingly illusionary "community of interests"

which, he had argued, he and his companies shared with the citizens of Hamilton.

CAROLYN E. GRAY

AO, F 2, ser.B-5-a, letter-book 9: 172–73, 276, 579–80; F 5; RG 8-1, 1901, file 710; 1902, file 1448; RG 22-205, nos.909, 3622; RG 24-10; RG 80-5-0-2, vol.2: f.28; RG 80-5-0-62, no.12381; RG 80-5-0-103, no.12466. Hamilton Board of Education Arch. (Hamilton, Ont.), Board of School Trustees, minutes, 1868–84. Hamilton Public Library, Special Coll. Dept., Hamilton city records, RG 6, ser.N (city clerk's dept., misc. papers), railway papers, petitions of Cannon Street ratepayers re the Hamilton Radial Railway, 15, 21, 26 Nov., 8 Dec. 1894. Hydro One Inc. Corporate Arch. (Toronto), Dominion Power and Transmission papers. LAC, MG 26, G; MG 27, I, F7; RG 46, 1070, 1087, 1089–91. Royal Hamilton Light Infantry Arch., J. M. Gibson papers; Scrapbooks, 1875–95. UTA, B1965-0014/004, 1 Oct. 1879; 16 Oct. 1880; 28 Feb. 1883; 1 Oct. 1884; 27 March 1885; 26 March 1887; 26–27 Sept., 4 Oct. 1889. Wentworth Land Registry Office (Hamilton), Copy books, City of Hamilton (mfm.). *Daily Times* (Hamilton), 1880–1920. *Hamilton Herald*, 1889–1929. *Hamilton Spectator*, 1870–1929. *Palladium of Labor* (Hamilton), 18 Aug. 1883–18 Dec. 1886. *Canadian annual rev.*, 1901–29. *Canadian men and women of the time* (Morgan; 1898 and 1912). *Cyclopædia of Canadian biog.* (Rose and Charlesworth), vol.3. J. E. Middleton and Fred Landon, *The province of Ontario: a history, 1615–1927* (5v., Toronto, 1927–[28]), 3: 52–54. *Standard dict. of Canadian biog.* (Roberts and Tunnell).

GLASGOW, ROBERT POLLOCK, bookseller and publisher; b. 3 Sept. 1875 near Shipton, Que., son of William Glasgow and Helen Tough; m. 16 June 1897 Louise Campbell Barter in Fredericton, and they had two daughters and two sons; d. 5 April 1922 in New York City.

Robert Glasgow's father immigrated to the Eastern Townships from County Londonderry (Northern Ireland); he settled first in Sherbrooke and then, in 1874, he acquired a farm near Shipton. His death when Robert was 12 brought the boy's public school education to an end: as the eldest of six children, he had to find work to help support his family.

By the age of 15 Glasgow was canvassing the local countryside, peddling books published by subscription. He continued in this business, which presented a serious challenge to traditional bookselling, through his twenties. He worked briefly for the Bradley-Garretson Company Limited (Brantford, Ont.) and Morang and Company (Toronto), and then represented R. S. Peale and Company (New York), selling Charles Dudley Warner's *Library of the world's best literature* in Australia and the *Encyclopedia Americana* in the United States and Canada. In 1906 he became a sales agent for George Nathaniel Morang*'s *Makers of Canada*, a 20-volume series published by subscription between 1903 and 1908 in Toronto. Designed to provide a history of Canada through studies of its major figures, the series, though of uneven quality, sold well.

By 1907 Glasgow had moved to Toronto, where, in addition to pushing *Makers*, he briefly took on bread-and-butter work as a departmental manager for *Scientific American* (New York). He was convinced by his involvement with *Makers* that a market existed for books on Canadian history, and although the vogue for subscription publication was over, he saw its usefulness for selling prestigious releases. By 1909 he was planning a new, multi-volume history of Canada. With Arthur H. Brook as vice-president, he founded the publishing and bookselling firm of United Editors Limited and secured two historical experts, civil service commissioner Adam Shortt* and dominion archivist Arthur George Doughty*, as the series' general editors. In 1911 a memorandum of agreement was signed by the contributors. Within a year United Editors had been reorganized as the Publishers' Association of Canada Limited, with Glasgow still as president, to help finance *Canada and its provinces; a history of the Canadian people and their institutions by one hundred associates*, which appeared in 23 volumes between 1913 and 1917. In 1914 responsibility for its publication shifted to the newly formed Glasgow, Brook and Company. (Between about 1911 and 1915 Glasgow also ran a general publishing business, R. P. Glasgow and Company, out of the same office.)

A milestone in Canadian historiography and still an invaluable reference, *Canada and its provinces* was the most comprehensive survey to appear to that time. Shortt and Doughty adopted the scientific, cooperative approach to writing advocated by Lord Acton in Britain, and they prided themselves on a rigorous use of primary sources, without the nationalistic moralizing that characterized much historical writing of the period. The volumes, beautifully printed at Edinburgh University Press, contained articles by more than 100 professional and amateur historians, journalists, and technical experts, who considered both national and regional history as well as Canada's current situation, with a strong emphasis on political and economic developments.

Undertaken as *Canada and its provinces* was being released, Glasgow's next project, *Chronicles of Canada*, approached the dominion's history in a less methodical, and more narrative and romantic, fashion. As editors Glasgow chose George MacKinnon Wrong*, professor of history at the University of Toronto, and Hugh Hornby Langton*, its librarian. Designed as a more popular project than *Canada*, *Chronicles* consisted of 32 "light, handy" volumes published by Glasgow, Brook between 1914 and 1916. Glasgow wrote to William Charles Henry Wood*, one of the contributors: "What we want for this series is straightway narrative – sequential and clear – not discussion or argument – no preaching, or direct teaching

either. . . . In this way we both preach and teach without seeming to do so and we gain our point." In an advertisement the publishers promised true stories "from human life, told clearly and vividly" and they offered prospective subscribers a free sample book of chapters drawn from the works.

Glasgow's care in production and marketing ensured economic success. He was prepared to leave accuracy to the historians, but in terms of the "organization and construction" of books, he told Wrong, "I have never found anyone who could handle this as well as I can myself." Wrong agreed: Glasgow "is a coming man in the publishing world, with good ideas, and a high integrity," he assured Sir John Stephen WILLISON. "He knows how to sell books and make them pay." Textually, *Chronicles* was a return to the unevenness of *Makers*; many of the manuscripts had been substantially edited or rewritten, but the resulting volumes remained inconsistent. In January 1914 Glasgow wrote in a burst of frustration to Langton: "Truly Canada has more half-baked editors and authors than any other country of the English-speaking world." Yet a month later he could write to Wrong: "I know that these, even, are the best Canadian writing of history we have had, & I have no fear of the verdict of Canadian readers on these volumes."

In 1916 Glasgow's career shifted to the United States, though he would maintain some publishing interest in Toronto. According to his obituary in the Toronto *Globe*, during the war he found the field in Canada "fully occupied." In New York he formed the United States Publishers' Association to produce an expanded edition of Warner's *Library*. His major project, however, was *Chronicles of America*. Following the format of *Chronicles of Canada*, this ambitious, 50-volume series was published jointly between 1918 and 1921 by Glasgow, Brook and Yale University Press. The project attracted eminent American historians as well as some Canadians. In recognition of Glasgow's contributions to the university and American historical literature, Yale awarded him an honorary MA in 1920.

Once *Chronicles of America* had appeared, work began on translating it to the relatively new medium of film. Glasgow became vice-president of the Chronicles of America Picture Corporation, which successfully produced a series of motion pictures of the same name. In April 1922, while working on this project in his office, he died of a heart attack; he had had some heart trouble the previous fall during a bout of influenza. A member of First Unitarian Church in Toronto and of All Angels' Episcopal Church in New York, he was interred in Mount Pleasant Cemetery, Toronto.

Despite his untimely death at age 46, Glasgow's career had been enormously productive. His publishing ventures, undertaken in a struggling industry, were ambitious and highly successful. He wrote nothing himself – his role in his projects was behind the scenes. Practical, entrepreneurial, and energetic, he was also well read and idealistic. He saw history in terms of nation building, a way to combat sectionalism and inculcate a sense of patriotism and citizenship. As one obituary noted, "He was a publisher, but never for profit only. There was in him combined the dreams of a man of vision and the capabilities of a man of action."

DANIELLE HAMELIN

The first edition of *Canada and its provinces*, published by subscription between 1913 and 1917, quickly sold out and was soon followed by the "Archives edition" and the "Edinburgh edition," both issued from 1914 to 1917. The *Chronicles of Canada* series, originally published between 1914 and 1916, was reprinted in 1922 and again in 1964.

ANQ-E, CE501-S93, 25 oct. 1875. Dalhousie Univ. Arch. (Halifax), MS 2-82 (A. McK. MacMechan papers). TRL, SC, Biog. scrapbooks, 4: 554–56. UTA, B1965-0014, H. H. Langton papers. Yale Univ. Library, Beinecke Rare Book and MS Library (New Haven, Conn.), Yale Univ. Press papers. *Globe*, 6 April 1922. Carl Berger, *The writing of Canadian history: aspects of English-Canadian historical writing since 1900* (Don Mills [Toronto], 1976). *Canadian annual rev.*, 1912, 1915. *Directory*, Toronto, 1907–22. *Literary history of Canada: Canadian literature in English*, ed. C. F. Klinck *et al.* (2nd ed., 4v., Toronto, 1976–90), 1. G. L. Parker, *The beginnings of the book trade in Canada* (Toronto, 1985). *Standard dict. of Canadian biog.* (Roberts and Tunnell), vol.1. I. E. Wilson, "Shortt and Doughty: the cultural role of the Public Archives of Canada" (MA thesis, Queen's Univ., Kingston, Ont., 1973).

GOHIER, ÉDOUARD (baptized **Benjamin-Édouard**), businessman, politician, and philanthropist; b. 27 April 1861 in Saint-Martin (Laval), Lower Canada, son of Benjamin Goyer, a farmer, and Célina Crevier; m. 2 April 1883 in the parish of Saint-Laurent, Que., Pomela Gosselin, daughter of Narcisse Gosselin, an innkeeper, and Philomène Saint-Aubin, and they had 13 children, eight of whom lived to adulthood; d. there 12 March 1923.

Born into a farming family that had settled in Saint-Laurent several decades earlier, Édouard Gohier spent the first years of his life in Saint-Martin and on the family farm on Chemin Côte-Vertu in the parish municipality of Saint-Laurent, where his father would serve as mayor from 1885 to 1890. Édouard completed the sixth year of studies (Rhetoric) at the Petit Séminaire de Sainte-Thérèse and afterwards learned a trade as a tailor of ready-made garments. In 1883, at the age of 22, he opened a dry goods shop in the parish of Saint-Laurent, which he sold in 1890. He then embarked on a career as a land and real estate developer by purchasing from his father, for $2,700, some parcels of land on which the town of Saint-Laurent would be built three years later. His business partner at

the time was Théophile Migneron (who, like Gohier himself, would become mayor of the town).

Gohier was among those who brought the town of Saint-Laurent into being on 27 Feb. 1893, and he would reside there with his family for the rest of his life. Elected mayor by acclamation on three occasions, he held this office from 25 April 1893 to 5 Feb. 1901, from 19 Jan. 1903 to 19 Jan. 1905, and from 7 Feb. 1911 to 4 Feb. 1913. Convinced that Saint-Laurent had geographical advantages, since it was at the heart of the island of Montreal and close to many roads, he obtained a charter authorizing the new town, among other things, to increase its borrowing power in order to develop the area and improve its infrastructure. Under Gohier's administration, Saint-Laurent changed considerably in appearance, becoming a small suburban town with modern urban services: a network of streets, public transit (1896), street lights (1900), and sewers and waterworks (1903). The town passed laws and municipal regulations and organized a fire protection service. In 1911 the Recorder's Court was opened, and the following year the first town hall and a fire station were built. Gohier's position as a landowner greatly facilitated the establishment of urban services; at the same time his position as mayor enabled him to make his land development business more profitable. In 1896, for instance, he provided, free of charge, the land on which a streetcar line was constructed. As a result the nearby building lots, which also belonged to him, became more desirable.

After serving for 12 years, Gohier was forced by health reasons to give up the mayoralty of Saint-Laurent. Meanwhile, in the provincial general elections of 1897 and 1904, he had tried to win a seat for the Conservative party in the riding of Jacques-Cartier, in which Saint-Laurent was located. He was defeated on both occasions, although his opponent in 1897, Joseph-Adolphe Chauret, won by only ten votes. Another member of his family was to leave his mark on the political history of Saint-Laurent. His son Édouard, a lumber merchant and land developer, would be mayor from 1928 to 1938 and from 1943 to 1949.

Gohier's start in real estate in 1890 had coincided with the rapid expansion of small suburban municipalities in various parts of the island of Montreal. The participants in this suburbanization movement were trying to persuade investors to buy vacant lots, but in order to do so they had to carry out certain improvements. Thanks to his position as mayor, Gohier was able to use this strategy in Saint-Laurent, where in 1896, for instance, he and his partner, Ludger Cousineau, put forward a proposal for a subdivision. The project, known as the Grande Allée de Florence, constituted the first plan for the town, which was built around a central artery (now Boulevard Décarie) where the streetcars ran. The economic problems that beset the country led to the dissolution of Gohier and Cousineau's company at the end of the 19th century, but this did not put an end to Gohier's land speculation, for he bought back the company's assets from its creditors.

In March 1907, in partnership with real estate agent Ucal-Henri Dandurand* and lawyer Joseph-Ulric Emard, Gohier founded the Compagnie des Boulevards de l'Île de Montréal, "for the purpose of buying and selling lots specially intended for building, and investing capital in public improvement firms." A few years after its inception, this company owned a large part of the land in the parish of Saint-Laurent and the village of Cartierville (Montreal). From 1908 to 1910 it also developed land in Bordeaux (Montreal), Ville Emard (Montreal), and the village of Sainte-Geneviève-de-Pierrefonds (Sainte-Geneviève). Gohier and his partners had an interest as well in the area near Mount Royal, where they purchased some of the land on which the new buildings of the Université de Montréal would be built in the 1930s. In 1911 the company sold to the Canadian Northern Land Company, for $600,000, a parcel of land on which part of the Town of Mount Royal would be built. This financial transaction was one of the largest the firm carried out. Gohier was also a director of the Northmount Land Company.

In view of the rapidity with which Gohier, alone or in partnership, completed speculative transactions, it is difficult to estimate the value of the real estate he traded. There is no doubt, however, that he profited handsomely from buying and selling land. He also showed foresight by purchasing vast tracts of land that he subdivided to increase his gains. From 1908 to 1912, the period when Gohier's career was at its peak, his speculative strategy proved highly rewarding. During that time the land value of some of his properties, especially in Cartierville, increased tenfold.

In 1913, however, Gohier would feel the impact of the economic recession, which substantially reduced the demand for new homes and sales of lots, and thereby led Montreal into a real estate crisis. In some suburban localities, moreover, the population had not reached the anticipated levels. As an example, Saint-Laurent had gone from 1,225 in 1893 to 1,860 in 1911, while the land area of the municipality had doubled with the annexation of parts of the parish in 1901 and 1908. In other words, the increase in population had not kept pace with the increase in land area and the rise in the value of real estate. Thus Gohier was put in a precarious financial situation, given the loans he had to repay. The war years worsened his plight, and he would never manage to resume his activities as a speculator.

In March 1914 the federal government appointed Gohier to the Georgian Bay Canal Commission, which was set up to promote a plan for constructing a canal to link Montreal, Ottawa, and Georgian Bay by way of the Ottawa River. He was also appointed to the Commission of Conservation [see Sir Clifford SIFTON]. Since he was neither a specialist on environmental issues nor a scientist, he played a secondary role in these bodies.

Édouard Gohier was known for his practical turn of mind and charitable spirit, his business sense, and his integrity. A man of his time, he took part in modernizing urban space, while remaining attached to the values of Catholicism. A fervent Roman Catholic and patriot, he made many gifts to the church for the purpose of creating closed retreat houses (in particular the Villa Saint-Martin, which was opened in 1913), whose tranquillity he himself appreciated. His contemporaries recognized him also for his great generosity, his modesty, and his enthusiasm for the many charitable causes that were dear to his heart: help for the destitute, the sick, the dying, and those on retreat, and the propagation of Christian and nationalist values (such as the preservation of the faith and traditions, as well as the economic development of the province). His patronage also included a contribution in 1911 to the founding of the École Sociale Populaire [see Joseph-Papin Archambault*]. He was a member of the Society of St Vincent de Paul and a trustee of Notre-Dame Hospital in Montreal and of the Hôpital Notre-Dame-de-l'Espérance in Saint-Laurent. One of the founders of Le Devoir in 1910, he was also a director of this paper and of the Imprimerie Populaire Limitée (where Le Devoir was printed). According to an article it published on 14 March 1923, Gohier, who reputedly had "slight differences of opinion on minor issues" with the other founders, was "a fine example of a Canadian, with a keen intellect [and] a large and generous nature: what the English call a big-minded, big-hearted man."

CLAIRE POITRAS

ANQ-M, CE601-S44, 2 avril 1883; CE601-S48, 28 avril 1861. Arch. de la Ville de Saint-Laurent, Qué., Fonds institutionnel de la paroisse et de la ville de Saint-Laurent, 1788–1965, 11a/6, plans; 11b/2, lots 409-137 and 409-137a, 1890–1938. Palais de Justice, Montréal, Cour supérieure, Greffes, Hercule Gohier, 25 juin 1901; 13 sept. 1907; 8 avril 1908; 22 févr. 1910; 24 juin 1913; 2 mars 1914; 13 avril 1917; 28 mai, 21 juin 1923. VM-DGDA, P12, Rôles d'évaluation, 1908–12. Le Devoir, 13–14 mars 1923. La Presse, 13 mars 1923. J.-P. Archambault, Figures catholiques (Montréal, 1950), 76–94. W. H. Atherton, Montréal, 1534–1914 (3v., Montreal, 1914), 3. M. F. Girard, L'écologisme retrouvé: essor et déclin de la Commission de la conservation du Canada: 1909–1921 (Ottawa, 1994). Linteau, Hist. de Montréal. Montréal fin-de-siècle; histoire de la métropole du Canada au dix-neuvième siècle (Montréal, 1899), 193–94. Mario Nadon, Saint-Laurent mayors and city councils: a history worth discovering ([Saint-Laurent, 1993]); Les rues de Saint-Laurent, répertoire toponymique: un patrimoine à découvrir ([Saint-Laurent, 1992]). Qué., Statuts, 1907, c.94. Robert Rumilly, Histoire de Saint-Laurent (Montréal, 1969).

GOOD, HENRY JOHN PRESCOTT WIL-SHERE, sportsman and newspaperman; b. 22 Nov. 1848 in Solihull, England, son of John Presly Good and Clara Louisa Rogers; m. 20 Nov. 1873 Helen Mar Clute in Yorkville (Toronto), and they had three sons and two daughters; d. 31 Aug. 1927 in Toronto.

A pioneer sports leader and writer, Henry J. P. Good linked two of the principal institutions that gave Canada's burgeoning cities their public discourse, men's sports and newspapers. After private tuition in Shoreham and some time at King's College in England (which King's College is uncertain, but he was a successful rower there), he immigrated to Canada in 1869. He quickly established himself as a prominent organizer in Toronto's flourishing sports scene and as an ambitious newspaperman. Good helped found the Canadian Association of Amateur Oarsmen in 1880 and was also closely associated with the career of professional rower Edward Hanlan*, whose matches, bets, and victory parades he arranged. One episode solidified Good's renown. In 1882, when Hanlan defended his world championship against Edward Trickett in England, Good placed some $40,000 in Toronto wagers with London bookies. Hanlan won, but unknown to the betters was the bookies' practice of paying out only on Mondays, in this case a full week after the race. According to Robert S. Hunter, "Mr. Good made his reputation as an orator on those horrible intervening days, endeavouring to account for his inability to pay off the speculators." To make matters worse, newspaper colleague Philip Dansken Ross* recalled, just when Good was about to distribute the winnings at a gathering of the betters – "he had an eye for the spectacular" and wanted "to make an occasion" – an unexpected telegram arrived from Hanlan demanding a share.

In the late 1880s, as a senior member of the Toronto Lacrosse Club, Good helped shift the power in that sport from Montreal, where William George Beers* had first codified the modern game, to Toronto through the creation of the Canadian Lacrosse Association. Good served as its president in 1890–91. He was active as well in the Canadian National Bureau of Breeding Limited and the Toronto Open-Air Parade Association, both of which promoted equestrianism, and in the Canadian Bowlers' Association.

Good had begun work in Toronto in 1872 as a proof-reader for John Ross Robertson*'s *Daily Telegraph*. By November 1873 he had moved to the *Mail*, which, since 1 April 1872, had been publishing weekly, well-informed collections of "Sporting Intelligence" on a single page. Despite the growing popularity of sports, most daily newspapers provided only brief notes scattered throughout their pages. The most extensive coverage was obtained in weeklies and monthlies such as the *National Police Gazette* and *Harper's*, both from New York City. Good advanced

at the *Mail* from proof-reader to reporter to night editor (1878), but he was likely responsible for the sports section from an early date, possibly even from its start. At the request of managing editor Thomas Charles Patteson he became the *Mail*'s full-time sports editor, North America's first in the estimate of both the *Globe* and journalist Hector Willoughby Charlesworth*. Under Christopher William Bunting* the entire paper was redesigned with larger stereotyped print and organized sections throughout; it appeared in its "new shape and dress" on 2 Aug. 1880. Good's section, "Sports and Pastimes," contained the latest news and gossip about rowing, horse racing, baseball, rifle shooting, lacrosse, cricket, distance running, cycling, and swimming. Without bylines, which did not become widespread until after World War I, it is impossible to tell what Good actually wrote, but the style is expansive, gracious, and authoritative.

In the years to follow, Good would move from paper to paper in Toronto, sometimes serving as sports editor (*Mail*, 1880–83; *Empire*, 1889–92) or general editor (*Telegram*, 1884; *Mail*, 1887–88; *World* and *Sunday World*, 1894–95; 1897–1909), but he always wrote about sports. In 1885 he was assistant editor of Edmund King Dodds's *Canadian Sportsman and Live Stock Journal* and in 1896, with John F. Snetsinger, he put out a weekly called *Sport*. After the turn of the century, he began writing under his own byline, first as Pop for the *World* and then as H. J. P. Good. About 1901, evidently as a freelancer, he joined Richard Thomas Lancefield in editing a memorial piece on Queen Victoria.

After he left the *World*, he tried stints in 1910 as manager of the Dominion Exhibition in Saint John and of a private venture, the Good Correspondence, Reporting, and Publishing Bureau, but he soon returned to what he did best, sports writing. During the last years of his life, he became known to a new audience as a popular historian of Canadian sport, with articles in the *Toronto Star Weekly* that drew on his recollections and records. Then as now, freelance writing was a precarious existence. Despite his Albany Club membership and upper-class connections, he and his family moved frequently and when he died of arteriosclerosis in 1927 he was virtually penniless. His son Charles Henry had followed him into a career in newspapers, becoming one of the city's best known baseball writers.

Throughout his long career, Good stressed three values that have been mainstays of Canadian amateur sport: purposeful recreation, respectable masculinity, and nationalism. He promoted sports for the health, the civic virtues, and the friendships that they encourage. Despite his involvement with Hanlan, he often bemoaned professionalism as "social degradation" for participants and "physical degeneration" for spectators. He abhorred brawling in hockey and had a low opinion of boxing. Probably the most distinctive feature of Good's writing was his Canadianism. He covered not just Ontario sports, but the prospects and achievements of athletes from the Maritimes, Quebec, and the west, and of immigrants and the First Nations. His columns were replete with suggestions for boosting home-grown talent. He regularly regaled his readers with Canadian victories abroad, and complained when outstanding athletes such as the Toronto Lacrosse Club's star runner, George Washington Orton, went to the United States. (Orton was the first Canadian to win an Olympic gold medal, in the steeplechase in 1900, but he did so in the uniform of the University of Pennsylvania.) Success in sports was a barometer of national vitality, Good argued, and Canada should seek to become one of the foremost of nations.

BRUCE KIDD

Along with R. T. Lancefield, Henry J. P. W. Good edited *Victoria, her life and reign* (Toronto, 1901). George William Ross* provided an introduction to this book.

AO, RG 22-305, no.57572; RG 80-2-0-106, no.36618; RG 80-5-0-47, no.14276. *Globe*, 2–3 Sept. 1927. *Mail* (Toronto), 1872–83, esp. 21 Nov. 1873. *Toronto Daily Star*, 1–2 Sept. 1927. *Toronto Star Weekly*, 1923–24. *Toronto Sunday World*, 1900–9. *Canadian Courier* (Toronto), 1907–8. *Canadian men and women of the time* (Morgan; 1912). *Canadian who's who*, 1910. H. [W.] Charlesworth, *Candid chronicles: leaves from the note book of a Canadian journalist* (Toronto, 1925). *Directory*, Toronto, 1872/73–1927. R. S. Hunter, *Rowing in Canada since 1848...* (Hamilton, Ont., 1933). P. D. Ross, *Retrospects of a newspaper person* (Toronto, 1931). Paul Rutherford, *A Victorian authority: the daily press in late nineteenth-century Canada* (Toronto, 1982).

GOOD, JAMES WILFORD, physician, professor, and health officer; b. December 1852 in Kincardine, Upper Canada, son of John Good and Isabella Anderson; d. unmarried 1 Sept. 1926 in Vancouver, and was buried in Brandon, Man.

James Wilford Good graduated MB in 1877 from Trinity Medical School, Toronto, and took postgraduate medical studies in Edinburgh. In 1879 he went to Winnipeg and became associated with James Robert Jones, a physician and neurologist. Appointed a physician at the Winnipeg General Hospital and at the Hôpital de Saint-Boniface, Good would later practise general surgery at those hospitals. After studying diseases of the eyes, ears, nose, and throat in Vienna, he became the first ophthalmologist to practise in western Canada. From about 1893 to 1897 he would be associated in a private ophthalmological practice with Gordon BELL.

In 1883 Good was a founding member of the Manitoba Medical College in Winnipeg and that same year he became professor of clinical surgery and lecturer in ophthalmology and otology there. Four years later he succeeded Dr James Kerr as dean of the college; he held the post to 1898. In 1890 he had been named second vice-president of a committee convened to form a provincial medical association. The actual formation of the association would be delayed until 8 Oct. 1908.

In 1898, during the gold rush in the Yukon, Good left for Dawson. He established a practice there and later the board of health, chaired by his friend Superintendent Samuel Benfield Steele* of the North-West Mounted Police, appointed him medical health officer for the town and inspector for the Lower Yukon district. Along with Dr Alfred Thompson and the Reverend Andrew Shaw Grant, who was also a physician, he tackled the problems of typhoid fever and scurvy that were rampant in the area. The doctors serviced St Mary's Hospital, the Good Samaritan Hospital, which Grant had founded, and the mounted police hospital. From time to time members of the Victorian Order of Nurses from nearby Fort Selkirk were called in to assist them.

Good returned to practise ophthalmology in Winnipeg on 16 Dec. 1900 and became associated with Dr Thomas Turnbull. He resumed teaching at the Manitoba Medical College, where he was professor of theoretical ophthalmology and otology. His lectures and clinics were said to be entertaining and combined practical knowledge with anecdotes from his long experience. They were presented solemnly, but also contained some sparkling wit. A humorist, Good gave public lectures at the medical college and frequently spoke at student banquets.

At the start of World War I, Good was deemed too old to be in active service, but he circumvented this obstacle by accepting a post under the French Red Cross and served at the Ulster Volunteer Hospital in Paris in 1916. After six months he returned to Winnipeg. He then went overseas again in 1917 as a specialist with the honorary rank of major in the Canadian Army Medical Corps and was posted to a surgical centre specializing in facial wounds at Westcliffe, England.

Throughout his life Good had travelled widely. In addition to Europe and South America, he visited India, where he observed Lieutenant-Colonel Henry Smith perform cataract surgery at Jullundur. He later invited Smith to demonstrate his cataract operation at the Winnipeg General Hospital. With the discovery of radium treatment for cancer [*see* William Henry Beaufort AIKINS], he purchased a supply of radium and treated laryngeal cancer, the first to do so in western Canada.

After visiting the Calgary Stampede, Good took up horseback riding, dressed as a cowboy. To maintain his physique he began boxing and hired a former prizefighter as a sparring partner; on receiving a heavy punch that knocked him out and prevented him from working for a week, he gave up this athletic pursuit.

Later, he played golf with two sets of clubs, right- and left-handed. He would alternate with each stroke, stating that he had more balanced exercise for his muscles while golfing in this manner. He also played billiards.

In 1921 Good moved to Vancouver. He had accumulated considerable wealth and after his death five years later it was distributed to the sanatorium in Ninette, Man., the Children's Home of Winnipeg, and a senior citizens' home. Good Street in Winnipeg was named in his honour.

I. I. MAYBA

College of Physicians and Surgeons of Manitoba (Winnipeg), Record of registration, 1878. Man., Legislative Library (Winnipeg), Biog. scrapbooks. Univ. of Manitoba, Faculty of Medicine Arch. (Winnipeg), 21.2.3 (Manitoba Medical College founders); 21.9, J. W. Good file. Univ. of Manitoba Libraries, Neil John Maclean Health Sciences Library (Winnipeg), L. G. Bell, "Fox Lake: an informal history" (typescript, Winnipeg, n.d.). *Manitoba Free Press*, 20 May 1890, 17 Jan. 1917. E. M. Peplow, "Winnipeg's first medical specialist," *Winnipeg Free Press*, 3 Dec. 1938. Harry Shave, "Early doctor, pioneer banker," *Winnipeg Free Press*, 10 May 1963. *Winnipeg Free Press*, 16 Dec. 1960. Jack Bennest, "Dr. James Wilford Good, M.D.: the west's first eye specialist," *Generations* (Winnipeg), 21 (September 1996), no.3: 6. Can., North-West Mounted Police, *Report* (Ottawa), 1900, app.G. A. J. Douglas, "Dr. J. W. Good," *Univ. of Manitoba Medical Journal* (Winnipeg), 1 (1929–30): 150–51. C. C. Ferguson, *One hundred years of surgery, 1883–1983: professors of surgery, the University of Manitoba* (Winnipeg, 1983). J. J. Heagerty, *Four centuries of medical history in Canada and a sketch of the medical history of Newfoundland* (2v., Toronto, 1928). Ross Mitchell, *Medicine in Manitoba; the story of its beginnings* ([Winnipeg, 1955?]). E. W. Montgomery, "J. W. Good, the most unforgettable character I have known," *Manitoba Medical Rev.* (Winnipeg), 23 (February 1943): 33–37. S. B. Steele, *Forty years in Canada: reminiscences of the great north-west . . .* , ed. M. G. Niblett (Toronto and London, 1915; repr. 1972). J. O. Todd, "Doctor J. W. Good and Manitoba Medical College," *Univ. of Manitoba Quarterly* (Winnipeg), 2, no.1 (December 1927): 31–32. Univ. of Manitoba, *The centennial program, 1883–1983, the Manitoba Medical College, 1883–1919, becoming the faculty of medicine, the University of Manitoba, 1919–1983* ([Winnipeg], 1983).

GORDON, DANIEL MINER, Presbyterian minister, author, and educator; b. 30 Jan. 1845 in Pictou, N.S., son of William Gordon and Amelia Miner; brother of Wilhelmina GORDON; m. 28 Sept. 1869 Eliza Simona MacLennan in Charlottetown, and they had three sons and three daughters, one of whom died in infancy; d. 31 Aug. 1925 in Kingston, Ont.

Daniel M. Gordon's father was born in Kildonan, Scotland, and came to Pictou with his family as a boy in 1816. At the time of his marriage in 1837, he was a prominent merchant in Pictou, a staunch conservative in politics, and an active elder of the Church of Scotland. He donated the land on which a manse was built

and became treasurer of a program that sent young men, including George Monro Grant*, to the University of Glasgow to train for the ministry. Gordon's mother was, by his own account, the most important personal and religious influence on him and he maintained an active correspondence with her throughout his life.

The second son in a prosperous family, Gordon had the educational advantages of early tutoring and was able to read at the age of four. At seven, he entered Pictou Academy, founded by Thomas McCulloch*, where he remained until, not yet fifteen, he was sent in 1859, at his father's expense, to Glasgow to study arts and then divinity. Like Grant, who returned to Nova Scotia a few months after his arrival, Gordon was much influenced by the famous Dr Norman Macleod of the Barony Church, Glasgow, and became president of the Conservative Club at the university. Unlike Grant, he was also exposed to the Christian idealism of John Caird, who was appointed to the chair of divinity in 1862. He attributed his own intellectual awakening to Caird and continued to read his teacher's work with appreciation until his death.

Not pressed by financial necessity to teach during his vacations, he passed the summers reading and travelling. One summer was spent in Berlin learning to speak and read German, and attending lectures. This sojourn was followed by a walking tour from Heidelberg to Milan; his classmate Daniel James Macdonnell* accompanied him for much of the way. Other Canadian friends included Charles Martin Grant, younger brother of George and later a missionary to India, with whom he shared accommodation in Glasgow for a year.

Having graduated MA in 1863 and BD three years later, he was licensed and ordained in 1866 by the Presbytery of Ayr and sent to Nova Scotia by the Colonial Committee of the Church of Scotland as a missionary. He preached for some months at St Paul's Church, Truro, and its attached mission stations before being called to St Andrew's, the oldest Protestant church in Ottawa, in 1867. The congregation included the engineer Sandford Fleming* and wealthy lumbermen such as Allan Gilmour* and Henry Franklin Bronson*. In 1869 he married Eliza, daughter of the Reverend John MacLennan*, in Prince Edward Island.

Besides his strong biblical preaching and pastoral work at St Andrew's, he was active in efforts to found a nurses' training school at the Protestant hospital in Ottawa. He served on committees of the Church of Scotland synod and on the board of trustees of Queen's College in Kingston and worked for the union of the various branches of Presbyterianism in Canada, which was achieved in 1875 [see William Caven*; William Snodgrass*]. In 1879 he accompanied George Mercer Dawson* as secretary of an expedition to explore the Peace River and Pine River passes as possible routes for the Pacific railway. His account of the journey was published the following year as *Mountain and prairie*.

One result of this experience was his urging the General Assembly of the Presbyterian Church in Canada to appoint a superintendent of missions for Manitoba and the North-West Territories. In 1881 James Robertson* was named to the position, a decision which was to result in the Presbyterian Church becoming the largest in western Canada at the time of Robertson's death in 1902. The move, however, left Knox Church, Winnipeg, vacant and in 1882 Gordon felt it his duty to leave the comforts of the national capital and accept a call to that congregation as Robertson's replacement.

The years in Winnipeg were hard on Gordon and his young family. In addition to his heavy pastoral work, he lectured on apologetics at Manitoba College and supported Robertson's energetic expansion of Presbyterianism as secretary of the Church and Manse Building Fund of Manitoba and the North-West. During the Riel rebellion in 1885 [*see* Louis Riel*] he served as a chaplain to the 90th (Winnipeg) Battalion of Rifles. Gordon's coolness under fire at Batoche (Sask.) made him popular with Major-General Frederick Dobson Middleton*'s men and earned him a reputation as "Fighting Dan Gordon." Yet he was not, by nature, a fighter. His gentle and irenic temper led to an awareness of the real grievances suffered by the Métis and Indians, and to shame at the church's lack of missionary zeal towards native people. He wrote to George Grant that they were "very much worse off by reason of the advent of the whites. . . . It is a bitter mockery on the Christian name for us to apply it to ourselves as a people when we have treated the Indian in such a way as to make him partake of our worse vices and vilest diseases, and do nothing more to help him than give him a bare pittance of food. I think if I were an Indian I would take all the risks of an uprising and have done with it."

Failing health prompted a move to St Andrew's Church, Halifax, in 1887. (Health continued to be a problem until, in 1889, the Victorian remedy of a trip around the world provided the needed rest.) Diminished pastoral responsibilities gave him time to acquaint himself with developments in the historical criticism of the Bible. He became a careful student of reverent biblical criticism and the works of scholars such as William Robertson Smith and Charles Augustus Briggs. He remained the minister of St Andrew's until 1894 when he moved from the board of the Presbyterian College in Halifax to the chair of systematic theology and apologetics there, succeeding Alexander McKnight*. Though Gordon was never an original scholar, he brought to the task a great wealth of pastoral experience, conservative instincts, and the habits

of careful and well-informed study. The pastoral emphasis is evident in his contributions to the school's publication, the *Theologue*. The most trusted of the Auld Kirk ministers within the Presbyterian Church in Canada, Gordon was elected moderator of the General Assembly in 1896. During the years in Halifax he presided as "King Arthur" over a Round Table of younger Presbyterians who were to become influential in 20th-century Canadian university life, including Walter Charles Murray*, Alfred Gandier, Clarence Mackinnon, Arthur Silver Morton*, and Robert Alexander Falconer*.

In 1902 Gordon was persuaded by Sandford Fleming, then chancellor of Queen's College, to become George Grant's successor as principal. The issue that had dominated the latter years of Grant's tenure was the secularization of the university. By 1900 Grant had come to the conclusion that Queen's had to sever its relationship with the Presbyterian Church if it was to receive the government and private funding needed to run a modern university, and had begun applying his legendary political skills towards that end. He had already won approval in principle for the change from the General Assembly, and a joint committee of the university and the assembly had drafted the necessary legislation before his death in 1902.

Initially supportive of the shift envisaged by Grant, Gordon lacked his predecessor's aptitude for public debate and shaping collective decisions. The 1903 assembly, swayed by a vision of Queen's as a national Presbyterian university and by the promise of a generous donation from John Charlton*, rejected the bill. Permission was, however, granted for the university to appeal to individual congregations to increase the endowment. Gordon acquiesced in this result and shouldered the years of strenuous effort that it took for him eventually to raise $400,000 – which his acquaintance Andrew Carnegie topped up to half a million.

More diplomat than fighter, Gordon sought consensus and trusted that free discussion would eventually result in unanimity. But the increasingly polarized debate over Queen's pitted the interests of the faculty against the hopes of those who wanted to maintain Presbyterian control of the institution that the church had founded but never enthusiastically supported. Even as the evidence accumulated that the church lacked the will and the resources to fund the faculties of arts, science, medicine, and education of a modern university, the controversy split Queen's board of trustees. Gordon was rebuffed twice more by the General Assembly before provincial legislation was finally passed in 1912 that divided the endowment and left the church in control of just the theological college.

Ten years of equivocation proved costly for the university. As a denominational institution, it was unable to participate in the pension scheme for professors established by the Carnegie Foundation for the Advancement of Teaching until the funds had already been allocated. Not only was this exclusion resented by the older members of the faculty, but the university found it difficult to retire old professors and to compete with other institutions for new staff. The delay also prevented anticipated support from the Ontario government for the faculty of arts until after World War I.

Besides attending to his administrative and fundraising responsibilities as principal, Gordon shaped the training of divinity students. Whatever the influence of the philosophical idealism associated with John Watson* and Samuel Walters Dyde on the campus, Gordon was a "religious conservative." As he explained in the *Queen's Quarterly*, the theological faculty strove to teach that "the interests of redemptive truth are paramount, the aim being to make all knowledge lead up to the knowledge of God and his purposes for men." Theological examinations centred on the nature of sin and theories of the Atonement. Gordon told those attending the alumni conference in 1907 that David Hume's scepticism about the possibility of miracles violating so-called "natural law" was unwarranted. "We must remember that we are not asked to accept the miracles as mere supernatural marvels but as works of the Person Jesus Christ. . . . Christ's miracles . . . help to interpret to us the living Christ, the image of the invisible God." Science dealt with observed information; faith marvelled in astonishment at God's involvement in history. Gordon is a good example of a minister who, although exposed to idealism and an admirer of John Caird, remained open to the possibility of miracle and firmly within the orthodox and evangelical camp.

Politically, Gordon was an imperial federationist who advocated improved communication and trade links between the various parts of the empire. He was an active member of the Canadian Defence League, which under the presidency of William Hamilton Merritt* urged universal voluntary military training, and supported the creation of an engineering cadet corps at Queen's in 1910 under his own motto, Fear God, Honour the King. He foresaw a conflict tied to clashing imperialisms. At an engineering dinner in December 1913 he urged increased enlistment in the corps and suggested that Queen's ought also to be able to supply one or two companies of infantry from the arts students and an efficient ambulance corps from the medical school, with a full supply of chaplains from the theological college. Gordon's enthusiasm for imperial defence was not shared by all at Queen's. An offer from Reuben Wells LEONARD to build a residence for students who enrolled in an officer-training program provoked organized opposition from Oscar Douglas Skelton*, then head of the political science department. But when war was declared, the 5th

(Kingston) Field Engineer Company from Queen's was ready and helped to prepare the base at Valcartier, Que., for the first contingent of the Canadian Expeditionary Force. Many of its members were also among the first unit from any Canadian university to get to the front. In 1914 Gordon was made an honorary colonel by Samuel HUGHES, minister of militia and defence, and he served on the cadet committee of the adjutant general's branch of Hughes's department. The following year he was created a CMG.

Gordon's view of the war was balanced and well founded. Two of his sons served as officers. The eldest, the Reverend Alexander MacLennan Gordon, was awarded the DSO as the senior chaplain of the 4th Canadian Division. The relationship between father and son was very close and their correspondence presents an interesting and theologically informed reading of the war. Unlike those clergy who baptized the war effort a glorious crusade or clung to an unyielding pacifism, Gordon was sufficiently sophisticated in his theology to distinguish between Christ and Caesar and the weapons and responsibilities of church and state. Like many, he hoped that the war might be a means of turning hearts from the unbounded pursuit of financial gain to considerations of service. He carried on correspondence with students at the front and wrote to bereaved parents. During the war, as enrolment at Queen's plummeted, Grant Hall and the adjoining Arts Building were converted into a convalescent hospital, and women, including Gordon's daughter Wilhelmina, began teaching for the first time.

Failing health finally prompted Gordon's retirement in 1917, 50 years after his ordination. His last years were spent with Wilhelmina, his wife having predeceased him in 1910. "The very heart and centre of her home," according to her daughter, Mrs Gordon had been intensely interested in her husband's work at Queen's and her sympathy and thoughtfulness had endeared her particularly to the female students. Gordon's retirement afforded him the time to write five volumes of unpublished but engagingly readable reminiscences. He also corresponded widely with those involved in church union, including former members of the Round Table. By the 1920s he was the only minister still alive who had actively participated in the union of all the Presbyterian churches in 1875 and in the early discussions about the possibilities for an organic union across denominational lines. He had briefly been the convenor of the church union committee after the death in 1911 of Principal William Patrick of Manitoba College, presented to the General Assembly the report of the congregational vote taken that year, and recommended against precipitate action without a greater degree of consensus. He continued a member of the committee until 1915.

As it appeared increasingly likely in the 1920s that the issue would be forced and legislation sought from parliament, he exerted his influence to promote the alternative of spiritual union and cooperation rather than an organic union purchased at the cost of disruption. While he deplored clergymen who derided, before parliamentary committees, the Westminster Confession to which they had given assent at ordination, and disapproved of boasting about the political influence of the new church, Gordon's main objection to union was not theological but to the aggressive tactics of its supporters and the violation of trust that he believed was at stake.

Once the disruption within the Presbyterian church had occurred in 1925, however, he wrote, just weeks before his death, to both Clarence Mackinnon in the new United Church and to Ephraim Scott*, moderator of the continuing Presbyterians, to urge reconciliation and cooperation in joint mission work. In the midst of all the rancour generated by church union, the attempt at peacemaking was typical of the man.

D. B. MACK

Daniel Miner Gordon's publications include *Mountain and prairie: a journey from Victoria to Winnipeg via Peace River Pass* (Montreal, 1880); "The spirit of theological inquiry," *Presbyterian Witness* (Halifax), 10 Nov. 1894; the following articles in the Presbyterian College's journal *Theologue* (Halifax): "Our summer school," 5 (March 1894): 82–86; "The young minister's library," 7 (February 1896): 69–77; "Some eminent preachers," 8 (April 1897): 137–45; "Spiritual diagnosis," 11 (April 1900): 133–45; and "Culture and religion," 12 (January 1901); and these articles in *Queen's Quarterly* (Kingston, Ont.): "The functions of a modern university," 10 (1902–3): 487–97; "Reminiscences of the N.W. rebellion campaign of 1885," 11 (1903–4): 3–20; "Queen's and the Assembly's commission": 187–90; "The installation address of Principal Gordon": 318–25; "The General Assembly and Queen's University," 13 (1905–6): 68–70; "An imperial intelligence union as a means of promoting the consolidation of the empire," 14 (1906–7): 125–33; "Political impurity once more": 149–52; "Miracles," 15 (1907–8), suppl.: 15–16; "Livingstone," 20 (1912–13): 347–67; and "Our late chancellor," a eulogy of Sir Sandford Fleming, 23 (1915–16): 111–23. Gordon's "Sermon, 21st January 1872, on the occasion of the last service in the old church" is reproduced in J. G. Macphail, *St. Andrew's Church, Ottawa: the first hundred years, 1828–1928* (Ottawa, 1931), 74–82.

QUA, Alex MacLennan Gordon fonds; Daniel Miner Gordon fonds; Wilhelmina Gordon fonds. E. J. Chambers, *The 90th Regiment: a regimental history of the 90th Regiment Winnipeg Rifles* (n.p., 1906). Duff Crerar, *Padres in no man's land: Canadian chaplains and the Great War* (Montreal and Kingston, 1995). Wilhelmina Gordon, *Daniel M. Gordon: his life* (Toronto and Halifax, 1941). J. G. Greenlee, *Sir Robert Falconer: a biography* (Toronto, 1988). John Macnaughton, "Principal Gordon," *Queen's Quarterly*, 10 (1902–3): 249. H. M. Neatby and F. W. Gibson, *Queen's University*, ed. F. W. Gibson and Roger Graham (2v., Kingston and Montreal, 1978–83), 1. [O. D. Skelton], "The approaching retirement of Principal Gordon," *Queen's Quarterly*, 24 (1916–17): 131–32. Daniel Strachan, "Rev. Daniel Miner Gordon, D.D., LL.D., C.M.G.," *Queen's Quarterly*, 25 (1917–18): 365–67. [R. B.] Taylor, "Principal Taylor's eulogy of late Dr. Gordon," *Queen's Quarterly*, 33 (1925–26): 111–13.

GORDON, WILHELMINA (Minnie) (Smith), churchworker and social reformer; b. 5 Feb. 1849 in Pictou, N.S., daughter of William Gordon and Amelia Miner; m. there 29 Oct. 1879 George Frederick Smith, and they had three daughters; d. 16 July 1925 in St Andrews, N.B.

Minnie Gordon, the daughter of a Pictou merchant, was brought up in a home that her brother Daniel Miner GORDON described as "very, very happy." A great influence was her mother, who undertook the children's religious training, and Minnie became, in the words of her brother, "a devout & active Christian." Her marriage in 1879 to a New Brunswick ship broker took her to Saint John, where she gradually moved from being an outsider to one possessing "the confidence of the community." Though raised a Presbyterian, she was with her husband a member of St John's (Stone) Anglican Church, a congregation that enjoyed a long evangelical tradition and over the years numbered several social reformers among its members. Minnie taught in the Sunday school at St John's and sat on committees of the Ladies' Society of Church Workers, which unanimously elected her president in 1891. She was also on the executive of the ladies' association of the Church of England Institute. Her husband, George, was equally active in the church, serving as a vestryman for 15 years.

Following the death of her husband on 6 March 1894, Smith continued to raise the family's three daughters. The task was eased somewhat by her inheritance of George's entire property, amounting to real estate worth $9,400 and a personal fortune of $71,600. The wealth also afforded her a measure of independence, and as her children grew older she devoted herself more to charitable activities. She freely gave her time and energy to many causes, and became involved in a number of organizations at both the local and the national levels.

Smith was a charter member of the Victorian Order of Nurses in Saint John when the branch was formed in 1899. She became its first vice-president and held the office until her death, helping guide the organization with a clear, incisive mind that could make solid decisions. Her contributions through the years were several, and included chairing committees, organizing events, and overseeing the establishment of a short-lived training school for nurses during the early 1920s. From 1905 to 1911 she represented the VON on the Local Council of Women.

The church continued to be a major interest. When in 1903 the diocese of Fredericton formed a chapter of the Woman's Auxiliary to the Missionary Society of the Church of England in Canada [*see* Roberta Elizabeth ODELL], she became first vice-president of the board; she served in this capacity until 1919, when she was elected president, an office she held until 1925. To these positions she brought, a later history noted, "a wise appreciation of the services of women." From 1911 to 1925 she was vice-president for the Maritime provinces of the dominion board as well. A life member of both bodies, she would leave $500 to the diocesan board in her will.

In February 1918 Smith was one of a select group of women invited to attend a national conference of women in Ottawa by the war committee of the federal cabinet. The conference sought to define a role for women on the home front and ultimately determined that "we can best serve the state at this time by simplicity of life and by concentrating energy on increased production and on thrift in all our ways." On her return Smith encouraged the VON in Saint John to eliminate refreshments from its meetings, a step that won praise from local newspapers.

Gordon died at her summer home in St Andrews in 1925 of uterine cancer. Her body was returned to Saint John for burial in Fernhill Cemetery. A tangible tribute was paid her with the donation by her daughters of a prayer desk and choir fronts in her memory to St John's Church. At a dedication service on 6 Sept. 1925 the rector, Archibald Lang Fleming*, praised "her keen intellect," "remarkably gracious spirit," and "tremendous capacity for work." Her niece Wilhelmina Gordon noted that she and her brother Daniel, a Presbyterian minister, had been much alike in many ways, and above all in "their sincere and serene religious life and their unostentatious devotion to their Master."

PETER J. MITHAM

Fernhill Cemetery Company (Saint John), Burial records, order for interment, Wilhelmina Smith. LAC, RG 31, C1, 1901, Saint John, Kings Ward: 18, dwelling 123. PANB, RS71/1894, G. F. Smith. Pictou-Antigonish Regional Library (New Glasgow, N.S.), "Alexander Gordon, tacksman of Dalcharn, 1732–1810." QUA, Daniel Miner Gordon fonds, reminiscences, vol.1; box 9, diary, 1925. Victorian Order of Nurses (Saint John), Arch., Minutes, 1919–25. *Daily Telegraph* (Saint John), 30 Oct. 1879. *Ottawa Citizen*, 5 March 1918. *Saint John Globe*, 5 March 1918, 17 July 1925. Mrs Willoughby Cummings [E. A. McC. Shortt], *Our story: some pages from the history of the Woman's Auxiliary to the Missionary Society of the Church of England in Canada, 1885 to 1929* (Toronto, [1929?]). *Directories*, N.B., 1889/90; Saint John, 1891/92. A. L. Fleming, *A book of remembrance; or, the history of St. John's Church, Saint John, New Brunswick* (Saint John, 1925). Wilhelmina Gordon, *Daniel M. Gordon: his life* (Toronto and Halifax, 1941). A. G. McIntyre, *Our first fifty years, 1903–1953; Woman's Auxiliary of the Church of England in Canada, Fredericton diocesan board* ([Fredericton?, 1953?]). J. P. MacPhie, *Pictonians at home and abroad: sketches of professional men and women of Pictou County; its history and institutions* (Boston, 1914). National Council of Women of Canada, *Year book* (Toronto), 1905–12. St John's Church, *Parish Notes* (Saint John), 1889, 1891–92; continued as *St. John's Church Record and Parish Notes*, 1892–93. J. V. Young, *Brief history of the Victorian Order of Nurses, Saint John, N.B., 1899–1963* (Saint John, 1963).

GOSLING, WILLIAM GILBERT, businessman, politician, and author; b. 8 Sept. 1863 in Paget Parish, Bermuda, second of the six sons of Charles Gray Gosling and Elizabeth Gilbert; m. 2 Jan. 1888, in Halifax, Harriette Armine Nutting* of Waterloo, Que., and they had two sons and two daughters; d. 5 Nov. 1930 in Paget Parish.

Gilbert Gosling received his early education at the Pembroke Grammar School in Hamilton, Bermuda. He arrived in St John's on 22 June 1881 to work as a clerk with the fish-exporting firm of Harvey and Company, whose owners had a long commercial and family connection with Bermuda [see Augustus William Harvey*]. Gosling was given charge of the wholesale side of the business and, as his future wife, Armine, would later write, "from the first he showed a . . . marked aptitude for it, setting himself with characteristic patience and thoroughness to master every detail connected with his work."

Not long after his arrival in St John's, he met Armine, the headmistress of the Church of England Girls' School there. They had a lengthy engagement, during which she returned to her native Canada for some time. In his leisure hours Gosling sought solace in reading. "I find it helps me a lot in my work," he told her. "It takes my mind off business troubles." Thus began his life-long passion for books and book collecting, which Armine shared. His other recreational pursuits included photography, painting, and golf.

Before 1900 Gosling's main interest was English literature, especially the works of Shakespeare, and his purchases reflected this preoccupation. In 1899 he published his first literary work, an article on *The tempest* in the London periodical *Literature*. Paid nine guineas for this piece, Gosling earned as well the respect of St John's author and judge Daniel Woodley Prowse*, who addressed him as "my literary brother." The money was naturally devoted to Gosling's library. He had become especially interested in rare and first editions, though he could seldom afford them.

In 1906, along with Prowse and others, Gosling helped to revive the Newfoundland Historical Society, which had been moribund since 1881. At this time as well he took up historical writing when Dr Wilfred Thomason Grenfell* asked him to contribute a chapter on the history of Labrador to a book he was publishing on his experiences as a physician there. The chapter became Gosling's own *Labrador: its discovery, exploration, and development* (London, 1910), which stands to this day as the most comprehensive work on its subject. Gosling drew upon documents he had obtained from both British and Canadian archives. Indeed, his research would prove invaluable to Sir Patrick Thomas MCGRATH, who in the 1920s prepared Newfoundland's case in its legal dispute with Canada over the ownership of Labrador. At the same time Gosling had undertaken a biography of Sir Humphrey Gilbert*, published in London in 1911.

Active in the local business community, Gosling in 1909 played a prominent role as organizing secretary in forming the Newfoundland Board of Trade, of which he became president in 1913. In that year as well he was made a director of Harvey and Company, an office he would retain until his retirement in 1927. His concern for Newfoundland's commercial interests led him to oppose the colony's confederation with Canada. In 1907 he had corresponded with the London *Spectator,* arguing the view of his fellow St John's merchants that the basis of Newfoundland's well-being was its freedom of trade. Newfoundland neither consumed what goods it produced nor produced what it consumed, and "must therefore have absolute freedom to sell in the highest and best market, and with the gold thus obtained to buy in the cheapest. To tie ourselves down to buy from any one country would be to sacrifice a portion of our national income." Gosling's standpoint was shaped by the years he had spent as a commercial traveller to Canada, the United States, Britain, and the European continent.

Gosling is best remembered for his contributions to the public life of his adopted city. In 1902 he had served as honorary secretary of a fund-raising committee for rebuilding the Anglican cathedral, part of which had been destroyed by fire in 1892. In 1908 he helped form, and became vice-president of, the Association for the Prevention of Consumption, which did much to encourage the battle against tuberculosis [*see* Ella Campbell*]. After 1911, however, his interests concentrated on municipal government.

He was greatly influenced by civic reform movements in Canada and the United States and their emphasis on administrative efficiency and social improvement. Using the prestige of his presidency, in December 1913 he had the Board of Trade organize a citizens' committee to ascertain what reforms could be effected in St John's, whose council dated from 1888. The result was that in 1914 the legislature replaced the elective council with a 12-man appointed commission. Under Gosling's chairmanship it governed the city for two years, instituting a number of reforms in the method of collecting and disbursing revenues and reorganizing the city's water and sewage services. It also drafted a new municipal charter, giving the council broader powers and more independence from the legislature. The legislature refused to pass this charter in 1916, however, claiming that more study was needed, and instead restored the elective council.

A civic election was thus held in June 1916, and Gosling was returned as mayor. The following year he succeeded in securing legislative authority for the city to initiate a public housing program and revise its system of taxation. In 1920–21 he was again made chair of an appointed commission, which administered St John's until the charter became law and provided for elected government. His years in local politics were difficult ones for Gosling. "Gone are the lighter avocations of former days, – the painting, the photographing, the adventures in search of old books," his wife had written to her sister in 1914, " – and when there are no meetings he spends his evenings absorbed in light literature dealing with the most approved methods of the disposal of garbage, and kindred topics." His health deteriorated, and in 1921 he declined public demands that he again stand for the mayoralty, withdrawing from civic life for both business and health reasons.

Gosling's efforts at civic reform represented one aspect of a larger social-reform impulse at work in Newfoundland during World War I. Its most obvious manifestation was the organization by William Ford Coaker* of the Fishermen's Protective Union in 1908 and its entry into active politics in 1913. What both reform elements held in common was a strong belief in improving social conditions, which was the subject of a congress held in St John's in October 1917 by local religious and political leaders and featuring Social Gospel reformers from Canada and the United States, among them John George SHEARER and Thomas Albert Moore* of Ontario. Mayor Gosling welcomed the participants, saying that he was a "social worker himself, in a measure, because the government of a city touched in hundreds of ways upon the lives of the people." Concerned about the "disgraceful rate of infant mortality in Newfoundland," Gosling had initiated efforts to promote a child welfare service, and in 1918 he helped to fund the salary of a community health nurse from his emoluments as mayor. After 1919 the Women's Patriotic Association, of which Armine was an executive member, took up fund-raising for this cause and its efforts led to the formation in 1921 of the Child Welfare Association under the presidency of Mary Meager Southcott*. Gosling also supported the women's suffrage movement in St John's, which included his wife as one of its strongest proponents [*see* Fannie KNOWLING]. The St John's Municipal Act of 1921 reflected this influence by giving women the right to vote in civic elections.

In September 1927 the Goslings retired to Bermuda, where Gilbert died in 1930. His wife later donated his extensive collection of books to the people of St John's to form the basis of the city's first public library, the Gosling Memorial Library, which opened in 1936. The establishment of just such a library had been one of Gosling's cherished dreams before his retirement from public life.

MELVIN BAKER

Evening Telegram (St John's), 8 Oct. 1917, 7 Nov. 1930. Melvin Baker, "The government of St. John's, Newfoundland, 1800–1921" (PHD thesis, Univ. of Western Ont., London, 1981), 367–71; "Prominent figures from our recent past: William Gilbert Gosling," *Newfoundland Quarterly* (St John's), 81 (1985–86), no.1: 43; "William Gilbert Gosling and the charter: St John's municipal politics, 1914–1921," *Newfoundland Quarterly*, 81, no.1: 21–28; and "William Gilbert Gosling and the establishment of the Child Welfare Association, 1917–1921," *Newfoundland Quarterly*, 77 (1981–82), no.4: 31–32 (the texts of the articles are also available on the author's website, *www.ucs.mun.ca/~melbaker/*). Melvin Baker and G. M. Story, "Book collectors in Newfoundland: the case of W. G. Gosling," in *"The book disease": Atlantic provinces book collectors*, ed. E. L. Swanick (Halifax, 1996), 83–92. [H.] A. N[utting] G[osling], *William Gilbert Gosling: a tribute* (New York, [1935]).

GOUIN, Sir LOMER (baptized **Joseph-Alfred-Lomer**), lawyer and politician; b. 19 March 1861 in Saint-Charles-des-Grondines (Grondines), Lower Canada, son of Joseph-Nérée Gouin, a physician, and Séraphine Fugère; m. first 24 May 1888 Élisa Mercier (d. 4 Sept. 1904), daughter of Honoré Mercier*, premier of Quebec, and Léopoldine Boivin, in the parish of Saint-Jacques, Montreal; of the five children born of their marriage, two sons reached adulthood; m. secondly 19 Sept. 1911 Alice Amos in the Roman Catholic cathedral in Montreal; they had no children; d. 28 March 1929 at Quebec and was buried 1 April in Notre-Dame-des-Neiges cemetery, Montreal.

Lomer Gouin's paternal ancestor Mathurin was born in 1638 in Poitou, France. He immigrated to New France in 1660, settled in Trois-Rivières, and died in Sainte-Anne-de-la-Pérade in 1710. His son Joseph was Lomer's direct forebear. After his father's death in 1872, Lomer went to live with an uncle, the protonotary Antoine-Némèse Gouin, in Sorel. That year he began his classical studies in this town, but he completed them in Lévis, where he excelled in oratorical contests on historical subjects with Adélard TURGEON and other friends. After enrolling in law at the Montreal branch of the Université Laval in 1881, he obtained his LLB in 1884. He was articled in Montreal to John Joseph Caldwell Abbott*, a future Conservative prime minister of Canada, and Toussaint-Antoine-Rodolphe Laflamme*, a member of the Institut Canadien in Montreal and a radical Liberal. Called to the bar in 1884, he remained active in law in Montreal throughout his political career, maintaining a full-time practice until at least 1897. His first partners were Siméon Pagnuelo, a well-known lawyer and prominent ultramontane, and Louis-Olivier TAILLON, who would later be a Conservative premier of Quebec. He would become an expert in cases concerning railways and contested elections.

From at least 1884, Gouin was also acquainted with Honoré Mercier, who was to be provincial premier from 1887 to 1891, and he visited his home in Montreal with such prominent moderate Liberals as Félix-Gabriel Marchand* and Laurent-Olivier DAVID. He also associated with radical Liberals, in particular the lawyer and journalist Godfroy LANGLOIS, who was a fellow member of the Club National. When Gouin became president of this Liberal political organization in Montreal in 1889, he supported Mercier, who had become his father-in-law the previous year and was now under attack from radical Liberals. In 1892 a disgraced and ruined Mercier would go back to the practice of law with two young lawyers, Gouin and Rodolphe Lemieux*, who were to remain lifelong friends. In articles Gouin wrote for *Le Clairon*, a Montreal weekly that had been launched by a group including Langlois and that appeared from December 1889 until May 1890, he showed his concern to reconcile all elements of the party, both moderates and those less so. For political and personal reasons, this reconciliation would become his overriding concern.

Gouin had his first experience in politics during the federal general election of 5 March 1891. As the Liberal candidate in the riding of Richelieu, he was defeated by Conservative cabinet minister Sir Hector-Louis Langevin*. In 1896 he and a group of Liberals that included Langlois, Christophe-Alphonse Geoffrion*, and Camille Piché founded *Le Signal*, a radical Montreal weekly. He won a seat in Montreal, Division No.2, in the provincial general election of 11 May 1897, and he would be re-elected by acclamation on 7 Dec. 1900. In spite of the support he had given his father-in-law, Gouin was perceived as a radical because of the people he associated with and the stands he had taken on certain issues; for example, he favoured the establishment of a ministry of education and wanted changes in Montreal's municipal administration. In 1898 he supported the Marchand government's bill on reforming public education, but it was voted down in the Legislative Council. However, Marchand had Gouin appointed to the Council of Public Instruction to satisfy the radicals. Gouin was also elected to represent the East ward on the Montreal city council, and he would serve in this position from February to November 1900.

Sir Wilfrid Laurier* was probably suspicious of Gouin's political radicalism and for several years their relationship was rather cool. In 1899, however, it became clear that Gouin supported Laurier's moderate policy on so-called "national" questions, which were now being pushed to the foreground by international events. When, in his presence, Henri Bourassa* informed Laurier that he could not accept the decision to send Canadian troops to South Africa, Gouin did not challenge the federal leader's decision. Later on, the struggle against the Nationalistes would bring the two leaders, who were already linked by their common party interests, closer together, and would strengthen their mutual confidence.

After the sudden death of Marchand in September 1900, Simon-Napoléon Parent* became leader of the Liberal party and premier, very likely at Laurier's insistence. The choice did not meet with unanimous approval. He was mayor of Quebec, had close ties to the business community, and was a skilful politician in organizing elections and handling patronage matters, but the party's radical wing, which would have preferred to have the province led by a true Liberal such as Joseph-Emery Robidoux, disapproved of him. The desire to allay this discontent may have been a factor in Gouin's appointment as commissioner of public works in October 1900 and as minister of colonization and public works in July 1901.

The radicals – in particular Langlois, who became the editor of Le Canada, a Liberal daily published in Montreal from April 1903 – were well disposed toward the new recruit. Gouin had appeared to support their arguments by opposing – albeit unsuccessfully – in 1901 certain clauses in bills aimed at favouring the Montreal Light, Heat and Power Company [see Louis-Joseph Forget*], which held a monopoly on the distribution of gas and electricity in Quebec; he would do so again in 1904. In 1901, as commissioner of public works, he had led the debate in the assembly on the Act respecting councils of conciliation and of arbitration for settling industrial disputes. The positions he took enabled him to deal sensitively with both the religious authorities and the business community. However, the Nationalistes were already suspicious of Gouin. Olivar Asselin*, his secretary, left him in 1903, criticizing him for his lack of zeal in proceeding with reforms in the field of colonization. In the pages of the Montreal weekly Le Nationaliste, which Asselin helped found in 1904, this fiery journalist would write many articles critical of the government.

At the end of 1904 and the beginning of 1905, a veritable palace revolution would oust Parent from the government and push Gouin into the premier's office. Parent, whose style of management and personal image drew increasing criticism within his own party, and whose integrity was being questioned by the opposition, is believed to have indicated that he would resign immediately after the federal election of 3 Nov. 1904, which kept Laurier in power. Instead, seeking to take advantage of an electoral climate that was favourable for the Liberals and thereby to strengthen his authority, he dissolved the Legislative Assembly and called an election for 25 November. The Conservative party was weakened and caught off guard by the announcement of a campaign that would last a scant three weeks. Its leader, Edmund James FLYNN, de-

nounced the hurried election call and declared that he would not participate officially in the contest. With the Conservatives running in only 24 ridings, the Liberals easily won the election, but dissension within the party itself broke out into the open. These fratricidal struggles worried Laurier, who had admitted, in a letter to Langlois on 1 April 1904, that Parent had to be replaced. This time, however, the federal Liberal leader would not be able to influence the provincial party's choice of a leader as he had done in 1900.

In the fall of 1904 Gouin was in mourning for his wife, Élisa Mercier, who had died in September. Nevertheless, he decided to oppose Parent more strenuously. For the November election he contrived to recruit several candidates from among the premier's opponents, and he discussed strategy with two cabinet ministers, Adélard Turgeon and William Alexander Weir, who were both hostile to Parent. Since 1901 Weir, like Gouin, had opposed the privileges granted by their own government to the Montreal Light, Heat and Power Company. This issue split the Liberal party. In municipal politics, these opponents of Parent supported the party's reformist faction, which was attacking Mayor Raymond Préfontaine*. The latter was a pillar of the Liberal elite and a friend of Laurier, but he was perceived as corrupt and as a friend of the trust headed by Louis-Joseph Forget, his nephew Rodolphe Forget*, and Herbert Samuel Holt*. Turgeon, who was increasingly dissatisfied with Parent's leadership, seemed to be afraid that Parent might hatch a plot to force him, as well as Gouin and Weir, to resign.

Having decided to strike hard, the three ministers submitted their resignations on 3 Feb. 1905, blaming Parent for not having consulted his cabinet before he made important decisions, such as on the dissolution of the assembly. They also declared that, despite having been re-elected, he did not enjoy the confidence of the voters. When Parent, now facing new accusations, delayed recalling parliament, his bitter political enemy Senator Philippe-Auguste Choquette* busied himself with rallying the MLAs who were hostile to the premier. During a meeting on 8 February at the Château Frontenac, a clear majority of the Liberal MLAs signed a petition calling for the premier's resignation. When the legislature finally opened on 2 March 1905, Parent brought up the accusations levelled against him "in connection with the administration of the Department of Crown Lands," rejected them, and called for an inquiry by a parliamentary committee. The committee's report exonerated the premier, who resigned on 21 March.

It was a good question who would replace him. Turgeon, who had an outgoing personality and was a fine speaker, declined. The lieutenant governor, Sir Louis-Amable Jetté*, then called on Gouin, who coveted the position and who was the candidate of the generally more progressive Montreal wing of the party, to form a cabinet. Gouin came to power thanks to the support of the Liberal party's reformist faction – those wanting changes in the field of education or seeking state control of public services such as electricity, especially in Montreal. But in his choice of ministers, he did not reward these progressive elements as much as they had hoped. His co-conspirators Weir and Turgeon were brought into the cabinet, but Louis Allard, a rural MLA whose chief qualification was his loyalty to Gouin, was awarded the important Department of Public Works and Labour. By the moderate program Gouin introduced, he gradually distanced himself from the progressives. In 1907, anxious to reconcile the supporters and opponents of Parent in order to fight more effectively against the nationalist threat, he would make room in his cabinet for Louis-Alexandre Taschereau*, a close friend of the former premier.

Gouin would be premier of Quebec from 1905 to 1920. During his term of office he benefited from generally favourable circumstances. Ideologically, he leaned towards classical liberalism, which called, for example, for the state to rely on private enterprise to encourage economic development. In any case the Quebec of his time was hardly in a position to act in any other way. For almost two decades, the Canadian provinces had been trying in vain to persuade the federal government to increase its annual grants to them. In 1902 Gouin, for whom this cause would become a hobby horse, had strongly supported Parent's request to this effect. But Laurier was not easily persuaded. Once he became premier, Gouin, with the backing of the other provinces, kept up his campaign unflaggingly. "We have been reduced to the point of not being able to administer the criminal justice system properly and of postponing the encouragement and improvements that the public education system requires," he complained in a letter to Laurier on 22 Nov. 1905. In the end, Laurier called an interprovincial conference in October 1906 at which he acceded to most of the provinces' demands. The Liberal press hailed Gouin as a worthy successor to Mercier, the defender of provincial autonomy. In 1907 Gouin approached the federal government for permission to extend the northern boundaries of Quebec and thus take over the district of Ungava. This territory would be annexed to the province under the name of Nouveau-Québec in 1912.

Like his predecessors Marchand and Parent, Gouin sought to attract English Canadian and especially American capital into his province to ensure its economic growth. His efforts to this effect were assisted by a greatly increased demand for the natural riches of Quebec (pulpwood, minerals, hydroelectric energy). On the other hand, Gouin was not opposed to certain well-aimed government initiatives that would enable the province to benefit even more from its resources. For example, in order to stimulate the production of

paper and create employment in 1910, he banned the export of pulpwood cut on crown lands. The United States countered by putting customs duties on imported paper, but Gouin was unshakeable, and a number of new paper mills were opened in the province. In 1910 he also set up the Quebec Streams Commission, which undertook the construction of works to regulate the flow of water in rivers harnessed to produce energy [see Simon-Napoléon Parent]. It was not supposed to compete with private enterprise, and Gouin refused to follow Ontario's lead in establishing public ownership of the hydroelectric industry [see Sir Adam BECK; Sir James Pliny Whitney*]. Economic growth made it possible to stabilize the province's finances. The larger federal grant, higher logging fees, the leasing of waterfalls, and the introduction of new permits and licences raised revenues from $5,340,000 in 1905–6 to $14,473,000 in 1919–20. The government could not only increase its expenditures during the same period from $5,012,000 to $13,503,000, but was able to balance its budget and even to declare modest surpluses year after year, while slightly reducing the province's per capita debt. This sound management won the enthusiastic approval of the business community.

Gouin had taken a keen interest in the development of education. He established many normal schools for girls (in particular, at Hull, Nicolet, Trois-Rivières, and Salaberry-de-Valleyfield), raised teachers' salaries, and provided much more funding to elementary schools. He especially emphasized the need to encourage technical and scientific education, and to that end in 1907 he personally steered through the assembly bills creating the Montreal and Quebec technical schools (with the object of providing a better grounding for young people heading for careers in industry), and the École des Hautes Études Commerciales de Montréal. In founding the latter establishment, the premier was carrying out the repeatedly expressed wishes of the Chambre de Commerce du District de Montréal, of which he himself had been a member, and of the party's radical faction, and was hoping to increase the participation of French Canadians in the province's economic development. The school began in 1910, on a modest scale, with 32 students and 12 professors. Gouin also founded the École Centrale de Préparation et d'Arpentage and the École Forestière, which opened in 1907 and 1910 respectively at the Université Laval at Quebec.

The increasing popularity of the automobile as a means of transportation led Gouin to create the Department of Highways in 1912 and to devote substantial amounts of money to this sector [see Joseph-Adolphe TESSIER]. He built and paved new provincial highways, and guaranteed loans for municipalities interested in building them in their jurisdictions.

Gouin also had to take a stand on a number of

highly controversial issues, including the prohibition of alcoholic beverages, a question on which Roman Catholics were divided. In 1908 he reduced the number of establishments serving alcohol in Montreal and Quebec and increased the fees for licences. He himself was opposed to total prohibition, preferring instead an educational campaign. After 1910, however, groups favouring prohibition, including some within the Catholic church, stepped up their pressure on the government, and it had to toughen its legislation. In 1919 a bill was passed imposing prohibition, with a few exceptions, but the law was unenforceable and was openly ridiculed. Feeling that the prohibition movement was losing momentum, Gouin moved back to a system of partial prohibition that permitted the sale of beer and wine.

Gouin had reorganized the municipal administration of Montreal by creating the board of commissioners in 1909. This new system of government was instituted following the recommendations of the royal commission to make a general and complete inquiry into the administration of the affairs of the city of Montreal [see Lawrence John CANNON] and after a referendum had been held. It was intended to reduce the patronage and corruption poisoning the municipal life of the metropolis. In 1918 Gouin's government would again get the city's charter amended, setting up the Administrative Commission of the City of Montreal with a mandate to manage the city's administration and straighten out its finances. Since this move appreciably diminished the powers of the city council and the mayor, it aroused the ire of the mayor of Montreal, Médéric Martin*. With Gouin as premier, the assembly had also modified the provincial voting system in 1912 to give the vote to almost all men aged 21 or over and eliminate the plural voting that allowed electors to cast a ballot in every electoral district in which they owned property. He categorically opposed women's suffrage. "Women do not vote in England," he said in 1915 to Carrie Matilda Derick*, the president of the Montreal Suffrage Association.

In implementing his policies, Gouin had to contend with the Conservative party in the Legislative Assembly. Weakened, however, by having a smaller number of MLAs and by a succession of leaders, and lacking a coherent program, the Conservatives were not managing to function effectively as the opposition. Outside parliament, however, Gouin had to reckon with powerful pressure groups. On the one hand, the Catholic clergy was worried that he might try to reduce the church's control over education. On the other hand, among workers there was beginning to be a demand for social reforms from the government, which they considered too ready to listen to employers. For their part, the Nationalistes, such as Omer Héroux* and Olivar Asselin, denounced Gouin's decisions related to colonization, accusing him of paying more atten-

tion to the demands of speculators and foreign capitalists than to the needs of the colonists.

On coming to power, Gouin had tried to calm the fears of the Catholic clergy. He promised Archbishop Paul Bruchési* of Montreal, with whom he developed a special relationship, that he would not secularize the educational system. In a speech on 11 Dec. 1905 at a banquet organized by the Liberals of the riding of Montreal, Division No.2, he declared: "We want neither to destroy nor to revolutionize; we want to improve and strengthen." Out of concern for the archbishop's opinion, he blocked the adoption of many bills (often introduced by Godfroy Langlois) aimed at creating a department of education, standardizing school textbooks, introducing compulsory education, requiring all teachers whether secular or religious to hold a certificate of competence, and democratizing the Montreal school system. He would put off until 1916 [see Joseph-Narcisse PERRAULT] the recommendations of the royal commission on the Catholic schools of Montreal, appointed in 1909 and chaired by Raoul Dandurand*. In their report, the lay members of the commission recommended the formation of a single school board in Montreal. Abbé Louis-Philippe Perrier dissented, expressing the position of the clergy, who preferred a decentralized system that was easier to influence. In 1913, when Gouin told the archbishop of Montreal that he was thinking of giving Langlois a foreign posting, Bruchési was delighted, and is said to have exclaimed, "Get that pest out of the country." In 1914, at the archbishop's urgent request, and following an exhausting campaign carried on by both the Nationalistes and the official organ of the archdiocese of Quebec, L'Action sociale, Gouin agreed to have the École des Hautes Études Commerciales affiliated with the Montreal branch of the Université Laval, an institution under the control of the clergy [see Jean Prévost*]. The school was able to maintain a de facto independence, however. Gouin made a point of involving members of the clergy in most official events and of appointing priests as colonization agents. Despite all this, L'Action sociale remained highly critical of Gouin and his government, to the point where the premier finally complained about it to Pope Pius X.

Opposition from the labour movement had remained marginal. The secretary of the Labour party, Albert Saint-Martin*, had run against Gouin in Montreal, Division No.2, in a by-election on 10 April 1905 and had won 13 per cent of the votes. Gouin promised that he would continue to be the workers' champion and immediately created a department of labour, attaching it to Public Works (which thereby became the Department of Public Works and Labour). He would also have a number of measures adopted – modest ones, on the whole – including one passed in 1909 providing for compensation in the case of accidents in the workplace, and another the following year making it illegal to employ children under the age of 16 if they could not read and write.

The Nationalistes were more of a problem for Gouin. The Ligue Nationaliste Canadienne [*see* Olivar Asselin], which had been founded in 1903 and had begun publishing an official newspaper, *Le Nationaliste*, the following year, had at first attacked Laurier's policies. But it also had concerns at the provincial level, so that, especially from 1907, under the leadership of their mentor Henri Bourassa the Nationalistes showed the Gouin government no mercy. Bourassa made a sensational entry into the Legislative Assembly by defeating the premier himself in the general election of 8 June 1908, in Montreal, Division No.2. Gouin, who had, however, won in the riding of Portneuf, wrote a letter to Laurier four days later in which he attributed his defeat to "the over-confidence of my organizers" and the receptiveness of the crowds whipped up by Bourassa. In 1908 and 1909 especially, the Nationalistes, who formed an alliance with the Conservatives, harshly denounced some of Gouin's policies. On the subject of colonization, they maintained that the timber limits granted to the logging companies hindered the settling of colonists on new land. In their view, the measures aimed at encouraging industrialization were first and foremost of benefit to foreigners and they called for an end to the sale of forests at bargain prices. They demanded reforms, including restrictions on the export of pulpwood and paper pulp, and made accusations of corruption. Outside the house, Jules Fournier*, who had been the editor of *Le Nationaliste* since 1908, led the attack until Gouin, in an effort to silence him, sued him for libel in 1909.

During the election campaign, however, Bourassa on 9 May 1916 would publish in his newspaper, *Le Devoir*, these highly flattering remarks about the party and the leader whom he had criticized so severely: "The Liberal party is something; Gouin is a somebody. The Quebec Conservative party is nothing any more; [Philémon] Cousineau [the new Conservative leader] is a nobody." What had happened to enable Gouin to overcome the nationalist opposition?

First of all, the Nationalistes considered that Gouin had implemented some important planks from their own program. He had had an embargo placed on the export of pulpwood from crown lands, raised the stumpage fees to force the big logging companies to pay more for their raw material, and substituted long-term leases for the outright sale of waterfalls. He had also encouraged colonization by creating some 50 new parishes and building roads and schools. In 1913 Abbé Ivanhoë Caron*, a priest and colonizer, praised the efforts made by the Gouin government in Abitibi, a region that Gouin visited the following year.

In the era of World War I things worked in Gouin's favour. By 1910 Bourassa and the Nationalistes were again giving priority to their federal concerns. After forming an alliance with the Conservative leader, Robert Laird Borden*, to defeat Laurier, they quickly became disillusioned with the war policy of the Canadian prime minister. Gouin supported Canada's participation in the war effort. On 15 Oct. 1914 he attended a large rally in Montreal's Parc Sohmer, where Laurier spoke about the duty of French Canadians towards their two mother countries. In 1915 and 1916 he continued to appeal for recruits and to work with the federal government in encouraging the military effort. But, like Laurier and the Nationalistes, he soon found himself with no choice but to oppose conscription strongly.

Gouin had also vigorously championed the struggle of the Franco-Ontarians against Regulation 17, a measure adopted in 1912 that severely limited the use of French as a language of instruction in Ontario schools [*see* Sir James Pliny Whitney]. Gouin raised this matter in 1913, during an audience with the pope. On 11 Jan. 1915 he delivered an important speech in which he asked the government of Ontario to demonstrate justice and generosity in its dealings with the province's francophone minority. Then, on 25 January, to give resounding support to the Franco-Ontarian cause he took part in a big demonstration at the Université Laval at Quebec, along with Cardinal Louis-Nazaire Bégin, the Nationaliste Armand La Vergne*, and a number of other dignitaries. In March 1916, under his guidance, a bill introduced by Antonin Galipeault, to authorize school commissions to make contributions from their funds for patriotic, national, or school purposes, was passed. (Gouin did not want his province to make a direct grant to the Franco-Ontarians, for fear of angering their government.)

In addition, Gouin contributed to the Bonne Entente movement, begun in 1916 by two Torontorians, John Milton Godfrey* and Arthur Hawkes, to promote harmonious relations as important between French- and English-speaking Canadians. In January 1917 Gouin was part of a delegation that went to Toronto and Hamilton, following a visit by an Ontario delegation to Montreal, Sherbrooke, Quebec, and Trois-Rivières. But during that year, when Laurier refused to form a coalition with the Conservatives to put into effect a policy of conscription, Gouin, who had likely also been approached by Borden, rejected the offer as well. The Quebec Liberals, headed by Gouin, were fiercely opposed to conscription. More than anyone else, it was Gouin who, for Laurier, led the campaign in Quebec preceding the general election of 17 Dec. 1917.

In December 1917, in the face of a frequently acerbic campaign in the English-Canadian press to denounce the so-called "disloyalty" of French Canadians and their rejection of compulsory military ser-

Gouin

vice, Gouin allowed one of his MLAs, Joseph-Napoléon Francœur, to present a notice of motion stating that the province of Quebec would be prepared to accept the breaking up of the confederation pact if the other provinces considered it an obstacle to the development of Canada. Gouin made a vigorous and memorable defence of confederation at that time. After reminding his listeners that the federal system was the only one suitable for Canada, that separatism was impossible, and that confederation had brought notable benefits, the premier declared his confidence that the storm would pass. He was proud, he said, to be called a Canadian, and proud of his country, Canada. This part of his speech drew very positive reviews in the anglophone press. But at the same time, Gouin made a point of recalling the sufferings of "our fathers" in the wake of insults and appeals to prejudices, and he declared that the slanders of the present moment were the work of a "small number" and not the majority of anglophones. These references were probably intended to satisfy the Nationalistes in particular. At the end of the speech, Francœur withdrew his motion, declaring that it had had "the desired effect." In 1937 he would admit, as the press reported on 10 December: "It was only a warning; I have never really wanted the province of Quebec to separate from the other eight provinces of the country."

At the end of the war, Gouin was at the height of his power. His authority within the Liberal party was uncontested, and there was almost no opposition, either inside or outside the Legislative Assembly. His compatriots increasingly viewed him as their main champion. Many considered him a possible successor to Laurier, whose health was failing and who was faced with increasing opposition in the ranks of his party. In 1918 Borden, aware of his government's extreme weakness in the province of Quebec, had made another unsuccessful attempt to persuade Gouin to join his Union government. Gouin certainly had much in common with the Conservatives on some questions. Although he was a Liberal, in governing his province his approach was conservative, he was close to the financial circles in Montreal, and he supported the tariff protection so dear to the Conservatives. But Gouin also knew that, given the conscription issue, he would be signing his political death warrant if he developed close ties with Borden.

The year 1919 brought important changes in Canadian politics. Laurier died in February. In western Canada and Ontario the United Farmers gained ground and fiercely opposed the protective tariff. In order to fight them, some Conservatives wondered whether the time had come to form an alliance with Quebec Liberals who favoured the tariff, starting with Gouin. In July Borden had another meeting with Gouin and two other Liberals, Ernest Lapointe* and Rodolphe Lemieux, who told him plainly that they

could not become part of a union government because of their province's opposition to conscription. Gouin also stressed the need to amend Regulation 17 in Ontario, a concession Borden was obviously powerless to grant. In any case, Gouin strongly opposed the Union government's policy of nationalizing railways.

Gouin put an end to these dealings by attending the Liberal convention in August. To be sure, the Liberal platform, with its reference to lower tariffs, worried the Montreal business community and its political friends, including Gouin and Lemieux. The co-chair of the convention, Gouin supported William Stevens FIELDING, who had been minister of finance in Laurier's government, in the race for the party leadership. Fielding was pro-tariff and, although he had supported conscription, he had never disowned Laurier or served in the Union government. The Quebec delegates were more in favour of William Lyon Mackenzie King*. Particularly concerned about bringing the western farmers back into the Liberal fold, King was prepared to agree to some relaxation of the tariff. He had been defeated in the general election of 1911, but had remained loyal to Laurier during the war. At Laurier's request, he had run as the Liberal candidate in the Ontario riding of York North in 1917, and had been defeated. He opposed conscription because he believed it posed a threat to national unity. King would never forgive Gouin for supporting Fielding.

In 1919, as well, Gouin had called a general election, two years before he had to, supposedly in an endeavour to win popular support for an ambitious and costly "program of reconstruction" (according to the account in *Le Devoir* of 10 June 1919) based on colonization and the development of hydroelectric power. It was becoming increasingly obvious that he wanted to relinquish the leadership of the government; in fact, his aim was to give his successor a strong mandate. The official opposition, led by Arthur Sauvé*, carried the stigma of the pro-conscription federal Conservatives. On election day, 23 June, 43 of the 81 Liberal candidates had no Conservative opponent; 74 Liberals and 5 Conservatives were elected. It was Gouin's last election campaign as premier. On 25 August he appointed Louis-Alexandre Taschereau, who seemed to represent a comfortable political choice, as attorney general. After serving for one session in the spring of 1920, Gouin gave a farewell speech on 21 June to the Young Liberals in Montreal, in which he reviewed his 15 years as premier. On 25 June he and Taschereau left for the Rivière Moisie and discussed the transfer of power. Gouin resigned on 8 July and Taschereau was summoned to replace him the following day.

During his years in provincial politics, Gouin had received many honours. France had made him a knight of the Legion of Honour in 1907 and a commander in 1920. He was awarded a KMG in 1908 and a KCMG in 1913. He became a grand officer of the

Order of Leopold II in 1912 and a commander in 1920. A number of universities conferred honorary LLDs on him.

A more trying period for Gouin began in 1920. During a brief stint as editor of *La Presse* (from August to December), he found it difficult to cope with the restrictions placed on him by its owner, Eugène Berthiaume, and the arrangement ended on a sour note. In July of that year Taschereau had appointed him to the Legislative Council for the division of Salaberry, but he resigned in October 1921 without having taken his seat. Then, at the request of King – who was under pressure to recruit such a high-profile candidate – Gouin entered federal politics. As the candidate in the riding of Laurier-Outremont he won an easy victory in the general election of 6 Dec. 1921. With 116 MPs out of a total of 235, the Liberals won the election but they had lost the support of the western farmers, who voted for the new Progressive party, which, with its 64 seats, was in second place. The Conservative Montreal *Gazette* predicted that Gouin, who headed a large block of Quebec MPs, would soon become the real leader of the Liberal party. During the campaign, there was another rumour that Gouin and Lemieux were plotting with Conservative prime minister Arthur Meighen* to unite the protectionist forces and enable Gouin to take power in Ottawa. King was furious and demanded a public show of support from the two Quebec Liberals. Lemieux complied with a letter published in the press, but Gouin simply sent indirect assurances of support. King continued to harbour doubts about the loyalty of his brilliant recruit.

Once the Liberals were in power, Gouin expected an important cabinet portfolio. King, who was worried mainly about the growing threat from the Progressives, knew that it was better for him to work closely with the Liberals from the Quebec City area, headed by Ernest Lapointe, than with the protectionist Liberals in Montreal. Maintaining ties with the former, who were relatively open to concessions in the matter of tariffs, would give him more opportunity to placate the farmers. Gouin asked King to give his province six ministers, four of them from Montreal. He pictured himself as minister of justice (a portfolio that King was planning to give to Lapointe), and president of the Privy Council, a prestigious office. The Montreal business community put similar pressure on King. The prime minister finally gave Gouin the most important portfolio, justice, but kept for himself the presidency of the Privy Council, in order, as he confided to Lapointe, not to put Canada's future in the hands of the Montreal financial magnates. In the end, the Montreal region had three ministers (Raoul Dandurand, Gouin, and James Alexander ROBB), as did the Quebec region (Henri-Sévérin Béland*, Jacques Bureau*, and Lapointe). For the moment, Gouin was doing well. Having failed in his attempt to

attract the Progressives into his cabinet, King could not afford to ignore the Montreal Liberals. In Gouin's case, the issue was merely postponed.

Gouin's career in federal politics was short. King never trusted him, for both personal and ideological reasons. He knew he had to get reduced tariffs and lower freight rates adopted in order to calm the farmers' revolt. Gouin objected to this policy and seems to have threatened more than once to resign. As time went on, he found himself more and more isolated. The younger Liberal MPs disliked his arrogance and his ties to the Montreal ruling class. On 16 Dec. 1923 King recorded in his diary that he judged the time had come to dissociate himself completely from the Montreal interests in order to move closer to the farmers. When Gouin sent him his letter of resignation soon afterwards, King eagerly accepted it and made it public on 3 Jan. 1924. As soon as he had left, King committed himself to lowering the tariff, and noted in his diary that he would never have been able to get cabinet agreement if Gouin had been there.

On leaving active political life, Gouin was able to devote more attention to his business affairs, which indeed he had never neglected, even during his time as premier. On 12 May 1919, his friend Georges-Élie AMYOT, who owned the Dominion Corset Company, stated in the Quebec newspaper *L'Événement* that Gouin had sold him a lot in Maisonneuve (Montreal) in 1911 for $100,000. "Is it scandalous," he concluded, "for a premier of Quebec to carry on business because he is the premier? On the contrary, I think we should congratulate ourselves on having a man in charge of our affairs who is able to look after his own and ours at the same time." During his years in politics, Gouin continued to practise law, and his office maintained close ties with a number of big companies in Montreal. While he was a cabinet minister in Ottawa, he was a director of many corporations, including the Bank of Montreal, the Montreal City and District Savings Bank, the Royal Trust Company, the Crédit Foncier Franco-Canadien, the Shawinigan Water and Power Company, the Laurentide Company Limited, the Montreal Light, Heat and Power Company, and the Mutual Life Assurance Company of Canada. In April 1922 the Liberal MP Andrew Ross McMaster introduced a motion in the House of Commons that would have prohibited cabinet ministers from serving on the boards of directors of corporations. The person targeted was obviously Gouin and the government had to intervene vigorously to get the motion withdrawn.

Gouin continued to take an interest in education. In 1920 the new Université de Montréal had invited him to chair its governing council. In 1924 Taschereau appointed him to head a commission to study, among other things, the advisability of creating a network of Jewish parochial schools. In 1926 the premier gave him the task of investigating the state of French-language Catholic education in Montreal.

After leaving the House of Commons, Gouin hoped to be given a seat in the Senate. Senator Dandurand interceded on his behalf, but King, and especially Lapointe, opposed the appointment. In 1926 Oswald Mayrand, Gaspard De Serres, Léon Trépanier, and J.-P.-Victorien Desaulniers made a vain attempt to persuade Gouin to run for the mayoralty of Montreal. He showed some interest, but because he did not wish to run against Médéric Martin, he made one stipulation: he wanted to be elected by acclamation. Dandurand tried again in 1927 to persuade King to appoint Gouin to the Senate, but Lapointe still objected. King nonetheless offered him the post of lieutenant governor of Quebec. Humiliated at having been denied a seat in the upper house, but by now seriously ill, Gouin agreed to become lieutenant governor. "It is not a question of honours, but of honour," he confided to one of his daughters-in-law. "I will go to Spencer Wood to die on my feet." He took office on 10 Jan. 1929. In March, during a visit to Montreal, Gouin suffered an attack of angina. On 28 March he went to parliament in ceremonial dress to perform his first official act as lieutenant governor – to give royal assent to the acts that had been passed and to prorogue the session. In the presence of Premier Taschereau, a number of ministers and MLAs, Lady Gouin, and a few close friends, he suffered another angina attack, collapsed in his office, received the last rites, and breathed his last. Thousands of people filed past his body in the chapel of rest at Spencer Wood, in Sillery, near Quebec. Messages of condolence poured in from all directions. The funeral took place in Notre-Dame basilica at Quebec on 1 April, after which a special train transported the casket to Montreal for burial.

Gouin was a taciturn, rather cold, and distant man. According to his friend Dandurand, he did not reveal his thoughts to anyone. He had no charisma and had little ability to stir up crowds. Because he was sensitive to criticism, some of his close friends thought he lacked self-confidence. In 1920 the *Canadian annual review* had referred to him admiringly as a "cool, calm and calculating" man, who appealed to people's intelligence rather than to their feelings. Somewhat authoritarian in style, Gouin kept a firm hold on the reins of the party and government. He saw to it that the Montreal Reform Club became the seat of the powerful Liberal machine, and in the house he gave his MLAs little leeway except on private members' bills. His two sons would also have political careers. Léon Mercier-Gouin would become a professor of law at the Université de Montréal and a senator, and Paul Gouin* would be one of the founders of the Action Libérale Nationale and the Bloc Populaire.

Sir Lomer Gouin was premier almost as long as Louis-Alexandre Taschereau and Maurice Le Noblet Duplessis*. But while their terms of office would end in great political upheavals, Gouin left the Liberal party stronger and more united at the end of his years than when he had found it in 1905. By encouraging the industrialization of the province and attaching great importance to education, he assuredly helped bring Quebec into the modern world.

RICHARD JONES

Several of Sir Lomer Gouin's speeches are available on microfiche and are listed in CIHM, *Reg*. The Lomer Gouin fonds at the LAC (MG 27, III, B4) is voluminous and there is a copy on microfilm at the ANQ-Q. The ANQ-Q holds a second collection of his papers, at P1000, D2348. Other fonds at these archives that contain useful documents are LAC, MG 26, G; H; J; MG 27, II, D10; E1; III, B3; and ANQ-Q, P198 and P350.

Gouin's public career between 1906 and 1921 may be traced in such printed sources as Que., Legislative Assembly, *Debates*, 1906–21; Can., House of Commons, *Debates*, 1906–21; and *Canadian annual rev.*, 1906–21. The memoirs of several politicians recall his life. Among them are R. L. Borden, *Robert Laird Borden: his memoirs*, ed. Heath Macquarrie (abridged ed., 2v., Toronto, [1969]), 2; P.-A. Choquette, *Un demi-siècle de vie politique* (Montréal, 1936); and Raoul Dandurand, *Les mémoires du sénateur Raoul Dandurand (1861–1942)*, Marcel Hamelin, édit. (Québec, 1967). Pertinent theses and dissertations include René Castonguay, "La motion Francœur (1917–1918)" (mémoire de MA, univ. de Montréal, 1989); Ruby Heap, "L'Église, l'état et l'enseignement primaire public catholique au Québec, 1897–1920" (thèse de PHD, univ. de Montréal, 1987); and Edwidge Munn, "Les relations entre Wilfrid Laurier et Lomer Gouin, de 1905 à 1908" (mémoire de MA, univ. de Montréal, 1985).

There are two articles that are entirely devoted to Gouin – P. A. Dutil, "The politics of progressivism in Quebec: the Gouin 'coup' revisited," *CHR*, 69 (1988): 441–65 and Bernard Weilbrenner, "Les idées politiques de Lomer Gouin," CHA, *Report*, 1965: 46–57 – and he figures prominently in a number of others: in F. W. Gibson, "The cabinet of 1921," in *Cabinet formation and bicultural relations: seven case studies*, ed. F. W. Gibson (Ottawa, 1970), 63–104; in Jean Hamelin *et al.*, "Les élections provinciales dans le Québec," *Cahiers de géographie de Québec* (Québec), 4 (1959–60): 5–207; and in three articles by Ruby Heap, "Libéralisme et éducation au Québec à la fin du XIXᵉ et au début du XXᵉ siècles," in *Combats libéraux au tournant du XXᵉ siècle*, sous la dir. d'Yvan Lamonde (Montréal, 1995), 99–118, "La Ligue de l'enseignement (1902–1904): héritage du passé et nouveaux défis," *RHAF*, 36 (1982–83): 339–73, and "Urbanisation et éducation: la centralisation scolaire à Montréal au début du XXᵉ siècle," CHA, *Hist. papers*, 1985: 132–55.

Aside from Jacques Gouin's brief study, *Sir Lomer Gouin* (Montréal-Nord, [1981?]), and the collection of articles by Gonzalve Desaulniers*, *Sir Lomer Gouin: sa vie, son œuvre* ([Montréal], 1923), Gouin has never been the subject of a biography. On the other hand, several specialized studies contain information about him and allow him to be better placed in context: Réal Bélanger, *Wilfrid Laurier; quand la politique devient passion* (Québec et Montréal, 1986); R. C. Brown, *Robert Laird Borden, a biography* (2v., Toronto,

1975–80), 2; René Castonguay, *Rodolphe Lemieux et le Parti libéral, 1866–1937: le chevalier du roi* (Sainte-Foy, Qué., 2000); R. MacG. Dawson and H. B. Neatby, *William Lyon Mackenzie King: a political biography* (3v., Toronto, 1958–76), 1–2; P. [A.] Dutil, *Devil's advocate: Godfroy Langlois and the politics of Liberal progressivism in Laurier's Quebec* (Montreal and Toronto, 1994); John English, *The decline of politics: the Conservatives and the party system, 1901–20* (Toronto, 1977); Roger Graham, *Arthur Meighen: a biography* (3v., Toronto, 1960–65), 1–2; Alain Lacombe, *Errol Bouchette, 1862–1912: un intellectuel* (Saint-Laurent, Qué., 1997); Claude Larivière, *Albert Saint-Martin, militant d'avant-garde, 1865–1947* (Laval, Qué., 1979); Joseph Levitt, *Henri Bourassa and the golden calf; the social program of the nationalists of Quebec (1900–1914)* (Ottawa, 1969); H. B. Neatby, *Laurier and a Liberal Quebec; a study in political management*, ed. R. T. Clippingdale (Toronto, 1973); Hélène Pelletier-Baillargeon, *Olivar Asselin et son temps* (2v. parus, [Montréal], 1996–); Yves Roby, *Les Québécois et les investissements américains (1918–1929)* (Québec, 1976); Fernande Roy, *Progrès, harmonie, liberté: le libéralisme des milieux d'affaires francophones de Montréal au tournant du siècle* (Montréal, 1988); three works by Robert Rumilly, *Henri Bourassa; la vie publique d'un grand Canadien* (Montréal, 1953); *Hist. de la prov. de Québec*, 8–30; *Histoire de l'École des hautes études commerciales de Montréal, 1907–1967* (Montréal, 1966); Adrien Thério, *Jules Fournier, journaliste de combat* (Montréal et Paris, 1954); B. L. Vigod, *Quebec before Duplessis: the political career of Louis-Alexandre Taschereau* (Kingston, Ont., and Montreal, 1986); and two works by Mason Wade, *The French Canadians, 1760–1945* (Toronto 1956); *The French Canadians, 1760–1967* (rev. ed. 2v., Toronto, 1968).

Other useful sources are ANQ-M, CE601-S33, 24 mai 1888; ANQ-Q, CE301-S9, 19 mars 1861; Rosario Gauthier, *Cathédrale Marie-Reine-du-Monde de Montréal: mariages, 1862–1964* (2v., [Saint-Jérôme, Qué.], 1993); *La Presse*, 6 sept. 1904.

GOWANLOCK, JENNY KIDD (Trout), schoolteacher, physician, and mother; b. 21 April 1841 in Kelso, Scotland, daughter of Andrew Gowanlock and Elizabeth Kidd, farmers; m. 25 Aug. 1865 Edward Trout in Stratford, Upper Canada, and they had by adoption one son and one daughter; d. 10 Nov. 1921 in Hollywood (Los Angeles).

Jenny Kidd Gowanlock was one of the women who first challenged men's exclusive hold on the medical profession in Canada. To some Victorians, the field of medicine appeared particularly appropriate for the female personality as they defined it, and so in this area women made early gains despite staunch opposition from most male doctors. Jenny's participation in the struggle to open new doors for women in the profession was inspired by feminism and by her Christian faith. "I hope to live to see the day when each larger town (at least) in Ont. will have one good true lady physician working *in His name*," she would write in 1881.

Jenny was six when she immigrated with her family to Ellice Township, Upper Canada. They developed a thriving ten-acre farm and regularly worshipped at Knox Presbyterian Church in nearby Stratford. She attended school in the town and in 1860 was accepted as an adult member of the Free Church. One year later Miss Gowanlock finished her training at the Normal School in Toronto, in about half the usual time, and from 1861 to 1865 she taught public school in the Stratford area.

There she met Edward Trout, who sold advertising for the Toronto *Leader* in the region. After an extended courtship they married and settled in Toronto. Edward prospered and in 1867 he and his brother John Malcolm founded a highly respected financial weekly, the *Monetary Times*. Mrs Trout did not fare as well: nervous disorders that suddenly set in after her marriage left her a semi-invalid barely able to move. She sought treatment through the new science of electrotherapy, and good results caused her to revive her childhood dream of pursuing medicine as a career.

Always encouraged and financially supported by her husband, in 1871–72 she took a one-year qualifying course at the Toronto School of Medicine. Both she and her classmate Emily Howard Stowe [Jennings*] passed, despite the active hostility of some professors and male students. No medical college in Canada was prepared to accept a woman as a regular full-time student, however, and Jenny, like Charlotte Ross [Whitehead*] of Montreal, attended the Woman's Medical College in Philadelphia, an institution noted for its Christian orientation. She received her MD in March 1875 and a month later passed with relative ease the licensing examinations of the College of Physicians and Surgeons of Ontario. She thus became the first woman doctor authorized to practise in Canada, and she would remain unique in that regard until 1880, when Emily Stowe was licensed.

At Toronto in July 1875 Dr Trout and her close personal friend Emily Amelia Tefft, another graduate of the Woman's Medical College, started their practice, which featured "special facilities for giving treatments to ladies by galvanic baths or electricity." Electrotherapy was highly regarded among late-Victorian physicians and in 1877 doctors Trout and Tefft launched the Medical and Electro-Therapeutic Institute in the three houses north of Jenny's home on Jarvis Street. Around 60 female patients lived at it and about 40 of them were treated each day. Eventually Trout and Tefft created branches in Hamilton and Brantford. The vast undertaking, although popular, proved to be a losing investment and its heavy personal demands wore down the always frail Dr Trout. Towards the end of 1882 she was forced to announce her retirement from the medical profession at the young age of 41.

This severe disappointment was mitigated by the rise of a new cause for her in 1883: the establishment of a women's medical college in Canada. Dr Michael Barrett* and five male colleagues at the Toronto

School of Medicine had, on their own initiative, formed themselves into the faculty of a prospective institution in that city. Trout was willing to endorse the move with both her influence and her money, but only if women constituted a majority of the trustees and filled at least some of the positions on the faculty. Barrett, who was opposed to having any female trustees at all, rejected these demands and Trout then threw her support to a more obliging group in Kingston which was organizing a school in affiliation with Queen's College. After the founding of the Women's Medical College was approved at a public meeting in Kingston on 8 June 1883, Trout became not only one of its trustees but also its principal benefactor, promising $200 a year for the next five years.

She was stunned by the news on 12 June that Barrett and his associates, assisted by Emily Stowe and the Canadian Women's Suffrage Association, had created the Woman's Medical College in Toronto. Barrett, obviously afraid that his plans would be pre-empted by the Kingston group, was now willing to accept women on both the board of trustees and the faculty. Edward Trout, representing his wife's interests, denounced Barrett's "complete change of heart" and claimed the Toronto action was grossly unfair to the Kingston college. Neither side would yield, however, and in October two women's medical colleges were launched.

There were not enough students. Bitter rivalry between the Kingston and Toronto colleges deeply divided the small and struggling community which the *Toronto Daily Mail* called the "lady medicos," and the competition for students was heightened in the 1890s with the opening to women of several Canadian medical faculties, including that of Bishop's College [*see* Francis Wayland Campbell*]. Strife did not end until 1894 when the two female schools united to form the Ontario Medical College for Women in the provincial capital. Dr Trout had served on the Kingston body's board of trustees until the end and had remained one of its principal financial patrons.

Trout's interest in medical matters was gradually overshadowed by other concerns. She became increasingly involved in Bible study and foreign missions, which many late-Victorian women found a liberating experience. Moreover, after a family tragedy the Trouts adopted their orphaned great-nephew and great-niece. She was also active, at some point in her career, in the temperance movement and in the Association for the Advancement of Women.

In 1908 the family moved to Hollywood, where Dr Trout died 13 years later. She had been significant in Canada as the country's first licensed female doctor, as a promoter of women's medical education on firm feminist principles, and as a quintessential Christian feminist.

PETER E. PAUL DEMBSKI

Jenny Kidd Gowanlock Trout's studies at the Woman's Medical College of Pennsylvania in Philadelphia included the preparation of a thesis on the medical uses of the opium poppy, "Papaver somniferum" (MD thesis, 1875).

Univ. of Waterloo Library, Special Coll. Dept. (Waterloo, Ont.), WA 10 (Elizabeth Smith Shortt fonds). Victoria Univ. Arch. (Toronto), Fonds 2083 (Victoria Univ., Cobourg, Ont., Dept. of Medicine fonds), 87.144V, 1os-1 (Toronto School of Medicine, student reg., 1858–75). *Daily British Whig* (Kingston, Ont.), 9 June, 3 Oct. 1883. *Globe*, 24 July 1875; 12, 15 May, 13 June, 2 Oct. 1883. *Mail* (Toronto), 16 April 1875, continued as *Toronto Daily Mail*, 14 May, 2 Oct. 1883. *World* (Toronto), 5 April 1883. G. F. Alsop, *History of the Woman's Medical College, Philadelphia, Pennsylvania, 1850–1950* (Philadelphia, 1950). P. E. P. Dembski, "Jenny Kidd Trout and the founding of the Women's Medical colleges at Kingston and Toronto," *OH*, 77 (1985): 183–206. V. [J.] Strong-Boag, "Canada's women doctors: feminism constrained," in *A not unreasonable claim: women and reform in Canada, 1880s–1920s*, ed. Linda Kealey (Toronto, 1979), 109–29; reissued in *Medicine in Canadian society: historical perspectives*, ed. S. E. D. Shortt (Montreal, 1981), 207–35. A. A. Travill, *Medicine at Queen's, 1854–1920: a peculiarly happy relationship* ([Kingston, 1988]). W. H. Trout, *Trout family history* (Milwaukee, Wis., 1916).

GRAFTON, GARTH. *See* DUNCAN, SARA JEAN-NETTE

GRAND, JAMES, businessman; b. 8 March 1857 in Yorkville (Toronto), son of James Grand, an architect, and Mary Ann ——; m. 8 March 1881 Elizabeth Jane Toy in Toronto, and they had three sons; d. there 7 Nov. 1921.

A co-founder of one of Canada's most successful stationery firms, James Grand was raised in Toronto by English-born Anglican parents. In the mid 1870s he was a clerk and salesman, possibly in the stationery business of his brother-in-law William Leitch MacGillivray. Between 1878 and 1882 Grand and Frederick Perry worked in partnership as printers and railway and mercantile stationers, after which Grand continued under his own name. Failing prospects, combined with responsibility for his wife and son, may have pushed him to tackle a new enterprise, though he was already fighting a serious illness (possibly scleroderma, which would eventually force his retirement). On 1 Aug. 1882 he opened a stationery supply firm on King Street. Grand found that Toronto's market was eager for a personal touch, which he provided by delivering goods right to the customer's door in a wheelbarrow. Business prospered so much that one year later, on 1 Aug. 1883, he signed a partnership agreement with Samuel Martin Toy, his brother-in-law and a bookkeeper, to form Grand and Toy, with a store at the corner of Leader Lane and Colborne Street.

Grand soon realized that businesses required not only paper goods but also a complete range of office supplies, including typewriting materials. The company thus expanded, and a new store was opened in August 1893 at Wellington and Jordan. Although Grand and Toy gained a name for quality products (its slogan from 1883 to 1990 was "If Its Good – We Have It"), the firm did not have a large customer base. In 1904 Toronto had over 20 stationery and office-supply concerns in the downtown area. The company's fortunes, however, changed almost overnight. On 19–20 April 1904 fire devastated the city's commercial core. Over 220 businesses were destroyed, including 23 printing, bookbinding, and lithographing concerns, among them Warwick Brothers and Rutter, W. J. Gage, Barber and Ellis, and Copp, Clark. "The stationery trade of Canada is ruined," Arthur Frederick Rutter ruefully told the *Globe*. By luck of location (one block east of the flames) and favourable winds, as well as the quick work of Grand's eldest son, Percy Frank, dousing sparks on the roof of their warehouse and store, Grand and Toy survived. In the aftermath of the fire, many businesses required a full stock of stationery and supplies. Grand and Toy was ready. Its sales were so intense during the rebuilding process that the partners handed out waste-paper baskets so that customers could fill their own orders. Heretofore grocers were the only merchants likely to have allowed any type of self-service.

The company expanded its clientele enormously over the following decade. Toy's death on 1 March 1906 left the firm under the sole control of the Grand family, who would run it until 1990. In 1911 James Grand had it incorporated and he opened an office-furniture department. In addition, to complement his profusely illustrated catalogues, he initiated *Office Talk*, a monthly promotional bulletin for his clients and employees. Within its pages, he demonstrated his sound knowledge of ethical business principles and offered futuristic articles on Toronto's need for an underground electric transit system, the transmission of business news by radio, and the place of ergonomics in the design of office equipment.

Grand continued as the titular president of Grand and Toy Limited until his death, though his poor health had caused him virtually to retire in 1913, when his son Percy, then vice-president, took over. Little is known of James Grand's private interests; by 1901 he and his wife had converted to Methodism. He died in 1921 at his residence at 28 Oriole Road, in the Deer Park neighbourhood, and was interred in St James' Cemetery. His estate, most of it in life insurance and stock, was valued at more than $210,500.

GAYLE M. COMEAU

AO, RG 22-305, no.44063; RG 80-5-0-104, no.13529; RG 80-8-0-804, no.6603. LAC, RG 31, C1, 1871, Toronto, St James' Ward, div.6: 75; 1901, Toronto, Ward 4, div.5: 9 (mfm. at AO). *Globe*, 2 March 1906, 8 Nov. 1921. Grand and Toy Limited, *Grand & Toy Limited: a century of service, 1882–1982* ([Toronto, 1982?]; copy in North York Central Library (Toronto), Canadiana Coll.); *Mail order catalogue of office supplies, printing and office furniture* (Toronto), 1924 (copy in TRL, SC). Michael McVean, *100 years for Grand & Toy Ltd., an all-Canadian celebration of success* ([Toronto, 1982?]; copy in North York Central Library, Canadiana Coll.). Nancy Rawson and Richard Tatton, *The great Toronto fire* (Erin, Ont., 1984).

GRANDIN, HENRI (named at birth **Henri-François**), Roman Catholic priest, Oblate of Mary Immaculate, and educator; b. 20 May 1853 in Sillé-le-Guillaume, France, son of Florent-Thomas Grandin, a butcher, and Modeste-Françoise Morin; nephew of Vital-Justin Grandin*; d. 16 Feb. 1923 in Paris.

Like his uncle, the bishop of St Albert (Alta), Henri Grandin attended the Petit Séminaire de Précigné and the Grand Séminaire du Mans. On the occasion of the Oblates' general chapter in France in 1873, Bishop Grandin spoke at the seminary attended by his nephew and persuaded the young man to accompany him to Canada. After his arrival the following year, Henri attended the noviciate of Notre-Dame-des-Anges at Lachine, Que., and he made his perpetual profession of faith on 27 May 1875. He then journeyed to St Albert, where he was ordained by his uncle on 30 November. The young priest celebrated his first mass the following day and his first high mass on 5 December.

Henri Grandin was immediately placed in charge of the minor seminary established by Bishop Grandin in St Albert; he also taught there. As an administrator, he demonstrated qualities that soon ensured his appointment to positions entailing more responsibility. In 1880 he was made superior of the Lac Ste Anne mission, where he provided instruction to novices who were completing their theological studies prior to ordination. Three years later he was appointed the first resident priest in Fort Edmonton (Edmonton) and curate of St Joachim's parish. In 1889 he became superior of the Lac la Biche mission, which had been transferred from Bishop Grandin's jurisdiction to that of Bishop Henri Faraud* of Athabasca-Mackenzie. The status of the mission had been a constant source of controversy between the two bishops, and Henri Grandin was sent there to ensure that the interests of the diocese of St Albert were protected when Faraud relinquished control. In 1897 he was named superior of the Saddle Lake district, and he later became temporary curate of Saint-Paul-des-Métis (St Paul, Alta), where he built a new church. He returned to Lac la Biche as superior for the years 1903–5.

In the latter year Bishop Émile-Joseph Legal* of St Albert decided that the Oblates serving in his diocese should have their own organization, distinct from that of the diocese, and he asked to be replaced as vicar of missions, that is, superior of all the Oblates in the diocese. Consequently, on 8 Sept. 1905 Grandin was appointed to this position. The following year, Bishop

Grandin

Albert Pascal of Saskatchewan also asked to be relieved of his responsibilities as vicar of missions, and Grandin assumed charge as well of the Oblates serving in the vicariate apostolic (soon to be the diocese of Prince Albert). When the Oblate province of Alberta-Saskatchewan was created in 1921, he would be appointed provincial.

As Oblate superior, Henri Grandin was responsible for, among other things, recruiting and preparing new members. To this end, he inaugurated the Juniorat de Saint-Jean l'Évangéliste in Pincher Creek, Alta, in 1908; two years later this institution was moved to Edmonton. He was also instrumental in establishing the Scholasticat de Marie-Immaculée in Edmonton in 1917 to enable western candidates for the priesthood to study in the west, rather than have to complete their theological and philosophical studies in Ottawa. Grandin had to deal with John Thomas McNally*, bishop of Calgary from 1913, who felt that there were too many French orders in his diocese. As part of his solution to what he regarded as the legacy of a "dead and useless past," McNally ordered the Oblates to vacate their parish in his episcopal city and St Patrick's parish in Lethbridge. The question of ethnicity also involved Grandin and McNally in a controversy over St Joseph's Industrial School for native students at Dunbow, which was having serious problems attracting and retaining pupils from southern Alberta. The school was under the jurisdiction of the Oblates, and McNally alleged that it was not being properly conducted because none of the staff was English-speaking or competent to teach that language. For his part, Grandin argued that some of the institution's problems resulted from the fact that the Department of Indian Affairs and its agents were not assisting the Oblates with recruitment. He would not bow to pressure from McNally to close the school, and he informed the bishop that he alone would have to make the decision as to the institution's future.

In his capacity as religious superior, Grandin devoted much time and energy to overseeing the efficient management of the Indian residential schools administered by the Oblates. He was aware of the necessity of maintaining harmonious relations between the missionaries attached to these institutions and the female religious communities who performed certain functions in the schools. As a missionary and an administrator, Grandin was also concerned with the welfare of the native populations served by the Oblates. He made representations to the federal authorities for the services of a doctor to treat the Indians and asked that the Oblates be provided with medicines and instructions on how to dispense them. In his report to the general chapter in 1908, Grandin expressed the fear that the native population in his vicariate was on the verge of extinction as a result of epidemics and diseases. He was supportive of continuing the Oblate ministry among the Métis, even when their economic and spiritual welfare declined as a result of contact with whites.

In the last years of his life Henri Grandin suffered ill health, and in January 1923 he returned to France to seek medical attention. He died in Paris after undergoing surgery and was buried in the Oblate vault in Montmartre. A skilled administrator, as evidenced by his many years as religious superior, he had also demonstrated a keen interest in education. Grandin was a warm and generous individual, and his personal charm endeared him to everyone who knew him. Unfortunately, he remains relatively unknown and his contribution largely ignored because he has been eclipsed by both his uncle and the legendary Albert Lacombe*.

RAYMOND HUEL

Arch. Départementales, Sarthe (Le Mans, France), État civil, Sillé-le-Guillaume, 20 mai 1853. Arch. of the Roman Catholic Diocese of Calgary, Bishop J. T. McNally papers. PAA, Arch. of the Oblates of Mary Immaculate, Prov. of Alberta-Saskatchewan, 71.220, items 3376, 7732; 84.400, items 883, 893–95, 898, 900. "Alberta et Saskatchewan," *Missions de la Congrégation des missionnaires oblats de Marie Immaculée* (Rome et Bar-le-Duc, France), 47 (1909): 133–34. P.-É. Breton, "Histoire du collège," in *Collège Saint-Jean: cinquantième anniversaire, 1911–1961*, ed. A. Duhaime (Edmonton, [1961]), 32–33. Gaston Carrière, *Dictionnaire biographique des oblats de Marie-Immaculée au Canada* (4v., Ottawa, 1976–89), 2: 105–6. *The diaries of Bishop Vital Grandin, 1875–1877*, trans. A. D. Ridge, ed. B. M. Owens and C. M. Roberto (Edmonton, 1989). "Feu le R.P. Henri Grandin, O.M.I.," *Les Cloches de Saint-Boniface* (Saint-Boniface [Winnipeg]), 22 (1923): 51–54. R.[-J.-A.] Huel, "La mission Notre-Dame-des-Victoires du lac la Biche et l'approvisionnement des missions du nord: le conflit entre Mgr V. Grandin et Mgr H. Faraud," in *Western Oblate Studies 1: proceedings of the first symposium on the history of the Oblates in western and northern Canada . . .*, ed. R.[-J.-A.] Huel *et al.* (Edmonton, 1990), 17–36. "Jubilé d'or du R.P. Gabillon, O.M.I.," *Missions de la Congrégation des missionnaires oblats de Marie Immaculée* (Rome), 65 (1931): 755–58. "Lettre du R.P. Leduc au P. Aubert," *Missions de la Congrégation des missionnaires oblats de Marie Immaculée* (Paris), 15 (1877): 297–306. "Oblations," *Missions de la Congrégation des missionnaires oblats de Marie Immaculée* (Paris), 14 (1876): 562–66. "Le premier siècle de Saint-Joachim," *Missions de la Congrégation des missionnaires oblats de Marie Immaculée* (Rome), 87 (1960): 70. "Le R.P. Grandin, vicaire des missions de Prince-Albert," *Missions de la Congrégation des missionnaires oblats de Marie Immaculée* (Rome et Bar-le-Duc), 44 (1906): 469. "Rapports au chapitre général de 1908: Alberta et Saskatchewan," *Missions de la Congrégation des missionnaires oblats de Marie Immaculée* (Rome et Bar-le-Duc), 47 (1909): 133–41. [E.] B. Titley, "Dunbow Indian Industrial School: an Oblate experiment in education," in *Western Oblate Studies 2: proceedings of the second symposium on the history of the Oblates in western and northern Canada . . .*, ed. R.[-J.-A.] Huel with Guy Lacombe

(Lewiston, N.Y., and Queenston, Ont., 1992), 95–113. M. B. Venini Byrne, *From the buffalo to the cross: a history of the Roman Catholic diocese of Calgary* (Calgary, 1973).

GRANDSAIGNES D'HAUTERIVES, HENRY DE, Vicomte de GRANDSAIGNES D'HAU-TERIVES (named at birth **Henri-Louis-Marie**), itinerant projectionist and cinema operator; b. 28 July 1869 in Pont-l'Abbé, France, son of Gustave de Grandsaignes d'Hauterives, Comte de Grandsaignes d'Hauterives, a customs collector, and Marie Tréourret de Kerstrat; m. first in June 1894 Charlotte Subé in Paris, and they had one son, Robert, who was the treasurer of the North Atlantic Treaty Organization (NATO) in 1950; m. secondly in 1922 in the same city Marguerite Holleville; d. there 26 Sept. 1929.

Henry de Grandsaignes d'Hauterives belonged to two distinguished families of the French nobility. On his mother's side he was a descendant of the Comte de Mirabeau, a writer and a great revolutionary leader; on his father's side he had a prestigious military ancestry. These families had been impoverished by the French revolution and the advent of the Republic, but, through shrewd investments and creative management, Henry's mother restored the family's fortunes and prestige by setting up one of the first commercial holiday resorts in Brittany. Becoming a solicitor in Paris after he had studied law in Poitiers, Henry soon went into debt because of an extravagant style of living which caused his wife to leave him in 1897. He then decided to set out for North America, bent on making his fortune in the fledgling cinema business. To this end, he went into partnership with his mother, who became the manager of Historiographe Compagnie, an itinerant cinema company.

The Vicomte and Comtesse d'Hauterives, as they were known in Canada, began presenting films in Montreal in October 1897 and they were among the first to offer this kind of entertainment. After several profitable months, they began a tour of Quebec towns in 1898; they drew audiences on obtaining the prior consent of the civil and religious authorities. They next went to Ontario and in 1899 they continued along the eastern seaboard of the United States, visiting New York, Boston, Atlantic City, N.J., and the neighbouring towns. Their tours soon extended to Bermuda and Saint-Pierre and Miquelon.

Until 1906 the province of Quebec was the main area of activity for Grandsaignes d'Hauterives and his mother. They returned there every fall for tours in the course of which they showed dozens of films (then of only a few minutes' duration) in theatres, schools, and parish halls. They used a projector called a Historiographe, which was operated by a crank that ran the film in front of a lens illuminated by a gas lamp. The shows were well known and praised for their high quality. They included the most recent French films,

especially historical ones, purchased from Charles Pathé and Georges Méliès and coloured by hand in a Parisian workshop. Grandsaignes d'Hauterives was famous as a "bonimenteur," the now obsolete occupation of providing an oral commentary on silent films. The journalists of the day almost unanimously praised his relevant and eloquent talks, which were given in both French and English during the shows.

However, the increase in the number of movie houses led Grandsaignes d'Hauterives and his mother to give up their tours. They ran movie houses in New York from 1906 to 1908, in St Louis, Mo., from 1908 to 1910, and in Bermuda and the islands of Saint-Pierre and Miquelon from 1910 to 1913. Their activities were eventually curtailed and then brought to an end by the monopolization of the American movie industry that forced operators to become part of networks with which neither the Vicomte nor his mother wished to be associated. They insisted on remaining independent and on operating their cinemas on a seasonal basis, but this approach did not fit commercial practices. After returning to France in 1913, without having made his fortune, Grandsaignes d'Hauterives worked as a civil servant in Rouen during the war and as a solicitor in Paris from 1920 until his death in 1929 (his mother had died in December 1920). During that period, he was better known for his worldly conviviality than for his professional activities.

A happy-go-lucky aristocrat who toiled as an obscure civil servant in France, Henry de Grandsaignes d'Hauterives had been a daring pioneer in the cinema industry in North America, travelling the continent to present a new type of show, which he popularized by enhancing the interest of early silent films with the excitement of fascinating oral narration. Throughout his years in North America he continued to offer French films to all kinds of audiences, maintaining his reputation as an outstanding cinema operator. Showing silent films with commentary, a practice he initiated in Quebec, lasted until 1930. Many people became acquainted with the cinema through his work.

GERMAIN LACASSE

This biography is based on contemporary newspaper accounts of Henry de Grandsaignes d'Hauterives's shows and on the correspondence of the Comtesse Marie de Grandsaignes d'Hauterives in the Arch. Départementales of Finistère (Quimper, France), dossier 60 J 67.

Arch. Départementales, Finistère, État civil, Pont-l'Abbé, 28 juill. 1869. Arch. Municipales, Paris, État civil, 28 sept. 1929. Germain Lacasse et Serge Duigou, *L'Historiographe (les débuts du spectacle cinématographique au Québec)* (Montréal, 1985); *Marie de Kerstrat, l'aristocrate du cinématographe* (Quimper, 1987).

GRANT, ROBERT HENRY, farmer and politician; b. 5 Aug. 1860 in Ottawa, eldest child of Robert Grant and Eliza Hardy; m. first 10 Jan. 1886 Sara Christiana Cuddie (d. 31 July 1887) in Perth, Ont.; m. secondly 17 June 1891 Sarah Maria Gourlay (d. 18 Feb. 1927) in Huntley Township, Ont., and they had six sons and three daughters; d. 26 Nov. 1930 near Hazeldean (Ottawa), Ont.

Following her husband's death in a fire in 1870, Eliza Grant moved with her children to Ottawa, where Robert Henry managed to obtain a secondary education. He spent some time at the University of Toronto and the Ontario Agricultural College in Guelph before taking over the family's large farm near Hazeldean in Goulbourn Township, where he also became active in local government. He represented Goulbourn on Carleton County Council from 1882 to 1891 and then served as county auditor for 12 years. In 1884 he was appointed a justice of the peace. The dominion government engaged him the following year to assist in evaluating land to be purchased for the Central Experimental Farm at Ottawa and in 1915 for the military base at Valcartier, Que. A freemason and member of St Paul's Anglican Church in Hazeldean, he served as secretary of a local cheese factory and telephone company, the Farmers' Institute of Carleton, and the Eastern Ontario and Western Quebec Plowmen's Association.

Though a long-time Conservative, Grant joined the United Farmers of Ontario, the agrarian movement formed in 1914. When it fielded candidates in the provincial election of October 1919, he reluctantly accepted the nomination for Carleton, an old Conservative constituency, and ran a solid, if understated, campaign. Grant accused his Tory opponent, fellow farmer Adam Holland Acres, of blind party loyalty and argued that all organizations, including legislatures, could be improved by the presence of farmers. He obtained a stunning majority; "Carleton Sells Birthright," proclaimed the *Carp Review* (Carp, Ont.). Provincially, the Farmers won more seats than any other party and, with 11 Independent Labor MPPs, they formed a coalition government. Grant sat on the committee that selected Ernest Charles Drury* as premier. Although early rumours placed Grant in the agriculture portfolio, Drury made him minister of education, to some extent because of his post-secondary experience. This nomination marked the first time that a Carleton MPP had been appointed to cabinet. Grant displayed typical modesty in an interview shortly after his appointment: "I was born a farmer, am a farmer and am nothing else. My farm has been my principal attraction and comfort despite the other activities in my life."

During his three-year tenure as minister, Grant performed competently but not spectacularly. From the beginning he emphasized the improvement of rural schools, a sector where he met with some success: the salaries of teachers were increased, a director of rural school organization was named (William John Karr),

and classes were begun at agricultural schools in Ridgetown and Kemptville. The government's efforts, however, to enforce the 1921 act that extended the age of compulsory attendance from 14 to 16 met with resistance from rural backbenchers, and school attendance fell off. Drury believed that Grant, rather than use his own judgement, too often deferred to his department's officials, who included such experienced authorities as Arthur Hugh Urquhart Colquhoun (deputy), Francis Walter Merchant* (industrial and technical education), and William Oliver CARSON (public libraries). Grant occasionally stood his ground. When Charles Vincent Massey* offered in 1920 to fund a commission on Ontario schools, Grant, because he had not been consulted, threatened to resign if Drury went ahead with the plan. Drury backed down, in part because the Farmers were wary of any external commission and of Massey because of his family's involvement in the implement business. On other important matters, Grant was either unable or unwilling to act upon Farmers' principles. Regulation 17, a measure passed by the former Conservative government of Sir James Pliny Whitney* to restrict the use of French in schools, was opposed by the Farmers, but Grant did not revoke it. Although he claimed inaction because of tensions between French- and English-speaking Catholics, the fact that his riding contained 87 Orange lodges was probably an important factor in his decision. The failure to rescind the regulation underscored the differences between the Farmers' rank-and-file members and their elected officials, who moderated or ignored several key planks of the party's platform.

In the election of June 1923, Grant again faced A. H. Acres, and was defeated. He returned to his farm and never ran again, though he continued to have an interest in education. He believed his Conservative successor as minister, George Howard Ferguson* of Kemptville (not far from Goulbourn), had a solid grasp of educational matters, and they corresponded. While Grant attended to his farm in the 1920s, his wife maintained her public profile. She was an honorary vice-president of the Ontario Federation of Home and School Associations, and in 1927 she represented the Federated Women's Institutes of Ontario at the annual meeting of the League of Nations Society in Canada. R. H. Grant died in 1930 and was buried in Maple Grove cemetery at Hazeldean.

Grant was fairly typical of the United Farmers returned in 1919 and the extent to which they diverged from other party members. He had believed that if farmers were elected, policies favourable to their calling would result. But, once at Queen's Park, the MPPs largely failed to satisfy the membership's desire for sweeping changes to the political, economic, and social systems that went beyond agricultural concerns.

KERRY BADGLEY

AO, RG 80-5-0-142, no.5994; RG 80-5-0-184, no.1976. LAC, RG 31, C1, 1871, Ottawa, Wellington Ward, div.1: 7; 1901, Goulbourn Township, Ont., div.5: 3. *Carp Review* (Carp, Ont.), 16, 23 Oct., 20 Nov. 1919; 7 June 1923; 24 Feb. 1927; 4 Dec. 1930. *Ottawa Evening Journal*, 27 Nov. 1930. Kerry Badgley, *Ringing in the common love of good: the United Farmers of Ontario, 1914–1926* (Montreal and Kingston, Ont., 2000). *Canadian annual rev.*, 1920: 540. E. C. Drury, *Farmer premier: memoirs of the Honourable E. C. Drury* (Toronto, 1966). C. M. Johnston, *E. C. Drury: agrarian idealist* (Toronto, 1986). K. M. Nicholson, "Policies of the Department of Education during the administration of Premier E. C. Drury, 1919–1923" (MA thesis, Univ. of Toronto, 1972). Peter Oliver, *G. Howard Ferguson: Ontario Tory* (Toronto and Buffalo, N.Y., 1977). Ont., Legislature, *Sessional papers*, reports of the minister of education, 1919–22. R. M. Stamp, *The schools of Ontario, 1876–1976* (Toronto, 1982).

GRASETT, HENRY JAMES, army and militia officer, and police chief; b. 18 June 1847 in Toronto, third son of Henry James Grasett* and Sarah Maria Stewart; m. 4 Oct. 1887 Alice Katharine Parke in Brompton (London), England; they had no children; d. 30 Sept. 1930 in Toronto.

Henry J. Grasett was born into a prominent Toronto family – his father was rector of St James' Cathedral. He attended a private school in Toronto and Leamington College in England. His military career began in Canada when he was not yet 19: in June 1866 he served in the Fenian campaign with the 2nd Battalion of Rifles (Queen's Own Rifles of Toronto) [*see* Alfred Booker*]. After entering the British army in September 1867, as an ensign in the 100th Foot (Royal Canadians), he spent time in England and Canada; when he retired in 1875, with the rank of lieutenant, he had been adjutant of the regiment for five years.

After returning to Toronto, Grasett became a partner in a firm of shipping and commission merchants. On 5 Nov. 1880 he was gazetted lieutenant-colonel and commander of the reorganized 10th Battalion of Infantry (later the Royal Grenadiers). Following the outbreak of the North-West resistance in 1885 [*see* Louis Riel*], this militia battalion was mobilized and saw action at Fish Creek and Batoche (Sask.), and against the Cree led by Big Bear [Mistahimaskwa*].

On the basis of his military accomplishments and family connections, Grasett succeeded Francis Collier Draper* as chief constable of the Toronto police on 1 Dec. 1886. Some politics may have been involved: the Board of Police Commissioners passed over deputy chief William E. Stuart, the political appointee of a former mayor. Grasett would head the force for 34 years, in contrast to the average tenure of less than four years in large American cities. Under Grasett the department grew – from 172 police to 662 by 1920; in composition, however, it remained heavily Anglo-Celtic. As a result of lobbying by moral reformers that focused on prostitution, a number of policewomen

were added in 1913. One of Grasett's first innovations was to arm the patrolmen, although, as an admirer of British policemen, he discouraged the use of firearms. As well, he supervised the reorganization of both the morality squad (under David Archibald*) and the detective department, the installation of a new electric call-box and signal system, and the acquisition of patrol wagons (1888), bicycles (1895), motorcycles for a traffic squad (1912), and motorized patrol wagons (1913). After 1917 mobility was increased by the greater use of automobiles, which themselves produced problems of traffic control.

Such developments helped make Grasett's department one of the most professional in Canada. It also became a powerful bureaucracy, charged not only with the preservation of law and order but also with regulatory functions such as licensing small businesses. In addition, it had to work with new agencies, among them the juvenile and women's courts. Training remained traditional, however, with an emphasis on military drill and learning on the streets. For years constables walked timed beats, and the merit-based system of pay and promotion was modelled on the British army's.

An important figure in North American police circles, Grasett served in the 1890s on the board of the Central Bureau of Identification in Chicago. This board was appointed by the National Association of Chiefs of Police, which in 1901 became the International Association of Chiefs of Police; Grasett was its vice-president in 1902. In 1905 he was involved, with Dominion Police commissioner Arthur Percy Sherwood* and others, in the formation of Canada's major police-lobby organization, the Chief Constables' Association of Canada. As its president in 1906, he spoke of how the police had become respectable in the eyes of the public. Under Grasett the Toronto department remained a driving force behind the CCAC.

In Toronto Grasett was a fairly popular and respected chief constable, despite criticisms before World War I. Moral reformers charged that prostitution was tolerated; Prohibitionists claimed that liquor laws were ignored or weakly prosecuted. To a large extent Grasett was shielded by the Board of Police Commissioners (the mayor, police magistrate, and county judge). When public debate called for direct municipal supervision, Grasett lobbied to preserve the autonomy of the police-commission system. Unlike his successors, he was careful to avoid inflammatory public statements, except during the war, when he spoke out vigorously against Toronto's foreign element.

Although crime actually declined between 1914 and 1918, Grasett was saddled with heavy responsibilities: war-time controls, monitoring aliens and radicals, enforcing the Ontario Temperance Act, and policing a large number of strikes. In the interest of

Gravel

patriotism and order, he banned outdoor anti-conscription meetings. When anti-foreigner riots broke out in August 1918, during a veterans' convention, his police intervened reluctantly, and then with force, generating bad publicity and an investigation. The inquiry exonerated the department as a whole, but led to the dismissal of two inspectors, a sergeant, and a constable. Grasett's greatest challenge, however, came from his own men, who were dissatisfied with wages, benefits, promotions, and disciplinary policies. In the fall of 1918 they organized a union in affiliation with the local Trades and Labor Council. The police strike that followed in December, combined with unrest among police in other Ontario centres, led to a provincial commission in 1919 headed by Sir William Ralph MEREDITH. During its hearings Grasett expressed disapproval of promotion by seniority, one of the bases of trade unionism. In late 1920 he retired as chief constable and was replaced by an officer who had risen from the ranks, Samuel James Dickson.

Grasett epitomized the patrician police leader of the era. He had much in common with long-time police magistrate and commissioner George Taylor DENISON, a fellow veteran of the Fenian campaign. Grasett had played an important role in the royal tour of 1901 and for his contributions to the war effort he was made a CMG in 1916. A Conservative in politics, he was an Anglican in religion and served for a number of years as a warden of St James' Cathedral and as a delegate to synods. He was socially active in several Toronto clubs, and belonged to the Canadian Military Institute and the Naval and Military Club of England.

Predeceased in 1926 by his wife, who passed on her inherited wealth, Grasett died of pneumonia at his home on Clarendon Avenue in 1930. He received a full police and military funeral, and was buried in St James' Cemetery. In eulogies that focused on his career in policing, city officials, mindful or not of events in 1918–19, spoke of a record of unblemished achievement. One-time mayor Thomas Langton Church* believed that "only those intimately connected with the police force could appreciate adequately his services," while Charles Alfred Maguire, a former controller and mayor, stated to the *Globe* that, in contrast to the experience of other cities, "no one had ever been able to attack the Toronto police force or its head."

GREG MARQUIS

AO, RG 22-305, nos.56821, 65543. *Globe,* 30 Sept.–2 Oct. 1930. *Toronto Daily Star,* 6–7 Sept. 1905. *World* (Toronto), 19 Oct. 1887. *Canadian annual rev.,* 1916: 802; 1918: 334–35, 586–87. *Canadian men and women of the time* (Morgan; 1898 and 1912). *Canadian Municipal Journal, and Telephone and Building News* (Montreal), 2 (1906): 387–88. *Canadian Police Bull.* (Toronto), December 1930. E. M. Chadwick, *Ontarian families: genealogies of United-Empire-Loyalist and other pioneer families of Upper Canada* (2v., Toronto, 1894–98; repr., 2v. in 1, Lambertville, N.J., [1970]), 2. T. E. Champion, *History of the 10th Royals and of the Royal Grenadiers, from the formation of the regiment until 1896* (Toronto, 1896). Chief Constables' Assoc. of Canada, *Proc. of the annual convention* (Toronto), 1912–31. International Assoc. of Chiefs of Police, *Annual session* (Washington), 1902. Greg Marquis, "The early twentieth-century Toronto police institution" (PHD thesis, Queen's Univ., Kingston, Ont., 1987); *Policing Canada's century: a history of the Canadian Association of Chiefs of Police* (Toronto, 1993). Middleton, *Municipality of Toronto,* vol.1: 178–80. Desmond Morton, *Mayor Howland: the citizens' candidate* (Toronto, 1973). *National encyclopedia of Canadian biography,* ed. J. E. Middleton and W. S. Downs (2v., Toronto, 1935–37), 1: 178–80. R. E. Riendeau, "Servicing the modern city, 1900–30," in *Forging a consensus: historical essays on Toronto,* ed. V. L. Russell (Toronto, 1984), 157–80. Toronto, Chief constable, *Annual report,* 1886–1920.

GRAVEL, LOUIS-PIERRE (baptized **Louis-Joseph-Cyriaque**), Roman Catholic priest, colonizing missionary, and office holder; b. 8 Aug. 1868 in Stanfold (Princeville), Que., son of Louis Gravel, a doctor, and Jessie Bettez; d. 10 Feb. 1926 in Montreal and was interred 18 February in the cemetery at Gravelbourg, Sask., where five brothers and a sister, whom he had persuaded to come and help in his colonizing work, are also buried.

Louis-Pierre Gravel, called Pietro by his friends, grew up in Arthabaskaville (Victoriaville), Que. Although his father belonged to its small circle of leading citizens (the best known being Wilfrid Laurier*), Gravel's large family was never well off and they were in even worse straits after his father's early death in 1888.

Louis-Pierre did his classical studies at the Séminaire de Trois-Rivières and the Séminaire de Nicolet. In the autumn of 1888 he entered the Grand Séminaire in Montreal and he later continued his theological studies at Nicolet. Bishop Elphège Gravel* of Nicolet, who was his father's first cousin, ordained him priest on 28 Aug. 1892. Louis-Pierre left soon after for New York, where a higher stipend than was supplied in Quebec enabled him to help support his mother, who had been left with eight children still to raise.

In New York Abbé Gravel ministered in the French Canadian parish of Saint-Jean-Baptiste from 1892 to 1901, and in the parish of Saint-Joseph from 1901 to 1906. A poet and musician in his spare time, a brilliant preacher devoted to his parishioners, he composed patriotic and religious songs in French, as well as sermons and tracts in English, which were published. He had just been named assistant priest in the suburb of Yonkers when he received a letter dated 28 July 1906 from the well-known Oblate missionary Zacharie LACASSE, requesting him, on behalf of Archbishop Adélard Langevin* of St Boniface (Winnipeg) to come to the Canadian west.

From his first days in the United States, Abbé Gravel had been able to observe for himself the poverty of many of the French Canadians who had emigrated south of the border. He saw in Langevin's request an opportunity to repatriate these exiles and help them benefit from the riches of the new provinces of Saskatchewan and Alberta, where the government was offering free land. At the end of September 1906 Gravel left for the west with his younger brother Émile. They stopped first in St Boniface; there Abbé Gravel was given a document authorizing him to found a parish "in the region of his choice." Accompanied by a guide, they examined prospects in southern Saskatchewan and located 1,600 acres of unsurveyed land in the fertile valley of the La Vieille River (Notukeu Creek), 80 miles southwest of Moose Jaw. The five or six French Canadian squatter families already in the area would be the first settlers of the new parish. On 22 Feb. 1907 Gravel was named an immigration agent for the Canadian government and obtained four townships for the future colony of Gravelbourg. Ottawa assigned the new settlement a post office in March 1907: Gravelbourg was officially founded.

Since the regional office of the Department of the Interior's dominion lands branch was located in Moose Jaw, on the railway line, Gravel made this town his base. In the fall and winter he went east, stopping in St Boniface to consult with the archbishop, in Ottawa to solicit assistance from the government, and in Montreal to schedule interviews and launch newspaper appeals. He undertook lecture tours on colonization throughout the province of Quebec, and visited New York and the New England states in order to repatriate Franco-Americans, recruiting settlers even on board the train. Spring and summer were spent on the prairies. He was most often in Moose Jaw, welcoming and directing his new recruits; sometimes he even accompanied them to the land they had been granted. Moreover, he dealt with the numerous problems brought to him by the settlers as well as by many priests including those of Notre-Dame d'Auvergne (Ponteix), Le Pinto (Meyronne), Lac à la Plume (Pelletier Lake), and Gull Lake. He was also involved in the villages of Courval, Dollard, Mazenod, and Lafleche; he thus contributed a great deal (often in ways others never suspected) to the establishment and development of a francophone settlement in southern Saskatchewan, of which Gravelbourg was the centre. His letters and reports to William Duncan SCOTT, the superintendent of immigration in Ottawa, and to his bishop give some idea of the prodigious amount of work accomplished by this energetic man.

On 18 March 1912, following the election of a Conservative government in Ottawa, Abbé Gravel, who was a fervent Liberal, lost his position. He still enjoyed the favour of the provincial Liberal government of Thomas Walter Scott*, however, and he decided to settle permanently in Gravelbourg. From the beginning, he had busied himself in obtaining essential services (wells, bridges, telegraph) for the settlement. He was also responsible for securing many other improvements, for example, a French-language land office in the village itself in 1910 and an immigration shed to house new settlers in 1911. There was still no railway, an essential for the development of the community and the surrounding area. The year 1913 saw the fruit of five years of requests to the railway companies and the various levels of government: on 20 September the first Canadian Northern train entered the Gravelbourg station. The village acquired the status of a rural municipality that year and became a town in 1917. In February 1918 Gravelbourg was made a judicial district.

These developments, however, did not satisfy Abbé Gravel. He wanted to make Gravelbourg the French and Catholic cultural centre of Saskatchewan. To achieve this goal, the little town had to have schools and religious institutions. It was through his initiative and determination, and his powers of persuasion, that in 1915 the Religious of Jesus and Mary of Sillery, Que., established themselves in Gravelbourg, where they founded a convent that Gravel served as chaplain and patron. His tenacity and spirit were also responsible for the establishment in 1918 of a college, of which he was procurator for a time, as well as for the founding in 1920 of an elementary school directed by the Oblate Missionaries of the Sacred Heart and of Mary Immaculate. Gravel certainly benefited from the essential support of Archbishop Olivier-Elzéar Mathieu of Regina, and the encouragement of parish priest Charles-Adrien Maillard, but he himself was the driving force. He had to approach the Religious of Jesus and Mary twice to persuade them to come, and in 1917 it was he who requested and obtained from the provincial government the charters authorizing the creation of two Catholic colleges, one English-language, the future Campion College of Regina, and the other French-language, the Collège Catholique de Gravelbourg, which would later be called Collège Mathieu.

On 23 Feb. 1923, after the Liberals had returned to power in Ottawa, Gravel was rehired as an immigration agent; in fact, he had hardly stopped doing this work. He was a builder in all senses of the word, and his papers include plans for an orphanage and an agricultural school. By 1909 he had begun thinking about establishing a hospital and from 1912 until 1925 he worked steadily toward this goal. Unfortunately, he would not live to see its completion. He had, however, prepared the way for his successors and he bequeathed a property to "the Corporation of the Gravelbourg hospital." He died suddenly, on 10 Feb. 1926 at the age of 57, while on a trip to Montreal. His body was transported to Gravelbourg. Though the church could seat 2,000, it could not accommodate all those who came to attend his funeral. The eulogy was delivered by Archbishop Mathieu.

Abbé Louis-Pierre Gravel devoted 20 years of his life to the cause of French, Catholic settlement. Like Father François-Xavier-Antoine Labelle*, to whom he has been compared, he lived and died for this cause. A monument erected to his memory in Gravelbourg in 1958 commemorates his work. The inscription reads: "Between 1906 and 1926 more than 10,000 Canadian citizens, many of whom were then living in the United States, answered the call of Reverend Louis-Pierre Gravel to make their homes on the broad plains of Saskatchewan where they built towns and established French-speaking cultural institutions." His most precious legacy remains Gravelbourg, which carries his name.

GHISLAINE GRAVEL BERNIER

A copy of the Gravel family fonds, the originals of which are in the author's possession, is available at ANQ-Q, ZQ137. It consists of 510 files on 20 microfilm reels; Father Louis-Pierre Gravel's papers make up the bulk of the collection (files 179–444, reels 9–18). A copy is also available at the Saskatchewan Arch. Board (Regina), R-9.48.

Additional material concerning Gravel is scattered among several collections, including the Arch. of the Diocese of Gravelbourg, Sask.; the Fonds Langevin in the Arch. de l'Archevêché de Saint-Boniface (Winnipeg); and the records from the period of O.-E. Mathieu's installation as bishop in 1911 in the Arch. of the Archdiocese of Regina. Material at the LAC includes Gravel's reports as immigration agent to the federal superintendent of immigration, W. D. Scott (MG 26, G: 13703–6 and RG 76, Acc. 1969/017, box 213, file 595025-2).

J. H. Archer, *Saskatchewan: a history* (Saskatoon, 1980). Adrien Chabot, *History of the diocese of Gravelbourg, 1930–1980* (n.p., 1981). *1915–1965, souvenirs: album souvenir pour marquer le cinquantième anniversaire de la fondation du couvent des religieuses de Jésus-Marie à Gravelbourg* ([Gravelbourg?, 1965?]). *Les Gravel*, Lucienne Gravel, édit. (Montréal, 1979). Georges Hébert, *Les débuts de Gravelbourg: son fondateur, ses pionniers, les institutions, 1905–1965* (Gravelbourg, 1965). *Heritage: Gravelbourg – district, 1906–1985* (Gravelbourg, 1987). *Historical sketches of the parishes of the diocese of Gravelbourg, Sask., on the occasion of its silver jubilee, 1930–1955* ([Gravelbourg, 1956]). Ernest Laforce, *Bâtisseurs de pays* (3v., Montréal, 1944–48). Richard Lapointe, *100 noms: petit dictionnaire biographique des Franco-Canadiens de la Saskatchewan* (Regina, 1988). Richard Lapointe and Lucille Tessier, *The francophones of Saskatchewan: a history*, trans. Lucille Tessier (Regina, 1986). Robert Painchaud, *Un rêve français dans le peuplement de la prairie* (Saint-Boniface [Winnipeg], 1987). *La Saskatchewan de A à Z*, Richard Lapointe, compil. (Regina, 1987).

GRAVES, MINARD WENTWORTH, farmer and manufacturer; b. 7 July 1858 in Port Lorne, N.S., son of Robert Graves and Harriet Bishop; m. 8 Sept. 1886 Florence Nightingale Winchester (1854–1937) in Stoney (Granville) Beach, N.S., and they had two sons and two daughters; d. 6 Jan. 1926 in Bridgetown, N.S.

According to an obituary, Minard W. Graves received "but a meagre common school education," probably at the one-room school in Port Lorne. In 1883 he purchased a farm in Upper Granville, and for the next 20 years he would regularly appear in official documents as "farmer" or "yeoman."

Like many other Annapolis valley farms of this period, Graves's property had an established orchard, and for a time apple growing was a minor sideline for him. However, the development of rapid steam transportation by sea, combined with the railway that had been built through the valley in the 1860s, opened a new era in fruit production, the benefits of which would be quickly seized by Graves. Beginning in the 1880s the vastly increased apple crop of Nova Scotia found a ready market, first in the United States and then in Great Britain. Yet increased production also meant larger quantities of substandard fruit, unfit for foreign markets. It was to this part of the crop that Graves turned his attention. For several years, using a small apple press, he experimented with the making of cider vinegar, finally producing nine barrels which he sold in Saint John.

One of the first to recognize that there was a market for processed apples, not merely the raw fruit, Graves gradually turned his full attention to vinegar production. In 1903 he moved his operations to Bridgetown, a few miles from his farm, and there established a plant containing initially eight vats, which he ran in association first with Fred E. Bath and then with Jacob W. Salter (as M. W. Graves and Company). In spite of a devastating fire in 1904, Graves's business prospered. In 1913 his plant was described in the Halifax *Morning Chronicle* as "one of the largest and best equipped in the Dominion," and by 1924 it was producing 400,000 barrels of vinegar a year, most of which was sold on the British market.

For some time Graves restricted his processing to cider vinegar, but he gradually expanded his operations, especially after his sons, Francis Mann and Owen Winchester, entered the firm (the three would incorporate the business as a limited company on 18 Feb. 1921, with a capitalization of $100,000). The production of dried apples, previously largely a home industry, soon became an important sideline. Evaporating plants were built in Bridgetown and several neighbouring communities; by 1925, 28,000 barrels of apples were being dried, most of which found a market in western Canada. The acquisition in 1922 of the Annapolis Valley Cyder Company Limited moved Graves into new areas, including canned apples, concentrate, and juice, and for a time carbonated beverages as well. Under Graves's sons, who carried on the business after his death, the company and its range of products continued to expand, encompassing additional plants in Berwick and Kentville and a wide variety of canned, and then frozen, vegetables. Although no longer owned by the Graves family, M. W. Graves and Company Limited is still a major producer of processed fruits and vegetables at the beginning of the 21st century.

Graves was an important leader in the development of the apple-processing business in Nova Scotia. Although apple production there increased dramatically during his active career, from an average of 284,000 bushels in the early 1880s to 5,389,000 bushels in 1923, the processed portion of the crop fluctuated from a low of 3.2 per cent to a high of 26.9 per cent. Most growers depended on the overseas market to absorb raw fruit. The powerful Fruit Growers' Association of Nova Scotia, founded in 1864 [*see* Andrew Hay Johnson*], focused its entire attention on this market, with its problems of shipping and quality control; virtually no mention of apple processing is to be found in the records of its proceedings. Significantly, Graves apparently never saw the advantage of joining this organization. The report produced in 1930 by the royal commission investigating the apple industry did not even address the issue of processing, so wedded was the larger community to the shipment of unprocessed fruit. It was, however, only the foresight of a few men such as Graves that kept even a segment of the apple industry alive in the Annapolis valley following the devastation of its foreign markets in the post–World War II period.

BARRY M. MOODY

Annapolis County Registry of Deeds (Lawrencetown, N.S.), Deeds, book 80: 676–77 (30 April 1883); book 86: 135–36 (1 Sept. 1886); book 95: 426–28 (17 Nov. 1891); book 123: 551–54 (13 Oct. 1903); book 126: 152–53 (25 June 1904); book 141: 401–4 (23 June 1909); book 184: 593–94 (28 May 1925). Bridgetown and Area Hist. Soc. (Bridgetown, N.S.), "The Graves families," comp. J. Dexter (MS); Obituary (no source), M. W. Graves. Macdonald Museum (Middleton, N.S.), Norwich Union insurance book, 47 (insurance policy). NSARM, RG 32, WB, Annapolis County. Riverside Cemetery (Bridgetown), Burial records, 607. *Halifax Herald*, 7 Jan. 1926. *Middleton Outlook*, 8 March 1904. *Morning Chronicle* (Halifax), 1 Jan. 1913. *Morning Herald* (Halifax), 17 Sept. 1886. *Weekly Monitor* (Bridgetown), 13 Jan. 1926. Margaret Conrad, "Apple blossom time in the Annapolis valley, 1880–1957," in *Atlantic Canada after confederation . . .*, comp. and ed. P. A. Buckner and David Frank (Fredericton, 1985), 351–76. Fruit Growers' Assoc. of Nova Scotia, *Annual report* (Kentville), 1905, 1910. Anne Hutten, *Valley gold: the story of the apple industry in Nova Scotia* (Halifax, 1981). M. W. Graves and Company Limited, *Our story* (Berwick, N.S., n.d.). N.S., Legislative Council, *Journal and proc.*, 1922, app.12: 9.

GRAY, ANN JANE. *See* POWELL

GRAY, ROBERT, manufacturer; b. 3 Feb. 1862 in Chatham, Upper Canada, son of William Gray and Ellen ——; m. 28 Dec. 1887 Margaret Haldane McLaren in Chatham, Ont., and they had a son and a daughter; d. there 31 March 1929.

Robert Gray was the eldest of the four children of a blacksmith who had immigrated with his wife from Roxburghshire, Scotland, in 1853. They settled in Chatham, where William Gray established a carriage-making business. In 1883 Robert and his brother, James Scott, were taken into the business, which became William Gray and Sons. The following year the 22-year-old Robert assumed control after his father slipped while disembarking from a train in Kingston and died. He rose steadily in Chatham's business community, and became the first president of the Board of Trade. On 5 Jan. 1899 William Gray and Sons Company Limited was incorporated.

Like many carriage producers, Gray believed the advent of the automobile was the beginning of the end of carriage making, but he also saw the construction of auto bodies as an extension of the artisanal production that characterized the carriage industry. Conservatively minded, he carefully integrated auto work into his enterprise. His firm built bodies for the Still Motor Car Company of Toronto in 1899 and for the Chatham Motor Car Company from 1906. Gray's interest in automobiles and the emerging industry would be keenly shared by his son, William Murray, who motorized a buggy in his teenage years. An owner of Detroit-made Fords, Gray Sr was an original investor in the Ford Motor Company of Canada Limited in 1904. He had offered a used Ford as partial payment, but was politely turned down by Gordon Morton MCGREGOR, the company's Canadian head, who needed cash more. Between 1906 and 1912 Gray would also make bodies for the Fords being assembled in Walkerville (Windsor); a strong booster of Chatham, he had tried to secure Ford work for other local companies, notably the foundry of McKeough and Trotter, and he was involved in bringing Chaplin Wheel, Dowsley Spring and Axle, and International Harvester to his native city. A shrewd businessman who would diversify his investments, in 1912 he discouraged his son from putting his savings of $6,250 into Ford stock, despite the substantial increase in value of his own shares.

Until 1916 Gray remained committed to developing his carriage business, of which automotive work was only one component. In 1907 he combined his sales force with that of the farm-equipment company of a partner in William Gray and Sons, Manson Campbell of Chatham, who had a strong distribution network in western Canada. A full merger on 24 Feb. 1911 created William Gray-Sons-Campbell Limited for the production of carriages, sleighs, fanning mills, cabinets, and auto bodies. William Gray and Sons would remain in business, but without the involvement of Robert's accountant brother, who died in 1911. By 1912 Gray's output had reached 15,000 wagons. When his main competitors in carriage making, Robert MCLAUGHLIN of Oshawa and James Brockett Tudhope of Orillia, expanded into making automobiles, Gray followed suit. He found an American partner to provide chassis, to beat the tariff on importing fully assembled automobiles. In October 1915 Gray and Josiah Dallas Dort, a Michigan carriage maker turned auto maker who was also president of a Canadian carriage company, created Gray-Dort Motors Limited. In the first year Gray imported fully assembled Dorts, but in 1916 he was building Gray-Dorts in Chatham. Though he ceased building carriages that year, he continued to use the Gray-Campbell network of distributors, which made his car particularly popular in Saskatchewan. Like McLaughlin, Gray was a transitional figure who had one foot planted in the old culture of carriages and personalized dealings. Known for his flexibility with customers, he once accepted a mare worth $150 as a trade-in on a Gray-Dort.

Marketed with an unassuming motto ("Own a Gray-Dort – You Will Like It"), Gray's auto became more popular in Canada than the Dort was in the United States. It was produced in various models over the years and was admired for its power, reliability, and ease of repair. Starting with a technically advanced automobile, Gray added such features as leather upholstery, a tilting steering wheel, optional wire wheels, and even a cigar lighter. The Gray-Dort sold in the mid-price range – the 1919 touring car cost $1,275, the sedan $3,000 – and followed the Mc-Laughlin-made Buicks and Chevrolets as Ford's main rivals in the Canadian market. By 1921 he was making 8,000 cars annually and employing up to 825 people, and according to Bill Gray, then vice-president of Gray-Dort, 60 per cent of each car was being manufactured in Canada. The company boasted three plants in Chatham, factory branches across Canada, and some 400 dealers; 23,000 Gray-Dorts were made between 1916 and 1923. Though little is known of Gray's day-to-day involvement, there is some evidence that the company resisted union activity and that Gray had other corporate associations. In 1920 he became a director of the Standard Bank of Canada.

In 1922 J. D. Dort decided to get out of the business. His operating costs were higher than those of his competitors in the United States, sales were low, and producers were feeling the economic downturn. His liquidation in 1924 devastated Gray's operation. Despite the degree of Canadian manufacture, it had relied on Dort engineering and design. Like many other Canadian auto makers, Robert Gray was not the master of his own destiny. In addition, pressure from Ford and General Motors made it impossible for such small companies as Gray-Dort to continue. In 1924,

with a debt of $1.2 million, it stopped making cars. By April of that year Robert Gray had left the firm, which some of its members unsuccessfully tried to keep going. Within months Bill had formed Colonial Traders Limited, to deal in automotive equipment and accessories.

Robert Gray's interests included the Presbyterian church and the Chatham Curling Club, and the family enjoyed a summer cottage on Lake Erie at Erieau. After an illness of six months, he died in 1929 at the age of 67. Although his shares in Gray-Dort and William Gray and Sons were deemed worthless at his death, these companies had been profitable in their heyday, and he was able to leave an estate valued at almost $595,000, much of it in war loans and stock in Chrysler and GM.

CÒREY LAROCQUE

The Chatham-Kent Museum in Chatham, Ont., has a Gray-Dort automobile and a strong archival collection of Gray-Dort files.

AO, F 149; RG 22-397, no.136-1929; RG 80-5-0-159, no.205469. Ont., Ministry of Consumer and Business Services, Companies and personal property security registration branch (Toronto), Dormant corporation files, TC 31828 (Gray-Dort Motors Limited). *Globe*, 1 April 1929. *Automotive Industries* (Philadelphia), 4 Sept. 1924: 464. *Canada Gazette*, 7 Jan. 1899: 1287; 25 Feb. 1911: 2798–99. *Canadian annual rev.*, 1920: 64. R. A. Collins, *A great way to go: the automobile in Canada* (Toronto, 1969). D. F. Davis, "Dependent motorization: Canada and the automobile to the 1930s," in *The development of Canadian capitalism: essays in business history*, ed. Douglas McCalla (Toronto, 1990), 191–218. Hugh Durnford and Glenn Baechler, *Cars of Canada* (Toronto, 1973). *Industrial Canada* (Toronto), 1911–24; May 1929: 150, 152. James Naylor, *The new democracy: challenging the social order in industrial Ontario, 1914–25* (Toronto, 1991).

GREEN, NATHAN, cigar maker and merchant; b. 12 June 1828 in Amsterdam; m. first Elizabeth Pizarro (d. 20 Oct. 1853), and they had one son; m. secondly Jane Hart (d. 17 Oct. 1889) in New York City, and they had two sons and three daughters; d. 26 April 1922 in Chicago.

Nathan Green moved to London in 1842 and learned the cigar-making trade with Moses Gompers. He then left for New York in the 1850s with his brothers-in-law Solomon Henry Hart and Henry Levy. England offered few opportunities for immigrant Jews; journeying to the New World opened up better prospects. While in New York, Green worked with and befriended fellow cigar maker Samuel Gompers, a relative of Moses's and later the founder of the American Federation of Labor.

By 1859 Green was living with his wife and children in Saint John, as the second Jewish family to make this city its home. They had been preceded by

Solomon Hart and his wife Alice Catharine Davis*, who had settled with their family in 1858; Henry Levy also resided in the city for a few years. Green's household in 1871 included his wife, six children, a female domestic servant, and a male apprentice. His home was imposing and had a billiard room. Until 1878 Green was one of a small Jewish community in Saint John that numbered no more than 15. In 1879 he participated in the first Rosh Hashana and Yom Kippur services held in the city. The second celebration almost did not happen: the *minyan*, or quorum, for public worship was ten males over the age of 13 but the community was one short until a Jewish visitor was located in a city hotel. Three years later the first Jewish wedding in the Maritime provinces was celebrated when Green's eldest son, Louis, married the Harts' daughter Elizabeth; they would become the parents of Solomon Hart Green*, a lawyer and MLA in Manitoba. The first Jewish burial in Saint John had occurred in 1873 after Nathan Green and others had purchased a plot of land for a cemetery (the remains of deceased members of the community had generally been conveyed to New York for interment). The burial ground was consecrated by a rabbi from Boston. The plot retains the name Green-Hart Cemetery and is the burial ground for the original settlers and their descendants.

Green's life in Saint John revolved around the cigar-manufacturing and wholesale and retail tobacco business he had established in 1861, the largest in the city. His home and store, located on Prince William Street, were destroyed in the great fire of 20–21 June 1877 [*see* Sylvester Zobieski Earle*], but he was reportedly back in business within 24 hours. Advertisements for his store indicated a wide range of merchandise for which he was the exclusive distributor. Those who approached it after 1880 were greeted by a carving of a Scotsman which stood on the street outside.

The first Jew in the Maritimes to belong to the masonic order, Green was listed as a member of St John's Lodge No.2 for many years and was at his death its oldest living member. He was also a philanthropist, known especially for his assistance to the county poorhouse and to impoverished immigrants arriving in the city. He was the last Saint John resident to receive the freedom of the city before confederation. This was a privilege paid for by those who intended to conduct business there and was recorded in the city's financial accounts as a form of business taxation.

In 1888, at the age of 59, Green disposed of the stock in his tobacco shop, then located on Charlotte Street, and retired with savings of $100,000. Believing that this sum would last him for the rest of his life, he moved with his wife, his son Solomon, and his daughters Sarah and Frances to Chicago, where members of the family were already established. The Greens' son Henry (Harry) had settled there in 1885 and had established a wholesale and retail tobacco business. Their daughter Elizabeth had married a Chicago resident in 1886 and two of Green's sisters were also living in the city. Green purchased a block of houses for himself and his family; there he resided for many years, first with his wife and after her death in 1889 with one of his daughters. For a time he was associated with Harry Green and Company, in which Solomon had become a partner. Despite the distance, he maintained close ties to the Jewish community in Saint John. His son Louis, who had remained in the city, annually purchased a train ticket for his father to visit. In 1899 Nathan sponsored two small prizes for the Saint John Hebrew School. Six years earlier he had hosted a reception for the City Cornet Band of Saint John, which performed at the Columbian exposition in Chicago. Green boasted of his love of travel and made the voyage across the Atlantic more than 70 times.

Nathan Green died in his sleep in Chicago, at the age of 93.

KATHERINE N. E. BIGGS-CRAFT

Fernhill Cemetery Company (Saint John), Burial records. LAC, RG 31, C1, 1871, Saint John County (mfm. at Saint John Regional Library). Saint John Jewish Hist. Museum Arch., Corr. from Richard Berger, 21 June 1988; Green–Hart–Isaacs family tree, comp. Phyllis Green (1976); Hart–Green family tree; Hist. of Jewish businesses, Saint John City directory, 1880–1989; Shaarei Zedek Cemetery database; Joseph Tanzman, "The story of the Jewish community of Saint John, N.B." (typescript, n.d.). Saint John Regional Library, Misc. index, SB (scrapbook) 18 (mfm.). *Jewish Times* (Montreal), 7 July, 22 Dec. 1899. *St. John Daily Sun*, 30 Sept. 1893. *St. John Daily Telegraph and Morning Journal*, 1 May 1871; continued as *Daily Telegraph*, 28 Sept. 1881, 16 Dec. 1896, and as *Telegraph-Journal*, 28 April 1926, 3 Feb. 1966. *Saint John Globe*, 11 Oct. 1882, 1903–13. Eli Boyaner, "The settlement and development of the Jewish community of Saint John," N.B. Hist. Soc., *Coll.* (Saint John), no.15 (1959): 79–86. *Directory*, Saint John, 1865/66–89/90. Grand Lodge of the Ancient and Honorable Fraternity of Free and Accepted Masons of N.B., *Proc.* (Saint John), 1868–88. *The Jew in Canada: a complete record of Canadian Jewry from the days of the French régime to the present time*, ed. A. D. Hart (Toronto and Montreal, 1926). Marcia Koven, *Weaving the past into the present: a glimpse into the 130 year history of the Saint John Jewish community* (Saint John, 1989). *The Lakeside annual directory of the city of Chicago* (Chicago), 1888–90. Sheva Medjuck, *Jews of Atlantic Canada* (St John's, 1986). S. E. Rosenberg, *The Jewish community in Canada* (2v., Toronto and Montreal, 1970–71), 1. *Vital statistics from N.B. newspapers* (Johnson), 27–83.

GREENFIELD. *See* MACDONELL

GRIER, SARAH HANNAH ROBERTA (Coome), founder and superior of the Sisters of St John the Divine; b. 28 Oct. 1837 in Carrying Place, Upper Canada, third daughter of John Grier and Eliza Lilias Geddes; m. 23 July 1859 Charles Horace Coome; d. 9 Feb. 1921 in Toronto.

Educated at home by her father, a high-church Anglican clergyman, Hannah Grier married a civil engineer working on the Grand Trunk Railway. For a time they resided in Kingston. In 1862 they moved to Britain, where Hannah was drawn to the mission work of the Anglican Sisters of St Mary. A fall during pregnancy resulted in the loss of her child and a long convalescence.

A year after their return to North America in 1877, Charles died in Chicago. Though Hannah contemplated going back to England "to offer her widowhood . . . to God's service," she remained with a nephew and a brother in Chicago, taking a position at the School of Decorative Art and executing embroidery and hangings for churches. She was on her way to enter the Sisters of St Mary in 1881 when, stopping in Toronto to visit her mother, she was approached about forming a sisterhood there.

Under the leadership of Georgina Broughall, wife of the rector of St Stephen-in-the-Fields Church, and the Reverend Ogden Pulteney Ford, organizational meetings were held between November 1881 and April 1882. In June, Hannah Coome and Amelia Elizabeth (Aimée) Hare entered the noviciate of the Sisters of St Mary in Peekskill, N.Y. Anxious to gain experience in nursing and social work, Hannah spent some time at their hospital and missions in New York City. Meanwhile steps were being taken in Toronto to raise an endowment.

After making her profession on 8 Sept. 1884 in Peekskill, Hannah founded the Sisterhood of St John the Divine in Toronto, taking up residence there at Bishop Strachan School, where her sister Rose Jane Elizabeth* was principal. In December, Hannah and Aimée Hare occupied a converted house on Robinson Street, in a receptive parish known for its high-church traditions, and began work: meals for the poor, a dispensary, Bible classes, visitations, the provision of clothing, and sewing for churches. Reaction to a Protestant sisterhood was mixed. Despite the support of Bishop Arthur Sweatman* and even the Orange order, some Anglicans found the sisters' black habits and religious practices too Catholic.

In the spring of 1885, during the North-West rebellion [see Darby Bergin*], Sweatman telegraphed Major-General John Wimburn Laurie to ask if volunteer nurses could serve. As a result of Laurie's response, requesting trained nurses under one head, the diocese directed the Reverend John Langtry to approach the Sisterhood of St John. Leaving three sisters in Toronto, Hannah, a novice (Aimée Hare), and two postulants joined three lay nurses in staffing a field hospital in Moose Jaw (Sask.), where, aided by Dr William Canniff*, they tended the wounded from Batoche and Fish Creek. For her work, Hannah received a service medal from the government.

Following their return in July, the sisters quickly set up St John's House on Euclid Avenue, the first surgical hospital for women in Toronto, and secured a staff of doctors. Over the next few years they progressed in several directions: a home for the aged (1886), an enlarged hospital and convent on Major Street (1888–89), incorporation of the order (with five sisters, 1889), a mission in Seaton Village north of Bloor Street (1890), and a system of lay associates and responsibility for Bishop Bethune College in Oshawa (1893). Though three British sisterhoods within the Church of England had established branches in Canada by 1900, the Sisters of St John remained the only Canadian order.

From the outset Hannah was insistent that they were never to beg for support, a condition that necessitated strong lay backing and periodic appeals. During her time as superior, the order was never large; the scope of their work often seemed to exceed their numbers. One result was the development of an extremely close religious community. Hannah was a pillar of strength who, though outwardly reserved, corresponded affectionately with sisters and novices when they were away. A shrewd financial administrator prone to overwork, she was compelled to take recuperative trips in 1889, 1894–95, and 1903. One of her last achievements was the opening in 1915 of a mission in the new east-end parish of All Hallows, where people were so well off, the sister-in-charge reported, "that we have to work persistently and patiently to get them to attend Church."

In June 1916 Hannah, at age 78, resigned as superior and was succeeded by her niece Dora Lilias Grier. She died in 1921 and was buried in St James' Cemetery. Today the sisterhood is best known for its rehabilitation hospital and retreat centres.

MURRAY W. NICOLSON

Toronto Daily Star, 10 Feb. 1921. P. F. Anson, *The call of the cloister: religious communities and kindred bodies in the Anglican communion* (London, 1958). *A memoir of the life and work of Hannah Grier Coome, mother-foundress of the Sisterhood of St. John the Divine, Toronto, Canada* (London, 1933). *Religious communities in the American Episcopal Church and in the Anglican Church of Canada* (rev. ed., New York, 1956; copy in the contributor's possession). *The Sisterhood of Saint John the Divine, 1884–1984* (4th revision, Willowdale [Toronto], 1984).

GRIMES, GEORGE FREDERICK ARTHUR, businessman, labour activist, and politician; b. 29 June 1877 in Channel (Channel–Port aux Basques), Nfld, son of William Grimes and Amelia White; m. 28 Aug. 1900 Annie Clarke in St John's, and they had seven daughters; d. there 10 Aug. 1929.

George F. A. Grimes's father was an outport police-man, who in 1878 was posted to his home town of Bri-gus, where he became a sergeant. When George was 12, the family moved to St John's for William to take up a posting as head constable (he would eventually rise to the rank of superintendent). George left school around this time. In 1890 he was an apprentice clerk in a dry-goods establishment. He would remain with this business until 1902, when he secured a much more favourable berth as manager of the book and statio-nery department for George Knowling Limited, one of the largest general retailers in St John's. Grimes con-tinued his education through private reading. He was active in the Cochrane Street Methodist congregation, as well as the Methodist College Literary Institute, a mainstay of the intellectual life of St John's. His prac-tical faith led him to a lifelong advocacy of temper-ance and also, it would seem, to socialism.

It is not known when Grimes began to identify with socialism. At his death contemporaries would note a long-standing interest in the "labour question," which may date from the unionization of the St John's waterfront in his young manhood. The Truckmen's Protective Union was founded in 1900 and the Long-shoremen's Protective Union in 1903. It was a period of labour activism in the city, including the "great sealers' strike" of 1902 [see Simeon Kelloway*]. Meanwhile, political philosophy and current events were common topics at the MCLI. Grimes's known associates at this time include Julia Salter* (subse-quently Julia Salter Earle, a labour and social activist). In 1906 Grimes was a founding member of the New-foundland Socialist Society, and in 1908 he was finan-cial secretary of the St John's Trades and Labour Council, newly formed by the mayor, labour lawyer Michael Patrick Gibbs*.

As one with both an intellectual and a practical interest in labour matters, Grimes must have followed keenly the formation of the Fishermen's Protective Union in 1908 by William Ford Coaker*. By 1911 the FPU had 12,500 members in 116 local councils and was a force to be reckoned with. Bent on reforming the system of supply to fishermen as the crucial first step in social change, Coaker incorporated the Fisher-men's Union Trading Company, commonly known as the Union Trading Company, to supply "cash stores" in the outports. Grimes's first known association with the FPU came in 1912. In March he spoke at a mass meeting it held in the capital, and when the UTC began operating from St John's premises in May, he was manager of the dry-goods department. He attended the annual convention that December where the FPU unveiled its Bonavista Platform and made plans for Union candidates to contest the coming gen-eral election.

The FPU had solid support in northern Newfound-land, yet the closest local council to St John's was at Grimes's boyhood home of Brigus, in the district of Port de Grave. Early in 1913 Grimes was selected as the Union candidate in this district, where his local connection helped him secure election in October. He was one of eight Unionists elected in alliance with Sir Robert BOND's Liberal party, and he soon came to be regarded as one of his party's most effective spokes-men in the opposition.

It was shortly after his election that the incident occurred which, perhaps more than any other, has secured Grimes a place in Newfoundland history: his "conversion" of the young Joseph Roberts Small-wood* to socialism. Smallwood relates that this came about as a result of a chance meeting at a dentist's office, probably early in 1914. The schoolboy ingenu-ously blurted to the politician that he was a socialist; Grimes asked a few questions and afterwards supplied young Smallwood with pamphlets. (Grimes's depic-tion in Wayne Johnston's historical novel *The colony of unrequited dreams* (1998) – persistent in the cause yet mild-mannered to a fault – is consistent with per-sonal recollections of him. However, the Smallwood character's disenchantment with his mentor is not consistent with Smallwood's lifelong respect for Grimes, whom he considered a true intellectual, gen-tleman, and socialist.)

Grimes's earnest, inoffensive air generally de-flected criticism of his proclaimed ideology. His years with Knowling's book department had bolstered his natural inclinations to make him one of the best-read residents of the capital. He was no revolutionary, being known in St John's as a man of solid family and a pillar of his church. Among those who were pre-pared to overlook Grimes's ideological idiosyncrasy was Coaker, who had publicly dissociated himself and the FPU from socialism.

In St John's, as elsewhere, the Great War saw an increased interest in labour politics. Grimes helped form the Newfoundland Socialist League in 1914 and in 1917 he was a frequent speaker at meetings which resulted in the formation of the Newfoundland Indus-trial Workers' Association [see Philip BENNETT]. The sole point of contact between city unions and the FPU, which also rejected any affiliation with the labour movement, Grimes helped organize an NIWA cooper-ative. He was a regular speaker in the House of Assembly, particularly in the debate over Prohibition in 1915–17. He had been a long-time advocate of women's suffrage (no doubt he knew well his former employer's daughter Fannie McNeil [KNOWLING]), in part because, as he said, "Prohibition would have been world-wide long ago, if women had a vote on it." In labour matters his voice was one of conciliation, favouring "machinery to prevent strikes" and, above all, "learning to know each others difficulties and becoming less suspicious."

In July 1917 Coaker and William Wesley Halfyard*,

another Unionist MHA, were invited by Sir Edward Patrick Morris* to sit in cabinet as part of an all-party National government, felt to be a necessary step in order to introduce conscription. There are indications that Grimes opposed the coalition, although he eventually fell into line behind Coaker. In April 1917, to pave the way for an accommodation with the FPU, the government had established a commission to investigate war profiteering. It recommended a board of food control, to which Grimes was appointed early in 1918.

Meanwhile the FPU was building a model town on the northeast coast, a centre for its various businesses. When the UTC moved its headquarters to Port Union in February 1918, Grimes went too, along with his wife and daughters. As in 1913, when his experience in debate had been crucial in establishing the credibility of the Union party, Grimes's knowledge of business and community affairs contributed to the success of both the UTC (which had 40 branch stores by 1918) and Port Union. In November 1919 Grimes ran for re-election, as part of a Union alliance with the Liberal Reform party of Richard Anderson Squires*. Although the Squires–Coaker combination carried the day, Grimes was defeated in Port de Grave by Sir John Chalker Crosbie*. Three weeks later he was selected secretary-treasurer of the Supreme Council of the FPU.

Out of public life during 1919–23, Grimes was able to devote his energies to the UTC at a time when its two principals, Coaker and Halfyard, had responsibilities in cabinet. By 1922, however, the "Coaker regulations," introduced when Coaker became minister of marine and fisheries to reform the marketing of fish, had been undermined and the whole Union agenda was in danger. Disillusioned, Grimes moved back to St John's, where he established a modest agency and wholesale business. He also resumed his leading place in the Cochrane Street congregation, and was elected secretary of the East End Methodist School Board and president of the MCLI.

As a general election came due in May 1923, Coaker determined that the FPU would stick with Squires. Grimes was returned as a member for Fogo – unlike Port de Grave, an area with deep Union support. Though he had stood as a Liberal, he was clearly pledged to Coaker. Squires was soon compelled to resign in the face of evidence of systematic misuse of public funds. William Robertson Warren then formed an administration, with Union support. Grimes was Warren's minister of marine and fisheries, outside cabinet, from 29 July 1923 to 2 May 1924, when the government collapsed as its Unionist faction pushed for the prosecution of Squires.

Grimes was returned to the assembly twice more. Elected as a Liberal-Progressive for Twillingate in June 1924, he became one of the more effective members of a fractured opposition, speaking out against the policies of Prime Minister Walter Stanley Monroe*. He was the Liberal member for Lewisporte from October 1928, serving also as deputy speaker of the house and as a member of the Board of Works.

The following summer Grimes died of an "apoplectic attack," while at work in his office on a Saturday night. He had contributed a great deal to the FPU movement in Newfoundland, including a grasp of parliamentary procedure, a respected intellect, and a St John's perspective. In return the FPU raised the bookish floorwalker to be a man of affairs. Looking back on the achievements of the FPU, Coaker identified Grimes as one of those men of "common sense and hidden ability" which the Union had brought into public life to the profit of the country.

ROBERT CUFF

[Information about G. F. A. Grimes was provided in interviews with the late J. R. Smallwood, 1981–82, and R. Carl Grimes, 1998. R.C.]

PANL, GN 30, 97; Parish records coll., Methodist/United Church, St John's, Cochrane Street. W. F. Coaker, "The passing of George Grimes" and "Past, present and future," *Fishermen's Advocate* (Port Union, Nfld), 16 Aug. 1929 and 27 July 1932. *Evening Telegram* (St John's), 12 Aug. 1929, 7 April 1933. Arthur Fox, "M.C.L.I. is one of North America's oldest debating clubs," in *The book of Newfoundland*, ed. J. R. Smallwood *et al.* (6v., St John's, 1937–75), 5: 400–3. I. D. H. McDonald, *"To each his own": William Coaker and the Fishermen's Protective Union in Newfoundland politics, 1908–1925*, ed. J. K. Hiller (St John's, 1987). Nfld, General Assembly, *Proc.*, 1914–30. J. R. Smallwood, *I chose Canada: the memoirs of the Honourable Joseph R. "Joey" Smallwood* (Toronto, 1973). G. H. Tucker, "The old N.I.W.A.," in *The book of Newfoundland*, 1: 279–81. *Who's who in and from Newfoundland* (St John's), 1927.

GUAY, JOSEPH-DOMINIQUE, journalist, farmer, politician, and businessman; b. 14 April 1866 in Chicoutimi, Lower Canada, son of Johnny (Jean) Guay, a merchant, and Marie-Émilie Tremblay; m. 2 Sept. 1889 Maria Morin in Saint-Louis-de-Métabetchouan (Chambord), Que., and they had six children; d. 18 Sept. 1925 in Chicoutimi.

Early in 1850 Joseph-Dominique Guay's family became one of the first to put down roots in the Saguenay region. He was the ninth of 11 children. His father, who served as mayor of Chicoutimi from 1863 to 1870, was considered the most important businessman in the region, next to William Price*. When he died in 1880 Johnny Guay would leave his widow a fortune of nearly $100,000. Until her death in 1904, Marie-Émilie, a talented, indeed formidable businesswoman, would see to it that the family wealth increased and that her children were educated and established in life. In 1873 Joseph-Dominique enrolled in the Petit Séminaire de Chicoutimi, with the intention of following in the footsteps of his godfather

Dominique Racine*, a future bishop of Chicoutimi, and teaching at the college. His academic results were apparently good, since he was awarded various honours. After completing a year of the two-year philosophy program at the Petit Séminaire de Québec in 1882–83, he began studying law in the office of his brother-in-law, Jean-Alfred Gagné, who was a lawyer in Chicoutimi and an MP. However, he abandoned his studies because of a set of circumstances related to his father's estate, his own temperament, and his personal predilection for business and journalism.

In August 1887 Guay began a career in journalism which he would pursue for some 20 years. With his brother Alphonse and his future brother-in-law Louis de Gonzague Belley, he founded *Le Progrès du Saguenay* (Chicoutimi). As a result of a gift from his mother on the occasion of his marriage to Maria Morin, he became its owner, editor, and publisher from 1889. Under his direction it became the most important newspaper and the largest printing plant in the region. As a journalist, Guay mainly covered election campaigns. He was a political organizer for the Conservative party and had been active in the 1887 federal election, travelling the length and breadth of the riding of Chicoutimi and Saguenay on behalf of its candidate, his brother-in-law Gagné. He did the same for Belley in the 1892 by-election.

Guay championed the building of the Quebec and Lake Saint John Railway, which would reach Roberval in 1888 and Chicoutimi in 1893 [*see* Horace Jansen Beemer*]. He made it his mission, first in his newspaper and later in his public life, to promote agricultural and industrial progress in the Saguenay region, the two being, in his opinion, inseparable and complementary. He had shown an early interest in agriculture, attending around 1878 a lecture on the dairy industry given by Édouard-André Barnard*, who was then editor of *Le Journal d'agriculture* (Montréal) and director of agriculture in the Department of Agriculture and Public Works. In 1887 Guay took part in the Quebec provincial exposition and won first prize in the horse category with a year-old colt.

As the operator of a farm his mother had given him and as a member of the Société d'Agriculture de Chicoutimi, Guay supported the conversion of agricultural operations to dairy farming. In the spring of 1893, with the backing of Bishop Michel-Thomas Labrecque* of Chicoutimi, he encouraged the creation of a mutual fire insurance company for the farming community. He also undertook a tour to promote the establishment of agricultural clubs. In his talks he advocated the improvement of crops, animals, and buildings, and he set an example himself by becoming one of the first to own a silo in the Saguenay region. In October he went with veterinarian Joseph-Alphonse COUTURE – who, among other things, had founded the École Vétérinaire de Québec in 1885 – to the Colum-

bian exposition in Chicago; while there he noted that Canadian cheese had an excellent reputation and that the British market was opening. In 1894, thanks to his network of contacts and his participation in the field, he was elected president of the Société d'Agriculture de Chicoutimi for the first time. He would continue to be one of its chief architects until 1924.

In 1897 Guay worked with the Société Générale des Éleveurs d'Animaux de Race Pure de la Province de Québec as president of the Canadian horse section. That year he bought his brother Victor's farm, which was one of the finest in the Saguenay region. By cultivating extensive acreage and raising a herd of 30 milk cows and a number of horses, he won a silver medal two years later at the competition for the Order of Agricultural Merit.

From 1895 to 1900 Guay was also a director of the Industrial Dairy Society of the Province of Quebec. Concerned about market standards, he persuaded cheese factory owners to upgrade their equipment and set common rules for the quality of milk as well as for the ripening and packaging of rounds of cheese. In June 1895 he accepted the presidency of a sales syndicate to export cheese directly to England, bypassing the Montreal market. Every two weeks an auction in Chicoutimi drew representatives of buyers from Montreal, Quebec, and the surrounding region. By making it possible for producers to be paid cash on delivery at the highest market price, this initiative not only helped the growth of local savings, but also led to a refrigerated warehouse being built and to the hiring of an inspector to grade the cheese. These improvements were responsible for the excellent reputation of the region's cheddar.

In 1895 Guay gained more influence over the development of the Saguenay region by running for mayor in Chicoutimi on a platform of urban modernization. He and four other fellow candidates won a crushing victory over the group running the previous administration, which had been under the thumb of Price Brothers and Company [*see* Sir William PRICE]. At the new council's first meeting, Guay was named mayor. In cooperation with the councillors, he put municipal finances in order. He undertook maintenance work on the streets, inaugurated an electrical system, and provided water service for the townspeople. Focusing on job creation and the growth of the economy, Guay sought to attract new industries by going in search of investors. One approach was to put advertisements in the province's large newspapers extolling the virtues of Chicoutimi. These measures proved unsuccessful and Guay, who was convinced that wood pulp was an "industry of the future," destined to "revolutionize the province" because of the growing demand for paper to print mass-circulation newspapers, then decided he would work to set up a factory.

Thus in 1896 Guay and a few partners founded the

Chicoutimi Pulp Company. The construction of the plant created a large work site and in July 1898 production of pulp began. The company soon made a name for itself on the British and American markets, thanks to the high quality of its machine-made pulp and the entrepreneurial spirit of its general manager, Julien-Édouard-Alfred Dubuc*. In 1898 it was cited as an example by *La Semaine commerciale* (Québec) for "dispelling the false claim that French Canadians are not suited for business." Two years later it won a gold medal at the universal exposition in Paris. Ushering in the era of heavy industry in the Saguenay and Lac-Saint-Jean region, the company contributed to the area's urbanization. Not only did the population of Chicoutimi increase from 2,000 to 5,000 between 1895 and 1902, but its light industry, commerce, and institutions also experienced unprecedented growth.

In 1902, following a trip to Bermuda for health reasons, Guay resigned as mayor and he would not become involved in public affairs again until 1922. Meanwhile he worked as a journalist, writing columns on hunting and fishing for *Le Progrès de Saguenay*, and he looked after his mother's estate. Along with his father-in-law, he worked to organize a supply of wood for the Chicoutimi Pulp Company, of which he remained a shareholder and co-director until 1909. A large-scale landowner whose properties would be evaluated at more than $42,000 in 1914, he was also particularly involved in real estate. He presided over the operations of the Château Saguenay, a 130-room hotel he had built in Chicoutimi in 1898 in partnership with Dubuc and protonotary François-Xavier Gosselin. The building and the surrounding neighbourhood were destroyed in a fire in 1912. Guay then converted another of his properties, located in the centre of the city, into a hotel. Like a true travel agent, he offered hunting and fishing expeditions to the tourists he welcomed as guests, as well as overseas cruises on behalf of the big ocean-going ship lines. In October 1922 he was again elected mayor of Chicoutimi, but a year later he abruptly terminated his second term of office because of a lengthy illness. He died on 18 Sept. 1925 at the age of 59 years and five months.

A man of vision who focused on his own region, Joseph-Dominique Guay, throughout his life, devoted his energies to the development of the milieu he came from. Forward-looking, he used his boldness, organizational skills, and personal and family capital to ensure the Saguenay region's entry into the industrial age. Circumstances did work in his favour; his success shows nevertheless that progress does not come by itself, without action and determination.

GASTON GAGNON

Material relating to Joseph-Dominique Guay in the ANQ-SLSJ includes the records of his baptism and marriage (CE201-S2, 15 avril 1866, and CE202-S5, 2 sept. 1889); entries in the minute-books of notaries T.-Z. Cloutier (CN201-S4), Jean Gagné (CN201-S5), Raymond Belleau (CN201-S9), and G.-A. Saint-Pierre (CN201-S10); the Coll. de la Soc. hist. du Saguenay (P2), S1, D161; and the Fonds Joseph-Dominique Guay (P161).

Arch. de la Ville de Chicoutimi, Qué., Reg. des délibérations du conseil de ville, 1895–1902, 1922–25. Arch. du Séminaire de Chicoutimi, Annales du séminaire de Chicoutimi, 1866–1925. *Alma mater* (Chicoutimi), 1916–25. *La Défense* (Chicoutimi), 1898–1905. *Le Journal* (Chicoutimi), 1899–1902. *Le Progrès du Saguenay* (Chicoutimi), 1887–1925, esp. 24 sept. 1925. *Le Protecteur du Saguenay* (Chicoutimi), 1896–98. *La Semaine commerciale* (Québec), 8 avril 1898. *Le Travailleur* (Chicoutimi), 1905–12. Gérard Bouchard, "Élites, entrepreneurship et conflits de pouvoir au Saguenay (1890–1920)," *Social Hist.* (Ottawa), 60 (1997): 267–99. *Directory*, counties of Chicoutimi and Lac-Saint-Jean, 1927. Raymond Laliberté, "Joseph-Dominique Guay (1866–1925)," *Saguenayensia* (Chicoutimi), 10 (1968): 89–92.

GUERIN, BELLELLE (baptized **Mary Ellen Gueren**), author and social activist; b. 24 Sept. 1849 in Montreal, eldest child and only daughter of Thomas Gueren and Mary Maguire; d. unmarried there 28 Jan. 1929.

The ancestors of Mary Ellen Gueren's father originated in France and immigrated to Ireland in the 1600s. In the 1830s Thomas came to Lower Canada from Clonbeg (Republic of Ireland) and settled in Montreal. He married Mary Maguire, also of Irish descent, in 1848. In addition to Mary Ellen, the couple had five sons, one of whom died in infancy. Initially a surveyor, Thomas became a civil engineer. In 1861, while her parents resided temporarily in Ottawa, Mary Ellen was enrolled as a student boarder at the Pensionnat Mont-Sainte-Marie established by the Congregation of Notre-Dame in Montreal. There, she pursued the French-language program in subjects such as music, art, grammar, elocution, and cooking. Little is known about her activities for a period of 20 years after she left the Pensionnat at age 17. She would later be described as having become an accomplished poet as well as the author of historical sketches of prominent women in New France, but no trace of these writings has been found. Perhaps during this time she adopted the name Bellelle Guerin, by which she would be known for the rest of her life.

In 1886 Bellelle took over the duties of raising the two young children of her brother James John Edmund after the death of his wife. The task occupied her for the next two decades. Her public career began in 1910, at age 61, with the election of James as mayor of Montreal. Bellelle acted as hostess for him, accompanied him to civic functions, and participated in such significant events as the International Eucharistic Congress, held in Montreal that year. This occasion was probably a catalytic moment for her. She was inspired by the suggestion of the visiting archbishop of Westminster, Francis Alphonsus Bourne, that she work to bring together the English-speaking Catholic women of Canada. About 1911 she published a tribute to a former mayor of Montreal, John Easton Mills, who had died in 1847 of typhus contracted while visiting the sick during an epidemic. "No greater hero is there," she said, "than he who sacrifices his life on the altar of duty for charity's sweet sake!" Her words presaged the motivating principle – the dedication of oneself to the welfare of others – that would soon mark the achievements for which she is best known.

By 1917 Bellelle had become president of the Catholic Women's Club, formerly the Ladies of Loyola Club. That June she wrote to Montreal's Roman Catholic archbishop, Paul Bruchési*, requesting his blessing for the formation of another Catholic women's group, a local chapter of the Catholic Women's League, an organization which already existed in Edmonton [see Katherine Angelina HUGHES], Boston, Chicago, and London, England. The Montreal CWL, Bellelle said, was meant to follow the model encouraged in England by Bourne and to unite English-speaking Catholic women for the purpose of "counsel, philanthropy and educational work in accordance with Catholic principles." Bruchési gave his "hearty approval," at the same time reminding Bellelle that "the French-speaking ladies of Montreal have a society with aims similar to the one you have in view, and which is known as the Fédération Nationale Saint-Jean-Baptiste [see Marie Lacoste*]." In November 1917 she called a meeting at which the Montreal branch of the CWL was founded, with herself as first president.

For the next three years Bellelle presided over the Montreal branch, which by 1920 would grow to 440 members. The league was organized into various departments: art and literature, civics and education, current events, home economics, music, the Loyola Convalescent Home (opened in 1914 by the Ladies of Loyola Club), the Community House, and the junior branch. At weekly afternoon meetings speakers addressed the women on such topics as "Canada's contribution to modern art," "Catholic women and the vote," and "Homemaking as a profession." Departments presented reports, the most crucial being that of the Loyola Convalescent Home, which in 1920–21 provided care for 125 patients at a daily cost of $1.10 per patient.

While the CWL continued to grow, Bellelle had been active in other organizations, particularly those connected with the war effort. She was the English-language editor of the bilingual *L'Aide à la France* (Montréal), published in 1918 to raise funds for soldiers and refugees in France and Belgium. In addition she worked with the Canadian Red Cross Society and the Canadian Patriotic Fund.

In June 1920, at Bellelle's instigation, a meeting was called in Montreal to consider the unification of branches of the CWL, which by then existed in most major cities across Canada. She was elected first dominion president of the national federation, the Catholic Women's League of Canada. The following year at the first national convention, held in Toronto, she expressed her belief in the future of the organization. "We may be said to be laying the cornerstone of an edifice that will arise fair and beautiful, strong and proud before the eyes of the world."

During her tenure as national president Bellelle saw the CWL become an important force for the integration of Catholic immigrants into the community, as well as an advocate for legislation affecting women, such as minimum wage acts and the Mothers' Allowance Act of Ontario. She promoted what she termed "Catholic feminism," which, according to her, called for a woman "to direct thought, to guard morals, and to carry her influence into the scale of justice whenever righteousness demands." Sometime after 1921 she changed the league's motto from *Laborare est orare* ("To labour is to pray") to the more inclusive and patriotic "For God and Canada." She also wrote English lyrics to "O Canada," composed in 1880 by Calixa Lavallée* with French lyrics by Adolphe-Basile Routhier*. As she later explained, "It was my earnest desire that we should all hear the same words, the same sentiments as well as the same beautiful melody as our French Canadian fellow citizens." Adopted by all league subdivisions and sung at the close of meetings, these lyrics were accepted by the Catholic committee of the Council of Public Instruction of the Province of Quebec in 1924, but they would not replace the more widely used version published by Robert Stanley Weir in 1908.

Bellelle's role in the CWL was recognized in 1922 at a meeting of the International Union of Catholic Women's Leagues in Rome, when she became the first woman in Canada to receive *La Croce Pro Ecclesia et Pontifice* from the papacy. She was also favoured with a letter praising her good works and with an apostolic benediction from the Vatican. By 1923 the national membership of the CWL had grown to 50,000. At the annual convention held in Halifax, Bellelle was made honorary president for life and Frances Lovering [MAHONY] was elected president.

Bellelle Guerin died in 1929 at age 79. That same year the Montreal branch of the CWL established an annual scholarship in her memory at Marianopolis College, a private college for women. She exemplified those women in Canadian society who acted on behalf of a vision based on faith, Catholic feminism, philanthropy, and patriotism.

MOLLY PULVER UNGAR and VICKY BACH

Guichon

Bellelle Guerin is the author of *John Easton Mills: the martyr mayor of Montreal* ([Montreal?, 1911?]).

ANQ-M, CE601-S51, 7 nov. 1848, 30 sept. 1849. Arch. de la Chancellerie de l'Archevêché de Montréal, 773.115 (Catholic Women's League of Canada/Plan national – Corr. générale, 1893–1925). Arch. de la Congrégation de Notre-Dame (Montréal), 312.560 (Mont-Sainte-Marie), nos.008, 161, 178–79, 257, 267. TRL, SC, Biog. files, vol.16: 719–21. *Canadian men and women of the time* (Morgan; 1898 and 1912). *"Except the Lord build the house . . .": a history of the Catholic Women's League of Canada, 1920–1990*, comp. V. J. Fall (Winnipeg, 1990). J. Hamelin *et al.*, *La presse québécoise*, vol.5. Ross Hamilton, *Prominent men of Canada, 1931–32* (Montreal, [1932?]). [D.-A. Lemire-Marsolais, dite Sainte-Henriette, et] Thérèse Lambert, dite Sainte-Marie-Médiatrice, *Histoire de la Congrégation de Notre-Dame* (11v. en 13 parus, Montréal, 1941–), 10. Sheila Ross, "'For God and Canada': the early years of the Catholic Women's League in Alberta," CCHA, *Hist. studies*, 62 (1996): 98–108. W*omen of Canada* (Montreal, 1930).

GUICHON, JOSEPH, rancher and entrepreneur; b. 22 Oct. 1843 in Chambéry, France, youngest of the five sons of Jean Guichon and Annette Veil; m. 11 Nov. 1878 Josephine Rey (d. 1929) in Keating, B.C., and they had four daughters and three sons; d. 30 April 1921 in Vancouver.

Joseph Guichon was a significant figure on the British Columbian ranching frontier in the 19th century. His considerable success in stock raising and, more important, in marshalling and consolidating land was overshadowed by the achievements of the neighbouring Douglas Lake Cattle Company (DLCC). Nevertheless, as an independent without large financial reserves Guichon was probably more typical of his ranching contemporaries in the interior of British Columbia.

Born in the Savoie region of southern France, Guichon left at the age of 14 for Paris, where he worked for a vintner or distiller. In 1862 he followed his brothers Charles, Laurent, and Pierre to the Cariboo goldfields of British Columbia via London, Liverpool, New York, Panama, and San Francisco. Travelling on a freighter carrying pioneers and sheep, he made his way from California to Portland, Oreg., and thence to the crown colonies of Vancouver Island and British Columbia, which he reached in March 1864. He hiked from the Fraser valley to Barkerville [*see* William Barker*], where he teamed up with three other prospectors. Despite a few lucrative strikes, Guichon's mining experience was a failure. He wintered in Victoria and returned to the interior in 1865, finding employment on the Ashcroft ranch managed by Charles Augustus SEMLIN and with a nearby Basque rancher named Minabarriet. The next year he hired on with Jean CAUX, known as Cataline, the French packer who provisioned the goldfields using the old Hudson's Bay Company brigade trails.

It was while wintering horses in the Nicola valley in 1866–67 that Guichon first became aware of the ranching potential of the district. His own small herd thrived on a homestead he obtained in the area of Savona's Ferry (Savona) in 1868. He subsequently took up land at Mamit Lake to the south where, along with his brother Laurent and a small number of francophones from both Quebec and France, he began to develop a farm. In the autumn of 1877 the geologist George Mercer Dawson* found Guichon growing "grain of all Sorts & potatoes with success," despite the high elevation. Around 1878 Laurent and Joseph relocated to Chapperon Lake, some 25 miles to the southeast, establishing their base of operations at the Home Ranch. Throughout the decade they each acquired additional properties in the valley.

Joseph married Josephine Rey in 1878 at Keating, near Victoria. Rey was also from Savoie, but the pair had met for the first time at Mamit Lake through mutual friends. Josephine arrived at the Home Ranch from Victoria in 1879 with their first-born, Lawrence Peter. A second Rey sister married Laurent that year, and the two families combined land resources in the Nicola valley area, forging a chain of grazing properties from Mamit Lake to Chapperon Lake.

Within a few years the Guichon ranch became centred to the east of Nicola Lake, on Lot 105 of Township 97 (which was surveyed in 1881 and where Joseph and his family moved in 1882). Its history was one of almost perpetual expansion, though not as rapid or as great as that of the DLCC. One of the first properties acquired by the syndicate that would become the DLCC was the Guichons' Chapperon ranch in 1883. The brothers divided the spoils so that Joseph retained some 1,400 head of livestock while Laurent retired to the coast with the cash proceeds. Joseph Guichon's headstart in ranching allowed him to take advantage before 1885 of the food demands of the construction crews on the Canadian Pacific Railway. His ranch was roughly equidistant from the divisional points at Kamloops to the north and Spences Bridge to the west. After 1885 he marketed his cattle mainly in the burgeoning town of Kamloops. Guichon's relationship with the DLCC was sometimes uneasy. Suffering from a lung ailment in the 1880s, he sought a cure in San Francisco; when he returned a short time later he found his 320 acres at nearby White Lake completely surrounded by the DLCC's new holdings. Not to be entirely outdone, Guichon gradually increased his own holdings in the Nicola valley and obtained leases to huge tracts of crown land. He expanded his spread to the north in the 1890s, acquired the Quilchena Ranch, hotel, and general store from Edward O'Rourke in 1904, and bought the Triangle Ranch in 1911 with $40,000 loaned to him by Joseph Blackbourne Greaves of the DLCC. By the time of his death the Guichon lands included nearly 40,000 acres of deeded land in addition to leases on over half a million acres of crown land.

Guichon repeatedly experimented with diversification. Around 1880 he obtained Percherons and Thoroughbreds which he raised for the North-West Mounted Police (and later the Royal Canadian Mounted Police) and the Vancouver police. He imported purebred Herefords from Quebec in 1894 to improve his cattle herd. In 1908 he replaced the old Quilchena roadhouse with the opulent Edwardian structure that still stands, using single Douglas fir studs that ran the full height of the structure. Later he incorporated fixtures rescued from the demolition of the first Hotel Vancouver in 1913. Additionally, he erected a new general store (the first stone building in the valley), raised sheep, and branched out into fox breeding. Not all of these efforts were successful. Like many local contemporaries, Guichon hoped that his hotel would both attract and profit from a CPR branch line. The railway never arrived, however, and in 1918 the hotel closed for more than 30 years, a victim of Prohibition and changing transportation routes and technologies.

Guichon retired in 1918, dividing his holdings among his seven children (according to French custom). Josephine and Joseph moved briefly to California before returning to British Columbia in 1919. Guichon died in Vancouver on 30 April 1921. Never at the centre of economic or political power, he had had close links to one of the largest agricultural businesses in North America (the DLCC) and connections with two provincial premiers (in addition to Semlin, he knew the family of George Anthony Walkem*). The lasting grandeur of his Quilchena operations is testimony to his personal ambition. The family name survives in the Gerard Guichon Ranch Limited and on the local map at Little Guichon Field, Mount Guichon, and the enormous, mineral-rich Guichon Batholith; Guichon Creek flows through what is idyllically known as "the Valley of Guichon."

JOHN DOUGLAS BELSHAW

Kamloops Museum and Arch. (Kamloops, B.C.), Vertical files, Guichon, Dr L. P. *Inland Sentinel* (Kamloops), 20 Jan. 1881, 15 April 1963. H. S. Cleasby, *The Nicola valley in review* ([Merritt, B.C., 1958]). G. M. Dawson, *The journals of George M. Dawson: British Columbia, 1875–1878*, ed. Douglas Cole and Bradley Lockner (2v., Vancouver, 1989), 2. Sandra Klein and Gerard Guichon, "The Guichon family," *Nicola Valley Hist. Quarterly* (Merritt), 11 (1993–94), no.1: 3–12. *Landmarks and branding irons: a guide to some historical ranches in the Nicola valley of British Columbia* (n.p., [1988?]). Nicola Valley Arch. Assoc., *Merritt & the Nicola valley: an illustrated history* (Merritt, 1989). N. G. Woolliams, *Cattle ranch: the story of the Douglas Lake Cattle Company* (Vancouver, 1979).

GWATKIN, Sir WILLOUGHBY GARNONS, army officer; b. 11 Aug. 1859 in Twickenham (London), England, son of Frederick Gwatkin, a solicitor, and Louisa Isabella Stapleton; m. 23 June 1888 Edith Campbell Rowley in Hurst, Lancashire, England; d. 2 Feb. 1925 in Twickenham.

Educated at Shrewsbury School, King's College, Cambridge, and the Royal Military College, Sandhurst, Willoughby Gwatkin was commissioned in the Manchester Regiment in 1882. He served as adjutant of his battalion from 1888 to 1892, was promoted captain in 1890, and passed the Staff College, Camberley, in 1895. In March 1899, after a short period on the staff in Egypt, he went to the War Office, where he served for a time in Colonel Percy Henry Noel Lake*'s celebrated mobilization section. In 1900 he became a major. On 31 Oct. 1903 he returned to regimental service in South Africa, a vital experience for an ambitious officer.

In 1905 Lake, now chief of the general staff (CGS) in Canada, summoned Gwatkin as director of operations and staff duties to develop plans and procedures for a militia that was becoming an army [*see* Sir Frederick William Borden*]. The following year Gwatkin brought over 250 disbanded veterans from his old regiment as volunteers for Canada's expanding Permanent Force. He remained Lake's right-hand man until 20 Oct. 1909. He then went back to England with the rank of colonel to serve as general staff officer, 1st grade, at Eastern Command.

In the summer of 1911 Gwatkin returned to Ottawa as general staff officer, mobilization. Though he believed that war with the United States was "very remote," he developed a plan that expanded militia strength in the vulnerable Canadian west. A European war was more likely, and Gwatkin prepared a proposal for an infantry division and a mounted brigade to serve in "a civilized country with a temperate climate." He also pressed discreetly for an interdepartmental committee to coordinate war planning. The committee, headed by Sir Joseph POPE, would barely complete Canada's War Book by the summer of 1914.

The Conservative victory in the federal election of 1911 gave Gwatkin a new political master, Colonel Samuel HUGHES, a militia officer with a pronounced distaste for British officers and regular soldiers. By the summer of 1913 Gwatkin's superior, Major-General Colin John Mackenzie, had fallen victim to Hughes. When the War Office tried to negotiate better terms for a successor, on 1 Nov. 1913 Hughes simply promoted Gwatkin. For fear of losing any rational influence in the Department of Militia and Defence, Gwatkin determined to get along with Hughes. More peremptory decisions by the minister soon followed. On the outbreak of war in August 1914, Hughes scrapped Gwatkin's mobilization plan, summoned volunteers to Valcartier, Que., and proceeded to organize his own contingent, choosing officers, organizing units, and making all the decisions himself. Then he

Gye

left for London to demand the right to command Canadians in the field. In his absence Gwatkin managed to use his plan to organize a second contingent for the Canadian Expeditionary Force.

Gwatkin appealed to be allowed to rejoin the British army; the War Office promoted him major-general (26 Feb. 1916) and left him in Ottawa. By working incredible hours Gwatkin kept militia headquarters functioning. His increasingly erratic minister was a bigger strain. Could military schools be reserved for would-be CEF officers? No, declared Hughes, everyone who applied must be trained. Hughes insisted on naming colonels and creating new battalions, a procedure that brought quick results but ultimately wasted men, money, and morale. Though responsible for recruiting and training hundreds of thousands of men, Gwatkin was kept in ignorance of overseas tactics and techniques. His wisest advice was that Canada's manpower commitments reflect the availability of volunteers – two or three divisions. Hughes insisted that Canadians would fill six or even eight divisions.

By mid 1916 an exhausted Gwatkin was close to the limit of his extraordinary stock of tact and patience. A confidant, Charles Frederick Hamilton*, believed that only the belated dismissal of Hughes prevented his resignation. Gwatkin soldiered on under Sir Albert Edward KEMP and the Unionist ministers of militia, Major-General Sydney Chilton Mewburn and Hugh Guthrie*. Having planned and managed, as best he could, the wartime expansion of the CEF, Gwatkin also had to oversee its repatriation, demobilization, and reorganization as a peacetime force. His plans, submitted in 1917, would have established a permanent army of 20,000, strong coastal garrisons, and universal military service. The British also held him responsible for the imperial operation in Siberia, where two British battalions came under Canadian command at Vladivostok. He retired as CGS in 1920 with a KCMG.

During the war Gwatkin had opposed a separate Canadian air force, but his encyclopedic mind foresaw the problems and possibilities of post-war aviation. Mindful of his ideas and his weariness, and having the CEF's leaders to employ, the government appointed him air vice-marshal and inspector-general of the Canadian Air Force. Gwatkin saw the impossibility of maintaining a real air force on a part-time "militia" basis, as the government proposed, and understood the potential of aviation as a servant of many branches of government. His prestige won the infant CAF its own ranks and uniforms. He joined Sir Arthur William Currie*; the inspector-general of the militia,

Major-General James Howden MacBrien*, his successor as CGS, and Sir Eugène Fiset*, the deputy minister of militia, in successfully urging that all of Canada's defence services be united in a single department of national defence. At the same time he fought the army to give the CAF the same independence as the post-war Royal Air Force had in Britain. As a final service to Canada, Gwatkin brought his knowledge of heraldry to the committee that designed the new Arms of Canada in 1919–20.

After his retirement in 1922 Gwatkin stayed on in Ottawa, intending to divide his time between Canada and England. He went back to London in the summer of 1924 when he was made colonel of his old regiment, but his friends there knew he was failing and they were not surprised that he died at St John's Hospital in Twickenham after being admitted for sciatica. His long wartime hours of work, often while he was suffering severe stomach pains, had shortened his life.

Outside Ottawa's narrow official circles, few knew Gwatkin. Those who recalled him, as did Charles Hamilton, remembered "a man of unusual cultivation and of wide intellectual interests," whose writing extended to Canadian ornithology, traces of the Basques in Canada, and anonymous contributions of Latin and macaronic verse to scholarly journals. Gwatkin's judgements, sometimes brutal, often shrewd, were rendered with a rare brevity and precision. In a city of myopic politics, he saw farther than most.

DESMOND MORTON

Erindale College, Univ. of Toronto (Mississauga, Ont.), Desmond Morton, Canadian Expeditionary Force research files, Donald MacKinnon papers, MacKinnon to parents, 14 Oct. 1915. Gazette (Montreal), 25 March 1922. Times (London), 27 June 1888, 4 Feb. 1925. Cyclopædia of Canadian biog. (Rose and Charlesworth), vol.3. G.B., War Office, The monthly army list (London), 1900–5. C. F. Hamilton, "Lieut.-General Sir Willoughby Gwatkin: an appreciation," Canadian Defence Quarterly (Ottawa), 2 (1924–25): 226–30. S. J. Harris, Canadian brass: the making of a professional army, 1860–1939 (Toronto, 1988). R. G. Haycock, Sam Hughes: the public career of a controversial Canadian, 1885–1916 (Waterloo, Ont., 1986). Desmond Morton, A peculiar kind of politics: Canada's overseas ministry in the First World War (Toronto, 1982); When your number's up: the Canadian soldier in the First World War (Toronto, 1993). Nicholson, CEF. The official history of the Royal Canadian Air Force (3v. to date, [Toronto and Ottawa], 1980–), 2 (W. A. B. Douglas, The creation of a national air force, 1986).

GYE, EMMA. See LAJEUNESSE

H

HALPERN, ISAAC, rag dealer, butcher, and Jewish religious leader; b. 10 July 1860 in Galicia, a province of the Austrian empire; m. before 1877 Fanny Singer, and they had three sons and three daughters; d. 7 July 1922 in Toronto.

Isaac Halpern came to Toronto from New York in 1888 or 1889, shortly after he had emigrated from Austria. If he was like other East European Jews arriving in Toronto in the 1880s and 1890s, he was close to being destitute. Collecting rags, which were used mostly for making paper, required little capital and offered a degree of independence for Jews wishing to observe holy days. In 1890 Halpern became a naturalized citizen and was joined by his family.

Although he was not an ordained rabbi, Halpern was highly learned in Jewish law and became the shochet (ritual slaughterer) for the Galician Jewish community in the city. Almost immediately upon his arrival, he had been among the founders of the Galician synagogue, Shomrai Shabboth. The congregation met first in a room on Richmond Street, then on Queen Street, and finally, in 1899, on Chestnut Street in St John's Ward, where the Halperns lived. Isaac acted as their spiritual leader until the arrival from Romania in 1901 of the Galician-born Joseph Weinreb, the first eastern European rabbi to serve in Toronto. Halpern was especially popular because he undertook to be the East Europeans' spokesman whenever the acculturated English Jews of Holy Blossom Temple became patronizing or attempted to speak for them. When the Duke and Duchess of Cornwall visited Toronto in 1901, he was a representative of the Jewish community at the formal greeting ceremony.

After 1901 Halpern appears to have given up his work as a butcher to focus on rabbinical duties at Chestnut Street Synagogue as well as at the Polish Jewish synagogue on nearby Elm Street. Religious and ethnic tensions existed among Toronto's Galician, Polish, Russian, and Lithuanian Jews; in 1906 the Galician congregation itself split over differing religious practices, largely according to place of origin in Galicia. The division even occasioned a riot. Halpern stayed with the congregation on Chestnut Street.

Several of his children continued to live at home after they had started work: Moses was a commercial traveller who with his brother Jacob, a butcher, started a soda-water manufactory, and Susan became a stenographer. Abraham, a student in 1913, would go on to become a prominent rabbi in the United States. Another daughter, Malca, a graduate in nursing from Mount Sinai Hospital in New York City, took charge about 1922 of the medical operations of the Federation of the Jewish Philanthropies in Toronto.

Isaac Halpern died of heart disease in July 1922 and was buried in the Jones Avenue Cemetery. The *Toronto Daily Star* described his passing as "a great loss to the Jewish community."

STEPHEN A. SPEISMAN

AO, RG 22-305, no.45794; RG 80-2-0-450, nos.2369, 3589. LAC, RG 31, C1, 1901, Toronto, Ward 3, div.10: 15 (mfm. at AO). *Evening Telegram* (Toronto), 8 July 1922. *Globe*, 8 July 1922. *Toronto Daily Star*, 8 July 1922. *Yiddisher Zhurnal/ Daily Hebrew Journal* (Toronto), 9 July 1922. *Directory*, Toronto, 1891–1922. Joseph Pope, *The tour of their royal highnesses the Duke and Duchess of Cornwall and York through the Dominion of Canada in the year 1901* (Ottawa, 1903). S. A. Speisman, *The Jews of Toronto: a history to 1937* (Toronto, 1979).

HAM, GEORGE HENRY, journalist, office holder, author, and railway publicity manager and lobbyist; b. 23 Aug. 1847 in Trent Port (Trenton), Upper Canada, son of John Vandal Ham and Eliza Anne Eleanor Clute; m. 24 Dec. 1870 Martha Helen Blow in Shannonville, Ont., and they had two daughters and three sons; d. 16 April 1926 in Montreal and was buried in Whitby, Ont.

George Ham was the son of a country doctor of United Empire Loyalist stock who gave up his medical practice to study law. In 1851 the Hams took up residence in Whitby, where George attended the Henry Street School and then the Whitby Grammar School. Dr Ham wanted his son to become a lawyer, but George baulked at the idea because, in his words, few of the lawyers he knew "had achieved high distinction and greatly accumulated wealth." Instead, he took up journalism, obtaining his first employment at the *Whitby Chronicle* in 1865. As a reporter, he showed considerable enterprise and talent. Failing health, however, prompted him to try his hand at a variety of other pursuits, one of which involved a stint as a sailor on schooners operated by his father-in-law in the early 1870s. In this, as in other lines of work, the gregarious Ham did not find what he was seeking. Nevertheless, the wide experience that he acquired would prove an invaluable asset.

After working briefly for newspapers in Guelph and Uxbridge and serving as a correspondent for the Toronto press, Ham set off in May 1875 for Winnipeg. There he obtained a job at the *Manitoba Free Press* as a compositor and began to write unsigned humorous articles. These attracted the attention of the paper's editor, William Fisher Luxton*, who, on learning the author's identity, promoted Ham to the editorial department. Ham soon rose to become city editor.

Hamilton

In late October 1879 Ham launched his own paper, the Winnipeg *Daily Tribune*. When it amalgamated a few months later with the *Daily Times*, another Winnipeg paper, he became managing editor of the joint publication. Ill health forced him to leave regular newspaper work in 1882 and to take up the less demanding occupation of registrar of deeds for Selkirk. He served in this capacity until about 1885. That year he acted as war correspondent for the *Toronto Daily Mail* during the North-West rebellion [*see* Louis Riel*]. Since he was invariably the first reporter to file his copy, his articles were the most widely quoted of any that originated from the front. In 1886 he was admitted to the Parliamentary Press Gallery in Ottawa as correspondent for the *Daily Times*. When parliament was in session, he would regularly attend the gallery's Saturday night banquets until their discontinuance in 1914. For 16 years he would sit beside Sir Wilfrid Laurier*, who became a great friend and admirer.

A pillar of the Winnipeg community, Ham had been elected to Winnipeg City Council as alderman for Ward 1 in 1883, 1884, and 1887. During the 1880s he also served as a school trustee and for some time between 1883 and 1885 as a commissioner under the McCarthy Act, the federal liquor licensing act. In 1888 Ham wrote and published his first book, *The new west*, a description of the region's potential. It and two subsequent works – *The flitting of the gods* (1906) and *Reminiscences of a raconteur* (1921) – are notable for the glimpses that they provide of his wit and philosophy.

It was not until he joined the Canadian Pacific Railway, however, that Ham found his true calling, that of "Ambassador-At-Large," one of several unofficial titles by which he became known. He was lured away from Winnipeg and his job with the *Manitoba Free Press*, which he had taken on in the late 1880s, by CPR president William Cornelius Van Horne*. On meeting Ham in July 1891, Van Horne hired him on the spot as a general passenger agent, to be based at CPR headquarters in Montreal. Two years later Ham was assigned the newly minted position of journalist – the inception of what would become known as the Canadian Pacific Press Bureau.

In his work for the CPR, Ham accompanied parties of newspaper reporters and other excursions across Canada, entertained special guests, spoke at public functions, and represented the company at expositions and fairs. He was particularly adept at the promotion of tourism and he became one of the most popular and best-known men in Canada. In 1904 he was elected honorary president of the newly founded Canadian Women's Press Club after he had arranged for the CPR to provide free transportation to 16 Canadian women journalists attending the Louisiana Purchase exposition. In later years he would quip that his job kept him "in umbrellas and valises [gifts from the groups he escorted]." He continued to fill publicity positions at the CPR's Montreal headquarters until 1913, when he was appointed special assistant to the president, acting as a lobbyist for the CPR. He remained with the railway until his death in 1926.

George Ham, with his large frame, trademark slouch hat, ill-fitting suit, and brilliant wit was one of the most colourful figures of his day. He was also a big-hearted, clever man, whose many talents found their fullest expression in the work that he did for the CPR. By just being himself he won many friends for the company and Canada and at the same time made his name synonymous with CPR tourism.

VALERIE KNOWLES

George Henry Ham is the author of: *The new west: extending from the Great Lakes across plain and mountain to the golden shores of the Pacific: wealth and growth, manufacturing and commercial interests, historical, statistical, biographical* (Winnipeg, 1888); *Our western heritage* ([Toronto, 1895?]); *The flitting of the gods: an authentic account of the great trek from Mount Olympus to the Canadian Rockies* ([Toronto?], 1906); *All's well, no blue ruin* (Montreal, [1914?]); *Reminiscences of a raconteur, between the '40s and the '20s* (Toronto, [1921]); and *The miracle man of Montreal* [biography of Alfred Bessette*, named Brother André] (Toronto, 1922).

AO, RG 22-264, no.376; RG 80-5-18, 17: 111. Canadian Pacific Arch. (Montreal), Newton MacTavish, "George Ham: sketch of a gentleman on whom the sun never sets" (typescript). *Gazette* (Montreal), 16, 19 April 1926. *Manitoba Free Press*, 17 April 1926. *Montreal Daily Star*, 16 April 1926. *Vancouver Daily Province*, 18 April 1926. *Canadian Railway and Marine World* (Toronto), May 1926. E. J. Hart, "See this world before the next," in *The CPR west: the iron road and the making of a nation*, ed. Hugh Dempsey (Vancouver and Toronto, 1984), 151–69; *The selling of Canada: the CPR and the beginnings of Canadian tourism* (Banff, Alta, 1983). *Standard dict. of Canadian biog.* (Roberts and Tunnell).

HAMILTON, DANIEL SALMON, Congregational minister and social worker; b. 8 March 1864 near Forest, Upper Canada, son of David Hamilton, a farmer, and Elizabeth Macpherson; m. 31 Dec. 1910 Edna Irene Walker, a teacher, in Odell, Middlesex County, Ont., and they had a daughter (who may have predeceased her father) and a son; d. 22 April 1929 in Winnipeg.

Daniel Salmon Hamilton was first educated at a public school in Forest and the Business College in Toronto. He then attended McGill University in Montreal. A well-known athlete, he played rugby with the McGill team, provincial champions. After obtaining a BA in 1892, he undertook theological studies at the Congregational College of Canada, also in Montreal, and graduated in 1894. He led his class easily, receiving the Barbour gold medal and the Calvary Church silver medal.

In 1894 and 1895 Hamilton served a Congregational church in Forest. Probably in the mid 1890s he undertook postgraduate studies in Christian sociology at the Chicago Theological Seminary with Graham Taylor. Under Taylor's tutelage he also did social settlement work. He then took up pastorates in Pointe-Saint-Charles (Montreal) (1898–1902) and London, Ont., at First Congregational Church (1902–8). He was particularly successful in London, where he developed a strong congregation. He became a member of the school board, served for four years as president of the London Temperance League, and was a councillor in the Royal Templars of Temperance. As a member of the local Charities Organization Board, he tried to develop an awareness among the public of its obligations toward the needy, but he did perhaps his best work as a member of the board of the Children's Aid Society.

Hamilton became a prominent figure in the councils of the Congregational Church and was president of the Western Association in Ontario. In favour of the proposed union of the Presbyterian, Methodist, and Congregational churches, he believed that amalgamation would increase the efficiency of church work. He served in 1906 as a member of the national joint committee on church union. In 1909 he went west to take charge of a church in Creelman, Sask., but finding the congregation divided on the issue of union, he left shortly afterwards. By June 1910 he had accepted a call as assistant at Central Congregational Church in Winnipeg. Active in the Congregational Church Extension Society of Western Canada, he had organized a congregation in Calgary in the spring of 1910. The following year he became superintendent of the society. Although he left this post and the ministry shortly afterwards, he would continue to be active in the church for many years. By 1925 he had served three terms as president of Central Church.

In 1911 Hamilton was appointed inspector of foster homes by Felix John Billiarde, the provincial superintendent of neglected and dependent children. Manitoba's initial child welfare legislation, the Children's Protection Act of 1898, had been established to protect children from abusive or incompetent parents and to keep society safe from delinquents. To the private orphanages and children's homes already existing the act had added the ostensibly private Children's Aid societies and a part-time, government-appointed superintendent, who provided services for children in regions not covered by these organizations. Billiarde, the first full-time superintendent, had been appointed early in 1908 in anticipation of the Juvenile Delinquents Act of that year; when the juvenile court was established, he was also made chief probation officer and he occasionally acted as judge. In 1910 he had been given powers to advise and supervise the Children's Aid societies and in 1912 he was authorized to oversee orphans' homes and asylums. Hamilton had been appointed to assist the overburdened superintendent. According to Billiarde, Hamilton's job required "a very large measure of discrimination and tact." The superintendent later reported that in selecting and visiting foster homes across the province, Hamilton travelled over 10,700 miles per year.

Hamilton succeeded Billiarde as superintendent in 1919. He made few changes in his predecessor's programs. The number of rural cases he investigated remained relatively constant (212 in 1921–22, 182 in 1922–23, and 232 in 1923–24) and the number of children brought into care increased (63, 92, and 93 respectively). The majority of these children were placed with Children's Aid societies; the rest were sent to various institutions. In addition he dealt with cases requiring the cooperation of other government bodies, oversaw relations with other child-care agencies, mediated disputes between agencies and vetted the quality of their work, investigated applications for adoption, assisted the general public, promoted the work of his office, collected statistics, and reported on all of the above to the government. Although he continued to hold the title of inspector, he gave no indication of visiting institutions or foster homes. He counted on public-spirited individuals to inform his office of any problems and sought to cultivate the recognition of local responsibility with regard to the needy.

The superintendent also had responsibilities under the Juvenile Delinquents Act, including occasionally acting as judge, cooperating with the chief school attendance officer, and helping to find employment for boys. In keeping with modern methods of juvenile work, Hamilton sought to "conserve rather than disrupt homes, and to reduce rather than increase institutional care," placing as many children as possible on probation rather than in jail.

In 1924 the government of John Bracken* proclaimed the Child Welfare Act. The original intention of the act, passed by the government of Tobias Crawford Norris* in 1922, had been to create a central department of public welfare coordinating all work in the province. The legislation, once amended and implemented under an economical government, combined the administration of child welfare with that of mothers' allowances and relegated child welfare programs to a position of secondary importance. Moreover, when the child welfare division of the new department was created in 1924, the former secretary of the Mothers' Allowance Commission, Alfred Percy Paget, was appointed director and Hamilton was given the subordinate position of chief inspector. He retired the following year.

Elected president of the Social Workers' Welfare Club of Winnipeg in 1925, Hamilton passed away in 1929 after an illness of three years. He was survived by his wife and son.

Hanrahan

During Daniel Salmon Hamilton's years of service, responsibility for the care of neglected children had continued to be gradually shifted from private charity to the provincial government. Much of the impetus for the transition came from government legislation, but some may be attributed to the work and enthusiasm of the first two superintendents. Hamilton had followed the pattern set down by his predecessor and extended his influence. Although he frequently lacked resources and the legislation under which he operated was not always adequate to meet the needs of the population, he had nonetheless helped to lay the foundations of the modern child welfare system in Manitoba.

LEN KAMINSKI

AO, RG 80-5-0-416, no.15348. *Winnipeg Tribune*, 2, 23 June 1910; 23 April 1929. Conference of the Joint Committee on Church Union, *Proceedings of the second conference . . . together with the reports of the sub-committees as adopted by the joint committee* (Toronto, 1906). "The Congregational churches of Canada: a statistical and historical summary," comp. Douglas Walkington (mimeograph, [Toronto], 1979; copy at UCC-C). *Directories*, London, Ont., 1902, 1908; Montreal, 1900–10. L. F. Hurl, "An analysis of social welfare policy: a case study of the development of child welfare policies and programmes in Manitoba, 1870–1924" (MSW thesis, Univ. of Man., Winnipeg, 1981); "The politics of child welfare in Manitoba, 1922–1924," *Manitoba Hist.* (Winnipeg), no.7 (spring 1984): 2–9. McGill Univ., *Annual calendar* (Montreal), 1889–92. Man., Dept. of Education, *Annual report* (Winnipeg), 1913–25. *Pioneers and prominent people of Manitoba*, ed. Walter McRaye (Winnipeg, 1925). P. T. Rooke and R. L. Schnell, *Discarding the asylum: from child rescue to the welfare state in English Canada (1800–1950)* (Lanham, Md, 1983). F. H. Schofield, *The story of Manitoba* (3v., Winnipeg, 1913). UCC, Conference of Manitoba, *Minutes* (n.p.), 1929.

HANRAHAN, FRANCIS, policeman; b. 21 Dec. 1870 in Fergusons Cove, N.S., son of Captain James Hanrahan, a pilot, and Mary Jane Smith; m. there 14 Sept. 1892 Mary Anne Hayes, and they had seven sons and four daughters who survived him; d. 30 March 1926 in Halifax.

Of Irish-Scottish parentage, Frank Hanrahan dedicated much of his life to the Halifax Police Department. In 1892, at the age of 21, he joined the force as a patrolman. He had previously worked as a fisherman in Halifax County but his marriage had no doubt caused him to seek a more stable form of employment. Hanrahan gradually rose through the hierarchy of the department. In 1906 he was promoted to the rank of detective and in 1907 he became deputy chief of police. After less than two years the department transferred him back to the detective branch, where he served as chief detective until 1917. That year he returned to the post of deputy chief and then in 1918 city council appointed him chief of police.

In his 32 years with the department, Hanrahan gained notoriety for his ability to solve crimes. The *Halifax Herald* claimed that his detective work "made his name known over the North American continent." On two occasions he worked closely with law enforcement officials in the United States and overseas to apprehend embezzlers, travelling to Colorado in 1909 and England in 1910 to escort suspects back to Halifax. His collaboration with Scotland Yard in the latter case bolstered his image at home to the point where he was regarded as among the "finest officials" in the city.

During his career Hanrahan oversaw 12 murder investigations, including that into the slaying of lawyer James Robinson Johnston*. Each resulted in the capture of the perpetrators and their subsequent convictions. Perhaps the most celebrated case involved the murder of Maud Delaney in August 1919. The police found her battered body lying in bed with her two-year-old son beside her. Hanrahan launched a province-wide search for her husband, John, the prime suspect in what the *Herald* called "one of the most brutal murders that has ever been committed in Nova Scotia." He eventually discovered Delaney hiding in a home in the city's south end. As chief, Hanrahan was actively involved in his department's ongoing efforts to maintain law and order in Halifax.

Hanrahan was deemed by many of his peers to be "one of [the] Best Chiefs We Have Had." His officers considered him a "strict disciplinarian" but fair, attributes that earned him the respect of most members of the department. Indeed, they greeted his resignation with regret. However, Hanrahan's tenure as chief was not without problems. Most Halifax police officers in the early part of the 20th century received inadequate training and pay. Although the chief outlined to all new recruits their responsibilities before sending them out on patrol, critics, including some patrolmen, argued that officers were ill-equipped to meet the challenges they faced. Similarly, patrolmen's wages did not match the professional stature sought by the department. In 1918 they earned between $750 and $850 per year depending on seniority. Next to their superior officers and some skilled workers, such as carpenters, they were underpaid, a fact that solidified their position as members of Halifax's working class.

Officers' low pay forced some to quit. In 1924, the year of Hanrahan's resignation, four men left to join the Canadian National Railways police. Hanrahan had lobbied the city council in 1918 for a substantial pay increase to attract "a class of men worthy of the city, fit for the duties of law enforcement and capable of coping with growing responsibilities," but with little success. As a result, morale on the force had plummeted. It was reported in 1924 that discontent over the city's "cutting" policy, designed to reduce the size of the force (and effectively ending some patrolmen's chances for promotion), permeated the rank and file.

Moreover, while Hanrahan was chief, the department, once "the pride of the Dominion," seemed to be in a state of disarray. Revelations to this effect emerged shortly after he stepped down in May. "All is not well with the police force in Halifax," cried the *Evening Mail*. While the paper did not impugn Hanrahan's integrity, or his career, it questioned "whether he has possessed the executive ability so necessary to the successful sustaining of the office of chief of police."

As Mayor John Murphy declared soon after Hanrahan had submitted his resignation, "I doubt if any department is in need of more careful study at the present time than the police." "There seems to be an impression," he continued, "that certain factions exist in the force and that this fact coupled with petty jealousies is tending to keep its efficiency below standard." Although not a direct criticism of Hanrahan, Murphy's words, combined with his call to reassess the department, cast doubt upon Hanrahan's abilities.

In one sense Murphy's observations were accurate. Hanrahan did not have an affinity for managerial duties. Instead, he concentrated on investigating crimes and overseeing the maintenance of law and order. Under his successors, the office of chief of police underwent a transformation, becoming more bureaucratized and more a public relations medium for the department than an agency representing the members of the force. This and other developments after 1924, such as the introduction of new technology, notably fingerprinting, led to the modernization and professionalization of the department.

When Hanrahan resigned he offered no reason for his decision, nor did he announce any immediate plans for his retirement. Although rumours began to circulate that he was to become "actively connected" with the soon-to-be established provincial police force, he never had the opportunity. In March 1926 he contracted influenza and bronchitis and died within a day. In addition to his 11 children, he was survived by 8 brothers and 3 sisters; his wife had predeceased him about 1915. Hanrahan's sudden death left many saddened at the loss of a "veteran" of the Halifax Police Department and a central figure in the city's efforts to preserve law and order.

MICHAEL BOUDREAU

NSARM, Churches, St Paul's Roman Catholic (Herring Cove), reg. of baptisms (mfm.); RG 32, M, Halifax County, no.362/1892. *Acadian Recorder* (Halifax), 31 March 1926. *Evening Echo* (Halifax), 28, 30 April 1924. *Evening Mail* (Halifax), 29 April 1924. *Halifax Herald*, 9 Jan. 1918; 16 Aug., 15 Oct. 1919; 29 April, 9 May 1924; 31 March 1926; 16 Jan. 1935. *Morning Chronicle* (Halifax), 2 May 1924, 31 March 1926. Michael Boudreau, "Crime and society in a city of order: Halifax, 1918–1935" (PHD thesis, Queen's Univ., Kingston, Ont., 1996). Halifax, City Council, *Annual report of the several departments of the civic government of Halifax, Nova Scotia* (Halifax), 1917/18, annual report of the chief of police. Peter McGahan, "Halifax Police Department, 1919–1924," Atlantic Institute of Criminology, *Report* (Halifax), no.14 (1989). Greg Marquis, *Policing Canada's century: a history of the Canadian Association of Chiefs of Police* (Toronto, 1993); "Working men in uniform: the early twentieth-century Toronto Police," *Social Hist.* (Ottawa), 20 (1987): 259–77.

HARDY, DAMAS. *See* LESAGE, DAMASE

HARRIS, JOHN WALTER, surveyor, tax assessor, JP, and author; b. 26 Feb. 1845 near Kemptville, Upper Canada, son of John Harris and Jane Jones; m. first 12 April 1876 Susan Elizabeth Smith (d. 1918) in Waltham, Iowa; they had no children who survived birth; m. secondly 15 June 1921 Annie Jane Millions, née Watson, in Winnipeg, Man.; they had no children; d. there 20 March 1926.

J. W. Harris's parents, John Harris and Jane Jones, were of Irish and Welsh descent respectively and were early settlers in Oxford Township, Upper Canada. After studies in civil engineering and surveying in Toronto, Harris secured his land surveyor's commission in 1866. He subsequently taught elementary school in Illinois and Iowa from 1868 to 1871. While in Iowa he obtained a first-grade teaching certificate and introduced a method of arithmetic he had devised known as the Lightning Calculator. During 1871–72 he was an investor in and operator of a lumber mill at Batchawana Bay, Ont., on the north shore of Lake Superior.

In mid July 1873 Harris accepted a post as a dominion surveyor in Manitoba. In this capacity he laid out Indian reserves north of Winnipeg, surveyed wood lots, unclaimed lands, and settlement areas along the Red and Assiniboine rivers, and planned the towns of Emerson and Selkirk. By the late 1870s, his practice had shifted from work for the federal government to work in the private sector and for the province.

Harris's association with the city of Winnipeg began on 10 Feb. 1879 when he was hired to prepare the annual tax assessment and collection rolls. He kept the job in 1880, lost it the next year after seeking a salary increase, but was rehired in early 1882 when two additional assessors were also appointed. From 18 Dec. 1882 to his retirement on 30 April 1916 he held the posts of assessment commissioner and city surveyor.

During Harris's tenure, the value of land, buildings, and other property multiplied many times over as Winnipeg grew in size and wealth. The responsibilities and resources of his office likewise expanded. Between 1893 and 1910 he implemented major changes in methods of assessing businesses. He also organized special block surveys in the early 1890s to ensure that the city's future development would be orderly and free of the errors that had caused so many property disputes in the past. He took every opportunity to consult with officials in eastern Canada and the United States on assessment matters, attended international conferences on taxation, and presented papers. Over time, he became a source of advice for others in the fields of assessment and urban planning.

Harris retained a private surveying practice into the early 1900s and actively furthered the profession's development. He was among the 11 surveyors who met in Winnipeg on 24 April 1874 to organize a provincial association, the first in Canada. The group was unable to gain legislative recognition in 1875, but a renewed effort in 1880–81 was successful. Harris was secretary of the Association of Provincial Land Surveyors from 1881 to early 1904 and its president in 1907 and 1916. He also was involved for more than 20 years on its board of examiners.

Ever entrepreneurial, Harris became a director of several local businesses and he frequently invested in mining ventures, land, rental properties, and agricultural enterprises, both in Canada and abroad. Some endeavours were profitable, others failed; none made him exceptionally wealthy, but he had a comfortable lifestyle. Among other activities, Harris became a justice of the peace in 1883. He supported the involvement of his first wife, Susan, in arts, social and animal welfare, hospital aid, and nursing organizations, but he was most prominent in sports and masonic circles. He planned many racecourses, laid out the Winnipeg Industrial Exhibition grounds, and often was a timer, judge, or referee at horse-racing, track, and other sporting events. Avidly interested in baseball, he helped run a local amateur league and a professional club, the Winnipeg Maroons. A long-time adherent of the Ancient Free and Accepted Masons, he served as a master and deputy master.

Harris's retirement from the city did not inaugurate a period of leisure. Instead, he plunged into the preparation of a manuscript on abbreviated methods of arithmetic, which he published in 1919. As part of his pension agreement with the city, he served on the Board of Valuation and Revision into the 1920s. He continued to participate in municipal tax reform and urban planning. He also managed his many investments and organized a library at the masonic temple.

Harris was physically imposing in presence, firm in his principles, demanding of himself and others, and always open to new ideas and challenges. His career and his business and personal relations had their share of controversy. He nonetheless garnered public praise and honours for his contributions to his profession and his community, including his formative role in the development of Winnipeg's civic administration.

DEBORAH M. LYON

John Walter Harris is the author of *The art of rapid compu-*

tation and simplification of the science of numbers . . . (Winnipeg, 1919).

AM, GR 393, I-2-6-17, file 17379; GR 549A, G4339, Y17: ff.526–27; MG 11, A20; MG 14, C74. City of Winnipeg, Arch. and records control branch, City Council, minutes, 1878–1911, 1914–16. *Manitoba Free Press*, 6, 14 May 1875; 28 Dec. 1878; 11, 13 Feb. 1879; 11, 25 Jan., 1–3, 15 Feb., 26 May, 23 June, 6 Sept., 6–7, 13 Dec. 1881; 24, 26, 31 Jan., 1, 14 Feb., 7 Nov., 19 Dec. 1882; 13 Dec. 1892; 15 Feb. 1902; 11, 13 Feb. 1908; 14, 16 Oct. 1915; 20, 25 Jan. 1916; 18 April, 5–14 Nov. 1917; 21, 23 Dec. 1918; 28 June 1919; 17 June 1921; 22, 24 March 1926. Edith Paterson, "The diary of J. W. Harris," *Winnipeg Free Press*, 1, 8 March 1969, *Leisure Magazine*; "J. W. Harris – land surveyor," *Winnipeg Free Press*, 22 Feb. 1969, *Leisure Magazine. Winnipeg Tribune*, 23 Aug. 1910; 13–14, 19 Oct. 1915; 20, 26 Dec. 1918; 21 June 1919; 16 June 1921; 22, 24 March 1926. George Bryce, *A history of Manitoba; its resources and people* (Toronto and Montreal, 1906). "J. W. Harris, M.L.S., D.L.S," *Canadian Surveyor* (Ottawa), 2 (1925–28), no.4: 15.

HARRIS, SAMUEL, fishing captain and businessman; b. 2 July 1850 in Grand Bank, Nfld, eldest son of Thomas Harris, a fisherman, and Eleanor Ann Foote, née Hickman; m. there first 6 Dec. 1875 Mary (Polly) Forsey (d. 1913), and they had four sons and six daughters (one son and three daughters died in infancy); m. there secondly 20 Sept. 1915 Harriet Marion Harding; they had no children; d. 20 April 1926 in Grand Bank.

In common with many boys of his age and social class in 19th-century Newfoundland, Samuel Harris received only the rudiments of an education before going to sea. At age 10 he boarded the *Billow*, a coaster engaged in the cod fishery belonging to his half-brother Morgan Foote. By age 22 he was captain of another of Foote's vessels, the *Jennie S. Foote*, a command he held for most of the 1870s.

By 1881 Harris had acquired fishing schooners of his own: the *Kitchener* and the *George C. Harris*. In the latter vessel he sailed in 1881 to the offshore banks, where foreign fleets had been operating for some time, and thus, it is claimed, ushered in the modern Newfoundland bank fishery. The venture proved to be lucrative, and the fishery soon expanded to include other vessel owners from Grand Bank and communities along Newfoundland's south coast.

After a ten-year partnership with his brother-in-law George Abraham Buffett in a retail outlet, in 1895 Harris established Samuel Harris Limited, a general merchandise and fish-exporting business. He remained a seagoing captain until 1898, after which he was content to manage his operations from shore. His business flourished: within the first 20 years of the new century branches had been formed in the nearby communities of Garnish and Lamaline and separate operations had been founded or purchased at Marystown, Change Islands, and Hermitage.

Harris acquired additional ships, vastly increasing

the amount of cod he could catch, cure, and export. He was also able to eliminate the St John's merchants, who usually bought the fish caught by outport fishermen. His ships returned from Europe and the West Indies with the holds full of salt for the next season, which further enlarged profit margins and reduced expenses. Many of these ships were tern (three-masted) schooners, built in Grand Bank especially for the deep-sea fishery. Harris owned and operated more than 60 schooners in the years between 1881 and 1926, 14 of which, in a grand show of patriotic fervour, were named for World War I military heroes.

In 1915 Harris turned much of the day-to-day operation of his business over to his eldest son, George. At that time the company was the largest and most prosperous fish business on the south coast, estimated to be worth $2,000,000; by 1919, as a result of the increased demand in European and Caribbean markets for salted cod during World War I, assets were valued at $4,000,000.

The end of the war brought a downturn in European markets. This, coupled with over-expansion during the war years, declining revenue (that Harris claimed was a direct consequence of new regulations governing the fishery introduced in 1920 by William Ford Coaker*, Newfoundland's minister of marine and fisheries), and the loss of at least eight schooners between 1919 and 1922, led to the company being placed in receivership in 1922 and declared bankrupt in 1923. It was taken over by a consortium of creditors, headed by the Bank of Nova Scotia, which restructured the firm as Samuel Harris Export Company Limited, with Harris as president and his son-in-law Percy Lee Carr as managing director.

A well-respected and influential figure in Grand Bank, Harris served for many years on its Board of Works, established in 1879 to direct improvements to the harbour. He gave liberally to the Methodist church, in both time and money, donating, for example, a large clock for the church's bell tower. He was committed to education, working hard to ensure that there were always teachers available for the community's school. Through the efforts of his first wife, Mary, who apparently originated the idea, he provided much of the money needed for the construction of Grand Bank's first hospital in 1900.

Samuel Harris was a generous community leader and benefactor, an astute businessman, and an advocate of hard work whose ability, industry, and sense of fair play were known throughout the island. He is recognized as the founder of the modern Newfoundland bank fishery, the economic mainstay of many of the island's fishing communities for the first half of the 20th century.

BERTRAM RIGGS

PANL, Parish records coll., Grand Bank Methodist Church (Grand Bank, Nfld), RBMB (photocopies). A. F. Buffett, "Grand Bank," Daily News (St John's), 23 June 1941. Evening Telegram (St John's), 22 April 1926. Bert Riggs, "Bound down from Grand Bank: Samuel Harris earned his nickname as the Father of the Bank Fishery," Telegram (St John's), 20 April 1999: 9. J. A. H. Carr, "Genealogical histories: the Samuel Harris family and the Percy Lee Carr family of Grand Bank, Newfoundland" (typescript, 1996; copy in the author's possession). Garfield Fizzard, Unto the sea: a history of Grand Bank ([Grand Bank], 1989). Charles Lench, "Grand Bank: an interesting outport," Newfoundland Quarterly (St John's), 12 (1912–13), no.3: 13–15. [R. C. Parsons], "Prominent figures from our recent past: Samuel Harris," Newfoundland Quarterly, 89 (1994–95), no.1: 34–35.

HARRIS, WILLIAM RICHARD, Roman Catholic priest and author; baptized 28 Feb. 1846 in Cork (Republic of Ireland), son of Richard Harris and Ellen Cotter; d. 5 March 1923 in Toronto.

William Richard Harris was always reticent about his family, even suppressing any mention that his sister Mary was Mother Jones, the famous American labour leader. The family may have settled in Toronto as early as 1853. Harris was first educated by the Brothers of the Christian Schools, and from 1860 to 1867 he took his classical studies at St Michael's College. Favoured by his bishop, John Joseph Lynch*, a fellow Irishman, he was sent to study philosophy and theology at the Collège de Sainte-Anne-de-la-Pocatière in Quebec. He taught English and belles-lettres at the college and earned a reputation as a formidable athlete.

In 1869 Lynch appointed Harris his secretary and took him to Rome for the opening of the first Vatican Council. There he completed his BD degree at the college of the Sacred Congregation of Propaganda and was ordained priest on 11 June 1870. The two men toured the continent before returning to Toronto. Harris would never forget his European experiences, which whetted his appetite for travel and adventure.

Harris subsequently served as assistant pastor and then pastor of St James in Colgan, Ont. (1870–75), rector of St Michael's Cathedral in Toronto (1875–76), and pastor of St John Chrysostom in Newmarket (1876–84). Energetic, ambitious, and committed to "square dealing" with his flock in financial matters, he was a building priest in an era when the erection of churches and schools was the summit of Catholic clerical success. At the same time he was thoroughly modern for his day. Believing that the prejudices transferred from the Old World had to die if Canada was to flourish as a nation, he made himself a leading example of ecumenical behaviour. In Newmarket he was an important patron of the local library and mechanics' institute, for in his view adults no less than their children should acquire an education to meet the demands of an emerging industrial world.

Harris's final parish appointment was as priest of St Catherine of Alexandria in St Catharines from 1884 to 1901, when he was also dean of St Catharines. His policies of openness in financial matters, church-related construction, and religious toleration were continued with even greater results. He printed two audited statements of the parish finances, erected a separate school with his own money, decorated and enlarged the church, collected funds to build the Canadian Lyceum and Athletic Club, which was open to all city athletes, and warned his parishioners, many of whom were Irish-born, not to be gulled into sectarian violence no matter the provocation. Responding quietly to one Presbyterian minister's attack on Catholicism, he wisely left it up to Presbyterians and the public at large to judge "the wisdom or expediency of a minister of the gospel of Christ scattering in the furrows of society the seeds of religious rancour and bitterness."

Before too long, Harris had acquired a public persona rare among the Catholic clergy of his day. He had transcended factionalism of all kinds, without sacrificing his own religious faith and Irish nationalism, in favour of a kind of public service that dovetailed with his own broader interests in continuing education and Irish Home Rule. In addition to being in great demand as a preacher, Harris was elected president of the Association of Mechanics' Institutes of Ontario for 1886, the first Catholic to serve in this capacity; delivered a paper to the Pan-American Congress of Religion and Education in Toronto in 1895; was invited to lecture before the St Catharines Historical Society; and in 1896 was one of the Canadian delegates at the Irish Race Convention in Dublin.

The St Catharines period witnessed the beginning of Harris's prolific writing career. That career, so central to his public reputation, would not have been possible without David Boyle*, head of the Canadian Institute Museum and Ontario's first professional archaeologist, whose excavation of a Neutral Indian site near Port Colborne in 1887 inspired Harris to begin writing about the natives and early French missionaries. His first scholarly article, "The Indian missions in western Canada" – western Canada, for Harris, meant Ontario – was published in 1892 and then expanded the next year into a book, *History of the early missions in western Canada* (Toronto). Eight articles followed by 1901, including "The Roman Catholic Church in Ontario," his contribution to John Castell HOPKINS's *Canada, an encyclopædia of the country,* as did his classic work of history and archaeology, *The Catholic Church in the Niagara peninsula, 1626–1895,* published in Toronto by William BRIGGS in 1895. This book earned him a place in the small but influential world of English Catholic letters and is the one book still in general circulation today. In recognition of his achievement, the University of Ottawa awarded him an honorary degree in 1896.

Just when Harris should have been enjoying the fruits of his success, a division took place in the parish over his handling of the finances. He had lost the trust of enough parishioners to ask Archbishop Denis O'Connor* for his unrestricted release from parish work, an exeat granted without question in April 1901. Harris soon set off on travels that were to last more than four years and take him to the Azores, the Caribbean, South and Central America, Mexico, and the southern United States. No idle tourist, he regularly contributed lengthy descriptions of his adventures to the *Toronto Daily Star.* These articles and other material were later compiled into three travel books of extraordinary quality: *Days and nights in the tropics* (Toronto, 1905), *By path and trail* (Chicago, 1908), and *Here and there in Mexico* (Chatham, Ont., [1920?]). They remain very readable, for Harris was a natural storyteller, obviously at ease with the world of the exotic and the bizarre.

By June 1905 Harris was living in Salt Lake City, where Bishop Lawrence Scanlan gave him the task of writing an official history of his diocese, published there in 1909 as *The Catholic Church in Utah.* Other undertakings included articles for *The Catholic encyclopedia,* regular contributions to the diocesan newspaper, and the publication of *By path and trail* and *Pioneers of the cross in Canada* (Toronto, 1912). When he was not writing, Harris was chaplain at Kearns St Ann's Orphanage and then at Judge Mercy Hospital.

In January 1913 Harris, who had returned to Canada, became chaplain of St John's Industrial School for Boys in Toronto. He also entered upon the most productive period in his life: he would write five books, 25 articles, and even some poetry. His reputation for religious tolerance in Protestant Toronto was almost legendary. He received two more honorary degrees, from the University of Toronto in 1916 and the Université Laval in 1920, and he was elected twice by acclamation as president of the Ontario Archaeological Association, in 1919 and 1920.

Harris's death on 5 March 1923 was given extensive coverage in all the Toronto newspapers. During his life his many books had received much positive publicity. Time, however, has not been kind to his oeuvre. Although his writing is strong in narrative and style, his lack of training in research, his uncritical acceptance of sources, and his fondness for superlatives combine to rank him as a gifted amateur. However, the sheer volume of his output and the beauty of much of his writing laid the foundation for later generations of scholars to write the history of Catholic Ontario.

MICHAEL POWER

Harris's first publication, "The Indian missions in western Canada," originally appeared in *Jubilee volume, 1842–1892:*

the archdiocese of Toronto and Archbishop Walsh, [ed. J. R. Teefy] (Toronto, 1892), 1–36. Bibliographies of his writings appear in R. J. Scollard, "Reverend William Richard Harris, 1846–1923," CCHA, *Study sessions,* no.41 (1974): 65–80, and Michael Power, "An introduction to the life and work of Dean Harris, 1847–1923," in *Catholics at the "Gathering Place": historical essays on the archdiocese of Toronto, 1841–1991,* ed. M. G. McGowan and B. P. Clarke (Toronto, 1993), 119–36. Two manuscripts by Harris, "Travel notes and autograph album" (1894–1902) and "Notes of foreign travel" (1900–7), are preserved in the Univ. of St Michael's College Library, Toronto.

Arch. of the Roman Catholic Archdiocese of Toronto, Clergy biog. and ministry database; SC, AB02.05(a–b), AB02.06. QUA, Lorne and Edith Pierce coll., Thomas O'Hagan, "Dean Harris" (1924). St Mary's [North Cathedral] (Cork, Republic of Ireland), RBMB, 28 Feb. 1846. Univ. of St Michael's College Arch., Records concerning W. R. Harris. *Canadian Freeman* (Toronto), 15 Sept. 1870. *Catholic Register* (Toronto), 23 June 1893. *Catholic Weekly Review* (Toronto), 17 Nov. 1888, 16 Feb. 1889, 17 May 1890. *Daily Mail and Empire,* 7 March 1923. *Evening Star* (St Catharines, Ont.), 1 June 1901, 29 Dec. 1904. *Globe,* 6 March 1923. *St. Catharines Standard,* 11 Feb. 1892, 17 Oct. 1896, 19 Jan. 1897, 29 Dec. 1910, 11 June 1920, 6 March 1923. *Toronto Daily Star,* 6 March 1923. *The Cathedral of St. Catherine of Alexandria 150th anniversary, 1832–1982* ([St Catharines, 1982]). *Cyclopædia of Canadian biog.* (Rose and Charlesworth), vol.2. *History and album of the Irish Race Convention, which met in Dublin the first three days of September, 1896 ...* (Dublin, [1897]). Gerald Killan, *David Boyle: from artisan to archaeologist* (Toronto, 1983). W. C. Noble, "An early O.A.S.," Ontario Archaeological Soc., *Arch Notes* (Toronto), 81 (1981), no.1: 9–10. Ontario Provincial Museum, *Annual archæological report* (Toronto), 1923: 140–41. *St Joseph Lilies* (Toronto), 11 (March 1923): 13. St Michael's College, *Year book* ([Toronto]), 14 (1923): 19.

HARRISS, CHARLES ALBERT EDWIN, musician, impresario, and educator; b. midnight 16–17 Dec. 1862 in London, England, son of Edwin Harriss, an organist, choir master, and concert manager, and Elizabeth Duff; m. 15 Sept. 1897 in Cobourg, Ont., Ella Frances Shoenberger, née Beatty (d. 1924), daughter of Dr John Beatty, a former professor at Victoria College there; they had no children; d. 31 July 1929 in Ottawa and was buried in Cobourg.

Charles Harriss was an ardent and outspoken British imperialist whose lifelong quest was to establish British musical excellence in Canada and in other parts of the empire. His persuasive personality, enthusiasm, organizational abilities, and varied musical talents, combined with his ambition, grandiose vision, and prominent social standing, ensured that the majority of his projects were realized.

Harriss first studied music with his father, and then was educated in the English cathedral tradition as an Ouseley scholar at St Michael's College, Tenbury, in the early or mid 1870s. After his initial church appointment as choir director at St John's in Wrexham, Wales, he was apprenticed with Frederick Davis

of Reading, near London, before becoming parish organist in Welshpool, Wales, in 1880. When Susan Agnes Bernard*, wife of Canadian prime minister Sir John A. Macdonald* asked the prominent British musician Sir Frederick Arthur Gore Ouseley to secure an organist for the Church of St Alban the Martyr in Ottawa, Harriss auditioned and obtained the position. He arrived in Ottawa in December 1882. He moved to Montreal the next year to become organist and choir master at Christ Church Cathedral, where he remained until 1886, when he succeeded his father in the same positions at the Church of St James the Apostle, also in Montreal; he would hold the posts to 1894. During his father's sojourn in Montreal from 1883 to 1885, the Harrisses gave joint recitals, taught privately, conducted choral groups, and managed concerts.

From around 1890 to 1898 Harriss was the Canadian agent for Nicholas Vert, a leading European impresario based in London. In this capacity he organized North American tours for such artists as Sir Charles Santley in 1891 and Emma Albani [LAJEUNESSE] in 1896. During this period he composed mainly religious and salon pieces which were published by leading Canadian, English, and American companies, and two major works for solo, chorus, and orchestra, namely *Daniel before the king,* a dramatic sacred cantata, and *Torquil,* based on a Scandinavian legend. The first work, written in 1884 and published by the American firm G. Schirmer in 1890, was premiered on 18 April 1890 by the Montreal Philharmonic Society conducted by Guillaume Couture*. *Torquil,* published as a piano-vocal score by the Toronto firm Whaley, Royce and Company Limited in 1896, was first performed on 22 May 1900 by Frederick Herbert Torrington*'s Festival Chorus, accompanied by the Boston Festival Orchestra, at Toronto's Massey Music Hall. His larger choral works show the influences of the oratorio tradition and of such composers as Mendelssohn and Wagner.

Harriss's focus on the production of large-scale works was facilitated by his marriage in 1897 to Ella Beatty, the widow of wealthy Ohio manufacturer George K. Shoenberger, who helped to obtain patronage and provide the necessary capital for his many ventures. In 1900 she bought Earnscliffe, Lady Macdonald's Ottawa residence, for $15,000. Notwithstanding her lavish renovation of the house, she maintained the Macdonalds' atmosphere in a number of rooms. She directed several musical associations in Canada. Their many prominent friends included Lady Minto, wife of Governor General Lord Minto [Elliot*]. Lady Minto regularly corresponded with Charles Harriss for over 20 years and he dedicated his *Festival mass* to her. This work was premiered at Notre-Dame Basilica in Ottawa in 1902 and included the 16-year-old Éva Gauthier* as one of the soloists.

In 1903 Harriss was appointed by McGill University honorary director of a system of musical examination centres which had been set up by McGill in conjunction with the Associated Board of the Royal Schools of Music in London. This appointment led to his being chosen the following year as the first director of the McGill Conservatorium of Music; he would hold the post to 1907. Harriss wanted to establish British standards of music education and examinations in Canada. His main objective was to promote musical reciprocity within the empire. Many Canadian music teachers considered the introduction of the associated board a one-sided affair, but its examinations were successfully implemented in spite of their protest.

Harriss's mission carried over into other activities, such as organizing concerts and conducting. He planned the Cycle of Music Festivals of the Dominion of Canada, featuring a British choral and orchestral repertoire conducted by Sir Alexander Campbell Mackenzie and performed by choruses in 15 cities across Canada. In 1905, with the sponsorship of Mackenzie, he became the first colonial musician to receive the Lambeth degree D.MUS., conferred by the archbishop of Canterbury. The next year he set up a Montreal choir, the Philharmonic Union, which performed his "choric idyll" *Pan* with the Pittsburgh Orchestra and in 1907 premiered his ballad *The sands of Dee*. During these years he extended his musical reciprocity to England, starting in 1906 with the Canadian Music Festival in London, which featured a performance of *Pan* with Pauline Donalda [Lightstone*], and continuing in 1907 with the Empire Day Concerts there. In 1908, also in London, Harriss conducted his second mass, *Coronation mass Edward VII*, which had premiered in Saint John in 1903; it was performed by the Sheffield Choir and the London Symphony Orchestra, with Gauthier again as one of the soloists. The same year he organized the Canadian tours of Sir John Frederick Bridge and of the Sheffield Choir under Henry Coward. His last Canadian tour featured His Majesty's Scots Guard Band in 1922. In 1909 he had set up the 4,500-voice Imperial Choir in London; it formed the basis of the mammoth 10,000-voice choir which performed at the Empire Day Concert in 1911 and as part of the peace celebrations at Hyde Park in 1919. He prepared the Musical Festival of the Empire, a musical tour of Australia, New Zealand, South Africa, Canada, and the United States which was held in 1911. Two years later he took 2,000 members of the Imperial Choir to perform at the International Exhibition in Ghent, Belgium. His last major undertaking was as music director of the British Empire Exhibition in Wembley (London) in 1924. He was offered a knighthood for his contribution to the empire, an honour which he surprisingly refused.

This indefatigable champion of closer cultural ties with Britain was described by the English musical scholar Percy Alfred Scholes as "a veritable musical Napoleon – always engaged in a tonal campaign somewhere at earth's service." Harriss received regular coverage of his compositions, recitals, and projects in the press and he used his extravagantly vocal public persona to create, organize, and invigorate musical institutions and concert activity across Canada and abroad. He successfully composed in the idiom of his time. Although his works did not survive him, they were published and probably performed to a greater extent than those of most of his Canadian contemporaries.

NADIA TURBIDE

[About half of Charles Albert Edwin Harriss's 125 known compositions have not been located, including two of his major works: *The admiral*, a comic opera composed around 1902, and *Canadian fantasie* for chorus and orchestra, which premiered in Ottawa in 1904. A detailed catalogue of Harriss's works can be found in the appendix of the author's MA thesis. The bulk of his manuscript scores, along with correspondence, the first chapter of a typescript autobiography, programs, and other materials, are held in the Harriss coll. at MUA, MG 3021. The LAC holds 13 volumes containing compositions, printed programs, scrapbooks, and miscellaneous items (MUS 11). The remainder of the collection in the LAC (MG 30, D15) includes correspondence, programs, and pamphlets. The most extensive analysis of Harriss's compositions appears in John Beckwith, "Choral music in Montreal circa 1900: three composers," *Univ. of Toronto Quarterly*, 63 (1994): 504–17. N.T.]

The Canadian musical heritage, ed. Elaine Keillor *et al.* (23v. in 18 to date, Ottawa, 1983–   ). "Dr. Charles Harriss," *Musical Times* (London), 50 (1909): 225–29. *Encyclopedia of music in Canada* (Kallmann *et al.*). A. C. Mackenzie, *A musician's narrative* (London, [1927]). *Musical Canada* (Toronto), November 1908. *The musical red book of Montreal . . .* , ed. B. K. Sandwell (Montreal, 1907). Tancrède Trudel, "Charles A. E. Harriss," *Le Canada artistique* (Montréal), 1, no.12 (décembre 1890): 193–94. Nadia Turbide, "Charles Albert Edwin Harriss: the McGill years" (MA thesis, McGill Univ. (Montreal), 1976).

HARTY, WILLIAM, businessman and politician; b. 8 March 1847 in Biddulph Township, Upper Canada, son of John Harty and Elizabeth Heenan; m. 1870 Catherine Mary Bermingham (d. 1889) of Ottawa, and they had two sons and a daughter; d. 1 April 1929 in Kingston, Ont.

The son of immigrants from Tipperary (Republic of Ireland), William Harty was educated in Kingston by the Roman Catholic Church, at first by the Brothers of the Christian Schools and then at Regiopolis College. While in his teens he joined the wholesale grocery firm there of his uncle James Harty and in 1868, after his uncle's death, he took it over. A member of the local Board of Trade, he rose to become its president in 1873. The following year he attended the meeting at Saint John of the Dominion Board of Trade, which rejected the proposals of George Brown*, a leading Reformer, for a reciprocity agreement with the United

States. The experience nonetheless confirmed Harty's affiliation with the Liberal party.

Success in the grocery business led Harty into other enterprises. From 1875 to 1879 he was a director and executive member of the Kingston and Pembroke Railway. Perhaps because of his success in this venture, he left the grocery trade in 1881 and helped set up the Kingston Charcoal and Iron Company. With other Kingstonians, he also gained control of the Canadian Locomotive and Engine Company. This business, which had originated as a foundry on Kingston's waterfront [see James Morton*], had moved its offices to Montreal and fallen on hard times. Harty's group included MPs George Airey Kirkpatrick* and Sir Richard John Cartwright* and two former mayors, John McKelvey and John Breden. They brought the offices back to Kingston, installed Harty as managing director, and operated the factory successfully for seven years before selling it to a Scottish firm, Dubs and Company. At this point Harty left and accepted a position as the general manager in Canada for the Equitable Life Assurance Society of the United States.

In his absence Canadian Locomotive again declined. The problems experienced by Dubs and Company eventually led the Bank of Montreal, its largest creditor, to have the courts appoint A. F. Riddell and Kennet William Blackwell as receivers. In 1900 they selected the offer of a group led by Harty, now an MLA, to take control and reopen the works. He joined with his brother-in-law Cornelius Bermingham and Michael John Haney, a Toronto engineer and fellow Liberal, to purchase the company for $60,000. An important part of this agreement was their commitment to upgrade the factory, which had fallen behind the industry standard. The resulting technical improvements and Harty's political connections brought new contracts, notably from the Intercolonial Railway and rail barons Donald Mann* and William MACKENZIE, and renewed the company's position as one of Kingston's largest employers. The partisan *Daily British Whig* trumpeted the news on 6 Nov. 1900 as a Liberal triumph: "Secured the works. Honourable William Harty is now in possession. Orders for 32 engines. Liberals only friend of working man after all." On 7 Feb. 1901 the firm was reincorporated as the Canadian Locomotive Company Limited. That year it faced a strike by the local machinists' union over the issue of ironworkers being assigned machinists' work. The dispute would drag on until 1905 but the use of replacement workers meant that production continued unabated.

Although Harty and his associates had great success in restoring the works to prominence, their relationship was strained by Harty's refusal as president to consider offers to participate by American investors and his determination to keep the company in Kingston. The friction between Harty and Bermingham was not resolved, and Harty never spoke to his brother-in-law again. In the aftermath, Haney and Bermingham opened a larger locomotive factory in Montreal, while retaining their positions in the Kingston firm. In 1911 Harty, though commercially well connected, lost control of Canadian Locomotive to a group of Toronto speculators led by Edward Æmilius Jarvis, and shortly thereafter he resigned. His sons would remain with the firm, each becoming president, John Joseph (Jock) in 1917 and William in 1924.

In addition to his career as an industrialist, Harty was extremely active in Kingston's politics. He had been elected as an alderman in 1879 and sat on the city's finance committee. A president of the local Reform Association, in 1892 he was elected to the Ontario legislature. His defeat in 1894 by one vote was overturned and he won the subsequent by-election in 1895, thanks in part to the intervention of Premier Sir Oliver Mowat*. This election too was overturned but in October 1895 Harty was returned by acclamation. In May 1894, though not well known throughout Ontario, he had been appointed commissioner of public works, largely to replace Christopher Finlay Fraser* as the Roman Catholic representative in the cabinet. Although he gave up this post in October 1899, he continued as a minister without portfolio and retained his seat until January 1902, when he moved to the federal House of Commons following a by-election in Kingston. A member of the manufacturers' deputation that in January 1911 opposed the government's adoption of reciprocity, he did not run in the reciprocity election in September. His view of politics is best revealed in his correspondence with Prime Minister Sir Wilfrid Laurier*. Much of the exchange consists of requests from Harty for financial aid for his locomotive company and continued tariff protection, and appeals from Laurier for financial and political support.

Following Harty's retirement in 1911, he remained publicly active as a trustee of Queen's University in Kingston and as chairman of the board of its School of Mining and Agriculture. His interest in education had earlier been reflected by the active role he and his wife had taken in the creation of the Women's Medical College at Queen's in 1883 [see Jenny Kidd GOWANLOCK]. In 1892 Harty had also accepted appointment to the senate of the University of Toronto. His later years were darkened by the loss of his elder son, John, of pneumonia in 1919. William Jr and his sister, Kathleen, survived their father, who died in 1929, leaving an estate worth more than a million dollars.

William Harty's life had been wrapped up in Kingston. He told electoral supporters in 1908 that his desire to reacquire Canadian Locomotive had been both personal and altruistic. At the time of the purchase he telegraphed Kingston that "in endeavoring to help myself I rejoice in being able to do something for my old employees of the Locomotive Works and for

Kingston." This sentiment neatly summarizes his approach to business and politics: the Limestone City brought him enormous success and he attempted to return the favour.

ANDREW THOMSON

AO, RG 22-159, no.4215. LAC, MG 26, G, Harty to Laurier, 11 Dec. 1903; Laurier to Harty, 14 Dec. 1903. *Daily British Whig* (Kingston, Ont.), 6 Nov. 1900. *Kingston Whig-Standard,* 1 April 1929. Katherine Bermingham Macklem, *The Berminghams of Kingston* (Kingston, 1977). *Canadian men and women of the time* (Morgan; 1912). *Cyclopædia of Canadian biog.* (Rose and Charlesworth), vol.1. Fritz Lehmann, "The Canadian Locomotive Company's response to three crises in the post–World War II era" (paper presented at the annual CHA meeting, Kingston, 1991). D. R. McQueen and W. D. Thomson, *Constructed in Kingston: a history of the Canadian Locomotive companies, 1854–1969* (Kingston, 2000). George Richardson, "The Canadian Locomotive Company," in *To preserve & defend: essays on Kingston in the nineteenth century,* ed. G. [J. J.] Tulchinsky (Montreal and London, 1976), 157–67. *Standard dict. of Canadian biog.* (Roberts and Tunnell). A. A. Travill, *Medicine at Queen's, 1854–1920: a peculiarly happy relationship* ([Kingston, 1988]).

HARVIE, ELIZA JANE. *See* CREIGHTON

HATHEWAY, WARREN FRANKLIN, businessman, social activist, politician, and author; b. 16 Sept. 1850 in Saint John, son of Thomas Gilbert Hatheway and Harriet E. Bates; m. first 28 Feb. 1880 Elizabeth Elsom Green in Dedham, Mass.; m. secondly 19 Feb. 1883 Ella Bertha Marven in Saint John, and they had two daughters; d. there 29 Oct. 1923.

The family of W. Frank Hatheway was well connected in the social, commercial, and political circles of New Brunswick. His paternal great-grandfather had commanded loyalist troops in the American revolution, and his grandfather Calvin Luther Hatheway* wrote a history of the province published in 1846. A cousin, George Luther Hatheway*, served as premier during 1871–72. The death of Hatheway's father in 1855 and his brother Charles E. in 1863 had stripped the family of its gentility, however. "We suddenly realized that we were quite poor . . . and [I] at once determined to go to work," he recalled. At 13 he left school and found employment as a clerk in the office of the Union Line steamers, managed in part by his brother Thomas, and from 1868 with the wholesale provisions firm of William Wallace Turnbull*, a relative by marriage, where he rose to become bookkeeper. These early experiences gave Hatheway an appreciation for the lot of the labouring classes as well as the skills needed to establish his own grocery business.

Hatheway embarked on a vigorous program of intellectual improvement during his time with Turnbull, studying the classical Latin authors to improve his speaking style, and learning French, Spanish, and German. He began to write for the press, too, submitting translations of Chateaubriand to the Saint John periodical *Stewart's Literary Quarterly Magazine* [*see* George Stewart*]. Verse under the pseudonyms Carey and Philip and articles signed O. M. also began appearing in the Saint John *Globe*. Together with some other young men he formed the Round Table Club, a forerunner of the Fortnightly Club, to discuss literary topics. Hatheway also learned guitar during this period and sang at Germain Street Baptist Church, though he was a lifelong member of St John's (Stone) Anglican Church. These activities were complemented by membership in the 62nd (Saint John) Battalion of Infantry, in which he attained the rank of captain in 1872.

The fire that devastated the city in June 1877 marked the turning point in Hatheway's career. He left Turnbull before the end of the year and established his own grocery firm on 1 Jan. 1878 with James Spurr Harding. It flourished, carrying sugar, flour, fish, and a variety of teas (the firm was one of the first in Canada to import tea directly from China). When the partnership was dissolved in 1887, the business was worth over $20,000. Hatheway continued on his own and by 1895 employed four salespeople to travel about the Maritimes. From 1887 he enabled his employees to share in the profits of his company, and when he made it a limited liability firm in 1908 he allowed several of them to become part-owners.

Hatheway's political sensibilities also awakened after 1877. "The new Canada appealed to my imagination," he stated, and moved perhaps as much by personal respect for his friend Samuel Leonard Tilley* as by national and economic reasons, he embraced the protectionist policy of Sir John A. Macdonald*'s Conservative government as a means to improve the welfare of workers. Though he would remain essentially a Conservative, he did not let party affiliation stand in the way of personal beliefs. The support given by Sir Charles Tupper*'s administration to Halifax over Saint John as the terminus of a recently inaugurated fast Atlantic mail service prompted Hatheway to break with the Conservatives in 1896. In the years before he returned to the Conservative fold in 1901 he discovered the freedom to advocate his socialist ideas.

The pamphlet *Poorhouse and palace* (1900), for example, advocated a system of graduated taxation exempting those earning less than $800 a year (Hatheway subsequently reduced the amount to $600 and then $400 in order to gain his point). He further demonstrated his socialist tendencies by spearheading the formation of the Fabian League in Saint John in April 1901. The organization encouraged the discussion of economic problems, especially issues concerning the working population. It was not a political body, but a card published later that year outlines a platform consistent with Hatheway's political agenda.

The Fabians sought public ownership of utilities and services, as well as of natural resources that could be monopolized by private interests. The league also established a board of arbitration to negotiate between employees and employers. Hatheway would continue to support Fabian aims as an MLA after 1908.

Hatheway's increasing political activity had led him to run in the provincial election of 1903 as a labour candidate for Saint John City. Unsuccessful, he "saw political expedience in playing the game more conventionally," according to G. H. Allaby, and in 1908 he stood as an official opposition (Conservative) candidate with labour backing, a strategy that took him to Fredericton. There he fought, largely without success, for a number of radical causes. Despite stiff opposition from members of his own party, now in power under John Douglas Hazen*, he was able to amend William PUGSLEY's Workmen's Compensation for Injuries Act of 1903 to secure the principle that employers were responsible for injuries incurred through the negligence or incompetence of fellow workers. The points he conceded to achieve this result cost him support among unionists and reformers until 1910 when he successfully pressed for a government bureau to monitor labour conditions throughout the province. Two years later he was instrumental in the passage of government amendments that brought the workmen's compensation legislation up to the standard he had campaigned for in 1908. These successes eclipse the failure of equally significant causes such as the enfranchisement of widows and unmarried women owning property or having an annual income of at least $400. His wife Ella, a suffragist and a founding member of the Women's Enfranchisement Association in Saint John [*see* Emma Sophia Skinner*], encouraged him in the latter campaign. The two also worked to establish the first kindergarten in Saint John.

Hatheway was ultimately overtaken by the acceptance among reform-minded elements of the population of his own radical ideas, a process evident by 1910. Following his decision not to run in the 1912 election – possibly because the government of James Kidd FLEMMING had denied him the office of first commissioner of labour – he continued to write on a variety of subjects that encouraged readers to know themselves and the world about them. He sought an economic, political, and social order that would make Canada strong. Though his books were rarely acknowledged in New Brunswick, they attracted some critical acclaim nationally. A deed of 83 acres of land to the labourers of Saint John in 1917 was a practical expression of the love of nature and commitment to workers evinced in his writing. Hatheway died of a stroke six years later.

PETER J. MITHAM

Warren Franklin Hatheway's publications include a poetry chapbook published under the pseudonym R. Belmont as *God and the doubter; At Partridge Island; Sunset on Nerepis River; and other verses* ([Saint John, 1896]), as well as several pamphlets and books issued under his own name: *Poorhouse and palace: a plea for a better distribution of wealth* [Saint John, 1900]; *Canadian nationality; The cry of labor; and other essays* (Toronto, 1906); *Injustice to New Brunswick: a few facts for thoughtful, impartial, liberal Liberals* (n.p., [c. 1908]; copy in the N.B. Museum, Saint John); *The reciprocity agreement: its effect on New Brunswick* ([Saint John], 1911); *Mr. W. Frank Hatheway's speech in support of the more complete education for the mechanic and farmer, given in the House of Assembly, Fredericton, N.B., March 19th, 1912* ([n.p., 1912]); *Why France lost Canada, and other essays and poems* (Toronto, 1915); *Trade after the war: a resumé of trade conditions in France, Italy and Great Britain before 1915, with suggestions as to expansion of Canada's trade after the war* ([Saint John, 1917]); and *Labor's just and reasonable demands: . . . should not these demands be granted? A review of what Australia and other countries have done, and what Canada must do* (Saint John, 1919). A selection of his writings edited by James Keith Chapman has been published under the title *Hair from a black stallion's tail* (Fredericton, 1986), and reissued, without the frontispiece photograph of Hatheway, as *Frank Hatheway's highways & byways: tales from 19th century wanderings in New Brunswick, the Gaspé, and Cape Breton* (Fredericton, 1986). Hatheway also contributed articles to several periodicals, including *Atlantic Monthly* (Boston), *Canadian Magazine*, *Contemporary Rev.* (London and New York), *Empire Rev.* (London), and *New England Magazine* (Boston).

Manuscript and archival material relating to Hatheway includes a typescript autobiography in A Case 39 at the Univ. of N.B. Library, Arch. and Special Coll. Dept., Fredericton, as well as a file of documents regarding his militia involvement and some biographical material at the N.B. Museum (Hatheway, W. F., CB DOC). Hatheway's marriage to Elizabeth Elsom Green is recorded in Saint John newspapers and the International geneal. index of the Church of Jesus Christ of Latter-day Saints, Geneal. Soc., but no further reference to her has been found.

An excellent obituary and editorial comment appeared in the *Saint John Globe*, 30 Oct. 1923: 2, 4. The other main biographical sources are Hatheway's entry in *Canadian men and women of the time* (Morgan; 1912) and Chapman's sketch in *Hair from a black stallion's tail*, 41–50. A critical consideration of Hatheway's work appears in G. H. Allaby, "New Brunswick prophets of radicalism, 1890–1914" (MA thesis, Univ. of N.B., 1972), 86–123.

HAUTERIVES. *See* GRANDSAIGNES

HAWKE, JOHN THOMAS, printer, journalist, and newspaper publisher; b. 30 April 1854 in Plymouth, England, son of John Peter Hawke, a cartman, and Mary Ann Harvey; m. October 1875 Della Thornton of Aylmer, Ont., and they had three daughters; d. 17 Feb. 1922 in Moncton, N.B.

Of Cornish descent, John Thomas Hawke claimed kinship with Admiral Sir Edward Hawke, hero of the battle of Quiberon Bay, a decisive British victory in

Hawke

the Seven Years' War, but this connection has not been substantiated. Little is known about his early life or where he learned the craft of typesetting, though he is said to have become a printer in Torquay. After emigrating to the United States in 1873, Hawke worked briefly as a compositor in the office of the *Rome Sentinel* in Rome, N.Y., before moving the same year to Ontario. There over the next decade and a half he was employed by various newspapers, rising from compositor to reporter for the St Thomas *Times*, legislative reporter for the Toronto *Leader*, reporter for the Ottawa *Citizen*, and member of the parliamentary staff and political correspondent for the Toronto *Globe* in Ottawa. From 1882 to 1885 he was managing news editor of the *Globe*, before moving to the Hamilton *Tribune*, a prohibitionist daily, as editor and then to editorship of the Ottawa *Free Press*, a position he held until 1887. In that year, with support from the federal Liberal party, Hawke purchased the *Daily Transcript* of Moncton, a move made to counter the dominance of the Conservative *Daily Times*, edited by Henry Thaddeus Stevens. He became editor and publisher of the Liberal paper on 1 June.

The following day in the *Transcript*, Hawke set out his views, which he was to promote through his newspaper and in other activities for the rest of his life. He would, the editorial stated, "adhere to the traditional lines and policy of liberal journalism . . . [since] the best interests of Canada are identified with advent of the Liberal Party to power." He argued for commercial union with the United States and against the current high tariffs. He expressed dismay at the "enormous increase in the number of Federal employees," noting that "a source of patronage is becoming . . . a menace to the existence of constitutional government." Hawke believed that members of the Senate should be elected. He also argued for the abolition of the New Brunswick Legislative Council, the provincial upper house, and he believed that the British North America Act should be amended to eliminate the office of the lieutenant governor, whose responsibilities should be assumed by the chief justice. He opposed the sale of intoxicating liquor and felt that the prohibition question should be decided by a direct vote of the people, not during an election. In conclusion, Hawke pledged that his newspaper would advance the interests of the Maritime provinces, New Brunswick, and especially the town of Moncton.

He was almost immediately involved in controversy. After the Conservative candidate, Josiah WOOD, defeated his Liberal opponent, Henry Robert Emmerson*, in Westmorland County during the federal election of 1887, Emmerson responded with a petition alleging that Conservative agents had been responsible for 500 acts of bribery and corruption in the course of the campaign. Such petitions had to be heard within six months of filing or they would expire. After judge

John James Fraser*, apparently misunderstanding the terms of this requirement, three times postponed the date of the hearing, Wood's counsel, Pierre-Amand Landry*, claimed on 22 October that the petition had expired, and Fraser so ruled. Emmerson appealed, and the full bench of the Supreme Court, which included Fraser, reversed the judge's earlier decision. In an editorial in the *Transcript* Hawke referred to "that distinguished judicial acrobat, Mr. Justice Pooh-Bah Fraser," an allusion to the popular Gilbert and Sullivan musical *The Mikado*. He went on to claim that the judge had been "manifestly inebriated on the bench" on a previous occasion. Hawke was summoned to Fredericton to show why he should not be charged with contempt of court. Despite a lengthy speech in his own defence, the Supreme Court concluded that he was guilty of contempt for implying that Fraser had taken bribes. He was given an opportunity to apologize, but refused. On 27 April 1888 he was sentenced to two months' imprisonment and a fine of $200. Hawke's arrest and sentence sparked lively discussion in many Canadian newspapers and a day-long debate in the House of Commons on 9 May on the issues of press freedom and the limits of judicial power. Having paid his fine and served his time in prison, he returned to Moncton to much acclaim.

Under Hawke's editorship, the *Transcript* flourished. In the early 1890s he built a new building for the newspaper, and by 1911 the coverage of the paper, now called the *Moncton Transcript,* was expanded to include more sports and community news. His financial success and political influence had increased appreciably as a result of the Liberal victory in Westmorland County in the federal election of 1896. Hawke obtained lucrative printing contracts for the Intercolonial Railway, which had its headquarters in Moncton, and he dispensed many of the railway's jobs from his newspaper office, rewarding Liberals and party donors. For a number of years Hawke also served as president of the local Liberal association.

Always desirous to promote the press and its interests, he was the first president of the New Brunswick Press Association from 1905 to 1907. After this organization merged with its Nova Scotia counterpart to form the Maritime Press Association, he served as secretary of the new group for the first three years of its existence. He also played a significant role in persuading the Maritime Press Association to join the Canadian Press Association in 1913. As well, Hawke was active in the community. In 1900 he became chair of the Moncton school board, a position he held until 1911. He pushed for legislation that would raise the age of school admission to six and argued vigorously for compulsory school attendance, noting in the board's annual report for 1908–9 the high incidence of petty crimes committed by juveniles in the Moncton area. Under his tenure the board also advocated the medical examination of schoolchildren. Its recommendations were energetically endorsed in Hawke's newspaper.

A strong supporter of the monarchy, Hawke attended the coronation of George V in 1911 as a delegate from Moncton. During World War I, always an effective speaker, he regularly addressed the fortnightly "patriotic meetings" held in the city. He was also active in the Canadian Patriotic Fund, established to aid families of Canadian servicemen, and in the Board of Trade of the Maritime Provinces. Other issues that he promoted included women's suffrage and Maritime union. On the question of union he wrote that "we stand at a disadvantage in this Morning Land of Canada because as three provinces we speak with differentiated voices." Through his many activities, John Thomas Hawke contributed in numerous ways to the city of Moncton and the province of New Brunswick.

ERIC L. SWANICK

John Thomas Hawke is the author of "The meeting was an excellent one," *Busy East of Canada* (Sackville, N.B.), 10 (1919–20), no.2: 24–25, "Moncton City and its future," *Busy East of Canada*, 8 (1917–18), no.[11]: 26–28, 60, and "The *Transcript*'s platform," *Daily Transcript* (Moncton, N.B.), 2 June 1887: [2].

GRO, Reg. of births, Plymouth, 30 April 1854. *Moncton Transcript*, 17–18, 20–21, 28 Feb. 1922. *Times & Transcript* (Moncton), 15 Aug. 1998; 16 Oct. 1999; 13 May, 15 July 2000. J. E. Belliveau, "Hawke of the *Transcript*: a forgotten hero of Canadian journalism," *Beaver* (Winnipeg), 77 (1997–98), no.4: 35–37; "Hawke of the *Transcript* . . . in Liberal homes he was a family deity," *Atlantic Advocate* (Fredericton), 65 (1974–75), no.7: 36–38; *The Monctonians* (2v., Hantsport, N.S., 1981–82). Can., House of Commons, *Debates*, 9 May 1888. J. A. Cooper, "The editors of the leading Canadian dailies," *Canadian Magazine* (Toronto), 12 (November 1898–April 1899): 336–52. *A history of Canadian journalism* . . . (2v., Toronto, 1908–59). H. B. Jefferson, "The great Pooh-Bah case," *Atlantic Advocate*, 54 (1963–64), no.1: 45–51. "Liberty of the press," *University Monthly* (Fredericton), 7 (1887–88), no.8: [1]–2. N.B., Dept. of Education, *Annual report of the schools of New Brunswick* (Fredericton), 1900–11. C. A. Pincombe and E. W. Larracey, *Resurgo: the history of Moncton* (2v., Moncton, 1990–91).

HAWTHORNTHWAITE, JAMES HURST, secretary, land agent, politician, and businessman; b. 1869 in County Westmeath (Republic of Ireland); m. 1890 Elizabeth (Ada) Bate, and they had eight children; d. 1 Nov. 1926 in Victoria.

Educated in England, James Hawthornthwaite went to British Columbia in the late 1880s. His early employers included the American consulate in Victoria, for which he worked as a secretary, and more important, the London-based New Vancouver Coal Mining and Land Company Limited, which operated collieries in Nanaimo. His position as real estate agent

with the NVCMLC introduced him to the intricacies of settlers' rights and competing mineral claims on Vancouver Island; a huge swath of the island had been ceded in 1886 to a coal-mining enterprise headed by Robert Dunsmuir*. Hawthornthwaite became a very public opponent of the Dunsmuir family.

The NVCMLC's long-time manager, Samuel Robins, was a dogged rival of the Dunsmuirs and one of a number of interesting local personalities who were Hawthornthwaite's political mentors. Robins enjoyed cordial relations with the Miners' and Mine Laborers' Protective Association, whose general secretary from the early 1890s, Ralph Smith*, also influenced Hawthornthwaite. Another mentor, Mark Bate, was a business associate of Robins and a former mayor of Nanaimo. In 1890 Hawthornthwaite cemented his alliance with Bate by marrying his daughter Elizabeth. Last, but not least, was Eugene Thornton Kingsley, whose doctrinaire socialist preachings would have a wide impact on the political life of the west coast.

In the depressed circumstances of the mid to late 1890s Hawthornthwaite was kept on for a time at the NVCMLC as night watchman. The Hawthornthwaites had a large and growing family; eight children would be born before the break-up of the marriage around 1912. A political opponent charged in 1908 that they were clothed "by charity," and that Hawthornthwaite was "no man at all." Whatever the truth of the matter, Hawthornthwaite's uncertain status within the Nanaimo elite helped push him into more radical positions. He had been first acclaimed to the Legislative Assembly as an independent Labour candidate for Nanaimo City in a by-election held on 18 Feb. 1901. In a Labour Day speech in Victoria that year he reportedly stated that the remedy to be applied to social ills "was socialism, pure and simple."

West coast socialism was, of course, neither pure nor simple. A populist campaign against the Dunsmuirs was its driving electoral force, as Vancouver Island became the nerve centre of the fledgling Socialist Party of British Columbia, founded in the summer of 1901, and later of the Vancouver-based Socialist Party of Canada. Hawthornthwaite and Kingsley were founding members of the SPC in 1904. James Dunsmuir*, who managed the family's coal-mining assets with an iron fist between 1889 and 1910, served as premier in 1900–2 and he continued in the limelight as lieutenant governor between 1906 and 1909. His arrogant assertion of managerial rights before the royal commission on industrial disputes in 1903 and his transparent conflicts of interest made him a convenient political target. Hawthornthwaite and another representative of the Nanaimo coalfields, Parker Williams, were returned in the provincial elections of 1903, 1907, and 1909 as revolutionary socialists committed to the anti-Dunsmuir cause. During the sessions of 1908 and 1909 they were joined by the mainland miners' representative, John McInnis. Unlike Hawthornthwaite and Williams, McInnis had not been elected on a SPC platform, but he deferred to Hawthornthwaite's parliamentary leadership as part of a province-wide and, indeed, nation-wide strategy to link the SPC with the miners' movement.

Hawthornthwaite's contributions were far more constructive than revolutionary and had included rudimentary farm security legislation in 1901 and a workmen's compensation act in 1902. When Conservative premier Richard McBride* took office in June 1903, he had only a small majority so he turned to Hawthornthwaite for support. Thus, Hawthornthwaite was able to push for additional legislation, including improved safety standards and labour reforms in the mining industry. The premier used members of the socialist caucus to sound out the opinion of the popular class on a narrow range of issues. In return, Hawthornthwaite and his associates eschewed detailed criticism of McBride's policies of development. There were limits to such arrangements. For example, McBride allowed members of the socialist caucus to lead the fight for women's suffrage, but applied no party discipline to bring it about, though he personally supported enfranchisement of women as part of his "white B.C." policy. In addition, administration of labour legislation sometimes made a mockery of the reforms enacted during McBride's premiership. Hawthornthwaite's correspondence shows that the enforcement by government officials of different parts of the Coal Mines Regulation Act depended on his persistent efforts and those of other elected officials. Nevertheless, and although accumulated grievances in the Vancouver Island coalfield would later boil over into violent confrontation, for a time the socialist alternative of a "strike at the ballot box," the slogan of the socialist *Western Clarion* (Vancouver), had unexampled success.

Their local base seemingly secured, SPC activists on Vancouver Island pulled out all the stops in a campaign from 1904 to 1908 to defeat Smith, who had abandoned his independent stance as a Labour MP to join the federal Liberal caucus of Sir Wilfrid Laurier*, and elect one of their own. The popular Hawthornthwaite resigned his provincial seat in 1908 to join the anti-Smith campaign. Some historians have suggested that the SPC's pacifist stance was the cause of his narrow defeat in Nanaimo in the federal general elections of that October. The riding included the naval base at Esquimalt, which would soon be transferred from Britain to the federal government. Hawthornthwaite regained his provincial seat in a by-election held on 12 Jan. 1909.

Hawthornthwaite, who had referred to himself as a "free miner" in 1908, turned his attention in 1911 to speculative enterprises such as a prospective pulp and paper mill at Cowichan Lake. It was an attempt, as he explained to Kingsley, his partner in the business, to "square us up with the world." His divided personal agenda became intolerable to some SPC members. In an internal fight that coincided with wider ideological schisms between purist and revisionist factions, he was expelled from the party in 1912. The Nanaimo local of the SPC went over as a body to the more moderate Social Democratic Party of Canada, but Hawthornthwaite did not represent it in the provincial elections of that year.

His business activities – and, very likely, his personal relationship with McBride, who was frequently in England – enabled Hawthornthwaite to travel to London and Europe on the eve of World War I. During the war he kept a low profile at his residence, Burleith House, in Victoria, acting in a potentially controversial role as a representative of German investors in British Columbia. He would later claim to have met the exiled Bolshevik leader Lenin during his travels and though this claim cannot be verified, the Bolshevik revolution in Russia evidently rekindled his political fires. The wartime break-up of what remained of the SPC coalition on Vancouver Island presented him with an opportunity to regain a seat in the provincial legislature; he was successful in a by-election held in Newcastle in January 1918. Hawthornthwaite's campaign was part of a movement in support of the Federated Labour Party, a new coalition supported by former SPC stalwarts such as Kingsley. The FLP movement was clearly a lightning rod for anti-war sentiment and general social unrest, full of rhetorical solidarity with Lenin and Bolshevism. Hawthornthwaite's third stint in the legislature was, not surprisingly, barren of personal achievement. He had no allies in the assembly and the Liberals under premiers Harlan Carey Brewster* and John OLIVER had no need of his support and no desire to let him influence legislation as he had in the pre-war years. Hawthornthwaite's problematic claim to represent Vancouver Island's "wage slaves" was successfully challenged by a working miner, Samuel Guthrie, in the general elections of October 1920. He continued to dabble in socialist politics as a sideline to business, but his effectiveness had come to an end with his defeat at the polls. The *Canadian annual review* of 1918 had described Hawthornthwaite as "a Miners' representative of the most radical type." By the time of his death in 1926, he was probably better known for his boosting of gold-mining properties in the Cassiar district, investments he had been promoting for a few years.

James Hurst Hawthornthwaite's legacies are hotly debated by historians. The pioneering socialists of British Columbia, of whom he was one of the most prominent, are viewed by some as a collection of charlatans who exploited class consciousness for personal gain, by others as architects of regional political identity, and by still others as prophets of social democratic values now widely accepted as part of the Canadian ethos. Even the briefest consideration of his multi-faceted career illuminates all of these arguments and helps anchor discussion in the history of ongoing struggles for western lands and resources.

ALLEN SEAGER

The author is grateful to Don Stewart of Vancouver, who allowed access to the Hawthornthwaite papers. These papers are now located at Simon Fraser Univ. Library, Special Coll. and Rare Books (Burnaby, B.C.), in the History of Western Canada Coll.

Lynn Bowen, *Three dollar dreams* (Lantzville, B.C., 1987). *Canadian annual rev.*, 1918. *Canadian men and women of the time* (Morgan; 1898 and 1912). *CPG*, 1901–20. *Electoral hist. of B.C.* [J.] M. Leier, *Rebel life: the life and times of Robert Gosden, revolutionary, mystic, labour spy* (Vancouver, 1999). A. B. McCormack, *Reformers, rebels, and revolutionaries: the western Canadian radical movement, 1899–1919* (Toronto and Buffalo, N.Y., 1977; repr. 1991).

HÉBERT, GAUDIOSE, shoemaking machine operator and trade union leader; b. 27 Sept. 1866 at Quebec, son of Alexandre Hébert, a rigger, and Philomène Lortie; m. there 2 July 1894 Malvina Laroche, and they had three children; d. there 17 Feb. 1923.

Gaudiose Hébert was born in Saint-Roch ward, to a French father and a French Canadian mother. One of 16 children in a family of modest means, he attended school until the age of 12, when he went to work in one of the many shoe and boot factories in Quebec's Lower Town and began to learn how to operate a shoemaking machine. At the end of the century he joined the Union des Cordonniers-Machinistes, a strong union which in 1899 became a member of the Fraternité des Cordonniers Unis de la Puissance du Canada. This exclusively Quebec federation also included the Montreal and Saint-Hyacinthe unions of shoemaking machine operators. Hébert was convinced that unions had to be organized to stop workers from being exploited. In the personal notebook in which he set down his impressions, he commented, "We had reached such a level of exploitation that we would have risked our lives in order to unite." He was a member of the union when the footwear manufacturers at Quebec, who were exasperated at having to negotiate with unions, declared a lockout in October 1900, demanding that all their employees appear before a notary to renounce membership in a labour organization. Some 3,850 men and women, including 1,800 union members, found themselves out of work.

Since the dispute was dragging on, Archbishop Louis-Nazaire BÉGIN of Quebec agreed to intervene, provided the two parties would undertake to abide by his decision. The ruling he handed down in January 1901 stipulated that the manufacturers must recognize the workers' right of association, the unions must let their constitutions be revised, and both parties must agree to bring future disputes to arbitration. The Union des Cordonniers-Machinistes, to which Hébert belonged, proved especially unwilling to submit its constitution to the archbishop for examination. It even called on the federal government to denounce this "abuse of power" [*see* Arthur MAROIS]. In the face of this refusal, Bégin released the manufacturers from their obligations, whereupon they issued an ultimatum to the machine operators: they would lose their jobs if their union did not revise its constitution. The union members gave in and could go back to work, but only after each had signed a notarized affidavit promising that they would no longer belong to any labour organization which did not have the archbishop's approval. All the unions also had to agree to have a chaplain attend their meetings. While it did recognize the workers' right of association, Bégin's verdict was the first step in the process of Catholicizing the Quebec boot and shoe workers' unions.

Hébert acceded to the notion of increasing clerical influence in union affairs. At the beginning of the 20th century he served on his union's executive and later as a delegate to the Central Trades and Labor Council of Quebec, the coordinating body of unions in the city. Around 1910 the question of uniform textbooks for public schools was creating sharp divisions in these unions; traditionally the national trade unions at Quebec (those not affiliated to an international union of American origin) and the international ones (those affiliated to an international union), which were nondenominational bodies, had always demanded that the government prescribe such books. They saw this requirement as a considerable saving for working-class families, who often had to buy new texts when their children changed schools. The Roman Catholic clergy were strongly opposed to uniformity, fearing it would lead to a situation where textbooks were chosen by the state. Hébert, who was a delegate from the Fraternité des Cordonniers to the Canadian Federation of Labor convention in Ottawa in 1910, defended the clerical position. The question was a significant factor in the split that occurred in the Central Trades and Labor Council of Quebec the following year. The Fraternité des Cordonniers joined the new Conseil Central National du District de Québec et de Lévis, which adopted a constitution specifying that its demands would be based on the directives of the Catholic Church. In a leaflet distributed during a strike in 1914, Hébert repeated that his union wanted above all to "act as a Christian subject to the church."

Following the establishment of an international union at Thetford Mines in the fall of 1915, the religious authorities at Quebec wanted to strengthen their hold on the city's unions. Abbé Maxime Fortin*, a young priest keenly interested in social questions,

465

undertook to turn them into true Catholic unions. He wisely deemed it necessary, as a first step, to impress upon certain labour leaders the principles of the church's social doctrine. To this end in November and December 1915 he organized a study circle open only to an elite group of union leaders, including Hébert. A year and a half later, judging that his teaching had borne fruit, he convened a meeting on 10 May 1917 of the members of the councils from most of the city's national unions with a view to their revising their constitutions and agreeing to the presence of a chaplain. The Central Trades and Labor Council gave its consent on 5 Feb. 1918 and a number of unions followed its example. Shortly thereafter the council merged with the district council to form the Conseil Central National des Métiers du District de Québec.

In order to broaden the reach of Catholic unionism, the council decided in 1918 to appoint a general organizer (probably paid by Action Sociale Catholique [see Paul-Eugène ROY]), and its choice fell on Hébert because of his skills as a speaker, his character, his experience, and "the Catholic way of thinking that inspired him." In two years, he reportedly brought more than 30 new unions into the fold of Catholic unionism. He was firmly convinced that the future of trade unionism lay in its religious orientation. "This is the kind of union that, where we are, has brought about our prosperity. We owe our entire success to the benevolent support of the church, acting through our devoted chaplains," he said in 1920. "Without the church, we have no one to guide us, and in our union the church is the chaplain." He believed that the church's assistance to the trade union movement might foster its development, especially in a context in which employers were fighting against its very existence.

In September 1918 the council held a three-day study session at Quebec to which all the Catholic and national trade unions of the province were invited. The meeting turned into a deliberative assembly, and Hébert was elected its chairman. He made a motion opposing uniform textbooks and free and compulsory schooling. The resolution, which repeated in its preamble some of the principles advocated by the Catholic clergy, objected to "any attempt to impose a system of secular schools on the province of Quebec," and expressed "confidence in the present direction of the department of public instruction." Adopted without dissent, the motion certainly gave great comfort to the religious authorities, who could now impress upon the government the fact that labour unions were no longer unanimous in supporting free and compulsory schooling. Moreover, a few months later a delegation from the Catholic unions presented the resolution to the government on the very day when delegates from the international unions were urging it to pass legislation to the opposite effect.

On 23 Sept. 1919 Hébert was elected president of the Conseil Central National des Métiers du District de Québec and general president of the Catholic trade unions at their convention in Trois-Rivières. The 120 delegates, who came from every part of the province, were working towards the formation of a central provincial body. Not only did they elect a permanent executive and vote on resolutions, but they gave their leaders the power to issue affiliation charters and to require a fee from the affiliated unions. As president, Hébert was a member of the delegation that went to Ottawa in January 1920 to meet with the federal minister of labour, Gideon Decker Robertson*, who did not look favourably upon Catholic unions. The fact that those unions had not been invited to take part in the National Industrial Conference of Dominion and Provincial Governments organized a little earlier by the federal government was described by Hébert as an offensive oversight. Robertson replied with a long diatribe in which he questioned the need for denominational unions and suggested working in harmony with the other labour organizations in the country. The fiery chaplain of the Catholic unions, Abbé Fortin, riposted that religion must be the cornerstone of unionism.

In June 1920 Hébert took part in the great labour demonstration in Parc Lafontaine in Montreal as part of the meetings of the Semaines Sociales du Canada begun by the Jesuits [see Joseph-Papin Archambault*]. Invited to speak along with Victor Morin, Henri Bourassa*, and Abbé Fortin, he stressed the two original principles of Catholic unionism: unions must not be run from outside the country and it was essential for them to reflect the religious ideals of the populace. At the convention of Catholic unions in Chicoutimi in July 1920, which was attended by more than 200 delegates, Hébert gave an account of his administration. After expressing his pleasure at the progress of Catholic unionism, he paid tribute to the beneficent influence of the chaplains and to the courage of the lay pioneers.

In the course of that year Gaudiose Hébert's health deteriorated. He put in an appearance at the founding convention of the Canadian and Catholic Confederation of Labour in Hull from 24 to 28 Sept. 1921, but only to announce his retirement. Had it not been for this decision, he would probably have been elected the first president of the new trade union organization. On 19 Aug. 1921 he had been named by the provincial government inspector of industrial establishments and public buildings for the Quebec region, but because he was suffering from asthma and general bronchial infection, he held this office only a few months. Before his death in 1923, the federal government appointed him to the Canadian committee at the League of Nations.

JACQUES ROUILLARD

ANQ-Q, CE301-S22, 27 sept. 1866; CE301-S96, 2 juill. 1894. *L'Action catholique* (Québec), 3 sept. 1918, 21 juill. 1920, 19 févr. 1923. *Le Soleil*, 19 févr. 1923. J.-P. Archambault, *Figures catholiques* (Montréal, 1950), 153–92. M.-A. Bluteau *et al.*, *Les cordonniers, artisans du cuir* (Montréal, 1980). Confédération des Travailleurs Catholiques du Canada, *Programme-souvenir du deuxième congrès . . .* (Québec, 1923). Aubert du Lac [Maxime Fortin], *L'œuvre d'une élite* (Québec, 1918). Jacques Rouillard, *Les syndicats nationaux au Québec, de 1900 à 1930* (Québec, 1979). Semaines Sociales du Canada, Section française, *Semaine sociale du Canada* (Montréal, 1920), 162–64.

HÉBERT DE LA ROUSSELIÈRE, MARIE (at birth she was called **Henriette-Anne-Florence-Marie**), named **Marie-Clémentine de Jésus-Hostie**, promoter of Eucharistic works; b. 12 May 1840 in Angers, France, daughter of Alfred-Augustin Hébert de La Rousselière and Marie-Clémentine Bodin Des Plantes (Desplantes); d. 3 Oct. 1924 at the Carmelite monastery in Angers.

Marie Hébert de La Rousselière was descended from a distinguished family of magistrates and notaries. When she was still very young, she and her sister Clémentine were given into the care of their maternal grandmother. Her life would be closely linked to that of her sister. In 1865, when Clémentine left to live in Paris after her marriage to André Brisset Des Nos, she accompanied the young couple.

At the Sanctuaire de l'Adoration on Rue Faubourg Saint-Jacques, Marie was fascinated by the preaching of Father Pierre-Julien Eymard, the founder of the Blessed Sacrament Fathers; this congregation was dedicated to glorifying Christ in the Eucharist by adoration of the Blessed Sacrament and discipleship. She recognized him as a perceptive confessor. In October 1879 she resolved "to organize a sort of chain of worshippers, consisting entirely of priests, wholly dedicated to the glory of Jesus the Sacrificial Victim." The plan was favourably received by the priests. In January 1881 the work, which had been taken over by the Blessed Sacrament Fathers, was approved by Pope Leo XIII under the name of the Association des Prêtres Adorateurs.

That year Marie found in Canada, in Father Cyrille Beaudry*, an enthusiastic promoter who in 1883 would become the North American director of the association. By 1913 it would be a worldwide body with 120,000 members. She also came into contact with the faithful from French parishes through the Œuvre de l'Exposition Mensuelle du Saint Sacrement and gave assistance to poor parishes through the Œuvre des Tirelires Eucharistiques. A tireless champion, she was in charge of the Bureau des Œuvres Eucharistiques in Paris.

Marie had come to know Father Beaudry through Brother Eugène Prévost*, who had joined the Blessed Sacrament Fathers in Brussels in 1881. A native of Saint-Jérôme, Que., Prévost was a friend of the curé François-Xavier-Antoine Labelle*. The two men had dreamed since 1881 of establishing a community of Blessed Sacrament Fathers in Canada, and with the support of Fathers Edmond Tenaillon and Louis Estévenon the project took shape. In the spring of 1885 and with the backing of Labelle, Marie boldly and persistently urged Bishop Édouard-Charles Fabre* of Montreal to build a large chapel in his city for the community. Fabre insisted that this was no time for such a move. The diocese was in a precarious financial state and there were already enough male congregations. His refusal was categorical.

Marie came to Montreal in June 1886 with the Brisset Des Nos family, who had decided to leave France because of the anticlericalism rampant there. For years she had been helping her sister Clémentine, whose health was frail, with the education of her children. She was fairly well off financially, since she and her sister had inherited their grandmother's chateau and had sold it two years before their departure. She was soon in Fabre's good graces. In this land where the tradition of the Eucharist had endured from the earliest days of settlement, she too organized a service of adoration in the parishes and communities. She launched the Œuvre de la Journée Réparatrice du Premier Vendredi and published many booklets and pamphlets on spiritual matters. In March 1890, feeling the time was ripe, she urged Father Albert Tesnières, the superior general of the Congregation of the Blessed Sacrament, and Father Prévost to hasten to Montreal and set up there a sanctuary for adoration. Fabre welcomed them, and on 1 July he personally displayed the Blessed Sacrament in the house purchased through the generosity of Marie and the family of Father Eugène Seers. This event marked the introduction of the congregation into Canada.

Marie's fascination with atonement inspired her to build a chapel on the property of the Brisset Des Nos family in Pointe-aux-Trembles (Montreal), and it was inaugurated on 25 May 1897. She asked Archbishop Paul Bruchési* to have it served by Dominicans, out of consideration for a nephew who had joined that community. In 1900 it was entrusted to the Blessed Sacrament Fathers. In 1913 Bruchési was to designate it a site of Eucharistic pilgrimage and in 1918 he would declare it an "accredited temple of atonement to the Sacred Heart." It has been served by the Capuchins since 1921. Ever attentive to works of atoning adoration and prayer for priests, Marie gave her unconditional support to the work of Abbé Alexis-Louis Mangin, who with Éléonore Potvin had founded the Servantes de Jésus-Marie at Masson (Masson-Angers) in 1895.

After the death of her sister Clémentine in December 1900, Marie Hébert de La Rousselière returned to France. In 1902 she took the veil of the Carmelites in

Helbronner

Angers, with the name of Marie-Clémentine de Jésus-Hostie. She died in 1924 at the age of 84, leaving works that still bear witness to her influence on the spiritual life of Canadians.

ÉDOUARD BUSSIÈRES

Marie Hébert de La Rousselière is the author of *Histoire du pèlerinage La Réparation au Sacré-Cœur; un écrit posthume*, P.-M. Hébert, édit. (Montréal, [1979?]).

Arch. de la Chancellerie de l'Archevêché de Montréal, RLF (Reg. des lettres de Mgr Fabre), 6: 43, 74, 86, 95, 104, 106, 168–69; 421.154 (dossier Antoine Labelle); 465.108 (Congrégation du Très-Saint-Sacrement), 885-1, 890-1. Arch. de la Congrégation du Très-Saint-Sacrement (Montréal), D-1, Fondation de Montréal; E-XV, Marie de La Rousselière; E-XVI, La Réparation; Aimé Côté, "Le Montréal des premiers jours," dans "Le livre du famille" (texte dactylographié, juin 1951). "Association des prêtres adorateurs, revue et approuvée par S. S. Léon XIII, le 25 janvier 1881," *Le Très Saint Sacrement* (Paris), 6 (1881–82): 464–67. Adrien Bergeron, "Mademoiselle de la Rousselière," *Le Sauveur* (Montréal), article running from vol.59 (juillet–août 1985): 7–8 to vol.61 (novembre–décembre 1987): 16–17. Léo Boismenu, "Mademoiselle de la Rousselière, en religion sœur Marie-Clémentine, du Carmel d'Angers (1838–1924)," *Annales des Prêtres-Adorateurs et de la Ligue sacerdotale de la communion* (Montréal), 27 (1924): 337–45. "Chronique et correspondance de l'Association des prêtres adorateurs," *Le Très Saint Sacrement*, 7 (1882–83): 445, 640, 643; 8 (1883–84): 150. André Guitton, *Pierre-Julien Eymard, 1811–1868; apôtre de l'eucharistie* (Paris et Montréal, 1992), 302–3. P.-M. Hébert, "La famille Brisset des Nos, de Dreux (Normandie) à Montréal," SGCF, *Mémoires*, 28 (1997): 243–59. Guy Laperrière, *Les congrégations religieuses: de la France au Québec, 1880–1914* (2v. parus, Sainte-Foy, Qué., 1996–), 1: 116–25. "Œuvre de l'exposition mensuelle," *Le Très Saint Sacrement*, 9 (1884–85): 830. *Une apôtre de l'eucharistie et de la réparation: Mlle Marie de la Rousselière, en religion "sœur Marie-Clémentine de Jésus-Hostie" du Carmel d'Angers, 1840–1924* (Angers, France, 1925; 2ᵉ éd., revue et augmentée par P.-M. Hébert, Montréal, [1996]).

HELBRONNER, JULES (baptized **Samson-Jules**), journalist, labour activist, office holder, and social reformer; b. 23 Dec. 1844 in Paris, son of Joseph Helbronner, a florist, and Caroline Alcan; m. sometime before 1875 Eugénie Meusnier in France, and they had a son and a daughter; d. 25 Nov. 1921 in Ottawa and was buried in Mount Royal Cemetery in Montreal.

Not much is known about Jules Helbronner's life before he came to Canada with his wife in 1874. They settled in Montreal and would have two children, Michel and Antoinette, born respectively in 1876 and 1880. Helbronner worked as a clerk and sales representative before setting up his own enterprise, Jules Helbronner and Company, which distributed Quina-Laroche quinine, mainly in Canada.

Helbronner went to work for the Montreal weekly *Le Moniteur du commerce* as assistant editor in 1882, and he became its editor-in-chief in 1884. He did not get on well with the owner and resigned shortly afterwards. On 20 Oct. 1884 he wrote his first labour column for *La Presse* under the pseudonym Jean-Baptiste Gagnepetit, and it would appear at very irregular intervals until 1894. Although nearly 350 of these articles were published, they dealt with a relatively limited number of topics. Following a strategy widely used in the Anglo-American press at that time, Helbronner regularly engaged in newspaper campaigns. For several weeks he would concentrate on one theme, such as early closing hours for shops, preventive vaccination, or the reform of the water tax, and he would even return to it at more or less frequent intervals. In his columns he supported the whole range of demands put forward by the North American labour movement, while maintaining his critical attitude towards workers' organizations. His vision of society was marked by organicism, a conviction widely held by social thinkers of his day. In his view, trade unionism provided workers with the essential means to defend their interests, but political action was also a route worth pursuing. This was why he supported labour candidates on a number of occasions, though he expressed reservations with regard to a genuine labour party. It seemed to him that workers' interests were better served in the short term by the existing political parties.

Helbronner was also active within the trade union movement. He joined the Knights of Labor in 1885 and helped draw up the program supported by three labour candidates in the Montreal region in the 1886 provincial election. He was an executive member of the Central Trades and Labor Council of Montreal and he would be made a life member of this body in 1889. From 1887 to 1889 he served on the royal commission on the relations of labour and capital [*see* James Sherrard Armstrong*], participating actively. He went on almost all its travels and wrote 5 of the 14 appendices of its minority report, those covering economy and the working class, unjust laws, strikes and arbitration, the payment and non-payment of wages, and the "sweating process." He set the tone for the minority report, which was disparagingly described by some as "capitalistic." It would have been more accurate to label it "philanthropic," since its authors, taking their inspiration from a consensual vision of society, proposed measures likely to integrate workers harmoniously into the economic system. As a delegate from the Canadian government to the universal exposition in Paris in 1889, Helbronner studied the condition of the working class in the various countries represented in the section on social economy.

After an absence of several years from day-to-day journalism because of his official duties, Helbronner signed an employment contract with *La Presse* in 1890 stipulating that he would deal with "civic" and labour issues. Having made a name for himself there as a columnist, he became the newspaper's editor-in-chief, a post he would hold almost continuously from 1892 to 1908. Although he produced most of his writings on labour issues over a period of some ten years, he maintained his interest in municipal affairs throughout his journalistic career. In one of his earliest press campaigns he had denounced the corvée, a regressive fiscal measure imposed on Montreal tenants which was abolished in 1886, thanks in part to his efforts. In 1904 a disagreement with the administrator of *La Presse*, Herménégilde Godin, forced him to leave the newspaper temporarily. This situation recurred in 1908 when, despite opposition from the paper's management, Helbronner strongly advocated the establishment of the royal commission to make a general and complete inquiry into the administration of the affairs of the city of Montreal [*see* Lawrence John CANNON], which began its work in April of the following year. In 1909 he joined *La Patrie*, where he was municipal affairs correspondent for several years. In 1916 he moved to Ottawa, probably to be closer to his daughter, who had been married since 1904 to Louvigny de Montigny*, a journalist, a writer, and since 1910 a translator for the Senate. Helbronner worked until 1920 as a clerk in the Department of Public Printing and Stationery in Ottawa, and he died in that city on 25 Nov. 1921. During his career as a journalist, he had written for many other Montreal periodicals, including *Le Journal du dimanche*, *Le Nationaliste*, *La Revue moderne*, and *Le Soir*.

Helbronner fiercely defended his Jewish heritage, as witness the many libel suits he brought against journalists of every socio-political stripe. He kept his own religious convictions to himself and clearly did not try to impose them on his children, since both of them were baptized and married – to French Canadian spouses – in the Roman Catholic faith. He personally identified with the French in Montreal, rather than with the Jewish community. He participated in the activities of the Chambre de Commerce Française in Montreal from 1887 to 1905 and was chairman of the Union Nationale Française from 1901 to 1909. Under his leadership, this charitable organization made outstanding progress. His achievements earned him the title of knight of the Legion of Honour in 1906.

Even after leaving *Le Moniteur du commerce*, Helbronner had continued to take an interest in the world of business. In 1887 he was one of the founders of the Montreal newspaper *Le Prix courant*, which specialized in business, finance, industry, real estate, and insurance. He left the newspaper at the beginning of the 1890s. His name also appeared on the membership list of the Chambre de Commerce du District de Montréal from 1886 to 1895, and he was a member of the committee in charge of its *Bulletin* from 1906 to 1908.

The question of workers' savings and provision for mutual benefits was one of Helbronner's favourite subjects. He devoted a number of columns to it and dealt with it in an appendix to the report presented in 1889 by the royal commission on the relations of labour and capital, as well as in his *Report on the social economy section of the Universal International Exposition of 1889 at Paris*, which was published in Ottawa in 1890. He also served on the boards of directors of several mutual benefit societies. In 1901, in a series of articles in *Les Débats* (a militant Montreal weekly founded in 1899 by Louvigny de Montigny and Paul de Martigny that from October 1900 bore the Liberal label), he exposed the shortage of reserves in the life annuity department of the Union Franco-Canadienne, an insurance company. This campaign, which he waged under the pseudonym of Julien Véronneau, gave rise to some widely publicized lawsuits between him and Louis-Gaspard Robillard, the company's president and the editor of *Le Pionnier*, which was then being published in Montreal. The affair came to an abrupt end when Robillard fled to the United States.

The importance of Jules Helbronner's service to the working class was widely recognized. A number of his contemporaries even credited him with the success of *La Presse*. While doubtless exaggerated, this claim was not groundless. Although the daily's commercial success from the mid 1890s was evidently the result of decisions taken by its owner, Trefflé Berthiaume*, the fact remains that during the 1880s Helbronner's column had greatly assisted in establishing the credibility of *La Presse* among working people. This was, however, a succès d'estime that had not increased the paper's circulation to any appreciable extent.

JEAN DE BONVILLE

[There is no known archival fonds solely for Jules Helbronner. Correspondence concerning him can be found in a few collections, in particular that of Trefflé Berthiaume (P207) at ANQ-M. Many indications of his disputes, notably with his employers, other journalists, a tenant, and the city of Montreal, can be found in the judicial archives of the District of Montreal, which are held at ANQ-M, T. The Fonds de la Légion d'Honneur at the Arch. Nationales (Paris), L1278060, contains a thin file on him. The Arch. Départementales, Seine (Paris), État civil, Paris, holds a copy of his birth certificate. The biographical dictionaries on Canadian Jews make no mention of Helbronner. Doubtless this lacuna is a sign that he defined himself as first and foremost a Frenchman and had tenuous links with the Jewish community in Montreal. He seems to have been brought back into the collective memory of Quebec Jews through the work of David Rome, who assembled a large file of documents that is held at the Canadian Jewish Congress National Arch. (Montreal), and who devoted a monograph to him – *On Jules Helbronner*, David Rome, comp., intro. Saul Hayes (Montreal, 1978).

Helbronner's significant contribution to newspapers spanned nearly 40 years; since much of it consists of columns and editorials, it can quite easily be identified. He engaged in numerous polemics that give indications of his personality and his journalistic endeavours. Fernande Roy takes up his career as a business correspondent in *Progrès, harmonie, liberté: le libéralisme des milieux d'affaires francophones de Montréal au tournant du siècle* (Montréal, 1988), as does Yves Saint-Germain in "The genesis of the French-language business press and journalists in Quebec, 1871–1914" (PHD thesis, Univ. of Delaware, Newark, 1975). On his labour column, the author's monograph *Jean-Baptiste Gagnepetit: les travailleurs montréalais à la fin du XIXe siècle* (Montréal, 1975) and Mélanie Méthot, "Jules Helbronner (1844–1921): père de la conscience ouvrière montréalaise et intellectuel engagé," *Mens* (Montréal), 2 (2001–2): 67–104, may be consulted.

As a member of the royal commission on the relations of labour and capital in Canada, Helbronner co-signed the minority report, in particular with Guillaume Boivin*, as well as several of its appendices: Can., Royal commission on the relations of labour and capital in Canada, *Report* (5v. in 6, Ottawa, 1889), first report, apps.C, H, I, L, O. Subsequently, as Canada's delegate to the universal exposition in Paris, he penned the voluminous *Report on the social economy section of the Universal International Exposition of 1889 at Paris* (Ottawa, 1890). Analysis of his contribution to the work of the royal commission can be found in *Canada investigates industrialism: the royal commission on the relations of labor and capital, 1889 (abridged)*, ed. G. [S.] Kealey (Toronto and Buffalo, N.Y., 1973), and in Fernand Harvey, *Révolution industrielle et travailleurs; une enquête sur les rapports entre le capital et le travail au Québec à la fin du 19e siècle* (Montréal, 1978). Marcel Pleau, in *Histoire de l'Union française, 1886–1945* (Montréal, 1985), gives an account of Helbronner's involvement in supporting French nationals in Montreal. J.DE B.]

Le Devoir, 26 nov. 1921. *Le Droit* (Ottawa), 26 nov. 1921. *La Patrie*, 26 nov. 1921. *La Presse*, 26 nov. 1921. *Canadian men and women of the time* (Morgan; 1898).

HENDRIE, Sir JOHN STRATHEARN, engineer, businessman, militia officer, politician, and office holder; b. 15 Aug. 1857 in Hamilton, Upper Canada, son of William Hendrie* and Margaret Walker; m. 2 April 1885 Lena Maude Henderson (d. 18 July 1928) in Kingston, Ont., and they had one daughter and two sons; d. 17 July 1923 in Baltimore, Md.

John S. Hendrie attended the Hamilton grammar school and in 1872 he was sent to Upper Canada College in Toronto, where he excelled in mathematics and rugby. On graduation he went to work for the Great Western Railway as a civil engineer. He joined his father and uncle in carting and engineering in the late 1870s, occasionally as a project engineer on lines in Ontario and Michigan. In 1895 he became manager and then vice-president of the Hamilton Bridge Works Company Limited, a reorganization of a firm started by his father to produce bridges, railway turntables, powerhouses, and sheds. By the first decade of the new century, its proficiency in structural steel had led it into the supply of equipment for the electrical power and telecommunications industries. Hendrie, who assumed the presidency after his father's death in 1906, became known for his "aggressive and skillful" managerial qualities. His business career also included service with the Bank of Hamilton – he became a director in 1903 and president in 1914 – and directorships in Great-West Life Assurance and Mercantile Trust.

His father's considerable success had made the family one of Hamilton's wealthiest. Within the city's civic culture, militia rank was a test of social respectability, and in December 1883 J. S. Hendrie was commissioned a captain in the Hamilton Field Battery. Promoted major in June 1894, he was chosen to command an artillery contingent at the celebration in 1897 of Queen Victoria's diamond jubilee in England. In September 1903 he was promoted lieutenant-colonel and given command of the 2nd Brigade of Artillery; he would retire in 1909. A president of the Ontario and Canadian artillery associations, in 1907 he was made a commander of the Royal Victorian Order. In addition, he had been a founder of the Hamilton Patriotic Fund in 1899, during the South African War, and served as its chairman from 1906 until it merged with the Canadian Patriotic Fund during World War I. The English Canadian search for national identity in an imperial context was expressed by a keen interest in the War of 1812. Hendrie's wife was vice-president in 1905 of the Women's Wentworth Historical Society [see Sara Galbraith Beemer*], which had long advocated the commemoration of the battle site at Stoney Creek. John's own efforts to create a park there, along with his militia service, led to his appointment to the National Battlefields Commission in 1908.

Meanwhile, Hendrie had entered politics. In December 1900, when Frank E. Walker, the Tory candidate and front runner in Hamilton's mayoralty race, dropped out, he was approached. Disinclined at first to accept the nomination – his reluctance was genuine, not feigned – he changed his mind, and turned his lack of political experience to advantage in a campaign where the municipal debt was a major issue. His reputation as an efficient businessman was cited by the pro-Tory *Hamilton Spectator* as his key credential, and Hendrie promised the application of "business methods" to the administration of Hamilton. Elected on 3 Jan. 1901, he cut both its debt and its taxes. The mayor generally served two terms, with an understanding between the Grits and the Tories that an incumbent could seek his second term unopposed. In the 1902 election, however, opposition came from socialist candidate William Barrett, who received a quarter of the votes. Though easily re-elected, Hendrie remained concerned about this support: "a capitalist looking for a place to locate a manufacturing concern will avoid a socialist city every time," he told the *Spectator*.

In anticipation of the provincial election on 29 May 1902, Hendrie was nominated as the Tory candidate for Hamilton West in preference to Edward Alexander Colquhoun, the sitting MPP. Hendrie handily defeated Colquhoun (who ran as an independent), Grit candidate Stephen Frederick Washington, and socialist Robert Roadhouse. Though the Liberal government of George William Ross* was returned, the Tories emerged as the party of Ontario's cities and in 1905 they swept the scandal-plagued Ross government from power. Premier James Pliny Whitney* offered Hendrie the position of minister of public works but he declined, preferring to serve as a minister without portfolio and chairman of the legislature's railway committee or, as the Toronto *Globe* put it, "virtually acting Minister of Railways."

Drawing on the principles of competent management that had earned him his reputation, in March 1906 Hendrie introduced two significant bills on railways and municipal affairs, both of which had engaged the drafting skills of former Conservative leader Sir William Ralph MEREDITH. The Ontario Railway Act, which regulated all aspects of operations and franchises, including those of a rising number of electric and privately owned lines, helped appease popular sentiment against William MACKENZIE's monopolistic Toronto Railway Company. The second, and related, act formed the semi-judicial Ontario Railway and Municipal Board and gave it unprecedented powers. Within months, under the chairmanship of James Leitch, it had made decisions on a range of issues, among them rates, accidents, strikes, assessments, utilities, and municipal financing. In February 1907 Hendrie continued his regulatory impulse by introducing legislation stripping provincial benefits from any public utility that had secured a federal charter. This aggressive bill drew him into a complex debate over provincial rights and the privileges sought by the Hamilton Radial Electric Railway, backed by a determined John Morison GIBSON. The bureaucratic instinct for government by specialistic tribunal that gave rise to the ORMB produced a long list of other agencies, boards, and commissions, which characterized the growth of the administrative state in 20th-century Ontario.

Another major achievement of the first Whitney government, again with a focus on government by expertise and the limitation of private interests, was the establishment in 1906 of the Hydro-Electric Power Commission of Ontario. Hendrie's part in its development was minor, and his attitude to the public ownership of electrical utilities was ambivalent. In Hamilton he had leaned towards private control; in the legislature he had sat on a select committee in 1903–4 to survey public opinion on the principle of municipal ownership. In 1906 he was appointed to the hydro commission to assuage private interests and to keep a

firm hand on the radical populism of its chairman, Adam BECK. Hendrie's insistence on a critical examination of many early projects was interpreted by Beck as personal animosity rather than a concern for diligence. There was likely an element of both. Hendrie had inherited from his father (and shared with his brothers) a love of horses – his entries won the King's Plate in 1909 and 1910. Beck too was an avid horseman, and their rivalry at meets and their dramatically different temperaments amplified their persistent conflict at Hydro.

Hendrie was returned in Hamilton West with declining majorities in the elections of 1908, 1911, and 1914. In September 1914 he succeeded his fellow Hamiltonian Sir John M. Gibson as lieutenant governor of Ontario. One reason for his selection was his personal wealth (his father had left an estate worth $2.3 million). His affluence enabled him to maintain a residence in Toronto until the completion there of a new government house, which the Hendries would occupy at the end of 1915. On the announcement of the king's birthday honours on 3 June 1915, Hendrie was created a KCMG. He frequently used his position to further the war effort. At the opening of the Canadian National Exhibition in August 1915, for instance, he reconfirmed his "life-long" belief in the militia; though he found the term conscription a "misnomer," he firmly supported "universal training and service for all." In addition, he continued to be involved in volunteer endeavours such as the Canadian Patriotic Fund, the Speakers' Patriotic League, and the Hamilton Recruiting League, and he chaired the provincial Organization of Resources Committee, established in 1916 to maximize Ontario's contribution to the war. In 1917 the University of Toronto recognized his work by awarding him a LLD. One of his last functions was a dinner for the Prince of Wales at Government House on 25 Aug. 1919. He retired from public life in November and returned to his Hamilton home, Strathearn, where he would continue to enjoy affiliations with local clubs, the masonic lodge, and the Presbyterian Church.

In July 1923 Hendrie travelled to Baltimore to undergo an operation for intestinal problems at Johns Hopkins Hospital. While recovering, he developed bronchial pneumonia, from which he died on the night of 17 July; his remains were returned to Ontario for burial in Hamilton Cemetery. Survived by his wife and their daughter and son (a war veteran), he left an estate worth almost $1.35 million.

Sir John S. Hendrie's resolve to bring business methods to government at the local and provincial levels reflected a desire to improve public administration through rigour and expertise. Though a leading industrialist in Hamilton, he was certainly not the most important Canadian of his age; many others were more powerful and more accomplished. His significance lies in his typicality of the urban elite who came of age after confederation. He was committed to an ideology of service that, in the words of historian John English, "created a scale to measure the quality of citizenship." Measured on this scale, Hendrie did well.

THOMAS H. FERNS

AO, RG 22-205, no.13103; RG 24; RG 80-5-0-133, no.3382. Hamilton Military Museum (Hamilton, Ont.), Hendrie papers. Hamilton Public Library, Special Coll. Dept. (Hamilton), Arch. file, Brown–Hendrie papers. *Globe*, 28 Sept. 1914. *Hamilton Spectator*, 8 Jan. 1902. R. M. Bray, "'Fighting as an ally': the English-Canadian patriotic response to the Great War," *CHR*, 61 (1980): 141–68. R. C. Brown and Ramsay Cook, *Canada, 1896–1921: a nation transformed* (Toronto, 1974). *Canadian annual rev.*, 1901–19. *Canadian men and women of the time* (Morgan; 1898 and 1912). J. H. Collinson and Mrs Bertie Smith, *The Recruiting League of Hamilton* ([Hamilton, 1918?]). Merrill Denison, *The people's power: the history of Ontario Hydro* ([Toronto], 1960). *DHB*, vol.2. John English, *The decline of politics: the Conservatives and the party system, 1901–20* (Toronto, 1977). T. H. Ferns, "The life and times of John Strathearn Hendrie, 1857–1923" (graduate research paper, Univ. of Toronto, 1991). C. W. Humphries, *"Honest enough to be bold": the life and times of Sir James Pliny Whitney* (Toronto, 1985). J. E. Middleton and Fred Landon, *The province of Ontario: a history, 1615–1927* (5v., Toronto, 1927–[28]), 3: 4–6. H. V. Nelles, *The politics of development: forests, mines & hydroelectric power in Ontario, 1849–1941* (Toronto, 1974). *Ontario and the First World War, 1914–1918; a collection of documents*, ed. and intro. B. M. Wilson (Toronto, 1977). W. R. Plewman, *Adam Beck and the Ontario Hydro* (Toronto, 1947).

HERBIN, JOHN FREDERIC, jeweller, author, optometrist, politician, historian, and promoter of Acadian heritage; b. 8 Feb. 1860 in Windsor, N.S., son of John Herbin and Marie-Marguerite Robichaud; m. 3 June 1897 Minnie Rounsefell Simson in Grand Pré, N.S., and they had five children, of whom two sons and two daughters survived infancy; d. 29 Dec. 1923 in Wolfville, N.S.

John Frederic Herbin's professional life was influenced by his Huguenot father, who, in the early 1850s, immigrated to Nova Scotia from Cambrai, France, allegedly because of political difficulties. Herbin's father was a watchmaker in Bedford and then in Windsor until 1870, when he moved with his family to Halifax to establish himself as a goldsmith. John Frederic had left school to assist in the family trades, reputedly making his first gold wedding band at age nine. The family returned to Windsor in 1877, where both father and son were watchmakers. In December 1882 Herbin followed his father to Colorado and New Mexico. After teaching school there until April 1884, he moved to Wolfville, N.S., where in 1885 he established Herbin Jewellers, a family business that would mark its 120th anniversary in 2005. He continued his studies, earning a BA degree at Acadia College in Wolfville from 1886 to 1890 and graduating with honours. In addition to running his business, he began teaching shorthand in 1891 and, after placing first in his class during a brief course at the Ontario Optical Institute in Toronto in 1896, added optometry to his professional ventures. Always public spirited, he served as a town councillor of Wolfville and in 1902–3 as its mayor.

It was as an author and public advocate of Acadian history and nationalism that Herbin best caught the imagination of his time. While at Acadia he had already begun publishing poetry and prose in the college paper, the *Acadia Athenæum*, and in local newspapers. Reputedly influenced by his Acadian mother's stories of her people's exile and return after the deportation of 1755 [*see* Charles Lawrence*], he began to make it his "mission to work and write," as he would explain to a Boston reporter in 1905, "to preserve for the interested the name and memory of my people, the terribly wronged Acadians." "I imagine," he noted, "the anguish of my great-great-grandfather as he was made to leave . . . and go away to a strange land. I can almost hear the crying of the mothers separated from their children, and I realize . . . the injustice and the awfulness of it all."

Canada, and other poems (Windsor, 1891), Herbin's first volume of poetry, struck a note of Canadian nationalism characteristic of other post-confederation poets. That year the literary editor of the New York *Independent*, poet William Bliss CARMAN, included Herbin's work in his periodical and wished "that every man in [Canada's] far borders should be as sturdy and loyal a son as you are." *The marshlands: a souvenir in song of the land of Evangeline*, which first appeared in Windsor in 1893, focused more intimately on the dykelands, seasonal rhythms, and Acadian iconography of the region. Subsequent editions, bound with Herbin's *The trail of the tide*, would be published by William BRIGGS of Toronto in 1899 and 1909.

Poets Charles George Douglas Roberts*, Theodore Harding Rand*, and Carman praised Herbin's handling of the sonnet form. American philosopher William James discerningly wrote from Cambridge, Mass., in 1897, "I don't know that I have ever met so complete a marriage of a man's soul with the land which he inhabits." Herbin most effectively translated to a wide reading public his personal research on Acadian genealogy, archaeological sites, roadways, aboiteau (dyke) systems, and artefacts through a series of local histories such as *Grand-Pré: a sketch of the Acadian occupation of the shores of the basin of Minas* (Toronto and Montreal, 1898), *The history of Grand-Pré: the home of Longfellow's "Evangeline"* (Toronto, 1900), and *The land of Evangeline: the authentic story of her country and her people* (Toronto, 1921). Publishing records for Briggs reveal 500 copies (400 paper, 100 cloth) of *The marshlands* for distribution in 1900 and runs of 1,000 copies of *The history of Grand-Pré* for the first edition in 1900 and the third in 1907. *The land of Evangeline*, bound with a copy of Longfellow's *Evangeline* and brought out by the Musson Book Company Limited, went through five editions and sold 15,000 copies in 1921. Herbin's romantic fiction, *The heir to Grand-Pré*, had a more modest run of 500 copies when published with Briggs in 1907 and the account was closed in 1914. His novel *Jen of the marshes*, which appeared in Boston in 1921, echoed his earlier local colour fiction by reconceptualizing the Evangeline figure as a modern heroine firmly rooted in the pastoral heritage of latter-day Grand Pré. Herbin's star-crossed English-French lovers are symbolically united at the conclusion of both novels, but his more obvious intention was to exploit romance so as to highlight the memory of his dispossessed ancestors.

By far the most enduring of Herbin's contributions to preserving the memory of pre-deportation Acadian culture was his success in 1907 in securing 14 acres of land on which the original Grand Pré community had stood and in spearheading the movement to establish a memorial park. Included among the list of projects which he had drawn up the previous year for the proposed park were the enclosing of the grounds, the erection of memorials to Longfellow, the Acadians, and Evangeline, the rebuilding of the Acadian church on its original site, the restoration of the priest's house, the Acadian well, and "the burying ground," the protection of the original Acadian willows, and the erection of bronze description plates. In a letter to Prime Minister Sir Wilfrid Laurier* on 25 June 1906, Herbin had explained that "international interest," "amity between our two leading Canadian peoples," and "pride and gratification" were the catalysts for the proposed $50,000 project and he invited Laurier to be a patron (with politicians Robert Laird Borden* and Sir Frederick William Borden*, both from the Minas Basin deportation area). Although F. W. Borden acknowledged Herbin to be a "thoroughly honest and honorable" man, he advised Laurier to withhold his patronage until he could assess the degree to which the restoration scheme was directed at attracting American tourists.

In November 1917, having also failed "to get the Acadians interested in the project," and concerned about potential desecration of the site, Herbin sold the land for $1,650 to the Dominion Atlantic Railway (leased to the Canadian Pacific Railway) for the creation of a park, stipulating that the location of the original Saint-Charles-des-Mines church be deeded to the Acadians for the erection of a memorial to their past. On 28 May 1919 the Société l'Assomption [*see* David-Vital LANDRY] took possession of the church site. The DAR, which as early as the 1890s had exploited the anti-modernism of the Evangeline myth for purposes of tourism, unveiled a statue of Evangeline (conceived by Louis-Philippe Hébert*) in the park in 1920. Herbin's poetic tribute to his ancestors, "The returned Acadian," had become the signature promotional poem of the DAR under the title "Evangeline's return." Before his sudden death in 1923 Herbin had an opportunity to witness the evolution of his dream when construction of the memorial church began (on completion it would include his collection of Acadian artefacts in its museum).

Perhaps because of his Protestant English-speaking background (he read French, but did not speak it) Herbin had difficulty throughout his life attracting Acadian support for his endeavours. He was finally recognized in an article published in *L'Évangéline* (Moncton) in 1924 and by a plaque added in 1925 to the commemorative stone cross that he had placed in the park in 1909. His promotion of the Grand Pré area (including postcards that he had produced commercially) continued to inform the marketing of tourism in the region as late as the 1930s, but it is as a torch keeper of the Acadian past through his literary work and his endeavours to promote a park at Grand Pré that he most effectively contributed to the nation-building spirit of both Acadians and Canadians during his lifetime.

GWENDOLYN DAVIES

Acadia Univ., Vaughan Memorial Library, Esther Clark Wright Arch. (Wolfville, N.S.), John Frederic Herbin fonds. Centre d'Études Acadiennes, Univ. de Moncton, N.-B., Fonds Placide Gaudet, 1.70-8. LAC, MG 26, G: 111544–48. UCC-C, Fonds 513/1, 83.061c, file 43-1os. "Dette de reconnaissance," *L'Évangéline* (Moncton), 7 mai 1925. *L'Évangéline*, 3 janv. 1924. *Sunday Herald* (Boston), 20 Aug. 1905. Blodwen Davies, "Wanted: a literary executor," *New Outlook* (Toronto), 30 Nov. 1927. Barbara Le Blanc, *Postcards from Acadie: Grand-Pré, Evangeline & the Acadian identity* (Kentville, N.S., 2003). Ian McKay, *The quest of the folk: antimodernism and cultural selection in twentieth-century Nova Scotia* (Montreal and Kingston, Ont., 1994). Harry Piers and D. C. Mackay, *Master goldsmiths and silversmiths of Nova Scotia and their marks*, ed. U. B. Thomson and A. M. Strachan (Halifax, 1948). L. D. Storr, "John Frederic Herbin: the re-creation of the past" (MA thesis, Acadia Univ., 1995).

HERDT, LOUIS-ANTHYME, engineer, professor, and scientific consultant; b. 14 June 1872 in Trouville-sur-Mer, France, son of John Herdt, a banker, and Hélène-Denise-Amélie Fleury de La Hussinière; m. 4 May 1897 Blanche Dugas (d. 1907), daughter of judge Calixte-Aimé Dugas, in Montreal, and they had two sons; d. there 11 April 1926.

Louis-Anthyme Herdt's family came to Montreal around 1880. As a Protestant, Louis-Anthyme at once began attending the prestigious High School of Montreal. In 1889 he entered McGill University, from which he graduated with a bachelor's degree in electrical engineering in 1893. When he was called up for military service in France, he took the opportunity to obtain further training as an engineer in Europe. As it turned out, he was excused from military service because he was partially deaf and he enrolled in the Montefiore Institute of Electrotechnics in Liège, Belgium. A year later he continued his studies at the École Supérieure d'Électricité in Paris. On returning to Montreal in 1895, Herdt was hired as a demonstrator in the department of electrical engineering at McGill. He became a lecturer in 1897 and the following year obtained his master's degree there. Teaching and research in the sciences at McGill were expanding significantly at the turn of the century. Thanks to the munificence of tobacco magnate Sir William Christopher Macdonald*, a number of buildings and laboratories specifically for the sciences, and especially the applied sciences, were erected on the university campus. In 1896, for instance, Macdonald gave $30,000 for the electrical engineering laboratory. It was under these exceptional circumstances that Herdt engaged in research, at a time when Quebec was on the verge of discovering its hydroelectric potential.

Herdt's first experiments in the new laboratory were focused on the performance of electrical motors and alternators. He was working at the time with Robert Bowie Owens, the professor principally developing electrical engineering at McGill. With Owens's assistance, Herdt perfected an invention that made it possible to guide ships through a canal. The ships had to be equipped at the bow with a device for detecting changes in a magnetic field generated by an underwater cable. The captain could then keep the ship on the course set by the cable, even in conditions of zero visibility. This invention, which was tested for the first time in 1904 on the St Lawrence in the presence of Raymond Préfontaine*, the minister of marine and fisheries, earned high praise for Herdt from the scientific community. It was not until World War I, however, that its full potential was revealed. Thanks to Herdt's invention, ships of the Royal Navy could be guided into English ports during the war. In 1907 Herdt became an assistant professor at McGill. Two years later he held the Macdonald chair of electrical engineering and succeeded Owens as head of the department, a position he retained for the rest of his life. The university recognized the importance of his scientific work by granting him a DSC in 1910.

At the end of the 19th century, wide-ranging economic changes forced provincial governments and municipalities to create new agencies to regulate the exploitation of natural resources and to coordinate the establishment of the main public utilities. Scientific consultants, of whom engineers certainly were the largest group, had to be recruited for commissions of inquiry, technical services, government departments,

and supervisory commissions. Herdt's interest in solving concrete problems in the field of electricity placed him in the front rank of the experts on whom these bodies called for assistance. In 1907 he was appointed to the Board of Consulting Engineers of the City of Winnipeg, which supervised work on the Pointe du Bois hydroelectric station. Whether it was to develop the hydroelectric potential of the Ottawa River or of New Brunswick, Herdt was approached for his opinion in order to inform decision-makers. He was a member of most of the public utility commissions in Montreal. In 1912 he was appointed by provincial order in council chair of the Electrical Commission of the City of Montreal, whose responsibilities included supervising the construction of underground conduits for the city's many electric cables. When the Quebec government created the Montreal Tramways Commission in 1916 to ensure some uniformity in the services and contracts of the Montreal Tramways Company, Herdt acted as consulting engineer. A 36-year agreement between the city and this corporation was signed in June 1918. The Montreal Tramways Commission then became a permanent agency and Herdt was appointed one of its two vice-presidents. Decisions on public transportation in Montreal would now come under the jurisdiction of this body, rather than that of a private company or of the city. In the same year Herdt went to the United States to study various metropolitan transportation systems.

Because of his involvement in public utilities and his scientific accomplishments, Herdt came to hold prestigious offices in national and international organizations. He was elected a member of the Canadian Society of Civil Engineers in 1899 and served as a member of its council from 1907. As a delegate to the International Electro-Technical Commission held in London, England, in June 1906, he helped define standards in the field of electricity. He was admitted to membership in the Royal Society of Canada in 1911.

When World War I broke out, Herdt went to France to take part in the war effort, but the French military authorities asked him to return to Canada, where his services would be more useful. Soon afterwards he became technical consultant to the French Artillery Mission in New York, overseeing the contracts it signed and the material it purchased from Canadian manufacturers for field telephones. The French government would award him the Legion of Honour in 1923 in recognition of his services.

In the mid 1920s, Louis-Anthyme Herdt began to experience health problems. He suffered from depression and was treated at the Royal Victoria Hospital. On Sunday, 11 April 1926, his son John Dougas noticed that his father, when leaving the house for his office at McGill University, as he did every Sunday, seemed back in form. A couple of hours later Herdt's body was found by one of the watchmen of the building. At the age of only 53, the renowned McGill professor and vice-chairman of the Montreal Tramways Commission had shot himself in the head, putting a tragic end to a brilliant scientific career. Over the years he had helped develop standards in a number of fields connected with the use of electricity. He had also distinguished himself as a technical consultant in the setting up of hydroelectric stations and had proved an important expert for public agencies charged with the regulation of recognized utilities.

ROBERT GAGNON

Louis-Anthyme Herdt is the author of: *Notes of polyphase equipments of some European high speed electric railways* ([Montreal?, 1902?]); *The use of electricity on the Lachine Canal* ([Montreal?, 1904?]); and *Electrolysis in the city of Winnipeg* (n.p., [1910?]). He also published several articles, notably in *Canadian Electrical News and Engineering Journal* (Toronto) and in Canadian Soc. of Civil Engineers, *Trans.* (Montreal). A partial list of his publications can be found in *Science and technology biblio.* (Richardson and Mac-Donald).

ANQ-M, CE601-S1, 4 mai 1897. Arch. Départementales, Calvados (Caen, France), État civil, Trouville-sur-Mer, 17 juin 1872. MUA, Reference Room Staff Index, Herdt, L.-A.; RG 49, scrapbooks and newspaper clippings, 1–6. *Montreal Daily Star*, 13 April 1926. Christopher Armstrong and H. V. Nelles, *Monopoly's moment: the organization and regulation of Canadian utilities, 1830–1930* (Philadelphia, 1986), 251–54. *Canadian men and women of the time* (Morgan; 1912). "Dr. Louis A. Herdt," *McGill News* (Montreal), 7, no.3 (June 1926): 29–30. R. C. Fetherstonhaugh, *McGill University at war, 1914–1918, 1939–1945* (Montreal, 1947). S. B. Frost, *McGill University: for the advancement of learning* (2v., Montreal, 1980–84), 2: 104. Robert Gagnon et A. J. Ross, *Histoire de l'École polytechnique, 1873–1990; la montée des ingénieurs francophones* (Montréal, 1991), 178–81. Linteau, *Hist. de Montréal*, 273. "Louis Anthyme Herdt," RSC, *Trans.*, 3rd ser., 20 (1926), proc.: xxi–xxiv. McGill Univ., *Annual report* (Montreal), 1894–1926.

HESPELER, WILLIAM (Wilhelm), businessman, office holder, politician, and JP; b. 29 Dec. 1830 in the Grand Duchy of Baden (Germany), second son of Johann Georg Hespeler and Anna Barbara Wick; m. first 21 Dec. 1854 Mary H. Keatchie (d. 1872) of Galt (Cambridge), Upper Canada, and they had three children, two of whom survived to adulthood; m. secondly 15 Dec. 1874 Mary Meyer (d. 1883) of Seaforth, Ont.; m. thirdly 6 April 1887 Catherine Robertson, née Keatchie (d. 1920), a sister of his first wife, in Port Arthur (Thunder Bay, Ont.); no children were born of the second or third marriages; d. 18 April 1921 in Vancouver.

William Hespeler grew up in a bourgeois household in Baden, his father a prosperous merchant and his mother related to Hungarian aristocracy. The family's nine children, two boys and seven girls, received extensive education in German, French, and English. They were steeped in the family's mercantile tradition and imbued with a sense of adventure which was tempered only by the inherent social conservatism of their class. The Hespelers believed not only in technological but also in political progress. Their hopes for democratic reform in Baden were dashed when the revolution of 1848 failed. The family valued service to the public and its members would frequently participate in civic and political affairs.

Through chain migration started by William's elder brother, Jacob, most of the family eventually came to settle in Upper Canada, in the area around Berlin (Kitchener) and Waterloo. In this largely German enclave, Hespeler, who arrived in 1850, demonstrated his willingness to reach beyond his ethnic and religious background (he was Lutheran) by marrying a Canadian-born woman of Scottish-Presbyterian descent. He soon proved his business acumen as well, working initially in his brother's milling, distilling, and general merchandising business in Preston (Cambridge). In 1854 he set up a similar business in Waterloo with George Randall. A few years later the partners built the Granite Mills and the Waterloo Distillery. By 1861 the flourishing business was producing 12,000 barrels of flour and 2,700 barrels of whiskey; it employed 15 men. Two years later William Roos joined the partnership.

In the 1870s Hespeler's career took a different turn. According to one account, Hespeler, a naturalized British subject, briefly served as a stretcher-bearer during the Franco-German war of 1870–71. He returned to Canada but by the spring of 1872 he had left his milling business in the care of an employee, Joseph Emm Seagram*, and had taken his ailing wife and two surviving children to Baden. On 2 Feb. 1872 he had been appointed special immigration agent for Germany by the Canadian government. With the help of shipping agents of the Allan Line [*see* Sir Hugh Allan*], he recruited new settlers, especially from the war-ravaged province of Alsace. That summer the Canadian government sent him to southern Russia, a region from which large numbers of German-speaking Mennonites wanted to immigrate. Despite considerable opposition from Russian authorities and little support from British diplomats, he arranged for several thousand Mennonites to move to Canada [*see* Gerhard Wiebe*].

Rewarded by the federal minister of agriculture, John Henry Pope*, with an appointment as dominion immigration agent for Manitoba and the North-West Territories (a position he would hold until 1882), the recently widowed Hespeler moved permanently to Winnipeg in 1873. Through his work in providing temporary shelter and emergency provisions as well as in directing newcomers to available lands, he had close dealings not only with the Mennonite settle-

Hespeler

ments but also with the early Icelandic settlements [*see* Jón Bjarnason*]; he was similarly involved in organizing relief for Jewish refugees [*see* Benjamin ZIMMERMAN]. Uncomfortable with the government's laissez-faire approach to the establishment of recent arrivals, he took a paternalistic view of aid. He did not mind combining the government's relief with his own economic self-interest as a grain merchant. He delighted in planning new settlements, such as Niverville, Man., and in exploring agricultural innovations. Together with his son he erected what is said to have been the first grain elevator in western Canada, in 1879. He deftly explored the entrepreneurial opportunities of the frontier, acquiring rural and city plots, dealing in mortgages and loans, and acting as a middleman between the Winnipeg business community and the Mennonite settlements. From 1886 to 1905 he would serve as manager of the Manitoba Land Company. He soon became known as an expert on western Canadian development.

By the mid 1870s, remarried and at his energetic best, Hespeler was proving his civic-mindedness in many ways. He was elected alderman for Winnipeg's South Ward in 1876 and 1878, joined the board of the Winnipeg General Hospital (he would serve as its president for more than a decade, starting in 1889), and on 25 Nov. 1876 was appointed to the provisional council of Keewatin to deal with the smallpox epidemic of 1876–77. By 1876 he had been appointed a justice of the peace. Involved in the Anglo-Saxon community of Winnipeg, he was also active among the city's small German population. His second wife was of German origin and he himself participated in German singing and social clubs in the late 1870s and mid 1880s.

When the German government sought an honorary consul for Winnipeg and the North-West Territories in 1882, Hespeler was a natural choice. This unsalaried position allowed him to pursue his business interests and it would help him overcome personal tragedies – the death of his second wife in 1883 and that of his daughter, Georgina Hope, wife of Augustus Meredith NANTON, in 1887. As consul, he maintained his connections with the growing German community of the city. In 1888, for example, he supported the establishment of a German Lutheran congregation in Winnipeg. The following year he was instrumental in setting up a German-language newspaper, the *Nordwesten*. Although the consular workload became increasingly heavy in the new century, he would stay on until July 1907. In 1903 he was rewarded with the German Order of the Red Eagle for 20 years of service.

At age 69 Hespeler moved into the political arena. His reputation for thoroughness and common sense and his close association with the Mennonite community won him the rural seat of Rosenfeld in the provincial general election of 7 Dec. 1899 as an independent candidate with Conservative leanings. Once elected, however, he declared himself against the government of Conservative premier Hugh John MACDONALD. On 29 March 1900 he became speaker of the Legislative Assembly, one of the earliest persons who were not born British subjects to hold this position in any legislative body in the British empire – but not the first, as has been claimed. Lacking vanity and a sense of self-importance, he left politics a few years later to make way for a younger person.

Hespeler's business activities had laid the foundation for considerable wealth that promised a comfortable old age with his third wife, Catherine. He continued to serve on the boards of numerous financial institutions and could have lived out his final years quietly enjoying the fruits of his labour in his luxurious apartment block in Fort Rouge (Winnipeg), designed for him by noted architect John D. Atchison in 1906. World War I intervened, however. Hespeler's German connections suddenly tainted the man and his achievements. He refused to be cowed by the nativist hostility of the period and devoted his energy to helping recent German immigrants who had lost their jobs. The city, and the rest of Canada, soon forgot him.

In his final months, after the death of his third wife in 1920, Hespeler moved to Vancouver to be with his son, Alfred. He died there and was buried in St John's Anglican cemetery in Winnipeg, among the city's pioneers. His obituary remembered him as a man "who was at one time so foremost in the life of the province."

ANGELIKA SAUER

AO, RG 80-5-0-42, no.2961. Man., Legislative Library (Winnipeg), Biog. scrapbooks. Univ. of Waterloo Library, Special Coll. Dept. (Waterloo, Ont.), GA 104 (Seagram Museum fonds), sousfonds 1 (Joseph E. Seagram and Sons, Ltd fonds); sousfonds 2 (Seagram family fonds). *Berliner Journal* (Berlin [Kitchener, Ont.]), 1858–72. *Dumfries Reformer* (Galt [Cambridge, Ont.]), 27 Dec. 1854. *Manitoba Free Press*, 19 April 1921. *Nordwesten* (Winnipeg), 1889–1921. *Winnipeg Tribune*, 15 April 1911, 29 May 1930. Alexander Begg and W. R. Nursey, *Ten years in Winnipeg: a narration of the principal events in the history of the city of Winnipeg from the year A.D. 1870 to the year A.D. 1879, inclusive* (Winnipeg, 1879). George Bryce, *A history of Manitoba: its resources and people* (Toronto and Montreal, 1906). Mrs George Bryce, [Marion Samuel], "Historical sketch of the charitable institutions of Winnipeg," Man., Hist. and Scientific Soc., *Trans.* (Winnipeg), no.54 (February 1899): 1–31. Can., Parl., *Sessional papers*, reports of the Dept. of Agriculture, 1871–82. Ernst Correll, "Mennonite immigration into Manitoba: sources and documents, 1872, 1873," *Mennonite Quarterly Rev.* (Goshen, Ind.), 11 (1937): 196–227, 267–83. *CPG*, 1901. Werner Entz, "William Hespeler, Manitoba's first German consul," *German-Canadian yearbook* (Toronto), 1 (1973): 149–52. Arthur Grenke, "The formation and early development of an urban ethnic community: a case study of the Germans in Winnipeg" (PHD thesis, Univ. of Man., Winnipeg, 1975). Angelika Sauer, "Ethnicity employed: William Hespeler and the Mennonites," *Journal of Mennonite Studies* (Winnipeg), 18 (2000): 82–94. W. H. E. Schmalz, "The Hespeler family," *Waterloo Hist. Soc., Annual report* (Kitchener), 57 (1969): 21–29. F. H. Schofield, *The story of Manitoba* (3v., Winnipeg, 1913).

HIESTER, MARY AUGUSTA CATHARINE (Reid), artist; b. 10 April 1854 in Reading, Pa, daughter of John Philip Hiester, a physician, and Caroline Amelia Musser; m. 13 May 1885 George Agnew Reid* in Philadelphia; they had no children; d. 4 Oct. 1921 in Toronto.

Mary Hiester's ancestors emigrated from Germany to the United States in the mid 18th century. Her father died when she was an infant, and about 1863 her mother took Mary and her sister, Caroline, to live with relatives in Beloit, Wis. After her mother's death in November 1875, Mary returned to Pennsylvania, where she lived in Reading with a cousin's family. She then attended the Philadelphia School of Design for Women in 1881–83 and enrolled (most likely on a part-time basis) at the Pennsylvania Academy of the Fine Arts in 1883–85, in classes taught by Thomas Pollock Anshutz and Thomas Eakins. It was at the academy that she met Canadian artist George Reid, a fellow student, whom she married in 1885.

The Reids honeymooned in Europe for four months, visiting London, Paris, Italy, and Spain. In Málaga they saw Mary's sister, who had converted from the family's Lutheran faith to Roman Catholicism and become a nun. On their return they settled in Toronto and established a studio at 31 King Street East, where they gave art lessons. The couple moved, probably in 1888, to quarters in the Toronto Arcade building on Yonge Street, in 1901 to a house on Indian Road, and finally in 1907 to Upland Cottage, a house designed by George in Wychwood Park, a pastoral community north of Toronto. In the spring of 1888 an auction of their work had raised enough money to finance a second trip to Britain and France, in 1888–89. Mary Reid enrolled in the Académie Colarossi in Paris, taking costume-study and life classes under Joseph Blanc, Pascal Dagnan-Bouveret, Gustave Courtois, and Jean-André Rixens. She studied there again in 1896, when the couple made an extensive tour of Gibraltar and Spain, which she described in three articles in *Massey's Magazine* (Toronto). They would make two more trips to Europe, in 1902 and 1910. In addition, the Reids spent every summer from 1891 to 1916 at Onteora, a private literary and artistic club in the Catskill Mountains near Tannersville, N.Y., where they had a house and a studio, both designed on arts and crafts principles by George. They spent their time painting and teaching, their studio having accommodation for ten students, some of whom came from as far away as Toronto.

Reid's oeuvre consists almost exclusively of easel paintings and a few surviving watercolours, but also includes a small number of *marouflée* landscape murals. The most admired of these murals was a view of the Humber River done for the town hall of Weston (Toronto) in 1912–13. She was, however, best known as a painter of floral still lifes, and by 1890 she was widely considered the pre-eminent flower painter in Canada. Critics particularly liked her sophisticated infusion of "character" into the straightforward botanical accuracy emphasized by most of her Canadian predecessors in this genre. As well, she regularly exhibited paintings of gardens, meadows, and other domesticated landscapes, night scenes, and, less frequently, studio interiors and figure studies. Along with a superficial examination of Impressionism, especially in her work of the 1880s and 1890s, she developed an enduring interest in a restricted range of colours to evoke a poetic subjectivity in her paintings, as in *A study in greys*, done about 1913. These were characteristics of the tonalist aesthetic found throughout North American art of the late 19th and early 20th centuries. Reid's attraction to such a palette was reinforced by the paintings of Diego Velázquez, which she had studied and admired in Madrid in 1896. Her work also incorporated elements from the aestheticism of American artist James Abbott McNeill Whistler. These included oriental motifs, which sometimes appear in her still lifes and interior scenes, for example in *Chrysanthemums: a Japanese arrangement* (painted around 1895), and the occasional use of titles to suggest parallels between visual art and music, as in her *Harmony in grey and yellow* (1897). More than most contemporaries, Reid produced work that exemplified the decorative sensibility that was also prevalent in North American art. In this respect she was supported by critics such as Hector Willoughby Charlesworth* of *Saturday Night*, who described Reid's paintings as "exquisitely refined." In explaining the idealized feminine sensitivity that he found in her works, however, he resorted to stereotype, emphasizing that she was a model of humble and gracious womanliness – the perfect helpmate to her more famous husband. Reid said or did little to contradict this image. "Nothing can tempt her to talk about her pictures," Marjory Jardine Ramsay MacMurchy* wrote in the *Globe* in 1910. Yet Reid clearly saw herself as a professional artist. This perception would be echoed in a memorial poem published in 1921 in the *Daily Mail and Empire* and reprinted in the *Canadian Theosophist* (Toronto): "Lived she to work and bless; / This was her heart's delight." In the absence of firmer documentation, however, little else can be said of Reid personally, and the two major portraits of her by her husband provide only tentative clues.

Reid had entered the artistic establishment of Toronto soon after settling there. Elected a member of the

Hilborn

Ontario Society of Artists in 1887, in 1907 she became only the second woman to serve on its executive committee. She was elected an associate of the Royal Canadian Academy of Arts in 1893 and a member of the Canadian Society of Applied Art in 1904. Although, in both Toronto and Onteora, she gave lessons to students, among them Mary Matilda (May) Riter Hamilton, her reputation was principally based upon her exhibited work. She contributed to the annual exhibitions of the OSA and the RCA almost every year between her arrival in Canada and her death, and participated in selected annual exhibitions at the Art Association of Montreal, the Women's Art Association of Canada, and the Canadian National Exhibition. She also showed at the Columbian exposition in Chicago (1893), the Pan-American exposition in Buffalo (1901), and the Louisiana Purchase exposition in St Louis (1904), with Mary Evelyn Wrinch at the galleries of the Art Metropole in Toronto (1912), and with her husband and Wrinch at the Royal Ontario Museum, in aid of the Red Cross Society during wartime (1915).

Following George's appointment in 1912 as principal of the Ontario College of Art, Reid, a member of its board, actively supported its development and life. She had been a fixture of the Toronto art scene for three decades when, in 1919, she began suffering from angina. At the time of her death two years later, many of her paintings were owned by private collectors and others had been acquired by the National Gallery of Canada and the government of Ontario. In 1922 a large retrospective was organized at the Art Gallery of Toronto, the first solo exhibition given there to a woman, and it was enthusiastically praised in the press. By then, however, the visual aesthetic embodied in Reid's art was becoming dated as Canadian artists moved on to new concerns.

BRIAN FOSS

Mary Hiester Reid's articles on her tour of Gibraltar and Spain were published, with illustrations by her husband, in *Massey's Magazine* (Toronto), 1 (January–June 1896): 297–308, 373–84; 3 (January–June 1897): 375–83. Two important portraits of her were painted by her husband: *Portrait of Mary Hiester Reid* (1885) at the National Gallery of Canada (Ottawa) and *Mary Hiester Reid* (1898) at the Art Gallery of Ontario (Toronto). In addition, she is pictured in George A. Reid's *Reverie* (c. 1885) at Museum London (London, Ont.), *Mortgaging the homestead* (1890) at the NGC, and *Sketch portraits of GAR and MHR* (1896) at the AGO. Her paintings *A study in greys* and *Chrysanthemums* are located at the AGO, and *Harmony* is in the Government of Ontario Art Coll., which was transferred to the AO in 2001. Other works by her are in the NGC, Museum London, the Robert McLaughlin Gallery (Oshawa, Ont.), the Agnes Etherington Art Centre, Queen's Univ. (Kingston, Ont.), the Art Gallery of Windsor, Ont., the Art Gallery of Hamilton, Ont., and the Edmonton Art Gallery.

Art Gallery of Ontario, Research Library and Arch., C. W. Jefferys papers, C. W. Jefferys, "The art of Mary Hiester Reid"; George Reid scrapbook. AO, F 1140, minute-books; RG 22-305, no.43899. Moore College of Art and Design (Philadelphia), Philadelphia School of Design for Women, student registration records. Pennsylvania Academy of the Fine Arts (Philadelphia), Records, school reg. of students, 1884–85 (mfm. in Arch. of American Art, Smithsonian Institution (Washington), reel no.62: 221–36); student reg. in antique and life classes, 1858–84 (reel no.62: 666–89). *Daily Mail and Empire*, 11 Oct. 1921. *Farmers' Sun* (Toronto), 24 Oct. 1922. *Globe*, 16 July 1910. Art Gallery of Toronto, *Memorial exhibition of paintings by Mary Hiester Reid, 1922* (Toronto, 1922). *Canadian Farmer, Dairyman and Stockbreeder* (Toronto), 30 Dec. 1922: 24. *Canadian men and women of the time* (Morgan; 1912). *Canadian Theosophist* (Toronto), 2 (1921–22), no.10: 144. V. E. C[lymer] Hill, *A genealogy of the Hiester family* (Lebanon, Pa, 1903). *Directory*, Toronto, 1887–1910. Brian Foss and Janice Anderson, *Quiet harmony: the art of Mary Hiester Reid* (exhibition catalogue, AGO, 2000). E. D. Gaillard, *Onteora: hills of the sky, 1887–1987* (n.p., 1987). Madge MacBeth, "Canadian women in the arts," *Maclean's* (Toronto), 27 (1914), no.12: 23. Muriel Miller Miner, *G. A. Reid, Canadian artist* (Toronto, 1946; rev. ed., *George Reid, a biography*, ed. I. R. Coutts, 1987). M. L. Montgomery, *History of Berks County in Pennsylvania* (Philadelphia, 1886), 595–96. *Saturday Night*, 19 Nov. 1898, 15 Oct. 1921, 21 Oct. 1922.

HILBORN, WILLIAM WILSON, horticulturist, author, and civil servant; b. 8 April 1849 in Yarmouth Township, Upper Canada, son of Levi Hilborn, a Quaker minister and farmer, and Dorothea Harvey; m. 5 May 1883 Johanna (Josie) Hartwig in Arkona, Ont., and they had two sons and two daughters; d. 10 Dec. 1921 in Mersea Township, Ont.

At the age of eight months, William Wilson Hilborn moved with his parents and grandparents to a farm in Lambton County, one mile west of the settlement that would become Arkona. He was educated privately by family members. From a young age he experimented with plants and shrubs, always trying to develop better varieties. At the time of his marriage in 1883 to Josie Hartwig, who had taught sign language to the deaf in Michigan, he purchased the adjoining farm and took up the culture of fruit. He began contributing articles on small fruits and their marketability to the *Canadian Horticulturist* [see Linus Woolverton*] and served as a divisional director of the Fruit Growers' Association of Ontario. The success of his work attracted the attention of William Saunders*, director of the Dominion Experimental Farms, who in November 1886 selected him to become the first horticulturist at the central farm in Ottawa. There Hilborn would work with such agricultural scientists as James Fletcher* and, when Saunders was away setting up new stations, he oversaw the developing farm.

Hilborn's intention, according to his horticultural report for 1887, was to promote fruits that could adapt to extreme Canadian weather conditions. Chosen too for their commercial potential, trees were imported from Russia and northern Europe for experimentation. The plantings in the spring of 1887 included 297 varieties of apples, 101 of pears, 72 of plums, and 71 of cherries, as well as 11 American varieties of peaches and apricot trees from Europe and China. Small fruits – grapes, currants, gooseberries, raspberries, blackberries, and strawberries – were also started. In 1889 the Department of Agriculture published, in both English and French, his practical report on strawberry culture.

Hilborn resigned his post in September 1889 and purchased a 70-acre farm near Leamington in Essex County, the most southerly part of Ontario, where the climate and soils were conducive to early yielding crops. Intending to concentrate on peach culture, he immediately made plans to plant different varieties. He began experimenting as well with gooseberries and currants from varieties he had grown in Ottawa. An energetic promoter, in January 1890 he addressed a meeting held in nearby Kingsville for the purpose of setting up the Essex County Horticultural Society. By December, Hilborn and Edward Maxson, a former head florist in the governor general's gardens in Ottawa, were advertising in the *Leamington Post* that they had erected large greenhouses for "the growth of choice greenhouse plants, gladioli and dahlia bulbs, fruits and early vegetables." Mail orders were accepted and the operation was soon shipping vegetables as far away as Quebec and Manitoba.

In December 1891 the managers of the Ontario Agricultural College and Experimental Farm in Guelph asked Hilborn to accompany them around the province to give lectures. Two years later the Fruit Growers' Association named Hilborn, dominion horticulturist John Craig, and Windsor fruit-grower Alexander McNeill to a committee "to devise a practical scheme for experimental horticulture, contemplating several small stations." In 1894 ten stations were established under the joint control of the association and the OAC. Hilborn was placed in charge of the southwestern station, at Leamington, where he specialized in peaches and strawberries. The firm of Morris and Wellington, which ran the Fonthill Nurseries in Niagara, was so attracted by the station that it bought a farm west of Leamington and sought Hilborn's help in an enterprise that involved planting 10,000 peach trees. The Lake Erie and Detroit River Railway put in a special siding to accommodate the shipment of the fruit expected from this farm.

Near the turn of the century, Hilborn had about 100 acres of peaches, plums, pears, and apricots under cultivation. The fruit-growing industry, especially peach culture, had spread rapidly through the southern portion of Essex on farms with sandy soils. In 1895 Hilborn's brother Joseph Lundy had settled in the area and had begun growing fruit, early vegetables, and

greenhouse crops. About 1898, according to one report, over 1,000 acres of orchards could be seen from Inglewood, W. W. Hilborn's new residence on the Talbot Road. In February 1899 Hilborn and other growers suffered major financial losses when severe frost destroyed most of their trees. Undeterred, Hilborn continued to work with peaches and other plants and small fruits. He had large fields of strawberries and raspberries, including his own variety of blackcap, the Hilborn raspberry, which was planted widely in Canada and the United States. As well, he had his greenhouse operation, grew flowers for sale, and with his wife provided floral arrangements for funerals. Family photographs of Hilborn, some taken in his fields, portray a broad-shouldered man of medium height and build with a weathered face.

Hilborn travelled widely to share his expertise. He prepared award-winning exhibits for international expositions in London, Chicago, and St Louis. A member of the Farmers' Institute staff of speakers for many years, he addressed meetings in nearly every county in Ontario. He judged fruit as far away as California, and both Hilborn and his son Chester Harvey adjudicated at fall fairs throughout western Ontario. At exhibitions and in business, he always stressed careful selection, top quality produce, precise grading and packing, and presentation in attractive containers.

In August 1912 Hilborn sold ten acres of his farm to the manager of the Windsor, Essex and Lake Shore Rapid Railway, which, according to the *Kingsville Reporter*, already had one peach orchard about to bear fruit. His remaining land was divided between his sons, Harvey and William Edward, but he retained a three-acre plot at his residence and turned it into a showplace with colourful flowers and ornate shrubs and trees of new and rare varieties. Despite this reduction of his farm, he continued to experiment and, with one of his sons, maintain a large greenhouse. In November 1917 W. W. Hilborn and Son leased its greenhouse to the Dominion Floral Company for the purpose of cultivating carnations and sweet peas "for the city trade." Four years later complications from cataract surgery led to Hilborn's death. He was buried in Lakeview Cemetery in Leamington.

A man of ambition and enthusiasm, W. W. Hilborn had enjoyed experimenting and developing new strains of plants, shrubs, and trees, an endeavour that gave him an expert knowledge of soils, climatic factors, fertilization, and entomology. Growing fruit for commercial ventures was also a driving force throughout his life. He was one of the earliest agriculturists in south Essex to promote the industry of growing vegetables and flowers under glass, now a prominent business in the area.

MADELINE HILBORN MALOTT and
MARILYN ARMSTRONG-REYNOLDS

Hobson

William Wilson Hilborn's contributions to the *Canadian Horticulturist* (St Catharines, Ont.; Toronto; etc.) are listed, along with other writings by him, in *Science and technology biblio.* (Richardson and MacDonald). His report on the growing of strawberries was published as *Strawberry culture* ([Ottawa, 1889]). A collection of family photographs is in the possession of a granddaughter, co-author Madeline Hilborn Malott of County Road 20, Kingsville, Ont.

AO, RG 80-8-0-812, no.12601. *Amherstburg Echo* (Amherstburg, Ont.), 1889–1917. *Kingsville Reporter*, 22 Aug. 1912. *Leamington Post* (Leamington, Ont.), 18 Dec. 1890, 15 Dec. 1921. T. H. Anstey, *One hundred harvests: research branch, Agriculture Canada, 1886–1986* (Ottawa, 1986). Can., Experimental farms service, *Fifty years of progress on Dominion Experimental Farms, 1886–1936* (Ottawa, 1939); Parl., *Sessional papers*, report of the minister of agriculture, app., report of Experimental Farms, 1887, 1889. *Commemorative biographical record of the county of Essex, Ontario . . .* (Toronto, 1905). B. S. Elliott, *The city beyond: a history of Nepean, birthplace of Canada's capital, 1792–1990* (Nepean, Ont., 1991). *Farmer's Advocate and Home Magazine* (London, Ont.), 1892: 630. N. F. Morrison, *Garden gateway to Canada: one hundred years of Windsor and Essex County, 1854–1954* (Toronto, 1954). Ont., Dept. of Agriculture, Fruit branch, *The fruits of Ontario* (Toronto, 1914); Legislature, *Sessional papers*, 1886, no.6; 1887, no.11; 1893, no.13; 1894, no.37; 1895, no.67; 1900, no.17; 1922, no.44: 19–20.

HOBSON, ROBERT, industrialist; b. 13 Aug. 1861 in Berlin (Kitchener), Upper Canada, son of Joseph Hobson and Elizabeth Laidlaw; m. 31 Oct. 1891 Mary Andrewina Wood in Hamilton, Ont., and they had a daughter; d. there 25 Feb. 1926.

Robert Hobson was born into a railway family. A native of Guelph Township, his father was a highly respected civil engineer who rose to become chief engineer of the Grand Trunk Railway and whose accomplishments included the St Clair Tunnel at Sarnia, Ont., and the rebuilding of Montreal's Victoria Bridge. After attending common schools in Berlin, Robert joined him in the construction department of the Great Western Railway. His family's social status and residence in Hamilton from 1875 brought him into the orbit of hardware merchant Andrew Trew Wood*, who stood at the centre of an ambitious group of capitalists. Hobson married his daughter, and in 1896 Wood turned to his son-in-law to help administer the Hamilton Blast Furnace Company, of which he was president. It had just begun smelting pig iron and though Hobson knew nothing about making iron and steel, he became the firm's secretary-treasurer in February 1896. He threw himself into the job, thus beginning a lifelong fascination with the industry, and soon impressed the board of directors with his managerial abilities. When the company merged with the local Ontario Rolling Mills to create the Hamilton Steel and Iron Company Limited in 1899, he became the new firm's secretary and assistant general manager, and he would take over as general manager in 1904.

The first steel was poured on 15 May 1900, but steel production was then a risky business in Canada. Unlike its giant competitors in Sault Ste Marie, Ont., and Sydney, N.S., the smaller Hamilton firm pursued a cautious policy of slow growth and diversification of products to serve many different markets. The company's plant in the city's suburban east end became a nucleus around which many large corporations established metalworking factories. Hobson would help attract a number of them, including International Harvester in 1902 and National Steel Car in 1913.

In 1910 an opportunity emerged to integrate the firm's primary production with the manufacturing of secondary products. That year the Montreal-based promoter William Maxwell Aitken* acquired options on the Montreal Rolling Mills and Dominion Wire Manufacturing and, rejecting a purchase offer from United States Steel, set out to organize a Canadian merger. He called together Charles Seward Wilcox, president of Hamilton Steel and Iron, Cyrus Albert BIRGE, president of a screw and tack company in Hamilton, and Lloyd Harris, head of Canada Bolt and Nut in Toronto. Out of their negotiations emerged the Steel Company of Canada Limited in June. Wilcox became president and Hobson general manager of this vastly bigger corporation; it established its headquarters in Hamilton, where Hobson provided the energy and skills needed to knit the new enterprise into a major corporate success, of which he would become president in 1916. For Hobson its emergence was marred only by the death of his daughter, Dorothy Wood, in April 1910 as a result of an automobile accident.

At the outbreak of World War I, Hobson was one of North America's most prominent steel men. With his corporation's rolling mills and finishing plants as assured consumers, he had been able to initiate a major expansion to create state-of-the-art facilities. Most important were the electrically powered mills completed in 1913 for breaking down steel ingots into blooms, bars, and rods. Increasingly Hobson and his plant supervisors were changing the complexion of the local labour force by recruiting large numbers of recent immigrants from southern and eastern Europe. By 1914 recession had hit the Steel Company, but when the war eventually brought a massively increased demand for steel, his company expanded again by adding a munitions department for turning out shells, for which it developed a special steel. In 1917 a rolling mill to produce sheet metal – vital for the growing automobile industry – was added and iron and coal properties were acquired in the United States. Known as Stelco from about 1915, the company emerged from the war as the largest, most diversified steel maker in Canada.

Hobson's management style was paternalistic and authoritarian. His affability apparently built allegiance among his white-collar staff, but he crushed all efforts by his blue-collar workers to form unions. At the end of the war, however, he recognized that Stelco had to appeal more directly for their loyalty, and a company magazine, safety program, and pension plan were instituted. As president, Hobson had a particular responsibility to scout out markets and sound out broader trends in the international capitalist economy. In this work he travelled widely in Britain, Europe, and North America to meet with powerful business-men. He also kept abreast of new developments in the industry by attending the annual meetings of the American Iron and Steel Institute, of which he had become a director by 1913. He was as well a fel-low of the Royal Colonial Institute in London and an active member of the American Institute of Mining Engineers.

Hobson had not restricted himself to the fortunes of one company. He participated in a tight web of inter-locking directorships in Hamilton, joining the boards of the Landed Banking and Loan Company and Tuck-ett Tobacco in 1910, the Bank of Hamilton in 1915, and Dominion Power and Transmission in 1917. A tall, genial, articulate man with a large white mous-tache and a jaunty air, he emerged as a leader when the business community wanted to express its collective concerns. In 1909 he was elected first chairman of the newly formed Hamilton branch of the Canadian Man-ufacturers' Association, and he served on its executive several times over the next decade. When the Ontario commissioner investigating workers' compensation, Sir William Ralph MEREDITH, visited Hamilton in 1912, Hobson took charge of presenting business's case. He also became the leading voice of the Hamil-ton Employers' Association, formed after the city's production of munitions was disrupted by a huge strike in June 1916.

Like many other capitalists of this period, Hobson moved comfortably too within the emerging national business elites centred in Montreal and Toronto. He personally invested on a national scale, and was added to the boards of the Canadian Locomotive Company in Kingston, Toronto General Trusts, North Star Oil and Refining in Calgary, and Canada Steamship Lines in Montreal, of which his brother, Joseph Irvine, was treasurer. He was unapologetic about this widening capitalist vision. In 1915, when rumours suggested the Bank of Hamilton was about to be taken over by the Royal Bank of Canada, he publicly defended, to loud protest from Hamilton politicians, small busi-nessmen, and labour leaders, the right of a local bank to merge into a larger corporate unit. The merger would be "in the public's interest," he proclaimed, since strong banks were a "national asset." Not sur-prisingly, he would have no qualms about joining the board of the Canadian Bank of Commerce when it absorbed the Bank of Hamilton in 1923. The federal government named him in September 1918 to the board formed to direct the beleaguered Canadian Northern Railway [see Sir William MACKENZIE], to which the Canadian Government (later Canadian National) Railways were added in November. It is unlikely that Hobson was dismayed when Andrew Ross McMaster rose in the House of Commons in 1921 to denounce the alleged interlocking director-ships held by four members of the Canadian National board: chairman David Blythe Hanna*, Hobson, Tho-mas Cantley*, and Edward Rogers Wood*.

Well before the war Hobson had emerged as a kind of industrial statesman who carried the concerns of the business community into the political realm. His skills brought him onto the executive council and the tariff and transportation committees of the CMA in 1901, to its Ontario vice-presidency in 1907, and to its national presidency in 1908. A long-time Liberal, he joined other Canadian industrialists in publicly denouncing Sir Wilfrid Laurier*'s reciprocity platform three years later; he served on the executive of the Canadian Home Market Association, the CMA's front organiza-tion for supporting the Conservative election cam-paign of 1911. Henceforth he gave his allegiance to the Conservatives. As late as 1920 he continued to maintain that the elimination of tariff protection would spell the end of Canada's steel industry.

Hobson may have reached the pinnacle of his influ-ence locally and nationally during the war. In Hamil-ton he was a director of the Canadian Patriotic Fund, and, as chair of its finance committee, he used his many connections to raise money to support the dependants of local men in the armed forces. He would remain active on the fund's local relief commit-tee until 1923. As a close friend of Conservative prime minister Sir Robert Laird Borden* and his finance minister, William Thomas White*, Hobson was not only consulted regularly, he was also recruited for the munition resources commission in 1915 and the new Honorary Advisory Council for Scientific and Indus-trial Research (later the National Research Council) a year later. In 1919 he was added to the executive of the Canadian Reconstruction Association, the national business organization that attempted to smooth the transition from war to peace and to promote class har-mony in the face of popular unrest.

Long an active member of Hamilton's Central Pres-byterian Church, the religious home of many in the local elite, Hobson served on its board of trustees. He had been a freemason since 1888, when he joined the Scottish rite as a member of the Murton Lodge of Per-fection, in which he held several offices, including inspector general of the Supreme Council. No prude, he enjoyed the masculine pleasures of his class. He was a director of the Hamilton Jockey Club and, despite an early football injury that left him with a permanent limp, he enjoyed outdoor sports in the

Hodgins

Hamilton Golf and Country, Tamahaac, and Caledon Mountain Trout clubs. Exuding bonhomie and a flair for sporty attire, he mixed business and pleasure in the exclusive lounges of his clubs in Hamilton, Montreal, Ottawa, and Toronto. Hamilton was shocked when he died suddenly of a brain haemorrhage in February 1926.

Robert Hobson was a new breed of industrialist in the early 20th century. No rags-to-riches entrepreneur, he entered middle management from the middle-class profession of engineering, honed his skills in a large corporation, exercised a leadership role within the Hamilton business community, and reached a level of influence that extended far beyond that steel town. With his acumen as a corporate administrator and his leadership abilities, he was a major player in planting a vital new industry, helping transform the nature of work inside Canadian factories, and generally bringing corporations to a central role in Canadian economic, social, and political life.

CRAIG HERON

AO, RG 22-205, no.14385; RG 80-5-0-191, no.12937; RG 80-8-0-904, no.35583. LAC, MG 28, I 230, 16: 1909–10; 17: 1915–20; 18: 1921–26; MG 30, A16. *Daily Times* (Hamilton, Ont.), 18 Feb. 1896. *Hamilton Herald,* 18 Sept. 1918, 26 Feb. 1926. *Hamilton Spectator,* 26 Feb. 1926. American Iron and Steel Institute, *Yearbook* (New York), 1912–26. *Annual financial rev.* (Toronto and Montreal), 1902: 113; 1910: 254; 1911: 190; 1916: 92, 329; 1917: 227, 418; 1920: 442, 567. R. C. Brown, *Robert Laird Borden: a biography* (2v., Toronto, 1975–80), 1: 190. *Canadian annual rev.,* 1903–26. *Canadian Engineer* (Toronto and Montreal), 7 (1899–1900): 141. *Canadian men and women of the time* (Morgan; 1912). Canadian Patriotic Fund, Hamilton and Wentworth Branch, *Five years of service, 1914–1918* ([Hamilton?, 1920?]). *DHB,* vol.3. D. B. Hanna, *Trains of recollection drawn from fifty years of railway service in Scotland and Canada,* ed. Arthur Hawkes (Toronto, 1924), 271. Craig Heron, "Working-class Hamilton, 1895–1930" (PHD thesis, Dalhousie Univ., Halifax, 1981); *Working in steel: the early years in Canada, 1883–1935* (Toronto, 1988). *Industrial Canada* (Toronto), 2 (1901–2): 12, 75, 101, 331; 3 (1902–3): 44; 4 (1903–4): 92; 6 (1905–6): 204–5, 637; 7 (1906–7): 266–68; 8 (1907–8): 209, 278. William Kilbourn, *The elements combined: a history of the Steel Company of Canada* (Toronto and Vancouver, 1960). J. E. Middleton and Fred Landon, *The province of Ontario: a history, 1615–1927* (5v., Toronto, 1927–[28]), 3: 61–63. Ont., Commission on laws relating to the liability of employers, *Final report on laws relating to the liability of employers to make compensation to their employees for injuries received in the course of their employment which are in force in other countries and second interim report on laws relating to the liability of employers,* commissioner W. R. Meredith (Toronto, 1913): 32–46. P. E. Rider, "The Imperial Munitions Board and its relationship to government, business, and labour, 1914–1920" (PHD thesis, Univ. of Toronto, 1974). Victor Ross and A. St L. Trigge, *A history of the Canadian Bank of Commerce, with an account of the other banks which now form part of its organization* (3v., Toronto, 1920–34), 3. Mel Thistle, *The inner ring: the early history of the National Research Council of Canada* (Toronto, 1966), 60. *Who's who and why,* 1914–16, 1921.

HODGINS, WILLIAM EGERTON, lawyer, civil servant, and army officer; b. 3 Oct. 1851 (some sources give 1850) in Toronto, eldest son of John George Hodgins* and Frances Rachel Doyle; m. first 23 June 1880 Caroline Seymour Clark (d. 28 Feb. 1881) in Cobourg, Ont.; m. secondly 30 Oct. 1883 Eleanor Jaffray Ritchie in Ottawa, and they had two sons and a daughter; d. there 27 Feb. 1930.

The son of a long-time deputy superintendent of education, William Egerton Hodgins appears to have enjoyed the privileges associated with being born to an upper middle class family. He was educated at Hellmuth College in London, Ont., and the University of Toronto (BA 1874, MA 1875). Admitted to the bar in 1877, he practised in Toronto and for a time in Bowmanville; in addition, he attempted to secure various public registrarships. His first wife, Carrie, died at childbirth in 1881. Following his remarriage, to a daughter of Chief Justice Sir William Johnston Ritchie*, he was hired as a barrister in November 1883 by the federal Department of Justice. One of his first assignments for its minister from 1885, John Sparrow David Thompson*, was the compilation and publication of documents on the allowance and disallowance of provincial and territorial legislation, a voluminous and useful work that Hodgins would later update.

At an early age he had also embarked on a military career. He entered the Toronto Military School in 1866 as a cadet, and served as a trooper during the Fenian raids. While at university, he joined the 2nd Battalion of Rifles (Queen's Own Rifles of Canada) and in 1877 he became a captain. Following his move to Ottawa, he transferred to the No.1 Battalion of Infantry (Governor General's Foot Guards); promoted major in 1890, he assumed command of the regiment in 1894, apparently with some reluctance since it was in a state of disarray. Even so, his tenure seems to have been without controversy, and he served as an aide-de-camp to a number of governors general. A member of the councils of the Dominion and Ontario rifle associations, from 1897 to 1903 he was secretary of the national organization. In 1903 he accepted appointment to the Permanent Force, a move that necessitated his retirement from the justice department; appointed colonel in 1909 and brigadier-general in 1914, he held a number of district commands.

In January 1915, during World War I, Hodgins was made acting adjutant-general in Ottawa, and in September he was promoted major-general. In September 1917, as a representative of the Department of Militia and Defence, he joined the demobilization committee of the Overseas Military Forces of Canada, based in

England and chaired by Sir Hugh Montagu Allan*. He threw himself into this work with characteristic zeal; he studied how other countries approached the problem and his reports were perceptive and comprehensive. In a draft report in February 1918 to the minister in Ottawa, Sydney Chilton Mewburn, Hodgins, maintaining that demobilization and repatriation were "inseparably allied," recommended two new government departments, for "reconstruction" and "pensions and invalids," and a central advisory committee. He was far removed, however, from the political negotiations that produced the Department of Soldiers' Civil Re-establishment that same month. Hodgins retired from service in March, and in June he was created a CMG. Both of his sons had also served with distinction in the war, and one, Frederick Owen, would die in 1924 as a consequence of disabilities resulting from the conflict.

A "splendid athlete" in his youth, Hodgins was an active member of the Royal Ottawa Golf Club, the Rideau Curling Club, and the local branch of the Royal Caledonian Curling Club. An Anglican, in Ottawa he attended St George's Church and then All Saints'; in 1920 he participated "whole-heartedly" in the Anglican "Forward Movement." He then began to slow down, though some recognition would still come his way. In 1925, for instance, the University of Toronto awarded him an LLD. Following his death after a brief illness in February 1930, it was reported in obituaries that he had held the record for the longest military service in Canada. Hodgins had performed competently in two very different careers, law and the military, which he favoured. He never attained the fame of some contemporary military figures, but he performed his tasks, a number of them quite onerous, with proficiency. He was apparently ill rewarded, for his estate consisted almost entirely of life insurance. Enormously popular in Ottawa, he was accorded one of the largest military funerals seen in the city for many years.

KERRY BADGLEY

During his time with the Department of Justice, William Egerton Hodgins compiled *Correspondence, reports of the ministers of justice and orders in council upon the subject of provincial legislation, 1867–1887* (2v., Ottawa, 1886–88). Volumes were subsequently compiled by him for the periods 1867–95, 1896–98, 1899–1900, and 1901–3.

AO, RG 22-354, no.14506; RG 80-5-0-92, no.7870; RG 80-8-0-71, no.13346. LAC, MG 26, H, 65; MG 30, E48; RG 13, 35, 39, 72, 74, 128; RG 25, 206: file M3/54; RG 31, C1, 1881, Bowmanville, Ont., div.1: 61 (mfm. at AO); RG 150, Acc. 1992-93/166, box 4411. UTA, A1973-0026/152(91). *Ottawa Evening Journal*, 28 Feb., 3 March 1930. Gordon Bale, *Chief Justice William Johnstone Ritchie: responsible government and judicial review* (Ottawa, 1991), 273. Can., Parl., *Sessional papers*, 1901, no.30: 4. *Canada Gazette*, 12 Oct. 1877: 384; 28 April 1883: 1781; 20 Oct. 1917: 1253.

Canadian annual rev., 1909, 1914, 1917. *Canadian men and women of the time* (Morgan; 1898 and 1912). *Directory*, Toronto, 1880–83. *Dominion annual reg.*, 1883: 185. Governor General's Foot Guards, *Steady the buttons two by two: Governor General's Foot Guards regimental history, 125th anniversary, 1872–1997*, comp. R. M. Foster *et al.* (Ottawa, 1999).

HOPKINS, JOHN CASTELL, bank clerk, author, and imperialist; b. 1 April 1864 in Dyersville, Iowa, eldest son of John Castell Hopkins and Triandra Phelia Boyd Heu-de-Bourck; m. 2 Oct. 1906 Annie Beatrice Mary Bonner in Toronto, and they had two daughters; d. there 5 Nov. 1923.

Of British parentage, Castell Hopkins moved as a child with his family to Bowmanville, Ont., where he completed his education. Between 1883 and about 1891 he worked as a clerk with the Imperial Bank of Canada, first in Bowmanville and from 1889 in Toronto. During the mid 1880s the British imperial tie became one of his abiding passions: in Ingersoll on 28 May 1886 he played a key role in the formation of the Ontario branch of the Imperial Federation League and in November 1888 he became an honorary secretary of the dominion League. During this period he set his sights too on a literary career; in February 1887 Goldwin Smith* of Toronto had applauded, but declined to contribute to, Hopkins's planned project to "diffuse correct information about the Colonies." Hopkins left banking to join the strongly imperial Toronto *Empire*, where he quickly moved from clerk to associate editor, a position he relinquished in 1894 to freelance full-time.

Hopkins did not possess a "hardy physique" but was a fast writer, one who allowed few distractions. An Anglican, he did not marry until 1906 (Annie Bonner, a Roman Catholic, was half his age). According to one biographer, his "life was one of great nervous activity" and "his literary output was probably larger than any other publicist in the Dominion." In a writing career that spanned three decades, he produced some 40 books and pamphlets, wrote extensively for newspapers, journals, and other publications in Canada and abroad, and coordinated and edited a number of series, including the first encyclopedia on Canada. Produced in six volumes between 1898 and 1900, this work, a good deal of it prepared by Hopkins himself, was meant to document authoritatively Canada's past and present; Canada "requires only to be known in order to be great," he wrote. In addition, each year between 1901 and 1923 he edited and wrote much of the ambitiously conceived, massively detailed, and still widely consulted *Canadian annual review of public affairs*, which he intended to be an impartial compendium of statistics, current events, speeches, and press opinions. He was assisted in this project by his wife.

A good deal of Hopkins's work reflected his strong attachment to British imperialist philosophy, a gospel that had a wide audience. Closely related and also evident was a romanticized sense of history and an acceptance of the popular idea of progress. For Hopkins these strands came together in a view of national development that stressed Canada's advancement under British guidance. The logical goal was membership in an imperial federation in which Canada would play a key role. Like most imperialists, Hopkins was suspicious of possible aggression by the United States and he loathed what he saw as its excessive democracy and materialism. He provided hagiographical depictions of groups who championed the British connection, such as the United Empire Loyalists and Canada's defenders in the War of 1812; chosen individuals such as Prime Minister Sir John Sparrow David Thompson* were squeezed into an imperial mould, regardless of their true sentiments. Similarly, in well-meant but condescending caricature, French Canadians were cast as loyal habitants. Hopkins took his imperialism very seriously, and did not hesitate to publicize its trappings. In 1910, for example, he issued a pamphlet on the origins of Empire Day in Canada (in which he gave credit to Sir George William Ross*, thus undermining the claim of Hamilton imperialist Clementina Fessenden [Trenholme*]).

Whatever the imperial crusade, Hopkins offered unqualified support. In *South Africa and the Boer-British war* . . . (Brantford, Ont., 1900) he upheld the cause by defending the liberty of Anglo Uitlanders against autocratic and cruel Dutch Boers. He went on to portray World War I as a struggle between British civilization and German authoritarianism, so that in such works as *The province of Ontario in the war* . . . (Toronto, 1919) he used his pen as a sword to rally Canadians. He came to celebrate the war years as Canada's coming of age within the international community, something demonstrated, he said, by the acceptance of Canadian delegations at the Paris Peace Conference in 1919 and the League of Nations. However, he insisted that this new status had been attained with Britain's support and thus did not adversely affect the dominion's commitment to the empire. He could not recognize that the nationalism generated by the war had, in fact, moved Canada away from Britain, a trend reinforced during the 1920s by a desire to avoid costly involvement in another European conflict. Furthermore, the United States had become Canada's pre-eminent trading partner. The declining influence of imperialism was also reflected in scholarly works that explained the essence of Canada by reference to theories centred on North America.

Most of Hopkins's work thus fell into obscurity after his death in 1923, little of it sustained by literary merit. Much had been written in haste, the result of professional need and journalistic energy. In a patronizing critique of one of his books, academic historian William Stewart Wallace* said its only use was "to lend an air of refinement to the parlours of many farmhouses throughout the countryside." Referring to Hopkins's deferential treatment of Thompson, which came out within two months of his death, historian P. B. Waite finds its language "flat, even flatulent" and the biography "for most purposes dead."

If, as Carl Berger suggests, Hopkins did not mix easily with such elite imperialists as George Taylor DENISON, he did correspond with most of Canada's leading imperialist thinkers, and important links were maintained through his many associations. A member of the Orange order, the Sons of England, and the council of the British Empire League, he was president in 1891–92 of the Toronto Young Men's Liberal Conservative Association and in 1910–11 of the Empire Club of Canada, which he had helped found in 1903. Connections were no doubt made too through his memberships in major historical societies and the Toronto-based Albany Club, Rosedale Golf Club, and Royal Canadian Yacht Club. He was, as well, a fellow of the Royal Statistical Society, the Royal Geographical Society, and the Royal Society of Literature of the United Kingdom.

Hopkins's books, pamphlets, and articles provide considerable insight into the imperialist mindset that so profoundly affected Canadian politics and society during the late 19th and early 20th centuries. Longer lasting in impact was the meticulous effort made by Hopkins to record contemporary history in his *Canadian annual review*, a project that was carried on by his wife from 1923 to 1936 and, after a long hiatus, was reborn in 1960.

JEFFREY A. KESHEN

There is no comprehensive listing of John Castell Hopkins's publications, but partial ones appear in Middleton, *Municipality of Toronto*, vol.2: 32–33, and in an MA paper prepared by the author, "The policies of Canada's chief press censor during the Great War" (MA memoir, Carleton Univ., Ottawa, 1986). Most of Hopkins's books and pamphlets have been made available on microfiche by the CIHM and are listed in its *Reg.*

Representative publications include *Canada and the empire; a study of imperial federation* (Toronto, 1890); *Canada and American aggression* ([Montreal, 1892]); *The maple leaf and the Union Jack: a brief study of the imperial connection* (Toronto, 1892); the entries for "D'Alton McCarthy," "Wm. Ralph Meredith," and "Charles H. Tupper," in *Men of the day: a Canadian portrait gallery*, ed. L.-H. Taché (32 ser. in 16v., Montreal, 1890–[94]), 14th, 20th, and 24th ser., respectively; *Life and work of Mr. Gladstone; a great and varied career* (Toronto and Brantford, 1895); *Life and work of the Rt. Hon. Sir John Thompson* . . . (Toronto, 1895); *Queen Victoria: her life and reign* . . . (Toronto and Brantford, 1896; another ed., Toronto, 1901); *The sword of Islam; or, suffering Armenia* . . . (Brantford and Toronto, 1896); *Progress of Canada in the nineteenth century* . . . (Toronto and Brantford, 1900); *The story of the dominion: four hun-*

dred years in the annals of a continent . . . (Philadelphia and Toronto, 1901); *The origin and history of Empire Day* (Toronto, 1910); *French Canada and the St. Lawrence; historic, picturesque and descriptive* (Toronto, 1913; repr., 1974); "The war of 1812–15," *OH*, 12 (1914): 42–57; and *Canada at war, a record of heroism and achievement, 1914–1918* (Toronto, 1919).

Hopkins also edited *Canada, an encyclopædia of the country: the Canadian dominion considered in its historic relations, its natural resources, its material progress, and its national development* (6v., Toronto, 1898–1900), to which he contributed numerous articles, among them "The imperial federation movement in Canada," 6: 53–57.

AO, F 102; RG 80-2-0-227, no.45365; RG 80-5-0-344, no.3324. LAC, MG 29, D35. *Globe*, 7 Nov. 1923. *Toronto Daily Star*, 6 Nov. 1923. *World* (Toronto), 3 Oct. 1906. Carl Berger, *The sense of power; studies in the ideas of Canadian imperialism, 1867–1914* (Toronto and Buffalo, N.Y., 1970). *Canadian men and women of the time* (Morgan; 1898 and 1912). *Canadian who's who*, 1910. *Directory*, Toronto, 1889–1900. *Encyclopaedia of Canadian biography . . .* , vol.3: 55. *The Oxford companion to Canadian history and literature*, ed. Norah Story (Toronto, 1967). *Standard dict. of Canadian biog.* (Roberts and Tunnell), vol.2. P. B. Waite, *The man from Halifax: Sir John Thompson, prime minister* (Toronto, 1985). *Who's who in Canada*, 1922.

HORNBY, JOHN, northern traveller and soldier; b. 21 Sept. 1880 in Church Minshull, England, youngest son of Albert Neilson Hornby and Ada Sara Ingram; d. unmarried 16 April 1927 on the Thelon River, N.W.T.

Jack Hornby's father, whose family were cotton magnates in Blackburn, Lancashire, captained England in both cricket and rugby. Herbert Ingram, his maternal grandfather, had owned the *Illustrated London News*. His brother Albert Henry led Lancashire's cricket team; his other brothers would predecease him: George in Africa in 1905 and Walter of wounds at the end of World War I. Like his father and brothers, he was educated at Harrow (1894–98). Afterwards he lived in Germany to learn the language as part of an uncompleted diplomatic training.

In 1904 Hornby came to Canada to visit a cousin, Cecil Armitstead, at Onoway, near Edmonton. After three years exploring and working in the Lac Ste Anne area of Alberta, he freighted for surveyors on the Grand Trunk Pacific Railway in 1907. His first journey into the Barren Ground of the North-West Territories began the next year, with a trading and hunting party led by fellow Englishman James Cosmo Dobrée Melvill. The group spent the winter on Great Bear Lake (1908–9), visited the Coppermine River district (1909–10), and wintered again on Great Bear (1910–11). This is when, as author George Whalley describes it, Hornby's "fatal devotion" to the Barren Ground began. Hornby subsequently connected himself to the missionary expedition of Jean-Baptiste Rouvière, an Oblate priest. In 1912 he travelled with Canadian engineer George Mellis Douglas to the Coppermine, a journey described by Douglas in *Lands forlorn . . .* (New York, 1914).

Following the outbreak of war in 1914, Hornby joined the 19th (Alberta) Dragoons as a private. He survived the first use of poison gas in warfare at Ypres (Ieper), Belgium, on 22 April 1915. In September he applied for a commission in the South Lancashire Regiment and was gazetted second lieutenant. In June 1916, shortly before the battle of the Somme, he received the Military Cross. Wounded in the back and shoulder during this battle, he was invalided to England. Once his injuries had healed, he walked out of a convalescent hospital near London and by September he had returned to Canada. In December he was decommissioned on account of ill health.

Funded by his mother, Hornby wandered in British Columbia and the north, trapping, hunting, and at times barely surviving. From 1923 to 1925 he explored and trapped in the Artillery Lake–Thelon River area with James Charles Critchell-Bullock, a retired British officer. After attending his father's funeral in England in December 1925, he came back to Canada in 1926 accompanied by a young cousin, Edgar Vernon Christian. Hornby took him and a former Royal Air Force officer, Harold Challoner Evan Adlard, into the Barren Ground to winter in the Thelon–Dubawnt River region. Though Hornby prided himself on being able to live off the land – an ability some questioned – the migrating caribou failed to come and, lacking sufficient supplies, the party starved to death in the spring of 1927. Christian, the last of the three to succumb, left a diary describing their experience. Their bodies, left alone by prospectors who discovered the party's cabin in July 1928, were buried nearby the following summer by the Royal Canadian Mounted Police.

What motivated John Hornby to lose himself in the north? Even before the Great War he had tried to winter there with inadequate supplies, but following the trauma he suffered in the war, which probably led to post-traumatic stress disorder, his desire to risk his life and the lives of others intensified. His sense of guilt over having survived the war was likely increased by the deaths of his two brothers and his father. By a cruel irony he took two younger men with him when he perished in 1927.

JOHN FERNS

E. [V.] Christian, *Unflinching: a diary of tragic adventure*, intro. and conclusion B. D. Roberts (London, 1937). *Death in the Barren Ground: Edgar Christian*, ed. George Whalley ([Ottawa], 1980). Clive Powell-Williams, *Cold burial: a true story of endurance and disaster* (New York, 2002). Malcolm Waldron, *Snow man: John Hornby in the Barren Lands* (Boston, 1931; repr., intro. Lawrence Millman, 1997). George Whalley, *The legend of John Hornby* (Toronto, 1962).

HORNER, RALPH CECIL, farmer, Methodist clergyman, revivalist, and holiness bishop; b. 22 Dec. 1853 near Shawville, Lower Canada, eldest son of James Horner and Ellen Richardson; m. 27 Nov. 1890 Annie E. McDonald in Ottawa, and they had at least four daughters and three sons; d. 12 Sept. 1921 near Ivanhoe, Ont.

Of Anglican, northern Irish descent, Ralph C. Horner was a third-generation farmer on the Quebec side of the Ottawa valley across from Renfrew. His father had died when he was 16, and he had been obliged to abandon his schooling to run the farm. Immediately after his spiritual conversion at a Methodist camp meeting nearby in July 1876, he received a second blessing of entire sanctification or complete holiness [see James Caughey*] and began to serve as a lay revivalist at religious gatherings in his neighbourhood. He testified to the gifts God had granted him, particularly holiness. He later achieved through prayer a third blessing from the Holy Spirit of a pentecostal "Tongue of Fire," which empowered him to evangelize. "The extra gift for soul winning has been the aggressive element in my experience," he wrote in his memoirs. "It brought all the dormant powers of my soul into activity, and energized all my faculties for efficiency in the vineyard of the Lord."

In 1882 Horner became a probationer in the Methodist Church of Canada to facilitate his labours as an evangelist – he always denied being called to regular pastoral duties. He served his first year on the Clarendon circuit south of Renfrew County, and from 1883 to 1885 he studied theology at Victoria University in Cobourg. During his last probationary appointment, in 1885–86 to Cobden and Locksley in Renfrew, he spent time in Philadelphia obtaining a bachelor of oratory from the National School of Elocution and Oratory. After a short but public disagreement with officials of the church's Montreal Conference over the nature of ordination – the Methodists had no irregular or special ordination to become an evangelist – he was ordained on 29 May 1887. Nevertheless, he was appointed one of the conference's evangelists for the next three years. The church had established the positions to avoid the disciplinary and theological difficulties often associated with independent, transient preachers. No revivalist could preach within a jurisdiction without permission from the conference and the local circuit.

With his highly emotional and enthusiastic preaching, emphasis on entire sanctification and the pentecostal third blessing, and reliance on wild physical manifestations such as shouting, crying, flailing about, and prostration, Horner was soon censored by his superiors and Methodists intent on keeping the denomination respectable. As well, he disobeyed established regulations by evangelizing wherever he decided he could be effective, even if his "flaming" revivals interfered with the work of the local clergy. To discipline him, the conference stationed him in 1890–91 to the Portage-du-Fort circuit, near Shawville. However, he hired a supply minister in July 1890 and continued his independent evangelism. Because he had converted thousands in the Ottawa valley and adjoining territories, and had also published several useful religious books, his unconventional conduct was overlooked and he was appointed a conference evangelist for 1891–92 and again for 1892–93. In November 1890 he had married the 23-year-old Annie McDonald, who had been an assistant in revivalist services he had visited and who would help him in his evangelism.

In 1893, in response to further complaints about Horner's conduct (including his hiring untrained and unlicensed lay preaching assistants) and at his own request, the conference's stationing committee left him without an appointment. With his lay preachers, Horner bought a former Baptist church in Ottawa in order to enlarge and formalize his work. The following year he was stationed to the Combermere circuit in Renfrew, but his refusal to go and his increasing unwillingness to follow the doctrine and discipline of the church forced it to depose him in 1895. Horner, whose religious tracts included studies of John Wesley and Methodist holiness, argued that the church opposed the preaching of the great Wesleyan doctrine of entire sanctification. Initially he had been supported by the conservative general superintendent, Albert Carman*, but Carman could never accept any repudiation of disciplinary authority. Moreover, the church's powerful liberal wing refused to condone Horner's excesses and criticisms of institutional Methodism.

By the early 1890s Horner had united with like-minded Methodist clergy, including Nelson Burns* and Albert Truax, and laity in espousing holiness principles. Among Methodists, in 1895 they reorganized the Canada Holiness Association (founded in 1879) to form the Christian Association. In 1894 Horner had become a member of the extreme holiness organization, the Wesleyan Methodist Connection of America; after his expulsion he unsuccessfully attempted to have it incorporated in Canada. In 1897 he founded the Holiness Movement Church in Canada, with himself as bishop. The church attracted several thousand disenchanted Methodists, Baptists, and other evangelical Christians in the Renfrew–Montreal–Kingston triangle. The denomination soon gained support as well in Ontario's Bruce peninsula and in western Canada, where many members migrated. It operated overseas missions (especially in Egypt) and opened a publishing house and seminary in the Horners' residence in Ottawa. Beginning in 1897, the denomination published the *Holiness Era* journal. In Ontario, Hornerites were normally farmers or workers who were facing rural depopulation or economic decline. They also felt threatened by aggressive Roman Catholicism and, like other conservative Protestants, they mistrusted liberal theological modernism.

To his followers, Horner's self-possessed style, espousal of holiness, and willingness to confront the apparently lax "professors of religion" were mesmerizing. In his sermons and writings he claimed to have known infusions of power that enabled him to convert sinners. Speaking about 1899 on a favourite passage, Micah 3:8 ("But truly I am full of power by the Spirit of the Lord"), he recalled his first experience: "On a Saturday evening, while in my tent waiting for a victory for the Sabbath, this text came, and with it a cyclone of power; I could not sit, stand or lie; I was in every shape and form, and the tent, 40 x 60, seemed too small to hold me. I longed to be outside to have room. . . . I preached the next day on 'Truly I am full of power.' All the opposers ran to the altar for mercy."

Horner always considered himself a faithful follower of Wesley and a defender of scriptural Christianity. Although not a premillennial Adventist, he believed the world should be prepared for the second coming. Most important, he argued that every sanctified person should seek the additional blessing of the pentecostal baptism of fire, which empowered the individual to prevail before God on behalf of sinners, and thereby help convert the world. Because Horner felt these standard Wesleyan principles were being violated, even within his own denomination, in 1916 the bald, white-bearded bishop and a substantial minority of members in the Holiness Movement Church formed the Standard Church of America, with headquarters and a publishing house in Brockville, Ont. Much of the division, in fact, had centred on Horner's style of episcopacy and his inability to accept advice from new generations of holiness leaders. During the early 20th century, many holiness congregations were breaking apart and re-forming around specific leaders and issues, including the implications of pentecostalism, especially speaking in tongues.

An evangelist to the end, Ralph C. Horner died in 1921 during a camp meeting he was conducting near Ivanhoe, Ont., north of Belleville. He was buried in Merivale Cemetery near Ottawa.

NEIL SEMPLE

Ralph Cecil Horner's publications include *Pentecost* (Toronto, 1891); *Notes on Boland; or, Mr. Wesley and the second work of grace* (Toronto, 1893); *Fragments from the feast; or, 18 sermons*, ed. E. T. Campbell (Belleville, Ont., 1902); *Bible doctrines* (2v., Ottawa, 1908–9); *The doctrines of the Standard Church of America defined and proved from Scripture . . .* (Brockville, Ont., n.d.); and *Ralph C. Horner, evangelist: reminiscences from his own pen; also reports of five typical sermons*, issued posthumously by his widow Annie E. [McDonald] Horner (Brockville, [1926?]). Issues of the *Holiness Era* (Ottawa) from 1897, 1899, and 1900 are available on microfilm at UCC-C.

ANQ-O, ZQ127/28, 13 juill. 1854. AO, RG 22-354, no.10387; RG 80-5-0-175, no.2132; RG 80-8-0-818, no.15841. LAC, RG 31, C1, 1901, Ottawa, Wellington Ward, div.9: 18 (mfm. at AO). *Ottawa Evening Journal*, 16 Sept. 1921. *Canadian men and women of the time* (Morgan; 1912). G. H. Cornish, *Cyclopædia of Methodism in Canada . . .* (2v., Toronto and Halifax, 1881–1903), 2. *Directory*, Ottawa, 1901. Marilyn Fardig Whiteley, "Cyclones of power/noisy display: the holiness conflict in the Methodist Church," Canadian Methodist Hist. Soc., *Papers* (Toronto), 11 (1997): 11–25. B. R. Ross, "Ralph Cecil Horner: a Methodist sectarian deposed, 1887–1895," Canadian Church Hist. Soc., *Journal* (Toronto), 19 (1977): 94–103. Neil Semple, *The Lord's dominion: the history of Canadian Methodism* (Montreal and Kingston, Ont., 1996).

HORNER, RALPH JOSEPH, conductor, composer, music teacher, and journalist; b. 28 April 1848 in Newport, Monmouthshire, Wales, son of James Horner and Sarah ——; m. there first 1869 Marianne Amelia Rowse (d. 1915), and they had three sons and a daughter; m. secondly 3 June 1920 Mrs Sarah Aily Carter in Winnipeg; d. 7 April 1926 in Winnipeg.

Although Ralph Horner's earliest proclivities were musical, he was apparently destined for a business career. Yet "the natural bent of his mind was so clearly manifested," a later biographical account states, "and his progress so rapid that at the age of eleven he officiated as pianist to the Newport Choral Society notwithstanding parental opposition."

From 1864 to 1867 Horner studied at the Leipzig Conservatory. After returning to London in 1868 he conducted choirs and operatic productions for the Peckham Choral Society and was choirmaster at St Mary's Church, Peckham. For seven years he directed the English Opera Company and also operas at Alexandra Palace, London. He taught piano, singing, and harmony at Camberwell (London) during 1869. From 1878 to 1888 he conducted operas composed by Gilbert and Sullivan throughout the British provinces. Following these successful tours he settled in Nottingham, where he led the Nottingham Amateur Orchestral Society, the Nottingham Operatic Society, and the Nottingham Philharmonic Choir. He lectured in music at University College in Nottingham for ten years. In 1893 he took a BM and in 1898 a DM, both at the University of Durham.

In 1906 Horner landed in North America and for a brief period he lived in New York City. In 1909 he arrived in Winnipeg. He was immediately named director of the Imperial Academy of Music and Arts, a position he held until 1911. As music editor from 1909 to 1914 of *Winnipeg Town Topics*, high society's weekly journal of cultural, musical, and artistic matters, he helped establish standards of taste for many Winnipeggers. From 1909 to 1912 he conducted the Winnipeg Oratorio Society. He also directed an opera troupe, which in 1911 presented his comic opera *The belles of Barcelona*. A charter member of the Men's Musical Club of Manitoba, he served as vice-president during its inaugural year, 1915–16. The club's mandate was the promotion, elevation, and extension of the "art of music." Members also discouraged and condemned any measures which would debase the standard of music in Manitoba. This objective befitted Horner's principles and status as well as the genteel aspirations of the amateur and professional artistic community carving a niche for itself within the rapidly growing metropolis of Winnipeg. The club would continue to perform Horner's work after he left it to serve as bandmaster in the 190th and 250th Infantry battalions during 1916–17. Following World War I he resumed teaching music in Winnipeg and he served as choirmaster of St Matthew's Church from 1921 to 1925. From about 1917 until his death he directed the Ralph Horner Opera Company in Winnipeg.

Horner's musical compositions were many and varied. They included operas (*Amy Robsart*, *The belles of Barcelona*, and *A fairy overture*), the *Intermezzo for orchestra in B major*, six operettas, two oratorios (*St. Peter's* and *David's first victory*), cantatas (including the dramatic cantata *Confucius*), many piano pieces, several anthems, and part-songs. Some of his approximately 100 songs were published by the firm Reeder, Weekes, and Ashdown.

A prominent member of social and musical circles for many years, Ralph Horner was described as "Winnipeg's grand old man of music, and one of her best known citizens," a reputation he well deserved.

DAVID LARSEN

Man., Dept. of Finance, Consumer and Corporate Affairs, Vital statistics (Winnipeg), no.1920-03126. *Manitoba Free Press*, 24 Sept. 1909, 8–9 April 1926. *Encyclopedia of music in Canada* (Kallmann *et al*.). G Sharp Major [G. S. Mathieson], *Crescendo; a business man's romance in music* (Winnipeg, [1935?]). *Pioneers and prominent people of Manitoba*, ed. Walter McRaye (Winnipeg, 1925). *Who's who and why*, 1921.

HOWARD, LEONORA ANNETTA (King), teacher and medical missionary; b. 17 March 1851 near Farmersville (Athens), Upper Canada, daughter of Peter Gilton Howard, a farmer, and Dorothy E. Carter; granddaughter of Dr Peter Howard*; m. 21 Aug. 1884 Alexander King in Tientsin (Tianjin, People's Republic of China); d. 30 June 1925 in Peitaiho (Beidaihe, People's Republic of China).

Educated in Soperton, near the family farm in Leeds County, Leonora Howard attended teachers' college in Syracuse, N.Y., and spent some years teaching in eastern Ontario, but she really wanted to be a physician. Because the Royal College of Physicians and Surgeons of Kingston would not accept women

for training, she applied to the medical school of the University of Michigan, which admitted her in 1872. She graduated with honours and an MD in 1876. The previous year she had applied to and been adopted by the Woman's Foreign Missionary Society of the American Methodist Episcopal Church. Perhaps she had been influenced by Adelaide Galliland, a member of Leonora's Methodist church in Soperton and the first Canadian woman to live in China, as the wife of an American missionary, Virgil Hart.

In 1877 Leonora was sent by the WFMS to China, where she took up residence in Peking (Beijing) to assist the American physician Lucinda L. Coombs, the first female doctor in China. After Coombs left the WFMS to marry in 1878, Leonora continued on her own and as an itinerant physician, operating from back doors, from broken-down inns, and even under trees in remote provincial villages. In August 1879 she was summoned to Tientsin by Li Hung-chang, the viceroy of Chihli province, to attend his wife, then recovering from serious illness.

Leonora was subsequently invited to remain – an extraordinary recognition of a westerner – and was given a portion of the memorial temple to statesman Tseng Kuo-fan in which to practise. Because of Lady Li's influence, the doors (and presumably the wallets) of many wealthy and aristocratic Chinese were opened to her. Shortly thereafter Li Hung-chang's mother left $1,000 for her work, a contribution said to be the first bequest to missionary endeavour from a Chinese woman. Leonora's prestige was further enhanced in 1880, when missionaries and news correspondents credited her with helping secure the Sino-American treaty negotiated by James Burrill Angell, the American ambassador to China and president of the University of Michigan.

In 1881 Leonora opened, in Tientsin, the WFMS-sponsored Isabella Fisher Hospital for Women and Children, named for an American benefactor. As a result of Leonora's efforts, the medical work of the WFMS's North China mission became centred in Tientsin rather than Peking. Leonora regretted that her group's evangelistic work did not keep pace with their medical work, though in reality she put less emphasis on conversion and fundamentalism than others did. In 1884 she married a widowed Scottish minister who had come to China in 1880, Alexander King of the London Missionary Society. Female missionaries who married were obliged to join their husband's organizations, but although Leonora had to resign from the WFMS, she was never officially attached to the LMS. She now worked almost exclusively for the Chinese, who called her Dr Ke Ye-da (Chinese for King). In 1885 she opened the Government Hospital for Women and Children, again sponsored by Lady Li.

Leonora and Alex took their allotted furlough in 1891 to travel to Canada and England. When war broke out between China and Japan over the tributary country of Korea in 1894, Leonora closed her hospitals to all but Chinese soldiers and sailors. For her heroic efforts this tall, slim physician was awarded the Imperial Order of the Double Dragon the following year, thus becoming the first western woman to be made a mandarin. During the Boxer rebellion of 1900, the Kings and three others were the only missionaries to remain and work in besieged Tientsin – the rest fled to Japan or home. In 1902, a year after the death of Leonora's mentor Li Hung-chang, the Kings went on just the second furlough of their careers: Alex returned to England and Scotland while Leonora, who loathed Britain's climate, took medical courses in Vienna.

In 1908 she opened China's first Government Medical School for Women in Tientsin, to teach Chinese women to become doctors and nurses. In 1915 a new Isabella Fisher Hospital was launched by the WFMS and a room was named in honour of Leonora King. Though she and her husband officially retired in 1917, they continued their "service of healing and love." Sometime during this period they adopted Agnes Clarke, the daughter of British missionaries who had died during a disturbance.

The Kings travelled to Canada again in 1923 to visit Leonora's family and look for a retirement property near Gananoque, in the county of her birth. Following her return to China to pack their belongings and close their houses, officials in Tientsin refused to let her practise any medicine. The reasons are unclear: perhaps she was being held to her retirement or was being sidelined by the new "China for the Chinese" attitude. Before she could leave she died of influenza at her country home in Peitaiho; her gravesite cannot be located. Alex King died in England in 1939.

MARGARET NEGODAEFF

Sources for Howard's life can be found in the author's full-length biography, *Honour due: the story of Dr. Leonora Howard King* (Ottawa, 1999).

HOYLES, NEWMAN WRIGHT, lawyer, educator, and Anglican layman; b. 14 March 1844 in St John's, son of Hugh William Hoyles* and Jean Liddell; m. 27 Nov. 1873 Georgina Martha Moffatt, daughter of Lewis Moffatt*, in Toronto, and they had two sons and two daughters; d. there 6 Nov. 1927.

A third-generation Newfoundlander, Newman Hoyles grew up in St John's, the son of a leading lawyer and future premier and chief justice. In 1858 his parents sent him for schooling, not to Britain, but to Upper Canada College in Toronto. After two years there, Hoyles attended King's College in Windsor, N.S., and Trinity College in Cambridge, England, where he took a BA in classics and won medals in rowing. Hoyles then pursued a legal career in Toronto.

Articled in 1869 and called to the bar three years later, he formed a partnership with James Bethune that grew into a prominent law firm, which included Charles Moss* and William Glenholme Falconbridge*. He was named QC by the Ontario government in 1889.

In 1894 Hoyles succeeded William Albert Reeve* as head of the law school run by the Law Society of Upper Canada – Ontario's only accredited law school – at Osgoode Hall in Toronto. Hoyles, whose partner Charles Moss had chaired the hiring committee, had been widely seen as the establishment candidate. He had declined to apply until the salary was raised by 25 per cent, to $5,000.

The school's program of morning lectures, followed by service "under articles" in local offices, was mandatory for would-be lawyers in Ontario. Innovations at Harvard and at Dalhousie University in Halifax [*see* Richard Chapman WELDON], however, had begun to establish the full-time, academic LLB as the standard credential for North American lawyers, so Osgoode Hall's training was controversial. Hoyles shared the conviction of the Law Society, which controlled the call to the bar, that no university program could adequately provide the practical training lawyers needed, and that a "learned and honourable" profession had to see to the education of its own. He believed all his life that schooling in arts or classics, followed by intense professional apprenticeship, produced the best lawyers.

In the early 20th century, when advocates of university law schools often favoured them as much for their potential to exclude socially undesirable elements from the profession as for their intellectual aspirations, Osgoode Hall accepted many students who had begun legal studies simply by finding lawyers willing to instruct them. Hoyles's opposition to academic control over legal credentials may have reflected an underlying liberalism as well as professional pride. Throughout his tenure (and until 1957), the Law Society treated university programs as worthwhile but held that they conferred no entitlement to be called to the bar. Hoyles thus rejected several overtures from the University of Toronto. Even while helping to keep Ontario universities out of professional education in law, he was a long-time member of the University of Toronto's senate, and he received an honorary LLD from Queen's College in Kingston in 1902.

Few innovations marked Hoyles's 29 years as principal. Though he lectured regularly, he published no legal scholarship of substance. A popular figure, nicknamed Daddy by his students, he was reported to be kindly, courteous, and helpful. It was during his tenure that Ontario's first women lawyers, notably Clara Brett MARTIN, and most of its early Jewish lawyers, among them Arthur Cohen*, entered the profession. In 1923 Hoyles called the entry of women the most important change seen during his principalship, though he doubted whether they would succeed "in the highest branches of law – in pleading in court." He retired in 1923, not quite 80 years old, and was succeeded by his deputy, the much more scholarly John Delatre Falconbridge*.

Hoyles's other lifelong commitment was Anglican evangelicalism. In Newfoundland his family had supported evangelical causes, but friends said his faith had been sparked in 1877 by the Toronto crusade of the Irish-born evangelist William Stephen Rainsford. At the time disputes between evangelicals and Anglo-Catholics were causing near-schism in the diocese of Toronto. The lay evangelicals, low church but not low society, were led by Samuel Hume Blake* and other social and professional colleagues of Hoyles who poured their organizing skills and funds into supporting "protestant" Anglicanism.

Hoyles did mission work in his parish (St Philip's), but his most visible contribution was service to evangelicals' institutional network. In 1877 he helped found the Protestant Episcopal Divinity School [see James Paterson Sheraton*], the evangelical alternative to Trinity College in Toronto, where his father-in-law was a council member. Religious-oriented organizations later supported by Hoyles included Bishop Ridley College in St Catharines and Havergal Ladies' College and the *Evangelical Churchman* in Toronto. He served for decades on the boards, and eventually as chairman or president, of these bodies. In 1904 he negotiated the merger of the Upper Canada Bible Society with other provincial societies to form the Canadian Bible Society, and he would serve as its national president until 1921. He was a frequent delegate to the General Synod of the Church of England in Canada, from its foundation in 1893 until 1908, and he represented the church and its missionary society at international congresses.

He and his family lived in Toronto's Annex district, on Lowther Avenue after 1892 and later on Huron Street. His elder son, Hugh Lewis, who had attended both University College and Osgoode Hall and was called to the bar in 1906, joined the Canadian army while practising law in Montreal and was killed in action in 1918. Family tradition suggests that, at the end of his life, Newman Hoyles was somewhat estranged from his widowed daughter-in-law, who had soon remarried. But his will, signed five months before his death in 1927 at age 83, was scrupulously fair in providing for his own widow, making small bequests to friends and relatives, and dividing the rest of his $45,000 estate among his three surviving children and Hugh's son and daughter. Obituaries of Hoyles stressed his absolute faith in the Bible and his "quiet," "unobtrusive," and "unswerving" service to Osgoode Hall and to the evangelical cause.

CHRISTOPHER MOORE

[Family traditions were kindly provided by John Hoyles of Ottawa, a great-grandson of the subject. C.M.]

AO, RG 22-305, no.58183. Law Soc. of Upper Canada Arch. (Toronto), 1–5 (Convocation, rolls), common roll, Michaelmas term, 1869; Curtis Cole, "A history of Osgoode Hall Law School, 1889–1989." *Globe*, 28 Nov. 1873. *Mail* (Toronto), 28 Nov. 1873. *Toronto Daily Star*, 26 Nov. 1923. Canadian Bible Soc., *Annual report* (Toronto), 1928. *Canadian men and women of the time* (Morgan; 1912). *The jubilee volume of Wycliffe College* (Toronto, 1927). Christopher Moore, *The Law Society of Upper Canada and Ontario's lawyers, 1797–1997* (Toronto, 1997). W. W. Pue, "Common law legal education in Canada's age of light, soap and water," *Manitoba Law Journal* (Winnipeg), 23 (1995): 654–88. *The roll of pupils of Upper Canada College, Toronto, January, 1830, to June, 1916*, ed. A. H. Young (Kingston, Ont., 1917).

HUARD, VICTOR-ALPHONSE (baptized **Joseph-Alphonse**) (until the beginning of the 1890s, he sometimes spelled his family name **Huart**), Roman Catholic priest, professor, school administrator, naturalist, author, editor, museum curator, and the first provincial entomologist of Quebec; b. 28 Feb. 1853 in Saint-Roch ward, Quebec, son of Laurent Huard, a joiner, and Ursule Thérien; d. 15 Oct. 1929 at Quebec.

Victor-Alphonse Huard attended the Petit Séminaire de Québec as a day student from 1863 to 1872, completing his classical studies with high standing. He began taking a particular interest in the natural sciences as a result of an event in June 1869. As he would later note in his book *La vie et l'œuvre de l'abbé Provancher*, which was published at Quebec in 1926, he was this naturalist's hiking companion on an outing in Montreal by students of the Séminaire de Québec. Léon Provancher* had just founded a journal at Quebec, *Le Naturaliste canadien*, to disseminate information about natural history in French Canada. A firm friendship developed between the young college student and the man who would become his mentor. Their correspondence, which commenced in 1872, was maintained without a break until Provancher's death in March 1892. In 1872 Huard began studying at the Grand Séminaire de Québec. He was granted the degree of BD in 1875 and would be ordained to the priesthood in the basilica of Notre-Dame at Quebec on 13 Aug. 1876.

Huard arrived in Chicoutimi on 6 Oct. 1875. Archbishop Elzéar-Alexandre Taschereau* of Quebec had invited him to go there and participate in the initial work of the seminary. Teachers were in short supply in the Saguenay region, which had only recently been opened to settlement [see Nicolas-Tolentin Hébert*]. Until 1893, when he would begin concentrating solely on the administration of the seminary, he would teach religion, languages, rhetoric, zoology, and geography. He took on other important offices as well, serving as the first director of the Grand Séminaire (1878–80) and as secretary (1880–89), prefect of studies (1881–

87), vice-superior (1892–96, 1899–1900), and superior (1896–99) of the Séminaire. Many additional tasks made heavy demands on his time: the founding of the Académie Saint-François-de-Sales (1877) and the organization of the library (1876–78, 1880–81) as well as of the bookstore (1880–94). He was also the promoter of the house orchestra, curator of the museum, annalist, and co-founder and co-editor of *L'Oiseau-mouche*, the student newspaper at the Petit Séminaire.

Huard made his passion for natural history an integral part of his duties. On 14 May 1876 he wrote in the seminary's annals: "Little children take part enthusiastically in the hunt for insects, which they capture by lifting up stones in the fields. Not a stone is to be found in all the surrounding grounds that has not been lifted. They have collected at least 500 beetles since the beginning of the month in this way." But his contribution to the field of natural science really took off in 1894, when Provancher's "disciple" – as he chose to call himself – resumed publication of *Le Naturaliste canadien,* which had ceased to appear in June 1891. At first, Huard managed to keep the magazine alive without a grant. The governments of Sir Lomer GOUIN and Louis-Alexandre Taschereau* would give him financial assistance from 1919. Huard's magazine was more modest and less technical than Provancher's had been, and it would remain so until about 1910. After that, as a result of contributors in the fields of geology, zoology, ornithology, microbiology, and entomology, *Le Naturaliste canadien* would become a popular magazine with varied and original content that Huard would publish without interruption until his death in 1929.

In 1901 Huard returned to live at Quebec, where he continued to popularize science by writing a number of textbooks. The first, published in 1905, was entitled *Traité élémentaire de zoologie et d'hygiène.* From 1907 to 1925, a series of short works for the use of educational institutions would be published and reissued at Quebec. These included the *Abrégé de zoologie,* the *Manuel des sciences usuelles* (written in part by Abbé Henri Simard), the *Abrégé de minéralogie,* the *Abrégé de botanique,* and the *Abrégé de géologie.* Their popularity, which held up, proved that Huard's textbooks met a need in the province's schools.

Over the years Huard acquired a name in the field of the natural sciences. In 1904 he became curator of the Musée de l'Instruction Publique. This office, which he would retain until 1927, let him keep an eye on the scientific collections that his mentor had sold in 1877 to the provincial Department of Public Works and Agriculture for the creation of the museum. From 1913 to 1916 Huard was the province's first titular entomologist.

Huard cherished great hopes as well. He wanted to complete the entomological work that Provancher had put aside after investigating five orders of insects, leaving the study of the lepidoptera, the diptera, and the aptera still undone. If Huard's project had materialized, it would have resulted in a ten-volume work. All his life, he wanted to undertake this task, but writing his textbooks kept him from it until the spring of 1927. In the end he had time to update only one of Provancher's manuscripts, which had been written in 1880 on "Les lépidoptères *lepidoptera.*" Huard published an expanded version of it at Quebec in 1929, under the general title *Faune entomologique de la province de Québec.* This volume on the diurnal lepidoptera was his only entomological publication on taxonomy, since his death occurred shortly afterwards. The study on moths that he was preparing at the time would never be published.

Huard had also been actively involved in the religious life of his day. Although a speech impediment of a slight stammer and shyness kept him from undertaking regular parish duties, they did not deprive him of talent as a communicator. In 1895, while living in Chicoutimi, he helped found *Le Messager de Saint-Antoine.* The following year he also began assisting with its English-language version. With Elzéar DE LAMARRE, he was co-editor of this monthly (in French and English) until he left Chicoutimi in 1901. On his return to Quebec, he became the editor of *La Semaine religieuse de Québec,* a weekly founded by Provancher in 1888, and he carried out this responsibility until August 1913.

In the field of religion, as in that of the natural sciences, Huard was awarded a number of prestigious honours. The Royal Society of Canada admitted him as a member of the section on biological and geological sciences on 27 May 1913, and in 1916 he was granted the degree of doctor of science *honoris causa* by the Université Laval. Given the Pro Ecclesia et Pontifice cross in 1903 and made an honorary canon of the metropolitan chapter of Quebec in 1915, he received a special apostolic blessing from Pius XI in 1924. The news of his final honour, an appointment as domestic prelate of the pope, arrived the day after his death.

An educator valued by his students, an able popular scientific writer, and a conscientious organizer, Victor-Alphonse Huard succeeded in reconciling his duties as professor, editor, curator, and man of religion. Because he had linked the work of the 19th-century naturalists and the scientific revival in French Canada at the dawn of the 20th century, experts consider him the successor to Provancher. A model both for the naturalists of his day and for scientists in the future, Huard stands out as a "diligent intellectual worker, a perfect gentleman, [and] accomplished priest." Such was the tribute Mgr Eugène Lapointe*, of the Séminaire de Chicoutimi, paid him shortly after his death.

MÉLANIE DESMEULES

Hubbard

[In addition to the works cited above, Victor-Alphonse Huard published several books and pamphlets, among them: *Impressions d'un passant: Amérique, Europe, Afrique* (Québec, 1906) and *Manuel théorique et pratique d'entomologie* (Québec, 1927). For the most part, his other works can be consulted on microfiche and are listed in the CIHM *Reg.* As curator of the Musée de l'Instruction Publique, Huard published in Que., Parl., *Sessional papers*, 1908–9, a report that covers the years 1893–1909 and, as entomologist in the Department of Agriculture, he published another report in Que., Parl., *Sessional papers*, 1912–13.

Huard is also the author of hundreds of articles which appear in the following periodicals between 1877 and 1929: *L'Abeille* (Québec), *L'Alma mater* (Chicoutimi, Qué.), *L'Almanach de l'Action sociale catholique* (Québec), the *BRH*, *Le Canada français* (Québec), *La Kermesse* (Québec), *Le Messager de Saint-Antoine* (Chicoutimi), *Le Naturaliste canadien* (Chicoutimi; Québec), *La Nouvelle-France* (Québec), *L'Oiseau-mouche* (Chicoutimi), *La Semaine religieuse de Québec*, and RSC, *Trans.*

Numerous documents concerning Huard are conserved at the Arch. du Séminaire de Chicoutimi, in the Abbé V.-A. Huard papers (C-11 and C-12) and in the general records of the Séminaire de Chicoutimi (C-20 and C-21). The first collection contains about 24,000 letters that he received, as well as various manuscripts of his works. It has not yet been processed, but researchers can consult a nominal index and a card catalogue that provides a guide to the 344 files. The second collection includes some portraits of Huard (C-20, fiche 587). Huard's scientific and religious library is held in the Salle Huard in the Arch. du Séminaire de Chicoutimi, where there are also volumes of newspaper clippings (of 500 pages each), which he classified under different categories: "Varia Saguenayensia" (15v.), "Varia Scientifica" (9v.), and "Varia de Variis" (70v.).

Huard's entomology collection, held at the Pavillon Louis-Jacques-Casault, is prominent among the Coll. de l'Univ. Laval.

At ANQ-SLSJ, in the Coll. de la Soc. Hist. du Saguenay (P2), there are copies of Huard's correspondence between 1875 and 1912 (S1, D1050), articles and handwritten notes (S1, D1206), a letter, dated 1896, from Charles Arnaud* to Huard (S2, D6), reports, along with other letters and articles (S2, D174), and his correspondence on the subject of *Le Naturaliste canadien* between 1866 and 1922 (S2, D316). The archives also has the correspondence that Huard conducted with François-Xavier Gosselin between 1888 and 1929 (P165).

There is no detailed biography of Huard. The following items are among the most useful for studying his life: *L'Action catholique* (Québec), 8 nov. 1929; *Le Devoir*, 15, 19 oct. 1929; Yvon Paré, "À la découverte de notre littérature," *Le Quotidien du Saguenay–Lac-Saint-Jean* (Chicoutimi), 1ᵉʳ sept. 1979; *La Semaine religieuse de Québec*, 12 août 1926; 17, 24 oct. 1929; 6 mars 1930; Yves Thériault, "Un exquis prosateur du siècle dernier," *La Patrie du dimanche* (Montréal), 20 déc. 1959; *BCF*, 1926; Luc Chartrand *et al.*, *Histoire des sciences au Québec* (Montréal, 1987); Raymond Desgagné, "Mgr Victor-Alph. Huard," *Saguenayensia* (Chicoutimi), 1 (1959): 102–4; Mélanie Desmeules, "Les années chicoutimiennes du *Naturaliste canadien*," *Saguenayensia*, 43 (2002), no.3: 19–21; Conrad Laforte, "Essai de bio-bibliographie de monseigneur Joseph-Victor-Alphonse Huard, P.D." (école de bibliothécaires, univ. de Montréal, 1949); Georges Maheux, "Feu le chanoine V.-A. Huard, 1853–1929," *Le Naturaliste canadien*, 57 (1930): 6–10; J.-M. Perron, "La course à relais du *Naturaliste canadien*," *Le Naturaliste canadien*, 125 (2001), no.2: 6–10; Adrien Robert, "Le chanoine V.-A. Huard, 1853–1929," Entomological Soc. of Que., *Annals* (Sainte-Foy, Que.), 6 (1960): 148–49; André Simard, *Les évêques et les prêtres séculiers au diocèse de Chicoutimi, 1878–1968; notices biographiques* (Chicoutimi, 1969), 569–71; RSC, *Trans.*, 3rd ser., 24 (1930), proc.: vi–vii. M.D.]

HUBBARD, MABEL GARDINER (Bell), homemaker, venture capitalist, and social reformer; b. 25 Nov. 1857 in Cambridge, Mass., second daughter of Gardiner Greene Hubbard and Gertrude Mercer McCurdy; m. there 11 July 1877 Alexander Graham BELL, and they had two sons, who died in infancy, and two daughters; d. 3 Jan. 1923 in Chevy Chase, Md, and was buried at Beinn Bhreagh, near Baddeck, N.S.

Mabel Hubbard was born into a rich, well-connected Massachusetts family. Her life and destiny were profoundly affected by deafness caused by scarlet fever at age five. It was the prevailing opinion in the United States that children who became deaf in their early years could not retain the ability to speak; signing was thus considered the best means of communication. To prevent Mabel from becoming mute, Gertrude Hubbard found tutors who could teach her to lip-read and reinforce her speech, so that much of the time her highly intelligent daughter was educated among hearing children. Mabel's father, a distinguished lawyer, played a leading role in securing a charter for the Clarke Institution for Deaf-Mutes at Northampton, where children were instructed in speech; he served as its first president. Though Mabel did not attend the school, at nine she testified before a committee of the Massachusetts legislature to aid the cause. Its members plied her with questions in history, geography, and arithmetic, which she answered with assurance; her voice, though not perfect, was intelligible, according to biographer Lilias M. Toward. Many years later, Mabel, whose triumph over her handicap had led her to conduct her life among hearing people, wrote to her daughter Elsie May commending the school: "Having taught you all my life to forget that I was deaf, I now want you to remember it, at least to the extent of looking on the Clarke School as a sort of family affair whose welfare is a family concern."

It was as a teacher of speech and the deaf that Alexander Graham Bell met Mabel Hubbard. One year out from Scotland, he had left Canada for Boston in 1871 to give a series of talks and he quickly became admired for his teaching techniques. He opened a school, lectured at Boston University's School of Oratory, and worked on inventions. "I both did and did not like him," Mabel wrote in her journal after her teacher Mary True brought her to meet him in 1873 to see if he

492

could improve her articulation. Her sentiments quickly became more positive; engaged in 1875, they married two years later, the telephone by then a reality. On the back of a family picture of Mabel are the words "The girl for whom the telephone was invented." The couple's touching and lively letters bear witness to a lifetime of loving companionship. While away in 1879 testifying in a lawsuit over the telephone, Bell implored her to make him write: "Make me describe and publish my ideas that I may at least obtain credit for them and that people may know that I am still alive and thinking. . . . You are the mistress of my heart and sharer of my thoughts . . . so I send you a few ideas – as they come to me – to be added to the list of unwritten inventions and upon my return to be written out by US." All their life together, Bell relied on her avowal, "I believe thoroughly in you, Alec dear."

It was on Cape Breton Island, N.S., where much of Bell's work after the telephone was accomplished, that the slender, gentle New Englander left her own legacy. The widely travelled family were residents of Washington but Bell disliked its summers. In 1885, with their daughters, the couple made their first summer trip to Baddeck, on the Bras d'Or lakes, and were delighted. "May it be long before fashionable people with their big hotels, big trunks and high charges find their way here," wrote Mabel on 17 September. They returned the following year – they would do so for the rest of their lives, sometimes spending six months at a time – and established themselves in a farmhouse on a property on the outskirts of Baddeck they called Crescent Grove. Bell then bought, parcel by parcel, the headland across the bay that he named Beinn Bhreagh (beautiful mountain). Here they constructed Cape Breton's biggest house and, eventually, miles of roads, wharves, workshops, and a laboratory. In time much of the population of Baddeck became involved in the experiments Bell conducted there. Granddaughter Dr Mabel Hubbard Grosvenor, who witnessed some of these activities as a child, told journalist Jocelyn Bethune, "We grew up with wonders – they seemed commonplace."

Bell's involvement in his work often set him apart. On occasion Mabel complained of "that work of yours of which I am so proud and yet so jealous," but she was tolerant of all his eccentricities and solitary habits. With his eyesight failing, he also needed assistance. When his work with large kites led to thoughts of powered flight, Mabel encouraged him and four young collaborators to set up a formal organization in 1907. She financed the group as the Aerial Experiment Association with $35,000 of her own money, thus becoming the North American aviation industry's first backer. Independently wealthy, she had been further enriched at the time of her marriage when Bell turned over to her all but ten shares in the Bell Tele-

phone Company. Mabel managed all the family's expenses. "Mr. Bell . . . didn't want to be bothered with petty cash and money and bills and Mrs. Bell was more than willing," recalled Edith (Polly) Mac-Mechan. "I was Mrs. Bell's secretary, so I paid the bills. That was fun, too – a great eye-opener for me as to what real money can do." A daughter of Halifax professor Archibald McKellar MacMechan*, Polly met her husband, Claude Congreve Dobson, in 1920 when he arrived with a British naval team to inspect the hydrofoil built by Bell and Frederick Walker (Casey) Baldwin*.

Particularly during earlier summers in Baddeck, before marriages and grandchildren claimed her attention, Mabel had participated vigorously in the community's life. The Bells brought new ideas and legitimized them by their personal involvement. Perhaps Mabel's favourite project was the establishment in 1891 of the Young Ladies Club of Baddeck, one of the first Canadian women's clubs. Founded "to stimulate knowledge and promote sociability," it drew inspiration from a similar type of club she had attended in Washington. A. G. Bell drew up its constitution and it continues to this day as the Bell Club. A former president, Jocelyn Bethune, maintained that, because of the strong religious and political affiliations of the times, in the area around Baddeck "there was not a lot of tolerance for a different point of view. . . . People moved in their own circles." At the club, however, "everybody was brought together in a friendly atmosphere which I think owed a lot to Mrs. Bell's ability to make people feel comfortable." After one meeting Mabel wrote, "There is nothing like real country life when you know how to manage it so that you have real sociability. I have more of this here than I do in Washington." Members met in their homes and each meeting featured an address by one of them. Since there was only one public library in Nova Scotia, in Halifax, they raised money to subscribe to newspapers and magazines. With George Kennan, a Washington friend and journalist who also summered in Baddeck, Mabel rallied support for a library. It became a reality when she bought a former Methodist church, named it Gertrude Hall after her mother, and donated it to the community. The Young Ladies Club also played a role in the development of a national home and school association. On 18 Dec. 1895, after Bell's talk to the club on the parents' organizations he had encouraged at American schools for the deaf, a group of interested women met at Baddeck Academy and formed a parents' association, the first in Canada.

In the 1890s Mabel's interests also encompassed handicrafts. Picking up on ideas made popular by the English arts and crafts movement, she tried to introduce better techniques and materials so that home crafts could generate significant income for rural women. It may have been her example that led her daughter Marian Hubbard (Daisy) to back the work of American occupational therapist Lillian Burke, who about 1927 helped Acadian women in the Chéticamp area of Cape Breton turn rug hooking into a source of profit. Baddeck recognized Mabel's contributions, and tradition has it that sometime in the 1890s, though women did not have the franchise, the town gave her the right to vote in local elections. (History does not relate whether it was exercised.)

Gardens were a lifelong interest for Mabel Bell. Older people remembered that on her walks through Baddeck she would lean over fences, look, and chat about what was growing. She oversaw the development of magnificent gardens at Beinn Bhreagh. After Daisy's marriage in 1905 to David Grandison Fairchild, the plant explorer for the United States Department of Agriculture who helped develop the Florida citrus industry, Mabel often grew unusual foreign plants. One was the edible udo, of Japanese origin, which had been thought to have potential as a cash crop. It never caught on because, unless it was cultivated and harvested with great care, it could taste like turpentine. Mabel was a generous donor of flowers and plants, and for years udo roots flourished in local gardens. Her delight with the outdoors extended as well to her participation in experiments at Beinn Bhreagh, to boating, and to excursions. Even in the months before her death she loved to camp out. As Daisy related, "She couldn't read our lips very well by firelight, so in the evenings she put cushions on the ground and read by the car headlights."

"Mother always did her own thinking," Daisy recalled in a letter to the Bell Club some years after Mabel's death, "and it is interesting . . . to realize what a completely original individual she was. I don't think it was just because her deafness saved her from the endless objections and criticisms that so many of us hear when we have a new idea to put over. She just knew what she thought would be fun or interesting or worth while to do and then tried to do it." Mabel Bell died of cancer at Daisy's home near Washington on 3 Jan. 1923, six months after her husband's passing, and is buried next to him on top of Beinn Bhreagh.

DOROTHY HARLEY EBER

The author wishes to thank Bell Club members Jocelyn Bethune and Nancy Langley of Baddeck, N.S., Ainsley MacFarlane of the Alexander Graham Bell National Historic Site there, and Judith Tulloch of Parks Canada in Halifax for providing information on Mabel Bell.

Alexander Graham Bell National Hist. Site of Canada, Bell Museum (Baddeck, N.S.), A. G. Bell family coll. Library of Congress, Manuscript Div. (Washington), 0030M, A. G. Bell family papers. New York Times, 4 Jan. 1923. D. H. Eber, Genius at work: images of Alexander Graham Bell (Toronto, 1982; repr., Halifax, 1991). From the records: the Bell Club treasures, comp. L. M. Toward and Sharon Mac-Donald (Baddeck, 1992). C. V. Madder, History, 1895–1963, the Canadian Home and School and Parent-Teacher Federation (Oshawa, Ont., 1964). L. M. Toward, Mabel Bell: Alexander's silent partner (Toronto, 1984).

HUGHES, KATHERINE (Catherine) ANGELINA, teacher, journalist, public servant, author, and Irish political activist; b. 12 Nov. 1876 in County Line (Emerald Junction), P.E.I., daughter of John Wellington Hughes, a merchant, and Annie Laurie O'Brien; d. 26 April 1925 in New York City.

Katherine Hughes was the second youngest of nine children in a close-knit, lower middle class, Irish Catholic family in which service on behalf of the church was highly valued. Her uncle Cornelius O'Brien* was archbishop of Halifax from 1883 until 1906. Hughes was educated in Charlottetown at Notre Dame Convent and at Prince of Wales College, from which she graduated with a first-class teacher's licence in 1892. Little is known about her early career. It is likely that she followed her family which had moved to Ottawa around 1890. Biographical sketches claim that she was involved in mission work for the "uplift" of natives in eastern and central Canada. In the summer of 1899 she was employed as teacher at the Mohawk reserve of Saint-Régis (Akwesasne). Two years later Hughes launched, with ecclesiastical support, the Catholic Indian Association, which sought to find employment outside reserves for graduates of Indian schools and, reflecting contemporary attitudes to natives, assimilate them.

By the time Hughes left Saint-Régis and the teaching profession to undertake "literary work" in 1902, she had already established a modest reputation as a writer. In stories published by the Catholic World (New York) and the Prince Edward Island Magazine (Charlottetown), she drew on her experiences amongst the natives, whom she presented in a sympathetic light. As the contributor of "Canadian forests and timber interests" in John Castell HOPKINS's Canada, an encyclopaedia of the country, she demonstrated her versatility and sureness in mastering assignments.

Employed by the Montreal Daily Star from 1903 to 1906, Hughes joined Kit Coleman [Ferguson*] and other female journalists travelling by train to the world fair at St Louis, Mo., in June 1904. A founding member of the Canadian Women's Press Club, which was established en route, Hughes, unlike many of her colleagues in that organization, did not graduate eventually to the social reform movement; she preferred instead, as did many Catholic women, to channel her energy into church-connected projects.

In 1906, the year in which she published her first book, a hagiographic study of her uncle, Hughes moved to Edmonton as a journalist on the Edmonton Bulletin, where her duties included reporting on sessions of the Alberta legislature. The Edmonton years were exceptionally busy ones in which Hughes displayed her ability not merely to adapt to a new environment but to succeed as administrator and organizer and to impress men of influence and power. Appointed first provincial archivist of Alberta in May 1908, she set about developing the Bureau of Archives. Seconded in 1909 to the premier's office, she served as private secretary to Alexander Cameron Rutherford* and to his successor, Arthur Lewis Watkins SIFTON. She renewed her acquaintance with Albert Lacombe*, the famous Catholic missionary, and agreed to write his biography. *Father Lacombe, the black-robe voyageur* was published in Toronto and New York to critical acclaim in 1911. Hughes remained active in the Canadian Women's Press Club and participated in the work of the Women's Canadian Club of Edmonton. In order to assist newly arrived Catholic immigrants, especially those from eastern Europe, she established the Catholic Women's League of Edmonton in November 1912, the first branch of an organization that was not launched nationally until 1920 [*see* Bellelle GUERIN] (when Lauretta Hughes Kneil, Katherine's sister, would be the organizing secretary).

A successful political insider in the era before women's suffrage – which she is on record as opposing in 1913 – she gave no inkling of the major change that was about to occur in the course of her career when, in September 1913, she transferred to London, England, to take up a position as assistant and secretary in the newly created office of the agent general for Alberta. Although she had displayed no interest in Irish affairs previously, Hughes made the acquaintance in London of prominent figures in the Irish cultural revival and political separatist movement. In the summer of 1914 she travelled to Ireland and, in her official capacity, met with Lord Aberdeen [Hamilton-Gordon*], lord lieutenant of Ireland, and Lady Aberdeen [Marjoribanks*]. However, in a private capacity she journeyed to Killarney to attend the annual weeklong cultural festival of the Gaelic League. Back in London, she set about learning the Irish language, probably under the direction of Pádraic Ó Conaire, the London-based Gaelic writer, with whom she coauthored *The cherry bird*, a play in English. She studied Irish history and literature, and commenced an in-depth examination of the economic advantages to Ireland of its political independence. Katherine Hughes, or Caitlín Ní Aodha, as she styled herself on occasion henceforth, was transformed from a loyal Canadian public servant to a committed supporter of Irish cultural renewal and of Irish separation from Britain.

Hughes was highly rated by Sir William Cornelius Van Horne*, who had provided a preface to the Lacombe biography, and she and the railway tycoon had agreed to collaborate on a series of books dealing with the Canadian Pacific Railway. When Van Horne

died in September 1915, Hughes was commissioned by Richard Benedict Van Horne to write his father's biography. Resigning her government position, she returned to Canada and, based in Montreal, spent much of the next few years travelling and collecting material for the biography and preparing a draft copy. However, she had not lessened her commitment to Ireland. In her trips around North America, she made contact with supporters of the Irish separatist movement. The Easter rising against British rule in 1916, and the subsequent execution of its leaders by the British authorities, caused her to increase her involvement in organized efforts for Irish independence. Frequently citing the sacrifice of Canadian soldiers on the battlefields of Europe on behalf of the liberation and rights of small nations, Hughes presented a carefully reasoned case for Irish self-determination in her 1917 monograph *Ireland* (Kingston, Ont.). Yet, in wartime Canada others viewed her championing of Irish independence as treason towards the British empire.

Upon presenting a draft of the Van Horne biography to R. B. Van Horne in August 1918, Hughes moved to Washington, D.C., where she established on behalf of the Irish Progressive League an organization to disseminate information and lobby politicians in support of Irish self-determination. With her immense experience as an administrator and valuable knowledge of the political process, she played an important role within the Friends of Irish Freedom, the umbrella organization for pro-Irish groups, in creating the blueprint which gradually transformed amateurish propaganda efforts into a professional publicity campaign.

Hughes spent late 1919 and early 1920 touring the southern states, preparing for the arrival of Eamon de Valera, president of the unilaterally declared "Irish Republic." A devotee of de Valera, she avoided much of the controversy that would arise between him and the Irish American leaders because she returned to Canada in May 1920 at his apparent request to mobilize Irish Canadian opinion. In conjunction with Robert Lindsay Crawford, an Irish-born journalist and former Orangeman, and under the watchful eye of the Royal Canadian Mounted Police – which reported to Arthur Sifton, now federal secretary of state – Hughes made preparations to launch the Self-Determination for Ireland League of Canada and Newfoundland. In choosing this benign title for the new organization, and in avoiding the use of the loaded terms "Freedom" or "Republic," the leaders sought to build a broad coalition of Irish Canadians, other ethnic groups, and social reformers.

In early July 1920 Hughes began a tour which took her from the Maritimes to the Pacific coast, back to Atlantic Canada, and on to the Dominion of Newfoundland. She established branches of the Self-Determination for Ireland League in most major urban centres, ensuring before she moved from one location to the next that she had left a strong committee, made up of respectable local business people and professional figures, to continue the work. Well received in eastern and central Canada, Hughes's activities attracted the attention of opponents in the west, although she was not a victim of physical violence as Crawford was.

In an atmosphere of hostility from the establishment and threats of violence, delegates representing the estimated 25,000 league members, and representatives of other bodies including the Société Saint-Jean-Baptiste, assembled in Ottawa for the league's first national convention on 16–17 Oct. 1920. Hughes was introduced "as the woman who had done more than any other for the cause of Ireland in Canada." However, by the time that the convention concluded, with Crawford elected as president of the league, Hughes knew that she had no further role to play in Canada. At de Valera's urging, she agreed to travel to Australia and New Zealand to set up sister organizations.

Hughes's commitment to travel to Australia coincided with publication of the biography of Van Horne. Though Walter Vaughan was credited as sole author, he admitted in the preface to *The life and work of Sir William Van Horne* (New York, 1920), "Much of this volume . . . is frankly based on Miss Hughes's material, and wherever it has been possible I have used and adapted her rough narrative." In reality, Vaughan's contribution was limited to editing Hughes's manuscript, for this published biography is merely a shorter and tighter version of the work she had researched and written.

Bitter and angry, and firmly convinced that she was being punished by the establishment, as personified by R. B. Van Horne, for her advocacy of Irish independence, but lacking resources to mount a legal challenge, Hughes headed to Australia. In February 1921 the Melbourne Catholic paper, the *Advocate*, reported her presence. In the following months Hughes, using the Canadian model, made contact with local activists, united disparate Irish groups, and successfully launched self-determination leagues in Australia and New Zealand.

After this campaign, Hughes travelled to Paris in September 1921 at de Valera's bidding to coordinate the Irish World Race Congress to which representatives of the Irish diaspora were invited. Scheduled for January 1922 and heralded as a major publicity event for the "Irish Republic," the congress was overtaken by political developments. The Anglo-Irish treaty of December 1921, which bestowed dominion status on a new Irish Free State and recognized the right of Northern Ireland to secede, divided Irish nationalists and set the scene for civil war.

Hughes returned to North America in April 1922 to find that the pro-Irish networks, reflecting splits within Ireland, had fragmented. Marked as an agitator

for whom Canada offered no future, she described herself in 1924 as "a once-upon-a-time Canadian." If not evidence that she had become a naturalized American citizen, her words suggest that she had turned her back, politically, psychologically, and emotionally, on her native country. Based in New York, she was dogged by ill-health and did not have steady employment. Politically, she remained loyal to the ideal of a fully independent Irish republic. When she died of cancer, Hughes was a lonely, marginalized figure, seeking solace in fanciful dreams of recreating the unity of purpose which had existed amongst Irish nationalists in the years after 1916. She is buried in an unmarked grave at St Raymond's cemetery in the Bronx.

A dynamic, highly talented, and intelligent person who left little documentation to help explain her motivation and the apparent contradictions in her character and in her career, Hughes showed an amazing ability to transcend social, political, and cultural barriers, to accommodate herself to her new surroundings – whether on an Indian reserve, in the west, or amongst Irish activists – and to thrive. Yet, while her circumstances changed dramatically and transformed the political insider into a political outcast, her strong Catholic faith and belief in causes remained the cornerstones in her life. Although there is no clear suggestion of a reformist agenda in her attitudes to the role of women or the plight of natives, her discovery of her ancestral homeland, her avid and extensive reading about Ireland, and her experiences as an Irish activist developed in her a strong anti-imperialist stand. The detached missionary work amongst the Indians was replaced by a pledge, both reasoned and passionate, of self-sacrifice on behalf of Ireland.

PÁDRAIG Ó SIADHAIL

Katherine Hughes's contribution on "Canadian forests and timber interests" appears in *Canada, an encyclopædia* (Hopkins), 5: 511–20, under the byline "Miss Catherine Hughes, of Ottawa." In addition to the publications cited in the biography, her writings include *Archbishop O'Brien: man and churchman* (Ottawa, 1906) and *English atrocities in Ireland; a compilation of facts from court and press records* (New York, [1920]).

American Irish Hist. Soc. (New York), D. F. Cohalan papers. City of New York Municipal Arch., Dept. of Records and Information Services, Death certificate. LAC, MG 27, II, D19, vols.9, 14; MG 28, I 232, vols.1–2, 11–12, 41, 43, 46; MG 30, D71. PAA, GR1974.350/81, 83–84; O.C. 325/08, O.C. 12/11, O.C. 759/13, O.C. 627/14; Arch. of the Oblates of Mary Immaculate, Prov. of Alberta-Saskatchewan, 71.220, items 6548–49. PARO, St Mary's Roman Catholic Church (Indian River, P.E.I.), Reg. of baptisms, 12 Nov. 1876. Richard Davis, "Irish nationalism in Manitoba, 1870–1922," in *The untold story: the Irish in Canada*, ed. Robert O'Driscoll and Lorna Reynolds (2v., Toronto, 1988), 1: 393–415; "The Self-Determination for Ireland leagues and the

Irish Race Convention in Paris, 1921–22," Tasmanian Hist. Research Assoc., *Papers and Proc.* (Hobart, Australia), 24 (1977). *Illustrated historical atlas of the province of Prince Edward Island* . . . ([Toronto], 1880; repr. Belleville, Ont., 1972). P. E. Magennis, "Catherine Hughes – a memory," *Catholic Bull. and Book Rev.* (Dublin), 15 (1925): 1045–54. Pádraig Ó Siadhail, "Katherine Hughes, Irish political activist," in *Edmonton: the life of a city*, ed. Bob Hesketh and Frances Swyripa (Edmonton, 1995), 78–87; "Ó Emerald go hÉirinn (Spléachadh ar bheatha is ar shaothar Katherine Hughes, 1876–1925)" [From Emerald to Ireland (A look at the life and works of Katherine Hughes, 1876–1925)], *Iris-leabhar Mhá Nuad* [Maynooth Journal] (Maynooth, Republic of Ire.), 1991: 13–39.

HUGHES, Sir SAMUEL, teacher, militia officer, newspaper proprietor, and politician; b. 8 Jan. 1853 in Darlington Township, Upper Canada, son of John Hughes and Caroline Laughlin; m. first 1872 Caroline J. Preston (d. 1873); m. secondly 5 May 1875 Mary Emily Burk in Darlington, and they had a son, Garnet Burk*, and two daughters; d. 24 Aug. 1921 in Lindsay, Ont.

Sam Hughes's father emigrated from Ireland to Durham County, Upper Canada, in the 1840s and made his living as a farmer and a schoolteacher. He married the daughter of a British artillery officer serving in the colony, and they raised a large family: four sons, of whom Sam was the third, and seven daughters. Sam took his early education in the public schools of Durham and at home, where he read widely with a special interest in travel accounts and military campaigns. As a young man, he developed a love of fishing, hunting, and organized sports; he became a competitive runner and a particularly aggressive lacrosse player. His fondness for hunting would continue throughout his life. He left school after his 16th birthday to become a primary teacher and to attend the Toronto Normal School, where he earned a first-class certificate.

In 1872 Hughes married Caroline Preston, one of his students and a daughter of a farmer in Manvers Township. Soon afterwards he found work with a railway company in Milwaukee, Wis. Caroline's sudden death a year later brought him back to Ontario to resume teaching, in Bowmanville, and then take up accounting. In 1875 he took a second wife, the daughter of Harvey William Burk, a well-to-do farmer who was also the Liberal MP for Durham West. Mary and Sam moved to Toronto, where his brother James Laughlin* was a school inspector. After a brief apprenticeship in law, Sam began teaching English and history at the Toronto Collegiate Institute. He took courses in history and modern languages at the University of Toronto on a part-time basis, earned a provincial school-inspector's certificate, and played lacrosse. His abiding interest, however, was the active militia, in which he would serve for more than half a century. He had joined a rifle company of the 45th (West Durham) Battalion of Infantry in 1866 and he climbed through its ranks to become a lieutenant in 1873 and captain and adjutant five years later.

In 1885 Hughes gave up teaching and purchased the *Victoria Warder*, a Conservative newspaper in Lindsay. As its editor and proprietor, he vigorously supported the Conservative party and, while it was in power in Ottawa under Sir John A. Macdonald*, he enjoyed the favour of government advertising in his paper. He founded the Victoria County Rifle Association and became a member of the Lindsay Board of Trade, the freemasons, the Oddfellows, and the Orange order. In 1888 he sat on the organizing committee of the Imperial Federation League, which championed the interests of British imperialism in Canadian affairs.

In Victoria South, a federal constituency where religion and politics were the most comfortable of bedfellows, Hughes, a Presbyterian turned Methodist, used the *Warder* to promote imperial centralization and a strident anticatholicism. As well, he maintained an unshakeable belief in the militia as a force better suited to Canada's requirements than the small, professional Permanent Force, which was commanded by a British officer. Hughes's positions, which sat well with the Conservatives of Victoria South, except for a small group of Roman Catholics, helped him rise to prominence in the local party organization. The opportunity to advance his ideas on a larger stage came in 1891 when he challenged the Liberal incumbent in Victoria North, John Augustus Barron, for his seat in the House of Commons. Hughes was badly beaten but he contested the election, won his case, and was returned in a by-election the next year. He would hold the seat (which became Victoria and Haliburton in 1903) until his retirement from politics in 1921.

Hughes was a backbencher in the troubled years after Macdonald's death in 1891, when four successive prime ministers struggled to keep the fractious Tory party together. The Manitoba school issue dominated the religious politics of these years [see D'Alton McCarthy*]. Hughes seldom missed an occasion to denounce the Catholic Church's promotion of separate schools in Manitoba. Just as frequent were his advocacy of the active militia and his outspoken criticism of the dominion's Permanent Force. In 1894 he engaged in a public feud with its general officer commanding, Major-General Ivor John Caradoc Herbert*, over Herbert's plan to make the force the core of Canada's defence. For his part, Herbert complained openly about Hughes's persistent efforts to use his elected position and his place in the West Durhams to get militia appointments for his Tory comrades.

Hughes supported Sir John Sparrow David Thompson* during his prime ministership, was unenthusiastic about Sir John Joseph Caldwell Abbott* and Sir Mackenzie Bowell*, and welcomed Sir Charles Tupper* when he returned from England to lead the Tories in the general election of 1896. On the Manitoba school issue Hughes favoured neither the remedial measures Thompson, Bowell, and Tupper had advanced nor the extremism of the opponents of remedial action in the Orange order [see Nathaniel Clarke Wallace*]. Distrustful of all organized churches as "the greatest enemy of civilization," he was an uncompromising champion of secular education controlled by the state. In the election the Liberal party, led by Wilfrid Laurier*, soundly defeated the Conservatives. Hughes held his seat by 338 votes.

Accustomed to the privileges of power, the Conservatives were now in opposition. It was a difficult time for Hughes. There was no patronage to bestow and the *Warder* was not a financial success. Nor were his efforts to sell a ventilating system for railway cars, as president of the Hughes Ventilator Car Company, the limited stock company that he had formed in 1894 along with William MACKENZIE, James Ross*, and other capitalists. In 1898 Hughes gave up the company and the *Warder* to pay off his debts. In later years his fortune would pick up, largely through highly rewarding investments in Standard Oil and Imperial Oil, but that recovery was far in the future. As the century came to a close, his business ventures were only sources of trouble. He found personal compensation in the militia where, in 1897, he had been given command of the 45th Battalion and promoted lieutenant-colonel.

Two years later, on the eve of the South African War, Hughes, as the 45th's commander, impetuously wrote to the colonial secretary, Joseph Chamberlain, and to the Canadian minister of militia and defence, Frederick William Borden*, offering to lead a regiment or brigade. With almost certain deliberation, he bypassed his superior officers and angered the GOC, Major-General Edward Thomas Henry HUTTON. In due course the government sent a volunteer force under a distinguished Permanent Force officer, Lieutenant-Colonel William Dillon OTTER, who wanted no part of Hughes because of his unruly nature and lack of "professional qualifications." Hughes nonetheless joined them, as a civilian.

Once in South Africa, in the spring of 1900, he used his influence with British friends to gain command of a small force of irregulars fighting behind the main line of battle, under a British lieutenant-general, Sir Charles Warren. In two brief campaigns Hughes had some success clearing out pockets of Boer resistance. He was proud of his display of leadership. In a series of letters to newspapers at home and in the Cape Colony he boasted of his exploits, continued his fulminations against Hutton, and criticized the competence of the senior British command. Together with his refusal

to carry out a crucial order from Warren, Hughes's outrageous letters swiftly led to his dismissal by the British army with orders to return to Canada. He was humiliated and angry. Blind to his own arrogance and wilful disregard for authority, he believed not just that he had been wrongfully dismissed, but that he had been denied not one but two Victoria Cross awards for his bravery. The episode hardened his lack of respect into a lasting distrust of professional soldiers, be they British or Canadian.

When the Tory caucus received Tupper's resignation as party leader in November 1900, Hughes was in Ottawa. He and the new leader chosen in February, Halifax lawyer Robert Laird Borden*, were very different men, but they would support each other for nearly a generation. Hughes had learned his politics in the 19th century, Borden was learning his in the 20th. The MP for Victoria North was a skilful practitioner of inflammatory rhetoric, back-room deals, and parish-pump patronage. Borden's speeches read like legal briefs. His goal was to rebuild the Conservative party with a future-oriented outlook; nevertheless, over his ten years as leader of the opposition, he depended heavily on old warriors such as Hughes. Many, including Hughes, resisted Borden's efforts to democratize the party's national organization, and there were open revolts against Borden, but Hughes was not part of them. However much he and his leader differed on party matters, however much he disliked the business-minded reformers whom Borden attracted into the party, he remained loyal. When Borden suffered personal defeat in 1904, Hughes was the first to offer him a seat, a favour he never forgot. In 1910 and 1911, when factions within caucus again challenged Borden's leadership, Hughes stood by him. Borden, Hughes told a crony in March 1911, was "very capable, but not a very good judge of men or tactics; and is gentle hearted as a girl."

In the early and middle years of the Laurier period, the government, led by its capable minister of militia and defence, Frederick Borden, had initiated a number of reforms designed to expand the militia and bring it directly under government control. Hughes, who encouraged the reforms, was especially interested in the Ross rifle, which the minister had adopted as the rifle for Canada's forces late in the South African War. The War Office was opposed to Canada having a rifle other than the Lee-Enfield, the standard imperial issue. Borden countered with a bipartisan selection committee of MPs, including Hughes, which vigorously "pumped" the Ross. Ultimately Hughes would become the fiercest champion of the Ross, a symbol of all the virtues he assigned to the volunteer citizen soldiers of the militia. And, ultimately, this championship would jeopardize his career in World War I.

In September 1911, after campaigning on the naval issue in Quebec, the reciprocity issue in English Canada, and Liberal corruption everywhere, R. L. Borden's party returned to power. Only four days after the votes were counted, Hughes wrote to Borden seeking appointment as minister of militia and defence. The prime minister read of Hughes's dark fears that others were conspiring against him, of his service to the party and to Borden, and of his distinguished military record. "In your coming Cabinet operations difficulties may from time to time arise," Hughes advised. "It strikes me that it might be that again, my tact, firmness and judgement might come in to help matters along." He concluded by telling Borden that "in my walks through life easy management of men has ever been one of my chief characteristics – and I get the name of bringing success and good luck to a cause." Men first elected just days before, and others from Borden's select group of "new style" politicians, were offered places in cabinet. Hughes, like another veteran of 19th-century political wars, George Eulas Foster*, waited. Finally, Borden summoned Hughes. "I impressed strongly upon him the mischievous and perverse character of his speech and conduct," Borden later recalled. "He broke down, admitted that he often acted impetuously, and assured me that if he were appointed I could rely on his judgment and good sense. This promise was undoubtedly sincere but his temperament was too strong for him. He was under constant illusions that enemies were working against him." Hughes was sworn in along with the rest of cabinet on 10 October.

Once in office he opposed Borden's attempts to reform the inside (Ottawa-based) civil service and strongly resisted having his department's spending brought under the control of the Department of Finance. He pestered Borden to have him promoted to the rank of major-general, and in 1912 Hughes forced through the Militia Council a general order allowing for such promotion of a civilian minister. Patronage in militia and defence was as old as the department itself, its muscle and bone in one of the most politically oriented departments of the pre-war government. This was Hughes's environment and one in which, he told the commons on 7 March 1913, "I am the boss while I am here." He worked tirelessly to build up the militia to unprecedented levels of strength, to improve equipment and training, to construct new armouries and drill-halls (59 by 1915), and to push for a second dominion arsenal, at Lindsay. At the same time, between 1911 and 1914, he ignored recommendations from his senior staff officers that the Permanent Force be expanded, to supervise the training of the growing militia. He evinced equal lack of interest in his staff's efforts to formulate defence plans. Steps to prepare a war book for Canada, to address anticipated hostilities in Europe, originated not with Hughes but with Sir Joseph POPE of the Department of External Affairs, in January 1914.

That spring Hughes's departmental budget was nearly twice what it had been in 1911. No Canadian could have imagined that a few months later the commons would pass (with scarcely any debate) an initial war appropriation of $50 million, that Hughes would take personal responsibility for raising more than 30,000 men for the Canadian Expeditionary Force, and that censorship would be instituted under his control [*see* Ernest John CHAMBERS].

In the beginning, Sam Hughes had a very good war. An expeditionary force was authorized by cabinet on 6 Aug. 1914 and Hughes, ignoring the mobilization plans prepared by his chief of staff, Colonel Willoughby Garnons GWATKIN, sent flurries of contradictory orders across the country. Instead of gathering the force at Petawawa, an established training site in Ontario, he ordered the men to report to Valcartier, an undeveloped site near Quebec City. His contractors, under the direction of William PRICE, had a huge camp ready there in less than three weeks; its first commander was Hughes's brother John. In late September, amidst more confusion, the 1st Division of the CEF began boarding hastily assembled transports at Quebec, several thousand men overstrength. It landed in England on 15 October. On the 22nd Hughes was finally gazetted major-general. To give him seniority of rank over his chief of staff, the promotion was backdated to 1912, when his appeal had started.

On his way to England to consult with the division's commander, Lieutenant-General Edwin Alfred Hervey ALDERSON, Hughes had announced in New York on the 7th that Canada "could send enough men to add the finishing touches to Germany without assistance either from England or France." In England, without Borden's knowledge, he appointed Colonel John Wallace Carson as his "special representative." Carson was joined by Sir William Maxwell Aitken*, another irregular appointment, as "Canada's eye-witness" in the first stage of a series of Hughes nominations that thoroughly confused the War Office.

By early November Hughes was back in Canada and recruiting for a second division was well underway. In January 1915, as the 2nd Division was preparing to embark [*see* Sir Samuel Benfield Steele*] and the 1st was in final training before going to the front, Hughes authorized recruitment for a third division. Voluntary recruiting continued successfully throughout 1915 but began to fall off sharply in the early months of 1916, after Borden had increased the level of Canada's force to 500,000. In the last six months of 1916 a mere 2,810 men were sent overseas.

Sam Hughes was everywhere, except in his office in Ottawa. Biographer Ronald G. Haycock notes that between August 1914 and November 1916 he was out of the country one-third of the time. When in Canada he rushed from one camp or speech to another, inspecting "his boys," promoting recruiting, making promises and issuing orders unknown to his department, and lashing out at a growing list of critics. They were, he told a crowd in London, Ont., "yelping like a puppy dog chasing an express train." "I am loved by millions," he assured his prime minister. Borden, who sincerely admired Hughes's work at Valcartier, defended his colleague, praising his energy and enthusiasm. On 24 Aug. 1915, on nomination from Colonial Secretary Bonar Law, Hughes was made a KCB (military) while in England with the prime minister. "He has earned it," Borden wrote in his diary.

But behind the scenes, Borden grew increasingly concerned about Hughes's management of Canada's military effort. Hughes continuously confused his roles as a senior militia officer and as a minister of the crown, and the latter always took second place. Borden had reprimanded him in December 1914 for running his department without informing or getting the approval of the Militia Council. In September 1915 he criticized him for his long absences from his office: "Your first duty is to administer your Department." Hughes untruthfully retorted that he met his subordinates "more than all the other Cabinet Ministers put together consult theirs," adding that "I, as the responsible Minister, and having an experience second to none in any Department and far superior to many, and generally being considered as endowed with some common sense, will certainly not delegate my responsibility to any subordinate officer in my Department, or to any Militia Council in my Department."

There were other problems – many of them. Overseas, though Hughes continually boasted of the superiority of Canadian equipment over British issue, Alderson had had to replace the 1st Division's boots (developed for use in the South African War), webbing, and other equipment before the troops left for the front. In their first battle in the Ypres (Ieper) salient, their Ross rifles failed. "It is nothing short of murder to send our men against the enemy with such a weapon," one officer reported. Alderson replaced the Ross with the Lee-Enfield in June, thus ensuring his status as an enemy of Sam Hughes.

Overseeing the expenditure at home of millions of dollars for supplies and equipment for recruitment and the CEF, Hughes had been joined by a committee of fellow cabinet ministers well tutored in the art of allocating patronage. Though Hughes was not responsible, there were scandals over the purchase of drugs, horses, and other materials. Two Conservative MPs turned out to be the culprits in the drugs and horses scandals and they were thrown out of caucus by Borden. In June 1915 he appointed Sir Charles Peers Davidson, former chief justice of the Superior Court of Quebec, to investigate purchasing. Meanwhile, Hughes's Shell Committee, formed in September 1914 to implement the manufacture of munitions in Canada for the Allied governments, struggled to get orders and, when it did, struggled to fill them. Ugly rumours abounded that financier-manufacturer John Wesley Allison, a Hughes crony and an honorary colonel, was profiting hugely from Shell Committee contracts. In April 1916 Sir William Ralph MEREDITH, chief justice of Ontario, and Lyman Poore Duff* of the Supreme Court of Canada constituted a commission to examine charges against Allison and the work of the Shell Committee.

Though the commission would exonerate Hughes, he was increasingly a problem. As the war grew in intensity and expense, as more and more men were shipped overseas, the voluntary spirit and pluck that characterized Hughes's leadership became out of place, inefficient, and outdated. On both the European front and the home front, professionalism and orderly management and execution were required. Hughes never understood or accepted the change that swirled about him. Gradually, the prime minister removed more and more of his responsibilities and placed them in other, more capable hands. In May 1915 the management of spending for supplies had been assigned to the newly formed War Purchasing Commission, chaired by Toronto manufacturer and MP Albert Edward KEMP. In November the Shell Committee was replaced by the Imperial Munitions Board, responsible to the British Ministry of Munitions and headed by Joseph Wesley Flavelle*, another Toronto businessman with an impeccable reputation. The following spring, during the Shell Committee investigation, Borden took over administration of Hughes's department. Then, in June 1916, he appointed Fleming Blanchard McCurdy*, a Nova Scotia MP and financier, as parliamentary secretary of the department to assist Hughes and "provide for continuity in the conduct of the Department's business and business policy."

After initial protests, Hughes took much of this takeover in stride. His attention by 1916 was almost solely concentrated on the overseas forces. At the front the Canadian Corps fought within the British armies. In England the CEF had an autonomous command structure but was in complete disarray. Hughes failed to straighten things out during a trip in March and April. Called home during the Shell Committee investigation, he made a whirlwind tour of eastern Canada – in Ontario he opened Camp Borden on 11 July – but he returned to England later that month. At the end of July Borden instructed him to send back his recommendations for approval by cabinet. Follow-up queries in August were ignored by Hughes.

"I do not mind fault-finding by my enemies," he wrote Borden on 1 September. "You have never known me fail you in anything yet," he boasted, but he was doing just that. Borden learned in the press on the 6th that Hughes had created a "Sub-Militia Council," with Major-General Carson as its president, in direct violation of Borden's instructions. It had met, in further violation, the day before. Hughes, at last, had gone too far. He was, Borden wrote, "wrong-headed and stupid as ever." Borden took his remaining responsibilities away, created the Ministry of Overseas Military Forces of Canada, and appointed his trusted friend Sir George Halsey Perley*, the acting high commissioner in London, as minister. Hughes was summoned home. When the new ministry was announced at the end of October, he wrote an "impertinent" letter to Borden criticizing his demands for constitutional and orderly procedures and accusing the prime minister of joining the nest of conspirators. On 9 Nov. 1916 Borden demanded his resignation. It was tendered two days later. Kemp replaced Hughes as minister of militia and defence. "The nightmare is over," Sir George Foster observed.

Hughes told Borden on the 15th that he had left cabinet "with regret, not on account of the office or anything special, outside of friendships which will last – but for the welfare of the soldiers," adding that "a kindly, watchful eye will be kept over them by your humble servant." He remained in parliament, keeping a watchful, not always kindly, eye on Borden. The following spring, apparently impatient that the prime minister had taken so long to introduce conscription, Hughes tried to drum up support for a conscriptionist third party, headed by himself. He failed. In the fall he opposed Borden's plan for a union government, but he then ran successfully as a Unionist candidate in the general election in December 1917. On 1 Oct. 1918, while the Canadian Corps was in a fierce battle at Cambrai, he wrote to Borden accusing its commander, Lieutenant-General Sir Arthur William Currie*, of the "needless massacre of our Canadian boys." In the debate over the throne speech the following March, Hughes, in a vicious attack on the Union government, his former colleagues, and Flavelle, made his letter public. Currie, he went on, had sacrificed the lives of even more Canadian soldiers in his attack on Mons and should be "tried summarily by court martial and punished so far as the law would allow." Hughes was protected from charges of libel by parliamentary privilege. Despite spirited defences of Currie in the days that followed, the ugly smear would persist until his vindication in a celebrated trial in 1928.

Hughes's shameful speech was, perhaps, the most outrageous act in his long public career of colourful and irresponsible behaviour. On 6 Oct. 1919 he stood up in the commons to proclaim that he had initiated or urged much of Canada's apparatus of war, including defensive trenches and numerous kinds and placements of weaponry. He was 66, bitter, and physically failing. The war had ruined both his career and his health. In the winter of 1915–16 he had been in hospital for some weeks; in March 1916 he advised Borden he was suffering from insomnia and had been told by his doctor that he had some marked irregularity in the

action of his heart. In 1917, after his dismissal from cabinet, he began building an impressive summer home, Glen Eagle, in Guilford Township in the Haliburton highlands, but whatever rest he got there did not help. By the fall of 1920 he was bedridden in Ottawa, diagnosed as a victim of the then lethal disease, pernicious anaemia. Major-General Sir Sam Hughes died at his home in Lindsay on 24 Aug. 1921, and was buried with full military honours.

ROBERT CRAIG BROWN

AO, RG 22-357, no.3322; RG 80-5-0-212, no.6180. LAC, MG 26, H; MG 27, II, D9. R. C. Brown, *Robert Laird Borden, a biography* (2v., Toronto, 1975–80). R. C. Brown and Donald Loveridge, "Unrequited faith: recruiting the CEF, 1914–1918," *Rev. internationale d'hist. militaire*, no.[54] (éd. canadienne, Ottawa, 1982): 53–79. Can., Parl., *Sessional papers*, 1915–19. *Canadian annual rev.*, 1914–19. John English, *The decline of politics: the Conservatives and the party system, 1901–20* (Toronto, 1977). J. L. Granatstein and J. M. Hitsman, *Broken promises: a history of conscription in Canada* (Toronto, 1977). R. G. Haycock, *Sam Hughes: the public career of a controversial Canadian, 1885–1916* (Waterloo, Ont., 1986). A. M. J. Hyatt, *General Sir Arthur Currie: a military biography* (Toronto, 1987). J. A. Keshen, *Propaganda and censorship during Canada's Great War* (Edmonton, 1996). Desmond Morton and J. L. Granatstein, *Marching to Armageddon: Canadians and the Great War, 1914–1919* (Toronto, 1989). Nicholson, *CEF.* Nila Reynolds, *In quest of yesterday* (3rd ed., Minden, Ont., 1973). R. J. Sharpe, *The last day, the last hour: the Currie libel trial* ([Toronto], 1988).

HULL, WILLIAM CHARLES JAMES ROPER, rancher, meat packer, businessman, and philanthropist; b. 20 Dec. 1856 at Childhay Farm, Broadwindsor, England, son of Arthur Hull and Honora James Berry; m. 29 Oct. 1903 Emmeline Mary Ellis, née Banister (d. 11 March 1953), in Davisburg (Alta); they had no children; d. 4 April 1925 in Calgary.

The son of a breeder of "high-class stock," William Roper Hull attended school in Dorchester and Bridport in Dorset. In 1873, along with his brother John Roper Hull, he left England for the interior of British Columbia, where their uncle William James Roper raised cattle near Kamloops. After travelling by steamer to Victoria via Panama, they boated up the Fraser River and reached Kamloops on foot. With little more than their personal effects, the brothers began ranching near Edith and Hull lakes and by 1880 were grazing cattle and horses. Three years later, when they found themselves with a surplus of horses, they drove 1,200 of them over the Crowsnest Pass to Calgary and sold them to the North-West Mounted Police and the North-West Cattle Company [see Frederick Smith Stimson*]. In 1886 the Hull brothers and a partner, Walter Pound Trounce, set up a butchering and livestock-trading business known as Hull, Trounce and

Hull

Company. William Hull and Trounce moved to Calgary to run its head office while John Hull remained in Kamloops. The partners were the first to integrate cattle raising, meat packing, and retailing on a large scale in Alberta. During their initial year they brought into the Alberta district the first consignment of cattle shipped by rail from the west; delivered at Calgary, it was sold to the McDermott and Ross Ranche. Over the course of 1886 Hull and Trounce ordered in a total of 500 horses and 3,000 cattle, selling two-thirds of them and utilizing the remainder to stock their first ranch, the 25, near Nanton.

Hull's arrival in Calgary coincided with the golden age of the western Canadian ranching frontier. From the early 1880s the human and bovine populations grew dramatically. Hull was able to purchase cattle and other livestock from area ranchers and farmers and sell the meat in town and in distant markets. In May 1887 his company obtained the profitable contract for supplying beef to the Pacific division of the Canadian Pacific Railway. It established butcher shops the following year at Banff, Donald, Revelstoke, and Kamloops, and later in Anthracite, Canmore, Golden, and Field.

About 1890 Trounce left the partnership, and William and John formed Hull Brothers and Company. By 1891 they were the largest butchering establishment in Calgary. They had a slaughterhouse on the Bow River and, in Calgary, a stone packing plant with refrigerated chilling rooms, a cold-storage area, and the company's Pioneer Meat Market, which sold a variety of fresh meat, poultry, and fish. From the beginning their main product was beef. To process it they designed a modern, partially mechanized system that involved cutting by hand and movement by steam hoist and conveyor. In the 1890s much of the meat was sold locally, though a considerable amount was shipped on CPR refrigerator cars to the brothers' shops in other locations. The Hulls also supplied the railway's dining cars and wholesale distributors throughout southern Alberta and British Columbia. W. R. Hull relied on small margins and high volume – he sometimes dropped his prices below cost to beat out competition.

Hull closely integrated his Pioneer market with his company's second ranch, a 4,000-acre operation south of Calgary on Fish Creek, in the Bow River valley, where close to 1,000 steers were regularly grazed and fed. The Hulls had first leased this land from Senator Théodore Robitaille* in 1887 and bought it in 1892. The Bow Valley Ranche became known for its experiments to find the best production techniques. W. R. Hull undertook irrigated farming on a large scale. In 1893 he spent $2,000 to construct a ditch off the Bow to water 500 acres of bottom land along Fish Creek; he estimated that he recouped the cost from the extra yields of oats and hay in the first year. Some three years later he ran a second ditch to water an additional 800 acres. The ranch, often referred to as Hull's Irrigation Farm, used modern raking and stacking machines to put up roughage. As one of the major agricultural showpieces in the North-West Territories, it played a role in helping the cattle industry move from crude, open-range ranching to intensive mixed farming. The ranch was also a visual showpiece. Hull seems initially to have used the 25 as his home, but after the log dwelling on the Bow ranch burned in 1895, he decided to replace it with a magnificent house as his main residence. Designed by James Llewellyn Wilson of Calgary, the two-storey mansion built the following year – it is now a restaurant in Fish Creek Provincial Park – was an excellent example of the Queen-Anne style in a rural setting. Its doorway was flanked by whale ribs, string quartets played on the lawn during extravagant garden parties, and upper-crust English gentlemen were frequent visitors.

The erection of Hull's residence coincided with the dissolution of his partnership with his brother. William took the Alberta end of their business and John the Kamloops holdings. In 1902 W. R. Hull sold the Bow Valley Ranche and his beef businesses to cattle king Patrick Burns* so that he could concentrate on other interests. With Alfred Ernest Cross*, William Edward Cochrane, and others, he had founded the Calgary Brewing and Malting Company in 1892. He was involved too in W. Roper Hull Limited, a ranching, farming, and insurance agency. As a property broker and owner, he made a major impact. Among his holdings were the 6,000-acre Oxley Ranch near Claresholm that he bought in 1903 and the 37,500-acre Walrond Cattle Ranch in the foothills north of Pincher Creek [see Duncan McNab McEachran], which he leased for a period beginning in 1909. In Calgary he had a number of substantial buildings constructed. His five commercial blocks included the Hull Opera House (1893) and the Grain Exchange (1908–10), and he put up office blocks in Edmonton, Medicine Hat, and Lethbridge. There can be little doubt that he made a great deal of his money through real-estate ventures – he seems to have had a gift for recognizing locations that would jump in value. For example, in Calgary, he paid $7,500 for a corner lot at 8th Avenue and Centre Street in 1886, put up a small butcher shop, and sold the property for twice the original price seven years later.

Perhaps more than anyone else, Hull symbolized the business and ranching aristocracy for which the early prairie west has become famous. He consistently used his wealth to shape an Old World social and cultural environment in southern Alberta. The opera house is a case in point. With a seating capacity of 1,000, it hosted operatic and theatrical presentations by famous touring companies, school concerts, fundraising productions, auction sales, and dances. In later years he continued the custom, started on his Bow

Valley Ranche, of turning his home into a centre for refined social activities. After selling the Bow to Burns, he required living quarters for himself and his new wife, a daughter of Albert Edward Banister, a veterinarian who had emigrated from Bridport to Davisburg to farm. Hull's second mansion, on the fringe of Calgary, was even grander than his first, on Fish Creek. Designed by Hodgson and Bates, the architects of the Grain Exchange, it was named Langmore after the Hull family home in England. It took two years to build and cost $12,000 and another $3,000 to furnish. Its style was European, but the setting was distinctly western. "When I first came here to live," Mrs Hull later remembered, "the prairie stretched away before us. There were not any fences and often we would sit and watch from our windows, riders jumping hurdles and practicing for the races." Eventually the grounds were landscaped and the garden parties held there were renowned. Such entertainments exuded the values and the lifestyles that Hull and many of his peers had brought to the west. In 1922 the Hulls returned to their former Bow residence, which was still owned by Patrick Burns, to help entertain Arthur Neville Chamberlain, a British MP and future prime minister, then on a tour of Canada.

W. R. Hull was a very capable businessman who also had a keen sense of social responsibility. At his death in 1925 he left instructions that a major portion of his $1.6 million estate should be set aside to build an orphanage. By the time of Mrs Hull's death in 1953 the value had risen to $5 million. Expected to be constructed before 1956, the William Roper Hull Home was not officially opened until 1962. Now known as Hull Child and Family Services, this agency operates, with the Calgary Board of Education, the William Roper Hull School, to provide programs for students with behavioural and emotional difficulties. Other organizations that benefited from Hull's estate include the Anglican diocese of Calgary, the Red Cross, and various hospitals.

WARREN M. ELOFSON

GA, M 8688/7; NA-14-1. GRO, Reg. of births, Netherbury, 20 Dec. 1856. Univ. of Birmingham Library, Special Coll. (Birmingham, Eng.), Chamberlain papers, [Arthur Neville Chamberlain's] travel journal, western Canadian trip, September–October, 1922. *Calgary Daily Tribune*, 11 Oct. 1893. *Calgary Herald*, 13 Feb. 1889; 3 March 1891; 13 Oct. 1923; 18 Nov. 1933; 21 Oct. 1996; 18 Jan. 1998; 5 Feb., 23 Sept. 2003. *Calgary News Telegram*, 11 Jan., 1 Nov. 1913. *Globe*, 17 Oct. 1891. *Pincher Creek Echo* (Pincher Creek, Alta), 23 Sept. 1997. Alberta Geneal. Soc., Edmonton branch, *Alberta: index to registration of births, marriages and deaths* . . . (1v. to date, Edmonton, 1995–), 1 (*1870 to 1905*): 262. Mary Balf, *Kamloops: a history of the district up to 1914* (Kamloops, B.C., 1969). *Canadian who's who*, 1910. *Commercial* (Winnipeg), 5 (1886–87): 667. L. V. Kelly, *The range men* (75th anniversary ed., High River, Alta, 1988). H. C. Klassen, *Eye on the future: business people in Calgary and the Bow valley, 1870–1900* (Calgary, 2002). A. O. MacRae, *History of the province of Alberta* (2v., [Calgary], 1912). *Newspaper reference book.* "Out of our past," comp. Kelly Untinen, *Sunday: Calgary Herald Magazine*, 3 March 1991: 5.

HUOT, CHARLES (baptized **Charles-Édouard-Masson**), painter, drawing teacher, and illustrator; b. 6 April 1855 at Quebec, son of Charles Huot, a merchant, and Aurélie Drolet; m. September 1885 Louise Schlachter in Belitz (Mecklenburg–Western Pomerania), Germany, and they had a daughter; d. 27 Jan. 1930 in Sillery, Que.

Hormisdas Magnan*, the painter's friend and first biographer, would note in 1932 that Charles Huot was said to have demonstrated talent for drawing very early on, copying landscapes from a book his father had given him. Charles entered the Collège de Sainte-Anne-de-la-Pocatière as a boarder in January 1866 at the age of ten; he would leave in July 1870, having completed his first year of commercial studies. His mother died on 26 September as he was entering the École Normale Laval in Quebec City. Few traces remain of the four years he spent in this institution, but various facts suggest that Huot was becoming increasingly interested in painting. First, the sale of a "very beautiful painting of animals done by M. Huot" at the auction of Cornelius Krieghoff*'s estate – which was reported in *Le Journal de Québec* on 19 May 1877 – implies that the aspiring painter and the master had met. Huot may have used the occasion of Krieghoff's final stay at Quebec (between 1870 and 1872) to take lessons, but there is no way to confirm this hypothesis. As well, Magnan revealed that the presentation of the Joseph-Légaré collection at the Université Laval in 1872 so fascinated Huot that he returned several times to examine some of the paintings. Huot learned and became a skilful painter, as his works from 1873 prove. He received his first official commission from Clément Vincelette, the superintendent of the Asile de Beauport, who wanted a painting of the institution and its outbuildings. The work, dated 2 Dec. 1873, was displayed in the window of a music shop owned by Robert Morgan on Rue de la Fabrique in Quebec City. From then on, the artist received encouragement. In June 1874 *La Minerve* would note that Antoine Plamondon*, "who, ordinarily, is quite harsh in his assessments, warmly praised this painting and fully acknowledged the artist's talent."

The success Huot achieved soon earned him the support of Abbé Pierre Lagacé, principal of the École Normale Laval, who set up a subscription committee chaired by architect Eugène-Étienne Taché* to send him to study in Europe. On 30 May 1874 *Le Journal de Québec* announced that $1,400 had been collected "to cover [the] travel costs and the expenses that a four-year stay in Paris will require." Huot left Quebec on 6 June, at the age of 19, to enter the studio of academic painter Alexandre Cabanel; he lived with the family of Gustave Lefèvre, principal of the École de Musique Classique et Religieuse Niedermeyer. On 16 March 1875 he was finally admitted to the École des Beaux-Arts, where he would do the classical academic program. An unpleasant surprise awaited him the following year, however: the subscribers withdrew their assistance, despite Abbé Lagacé's repeated requests. Huot thus had to pursue his studies while supporting himself, though Lefèvre did cover his room and board.

In 1876, participating in the Paris Salon for the first time, Huot received an honourable mention and four of his works were accepted for the annual exhibition of the École des Beaux-Arts. He thus prepared actively for the 1877 Salon, where he presented a skilfully executed oil on canvas, *Le bon Samaritain* (now held at the Musée Tavet-Delacourt, in Pontoise, France), which showed both his academic training and his progress. After finishing his studies at the École des Beaux-Arts, probably in 1879, he took part in the salons of 1881, 1882, 1884, and 1885. During these years Huot worked on various projects. In *La Presse* on 20 Jan. 1927, he would note: "I came first in the competition in which the prize was a commission . . . to reproduce a masterly work by Paul Beaudry [Baudry], 'Les Muses,' imitative of tapestry, which one can admire in the foyer of the Opéra. This project took me two years. Then I did illustrations for Charles Delagrave, Firmin Didot, Hachette." In 1881 he lived for a few months in a former residence of the Marquise de Sévigné, where he produced paintings of a decorative type for a Paris exhibition. An ageing Huot would take pleasure in telling certain anecdotes related to this sojourn, which Maurice Hébert would evoke in a poem entitled "Le soulier de satin; conte au coin du feu," published in *Le Canada français* (Québec) in May 1925.

Huot married a pastor's daughter, Louise Schlachter, in Belitz in September 1885. The following year, the chance to return home materialized when the Oblates of Mary Immaculate, who were thinking of entrusting him with the task of decorating the church of Saint-Sauveur, had him come to Quebec City. Huot arrived on 18 July, with the lustre of his studies in Paris and of 12 years spent in Europe. He hurried to exhibit a few works in Montreal, on Rue Notre-Dame, namely genre scenes – his favourite subjects – and a religious painting in the style of Eustache Le Sueur. Also on display was a drawing that had won him a silver medal in the spring at the second Blanc et Noir exhibition in Paris. While establishing new relationships, Huot tended his old ones by publicly thanking his patrons in *L'Étendard* (Montréal). In January 1887 the Oblates officially commissioned 13 paintings. A few days later Huot left to rejoin his wife in

Paris, intending to undertake his first large-scale project there. Instead, however, he moved in with his father-in-law in Neukrug (Mecklenburg–Western Pomerania), where his wife gave birth to their daughter. He had the use of a large studio for the painting of the five canvases that would decorate the vault of the church of Saint-Sauveur. The work progressed and by January 1888 Quebec's *Le Courrier du Canada* reported on the success enjoyed by Huot, who exhibited each work in Germany upon finishing it. The following October the paper mentioned that in the three days the painting *La fin du monde* was on view, "more than 3,000 people went to admire this masterpiece." The flattering remarks in the Rostock and Schwerin newspapers, which were quoted regularly in Quebec publications, created a favourable climate for Huot, who landed at Quebec with his wife and daughter on 28 Oct. 1889, with his five finished canvases. Unquestionably, the Saint-Sauveur undertaking launched the painter's career; he could count increasingly on influential connections. His fame spread through an article by Ernest Gagnon* in the *Revue canadienne* (Montréal), and then pieces in *L'Électeur* (Québec) by Louis Fréchette* (who, by 1890, suggested Huot for the job of decorating the provincial legislative building). The decor of the church of Saint-Sauveur was appreciated by Huot's contemporaries, who regarded him as a true artist. The present condition of the paintings and the loss of a portion of them make it difficult to evaluate the work, but they still give the impression of derivative academicism. Although the work has been criticized for its lack of unity, its monumental decor nonetheless constitutes an important example of the aesthetics flourishing at the turn of the 20th century.

Back at home, Huot set about building up a clientele. He first had to finish the eight other paintings commissioned for the church of Saint-Sauveur, which would be completed in May 1893. By the summer of 1890 he was doing portraits; in the autumn he opened a painting school in his home, located at the corner of Avenue de Salaberry and Rue Grande Allée. At about the same time, he was commissioned to do 18 paintings for the church of Saint-Joseph parish in Carleton, whose interior decor was finished in November 1892. In the years that followed, the parishes of Saint-Jean-Baptiste and Notre-Dame in Quebec City, the parish of La Nativité-de-Notre-Dame at Beauport, as well as the Sœurs de la Charité de Québec would purchase works from him. The painter also accepted certain projects that ensured him good visibility, for example, the creation of an *Apothéose de la charrue* for the festival of the Order of Agricultural Merit in 1890, and the photo-engraved reproduction of a drawing of the carnival of Quebec in 1894. Thousands of the latter would sell in Canada and 30,000 copies of it would be printed in New York. In 1894 Huot participated for the first time in the exhibition of the Art Association of Montreal, and he would be present again in 1908 and 1909. From 1895 he also taught freehand drawing at the École des Arts et Métiers at Quebec.

From 10 to 21 May 1900 Huot had a solo exhibition of some one hundred pieces at the legislative building, where, at least in 1898, he had his studio. The event earned him rave reviews, such as the one in *Le Courrier du Canada* on 22 May, highlighting the nationalist character of the works: "The first thing that strikes the visitor . . . is . . . the national, almost patriotic character of the works. . . . The perfume of Canadianism that they give off is exquisite." The landscapes and genre scenes inspired by the inhabitants of the Île d'Orléans, where Huot had spent his last few summers, were well received by people supporting clerical-nationalism. At the time, attachment to religion and to tradition dominated the discourse of French Canadians, who recognized themselves in and projected themselves into some of the subjects treated by the painter. These works should, in fact, be compared with the paintings of Horatio Walker* and Marc-Aurèle de Foy Suzor-Coté* that celebrate the traditional way of life. When Pierre-Georges Roy* published his book *L'île d'Orléans* in 1928 in Quebec City, he would recall this aspect of Huot's career by reproducing a few of the pieces shown in the 1900 exhibition. Also, the texts of Henri Beaudé, known as Henri d'Arles, would help publicize the painting *Le sanctus à la maison* (destroyed in the fire of February 1966 at Spencer Wood in Sillery, the official residence of the lieutenant governor of the province of Quebec); it would become extremely popular and inspire a poem by Pamphile Le May* (in *Les gouttelettes: sonnets,* an anthology published in Montreal in 1904). Towards the end of his life, in 1925, Huot was to recognize the importance of this work: in that year he presented it at the salon of the Royal Canadian Academy of Arts, even though he had participated in their exhibitions in 1902, 1903, and 1908.

From 1900 Huot regularly undertook contracts in the Saguenay region. He owed them largely to his cousin and friend Abbé Elzéar DE LAMARRE, who was then the chaplain of the Hôtel-Dieu Saint-Vallier in Chicoutimi. In the autumn he did a painting for its chapel. Then he created in wax a recumbent statue of St Anthony of Padua in the throes of death, a model sculptor Louis JOBIN would render in wood. In 1901 he painted a *Résurrection* for the church of Saint-Patrice parish in Rivière-du-Loup, to which, in 1903, he delivered stations of the cross that he had exhibited initially with the Ursulines of Quebec. One commission followed another: they came from the cathedral of Saint-François-Xavier in Chicoutimi, St Patrick's Church at Quebec, and the parish of Saint-Jérôme (Métabetchouan) in the Lac-Saint-Jean region. In addition, in 1903 *La Nouvelle-France* (Québec) printed a talk he

gave upon the death of painter James Tissot, and Beaudé published a work in New York entitled *Propos d'art* that was devoted to Huot.

Huot returned to Europe with his family in November 1903 and, after a brief stay in Germany, he went to Italy; in Rome he took classes with Francesco Gai at the Accademia di San Luca. He came back to Quebec City alone in June 1904. Immediately upon his return, the parish of Saint-Ambroise in Loretteville commissioned him to do four paintings, which were hung in the church the following spring. He then went to Chicoutimi, where he finished a canvas he had begun in Rome for the seminary chapel; the chapel was enhanced by a second work of his in the autumn. After selling a portrait of Pius X to the Séminaire de Québec, Huot rejoined his family in Brussels in May 1905. A perfectionist as a painter, he took classes again for seven months, this time with Jean Delville, senior professor at the Académie Royale des Sciences, des Lettres et des Beaux-Arts de Belgique. Little is known about this sojourn. There is no doubt, however, that Huot lived in Saint-Malo, France, in the spring of 1907 and that his wife died on 28 June at a nearby beach resort. Huot returned to Quebec City with his daughter in August; he set up his studio on Rue Saint-Jean and quietly resumed his activities. He produced a few illustrations for the 1907 edition of Le May's *Contes vrais* and drew the costumes and flags for the celebrations of Quebec's tercentenary in 1908.

In his prime, Huot received the commission that painters in the province of Quebec had dreamed of for decades: to produce a historical painting for the legislative building. On 16 Aug. 1910, having been selected by a committee composed of Thomas Chapais*, Eugène-Étienne Taché, and Ernest Myrand, Huot agreed to paint an oil on canvas whose subject would be *Le débat sur les langues: séance de l'Assemblée législative du Bas-Canada le 21 janvier 1793.* The canvas would be glued onto the wall above the speaker's chair in the chamber of the assembly. That Huot was awarded this contract was hardly surprising, for Quebec's intellectual elite had supported him from the outset of his career, and he also had useful connections in the political milieu. Chapais was a personal friend (they attended the Collège de Sainte-Anne-de-la-Pocatière at the same time) and Jules Tessier, a Quebec lawyer and politician, had already obtained a studio for him in the legislative building. In addition, his conservative aesthetic was entirely pleasing to his contemporaries. Huot worked for three years on this mural, the sketch for which was finished in February 1911. A few months later he went to France to complete his historical research and to do certain tasks deemed necessary to create the work. Back home in November, he set himself up at the Quebec Technical School until January 1913 and then began to paint directly on the canvas glued onto the wall of the chamber of the assembly. Unveiled on 11 November, the work was such a tremendous success that the government quickly gave him a new contract. This time he was to paint an allegory based on the theme of Quebec's motto, *Je me souviens*, to decorate the ceiling of the same room. Huot would spend years deciding on the composition of this work; he found it difficult to define its subject, which seemed neither to enthuse nor to inspire him. The painting would not be finished until December 1920.

While working on the sketches for *Je me souviens*, Huot accepted other commissions. In 1914 he drew an allegory of knowledge that would serve as the model for a stained-glass window in the legislative building's library. He painted stations of the cross for the Sœurs de Saint-Antoine de Padoue in Chicoutimi in 1915, did seven paintings for the church of Notre-Dame parish in Hébertville the following year, and produced a few illustrations for Ulric Barthe's work, *Similia similibus ou la guerre au Canada: essai romantique sur un sujet d'actualité*, which was published at Quebec in 1916. One project, however, held a special place in Huot's life between 1910 and 1920: the decoration of the chapel at the Ermitage San'Tonio (in Lac-Bouchette). Out of friendship for Abbé De Lamarre, who wanted to establish a pilgrimage site there, Huot did 22 paintings for the chapel during his summer holidays.

Huot was reducing his activities by 1920. In 1924, however, he drew the medal commemorating the tercentenary of the consecration of New France to St Joseph, which Alfred Laliberté* rendered in relief. At the age of 71, he enthusiastically accepted a final contract from the government: *Conseil souverain*, a depiction of the first meeting of that body to decorate the Legislative Council chamber. In order to gather information, he spent the spring of 1927 in Paris. Huot worked on this painting until his death on 27 Jan. 1930. It would be completed by two students from the École des Beaux-Arts in Montreal and in Quebec City under the supervision of their respective principals, Charles Maillard* and Henry Ivan Neilson*. In March 1930 the French government would posthumously name Huot an *officier de l'Instruction publique*.

Charles Huot had many students, including Edmond Lemoine and Louise Gignac. He was a respected and admired man, whose conservative aesthetic met the expectations of his contemporaries. Posterity would be harsher on him, however; he would be criticized for his academicism and his work as a copyist. In fact, Huot's oeuvre probably deserves to be re-evaluated in the light of new research and directions in the field of art history.

JOANNE CHAGNON

Several of Charles Huot's religious paintings have been destroyed in fires, but those in the churches of Saint-Sauveur (Quebec), Saint-Joseph (Carleton, Que.), Saint-Patrice (Rivière-du-Loup, Que.), and Notre-Dame (Hébertville, Que.) and in the chapel of Lac-Bouchette have survived. Examples of Huot's work are also found in Quebec City in the legislative building, the Musée National des Beaux-Arts du Québec, the National Commission of Battlefields, and the Museum of Civilization, Dépôt du Séminaire de Québec; the Musée du Saguenay–Lac-Saint-Jean in Chicoutimi, Que.; the Montreal Museum of Fine Arts; and the Centre for Research on French Canadian Culture and the National Gallery of Canada in Ottawa. Huot is the author of "Causerie artistique: l'œuvre de Tissot," *La Nouvelle-France* (Québec), 2 (1903): 188–92. Despite extensive research, it has proven impossible to locate his marriage record.

ANQ-Q, CE301-S1, 10 avril 1855. Centre for Research on French Canadian Culture, P 24 (fonds Charles-Huot). Musée National des Beaux-Arts du Québec, dossier Charles Huot; Fonds Gérard-Morisset, dossiers Charles Huot et paroisses. *L'Action sociale* (Québec), 22 juill. 1908, 2 févr. 1911. *Le Canadien* (Québec), 15 mai 1876. *Le Courrier du Canada* (Québec), 9 déc. 1873; 2 mars 1881; 8 janv., 8 oct. 1888; 28 oct. 1889; 8 nov. 1890; 22 mars, 11–12 juill., 16 nov. 1892; 23 mai 1893; 8 févr. 1894; 8–9, 12, 22–23 mai 1900. *Le Devoir*, 28 janv. 1930. *L'Électeur* (Québec), 27 nov., 13 déc. 1890; 11 juill. 1892; 12 févr., 25 juill. 1894. *L'Étendard* (Montréal), 30 nov. 1886, 14 juin 1901. *L'Événement*, 27 sept. 1870, 6 déc. 1873, 6 avril 1875, 15 mai 1876, 23 mai 1900, 16 nov. 1911, 28 janv. 1930. *Le Journal de Québec*, 30 mai 1874; 15 mai, 16 sept. 1876; 19 mai 1877. *La Minerve*, 6 juin 1874; 16 juill., 6 août 1886; 4 févr. 1887. *L'Opinion publique* (Montréal), 15 mars 1877. *La Presse*, 26 mai 1900, 8 avril 1913, 13 nov. 1920, 20 janv. 1927. *La Semaine commerciale* (Québec), 6 mai 1898. *Le Soleil*, 25 mai 1900, 12 févr. 1930. Sylvain Allaire, "Élèves canadiens dans les archives de l'École des beaux-arts et de l'École des arts décoratifs de Paris," *Journal of Canadian Art Hist.* (Montreal), 6 (1982), no.1: 98–111; "The Charles Huot paintings in Saint-Sauveur church, Quebec City," National Gallery of Canada, *Annual bull.*, 2 (1978–79): 17–30. Henri d'Arles [Henri Beaudé], *Pastels* (New York, 1905); *Propos d'art* (New York, 1903). Commission des Biens Culturels du Québec, *Les chemins de la mémoire* (3v., Montréal, 1990–99), vol.3 (*Biens mobiliers du Québec*, 1999). Robert Derome, "Charles Huot et la peinture d'histoire au Palais législatif de Québec (1883–1930)," National Gallery of Canada, *Bull.*, 27 (1976); "Charles Huot, peintre traditionnel?" *Vie des arts* (Montréal), no.85 (hiver 1976–77): 63–65. "Description de la chapelle de S. Antoine," *Le Messager de Saint-Antoine* (Chicoutimi), 7 (1901–2), no.10: 145–51. *Dictionnaire critique et documentaire des peintres, sculpteurs, dessinateurs et graveurs de tous les temps et de tous les pays* (nouv. éd., 10v., Paris, 1976), 5: 676. Ernest Gagnon, "M. Charles Huot et l'église de Saint-Sauveur," *Rev. canadienne* (Montréal), 26 (1890): 463–65. Maurice Hébert, "Le soulier de satin; conte au coin du feu," *Le Canada français* (Québec), 2e sér., 12 (1924–25): 673–81. Maurice d'Hesry, "Charles Huot et l'abbé Delamarre," *Saguenayensia* (Chicoutimi), 2 (1960): 129–33, 142–48; 3 (1961): 3–10. J.-S. Lesage, *Notes et esquisses québécoises; carnet d'un amateur* (Québec, 1925). Hormisdas Magnan, *Charles Huot, artiste-peintre, officier de l'Instruction publique: sa vie, sa carrière, ses œuvres, sa mort* (Québec, 1932). Raymond Montpetit, "Un exemple de peinture d'histoire au Québec:

Charles Huot à l'Assemblée nationale," *RHAF*, 31 (1977–78): 397–405. J.-R. Ostiguy, *Charles Huot* (Ottawa, 1979); "Charles Huot raconte les miracles de saint Antoine de Padoue," *Vie des arts*, no.87 (été 1977): 16–17.

HUTCHINGS, ELISHA FREDERICK, harness maker, businessman, and politician; b. 13 June 1855 in Newboro, Upper Canada, son of Elijah Hutchings and Harriet Gifford; m. there 3 Oct. 1882 Sarah Ann Denby, and they had three daughters and two sons; d. 14 April 1930 in Winnipeg.

The son of a farmer, Elisha Hutchings attended the country schools of Leeds County, Upper Canada, until age 15 when he was apprenticed to a harness maker. After completing his training in 1873, he plied his trade as a journeyman for three years before seeking his fortune in western Canada. Unimpressed with Winnipeg and short of cash, he was attracted to Edmonton by rumours of gold strikes. There he found occasional work at his trade and supplemented it with hunting and trapping. In the spring of 1877 he returned to Winnipeg.

Hutchings had planned to go into business, but the theft of his money and clothing forced him to take wage labour once again. He studied briefly at night at Alexander Begg*'s short-lived Manitoba Commercial College. He worked on his own account as a harness maker for a short time in 1878, but in 1879 he bought a junior partnership in Richard Stalker's harness-making business. By 1881 the firm had a retail and wholesale operation in Winnipeg under Hutchings's direction and a retail branch in Portage la Prairie under Stalker. It possessed capital of between $10,000 and $20,000. When Stalker died three years later, Hutchings purchased his interest.

Hutchings made brief incursions into municipal politics. He served two two-year terms as alderman, 1887–88 and 1894–95. As well, he ran unsuccessfully for mayor in 1900. Meanwhile, his business flourished with the settlement and growth of western Canada. In 1891 Dun, Wiman and Company reported its worth at between $75,000 and $125,000. By 1899 the extent of his investment had persuaded Hutchings to incorporate as the Great West Saddlery Company. The firm manufactured harnesses, saddles, trunks, and bags in Winnipeg and Calgary and ran a wholesale business in harness, saddlery, and hardware. As well, the company operated ten retail stores throughout the west and developed a significant export trade to South Africa, Australia, and New Zealand. By 1911 its assets were estimated at $750,000 to $1,000,000 and Hutchings himself was reputed to be worth $2,000,000, including his investments in several insurance and loan companies and building materials firms.

A major employer in Winnipeg, Hutchings had about 150 men by 1911. He actively recruited skilled workers in England. Disgruntled former employees disputed his claims of job opportunities and wrote home that his real goal was to depress wages and weaken organization among his workers. Hutchings routinely fired union men. In October 1911 he locked out ten employees who refused to sign a contract pledging not to start a union and not to belong to any association that supported strikes or promoted organization in his or any other business. When another 14 were fired for attending a protest meeting, the dismissed workers formed the Leather Workers' Union and declared a strike against Great West Saddlery. Early in December the company laid off workers in Calgary who refused to sign its employment contract. The labour disputes attracted attention in Winnipeg, where class lines were beginning to harden. The *Voice* (Winnipeg) condemned Hutchings for duping uninformed "foreign-speaking" workers into signing the contract. The Trades and Labor Council supported the strike, as did several local unions, which contributed strike funds.

The most controversial reaction came from the Winnipeg Ministerial Association. At the request of several employees, the association appointed a committee in October 1911 to investigate the dispute. Its report, issued the following month, emphasized that wages and factory conditions were not issues, but that the right of organization was. In response to the report, the reverends Charles William Gordon*, Salem Goldworth Bland*, and Fred Cook moved that the association condemn Hutchings for discriminating against union men. Although the Reverend James Shaver Woodsworth*, a member of the committee, argued for the adoption of a stronger resolution against the open shop, the majority favoured moderate censure. Even this resolution created a breach, since the Reverend David Christie of Westminster Presbyterian Church, where Hutchings was an office holder, resigned from the association. Pressure from the clergy did not move Hutchings and both the strike and the union collapsed.

In 1917 Hutchings again achieved national notoriety, this time for his attempts to seek an exemption from military service for his son Harold Gifford. His son, he argued before the appeal judge, was crucial to his plant's operations. Besides, he said, "I helped to build up this country not like some of these little one-horse men," and having established a successful business, "I want to hand it over to my son to keep." Hutchings claimed to be planning a shipbuilding operation in Vancouver and to be intending to leave the saddlery business under his son's management. It was charged that he had attempted to use his wealth in his son's cause and had declined to contribute to the Victory Loan unless exemption was granted. Hutchings denied these stories and won an apology, though witnesses testified to the Victory Loan incident before the appeal judge. Former employees, now in the military, denied that Harold played a significant role in the plant's operation. The exemption was rejected.

Great West Saddlery continued as a family business. Hutchings sold his interest in 1928, but remained active as president of the Equitable Trust Company and the Canada Loan and Mortgage Corporation. In the summer of 1929 he experienced heart difficulties, which caused his death the following April.

Shortly after his son's hearing, Hutchings was denounced by the *Manitoba Free Press* for the "ignorant arrogance of his purse-proud blatantly materialistic soul." In his business and in his public dealings, Hutchings claimed authority and privileges on the basis of his success and his wealth. In the extreme, his example attested to the growing social tensions in the city of Winnipeg.

DAVID G. BURLEY

Elisha Frederick Hutchings is the author of "Winnipeg's increase of manufactured products in 1912 has been over fifty per cent," *Dominion Magazine* (Toronto), December 1912: 27–28.

AO, RG 80-5-0-108, no.6061. GA, M 1469–71, PA 234, PA 330. LAC, RG 27, 299, no.3420. *Gazette* (Montreal), 5 Dec. 1917. *Manitoba Free Press*, 2 Aug. 1894; 22 Nov., 14–15, 17 Dec. 1917. *Saturday Post* (Winnipeg), 4 Nov. 1911. *Voice* (Winnipeg), 4, 11 March 1904; 13, 20, 27 Oct., 3, 10 Nov. 1911. *Winnipeg Telegram*, 29 Jan. 1910. *Winnipeg Tribune*, 22 June 1896, 14 April 1930. D. J. Bercuson, *Confrontation at Winnipeg: labour, industrial relations, and the general strike* (Montreal and London, 1974). George Bryce, *A history of Manitoba; its resources and people* (Toronto and Montreal, 1906). *Canadian album* (Cochrane and Hopkins), 3: 182. *The mercantile agency reference book . . .* (Montreal), 1901, 1911. *Winnipeg, Manitoba, and her industries* (Chicago and Winnipeg, 1882).

HUTTON, Sir EDWARD THOMAS HENRY, army officer; b. 6 Dec. 1848 in Torquay, England, son of Edward Thomas Hutton, a banker, and Jacintha Charlotte Eyre; m. 1 June 1889 Eleanor Mary Paulet (d. 27 March 1950) in Knightsbridge (London), England; they had no children; d. 4 Aug. 1923 in Chertsey, England.

Educated at Eton College, Edward Hutton joined the 60th Regiment as an ensign in 1867. Service in the Zulu War (1879), the Anglo-Boer War (1880–81), the Egyptian campaign (1882), and the Nile expedition (1884–85) brought promotion. Marriage to a cousin of the Marquess of Winchester, and membership in Lord Wolseley*'s coterie of careerist officers, provided influence. Within the Wolseley ring, Hutton made a "mounted infantry" his particular crusade. Promoted colonel and appointed aide-de-camp to Queen Victoria in 1892, the following year he became commandant of the military forces in New South Wales (Australia).

A driven officer with a fatal flair for public speaking, Hutton reformed the colony's headquarters staff,

created administrative support for its fighting units, and brought the military secretary under his command. As well, he advocated preparedness for imperial defence. His tactless promotion of increased defence commitments alienated the colony's hard-pressed government, and he was recalled in 1896, a hero to himself and his friends, and ready for a larger challenge. After brief service in Ireland, the challenge came in July 1898 when he was appointed general officer commanding the militia in Canada, where he attempted to replicate his New South Wales experiment. The appointment gave him the local rank of major-general. In late August the Huttons took up residence in Ottawa.

Hutton's allies in the War Office had protested the Colonial Office's attempt to block his selection. The Colonial Office acquiesced on the condition that he would be recalled should he prove troublesome. Wolseley and Sir Redvers Henry Buller, both of whom had served in Canada, warned him to flatter the colonials rather than abuse them. Hutton, however, was recalcitrant, confident that he was "the very humble instrument of an All-wise Providence." It helped to have his friend, the naïve and inexperienced Earl of Minto [Elliot*], appointed Canada's governor general that same year. Minto shared many of his causes.

Hutton's civilian master, the minister of militia and defence, Frederick William Borden*, supported the general's efforts to promote military service, reorganize the headquarters staff, improve training, encourage bilingualism, establish rigorous criteria for appointments and promotions, and create service units to support the fighting arms. He also backed Hutton's efforts to create a self-supporting force capable of serving as a "little Canadian Army in the field." Borden, however, objected to Hutton's pre-emptive, arrogant methods and his attempts to bring military administration under his exclusive control. Moreover, many of Borden's ministerial colleagues resented Hutton's public advocacy of imperial obligations, especially during the divisive debate that preceded Canada's participation in the South African War.

The minister and the general first quarrelled over the appointment of Napoléon Chevalier as medical officer at the infantry school in Saint-Jean (Saint-Jean-sur-Richelieu), Que. Hutton immediately sought the assistance of the newly arrived Minto, whose support fed his pretensions. A more tangled dispute in 1899 over the extension of Lieutenant-Colonel James DOMVILLE's command of the 8th (Princess Louise's New Brunswick) Regiment of Cavalry reflected poorly on all parties. Scornful of "ignorant civilians," Hutton and Minto tended to attribute every ministerial intervention to partisan politics, and they failed to see that Borden was the "most powerful force for reform in [Sir Wilfrid Laurier*]'s government."

Many Liberals, for their part, believed that Hutton

favoured Conservatives for militia appointments. His battle with Samuel HUGHES, a Conservative MP and a lieutenant-colonel in the Ontario militia, demonstrated that Hutton respected no man's politics, especially when they challenged his personal ambitions. Both were competent officers, but they were also vain and intemperate men who craved rank and saw war as a means to advancement. Their most violent altercation occurred over the leadership of whatever troops Canada might decide to send in the event of a war in South Africa. Hutton had set his heart upon commanding a combined force of Canadians and Australians, and he sought this goal by insisting on an official Canadian contingent. Hughes, fearing that Hutton had omitted him from a lead role in any contingent, offered to recruit and command a volunteer unit. Hutton, however, refused to transmit this offer to the British government, and in August 1899 he asked Minto to block any Canadian endorsement. Hughes struck back like a doomed man, denouncing Hutton and Minto and reminding them of the stupidities of British regulars through the ages. His communication left Hutton with the impression that he was slightly mad. In fact, Hughes resembled no one more than Hutton. After Hughes advertised for volunteers, Hutton charged him with violating the British Army Act, which forbade unauthorized recruitment, and threatened to remove him from his militia command. When Canada decided – on 13 October, two days after the outbreak of the South African War – to send an official contingent, Borden would intervene to permit Hughes to accompany it in civilian dress and seek military employment with some other unit, an unlikely chance owing to the vindictive correspondence from Minto and Hutton to senior British officers.

The government watched this public controversy with incredulity. Those in cabinet who opposed a contingent, including Joseph-Israël Tarte* and Richard William Scott*, were convinced that Hutton and Minto were in league with Colonial Secretary Joseph Chamberlain to force Canada to commit troops. They were wrong, however: there was no accord, and Hutton and Minto disagreed on the necessity of war. During the summer of 1899, Hutton worked "patriotism and military enthusiasm . . . to a white heat" in the militia camps; Minto remained equivocal until the outbreak of war. In the end, the decision to send troops was a reluctant, politically motivated capitulation to the strident demands of Canada's pro-war advocates. It was not helped, however, by rumours that Hutton had boasted he might have to overturn the government as he claimed to have done in New South Wales.

The crisis over the contingent further embittered Hutton's relationships with the government, and set the stage for his dismissal for insubordination. Antagonisms surfaced during the ceremonies marking the contingent's departure. At the Quebec garrison's banquet on 28 October for the officers, Hutton, intoxicated by his own rhetoric, predicted that Canada would send 50,000 to 100,000 men to defend the empire's integrity. This declaration appeared to repudiate the government's public promise that the 1,000-man contingent constituted no precedent for future contributions. The next day Hutton quarrelled with Borden and stomped off the parade square in a huff.

Meanwhile Hutton's disagreement with Lord William Frederick Ernest Seymour, the commander of the British troops in Halifax, had come to a head. What began in June 1899 as a petty issue of protocol grew into a personal vendetta. As the senior British officer in Canada, Seymour, in the event of war, was to assume command of the combined Canadian and British forces. Hutton refused to provide him with a secret report and routine information on British regulars in the Canadian militia. Such an exchange, he felt, would be an infringement on Canadian autonomy. When Seymour addressed him through Borden, Hutton appeared even more alarmed. Finally, Seymour appealed to Borden to help curtail Hutton's growing insubordination and sent the minister a secret memorandum condemning Hutton's behaviour while in command of the militia. Minto reported Seymour to the War Office. Its assessment would precipitate Seymour's resignation in 1900; a subsequent military inquiry would uphold him.

As the war continued, Hutton became increasingly erratic. Even Minto quarrelled with him over the composition of a second contingent. Hutton was determined to recruit mounted men from the militia cavalry, confident that their success would reflect favourably on his command. Minto suggested recruits from the northwest who could ride and shoot and had experience with rough terrain. In despair, he explained to his War Office friend Lord Lansdowne [PETTY-FITZMAURICE] how unreasonable Hutton had become: "He can not get it out of his head the popular effect of the organization and thinks a great deal about the hats they are to wear." Minto even asked Prime Minister Laurier to intervene.

A minor dispute over the purchasing of horses for the second contingent hastened Hutton's break with the government in January 1900. After he had refused to supply information, Borden secured cabinet's approval to dismiss the general. Minto foolishly considered forcing his government's resignation over the issue. When Laurier remained adamant, Minto informed the Colonial Office of his plans. Its reaction was immediate. Convinced that Hutton was "unfit by temperament and manners" for his position, it recalled him, effective 12 February.

Hutton's friends in the War Office found him a place in South Africa as commanding officer of the 1st Mounted Infantry Brigade. Composed largely of Canadian, Australian, and New Zealand troops, it resembled Hutton's initial dream. Canadian troops detested him, however, and the feeling appeared mutual. Hutton described them as the worst thieves in the British army; on one occasion they had stolen his horse. The Canadians soon discovered their poor opinion of Hutton was shared by British officers, who dismissed him as "a bit of a crank and somewhat impractical."

Created a KCMG in 1900, the following year Hutton became the first GOC land forces of the new Commonwealth of Australia. His mission and his methods were familiar as he strove to create, often in the face of political opposition, an integrated, well-equipped garrison and field force prepared for service at home and abroad. He consolidated the state militias and drafted a national defence policy. Its revision in 1904, to replace the position of GOC with an army council, precipitated his resignation, an issue brought to a head by a quarrel over payment for a secret cable. When this incident reached the War Office, its secretary of state noted his reluctance to recall Hutton since he "cannot keep his mouth shut, and would talk us into a difficulty every week." After necessity had forced the secretary's hand, the War Office made Hutton commander of the 3rd British Division. Before his retirement in 1907 he was promoted lieutenant-general, and in 1912 he was made a KCB. Although he returned for service during the Great War, to organize and command the 21st Division, in 1915 a riding accident restored him to retirement. He died eight years later at Fox Hills, his home in Chertsey, and was buried in nearby Lyne.

A man of great energy, ambition, and organizational ability, and committed to defending the imperial estate, Hutton regarded the colonies as a laboratory for experiments in civil-military relations and a means of personal advancement. His vanity, passion for public speaking, scorn for civilians, disregard for democratic institutions, and lack of tact proved fatal liabilities, and made him appear to be, in the estimate of one former GOC, a "dangerous martinet." His turbulent career undermined the imperial influence in Canadian defence and argued for the appointment of a Canadian to command the militia.

CARMAN MILLER

British Library (London), Add. MSS 50078–114 (Hutton papers); Add. MSS 50275–357 (Arnold-Forster papers). LAC, MG 26, G; MG 27, II, B1; MG 30, E242. NSARM, MG 2. *Australian dictionary of biography*, ed. Douglas Pike *et al.* (16v. and an index to date, Melbourne, 1966–), 9. Stephen Clarke, "'Manufacturing spontaneity'? The role of the commandant in the colonial offers of troops to the South African War," in *The Boer War: army, nation and empire: the 1999 Chief of Army/Australian War Memorial military history conference*, ed. Peter Dennis and Jeffrey Grey (Canberra, Australia, 2000), 129–50. R. G. Haycock, *Sam Hughes: the public career of a controversial Canadian, 1885–1916* (Waterloo, Ont., 1986). Carman Miller, *The Canadian career of the fourth Earl of Minto: the education of a viceroy* (Waterloo, 1980); *Painting the map red: Canada and the South African War, 1899–1902* (Montreal and Kingston, Ont., 1993). Desmond Morton, *Ministers and generals: politics and the Canadian militia, 1868–1904* (Toronto and Buffalo, N.Y., 1970). R. A. Preston, *Canada and "Imperial Defense"; a study of the origins of the British Commonwealth's defense organization, 1867–1919* (Toronto and Durham, N.C., 1967).

HYMAS, SARAH (Bates; Daines), Mormon community leader; b. 6 Dec. 1841 in Rayleigh, England, fourth of the eight children of William Hymas and Mary Ann Atkins; m. first 16 Nov. 1862 Ormus Ephraim Bates in Salt Lake City (Utah), and they had five children, two of whom died young; m. secondly 5 April 1875 Robert Daines in Hyde Park (Utah), and they had a daughter and a son; d. 27 Nov. 1929 in Cardston, Alta.

At age 10, Sarah Hymas began to work for a living. When she was 16, Charles W. Penrose, an apostle of the Church of Jesus Christ of Latter-day Saints, converted her and all but one of her family to Mormonism. In 1861 Hymas and most of the family immigrated to the United States. They worked in Brooklyn (New York City) for a year to pay their way to Salt Lake City, which they reached on 26 Sept. 1862.

Before the practice of having more than one wife at a time was officially abandoned by their church in 1890, many Mormons accepted plural marriage as a divinely inspired teaching of Mormon patriarch Joseph Smith. In Salt Lake City, Sarah became the sixth concurrent wife of pioneer farmer, miner, and stockraiser O. E. Bates. After he died in 1873, she became the fourth wife of Robert Daines, the leader or bishop of the Hyde Park Ward. (A ward was a unit of the church comparable to a congregation; several wards composed a stake.)

The escalation of federal anti-polygamy laws in the 1880s forced Mormon polygamists to look for a refuge. Daines was one of a group of men, headed by Charles Ora Card*, who escaped the threat of imprisonment by immigrating to Lee's Creek (Cardston), in southwestern Alberta. While Daines's other families remained behind – he hoped to bring them to Canada eventually, without controversy – he, Sarah, and their children travelled north by wagon train, accompanied by one other Mormon family. Sarah tackled the rigours of cross-country travel and handled tasks that ordinarily fell to men, such as driving and repairing the wagon. They arrived in the fall of 1887.

Despite the vehement anti-Mormon sentiment expressed by some Canadian politicians and journalists, these pioneer families thrived, in part because of their agricultural skills, most notably in irrigation. Hymas was crucial to the development of the community's fledgling social and cultural infrastructure. Her home accommodated religious services, public meetings, and musical and theatrical evenings. During the first winter, she helped deliver the first white child born at Lee's Creek, Zina Alberta Woolf. She also played important roles in the newly created Cardston Ward: in 1887–88 she was the founding president of its Primary Association, which taught children about the Mormon religion, and secretary of the Relief Society, a traditional Mormon women's organization devoted to charitable work, sewing, testimony, and scriptural study.

Robert Daines returned to Hyde Park in the fall of 1888. The next year Hymas followed, to help her co-wives care for him in his failing health. In June 1894, after his death, she came back to Cardston. The following year she would celebrate the marriage of her daughter Sarah Annie Daines to Chauncey Edgar Snow, a prominent local businessman. She served as president of the ward relief society from 1894 to 1910, and was treasurer of the stake relief society from 1910. By 1929 she was the oldest survivor of the 1887 pioneers. Her years of dedication to church and community had earned her the affectionate and respectful title of Aunt or Grandma Daines.

SIRI LOUIE

International Soc. Daughters of Utah Pioneers (Salt Lake City), E. P. and D. E. Haddock, "History of Sarah Hymas Bates Daines," 17 May 1968; "History of Sarah Hymas," 20 April 1973. *Lethbridge News* (Lethbridge, Alta), 18 Sept. 1895. *News* (Cardston, Alta), 5 Dec. 1929. J. E. W. Bates and Z. A. W. Hickman, *Founding of Cardston and vicinity* (n.p., 1974). M. U. Beecher, "Mormon women in southern Alberta: the pioneer years," in *The Mormon presence in Canada*, ed. B. Y. Card *et al.* (Edmonton, 1990), 211–30. [C. O. Card], *The diaries of Charles Ora Card: the Canadian years, 1886–1903*, ed. D. G. Godfrey and B. Y. Card (Salt Lake City, 1993). Brian Champion, "Mormon polygamy: parliamentary comments, 1889–90," *Alberta Hist.* (Calgary), 35 (1987), no.2: 10–17. *Chief Mountain country: a history of Cardston and district*, ed. Keith Shaw and Beryl Bectell (2v., Cardston and Calgary, 1978–87). Dan Erickson, "Alberta polygamists? The Canadian climate and response to the introduction of Mormonism's 'peculiar institution,'" *Pacific Northwest Quarterly* (Seattle, Wash.), 86 (1995): 155–64.

I

IDINGTON, JOHN, lawyer and judge; b. 14 Oct. 1840 in Puslinch Township, Upper Canada, eldest child of Peter Idington, a farmer, and Catherine Stewart; m. 25 Sept. 1866 Margaret Colcleugh in Mount Forest, Upper Canada, and they had 11 children; d. 7 Feb. 1928 in Ottawa.

John Idington's parents were among the Scottish pioneers of Puslinch, south of Guelph. The family moved to a farm in Waterloo County near Fisher's Mills in 1853. An able student, John received a thorough education at William Tassie*'s school in Galt (Cambridge). In 1864 he graduated from the University of Toronto with an LLB, was called to the bar, and started practice in Stratford with Robert MacFarlane, the MLA for Perth and a fellow Liberal. MacFarlane's death in 1872 left Idington with a large practice in a community that was expanding rapidly, partly as a result of the location there of the Grand Trunk Railway shops in 1871. He was created a provincial QC in 1876 and a dominion QC in 1885. In 1879, the year he became crown attorney and clerk of the peace for Perth County, he began construction of a substantial brick office building, a sure sign of his success.

A key supporter of Stratford's incorporation as a city in March 1885, Idington delivered the main oration at a great banquet celebrating the event on 22 July. By this time he had also gained notoriety for his attempt, as a parent and school trustee, to discredit the principal who had set one of his sons back a grade. Other trustees distanced themselves, but Idington persisted, to the point of involving the minister of education, George William Ross*. The vendetta revealed Idington's stubborn determination and willingness to stand alone. On 18 Jan. 1886 he became the city's solicitor, a post he would hold until his appointment to the bench; the following year he was elected first president of the Perth County Law Society. From 1891 to 1904 he was a bencher of the Law Society of Upper Canada, and in 1894–95 he was president of the Western Bar Association. Among the benchers, Idington was an early supporter of Clara Brett MARTIN; his motion of 13 Sept. 1892 would have led to her admission as the first female member of the society but it was rejected by a vote of 9 to 4.

As city solicitor and crown attorney, Idington gained wide experience. In 1891 ratepayers from Stratford's Romeo Ward presented him with a gold-headed cane as thanks for obtaining the conviction of a woman who ran a brothel. He prosecuted as well in a number of notable murder trials, including that in 1894 of Amédée (Almeda) Chattelle, who had brutally slain and carved up a young girl. Over the years Idington had a number of partners in private practice but each moved on, indicating perhaps that he was difficult to work with.

In March 1904 the Liberal government of Sir Wilfrid Laurier* appointed Idington to the provincial High Court of Justice in Toronto. Less than 11 months later, on 10 Feb. 1905, he was elevated to the Supreme Court of Canada. Lawyers have been appointed directly from practice, but no sitting judge has received such quick promotion. An excellent judicial record could hardly be the explanation – Idington had had little time to prove himself. The *Canada Law Journal* (Toronto) probably reflected the true reason: "Having so recently severed his connection with his former place of abode at Stratford, he naturally would have less hesitation in going to Ottawa than many others." This explanation suggests that the court did not enjoy sufficient prestige to compensate for the inconvenience of a move to the national capital. At the time the court was not, in fact, "supreme": its judgements could be appealed to the Judicial Committee of the Privy Council in England; important cases could go straight there from provincial appellate courts, some of which were felt to be as strong as the Supreme Court; and it was experiencing a high turnover of justices. Moreover, in 1905 Ottawa lacked a large legal fraternity and the amenities of bigger cities.

On the bench Idington displayed industry and marked individuality, and became known for his wit. He rendered dissenting opinions in a great many cases – more than any other judge to the present time. Although legal scholar Ian Bushnell regards him simply as a renegade whose judgements had a "discordant quality," several of his dissents have merit as important interpretations of fundamental functions and rights in law and government. In 1910, for instance, the Laurier government asked the Supreme Court to determine whether the parliament of Canada could impose on the court the duty to answer reference questions not related to actual or intended federal legislation. The majority of judges said parliament could do so; dissenting, Idington addressed a core issue, the imposition of political function: "If we degrade this court by imposing upon it duties that cannot be held judicial but merely advisory . . . , we destroy a fundamental principle of our government." Moreover, since provincial and private rights could be affected by a reference, he contended that it amounted to taking away rights without the due process of law.

In *Quong-Wing v. the King* (1914) the court tested the validity of a Saskatchewan statute that prohibited the employment of white females in businesses owned or managed by an "Oriental person." Born in China but a naturalized British subject, Quong Wing operated a restaurant in Moose Jaw and employed two white waitresses. His conviction was appealed to the Supreme Court, which, as precedents, had to consider conflicting decisions of the JCPC. In *Union Colliery Company of British Columbia v. Bryden* (1899) it had held invalid a British Columbia statute prohibiting the employment of Chinese in coalmines because the law infringed federal power over aliens and naturalized citizens [*see* John Bryden*]. In *Cunningham v. Tomey Homma* (1903), however, it upheld British Columbia's Provincial Elections Act, which prohibited any "Chinaman, Japanese, or Indian" from voting. The majority of the Supreme Court followed *Tomey Homma*. Incensed by the discriminatory legislation, Idington disagreed, stating that "equal freedom and equal opportunity before the law . . . are not to be impaired by the whims of a legislature" and that the "legislation is but a piece of the product of the mode of thought that begot and maintained slavery." From parliament's jurisdiction over aliens and naturalization, Idington inferred the power to guarantee equality for naturalized subjects. Historian James W. St G. Walker has written that "if Idington's implied Bill of Rights was too radical, *Bryden* was available to squelch a law that was openly discriminatory." Few judges have their dissenting judgements favourably commended as progressive after the lapse of more than 80 years.

In 1917, during wartime, the Military Service Act instituted conscription and established exemptions, one being for farm workers. As the need for troops increased, the cabinet, acting under the War Measures Act, passed orders in council in April 1918 purporting to cancel these exemptions. George Edwin Gray, a northern Ontario farmer, refused to report for duty; when arrested, he brought a writ of habeas corpus. The issue, as it came before the Supreme Court in July, was whether the government could amend a statute through order in council under the War Measures Act. Four of the six judges upheld such delegation of legislative power. In objecting, Idington stated that "a wholesale surrender of the will of the people to any autocratic power is exactly what we are fighting against." His opinion is echoed in the work of modern-day constitutional expert Peter W. Hogg: if the War Measures Act is not "unconstitutional abdication . . . it is not easy to imagine the kind of delegation that would be unconstitutional."

In many constitutional cases Idington tended to take a strong provincialist position. In *Re Board of Commerce* (1920) the court split on the validity of federal legislation to control prices, with the issue being whether such control fell within federal competence under the "trade and commerce" power of the British North America Act or within provincial competence under "property and civil rights." Idington, who along with Lyman Poore Duff* and Louis-Philippe BRODEUR held the legislation invalid, said: "Our Confederation Act was not intended to be a mere sham, but an instrument of government intended to assign to the provincial legislatures some absolute rights, and of these none were supposed to be more precious than those over property and civil rights." In his dislike of many forms of regulation, he revealed himself as a laissez-faire liberal. Duff later remarked on his passion for justice; jurist Eugene LAFLEUR, who frequently appeared before Idington in court, noted that the depth of his convictions made him almost a terrifying figure to counsel who supported what he believed to be the weaker cause.

With the appointment of Sir Louis Henry DAVIES as chief justice on 23 Oct. 1918, Idington became the senior puisne judge. On 11 Aug. 1921, with the chief in Britain, he administered the oath of office to Governor General Lord Byng*. After trying to persuade Lafleur to accept the chief justiceship following Davies's death in 1924, Prime Minister William Lyon Mackenzie King* appointed Francis Alexander Anglin*, passing over the more senior Idington and Duff. In his diary King wrote that "Idington will be disappointed not being made C.J. but he is 86 years of age and senile." He was, in fact, approaching 84; whether he was disappointed or not, Duff certainly was.

In 1926 Minister of Justice Ernest Lapointe* asked for Idington's resignation since he had been absent from the court for extended periods in 1925 and 1926. Whatever his reply, he clung to office. The Liberal government had been considering mandatory retirement for judges of the Supreme and Exchequer courts, and Idington's refusal to go provided the catalyst. Legislation was enacted, effective 31 March 1927, requiring retirement at age 75. Idington was thus forced to step down that day. On 5 October his wife passed away and four months later he died, leaving a modest estate of $41,842. Survived by four sons and four daughters, he was buried in Avondale Cemetery in Stratford.

GORDON BALE

AO, RG 80-27-2, 79: 183. *Beacon Herald* (Stratford, Ont.),

14 April 1956, 3 July 1971, 26 Aug. 1978, 17 July 1982. *Globe*, 6 Oct. 1927, 8 Feb. 1928. *Guelph Mercury* (Guelph, Ont.), 11 Oct. 1866. Ian Bushnell, *The captive court: a study of the Supreme Court of Canada* (Montreal and Kingston, Ont., 1992). *Canada Law Journal* (Toronto), 40 (1904): 209; 41 (1905): 206–7. *Canadian Bar Rev.* (Toronto), 6 (1928): 142–43. *Canadian Law Times* (Toronto), 24 (1904): 114–15; 25 (1905): 164. *Canadian men and women of the time* (Morgan; 1898 and 1912). W. A. Craik, "Canada's Supreme Court at work," *Maclean's* (Toronto), 27 (1913–14), no.5: 13–16, 137–38. *Cunningham v. Tomey Homma*, [1903] *Law Reports, Appeal Cases* (London): 151–57 (Privy Council). J. G. Hodgins, *The Stratford case: Idington vs. McBride; report of the commissioner . . .* (Toronto, 1887). P. W. Hogg, *Constitutional law of Canada* (4th ed., Scarborough [Toronto], 1997). William Johnston, *History of the county of Perth from 1825 to 1902* (Stratford, 1903; repr. 1976). W. L. M. King, *The Mackenzie King diaries, 1893–1931* (microfiche ed., Toronto, 1973), 12 Sept. 1924. Adelaide Leitch, *Floodtides of fortune: the story of Stratford and the progress of the city through two centuries* (Stratford, 1980). *Quong-Wing v. the King* (1914), *Canada Supreme Court Reports*, 49: 440–69; *Re George Edwin Gray* (1918), 57: 150–83. *Re Board of Commerce* (1920), *Canada Supreme Court Reports* (Ottawa), 60: 456–522; *Re marriage laws* (1912), 46: 132–456; *Re references by the governor-general in council* (1910), 43: 536–94. *Saturday Night*, 18 Feb. 1928: 2. J. G. Snell and Frederick Vaughan, *The Supreme Court of Canada: history of the institution* ([Toronto], 1985). *Union Colliery Company of British Columbia v. Bryden*, [1899] *Law Reports, Appeal Cases*: 580–88. J. W. St G. Walker, *"Race," rights and the law in the Supreme Court of Canada: historical case studies* ([Toronto and Waterloo, Ont.], 1997). Waterloo Hist. Soc., *Annual report* (Kitchener, Ont.), 1 (1913): 38.

IGNATIA, Mother; IGNATIUS, Sister. *See* CAMPBELL

IRISH NELLIE. *See* CASHMAN, ELLEN

ISSAUREL, BÉATRICE. *See* LA PALME

J

JARVIS, WILLIAM MUNSON, barrister, insurance agent, and author; b. 9 Oct. 1838 in Saint John, son of William Jarvis and Mary Caroline Boyd; m. first 14 May 1861 Jane Hope Beer in Sussex, N.B., and they had two sons and a daughter; m. secondly 20 April 1868 Mary Lucretia Scovil in Saint John, and they had two daughters; d. there 17 Sept. 1921.

William Munson Jarvis was the grandson of Munson Jarvis*, a loyalist merchant and politician in Saint John. His father was also a successful merchant. As befitted his status, William Jarvis undoubtedly pro-

vided his son with private tutors before sending him to the elite Saint John Grammar School. Here, from 1848 to 1854, William Munson faced a challenging curriculum consisting of natural philosophy and modern and classical languages; he apparently excelled in Greek, Latin, and mathematics. From the late 1850s Jarvis was a member of the Church of England Young Men's Society. By 1860 he had also joined the Chatham Club, a society of young men who routinely met for conversation and debate.

Between the years 1860 and 1864 Jarvis established the foundation of his personal and professional life. In May 1861, a month after his admission as an attorney, he married Jane Hope Beer. In a poignant recollection penned after her untimely death, he recalled fondly their two-month wedding trip to New York City, Niagara Falls, and finally Charlottetown, where they visited the children of his late uncle Edward James Jarvis*. After returning to Saint John, Jarvis and his bride settled in with his mother in his boyhood home. The extended household also included his mother's three sisters and a few of her nephews. Nevertheless, Jarvis did not begin to build a residence until 1863, the year in which he became a barrister. The young couple, now with two children, moved into their new home in Portland (Saint John) at Christmas 1864. Their marital happiness was short-lived. Soon after the birth of a third child in 1866, Mrs Jarvis died. She had asked that "her little one" be named Frank, to which Jarvis had replied that his second name should be her own, Hope.

A widower at 27, Jarvis relied on his ageing mother and his late wife's sister Eleanor (Ellen) James Beer for much of the children's care. During her last days his wife had also asked him to find another mother for her children, and in 1868 he married Mary Lucretia Scovil. Three years later he was serving on the Portland town council, having earlier that year prepared its charter of incorporation. His life had begun to return to a happy state, but once again he experienced tragedy with his wife's premature death in 1873. He did not remarry. With the assistance of servants and family he assumed the solitary responsibility of raising five children.

Jarvis's professional life mirrored the events of his day. As a young man during the Fenian raid of 1866, he had been a member of the volunteer militia, and he would attain the rank of lieutenant-colonel. By the mid 1870s he had been made the general agent for the Maritime provinces of the Liverpool and London and Globe Insurance Company. It is unclear which occupation – law or insurance – provided him with most of his living but probably his insurance business drew substantially on his legal knowledge. The great fire of June 1877 in Saint John occurred while he was still building his career, and his attention would be focused for more than 20 years on its after-effects. His work involved petitioning various agencies on behalf of clients for the reissuance of bonds to replace those which had been destroyed. He continued to handle the investment accounts of a number of aunts and uncles, some of whom had removed to England following the fire. By 1888 he was the president of the New Brunswick Board of Fire Underwriters. He would serve as president of the Board of Trade of the Maritime Provinces in 1898 and of the Saint John Board of Trade in 1902–3.

Jarvis was a fairly prolific essayist. As a young lawyer, he had written a paper entitled "The title to the soil and early history of the territory of New Brunswick." Most of his essays centred on the Church of England in New Brunswick and included such topics as clergy appointments, church governance, financial support for church initiatives, Sunday school programs, and, perhaps most significant, the impact of the Oxford Movement, which had attempted to steer a course for the Church of England between Roman Catholicism and evangelicalism. Jarvis, apparently a deeply religious man, directed his attention to the liturgical and doctrinal differences between Anglicans and Catholics. For him, as for others, matters came to a head in 1880 and 1881 with the proposed establishment in Portland of the Mission Chapel, promoted by parishioners of St Paul's (Valley) Church, such as Isaac Allen Jack*, who wished to see a "local expression of the Anglican church revival." Jarvis agreed with the formal protest sent in May 1881 to Bishop John Medley* and to the Reverend John Metcalf Davenport*, who had been asked to take charge of the projected church. The bishop, however, supported the chapel, which opened in January 1882.

Jarvis and others who were sceptical of the Oxford Movement may have viewed the chapel initially as more Roman Catholic than Anglican and therefore as potentially subversive doctrinally. In one of his essays Jarvis questioned the Catholic tenet in which "the intercession of the blessed virgin mary is allowed . . . practically to supercede the mediation of Him whom St. Paul terms 'the one mediator between . . . God and man.'" He urged Catholics to embrace Anglicanism because they would find their "own prayers" translated into English, a language they could understand, and would thus more fully participate in church services. Eventually Jarvis and most of the city's Anglican clergy accepted the Mission Chapel, in part because of Davenport's public pronouncements on what he claimed was the utter doctrinal corruption of the Roman Catholic Church in promulgating the dogma of the Immaculate Conception.

Testimonials at Jarvis's death in 1921 reveal the esteem in which he was generally held. Perhaps in the small city that was Saint John in the late 19th and early 20th centuries these commentaries reflected an unspoken appreciation of a man admired not only for his professional achievements but also for having borne the challenges of raising his children alone and the sorrow of having to commit his son Frank Hope to the Provincial Lunatic Asylum, where he would reside until his death more than 50 years later.

ELIZABETH W. MCGAHAN

N.B. Museum (Saint John), "Family tree of Stephen Jarvis of Huntington, L.I., New York" (MS); Jarvis family papers; Vert. file, circular, genealogy of the Jarvis family. PANB, RS140.

Saint John Regional Library, "Biographical data relating to New Brunswick families, especially of loyalist descent," comp. D. R. Jack (4v., typescript; copy at the N.B. Museum). *Evening Times and Star* (Saint John), 1921. *Saint John Globe*, 1921. *Biographical review . . . of leading citizens of the province of New Brunswick*, ed. I. A. Jack (Boston, 1900). J. M. Davenport, *Messiah (God incarnate) not Messiah's mother the "bruiser of the serpent's head" . . . with a concise exposure of Mr. R. F. Quigley's errors and controversial tactics . . .* (Saint John, 1891). *Directory*, Saint John, 1865/66–74/75. *History of the Mission Church of S. John Baptist, Saint John, N.B., 1882–1932* (Saint John, 1932).

JEFFERS, FRANCES. *See* MAHONY

JENKINS, MARGARET. *See* TOWNSEND

JENKINS, STEPHEN RICE, physician, militia officer, politician, and office holder; b. 12 Nov. 1858 in Charlottetown, son of John Theophilus Jenkins and Jessica Esther Carson Rice; m. 7 Oct. 1886 Ellen Josephine Sweeney, and they had seven daughters and four sons (a daughter and a son did not reach adulthood); d. 15 Sept. 1929 in Charlottetown.

Stephen Jenkins came from a notable Prince Edward Island family – the Anglican clergyman Theophilus Desbrisay* was a great-grandfather – and he would be the fourth in a line of five generations of Jenkins doctors. His father, a Crimean War veteran and the first physician born on the Island to practise there, was elected to the House of Assembly and the House of Commons. In many ways, Stephen Jenkins's career would mirror his father's: he would take up medicine, serve in the military, and enter politics. He diverged from family conventions only by leaving the Church of England and converting to Roman Catholicism before his marriage.

Jenkins was educated at St Peter's Boys' School in Charlottetown and King's College in Windsor, N.S. After receiving preliminary medical training from his father, he studied medicine at the University of Pennsylvania. He graduated with honours in 1884 and was then engaged as house surgeon at Blockley Hospital in Philadelphia. In 1885 he returned to the Island, where he practised briefly in Tignish before settling in Cardigan. During the smallpox epidemic in the fall of 1885 he was put in charge of a quarantine hospital in Charlottetown. He moved to the city with his family in 1888, the same year he was commissioned surgeon in the 4th Prince Edward Island Provisional Garrison Artillery Brigade. In 1904 he would be made its honorary lieutenant-colonel. He also tried his hand at provincial politics. Defeated in 1900, he was elected in Charlottetown as a Conservative in 1912 and again in 1915. He served as a minister without portfolio during his second term, in the administration of John Alexander Mathieson*, and as chief aide-de-camp to three lieutenant governors. During World War I he entered the Canadian Army Medical Corps, and from March 1915 to April 1919 he was in charge of the Rockhead Military Hospital in Halifax. In 1918 he was instrumental in having a veterans' hospital established in Charlottetown; it was named in honour of nursing sister Rena Maude McLean* and for a time the medical officer in charge was his son John Stephen.

Taking up active service in the prime of his career probably meant significant financial loss for Jenkins. Recognized as having the largest medical and surgical practice on the Island, he was the only physician to serve at both of its major hospitals; at the time of his death he was senior staff surgeon at the Prince Edward Island Hospital and chief of staff at the Charlottetown Hospital. He normally took hospital rounds and performed surgery in the mornings, and then kept office hours and made house calls. Nights were spent reading medical journals, as he attempted to keep abreast of the latest advances. Later in life, he would take holidays to tour hospitals in London and Vienna.

Jenkins worked steadily to bolster a range of professional organizations. A member of the first Dominion Medical Council, registrar of the Prince Edward Island Medical Council, and a fellow of the American College of Surgeons, he served as president in 1906 of the Maritime Medical Association, chair in 1922 of the Island branch of the American Society for the Control of Cancer, and president in 1928–29 of the Canadian Medical Association. He regularly reported cases at meetings of the provincial medical association, and was active in local committees on cancer research and social hygiene. Concerned with preventive medicine and public health, he helped establish and served as secretary of the provincial Red Cross Society. For a time he was president as well of the Anti-Tuberculosis Society. Jenkins's professional status also afforded him a role in civic development. He helped foster the local economy as a member of the Charlottetown Club and promoted educational standards and healthy school environments during his 30 years on the city's school board. A member of the Catholic Mutual Benefit Association and the Phi Gamma Delta fraternity, he founded the Free Dispensary for the Poor and continued the Jenkins Coal Fund, a charity initiated by his father.

This broad involvement did not leave Jenkins much time for his large family – it was Ellen Jenkins who provided the structure in their household. The busy, often absent doctor could still be an indulgent father, one whose kindliness spilled over into his professional role. His daughters recall him, in emergencies, taking patients (and once an entire family) into their home. The demands of work meant that he could be inattentive to his own health. In 1902, for instance, he lost an eye when an infection went untreated. The stresses could also manifest themselves in bursts of temper. It was not uncommon for him, if vexed by some aspect of an operation, to fling a piece of surgical equipment across the room and then carry on. But there was recompense. As he grew older, his flourishing practice allowed him to hire younger doctors to assist him, keep his family in a grand house (Brighton Villa), and spend some leisure time at golf, curling, and tennis.

For Jenkins, "a man of keen intellect and indefatigable energy," general practice demanded an enormous amount of talent and time, whatever its return. He did not focus on any one specialty, but mastered many. As a colleague would observe in his eulogy, it was through general medicine that he "climbed to the highest pinnacle in his profession." Jenkins died of pneumonia in 1929 following a brief illness. His passing was peaceful – city council had closed his street so the esteemed doctor could rest. His medical peers regarded him as "the ideal physician," in true Oslerian tradition, just as his community remembered him as "that perfect citizen."

SASHA MULLALLY

A photograph of Stephen Rice Jenkins performing surgery in the operating room of the Charlottetown Hospital is found in PARO, Acc. 2320/32-12.

PARO, P.E.I. Geneal. Soc. coll., family files, Jenkins family, Hilda Jenkins and Margaret Jenkins Taylor, "The Jenkins family: five generations of doctors" (summer 1975). People's Catholic Cemetery (Charlottetown), Tombstone no.671. *Charlottetown Guardian*, 16, 18 Sept. 1929. *Examiner* (Charlottetown), 2 May 1884. *Patriot* (Charlottetown), 16 Sept. 1929. D. O. Baldwin, "Smallpox management on Prince Edward Island, 1820–1940: from neglect to fulfillment," *Canadian Bull. of Medical Hist.* ([Waterloo, Ont.]), 2 (1985): 147–81. Marcia Bruner, "Early practitioners of P.E.I.," *Doctor's Rev.* ([Montreal]), 5 (October 1987): 86–91. *Canadian Medical rev.*, 1922. Canadian Medical Assoc., *Journal* (Toronto), 21 (July–December 1929): 620–21. *CPG*, 1915–17. *Cyclopædia of Canadian biog.* (Rose and Charlesworth), vol.3. *Maple Leaf* (Oakland, Calif.), 22 (December 1929): 383. *Past and present of Prince Edward Island . . .* , ed. D. A. MacKinnon and A. B. Warburton (Charlottetown, [1906]), 478–79. I. L. Rogers, *Charlottetown: the life in its buildings* (Charlottetown, 1983). W. L. Whelan, "The Jenkins of Charlottetown," Canadian Medical Assoc., *Journal*, 155 (July–December 1996): 445–47.

JENNINGS, MILTON ROBBINS, newspaperman; b. 4 March 1874 in Warsaw, N.Y., son of Edward M. Jennings and Mary Eliza Robbins; m. 1905 Carolyn Louise Sheldon of Buffalo, N.Y.; they had no children; d. 16 Feb. 1921 in Victoria.

The son of a prominent businessman and Civil War veteran, Milton R. (Bob) Jennings began his career as a reporter in Rochester and Buffalo between 1890 and 1894, while he was at the University of Rochester taking his AB. He worked for the *Montreal Herald* in 1894–95, then operated an advertising agency, and returned to the United States in 1896 as advertising manager of the *Washington Times*. From May 1897 he

and a partner ran the Merchants' Cut Service. In July 1898, during the Spanish-American War, he enlisted with the 202nd New York Volunteers and later he served in Cuba, where he also acted as a correspondent. He joined the *Daily Mail and Empire* in Toronto as circulation manager in 1899 and the advertising department of the *Evening Telegram* in 1903. For a time in 1905–9 he participated in contracting and mining ventures in Nevada and the Cobalt region of northern Ontario.

A former Toronto acquaintance, James Hossack Woods of the *Calgary Herald*, which was owned by William Southam*, secured an option on the *Edmonton Evening Journal* in 1909 and brought Jennings west as its editor and managing director. Acting on changes recommended by management consultant Albert Haynes, the Southams reorganized the Journal Company in 1911 and absorbed it the following year. From the time Jennings's name had first appeared in the Conservative paper's masthead, on 17 June 1909, he demonstrated a pro-business tone. In addition to joining the Rotary Club and St George's Society, he served on Edmonton's Board of Trade in various offices, including president (1918). In the municipal election of 1917, in a bid to sustain the city's finances, he helped loosen the Southams' preference for limited taxation and backed a new levy on business. Quick to understand the promotional value of aviation, in June 1919 he hired the firm of Elgin Court May and Wilfrid Reid (Wop) May* to fly bundles of the *Journal* to Wetaskiwin on the first commercial flight from Edmonton. Recognition came too from his keen sponsorship of the Edmonton Newsboys' Band, organized in 1913 by news-stand owner John (Mike) Michaels.

In the field of journalism, in 1913 Jennings was involved in the reorganization of the Canadian Press Association and served as president of the Alberta and Eastern British Columbia Press Association. Five years later, during World War I, he toured the western front with other Canadian Press members. In 1919–20 he was first president of the Canadian Daily Newspapers Association. When delegates to the Imperial Press Conference of 1920 crossed Canada, he helped organize their visit to Edmonton and Jasper. Other wartime activities included his recruitment for the navy of men from Alberta's rivers, participation in the Red Cross and Canadian Patriotic funds, and chairmanship of the Belgian Relief Committee of Northern Alberta and the local hospital committee for returned soldiers. Subsequently he served as president of the Navy League's Edmonton branch.

Jennings died in February 1921 in Victoria, where he was recuperating after treatment in Portland, Oreg., for an illness of several months' duration. He was buried in Edmonton Cemetery, and the Alberta legislature closed on 22 February in his honour. William Southam called him "a Canadian newspaperman of outstanding ability, vision, humanity and idealism who can ill be spared in these troublous times." Journalists from around the world sent condolences and contributed to a fund for a memorial window in Christ Church (Anglican), which Jennings had attended.

KATHRYN IVANY

City of Edmonton Arch., MS 324 (Edmonton Newsboys' Band fonds), Class 1, Scrapbook: 36, 43, 52. Univ. of Rochester, Rush Rhees Library, Dept. of Rare Books and Special Coll. (Rochester, N.Y.), Alumni files, M. R. Jennings. *Edmonton Journal*, 16–17 Feb. 1921. Charles Bruce, *News and the Southams* (Toronto, 1968). *Canadian annual rev.*, 1919–21. *Directory*, Toronto, 1901–6. *History of Wyoming County, N.Y., with illustrations, biographical sketches and portraits of some pioneers and prominent residents* (New York, 1880). Dennis Person and Carin Routledge, *Edmonton: portrait of a city* (Edmonton, 1981). Minko Sotiron, *From politics to profit: the commercialization of Canadian daily newspapers, 1890–1920* (Montreal and Kingston, Ont., 1997). G. M. Strathern, *Alberta newspapers, 1880–1982* (Edmonton, 1988). *Who's who and why*, 1919/20.

JETTÉ, JULES, professor, Jesuit missionary, ethnographer, and specialist in the Koyukon language; b. 30 Sept. 1864 in Montreal, son of Louis-Amable Jetté* and Berthilde Laflamme; d. 4 Feb. 1927 in Akulurak, Alaska.

Jules Jetté was born into a well-to-do Montreal family. His mother was the daughter of a rich merchant of that city. His father, who was a lawyer, became a leader of the young Liberals in the Parti National. After spending a few years in Ottawa as an MP, he was appointed to the bench and he later became lieutenant governor of Quebec. Jules attended the Petit Séminaire de Montréal from 1874 to 1880, and then studied at the Collège Sainte-Marie, where he spent two years in the Philosophy program but did not finish it. In 1882 he entered the Society of Jesus. He began his noviciate on 1 September in Sault-au-Récollet (Montreal) and finished it in September 1884, when he took his final vows. A long period of intellectual training followed, which he completed in 1898, despite the difficulties caused by migraines and other health problems. Jetté had applied himself initially to studying the natural sciences, numerous languages (Latin, Greek, Italian, Spanish, English), and French literature, in all of which he was successful. After teaching a few courses in mathematics at the Scolasticat de l'Immaculée-Conception in Montreal in his spare time, and serving as science monitor at the Collège Sainte-Marie from 1885 to 1887, he left Sault-au-Récollet in the summer of 1888 and went to the Université d'Angers, in France, seeking a degree in mathematics. Although he had some difficulty coping with this first separation from his native land, the experience whetted his curiosity about ethnography. He eventually abandoned

mathematics for metaphysics, but failed the examination for his degree and returned to Canada in September 1890. After a brief stay at the scholasticate, he was sent to the Collège de Saint-Boniface in Manitoba, where he taught mathematics and science until 1892. In the course of these years he became firmly convinced of his missionary vocation, and he prepared for it by accompanying students when they went out on snowshoes and by taking an interest in the northern missions. On his return to the Scolasticat de l'Immaculée-Conception he completed the Philosophy program and took courses in theology.

In May 1896 Jetté was ordained to the priesthood by Archbishop Édouard-Charles Fabre* in Le Gesù, the church adjoining the Collège Sainte-Marie. As a result of increasingly severe migraines he was, however, excused from the final year of theology. In the summer of 1896 he served as bursar at the noviciate of the Society of Jesus (Maison Saint-Joseph) in Sault-au-Récollet, but in 1897 a visit by Father John Baptiste René, the prefect apostolic of the Alaska mission, prompted him to ask that he be sent there as a missionary. Rome granted his request on 18 May 1898 and Father François-Xavier Renaud, the superior of the Jesuits in Canada at the time, notified him of his appointment.

Father Jetté's stay in Alaska would stretch over nearly 30 years, from 1898 to 1927, with a brief interlude in Canada. During his first journey, which would last until 1903, he had various learning experiences. He went first to San Francisco, which he left on 13 June 1898. After two weeks at sea he stopped at St Michael Mission, north of the Yukon River estuary in Alaska, and spent three months there – long enough to build a boat. He then travelled up the Yukon as far as the village of Nulato, north of Holy Cross, where Father Charles John Seghers* had been murdered on 28 Nov. 1886, while founding a mission. By the end of September he was beginning his first pastoral rounds. On foot, by sled, or by boat, he covered enormous distances to visit the aboriginal camps scattered across the interior of the country and on the banks of the river. He continued the missionary work using his predecessors' methods, which sought to gain the confidence of the natives principally through the education of the children and through singing lessons. Jetté's regular correspondence with his mother and his articles for the Jesuit periodical *Woodstock Letters* (Woodstock, Md) show how well he had adapted to local traditions and to the diet of the indigenous people. He even learned their language, Koyukon. Semi-nomadic hunters belonging to the Athapaskan language group, these natives practised shamanism, which the missionary, with the ethnocentrism common to his time, considered full of superstition.

Jetté returned to Canada in July 1903. He travelled by train from Seattle, Wash., to Montreal, and even journeyed as far as Quebec to visit his family. He then went back to the Collège de Saint-Boniface for a year's rest. An indefatigable worker, he again taught mathematics there, while finishing a collection of prayers, songs, and devotions in Koyukon, which he published in Winnipeg in 1904 under the title *Yoyit rokanaga: nulator roka do-daletloye.*

Jetté's second trip to Alaska – one from which he would not return to Canada – was more eventful. After leaving Seattle in the summer of 1904, he stopped over at Nulato and then continued to Fairbanks the following year. He found his work there very difficult because of the severe ravages caused by alcohol among the parishioners. Father Jetté succeeded in converting many Protestants to Catholicism at Kokrines, to which he was assigned from 1907 to 1913, and in the surrounding villages, among them Mouse Point. However, the opening of a mining centre in the Ruby region around 1908 marked the beginning of a frustrating period that lasted until 1913, during which the missionary waged a bitter struggle against the whisky traders.

The submission of a paper to the 15th International Congress of Americanists, held at Quebec in 1906, marked the beginning of Jetté's career as an ethnographer. He later published a number of articles on the social organization and religious traditions of the Koyukons in such periodicals as the *Journal* (London) of the Royal Anthropological Institute of Great Britain and Ireland in 1907, 1908, and 1909, *Man* (London) in the same years, and *Anthropos* (Vienna) in 1911 and 1913. He was also the author of a huge dictionary of some 30,000 words, which remained unpublished until 2000. Jetté made a considerable contribution to ethnography that was of excellent quality, to judge by the praise of anthropologists such as Frederica De Laguna and linguists such as Michael E. Krauss.

In May 1913, following the sudden departure of Father Crispino Rossi, Jetté was recalled to Nulato, where he acted as superior for a year. From 1914 to 1922 he lived in the Tanana region, a bit farther north on the Yukon River. In addition to his pastoral work among the aboriginals and whites, he pursued his studies in linguistics. In 1916 he did substitute work on a number of occasions in Ruby and Kokrines, but his missionary activities were suddenly interrupted in 1922 by a serious hernia. Treated at the Fairbanks hospital, he was sent to Seattle to convalesce in October 1923. Despite these difficulties, he used his time to teach French in a college and to begin writing a history of Christian missionary work in Alaska from 1741 to 1877. In the summer of 1925 he obtained permission to return there, and he served as chaplain to the Fairbanks hospital. In July 1926 he took up residence at the mission in Holy Cross, where he was asked to preach at the nuns' annual retreat. Having a talent for ethnology and for learning languages, the missionary set out on a journey through the region. In

mid July he was in Akulurak, another Jesuit mission looking out over the Bering Sea. He spent several weeks there, along with Father Martin Lonneux, cooking and maintaining the mission, which was attended mainly by Yupiks (Alaskan Inuit). Their language became a new passion for Father Jetté, but on 4 Feb. 1927 he died of exhaustion.

Although not widely known outside Alaska, Jules Jetté remains a missionary to be reckoned with in the history of Jesuit evangelization in that region. His linguistic and ethnological contribution is still indispensable for understanding the oral tradition of the Koyukons. Persistent, meticulous, and discerning in his work – a man ahead of his time – Jetté was a linguist who succeeded in highlighting regional variations and linking language and culture.

FRÉDÉRIC LAUGRAND

Jules Jetté's dictionary was completed by Eliza Jones and published as *Koyukon Athabaskan dictionary* (Fairbanks, Alaska, 2000).

ANQ-M, CE601-S51, 1er oct. 1864. Arch. de la Compagnie de Jésus, Prov. du Canada Français (Saint-Jérôme, Qué.), BO-27 (Théophile Hudon); BO-44 (Jules Jetté). *Le Devoir,* 3 mars 1927. R. C. Carriker *et al., Guide to the microfilm edition of the Oregon Province archives of the Society of Jesus Indian language collection: the Alaska native languages* (Spokane, Wash., 1976). Antonio Dragon, *Enseveli dans les neiges: le père Jules Jetté* (Montréal, [1951]). L. L. Renner, "Julius Jetté: distinguished scholar in Alaska," *Alaska Journal* (Anchorage, Alaska), 5 (1975): 239–47. L. L. Renner and D. J. Ray, *Pioneer missionary to the Bering Strait Eskimos: Bellarmine Lafortune, s.j.* (Portland, Oreg., 1979). Angel Santos, *Jesuitas en el Polo Norte: la mision de Alaska* (Madrid, 1943). George St. Hilaire, "Julius Jetté, s.j.: language and ethnology scholar of the Yukon," *Nouvelle Rev. de science missionnaire* (Beckenried, Switzerland), 14 (1958): 241–52.

JOBIN, LOUIS (baptized **Louis-Jean-Baptiste**), sculptor, statuary, gilder, and inventor; b. 26 Oct. 1845 in Saint-Raymond, Lower Canada, son of Jean-Baptiste Jobin, a farmer, and Luce Dion; m. *c.* 1869 Marie-Flore Marticotte, and they adopted a daughter named Éva; d. 11 March 1928 in Sainte-Anne-de-Beaupré, Que.

Louis Jobin was the first child born to Jean-Baptiste Jobin and Luce Dion, who had married in January 1845 in Pointe-aux-Trembles (Neuville), and then moved to Saint-Raymond in the Portneuf region. In 1847 the Jobins returned to Pointe-aux-Trembles but two years later they went to the village of Petit-Capsa (later part of Pont-Rouge). Little is known about Louis's childhood and youth except that he received a fairly good education. When he was about 14 or 15 years old he began working with an uncle, a woodcarver living at Quebec who was employed in the shipbuilding industry.

In 1865 Jobin entered the workshop of François-Xavier Berlinguet*, a celebrated Quebec wood-carver. Since there was no art school, the only way of learning the trade at that time was through a traditional apprenticeship to a master artisan. In the course of this broad training, Jobin created liturgical furniture (the altars of Sainte-Marie in Beauce), figureheads, commercial signs, ornaments, British coats of arms, and other works, most of which have now disappeared. His natural talent ensured that he soon became known for both secular and religious statuary. His *Self-portrait*, a polychrome relief now in the Canadian Museum of Civilization in Hull, dates from this period.

After a three-year apprenticeship with Berlinguet, Jobin left for New York, where he honed his skills in carving signs and figureheads. For more than a year he was employed as a carver at a number of workshops in lower Manhattan. He was first taken on as an assistant by William Boulton, a marble carver from London, England, who specialized in statues to be used as signs for tobacconists' shops. He then worked for some Germans, in all likelihood at the firm of Simon Strauss, who advertised himself as a "Carver of Figures for Segar Stores." At both places Jobin turned to good account his talents as a rougher and carver of statues.

Early in 1870 Jobin moved to Rue Notre-Dame in Montreal, where a number of sculptors had their studios. According to the 1871 census, he lived with Marie-Flore Marticotte, his new 30-year-old wife, and Narcisse Jobin, his younger brother, who was then a carver's apprentice. During his five years in Montreal, he worked for himself in his own shop. In order to meet the competition and build up his reputation, he had to accept all kinds of orders, but only a few examples of his work remain.

It was mainly because of the various markets for secular sculpture that Jobin was able to earn his living during his early days in Montreal. He produced numerous figureheads for a Captain MacNeil, including one for the vessel *Chief Angus*. He carved a number of signs, in relief or in the round, depicting animals (a *Hanging sheep* for a tailor) as well as life-size human figures (a *Lawyer* for a law office and a *Sailor* for a tobacco merchant). According to an advertisement first carried in *La Minerve* on 4 June 1870, he had on display statues to be used as garden ornaments or as signs for tobacco merchants ("Indians and little Negroes," as he put it). In the field of religious art, Jobin's creations ranged from cabinetwork (the altar of the church of Saint-Pierre-Apôtre in Montreal) to representational sculpture. Of the few reliefs he produced that have been traced, three date from this period: *Apparition of Our Lady of Lourdes* for the church at Sault-au-Recollet (Montreal), *Holy Family* for the Carmelite monastery in Montreal, and *Good shepherd* (now in the National Gallery of Canada in Ottawa). A few sculptures in the round also bear witness to his skill in statuary. It was in his Montreal workshop that he began to specialize in the production of religious statues. Given a declining demand for sculpture for vessels – due to the advent of the steamer and the metal ship – and keen competition in the field of religious statuary, Jobin eventually had a hard time making a living at his trade in Montreal. In the fall of 1875 he closed his workshop and moved to Quebec.

On arrival in the capital, Jobin went into partnership for a year with Charles Marcotte as "merchants and wood-carvers." He lived at various addresses in Saint-Jean ward before settling in 1878 at the corner of Rue Burton and Rue de Claire-Fontaine, where he had a house built for himself. A fire on 8 June 1881 in that *faubourg* destroyed his workshop, but he reopened it the following year at the same place. For a year he also had a shop on Rue Saint-Jean, where he sold his statues. Jobin regularly worked outdoors, attracting both passers-by and journalists. He hired assistants to produce furniture and ornamental work, in particular, and trained apprentices, including Henri Angers, who was with him from 1889 to 1893 and helped him create the monument to *Saint Ignatius of Loyola* for the Villa Manrèse at Quebec.

Jobin's competitors included many local artists – amongst them wood-carver Jean-Baptiste Côté* and especially Italian sculptor and caster Michele Rigali* – but he also had to contend with imported items of foreign manufacture now on the market. He advertised regularly in *Le Courrier du Canada* (Québec). These advertisements contain much information about the development of his career and work. At first Jobin offered a wide variety of statues and was ready to create, repair, or decorate altars, statues, and ornaments to order. Devoting himself increasingly to religious statuary "after the best European models," Jobin began in 1881 to concentrate on what was to become his specialty: "lead-coated wooden statues for outdoor use" – figures sheeted in metal by a process of embossing and punching. In 1877 he displayed a *Saint Joseph* in the window of *Le Courrier du Canada* and three other statues at the Quebec provincial exhibition, at which he was awarded a "special prize."

Religious statuary, then, proved Jobin's most lucrative market. The artist found clients among the clergy, religious communities, architects active as contractors (Ferdinand Villeneuve*, David Ouellet*, Joseph-Ferdinand Peachy*), and ordinary citizens. While some *fabriques*, such as those of Saint-Charles parish (in Bellechasse) and Sainte-Jeanne (in Pont-Rouge), purchased a good many statues at various times, others commissioned imposing decorative groupings to embellish the interior (32 statues for Saint-Henri, near Lévis, 1878–84; 17 statues for Saint-Patrice, in Rivière-du-Loup, 1894–95) or the exterior (six statues for Saint-Thomas in Montmagny, 1890). In 1894 Jobin delivered eight statues for the high altar in the church of Saint-Michel (Saint-Michel-de-Bellechasse). In 1894 and 1895 he produced 16 busts for the Séminaire de Québec. These imposing ensembles are among his most noteworthy religious works. Closely linked to the major devotions, which were themselves widely disseminated by contemporary popular imagery (the Sacred Heart, the Virgin Mary, St Joseph, St Anne, Calvary, and patron saints and angels of all kinds), many religious statues were also commissioned by individuals for diverse purposes such as thanksgiving, protection, or commemoration. A notable example was his *Our Lady of the Saguenay*, a huge ex-voto, almost 25 feet, created in 1880–81 for commercial traveller Charles-Napoléon Robitaille which was erected on Cap Trinité. Its history is truly an epic. Jobin also became renowned as an expert carver of Christ on the Cross and calvaries. He even received a commission from New Brunswick (a *Calvary* with six human figures for Richibucto, 1879 and 1884). On the whole, the statues Jobin produced, which were dictated by the tastes and needs of his clients, bore a strong resemblance to the mass-produced plasters of his competitors. With his *Our Lady of the Saguenay*, however, he began to concentrate on the new market for large-scale, metal-clad outdoor statuary (*Saint Louis*, for the church of Lotbinière in 1888). Jobin's reputation in this field even brought him some orders from the United States; the Brothers of the Christian Schools in 1889 purchased a *Saint Jean-Baptiste de La Salle* for their school in Ammendale, Md.

Despite this increasing specialization, Jobin still turned out sculpture for vessels and carved signs (figures of Amerindians and of all kinds of animals), designed liturgical furniture (altars at Cap-Chat in 1885 and Pointe-aux-Trembles in 1886), and supervised woodworking and ornamentation (interior decoration for the chapel of the Hôtel-Dieu du Sacré-Cœur de Jésus at Quebec, 1879). He also produced a few unusual works, such as a carved *Coleoptera* for naturalist Léon Provancher*, and in 1894 he invented a device for opening and closing the slats of window blinds without opening the windows. For the Saint-Jean-Baptiste festivities at Quebec in 1880, he helped create at least two banners and four floats bearing statues, including the one representing agriculture, which featured a *Ceres* (now in the Musée National des Beaux-Arts du Québec at Quebec). During the first winter carnivals in the capital, in 1894 and 1896, Jobin carved a few ice sculptures, including a replica of the Statue of Liberty, thereby becoming a pioneer in this technique in the province. In the spring of 1896 his studio again burned down. He sold his house and moved, penniless, to Sainte-Anne-de-Beaupré, one of the most famous places of pilgrimage in North America. There he would carry out a number of commissions for the basilica and build up his religious clientele.

At first Jobin lived in a small dwelling adjoining a workshop, but in 1901 he bought a lot on Chemin Royal and had a house built there. He set up his new shop in the basement and decorated the exterior with numerous statues. He again hired a few apprentices and assistants. In 1901, to complete the interior decor of Saint-Louis-de-l'Isle-aux-Coudres (including the retable, high altar, and side altar), he hired Régis Perron, a local carpenter who would later follow the master artisan to Sainte-Anne-de-Beaupré. In 1907, after the death of his wife, Jobin took in his nephew, Édouard Marcotte, who would become his chief assistant, as well as an eccentric inventor and sculptor named Octave Morel, who would later die in his house.

At the beginning of his stay in Sainte-Anne-de-Beaupré, Jobin again gave his attention to church ornamentation and to making liturgical furniture. Around 1898, for example, the sculptor created various works in the old basilica of Sainte-Anne-de-Beaupré (among other things, altars and ornaments for the side chapels and canopies for the episcopal thrones). In the secular field, he would produce only five more statues: a *Neptune* and a *Wolfe* for two commercial buildings at Quebec (1901), a bust of *Champlain* for the capital's tercentenary (1908), and a *Frontenac* and a *Lord Elgin* for the Séminaire Saint-Charles-Borromée in Sherbrooke (1913). By specializing in statues "overlaid with metal, impervious to seasonal inclement weather," Jobin held pride of place, as a wood-carver, in the market for exterior religious and monumental statuary. Designed to stand in the open air, his works imitated, moreover, the bronzes of his competitors. The sculptor's last two account books, which cover the years 1913–25, list some 240 commissions for religious statues, for the most part of considerable size. In this period, and especially during World War I, he would become the Quebec specialist in monuments to the Sacred Heart and in calvaries with one, three, or six human figures (Ermitage San'Tonio at Lac-Bouchette, 1918), themes which were often commissioned as ex-votos and which would constitute 40 per cent of his output.

At Sainte-Anne-de-Beaupré, Jobin acquired a significantly larger and more diverse clientele. He became the leading supplier of religious statues for architect-contractors, for retailers of religious articles, and even for other sculptors, such as Louis Caron of Nicolet, Joseph Villeneuve and Joseph Saint-Hilaire of Saint-Romuald, and François-Pierre Gauvin of Quebec. Several *fabriques* (Saint-Georges-de-Windsor and Sainte-Perpétue in the Nicolet region; Chute-à-Blondeau and St-Eugène in Ontario) and religious communities (Redemptorists and Franciscan Missionaries of Mary in Sainte-Anne-de-Beaupré) also purchased a number of works. Jobin created a dozen groupings, consisting of three to five statues each, to decorate church façades (Saint-Casimir in the Portneuf region in 1899, and Saint-Dominique in Jonquière in

1913). Living very close to the railway, Jobin also shipped many works to tourists and pilgrims who came from all over Canada and even from the United States.

Jobin's everyday work at Sainte-Anne-de-Beaupré is generally of rather average quality because of technical and aesthetic factors, but also because of the modest price of the statues and the short time allowed for completion of a large number of works. When clients agreed to pay their true value, however, the sculptor succeeded in executing exceptional works. Three illustrations are the recumbent statue of *Saint Anthony of Padua* in the chapel of the Hôtel-Dieu Saint-Vallier in Chicoutimi (1900), with its unusual subject and model; the *Angel with trumpet* on the organ case of the church in Plessisville (1902), a masterpiece of delicacy and elegance; and the equestrian monument of *Saint George slaying the dragon* for the parish of Saint-Georges in Beauce (1909), the most complex work the artist ever created.

There was a marked decline in Jobin's output around 1920, when he reached the age of 75. At the same time a number of prominent people rediscovered "the old sculptor on the Beaupré shore," and their accounts, while invaluable, depict the artist sometimes as an exotic or folk figure, sometimes as a romantic and legendary one. They included journalist Victoria Hayward and photographer Edith S. Watson; writer Frank Oliver Call; painter John Young Johnstone; ethnographer Marius Barbeau* of the Victoria Memorial Museum in Ottawa (which in 1927 became the National Museum of Canada), accompanied by two painters from the Group of Seven, Arthur Lismer* and Alexander Young Jackson*; and writer and journalist Damase Potvin*. At the end of 1925, after shipping one final work to Florida, the sculptor gave all his property, including his statues and tools, to his nephew, and retired. It was only then that museums and collectors began to purchase his sculptures and that the first exhibits of his works were held at the Art Gallery of Toronto (Art Gallery of Ontario) and the Château Frontenac at Quebec. On 11 March 1928 the artist died in poverty but famous because of the many articles about him published in newspapers in Quebec and in English Canada during the 1920s.

More than any other sculptor of his day, Louis Jobin demonstrated an unusual adaptability and sensitivity to the needs of his milieu and the dictates of the marketplace, which was shaped by pressures of competition and of nascent industrialization. In the province of Quebec, he was one of the most famous and prolific sculptors of his time and he is now considered one of the most outstanding figures in the history of this art. During his 60-year career he produced at least 1,000 sculptures, which are now to be found across North America. Despite his traditional and non-academic background, he is seen as a fully fledged artist. When he was living at Quebec, he was from the outset the sculptor favoured by the press, and columnists never stopped praising his talent and his creations. Some of his works, such as the *Our Lady of the Saguenay*, are real technical feats. Others, such as the statues at Saint-Henri and Saint-Patrice, are among the masterpieces of early sculpture in Quebec. Spanning the 19th and 20th centuries and linking the traditional and the modern, the career and output of Louis Jobin stand as a milestone in the evolution of Quebec sculpture.

MARIO BÉLAND

[Louis Jobin was the subject of a major retrospective at the Musée National des Beaux-Arts du Québec during the summer of 1986. The exhibition was accompanied by the publication of a monograph by Mario Béland entitled *Louis Jobin, master sculptor* (Quebec, 1986). Of its 210 illustrations, 59 present a selection of Jobin's sculptures and another 59 concern his studio pieces, his tools, and other items. The work contains a historical essay, a chronological summary, a list of exhibitions, and a bibliography. Also valuable are Mario Béland, "Les trente premières années du sculpteur Louis Jobin (1845–1928): formation et premier atelier" (mémoire de MA, univ. Laval, Québec, 1984), and especially the same author's "Louis Jobin (1845–1928) et le marché de la sculpture au Québec" (thèse de PHD, univ. Laval, 1991). The doctoral disseration includes a detailed chronology and an exhaustive bibliography divided into several sections: archives and manuscript sources, printed sources, reference works and research guides, specialized publications, and newspaper and journal articles. In addition it contains four appendices: references to Louis Jobin in the Quebec and Montreal directories between 1860 and 1896; announcements in *La Minerve* (Montréal), from 4 June to 7 Sept. 1870 and *Le Courrier du Canada* (Québec) between 5 May 1876 and 30 Jan. 1896; order-books (1913–26); and 12 extracts from various journals (1873–1900).

Examples of Jobin's work are to be found in most art galleries in Quebec and Ontario. There are numerous photographic portraits of him, taken at different periods, as well as sketches drawn by Arthur Lismer in 1925 and a canvas painted by John Young Johnstone around 1920. Most of these images show the sculptor working in his studio or posing beside his statues.

Despite intensive research, the place and date of Jobin's marriage have not been identified. His baptismal record is available at ANQ-Q, CE301-S53, 4 déc. 1845. Given the extensive bibliography provided in the author's thesis, only a few additional publications issued since 1991 are cited here: Mario Béland, "Les monuments de bois: ces autres disparus," *Continuité* (Québec), 49 (hiver–printemps 1991): 33–37, and "Aux origines de la sculpture sur glace," *Continuité*, 59 (hiver 1994): 18–20; and Karel, *Dict. des artistes*. M.B.]

JOHNSON, ALICE JANE. *See* STERLING

JOHNSON, ARTHUR JUKES, physician and coroner; b. 20 Aug. 1848 in Yorkville (Toronto), son of William Arthur Johnson* and Laura Eliza Jukes; m. 14 July 1887 Sophia Maud Elliot Widder in Goderich, Ont., and they had two sons and a daughter; d. 9 June 1921 in Toronto.

Johnson

Born in Yorkville while his father was a divinity student, Jukes Johnson spent most of his childhood years moving between Cobourg, Yorkville, and eventually Weston (Toronto), where W. A. Johnson was named rector of St Philip's Church in 1856. His grandfathers had known each other in India, and both his parents had been born there. Lieutenant-Colonel John Johnson was an officer in the East India Company who held the position of aide-de-camp to the Duke of Wellington before emigrating to the Niagara District of Upper Canada in the 1830s; Dr Arthur Jukes served as an inspector of hospitals in India.

Johnson received his early education at Toronto's Model Grammar School and then at Trinity College School in Weston, which had been founded by his father. After attending Trinity College, Toronto, in 1866–67, probably enrolled in the arts program, Johnson turned to the study of medicine. He was most likely influenced by the example of his grandfather Jukes and by his own father's novice practice in the field. W. A. Johnson had studied some medicine at Guy's Hospital in London, England, and was medical adviser to his Weston church community.

Johnson graduated from the University of Toronto with an MB in 1870. He would receive a second MB, *ad eundem*, from Trinity in 1892. Following graduation, he spent about two years in Britain, where his mother's brothers were physicians. He took up postgraduate work and in 1871 was awarded membership in the Royal College of Surgeons of England. He worked as a surgeon at St Thomas's Hospital in London. Johnson would become a member of the Pathological Society of London and a fellow of the Obstetrical Society of London and the Royal Microscopical Society.

After returning to Toronto in 1873, Johnson registered with the College of Physicians and Surgeons of Ontario and established a practice at 1 William Street (Yorkville Avenue). Two years later he became a coroner for York County. He was soon associated with the leading medical men of Toronto, including James Bovell*, Edward Mulberry Hodder*, and Cornelius James Philbrick, with whom, an obituary would state, he was "practically, if not actually, in partnership." By 1885 he had built a combined house and office at 52 Bloor Street West in Toronto, where he would live until his death.

Johnson had taken a keen interest in pathology when he returned to Canada and worked for some time as a pathologist at Toronto General Hospital. His expert knowledge in medical jurisprudence, coroner's experience, and reputation as being an independent in politics would lead to his appointment by the province as the first chief coroner of Toronto in June 1903. In this position Johnson's duties were to supervise 30 associate coroners and to decide when there was to be an investigation into a death in the city. He headed inquests into fatalities resulting from train, car, and streetcar accidents or mishaps in the workplace, as well as deaths involving criminal action, and he had the power to issue arrest warrants.

As a coroner, Johnson provided evidence for the crown in many criminal trials in the Toronto area and throughout the province. He was involved in 1890 in the Reginald Birchall* case, prosecuted by Britton Bath Osler*, brother of Johnson's former schoolmate and fellow doctor William Osler*. In the famed Hyams brothers case of 1895–96 he contributed again as part of Osler's prosecution team. The case revolved around the body of young William Chinook (Willie) Wells, who had died, apparently from an industrial accident, in 1893. Wells's body was exhumed under orders from a Toronto coroner in 1895 when his sister revealed that a large insurance policy on her brother had been made out to her by her husband, Harry Place Hyams. Re-examination of the skull by Johnson and others brought Harry and his brother Dallas Theodore to trial on murder charges. Johnson was a witness for the prosecution, but the Hyamses were discharged in the end. In another case prosecuted by Osler, Olive Adele Sternaman was accused in 1897 of administering arsenic to her second husband, George H. Sternaman. Johnson, an expert in poisons, was the chief medical witness, heading the prosecution's team of five doctors. Sternaman was convicted of murder, but acquitted the following year on appeal.

Johnson had a strong ideal of community service and was for many years an active member of the College of Physicians and Surgeons, sitting on its council in 1890–95 and 1903–21 and acting on the printing, education, registration, complaints, and property committees. He was also a consulting surgeon to Toronto General, St John's, and St Michael's hospitals. His academic contributions included service as a lecturer and examiner at Trinity College and Toronto General, membership on the board of governors of Trinity College School (1902–21), and a book, *Inquests and investigations: a practical guide for the use of coroners holding inquests in Ontario . . .* (Toronto, 1911). Jukes Johnson died of pancreatic cancer in June 1921 at his home in Toronto. A member of St Thomas's Anglican Church, he was buried in St James' Cemetery. In his will he left $5,000 to establish a hospital at Trinity College School as a memorial to his father.

ROSEMARY WAGNER

Anglican Church of Canada, Diocese of Toronto Arch., Clergy cards, W. A. Johnson. AO, RG 22-305, no.43320; RG 80-5-0-150, no.4935; RG 80-8-0-802, no.4123. Trinity College Arch. (Toronto), 985-002 (Office of Convocation); 990-0053/074; 996-0025/001 (Office of the Registrar). UTA, A1973-0026/179(55). *Toronto Star: pages of the past* (searchable online version of the newspaper, 1894–1999; available at TRL). *Canadian Practitioner and Medical Rev.* (Toronto), 46 (1921): 235. William Canniff, *The medical pro-*

fession in Upper Canada, 1783–1850 . . . (Toronto, 1894; repr. 1980). H. [W.] Charlesworth, *Candid chronicles: leaves from the note book of a Canadian journalist* (Toronto, 1925); *More candid chronicles: further leaves from the note book of a Canadian journalist* (Toronto, 1928). College of Physicians and Surgeons of Ontario, *Annual announcement* (Toronto), 1890/91–1920/21; *Published Ontario medical register* (Toronto), 1887, 1892, 1903. *Commemorative biographical record of the county of York* . . . (Toronto, 1907). F. D. Cruickshank and J[oseph] Nason, *History of Weston* (Weston, [Toronto], 1983). *Directory*, Toronto, 1873–1921. *Grand heritage: a history of Dunnville and the townships of Canborough, Dunn, Moulton, Sherbrooke and South Cayuga*, ed. Cheryl MacDonald (Dunnville, Ont., 1992). *List of magistrates in and for the county of York* (Toronto, 1880). Trinity Univ., *Year book* (Toronto), 1902–3. Toronto, City Council, *Minutes of proc.*, 1903.

JOHNSON, PHELPS, engineer; b. 23 Oct. 1849 in Warwick, N.Y., son of William H. Johnson and Eliza Phelps; d. unmarried 20 Feb. 1926 in Montreal.

Educated in public schools in Springfield, Mass., and at Goldthwaites Academy, a private school in Longmeadow, Phelps Johnson began his engineering career in March 1867 with the R. F. Hawkins Iron Works in Springfield. He started as a draftsman and later he became an assistant engineer. From 1879 to 1881 he was an assistant engineer with the Wrought Iron Bridge Company of Canton, Ohio. The firm's vice-president, Job Abbott*, left in 1880 to become president and chief engineer of the Toronto Bridge Company and in February 1882 Johnson joined the Toronto firm. That same year Abbott, Johnson, and others obtained a federal charter to establish the Dominion Bridge Company Limited, a firm with much wider powers than Toronto Bridge. In May 1883, after Dominion Bridge had purchased Toronto Bridge, Johnson was appointed manager and engineer of the Toronto works. When the Toronto operations closed five years later, Johnson moved to the company's main office near Lachine, Que., as chief engineer. While Dominion Bridge developed into the largest steel construction firm in Canada, he held the posts of general manager (1892–1904), director (1903–26), general manager and chief engineer (1904–19), managing director (1910–13), and president (1913–19). After his retirement in January 1919, he remained a member of the firm's executive committee until his death.

During his tenure with Dominion Bridge, Johnson presided over the construction of many important structures, such as, in 1886, the Lachine Bridge which crossed the St Lawrence River for the Canadian Pacific Railway and, in 1915, a cantilever bridge over the Reversing Falls in Saint John. He was consulted frequently on engineering problems, especially those relating to the design and construction of bridges.

Johnson's greatest achievement was the rebuilding of the Quebec Bridge. The first attempt to span the St Lawrence near Quebec City, to permit the crossing of the main line of the National Transcontinental Railway, had ended tragically on 29 Aug. 1907. The bridge, nearly completed by the Phoenix Bridge Company of Phoenixville, Pa, for the Quebec Bridge and Railway Company [*see* Simon-Napoléon Parent*], collapsed, killing 75 of the 85 men working on the structure. It was one of the world's most spectacular engineering disasters. A royal commission, established two days later, blamed the accident on faulty design and inadequate supervision. The federal government nationalized the project and appointed a board of engineers to oversee the rebuilding. After extensive consultations with experts, including Johnson, the board produced a new set of specifications.

The St Lawrence Bridge Company, a partnership between Dominion Bridge and the Canadian Bridge Company, was formed in 1911 with Johnson at its head, to pool the resources of the two firms and to keep the project Canadian. On 4 April 1911 St Lawrence Bridge was awarded the contract, based on one of several designs by Johnson which the firm had submitted. With its heavy 1,800-foot span, the new bridge presented unprecedented engineering problems, which he solved with an innovative K-truss bracing system. Working under Johnson's direction, chief engineer George Herrick Duggan built the structure, but not without serious mishap. On 11 Sept. 1916, as the 640-foot, 5,000-ton centre span was being hoisted into place, a hydraulic jack slipped and the span fell into the river, killing 13 men. A new piece was made and was secured in place the following year. Fully completed on 21 Aug. 1918, the bridge, the largest in Canada and the longest cantilever span in the world, was officially opened on 22 Aug. 1919 by the Prince of Wales. According to the *Canadian Engineer*, it was "the most remarkable steel structure ever built." The entire enterprise cost approximately $35,000,000.

Johnson was not only a leading engineer, he was also a leader of his profession. Elected a member of the American Society of Civil Engineers in 1891 and of the Canadian Society of Civil Engineers in 1893, he served as one of the Canadian society's councillors from 1904 to 1906 and from 1910 to 1912, as vice-president in 1907, and as president in 1913. In his presidential address of 1914, he explained that the status of engineers could best be improved by raising the standards of their practice through the exchange of professional knowledge. He staunchly opposed the use of collective action to coerce employers or to restrict competitions to Canadian engineers, actions which he thought would bring the profession into public disrepute.

Although a member of the St James, Engineers', and Royal St Lawrence Yacht clubs – some of Montreal's most important English-speaking clubs – Johnson, a bachelor, participated little in Montreal's active social life, dedicating himself instead to his business and professional interests. In recognition of his achievements, particularly his role in building the Quebec Bridge, McGill University conferred an honorary LLD on him in 1921.

For more than a quarter century, Phelps Johnson occupied an important position in business and engineering. As a management engineer, he helped to make the Dominion Bridge Company profitable; at the same time, he directed the construction of crucial rail and highway bridges that bound Canada together. He was honoured throughout North America for his original solutions to difficult steel construction problems. When he died, the *Engineering News-Record* of New York praised him as "the most widely known and respected engineer in the Dominion."

J. RODNEY MILLARD

Although he was an important figure in Canadian engineering history, there is comparatively little source material on Phelps Johnson. His application for membership in the Canadian Soc. of Civil Engineers is missing from the papers of the Engineering Institute of Canada (Montreal). Johnson's presidential address to the Canadian Soc. of Civil Engineers appears in its *Trans.* (Montreal), 28 (1914): 102–6.

American Soc. of Civil Engineers, *Trans.* (New York), 90 (1927): 1176–78. *Canadian men and women of the time* (Morgan; 1912). *Canadian Railway and Marine World* (Toronto), October 1917: 400–2; March 1926: 135. G. H. Duggan, *The Quebec Bridge: notes on the work of the St. Lawrence Bridge Company, in preparing the accepted design for the construction of the superstructure* ([Quebec?, 1918?]). *Engineering Journal* (Montreal), 9 (1926): 168; 20 (1937): 288. *Engineering News-Record* (New York), 96 (January–June 1926): 376–77. J. W. Leonard, *Who's who in engineering: a biographical dictionary of contemporaries, 1925* (2nd ed., 2v., New York, 1925). W. D. Middleton, *The bridge at Québec* (Bloomington, Ind., 2001). J. R. Millard, *The master spirit of the age: Canadian engineers and the politics of professionalism, 1887–1922* (Toronto, 1988). "The Quebec Bridge," *Canadian Engineer* (Toronto), 33 (July–December 1917): 264–66. *The Quebec Bridge over the St. Lawrence River near the city of Quebec on the line of the Canadian National Railways: report of the government board of engineers* (2v., Ottawa, 1919). C. R. Young, "Bridge building," *Engineering Journal*, 20: 486.

JOHNSON, THOMAS HERMAN (Hermann), lawyer and politician; b. 12 Feb. 1870 in Héðinshöfði, Iceland, son of John Johnson (Jón Björnsson) and Margrét Sigríður Bjarnadóttir; m. 21 June 1898, in Winnipeg, Aurora Frederickson of Glenboro, Man., and they had one daughter and two sons; d. 20 May 1927 in Winnipeg.

Thomas Herman Johnson moved with his parents to Gimli (Man.) in 1879. Gimli was the main village in New Iceland, an ethnic reserve created in 1875 by the federal government on the west side of Lake Winnipeg [see Jón Bjarnason*]. The family moved to Winnipeg

in 1881 and then in 1886 to the Argyle settlement, an Icelandic district (not a reserve) near Glenboro, about 150 kilometres southwest of Winnipeg. In 1898 Johnson would marry Aurora Frederickson, the daughter of a prominent Icelandic merchant who had moved to Glenboro in 1886.

In 1888 Johnson obtained a teacher's certificate and started work in a school in the Argyle district. For him, as for many young men of his time, teaching was only a temporary pursuit. In 1890 he enrolled at Gustavus Adolphus College, a Lutheran institution in St Peter, Minn. He financed his studies by teaching school in the summers and received a BA in 1895. That year he began to study law with the Winnipeg firm of Richards and Bradshaw. In 1900 he was called to the bar, the first lawyer in Canada of Icelandic descent. He soon became a partner in Rothwell, Johnson and Bergman (after 1924 Johnson and Bergman) and was successful in the profession. Eventually, he became the chief legal counsel in Winnipeg for the Hudson's Bay Company and he would be appointed KC in 1919.

From a young age Johnson was both interested in politics and sympathetic to the Liberal party. He gained a seat on the Winnipeg School Board in 1904 and in March 1907 he successfully ran as a Liberal in the provincial election. For the next 15 years he represented Winnipeg in the Legislative Assembly. When Johnson was first elected, the Liberals formed the opposition to the Conservative government of Rodmond Palen Roblin*. After 1907 they gained increasing support from advocates of reform as well as from voters who believed that the Roblin machine not only took partisan politics to ridiculous lengths but probably was also corrupt. Finally, in 1915, led by Tobias Crawford Norris*, who relied heavily on Johnson (he could be nastier and more sarcastic than Norris), they were able to expose a major scandal over the construction of the new legislative building. Roblin resigned on 12 May. The Liberals took office, quickly called an election, and were rewarded with 42 of the 49 seats in the assembly.

The first person of Icelandic descent to become a cabinet minister in Canada, Johnson served from May 1915 to November 1917 as minister of public works, from November 1917 to June 1922 as attorney general and minister of telephones and telegraphs, and during part of 1916 as acting premier. The government of 1915–20 was one of the most important administrations in the history of Manitoba. Among its major initiatives were two Prohibition measures. The Manitoba Temperance Act, passed in 1916, banned the manufacture and sale of alcohol in the province except by druggists on prescription. The second act, passed in 1920, prohibited the importation of alcoholic beverages. Initiatives of immense consequence were taken in education: school attendance became compulsory, English was made the sole language of instruction in public schools, and the government took greater control over, and provided more money for, the University of Manitoba. Significant political reforms included the Initiative and Referendum Act (which was declared *ultra vires*), the creation of a civil service commission, the introduction of measures to publicize and limit amounts spent on elections, and the establishment of Winnipeg as one large constituency with 10 members, elected by proportional representation. Many reforms benefited women: the Dower Act, the creation of a board to fix minimum wages for female employees, and legislation to give women the right to vote in provincial elections and to hold political office. There were also measures to give farmers easier access to credit, improve the public health system [*see* James William ARMSTRONG], upgrade the emerging provincial road system, and provide hydro-electric power to rural communities.

Johnson was philosophically and emotionally committed to his government's program, which he and the other members thought was supported by the vast majority of Manitobans. Yet in the provincial election of 1920 the Liberals took only 21 of the 55 seats and their popular vote dropped to 36 per cent from the 54 per cent of 1915. Opposition to the Liberals had developed because of the government's increased expenditures and disappointment over its indecisive approach to the Winnipeg General Strike of 1919 [*see* Mike Sokolowiski*]. In addition, most ethnic and religious minorities protested against its educational reforms and Prohibition. The two most important reasons for the decline of the Liberals were, however, the divisions within the party itself caused in 1917, when Johnson and other government members supported conscription and the Union government of Sir Robert Laird Borden*, and the demand on the part of farmers for independent candidates.

From 1920 to 1922 Johnson was attorney general in a minority Liberal administration. This government could introduce little new legislation because of the resistance or anticipated resistance of opposition parties and various groups in the legislature. In 1922 Johnson successfully completed the civil suit the province had initiated in 1916 against Thomas Kelly and Sons, the contractors of the legislative buildings, but after the government was defeated in the house he decided not to run in the election of that year. He devoted his energies to his law practice.

During his years in politics Johnson had been an important and highly visible member of Manitoba's Icelandic community. He and his wife were strong supporters of, and sang in the choir of, Winnipeg's First Lutheran Church, which had an essentially Icelandic congregation. In 1925 Christian X, King of Denmark and Iceland, awarded him the prestigious Grand Cross of the Knights of the Order of the Falcon, given to natives of Iceland who serve their country

with distinction. That year, at the Norse-American Centennial Celebration held in St Paul, Minn., Johnson was made a knight of the Order of St Olaf by Haakon VII, King of Norway. When he died in 1927 a local newspaper referred to him as "the most distinguished member of his race in Western Canada."

At the end of World War I Johnson had contracted the Spanish influenza that had spread rapidly through Canada. He was never really strong thereafter. He had a serious operation, probably for cancer, in 1926. He seemed to recover well, but died rather unexpectedly in May 1927. By then Manitobans had become aware that 1930 would mark the 1,000th anniversary of the founding of the Icelandic parliament. To recognize the important part played by Icelanders in the development of Manitoba, the government of John Bracken* donated a bronze portrait of Johnson. It was unveiled in Reykjavík, Iceland, in June 1930.

MORRIS MOTT

AM, MG 14, B44, box 5, file 9. Man., Legislative Library (Winnipeg), Biog. scrapbooks, Manitoba hist. scrapbooks, political scrapbooks. Univ. of Man. Libraries, Dept. of Arch. and Special Coll. (Winnipeg), J. W. Dafoe fonds. *Lögberg* [Mount of Laws] (Winnipeg), 26 May 1927. Marilyn Baker, *Symbol in stone: the art and politics of a public building: Manitoba's third legislative building* (Winnipeg, 1986). Flora Benson, "Aurora Frederickson Johnson," Lutheran Women's League of Manitoba, *Árdís* (Winnipeg), 22 (1954): 72. *Canadian annual rev.*, 1907–22. *CPG*, 1914–23. L. J. Fisk, "Controversy on the prairies: issues in the general provincial elections of Manitoba, 1870–1969" (PHD thesis, Univ. of Alta, Edmonton, 1975). A. I. Inglis, "Some political factors in the demise of the Roblin government: 1915" (MA thesis, Univ. of Man., 1968). W[ilhelm] Kristjanson, *The Icelandic people in Manitoba: a Manitoba saga* (Winnipeg, 1965). D. H. Laycock, *Populism and democratic thought in the Canadian prairies, 1910 to 1945* (Toronto, 1990). W. L. Morton, *Manitoba: a history* (Toronto, 1957); *The Progressive party in Canada* (Toronto, 1950). Lionel Orlikow, "The reform movement in Manitoba, 1910–1915," in *Historical essays on the prairie provinces*, ed. Donald Swainson (Toronto and Montreal, 1970), 215–29. P. F. Sharp, *The agrarian revolt in western Canada: a survey showing American parallels* (Minneapolis, Minn., 1948). *Vestur-Íslenzkar æviskrár* [Icelandic-American genealogies], ed. Benjamin Kristjánsson (4v., Akureyri, Iceland, 1961–72).

JOHNSTONE, ISABEL (at birth she was named Isabella Johnston), nurse and hospital superintendent; b. 15 Dec. 1872 in Guelph, Ont., eldest daughter of John Johnston, a carpenter, and Ann McPherson; d. unmarried 4 June 1923 in Fort William (Thunder Bay), Ont.

Isabel Johnstone's parents were born in Scotland. After her father had died of tuberculosis early in 1878 at age 30, her mother raised Isabel and her younger siblings, Margaret A., John, and Jessie, in Guelph, where she had ties with relatives and the Presbyterian

Church. The family does not appear in the census records, however, until 1891: Isabel as a milliner, John as an apprentice tailor, and their mother as a seamstress in a woollen mill. Margaret drowned in 1900, and the only members listed in 1901 are Isabel's mother and Jessie, a stenographer. In 1905 Jessie married William John Dollery, a machinist for the Canadian Pacific Railway in Fort William.

In 1907 Isabel moved there to train as a nurse at the John McKellar Memorial Hospital, built in 1903 in memory of John McKellar*. Before its erection nursing services had been provided by the Victorian Order of Nurses, one of whose members, Christina Banks, became the hospital's first superintendent. After its School of Nursing opened in 1904, most of the hospital's employees were students. The hospital's board and Ladies' Aid arranged for donations of furnishings, equipment, and capital, and a new wing was added to the hospital in 1909, at which time it was renamed McKellar General Hospital. The students worked 12-hour shifts with a half day off each week and lived in the hospital until a residence was built in 1911.

By the time Isabel had graduated, in 1910, McKellar's capacity had more than tripled, from 35 beds to 120. She joined a staff of 5 graduate nurses, 14 students, and 2 interns. In April 1913, after working as head nurse of the surgical ward and then as operating-room supervisor, she was appointed superintendent. Because her quarters were in the hospital, she was able to devote all her energy to its operation and her beloved students. She interviewed all applicants personally and arranged for their practical and formal education. (It is on a student's acceptance form that her only known signature, Isabel Johnstone, appears.) According to graduates, she was a motherly, well-built woman with a pleasant face, but she could be firm when necessary. Despite many challenges, under her supervision the number of graduate nurses doubled, the enrolment at the School of Nursing quadrupled, and another wing was built. The crowning achievement was the hospital's accreditation by the province in 1922.

Unfortunately, in June of that year Isabel Johnstone underwent surgery for breast cancer in Rochester, N.Y. She died at the age of 50, just before the class of 1923 graduated. It was a sad troop of uniformed nurses and students that paraded to St Andrew's Presbyterian Church for the funeral of their role model.

The chairman of the hospital board praised her efficiency and devotion to duty, and flags on public buildings flew at half mast. A second service was held in Guelph at 126 Palmer Street, Isabel's childhood home, before her burial in the family plot at Woodlawn Cemetery.

She was not forgotten. Jane Hogarth, a McKellar graduate who had been appointed assistant during Isabel's illness, founded the McKellar Alumnae Association in her honour and raised funds to furnish a ward in her name. Although the ward has not survived, the alumnae continue to hold annual banquets.

Isabel Johnstone was representative of the many women whose contributions influenced Canada's social development at the local level. During her 16 years at McKellar General, the hospital not only achieved accreditation but also reflected the high standards she helped set for its School of Nursing. McKellar graduated 1,100 nurses between 1907 and 1971, when the responsibility for training nurses was transferred to Ontario's Department of Education.

ELINOR BARR

[Isabel Johnstone's paper trail consists of little more than her signature on a student's acceptance form. Her family does not appear in the census records for Guelph, Ont., until 1891. Death notices and obituaries yielded some information, but hospital records are virtually non-existent. The main sources for her life, including the student nurses' yearbook *Iridos* (Fort William [Thunder Bay], Ont.), are found among the archival holdings of the Thunder Bay Hist. Museum Soc. Certain aspects of Isabel's character were confirmed by two 1923 McKellar graduates, the late Jessie McLaren Hamilton of Thunder Bay, and the late Mary Sideen Berglund of Ignace, Ont. E.B.]

AO, RG 80-2-0-42, no.24122. LAC, RG 31, C1, Guelph, 1891, 1901. Thunder Bay Hist. Museum Soc., Jane Hogarth, Address given at the 60th anniversary banquet of McKellar Nursing School, 2 June 1964 (typescript, [1964]), and "A history of McKellar General Hospital" (typescript, n.d.); Jane Hogarth biog. file (includes acceptance form bearing Isabel Johnstone's signature); Olga Jagodnik, interview with Jane Hogarth, 6 April 1977 (transcript); McKellar Nursing School Alumnae coll., minute-books and class photographs. *Daily Times-Journal* (Fort William), 4–5 June 1923. *Guelph Mercury*, 6, 8 June 1923. *Canadian Nurse and Hospital Rev.* (Toronto), 19 (1923): 425. *Directory,* Fort William and Port Arthur [Thunder Bay], 1910–14/15. *Iridos*, 1926, 1951.

K

KABURAGI, GORO, Methodist minister and newspaper publisher and editor; b. 27 Dec. 1867 in Katori county, Chiba prefecture, Japan; m. 1897 Kaoru Ishiwara, and they had at least one son; d. 14 May 1926 in

Nagoya and was buried in Yamakura village, Chiba prefecture.

Goro Kaburagi's background was quite different from that of most Japanese immigrants to Canada, who were mainly farmers, fishermen, and day labourers. He was likely of the samurai class and had attended the Imperial College of Forestry in Tokyo and Northwestern University in Evanston, Ill. In 1895 he had been granted a B.PHIL. from Upper Iowa University in Fayette, Iowa; four years later he would obtain an MA from the same institution. His excellent command of English enabled him to be of considerable assistance to Japanese immigrants in North America.

Having been admitted to the Methodist ministry, probably in the mid 1890s, Kaburagi served a congregation in Fayette in 1895. The following year he was leading a congregation of the Methodist Episcopal Church in Columbus, Ohio, when he was invited by the Japanese Christian Endeavour Society to minister to Japanese immigrants in British Columbia. In 1895 the society had opened a mission at the corner of Pender and Abbott streets in Vancouver. It soon realized the necessity of having a Japanese-speaking minister and approached Kaburagi, who probably returned briefly to Japan before proceeding to Canada in August 1896. Soon after he started his work in 1897, he found the management of an independent mission "difficult," so he appealed successfully to the Methodist Church of Canada for support. In 1903 three city lots were purchased at the corner of Jackson and Powell streets in Vancouver and in September 1906 the Japanese Methodist Church (later Powell Street United Church) was dedicated. It had night-school classrooms as well as dormitories for single men on the upper floors.

Kaburagi's activities went beyond preaching. He led his community in its struggle for civil rights. In 1895 the Legislative Assembly of British Columbia had amended the Provincial Voters' Act and denied the franchise to the Japanese, the Chinese, and East Indians. They were also denied the right to vote in municipal and federal elections since voters' lists for these elections were based on the provincial list. In addition, certain sectors of the provincial civil service and numerous professions required that their members be on the voters' lists, so the amendment effectively barred the Japanese and others from many fields of employment. Kaburagi was a leader of the group that sent Tomekichi Homma to the courts in 1900 to challenge the legislation. Although the Supreme Court of British Columbia and the Supreme Court of Canada ruled that the amendment was *ultra vires* of the provincial legislature, those decisions were overturned by the Judicial Committee of the Privy Council in 1902.

With the help of the Japanese consul, in 1902 Kaburagi started an elementary school for children of Japanese ancestry. Taught by two trained teachers from Japan, it became the Vancouver Japanese School in 1906 and followed the same curriculum as the schools in Japan, with the addition of courses on the English language.

In order to spread his religious and social beliefs to a greater number of Japanese immigrants, Kaburagi had started the *Bankuba Shuho* [Vancouver Weekly] on July 1897. It was renamed the *Kanada Shinpo* [Canada News] in November 1903. On 1 March 1904 it became the first Japanese daily in Canada and Kaburagi was its full-time editor. The paper preached temperance and opposed gambling and prostitution – vices to which many Japanese immigrants had succumbed. It also encouraged assimilation with the mainstream of society. These goals were to be attained by learning English, moving away from the Powell Street community, eating western food, attending church, and competing as equals with white labourers. In the prevailing "boss" system, early immigrants who had some knowledge of English had become labour contractors, providing Japanese labourers to white businesses at lower wages. These contractors had gradually become the elite of the Japanese community. They had also attached themselves to the Japanese consulate in Vancouver. A pacifist who believed in the equality of all peoples, Kaburagi opposed the new imperialism that had developed in Japan after its victory in the Russo-Japanese War of 1904–5 and thus disagreed with the Japanese consulate which espoused it. In 1907 the consulate backed the publication of another Japanese newspaper, the *Tairiku Nippō/Continental News* to counter the influence of the *Kanada Shinpo*. In addition to his disagreements with the consul, by mid 1907 Kaburagi was also having differences with his congregation because of his pacifist stance. Kaburagi lost his ministry and the Reverend Yoshi Ono took his place. A number of Kaburagi's friends, including his wife's younger brother, Dr Meinosuke Ishiwara, a popular physician whom he had encouraged to come to Vancouver, left the church with him.

Undaunted by these setbacks, Kaburagi continued publishing his views in the *Kanada Shinpo*. He also pursued his dream of creating a Japanese garden on a three-acre plot at 21st Street and St George Avenue in North Vancouver. A young Christian student, Senji Yamamoto, spent a summer in 1907 leading a crew that cleared the virgin land. It appears that the project was never completed.

According to Yamamoto, Kaburagi and his wife lived in a "completely western-style house" at 428 Cordova Street East, one block from the commercial centre of the Japanese community. His home was always open to his fellow Japanese, especially to the young. Yamamoto had initially lived with the

Kanaka

Kaburagis when he came to Canada and often mentioned their kindness in his diaries and letters to his parents. Kaburagi influenced and assisted many others. Jinsaburo Oikawa, a pioneer immigrant from the Miyagi prefecture who would bring many of his fellow villagers to Canada and set up communal colonies on two islands in the Fraser River, had met Kaburagi aboard ship on his first trip to Canada. Kaburagi had stressed to Oikawa the need to learn English and had begun lessons on board. He later helped Oikawa with his land transactions.

Little is known of Kaburagi's later activities except that he continued his association with the *Kanada Shinpo*. In 1915 the Canadian Japanese Volunteer Corps was organized for military service overseas [*see* Yoichi Kamakura*]. Yasushi Yamazaki, chairman of the Canadian Japanese Association and editor of the *Tairiku Nippō*, had persuaded members of the association to sponsor the corps to "bring glory and honour to the Japanese Canadian community and lead to full citizenship rights." When Kaburagi dared to question the efficacy of the program, the volunteers vandalized his newspaper office in March 1916 and forced him to seek the protection of the police.

Although the exact details are not clear, Kaburagi apparently passed on the newspaper to a colleague and went back to Japan. He may have returned to Vancouver for some time during the early 1920s. He died in Japan in 1926 and left an estate, including land and cash in Canada and Japan, evaluated at over $18,000. Although his strong religious, moral, and social opinions were contrary to those held by many of his fellow countrymen, Goro Kaburagi is still remembered as an influential community leader who contributed substantially to the lives of the early Japanese immigrants to Canada.

MIDGE AYUKAWA

BCA, GR-1415, file 11774. Ken Adachi, *The enemy that never was: a history of the Japanese Canadians* (Toronto, 1976). Peter Duus, "The takeoff point of Japanese imperialism," in *Japan examined: perspectives on modern Japanese history*, ed. Harry Wray and Hilary Conroy (Honolulu, 1983). Roy Ito, *Stories of my people: a Japanese Canadian journal* (Hamilton, Ont., 1994). *Kanada Nikkeijin Godo Kyokai shi, 1892–1959* [A history of the Japanese congregations of the United Church of Canada, 1892–1959] (Toronto, 1961). Kenneth Matsugu, "A brief history of the Japanese United Church of Canada," in *A centennial legacy: history of the Japanese Christian missions in North America, 1877–1977*, comp. Sumio Koga (Chicago, 1977). Tadashi Mitsui, "The ministry of the United Church of Canada amongst Japanese Canadians in British Columbia, 1892–1949" (M.S.T. thesis, Union College of B.C., Vancouver, 1965). Mark Mullins, *Religious minorities in Canada: a sociological study of the Japanese experience* (Lewiston, N.Y., and Queenston, Ont., 1989). Nakayama Jinshiro, *Kanada doho hatten taikan* [Encyclopedia of the Japanese in Canada] (Tokyo, [1929]). Nitta Jiro, *Mikkosen Suian Maru* [The secret journey of the Suian Maru] (Tokyo, 1979). P. E. Roy, *A white man's province: British Columbia politicians and Chinese and Japanese immigrants, 1858–1914* (Vancouver, 1989). Sasaki Toshiji, *Yamamoto Senji* (2v., Tokyo, 1998), 1. Shinpo Mitsuru, *Kanada Nihonjin imin monogatari* [Tales of Japanese immigrants in Canada] (Tokyo, 1986). Shinpo Mitsuru *et al.*, *Kanada no Nihongo shinbun: minzoku ido no shakaishi* [Japanese-language newspapers in Canada] (Tokyo, 1991). Toyo Takata, *Nikkei legacy: the story of Japanese Canadians from settlement to today* (Toronto, 1983).

KANAKA, Inuit hunter and trader; b. about 1855 in Baffin Island (Nunavut), possibly near Cape Haven; m. Kumiapik (Ky-mi-a-pik), and they had at least one son and a daughter; d. 25 Aug. 1925 near Cape Mercy (Nunavut).

Kanaka was born on the brink of one great transformation in southern Baffin and he played a part in two more. For centuries the economy of the region revolved around the seasonal hunting by the Inuit of caribou, seals, walrus, and other game. Until the 1840s encounters with Europeans were limited to occasional trade with passing ships, chiefly those of the Hudson's Bay Company. The bowhead whale, which was also hunted though with great difficulty, drew British and American whalers [*see* Eenoolooapik*; William Penny*]. In 1851–52 the crew of an American vessel first wintered in Cumberland Sound; the venture was profitable and wintering became common. The Oqomiut, as the Inuit people there are known, began hunting for the incomers but the opportunity came at the cost of a heavy loss of population due to epidemics. These changes were followed by a seasonal reorientation around three whaling stations, one at Cape Haven on Hudson Strait and two in Cumberland Sound at Blacklead and Kekerten islands.

Kanaka was probably born within five years of the whalers' first wintering. Incomers later perpetuated a rumour that his father was a "Portugee," a black Azorean aboard a Massachusetts whaler. This claim helps confirm his reported date of birth. Such circumstances did not affect an individual's place in society. One can be sure that he was named for a cherished kinsman and lived in a skin tent in summer and fall and in an igloo, sometimes on the sea ice, in winter. Kanaka, who excelled in hunting and leadership, was apparently respected by the people at the whaling stations; it was at Blacklead that he would enter the written record.

After the economic and demographic shocks of the 1850s and 1860s, it is surprising that the next transformation, a religious one, was so long in coming. In 1894 the whalers brought the first missionary, Anglican priest Edmund James PECK, to Blacklead. He introduced the gospel in the Inuktitut syllabics he had adapted in Ungava (Que.) and the appeal of this native writing system proved irresistible. By 1903 the struggle between converts and traditionalists was approaching a crisis; mission sources identify Kanaka at Blacklead and Ohitok at Kekerten as the shamans leading the resistance. No confrontations took place, however, and Kanaka soon converted. When Peck was travelling on the sea ice early in 1903, Kanaka hospitably received him in his igloo. During a later encounter on the walrus-hunting grounds, he unexpectedly proposed that Peck conduct a prayer service.

On 22 July 1903 Kanaka and Ohitok left to work at a new station at Igarjuak on Pond Inlet in northern Baffin. They were part of the two crews of whaleboatmen who had come to terms with a Scottish company to move with their families to a region where whales were still relatively abundant but where the local Inuit, the Tununirmiut, were not engaged to hunt them. (A zealous young Christian girl in the same party would lay the foundations of Christianity there.) Economically the venture came too late: only three bowheads were caught in seven years, though the returns did include polar bears, Arctic foxes, ringed seals, and walrus hides and tusks. None of this trade demanded the special skills of the incomers, and for six months in 1906–7 Kanaka was one of the Inuit who also hunted and guided for the government expedition of Joseph-Elzéar Bernier*. By 1910 the station was closed and Kanaka returned south, settling at the whalers' rock-nosing (inshore-whaling) harbour of Kivitoo.

Here Kanaka continued his long connection with Scottish whaler James S. Mutch, who had spent much of his life in Cumberland Sound, established the Igarjuak station, and commanded or piloted vessels for the London-based Sabellum Trading Company [*see* NIAQUTIAQ]. It is possible in the logbooks to follow their connection from 1903 to Mutch's retirement in the 1920s, as the two old whalers met almost every year. Kanaka was being given trade goods and provisions by 1911, and in 1913 he moved to Cape Mercy on Cumberland Sound, where he assembled two prefabricated houses as trading stations. These also provided a base for an innovative venture to pack Arctic char – many over a metre long, from coastal rivers and fjords – for export to Britain. In 1916 Kanaka accompanied the *Erme* to Kivitoo, where he helped set up another station and worked at carpentry and blacksmithing to refit the vessel for its return voyage, which would include a detour to take him back to Cape Mercy, his trading base for another nine years. Goods were picked up or dropped off annually by one schooner or another from Scotland. For a few years his harbour appeared on government maps as Kanacker or Kanacker Inlet, though the name was never officially adopted.

Kanaka took part at Cape Mercy in the third transformation of his lifetime: the movement from the whaler-Inuit relationship to the stricter, debt-and-barter arrangement with the monopolistic HBC. From its post at Cape Dorset it thrust hard in 1921 into the east-erly territory served by the whaling concerns. The first HBC trader at Pangnirtung resolved to "break . . . like dogs" any Inuit who remained loyal to the whalers. Two of the three independent firms sold out, leaving Sabellum to wither and abandon its posts in 1927. For a time Kanaka remained an active trader and traveller who made an annual circuit of all the rival posts between Kivitoo and the mouth of Cumberland Sound.

In August 1925 he welcomed to his station another newcomer, Sergeant J. E. F. Wight of the Royal Canadian Mounted Police. Hale enough to tour the sound in March, Kanaka was now bedridden with tuberculosis. He dictated a will to Wight, and then signed it in syllabics. Written as a letter to the master of the supply vessel, it asked for his wife to be appointed post manager and for their son, Padlooapik, to take over the responsibilities of hunting and preparing the skins.

Kanaka lived to an unusual degree on the borders of two cultures, so it needs to be emphasized that his story is told from only one side, the written records of Euro-Canadians. He almost certainly could speak the pidgin English common in Cumberland Sound in the 1880s but which died out with his generation. A reputed shaman turned Anglican, he bridged the two forms of belief without, one may suppose, discarding core ethical values. He was true to the customs of the new whaling economy, in which Inuit traders carried on the traditions of whaleboat leaders of former eras and acted as brokers between the British suppliers and their own people. Maintaining this blend into the 1920s was Kanaka's special contribution to Baffin Island and Canadian history.

Philip Goldring

Dartmouth College, Rauner Special Coll. Library (Hanover, N.H.), MSS-122, logbooks of the ship *Rosie*, 1924–25, 21 Sept. 1925. LAC, RG 85, 64, file 164-1 (1); 1044, file 540-3 (3A). William Barr, "The *McLellan*: an eyewitness account," *Beaver* (Winnipeg), 66 (1986–87), no.3: 60–61. *Church Missionary Gleaner* (London), 1 Jan. 1914. Philip Goldring, "Goldring's post[s]cript," *Beaver*, 66, no.3: 61; "Inuit economic responses to Euro-American contacts: southeast Baffin Island, 1824–1940," in *Interpreting Canada's north: selected readings*, ed. K. S. Coates and W. R. Morrison (Toronto, 1989), 252–77; "The last voyage of the *McLellan*," *Beaver*, 66, no.1: 39–44. J. S. Mutch, "Whaling in Ponds Bay," in *Boas anniversary volume: anthropological papers written in honor of Franz Boas . . . presented to him on the twenty-fifth anniversary of his doctorate, ninth of August, nineteen hundred and six*, ed. Berthold Laufer (New York, 1906), 485–500.

KAPITIKOW. *See* Peyasiw-awasis

K'AYAX. *See* Sganism Sm'oogit

KEEFER, FRANCIS HENRY, lawyer, politician, and office holder; b. 24 July 1860 in Strathroy, Upper

Keefer

Canada, son of James Keefer, a merchant and village reeve, and Maria Cook; m. first January 1884 Annie Frances Daby (Daley, Davey) (d. 1915), and they had two daughters, one of whom died young, and two sons; m. secondly 15 Aug. 1917 Margaret Wilhemina Keefer in Toronto; d. there 4 Dec. 1928.

Frank Keefer received his early education at Strathroy Grammar School and Upper Canada College before attending the University of Toronto (BA 1881; MA, LLB 1882). In 1883 he moved to Prince Arthur's Landing (Port Arthur, now Thunder Bay), where the *Weekly Herald and Lake Superior Mining Journal* described him as a metallurgist. After his call to the bar in 1884 he joined the law practice there of his brother Thomas Alexander Keefer and Edward Robert Cameron, who soon left. The brothers combined their legal work with an interest in mining. In 1889 Frank also assumed the responsibilities of solicitor for Port Arthur, a position he would hold until 1910. Named a federal QC in 1897 and a provincial KC in 1907, he was socially active as a member of the Foresters, the Oddfellows, and the Port Arthur Club, and was a delegate to the General Synod of the Church of England in Canada.

An able advocate, Keefer acquired a continental perspective on questions relating to transportation and natural resources. His passionate interest in shipping and waterways was refined through his work as counsel before the International Waterways Commission [*see* Sir George Christie Gibbons*] for both the federal and the Ontario governments. His interest stemmed too from family linkages: he was a grandson of George Keefer*, the first president of the Welland Canal Company and founder of Thorold, Ont.

After settling in Port Arthur, Keefer had also immersed himself in politics. As secretary of the Liberal-Conservative Association of West Algoma, for example, he advised Prime Minister Sir John A. Macdonald* in 1891 that feelings were against the renomination of Simon James Dawson*. Seeking election himself in 1908, he was defeated by James Conmee*. He eventually sat as the Unionist-Conservative MP for Port Arthur and Kenora from 1917 to 1921.

While in Ottawa, Keefer acted as counsel and adviser to the federal Food Board and, from 1918 to 1920, he was parliamentary under-secretary of state for external affairs. During the House of Commons' consideration of margarine as a wartime substitute for butter, Keefer, reflecting perhaps an understanding acquired at the Food Board, advanced the strongest pro-margarine position against the protests of the dairy industry. The representative of a riding that accommodated three transcontinental railways and nine railway divisional points, he also championed the adoption by the government railways of workers' compensation provisions equivalent to those in effect on private lines. As well, he promoted voting mechanisms to ensure that railwaymen would not be disenfranchised if work took them away before polls opened.

Keefer's most extended interventions were made on behalf of international trade with the West Indies and the improvement of the Great Lakes–St Lawrence waterways. He viewed deeper shipping channels as an important means to lower the costs of transporting wheat and minerals, and to reduce Canadian dependency on American coal. In a circumstance that he described in 1921 as "most unenviable," he found himself at odds with his government in connection with the statutory creation of the Lake of the Woods Control Board, a water and power regulatory body that seemed to favour the needs of Winnipeg. He considered the measure ill-advised and asserted northwestern Ontario's interests accordingly. "Winnipeg is a very big city," he acknowledged, "but I do not think it should have the right, by way of legislation or otherwise, to take away the rights of the little town of Kenora without either consultation, negotiation or compensation."

As early as November 1920 Keefer was openly advocating the formation of a new northwestern province, Superior. It may have been his willingness to defend northern interests against his own government's policy that attracted the attention of Ontario Conservative leader George Howard Ferguson*, who recruited the former MP for the provincial election of June 1923, which the Tories swept. Returned in Port Arthur, Keefer would represent the riding until his defeat in 1926. A month after the contest he was made legislative secretary for northern Ontario, and he eventually succeeded in having Port Arthur made the northwest headquarters of the Department of Lands and Forests. These achievements no doubt provided some satisfaction to a man who had once remarked that "we in the North country are fighting against the difficulties of nature, and I feel that in this matter we should receive the most sympathetic consideration."

Keefer acted as a watchdog for Ontario on matters connected with the St Lawrence. This responsibility, though consistent with his commitment to a deep waterway system, produced some friction with Premier Ferguson, who did not wish to see Ontario's hydroelectric plans encumbered by a canal proposal. Attention to the St Lawrence also saw Keefer continue his efforts against "the Chicago steal" – the unauthorized diversion of Lake Michigan waters to the Gulf of Mexico. He monitored Chicago's machinations with particular reference to the interests of the Great Lakes Harbours Association of Canada and the United States, and repeatedly advised senior political figures in Ottawa that the development of the St Lawrence was the key to creating Canadian-American alliances capable of resolving the Chicago situation. In 1927 Keefer recognized the opportunity to tie the waterways issue to the historical canal interest of his family and that of Prime Minister William Lyon Mackenzie

King*: "Exactly one hundred years ago your grandfather, [William Lyon Mackenzie*], and mine were directors of the Welland Canal Company and opened that Canal for traffic. . . . It has just struck me how befitting it would be, if his grandson, and as Prime Minister of Canada, could bring to pass . . . the understanding with the government of the United States to do the same thing with the St. Lawrence."

Appointed public trustee for the province of Ontario in May 1928, Keefer had just begun to make his influence felt in this position when he died of a heart attack at his Toronto home in December. He was buried in Lakeview Cemetery in Thorold, where a son lived and where he had long held an interest in local history and St John's Anglican Church.

JAMIE BENIDICKSON

Francis Henry Keefer is the author of *Beaverdams* (Thorold, Ont., 1914).

AO, RG 80-5-0-917, no.4133. LAC, MG 26, I. *Thorold Post*, 6, 13, 27 Dec. 1928. *Toronto Daily Star*, 5 Dec. 1928. *Weekly Herald and Lake Superior Mining Journal* (Port Arthur [Thunder Bay], Ont.), 3 April 1884, 24 Jan. 1885. Christopher Armstrong, *The politics of federalism: Ontario's relations with the federal government, 1867–1942* (Toronto, 1981). Can., House of Commons, *Debates*, 2 April 1919: 1083–85; 31 May 1921: 4184–98. *Canada Law Journal* (Toronto), 20 (1884): 356, 391. *Canadian annual rev.*, 1917–27/28. *Canadian directory of parl.* (Johnson). *Canadian men and women of the time* (Morgan; 1912). E. M. Chadwick, *Ontarian families: genealogies of United-Empire-Loyalist and other pioneer families of Upper Canada* (2v., Toronto, 1894–98; repr., 2v. in 1, Lambertville, N.J., [1970]), 2. Alexander Fraser, *A history of Ontario: its resources and development* (2v., Toronto, 1907), 2: 796–98. W. H. Heick, *A propensity to protect: butter, margarine and the rise of urban culture in Canada* (Waterloo, Ont., 1991). John Hilliker and Donald Barry, *Canada's Department of External Affairs* (2v., Montreal and Kingston, Ont., 1990–95), 1. Peter Oliver, *G. Howard Ferguson: Ontario Tory* (Toronto, 1977). *Who's who in Canada*, 1925/26.

KELLY, ROBERT, wholesale merchant and political activist; b. *c.* 1861 in Russell Township, Upper Canada, third son of James Kelly and Sarah Ann Mills; m. 1892 Lillian Catherine Craig (d. 1952), and they had a son and a daughter; d. 22 June 1922 in Point Grey (Vancouver).

The son of an Irish tailor, Robert Kelly was educated in the public schools of Russell Township. At age 16 he became an errand boy in William Petrie's general store in Russell. A few years later he was promoted to clerk and also worked as a telegraph operator. In 1884, after seven years' service, he became manager of a branch store and telegraph office in Finch Township.

In 1886 Kelly travelled to Vancouver, but did not find an opening to his liking. He went on to California and took up a position as manager of a general store and telegraph office in McPherson, just south of Los Angeles. After returning to Vancouver in 1887, he established a wholesale fruit and provision business with William James McMillan on Water Street in the heart of the city's new wholesale and warehouse district. He left the partnership in 1889 and became a travelling salesman for Oppenheimer Brothers, the wholesale grocery firm of Isaac and David* Oppenheimer. While working for the firm, he made many contacts and became familiar with business opportunities throughout the Pacific northwest. In 1895 he left Oppenheimer Brothers and joined William Goldsworth Braid to form Braid, Kelly and Company, wholesale grocers specializing in tea and coffee. The partnership flourished, but lasted less than a year, since the brash, aggressive nature of the short, stocky Kelly did not agree with the staid, conservative Braid.

In early 1896 Frank Ross Douglas, a native of Lachute, Que., arrived in Vancouver seeking investment opportunities. An easygoing, cheerful, and tactful man, Douglas would be described a few months later by the *Vancouver Daily World* as "an able and progressive business man." He soon met Kelly and in March, despite their differing personalities, they formed Kelly, Douglas and Company, wholesale grocers and tea importers. With $14,500 in capital and an $8,000 line of credit, they rented a warehouse and office on Water Street. Kelly acted as managing director of the company while Douglas travelled throughout the province securing customers. Though British Columbia was in the midst of an economic depression, Kelly's intimate knowledge of the wholesale grocery business and the firm's strategic location at the hub of the province's new marine and railway transportation systems ensured the company's success.

Kelly's strong support of the Liberal party enhanced the firm's fortunes. When in 1896 the Reverend George Ritchie Maxwell* became a candidate for the federal riding of Burrard, but could not meet his campaign expenses, Kelly agreed to help. He provided Maxwell with funds on the understanding that, if he won, he would direct government patronage to Kelly, Douglas. Maxwell was successful and when the Klondike gold rush began in 1897, the company received many large orders for supplies from the new Liberal government of Sir Wilfrid Laurier*.

In the ensuing years, Douglas spent each summer visiting the Klondike to meet clients and secure orders. Business was good, but on 15 Aug. 1901 he drowned when the *Islander*, the steamer on which he was travelling, hit an iceberg and sank in Lynn Canal, Alaska. Kelly carried on the business himself until August 1904, when he sold a 20 per cent interest in the company to Edward Douglas, an elder brother of Frank. Under the two men the company entered a period of rapid expansion.

British Columbia's population doubled in the years

531

between 1901 and 1911. This growth, coupled with the continued patronage of the Laurier government and the firm's advantageous position in Vancouver, brought increased business and profits to Kelly, Douglas. The company supplied many small grocers across the province, as well as major department stores, mining and logging camps, and various work gangs. The company's Nabob brand was registered in 1905 and soon became synonymous with high-quality pre-packaged teas and coffees. In 1906 the firm was reorganized as a limited liability company with a capital of $500,000. An extensive nine-storey warehouse was built on Water Street. The Kelly Confection Company Limited was established that year to market confectioneries. In 1909 Kelly, Douglas had 30 employees in its warehouse and 10 travelling salesmen. The following year the authorized capital was raised to $1,000,000 and branches had been established in all the major urban centres of the province. In 1911 the firm registered sales of over $4,500,000. It was one of the largest of its kind west of Winnipeg.

Kelly exerted much back-room political influence in British Columbia. In 1905 Vancouver Liberals had put his name forward as a candidate for the Senate. This gesture provoked the Conservative Victoria *Daily Colonist* into publishing a lengthy editorial that labelled Kelly "the Tammany leader," a man "who gets what he wants every time," and one who aimed to be "the political dictator of his party in this province." When asked by the *Vancouver Daily Province* to comment on the *Colonist*'s remarks, Kelly stated that it was merely "good advertising."

In addition to his wholesale grocery business, Kelly invested in a number of other firms and had substantial interests in the lumber and salmon-canning industries. Despite the severe business depression that prevailed in British Columbia from 1912 to the end of World War I, Kelly, Douglas and Company remained profitable. At the end of the war Kelly's health began to fail and he took a year's leave of absence from the management of the firm. His health did not improve and he died at his home in Point Grey on 22 June 1922 from cirrhosis of the liver.

Robert Kelly's many mercantile skills and political ties in the booming economy of British Columbia before World War I had quickly made him both a political power-broker and a business leader in the province.

BRAD R. MORRISON and
CHRISTOPHER J. P. HANNA

BCA, GR-2951, nos.1922-09-300764, 1952-09-003965. City of Vancouver Arch., Add. MSS 54 (J. S. Matthews coll.), topical files, Kelly, Douglas and Co. Ltd. (02437). LAC, RG 31, C1, 1861, 1871, 1881, Russell Township, Ont.; 1901, Burrard, B.C., dist.D8. *Daily Colonist* (Victoria), 29 Dec. 1905, 23 June 1922. *Vancouver Daily News-Advertiser*, 3 Oct. 1897. *Vancouver Daily Province*, 29 Dec. 1905, 13 March 1906, 11 Dec. 1948. *Vancouver Daily World*, 20 June 1896 (souvenir ed.). *Vancouver News-Herald*, 11 Dec. 1948. *Vancouver Sun*, 23 June 1921, 17 Aug. 1953. *Victoria Daily Times*, 22 June 1922. *Canadian who's who*, 1910. Bill Davies, *From sourdough to superstore: the Kelly, Douglas story* (Vancouver, 1990). *Directories*, Carleton County, Ont., 1884; B.C., 1889–95; Ont., 1884–89; Ottawa, 1866–67, 1870–73; Vancouver, 1888, 1896. R. E. Gosnell, *A history o[f] British Columbia* (n.p., 1906). *Newspaper reference book*. E. O. S. Scholefield and F. W. Howay, *British Columbia from the earliest times to the present* (4v., Vancouver, 1914), 3. *Who's who in western Canada . . .* (Vancouver), 1913.

KEMP, Sir ALBERT EDWARD, businessman and politician; b. 11 Aug. 1858 near Clarenceville (Saint-Georges-de-Clarenceville), Lower Canada, son of Robert Kemp and Sarah Ann Bush, widow of John Derick; m. first 21 Aug. 1879 Celia Amanda Wilson in Montreal, and they had three daughters; m. secondly 3 March 1925, in Toronto, Virginia Norton, widow of Norman Copping, and they had a daughter; d. 12 Aug. 1929 near Bobcaygeon, Ont.

Edward Kemp's father was an immigrant from Yorkshire, England; his mother was Canadian-born. Raised near the Eastern Townships village of Clarenceville, where he attended school, Edward later studied at the academy in Lacolle, excelling in mathematics, but he did not finish. His real interest was business; at 16 he sought a share of his father's mercantile and farming ventures. Rebuffed, he left home, according to a later account, "somewhat surreptitiously one morning while the family was preparing for prayers." He headed to Montreal and took various jobs until he found employment as a "general servant" in a hardware store. Recognized for his arithmetical aptitude, he eagerly accepted an offer to be its bookkeeper and he spent four years learning the business methods that would serve him well in later life.

At 20 Kemp had two ambitions: to start his own business and to marry his Montreal sweetheart. But Celia Wilson's father was cool to the match because Kemp was young and unproven in the world of enterprise. Celia persuaded him to write to her suitor, explaining his concerns. Kemp replied immediately, hoping to allay the misgivings. The approach worked, and on 31 Jan. 1879 Kemp presented Celia with an engagement ring. A month later, he and a partner opened a manufacturing and retailing shop on St Catherine Street (Rue Sainte-Catherine), offering stoves and ranges and tin, japanned, and galvanized-iron wares.

Celia and Edward were married in August at Wesley Congregational Church. The support of her family and in-laws was critical to the success of her marriage to a man driven by entrepreneurial ambition. The toll was heavy. Once, not finding Edward in his shop on a visit, Celia scribbled: "Couldn't you let me see you for a few moments before Sunday. You have no idea how lonesome I seem." The shop was successful but Kemp wanted more. In 1885 he and Celia moved to Toronto, where he entered into partnership with Thomas McDonald, owner of the struggling Dominion Tin and Stamping Works at Gerrard and River streets. His business skill and bookkeeper's eye for efficiencies turned the operation around. Also productive were his efforts to cultivate a network of friends and contacts through the Board of Trade, the Canadian Manufacturers' Association, clubs, and the British Empire League, where he found like-minded young men who were connected to some of the city's largest banks, law firms, manufacturers, and merchants.

Despite their success, Kemp's relationship with his partner broke down. He confessed to an uncle that McDonald was known to "get men in this business who were capable of getting it into shape for him and then regardless of obligation make it so hot for them that they would willingly sacrifice their interests and get out." McDonald underestimated Kemp, who rallied their employees and warned McDonald that attempts to force him out would produce a rival operation headed by himself and staffed by their workers. In 1888 he bought out McDonald and formed the Kemp Manufacturing Company with his younger brother, William Arthur, who had left the lumber trade in Quebec to apply his inventive and marketing talents in Toronto. William's one-piece furnace pipe would bring fortune to the brothers. Their expanded operations and growing national reputation, through William's sales efforts, led to plants in Montreal and Winnipeg. In 1911 they reorganized their business as the Sheet Metal Products Company of Canada Limited, whose "goods found ready market in all parts of the Dominion, driving the United States' products from the market and competing with them for supremacy in the export trade."

Kemp's acumen and partnership with William had been primary factors in the prosperity of Kemp Manufacturing. A healthy dose of tariff protection had also contributed. Kemp eagerly endorsed the Conservative government's National Policy but believed it could be refined. With an introduction from the CMA's secretary, in 1889 he tried to get customs minister Mackenzie Bowell* to reduce the tariff on iron, his firm's raw material. He failed but did not give up. After the death of Prime Minister Sir John A. Macdonald*, he vigorously supported the Tories through their troubled times in the 1890s, all the while promoting stronger protection.

By 1900 Kemp was a recognized figure among the "better elements" of Toronto society. A member of Sherbourne Street Methodist Church, along with other prominent businessmen, he was president of the CMA in 1895 and 1896, and of the Board of Trade in 1899 and 1900. He continued to nurture friendships with top bankers and was doing important work for the Victorian Order of Nurses. As well, his wealth and influence were prized assets for the tattered Conservative party during the early years of Liberal government under Wilfrid Laurier*. Amid demands to rebuild the Tory machine, lamentations over Laurier's response to the South African War, Liberal disposition to free trade, and pressure from Conservative leader Sir Charles Tupper*, he left Kemp Manufacturing in William's care and launched his own political career, his sights set on the federal election of November 1900. Toronto lawyer Edmund James BRISTOL, an executive member of the Ontario Conservative Association, secured his nomination in Toronto East.

Kemp won. Years later the *Globe* said of him that in the House of Commons he was "never inclined to overwork Hansard." But he did speak on major issues, such as the budget, the prospects of an imperial preferential tariff, the settlement of the war, and transcontinental railways. Robert Laird Borden*, the Halifax lawyer who had succeeded Tupper in 1901, liked Kemp's steady disposition, his wealth and status in Toronto's Tory circles, and his support for Borden's own efforts to reform the Conservative party. Borden also admired the broad, national perspective displayed by Kemp – and by other progressive business figures whom he wanted to bring into federal Conservatism. Kemp extolled Canada's business opportunities and argued that economic prosperity would promote harmony between classes and cultures. Mindful perhaps of the absence of strong Conservative lieutenants in Quebec, he emphasized the mutual interests of the French and the English in public life, encouraged English Canadians to take a sanguine view of Quebec, and reproached "mischievous" politicians who inflamed tension for their own ends. "The best way . . . to draw the English and French speaking elements nearer each other," he would argue in a letter to Olivar Asselin* in 1905, "is to cease . . . discussing the question."

On the pragmatic level in Kemp's riding, constituents sought work from the wealthy MP and party members solicited favours. In the election of 1904 Kemp improved his margin of victory. Still, his relationship with ordinary voters was distant, and he had again depended on his party's elite to secure his nomination. A serious man of prideful bearing, he had no gift for the common touch; meeting constituents was not an opportunity for Kemp but a necessary chore. He never liked glad-handing, though only a few penetrative minds discerned the truth behind his handshake.

In the run-up to the election of 1908, Kemp paid little heed to the nomination process and a dispute arose over the Conservative candidacy. Some mem-

533

bers grumbled that Kemp's nomination was again being engineered by outsiders, behind the walls of Toronto's Albany Club. As a result, an independent Conservative, Joseph Russell, was nominated in addition to Kemp, who suddenly found his commercial prominence a liability with some working-class Tories. They charged that he employed Macedonians at the expense of Canadians and paid his workers pitiful wages while Russell, a brick maker, offered pay that allowed workers to "live in houses of their own, and not herd a dozen into a room." Kemp lost to Russell; nationally the Conservatives fell victim to Laurier's Liberals for a fourth time. The defeat struck the Ontario wing hard. Its chief organizer, John Stewart Carstairs, would later tell Borden that "it was only through the generous assistance of Mr. A. E. Kemp that we were rescued from the debts that had accumulated."

Kemp threw himself into reorganizing the Ontario machine. He used his influence and business connections to rally opposition to Laurier's naval policy and to reciprocity with the United States. While making the usual allegations that the Liberals were running a corrupt regime, he and a supportive Premier Sir James Pliny Whitney* recruited wealthy Ontario Liberals opposed to reciprocity and helped drive Laurier from power in September 1911. Borden, acutely aware of Kemp's role in the campaign, made him a minister without portfolio in his first cabinet. Kemp's mandate was to investigate government purchasing. He discovered that there was no common system and that expenditures were being made in uncontrolled and sometimes unexplained ways. At the riding level in Toronto, Kemp developed a business-like process to distribute the spoils of electoral success. Constituents' requests were screened by a committee which then forwarded a list of potential benefactors to Kemp and other local MPs who had jobs to dispense in the Post Office and other departments. By the outbreak of World War I, Kemp had added a thorough knowledge of patronage and government expenditure to his managerial skills.

The war created huge demands for material to support, by the end, over 400,000 Canadian soldiers at the front. War appropriations during the conflict totalled more than $1 billion. In the early months of the conflict most of the money was spent by Colonel Samuel HUGHES, the flamboyant minister of militia and defence. By April 1915 his department was in chaos, its Militia Council unconsulted and Hughes often absent and making commitments with overweening confidence and contempt for orderly procedure. Rumours of mismanaged contracts for munitions and other material spread like wildfire; two Tory MPs were dismissed for "gross profiteering" and investigatory commissions were set up. In May, Borden removed Hughes from his responsibilities for spending war

allocations, placed them in the hands of deputy minister Eugène Fiset*, and, to clean up the mess, appointed Kemp chair of the newly formed War Purchasing Commission. It was a bad time for Kemp – he and Celia had just lost a grandchild in the sinking of the *Lusitania* – but it was a challenge he could not refuse. His talents and nature were the exact opposite of Hughes's and he disliked the brash politics of favouritism that Hughes had practised with such flourish. Under Kemp's leadership the commission shifted expenditure away from what was good for the party to what was good for the war effort. A systematic tendering process was established, contracts were issued to proven suppliers, and patronage was restricted to contractors who could deliver quality material. Behind the scenes William Kemp offered technical expertise and kept his eye on affairs in Toronto East. As more and more soldiers went overseas, and as war appropriations grew and grew again, from $166 million in the fiscal year 1915–16 to $306 million in 1916–17, much of the work had to be delegated to Kemp's co-commissioners, George Frederick GALT and Hormisdas Laporte*, and their staff. Still, for Kemp the burden was heavy: it left him seriously ill by May 1916 and forced him into a period of recovery.

In November, Hughes was in deeper trouble still over the confused military administration of the Canadian Expeditionary Force in London and his defiance of Borden's instructions. The prime minister demanded his resignation and called on Kemp to put the Department of Militia and Defence back in order; he became minister on 23 November. In a private note on 5 Jan. 1917 to Sir George Halsey Perley*, another trusted lieutenant, who had gone to London as high commissioner and was now minister of overseas military forces, Kemp confessed that he found the department in a "remarkable condition of affairs" and that the "adjustment of nearly every difficult decision had been postponed and the stream was blocked."

Kemp turned to solving the problems, counselling patience, delegating duties to the ablest men he could find, and ending the one-man show that had been Hughes's downfall at home and then overseas. Dismayed as he was, he had some sympathy for Sir Sam and no time for recriminations. He reported that he had admonished a senior officer and bitter critic of Hughes to "have a little more regard for those whose honesty of purpose, although they may have made some mistakes, was no less sincere than his own." At the same time Kemp was creating a professional, efficient operation to implement the day-to-day administrative routine he had designed. For his service he was made a KCMG; announced in the king's New Year's honours of 1917, it was conferred on 13 Feb. 1917. The following month he announced a "Canadian Defence Force," to increase the militia ranks for home defence in order to free up troops for overseas service.

The plan was largely a failure; "voluntary enlistment has about reached its limit," he confessed to Borden in April. Like many of his cabinet colleagues, he came to realize that conscription was inevitable.

His tenure in Militia and Defence was short-lived. In October he became minister of overseas military forces in Borden's new Union government. He replaced Perley, who had started to build a sound administration but wanted to resume his post as high commissioner. In the general election in December, Kemp won handily and the Unionists returned to power on a conscription platform, which deeply divided the nation.

Kemp's work in England, where he arrived in January 1918, was the second part of his reform mission. Close to field operations and British headquarters, he was besieged by Tories and others wanting assistance for friends and family in the war. Despite such distractions, he concentrated on rebuilding relations with the British that Hughes had nearly destroyed. Prime Minister David Lloyd George knew that the British armies needed more soldiers from the dominion. Unlike his predecessor, Herbert Henry Asquith, he recognized that in return the Canadians, in Ottawa and in London, would have to have a greater share in wartime decision making. That spring Kemp joined Borden at the meetings of the imperial war cabinet. As well, he carried on the managerial reform of the overseas forces. He formed, in April, and chaired the Overseas Military Council, which was similar to the Militia Council in Ottawa, and imposed his authority over the administrative control of the CEF. As part of this change, the position of general officer commanding in England was abolished and Lieutenant-General Sir Richard Ernest William Turner* assumed the new post of chief of general staff. In addition, Kemp persuaded the War Office to establish, in July, a Canadian section at General Headquarters in France that would oversee the troops and serve as the link between the Canadian Corps and the overseas ministry. This section was headed by Brigadier-General John Fletcher Leopold Embury*.

In May, persuaded by the advice of Turner and other senior officers and reversing his earlier opposition, Kemp had lent his support to the formation of the Canadian Air Force. It was just being organized when fighting stopped in November 1918 and it would be disbanded the following year. With the war's end, demobilizing Canada's troops and getting them home became Kemp's top priority. Because the armistice had come unexpectedly, most of the planning to move close to half a million soldiers, in the midst of a huge shortage of shipping, posed an enormous challenge. It kept Kemp in England until 1920, when the overseas ministry was terminated. His long service as the government's "repairman" of wartime administration was over. Kemp was then in his sixties, exhausted by a

series of demanding assignments. He nonetheless served out his term, including time, from July 1920, as a minister without portfolio in the short-lived government of Arthur Meighen*. In August 1920, in a final gesture of personal wartime abstention, he returned to the government cheques totalling more than $25,000, his ministerial salary during the war. Appointed to the Senate in November 1921, he did not run in December's general election.

The contest signalled a new era in politics: William Lyon Mackenzie King*, the Liberal leader since 1919, won the election. Kemp was now the grand old man of Ontario Conservative politics. He acted as one of Meighen's advisers and returned to work at Sheet Metal Products. It too was a different place, his trusted brother having passed away in 1919. At Castle Frank, his palatial home overlooking the Don River valley, Kemp found comfort in his wife's companionship, but Celia died on 20 Jan. 1924 following surgery. A year later Kemp quietly married Virginia Copping, a young widow with two daughters. He kept up his interest in Tory politics, made the occasional speech, retained some directorships, and continued his support of charitable causes, including church work and the Young Men's Christian Association. In October 1927 Sheet Metal Products merged with McClary Manufacturing [see John McClary] and Thomas Davidson Manufacturing Company Limited of Montreal to form General Steel Wares Limited, a combination that reputedly netted Kemp more than $3 million. On 11 Aug. 1929 he celebrated his birthday with a round of golf, a favourite pastime, on the private course of Missisquoi, his summer home on Pigeon Lake near Bobcaygeon. Early the next morning he died, according to the press, of an attack of acute indigestion. Buried in Mount Pleasant Cemetery in Toronto, he left an estate worth more than $7,700,000.

Kemp had begun his career as an ambitious businessman whose accounting and managerial expertise turned his partnership in Montreal to success. Repetition of this pattern in Toronto opened doors to the homes and friendships of the cloistered, often smug business and political elites of late colonial Toronto. At the dawn of the new century Kemp won a seat in parliament and soon found himself a leader in the Conservative party in Ontario. His service and pocketbook, many acknowledged, kept the Ontario wing healthy in the lean years of the Laurier era. In 1911 Kemp joined George Perley as Borden's choices for cabinet. Both were wealthy businessmen, skilled administrators with more talent for the management of affairs than for rough-and-tumble constituency politics. Both carried out personal assignments for the prime minister before and during the Great War. One account said of Kemp that he was "seldom on parade, but seldom inactive and never inefficient." Kemp himself once attributed his success to energy and application. In effect, he was the ex officio minister of efficiency in Borden's governments.

JOHN A. TURLEY-EWART and
ROBERT CRAIG BROWN

ANQ-E, CE502-S75, 21 mai 1856; ANQ-M, CE601-S150, 21 août 1879. AO, F 68, MU 284, box 2; RG 8-5, container 5; RG 22-305, no.62898. LAC, MG 27, II, D9. TRL, SC, Biog. scrapbooks (copy at AO). *Financial Post* (Toronto), 27 June 1924. *Globe*, 29 Dec. 1915, 24 Nov. 1916. *Toronto Daily Star*, 21 Jan. 1924, 4 March 1925, 12 Aug. 1929. R. C. Brown, *Robert Laird Borden: a biography* (2v., Toronto, 1975–80). R. C. Brown and Ramsay Cook, *Canada, 1896– 1921: a nation transformed* (Toronto, 1974). Can., Ministry of Overseas Military Forces, *Report* (London, 1918); Parl., *Debates*, 19 March 1901; 15, 23 April 1902; 19 April, 19 Aug. 1903. *Canadian annual rev. CPG*, 1918. *Directory*, Toronto, 1886–1929. John English, *The decline of politics: the Conservatives and the party system, 1901–20* (Toronto, 1977). Middleton, *Municipality of Toronto*, vol.2: 1–2, 38– 39. Desmond Morton, *Canada and war: a military and political history* (Toronto, 1981). Desmond Morton and J. L. Granatstein, *Marching to Armageddon: Canadians and the Great War, 1914–1919* (Toronto, 1989). *The official history of the Royal Canadian Air Force* (3v. to date, [Toronto and Ottawa, 1980–]), vol.1 (S. F. Wise, *Canadian airmen and the First World War*, 1980). *Standard dict. of Canadian biog.* (Roberts and Tunnell), vol.1.

KENDALL, GEORGE WASHINGTON, known as **George Kennedy**, wrestler and sports promoter; b. 29 Dec. 1881 in Montreal and baptized there 25 Dec. 1882, son of George Hiram Kendall, an industrialist, and Jane McClosky (McCluskey, McKlosky); m. 1 June 1907 Myrtle Agnes Pagels in Montreal, and they had two daughters, one of whom died before the age of one; d. 19 Oct. 1921 in Montreal.

The son of a Scottish Protestant father and an Irish Catholic mother, George Washington Kendall studied at the High School of Montreal and then attended the Collège de Saint-Laurent for at least the year 1899– 1900. By 1901 he was said to be the Canadian amateur lightweight wrestling champion. Kendall was training at that time in the gymnasium and under the direction of Dr Joseph-Pierre GADBOIS, who would become his friend and business partner. Because his father, who was a pillar of the Baptist denomination in Montreal, disapproved of his choice of career, Kendall took the name George Kennedy, under which he would work all his life. From 1901 to 1903 he dominated his class on the Canadian wrestling scene. After losing to Eugène Tremblay on 3 April 1903, he left wrestling for a career as a sports promoter. He became Tremblay's principal trainer, and his skilful direction enabled Tremblay to win the world lightweight championship by defeating the American George Bothner in Montreal in 1905.

That year Kendall and Gadbois founded the Club Athlétique Canadien (CAC), an organization incorporated on 22 Sept. 1908 that had mostly French-speaking shareholders. The club invested first in wrestling and then in hockey, baseball, lacrosse, and other sports. Under Kendall's impetus it became the most powerful professional sports organization in the province, proof of his organizing abilities and business flair. For him, sports were first and foremost a business that had to show a profit. In 1910, when the club's share capital increased from $25,000 to $100,000, it had some 116 shareholders. Kendall managed to combine French Canadian patriotic pride with his own financial interests, and he skilfully joined forces with the press. By 1909 he was busily promoting the construction of a gymnasium in the east end of Montreal. The building opened on 10 March 1911, and besides a modern gymnasium, it had billiard and pool tables, bowling alleys with automatic pinsetters, a handball court, showers, a sauna, and a massage room. A smoking room was added the following year, as well as a reading room with "all the major Canadian and American daily papers and the main sports magazines," as *La Presse* noted. There were plans to add a swimming pool and to buy land for an automobile racetrack and a baseball and lacrosse field, but they were wrecked when the building was damaged by fire on 21 Jan. 1914. The CAC's financial situation, already weakened by an unfortunate venture into the world of lacrosse, was badly affected. Probably as a result Kendall on 10 March 1916 created the Canadian Hockey Club Incorporated, a new company having the same aims and substantially the same directors as the former CAC, with Kendall as principal shareholder.

Through these two companies and Kendall himself, Montreal became one of the most important wrestling centres in North America from 1905 to 1920. He made contact with the top wrestling promoter in France, Léon Dumont, and became friends with the American promoter Jack Curley, who was nicknamed "the czar of wrestling." He met managers and wrestlers, negotiated contracts, ironed out financial and material difficulties, travelled throughout the United States, and went to Europe and even to Turkey in search of new athletes. His knowledge of French encouraged Belgian and French wrestlers who wanted to break into the North American market to hire him as their manager. On 24 May 1913 Kendall staged a sports event that would stand for years as the most important of its kind in the history of Montreal: the fight between Stanislaus Zbysko of Poland and Constant Le Marin of Belgium for the world heavyweight championship. More than 10,000 people watched the match. That year he set up two American circuits, one in the east and one in the west. In 1913 he also arranged with promoters in Paris to bring the best American wrestlers to the French capital. The war would put a stop to this project. On 22 April 1920 he organized a match in Montreal between the world heavyweight champion, Joseph James Stecher of the United States, and the European champion, Salvatore Chevalier of France. In Quebec the CAC, and later the Canadian Hockey Club Incorporated, brought the top wrestlers to 20 or more towns and villages, stimulating interest and sparking an increase in the number of wrestlers and wrestling arenas.

In 1908 Kendall had begun investing in boxing, a sport that had a bad press at the time. A Canadian law, passed in 1881, had banned professional fights and Montreal had adopted a similar regulation in 1887. Fights were held in public anyway, but the police were watchful. This situation prompted the CAC to encourage boxing fans to become members of the club, where bouts would be held in private under the guise of exhibition matches. Kendall counted on thereby acquiring the means to hire good American boxers, but the fire at the CAC delayed his plans. The war changed attitudes, however, and boxing was now seen as an excellent way to prepare soldiers for combat. Kendall took advantage of this change and succeeded in attracting "boxers of note" to Montreal including Joe Jeannette of Martinique on 26 Feb. 1915. A few weeks later he obtained from Jack Curley the exclusive distribution rights in Quebec for the film of the fight for the world heavyweight championship between the black boxer John Arthur (Jack) Johnson and Jess Willard, the "white hope." In June 1916, following a match between two professionals held in public in Montreal, the Canadian Vigilance Association lodged a complaint and he had to appear in municipal court. He won his case and, thanks to this victory, boxing was legalized. From 1916 to 1920 Kendall brought in excellent boxers under the auspices of the Canadian Hockey Club Incorporated. The appearance in Montreal on 15 May 1920 of Georges Carpentier of France, the famous European middleweight champion, was his last master stroke.

Of all his many accomplishments, Kendall was best known for his role as manager of the Canadiens hockey club. As early as 1908 he and Gadbois had wanted to organize an exclusively French Canadian senior hockey team. The plan was, however, realized by John Ambrose O'Brien, who in December 1909 founded the Canadiens: the team was immediately accepted into the National Hockey Association of Canada. Nearly a year later Kendall protested on behalf of the CAC, claiming that the name "Canadien" was its property. On 12 Nov. 1910 he purchased the franchise for $7,500. Under his management the reorganized Canadiens showed a profit of $4,000 in their first season, more than was made by any other team in the association. Kendall succeeded in using French Canadian national sentiments to stimulate competition and increase the number of spectators, but the club's main function, in his view, was to pay dividends to its shareholders. In November 1912 he sought and received permission from the association to hire English-speaking players to improve the team's performance; some people accused him of "polluting" the club's distinctive character. A three-time winner of the association championship, the team won its first Stanley Cup in March 1916 [see Georges VÉZINA]. From 26 Nov. 1917 the team played in the National Hockey League, which replaced the National Hockey Association of Canada and which Kendall had helped organize. Unfortunately, in March 1919, when the Canadiens were playing in Seattle against the Metropolitans for the Stanley Cup, the Spanish influenza took its toll of the players. Defenceman Joseph Henry Hall died and Kendall contracted a severe case of the disease. He remained in precarious health, but he would continue to manage the Canadiens until his death in October 1921. On 4 November his widow sold the club's franchise for $11,000 to a financial syndicate consisting of Léo Dandurand, Joseph Cattarinich, and Louis Létourneau.

Apart from wrestling, boxing, and hockey, Kendall had tried, through the CAC, to develop a number of other sports. In 1904 he made an unsuccessful attempt to introduce bullfighting to Montreal. In 1911 he put together a short-lived but powerful baseball team. From 1911 to 1914 he managed the Canadians lacrosse team. Also known as the Irish Canadians, this team played in the Dominion Lacrosse Union, of which he had been a founder. In October 1911 Kendall was among the promoters of one of the first flying competitions held in Quebec. He organized foot races in 1912, and soccer matches in 1913. He had also considered setting up a handball league, and was the owner of the most modern bowling alley in Montreal, the Windsor Bowling Club, which was built in 1914.

George Washington Kendall enjoyed spending summers with his wife and daughter at his farm near Sainte-Agathe-des-Monts. But this dynamic man had never completely recovered from the Spanish influenza and in the spring of 1921 he collapsed. In the hope of restoring his health, he went to his farm and to Atlantic City, N.J., to rest. Excellent American and Canadian doctors tried in vain to come to grips with his baffling illness. The premature death, at the age of 39, of this pillar of professional sport in Canada early in the 20th century left a great hole in the sporting world of that period.

GILLES JANSON

[This article was assembled largely from newspaper accounts, particularly those in *La Presse*, which was examined systematically for the period 1900–21. Information was also drawn from *Le Canada* (Montréal), 30 oct. 1910; 13 mars 1911; 3, 13, 15 mai, 27 sept., 10, 28 oct., 5, 20, 22 nov., 2–3, 11 déc. 1918; 15 mars 1919; 20–22, 28 oct., 3 nov. 1921; *Le Devoir*, 13, 24 janv., 17 févr., 8, 17, 21, 29 mars, 2,

Kennedy

8, 23 avril, 20 oct., 4, 10–11, 14 nov., 9, 13 déc. 1910; 14 févr., 4 mars, 2 nov. 1911; 16 févr. 1912; 23 janv. 1914; 30 sept., 8–9, 19, 26 oct., 11, 20, 25 nov., 5, 10, 12, 16 déc. 1918; 19, 21, 28 oct., 3 nov. 1921; *Gazette* (Montreal), 31 March 1914; 20, 22 Oct. 1921; *Montreal Daily Herald*, 7 Oct., 9, 12, 22 Nov. 1910; *Montreal Daily Star*, 7 Nov. 1908, 30 March 1914, 19–20 Oct. 1921; *Montreal Herald*, 19–20 Oct. 1921; *Le Nationaliste* (Montréal), 5, 12, 26 mars 1911; 8 mars 1914; *La Patrie*, 9–10, 13 mars, 19, 21, 24–25, 28 oct. 1921; and *Le Soleil*, 15 oct. 1908, 26 avril 1909, 18 mars 1911. G.J.]

ANQ-M, CE601-S60, 25 déc. 1882; TP11, S2, SS2, SSS1, dossier 2963 (1908) (C. Y. Rogers *c.* George Kennedy, alias George Kendall). Arch. des Pères de Sainte-Croix (Montréal), D1 (fonds du collège de Saint-Laurent), annuaires. BCM-G, RBMS, St Patrick (Montréal), 1er juin 1907. Rosaire Barrette, *Léo Dandurand, sportsman* (Ottawa, 1952), 105–10, 155, 180, 201–2. François Black, *Habitants et glorieux: les Canadiens de 1909 à 1960* (Laval, Qué., 1997), 17–47, 133–35. Line Bonneau et Taïeb Hafsi, *Sam Pollock et le Canadien de Montréal* ([Sainte-Foy, Qué.], 1996), 21–40. [Pat Calabria *et al.*], *The official National Hockey League Stanley Cup centennial book*, ed. Dan Diamond (Montreal, 1992). Michel Chemin, *La loi du ring* ([Paris], 1993), 44–59. *Directory*, Montreal, 1912–13, 1915–16, 1918–19. Chrys Goyens and Allan Turowetz, *Lions in winter* (Scarborough [Toronto], 1986). Donald Guay, *L'histoire du hockey au Québec; origine et développement d'un phénomène culturel* (Chicoutimi, Qué., 1990), 256–74. Graeme Kent, *A pictorial history of wrestling* (London, 1968), 128–83. Charles Mayer, *L'épopée des Canadiens de Georges Vézina à Maurice Richard: 46 ans d'histoire, 1909–1955* (Montréal, [1956?]). Claude Mouton, *The Montreal Canadiens: a hockey dynasty* (Toronto, 1980). Andy O'Brien, *Fire-wagon hockey: the story of the Montreal Canadiens* ([Toronto, 1967]). Alexis Philonenko, *Histoire de la boxe* (Paris, 1991), 155–267. *Quebec Official Gazette*, 1908: 1601–2; 1916: 880. Maurice Richard and Stan Fischler, *The flying Frenchmen: hockey's greatest dynasty* (New York, [1971]).

KENNEDY, Sir JOHN, engineer; b. 26 Sept. 1838 in Spencerville, Upper Canada, eldest son of William Kennedy and Agnes Stark; m. 14 Aug. 1865 Louisa Charlotte Scott in Montreal, and they had two sons who predeceased him and two daughters (one of whom married Sir Herbert Brown Ames*); d. 25 Oct. 1921 in Montreal.

The son of a Scottish millwright who came to Upper Canada in 1832, John Kennedy was educated at the grammar school in Bytown (Ottawa), by private tuition, and at McGill College in Montreal. He began his professional career in 1853 under Thomas Coltrin Keefer*, working on channel and harbour improvements, on waterworks in Montreal, Ottawa, and Hamilton, and on other projects. In 1863 he was appointed assistant city surveyor in Montreal and a few years later he was promoted deputy city surveyor. He resigned in 1867 to become manager of the Hull Iron Mining and Manufacturing Company's iron mines and new smelting works at Ironside, Que. Having taught himself chemistry, he ran the company successfully, but concluded that there was no future in smelting iron with wood charcoal. He then joined his family's thriving iron foundry and machine shop, Wm. Kennedy and Sons, in Owen Sound, Ont.

In 1871 Kennedy returned to civil engineering as divisional engineer on the Wellington, Grey and Bruce branch of Canada's largest railway system, the Great Western. Within three years he was promoted chief engineer of the entire railway, then the highest paid engineering position in Canada. He completed a rail link between Fort Erie and Glencoe, Ont. (the Canada Air line), built some minor branches, and laid the first double track in Canada, between Glencoe and Windsor.

In 1875 Kennedy accepted the newly created post of chief engineer of the Montreal Harbour Commission. He would hold this office for nearly 33 years and would make his professional reputation by developing the modern port of Montreal and by deepening the St Lawrence ship channel between Montreal and Quebec. When Kennedy took up the post, the port was small and in poor condition. It had narrow wooden wharves, shallow basins, temporary wooden sheds, and no grain elevators. A plan to improve it was put aside in 1877; approval to enlarge the port was not granted until 1891. A year later Kennedy began construction on a guard pier, or breakwater, which enclosed a mile-and-a-half-wide harbour basin at the mouth of the Lachine Canal. This pier protected the harbour and the city from floods caused by ice jams. Kennedy then deepened the harbour basins to 30 feet and, against strong opposition, built three massive 1,000-foot-long, 300-foot-wide piers – the Jacques Cartier (1898–99), the Alexandra (1899–1901), and the King Edward (1901–2). An elevator, designed to deliver grain directly to ships by an elaborate conveyor system, was erected in the centre of the harbour between 1903 and 1904. Wharves on shore were raised and protected, and 14 steel-and-concrete two-storey freight sheds were built (1904–8). Piers, wharves, and harbour approaches were paved and a modern electric light and telephone system was installed. The Grand Trunk's track on the docks was replaced with the commission's extensive electric railway (1907). Other improvements followed. Kennedy was far-sighted enough to have made allowances for future growth.

For 18 of the 33 years that Kennedy was chief engineer of the harbour commission, he was also chief engineer of the St Lawrence ship channel between Montreal and Quebec. By 1887 he had deepened it from 20 to 27½ feet, employing dredges of his own design, some of which would be used the world over. The deeper channel allowed larger ocean ships to reach Montreal, helping to make the port the biggest and most important in Canada. The improved harbour facilities fostered Montreal's industrialization and made the city Canada's principal transportation centre, as well as the world's largest grain port by the mid 1920s.

In 1899 Kennedy's eyesight began to fail, as his father's had before him. Consultations with specialists in the United States and Great Britain were not encouraging and in 1906 he had an operation to preserve what sight he had; it was not a success and he suffered neuralgic pain for the rest of his life. Totally blind in 1907, he resigned as chief engineer and was appointed consulting engineer to the commission, a post he held until his death. Although blind, he continued to ride his horses and practise engineering, designing, for example, the world's largest dipper dredge for the St Lawrence and Pier No.2 in Halifax harbour for the federal government.

Kennedy had been appointed to a number of federal commissions: on the leasing of water-power on the Lachine Canal (1886); on the causes of the flooding of Montreal the same year; on the advisability of extending the Trent Canal (1887); and on enlarging the Cornwall Canal (1891). A staunch advocate of private enterprise, in 1916 he and other leading engineers from Montreal persuaded the city to abandon plans for an aqueduct and a hydroelectric power scheme. Similarly, a year later, he was among the prominent engineers who advised the government of Ontario not to proceed with an electric railway between Port Credit and St Catharines, Ont. Their report, together with other factors, eventually killed Sir Adam BECK's scheme for a government-owned high-speed radial railway system centred on Toronto. Kennedy also acted as an arbitrator, or consulting engineer, on a variety of engineering projects and gave advice on mining and industrial works.

Kennedy was a member of the leading British and American engineering societies: the Institution of Civil Engineers of Great Britain and, from 1875, the American Society of Civil Engineers. The first Canadian to become a councillor of the ICE, he served for many years as a director of the ASCE. In 1887 he was one of 19 founding members of the Canadian Society of Civil Engineers (renamed the Engineering Institute of Canada in 1918), Canada's first national professional engineering society. He sat for several years on the CSCE's council, was elected president in 1892, and was made an honorary member in 1907.

Together with other older, prominent engineers, Kennedy controlled the CSCE's executive until the end of World War I. A tireless promoter of the welfare of engineers, he had nevertheless opposed Alan Macdougall*'s attempt in 1887 to have the CSCE incorporated as a self-governing licensing and regulatory body. Kennedy believed that the status of engineers could be improved only by raising the standard of engineering practice through the exchange of profes-

sional knowledge. Although Macdougall's plan would eventually succeed with the creation of provincial licensing associations, beginning in Manitoba in 1896, Kennedy and his colleagues greatly influenced the style of engineering professionalism in Canada.

In recognition of his service to Canada, Kennedy was made a knight bachelor in 1916. McGill conferred a LLD on him the following year and in 1921 McMaster University in Toronto honoured him with a DCL. Kennedy was a member of the University Club in Montreal, a director of the Young Men's Christian Association, and a director of the Montreal Association for the Blind, in which capacity he was a founder of the School for the Blind. He was active in religious and social reform work through the Olivet Baptist Church in Montreal.

A major figure in the professionalization of Canadian engineers, Kennedy had a full and varied career few of his colleagues equalled. With other engineers, he helped transform Canada into a modern, urban-industrial nation by building the country's most important civil and mechanical infrastructures. When he died, the Engineering Institute of Canada referred to him as the "dean of the engineering profession in Canada."

J. RODNEY MILLARD

[Sir John Kennedy's publications concern his activities as a professional engineer. These include his reports to the Montreal Harbour Commission, published on an irregular basis between 1875 and 1910 in Can., Parl., *Sessional papers*. See especially 1900, no.11b; 1903, no.23; 1905, no.23; 1906–7, no.23; and 1910, no.2. Three reports written or co-written by Kennedy on proposed engineering works are available in the CIHM, *Reg.*, and a major article by Kennedy on "The Montreal waterworks" was published in *Canadian Engineer* (Toronto), 3 (1895–96): 268–72. His presidential address to the Canadian Society of Civil Engineers appears in its *Trans.* (Montreal), 7 (1895): 12–15.

Although Kennedy was a major figure in Canadian engineering history, there is little source material on him. For instance, his application for membership in the Canadian Society of Civil Engineers is not among the papers of the Engineering Institute of Canada. Articles or obituaries appear in the following engineering journals: *Canadian Engineer*, 14 (1907): 19–20; 41 (July–December 1921): 6; 45 (July–December 1923): 423–26, 435; *Canadian Railway and Marine World* (Toronto), November 1921: 582; *Contract Record and Engineering Rev.* (Toronto), 35 (1921): 962; Engineering Institute of Canada, *Journal* (Montreal), 4 (1921): 581–82; *Engineering Journal* (Montreal), 20 (1937): 284; *Engineering News-Record* (New York), 87 (July–December 1921): 749; L. E. Jones, "Delineations of destiny – John Kennedy," *Professional Engineer & Engineering Digest* (Toronto), 29 (1968), no.5: 30; *Railway and Shipping World* (Toronto), December 1899: 363–65; February 1900: 52–53; September 1903: 322–24; November 1903: 395; April 1904: 137.

Additional information can be found in the obituaries

which appeared on 25 Oct. 1921 in the *Ottawa Citizen*, the *Montreal Daily Star*, and the *Toronto Daily Star*; in his marriage registration in ANQ-M, CE601-S85, 14 août 1865; in the *Standard dict. of Canadian biog.* (Roberts and Tunnell); and in J. R. Millard, *The master spirit of the age: Canadian engineers and the politics of professionalism, 1887–1922* (Toronto, 1988). J.R.M.]

KENNEDY, WILLIAM COSTELLO, businessman and politician; b. 27 Aug. 1868 in Ottawa, son of William Kennedy and Julia Costello; m. 8 May 1907 Glencora Bolton in Detroit; they had no children; d. 17 Jan. 1923 in Naples, Fla, and was buried in Windsor, Ont.

Sometime before 1871 William C. Kennedy moved with his family to Toronto, where his father, a bookkeeper, became a messenger at the Legislative Assembly. He attended separate schools and De La Salle Institute and was a page in the legislature. In 1887 he joined the London and Canadian Loan and Agency Company as a clerk. A natural athlete and a member of the Toronto Rowing Club, he developed into one of the city's best-known oarsmen as well as a skilled lacrosse player.

In 1897 Kennedy accepted an offer of employment in the oil and gas industry of southwest Ontario, which, though new to him, proved to be a fertile field for his instincts for making money. Shrewd and disciplined, he was secretary-treasurer of the United Gas and Oil Company of Ontario Limited (incorporated in 1900) and, from 1908 to 1917, president of the Windsor Gas Company Limited. Kennedy invested in various commercial interests on both sides of the Detroit River – for some years before 1910 he lived in Detroit – and he was possibly involved in the development of the Oklahoma oil industry. He gained recognition from his participation in public life as well as from business. Twice elected to the presidency of the Windsor Board of Trade (1909 and 1910), he was a trustee of the Board of Education (1913–18) and sat on the council of the neighbouring municipality of Ojibway (1913–23). In addition, he was a founder and treasurer of the Children's Aid Society in Windsor, and a prominent member of St Alphonsus' Roman Catholic Church.

Kennedy's first foray into federal politics occurred in 1911, when he ran for the Liberal nomination in Essex North. A deadlock at the convention ended only when Kennedy persuaded his main rival that they should both step down in favour of a compromise candidate (who in the end lost to his Conservative opponent). Talk of an election in 1915 prompted the Liberals unanimously to choose Kennedy, but no contest was held because of World War I, and he had to wait until the writ was dropped in late 1917. His opponent was Ernest Solomon Wigle, a Conservative Unionist and former commander of the 99th Infantry

Battalion. Although he was a popular threat to Kennedy as a military man who had served overseas, the biggest concern facing any Liberal candidate in English-speaking Canada was conscription, which had been introduced that August by Sir Robert Laird Borden*'s Union government over the opposition of Sir Wilfrid Laurier*. Ever the Liberal loyalist, Kennedy supported Laurier as his leader, but he left himself room to manoeuvre. Although he was consistently critical of the government's application of the Military Service Act, especially to farmers, he did not attack the act itself since he believed that conscription was the best way to end the war.

During the campaign, Kennedy endured taunts of disloyalty and the likelihood of a large military vote for Wigle. His own candidacy, however, had behind it the high-powered, severely patriotic Victory Loan drive led by Gordon Morton McGregor, head of the local Ford plant and a strong Laurier Liberal. Kennedy won by 446 votes. Laurier made him the opposition's finance critic, a natural fit for a businessman of his calibre. Though he had little taste for combative behaviour in the House of Commons, the assignment allowed him to flourish as a novice parliamentarian and to hone his skills as a presenter of fact. In his first speech in the commons, which was devoted to the budget of 1918, Kennedy displayed his brilliant mind for figures. He exposed the exorbitant expense of raising Victory Loans, defended the working man by criticizing recent bank mergers and the proposed tax on tea, and, with devastating wit, castigated the special interests that were courting cabinet and scorned finance minister Sir William Thomas White* for living in the United States. While serving as finance critic, he attended as well to his constituency. It was through his effort, for instance, that Windsor-area residents working in Detroit were exempted from American income taxes imposed on them in 1919.

Following Laurier's death in February 1919, Kennedy supported William Lyon Mackenzie King*'s winning bid for the party leadership. The two soon formed "a close and confidential friendship." Kennedy remained finance critic and helped to organize King's tour of western Canada in 1920. In the election of December 1921 the Liberals gained power. In Essex North, a campaign dominated by Gordon McGregor's vehement defence of Liberal tariff policy helped sweep Kennedy to a remarkable 7,195-vote majority. King was so determined to give him a portfolio – he initially lined him up for public works – that he took the unusual step of placing two Ontario Catholics in cabinet, Kennedy as minister of railways and canals and Charles Murphy* as postmaster general. Despite his limited experience in the commons, Kennedy had the advantage of having no ties to the railway interests.

In a ministry overflowing with political landmines, he had to find his way through a range of nagging issues, including demands for lower freight rates, the renewal of the Crowsnest Pass agreement, and the threat of a nation-wide rail strike. These questions, however, paled in comparison with his primary task: implementing the Canadian National Railways Act of 1919. He undertook a three-week tour of Canada's lines in January 1922 and submitted his report in March. The following month he made his statement on railway conditions and policy; aided by an acquiescent commons, he performed flawlessly. His chief triumph as minister was to initiate the processes that led to the proper functioning of the Canadian National. This goal necessitated the careful amalgamation of more than 22,000 miles of track, previously run by the Canadian Northern, the Canadian Government Railways, the Grand Trunk, and the Grand Trunk Pacific, and the establishment of a single board of directors. Kennedy's choice for the CN's first president, in October 1922, was Sir Henry Worth Thornton*.

On 25 August Kennedy had undergone surgery for an undisclosed problem at the Royal Victoria Hospital in Montreal. A second operation a month later largely forced him out of political circulation. One of his last acts was a letter to King on 30 December stressing the opposition of western Ontario Liberals to any material change in the tariff. To recuperate Kennedy went to Stratford, Ont., where two sisters lived, and then to Florida. His unexpected death there on 17 Jan. 1923 shocked the political establishment. The prime minister and his entire cabinet, as well as opposition leader Arthur Meighen*, attended Kennedy's requiem at St Alphonsus' Church in Windsor, where Father Charles Edward Coughlin, later known as the radio priest, delivered the eulogy.

According to the Toronto *Globe*, Kennedy had been "the administrative hope of the Liberal party. He had the persistence, the clear thinking, the business experience, the sound judgment necessary to the solution of the country's biggest problems." Only 54 at his death, he might have become a great minister.

MICHAEL POWER

AO, RG 22-311, no.1923/117. City of Windsor Municipal Arch. (Windsor, Ont.), RG 5, BI-1/1/2: 184 (Ojibway, special council meeting, 22 Jan. 1923). LAC, RG 31, C1, 1871, Toronto, St Patrick's Ward, div.1: 106. *Border Cities Star* (Windsor), 11 Sept. 1918; 1–22 March 1919; 27 April 1920; 23 Nov.–7 Dec. 1921; 19 Jan. 1923. *Evening Record* (Windsor), 8 May 1907; 10 May 1915; 16, 23, 26 Nov. 1917. *Globe*, 10 May 1915, 18 Jan. 1923. [Glencora Bolton Kennedy], *In memory of the late Hon. William Costello Kennedy, P.C., M.P.* (n.p., [1923?]; copy in Univ. of Windsor Arch.). Can., House of Commons, *Debates*, 2 May 1918, 16 June 1919, 21 May 1920, 14 May 1921. *Canadian annual rev.*, 1920: 431; 1922: 306, 468–97. *CPG*, 1922. *Cyclopædia of Canadian biog.* (Rose and Charlesworth), vol.3. R. MacG. Dawson and H. B. Neatby, *William Lyon Mackenzie King: a political biography* (3v., Toronto, 1958–76), 1. *Directory*, Windsor, 1903–16.

KILPATRICK, THOMAS BUCHANAN, Presbyterian minister, author, university professor, and social reformer; b. 27 Sept. 1857 in Glasgow, son of Daniel Ross Kilpatrick and Elizabeth Margaret Ritchie; m. first 21 April 1885 Anna M. K. Orr in Edinburgh, and they had a son and two daughters; m. there secondly 27 June 1899 Jane M. Binnie; d. 20 March 1930 in Toronto.

Thomas B. Kilpatrick was born into a Free Church family. His father, a minister in working-class Glasgow, was a leader of the evangelical revival there in 1859. Kilpatrick studied at the Glasgow Academy and the University of Glasgow, where leading British idealist philosopher Edward Caird reputedly considered him one of his finest students. He graduated in 1877 with first-class honours in mental philosophy. Kilpatrick graduated next in 1881 from the Free Church College in Glasgow; he then pursued further studies at the University of Jena in Germany. In 1882 he was ordained to the parish of Burntisland in Fife, Scotland. Free Church family connections ran deep for Kilpatrick. His first wife was the daughter of Free Church minister George Orr; his second wife was the daughter of Professor William Binnie of the Free Church College in Aberdeen.

Kilpatrick's first published work appeared in *Essays in philosophical criticism* (London, 1883), which featured a new generation of philosophers educated by Caird and Thomas Hill Green of Oxford. The writers sought to apply idealist thinking to the most pressing problems in science, ethics, and religion. Kilpatrick's essay dealt with the pessimism created by contemporary, individualistic philosophies that left people feeling alone, separated from God, nature, and each other. The task of religion was to proclaim the hope provided by the supreme principle of love. This principle, in Kilpatrick's estimation, reached its ultimate expression in Christianity. Throughout his career he sought to promote this interpretation in the classroom, print, parish life, and church committees.

In 1888 Kilpatrick moved to Ferryhill Free Church in Aberdeen. The congregation almost doubled in size during his 11 years there and he gained a reputation for convincing the younger generation of the validity of Christian claims. He continued to write, and turned his attention to popular theology and ethics. In 1888 he edited a collection of sermons by English apologist Joseph Butler for a series of handbooks aimed at Bible classes and private students. His *Christian character: a study in New Testament morality* (Edinburgh, 1899) appeared in a series of Bible-class primers designed to make the results of scholarly study and progressive biblical and theological thought accessible to intelligent readers.

By the time Kilpatrick lectured during the summer session of 1898 at Manitoba College in Winnipeg, he was recognized as an important interpreter of the more traditional wing of the back-to-Christ movement in theology. This school of thought sought to reinterpret, not reject, traditional affirmations in the light of modern scholarship. It focused on the person of Christ rather than on doctrines or creeds, but found in the historical Christ one who was aware of his divinity and who was declared by the Resurrection to be the Son of God. This thinking harmonized an evangelistic piety, an idealistic world-view, and a devout approach to biblical criticism.

In 1899 Kilpatrick received an honorary doctorate from the Free Church College and accepted the invitation of Manitoba College to become professor of systematic theology and apologetics and a joint lecturer in philosophy. During his tenure there an influential group of Protestant ministers, including Principal William Patrick (who had followed Kilpatrick from Scotland in 1900) and Charles William Gordon*, promoted the idea of uniting Protestantism in Canada to ensure the continuing influence of Christianity in a rapidly changing dominion, especially in the cities and in the west. Kilpatrick's enthusiastic support for church union rested on his belief that the context of a new country offered possibilities to create a synthesis of the best of the past through historical evolution guided by the spirit of God. In his view, the best was distinctly moral and Protestant. During debates over the Prohibition referendum in Manitoba in 1902, he publicly supported the Dominion Alliance for the Total Suppression of the Liquor Trade. The church had a duty to help purify politics, he later maintained. In his promotion in 1904 of a grand design for education in Canada, he was forced reluctantly to recognize the constitutional reality of separate schools. In a discussion in 1907 about Mormon immigration, he stated that "the greatest grief in Alberta is the Mormon settlement."

In 1905 Kilpatrick had carried his vision of church unity to the University of Toronto's Knox College, where he had been appointed professor of systematic theology. He and Principal Alfred Gandier formed the continuing core of Knox's faculty over the time it took Canadian Presbyterians, Methodists, and Congregationalists to work through the details and the battles involved in creating the United Church of Canada in 1925. At the same time Kilpatrick continued to venture opinions on public matters and write popular theology. For a series of dictionaries and encyclopedias edited by James Hastings, he authored articles on conscience, philosophy, the character of Christ, the Incarnation, the anger of God, benevolence, salvation, soteriology, and suffering. In addition, he published *New Testament evangelism* (Toronto, 1911), a set of lectures he gave to the Knox alumni conference of 1910, with appendices by John George SHEARER, secretary of the Board of Social Service and Evangelism of the Presbyterian Church in Canada. This book was designed to advance the church's program for liberal evangelism, which combined traditional evangelistic appeal with the promotion of progressive social reform. Kilpatrick's social ethic embraced Victorian middle-class values as applied to the new conditions of immigration, industrialization, and urbanization in Canada. He was an influential member of Shearer's board for many years, participated in a number of evangelistic campaigns, and taught the course on evangelism at Knox. In recognition of his work, he was made a doctor of sacred theology in 1910 by the Hartford Theological Seminary in Connecticut.

Kilpatrick believed that his ideal of an integrated and unified nation required a united Protestantism. Separation should cease, he argued, unless the maintenance of some vital element of Christian salvation was at issue. He sat on the joint committee on church union from 1906 to 1925, and was an influential member of the committee that drafted the doctrinal section of the Basis of Union. In 1919 he wrote that the church needed to consolidate its resources to serve God, not as a machine, but as "an organic whole, a living organism, a spiritual community, whose creative centre is Christ, whose vital power is the Divine spirit, whose members are held together by one faith and love." Especially in the aftermath of World War I, he believed, the ideals of the church needed strong and unified promotion. "War-devastated, distracted by animosities, misled by statesmen, disillusioned as to democracy, rendered desperate by failure of schemes and plans, treaties and conventions, alliances and leagues, the world needs that God ... who is Love," he would write in 1928.

With the creation of the United Church, Kilpatrick and his professorial colleagues left Knox and moved to the college of the new church, eventually named Emmanuel College. Ill health, however, led to his retirement in 1926. He died four years later at his home at 134 St George Street, near the university, from which all three of his children had graduated. Elizabeth Margaret Ritchie, after service overseas as a nurse in 1918–19, taught at Branksome Hall girls' school in Toronto; Dorothy Hamilton, following several years as a missionary in India, became a dean of women at the university; and George Gordon Dinwiddie, a chaplain during the war, later served as principal of the United Theological College in Montreal.

BRIAN J. FRASER

Thomas Buchanan Kilpatrick's publications include "Pessimism and the religious consciousness," in *Essays in philosophical criticism*, ed. Andrew Seth [Pringle-Pattison] and R. B. Haldane (London, 1883), 246–77; *Counsels to a young missioner* (Toronto, 1909); *The Kootenay campaign: evangelism and moral reform, April and May, 1909*, co-written with J. G. Shearer (Toronto, 1910); "William Patrick: 1852–1911; an appreciation," *Presbyterian* (Toronto), new ser., 19 (July–

December 1911): 359–60; "The end of a long ministry," *Presbyterian*, new ser., 25 (July–December 1914): 175; "The church in the twentieth century," *Constructive Quarterly* (New York), 7 (1919): 400–33; and *Our common faith; with a brief history of the church union movement in Canada* by *Kenneth H. Cousland* (Toronto, 1928). In addition, he edited Joseph Butler, *Sermons: sermons I, II, III, upon human nature, or man considered as a moral agent* (Edinburgh, [1888]), and contributed a number of entries to the following theological reference works edited by James Hastings: *A dictionary of Christ and the Gospels* (2v., Edinburgh, 1906–8), 1: 281–91, 796–813; *A dictionary of the Bible; dealing with its language, literature, and contents, including the biblical theology* (5v., Edinburgh, 1906), 1: 468–75; 3: 848–54; *Encyclopædia of religion and ethics* (13v., Edinburgh, 1908–26), 1: 477–82; 2: 474–79; 11: 110–31, 694–725; 12: 1–10.

AO, RG 22-305, no.65419. General Register Office for Scotland (Edinburgh), Blythswood (Glasgow), reg. of births, 27 Sept. 1857; Newington (Edinburgh), reg. of marriages, 21 April 1885; St Andrew (Edinburgh), reg. of marriages, 27 June 1899. UTA, A1973-0026/201(38)–(40). *Globe*, 22 March 1930. *Canadian annual rev.*, 1902, 1907. *Canadian men and women of the time* (Morgan; 1912). B. J. Fraser, "Christianizing the social order: T. B. Kilpatrick's theological vision of the United Church of Canada," *Toronto Journal of Theology*, 12 (1996): 189–200; *Church, college, and clergy: a history of theological education at Knox College, Toronto, 1844–1994* (Montreal and Kingston, Ont., 1995); *The social uplifters: Presbyterian progressives and the Social Gospel in Canada, 1875–1915* (Waterloo, Ont., 1988). *Standard dict. of Canadian biog.* (Roberts and Tunnell). *Univ. of Toronto Monthly*, 30 (1929–30): 376.

KING, GEORGE GERALD, businessman and politician; b. 11 Dec. 1836 in White's Corner (Springfield, Kings County), N.B., son of Malcolm King and Elizabeth Hickson; m. 28 Oct. 1860 Esther Briggs (d. 29 Jan. 1907), and they had five daughters, two of whom died in infancy, and four sons; d. 28 April 1928 in Edmonton.

After leaving school at 13, George Gerald King was employed by White Brothers of Sussex, where his duties were "to count the eggs and sweep the store." Six years later he decided to seek his fortune in Upper Canada but turned down a job in a grocery store when he learned that he would be required to sell liquor; instead he returned to Sussex. The Whites recommended him to Daniel Briggs of nearby Salmon River, who needed a clerk, and four years after starting work with Briggs, King married his employer's sister. Eventually he took over the business. Realizing that Salmon River was a backwater, he built a general store and a sawmill 12 miles south, at what is now the centre of Chipman. He operated the business as G. G. and W. C. King, in partnership with his brother. After William C. King died, it was reorganized as the King Lumber Company. With coalmines and lumbering operations nearby, in which George King had substantial interests, the settlement of Chipman flourished.

His extensive trade with the United States in shingles, laths, and other wood products made King a supporter of free trade. He built four schooners to facilitate these exports and strongly promoted railway transportation. Through his Liberal connections, he became a commissioner of the Central Railway, which ran through Chipman. King twice served as president of the New Brunswick Liberal Association, in 1887 and 1896. He was also a member of the Queens County Council and its warden in 1876–77.

King first entered federal politics in the election of 1878, when he won the Queens seat for the Liberals; he was re-elected four years later. But in the two following elections he became embroiled in the savage parish-pump politicking that characterized New Brunswick in these years. In 1887 he ran against Conservative George Frederick Baird, a Saint John lawyer, and received 61 votes more than Baird. To the amazement of many, however, the returning officer, John R. Dunn, ruled King's election invalid on the grounds that his deposit had not been paid by his official agent, and declared Baird elected by acclamation. King sought a recount in court, but Baird argued that there were no ballots to count since there had been no election. Judge William Henry Tuck* of the Supreme Court decided in Baird's favour. John Valentine Ellis*, the Liberal MP for Saint John, in an editorial in the *Saint John Globe* that earned him a contempt of court charge, accused Tuck of partisanship and called his conduct "a scandal and an outrage of the most abominable character."

The "dirty election" in Queens caused a national furore and lengthy debate in the House of Commons. The issue was referred to the standing committee on privileges and elections, and Dunn was summoned to appear before the bar of the house to explain his decision. The committee concluded that the matter more properly belonged under the Dominion Controverted Elections Act. Baird announced that, regardless of the committee's finding, he would resign. A by-election was held in January 1888, generously supplied with both money and liquor. Baird won by a 111-vote margin, but stories of stuffed ballot boxes and voter irregularities were rampant. King challenged the outcome in court under the controverted elections act. He lost, and Baird again took his seat in the commons.

The King–Baird enmity continued into the 1891 federal election. King initially won the contest by 29 votes, but his joy was short-lived. Baird claimed that King's agents had bribed 30 voters, and King counterattacked with a similar charge. The case went before Supreme Court judge Acalus Lockwood Palmer. Baird and King agreed to abide by the court's decision, and both admitted bribery by their agents. But while Baird complied with the law and submitted the names of those bribed, King did not, and the judge reduced his votes, giving Baird the majority.

Redistribution in the 1890s resulted in the new

riding of Sunbury and Queens. King was returned in the federal election of 1896, in which Wilfrid Laurier*'s Liberals triumphed. When Laurier offered a cabinet post to New Brunswick premier Andrew George Blair*, King resigned to allow Blair to enter the commons in a by-election. On 18 December he was rewarded with a summons to the Senate, where he would remain for 31 years.

As a member of parliament, King had focused on New Brunswick issues. He supported government dredging of waterways in his constituency and was critical of Sir John A. Macdonald*'s National Policy as detrimental to the province's industries. He contended that the Maritime provinces were not getting their fair share of immigration, which was being directed to western Canada. When the federal government considered extending the franchise to the native peoples, King expressed his outrage.

He rarely spoke in the Senate, though he did address the upper house at length on 17 June 1904 in support of an all-Canadian route for the National Transcontinental Railway, through Edmundston, N.B., and southeast to Moncton, where it would connect with the Intercolonial. He argued that the connection with Moncton would encourage more Canadian grain and other freight to be handled through Saint John and Halifax, rather than Portland, Maine, and Boston. When it looked as if the railway might go through Salmon Creek instead of Chipman, King used his political influence to have it rerouted through his home community, even though a high bridge would have to be constructed.

George Gerald King lived long enough to see two of his sons elected to public office: George Herbert as a member of the New Brunswick legislature for Queens and James Horace* first to the British Columbia legislature and then to the House of Commons (he would eventually hold a cabinet post and a seat in the Senate). When he died in 1928, King was living with one of his daughters in Edmonton; aged 91, he was the oldest member of the upper house.

WENDELL E. FULTON

PANB, MC 1156. Frank Baird, *History of the parish of Chipman* (Sackville, N.B., 1946). Can., House of Commons, *Debates*; Senate, *Debates*. *Canadian directory of parl.* (Johnson). *Canadian men and women of the time* (Morgan; 1898 and 1912). F. A. McGrand, *Backward glances at Sunbury and Queens* (Fredericton, 1967). *Prominent people of New Brunswick ...*, comp. C. H. McLean ([Saint John], 1937).

KING, LEONORA ANNETTA. *See* HOWARD

KLOTZ, OTTO JULIUS, surveyor, civil servant, astronomer, and author; b. 31 March 1852 in Preston (Cambridge), Upper Canada, son of Otto Klotz and

Elise (Elizabeth) Wilhelm; m. 4 Dec. 1873 Marie C. Widenmann (Wiedeman), and they had three sons and a daughter; d. 28 Dec. 1923 in Ottawa.

Otto Klotz Sr immigrated from Kiel (Germany) to New York City in 1837 and then settled in Preston. Married in 1839 to the German-born daughter of a Wilmot Township farmer, he became a successful brewer, innkeeper, court clerk, and educationist. Otto J. Klotz attended Galt Grammar School and in 1869 entered the University of Toronto on a scholarship. Dissatisfied with its training in science, he transferred in 1870 to the University of Michigan in Ann Arbor, where he studied with astronomer James Craig Watson*. While there he met his future wife, the daughter of the German consul. After graduating as a civil engineer in 1872, he returned to Preston to practise as a surveyor. He quickly obtained his qualifications as a dominion land surveyor and, on 19 Nov. 1877, the more coveted designation of dominion topographical surveyor.

Klotz joined the federal Department of the Interior as a contract surveyor in 1879. His early work was on the prairies, although he led an expedition in 1884 to search for possible ports on Hudson Bay for a railway terminus [*see* Andrew Robertson Gordon*]. Beginning in 1885, he surveyed sections of the Canadian Pacific Railway belt through British Columbia. In order to tie these surveys to the prairie grid, astronomical observations for latitude and longitude were required. Since no trans-Canada telegraph line existed, he chose Seattle as his astronomical base, and, by employing western telegraphs to convey stellar readings from other points, he moved inland from Victoria to Revelstoke. In 1889 the federal government dispatched him to the Alaska panhandle to look into American infringement on reputed British territory. Klotz supported the American position on the inland boundary of the panhandle, so, when the international boundary commission was nominated in 1892, it was William Frederick King*, not Klotz, who obtained the British government's post.

Klotz had worked with both King, the chief inspector of surveys for the interior department, and Édouard DEVILLE, the surveyor general, during many years of western surveying. In 1890, when King became chief astronomer, he and Deville established a small observatory in Ottawa and they wanted Klotz, who still lived in Preston in the winter, on their staff. He moved to Ottawa in 1892 but continued to do fieldwork; in 1893–94, for instance, he performed surveys in the area of the Unuk River and the Bradfield Canal in the Alaska panhandle. In 1896 he formally entered the permanent civil service as a chief clerk and astronomer. He was deeply involved with King in the organization of the Dominion Observatory in the late 1890s, though they had strong differences of opinion about its site and nature. While it was being constructed, Klotz travelled to the South Pacific in 1903–

4 to determine the longitudes of points along the All-Red cable line, which connected Vancouver with Australia and New Zealand. By the time of his return, the observatory was nearly ready.

During the next decade, Klotz's work centred on geophysics, an area in which he had no training but great interest. He had already made magnetic observations during his Hudson Bay trek and had undertaken gravity measurements in Canada in 1902 and in the South Pacific. From 1907 he directed a Canada-wide magnetic survey (a field survey to measure local values of magnetic declination, dip, and strength, which were then compared to observatory standards). He was drawn particularly to the new science of seismology, where he developed the sub-field of microseisms. Following the San Francisco earthquake of 1906, the American Association for the Advancement of Science formed a seismology committee, which included Klotz, who persuaded the Canadian government to join the International Seismological Association in 1907 and who would represent Canada at several international seismological conferences. Thanks to Klotz, who was made assistant chief astronomer on 1 April 1911, the Dominion Observatory became one of the most important seismological stations in the world; it issued bulletins on earthquakes and set up seismographs throughout Canada.

When King died in 1916, Klotz was his likely successor, but strong anti-German feeling in the midst of war precluded his immediate appointment. Both the observatory and the Geodetic Survey of Canada were directed by King's former, non-scientist secretary, Wilbert Simpson, for nearly a year and a half. Internal division was rife, and morale plummeted. In the summer of 1917 the entire scientific staff signed a memorandum to interior minister William James Roche* in support of Klotz, whose appointment as chief astronomer came in September. During the interregnum, the sprawling astronomical branch, including the observatory, the Geodetic Survey, the boundary surveys, and the new Dominion Astrophysical Observatory in Victoria, had broken into separate organizations. Klotz's early administration was bedevilled by friction with Noel John Ogilvie of the Geodetic Survey and John Stanley Plaskett* of the Victoria observatory. The loss of staff under both Simpson and Klotz required some reorganization, particularly in the geophysical sections. When Canada joined the new International Geodetic and Geophysical Union and the International Astronomical Union, the national committees that were set up had Klotz as an ex officio member. At the first meetings of both organizations, in Rome in 1922, he went as one of Canada's official representatives. During his last year in office, heart trouble curtailed his ability to work. He died in December 1923, and was survived by his wife and two sons, one of whom, Oskar*, was a renowned pathologist.

Otto Klotz appears to have been a strong personality; many liked him, others were quite repelled. He had a high opinion of himself and did not suffer fools gladly. Musical interests helped fill his spare time. His wife, Marie, caused him some concern early in the war on account of her pro-German pronouncements, but theirs seems to have been a solid relationship.

Professionally Klotz had been a lifelong organizer. He was the first president of the Association of Dominion Land Surveyors (1882–86) and was prominent in the formation of the surveyors' associations of Manitoba and Ontario. A DLS examiner in British Columbia from 1885, he served on the examining board for dominion surveyors between 1887 and his death. In addition, he was president of the Association of Mechanics' Institutes of Ontario in 1884–85. In Ottawa, he was considered the founder of the Carnegie Library, and he served as president of both the Canadian Club and the Ottawa Literary and Scientific Society. A fellow of the Royal Society of Canada, the American Association for the Advancement of Science, and the Royal Astronomical Society in England, he was president of the Royal Astronomical Society of Canada (1908), vice-president of the American Astronomical Society (1920), and president of the Seismological Society of America (1920). He was awarded honorary LLDs by the University of Toronto (1904) and the University of Pittsburgh (1916) and a D.SC. by the University of Michigan (1913). Besides his official reports, which were often loaded with detailed calculations, he authored nearly 100 papers, many of a popular nature, and he was a gifted speaker on scientific matters. According to his obituary in the *Ottawa Citizen*, "His public lectures had a breeziness and charm that put him in instant touch with his audiences."

Klotz headed the Dominion Observatory for too short a period to make any lasting organizational changes, but his development of geophysics – a field one might not have expected in an astronomical institution – laid the groundwork for the later eminence of the Canadian government's geophysical research.

RICHARD A. JARRELL

Papers relating to Otto Julius Klotz's career are in LAC, MG 30, B13. The most important part of this collection is his diaries, which run unbroken from 1866 to his death. Photographs of Klotz in the LAC include PA-12295, PA-27800, PA-43037, and C-131090. His official reports as a surveyor are found in the annual reports (available in Can., Parl., *Sessional papers*) of the Dept. of the Interior, which also include those he wrote as chief astronomer, and in the *Pubs.* of the Dominion Observatory. Between 1905 and 1921 he contributed some 50 articles to the Royal Astronomical Soc. of Canada, *Journal* (Toronto), most of a popular nature on geophysical matters.

AO, RG 22-354, no.11510; RG 80-8-0-161, no.17966; RG 80-8-0-915, no.11278. LAC, RG 2, 4, vol.49, no.2756.

Knott

Galt Reporter (Galt, Ont.), 8 July 1892. *Ottawa Citizen*, 29 Dec. 1923. Can., Parl., *Sessional papers*, 1898, no.16b: 20; 1914, no.25, pt.III: 49; 1918, no.30; 1919, no.30: 182. *Canadian men and women of the time* (Morgan; 1898 and 1912). J. H. Hodgson, *The heavens above and the earth beneath: a history of the dominion observatories* (2v., Ottawa, 1989–94), 1. R. A. Jarrell, *The cold light of dawn: a history of Canadian astronomy* (Toronto, 1988). J. E. Middleton and Fred Landon, *The province of Ontario: a history, 1615–1927* (5v., Toronto, 1927–[28]), 3: 171–74. R. M. Stewart, "Dr Otto Klotz," Royal Astronomical Soc. of Canada, *Journal* (Toronto), 18 (1924): 1–8. D. W. Thomson, *Men and meridians: the history of surveying and mapping in Canada* (3v., Ottawa, 1966–69), 2–3. *Who's who in Canada*, 1922.

KNOTT, CAROLINE SARAH (Tate), Methodist lay missionary and teacher; b. 1842 in London, England, eldest daughter of John Knott, a piano maker, and Caroline Sarah ——; m. 24 Oct. 1879 the Reverend Charles Montgomery Tate in Fort Simpson (Lax Kw'alaams), B.C.; d. 7 May 1930 in Victoria.

Caroline Knott came to Upper Canada with her family from England in 1856 or early in 1857. Shortly after their arrival in Hamilton, Caroline's mother died, leaving her in charge of seven brothers and sisters. When they grew up, she applied to the general committee of the Wesleyan Methodist Missionary Society for mission work. She was posted as a schoolteacher to aboriginal children, first at Rice Lake and then at Sault Ste Marie. When the call came for teachers to go to the Methodist mission at Fort Simpson in 1875, Caroline responded and was chosen, despite the fact that she was already 33 and was somewhat older than most applicants. At Fort Simpson she established herself as a good worker, winning the esteem of prominent Methodist missionary Thomas Crosby*. Four years after her arrival, she met and married Charles Tate. Together they embarked on over 31 years of missionary service, the longest of any couple in British Columbia, including postings at Bella Bella, Rivers Inlet, Burrard Inlet, Clayoquot, and Chilliwack.

Caroline Tate was both remarkable and typical of her time. The mere fact that her missionary career lasted so long indicates incredible fortitude and faith. Historian Rosemary Gagan has argued that home mission work, particularly among the First Nations, was often more physically and psychologically demanding than similar work in Asia. The majority of home missionaries left their jobs within five years and few continued until their retirement. Even at the time of her marriage, Caroline had outlasted many of her contemporaries in Fort Simpson. In total, she worked as a missionary among the First Nations for over 35 years and spent an additional 15 years in church organizations in Victoria. In many of her attitudes towards her work and towards the indigenous peoples with whom she associated, however, she was typical of her time.

As a missionary, Caroline lived an adventurous life for which little in her previous experience would have prepared her. She worked at a time of high mortality among the First Nations and so witnessed countless epidemics and deaths. Always reliant on the goodwill of aboriginal leaders for their survival, the Tates boarded in traditional longhouses, travelled in canoes over the ocean, and, when they reached a new posting, often had to build the mission from the ground up. On their arrival at Bella Bella in 1881, for instance, the crew of the steamer *Princess Louise* made a raft out of the lumber the Tates had brought to construct a house and a church and set them adrift on it as they approached the village. The Heiltsuk chief Humcheet organized a party to rescue the missionaries and welcomed them into his home. While other missionaries soon tired of the damp isolation of the northwest coast, the Tates endured.

Despite her many varied experiences in the field, Caroline Tate shared the negative attitudes towards aboriginal peoples then common among missionaries. Like them, she disdained aboriginal culture, particularly the feasting rituals associated with marriage and death. She approached indigenous healers with fear and loathing. Her attitudes towards women were mixed. She frequently blamed the deaths of children on what she saw as the poor housekeeping skills of their mothers. Yet she also viewed herself as saving indigenous women from a misogynist culture. On a speaking tour of Ontario in 1897 she reported to audiences of the Woman's Missionary Society and the Woman's Christian Temperance Union that only the work of missionaries saved the lives and honour of aboriginal women and children. Though Indian agents and others rightly disputed her claims, she reported that infanticide was widespread, that children were sold into marriage, and that widows were often killed or maimed. She supported the ban on the potlatch on the grounds that the traditional feasting abused women by forcing them to generate wealth by prostitution. Her diary is replete with references to her efforts to disrupt aboriginal funerary practices with prayer and singing. She reports few aboriginal women friends, although her husband's diary frequently refers to indigenous men he respected and relied on. Her fear of aboriginal culture never abated and fuelled her work to replace it with Christianity.

Like many other missionaries, Tate believed that cultural change could best be accomplished by removing children from their families. At Chilliwack she started to take into her home aboriginal girls who were orphaned or who were estranged from their community. Out of this endeavour emerged the Coqualeetza Home (later the Coqualeetza Institute), a Methodist boarding school which opened in 1889 on Stó:lo land at Sardis. Like that of many residential schools, Coqualeetza's legacy is mixed. It was not immune from the cultural, emotional, and physical abuse that plagued other institutes. A report issued in 1905, after the Tates had moved on to another post, stated that over 20 per cent of Coqualeetza graduates died shortly after they left the school and pointed to poor institutional conditions as the cause. Yet the institute also helped produce a generation of aboriginal leaders in the province, of whom Haida chief Peter Kelly* is the most prominent example.

The Tates retired to Victoria in 1910. Caroline Tate remained active in church work until 1925, becoming the first member of the Woman's Missionary Society of the Methodist Church of British Columbia. She died in 1930. Charles Tate died three years later.

MARY-ELLEN KELM

AO, RG 22-205, no.2073. BCA, MS-0303. British Columbia Vital Statistics Agency (Victoria), Marriage registration records, 1872–1925 (mfm. at Victoria Geneal. Soc.). LAC, RG 10, 6422, file 869-1, pt.1; RG 31, C1, 1861, Hamilton, [Ont.], St Lawrence Ward: 368; 1871, Hamilton, St Andrew's Ward, div.1: 65. *New Outlook* (Toronto), 4 June 1930. *Victoria Daily Times*, 7 May 1930. *Directory*, Hamilton, 1858, 1862–63. R. R. Gagan, *A sensitive independence: Canadian Methodist women missionaries in Canada and the Orient, 1881–1925* (Montreal and Kingston, Ont., 1992). Jan Gould, *Women of British Columbia* (Saanichton, B.C., 1975). C. M. Tate, "A story of missionary adventure," *Western Recorder* (Victoria), December 1929: 20–22. *Western Recorder*, May 1930. Margaret Whitehead, "Women were made for such things: women missionaries in British Columbia, 1850s–1940s," *Atlantis* (Wolfville, N.S.), 14 (1988–89): 141–50.

KNOWLING, FANNIE (Fanny) (McNeil), suffragist and artist; b. 14 March 1869 in St John's, one of the ten children of George Knowling and Elizabeth Upham; m. there 5 July 1899 Hector McNeil, and they had one son, who died in infancy, and two daughters; d. there 23 Feb. 1928.

Fannie Knowling grew up in an affluent and enlightened family. Her father, a native of Devon, was a prosperous St John's merchant and a member of the Legislative Council from 1897 to 1923. Both he and his wife, also from Devon, were early supporters of women's suffrage. Some of Fannie's school years were spent in England, where she may have received formal art instruction. Her "gifted brush" and interest in art were constants. In 1925 she and fellow artist Albert Edward Harris would begin organizing exhibitions of local and foreign art, ventures that grew into the formation of the Newfoundland Society of Art, of which she was the first president.

Following her marriage in 1899 to Hector McNeil, a native of Scotland and paymaster of the Newfoundland Railway, she steadily became an activist in social causes such as child welfare and health services, and in intellectual interests such as the Ladies' Reading Room and Current Events Club. This association (later renamed the Old Colony Club) was founded in 1909 by a group of middle-class St John's women, among them Harriette Armine Gosling [Nutting*] (wife of William Gilbert GOSLING), and was devoted "solely to the mental refreshment of women, in the shape of a reading-room, containing a well-selected assortment of leading magazines and papers." On Saturday afternoons the reading-room became the Current Events Club, to which "Prominent Citizens" were invited to lecture. From the outset women's suffrage was a topic of debate. A member later recalled: "One day Mrs. McNeil was arranging the magazines and asked what we were discussing. We told her and from that time onwards she became our leader and the greatest worker for the cause." In 1920 suffragists of the club, energized by victories won elsewhere, formed the Women's Franchise League (sometimes known as the Women's Suffrage League and the Committee for the Enfranchisement of Women) and launched a campaign to secure the vote for women, a revival of an earlier attempt in the 1890s.

As secretary of the League, Fannie was supported by her husband, Hector. When threatened with dismissal by the anti-suffrage government of Sir Richard Anderson Squires*, this quiet man was reported as saying, "I told him he could jolly well go to the devil." By this time the McNeil home had become the headquarters of a vigorous campaign which saw systematic lobbying of politicians, a blitz of letters to publicize the cause, debates and rallies, and the collection of 20,000 signatures on an island-wide petition. Recalled a contemporary: "Mrs. McNeil was a great favourite. She never lost her head. Was utterly natural and sincere. The crowd loved her."

The League's chief antagonist was Squires. All through 1920 and 1921 he equivocated, his government defeating the necessary legislation for the vote in 1920 but promising to reconsider it in six months' time, when it was allowed to die in committee. The League's leadership pressed on, however, and achieved victory on 9 March 1925 when a new prime minister, Walter Stanley Monroe*, piloted through the House of Assembly legislation giving Newfoundland women of 25 years or older the right to vote for, and stand as, candidates in general elections (the voting age for men was 21, an inequality that remained until 1946). The Women's Franchise League held a victory banquet and disbanded in triumph. The first opportunity for women to stand for election came in the St John's municipal contest of December 1925. Three women put themselves forward – Fannie McNeil and May Kennedy, who ran for the newly formed Women's Party, and Julia Salter* Earle, a labour candidate – but all three were defeated. The first general election in which women could vote would take place in 1928.

Fannie McNeil died of cancer on 23 Feb. 1928 and

was buried in the General Protestant Cemetery in St John's. An obituary tribute said, "To her in supreme measure was due the placing of the Woman Franchise Act on the Statute Book, resulting from a campaign conducted in a manner unexcelled in any land."

ANNE HART

Centre for Newfoundland Studies, Memorial Univ. of Nfld (St John's), Arch., MF-157 (Sir Richard Squires papers). *Daily News* (St John's), 24–25 Feb. 1928. [Agnes Ayre], "Current Events Club – woman suffrage – Newfoundland Society of Art," in *The book of Newfoundland*, ed. J. R. Smallwood *et al.* (6v., St John's, 1937–75; vols.1–2 repr. [1968] and 1979), 1: 199–201. T. [L.] Bishop, "Newfoundland's struggle for the women's franchise" (course paper, Memorial Univ. of Nfld, 1982). *Distaff* (St John's), 1916: 18. *DNLB* (Cuff *et al.*). M. I. Duley, "'The radius of her influence for good': the rise and triumph of the women's suffrage movement in Newfoundland, 1909–1925," in *Pursuing equality: historical perspectives on women in Newfoundland and Labrador*, ed. Linda Kealey (St John's, 1993), 14–65; *Where once our mothers stood we stand: women's suffrage in Newfoundland, 1890–1925* (Charlottetown, 1993). Nfld, *Acts*, 1925: c.7. Janice O'Brien, "Woman's suffrage in Newfoundland: a determined goal" (course paper, Memorial Univ. of Nfld, 1982). Gaynor Rowe, "The woman suffrage movement in Newfoundland" (course paper, Memorial Univ. of Nfld, 1973).

L

LACASSE, ZACHARIE (baptized **Pierre-Zacharie Cassé**), Roman Catholic priest, Oblate of Mary Immaculate, missionary, colonizer, preacher, and author; b. 9 March 1845 in Saint-Jacques-de-l'Achigan (Saint-Jacques), Lower Canada, son of Joseph Cassé, a farmer, and Marguerite Mirault; d. 28 Feb. 1921 in Gravelbourg, Sask., and was buried in Lebret, Sask.

Zacharie Lacasse was born into a poor and devout family. A difficult child, he was known as an unruly, mischievous, and not overly talented pupil. From 1857 to 1865 he did his classical studies at the Collège de L'Assomption, in Quebec, where Wilfrid Laurier* was also a student. He entered the noviciate of the Oblates of Mary Immaculate in Lachine on 28 Aug. 1869 and made his perpetual vows on 29 Aug. 1871. After completing his theological studies at the University of Ottawa, he was ordained to the priesthood on 27 April 1873 by Bishop Joseph-Bruno Guigues*. Within a few weeks Lacasse left Ottawa to minister among the Montagnais and French Canadians in the region of Betsiamites in the province of Quebec. From there he travelled to the interior of Labrador. He spent the winter of 1875–76 at Baie des Esquimaux (Hamilton Inlet); there he came in contact with Naskapi and Inuit and began learning Inuktitut. He reportedly compiled a dictionary for this language that was lost when the whaling ship transporting his luggage sank. In 1880 he went as far as Fort Chimo (Kuujjuaq), Que., on Ungava Bay.

That year, at the request of Archbishop Elzéar-Alexandre Taschereau* of Quebec, Lacasse agreed to turn his energies to colonization. He continued doing this work until 1883, especially in the area that would become the township of Normandin in the Lac-Saint-Jean region, and in the Beauce, within the parishes of Saint-Prosper and Saint-Zacharie (named in his honour). He is thought to have associated at that time with Arthur Dansereau*, Joseph-Israël Tarte*, and Jules-Paul Tardivel*, and to have persuaded Tardivel to found in 1881 the ultramontane Quebec newspaper *La Vérité*, to which he contributed. His evangelical activities were not confined to his preaching; he also took pen in hand to disseminate clerical-nationalist ideas among a larger number of believers. The apostolic writings he began to publish at that time would meet with extraordinary popular success. His first "mine," to use his own expression, came out at Quebec in 1880 under the title *Une mine produisant l'or et l'argent, découverte et mise en réserve pour les cultivateurs seuls*. Written from a moralistic stance, this work sought to check emigration to the United States. Lacasse proposed a system in which missionaries acting as colonization agents would recruit patrons, who would provide the financial aid new settlers needed. Settlers, in turn, would have to work a certain number of hours for their benefactor. Lacasse also set out a scheme for dividing the land that would keep the inhabitants close together rather than isolated on widely separated parcels of land; as well, he presented a plan for constructing roads and railways and offered practical advice about cultivating the soil. This volume went through seven editions in one year, and it was soon followed by *Une mine de pierres détachées à l'usage des cultivateurs*, which was brought out at Quebec in 1881. This somewhat autobiographical essay linked working on the land and being a good Catholic, and it emphasized the importance, in farming, of taking care not to exhaust the soil. In the volume Lacasse spoke out against, among other things, intemperance, luxury, freemasonry, and unsavoury reading material. He tried to encourage farmers to show their faith by paying the tithe, and to convince them that the Roman Catholic religion was superior to all others. "Remember this, my good country folk: on the day you no longer want to be the friends of the clergy, you will be the slaves of libertines. The choice is yours."

In 1883 Lacasse received a new assignment. He was attached to the Montreal house and preached at retreats in Canada and the United States. He would remain in this new field of evangelism until 1896. According to his contemporaries, he had the gift of eloquence, a sense of irony and earthy humour, and quick repartee, and he larded his talks with amusing stories and puns that appealed to the general public. His written pieces, set out as conversations, were highly representative of his preaching. During these years, his publications once again enhanced his fame. Lacasse's *Une nouvelle mine; le prêtre et ses détracteurs*, published in Montreal in 1892, was an apologia for the Roman Catholic clergy in Canada; 32,000 copies reportedly were quickly sold. The following year, *Une quatrième mine; dans le camp ennemi* came out in Montreal. It denounced the "enemies of religion" and especially a few "irreligious journalists." Lacasse took aim at the French anticlericals, whom he referred to as *francissons*, and he also attacked, among others, the Alliance Française. This essay, which Louis Fréchette* lost no opportunity to revile, aroused the ire of liberals and touched off a major debate in the media. Lacasse attacked Laurent-Olivier DAVID, president of the Association Saint-Jean-Baptiste de Montréal, and Charles-Horace Saint-Louis, a lawyer for the Montreal *Canada-Revue*, who had brought suit against Archbishop Édouard-Charles Fabre* for having placed the newspaper under an interdict. His polemics described Saint-Louis as a renegade, an enemy of the church, a bad Catholic, and a citizen unworthy of being numbered among his compatriots. Saint-Louis sued Lacasse for libel, claiming damages of 25,000 "francs," but the case was stillborn, for the plaintiff apparently withdrew his complaint in the face of the defendant's pugnacious attitude. In 1895 Lacasse returned to the fray with *Une cinquième mine; autour du drapeau*, a defence of Christianity published in Montreal. The fourth "mine" had met with some disapproval from Archbishop Fabre, however, and he followed the new one with keen interest. It seems that in the wake of the stir Lacasse occasioned by his writings, his superiors decided to send him to western Canada.

Thus in 1896 Lacasse left Quebec for St Boniface (Winnipeg). In 1897–98 he was in charge of the parish of Sainte-Marie in Winnipeg. He took to the road again in 1900 to preach at retreats in North Dakota. From November 1902 to March 1903 he was interim curé in the parish of Saint-Jean-Baptiste in Duluth, Minn. In 1905 he was recalled to St Boniface, where

he helped set up the Juniorat de la Sainte-Famille, a minor seminary for young people wishing to enter the religious life, and he served as its director in 1905–6. He also wrote articles for *L'Ami du foyer*, a periodical published by the Oblates of Mary Immaculate, notably "Les légendes du peuple canadien à l'ombre de la croix," a series of some 40 articles which came out between 1905 and 1918. After taking part as a theologian in the first Plenary Council at Quebec in 1909, he returned to Duluth and resumed his preaching tours, travelling as far as Wisconsin. In both western Canada and Minnesota, Lacasse became involved in intrigues and local polemics. In 1918, for example, Bishop Timothy Corbett of Crookston, Minn., accused him of slander in connection with a controversy concerning the enlargement of a hospital in Duluth.

In 1919 Zacharie Lacasse returned to the Juniorat de la Sainte-Famille. In 1920 his superiors appointed him spiritual director of the newly opened college in Gravelbourg, where he died on 28 Feb. 1921 of a heart ailment aggravated by diabetes. The previous year, he had published his autobiography in St Boniface. Its title, *Une mine de souvenirs*, recalls the works that made him the epitome of popular writing on ultramontane doctrines and teachings. Close to the land by birth and an eloquent preacher, he unconditionally advocated the doctrines of intransigent Roman Catholics. His intention was to make known the truth and defend it, as well as to condemn and deplore the errors denounced by Pope Pius IX in the Syllabus of December 1864.

GILLES LESAGE

In addition to the works already mentioned, Zacharie Lacasse's publications include *Trois contes sauvages* (Québec, 1882); *Difficulté scolaire de Manitoba par questions et réponses à la portée de tous* (Québec, 1897); and, under the pseudonym of Jean Des Prairies, *Une visite dans les écoles du Manitoba* (Montréal, 1897).

Researchers can find a voluminous file on Father Lacasse at the Arch. Deschâtelets, Oblats de Marie-Immaculée, Ottawa (HEC 2130.Z16C), including letters, an "Essai de bio-bibliographie: le révérend père Zacharie Lacasse, O.M.I." by Huguette Renaud (typescript, 1953) (Z16C26ex.1), and "Le R.P. Zacharie Lacasse, O.M.I." by Normand Lafleur (typescript) (Z16C4). Father Lacasse's baptismal record is at ANQ-M, CE605-S31, 10 mars 1845. The journal *Missions de la Congrégation des missionnaires oblats de Marie Immaculée* (Marseille, etc.) contains, among other items, letters and reports prepared by Lacasse during his years of service as a missionary; this material can be located by consulting its general index.

Les Cloches de Saint-Boniface (Saint-Boniface [Winnipeg]), 18 (1919): 19–20, 274; 20 (1921): 44–47. *Le Devoir*, 1er mars 1921. *La Liberté* (Saint-Boniface), 12 oct. 1932. *Le Monde* (Montréal), 27 oct., 15 déc. 1893. *L'Oiseau-mouche* (Chicoutimi, Qué.), 11 nov. 1893. *La Patrie*, 18 nov. 1893; 19 févr., 21 juill. 1894. *Le Patriote de l'Ouest* (Prince Albert, Sask.), 2 mars 1921. J.-B.-A. Allaire, *Dictionnaire biogra-*

phique du clergé canadien-français (6v., Montréal et Saint-Hyacinthe, Qué., 1908–34). Marcel Bernad, *Bibliographie des missionnaires oblats de Marie Immaculée* (Liège, Belgique, 1922). Gaston Carrière, *Dictionnaire biographique des oblats de Marie-Immaculée au Canada* (4v., Ottawa, 1976–89), 2: 217–18; 3: 47–48; *Histoire documentaire de la Congrégation des missionnaires oblats de Marie-Immaculée dans l'est du Canada* (12v., Ottawa, 1957–75), 8. Ernest Cyr, *Le révérend père Zacharie Lacasse, O.M.I.: conférence donnée sous les auspices de l'Union canadienne à Saint-Boniface, le 6 novembre 1924* (Lyon, France, et Saint-Boniface, 1925). Lionel Dorge, *Introduction à l'étude des Franco-Manitobains; essai historique et bibliographique* (Saint-Boniface, 1973). *Esquisses: la ville de Duluth; l'Église catholique et la colonie franco-américaine à Duluth* (Duluth, Minn., 1910). Arthur Joyal, "Un missionnaire patriote: le R.P. Zacharie Lacasse, O.M.I.," *Almanach de la langue française* (Montréal), 7 (1922): 76–80. Le Jeune, *Dictionnaire*. Josaphat Magnan, "Il faisait rire, pour faire du bien," *L'Ami du foyer* (Saint-Boniface), 52 (1956), no.3: 12; no.4: 13. A.-C. Morin, *Dans la maison du père; nécrologie sacerdotale du diocèse de Rimouski, 1867–1967* (Rimouski, Qué., 1967). J.-P. Tardivel, *Mélanges ou recueil d'études religieuses, sociales, politiques et littéraires* (3v., Québec, 1887–1903), 2: v–vii.

LACOSTE, Sir ALEXANDRE (baptized **Alphonse-Charles-Alexandre**), lawyer, professor, politician, and judge; b. 13 Jan. 1842 in Boucherville, Lower Canada, son of Louis Lacoste*, a notary and politician, and Marie-Antoinette-Thaïs Proulx; m. 8 May 1866 Marie-Louise Globensky in Montreal, and they had at least seven daughters and three sons; d. 17 Aug. 1923 in Montreal and was buried 21 August in Notre-Dame-des-Neiges cemetery there.

Alexandre Lacoste did his classical studies at the Séminaire de Saint-Hyacinthe, where he enrolled in 1851. His father's reputation as one of the most highly regarded legal practitioners of his time no doubt drew him to a career in law. After studying at the law faculty of the Université Laval at Quebec in 1858–59, he attended the law school of the Collège Sainte-Marie in Montreal, which was directed by François-Maximilien Bibaud*; there he obtained an LLB. He entered the law office of Pierre Moreau, Gédéon Ouimet*, and Joseph-Adolphe Chapleau* as a clerk. In February 1863 he passed the bar entrance examination brilliantly.

Lacoste practised as a lawyer solely in Montreal. From 1863 to 1891 he was a partner, in turn, with Isaïe-A. Jodoin, Charles-André Leblanc*, Francis Cassidy*, William D. Drummond, Benjamin-A. Globensky, Toussaint Brosseau, François-Joseph Bisaillon, and his son-in-law Henri Gérin-Lajoie. He served as *bâtonnier* of the Montreal bar from 1879 to 1881. Working in particular in commercial law, real estate law, and estate law, he built up a heterogeneous clientele. As a result of the connections he formed in the business world, he sat on a number of boards of direc-

tors, including those of the Manitoba Assurance Company and the Liverpool and London and Globe Insurance Company. He also became chairman of the board of control of the Banque Provinciale du Canada. Because of his activities within the Conservative party, he frequently represented politicians involved in contested elections. In 1882 the provincial government retained him as counsel and negotiator in the sale of the Quebec, Montreal, Ottawa and Occidental Railway to the Canadian Pacific Railway and the syndicate put together by Louis-Adélard Senécal* [*see* Sir Joseph-Adolphe Chapleau], who happened to be one of his clients. He appeared on a number of occasions before Canadian courts at different levels. He also went to London, England, to represent various clients before the Judicial Committee of the Privy Council.

Lacoste was one of the first professors in the law faculty of the Montreal branch of the Université Laval. As was customary, he was granted an honorary LLD when he took up his duties in December 1879. He held the chair of commercial law and maritime law for the rest of his life. At the time he received his appointments, the expansion of the Université Laval to Montreal [*see* Édouard-Charles Fabre*] was meeting with opposition. There were those who questioned its right to open a branch there on the basis of the prerogatives granted in its royal charter. The university undertook to put an end to the controversy by asking the Legislative Assembly to intervene. In 1881 the rector, Thomas-Étienne Hamel, and Lacoste appeared before the committee on private members' bills and successfully defended a measure confirming the university's powers [*see* Chapleau].

Although Lacoste, who was a moderate conservative, was interested in politics, he never sought to become an elected representative. He preferred to carry on his well-established law practice, while exerting influence within the Conservative party, where he helped to resolve thorny matters. Following the Tanneries scandal in 1874, for example, he was among those who concluded that Premier Gédéon Ouimet would have to resign. In 1880 he and a group that included Joseph Tassé*, Louis-Aimé Gélinas, and Jean-Baptiste Renaud* purchased the Conservative newspaper *La Minerve*. He was appointed to the Legislative Council to represent the division of Mille-Isles in 1882. Chapleau, to whom he was apparently an adviser, was premier at the time. Lacoste remained a legislative councillor until December 1883, and in January 1884 he entered the Senate to represent the division of Lorimier. Parliamentary life held little attraction for him. He rarely took the floor in the Senate and his speeches there were far from noteworthy. He concentrated his energy mainly on the work of the committee studying private members' bills.

In 1891, after serving for several months as speaker

of the upper house, Lacoste became chief justice of the Court of Queen's Bench for the province of Quebec, replacing Sir Antoine-Aimé Dorion*. On accepting this prestigious appointment, however, he found that his income was reduced, especially since he stopped practising law at the same time. It was probably for this reason that he would continue to hold company directorships until the federal government forbade the judiciary to do so. According to the law reports, Lacoste frequently wrote the reasons behind the rulings on cases appealed to the Court of Queen's Bench. His judgements were rigorous and concise, but offered scant scholarly elaboration. Unlike some of his colleagues, he confined himself to the arguments raised by the parties to a case.

At the end of the 19th century the administration of justice, in particular its high cost and the unequal division of work among the judges, was widely criticized. Around 1892 Lacoste drew up a plan for judicial reform. He proposed that the judges of the Superior Court be grouped together in large urban centres in order to share the burden more equally, work in a more collegial way, and thus develop a more coherent jurisprudence. Thomas Chase-Casgrain* introduced a bill incorporating Lacoste's suggestions in February 1893, but it did not pass.

In 1907 Lacoste resigned from the bench and returned to the practice of law with his sons Paul and Alexandre. Shortly afterwards he agreed to become president of the Conservative Association of Montreal, a move that drew sharp criticism from his political opponents, including Prime Minister Sir Wilfrid Laurier*, who considered such conduct unacceptable in someone receiving a government pension.

An open-minded man, Lacoste likely encouraged his daughters to participate in social life. Their mother, a ready supporter of charities who for more than 30 years kept a diary chronicling the developments in their life as a middle-class Montreal family, certainly also encouraged such activity. Marie* and Thaïs, who taught themselves the rudiments of law, campaigned for more civil rights for women through their lectures and writings; Justine founded the Hôpital Sainte-Justine in Montreal in 1907. Interested in matters relating to education, Lacoste collaborated, in particular, in a series of lectures on ordinary law for teachers that was organized by Marie in 1905.

Over the years, Lacoste received many honours. He was named a QC by the provincial government in 1876 and by the federal government in 1880. In 1892 he was made a KCMG. Bishop's College gave him an honorary doctorate in 1895.

Alexandre Lacoste remained firmly attached to a rational approach to the law, as Laurent-Olivier DAVID recalled in *Au soir de la vie*: "Nothing brilliant, little polish in his arguments in court or his judicial decisions, but plenty of logic, force, and clarity." In

this respect, he was the model of the kind of lawyer who would increasingly be seen at the beginning of the 20th century. His character traits, his passion for the law, and his success no doubt explain why he was unwilling to sacrifice his professional career in order to hold prominent offices in the world of politics. Despite this reluctance, he agreed to sit in the upper houses of the province and the country. Close to the seat of power, he played a role as an influential, but discreet, adviser to the Conservative party.

SYLVIO NORMAND

ANQ-M, CE601-S22, 13 janv. 1842; CE601-S51, 8 mai 1866; P76. *Le Canada* (Montréal), 18 août 1923. *Le Devoir*, 21 janv. 1919, 17 août 1923. *Gazette* (Montreal), 24 Oct. 1908; 18, 23 Aug. 1923. *Montreal Daily Star*, 17 Aug. 1923. *La Patrie*, 17–18, 21 août 1923. *La Presse*, 17 août 1923. F.-J. Audet, *Les juges en chef de la province de Québec, 1764–1924* (Québec, 1927). L.-P. Audet, *Histoire de l'enseignement au Québec* (2v., Montréal et Toronto, 1971), 2. *BCF*, 1920: 23. [F.-M.] Bibaud, *Supplément à la "Notice historique sur l'enseignement du droit"* ([Montréal?, 1862?]). Can., Senate, *Debates*, 1884–91; *Journals*, 1884–91. *Canada Gazette*, 16 Oct. 1880: 419; 22 Oct. 1892: 767; 25 March 1893: 1767; 10 April 1897: 2015. *Canadian directory of parl.* (Johnson). *CPG*, 1887, 1897. L.-O. David, *Au soir de la vie* (Montréal, [1924]). *Directory*, Montreal, 1863–91. *DPQ*. A[lfred] D[uclos] De Celles, "Sir Alexandre Lacoste," trans. Mrs Carroll Ryan [M. A. McIver], in *Men of the day: a Canadian portrait gallery*, ed. L.-H. Taché (32 ser. in 16v., Montreal, 1890–[94]), 18th ser.: 273–82. [Édouard Fabre] Surveyer, "Sir Alexandre Lacoste," *Canadian Bar Rev.* (Toronto), 1 (1923): 757–62. T.-É. Hamel et Alexandre Lacoste, *Plaidoyers de MM. Hamel et Lacoste devant le comité des bills privés en faveur de l'université Laval les 20, 21, 27 et 28 mai 1881* (Québec, 1881). Jean Hétu, *Album souvenir, 1878–1978; centenaire de la faculté de droit de l'université de Montréal* (Montréal, 1978). Nicholas Kasirer, "Apostolat juridique: teaching everyday law in the life of Marie Lacoste Gérin-Lajoie (1867–1945)," *Osgoode Hall Law Journal* (Toronto), 30 (1992): 427–70. J.-J. Lefebvre, "Tableau alphabétique des avocats de la province de Québec, 1850–1868," *La Rev. du Barreau de la prov. de Québec* (Montréal), 21 (1961): 314–32. *Prominent men of Canada: a collection of persons distinguished in professional and political life, and in the commerce and industry of Canada*, ed. G. M. Adam (Toronto, 1892). Qué., Parl., *Doc. de la session*, réponses aux adresses, no.13, 1888. *Quebec Official Gazette*, 1876: 488. *Quebec Official Reports: King's Bench* (Quebec), 1892–1907. G.-É. Rinfret, *Histoire du barreau de Montréal* (Cowansville, Qué., 1989). P.-G. Roy, *Les juges de la prov. de Québec*. Rumilly, *Hist. de la prov. de Québec*, vols.2–26. [F.-]X.-A. Trudel *et al.*, *Réplique aux plaidoyers de MM. Hamel et Lacoste: Rome 25 septembre 1881* ([Rome?, 1882?]). Gustave Turcotte, *Le Conseil législatif de Québec, 1774–1933* (Beauceville, Qué., 1933). Univ. Laval, *Annuaire*, 1859–60, 1880–81.

LAFLEUR, EUGENE, lawyer and university professor; b. 12 April 1856 in Longueuil, Lower Canada, eldest son of the Reverend Theodore Lafleur and Adele Voruz; m. 16 March 1896 a first cousin, Marie-Alice Voruz, in Geneva, Switzerland, and they had two sons and two daughters; d. 29 April 1930 in Ottawa.

Eugene Lafleur was of Swiss lineage on his mother's side of the family. His father's ancestors, of Swiss or French origin, had settled in New France before 1700. Lafleur was raised a Baptist, but in adulthood he joined the Church of England. His father, an influential member of the Grande-Ligne mission [see Henriette Odin*], ministered in Longueuil and then in the Eastern Townships before moving his family to Montreal when Eugene was 14. Although raised in an English-speaking household, Lafleur was markedly proficient in French. He enrolled in the classical program of the High School of Montreal in 1870 and became an outstanding student. After graduation he entered McGill College, took his BA in 1877 at age 21, and was graduated BCL in 1880, winning the gold medal for the highest standing in mental and moral philosophy. He was called to the bar of the province of Quebec the following year. Thus began an illustrious career that would last nearly 50 years. He served as a bencher of the Quebec bar between 1894 and 1897, was created QC in 1899, became *bâtonnier* of the Montreal bar and of the province in 1905–6, and was the acknowledged leader of the legal profession in Canada during the last 20 years of his life.

In 1890 Lafleur had accepted the post of professor of civil law at McGill. He developed a deep interest in conflicts of laws (international disputes between individuals), becoming a Canadian pioneer in the field. His reputation was enhanced by the publication in 1898 of a gracefully written text on the subject, the first by a Canadian author. That same year he became professor of international law and he taught until 1909. He resumed his professorship in 1912 and taught public international law (disputes between nations) until 1921, when he retired. McGill conferred on him an honorary LLD in October 1921, and he held the title of emeritus professor of law until 1929. In 1911 he had been appointed chairman of a tribunal of arbitration set up by the United States and Mexico to settle a long-standing dispute between the two nations over ownership of a strategically located piece of land, the Chamizal, at El Paso, Tex., and Juárez, Mexico, left exposed by a shift in the course of the Rio Grande. Lafleur, joined by his Mexican colleague, ruled in favour of Mexico, the American commissioner dissenting.

Lafleur was, however, first and foremost an advocate, pleading clients' causes in court. In 1885 he had taken a partner and founded the firm that still continues as the Montreal office of McCarthy Tétrault. One of his articled students was Aimé Geoffrion*, another luminary of the bar. Lafleur did mainly trial work in his earlier years, but with age and experience he preferred the appellate courts, where one could dispassionately analyse legal issues. He firmly believed that the role of the advocate was not subservient to that of judges and that bench and bar together should respectfully seek solutions to legal problems. As his reputation widened, he began to confine himself to appeals in the Supreme Court of Canada and the Judicial Committee of the Privy Council. Probably no other Canadian lawyer to this day appeared in the Supreme Court as often as he did; the published reports show him there on just under 300 cases, but there were many unrecorded appearances during the preliminary stages of appeals. He argued before the Privy Council in London on at least 30 recorded cases and an unknown number of unrecorded occasions.

Although he took cases covering the whole spectrum of law, he achieved a national reputation, primarily as a constitutional lawyer and, secondly, as a lawyer engaged in freight rate litigation. In his time, a constitutional lawyer was concerned with the distribution of legislative powers between the federal and provincial governments set forth in the British North America Act. Although the broad lines of interpretation of the act tended to favour provincial rights when a competing interest with Ottawa was involved, wide areas of jurisdiction were still to be settled as Canada became more and more industrialized. This change in the economy, combined with increasing governmental intrusion into trade and commerce, was reflected in disputes between the provinces and Ottawa about regulatory jurisdiction over such matters as business enterprises and commercial corporations and over the development of water resources for commercial use, a provincial field, as opposed to their use for navigation, a field of federal jurisdiction. The development of water resources was of particular concern to Quebec, to whose governments Lafleur gave advice over many years. The regulation by the Board of Railway Commissioners of rates set by railways moving goods across provincial boundaries and the application of the Crowsnest Pass agreement to grain shipments formed, in Lafleur's lifetime, the most important commercial litigation in the country. During his last 20 years there was hardly a case of consequence concerning constitutional law or freight rate litigation that did not involve him.

Two prime ministers offered Lafleur judicial appointment. In 1907 Sir Wilfrid Laurier* urged him to accept a seat on the Court of King's Bench in Quebec, but he declined. In 1924, after the death of Sir Louis Henry DAVIES, chief justice of Canada, Prime Minister William Lyon Mackenzie King* did his utmost to persuade Lafleur to accept the chief justiceship. Again, no inducements could sway Lafleur, whose stated ground of refusal was his age. In reality, Lafleur preferred the life of an advocate; as he told a colleague, he loved "the smell of powder."

Lafleur's decision was also prompted in part by financial reasons – he enjoyed a handsome income, far greater than that which he would have earned as chief justice – and by his reluctance to leave Montreal for Ottawa. He lived comfortably in a large house on Rue Peel, where he maintained a horse and stable. Weather permitting, he rode on the slopes of Mount Royal before breakfast. He enjoyed his membership in the University Club in Montreal, of which he was president for 1922–23, and, with friends of like minds, he cultivated literary and theatrical pursuits.

Late in April 1930 he went to Ottawa to put the finishing touches to his submission in an appeal to the Supreme Court. Soon after his arrival he came down with a heavy cold which turned into pneumonia; he died, unexpectedly, on 29 April. After a funeral service at Christ Church Cathedral in Montreal on 2 May, he was buried in Mount Royal Cemetery.

Lafleur possessed all the talents which make for a highly competent advocate: a retentive memory, a capacity for sustained concentration, an extensive knowledge of many areas of the law, and the ability to divine the thinking of judges so as to turn them in his clients' favour. These, and others, are obvious, but he possessed less easily defined skills which lifted him above the level of a superior advocate to that of a great one. He spoke spontaneously in both languages with elegant turns of phrase. When in court he used the briefest of notes, which belied the extent of his underlying preparation. He was invariably courteous to the judiciary and legal opponents alike. He was even-tempered, patient, and thoughtful, free of theatrics and pyrotechnics. There was, over and above even those attributes, a further distinction rooted in his character, an absolute integrity. The Privy Council adverted to this in paying tribute to him in its proceedings on 1 May.

During Lafleur's time the gap between Roman Catholics and Protestants was far wider and of far greater significance than it is today. Lafleur was an anomaly, a Protestant of foreign background, yet a member of both the French Canadian and the English Canadian establishments. In fact, he was truly bilingual, bilegal, and bicultural, but single-mindedly Canadian.

DAVID RICARDO WILLIAMS

Eugene Lafleur is the author of *The conflict of laws in the province of Quebec* (Montreal, 1898) and *International law and the present war* ([Toronto, 1915?]).

BCA, GR-1323, nos.244/10, 2599/10, 4263/10, 4264/10 (mfm.). McCarthy Tétrault (Montreal), "Clarkson Tétrault Avocats, barristers, and solicitors" (typescript, 1985); Daybook, 1919–29 (fees and drawings); W. J. Henderson, "Recollections" (typescript, 1948); A. K. Hugessen, "Reminiscences" (typescript, 1963); Indenture of clerkship, 16 Jan. 1878; Judicial Committee of the Privy Council, proc., 1 May 1930; W. L. M. King to Eugene Lafleur, 8–9 Sept. 1924 (mfm. at LAC); Opinion books, 1 (1885)–19 (1934); Thomas Shaughnessy, "Clarkson Tétrault" (typescript, 1981); Testimonial, 8 Jan. 1881. LAC, MG 26, J1, 102: 86522 (mfm.); J13, 4–5, 11 mai, 12 sept. 1924. Private arch., R. E. Parsons (Montreal), High School of Montreal, reports of the attendance, progress and conduct of Eugene Lafleur, 31 Jan., 15 April 1871; 31 Jan. 1872; letters from the État Civil de la Ville de Genève to Marie-Alice Voruz, 2 mars 1896, and to Eugene Lafleur, 7 mars 1896. *Gazette* (Montreal), 30 April 1930. *Montreal Daily Star*, 30 April, 1–3 May 1930. *Times* (London), 30 April, 1–2 May 1930. *Canada Supreme Court Reports* (Ottawa), 1890–1930. *Canadian men and women of the time* (Morgan; 1912). *Canadian Railway Cases* (Toronto), 17 (1913–15): 123–231. *Eugène Lafleur: l'homme et l'avocat* (Montréal, [1934]). E. A. Forsey, *A life on the fringe: the memoirs of Eugene Forsey* (Toronto, 1990). *Law Reports, Appeal Cases* (London), 1900–30. J. E. Mueller, *Restless river: international law and the behavior of the Rio Grande* (El Paso, Tex., 1975). D. R. Williams, *Just lawyers: seven portraits* (Toronto, 1995).

LAJEUNESSE, EMMA (also called **Marie-Louise-Cécile-Emma**) **(Gye)**, known as **Emma Albani**, singer, pianist, harpist, and teacher; b. 1 Nov. 1847 in Chambly, Lower Canada, daughter of Joseph Lajeunesse, a music teacher, and Mélina Mignault; m. 6 Aug. 1878 Ernest Gye in London, England, and they had one son; d. there 3 April 1930.

Emma Lajeunesse's parents were musicians who recognized their daughter's exceptional talent very early in her life. Her mother first taught her to play the piano, but it was her father, a pianist, harpist, organist, and violinist, who saw to it that she received a full musical education. After his wife's death in 1856, Joseph Lajeunesse was hired to teach music at the convent of the Religious of the Sacred Heart in Sault-au-Récollet (Montreal), where his daughters Emma and Cornélia (also called Nellie) enrolled as boarders and received a sound general education. Attending from 1858 to 1865, Emma reportedly had Charles-Gustave Smith* as one of her teachers there. Both girls were musicians and occasionally performed in public. Emma, who sang, composed, and played the piano and harp, had given her first concert on 15 Sept. 1856 at the Mechanics' Institute in Montreal. She was eight years old, and the critics marvelled at this child, recognizing her as a prodigy. On 16 Sept. 1862, the day after another concert that the now 14-year-old Emma gave at the same place, *La Minerve* described her voice as "sent from heaven." She also sang in Chambly, Saint-Jean (Saint-Jean-sur-Richelieu), L'Assomption, Sorel, Industrie (Joliette), and Terrebonne.

Joseph Lajeunesse was aware of Emma's exceptional talent and sought to encourage it. He tried to raise enough money to send her for studies in Paris. Faced with an indifferent community uninterested in the development of musical talent, he left Montreal, probably in 1865, and set out with his family for New

Lajeunesse

York State, stopping at several towns, including Saratoga Springs and Johnstown, where his daughters performed. In Albany, Emma was hired as soloist for the parish church of St Joseph, where for three years she sang, played the organ, and directed the choir. She also worked at composing vocal scores, as well as pieces for solo piano, two pianos, and harp. In 1868, with her father's savings, the encouragement of Bishop John Joseph Conroy of Albany, and financial assistance from the parishioners, Emma was able to go to Paris, where she studied singing with Gilbert-Louis Duprez, the famous French tenor, who had created the role of Edgardo in Donizetti's *Lucia di Lammermoor*. Not long after her lessons with him began, Duprez is said to have remarked, "She has a beautiful voice and ardour. She is of the kind of wood from which fine flutes are made." Unfortunately, he fell ill a few months later. Emma continued her studies for a year in Milan, Italy, with the eminent voice teacher Francesco Lamperti. The solid technique she learned from him, along with her rigid discipline, kept her in good vocal health and enabled her to alternate between light and dramatic roles for many years.

Soon short of money, Emma went looking for work, and thus obtained her first engagements in Messina during the 1869–70 season. She sang the roles of Oscar in Verdi's *Un ballo in maschera*, Amina in Bellini's *La sonnambula* (her lucky role), and Alina in Donizetti's *Alina, regina di Golconda*. It was the custom in operatic circles for singers to adopt stage names. Emma unhesitatingly followed the advice of her elocution teacher, Delorenzi, and took the stage name of Albani for her Italian debut, thereby perpetuating the name of an old Italian family of which only one member was still alive. From the time of her debut in Messina, she realized that to portray historical characters it was not enough to sing well. To broaden her cultural awareness, she visited museums and read widely. Her first brilliant successes gave her an entrée to theatres in Florence, Italy, in Malta, and in London. Albani had her first engagement at the Royal Italian Opera – the name taken in 1847 by Covent Garden in London – on 2 April 1872, and was a great success in the role of Amina. She was the first Canadian woman to perform in this prestigious opera house and would remain with it until 1896.

Albani's London debut launched her firmly on her career. From then on she was in demand by the most famous theatres in Europe and North America. London, Paris, Berlin, Vienna, Brussels, Venice, New York, Moscow, St Petersburg, and other cities welcomed and applauded her. Her light voice, her stage presence, her mastery of mezza voce singing, her perfect technique, and her ability to trill (Lamperti reportedly even dedicated a treatise on the art of trilling to her) made her the ideal interpreter of bel canto, which then held sway in opera houses. As time went on, she would develop a fuller and more robust chest voice, enabling her to sing more dramatic roles. The Sicilians nicknamed her "Bellini's daughter" for her performances of that composer's works. Her repertoire included Amina in *La sonnambula* and Elvira in *I Puritani* by Bellini, Lucia in *Lucia di Lammermoor* and Linda in *Linda di Chamounix* by Donizetti, Gilda in Verdi's *Rigoletto*, and Rosina in Rossini's *Il barbiere di Siviglia*. She was tall and slender, with blue eyes and a pale complexion, and the critics emphasized her serenity and her exceptional powers of concentration.

In the 1870s Albani went to Moscow and St Petersburg, where she sang in the Alexander theatre in the presence of Tsar Alexander II of Russia. In 1874, a memorable year for the singer, she was honoured with an invitation to Windsor Castle to give a private recital for Queen Victoria. This was the first of a series of occasions on which Albani would perform for reigning monarchs, but it was also the beginning of a friendship between the two women, who would visit each other regularly until Victoria's death in 1901. Albani would even sing at the funeral of the monarch, whose diary contains references to the singer's dignified bearing, friendliness, and kindness. In November 1874 Albani went on tour in the United States, where she performed her first Wagnerian role – Elsa in *Lohengrin* – at the Academy of Music in New York. A role she created at the Royal Italian Opera the following year, it brought her one of her greatest triumphs. Year by year her repertoire grew. She played Lady Harriet in Flotow's *Martha*, Juliette in Gounod's *Roméo et Juliette*, Inès in Meyerbeer's *L'Africaine*, Ophélie in Thomas's *Hamlet*, and Mignon in *Mignon* by the same composer, and she took Wagnerian roles such as Eva in *Die Meistersinger von Nürnberg*, Senta in *Der fliegende Holländer*, Elisabeth in *Tannhäuser*, and Isolde in *Tristan und Isolde*.

During the final years of the century the glory of bel canto faded and new styles emerged, including that of performing operas in their original languages rather than, as previously, in Italian. Albani did not resist this change and would sing Wagner in German – not surprising for a multilingual perfectionist who spoke French, English, Italian, and German. Beyond the confines of Germany, she became one of the most sought-after Wagnerian performers of her time.

From the beginning Albani's career was marked by privileged meetings and friendships. In 1872 she worked at the role of Mignon with Thomas. She would sing under Sullivan in 1880, Gounod in 1882, and Dvořák in 1885, in performances of their own works. Flotow would write his opera *Alma l'incantatrice* especially for her in 1878. Gounod would do the same in 1885 with his oratorio *Mors et vita*. In 1886 Liszt would hear her in London in his oratoria *Die Legende von der heiligen Elisabeth*. In 1893 she would move Brahms to tears with her rendition of the solo from his *Deutsches Requiem*. These titles illustrate an important facet of Albani's career: she was a highly skilled singer experienced in oratorio and recital. In England she performed at famous festivals (Leeds, Birmingham, Norwich, Bristol, Liverpool) and at gala events. For instance, at the Crystal Palace in London in 1877, she sang in Handel's *Messiah* before an audience of 20,000.

From 1876 Albani always had her sister Cornélia by her side. Also a talented pianist, Cornélia had studied in Germany and then had taught music to the children of the royal family of Spain. All her life (she would die not long after Emma), she was her famous sister's accompanist and companion. Emma married Ernest Gye, the son of the director of the Royal Italian Opera, on 6 Aug. 1878. Following his father's death as a result of an accident, he took over this position from 1878 to 1885. He would become his wife's impresario. Their son, Ernest Frederick (b. 4 June 1879), would have a prominent diplomatic career and would die in London in 1955.

In 1880, while playing Lucia (*Lucia di Lammermoor*) and Gilda (*Rigoletto*) at La Scala in Milan, Italy, Albani suffered one of her rare setbacks. Not only was she facing an audience hostile to the presence of non-Italian singers in this theatre, but on that evening she was not in good voice and failed to impress her listeners. The incident did no damage to her reputation, however. Her career even broadened, since she performed in cities she had not previously visited. In 1883, under the auspices of impresario James Henry Mapleson, she and Adelina Patti undertook a long tour in the United States during which the two singers shared the limelight. Chicago, Washington, Baltimore, and New York welcomed them. In the same year Emma returned to Canada to give concerts after an absence of some 20 years. When she arrived in Montreal, 10,000 people were waiting to greet her and pay homage to her. It was on this occasion that poet Louis Fréchette* wrote "À Mme Albani (Emma Lajeunesse)," which was published, among other places, in *La Patrie* on 28 March 1883. For her first concerts in Montreal, Albani was accompanied by violinist Alfred DE SÈVE. She remained attached to her native country and returned nine times between 1883 and 1906 for tours that took her from one end of Canada to the other. During her first Canadian tours, she only gave recitals. It was not until 1890 that she performed in two complete operas at the Academy of Music in Montreal, *Lucia di Lammermoor* and Verdi's *La traviata*. That year she lent her support to a benefit concert for Notre-Dame Hospital. At the Victoria Skating Rink an audience of 6,000 cheered her, as well as pianist and composer Salomon Mazurette, violinist De Sève, and the Montreal City Band under the direction of Ernest Lavigne*. Albani was always generous to charitable organizations.

It was in 1890, too, that Albani's career reached its peak when she gave a spirited performance at the most famous and respected opera house in North America, the Metropolitan Opera in New York. She became the first French Canadian woman to perform in this theatre when she sang the role of Desdemona in Verdi's *Otello*, a work that marks an important stage in the history of Italian opera. In July 1891 she also became the first to sing the role at the Royal Italian Opera. This high point was followed by other significant occasions. In the course of the 1890s the singer worked alongside famous performers in Europe, such as the brothers Jean and Édouard de Reszke and musicians Pablo de Sarasate and Ignacy Jan Paderewski. Her stage career ended in July 1896 at the Royal Opera House (as the Royal Italian Opera had been renamed in 1892), where, except for four years, she had had top billing since 1872. After her triumph in the role of Isolde (*Tristan und Isolde*), she made her farewell appearance as Valentine in Meyerbeer's *Les Huguenots*. The changing tastes of the theatre's various directors had obliged her to demonstrate a high degree of flexibility and stylistic diversity. Her eminence as a singer came primarily as a result of her association with this opera house, which was one of the most famous of its day.

Albani still sang in recitals. In 1901 she travelled across Canada from Halifax to Vancouver. Wherever she went Canadians acclaimed her as the "queen of song." Accompanied by a few musicians, she continued to go on tour: South Africa (1898, 1899, 1904), Australia (1898, 1907), Ceylon (Sri Lanka) (1907), India (1907), and New Zealand (1907). In 1906 she made her farewell Canadian tour, accompanied by the young Canadian singer Éva Gauthier*. During the same period, from 1904 to 1907, she is believed to have recorded nine titles, some of which have been remastered and are again available in the 21st century. Her career came to an end before a crowd of 10,000 at the Royal Albert Hall in London on 14 Oct. 1911, the year her memoirs were published in that city under the title *Forty years of song*.

The last years of Albani's life were clouded by financial difficulties that forced her to teach and occasionally to perform in music halls. Her plight, as a result of the war and bad investments, was such that in 1920 the British government voted her an annual pension of £100 to provide some relief. In 1925, on the initiative of the Australian singer Nellie Melba, a great benefit concert was organized for her. Reports of her penury reached Montreal, where *La Presse* sponsored a recital on 28 May 1925 in the Théâtre Saint-Denis to raise money for the singer; more than $4,000 was collected. The Canadian and Quebec governments were urged to come to her assistance, but they declined to contribute on the grounds that Albani was more a British subject than a Canadian citizen (she had lived in London since 1872). She was widowed in 1925 and died on 3 April 1930 at her home on Tregunter Road, Kensington (London).

Recognized for her work both on stage and in recital, Emma Albani had a repertoire that included 43 roles in 40 Italian, French, and German operas. One of the opera stars of her generation, on an equal footing with her contemporaries Jenny Lind, Adelina Patti, and Nellie Melba, she had a dazzling career for nearly 40 years, winning the admiration of the international musical world. She worked hard and quickly, and with her exceptional voice she used her talent in the service of the music of her day. She was the first of a number of Canadian singers to perform on the great opera stages, preparing the way for artists such as Jeanne Maubourg* (Roberval), François-Xavier Mercier, Béatrice LA PALME (Issaurel), Pauline Donalda [Lightstone*], and Joseph Rouleau, and more particularly Sarah Fischer*, her pupil, and Éva Gauthier, who worked with her. She received many awards, including the gold Beethoven Medal (given by the Royal Philharmonic Society of London) and the medal of honour commemorating Queen Victoria's jubilee in 1897. In 1925 she was made a dame commander of the Order of the British Empire.

PIERRE VACHON

Emma Lajeunesse is the author of *Forty years of song* (London, 1911; repr. New York, 1977); Gilles Potvin published a translation under the title *Mémoires d'Emma Albani; l'éblouissante carrière de la plus grande cantatrice québécoise* (Montréal, 1972). Despite extensive searching, Emma Lajeunesse's baptismal certificate could not be found. The most reliable document on the subject of her birth, cited in Hélène Charbonneau, *L'Albani: sa carrière artistique et triomphale* (Montréal, [1938]), is the register of the convent of the Religious of the Sacred Heart, which lists Albani's birth date as 1 Nov. 1847. A copy of her marriage certificate is in the Fonds Gilles-Potvin cited below.
    Arch. de la Ville de Chambly, Qué., FA (fonds Albani). Arch. de l'Univ. de Montréal, P 279 (fonds Arthur-Prévost); P 299 (fonds Gilles-Potvin). LAC, MG 26, G; J1; MG 30, D178; D207; MUS 10. "Albani," *L'Album musical* (Montréal), mars 1883: 17–19. *Catalogue of Canadian composers*, ed. Helmut Kallmann (2nd ed., Toronto, 1952; repr. St Clair Shores, Mich., 1972), 144. M.-B. Clément, "Albani," *BRH*, 55 (1949): 199–210; "Les concerts à Montréal de madame Albani," *BRH*, 53 (1947): 364–72. *Dictionnaire biographique des musiciens canadiens* (2e éd., Lachine, Qué., 1935). *Encyclopedia of music in Canada* (Kallmann *et al.*). Romain Gour, "Albani (Emma Lajeunesse), reine du chant (1847–1930)," *Qui?* (Montréal), 1 (1949–50): 3–20. Helmut Kallmann, *A history of music in Canada, 1534–1914* (Toronto and London, 1960; repr. [Toronto], 1987). Napoléon Legendre, *Albani (Emma Lajeunesse)* (Québec, 1874). Cheryl MacDonald, *Emma Albani: Victorian diva* (Toronto, 1984). Renée Maheu, "Les grandes voix du Québec," *Cap-aux-Diamants* (Québec), no.35 (automne 1993): 10–14. É.-Z. Massicotte, "La famille d'Albani," *BRH*, 37 (1931): 660–69, 713.

The new Grove dictionary of music and musicians, ed. Stanley Sadie (6th ed., 20v., London, 1980), 1: 196–97; 5: 7. *The new Grove dictionary of opera*, ed. Stanley Sadie (4v., London and New York, 1992), 1: 49, 1000; 3: 918; 4: 76. Gilles Potvin, "Emma Albani," *Opera Canada* (Toronto), 23 (1982), no.4: 20–21; "Emma Albani (1847–1930)," ARMuQ [Assoc. pour l'Avancement de la Recherche en Musique du Québec], *Cahiers* (Québec), 7 (1988): 46–64; "Emma Albani dans *I Puritani* au siècle dernier: un succès pyramidal et des déluges de fleurs," *Aria* (Montréal) 10 (1987), no.1: 7. Pierre Vachon, *Emma Albani* (Montréal, 2000).

LAJOIE, JEANNE (baptized **Marie-Jeanne-Alberta**), teacher; b. 2 Feb. 1899 in Lefaivre, Ont., one of the 12 children of Damien Lajoie, a joiner, and Alexina Proulx; d. unmarried 2 March 1930 in Montreal.

Marie-Jeanne Lajoie (as she was called until about 1922) did not start attending school until she was eight because of poor health. Illness would later prevent her from writing her high-school entrance examinations. Nonetheless, at 13 she began taking piano lessons and at 15 she obtained a diploma in stenography from an academy in Montreal. In 1919 she became housekeeper for her brother Élias, the parish priest at Vars, Ont. Her objective was to be a teacher and in 1921 she was hired to take over, from February to June, a class with four students in a separate school in the Sudbury district near Warren. She went next to a public school near Azilda, where she had some 60 students, before moving to a school at Naughton in September 1922. She left, however, at the end of October, fatigued and complaining of depression. In March 1923, having recovered from what she called a "breakdown," she took on a class at Blezard Valley. At the English-French summer model school in Ottawa in 1922, she had obtained an English-French district certificate, which qualified her to teach for a year in a dual-language school. In the summer of 1923 she attended a month-long academic course at the English-French model school in Vankleek Hill. That September, shortly before her certificate was renewed, she accepted a position to teach French at St John School, one of two separate schools (neither of them officially designated as bilingual) in Pembroke, an Ottawa valley town with a large francophone population.

St John School, where the majority of students were French-speaking, had been opened in early 1923 as a result of a campaign by the Cercle Lorrain. (Formed in 1916 and named for Narcisse-Zéphirin Lorrain, the first Roman Catholic bishop of Pembroke, this society promoted the interests of local francophones.) Under the provisions of and amendments to the province's Regulation 17 [*see* Sir James Pliny Whitney*], French could not be used in the school as a language of communication and instruction beyond form 1 except by permission from inspectors. French reading, grammar, and composition could be subjects of study in forms 1 to 4 but for no more than one hour per day. Jeanne was hired to teach a regular class of some 30 French-speaking students and to provide one hour of instruction in French to a rotating group of students, also French-speaking, from other classes. Her arrival was not entirely welcome: the principal of the school, which was supervised by the Sisters of St Joseph, immediately told her it was "foolish" to teach children two languages. A few weeks later the inspector recommended to Pembroke's school board that Jeanne's classes be turned over to another teacher, a more highly qualified anglophone sister who also held an English-French certificate and who, despite lacking a mastery of French, had taught it the previous year. Bowing to pressure, in October 1923 the board decided to dismiss Jeanne. There is little doubt she had fuelled the controversy by seeking to teach in French for periods longer than allowed by Regulation 17.

The decision was not well received among the parents and other francophones in Pembroke. Jeanne's cause was also taken up by the Association Canadienne-Française d'Éducation d'Ontario [see Napoléon-Antoine Belcourt*]; a spokesman commented privately on 10 October to Alfred Longpré, the president of the Cercle Lorrain, that "this provocation cannot be allowed to pass without the French Canadians of Pembroke protesting very strongly." Jeanne had written to the ACFEO on 6 October setting out her version of events and her letter was printed anonymously in the Ottawa newspaper Le Droit. When a petition and other protests did not result in the reversal of the school board's decision, several hundred people decided, at a meeting sponsored by the Cercle Lorrain, to follow the example of Franco-Ontarians in Green Valley (in Glengarry County) in 1916 and establish a "free" school outside government control, with Jeanne as its teacher. On 6 November, after speeches by representatives from the Cercle and the ACFEO, by Montreal editor Omer Héroux*, and by Jeanne herself, the École Jeanne-d'Arc opened with more than 50 students in the dining room of a private home. Jeanne, who according to Héroux "had lifted the courage" of the francophones in Pembroke, had become a symbol of the resistance offered to what was perceived as the persecution of Franco-Ontarians.

The school survived by means of donations received from organizations such as the Association Catholique de la Jeunesse Canadienne-Française and the Union Saint-Joseph du Canada and from individuals, many of them responding to appeals made especially in Le Droit and Heroux's Le Devoir. Later in November a new home was purchased for the school and in February 1924 another teacher was hired. In addition to giving speeches in support of the school, Jeanne raised money while on summer holidays in Montreal. Her reputation as a teacher was recognized when she was offered the principalship of a school in Windsor, Ont., in May 1925. She refused, saying her work was in Pembroke.

The protest by francophones in Pembroke reflected events in many parts of Ontario. A large number of French-instruction schools, especially in Ottawa and the rural areas of Prescott and Russell counties, had openly resisted Regulation 17. The ACFEO continued to oppose the regulation, which would be shelved by the province in 1927, but by then Jeanne was no longer in the front ranks of the resistance.

Her health had taken a turn for the worse. In September 1926 she entered the Hôpital du Sacré-Cœur in Cartierville (Montreal), diagnosed with tuberculosis. She never recovered and died on 2 March 1930. The "heroine of Pembroke" was not forgotten. Originally interred in a pauper's grave in the Notre-Dame-des-Neiges cemetery in Montreal, she was reburied and given a new headstone. Abbé Lionel Groulx* said in 1940 that she was of the "spiritual family of Joan of Arc" and that with her name, Jeanne, she "could be called the Maid of Pembroke." Pilgrimages were made to her tomb in the 1940s and she was the subject of allegorical floats in Saint-Jean-Baptiste day parades. In the last half of the 20th century, some French-language schools in Ontario were named in her honour, the story of her struggle was the subject of at least three plays, and her actions were cited as exemplary for those anxious about the survival of the French language in Ontario.

HENRI PILON

There are photographs of Jeanne Lajoie in Dictionnaire de l'Amérique française; francophonie nord-américaine hors Québec, Charles Dufresne et al., édit. (Ottawa, 1988), and in La Patrie, 7 nov. 1923.

AO, RG 2-102-0-3; RG 80-2-0-499, no.32793. Centre for Research on French Canadian Culture (Ottawa), C2 (Fonds Association canadienne-française de l'Ontario), /21/5: corr., rapports, 1922; /21/8: rapports, résolutions, 1926; /101/9: corr., résolution, loi, 1923–24; /183/22: Lajoie, Jeanne; /186/9: Longpré, Alfred; /211/4: corr., juillet–octobre 1923; /212/1–2: corr., février–décembre 1924; /212/4–5: corr., 1925–26; /212/6: corr. et coupures de presse, 1927; Edmond Clouthier, "Quinze années de lutte! 1910–1925: catéchisme de la question scolaire ontarienne" (texte dactylographié, [1925]). LAC, RG 31, C1, 1901, Alfred Township, Ont., div.4: 2 (mfm. at AO). Le Droit (Ottawa), septembre 1923–décembre 1924, 6 mars 1930. P.-F. Sylvestre, "Naissance de Jeanne Lajoie, la 'pucelle de Pembroke,'" L'Express (Toronto), 3–9 févr. 2004: 3. Robert Choquette, Language and religion: a history of English-French conflict in Ontario (Ottawa, 1975). Alfred Longpré, L'éveil de la race: un épisode de la résistance franco-ontarienne, Pembroke, 1923–27 ([Pembroke, Ont., 1930]). Peter Oliver, Public & private persons: the Ontario political culture, 1914–1934 (Toronto and Vancouver, 1975), 92–124. Frère Urbain-Marie [J.-A. Delisle], Jeanne Lajoie: l'héroïne de Pembroke (Laprairie, Qué., [1942?]). F. A. Walker, Catholic education and politics in Ontario . . . (3v., Toronto, 1955–87; vols.1–2 repr. 1976), 2.

Laksi

LAKSI, SLME'N. *See* LONECLOUD, JERRY

LANDRY, DAVID-VITAL, doctor, politician, farmer, and office holder; b. 14 July 1866 in Memramcook, N.B., son of Vital-J. Landry and Mathilde-D. Cormier; m. 6 Oct. 1896 Annie-Marie Michaud in St Leonard, N.B., and they had three sons and five daughters; d. 18 Dec. 1929 in Bathurst, N.B.

David-Vital Landry attended public school and the College of Saint Joseph [*see* Camille Lefebvre*] in Memramcook. In 1892 he graduated MD with highest honours from the Université Laval in Montreal. He had taught briefly in the public school system of New Brunswick before finishing his medical degree; he practised medicine from 1892 to 1894 in Memramcook and then in Buctouche, where he would reside until his death.

A municipal councillor for the parish of Wellington in 1900–1, Landry was elected as a Conservative for Kent in the provincial general election of 3 March 1908. He was named commissioner for agriculture in John Douglas Hazen*'s government on 24 March and he won the subsequent by-election by acclamation on 7 April. His appointment was not surprising; although Acadian influence in provincial politics was waning at the time, he was a prominent local figure and he owned a productive farm in Buctouche. In later years he would successfully raise black foxes.

As head of the department, Landry chaired a commission established in 1908 to investigate the state of agriculture in the province, attending hearings in many small rural communities. He actively promoted education through the development of agricultural societies and the appointment of a provincial horticultural expert. He also sought to improve rural life, proposing more telephones, fewer automobiles, increased immigration to New Brunswick, and the release of more government lands for colonization. His stand on immigration left him vulnerable to criticism from Acadians, who feared the introduction of anglophone settlers into their regions. In addition, he faced questions in the assembly about patronage and the expenses his department had incurred in importing Kentucky horses. He was, nonetheless, reappointed to his cabinet post by Hazen's successor, Premier James Kidd FLEMMING, on 16 Oct. 1911.

Despite the efforts of Liberal Peter John Veniot*, the rising star of Acadian politics, to hold him accountable for his government's actions, particularly on the issue of patronage, Landry successfully contested the general election of June 1912. That year the title of his portfolio was changed to minister of agriculture. On 22 Jan. 1914 he resigned the post on his nomination as provincial secretary-treasurer. He does not appear to have been personally involved in the major scandal that led to Flemming's resignation as premier in early December. He continued as secretary-treasurer under Conservative premier George Johnson Clarke, but maintained an interest in promoting agriculture, especially among Acadians. In 1915 he urged Monsignor Marcel-François Richard* to start an agricultural college in Rogersville. Although he was the senior member of the Clarke government, it was clear that he could not deliver the Acadian vote. The Liberal opposition consisted of only two members and both were Acadian; the traditional Conservative hold over francophones in New Brunswick was gradually eroding. This situation may have prevented his appointment as interim premier in February 1917, when an election was pending and Clarke became too ill to continue. Landry retained his post as secretary-treasurer under the new premier, Conservative James Alexander Murray.

An enthusiastic supporter of the formation of an Acadian battalion in World War I, Landry seems to have been silent on the question of military conscription. His discretion, his reported disgust at the scandals that plagued successive Conservative governments, and a well-fought campaign did not, however, prevent his going down to defeat, along with his party, in the general election of 24 Feb. 1917. He resigned with Murray's administration on 29 March. The anglophone hostility directed at Acadians because of their supposed failure to support the war effort and the unpopularity of the Conservatives, involved in scandals, meant that he had had little chance of re-election. He ran again in Kent in October 1920, as a candidate of the United Farmers of New Brunswick, but was defeated.

Landry identified with his fellow francophones, wrote some patriotic poems for the Acadian press, and supported the traditional view of his people's history as a struggle for survival. In Saint-Louis de Kent in 1911, at the first Acadian teachers' institute, he had announced government sponsorship of the first French-language Canadian history textbook for the province's public schools, written by Philéas-Frédéric Bourgeois*. Pressure from Landry and from the two Acadian school inspectors, Jean-Flavien Doucet and Charles-D. Hébert, had probably influenced Conservative policy on this issue. Acadians subsequently criticized the government for having delayed the book's introduction until 1914.

A member of the Société l'Assomption [*see* Rémi Benoît*], almost from its beginning, in 1904 Landry had founded the first branch in Canada of this mutual benefit society. He actively promoted its scholarship program and served on its executive in various capacities from 1904 until 1927, including from 1913 to 1919 as president. In 1917 he was president of a committee it formed to purchase the land in Grand Pré, N.S., that had been the site of Saint-Charles-des-Mines church, from which Lieutenant-Colonel John

Winslow* had announced the deportation of the Acadians of the region in 1755. The committee planned to create a park and erect a commemorative church. Landry had also been active in the Société Nationale de l'Assomption [see Pascal Poirier*], notably as a councillor and vice-president in 1907. In 1921 he presided over a congress of the national society in Church Point, N.S., which gave momentum to a massive fund-raising campaign for the commemorative church.

In 1925 there were rumours that the Conservatives might use Landry to muster Acadian support against Veniot, who had become premier two years earlier. Landry's efforts to identify himself as the real defender of Acadian nationalism, since he supported the Société l'Assomption while Veniot was not even a member, appear to have embarrassed other members of the society. He was defeated in the provincial general election of August 1925. Two years later he was rewarded with a patronage post as health officer for the northern counties.

Landry died suddenly in Bathurst in 1929, just before he was to preside at a meeting of the board of health. In spite of his Conservative politics, he had served for several years as a conscientious director of the more Liberal *L'Évangéline* without attempting to impose his views. He had also been a member of the League of Nations Society in Canada and a supporter of the temperance movement.

Known for his oratorical skills and his diligent attention to his work, David-Vital Landry had maintained a reputation for honesty throughout his career, amid numerous political scandals. During a period when many Acadians were moving towards the Liberal party, he had given francophones a continued presence among the Conservatives.

SHEILA ANDREW

PANB, MC 1156, 9; RS657P3, F4761 (mfm.). Centre d'Études Acadiennes, Univ. de Moncton, N.-B., Fonds R.-A. Arsenault, 506.1-1; Fonds M.-F. Richard, 8.2-18. *L'Évangéline* (Weymouth Bridge, N.-É.), 1er oct. 1896; (Moncton), 1er, 22 mai, 12, 19 juin 1912; 30 mars 1916; 28 févr. 1917; 22 août 1921; 24 juill., 4, 18 déc. 1924; 5 févr., 7, 14 mai 1925; 26 déc. 1929. *Moncton Transcript*, 1 March 1916. *Le Moniteur acadien* (Shédiac, N.-B.), 3 sept. 1908; 15 avril, 13 mai, 12 août 1909. *CPG*, 1908–25. *Cyclopædia of Canadian biog.* (Rose and Charlesworth), vol.3. A. T. Doyle, *Front benches & back rooms: a story of corruption, muckraking, raw partisanship and intrigue in New Brunswick* (Toronto, 1976). A.-J. Léger, *Les grandes lignes de l'histoire de la Société l'Assomption* (Québec, 1933). A.-J. Savoie, "Education in Acadia: 1604–1970," in *The Acadians of the Maritimes: thematic studies*, ed. Jean Daigle (Moncton, 1982), 383–427; *Un siècle de revendications scolaires au Nouveau-Brunswick, 1871–1971* (2v., [Edmundston, N.-B.], 1978–80). Univ. Laval, *Annuaire*, 1893–94. [J.] R. [H.] Wilbur, *The rise of French New Brunswick* (Halifax, 1989).

LANE, GEORGE, rancher and farmer; b. 6 March 1856 in Boonville, southwest of Des Moines, Iowa, son of Joseph William Lane, a farmer, and Julia Pidgeon; m. 24 Dec. 1885 Elizabeth Sexsmith in Calgary, and they had four daughters and four sons; d. 24 Sept. 1925 at the Bar U Ranch, near Pekisko, Alta.

George Lane's career seems almost too much like a romantic stereotype to be real. At age 16 he followed his father to the goldfields of Montana. Later he was a dispatch rider and a scout for the United States army. During his twenties he served an apprenticeship on several of the best-run ranches in Montana.

In 1884 Lane moved to the District of Alberta to take up the job of foreman on the North-West Cattle Company's Bar U Ranch [see Frederick Smith Stimson*]. He thus became one of the handful of experienced American cowboys guiding day-to-day work on the ranches which pioneered large-scale commercial operations in Canada. A master of the cowboy's skills, he also showed unusual leadership abilities.

Lane left the Bar U in 1887 and for several years acted as an independent cattle buyer. By 1893 he was purchasing for the Winnipeg firm of James Thomas Gordon and Robert Ironside*, and in 1897 he became a partner in Gordon, Ironside, and Fares. He emerged as a "cattle king" during the first decade of the 20th century. In 1902 he and his partners purchased the Bar U Ranch from the family of the late Andrew Allan* in one of the biggest deals that the foothills country had ever seen. He already owned the YT Ranch on the Little Bow River and the Willow Creek Ranch in the Porcupine Hills. He managed them as cow-calf operations and intensified production by putting up quantities of hay, using pure-bred bulls, regulating the calving season, and experimenting with irrigation. He also made use of the huge expanses of short grass prairie, between the Bow River and the Red Deer, which had yet to be affected by farm settlement. Here his operations employed the more risky methods of the open range, with cattle being turned loose to graze on ungranted land under a minimum of supervision. It was estimated that Lane ran from 16,000 to 18,000 head on his various properties.

Even as his cattle-ranching enterprises increased in scope and variety, Lane was evaluating the vigour with which homestead settlement was encroaching on the range. Far from seeing it as a threat, he viewed it as inevitable and sought to profit from it. He argued that farmers would need enormous numbers of draught horses, and set about meeting this demand. During the first two decades of the century, Lane built up the largest pure-bred Percheron stud in the world. He journeyed to France and brought back prizewinners of the breed, both classic mares and sleek powerful stallions weighing more than a ton each. The Bar U show team was made up of six perfectly matched dappled greys, but others were almost pure white or black, some with white blazes. For more than a decade Lane's Percherons dominated the show rings of the Pacific northwest, and his Bar U Ranch became internationally famous.

Always an advocate of mixed farming, Lane began to balance his ranching endeavours with wheat growing. In 1913 he bought the Namaka Farms, about 10,000 acres altogether. By 1915 he was vying with Charles Sherwood Noble* for the title of largest grain producer in the province of Alberta. As long as prices remained high and sufficient rain fell, the huge overheads incurred for machinery and labour were justified. However, the record yields of 1916 were followed by a dry cycle. Lane was badly overextended, and the enormous property reverted to the Dominion Bank in 1922.

As Lane's holdings increased, he had become an influential voice for stockmen. On several occasions he went to Ottawa to represent the cattlemen's interest. One of the first members of the Western Stock Growers' Association, he was a vice-president from 1903 to 1911 and president for 1913 and 1914. A Liberal, he was elected to the Legislative Assembly in 1913 but resigned his seat to allow a defeated cabinet minister to run. In 1919 he was instrumental in establishing a new and effective lobby group, the Cattlemen's Protective Association of Western Canada. He was also active in the Alberta Horse Breeders' Association and was a founding member of the Canadian Percheron Horse Breeders' Association.

In spite of his somewhat taciturn nature, Lane was sought out by the press for his views on a variety of matters. His unshakeable confidence in the future of western Canada and his belief that Alberta was the greatest farming and ranching country in the world were repeatedly noted and had a considerable effect on immigration and investment. Such was his profile that one old neighbour, on hearing of Lane's demise in 1925, lamented, "The country's gone plumb to hell – Wheat under two dollars and George Lane dead!"

Lane is remembered best in western Canada for two somewhat incidental associations. Along with Patrick Burns*, Alfred Ernest Cross*, and Archibald James McLean*, he put up the money for the first Calgary Stampede in 1912. His other claim on the popular imagination is his connection with Edward, Prince of Wales. When the prince intimated that he would like to see a "real ranch" on his cross-Canada tour in 1919, it was natural that he should be brought to visit George Lane's Bar U, and he enjoyed his stay so much that, with Lane's help, he purchased a small neighbouring ranch.

After Lane's death the Bar U was bought by Patrick Burns. Many of its buildings survived into the late 20th century. In 1991 the ranch headquarters site, comprising more than 30 historic structures, including two barns which date back to the 1880s, was acquired

by the Canadian government to commemorate the history of ranching. The Bar U Ranch National Historic Site is open to the public at Longview.

SIMON M. EVANS

Canadian Heritage, Parks Canada, Western Canada Service Centre, S. M. Evans, "George Lane: notes on a life" (research paper, Calgary, 1993); "George Lane: purebred horse breeder" (research paper, Calgary, 1994). GA, M 651, Elizabeth Sexsmith Lane, "A brief sketch of memories of my family" (1945). Wayne Dinsmore, "Development of the Percheron horse in Canada," Nor'-West Farmer (Winnipeg), 20 Feb. 1917. Edward Brado, Cattle kingdom: early ranching in Alberta (Vancouver, 1984). D. H. Breen, The Canadian prairie west and the ranching frontier, 1874–1924 (Toronto, 1983). Leaves from the medicine tree . . . (Lethbridge, Alta, 1960). [J. W.] G. MacEwan, Heavy horses: highlights of their history (Saskatoon, 1986). "A pioneer stockman," Farm and Ranch Rev. (Calgary), 20 Sept. 1922. Norman Rankin, "The boss of the Bar U," Canada Monthly (London, Ont.), 9 (1910–11): 323–33. C. I. Ritchie, "George Lane – one of the Big Four," Canadian Cattlemen (Winnipeg), September 1940. Bruce Roy, "The Bar U Percherons," Horses All (Calgary), January 1980.

LANGLOIS, GODFROY (baptized **Joseph-Ernest-Godefroi**), journalist, newspaper editor, freemason, politician, and agent general for the province of Quebec in Brussels; b. 26 Dec. 1866 in Sainte-Scholastique (Mirabel), Lower Canada, son of Joseph Langlois and Olympe Clément (Proulx, dit Clément); m. 24 Jan. 1900 Marie-Louise Hirbour in Montreal, and they had one daughter; d. 6 April 1928 in Brussels, and was buried on 28 July in Sainte-Scholastique.

Godfroy Langlois's father was a merchant and politician of considerable importance in Sainte-Scholastique. After elementary school, Godfroy was enrolled at the Petit Séminaire de Sainte-Thérèse in the fall of 1881. For reasons that are unclear, he left in June 1884 and entered the Collège de Saint-Laurent, near Montreal. He graduated gold medallist in June 1887. That September he entered the law school of the Université Laval in Montreal. Bored by the academic approach to law, he chose to pursue his legal studies as a clerk in the prestigious practice of Raymond Préfontaine* and Pierre-Eugène Lafontaine*. A few months later he moved to the firm of Toussaint-Antoine-Rodolphe Laflamme*, a prominent Rouge.

Laflamme proved to be influential. He advised Langlois to abandon law and to pursue instead a career in journalism. In December 1889 Langlois launched Le Clairon in Montreal with three other collaborators. The weekly quickly attracted attention, but could not find its niche and ceased publication in March 1890.

Langlois immediately accepted an invitation from Honoré Beaugrand* to work at La Patrie. On 6 November, while still at La Patrie, he launched

L'Écho des Deux-Montagnes (Sainte-Scholastique) with lawyer Joseph-Dominique Leduc. His bold sense of liberalism flourished in this weekly, where he defined the contours of his "radicalism" more succinctly, addressing issues such as annexationism, educational reform, politics, and the abuses committed by the clergy. Édouard-Charles Fabre*, archbishop of Montreal, reacted to Langlois's increasingly hostile attacks by banning *L'Écho* on 11 Nov. 1892. Langlois obstinately resumed his criticism two weeks later in a new publication, *La Liberté* (Sainte-Scholastique), laid out exactly as *L'Écho* had been, with the same number of pages, the same sponsors, and the same bylines. Educational reform assumed sovereign importance in the newspaper, as it would throughout Langlois's career. "[The] masses must be enlightened," he wrote, "they must know of the progress being made and they must have the tools to compete."

Langlois continued at *La Patrie* until December 1893, when he accepted an offer to join *Le Monde* (Montréal) as assistant editor. *Le Monde* had been purchased by a consortium of businessmen who were eager to reorient the traditionally ultramontane daily. Under the new management, its editorial comments were few and moderate in tone, hardly in keeping with Langlois's style. The experience in administration which he gained there would nevertheless benefit his career.

On 24 Oct. 1895 *La Liberté* appeared for the last time. The following day Beaugrand announced that Langlois would become managing editor of *La Patrie*. Félix-Gabriel Marchand*, leader of the Liberal opposition in Quebec, was infuriated by the appointment of Langlois. Federal Liberal leader Wilfrid Laurier*, who was also concerned about the rising tide of radicalism, especially in the light of his preparations for the imminent elections, was equally angered. Beaugrand stood his ground, however, and Langlois remained.

Langlois also found a fertile ground for his advanced liberalism in freemasonry. He joined the Cœurs-Unis Lodge No.45 in Montreal in December 1895. Freemasonry in Quebec at the time was dominated by the Grand Lodge of Canada and the Grand Lodge of Quebec, both of which were affiliated with British masonry. The Cœurs-Unis Lodge was a chapter of the Quebec organization. On 12 April 1896 a meeting of the Cœurs-Unis was called to ask for an alliance with the Grand Orient in France. Langlois joined the committee that petitioned for a new constitution and he proposed a name for the new lodge, L'Emancipation, that was immediately accepted.

Although enthusiasm for the lodge was strong in its first year, its handful of members met only sporadically after 1899. Langlois nevertheless remained a staunch member, rising to the presidency in 1901. An inspection report submitted to the Grand Orient in early 1903 made particular mention of his "energy" and "deep conviction." Langlois was often publicly accused of being a freemason, a charge he never denied but often mocked. His marriage in the Roman Catholic Church and the baptism of his child there certainly colour the principles he harboured as a freemason.

On 4 Feb. 1897 Joseph-Israël Tarte* had purchased *La Patrie* from Beaugrand. Four days later Langlois officially penned his first comment as editor-in-chief. Fortified by his promotion, he submitted his name for the Liberal candidacy in the provincial riding of Deux-Montagnes. He was supported by local Liberal leaders, but Marchand intervened and disallowed his candidacy. About two months after Langlois became editor-in-chief Tarte demoted him to make room for the rising star in Liberal ranks, Henri Bourassa*. The new editorial director's politics could not have been more dissimilar, but Langlois's supporters rallied and Bourassa was forced to leave after a few days. Langlois's stature as a leading spokesman of the unofficial progressive faction of the Liberal party was becoming clear.

A co-worker, Charles Robillard, remembered Langlois's endearing personal qualities. "Of great simplicity, warm, affable, and obliging, a friend of the good clean joke, he knew how to bring a gaiety to everyday conversation. ... The intransigence of his principles was forgotten when in close company, and colleagues saw before them only the most humble and charming of men." Just over five feet tall, he was always slightly corpulent. He had clear blue eyes and had sported a pince-nez since he was in his early twenties. As soon as he could grow one, he had worn a moustache.

In November 1901 Langlois articulated the need for an organization to promote educational reform. The Ligue de l'Enseignement was officially founded in Montreal on 9 Oct. 1902. Its name deliberately evoked that of the Ligue Française de l'Enseignement and its members were drawn mainly from the progressive wing of the Liberal party. Langlois was named vice-president and secretary. The program he submitted, which was approved on 21 Nov. 1902, included improved salaries and qualifications for schoolteachers, increased government subsidies, the enforcement of current educational legislation, the building of clean, "sanitary" schools, and the centralization of the Catholic school system's administration.

In January 1903 Tarte broke the ties between *La Patrie* and the Liberal party. Laurier had long anticipated the loss of the daily and had struck a committee after Tarte's departure from cabinet in October 1902 to look into the question of launching a new paper. Senator Frédéric-Ligori Béïque* offered the necessary capital. After much deliberation, Laurier met with Langlois to discuss the tone and orientation of the new publication. There was much opposition within the party to Langlois's appointment, but armed with Langlois's guarantee that the paper would remain loyal, Laurier approved the preparations for a morning publication that would be called *Le Canada*.

Langlois quickly dedicated the newspaper, launched in April 1903, to educational and municipal reform, and mounted a campaign against the privileges of the Montreal Light, Heat and Power Company [*see* Louis-Joseph Forget*]. He took his crusade for good government into the provincial Liberal party during the elections in the fall of 1904. Although *Le Canada* did its duty by pledging its support to Premier Simon-Napoléon Parent* in its editorial of 7 November, that same night Langlois mobilized his supporters against the government. The Liberals in Division No.3 in Montreal met to reaffirm the nomination of the incumbent, Henri-Benjamin Rainville, the *bête noire* of all progressive Liberals. The meeting ended in an impasse and when it resumed the following evening Langlois was nominated. He presented himself as "the champion of people's rights against the 'trusts' who have crushed and intimidated us," and promised to pay particular attention to the issues of colonization and public education.

Langlois's campaign shook the Parent administration to the core. He was elected, defeating Rainville, who ran as an independent Liberal. The Liberal party was thrown into disarray. In February 1905 Langlois supported the three cabinet ministers, Lomer GOUIN, William Alexander Weir, and Adélard TURGEON, who resigned in protest against Parent's authoritarian methods and precipitated his resignation as premier the following month.

Taking to his work as a member of the assembly with great enthusiasm, Langlois pressed the new Liberal government under Gouin to enact reforms in the field of education and in matters relating to Montreal. He would hold his seat, renamed Montreal–Saint-Louis in 1912, until 1914 and over the years some of his ideas would meet with success. He argued for a public utilities commission, proposed that a board of control be added to Montreal's administrative structure (as he suggested, a referendum was held on the question), and lobbied for a royal commission to examine Montreal's administration [*see* Lawrence John CANNON]. All these reforms were adopted.

In matters of education Langlois's demands were wide-ranging and triggered bitter debates with Bourassa in the assembly. His focus was the unification of Catholic school boards on Montreal Island, the election of school commissioners, and the creation of a royal commission on education. Gouin ordered the creation of the royal commission with respect to the Catholic schools of Montreal in July 1909, chaired by Raoul Dandurand*.

At the same time, Langlois's idea of liberalism moved considerably to the left in *Le Canada*. A convinced francophile, he turned to France for inspiration in rethinking Canadian liberalism. French liberalism at the time was taken by the idea of *solidarisme*, a blend of beliefs in capitalism and a limited welfare state that gave pride of place to educational reform. Langlois's thinking strongly resembled that ideology. "The beaten path was repugnant to him," remembered Robillard. "He ventured in new, audacious directions, at the risk of frightening important groups of the party he wanted to serve."

Langlois's constant criticism of Quebec's church-dominated educational system irritated Archbishop Paul Bruchési*, who repeatedly made his views known to Laurier. Coincidentally, the leadership of the Liberal party grew exasperated with Langlois's divisive activities at the provincial and municipal levels. "[*Le Canada*] has ceased to be the organ of the party in Ottawa and in Quebec; it has become . . . the organ of Langlois," a resentful Béïque told Laurier in 1909. Laurier concurred, but confided to Béïque his "hesitation to break with the radical group of our party."

An agreement was finally reached on Christmas Eve 1909 and Langlois was removed as editor of *Le Canada* a week later. He was named secretary to the International Joint Commission [*see* Sir George Christie Gibbons*], a position he never formally assumed. Instead, he founded a new weekly to encourage educational and municipal reform. Just as Bourassa launched *Le Devoir* in mid January 1910, Langlois's *Le Pays*, named after the old Rouge journal, hit the stands.

Langlois was bitterly disillusioned with the party leadership and had come to the conclusion that radical action was necessary; stop-gap measures and piecemeal reforms only threatened real change. *Le Pays* was a last-ditch attempt to reaffirm principles most held to be lost. It proved to be both a continuation of and a new departure from his ideas of Liberal progressivism as they had been expressed in *Le Canada*. He embraced the trade union movement as never before and demanded open discussion of socialism. He rejected the authority of the church and denounced nationalism as an artificial fabrication of reactionaries. He was open to the suggestion that liberalism had much to learn from other ideologies and diligently applied himself and his readers to a study of the alternatives. His conclusions were, in the end, predictable: to survive, liberalism had to be radical.

On 29 Sept. 1913 Archbishop Bruchési officially barred Catholics from reading *Le Pays*. The paper's response, "Toujours debout," encapsulated the essence of Langlois's thought and was issued as a pamphlet in English and in French. Langlois attacked the hegemony of clerico-nationalistic thinking and, mocking Bruchési's words, boldly continued to publish *Le Pays*.

Relations were tense between Gouin and Langlois as Gouin tried to distance the inveterate radical. The occasion finally arose when the Quebec government decided to open an office in Brussels to encourage trade with French-speaking countries and Langlois sought the opportunity to represent the province. On 14 May 1914 his appointment as Quebec's agent general in Brussels at a salary of $6,000 per year was confirmed. He quit *Le Pays* and resigned his seat in the legislature. On 22 June the Club Canadien offered a banquet in his honour. He left Montreal with his family soon after.

Europe was slowly being engulfed in war, so Langlois made arrangements with the Quebec government to settle in Paris for a time. Contacts between him and Quebec were minimal at least until 1917. Putting old differences aside, Laurier asked Langlois that November to represent the opposition in the monitoring of the Canadian election overseas. Langlois accepted. He formally assumed his position as Quebec's agent general in Brussels in 1919 and only returned to Canada in 1921 for a brief visit.

At the end of 1927 Langlois became ill and he died of cirrhosis of the liver just over three months later in Brussels. A year earlier he had revised his will and reaffirmed his renunciation of Catholicism by asking to be cremated. His wish was not granted. His remains were transported back to Canada, a funeral mass was sung in the church at Sainte-Scholastique, and he was buried in its cemetery.

Godfroy Langlois was one of the most important journalists of his generation and one of the most progressive thinkers in the Liberal party in Quebec. A free-thinker par excellence, he worked and argued for a better democracy that would welcome new ideas. His campaign for reform in municipal government and education and against hydroelectric trusts placed him in the forefront of a small but influential group of activists who believed that Quebec's future could be guaranteed only by energetic state involvement in key issues.

PATRICE A. DUTIL

[Godfroy Langlois published a few pamphlets outlining various aspects of his thought: *La république de 1848* (Montréal, 1897); *Sus au Sénat* ([Montréal], 1898); *L'uniformité des livres: deux discours . . .* ([Québec?, 1908?]); and *Toujours debout: le mandement de Mgr Bruchési et la réponse du "Pays"* (Montréal, 1913), translated as *Still on deck: the answer of "Le Pays" to Archbishop Bruchesi's mandement* (Montreal, 1913).

This biography is based on the author's study *Devil's advocate: Godfroy Langlois and the politics of Liberal progressivism in Laurier's Quebec* (Montreal and Toronto, 1994), translated as *L'avocat du diable: Godfroy Langlois et la politique du libéralisme progressiste à l'époque de Laurier*, Madeleine Hébert, trad. (Montréal, 1995). P.A.D.]

ANQ-M, CE606-S22, 30 déc. 1866. Charles Robillard, "Réminiscences d'un vieux journaliste; Galerie nationale: Godfroy Langlois," *La Patrie* (Montréal), 10 janv. 1943.

LANSDOWNE, Marquess of. *See* PETTY-FITZMAU-RICE

LA PALME, BÉATRICE (baptized **Marie-Anne-Béatrice-Alice**) (**Issaurel**), violinist, soprano, and teacher; b. 27 July 1878 in Belœil, Que., daughter of Alexandre Lapalme, a farmer, and Marie-Praxède Le Testu; m. 14 Oct. 1908 Salvator Issaurel in Paris; they had no children; d. 8 Jan. 1921 in Montreal.

In 1881 Béatrice La Palme's family moved to Montreal, where her father worked as a real estate agent and building contractor. Béatrice received her elementary schooling in Hochelaga (Montreal) at the boarding-school run by the Sisters of the Holy Names of Jesus and Mary, and continued her studies at their academy on Rue Cherrier. Introduced to music by her mother and by the nuns, she took lessons from Alexis Contant* and then studied the violin with Charles Lejeune and Frantz Jehin-Prume*. She gave her first recital, with Joseph Saucier* as accompanist, on 5 March 1894. In 1895 she was the first person to receive the Strathcona Scholarship (established that year by Donald Alexander Smith*, who became Baron Strathcona and Mount Royal) and it enabled her to attend the Royal College of Music in England for five years. There she studied the violin with the Spanish violinist Enrique Fernández Arbós and began voice lessons with Gustave García. In 1900 she became the first French Canadian woman to be made a corresponding member of the Royal College of Music. After returning to Montreal that year, on 11 October she gave a concert with both violin and vocal numbers. She went back to England and, on the advice of Emma Albani [LAJEUNESSE], thereafter devoted herself exclusively to singing, which she continued to study with Nelly Rowe, a student of Mme Mathilde Marchesi.

Béatrice La Palme presented a vocal recital in Montreal on 17 Oct. 1902, accompanied by Bernadette Dufresne. On 18 July 1903 she began her international career as a soprano at the Royal Opera House in London, performing the role of Musetta in Puccini's *La Bohème*. She sang in Lyons, France, during the 1903–4 season and in Royan in the summer of 1904. From September 1905 her career also took her to the Opéra-Comique in Paris, where one of her partners was the French tenor Salvator Issaurel, with whom she had sung in Royan. They were married in 1908 in the church of Notre-Dame-de-Lorette in Paris. Béatrice played many roles in France and in England, where she sang under the baton of Thomas Beecham.

The Issaurels moved to Montreal in July 1911. Béatrice gave a recital at the Monument National on 2 Oct. 1911 (and another the following day at Quebec). Her program included pieces by Gounod, Massenet, Debussy, and Fauré, and several works of the Canadian composer Alfred Laliberté. On this occasion Mayor James John Edmund Guerin presented her

Lapointe

with a silver cup to recognize "the Canadian artist who has had such success abroad." That year, she joined the troupe of the Montreal Opera Company, which had been founded in 1910 by Frank Stephen Meighen and Albert Clerk-Jeannotte. The company went bankrupt in 1913, and in November she moved to the Century Opera House in New York, but the uncertain climate created by the war in Europe led her to return to Montreal at the end of 1914. Teaching in the studio that she and her husband had opened in 1911 now became her focus. She gave a final recital with Salvator at the Ritz-Carlton Hotel in Montreal on 14 Nov. 1919. The program included works by Fauré, Saint-Saëns, Mozart, Grétry, and Debussy, as well as the famous love-duet "Duo de la rencontre" from Massenet's *Manon*. She died prematurely on 8 Jan. 1921 at the age of 42. The funeral was held four days later in the church of Saint-Léon in Westmount.

Béatrice La Palme was the first Canadian female singer after Emma Albani to make a name for herself on the European and American musical scenes. She was remembered by her many students – including Camille Bernard, Graziella Dumaine, and Flora (Fleurette) Contant (a daughter of Alexis Contant) – as a great artist, demanding teacher, and warm person. She and her husband were pioneers in establishing a vocal school in Quebec. Salvator Issaurel continued to teach until his death in 1944. It was in his studio that Pierrette Alarie and Léopold Simoneau, two singers who would have international careers both individually and as a couple, first met.

MARIE-THÉRÈSE LEFEBVRE

ANQ-M, CE601-S49, 28 juill. 1878. *Le Devoir*, 10, 12, 15 janv. 1921. *La Presse*, 10 janv. 1921. *Encyclopedia of music in Canada* (Kallmann *et al.*). Romain Gour, *La Palme-Issaurel; biographie critique* (Montréal, 1948). Hélène Paul, "Béatrice La Palme (1878–1921); une superbe voix au service de l'enseignement du chant lyrique," in *Ces femmes qui ont bâti Montréal*, sous la dir. de Maryse Darsigny *et al.* (Montréal, [1994]), 168–70.

LAPOINTE, ALEXIS, known as **Alexis le Trotteur**, maker of bake-ovens, labourer, runner, and popular figure; b. 4 June 1860 in La Malbaie, Lower Canada, son of François Lapointe, a farmer, and Adelphine Tremblay, *dit* Picoté; d. unmarried 12 Jan. 1924 in Saint-Joseph-d'Alma (Alma), Que., and was buried 16 January in La Malbaie.

Alexis Lapointe, known as Alexis le Trotteur, was the eighth in a family of 14 children. His maternal grandfather, Alexis Tremblay*, *dit* Picoté, was a leading member of the Société des Entrepreneurs des Pinières du Saguenay (later known as the Société des Vingt et Un), which opened up the Saguenay region to colonization in the spring of 1838.

Alexis had a Christian upbringing in modest circumstances and his education at home was certainly comparable to that of other farmers' sons in his day. His schooling, on the other hand, was rudimentary. Naive and not overly intelligent, he likely attended the local school for a year at most. He could recognize coins fairly well but was easily deceived. Since no document in his handwriting has ever been found, probably, unlike his parents, he could neither read nor write. Throughout his life he would have the mind of a child, but this would not keep him from being witty and cunning at times. His greenish eyes were unusual, having a pale line around the iris, and hence mixed hues.

By his own efforts and almost without being aware of it, Alexis very early in life developed a potential for competitive running, having been endowed with the right body and frame. He so enhanced his ability to run long distances that he was to accomplish feats never before considered possible. As an adult, he would be of average height (about five feet seven inches) and rather stocky. His powerful rib cage, broad shoulders, abnormally long arms, muscular thighs, and bony, pointed knees would certainly give him an athletic appearance.

Lapointe earned his living as a handyman in the Charlevoix, Saguenay, and Lac-Saint-Jean regions, mainly in sawmills and logging camps and on farms. After the death of his mother on 13 April 1890, he went to the Matapédia valley, where the lumber trade was flourishing. During the ten years he spent south of the St Lawrence, he ventured as far as Maine and Vermont, where he worked in lumber camps. When he returned to La Malbaie around 1900, he discovered a new trade for himself, that of making bake-ovens. It was one at which he excelled and he worked in a special way. Few people mixed clay and water with their feet, dancing and stamping in the trough, or added a magic potion to give the hearth its very own character. Because of his trade, he had to go from village to village. Always on the move, he never stayed more than one season in the same place.

In all the regions he travelled through, Lapointe also performed in public as an entertainer. A musician, he played the harmonica, the Jew's harp, or simply a comb (covered with birchbark or thin paper). Many people attending dances were astonished at the frenzied jigs he played for hours on end. Over the years he increasingly took on the identity of horses, whinnying, kicking, stamping his feet, whipping himself, wearing a harness, running, and even chewing on oats. This was the way he gained popularity. Little by little, people began to notice him, point at him, laugh at his feats, and make fun of them. At the age of 26 he would compete with the best trotters, leap over cedar fences, run races with trains, and even challenge ships. Although the stories of Lapointe's exploits, which were largely reported by eyewitnesses, would be coloured by legend as the years went by, they would retain a considerable element of truth. Examination of his skeletal remains in fact revealed the stuff of a champion. As a result of his running and jumping, his ceaseless dancing, and the way he lived, worked, and travelled, Alexis le Trotteur was in prime physical shape. Like many others, he probably could have made a good showing in the marathon held at Athens in 1896, during the first Olympic Games of modern times.

Although Lapointe fell madly in love with anyone wearing a skirt and having long hair, he never married. And yet he proposed to a dozen women, always proceeding in the same way, by proffering a letter that indicated he owned goods and property north of Lac Saint-Jean. His demonstrations of affection for the women he desired were always those of a somewhat eccentric teenager whom no one ever took seriously.

Lapointe was killed in an accident when a flatcar struck him as he was wandering along one of the railway tracks on a bridge across the Rivière La Grande Décharge. He had been doing various odd jobs at the time for the Quebec Development Company Limited, which was in charge of building a large hydroelectric dam between Alma and Île Maligne, in the Lac-Saint-Jean region [*see* Sir William PRICE].

Running, entertaining people, telling stories, enlivening evening parties, building bake-ovens, making jokes, and playing tricks – such was the world of Alexis Lapointe, to whom Marius Barbeau*, among others, would devote several studies. An imaginative man, he was often seen as eccentric. With no goal in life, he was content to live for the present moment. He seemed to cherish the conviction that there would always be doors open to welcome him, lumber camps where he could serve as a kitchen boy, farms and sawmills where he could find temporary work. By carrying on these repetitive activities in many places, Alexis le Trotteur transformed what might have been a banal existence into a life so astonishing that it enriched people's fantasies.

JEAN-CLAUDE LAROUCHE

ANQ-Q, CE304-S3, 4 juin 1860. ANQ-SLSJ, P18. Marius Barbeau, "Alexis le Trotteur," *Le Canada français* (Québec), 2ᵉ sér., 27 (1939–40): 881–91; *The Kingdom of Saguenay* (Toronto, 1936); *Le Saguenay légendaire* (Montréal, 1967). Marjolaine Bouchard, *Le cheval du Nord* (Chicoutimi, Qué., 1999). J.-C. Larouche, *Alexis le Trotteur* (Montréal, 1971; 2ᵉ éd., Chicoutimi, 1987); *Alexis le Trotteur: athlète ou centaure?* (Saint-Nazaire-de-Chicoutimi, Qué., 1977).

LAPORTE, MARIE-ANNE, factory worker, store clerk, and labour activist; b. 11 Oct. 1871 in the parish of Saint-Liguori, Que., daughter of Urgel Laporte, a day labourer, and Marie-Louise Perrault; d. unmarried 26 Nov. 1929 in Montreal and was buried in L'Assomption, Que.

Very little is known about Marie-Anne Laporte's early life. She is believed to have arrived in the village of Hochelaga (Montreal) with her parents when she was quite young. It is thought that she worked at first as a weaver in a cotton mill, and then as a store clerk for Joseph-Wilbrod Moreau, the owner of a large retail business established in Hochelaga around 1897. From about 1910 and for much of her life, Marie-Anne Laporte devoted considerable energy to the Fédération Nationale Saint-Jean-Baptiste. She would make her most significant contribution, however, to the Association Professionnelle des Employées de Magasins, of which she was to be elected vice-president around 1916 and president in 1923. Although she relinquished the presidency of the organization in December 1925 for reasons of health, she would remain on its board of directors until 1928.

The Association Professionnelle des Demoiselles de Magasins was formed in the fall of 1906 and became affiliated with the Fédération Nationale Saint-Jean-Baptiste in 1907, the year that organization was founded [*see* Marie Lacoste*]. In April 1909 its name was changed to Association Professionnelle des Employées de Magasins. The federation sought to encourage the formation of professional associations rather than trade unions. Although the two kinds of organization were alike in seeking to protect the economic interests of their members, associations affiliated with the federation differed because they wanted to prepare them for their role in the family and in society. The aim of the Association Professionnelle des Employées de Magasins was to bring together the French Canadian Catholic saleswomen in Montreal, but from 1927 it would accept "persons other than saleswomen working at the counter" as members. Its motto was "Work, honesty, kindness." Its efforts to foster the intellectual and moral development of working women – most of whom were young – and to defend their professional interests reflected closely the social doctrine of the Roman Catholic Church and the tenets of the federation. Its chief activities included offering members free evening courses in diction, sewing, the art of cooking, hygiene, fashion, singing, bookkeeping, and English. The association also maintained a library, organized cultural activities (including a choir), and held monthly meetings. In addition, it had an emergency fund that enabled members to receive free medical care and compensation for lost wages in case of illness. In 1927 an employment agency would be set up as well.

Like the federation, the association advocated measures to improve the daily lives of working women. Among other things, it made attempts – which usually proved fruitless – to ensure enforcement of the law (passed in 1908) requiring "bosses" to provide seats for "girls and women employed in stores." Around 1915, on the initiative of Marie-Louise Brodeur [MARMETTE], it encouraged the formation of a league of women shoppers, with the objective of patronizing merchants who offered goods that were "irreproachable" in both value and quality and provided their female employees with the best working conditions in terms of hygiene, comfort, wages, and working hours. From 1917 it also tried to encourage women shoppers to do their shopping early during holiday periods so that store clerks would not be swamped at the last minute. On several occasions the association asked that stores be closed early. One such request, made in 1917 to the merchants in the east end of the city, would lead in 1919 and 1920 to a six-o'clock closing time on Saturdays during July and August. The Women's Minimum Wage Act was passed in 1919 to meet the needs of female employees in industrial plants, and, with the backing of the association, the Fédération Nationale Saint-Jean-Baptiste demanded that female store employees be included in the categories of working women covered by the law (a goal achieved in 1934).

From 1906 to 1921 the Association Professionnelle des Employées de Magasins recruited 973 members. Although it had 200 members in 1911, its membership had dropped to 59 by 1929–30. The cause may have been the founding in 1918 of the Syndicat Catholique et National des Employés de Magasins (which, in fact, cooperated with the association) and possibly of other unions. There seems to have been a slight improvement later: in 1937–38 the association would have 125 members, and it was to pursue its activities at least until the 1960s.

Marie-Anne Laporte died on 26 Nov. 1929. The federation's publication, *La Bonne Parole*, paid homage to her in its December issue. "What an example for women employed in stores. . . . And how she worked to improve the lot of those who earn their living as she earned hers!"

MICHELLE COMEAU

AC, Joliette, État civil, Catholiques, L'Assomption, 29 nov. 1929. ANQ-M, CE601-S51, 1er févr. 1899; CE605-S36, 12 oct. 1871; P120. LAC, RG 31, C1, 1871, Saint-Liguori, Que.; 1881, Hochelaga, village, Que.; 1891, 1901, Montréal, Hochelaga ward. "Beau mouvement philant[h]ropique," *La Patrie*, 20 févr. 1915. *Le Devoir*, 28 nov. 1929. *La Presse*, 27 nov. 1929. *La Bonne Parole* (Montréal), 1 (1913)–18 (1930), esp. "Mlle Marie-Anne Laporte," 17 (1929), no.12: 8. *Le Duprex* (Montréal), 4 (1929–30), esp. Églantine Phaneuf, "Une perte pour l'Association des employées de magasins," 87. Nadia Fahmy-Eid et Lucie Piché, *Si le travail m'était conté . . . autrement; les travailleuses de la CTCC-CSN: quelques fragments d'histoire, 1921–1976* ([Montréal], 1987). Marie Gérin-Lajoie, "Le syndicalisme féminin," in *Québécoises du 20e siècle: les étapes de la libération féminine au Québec, 1900–1974*, Michèle Jean, édit. (2e éd.,

Montréal, 1977). Karine Hébert, "Une organisation maternaliste au Québec: la Fédération nationale Saint-Jean-Baptiste et la bataille pour le vote des femmes," *RHAF*, 52 (1998–99): 315–44. Marie [Lacoste] Gérin-Lajoie, *La Fédération nationale Saint-Jean-Baptiste et ses associations professionnelles* (Montréal, 1911). Marie Lavigne *et al.*, "La Fédération nationale Saint-Jean-Baptiste et les revendications féministes au début du 20e siècle," in *Travailleuses et féministes: les femmes dans la société québécoise*, sous la dir. de Marie Lavigne et Yolande Pinard (Montréal, 1983), 199–216. *La paroisse de L'Assomption: répertoire des sépultures, 1800–1980*, Maurice Perreault, compil. (Ottawa, 1983). Yolande Pinard, "Le féminisme à Montréal au commencement du XXe siècle (1893–1920)" (mémoire de MA, univ. du Québec à Montréal, 1976). "Rapport de l'Association des employées de magasins," in Fédération Nationale Saint-Jean-Baptiste, *Recueil des œuvres fédérées ou l'Action des Canadiennes-françaises* (Montréal, 1911), 140–46.

LA RIVIÈRE, ALPHONSE-ALFRED-CLÉMENT (baptized **Alfred-Alphonse**), businessman, civil servant, newspaper owner, and politician; b. 24 July 1842 in Montreal, son of Abraham Clément, *dit* La Rivière, a carriage maker, and Adélaïde Mercil; m. there 4 Feb. 1867 Marie-Melvina Bourdeau (d. 1885), and they had 13 children, 4 of whom survived him; d. 20 Sept. 1925 in St Boniface (Winnipeg).

Alphonse-Alfred-Clément La Rivière entered the Jesuits' Collège Sainte-Marie in Montreal in 1855 and the École Normale Jacques-Cartier in 1857. After his studies there he trained at the School of Military Instruction of Montreal. Following his graduation in 1866, he established a wholesale and retail hardware business in Montreal, which he ran until it failed in 1871. During this period, he served in the militia and was active in a number of cultural and social organizations, including the Cercle Saint-Pierre, founded by the Oblates of Mary Immaculate to provide morally healthy recreational and cultural facilities for Montrealers. La Rivière became its first president in 1869. He was also prominent in several trade associations and, as president of a subcommittee of the Council of Arts and Manufactures of the Province of Quebec, he was instrumental in organizing the Quebec provincial exhibition in 1871.

After the failure of his business in 1871, La Rivière accepted a position with the Dominion Lands Office in Winnipeg, encouraged by Bishop Alexandre-Antonin Taché* of St Boniface, who was eager to attract educated French Canadians to lead Manitoba's francophone community. His salary was disappointingly small: he complained that he could not bring his family from Montreal unless the government paid their way, and even then they had to share a house with another recruit from Quebec, the lawyer Joseph Dubuc*, and his wife.

When La Rivière arrived in St Boniface on 27 Oct. 1871, provincial and local institutions were being set up and the francophones in particular, still almost half of Manitoba's population but facing a massive immigration of anglophone settlers, needed professionals and businessmen as leaders. La Rivière quickly became involved in the community. He participated in the founding of the Société Saint-Jean-Baptiste in December 1871 and was among the notables who congratulated Taché the following month on his elevation to archbishop.

As part of the French-speaking elite, La Rivière naturally became involved in politics. He supported efforts to obtain an amnesty for Louis Riel* and other Métis who had participated in the 1869–70 Red River uprising and particularly in the killing of Thomas Scott*. In September 1872 he and Dubuc joined Joseph Royal* and Marc-Amable Girard* (two other recruits from Quebec) in helping to persuade Riel to withdraw his candidacy for a House of Commons seat in favour of Sir George-Étienne Cartier*, who had just been defeated in his own riding of Montreal East. They wanted Cartier to show his gratitude by obtaining an amnesty, but he died in May 1873. La Rivière and the others then nominated Riel, who was acclaimed in a by-election that October. Despite this show of confidence by the voters, who repeated it in the general election of 1874, no amnesty was announced. When Riel was expelled from the commons in April 1874, La Rivière became discouraged, believing that the Métis leader's candidacies were counterproductive. This attitude, however, earned him the antipathy of Riel's Quebec supporters (some of whom suspected him of wanting Riel's seat) as well as of the Manitoba Métis. He would antagonize the former again in 1885 by opposing the Quebec movement of protest against Riel's execution – a protest which, he feared, would provoke a dangerous backlash against French Canadians in the west.

In 1874 La Rivière became involved in conflicts with his superiors in the Dominion Lands Office and with Antoine-Aimé Dorion*, minister of justice in the new Liberal government of Alexander Mackenzie* and leader of the Quebec caucus in the House of Commons. By 1875 he had lost his job. He had already begun speculating in land, however, and had launched a real estate business. He had also joined Taché and others in efforts to promote the settlement of French Canadians in Manitoba. In 1874 La Rivière took the leading role in founding the Société de Colonisation de Manitoba, whose first president he became. Expecting a large number of French Canadians to move to the west and wanting to locate them within a consolidated community, he applied to the federal government for a reserve adjacent to the one already set aside for the Métis. The government was slow to respond and when the land was finally granted, it was not in the desired location. In any case, few French Canadians were drawn to Manitoba. La Rivière would work continually over the next 37 years to attract fran-

cophones from Europe as well as from Quebec and New England, but the number who came was never enough to preserve Manitoba's linguistic balance in the face of the massive immigration of anglophones.

La Rivière entered the Legislative Assembly of Manitoba as the member for St Boniface after the general election of December 1878. He was soon caught up in controversy. The relative strength of Manitoba's francophones had declined from about half to 15 per cent of the population during the 1870s, as large numbers of anglophone settlers arrived. French-speaking politicians had tried to compensate by forming a united block whose weight could be decisive in alliance with one anglophone party or another. However, Royal, who led the French caucus, believed that the position of the francophone population could never be properly secured unless it could gain acceptance of the principle that all governments must be supported by a majority of the MLAs within each of the two linguistic groups. When La Rivière came to the assembly, Royal had just entered the government of John Norquay*, although it did not have a majority of anglophone members behind it. In May 1879 Royal presented Norquay with an ultimatum: he must obtain a majority among the English or lose the support of the French. At the same time, La Rivière approached another anglophone, Thomas Scott, about forming an alliance to replace Norquay.

Norquay, however, outmanoeuvred them all. Overnight he formed a new coalition of anglophone members and demanded the resignation of his two French-speaking ministers, Royal and the Métis Pierre Delorme*. He then introduced legislation to abolish the use of French in the printing of public records. Only the refusal of the French Canadian lieutenant governor, Joseph-Édouard Cauchon*, to sign the bill prevented it from becoming law.

La Rivière's role in the crisis earned him the resentment of Norquay, who accused him of having conspired for months beforehand. Nevertheless, by November 1881 he had been sufficiently forgiven to be brought into the cabinet as provincial secretary. In September 1883 he took over the ministry of agriculture, statistics, and health, in August 1886 he became provincial treasurer, and in June 1887 he was appointed provincial land commissioner.

Meanwhile, La Rivière had gone into journalism. In October 1881 he had purchased Royal's *Le Métis* (which he would control until the end of 1897) and had changed its name to *Le Manitoba,* promising that it would be a "vigilant sentinel" protecting the rights of the "French" population. It was, in fact, a strong defender of the French language in Manitoba, but La Rivière's conception of Frenchness went beyond language. The graduate of an ultramontane college, closely associated with an ultramontane archbishop, he wanted his paper to be "entirely devoted to the

La Rivière

interest of religion" – and ethnicity. "Unity of origin, unity of language, unity of manners and habits": these were the elements of "a strong nationality." His ethnic and religious conception of nationality inspired La Rivière's continued advocacy of French Canadian settlement – and perhaps, too, his opposition to some other groups. When the first Jewish refugees from Russian pogroms arrived in 1882 [*see* Benjamin ZIMMERMAN], *Le Manitoba* was the only local newspaper to oppose their settlement in the province. Wherever Jews settled, the paper warned, it was "to seize the wealth of the country and to plunder the inhabitants."

La Rivière's career in provincial politics ended in controversy in 1887. Late in the year he had met with Prime Minister Sir John A. Macdonald* and thought he had obtained his approval for a transfer of federal lands to the Winnipeg and Hudson Bay Railway. The lands were to serve as security for bonds the province wanted to issue to pay the railway's contractors. La Rivière issued the bonds, but Macdonald denied that he had approved the transfer. Without the land, Manitoba's books were in disarray. Accused of serious improprieties in their handling of provincial finances, La Rivière and Norquay resigned in late December and less than a month later the Liberals, under Thomas Greenway*, came to power for the first time in Manitoba's history. Federal Conservatives blamed Norquay and La Rivière for handing Manitoba over to the Liberals. Royal – now an MP – was particularly harsh, calling La Rivière "the evil genius" whose financial misdeeds had brought disaster to the party. Yet when Royal was appointed lieutenant governor of the North-West Territories in 1888, it was La Rivière who replaced him as federal member for Provencher after a by-election in January 1889.

La Rivière was not very active in Ottawa. Although he obtained federal funding for new efforts to attract francophone settlers to Manitoba, he did not play a prominent role in the House of Commons. He spoke twice on the bill introduced by D'Alton McCarthy* in 1890 to abolish the official use of French in the North-West Territories, but, in the end, he supported an amendment which allowed the territorial assembly to decide the issue. He spoke again in 1895 and 1896, in support of measures to restore the public funding for Manitoba's Roman Catholic schools which Greenway's government had abolished in 1890, but all in all he proved a weak champion for Manitoba's Catholics. Father Albert Lacombe*, sent to Ottawa in late 1895 to lobby for remedial action, complained to Taché's successor, Archbishop Adélard Langevin*, that nothing was to be expected of La Rivière or of Senator Thomas-Alfred Bernier*. "Without energy or the necessary ability, what kind of a fight can they possibly put up?" In the end, La Rivière compromised again, accepting what he considered an inadequate remedial bill and urging Langevin to do the same.

Despite his ineffectiveness, La Rivière retained the Provencher seat until 1904. From 1905 to 1911 he worked in Montreal as Manitoba's agent to recruit settlers from eastern Canada and New England. When the Conservatives came back into power in 1911 under Robert Laird Borden*, La Rivière was made a senator. He was less active in the Senate than in the House of Commons and more willing to follow the government line even when it went against French Canadian or Catholic interests. He supported a bill to annex the District of Keewatin to Manitoba in 1912, though it would mean a loss of school rights for Catholics in the region and was strongly opposed by French Canadian nationalists [*see* George Robson COLDWELL]. In 1917, when the Borden government introduced legislation for conscription – a measure overwhelmingly rejected by French Canadians – he remained docile. He said nothing during the debate and then quietly voted in favour of the bill. It was his last political act. He withdrew to his home in St Boniface and on 29 August, the day the bill became law, he resigned from the Senate. Age and ill health were the reasons he gave, but Montreal's nationalist newspaper, *Le Devoir*, thought the anger he had provoked by his vote on conscription was probably the real cause.

La Rivière had never been a great leader. In a society more mature than the Manitoba of the 1870s and 1880s he might never have attained the prominence he did. Even there, he seemed always to be the next in line after his better-known colleagues, Royal, Dubuc, and Girard. He followed Royal as mayor of St Boniface (1881) and Dubuc and Royal as superintendent of Manitoba's Catholic schools (1879), as MP for Provencher, and as president of the Société Saint-Jean-Baptiste. Later he followed Girard and Bernier in the Senate. In this way, he left his mark on Manitoba's history. It was a modest one, however, and when he died at home in St Boniface, the newspapers spared only a few paragraphs to take notice.

A. I. SILVER

There is no known collection of La Rivière papers in any Canadian repository. The odd letter may be found in the papers of the politicians with whom he had contact, such as Sir George-Étienne Cartier (LAC, MG 27, I, D4), but the most significant body of correspondence is probably that at the Arch. de la Soc. Hist. de Saint-Boniface [Winnipeg], in the Fonds de la Corporation Archiépiscopale Catholique Romaine. It includes 62 letters in the Série Taché, mostly from La Rivière to Taché, and 110 letters in the Série Langevin. No books have been written about La Rivière and his name rarely appears in works on the history of Manitoba. P. [E.] Crunican, *Priests and politicians: Manitoba schools and the election of 1896* (Toronto and Buffalo, N.Y., 1974), and Robert Painchaud, *Un rêve français dans le peuplement de la Prairie* (Saint-Boniface [Winnipeg], 1986), give an indication of his role in history. A chapter in M. S. MacGregor [and A.-A. Taché], *Some letters from Archbishop Taché on the Manitoba school question* (Toronto, 1967), throws light on his ineffectiveness in business as well as in politics. Short notices in the *Canadian directory of parl.* (Johnson), *Canadian men and women of the time* (Morgan; 1898 and 1912), the *CPG*, 1878–1927, and A.-G. Morice, *Dictionnaire historique des Canadiens et des Métis français de l'Ouest* (Québec et Montréal, 1908), provide basic biographical information. The *Manitoba Free Press*, a Liberal newspaper, was generally hostile to the Conservative La Rivière, but it is the most important Manitoba paper. The most abundant and sympathetic source on La Rivière is his own newspaper, *Le Manitoba* (Saint-Boniface), which was published until 1925. Unfortunately only the issues to 1900 have been microfilmed and are widely available. The *Index du journal "le Manitoba" (1881–1925)* (Saint-Boniface, 1982) provides numerous references to him, but it also leaves out many more.

A speech delivered by La Rivière before the Legislative Assembly of Manitoba is included in L. M. Jones *et al.*, *The budget . . .* ([Winnipeg?, 1888?]). Other speeches by him can be found in the *Debates* of the Canadian House of Commons and Senate.

ANQ-M, CE601-S51, 25 juill. 1842, 4 févr. 1867. *Le Métis* (Saint-Boniface), 2 nov., 14 déc. 1871; 27 janv. 1872; 17 mai 1877. *Directories*, Man., 1877–78; Montreal, 1842, 1869–72; Winnipeg, 1880–84.

LARKIN, PETER CHARLES, businessman and diplomat; b. 14 May 1855 in Montreal, son of Michael Larkin and Sarah McGill; m. 27 June 1883 Hannah Jean Ross in Cobourg, Ont., and they had one son and one daughter; d. 3 Feb. 1930 in London, England.

Peter Larkin always gave his date of birth incorrectly as 13 May 1856. Little is known about his early life and upbringing in what undoubtedly were modest circumstances. His father, a bricklayer, died when he was seven; his mother worked as a charwoman. He received his primary education in Montreal, and is said to have had some training in Toronto. Perhaps this occurred in the evenings after he moved there in his twenties. Young Peter's business career had begun when he went to work at age 13 for a retail grocer. By 1875–76 Montreal directories listed him as a bookkeeper for an unnamed employer. About 1877 he joined Tiffin Brothers, a grocery wholesaler in Montreal, as a commercial traveller calling on customers from Halifax to Winnipeg. At the time of his marriage he was based in Toronto.

In 1889 he left Tiffin Brothers to start his own business in Toronto as a tea broker and wholesaler of sugar, dried fruits, and nuts. An early indication of his commercial ability and shrewdness came two years later after he had fallen out with the city's Wholesale Grocers' Guild over his refusal to maintain the prices for granulated sugar its members had agreed upon. They were unable to match either the lower expenses he achieved by stocking a narrow line of high-volume items or the flexibility he gained by using public warehouses. Larkin's main interest, however, remained the tea trade, and soon it demanded almost his entire attention.

Beginning in the 1880s public taste in Britain, and in Canada, turned away markedly from the increasingly adulterated green teas of China and Japan toward the more robust black teas of India and Ceylon (Sri Lanka). Between 1882 and 1892 imports of China tea into Britain declined from 114 million pounds to 34, while imports from the Indian subcontinent rose from 31.5 million to 173. As well, the old way of selling tea, from open, lead-lined chests where it was prone to absorb strong odours in a grocer's shop, began to be superseded about 1890 by its sale in small, sealed, lead-foil packets.

Although Larkin was neither the first to introduce India and Ceylon teas to Canada nor the first to supply them in packets, he was in the vanguard of innovators and certainly the earliest importer to mix his own blends, which were marketed with a skill and drive unmatched by his competitors. As early as 1891 he advertised Ceylon tea in 50-pound chests to the grocery trade. A year later he refined his line by blending Ceylon teas and offering them to grocers in pound and half-pound packages as the Golden Teapot Blend from "The Salada Tea Co., L'td., Ceylon." No evidence has been found that this company, said to be named for a tea-growing district in India, was other than Larkin's invention. All mention of Golden Teapot Blend was soon dropped and Salada went on to become one of the strongest brand names in the Canadian and American markets.

Larkin's marketing strategy was to appoint agents to sell his product and to support them with extensive newspaper publicity. "In advertising," he said, "be sure you have the right article first, then don't spare the printer's ink." As of May 1893 more than 200 Toronto grocers stocked Salada. A year later, when sales in the city had grown to exceed those of all other packaged teas combined, Larkin turned his attention outside Toronto and rapidly signed up grocers throughout southern Ontario. Week after week the *Canadian Grocer* (Toronto) reported, like a railway conductor calling out stops, the towns where agents had been appointed. His next target was Montreal, where, within four months, some 225 accounts had been opened. By May 1895 Larkin boasted nearly 2,000 agents in eastern Canada; sales volumes were more than double those of the year before. With the opening of a wholesale depot in Vancouver in 1896, Salada gained national distribution. Backed by advertising in some 340 daily and weekly newspapers, it quickly captured about 75 per cent of the sales of packaged tea in the country.

As his brand's share of its market neared saturation, Larkin had a choice, either of slower growth as packaged tea made inroads on bulk sales, which still accounted for 85 per cent of Canada's black-tea market, or of expanding to the United States. He chose the latter, though per capita consumption of tea there was much lower than in Canada. His first American branch opened in Buffalo, N.Y., in mid 1896; others followed in quick succession in Pittsburgh, Boston, Rochester, and Detroit. The hub of his American business, however, was Boston. By early 1898 more than 500 grocers in that city and its suburbs were handling Salada.

Until 1900 Larkin's business – styled P. C. Larkin and Company, but usually known as the Salada Tea Company – was organized as a sole proprietorship. In that year the Salada Tea Company Limited was incorporated with 40,000 shares having a par value of $10 each. Larkin held all the shares except those needed by his wife and accountant to qualify as directors. Salada's offices and factory were then at 32 Yonge Street, Toronto, in a building acquired in 1898 after fire had damaged Larkin's previous quarters and stock. His income from tea was augmented by sales of his patented invention, the Ideal tea packer, which enabled three men to turn out 20,000 half-pound packages of tea per week. Even competitors such as Thomas J. Lipton Company acquired Ideal packers for their own use. By 1899, when Larkin was invited to join George Albertus Cox*, William Mulock*, Timothy Eaton* and others in buying shares to support Joseph E. Atkinson*'s bid for control of the *Toronto Daily Star,* it was clear he had become a wealthy man. A few years later he was said to be the "heaviest insured man" in Canada.

Earlier, in the mid 1890s when Atkinson was the Toronto *Globe*'s Ottawa correspondent, he had interviewed Larkin about the Liberal party's policy of unrestricted reciprocity. Likely the tea merchant's opinion was sought not only because he was a leading businessman but also because he was a known supporter of the party and its charismatic leader, Wilfrid Laurier*. While Larkin might doubt as late as 1899 that Laurier would remember him from their few previous contacts, this uncertainty was unwarranted by September 1905, when Larkin became treasurer of the General Reform Association of Ontario, a position he would hold for several years. In 1909 he helped found the Ontario Club, the party's chief social establishment in Toronto; he was its president in 1911–12. Following the Imperial Conference of 1911, which recommended a British royal commission on the natural resources, trade, and legislation of the dominions, he was appointed Canada's representative on the commission. Barely two months later, after the Liberals were soundly defeated in a general election by Robert Laird Borden*'s Conservatives, George Eulas Foster*, the new minister of trade and commerce, lost no time in replacing Larkin.

Larkin's essentially benevolent view of life had been reflected in the other endeavours in which he was active during the century's first decade. In 1904, on the initiative of Joseph Wesley Flavelle*, chairman of the Toronto General Hospital, Larkin was appointed to its board of trustees. For 17 years he would throw himself into the hospital's affairs as a member of several committees and as vice-chairman of the board, retiring with Flavelle only after the large new hospital built near Queen's Park had been finished and was free of debt. In 1909 Larkin became president of the Toronto League for the Prevention of Tuberculosis; he served in this capacity for 20 years and gave heavily of his time and funds to its work. In addition, he was credited in obituaries with being the first prominent person to advocate a system of old-age pensions, which took shape in parliament as the Government Annuities Act of 1908.

For all Larkin's involvement in politics, he was more comfortable as a power behind the throne rather than on it. Before the Liberals lost office in 1911, he was often spoken of as a possible senator. As Laurier went about rebuilding the party after the election, the two men became close friends. When Laurier visited Toronto he usually stayed at the Larkins' house on Elm Avenue in Rosedale. After the conscription issue split the country in 1917, Larkin was one of the few Ontario Liberals who backed their leader in opposing forced military service. He even resigned over the issue from the board of the *Globe*, where he had sat for almost ten years. Yet when it was suggested that he contest a seat in the election of December 1917, he declined on the grounds that his business could hardly do without him.

Larkin had a point. Though exact figures are not available, Salada Tea's volume had increased between five and ten times since 1900. He prided himself on being known as "The Tea King of America," in tribute to the company's domination of markets north and south of the border. Soon after World War I broke out, however, an embargo on tea exports from England made the company dependent on shipments direct from Ceylon and India, which took three months to arrive. To protect against any interruption in its supplies, Salada bought in unusually large quantities, borrowing heavily from its bankers to finance the purchases. Five or six years before the war Larkin had begun to turn over the day-to-day management of his company to his son, Gerald Ross, but when Gerald and more than two dozen key employees enlisted to fight in Europe, Larkin was forced to resume detailed charge. At one point his tea-taster in Boston joined up and he had to take the man's place for a while.

In the aftermath of the 1917 election, which was a disaster for the Liberals, Laurier again set about reviving his party, though illness began to hobble him the following summer. One of the last letters he received before his death in February 1919 came from Larkin asking if a seat in parliament could be found for William Lyon Mackenzie King*, who had been defeated in the election (despite Larkin's financial backing), to avoid losing his talents to the United States. As events unfolded, King was chosen to succeed Laurier as leader in August, and he was returned to the House of Commons in a by-election two months later. He then led the opposition until the Liberals squeaked into office in December 1921.

One of King's first acts in power was to make Larkin Canada's high commissioner in London in place of Sir George Halsey Perley*, who had retired after the election. The appointment, the highest within the gift of the government, was gazetted on 10 Feb. 1922, when Larkin was also sworn in as a privy councillor for Canada. In offering him the post, King had played down his influence by saying he was only carrying out Laurier's wish and expressed belief that "there is nothing too good for our friend Larkin." Although there were some grumblings – George MacKinnon Wrong* of the University of Toronto had advised King not to pick someone with such limited formal education – on the whole bipartisan approval greeted the appointment. Larkin was thought by most to have the intelligence and urbanity to do Canada credit, as well as a business reputation the British would respect. He was tall and patrician, with coal-black eyes, a full, white moustache, and a well-formed head that had been bald since his thirties. Known for being particularly well-dressed, he usually wore formal attire with a black silk hat. Asked to describe himself, he said he was a "plain, blunt man," like Mark Antony, but drew attention to his literary tastes, the experience he had gained from travelling to Europe annually for many years, and his considerable knowledge of art and architecture. The prime minister had benefited from Larkin's interest in the decorative arts after Lady Laurier left her house in Ottawa to the Liberal party as an official residence for its leader. Larkin contributed heavily to the costs of renovation and provided much of the furniture for the public rooms from a stock of Adam, Hepplewhite, and Sheraton pieces he had gathered in a Montreal warehouse. His involvement foreshadowed his role in creating Canada House in London.

When Larkin was appointed, it was made clear that the high commissioner would communicate directly with the prime minister on all matters of public policy, and avoid any gatherings of British officials and high commissioners that might pull Canada into a commitment to British foreign policy. Larkin was later quoted as saying, "The people of Canada think the high commissioner for Canada is a person of some importance in London. He is not." Since he shared King's sense of Canadian autonomy and his mistrust of the British government, Larkin was quite willing to conform to his prime minister's expectations. This understanding reflected not only the similarity of views and close ties between the two men, but also King's desire to exercise control over matters at a time when Canada's relationships with Britain and the other dominions

were being redefined. To reinforce the chain of command, an order in council was passed concurrent with Larkin's appointment placing all agencies of the Canadian government in the United Kingdom under the high commissioner. On 23 April, barely two weeks after Larkin arrived in Britain, he wrote to King proposing that things be taken to their logical conclusion by concentrating all operations under one roof. The proposal soon became mixed up in the simmering issue of whether provincial agents general in London would be recognized as equals to the high commissioner in matters where the British North America Act accorded powers to the provinces. After Frederick Coate WADE, British Columbia's aggressive agent general, was found to be using his influence against the sale of his province's well-located quarters to the Canadian government, which already leased part of it, King wrote Larkin on 22 June 1922 that he was not inclined "to go particularly out of my way towards seeking any added status for the representatives of the provinces in London." Finding an alternative site took Larkin another year, but the delay was well worth the wait when he secured from the Union Club its distinguished building on Trafalgar Square. Canada House was opened by King George V on 29 June 1925. The consolidation there of Canadian offices soon strained relations with the trade commissioners in Britain of the Department of Trade and Commerce, in part because the move facilitated Larkin's periodic interference in trade matters.

Meanwhile, there were other issues demanding the high commissioner's attention, including the lifting of a 30-year embargo on the importation of live cattle into Britain, settling Britain's war debt to Canada, and preparations for the British Empire exhibitions of 1924 and 1925. In addition, the high commissionship committed the Larkins to incessant socializing. Jean Larkin's contribution was the hosting of weekly receptions in their residence at Lancaster Gate, London. That King was grateful for such diligent work, not to mention Peter Larkin's financial support, is clear from the long and sentimental letter the prime minister, exhausted by constitutional tilting with Governor General Lord Byng*, wrote Larkin on New Year's Eve 1926. "I have no living friend for whom I have a greater or truer regard than for yourself," King told him. Although Larkin would continue to serve for another four years, until his death, King's words were a fitting tribute to his work as high commissioner.

Larkin died of a heart attack in 1930. After a memorial service at Christchurch, Lancaster Gate, his cremated remains were returned to Toronto for burial. Subsequently, uncashed cheques for his salary from the government were found in his desk. With an income said to have reached $650,000 annually from the Salada Tea Company, which during the 1920s had grown under Gerald Larkin's management to be the

La Rocque

third-largest supplier of teas in the world, Peter Larkin had asked no more from his country than the honour of serving it.

STEPHEN A. OTTO

ANQ-M, CE601–S51, 20 mai 1855. AO, F 749; RG 8-1-1, file 4408; RG 55-1, 58: 98; RG 80-3-2-31, no.901673; RG 80-5-0-118, no.8616. City of Toronto Arch., RG 5, F (assessment rolls), sub-ser.1, 1834–1951, St Lawrence Ward, 1 Oct. 1889. LAC, MG 26, G, 32019–22, 197578–80, 202509–12; J1, 20: 18664–65; 76: 64254, 64256–57, 64283–85, 64361, 64462; 133: 113612–16; MG 27, III, E1; RG 32, C2, 331, file 1856. *Evening Telegram* (Toronto), 4 Feb. 1930. *Gazette* (Montreal), 3–4, 6 Feb. 1930. *Globe*, 4 Feb. 1930. *Montreal Daily Star*, 10 Feb. 1922. *Toronto Daily Star*, 3 Jan. 1931. *Canadian annual rev.*, 1905, 1922. *Canadian Grocer* (Toronto), 1890–98. *Canadian men and women of the time* (Morgan; 1912). R. MacG. Dawson and H. B. Neatby, *William Lyon Mackenzie King: a political biography* (3v., Toronto, 1958–76), 2: 40–41. *Directory*, Montreal, 1854–62/63, 1867/68, 1875/76–76/77. Nancy Gelber, *Canada in London: an unofficial glimpse of Canada's sixteen high commissioners, 1880–1980* (London, [1980]). Ross Harkness, *J. E. Atkinson of the "Star"* (Toronto, 1963). O. M. Hill, *Canada's salesman to the world: the Department of Trade and Commerce, 1892–1939* (Montreal and London, 1977). [C.] V. Massey, *What's past is prologue: the memoirs of the Right Honourable Vincent Massey, C.H.* (Toronto, 1963). Middleton, *Municipality of Toronto*, vol.2: 783. Peter Oliver, *G. Howard Ferguson: Ontario Tory* (Toronto and Buffalo, N.Y., 1977). J. E. Saunders, "The Honourable Peter Charles Larkin, collector, philanthropist, and fifth high commissioner for Canada in London: a study on Canadian collecting in the decorative arts" (MA thesis, Bard Graduate Center for Studies in the Decorative Arts, New York, 1999).

LA ROCQUE, PAUL (baptized **Paul-Toussaint**, he signed **Paul LaRocque**), Roman Catholic priest and bishop; b. 27 Oct. 1846 in Sainte-Marie-de-Monnoir (Marieville), Lower Canada, son of Albert Larocque, a farmer, and Geneviève Dagneau; d. 15 Aug. 1926 in Sherbrooke, Que.

Paul La Rocque came from a family that included several prominent members of the Catholic clergy. Two of his father's cousins were bishops of Saint-Hyacinthe, Joseph* from 1860 to 1866 and Charles* from 1866 to 1875. Paul's younger brother Charles was the first curé of Saint-Louis-de-France in Montreal (1888–1904), and a sister became a nun with the Sisters Adorers of the Precious Blood. Paul himself was made the second bishop of Sherbrooke. Yet his father had been unable to sign his name at Paul's baptism.

Paul La Rocque first attended the Petit Séminaire de Sainte-Thérèse in 1858–59. Following a period at the Séminaire de Saint-Hyacinthe from 1859 to 1862, he returned to it to complete his classical studies and he donned the soutane there in 1865. With his delicate constitution (he suffered from poor health all his life), he was "ordained to die," as the saying went, by

Bishop Charles La Rocque at the Hôtel-Dieu in Montreal on 9 May 1869. He was then sent as a missionary to Key West, Fla, to build up his strength. La Rocque spent more than ten years there working with the Cubans and blacks who inhabited the island. This period in Florida enabled him to acquire a command of English that would prove extremely useful to him in his future diocese. Back in Saint-Hyacinthe in 1880, he was immediately sent by his bishop, Louis-Zéphirin Moreau*, to study in Rome, where he earned doctorates in theology and canon law. La Rocque returned to Saint-Hyacinthe in 1884 and a year later was appointed curé of the cathedral, succeeding Elphège Gravel*, who had been chosen as the first bishop of Nicolet. Saint-Hyacinthe was at that time (and would remain) a veritable seedbed of future bishops.

It was in 1893 that La Rocque became the second bishop of Sherbrooke, succeeding Antoine Racine*. Consecrated there on 30 November, he would remain at the head of the diocese until his death 32 years later. The period in which he held episcopal office coincided with a time of expansion for the Catholic Church in the Eastern Townships. The decennial reports La Rocque sent to Rome noted the growth of the Catholic population. It rose from 60,000 to 105,000 between 1896 and 1924, years which saw the non-Catholic population decline from 43,000 to 32,000; the ranks of secular priests increased from 90 to 177, and 37 new parishes were established, bringing their total number to 91 by 1924. La Rocque toured these parishes every three years. During his pastoral visits, which lasted more than a month, he confirmed the children, who would never forget his long white beard, doubtless a holdover from his missionary days. From 1910 La Rocque frequently spoke about the "petits chevaliers de la tempérance," the newly confirmed boys to whom he awarded the Cross of Temperance once they had promised "to abstain from every kind of intoxicating drink until the age of 21," as he put it to the curés of his diocese. At the pastoral level the bishop, who in all other respects maintained excellent relations with those whom he referred to as "our separated brothers," vigorously opposed both mixed marriages and the practice of Catholic children attending Protestant schools.

The growth of the Catholic Church led to the establishment of various new charities and institutions and the consolidation of existing ones, such as the Séminaire Saint-Charles-Borromée, which was adjacent to the bishop's residence. Destroyed by fire on 30 Dec. 1897, the seminary was rebuilt and inaugurated in June 1900 by the apostolic delegate, Mgr Diomede Falconio. Among the religious bodies he welcomed, La Rocque was particularly supportive of the contemplative orders: the Sisters Adorers of the Precious Blood (1895) and the Servants of the Blessed Sacrament (1925) in Sherbrooke, and the Benedictines

(1912) in Saint-Benoît-du-Lac [*see* Pierre-Paul Vannier*]. He was on the verge of losing the last order at the end of World War I, but managed to keep them in 1919. Two other female orders established their mother houses within his diocese. The Little Sisters of the Holy Family, founded by Élodie Paradis*, named Mother Marie-Léonie, arrived in Sherbrooke in 1895 and spread rapidly; they devoted themselves to "the manual tasks required for the material care of the interior of seminaries, colleges, [and] episcopal houses." In his pastoral letter of 28 Jan. 1896, which gave this community canonical recognition, La Rocque specified that the sisters should "confine themselves to this work and never deviate from it." In 1919, in Lennoxville, Florina Gervais, named Marie du Sacré-Cœur, founded the community of the Missionary Sisters of Notre Dame des Anges, which was devoted to fostering among young Chinese girls the vocations of catechist and nun. In 1920 the Franciscans also set up their noviciate in Lennoxville, following the lead of the Redemptorists; the bishop had put the Redemptorists in charge of a Sherbrooke parish which in 1913 had become known as Notre-Dame-du-Perpétuel-Secours.

La Rocque was also interested in education. There already were several teaching communities in his diocese, among which the most important numerically were the Congregation of Notre-Dame, the Sisters of the Presentation of Mary, and the Brothers of the Sacred Heart. In 1907 he managed to attract the Filles de la Charité du Sacré-Cœur de Jésus. To develop hospitals and other charitable institutions he had to negotiate with the Sœurs de la Charité de Saint-Hyacinthe (Grey Nuns), who had been responsible for the Hospice du Sacré-Cœur in Sherbrooke since 1875. These discussions drew him into a lengthy conflict with the sisters lasting from 1895 to 1905, because he wanted to establish a mother house in Sherbrooke. The sisters refused and took their case right up to the Holy See in Rome, which ruled in their favour. Good relations were re-established when the bishop's second cousin Mother Mathilde Davignon became the superior general at Saint-Hyacinthe in 1905.

La Rocque spent almost a year in Rome, from November 1904 to October 1905, to settle this affair. It was his second *ad limina* visit, and he was accompanied by his vicar general, Hubert-Olivier Chalifoux, who hailed from Saint-Hyacinthe. On the occasion of his third and final *ad limina* visit in 1914, La Rocque, who was ill at the time, managed to persuade Benedict XV to appoint Chalifoux auxiliary bishop of Sherbrooke, despite the opposition of the apostolic delegate, Mgr Pellegrino Francesco Stagni. Chalifoux in May 1919 organized the celebrations to honour La Rocque's 25 years of service as bishop and 50 years as a priest, marking the high point of his episcopate. On this occasion the clergy and the faithful presented him with an offering that amounted to $34,305.64 when the subscription ended on 30 June 1920. It was also in 1919 that the bishop inaugurated his cathedral, the Pauline chapel (actually the basement of the future cathedral), and, most significantly, his new bishop's house, a veritable episcopal palace that was the work of architect Louis-Napoléon Audet. The chapel, which was dedicated to the Blessed Virgin, would be decorated by Ozias Leduc*.

In 1922 La Rocque lost his faithful companion, Bishop Chalifoux, who had been ill for three years. Alphonse-Osias Gagnon, the superior of the seminary, was chosen as his auxiliary in 1923; he would later become his successor (1927–41). In the last years of his life La Rocque devoted himself mainly to new Catholic initiatives: a weekly newspaper (*Le Messager de Saint-Michel de Sherbrooke*, in 1917), Catholic and national labour unions, closed retreats (the Villa Saint-Alphonse, 1923), and the Semaine Sociale (1924). He died in 1926, widely venerated.

La Rocque had taken little part in the great national debates, although he strongly endorsed the bishops' stand on the Manitoba schools question [*see* Thomas Greenway*]. He was an ardent and steadfast supporter of Franco-Ontarians; in 1916 a subscription "for our brothers, the *wounded* of Ontario" [*see* Charles Hugh GAUTHIER], raised $2,055, the highest sum collected in the diocese up to that point. Characteristically for the period, his spirituality was based on devotion to the Sacred Heart as well as to the Virgin Mary, love of the Eucharist, and veneration of the papacy, as witnessed his heartfelt greeting to Mgr Stagni, the pope's representative, when he travelled around the diocese in 1913.

Because of his poor health, La Rocque did not take the usual path of Quebec bishops. His ten years in Key West had given him a tolerant approach that proved valuable to him throughout his episcopate. He successfully ensured the growth of the Catholic diocese of Sherbrooke. An embodiment of the good bishop, loved by all, "the magnificent and splendid Mgr Paul LaRocque" – as one of his successors, Bishop Philippe Desranleau*, would describe him – fully lived up to his motto, *Omnibus omnia factus sum* ("I made myself all things to all people").

GUY LAPERRIÈRE

[The main documents concerning Paul La Rocque are found in the Arch. de l'Archevêché de Sherbrooke, Qué. Its archival collections are in two separate locations: the Service des Archives (Historiques) holds the La Rocque fonds (P4), which contains important correspondence, while the Chancellerie houses the administrative files and the register of letters. Both the collections are so voluminous that the author was able to consult only a small part of each. The bishop's pastoral thought is condensed in his *Mandements, lettres pastorales, circulaires et autres documents publiés dans le diocèse de Sherbrooke* (24v., Sherbrooke, 1874–1967), 4–9.

La Rousselière

A selection of the numerous works on La Rocque includes the following items: É.-J.[-A.] Auclair, *Mgr Paul LaRocque, deuxième évêque de Sherbrooke* ([Saint-Gérard, Qué.], 1930); "Les trois évêques Larocque," SCHEC, *Rapport*, 13 (1945–46): 11–17; P.-J.-A. Lefebvre, *Monseigneur Paul LaRocque, deuxième évêque de Sherbrooke: souvenir de 1893–94* (Montréal, 1894); "Mgr Paul-Stanislas LaRocque," Séminaire Saint-Charles-Borromée, *Annuaire* (Sherbrooke), 1926–27: 341–65; Dolor Biron, *Jubilé d'argent et d'or de Monseigneur Paul LaRocque, évêque de Sherbrooke, mai 1919: 1869–1919, 1893–1918* ([Sherbrooke?, 1919?]); C.-J. Roy, *Visite de S.E. Monseigneur Stagni, délégué apostolique au Canada et à Terreneuve, dans les Cantons de l'Est: compte rendu des fêtes . . .* (Québec, 1914); *Obituaire du clergé, 1874–1993: archidiocèse de Sherbrooke* (Sherbrooke, 1993?), 38; Laurier Lacroix, "La décoration religieuse d'Ozias Leduc à l'évêché de Sherbrooke" (mémoire de MA, univ. de Montréal, 1973); [Philippe Desranleau], *La chaire de Mgr Desranleau: extraits de sermons, conférences, causeries, allocutions du premier archevêque de Sherbrooke*, L.-C. O'Neil, compil. (Sherbrooke, [1953]), 33. G.L.]

LA ROUSSELIÈRE. *See* HÉBERT

LASSALLE, EUGÈNE (baptized **Eugène-Jean-Baptiste**), actor, school administrator, professor, and author; b. 20 May 1859 in Saint-André-de-Cubzac, France, son of Jean-Prosper Lassalle, a collector of indirect taxes, and Mélanie Barthèlémy; m. first Onésime Fouré (d. in France); m. secondly 16 March 1908 Marie-Louise Doëlling, widow of Antonin-François Landreau, in Montreal; one son survived him; d. 1 March 1929 in Montreal.

After studying at the Petit Séminaire de Bordeaux, Eugène Lassalle made his theatrical debut in Angers in 1877 under the direction of actor Émile Marck. He continued his career in France from 1878 to 1886 and then directed French theatrical and operatic companies from the Balkans to Central Asia for the next seven years. In 1898 he would be given the title of *officier d'académie* for his work in disseminating French culture abroad.

After returning to France in 1893, Lassalle performed first at the Grand-Théâtre in Bordeaux, and then at Le Havre, Reims, Montpellier, and Paris. On 14 Aug. 1906 he signed a three-month contract with the Compagnie des Théâtres de Montréal (better known as the Théâtre des Nouveautés), whose artistic director was Jean Prévost. He was offered a salary of 1,800 francs (about $360) a month, which was apparently the going rate for a leading role in Montreal at that time. He began performing there on 3 September in the role of Mathis in *Le juif polonais*, by Émile Erckmann and Alexandre Chatrian. The next day *La Patrie* wrote: "M. Lassalle is an artist of great merit. He literally takes hold of his audience [and] makes them shiver with excitement." The Théâtre des Nouveautés extended the contract to 2 May 1907, but a dispute arose between Lassalle and the management,

who wanted him to play Scarpia in Victorien Sardou's *La Tosca*, a role with which he was not familiar. The theatre rejected the alternative solutions he proposed and dismissed him on 6 April 1907. He took his case to court and eventually won a settlement of $110 from his former employer.

Lassalle now abandoned his acting career. In the fall of 1907 he set up a school of elocution in Montreal, with support from representatives of the city's political, literary, and media circles, including legislative councillors Trefflé Berthiaume* and Jean-Damien Rolland, Montreal mayor Louis Payette, writer Jean Charbonneau, and journalists Godfroy LANGLOIS and Ernest Tremblay. The school's founding took place in the context of a major campaign to improve the quality of French spoken in Quebec, a campaign energetically led by *Le Nationaliste*, a Montreal newspaper under the editorship of Olivar Asselin*. On 3 April 1908 the province granted letters patent to the Conservatoire Lassalle, "a national school of elocution, french diction, and of the dramatic art." The government of Lomer GOUIN considered that it was an educational endeavour of national scope, and awarded the institution a large annual grant, which would enable it to offer its courses free of charge. From its first year of operation, the school had dozens of students, including Juliette Béliveau, Camillien Houde*, Paul Coutlée, and Laura Lussier. The courses dealt mainly with diction and elocution and were given three evenings a week. As a practical exercise, Lassalle and his students produced the great French classics that were too seldom seen in the province's theatres, such as Jean Racine's *Athalie* (1908) and *Britannicus* (1913). For this new championing and presenting of French culture abroad, the French government awarded him the title of *officier de l'Instruction publique* in 1911. Lassalle also taught elocution at the Petit Séminaire de Montréal from 1913 to 1916 and in 1918.

Lassalle even became an author, producing, among other things, his own version of the Passion of Christ in 1926 and 1927, with professional actors. He had been experiencing health problems for several years, however. He died at his home on 1 March 1929, at the age of 69.

An editorial in *La Patrie* paid tribute to his contribution. "Professor Lassalle's work was not solely a matter of promoting correct oral French. The students at his school drew from the store-house of French literature as a whole and thereby could not help acquiring the attitude of our overseas cousins, which strives for clarity and irony." From 1929 to 1988 the conservatory was guided in turn by Lassalle's wife, his stepson Georges Landreau, and Georges's daughter Marcelle Landreau (who was better known by her stage name of Nicole Germain). It would celebrate its 90th anniversary in 1998. Now a private school, it graduated many classes of elocution teachers. It also provided the province of Quebec with its first professional theatre school (where numerous actors would learn their trade), some 40 years before the opening of the Institute of Music and Dramatic Art of the Province of Quebec.

MIREILLE BARRIÈRE

Eugène Lassalle is the author of *Influence du théâtre français à l'étranger* (Athènes, 1887); *L'opérette française en Asie centrale, récit du voyage de la première troupe française dans la Transcaspienne et le Turkestan* (Tiflis [Tbilissi, Géorgie], 1891); *De Batoum au Thibet* (Tiflis, 1892); *L'art de mettre en scène* (Bruxelles, 1896); *Les monologues Lassalle sérieux et comiques, recueil pour dames, messieurs, jeunes filles, jeunes gens, fillettes et petits garçons, choisis parmi les auteurs français et canadiens-français* (Montréal, 1914); *Comédiens et amateurs; le théâtre et ses dessous* (Montréal, 1919); and *Aimons, rions, chantons en France et au Canada; méli-mélo* (Paris, [1924?]). In 1926 he also wrote and produced *La Passion*, a religious drama having 100 characters and walk-ons and a 30-voice mixed chorus, a work that was apparently never published.

ANQ-M, P565; TP11, S2, SS2, SSS1, dossier 966 (1908) (E.-J.-B. Lassalle *c.* Cie des théâtres de Montréal). Arch. Départementales, Gironde (Bordeaux), État civil, Saint-André-de-Cubzac, 30 mai 1859. Bibliothèque Nationale du Québec (Montréal), Div. des coll. spéciales, Programmes de théâtre, 6.5 (théâtre des Nouveautés), saison 1906–7. *Le Devoir*, 28 mai 1913. *Le Passe-Temps* (Montréal), 22 févr. 1908. *La Patrie*, 4 sept. 1906, 2 mars 1929. *La Presse*, 9 avril, 6, 13 juin 1908; 29 mars 1927. *BCF*, 1924. Baudoin Burger, "Les spectacles dramatiques en Nouvelle-France (1606–1760)," *Arch. des lettres canadiennes* (Montréal), 5 (1976): 44. Jean Charbonneau, *Discours ... à l'occasion du Xe anniversaire du conservatoire Lassalle en la salle de la bibliothèque Saint-Sulpice le 3 décembre 1916* (Montréal, 1917). *DOLQ*, vol.2. *Historique du conservatoire Lassalle, école gratuite d'élocution française: incorporé le 3 avril 1908, reconnu d'utilité publique par le ministère des Affaires étrangères de la République française et par le gouvernement de la province de Québec* ([Montréal, 1919?]). Georges Landreau, *Le conservatoire Lassalle présente les diverses maladies de notre langage* ([Montréal?], 1960). Petit Séminaire de Montréal, *Distribution des prix*, 1913–16, 1918. G.-É. Rinfret, *Le théâtre canadien d'expression française: répertoire analytique des origines à nos jours* (4v., [Montréal], 1975–78), 2: 312.

LASSANDRO, FLORENCE. *See* COSTANZO

LAVERGNE, ÉMILIE. *See* BARTHE

LAWLER (Lawlor), ELIZABETH GERTRUDE, educator and social advocate; b. in Boston, third daughter of John Lawlor and Ann Leighton; d. unmarried 21 July 1929 in Toronto.

The date of Gertrude Lawler's birth is uncertain: 1866 and 1867 are possibilities and the census of 1901 gives 28 Dec. 1871. Her familial connections in Canada included three Roman Catholic priests: her great-great-uncle Edmund Burke* (a vicar apostolic of Nova Scotia), her great-uncle John Carroll of Toronto and Chicago, and her uncle Edmund Burke Lawlor of Toronto. Gertrude began her education in Boston. After she moved to Toronto as a child in 1879, she attended public schools there and was the recipient of the Jesse Ketchum prize. Yet throughout her life she regarded St Joseph's Academy, run by the Sisters of St Joseph in Toronto, as the school of her formation. When she graduated in June 1882 she was the valedictorian and recipient of the academy's gold medals for proficiency and English literature. In addition to her pursuits there, she studied fine arts, elocution, and vocal and instrumental music (she took church organ with Frederick Herbert Torrington*).

During the time Lawler attended St Joseph's, it was not certified to present pupils for matriculation examination. With the encouragement of inspector James Laughlin Hughes*, she wrote her examinations at Toronto Collegiate Institute. (Her success encouraged the Sisters of St Joseph to amend their curriculum to meet provincial requirements and henceforth present their pupils at their own site.) A brilliant student, in 1886 Lawler entered the University of Toronto, where she received many awards and graduated with a BA in 1890. She took her MA in 1892 in honour mathematics, "being the first woman in Canada to take such standing in this department," according to her graduate records.

Lawler had a highly successful career as a secondary-school teacher. Having gained a professional certificate, in 1890 she was appointed to Stratford Collegiate Institute; two years later she joined the newly founded Harbord Street Collegiate Institute in Toronto, where she lived with her uncle E. B. Lawlor. From the outset of her teaching career, she was proud of the fact that she always received the same salary as a man would have been paid. She acquired specialist certificates in English, French, German, and mathematics, but it was as an English teacher and director of Shakespearean plays that she was most fondly remembered. "Filled with a deep patriotism," one biographer recalled, "she always maintained that it is essential to keep the Dominion truly British in language, education and ideals; and it was this deep feeling which made her teaching of the English language a living thing to her students." Business tycoon Willard Garfield Weston* was not alone in declaring her his favourite teacher. Her love of English also inspired many students beyond her high school. She served in the university's faculty of education as a lecturer and examiner in methods in English (1908–10), and edited several textbooks, including works by Shakespeare, Tennyson, Arnold, and Browning.

During her 26 years at Harbord, Lawler became enormously popular. "Reticent and dignified of person," according to some who knew her, "she was a model of graciousness and decorum." In 1906 news of her possible transfer brought a deputation of parents to a meeting of the Board of Education that resulted in her remaining at Harbord. She received attention again in 1914 when she was reported to be the leading candidate for the principalship of Jarvis Street Collegiate Institute. Although her qualifications and experience were celebrated by the press and her colleagues, she was unsuccessful; the *Globe* wondered if sexual discrimination was the reason. During World War I she worked closely with Harbord principal Edward William Hagarty, who also commanded the 201st Battalion, to establish an auxiliary for this unit. Ill health caused her to retire in 1918, but she would maintain her association with Harbord as honorary president of its Alumni Association.

Lawler steadfastly fostered the creation of bonds between students and their schools. A lifelong supporter of her own alma maters, she was first president of the St Joseph's Alumnae Association in 1911 and founding editor a year later of the *St Joseph Lilies*, a literary and alumnae magazine. She was a member as well of the International Federation of Catholic Alumnae, an organization of convent-school graduates, and, within the University of Toronto, an executive member of its Alumnae Association, an associate editor of the *University of Toronto Monthly*, and from 1910 a member of its senate. Such involvement is striking since, in addition to teaching, Lawler belonged over time to a host of other organizations, among them the League of Nations Society in Canada, the Dickens Fellowship, the University Women's Club, Ontario's Committee of Education Films, the Canadian Red Cross, and the Pure English Society of Chiswell.

Once she left teaching, Lawler's attention focused on the needs of women and children. She was especially active in the Catholic Women's League of Canada [*see* Bellelle GUERIN]; at its organizational meeting in Montreal in June 1920 she was appointed a vice-president. Re-elected at the 1921 convention, she served as well as president of the Toronto division and as a representative in 1921 to the International Union of Catholic Women's Leagues. At the 1922 convention she moved that the CWL adopt, as a national undertaking, the work of the Sisters of Service, a religious community formed in Toronto that year for "the preservation of the Faith and Nationalization of New Canadians." She subsequently headed the league's Sisters of Service committee in its initial phase.

Lawler's interest in public welfare led her to an active role as well on the Social Service Council of Ontario and Toronto's Social Hygiene Council. Indefatigable, she convened a building-fund drive for Women's College Hospital in Toronto, and in 1920–27 chaired the local Mothers' Allowance Board, in which her leadership was highly praised. In 1922 she was a delegate to the international convention held under the auspices of the United States League of Women Voters. Lawler's abundant contributions were

recognized by religious and secular institutions alike: in 1925 she was awarded a papal medal by Pius XI "for distinguished services to education and religious work" and two years later the University of Toronto granted her an honorary LLD. Following her death from cancer in 1929, scholarships were established in her name at both the university and St Joseph's Academy. Buried in Mount Hope Cemetery, she was survived by a niece and two sisters, Annie Lee Lawler of Toronto, to whom she left her modest estate, and Mary E. Walsh of Boston.

Gertrude Lawler was a pioneering woman in many fields, in secondary and post-secondary education, in the advocacy of equal pay for work of equal value (especially in education), and in the structuring of non-denominational and interdenominational agencies to address social justice. She represents an emerging tradition: a woman of strong conviction who, while practising her faith openly and supporting church-based organizations, spent her professional life in the sphere of public education and who divided her volunteer time between denominational and secular charitable activities.

ELIZABETH M. SMYTH

There are several portraits of Elizabeth Gertrude Lawler, including one in the student library of St Joseph's College Residence, Univ. of St Michael's College, Univ. of Toronto, and miniatures at the Sisters of St Joseph of Toronto Arch.

Textbooks edited by Lawler include *Shakespeare's "The merchant of Venice"* (Toronto, 1906), *Shakespeare's "A midsummer-night's dream"* (Toronto, 1909), and, as assistant to Alfred Henry Reynar, *Select poems of Alfred Tennyson, with memoir, introduction, and annotations* (Toronto, 1903). She is also credited with editing a collection of works by Arnold, Browning, and Tennyson, but no copies of this textbook have been located.

AO, RG 22-305, no.62766. Harbord Collegiate Institute Arch. (Toronto), Gertrude Lawler file. Mount Hope Cemetery (Toronto), Burial card, interment no.16142. LAC, RG 31, C1, 1901, Toronto, Ward 2, div.31: 4 (mfm. at AO). Sisters of St Joseph of Toronto Arch., box 5, St Joseph's Academy, reg., 1859–1920, 13 April 1882; Gertrude Lawler file. UTA, A1973-0026/221(92). *Evening Telegram* (Toronto), 21 July 1929. *Globe*, 22 July 1929. *Canadian League* (Toronto), 1921–22 (copies in the Catholic Women's League of Canada Arch., Winnipeg). *St Joseph Lilies* (Toronto), 1 (1912–13), no.4: 72–74 (copies in Sisters of St Joseph of Toronto Arch.). E. M. Smyth, "The lessons of religion and science: the congregation of the Sisters of St. Joseph and St. Joseph's Academy, Toronto, 1854–1911" (ED.D. thesis, Univ. of Toronto, 1989). *Standard dict. of Canadian biog.* (Roberts and Tunnell). *Women of Canada* (Montreal, 1930).

LECOQ, CHARLES (baptized **Isaïe-Marie-Charles**), Roman Catholic priest, Sulpician, teacher, and superior; b. 4 Nov. 1846 in Nantes, France, son of Isaïe Lecoq, a shipyard worker, and Rose-Angèle Maunoury; d. 6 April 1926 in Montreal.

Charles Lecoq was a brilliant student in the classical program at the Lycée Impérial in Nantes from 1855 to 1863, and he continued his education at the Séminaire de Nantes, which was run by the Sulpicians, until 1868. Ordained deacon on 19 Dec. 1868 when not yet old enough to be priested, he did his solitude (Sulpician noviciate) in 1869–70 and received ordination to the priesthood on 24 Sept. 1870.

Lecoq began his career in France as a professor of philosophy at the Séminaire d'Issy-les-Moulineaux, where he taught from 1870 to 1876. While there, he became known as an excellent professor who was scrupulously orthodox and who rejected Cartesianism. He also showed exceptional courage in the disturbances of 1871 under the Paris Commune, at the time the Communards occupied the seminary in April and May, forcing the Sulpicians to flee under heavy gunfire and to take refuge in a building at the far end of their property.

Designated for missionary work, Lecoq arrived in Montreal on 19 Aug. 1876. His assignment was to organize the autonomous "philosophy" program for students from the Petit Séminaire de Montréal which was housed in the east end of a large building begun in 1854, but was not integrated into the Grand Séminaire in the west end. He was the superior of the Séminaire de Philosophie until 1881, when he was appointed superior of the Grand Séminaire. He served in this capacity until 1903, while continuing to teach courses, including *diaconales* (sexual ethics) and canon law. Since the Grand Séminaire had become the faculty of theology of the Université Laval in Montreal in April 1878, he was also dean of this faculty from 1882 to 1904. The seminarians had a high regard for him because of his exemplary life, clear theological thinking, and fatherly devotion. By their content and conviction, Lecoq's lectures, which were informed by his vast erudition in religious and secular matters, revealed surprising spiritual dimensions in every subject covered.

During his 22 years as head of the Grand Séminaire, Lecoq carried out a number of major projects. In 1894 he moved the Séminaire de Philosophie to a new building on Chemin de la Côte-des-Neiges. In 1900 he began the reconstruction of the chapel of the Grand Séminaire, the masterpiece of architect Jean-Omer Marchand*, and from 1900 to 1902 he had the west side of the seminary enlarged.

On 3 Dec. 1902 Lecoq was elected superior of the Sulpicians in Montreal, succeeding Louis-Frédéric Colin*, who had died in November. In 1907 he had to account for the costs of reconstructing the chapel of the Grand Séminaire. He was secretary of the first Plenary Council held at Quebec in 1909. At the request of Archbishop Paul Bruchési* of Montreal, he organized the founding of the École Sacerdotale Saint-Jean-l'Évangéliste (1911), a *petit séminaire* in the strict sense of the words. He also oversaw the construction of the Bibliothèque Saint-Sulpice (subsequently the Bibliothèque Nationale du Québec) on Rue Saint-Denis, which was built from plans drawn up by architect Eugène Payette and was opened to the public in 1915.

Lecoq was the last Sulpician from France to head Saint-Sulpice in Canada. Since his Canadian colleagues were demanding more administrative positions, he humbly accepted the decree of the general council in Paris in 1908, which stipulated that there must be "an equal number of Canadian and French" members on the two boards (one consisting of 12 assistants and the other of four *consulteurs* or advisers). The transition took place at a time of Lecoq's choosing, and when he resigned because of a serious illness in 1917, Narcisse-Amable Troie*, a Canadian, was elected to succeed him.

In his retirement, Lecoq became the ecclesiastical superior of the Sisters of Charity (Grey Nuns) of the Hôpital Général in Montreal. As their spiritual director, he developed close ties with many of them, which more than 850 letters show to be the case. The last years of his life were clouded by two ailments, diabetes and facial neuritis of the trigeminal nerve, from which he had suffered since 1914 and which had sent him frequently to hospital. He spent his leisure working on an annotated version of the New Testament, which he translated from the Greek.

Charles Lecoq was a priest of exceptional merit; the eulogies published after his death emphasized that he was a brilliant man possessed of a prodigious memory, a broad humanist education, and competent, sound theological judgement, who dedicated himself to almost absolute poverty, deep humility, fervent union with God, and untiring charity towards his fellow human beings. Although neither a great orator nor a far-sighted administrator, he is remembered for having been a priest to the very depths of his being, in all places and circumstances.

ALCIDE LAPLANTE

Arch. de la Compagnie de Saint-Sulpice (Paris), Dossier 18 C 3 (corr. passive de M. Garriguet); Sect.N, dossier Vigourel. Arch. Départementales, Loire-Atlantique (Nantes, France), État civil, Nantes, 6 févr. 1843, 4 nov. 1846. Arch. du Séminaire de Saint-Sulpice (Montréal), Voûte 2, armoire 6, boîte 127 (consulteurs); armoire 7, tiroirs 148–49, cartons 66–68 (lettres et fascicules d'œuvres manuscrites). *L'Action catholique* (Québec), 8 avril 1926. *Le Devoir*, 7–8 avril 1926, 2 déc. 1939. J.-B.-A. Allaire, *Dictionnaire biographique du clergé canadien-français* (6v., Montréal et Saint-Hyacinthe, Qué., 1908–34). Émile Boucher, "L'œuvre sulpicienne de la formation cléricale, les supérieurs du grand séminaire," *Le Séminaire* (Montréal), 22 (1957): 317–28. Ægidius Fauteux, *Monsieur Lecoq: souvenirs d'un ancien séminariste* (Montréal, 1927). Barthélemi Gattet, "M. Charles-I. Lecoq, P.S.S.," *Le Séminaire*, 5 (1940): 48–49. Henri Gauthier, *Une âme sacerdotale: Charles Lecoq, prêtre de Saint-Sulpice, 1846–1926* (Montréal, 1939). Bruno Harel, "Le grand séminaire de 1840 à 1940: une période d'établissement et de rayonnement," in *Le grand séminaire de Montréal de 1840 à 1990: 150 années au service de la formation des prêtres,* sous la dir. de Rolland Litalien (Montréal, 1990), 93–103. Josette Michaud et Bruno Harel, *Le séminaire de Saint-Sulpice de Montréal* ([Montréal], 1990). *Les prêtres de Saint-Sulpice au Canada: grandes figures de leur histoire* (Sainte-Foy, Qué., 1992), 360–64.

LEE MONG KOW (**Li Mengjiu** in Mandarin), interpreter and school principal; b. 2 Dec. 1861 in Panyu county, Guangdong province (People's Republic of China); he had at least one wife, and six sons and six daughters; d. 9 May 1924 in Hong Kong.

Lee Mong Kow's family was probably relatively well-to-do. His mother, Lee Quan Sze, widowed at age 22, saw to her son's education. Once he had grown, she pursued charitable activities, gaining considerable prominence in China and North America. Poor families did not have the financial resources to educate sons or to enable widows to avoid remarrying.

It is not clear when Lee entered Canada, but he most likely arrived around 1880. Initially he worked as a labourer in Esquimalt, B.C., and then by "studying and saving" he became a tailor. In 1882 he moved to Victoria. He may have worked as an interpreter on an ad hoc basis before his appointment as chief interpreter for the Chinese immigration services of the Department of Customs in November 1889. Although responsibility for Chinese immigration would change ministries, he would continue as chief interpreter until 1920. During his tenure he oversaw the entry of thousands of Chinese into Canada and earned a reputation for honesty and integrity.

One of the few members of Victoria's Chinese community whose activities were discussed in the province's English-language press, Lee first came to public notice as a witness for the royal commission to investigate Chinese and Japanese immigration into British Columbia, appointed in 1900. On this occasion he testified to the importation of Chinese prostitutes. His comments illustrate his role as cross-cultural interpreter. When asked whether he knew of Chinese women who had been sold into slavery as prostitutes, he replied that he knew of three cases of "Chinese women coming here who might be called slaves by the white people, but in China we do not call them slaves." He explained that men paid the passage money and head taxes of women who wanted to come to Canada but could not afford it. The women agreed to work as prostitutes in order to pay back the costs plus seven per cent interest within an agreed period of time.

Lee's prominence in the Chinese community of Victoria was noted by the Chinese government, which in 1907 awarded him fourth-class honours, described by the *Daily Colonist* (Victoria) as equivalent to a KCMG. The following year the paper reported on a combined business and pleasure trip he took to eastern Canada. In an era of considerable discrimination against the Chinese, he had the social and financial capital to ensure that his rights were respected. In 1906 the *Vancouver Daily World* had claimed that he was in the process of buying one of the province's newspapers, in contravention of laws governing such matters. The *World* had to issue an official apology after being contacted by his solicitors. In 1908 he threatened the city of Victoria with a lawsuit over a disputed building permit. In 1909, in the midst of a dispute over the enrolment of Chinese children in Victoria schools, including the establishment of a racially segregated class, he applied for and received a permit for three of his children to attend the unsegregated North Ward School.

Possibly because of his work with the federal government, Lee appears to have been less active in the political life of Victoria than other members of the Chinese elite. His absence may have been related to the fact that he belonged to a minority within the Cantonese-speaking community in Canada. Most Chinese in British Columbia were from Siyi, a region of four adjacent counties in the Canton (Guangzhou) delta, where a sub-dialect of Cantonese was spoken. Lee came from Panyu, a county close to Canton, where people spoke the standard form of Cantonese. His origins may have made him an outsider given the overlapping loyalties of birthplace and lineage that shaped so much of the political life of overseas Chinese communities. On the other hand, he seems to have had social ties to people such as Yip On, the chief organizer of the Chinese Empire Reform Association, one of the main political movements of the era. This association in turn would have linked him to Vancouver businessman YIP SANG. Lee did not become caught up in the immigration scandal of 1910–11, examined by the royal commission appointed to investigate alleged Chinese frauds and opium smuggling on the Pacific coast. The commission recommended that criminal charges be laid against Yip On.

Lee's leadership is most evident in the field of education. He was likely one of the prime movers behind the establishment of the Le Qun Yishu, the first Chinese-language elementary school in Canada, and he became its first principal. Opened in 1899, the school enrolled 100 Chinese students and was entirely supported by voluntary subscriptions. According to the *Daily Colonist,* a spokesperson, probably Lee himself, explained that it had been established because "we are Chinamen, no matter where we go and find that, in view of the international relations now opening up, it is necessary to have an education in Chinese as well as in English." In 1908 the school was brought under the control of the Chinese Consolidated Benevolent Association, the leading Chinese community organization, and it was reorganized the following year as the Chinese Imperial School with funding from the Chinese government. It became the Chinese Public School in 1913, when the Victoria School Board arranged with Lee to accommodate two of its own segregated classes for Chinese pupils there. Chinese children attended English-language classes under the jurisdiction of the board during the day and Chinese-language classes under the control of the association at night. This arrangement continued until 1915, when the board was unable to secure a reduction in the rent for the rooms. Lee's address to the students at the first graduation, in 1915, noted that the institution was the largest Chinese school in Canada. He pointed out that in addition to their studies in the "Westerner's schools," the students had achieved "a Chinese national standard." They had met certification requirements for elementary school graduates set by the Chinese ministry of education. The school would still offer classes in Chinese at the beginning of the 21st century.

In 1920 Lee moved to Hong Kong to become the Chinese agent for Canadian Pacific Ocean Services Limited. Apparently, he became sick shortly afterwards and he passed away in May 1924 after an extended illness. At his death, Lee Mong Kow may have been more prominent in the eyes of Anglo-European Canadians than in those of Chinese Canadians. His death was front-page news in the English-language press, an unusual recognition for someone of Chinese origin in the highly racially stratified and racist society of the time. Vancouver's *Dahan Gongbao* [Chinese Times], the only Chinese newspaper preserved from this period, had only a short report on his death.

TIMOTHY J. STANLEY

School District 61 Educational Heritage Arch. and Museum (Victoria), Victoria School District, trustees' meetings, minute-books, 1905–10: 112; 1911–14: 440. *Dahan Gongbao* [Chinese Times] (Vancouver), 22, 24 March, 13 July 1915. *Daily Colonist* (Victoria), 18 Jan. 1899, 9 Sept. 1906, 15 April 1907, 8 Oct. 1908. *Victoria Daily Times*, 1 Sept. 1908, 10 May 1924. Lim Bang, "Weibu Zhonghua Huiguan zhi yuange ji qiaoxiao chuanli zhi yuanqi" [The origins of the Victoria Chinese Consolidated Benevolent Association and the reasons for the creation of overseas schools], in *Jianada Weiduoli Zhonghua Huiguan chengli qishiwu, Huaqiao Xuexiao chengli liushi–zhounian jinian tekan* [Seventy-fifth anniversary of the Victorian Canadian Chinese Consolidated Benevolent Association and the sixtieth anniversary of the Overseas Chinese School, special memorial publication], ed. D. T. H. Lee [Lee T'ung-hai] (Victoria, 1960), pt.IV: 1–5. Can., Parl., *Sessional papers*, 1909, no.30; Royal commission on Chinese and Japanese immigration, *Report* (Ottawa, 1902; repr. New York, 1978); Royal commission appointed to investigate alleged Chinese frauds and opium smuggling on the Pacific coast, *Report* (Ottawa, 1913). A. B. Chan,

Gold Mountain: the Chinese in the new world (Vancouver, 1983). Harry Con *et al.*, *From China to Canada: a history of the Chinese communities in Canada*, ed. Edgar Wickberg (Toronto, 1982; repr. 1988). C. D. Lai, "Home county and clan origins of overseas Chinese in Canada in the early 1880s," *BC Studies* (Vancouver), no.27 (fall 1975): 3–29. T. J. Stanley, "'Chinamen, wherever we go': Chinese nationalism and Guangdong merchants in British Columbia, 1871–1911," *CHR*, 77 (1996): 475–503.

LEGARÉ, PIERRE-THÉOPHILE, merchant, industrialist, and philanthropist; b. 12 Feb. 1851 in Charlesbourg, Lower Canada, eldest child of Pierre Legaré, a blacksmith and farmer, and Eulalie Renault; m. first 24 July 1876 Camile Bédard (d. 1902) in Charlesbourg, Que., and they adopted at least three daughters, in addition to taking in orphans; m. secondly 10 Feb. 1903 Ethel Caroline Griffith in Ottawa, and they had a son and a daughter; d. 2 July 1926 at his summer residence in Saint-Benoît-Abbé (Packington), Que., and was buried in Notre-Dame de Belmont cemetery at Sainte-Foy, Que.

Pierre-Théophile Legaré attended the parish school and then in 1861 enrolled in the Petit Séminaire de Québec. In February 1866 he began a commercial course at the Collège de Sainte-Anne-de-la-Pocatière and he continued his studies the following year at the Académie Commerciale de Québec. In 1871 he took some "industrial" training in the United States.

Legaré first went into partnership with his father in a small plough factory in Charlesbourg, which had probably been opened in the late 1860s. The partnership is believed to have lasted until 1877, when Pierre-Théophile took over the business in his own name and moved to Rue Saint-Vallier in Saint-Sauveur (Quebec City). In 1879 he became a representative for the G. M. Cossitt and Brother Company of Brockville, Ont., which specialized in manufacturing agricultural implements. Not long thereafter, he began making horse-drawn carriages, but his enterprise was completely destroyed by a fire that levelled a third of Saint-Sauveur on 16 May 1889.

To make a new start in business, Legaré went into partnership with Montreal merchant Robert Johnston Latimer on 17 Jan. 1890. The firm of Latimer et Legaré specialized in the sale of ploughs, carriages, and various kinds of machinery. In addition to the store on Rue Saint-Vallier, it had another on Rue Saint-Paul in Quebec's Lower Town. The partnership would end on 1 Nov. 1896; Legaré would become the sole owner of the business, then known as P. T. Legaré and estimated to be worth between $20,000 and $35,000.

Legaré quite logically was also interested in agriculture and its improvement. With his father and other partners, he invested in a butter factory in Charlesbourg and helped organize the Quebec Provincial Exposition. As the 1890s progressed, however, his commercial activities expanded. For example, he and Latimer could afford to hire employees, two of whom would leave a strong mark on the firm's history. Joseph-Herman Fortier began working for Latimer et Legaré as a stenographer in 1893 and his role would be particularly important; his brother, Pierre-Wilfrid Fortier, was hired in 1895 as a typist. They were both graduates of the Académie Commerciale de Québec and soon became part of Legaré's family by marrying his sisters-in-law. Joseph-Herman was the "guiding spirit" of the enterprise after Legaré put him in charge of its finances in 1903. That year the brothers were invited to become equal partners with the founder. The firm of P. T. Legaré now began its territorial expansion by opening branches and agencies in many Quebec towns. It was one of the first chain stores established in Canada.

The branches multiplied so rapidly that by 1910 there were 11, and from then on progress was phenomenal. The business now became a limited company, P. T. Legaré Limited, with an estimated value of about $100,000, which would increase to more than $1,000,000 by 1920. Up-to-date marketing techniques were used: advertisements in mass-circulation newspapers, a catalogue and mail-order service, and sales on credit. P. T. Legaré Limited sold everything: farm machinery of various kinds, horse-drawn carriages, and household goods (such as furniture, wood stoves, refrigerators, washing machines, and musical instruments).

Legaré and his partners also became manufacturers. In 1916 they purchased the Percival Plow and Stove Company Limited in Merrickville, Ont., and the following year they founded the Dominion Carriage Company Limited, located in Montreal East. This firm, which would remain in business until 1 Dec. 1924, became one of the largest manufacturers of horse-drawn carriages in the country. It was the popularity of the automobile that led the partners to close it down.

Legaré and the Fortier brothers adapted to the advance of technology and to the market and they set up a large sales network for automobiles. Founded in 1911, their firm was known at first as the Compagnie d'Automobiles de Montréal, but changed its name to Legaré Automobile and Supply Company Limited in 1917. With Montreal and Quebec as its main places of business, it extended its network of branches to most of the small towns in the province. For a time it was the largest automobile and supply company in the country.

In 1921 Legaré and his partners obtained a federal charter and issued bonds to a total value of $1,200,000. That year the combined turnover of their businesses exceeded $12 million. At the time of its founder's death (which occurred at the peak of its success), P. T. Legaré Limited alone had more than 50 stores and about 1,000 local agencies in Quebec, northeastern New Brunswick, and eastern Ontario. The Toronto *Financial Post* went so far as to declare in 1925 that the catalogue of P. T. Legaré Limited "is next to the bible in French Canada."

After Legaré's death in 1926, the company would continue to expand with Joseph-Herman Fortier as its president. It would be pushed into bankruptcy in 1935, however, by the combined effects of the depression and the fraudulent dealings of its chief officers. Fortier, his brother, and a former member of the management would be sued for fraud and sent to prison. Although the business was restructured after the bankruptcy, it would gradually decrease in importance in the decades ahead. The Legaré banner would not, however, disappear from the commercial landscape in the province of Quebec until 1998.

Although he was often urged to take up politics, Legaré made only one brief foray into it. In 1888 he was elected alderman of the municipality of Saint-Sauveur parish, barely a year before it would be annexed to Quebec City by a referendum. Though a Conservative, Legaré did not seem to be embarrassed by the fact that his principal partner, Joseph-Herman Fortier, supported the Liberals.

After living for much of his life on Rue Saint-Vallier in Saint-Sauveur, Legaré decided in 1912 to join the middle-class citizens of the capital on the Grande Allée, and he built a magnificent Victorian-style residence there. Thanks to his wealth, Legaré also became a philanthropist. On many occasions he gave substantial donations to the Université Laval, with which he had business dealings, including a gift of $25,000 in 1920, and to the parish of Saint-Cœur-de-Marie, contributing, for example, $15,000 in 1919 when the church was being built.

Pierre-Théophile Legaré possessed great entrepreneurial skills. He made his fortune through the timely development of two large networks of stores and the creation of manufacturing enterprises to supply his commercial activities. From modest beginnings, he became one of the most important self-made men of his day in Quebec.

ANTONIO LECHASSEUR

[The author wishes to thank Guy Legaré, grandson of Pierre-Théophile Legaré, Yves Tremblay, Raynald Lessard, Marc Vallières, and Mme Sylvie Tremblay for their valuable assistance over the course of his research. A.L.]

ANQ-Q, CE301-S7, 12 févr. 1851, 24 juill. 1876; CT301-S1, 10 avril 1928; TP11, S1, SS10, SSS1, mars 1935, no.2964F; SS20, SSS48, 17 janv. 1890, no.4432; 9 mars 1891, no.4591; 11 nov. 1896, no.6035; 10 mars 1903, no.37; 25 oct. 1910, nos.253–54; 20 avril 1918, no.355. AVQ, M1-1; M2; QA5, rôles d'évaluation. Arch. de l'Univ. Laval (Québec), P136 (fonds Joseph-Ernest-Grégoire), C2/3, discours de 1935. Arch. paroissiales, Sacré-Cœur (Ottawa),

RBMS, 10 févr. 1903. MCQ-FSQ, SME 2.2/55/22d., 16 juill. 1897; 9/15/45, 29 mars 1920; 9/15/46, 16 juin 1920; 9/15/65, 28 sept. 1920; 9/189/51, 21 avril 1920; 9/190/63, 18 mai 1921. LAC, MG 26, G: 23908–9, 56658–62, 86948–50; I: 67226, 89548–51; RG 17, AI, 900: 115816; RG 31, C1, 1851, 1861, 1871, 1881, 1891, 1901, Quebec City; RG 95, ser.1, 1375, 1612, 1791; RG 125, 705, file 6588. Private arch., Guy Legaré (Le Bic, Qué.), papiers de la famille Legaré. *L'Action catholique* (Québec), 30 juin, 3, 5–6 juill. 1926. *L'Événement*, 16 mai 1889, 14 févr. 1921, 7 juill. 1926. *La Presse*, 17 janv. 1920. *Le Soleil*, 26 juin 1902; 3 mars 1903; 3, 5–6 juill. 1926. *Annuaire du commerce et de l'industrie de Québec* . . . (Québec), 1873. *Bradstreet Commercial Report* (New York), 1881–1933. C. H. Cheasley, *The chain store movement in Canada* (Montreal, [1930]), 57–78. *Directories*, Quebec, 1873–74, 1880–90, 1916–24; Quebec and Lévis, 1875–79, 1890–1916, 1924–39. J. Hamelin *et al.*, *La presse québécoise*, vols.2, 6. *Index to "The Financial Post," 1907–1948*, comp. and ed. G. R. Adshead (Toronto, [1990]) (contains numerous references to Legaré). P. T. Legaré Limitée, *Catalogue no.44* (Québec et Montréal, 1920). Michel Lessard, "L'empire P. T. Legaré Limitée," *Cap-aux-Diamants* (Québec), 40 (hiver 1995): 34–37; *Objets anciens du Québec* (2v. parus, [Montréal], 1994–). David Monod, *Store wars: shopkeepers and the culture of mass marketing, 1890–1939* (Toronto, 1996), 124. Univ. Laval, *Annuaire*, 1911/12: 177. *Who's who and why*, 1915/16. *Who's who in Canada*, 1925/26.

LEHMAN, BERTHA (Rosenthal), philanthropist and Jewish communal leader; b. 2 Aug. 1849 (some sources give the year as 1850 or 1852) in Berlin, daughter of Lewis Lehman; m. 27 March 1867 Aaron Rosenthal, and they had five sons; d. 10 Dec. 1922 in Ottawa.

Bertha Lehman met and married Aaron Rosenthal while on a visit to Australia. He had left Prussia at 13, travelled through India and Ceylon (Sri Lanka), and was in Australia at the time of the gold rush in the 1850s. After living in England in the early 1870s, the Rosenthals immigrated to Canada in 1874, settling in Montreal, where Aaron established Rosenthal, Benjamin and Company, wholesale jewellers. They moved in 1878 to Ottawa, where Aaron opened a jewellery shop. In 1911, two years after Aaron's death, his business was sold to Henry Birks and Sons Limited [*see* Henry BIRKS].

The Rosenthals, along with the family of Moses BILSKY, were among the founders of Ottawa's Jewish community. During the 1870s and 1880s it had been necessary to gather Jews from the Ottawa valley, western Quebec, and eastern Ontario to form a *minyan* (quorum) for holiday prayers. Between 1891 and 1901, however, the number in Ottawa grew from 46 to 398, most of them immigrants from Russia and Lithuania; in the next decade the Jewish population would more than quadruple. Thus by the early 1890s there were sufficient numbers to establish the Adath Jeshurun congregation, commonly known as the King

Edward Avenue *shul*. Its Ladies Auxiliary Society, under Bertha's leadership, organized musical entertainment on festivals such as Hanukkah and Purim. In 1904 Aaron laid the cornerstone of its new oriental-style synagogue.

Bertha's early presence, financial means, and organizational acumen gave her the social status necessary to head up efforts on behalf of immigrants. Concentrated in Lower Town and the By Ward Market area, most of the newcomers worked as pedlars, hawkers, petty merchants, and craftspeople. Many, arriving in poverty, were aided by the Ottawa Ladies' Hebrew Benevolent Society, established in 1898 and the city's first (and for some time only) Jewish charity. Bertha was its founding president, and would serve in this capacity until her death. The society, which operated without civic assistance, raised funds through donations, concerts, and such projects as the *Economical cook book* (Ottawa, 1915), the first book of Jewish recipes to be produced for a fund-raiser in Canada. She served as well as honorary president of the Ottawa Hebrew Ladies Sewing Circle, which provided clothing.

A biographer noted that her "charities and sympathies . . . knew no creed." She was involved in several Gentile institutions, among them the Perley Home for Incurables and the Ottawa General Hospital. She organized assistance too for soldiers' families during the 1914–18 war. The Disraeli Chapter of the Imperial Order Daughters of the Empire, founded in July 1918, grew out of a Canadian Red Cross sewing circle Bertha had established in 1910. This chapter, which furnished a recreation room for veterans, aided the children of fallen soldiers, and raised money for the Red Cross, ceased operation in 1923 when the last sponsored child had completed his training at the Ottawa Technical High School.

A symbol of the success of both family and community, the Rosenthals' son Samuel became a local sports hero and the first Jew to hold municipal office in Ottawa. Elected as an alderman in 1902, he sat for four terms, was returned again in 1921, and also served as a magistrate.

Bertha Rosenthal died of pneumonia in 1922. On the sabbath eve in traditional homes, Jews praise their wives and mothers by reciting Prov. 31:10–31, which describes the virtuous woman who creates a safe home for her family and reaches out to the needy. Rosenthal capably fit this description. Her life encompassed the establishment of a Jewish community in Canada's capital and the emergence there of a sense of Jewish womanhood. Her philanthropic work brought comfort. At the same time, her efforts during wartime drew Ottawa's Jews closer to the mainstream Canadian and British imperial communities.

DAVID KIMMEL

Le Jeune

AO, RG 22-354, no.10955; RG 80-8-0-864, no.10838. LAC, RG 31, C1, 1901, Ottawa, Central Ward, div.2: 24–25. Ottawa Jewish Arch., Max Bookman papers; Congregation Adath Jeshurun papers, Ladies Auxiliary Soc. of the King Edward Avenue Synagogue and Minutes ser.; Dribbin–Berman corr., 1992. Ottawa Public Library, Special Coll., Biog. scrapbook 144. *Canadian Jewish Times* (Montreal), 8 Oct., 24 Dec. 1909; 18 Feb., 25 March, 25 Oct. 1910; 18 April 1913. A. W. Margosches, "Reminiscences of Jewish life in Ottawa," *Ottawa Hebrew News* (September 1934). *Ottawa Citizen*, 2 Oct. 1909, 12 Dec. 1922, 25 Sept. 1948, 31 Aug. 1956. *Ottawa Journal*, 22 Jan. 1972. J. J. Price, "Jews of Canada: the first Jewish settler of Ottawa," *American Israelite* (Cincinnati, Ohio), 10 Aug. 1916 (repr. in Max Bookman, "Excerpts . . . ," *infra*). I. [M.] Abella, *A coat of many colours: two centuries of Jewish life in Canada* (Toronto, 1990). *A biographical dictionary of Canadian Jewry, 1909–1914, from "The Canadian Jewish Times"*, comp. L. F. Tapper (Teaneck, N.J., [1992]). Max Bookman, "Excerpts from a history of the Jew in Canada's capital," in *Canadian Jewish reference book and directory*, comp. Eli Gottesman (Montreal, 1963), 387–405. *Directory*, Ottawa, 1878–1930. Bernard Figler, *Lillian and Archie Freiman: biographies* (Montreal, 1962). Ruth Gay, *The Jews of Germany: a historical portrait* (New Haven, Conn., 1992). A. R. George, *The house of Birks: a history of Henry Birks and Sons* ([Montreal?], 1946). Arthur Hertzberg, *The Jews in America: four centuries of an uneasy encounter; a history* (New York, 1989). *The Jew in Canada: a complete record of Canadian Jewry from the days of the French régime to the present time*, ed. A. D. Hart (Toronto and Montreal, 1926). Eva Taylor and James Kennedy, *Ottawa's Britannia* (Ottawa, 1983). G. [J. J.] Tulchinsky, *Taking root: the origins of the Canadian Jewish community* (Toronto, 1992).

LE JEUNE, JEAN-MARIE-RAPHAËL (named at birth **Jean-Marie**), Roman Catholic priest, Oblate of Mary Immaculate, missionary, linguist, author, and newspaper publisher; b. 12 April 1855 in Pleyber-Christ, France, one of the three sons of Pierre Le Jeune, a merchant, and Marie-Françoise Breton; d. 21 Nov. 1930 in New Westminster, B.C.

Jean-Marie-Raphaël Le Jeune, whose brothers, Louis* and Yves-Marie, would also become Oblate priests, entered the Oblate seminary in Nancy, France, on 10 Dec. 1873 and took his perpetual vows on 12 Dec. 1875 at the scholasticate of Autun, where he was ordained on 7 June 1879. He volunteered for service in British Columbia and, accompanied by the newly ordained Eugène-Casimir CHIROUSE, he arrived in New Westminster – the Oblate headquarters in the province – in October 1879. He wintered there under the supervision of Bishop Paul Durieu*, learning Chinook Jargon, a pidgin containing Chinookan, Nootkan, French, and English words which was used by the Oblates to communicate with natives who spoke a variety of languages. Le Jeune spent the summer of 1880 in the Fraser Canyon learning native languages and in the fall he was sent to St Mary's mission in the lower Fraser valley, where he was stationed for the next two years.

Assigned in 1882 to St Louis's mission in Kamloops, Le Jeune arrived on 17 October with a printing press, probably intending to publish works in native languages. Charged primarily with the proselytization of native people in the region, he was also posted in 1885 and 1887 to the railway district, the Canadian Pacific Railway's territory from Kamloops east to the summit of the Rocky Mountains; it took three to four months to traverse the region. In 1891 Le Jeune became the rector of St Joseph's Church on the Kamloops Reserve and in November 1893 he succeeded Father Jean-Marie-J. Le Jacq as superior of St Louis's mission. There he would remain until 1929, when he transferred to New Westminster owing to ill health and old age.

Le Jeune was very active among the native people of the region. He successfully encouraged the construction of chapels and was deeply involved in retreats which could be attended by 2,000 to 3,000 natives. These retreats reflected the Oblate belief that when proselytizing natives one could "better speak to their hearts by [appealing to] their eyes." Elaborate visual spectacles featuring exhibitions of Christ's Passion enacted by natives, penitential parades, expositions of the Eucharist, and first communions were organized by the Oblates. In 1892, such a retreat was held at St Mary's mission and Le Jeune and Durieu had started planning for it two years earlier. Their correspondence testifies to the organization such an event required: transportation of natives had to be arranged, each band's food had to be gathered and transported "so that our meetings will not be potlatches," and decorations and props had to be acquired or built.

Le Jeune was an apt student of native languages. In 1922 he would tell the Kamloops Rotary Club that he "could swear in 22 languages." His most lasting material accomplishments stem from his linguistic talent. In 1890 he had set about adapting the Duployan system of shorthand (developed in France by Émile Duployé) to the sounds of Chinook Jargon. He was considerably aided in this project by Durieu, who urged him to see that the stenographic system was as true to the jargon's pronunciation as possible. Le Jeune's first pupil was Charlie Alexis Mayous, who was able to learn the system rapidly. Mayous wintered at the Coldwater Reserve in 1890–91 and taught many others the shorthand. Literacy in the Duployan system seems to have spread quickly among native people in the district and on 2 May 1891 Le Jeune launched the first edition of what he would later describe as "the strangest newspaper in the world," the *Kamloops Wawa* [Talk of Kamloops]. This illustrated, mimeographed periodical, written in Chinook Jargon and English, contained information on local affairs as well as international news of religious importance. It was published regularly through to December 1904 and occasionally up until 1917. Its success is evident from its circulation numbers, which peaked at 3,000 copies per edition.

In 1904 Le Jeune visited Europe, accompanied by chiefs Louis Clexlixqen* of Kamloops and Johnnie Chilleheetsa of Douglas Lake. The two native men took part in an exhibition of stenography, at which they received three gold and five silver medals. They also met Pope Pius X and were received at Buckingham Palace by King Edward VII.

Le Jeune was the author of numerous pamphlets and educational works, such as *Practical Chinook vocabulary . . .* (Kamloops, 1886), *Prayers in the Okanagan language* (Kamloops, 1893), and *Chinook rudiments* (Kamloops, 1924). His linguistic abilities are evidenced in the Oblate *Polyglott manual of prayers* (12v. in 1, Kamloops, 1896–[97]): he was responsible for eight of the eleven dialects represented therein.

Jean-Marie-Raphaël Le Jeune was a kind man with a sense of humour, who seems to have been very popular with the native people of his district. Interviews with natives on the Kamloops Reserve in 1947 elicited a common response: "Invariably their faces lighted up with pleasure as they replied, 'Yes, we remember him well, He was a great and good man.'" He died in 1930 and was buried at the Oblate cemetery in Mission.

LYNN BLAKE

Aside from the works mentioned above, Jean-Marie-Raphaël Le Jeune published many others, some in several editions. The catalogue of the LAC, which can be consulted on the Internet, lists 109 entries under the name of Le Jeune. The CIHM's *Reg.* also mentions a number of his publications.

Arch. Départementales, Finistère (Quimper, France), État civil, Pleyber-Christ, 16 juin 1854. Arch. Deschâtelets, Oblats de Marie-Immaculée (Ottawa), HPK 5301-20 (brochures, articles, études et corr. de J.-M.-R. Le Jeune). *Kamloops Sentinel* (Kamloops, B.C.), 29 Dec. 1922. L. A. Blake, "Let the cross take possession of the earth: missionary geographies of power in nineteenth-century British Columbia" (PHD thesis, Univ. of B.C., Vancouver, 1998). Gaston Carrière, *Dictionnaire biographique des oblats de Marie-Immaculée au Canada* (4v., Ottawa, 1976–89), 2: 305–6. R. V. Grant, "Chinook Jargon," *International Journal of American Linguistics* (Baltimore, Md), 11 (1945): 225–33. W. H. Gurney, *The work of Reverend Father J. M. R. Le Jeune, O.M.I.* ([Vancouver], 1948). *Missions de la Congrégation des missionnaires oblats de Marie Immaculée* (Liège, Belgique), 43 (1905): 242–43. *Month* (London), June 1892. *Les oblats de Marie Immaculée en Orégon, 1847–1860: documents d'archives*, Paul Drouin, édit. (3v., Ottawa, 1992).

LEMOINE, MARIE-LOUISE-THÉRÈSE, named **Marie-Joseph de Jésus**, founder and abbess of the first monastery of Poor Clares in Canada; b. 25 Aug. 1858 in Daon, France, daughter of Stanislas Lemoine

and Colette Lemoine; d. 8 July 1925 in Salaberry-de-Valleyfield, Que.

Marie-Louise-Thérèse Lemoine attended the boarding school of the Sœurs de la Charité de Notre-Dame d'Évron between the ages of 6 and 14, and attracted attention for her piety and her ability to learn quickly. After a sheltered adolescence within the family circle – her widowed mother made flowers and liturgical decorations – she became a lady's companion at 19. She applied for admission to the monastery of the Poor Clares in Lourdes in 1884 and took her final vows on 16 Sept. 1886. After performing various duties at the monastery, she became mistress of novices in 1897 and participated in making the decisions related to the founding of a monastery of Poor Clares in Canada.

At the time Mother Marie des Anges, the abbess of Lourdes, was being urged by a number of people to found a monastery in Montreal. Among them were the Franciscans, who had been established in the city since 1890; the Poor Clares formed the contemplative branch of this order. The Franciscans had stirred the interest of many young women in Canada, and a large number had become novices in Lourdes, though only three would persevere in their vocation. When Archbishop Édouard-Charles Fabre*, and later Archbishop Paul Bruchési*, refused to allow a new contemplative congregation to come to Montreal – the Carmelites from Reims, France, had moved there in 1875 [see Antoine-Nicolas Braun*] – an approach was made to Bishop Joseph-Médard EMARD of the diocese of Valleyfield, who agreed to accept the Poor Clares. In 1899 Sister Marie-Joseph de Jésus was chosen to direct the work of founding the community. "She seems to me suitable in every respect because of her experience, her great faith, [and] her kindness," Mother Marie des Anges observed. However, the project required funds, which were hard to find. The dangers threatening religious congregations in France in 1902 [see Gustave Blanche*] hastened a decision, and in April a group of five nuns that included the three Canadians, under the guidance of Sister Marie-Joseph de Jésus, left for Salaberry-de-Valleyfield. On their arrival the Poor Clares were taken in by the Little Sisters of the Holy Family until their monastery was ready. On 10 August, in the course of a spectacular ceremony, the Poor Clares were taken in procession by horse-drawn carriages to their monastery on the other side of the bay that divides the town. More than 5,000 people crowded around to witness the five recluses renew their vows at the foot of an open-air altar. The people of Salaberry-de-Valleyfield would show a lasting affection for "their" Poor Clares. "Far from having to suffer extreme poverty," as the abbess of Lourdes had feared, "the dear children had rather to ward off the excess of Canadian charity."

The new abbess now undertook to embed the rule

of St Clare of Assisi and the constitutions of St Colette in Canadian soil, "requirements that are not incompatible with the rigorous Canadian climate." The observance of the rule was hard: "continual abstinence, fasting throughout the year, bare feet, rising at night, no undergarments." There were many candidates, and the abbess had to be extremely vigilant to be sure that they were serious about their calling. She found a supporter in Abbé Joseph-Charles Allard, the vicar general of the diocese, with whom she carried on a steady correspondence. In 1906 she asked his permission to hold regular elections so as to apportion offices among the nuns in an orderly way. "There is a difference or hierarchy in the offices," she pointed out. "Otherwise, everything tends to turn into little republics where everyone gives orders and no one knows how to obey any more!" She complained that she was "always bogged down in material questions": construction of a larger monastery in 1907, of the chapel in 1912, and of the cloister wall in 1921. She supervised the making and ornamentation of sacerdotal vestments, a craft that provided a living for the cloistered nuns. For a time glaucoma prevented her from reading and writing, but she was miraculously cured in 1917, according to her own account, by the intervention of the late Father Frédéric Janssoone*, a famous Franciscan who had canvassed every parish in the diocese to raise money for the Poor Clares.

When she fell ill in 1922, Mother Marie-Joseph de Jésus continued to carry out her responsibilities. With the publication in Rome in 1924 of *Nuper Edito*, which allowed French cloistered nuns to take their solemn vows – something they had been forbidden to do since the French revolution – she decided to send a petition to Rome. The rescript granting authorization reached her on 8 May 1925, and Mother Marie-Joseph de Jésus, along with 30 nuns from the monastery, took her solemn vows on 30 May. She died less than two months later, leaving a well-established congregation to the new abbess, Marie Hurtibise, named Marie Saint-Paul de Jésus; one of the Canadians associated with its founding, she would remain in office until 1956.

MICHELINE DUMONT

The Arch. des Clarisses de Valleyfield (Salaberry-de-Valleyfield, Qué.) is the best resource for the life of Mother Marie-Joseph de Jésus. It holds, among other items, "Préliminaires de la fondation de Valleyfield," a 190-page manuscript drawn up by Mother Marie des Anges around 1905, which contains all of the pertinent information about the founding of the abbey; the correspondence of Marie-Joseph de Jésus; and a "Journal de voyage" by the subject, along with personal documents and her "Autobiographie" (birth to age 19), written at the request of her spiritual adviser. Useful as well are Premier reg. and Chroniques.

Arch. Départementales, Mayenne (Laval, France), État civil, Daon, 25 août 1858. *Bulletin paroissial de Valleyfield*, août 1925: 227. *Almanach de saint François d'Assise* (Québec), 1927: 16–19. Guy Laperrière, *Les congrégations religieuses: de la France au Québec, 1880–1914* (2v. parus, Sainte-Foy, Qué., 1996–), 2. Marie-Cécile de Jésus [Mlle Mongeau], "La très révérende mère Marie-Joseph-de-Jésus, fondatrice et 1ère abbesse des Pauvres Clarisses de Valleyfield," *La Rev. franciscaine* (Montréal), 41 (1925), no.9: 338–41; no.10: [3]81–83; no.11: [5]94–97.

LEONARD, BERNARD, painter, glazier, merchant, interior decorator, manufacturer, and politician; b. 1841 in Enniskillen (Northern Ireland), son of Bernard Leonard and Mary McKenna; m. 7 Feb. 1871 Catherine (Kate) Kirwin (Kerwin) at Quebec, and they had eight children; d. there 20 March 1924.

Bernard Leonard immigrated to Quebec with his family in 1846. His schooling was of short duration. In his youth he was trained as a painter by his compatriot Charles McDonald, a painter and dealer in hardware, wallpaper, and carpets, and he worked for him from 1863 until 1869, when he went into business on his own at 8 Rue de la Fabrique. Leonard first gained fame for his decorative painting (in particular the decor he installed in the Music Hall in November 1871 on the occasion of a ball to mark the departure of the 60th Foot, as well as the murals he painted for the Quebec legislative building in 1883) and even for his signs, which won a prize at the Quebec provincial exhibition in 1877. Over the years he became interested in other areas. By 1876, for example, he was advertising himself as a glazier and importer of wallpaper and earthenware.

Three years later, a sensible businessman, he set up shop permanently on Rue Saint-Jean, the major commercial thoroughfare of Quebec's Upper Town. A sign bearing his name, mounted under the cornice, still identifies what is now no.1117 as his premises. The purchase of this building in 1889 marked an important turning point for his business: in that year his eldest son, John Kirwin, fresh out of the Académie Commerciale de Québec, took his place in the family company, B. Leonard, which now had some 40 employees. John Kirwin became a partner in his father's firm in 1895, and the following year also joined forces with his brother Bernard James to form Leonard Brothers, which owned the Quebec Shoe Store, a high-quality footwear shop a few doors away from the B. Leonard store. In 1900 William Henry, the artist in the family, came into the business as assistant to Wallace J. Fischer, an English stained-glass artist. Fischer had been hired to set up a stained-glass window factory in 1896–97 and to take charge of the painted decorations. Some ten years later B. Leonard had 150 workers. When Fischer left around 1921, William Henry assumed responsibility for the workshop and the store on Rue Saint-Jean. After their father's death, the Leonard brothers would concentrate more on interior decorating and stained-glass windows and discontinue the sale of wallpaper, pigment, varnish, and paint. On William Henry's death in 1940, the factory would cease to exist and the company would be purchased by Ernest Legault, who would give it up around 1948.

The establishment of the factory at 31 Rue Saint-Stanislas, close to the store that already had been recognized as the largest wallpaper retailer in eastern Canada, is an indication of the Leonard family's entrepreneurial spirit. According to the 1891 census, there were only three "stained-glass window factories" in the province of Quebec, all of them in Montreal. Bernard Leonard and his eldest son wanted, it would seem, to take advantage of the current mania for stained-glass windows to add a promising sector to their business and to get ahead of the competition by employing a true stained-glass artist who could design and create large works that were consistent in both construction and iconography. Fischer had learned his trade in England, France, and Germany, as can be seen from his work, especially the religious windows he produced between 1897 and 1921. The 41 stained-glass windows of the church of Saint-Jean-Baptiste at Quebec, installed between 1897 and 1912, constitute the largest contract Fischer carried out for the B. Leonard company. As well, at Quebec he made the windows for the chapels of the seminary, the Ursulines, the Augustines, and the Congrégation des Hommes de la Haute Ville, and some of the commemorative windows in St Matthew's, Chalmers Free, and Wesley Methodist churches, the Baptist church, and others. To these approximately 100 windows that remain in their original setting must be added those that were destroyed or moved, including the ones in the former chapel of Notre-Dame-du-Chemin, which since 1986 have been safely lodged in the church in Amqui. Stained-glass windows by Fischer are still in place at Cacouna, Chicoutimi, Deschambault, and Saint-Isidore (near Quebec), on the Île d'Orléans, and in other parts of the province. In addition to religious windows, B. Leonard designed and produced many stained-glass windows for public buildings, businesses, and residences of wealthy merchants at Quebec and even in Montreal. Most of these are no longer extant, or cannot be positively identified since the company's works were seldom signed. Like the interior decorations, they have fallen victim to fashion and periodic renovations, or, in some cases, to demolition.

Having guaranteed the future of his sons by bringing them into the business, Bernard Leonard devoted himself increasingly to other activities. He became involved in mining exploration and in 1907 was vice-president of the Chibougamoo Mining Company Limited and the Great Northern Gold Fields Company. He was also active in municipal affairs. Between 1890 and 1906 he was elected alderman of Saint-Louis

ward six times, and he served on the municipal health, water, fire, and other committees. He certainly turned this experience to good advantage as president of the Industrial Life Insurance Company, which was founded in 1904 at his home on Rue Grande Allée with the participation of legislative councillor Némèse Garneau*, merchant Gaspard Le Moine, and his son John Kirwin. Incorporated in May 1905, it was authorized to write policies for accident, health, and life insurance. From 1905 to 1922 Bernard Leonard was elected president every year and the firm grew steadily. In 1906 two offices were opened in Montreal and another in Drummondville. The net value of the policies in force rose from $4,764.55 at the end of 1906 to $453,348.11 on 31 Dec. 1921. In February 1922 John Kirwin succeeded his father as president, an office he would retain until 1944, when Esmond, Bernard's youngest son, would take over. Esmond would finally dispose of his shares in 1950, thereby putting an end to the Leonard family's association with the business. A portrait of Bernard Leonard, painted in 1930 by Lucien-Raoul-Jean Martial and still kept at Quebec in the building of what is now the Industrial Alliance Life Insurance Company, is a reminder of this connection.

According to the *Album biographique des membres du conseil de ville de Québec*, published by Léon Lortie, Bernard Leonard was the president, around 1895, of two Irish organizations in the city, the Irish Catholic Benevolent Society and St Patrick's Literary Institute of Quebec. But it was mainly by his good taste, together with his undeniable business sense, that he made a reputation for himself. He trained many artists and decorators. To have worked for his company was a guarantee of success, as *La Semaine commerciale* pointed out in March 1900, when the Simard brothers opened a store in Quebec's Lower Town: "These gentlemen have spent ten years in the employ of the . . . Leonard company as painters [and] decorators, tapestry workers, etc. Given such a record of service, it seems to us unnecessary to recommend them."

GINETTE LAROCHE

ANQ-Q, CE301-S98, 7 févr. 1871. AVQ, QP1-4, 41/0002. Industrial Alliance Life Insurance Company (Quebec), Minutes of the directors' meetings, 1905–30; Minutes of the shareholders' meetings and financial statements, 1905–30. *L'Action catholique* (Québec), 21 mars 1924, 17 juin 1940. *Daily Telegraph* (Quebec), 1 Jan. 1900. *L'Événement*, 21 mars 1924. *Montreal Herald*, 8 Nov. 1890. *La Semaine commerciale* (Québec), 22 déc. 1899, 9 mars 1900. *Canada ecclésiastique*, 1914–20. *The Canadian trade review: an illustrated descriptive edition of the city of Quebec and district, treating of their history, resources, industries, scenery and waterfalls* ([Montreal?, 1908?]), 65, 87. *Directories*, Quebec, 1863–89; Quebec and Lévis, 1890–1950. Jacques Lapointe, "Monographie de l'Industrielle, cie d'assurance-vie" (mémoire de M.SC.C., univ. Laval, Québec, 1950). Ginette Laroche, "Des vitraux 'made in Quebec,'" *Cap-aux-Diamants* (Québec), 2 (1986–87), no.3: 7–9; *Stained-glass windows* (Quebec, 1999). Léon Lortie, *Album biographique des membres du conseil de ville de Québec, 1894–95* (Québec, 1895). *"La Semaine commerciale"; dépouillement de la 'colonne de l'entrepreneur' 1894 à 1913: le Vieux-Québec, le faubourg Saint-Jean, la Grande-Allée*, Robert Caron, compil. (Québec, 1983). *Une page d'histoire de Québec; magnifique essor industriel* ([Montréal, 1955]), 476–82.

LEONARD, REUBEN WELLS, engineer, militia officer, mining magnate, civil servant, and philanthropist; b. 21 Feb. 1860 in Brantford, Upper Canada, son of Francis Henry Leonard, a businessman and civic official, and Mary Elizabeth Catton; m. 11 Oct. 1889 Kate Rowlands (d. 12 Sept. 1935), granddaughter of James Lesslie*, in Kingston, Ont.; d. 17 Dec. 1930 in St Catharines, Ont.

Reuben W. Leonard attended Brantford Collegiate Institute, and following a short stint as a teacher in Brant County he entered the Royal Military College of Canada in Kingston to study civil engineering. He graduated in 1883 as the bronze medallist in a class of 23 cadets, and for the next two years worked as an engineer for the Canadian Pacific Railway (leaving temporarily to serve in the militia during the North-West rebellion of 1885 [see Louis Riel*]). His engineering career then took off. In the period from 1886 to early 1906 he was involved mainly in railway and hydroelectric projects in central and eastern Canada. Among these, his crowning achievement was the construction of the first Niagara Falls power station, in 1892–93.

In 1905 Leonard's life would take a dramatic turn. A grubstaking venture in northern Ontario led that year to the acquisition of a mineral-rich claim in the centre of Cobalt. These mines contained cobalt (co), nickel (ni), silver (ag), and arsenic (as) and so the business was named Coniagas Mines Limited; Leonard served as its president and general manager. In 1908 he established and became president of the Coniagas Reduction Company Limited in Thorold, where the ores were processed. In nearby St Catharines, Leonard and his wife built a stately home, Springbank, which overlooked the old Welland Canal. The Leonards had no children, but a nephew, Arthur Leonard Bishop*, came from Brantford to St Catharines to attend school; he became their ward, and later heir to the Leonard fortune.

Leonard was a successful businessman and a renowned philanthropist, giving extensively to educational institutions, churches (low-church Anglican), hospitals, and other causes. It became lore that he viewed his great wealth as a public trust. Leonard was appointed to boards of governance at the University of Toronto, Wycliffe College in Toronto, Ridley College in St Catharines, the School of Mining and Agriculture and Queen's University in Kingston, and the Khaki University of Canada. Keenly interested in imperial politics, he served on the Canadian executive of the Round Table, a study group devoted to the reorganization of the British empire. Kate Leonard was similarly active, prominent in such institutions as the Imperial Order Daughters of the Empire, the Victorian Order of Nurses, and the Young Women's Christian Association.

In 1911 Leonard was appointed by Prime Minister Robert Laird Borden* to succeed Simon-Napoléon Parent* as chairman of the Transcontinental Railway Commission, where he spent three years diligently overseeing the construction of the line from Moncton, N.B., to Winnipeg. When the war broke out Leonard committed himself to aiding the cause: not content to stay safely at home, he spent several months in Europe in 1915; as a major in the Corps of Guides – he had joined in 1904 and would become a lieutenant-colonel in September 1915 – he monitored anti-British sentiment in the United States; as an executive of the Win-the-War movement, he lobbied for the formation of the Union government in 1917. He gave generously to support the war effort and helped to raise funds through such agencies as the Canadian Patriotic Fund.

Following the armistice Leonard continued with an array of philanthropic activities. He served a year as president of the Engineering Institute of Canada in 1919–20 and was appointed in 1920 to the Canadian Battlefields Memorials Commission. However, he rejected an invitation to join the League of Nations Society in Canada. The League was doomed to fail, he argued, because it did not acknowledge the vast and ineradicable differences that existed among races. Coniagas also demanded his attention. The price of silver, the main ore, began to recover after the war. In 1919 a bitter strike halted production for seven weeks, as Leonard and the other mine owners in the Cobalt region successfully prevented the unionization of the miners. Leonard's disdain for unions was manifested not only at Coniagas, but also at the University of Toronto, where as a member of the board of governors he tenaciously assailed Robert Morrison MacIver, a professor in the department of political economy who was known for his pro-labour views.

Through the Round Table, Leonard had become acquainted with the English writer Lionel George Curtis. In 1923 Leonard purchased a historic home in the centre of London, Chatham House, which he donated to Curtis's new project, the British (later Royal) Institute of International Affairs. In that same year Leonard extensively revised the terms of an educational trust he had established in 1916 primarily to assist the sons of clergymen, teachers, and war veterans. These terms had been expanded in 1920 and now took their final form, when the fund was increased to

$500,000. The trust recitals explain Leonard's deeply held ideologies. He believed in the natural superiority of "the White Race," and in the importance of Christianity and the British empire in ensuring the progress of civilization. Hence bursaries were made available to students who were white, British subjects, and Protestant. In addition, no more than one-quarter of the moneys could be awarded to females. Leonard's goal was to provide financial assistance to needy students who showed the promise of becoming leading citizens of the empire.

These benefactions marked the climax of Leonard's public life and by the end of 1923 he had become well known in Canada and England. The denouement soon followed. Leonard began suffering symptoms of a neurological disorder now believed to have been Parkinson's disease. As his health declined, he made an extensive series of donations including large capital grants to Ridley and Wycliffe colleges. He also received a number of tributes and honours, including a doctorate from Queen's University, conferred in October 1930. Leonard died just six weeks later; even after 20 years of assiduous philanthropy, he left an estate in excess of $4.5 million.

Gifts such as Chatham House stand as enduring memorials. However, it is the Leonard Foundation that serves as the most significant legacy of the man and his times. A relic of the 1920s, the trust's exclusionary criteria provoked public concern starting in the 1950s. Though Leonard was celebrated in life as a Canadian patriot and philanthropist, his racist beliefs came under scrutiny as the controversy over the trust escalated. A complaint filed against the foundation under the Ontario Human Rights Code in 1986 prompted litigation. In 1990 the Ontario Court of Appeal held that the terms relating to race, religion, nationality, and gender were contrary to law.

BRUCE ZIFF

Reuben Wells Leonard's personal papers have not surfaced. It is believed that on his death they were taken by his personal secretary, Henry Collins, with a view to preparing a biography. This work never materialized.

A complete bibliography for Leonard's life, including the available primary sources, may be found in the author's *Unforeseen legacies: Reuben Wells Leonard and the Leonard Foundation trust* (Toronto, 2000), which also reproduces the Leonard Foundation trust deed, dated 28 Dec. 1923. Among the most pertinent sources are *Cyclopædia of Canadian biog.* (Rose and Charlesworth), vol.3; [R. W. Leonard], "Retiring president's address," Engineering Institute of Canada, *Journal* (Montreal), 3 (1920): 78–84; Re Canada Trust Co. and Ontario Human Rights Commission . . . (1990), *Dominion Law Reports* (Aurora, Ont.), 4th ser., 69: 321–56; and *Standard dict. of Canadian biog.* (Roberts and Tunnell).

LÉPINE, AMBROISE-DYDIME, farmer, Métis leader, and politician; b. 18 March 1840 in St Boni-face (Winnipeg), fifth of the six children of Jean-Baptiste Lépine and Julie Henry; m. there 12 Jan. 1859 Cécile Marion, and they had 14 children, six of whom survived him; d. there 8 June 1923.

Ambroise Lépine's father, an engagé of the Hudson's Bay Company, was born in Saint-Jacques-de-l'Achigan (Saint-Jacques), Lower Canada, to Joseph Chevaudier, *dit* Lépine, and Marie-Anne Pellerin. His mother, the daughter of an English fur trader and an Indian woman, was a native of Ste Agathe (Man.). Lépine was educated at the Collège de Saint-Boniface. After his marriage to Cécile Marion, who was of French Canadian and Métis descent, the couple began farming in St Boniface on river lot 119. Lépine supplemented his income with freighting and hunting.

There is no evidence that Lépine was politically active prior to 1869, when the forthcoming transfer of Rupert's Land from the HBC to Canada was announced. On his return to the Red River settlement (Man.) on 30 October from a freighting expedition to Fort Pitt (Sask.), he learned that the Métis, led by Louis Riel*, had taken steps to delay the transfer and force the Canadian government to negotiate the terms of union with the colony's inhabitants. Apparently asked by Riel if he was "for or against the Métis," Lépine replied that he was in favour of Métis rights. Riel immediately ordered him, with 14 others, to ride to Pembina (N.Dak.) to turn back the lieutenant governor designate, William McDougall*, at the border. On 7 December, on Riel's orders, he led 100 Métis in the capture of Canadians who were garrisoned in the house of one of their leaders, John Christian Schultz*. On 8 Jan. 1870 Riel's provisional government appointed Lépine adjutant general to administer justice in the settlement. A few weeks later Lépine was also elected to represent St Boniface in a convention of 40 representatives of the settlement and he was subsequently appointed head of the military council, a subcommittee of the convention.

A contemporary speculated that Riel chose Lépine as his military chief because of the respect he commanded among the Métis tripmen and buffalo hunters. The Reverend Roderick George MacBeth* described Lépine as a man of prodigious strength, "standing fully six feet three and built in splendid proportion." Reputedly a skilled plainsman, he was assumed to have been the natural leader of the soldiers of the resistance. This assessment does not bear careful scrutiny, however. There is no evidence that Lépine was a buffalo hunter and in March 1870 diarist Alexander Begg* noted that there was open revolt amongst the Métis over Lépine's conduct. Riel patched up the affair, but ordered him not to be so overbearing. A more convincing explanation for Lépine's advancement in the Riel party involves his loyalty to Riel and their close personal and family ties. Furthermore, Lépine was allied with the Roman Catholic Church and many of Riel's most trusted advisers during 1869–70 were Catholic priests.

In mid February 1870 Lépine and a group of Métis arrested Major Charles Arkoll Boulton* and a number of men after their plan to capture Upper Fort Garry (Winnipeg) aborted. Among the prisoners was Thomas Scott*, whose behaviour soon angered his Métis guards. Riel ordered Scott court martialled on 3 March. As the military leader, Lépine headed the tribunal that tried Scott and found him guilty of rebelling against the government and it was he who declared that Scott should be executed. It was Riel, however, who turned down all pleas to spare Scott's life.

Scott's execution would have profound repercussions for both Riel and Lépine. When they later became fearful about reaction to the execution, especially in Protestant Ontario, they were assured by Bishop Alexandre-Antonin Taché* that an amnesty would be granted covering all the events of the resistance. The arrival of the troops led by Colonel Garnet Joseph Wolseley* on 24 Aug. 1870, along with warnings that their lives were in danger, persuaded Riel and Lépine to flee. They eventually ended up at the Catholic mission of St Joseph (N.Dak.), but over the next year they would move back and forth across the boundary, causing a good deal of excitement in the Red River settlement.

In October 1871 Lépine was chosen captain of the troops from St Boniface who volunteered to defend the settlement against the Fenian invasion led by William Bernard O'Donoghue*. He hoped that these loyal actions would result in amnesty, but it was not forthcoming. Although the government had little interest in bringing him and Riel to trial, fearing the uproar that such a move would cause throughout the country, certain individuals wanted vengeance. Given the increasing danger of their arrest, he and Riel were persuaded by Taché to go into voluntary exile in the United States. Lépine was unhappy there. Alternately bored and afraid for his life, he also worried about the welfare of his family and by May 1873 had resolved to go home.

Back in Manitoba, Lépine returned to his farm. His arrest on 17 September on the charge of murdering Scott was the initiative of two Canadians who had been imprisoned by the Métis during the troubles and it caused a great stir in Manitoba. The trial was delayed several times since the judges were unwilling or unable to decide if the Court of Queen's Bench had jurisdiction to try the case. The matter was settled in June 1874 by the newly appointed provincial chief justice, Edmund Burke Wood*, who released Lépine on $8,000 bail.

The trial, which began on 13 October, lasted until 4 November, when the jury, consisting of six French- and six English-speaking members, returned a verdict of guilty with the recommendation of mercy. Wood,

comparing the execution of Scott to a "savage atrocity," sentenced Lépine to death by hanging. The conviction and sentencing elicited great excitement and indignation in Red River and the rest of Canada. *Le Nouveau Monde* (Montréal) [*see* Alphonse Desjardins*] demanded that the federal French Canadian ministers secure a pardon or resign their seats, and the Legislative Assembly of Quebec passed a unanimous resolution asking for amnesty. The federal Liberal government of Alexander Mackenzie* turned the matter over to the governor general, Lord Dufferin [Blackwood*], hoping that the intervention of the imperial authorities would be useful in reconciling the Orange faction in Ontario to a policy of clemency. Dufferin eventually decided that Lépine's sentence should be commuted to two years in prison along with the forfeiture of his civil rights. A few months later, in April 1875, both Riel and Lépine were offered an amnesty on the condition that they accept a five-year banishment from Canada. Unlike Riel, Lépine refused the offer, choosing to serve out the balance of his sentence.

After his release from prison on 26 Oct. 1876 Lépine maintained close contact with Riel and Taché and remained active in Manitoba's French-speaking community. In 1871 he had participated in the formation of the Union Saint-Alexandre to protect Métis interests in the new province and in 1878 he was elected vice-president of the Société Saint-Jean-Baptiste. The following year, when Riel tried to enlist him in the project of uniting the Métis and Indians of the northwest into a confederacy, he travelled to Montana Territory to meet with Riel. Although he spent the winter with the Métis of the region, he took the advice of Taché, who was worried about possible trouble in the northwest, and left before seeing Riel. This decision, and his siding with Taché over the Métis leader, seems to have been a turning point. From then on he stayed out of Métis politics.

The Lépine family remained in St Boniface until 1882 when they moved to Grande Pointe, nine miles southeast of Winnipeg. After a fire destroyed their farm there in 1891, they settled amongst relatives and friends at Oak Lake. Lépine's prospects did not improve. Poor harvests left his family nearly penniless and English-speaking settlers soon overwhelmed the Métis community. By 1902 he was homesteading near Forget (Sask.), close to his sons. In 1908 his wife, Cécile, died and he moved in with his children.

In 1909 the *Winnipeg Evening Telegram* reported that Lépine, impecunious, was in Winnipeg and was willing to disclose the location of Thomas Scott's body for money. Lépine at this time also maintained that Roman Catholic priests Jean-Marie-Joseph Lestanc and Noël-Joseph Ritchot* had advised Riel to execute Scott. The church was quick to reject these allegations and silence Lépine, who then denied that he had ever offered to reveal the location of Scott's body. Sometime after 1909 he sold his land near Forget and bought a summer resort in Quibell, Ont., near Lake of the Woods. He lived there with a granddaughter. Shortly before his death Lépine had his civil rights restored and he moved back to St Boniface. He died at the Hôpital de Saint-Boniface in 1923. His funeral was attended by the former premier of the province, Sir Rodmond Palen Roblin*, and other dignitaries and he was buried in the St Boniface cemetery next to Riel.

Ambroise-Dydime Lépine played a major role in the events of 1869–70, but his contribution was of a different order than that of Riel. Not a natural politician or a strategist, Lépine was a loyal follower of Riel and the church. When the interests of Riel and the church began to diverge in 1879, he sided with Taché and the church. He had, he said, risked his life once for the Métis cause and was not willing to do so again. He did continue to work for the Métis in other ways, helping to establish the historical committee of the Union Nationale Métisse Saint-Joseph du Manitoba in 1909, which would spearhead the drive to publish Auguste-Henri de Trémaudan's *Histoire de la nation métisse dans l'Ouest canadien* in 1935.

GERHARD J. ENS

AM, HBCA, E.6/2; MG 3, B19; D1; D2; P 4895, Émile Lépine fonds, file 2. Arch. de la Soc. Hist. de Saint-Boniface (Winnipeg), Dossiers généalogiques; Fonds de la Corporation archiépiscopale catholique romaine, sér. Langevin; sér. Taché. LAC, RG 15, 1322. *Manitoba Free Press*, 9 March 1909. *Le Métis* (Saint-Boniface [Winnipeg]), 30 nov. 1872. *Winnipeg Evening Telegram*, 8, 11 Feb. 1909. Alexander Begg, *Alexander Begg's Red River journal and other papers relative to the Red River resistance of 1869–1870*, ed. W. L. Morton (Toronto, 1956). Alexander Begg and W. R. Nursey, *Ten years in Winnipeg: a narration of the principal events in the history of the city of Winnipeg from the year A.D. 1870 to the year A.D. 1879, inclusive* (Winnipeg, 1879). J. M. Bumsted, "The trial of Ambroise Lépine," *Beaver* (Winnipeg), 77 (1997–98), no.2: 9–19. Can., House of Commons, Select committee on the causes of the difficulties in the North-West Territory in 1869–70, *Report* (Ottawa, 1874). *The Canadian north-west, its early development and legislative records . . .*, ed. E. H. Oliver (2v., Ottawa, 1914–15). *Dufferin–Carnarvon correspondence, 1874–1878*, ed. C. W. de Kiewiet and F. H. Underhill (Toronto, 1955; repr. New York, 1969). J. A. Kerr, "'I helped capture Ambroise Lépine,'" *Canadian Magazine*, 79 (January–May 1933), no.5: 13, 40–41. Constance Kerr Sissons, *John Kerr* (Toronto, 1946). Denys Lamy, "Ambroise-Didyme Lépine," *Les Cloches de Saint-Boniface* (Saint-Boniface), 22 (1923): 114–16. R. G. MacBeth, *The making of the Canadian west: being the reminiscences of an eye-witness* (Toronto, 1898). *Preliminary investigation and trial of Ambroise D. Lepine for the murder of Thomas Scott . . .*, comp. G. B. Elliott and E. F. T. Brokovski (Montreal, 1874). Louis Riel, *The complete writings of Louis Riel*, ed. G. F. G. Stanley (5v., Edmonton, 1985). G. F. G. Stanley, *Louis Riel* (Toronto, 1963).

LESAGE, DAMASE (baptized **Damas Hardy**), piano manufacturer; b. 28 March 1849 in Sainte-Thérèse-de-Blainville (Sainte-Thérèse), Lower Canada, son of Janvier Hardy, a farmer, and Florentine Ouimet; m. there 14 May 1872 Isabella King (d. 1924), and they had 16 children, 12 of whom died in infancy; d. there 21 Sept. 1923.

The name Lesage first appeared with the fourth generation of Hardys in New France, when Rose Matte, the widow of François de Sales Hardy, married Joseph Lesage in 1754. Lesage adopted Hardy's three sons; some of the descendants took the name of Hardy, others Lesage, or else the double name Hardy, *dit* Lesage. Damase Lesage himself used the name Hardy until at least 1891.

Little is known of Lesage's life before the 1890s. At the time of his marriage in 1872, he called himself a farmer. He apparently also worked as a carpenter for the Canadian Pacific Railway. In 1891, at age of 42, he set up in business with two former employees of Thomas-Ferdinand-Guildor Foisy, a piano maker who had been established in Sainte-Thérèse-de-Blainville since 1888. With his wife's encouragement and $10,000 derived from the sale of two farms, he invested in a firm called Canadian Piano Manufacturing, which he founded on 22 March 1892, in partnership with two cabinetmakers, Rodrigue Légaré and Joseph Desjardins. The firm built two pianos a week, which seems a good rate of production for the period. However, on 20 October Lesage was given the task of winding up the company. He decided to launch the Compagnie Canadienne de Pianos de Sainte-Thérèse-de-Blainville in partnership with cabinetmaker Procule Piché on 9 November; they would remain in business together for 12 years. On 1 May 1905 Lesage made his son Adélard, who had worked for the firm since its opening, a partner. In the years that followed up to 500 pianos were produced annually. The Lesages became one of the largest suppliers of pianos in the province; their clients included the Montreal firms of Charles William Lindsay, Alexander Parker Willis*, and Edmond Archambault*. In 1907, with a view to building its own instruments, the Willis Piano Company Limited acquired a majority holding in the Lesage business. This partnership does not, however, seem to have benefited the Lesages, since Adélard sold his shares to the Willis family in 1911 and set up his own company, A. Lesage, in which he was joined by his sons Jacques-Paul and Jules, and a bit later Gérard. Damase Lesage retired in 1912 and it fell to Adélard to continue his work.

Despite a difficult economic climate, the ensuing years were prosperous; the factory was enlarged twice, in 1916 and again in 1926. Moreover, within ten years, the house of Lesage acquired three other piano manufacturing companies: Craig Piano Company of Montreal in 1930, Bell Piano and Organ Company of

Lesaulnier

Guelph, Ont., in 1934, and Weber Piano Company Limited of Kingston in 1939. In addition to instruments sold under its own name, the Lesage factory made pianos with the brand names of Bell, Mendelssohn, Schumann, and Belmont. In 1942 the company became Lesage Pianos Limited, with Jacques-Paul Lesage as its president. In this period, the family business, with its motto "Now is the time to think positive," had an excellent reputation both locally and on an international scale: Lesage pianos were exported to Australia, New Zealand, South America, and Europe. Fine workmanship, the most modern equipment, and the excellence of its products seem to have been the basis of the firm's success. From the 1950s, however, the company felt the effects of foreign competition, particularly from Japan and Korea. In the 1980s the recession and the rise in interest rates caused serious problems and the owners ultimately sold the business to PSC Management, a Canadian consortium belonging to Grant Clark. Attempts were made to relaunch the product, but they failed. The firm of Lesage Pianos Limited finally closed in early 1987.

For almost a century the Lesage family made an important contribution to the piano manufacturing industry, thanks to the entrepreneurial spirit of Damase Lesage. He put all his energy into the business and played little part in the political, social, or religious life of Sainte-Thérèse-de-Blainville, except as a churchwarden in 1903. Despite a periodically sluggish economy, the company he founded produced many fine instruments and added lustre to the piano manufacturing industry in Canada.

CAROLE GRÉGOIRE

ANQ-M, CE606-S25, 28 mars 1849, 14 mai 1872; TP11, S2, SS20, SSS48, vol.46-o, 3 mars 1936, no.495; S22, SS20, SSS48, 16 avril 1892, no.160; 28 oct. 1892, no.180; 9 janv. 1893, no.187; 21 déc. 1904, no.188; 3 juill. 1905, no.211. *L'Avenir du Nord* (Saint-Jérôme, Qué.), 25 sept. 1923. J.-P. Charbonneau, "Les nouveaux propriétaires ferment les Pianos Lesage," *La Presse*, 28 avril 1987. *Le Devoir*, 6 juin 1925. Robert Gibbens, "Lesage Pianos' future better despite two very tough years," *Globe and Mail*, 11 April 1983. Jacques Roy, "This piano-maker keys on European market," *Gazette* (Montreal), 1 May 1982. *La Voix des Mille-Îles* (Sainte-Thérèse-de-Blainville [Sainte-Thérèse], Qué.), 15 août 1941. *Encyclopedia of music in Canada* (Kallmann *et al.*), 744, 1053–55. Wayne Kelly, *Downright upright: a history of the Canadian piano industry* (Toronto, 1991). Soc. Hist. de Sainte-Thérèse-de-Blainville, *Cahiers hist.: histoire de Sainte-Thérèse* ([Joliette, Qué.], 1940).

LESAULNIER, AURÉLIE, first superior in Quebec of the Daughters of the Heart of Mary; b. 16 Jan. 1834 in Paris; d. 2 Feb. 1922 in Caughnawaga (Kahnawake), Que.

Little is known about the life of Aurélie Lesaulnier before 1870, when at the age of 36 she entered the Daughters of the Heart of Mary as a postulant. She took her vows in Paris in 1877. This late decision was typical of postulants in this very special congregation, which had been founded in 1790, during the French revolution, by the Jesuit Pierre-Joseph Picot de Clorivière and Marie-Adélaïde Champion de Cicé to fill the void left by the banning of religious congregations at that time. Its members had no habit, religious name, or convent. It was a kind of underground congregation whose spiritual gifts were not "devoted to a particular work of charity . . . , no other purpose being in their minds than the spiritual and temporal welfare of neighbours." Each community group formed a "meeting" in which a few "friends" worked, often without the knowledge of their families, because of the secrecy surrounding the very existence of the Daughters of the Heart of Mary. (This secrecy was not lifted until 1957.) The congregation almost always acted within the sphere of influence of the Jesuits and it began to develop internationally towards the mid 1840s. Having spread to Great Britain and Ireland by 1846, it had members in the United States in 1851, Italy in 1858, the Great Lakes region of Canada in 1862, and Belgium in 1866. It engaged in a variety of charitable works: schools, sewing workrooms, orphanages, youth clubs, catechism classes, libraries, workshops, safe houses for girls, retreat houses, missions, women's associations, home visits to the sick, and hospitals. From 1877 Aurélie Lesaulnier held various jobs in France, including positions of responsibility. She was mistress of novices in Lyons in 1888 and assistant in Dijon in 1889; two years later she replaced the superior in Orléans. In 1894, at the age of 60, she was sent to Buffalo, in the United States, as a teacher; the assistant general of the Daughters of the Heart of Mary observed, however, that "her English is poor and she would probably do better in a country where French is spoken."

During this period, Abbé Henri-Raymond Casgrain*, who was visiting Paris, was asked by the congregation's leaders to write its history. One of its members, Anne de Tanquerel, was assigned to him as a secretary, first in Paris during the winter of 1897–98, and then at Quebec from 24 April 1899. The congregation, along with Archbishop Louis-Nazaire BÉGIN of Quebec, was considering opening a meeting in that city. Anne de Tanquerel brought together some ten postulants there. It was the provincial of North America, Adèle Senil (the widow Perronno), who decided to send Lesaulnier as superior in 1899. No preparations had been made in this new location, and she devoted "all her income" and her motherly personality to the task. The new superior quickly organized a number of charitable works: visits to the sick, a sewing workroom, an employment office, and most important of all, in 1906, a safe house at 6 Côte du Palais. Founded to take in girls from the countryside who came to find work as domestic servants, the Œuvre de la Protection de la Jeune Fille would place more than 5,000 of them over the next three decades. Lesaulnier also looked after the religious instruction of the new recruits. The women who supported the charity came from the highest ranks of society.

Despite her advanced age, Lesaulnier was sent to Montréal in 1907 to open a new meeting. Archbishop Paul Bruchési* of Montréal was opposed at first to having the Daughters of the Heart of Mary. At the beginning of the century many French congregations had asked to settle in his archdiocese. There were numerous discussions about whom the Canadian houses would be responsible to – the superior general of the Daughters of the Heart of Mary wanted them under the authority of the province of New York, but Bruchési preferred the province of Paris. In the end, the archbishop accepted the proposal, probably because of the financial and canonical independence of the congregation, which was under papal authority.

The meeting led by Aurélie Lesaulnier in Montréal had only two or three members at first, but by 1909 there were 19 novices. It devoted itself to various charitable works in the parish of L'Immaculée-Conception, which was under the direction of the Jesuits. These included catechism for mentally retarded children, adult education, visits to hospital patients, closed retreat houses, and attendance at courts where young offenders were tried. The church officials with whom she dealt were delighted with her intelligence and education. Archbishop Bégin would declare that "one rarely met a woman as spiritual and as well-informed."

In 1912 Aurélie Lesaulnier was finally relieved of her responsibilities. The Daughters of the Heart of Mary now had about 40 members in the province of Quebec. She chose to retire to the hospital in Caughnawaga, which had been founded in 1905 by Adèle Perronno. For ten years she continued to make herself useful by visiting the sick, copying manuscripts for the province's two meetings, and carrying on an extensive correspondence. Blind and ill, she lived quietly until her death on 2 Feb. 1922, the anniversary of her profession as a religious.

MICHELINE DUMONT

Arch. de la Soc. des Filles du Cœur de Marie (Montréal), Albums de photographies; Annales de Montréal, 1907–13; Dossiers de correspondance; Lettres annuelles, 1898–1914; Montréal-historique; Notice nécrologique d'Aurélie Lesaulnier; Procès-verbaux des conseils, 1904–16; Renouvellement des vœux. L'Action catholique (Québec), 3 févr. 1922. H.-R. Casgrain et les Filles du Cœur de Marie, La Société des Filles du cœur de Marie … (5v., Paris, 1899–1964). Guy Laperrière, Les congrégations religieuses: de la France au Québec, 1880–1914 (2v. parus, Sainte-Foy, Qué., 1996–   ), 1: 143–45. "L'Œuvre de la protection de la jeune fille, no 6, côte du Palais, Québec," Almanach de l'Action sociale catholique (Québec), 2 (1918): 98–99. "La Société des Filles du cœur immaculé de Marie: le foyer de l'Œuvre de protection des jeunes filles," La Semaine religieuse de Québec, 7 déc. 1960: 233–36.

LESPÉRANCE, ZOTIQUE, leather cutter and labour organizer; b. 22 Nov. 1865, son of Jacques Lespérance (Talon, dit Lespérance) and Angélique Brabant; m. 20 June 1899 Élizabeth Lamarche in Montréal, and they had four children; d. there 29 May 1929.

A leather cutter by trade, Zotique Lespérance worked in boot and shoe factories in Montréal. In the 1880s he was introduced to trade unionism through the Knights of Labor, an American organization that was increasingly becoming solidly established in Quebec. In August 1894 Lespérance and several other cutters left their assembly of Knights to form an autonomous union of leather cutters. In January 1901 this union joined an American one, the Boot and Shoe Workers' Union (of which it formed Local 249), and Lespérance became its business agent. In charge of recruiting members and ensuring implementation of collective labour agreements, he had his work cut out for him in the metropolis, for there was intense rivalry with the national footwear unions, which in November established the Canadian Federation of Shoe Workers in order to unite all such workers of Canada. According to Lespérance, "The International [union] is superior because in it neither religion nor borders nor differences of race matter." From 1905 he served as the business agent and organizer of the joint council of the Montreal shoe workers' unions that were affiliated with the Boot and Shoe Workers' Union. On 1 April 1905 he was also named a member of the general management of this union, an office he would hold for the rest of his life. The Montreal boot and shoe workers' unions affiliated with it had about 300 members in 1907. This number increased appreciably with the disappearance of the Canadian Federation of Shoe Workers in 1911; it fluctuated between 1,200 and 1,500 from World War I to 1930.

Lespérance crossed swords with the Roman Catholic clergy in 1912 during a lockout at Tebbutt Shoe and Leather Company Limited, a factory in Trois-Rivières. In October its owner, J. T. Tebbutt, dismissed all those who had just formed a union affiliated with the Boot and Shoe Workers' Union when they asked for a salary increase. He refused to meet with Lespérance, who had come to find common ground. Having tried unsuccessfully to recruit workers in Quebec City and in Montreal, Tebbutt looked to the local clergy to persuade the employees to return to work. The parish priest showed sympathy for the workers' demands, but the bishop of Trois-Rivières, François-Xavier Cloutier*, reacted very differently: he decided to set up Catholic trade unions "to tear [the] workers from the grip of the non-confessional unions." The international union collapsed the following month. The bishop's decision marked the beginning of the establishment of Catholic trade unionism in Trois-Rivières. This movement would spread to the footwear unions in Quebec City and Montreal a few years later [see Gaudiose HÉBERT]. Lespérance, who would be general organizer of the Boot and Shoe Workers' Union from at least 1918, undoubtedly had brushes with these unions. Like the other leaders of international unions of the time, he surely experienced how difficult it was to fight organizations backed by the Catholic clergy.

Also like a good many of these leaders, Lespérance was interested in the political dimension of trade unionism. Active within the Montreal Trades and Labor Council, which defended the rights of unionized workers in their dealings with municipal governments, he on several occasions between 1910 and 1916 served on the executive committee for the province of Quebec of the Trades and Labor Congress of Canada, a committee responsible for presenting the organization's grievances to the provincial government. In addition, he held the office of delegate of the Montreal Trades and Labor Council to the Labour party [see Alphonse VERVILLE] in 1908, and the party's general committee supported his candidacy for alderman of Longue-Pointe ward in 1914; he was, however, defeated. Of all the reforms called for by the international unions, the one Lespérance was particularly concerned about was that workers' sons and daughters have better access to public education. He had been on the committee that had prepared the Labour party's memorandum to the royal commission with respect to the Catholic schools of Montreal in 1909. In it the party proposed free schools, standardized textbooks, a single school board in Montreal, and the creation of a department of public instruction. On 29 May 1917 Lespérance was named a member of the new library commission that was charged with choosing books, journals, newspapers, and other materials to be held by the Civic Library.

A committed trade unionist throughout his life, Zotique Lespérance can be considered an important figure in the establishment of international trade unionism in Quebec at the outset of the 20th century. Upon his death, *Le Monde ouvrier* (Montréal), to which he had been a faithful contributor, stressed that he had toiled "all his life in the interest of the working class" and that his "sound and level-headed judgement" earned him "nothing but friends both in the ranks of labour and in the other spheres of society."

JACQUES ROUILLARD

ANQ-M, CE601-S15, 20 juin 1899. BCM-G, RBMS, Notre-Dame de Montréal, 20 mars 1902, 11 nov. 1903, 17 juin 1906; Sacré-Cœur de Jésus (Montréal), 22 juill. 1901, 28 sept. 1902; Sainte-Brigide (Montréal), 10 mai 1907; Saint-Louis-de-France (Montréal), 12 nov. 1903 (mfm.). VM-DGDA, VM1, procès-verbaux du Bureau des commissaires, 29 mai 1917; VM6, règlement 624. *Le Monde ouvrier* (Montréal), 1er juin 1929, 31 août 1935. *La Patrie*, 1er avril 1903, 6 août 1907, 4 juin 1909. Éric Leroux, "Les syndicats internationaux et la commission royale d'enquête sur l'éducation de 1909–1910," RCHTQ [Regroupement des Chercheurs-Chercheuses en Hist. des Travailleurs et Travailleuses du Québec], *Bull.* (Montréal), 23 (1977), no.1: 5–28. Jacques Rouillard, "Implantation et expansion de l'Union internationale des travailleurs en chaussures au Québec de 1900 à 1940," *RHAF*, 36 (1982–83): 75–105; *Les syndicats nationaux au Québec, de 1900 à 1930* (Québec, 1979), 56–65, 106–11, 191–93. Robert Tremblay, "Répertoire biographique du mouvement ouvrier québécois, 1880–1914" (rapport postdoctoral, univ. du Québec à Montréal, 1995), 69–70.

LESSARD, FRANÇOIS-LOUIS (baptized **Louis-François-Guillaume**), militia and army officer; b. 9 Dec. 1860 at Quebec, son of Louis-Napoléon Lessard and Jane Felicity McCutcheon; m. there 25 April 1882 Marie Florence Lee, and they had three daughters; d. 7 Aug. 1927 in Meadowvale (Mississauga), Ont.

François-Louis Lessard's father was a secretary with the Quebec Permanent Building Society; his mother was of Scottish background. Known to his friends as Louis, Lessard was educated at the Collège Saint-Thomas in Montmagny and the Académie Commerciale de Québec. According to an obituary, he "spent some years in business" before concentrating on a military career. As with many other francophone political and military leaders of the time, he was exposed throughout his early life to both British and French cultures. He joined the Quebec Volunteer Militia Cavalry Squadron as a private in 1878; two years later he entered the School of Gunnery (B Battery, Garrison Artillery) as an officer. In 1884 he transferred to the 65th Battalion of Rifles (Mount Royal Rifles) and then to the Cavalry School Corps (Royal Canadian Dragoons), one of the original Permanent Force units. Lessard's first active service, during the North-West campaign of 1885 [see Sir Frederick Dobson Middleton*], was limited to protecting supply lines and his cavalry unit never came under fire. Increasingly recognized as a trainer and an administrator, he was promoted captain (1888), major in command of A Squadron of the RCD at Toronto (1894), inspector of cavalry for Canada (1896), and lieutenant-colonel (1899).

When Prime Minister Sir Wilfrid Laurier* announced a contribution of volunteers for the South African War in October 1899, Lessard led the calls for recruits in Quebec. He could not join the first contingent [see Sir William Dillon OTTER], which consisted of infantry, but he volunteered for special service and sailed with it to Cape Town. He found employment on the staff of the imperial cavalry commander, John

Denton Pinkstone French, and participated in the relief of Kimberley. After British leaders asked for a second Canadian contingent, with mounted troops, two battalions of the Canadian Mounted Rifles arrived in March 1900. Lessard took charge of the 1st Battalion, which he helped rename the Royal Canadian Dragoons (underlining its relationship to the Permanent Force was perhaps one of his considerations), and he led it through 27 engagements. In October he was placed in temporary command of Major-General Horace Lockwood Smith-Dorrien's mounted troops clearing the Belfast district.

One of the best-known battles involving Canadians occurred at Liliefontein, when Smith-Dorrien led an expedition to disperse a Boer commando laagered in the area of Witkloof. The strength of the Boer forces and his own lack of mobility forced Smith-Dorrien to return to Belfast, leaving Lessard's Dragoons and Lieutenant Edward Whipple Bancroft MORRISON's guns to cover the retreat on 7 November. Although a few individuals criticized Lessard's performance, Smith-Dorrien described him as an able commander who displayed "the greatest gallantry." Historians have recognized his participation as courageous and decisive and the RCD as one of the best units on either side. Lessard's actions would seem to have helped his career; he received several honours, including the CB. After his return to Canada in 1901 and the disbandment of the Dragoons, he continued to command the original RCD in Toronto, in addition to resuming his role as inspector of cavalry. Lessard's regiment was the model for the cavalry school at Stanley Barracks in Toronto. The courses he conducted there for the militia greatly influenced the development of cavalry in eastern Canada. Many benefited too from the lectures and courses he gave on staff duties, military law, tactics and strategy, and topography at the Canadian Military Institute and elsewhere during the years he was stationed in Toronto. In 1907 he was promoted colonel and made adjutant general of militia; he became brigadier-general in 1911 and major-general a year later.

When war broke out in 1914, many considered Lessard the ideal candidate to lead the 1st Canadian Division overseas. The command, however, went to Lieutenant-General Edwin Alfred Hervey ALDERSON. Even before the war Lessard's differences with Samuel HUGHES, the minister of militia and defence, had become a serious obstacle to his advancement. Hughes favoured the role of citizen volunteers at the expense of Permanent Force soldiers, whom he believed should be relegated to instructional roles. In April 1912 Lessard helped foil Hughes's first attempt to promote himself major-general. As a result, he was removed as adjutant general and sent to command Military District No.2 (Toronto and central Ontario). This is the position he held in August 1914; in December he was made inspector general of militia for eastern Canada. Lessard had several more confrontations with Hughes, while continuing to receive praise for his administrative skills. For six months in 1916 he went overseas to report on training in the Canadian forces. His findings highlighted the problems in Hughes's system of recruitment and training [see Onésime Readman*] and he recommended improvements that would help Canadians integrate more easily into units in the field. In particular, he hoped to see more input from non-commissioned officers. Hughes took no action but his replacement, Albert Edward KEMP, implemented many of Lessard's recommendations.

Prior to the highly controversial introduction of conscription in 1917, Lessard toured Quebec campaigning for recruits. During the last year of the war, in addition to his duties as inspector general, he dealt with two difficult situations. He was appointed temporary commander of Military District No.6 and fortress commander at Halifax, where his main task was to apply Ottawa's plans to reduce the garrison (to free up reinforcements) and increase fighting efficiency. Then in late March 1918 he was directed to restore order in Quebec City after anti-conscription riots had broken out. He was harshly criticized by some for the intervention on 1 April that left 30 to 75 civilians injured and 4 dead, including 14-year-old Georges Demeule*. Others noted that posters had cautioned the public against unlawful assemblies and that the soldiers had used restraint while being bombarded with projectiles until some rioters opened fire. Only then, after several soldiers had been wounded, did Lessard order the use of rifles and machine-guns. Before the intervention he had published warnings that "every measure" would be taken "to maintain order and peace."

In June 1919 Lessard retired to a small farm west of Toronto, at Meadowvale. The former cavalry officer raised horses and judged at horse shows. Throughout his career his leisure interests had largely been defined by his profession. Elected president of the Canadian Military Institute in 1904, he belonged to the hunt clubs of both Ottawa and Toronto, and when the Polo Club of Toronto was established in 1901, he brought 26 ponies from Calgary. The *Globe* noted that he always possessed the élan that went with being a cavalryman. His family life, however, is obscure. A friend explained in 1898 that Lessard's wife was rarely seen in public because of a "painful malady"; she died in June 1924, possibly in Quebec. One of their daughters also passed away, and another was cared for in a children's home in Quebec City. Lessard himself died of stomach cancer in 1927; a Roman Catholic, he was buried in Mount Hope Cemetery in Toronto. He was remembered as an extremely popular soldier, a stern but just disciplinarian, and, in the words of militia minister Sydney Chilton Mewburn, "a fine type of Canadian citizen."

JOHN MACFARLANE

ANQ-Q, CE301-S1, 25 avril 1882; CE301-S22, 9 déc. 1860; E17, dossier 1661 (1918) (versement 1960-01-036/361). AO, RG 22-359, no.4680; RG 80-8-0-1072, no.26626. LAC, MG 29, D61: 4929–30; MG 30, E41; E339, A. E. Hilder, "Comrades all," 58–73 (photocopies); RG 9, II, A2, 9; A3, 32; RG 24, 2323, HQS 66-10; RG 150, Acc. 1992–93/166. *Conservator* (Brampton, Ont.), 11 Aug. 1927. *Globe*, 8 Aug. 1927. *La Patrie*, 14 oct. 1899. *La Presse*, 9 oct. 1899. *Toronto Daily Star*, 8 Aug. 1927. Can., Dept. of National Defence, Directorate of Hist. and Heritage, Hist. Resource Centre (Ottawa), 71/246 (C. G. Power, Account of riots in Quebec City); Parl., *Sessional papers*, 1901, no.35a. *Canadian annual rev.*, 1904, 1917. *Canadian men and women of the time* (Morgan; 1912). J. F. C[ummins], "A distinguished Canadian cavalry officer: Major-General F. L. Lessard, C.B.," *Canadian Defence Quarterly* (Ottawa), 3 (1925–26): 128–31. A. F. Duguid, *Official history of the Canadian forces in the Great War, 1914–1919* (only 1v. in 2 pts. [1914–September 1915] was published, Ottawa, 1938). Brereton Greenhous, *Dragoon: the centennial history of the Royal Canadian Dragoons, 1883–1983* (Belleville, Ont., 1983). R. G. Haycock, *Sam Hughes: the public career of a controversial Canadian, 1885–1916* (Waterloo, Ont., 1986). John MacFarlane, "The right stuff? Evaluating the performance of Lieutenant-Colonel F.-L. Lessard in South Africa and his failure to receive a senior command position with the CEF in 1914," *Canadian Military Hist.* (Waterloo), 8 (1999), no.3: 48–58. Carman Miller, *Painting the map red: Canada and the South African War, 1899–1902* (Montreal and Kingston, Ont., 1993). Jean Provencher, *Québec sous la loi des mesures de guerre, 1918* ([Trois-Rivières], 1971). R. F. Sarty, "Silent sentry: a military and political history of Canadian coast defence, 1860–1945" (PHD thesis, 2v., Univ. of Toronto, 1983), 326–35.

LE VASSEUR, NAZAIRE (baptized **Louis-Nazaire-Zéphirin**), journalist, office holder, soldier, musician, and writer; b. 6 Feb. 1848 at Quebec, son of Zéphirin Levasseur and Madeleine Langevin; m. there 5 June 1872 Phédora Venner, and they had four children, including Irma*, the first French Canadian woman physician in the province of Quebec; d. 8 Nov. 1927 at Quebec.

Nazaire Le Vasseur grew up in a business world in which, as he would later recall in his *Réminiscences d'antan*, hospitality was "open-ended and bountiful" and cultivation of the arts was encouraged. His father, who was at that time manager of a shipyard, was an amateur musician, and the family home was "a meeting place for intellectuals" where many leading figures of the day gathered. They included merchant Abraham Hamel, brother of painter Théophile Hamel*, the family of notary Louis-Édouard Glackmeyer*, pianist Charles Sabatier [Wugk*], and French composer and organist Marie-Hippolyte-Antoine Dessane*. The eldest of three children, Le Vasseur began to take music lessons with Dessane by the time he was five, and over the years he would study piano, cello, violin, flute, and organ.

After completing classical studies undertaken at the Petit Séminaire de Québec from 1857 to 1866, Le Vasseur enrolled in the faculty of medicine at the Université Laval, but after three years, as he himself indicated, his family's financial difficulties obliged him to withdraw (although his name is not on the list of students enrolled for 1868–69). He then joined the staff of *L'Événement*, a newspaper recently founded by Hector Fabre*, on which he worked in succession as chief reporter, assistant editor, and finally editor until 1878. As a journalist, he came in contact with many leading political figures, to whom he gave advice or support in electoral campaigns, as he did for Wilfrid Laurier* in 1877. Le Vasseur's marriage in 1872 to the daughter of a banker had confirmed his social success.

On 2 Oct. 1878 Le Vasseur became a gas and gas meter inspector for the federal government, a position he was to hold until 1915. At the same time he maintained his interest in journalism. In April 1883 he founded an evening newspaper, *La Presse*, but publication ceased after the first issue because of inadequate funding. Eleven years later, he and Émile La Salle launched *La Revue commerciale*, a paper quickly replaced in August 1894 by *La Semaine commerciale*, in which Le Vasseur would continue to publish articles until 1904. He was also a regular contributor to *L'Événement*. Despite all these activities, he found time to enlist as a militiaman in the 9th Battalion Volunteer Militia Rifles; he took part in the 1885 North-West expedition against Louis Riel*'s Métis, which earned him promotion to the rank of major on his return. Between 1898 and 1913 he was the consul in Quebec for several Central and South American countries, including Nicaragua, Guatemala, Brazil, and Chile.

In 1877 Le Vasseur had been one of the founding members of the Geographical Society of Quebec. Known for his "insatiable intellectual curiosity," as the *Bulletin* of the society put it, he published nearly 50 articles between 1883 and 1921 on topics as diverse as Lake Winnipeg, the Mackenzie River basin, Halley's comet, and Russia. He served as the society's assistant recording secretary in 1880 and subsequently as vice-president in 1889, honorary president in 1896 ("in recognition of services rendered to the society"), and president from 1898 to 1905. By 1895 he was closely connected with Captain Joseph-Elzéar Bernier*; through the Geographical Society and by organizing fund-raising campaigns, he would help Bernier carry out his expeditions to the North Pole between 1904 and 1911. In 1893 Le Vasseur was also one of the founding members of the Cercle des Dix, a Quebec society which included writers, musicians, and journalists such as Napoléon Legendre*, Narcisse-Henri-Édouard Faucher* de Saint-Maurice, and James MacPherson Le Moine*.

Le Vasseur also took part in the musical life of Quebec. He succeeded his teacher Dessane as organist of Saint-Roch, from 1873 to 1881; together, they had founded the Société Musicale Sainte-Cécile of the church of Saint-Roch in 1869. As conductor of this choir from 1873 to 1885, Le Vasseur performed masses by Haydn, Rossini, and Gounod, as well as Félicien David's opera *La perle du Brésil*; Le Vasseur's wife, who was a singer, was a soloist in some of these concerts. He was secretary of the Quebec Harmonic Society in 1870, and the following year he was co-founder and violinist of the Septuor Haydn, which in 1903 formed the nucleus of the Société Symphonique de Québec (the future Quebec Symphony Orchestra) [*see* Joseph VÉZINA]; Le Vasseur played the double bass in this new orchestra between 1903 and 1907. When he died, his fellow musicians, at one of their meetings, would lament the passing of a "pioneer worker who has contributed so much to the success of the society." In 1880 he succeeded Calixa Lavallée* as director of a choir known as the Quatuor Vocal de Québec and in the same year he was secretary of the organizing committee for the Saint-Jean-Baptiste celebrations in Quebec, during which "O Canada" was given its first performance. In 1887 Le Vasseur was named a member of the Académie de Musique de Québec, which aimed principally to foster interest in music and better regulate musical education; he thus made a mark in the leading musical organizations of the province of Québec.

Despite badly failing eyesight from 1908, Le Vasseur – "with two pairs of glasses on his nose," as Edmond Chassé, news editor of *L'Événement*, noted – continued to write for the *Bulletin* of the Geographical Society of Quebec. He had been thinking since 1881 of undertaking a history of music in Quebec; between 1919 and 1922 this project took form in a series of some 40 articles published in the journal *La Musique*. Although they contain a number of gaps and errors, as musicologist Vivianne Émond has pointed out, these essays, which were enlivened by personal reminiscences, served for many years as a primary reference source for historians of music in Quebec, particularly with regard to the 19th century. In 1925 Le Vasseur wrote the biography of his friend Ferdinand-Philéas Canac-Marquis, in which, however, anecdotes about the surgeon's life and his travels figure more prominently than his contributions to science. Two other books, *Têtes et figures* and *Réminiscences d'antan*, published in 1920 and 1926 respectively, show that Le Vasseur had a fine sense of style and a gift for story-telling; in the case of *Têtes et figures*, vivid imagination and knowledge of French Canadian customs are skilfully blended.

Nazaire Le Vasseur died in an unpretentious board-ing house in old Quebec. His funeral, held with due solemnity in the basilica of Notre-Dame, was attended by many dignitaries, magistrates, soldiers, and musicians, marking the prestige and influence enjoyed by this passionate and sympathetic scholar. For almost half a century, he had been omnipresent in the cultural, social, and political life of Quebec. A man of wide culture and great intellectual curiosity, a gifted writer, he served on many a committee, founded or co-founded numerous associations, and built up a network of friends who shared his tastes and passions. Having lived since childhood in an artistic milieu, he remained active as a musician throughout his life. Although an amateur, through his activities as a performer, historian, and journalist, he helped lay the foundations of musical life in Quebec City, a contribution for which posterity can be grateful.

IRÈNE BRISSON

In addition to his articles in *L'Événement*, *Le Soleil*, *La Semaine commerciale* (Québec), *La Musique* (Québec), and the *Bull.* (Québec) of the Soc. de Géographie de Québec, Nazaire Le Vasseur is the author of *Honorable Ph.-Aug. Choquette, ancien sénateur, juge de la Cour des sessions de la paix, Québec* (Québec, 1920); *Têtes et figures* (Québec, 1920); *Ferdinand-Philéas Canac-Marquis, médecin-chirur-gien: esquisse biographique* (Québec, 1925); and *Réminiscences d'antan; Québec il y a 70 ans* ([Québec, 1926]). He collaborated with Narcisse-Henri-Édouard Faucher de Saint-Maurice and Joseph-Étienne-Eugène Marmette on *Le Canada et les Basques* (Québec, 1879). At the time of his death, he left in manuscript form a translation of Napoléon-Alexandre COMEAU's *Life and sport on the north shore of the lower St. Lawrence and gulf* (Quebec, 1909); it would be published in Quebec in 1945 as *La vie et le sport sur la Côte Nord du bas Saint-Laurent et du golfe*, and reprinted in 1983. He also translated *The trail of the sword* (New York, 1894) by the Canadian Horatio Gilbert George Parker* under the title *Femme, ou sabre* ([Québec], 1898).

As a composer, Le Vasseur left some salon music and occasional pieces appealing to contemporary tastes, mentioned by Gilles Potvin in *Encyclopedia of music in Canada* (Kallmann *et al.*), 748.

ANQ-Q, CE301-S22, 7 févr. 1848, 5 juin 1872; P152. LAC, MG 30, B21. F.-X. Chouinard, "In memoriam: le major Nazaire Le Vasseur," Soc. de Géographie de Québec, *Bull.*, 21 (1927): 193–200. *DOLQ*, vol.2. Vivianne Émond, "'Musique et musiciens à Québec: souvenirs d'un amateur' de Nazaire LeVasseur (1848–1927): étude critique" (mémoire de M.MUS., univ. Laval, 1986). Robert Germain, "Sur tous les claviers . . . Louis-Nazaire Levasseur," *Cap-aux-Diamants* (Québec), 5 (1989–90), no.2: 41–44. Christian Morissonneau, *La Société de géographie de Québec, 1877–1970* (Québec, 1971), 53–55, 258. Victor Morin, "Les Dix," *Cahiers des Dix*, 1 (1936): 22–25.

LEW, DAVID HUNG CHANG (also known as **Lew Hung Chang** (**Liao Hungxiang** in Mandarin), but he frequently signed his correspondence in English **David C. Lew**), interpreter and legal adviser;

Lew

b. *c.* 1886 in China; d. unmarried 23 Sept. 1924 in Vancouver.

At the time of his murder in broad daylight on the streets of Vancouver's Chinatown, allegedly at the hands of another Chinese, David C. Lew was linked in police reports to the shadowy world of Chinese politics and tong wars. An examination of his life suggests a different picture. Like a handful of other Chinese in Canada, he used his considerable language skills to make a living as an intermediary between Canadian authorities and migrants from China.

Lew likely arrived in Canada when he was 13 or 14. The son of a prominent merchant, he attended public school in British Columbia, where he learned the English language and Canadian customs. His English was apparently excellent. One contemporary newspaper account noted that "to hear him talk one would almost imagine he was a born Canadian." Lew's own writings demonstrate a high degree of fluency with only occasional grammatical lapses.

Although he probably qualified as a lawyer, Lew was never able to practise. Members of the British Columbia bar had to appear on the provincial voters' list and between 1872 and 1947 all those of "Chinese race" were banned from voting in the province. (In 1945 the franchise was extended to those who were serving or who had served in the Canadian military.) As was common among Chinese who had legal training, Lew had a working relationship with a white lawyer, William Wallace Burns McInnes, acting as an interpreter and adviser for Chinese clients. This arrangement allowed him to practise unofficially, but he could not sign official documents or plead in court. He represented clients in a variety of matters. For example, in 1908 he corresponded with a lawyer on behalf of a man who had bought property in Steveston and had been warned by the local chief of police that he would be fined if his tenants engaged in prostitution or gambling. With the lawyer's assistance, Lew was able to ensure that his client would not be liable for his tenants' actions. Lew also acted as a court interpreter in British Columbia and other provinces and assisted in police investigations. In 1909 he explained to police chief John C. McRae of Winnipeg, after a member of that city's Chinese community had been murdered, that "there is very little chance of doing much without some fearless and independent interpreter." In 1924 Lew would act as legal representative for Wong Foon Sing, the houseboy suspected of having murdered nursemaid Janet Kennedy Smith.

Lew was not above using his role as a go-between for personal gain. A promissory note written in 1908 indicates that he was prepared to pay $1,500 in "legal fees" if he were appointed interpreter for the customs and immigration office in the port of Vancouver. Two other letters suggest that he was involved in a scheme with lawyer Joseph Ambrose Russell, MP Robert George Macpherson, and another person (likely merchant Robert Kelly) to move Chinese through the port in return for $100 per person. The scheme may have involved the use of falsified documents to identify the immigrants as merchants or students, categories exempt from the $500 head tax then applicable.

In 1910–11 Lew's role as a middleman put him at the centre of a controversy. During his testimony before the royal commission appointed to investigate alleged Chinese frauds and opium smuggling on the Pacific coast, presided over by judge Denis Murphy, Lew claimed that he was the instigator of the inquiry. He stated that he had first expressed his concerns about immigration frauds to the deputy minister of labour, William Lyon Mackenzie King*, in 1908 and that he had also supplied information to lawyer Thomas Robert Edward MacInnes, who was employed by the federal government to advise it on immigration legislation. In June 1910, apparently at his own expense, Lew had gone to Ottawa to present his allegations to the deputy minister of trade and commerce and chief controller of Chinese immigration, Francis Charles Trench O'Hara. Lew charged that the Chinese interpreter for the immigration authorities at Vancouver, Yip On, was part of an immigrant smuggling ring. According to Lew, Yip received payments from people with fraudulent papers and translated their answers to questions from immigration officials in such a way as to allay suspicion. The star witness at the inquiry, he testified that he and federal officials had boarded a ship coming to Vancouver and had tricked passengers into handing over letters about the scheme intended for Yip On. Meanwhile, Yip On's lawyers claimed that their client was the victim of a conspiracy by Lew and his associates, who were the ones involved in a smuggling scheme. Their accusations may have been correct. Justice Murphy identified Lew as an associate of Chang Toy, the passenger agent for the Blue Funnel Line. Chang was an intense rival of Yip Sang, the passenger agent for the Canadian Pacific Railway's steamship line and an uncle of Yip On. A letter to O'Hara from Methodist missionary Tom Chue Thom dated 1910 was produced before the commission. It described a serious conflict in Vancouver's Chinatown between two competing factions, one of which included Lew. Thom described Lew as "Not a Moral man," but also stated that "he do Good service to your Government which no other Chinaman dare to do it." Murphy found that Lew and his non-Chinese associates had engaged in "an intrigue . . . to establish some sort of connection with the administration of the Chinese Restriction Act at the Port of Vancouver by obtaining control of the position of Chinese interpreter, and possibly in other ways. Its object to serve some personal advantage." Murphy did not have sufficient evidence to recommend criminal charges against Lew, although he did recommend them against

Yip On. He justified the commission's reliance on Lew, noting that "the Chinese communities at the coast constitute an *imperium in imperio*, and it is hopeless for white people to attempt to obtain information of value . . . unless the co-operation of at least one well informed Chinaman can be secured. Mr. Lew was the only such person willing to assist so far as the Commission was aware. . . . In justice to him it must be said that he rendered much valuable aid."

Lew's work for the police and other authorities may have made him powerful enemies within the Chinese community and could well have caused his death. After he was shot, newspapers reported that the police were carefully watching the tongs in Chinatown and were going to observe his funeral closely. The police linked Lew to what they described as competition between different tongs over gambling revenues. Modern scholarship suggests that the concern over tong wars was exaggerated. In the racially divided world of British Columbia, the police could have known of such activities only by relying on go-betweens and, as Lew's personal history suggests, go-betweens were not simply neutral interpreters; they had interests of their own. His murderer was never found.

TIMOTHY J. STANLEY

BCA, E/D/L58; GR-1415, file 09847; GR-2951, no.1924-09-331092 (mfm.). *Regina Standard*, 21 Feb. 1906. *Vancouver Daily Province*, 11 Jan. 1911, 25 Oct. 1924. *Vancouver Daily World*, 7, 12 Jan. 1911. *Vancouver Morning Sun*, 25 Sept. 1924. K. J. Anderson, *Vancouver's Chinatown: racial discourse in Canada, 1875–1980* (Montreal and Kingston, Ont., 1991). Can., Royal commission appointed to investigate alleged Chinese frauds and opium smuggling on the Pacific coast, *Report* (Ottawa, 1913). Harry Con *et al.*, *From China to Canada: a history of the Chinese communities in Canada*, ed. Edgar Wickberg (Toronto, 1982; repr. 1988). L. E. A. Ma, *Revolutionaries, monarchists, and Chinatowns: Chinese politics in the Americas and the 1911 revolution* (Honolulu, 1990).

LI MENGJIU. *See* LEE MONG KOW

LINDLEY, SARAH (Crease, Lady Crease), artist, socialite, and diarist; b. 30 Nov. 1826 in Acton (London), England, eldest daughter of John Lindley and Sarah Freestone; m. there 27 April 1853 Henry Pering Pellew Crease*, and they had three sons and four daughters; d. 10 Dec. 1922 in Victoria.

The eldest daughter of a distinguished botanist, university professor, and author, Sarah Lindley grew up in an environment steeped in plant lore and scientific curiosity, with an emphasis on gardening, horticulture, and specimen collecting. As a young girl, she attended Mrs Gee's school in Hendon (London) and received private art lessons from family friend and noted portraitist Charles Fox. Inspiration and instruction in botanical illustration with watercolours came from Sarah Ann Drake, chief illustrator in her father's employ. Fox taught watercolour and pencil sketching and introduced Sarah to woodblock printing and copperplate engraving. These techniques would be crucial to her later work, allowing her to translate her sketches into a publishable format. Between 1842 and 1858 she produced pen-and-ink botanical illustrations to accompany her father's numerous publications, notably the *Gardeners' Chronicle* (London), which he helped to found in 1841 and would edit until his death in 1865, and *The vegetable kingdom* . . . (London, 1846). Many of these sketches she also translated into woodblock prints. She was thus able to study botany and earn pocket money, yet she remained in the separate sphere of domestic life as a female dependent.

In 1848 Sarah met a law student and friend of her brother, Henry Pering Pellew Crease. They became engaged in June 1849, but the engagement was not publicly announced since Crease was obliged to travel with his family to Upper Canada immediately after taking his bar exams in July. During their separation Crease attempted to find suitable employment. John Lindley would not compromise in his expectations for his daughter. Sarah and Henry corresponded continuously over a period of almost 18 months. Her charming letters shyly reveal the thoughts and emotions of a young woman in love.

Crease returned to England in December 1850 and the couple eventually married on 27 April 1853. After setting up a household in Notting Hill (London), he became a mining manager in Cornwall; his family moved there in 1856. Following his resignation in 1857, he left England and the next year he settled in Vancouver Island, where he became a barrister. Sarah arrived with their three daughters in February 1860.

The family lived in Victoria until 1862. Crease had been appointed attorney general of the mainland colony of British Columbia in October 1861, so they moved to New Westminster, the capital, and resided at Ince Cottage. They remained there until 1868, when they returned to Victoria. Financial uncertainty plagued the family, but in 1872 they began to construct Pentrelew, an Italianate-style country house, which would soon be surrounded by lush gardens.

Over an 18-year period, from 1854 to 1872, Sarah bore seven children, the youngest when she was 45. She coped with their measles, mumps, diphtheria, and scarlet fever, but still three children would predecease her. Henry Hooker, born in 1869, died a year after his birth. Barbara Lindley would die in 1883, after many years of indifferent health, and in 1915 Mary Maberly would die of cancer. Sarah loved her family, but was a strict disciplinarian who set high moral standards.

Because of her husband's prominent position – he had been appointed a judge in 1870 – Sarah and her family were part of the immigrant social elite. Despite continued worry over finances, the family maintained a façade of genteel, cultured living and participated in a wide variety of activities. The sons completed their education in England and the daughters travelled there to attend art classes, meet relatives, and further their social connections. Until 1875 Sarah employed domestic help only sporadically, assuming the principal load of household responsibilities and training her daughters to share in the duties. In the evenings she assisted her husband in his business affairs by performing the role of clerk, copying his correspondence and assisting with accounts. This unpaid labour was an economic necessity. Unfortunately, it strained her eyesight.

As befitted her role as a social leader, Sarah immersed herself in charitable works. Both she and her husband were generous financial supporters of the Church of England, contributing whenever possible to special projects. Never in a position of complete financial security, Sarah often preferred to volunteer her time and lend her name to charitable causes rather than donate funds. Thus she taught Sunday school for over a decade, worked on committees to establish a women's infirmary, served from 1899 to 1901 on the women's auxiliary to raise funds for the Royal Jubilee Hospital, was a founding member in 1894 and honorary president of the Local Council of Women of Victoria and Vancouver Island, and in 1910 became patron of the Island Arts and Crafts Society.

Sarah's art occupied a prominent part of her leisure time. In 1860 she had executed a series of 12 watercolours depicting the Hudson's Bay Company fort and the town of Victoria; they remain important historical documents. These detailed and realistic paintings received a wide audience on their initial showing in 1862 at the International Exhibition in London, where they were labelled "the work of a colonial amateur." Two of the sketches were later translated into lithographs to illustrate Richard Charles Mayne's *Four years in British Columbia and Vancouver Island . . .* (London, 1862) and they would be reproduced in numerous publications over the years. In 1862 she sketched landscapes of New Westminster, Hope, Yale, and the Fraser River and a decade later she documented the house and gardens of Pentrelew. Her sketches in 1877 of the newly consecrated St Andrew's Church at Comox and of the Courtenay River were made into woodblock prints for the Church of England's annual report on British Columbia's missions. By the late 1870s her artistic activity had diminished and it soon ceased as failing eyesight (eventually diagnosed as glaucoma), compounded by years of eye strain, impaired her abilities. In 1880 she accompanied her husband on circuit during a three-month trip from New Westminster to the Cariboo region. Her daily diary remains an important record of travel in the province, containing details of events,

people, and landscapes. Sarah became Lady Crease in 1896, when her husband was knighted. Henry Crease retired that year and the social obligations of public life ceased. Until 1919, when she broke a hip, she remained active in community works and corresponded with friends and family around the world.

Ever the communicator, Sarah Crease left an impressive legacy. Several hundred of her ink, pencil, and watercolour works are extant, a prodigious and outstanding body of sketches. Together with her voluminous correspondence and numerous diaries, these records provide unparalleled documentation of British Columbia's colonial and post-confederation immigrant society.

KATHRYN BRIDGE

Sarah Lindley's voluminous correspondence and her diaries can be found in the BCA (MS-0054; MS-0055; MS-0056; MS-2879), together with over 400 of her paintings and sketches. She transmitted her love of record-keeping to her children, whose works of art, letters, and diaries are also held at the BCA.

K. A. Bridge, *Henry & self: the private life of Sarah Crease, 1826–1922* (Victoria, 1996); "Lindley documents in the British Columbia Archives," in *John Lindley (1799–1865): gardener-botanist and pioneer orchidologist: bicentenary celebration volume*, ed. W. T. Stearn (Suffolk, Eng., 1999), 191–92; "Two Victorian gentlewomen in the colonies of Vancouver Island and British Columbia: Eleanor Hill Fellows and Sarah Lindley Crease" (MA thesis, Univ. of Victoria, 1984). C. B. Johnson-Dean, "The Crease family and the arts in Victoria, British Columbia" (MA thesis, Univ. of Victoria, 1981); *The Crease family archives: a record of settlement and service in British Columbia* (Victoria, 1982).

LITTLE STANDING BUFFALO. *See* MATOKINA-JIN

LITTLE, JOHN MASON, surgeon and hospital administrator; b. 9 June 1875 in Boston, son of John Mason Little and Helen Beal; m. 24 Sept. 1911 Ruth Esther Keese in St Anthony, Nfld, and they had five sons and one daughter; d. 23 March 1926 in Brookline, Mass.

A tension between the privileges of a genteel mercantile family and the desire for personal accomplishment governed the life of Dr John Mason Little. His father, a businessman in dry goods and textiles, managed the considerable real-estate properties of his own father, and in 1916 he constructed the Little Building, a 12-storey edifice in downtown Boston. His mother's family were founders of the Second National Bank of Boston. Little attended the Noble and Greenough School in Dedham until 1893, and in 1897 he took his AB at Harvard University. He then proceeded to its medical school, where he distinguished himself in surgery and earned his MD in 1901. After an internship at the Massachusetts General Hospital, he travelled and studied in Europe; he returned a year later to enter private practice with a classmate, Fred Townsley Murphy. He would also assist his former instructor, surgical pioneer Samuel Jason Mixter, at Massachusetts General.

Little's early career seems to have been marked by self-indulgence. In 1907 he attempted to "cure" himself by volunteering to serve with the medical mission founded by Dr Wilfred Thomason Grenfell* at St Anthony, Nfld. Grenfell required a sound hospital administrator and a surgeon to carry out a full range of procedures, especially those associated with tuberculosis, the most devastating affliction in the colony. A keen outdoorsman as well as a bon vivant, Little revelled in the physical demands of the job, patrolling the Northern Peninsula by dog team in winter and sailing along the Labrador coast in summer. In short order, he gained recognition as one of the most competent surgeons in Newfoundland and transformed a pioneer hospital into a centre for advanced work. He wrote his mother with some self-satisfaction in June 1908, "I have not a doubt whatsoever that should I want to stay here I could have the whole surgical practice of Newfoundland in a not very long time." Later that year, fearing that he would be lured to a more lucrative practice, Grenfell broke his fundamental rules of voluntary involvement and primary commitment to mission work and offered Little (a Unitarian) an annual salary of $1,000, which he accepted on the understanding that he would not have to participate in the mission's religious activities.

Little now devoted himself to advanced surgical procedures he would not have had an opportunity to undertake had he remained in Boston. In one celebrated case, he performed a craniotomy on an epileptic patient, identified the epileptogenic focus by electrical stimulation, and removed the affected area, a portion of the motor cortex. Despite his surgical interests, he recognized, as did Grenfell, the greater need to concentrate on problems of public health, especially the prevalence of ailments, such as beriberi, caused by dietary deficiencies. Beriberi had first been identified as a tropical disease associated with a diet based on polished rice, but in northern regions, where wholewheat flour was often rejected as inferior, the same deficiency was seen to be produced by a heavy consumption of bleached flour. Though the theory of organic trace nutrients was still emerging in 1912, Little clearly understood it. On his suggestion, William Richard Ohler conducted experiments at Harvard in 1913 and 1914 which showed that chickens fed with white bread developed polyneuritis. Ohler concluded that, in a diet restricted to milled flour, necessary vitamins were absent and the chickens' condition developed in a fashion similar to beriberi.

Almost from the beginning of his stay in St Anthony, Little had disagreed with Grenfell over the priorities of the mission and its weak organization. At the same time he did not share Grenfell's necessary interest in promotion and fund-raising, though he would raise the money for a new surgical wing in 1910. When Grenfell published some of Little's letters home without his permission, the surgeon expressed his frustration to his mother in June 1909: "I quite understand Dr. Grenfell's attitude about advertising his work, and he is so constituted, and is so really simple that there is no harm about it, only good for other people and for the work. But I am not like Dr. Grenfell and cannot appear as a tin hero any more than I can lead prayers."

By 1917 Little was ready to re-enter the medical community in Boston, where his father was prepared to back him. In addition to his differences with Grenfell, he had not been well for two years. The physical demands of his work had become increasingly difficult, and he had a growing family to consider. He tendered his resignation in June 1917 and left in October with his wife, an American who had taught at St Anthony, and their four children. He was subsequently appointed surgeon to outpatients at Massachusetts General, visiting surgeon to the Long Island Hospital, and instructor in surgical technique at the Harvard Medical School. He later became medical examiner of the New England Mutual Life Insurance Company and chief surgeon of the Boston and Albany Railroad. A fellow of the American Medical Association, he could not abandon the Grenfell mission altogether: he served as a director and president of the New England Grenfell Association and as a director of the International Grenfell Association. Tragically, he also developed a heart condition which he kept secret, even from his immediate family, and in the spring of 1926, at age 50, he died suddenly of pulmonary embolism combined with an inflammation of the heart muscle. His ashes were returned to St Anthony, where they were sealed in a rock face on Fox Farm Hill, overlooking the scene of his most productive and satisfying years.

RONALD ROMPKEY

The author is grateful for family history provided by John Mason Little's grandson Thomas Mayhew Smith of Cambridge, Mass., who holds a collection of Little's correspondence.

Little's publications include two articles in the *Boston Medical and Surgical Journal*, "Kallak, an endemic pustular dermatitis" and "A winter's work in a subarctic climate" (158 (1908): 253–55 and 996–97 respectively); and three in the American Medical Assoc., *Journal* (Chicago), "Medical conditions on the Labrador coast and north Newfoundland," "Beriberi caused by fine white flour," and "Beriberi," (50 (January–June 1908): 1037–39, 58 (January–June 1912): 2029–30, and 63 (July–December 1914): 1287–90 respectively); and "From the records," *Grenfell Clinical Quarterly* (St Anthony, Nfld), 4 (1987–88), no.1: 17–22, which is a record of a case of epilepsy in one of Little's patients, transcribed in its entirety.

Mass., Secretary of the Commonwealth, Arch. Div., Registry of vital records and statistics (Boston), Birth certificate, 9 June 1875; State Dept. of Public Health, Registry of vital records and statistics (Boston), Death certificate, 23 March 1926. PANL, GN 30, marriage records, 1891–1922: 24 Sept. 1911. Yale Univ. Library, MSS and Arch. (New Haven, Conn.), Wilfred Thomason Grenfell papers. *New York Times*, 25 March 1926. American Medical Assoc., *Journal*, 86 (January–June 1926): 1381. D. N. B[lakely], "John Mason Little, M.D.," *Boston Medical and Surgical Journal*, 194 (1926): 652–53. *Encyclopedia of Nfld* (Smallwood et al.), 3: 345. *Graduates and members of the Graduates Association, 1867–1950* ([Dedham, Mass., 1950]). Harvard Univ., *Quinquennial catalogue of the officers and graduates, 1636–1930* (Cambridge, 1930). W. R. Ohler, "Experimental polyneuritis: effects of exclusive diet of wheat flour, in the form of ordinary bread, on fowls," *Journal of Medical Research* (Boston), 31 (1914–15): 239–46. Ronald Rompkey, *Grenfell of Labrador: a biography* (Toronto, 1991).

LIVINGSTON, GERTRUDE ELIZABETH (Nora), hospital and nursing school administrator; b. 17 May 1848 in Sault Ste Marie, Mich., daughter of John Livingston and Margaret ——; d. unmarried 24 July 1927 in Val-Morin, Que.

Little is known about the childhood and youth of Gertrude Elizabeth Livingston, who was called Nora. At the time of the 1850 census in Michigan, her father listed himself as a merchant in Sault Ste Marie. He is also known to have been a captain in the British army. When he retired, he moved with his family to Como (Hudson) on Lac des Deux Montagnes in the province of Quebec. Nora left home to train as a nurse at the New York Hospital's Training School for Nurses. A few years later she received her diploma from this institution, which was renowned for its teaching and was then the school preferred by people in North America who were not in religious orders.

Before hiring Miss Livingston in 1890, the management of the Montreal General Hospital had made several attempts to recruit a competent and efficient superintendent to take charge of the hospital's overall administration. However, there were differences of opinion within their ranks about the division of duties between the general superintendent and the head nurse, or matron. Responsibility for nursing care and for the supervision of all employees except the physicians was assigned in turn to one or the other, depending on their qualifications. From 1875 to 1877 Maria Machin, the superintendent at St Thomas's Hospital in London, England, had tried in vain to organize its nursing care. Sent by Florence Nightingale – a pioneer in the training of hospital nursing personnel – at the request of the Montreal General Hospital, Machin had also done her best to establish rules of hygiene and order for it, considering it badly organized and insalubrious. From 1877 to 1887 the medical superintendent had provided training for the nurses by practical demonstrations, while the head nurse was responsible for

their supervision, among other things. During these years, the nurses' difficult work and precarious living conditions resulted in much turnover of staff. The heavy burden of domestic tasks (housecleaning in the wards, strict attention to cleanliness), as well as personal care-giving and the lack of living space were, for example, obvious problems. Furthermore, since Canada had few schools for nurses [see Theophilus Mack*; Charles O'Reilly*], young women attracted to the profession often went to the United States to complete their training. The resignation in 1889 of the hospital's superintendent, however, would clear the way for someone who would take the situation in hand.

Nora Livingston was working as a registered nurse at the New York Hospital when, on the advice of a family friend, Francis John Shepherd, who was a surgeon at the Montreal General Hospital, she applied for the position of its superintendent. Before accepting the appointment she was eventually offered, she set down her conditions: two experienced nurses of her own choosing would work with her, and her duties would not include any domestic tasks. Her employment began on 20 Feb. 1890 at an annual salary of $800. The hospital had 165 beds at the time and she was responsible for 30 to 35 nurses. She promptly rearranged the duties of the staff and made preparations to open a school for nurses of which she would be in charge, at the behest of the hospital's medical board. The first students arrived on 1 April 1890. In July she reported that 30 were already enrolled, chosen from among 180 applicants. After a probationary period of two months, the candidates studied for two years, and then received their diplomas as nurses. The first graduation ceremony was held in April 1891, for six nurses whose experience had enabled them to complete the course in one year. For this occasion, she followed the example of physicians and instituted a code of ethics requiring the new nurses to take an oath (a practice rare in Canada at the time, but found in the United States).

In 1894, following a proposal made by an American nursing school and in response to pressure in favour of giving professional status to nurses, the duration of the course was increased by a year and a committee was set up to coordinate its content. In 1899 the superintendent and the medical board drew up a definitive training program that established the length and sequence of courses over the three years and provided for the monitoring of every student. The teaching was done by the superintendent, assisted by two registered nurses, and by members of the medical board. The hospital would not hire a full-time teacher for the school, Flora Madeline SHAW, until 1906.

At the hospital, Livingston looked after all matters related to the nurses: their training, recruitment, dismissals, working conditions, and similar concerns, although in such matters as the discharging or hiring of a nurse, she had to obtain the prior agreement of the board of governors. She had a great deal of authority over nurses and nursing care.

As one of the leading members of her profession, Livingston had a lofty concept of her mission and took care to see that the hospital's school acquired an enviable reputation all across Canada. The selection of students, sound training, and strict discipline in work and life were her means to this end. In 1910 she objected to the fact that candidates from other establishments were coming only for the final part of their training. According to the minutes of the management committee meeting of 6 April, to allow this practice "might give the public the idea that the graduates of such institutions possessed equivalent standing to our own nurses. . . . To place the stamps of the Hospital's Training School upon diplomas of minor institutions would tend to induce prospective applicants to enter those institutions offering the least resistance." Livingston insisted that candidates have a superior academic background. She imposed Draconian rules of conduct on the students and nurses hired by the hospital, and she regulated conditions of work and training as well as rest periods, stipulating a precise bedtime, a fixed number of visits outside the hospital, the wearing of a uniform, and so on. Any violation of discipline was generally punished severely. On several occasions recalcitrant nurses were dismissed from the school or suspended for several months.

The management of the hospital recognized Livingston's competence. In 1903 she even got them to agree that only its own graduates could work in its private wards, unless there were exceptional circumstances. The 1910 rules for the employees gave full authority to the superintendent – a further indication of its confidence in her.

By reorganizing the work, gradually encouraging the appointment of nurses to positions of responsibility, and establishing specific duties, Livingston helped to define the proper functions of a nurse. In 1890, for example, with the agreement of the board of governors, she hired a boy to carry medicine from one ward to another. In 1894 the nurse in charge of the scarlet fever department managed to get a housekeeping assistant hired. These temporary employees freed the nursing staff from duties not directly related to the care of patients. In this way, the Montreal General Hospital's school built a solid reputation both in the English-language hospitals of Quebec and in the rest of Canada. Affiliated to McGill University's faculty of medicine, it ushered in a new era in nursing care.

After some 30 years of service to the hospital, Nora Livingston had achieved her objectives. She received many marks of distinction and was recognized as a pioneer by her profession. In 1905 the Livingston Club was founded in her honour, as was the Nora Livingston Scholarship Fund in 1940. Nursing was now

distinguished from domestic tasks, nurses were trained in an appropriate school, and the care of patients was the exclusive responsibility of a superintendent determined to impose extremely strict professional standards. Livingston had played a decisive role in the development of the nursing profession. The model she had established at the Montreal General Hospital would later become a guide for smaller hospitals elsewhere in the province and throughout the country that wanted to set up such a structure.

YOLANDE COHEN

Despite extensive research, no original record of Gertrude Elizabeth Livingston's birth record has been found.

MUA, MG 3099; RG 96, c.23, c.26–34, c.37, c.405, c.421. *Gazette* (Montreal), 25 July 1927. Yolande Cohen et Michèle Dagenais, "Le métier d'infirmière: savoirs féminins et reconnaissance professionnelle," *RHAF*, 41 (1987–88): 155–77. D. MacL. Jensen, *History and trends of professional nursing* (9th ed., St Louis, Mo, 1950). H. E. MacDermot, *History of the School of Nursing of the Montreal General Hospital* (Montreal, 1940; repr. 1961). Barbara Melosh, *"The physician's hand": work, culture and conflict in American nursing* (Philadelphia, 1982). *Michigan 1850 census index*, ed. R. V. Jackson and G. R. Teeples (Bountiful, Utah, 1978).

LOCHHEAD, WILLIAM, professor, biologist, educator, author, and editor; b. 3 April 1864 in Elma Township, Upper Canada, fourth son of William Lochhead, a farmer, and Helen Campbell; m. 14 Aug. 1889 Lillias Grant in Windsor, Ont., and they had one son; d. 26 March 1927 in Sainte-Anne-de-Bellevue, Que.

The son of a Scottish settler, William Lochhead was raised on a farm in Elma Township and received his secondary education at Listowel High School. In 1881 he enrolled at McGill College, where one of his professors, John William Dawson*, introduced him to geology and zoology. After graduating with a BA with honours in natural science in 1885, he entered the Kingston Training Institute. He was thus able to earn a teaching certificate, and he taught science at the collegiate institutes of Perth and Galt (Cambridge), Ont., from 1886 to 1894. His career was interrupted, first in 1886, when he received a scholarship to study geology at Cornell University in New York State, and in 1894 and 1895, when he enrolled there again to take a master's degree in science. On his return to Ontario he resumed teaching, at Napanee and then in London. In 1898 the Ontario Agricultural College in Guelph hired him as a professor and head of the department of biology and geology.

While holding these positions, Lochhead was called to act as an adviser to the provincial government and to publish extension bulletins on problems related to the protection of crops. In the late 19th century, governments were trying to provide technical support for farmers and thereby to put on a sound

Lochhead

basis the rapid growth of commercial agriculture. This concern led to such measures as the establishment of an experimental farm system by the federal Department of Agriculture and of agricultural schools by provincial governments. These initiatives also answered the needs of farmers concerned about the profitability of their operations, which were threatened by crop pests such as insects, plant diseases, and weeds [see James Fletcher*; William Saunders*].

Lochhead's activities went beyond providing farmers with training and information. He was also interested in education, especially the teaching of natural history in rural schools. This concern exactly fitted the objectives of an education project being developed by Montreal businessman Sir William Christopher Macdonald* in cooperation with James Wilson ROBERTSON, the dominion commissioner of agriculture and dairying. The two men sought in particular to improve the quality of education in rural areas with the consolidation of schools and the introduction of a curriculum centred on manual training and the study of nature. Thanks to Macdonald's wealth, rural schools were consolidated in a number of provinces, and in 1904 the Ontario Agricultural College officially inaugurated on its campus the Macdonald Institute [see Adelaide Sophia Hunter*] for training teachers in home economics, nature study, and industrial arts. During the institute's first year, Lochhead served as head of the department of natural history. In 1905 Robertson asked him to leave his post in Guelph and help set up a second institute that Macdonald wanted to establish for the rural anglophone population of Quebec. This project led to the creation of Macdonald College in Sainte-Anne-de-Bellevue. Lochhead helped organize the college and set the curriculum, and he was on its teaching staff from its inauguration in November 1907. Head of the biology department, he taught botany, genetics, geology, and zoology. When the department was split in 1921, Lochhead was made head of the department of entomology and zoology and no longer taught botany, which became a separate department. He could now devote himself to what had become his main field of interest from his earliest days in Guelph: economic entomology or the science of insect control.

During his career as professor at Macdonald College, Lochhead wrote a number of introductory textbooks, including Class book of economic entomology, with special reference to the economic insects of the northern United States and Canada, published in 1919, which was used in classrooms in Canada and the United States for many years. Although these works, as well as articles published in the annual reports of entomological and natural history societies, were not the product of original scientific research, Lochhead kept abreast of recent developments in the field of biology. His writings on heredity, for instance, dealt with the rediscovery at the turn of the 20th century of Mendelian laws (of hybridization) and their effect on the Darwinian theory of evolution, while a number of his articles touched on problems related to the ecology of insects.

These theoretical considerations were matched by practical concerns. In 1908 Lochhead founded the Quebec Society for the Protection of Plants from Insects and Fungous Diseases. It sought to bring together professionals and amateurs interested in economic entomology and phytopathology in order to promote these sciences and disseminate information about crop protection to farmers. From 1908 to 1920 Lochhead edited the monthly Journal of Agriculture and Horticulture, which was published by the Quebec Department of Agriculture. He also tried to persuade the federal Department of Agriculture to set up an entomology laboratory at Macdonald College so that qualified researchers could be trained for governmental entomological services. Although the department did not give its approval for this project, Lochhead nevertheless managed to train a number of entomologists who held important offices in the Canadian and American civil services as well as posts in Canadian universities.

Ill health forced Lochhead to give up his teaching position for a few months in 1921. When he did not get better he had to resign on 31 August 1925. Macdonald College made him a professor emeritus of entomology and zoology. After his death from a heart ailment on 26 March 1927, there were many eulogies in scientific periodicals in the United States and Canada. Lochhead had been active in numerous scientific societies in North America. A member of the American Entomological Society and the American Association of Economic Entomologists, he was elected a fellow of the American Association for the Advancement of Science in 1906. President of the Entomological Society of Ontario from 1902 to 1904, he had been vice-president from 1908 to 1909 of the American Nature Study Society, of which he was a charter member. From 1908 to 1925 he served as president of the Quebec Society for the Protection of Plants.

William Lochhead had a great interest in the practice of research, which he passed on to his students by introducing laboratory teaching at the Ontario Agricultural College and setting up a program of advanced studies in entomology at Macdonald College, but he worked first and foremost at educating farmers and students. His scientific and teaching career fitted into a reform movement to improve education in rural areas and came at a time when agricultural research was beginning to take shape. As self-taught people were giving way to scientists, Lochhead made such a transition possible.

STÉPHANE CASTONGUAY

A list of articles published by William Lochhead up to 1914 is available in *Science and technology biblio.* (Richardson and MacDonald). Several other items appeared in the annual reports of the Que. Soc. for the Protection of Plants, the Entomological Soc. of Ontario (Toronto), the Pomological and Fruit Growing Soc. of the Prov. of Quebec (Quebec), and the Ottawa Field-Naturalists' Club. Lochhead also published articles in American journals such as the *Nature Study Rev.* (Ithaca, N.Y.). A tribute by Father Léopold, director of the Institut Agrocole d'Oka and a close friend of Lochhead, appears as "The life of Professor William Lochhead" in Entomological Soc. of Ontario, *Annual report*, 58 (1928): 86–91; it includes the titles of the Ontario Dept. of Agriculture and Ontario Agricultural College bulletins prepared by Lochhead and a list of the articles he published in the annual reports of the Quebec Soc. for the Protection of Plants.

Lochhead published an entomological guide during the San José scale infestation at the end of the 19th century: *The San José and other scale insects: prepared for the use of fruit growers and scale inspectors* (Toronto, 1900). He also prepared a guide for teachers of natural history, *Outlines of nature studies* (Toronto, 1905), as well as various manuals intended for the use of his students: *Modern biological laws and theories relating to animal & plant breeding* (Montreal, 1911); *An introduction to heredity and genetics; a study of the modern biological laws and theories relating to animal and plant breeding* ([Sainte-Anne-de-Bellevue, Qué., 1920]); with W. P. Fraser, *Economic grasses: their habits, structure and identification; for use in the biology laboratories, Macdonald College* (Sainte-Anne-de-Bellevue, 1915); *A synopsis of economic entomology* ([Sainte-Anne-de-Bellevue, 1919]); and *Class book of economic entomology, with special reference to the economic insects of the northern United States and Canada* (Philadelphia, 1919). His master's thesis was "Proglacial drainage of the Upper Cayuga Basin" (M.SC. thesis, Cornell Univ., Ithaca, 1895).

AO, RG 80-5-0-167, no.3324. Cornell Univ. Library, Div. of Rare and MS Coll., American Nature Study Soc. records, no.2195; Deceased alumni files, no.41-2-877. LAC, RG 17, BII, 2, 3044, file 40-5-37 (1). MUA, MG 1049; RG 43, administrative records, 3, file 139; 5, file 225; 9, Lochhead file; 12, file 515. A. D. Baker, "William Lochhead, 1864–1928," *Entomology Newsletter* (Ottawa), 34 (1956), no.5: 2–3. Luc Chartrand et al., *Histoire des sciences au Québec* (Montréal, 1987). R. H. Estey, *Essays on the early history of plant pathology and mycology in Canada* (Montreal, 1994). D. K. McE. Kevan, *The department of entomology, McGill University: a history to 1978* (Sainte-Anne-de-Bellevue, 1979). A. J. Madill, *History of agricultural education in Ontario* (Toronto, 1930). Ontario Agricultural College and Experimental Farm, *Annual report* (Toronto), 1898–1905. J. F. Snell, *Macdonald College of McGill University: a history from 1904–1955* (Montreal, 1963). Neil Sutherland, *Children in English-Canadian society: framing the twentieth-century consensus* (Toronto, 1976).

LOGGIE, ANDREW, businessman; b. 14 July 1848 in Black Brook (Loggieville), N.B., son of Alexander Loggie and Georgina Gray Jardine; d. unmarried 23 July 1928 in Dalhousie, N.B.

Andrew Loggie was a great-grandson of Robert Logie (Loggie), a fisherman from the River Spey in Morayshire, Scotland, who emigrated with his wife and several children around 1780 and settled on the south side of Miramichi Bay, N.B. Over the generations, various descendants became involved in the commercial fishery in the bay and the Gulf of St Lawrence; Loggie and Anderson, A. and D. Loggie Company, W. S. Loggie Company, and A. and R. Loggie Company were among the firms that carried the family name. The fishery had been one of the leading industries of the Miramichi area ever since William Davidson* and John Cort received a 100,000-acre township grant on the river in 1765, with fishing rights attached. During the first 100 years, fish were salted or canned before being shipped, but the network of railways that came into being in the second half of the 19th century enabled merchants to deliver fresh fish to the larger ports for shipment overseas or directly to markets in the United States. Between 1870 and 1900 there was rapid growth in the volume of fish exported from New Brunswick, much of it in a fresh or fresh-frozen state.

In the mid 1870s Andrew Loggie and his brother Robert, who had a small general store at Black Brook, entered the fish packing and shipping business on an ambitious scale. The Miramichi was famous for Atlantic salmon, but they concentrated on shipping fresh-frozen smelts to the United States. By 1879 they were among the leading suppliers of this product in the region and one of the top five shippers of fish from Chatham and Newcastle. In 1881 they incorporated as the A. and R. Loggie Company, with Andrew and Robert as president and vice-president respectively. Later their younger brother Francis Peabody became a partner and secretary-treasurer.

Before the end of the 1880s the company was one of the largest packers and exporters of fish in Atlantic Canada. On the merchandising side, it also grew rapidly, opening general stores at Black Brook, Dalhousie, Richibucto, and elsewhere. In the years that followed, the firm continued not only to expand but to diversify. Although its home base was still at Black Brook, or Loggieville as it became known in 1895, business was now being conducted all over northeastern New Brunswick, as well as in Quebec, Nova Scotia, Maine, and Vermont.

From northern New Brunswick, the company exported 4,000,000 pounds of fresh and frozen salmon annually, much of it to Britain and Germany. Lesser quantities of mackerel and other kinds of fresh and fresh-frozen fish were shipped to both European and North American destinations from ports along the coast of the Gulf of St Lawrence in New Brunswick and Nova Scotia. Each year, about 300,000 pounds of clams were canned for export at a plant at Inkerman, N.B. A million tins of smelts, 60,000 pounds of canned lobster, and 80,000 pounds of finnan haddie packed in boxes rounded out the annual shipments of

Lonecloud

sea products. Most of the canning and packaging was done under the company's Eagle Brand label. The Loggies were primarily buyers rather than harvesters, but they owned a back-up fleet of 25 fishing vessels and a variety of other commercial watercraft.

Given these facts, it is surprising to learn from an 1904 article in the *Miramichi Advance* that the company's largest output was no longer in fish. The Loggies then had 13 huge ice houses at different locations in New Brunswick, Nova Scotia, and Quebec in which, in addition to fish, they stored large quantities of beef, pork, poultry, and game birds. They were a major producer of wild blueberries, for which they operated three canneries in New Brunswick, six in Quebec, and one in Vermont. They also canned vegetables and other fruit. In all, they owned 17 canneries in two provinces and two states. At Loggieville they operated a can and box factory and an electricity generating plant, from which they sold surplus energy to customers in the village. They had a number of unrelated business interests as well, such as fox ranching and river and harbour dredging.

Besides heading up the family firm, Andrew Loggie acted as Loggieville's postmaster for 33 years, starting in 1877. He resigned the office in 1910, when he moved to Dalhousie for business reasons, but he retained the presidency of the A. and R. Loggie Company until his death in 1928, at age 80. The press reported that he left an estate valued at more than $750,000, mostly in "cash in the bank." His successor as president was his brother Robert, who had been based at Loggieville throughout. Robert lived until 1940, surviving his younger brother Frank by one year. These men also left large personal estates.

A. and R. Loggie was successful as long as its founders were alive and was continued as a family-owned business until 1945. The firm was then sold with its corporate name intact. It rapidly declined in importance, but scored a first in 1953 when it introduced pre-cooked fish to the Canadian market. The company was producing 78,000 fish sticks a day in 1958, the year before it was acquired by Eagle Fisheries, a subsidiary of National Sea Products Limited.

W. D. Hamilton

PANB, MC80/743; RS141C5, F18932, no.429030. "A. & R. Loggie: the king canners and fresh fish exporters of eastern Canada," *Miramichi Advance* (Chatham, N.B.), 10 Nov. 1904. [This article is particularly valuable, thanks to the fact that the editor of the paper, David George Smith, was fishery commissioner for New Brunswick and had a keen personal interest in the subject. w.d.h.] *Commercial and the World* (Chatham), 17 Feb. 1955, 6 Feb. 1958, 2 April 1959. *North Shore Leader* (Newcastle, N.B.), 27 July 1928. *Union Advocate* (Newcastle), 14 Jan. 1880, 19 Sept. 1928. J. A. Fraser, *A history of the W. S. Loggie Co. Ltd., 1873–1973* (Fredericton, 1973); *Loggieville: child of Miramichi* (Fredericton, 1973). W. D. Hamilton, *Dictionary of Miramichi biography; biographical sketches of men and women born before 1900 who played a part in public life on the Miramichi: Northumberland County, New Brunswick, Canada* (Saint John, 1997). LAC, "Post offices and postmasters database:" *www.collectionscanada.ca/archivianet/0201_e.html* (consulted 27 Oct. 2002).

LONECLOUD, JERRY (his birth-name was **Germain Bartlett Alexis** and sometimes he used **Jerry Bartlett**; known in Micmac (Mi'kmaq) as **Slme'n Laksi (Haselmah Luxcey)**), guide, lumberer, showman, herbalist, Micmac (Mi'kmaw) sub-chief, and folklorist; b. 4 July 1854 in Belfast, Maine, son of Abram Bartlett Alexis of Shelburne County, N.S., and Mary Ann Toma (Thomas) of St Croix, N.S.; m. 1888 in Kentville, N.S., Mary Elizabeth Paul of Fredericton, and they had four daughters, two sons, and two children who died in infancy; he also had a son by an unknown mother; d. 16 April 1930 in Halifax.

Jerry Lonecloud was born in 1854 into a Micmac family of herbalists who travelled through British North America and the northeast United States, making and selling remedies. His father provided recipes to the bottlers of Dr Morse's Indian Root Pills. His family canoed the Great Lakes when he was a child, and once took the Erie Canal to New York City, where they camped in an alder swamp at the site of the future Brooklyn Bridge. When the Civil War began, Lonecloud's father joined the Union army. As one of the volunteers who tracked and captured John Wilkes Booth, Abraham Lincoln's assassin, he went to New York in 1866 to collect his share of the reward money, and he was murdered there. Lonecloud's mother died shortly afterwards, in Vermont, leaving him to care for his sister and two younger brothers. He got them safely home to Nova Scotia.

Jerry made a living there guiding and lumbering until a talent scout for Healy and Bigelow's Wild West Show recruited him to return to the States early in the 1880s. He was then living at Bear River. As a so-called medicine man with Healy and Bigelow, he was given the name "Dr. Lone Cloud." He performed as a sharpshooter, helped prepare the Kickapoo Indian Sagwa patent remedy, and peddled it as far away as South America. Eventually he left to perform with Buffalo Bill Cody's show, but he deserted it when Cody prepared to visit England. Highlights from this part of his life, in 1885, were a visit to Niagara Falls and the funeral of President Ulysses S. Grant in New York.

After another spell with Healy and Bigelow's outfit, Lonecloud formed his own company, the Kiowa Medicine Show, which played little towns throughout New England. It failed, but he later put together a show in Maritime Canada, giving dramatizations of Captain John Smith and Pocahontas and similar

"Indian" entertainments. He married his 17-year-old co-star, Elizabeth Paul, a young Maliseet who had joined the show. "I liked her ways," he explained. "There was no more to it. I hired her brother, and she wanted to come." Lonecloud would continue to lecture and perform sporadically in Nova Scotia for much of the rest of his life, often assisted by his family. "I was a showman," he would relate with pride.

In 1890 Lonecloud took Elizabeth and their children to Liscomb Mills, N.S., where he worked as a prospector, herbalist, logger, and guide to sportsmen. He came to have a comprehensive knowledge of the province, hunting all over it during the next 20 years. In 1910 an affair with a married woman in the Liscomb neighbourhood became public when she bore him a son. Separating from his wife, he moved to Halifax. There he acted as an advocate for the Micmac, writing endless letters to Indian agents in Nova Scotia and Ottawa on property rights and other matters. He was elected captain and then sub-chief for Halifax County, and became, possibly through self-appointment, "Chief Medicine Man" for the county and later for all of Nova Scotia and Prince Edward Island.

While living in Halifax, he initiated the two greatest contributions of his life, both in the preservation of Micmac culture. In 1910 he met Harry Piers*, curator of the Provincial Museum, and began passing on oral histories, folk tales, and over 200 cultural and natural history specimens, including photographs, traditional clothing, birds, and plants. In addition, he made replicas of unobtainable Micmac items and, building on the work of Silas Tertius Rand*, Father Pacifique [Buisson*], and other early ethnologists, he contributed to a wider knowledge of his language by teaching Piers Micmac place-names and vocabulary. Piers, who had many Micmac informants, frequently commented in his notes on Lonecloud's broad intelligence, how he was "possessed of a fund of information. . . . I always found him frank, loyal, and he had a razor-keen sense of humour. He was familiar with every brook, river and lake from Windsor to Canso." In return, Piers, who erroneously believed that Lonecloud's first name derived from Jeremiah, drafted some of his formal correspondence, including a number of petitions to the Department of Indian Affairs.

At some point before 1917 Lonecloud's wife and family rejoined him. They lived in a Micmac shantytown at Tufts Cove, northwest of Dartmouth across the harbour from Halifax. Tragedy struck on 6 December of that year, when the ammunition ship *Mont Blanc* exploded, destroying much of Halifax-Dartmouth and killing Lonecloud's daughters Rosie and Hannah. His possessions gone and blind in one eye, Lonecloud was hard put to support his family. He made baskets, snowshoes, moose calls, and caps for sale, and until 1929 he continued to travel the province collecting items to sell to the museum. In April 1930 he became ill and died; he was buried in St Peter's Roman Catholic Cemetery in Dartmouth.

Lonecloud left an even greater legacy than the material he passed on to Piers. Between 1923 and 1929 he had given a series of interviews, unpublished until 2002, to reporter Clarissa (Clara) Archibald Dennis of Halifax. She recorded his life story, thus creating the earliest known Micmac autobiography. Lonecloud poured out a lifetime of recollections, tales, and customs in a style that was folksy with flashes of poetry. In Lonecloud's story of creatures before the Flood, Pollywog explained in verse his presence beside a lake: "I am going down / Into the water / Where there are no stars." Dense with data and vivid with life, this material is an enormous contribution to our knowledge of Micmac culture since much of what Jerry Lonecloud told Dennis is not available from any other source. Ethnographer of the Micmac nation could rightly have been his epitaph, his final honour.

RUTH HOLMES WHITEHEAD

Photographic portraits of Jerry Lonecloud, and portraits of others collected by him, are found in "The Mi'kmaq portraits coll.," comp. R. H. Whitehead: *museum.gov.ns.ca/mikmaq/index.htm* (consulted 3 Jan. 2005). Another photograph of Lonecloud is in the collections of the Geological Survey of Canada (Ottawa), N-24253 (Mi'kmaq at a geological congress), 21 July 1913. The Harry Piers papers are in the N.S. Museum Library (Halifax).

N.S. Museum, Hist. section, Mi'kmaw heritage resource files, Ruth Legge to Ruth Whitehead, taped interview and transcript, September 1995. "Jerry Lonecloud and the Nova Scotia Museum: information acquired by the Nova Scotia Museum from Jerry Lonecloud, 1910–1930," ed. R. H. Whitehead: *museum.gov.ns.ca/resources/lonecloud.htm* (consulted 3 Jan. 2005). *The old man told us: excerpts from Micmac history, 1500–1950*, comp. R. H. Whitehead (Halifax, 1991). R. H. Whitehead, *Harry Piers papers in the Nova Scotia Museum* (3v., Halifax, 2003); *Tracking Doctor Lonecloud: showman to legend keeper, including the memoir of Jerry Lonecloud* (Fredericton and Halifax, 2002).

LONGLEY, JAMES WILBERFORCE, journalist, lawyer, politician, judge, and author; b. 4 Jan. 1849 in Paradise, N.S., youngest and only surviving child of Israel Longley and Frances Manning; grandson of Edward Manning*; m. first 3 Sept. 1877 Annie Brown (Browne) (d. 1899) in Middleton, N.S., and they had two sons and two daughters; m. secondly 4 April 1901 Lois Elizabeth Fletcher (d. 1958) in Binkley, Kent, England, and they had three sons; d. 16 March 1922 in Halifax.

J. W. Longley's New England Planter ancestor settled in Nova Scotia's Annapolis County about 1760. Raised on a farm, Longley was educated at the grammar school in Paradise and at Horton Academy in

Wolfville. In 1867 he matriculated at Acadia College, where he graduated BA in 1871 (MA 1877, DCL 1897). In the autumn of 1871 he moved to Halifax and began the study of law with Hiram Blanchard*. Called to the bar in 1875, Longley was already working as a journalist, having two years earlier become chief editorial writer for Halifax's independent liberal organ, the *Acadian Recorder* [*see* Henry Dugwell Blackadar*]. In 1887 he would be made managing editor of the Halifax *Morning Chronicle*, Nova Scotia's chief Liberal newspaper. From 1875 to 1882 he practised law in Halifax, but as Benjamin Russell*, a fellow barrister and judge, would candidly observe, Longley's heart "was not in the profession." Politics was his forte and obsessive love; law was but the stepping stone to preferment.

From childhood Longley was inured to partisan politics, attending his first political meeting at age ten. His father stood unsuccessfully for the provincial Liberals, and his uncle Avard Longley* was a Conservative MHA and later an MP. Longley himself gave his first political speech, on the anti-confederate Liberal platform, in 1867. In 1882 he was first elected to represent Annapolis County in the House of Assembly, and he would continue to do so for the next 23 years, apart from a brief hiatus in 1896. He served William Stevens FIELDING as minister without portfolio in 1884–86 and from 1886 as attorney general, a post he was to hold until his appointment to the Supreme Court of Nova Scotia on 13 June 1905. Longley's only foray into dominion politics occurred in June 1896, when he resigned his seat at Annapolis to contest the riding federally. He came within 200 votes of defeating the incumbent Conservative, an outcome that mirrored the close results in Nova Scotia, where the Liberals and Conservatives each took ten seats. But for this setback, he might have become premier. When in April Fielding had floated with his caucus the idea of entering federal politics, Longley had had the most support as his successor. As it was, Fielding was able to use Longley's defeat to ensure that his own preferred heir, George Henry MURRAY, became party leader in July. Murray retained Longley as attorney general and also made him commissioner of crown lands, a post which some felt demeaned the senior law officer of the crown.

Given his long tenure as attorney general, Longley's record was not particularly noteworthy. A high point for him was his appearance in England before the Judicial Committee of the Privy Council in 1895, when he argued that the decisions of the Nova Scotia courts should be overturned in a matter concerning the power of the House of Assembly to imprison for contempt. The JCPC agreed that a provincial statute authorizing this power was valid and that it had been properly invoked in the instant case. One of Longley's first pieces of legislation had empowered the attorney general, rather than judges of the Supreme Court, to appoint lawyers to carry on criminal prosecutions in the counties. An act of 1888 provided a standard process for the incorporation of towns. A number of reforms arose in response to Nova Scotia's industrial revolution of the 1880s and 1890s. A major revision of company law was undertaken in 1900, at the same time that the employer's common-law defence of contributory negligence was abolished in suits by employees for workplace accidents. The province's first factories act was passed in 1901, regulating the employment of women and children and requiring some safety measures, but it was a rather tentative effort. One of the most notable legacies of the Longley era was the plethora of new legislation dealing with children, which also included laws providing for the reform of juvenile offenders, forbidding the provision of tobacco and opium to children, regulating their hours of work, instituting equal custody rights for parents, licensing nursing homes for infants, and permitting adoption.

During these years Longley suffered the death of his own favourite child, Frances Mary, aged 13, in June 1898. It was followed by that of Mrs Longley in October 1899. These losses profoundly saddened but did not demoralize him. Eighteen months after his wife's death he remarried in England, his second wife being some 23 years his junior. He would have three more children.

Longley had vacillated for some time on the question of repeal of confederation, which had been championed by Fielding in the provincial election of 1886, before finally rejecting the idea. More a pan-Americanist than a Canadian nationalist, he favoured unrestricted reciprocity extending across both North and South America, a position that made him possibly the earliest Canadian exponent of a hemispheric free-trade agreement. The solution to the economic disequilibrium induced by confederation was regionalism, and that meant Maritime union, of which Longley was among the first advocates. The solution to Britain's sacrifice of Canadian interests was for Canada to cut the imperial knot and enter into a continental partnership with the United States. George Monro Grant* suspected that Longley was an annexationist, an opinion with which Benjamin Russell, who had also become active in Liberal politics and was certainly in a position to know, agreed. Longley travelled regularly in the United States and knew many of the business and political leaders of the eastern region, including Erastus Wiman*, the Canadian-born New Yorker who led the movement for commercial union between the two countries. Rare enough among Canadian public figures of the day, Longley admired American political institutions, believing that "in the main, the United States have worked out the problem of popular government with most wonderful results." A radical Liberal, Longley favoured abolition of the Senate and tried unsuccessfully to rid Nova Scotia of its upper house.

Yet ideologically Longley was a bundle of contradictions. Historian Colin D. Howell describes him as "an unreconstructed opponent of powerful labour unions and female emancipation." There was no progress on either of these fronts during the nearly 20 years that Longley served as attorney general. So agitated was he by women's suffrage that in 1918, when the enfranchisement bill was finally about to pass, Longley, 13 years out of politics, went to the gallery of the House of Assembly to loom over the proceedings. In spite of his professed admiration for American-style popular government, he had constantly opposed attempts to widen the provincial franchise, stating in 1885 that a property qualification was necessary "until a degree of intelligence is reached that has not been reached yet in this country."

Longley was a difficult, egotistical individual whose unattractive personality prevented his rising higher in politics. A member of his own party described him as "conceited, unlovable and unbearable." Family tradition has preserved an incident particularly revealing of Longley's hauteur. Attending a dinner at which Mark Twain was also present, Longley rose and left the room when Twain rather than he himself was called on to speak first. Had the Liberals not been in power in Ottawa and had Fielding not been a powerful minister in Sir Wilfrid Laurier*'s cabinet, Longley would never have secured a position on the Supreme Court of Nova Scotia in 1905 in succession to Robert Linton Weatherbe*, who had been made chief justice. Seven-eighths of the bar, Fielding was told, opposed the appointment. Longley's 17 years on the bench were unremarkable, though he earned some respect when one of his early decisions, involving a dispute over the quality of coal delivered by the Dominion Coal Company to the Dominion Iron and Steel Company, was upheld by the JCPC. In 1915 he presided over the first trial of Harry Allen for the murder of black lawyer James Robinson Johnston*, which was set aside as a result of errors in his charge to the jury. While on the bench Longley occasionally chaired conciliation panels in industrial disputes under William Lyon Mackenzie King*'s federal legislation of 1907.

Longley was a frequent public speaker and prolific writer, especially on historical and political subjects. Elected a fellow of the Royal Society of Canada in 1898, a rare honour for an active politician, he became its vice-president in 1916 and honorary president in 1917. President of the Nova Scotia Historical Society from 1897 to 1905, he played a major role in the 1899 sesquicentenary of the founding of Halifax, which was grandly celebrated, and in the tercentenary of Annapolis Royal in 1904. Longley was elected a cor-

responding member of the Massachusetts Historical Society in 1908. He was also president of the Nova Scotia Exhibition Commission, 1896–1910, and of the Charitable Irish Society of Halifax, 1909–12. An Irish descendant on his mother's side, he was a warm supporter of Home Rule; he lived long enough to see Ireland engulfed in civil war. Longley was the author of the first important book-length study of Joseph Howe* and of a biography of Sir Charles Tupper*, but his historical scholarship has not stood the test of time. He took for his model the American historian Charles Francis Adams, after whom he named the youngest son of his second marriage.

BARRY CAHILL and PHILIP GIRARD

An oil portrait of J. W. Longley by Alfred T. Barrett hangs in the Law Courts Building in Halifax.

[J. W. Longley was the compiler of *The trial of Peter Mailman for the murder of his wife at Lunenburg, N.S. . . .* (Halifax, 1874) and the author of *Love* (Toronto, 1898), *Joseph Howe* (Toronto, 1904) and *Sir Charles Tupper* (Toronto, 1916). A list of his extensive periodical writings may be found in H. G. Morse, "Acadia authors: a bibliography," *Acadia Bull.* (Wolfville, N.S.), 11 (1922), no.11. The chief source of information about Longley's early life and political career is his memoirs, "Reminiscences political and otherwise," published as a five-part series in *Canadian Magazine*, 55 (May–October 1920): 443–50; 56 (November 1920–April 1921): 60–67; 147–53; 210–16; 309–13. His personal papers, which would have contained the manuscript of an unpublished novel as well as of his incomplete multi-volume political history of Canada, were unintentionally destroyed after his widow's death in 1958. B.C. and P.G.]

AO, F 2. Halifax County Court of Probate (Halifax), Estate papers, no.10164. LAC, MG 26, G (mfm. at NSARM). NSARM, MG 2, 422–541, 784–90(B). *Morning Chronicle* (Halifax), 17 March 1922. J. M. Beck, *Politics of Nova Scotia* (2v., Tantallon, N.S., 1985–88). *Biographical review . . . of leading citizens of the province of Nova Scotia*, ed. Harry Piers (Boston, 1900). *Canadian annual rev.*, 1901–10. *Canadian men and women of the time* (Morgan; 1898 and 1912). *Dominion annual reg.*, 1884–86. John Doull, *Sketches of attorney generals of Nova Scotia, 1750–1926* (Halifax, 1964). Philip Girard, "The Supreme Court of Nova Scotia, responsible government, and the quest for legitimacy, 1850–1920," *Dalhousie Law Journal* (Halifax), 17 (1994): 429–57. D. C. Harvey, "Fielding's call to Ottawa," *Dalhousie Rev.* (Halifax), 28 (1948–49), no.4: 369–85. C. D. Howell, "Repeal, reciprocity, and commercial union in Nova Scotian politics, 1886–1887" (MA thesis, Dalhousie Univ., Halifax, 1967). K. M. McLaughlin, "The Canadian general election of 1896 in Nova Scotia" (MA thesis, Dalhousie Univ., 1967); "Race, religion and politics: the election of 1896 in Canada" (PHD thesis, Univ. of Toronto, 1974); "W. S. Fielding and the Liberal party in Nova Scotia, 1891–1896," *Acadiensis* (Fredericton), 3 (1973–74), no.2: 65–79. RSC, *Trans.*, 1898–1922.

LOUGHEED, Sir JAMES ALEXANDER, carpenter, lawyer, businessman, and politician; b. 1 Sept.

Lougheed

1854 in Brampton, Upper Canada, son of John Lougheed and Mary Ann Alexander; m. 16 Sept. 1884 Isabella (Belle) Clarke Hardisty in Fort Calgary (Calgary), and they had four sons and two daughters; d. 2 Nov. 1925 in Ottawa.

James Lougheed's family was of Protestant Irish descent, his father being born in Upper Canada and his mother in Ireland. When James was two or three they moved from Peel County to Toronto. The young boy grew up in Cabbagetown, the poorer eastern section of the city. The family were of modest means; in James's teenaged years they rented a small frame house at the junction of Queen and River streets, near the Don River. James attended the Park Street School. According to his obituary in the *Calgary Herald*, Lougheed often attributed his success to the early influence of his mother, a devout and active worker at Berkeley Street Methodist Church. She sent him to two Sunday schools: Little Trinity Anglican in the morning and Berkeley Street in the afternoon. It was a strict upbringing. Berkeley Street Methodists, his lifelong friend Emerson Coatsworth would later comment, "did not play cards or dance. We did not attend the theatre or the races." Lougheed and Coatsworth shared Orange connections as well. In 1936 James's first cousins Jane and Elizabeth Lougheed would remember that while a stripling he had been a chaplain in the Orange Young Britons – he "wore a white gown and carried a Bible at Parades."

James's father intended that his sons follow him into carpentry and the building trade, which James did after leaving school. In 1869 the firm for which James worked also employed William PEARCE, a surveyor and later a prominent Calgarian. After Lougheed's death in 1925, Pearce would recall his acquaintance with him in 1869–70: "He was then a very young man, in fact he was regarded as a boy, but he was always very industrious and aggressive."

Although his father may have been pleased with his progress, his mother was not. She wanted him to consider options other than the building trades. She encouraged him, after he had left school, to continue attending the two churches on Sunday. At Little Trinity he came to know Samuel Hume Blake*, a distinguished layman and eminent lawyer, after volunteering to become the church's assistant librarian. Blake took a liking to the clever young man, and once said to him: "Boy you have too good a head to be a carpenter, why don't you take up law?" James relished the idea and went back to school; he chose Weston High School, west of Toronto. Upon his return to Cabbagetown, he and Coatsworth prepared together for their matriculation exams for entrance to Osgoode Hall, which they passed in 1875. In 1876 or 1877 Lougheed was articled to the local law firm of Beaty, Hamilton, and Cassels, and in May 1881 he would be sworn in as a solicitor.

Following his return to Toronto, James, his younger brother Samuel, Coatsworth, and six others formed the Awascal Literary Society at Berkeley Methodist Church. All that survives of this club is a financial account by treasurer Coatsworth of an oyster supper held on 30 Dec. 1876. Before his death in 1925, Lougheed told a reporter that it was at the Awascal society that he had received his "early training as a speaker." He may well have put this training to use in 1878, when, as a member of the Young Men's Conservative Club, he fought hard in the successful campaign to return Sir John A. Macdonald* to power. It was not surprising, given his Orange background, that he identified with the Conservatives. According to his cousins, his political interests had always run deep and he had often spent his spare time attending the provincial parliament, "where he liked to listen to the speeches."

In January 1882 Lougheed, now a practising lawyer, decided to move with his brother Sam to Winnipeg. A year later, following the Canadian Pacific Railway's construction teams, James moved farther west to Medicine Hat (Alta). Then, just before the rails reached the hamlet of Fort Calgary in August 1883, he and Sam moved there. Lougheed's marriage to Belle Hardisty, the daughter of the late William Lucas Hardisty*, a Hudson's Bay Company chief factor in the Mackenzie River district, and his wife, Mary, an English-speaking mixed-blood woman, solidified James's links with the west. Belle had received a good education, at Mathilda Davis*'s school in St Andrews (Man.) and then at the Wesleyan Female College in Hamilton, Ont. James met her in Fort Calgary while she was visiting her uncle Richard Charles Hardisty*, chief factor of the HBC's Upper Saskatchewan district. Through this marriage Lougheed acquired a close connection to both Richard Hardisty, the richest man in the North-West Territories, and Donald Alexander Smith*, his wife's uncle by marriage and soon to be one of the wealthiest men in Canada.

James's legal practice thrived. The CPR soon became one of his most important clients. In 1887 he formed a partnership with Peter McCarthy and two years later he became a dominion QC. In 1911 he would add to his legal business a brokerage firm, Lougheed and Taylor Limited. As well, beginning in the 1880s, he made good investments in Calgary real estate, building many rental properties in the downtown area. His show-piece, the Lougheed Building, an office block that included a 1,500-seat theatre, the Sherman Grand, was completed in 1912. In 1891–92 the Lougheeds had erected a magnificent sandstone mansion, Beaulieu, in southwest Calgary. The Duke of Connaught, the governor general of Canada, would stay here with his family in 1912 and the Lougheeds held a huge garden party for the Prince of Wales in

1919. And it was at Beaulieu that Belle Lougheed, Calgary's principal hostess, raised their children. She also took an active part in a good number of community organizations. For example, she was the first treasurer of the Women's Hospital Aid Society (1890), vice-president for the Alberta district of the National Council of Women of Canada (1896), first vice-regent of the Colonel Macleod Chapter of the Imperial Order Daughters of the Empire (1909), first president of the Women's Pioneer Association of Southern Alberta (1922), and first president of the Calgary branch of the Victorian Order of Nurses.

In many ways Lougheed seemed far removed from his humble Toronto origins. He took no part in the Orange lodge in Alberta and never talked about his Cabbagetown roots; moreover, contrary to his Berkeley Street Methodist teachings, he and his wife hosted dances in their mansion and developed a strong interest in the theatre. As Maynard J. Joiner, the Grand's manager in the mid 1920s, said of James Lougheed, "Whenever in the city one of his greatest delights was to be present at one of our performances."

Shortly after his arrival in Alberta the former Torontonian had become a strong champion for western interests. Charles Edward Dudley Wood, the editor of the *Fort Macleod Gazette*, wrote of him in late 1890, "He is an Alberta man first, last and everytime." After Senator Richard Hardisty died in 1889, Lougheed was selected as his successor. Called to the Senate on 10 Dec. 1889, he became, at 35, its youngest member. In addition to his relationship to Hardisty and Smith, he was a personal friend of interior minister Edgar Dewdney*. He had met Sir John A. Macdonald in Calgary in 1886, had been consistently loyal to the prime minister amidst the volatile western politics of the 1880s, and was a prominent investor in the Conservative *Calgary Herald*. The Reverend Leonard Gaetz, a leading Tory in the Red Deer district, had spoken for many when he wrote in October 1889, "Mr. Lougheed is incomparably the best name we can offer. He is a gentleman of culture, ability & position with thorough knowledge of and faith in Alberta, a Conservative of the Conservatives, a good address, and will make I believe a first class representative." Lougheed subsequently moved back and forth between Calgary and Ottawa. To give him more time to look after his extensive political and business interests, he would persuade Richard Bedford Bennett*, a young New Brunswick lawyer, to join his law firm. Bennett arrived in January 1897 and they would work together for over two decades, until Lougheed's attempt to dissolve their partnership without Bennett's agreement caused a bitter quarrel and separation in 1922.

During the 1890s Lougheed emerged in the Senate as a true representative of the west and an advocate of provincial status. Frequently he educated his colleagues concerning the nature of the region and its institutions, about the impact there of past legislation, and on the need to ensure that the west was fully comprehended in various statutes. He spoke often enough to be noticed, yet avoided challenging the Senate's seasoned gladiators. He also used his considerable legal skills to improve legislation, especially in the committee stage of detailed consideration. Gradually he broadened his perspective, learning to speak from a national as well as a western perspective. His sheer ability, diplomacy, and geniality won him respect. In 1906 he was elected by his colleagues to succeed Sir Mackenzie Bowell* as the Conservative leader in the Senate, a position he would occupy until his death.

With respect to the Autonomy Bills, introduced in the House of Commons in February 1905 to create the provinces of Alberta and Saskatchewan, Lougheed had been predictably partisan, particularly concerning the education clauses. Better to forgo provincial status, he remarked darkly in an interview in Winnipeg on 27 February, than to have the hands of the new provinces "tied for all time to come on this question of Education." It was not a "sectional" or regional issue; rather, it was a constitutional one, "a deliberate assault on Provincial rights, the fundamental basis of our political fabric." He also denounced the federal government's gerrymander of seats in the new provinces, intended to produce strong Liberal majorities in the new provincial legislatures. His objections naturally were ignored by the Liberal government.

From 1911, when the Conservatives came to power, to 1921 Lougheed was the government leader in the Upper Chamber and a member of cabinet. For at least the first five of these years his diplomatic skills were tested to the full as he had to try to steer the legislation of the government of Robert Laird Borden* through the Senate while the Conservatives had a minority of seats there. As long as Sir Wilfrid Laurier*'s Liberals held the majority, they could and did defeat numerous measures. From about 1917 Lougheed was able to command a majority most of the time, though it was not always reliable given the independent-mindedness of some senators.

Within cabinet he served as a minister without portfolio (October 1911–February 1918), minister of soldiers' civil re-establishment (February 1918–July 1920), and then, under Arthur Meighen*, minister of the interior (July 1920–December 1921), to which portfolio Indian affairs and mines were added. During most of this ten-year period he was the sole member of the Upper Chamber who could speak for the cabinet, and as such he had to master the full range of government legislation – a task required of no minister in the commons.

Lougheed was thoroughly conservative in his views, beginning with the role of the Senate. "This is a revising body," he remarked in 1904; its duty was to keep a rein on popular enthusiasms and "to check hasty legislation." In debates he favoured business and free enterprise. "Parliament exists, not for the purpose of wrecking the interests of the producer," he said in 1918, "but rather to protect them." He deplored excessive taxation and the "paternalism" of subsidies and protective tariffs. In 1897 he had objected to a bill to create the Victoria Day holiday on the ground of loss of business. He contended that outsiders provoked much of the labour trouble in Canada, and in 1903 tried to have the Criminal Code amended "to prevent alien agitators from coming into Canada and organizing strikes." Following the Winnipeg General Strike in 1919 [see Mike Sokolowiski*], he strongly supported the government's anti-sedition legislation.

Lougheed also shared common western conservative views about Canada's native peoples and immigrants. Canada, in his opinion, had by far the best record of any country of dealing with its indigenous peoples. He firmly believed that they required strong, paternal supervision and must not be allowed to impede progress. While in opposition he had wanted the government to take it upon itself to sell Indian lands, especially when they were located close to settlements, which he thought demoralized the natives. After his own party came to power, he strongly backed its 1914 measure to initiate sales. In 1920 he fully supported a Conservative bill to force compulsory enfranchisement or the elimination of Indian status under the Indian Act. Two years later he strenuously opposed as "retrograde and reactionary" the decision of the new Liberal government of William Lyon Mackenzie King* to repeal compulsory enfranchisement. Lougheed had been uncharacteristically extreme – though entirely representative of his fellow Alberta Conservatives – in denouncing the immigration policy of the Laurier government. "We will have the very excrescence of European immigration placed on our shores," he huffed. Miraculously, however, under the Borden government, immigrants became subjects of Lougheed's praise.

In 1910 Lougheed, an admirer of the British empire, had opposed Laurier's Naval Service Bill. It provided, he thought, inadequate help to Britain in the emergency of the European naval race and he feared that establishing a separate Canadian navy would lead to the severance of Canada from the empire. His proposed amendment, to submit the question to the country, was defeated by the Liberal majority. In 1913 the Borden government used closure to force its Naval Aid Bill, intended to give Britain $35 million for construction, through the commons. Lougheed negotiated an arrangement with Senate Liberal leader Sir George William Ross* to amend the legislation to provide for an appropriation for a Canadian navy, in return for passage of the bill. Enraged by the government's use of closure, however, Laurier and most of the Liberal senators were determined to defeat the measure.

Nonetheless, Lougheed introduced it. He outlined the government's case in impressive detail in the longest speech of his career, nearly three hours, but the Senate killed the bill by passing an amendment similar to Lougheed's in 1910 – that the naval policy be put to the people.

Upon the outbreak of war in 1914, Lougheed exhibited a restrained commitment to seeing the "dominions . . . march in step with the armies of the empire." But with his son Clarence Hardisty serving overseas, his response to the war, like that of many other Canadians, became personal and emotional. By 1916 he was convinced that Germany meant to convert Canada "into a trans-Atlantic Germany." Thus the war was a struggle for national survival and the Military Service Act of 1917 was an "extraordinary" law necessary for "the preservation of the state." He rejected the idea of a referendum on conscription: why should the government ask the opinion of pacifists, slackers, and socialists, men who "proclaim their disloyalty from the house tops"? When Senator Philippe-Auguste Choquette* requested that implementation of conscription be suspended until after the 1917 election, Lougheed responded vehemently, "I propose that any member of this House who preaches sedition, as this honourable gentleman is doing, will not be heard by this House." He observed, during his introduction of the War-time Elections Bill in 1917, that the emergency justified setting aside some venerated traditions. The essential principle of the bill, he said, was "if a man objects to fight he should not be permitted to vote." Clearly winning a war to preserve democracy justified, for Lougheed, limiting the democratic rights of many Canadians.

As the war proceeded, Lougheed assumed increasing responsibilities for the government, in recognition of which he would be made KCMG on 3 June 1916. In June–September 1915 he was acting minister of militia and defence in the absence of Samuel HUGHES. He found the department in chaotic disarray, and spent much time trying to get shell production properly coordinated between Canada and Great Britain. He also raised donations from the public for machine guns. In response to complaints concerning the treatment of returned wounded soldiers, the government in June 1915 established the Military Hospitals Commission; on 3 July Lougheed became its chair. It supervised hospitals and other long-term care facilities, retrained and helped find employment for those able to work, coordinated the effort with the provinces, and solicited public support. In October Borden also asked Lougheed to chair the Commission on Natural Resources, which was expected to solve the problem of unemployment by suggesting methods for improving agriculture and the marketing of goods internally and abroad, locating land for agricultural development, and considering how returned soldiers might be employed and how more capital might be raised for both agriculture and manufacturing. A plan for soldier settlement suggested by the commission in 1916 had little appeal, so the government devised quite a different scheme the following year. In 1918 the work of the Military Hospitals Commission was divided between two departments: the militia department took over most of the military hospitals, while the new Department of Soldiers' Civil Re-establishment assumed the remaining duties of the commission and planned for demobilization and the reabsorption of soldiers into society and the economy. From July 1920 to September 1921, Lougheed, in addition to performing his duties as interior minister, would serve as acting minister of soldiers' civil re-establishment. Historians Desmond Morton and Glenn Wright, though they recognize Lougheed's role in establishing the Military Hospitals Commission and the new department, contend that he was chronically indifferent to the affairs of the commission and to veterans' problems generally.

In 1919 Lougheed played a prominent role in the Senate's consideration of two important post-war measures, one external, one domestic. In presenting the Treaty of Versailles for ratification, he noted that Canada had made a significant advance in international status as a signatory and as a member of the League of Nations. He argued in favour of article 10 of the league's covenant, which bound members to support the territorial integrity of other member nations when under attack. Apparently he was unaware that Borden and his Canadian colleagues at Paris, fearful of involvement in future European wars, had tried to eliminate or modify the article throughout the negotiations leading to the treaty and would continue to do so thereafter. On the home front, Lougheed shepherded through the Senate the contentious Grand Trunk Railway acquisition bill, designed to round out the government's accumulation of bankrupt railways that would lead to the formation of the Canadian National Railways. Even senators opposed to the bill recognized his introductory speech as "a brilliant oration." The real work, however, was accomplished in committee, where Lougheed demonstrated mature diplomacy and leadership. Still, since several Conservative senators were passionately opposed to government ownership, the bill carried only by the narrow margin of 39 to 35.

In the fall of 1920, while interior minister in the short-lived Meighen administration, Lougheed was responsible for amending existing policy when he opened the crown forest reserves on the eastern slopes of the Rocky Mountains to petroleum exploration, a change long desired by Calgary oilmen but previously resisted by the interior department. The new policy required that a leased area be divided into two equal parts, one of which would generate revenue for the crown. This policy, further modified after the discovery of oil at Leduc in 1947, ultimately became the means by which vast sums were transferred to Alberta's treasury. Lougheed was instrumental as well, in 1921, in passing the legislation that killed the Commission of Conservation, established in 1909 [*see* James WHITE]. Resentful of the powers it had exercised at arm's length from government control, he claimed that it had duplicated the work of at least six government departments and that its abolition would save some $250,000 annually. Shortly thereafter he supported a bill to establish "a National Research Institute," which would allow the government to centralize all its scientific and research work in Ottawa and to place it under ministerial control [*see* Robert Fulford RUTTAN]. This bill, however, failed to pass.

After the defeat of the Meighen government by the Liberals under King later in 1921, Lougheed continued to lead the Conservatives in the Senate. The new government was just shy of a majority in the commons, and the Conservative majority in the Senate had no intention of being cooperative. Among the measures rejected was the Canadian National Railways construction bill in 1923, during a session marked by unusually aggressive partisanship as the parties tried to position themselves for the next election.

Lougheed was seriously ill early in 1925, but he seemed to be recovered when he returned to his duties in May. In July, anticipating an election call, Meighen summoned him back to Ottawa again to assist with electoral organization, a task, along with patronage, at which the Calgary senator had always excelled. The work continued into the fall when, during the coldest October then on record for the nation's capital, Lougheed contracted bronchitis, which turned to pneumonia. He succumbed on 2 November in the Ottawa Civic Hospital, and was buried in Calgary on the 8th. In the year of his death a village in central Alberta was renamed Lougheed in his honour. A small peak west of Banff was named after him as well, in 1926, but two years later the name was transferred to a larger, more accessible peak on the edge of the Rocky Mountains near Canmore. Earlier, in 1916, Vilhjalmur Stefansson* had explored one of the Queen Elizabeth Islands, in what is now Nunavut, and designated it Lougheed Island.

Sir James Lougheed was a true Victorian believer in hard work and the idea of progress. Thanks to the timing of his arrival in Calgary, his training as a carpenter and a lawyer, and his marriage to a woman whose family had power and wealth in the northwest, this ambitious and capable Torontonian became the dominant business and political figure in Calgary at the turn of the century. He also served most competently on the national level as a cabinet minister and a party leader in the Senate, which, in his day, largely represented an aristocracy of business and the law. In many respects Lougheed was the exemplar of the ideals of the Senate; perhaps only Raoul Dandurand* commanded equal regard. Not only had Lougheed risen above his background, he had also acquired and honed the industriousness, the courtly manners, and the political skills that enabled him to reach a position of leadership and respect among his peers and the wider public.

DAVID J. HALL and DONALD B. SMITH

[One of Lougheed's boyhood books, Thomas Pelham Dale's *A life's motto illustrated by biographical examples* (London, [1869]), is held by the Lougheed House Conservation Society, which looks after the Lougheed mansion and gardens in Calgary. The motto, from Ecclesiastes, is "Whatsoever thy hand findeth to do, do it with thy might; for there is no work, nor device, nor knowledge, nor wisdom, in the grave, whither thou goest." The book contains the handwritten inscription "Presented to James A. Lougheed for punctuality and attention at Trinity Sunday School from his teacher, October 15, 1869." Lougheed must have valued this book highly since he kept it all his life and passed it on to his eldest son, Clarence, a lawyer with Lougheed and Taylor.

The authors wish to thank Professor David H. Breen of the University of British Columbia for his comments on the issue of crown reserves. D.J.H. and D.B.S.]

AO, F 332, 3 April 1936. GA, M 927; M 928; M 4843, files 13–14. Glenbow Library (Calgary), James Lougheed file. LAC, MG 26, A; G; H; I; K. Private arch., Jamie Coatsworth (Toronto), "Awascal Literary Soc., Toronto, Dec. 30/[18]76: 'Report of oyster supper.'" *Calgary Albertan*, 3, 10 Nov. 1925. *Calgary Herald*, 21 March 1922; 1 Sept., 2–3 Nov. 1925; 8 July 1950; 15 June 1997; 29 May 1999. *Globe*, 23 Feb. 1918. *Mail and Empire* (Toronto), 14 March 1936. *Manitoba Free Press* (Winnipeg), 11 Aug. 1924. *Morning Albertan* (Calgary), 15 Sept. 1919. *Ottawa Citizen*, 2–3 Nov. 1925. Norman Anick, *Sir James Alexander Lougheed* ([Ottawa], 1991). R. L. Borden, *Robert Laird Borden: his memoirs*, ed. Henry Borden (2v., Toronto, 1938). D. [H.] Breen, *Alberta's petroleum industry and the Conservation Board* (Edmonton, 1993); *The Canadian prairie west and the ranching frontier, 1874–1924* (Toronto, 1983). Can., Parl., *Sessional papers*; Senate, *Debates*, 1890–1926. *Canadian annual rev.*, 1901–25. *Canadian men and women of the time* (Morgan; 1898 and 1912). Raoul Dandurand, *Les mémoires du sénateur Raoul Dandurand (1861–1942)*, Marcel Hamelin, édit. (Québec, 1967). Janet Foster, *Working for wildlife: the beginning of preservation in Canada* (Toronto, 1978). H. F. Gadsby, "The Borden cabinet – X: the government leader in the Senate," *Canadian Liberal Monthly* (Ottawa), 1 (1913–14): 123. M. F. Girard, *L'écologisme retrouvé: essor et déclin de la Commission de la conservation du Canada* (Ottawa, 1994). "James Lougheed of Britannia," comp. Jopie Loughead *et al.* (typescript, n.p., 1998; copy in the authors' possession). A. O. Jennings, "Lougheed & Taylor, Limited, financial brokers," in *Calgary, Alberta, merchants and manufacturers record: the manufacturing, jobbing and commercial center of the Canadian west* ([Calgary, 1911]), 98–99. Madeleine Johnson, "Lady Isabella Lougheed" (research report, [Calgary?], 1996; copy at Lougheed House Conservation Soc. arch.). H. C. Klassen,

"Lawyers, finance and economic development in southwestern Alberta, 1884 to 1920," in *Essays in the history of Canadian law*, ed. D. H. Flaherty *et al.* (8v. to date, [Toronto], 1981–), vol.4 (*Beyond the law: lawyers and business in Canada, 1830 to 1930*, ed. Carol Wilton, 1990), 298–319. M. C. McKenna, "Sir James Alexander Lougheed: Calgary's first senator and city builder," in *Citymakers: Calgarians after the frontier*, ed. Max Foran and S. S. Jameson (Calgary, 1987), 95–116. Desmond Morton, "'Noblest and best': retraining Canada's war disabled, 1915–23," *Journal of Canadian Studies* (Peterborough, Ont.), 16 (1981), nos.3–4: 75–85. Desmond Morton and Glenn Wright, *Winning the second battle: Canadian veterans and the return to civilian life, 1915–1930* (Toronto, 1987). *Prominent men of Canada: a collection of persons distinguished in professional and political life, and in the commerce and industry of Canada*, ed. G. M. Adam (Toronto, 1892), 118–19. W. K. Regular, "Regionalism, nationalism and the Canadian character: the Senate career of James A. Lougheed, 1890–1905" (BA dissertation, Memorial Univ. of Nfld, St John's, 1978). John Richards and Larry Pratt, "Oil and social class: the making of the new west," in *Riel to reform: a history of protest in western Canada*, ed. George Melnyk (Saskatoon, 1992), 224–44. G. H. W. Richardson, "The Conservative party in the provisional district of Alberta, 1887–1905" (MA thesis, Univ. of Alta, Edmonton, 1977).

LOVERING, FRANCES. *See* MAHONY

LOWERY, ROBERT THORNTON, newspaper publisher, editor, and printer; b. 12 April 1859 in Halton County, Upper Canada, son of William L. Lowery and Mary Ann Mills; d. unmarried 20 May 1921 in Grand Forks, B.C.

Following an education in private and public schools, Bob Lowery began working for a Toronto printing office in 1876. His first newspaper venture, in Petrolia, Ont., began on 20 March 1879, when with his brothers William M. and Samuel M. he published the *Petrolea Topic*. The brothers also dealt in books and stationery. Although they sold the paper around 1886, they continued the stationery business for another year. Bob then drifted westward, first to Sault Ste Marie, where he stayed for several years, and, in 1891, to British Columbia.

On 12 May 1893 Lowery launched his first British Columbia newspaper, the *Kaslo Claim*. The untimely collapse of silver prices in the United States placed a severe strain on the Kootenay mining industry and this, in turn, forced him to cease publication in just over three months. The front page of the last issue, bordered in black, featured a tombstone to the memory of the *Claim*. Lowery also identified merchants with overdue accounts by displaying their advertisements upside down (unpaid) or sideways (partially paid).

The lifespan of a weekly newspaper in a mining community was often short, so in the years that followed Lowery moved frequently. Often owning more than one paper at a time, he hired editors and managers for those that he did not personally supervise. He also printed newspapers owned by others. In Kaslo, Nakusp, New Denver, Sandon, Rossland, Slocan, Vancouver, Nelson, Poplar Creek, Fernie, Greenwood, and Princeton, his controversial newspapers championed various causes, such as improved working conditions and better wages for miners, with wry wit and acid humour. Like Calgary journalist Robert Chambers EDWARDS, he was often critical of commercial, political, or religious bureaucrats and their organizations. Of the Canadian Pacific Railway he once wrote that it was "a wonderfully safe road to travel on, and seldom kills a passenger, although occasionally some one dies of heart failure after looking at their freight charges."

Constantly reminding readers to honour their subscriptions, Lowery claimed that "one of the noblest works of God is the man who always pays the Printer." A cartoon that appeared almost weekly in the *Ledge,* published in New Denver, Nelson, and Fernie between 1900 and 1905, shows an unconcerned Lowery sitting at his desk with money scattered on the floor, but the weapons on the wall and his bulldog ripping the arm off a delinquent subscriber suggest another attitude. As a last resort, Lowery would play a game of poker to raise enough capital to pay his expenses. His enjoyment of whiskey and poker, combined with his smart dress and military bearing, may have been responsible for his being given the title Colonel.

Lowery's Claim, a polemical monthly started in June 1901 in New Denver and "devoted to Truth and Humor," was banned from sale on CPR trains in December because of its criticism of the company. In January 1903 it was denied postal service after the authorities, who had received complaints, deemed its contents indecent and offensive. The Post Office Department reinstated service one month later after a repentant Lowery pledged to reform his ways. By August 1906, however, *Lowery's Claim* was permanently banned from Canada's mails and the following month its editor published the last issue.

Like his newspaper colleague John Houston*, Colonel Bob paid the price for tackling the establishment. After the collapse of *Lowery's Claim*, he focused on the *Ledge*, then being printed in Greenwood. He remained there until admitted to the Grand Forks hospital, where he stayed for over a year. His dying wish was to be buried in Nelson, by members of the Kootenay Pioneers' Association. He succumbed to chronic nephritis and was buried in an unmarked grave in the Anglican section of Nelson Memorial Park Cemetery. Only a fraction over five feet tall, Bob Lowery had loomed large among the newspaper publishers of British Columbia for more than a quarter of a century.

R. J. WELWOOD

[The numerous newspapers Robert Thornton Lowery published and edited between 1879 and 1920 are one of the most important sources of information on his life and career. A list can be found in the author's article "The wit and wisdom of 'Colonel' Bob Lowery," Boundary Hist. Soc., *Report* (Grand Forks, B.C.), 14 (2001): 113–24 and another is in the Lowery file at the DCB. Particularly useful for this biography were the following Lowery publications: *Ledge* (New Denver, Nelson, Fernie, and Greenwood, B.C.), 1893–1920 (mfm. and originals at the Selkirk College Library, Castlegar, B.C.); *Float* (New Denver and Nelson), 1 (1903–4), no.1 (copies at the Selkirk College Library); and *Lowery's Claim* (New Denver, Vancouver, and Nelson), June 1901–September 1906 (mfm. and originals at the Selkirk College Library and originals at the Kootenay Lake Arch., Kaslo, B.C.). R.J.W.]

BCA, S/F/L95. *Ledge* (Greenwood), 26 May 1921. B. A. Little, "Robert T. Lowery: editor, publisher & printer," *British Columbia Hist. News* (Victoria), 31 (1997–98), no.2: 18–23. George Ryga, *Ploughmen of the glacier: a play* (Vancouver, 1977; Lowery is one of the characters in this play). R. [J.] Welwood, "Lowery PO'd or Colonel Bob twice cancelled by the Post Office," *British Columbia Hist. News*, 32 (1998–99), no.1: 2–5. *Who's who in western Canada . . .* (Vancouver), 1911.

LOZEAU, ALBERT (baptized **Charles-Joseph-Albert**), poet; b. 23 June 1878 in Montreal, son of Joseph Lozeau and Adèle Gauthier; d. there 24 March 1924.

Albert Lozeau was the eldest of 11 children, seven of whom lived past infancy. His father pursued an honourable career as a civil servant at the Superior Court. Immobilized by illness, Lozeau would spend almost his entire life under his mother's care in the village of Saint-Jean-Baptiste, north of Square Saint-Louis (now in the heart of Montreal), to which his parents had moved in 1877, shortly after their marriage.

Lozeau enrolled in the Académie Saint-Jean-Baptiste in Montreal in 1886. Five years later, at the point when he was completing a commercial course, his studies were interrupted by an accident while he was playing. In 1892 the poet suffered the first attacks of the illness that would mark his life: he became progressively paralysed by Pott's disease, tubercular arthritis of the spine. From 1896 to 1904 he was confined to bed, hunched up by the disease. This was how he would write his first poems, on a small board placed on his knees. "I spent nine years with my feet at the same level as my head: that taught me humility. I wrote rhymes to kill time, which was killing me in turn," he asserted in a letter quoted in the preface to his first collection of poetry. According to his friend journalist Omer Héroux*, "Lozeau saw only as much of the outside world as could be glimpsed from his bed through his bedroom window. . . . And yet I never heard him breathe a complaint, express a bitter thought, [or] say that life was painful."

After the onset of his illness, Lozeau could continue his studies only sporadically. He delved into literature on his own, however, with books brought to him by his friends, and soon he was contributing to various newspapers. In 1900 the collective anthology of the École Littéraire de Montréal, *Les soirées du château de Ramezay*, included seven of his poems. Although his condition prevented him from participating in the group's activities, Lozeau was officially a member from 1904 to 1907. A series of surgical operations, beginning in 1903, enabled him to sit in a padded chair, so that on fine days he could go out onto the balcony of his family's house on Avenue Laval. He was a regular contributor to *Le Nationaliste, Le Canada*, and a number of other Montreal periodicals. In 1907, through the good offices of the French critic Charles ab der Halden, he published his first collection of poems, entitled *L'âme solitaire*, in Paris and Montreal. He received excellent reviews from the critics and enjoyed such success that a second edition came out in 1908. A new poetry had been discovered in Quebec, new in its insistence on subjectivity and in its quest for new rhythms: "My heart now stands open like a door. / It awaits you, my Beloved; will you come in?"

Lozeau became a well-known poet who through his articles and poems played a role in the literary life of his time. With a poem entitled "Canada," he was one of the winners of the competition "Poètes de clocher" organized by *Les Annales politiques et littéraires* in Paris in 1907. He was elected a member of the Royal Society of Canada in 1911. On 11 June 1912 *La Patrie* (Montréal) reported that the French government had made him an *officier d'académie*. This fame aroused jealousy. However, a group of friends and writers met regularly at his home. "His room for a long time was a special meeting-place where we would go to share our dreams and our youthful ambitions," Madeleine [Anne-Marie Gleason*] would write in *La Revue moderne* (Montréal) immediately after his death. "Gathered around the poet, we would spend long hours discussing literature and art. He guided the conversation, steered it, gave it a worthwhile goal. And we would go out with our hearts refreshed and our souls uplifted." Charles Gill*, Albert Milette, Louis-Joseph Doucet*, and Abbé Joseph-Marie Melançon*, known as Lucien Rainier, were frequent visitors.

From 1910 Lozeau regularly contributed poetry and prose to *Le Devoir*, which Henri Bourrassa* had just founded. In particular, he wrote short topical prose pieces under the heading "Billets du soir" in which he commented in a familiar and humorous way on the weather or daily happenings. These writings were published in Montreal in three volumes from 1911 to 1918, under the title *Billets du soir*. In 1912 Lozeau's second collection of poems, *Le miroir des jours*, came out, also in Montreal. It would be his most polished work, showing a mastery of symbolist versification in poetry that was touching, erudite, and refined: "The dust of the hour and the ashes of the day / Float at eventide in a thin haze." Once again, the work was well received. French critic Auguste Dorchain placed its author in the front ranks of contemporary poets writing in French.

During World War I, Lozeau's work took a new turn. He contributed some patriotic and religious poems to *Le Devoir* which were put together in *Lauriers et feuilles d'érable*, a collection published in Montreal in 1916. In the dispute between the exotic and the regional, which occupied the literary circles of his day, Lozeau had long maintained a neutral position, acknowledging the right of each to its own genius and its own freedom. This was the point of view he defended in an article entitled "Le régionalisme littéraire, opinions et théories," which he published in the *Transactions* of the Royal Society of Canada in 1921. Ultimately, however, he would adopt a more "nationalist" view of literature: at the end of his life he would place literature at the service of patriotism – "Les lettres au service de l'idée patriotique," as he put it in the title of an article in the *Almanach de la langue française* (Montréal) in 1924.

Albert Lozeau died of a stroke on 24 March 1924. He had been working on a revised edition of his poetical works. His *Poésies complètes* would be published in three volumes at Montreal in 1925 and 1926. It contains a number of previously unpublished poems collected under the title "Les images du pays." Lozeau ranks with Émile Nelligan* as the greatest Quebec poet of the early 20th century because he went against the current of his time to create an *intimiste* and musical poetry. His work provides a detailed and emotional analysis of the stirrings of inner feelings and spirituality in a human being immobilized at his window, watching life outside it go by.

MICHEL LEMAIRE

A selection of Lozeau's writings has been published in the series "Classiques canadiens" as *Albert Lozeau*, Yves de Margerie, édit. (Montréal et Paris, 1958).

ANQ-M, CE601-S35, 23 juin 1878. Bibliothèque Nationale du Québec (Montréal), MSS-384 (fonds Albert-Lozeau). *Le Devoir*, 25 mars 1924. Jacques Lambert, "La séduction du temps intérieur; trajet d'Albert Lozeau jusqu'à 'L'âme solitaire'" (mémoire de MA, univ. du Québec à Trois-Rivières, 1994). Madeleine [A.-M. Gleason], "Un grand poète canadien: Albert Lozeau," *La Rev. moderne* (Montréal), 5 (1924), no.7: 7. Yves de Margerie, "Albert Lozeau et l'École littéraire de Montréal," in *L'École littéraire de Montréal*, sous la dir. de Paul Wyczynski *et al.* (2e éd., Montréal, 1972), 212–54. J.-M. Melançon, "Albert Lozeau; notes et souvenirs," *L'Action française* (Montréal), 11 (1924): 273–90. Jeanne d'Arc Séguin, named Saint-Jean-de-Sienne, "Le sentiment de la nature chez Lozeau" (thèse de PHD, univ. d'Ottawa, 1963).

LUXCEY, HASELMAH. *See* LONECLOUD, JERRY

M

McARTHUR, JOHN DUNCAN, railway contractor, lumberman, and businessman; b. 25 June 1854 in Lancaster, Upper Canada; m. there January 1889 Mary McIntosh; they had no children; d. 10 Jan. 1927 in Winnipeg.

John Duncan McArthur received his schooling in Glengarry County and spent several years on his father's farm before moving west in 1879. He found work with a special "flying gang" that maintained Winnipeg's first rail connections with the outside world, via St Paul and Minneapolis, Minn.

When the Canadian Pacific Railway syndicate began construction of its main line in 1881, McArthur obtained a number of subcontracts, first in heavy rock cutting between Winnipeg and Fort William (Thunder Bay, Ont.) and then with contractors building the line on the prairies. After 1883 he secured several contracts from James Ross* for work on the mountain section of the CPR.

In 1888 McArthur achieved notoriety when he signed a contract for the construction of the Red River Valley Railway from Winnipeg to Emerson, Man. This railway had been chartered by the Manitoba government of John Norquay* the previous year and was to run south to join with the Northern Pacific Railroad. Provincial politicians hoped that the creation of a line to compete with the CPR would result in significantly lower freight charges. The federal government of Sir John A. Macdonald* disallowed the provincial legislation, but the Manitoba government proceeded with construction of the railway, which was leased to a subsidiary of the Northern Pacific, the Northern Pacific and Manitoba. There were several tense and colourful confrontations between CPR crews under superintendent William Whyte*, supported by the federal government, and McArthur's construction workers, who were reinforced by specially sworn provincial constables, over the right of the Manitoba railway to cross the CPR line. A snowstorm halted construction in the fall of 1888. The matter was referred to the courts, which decided in favour of Manitoba, and construction resumed in 1889. In the midst of this turmoil McArthur returned to his native Glengarry County, where he married Mary McIntosh.

There was a lull in Canadian railway construction from 1889 until 1897, when the CPR secured federal subsidies for the building of a branch line from Lethbridge, Alta, to Nelson, B.C., popularly known as the Crow's Nest Pass Railway. McArthur obtained the contract. His work satisfied CPR officials, but got him into serious difficulties because of widely publicized allegations regarding his treatment of his crews. Press reports and complaints from social reformers,

often based on first-hand accounts by disgruntled workers, suggested that he and other contractors on the line failed to take appropriate safety measures or to provide suitable living conditions and medical care (in spite of the fact that deductions were made from workers' pay to cover the cost of medical treatment). The incidence of accidents and illness lent credence to these complaints and resulted in the appointment in 1898 of a federal commission of inquiry chaired by judge Calixte-Aimé Dugas. The commission gathered evidence of dubious employment practices in McArthur's business, and in the railway contracting business generally. It made numerous recommendations, but no charges seem to have been laid.

After completing work on the Crow's Nest line, McArthur obtained a contract from the promoters of the Canadian Northern Railway, William Mackenzie and Donald Mann*. Attempts to provide links at Edmonton between their lines north and south of the North Saskatchewan River resulted in physical confrontations between CPR employees and McArthur's construction workers which were reminiscent of those in Manitoba.

In 1903 the federal government of Sir Wilfrid Laurier* introduced legislation calling for a second transcontinental railway, to be constructed in two sections. When the Grand Trunk Pacific Railway Company [*see* Charles Melville Hays*], which was to build the section from Winnipeg to the Pacific, began construction on the prairies, McArthur secured some work, while completing old contracts and negotiating new ones with the Canadian Northern and the CPR. The federal government had agreed to build, and then lease to the GTPR, the eastern section from Winnipeg to Moncton, N.B. McArthur's most profitable and most controversial contract, signed in 1905, was for construction of the critically important mileage from Winnipeg to Superior Junction, in northern Ontario. His bid, which left blank 48 of the 101 items on the application form, has been described by CPR historian George Roy Stevens as "grossly irregular." The incomplete bid was for $33,073 per mile, which was three per cent below the costs estimated by the government. In the end he was paid $78,745 per mile, this in spite of the fact that he failed to meet construction deadlines. Difficulties caused by muskeg and heavy rock work, and hence changes in the classifications of work done, were blamed for the higher costs. His failure to complete the work on time proved extremely expensive for the Grand Trunk Pacific because the entire line could not be opened for through traffic as quickly as originally planned. Few railways in Canadian history have as sorry a record of government incompetence and alleged political corruption and patronage as does the National Transcontinental Railway; McArthur's contract, completed in August 1910, is often cited as an example of what went wrong.

The delays in completing the route from Winnipeg to Superior Junction were in part due to the fact that McArthur was at the same time working on a number of smaller contracts with the other major railways which exacted more stringent penalties if work was not completed on time. In addition, he took up two large new projects. The first of these involved railways in northern Alberta, for which the provincial government of Arthur Lewis Watkins SIFTON was willing to provide generous financial assistance. In 1911 McArthur gained control of the Edmonton, Dunvegan and British Columbia Railway, which was to provide service to the Peace River country, and he became both its promoter and its contractor. In addition, in 1913 he obtained a contract to build the Alberta and Great Waterways Railway. Owing to the exigencies of World War I, McArthur was unable to raise the money needed to complete construction of the EDBCR. The Alberta government was forced to take it over in 1920, but not before it had earned the nickname Extremely Dangerous and Badly Constructed. McArthur got paid for the work completed and the materials and equipment left behind. The problems documented by the commission of 1898 were also evident on these later contracts, although they received much less publicity.

While still busy building the line from Winnipeg to Superior Junction and already heavily committed in northern Alberta, McArthur signed another large and difficult contract, this time to build from The Pas, Man., to Port Nelson on the western shore of Hudson Bay. This too was a federal government project, sanctioned by the Liberals just before their defeat in the election of 1911. The new Conservative government of Robert Laird Borden* first stopped, but then approved and extended the terms of McArthur's contract. At the close of the construction season of 1914, rails had been laid on the first 214 miles of the new line, but the financial difficulties of wartime, a fire which destroyed McArthur's track-laying outfit, and growing uneasiness regarding the suitability of the proposed harbour facilities at Nelson resulted in a halt when construction reached mile 333 in December 1917. In 1919 the federal government cancelled the contract. Canadian National Railways took possession of McArthur's remaining equipment and supplies for use elsewhere on their system. A decade later the route was changed and the Hudson Bay Railway was built to Churchill, Man., in 1930–31.

McArthur was also a promoter of lumbering operations and the manufacture of pulp and paper. Early in his career he had secured large timber leases in the Birtle and Lac du Bonnet regions of Manitoba. Later he obtained similar rights in British Columbia. Initially he engaged mainly in lumbering operations, but toward the end of his career he became active in the pulp and paper industry. He was instrumental in the organization of the Manitoba Pulp and Paper Company, which at the time of his death had almost completed construction of a huge mill and hydroelectric generating plant at Pine Falls. He was also interested in a second large pulp and paper mill near Prince George, B.C., was involved in a smaller mining and lumbering operation near Moyie, B.C., and had extensive real estate holdings, particularly in the Winnipeg area.

After unsuccessfully seeking treatment in the United States for pernicious anaemia and related complications, John Duncan McArthur returned to Winnipeg and died there early in 1927. He was one of western Canada's greatest railway contractors, having built over 2,833 miles of track, but he was also one of its most controversial.

THEODORE D. REGEHR

Manitoba Free Press, 11 Jan. 1927. J. A. Eagle, "J. D. McArthur and the Peace River Railway," *Alberta Hist.* (Calgary), 29 (1981), no.4: 33–39. H. A. Fleming, *Canada's Arctic outlet: a history of the Hudson Bay Railway* (Berkeley, Calif., 1957; repr. Westport, Conn., 1978). T. D. Regehr, *The Canadian Northern Railway, pioneer road of the northern prairies, 1895–1918* (Toronto, 1976); "The National Policy and Manitoba railway legislation, 1879–1888" (MA thesis, Carleton Univ., Ottawa, 1963). G. R. Stevens, *Canadian National Railways* (2v., Toronto and Vancouver, 1960–62). A. B. Woywitka, "Strike at Waterways," *Alberta Hist. Rev.* (Calgary), 20 (1972), no.4: 1–5.

McARTHUR, PETER GILCHRIST, writer and farmer; b. 10 March 1866 in Ekfrid Township, Upper Canada, son of Peter McArthur and Catherine McLennan; m. 11 Sept. 1895 Mabel Clara Haywood-Waters in Niagara (Niagara-on-the-Lake), Ont., and they had four sons and a daughter; d. 28 Oct. 1924 in London, Ont., and was buried in Ekfrid.

Raised on a farm by Scottish-born Presbyterian parents, Peter McArthur would become a lifelong spokesman for the values he believed were implicit in a pioneer's way of life. Upon graduating from the collegiate in nearby Strathroy in 1887, he attended the model school there and taught briefly. The following year he entered the University of Toronto, where his character and determination to resist hazing impressed President Sir Daniel Wilson*. His ambition was to be a writer, hence he submitted jokes to John Wilson BENGOUGH's *Grip* and in 1889 left university to be a reporter with the *Toronto Daily Mail*.

McArthur moved to New York City in 1890 to hone his craft freelance. He quickly fitted in with the Canadian expatriate artistic community there, which included poets Charles George Douglas Roberts* and William Bliss CARMAN, poet-artist Duncan A. McKellar, and Jay Hambidge, an illustrator who studied proportion in art and mathematical formulae in nature. He referred to the group as "the commune." Two of them, Carman and printer Calvert Bowyer Vaux, would correspond with McArthur throughout his life, and in 1921 McArthur would organize Carman's Canadian reading tour. Besides contributing articles, poems, and humorous items to such publications as *Life*, *Puck*, and *Atlantic Monthly*, McArthur, as editor of the New York *Truth* from 1895 to 1897, published work by Roberts, Carman, Stephen Butler Leacock*, and Duncan Campbell Scott*. It was while he was living in Brooklyn in 1895 that he married Mabel Haywood-Waters, at St Mark's Anglican Church in Niagara.

In 1902 McArthur went to London, England, with his family to edit a magazine that would express Hambidge's "aesthetics of dynamic symmetry." It did not materialize so he turned to other projects there: contributing to *Punch*, working with William Thomas Stead on the *Review of Reviews* and the *Daily Paper*, and writing *To be taken with salt: being an essay on teaching one's grandmother to suck eggs* (1903), a satire that reflects a colonial's view of imperial society. In 1904 the McArthurs came back to New York, where Peter, as a partner in an advertising agency, wrote short fictional works that conclude with product endorsements, and, as a freelance writer, produced *The prodigal, and other poems* (1907), in which several items anticipate a return to rural life. Shortly thereafter he left the uncertainties of business, moved to Niagara, and in 1908 took his family to Ekfrid, where his father had left him land. He would live there for the rest of his life, carrying on a small mixed-farming operation, not for wealth but for physical well-being and spiritual nourishment (in addition to that gained as a member of St John's Anglican Church). His enterprise, similar to the one in Henry David Thoreau's *Walden*, allowed him to relish and describe the natural world and rural activity, and to interpret them in a philosophical spirit. His persistent focus on the common man emerged easily from his spiritual analysis of nature. In one unpublished essay, which challenged Richard Maurice Bucke*'s championship of Walt Whitman as the prime example of cosmic consciousness, McArthur held that cosmic consciousness "is possessed by men of all description" and that Whitman's real glory lay in his intent "to help every man to develop the possibilities of his own nature."

McArthur's preferred place for thinking and writing was a tent in his woodlot. From 29 May 1909 until his death he revealed his manifold interests in articles for the Toronto *Globe*, and between 1910 and 1917 he contributed as well to the *Farmer's Advocate and Home Magazine* (London, Ont.). Selections from these sources were published in Toronto as *In pastures green* (1915) and *The red cow and her friends* (1919). His reputation rests mainly on these essays, and on occasional poems, but McArthur was a prolific writer. Between 1910 and 1912 he published eight numbers of *Ourselves: a Magazine for Cheerful Canadians* (St Thomas, Ont.), a largely humorous and satirical journal that includes critiques of some of his favourite targets: big business, the Canadian banking system, politicians, and the staleness of imperial society. His poems and stories also appeared from time to time in other Canadian and American periodicals and newspapers. In 1919 he compiled a eulogistic and anecdotal biography of Liberal prime minister Sir Wilfrid Laurier* and in 1923 he would undertake a study of Stephen Leacock for Lorne Albert Pierce*'s *Makers of Canadian literature* series. *The affable stranger* (Toronto, 1920), a collection of essays, is the product of McArthur's observations during travels in Canada and the northeastern United States after World War I. Through a sceptical and conservative lens, and with repeated assertion of the validity of pioneer values, he examines contemporary economy, organizations, social movements, and differences between the Old and the New World. He also returned to commerce as a theme, writing tracts and poems on life insurance as a means to reform society in the interests of the common man. *A chant of Mammonism* (Waterloo, Ont., [1922]), for example, predicts the demise of the capitalist as the financial power of mutual life insurance companies grows.

Much of McArthur's work gives evidence of haste, the biography of Laurier being a notable example. Hence, he has been charged by critics with carelessness and stylistic unevenness. F. W. Watt, in his examination of McArthur and the "agrarian myth," asserts that his work rarely emerges from "journalistic dross." To some extent these defects may be forgiven in the light of McArthur's observation about Leacock, that the pressure exerted by publishers may have limited the development of his powers. In McArthur's case, the demands of his farm and semi-weekly newspaper columns strained the quality of his prose. Any unevenness or lack of cohesion also stems from his use of various styles and tones, and the wide range of his interests: natural history, farming, theosophy, depersonalization caused by urban life and technological development, the evils of big business and politicians, and "the over-organization of humanity for profit," especially during the war.

Despite this diversity, there are unifying themes in McArthur's work. He consistently espoused the idea of a New World democracy that was epitomized in the cooperative individualism of the pioneers. Out of this model came his articulation of the interests of the "common man" and his emphasis on "brotherhood," notions that found their best political expression, he believed, in the liberalism of Laurier. Idealistically, he urged people to cease being pawns of exploitive organizations and capitalist greed, and to return to the land for lives of self-reliance and mutual support. That his advocacy was widely admired is testified to by the numerous obituaries of "the Sage of Ekfrid" that appeared in newspapers and journals throughout Canada and United States after his death. He died in 1924 following surgery at the Victoria Hospital in London.

CARL P. BALLSTADT

Peter McArthur's writings are listed in W. A. Deacon, *Peter McArthur* (Toronto, [1923?]) and Alec Lucas, *Peter McArthur* (Boston, [1975]). In addition, he wrote "Public opinion and political life," in *The new era in Canada; essays dealing with the upbuilding of the Canadian commonwealth*, ed. J. O. Miller (Toronto, 1917), 331–45. A selection of his works by Alec Lucas has been published as *The best of Peter McArthur* (Toronto, 1967). McArthur's manuscripts, along with many other papers and his lantern slides, can be found in Univ. of Western Ont. Arch., J. J. Talman Regional Coll. (London), B4291–94.

AO, F 977-4, Eddie Cemetery (Ekfrid Township, Ont.), nos.90–91 (mfm.); F 978, St Mark's Anglican Church, Niagara [Niagara-on-the-Lake, Ont.], RBMB, 11 Sept. 1895 (mfm.); RG 80-5-0-226, no.7378; RG 80-8-0-966, no.21243. UTA, B1965-0014/004(02). *Glencoe Transcript* (Glencoe, Ont.), 12, 19 Sept. 1895; 7 Jan. 1904. *London Evening Advertiser*, 29 Oct. 1924. *Canadian men and women of the time* (Morgan; 1898 and 1912). Brandon Conron, "Essays (1880–1920)," in *Literary history of Canada: Canadian literature in English*, ed. C. F. Klinck *et al.* (Toronto, 1965), 340–46. F. W. Watt, "Peter McArthur and the agrarian myth," *Queen's Quarterly* (Kingston, Ont.), 67 (1960–61): 245–57.

McCARTHY, MAITLAND STEWART, lawyer, politician, and judge; b. 5 Feb. 1872 in Orangeville, Ont., son of Thomas Anthony Maitland McCarthy and Jennie Frances Stewart; m. 26 May 1900 Eva Florence Watson in Hamilton, Ont., and they had two sons and a daughter; d. 17 May 1930 in Montreal and was buried in Orangeville.

Born of Irish parents, Maitland McCarthy followed family members into a career in law; both his paternal grandfather and his uncle D'Alton McCarthy* were lawyers, and his father was a county court judge in Orangeville. He attended Trinity College School in Port Hope, Ont., and Trinity University in Toronto (BA 1893, MA 1895, LLB 1896). Called to the bar in 1897, he practised in Sarnia, where he also became active in the local Conservative association. In September 1903 he moved to Calgary. Admitted to the bar of the North-West Territories in October, he soon formed a partnership with William Legh Walsh*, who had once worked in Orangeville.

McCarthy entered politics within a year of his arrival in Calgary. He was elected to the House of Commons for Calgary in 1904 and again in 1908 but he did not run in 1911. A major speaker in the house, he was noted for his constant attendance and attention to details in legislation. During the Conservatives' attack in 1905 on the education sections of the Autonomy Bills, for the creation of the provinces of Alberta and Saskatchewan, McCarthy "treated the constitutional question with penetrating subtlety," in the estimate of one historian. In February 1909 he was offered the leadership of the Conservatives in Alberta but declined.

After leaving parliament, McCarthy joined the Edmonton law firm of Eddinton and Hanna. He became one of the leading members of the Edmonton Bar Association, and revelled in its social affairs. Named KC on 19 March 1913, he was appointed to the Supreme Court of Alberta on 11 July 1914 and to its newly formed trial division on 15 Sept. 1921.

On the bench, McCarthy was regarded as a wise observer of human action. He spoke slowly, with a sense of humour; a generalist, he gave more weight to common sense than to legal technicality. According to one associate, he became a heavy drinker and could forget his legal training; another believed he could have been one of the most brilliant legal minds of his time. Although he did not write many judgements that furthered the jurisprudence of the court, he authored important precedents in such areas as the extent of contributory negligence in personal accidents, corporate negligence, and the rules of evidence. He valued precise judicial writing and did not hesitate to dissent. Several of his major decisions involved the Canadian Pacific and Grand Trunk railways. His most noteworthy judgement was *The King v. Wilson* (1919), where he overturned a decision for criminal misconduct against an automobile driver, and narrowed the parameters of personal liability for drivers encountering cyclists and pedestrians on the roadways.

Throughout his legal career McCarthy was active in outdoor sports, the Anglican church, and his community. He was a governor of Trinity College School and Western Canada College in Calgary, a chairman of the Alcoholics Anonymous Association of Alberta and the Amateur Athletic Association for Alberta, and a member of the Central Olympic Committee in 1908. He held memberships too in the Calgary and Ranchmen's clubs and the Rideau Club in Ottawa.

Maitland McCarthy retired from the bench because of health problems on 3 May 1926. He died in Montreal four years later while on vacation.

LOUIS A. KNAFLA

[Biographical information about Maitland Stewart McCarthy can be found in *Canadian men and women of the time* (Morgan; 1912), *Canadian directory of parl.* (Johnson), *Canadian who's who*, 1910, and *Who's who and why*, 1917/18. Obituaries are in the *Calgary Herald* and the *Edmonton*

Journal, both on 19 May 1930. There are no extant family manuscripts or legal files.

There is a photograph and a short legal biography of McCarthy in L. [A.] Knafla and Richard Klumpenhouwer, *Lords of the western bench: a biographical history of the supreme and district courts of Alberta, 1876–1990* (Calgary, 1997), 114–15. McCarthy's written judgements can be found from time to time in the *Alberta Law Reports* (Toronto), *Western Law Reporter* (Toronto), and *Western Weekly Reports* (Calgary) for 1914 to 1925. Judgements by McCarthy are also recorded in the civil trial books at the PAA, GR1979.266. Contemporary opinions are expressed in interviews of John Edward Annand Macleod and George Wilbert Skene, on tape at the GA, M 3983. L.A.K.]

AO, RG 80-5-0-286, no.17593. *Edmonton Journal*, 28 May 1930. *CPG*, 1905. M. R. Lupul, *The Roman Catholic Church and the North-West school question: a study in church-state relations in western Canada, 1875–1905* (Toronto, 1974).

McCAUL, CHARLES COURSOLLES, lawyer and author; b. 17 Feb. 1858 in Toronto, third son of the Reverend John McCaul* and Emily Augusta Jones; m. first 12 May 1887 Frances Greenwood in Lethbridge (Alta), and they had a son and two daughters; m. secondly 1921 Eugenie Marie Lachapelle; they had no children; d. 10 Aug. 1928 in Edmonton.

Charles Coursolles McCaul came from a distinguished family: his father was president of University College in Toronto and his mother was a daughter of Jonas Jones*, a judge. He attended Upper Canada College and the University of Toronto, from which he graduated in 1879 with a BA, a prize in classics, and a silver medal in natural science. After attending Osgoode Hall, he was called to the Ontario bar in February 1883, but, drawn west by the Canadian Pacific Railway, he left in July for the North-West Territories.

McCaul settled for a year at North Fork Ranch near Fort Macleod (Alta). He helped run it and enjoyed riding and fishing. In 1885 he set up his law practice in town, and in June 1886 he was one of the first lawyers to be enrolled in the Law Society of the North-West Territories. Most of his business was as a proctor and notary. Active on town council, he assisted in drafting its charter and by-laws, and moved a petition for the erection of a courthouse. In addition, he served as solicitor of the South-Western Stock Association [*see* Frederick Smith Stimson*].

After his marriage in 1887, McCaul moved to Lethbridge, where he opened a practice on 31 May 1888 with Frederick William Gordon Haultain*, with whom he had graduated from university. Haultain, who had been elected to the territorial assembly, left the practice in January 1890. Named QC that summer, McCaul was in partnership with Thomas William Clarke from July 1891 to January 1892. By September 1891 he had moved to Calgary, where he joined the firm of James Alexander LOUGHEED; he was a partner with Costigan and Bangs by 1894 and then with James Short.

McCaul was quite active in community and legal circles in the late 1880s and 1890s. He was a founding member in 1889 of the Lethbridge Board of Trade and Civic Committee, drafted the papers for the creation in 1890 of the Lethbridge Waterworks and Electric Light Company Limited, and established the Lethbridge Turf and Athletic Association. A bencher and examiner for the law society, he edited the *Territories Law Reports* (Toronto) in 1897–98 and served on the commission to revise the territorial ordinances in 1898. One of the first members of the Calgary Bar Association, which often met in his office, he chaired it and sat on numerous committees and commissions. Earlier he had helped form the Lethbridge Scientific and Historical Society. His addresses to this society emphasized the need to study the climate, geology, and history of the region, which he saw as full of life and romance. He also noted the destruction of native life and its artefacts. Perhaps such interests, along with his inability to stay put, led him to leave Alberta for the Yukon gold rush in October 1899.

In Dawson, McCaul joined the firm of White and Davey. His diary for the period November 1899–April 1900, which scarcely mentions legal matters, focuses on civic affairs, social life, and mining and exploration. But Dawson could not hold McCaul either: he left for San Francisco later that spring, and then travelled throughout Europe, without his wife. They returned to Dawson briefly in 1901; by the spring of 1902 they were in Vancouver, where he was in partnership with Ernest John Deacon. The firm was dissolved because of McCaul's ill health the following year. After more travels in England and France, in 1905 he went back to San Francisco, where he was admitted to practise. Within a year, he was once again in Fort Macleod and then, in 1907, he settled in Edmonton. He seems to have had domestic problems with his wife – in 1921 he would marry a nurse from Beaumont, Alta.

McCaul could never keep his law partners. Admitted to the Law Society of Alberta on 16 Sept. 1907, for the next 20 years he practised with George C. Valens, George W. Archibald, Friedman and Lieberman, and, finally, Stanton and Smith. From 1927 he was on his own. In his last few years, in poor health, he allowed his practice to dwindle while he travelled to London and Paris, his wife, and nurse, beside him.

Contemporaries noted McCaul's sociability and keen mind. He joined the city club and Anglican church in every place he lived. Talented but restless, he had a flair for the literate and elegant appeal that could touch the hearts of jurors as well as readers. Several of his opening and closing addresses in the few criminal trials that he prosecuted or defended were published privately. Legal historian Wilbur Fee Bowker considers McCaul to be one of the province's "great counsel."

McCauley

McCaul's most important legacy is his publications – surprisingly, since few lawyers of his era became writers. In 1896 he compiled, with Horace Harvey*, a guide to the ordinances of the North-West Territories. He followed up his work on the *Territories Law Reports* by editing the *Alberta Law Reports* (Toronto) in 1907–8. In addition, he wrote on foreign judgements for the *Law Quarterly Review* (London) and produced several jurisprudential articles for the *Canadian Law Times* (Toronto). His major work, which came out in 1910, was on vendors and purchasers of real estate, but more interesting were his scientific and historical writings. "South Alberta, and the climatic effects of the chinook wind," published in 1888, remains a classic. McCaul's 1884 article on the constitutional status of the territories was the first study of proclamations, statutes, and judicial precedents there. His insightful piece of 1925 on the leaders of the bench and the bar in the west is the first historical survey of his generation of lawyers.

McCaul died at his home in Edmonton in 1928.

Louis A. Knafla

[A short biography of Charles Coursolles McCaul can be found in A. D. Ridge, "C. C. McCaul, pioneer lawyer," *Alberta Hist. Rev.* (Calgary), 21 (1973), no.1: 21–25. Other sources of biographical information are *Canadian men and women of the time* (Morgan; 1898 and 1912), *Who's who and why*, 1917/18 and 1919/20, and PAA, PR1981.356/SE. His obituary appeared in the *Edmonton Journal*, 11 Aug. 1928.

McCaul's major published writings include *Ready reference guide to the ordinances of the North-West Territories . . .* (Toronto, 1896); "The constitutional status of the North-West Territories of Canada," *Canadian Law Times* (Toronto), 4 (1884): 1–15, 49–61; "Notes on the Territories Real Property Act," *Canadian Law Times*, 9 (1889): 25–40, 53–59 (written with John Campbell Ferrie Bown); "South Alberta, and the climatic effects of the chinook wind," *American Meteorological Journal* (Ann Arbor, Mich.), 5 (1888–89): 145–59; "Addenda to the article on 'The climate of South Alberta,'" in the August number," *ibid.*: 362–69; *Notes on the remedies of vendors and purchasers of real estate with special reference to instalment-plan agreements, rescission, determination, relief against forfeiture* (Toronto, 1910); *Address in opening the case for the prosecution of Sinnisiak, an Eskimo charged with murder, before the Hon. Chief Justice Harvey and a jury, at Edmonton, Alberta, August 14th, 1917* ([n.p.], 1917); and "Precursors of the bench and bar in the western provinces," *Canadian Bar Rev.* (Toronto), 3 (1925): 25–40. McCaul's published writings were cited widely by contemporaries.

The most revealing work is McCaul's Yukon diary of 1899–1900 in PAA, PR1971.338. Recollections of his early years may be found in GA in the diary and correspondence of Mrs Ella Inderwick, M 559, and in the papers of F. W. G. Haultain, M 495. McCaul's name appears frequently in the minute books, 1890–1904, of the Calgary Bar Association in GA, M 1925. The record of his litigation, however, is weak, with the exception of some isolated cases in the *Territories Law Reports* (Toronto), 1900–7, and the *Alberta Law Reports* (Toronto), 1907–28. L.A.K.]

Toronto Daily Mail, 20 May 1887. "The chinook winds," *American Meteorological Journal*, 5: 186–88. Alex Johnston, *Lethbridge, from coal town to commercial centre: a business history*, ed. Irma Dogterom and L. G. Ellis (Lethbridge, Alta, 1997).

McCAULEY, MATTHEW, businessman, farmer, politician, and penitentiary warden; b. 11 June 1850 near Sydenham (Owen Sound), Upper Canada, son of Alexander McCauley and Eleanor Latimer; m. first 1875 Matilda Susannah Benson (d. 1896) in Winnipeg, and they had two sons and six daughters; m. secondly 27 March 1900 Annie Cookson in Edmonton, and they had two daughters and two sons; d. 26 Oct. 1930 near Sexsmith, Alta.

Matt McCauley grew up on a farm near Owen Sound, but at the age of 21 he left Ontario for Upper Fort Garry (Winnipeg), where he worked at various jobs until he established a cartage business in 1874. Five years later he and his family travelled by ox cart to Fort Edmonton (Edmonton) and took up a farm near Fort Saskatchewan (Alta). They moved into Edmonton in 1881. There McCauley established the business that would become the Edmonton Cartage Company.

Over the following three decades he would involve himself in virtually every aspect of public life in the small but growing community. He helped to establish and served on the public school board, was a member of the Home Guard during the 1885 uprising led by Louis Riel*, founded the Edmonton Board of Trade and the Edmonton Agricultural Society, served as the first mayor for the town of Edmonton and as a councillor, sat in the territorial and provincial assemblies, and eventually became warden of the Alberta penitentiary. He was also involved with the masonic lodge and a founder of the Royal Curling Club.

In 1881 McCauley was the driving force behind the establishment of the first public school in the community. With the support of Frank Oliver*, editor of the *Edmonton Bulletin*, he persuaded the Hudson's Bay Company to provide a lot for the school and raised funds by subscription to pay for its construction and the teacher's salary. He and the other trustees constantly found themselves short of money, however, as the territorial school grants and residents' pledges failed to materialize. The citizens resorted to organizing minstrel shows and renting out the school to raise the money needed to settle with the contractor, buy supplies, and lease a heater.

The North-West Territories School Ordinance of 1884 made it possible for the residents of Edmonton to establish a public school district, and a plebiscite to approve its incorporation was held on 21 December that year. Despite the support of local leaders such as McCauley and Oliver, there was considerable opposition from the HBC and other large landowners, who did not wish to pay taxes to support a public school. Both sides put considerable effort and ingenuity into getting voters out for the plebiscite. In the end, returning officer McCauley was pleased to announce the results: 54 votes to 43 in favour of incorporation. He would serve as chairman of the board or trustee for 15 years.

McCauley's involvement in a public vigilance committee in 1882 helped to further his reputation as a champion of local residents. By this time several settlers had built houses along the cliffs overlooking the North Saskatchewan River, but because the federal government had not completed a survey, they could not establish legal title to the land they occupied. Newcomers to the settlement started to build on land that was already occupied and resisted attempts to persuade them to move elsewhere. McCauley and some others therefore took matters into their own hands and threw the newly built shacks over the cliffs into the valley below.

In 1892, when the town of Edmonton was incorporated, McCauley was chosen its first mayor by acclamation; he was re-elected in 1893 and 1894. The burning issue in these years was the need for a railway link. The Canadian Pacific Railway had bypassed Edmonton when it took a southern route through the territory, and the Calgary and Edmonton Railway, which had been intended to connect the two towns, terminated at Strathcona (now southern Edmonton) in 1891, failing to cross the North Saskatchewan River. Mayor McCauley went to Ottawa three years later and lobbied politicians on both sides of the House of Commons to support the construction of a bridge over the river. It was finally completed in 1900.

Meanwhile, community leaders in Strathcona argued that because the railway ended there, the other services required by settlers arriving in the area, including the dominion land titles office, should be moved from Jasper Avenue in Edmonton to Strathcona. On 18 June 1892 McCauley called up a "home guard" and surrounded the land agent and his men, who were in the midst of moving the office to the south side of the river. He and his supporters forced a delay by unhitching the horses and removing the wagon's wheels. Telegrams were sent to Edgar Dewdney*, the minister of the interior in Ottawa, demanding that the order to move the office be rescinded. Dewdney initially responded by directing Superintendent Arthur Henry Griesbach of the North-West Mounted Police to take his troop from Fort Saskatchewan to Edmonton and effect the removal, but McCauley met the detachment and reiterated his demand for more time. On 20 June he received a telegram from Dewdney assuring him that it had never been the government's intention to move the office permanently, only to set up a temporary branch in Strathcona to deal with the expected influx of new settlers. The office remained on Jasper Avenue, and McCauley reinforced his reputation as a stern defender of the interests of Edmonton's citizens. He maintained this position while serving as the Liberal member for Edmonton in the Legislative Assembly of the North-West Territories from 1896 to 1902.

In the latter year McCauley and his family left the town to take up a farm near Tofield, but he was drawn back into politics when the province of Alberta was created in 1905. He was persuaded to run for the Vermilion district northeast of Edmonton and won the seat. However, he served only during the first session and then was rewarded for his loyalty to the Liberals by being appointed warden of the Alberta penitentiary, established in Edmonton the following year. As warden, McCauley worked to make the facility largely self-sufficient. By 1908 prisoners were manufacturing bricks and crushing stone for concrete. They were also making their own clothing, shoes, and tools, and gardening and producing much of their own food. Two years later the prison had its own coalmine.

Following the election of a Conservative government in Ottawa in 1911, McCauley lost his position as warden of the penitentiary. He moved to Penticton, B.C., where he ran an orchard for 14 years. Then at the age of 75 he took up a homestead in the Peace River district of Alberta near Sexsmith. He died there at the age of 80 and was buried in Edmonton. A public school and a plaza in the city are named in his honour.

AMY VON HEYKING

Alta Legislature Library (Edmonton), Scrapbook *Hansard*, March–May 1906 (mfm.). City of Edmonton Arch., MS 320 (Matt McCauley fonds); Newspaper clipping files, Edmonton Penitentiary clippings; Matt McCauley clippings; RG 8 (Edmonton Town Council), minute-books, 1892–94. Edmonton Public Schools Arch. and Museum, Edmonton School District No.7 fonds, reference file: McCauley, Matthew, minute-books, 1885–1902. Jim Blower, "Matthew McCauley," *Alberta Hist. Rev.* (Calgary), 20 (1972), no.1: 11–17. M. A. Kostek, *A century and ten: the history of Edmonton public schools* (Edmonton, 1992). J. G. MacGregor, *Edmonton: a history* (Edmonton, 1967; 2nd ed., 1975). Alex Mair, *Gateway city* (Calgary, 2000). North-West Territories, Legislative Assembly, *Journals* (Regina), 1896–1902.

McCLARY, JOHN, manufacturer; b. 2 Jan. 1829 in Westminster Township, Upper Canada, son of John McClary and Sarah Stark; m. first 1853 Mary Ann Drake (d. 1862), and they had two daughters; m. secondly 1866 Mary Jane Pavey (d. 1909); d. 11 Dec. 1921 in London, Ont.

A native of New Hampshire, John McClary Sr married in Pennsylvania and about 1817 settled with his family in Westminster. Since John Jr was the 11th of 12 children, his future lay away from the family farm. An older brother, Oliver, trained him as a tinsmith and in 1849 John went to work for him in nearby London. John left for California the following year when, as he later recalled, "gold fever set in." In San Francisco he decided that, amidst the thousands of seekers, a tin-smith could profit, so he established a shop. In 1851 his business was burned out and, after an unsuccessful try for gold, he returned to London.

The brothers formally resumed business together as J. and O. McClary on 1 Jan. 1852, and moved to expand. They added a foundry to make stoves, which would become their mainstay, and hired others to sell their products. John even visited the factory of the Meriden Britannia tin company in Connecticut to study the latest developments in the trade. In 1871 they created a limited liability company, McClary Manufacturing, with the stated intention of producing stoves, tin, copper, and pressed wares, agricultural implements, and other ironware and machinery. Aided by the protectionist National Policy, the firm introduced new lines, including a profitable range of enamelware in 1880, and established warehouses in Toronto and Montreal (1879), Winnipeg (1880), Vancouver (1894), Saint John (1901), and Hamilton (1902). In 1882 the company had secured a dominion charter and within two years it was exporting to Britain, the West Indies, and Australia. Its rapid rebuilding after a fire in 1888 led the *London Advertiser* to exclaim "there is probably no firm in Canada that has such a reputation for hustling." Following Oliver McClary's death in 1902 John ran the business on his own. A state-of-the-art factory completed in 1904 to replace the foundry facilitated new models of stoves and furnaces.

During these decades of growth John McClary had become involved in other businesses, notably as a director and vice-president of the Ontario Loan and Debenture Company and the London Life Insurance Company. As well, he was a founding director of the London and Western Trusts Company Limited. He invested widely, but McClary Manufacturing would remain his focus. One of London's more prominent industrialists, he was active in 1881 in the formation of the Merchants' and Manufacturers' Exchange and then of the Board of Trade.

McClary's relations with labour were shaped in the 1880s through encounters with the aggressive iron-moulders' union. An unsuccessful strike in 1882 left the firm non-union; in 1885 renewed resistance, supported by the Knights of Labor, produced dismissals. Four years later McClary gave a defensive explanation of the affair before the royal commission on the relations of labour and capital, which also pressed him for answers on price-fixing by the Stove Manufacturers' Association, to which he belonged. McClary and the moulders clashed again in a vehement strike in 1905–6, which led to a long feud; in 1909 unionists were still boycotting his products.

A different image of McClary emerged in sympathetic manufacturers' journals and promotional pieces on London. In 1906 *Industrial Canada* (Toronto) called him "an ideal employer of labour." "Although he runs an open shop, complaints from employees receive the quickest attention." Examples of his concern included the employees' benefit society founded in 1882 and the welfare department set up in 1910. This paternalism was continued after McClary's death by his son-in-law William Moir Gartshore, who assumed control of the company. Its merger in 1927 into General Steel Wares Limited of Toronto ended the family connection.

A Methodist and an ardent imperialist, McClary had been a staunch Conservative. Though he never held elected office, he wrote frequently to newspapers and public figures to express his views. His heavy-handed opposition to the free trade agreement of 1911 attracted particular attention. In its obituary the *Advertiser* noted his passion for "questions of the day." His style of hands-on management in business was becoming outdated when he died, but the presence of McClary employees and trust company representatives as pall-bearers at his funeral suggests the wide respect he had nonetheless enjoyed.

ANDREW THOMSON

AO, RG 8-1-1, 589/1871; RG 55-17-33, no.81. Univ. of Western Ont. Arch., J. J. Talman Regional Coll. (London), McClary family papers, ser.II-C-1. *London Advertiser* (London, Ont.), 7 Jan. 1889, 12–13 Dec. 1921. *Canada investigates industrialism: the royal commission on the relations of labor and capital, 1889 (abridged)*, ed. G. [S.] Kealey (Toronto and Buffalo, N.Y., 1973). *History of the county of Middlesex ...* (Toronto and London, 1889; repr., intro. D. [J.] Brock, Belleville, Ont., 1972). G. S. Kealey and B. D. Palmer, *Dreaming of what might be: the Knights of Labor in Ontario, 1880–1900* (Cambridge, Eng., and New York, 1982). *Leaves from a lifetime; being a brief history of the Gartshore family in Scotland; of the Gartshore and Moir families, as pioneers in early days in Ontario; and of the life and reminiscences to date of William Moir Gartshore*, ed. Margaret Wade (London, [1929]). B. D. Palmer, *A culture in conflict: skilled workers and industrial capitalism in Hamilton, Ontario, 1860–1914* (Montreal, 1979). B. S. Scott, "The economic and industrial history of the city of London, Canada, from the building of the first railway, 1855, to the present, 1930" (MA thesis, Univ. of Western Ont., 1930). N. Z. Tausky and L. D. DiStefano, *Victorian architecture in London and southwestern Ontario: symbols of aspiration* (Toronto, 1986).

McCORD, DAVID ROSS, lawyer, alderman, and museum founder; b. 18 March 1844 in Montreal, fourth child of John Samuel McCord, a lawyer, and Anne Ross; m. 21 Aug. 1878 Letitia Caroline Chambers (d. 1928) in Toronto; they had no children; d. 12 April 1930 in Guelph, Ont., of myocardial failure.

Descended on his paternal and maternal sides from three generations of merchants, landowners, and jurists [*see* Thomas McCord*], David Ross McCord was raised in a family which valued both science and art. John Samuel McCord, who became a judge shortly after David's birth, instilled a love of science in his children, provided them with a classical education, and insisted that they learn to speak French. Mrs McCord was fluently bilingual. Collecting was part of the family culture. David's father was a connoisseur of art and his mother was an accomplished watercolour artist. Both she and David were taught drawing by James D. Duncan*.

McCord attended the High School of Montreal and then McGill College (BA 1863; MA, BCL 1867). He articled with the firm of Charles-André Leblanc* and Francis Cassidy* and was called to the bar in 1868. He practised alone, except for 1879–80, when he was in partnership with Joseph Doutre* and Moïse Branchaud, and he acted for the city of Montreal as well as for various institutions. He represented the descendants of Sir William* and Sir John* Johnson in their attempt to gain compensation from the American government for lands in New York State which had been confiscated after the American revolution. In 1895 he would be named a QC.

Continuing his father's involvement in the Church of England, freemasonry, and the militia, McCord was a member of Christ Church Cathedral and St Paul's Lodge and a lieutenant in the reserves. He was also active in urban reform, pursuing in particular issues of health and public sanitation as an alderman for Centre Ward from 1874 to 1882. In this work he met his future wife, Letitia Caroline Chambers, matron of the civic smallpox hospital. They were married despite the disapproval of his sisters, who had little regard for the occupation of nursing. His wife was a poet whose strongly imperialist verse would be published in *Poems and songs on the South African War . . .* (Montreal, 1901), edited by John Douglas Borthwick.

From about the 1880s, McCord's chief interest was the collecting of material relating to the history of Canada, in which endeavour his wife acted as his assistant. The theoretical basis for his collection provides insight into the intellectual milieu in which his family ties and his research interests had placed him. In a climate of anxiety about the young country's future, he, like other Canadian imperialists, turned to history to define, build, and defend the nation's place within the empire. He read broadly in current works of history and literature in both French and English. He appreciated Quebec historians François-Xavier Garneau* and Henri-Raymond Casgrain*, who idealized the history of New France by emphasizing the conservative, agrarian, hierarchical, and religious nature of early French Canada. He chose themes recognizable to those who shared his imperialist views: Canada's

native cultures, the conquest of New France, the Seven Years' War and Canada's involvement in war, Catholic and Protestant church leaders who played a prominent role in building the country, romantic heroes of the fur trade, and Canadian scientists whose discoveries benefited the country and made it known abroad. His collection also reflected Montreal's role in the development of Canada. Chosen mainly for their association with individuals, McCord's acquisitions personified the events in Canadian history. He amassed his collection of roughly 18,000 artefacts from a variety of sources: his family, purchases, and donations obtained by sending flattering letters of appeal. In 1919, when he presented it to McGill University with an endowment, it was the largest collection of its kind in Canada. McCord's friend and lawyer William Douw Lighthall* and McGill's librarian, Charles Henry Gould*, had been instrumental in ensuring that the collection was acquired by McGill.

On 13 Oct. 1921 the McCord National Museum was officially opened. In its initial displays, McCord treated the leaders of Canada's Christian traditions as spiritual pioneers, focusing on the theme of struggle and exhibiting the broadest range of objects, from early printed pamphlets, letters, portraits, and regalia to elements of church architecture which had been discarded during renovations. In collecting native material McCord had read the works of ethnologist Daniel Wilson*, geologist John William Dawson*, and philologist and ethnologist Horatio Emmons Hale*. Influenced by these three men who, according to anthropologist Bruce Graham Trigger, rejected "what modern anthropologists regard as some of the most abhorrent views of nineteenth-century anthropologists," McCord hoped that his ethnological acquisitions "would stand unrivalled on the continent" as a testimony to "the skill and industry" of the native peoples. Prizing older material which reflected life before European contact, he also acquired a range of more recent artefacts for comparative purposes. Among the more spectacular items were his Micmac (Mi'kmaw) collection, an Iroquoian-type early-19th-century headdress believed to have been worn by the Shawnee leader Tecumseh*, an early Athapaskan jacket with quillwork decoration, and a significant collection of trade silver.

McCord referred to his paintings, prints, and drawings as visual records of the country's progress. The initial displays drew on his collection of important family portraits by William Berczy*, Louis Dulongpré*, Frederick W. Lock, and James D. Duncan. He added his mother's flower paintings and Duncan's scenes of Montreal which his father had commissioned in 1831. He asked Henry Richard S. Bunnett to paint historic sites which he felt were destined to disappear. His most famous acquisitions are probably *The negress* (1786) by François Malepart* de Beaucourt, George Townshend*'s watercolour portrait of General James Wolfe* (the only known image drawn from life), a series of cartoons of Wolfe by Townshend, and 31 watercolours by William George Richardson Hind* executed during an expedition to British Columbia in 1862.

The collection's material on western and northern expansion and exploration symbolized the romantic lure of the fur trade and the struggle to open up the country in the face of overwhelming obstacles. Maps, prints, silver, journals, and letters conjured up vast expanses of territory. Minutes of the Beaver Club, medals and portraits of its members, among them Isaac Todd*, Joseph Frobisher*, and James McGill*, and diaries of Arctic explorer Sir George Back* were among his prized possessions.

McCord believed that war refined the individual and the nation, providing national myths of heroism and sacrifice. Portraits, prints, paintings, uniforms, and weapons represented every battle, internal and external, in which Canadians had fought. He viewed the War of 1812 as Canada's war of independence, in which native people and French and English Canadians fought alongside British regulars to defeat the invading Americans.

The considerable estate McCord had inherited had helped to finance his acquisitions, but his management of it during the period from 1870 to 1900 was, according to 20th-century historians, "marked above all by a remarkable inattention to legal obligations, often with costly consequences." By the early 1900s, possibly earlier, McCord was experiencing financial difficulties. Later he suffered from arteriosclerosis, which led to mental deterioration. In early June 1922 Lighthall recommended interdiction (a legal restraint imposed on a person incapable of managing his or her own affairs) to McCord's wife. It was granted on 29 June. In September McCord was admitted to the Protestant Hospital for the Insane in Verdun and the following year he became a patient at the Homewood Sanitarium in Guelph, where he remained, except for brief visits to Montreal, until his death.

David Ross McCord's views on Canadian history were similar to those of many contemporaries who shared his enthusiasm for preserving the landmarks of their country's past. He stands out among his peers, however, in three areas: the documentation of his artefacts (he accumulated 626 files of correspondence with donors or dealers, research notes, and bills), the obsessiveness of his collecting, and, finally, the comprehensiveness of his collection (he had also acquired thousands of books and pamphlets). He left to his university and future generations an invaluable legacy to serve in the interpretation and reinterpretation of Canadian history.

PAMELA MILLER

David Ross McCord's papers are preserved in the McCord family fonds at the McCord Museum of Canadian Hist. (Montreal), 13 metres of records comprising his family's papers and documentation concerning his activities as a collector. An inventory, *McCord family papers, 1766–1945,* comp. P. J. Miller (2v., Montreal, 1986), has been published by the museum. Another important source is P. [J.] Miller *et al., The McCord family: a passionate vision* (Montreal, 1992), a catalogue prepared for an exhibition at the McCord Museum. It examines the history of the family, studies each of McCord's collections, and contains a select bibliography.

B. G. Trigger, *Natives and newcomers: Canada's "Heroic Age" reconsidered* (Montreal, 1985). D. A. Wright, "Remembering war in imperial Canada: David Ross McCord and the McCord National Museum," *Fontanus* (Montreal), 9 (1996): 97–104; "W. D. Lighthall and David Ross McCord: anti-modernism and English-Canadian imperialism, 1880s–1918," *Journal of Canadian Studies* (Peterborough, Ont.), 32 (1997–98), no.2: 134–53.

McCREA, FRANCIS (Francis Nelson), lumber merchant, manufacturer, and politician; b. 14 Jan. 1852 in the township of Durham, Lower Canada, son of Francis McCrea, a farmer, and Eliza Nelson; m. first Elizabeth Church (d. 1876); m. secondly 11 Nov. 1882 Judith Fanny Ella Wakefield in South Durham (Durham-Sud), Que., and they had ten children; d. 30 Oct. 1926 in Sherbrooke, Que.

Francis McCrea was born to Irish parents who worked a small farm in the Eastern Townships and he grew up there as part of a large family. He is believed to have received only a rudimentary education. He began a long and fruitful career as a self-made man in the mid 1870s, while employed as a labourer in the lumbering operations of Charles Church, of South Durham. This period was clouded, however, by the deaths in 1876 of his first child and then of his young wife, who was the niece of Charles Church. In 1881, the year before his second marriage, the 29-year-old McCrea appears in the census as a merchant living with a carpenter and his wife in South Durham. A little later he is described as a supplier of wood and fuel to the Canada Paper Company in Windsor Mills (Windsor). Listed in the 1891 census for South Durham as a merchant, McCrea already seemed reasonably well off, with two servants in the house to cater to a second family that included three young children. At the time, he had 15 people working for him. McCrea moved to Sherbrooke, a large regional centre, in 1901, and soon took his place among its most prosperous citizens, as the luxurious residence he built in the northern part of the city shortly before 1909 shows. In partnership with others, he bought or founded lumbering firms such as the Lotbinière Lumber Company and the Sherbrooke Lumber Company (which received its letters patent in 1903). It was, however, with his arrival at the Brompton Pulp and Paper Company, probably in 1907, that he was able to move up to a position among the leaders of the middle class in the Eastern Townships.

Brompton Pulp and Paper, which had been founded partly by American capital, was then on the way to becoming an important component of the region's economy, with its plants in Bromptonville and East Angus, its control of the water resources of the Rivière Saint-François, and its hold on extensive timber limits. McCrea would be its president until his death in 1926. In 1920 Brompton Pulp and Paper produced wood pulp, newsprint, kraft paper, and cardboard. The Bromptonville plant was the third largest pulp maker in Canada in 1910, and the plant in East Angus, which was the first in Canada to supply sulphate pulp and kraft paper, was the third largest manufacturer of paper in the province of Quebec in 1920. What is interesting about the company's success is the fact that some entrepreneurs from the region (albeit in partnership with businessmen from the United States) were able to resist the pressure of monopoly capitalism, especially Montreal-based, during the early decades of the 20th century by concentrating on the exploitation of forest resources. At that very time, other sizeable firms, developed at the outset mainly by local elites (the Paton Manufacturing Company of Sherbrooke, the Eastern Townships Bank), had succumbed or were succumbing to that pressure. Although it did very well during World War I, Brompton Pulp and Paper would find itself in difficulty at the end of the 1920s, very likely because of the price war in the paper industry and the advent of plants with greater production capacity. It would merge with other firms in 1930 to form the St Lawrence Corporation.

Like the rest of the elite in his time, McCrea was notable for the many interests in which he was involved. In addition to being associated with numerous firms at the same time (he was president of five companies and vice-president of two others in 1917), he was active in politics. He was mayor of South Durham for about ten years at the end of the 19th century, and he was the Conservative candidate for Drummond in the provincial election of 1900, in which he was defeated. Eventually he represented Sherbrooke as a Liberal MP for nearly 14 years, winning consecutively in the elections of 1911, 1917, and 1921. His political role on the federal scene proved minor on the whole, but his speeches in the house provide much information about his concerns and thinking. As an entrepreneur who had started with nothing, McCrea was a staunch supporter of economic liberalism. He based his views on his own experience, as this statement made in 1922 shows: "When I left my father's farm I went out as a labouring man, and without friends, without money, without anything to recommend me to the world. If I have had some degree of success it has been by putting into practice what I am now preaching to others; it has been the result of thrift

and industry, of taking care of my money and not spending more than I earned." In his eyes, work was the cure-all for a "difficult situation." Doubtless it was for this reason that he had little sympathy for the unemployed in 1922. "I had been told there are 250,000 idle men," he said, and he wondered "what those men are looking for? Are they looking for work, or is it 'positions' they want?" In the same vein, he protested against changes in working conditions, especially against shortening the working day and raising the cost of labour. As a paper manufacturer well aware of his own interests, he spoke out in the house during World War I against regulation of the price of newsprint (below the cost of its production, according to him) and he frequently denounced the existing railway freight rates (which he considered excessive).

As the MP for a riding whose central city, Sherbrooke, was largely French-speaking, McCrea came to the defence of French Canadians during the conscription crisis of 1917 [*see* Sir Robert Laird Borden*], condemning in the house the attitude taken by Ontario. "The war had hardly commenced before Ontario was hurling insult at them about being slackers, and not enlisting. . . . I think if they had spent part of the time in trying to do justice to the minority in Ontario, by granting them the right to teach their children in their own language . . ., they would have accomplished more in the direction of recruiting." Yet towards the end of his career in federal politics, he had a difference of opinion with his party, which was then in power, in particular about customs duties, for he was a protectionist. McCrea voted against the government on several occasions, with the result that he ran in the 1925 election as an independent. He withdrew from the race before election day, however, and he died the following year.

Francis McCrea was one of the last illustrious representatives of a native-born, English-speaking middle class in the Eastern Townships that owed its influence to the accumulation of important political and economic positions. He occupied a strategic position for many years, and it is noteworthy that he did so until the mid 1920s, even while the rise of monopoly capitalism was increasingly bringing the Eastern Townships' economic assets under the control of capital from outside the region.

THIERRY NOOTENS

ANQ-MBF, CE402-S74, 14 mars 1852; CE403-S22, 31 août 1876, 11 nov. 1882. LAC, MG 26, I, 91, 134; RG 31, C1, 1851, 1861, 1871, 1881, 1891, Durham and South Durham, Que. Sherbrooke Hist. Soc. (Sherbrooke, Que.), IP 464 (McCrea family papers). Ville de Sherbrooke, Div. du greffe, Rôles d'évaluation, Sherbrooke, 1905, 1911. *Sherbrooke Daily Record*, 23 March 1911, 27 Oct. 1925, 30 Oct. 1926. *La Tribune* (Sherbrooke), 15 mai 1930. "Attractive residence at Sherbrooke, Que.," *Contract Record* (Toronto), 23 (1909), no.19: 57–60. Can., House of Commons, *Debates*, 1911–25. "Death of Frank N. McCrea," *Canada Lumberman* (Toronto), 46 (1926), no.22: 46. J.-P. Kesteman *et al.*, *Histoire des Cantons de l'Est* (Sainte-Foy, Qué., 1998). *Men of today in the Eastern Townships*, intro. V. E. Morrill, comp. E. G. Pierce (Sherbrooke, 1917), 219–20. Thierry Nootens, "Men of today in the Eastern Townships, 1917: les notables sherbrookois à la fin de la Première Guerre mondiale," *Rev. d'études des Cantons de l'Est* (Lennoxville, Qué.), no.11 (automne 1997): 85–111. Gilles Piédalue, "Les groupes financiers et la guerre du papier au Canada, 1920–1930," *RHAF*, 30 (1976–77): 223–58. Ronald Rudin, "The transformation of the Eastern Townships of Richard William Heneker, 1855–1902," *Journal of Canadian Studies* (Peterborough, Ont.), 19 (1984–85), no.3: 32–49. *The storied province of Quebec; past and present*, ed. W. [C. H.] Wood *et al.* (5v., Toronto, 1931–32), 5: 572–73.

McCULLY, LAURA ELIZABETH, feminist, poet, journalist, and independent woman; b. 17 March 1886 in Toronto, one of three surviving children of Samuel Edward McCully, MD, and Helen Fitzgibbon; greatniece of Jonathan McCully*, a Father of Confederation; d. 7 July 1924 in Toronto.

Through her commitment to political equality for women and a life dedicated to work, public expression, and social reform, Laura McCully epitomizes the aspirations of many first-wave feminists. Although she was never a national figure in the manner of Helen Letitia McClung [Mooney*], she was well known in Toronto. Her career demonstrates that early feminism, which has sometimes been dismissed as too limited in its goals and too middle-class in its perspective, was a complex movement composed of women with a variety of views and experiences.

McCully's public expression began in childhood. She was a regular contributor of poetry and correspondence to the "Children's corner" of the Toronto *Daily Mail and Empire* and was profiled in *Harper's Bazaar* (New York) in 1899. She continued to write poetry throughout her life, publishing two volumes, *Mary Magdalene, and other poems* (Toronto, 1914) and *Bird of dawn, and other lyrics* (1919). The verse interweaves her love of the classical and of nature with her political views, moral perspective, and thoughts on the human condition. Her poem "Cassandra," for example, builds on the classical story to reflect her own views of life's quest:

Knowledge is pain, and love and life are pain
And every upward impulse from the clay
Is pain, and but by pain we have no growth.

Her work was sufficiently well known to be included in the first edition of John William Garvin*'s anthology *Canadian poets* (Toronto, 1916) and in the revised edition a decade later.

McCully was part of the first generation of Canadian women for whom the doors to university education were opening. After early studies at Deer Park Public School and Jarvis Street Collegiate Institute in Toronto, she obtained a BA in 1907 and an MA in 1908 from the University of Toronto. Her master's thesis, entitled "A critical study of Milton's theory of divorce," raises issues relating to the impact on women and children of divorce laws intended to favour men. The bitter separation of her own parents in the 1890s may have influenced her views. In 1909 McCully received a fellowship to study Anglo-Saxon at Yale University in New Haven, Conn. Reporting the event, the Toronto *World* of 2 October noted that this was "an honor that university has rarely accorded to a woman." It is not clear why McCully returned to Toronto in 1910 without completing her studies, but it is possible that court proceedings between her estranged parents were among the reasons.

The commitment McCully made to women's suffrage and feminism had emerged during her undergraduate years. She aligned herself with those who viewed votes for women as an equal right to be extended to them as human beings, not simply as a reward for their maternity. She sympathized with the militant tactics used by some British suffragists, although she did not believe them necessary in Canada. The image of women who could fight for a cause, stand firm against injustice, and make personal sacrifices inspired her. To advance the movement, she wrote about women's rights, participated in the first open-air suffrage rallies, including one in Orillia on 9 Aug. 1908, and was an active member of the Canadian Women's Suffrage Association. In an article published by *Maclean's* (Toronto) in January 1912, entitled "What women want," she described the desire for suffrage in part as a by-product of increased education, noting that after they began obtaining access to professions, women realized "however important education and the emancipation of the body, no human being is complete without the legal status of a citizen." In her writing and poetry, McCully discussed the inequality women faced. Single throughout her life, she reflected on the difficulties for those who sought to define themselves outside the accepted societal norm of wife and mother. Although she sometimes echoed the biases of the English Canadian community of which she was a part, writing, for example, that the female vote was needed to bolster Canadian voices against those of foreigners, her general approach to women's equality was to expand the horizons of all women.

The declaration of World War I created a moral dilemma for McCully, as it did for many suffragists. Although they viewed the war as evidence of the failure of male politics, only a few suffragists were able to maintain their pre-war pacifist beliefs in the face of the perceived threat to civilization. What separated

McCully from most suffragists who supported a role for women in winning the war was her ardent belief that they should have the right to bear arms during the crisis, or at least serve in an auxiliary military force. In 1915 she joined the Women's Home Guard to train with a view to relieving men for active duty. When the guard was ridiculed in the press, McCully responded with an April 1916 article in *Maclean's* entitled "The woman soldier: a by-product of the war." She disputed that gender differences were relevant to the issue, stressing the absolute necessity of using women to support the war effort.

By late 1916 McCully's active public life had begun to unravel. Diabetes and mental illness diagnosed as dementia praecox resulted in several hospital admissions between 1917 and 1923, a suicide attempt in 1917, and a descent into poverty. The thoughts that plagued McCully during these last years of her life are particularly poignant because they highlight doubts and fears that existed in a woman who seemed so strong. She became convinced that her reputation was being ruined by false allegations of pregnancy. She thought she was at risk of being forced into prostitution. She believed that others were taking credit for her poetry. Although the tone of McCully's comments was distorted, the nature of her fears reveals the vulnerability of women generally, and in particular single women who were leading lives for which precedents and role models were few.

McCully was committed to hospital for the last time in March 1923 and she died there on 7 July 1924 of complications from her diabetes. She was 38 years old. Toronto newspapers marked the passing of "one of the most brilliant of Toronto University graduates," "a young poet of remarkable ability," and "one of Toronto's most enthusiastic suffrage workers when it was an unfashionable thing."

In a society where most women's lives were preordained from cradle to grave, Laura McCully challenged established views of who women could aspire to be. Although her middle-class background may have made it easier for her to take the first steps toward education and work, what is significant is that she used her education to lead an unashamedly public life devoted to reform and women's rights.

Sophia Sperdakos

Further details concerning Laura Elizabeth McCully's life can be found in the author's exhaustively researched article "'For the joy of the working': Laura Elizabeth McCully, first-wave feminist," *OH*, 84 (1992): 283–314.

Additional poems by McCully appear in the *Univ. of Toronto Monthly*, 25 (1924–25) and in the university's newspaper, the *Varsity* (Toronto), between 1903 and 1908. A copy of her essay "The woman suffrage movement in Canada," published in an unidentified magazine in or around November 1914, is preserved in Univ. of Toronto Library, Thomas Fisher Rare Book Library, MS coll. 51 (Flora MacDonald Denison papers), box 8A. Her views on the war and the Women's Home Guard can be found in the Toronto *News*, 31 Aug. 1915.

AO, F 719; RG 10-20-B-2, no.16148; RG 10-20-G-1, no.1411. UTA, A1973-0026/258(56); T1979-0077(31).

McCURDY, ARTHUR WILLIAMS, businessman, editor, private secretary, photographer, inventor, and astronomer; b. 13 April 1856 in Truro, N.S., seventh child of David McCurdy and Mary Archibald; m. first 20 Sept. 1881 Lucy O'Brien in Windsor, N.S., and they had three sons and a daughter; m. secondly 2 Oct. 1902 Hattie Maria Mace in Montreal, and they had two daughters and a son; d. 1923 in Washington, D.C.

Arthur McCurdy was born to a prominent Nova Scotian family that traced its lineage back to a son of Daniel McCurdy of Ballykelly (Northern Ireland). This son (Arthur's great-grandfather), Alexander "the Pioneer," immigrated to Windsor, N.S., in 1765 after his marriage to Jennet Guthrie; they subsequently lived in Londonderry before acquiring a farm in Onslow. McCurdy's Presbyterian roots originate with this Alexander, a church elder for 20 years. His paternal grandfather, James, married into the Archibald family of Truro, as did his father.

McCurdy was nine when his father sold the Onslow farm and moved to Baddeck to take over the store established by his son-in-law Angus Tupper, who had died. After finishing public school, Arthur attended the collegiate institute in Whitby, Ont. He was articled as a law clerk for four years in a relative's firm, W. H. and A. Blanchard in Windsor, but he did not take the bar examinations. Instead, he returned to Baddeck to join the family enterprise, D. McCurdy and Son, from which his father's attention was diverted in 1873 by his election to the provincial legislature. A year after his marriage in 1881, Arthur acquired his father's share and, with his brother William Fraser, expanded the business by building a new wharf, opening a meat-curing operation, and starting the *Island Reporter*, which Arthur edited.

A life-changing event occurred when he met the inventor of the telephone during the visit of Alexander Graham Bell and his wife, Mabel Gardiner Hubbard, to Baddeck in the late summer of 1885. The McCurdys were early users of Bell's device: William had bought sets to link the store with his home and his father's. Family lore has it that Arthur was having difficulty with the store phone one day when a stranger walked over and repaired it. "How did you know how to fix that?" asked McCurdy. "My name is Alexander Graham Bell," replied the visitor. Bell was so taken by Baddeck that, on his return to his home in Washington, he wrote to Mrs Kate M. Dunlop of the Telegraph House hotel, where he had stayed, to say that he and his wife wished to return the next year and acquire a cottage. She recommended Arthur as an agent; the Bells' first purchase was a farm home on Crescent Grove, next door to his parents. Bell and McCurdy became fast friends – they played chess and each had ceaseless curiosity and a love of invention.

At the same time, McCurdy's family was growing. His third child, John Alexander Douglas*, was born in 1886. But Cape Breton was entering a period of economic decline, which precipitated the failure of the McCurdy business in 1887. Fortunately, Arthur was offered employment by Bell as his private secretary, and for the next 15 years he would divide his time between Baddeck and Washington. Both Bell and Mabel developed a special bond with the young man. Enthusiastic and driven by a boundless energy, McCurdy cut a striking figure – he was tall and had a prominent moustache and Vandyke beard. An inveterate outdoorsman, he led the Bells on camping trips and taught them how to use snowshoes and shoot. On one visit to a Micmac (Mi'kmaw) village, he photographed them next to two tepees, adjacent to newly constructed telephone poles. Daisy Bell later recalled that he gave her parents "a kind of young friendship that they never had with anyone else. . . . they did things with him that they could never have done without him."

They soon outgrew their first residence. Bell had fallen in love with Red Head peninsula, on Baddeck Bay, and he tasked McCurdy to acquire the property and 50 adjacent acres. Together they designed The Lodge, the Bells' rustic home on the point. The association deepened following the death of Lucy McCurdy on 25 March 1888, a week after the birth of another son. Although their children were brought up by Arthur's sister Georgina, they became part of the Bells' extended family. The McCurdys could also claim a relationship through Mabel's mother, Gertrude Mercer McCurdy.

Bell broadened Arthur's duties in 1889 when he reopened his Washington-based laboratory with McCurdy as one of two assistants. In addition to working on experiments, he took daily dictation of Bell's thoughts in "Lab Notes" and "Home Notes," designated by where each book was kept. "You are my private secretary and Alter Ego to the world," Bell told him in a letter in December 1896. The same exchange revealed that Bell's office habits could be a source of irritation. "Our work," he wrote, "is actually in a chaotic condition. . . . This is entirely my own fault, and I sympathize with you in having to work with such an unsystematic man as myself." McCurdy responded on 28 January with some strong suggestions to Bell to rectify this disarray: "1. You [must] come to the office in some sort of season, and not put off office work until three or four o'clock and in the afternoon. 2. Don't take letters away from the files of the office and expect me to find them when wanted. 3. Don't take unanswered letters away, and expect me to answer them."

Along with his administrative duties, McCurdy was the first employee to record visually the inventor's experiments and activities. Like Bell, he embraced the art and science of photography. He took one of the most famous images of Alexander and Mabel, holding hands during a visit in 1898 to Sable Island, N.S.

In 1899 McCurdy's love of photography led to the development of one of his own successful inventions. His small portable tank for developing film in daytime, dubbed the Ebedec (the Indian name for Baddeck), has been used by generations of photographers. With financial assistance from Bell, he spent three years commercializing it. After obtaining a United States patent in 1902, he sold the rights to Eastman Kodak. The first model, which he presented to Mabel, is now in the Bell Museum at Baddeck. He left Bell's employ in 1902 to pursue invention full-time, including a method of printing statistical maps using interchangeable "map type." Some months later he married Hattie Mace of Sydenham, Ont., a niece of Bell's stepmother, and they moved to Toronto, where their first child was born in 1903. That same year he was awarded the John Scott premium and medal of the Franklin Institute in Philadelphia for his success in invention. A second child was born in 1905 in Baddeck, where, in the summer of 1906, McCurdy's son Douglas, an engineering student at the University of Toronto, began helping Bell design and fly heavier-than-air craft. The Bells adored Douglas and had tried to adopt him after his mother's death.

By then, McCurdy had moved his family to British Columbia and set up a laboratory at his country home outside Victoria. He continued to photograph and was active in community affairs; named the first president of the local Canadian Club in 1907, he also pursued his keen interest in nature. For instance, he wrote about Victoria's climate for the *National Geographic Magazine* (Washington) in 1907. As president of the Natural History Society of British Columbia, he promoted the establishment of a federal observatory and seismological and meteorological research station, built on Gonzales Hill north of the city in 1913 and headed by Francis Napier Denison*. On 6 March 1914 he chaired a meeting and lecture by federal astronomer John Stanley Plaskett*, at which time the Victoria centre of the Royal Astronomical Society of Canada was organized with Denison as president and McCurdy as vice-president. Through his connection to Denison, he lobbied Ottawa to construct a major astronomical facility on Vancouver Island [see William Frederick King*]. Begun on Little Saanich Mountain near Victoria in mid 1915 and opened two years later under Plaskett's direction, the Dominion Astrophysical Observatory was to house a 72-inch reflecting telescope; installed by May 1918, it was, for a few months, the largest in the world until superseded by the 100-inch instrument at Mount Wilson, Calif.

In 1916 McCurdy had run for a seat in British Columbia's legislature as the Liberal candidate in the riding of Esquimalt. Although he was declared elected on 21 November by a two-vote margin over Conservative candidate Robert Henry Pooley, he resigned over alleged irregularities in taking the soldiers' vote. Pooley emerged from a recount with a two-vote victory.

McCurdy died at his Washington home of heart failure in 1923. "He interested himself in the things of life which count," stated one obituary, and had a "life well spent."

LAWRENCE SURTEES

Correspondence between Arthur Williams McCurdy and Alexander Graham Bell is found in the A. G. Bell family papers (0330M) at the Library of Congress, Manuscript Div., in Washington. The finding aid to this enormous collection, as well as much of Bell's correspondence, including that with McCurdy between 1889 and 1903, is available on the internet. Many of the photographs taken by McCurdy for Bell are housed in the G. H. Grosvenor coll. in the Library of Congress, Prints and Photographs Div. The Bell Museum at the Alexander Graham Bell National Hist. Site of Canada in Baddeck, N.S., has the journals known as "Home Notes," vols.1–135, and "Lab Notes," vols.1–75. McCurdy is the author of "Factors which modify the climate of Victoria," *National Geographic Magazine* (Washington), 18 (1907): 345–48. The year of his death is based on a clipping of an otherwise undated obituary from the *Daily Colonist* (Victoria), 1923.

BCM-G, RBMB, St George's Anglican Church (Montreal), 2 Oct. 1902. R. P. Broughton, *Looking up: a history of the Royal Astronomical Society of Canada* (Toronto, 1994). R. V. Bruce, *Bell: Alexander Graham Bell and the conquest of solitude* (Boston, 1973). *Genealogical record & biographical sketches of the McCurdys of Nova Scotia*, comp. H. P. Blanchard (London, 1930). E. S. Grosvenor and Morgan Wesson, *Alexander Graham Bell: the life and times of the man who invented the telephone* (New York, 1997). Dorothy Harley Eber, *Genius at work: images of Alexander Graham Bell* (New York, 1982). J. H. Parkin, *Bell and Baldwin: their development of aerodromes and hydrodromes at Baddeck, Nova Scotia* (Toronto, 1964). A. D. Watson, "Astronomy in Canada," Royal Astronomical Soc. of Canada, *Journal* (Toronto), 11 (1917): [47]–78.

MACDONALD, Sir HUGH JOHN, lawyer, militia officer, politician, and police magistrate; b. 13 March 1850 in Kingston, Upper Canada, only surviving son of John A. Macdonald* and Isabella Clark; m. first 1 June 1876 Mary Jean King, née Murray (d. 1881), and they had a daughter; m. secondly 23 April 1883 Agnes Gertrude Vankoughnet in Toronto, and they had a son who died young; d. 29 March 1929 in Winnipeg.

Hugh Macdonald grew up in Kingston and in Toronto, where his family moved in 1856. His father, who had become attorney general of the province two years earlier, was frequently absent. Following the death of his mother in 1857 he returned to Kingston and spent his formative years in the care of his father's sister Margaret and her husband, the Reverend James Williamson*. A Presbyterian minister and professor at Queen's College, Williamson imparted to Hugh a ritual anti-Catholicism and he instilled in him a streak of intolerance which was missing in his father. Hugh would keep these views to himself, revealing them only rarely in private correspondence with Williamson.

Macdonald was educated at the Queen's College School in Kingston and at the University of Toronto, from which he graduated BA in 1869. He then studied law, first in Ottawa and later with Robert Alexander Harrison* in Toronto. After he was called to the bar in 1872, he practised, usually in partnership with his father, in Toronto and Kingston.

At an early age Macdonald had shown an interest in the militia and he saw active service on three occasions. He spent the summer of 1866 with the 14th Battalion Volunteer Militia Rifles near Cornwall in anticipation of a Fenian invasion. In 1870 he joined the expedition of Colonel Garnet Joseph Wolseley* and made the trek to the Red River settlement (Man.) as an ensign in the 16th Company of the 1st (Ontario) Battalion of Rifles. During the North-West rebellion in 1885 [*see* Louis Riel*] he would serve as lieutenant in the 90th (Winnipeg) Battalion of Rifles, a unit he helped to organize. He saw action at Fish Creek (Sask.).

In 1882 Macdonald moved to Winnipeg, perhaps for personal reasons after the death of his first wife or because of the possibilities the west offered to well-connected lawyers. For the next 30 years he practised there in partnership with James Stewart Tupper, a son of his father's colleague Sir Charles Tupper*, and with a variety of others. He would be named a QC in 1890. Throughout the 1880s he was an informal agent in Manitoba for his father, now prime minister of Canada. During the 1890s he took a more active part in both national and provincial politics. In the federal general election of 1891 he reluctantly accepted the Conservative nomination in Winnipeg and he won the constituency with a majority of 500 votes. Up to that time he had been known as Hugh and signed Hugh J. During the campaign, newspaper advertisements referred to him as Hugh John (thus emphasizing the link to his father) and he was known by those names ever after. He resigned his seat on 4 May 1893. Although he claimed the primary reason for his resignation was financial, there were several others. One was his shy and retiring nature combined with a distaste for public life. A second was his determination to elude the shadow of his illustrious father. Equally important were his views on important issues facing the federal Conservative government. He had supported the laws the provincial Liberal government of Thomas Greenway* had passed abolishing the official use of the French language and ending public support for denominational schools. He thus opposed the federal government's commitment to redress the injuries suffered by the Catholic minority in Manitoba.

In late 1894 Macdonald declined the entreaties of Prime Minister Mackenzie Bowell* that he return to political life in the interests of the Conservative party. Two years later, however, he acceded to a similar request from Prime Minister Sir Charles Tupper. What enabled Tupper to succeed where Bowell had failed was his own insistence, the efforts of his son James Stewart, and Macdonald's own respect for the prime minister. On 1 May 1896 Macdonald joined the short-lived Tupper government as minister of the interior and superintendent general of Indian affairs. In the federal general election held in June he again won in Winnipeg, but he resigned his government posts with Tupper in July and was unseated by judicial decision the following year after a formal protest by his opponent, Joseph MARTIN. He did not contest the ensuing by-election. After the election of June 1896, an element in the Conservative party regarded him as a possible future leader.

In March 1897 Macdonald took on the leadership of the Manitoba Conservatives. The party hierarchy, local and federal, arranged this move, perhaps to give him political experience and to keep him in the public eye. In the provincial election of 7 Dec. 1899 he led the party to a narrow victory and won by 60 votes in his own riding of Winnipeg South. In its first year his administration enacted laws to tax corporations, reform the franchise, and reduce expenditures. The most important legislation was the Liquor Act drafted by James Albert Manning AIKINS to outlaw the sale of intoxicating beverages.

At the end of his first legislative session Macdonald resigned as premier and as a member of the assembly. He had done his part for the provincial Conservatives, many of whom wished him to make way for the return of Rodmond Palen Roblin* as party leader. At the same time, the federal party thought he had more use in their sphere. Tupper and Roblin, among others, persuaded him to contest Brandon in the federal general election of 1900, apparently believing that the incumbent, Clifford SIFTON, was vulnerable. In 1899 Conservatives had won 9 of the 12 provincial seats in Sifton's federal riding and their organization hoped that with the right candidate they could be successful again. The federal Tories also thought that a contest against Sifton would test Macdonald's leadership potential. Sifton won Brandon with a decisive majority, however, and Macdonald withdrew from public life again.

For the next decade, Macdonald practised law. Then, in December 1911 the Roblin government appointed him Winnipeg's police magistrate, a position he would hold for the remainder of his life. On 11 June 1913 he was made a knight bachelor. Two years later he was a member of the commission chaired by judge Thomas Graham Mathers which investigated charges of financial irregularities in the construction of Manitoba's legislative buildings. The commission unanimously found Roblin and several of his colleagues guilty of conspiracy to defraud the province. During the labour unrest of 1917–18, Macdonald opposed the unionization of the police force and stood in the front line of reaction during the Winnipeg General Strike of 1919 [see Mike Sokolowiski*]. In its aftermath he favoured the wholesale deportation of "undesirable aliens." He survived the amputation of a leg in 1927, but two years later he would not consent to a second amputation. Infection led to his death on 29 March 1929.

As a politician, Hugh John Macdonald was of only secondary importance. His principal value lay in the surname he had inherited. Ironically, he had grown up apart from his father and thus did not share the tolerant views long associated with the Macdonald name. When the Conservative party called on the Old Chieftain's heir, it found not another John A. but a second James Williamson. Throughout his life he had tried in vain to escape the comparisons to his father. In the end, his loyalty to the party and to the memory of his father overcame his natural aversion to public life, with consequences which were often not in his own best interests. In his public careers his sometimes romantic, often meticulous, and always courteous manner contributed to the popular affection he enjoyed.

HAL J. GUEST

AO, RG 80-5-0-70, no.12878; RG 80-5-0-122, no.14879. LAC, MG 26, A; D; F; MG 27, II, D15 (mfm. at Univ. of Man. Libraries, Winnipeg). QUA, James Williamson fonds. *Manitoba Free Press*, 1883–1929. *Winnipeg Telegram*, 1899–1920. *Winnipeg Tribune*, 1891–1929. *Affectionately yours; the letters of Sir John A. Macdonald and his family*, ed. and intro. J. K. Johnson (Toronto, 1969). H. J. Guest, "The Old Man's son: Sir Hugh John Macdonald," Man., Hist. and Scientific Soc., *Papers* (Winnipeg), 3rd ser., no.29 (1972–73): 49–67; "Reluctant politician: a biography of Sir Hugh John Macdonald" (MA thesis, Univ. of Man., 1973). G. P. Macleod, "Sir Hugh John Macdonald," Man., Hist. and Scientific Soc., *Papers*, 3rd ser., no.14 (1957–58): 33–53. R. St G. Stubbs, *Lawyers and laymen of western Canada* (Toronto, 1939).

MACDONALD, JAMES ALEXANDER, editor, Presbyterian minister, school principal, orator, social reformer, and author; b. 22 Jan. 1862 in East Williams Township, Upper Canada, son of John Alexander Macdonald, a farmer, and Jane Grant; m. 11 June 1890 Grace Lumsden Christian in Oil City, Ont., and they had two sons and a daughter; d. 14 May 1923 in Toronto.

James A. Macdonald traced his ancestry to Glen Urquhart in the Highlands of Scotland. His great-great-grandfather had survived the battle of Culloden in 1746, immigrated to North Carolina, and fought with his sons on the side of the British in the American revolution. The family subsequently moved to Pictou County, N.S., and then to East Williams. Gaelic was the first language for many in the community where Macdonald grew up. The congregation he attended was a Free Church that stayed out of the Presbyterian unions of 1861 and 1875 to remain true to the principle of Christ's headship over both church and state. Throughout his youth Macdonald was nonetheless influenced by the Presbyterian tradition in southwestern Ontario that was closely allied with the political Liberalism of George Brown*, Oliver Mowat*, and the Toronto *Globe*.

Macdonald attended school in East Williams and the collegiate institutes in Hamilton and Toronto. In 1878 he entered the University of Toronto, where George Paxton Young*, professor of mental and moral philosophy, made the greatest impression on him with his emphasis on critical thinking and Christian belief. From 1883 to 1887 he studied at Knox College in Toronto; its principal, William Caven*, also had a lasting influence on Macdonald. In a period of theological turmoil, when men of learning were calling upon the church to prove the fundamental truths of Christianity, Macdonald found in him a mentor who accepted devout biblical criticism and cautious theological reformulation "without either undue elation or anxious fear." He took from Caven's teaching "a strong, positive, evangelical Christianity," whose purpose was to engage the challenge of modern thought. Caven deepened for Macdonald the integration of social and political activism and Christianity that characterized the liberalism of Brown and Mowat.

Macdonald began his career in journalism at Knox. In 1885 he joined the editorial staff of the *Knox College Monthly*, established in 1883 to disseminate college news and debate the faith. Under Macdonald's leadership until 1892, the *Monthly* greatly expanded its size, subscription list, and reputation. He discussed the most pressing questions of biblical and theological thought and modern research methods, and began to pay attention to missions in the Canadian west and overseas. He explored the application of Christian principles to the social problems that were emerging with immigration and urbanization. As well, he reviewed theological and devotional literature and commended those writers who defended traditional doctrines in new ways. After graduating in 1887 and winning the Fischer Scholarship in systematic theology, he continued to edit the *Monthly* and served as the college's librarian.

Macdonald's commitment to a progressive interpretation of evangelicalism was solidified on a visit in 1888–89 to Scotland, where he attracted the notice of newspapers in Edinburgh for his prowess in the pulpit and on the speaker's platform. Old Testament scholar George Adam Smith, New Testament expert Marcus Dods, theologian Alexander Balmain Bruce, and natural scientist Henry Drummond were particularly influential on him, and their fight for progressive evangelicalism was followed closely in the *Monthly* and in Macdonald's subsequent papers. Macdonald's ardent Scottishness bolstered his interests. A member of the Gaelic Society of Toronto since 1887, he bemoaned the death of the language among ministers. In the *Monthly* in 1888 he had insisted that the preacher and the orator needed the "mystic element," a feature he associated with his Celtic heritage. His friend Sir Robert Alexander Falconer* would note in an obituary that "Celtic fire" marked his oratory. Alfred Gandier, a room-mate in Edinburgh and a close colleague while principal of Knox, said he had "the Highlander's mysticism and his deep religious nature."

In 1891 Macdonald was ordained and appointed to Knox Presbyterian Church in St Thomas, Ont. The following year he resigned from the *Monthly*, though he continued to write and edit. Most notably, he edited *From far Formosa* . . . (Toronto, 1896), the biography of missionary George Leslie Mackay*. A serious student of preaching, Macdonald had claimed in the *Monthly* that the early preachers who took their bearings from the doctrine of the Atonement, such as the apostle Paul, Luther, and Calvin, were "the tide-marks of Christian progress." Preaching combined "a sympathetic soul, the poet's brooding spirit, [and] the prophet's master-passion." In St Thomas his reputation as a speaker grew. The venues for his oratory included congregations throughout the Anglo-American world, church and peace conferences, men's organizations, business and professional associations, civic and service clubs, and universities. His topic, with a multitude of variations, was the Christianization of civilization. Christ's love, standard of service, and goal of universal brotherhood, Macdonald would tell the Canadian National Missionary Congress of 1909, would redeem public life from "shoddy sentiment in public speech and from dishonesty in public office and from all forms of graft and malfeasance in public service . . . [and] from the pagan ideals that have made it sordid and mean." Liberty, democracy, and internationalism would promote these ends. By the time of his death, Macdonald was reputed to have spoken to more people outside the dominion than any other Canadian of his generation.

In 1896 Macdonald returned to Toronto to become principal of the Presbyterian Ladies' College (a position he would hold for five years) and, more significantly, edit the *Westminster*, a new Presbyterian monthly that sought to apply Christian principles to every dimension of life. Its publisher, the Westminster

631

Company, was incorporated in 1897 under the presidency of Christopher Blackett Robinson, and by 1902 it had acquired and consolidated a number of smaller journals to create the weekly *Presbyterian* and to expand the *Westminster*. In his editorial work on both Macdonald displayed the moral optimism and belief in social renewal that he brought to all his efforts. His enthusiasm and related liberal sentiment are caught in his publication in *Westminster* in October 1897 of a poem by Presbyterian radical John Wilson BENGOUGH, who saw in the newly elected Liberal prime minister, Sir Wilfrid Laurier*, the "ruling hand of God"

As the tribes of old beheld it
  On the wide Egyptian plain,
Bringing gracious peace and union
  Out of long-borne strife and pain.

The Westminster Company also began to publish popular fiction and devotional literature. Its most famous author was the Reverend Charles William Gordon* of Winnipeg, a Knox classmate and co-editor with Macdonald of the *Knox College Monthly* in the 1880s. Macdonald encouraged Gordon to rework some of his earlier writings in the *Monthly* as fiction, to be published in the *Westminster* to promote the cause of missions in western Canada. The result was the early chapters of *Black Rock: a tale of the Selkirks* (Toronto, 1898), the first of Gordon's several best-selling novels under the pen-name Ralph Connor. Its success, and his own writing, may have helped motivate Macdonald to join in the formation of the Canadian Authors' Club in 1899. Another classmate and *Monthly* editor who came to work with him was the Reverend Robert Haddow; with western representative Malcolm McGregor, Haddow took over the direction of the *Presbyterian* and the *Westminster* when Macdonald accepted the invitation to become managing editor of the *Globe* on 1 Jan. 1903.

Macdonald's move to Canada's largest daily newspaper, and the Liberal party's chief journal in Ontario, surprised many. The *Globe*'s board, chaired by owner Robert Jaffray* and including Methodist layman Newton Wesley Rowell*, felt that Macdonald would uphold the paper's Liberal and evangelical traditions. In a final editorial in the *Presbyterian*, on 10 Jan. 1903, Macdonald insisted that the *Globe* was not simply "a party organ, but also a great paper, true in motive and purpose to the ethical principles and moral truths underlying all sound politics and high service." One of his models as he moved into secular publishing was British journalist, social reformer, and peace activist William Thomas Stead. The *Globe*'s directors were undoubtedly aware of Macdonald's own involvement in public affairs, most recently in support of Prohibition in the provincial referendum of December 1902.

The provincial Liberal government, in power since 1872, was led by an ageing George William Ross*. Internal tensions and charges of corruption marked his administration as Macdonald assumed his editorial duties. On 9 Nov. 1903 Macdonald attacked the decay of the ship of state: "There is but one thing open to the Liberals of Ontario, and that thing is their first and most pressing duty. The barnacles on the ship must be treated with an iron hand." Late in the election campaign that led to the defeat of the government in January 1905, Macdonald articulated his attitudes to party loyalty in another lead editorial. The *Globe* sought the public good, and supported those men and measures that served it best. These were found most frequently in the Liberal ranks, but the notion that the paper was obligated to support anything done by Liberal leaders was "offensive to every self-respecting newspaperman." On the federal level, the issue that most strained the bonds of loyalty for Macdonald and the *Globe* was the Autonomy Bills of 1905 and their educational clauses. Laurier wanted to extend the right of Roman Catholics to separate schools in the new provinces of Alberta and Saskatchewan. Macdonald and the *Globe*, speaking for many Ontario Protestants, stood on the Liberal doctrine of provincial rights and insisted that the new provinces should determine their own school policies. Macdonald's zeal for public and political purity led to what journalist Hector Willoughby Charlesworth* described as "slanderous invective," which resulted in a string of libel suits from Conservative politicians attacked in the *Globe*. The most celebrated case, that of George Eulas Foster*, the veteran MP accused in 1908 of pocketing profits illegally from business dealings, ended with Macdonald's acquittal in 1910.

His tenure as editor (1903–15) was a period of intense activity and public engagement. He seemed to be constantly writing, speaking, and taking on new responsibilities. In journalism, he served as a director of the Canadian Associated Press and in 1909 he attended the Imperial Press Conference in Britain, where he was most struck by the unemployed and the destitute – the "human sediment" – of the large cities. Appointed in 1906 to the University of Toronto's newly reorganized board of governors, he helped bring in Falconer as president in 1907; he received honorary doctorates from the universities of Glasgow (1909) and Edinburgh (1911), as well as Oberlin College in Ohio (1915). By 1912 he was a trustee of the Toronto General Hospital and a vice-president of the Toronto Conservatory of Music; he sat on the board of management of Knox College and the executive committee of the Dominion Alliance for the Total Suppression of the Liquor Traffic. He also remained active in church affairs within his own denomination and throughout the ecumenical networks. He was a founding member of the Board of Moral and Social Reform of the Presbyterian Church in 1907. That same year, he and C. W. Gordon introduced the Presbyterian Brotherhood to Canada as a means of mobilizing laymen. The same motive prompted Macdonald's involvement in the Laymen's Missionary Movement. A strong supporter of church union since the 1880s, he used his papers to further that cause. Such broad engagement could not be sustained without criticism. Some contemporaries found him overbearing. The Methodist *Christian Guardian* wondered how a Prohibitionist could justify liquor advertising in the *Globe*. In 1913 Toronto meat packer Joseph Wesley Flavelle*, whom Macdonald had once attacked as a monopolist, found in the reverend editor's support for Laurier's naval platform a transparently dishonest kind of partisan Christianity. Still, Macdonald's position at the *Globe*, convincing oratory, and public involvement made him the most influential clergyman of his generation in Canadian life.

In 1911 the Ontario Liberal leadership had been assumed by N. W. Rowell, a supportive colleague of Macdonald in moral and social reform movements, the promotion of missions, and the church union debate. Rowell in turn enjoyed Macdonald's backing in his reorganization of the Liberals, his stance on temperance, and his campaign in 1911 for reciprocity, an issue that split Toronto's Liberals and cost Laurier re-election. Macdonald's support ended with World War I. While Rowell moved to strengthen the war effort, Macdonald's moderate pacifism led him to a hesitant support and a critical view of Britain's role in encouraging militarism. His mild endorsement and peaceful rhetoric sprang from a need to preserve democratic tradition. "At bottom the war now involving all Europe and menacing the world," he wrote in the *Globe* on 4 Aug. 1914, "is humanity's own life struggle, the struggle for freedom, for national integrity, for free citizenship in a free democracy of the nations. It is the old struggle of the spirit of humanity, liberated and impassioned, against arrogant and privileged autocracy." At the same time, Macdonald's presence exerted a moderating influence on the *Globe*'s response to the war; his editorials that fall discouraged the fanning of anti-German sympathies among the dominion's young people.

Macdonald left the *Globe* suddenly on 24 Nov. 1915, claiming he wanted freedom to pursue literary and other endeavours. His *Democracy and the nations: a Canadian view* had come out in Toronto that year; Canadian reviewers found his championship of American democracy "problematical." His resignation, in fact, came at the end of a heated controversy in the Toronto papers over his participation in peace rallies in the United States and his ties with American leaders who opposed any involvement in the war effort. From 1911 he had been a director of the Boston-based World Peace Foundation, founded by pub-

lisher Edwin Ginn. Macdonald's denunciation of "arrogant Imperialism" in Philadelphia in October 1914 was a typical tirade. His anti-war address in Detroit in April 1915 was met with the "spontaneous" gift of a motor car from automobile giant and anti-war activist Henry Ford. Macdonald's acceptance of this present, his soft-pedalling in the *Globe* of Ford's opposition to American support for the Allied war loan, and his continuing pacifism (at a time of growing war fervour in Canada), combined with discontent among *Globe* staff and directors over his inattention to business and frequent absences on speaking tours, led to a showdown with the board. Even advertisers were upset. Ford's rival in the Canadian market, the McLaughlin Motor Car Company [*see* Robert MCLAUGHLIN], was stated by *Globe* reporter Melvin Ormond Hammond to have pulled its advertising until Macdonald was removed. When he resigned, there was evidently considerable satisfaction among the staff. "Most of them," Hammond diarized, "dislike if not despise Macdonald for his shirking of work, as it appears to them, and for his hogging of the lime light." Thomas Stewart Lyon, who had overseen day-to-day operations of the paper during most of Macdonald's tenure, replaced him.

Macdonald continued to write for the *Globe* and other publications and speak on a regular basis, frequently in the United States, which would not enter the war until the spring of 1917. At the same time his wife, Grace, was an active participant in Red Cross work and a member of the Ontario Women's Liberal Association, which in May 1917 passed a motion of no-confidence in the Conservative government's conduct of the war. Macdonald's growing conviction that German aggression had to be stopped did not prevent him from constantly emphasizing that the primary purpose of the war effort was to restore peace. He remained critical of the militarism and the jingoism on both sides. He saw peace emerging from a continental war effort. In a speech in New York in January 1916, he had urged such a unified response: "for North America not to rise to the tragic solemnity of the hour – that would be for this generation of Americans to renounce their Pilgrim fathers, to repudiate Washington, to prove unworthy of Montcalm and Wolfe." In 1917 he delivered the Cole Lectures at Vanderbilt University in Tennessee. Published that year in Toronto as *The North American idea*, they expressed his mature thoughts on liberty, democracy, and international peace. He held up the relationship of Canada and the United States as an example of international neighbourliness. The North American "idea" was the right of a free people to govern themselves, and he urged Canadians to enlist and fight in its defence. Macdonald traced the origins of the idea to the Celtic strain in British, American, and Canadian life and found its most valuable quality in loyalty to oaths.

Macdonald

Moral obligation in public life was the key issue in the fight against German autocracy and militarism, he argued, just as he had in editorials at the beginning of the war. The conflict had to be joined, he told his audience at Vanderbilt, but the motives had to be clear and pure. Prior to and throughout the war, he had reservations about the motives of Britain as well as Germany. Shortly after speaking at Vanderbilt, he experienced a series of physical and mental breakdowns, which forced his retirement.

Materialism and militarism, in Macdonald's analysis, were the primary forces impeding the triumph of righteousness in public affairs. His sense of vocation in promoting this goal was shaped by a prophetic moral imagination and a Celtic spirituality. These influences led to his advocacy of a progressive Christianity as the solution to the world's problems, but the war destroyed the underpinnings and credibility of his ideas. Macdonald's breakdowns in 1917, which led to his death in 1923, resulted in part from the toll of his travels but also from his despair at the return of barbarism and the failure of his beloved vision of Christianizing civilization through liberty, democracy, and internationalism.

BRIAN J. FRASER

James Alexander Macdonald's publications include "A biographical sketch," in William Caven, *Christ's teaching concerning the last things, and other papers* (London and Toronto, 1908), xiii–xxxii; "The Christianization of our civilization," in Canadian National Missionary Congress, *Canada's missionary congress: addresses delivered at the Canadian National Missionary Congress, held in Toronto, March 31 to April 4, 1909, with reports of committees* (Toronto, 1909), 115–21; *What a newspaper man saw in Britain* (Toronto, 1909); and *William T. Stead and his peace message* (Boston, 1912).

AO, F 1075-3, [M. O. Hammond], "Ninety years of the *Globe*" (typescript, [1934]); F 1075-5, 23–24 Nov. 1915; RG 80-5-0-178, no.6119; RG 80-8-0-910, no.4243. UCC-C, Biog. file. *Globe*, 9 Nov. 1903, 15 May 1923. Michael Bliss, *A Canadian millionaire: the life and business times of Sir Joseph Flavelle, bart., 1858–1939* (Toronto, 1978). *Canadian annual rev.*, 1901–20. *Canadian men and women of the time* (Morgan; 1898 and 1912). H. [W.] Charlesworth, *Candid chronicles: leaves from the note book of a Canadian journalist* (Toronto, 1925), 210; *More candid chronicles: further leaves from the note book of a Canadian journalist* (Toronto, 1928), 122. B. J. Fraser, *Church, college, and clergy: a history of theological education at Knox College, Toronto, 1844–1994* (Montreal and Kingston, Ont., 1995); "Peacemaking among Presbyterians in Canada, 1900–1945," in *Peace, war and God's justice*, ed. T. D. Parker and B. J. Fraser (Toronto, 1989), 126–31; *The social uplifters: Presbyterian progressives and the Social Gospel in Canada, 1875–1915* (Waterloo, Ont., 1988). *Knox College Monthly* (Toronto), 1 (1883)–5 (1887); continued as *Knox College Monthly and Presbyterian Magazine*, 6 (1887)–20 (1896). J. P. MacPhie, *Pictonians at home and abroad: sketches of professional men and women of Pictou County; its history and institutions* (Boston, 1914). *Outlook* (New York), 30 May 1923. D. M. Page, "Canada as the exponent of North American idealism," *American Rev. of Canadian Studies* (Washington), 3 (1973), no.2: 30–46. Margaret Prang, *N. W. Rowell, Ontario nationalist* (Toronto and Buffalo, N.Y., 1975). *Presbyterian* (Toronto), new ser., 1 (July–December 1902): 5; 2 (January–June 1903): 37–38. J. D. Rabb, "Canadian idealism, philosophical federalism, and world peace," *Dialogue* ([Waterloo]), 25 (1986): 93–103. T. P. Socknat, *Witness against war: pacifism in Canada, 1900–1945* (Toronto, 1987). *Westminster* (Toronto), new ser., 3 (July–December 1897): 293, 406–7; 9 (July–December 1900): 686–87; 13 (January–June 1902): 603. World Peace Foundation, *The World Peace Foundation: its present activities* (Boston, 1912).

MACDONALD, JOHN KAY, office holder, businessman, and philanthropist; b. 12 Oct. 1837 in Edinburgh, youngest son of Donald Macdonald and Elizabeth MacKay; m. 4 Dec. 1867 Charlotte Emily Perley (d. 26 Aug. 1902) in Burford Township, Ont., and they had three sons and one daughter; d. 4 July 1928 in Toronto.

John K. Macdonald's parents moved from their native Caithness to Edinburgh, where his father was a dairy farmer. The youngest of ten children, John recalled the building of the memorial to Sir Walter Scott but remembered little else of his birthplace before he was sent to join his family in 1845 on a farm in Chinguacousy Township, northwest of Toronto. He attended grammar school in Weston (Toronto), worked on the farm, and then, hoping to become a Presbyterian missioner, entered Knox College in Toronto. In 1863, after one session, he opted for financial administration, as assistant to James Scott Howard*, treasurer of the United Counties of York and Peel. He succeeded Howard in 1866. Following Peel's separation a year later, he continued as treasurer of York (with offices in Toronto) and was appointed a justice of the peace.

Macdonald was apparently drawn to the study of life insurance in 1869, soon after the federal government had begun regulating the industry. This governance created openings for Canadian companies when a number of American and British firms, faced with maintaining assets in Canada to cover their liabilities, chose to leave instead. As county treasurer, Macdonald understood finance, but he also saw provision for others through insurance as an instrument of social benevolence, a near-religious credence that would never waver. Begun as the Dominion Life Association – its name changed in March 1871 in the process of parliamentary incorporation – the Confederation Life Association was the creation of Macdonald and a group of high-profile business figures. The founding president was finance minister Sir Francis Hincks*, with Lieutenant Governor William Pearce Howland*

and Senator William McMaster* as vice-presidents. Named provisional manager in April, Macdonald was pushed to the brink of personal collapse by the organizational burdens: heavy correspondence, chronic eye strain, actuarial preparations, capitalization, travels to Quebec, New Brunswick, and Nova Scotia, and vindictive opposition from John Malcolm Trout, a commercial editor who had been cut out of the controlling clique. In addition, he still held the treasurership of York and troublesome investments he had made in mining operations in Nova Scotia. Although he resigned in July, to be replaced by William McCabe*, Macdonald continued a presence at Confederation Life, which began business in November. He reviewed this business, took out the first policy, was elected a director in December 1872 and a vice-president a year later, and was back with new energy as acting manager in September 1874. Confirmed as manager early the next year, in July he moved the company's offices from the Masonic Hall on Toronto Street to the nearby Temple Chambers. By this time he had begun his pattern of recuperative trips to the northern bush, "to comfort and rough it" in Muskoka he told his brother Daniel.

For the next two decades, the management of Confederation Life rested heavily on Macdonald's shoulders as it moved to establish a place among such competitors as Canada Life (established 1847), Sun Life (1865), London Life (1874), and Mutual Life (1874). He made inspection tours of the provinces and territories, built up networks of agents, and spread the gospel of insurance. Some regions required more work than others: "our cause seems virtually dead" in New Brunswick, he lamented in 1877, but adjustments in the Quebec City area had improved business there. The supervision of district agents required much of Macdonald's time, the firm application of his temperance principles, and a readiness to jettison the errant or the unproductive. After company actuary Professor John Bradford Cherriman* left in 1875 to become federal superintendent of insurance, Macdonald continued their frank exchanges on insurance matters. Ever blunt, he made no secret of his dislike for Cherriman's early "industrial scheme" for insuring clerks, artisans, and mechanics, favoured reduced rates for clergymen, and in 1880 toyed with the idea of replacing medical examinations with "stiff warranties." The company's investments were conservatively sound, mortgages and municipal debentures mostly, and there Macdonald's knowledge as a county treasurer was beneficial. Though rarely innovative, Confederation Life proved successful: by early 1877, with 5,177 policies and $7,339,167 in insurance in force, it trailed only Sun Life, where Robertson Macaulay* was secretary. Overall, American companies dominated. Macdonald's own circumstances improved too; in 1881 he was able to withdraw from his ventures in Nova Scotia.

Macdonald's conduct, professionally and personally, was infused with Christian impulse. His letter-books reveal a no-nonsense businessman who could easily dismiss gratuitous requests for financial aid, but who could also, fairly and quietly, dispense charity and practical counsel to agents, family, and friends in genuine need. He would later be justly described as "a veteran of Toronto's business life and in equal degree a veteran of the Cross." A director from 1866 of the Upper Canada Religious Tract and Book Society, he faithfully looked for opportunities to spread the Word; in 1873 he encouraged the society to consider the lumbermen in the region north of Peterborough. Starting as treasurer of the Young Men's Christian Association of Toronto in 1866, he also served terms as a vice-president and on its building fund committee. Fully supportive of his ministries, and with him a member of Westminster Presbyterian Church on Bloor Street, his wife was president of the Young Women's Christian Association. In 1882 he joined the committee of the Presbyterian Aged and Infirm Ministers' Fund, and five years later he was appointed its convenor. Not surprisingly, he backed broad Protestant causes. He succeeded the Reverend William Caven* in December 1890 as president of the Equal Rights Association, but enjoyed little of Caven's prestige, and in December 1891 he took the religious high-road as the doxology-singing leader of the Sabbatarian opposition to Sunday streetcars in Toronto. He juggled such causes along with his work and family duties – he and Charlotte suffered the accidental death of a son in 1887 – but for reasons of appearance in business he refrained from going public with his political Conservatism.

By the early 1890s Toronto teemed with agents for a hundred or so insurance companies, ready to cover a myriad of standard and specialized losses: life, accident, and fire but also cyclones, employer's liability, livestock, marine, commercial guarantees, and plate glass. J. K. Macdonald's grand project was the erection in 1889–92 of the red stone and brick Confederation Life Building at Yonge and Richmond streets. This bold, spacious structure gave the company an architectural presence to equal that of Canada Life and Western Assurance, though all would soon be outdone by the Temple Building of the fraternal order of Foresters. Even with a host of other institutional and legal responsibilities, including his executorship of his brother's estate and the heavily litigated Baldwin estate, Macdonald relished coordinating contractors' bids, watching the building rise, and fending off criticism of Confederation Life as a commercial landlord. One of the first tenants was the newly founded Toronto Children's Aid Society; Macdonald replaced John Joseph Kelso* as its president in 1892 and immediately brought his style of officious management to bear on the cause of children's welfare.

In a letter of 1899 to an ill acquaintance in

Macdonald

Hanover, Ont., who Macdonald hoped was ready to meet his Maker, he determined "that a portion of my time shall be reserved for religious and philanthropic work." This he did, to great public benefit, but the manner of his assistance differed little from his disciplined control of Confederation Life. In 1899 he advised its cashier in Winnipeg to read Isaiah for personal guidance. In 1901–2 he unceremoniously pressured his company's decrepit president, Sir W. P. Howland, into resignation; within years, he was kindly looking after the property interests of Lady Howland, from whom Sir William had separated. In his various public offices, he took an aggressive interest in finances; he demanded and got accountability. At the Children's Aid Society, where he encountered untold situations of abject abuse and poverty, he took a direct hand in the care of several wards. After separating a brother and sister from their mother in 1904, he refused to tell her of their whereabouts: "You are utterly unable to look after them." He dismissed the superintendent of the society's Shelter in 1902 and the society's secretary, J. Stuart Coleman, in 1906, and took on the city over its reduced funding of the society. As president of St Andrew's College in Toronto, he did not hesitate to probe the mental stability of its principal, the Reverend George Bruce, and initiate his dismissal. Macdonald himself resigned in February 1900 when his own son Donald Bruce was appointed to the principalship. He resigned too as president of the Upper Canada Bible Society, in 1901, but his responsibilities remained heavy. In 1896 he had become president of the religious tract and book society, whose sailors' mission on the Great Lakes was one of his favourite projects. Within the Presbyterian Church, he exceeded his reach when he helped set up an independent mission in India for the Reverend John Wilkie; in 1903–4 he had to stand up for this trouble-making missionary before the Foreign Missions Committee.

One of Macdonald's few recreational distractions, by about 1897, was Loch Helen, his summer home and farm near Long Bay on Manitoulin Island, where he also fished and hunted. This camp too he managed closely from his desk in the off-season. In August 1902 he was badly shaken by the slow death of his wife from throat cancer at Cona Lodge, their home on Charles Street East. Hours before her passing he was dictating business letters while waiting at her bedside, "expecting that at any moment it may please God to take the spirit from the body." In September, leaving the "dark shadow that has fallen upon our household," Macdonald, with one of his sons and his daughter, Charlotte Helen, took a train trip to Halifax. In 1904, at age 66 and again with an attentive Helen, he made his first trip back to the old country. Meanwhile he spent some time and letters musing on his Scottish origins; according to his father, he told Gaelic scholar

Alexander MacLean SINCLAIR, the family had come to Caithness from "the Isles."

As managing director of Confederation Life, Macdonald continued to oversee its daily operations. He was assisted by his nephew William Campbell Macdonald as actuary and in 1898 his younger son, Charles Strange, joined the company. Routine business included searching out mortgage securities and bidding on municipal debentures (for investment purposes) and supervising and intensifying field operations. By 1896 the opportunity to secure a substantial amount of reinsurance business in the West Indies was attracting the company's attention, though it would not branch out there and to Mexico until 1901. Macdonald would spend two months in the Caribbean on business in 1906. Extremely aggressive competition blocked its expansion in the United States and Britain until even later. In Canada, Confederation Life trailed Canada Life, Mutual Life, and Sun Life in terms of volume, innovation, and such practices as insuring the young, issuing investment bonds, and eliminating restrictions on residence, travel, and occupation. In 1895, in the midst of an industry-wide slump, Macdonald had dropped his company's interest rates on policies and reserves, a precedent that earned him the enmity of other managers, despite his role as a founder of the Canadian Life Managers' Association the year before. Within his company, in 1896 he began "loading" or increasing premiums to meet higher risks but also, he would later admit under examination, to increase profits.

In 1899 a new insurance act widened the range of investment possibilities open to Canadian companies, a regulatory change that would release into Canadian markets a flood of new investment capital. Despite the limitations still in effect under his company's original charter, and unconscious of any ethical concerns, Macdonald (like other managers) immediately initiated a buying spree, largely in utility and industrial securities and fully supported by his board of directors, which now included such unhesitating capitalists as Wilmot Deloui Matthews*.

New York State's investigation of the insurance industry in 1905 sent a mild tremor through executives in Canada, but here federal and provincial regulation [see John Howard Hunter*] curbed the wildest excesses and infringements. In the federal royal commission on life insurance of 1906, which exposed Canadian companies to intense scrutiny, full measure was taken of Macdonald's management and style. Examined on 28 May 1906, he confirmed a complex series of unauthorized and speculative investments between 1900 and 1905, purchases on margin, the elimination of revealing transactions from his company's statements to the government, concentration of control, and a trail of personal borrowing. The business was legitimate – the brokers used by Macdonald, including Pellatt and Pellatt and Osler and Hammond, were reputable; Edmund Boyd OSLER sat on the Confederation Life board. The commissioners, however, held up pure fiduciary principle as a standard, and under examination Macdonald reacted. He displayed memory failure and impatiently sparred with counsel. This was not the sort of conduct he wanted the public to witness, but the Toronto press did not cooperate; the *World* wondered how such an upstanding citizen could bend the law. In Macdonald's report on the commission to his company's agents the following November, he presented a clean finding: there had been no graft and the securities in question were all sound, without "the remotest possibility of loss." He emerged unblemished, but there would be no more investment bingeing.

Putting the "serious misunderstandings" caused by the commission behind him, Macdonald returned to work and his philanthropic commitments. In the glow of his charitable work, negative impressions of his tight control of Confederation Life faded. He continued as president of the Children's Aid Society, though his relations with J. J. Kelso, then provincial superintendent of neglected and dependent children, became strained. Kelso thought that the society could do more and that Macdonald resented interference, and in 1916 he would take his concerns before the National Council of Women of Canada and the city's board of control. Later that year the society allocated funds to improve its children's shelter. Macdonald remained president until 1921. As well, he served as a vice-president of the Lord's Day Alliance and on the boards of Knox College, St Margaret's College, and the Working Boys' Home. At Confederation Life, he replaced William Henry Beatty* as president in January 1912. Their relations had not always been smooth: in 1901, when Beatty was vice-president, he felt that if agents were expected to collect interest, they should be bonded, and he pressed Macdonald on the matter, only to receive a heated rebuff. After 1912 Macdonald carried on as managing director, a position assumed by his nephew in January 1914. Following W. C. Macdonald's tragic death at Union Station in January 1917 amid the tumult of wartime troop departures, Macdonald resumed the function, which would be taken over by his son in January 1920, when he also stepped down as county treasurer. The death of his daughter the year before was stoically endured. Through no concerted effort of his own, and possibly as a result of Canadians' anxieties following the war, Macdonald's best year in insurance occurred after 1918, when new business shot up from $17,668,072 to $30,652,751.

The acknowledged "dean of life insurance in Canada" continued to maintain an office at Confederation Life, which he visited daily until his death at the age of 90. With his white, centre-parted hair, moustache, and wire glasses, he was a familiar figure walking up and down Yonge Street. His dry humour was rarely witnessed in public. In 1900 he advised an ailing Stuart Coleman that his penchant for writing tediously long letters was what made him sick. When asked once about his stamina, he replied that, as head of the aged and infirm ministers' fund, he had a lot of old Presbyterian pastors praying for him. Felled by a heart attack on 4 July 1928, he was buried in Mount Pleasant Cemetery; his home was sold to the Children's Aid Society for use as a shelter. In its editorial eulogy, the *Toronto Daily Star* lauded John K. Macdonald, the late George Albertus Cox* of Canada Life, and Robertson Macaulay of Sun Life as the three great heads of insurance in Canada.

DAVID ROBERTS

AO, RG 22-305, no.59917; RG 80-8-0-1086, no.5043; RG 80-27-2, 1: 207. General Register Office for Scotland (Edinburgh), Reg. of births, Edinburgh, 12 Oct. 1837. LAC, MG 28, III 126. *Toronto Daily Star*, 27 Aug. 1902, 4–5 July 1928. Can., Parl., *Sessional papers*, reports of the superintendent of insurance, 1875–1921; Royal commission on life insurance, *Minutes of evidence* (4v., Ottawa, 1907); *Report* (Ottawa, 1907). *Canadian annual rev.*, 1911, suppl.: 39–48. *Canadian men and women of the time* (Morgan; 1898 and 1912). Children's Aid Soc. of Toronto, *Annual report* ([Toronto]), 1892–1900. *Commemorative biographical record of the county of York...* (Toronto, 1907). Confederation Life Assoc., *75 years of service, 1871–1946* (Toronto, [1946?]). Morton Keller, *The life insurance enterprise, 1885–1910: a study in the limits of corporate power* (Cambridge, Mass., 1963). Middleton, *Municipality of Toronto*, vol.3: 110–11. Toronto Young Men's Christian Assoc., *Annual report* (Toronto), 1865–71/72. *Who's who in Canada*, 1922.

MACDONELL (Greenfield), JOHN ALEXANDER, lawyer, political organizer, militia officer, and author; b. 23 June 1851 in Kingston, Upper Canada, son of Archibald John Macdonell (Greenfield), a barrister, and Mary Ann Catherine Innes; m. 3 Sept. 1879 Isabel Sophie Crawford in Toronto; they had no surviving children; d. 11 April 1930 in Alexandria, Ont.

A native of Glengarry County in eastern Upper Canada, John Alexander Macdonell's father practised law in Kingston and was John A. Macdonald*'s partner from 1855. After he died in 1864, Macdonald mentored the lad, giving him a clerkship in his office. Macdonell's work in the 1870s for the provincial chief justice and chancellor brought experience in electoral cases. He received further training under Christopher Robinson* in Toronto; called to the bar in 1875, he would practise there until 1888. In 1879 he confirmed his affiliation with eastern Ontario by marrying a daughter of John Willoughby Crawford*, a former lieutenant governor with ties to Brockville.

His fierce loyalty to Macdonald, who had become prime minister in 1867, and close understanding of the politics of eastern Ontario, where Scottish names abounded, made him a natural organizer, a fitting partner for such regional leaders in parliament as Alexander Campbell* and John Graham Haggart*. Macdonell helped work the Tory convention of 1874 in Toronto, which was intended to reconstitute the party after the Pacific Scandal and its turnover of power to the Liberals. In 1877 he organized party associations in the St Lawrence River constituencies and became secretary of the Toronto Liberal-Conservative Association. Early the following year Macdonald asked the 26-year-old Jack Macdonell – he was also commonly called Jack Greenfield – to become political secretary of the Toronto-based United Empire Club, the core political/social organization of the reviving Conservatives. As Macdonald's back-room man in Ontario, he was promised a war chest of $10,000, though fundraiser Charles Tupper* pulled together only about half that. In the election campaign of 1878 Macdonell arranged itineraries for leading politicians, including speakers for the Conservatives' front group, the Dominion National League. In addition, he dispensed organizational advice to candidates and oversaw the distribution of more than 400,000 campaign documents through the club. The Conservatives returned to power and virtually swept eastern Ontario.

Macdonell's intense partisanship was no more evident than during an episode in the House of Commons on 10 May 1879. Admitted to a seat near the speaker, he abused Lucius Seth Huntington* as a "cheat and swindler," clearly referring to his role in breaking open the Pacific Scandal, and was ejected three times. He was later forced to apologize to the house for this scandalous behaviour. In Toronto he worked after the 1878 victory in a legal partnership with James Joseph Foy, another major organizer, and Tupper's son James Stewart. Although he had asked for the government's legal business in eastern Ontario as a reward for his political achievements, he actually took a considerable share of the business in Toronto. Following the financial collapse of the United Empire Club, he was closely involved with establishing the replacement Albany Club in 1882 and he maintained a strong interest in patronage. After recovering from a severe illness in 1887, at which point he was evidently in practice alone, he requested (and had his friends press for) the county judgeship of Prescott and Russell, adjacent to Glengarry, but it appears that the illness may have permanently damaged his speaking ability and he did not receive the post.

In 1888 Macdonell moved to Glengarry where, in Alexandria, he formed a partnership with Francis T. Costello, a Liberal. In time they acted as solicitors for the Roman Catholic diocese of Alexandria [see Alexander Macdonell*] and the local Bank of Ottawa and seem to have taken on much government business. In 1889 the federal minister of justice, Sir John Sparrow

David Thompson*, found Macdonell's billings excessive and his request for advances inappropriate. The combative Macdonell, who claimed he needed the money because of a return of illness, threatened to sue. This altercation may have cooled his political ardour, but he laboured vigorously in the election of 1891. Macdonald's death that year and the changing demographics of eastern Ontario, where Scottish dominance subsided with the growth of a Canadian-born population, reduced Macdonell's clout. He also had problems with Roderick (R.) McLennan*, the Conservative incumbent of Glengarry from 1891 to 1900, but he maintained his secretaryship of the Glengarry Liberal-Conservative Association and would continue to do so until 1912. His wife too "made her influence felt on the Conservative side in more than one election" in Glengarry, which turned Liberal in 1900. With the possibility of the Conservatives regaining power nationally in 1911, Macdonell worked hard in eastern Ontario. In 1917 he connived with Costello to bring Glengarry into Sir Robert Laird Borden*'s Union government. After 1918 his political activity seems to have declined sharply. Costello was appointed county judge in 1929 and Macdonell then briefly partnered with a cousin, Donald Alexander Macdonald.

Macdonell publicly described himself as an "indifferent lawyer." He certainly used his political and religious connections to bolster his legal career. Given his extensive service to the Conservatives, he naturally recommended others for positions and occasionally sought plum posts for himself. After his efforts in 1891, his hopes went as high as a senatorship, a goal he returned to when he supported Borden's Union government. Most of his patronage efforts went to aid others, however. His crowning attainment had been his lobby for a senatorship in 1884 for Dr Donald McMillan who, Macdonell noted, "has in the Eastern District over *seven thousand blood relations* including those of the third degree."

Macdonell's interests were largely bounded by his regional and Highland background. He collected and in his will left to a family representative, for keeping and distribution, historical and military items stretching back to the battle of Culloden in 1746 and including a treasured correspondence with Macdonald. His fascination with the military was displayed as well in his captaincy in the 59th (Stormont and Glengarry) Battalion of Infantry between 1888 and 1897, in an article on General Sir Isaac Brock*, and in his history of Glengarry, where care was lavished on the military exploits of eastern Ontario Highlanders. He wanted battleground cairns erected to mark the War of 1812, in which his great-grandfather Alexander Macdonell of Greenfield and two great-uncles, John Macdonell* (Greenfield) (an aide-de-camp to Brock) and Donald Macdonell* (Greenfield), had served. His strong Catholic faith was exhibited in his memoir of Bishop

Alexander McDonell*, a one-time chaplain of the Glengarry Light Infantry Fencibles. Deeply conservative, Macdonell believed strongly in hierarchy: in 1904 he attempted to form a second Glengarry regiment in which the officers were to be only landed gentry and professional men. His vanity was assuaged in 1912 when the minister of militia and defence, Samuel HUGHES, appointed him to the department's cadet corps committee with the honorary rank of lieutenant-colonel. Macdonell's upright posture and groomed beard projected his military bearing and forceful character. Especially engaged in charitable activities during World War I, he also enjoyed his garden; his wife tended to music, elocution, and horsemanship.

In declining health for two years, Jack Greenfield nonetheless visited his office regularly until shortly before his death. Isabel Macdonell, who lived in the town of Prescott in 1903, had at the time of his passing a residence in Brockville, where she held some of his furniture and much of his library, though these were bequeathed to a grand-nephew. Isabel received nothing, but, with some of his close friends, she was at his deathbed. It could not have been easy to live with a man of sometimes choleric passion and a prodigious capacity for drink, though his rough good humour and loyalty made him well liked, as the many funerary visitors attested. He was buried in the Catholic cemetery at St Raphaels.

BEN FORSTER

John Alexander Macdonell (Greenfield) is the author of *A sketch of the life of the Honourable and Right Reverend Alexander Macdonell* . . . ([Alexandria, Ont.], 1890), *Sketches illustrating the early settlement and history of Glengarry in Canada, relating principally to the Revolutionary War of 1775–83, the War of 1812–14 and the rebellion of 1837–8* . . . (Montreal, 1893), and "Major General Sir Isaac Brock, K.B.," Ont. Hist. Soc., *Papers and Records* (later *OH*), 10 (1913): 5–32. His papers can be found in NA, MG 27, I, I15. His will is published in Glengarry Hist. Soc., *Glengarry Hist. Research Notes* (Williamstown, Ont.), no.1 (1992).

AO, F 978, St Mary's Roman Catholic Cathedral, Kingston, Ont., RBMB; RG 80-5-0-87, no.12835. LAC, MG 26, A; F; H; MG 27, I, C2; E8. *Glengarry News* (Alexandria), 18 April 1930. *Globe*, 26 Aug. 1878; 12 May 1879; 6 June, 19 Nov. 1887; 17 March 1892. *Ottawa Free Press*, 22 Oct. 1878. William Boss, *The Stormont, Dundas and Glengarry Highlanders, 1783–1951* (Ottawa, 1952). *Canada Gazette*, 15 Feb. 1890: 1645. *Canadian men and women of the time* (Morgan; 1898 and 1912). E. M. Chadwick, *Ontarian families: genealogies of United-Empire-Loyalist and other pioneer families of Upper Canada* (2v., Toronto, 1894–98; repr., 2v. in 1, Lambertville, N.J., [1970]), 1: 9–10. Ben Forster, *A conjunction of interests: business, politics and tariffs, 1825–1879* (Toronto, 1986); "A Conservative heart: the United Empire Club, 1874–1882," *OH*, 78 (1986): 83–104. J. G. Harkness, *Stormont, Dundas and Glengarry; a history, 1784–1945* (Oshawa, Ont., 1946). *Types of Canadian women* . . . , ed. H. J. Morgan (Toronto, 1903), 217.

McEACHRAN, DUNCAN McNAB, veterinarian, professor, author, school administrator, inspector, and stockbreeder; b. 27 Oct. 1841 in Campbeltown, Scotland, son of David McEachran and Jean Blackney; m. 9 June 1868 Esther Plaskett in East Zorra Township, Ont., and they had two daughters; d. 13 Oct. 1924 in Ormstown, Que.

After studying at the Free Church Grammar School in Campbeltown, Duncan McNab McEachran was admitted to the renowned Edinburgh Veterinary College in 1858. He graduated in 1861 and soon received his licence to practise from the Royal College of Veterinary Surgeons, of which he would be made an associate in 1873. In the fall of 1862 he immigrated to Upper Canada and settled in Woodstock, where he opened a private practice. In 1863 veterinarian Andrew Smith*, who had attended Edinburgh Veterinary College with him, asked him to help set up the Upper Canada Veterinary School (later the Ontario Veterinary College) in Toronto and to teach materia medica there. The two men also did their best to promote their field of study among farmers and politicians through lectures and newspaper articles. In 1867 they would publish in Toronto the first veterinary textbook in Canada for farmers, *The Canadian horse and his diseases*. McEachran would also write numerous articles and reports on the major infectious diseases affecting the country's livestock. The two men soon parted, however, over a disagreement about teaching methods. In 1865 McEachran decided to open a private practice in Montreal, where he settled permanently the following year. He was to set up the province's first school of veterinary medicine there. Canadian agriculture was already specializing, with stockbreeding and the dairy industry being the new directions. This trend, along with the growth of horse-drawn traffic in the metropolis, the increase in livestock, and the lack of qualified farriers, conduced to the introduction of veterinary education and the professional training of future practitioners.

Since he enjoyed an excellent reputation, McEachran managed to persuade the president of the Board of Agriculture of Lower Canada, Thomas Edmund Campbell*, that setting up such a school might further the economic development of the province. Having obtained a grant of $300 from Campbell and the support of both the principal of McGill College, John William Dawson*, and the dean of its faculty of medicine, George William Campbell*, McEachran founded the Montreal Veterinary College in 1866. Classes began on 26 September in a small residence at the corner of Rue Craig (Rue Saint-Antoine) and Rue de Bleury. McEachran had set himself the goal of making his veterinary school, which was the third in North America to associate itself closely with an institution of higher learning, an active part of McGill College. At that time American and British veterinary schools had no admission test, but McEachran instituted an entrance examination and insisted that students attend three six-month sessions instead of the two that were required at the other veterinary schools. He also established a bold program and high standards for graduation. The beginnings were modest; from 1866 to 1875 only ten students would earn a diploma. Although there were not many of them, they benefited from an advanced scientific training. They took courses in anatomy, dissection, materia medica, medicine, surgery, and veterinary obstetrics, as well as others given by the McGill faculty of medicine in physiology, pathology, histology, chemistry, and botany (over a three-year period). Clinical classes, conducted in the infirmary as well as at the main stables and butcher shops in the city, introduced them to the procedures of anatomical and clinical medicine. In 1875 the Montreal Veterinary College would begin to expand more rapidly. McEachran had a larger building erected at his own expense at 6 Avenue Union, to house a new infirmary for the clinical study of horses, as well as a laboratory, pharmacy, library, and museum where he displayed prepared specimens acquired in the course of his many trips to Europe. Such progressive measures earned him praise, and his school was soon considered one of the best, if not the very best, in North America.

In 1872 the authorities of New York City invited McEachran, as an expert, to find ways of combating a severe influenza epidemic that was affecting 30,000 horses and paralysing the city's transportation system. He would, in fact, make many visits to the United States to carry out research into certain epizootic diseases raging in the eastern states. Anxious to develop at the Montreal Veterinary College the experimental study of animal diseases in North America, McEachran joined forces in 1874 with Dr William Osler*, who would become an outstanding figure in medical science. Recently returned from a course of studies in Europe, Osler introduced the students of veterinary medicine to zoonoses (animal diseases transmissible to humans, such as hog cholera and trichinosis) and to entozoology (the study of the many parasites affecting domestic animals). With McEachran's consent, Osler set up a laboratory for pathological and microscopic demonstrations and initiated the first research in Canada in comparative pathology. The two men shared the same avant-garde philosophy of medical teaching. They considered human medicine and veterinary medicine to be complementary and based on the same fundamental principles. Students at the Montreal Veterinary College therefore had to take some courses in common with their colleagues in the medical faculty and write the same examinations. They not only left the college with an excellent training, but they also had the option of turning to a career in human medicine by taking only one additional year at the McGill faculty of medicine.

With a grant of $1,000 from the Council of Agriculture of the Province of Quebec, McEachran in 1877 set up the French section of the Montreal Veterinary College, thereby becoming the first person outside France to provide veterinary training in French. The structure of the program was identical to that of the English section. The veterinary courses were taught by French-speaking graduates of the college, including Orphir Bruneau and Joseph-Alphonse COUTURE, who were joined two years later by Victor-Théodule Daubigny*. McEachran himself taught there. The Montreal School of Medicine and Surgery (then affiliated with Victoria College in Cobourg, Ont.) was responsible for the medical curriculum. The excellence of instruction was universally recognized, but at the request of the provincial government the French section had to give way in 1885 to two new French-language schools, the École Vétérinaire de Québec, set up and operated by Couture, and the École de Médecine Vétérinaire Française de Montréal, founded by Bruneau and Daubigny. McEachran must be given credit for having strongly encouraged the development of French-language veterinary medicine following a university teaching model that would be a milestone.

The existing affiliation took concrete shape in 1889 when the Montreal Veterinary College became the faculty of comparative medicine and veterinary science (a name suggested by Osler) of McGill University. Pleased with this integration, McEachran accepted the office of dean (which he would hold until 1903) and instituted a program leading to a doctorate in veterinary science. McGill conferred on him the honorary degree of doctor of veterinary surgery in 1890, appointed him professor emeritus in 1905, and awarded him a second honorary degree, an LLD, in 1909. Anxious to keep pace with the latest advances in medical knowledge, McEachran raised the requirements for the program by adding lessons in comparative pathology and in bacteriology taught by Dr Wyatt Galt Johnston* and Dr John George Adami, as well as, among others, courses in zoology and cynology. The faculty was acknowledged, by such periodicals as *Chicago Field* and *Turf, Field and Farm* (New York), to be one of the best institutions in North America, and it attracted students from several countries to Montreal. Graduates of the school would practise in the United States, Great Britain, Japan, South Africa, and the West Indies.

Despite this enviable record, the faculty found itself in a difficult situation by the beginning of the 20th century. From 1890 to 1902 the number of students admitted dropped from 50 to 15. This decline was due not only to inadequate financial support from governments and from McGill, but especially to competition from smaller schools with lower admission standards and less demanding courses of study. In the event, the enormously popular Ontario Veterinary College had 3,365 graduates between 1863 and 1908, compared to the Montreal school's 315 (from both French and English sections) between 1866 and 1902. In 1903 the faculty was forced to close. Despite its brief existence, it had contributed greatly to the development of the teaching and practice of veterinary science. Its pedagogical philosophy, which was based on the similarity between human and animal medicine, as well as on instruction in basic science combined with clinical experience, anticipated the teaching model that most Western schools of veterinary medicine would adopt after World War I.

McEachran's activities were not confined to the field of education. From 22 June 1877 to 27 Aug. 1886 he served as veterinarian to the Volunteer Militia Field Battery of Artillery of Montreal. This work was, however, of slight importance in comparison to his involvement in the organization of the first system of animal quarantine in Canada. The rise in British demand for animals, the increasing volume of international trade by transatlantic steamer, and the threat of an outbreak of foot-and-mouth disease (present in Great Britain at that time) had prompted the federal government to institute a policy of systematic inspection for animals entering or leaving Canada. McEachran was put in charge of this program, and in 1876 he had become chief inspector of livestock. He assigned the province's best veterinarians to the port of Lévis, where what was probably the first animal quarantine station in North America opened that year; their job was to monitor the movement of cattle, sheep, hogs, and horses, which were often suffering from infectious diseases. Quarantine stations were also opened in Halifax and Saint John in 1876 and, following the growth of the trade in animals at the beginning of the 20th century, more than 20 more were established in Canada, from Pictou, N.S., to Nelson, B.C. Influenced by this type of preventive model, the United States would also set up such stations.

McEachran was recognized by the country's political leaders and in 1885 he became the first chief veterinary inspector for the government of Canada (a part-time position). He oversaw the enforcement of the Act respecting infectious or contagious diseases affecting animals, passed that year. This statute significantly strengthened measures for controlling infectious animal diseases by imposing new sanitary constraints on the owners of livestock, by giving expanded powers to veterinary inspectors, by specifying the standards for slaughtering infected animals, and by widening the powers for prohibiting the importation of suspect animals. McEachran also supervised the creation of a state apparatus that had several objectives, including the introduction of an animal and food inspection network and the supervision of the labora-tories in which veterinarians and other scientists carried out experimental studies of animal diseases. He was responsible as well for ordering the slaughter of herds declared contagious, so as to prevent a heavy toll on livestock. Aware of the complaints of breeders, who suffered substantial financial losses in such cases, he made a point of obtaining their cooperation. He tried to get them compensation from the federal government for their slaughtered herds. When trade disputes arose over the export of cattle, he refuted in detail British allegations to the effect that there were endemic animal diseases such as anthrax, bovine pleuropneumonia (especially in 1892), and Texas fever in Canada. Two research laboratories were set up while he was chief inspector, one in Stellarton, N.S., in 1891, and the other in Outremont, Que., in 1897. Having ensured that the animal inspection system was firmly established, McEachran resigned in 1902, but he remained an honorary consultant to the federal government. His successor, John Gunion RUTHERFORD, who was to interest himself particularly in the health of animals branch (it would become the Canadian Food Inspection Agency in 1997), carried on the work McEachran had begun.

In McEachran's view, scientific activities, and in particular laboratory sciences, were the royal road to the development of veterinary medicine. By 1882 McEachran had embraced Louis Pasteur's theory and the new discoveries in bacteriology. He took part in 1893 in the Montreal Medico-Chirurgical Society's investigations into infectious diseases. In 1895 he became one of the first to introduce into Canada the tuberculin test, a method of detecting bovine tuberculosis developed by German bacteriologist Robert Koch. He also encouraged the organization of research projects on this disease at the Outremont experimental station. As a member of the Milk Commission of the Montreal Medical-Chirurgical Society, he recommended to the city of Montreal in 1900 – some 20 years before the idea was put in practice – that it set up a system for supervising the production and distribution of milk. He represented Canada at many international gatherings, including the International Congress on Tuberculosis held in London, England, in 1901.

McEachran was an activist who, like his former colleague Andrew Smith, hoped to raise not only the intellectual and professional qualifications of veterinarians, but also their standing in society. It was with this goal in mind that in 1875 he helped found the Montreal Veterinary Surgeons Association, which sought to improve the training of graduate veterinarians, intensify the struggle against charlatans, and make farmers aware of the effectiveness of veterinarians. In 1876 McEachran began lobbying the American Veterinary Medical Association, through articles in the *American Veterinary Review* and the *United*

McEachran

States Veterinary Journal (published respectively at Schaumburg and Chicago in Illinois) for better courses of study and greater recognition of the profession. In the late 1870s he wrote a veterinary column for *Le Journal d'agriculture* (Montréal). From 1885 he was also part of a group urging the provincial government to give graduate veterinarians the exclusive right to treat animals. The message was heard, and an act passed in 1902 would create the Board of Veterinary Surgeons of the Province of Quebec. In 1888 he became a member of the Society for the Study of Comparative Psychology.

Keenly interested in stockbreeding and attracted by its potential profits, McEachran helped found the two biggest ranches in Canada at the end of the 19th century. In 1881, after going on horseback to the foot of the Rockies (an account of the trip was published in the Montreal *Gazette* that year), he joined with Senator Matthew Henry Cochrane*, of Compton, Que., in starting the Cochrane Ranche Company Limited. The first of a dozen large companies organized by capitalists from England or eastern Canada to set up livestock farms in southern Alberta, it came into being through a Canadian government program for leasing grazing land cheaply. After two years as vice-president and general manager of the company, which owned four ranches west of Fort Calgary, McEachran resigned in the wake of technical and financial problems. He then accepted a more lucrative position as general manager of the Walrond Cattle Ranch Limited, which was owned by British businessman Sir John Walrond and located a little farther south in Alberta, near Pincher Creek. The two companies each leased more than 200,000 acres of land and raised about 10,000 head of Hereford and Polled Angus cattle. Their founders counted on using the Canadian Pacific Railway, then under construction, to ship their animals to markets in eastern Canada and Great Britain. McEachran offered his experience as a veterinarian, visiting the site at least twice a year to inspect the operation. He also supervised the ranch managers from his base in Montreal. The head office of Walrond Cattle Ranch Limited remained in England until 1898, when the New Walrond Ranche Company Limited was formed, with McEachran becoming president and general manager. The enterprise ceased operations in 1908 after several years of financial losses. Its entire herd was purchased by stockbreeder Patrick Burns*.

In view of his keen interest in horses and knowledge of their ways, McEachran served as an equestrian judge at the National Horse Show in New York in 1891 and 1892 and at the Columbian exposition in Chicago in 1893. He was also a member of the Montreal Hunt Club, the Forest and Stream Club in Dorval, and the influential St James Club in Montreal. In 1909, when he was nearly 70 years old, he gave up his residence on Avenue Union in Montreal and moved into a magnificent villa in Ormstown, southwest of the city. He operated a dairy farm and raised Clydesdale horses on more than 200 acres of fertile land on the Rivière Châteauguay. In 1916 his farm won a silver medal in the Agricultural Merit competition in Quebec.

Duncan McNab McEachran may be considered a typical builder of Canada during the latter half of the 19th century. An educated Scot determined to carve out a place for himself in the country, he had the energy to provide it with competent professionals. His ambition attracted some criticism, since he was occasionally headstrong and inflexible. He was nevertheless a decisive and productive man. The advancement of veterinary medicine and the services he and his students were able to render to society are surely among his finest achievements. The Montreal Veterinary College provided its graduates with a scientific education that enabled them to participate in the progress of this vast country by ensuring the development of animal husbandry so as to provide food for cities with rapidly expanding populations, looking after the health of the horses on which highway traffic was still largely dependent, caring for the military cavalry, and safeguarding public health. By the end of his career McEachran had, through his efforts in the fields of education and the prevention and treatment of animal diseases, helped improve the health of the country's herds and rid them almost entirely of contagious diseases.

DENIS GOULET and FRÉDÉRIC JEAN

In addition to the book he wrote with Andrew Smith, Duncan McNab McEachran published several monographs and articles: *Bulletin on typhoid fever in horses, improperly called influenza* (Ottawa, 1901); *Hog cholera and swine plague and verminous broncho-pneumonia* (Ottawa, 1899); *Maladie du coït (equine syphillis)* (Ottawa, 1901); "On the intercommunicability of tuberculosis from animals to man and from man to animals," *Montreal Medical Journal*, 21 (1892–93): 801–12; "On the prevention of tuberculosis in animals," *Montreal Medical Journal*, 28 (1899): 410–22; *Opening address; Society of Comparative Psychology (in connection with the Montreal Veterinary College)* (Montreal, 1888); "Osler and the Montreal Veterinary College," in *Sir William Osler memorial number* ([Toronto], 1920): 35–38; *Tuberculosis in cattle* (Ottawa, 1900); and "Veterinary education," *American Veterinary Rev.* (Schaumburg, Ill.), 1 (1877): 12–13, 45–50, 85–92, 113–115. He also prepared all the reports of the Montreal Veterinary College from 1866 to 1903, published under the title *Annual announcement*, as well as numerous other reports for the provincial and federal governments: Que., Parl., *Sessional papers*, report of the commissioner of agriculture and public works (commissioner of agriculture and colonization; commissioner of agriculture), 1872–1904; Can., Parl., *Sessional papers*, reports of the minister of agriculture, 1874–1910. McEachran is also the author of several travel accounts – *Impressions of pioneers, of Alberta as a ranching country, commencing 1881* (Ormstown, Que.,

[1916?]), *A journey over the plains: from Fort Benton to Bow River and back* (Montreal, 1881), *Notes of a trip to Bow River, North-West Territories* (Montreal, 1881), and *Report of a visit to Great Britain and the continent of Europe in the winter of 1897–98* (Ottawa, 1898) – and of an unpublished report, "Sanitary measures in preventing disease in the U.S. and Canada," presented to the United States Veterinary Medical Assoc., Philadelphia, 1876.

AO, RG 80-27-2, 50: 92. MUA, 99-2; 923, 1. Private arch., A. B. McCullough (Ottawa), "The Walrond Ranche: a financial history" (1998); George Thomson (Lochmaben, Scot.), "Professor Duncan McNab McEachran, 1841–1924: a biography" (typescript). *Gazette* (Montreal), 14 Oct. 1924. T. W. M. Cameron, "Veterinary education in Canada," *Veterinary Journal and Annals of Comparative Pathology* (London), 93 (1937): 102–6. *Canadian men and women of the time* (Morgan; 1898 and 1912). *Cyclopædia of Canadian biog.* (Rose and Charlesworth), vol.2. F. T. Daubigny, "The teaching of veterinary science in the province of Quebec," American Veterinary Medical Assoc., *Journal* (Schaumburg), 18 (April–September 1924): 14–20. T. W. Dukes, "Veterinary history: early Canadian microscopists with associations to veterinary medicine," *Canadian Veterinary Journal* (Ottawa), 34 (1993): 241–45. T. [W.] Dukes and Norman McAninch, "Health of animals branch, Agriculture Canada: a look at the past," *Canadian Veterinary Journal*, 33 (1992): 58–64. S. B. Frost, *McGill University: for the advancement of learning* (2v., Montreal, 1980–84). Denis Goulet et André Paradis, *Trois siècles d'histoire médicale au Québec; chronologie des institutions et des pratiques (1639–1939)* (Montréal, 1992). Orlan Hall, "Progress of tuberculosis eradication in Canada," *Canadian Journal of Comparative Medicine and Veterinary Science* (Gardenvale, Que.), 3 (1939), no.2: 47–50. Frédéric Jean, "L'empoisonnement par le lait: l'impact de la campagne du lait pur sur la lutte à la mortalité infantile au Québec, 1830–1930: le cas de Montréal" (thèse de MA, univ. de Sherbrooke, Qué., 1999). McGill Univ., *Annual report* (Montreal), 1890–1903. C. A. Mitchell, *A note on the early history of veterinary science in Canada* (Gardenvale, 1940). "Montreal Veterinary Medical Association," *Veterinary Journal and Annals of Comparative Pathology*, 4 (1877): 140–41. V. A. Moore, "Duncan McEachran and the McGill faculty of comparative medicine," American Veterinary Medical Assoc., *Journal*, 13 (October 1921–March 1922): 625–38. "Necrology: Duncan McEachran," American Veterinary Medical Assoc., *Journal*, 19 (October 1924–March 1925): 265. Michel Pepin, *Histoire et petites histoires des vétérinaires du Québec* ([Montréal], 1986). J. F. Smithcors, *The veterinarian in America, 1625–1975* (Santa Barbara, Calif., 1975). P. M. Teigen, "The establishment of the Montreal Veterinary College, 1866/67–1874/75," *Canadian Veterinary Journal*, 29 (1988): 185–89. Sandra Vokaty, "The adventures of Dr. Duncan McNab McEachran in western Canada," *Canadian Veterinary Journal*, 20 (1979): 149–56. *Who's who and why*, 1914.

MCGRATH, Sir PATRICK THOMAS, journalist, office holder, author, and politician; b. 16 Dec. 1868 in St John's, eldest son of William McGrath and Mary Bermingham; d. there unmarried 14 June 1929.

From birth, Patrick T. McGrath suffered from a nervous tremor, with one side of his body being par-

tially paralysed. He was educated in St John's by the Brothers of the Christian Schools of Ireland, leaving at the age of 14 to work as a clerk with T. McMurdo and Company, a firm of druggists. Because of his indifferent health P. T., as he was known, was drawn to outdoor employment, and in 1891 he began work as a reporter for the St John's *Evening Herald*. In 1894 he would become Newfoundland correspondent for the London *Times*, and he would later write for other newspapers and magazines in England, Canada, and the United States.

In Newfoundland, success in journalism lay in alliances with local politicians, and McGrath was a skilful spokesman for those he supported. During the general election of 1893 he was interim editor of the *Evening Herald*, which backed the Tory opposition led by Moses Monroe* and Walter Baine Grieve. He was appointed editor the next year. McGrath was a "fearless individual," "scurrilous," and "hated by many," Peter John Cashin*, son of Sir Michael Patrick CASHIN and a politician himself by the 1920s, would recall in 1967. McGrath was attacked physically on several occasions and at one point was apparently forced "to get a bodyguard with a license to carry a gun."

Following a holiday in Canada in early 1895, McGrath wrote several articles in the *Evening Herald* favourable to the country and later in the year he actively promoted Newfoundland's unsuccessful efforts to negotiate a political union with Canada. In the general election of 1897 he was instrumental in helping Conservative leader Sir James Spearman Winter* defeat Sir William Vallance Whiteway*. He was private secretary to Winter in 1898 when the latter attended the Anglo-American joint high commission at Quebec to discuss the Atlantic fisheries. His selection reflected not only partisanship, but also his knowledge of fishery disputes involving France, the United States, and Britain, about which he had written for several foreign magazines. In the early 1900s he would help the Newfoundland government prepare its case in similar conflicts with both France and the United States.

From 1897 to 1900 McGrath was assistant clerk of the House of Assembly. In the 1900 election he supported Liberal leader Robert BOND and, after Bond became premier, he was appointed clerk of the house in 1901. When St John's West MHA Edward Patrick Morris* split with Bond six years later and formed the People's party, McGrath left the *Evening Herald* and launched the *Evening Chronicle* to support him. In the election of 1908, which ended in a tie, he acted as chief propagandist for Morris, and he did so again in 1909 when Morris won a clear victory. He retained his position as clerk of the assembly until his appointment in 1912 to the Legislative Council. As a councillor, he proved an able and knowledgeable debater. He placed his talents at the disposal of the administrations he supported and was often asked to prepare budget speeches. He became president of the council in 1915.

In 1911 he had published in London *Newfoundland in 1911 . . .*, an optimistic review of political, social, and economic conditions on the island. The book praised the policies of the Morris government and the business practices of William Duff REID and his brothers, the owners of the Newfoundland Railway and the holders of large land, timber, and mineral concessions in the colony. The following year McGrath's Chronicle Publishing Company purchased the *Evening Herald* and he merged the *Chronicle* with it. He became president of the new company and editor of the *Herald*. In 1913 the Morris government won re-election, but faced a stronger opposition in a coalition of Liberals and Unionists, the latter being followers of William Ford Coaker*, who had founded the Fishermen's Protective Union in 1908. From 1912 until he left the *Herald* in 1920 McGrath was one of Coaker's harshest critics.

During Morris's absences from Newfoundland on government business, McGrath kept him apprised of events in the colony. His letters, particularly for the years 1911 to 1914, are valuable for their comments on local political and social life. During World War I McGrath was honorary secretary of the Newfoundland Patriotic Fund and finance secretary of the Newfoundland Regiment. He helped to organize the Board of Pension Commissioners for Newfoundland, which administered war pensions, and served as its first chairman. In 1917 he presided over the government commission which investigated the high cost of living, and he became chair of the Food Control Board that was subsequently established. A supporter of conscription in 1918, he received a knighthood that year for his contributions to the war effort. He found the cynical local response to this honour disheartening. "But one has to be big enough to disregard these 'flea-bites,'" he wrote to a friend.

In the 1919 general election McGrath supported the Liberal-Progressive party headed by Sir Michael Cashin, which lost to an alliance of Liberals led by Richard Anderson Squires* and Unionists under Coaker. With the change in government, he resigned the presidency of the Legislative Council. In 1920 Prime Minister Squires, recognizing McGrath's historical knowledge and skills, offered him the task of researching Newfoundland's claim in its dispute with Canada over the ownership of Labrador. After consulting with Cashin, McGrath resigned from the *Evening Herald* (which ceased publication later in the year) to undertake this work. His extensive investigations in British, Canadian, and American archives played a key role in forming the legal case which resulted in 1927 in a decision in Newfoundland's favour by the Judicial Committee of the Privy Council in Britain.

From 1925 until his death McGrath again served as president of the Legislative Council. He occasionally represented Newfoundland at international conferences as well, but he was mainly occupied in giving public lectures and writing articles on the boundary dispute and on confederation. He had been a lifelong confederate but had kept his views on the subject muted during the heyday of his journalistic career after 1895.

MELVIN BAKER

Centre for Newfoundland Studies, Memorial Univ. of Nfld, Arch. (St John's), COLL-175 (P. T. McGrath papers), McGrath to E. P. Morris, 13, 20, 28 June, 4, 13 July 1911; McGrath to J. E. J. Fox, 8 April 1918. "Articles by Sir P. T. McGrath," comp. Melvin Baker (photocopy, [St John's, 1973]; copy in Centre for Newfoundland Studies). Melvin Baker, "Prominent figures from our recent past: Patrick Thomas McGrath, [1868–1928]," *Newfoundland Quarterly* (St John's), 87 (1992–93), no.4: 37–38 (text also available on the author's website: *www.ucs.mun.ca/~melbaker/*); "Sir Patrick Thomas McGrath: a brief bibliography of his writings" (typescript, [St John's, 1974]; copy in Centre for Newfoundland Studies). P. [J.] Cashin, "Sir Patrick McGrath, a biography" (Canadian Broadcasting Corporation radio broadcast, St John's, 1967; transcript in Centre for Newfoundland Studies). I. D. H. McDonald, *"To each his own": William Coaker and the Fishermen's Protective Union in Newfoundland politics, 1908–1925*, ed. J. K. Hiller (St John's, 1987). *Newfoundland Quarterly*, 29 (1929–30), no.1: 16. B. J. Pippy, "Sir Patrick McGrath: a biographical essay" (BA thesis, Memorial Univ. of Nfld, 1992).

McGREGOR, GORDON MORTON, manufacturer and civic officer; b. 18 Jan. 1873 near Windsor, Ont., second son of William McGregor and Jessie Lathrup Peden; m. 2 Nov. 1898 Harriet (Hattie) Dodds in Detroit, and they had three daughters and two sons; d. 11 March 1922 in Montreal and was buried in Windsor.

Gordon M. McGregor was born at his family's home south of Windsor, on the Detroit River. His father had a chequered career in business and as mayor of Windsor and Liberal MP for Essex. Reared in a Scottish Presbyterian family, Gordon was educated in Windsor and Winnipeg, where the McGregors lived for a time. He worked for a men's clothing store in Detroit and then with his father in a real estate and insurance agency in Windsor. By 1897 he was becoming active in Liberal politics. Known for his singing voice and socializing, he married the daughter of a wholesale druggist in Detroit, where he also kept the books for the Photokrome Company. In 1902, when McGregor Sr became collector of customs, he was installed with no experience as manager of the wagon works in Walkerville (Windsor) that his father and banker John Curry had acquired.

There McGregor witnessed four converging trends: the proliferation of American branch plants to bypass

Canadian tariffs; the growth of machine trades related to the bicycle craze; the birth of an automotive industry in Michigan; and the decline of the wagon works following William McGregor's death in 1903. Unable as president to sustain production, Gordon watched its debt climb and work stop in July 1904. As early as January apparently, under pressure from Curry to reduce obligations, he had been thinking of reusing the factory as a branch of an automotive firm. He gambled on Henry Ford of Detroit, who faced a patent lawsuit but had achieved startling success with gasoline-powered runabouts. Initially uninterested, Ford, who likely came to admire McGregor's underlying hardness, soon saw his overture as an opportunity to expand and exploit Canada's access to imperial markets. He had already tested the waters. In 1903 Canada Cycle and Motor in Toronto began selling his first model and in the spring of 1904 he made a promotional trip into Ontario. Though McGregor was confident that a branch would enjoy support from the federal Liberal government, which raised the tariff on automobiles, his plan was risky: the market was unformed and finding capital was a huge challenge. Still, bolstered with promises of extra stock he had shrewdly demanded as compensation, McGregor raised $125,000. On 10 August, an agreement was concluded; in a key exchange, Ford would share his patents and plans. At the inaugural meeting of the Ford Motor Company of Canada Limited on the 29th, McGregor was made managing secretary.

By year's end 25 Model Cs had been assembled in Walkerville from chassis made in Michigan and advertising was appearing in Canadian sources. At the Madison Square Garden car show in New York in January 1905, McGregor witnessed the power of bold displays; he would have recognized too the modesty of his own operation. He exhibited at CCM's little show in February, he held a second job, and finding sales agents and producers for parts in Ontario was a slow process. At the same time, the Windsor *Evening Record* started to champion both the fledgling industry and McGregor.

In 1906 he dutifully backed Ford's venture into the luxury car field, but it was with the overlapping production of the Model N that the organization returned to its originator's quest for a "light, low-priced car." There were sales from Vancouver to Fredericton. Sent to Walkerville that year to manage production, George Dickert would remember McGregor as a pleasant, persuasive man bent on "peddling." The atmosphere at Walkerville struck visitors as casual, but groundwork was being laid. Production climbed to 327 vehicles in 1907. That year, at the Toronto Industrial Exhibition (later the Canadian National Exhibition), McGregor showed for the first time apart from CCM, which Thomas Alexander Russell* had taken over to make a purely Canadian automobile. McGregor understood

that his firm had a dual identity: it was promoted as Canadian within the dominion, while in the United States and some British territories, where American consuls were big boosters, the Detroit affiliation was highlighted. When he began exporting in 1906, to Australia, New Zealand, and Natal (South Africa), he utilized Ford Detroit's shippers.

By 1907–8 his gamble was succeeding. His salary was increased, he bought in stock from nervous investors, payments to the old wagon company were met, and he ventured further into public life. With others he tried in 1906 to revive Windsor's defunct board of trade; in 1908 he chaired the board formed to build First Presbyterian Church in Walkerville. Most satisfying was the maturation of the automobile industry, including the emergence of a trade press and show entrepreneurs, notably Robert Miller Jaffray. McGregor, who saw Canada's regions taking to the automobile in different ways, was most troubled by the trend among provinces and municipalities to regulate its use. Like his testers, with their upsetting noise and fumes, he liked to drive fast. In 1908 he joined other automakers and officials of the newly formed Ontario Motor League – possibly the earliest such lobby in Canada – to ask a committee of the legislature to curtail regulatory amendments. Their worries were unfounded: controls were routinely violated as the public came to terms with the "devil wagon." Moreover, regulation tended to lead to calls for better roads, a movement supported by McGregor. At the end of September he reported annual profits of more than $18,500.

Announced by Ford Canada that fall, the utterly utilitarian Model T would make McGregor, and revolutionize transportation in Canada by breaking down time and distance. Specifications began arriving in February 1909 and chassis in March; Canadian-made bodies and other components were used from the start. Between August and January 1910, in concert with Ford Detroit's development of its own foreign markets, McGregor went to Australia, New Zealand, India, and Ceylon (Sri Lanka) to consolidate his networks. At home the Border Cities (Windsor, Walkerville, Sandwich, and Ojibway) began blossoming as Canada's centre of automotive and parts manufacture. In 1910 and 1911–12 McGregor undertook expansions in cutting-edge reinforced concrete; the large machine tools essential to mass production followed; the first "power conveyor" appeared about 1911. For the rest of his career he would be engaged in rounds of structural and mechanical change. During the surge in production from 1,280 in 1910 to 6,388 in 1912, his company was reincorporated in 1911 under a federal charter.

A photograph of a bespectacled McGregor taken about this time in Detroit exudes affluence. In 1910 he bought a cottage lot near Kingsville, a summer retreat on Lake Erie. The next year, he and some neighbours

McGregor

leaned on the town to annex their area and give it water and fire protection. Socially ambitious, he belonged to the Oak Ridge Golf Club, which was incorporated as the Essex Golf and Country Club in 1910. The reciprocity debate and election of 1911 tested his politics. Conscious of the tariff's role in fostering industry, the Walkerville Board of Trade opposed reciprocity; so too did such Liberal automakers as Russell and Robert McLaughlin of Oshawa. McGregor, however, thought it the "best proposition" Canada ever faced, a partisan position he could afford to adopt: the tariff on cars would be reduced minimally and his markets would not be threatened. When Prime Minister Sir Wilfrid Laurier* visited in September, McGregor proudly chauffeured him in a parade and went on stage for the ensuing speeches. Even with the Liberals' defeat, he came to master back-room politicking (with a reach that extended to the House of Commons) and he gained status. He purchased a stately house in Windsor in 1912, some commercial blocks, and a property for a showcase Ford dealership.

The real challenge facing McGregor's company was the need for a national distribution network to absorb the ever-increasing numbers of new Ford automobiles (11,584 in 1912–13). He assigned the task to Augustin Neil Lawrence, the bright young sales manager who, in consultation with McGregor and assistant manager Wallace Ronald Campbell, devised a "formula for organized selling." Representatives drove through every rural and urban section of the country, methodically charting their economic and physical condition and then calculating targets for sales and dealer recruitment. As part of this marketing tour de force, advertising was revamped (some of it quite unlike Ford Detroit's) and in 1913 the assertive *Ford Sales Bulletin* (for dealers) and the Canadian *Ford Times* were launched.

Ever-faster assembly line production, which was at the core of Ford Canada's drive to meet its targets and backlogs of orders, led to high turnover and new demands in labour relations. In a traditional manner, McGregor supported employee clubs and sports teams. Faced with a housing shortage, he applied to town council in 1912 for permission to house his workers in tents. A different test of his corporate sympathies came in April 1913 when, despite his opposition, Arsas Drouillard successfully applied for a licence to open a tavern near Ford's gates. Unwilling to bend, McGregor had the licence vetoed by provincial secretary William John Hanna*, who was also a director of Imperial Oil, which supplied Ford Canada. He then proceeded confidently in May into litigation over the stock promised him in 1904, a case that would go to the Judicial Committee of the Privy Council in England. The *Evening Record*'s report of his initial testimony stressed his early struggle and manly "perseverance" – the start of fabricated legend.

McGregor was beginning to become known on the national scene. In September 1913 he attended the annual meeting of the Canadian Manufacturers' Association in Halifax. Foundry and machine journals noted his achievements, but until after the war he received little personal attention in the daily press. The American *Ford Times* gave coverage to his markets – they held an exotic appeal – but in a "Ford family" way it grouped his operation with the American organization. He was highlighted in the *Times*' poems and cartoons, wonderfully so, but never in the Canadian *Ford Times*, where deference to Henry Ford and his homespun philosophies was de rigueur. Locally he continued to make a name for himself. He backed the short-lived Ontario Border Development Bureau in 1913 and led the successful drive to bring Ontario Hydro to Walkerville.

In a manner that would become standard, McGregor carefully orchestrated the shareholders' meeting of October 1913. The disappointing decision to withhold a dividend, he explained with mock gravity, was due to the company's "financial situation." The *Evening Record* was led to suggest that, as in 1904, he was hard-pressed. In fact, he needed to conserve funds to institute the shorter nine-hour day and pay raises and bonuses already implemented at Ford Detroit to curb turnover and early signs of labour militancy. Nonetheless, business boomed and, following the "American policy," final assembly and costs were shifted to the branches, relieving pressure on the main plant at Ford City, which had been carved out of Walkerville. Dealers were forced to take early deliveries. Similar pressure was exerted overseas; in the instance of British Honduras (Belize), Lawrence lambasted the federal Department of Trade and Commerce in 1914 (even after the outbreak of war) for failing to provide adequate information on roads and market potential. Against this backdrop of growth – 38 per cent of the cars registered in Canada in 1914 were Fords – McGregor and his wife enjoyed social and golfing engagements, corporate gatherings, and vacations at American resorts; the loss of a young son in January 1914 was stoically endured.

In the opening months of World War I, he was positioned to become the most important cog in the Border Cities' civilian war effort. Adhering to America's neutrality (until 1917) and Henry Ford's personal anti-war stance, Ford Detroit initially made no war materials. McGregor followed suit. Instead, he built the "Made in Canada" theme, which had been in play in industry for years, into a brilliant marketing tool that linked greater production, the T's growing Canadian content, and patriotic conviction. Between October 1914 and March 1915 his plant was "practically at a shut down" but only because another addition was being built. The ethos of "efficiency" in production and sales had moral as well as patriotic implications. In April, after talks with Ford and Ford's secretary-manager, James Joseph Couzens (a native of Chatham, Ont.), McGregor introduced a $4/eight-hour day. This "profit-sharing" plan came laden not with formulations for future profits but with qualifying conditions for upright lifestyles supervised by new "sociological" and centralized employment departments. A range of authorities, especially the National Civic Federation in New York, categorized the plan as a blatant wage hike.

In June 1915 the Border Cities were rocked by a detonation of planted explosives at a garment shop that was making uniforms. Fearful of similar sabotage, McGregor said nothing of the Pinkerton detectives he privately hired between July and January to investigate "suspected depredations" at his factory. Just as problematic was Henry Ford's cavalier treatment of his Canadian company. His unfulfilled promise to build a tractor plant locally left McGregor vulnerable to poaching of the Ford name for tractors and forced him to solicit legal opinion on whether his 1904 agreement allowed him to manufacture them – it did not. It was over the war, however, that Ford emerged as a publicist's nightmare. His half-baked pronouncements struck raw nerves in Ontario. Embarrassed and threatened with boycotts by municipal buyers, McGregor, who would never adapt easily to negative publicity, replied that his 78-per-cent-Canadian-owned company was "absolutely with the allies." He persuaded Ford to make conciliatory noises and donate to the Red Cross, though Ford was not one to be coerced. "All the boycotts that Canadian politicians are threatening will have nothing to do with the public demand for Ford cars," he told the Toronto Globe. Fortunately for McGregor, reaction to Ford's "peace ship" and dream of a peace conference did not focus on Ford Canada. Moreover, dominated by Ford personnel, the Ford City branch of the Canadian Patriotic Fund that McGregor had helped organize was one of several successes for him. He had an alderman lobby Toronto's board of control, he generously funded the enlargement of the Essex golf club, a stunning 100-per-cent dividend was declared, and the JCPC confirmed his claim to the Ford shares, now worth some $200,000. In December he felt able to shake off his parent company's disinclination for philanthropy and ask Couzens, who had parted ways with Ford in an ugly separation in October, to help the Essex Health Association, which needed money for its sanatorium. Couzens turned him down, bluntly.

In February 1916 McGregor went to Ottawa to talk to officials about the federal budget, specifically the proposed tax on excess business profits. Initially supportive (compliance looked good), he came to dislike this tax intensely and greedily. More troublesome, as his firm struggled to move 18,771 autos in 1915 and 32,646 in 1916, was the wartime congestion on Canada's railways. Amazingly, McGregor did not back

off. Production was boosted; in 1917 Ford was Canada's only exporter of cars. Company-sponsored newsreels and travelogues (many with Model Ts in imperial settings) took Ford into the culture of popular film across Canada and heralded Windsor as its automotive hub. An unusual puff in the Canadian Motorist (Toronto) in 1916 focused on "McGregor of Ford." In 1917 his office would take over all newspaper advertising from the dealers.

McGregor's industrial activities precluded military involvement, but he fully supported the martial efforts of his brother Walter Leishman, who in 1916 became lieutenant-colonel of the 241st Infantry Battalion (the Canadian Scottish Borderers), a unit the family wanted to attire in McGregor tartan. He was also restrained by increasing civic involvement. In 1916 he became the elected member for Ford City in the new Essex Border Utilities Commission, which was authorized by provincial statute to create a regional water and sewage system. The following year he became its chair. Almost immediately, common cause fell victim to opposing interests among the existing municipal commissions and councillors resentful of regional oversight, cost apportionments, and McGregor's corporate manner. Support came from the like-minded Border Chamber of Commerce, formed in January from the Windsor Board of Trade. McGregor was made a director in March and named to the labour committee.

These civic initiatives and squabbles faded in importance before gloomy war news and the unrestrained spread locally of manufacturers, including such new branches as Champion Spark Plug. Reports of revolutionary Russia sowed fears of Bolshevism and intensified antagonisms toward European workers, concerns shared by Ford Canada. In the fall of 1917 another phase of national fund-raising for the war, the Victory Loans, took McGregor to a new level of engagement. He was the natural choice to head the campaign in Essex: he had the connections, the organizational skills, and corporate resources. Ford accountants handled the finances, McGregor's film crews were everywhere, and employees were expected to subscribe. The drive included mass meetings, fireworks, John Philip Sousa's Marine Band from the United States, vaudevillian entertainments, and constantly elevated targets. McGregor raised $4,915,000, a figure exceeded only by the amounts raised in Toronto, Hamilton, Ottawa, and London.

The much-lauded campaign added to his civic weight. Within the EBUC, in early 1918 he moved debate forward slowly, in part by underlining the pollution found by the International Joint Commission. His private assets were bolstered by his purchase and reorganization, with others, of National Spring and Wire, which made fencing and seats for Fords. In April, on the question of adopting the federally initiated daylight saving, many factories, labour groups, and municipal councils followed Ford Canada's resistance, but when the tone-setting McGregor inexplicably reversed its position, all fell into line. In July the governor general, the Duke of Devonshire, marvelled at his plant, as all visitors did.

Watching for spillover into Canada, McGregor monitored the war's impact on the American automotive industry. In 1917 the powerful National Automobile Chamber of Commerce had resisted attempts to reduce the production of passenger cars and supplies of steel. Worried that the Canadian government would impose restrictions, in January 1918 McGregor brought together, for "co-operative action," 34 automotive, parts, and tire producers to form the Automotive Industries of Canada, of which he became first president. It weakly emulated the NACC model; some effort went into cancelling automobile shows (except for the CNE) as a gesture of restraint. McGregor could be more effective on his own. In February he successfully lobbied the new War Trade Board in Ottawa to forgo a tax on all motor cars and adopt instead, in June, a tax on imports alone and the stoppage of luxury imports. On steel, it was the Canadian Ford, Chalmers, and Studebaker firms in the Border Cities and branches of other heavy industries that persuaded the American War Industries Board to lift its embargo on exports. Supplies of steel nevertheless remained restricted and production at Ford Canada dropped, though its revenues were boosted by the start of manufacture of trucks, the sale of parts and Fordson tractors, and, in step with Ford Detroit in February, a price increase on Model Ts, which sparked consumer angst.

What McGregor could not control fully was the fundamental shifts among the autoworkers. The chamber of commerce, where he became vice-president and other Ford officers held sway, could address such recurring concerns as the cross-border taxation of commuting workers and gain popularity by jabbing immigrants. In the auto plants, declining work because of material shortages bred trouble; at the same time, governments in both countries relaxed limits on union activity. In the Border Cities before the era of lasting auto unions, it was the International Association of Machinists that had the strongest presence. On 28 June 1918 a delegation filed into McGregor's office and, emboldened by a membership drive, strikes in Toronto and Detroit, and wage increases in Detroit, tabled a petition for a $5/eight-hour day. Dissatisfaction was voiced too, backed by employees returning from the war, over Ford's use of Europeans, though few would do the work they did in the barely tolerable heat-treating shops. When McGregor locked out his workers on 6 July, both sides rushed to secure the support of federal labour minister Thomas Wilson Crothers. The IAM claimed, correctly, that the lockout was illegal and that McGregor, contrary to his profes-

sions and even as he rejected war production for Canada, had been turning out parts for the tanks and warships being made by Ford Detroit. Ottawa, however, refused to recognize the disruption as anything more than a lay-off. On 12 August – most suspected McGregor had been holding the Detroit-set wage increase in reserve – he calculatingly conceded.

McGregor's public profile could not have been greater – in his golf club (where he was president in 1917–18), in the debate on water and sewers, as chair for the organization of a manufacturers' section in the chamber of commerce, and in September 1918 in Toronto at the annual meeting of the AIC. Scant attention was paid to the *Canadian Motorist*'s complaints about his attempts to shut down shows for the duration of the war, which was winding down in any case, or to criticism in the press of Ford's reversal on pricing. After the lockout, McGregor moved to restore Ford's place in the war effort. Of the Ford-made films circulated by the Department of Trade and Commerce, one, dedicated to the Canada Food Board, merged footage on the Greater Production movement, the Border Manufacturers' Farmers Association, Fordson tractors, and good roads.

In the Victory Loan drive of October–November, McGregor once again devised a campaign brimming with theatricality. Reports of him announcing the armistice at campaign headquarters, and then jumping on a chair to lead the crowd in singing "Praise God from whom all blessings flow," present a stirring image. An outbreak of influenza produced only a temporary obstacle to the drive, and it would be some time before evidence of payment defaults and of embezzlement by a Ford accountant would surface. During the post-war years, McGregor had more serious problems. Both the EBUC and the chamber of commerce faced continued opposition. In January 1919 Windsor gained four labour councillors, including Archibald Hooper, a railway machinist and scrappy IAM mouthpiece who attacked the chamber over promotions that ensured neither housing nor jobs. McGregor and the EBUC attracted his particular ire. Bickering intensified as opposing technical plans were exchanged, though voter turnouts on related by-laws suggest low public concern. The commission, however, had the backing of the Ontario Railway and Municipal Board, and in July the province gave the EBUC additional power as a regional board of health.

As Ford Canada headed into an industry-wide post-war slump, McGregor, a master of corporate spin, remained optimistic. A wage increase in May and his initiation of an employees' welfare and housing fund in September may have forestalled IAM action. He had been re-elected president of the AIC, where he got on well with vice-president Robert Samuel McLaughlin* of General Motors of Canada, which gained ground on Ford through its heavy manufacturing plant in Walkerville. In October, Ford Canada responded by taking over Dominion Forge and Stamping, an important supplier. The previous month McGregor had gone to Ottawa as an employers' delegate to the National Industrial Conference, but he did not deem it important. Praise for Henry Ford, not criticism, came from labour. McGregor ran off statements about profit-sharing, said industry had done enough to improve living conditions, and complained about his troubles with labour in Australia.

The call for him to head the final Victory campaign in October–November 1919 was predictable, but he begged off. Though he claimed to be busy with private business, which now included a hotel company, he knew that patriotic enthusiasms had been superseded by cost-of-living concerns and a collapse of charitable giving – he had tried unsuccessfully to mount a drive to fund a hospital for the Salvation Army. Always thrilled at the prospect of hosting aristocracy, however, he took on the social arrangements for the visit of the Prince of Wales in October, a task that included the contentious paring of guest lists. Back-to-back elections, provincial in October and municipal in January 1920, involved him in a political role, aggressively prominent but never a candidate save for the EBUC. Supported by his coterie, Windsor's Liberal candidate (and McGregor's former pastor) survived the sweep of the United Farmers of Ontario. McGregor declined to run for mayor of Windsor but readily agreed to serve as president of the new Municipal Electors' Association, which briefly crystallized the progressive urge of businessmen to reform municipal politics based on experiments in the United States. Windsor's labour councillors resented this heady, undemocratic challenge, which seemed like Ford on the hustings. McGregor took the lead in nominating aldermanic candidates; for the water boards he wanted sympathetic nominees. Sewage politics could be gritty. At a meeting he chaired on 30 December in a Jewish school, candidate Charles Robert Tuson (a former mayor and an adversary on the sewage issue) was side-swiped by the accusation that he had registered restrictions prohibiting the sale of properties to Jews. In 1920 McGregor was reappointed chair of the EBUC. In March he threw a "bombshell" into its proceedings when he took its secretary away to become advertising manager of Ford Canada. He expended more charitable effort on his wife's campaign to rebuild the sanatorium of the Essex Health Association.

That fall, McGregor's gang appeared in strength at the CNE along with Henry Ford and his secretary, Ernest Gustav Liebold. Ford Canada did not suffer as acutely as its parent in the slump of the early 1920s, but McGregor still had to be careful, if not manipulative. In 1919 and again the next year he had delayed expansion; publicly he blamed the burden of federal taxes. At the same time he took accounting steps to shield his firm's true cash balances from the prying eyes of government and labour; he had his traffic manager challenge railway rates; and at a later point he probably took part in an arrangement between Canadian and American car makers to block the export of Canadian-made automobiles except for Fords. In 1920 he endured a number of personal difficulties. His mother and a sister died, and in November, after attending a directors' meeting of the Merchants' Bank of Canada in Montreal, he underwent surgery, reportedly for appendicitis.

While McGregor was recuperating, the hearings of the federal commission on tariffs re-opened debate on Ford Canada's prices. With his imprimatur, on 30 November assistant manager W. R. Campbell stepped up to refute claims that Ford was taking advantage of protection to maintain prices that exceeded the cost of Fords in the United States. Smaller scales of manufacture dictated different costs, he contended, but this argument was offset by testimony from other automobile executives and representatives from farmers' groups. Politically the Ford position changed no minds, and in perceptions of Ford there may have been other biases at work. Beyond the commission the Border Cities had a hard time explaining their affinity with Detroit: "It would almost seem that we are here in a little kingdom of our own and to some extent apart and away from the outer world," industrial commissioner F. Maclure Sclanders speculated in *Canadian Machinery and Manufacturing News* (Toronto).

A weakened McGregor returned to Windsor in January 1921, only to witness a flare-up of utility politics and more attacks on the chamber of commerce and his own "dictatorial" interventions. His response is obscure, but Archibald Hooper, who headed Windsor's campaign to withdraw from the EBUC, mysteriously lost his railway job and Queen's Park rejected Windsor's application. After offering some conciliation, McGregor, on his doctors' advice, resigned from the EBUC in March. For almost five years he had pushed an agenda, unique in Ontario, on the important if lacklustre issues of regional planning. Business concerns were just as taxing. When he was not occupied with petty requests from Henry Ford – his information on the banking of Ford's personal funds in Canada also shed light on Ford Canada's own strategic use of banks – there were corporate problems to face. He authorized advertising in response to competition from GM and company resistance to actions by dealers over excise tax refunds and over price cuts on tires as a result of Ford's pressure on suppliers. In April he began losing key personnel in reaction to the economy, Henry Ford's purges, and a possible shift in the balance of control between McGregor and Campbell, whom Ford had tried to lure to Detroit.

McGregor spent time that spring at a West Virginian resort and then at his cottage. A photograph shows him with a cane, overweight but nattily attired as always. Back at home, he worked on committees for a public golf course and the health association's sanatorium. That fall he did more jobs for Henry Ford, catering to his interests in water-power in Ontario and railways, and, with threats of court action, protecting Ford's Canadian dividends and salary from local assessment. In addition, he went along with the anti-Semitism espoused by Ford's *Dearborn Independent*, had his staff distribute copies of extracts published as *The international Jew: the world's foremost problem* (1920–21), and reported to Liebold on Jewish activity in Windsor. He was not alone in such condonation: the Woman's Christian Temperance Union, for one, reprinted anti-Jewish material from the *Independent* in its newspaper.

In late 1921 McGregor's attention was again sidetracked by the price issue. Despite his company's slashing of prices in September and a revival in demand, the question was taken up by William Edgar Raney*, Ontario's pugnacious attorney general. In the campaign leading up to the federal election of December, Raney threw his weight behind the Progressives and their agrarian, anti-protection platform. In a speech on 18 November he lashed out at the tariff on automobiles, higher prices, and the presumed complicity of Ford Canada. The address spread rapidly among Canadian newspapers. Unable to resist, and in a strong performance for an ailing man, McGregor thrust himself into the campaigns in Essex North and South. Audiences were amused by his characteristic gibes and numbed by his convoluted economics. The Liberals won overwhelming majorities.

McGregor could still handle an appreciable workload, including complex planning for a major plant expansion. In January 1922 Ford Canada announced its return to full-time production and the launch of its "greatest sales campaign ever," for its enclosed coupes and sedans – the company never treated the T as an unchanging model. After meetings in Montreal on a takeover of the Merchants' Bank, McGregor fielded more menial requests from Ford and Liebold. The *Border Cities Star*, as the *Evening Record* had become, had long granted McGregor a revered place in "Motoropolis," though this reputation could be at odds with the opinions of consumers, agrarian radicals, labour journals, and lesser auto executives with independent views. In January 1922, for example, the wife of a Walkerville plumber told Henry Ford in a blistering letter that she desperately wanted a used Ford, but resented their exorbitant price and the profiteering of such "millionars" as McGregor. On 4 March McGregor visited his oak-lined office for the last time. Feeling unwell, he was X-rayed and sent to Montreal's Royal Victoria Hospital, where he died.

The *Star* announced his passing in headlines of a size rarely seen, even during the war. The cause of death was reported as intestinal trouble arising from an old injury suffered in a railway accident; the family believed it was cancer; pathological study points to a rare blood-vessel disorder. McGregor's mammoth funeral was attended by the automotive elite; his canonization in the *Star* reached full definition. The bulk of his estate, which was valued at more than $1,235,500, went to his widow, whose social withdrawal ended when she returned to renovating St Andrew's Church in Windsor, a project she and Gordon had planned. Not surprisingly, Ford Canada was identified as his "greatest work." Campbell assumed direction there to complete the expansion planned to meet the hurtful "competition" of the parent company. Between April and June 1922 the *Star* published a series on the regional and national impact of Ford Canada, a summary, the timing suggests, of McGregor's legacy. In the midst of this series, a blustery portrayal elevated him to an iconic level. In the search for a speedy form of road transportation to open up the country, "Henry Ford solved the problem for the world. The late Gordon McGregor solved it for Canada." Even allowing for his company's minimal technological contribution and the vital work of his department heads, there is some merit in this claim when one equates him with his cars.

DAVID ROBERTS

AO, F 149; RG 8-1-1, 4352/1904, 2856/1905, 1937/1906. Benson Ford Research Center (Dearborn, Mich.), Acc. 65 (reminiscences of various Ford employees), box 130; Acc. 285 (Henry Ford, office papers [Dearborn]), box 9, file 14; box 28, file 9; box 57, file 10; Acc. 384 (L. J. Thompson research papers), box 1, "Philanthropies" [of Henry and Clara Ford] and "Properties – Sandwich, Ont." Ford Motor Company of Canada Limited, Hist. Dept. (Oakville, Ont.), Documentation in unmarked boxes; G. M. McGregor file; Legal Dept., Corporate minute-books, 1 (1904–11); 2 (1911–25). LAC, RG 36, ser.8, 5: 786–819; 9: 1304–1450; 15: 2221–32; 23: 4312–34. Library of Congress, Manuscript Div. (Washington), James Couzens papers. Univ. of Windsor Arch. (Windsor, Ont.), 97-002 (Ford Motor Company of Canada Limited), boxes 2–5, 7. *Border Cities Star* (Windsor), 1918–23. *Evening Record* (Windsor), 1895–1918. *Industrial Banner* (Toronto), 1918. *Canadian Machinery and Manufacturing News* (Toronto), 1909–21. *Canadian Motorist* (Toronto), 1914–22. D. F. Davis, *Conspicuous production: automobiles and elites in Detroit, 1899–1933* (Philadelphia, 1988). Hugh Durnford and Glenn Baechler, *Cars of Canada* (Toronto, 1973). *Ford Graphic* (Windsor), 7, no.15 (17 Aug. 1954), golden jubilee suppl. *Ford Sales Bull.* (Ford City [Windsor]), 1913–15. *Ford Times* (Ford City), 1913–18. *Industrial Canada* (Toronto), 1904–25. J. C. Keith, *Windsor Utilities Commission and its antecedent commissions . . .* (Windsor, 1957). G. S. May, *A most unique machine: the Michigan origins of the American automobile industry* (Grand Rapids, Mich., 1975). Kevin Mowle, "The Canadian 'T' – Made in Canada" series, *Old Autos* (Bothwell, Ont.), 4 March 1996–3 Nov. 1997. James Naylor, *The* new democracy: challenging the social order in industrial Ontario, 1914–25 (Toronto, 1991). Tom Traves, "The development of the Ontario automobile industry to 1939," in I. M. Drummond et al., Progress without planning: the economic history of Ontario from confederation to the Second World War (Toronto, 1987), 208–23; The state and enterprise: Canadian manufacturers and the federal government, 1917–1931 (Toronto, 1979). Mira Wilkins and F. E. Hill, American business abroad: Ford on six continents, intro. Allan Nevins (Detroit, 1964).

MACHAR, AGNES MAULE, author and social reformer; b. 23 Jan. 1837 in Kingston, Upper Canada, daughter of John Machar* and Margaret Sim; d. there unmarried 24 Jan. 1927.

John Machar, a Church of Scotland clergyman, left Scotland for Kingston in 1827 to become pastor of St Andrew's Church. He helped found Queen's College and was its principal from 1846 to 1853. His wife, herself the daughter of a Scottish clergyman, had joined him following their marriage in Montreal in 1832. Their first child lived only briefly; Agnes was born in 1837 and her brother, John Maule, four years later. Except for a year in a Montreal boarding school, she was educated by her father, who possessed an excellent library. Before she was ten he was instructing her in Latin and Greek; French, German, and Italian followed. Agnes throve on this regime, her precociousness in the study complemented by a love of the outdoors. After her father's death in 1863, she remained with her mother, a leader in good works who died in 1883. Agnes then moved in with her married brother, and she stayed on in his house on Sydenham Street following his passing in 1899.

Despite her residence in a small colonial city, Machar had the benefits of a rich social and intellectual milieu. Along with the sources of stimulation available to her as a youth in the manse, there were those that had come from her parents' acquaintances, among them politicians John A. Macdonald* and Richard John Cartwright*; Queen's professor George Romanes, whose son George John would achieve fame in England as an associate of Charles Darwin; and cleric Joseph Antisell Allen and his son Charles Grant Blairfindie, who would make his mark as a novelist and popularizer of Darwinian science, and whose sister Caroline Elizabeth became Agnes's sister-in-law in 1879. Later, as a well-known author, Agnes developed her own circle and, especially at Ferncliff, her summer home in Gananoque near the Thousand Islands, she hosted international figures who shared her interest in literature, religion, and science. On her travels she came to know some of the era's famous writers, including the one she most admired, Quaker poet John Greenleaf Whittier. Among prominent Presbyterians she seems to have been closest to Daniel James Macdonnell*, an intimate of her family from his days at Queen's, and George Monro Grant*, its

principal from 1877 to 1902. A key figure in Canada's small community of literary and artistic women, and something of a mentor to its younger members, she decried the neglect and premature death in 1887 of Isabella Valancy Crawford*; on happier occasions, she welcomed Emily Pauline Johnson* and other women writers to Ferncliff, which Grant Allen publicized so well in Longman's Magazine (London).

Agnes Machar had the time, wit, and vigour to turn her opportunities to good account in a stream of publications. These began anonymously in childhood; her first book, a memorial to a janitor at Queen's, appeared in 1859. The last three decades of the century were her most prolific. Her career could be said to have been launched by her prize-winning novel Katie Johnstone's cross: a Canadian tale (Toronto, 1870). Often writing under the pseudonym Fidelis, she subsequently produced a memorial to her father, at least eight novels, and numerous poems and essays. She also wrote or collaborated on six works of popular history, in addition to other publications. Her poetry appeared in American, British, and Canadian periodicals, a selection being published as Lays of the "True North," and other Canadian poems (London and Toronto, 1899). Patriotic and imperial themes informed much of her verse, but the natural beauty surrounding Ferncliff was her joy and most frequent inspiration. Generations of Canadian schoolchildren encountered her verse in their readers. This exposure, and the fact that her poems and novels won prizes and, like her histories, were often reissued, testifies to the degree to which her work struck a chord with contemporaries. Many of her essays can still be read with profit. The range of her interests can best be sampled from the pieces printed in the dominion's leading intellectual journal, the Canadian Monthly and National Review/Rose-Belford's Canadian Monthly and National Review, between 1872 and 1882 and in the Toronto Week in 1883–96.

Written for Sunday school libraries, Katie Johnstone's cross had introduced a classic Machar figure to Canadian literature: the girl or young woman whose faith, moral standards, and good works inspire errant males to turn from wrongdoing or recover their Christian belief. Shifting later in the decade to adult readers in a series of essays in the Canadian Monthly, Machar rose to the challenge of defending the Christian faith against the onslaughts of scientific rationalism and higher criticism. She did not insist on unchanging views of creation and the Bible; rather, she asked orthodox Christians and those on the brink of scepticism to accept evolutionary theory and critical readings of the Bible as the means to a new and fuller understanding of God's work. She may not have won many over, but she did win respect. In 1876 secularist and skilled controversialist William Dawson LeSueur* declared that, of those who had questioned his arguments in the *Canadian Monthly* on the efficacy of prayer, Machar had given the most satisfactory response. Although she regarded Christianity as the "fullest revelation" of God and personally remained within the Presbyterian fold, her theological liberalism did allow for a sympathetic interest in other religions, particularly Buddhism.

Machar's defence of Christianity also sought to make it socially relevant, especially in terms of what a Christian society owed to the poor in the new industrial age. Her thinking here showed considerable development. In an essay in 1879 she recommended measures to assist the urban poor, including Prohibition, state-funded work programs, and refuges. She worried, however, that if the churches became almoners to the largely unchurched poor they might encourage hypocrisy and pauperization. In the years that followed, when economic depression was accentuating poverty, her experience and wide reading, which included American Social Gospel literature, *In darkest England and the way out* by the Salvation Army's William Booth, and the 1889 *Report* of the royal commission on the relations of labour and capital, led her to a broader perspective. She now maintained that the real hypocrisy lay in churches that preached to the poor about their souls while disregarding their bodily needs. Privileged Christians needed to recognize that the poor had a right to work, justice, and the means to rise above subsistence.

Machar delivered this message most fully (if not as forcefully as in some of her articles) in *Roland Graeme: knight* ... (Montreal, 1892). In this well-received novel, orthodox Christians applaud a mill owner who gives $5,000 to the church even as they ignore the miserable dwellings in which he houses his workers and the grim factory where they toil for wages he threatens to reduce. Challenging this villain and a complacent clergyman is a crusading journalist, Roland, who espouses "Christian socialism." He joins the Knights of Labor and stands by the workers when they strike. Inspired by a minister who is the clergyman's opposite and by Nora, a female paradigm of applied Christianity, he recovers his faith and develops a new attitude to the urban poor. Cautious in its ending and unoriginal in its message, the book was nonetheless a pioneering Social Gospel novel, even somewhat radical in having as its hero a member of a controversial labour organization. Roland was perhaps based in part on Machar's barrister brother, who sympathized with the Knights and the reformist views of Henry George.

Though the elderly poor did not figure significantly in *Roland Graeme*, they became a source of particular concern for Machar. In a paper presented to the National Council of Women of Canada in 1895, she recommended that homes be established for them, by the state if necessary, and that the homes be "as little

regarded as *charity* for the veteran in the *industrial* army, as is the pension of the old soldier." Moreover, Prohibitionist though she was – three of her essays on temperance had appeared in the *Canadian Monthly* in 1877 – she wanted the housing to be sufficiently homelike to allow for, it seemed, the occasional drink. In the end, it was elderly women whom she would assist directly, by leaving a bequest to establish the Agnes Maule Machar Home "for old ladies past earning their own livelihood." Opened in Kingston by the Local Council of Women in 1930, it still functions.

Like many other English Canadians, Machar was a proud nationalist and imperialist. She took little interest in the mechanics of nation-building, instead promoting a vision with high moral purpose, purged of sordid party politics and "racial" tension. This vision was evident as early as 1875 in "Lost and won: a story of Canadian life," a novel serialized in the *Canadian Monthly* and so apropos that Machar and her publisher took care to assert that no reference was being made to contemporary political events, then still tainted by the Pacific Scandal. In 1879 she used a Dominion Day poem to suggest that, as leaders of a young nation where the "waxen mould" was still soft, Canada's politicians had the opportunity to set a moral example. Few of them took note, but parliamentary expert John George Bourinot* was so enamoured of this lofty idea 16 years later that he used a stanza of the poem to conclude his *How Canada is governed* ... (Toronto). Reviewers applauded.

Machar's interpretation of Canada's history was deployed to this same visionary end, and to promote patriotism. Though she was by no means unique among English/Protestant writers in her celebration of French Canada's past, her efforts are noteworthy because they were directed towards children as well as adults, were made through poetry and fiction as well as "factual" narratives, and were intended to mitigate French-English tensions. When her *Stories of New France* ... , written in two parts with Thomas Guthrie Marquis* penning the second, was published in Boston in 1890, in the wake of Quebec's controversial Jesuits' Estates Act, reviewers who recognized the book's moderating purpose praised its timeliness. As history, Machar's part is a light, unexceptional retelling of the stories of Samuel de Champlain*, Jacques Cartier*, Huronia, and the like. Occasionally she left the relatively safe terrain of history to address contemporary issues directly, as in her poem "Quebec to Ontario, a plea for the life of Riel, September 1885" and in letters advocating clemency for Louis Riel* in the *Canada Presbyterian* (Toronto). In taking this position she swam against a strong current, as is evidenced by letters of chastisement in the latter. In her last literary effort at crisis management, *Young soldier hearts of France: a wreath of immortelles* (Toronto, 1919), produced in her eighties, she edited and translated the letters of gallant French soldiers who had died in World War I. Given the state of relations between French-speaking Canada and the rest of the dominion, her gesture was sadly naive but wonderfully consistent.

Machar took a similar visionary approach to the British empire and Canada's place within it. The empire had flourished because it fulfilled a "Divine purpose." Admittedly for some it was a source of material aggrandisement or chauvinistic pride (shallow young Englishmen are stock figures in Machar's fiction). But it was here that Canada could play a role, by calling Britain back to its ancient ideals and function as the moral jewel in the imperial crown. Formal ties such as a Canadian presence in an imperial parliament did not interest Machar – spiritual and cultural links that required no institutional structures were her concern. Until 1913, when she published *Stories of the British empire* . . . (London and Toronto), verse was her main vehicle for promoting such links. *Lays of the "True North"* of 1899 began with the poem that had won her the *Week*'s prize for the best verse commemorating Queen Victoria's jubilee in 1887. The poem touched on what Machar saw as the most important imperial task, advancing the spread of Christianity. This spiritual aspect allowed her to work without national constraint for one of her abiding goals, closer ties between Britain, Canada, and the United States, and the undermining of what the *Week* called "Yankeephobia." Her aim led her to positions that were decidedly unusual for a nationalist/imperialist: yes to reciprocity with the United States in 1891 but no to an imperial trade *zollverein* two years later, and a resounding no to Canada's stand in the Bering Sea dispute, where Machar's environmental concerns confirmed her belief that the Americans were right in trying to halt pelagic sealing [*see* Clarence Nelson Cox*].

As a feminist, Machar was chiefly concerned with education and paid work. She challenged prevailing arguments that higher education would unsex women, maintaining instead that it would allow them to develop their God-given talents, make them better Christians, wives, and mothers, and, if marriage did not fall "naturally to their lot," assist them to earn "an honourable competence." Like most of her contemporaries, she assumed that married women should ideally be full-time homemakers, yet she recognized that it was often necessary for poor women to work. In essays and in a resolution presented to the National Council of Women in 1896, she called for legislation to improve the conditions of work for women and children in shops and factories. Her advocacy of shorter hours for female factory workers was challenged by Carrie Matilda Derick*, a lecturer at McGill University and a prominent council member, who maintained that such legislation was inconsistent with women's calls for equality of opportunity with men. Although Machar seems not to have pressed the council to lobby for equal pay for women, she did make adequate remuneration an issue in her writing.

Machar's organizational ties reflected her interests. In the 1880s she was treasurer of the Kingston wing of the Presbyterian Woman's Foreign Missionary Society and in the 1890s she sat on the executives of the Local Council of Women and the national body. She served as president of the Kingston Humane Society and as secretary of the local Young Women's Christian Association, and was a founder of the Canadian Audubon Society. During the first decade of the new century she was a founding member of the Canadian Women's Press Club, a vice-president of the Canadian Society of Authors, and a member of the Kingston branch of the Women's Art Association of Canada. Her intellectual gifts and literary accomplishments would certainly have qualified her for membership in such organizations as the Royal Society of Canada, but her gender kept her out. And she seems not to have belonged to the Woman's Christian Temperance Union, despite her support for Prohibition.

Though widely travelled, Machar never lived extravagantly, and she appears to have carefully managed her income from writing. When she died in 1927, she left an estate worth about $52,800, most of it in mortgages. To her "faithful friend and helper" Matilda Speers she bequeathed an annuity; Ferncliff she gave to two other close friends, T. G. Marquis and Lawson Powers Chambers, a Queen's graduate and professor of philosophy at Washington University in St Louis, Mo.

An exemplar of the theological liberalism and socially oriented Christianity present in late Victorian Canada, and of the national and imperial zeal that preoccupied many of its writers, Machar was nonetheless unusual in the range of issues she addressed and in some of the apparently paradoxical positions she adopted. Yet in keeping with her pseudonym, Fidelis, she was remarkably consistent. A century after her heyday, scholars may cringe at her poetic references to the "dusky Hindoo," the "low-browed savage," and the "hardy Indian," all succumbing willingly to the "hope and progress" brought by Victoria's Christian empire. In the end, however, most of those who have studied her career probably share the fond assessment of Alfred Edward Prince of Queen's, in 1934, that Agnes Machar had lived a large-hearted life and died "rich in character, rich in achievement."

RUTH COMPTON BROUWER

[No collection of Agnes Maule Machar's papers has been located. Some of her correspondence is available in the Louisa Murray fonds in York Univ. Libraries, Arch. and Special Coll. (Toronto); the Helena Coleman papers, file 152, in Victoria Univ. Library, Special Coll. (Toronto); and the George Monro Grant papers in LAC, MG 29, D38. Her estate file is in AO, RG 22-159, no.3867. Information on her background can be found in *Memorials of the life and ministry of the Rev. John Machar, D.D., late minister of St. Andrew's Church, Kingston* (Toronto, 1873), compiled by members of the family and edited by Agnes, and in John Machar's biog. file at the UCC-C.

Machar's first book, published anonymously, was *Faithful unto death, a memorial of John Anderson, late janitor of Queen's College, Kingston, C.W.* (Kingston, [Ont.], 1859). Her novels include *Katie Johnstone's cross: a Canadian tale* (Toronto, 1870); *Lucy Raymond, or, the children's watch-word* (Toronto, [1871?]); *For king and country: a story of 1812* (Toronto, 1874; originally serialized in the *Canadian Monthly and National Rev.*, Toronto); "Lost and won" (serialized in the *Canadian Monthly* in 1875 but not subsequently published, although journalist and poet Thomas O'Hagan regarded it as one of her two best novels: *see* O'Hagan, *infra*); *Marjorie's Canadian winter, a story of the northern lights* (Boston, 1892; repr. Toronto, 1906); *Roland Graeme: knight* (reprinted in Toronto in 1906 and again in 1996; the modern reprint, including an introduction by Carole Gerson, was issued as part of the *Early Canadian women writers* series); *Down the river to the sea* (New York, 1894); and *The heir of Fairmount Grange* (London and Toronto, [1895]). *The quest of the fatal river* (Toronto, 1904) is attributed to Machar in several sources including Wallace, *Macmillan dict.*, and the *Canadian annual rev.*, 1904: xiv, but researchers have been unable to locate any copies. A memorial entitled *Mère Marie-Rose, fondatrice de la Congrégation des SS. Noms de Jésus et de Marie au Canada* (Montréal, 1895), which is attributed to Machar in some libraries because its author also used the pseudonym Fidelis, was in fact written by Jules-Henri Prétot.

Besides *Lays of the "True North"* (a second enlarged edition of which was issued at London and Toronto in 1902), there are several more specialized collections of Machar's poems, including *The Thousand Islands* (Toronto, 1935), assembled after her death by Thomas Guthrie Marquis and published in the *Ryerson poetry chap-book* series. In addition to those discussed in the text, Machar's historical works include *The story of old Kingston* (Toronto, 1908). Her work as a historian is discussed in D. M. Hallman, "Cultivating a love of Canada: Agnes Maule Machar, 1837–1927," in *Creating historical memory: English Canadian women and the work of history*, ed. Alison Prentice and Beverley Boutilier (Vancouver, 1997), 25–50.

More extensive lists of Machar's publications can be found in Nancy Miller Chenier, "Agnes Maule Machar: her life, her social concerns, and a preliminary bibliography of her writing" (MA research essay, Carleton Univ., Ottawa, 1977), and in D. M. Hallman, "Religion and gender in the writing and work of Agnes Maule Machar" (PHD thesis, Univ. of Toronto, 1994). Her contributions to the *Canadian Monthly* and its successor, *Rose-Belford's Canadian Monthly and National Rev.*, are listed in the *Index* compiled by Marilyn G. Flitton (Toronto, 1976).

Among the sketches of Machar written during or just after her lifetime, and useful for identifying her Canadian and international circle of friends, are A. E. Wetherald, "Some Canadian literary women – II: Fidelis," *Week* (Toronto), 5 April 1888: 300–1; Thomas O'Hagan, "Some Canadian women writers," *Week*, 25 Sept. 1896: 1050–53; L. A. Guild, "Canadian celebrities, no.73: Agnes Maule Machar (Fidelis)," *Canadian Magazine*, 27 (May–October 1906): 499–501; F. L. MacCallum, "Agnes Maule Machar," *Canadian Magazine*, 62 (November 1923–April 1924): 354–56; Robert William Cumberland's tributes in the *Queen's Quarterly* (Kingston), 34 (1926–27): 331–39, and *Willisons Monthly* (Toronto), 3 (1927–28): 34–37; and the entry by Alfred Edward Prince in *Standard dict. of Canadian biog.* (Roberts and Tunnell), vol.1.

Recent secondary sources on Machar by historians include M[ary] Vipond, "Blessed are the peacemakers: the labour question in Canadian Social Gospel fiction," *Journal of Canadian Studies* (Peterborough, Ont.), 10 (1975), no.3: 32–43; Ruth Compton Brouwer, "The 'between-age' Christianity of Agnes Machar," *CHR*, 65 (1984): 347–70, and "Moral nationalism in Victorian Canada: the case of Agnes Machar," *Journal of Canadian Studies*, 20 (1985–86), no.1: 90–108; Ramsay Cook, *The regenerators: social criticism in late Victorian English Canada* (Toronto, 1985); and Constance Backhouse, *Petticoats and prejudice: women and law in nineteenth-century Canada* ([Toronto], 1991). A study from a literary perspective is Carole Gerson, "Three writers of Victorian Canada," in *Canadian writers and their works*, ed. Robert Leckie *et al.* (24v. in 2 ser., Toronto, 1983–96), fiction ser., 1 (1983): 195–256. R.C.B.]

McINTOSH, ELIZA ANN (Reid), social reformer; b. 30 Oct. 1841 in Montreal, daughter of Nicholas McIntosh, a cabinetmaker, and Margaret Brown; m. there 12 Sept. 1867 Robert Reid, and they had one daughter; d. there 8 Jan. 1926.

The increased public involvement of women and the rise of feminism were closely linked to the urban reform movement that began to take shape in Canadian cities around 1880. It was in this context that Eliza Ann Reid, about whom little is known before the 1890s, would win renown through her dynamism and innovative spirit. The daughter of a Montreal furniture maker, she probably received an education comparable to that of her sister, Frances Ramsay, who studied with private teachers and attended lectures given under the auspices of the Montreal Ladies' Educational Association. Frances was to marry George Washington Stephens* in 1878 or 1879 and, like her sister, would be active in various women's associations. In 1867 Eliza Ann married Robert Reid, a man of Scottish origins who prospered with the stone-carving firm he established in Montreal.

In 1892 Eliza Ann founded one of the first women's associations in Canada, the Montreal Women's Club, drawing her inspiration from similar organizations in a number of American cities. The club's objectives were broad: it sought to promote the cultural, scientific, and social development of its members. A feminist orientation clearly coloured its activities. It was concerned particularly about the lack of women on school and hospital boards, and on several university faculties. It fought this discrimination by sending petitions to the provincial government and to the relevant authorities, as well as by organizing lectures on themes such as education, law, and women at work, addressing in particular the academic programs to which women had access, their legal status in the province of Quebec, and their presence in the business world. Among the notable members of the Montreal Women's Club were Carrie Matilda Derick*, Lady Drummond [Parker*], Octavia Grace Ritchie*, and the president's own daughter, Helen Richmond Young Reid*. Eliza Ann Reid remained at the head of this association until her resignation in 1902.

In 1893, when the Local Council of Women (the Montreal branch of the National Council of Women of Canada) was founded [*see* Ishbel Maria Marjoribanks*], the Montreal Women's Club became affiliated with this new federation of women's associations in the city. Eliza Ann was then made a vice-president of the Local Council and she remained on its board until at least 1924 (acting as an honorary member during the last few years). In her work within this federation, she came into contact with several renowned feminists of the Montreal bourgeoisie, including francophones Marguerite Thibaudeau [Lamothe*], Joséphine Dandurand [MARCHAND], and Marie Gérin-Lajoie [Lacoste*]. At the national level, she served on a committee studying the legal protection of women and children.

The activities of the Montreal Local Council of Women were related to a number of the themes already espoused by the Montreal Women's Club; the Local Council, however, had greater means and more members to devote to the defence of its causes. Its strengths no doubt explain Eliza Ann's long-lasting commitment to this organization, which made a name for itself through campaigns raising awareness and achievements in public health (by combating infant mortality), education (by distributing pamphlets to mothers), and culture (by presenting concerts and promoting the arts). Advocating a social feminism that still accepted the idea of a natural distinction between the roles of men and women, the association nonetheless helped broaden the rights and privileges of female citizens. Thus it was as wives and mothers that women were urged to demand, for example, the vote and access to higher education and the liberal professions. In this spirit, Eliza Ann encouraged her own daughter to seek admission to McGill College's faculty of arts from the principal himself, John William Dawson*, even though women did not as yet have the right to attend this institution. Helen would follow in her mother's footsteps, being active in the Local Council of Women, figuring among the first women to obtain a BA from McGill University, and contributing to, among other things, the establishment of the McGill School for Graduate Nurses.

Along with her daughter, Eliza Ann served during the 1920s on the board of directors of the Victorian Order of Nurses, an organization that sought to disseminate principles of hygiene, particularly to mothers and young children, and that also helped gain recognition for the nursing profession.

Eliza Ann, who supported commercial reciprocity with the United States [*see* William Stevens FIELDING; Sir Wilfrid Laurier*], gave her political allegiance to the Liberal party. Her religious fervour led her to devote herself to promoting the growth and influence of the Unitarian faith, of which she was an active member. She was on the advisory committee and the board of Montreal's Church of the Messiah.

Firmly convinced that women needed to participate more fully in public affairs, Eliza Ann preached by example. Thus, as a Montrealer she took part in a number of initiatives, among them the improvement of housing in poor neighbourhoods and urban development reforms such as the building of parks, public playgrounds, and public baths, and the upgrading of the water supply, lighting, and public transportation (tramways) services. Following the example of her reformist colleagues, Eliza Ann also concerned herself with urban crime, the fate of prisoners, and prison reform. Involved as well in the fight against alcoholism, she advocated public intervention in this problem and demanded that the city of Montreal grant fewer liquor licences. She also recommended stricter control over the entry of immigrants into Canada.

Upon her death on 8 Jan. 1926, several prominent figures paid tribute to Eliza Ann Reid as a remarkable Montrealer and a Canadian pioneer in organizing women's clubs and promoting women's rights.

LOUISE BIENVENUE

ANQ-M, CE601-S126, 17 janv. 1842; S132, 12 sept. 1867. Victorian Order of Nurses for Canada, Arch. (Montreal), Minutes, 1898–1925. *Gazette* (Montreal), 9, 11–12 Jan. 1926. *Canadian men and women of the time* (Morgan; 1912). Elizabeth Collard, "Montreal cabinetmakers and chairmakers, 1800–1850: a checklist," *Antiques* (New York), 105 (January–June 1974): 1132–46. Margaret Gillett, *We walked very warily: a history of women at McGill* (Montreal, 1981). N. E. S. Griffiths, *The splendid vision: centennial history of the National Council of Women of Canada, 1893–1993* (Ottawa, 1993). Local Council of Women [of Montreal], *Annual report*, 1897–1923; *Montreal Local Council of Women: 21st anniversary, 1893–1915* ([Montreal?, 1915?]). Montreal Women's Club, *Report*, 1893–95, 1898–99, 1900–1. Juliette Patterson, "Helen Reid; l'accès des femmes à l'université: une cause familiale," in *Ces femmes qui ont bâti Montréal*, sous la dir. de Maryse Darsigny *et al.* (Montréal, [1994]), 115–16. Yolande Pinard, "Les débuts du mouvement des femmes à Montréal, 1893–1902," in *Travailleuses et féministes: les femmes dans la société québécoise*, sous la dir. de Marie Lavigne et Yolande Pinard (Montréal, 1983), 177–98. V. J. Strong-Boag, *The parliament of women: the National Council of Women of Canada, 1893–1929* (Ottawa, 1976).

MacKAY, ALEXANDER HOWARD, educator and scientist; b. 19 May 1848 in Plainfield, N.S., son of John MacKay and Barbara MacLean; m. 26 Oct. 1882 Maude Augusta Johnston, daughter of Dr George Moir Johnston*, in Pictou, N.S., and they had one son and one daughter; d. 19 May 1929 in Dartmouth, N.S., and was buried in Scotsburn, N.S.

Alexander Howard MacKay grew up in rural Pictou County, attended local public schools, and graduated from the Pictou Academy in 1865. After a few months of teaching, he enrolled at the Normal School in Truro. In 1869 – having presumably resumed his teaching career in the interim – he began work towards a BA at Dalhousie University in Halifax. The following year he became the editor of the *Dalhousie Gazette*, a position he held until his graduation in 1873 with honours in mathematics and physics. In 1880 he would receive a BSC from the University of Halifax with honours in biology.

In May 1873 MacKay was appointed principal of the Annapolis Academy, but in November he returned to the Pictou Academy to begin a 16-year career as principal. There he strengthened the science program, organized the Pictou Academy Scientific Association, and pursued his own botanical and zoological research. In 1889 he became principal of the Halifax Academy (he was replaced in Pictou by Robert MACLELLAN). He was also active in professional bodies such as the Provincial Educational Association of Nova Scotia, founded the Summer School of Science for teachers in 1887, and served from 1887 to 1891 as Nova Scotia editor of the *Educational Review* (Saint John) [*see* George Upham Hay*].

In 1891 MacKay began a 35-year term as superintendent of education for Nova Scotia. Throughout it, he constantly urged the provincial Council of Public Instruction and local school trustees to reform the curriculum and to hire trained teachers. Despite years of crusading, he met with little success in improving the educational attainments of the teachers. In 1905 he claimed that part of the problem was the Nova Scotian "idolatry of the principle of self-government," which gave school trustees too much power in hiring, but more generally he emphasized that, as he said in 1912, "the great need is simply a larger wage." When he retired in 1926, to be succeeded by Henry Fraser Munro*, fewer than ten per cent of teachers in the province had completed high school and one year of Normal School.

MacKay met with greater success in his campaign for reshaping the curriculum. In sharp contrast to his predecessor, David ALLISON, he favoured improved science programs and manual training over a classical curriculum. He used special conditional grants to encourage the teaching of manual arts, temperance, hygiene, domestic science, and agricultural chemistry and also to promote consolidation of rural schools.

Whenever possible, he took advantage of national programs to support his reforms, tapping into the Strathcona Trust for physical education and funding provided by the federal government for agricultural instruction and technical education.

Concerned about rural depopulation, MacKay developed rural-science programs that he believed would address the problem by encouraging children's scientific interest in nature. In addition to providing training and classroom materials for teachers, he instituted an unusual program of phenological observation for rural schoolchildren. This scheme required students to note the first appearance of botanical phenomena during the year and to provide the information to the teacher, who in turn submitted it along with the school's attendance register at the end of each year. The Nova Scotia Museum of Natural History holds MacKay's collection of these phenological reports from 1898 to 1923, and in the 1990s the observations were of considerable interest to scientists concerned with climatic change in Canada.

MacKay repeatedly emphasized his belief that it was the role of public schools to train industrial workers, and enthusiastically joined allies in the Nova Scotian Institute of Science and the Mining Society of Nova Scotia in the campaign for technical education that resulted in the provincial Technical Education Act of 1907. MacKay, as superintendent of education, became responsible for the Department of Technical Education, which included the Nova Scotia Technical College (a post-secondary institution for the training of professional engineers), the system of night schools for miners in existence since 1889 [*see* Edwin Gilpin*], and evening technical programs around the province.

Throughout his life MacKay continued his scientific studies, and his work on the flora and fauna of his own province, especially lichens, diatoms (plankton), where he collaborated with Loring Woart BAILEY, and freshwater sponges, earned him respect from other Canadian scientists. By 1876 he had already developed a herbarium of native plants, which was consulted by Andrew Walker Herdman Lindsay for his catalogue of Nova Scotia flora. His first major scientific article was published in 1881; by 1894 the Royal Society of Canada, to which he had been elected in 1888, listed more than 30 scientific and educational works by him in its bibliography. From about 1908 until his death he edited the *Proceedings and Transactions* of the Nova Scotian Institute of Science, of which he was president in 1899–1902. He also taught biology at Dalhousie for a time.

Most of MacKay's many activities related to his interest in education and science. He was president of the Dominion Educational Association from 1895 to 1898, and he represented Nova Scotia at imperial education conferences in 1907 and 1911. In 1909 he was vice-president of the Simplified Spelling Board of

New York and in 1912 he was made an honorary colonel and a member of a dominion cadet committee for his work in promoting military drill in the public schools. He served on the board of governors of Dalhousie from 1888 to 1927 and he represented the university on the board of the Marine Biological Stations of Canada and its successor, the Biological Board of Canada, from 1898 to 1926. He was awarded an honorary doctorate by Dalhousie in 1892 and by St Francis Xavier College, Antigonish, in 1905. He was a director or board member of a number of educational institutions in Halifax, including the Presbyterian College, the Halifax Ladies' College, and the Victoria School of Art and Design, which he served as president from 1908 to 1924. Active in the North British Society, of which he was president in 1894, he served as vice-president of the Nova Scotia Historical Society from 1896 to 1902 and as president of the Halifax Canadian Club in 1912–13.

Alexander Howard MacKay's career spanned an important era in Nova Scotian history, one that began with high hopes for a modern industrial future based on the application of science to natural resources and ended in economic depression, large-scale out-migration, and pessimism. MacKay imagined an orderly world in which professionally trained teachers brought scientific education to students across the province, resources were systematically developed, spelling was simplified, weights and measures were based on the decimal system, and the nations of the world worked together for justice and peace. The lasting institutional legacy of MacKay, and those who shared his scientific, economic, and educational vision, was the Nova Scotia Technical College. Later named the Technical University of Nova Scotia, it merged with Dalhousie in 1997 and is now known as DalTech.

JANET GUILDFORD

Alexander Howard MacKay is the author of "Leading to technical education," Mining Soc. of Nova Scotia, *Journal* (Halifax), 7 (1902–3): 49–54. Other of his publications may be found in "Bibliography of the members of the Royal Society of Canada," comp. J. G. Bourinot, RSC, *Trans.*, 1st ser., 12 (1894), proc.: 57, and *Science and technology biblio.* (Richardson and MacDonald).

Halifax County Court of Probate (Halifax), Estate papers, no.12010. NSARM, RG 14, 69, minute-book, 1862–1916. *Annals, North British Society, Halifax, Nova Scotia, with portraits and biographical notes, 1768–1903*, comp. J. S. Macdonald ([3rd ed.], Halifax, 1905). K. A. Balcom, "From recruitment to retirement: female teachers in the public schools of late nineteenth century Halifax" (MA thesis, Dalhousie Univ., Halifax, 1993). Janet Guildford, "'Separate spheres': the feminization of public school teaching in Nova Scotia, 1838–1880," *Acadiensis* (Fredericton), 22 (1992–93), no.1: 44–64; "Technical education in Nova Scotia, 1880–1930" (MA thesis, Dalhousie Univ., 1983). D. C. Harvey, *An introduction to the history of Dalhousie University* (Halifax,

1938). John McDonald, *A catalogue of the A. H. MacKay lichen collection with a short biography of A. H. MacKay* (Halifax, 1973). J. M. Norman, *Loran Arthur DeWolfe and the reform of education in Nova Scotia, 1891–1959* (Truro, N.S., [1989]). Nova Scotian Institute of Science, *Proc. and Trans.* (Halifax), 17 (1930): xlvii–liii. N. M. Sheehan, "Alexander H. MacKay: social and educational reformer," in *Profiles of Canadian educators*, ed. R. S. Patterson *et al.* ([Toronto], 1974), 253–70. Donald Soucy and Harold Pearse, *The first hundred years: a history of the Nova Scotia College of Art and Design* (Fredericton, 1993).

MACKAY, ISABEL ECCLESTONE. *See* MACPHERSON

MACKAY, JOHN ALEXANDER, Church of England priest, educator, and translator; b. 14 July 1838 in Mistassini (Moose Factory, Ont.), tenth of the twelve children of William McKay and Mary Bunn, who were both of mixed blood; brother of Joseph William McKay*; m. 4 Aug. 1864 Margaret Drever in Red River (Man.), and they had five daughters and one son; d. 26 Nov. 1923 in Battleford, Sask., and was buried in Prince Albert, Sask.

The son and grandson of Hudson's Bay Company men, John A. Mackay eschewed a career in the fur trade in favour of mission work. He received his initial training as a catechist under the Reverend John Horden* at Mistassini and then continued his studies in the late 1850s at St John's College in Red River. His ordination as a priest on 29 May 1862 was part of the mid-19th-century attempt of the Church Missionary Society to create an indigenous native clergy in Rupert's Land [*see* James Settee*; Thomas Vincent*].

Mackay went first to York Factory (Man.) (1862–64), moved to The Pas (1864–65), and then transferred to Stanley Mission (Sask.) (1865–76), the site of a massive, Gothic Revival–style church, the oldest structure in Saskatchewan today, on the English (upper Churchill) River north of Lac la Ronge. His journal demonstrates that his duties at Stanley went well beyond ministering to the local population. Not only did he travel extensively in all seasons through present-day northeastern Saskatchewan in an effort to convert the local aboriginal population, but he ran a 15-acre agricultural operation, including a mill, that made the mission almost self-sufficient. He also used a small printing press to begin to produce Cree translations of the Scriptures and religious services. In fact, there was little that the priest could not turn his hand to, a talent that was surpassed only by his capacity for northern travel. He was an imposing figure. With his flashing eyes, bushy eyebrows, and long clerical garb, he looked every part the prophet and reportedly feared no one but God.

In the fall of 1876 Dr John McLean*, the first Anglican bishop of Saskatchewan, invited Mackay to accompany him on a tour of the new diocese from

Prince Albert to Fort Edmonton (Alta); the pair conducted the first Anglican service in Battleford in the local telegraph office on New Year's Day 1877. Thereafter, Mackay worked briefly in the Fort Carlton (Sask.) and Nepowewin (Nipawin) districts before being sent back to Battleford by McLean in September 1877 to build a church there. Mackay worked largely with the local native population for the next two years and established a mission on the Red Pheasant Indian Reserve.

Bishop McLean had sent Mackay to Battleford apparently as part of a larger scheme to found a divinity college in the new capital of the North-West Territories. But in November 1879 McLean decided to open Emmanuel College in Prince Albert to train native missionaries and catechists for work in the territories. Mackay was one of the original staff members and taught Cree grammar and composition – an unprecedented educational experiment. In 1882 Mackay was named archdeacon and two years later he left the college for The Pas to supervise CMS activities in the Cumberland district. He returned to Battleford in the fall of 1885. Early the next year the Department of Indian Affairs appointed him its agent there. The department was worried about Indian behaviour in the aftermath of the North-West rebellion – there were ten reserves in the immediate Battleford area – and believed that Mackay would have a calming influence on the situation. This assignment lasted until 1887 when Mackay assumed a new role at Emmanuel. McLean's successor, Bishop William Cyprian Pinkham, believed that the college, which had secured university status in 1883, was best suited as an Indian boarding school and called on Mackay to serve as the new principal. Indian Affairs, however, used Mackay one more time, in February 1889 when as translator he persuaded the Montreal Lake and Lac la Ronge Cree to sign an adhesion to Treaty No.6.

During his 13 years at Emmanuel, Mackay continued to serve as Cree tutor. He translated the Bible, the Book of Common Prayer, and the hymn book into Cree, as well as prepared revised editions of the prayer book translated by James Hunter* and his wife, Jean Ross, and Horden's grammar in the Plains Cree dialect. He also vigorously pursued his evangelical work. Indeed, he could be rather territorial. When Mackay learned, for example, that the Oblates of Mary Immaculate wanted to re-establish a school on the Thunderchild Indian Reserve in 1891 [see PEYASIW-AWASIS], he reminded the Indian commissioner that the Anglicans had been there first and had always faithfully served the interests of the department. This uncompromising zeal ultimately led to his appointment as superintendent of Indian missions for the diocese of Saskatchewan in 1900. In this capacity, he supervised the building of churches and schools and hired staff; he also undertook gruelling annual inspec-

tion trips through northern Saskatchewan, even when he was well past retirement age.

Perhaps the best example of his determination to further the work of the church was his rescue of the abandoned day school on the Little Pine Indian Reserve. In 1921 he struck a deal with the deputy superintendent general of Indian affairs, Duncan Campbell Scott*. He offered to rebuild the school and provide the operating funds out of his own pocket; if after one year the school was considered a success, then Indian Affairs would take it over. It was Mackay's last challenge and last victory. He died in Battleford in November 1923 while working on a Cree dictionary. The Reverend Edward Ahenakew* remembered him as "a father to our race, not indulgent, but kindly and wise . . . a true and honest man. When need arose for determined action, he was far from wanting."

W. A. WAISER

John Alexander Mackay's publications are listed in *Biblio. of the prairie prov.* (Peel). His diary for 1870–72 has been published as "The journal of the Reverend J. A. Mackay, Stanley Mission, 1870–72," *Saskatchewan Hist.* (Saskatoon), 16 (1963): 95–113.

Saskatchewan Arch. Board (Saskatoon), S-A113 V (Campbell Innes fonds, J. A. Mackay papers). Edward Ahenakew, "Little Pine: an Indian day school," ed. R. M. Buck, *Saskatchewan Hist.*, 18 (1965): 55–62; *Voices of the Plains Cree*, ed. R. M. Buck (Regina, 1995). Arlean McPherson, *The Battlefords: a history* (Battleford and North Battleford, Sask., 1967). J. E. Murray, "The early history of Emmanuel College," *Saskatchewan Hist.*, 9 (1956): 81–101. Eleanor Shepphird Matheson, "The journal of Eleanor Shepphird Matheson, 1920," ed. R. M. Buck, *Saskatchewan Hist.*, 22 (1969): 66–72, 109–17.

McKAY, WILLIAM JAMES, Baptist pastor and editor; b. 27 Oct. 1858 in Beamsville, Upper Canada, son of Alexander John McKay and Susan McCordick; brother of Alexander Charles*; m. 9 Nov. 1888 Mary Emily Evans in Toronto, and they had two daughters and one son who survived their father; d. there 12 April 1922.

W. J. McKay was first educated in Grimsby's public and high schools and at the Canadian Literary Institute in Woodstock. After graduating from the University of Toronto in 1884 with a BA and the prize in oriental (biblical) languages, he enrolled in the Toronto Baptist College. In 1887 he completed its course in theology, winning a church history scholarship in competition with students of all North American Baptist colleges; five years later he would earn the first BD degree granted by McMaster University. Ordained in 1888, McKay served pastorates in London, Toronto, and Stratford. His preaching abilities and brilliant scholastic record earned him the presidency of the Baptist Convention of Ontario and Quebec for 1903–4. Immediately after leaving this office McKay was appointed editor of the denominational newspaper, the *Canadian Baptist* (Toronto).

From 1882 to 1888 Ebenezer William Dadson* had used this journal to promote the reformist principles of the Social Gospel that progressives drew from the Sermon on the Mount. Dadson's successor as editor, James Edward Wells*, had continued this advocacy. He supported the cause of trade unionism against industrial capitalism so openly that after his death in 1898 recourse was had to editorial committees, which operated the newspaper until 1904 with George R. Roberts as business and later also editorial manager. This corporate endeavour proving unsatisfactory, McKay was given full editorial control of the *Baptist* in May 1904; he would become business manager as well in 1916.

In McKay's first months as editor he called for purity in politics, deplored poverty in the midst of plenty, and asked Baptists to be "not too discriminating" in their charity. Soon, however, his editorials differed little from Roberts's, which had defended industrial capitalism by charging that wage contracts protected incompetence. By 1905 editorial references to social issues had disappeared from the newspaper. From the closing weeks of 1909, however, the editorial column repeatedly advocated "practical Christianity," calling for home missions and the evangelization of recent immigrants into urban areas such as Toronto where 45 languages were now spoken. McKay even advocated interdenominational cooperation to cope with this perceived "new Canadian" threat to the Canadian way of life.

McKay's years as editor coincided with intensifying theological conflict among provincial Baptists, between the orthodox evangelical fundamentalism represented by such men as Elmore Harris and the liberal theology supposedly taught at McMaster. A theological conservative himself, though less rigid than Harris, McKay believed that Baptists were unresponsive to the "new theology." Early in 1910 he published an editorial entitled "Another gospel?" in which he insisted that the gospel of personal salvation was all that the world needed. Immediately thereafter, however, he admitted that the *Baptist* had its critics, naming Harris as prominent among them. Soon afterwards the increased influence of the fundamentalists was revealed by the arrival in Toronto of a new pastor, Thomas Todhunter Shields*, who like Harris lacked formal training in theology. The *Baptist* did not identify the sources of these tensions, but McKay's minor crisis coincided with the appearance in the United States of the first volumes of *The fundamentals: a testimony to the truth*, a series of 12 tracts written by evangelical leaders, and with the height of Harris's attack on McMaster for modernist teachings by Professor Isaac George Matthews.

During the remainder of 1910, while the Matthews case raged, and in 1911 and 1912 the *Baptist* avoided any comment that might be interpreted as theological liberalism. Early in 1913, however, a little more than a year after Harris's death, it showed renewed interest in the Social Gospel, "a gospel of a saved society as well as a gospel of saved individuals." To judge by the various projects it supported, such as the establishment of social service committees in every congregation, practical Christianity was now popular. The following year, on 30 July, McKay reprinted an article from the *British Weekly* (London) asserting the Christian duty to preach the gospel of love and mercy, and to add simultaneously the gospel of a better day. Such a full gospel, the *Weekly* argued, must "satisfy the famine for righteousness and the hunger for the long-deferred justice of God." McKay noted that the editorial "expresses in general our own thought of the Social Service problem."

Two days before this Social Gospel credo appeared the first shot in World War I had been fired in Sarajevo (Bosnia and Herzegovina). McKay promptly announced that the war was Canada's as well as Britain's, in defence of civilization. He would later suggest that there should be a fighting battalion of Canadian preachers. Talk about social justice and the here-and-now Kingdom of God was soon drowned in global conflict, but the theological differences of conservative fundamentalists and modernist higher critics reappeared with the peace. In 1919, when an anonymous editorial in the *Baptist* attacked the doctrine of biblical inerrancy, Shields presented a strong condemnatory resolution to the annual convention. Although McKay was not the author of this editorial, he accepted responsibility for it. Shields's strong motion passed, but the convention also expressed complete confidence in McKay's editorship. Because of his reputation for piety and sound judgement, McKay had surmounted controversies about higher criticism and modernism; he insisted that the real issue was not individual *versus* social salvation, but individual *and* social salvation as epitomized in the phrase "full Gospel." After his death the *Christian Guardian* (Toronto) commented on his skill "in adjusting rival elements in his constituency so as to prevent a clash."

Under McKay's management between 1916 and 1921 circulation of the *Baptist* increased by more than a third, advertising grew by a larger amount, total income doubled, and profits from job printing more than doubled. In addition to fulfilling his editorial duties McKay was a member of a number of the convention's committees, including that on church union, which he and the convention opposed. He served as well as a senator of McMaster; he had supported the university in its early years in both teaching and administration and it had awarded him an honorary LLD in 1907. He was also a director of the Moral and

Social Reform Council of Canada and of the Ontario branch of the Dominion Alliance for the Total Suppression of the Liquor Traffic. While still editor of the *Baptist*, McKay died of uraemia in Toronto on 12 April 1922.

JOHN S. MOIR

No private papers of W. J. McKay appear to have survived, and the only primary source of information is the files of the *Canadian Baptist* (Toronto), 1882–1922.

AO, RG 80-5-0-165, no.14539. UTA, A1973-0026/277(11). *Canadian men and women of the time* (Morgan; 1912). G. G. Harrop, "The era of the 'great preacher' among Canadian Baptists: a comparative study of W. A. Cameron, John J. MacNeill and T. T. Shields as preachers," *Foundations: a Baptist Journal of History, Theology, and Ministry* ([Rochester, N.Y.]), 23 (1980): 57–70. C. M. Johnston, *McMaster University* (2v., Toronto, 1976–81), 1. J. S. Moir, "*The Canadian Baptist* and the Social Gospel movement, 1879–1914," in *Baptists in Canada: search for identity amidst diversity*, ed. J. K. Zeman (Burlington, Ont., 1980), 147–59. L. K. Tarr, *Shields of Canada: T. T. Shields (1873–1955)* (Grand Rapids, Mich., 1967). H. U. Trinier, *A century of service: story of "The Canadian Baptist," 1854–1954* ([Toronto, 1958]).

McKEAN, GEORGE BURDON, army officer and author; b. 4 July 1888 in Willington, County Durham, England, son of James McKean, a furniture broker, and Jane Ann Henderson; m. first 1915 Isabel Hall; m. secondly Constance ——, and they had a daughter; d. 28 Nov. 1926 in Potters Bar, England.

His parents deceased, George McKean immigrated to Canada at the age of 14 in 1902 to join his elder brother, J. W. McKean, who farmed near Lethbridge (Alta). After some years of ranching and farming, in 1912 he enrolled at Robertson College, the Presbyterian theological school in Edmonton. During summers he served as a student missionary at Hardieville and Athabasca Landing (Athabasca), and in 1912–14 as assistant minister at Robertson Church in Edmonton. In 1913 he organized the first Boy Scout troop in this church. He may have had some question about his vocation, however, because, on joining the Canadian Expeditionary Force during World War I, he gave his occupation as schoolteacher.

After being turned down three times, he enlisted in Edmonton on 23 Jan. 1915 as a private in the 51st Infantry Battalion. Possibly his small size had been an obstacle: he was five feet six inches in height and 120 pounds. He went to Britain as a sergeant in April 1916 and, after transferring to the 14th Infantry Battalion (the Royal Montreal Regiment), was sent to France as a private in June. When he won the Military Medal at Bully-Grenay, near Lens, he had advanced to corporal and was recommended for a commission, which he obtained in April 1917.

Perhaps because of his size, and his aptitude, Mc-

Kean was often assigned to scouting duties, creeping across no man's land and reporting on the enemy. "It was the pure love of adventure that attracted me to scouting," he later wrote, adding that the appeal had roots in his involvement with the Boy Scouts. On the night of 27–28 April 1918, near Gavrelle, the Canadians encountered stiff opposition; artillery could not be called in because the Germans were too close to the front line. With his patrol held up by grenades and rifle fire, Lieutenant McKean determined that this resistance had to be wiped out. Revolver in hand, he dived over a barricade of barbed wire and crashed into a German soldier, whom he shot. When another rushed at him with his bayonet, he killed him too. His men then joined him, and they charged along the trench. The Germans, who fled into a dugout, were dispatched with a Mills bomb. The citation for the Victoria Cross awarded McKean for this action reads: "This officer's splendid bravery and dash undoubtedly saved many lives. . . . His leadership at all times has been beyond praise." When she learned of this decoration, Isabel McKean, who had married George just before he enlisted, was "keenly pleased." At the time she was working as a private secretary in the office of Major J. M. Carson, the military registrar in Calgary. McKean was awarded the Military Cross for his part in an action in September at Cagnicourt, where he and his scouts led the battalion forward, sent back accurate reports, and captured a "party of the enemy over a hundred strong." McKean's "conduct throughout was magnificent," read his citation.

Severely wounded in this engagement and invalided to England, he was unable to rejoin his regiment before the end of the war. During his convalescence, while he was reportedly still suffering shock, his portrait was painted by Frederick Horsman Varley*, one of Canada's war artists. Of this haunting work, the artist's son Peter writes, "In his characterization of McKean, Varley caught the numbed horror of his shattered soul: rigid, staring, one eye showing a wild defiance, almost rage; the other guarded, cynical, hiding a storm of hatred." While recovering McKean also prepared for popular consumption a book on his war experiences, *Scouting thrills* (1919). He would later draw on his time in Canada for a juvenile book, *Making good: a story of northwest Canada* (1921), an account of two English lads' adventures ranching in Alberta.

Following his release from hospital, in February 1919 McKean, with the rank of acting captain, was put in charge of the Bureau of Information at the Khaki University of Canada in London, an educational scheme initiated by the Young Men's Christian Association of Canada to prepare soldiers for civilian life. He retired from the forces in July and subsequently settled near Brighton. In 1926 the sawmill he was operating at Cuffley, north of London, flew apart and a piece of blade fractured his skull. He died at nearby Potters Bar Cottage Hospital and was buried in Brighton Extra-Mural Cemetery. His medals and portrait are held by the Canadian War Museum, Ottawa.

JAMES ERNEST NIX

George Burdon McKean is the author of *Scouting thrills* (Toronto and New York, 1919) and *Making good: a story of northwest Canada* (Toronto and London, 1921).

Canadian War Museum Arch. (Ottawa), File on decorations of G. B. McKean. GRO, Reg. of births, Willington, County Durham, 4 July 1888. LAC, RG 150, Acc. 1992–93/166, file 436568. *Beaver* (London), 22 March 1919. *Edmonton Journal*, 29 June 1918, 11 Nov. 1996. *Lethbridge Herald* (Lethbridge, Alta), 1 Dec. 1926. *Morning Bulletin* (Edmonton), 1 July 1918. *Ottawa Citizen*, 28 March 1979. *Presbyterian and Westminster* (Toronto), 18 July 1918. *Times* (London), 29 June 1918, 29 Nov. 1926. W. A. Bishop, *Our bravest and best: the stories of Canada's Victoria Cross winners* (Toronto, 1995). *F. H. Varley: a centennial exhibition*, comp. Christopher Varley (Edmonton, 1981), 34. *The register of the Victoria Cross* (rev. ed., Cheltenham, Eng., 1988). *The Royal Montreal Regiment: 14th Battalion, C.E.F., 1914–1925*, ed. R. C. Fetherstonhaugh (Montreal, 1927). Peter Varley, *Frederick H. Varley* (Toronto, 1983).

McKELLAR, HUGH, teacher, farmer, civil servant, and publisher; b. 11 Dec. 1849 in East Zorra Township, Upper Canada, son of John McKellar and Agnes ——; m. 19 June 1894 Cassie Marie Sherrard in Pointe-du-Chêne, N.B., and they had two daughters; d. 28 Oct. 1929 in Moose Jaw, Sask.

Hugh McKellar was raised and nurtured in the agricultural community of Oxford County. His early education there was followed by study at the Galt Grammar School under William Tassie*. Unable to obtain teacher training because he was not yet 18, he taught in Huron County before enrolling at the Toronto Normal School. Accredited in 1870, he pursued his career in the public schools of East Zorra (1870–73), Paisley (1873–76), and Teeswater (1876–80).

By 1880 the federal government was vigorously extolling the merits of settling in western Canada. These urgings induced McKellar to leave education and go west. He homesteaded near Clearwater, Man., but he also travelled widely to become familiar with the soils, topography, vegetation, and climate of the province. During these trips he met many prominent government officials. In 1890 Manitoba's Liberal premier, Thomas Greenway*, selected him to be the province's immigration officer in Winnipeg, responsible for directing prospective settlers to suitable land. To stem the exodus of disillusioned farmers from the Maritimes to the United States, Greenway next sent McKellar to man an office in Moncton: it was hoped he could persuade the farmers to locate in western Canada, where good land was freely available. This office was jointly promoted by Manitoba and the Canadian Pacific Railway.

McKellar's stay in Moncton lasted only six months because he was recalled to Winnipeg by Greenway to become the chief clerk (deputy minister) of agriculture after the death of J. W. Bartlett in April 1892. He would serve in this capacity under three premiers (Greenway, Hugh John MACDONALD, and Rodmond Palen Roblin*). During his tenure (1892–1904), the *Moose Jaw Evening Times* would recall, he was always "preaching the gospel of permanent homes to the farmers and new settlers, urging them to look upon the west as a place to live and in which their children after them would make their homes, rather than a place to make money in, and then leave."

As chief clerk, McKellar had a duty to become acquainted with all the current problems in agriculture on the prairies. He became knowledgeable about injurious insects, especially grasshoppers. Along with dominion entomologist James Fletcher*, he conducted vigorous campaigns to control such plague insects. It was during these attempts that he came to assist Norman Criddle*, a farmer and entomologist at Aweme, Man., in demonstrating the superiority of poisonous bait over such mechanical implements as the "hopper-dozer," and in developing the "Criddle Mixture," a combination of arsenic (McKellar arranged for the supplies of poison) and horse manure that grasshoppers found irresistible. "Thus, in this way, as well as in others," Criddle would conclude in the *Canadian Entomologist* (London, Ont.), "he had a direct influence on the progress of economic entomology and for this reason, if for no other, his name is worthy of a place in its annals."

A new opportunity to advance the settlement of western Canada came to McKellar in 1905, when he accepted the position of secretary and commissioner of the Board of Trade at Moose Jaw. He would hold the post until 1919. Convinced that the west had to be filled with settlers to achieve prosperity, he worked diligently to promote Moose Jaw as the "buckle of the greatest wheat belt in the world" (in the words of a board publication in 1913) and to persuade immigrants that success lay in agriculture. He advised hundreds of farmers of the best districts in which to settle, especially the area that in the first decade of the 1900s showed the greatest development: south of Moose Jaw to the border and north to the South Saskatchewan River. Along with Angus Mackay* of the federal experimental farm at Indian Head, he determinedly propounded the sale of an extra quarter-section to homesteaders at $3 per acre to increase their holdings and ensure a viable base for grain production.

To give stronger voice to his promotions, in 1910 McKellar had become the founder, editor, and publisher of the *Saskatchewan Farmer* (Regina), in which he advocated weed-free summer-fallow, pure seed, weed control, mixed farming, tree planting, and a good farm garden. Although he sold the paper in

Mackenzie

1922, he continued as a joint editor for another two years and in 1928 he founded the *Agricultural Review* (Moose Jaw), which was dedicated to the betterment of farming in western Canada.

Hugh McKellar's activities also included executive positions with the Southern Saskatchewan Cooperative Stockyards, the Association of Saskatchewan Agricultural Societies, the Saskatchewan Livestock Association, and the Saskatchewan Registered Seed Growers Association. A staunch Liberal and an elder of St Andrew's Presbyterian Church in Moose Jaw, he died there in October 1929 at his home at 204 Stadacona Street West, and was remembered by William John Finley Warren, president of the Moose Jaw Agricultural Society, as "at all times a ready and willing worker for the advancement of agriculture."

PAUL W. RIEGERT

Hugh McKellar is the author of *Extended notes of an address on the geography of Manitoba* (Winnipeg, 1895).

Moose Jaw Evening Times (Moose Jaw, Sask.), 24, 28 Oct. 1929. *Regina Leader*, 24, 28 Oct. 1929. *Biblio. of the prairie prov.* (Peel). *Canadian Entomologist* (London, Ont.), 61 (1930): 288. *Historical directory of Saskatchewan newspapers, 1878–1983*, comp. Christine MacDonald (Regina and Saskatoon, 1994). *Vital statistics from N.B. newspapers* (Johnson), 92, no.2954. *Who's who in western Canada . . .* (Vancouver), 1912.

MACKENZIE, JOHN JOSEPH, scientist, civil servant, professor, and army officer; b. 24 March 1865 in St Thomas, Upper Canada, son of Donald Kennedy Mackenzie, a merchant, and Mary McAdam; m. 2 June 1892 Agnes Kathleen Rogers in Toronto; they had no children; d. 1 Aug. 1922 in Gravenhurst, Ont.

Of Scottish parentage, John J. Mackenzie was educated at St Thomas Collegiate Institute. Through "great sacrifice" by his father, in 1882 he entered University College in Toronto, where he soon came "under the spell" of science in the biology lectures of Robert Ramsay Wright*. Among the first to graduate from Wright's honours program in natural sciences at the University of Toronto, in 1886, Mackenzie contemplated a career in that field at a time when the "scientific point of view had not begun to prevail."

On the advice of Professor Archibald Byron Macallum*, he went to Germany for graduate work. He studied physiology at the University of Leipzig and bacteriology at the University of Berlin. Because there was little funding for biological research in Ontario, Mackenzie, at the urging of his instructors in Toronto, had also studied anatomy at Leipzig in preparation for a medical degree, "to provide him with the choice of an alternative career." Of note, in light of his future work, were his biological studies at Berlin, particularly his research in bacteriology at the Koch Institute. While in Europe he also developed a mastery of French and German, which allowed him, Ramsay Wright observed, to acquire an "extensive knowledge of modern pathology."

Mackenzie returned to Toronto in 1888. After completing a two-year fellowship in biology at the university, he faced the harsh reality of trying to earn a living from research. His wife later wrote that, having no interest in practising medicine but "wishing to marry," he was "forced" in 1890 to accept a position with the Ontario public service, as first bacteriologist of the Provincial Board of Health [*see* John Joseph Cassidy*]. The appointment put him in the midst of a small band of public-health reformers who, armed with the germ theory of disease and the microscope, would struggle for decades against political and public indifference. Mackenzie's laboratory – the second such facility in Canada, the first having been established in Quebec in 1887 – was located in the board's offices above a store on Yonge Street; in 1893 it moved to the university. The cost of operating the laboratory came from an appropriation in the Department of Agriculture for the investigation of diseases in animals. With obvious frustration, Mackenzie later noted that it was "easier to get legislation to expend money upon animal husbandry than upon the protection of human life."

Mackenzie faced a formidable task. By 1897 he was trying, in the words of board secretary Peter Henderson Bryce*, to undertake "work for almost all the 800 municipalities in a province of 2,250,000." Consequently, it was impossible for the laboratory "to do more than touch the fringe of the routine practical work" in the face, that year, of 10,000 cases of diphtheria, 5,000 or more of tuberculosis, and 1,432 of typhoid. Overwhelmed, Mackenzie did almost everything, from preparing media and solutions to examining thousands of specimens under his microscope. Still, over the course of this heavily repetitive work, he initiated many procedures, such as diphtheria swabs and the tuberculin testing of cattle. In addition, his systematic bacteriological and chemical examination of human and municipal-water samples, for evidence of tuberculosis and typhoid, was copied by other governmental laboratories in North America.

Despite the monotony, Mackenzie's scientific curiosity remained active, and it produced some impressive results. For instance, in 1894 he was an early observer of the degenerative impact of rabies on nerve-cell tissue: "I saw the structures afterwards described as 'Negri bodies' in the brains of rabbits dying from rabies, in dogs and in the brain of a child who had died of rabies in Hamilton." He also used his laboratory to study infectious micro-organisms, especially those causing diphtheria. More than just a researcher, Mackenzie advocated the use of diphtheria antitoxin and in 1895 he imported a supply from the Institut Pasteur in Paris for distribution to doctors treating children. This action, his wife recalled, "gained him some abuse" from critics of the use on humans of biological products from animals.

Mackenzie's "growing discontent" with his job gradually led to his return to the university. While working at the laboratory, he also taught, for the Royal College of Dental Surgeons of Ontario and the faculty of medicine, and studied medicine at night. He received his MB from the university in 1899. On 23 July 1900 he resigned his provincial position and joined the faculty as professor of pathology and bacteriology. Here his career as a researcher blossomed. His goal was simple – "to make pathology a bridge between clinic and laboratory" – and he firmly believed in research in hospitals. He approached, he once said in an address, the "disease phenomena from the broader biological standpoint, in contrast to the older methods of viewing them from the narrow aspect of human pathological anatomy." Elected in 1909 a fellow of the Royal Society of Canada and president of the Canadian Institute, he belonged to numerous scientific bodies, among them the Canadian Public Health Association, the American Association of Pathologists and Bacteriologists, and the Pathological Society of Great Britain and Ireland. In 1912–16 he and a colleague, Thomas Gregor Brodie, investigated the physiology and histology of the kidney; a portion of their work was published in the *Proceedings* of the Royal Society of London. In total Mackenzie published over 30 papers based on his own research. Among those who knew this tall (six feet, six inches), somewhat reserved authority, he was distinguished too by his "charming personality," "wide culture," and enthusiasm for golf and travel.

During World War I Mackenzie joined No.4 Canadian General Hospital, becoming a captain in April 1915 and head of its laboratory. Staffed largely from Toronto's hospitals and the university, the unit went overseas the following month. From November to August 1916 Mackenzie served with it at Salonica (Thessaloníki), Greece, where his work on severe dysentery led to improved treatment. Exposed to taxing field conditions, he contracted a heart infection that stayed with him when he returned to teaching in Toronto. In 1922 he died in Muskoka, where he and his wife summered, and was buried in Lakeview Cemetery in Gravenhurst.

PAUL ADOLPHUS BATOR

John Joseph Mackenzie's publications include "A preliminary list of algae collected in the neighbourhood of Toronto," Canadian Institute, *Proc.* (Toronto), 7 (1889–90): 270–74; "A case of acute phlegmonous gastritis," *Canada Lancet* (Toronto), 40 (1906–7): 491–94; "Ultramicroscopic organisms" and "Presidential address: human evolution and human disease," Canadian Institute, *Trans.*, 8 (1904–9): 53–62 and 535–47; and "Chairman's address," *Public Health Journal*

(Toronto), 10 (1919): 265–69. A report on his research with T. G. Brodie appears under the title "On changes in the glomerules and tubules of the kidney accompanying activity," in Royal Soc. of London, *Proc.*, ser.B, 87 (1914): 593–609. The best summary of Mackenzie's annual work for the Provincial Board of Health is found in his "Report of the laboratory work for the board for 1899," in its *Annual report* (Toronto), 1899: 29–32 (also published in Ont., Legislature, *Sessional papers*, 1900, no.32).

Mackenzie's wartime letters were published posthumously as *Number 4 Canadian Hospital: the letters of Professor J. J. Mackenzie from the Salonika front, with a memoir by his wife, Kathleen Cuffe Mackenzie* (Toronto, 1933).

AO, RG 22-305, no.45752; RG 80-5-0-201, no.14508. UTA, A1973-0026/279(70). P. A. Bator with A. J. Rhodes, *Within reach of everyone: a history of the University School of Hygiene and the Connaught Laboratories* (2v., Ottawa, 1990–95). *Canadian men and women of the time* (Morgan; 1912). A. B. Macallum, "J. J. Mackenzie – an appreciation," *Univ. of Toronto Monthly*, 23 (1922–23): 8. J. W. S. McCullough, "Early history of public health in Upper and Lower Canada," *Canadian Journal of Medicine and Surgery* (Toronto), 51 (January–June 1922): 60–84. Ont., Provincial Board of Health, *Annual report*, 1890–1900. RSC, *Trans.*, 3rd ser., 17 (1923), proc.: iv–vii.

MACKENZIE, Sir WILLIAM, railway contractor and entrepreneur; b. 17 Oct. 1849 (he claimed 30 October) in Eldon Township, Upper Canada, fifth son of John Mackenzie, a farmer, and Mary McLauchlan; m. 8 July 1872 Margaret Merry (d. 1917) in Lindsay, Ont., and they had three sons and six daughters; d. 5 Dec. 1923 in Toronto and was buried near Kirkfield, Ont.

A son of Scottish-born Presbyterian immigrants, William Mackenzie was educated at elementary schools in Bolsover and Kirkfield, and at the Lindsay grammar school. After teaching for one or perhaps two years, he helped operate a small general store in Kirkfield for a short while. At about the time of his marriage in 1872 to Margaret Merry, a Roman Catholic, he joined his brothers' contracting company. Beginning in 1874, he and Alexander, one of the brothers, obtained contracts to provide timber and to build bridges and other wooden structures for the Victoria Railway, a local colonization line being laid north from Lindsay. While working on it he became familiar with promoter George Laidlaw*, chief engineer and general manager James Ross*, and an ambitious young surveyor-office boy, Herbert Samuel Holt*. Mackenzie distinguished himself by completing his contracts on time and within estimate. He, Ross, and Holt then obtained work on another Laidlaw line in Ontario, the Credit Valley Railway. Mackenzie's contracts, again for timber, bridges, and buildings, once more proved profitable. During return visits to Kirkfield the rising young builder forayed into local politics: he served as a councillor for Eldon Township (1876–77) and as reeve (1880–81).

Mackenzie

Mackenzie's situation changed after the dominion government signed a contract in October 1880 for a railway to the Pacific coast. Work began in 1881. Mackenzie visited western Canada for the first time the next year – like several other Ontarians he apparently hoped to obtain contracts on the new railway, but he failed to get any. James Jerome Hill*, the only member of the Canadian Pacific Railway syndicate with practical experience in construction, arranged the early contracts and he preferred large, financially stable American operators. By the end of the 1883 season, however, increased tensions between Hill and William Cornelius Van Horne*, the CPR's general manager, together with financial and organizational problems, led to major changes in the company's contracting procedures. James Ross was named manager of construction for the mountain section, and Herbert Holt became his superintendent. Ross and Holt divided the route into numerous small contracts and subcontracts, making it possible for contractors with limited backing to get work. This change, and the fact that Ross and Holt had worked with Mackenzie in Ontario, resulted in a series of contracts under which Mackenzie supplied timber and built bridges, stations, and other wooden structures for the CPR in 1884.

On his first contract Mackenzie demonstrated unusual financial talent. He did not have sufficient funds to purchase appropriate equipment. Instead, he returned to Eldon and scoured the countryside for available horses and other necessities; among his finds was an abandoned sawmill, which was dismantled and moved to Mackenzie's work site in British Columbia. He gave little or nothing immediately, but promised payment in full after he was paid for his contract. The outfit he put together, not altogether suited to work in the mountains, was disdainfully referred to by other contractors as "The Farmer Outfit." Most of the workmen were also recruited in Mackenzie's home community and were sometimes dubbed the "Eldon reserve." They too were prepared to wait for at least a portion of their wages. But they got the job done, earning Mackenzie a reputation as a contractor who completed work on time and within budget. It was during the 1884 season too that Mackenzie met his future partner, Donald Mann*, a bluff, masterful railway builder who held contracts for roadbeds. The following year Mackenzie was rewarded with a much larger project: to supply all the timber and erect a huge trestle bridge across the Mountain Creek gorge in the Beaver River valley in British Columbia. Designed by W. A. Doans, the bridge rose 150 feet and was 1,070 feet in length, reputedly one of the largest wooden trestles ever built.

Although the last spike was driven on 7 Nov. 1885, construction did not halt. Expedients had been adopted to make the official opening possible and most of the builders still had work to do on their contracts in 1886. Mackenzie also obtained new contracts, to construct heavy timber enclosures to protect sections of line in the mountains against snow slides. His projects kept him in British Columbia throughout most of the season. Ross, Holt, and Mann, who too had unfinished work, contracted as well in 1886 to build the first 40 miles between Winnipeg and Hudson Bay of a proposed railway (later renamed the Winnipeg Great Northern) that might serve as a CPR feeder and an alternative shipping route to overseas markets.

Subsequent projects eventually brought the four men together. In 1887 Mackenzie, Mann, and Holt all secured contracts on a new CPR project: the "Short Line" across Maine to Bangor, with an extension to Saint John. Mackenzie and Mann, who held adjacent contracts, decided in March 1887 to merge. Their work proved more difficult than anticipated and they would barely break even on their first venture as partners. In 1888 Ross obtained a general contract for the construction of the Qu'Appelle, Long Lake and Saskatchewan Railroad north from the CPR at Regina to Saskatoon and Prince Albert. Mackenzie, Mann, and Holt joined him in this undertaking. Even before it was finished, profitably and on time, the partners obtained another contract, for a line from the CPR at Calgary northward to Edmonton and southward to Fort Macleod. On both of these projects Ross was in charge, Mann did the clearing, brushing, and grading, Mackenzie handled the bridges and other wooden structures, and Holt laid the tracks. By 1888 Mackenzie was sufficiently well off that he built an impressive brick house in Kirkfield.

The foursome worked well together, but after 1890 there were no large construction contracts for steam railways in sight. There were, however, new opportunities to build urban railways utilizing new electrical technology. Mackenzie, Holt, and Ross all had considerable experience with various power systems, and they realized that the electrification of urban tramways offered new contracting and promotional opportunities. Mackenzie returned to Toronto, where he had already begun to branch out in 1889 as president of the Charles J. Smith coal and wood company. In 1891 he joined a syndicate which acquired control of Toronto's horse-drawn trolley system, and obtained from that syndicate the construction contract for the electrification of the system. Ross and Holt became involved in the electrification of trams in Montreal, as did Mann in Winnipeg. (The four would often hold shares in each other's street-railway companies.) Substantial sums were reputedly spent to bribe Toronto city officials and politicians so that Mackenzie's group obtained a 30-year franchise for running the street railway. In April 1892 it was incorporated as the Toronto Railway Company, with interim financing from the Canadian Bank of Commerce, George

Albertus Cox*, and others. Mackenzie, as contractor, received payment in cash to cover his costs. When the work was completed, he was given company shares for the balance due and he became president of the concern. He had gained control of the railway without investing much of his own money. The manner in which he had done so raised suspicions of corruption, while the building and operating tactics of the company provoked public anger. During construction, for instance, he had gained notoriety over the placement of hydroelectric poles and the tearing up and, it was claimed, inadequate repaving of roads. Once the system opened, Mackenzie and other officials became embroiled in a bitter debate in 1893, mainly with religious leaders, when the company decided to run cars on Sunday. Reduced ticket prices and easier transfer arrangements, however, earned it considerable goodwill.

The new electrical and traction technology was risky, but under Mackenzie's leadership the Toronto Railway and affiliated electrical companies turned handsome profits. In 1896 Margaret Mackenzie bought land for a large summer home on Balsam Lake near Kirkfield and a year later William purchased Benvenuto, a mansion in Toronto. He fitted easily into Toronto's early-20th-century nouveaux riches, and he and his wife became important patrons and collectors of Canadian landscape art. For him, and other promoters in the utilities field, success opened up further opportunities in Canada and abroad [see Frederick Stark Pearson*]. They developed technological, financial, promotional, and political expertise that took them not only to numerous other Canadian cities but also to Mexico, Brazil, the Caribbean, Britain, and even China. Mackenzie's investment in street railways and utilities in Brazil in 1899 was the start of a major international venture. In Ontario, the franchise on Niagara Falls power secured in 1903 by the Electrical Development Company of Ontario Limited, controlled by Mackenzie, Frederic Thomas NICHOLLS, and Henry Mill Pellatt*, would make them key combatants against Adam BECK and other champions of a publicly owned system of distributing electricity.

In the 1890s unfinished business in western Canada had drawn Mackenzie into an even greater project, and his crowning achievement: the Canadian Northern Railway. The line from Winnipeg to Hudson Bay had encountered financial and political difficulties. Unpaid, Ross and Holt apparently lost interest but Mann hoped to salvage something from an adjoining line (the Lake Manitoba Railway and Canal, incorporated in 1889), which carried the promise of a federal land grant and a postal contract. He contacted Mackenzie, and together they devised a plan whereby the line would be deflected northwest to tap the rich agricultural area around Dauphin, Man. In 1895 they persuaded the Manitoba government of Thomas

Greenway* to guarantee the bonds issued by the railway. With funds from their sale, loans from the Canadian Bank of Commerce, and the hope of land subsidies and mail contracts, the private partnership of Mackenzie, Mann and Company built 125 miles of the LMRC in 1896. In December 1898 it and the Winnipeg Great Northern were amalgamated to form the Canadian Northern, with Nicholls as president; the new railway's federal charter was obtained in July 1899.

The Canadian Northern differed in its construction and operation from other prairie railways. Mackenzie and Mann had agreed that, in return for a provincial guarantee of its bonds, they would reduce freight rates and submit their rate schedules for approval to the Manitoba government. They were confident that it would not impose unreasonable rates because the province would be liable if the railway could not pay interest and principal on the guaranteed bonds. The arrangement, however, demanded extreme economies. The region was only sparsely settled and would not generate much traffic in the early years. The railway was therefore built as cheaply as possible, albeit with a promise that it would be improved when there was more traffic. Most of the Canadian Northern's early rolling stock was obsolete equipment obtained from the junkyards of wealthier American railways. Service was slow and breakdowns occurred often. But the Dauphin region finally had desperately needed rail service, which the CPR had been unwilling to provide. What really endeared the little railway to its patrons was the low rates it charged for freight.

The railway also initiated aggressive policies to increase the volume of traffic. It followed the example of the LMRC's general manager, David Blythe Hanna*, who, when local farmers lacked good seed grain, had purchased several carloads and sold it to them at cost in 1897. There were similar responses to other shortages. On occasions when major suppliers refused to grant individual farmers volume discounts, the Canadian Northern bought the materials in sufficient volume to obtain the discounts and passed the savings on to the farmers. While the CPR accepted only grain shipped from elevators, the Canadian Northern was willing to allow farmers to load their grain directly into its cars, thus saving elevator charges. Other accommodations included unscheduled stops to pick up freight wherever it was offered. As a result, the railway came to be regarded as "the Farmers' Friend" and was described as "the West's own product to meet the West's own needs." What made its service even better was the fact that when Mackenzie and Mann lowered their rates, the CPR had little choice but to follow suit if it was to remain competitive and avoid even greater clamour for more government assistance for new Mackenzie and Mann lines.

Mackenzie

In 1900 the American-based Northern Pacific, which had built lines in Manitoba, decided to sell them after years of poor returns. A proposed sale to the CPR, however, roused strong opposition and provided Mackenzie with an opportunity to make a daring counterproposal in 1901. The Canadian Northern was not in a financial position to purchase the lines, but Mackenzie suggested that the Manitoba government lease them and then reassign the lease to the Canadian Northern. In a much more significant move, he also promised drastic rate reductions on grain from Winnipeg to the Lakehead if the government would guarantee bonds to finance the construction of an extension over that stretch. Effective railway competition would thus be established from the prairies to the Lakehead, where water transport and then traffic exchanges with the Grand Trunk Railway would give the Canadian Northern access to eastern Canada. Through an assembly of charters that had actually begun in 1897, Mackenzie and Mann were able to complete a new line to Port Arthur (Thunder Bay), Ont., by the end of 1901.

Mackenzie and Mann held the construction contracts for all the lines under the Canadian Northern umbrella. Their costs were paid from the proceeds of bond sales, and in lieu of profits they took Canadian Northern shares. In 1902 they incorporated their construction interests as Mackenzie, Mann and Company Limited. This move was intended to circumvent the provision in the Railway Act that prevented contractors on a railway from serving as its officers. The new company could henceforth acquire Canadian Northern contracts, and Mackenzie and Mann were both legally free to become officers. Consequently, in March 1902 Mackenzie became president of the Canadian Northern Railway, responsible for finances and with his headquarters in Toronto, where he lived. As vice-president, Mann would award construction contracts and deal with governments west of Ontario.

The success of their strategy depended on bond sales. To expand their system they acquired the charters of numerous small lines, some with valuable land subsidies and mail contracts; other railways were chartered provincially so they could receive the local government's bond guarantees. Such backing facilitated sales, in which Mackenzie excelled. Although he could be domineering, he impressed colleagues, financiers, and politicians by his energy and assurance. He established close ties with leading Toronto financiers, particularly those associated with the Canadian Bank of Commerce, most notably Byron Edmund WALKER, but his most important and difficult work involved the selling of bonds to British investors. He approached this task with the zeal of an itinerant evangelist, making numerous transatlantic crossings (often accompanied by one or more of his charming daughters). Assisted by Robert Montgomery Horne-Payne,

a brilliant British financier, he not only made contact with leading underwriters in London but also went out into the countryside to sell bonds. Horne-Payne had the uncanny ability to assess how much money there was in a community for investment, which he and Mackenzie then systematically extracted. Both men had seemingly boundless faith in the future development of Canada, and the central role which the Canadian Northern could play in that development.

Mackenzie was a man of broad vision, not much interested in details. He was exceptionally fortunate in the legal services provided in Toronto by Zebulon Aiton Lash*, a former federal deputy minister of justice and a partner in Blake, Lash, and Cassels, one of Canada's most prestigious law firms. Lash drew up the necessary contracts and documents, which provided excellent protection for Mackenzie and the Canadian Northern and in many cases introduced innovative features in corporate structuring. Lash made sure that the documents were filed and payments made on time – an important concern since the normal state of Mackenzie's own office was chaotic, cluttered with piles of bills and other business, which Mackenzie was apt to ignore in the press of daily work. Mackenzie's bargaining tactics often had a rough frontier-like quality, devoid of diplomacy. He would approve an agreement in principle and then look to Lash to put it into the appropriate language. Lash made sure too that the company's financial records met legal requirements, although the overly optimistic accounts, with low figures for depreciation, may have prevented him, when combined with Mackenzie's unbounded confidence, from recognizing the warning signals that Canada's economic boom might be coming to an end.

Contrary to early predictions, the prairie lines built by Mackenzie and Mann had operated at a profit from the beginning. The main reason for their success was the tremendous increase in immigration and settlement and hence in the volume of rail traffic in western Canada. This growth allowed Mackenzie and Mann to improve substantially their main lines and to build many new branches – theirs was the railway of the northern prairies. They understood the needs and interests of prairie farmers, adapted operations to local circumstances, and set freight rates at levels that earned them much goodwill. In recognition of their contribution to the development of western Canada, they would both be knighted on 1 Jan. 1911.

It is not clear when William Mackenzie and Donald Mann made the transition from western contractors to national entrepreneurs. Before 1901 it was widely believed that they were simply building urban street railways and prairie lines with the intention of selling them at a profit to the CPR or another prospective transcontinental. The presence on the Toronto Railway board of W. C. Van Horne, now the CPR's president, and the employment of his son on Canadian Northern construction projects lent credence to allegations, by Northern Pacific officials among others, that Mackenzie and Mann were merely a front for the CPR. They seemed to acquire charters and build lines in an uncoordinated way.

Associates later regarded the 1901 agreement with the Manitoba government as the turning point when Mackenzie and Mann first entertained ambitions to build their own transcontinental. Others have suggested that the turn happened only in 1903 when the Grand Trunk decided to move into western Canada and tried to take over the Canadian Northern, but was rebuffed. The federal government had agreed to assist the Grand Trunk Pacific, headed by Charles Melville Hays*, but this support softened when it became clear that the Grand Trunk would not retain the low Canadian Northern rates on grain moving to the Lakehead. At the same time, Mackenzie and Mann's resistance to Grand Trunk incursion was significantly strengthened by cabinet's promise, facilitated by Clifford SIFTON, to guarantee Canadian Northern lines to Edmonton and Prince Albert.

Mackenzie and other senior Canadian Northern officials later insisted that the Grand Trunk's move westward made the transcontinental expansion of the Canadian Northern inevitable if it was to remain competitive. They had recognized that eastern connections had to be secured when they became available, a process that started in earnest with the acquisition in 1903 of the Great Northern Railway, which gave them vital access to a system across Quebec. Mackenzie and Mann moved closer to their transcontinental goal in 1909 when the government of British Columbia provided bond guarantees for the building of a Canadian Northern subsidiary from Alberta to Vancouver. At the same time Saskatchewan and Alberta, for the first time, offered guarantees to facilitate construction of a network of new branches. Mackenzie and Mann had also obtained charters, and in some cases government assistance, to build railways that served local needs, but were also situated to become parts of a transcontinental system.

In Mackenzie's bold surge as a national entrepreneur, a succession of major business deals kept pace with railway assembly. Ventures in Pacific whaling, insurance, lumber, ore mining, meat packing, brewing, retailing, and foreign utilities, among others, consolidated the position of Mackenzie, Mann as a preeminent Canadian holding company. Other initiatives were clearly linked to the Canadian Northern's expansion, such as Mackenzie and Mann's acquisition in 1910 of the Brazeau coalfields in Alberta and the coal operations of James Dunsmuir* on Vancouver Island. In Britain that year to launch the service of the Canadian Northern Steamship Company, the masterful Mackenzie, at the peak of his influence, secured financing worth an extraordinary $40,700,000, much of it destined for railway construction.

The final link in his transcontinental system fell into place only in 1911, when the embattled federal Liberals, fighting an election on a proposed reciprocity treaty with the United States which critics argued would divert much Canadian trade southward, tried in May to demonstrate their commitment to east-west trade by guaranteeing a proposed Canadian Northern line north of Lake Superior. The results, however, would be tragic for the two new transcontinentals: the Canadian Northern was unable to establish an adequate traffic base in eastern Canada while the Grand Trunk Pacific failed to do so in the west.

Shortly after the federal guarantee, Mackenzie and Mann began to encounter serious financial problems. In 1912 a crisis in the financial markets, triggered in part by fears of a European war, made it more difficult and expensive to sell the railway's bonds. The crisis came just as the Canadian Northern was facing costly construction in the Rockies and north of Superior. At the same time restrictions on emigration by European governments sharply reduced settlement in western Canada. Then, following the outbreak of war in 1914, the availability of rolling stock, supplies, and workers became problematic. Mackenzie and Mann tried to reduce costs, but they were determined to complete, open, and equip the Canadian Northern's transcontinental line. The last spike was driven by Mackenzie in an unofficial ceremony at Basque, B.C., on 23 Jan. 1915; the final mileage had been hastily thrown together in a desperate effort to give the railway greater credibility. Much additional construction remained to be done that year, and it was only in late August that a train carrying a small party including railway and bank officials made what amounted to the inaugural trip from Toronto to Vancouver. Two months later a special excursion train, hosted by Mackenzie, took a large press corps, politicians, businessmen, and other dignitaries from Quebec City to Vancouver. The celebrations were lavish, but they could not mask a harsh reality. The Canadian Northern could not survive the war without massive government assistance, which federal politicians found almost impossible to justify in the face of more urgent wartime needs. The government of Sir Robert Laird Borden* provided interim aid [see John Dowsley REID] and then in 1916 set up a royal commission to recommend long-term solutions to the country's railway problems. In the end Ottawa decided to take over and merge the two financially embarrassed transcontinentals.

A devastated Mackenzie fought hard to maintain control of the Canadian Northern, his largest and most cherished venture, but on 1 Oct. 1917 the Union government, Mackenzie, Mann and Company Limited, and the Canadian Bank of Commerce signed an agreement whereby the government would acquire the

Canadian Northern common shares in private hands. The price for the shares, almost all of which were held by Mackenzie and Mann, would be arbitrated. The amount awarded by the board of arbitration in its report of 25 May 1918 ($10,800,000) was barely sufficient to discharge their indebtedness to the bank.

Mackenzie remained active in numerous business operations even after the loss of the Canadian Northern. International financial hardships following the war depressed the value of his stock in Canadian and Latin American electrical and traction companies and of the many lumber, coal, real estate, mining, manufacturing, insurance, and financial operations in which he was interested. In 1920–21 he gave up his hydroelectric interests and his street railways in the Toronto area. Though he was able to maintain an affluent lifestyle at Benvenuto and at the family's homes in the Kirkfield area, the complicated estate he left at his death was, for a one-time magnate, relatively modest.

Sir William Mackenzie suffered an apparent heart attack in October 1923 and he died on 5 December. In life he had been one of Canada's most colourful and controversial railway promoters and entrepreneurs. In the opinion of Sir Edmund Walker, the banker with whom he had many dealings, he seemed "like the railway, driven by a steam engine." Mackenzie was, perhaps, too optimistic in his assessment of the economic prospects of Canada, particularly western Canada. His rapid rise to wealth and fame had the appearance of a meteor blazing a bright trail through the skies of the Canadian business world, but this meteor had burned itself out several years before Mackenzie's body was committed to the earth near his home town of Kirkfield.

THEODORE D. REGEHR

[The primary sources for Sir William Mackenzie and the Canadian Northern are given in the author's study *The Canadian Northern Railway, pioneer road of the northern prairies, 1895–1918* (Toronto, 1976). Mackenzie left virtually no private papers, a paucity that is admirably compensated for in R. B. Fleming, *The railway king of Canada: Sir William Mackenzie, 1849–1923* (Vancouver, 1991). Obituary notices appear in the *Canadian Railway and Marine World* (Toronto) and in several Toronto and Montreal newspapers. Other useful works include Christopher Armstrong and H. V. Nelles, *Monopoly's moment: the organization and regulation of Canadian utilities, 1830–1930* (Philadelphia, 1986), and *Southern exposure: Canadian promoters in Latin America and the Caribbean, 1896–1930* (Toronto, 1988); *Canadian men and women of the time* (Morgan; 1912); *Encyclopaedia of Canadian biography . . .* ; Duncan McDowall, *The Light: Brazilian Traction, Light and Power Company Limited, 1899–1945* (Toronto, 1988); *Standard dict. of Canadian biog.* (Roberts and Tunnell); and G. R. Stevens, *Canadian National Railways* (2v., Toronto and Vancouver, 1960–62), 2. T.D.R.]

MacKINNON, DONALD ALEXANDER, teacher, lawyer, politician, and author; b. 22 Feb. 1863 in Uigg, P.E.I., son of William MacKinnon and Catherine Nicholson; m. 17 Oct. 1892, in Charlottetown, Adelaide Beatrice Louise Owen (d. 1912) of Georgetown, P.E.I., and they had two sons and one daughter; d. 20 April 1928 in Charlottetown.

Donald A. MacKinnon was of Scots stock: his father had been born in Scotland and his mother was a descendant of settlers who had come to Prince Edward Island in 1803 with the Earl of Selkirk [Douglas*]. Donald attended the Uigg grammar school and, on completing his education there, taught in rural districts, beginning at the age of 14 if not earlier. By 1880 he had enrolled at Prince of Wales College in Charlottetown. After his graduation he received a first-class teaching licence and worked in several locations until 1882 when he began articles with Charlottetown barrister Malcolm McLeod. Taking advantage of changes to legislation which allowed time spent at approved law schools to count as part of the articling period, he attended Dalhousie law school in Halifax from 1885 to 1887 and received an LLB. He was called to the Island bar as an attorney in 1887 and as a barrister the following year.

MacKinnon opened a legal practice in Georgetown in 1887 and remained there until 1897, when he moved back to Charlottetown and began a partnership with Alexander Bannerman WARBURTON. The firm, which had offices in Summerside and Montague Bridge (Montague) as well, was short-lived because Warburton was called to the bench in 1898. Later law partners were Edward Bayfield Williams and Robert Neil McNeill. Named a QC in 1899, MacKinnon became president of the Law Society of Prince Edward Island the following year. He was also law agent for the dominion minister of justice in the province.

MacKinnon's political career had begun in 1893 when he was elected as a Liberal for 4th Kings in the newly constituted Legislative Assembly [see Neil McLeod*]. Re-elected in 1897, he was named attorney general in the government of Donald Farquharson* in 1899, but when he returned to the electorate that year as a consequence of taking office he was, unusually, opposed and defeated. In 1900 he entered dominion politics and ran in Queens East. Although he received the majority of the votes, the result was declared void for "corrupt practices" and a new election ordered which took place in March 1901 and which MacKinnon won by a larger majority. He sat until the dissolution but was not a candidate in the 1904 election. In June of that year he had complained to Prime Minister Sir Wilfrid Laurier* that his finances were not sufficient for politics and had indicated his desire to be made lieutenant governor of Prince Edward Island. In October 1904 the appointment came to him at the comparatively young age of

41. He held the position until May 1910. MacKinnon was again elected to the dominion parliament in 1921, representing Queens, and he sat until 1925. He did not contest the 1925 election.

In addition to his legal practice MacKinnon was involved in a number of business ventures, among them the Three Rivers Steamship Company and the Prince Edward Island Electric Company, of which he was president. His interests included the Boy Scouts, an organization he served as provincial commissioner, and writing. He was a contributor to the *Prince Edward Island Magazine* and in 1906, in partnership with Warburton, he edited *Past and present of Prince Edward Island*, an encyclopedic volume containing historical essays and biographical sketches. MacKinnon's contributions included articles on the fisheries, Queens County, geology, and the constitution. The volume continues to be useful for research. It was not, however, mentioned in obituaries, which concentrated on MacKinnon's political service, specifically mentioning his success in obtaining a branch line of the Prince Edward Island Railway that had benefited his district.

HARRY TINSON HOLMAN

The PARO holds a large collection of records relating to Donald Alexander MacKinnon's law firm, at Acc. 2947, including papers concerning the Three Rivers Steamship Company, as well as some material from his term as lieutenant governor.

MacKinnon's contributions to the *Prince Edward Island Magazine* (Charlottetown) include "Industrial progress in Prince Edward Island," 4 (1902–3): 342–46. In addition he prepared several articles for *Past and present of Prince Edward Island . . .* , the volume which he co-edited with Alexander Bannerman Warburton (Charlottetown, [1906]). MacKinnon's biography, which he probably wrote himself, appears on p.397a.

LAC, MG 26, G, MacKinnon to Laurier, 3 June 1904. PARO, Montague United Church (Montague, P.E.I.), Reg. of baptisms; RG 6.1, ser.3, subser.1, vol.6, 11 Oct. 1899; RG 19, ser.3, subser.1, 17 Oct. 1892. *Morning Guardian* (Charlottetown), 11 Oct., 14 Dec. 1899; continued as *Charlottetown Guardian*, 21 April 1928. *Patriot* (Charlottetown), 20 April 1928. *Canadian directory of parl.* (Johnson). *Canadian men and women of the time* (Morgan; 1912). *Newspaper reference book*. P.E.I., Board of Education, *Annual report* (Charlottetown), 1878–80. *Prominent people of the Maritime provinces* (Montreal, 1922).

MACKINTOSH, JAMES CROSSKILL, banker, stockbroker, and politician; b. 1 Feb. 1839 in Halifax, son of John Mackintosh and Mary Catherine Crosskill; brother of Kate MACKINTOSH; m. there 15 April 1869 Emma Isabel Grant, and they had two daughters and two sons; d. there 8 May 1924.

J. C. Mackintosh's father emigrated from Inverness, Scotland, and became one of Halifax's best-known Scotsmen – no small feat in a city full of successful Scottish immigrants. Although a native Nova Scotian, his mother was also of Scottish descent, and Mackintosh had a strict Presbyterian upbringing, attending St John's School and the Free Church Academy. In later life he would devote much of his spare time to religious pursuits. He became first president of the Halifax Young Men's Christian Association as well as a member of the board of management of the Presbyterian College. In addition, he was one of the founders in 1871 of Fort Massey Presbyterian Church, where he served as elder, clerk of session, chairman of the managing committee, trustee, secretary-treasurer, and member of the choir. One of the church's volunteer teachers, he was also superintendent of its Sunday school for a time.

After leaving school at 16, Mackintosh had joined the Bank of Nova Scotia as a senior clerk and begun his apprenticeship as an accountant. Two years later, in 1857, he in fact became the bank's official accountant – the first person to hold such a title in the organization – and his annual salary was raised from £100 to £125. Mackintosh remained at the bank for the next 18 years, during which time he developed a reputation for superior workmanship. In 1870 he alerted President Mather Byles Almon* and the board of directors to a defalcation by the bank's cashier (general manager), James Forman*, of some $315,000, an enormous amount of money at the time. Soon afterwards, he was promoted to deputy cashier. Although no descriptions of Mackintosh are available from this period, he appears to have been a serious and hard-working young man with a strict, perhaps even ascetic, Presbyterian ethos.

In 1873 Mackintosh left the Bank of Nova Scotia to set up his own business with Mather Byles Almon, son and namesake of the bank's past president. Styled as bankers, brokers, and financial agents, the firm went into the retailing of securities, a line of business that had only recently opened up. According to one early description, Almon and Mackintosh was organized "on the same principles as a chartered Bank" in that deposits were taken and interest paid, loans and promissory notes negotiated, and drafts drawn against shipments of merchandise. But the main activity was the buying and selling of local as well as national and American stocks and bonds.

The firm seemed to do well but the partners soon split up, Almon going into life insurance and Mackintosh continuing the brokerage and banking business under the title of J. C. Mackintosh and Company. Now on his own, he pushed into the relatively new business of selling the securities of local industrial and utility firms in addition to well-accepted government, railway, and municipal bonds. From its head office in Halifax, the firm eventually set up branches in Fredericton, Saint John, New Glasgow, N.S., and Montreal.

Stocks and bonds were purchased on all the major exchanges, including the Montreal Stock Exchange, where Mackintosh was a full member, and were resold to customers throughout eastern Canada.

By at least 1912 J. C. Mackintosh and Company was enough of a presence to begin distributing an annual multi-page *Investor's manual for the Maritime provinces of Canada*. Judging by this publication, Mackintosh catered to the more conservative of the region's investors, providing good if unremarkable returns on solid investments. He avoided the inherently riskier business of sponsoring new issues or providing capital to brand-new enterprises. He was, in other words, a stockbroker rather than an investment banker. In fact, he very much disliked the flamboyant and "get-rich-quick" style, to say nothing of the more speculative tendency, of younger financiers such as William Maxwell Aitken*. In one infamous incident he tried to push Aitken out of his privileged position in John Fitzwilliam Stairs*'s funeral procession, presumably incensed by the young man's standing with both Stairs and his immediate family.

As busy as Mackintosh must have been in building up his business, he nonetheless found time for civic duties. In 1878 he was elected to Halifax City Council, and he remained an alderman until 1884 when he was elected mayor. During three annual terms as mayor he spearheaded major public works projects including a dry dock and a regular ferry service between Dartmouth and Halifax. He also completely reformed Halifax's antiquated tax system, moving from a tax on residents to a tax on property.

In politics Mackintosh was an ardent Conservative and imperialist. He supported the National Policy and promoted the concept of imperial federation as a member of the Navy League. Proud of his Scottish heritage, he was active in the North British Society. First elected to it in 1859, he filled a number of roles including secretary, senior assistant, and president. In 1895 he was made a "Perpetual Member." By the time of his death he had set a new record for length of membership in the society – 66 years.

Mackintosh was also a Victorian moralist who felt it was his God-given responsibility to volunteer dozens of hours each week to worthy causes. Aside from his Sunday-school and YMCA involvement, he was an active member and eventually president of the Nova Scotia Society for the Prevention of Cruelty [*see* John Naylor*], one of the first organizations in Canada to promote child-protection legislation and to shelter wives from abusive husbands. In addition, he served for a time as vice-president of the Halifax School for the Blind [*see* Sir Charles Frederick FRASER], a member of the executive committee of the Moral Reform Association, and treasurer of the Children's Aid Society. He also sat on the board of governors of Dalhousie University from 1905 to 1919. His

wife was active in the Halifax Local Council of Women, of which she was first president, and in such benevolent institutions as the Halifax Infants' Home and the Home for the Aged.

Despite failing health Mackintosh clung to his business until 1922 when he was forced to turn over the reins to his son Alexander Forrester and his son-in-law John E. Wood, both of whom worked as brokers in the firm. His sincere hope was that the company would carry on after his death. It was not to be. Mackintosh succumbed to old age and illness on 8 May 1924 and the firm he had worked so hard to build was sold to a Montreal-based investment broker before the end of the year.

GREGORY P. MARCHILDON and BARRY CAHILL

Halifax County Court of Probate (Halifax), Estate papers, no.10722. NSARM, MG 1, 1731. *British Colonist* (Halifax), 17 April 1869. *Evening Echo* (Halifax), 9 May 1924. *Presbyterian Witness* (Halifax), 21 March 1857: 42–43. *Annals, North British Society of Halifax, 1924–1949* (Halifax, 1949), 10–11. *Canada Gazette*, 29 Nov. 1924: 1603–4. *Canadian men and women of the time* (Morgan; 1912). Dalhousie College and Univ., *Calendar* (Halifax), 1905/6. Dalhousie Univ., *President's report* (Halifax), 1918/19. *History of the Bank of Nova Scotia, 1832–1900, together with copies of annual statements* ([Halifax, 1901]). J. C. Mackintosh and Company, *The investor's manual for the Maritime provinces of Canada* (Halifax), 1912 (copy in NSARM, Library, Vert. file). G. P. Marchildon, *Profits and politics: Beaverbrook and the Gilded Age of Canadian finance* (Toronto, 1996). Joseph Schull and J. D. Gibson, *The Scotiabank story: a history of the Bank of Nova Scotia, 1832–1982* (Toronto, 1982). D. M. Sinclair, *Fort Massey Church, Halifax, Nova Scotia, 1871–1971: a century of witness* ([Halifax, 1971]). G. A. White, *Halifax and its business . . .* ([Halifax, 1876]).

MACKINTOSH, KATE, teacher and musician; b. 24 Feb. 1853 in Halifax, daughter of John Mackintosh and Mary Catherine Crosskill; d. there unmarried 8 Sept. 1923.

Kate Mackintosh's father died when she was four, leaving a large family in some disarray; otherwise, nothing is known of her formative years. In 1870 she graduated from the Normal School in Truro with a "Superior" standing and a first-class grade B licence. She was hired by Halifax's Board of School Commissioners at $280 per annum and assigned to the Brunswick Street school for girls, the beginning of a 46-year career in the classroom.

Mackintosh soon attracted attention for outstanding ability. As early as 1876 she was commended for producing, with the principal at Brunswick Street, Catherine Miller, "more than 100 girls . . . creditably advanced in Geometry and Algebra." In 1881 supervisor Benjamin Curren, an ardent classicist, thought "the very creditable examination of [her] class in Latin . . . worthy of special mention." By the early

1880s Miller and Mackintosh had developed at Brunswick Street an advanced curriculum for senior girls, who were otherwise excluded from the few high-school programs then available in Halifax. According to the board's annual report, the school achieved "its greatest success in the preparation of young ladies who wished to secure teachers' licences. They rarely failed in their examinations, and when they became teachers they carried into their work much of Miss Miller's conscientious, untiring industry and gentle spirit energized by Miss Mackintosh's enthusiasm." The unspoken economy of scale was that women hired with these minimum qualifications required only minimum remuneration.

In 1885 Halifax Academy opened as the city's first dedicated, co-educational high school. Mackintosh, now holding a grade A licence and reputedly the first woman in Nova Scotia to achieve this qualification, was immediately appointed to teach history, grammar, physiology, and paedeutics (the science of education). Class enrolments averaged 68 by the mid 1890s, although chronic problems of attendance reduced the daily ratios. Mackintosh was applauded for her ability "with such perfect ease [to] control . . . large mixed classes, and inspire them all with the highest enthusiasm . . . self-respect, and . . . noble motives." Despite her achievements and seniority – and the fact that her brother James Crosskill MACKINTOSH was the city's mayor – further professional advancement was not possible for her; the school board remained biased in favour of university-educated men. There were, however, compensations. From 1888 Mackintosh was the highest-paid woman teacher in the city, her salary culminating in 1914–16 at $1,100 per annum. She was also one of the few women to penetrate the leadership of professional organizations. In the 1880s she served for three terms on the executive committee of the Provincial Educational Association of Nova Scotia and sat as well on its committee examining primary education. From its foundation in 1907 to at least 1913 she was a member of the board of management of the Halifax Teachers' Pension System. She retired from teaching on 30 March 1916.

Mackintosh's contribution to Halifax life extended far beyond the classroom. Somewhere in her youth she had learned to play the pipe organ, and from at least 1887 she served as organist at Brunswick Street Methodist Church. From 1891 she was both organist and choir director, presiding over newly installed equipment which she had helped to select during a visit to New York City. Under her guidance the church was acclaimed as having the best choir in Halifax. Such pre-eminence did not come cheaply. In addition to Mackintosh, who received an annual honorarium of $300, there were three paid soloists. Eventually the congregation could no longer sustain the expense; in 1916 the choir was reduced and the organist discreetly replaced.

During the 1890s, following specialized training at the Halifax Conservatory of Music [*see* Charles Henry PORTER], Mackintosh gained recognition as a musical composer and arranger, the first woman in Nova Scotia known to have achieved such distinction. Although her talent was minor, she won praise for her arrangements of standard hymns, 17 of which were compiled as *Tunes to favorite hymns*; her setting for "Nearer, my God, to Thee" was included in the hymnal of the Methodist Church of Canada. Mackintosh reputedly continued to compose until her death, but little remains beyond patriotic pieces such as *Our Canada* and *Mother-land beyond the sea*, both published in 1897. Her obituary in the Halifax *Evening Echo* made the large claim that the latter was "sung in every school and played by every band throughout the Empire during the days of Queen Victoria's Diamond Jubilee." This was puffery, but the piece was definitely performed in Halifax under Kate's direction, by 6,000 schoolchildren who massed at the Exhibition Building during the visit of Governor General Lord Aberdeen [Hamilton-Gordon*] and Lady Aberdeen [Marjoribanks*] in May 1897. The event was long remembered locally as "the grandest part" of the jubilee celebrations.

This work with schoolchildren notwithstanding, Mackintosh believed, as she wrote in the *Halifax Herald* in 1912, that it was "useless to look to the schools to provide good training in music . . . [since] the curriculum is already over-crowded." Instead, noting that music "tends to elevate, morally and socially, the whole community," she called for churches, musical clubs, and amateur musicians to cultivate a love of music in the young. Her interests found natural expression in the Ladies' Musical Club of Halifax, of which she was a founding member in 1905. She served six terms as president, and was largely responsible for shaping the organization as a vehicle for fostering "a more perfect knowledge and understanding of vocal and instrumental music, and of musical literature."

Following her retirement, Mackintosh devoted herself to the Halifax Women's Club, described by the *Herald* as "the child of her vision and will." Founded around 1920, with Mackintosh as president, the club had as its objective the establishment of a self-sustaining residence for unmarried women employed in the city's clerical and paraprofessional workforce. The residence was maintained for some years, but much of the impetus died with Mackintosh and the initiative lapsed about 1926.

In death Mackintosh was eulogized as "the best known woman in the province of Nova Scotia." She had been a mentor to nearly three generations of young people and a significant contributor to the local and national musical communities. Although her estate was valued at less than $200, this modest legacy reflected not so much the straitened circumstances of so many early women professionals, but instead a richness and generosity of spirit, expressed through devotion to music and the liberal arts, travel, close friendships, and the desire to influence and improve the lives of women.

LOIS K. YORKE

[A fine photographic portrait of Kate Mackintosh is held at the NSARM.

The only article which Mackintosh is known to have written is "The future of music in Nova Scotia," *Halifax Herald*, 31 Dec. 1912. Her extant sheet music includes "The Halifax Herald march," in the *Halifax Herald*, 1 Oct. 1895, woman's extra: 13; *Our Canada: patriotic song*, lyrics by Edward Lawson Fenerty (Toronto, 1897; copy in NSARM, Oversize vert. file, 23, no.13); *Mother-land beyond the sea* (Halifax, 1897; copy in NSARM, MG 31, 26, no.13); and *Diamond Jubilee; the army of the Lord*, lyrics by J. T. Burgess (n.p., 1897; copy in NSARM, Vert. file, 98, no.12). A booklet of compositions by Mackintosh, *Tunes to favorite hymns* (Toronto, n.d.), includes 17 pieces and identifies her as organist of Brunswick Street Methodist Church, Halifax. L.K.Y.]

Brunswick Street United Church (Halifax), Minutes of trustees, 1885–1949. Halifax County Court of Probate (Halifax), Estate papers, no.10706. LAC, RG 31, C1, 1901, Halifax, Ward 2. NSARM, MG 20, 183; RG 14, 69, minutebook, 1862–1916. *Acadian Recorder* (Halifax), 10 Sept. 1923. *Evening Echo* (Halifax), 10 Sept. 1923. *Evening Mail* (Halifax), 10 Sept. 1923. *Halifax Herald*, 10–11 Sept. 1923. K. A. Balcom, "From recruitment to retirement: female teachers in the public schools of late nineteenth century Halifax" (MA thesis, Dalhousie Univ., Halifax, 1993). Board of School Commissioners for the City of Halifax, *Report*, 1870–1916/17. M. I. Campbell, *No other foundation: the history of Brunswick Street United Church and Mission with its Methodist inheritance* (Hantsport, N.S., 1984). *Directory*, Halifax, 1870–1927. Halifax Ladies' College and Conservatory of Music, [*Calendar*] ([Halifax]), 1888–95. *Musical Halifax* (Halifax), 1903/4.

McLAGAN, SARA ANNE. *See* MACLURE

McLAUGHLIN, ROBERT, manufacturer, office holder, and politician; b. 16 Nov. 1836 in Cavan Township, Upper Canada, eldest son of John McLaughlin and Eliza Rusk; m. first 5 Feb. 1864 Mary Smith (d. 1877), and they had two daughters and three sons, including John James* and Robert Samuel*; m. secondly 17 Jan. 1878 Sarah Jane Parr (d. 1899) in Oshawa, Ont.; m. thirdly 17 Dec. 1901 Eleanor McCulloch, née Smith (d. 1930), in East Whitby Township, Ont.; d. 23 Nov. 1921 in Oshawa.

Born on a farm near Millbrook of Irish Presbyterian immigrants, Robert McLaughlin moved with his family in 1837 to a lot near Tyrone, in Darlington Township, where he attended the local log school. His father wanted him to farm, but he preferred woodworking; his production of axe-handles and whiffletrees led him, guided by old issues of the *Coachmakers' Illus-*

trated Monthly Magazine (Columbus, Ohio), to make his first cutters in 1863–64. In 1869 he moved to the village of Enniskillen, where he built a carriage works, which, in 1871 at least, he operated in partnership with Daniel Kernick. A participant as a youth in daily readings of the Bible with his family, in Enniskillen he taught Sunday school in the Presbyterian church.

Attentive to his accounts and the quality of his materials, McLaughlin achieved modest prosperity, though competing with cheap, machine-made American imports in the 1870s was "an uphill fight," according to *Industrial Canada* (Toronto). By mid 1877 he had concluded that moving to a larger centre would be necessary for continued growth, and to provide a fresh start for his family. In March 1877 his wife had died of consumption, leaving him with five children, whose life worsened when their busy father married the tyrannical Sarah Jane Parr, apparently an employee in their household. It is impossible to say how long it took Robert to admit her harmful impact.

By January 1878 the McLaughlins had relocated to Oshawa, on Lake Ontario and near the Grand Trunk Railway. Local competitors, even relatives, doubted Robert's chances of success, but his sale of some land and a loan from the local Western Bank of Canada, whose president was also one of his iron suppliers, allowed him to build the Oshawa Carriage Works, a three-storey brick factory. Expansion of the company, which became known as McLaughlin Carriage about 1884, was facilitated by careful costing, new designs (some influenced by *Carriage Monthly*, a Philadelphia journal), and aggressive marketing, especially of the gear (the front-end turning and coupling mechanism) McLaughlin had first patented in 1880. His letter-books for the late 1870s and the 1880s show the square-dealing McLaughlin in his element: selling, coordinating orders of wood and hardware, resolving disputes, hiring and firing, protecting his patents (and buying others), refining carriage mechanisms, tabulating the credit ratings of potential retailers across Canada, and pushing and humouring agents in the field. "Don't stay to talk to doubtful marks, go for the good ones," he advised a company traveller who was working Ontario in 1886. In areas where he had no agents, he quietly placed one of his "best buggies" to attract interest. Only rarely do personal matters intrude in this correspondence, in occasional letters to his ageing father and one in January 1885 to his eldest son John, a pharmacy student in Toronto, admonishing him to wear underclothes, for better health.

The continued growth in the 1890s of the mostly wholesale business of McLaughlin Carriage is all the more impressive given that the trade in Ontario experienced some decline in this decade, McLaughlin's pieces were not the cheapest, and Robert Lindsay Torrance (head of J. B. Armstrong and Company) of Guelph, Robert GRAY of Chatham, and James Brockett Tudhope of Orillia all offered serious competition. Using a catchy motto ("One grade only, and that the best"), warranties, and easily recognized trademarks, McLaughlin promoted his works in his catalogues as "the best equipped and most extensive Factory in the Dominion." An attempted partnership in 1889 involving his son John had not worked out, but McLaughlin made his other boys junior partners in 1892: George William, who had entered the works as an apprentice in 1885, was quiet and steady; Sam, who began in upholstery in 1887 and moved up to design, was outgoing and restless. In December 1896 (by which time their stepmother had left, evidently under pressure from the whole family), George was sent to Saint John to open the firm's first branch and find retailers in the Maritimes. By 1899 McLaughlin had an annual output of 2,500 cutters and sleighs and an equal number of carriages, in a wide array of models. Thin rubber tires began appearing on models in 1901 and two years later fenders and bicycle-style wire wheels with pneumatic tires were offered. Around 1908 his catalogues became bilingual.

In Oshawa the abstemious McLaughlin had established a daunting presence: he was a member of the town's first board of health (1884) and its first board of water commissioners (1904), a school trustee and municipal councillor, mayor in 1899, a supporter of the Salvation Army, first president of the local Young Men's Christian Association, a freemason and a Templar, and an elder in St Andrew's Presbyterian Church. Behind a front of modesty lay a calculating businessman. As is evidenced by his caustic letters in the local press, he did not treat critics lightly, nor did he tolerate lax or intemperate workers. To move his vehicles more efficiently to the Grand Trunk's main line, he invested in the construction in 1895 of the Oshawa Railway, which local ratepayers strenuously opposed. After fire destroyed his works in December 1899, numerous towns jostled to land his business; McLaughlin accepted space in Gananoque, near two of his main suppliers, Gananoque Spring and Axle and George Gillies's forgery. McLaughlin's professed loyalty to Oshawa and its unabashed offer of a $50,000 loan to finance rebuilding, which McLaughlin (though heavily insured) took after resigning as mayor, brought the business back. He also seized the opportunity to renegotiate his freight rates with the Grand Trunk. By November 1900 a new factory had been completed. Additional buildings would be needed over the following decade, the cornerstone for one being laid in October 1902 by the Liberal minister of public works, Joseph-Israël Tarte*.

The previous year the now widowed McLaughlin was living on Colborne Street with a servant and his 34-year-old daughter Mary Jane. Though he had never indulged his daughters, and Mary Jane had run away from home in her youth, they adored their father. His remarriage in 1901 was welcomed by the family, who liked Eleanor McCulloch and whatever comfort she restored to McLaughlin's life. In his sixties he showed no sign of slowing down or of giving way to the new, automotive form of transportation. Boosted as the largest carriage maker in the British empire – its output would reach more than 14,000 units in 1904 – the McLaughlin Carriage Company Limited was provincially incorporated on 7 Aug. 1901. In February 1903, when 263 carriage workers struck for union recognition and a wage increase, a comfortably positioned McLaughlin opened his books to show that they were the highest paid employees in Oshawa, and the strike petered out. Automobiles were initially treated with disdain. Company calendars for 1903–6 depict high-stepping horses and carriages overtaking crashed motor cars and injured drivers. Sam nevertheless caught the fever: in 1904–5 he excitedly explored the prospect of making automobiles in Oshawa, and his purchase in Toronto in 1906 of an American-made, two-cylinder Buick focused his search.

A business plan worked out by Sam and George was, to their surprise, approved by the elder McLaughlin, who, Sam later explained, now thought automobiles would be a worthwhile sideline. Robert McLaughlin most likely had a hand in drafting the contract offered three Detroit tradesmen in February 1907 to come as foremen to build "elegant and marketable" autos using American chassis. This arrangement collapsed, as did another that summer to bring in an American engineer to make parts and import others for a prototype. Sam, who with George had already borrowed heavily and started advertising, quickly struck a deal for the purchase of chassis from the Buick Motor Company of Michigan, which was eager to capitalize on the McLaughlins' situation and the Canadian tariff breaks on imported parts. This branch-plant deal was formally accepted on 3 Oct. 1907 by Robert McLaughlin as president of McLaughlin Carriage. On 20 November the McLaughlin Motor Car Company Limited was provincially incorporated with Sam as president and George as vice-president, though their father held the controlling interest. Starting with a payroll of three under the management of E. W. Drew, the new company assembled 154 McLaughlin-Buicks in 1908; their debut at the Toronto automobile show in March of that year received only modest recognition. The McLaughlins made the bodies, which reflected a carriage-craft origin, especially in their folding tops and finely finished mahogany panelling and windshield frames. The McLaughlin-Buicks fell into a medium-price sector, closer to Oldsmobiles than to the cheap Fords being assembled in Walkerville (Windsor), Ont. [see Gordon Morton MCGREGOR]. In a market where all domestic producers offered some statement of Canadian origin, McLaughlin Sr did not hesitate to let his carriage company's reputation enter the early advertising for McLaughlin-Buicks.

With carriage and automobile production gradually climbing, McLaughlin properly credited his sons, but he still put in long hours at work. In addition, in 1907 he had joined the Western Bank as a director. The Governor, as he was called, rarely took vacations and generally remained aloof publicly, preferring to fraternize (and spit tobacco) on his shop floors. Only the family knew the extent of his warmth, gentle humour, and kindly gestures. His recreations were limited to his grandchildren, his dog, landscape painting, and his player-piano (Scottish tunes were his favourites); if he did not like the programmed sound of pieces, he would remove and alter the music rolls. In his art, amateurish and repetitive though it was, the one-time carriage painter could still display a workmanlike handling of colours. A Liberal in politics and a member of the executive council of the Canadian Manufacturers' Association, he followed national developments in the realm of trade. He had been described in the *Canadian album* in 1893 as "a Reformer who is not afraid of competition from manufacturers south of the Boundary Line, and believes in gradual tariff reform, looking toward free trade." Over time he reversed himself. After years of benefiting from Canada's protective tariffs, on carriages and then automobiles, he felt strongly about the shift of the Liberal government of Sir Wilfrid Laurier* in 1910–11 towards reciprocal trade with the United States. Canadian auto makers were split on the issue; McLaughlin, like most, was convinced that his firm would suffer.

In June 1910 he politely asked Laurier to maintain existing tariffs. He shared with him two letters he had written to the editor of the Toronto *Globe*, James Alexander MACDONALD, in opposition to reciprocity. The first was a detailed argument for continuing the tariff structure. Not wishing to tangle openly with the "free traders," he told Macdonald in his covering letter that he did not want to publish what he had written, but he did want to make a case. The government's announcement of talks with the Americans, he claimed, had cost him a half-million dollar investment in Oshawa by an unnamed but "very wealthy Auto Car Company" in the United States. Even if it was true about the withdrawal – the loquacious Sam would never mention it – it failed to move the prime minister, who, inundated with grievances from other industrialists, merely thanked McLaughlin for his opinion. In January 1911 McLaughlin was part of the delegation of "representative manufacturers" who waited upon the government, again to no effect. In September he attacked Laurier's free-trade policy on the front page of the *Globe* and threatened to leave the party. In the event, the Liberals went down to defeat days later, reciprocity died, and McLaughlin and other members of the CMA resumed a more relaxed consideration of

industrial concerns. In November McLaughlin became its Ontario vice-president.

Between 1912 and 1915 he carefully gauged both the decline of carriage sales and Sam's ongoing pains to attract the attention and respect of kingpins in the fast-moving American auto industry. To allow for the production of the highly marketable Chevrolet, an addition lined up by Sam (possibly without his father's knowledge), McLaughlin agreed in 1915 to dispose of the carriage company's business, again to the mild surprise of his sons. Recognizing the opportunity for clear transitions, McLaughlin was probably relieved too: he was determined not to see his sons shackled, Carriage Factories Limited (Tudhope's firm in Orillia) was a willing buyer, and, as is evident from his explanation to his carriage agents in November 1915, he was not blind to the inroads made by the gasoline engine. McLaughlin Carriage nonetheless continued as the holding company and McLaughlin Sr remained its nominal president. Though he was not a natural car man (despite his admitted "mechanical turn"), he still had some practical involvement, as buyer of the wood that went into the auto bodies. When his sons pressured him about 1916 to give up this role, he became irritated – he was the head, he knew woods inside out, and he still knew how to marshal support in the "Manchester of Canada," as Oshawa styled itself. In August 1916, when his works were being expanded for the assembly of Chevrolets, he signed an agreement on behalf of McLaughlin Carriage whereby the city agreed to fix the company's assessment and facilitate better railway shipping.

Automobiles apparently did not excite the unimpressionable McLaughlin. When Sam took him for a ride in a model with raised windows, a granddaughter recalled, the Governor's habit of turning aside to spit tobacco juice produced a mess unnoticed by the bespectacled gentleman with the white beard. In November 1918 McLaughlin Carriage, McLaughlin Motor Car, and the Chevrolet Motor Car Company of Canada Limited were formally taken over by General Motors, though how McLaughlin, then nearing 82 and out of the negotiations, felt about the loss of his business is uncertain. He retained an office – he painted there as well as at home – and would have been aware of GM's methodical replacement of executives, expansion of the Oshawa works, and construction of a motor plant in Walkerville. Birthday banquets in 1919 and 1920 kept him in touch with carriage-making old-timers. In November 1919 he was genuinely pleased to reminisce with a *Globe* reporter, who unwittingly brought out McLaughlin's commitment to ongoing learning, a factor perhaps in his industrial evolution. One of his last public appearances in Oshawa was at the opening on 25 Sept. 1920 of Lakeview Park, which he donated to the city.

McLaughlin had not seemed ill for long before he

died in November 1921 of colon cancer. From his deathbed he consoled his fearful grandchildren and bid farewell to veteran carriagemen. Press coverage of his passing ranged from the banner headlines of the *Oshawa Reformer* to the brief notice in *Automotive Industries* (New York), date line Detroit. Dignitaries from across Canada descended on Oshawa for the funeral, factories and stores closed, and a line of McLaughlin-Buicks conveyed the floral tributes from St Andrew's Church to Union Cemetery. McLaughlin left an estate valued at $496,288, much of it in shares in GM, the Goodyear Tire and Rubber Company of Canada, and the Robert Simpson Company. Under the terms of his will he compensated his daughters for their small share in the sale to GM, and bequests were made to the Muskoka Cottage Sanatorium near Gravenhurst, the Queen Mary Hospital for consumptive children at Weston (Toronto), the Oshawa General Hospital, and the Children's Shelter of Ontario County, also in Oshawa. After 1921 McLaughlin underwent a kind of corporate sanctification, hastened by George and Sam's gifts as raconteurs and by Oshawa's continued reverence.

DAVID ROBERTS

Restored examples of Robert McLaughlin's carriages and sleighs may be seen in Oshawa, Ont., at Parkwood Estate and the Canadian Automotive Museum, which also has a few McLaughlin-Buick automobiles. Oil paintings by McLaughlin are held by Parkwood and the Robert McLaughlin Gallery in Oshawa. Excellent photographs of Robert McLaughlin are in the possession of a great-granddaughter, Mary Patricia Bishop, of Toronto.

AO, C 88, sect.A (mfm.); RG 22-264, no.6524; RG 80-5-0-74, no.7794; RG 80-5-0-293, no.13178; RG 80-8-0-831, no.24607; RG 80-27-2, 42: 37. LAC, MG 26, G: 172585–90. QUA, McLaughlin Carriage Works fonds; George William McLaughlin fonds. *Canadian album* (Cochrane and Hopkins), 2: 89. D. S. Hoig, *Reminiscences and recollections: an interesting pen picture of early days, characters and events in Oshawa* (Oshawa, 1933). M. McI. Hood, *Oshawa . . . a history of "Canada's motor city"* (Oshawa, 1968). *Industrial Canada* (Toronto), 1904–21. Dorothy McLaughlin Henderson, *Robert McLaughlin: carriage builder* (Toronto, 1972). *Ontario Gazette* (Toronto), 1901: 900; 1907: 1308–9. Heather Robertson, *Driving force: the McLaughlin family and the age of the car* (Toronto, 1995). Sue Warren, "Conservation of an early 20th century McLaughlin piano box buggy": *www.sciencetech.technomuses.ca/english/collection/ box_buggy_cons.cfm* (consulted 28 April 2005).

McLEAN, AMELIA ANNE (Paget), linguist and author; b. 15 July 1867 at Fort Simpson (N.W.T.), daughter of William James MCLEAN and Helen Hunter Murray; m. 31 July 1899 Frederick Henry Paget in Winnipeg, and they had a daughter; d. 10 July 1922 in Ottawa.

Amelia McLean's family had roots steeped in fur trade history. Her mother was the daughter of Alexander Hunter Murray*, a chief trader with the Hudson's Bay Company. It was at Fort Simpson that Helen met and married W. J. McLean, a native of the Isle of Lewis, Scotland, who had joined the HBC in 1859. Amelia, the eldest of their 12 children, spent her earliest years at Fort Liard (N.W.T.). In 1873 her father was transferred to Fort Qu'Appelle (Sask.), where his family joined him the following year.

The McLeans arrived at a time of critical change for the aboriginal people of the district because of the collapse of the buffalo economy, treaties, and settlement on reserves. Treaty No.4, which Helen McLean signed as a witness, was made at Fort Qu'Appelle in September 1874. Amelia and her siblings became well acquainted with the Plains Cree and the Saulteaux, forming friendships and attending special ceremonies. Amelia was particularly gifted at languages – she would, for example, translate popular songs into Cree and Saulteaux. During some of the family's years at Fort Qu'Appelle, she attended St John's College Ladies' School in Winnipeg.

Posted in 1882–83 to Fort Ellice and then Île-à-la-Crosse, in 1884 W. J. McLean was assigned to Fort Pitt on the Saskatchewan River, in the territory of the Woods Cree. Amelia and the family joined him later that year, their arrival coinciding with the move of Plains Cree chief Big Bear [Mistahimaskwa*] and his followers into the district. He had only agreed to take treaty in 1882, following years of meagre subsistence for his people, and the winter of 1884–85 was one of great want and discontent. On 3 April 1885 the McLeans and the other residents of Fort Pitt learned that members of Big Bear's band had killed nine men at Frog Lake (Alta); a week before, an encounter at Duck Lake between the North-West Mounted Police and the Métis had left 15 dead.

Early in April non-aboriginal people from surrounding settlements sought refuge in Fort Pitt, which housed a NWMP detachment under the command of Francis Jeffrey Dickens*. The three eldest McLean girls, and one of their brothers, took turns at sentry duty. (An illustration in the *Montreal Daily Star* on 23 May would bear the caption "Noble women on the defensive. The Misses McLean show great courage, each one, Rifle in hand, Stands at a Loophole.") On 13 April the fort was surrounded by Big Bear and about 250 men; the next day W. J. McLean was requested to meet them. Consultation stopped when the Cree believed they were being attacked as three scouts tried to gallop through for the safety of the fort. One was killed; another, wounded, was brought into the fort while Amelia and others provided covering fire; the third escaped but was later taken by the Cree. Three Cree were also killed. Concerned about their father, Amelia and her sister Katherine (Kitty) left the fort and walked into the Cree camp unescorted. According to family accounts, some of the Cree, astonished at the girls' nerve, asked if they were not scared. The 17-year-old Amelia replied, in perfect Cree: "Why should we be afraid of you. We have lived together as brothers and sisters for many years. We speak the same language. Why should we be afraid of you?" Under her father's leadership, the remaining residents of Fort Pitt – the police had escaped – agreed to evacuate it under the custody of Big Bear. The group travelled to Frog Lake and then to Frenchman Butte, where there was a confrontation with the pursuing field force of Thomas Bland STRANGE. The camp fled, only to face another encounter, with NWMP scouts under Samuel Benfield Steele*. In mid June the McLeans were allowed to leave and on the 24th they arrived back at Fort Pitt.

During their months with the Cree, rumours had circulated that the older McLean girls were being mistreated, that they had been made the "slaves of the lesser chiefs" and had suffered the "final outrage." None of these stories was true, though there had been threatening behaviour from individuals as camp discipline deteriorated. Newspapers of the day commented at length on the girls, who were described as "plucky enough for life guardsmen," and Amelia was singled out for shouldering her Winchester at Fort Pitt. According to one account, she "would not have believed the endurance they all manifested possible, but now that the captivity is over she looks back at most of it with enjoyment."

In the American west, women like the McLean sisters might have enjoyed greater notoriety, perhaps in the style of Annie Oakley. Amelia, however, returned to a quiet life at Lower Fort Garry, Man., where her father was in charge from 1886 to 1893. During these years, with linguistic skills that were highly valued, she did some work for the federal Department of Indian Affairs. Its chief accountant and superintendent of Indian education, Duncan Campbell Scott*, who was also a published poet, later wrote that "she was gifted with a language-sense which made possible a knowledge of the subtlest peculiarities of two languages, the Cree and Ojibwa, both highly expressive, but the last eminently flexible and poetic." In 1899 she married Frederick Paget and moved to Ottawa. A clerk in Scott's offices, Paget was also useful to his department for his advice on western Indians (he had been a chief clerk at the Indian office in Regina and an assistant to the Indian commissioner). In this regard Amelia would have been an asset as well.

In 1906, in response to a special request from Governor General Lord Grey*, she received a commission from the department to travel among the Plains Indians and interview elders concerning their history, customs, and folklore. She visited the File Hills, Moose Mountain, Muscowpetung, and Crooked Lake agen-

cies in Saskatchewan in the fall of 1906, and met extensively with friends from her Qu'Appelle years. She required neither a driver nor, except when meeting with the Assiniboin, an interpreter, and she camped out unless the weather was poor. Her method was to gather together several elders: when one began telling his or her narrative, the others would corroborate, make corrections, and add detail. She was aware that beliefs limited the telling of fictitious stories to the winter – only actual happenings were recited in the long summer evenings – so she intended more trips, but it is unclear whether any took place. Her small commission was an unusual expenditure for the normally parsimonious government, but, as Scott would explain in his introduction to the resulting book, *The people of the plains* (Toronto, 1909), the project was motivated by a belief that ancient customs and manners were disappearing. He may also have found Amelia's insights useful to his poetry. She knew a great deal about the places and some of the individuals he wrote about, such as hunter/runner Akoose of the Crooked Lake agency and his father Qui-witch.

Amelia Paget's *People of the plains* is a remarkable and unconventional book. It contains none of the pejorative, negative descriptions of Indian habits and characteristics typically featured in other publications of the time (and before), including the work of Egerton Ryerson Young*. Paget's focus is the Plains Cree and the Saulteaux. She stresses that, before the arrival of immigrants, they led an ideal existence since they were a wealthy people who had all they desired and a nourishing diet, experienced no sickness, and lived in roomy tepees. After describing their modes of travel and how camping places were chosen and tepees constructed, she writes that "such an encampment amid beautiful scenery, astir with prosperous and contented Indians, must have been a most striking illustration of the Indians' own idea of the wonderful love and care bestowed upon them by the Great Spirit." She argues that it is unfair to call them heathens, and provides evidence of their complex religious beliefs. In her detailed descriptions of their ceremonies and dances, she distinguishes between those that were solemn and those intended to cause merriment. The book also contains accounts of the vanished buffalo hunt, warfare, burial customs, poetry, music, legends, and humour.

The way in which Paget undermines dominant stereotypes is most evident in her descriptions of women. Having talked with female elders who had observed "all the triumphs and trials" of their bands, she could maintain that the "popular idea of the poor Indian woman doing all the hard work has too often been overdrawn." The practice of polygamy is presented sympathetically: the wives "called each other 'sister,' and ... divided their labours equally, and tried in every way to cultivate mutual forbearance."

Paget's descriptions of Cree and Saulteaux life challenged conventional assumptions to such an extent that, in his introduction, Scott found it necessary to explain why the book had a "tone of championship for all Indians" and to account for the "idealistic tendency which places everything in a high and favorable aspect." He suggests that her early experiences, including her months with the Cree in 1885, had caused her to have a glowing view of bygone days and to ignore any "hardship and squalor, starvation, inhumanity and superstition in this aboriginal life." Paget had little say over the final appearance of her book. Scott edited it and corresponded with the publisher about the title, design, and illustrations. Her original title, which was in Cree or Saulteaux, and her design for the cover, drawn by one of her sisters, were both rejected.

The public was not entirely prepared for the point of view expressed in *People of the plains*, and it received mixed responses. Some appreciated the author's "first-hand information" and tendency to upset "popular superstitions." Others, however, found her account too much of a departure from the deeply embedded stereotypes of the day. The reviewer for the *Montreal Standard*, for instance, commented that "even when free from contact with the white man they were not exactly the Arcadian shepherds and shepherdesses that Mrs. Paget presents . . . the cruelty, the squalor, the dirt are glossed over. It is too late in the day for any Fenimore Cooper romance of the redskin."

Amelia McLean Paget died on 10 July 1922 in Ottawa following a four-year decline caused by pernicious anaemia. Her funeral took place at her father's home in Winnipeg and she was buried there in St John's cemetery.

SARAH A. CARTER

Amelia Anne McLean Paget is the author of *The people of the plains*, ed. and intro. D. C. Scott (Toronto, 1909). "The last hostage," by Duncan McLean, the subject's brother, as told to Eric Wells, is in *Weekend Magazine* (Montreal, etc.), 18 (1968), nos.32–33.

AO, RG 80-8-0-864, no.10132. LAC, RG 10, 4018, file 276916; RG 31, C1, 1901, Ottawa, St George's Ward, div.7: 14. Man., Dept. of Finance, Consumer and Corporate Affairs, Vital statistics (Winnipeg), no.1899-002441. *Calgary Herald*, 23 Oct. 1906. *Manitoba Free Press* (Winnipeg), 11, 14 July 1922. *Manitoba Morning Free Press* (Winnipeg), 21 Sept. 1909. *Montreal Daily Star*, 23 May, 23 June 1885. *Montreal Standard*, 9 Oct. 1909. *Ottawa Evening Journal*, 11 July 1922. *Patriot* (Charlottetown), 27 June 1885. Sarah Carter, "Amelia McLean Paget and *The people of the plains*" in *Good intentions in colonial Canada: the quest for "fair play" in aboriginal relations*, ed. Celia Haig-Brown and David Nock (Vancouver, forthcoming); *Capturing women: the manipulation of cultural imagery in Canada's prairie west* (Montreal and Kingston, Ont., 1997). *The Frog Lake "massacre": personal perspectives on ethnic conflict*, ed. Stuart Hughes (Toronto, 1976). Duncan McLean, "On the twilight trail of the fading west," *Nor'-Wester* (Winnipeg), centennial ed. (1970): 36–46 (includes a family photo taken about 1893). E. M. McLean, "The siege of Fort Pitt," *Beaver* (Winnipeg), outfit 277 (December 1946): 22–25; "Prisoners of the Indians," outfit 278 (June 1947): 14–17; "Our captivity ended," outfit 278 (September 1947): 38–42. Kitty [Katherine] McLean, "The adventures of Kitty," *Nor'-Wester*, centennial ed.: 37–38, 40–44, 46. W. J. McLean, "Tragic events at Frog Lake and Fort Pitt during the North West rebellion," *Manitoba Pageant* (Winnipeg), 17 (1971–72), no.2: 2–9; no.3: 19–24; 18 (1972–73), no.1: 22–24; no.2: 4–8; no.3: 11–16.

MACLEAN, JOHN (until about 1890 he spelled his family name **McLean**), Methodist missionary, author, office holder, newspaper editor, archivist, and librarian; b. 30 Oct. 1851 in Kilmarnock, Scotland, son of John McLean and Alice ——; m. 10 June 1880 Sarah Anne Barker in Guelph, Ont., and they had six children; d. 7 March 1928 in Winnipeg.

John Maclean pursued his education throughout his life. After attending an academy in Dumbarton, Scotland, he came to Canada in 1873. He was received on trial as a minister of the Methodist Church of Canada in 1875 and spent two years northwest of London, Ont., before entering Victoria College, Cobourg, where he earned a BA (1882) and an MA (1887). He went on to obtain a PHD in church history from Illinois Wesleyan University in Bloomington in 1888 and an LLB from the University of Manitoba in 1926. His doctoral degree made him the target of jealous criticism; some complained that his studying led him to neglect his mission. Maclean proceeded undaunted.

In 1880, after his ordination on 6 June and his wedding four days later, Maclean and his wife left for a new Methodist mission near Fort Macleod (Alta). They spent nine years among the Blood Indians, the North-West Mounted Police, and settlers; Maclean's circuit comprised almost all of what is now southern Alberta. There, he learned the languages of many native groups of the foothills. Settlement and the drive to create Indian reserves and industrial schools in the west during the last quarter of the 19th century spawned competition among missionaries. Maclean plunged into an unpleasant rivalry with Samuel Trivett of the Church Missionary Society which lasted until his departure in 1889. At the mission Maclean experienced mixed reactions from the Blood, who welcomed his offerings of food, clothing, and education, but who sometimes destroyed his property.

In 1886 Maclean had been appointed public school inspector for a territory extending from Medicine Hat to the Rockies and from Fort Macleod to the United States. He resigned this post after joining the Board of Education of the North-West Territories on 2 Dec. 1887. Two years later Maclean was appointed a member of the board of examiners for teachers and after accepting a charge in Moose Jaw (Sask.), he moved there with his young family; they stayed until 1892. Maclean also held posts within the church. The Manitoba and North-West Conference elected him journal secretary (1888–91) and secretary (1892); he would become president in 1895. In addition, he would serve as president of the Prohibitory League in 1898.

Along with a small group of unconventional missionaries such as Silas Tertius Rand*, Émile Petitot*, and Adrien-Gabriel Morice*, Maclean had a keen interest in Indian culture and ethnology. He corresponded with such early ethnologists as Horatio Emmons Hale*, Franz Boas*, and James Constantine Pilling, with the British Association on North-West Indian Tribes from 1882 to 1888, and for many years with the bureau of ethnology of the Smithsonian Institution in Washington, D.C., on the languages and literature of the native peoples of the west. His contemporaries thought him well informed on the languages, culture, and social and political life of the Plains Indians. At his death three of his books, *The Indians: their manners and customs* (Toronto, 1889), *The Blackfoot language* ([Toronto?, 1896?]), and *Canadian savage folk: the native tribes of Canada* (Toronto, 1896), were considered the best on their subjects. Besides his many works on native peoples and missionaries, some of which were published under the pseudonym Robin Rustler, he published numerous ethnological pamphlets and he was a regular contributor to the Hudson's Bay Company's magazine *Beaver* (Winnipeg) from 1924 to 1927.

Although Maclean clearly adhered to contemporary theories about the vanishing Indian and was later criticized for superficial fieldwork, he treated native peoples as humans who were capable of spiritual depth and sincerity. On 10 April 1889, for example, he wrote to his wife: "Listening to the song and story of my dusky friends my heart is bounding with delight. . . . Like innocent children they asked me whether or not I had seen any buffalo. . . . The shadows are falling over their pathway. . . . And they bow to the inevitable lot imposed upon them by the white race . . . [they] await the time when the Great Spirit shall call [them] away."

Maclean subsequently served at Port Arthur (Thunder Bay, Ont.) (1892–95), Neepawa, Man. (1896–1900), and Carman, Man. (1901–2). During those years he wrote a series of religious tracts. In 1902 he moved to Halifax, where he was editor of the *Wesleyan* for four years; he then returned west and was stationed at Morden, Man., until 1911. That year Maclean was sent to the small, struggling Bethel mission in Winnipeg. There, he and Sarah worked until 1919 among Winnipeg's English-speaking poor, providing social, legal, medical, and other relief services. At Bethel, which was renamed the Maclean mission in 1918, the couple established a Sunday school and

built a community centre, where an orchestra played a free concert every Saturday night.

In 1918 Maclean accepted the position of chief archivist of the Methodist Church at Wesley College, Winnipeg, a position which, from 1922, he held concurrently with that of chief librarian at the college. He would retain both posts until 1928. As archivist, he was especially interested in documenting the early history of the Methodist and Presbyterian denominations. He was active in many scientific and literary societies, including the Canadian Institute, the American Association for the Advancement of Science, the American Folk-Lore Society, the Historical and Scientific Society of Manitoba, and the Ontario Historical Society.

The 1920s were difficult for Maclean. The Winnipeg General Strike of 1919 had upset him greatly; he feared it to be the start of a revolution that was contemplated for the whole dominion. He was especially critical of the Social Gospel movement, believing that James Shaver Woodsworth* was supporting "Bolsheviks." As the 1920s went on, despite his optimism over church union, he was pessimistic about what he viewed as the decline of Methodism. After his death in 1928 John Maclean was warmly remembered as a committed and passionate man who devoted himself completely to scholarship, especially on native languages and culture, and to the church.

SUSAN GRAY

John Maclean is the author of numerous works, some of which went through several editions. The online catalogue of the LAC has 80 entries under his name. A number of his publications can also be found in CIHM, *Reg.*

AO, RG 80-5-0-94, no.11978. LAC, MG 29, D65. UCC, Manitoba and Northwestern Ontario Conference Arch. (Winnipeg), Vert. file, John Maclean. UCC-C, Biog. file; Fonds 3270. *Winnipeg Tribune*, 19 May 1926. *Canadian men and women of the time* (Morgan; 1898 and 1912). G. H. Cornish, *Cyclopædia of Methodism in Canada* . . . (2v., Toronto and Halifax, 1881–1903). J. W. Grant, *Moon of wintertime: missionaries and the Indians of Canada in encounter since 1534* (Toronto, 1984).

MACLEAN, WILLIAM FINDLAY, newspaperman and politician; b. 10 Aug. 1854 in Ancaster, Upper Canada, eldest son of John Maclean, a journalist, and Isabella Findlay; m. 3 June 1885 Catherine Gwynne Lewis in Toronto, and they had a son and a daughter; d. 7 Dec. 1929 near Toronto.

Of Scottish background, William Findlay Maclean was educated at schools in Hamilton and at the University of Toronto (BA 1880). He followed his father's career path and strong protectionist views. In the early 1870s he was a copyboy and writer for the Hamilton *Times*; in 1875 he became parliamentary correspondent for the Toronto *Liberal* [*see* John Cameron*] and then joined the *Globe* as John Gordon Brown's secretary and city editor.

Maclean's journalistic and political interests were closely intertwined. In August 1880 he and *Globe* reporter Albert Horton founded the *World* to support Liberal candidate Peter Ryan in a local by-election. After Maclean bought out Horton in October 1881, the paper would become a family affair, with his father, his brothers (James Hector, John, and Wallace), and eventually his son (Hugh John) working on it. It emulated the local papers founded by John Ross Robertson*, who had introduced the American-style "penny" press for the mass market. Bright and iconoclastic, the *World* gave Torontonians a taste of the populist crusades and sensationalism pioneered by the *New York Herald*. The new one-cent daily had an immediate impact; some found it the "editorially boldest," others viewed it as decidedly downscale.

The *World*'s irreverence, noisy exposés of civic corruption, skilful skirting of libel, and opposition to the religious establishment made it the favourite of Toronto's trolley-travelling working class. Maclean tweaked Sabbatarian sensitivity in 1891 by establishing the weekly *Sunday World*. In addition, persistent campaigning by the *World* from 1894 helped lead to the referendum of 1897 that allowed streetcars on Sundays. When Maclean entered the fray in 1907 in support of a municipally owned electrical utility to compete with Toronto Electric Light, he spoke from a strong populist base, reinforced by the brilliant cartoon work of Samuel Hunter*. Maclean's espousal of public interest spread through his training of such prominent newsmen as Hector Willoughby Charlesworth*, Joseph E. Atkinson*, and John Bayne Maclean*. Charlesworth remembered "W. F." (others called him Billy) taking on any task – sweeping, hefting newsprint, "grinding out little witty paragraphs shrewd as rapier thrusts."

Maclean's populist inclinations had probably hastened his entry into politics. Initially the *World* had identified itself as an "Independent Liberal" journal, but by the mid 1880s it was criticizing Ontario's Liberal premier, Oliver Mowat*, over liquor licensing and other issues. Maclean ran unsuccessfully for the provincial legislature in 1890 as a Conservative in Wentworth North. Federally the following year he almost upset former prime minister Alexander Mackenzie* in York East. Victorious in the by-election there on 11 May 1892, he was repeatedly re-elected in this Toronto-area riding and, from 1904, in York South.

In the House of Commons, he was as mercurial as he was at his newspaper. Nominally a Conservative, particularly on the protective tariff, he gained a reputation for unpredictable independence. As early as 1894 some Conservatives called him the "man with the knife" because of his role in breaking the news of

Prime Minister Sir John Sparrow David Thompson*'s serious state of health. Maclean's attempts to undermine Ontario Conservative leader James Pliny Whitney* and then federal leader Robert Laird Borden*, combined with rumours of his involvement in starting new parties, led the *Daily Mail and Empire* to read him out of the party in 1905. He subsequently ran as an independent Conservative. In 1907 his connivance to help the Liberal government of Sir Wilfrid Laurier* led to his acclamation the following year; at his nomination he lashed out at big business, appeared to befriend labour, and posted himself as the harbinger of "new ideas and new things for my party's platform. . . . The party system's all right, but I am not a machine." Conservative distrust deepened when he supported Laurier's naval policy in 1910. In 1926 the maverick MP was defeated by a bona fide Conservative, Robert Henry McGregor.

If Maclean's independence cost him respect, his 34 years as a backbencher and unrelenting promotion of radical causes gained him notoriety. His favourite demands included a "Bank of Canada," a national currency, the public ownership of railways, hydroelectricity, and telephones, and a uniform passenger rate on trains. His nationalism, expressed in his opposition to reciprocity and his calls for a Canadian-made constitution and a Canadian head of state, could occasionally take an eccentric turn. He argued, for example, that Hudson Bay should be renamed "Canada's Sea." In 1902, in the midst of his federal career, he had contested the mayoralty of Toronto. Dismissed by incumbent Oliver Aiken Howland as a bid to "revolutionize everything," Maclean's platform embraced public ownership, a doubtful concern for labour, and a vigorous hostility to big corporations and monopoly. He managed to poll 8,816 votes to Howland's 13,424, a result that reflected his perennial popularity.

Maclean's political career was further hobbled because, as the *Globe* pointed out, he was the "poorest of business men." The *World* always teetered on the edge of bankruptcy. This precarious state led Maclean to some questionable practices, giving the impression that his editorial views were for sale; in 1887 Prime Minister Sir John A. Macdonald* had been advised that he could be bought for $10,000. Though he remained stubbornly independent, his advocacy of some causes was tainted by self-interest. He accepted money from a grateful Toronto Railway Company after the successful Sunday battle. In 1911 the *Globe* claimed that the *World* had solicited deposits for the "rotten" Farmers Bank of Canada in exchange for its financial support. Later, Maclean's campaign for the construction of a viaduct over the Don River in Toronto was compromised by his ownership of Donlands, his farm west of the valley.

The decline of the financially troubled *World*, which was sold to the *Daily Mail and Empire* in 1921, was attributed by Hector Charlesworth to "the divided ambition of its chief," his constant shift between the editor's desk and the "turmoils" of politics. At his death the *Globe* would conclude, "That quality of independence which had made him shine in journalism also made him a personality in Parliament, but it finally spelled his political ruin." Maclean died in 1929 in York Township at Bayview, the home of his daughter and son-in-law, Henry Arthur Sifton, and was buried in the cemetery of St John's Anglican Church, York Mills (Toronto).

MINKO SOTIRON

Examples of William Findlay Maclean's opinions on issues of the day can be found in two of his published commentaries, "Canada first – empire next," *World* (Toronto), 22 Feb. 1907, and "Some of Canada's near-by problems," *Canadian Forum* (Toronto), 6 (1925–26): 173–75.

AO, RG 22-305, no.63800; RG 80-5-0-139, no.13795. LAC, MG 26, G: 128184; MG 27, III, C9. *Daily Mail and Empire*, 7 Dec. 1929. *Globe*, 9 Dec. 1929. *Manitoba Free Press*, 9 Dec. 1929. *World*, 1880–1921. Christopher Armstrong and H. V. Nelles, *The revenge of the Methodist bicycle company: Sunday streetcars and municipal reform in Toronto, 1887–1897* (Toronto, 1977); "The rise of civic populism in Toronto, 1870–1920," in *Forging a consensus: historical essays on Toronto*, ed. V. L. Russell (Toronto, 1984), 192–237. Can., House of Commons, *Debates*, 1892–1926. *Canadian annual rev.*, 1902, 1908, 1911. *Canadian men and women of the time* (Morgan; 1898 and 1912). F. S. Chalmers, *A gentleman of the press* (Toronto and New York, 1969). H. [W.] Charlesworth, *Candid chronicles: leaves from the note book of a Canadian journalist* (Toronto, 1925). Ross Harkness, *J. E. Atkinson of the "Star"* (Toronto, 1963). [J.] S. Roe, "In harness under 'W. F.,'" *Saturday Night*, 21 Dec. 1929: 5. Paul Rutherford, *A Victorian authority: the daily press in late nineteenth-century Canada* (Toronto, 1982). Minko Sotiron, *From politics to profits: the commercialization of Canadian daily newspapers, 1890–1920* (Montreal and Kingston, Ont., 1997).

McLEAN, WILLIAM JAMES (Big Bear), fur trader; b. 27 Oct. 1841 on the Isle of Lewis, Scotland, son of Angus McLean and Ann McRae; m. 23 Aug. 1866, at Fort Simpson (N.W.T.), Helen Hunter Murray, daughter of Alexander Hunter Murray*, and they had six daughters, including AMELIA ANNE, and six sons; d. 12 Nov. 1929 in Winnipeg.

W. J. McLean joined the Hudson's Bay Company in 1859 at the age of 18. He worked until 1864 as an apprentice clerk successively at York Factory (Man.), Lower Fort Garry (Man.), and Fort Norman (N.W.T.). In 1864 he was transferred to Fort Liard (N.W.T.), where he became clerk-in-charge. From 1873 to 1882 McLean was stationed at Fort Qu'Appelle (Sask.); there he was promoted chief trader and played a role in the conclusion of Treaty No.4 [see David Laird*]. After service in 1882–83 at Fort Ellice, Man., in 1883–84 he was chief trader at Île-à-la-Crosse (Sask.),

on the English (upper Churchill) River, and in 1884–85 he was stationed at Fort Pitt, on the Saskatchewan River. Thus, although McLean was a newcomer to Fort Pitt when the tumultuous events of 1885 erupted, he was not new to the northwest or to negotiating with native peoples.

The events that earned him the nickname Big Bear McLean occurred in rapid succession from April to June 1885. Early in the morning of 3 April McLean learned from farming instructor George Gwynn Mann and others coming to Fort Pitt for protection that nine settlers had been shot and killed at Frog Lake (Alta) on the previous morning by members of the Cree band led by Big Bear [Mistahimaskwa*]. McLean immediately organized the inhabitants of Fort Pitt, including Inspector Francis Jeffrey Dickens* and 23 North-West Mounted Police, to barricade and defend it against an expected attack ("I did not sleep two hours out of every twenty-four," McLean would later write). Nothing happened until 13 April, when Big Bear and about 250 Cree arrived at the fort. They asked that McLean speak with the chiefs the following day. McLean agreed, "in hope of being of some service to the Country and to those who were unfortunately so precariously situated with myself at Pitt."

Negotiations began cordially. According to McLean, both the Plains and the Woods Cree indicated that although they had no objection to the HBC's presence in their lands (and in fact did not want the company to leave), they were interested in driving out "the Government" and "his" adjuncts, the "Red Coats" or mounted police. McLean attempted to convince them that taking on the government and settlers was both "hopeless" and "dangerous." Wandering Spirit [Kapapamahchakwew*], armed and speaking for the Plains Cree, insisted that his words came too late, and that he must obey them and remain in their camp. According to his earliest report, McLean "felt wretched and helpless, filled with remorse at my falling a victim to the misplaced confidence and hope which I held but a few hours past of being able to convince the Indians of their errors and folly." Talks were interrupted by two NWMP scouts and one civilian galloping through the camp; they had been sent out the previous day by Inspector Dickens to look for Big Bear's men. Interpreting their presence as an attack, the Cree retaliated, killing one man and wounding another, while the third escaped. Wandering Spirit told McLean that he must swear to remain with the Cree and assured him that he would not be killed, nor would his family be hurt, saying "I know your tongue is straight." McLean agreed, and negotiated as best he could for the safety of the others at the fort, who also were to come to the Cree camp, and for the safe departure of Dickens and his men. William Bleasdell Cameron*'s account, *Blood red the sun*, reprinting a note from Big Bear to Sergeant John A. Martin of the

NWMP on 14 April, suggests that the decision to allow the police to leave had already been made. The police departed down the Saskatchewan River in a scow that had been hastily built in the preceding days, and McLean's family, the HBC servants, and all who had taken refuge at Fort Pitt joined Big Bear's camp. McLean's reports of these events reveal his feelings of impotence, but also his alertness to practical concessions that could still be gained.

McLean, his wife (pregnant with their tenth child), and their nine children remained with the Cree until mid June, when they were released by the Woods Cree, who had split off from the Plains Cree. By this time all others held by Big Bear's camp had been released or had escaped. On 24 June the McLeans finally arrived back at Fort Pitt. During the family's captivity, they had survived the battles of Frenchman Butte and Loon Lake as the Cree clashed with pursuing NWMP. According to his reports, McLean worked with various friendly Woods Cree and Riding Mountain Cree to prevent Big Bear's men from joining with Poundmaker [Pītikwahanapiwīyin*] at Battleford and Louis Riel* at Batoche.

In emerging from these events, McLean had to account, in the claims of the HBC against the Canadian government, for his role in the loss of Fort Pitt (which was looted, and later burned). His story differs from that of Inspector Dickens, an officer not known for his competence. According to McLean, when the Cree first arrived at Fort Pitt on 13 April he and Dickens had agreed it was important that McLean go to the Cree camp to talk, as the Cree had requested. Once there, he was told that the presence of the NWMP put everyone at Fort Pitt in jeopardy; unless they left, the Cree would burn the occupied fort. In his reports McLean implies that Dickens had shown lack of judgement in sending out inexperienced scouts who missed the movements of the Cree and stumbled into their camp, jeopardizing negotiations. Mrs McLean had helped an indecisive Dickens by recommending the HBC scow and by waiting until the NWMP had safely left Fort Pitt before joining the Cree camp.

According to Dickens, the NWMP initially refused to leave Fort Pitt unless the Cree dispersed. McLean, without consultation, agreed to talks, thereby becoming entrapped in the Cree camp, where his family and other civilians decided to join him. With no civilians left to guard, Dickens was free to "look to the safety of my own men" and leave the fort; he blamed "the surrender of the civilians" on "the pusillanimity of Mr. Maclean." Some newspaper accounts of the time also censured McLean. New settlers and those unused to relations with native people (Dickens was famed for his lack of tact in such dealings) saw negotiating with them as a concession. McLean, however, as an experienced HBC trader, would have thought it natural to meet and talk with them. The Cree, in turn, respected his advice (even if they were not always interested in following it) and his willingness to keep his word.

After the events of 1885, McLean became chief trader at Fort Alexander, Man.; he then served as chief trader in charge of the Lake Winnipeg district at Lower Fort Garry from 1886 until he retired in 1892. In 1893 he was called upon by John Christian Schultz*, lieutenant governor of Manitoba, to undertake a confidential survey of the District of Keewatin. McLean reported on the use of alcohol and criminal activity (there was little of either), the condition of non-treaty indigenous peoples, forest fires, and fishing regulations. His main concern was the preservation of fur-bearing animals, whose rapid decline was affecting the survival of the natives. He recommended that a system for the protection of moose, bear, and beaver, not just in Keewatin but throughout the northwest, be brought before parliament. Letters to his brother Duncan in 1899 indicate that he was involved in leading a party in exploring for gold in the Yukon, using his past experience and native contacts during his time as an HBC clerk at Fort Liard. In 1901 McLean read before the Historical and Scientific Society of Manitoba a paper entitled "Notes and observations of travels on the Athabasca and Slave lake regions in 1899." In it, he makes only one brief mention of "enormous mineral deposits," focusing mainly on the rugged scenery of the northeastern part of Great Slave Lake (so remote and silent, he comments, that it seems "nature had ceased to exist"), the "profusion" of fish, and the hunting of the caribou on their annual summer migration through the area. At the ruins of Fort Reliance (N.W.T.), McLean muses over the history of explorers in the region, and imagines a future in which "sportsmen and tourists" from Europe and the United States make it "an annual resort."

Little is known of his subsequent activities. An obituary in the *Beaver* in December 1929 noted that McLean was still active with the Department of Indian Affairs in Winnipeg at the time of his death.

LALLY GRAUER

William James McLean's "Notes and observations of travels on the Athabasca and Slave lake regions in 1899" appears in Man., Hist. and Scientific Soc., *Trans.* (Winnipeg), no.58 (1901).

AM, HBCA, D.20/35/1b, ff.134–58; E.218. Bob Beal and R. [C.] Macleod, *Prairie fire: the 1885 North-West rebellion* (Edmonton, 1984; repr. Toronto, 1994). W. B. Cameron, *Blood red the sun* (rev. ed., Calgary, 1950). F. J. Dickens, "Report of Inspector Dickens, North-West Mounted Police," in *Settlers and rebels: being the official reports to parliament of the activities of the Royal North-West Mounted Police Force from 1882–1885* (Toronto, 1973), 78–80. Robert Watson, "Late chief trader W. J. McLean," *Beaver* (Winnipeg), outfit 260 (December 1929): 315–16.

Maclellan

MACLELLAN, ROBERT, educator; b. 14 July 1849 in Durham, N.S., second son and sixth child of John Maclellan, a farmer, and Helen Hogg; m. 1 Jan. 1887 Martha Maria Fraser in Scotsburn, N.S., and they had three sons and a daughter; d. 12 July 1922 in Pictou, N.S.

Robert Maclellan's great-grandfather Anthony Maclellan and his family shipped in 1775 from Balcary, Scotland, on the *Lovely Nelly* bound for St John's (Prince Edward) Island. The following year the Maclellans relocated to West River (Durham) in Pictou County, N.S. Over the generations the family farmed; in 1871 John Maclellan owned an 80-acre operation. Robert attended school at Durham, Pictou Academy in Pictou, and, in 1871–72, Dalhousie College in Halifax, where he captured the gold medal in mathematics and rhetoric and the second prize in classics. He also proved to be a fair player in football and lacrosse. In the fall of 1872 an opportunity to teach arose and he took the position, at Upper Green Hill (Greenhill) in Pictou County.

The following year Maclellan was employed in the preparatory department of Pictou Academy. In 1876 he became its English and classics master, a position he retained until the spring of 1883, when he resigned to become the inspector of schools for the district of Pictou and South Colchester. On 8 July 1889 he was appointed classical master and principal of Pictou Academy, succeeding (as principal) Alexander Howard MACKAY, a strong disciplinarian. At the time the academy's enrolment of 245 made it the largest such institution in the province, and one of the most influential. Under MacKay's regime it had been used as a model to build a centralized provincial system of education, with a standardized curriculum, graded classes, and provincially controlled teachers' examinations and licences. The secondary level of schooling at the academy was marked by wide access and rigorous examination.

Maclellan had not been the first pick of the academy's board – it had wanted Ebenezer Mackay – but in the event he continued the exceptional leadership of his predecessor. When the building burned down in 1895, Maclellan and the board were able to have a three-storey structure erected within two years. Its library, science laboratory, and Convocation Hall were considered foremost in the province. In 1897 the British Association for the Advancement of Science praised the academy's extensive collection of specimens. During Maclellan's tenure, graduates led the province in matriculation examinations for entry to Dalhousie (1890–93), in the number of graduate students there (1895), and in marks achieved by fourth-year students in Nova Scotia (1912). As well, an academy student, Frank Parker Day, secured a Rhodes scholarship in 1905. The Pictou Academy Alumni Association was formed in 1893 to retain graduates'

interest; it raised money and offered a number of medals and prizes to foster academic excellence. In order to temper this meritocratic academic thrust, Maclellan introduced social and athletic activities in 1898–99. His support of student pleas for lighter workloads led to provincial curricular revisions in 1908. He also promoted the successful centenary celebrations at Pictou Academy in 1916.

Maclellan's style of leadership was more subtle than the authoritarian manner of MacKay. For instance, he opted to suspend rather than expel two students found guilty of public intoxication. Later, faced with demands that a staff member be fired, he quietly obtained a resignation through a three-month severance package. At the school socials he emphasized respectability and the deportment of "true gentlemen and ladies." His efforts to foster cooperation and a cohesive school culture were well suited to students from the town of Pictou, but they had a limited effect on those who, beginning in 1890, commuted by train from New Glasgow. They and rural students from elsewhere in the county, as well as several female students, felt increasingly alienated. Elizabeth Tibbel, a rural student who enjoyed the art program and wrote poetry, never showed her poems to the teaching masters because she lacked the courage to do so. In another example, from 1913, the academy's board denied the request of female students to use Convocation Hall to play basketball, in imitation of their male colleagues, who had begun using the Young Men's Christian Association for gymnasium classes two years before. The school culture changed even more during World War I, when the myth of a virtuous Scottish past, which emerged from a stirring address delivered during the centennial celebrations of 1916 by Arthur Stanley Mackenzie*, president of Dalhousie, combined with wartime realities to create a new sense of community within the academy.

Maclellan's three-decade tenure would be largely marked by consensus and conciliation, a situation that resulted in his immense popularity with both students and staff. The rigorous academic training he promoted allowed many talented young men to flourish in their professions. The gold medal students who would leave their mark on the nation included Henry Fraser Munro* (1893), later a superintendent of schools for Nova Scotia, James McGregor Stewart* (1906), a lawyer, financier, and close friend of Maclellan, and John Hamilton Lane Johnstone (1908) and George Hugh Henderson (1910), the Dalhousie professors who developed a method during World War II to degauss vessels to protect them from magnetic mines. Many other students used their programs to gain access to the teaching profession and to improve their licences. Under Maclellan's able leadership, the academy continued to foster academic excellence and a middle-class cultural ethos, which spread throughout

Pictou County and beyond. Little wonder that scholars have observed that he "re-established a genuine love of learning in the institution."

In 1908 Maclellan was awarded an honorary LLD by Dalhousie. The staff and former staff of Pictou Academy presented him with a silver loving cup in recognition of the honour. In 1916, during the centennial celebrations, he was tendered a dinner which lasted six hours. From 1914 Maclellan had begun to suffer from indifferent health. He submitted his resignation on 11 Feb. 1919; three years later he was dead. His funeral was held at First Presbyterian Church in Pictou under the direction of the Oddfellows' Eastern Star Lodge No.1. Buried in Haliburton Cemetery, he was survived by a son and a daughter and two brothers, James of Rogers Hill and William Edward, a postal superintendent and author. A final tribute to Robert Maclellan came in 1933 when an anonymous donor (likely James McGregor Stewart) established a scholarship in his name. At the time he was described by the *Pictou Advocate* as "a most inspiring teacher of the humanities and a delightful companion."

ALLAN C. DUNLOP and B. ANNE WOOD

A photograph and a plaque honouring Robert Maclellan hang on the walls of Pictou Academy in Pictou, N.S.

NSARM, Pictou (town), board of school commissioners, minutes of meetings, 1889–1919 (mfm.13278). *Halifax Herald*, 13 July 1922. *Pictou Advocate*, 5 May 1908, 6 Dec. 1913, 21 July 1922. *Journal of Education* (Halifax), 3rd ser., 10 (1920–22), no.6. C. J. W. Kedy, "Pictou Academy from its founding to the present: an important narrative in the history of education in the province of Nova Scotia" (M.ED thesis, Mount Allison Univ., Sackville, N.B., 1933). J. P. MacPhie, *Pictonians at home and abroad* (Boston, 1914). B. A. Wood, "Constructing Nova Scotia's 'Scotchness': the centenary celebrations of Pictou Academy in 1916," *Hist. Studies in Education* (London, Ont.), 6 (1994): 281–302; *Pictou Academy in the nineteenth century* (Pictou, 1997); "Pictou Academy: promoting 'schooled subjectivities' in 19th-century Nova Scotia," *Acadiensis* (Fredericton), 28 (1998–99), no.2: 41–57.

McLENNAN, ROBERT PURVES, tinsmith, businessman, politician, and banker; b. 7 Dec. 1861 in Pictou, N.S., seventh of the ten children of James Purves McLennan, a painter, and Eliza Anne Harrington; m. 23 Nov. 1887 Bessie Archibald McKenzie in River John, N.S., and they had ten children, nine of whom survived infancy; d. 27 July 1927 in Vancouver.

Robert Purves McLennan attended Pictou Academy until he was 15, at which time he left to learn the tinsmithing trade and hardware business. In 1882 he went to Winnipeg, then in the midst of a boom, and worked as a tinsmith. When the boom collapsed he returned to Nova Scotia for a brief visit before moving to Victoria, where he arrived in September 1884. There he opened a shop, making galvanized iron cor-

nices and installing tin roofing. The following year he invited Edward John McFeely, whom he had met in Winnipeg, to join him in business. The firm of McLennan and McFeely prospered, becoming dealers in stoves and tinware in addition to carrying on its roofing work.

By May 1886 McLennan and McFeely had expanded to Vancouver. The fire of 13 June which destroyed most of the town spared their building, then under construction, and shortly afterwards the company began to build stoves and deal in other metal wares. During the next few years it added many hardware and house-furnishing lines and advertised as general roofers, plumbers, and gas fitters. The firm's involvement in roofing, plumbing, and stove making was phased out in the early 1890s in order for it to focus on wholesale and retail activities. In 1891 McLennan, in Victoria, employed 13 persons and McFeely, in Vancouver, 17.

Victoria experienced a business slump in 1893. McLennan and McFeely decided to sell their business there and concentrate on Vancouver. By 1895 McLennan had moved to Vancouver with his family. McLennan, McFeely and Company Limited Liability was incorporated on 3 April 1895 with an authorized capital of $150,000 in 1,500 shares. The partners' wives held the largest number of shares, 351 each, while their husbands held 39 each. McFeely was named president and McLennan vice-president.

In 1898, a year after the beginning of the Klondike gold rush, McLennan took a load of merchandise to Dawson, Y.T., reportedly planning to stay for only several weeks. He remained five years. The firm was successful there and quickly rebuilt after losing a building worth $12,000 and stock valued at $6,000 in the fire of 26 April 1899. During 1899 and 1900 it had branches in Atlin and Bennett, in northern British Columbia. In the summer of 1900 the partners shipped to Dawson over 800 tons of merchandise worth $200,000, on which they paid $115,000 in freight charges.

While in Dawson, McLennan became involved in several other enterprises. In 1900 he was the principal shareholder in the Ridge Cable Company; a partner, Hill M. Henning, managed the operation. That same year he served as president of the Dawson City Water and Power Company Limited. In October 1902 McLennan and McFeely sold its retail hardware business in Dawson to the Yukon Hardware Company, formed that year. McLennan then concentrated on the wholesale trade. In January 1903, strongly supported by the *Daily Klondike Nugget*, he was elected the second mayor of Dawson. He served one term, during a period when the city was in decline, and did not seek re-election. Although he left for Vancouver in early 1904, the company continued in Dawson for some time afterwards.

In March 1904 McLennan and McFeely purchased land in Vancouver along Cordova Street East for $40,000. The five-storey building it erected would be outgrown by 1911. The firm raised its capital in 1905 to $500,000 and again in 1909 to $1,000,000. The partners' wives were still the largest shareholders. In 1913 the company was restructured in order to expand its capital to $5,000,000.

Elected vice-president of the Vancouver Board of Trade in 1905, McLennan served as president in 1906–7 and remained on its council until 1912. He had also been elected a trustee of the Vancouver School Board in 1905 and he served two two-year terms. A lifelong Liberal, he contested the provincial general election of 2 Feb. 1907 in the five-member riding of Vancouver City. After a hard-fought campaign, he took sixth place, behind five Conservatives. That year he became a member of the Royal Institution for the Advancement of Learning of British Columbia, which sought to establish a co-educational college connected to McGill University.

Along with other Vancouver businessmen who felt that Canada's central banks were not adequately supporting British Columbia's industry and commerce, McLennan promoted the Chartered Bank of British Columbia in 1907. The group combined in 1908 with another seeking the same goals and the Bank of Vancouver was incorporated on 3 April with a capital stock of $2,000,000. It opened two years later under McLennan's presidency. Although financially very strong, the directors lacked banking experience. Difficult economic conditions started in the autumn of 1912 and were followed by the withdrawal from the province of British capital, lengthy coal strikes, and, in 1913, rumours of impending war. Investment dried up, real estate speculation ceased, and construction halted. The bank had expanded too quickly and had some problematic loans. The collapse of the Dominion Trust Company in October 1914 was a crushing blow, since public confidence in financial institutions faltered. Depositors fled the bank, which suspended payment on 14 December.

In 1912 McLennan had purchased a farm of approximately 335 acres on Gambier Island, in Howe Sound, and from then until his death he may have spent much of his time and wealth improving it. His interest in the farm led to his involvement with the Vancouver Exhibition Association, of which he was president in 1927. In 1925 McLennan had campaigned as a Liberal in the federal riding of Vancouver-Burrard, pointing out that the Liberal government of Prime Minister William Lyon Mackenzie King* had lowered freight rates and provided grain elevators and permanent docks. He was defeated by Conservative John Arthur Clark. He died in 1927 after an operation to remove a gallstone, leaving an estate with a final net value of $191,483. McFeely, his partner of more than 40 years, died ten months later. In 1928 the firm became known as McLennan, McFeely and Prior Limited.

An enterprising and energetic businessman who was willing to take risks, Robert Purves McLennan founded a business that would continue until the 1960s to be a landmark for many British Columbians. Civic-minded, he had sought to improve the communities in which he lived. He achieved great financial success, perhaps at the expense of his relations with his family, with whom he was not close.

RONALD GREENE

BCA, GR-1415, file 12346; GR-1422, file 7739; GR-1438, files A16568, BC00226; GR-2951, no.1927-09-383900 (mfm.). LAC, RG 19, 228, file 616-2; RG 31, C1, 1871, Pictou, N.S., subdist.F, subdiv.1: 42; 1881, Pictou, subdist.F: 74, 75; 1891, Victoria, James Bay Ward: 12; 1901, Vancouver, subdist.D, subdiv.7: 1; Dawson, Y.T., subdist.F, subdiv.14: 3. Private arch., R. P. McLennan (Surrey, B.C.), Family bible. *Daily Colonist* (Victoria), 9 July 1885, 4 Dec. 1887, 11 Dec. 1894, 5 April 1895, 22 Dec. 1907. *Daily Klondike Nugget* (Dawson), 6 Dec. 1900; 3 Jan., 5 Feb. 1901; 6 Oct., 29 Dec. 1902; 6 Jan. 1903. *Dawson Daily News* (Dawson), September 1899, special mining ed. *Klondike Nugget* (Dawson), 29 April 1899. *Monetary Times* (Toronto), 21 Dec. 1907; 14 March 1908; 25 Jan. 1913; 16 Jan., 27 March, 8 Dec. 1914. *Vancouver Daily Advertiser*, 8 May, 5 July 1886. *Vancouver Daily Province*, 1904–27. *Vancouver Morning Sun*, 19 Sept., 9, 30 Oct. 1925; continued as *Evening Sun*, 28, 31 July 1927. B.C., Legislative Assembly, *Sessional papers*, reports on public schools, 1902/3–1905/6. *Canadian annual rev.*, 1906. *Directory*, Alaska–Yukon, 1903, 1907–8; B.C., 1884–1910; Dawson, 1901; Vancouver, 1887–90, 1896, 1899–1900, 1905–11. *Electoral hist. of B.C.* E. O. S. Scholefield and F. W. Howay, *British Columbia from the earliest times to the present* (4v., Vancouver, 1914), 4. Vancouver Board of Trade, *Annual report*, 1904/5–1912/13.

McLEOD, HENRY COLLINGWOOD, banker and yachtsman; b. 9 March 1851 in New London, P.E.I., son of John McLeod and Annabella Mackay; m. first 9 March 1875 Elizabeth Sarah Davison, and they had two daughters and a son; m. secondly 7 Sept. 1882 Ada Gordon in Georgetown, P.E.I., and they had two daughters and a son; d. 19 Dec. 1926 in Camden, S.C., and was buried in Minneapolis, Minn.

"The battles of his life were with other bankers on banking matters." With these words the Toronto *Globe* summed up Henry C. McLeod, who managed the Bank of Nova Scotia between 1897 and 1910, a critical period during which the bank established itself in central and western Canada. When he aired his dissident views and disputes with competitors, exposing in the press what propriety compelled others to reserve for backrooms, he gave the public cause to question rather than defer to their bankers. A candid and uncompromising attitude alarmed allies and irritated the Canadian Bankers' Association, the Department of Finance in Ottawa, and the financial press. McLeod's activism was inspired by a genuine concern about the consequences of bank failures. At the same time he recognized opportunity in the unease that such failures caused the public. McLeod employed the press to publicize the Bank of Nova Scotia's pioneering use of external auditors, turning the banking system's weakness, secretive management, to his advantage and ensuring the bank a reputation for the highest standards of prudence. This was McLeod's critical feat, securing a new market for the Bank of Nova Scotia by attaining the people's trust when trust was all important.

McLeod was the son of a ship's captain in Prince Edward Island, and his thoughts were never far from sailing and the "mid-Atlantic's pure breezes." Educated at local schools, he read law for three years while employed as an attorney's clerk in Charlottetown. In 1872, however, he opted for a business career, joining a firm of commission merchants as an accountant. A year later he entered the service of the small Merchants' Bank of Prince Edward Island in Charlottetown; he worked there as an accountant until 1875, when he was made manager of the Georgetown branch. His advancement brought social status and the liberty to marry, a step the etiquette of banking discouraged until an income to support a family had been secured. He married Sarah Davison and within a few years was the father of two girls and a boy. The family's quiet life was tragically disrupted in 1881 when Sarah died quite suddenly. Widowed with three small children to tend, McLeod faced the most difficult time of his life. A year passed before he married Ada Gordon. He then left his native province for Amherst, N.S., where he joined the Bank of Nova Scotia as its local agent. Over the next few years he and Ada would add three children to Ada's ready-made family.

The cashier (general manager) of the Bank of Nova Scotia was Thomas Fyshe*, a cantankerous Scot with little time for agents who operated outside the bounds of prudence. In Amherst, McLeod proved an able manager worthy of Fyshe's confidence. When McLeod assumed his duties the bank was confined to the Maritimes, where competition for deposits was fierce. Banks also fought for customers they could safely lend their deposits to, and when clients appeared in short supply a quest for new markets began. In 1882 Fyshe's search led him to Winnipeg for a share of that city's booming economy. The timing was unfortunate. Winnipeg's wave of prosperity crested, as did the careers of the local managers who had been too anxious to lend out the bank's money.

In 1884 McLeod was sent to Winnipeg with orders to dispatch the manager and wind up what was an embarrassing moment in the bank's history. En route he stopped in Minneapolis and was surprised by the opportunity that lay waiting for a bank willing to serve the many millers who looked to local banks for loans only to find few able to accommodate their needs. After completing his Winnipeg duties and returning to Halifax in 1885, McLeod persuaded Fyshe that Minneapolis was a good prospect. Later that year he went west for a second time, to open the Minneapolis branch, and was joined by his friend and the inspector of the Bank of Nova Scotia, James Berwick Forgan. Both men were excited by the opportunity that the new agency offered. Forgan wanted to run it and knew that he could have it because Fyshe had promised him a branch of his choosing after he refused the general manager's job at a competing bank in Halifax. He therefore proposed that he and McLeod switch jobs. Fyshe was initially reluctant, however, and the exchange occurred only after McLeod had threatened resignation. He was too valuable to lose.

Competition in the Maritimes was a constant irritant for Fyshe, but it was no less a problem in the western United States, where well-trained Canadian bankers were in demand. In 1887 Forgan joined the Northwestern National Bank of Minneapolis and McLeod returned to the city to protect the Bank of Nova Scotia's interests. Now, instead of making deals with his old friend, he battled him for business. Forgan, it seems, did not come out on top. McLeod built a profitable loan business between the bank and local American banks in which its advances were secured against gilt-edged securities. (He also acquired a keen sense of the American animosity for bankers, a feature of the country's political culture alien to Canada at the time.) The Northwestern felt the pinch of his presence and in 1892 tried to lure him to its side, as it had Forgan, offering a salary of $7,500 a year. With Forgan having defected and with an enviable record in hand, McLeod possessed the leverage needed to demand a similar offer from his employer. In September the bank's board of directors quickly agreed. McLeod then closed the Minneapolis office and opened an agency in Chicago, where he remained until 1897. In that year Fyshe accepted the job of joint general manager at the much larger Merchants' Bank of Canada, based in Montreal. The door was thus opened for McLeod to take charge of the Bank of Nova Scotia and lead its expansion in central and western Canada. He was appointed cashier on 25 June 1897. Just five months later he established a branch in Toronto, and in January 1899, as general manager (the title had changed in 1898), he reopened the Winnipeg branch.

Relatively unknown nationally and lacking the stature of his predecessor, McLeod differed from Fyshe in other ways as well. Despite his surly persona, Fyshe had long advocated cooperation between banks and he had been one of the principal founders of the CBA in 1891. McLeod did not possess the same proclivity and made his position painfully clear in 1899 when he threatened to scuttle a loose agreement between the Department of Finance and the larger banks to pay no more than three per cent for deposits. What had provoked McLeod's ire was the treatment his Winnipeg manager had received at the hands of the local subsection of the CBA, which accused him of soliciting the business of other bankers in Winnipeg, conduct it considered "unprofessional, improper and unsafe." McLeod vigorously denied the subsection's power to censure members of the association, "much less to pass resolutions calculated to prejudice public opinion to the disadvantage of a member." Frustrated when the CBA did no more than acknowledge his complaint, McLeod announced in July that the Bank of Nova Scotia would withdraw from the association and "from all regulations and agreements connected therewith." This threat prompted the general manager of the Canadian Bank of Commerce, Byron Edmund WALKER, to try to appease McLeod, but McLeod would not be moved unless given an apology on terms he dictated. In desperation, Walker wrote to the deputy minister of finance, John Mortimer Courtney*, pleading for the intervention of minister William Stevens FIELDING to prevent McLeod from abandoning the agreement on deposit rates, saying it would "embarrass the government and must inevitably lead to an upward movement in deposit rates over the entire country." McLeod kept his pledge to withdraw from the CBA. He did not, however, raise rates; he preferred toying with the association's more excitable general managers by letting them think he would.

Within the Bank of Nova Scotia important changes were underway while this dispute continued. McLeod's enthusiasm for central and western Canada began to pay dividends, but the bank's growth in these regions was hampered by the delays attending long-distance management from Halifax. At the start of 1900 it was determined that the head office would move to Toronto. McLeod left Halifax in April to take charge, sailing his cutter the *Gloria* alone and arriving in Toronto in a manner symbolic of the bank's heritage as much as the independence of his character. At the bank he did not mask the stress of his job well and was known for his short temper. He did, however, continue to prove himself a creative thinker, introducing in 1901 the "unit system of work," which measured the labour involved in various aspects of the bank's operations and recognized those officers who were most efficient.

Both McLeod's temper and his creative abilities had been put to the test early in 1900 when he learned of the proposed incorporation of the CBA. The move had been suggested by the Department of Finance and was eagerly supported by the association's main backers, who had long complained that the organization was not powerful enough to impose conservative methods on its members, or interest-rate and other

agreements that were deemed necessary. The CBA was to have power over the country's clearing houses, an essential means of monitoring and influencing the management of banks, and regulatory control over the banks' circulation. For McLeod, the proposed arrangement was "nothing short of coercion." He protested the association's right to inspect the accounts of the Bank of Nova Scotia even though it was not a member and maintained that incorporation would give the CBA "all the attributes of a trust." "If the Association persists and succeeds in its purpose," he told its president, Edward Seaborne Clouston*, "the likely result will be . . . an aversion by the public to banking interests similar to that in the United States which has resulted in . . . Banks being taxed out of existence and in making the adoption of banking reforms a matter which no political party dare attempt." McLeod reasoned that if conservative, prudent banking was the objective, government inspection of banks was the best answer. He took his views to the press and to the House of Commons, where Robert Laird Borden*, a leading Conservative, championed his cause and obliged the Liberal whip to enforce the finance minister's wishes.

As the incorporated CBA assumed responsibility for the banks' circulation, it had to deal with a watchful critic in McLeod. Most hoped that the renegade banker would quietly go away. Instead, in 1902 he launched a campaign calling for fixed reserves to protect depositors from unscrupulous and imprudent bankers as well as government inspection to ensure that such reserves were maintained. From figures given in the banks' monthly returns to the Department of Finance, McLeod demonstrated the continuing decline, since the 1880s, in their reserves. He was fighting a losing battle. The same demand had been made, by J. M. Courtney among others, and rejected during the 1890 revision of the Bank Act. Disappointed, McLeod concluded that if he was to enjoy any influence with fellow bankers, the Bank of Nova Scotia would have to renew its membership in the CBA, which it did in 1902. His hopes, however, were misplaced. At CBA meetings he could not even count on anyone seconding his motions to discuss matters that interested him.

The CBA's efforts to stifle McLeod ultimately proved unwise. The issues he wanted addressed soon emerged as issues the public wanted settled in the aftermath of several bank failures. During most of this period the financial press had downplayed McLeod's concerns. Toronto's *Monetary Times* described outside inspection as a "delusive panacea." Even finance minister Fielding mocked McLeod, calling his ideas "poppycock." Papers such as the *Globe*, the Toronto *World*, and the *Montreal Witness* were more sympathetic. So were advocates of banking reform in the House of Commons, who commended McLeod and the Bank of Nova Scotia for considering the public's interest and leading the way, after the Ontario Bank failed in 1906, on external examination. One of the more perceptive banks, Montreal's Molsons Bank, recognized the advantage accruing to McLeod as he championed inspection and followed his lead, albeit quietly. The majority of bankers as well as the CBA remained publicly opposed. As time passed and 1908 brought three bank failures, their position became increasingly untenable. The weight of public sentiment cracked the resistance of the *Monetary Times*, which threw its support to outside inspection conducted by the CBA. McLeod exploited the rising tide of concern in 1909 when he released a pamphlet on bank inspection reiterating the arguments he had made over the years and unsuccessfully challenging the CBA to answer popular cries for reform.

By the end of 1909 McLeod had been embroiled in this public dispute for seven years. His deep involvement had not, however, prevented him from aggressively pursuing the expansion of his bank. Branches had been established in Edmonton, Calgary, Vancouver, Regina, and Saskatoon, and many more were added in Ontario and the Maritimes. Altogether some 50 branches were opened during the course of his tenure as general manager. But in spite of his success – the bank's assets had more than tripled and its stock, up by $80 a share, had taken first place among Canadian bank stocks – he was growing weary of the public struggle for bank reform. His main source of happiness in 1909 was found aboard the *Amorita*, which he sailed to victory in a race between New York and Bermuda. By January 1910 he had decided that sailing was more satisfying than banking. He submitted his resignation; however, he could not remain aloof from Canadian banking for long, even after moving to Montclair, N.J. It was there that he had his papers shipped from the Bank of Nova Scotia so that he could continue his magnum opus – a statistical tell-all documenting the growing weakness of Canada's banks and reinforcing his support for government inspection. In 1913 he was called back to Canada to give testimony before the parliamentary committee considering changes to the Bank Act. He won what some considered a partial victory when the government introduced provisions for a shareholders' audit, but it took the disastrous failure of the Home Bank of Canada in 1923 to bring about government inspection. The office of inspector general of banks was created the following year.

McLeod's retirement years were darkened in 1917 by the loss of his younger son, Norwood, who like so many of his generation perished overseas during the war. He spent his time writing articles on banking and working on his book, which had grown to a thousand pages by 1924. He complained about the frailty that old age brings but enjoyed shows over the modern radio. At 75 he suffered a fatal heart attack in South Carolina at his winter home by the sea. His wife survived him by nine years, dying in Toronto in 1935.

JOHN A. TURLEY-EWART

Canadian Bankers' Assoc. Arch. (Toronto), Executive council, minutes, May 1902. First National Bank of Chicago Arch., J. B. Forgan papers, McLeod to Sir John Aird, 19 Jan. 1924; Forgan to McLeod, 19 June 1924; McLeod to Forgan, 16, 22 June, 18 Aug. 1924. LAC, RG 19, 3193, file 11889; 3197, file 12110. Scotiabank Group Arch. (Toronto), Bank of Nova Scotia coll., I.4.b2, McLeod to general managers of the banks of Canada, 24 April 1902; Directors' minute-books, 13 Sept. 1892; Thomas Fyshe letter-books, Fyshe to T. V. Macdonald, 29 Feb. 1888; Fyshe to McLeod, 17 May 1888; Jane Nokes, "Henry Collingwood McLeod" (typescript, 1973). TRL, SC, Biog. scrapbooks, 7: 272. Univ. of Toronto Library, Thomas Fisher Rare Book Library, MS coll. 1 (B. E. Walker papers), box 19, file 22, Walker to J. M. Courtney, 22 Dec. 1899. *Globe*, 20 Dec. 1926. *Monetary Times* (Toronto), 15 Dec. 1906, 11 July 1908. Dan Bunbury, "The public purse and state finance: government savings banks in the era of nation building, 1867–1900," *CHR*, 78 (1997): 566–98. Can., House of Commons, *Debates*, 1907–8: 4248–314. *Canadian Journal of Commerce* (Montreal), 10 Dec. 1909. H. V. Cann, *Pages from a banker's journal* (n.p., 1933; copy in LAC). Thomas Fyshe, "The growth of corporations; the beneficial results to society which will probably accrue from it, and its effect on credit and banking," Canadian Bankers' Assoc., *Journal* (Toronto), 2 (1894–95): 197–203. Joseph Schull and J. D. Gibson, *The Scotiabank story: a history of the Bank of Nova Scotia, 1832–1982* (Toronto, 1982).

MACLURE, SAMUEL, telegraph operator, artist, and architect: b. 11 April 1860 in Sapperton (New Westminster, B.C.), son of John Cunningham Maclure and Martha McIntyre; m. 10 Aug. 1889 Margaret Catherine (Daisy) Simpson, and they had four daughters, one of whom died shortly after birth; d. 8 Aug. 1929 in Victoria.

Reputedly the first white child born in New Westminster, Sam Maclure was the eldest son of John Maclure, a Scottish surveyor who had come to British Columbia with the Royal Engineers [*see* Richard Clement Moody*]. Raised on the family homestead at Matsqui, Sam was educated in area schools and at Victoria's high school. He was intent on pursuing art. After some time working as a telegraph operator and government agent, in 1884–85 he attended the Spring Garden Institute in Philadelphia, where he was most taken with architecture. Financial problems cut short his stay, however, and he returned to British Columbia. Supporting himself as a telegrapher for the Esquimalt and Nanaimo Railway, he studied architecture at home and produced watercolour paintings for sale. Art was more than a hobby – as an architect Maclure would produce meticulous presentation drawings and garden plats. His landscapes would evolve from harsh, linear depiction to a freer impressionistic style in which he brilliantly captured watery reflection, refracted light, and the aerial effects of mist, all of which have become a commonplace of the British Columbia artistic tradition.

In 1889 Maclure joined architect Charles Henry Clow in New Westminster. Two years later he established a brief partnership with Richard P. Sharp. Maclure's surviving residential commissions from this period exhibit prevailing High Victorian tastes and were evidently based on pattern-books. His elopement and marriage to Daisy Simpson, at the house of his sister SARA ANNE in Vancouver, may have generated more excitement than his conventional architecture.

Maclure opened a practice in Victoria in 1892. His first major project, the Temple Building for merchant Robert Ward (1893), reflects the Chicago School style. Commercial work, however, was not to form the core of his early output. Among his most successful designs were variations of the alpine house, which adapted the arts-and-crafts form to the steep slopes of Victoria's Rockland area. Rigid symmetrical planning was a distinctive feature of these small, shingle-style bungalows, including his own house of 1899. In 1900 Maclure broke through to the patronage of Victoria's commercial and political elite with the residence he designed for Robin Dunsmuir, a son of James Dunsmuir*. It brought him many lucrative commissions, including Government House (1901–3), a project he shared with Victoria's leading institutional architect, Francis Mawson Rattenbury*, and James Dunsmuir's Hatley Park residence (1907–8). His collaboration with Rattenbury would continue in the design of buildings for the Bank of Montreal in developing towns in the interior.

The period 1900–14 was the high point of Maclure's practice. In addition to his grand projects, he executed numerous more modest residential commissions. For small cottages he utilized board-and-batten cladding or sometimes slabs of unbarked fir. His larger houses were characterized by superb, dramatic staircases and halls backlit with banks of stained glass. Maclure's difficulty in retaining contractors to execute his meticulously detailed designs was an indication of both his insistence on high-quality materials and workmanship and his close supervision. He took pains in selecting sites, and could display admirable tact in dealing with demanding clients. Although his commissions reflected the influence of arts-and-crafts and shingle-style practitioners – his materials and axial planning show an affinity with the work of Wilson Eyre, whose circle he may have known in Philadelphia – Maclure catered more and more to the English revivalist tastes of his clientele. As a result his houses began to incorporate, in a robust, vernacular fashion, elements of the Queen-Anne style: half-timbered surfaces, tall chimney stacks, and complex roofscapes, notably, for instance, in the houses done in Victoria for wholesale merchant Biggerstaff Wilson (1905) and Charles Fox Todd (1907), son of salmon canner Jacob Hunter Todd*.

In 1903 Maclure had taken on as a draftsman Cecil Croker Fox, a former student of the premier British arts-and-crafts architect, Charles Francis Annesley Voysey. By 1905, to accommodate his growing business in Vancouver, Maclure had gone into partnership with Fox and they opened an office there, which Fox ran until he went off to war in 1915. After his death the following year, a loss that devastated Maclure, the office was closed. During their years together many Voysey elements had appeared in Maclure's commissions, particularly in his smaller houses but most obviously in the work of the Vancouver office, which provided many estate-style houses for the prestigious Shaughnessy Heights and Point Grey areas, often in association with landscape architects such as Thomas Hayton Mawson.

During the war, a lack of work produced some financial hardship for Maclure, who, one employee recalled, resorted on occasion to selling his paintings. In the following years, with the decline of wealth and social grandeur in Victoria, large commissions became rare. Maclure was able, however, to reopen his Vancouver office in 1920, and subsequently he turned increasingly to the neo-Georgian idiom. His most flamboyant commission in this style, a house in Victoria's exclusive Oak Bay neighbourhood for lumber baron Robert William Gibson, had been taken over from Rattenbury and completed in 1919. Among the few other outstanding buildings from Maclure's post-war practice is the rustic-style house executed for newspaper magnate Walter Cameron NICHOL in Sidney (1925). By this time Maclure's landscape designs had gained a reputation, with many plans being produced for Jennie Foster Butchart's famous public garden project near Victoria. Maclure died in 1929 following a prostate operation, and his ashes were taken to Matsqui. His practice in Victoria was liquidated but the Vancouver branch was continued by his partner there, Ross Anthony Lort.

Though not given to extensive travel, Maclure had always kept in touch with the outside world. There were occasional trips to San Francisco; Kirtland Kelsey Cutter, an architect in Spokane, Wash., was a close friend; and the Dunsmuirs paid for Sam and Daisy to go England to select furniture for Hatley Park. A sensitive family man and an Anglican, Maclure was renowned as an extremely generous, kind, and cultured individual, well-versed in music and literature; his wife was an accomplished pianist and a portrait painter. Both were founding members in 1909 of the Vancouver Island Arts and Crafts Society. Maclure's work was published in the *Canadian Architect and Builder* (Toronto), *Craftsman* (Eastwood,

N.Y.), *Studio* (London), and *Country Life* (New York), journals that often brought him fresh ideas. He is reputed to have corresponded with architectural modernist Frank Lloyd Wright. Certainly there is much evidence of Wright in the broad overhangs of Maclure's roofs and in his studied, geometric treatment of wall surfaces.

Sam Maclure is probably the most notable of Victoria's architects for the quality, originality, and quantity of his work – over 350 documented commissions. So powerful was his influence that numerous schools and other public buildings in British Columbia continued to bear his characteristic hallmarks, a mixture of the shingle style and English revival, well into the 1930s. His oeuvre, especially his use of half-timbering, still sets the architectural tone of Rockland and Uplands Estates in Victoria and Shaughnessy Heights and Point Grey in Vancouver.

MARTIN SEGGER

Paintings by Samuel Maclure are found in the Art Gallery of Greater Victoria, the BCA, and the Maltwood Art Museum and Gallery, Univ. of Victoria. The bulk of his architectural plans and drawings are held in the Univ. of Victoria Arch. and Special Coll., SC075 (Samuel Maclure fonds). Details of this collection are provided in D. R. Chamberlin, *Samuel Maclure: architectural drawings in the University of Victoria Archives; a catalogue*, intro. Martin Segger (Victoria, 1995).

BCA, CM-B308; CM-B944, sh.1–sh.4; CM-B1641, sh.1–sh.2; PDP00153–55, PDP00161–66, PDP01844, PDP03218, PDP03629–30, PDP03773; VF87, frames 0389, 0404, 0415, 0418. City of Vancouver Arch., Add. MSS 301 (Historic sites project); Add. MSS 314 (Janet Bingham coll.); Add. MSS 713 (Richard B. Gilman coll.); Add. MSS 1015 (R. A. Lort architect fonds); CVA 106-1 (photograph of Samuel Maclure); J. S. Matthews news clippings coll., M6015 (Maclure, Samuel); Port P984 N449 (group photograph of Maclure, McColl, and McLagan families, 1900). City of Victoria Arch., 98403-31 (Bakshish Gill, "A partial inventory of the buildings erected between 1918 & 1939," March 1983); Demolished building plans, 2-0685, 0733, 0763–64; PR 127 (R. A. Lort fonds). *Daily Colonist* (Victoria), 9, 25 Aug. 1929. R. A. Lort, "Castle in the country," *Daily Colonist*, 6 March 1960. Janet Bingham, *Samuel Maclure, architect* (Ganges, B.C., 1985). "A house in Vancouver that shows English traditions blended with the frank expression of western life," *Craftsman* (New York), 13 (October 1907–March 1908): 675–81. R. [A.] Lort, "Samuel Maclure, MRAIC, 1860–1929," Royal Architectural Institute of Canada, *Journal* (Toronto), 35 (1958): 114–15. P. E. Nobbs, "Some developments in Canadian architecture," *Country Life* (New York), 43 (1922–23), no.3: 35–41. "Recent designs in domestic architecture," *International Studio* (New York), 36 (November 1908–February 1909): 124–26. E. O. S. Scholefield and F. W. Howay, *British Columbia from the earliest times to the present* (4v., Vancouver, 1914), 4: 1063–64. Martin Segger, *The buildings of Samuel Maclure: in search of appropriate form* (Victoria, 1986). Martin Segger and Douglas Franklin, *Exploring Victoria's architecture* (Victoria, 1996). Carolyn Smyly, "The Maclure tradition," *Western Living* (Vancouver), 8 (1978), no.6.

MACLURE, SARA ANNE (McLagan), telegrapher, homemaker, newspaper publisher, journalist, and social reformer; b. *c.* 1856 in Belfast (Northern Ireland), daughter of John Cunningham Maclure and Martha McIntyre; m. 11 Dec. 1884 John Campbell McLagan, a widower, in Victoria, and they had three daughters and one son; d. 20 March 1924 in Vancouver.

Sara Maclure was not quite three when she arrived in British Columbia in April 1859 with her infant sister, Susan Elizabeth, and her mother, Martha. The trio had sailed from Belfast to be reunited with the children's father, sent to the colony the previous year as a surveyor with the Royal Engineers. On completion of his service, he signed on as a surveyor for the Collins Overland Telegraph Company, which was to build a line through British Columbia to Siberia in order to connect North America with Europe. When this enterprise was abandoned in 1866 after the Atlantic cable was laid [*see* Frederic Newton Gisborne*], he took up a land grant on the Matsqui prairie in the Fraser valley. Hoping to improve his growing family's financial prospects, he chose a site at the junction of two Western Union Telegraph Company lines and established a repeater station in the family parlour. Sara proved an apt pupil and quickly became an accomplished telegrapher. At 15 she was placed on the company's payroll as regular operator of the Matsqui office, responsible for sending and receiving messages, including all the press dispatches from the United States. The following year she noted in her diary that she had been appointed "tester and manager of repairs from New Westminster to Yale," sending out men to maintain the lines. In 1875, as a first-class Morse operator, she was promoted to the Victoria office. For several years before her resignation in October 1884, she was office manager, an atypical post for a woman.

Sara's resignation reflected the common practice of the period that women relinquish a salaried position on their marriage. Her husband, John Campbell McLagan, was a printer who had assisted in establishing the *Victoria Daily Times* earlier the same year. In 1888 McLagan began the *Vancouver Daily World* with capital borrowed by his wife from prominent industrialist James Dunsmuir*. The couple moved to Vancouver. How much Sara was involved with the running of the paper during her husband's lifetime is not clear. She was no doubt influential in persuading him to retain her brother SAMUEL to design new premises for the business in 1892. She occasionally "sat on the wire" for the paper, especially on important occasions such as elections. Her level of commitment changed with her husband's illness and his death in April 1901. Sara McLagan assumed control, functioning as publisher, managing editor, editorial writer, and sometime reporter. The introduction of a woman's page as a regular feature coincided with her assumption of ownership. These Saturday pages provided lively and well written commentaries on health, childcare, nutrition, women's clubs, local politics, and other matters. Her determination to oversee directly the continued success of the largest daily paper west of Winnipeg sometimes provoked opposition from staff who resented her interference. At one point, she became involved in a court battle with the local of the International Typographical Union to affirm her right as publisher to proof-read the paper. Despite this turmoil, the paper flourished under her direction and she sold it to a group headed by Vancouver businessman Louis Denison Taylor* for $65,000 in 1905. She continued from time to time to write copy and she edited, by invitation, special women's issues of Vancouver papers. She maintained her membership in the Canadian Women's Press Club, which she had helped to found with other women journalists covering the Louisiana Purchase exposition in 1904, and was a founding member of the British Columbia Institute of Journalists.

Like many middle-class women of her era, Sara participated in organizations designed to improve the quality of life. The centrepiece of her work was the Local Council of Women of Vancouver. A founding member in 1894, she served as treasurer (1895–97) and president (1898–1900). During her presidency she initiated the formation of a branch in New Westminster to help families in the city whose lives had been devastated by fire in 1898. As provincial vice-president of the National Council of Women of Canada from 1903 to 1907, she advocated greater rights and better conditions for British Columbia's women and children, including women's suffrage. Her desire to improve women's opportunities in the workplace led her to serve in the professions and careers department of the National Council.

While president of the local council, Sara had worked with Lady Aberdeen [Marjoribanks*] in support of the Victorian Order of Nurses. During her tenure, the council established a training home for nurses in the city and formed a chapter of the VON. She served as the chapter's secretary from 1898 to 1901 and as president from 1902 to 1906. She was also a charter member of the Vancouver General Hospital Women's Auxiliary in 1902 and she urged the construction of a hospital for aged and infirm women.

Some of Sara's volunteer work reflected other interests. In recognition of her efforts in 1894 to found the city's first cultural society, the Art, Historical and Scientific Association of Vancouver, and her service as its president in 1903, she was made an honorary life member. She had served on the committees that initiated the Vancouver branches of the Young Men's Christian Association in 1886 and the Young Women's Christian Association in 1897–98 and was a founding member of a club, the Athenaeum, and the Vancouver chapter of the Imperial Order Daughters of the Empire. In 1911, soon after its establishment, she joined the Georgian Club, a Vancouver women's organization.

Although Sara spent much of her life in the public eye, the private sphere also compelled her attention, as the mother of four children and stepmother to her husband's son from his first marriage. In 1908 she had returned to her parental home, Hazelbrae, in the Fraser valley to assist her recently widowed mother, oversee the management of the family farm, and support her brother John Charles in his brickworks at Clayburn. His initial missteps substantially depleted her finances. Never one to accept setbacks passively, she took advantage of wartime shortages of manpower and returned to telegraphy in 1916 while living for a short time with a daughter in California. The war exacted a heavy toll on her, with the death overseas of her only son, Patrick Douglas Maclure, in 1917 and a son-in-law on Armistice Day. Following World War I she arranged through a journalist friend, Julia Wilmotte Henshaw [Henderson*], to be appointed to the British Red Cross to assist the wounded and sick in France. Afterwards, she returned to Vancouver, where she remained until her death in 1924.

A pioneering "can do" spirit infused many of Sara McLagan's deeds. Despite the rhetoric of the period concerning separate spheres, she tackled tasks customarily assumed by men and succeeded. Within the sphere to which society would normally have restricted her, she fulfilled her roles as daughter, wife, mother, and maternal feminist. Generations of Vancouverites benefited from her many community endeavours.

LINDA L. HALE

BCA, GR-2951, no.1924-09-332253 (mfm.); GR-2962, no.1884-09-002716 (mfm.). City of Vancouver Arch., Add. MSS 54 (J. S. Matthews coll.), topical files, McLagan, J. C. [and] McLagan, Mrs J. C. (02939); Add. MSS 396 (Canadian Women's Press Club fonds). LAC, MG 28, I 232, 1. New Westminster Museum Arch. (New Westminster, B.C.), Sara Anne Maclure fonds. Univ. of B.C. Library, Rare Books and Special Coll. (Vancouver), Vancouver Council of Women records, box 3, files 1, 3; Vancouver Young Women's Christian Assoc. fonds. *Vancouver Daily Province*, 21 March 1924. *Vancouver Daily World*, 1888–1905. *Vancouver Evening Sun*, 21 March 1924. J. D. Adams, "Clayburn: a study of its brick industry, its architecture, and its preservation" (M.MUSEOL. thesis, Univ. of Toronto, 1976). Art, Hist. and Scientific Assoc. of Vancouver, *Museum Notes*, 1 (June 1926), no.2: 9. Marjory Lang and Linda Hale, "Women of *The World* and other dailies: the lives and times of Vancouver newspaperwomen in the first quarter of the twentieth century," *BC Studies* (Vancouver), no.85 (spring 1990): 3–23. D. A. McGregor, "Adventures of Vancouver newspapers: 1892–1926," *British Columbia Hist. Quarterly* (Victoria), 10 (1946): 89–142. National Council of Women of Canada, *Women of Canada: their life and work; compiled . . . for distribution at the Paris international exhibition, 1900* ([Montreal?, 1900]; repr. [Ottawa], 1975). E. O. S. Scholefield and F. W. Howay, *British Columbia from the earliest times to the present* (4v., Vancouver, 1914), 4: 1191. *Who's who in western Canada . . .* (Vancouver), 1912.

MCNEIL, FANNIE. *See* KNOWLING

MACPHERSON, ISABEL ECCLESTONE (Mackay), author; b. 24 Nov. 1875 in Woodstock, Ont., third daughter of Donald MacLeod MacPherson, a marble cutter, and Priscilla Eliza Ecclestone; m. there 22 April 1895 Peter John Mackay, and they had three daughters; d. 15 Aug. 1928 in Vancouver.

Noted for her warmth and ambition to achieve, Isabel (Belle) MacPherson grew up in the Scots community of Oxford County, Ont., where she won prizes in Highland dancing. She was educated at Woodstock Collegiate Institute, and her first work appeared in school publications. At 15 she began publishing poems and short stories in Canadian newspapers and magazines. From 1890 to 1900, under the pseudonym Heather, she was a staff contributor to the Woodstock *Daily Express. Miss Witterly's China* (Toronto, [1896]), a magazine story reprinted in pamphlet form for the Woman's Missionary Society of the Methodist Church, and *Pansies for thoughts* (1898), poems printed by the Woodstock Public Library, were her first books. Her work reached a wider audience through inclusion in *Selections from Scottish Canadian poets* (Toronto, 1900) and especially upon its collection in *Between the lights* (Toronto, 1904), published by William BRIGGS. Her reputation was firmly established when she won the Toronto *Globe*'s prize for the best poem on a Canadian historical subject in 1907 and again in 1910.

Marriage in 1895, births in 1902 and 1904, and the family's move to Vancouver in 1909, when Peter Mackay became chief reporter (stenographer) of the British Columbia Supreme Court, did not slow Isabel's career. Fees from her writing paid for a housekeeper, who freed her for literary activity. Her daughters, who would remember her playfulness and absentmindedness, were the first audience for the many poems and stories she contributed to periodicals for young people. A selection of her poems republished in *The shining ship, and other verse for children* (Toronto, 1918) confirmed Mackay's name as a lyric poet with a good rhythmic sense. It would be hailed as a "Canadian classic" in 1930, though an American reviewer in 1918 thought it imitated Robert Louis Stevenson with "a halting, shambling gait." Mackay's most enduring work has been this poetry of childhood, which was included in school readers until 1967.

The move to Vancouver had "a stimulating effect" on Mackay, as she had predicted it would in the *Canadian Bookman* (Toronto) in April 1909. "Thin ice," serialized the following year in the *Canadian Courier* (Toronto), marked her shift to longer fiction. Prose, she later observed, "is good mental training and not dependent upon a moment's mental exaltation." Her literary circle expanded through the Canadian Women's Press Club, a major force in the struggles of first-wave feminism; she was the founding president of the club's branch in Vancouver in 1910 and in 1913–16 she served as vice-president for British Columbia and Alberta. In an era when the "new woman" sought equality in the public sphere, journalism and literature were the favoured professions. Mackay's feminism was low-key – a review of Olive Schreiner's classic *Woman and labour* in March 1912 in the women's weekly the *Chronicle* or a casual remark about women's suffrage in the dialogue of a character in *The window-gazer* (Toronto) in 1921 – but feminism did inform her fiction, where she examined the psychological dynamics of power in families and other relationships.

Through her circle Mackay established intimate friendships with two of the foremost poets of her generation, Emily Pauline Johnson* and Marjorie Lowry Christie PICKTHALL. She helped nurse them during their final illnesses and facilitated production of their last books, as an executive of the trust fund that supported Johnson through the publication of her *Legends of Vancouver* (1911) and as hostess to Pickthall at Mackay's summer camp on Boundary Bay, south of Vancouver. In an appreciation of Pickthall, Mackay made her only explicit pronouncements on poetics: in seeing poetry as a mystical escape from everyday constraints, her views were typical of late-Victorian romanticism. It was laughter, however, that cemented friendship. Johnson had an "excellent sense of humour," Mackay wrote, and it helped balance her "differing legacies": the emotion of Amerindian oral eloquence with the literary sensibility of the European tradition. Mackay's narrative model in *Indian nights* (Toronto, 1930) is indebted to Johnson's "translation" of both the method and the content of Indian legends into English story form.

Over the course of her career, Mackay too was known for her humour, as well as for her "philosophic turn of mind" and a "note of yearning" balanced with a "concreteness of sensuous impressions." These qualities were evident in *Fires of driftwood* (Toronto, 1922). Inspired by the Boundary Bay campfires, it shows Pickthall's influence in the title poem – a rare experiment in free verse – and in the final elegy. In the only critical study of Mackay's work, written in 1942, Louis Dudek sees in the title poem a "strange magical flavour" that might have made Mackay "outstanding" had she been consistent and able to sustain an emotion or to accord idea and form as she did in the subtle rhythm of "Fear," another of her poems. Instead, most of her poetry is marred by fanciful flights, "light personification," "superficial symbolism," and jingling rhymes, characteristics that Dudek, from his tough imagist stance, dismisses as "eternally feminine." In the dominant spirit of literary nationalism of the day, however, author-historian Roderick George Mac-Beth* hailed Mackay, Johnson, and Pickthall in 1928 as "talented daughters of the Dominion," praising them for not leaving the country as many male writers had done. Nonetheless, lacking the "fiery sincerity" (Mackay's words) and dramatic flare of Johnson's work or the polished craftmanship of Pickthall's, Mackay's poetry is primarily of historical interest.

Although contemporary critics thought her poetry was her best work, they acknowledged that she was better known as a novelist. Written in the popular forms of the day, her fiction was reasonably well received. The Woodstock *Daily Sentinel-Review* judged her first novel, *The house of windows* (London and Toronto, 1912), "a book of promise rather than complete achievement." Set in a department store, it shows the exploitation of working-class women in a mode of social realism, and both the London *Athenæum* and the *New York Times* commented on the originality of the topic and the vividness of the *mise en scène*. However, a melodramatic plot that terminates in three engagements turns the book into a romance. Love conquers all as Mackay, wary of what editor Melvin Ormond Hammond, in a letter of rejection in 1908, called her "heterodox opinions," bows to propriety and a reading public seeking uplift. *Up the hill and over* (Toronto, 1917), which features an all-female family held together by one meagre salary, likewise received mixed reviews. The *Canadian Courier* claimed that "insanity" was fitting material for "students of morbid psychology," but not for fiction. Yet the *Times Literary Supplement* (London) praised the "well-studied picture of a woman who has yielded to the curse of drugs." The *Canadian Magazine* aptly compared Mackay's illumination of commonplace happenings in an obscure Ontario town with Mary Wilkins Freeman's "local colour fiction" set in New England. This regionalism was a favoured genre of women's writing, as feminist critics have subsequently shown. From a small town Mackay moved to the city with *Mist of morning* (Toronto and New York, 1919). Although many Canadian novelists of the period condemned urban life as immoral, Mackay treated it more positively in this novel. First serialized in *Canadian Magazine*, the work, in the estimate of John Daniel Logan and Donald Graham French, is a "curious" mixture of the "imaginative novel," which focuses on a protagonist with great dreams living in a Toronto rooming house, and the "realistic romance," which ends with declarations of love on the eve of World War I.

In her next two novels, both well received critically though for different reasons, Mackay returned to local colour realism, but with sharpened psychological analysis. *The window-gazer* describes the unusual relationship between a professor, shell-shocked during the war, who is studying the psychology of primi-

tive peoples, and a woman whose violent father is a scholar of Amerindian folklore resident on an island near Vancouver. The *Canadian Bookman* noted the novel for its improvement in plotting and characterization, while the *Times Literary Supplement* and the *New York Times Book Review* praised Mackay's artistry that sustains "a mood of humour" directed at religious and social proprieties. Mackay's focus in *The window-gazer*, as in *Blencarrow* (Toronto, 1926), is less on social manners than on mental states. The work of Sigmund Freud and William James on mental experience interested her and she gathered material in her notebooks on insanity and diseases of memory. Generally acknowledged her best novel, *Blencarrow* anatomizes the varieties of love as it records generational changes in a small town not unlike Woodstock, through the experiences of a group of boys and girls growing up together. A second plot centres on a family who have fallen from fortune because of the father's drinking. His abusive behaviour makes their lives unbearable. Mackay was ahead of her time in treating domestic violence, but her modernism was overlooked by Canadian reviewers who read her work within the frame of cultural nationalism. They praised the "depth" of characterization and "atmosphere" in her portrait of the town to claim this genre as the definitive form of the "Canadian novel."

Buoyed by the active little theatre movement in Canada in the 1920s, Mackay wrote a number of plays. Her skill at "snappy dialogue" contributed to her success as a playwright, as well as a novelist, and she won many prizes. *The last cache* (New York, 1927), first presented at Hart House Theatre in Toronto on 16 May 1927, was described by Lawrence Mason in the *Globe* as a "clever" sketch and "a grim little revelation of human weakness." A modern audience would be troubled by the over-reliance on coincidence in plotting and the stereotypical treatment of Chinese and Indian characters. Mackay's *The second lie* (Toronto, 1926), which literary historian Michael Tait dismisses as "negligible," is possibly her best writing, a sustained treatment of domestic violence in tightly structured dialogue. Charles Vincent Massey*, who played the role of the tyrannizing husband in 1921, later wrote perceptively that it was "a sketch in the manner of the 'Grand Guignol.'" *Goblin gold* (New York and Toronto, 1933), a comedy in which a relative rescues a mother-led family from genteel poverty in an urban tenement after he strikes gold, was posthumously given a governor general's prize in 1929. In her lifetime she had received other recognition of her work. In 1926 she was selected president of the British Columbia branch of the Canadian Authors Association. Two years later she won the prize of the Imperial Order Daughters of the Empire for her short story "Initials only," a field where she might have done more had not death intervened.

Isabel Mackay's writing was constrained by the lingering puritanism and philistinism that shaped her treatment of modernist topics such as urban malaise and sexuality. Writing for the market place, she was responsive to its norms and so was praised for material that was "interesting but not decadent." Although her work is forgotten today, she was a prominent member of a dynamic women's literary community in the early 20th century. Her obituary on the front page of the *Globe*, following her death from cancer in 1928 at age 52, testified to contemporary recognition of her writing and work in literary organizations.

BARBARA GODARD

The main collection of Mackay papers, including her publications, clippings, and copies of much of the material located in other archives, is housed in the Lady Aberdeen coll. at the Univ. of Waterloo Library, Special Coll. Dept. (Waterloo, Ont.), WA 18. Scattered letters and manuscripts are in Acadia Univ., Vaughan Memorial Library, Esther Clark Wright Arch. (Wolfville, N.S.); BCA, MS-2367; the Lorne and Edith Pierce coll. in QUA; and in the Univ. of B.C. Library, Rare Books and Special Coll. (Vancouver), I. E. Mackay papers. Mackay's birth and marriage records are in AO, RG 80-2-0-69, no.15412, and RG 80-5-0-227, no.9376. An extensive list of her published and unpublished writing has been issued as *Isabel Ecclestone Mackay bibliography*, comp. Susan Bellingham (Waterloo, 1987).

Biographical entries on Mackay are found in various standard reference works including *The Oxford companion to Canadian history and literature*, ed. Norah Story (Toronto, 1967), and the *Dictionary of literary biography* (317v. to date, Detroit, 1978–   ), 92 (*Canadian writers, 1890–1920*, ed. W. H. New, 1990).

McRAE, JOHN C., policeman and chief of police; b. 4 March 1859 in Carleton County, Upper Canada, son of Alexander McRae, a farmer, and Ann Conley; m. —— Frizzell, and they had two sons and two daughters who survived him; d. 19 July 1921 in Winnipeg.

A Scots Presbyterian, John McRae (the date and reason he assumed the middle initial are not known) was 20 when he left Ontario to homestead in the small southwestern Manitoba community of Minnedosa; he remained there only a few months before moving to Winnipeg. He joined the city's police force in 1881. Five years later he was promoted sergeant and he became Winnipeg's third chief constable in 1887.

McRae's rapid rise and his fame as a police officer were due in large measure to his apprehension of a number of high-profile criminals. In 1885 he had pursued Bulldog Kelly all the way into the United States before arresting the alleged murderer and returning him to Manitoba. Two years later, while attempting to detain one of the province's most notorious cattle rustlers, Joseph Fant, he was shot in the groin. Both the chase and the lengthy trial that followed the fugitive's arrest solidified his already notable reputation for

bravery. In 1889 he gained even further recognition when he single-handedly captured Martin Burke, one of the men responsible for the murder of Chicago doctor Patrick Henry Cronin, a homicide immortalized in Henry M. Hunt's *Crime of the century*. An imposing figure who did not make friends readily, McRae was nonetheless well regarded by the police force and the general public.

Despite a well-earned reputation for integrity, McRae received considerable criticism for his role in re-establishing a segregated red-light district in Winnipeg in 1909. A campaign in late 1903 led by the Reverend Frederic Beal DU VAL had succeeded in abolishing the city's policy of tolerating prostitutes in a segregated area. In 1904 the police had raided and closed the district. Prostitution continued to increase, however, and McRae did not have enough men to deal with it, especially since it spread throughout the city. In 1909 the Winnipeg Police Commission decided to leave the regulation of brothels to McRae's discretion, tacitly accepting that he would reintroduce segregation in an attempt to control the problem. The following year, in a series of articles in Toronto newspapers, a prominent Presbyterian minister and national secretary of the Moral and Social Reform Council of Canada, the Reverend John George SHEARER, accused Winnipeg of being the vice capital of the nation and implied that its police officials were guilty of graft. A commission established late in 1910 to investigate the charges exonerated McRae from any wrongdoing, but also found that the more than 50 houses of prostitution in the city existed because their presence was sanctioned by the police chief.

In 1911 McRae resigned as chief. With an annual pension of $2,485 the *Winnipeg Telegram* regarded him as being "comparatively a poor man." Largely uneducated, McRae had worked hard to improve both himself and the police force during his 24-year tenure as chief, the longest in Winnipeg's history. The force had expanded significantly during that period, from 13 men when he took office to over 108 men when he retired. He had seen to the construction of a new headquarters (1908) and two sub-stations (1911) and is credited with the introduction of a pension system, a variety of new investigative techniques, a motorcycle patrol, and North America's first police signal system (with 158 call boxes).

Two years after his retirement, McRae became one of the first recipients in Canada of the King's Police Medal, awarded for exceptional courage, skill, and distinguished service. He came out of retirement briefly in 1915 to act as a special commissioner for the provincial police during the investigation and prosecutions associated with the scandal over the construction of the Manitoba legislative buildings involving the premier, Sir Rodmond Palen Roblin*, the minister of education, George Robson COLDWELL, and others. He was

Magill

62 and in poor health when he died at his Winnipeg home in 1921. He left an estate of just under $64,000.

Dale Brawn

John C. McRae published an article entitled "I remember" in the *Winnipeg Telegram*, 25 Dec. 1911.

AM, ATG 25, file 13840; AMLJH, P 1359, file A0044. LAC, RG 6, D1, 359, file 114-2-k1-1, pt. 2. *Manitoba Free Press*, 24 Feb., 18 March 1886; 10–11 Jan., 1 Feb., 12 Nov. 1887; 17 June 1889; 10 June 1911; 2 Jan. 1913; 19–20, 22 July 1921. *Winnipeg Telegram*, 10 June 1911, 20 Sept. 1915. *Winnipeg Tribune*, 19 July 1921. A. F. J. Artibise, *Winnipeg: a social history of urban growth, 1874–1914* (Montreal and London, 1975). *Canadian annual rev.*, 1915. B. E. Chaffey, "Regina vs. Fant, a tale of fifty years ago," *Manitoba Bar News* (Winnipeg), 9 (1936–37): 327–29, 331–32. Joy Cooper, "Red lights of Winnipeg," Man., Hist. and Scientific Soc., *Papers* (Winnipeg), 3rd ser., no.27 (1970–71): 61–74. *Gateway city: documents on the city of Winnipeg, 1873–1913*, ed. and intro. A. F. J. Artibise (Winnipeg, 1979), 207–23. H. M. Hunt, *The crime of the century, or, the assassination of Dr. Patrick Henry Cronin: a complete and authentic history of the greatest of modern conspiracies* ([Chicago, 1889]). Robert Hutchison, *A century of service: a history of the Winnipeg police force, 1874–1974* (Winnipeg, 1974). *The Queen v. Cloutier* (1898), *Manitoba Reports* (Winnipeg), 12 (1897–99): 183–89. H. A. Robson, *Judge Robson on segregation or toleration of vice . . . the report of the Social Vice Commission, Winnipeg, January 11th, 1911* (Toronto, [1911?]). Jack Templeman, *From force to service: a pictorial history of the Winnipeg Police Department: 125th anniversary* (Winnipeg, 1998).

MAGILL, ROBERT, university professor, political economist, office holder, and secretary of the Winnipeg Grain and Produce Exchange; b. 23 May 1871 in Drumlee (Northern Ireland), fifth child of Robert Magill and Susan Shilladay; m. 14 April 1905 Susan Isabella Stairs, daughter of Edward Stairs and granddaughter of William James Stairs*, in Halifax, and they had three daughters and a son; d. 15 Jan. 1930 in Battle Creek, Mich.

Robert Magill's father was the farmer of a large estate that had been granted to the family two centuries earlier. He died when Magill was only four years old. In 1886, at age 15, Magill went to Belfast to apprentice as a wholesale linen merchant, but his father had left enough money to send his sons to college and the life of a scholar appealed to him more. He enrolled in 1890 at Queen's College, Royal University of Ireland, in Belfast, and graduated in 1894, obtaining a BA with first-class honours. A year later he received an MA from the Royal University in mental and moral science, again achieving first-class honours and also taking a gold medal for "highly distinguished answering." He followed this with a year of theological training at the Presbyterian College (Assembly's College) in Belfast and in 1897 was awarded a bursary for "Pulpit Eloquence." At the same time he worked as a tutor and then lectured in mental and moral science at Victoria College, a grammar school for girls, where he was popular with his students.

Magill attended the University of Jena in Germany for two years. In 1899 he was awarded a doctorate after completing a dissertation on the writings of the British philosopher Henry Sidgwick. Described by a colleague in Germany as a "capital raconteur" with a good sense of humour and a keen mind, Magill was a serious scholar, but he also enjoyed a bit of fun. A character based on him, known as "the Dr," would appear in the novel *The discard . . .* (Toronto, 1919) by Alexander Charles Stewart, who had been born in County Down like Magill and was a friend to the Magill family. In the book, the Dr appropriately is "a bright chap and a good old skate," possessing a brilliant mind, "with a vision wider than the mental prairies and mountain foot-hills."

After returning to Ireland in 1900 Magill was ordained a minister at the Magee Theological College in Londonderry (Northern Ireland). For nearly three years he served the small congregation of 260 families in Maghera. Seeking better opportunities, he immigrated in 1903 to Canada, where he had received a teaching appointment as a professor of philosophy at the Presbyterian College in Halifax. Beginning in 1904, he lectured as well at Dalhousie University, although without being paid a salary. In 1907 Magill succeeded Dr Robert Alexander Falconer* as principal of the Presbyterian College, but he still kept lecturing at Dalhousie. Finally, Dalhousie offered him the George Munro chair of philosophy. He took up his new position in September 1909 at a salary of $2,500 per year. By 1912 he was also teaching in the budding field of political economy.

Magill was representative of a new breed of academics in the country who believed they could contribute as much to Canadian society outside the classroom as in it. Through his father-in-law, Edward Stairs, a prominent Halifax businessman, he met and impressed the right people. In 1908 he was appointed by the provincial Liberal government of George Henry Murray as chairman of the commission on hours of labour. Outspoken, he did not hesitate to suggest in his report that "a man could do as much good work in an eight-hour as in a ten-hour day."

Magill's initiation into the grain trade came in 1910. On the advice of Walter Charles Murray*, the president of the University of Saskatchewan and formerly a professor at Dalhousie, Thomas Walter Scott*, the premier of Saskatchewan, appointed him chairman of a commission on grain elevators. Farmers in the province were pressing the provincial government to assume ownership of country elevators as a means of breaking the power of the large private firms [*see* Frederick William Green*]. After a thorough investigation, the commission advised against public ownership and in favour of a provincial loan to a farmer-operated cooperative elevator company. It was a politically safe solution for Scott, who called the report a "masterpiece." Magill was awarded $500 for his efforts and had established a name for himself as something of a grain expert.

In 1912 Magill was the obvious choice to head the new Board of Grain Commissioners for Canada, set up by the federal Conservative government of Robert Laird Borden* to supervise the transportation and inspection of grain. He was reluctant to leave Dalhousie and outings to the golf course, but he confidently took charge of his new responsibilities at the BGC's office in Fort William (Thunder Bay), Ont. He quickly became the federal government's chief adviser on Canadian grain policy and was popular with farmers and grain businessmen alike – an amazing accomplishment in itself. Still, he found the job, as he later put it, "more troublesome than many imagined." When World War I broke out, Magill wrote to Samuel HUGHES, the minister of militia and defence, offering to join the Canadian Expeditionary Force. The idea of the scholarly Magill in the trenches must have amused Hughes. He told Magill that he could best help "the boys" by "getting good grain" to feed them.

As chairman of the BGC, Magill impressed many members of the Winnipeg Grain and Produce Exchange, who were searching for a new secretary to manage their office and affairs after the resignation of Charles Napier Bell*. Again Magill was a natural choice. Despite a request from the minister of trade and commerce, George Eulas Foster*, that he stay at the BGC, Magill made the move to Winnipeg with his family in late November 1916. He was immediately caught up in the crisis precipitated by the poor wheat crop of 1916 and the British demand for large quantities of Canadian grain.

As an executive of the exchange, Magill became an ardent supporter of and spokesman for the open market, but even he was forced to concede to Foster that this marketing system which had evolved under "conditions of peace" required "modification during the period of war." To this end he informed Foster, who was preparing plans for a wartime grain marketing board, that the exchange was willing to cooperate. Such a board, he told the minister, "should consist of men who know how grain is gathered, transported, marketed and distributed." On 11 June 1917 his overtures were acknowledged by his appointment as chairman of the 12-man Board of Grain Supervisors of Canada that marked the beginning of the federal government's direct involvement in the Canadian grain industry.

Until the end of its term in 1919 the BGS regulated wheat prices and directed wheat distribution and export. Magill explained to Foster that his role as chairman "frequently puts me in a position of antago-

nism with men who are paying me the salary on which I live as secretary of the exchange." He submitted his resignation as chairman in October 1918, but Foster as well as the executive council of the exchange persuaded him to stay on. The Winnipeg grain men, in particular, were fearful of what might happen if a leader of the farm movement was elevated to the BGS's chairmanship. Reluctantly, Magill agreed to remain in his government position, but he worked as well to gain support for the reopening of the wheat market. His efforts were especially evident during his role as the exchange's representative at the Canadian trade mission in London in December 1918. The government did create a wheat board for the crop of 1919–20, but allowed the open market to operate again the following year.

During the 1920s Magill was kept busy defending the interests of the private grain trade, appearing as a witness at the proceedings of parliamentary committees and royal commissions. He became as frustrated with the inquiries as all grain men did. In an article written in 1921 he noted that "all these investigations have resulted in practically nothing in the way of disclosures of illegalities and criminalities on the part of the grain trade." He equally spent a great deal of time arguing with sceptical farmers about the benefits they received under an open market system as opposed to the dividends given to them by new prairie wheat pools or cooperatives established in 1923 and 1924.

In 1929 Magill sought treatment for heart trouble at a sanatorium in Battle Creek, Mich. He died there the following year at age 58 from arteriosclerosis. His death was a great loss to the Winnipeg grain community. "What is there to say at the passing of a man with the brilliant mind and great attainment of a man like Dr. Magill?" asked Ernest Seaforth Parker, the exchange's vice-president.

The *Winnipeg Tribune* offered this fitting eulogy: "The grain trade, in one way or another, is Canada's most important and most complex business and represents Canada's greatest contribution to world economics. It is a simple fact to say that no man knew the grain trade so thoroughly, in all its complexities, as Dr. Magill." Indeed, in an era frequently characterized by confrontation and dispute over Canadian agricultural policy, Robert Magill provided a calming and wise influence. Even western farmers, traditional opponents of the private grain trade and the exchange, although they did not agree with him, came to appreciate his integrity and his professional efforts on their behalf. As a sign of respect, the exchange closed the market on 18 January.

ALLAN LEVINE

Robert Magill is the author of *Grain inspection in Canada* (Ottawa, 1914), *The wheat situation* (Winnipeg, 1920; copy in the Winnipeg Commodity Exchange Library), "Private business and royal commissions," *Dalhousie Rev.* (Halifax), 1 (1921–22): 233–42, and *A prophecy comes true* ([Winnipeg, 1930]).

LAC, MG 27, II, D7; MG 28, III 82, 50; MG 30, E299. *Manitoba Free Press*, 15 Jan. 1930. *Winnipeg Tribune*, 16 Jan. 1930. A. [G.] Levine, *The exchange: 100 years of trading grain in Winnipeg* (Winnipeg, 1987). C. F. Wilson, *A century of Canadian grain: government policy to 1951* (Saskatoon, 1978).

MAHONY, FRANCES (Jeffers; Lovering), social activist; b. *c.* 1863 or 1 Nov. 1868 in New York City, daughter of Daniel Mahony and Frances Higgins; m. first 22 Nov. 1886 Charles Jeffers (Jefferis) in Toronto; m. there secondly 21 Oct. 1896 William Henry Lovering; she had no children; d. 26 March 1926 in Hamilton, Ont.

Frances Higgins, who had immigrated from Ireland to the United States in 1837, married Daniel Mahony and they had four children. Their only daughter, Frances (Fannie), was born shortly before her father's death. By 1874 the young girl and her mother had come to Toronto, where they lived with an uncle, Patrick Higgins, a shoemaker. Frances attended Loretto Abbey, a Catholic school for girls that offered a curriculum in both English and French. She graduated with a gold medal in 1884 and two years later married Charles Jeffers, a business clerk, who died of pneumonia in 1889. After studying at a Toronto business college, she worked for Brown Brothers Company, nurserymen, where she eventually became office manager. In 1896 she married a lawyer, William Henry Lovering, and went to live in Hamilton. An active member of St Joseph's and St Mary's parish churches, she continued, as a member of Hamilton's Alliance Française and a pianist in the Duet Club, interests initiated by her early education.

World War I was the catalyst for Frances Lovering's involvement in public life, and henceforth her activities would be devoted mainly to patriotic work, social welfare, and Catholicism. Fluently bilingual, in 1915 she led a committee of local French Canadians and members of the Alliance Française to form a branch of the Secours National. Its president until 1923, she was the prime mover behind extensive efforts to "assist needy persons in France." Hamiltonians could subscribe to adopt French children as "godsons" or send help to Mont-Saint-Eloi, the community's adopted town in France. Among the fundraising events, the "entertainment" at Niagara Falls in 1916, where Sarah Bernhardt appeared, netted $300 in one evening. By the end of 1919 Hamilton's Secours National had sent $42,839 to France in addition to 10 trucks and 3,097 cases of food, clothing, and hospital supplies.

During the war Lovering worked with her husband for the Canadian Patriotic Fund and, through St Mary's Benevolent Society, she mobilized the women of St Mary's parish to send aid to Canadian soldiers overseas. In 1917, perhaps in answer to a perceived need for a Catholic organization for women who wanted to contribute religious as well as patriotic work, she helped found the Catholic Women's Guild of Hamilton. Three years later a national association, the Catholic Women's League of Canada, was organized under the presidency of Bellelle GUERIN, with Lovering as honorary treasurer. A vice-president in 1922, in charge of social welfare, Lovering was elected president at the league's convention in Halifax in 1923 and at Edmonton in 1924. By her retirement the following year, the CWL had 40,000 members.

For Lovering the CWL provided a coordinated public voice on matters that affected all women, and Catholics in particular. Catholic women, she predicted, would use their recently acquired voting rights to influence beneficial legislation and discourage laws antithetical to Catholicism. Lovering applauded, for instance, the steps that Ontario had taken to amend the Separate Schools Act to allow for the surgical treatment of pupils at public expense (health officials in public schools already had authority to act in cases of tonsillitis and other afflictions). She viewed with alarm the federal government's proposed relaxation of divorce law, advising CWL members to use the power of public opinion to continue its delay. In 1921, at the CWL's first annual convention, she praised such initiatives in Ontario as the Mothers' Allowance Act, the Minimum Wage Board, and new regulations for film censorship, all undertaken by the government of Ernest Charles Drury*. Among the other issues of social welfare that concerned the league were the care and training of "mental defectives," the condition of pregnant women in prisons, and venereal disease. At the local level members visited hospitals and homes of refuge and for the aged, bringing food, magazines, and religious articles, and each October Catholic families were canvassed on behalf of the Orphanage Guild in Hamilton.

Lovering advocated a revitalized Catholicism as expressed in the ideas of the Catholic Truth Society, of which she was a vice-president from 1923 to 1925. Addressing a CWL convention in Montreal in 1924, she called on Catholic women "to restore men to discipline and self-control and to reconcile women to home and its duties." She warned against a society seemingly "discontented with life, and mad with the unrestricted love of pleasure." In her valedictory speech of 11 June 1925 at the league's annual convention in Hamilton, she based her remarks on biblical text. Women, she said, had had no place in society until they had been emancipated by Christ's words: "Son, behold your mother." Christianity had therefore freed women, making them their husbands' "partners" instead of "toys and slaves." Marriage was the basis of society, and Catholic women should resist easier divorce, birth control, the desire for political office, and theories of "ultra-feminism" that would "make a woman sexless, with none of the natural charms of womanhood."

As part of her league-related activities in the 1920s, Lovering served as vice-chair of the National Travellers' Aid Committee for Ontario, which looked after – with some moral overtone – Catholic women in transit or away from home. As well, she was a director of the Central Bureau of Social Agencies, sat on the Canadian Council on Child Welfare with Charlotte Elizabeth Hazeltyne Whitton* and other pioneers in this field, and was active in both the Social Hygiene Council for Canada and the Big Sisters Association of Canada.

Early in 1926, following her return with her husband from a Big Brothers and Big Sisters convention in Chicago, Lovering fell ill and died; she was buried in Holy Sepulchre Cemetery in Burlington, Ont. Her life of service had often been recognized. For her work on behalf of the Secours National the French government awarded her the Medaille d'Honneur (1917) and the Medaille de la Reconnaissance Française (1921); for her religious work the papacy gave her *La Croce Pro Ecclesia et Pontifice* (1925) and *La Medaglia Benemerenti* (1926). Shortly after her death she was made a chevalier of France's Legion of Honour, the only woman in Canada to have been granted this tribute.

In the early years of the 20th century, Frances Lovering and others like her in Catholic women's organizations, such as the CWL, reflected a general sense of nationalism and the newly found public voice of feminism and suffragism. Specifically they addressed the need to redefine and reaffirm the place of Catholicism in an increasingly secularized environment.

MOLLY PULVER UNGAR and VICKY BACH

AO, RG 80-5-0-156, no.13781; RG 80-5-0-241, no.15755; RG 80-8-0-136, no.16301. Hamilton Public Library, Special Coll. Dept. (Hamilton, Ont.), Clipping files, Hamilton biog.; Hamilton – organizations and societies – Secours National; Scrapbooks, *Herald*, vol.W2. Institute of the Blessed Virgin Mary North America Arch., Loretto Abbey (Toronto), "Memorandum re: Frances Mahony Lovering"; Student reg. LAC, RG 31, C1, 1901, Hamilton, Ward 1, div.2: 5. TRL, SC, Biog. scrapbooks, vol.16. *Hamilton Spectator*, 24 May 1915; 8 Nov. 1916; 20, 27 Oct. 1917; 20 Nov. 1918; 2, 4 July 1921; 27 March 1926. *News* (Toronto), 24 Nov. 1886. *World* (Toronto), 3 May 1889. *Canadian League* (Toronto), 4 (August 1924), 5 (July 1925). *Cathedral Magazine* (Hamilton), March 1917; October 1919; July, September 1920; November 1921; January 1922; December 1925; February, May 1926 (copies in Cathedral of Christ the King Arch., Hamilton). *DHB*, vol.3. *Directories*, Hamilton, 1900–1; Toronto, 1866–95. Hamilton Local Council of Women, *Fifty years of activity, 1893–1943; commemorating the golden anniversary of Hamilton Local Council of Women* ([Hamilton, 1944]). J. E. Middleton and Fred Landon, *The province of Ontario: a history, 1615–1927* (5v., Toronto, 1927–[28]), 4: 347–48.

MAIR, CHARLES, businessman, author, and office holder; b. 21 Sept. 1838 in Lanark, Upper Canada, youngest child of James Mair and Margaret Holmes; m. 8 Sept. 1869 Elizabeth Louise McKenney in the Red River settlement (Man.), and they had five daughters and two sons; d. 7 July 1927 in Victoria.

Throughout his life, Charles Mair, the "warrior bard," considered it his patriotic duty to crusade for Canada. He attributed this conviction to his origin in the Ottawa valley "in its primitive day." His paternal grandfather had come to Lanark in 1824 at age 78 and established two general stores; in 1831 his son and daughter-in-law left Scotland to join him in the merchant and timber trade. In his memoirs Mair would recall the romance and drama of the trade: "I loved the river life, the great pineries in winter, where the timber was felled and squared." He disliked the discipline of the schoolmaster in Lanark and his years at the Perth Grammar School, but he recalled the pastimes enjoyed by the villagers as idyllic: shinty on ice, games, trapping, making maple syrup, and visiting Indian encampments. This love of living close to the natural environment would remain with him, as would the anxiety of a second recollection: the conspicuous presence of disabled war pensioners, who conducted regular militia exercises for the young men in Lanark to guard against American invasion. Much of Mair's career would unfold as a loyalist campaign for a strong dominion.

Though his father intended him to study medicine at Queen's College in Kingston, Mair left after one year (1856–57) to help with the family's troubled businesses in Lanark. He worked as a clerk for ten years, and began publishing poems in newspapers and journals. He returned to Queen's in 1867, but, as he later recalled, "there is no such thing as free will; destiny rules." During this year of study he completed the manuscript for his first book, *Dreamland and other poems* (Montreal, 1868). After the spring term in 1868 he went to Ottawa, where his publisher was having it printed. He mixed there with a civil servant and writer he had met in 1864, Henry James Morgan*, who introduced him to three young lawyers interested in the challenges facing the new dominion, George Taylor DENISON, William Alexander Foster*, and Robert Grant Haliburton*. Together they organized the overtly nationalistic Canada First movement, which began as a small social group.

Through Morgan, Mair caught the attention of William McDougall*, the MP for Lanark North and minister of public works in the cabinet of Sir John A. Macdonald*. McDougall offered Mair a summer job as his research secretary to help the new Canadian government in its effort to annex the western territories controlled by the Hudson's Bay Company. Pleased with Mair's work, he chose him as his secretary for the mission to London to negotiate the transfer, but when Mair's sister in St Catharines fell ill, Mair went instead to visit her. At the point of leaving in October, McDougall appointed him paymaster for the construction of a road from Lake of the Woods to Upper Fort Garry (Winnipeg) [see John Allan Snow*]. Though Mair feared the job would interfere with his studies, he understood that McDougall was offering him the opportunity to "describe the country, a sealed book as yet to the Canadian people," a chance that could involve the poet directly in the patriotic positioning of Canada First. Toronto *Globe* editor George Brown*, who shared McDougall's transcontinental vision, hired Mair as a correspondent to inspire eastern interest in the northwest frontier.

Mair left just as *Dreamland* was published. It demonstrates a conventional colonial approach to poetry. Such poems as "August" succeed in their attention to natural detail: descriptions of the blueflies, the milkmaids, and the "ribby-lean" cattle in parched fields anticipate the mature nature poetry of Archibald Lampman*. But too often he wrote not of the timberlands he knew but of a dreamland weakly modelled upon the romantic flights of Keats. He would return throughout his career to variations of this dream of a heavenly realm that is sustained (as in "Dreamland") until dashed by the corruption of "brawling mammonists." Amidst reviewers of the book, many of whom lauded Mair for giving voice to a new land, there were two Canadian critics to whom he paid respectful attention. The first was the established poet Charles Sangster*, who referred to Canada's sophisticated literary tradition as one that was habitually overlooked in the popular press, which naively greeted each new poet as the first songster to "view our songless shores." The second was Mair's fellow Canada First advocate R. G. Haliburton, who urged Mair to Canadianize his subject matter, to look to the prairie rather than Milton for inspiration. Mair would take this criticism to heart, but in November 1868 he shifted to prose for his contributions to the *Globe*. These columns, which begin with his trip to Upper Fort Garry, provide a romantic account of the grandeur of the prairie – its vistas, wildlife, idyllic settlements, and loamy fields that entice the Canadian pioneer to pursue "the path of empire and the garden of the world." Mair includes equally vivid descriptions of the outrageous characters of the frontier, among them the spinners of tales, the corrupt bureaucrats from American bordertowns, and the back-biting "halfbreeds" at the Canadian outposts. By seeming to convey the impression that any enterprising immigrant could succeed amid these people, Mair's columns caused a furore in Red River. The Métis wife of Andrew Graham Ballenden Bannatyne* took exception to his account of the tension between mixed-blood and white wives at a dinner given by Alexander Begg*. As a result she slapped and whipped Mair in public. This incident

would lead to the first *roman-à-clef* set in the west, Begg's *'Dot it down'* . . . (Toronto, 1871), which presents a caricature of Mair as a self-important Upper Canadian flirt who dots down his sneering observations about the west. Mair's prose, and the reaction to it, obscured his road work, which drew more resentment. With bison scarce and crops levelled by grasshoppers in 1868, the Métis of Red River needed work on his crew, but the same Métis soon accused him of purchasing (from the Cree) land they had claimed.

Mair was also being drawn into conflict through his friendship with John Christian Schultz*, the businessman who angered both the Métis and the HBC with his advocacy of provincial status for the Red River settlement. Mair had fallen in love with Schultz's 19-year-old niece, Eliza McKenney, who had adventured out from Amherstburg, Ont. They were married in September 1869 and, for their honeymoon, they rode south to Minnesota to meet William McDougall, then on his way to Red River as lieutenant governor designate of the North-West Territories.

Despite the growing unrest among the Métis, who blocked McDougall's entry, the Mairs were determined to return to Red River, and were imprisoned for a time by the followers of Louis Riel*, some of whom Mair had employed. When the newly-weds were released and eventually reached Upper Fort Garry, they found it occupied and retreated to Schultz's warehouse, where they held out until mid December, the same month that Riel proclaimed a provisional government. Jailed again, without his wife, Mair was sentenced to be executed. After escaping with Schultz, he met briefly with Eliza until, with a bounty on his head, he fled through blizzards to St Paul, Minn. When Mair and Schultz arrived at the railway station in Toronto in April 1870, they were greeted by a crowd of 5,000; at a reception in St Lawrence Hall they spoke about the Métis insurrection. Although Macdonald's administration sought to play down the events, Mair and Schultz, with the help of Canada First advocate George Denison, campaigned for Riel's ouster. Mair and Denison believed their efforts were responsible for Ottawa's dispatch of troops under Garnet Joseph Wolseley*.

Eliza Mair's ordeal had been no less dramatic. When the guards failed to track down her husband, Riel ordered her seized, but she was hidden by the wife of the Reverend Henry George. On 4 March, the day the Métis executed Thomas Scott*, Eliza, then five months pregnant, risked capture when she searched Schultz's occupied house for the manuscripts of Charles's poetry. Riel had sacked it, however, and the papers were lost. Mair had spent five years on "Zardust and Sélima," a poem he believed would establish his reputation, and he did not feel he could reproduce it; the loss of his manuscripts, he lamented, "broke my literary heart." Still separated from her exiled husband,

Eliza gave birth to their first child in July in Winnipeg. Mair did not see them until October.

With a family to support and his manuscripts destroyed, he settled in Portage la Prairie, Man., to work as a general-store merchant and fur trader. During his seven years in what he considered the gateway to the frontier, he served as the Manitoba agent for the North West Emigration Aid Society, which he had established with his Canada First associates. In articles in 1875 for the *Canadian Monthly and National Review* (Toronto) [*see* Graeme Mercer Adam*], he articulated their vision of the west's development within the British empire: the "boundless ocean of land . . . waiting with majestic patience for the flocks and the fields, the schools, the churches, the Christian faith and love of freedom of the coming men." The rest of his articles comprise an aggressive statement of Anglo-Saxon ethnic nationalism in keeping with Canada First and other remarks made by Mair, who advocated a specifically Protestant immigration that would sweep aside the Roman Catholic Métis as well as the natives.

In 1877, with Portage la Prairie failing to develop commercially, the family moved to Prince Albert (Sask.). Here Mair built a store and continued to promote, in the *Prince Albert Times and Saskatchewan Review*, which he helped found, the need for immigrants to ensure that Canada would fulfil its imperial destiny. Such prominence kept him a target of Métis resentment. By mid 1882, fearing Riel's return, he had taken his family to Windsor, Ont., but he maintained his business in Prince Albert by wintering there for the next two years. His summer work was of a different kind. Situated close to Eliza's mother in Amherstburg, Windsor was also an ideal location for the research needed for his return to poetry, in the form of an inspirational national epic. For his subject he selected the Shawnee leader Tecumseh*, who had died in the War of 1812, which he viewed as "the turning point of Canada's destiny." Written as a blank-verse play, *Tecumseh: a drama* (Toronto, 1886) would be his greatest literary accomplishment. It would honour not only the heroic principles on which the dominion was founded, but also the Indians, the "sensible, intelligent" race he had known as a boy and in the northwest. He hoped his poem would help shape a different destiny, in Canada, for a people so "villainously wronged" by the Americans. In the summer of 1882 Mair had begun examining the sites in southwestern Ontario where Tecumseh had faced the American invaders – the quiet fields where Tecumseh had supposedly grown corn and the battlefields where stone tomahawks and the bones of warriors could still be found. After his "semi-savage life" in the northwest, Mair was now composing and sharing drafts within a community of literary sympathizers.

Mair had been writing full-time for more than a year when news of the North-West uprising interrupted his work in March 1885. Some of his friends were killed in the clash between the Métis and police at Duck Lake (Sask.) [*see* Lief Newry Fitzroy Crozier*], and he felt duty-bound to enlist in the militia against his nemesis, Riel. As quartermaster in Denison's unit, the Governor General's Body Guard, he was stationed at Humboldt, where the troops quietly guarded a telegraph station. Back in Windsor in July, after the rebellion had been suppressed, he was intent on completing his poem, but his campaign for Riel's execution shattered his focus. Riel was hanged in November and Mair finished his poem by the end of December. On 12 Feb. 1886 he proudly sent a copy of *Tecumseh* to Eliza. When he and other members of the Governor General's Body Guard were presented with North West Canada medals on 24 May in Toronto, by the wife of Lieutenant Governor John Beverley Robinson*, Mair was dubbed the "warrior bard."

Tecumseh, which Mair introduces as the "high ideal" of a "United Empire," contrasts the Canadian tradition of cooperative self-sacrifice for the good of the community with the American tradition of divisive self-interest. Mair identifies both Tecumseh and British general Sir Isaac Brock* as exemplars of self-sacrifice. A Shakespearean model is effective in his description of the northwest (which Tecumseh visits) as an ocean with shoreless prairies and waves of bison, and in his depiction of American ruffians whose slang draws on Thomas Chandler Haliburton*'s Yankee pedlar. Though *Tecumseh* was composed as a closet play, Mair confessed he entertained notions that it might be staged. It did receive many reviews. His representation of the native received gratifying endorsement by Mohawk poet Emily Pauline Johnson* in the Toronto *World*: "Mair avoids the usual commonplaces used in describing Indians by those who have never met or mixed with them." The *Globe* praised the play with a lofty comparison: "As the play of *Henry V* was a song of triumph to the English of Shakespeare's time, so is this a song of triumph for the Canadians of today." However, Mair would overdo his nationalist intentions: in *Tecumseh: a drama, and Canadian poems* (Toronto, 1901) he tries to Canadianize his earliest pieces by replacing medieval knights with the warriors and heroines of 1812.

At the height of his literary career, Mair and his family moved back in the summer of 1886 to Prince Albert, where he became active as a storekeeper, rancher, postmaster, and real-estate agent. He planned to write an even more ambitious drama, on the British conquest of Canada, but managed only to publish occasional poems. One of them, "The last bison," which appeared in *Dominion Illustrated* (Montreal) in 1888, identifies a concern Mair would pursue in prose. His impassioned essay on "The American bison . . . with reference to its threatened extinction and possible

Mair

preservation," published in 1890 in the *Transactions* of the Royal Society of Canada, to which he had been elected the previous year, may have been a factor in the federal government's attempts in 1898–99 to establish a herd in Rocky Mountains Park at Banff (Alta). In 1893 Mair left Prince Albert for St Paul. There he encouraged immigrants to move on to the northwest, and he visited Chicago to set up a Canadian exhibit at the Columbian exposition. He located next in Kelowna, B.C., where he opened a store, but he grew increasingly despondent until, in 1898, interior minister Clifford SIFTON appointed him as a travelling immigration agent, based initially in Winnipeg. Helping immigrants settle on the frontier fitted Mair's interests; he played some role, for instance, in the selection of land in the Swan River district (Sask.) by Doukhobor agents in late 1898. A four-month interruption of work in 1899 was another perfectly suited opportunity: he was granted leave to serve as English secretary of the commission established to deal with the land claims of the mixed-blood population of the northern region being transferred under Treaty No.8 [*see* James Andrew Joseph McKenna*]. His book on the commission's expedition, published in Toronto in 1908 and his major work of prose, is introduced as an Arcadian narrative and a plea for Canada to protect the primitive customs and traditions of an innocent people from the corrupt civilization of HBC traders and Klondike gold seekers. He contextualizes his journey in the early exploration narratives of Sir Alexander Mackenzie* and Sir George Simpson*, and focuses on the changes that had occurred during the 19th century as his party passed the ruins of forts and followed old buffalo paths and wallows overgrown with strawberry vines and saskatoon clumps. Mair was surprised to encounter, instead of the picturesque "savage types" of old, groups of natives in "store-clothes." *Through the Mackenzie basin: a narrative of the Athabasca and Peace River treaty expedition of 1899* marks the culmination of his long campaign for a northern dominion as a bulwark against American expansion.

During his years as an immigration agent, Mair gathered material for a book about the Red River uprising of 1869–70, but the research was difficult after his transfer from Winnipeg to Lethbridge (Alta) in 1903 and subsequently to Coutts and then Fort Steele, B.C. His time in Lethbridge was especially hard: he lost his daughter Elizabeth to typhoid in 1904 and his beloved wife died from a cerebral haemorrhage in 1906 while visiting their daughter Maude Louise in Victoria. When his request for a transfer to the archives branch in Ottawa was denied, he abandoned the Red River project, though some of his recollections were published as interviews.

Mair retired from the immigration office at Fort Steele in 1921 at age 83. He lived with his daughter Fanny George in Calgary until he moved to a retirement home in Victoria. In 1924 he was awarded an LLD by Queen's University. Another honour, long in the works, was the volume of his poetry, prose, and memoirs edited by John William Garvin* and released in April 1927 as a tribute to the old warrior bard. After celebrating the diamond jubilee of Canada on Dominion Day by sending a telegram to the Canadian Authors Association, Mair died on 7 July. He was buried beside Eliza in Ross Bay Cemetery in Victoria.

The extravagant claims by Garvin and Robert Winkworth Norwood* in the tribute volume that Mair was Canada's greatest poet were ill founded, but his considerable achievements have since been neglected or disparaged. Though his role as a founding member of the Canada First movement and his campaign for frontier immigration led him into conflict with the Métis, Mair's negative reputation for his imperialist stance might be measured against his later successes as an immigration agent and his well-meaning praise for the dignity of the native peoples. Mair's part in promoting a sanctuary for bison places him among our first conservationists. A scholarly edition of his prose is needed to bring together his Red River correspondence, "The American bison," and *Through the Mackenzie basin* for further scrutiny of his ideology. His *Tecumseh* is a major contribution to our 19th-century literary heritage, wherein the War of 1812 is the central event of Canadian history. Among the many literary treatments of this war, including works by Sangster, John Richardson*, and Sarah Anne Curzon [Vincent*], *Tecumseh* stands as the most accomplished.

DAVID LATHAM

Charles Mair's papers are at QUA. Bibliographies of his writings are in *Tecumseh: a drama, and Canadian poems; Dreamland and other poems; The American bison; Through the Mackenzie basin; Memoirs and reminiscences*, ed. J. W. Garvin, intro. R. [W.] Norwood (Toronto, 1926), in Norman Shrive's excellent biography, *Charles Mair, literary nationalist* (Toronto, 1965), and in Shrive's *The voice of the Burdash: Charles Mair and the divided mind in Canadian literature* (London, Ont., 1995). Mair's Red River articles in the *Globe*, some first published in the *Perth Courier* (Perth, Ont.), appeared on 14, 27 Dec. 1868; 4 Jan., 16 Feb., 28 May 1869. His two articles for the *Canadian Monthly and National Rev.* (Toronto) are "The new Canada: its natural features and climate," 8 (July–December 1875): 1–8 and "The new Canada: its resources and productions," 8: 156–64. "The last bison" was printed in *Dominion Illustrated* (Montreal), 1 (1888): 155 and "The American bison . . . with reference to its threatened extinction and possible preservation" was published in RSC, *Trans.*, 1st ser., 8 (1890), sect.II: 93–108. The reviews of Mair's works by Sangster, Haliburton, and Johnson appeared respectively in the *Times* (Ottawa), 10 Feb. 1869, *Evening Reporter and Tri-Weekly Times* (Halifax), 13 July 1869, and *World* (Toronto), 22 March 1892. The *Globe* reviewed *Tecumseh* on 20 Feb. 1886.

Useful insight into Mair's ideology, writings, and career may be found in C. C. Berger, *The sense of power; studies in* the ideas of Canadian imperialism, 1867–1914 (Toronto and Buffalo, N.Y., 1970); Leslie Monkman, "Charles Mair," in *Profiles in Canadian literature*, ed. J. M. Heath (6v., Toronto, 1980–91), 5: 49–56; Fred Cogswell, "Charles Mair," in *Canadian writers and their works*, ed. Robert Lecker et al., intro. George Woodcock (24v. in 2 ser., Toronto, 1983–96), poetry ser., 1 (1988): 119–55; Leslie Monkman, *A native heritage: images of the Indian in English-Canadian literature* (Toronto, 1981); and the introduction by D. W. Leonard and Brian Calliou to *Through the Mackenzie basin: an account of the signing of Treaty No.8 and the scrip commission, 1899* (Edmonton, 1999).

MALLORY, CALEB ALVORD, farmer, politician, and agrarian activist; b. 30 Sept. 1841 near Cobourg, Upper Canada, son of Caleb Robin Mallory (Mallery) and Harriet L. ——; m. first 9 Oct. 1866 Harriet Ann DeFurlong (d. 1902) of Warkworth, Ont., and they had five sons and two daughters; m. secondly Margaret Ann Berry (d. 1918); d. 6 Dec. 1926 near Cobourg and was buried in Grafton, Ont.

The eldest of seven children, Caleb A. Mallory was born and spent his life in Northumberland County. His father was a farmer who also became involved in a variety of commercial ventures. After receiving primary and secondary education, Mallory, a Methodist, attended Victoria College in Cobourg, but illness forced him to leave before he completed his studies. He purchased land near Warkworth in Percy Township in 1863 and cleared a farm. At various times he served as a township councillor, deputy reeve, and reeve, and in 1888 he was chosen warden of the United Counties of Northumberland and Durham.

A member of the Patrons of Husbandry, Mallory was drawn to the Patrons of Industry, an agrarian body founded in Michigan in 1887. County units of this organization were formed in Ontario and in February 1890 Mallory and other local delegates gathered in Sarnia to form a grand association in affiliation with the American body. Mallory was elected vice-president, a position he retained in the autonomous association organized in London in September 1891. The following year he became president, in which office he served until 1898. Using the elevated rhetoric of agrarian and urban radicalism, the Patrons of Industry called for sweeping reforms, including the elimination of tariffs on "the necessaries of life," enhanced democratic mechanisms, and "purity" in public life. During his tenure Mallory, in eloquent, well-publicized speeches, called upon farmers to renounce their old Conservative and Liberal party allegiances, to fight against monopolies and other corrupt business practices, and to build a more egalitarian and democratic society. The Patrons also established or supported several cooperative enterprises, including a binder-twine factory at Brantford and a salt company at Kincardine, and formed an alliance with the *Canada Farmers' Sun* (London, Ont.; Toronto), begun by George Weston Wrigley* in 1892. For a short time in the mid 1890s Mallory was president of the Sun Publishing Company.

Initially the Patrons enjoyed strong popularity, with a reported membership of 35,000 in Ontario and Quebec by 1893. In the Ontario provincial election a year later they fielded candidates in some 50 constituencies. To the surprise of many, the Patrons captured 17 seats and came close to winning 20 more. They appeared destined to present a strong challenge to the old parties, though their leader in the legislature, Joseph Langford Haycock, proved ineffectual. The Patrons never really became adept at parliamentary politics.

In 1895–96 Mallory, a former Liberal, participated in two secret attempts to collude with the federal Liberals. In 1895 his brother Albert Ethanan, a physician in Colborne, Ont., informed party leader Wilfrid Laurier* that a "person high up in the Councils of the Patrons" (almost certainly Caleb) wanted to work out an electoral arrangement whereby Liberals would not field candidates in ridings where Patrons' nominees were likely to win, and vice versa, thus preventing Conservative victories as a result of split voting. But no agreement was reached.

The second bid to trade off ridings, this time involving Liberal brokers and Caleb Mallory directly, became public knowledge. Mallory weakly defended his actions by pointing out that the Liberals had eventually backed out of the arrangement. The fact, however, that he had secretly negotiated with both the Liberals and parliamentary maverick D'Alton McCarthy* further demoralized the Patrons movement, which was struggling through internal divisions and failed attempts to join with urban labourites. His actions also fuelled charges that the Patrons were not the independent political force they purported to be but were merely disguised Liberals. In what undoubtedly was a sincere effort to obtain a presence in the House of Commons and deny seats to the protectionist Conservatives, Mallory, in the minds of many members, particularly secretary-treasurer L. A. Welch, had committed an unpardonable sin: he had connived with one of the vilified and patronage-ridden old parties.

Mallory nonetheless managed to retain credibility and the leadership of the movement. He contested the riding of Northumberland East in the federal election of June 1896 and publicly encouraged Patrons' locals elsewhere to endorse candidates; he lost by a narrow margin to his Conservative opponent, Edward Cochrane*. By this time, however, the Patrons were in irreversible decline and, overwhelmed by the Manitoba school question and other major political issues, they managed to elect only three MPs.

In an attempt to revitalize the farmers' movement in Ontario, Mallory and other leading agrarians formed the Farmers' Association of Ontario in September 1902. Its purpose was to press for legislation that benefited farmers. At the inaugural meeting in Toronto, which he chaired, Mallory was elected president, but he remained in the position for only a year. Though still vehemently opposed to protective tariffs that favoured manufacturers, he seemed content to pass the lead to such younger activists as James Lockie Wilson, James J. Morrison*, and Ernest Charles Drury*. In his sixties, he had probably lost much of the energy he had exhibited in the formative years of the Patrons, though around 1909–10 he played some role in the formation of the Canadian Council of Agriculture, for which he was honoured in the *Weekly Sun* (Toronto).

By the early 1900s Mallory had moved from Percy to the farm east of Cobourg where he had been born. Tragedy struck on 10 Dec. 1902 when the cutter carrying him and his wife was hit by a train. She died instantly and Mallory suffered severe injuries, though he recovered quickly. A freemason and a member of the Grafton United Church, he quietly lived out his final years at Maple Grove, the family homestead. Through his farm he recouped the losses he had incurred when he was preoccupied with Patrons business.

At the time of his death in 1926, Mallory was a largely forgotten figure in Ontario's agrarian movement. There appears to have been no tribute to him in the *Farmers' Sun* (Toronto), by then the official newspaper of the United Farmers of Ontario. Even so, his contributions to agrarian populism had been substantial. His thoughtful attacks on blind party loyalty, high tariffs, and monopolies, and his appeals for a more democratic and egalitarian Canada, had struck responsive chords in many who heard or read his words. Moreover, the Ontario farm leaders who succeeded him, including Drury, Morrison, and William Charles Good*, were all indebted to the ground-breaking work undertaken by the Patrons under Mallory's capable, if occasionally contradictory, direction.

KERRY BADGLEY

Caleb Alvord Mallory is the author of "The Patrons of Industry Order," in *Canada, an encyclopaedia* (Hopkins), 5: 100–5.

AO, F 179; RG 22-191, no.10947; RG 80-8-0-677, no.29182; RG 80-27-2, 39: 47–48. LAC, MG 26, G: 3548–51, 3561–63; RG 31, C1, 1871, Hamilton Township, Ont., div.1: 66. Northumberland East Land Registry Office (Colborne, Ont.), Percy Township, deeds, 1862–69: 231–32 (mfm. at AO). TRL, SC, Biog. scrapbooks, 12: 18. *Canada Farmers' Sun* (London, Ont.; Toronto), 7 Feb., 7 March 1893; 27 May 1896. *Cobourg World* (Cobourg, Ont.), 12 Dec. 1902, 21 June 1918, 9 Dec. 1926. *London Free Press*, 30 May, 6 June 1896. *Weekly Sun* (Toronto), 17 Dec. 1902. *Canadian annual rev.*, 1903: 85, 442. *Canadian men and women of the time* (Morgan; 1898 and 1912). Farmers' Assoc., *The Farmers' Association: grounds on which it seeks the cooperation of all farmers* ([Toronto, 1903]); *The Farmers' Association: origin and purpose of the organization* (Toronto, n.d.; copy in AO, Pamphlet coll., n.d., F, no.2). *From a farmer's standpoint* (n.p., 1904; copy in AO, Pamphlet coll., 1904, no.25). W. C. Good, *Farmer citizen: my fifty years in the Canadian farmers' movement* (Toronto, 1958). Patrons of Industry of North America, Grand Assoc. of Ontario, *Minutes of the annual meeting* (Strathroy), 1893–95. S. E. D. Shortt, "Social change and political crisis in rural Ontario: the Patrons of Industry, 1889–1896," in *Oliver Mowat's Ontario: papers presented to the Oliver Mowat colloquium, Queen's University, November 25–26, 1970*, ed. Donald Swainson (Toronto, 1972), 211–35. L. A. Wood, *A history of farmers' movements in Canada* (Toronto, 1924; repr., intro. F. J. K. Griezic, Toronto and Buffalo, N.Y., 1975).

MARCHAND, CHARLES (baptized **Joseph-Charles-Édouard**), office holder, baritone, folklorist, journalist, and artistic director; b. 8 May 1890 in Saint-Paul-l'Ermite (Le Gardeur), Que., son of Sévère-Gaspard Marchand, a mechanic, and Zoé Quintal; m. 19 Oct. 1912 Marie-Anita Reinhardt in Hull, Que.; three sons and one daughter survived him; d. 1 May 1930 in Montreal.

Charles Marchand attended the Collège de L'Assomption from 1902 to 1906, and then completed his classical studies at the Collège Bourget in Rigaud. In 1910 he moved to Hull and found employment with the federal Department of the Interior. It was through this position (which he would leave around 1918 to devote himself to singing and to folklore) that he met Fortunat Champagne, who would become a colleague.

Marchand made his first public appearance in Ottawa in 1910, as a member of the cast of the play *Fleur d'ajonc* by Théodore Botrel, who was a popular entertainer in French Canada at that time. Next he used his baritone voice for the benefit of parish charities, performing without pay at various events. His repertoire showed some similarity to that of Botrel, who highlighted rustic and Catholic Breton songs, but it gradually came to reflect the concrete realities of French Canadian life. In 1915 he began working with Oscar O'Brien*, who would arrange some 150 pieces for him, and with Maurice Morisset, who would write some of his songs. Marchand made his professional debut in Montreal on 12 March 1919 at the Salle Lafontaine.

Marchand gave his first important performance in May of the following year, when he was accompanied by harmonica players and fiddlers in traditional costume. The event took place at the Monument National in Montreal, the city to which he had recently moved; he is said to have studied singing there, with Jean Riddez and Max Pantaleieff. Alexandre D'Aragon, in an article on Marchand in the Saint-Jérôme paper *L'Action musicale, littéraire et artistique* on 14 May 1932, would emphasize his fine "timbre" and his "warmth in communicating." These gifts, along with the raftsman's costume and ceinture fléchée he wore when he performed his rousing songs, would make Marchand an emblem of the French Canada of his day.

Marchand, O'Brien, and Morisset, along with pianist Ernest Patience, founded a musical movement named the Carillon Canadien on 31 Jan. 1922. From 1922 to 1925 Marchand toured Quebec and visited parts of Ontario and a few towns in western Canada and in New England. He became editor of *Le Carillon*, which was published in Montreal from May 1926 to March 1927, when it merged with *La Lyre*. The periodical described itself as a theatrical, musical, and literary magazine seeking to promote "la bonne chanson." The publishing house Le Carillon brought out the songs by Morisset and O'Brien that Marchand performed.

For the celebrations held in Ottawa in 1927 to mark the 60th anniversary of confederation, Marchand put together a quartet. The Bytown Troubadours – Marchand, Émile Boucher, Miville Belleau, and Fortunat Champagne – went on tour in Canada as well as in the United States, and their repertoire included songs translated into English by John Murray Gibbon. In 1927, 1928, and 1930 the quartet was on the program of the Canadian Folk Song and Handicraft Festival, which was held in those years mainly in the Château Frontenac at Quebec. This series of festivals was organized by Gibbon, who was the publicity director in Canada for the Canadian Pacific Railway; the company sponsored the event, which took place at various CPR hotels from 1927 to 1931. Marchand took over part of the artistic direction of the festival in 1928. He was also involved in organizing the event in 1930, but it was postponed because of his sudden and premature death.

Charles Marchand helped gain recognition for the oral tradition by performing the repertoire that Marius Barbeau* had assembled; Marchand contributed to Barbeau's efforts. Besides Morisset and O'Brien, his colleagues included songwriters Pierre Dupaigne, Lucien Sirois, Hector Nadeau, and Robert Choquette*, as well as musician Hector Latour. From 1922 to 1926 he made many solo recordings for Edison and Columbia in New York and the Starr studios in Montreal. Marchand helped bring French Canadian songs into the cause of "la bonne chanson," which until then had consisted mainly of Botrel's work.

JEAN-NICOLAS DE SURMONT

AC, Hull, État civil, Catholiques, Notre-Dame-de-Grâce (Hull), 19 oct. 1912. ANQ-M, CE605-S33, 8 mai 1890. *Le Devoir*, 2 mai 1930. *Dictionnaire biographique des musiciens canadiens* (2ᵉ éd., Lachine, Qué., 1935). *Encyclopedia of music in Canada* (Kallmann *et al.*). Gabriel Labbé, *Les pionniers du disque folklorique québécois, 1920–1950* (Montréal, 1977). Bruno Roy, *Panorama de la chanson au Québec* ([Montréal], 1977). Soc. Hist. de Montréal et Soc. de Folklore d'Amérique (section de Québec), *Veillées du bon vieux temps à la Bibliothèque Saint-Sulpice, à Montréal, les 18 mars et 24 avril 1919* (Montréal, [1920]).

MARCHAND, JOSÉPHINE (baptized **Joséphine-Hersélie-Henriette**) (**Dandurand**), journalist, writer, lecturer, and feminist activist; b. 5 Dec. 1861 in Saint-Jean (Saint-Jean-sur-Richelieu), Lower Canada, daughter of Félix-Gabriel Marchand* and Hersélie Turgeon; m. there 12 Jan. 1886 Raoul Dandurand*, and they had one daughter; d. 2 March 1925 in Montreal and was buried there in Notre-Dame-des-Neiges cemetery.

One of a family of 11 children, Joséphine Marchand spent her early years in Saint-Jean. Because she was fidgety, she was nicknamed Froufrou, but in her adult years she would be calm and reserved. Her father, Félix-Gabriel, was a notary by training. In 1860, with Charles Laberge* and Isaac Bourguignon, he had founded a Liberal semi-weekly in Saint-Jean known as *Le Franco-Canadien*. From 1867 he represented the riding of Saint-Jean in the Legislative Assembly. After pursuing a career both in politics and in letters, he would become premier of Quebec on 24 May 1897. Joséphine's mother, Hersélie, had been educated at the Couvent de Saint-Roch at Quebec, and loved to read. She unquestionably belonged to one of the most prominent Quebec families of the time.

In this privileged environment, Joséphine acquired a taste for literature very early. Educated in her native city, with the Sisters of the Congregation of Notre-Dame, she was a talented pupil, and is thought to have won a prize for English literature. She adored the French language, but also mastered English, which she would sometimes use in her private diary and in public lectures. Arthur Buies*, Louis Fréchette*, and Benjamin SULTE were among her favourite Canadian writers, and among French ones she was especially fond of Alphonse de Lamartine, Victor Hugo, and Guy de Maupassant. She also read Spanish and English literature.

Joséphine Marchand began to write for publication in 1879. Over the next 12 years her work, usually in the form of short stories and tales, would appear in *Le Franco-Canadien*, of which her father was editor, and the Montreal newspapers *La Patrie* and *L'Opinion publique*; Honoré Mercier*, a family friend, insisted on representing her in her dealings with the latter. Her private diary, begun at the age of 17, is a valuable document, both for the information it contains and for the picture it provides of her. (Her husband would be unaware of its existence until after her death.) Among other things, the young woman tells of the curiosity her by-line aroused. In truth, at the time she began writing few women were trying their hand at literary endeavours in French Canada. Until then, Félicité ANGERS, known as Laure Conan, had been almost the only one. From the outset of Joséphine's career, her father, who was her first reader and critic, acknowledged that she showed a certain facility of expression, but he maintained, according to her private diary, that she would have to "work very seriously to eliminate many stylistic shortcomings."

On 12 Jan. 1886, in the parish of Saint-Jean-l'Évangéliste in Saint-Jean, Joséphine Marchand married Raoul Dandurand, who described himself at the time as a gentleman and lawyer. For their honeymoon they went to New York. Their only daughter, Gabrielle, was born in December of that year. In 1891 they would use all their ready money ($2,000) for a five-month stay in Europe. Over the years Joséphine would take at least six more trips overseas, travelling to France, England, Germany, Austria, and Italy. A Liberal in politics, Raoul Dandurand was appointed to the Senate in 1898, assuming a heavy responsibility for a young man of 36. In his memoirs, which were to be published in 1967, he told of Joséphine's influence, claiming that he would not have been made a senator had it not been for her prestige and the affection she inspired in the people who met her.

Joséphine Dandurand enjoyed great success with her writing. In 1888 a performance of "Quand on s'aime, on se marie" at the Académie de Musique de Québec aroused public interest. This one-act comedy in prose would come out in 1896 with the title *Rancune*. In 1889 she published *Contes de Noël* under the pseudonym Josette, which she had been using since she began to write. With a preface by Fréchette, it was a collection of eight stories that had previously appeared in magazines. According to Fréchette – a man of his times – the style of the stories revealed "the author's femininity" hidden behind the pseudonym. She then brought out two short children's plays, *Ce que pensent les fleurs* in 1895 and *La carte postale* the following year. All four of these works were published in Montreal.

In January 1893 Dandurand founded *Le Coin du feu* in Montreal. With the inauguration of this monthly magazine she established a secure place for herself in the field of journalism. *Le Coin du feu* was the first French-language periodical in Canada edited by a woman and intended specifically for women. Although she could occasionally count on prestigious contributors – Félicité Angers, Marie Gérin-Lajoie [Lacoste*], Jules Simon, and Paul Bourget – as founder and editor she herself produced much of the material: a leading column signed with her married name, Mme Dandurand; columns titled "Travers sociaux," signed Marie Vieuxtemps and devoted to dissecting the shortcomings of middle-class society; and the articles by Météore, in which she dealt with literature and the French language. This forum enabled her to explore her favourite topics, including literature, family relationships, feminism, the intellectual awakening of women, and politics. In December 1893, for example, she published the opinions of a number of people, including her mother, Félicité Angers, Joseph-Israël Tarte*, and Arthur Buies, on

the subject of women's suffrage. Regular columns on cooking, fashion, hygiene, and health, as well as articles for children, poems, and illustrations, were included in the 30-odd pages of each number.

In the last issue of *Le Coin du feu,* which appeared in December 1896, Dandurand published an appeal for a flourishing women's press. "For the experiment has been done. A women's publication dealing with private family concerns – material as well as intellectual and moral – is timely and desirable in our society." In order to justify this opinion, she mentioned her "inability to devote to journalism all the time and effort necessary for this difficult profession." She then began writing for other Montreal publications, including *Le Monde illustré* (1898–1900), *Le Journal de Françoise* (1902–9), and *La Revue moderne* (1920–21). In 1901, in Montreal, she assembled 44 of her early newspaper items and two lectures in an anthology to which she gave the title *Nos travers.* This volume would be republished in 1924.

Along with her activities as a woman of letters, Dandurand was involved in a number of organizations. In the spring of 1894 she began a career as a public speaker, in English, at the first annual congress of the National Council of Women of Canada, which was held in Ottawa. At the conclusion of her talk on literary clubs, she expressed a wish for closer harmony between Canada's two linguistic groups. She subsequently became very active as a speaker and her eloquence even earned her the nickname "the female Laurier." She would be provincial vice-president of the National Council of Women of Canada (1912–13, 1917–19); within its Montreal branch she held the offices of vice-president (1895–96, 1900–1, 1906–7), member of the presidential board (1903–7), and honorary vice-president (1918–21). In 1898 she founded the Œuvre des Livres Gratuits, which provided reading matter for teachers in remote areas and people from underprivileged backgrounds. In March that year the French government awarded her the title of *officier d'académie*, in recognition of her defence of French culture in North America. Along with her fellow writer Robertine Barry*, known as Françoise, she represented Canadian women at the universal exposition in Paris in the summer of 1900. She was also one of the patronesses who in 1902 founded the women's section of the Association Saint-Jean-Baptiste de Montréal [*see* Jeanne ANCTIL].

The feminist movement "is an awakening of women to responsibility. . . . In the land as in the family, the voice of women must communicate the reassuring words that recall [us] to duty and to humanity," declared Dandurand in the course of a lecture reprinted in *Nos travers.* At the heart of her feminism was above all the responsibility to develop the mind. This was the goal of her various undertakings, and indeed of her marriage, to which she chose to give the motto

"Knowledge, intelligence before love!" After 1907, already overtaken by illness, she slowed the pace of her activities and less and less often wrote columns. Familiar with the world of politics, she remained closely associated with the work of her husband, who had been appointed speaker of the Senate in 1905. Astute and ambitious, she was also able to use her influence with key individuals, including Sir Wilfrid Laurier*, to advance Raoul Dandurand's career. Active all her life, she died in Montreal on 2 March 1925, following a lengthy illness, at the age of 63.

LINE GOSSELIN

[In addition to the works mentioned above, Joséphine Marchand (Dandurand) is the author of the chapter "French Canadian customs" in National Council of Women of Canada, *Women of Canada: their life and work; compiled . . . for distribution at the Paris international exhibition, 1900* ([Montreal?, 1900]; repr. [Ottawa], 1975), 22–30. She is also the author of a lecture, "Le français dans nos relations sociales," published in *Premier congrès de la langue française au Canada, Québec, 24–30 juin 1912: compte rendu* (Québec, 1913), pp.537–40. For many years she kept a diary which has been published as *Journal intime, 1879–1900*, Edmond Robillard, édit. (Lachine, Qué., 2000); the original is in LAC, MG 27, III, B3. Joséphine Marchand also wrote articles in various periodicals; beyond those mentioned in the biography, they include *Le Journal du dimanche* (Montréal), 1884, *Le Canada artistique* (Montréal), 1890, *L'Alliance nationale* (Montréal), 1899, and *La Bonne Parole* (Montréal), 1920. The contributor has compiled a partial list of Marchand's articles, a copy of which is available at the DCB. An inventory of her writings also appears in Laurette Cloutier, "Bio-bibliographie de madame Raoul Dandurand (née Joséphine Marchand)" (école de bibliothécaires, univ. de Montréal, 1942). L.G.]

ANQ-M, CE604-S10, 6 déc. 1861, 12 janv. 1886. ANQ-Q, P174. *Gazette* (Montréal), 3 March 1925. *La Patrie*, 31 mai 1902. Anita, "Mme Dandurand," *La Bonne Parole*, 14 (1926), no.2: 10. *BCF*, 1923: 157. Georges Bellerive, *Brèves apologies de nos auteurs féminins* (Québec, 1920). *Canadian men and women of the time* (Morgan; 1912). Raoul Dandurand, *Les mémoires du sénateur Raoul Dandurand (1861–1942)*, Marcel Hamelin, édit. (Québec, 1967). La Directrice [Robertine Barry], "Madame la présidente du Sénat," *Le Journal de Françoise* (Montréal), 3 (1904–5): 611. *DOLQ*, 2: 775–76. Sylvain Forêt, "Bibliographie; littérature canadienne," *Le Canada artistique*, 1, no.1 (prospectus, décembre 1889): 8–9. Lionel Fortin, *Félix-Gabriel Marchand* (Saint-Jean-sur-Richelieu, Qué., 1979). Françoise [Robertine Barry], "French Canadian women in literature," in *Women of Canada: their life and work*, 190–97. Hamel *et al.*, *DALFAN*, 361–62. Madeleine [A.-M.] Gleason-Huguenin, *Portraits de femmes* ([Montréal], 1938), 98–99. Yolande Pinard, "Les débuts du mouvement des femmes à Montréal, 1893–1902," in *Travailleuses et féministes: les femmes dans la société québécoise*, sous la dir. de Marie Lavigne et Yolande Pinard (Montréal, 1983), 177–98. Diane Thibeault, "Premières brèches dans l'idéologie des deux sphères: Joséphine Marchand-Dandurand et Robertine Barry, deux journalistes montréalaises de la fin du XIXe siècle" (thèse de MA, univ. d'Ottawa, 1981).

MARIE-ANNE-DE-JÉSUS. *See* BIBEAU

MARIE-CLÉMENTINE DE JÉSUS-HOSTIE. *See* HÉBERT DE LA ROUSSELIÈRE

MARIE DE SAINT-BASILE. *See* BERTRAND

MARIE-JOSEPH DE JÉSUS. *See* LEMOINE

MARIE-SAINT-DAVID. *See* TEYSSÈDRE

MARIE SAINTE-CÉCILE-DE-ROME. *See* BÉLANGER

MARK, FRANCES. *See* NICKAWA

MARLATT, WENONAH, YWCA general secretary and office holder; b. 18 Jan. 1883 in Portage la Prairie, Man., daughter of Samuel Reid Marlatt, a civil servant, and Elisabeth Whimster; d. unmarried 16 May 1930 in Victoria.

About 1915 Wenonah Marlatt, who was in her early thirties, settled in Victoria. In 1916 she applied for the position of general secretary of the local Young Women's Christian Association at a salary of $50 per month and was accepted. In her report for April 1917 she hinted at her heavy responsibilities and expressed an interest in working with young women. "Down in the park any evening one may see many many half grown girls . . . and one realizes how their energies might be deviated into safer channels through an effective programme. This teen age girls work appeals to me just now as the greatest necessity of the association." She added that her job as general secretary "is often baffling in its variety – During the past month, I have been called upon to act as a Matrimonial agent, I have been fearful of having to appear in Court, in a wage question and I wonder I have not more grey hairs when I consider the soaring prices of food."

On 13 Dec. 1918 Marlatt resigned; although her reason is not recorded in the YWCA's minutes, she was likely exhausted and may have wished to pursue women's labour issues more intently. Her expertise in the area of women's wages and labour concerns was by this time acknowledged. According to the *Daily Colonist* (Victoria), that same year the newly formed Minimum Wage Board, which included judge Helen Gregory* MacGill and the deputy minister of labour, J. D. McNiven, sought her help in establishing "from $30 to $35 per month as the lowest sum at which a working girl could be expected to procure board and lodging."

In December 1918 the provincial Department of Labour made plans to open a labour bureau in Victoria, one of a nationwide network of employment offices. The bureau was a result of federal legislation and a dominion-provincial conference held on 19–22 Nov. 1918; Ottawa agreed to pay half the operating costs of the provincial bureaux. The Victoria office, advertised in local papers as being "at the service of all persons seeking employment and of employers seeking help," opened in January 1919. It consisted of a male and a female department. The provincial government appointed Marlatt to head the female department on 7 Feb. 1919. The *Victoria Daily Times* pointed out that "in dealing with labor matters," she had "proved her organizing ability during the summer of the two last years" when she organized female labourers to pick fruit on the mainland.

In 1921 Marlatt spoke to the newly formed Kumtuks Club, a businesswomen's group that made the exercise of the franchise a qualification of membership. There she deplored "the inefficiency of the present-day youth when seeking employment without any specific qualification or training," and urged girls to develop a "wider knowledge of the household arts." Marlatt also joined the club.

Although many post-war labour problems stemmed from the influx of jobless soldiers, labour bureaux were intended to counter the difficulties of general unemployment. Women's employment needs were also escalating, as was the demand for female employees. The Department of Labour's report for 1919 shows 729 female applicants looking for work in Victoria, 957 employers seeking to fill posts, and 558 placements. In 1920 the women's office reported 2,346 applicants, 2,770 employers with positions to fill, and 1,230 placements. Marlatt was a first-hand witness to the province's growing labour problems and to the needs of female employees. "A woman of much sympathy and tact," noted the *Victoria Daily Times* at her death, "her relations both with applicants seeking employment and would-be employers were of the happiest and won for her widespread esteem."

After a short illness Marlatt died in St Joseph's Hospital in Victoria at age 47. The *Daily Colonist* noted that she left behind a "host of friends among the business and professional women of the city." Her career and community involvement in Victoria demonstrated her administrative skills and her particular interest in matters of female employment.

MELANIE BUDDLE

BCA, MS-0215, 1–3. LAC, RG 31, C1, 1901, Portage-la-Prairie, Man., dist.8, subdist.L, subdiv.2: 8. *Daily Colonist* (Victoria), 8 Sept., 19–20, 28 Dec. 1918; 1, 7 Jan., 8 Feb. 1919; 7, 12, 25 Oct. 1921; 17 May 1930. *Victoria Daily Times*, 7 Feb. 1919; 18, 21 Oct. 1921; 17 May 1930. B.C., Legislative Assembly, *Sessional papers*, reports of the Dept. of Labour, 1918–20.

MARMETTE, MARIE-LOUISE (baptized **Marie-Louise-Joséphine-Esther-Eliza**) (**Brodeur**), known as **Louyse de Bienville** (she also used the pseudonym **Domino Noir**), author and lecturer; b. 29 March 1870 at Quebec, daughter of Joseph-Étienne-Eugène Marmette and Marie-Joséphine Garneau; m. 6 July 1892 Donat Brodeur (d. 1920) in Ottawa, and they had three sons and five daughters, one of whom died in infancy; d. 2 May 1928 in Montreal.

Marie-Louise Marmette, the only surviving child of the four born to her parents, came from a literary family. The historian François-Xavier Garneau* was her maternal grandfather; her father was a prolific writer who, in 1884, helped found the Cercle des Dix, an Ottawa literary society. Indeed, it was the title of one of the latter's novels, *François de Bienville*, published in Quebec the year she was born, that inspired Marie-Louise to adopt the pen-name she would use most frequently, Louyse de Bienville. In later life she recalled that, when she was still a child, her father had taken her with him to several Quebec literary salons.

Schooled by the Ursulines in Quebec from 1880 to 1882, Marie-Louise was then taught by the nuns of the Congregation of Notre-Dame in Ottawa. She is also thought to have studied literature in Paris, where her family was obliged to make several stays on account of her father's position as an archivist for the federal government. According to her daughter Marguerite, Marie-Louise spent four years in all in the City of Light and thus developed a fondness for French culture. In the summer of 1892, in Ottawa, she married Donat Brodeur, a lawyer. They would subsequently settle in Montreal and have eight children.

Marie-Louise pursued a literary career that is still little known in detail. Between 1902 and 1909 she wrote articles for the *Journal de Françoise*, a Montreal newspaper founded by Robertine Barry*, who was known as Françoise; they were probably among her earliest contributions to periodicals. This association with the women's press in Montreal continued between 1913 and 1915 in the pages of *Pour vous mesdames*, a magazine founded and run by Georgine Bélanger*, who wrote under the name Gaétane de Montreuil. From 1913 to 1916 Brodeur also published articles in *La Bonne Parole*, the organ of the Fédération Nationale Saint-Jean-Baptiste, in which she was active. In particular she gave lectures at the monthly meetings of the Association Professionnelle des Employées de Manufactures and the Association Professionnelle des Employées de Magasins [*see* Marie-Anne LAPORTE], organizations that were sponsored by the federation. In 1920 and 1924 two pieces she wrote appeared in *La Revue moderne*, the journal whose editor was Anne-Marie Gleason*, known as Madeleine. At the same time, Brodeur published articles in newspapers of more general interest, including *Le Temps* of Ottawa, the Montreal paper *Le Pays*, *Le Courrier de Montmagny*, and Quebec's *Le Soleil*. But she would never publish a book.

Brodeur tried her hand at various literary genres,

including newspaper columns on current affairs and literature, biography, novellas, short stories, and poetry. While fascinated by the great figures of the past (from Joan of Arc to her ancestor François-Xavier Garneau), she also occasionally wrote about the state of Canadian literature, as well as about the advent of feminism, which was "one of the developments – the most important – that do honour to humanity," as she noted in *Pour vous mesdames* in October 1913. Always an avid follower of current affairs, she was interested in World War I, partly, of course, as a mother – her three sons having enlisted – but also as a journalist who published several "Pages de guerre" in *Pour vous mesdames* in October 1914 and *La Bonne Parole* in February, March, May, and June 1916. Filled with admiration for the courage shown by the women of France during this struggle, she declared in June 1916 that "a nation made more glorious by such women will never be conquered." When a daily column in *La Presse* invited opinions on the issue of female suffrage, on 18 Jan. 1919 Brodeur unequivocally demanded that women be accorded the right to vote, as well as "its liberal use."

Despite a distinguished career that lasted almost 25 years, Marie-Louise Brodeur has not enjoyed the ongoing fame of a Françoise or a Madeleine. The fact that her writing is scattered in various periodicals doubtless helps account for this neglect. After her death, her daughter Marguerite collected about 30 of her pieces and published them as a book entitled *Figures et paysages* (Montréal, 1931). By this posthumous volume, announced as the first in a series of four, she hoped to pay a well-deserved tribute to her mother. Unfortunately for the historian, there were no further volumes.

LINE GOSSELIN

[The author has compiled a complete list of the articles by Marie-Louise Marmette that appear in *Le Journal de Françoise*, *Pour vous mesdames*, *La Bonne Parole*, and *La Rev. moderne*, all published in Montreal. It is not exhaustive with respect to *La Bonne Parole* because the author was unable to consult the first volume. A copy of this list is available at the DCB. L.G.]

ANQ-Q, CE301-S1, 29 mars 1870. *Le Devoir*, 3 mai 1928, 21 mai 1932. *BCF*, 1923: 243. Georges Bellerive, *Brèves apologies de nos auteurs féminins* (Québec, 1920). *DOLQ*, 2: 493–94. Madeleine [A.-M.] Gleason-Huguenin, *Portraits de femmes* ([Montréal], 1938), 65. Hamel *et al.*, *DALFAN*, 946–47. J. Hamelin *et al.*, *La presse québécoise*, 4: 347. Roger Le Moine, *Joseph Marmette, sa vie, son œuvre, suivi de "À travers la vie, roman de mœurs canadiennes" de Joseph Marmette* (Québec, 1968). *Mariages de la paroisse Sacré-Cœur, Ottawa (1889–1975)*, Julien Hamelin, compil. (Ottawa, s.d.), 24. Gaétane de Montreuil [Georgine Bélanger], "Mme Donat Brodeur," *Pour vous mesdames*, 1 (1913–14): 202–3. M.-E. Vézina, "In memoriam," *La Rev. moderne*, 9 (1928), no.6: 17.

MAROIS, ARTHUR, bricklayer and trade union leader; b. 1 Nov. 1872 at Quebec, son of Ferdinand Marois, a mason, and Marie-Anne Juneau; m. there first 1 Feb. 1892 Adiana Langlois; m. there secondly 24 Oct. 1921 Émélie Bouret, widow of Gaudiose Langlois; four sons and one daughter survived him; d. 27 June 1928 at Quebec.

A bricklayer in Quebec City, Arthur Marois was introduced to trade unionism at a very early age by his father, who had founded a bricklayers' union there in 1880. In the 1890s he belonged to the Union Nationale des Briqueteurs, Plâtriers et Maçons de Québec and was its secretary. Subsequently he became a member of the Union Secourable et Protectrice des Journaliers, which elected him a delegate to the Central Trades and Labor Council (CTLC) of Quebec. At the end of the 19th century he joined the Feuille d'Érable Assembly 1160 of the Knights of Labor, "largely," he would write, "to learn about the organization where I felt the leaders [were]." He had a good opinion of the Knights of Labor, who impressed him with their concern for the "moral and intellectual" advancement of the working class. He did not at that time take umbrage at the organization's American origins, since its leaders left the assemblies considerable autonomy. On the other hand, the condemnation of the Knights of Labor by the archbishop of Quebec, Elzéar-Alexandre Taschereau*, in 1885 had left him with a bitter taste. "Instead of doing the same thing as the American clergy, who not only gather information but sympathize with the workers, ours ... learned only what the gossipmongers reported to them," he would point out in March 1917 in a letter to Alfred Charpentier*, the future president of the Confédération des Travailleurs Catholiques du Canada. Many members had at that time left the Knights of Labor and, according to Marois, the organization did not recover from the blow in Quebec City. From this experience he retained the conviction that the clergy understood nothing about labour issues and that they should not interfere in union affairs.

In 1898 Marois was elected president of the CTLC of Quebec, an office he held until 1901. Established in 1889, the council had a good many Quebec unions affiliated to it; its main role was to represent them on the municipal scene while serving as a forum for discussion of matters affecting the interests of the working class. In September 1900 Marois founded *Le Bulletin mensuel du travail*, Quebec City's first trade union newspaper, which took as its mission "to back and defend programs of organized labour." This monthly, which later became a weekly and which remained in publication until December 1903, sought in particular to support shoemakers' unions in their struggle to be recognized by factory owners. The members of these unions were the victims of a general lockout in October 1900 and, seeing that the conflict was dragging on, the parties agreed to resort to the arbitration of Archbishop Louis-Nazaire BÉGIN of Quebec [see Gaudiose HÉBERT]. One of the three unions affected, the Union des Cordonniers-Machinistes, was, however, particularly reluctant to subject its constitution to the archbishop's examination, as he required, for its leaders deemed that he was overstepping his authority. Marois, then still president of the CTLC, backed the shoemaking machine operators. Like them, he found it hard to understand why "the ecclesiastical authority would have become the competent court for imposing its judgements in purely civil matters." He saw in this development "the manifest, and equally unfortunate, coalition of clerical power and capitalist forces, to enslave poor workers." On 29 Nov. 1901 he sent a voluminous file on this matter to the federal Department of Labour, judging that the cause affected all Canadian workers and all those concerned about civil liberties. "The question," he wrote, "is to know whether from now on everything will have to be subjected to ecclesiastical jurisdiction: finance, commerce, industry, agriculture, work, contracts, our various daily transactions. . . . Do the laws of Canada give bishops the power to bring back the horrors of the Inquisition in their respective dioceses as soon as they can find laymen interested in acting as their secular arm to implement their decisions?" Henry Albert Harper*, the deputy minister, replied cautiously that in his opinion the union should respect the archbishop's decision and that the Department of Labour could not intervene in the conflict. The episode reinforced Marois's opinion that the Catholic clergy should stay far away from union affairs. In March 1917 he would write to Alfred Charpentier: "I fully profess my faith in the Catholic Church, I have all the proper respect for the ministers of God in the teaching of dogmas, but I absolutely deny their fitness in labour matters; with very rare exceptions they do not know the first thing about them, and if you had been permitted, as I was one day, to have a private discussion with His Eminence Cardinal Bégin, and on various occasions with some of our parish priests about the condition of the workers in our country you would, like me, be able to appreciate their mentality and their autocracy, even though for the most part they are workers' sons themselves."

Though he did not much value clerical authority where unions were concerned, Marois nonetheless did not favour workers joining international unions, which were experiencing tremendous expansion in Quebec at the beginning of the 20th century. He reproached the international unions for having "a point of view" that was "Americanizing [and] dominating" and for draining the dues of Canadians into a country "where gold flows." He sought to group workers into purely national unions, judging that

Canadians themselves should determine the direction of their trade union movement. Defiant, he submitted this proposal in 1913 to a meeting of union members from the province of Quebec who belonged to the Bricklayers, Masons, and Plasterers' International Union of America. He suggested to them that they disaffiliate their unions from this organization and that they found a national federation which, once well established in Quebec, could expand across the country. Taking advantage of a wave of discontent with "the International" among his colleagues, he initiated the process in Quebec City in July 1916 by founding the Union Canadienne des Briqueteurs, Maçons et Plâtriers. Two years later the bricklayers of Montreal left their international union and joined the Quebec bricklayers in forming on 24 Nov. 1918 the Canadian Federation of Bricklayers, Masons and Plasterers, which, it was hoped, would spread through Quebec and the rest of Canada. Marois became its secretary-treasurer. The federation gained members in other cities within the province of Quebec and for a time had three unions in Ontario. Eager to "cast off the American yoke" and to give the unions back their national autonomy, it affiliated with the Canadian Federation of Labor, a purely Canadian body, in 1920. However, English Canada responded poorly and the movement remained rather marginal in Canada.

From the time of World War I, national trade unionism also suffered strong competition in Quebec from Catholic unions, which wanted national scope as well. Marois was asked to support turning national unions into Catholic ones, notably by Charpentier, but he refused, not having forgotten the distressing episodes of the early 1900s. He still did not see the need for mixing religion with trade unionism, whose function he held to be purely material. In his view, labour relations were based fundamentally on a balance of power and it was utopian for Catholic trade unionism to want to change their nature. In his letters to Charpentier in 1917 Marois had occasionally intimated that he would be prepared to accept the Catholicizing of the unions but only after they had assumed a national structure for at least 25 years. Delegated by the Union Canadienne des Briqueteurs, Maçons et Plâtriers, which still refused to become a Catholic body, he nevertheless attended the first congress held to prepare for the founding of the Confédération des Travailleurs Catholiques du Canada in Quebec City in 1918. He was not able to participate in the Chicoutimi congress in 1920, however, for only truly Catholic unions were admitted [see Maxime Fortin*].

From 1920 Arthur Marois held the office of secretary of the Fédération des Travailleurs du Bâtiment du Canada, which was linked to the Canadian Federation of Labor. Tenacious and determined, he remained faithful to his principles: a purely Canadian trade unionism that was open to workers of every religious denomination and that separated religion from union activity.

JACQUES ROUILLARD

AC, Québec, État civil, Catholiques, Saint-Roch (Québec), 24 oct. 1921. ANQ-Q, CE301-S96, 1er nov. 1872, 1er févr. 1892. Arch. de l'Univ. Laval (Québec), P212 (fonds Alfred Charpentier), 1/1 (corr. avec Arthur Marois). *Le Bulletin mensuel du travail* (Québec), 1er sept. 1900. *Le Soleil*, 27 juin 1928. Alfred Charpentier, *Ma conversion au syndicalisme catholique* (Montréal, 1946); "Malheureuse aventure d'une ex-'Union canadienne,'" in *Programme-souvenir; fête du travail des syndicats catholiques nationaux* (Montréal, 1930), 10–23. Jacques Rouillard, *Les syndicats nationaux au Québec, de 1900 à 1930* (Québec, 1979).

MARSAN, ISIDORE-JOSEPH-AMÉDÉE, teacher, farm manager, agricultural lecturer, and educational administrator; b. 19 July 1844 in Saint-Roch-de-l'Achigan, Lower Canada, son of Isidore Marsan, *dit* Lapierre, a farmer, and Félonise Poitras; m. 11 July 1871 Marie-Elmire-Ernestine Viger in L'Assomption, Que., and they had twelve children, eight of whom survived him; d. there 25 April 1924.

Isidore-Joseph-Amédée Marsan did his classical studies at the Collège de L'Assomption from 1859 to 1866. He began articling in law, but then decided to enrol in the École d'Agriculture de Sainte-Anne-de-la-Pocatière on the advice of notary Louis Archambeault*, the MLA for L'Assomption who would serve as commissioner of agriculture and public works in the cabinets of Pierre-Joseph-Olivier Chauveau* (1867–73) and Gédéon Ouimet* (1873–74). After attending this establishment for a year, he began his teaching career at the new École d'Agriculture de L'Assomption. It was started in the fall of 1867 by the authorities of the Collège de L'Assomption and was subsidized by the provincial government [*see* Pierre-Urgel Archambault*]. Marsan was already on staff at the school when the Board of Agriculture of Lower Canada, on 11 March 1868, granted him a certificate as a teacher of agriculture. In addition to this subject, he taught geometry and arithmetic. In 1876 he was also put in charge of managing the Ferme Du Portage, 200 *arpents* of land adjoining the school; he would give up this responsibility in October 1895. Marsan had held both positions simultaneously because the government subsidy was insufficient to cover the cost of hiring a manager. His total salary at the time was $800 from an annual budget of $2,000. The school's staff included a principal, a vice-principal, teachers of English, agricultural law, and veterinary medicine, an instructor, and a field assistant. The aim of the program was primarily to train farmers' sons, aged 15 and over, to farm in an informed way and to have them spread their knowledge of farming principles in the rural regions; it was a two-year course for those with

sufficient education. However, Félix-Gabriel Marchand*'s Liberal government wanted to centralize the teaching of agriculture in Sainte-Anne-de-la-Pocatière (La Pocatière) and Oka and thus the school closed in 1899. During its 32 years, 626 students attended this establishment, where Marsan was the only teacher of agriculture.

In addition to teaching, Marsan accepted various other responsibilities at local, regional, and provincial levels. He was churchwarden, municipal councillor, and deputy mayor of L'Assomption, as well as secretary-treasurer of the county's agricultural society, an office he held for 46 years; he would also be secretary-treasurer of the town's school board from 1907. As an agriculture teacher, in 1868 he automatically became a member of the Board of Agriculture of Lower Canada, which had been established by the government in 1852 to assist the commissioner of agriculture and public works, and he sat until 1896 on the Council of Agriculture, which replaced the board. Appointed an agricultural lecturer in 1892, he was named secretary of the judges for the competition of the Order of Agricultural Merit in 1900; he would retain this office for the rest of his life. Obliged by his duties to visit the various regions of Quebec, he acquired a wealth of knowledge about the soils and the state of agriculture in the province, which he was able to share with his students.

At the beginning of the 1903–4 school year, Marsan joined the staff of the École d'Agriculture d'Oka, which had been founded by the Trappists in 1893 [*see* Pierre Oger*]. Recruited as a lecturer, he became a full professor and then scientific director in 1908, when the school became an institute affiliated with the Université Laval in Montreal. Despite its university status, the Institut Agricole d'Oka could not offer its staff very good working conditions. Since there was no housing on the premises, the lay professors had to live in the village about two miles away. As director, Marsan was paid directly by the Department of Agriculture.

A professor and director until 1921, Marsan, along with his colleagues, was to train Quebec's first generation of agronomists. According to his former students, he was a highly talented teacher. An interesting and persuasive speaker, he filled his lectures with examples gleaned during his visits to farmers across the province. Concerned to make his teaching concrete, he also took his classes on field-study trips to Oka and the surrounding areas. He was very approachable.

A man of science, Marsan nonetheless retained a traditional view of agriculture. While favouring intensive cultivation of the soil by new and better farming methods, he wanted families to strive for self-sufficiency; he felt that goods consumed in the home should as far as possible be produced on the farm, rather than bought at a store. He also believed that farming should improve family life.

Isidore-Joseph-Amédée Marsan worked tirelessly for more than a half-century without being justly remunerated for his services to the province. He obtained honours – the first doctorate in agricultural sciences in Quebec in 1916, awarded by the Université Laval, and the special certificate of exceptional merit of the Order of Agricultural Merit in 1921 – but reportedly he died poor. A monument to him was erected in front of the Collège de L'Assomption in 1926.

JACQUES SAINT-PIERRE

ANQ-M, CE605-S12, 19 juill. 1844; S14, 11 juill. 1871. *Le Devoir*, 25 avril 1924. *BCF*, 1922. Georges Boulanger, "Gloire à M. I. J. A. Marsan," *Le Journal d'agriculture* (Montréal), 30 (1926–27), no.4: 56. J.-C. Chapais, "Notes historiques sur les écoles d'agriculture dans Québec," *Rev. canadienne* (Montréal), 70 (janvier–juin 1916): 426–34, 520–27; "Le premier Docteur es-sciences agricoles canadien-français," *Le Journal d'agriculture et d'horticulture illustré* (Montréal), 20 (1916), no.1: 1–2. École d'Agriculture de L'Assomption, *Rapport . . . au Conseil d'agriculture P.Q. pour l'année 1876–1877* (s.l., [1877?]). "J. A. Marsan, 1844–1924," *Le Journal d'agriculture*, 27 (1923–24), no.11: 161, 174. Bruno Jean, *Les idéologies éducatives agricoles (1860–1890) et l'origine de l'agronomie québécoise* (Québec, 1977). Père Louis-Marie, *L'Institut d'Oka: cinquantenaire, 1893–1943; école agricole, institut agronomique, école de médecine vétérinaire* ([Oka, Qué., 1944]). J.-C. Magnan, *Le monde agricole* (Montréal, 1972), 52–53. Réjean Olivier, *La petite histoire du collège de L'Assomption: chroniques parues dans le "Joliette-Journal" de janvier à juin 1980* (L'Assomption, Qué., 1980). Qué., Assemblée Législative, *Débats*, 1924: 333–39.

MARTIN, CLARA BRETT, lawyer and office holder; b. 25 Jan. 1874 in Toronto, daughter of Abraham Martin and Elizabeth Brett; d. there unmarried 31 Oct. 1923.

Clara Brett Martin was the youngest of the 12 children of Anglican Irish farmers in Mono Township. The family, who moved to Toronto in the early 1870s, prized schooling: Clara's father had been a township superintendent of education and at least three of her siblings became teachers. In an era when less than one per cent of the Canadian population undertook post-secondary education, all of the Martin children spent some time at university. Clara entered Toronto's Trinity College in 1888, a mere three years after it had begun to admit females. Women's efforts to enrol in universities inspired considerable controversy at the time; physicians speculated that higher education would weaken them physically and mentally. Defying all predictions, the young Clara, who would later be pronounced attractive, graceful, and possessed of "treasured feminine charms," majored in mathematics

and graduated with a BA and high honours on 27 June 1890, at the age of 16.

In Hilary term 1891 Martin petitioned the Law Society of Upper Canada to admit her as its first female student-at-law. A committee chaired by Samuel Hume Blake* refused her request in June and advised that she should seek legislative clarification of women's access to the profession. William Douglas Balfour*, the MPP for Essex South, introduced a bill in March 1892 stipulating that women be admitted to the practice of law. The bill was subjected to a blistering attack from opposition leader William Ralph MEREDITH. Nature, he insisted, dictated that admission to law would prove "disastrous to the best interests of women," and he conjectured that fashion-conscious women would never want to wear the same official robes as male litigators. Martin found support in many powerful quarters, however, including Dr Emily Howard Stowe [Jennings*], a leading proponent of the women's movement, and Oliver Mowat*, Ontario's premier and attorney general. In the end a compromise statute was enacted on 13 April 1892 that gave the society the discretionary power to admit women to the level of solicitor.

The recalcitrant benchers of the society met five months later, deliberated over the permissive wording of the legislation, and then voted to deny Martin's application of 21 June on the grounds that it was "inexpedient" to frame rules for admitting women. Mowat appeared before the society's convocation on 9 December to argue Martin's case. After a heated discussion, the vote on the motion for admission came out as a tie. Chair Æmilius Irving* broke the impasse in favour of the motion, prompting the *Western Law Times of Canada* (Winnipeg) to regret that the entry of women had been occasioned by a single vote, which represented neither "the wishes of a large majority of the profession" nor the will of the benchers "if they only had the manliness to speak out."

Martin began articling in June 1893 with the Toronto firm of Mulock, Miller, Crowther, and Montgomery, but the unpleasant treatment she received there from her articling peers and the firm's secretaries forced her to switch to Blake, Lash, and Cassels. Sitting through lectures at Osgoode Hall was no easier: students hissed when she entered the room and some lecturers attempted to humiliate her by emphasizing points relating to sex. Martin passed her examinations handily despite this abuse, and she would go on to obtain a BCL from Trinity in 1897 and an LLB from the University of Toronto in 1899.

Eligible to be admitted as a solicitor in June 1896, she chose instead, while completing her articles, to join battle once more with the Law Society and seek admission as both a barrister and a solicitor. The widespread lobbying required for yet another legislative enactment elicited support from Lady Aberdeen

[Marjoribanks*] (the wife of the governor general) and the members of the National Council of Women of Canada and the International Council of Women. In March 1895 William Bruce Wood, the MPP for Brant North, brought in a bill to permit the society to admit women as barristers. After considerable debate over the dangers female litigators might pose to the "homes and womanhood of Ontario," the measure passed, and received royal assent on 16 April. The society continued to drag its feet, first exercising its discretion to refuse Martin's call as a barrister, and then sending the matter to committee. The benchers finally caved in to pressure from Mowat and a skilfully mounted public lobby. On 2 Feb. 1897, at 23, Clara Brett Martin was admitted as a barrister and a solicitor, the first woman in the British empire to achieve such status.

She began practice with the Toronto firm of Shilton, Wallbridge and Company, became a partner in 1901, and left to set up her own office in 1906. Her practice centred on wills, real estate, and family law. The profession she had joined was viciously anti-Semitic, and she shared much of its hostility to Jews. One of the few surviving letters from her business files is a missive in 1915 to Edward Bayly, solicitor to the attorney general's department, in which she accused certain Jewish realtors of transferring property titles improperly and misleading some of her clients about outstanding claims. She asked that the registry act be amended to prevent "such scandalous work" by Jewish "foreigners."

A frequent lecturer to women's organizations, Martin hired a number of female articling students and joined with advocates of women's rights to lobby for female suffrage and a separate court for women within the Toronto Police Court. In an article written for the National Council of Women in 1900, she attacked the dual standard of sexuality in law, in particular the legal disadvantages of married women and the supremacy of paternal rights in cases involving child custody. Law and women's rights, however, were not her only interests. In the 1890s, while living on Homewood Avenue with her mother and brother Robert Thomas, a school principal, she had joined her family's long-running involvement in education. She was a member of the Toronto Collegiate Institute Board in 1896–99 and of the Public School Board in 1901–10. During her time with these boards she achieved a reputation as a path-breaker in the field of equal intellectual rights for women. In 1920 she ran as an aldermanic candidate in Ward 2 but was narrowly defeated.

Clara Brett Martin died at age 49 of a heart attack at her home on Roxborough Street East and was buried in St James' Cemetery. She had bequeathed her property to her unmarried sister Fanny. Extensive obituaries in Toronto newspapers lamented her passing as the loss of a trailblazer for women in professional life.

CONSTANCE BACKHOUSE

Family information concerning Clara Brett Martin was supplied to the author in a letter of 9 Aug. 1984 from Betty L. Hall of Lockport, N.Y., a great-niece of the subject. The issue of Martin's anti-Semitism is discussed in a series of articles in the *Canadian Journal of Women and the Law* (Ottawa), 5 (1992): 263–356.

Martin's publications include "Legal status of women in the provinces of the Dominion of Canada (except the province of Quebec)," in National Council of Women of Canada, *Women of Canada: their life and work; compiled . . . for distribution at the Paris international exhibition, 1900* ([Montreal?, 1900]; repr. [Ottawa], 1975), 34–40, and "Women in law," an undated clipping from the *Illustrated Buffalo Herald* (Buffalo, N.Y.) preserved in Martin's file in the archives of the Women's Law Assoc. of Ontario, Toronto.

AO, RG 80-8-0-912, no.6854. Toronto Board of Education, Records, Arch., and Museum, Toronto Collegiate Institute Board, minutes, 1896–98; Toronto Public School Board, minutes, 1901–10. *Evening Telegram* (Toronto), 31 Oct., 1 Nov. 1923. *Globe*, 18 Feb. 1910, 1–2 Nov. 1923. *Toronto Daily Star*, 24 April 1914, 1 Nov. 1923. Alexandra Anderson, "The first woman lawyer in Canada: Clara Brett Martin," *Canadian Women's Studies* ([Toronto]), 2 (1980), no.4: 9–11. Constance Backhouse, *Petticoats and prejudice: women and law in nineteenth-century Canada* ([Toronto], 1991), 293–326; "'To open the way for others of my sex': Clara Brett Martin's career as Canada's first woman lawyer," *Canadian Journal of Women and the Law*, 1 (1985–86): 1–41. Isabel Bassett, *The parlour rebellion: profiles in the struggle for women's rights* (Toronto, 1975). *Canadian men and women of the time* (Morgan; 1912). *Directory*, Toronto, 1888–1923. "Laws affecting women in Ontario," *Canadian White Ribbon Tidings* (London, Ont.), 1 Aug. 1912: 2258–59. Theresa Roth, "Clara Brett Martin – Canada's pioneer woman lawyer," Law Soc. of Upper Canada, *Gazette* (Toronto), 18 (1984): 323–40. H. R. S. Ryan, "A pilgrim's progress" (transcript, n.d.; copy in QUA). *Types of Canadian women . . .* , ed. H. J. Morgan (Toronto, 1903).

MARTIN, JOSEPH, teacher, lawyer, politician, and businessman; b. 24 Sept. 1852 in Milton, Upper Canada, son of Edward Martin, a miller, and Mary Ann Fleming; m. 2 Sept. 1881, in Ottawa, Elizabeth Jane (Eliza) Reilly (d. 1913), widow of George Washington Eaton; they had no children; d. 2 March 1923 in Vancouver.

Joseph Martin went to school in Milton until 1865. That year his family moved to Michigan, where he then worked as a telegrapher. He was briefly involved with the Patrons of Husbandry, a farmers' protest movement, before entering the Michigan State Normal School in Ypsilanti in 1872. The following year he transferred to the Normal School in Toronto, from which he was expelled in 1874 for unruly behaviour. His quarrelsome nature and his tendency to resort to his fists to settle disputes would soon earn him the nickname Fighting Joe. Suspicious in nature and with a capacity for pettiness, he would be known throughout his career for his feisty, combative spirit. He would also demonstrate considerable eagerness to advance his own interests.

After his expulsion, Martin taught school in Ottawa for three years on a second-class certificate; there he embraced liberalism and developed strong anti-French sentiments. In 1877 he entered the University of Toronto, but he left two years later without a degree. On his return to Ottawa, he began his articles for law. In 1881 he married Eliza Eaton and became a stepfather to her young daughter, Irma Livingstone Eaton. His additional responsibilities prompted him to make a new beginning in Manitoba. In late 1881 he arrived with his family in Winnipeg, but thinking that Portage la Prairie held out more immediate prospects, they moved there early in 1882. Martin was admitted to the Manitoba bar late in the summer. He established a successful legal practice and took an articling student, Smith Curtis, who would later become his partner. A prominent figure, Martin was soon drawn into provincial politics as part of the growing opposition to Premier John Norquay*.

In January 1883 Martin contested Portage la Prairie as a supporter of Thomas Greenway*'s Provincial Rights party, which would form the nucleus of the provincial Liberal party shortly after the election. He won narrowly, but the results were overturned. Successful in the by-election of May 1883, he would hold the seat until 1891. His feistiness made him effective in opposition; he was a skilful debater with a biting wit. He took a leading role in the assembly, criticizing Norquay and the Canadian Pacific Railway's monopoly in the west. His attacks became harsher as Prime Minister Sir John A. Macdonald* began to disallow railway charters that had been passed by the provincial legislature. On 19 Jan. 1888 Greenway formed the first frankly party government in the province. Martin was installed as attorney general and commissioner of railways.

When the CPR abandoned its monopoly a few months later, Greenway seized the credit and the occasion to call a general election for July; he won a smashing victory. Pressure was now on the new ministry to provide an alternative to the CPR. Martin and Greenway had few choices. They opted later that month to sell the unfinished Red River Valley Railway to American railway builder Henry Villard, who would complete the line to Winnipeg and link it to his Northern Pacific Railroad. The unsatisfactory deal irritated Winnipeg Liberals who had promoted another railway, disappointed farmers who had expected more substantial rate reductions, and might have created considerable political difficulty for Martin and his colleagues if the Manitoba school question had not intervened. Historians have speculated that the controversial school legislation was intended to distract voters from the unpopular railway agreement.

Although Martin was only one of several key figures in the school question, he played a role that was typically provocative. At a public meeting in Portage la Prairie on 5 Aug. 1889 he followed Ontario MP D'Alton McCarthy*'s attack on Quebec and French-language rights with an excited announcement that the Greenway government would reform the dual public school system and end government printing in French. He admitted, almost contritely, to Greenway the next day that he might have been carried away by the occasion and by his knowledge that the Liberal caucus had already decided to act on the school matter. Greenway could have disavowed Martin's declarations. He chose to proceed.

Martin introduced the new school legislation early in 1890 and thus set in motion a political upheaval that would last over a decade. He probably benefited initially from the popularity of the measures; at the same time, however, he was under severe attack from the *Manitoba Free Press* for conspiring to rig land sales in Portage la Prairie, a charge he chose, perhaps wisely, to leave unanswered. In December his new school legislation faced a legal challenge from Winnipeg ratepayer John Kelly Barrett*, who refused to pay his school taxes. Martin successfully represented the interests of the provincial government when the case went before the Court of Queen's Bench.

Meanwhile, Martin's influence in Manitoba was on the wane and his constant quarrels with local notables made him a political liability. Seeking a new political arena, he resigned his provincial seat in February 1891 in order to contest Selkirk, unsuccessfully, in the federal general election of March. He regained his provincial seat in the by-election held later that month to fill the vacancy. In mid April he resigned as attorney general and went back to his law practice and to a milling business he had opened in Portage la Prairie. He represented Manitoba in the Barrett case, on appeal before the Supreme Court of Canada and in London before the Judicial Committee of the Privy Council, where the provincial legislation was upheld in a decision rendered on 30 July 1892.

Surprisingly, Martin won the traditionally Conservative riding of Winnipeg in a federal by-election held in November 1893. He did not fit easily into the Liberal caucus. His free trade sentiments rubbed against the party's increasingly flexible position on the tariff and his French Canadian colleagues resented the role he had played in the school question. Liberal leader Wilfrid Laurier* succeeded in moderating the fiery Manitoban's slashing style. Martin took part in the long filibuster in 1896 which finally forced Conservative party leader Sir Charles Tupper* to withdraw the government's remedial school legislation and call a general election for June. Despite the rising prospects of the Liberals, Martin lost his seat. He hoped that Laurier, now prime minister, would appoint him minister of the interior nonetheless, but Clifford SIFTON, the new Liberal master of the west, was chosen and Martin, without much justification, felt he had been betrayed.

In a rather extraordinary turn of events, Martin was offered a position by the CPR, probably to neutralize him. Even more curiously, he accepted and became the company's solicitor in British Columbia. The British Columbia press did not put out a welcome mat. One editor, John Houston*, urged Manitobans to keep Martin "and send on your blizzard." Only Hewitt BOSTOCK's *Province* (Victoria) seemed to look favourably on his coming. Martin arrived in Vancouver on 5 March 1897 and was soon in practice. His legal career was not without controversy. For example, in 1899 the benchers suspended him for a week for prosecuting in a civil suit on the understanding that if he won, he would receive part of the proceeds. This practice of champerty, which he had legalized in Manitoba, was contrary to the regulations of the Law Society of British Columbia. He pressed for its legalization and in 1901 the assembly would pass the necessary amendments to the Legal Professions Act.

Martin wasted little time in getting into politics. British Columbians supported Liberals or Conservatives federally but eschewed party lines provincially. Until 1903 provincial governments would be loose coalitions. Candidates presented themselves as supporters of the government or the opposition. During the provincial election of 1898 Martin ran successfully in Vancouver as an opposition candidate, criticizing the government of John Herbert TURNER and its links with railway and mining magnates Daniel Chase Corbin*, Frederick Augustus Heinze, and James Dunsmuir*. He initially rejected Charles Augustus SEMLIN's offer of the attorney generalship, perhaps because he hoped to become leader of the new administration, but changed his mind and accepted.

As attorney general and acting minister of education from 15 Aug. 1898, Martin introduced some reforms, of which the most important was the implementation of the Torrens system of land registration [*see* Louis William Coutlée*]. He had difficulty being a team player, however, and his propensity to change his mind made him unpredictable. His blurring of the distinction between his public and private responsibilities brought him into conflict with his legal clients and with his cabinet colleagues, especially the minister of finance, Francis Lovett Carter-Cotton*. Semlin soon lost faith in Martin. On 1 July 1899 he asked him to resign, reportedly because he had neglected departmental business to work on his own legal practice, had revealed cabinet's private business, and, "while the worse for liquor," had lost his temper when heckled by irate mine owners at a banquet in Rossland. Martin

resigned as attorney general and "vowed vengeance" on those responsible for his overthrow, especially Carter-Cotton.

Early in the next session, Martin seemed to have become reconciled with his former political foe Dunsmuir. He attacked Semlin's government on various issues and in late February 1900, despite his promise to support a government-sponsored redistribution bill, he joined with the opposition to defeat the legislation and the Semlin administration. A few days later Lieutenant Governor Thomas Robert McInnes asked Martin to form a government; he accepted and took office on 28 February. On 1 March 1900 members dropped their usual differences and almost unanimously voted no confidence in Martin. Nevertheless he prepared his election platform. Among its most important points, he endorsed government ownership of railways and undertook to arrange for construction of the Coast-Kootenay Railway. Recognizing labour problems in the Kootenay mines, he accepted the principle of the eight-hour day. He also promised to re-enact a statute concerning Asian labour that had been disallowed by the federal government. Although the executive of the Vancouver Liberal Association quickly endorsed his policies, the executive of the provincial association unanimously opposed his premiership and the introduction of party lines.

In forming his cabinet Martin attempted to appoint only Liberals. Initially, he named Smith Curtis, his old friend and former legal partner from Portage la Prairie, minister of mines, and James Stuart Yates of Victoria commissioner of both lands and public works. Neither had a seat in the assembly. As weeks passed, even some of Martin's friends complained of his failure to complete the cabinet. The appointment of George Washington Beebe, a Fraser valley farmer with no previous legislative experience, as provincial secretary drew little attention, but a few Liberals called the selection of another unknown, Cory Spencer Ryder, a small shopkeeper, as minister of finance and agriculture "an insult to the intelligence of the people." As criticism of Ryder's incompetence mounted, Martin replaced him with the more creditable John Cunningham Brown, the postmaster from New Westminster. Shortly thereafter, Martin called an election for 9 June. Despite a vigorous campaign, he and his forces were overwhelmingly defeated. He won in Vancouver, but lost in Victoria, where he had also run. Only five of his followers were elected. McInnes called on Dunsmuir to form an administration.

Martin became de facto the leader of the opposition. By the spring of 1901 the press noted evidence of "extreme friendliness" between him and Dunsmuir. He spoke in favour of the government's railway legislation, but dismissed as "poppycock" suggestions that he "was the guiding spirit of the administration." Although his position within the Liberal party continued to be contested, the provincial Liberal convention of February 1902 unanimously adopted the party lines he favoured and elected him leader. As such, he claimed to be the leader of the opposition in the assembly, an assertion that led to a shoving match that same month with Conservative Richard McBride*, the other claimant to the title, over physical possession of the opposition leader's chair in the chamber. Nevertheless, Martin continued to cooperate with the Dunsmuir government since he believed it was better than a strictly Conservative administration, which might be formed if Dunsmuir were defeated. His fears were confirmed in November when Dunsmuir resigned and was replaced by Edward Gawler Prior, a well-known Conservative.

On 3 June 1903 Martin relinquished the Liberal leadership. He believed Vancouver Liberals were planning to depose him. Moreover, he had just been released from hospital after a painful operation on his leg (a childhood injury had left him with a slight limp). For him, the loss of his seat in Vancouver during the general election of 3 October was anti-climactic. The Vancouver electorate was tiring of his brand of politics; they elected a solid slate of Conservatives. The next day Martin told reporters of the *Vancouver Daily Province* that he had quit "for all time" because he was "disgusted with politics" and "so much abuse from my enemies and so little thanks from my friends." The second part of the statement was probably true; the first was not. Martin turned his attention to the federal field. In 1905 he dropped his Liberal affiliation, explaining that Laurier's attempt to impose separate schools on the new provinces of Alberta and Saskatchewan meant that the Liberals "no longer believe in provincial rights." Like most British Columbian politicians of his day, he strongly opposed the presence of Asians. In 1908 he ran unsuccessfully as the candidate of the Asiatic Exclusion League in the federal constituency of Vancouver City. In private life, he inserted covenants on property he owned in the Hastings (Vancouver) townsite forbidding its sale or lease to Asians.

Martin had retained his legal practice and continued to have a variety of clients, including the city of Vancouver which, in April 1905, had appointed him counsel at $2,500 per year. It was not a full-time job; he was consulted only in important cases. In December he resigned to become general counsel in British Columbia for the Great Northern Railroad and its subsidiary, the Vancouver, Westminster and Yukon Railway. He also presented the Vancouver Board of Trade's case against CPR freight rates to the Board of Railway Commissioners early in 1906.

Although his legal practice and his heavy investments in real estate earned him a comfortable income, Martin was obviously not happy with his situation in British Columbia. Early in 1909 he announced that he was leaving to spend the rest of his days in London,

England, because "there is nothing there a person can not have." The *Vancouver Daily Province* praised his "undoubted ability for affairs" and "integrity of purpose" but noted that his "defects of temper" "made him almost impossible as a member of any government and a constant source of disquiet, if not of confusion, as a member of a party."

Within days of arriving in Britain, Martin had secured the Liberal nomination for a by-election in Warwickshire, Stratford-on-Avon Division, where he called for abolition of the House of Lords, votes for women, a land tax, and free trade. He did not win but made such an impression that he got the Liberal nomination in St Pancras, East Division, for the general election of 1910. He won. In the British House of Commons he appears to have shown many of the same characteristics he had demonstrated in Canada. Nevertheless, he would remain a member of the house until the dissolution of the war-extended parliament in 1918.

Martin did not stay in London, however. In 1914 he had returned to Vancouver and had begun attacking the provincial Liberal party, then in opposition. He ran as an independent in the provincial election of 1920 in Vancouver and lost, but not badly. In the meantime, the improving values of his real estate holdings in British Columbia had let him "redeem his promise to his constituents [in St Pancras] to return whenever he could." By the early 1920s his health was failing. He died in Vancouver on 2 March 1923. The immediate cause of death was influenza, complicated by diabetes. Ironically, he had just begun to take the newly discovered insulin treatment. As the *Victoria Daily Times* noted, "The fact that during the last few years of his life he played no very active part in politics was due to no fault of his own, but rather to his sinister record as a disruptive force, which made all parties fear his support as much as his opposition." To the end, Fighting Joe Martin remained a stormy petrel in politics.

J. E. REA and PATRICIA E. ROY

Several of Joseph Martin's speeches have been published; a list of these can be found in CIHM, *Reg.*

AM, GR 1662. AO, RG 80-2-0-64, no.2388; RG 80-5-0-96, no.2040. BCA, E/D/M362; VF90, frames 0006–0084. LAC, MG 26, G. *Daily Colonist* (Victoria), 29 May, 28 June, 5 July 1898; 2, 11 May, 6, 10 June, 4–6, 9 July, 9, 15 Aug., 6 Sept. 1899; 11 Jan., 24, 28 Feb., 2, 11 March 1900. *Daily Columbian* (New Westminster, B.C.), 26–27 April 1900; 8 May, 4 Sept. 1901; 8 Feb. 1902. *Daily News-Advertiser* (Vancouver), 18 June, 6 July 1898; 24 Jan. 1899; 1–2, 10 March, 7 April, 4, 12–13, 18 May 1900; 5 May 1901. *Manitoba Free Press*, 1882–97. *Province* (Victoria), 31 Oct. 1896, 30 Oct. 1897; (Vancouver), 10, 21, 30 May, 15, 22, 26 June, 11, 13, 15, 18 Aug. 1898; 19 Jan., 9, 15 May, 5, 28 July, 5 Sept. 1899; 8, 16 Jan. 1900. *Vancouver Daily Province*, 10 Feb., 5 April, 18 May 1900; 8 Feb., 7 May, 5, 7, 16 Sept., 11, 18 Oct. 1901; 24 Feb., 22 May 1902; 17 March, 20, 23 April,

3 June, 5 Oct. 1903; 15 April, 15 Sept., 7 Dec. 1905; 5 Jan., 11 July 1906; 27 Feb., 24 March, 13 April, 3 May 1909; 24 March 1910. *Vancouver News-Herald*, 8 Aug. 1939. *Vancouver Semi-Weekly World*, 24 Sept. 1896; 24 June 1898; 2, 6 March, 4 April 1900. *Vancouver Sun*, 12 Feb. 1922, 3 March 1923. *Victoria Daily Times*, 8 Jan., 15 Feb., 2, 8 March, 6, 19 April, 6 May, 8 June 1900; 24 April 1901; 29 Aug. 1916; 31 Jan. 1917; 2 March 1923. *Winnipeg Tribune*, 1890–97. P. [J.] Brock, *Fighting Joe Martin, founder of the Liberal party in the west: a blow-by-blow account* (Toronto, 1981). *Canadian men and women of the time* (Morgan; 1898 and 1912). *CPG*, 1883–1920. *Electoral hist. of B.C.* D. J. Hall, *Clifford Sifton* (2v., Vancouver and London, 1981–85). J. A. Hilts, "The political career of Thomas Greenway" (PHD thesis, Univ. of Man., Winnipeg, 1974). J. R. Miller, "D'Alton McCarthy, equal rights, and the origins of the Manitoba school question," *CHR*, 54 (1973): 369–92. P. E. Roy, *A white man's province: British Columbia politicians and Chinese and Japanese immigrants, 1858–1914* (Vancouver, 1989). *Who's who of British members of parliament . . .* , ed. Michael Stanton and Stephen Lees (4v., Brighton, Eng., and Atlantic Highlands, N.J., 1976–81), 2.

MARY CLARE, Sister. *See* CONNOLLY

MASSICOTTE, EDMOND-JOSEPH (baptized **Joseph-Edmond**), artist and illustrator; b. 1 Dec. 1875 in Sainte-Cunégonde (Montreal), son of Édouard Massicotte, a shoemaker, and Adèle Bertrand; m. 3 Feb. 1914 Aldine Émond in Montreal, and they had one daughter; d. there 1 March 1929.

Edmond-Joseph Massicotte took commercial courses and had his first lessons in drawing and painting with the Brothers of the Christian Schools in Sainte-Cunégonde. He then studied with Edmond Dyonnet at the Council of Arts and Manufactures of the Province of Quebec in Montreal from 1892 to about 1895, and finally with William BRYMNER at the school run by the Art Association of Montreal. On 15 Oct. 1892 the Montreal magazine *Le Monde illustré* published his first illustration, which accompanied a poem entitled "Le glaneur" that had been written by his brother, Édouard-Zotique*. Thus began, on the theme of the land, the close collaboration between the Massicotte brothers. Before confining himself to the role of portraying habitants, however, Edmond-Joseph would become the spearhead of a particular kind of modernism.

The international style known as art nouveau, in which sinuous lines convey the sensuous charms of human figures, would strongly influence Edmond-Joseph's early work. His rapid conversion was probably due to Édouard-Zotique, who was then described as a "young barbarian" because of his attachment to the European symbolist movement. The decorated title and allegorical figure the illustrator drew around 1895 for the cover of *L'Écho des jeunes*, a magazine launched in Sainte-Cunégonde in 1891 (to which Édouard-Zotique contributed), seemed the emblem of the direction that the visual arts would take, alongside the new Quebec literature, with its "decadent" inspiration. Although Édouard-Zotique's literary revolt was of short duration, Edmond-Joseph would spend another dozen years in mastering a modernism that would be useful in his work as an illustrator.

Massicotte was probably the only graphic artist in the province of Quebec to espouse the art nouveau movement at the time when it was flourishing in Europe. A number of followers subsequently appeared, including his fellow students in Sainte-Cunégonde, Henri Fabien and Georges Latour, his colleagues Raoul Barré and Albert-Samuel Brodeur at *Le Passe-Temps* (Montreal), Paul Caron, with whom he worked at *Le Monde illustré*, and even, for a short time, the traditionalist Henri Julien*.

The success of art nouveau in Montreal was the more remarkable given that Massicotte's eye and hand provided only sporadic support to the cause. His main ambition lay elsewhere. On 3 March 1900 he made a point of listing in *Le Passe-Temps* the illustrators whom he admired: first, the Americans Charles Dana Gibson, a prolific artist, and Charles Stanley Reinhart; among the French, Gustave-Henri Marchetti and Jean-André Castaigne as well as Alfons Mucha (a Czech by birth); and lastly his compatriot Julien.

Except for Mucha, the illustrators Massicotte so admired were not part of the art nouveau movement, but rather fashionable graphic artists of their times. They were witty and even daring, and their concept of style had more to do with their subject than with the actual drawing. What they all had in common was technical virtuosity, and their favourite milieu was high society. Massicotte's pencil was guided as well by the pursuit of virtuosity and social elegance. The bourgeois types he sketched – mostly friends or family members – were reminiscent of Gibson's. These elegant figures, hundreds of whom can be found in the artist's sketch books, were often used in designing advertisements. Nevertheless, a set of working-class and rural themes also evolved in his portfolio. Before adopting Julien's traditionalist realism, then, Massicotte was torn between Mucha's austerity and symmetry and Gibson's modern elegance.

Massicotte was prolific. By the beginning of the 20th century, some 1,000 of his designs and compositions graced publications in Montreal. In addition to illustrating newspapers, literary works, and promotional materials, he did amusing drawings, especially for *Le Canard*, a humorous Montreal newspaper, from 1896 to 1898. During his ten years at *Le Monde illustré*, from 1892 to 1902, he published 237 drawings, including several caricatures. The spectacular title pages Massicotte created for it from the fall of 1900 to Easter 1901 – at least three of which were directly inspired by Mucha – seemed to proclaim that the magazine (under the editorship of Édouard-Zotique) had

715

adopted the modernism of the new century. This series marked the high point of the art nouveau style in the artist's work, but it was also the catalyst of the movement – which he himself would soon abandon – in illustrated publications in Quebec. To judge from his less daring use of art nouveau, his voluptuous human forms probably offended public sensibilities. From 1895 to 1910 Massicotte contributed occasionally to *Le Passe-Temps*, producing portraits, illustrations, and impressions of theatrical performances, sketched on the spot and referred to as "illustrated theatre." He abandoned the latter in 1902, just as he was beginning a series of "Canadian types" in *Le Passe-Temps*.

By that year Massicotte's venture into utterly pure art nouveau had come to an end. He would henceforth strive for synthesis, a desire to reconcile the new and the old which would remain with him until 1908. Some of the drawings he did for the Montreal magazine *L'Album universel* (the name adopted by *Le Monde illustré* in 1902), where he worked until 1910, reveal an attempt to combine modernist style and traditional design. One example is the cover page of the 18 April 1903 issue of *Les Sucres*, a composition marked by a strong graphic statement whose flattened perspective is similar to the American poster style.

In 1909 Massicotte succeeded Julien, who had died the previous year, at the Montreal publication *Almanach du peuple*, for which he would draw more than 150 illustrations by 1929. This event marked a significant turn in his career as an illustrator; he now became the leading interpreter of traditional Quebec life. His brother clearly played a major role in this phase too, since the search for cultural authenticity in his works relied on the research done by Édouard-Zotique, who was a historian and folklorist.

Massicotte's fame rests primarily on the 12 plates he published in Montreal in 1923 under the title *Nos Canadiens d'autrefois*. Most of them had already appeared in the *Almanach du peuple*, and they were now supplemented by commentaries from such prominent writers as Albert Ferland*, Lionel Groulx*, and Marius Barbeau*. Five others, intended for a second volume that had not been completed at the time of Massicotte's death, were added to them. The title of any one of them suffices to evoke a familiar picture, for example *La bénédiction du jour de l'An* and *Le retour de la messe de minuit*. Massicotte achieved the elegant simplicity of these plates by purging his artistic vocabulary of modernistic fantasy. He was indebted to modernism, however, for their incisive graphic expression, which brought about such a fine marriage of line and motif.

Edmond-Joseph Massicotte died at the age of 53 following an attack of paralysis. Since the taste for traditional rural imagery was already fading at the time, he probably had no inkling of how durable his contribution would be. Having left no paintings to speak of,

Massicotte has not yet taken his rightful place in art history.

DAVID KAREL

An inventory of Edmond-Joseph Massicotte's promotional illustrations has yet to be compiled. It is known, for instance, that between 1906 and 1908 he prepared numerous advertisements for the Merchants Awning Company Limited.

Massicotte illustrated several books apart from his brother Édouard-Zotique's *La cité de Sainte-Cunégonde de Montréal: notes et souvenirs* (Montréal, 1893). The first was Wenceslas-Eugène Dick's *Un drame au Labrador* (Montréal, [1897?]), where his style is reminiscent of late European realism. In 1899 in Montréal, Édouard-Zotique's *Monographies de plantes canadiennes, suivies de croquis champêtres et d'un calendrier de la flore de la province de Québec* was published, illustrated by Edmond-Joseph with quasi-scientific precision in mind. In the same vein were Massicotte's drawings for his brother's book *Cent fleurs de mon herbier: études sur le monde végétal à la portée de tous, suivies d'un calendrier de la flore de la province de Québec* (Montréal, 1906); here he republished the illustrations that had originally appeared in the series *Nos fleurs canadiennes* in *Le Monde illustré* (Montréal) between 30 July 1893 and 22 June 1901. In addition, he prepared four drawings for Pamphile Le May*'s *Contes vrais* (2ᵉ éd., Montréal, 1907), drew 16 pen portraits for his brother's book *Conteurs canadiens-français du XIXᵉ siècle* (Montréal, 1902), provided for publication a set of illustrations for a novel by Laure Conan [Félicité ANGERS], *À l'œuvre et à l'épreuve* (3ᵉ éd., Montréal, 1914), created 22 illustrations for Auguste Tressol, named Brother Théodule, *Mes premières leçons de rédaction* (Montréal, 1914), and illustrated *Récits laurentiens* (Montréal, 1919) and *Croquis laurentiens* (Montréal, 1920) by Brother Marie-Victorin [Conrad Kirouac*] and Constant DOYON's *Au régime de l'eau* (Québec, 1919).

Massicotte also contributed to the *Almanach Rolland agricole, commercial et des familles de la compagnie J.-B. Rolland & fils* (Montréal), 1915–28, the *Almanach de l'Action sociale catholique* (Québec), 1918–24, and the *Annuaire Granger pour la jeunesse* (Montréal), 1926–29.

The publication of Bernard Genest's study *Massicotte et son temps* (Montréal, 1979) attests to renewed interest in the traditional aspect of Massicotte's work, and the awareness of his contribution to modernism is evidenced in Pierre Landry, "L'apport de l'Art nouveau aux arts graphiques, au Québec, de 1898 à 1910" (thèse de MA, univ. Laval, Québec, 1983).

Massicotte's works are available in the LAC's Documentary Art and Photography Div., 03391 and 120-080260-8 (the latter's inventory includes 300 items); the Musée Louis-Hémon (Péribonka, Qué.), which holds around 50 of his drawings (primarily buildings, historical figures, and anatomical studies); the Musée de la Ville de Lachine, Qué., which has 5 drawings; and the Musée National des Beaux-Arts du Québec, where the E.-J. Massicotte file conserves his 17 notebooks (dated for the most part between 1897 and 1918), containing 1,655 drawings, and 27 prints. Several other institutions hold collections of Massicotte's engravings and illustrations, among them the Musée Pierre-Boucher (Trois-Rivières, Qué.), the Musée d'Art de Joliette, Qué. (one drawing and several prints), and the McCord Museum of Canadian Hist. in Montreal (one drawing and several prints).

ANQ-M, CE601-S19, 2 déc. 1875. BCM-G, RBMS, Saint-Pierre-Apôtre (Montréal), 3 févr. 1914. *Le Devoir*, 2, 4 mars 1929.

MATHESON, JOHN, farmer; b. 29 Jan. 1838 at Big Bras d'Or, N.S., son of Hugh Matheson and Margaret McKenzie; m. first *c.* 1864 Sarah Fraser in Kincardine Township, Upper Canada, and they had one daughter; m. there secondly 7 Jan. 1869 Margaret McLennan, and they had two daughters and seven sons; d. there 29 July 1922.

Born on Cape Breton Island, John Matheson was the eldest of nine children of Scots Presbyterian parents. His father, a native of Assynt, Scotland, came to the Maritimes as part of the Highland diaspora; his mother was from Millbrook, near Pictou, N.S. Likely discouraged by poor soil and famine conditions on the Island, the Mathesons emigrated in 1852 to the recently surveyed Kincardine Township on the Bruce peninsula, part of the last settlement frontier in southern Upper Canada. John helped his family make a farm out of its thick, primeval forest – cutting trees, removing stumps, planting early crops, and erecting a home and outbuildings. The Mathesons survived the drought of 1858 and the resultant hunger of 1859, and John's father took out the crown deed on the farm in 1861.

In the following year John struck out on his own, purchasing a 50-acre property a mile to the southeast. He married a neighbour, Sarah Fraser, but she died in 1865, likely after childbirth; their daughter survived to be raised by John's parents. There is no record of his response to this tragedy. He forged on with his settlement duties, assisted by his brother Donald, who was working an adjacent lot. Having proved up, John married Margaret McLennan of nearby Ashfield Township in 1869.

After John expanded his farm by 25 acres in 1871, it remained stable for the next quarter-century. Life, however, was transformed by the arrival of nine children between 1869 and 1885. With the help of his family, he ran a mixed operation that was typical of the middling farms in his neighbourhood, producing crops such as peas, oats, and spring and fall wheat; a few head of cattle, sheep, and hogs for sale and home consumption; milk for butter and, in the 1890s, for the local cheese factory; root crops for the stock; wood from his wood lot; and vegetables, apples, and maple syrup. By diversifying, the Mathesons insulated themselves against failure in any area while providing food for a comfortable subsistence, even in the agricultural depression of the 1890s and the local drought in mid decade. Despite these difficult conditions, the family's reliance on its own labour meant that it was able to add a stone foundation to the barn in 1893 and brick the house the following year.

John Matheson negotiated a daring expansion in the early summer of 1896. Concluding that his family was "falling behind every day" – he had had only $2.50 in the house at the beginning of the year – he decided to purchase the neighbouring parcel of 50 acres that he had been working on shares, in the hope that the gains from additional crops would more than compensate for the interest on the parcel's mortgage. The gamble succeeded: a banner growing season and better-fed cows brought increased revenue from the cheese factory and a crop of grain and peas that literally spilled out of the barn. By the turn of the century the farm had moved ahead of its middling rank, with over 20 cattle and about a dozen hogs. Coming on the cusp of improved agricultural conditions in Ontario, the acquisition of 1896 had set the stage for further expansions that allowed for more improvements (a new barn and well, and the plastering of the house), prosperity for the rest of John's life, and the placement of two sons on the land. His hard work and business sense might make his success seem like a classic triumph of yeoman individualism. In fact, it was marked by a careful negotiation of responsibilities and rewards among the family. John's long days in his fields, barn, and wood lot depended entirely on Margaret's raising of their children, tending of the garden, and shrewd management of the household, and on the help of his sons and daughters, even after the non-inheriting children had begun to set out on their own.

The key to the latter group's participation was education. Perhaps motivated by a Scots Presbyterian faith in the value of schooling, John, himself a reader of books and newspapers, ensured that his children all graduated from high school. Further, the five non-inheriting boys received university educations that facilitated their economic independence: two became Presbyterian ministers, one was an actuary, and two taught in universities. One daughter trained at the conservatory in London, Ont., and gave piano lessons before her marriage; the other became a nurse after a failed engagement and would care for her parents until their deaths.

The cash-poor Mathesons managed this remarkable feat by having the children stage their departures so that, at any given time, a few boys and at least one girl were on hand to help at home. All the boys but one, whose negligence was criticized by his siblings, returned on summer holidays to assist with repairs and the harvest. The farm thus received the labour required to produce a pleasant standard of living for those who stayed and the resources needed to support the careers of the migrants. John fostered his children's interest by corresponding and consulting with them about farm operations and major projects. Once established, they sent money home or to younger siblings. Contrary to bleak contemporary and historical accounts of the "rural depopulation" of Ontario, the Matheson children remained integrated into the life

Mathison

and economy of the home farm long after their initial departures.

Ethnic and religious ties also bound the family together. They lived in what was, by 1901, the largest "Scotch block" in the province, a region that extended from Point Clark to Southampton along Lake Huron and back into Bruce and northern Huron counties. The Mathesons attended Gaelic services at the local Presbyterian church, where John was an elder; he and Margaret encouraged their children's engagement as ministers, members of church assemblies, and active churchgoers. By insisting that he be addressed in Gaelic at home, John raised them to be bilingual Scots who sought out Gaelic-speaking communities elsewhere in Ontario and Manitoba. One son became a noted Gaelic linguist, another was a founding member of the Kincardine pipe band. John thus helped to perpetuate a distinctive Scottish culture in Canada well into the 20th century.

A wonderful photograph of John in 1901 shows him with the strong upper body and arthritic hands of an ageing farmer, and the white beard of a patriarch, seated beside Margaret and surrounded by their entire family, the last time that everyone was together. Slowed by rheumatism and dizziness in his sixties and seventies, he gradually handed over farm operations to his son Charles, informally at the start of the century and then through a sale of property in 1919, two years after Margaret's death. Appropriately, when he died, he left his possessions and control of Charles's mortgage to his daughter Grace, who had cared for him. It was a final act of reciprocity in a life marked by such acts.

ADAM CRERAR

AO, D 217, Kincardine Township, assessment rolls, 1880, 1885, 1890, 1894, 1899; collectors' rolls, 1895; RG 1-57-1-5: 439; RG 22-358, no.6844; RG 61-3-1, Kincardine Township, concession 6, lots 8 and 9; concession 7, lot 8 and western half of lot 9; concession 9, lot 3; RG 80-8-0-861, no.8515. UCC-C, 3260. Adam Crerar, "Ties that bind: farming, agrarian ideals, and life in Ontario, 1890–1930" (PHD thesis, Univ. of Toronto, 1999). Chad Gaffield, "Children, schooling, and family reproduction in nineteenth-century Ontario," CHR, 72 (1991): 157–91. Murdock Matheson, Looking backward over my fifty years in Saskatchewan (n.p., 1960). Norman Robertson, The history of the county of Bruce . . . , ed. N. R. Shaw (Toronto, 1906); continued by Norman McLeod, The history of the county of Bruce . . . 1907–1968 . . . (Owen Sound, Ont., 1969). Toil, tears & triumph: a history of Kincardine Township, ed. W. H. Fletcher (Kincardine, Ont., 1990). W. R. Young, "Conscription, rural depopulation, and the farmers of Ontario, 1917–19," CHR, 53 (1972): 289–320.

MATHISON, ROBERT, newspaperman, office holder, educator of the deaf, and administrator of a fraternal order; b. 9 June 1843 in Kingston, Upper Canada, son of George Mathison and Anne Miller; m. before 1863 Isabella Christie (d. 1923) of Hamilton, Upper Canada, and they had two daughters and two sons; d. 30 July 1924 in Toronto.

Of Scottish-Irish parentage, Robert Mathison was educated in Woodstock and Brantford. He worked as a reporter for the Hamilton Times; by 1871 he was co-editor/proprietor of the Brantford Weekly Expositor and secretary-treasurer of the Canadian Press Association. He then moved into provincial positions: bursar of the London Asylum for the Insane in 1872 and manager of industries and bursar at the Central Prison in Toronto in 1878.

In September 1879 Mathison succeeded Dr Wesley Jones Palmer as superintendent of the Ontario Institution for the Education and Instruction of the Deaf and Dumb in Belleville. The first in a line of political appointees there, he had no notable acquaintance with educating the deaf. According to the school's official report of 1880, the government believed that his "varied knowledge and experience of public institution management . . . , combined with his well known administrative ability, eminently fitted him for the position of executive head." Administered through the office of John Woodburn Langmuir*, provincial inspector of prisons, asylums, and public charities, the institution had been opened in 1870 to "impart a general education as well as instruction in some professional or manual art" to the deaf. When Mathison arrived, according to one obituary, he found it "ill arranged, disorganized and classed with penal institutions and those for the insane." No attempt had been made to categorize students and no set curriculum existed. One of his first tasks was to have the students graded and courses of study and timetables put into operation.

Mathison was superintendent for 27 years. Whatever his shortcomings in 1879, he became a serious student of educating the deaf and visited similar institutions abroad. A vice-president of the Association of American Instructors for the Deaf, he was joined in his work in Belleville by his daughter Annie, who taught oral articulation. One of his greatest achievements, he believed, was to have the responsibility for his institution shifted in 1905 to the Department of Education, a move urged upon him by the deaf community. The bureaucratic alignment with prisons and asylums had lent a "stigma of inferiority" to the deaf population and led to an association "in the public mind, with the criminal incorrigibles and mentally defective classes." Other concerns raised by Mathison as superintendent included extending the school term from 7 years to 10 or 12, the costs to parents, and the granting of diplomas. In the debate over the causes of deafness, he disputed the theory of Alexander Graham BELL that deaf parents produced deaf offspring.

Two interrelated issues in particular dominated

718

Mathison's annual reports: the method of instruction and the purpose of educating the deaf. Mathison had inherited an entrenched system of manual teaching (sign-language with writing) [*see* Duncan Wendell McDermid*]. He used his reports to explore the potential of both oralism (speech, lip-reading, and writing), the method propounded by the European community, and the combined method (sign-language for instruction, with articulation for those who demonstrated aptitude), the system proposed by moderate American educator Edward Miner Gallaudet. By 1892 Mathison had firmly aligned himself and his institution with the combined system, and was focusing on the development of manners and morals and on industrial training. (The oralists emphasized academic work and intellectual development.) According to Mathison, the primary object of establishing schools for deaf children was "the cultivation of their minds, to teach them the ordinary branches of knowledge taught in the common schools of the country." The secondary motive was to "have them taught . . . such trades and industries as might prove of advantage to them after leaving school." The occupations taught (with varying success) included printing, shoemaking, carpentering, baking, and barbering for the boys, and tailoring, dressmaking, sewing, and housekeeping for the girls. In 1897 Mathison was able to note that many former pupils were "well off, others are in comfortable circumstances, few are a burden on their relatives, and none of them are in gaol as prisoners."

During his tenure Mathison worked actively for the wider deaf community. He supported its efforts in 1886 to organize the Ontario Deaf-Mute Association, of which he was made honorary president, and to form other bodies for the deaf, such as the Brigden Literary, Maple Leaf Reading and Debating, and Dorcas Sewing clubs, most of them in Toronto. In 1893, in recognition of his contributions, the Columbia Institution for the Instruction of the Deaf and Dumb, in Washington, awarded him an honorary MA.

In November 1906 Mathison left the Ontario Institution. In his last report he noted that he had given himself to his work "with entire devotion" and took great satisfaction from knowing "that I may have aided in some degree in bringing a little more of brightness and joy into the lives of our silent ones." Why he left when he did is not clear; his departure may have had something to do with two negative evaluations. In 1906 British specialist James Kerr Love visited the institution and found little oral work since Mathison's purpose was "to make his deaf children earn a living in a country where labor is plentiful and workmen scarce." A separate government investigation found the system of oral instruction at the school defective and recommended radical changes in its methods. The teaching of articulation was seen to be handicapped, however, not by Mathison's philosophy but by the failure to give

him "the support he deserved" and by too few teachers and insufficient accommodations. His successor, Charles Bernard Coughlin, embraced the oral method, which would be officially adopted by 1912.

After his resignation Mathison moved with his family to Toronto, where he became treasurer and later secretary of the Independent Order of Foresters, which he had joined in 1883. He retired in 1921. A Baptist and a member of the Oddfellows, the National Club, and the Royal Canadian Yacht Club, he passed away in Toronto in 1924 from an apoplectic stroke. Shortly before his death, an oil portrait of him by John Wycliffe Lowes Forster* had been unveiled at the Belleville school by the Ontario Association of the Deaf.

NANCY KIEFER

AO, RG 10-20-C-4-1; RG 22-305, no.50452; RG 63-A-10, 836, file 6, J. W. Langmuir to Mathison, 4 Oct. 1879; Mathison to Langmuir, 7 Oct. 1879. Univ. of Western Ont. Arch., J. J. Talman Regional Coll. (London), R. M. Bucke coll., medical superintendent's journal, vol.3 (1877–84). *Globe*, 8 Oct. 1923, 13 July 1924. *London Advertiser*, 15 March 1878. *Canadian men and women of the time* (Morgan; 1912). *Canadian who's who*, 1910. C. F. Carbin, *Deaf heritage in Canada: a distinctive, diverse, and enduring culture*, ed. D. L. Smith (Toronto, 1996). Ont., Legislature, *Sessional papers*, reports of the Ontario Institution for the Education of the Deaf and Dumb, Belleville, 1880–1907/8 (the institution's reports for 1880–81 are found in the reports of the inspector of prisons and public charities). *Saturday Night*, 27 Aug. 1898. M. A. Winzer, "Education, urbanization and the deaf community: a case study of Toronto, 1870–1900," in *Deaf history unveiled: interpretations from the new scholarship*, ed. J. V. Van Cleve (Washington, 1993); "An examination of some selected factors that affected the education and socialization of the deaf of Ontario, 1870–1900" (ED.D. thesis, Univ. of Toronto, 1981); *The history of special education: from isolation to integration* (Washington, 1993).

MATOKINAJIN (meaning "bear that comes and stands"; also called **Little Standing Buffalo**), Santee Sioux chief; b. 1846, son of Standing Buffalo [Tatanka-najin*]; d. 21 June 1921 in Fort Qu'Appelle, Sask.

Matokinajin was born in the region of North America that became the Minnesota and Dakota territories. Details of his childhood remain obscure. In 1862, after several decades of maladministered treaties, the Sioux in the eastern part of the region were left destitute with no lands in Minnesota and relegated to temporary reservations. Finally, when annuities became further delayed by the Civil War, some Sioux (or, more correctly, Dakota) seized food and clothing and began a resistance, killing settlers. Tatanka-najin's band, the most westerly of the eastern Dakota, was not part of the fighting and he gathered many who were fleeing and led them west and north, eventually into

British territory. In this diaspora, all sorts of bands were dissolving and others were being created in the flight onto the prairies.

Upon Tatanka-najin's death on 5 June 1871, and following the family tradition of his father and grandfather, Matokinajin took the name of his great-grandfather Standing Buffalo. Known as Little Standing Buffalo, he became the leader of a portion of his father's northern Sisseton and Wahpeton followers. In 1872, when his band was living at Wood Mountain (Sask.), he travelled to Winnipeg, visiting other Wahpeton and Santee on his way, and met with Lieutenant Governor Alexander Morris* to discuss his desire for a reserve. He declared his loyalty to Britain, and his request was forwarded to Ottawa in December. When treaty commissioners arrived at Fort Qu'Appelle to meet with the Plains Cree and the Saulteaux, they talked as well on 16 Sept. 1874 with Sioux leaders including Little Standing Buffalo, who confirmed his resistance to moving east into Manitoba or back to the United States, a position he restated a year later to commissioner William Joseph Christie*.

The arrival of Sitting Bull [Ta-tanka I-yotank*] in May 1877, in flight before the American army, forced many refugee Sioux to choose sides. Though the record is scanty, Little Standing Buffalo and most of his followers appear to have stayed far away from the Sitting Bull groups in their efforts to press their claim to remain in Canada. Deprivation became the norm in the absence of buffalo, and in the spring of 1877 Little Standing Buffalo found Lieutenant Governor David Laird* at Fort Pelly (Sask.) and stated his preference for a reserve that included the Jumping Deer Creek coulee northwest of Fort Qu'Appelle. This time the request was granted, on 22 Jan. 1878, and Standing Buffalo Reserve was formed. Seed and some implements were supplied by federal authorities, but no more tangible help with housing or farming was forthcoming as the Sisseton-Wahpeton shifted from the hunt to agriculture and wage labour for settlers. Some women also sold handicrafts at rail stops while others worked as domestics and cooks. American attempts in 1882–83 to induce Indians to return were countered by Canadian insistence that troops could not cross the border to lure or pursue them.

In 1885 events were already converging in the move toward rebellion [see Louis Riel*]. Disappointment among various tribal constituencies about the problematic implementation of the prairie treaties gave cause to some Indian groups to join in the Métis resistance [see Kāpeyakwāskonam*]. The Sisseton-Wahpeton led by Wapahaska (White Cap) were intimidated by Métis forces into joining as hostilities came to their doorstep, but the Standing Buffalo band remained far from the fighting and at peace. Not allowed into treaties, the refugee Sioux were destitute but grateful for sanctuary in Canada. As settlers flooded into the region, change affected the reserve. A Roman Catholic boarding school operated from 1886 until 1895, when children needing education were sent to Father Joseph Hugonard*'s establishment in nearby Lebret. By 1900 the band numbered 220, and most of the families had moved to the benchland above the coulee to take up agriculture in a serious way, producing oats, wheat, corn, and potatoes, sometimes with surplus to sell. Tightening supervision by the Indian department, including the suppression of ceremony, produced vigorous complaints from Little Standing Buffalo in 1903, but to no avail.

Little Standing Buffalo was aware of the manner in which the eastern Sioux had been punished for the outbreak of 1862 in the United States, and he sought a way to join eastern Sioux efforts for the restoration of the suspended annuities. In 1914 Frank Abbott of the American Department of the Interior, who visited him to discuss recovery, reported that his band received no assistance other than some implements, seed, and education, but that there was little hope they would ever obtain American compensation.

In the last years of his life, Little Standing Buffalo went by the name Louis Philippe Abelard. He lost a grandson in the World War I, and was overcome with grief. In 1920–21, to strengthen his band's economy, he and his son Julius asked Ottawa for the return of hay-lands being shared with the Cree, but no action was taken by the time of Little Standing Buffalo's death in 1921. He had been chief for 50 years.

DAVID REED MILLER

Mark Diedrich, *The odyssey of Chief Standing Buffalo and the Northern Sisseton Sioux* (Minneapolis, 1988). P. D. Elias, *The Dakota of the Canadian northwest: lessons for survival* (Regina, 2002). Gontran Laviolette, *The Dakota Sioux in Canada* (Winnipeg, 1991).

MATTHEW, GEORGE FREDERIC, office holder, geologist, palaeontologist, curator, and author; b. 12 Aug. 1837 in Saint John, son of George Matthew and Deborah Eliza Harris; m. 15 April 1868 Katherine Mary Diller in Brooklyn (New York City), and they had six sons and two daughters; d. 14 April 1923 in Hastings-on-Hudson, N.Y., and was buried in Gondola Point, N.B.

George Matthew lived in Saint John at a time when the city was a busy port and an important centre in eastern Canada. He attended the Saint John Grammar School and entered public service on 1 May 1853 as a clerk in the provincial Treasury Department, which merged with the federal Department of Customs after confederation. He would be appointed chief clerk of the Saint John customs service on 28 May 1879 and surveyor of customs on 1 July 1893, a position he held until his retirement in 1915. His friends believed that but for political considerations he would have been made collector of the port.

Even though Matthew did not attend university, the intellectual atmosphere in Saint John supported his interest in natural history, and its complicated geology challenged his curiosity. In 1857, at age 20, he helped found the Steinhammer Club, comprised of five young men interested in local geology. They were possibly inspired by the presence of Abraham Gesner*'s geological collection in the museum of the Mechanics' Institute. Matthew entered on the study of New Brunswick geology at an opportune time. John William Dawson* was then preparing a revised edition of his *Acadian geology . . .* (1855), which was to include New Brunswick. Dawson became interested in the Steinhammer Club, especially the work of Matthew and Charles Frederick Hartt*, who provided information used in his revision (1868) and in earlier papers on the Carboniferous and Devonian flora of New Brunswick. As Canada's foremost geologist, Dawson likely had considerable influence on Matthew. At his suggestion, the Natural History Society of New Brunswick (NHSNB) was established in Saint John in 1862. A charter member, Matthew became the society's first curator.

Soon after, Matthew's friend Professor Loring Woart BAILEY of the University of New Brunswick began geological mapping of the province with the assistance of Matthew and Hartt. Following confederation the Geological Survey of Canada extended its operation to the Maritimes, and in 1868 its director, Sir William Edmond Logan*, met with Bailey and Matthew to discuss the work. Between 1864 and 1880 Matthew, jointly with Bailey or with Bailey and GSC geologist Robert Wheelock Ells, published numerous reports and maps on New Brunswick geology. Matthew would work as a temporary palaeontologist for the GSC until 1901, occasionally recovering expenses and supplementing his salary. In addition to preparing reports, he acted as the survey's expert in Cambrian geology, assisting in the identification and classification of Cambrian specimens and in the arrangement of the GSC's museum.

In 1882 the NHSNB, which had been moribund for some years, started publishing a *Bulletin*. Matthew paid for the printing of the second number and became a regular contributor. That same year the Royal Society of Canada began meeting in Ottawa. Dawson, its first president, selected Matthew as one of the charter members representing the geological and biological sciences. In 1889 Matthew became president of the NHSNB, an office he held until 1895 (when he was succeeded by George Upham Hay*), and in 1891–92 he was president of his section of the RSC. He published over 200 papers and corresponded with geologists across North America, Britain, and Europe. His first paper, in the *Canadian Naturalist and Geologist*

(Montreal) for 1863, reported on the geology of Saint John County. His writings were mostly descriptive accounts of new species; however, he also contributed papers synthesizing regional geology. His interests ranged from Quaternary climate and archaeology to Precambrian palaeontology. Although at the time religion strongly influenced geologists, Matthew, an Anglican, did not mention religion or Darwinism in his writings, as Dawson often did.

Saint John's complex geology provided a lifetime of research. Within miles of home were Precambrian stromatolites, for which in 1890 Matthew provided the first scientific description. From local Cambrian shales, he was among the first palaeontologists to recognize a sub-trilobitic interval in the Lower Cambrian. In 1899 he summarized the "Etcheminian series" and accurately described small shelly fossils. Although American palaeontologist Charles Doolittle Walcott prevailed in dismissing the Etcheminian and included these fossils in his Lower Cambrian series, areas where the Etcheminian was originally recognized provide a standard reference for Cambrian correlation. Nearby at "Fern Ledges" Matthew studied fossil plants, insects, and trackways. After a Carboniferous age was established for these rocks, Matthew argued that fossil interpretations needed revision since the stratigraphy necessitated a Devonian age. His claim illustrated his devotion to the earlier work of Dawson and Bailey. Bailey said that Matthew, in his eighties, still determined to prove an older age for these rocks, walked the Bay of Fundy coastline to Maine to relate his observations to those made by American geologists.

By the 1890s Matthew had made himself a well-established member of the geoscience community, although still an amateur. The Université Laval conferred a DSC on him in 1894 and the University of New Brunswick bestowed two honorary degrees, MA in 1878 and LLD in 1897. In 1917 Matthew was awarded the Murchison Medal by the Geological Society of London.

Matthew devoted much time to research, but also to the NHSNB. In his first year as president he served on standing committees for geology, the library, essays and lectures, publications, the meeting hall, and the press – a typical commitment for him. He also enriched the museum through the collection and exchange of specimens. His wife, Katherine, was a long-time president and active member of the society's ladies' association. Their eldest son, William Diller, often accompanied his father in the field and became a famous vertebrate palaeontologist at the American Museum of Natural History in New York.

Matthew described more than 350 new species of fossil plants and animals. Although his work has been revised, much remains valid and attests to his excellence as a scientist with a keen sense of observation and an untiring spirit. He died in 1923 at William's home in Hastings-on-Hudson, where he and Katherine had gone to live two years before.

RANDALL F. MILLER

A listing of over 200 of Matthew's publications appears in Ed Landing and R. F. Miller, "Bibliography of George Frederick Matthew," New York State Museum, *Bull.* (Albany), no.463 (1988): 77–80, and about 150 in *Science and technology biblio.* (Richardson and MacDonald). His writings include "Sketch of the history of the Natural History Society of New Brunswick," N.B., Natural Hist. Soc., *Bull.* (Saint John), no.30 (1912): 457–74.

N.B. Museum (Saint John), F1, item 1-5 (H. Ami to G. F. Matthew, 27 Jan. 1888); G. F. Matthew corr., esp. G. M. Dawson to Matthew, 11 Jan. 1898 and 23 May 1900. *Daily Telegraph and the Sun* (Saint John), 8 Oct. 1921. *Saint John Globe*, 30 April 1903; 8 Oct. 1921; 18, 21 April, 12 May 1923. *St. John Morning Telegraph* (Saint John), 21 April 1868. L. W. Bailey, "George F. Matthew," RSC, *Trans.*, 3rd ser., 17 (1923), proc.: vii–x. W. D. Matthew, "Memorial of George F. Matthew," Geological Soc. of America, *Bull.* (New York), 35 (1924): 181–82. R. F. Miller, "George Frederic Matthew (1837–1923)," in *Trace fossils, small shelly fossils and the Precambrian–Cambrian boundary: proceedings, August 8–18, 1987, Memorial University*, ed. Ed Landing *et al.*, New York State Museum, *Bull.*, no.463: 4–7; "George Frederic Matthew: Victorian science in Saint John," *NBM News* (Saint John), August–September 1987: 1–28. R. F. Miller and D. N. Buhay, "Life and letters of George Frederic Matthew: geologist and palaeontologist; an annotated list of Matthew's geological correspondence in the New Brunswick Museum library and archives," N.B. Museum, *Pubs. in Natural Science* (Saint John), no.8 (1990); "The Steinhammer Club: geology and a foundation for a natural history society in New Brunswick," *Geoscience Canada* (St John's), 15 (1988): 221–26.

MAUNSELL, EDWARD HERBERT, NWMP officer and rancher; b. 14 Oct. 1855 in Ballywilliam, County Limerick (Republic of Ireland), son of Frederick Maunsell and Louise Herbert; m. 10 Aug. 1886 Jeanette Ryan of Tipperary (Republic of Ireland), and they had two daughters and one son; d. 11 Nov. 1923 in Lethbridge, Alta.

Edward Maunsell was educated in Ireland and came to Canada in 1874, where he immediately joined the North-West Mounted Police. Assigned to D Division, he took part in the Long March from Dufferin, Man., to the Sweet Grass Hills (Alta/Mont.). He was with the section of the force under Commissioner George Arthur FRENCH that returned to Manitoba, but in 1876 he was transferred to Fort Macleod (Alta). After completing his three-year term in 1877 he went back to Ireland. His familiarity with cattle raising had enabled him to recognize the potential for ranching in the foothills of the Rocky Mountains. He returned to North America, and when his elder brother George Wyndham obtained his discharge

from the NWMP in 1878, they undertook to become ranchers.

At that time, since no cattle were available in what is now southern Alberta, the brothers contracted with a Montana firm to deliver 103 head to them in the summer of 1879. Meanwhile, they earned a living near Fort Macleod by growing oats, cutting rails, and filling hay contracts for the mounted police. After receiving the cattle, the Maunsells learned that the land would not be opened to settlement for at least a year, and they worried that starving Indians would slaughter their herds [*see* Isapo-muxika*]. In the autumn round-up, when they discovered that nearly half their animals had strayed or been killed, with other cattle owners they sent their remaining stock to Montana. By the time the cattle were brought back in 1881, the herd had been further reduced through theft and mismanagement.

A third brother, Henry Frederick, joined Edward and George in 1881, and Maunsell Brothers took homesteads and a lease of 6,500 acres immediately west of Fort Macleod. Initially they prospered, but the terrible winter of 1886–87 ravaged their herd. As a result, George left the partnership to establish his own ranch, while Edward and Harry, as his younger brother was known, remained at the original site. In their partnership, Edward was in charge of the Ivy Ranch (named for his IV brand) and Harry ran the adjacent farm.

In Maunsell's opinion, the government's leasing policy for grazing land greatly favoured the huge ranch companies [*see* Matthew Henry Cochrane*; Frederick Smith Stimson*] and the only way to compete was to expand. Over the years, he became one of the leading cattlemen of the southern District of Alberta. In 1900 he leased the entire Peigan Indian Reserve and in 1901 he added 700 cattle to his herd when he bought out a neighbouring rancher. To increase further the size of his holdings, he entered into partnership with John Cowdry, a private banker in Fort Macleod. They purchased a 200,000-acre grazing lease west of Medicine Hat at Grassy Lake for $100,000 and when the historic Cochrane Ranche was sold to the Church of Jesus Christ of Latter-day Saints in 1905, Maunsell bought its entire herd for $240,000. At its peak, about 1910, the Maunsell ranch had some 15,000 cattle and shipped entire trainloads to the Chicago market.

Changes in its fortunes occurred in the 1910s. The federal government cancelled the Grassy Lake lease without notice, and although the subsequent lawsuit would be settled in favour of Maunsell, thousands of cattle had had to be sold at a tremendous loss. Maunsell suffered a personal blow in 1917 when his son, Frederick William Edward, was killed in France at Vimy Ridge and another in 1919 when his brother George died. The ranching operation experienced further reverses with the destruction of hundreds of stock in the harsh winter of 1919–20 and termination of the lease on the Peigan reserve. The Ivy Ranch was reduced to its freehold land.

In addition to ranching, Edward Maunsell was active in the community. An unsuccessful Liberal candidate for the Legislative Assembly of Alberta in 1910, he served as president of the Macleod Old Timers Association and took an interest in local history and place names. On 13 Oct. 1923, less than a month before his death, the *Calgary Daily Herald* published a long account of his adventures in the times before the arrival of the large ranch companies. His anecdotes, with their stories of danger and hardship, their humour, and their appreciation of character, bring to life the brief days of the frontier in southern Alberta.

HUGH A. DEMPSEY

"Epic of the west unfolded by pioneer of '70s," *Calgary Daily Herald*, 13 Oct. 1923. *Lethbridge Herald* (Lethbridge, Alta), 6 Jan., 13 Nov. 1923. Alberta Geneal. Soc. (Edmonton), "Master name index." John Blue, *Alberta, past and present, historical and biographical* (3v., Chicago, 1924), 2: 102–4. *Fort Macleod – our colourful past: a history of the town of Fort Macleod, from 1874 to 1924* (Fort Macleod, Alta, 1977), 341–42. A. O. MacRae, *History of the province of Alberta* (2v., [Calgary], 1912), 2: 692. "The west of Edward Maunsell," ed. H. A. Dempsey, *Alberta Hist.* (Calgary), 34 (1986), no.4: 1–17; 35 (1987), no.1: 13–26.

MAVOR, JAMES, economist, professor, and author; b. 8 Dec. 1854 in Stranraer, Scotland, son of James Mavor, a Free Church minister and teacher, and Mary Ann Taylor Bridie; m. 16 Jan. 1883 Christina Jane Gordon Watt (d. 1934) in Glasgow, and they had two sons and two daughters, including Dora*; d. there 31 Oct. 1925.

The eldest surviving child in a large family, James Mavor was compelled to leave the High School of Glasgow at an early age. Apprenticed to a dry-salter in 1868, he undertook evening courses at the Andersonian Institution. In 1874 he began formal studies at the University of Glasgow, where he was influenced by idealist philosopher Edward Caird, but these ended in 1876, before a degree was awarded, because of a bout with typhoid fever. Mavor nonetheless forged an eclectic career for himself in Glasgow as a businessman, teacher, editor, and social reformer. He edited the short-lived *Scottish Art Review* (Glasgow; London) and was on the staff of the technologically oriented *Industries* (London). He also worked on behalf of the poor with the Kyrle Society and was a founding member of the Glasgow Workmen's Dwellings Company Limited, which strove to provide affordable, sanitary housing for working people. Appointed lecturer in political economy and statistics at St Mungo's College in Glasgow in 1888, he lectured as well at the Glasgow Athenaeum and in the extension programs of Edinburgh and Glasgow universities; he also delivered popular courses on political science to various organizations. Mavor quickly gained a reputation as an authority on forms of social and industrial organization.

Looking for a more critical approach to explain the destructive effects of industrialization and urbanization on Glasgow's poor, Mavor actively participated in a number of socialist organizations including the Fabian Society, the Social Democratic Federation, and the Socialist League. He became acquainted with some of the key figures in the socialist scene in England and Scotland in the late 19th century, among them George Bernard Shaw, Sidney and Beatrice Webb, Patrick Geddes, and William Morris. In his 1898 play *Candida*, Shaw named one of the lead characters James Mavor Morell in his honour. Ultimately, however, the authoritarian tendencies of socialist leaders and his own conventional approach to economics led him to reject the Marxian theory of value and the effectiveness of socialist analyses of contemporary problems.

In 1892, on the recommendation of William James Ashley, the first professor of political economy at the University of Toronto, Mavor was appointed to succeed him as chair of the political science department, a position he would occupy until his retirement in 1923. He continued the department's emphasis on empirical research into existing conditions, believing that political economy could provide contextual understandings to further social progress. During his tenure he was instrumental in shaping the department into its modern form, in the process initiating distinct streams of study in commerce and finance, and providing the intellectual climate for such future disciplines as social work and sociology. The department trained leaders for positions in government, business, and philanthropic initiatives; among a number of prominent graduates were Samuel Morley Wickett*, a pioneer in Canadian urban studies, and Robert Hamilton Coats*, the first dominion statistician. Mavor began the trend within universities of social science researchers contracting their services to governments and outside agencies. For example, in 1899 he was asked by Clifton SIFTON, minister of the interior, to inquire into the progress of the settlement of Russian Doukhobors in western Canada. The previous year, at the request of his friend Prince Kropotkin, Mavor had persuaded Sifton to allow the Doukhobors to immigrate, and he would remain their staunch supporter, developing friendships with Count Tolstoy and Peter Vasil'evich VERIGIN, their spiritual leader. In 1899 as well he prepared a report for Sifton on potential European immigration to Canada. Mavor's most controversial study was that commissioned by the British Board of Trade in 1903 on the settlement and economic prospects of the Canadian west; his conclusion that Canada could not fully supply Britain's need for wheat in the immediate future was roundly condemned in both the British and the Canadian press. He subsequently devoted more time to his own wide-ranging research. In 1914 he published his most important study, the well-reviewed *Economic history of Russia*. Among his later works – a number hostile to public ownership – was *Niagara in politics*, an attack on Ontario Hydro and its chairman, Sir Adam BECK, that was paid for by private-power interests in the United States.

Mavor's activities extended beyond academe. He fashioned himself as an aesthetic theorist, art historian, connoisseur, and patron of the arts (including literature and drama). Among those whose work he promoted were artists Homer Ransford Watson* and Horatio Walker* and writers Marjorie Lowry Christie PICKTHALL and Ernest Thompson Seton*. He became involved in many aspects of Toronto's cultural and educational edification, working with Byron Edmund WALKER and others to found the Art Museum of Toronto and the Royal Ontario Museum; he was also active in the city beautification initiatives of the Toronto Guild of Civic Art. Mavor lectured and wrote extensively on the potential of art, his work appearing in such important publications as the *Year Book of Canadian Art* and the *Canadian Magazine*, both of Toronto. Increasingly recognized as an authority, in 1897 (less than five years after his arrival) he was asked by John Castell HOPKINS to write an article for his projected encyclopedia on "the Progress and Position of Art in Canada," an essay that for whatever reason did not appear. In 1897 he organized local artists, among them George Agnew Reid* and his wife, Mary Augusta Catharine HIESTER, to prepare sketches of the costumes worn at the Victorian Era Ball; these were published the following year in a commemorative volume.

Mavor's impact on the university was controversial, for he was seen as an eccentric dabbler. As early as 1895 he was implicated in a student strike over favouritism in appointments and matters of discipline [*see* William DALE]; questions arose about the authenticity of his credentials, his rambling lecture style, and his general academic fitness. William Lyon Mackenzie King*, an undergraduate in the political science department and a leader of the strike, was particularly antagonistic towards Mavor, especially after King was denied a prestigious fellowship. Though many of these conflicts were rooted in university politics and personal relations, it is notable that Mavor's detractors consistently fed the notion of "academic unsuitability" – a judgement drawing heavily on the professor's unpopularity – by emphasizing his dual interests in what a *Toronto Daily Star* article of 7 Nov. 1925 termed "Bohemia . . . [and] Collegia." His own disputatious attitude can be explained in part by his assess-

ment of Toronto as a colonial backwater and its inhabitants as minor players of limited intellect. In the preface to his memoirs, *My windows on the street of the world* (2v., London and Toronto, 1923), Mavor would still refer to Toronto as the "New World." Nevertheless, his achievements were recognized by the university, which granted him an honorary PHD in 1912. In 1926 Oscar Pelham Edgar*, in a eulogy on behalf of the Royal Society of Canada, to which Mavor had been elected in 1914, neatly captured his contribution to academia: "No professor has ever done more towards enlarging the boundaries of University life and to relieve it from the imputation of cloistral aloofness and academic pedantry."

Mavor died in Glasgow in 1925, en route to visit friends in Montpellier, France.

E. LISA PANAYOTIDIS

The largest collection of James Mavor's papers is housed in the Univ. of Toronto Library, Thomas Fisher Rare Book Library, MS coll. 119 (James Mavor papers). Additional resources are located in LAC, MG 29, C16; UTA, A1967-0007 and A1976-0025, box 2, files 3, 7; the Mavor fonds in York Univ. Libraries, Arch. and Special Coll. (Toronto), F0351; and the Art Gallery of Toronto correspondence and other collections in the Art Gallery of Ontario, Research Library and Arch. (Toronto). A detailed listing of these and other primary materials relating to Mavor is provided in *Guide to the papers of James Mavor*, compiled by D. A. Signori for the Fisher Library in 1989.

Mavor was a prolific author. His books appear in the standard catalogues, but there is no complete bibliography of his articles. Many are noted in the *Guide* to his papers, which does not, however, provide publication information. Partial listings appear in Bowker and in Shortt, *infra*. Of the works mentioned in the text, *An economic history of Russia* was published in two volumes in London in 1914 (a second edition appeared in 1925 and was reprinted in New York in 1965); *Niagara in politics: a critical account of the Ontario Hydro-Electric Commission* was issued in New York in 1925; and Mavor's *North west of Canada: report to the Board of Trade on the north west of Canada, with special reference to wheat production for export* was published as G.B., Parl., Command paper, 1905, 54, [C. 2628]. See also *Book of the Victorian Era Ball, given at Toronto on the twenty eighth of December, MDCCCXCVII* (Toronto, 1898).

General Register Office for Scotland (Edinburgh), Kelvin (Glasgow), reg. of marriages, 16 Jan. 1883. A. F. Bowker, "Truly useful men: Maurice Hutton, George Wrong, James Mavor and the University of Toronto, 1880–1927" (PHD thesis, Univ. of Toronto, 1975). Augustus Bridle, *Sons of Canada: short studies of characteristic Canadians* (Toronto, 1916). S. Z. Burke, *Seeking the highest good: social service and gender at the University of Toronto, 1888–1937* (Toronto, 1996). *Canadian men and women of the time* (Morgan; 1898). I. M. Drummond, assisted by William Kaplan, *Political economy at the University of Toronto: a history of the department, 1888–1982* (Toronto, 1983). [O. P. Edgar], "James Mavor," RSC, *Trans.*, 3rd ser., 20 (1926), proc.: xiii–xvi. J. B. Glasier, *William Morris and the early days of the* socialist movement; being reminiscences of Morris' work as a propagandist . . . (London, 1921). *James Mavor and his world: an exhibition of books and papers selected from the James Mavor collection, June–July 1975*, comp. Rachel Grover and F. W. M. Moore (Toronto, 1975). J. M. Moore, "Why 'James Mavor' Morell?" *Shaw Rev.* (University Park, Pa), 23 (1980): 48–51. Mavor Moore, *Reinventing myself: memoirs* (Toronto, 1994). E. L. Panayotidis, "James Mavor: cultural ambassador and aesthetic educator to Toronto's élite," *Journal of Pre-Raphaelite Studies* (Tempe, Ariz.), new ser., 6/7 (fall/spring 1997/98): 161–73. Rosalind Pepall, "Under the spell of Morris: a Canadian perspective," in *The earthly paradise: arts and crafts by William Morris and his circle from Canadian collections*, ed. K. A. Lochnan (Toronto, 1993), 19–35. S. E. D. Shortt, *The search for an ideal: six Canadian intellectuals and their convictions in an age of transition, 1890–1930* (Toronto and Buffalo, N.Y., 1976).

MAXWELL, EDWARD, architect; b. 31 Dec. 1867 in Montreal, son of Edward John Maxwell, a lumber dealer, and Johan Macbean; m. 15 Dec. 1896 Elizabeth Ellen Aitchison in Potsdam, N.Y., and they had four children; d. 14 Nov. 1923 in Montreal.

Edward Maxwell's paternal grandfather was a Scottish joiner and carpenter who immigrated to Montreal in 1829. His son Edward John became a builder and in 1862 founded E. J. Maxwell and Company, lumber dealers specializing in hardwoods, a business that would remain in the family until the 1970s. Edward John's two sons, Edward and William Sutherland, would both become architects. When Edward embarked on his career in the 1880s, there were no formal programs of study in Canada and only a handful of professional schools in the United States. Thus, after graduating from the High School of Montreal at age 14, Edward followed the traditional route by apprenticing with a local architect, Alexander Francis DUNLOP. Yet apprenticeship was less than satisfactory. Speaking to fellow architects in 1891, Alexander Cowper Hutchison, a leader of the profession in Montreal, would note that "heretofore the study of architecture in any of our offices has been something of a farce." To augment his education Edward set off for Boston, then the dominant centre for architecture in the United States. In suburban Brookline were the homes and offices of America's most famous architect, Henry Hobson Richardson (who died in 1886), and his frequent collaborator, landscape architect Frederick Law Olmsted. By 1888 Maxwell was working for Shepley, Rutan, and Coolidge, the partnership that completed Richardson's unfinished works. He remained there until 1891. Richardson's influence on him was profound, as it was on countless young architects of the time.

When, in the fall of 1890, a competition was organized for the design of Montreal's proposed new Board of Trade building, local architects were dismayed to learn that six firms from the United States had been requested to submit designs for which they would each be paid $300 expenses, but that no Canadians had been invited to participate. Those Canadians who wished to compete would not be compensated. This biased competition benefited Maxwell, for Shepley, Rutan, and Coolidge received the commission and in 1891 sent him to Montreal to supervise the work. Admitted to the Province of Quebec Association of Architects that same year, Maxwell quickly caught the eye of Montreal's powerful business elite. By the following year he had resigned from the Shepley firm and had set up his own office, although he continued to supervise the Board of Trade project. The city's industrialists, transportation magnates, and financiers would be the mainstay of his practice until his death.

Maxwell's first commercial building was an important one: Henry BIRKS's four-storey store and office, built in 1892–94 on Phillips square in what would soon become the city's new retail district. Not surprisingly, its design borrowed heavily from that of the Montreal Board of Trade building, which itself combined the Richardsonian Romanesque manner with Italian Renaissance influences that had gained attention in the 1880s, spearheaded by the New York firm of McKim, Mead, and White. In general, Maxwell's commercial work of the 1890s, including the Birks store with its round-arched openings, colourful, richly-textured stone, and heavy overhanging cornice, follows the pattern learned from Shepley, Rutan, and Coolidge.

William Maxwell, a gifted draftsman, gained his earliest architectural experience working in his brother's office in the 1890s, but, like Edward, he also journeyed to Boston. Between September 1895 and May 1898 he was employed there by Winslow and Wetherel, a firm well known for its large hotels and commercial buildings, as well as for its domestic work. More important were the months commencing in the fall of 1899 that he spent in Paris with Jean-Louis Pascal, director of one of the leading ateliers associated with the École des Beaux-Arts. Before he returned to Montreal in late 1900, he had acquired expertise in the logical, systematic planning espoused by the École and in the lavish neo-Renaissance and baroque detailing that characterized current French design. He would probably also have seen art nouveau work in the decorative arts exhibits at the universal exposition of 1900 in Paris, which he attended. In 1902 William became Edward's partner, replacing George Cutler Shattuck, who had been associated with Edward since 1899. The brothers would practise together until Edward's death in 1923.

Grand urban mansions had been among Edward's earliest commissions. Between 1892 and the onset of World War I, the firm would design more than 30 houses in the area of Montreal known as the Square Mile, where the city's wealthiest lived, and over 20 in contiguous Westmount, where the brothers had grown up. Stylistically these homes reflect the changing fashions that appealed to some of Canada's richest men, such as the Château-style house (1893–94) of Edward Seaborne Clouston*, general manager of the Bank of Montreal, the Queen-Anne mansion (1894) of his successor, Henry Vincent MEREDITH, and the opulent French neo-baroque pile (1901–2) of Charles Rudolph Hosmer, manager of the Canadian Pacific Railway's telegraph system.

Reflecting their owners' admiration of high-style homes in Boston and New York, these Maxwell houses are important not only as social records but for their craftsmanship. The Maxwell firm was an important patron of local artists, artisans, and suppliers who could provide the interior and exterior ornamentation demanded by affluent clients. Indeed, like the New York firm McKim, Mead, and White, the Maxwells were frequently required to supply furniture, wallcoverings, carpets, and even antiques to decorate the rooms they designed. The respected Montreal firm of Castle and Son provided stained and leaded glass, fine cabinetry, and interior furnishings. One of England's leading groups of craftsmen, the Bromsgrove Guild of Applied Arts, would open an office in Montreal in 1911, followed by a workshop, thanks in part to these architects' patronage.

Both Maxwell brothers were closely tied to Montreal's artistic community. Edward was a long-time member of the Art Association of Montreal, in company with many of his wealthy clients. William belonged to the Pen and Pencil Club of Montreal and the Canadian Handicrafts Guild. He helped to found the Arts Club of Montreal in 1912, served as its first president, and fitted up its premises. Two of the club's members, painter Maurice Galbraith Cullen* and sculptor George William Hill*, were among the brothers' close friends. Hill had collaborated with the Maxwells from 1894 and he would continue until World War I, providing exterior sculpture and woodcarving and furniture for interiors. Both Maxwells were elected members of the Royal Canadian Academy of Arts, Edward in 1908 and William in 1914, and participated in its exhibitions (showing architectural designs and watercolours). They would serve on the academy's council, Edward in 1910–12 and 1915–20 and William in 1916–18, 1921–23, and 1926–37.

There were many houses, large and small, which the Maxwell firm designed as vacation homes. Some, such as those for stockbroker Louis-Joseph Forget* and CPR financier and banker Richard Bladworth ANGUS, dating from just before and after 1900, were among Canada's grandest country estates – modelled, as was the most opulent of American examples, George Washington Vanderbilt's Biltmore in North Carolina, on the châteaux of the Loire. Like Biltmore, both Canadian projects involved landscape designs from the Olmsted firm of Brookline. Both estates

were located on the rural western tip of the island of Montreal. Other, less ostentatious houses were designed for sites in the Laurentians, some in the rustic Adirondack style that had developed earlier in northern New York State. Seaside houses in such fashionable watering places as St Andrews, N.B., show the influence of the American shingle style of Richardson and his followers.

One of the handsomest structures designed by Edward for a seaside estate is a splendid barn for CPR president Sir William Cornelius Van Horne* situated on Ministers Island, near St Andrews. There, Van Horne kept a prize herd of Dutch Belted cattle. The barn has remarkable timber framing in addition to its fine exterior of wood and fieldstone. Van Horne, an amateur architect, may have assisted Edward; he had certainly begun designing the house on his estate, but had ultimately called on Edward to help him, perhaps with the original building and certainly with several additions from 1899 onwards. Edward must have admired the dynamic Van Horne, for he built himself a country retreat on 160 acres he purchased in 1908 in Baie-d'Urfé on the island of Montreal; there he kept a choice herd of Jersey cattle. Like many of his clients, he also had a summer home in St Andrews. Tillietudlem was constructed around 1900. Again like so many of their clients, both brothers owned homes in Montreal's Square Mile, which they designed themselves.

Edward's skills as an architect were especially appreciated by the men who directed the CPR and its related enterprises. The CPR had become a client in 1897, when Edward had been asked to complete a grand western terminus in Vancouver for the transcontinental railway. Three years later he designed a large addition to the CPR's headquarters, Windsor Station, in Montreal. Over the years the firm would design stations and hotels across the dominion which would be landmarks in their time. Among the most notable are the station in Winnipeg and its accompanying hotel, the Royal Alexandra (1904–6), the 350-room Palliser Hotel (1911–14) in Calgary, and the central tower and additional wings (1920–24) that transformed the Château Frontenac in Quebec City into a Canadian icon. For the additions to the Château, the Montreal branch of the Bromsgrove Guild would later advertise that it had provided "all the modelling for all ornamental work in wood, iron, bronze, plaster and stone . . . as well as many items of special furniture."

These stations and hotels had followed the shift in design that had been evident in the firm's output as a whole, from Edward's late-Victorian picturesque work inspired by the New England stations of Richardson and his successor, Shepley, Rutan, and Coolidge, to the confident *beaux-arts* classicism that William had introduced when he became a partner in 1902. Railway commissions had helped raise the status of the Maxwell office across Canada, but the advent of William as a partner had also been important, bringing expertise in newer fashions and design that ensured the firm's continuing success throughout the first quarter of the 20th century. Art nouveau seems to have been too extreme for the Maxwells' conservative clientele for there is only the slightest trace of this fashion in the odd, sharply pointed dormers and segmental arched window heads and main entrance of the Angus country house in Senneville (1902–3) or in the sophisticated townhouse (1907–8) designed for Richard Ramsay Mitchell in Westmount. Interestingly, the most conspicuous example of this fashion, a proposal dated 1903 for a mansion in Montreal for John Kenneth Leveson Ross, son of the CPR contractor James Ross*, was rejected in favour of the stately exercise in neo-baroque classicism that was built in 1908–9 and which resembles the end pavilions of the Saskatchewan Legislative Building (1908–12) in Regina, also designed by the Maxwells.

William's *beaux-arts* approach served the firm well as it entered numerous competitions and dealt with important and complex commissions in the 20th century. In 1907 the Maxwells won the competition, open to all Canadian architects, for the Justice and Departmental buildings in Ottawa. Although their scheme was never built, the project enhanced their reputation. Their prestige was further augmented a year later when their design for the Saskatchewan Legislative Building was chosen in a limited, international competition. This major success was quickly followed by another: their winning design for a new gallery for the Art Association of Montreal (later renamed the Montreal Museum of Fine Arts) (1911–12). Other notable works in Montreal during this period were the Church of the Messiah (1906–8) and the High School of Montreal (1912–14). The last great project the two brothers undertook together, the enlargement of the Château Frontenac, completed a year after Edward's death, marked a summation. While maintaining the picturesque Château mode of the original building, the new work benefited from the two great axes of its plan, which gave a classical order to its varied parts, a perfect melding of the two Maxwells' talents.

Following Edward's death, Gordon MacLeod Pitts, an architect in the Maxwell office, became William's partner. The firm soon lost momentum, however. The brothers had complemented each other, not only as architects, but also as personalities. William was the more reserved, happiest in the company of artists, while Edward had been skilled at business and had pursued an active social life. In 1940 William moved to Haifa (Hefa), Israel, to be with his only child, Mary Maxwell Rabbani, who had married the head of the Baha'i faith. There, he designed his most unusual building, the gold-domed superstructure (1948–53) for the Shrine of the Bab, a major pilgrimage site for

Baha'is around the world. Spectacularly sited on the slopes of Mount Carmel, the arcaded, marble and granite structure was a fitting conclusion to his career, epitomizing grand *beaux-arts* design. In 1951, suffering from ill health, he returned to Montreal and died there the next year.

The Maxwell office had been one of the most important in the history of Canadian architecture. Although they came to their profession at a time when Canadian architects lacked adequate training opportunities and status, the two brothers created the largest and most successful firm in the country during the early part of the 20th century. They kept abreast of change, providing clients with a variety of building types in a range of fashionable styles. Edward's business and organizational abilities enabled the office to grow and handle large commissions, while William's collegiality and atelier experience made it an important and effective training place. Among the draughtsmen who would later become respected Canadian architects were John Smith Archibald*, David Robertson Brown, David Huron MacFarlane, Kenneth Guscotte Rea, and Charles Jewett Saxe. Not only did Edward and William Maxwell themselves benefit from their success, but so, too, did the Canadian profession as a whole.

SUSAN WAGG

The papers of Edward Maxwell, his brother William Sutherland, and their various partnerships are held in the John Bland Canadian Architecture Coll. of the Blackader-Lauterman Library of Architecture and Art, McGill Univ. Libraries (Montreal), Acc. no.2. They contain documentation for over 700 projects and include more than 16,200 plans and drawings, as well as personal correspondence, business papers, journals, notebooks, scrapbooks, clippings, photographs, fabric swatches, and artefacts. Significant new material has been added to the collection since the publication of *Edward & W. S. Maxwell: a guide to the archive*, ed. Irena Murray (Montreal, 1986). Throughout their lives, both Maxwells were avid book collectors, especially of works on art and architecture, including rare or limited editions. William's collection alone is thought to have totalled between 3,500 and 4,000 volumes. Part of the collections has been preserved and these items are listed in *The libraries of Edward and W. S. Maxwell in the collection of the Blackader-Lauterman Library of Art and Art, McGill University*, comp. Cindy Campbell *et al.*, intro. Irena Murray (Montreal, 1991). Numerous archival documents, photographs, and essays on the Maxwells have been placed on the Web as part of the digital collection "The architecture of Edward & W. S. Maxwell: the Canadian legacy" at *cac.mcgill.ca/maxwells/*.

ANQ-M, CE601-S126, 30 avril 1861. BCM-G, RBMB, Knox Presbyterian Church (Montreal), 9 Jan. 1869. *Gazette* (Montreal), 14–15 Nov. 1923. *Montreal Daily Star*, 14 Nov. 1923. *The architecture of Edward & W. S. Maxwell* (exhibition catalogue, Montreal Museum of Fine Arts, 1991). Kelly Crossman, *Architecture in transition: from art to practice, 1885–1906* (Kingston, Ont., and Montreal, 1987). France Gagnon-Pratte, *Country houses for Montrealers,*

1892–1924: the architecture of E. and W. S. Maxwell (Montreal, 1987). R. M. Pepall, Montréal, 1912: building a beaux-arts museum (exhibition catalogue, Montreal Museum of Fine Arts, 1986). "Province of Quebec Association of Architects," Canadian Architect and Builder (Toronto), 4 (1891): 88, 90–91. Royal Canadian Academy of Arts; exhibitions and members, 1880–1979, comp. E. de R. McMann (Toronto, 1981). The storied province of Quebec; past and present, ed. W. [C. H.] Wood et al. (5v., Toronto, 1931–32).

MAXWELL, SUSANNAH AUGUSTA. See STOKES

MELANSON, NATHALIE (Bourgeois), mystic; b. c. 1842 in Memramcook, N.B., daughter of François Melanson and Marie Le Blanc; m. 21 Jan. 1865 Denis-L. Bourgeois, a farmer, in Saint-Anselme, N.B., and they had two sons and two daughters; d. 24 Sept. 1923 in Scoudouc, N.B.

Nathalie Melanson lived in the farming community of Scoudouc, where her parents, from nearby Memramcook, had settled. Founded in 1809, Scoudouc would not become a parish until 1907. It was therefore administered by priests from Memramcook, Saint-Anselme, or Shediac. The Holy Cross Fathers, who had founded the College of Saint Joseph in Memramcook in 1864 [see Camille Lefebvre*], had a profound effect on Melanson. Father Louis-Joseph-Octave Lecours, who was in charge of the Scoudouc mission for 24 years, until 1892, promoted the devotion to the rosary there, enrolling many of his flock in the Archconfraternity of the Holy Rosary. Melanson was a devout member of this organization, and of the Archconfraternity of the Blessed Sacrament, and she was also a member of the Société Saint-Joseph, an organization run by the Holy Cross Fathers. According to a history of the parish of Scoudouc, Melanson, who became known locally as Mother Nathalie, had great respect for Father Lecours, and served him dinner every Sunday after mass.

Melanson is remembered especially for her role in the supposed apparitions of the Virgin Mary in the local school at Scoudouc. When a group of children between the ages of seven and eleven reported seeing and hearing the Virgin in the fall of 1893, Melanson was one of the few adults who also claimed to have had supernatural visions. Her testimony regarding the apparitions makes up an important part of a book by Philéas-Frédéric Bourgeois* entitled L'école aux apparitions mystérieuses (1896). In this study Bourgeois presents the people of Scoudouc as being devout churchgoers who gathered each Sunday to recite the rosary, and who held frequent processions in honour of the Virgin Mary.

Nathalie Melanson was at the centre of religious life in her community and found herself in a delicate position at the time of the apparitions. Scoudouc had been tied to the parish of Shediac a year before the events began to unfold. The assistant priest there,

Pierre-Paul Dufour, was sceptical about the apparitions and ordered that the children be kept away from school until their imaginations had calmed down. He also asked Melanson to stay away, and she was not permitted to return to the school for about a year and a half. When she did enter it again, the manifestations resumed. In 1896 she reported to P.-F. Bourgeois that she was happy that her visions of the Virgin Mary and the Christ child would be written down in detail, she herself being illiterate.

During the time of the apparitions, the members of the church who strongly believed in them resented the negative attitude taken by the assistant priest and the curé at Shediac. They remained obedient to the religious authorities, however. P.-F. Bourgeois also found himself in a difficult position, having published an inquiry into the apparitions without a mandate from the Church, and his book was banned in some New Brunswick parishes.

Nathalie Melanson remained true to her testimony until her death in 1923: a funeral notice in the newspaper L'Évangéline states that she died convinced she had seen the Virgin Mary. Her story provides an example of the complex role played by mysticism in French Canadian society. One of the most devout Catholics in her area, Melanson found herself in the middle of a controversy that led to her being reprimanded by the Church she served so faithfully.

RONALD LABELLE

Centre d'Études Acadiennes, Univ. de Moncton, N.-B., Fonds Alice Léger. L'Évangéline (Moncton), 11 oct. 1923: 8. P.-F. Bourgeois, L'école aux apparitions mystérieuses (Montréal, 1896). J.-A. L'Archevêque, Histoire de la paroisse St-Jacques-le-Majeur, Scoudouc, N.-B., diocèse de Saint-Jean (s.l., 1932). Ronald Labelle, "Philias-Frédéric Bourgeois: précurseur de l'ethnologie acadienne," Francophonies d'Amérique (Ottawa), no.2 (1992): 5–11.

MELANSON, OLIVIER-MAXIMIN, businessman and politician; b. 2 July 1854 in Haute-Aboujagane, N.B., son of Maximin Melanson and Julie Le Blanc; m. February 1878 Marguerite Boudreau in Barachois, N.B., and they had 11 children; d. 7 July 1926 in Moncton, N.B., and was buried in nearby Shediac.

Olivier-Maximin Melanson studied at the elementary school in his native village. Like many other farmers' sons, he was unable to continue his schooling for lack of money. The favourable economic climate probably encouraged him to undertake a career in business, which, until then, had been virtually restricted to an English-speaking elite. He settled in Shediac. With a salt-water port close by, rapidly expanding railway services, and abundant natural resources, this village in the 1870s was well on the way to becoming an important centre for exporting products such as lumber, potatoes, fish, and lobster to the United States, Europe, and the West Indies.

At the beginning of the 1870s, Melanson worked there as a clerk in a store owned by Fidèle Poirier, a brother of the future senator Pascal Poirier*. This experience with the first Acadian merchant in Shediac was evidently beneficial, since he became co-owner with one of Poirier's sons, André, of a general store in 1873. The following year he opened his own store, which proved so profitable that he was able to buy a large number of parcels of agricultural land as well as numerous lobster processing plants. This diversification enabled him to survive periods of stress and economic difficulty. For many years Melanson was one of the leading exporters of potatoes and eggs from southeastern New Brunswick. In 1887, for example, he shipped 40,000 dozen eggs by rail, enough to fill 45 rail cars, each holding $200 to $300 worth of goods. To remain competitive, he adopted some of the practices of his rivals. For many years the most important of these was Chesley Tait, who was the first to develop the potato industry in the Shediac region. To facilitate the export of his merchandise, Melanson built large potato storehouses near the railway lines. A typical storehouse might have been a storey and a half high, 60 feet long, and 35 feet wide. He paid his employees in wooden or cardboard tokens, redeemable only at his store. The value of his company's capital increased from $1,000 in 1881 to $99,000 in 1910. Melanson's career was so successful financially that at the time of his death, Placide GAUDET would refer to him as the first Acadian millionaire.

Melanson was also active in politics. He made an unsuccessful attempt in 1881 to win a seat on the Westmorland County Council. He had more success in 1903, when he became a municipal councillor in Shediac, which had been incorporated as a town in that year. His objective at the time was to promote the interests of his fellow Acadians.

On the provincial scene, Melanson was one of the first Acadians from the southeast to run for election in the riding of Westmorland, to win the seat, and to give speeches in French in the Legislative Assembly. A Conservative in politics, he was successful in the general elections of 20 Jan. 1890, 18 Feb. 1899, and 20 June 1912. He was defeated on 22 Oct. 1892, 28 Feb. 1903, and 3 March 1908. He was not a candidate in the 1895 election. On 4 March 1914 he became deputy speaker of the Legislative Assembly, replacing Walter Brittain Dickson, who was absent because of illness. On Dickson's death, Melanson took over his position on 9 March 1916, becoming the second Acadian in the Maritime provinces to hold such an office, after Stanislaus Francis Perry*, who had been speaker of the Prince Edward Island Assembly in 1873–74. When a general election was called in New Brunswick in 1917, Melanson bowed out of political life, citing medical

reasons. Thereafter, he devoted himself to his business activities, which his children carried on after his death.

A self-educated merchant and politician, Olivier-Maximin Melanson bore witness to the dynamism and strength of will shown by the Acadians of the late 19th and early 20th centuries. They laid the bases for economic success and political involvement, which hitherto had been mainly restricted to the English-speaking community. From then on, they could look forward to a promising future in New Brunswick.

LEWIS LEBLANC

PANB, MC 1156; RS141A1b, F18776, 30 July 1887 (mfm.); RS141C5.46, F18949, 7 July 1926 (mfm.). *L'Évangéline* (Moncton, N.-B.), 8, 15 juill. 1926. J. E. Belliveau, *Running far in: the story of Shediac* (Windsor, N.S., 1977). Régis Brun, *Shediac: l'histoire se raconte* (Sackville, N.-B., 1994). Diane Myles, *Speakers of the Legislative Assembly, Province of New Brunswick, 1786–1985* (Fredericton, 1986). *Vital statistics from N.B. newspapers* (Johnson), vols.43, 46.

MENISSINO (Menissinowinnini). *See* SHINGWAUK, GEORGE

MERCIER, OSCAR-FÉLIX, physician, surgeon, professor, and hospital administrator; b. 1 Dec. 1866 in Montreal, son of Joseph Mercier, a carter, and Zoé Gauthier; m. there 4 June 1895 Alexina Rolland, and they had one son and two daughters; d. there 26 July 1929.

After primary schooling at the École Modèle Jacques-Cartier in Montreal, Oscar-Félix Mercier went on to obtain his classical education at the Petit Séminaire de Montréal, where he enrolled in 1879, and then at the Collège Sainte-Marie. A brilliant and disciplined pupil, he took up the study of medicine at the Université Laval in Montreal in 1886. He obtained his MD in 1890 and was licensed to practise by the College of Physicians and Surgeons of the Province of Quebec on 14 May that year. Soon after, he went to Paris for further training as a surgeon. For two years he attended the clinic of Dr Paul Reclus, where he was introduced to the antiseptic and aseptic techniques recommended by French surgeons Octave Terrillon and Louis-Félix Terrier, who were pioneers in aseptic surgical methods. He became aware of the efficacy of autoclaves in sterilizing water, instruments, and surgical dressings. He also learned the new techniques of local anaesthesia, including the use of cocaine.

On his return to Montreal in 1892, Mercier went to work at Notre-Dame Hospital as assistant surgeon to Dr Alfred-T. Brosseau. He continued in this capacity until 1899, when he became acting chief of surgery at the hospital, replacing Brosseau. His position was made permanent the following year. The contrast between master and assistant was striking. A gruff and withdrawn man at the end of his career, Brosseau operated using traditional procedures that combined dexterity with quick motions. A young and inquisitive surgeon interested in medical bacteriology and new techniques, Mercier favoured closely linking laboratory sciences and medicine. Despite the sometimes sharp tensions between the two, Mercier was able to obtain from the authorities at Notre-Dame Hospital the support he needed to introduce new surgical procedures.

Mercier was one of the pioneers in the introduction of aseptic methods into surgery. He used the most recent discoveries in general and local anaesthesia and operated on patients according to a strict protocol. On visits to Paris in 1896, 1920, and 1924, he learned about the rapid development of bacteriology. In the fall of 1896, for example, he enrolled in a course in "microbial technique" taught by Émile Roux and Élie Metchnikoff (who would be awarded the Nobel Prize for medicine in 1908) in the laboratories of the Institut Pasteur. He was introduced at that time to research on the suppuration of wounds, including the role played by staphylococci and streptococci in post-operative infections. He also became aware of the first data obtained through immunology, such as the processes of virulence and phagocytosis. Mercier brought back from Paris various procedures for disinfection by physical means (boiling water, dry heat, moist heat, and steam sterilizers) and by chemical means (various antiseptics). In short, he was one of the first Canadian surgeons to receive adequate theoretical and practical training in microbial techniques as applied to surgery. With his rigorous method of surgical asepsis, he successfully performed abdominal operations, including herniotomies and appendectomies, which until then had been very dangerous.

After Mercier became chief of surgery in 1899, the reforms already introduced were consolidated and surgical practice was modernized at an accelerated pace. Under his leadership, extremely stringent measures of asepsis and tight controls on anaesthesia were put into effect. In addition, operating schedules and access to the operating room became stricter, the teaching of pathology there was forbidden, the staff received appropriate training, more effective instruments were acquired, and a recovery room was installed. The operating room and its annexes also underwent significant changes with the introduction of a mechanical operating table, dressing sterilizer, autoclave, and glass trays for holding sterile probes, compresses, and dressings. In 1913 Mercier promoted the establishment of an anaesthesia department under the direction of a chief anaesthetist and his assistants that would be responsible for instituting regular examination of patients, setting rigid timetables, recommending the purchase of equipment, and applying new techniques, such as the use of nitrous oxide in addition to chloroform (from 1919). His efforts would result in a significant reduction in infections and post-operative deaths, despite an increase in risky surgical procedures.

Mercier's interest in furthering medical science led him to promote improvements, not only in the operating room, but also in the laboratories at Notre-Dame Hospital. An excellent clinician and highly gifted diagnostician, he always emphasized the need to link clinical examination at the patient's bed with anatomical and pathological examination, using the methods provided by technical and scientific innovations. While continuing to use the traditional procedures of questioning, auscultation, percussion, palpation, and chemical urinalysis, he adopted a series of new clinical approaches recently created by medical technology, including radioscopic examination, bacteriological examination of sputum, exploratory extractions of fluid by syringe for laboratory analysis, electric cautery, the injection of antitetanus serum, and the use of cocaine as a local anaesthetic. He had also helped promote the plan to build a new hospital. Until it was opened, Notre-Dame Hospital was located in what had been Donegana's Hotel, near the Château Ramezay on Rue Notre-Dame. In 1901 the hospital authorities decided to erect a new structure on Rue Sherbrooke. The following year Mercier was a member of the committee responsible for supervising the building plans. Various problems delayed the project. Construction was under way when Mercier, after years of intense medical activity at the hospital, was appointed superintendent in 1918. In this capacity he made sure the work undertaken conformed to the construction standards of a modern, functional hospital. It was not until 1924 that the new $1.5 million building was opened. Mercier resigned as superintendent the following year, but he stayed on as chief of surgery for the rest of his life.

Through his teaching, his scientific papers, and his articles, Mercier assisted in a major way in disseminating the theoretical and practical implications of bacteriology in the field of surgery. Along with his work as a surgeon and administrator, he devoted considerable time to teaching. In 1893 he became an associate professor of surgery at the Montreal School of Medicine and Surgery, which was the faculty of medicine of the Université Laval in Montreal. He was appointed professor of clinical surgery in 1905 and joined the council of the faculty of medicine in 1913; he would hold both offices until the end of his life. To provide adequate theoretical and practical training for the staff who worked in the operating room, he had helped found a school for nurses at Notre-Dame Hospital [see Élodie Mailloux*] in 1897. His son, Oscar, would become an associate professor of surgery in the same faculty in 1927 and would be a prominent surgeon at Notre-Dame Hospital.

Mercier was very active in many professional associations. He contributed greatly to the revival of the

Société Médicale de Montréal in 1900 and served as its president for the year 1903–4. In 1904 he directed the surgical section of the second congress of the Association des Médecins de Langue Française de l'Amérique du Nord, held in Montreal. One of the founders of the Société de Chirurgie de Montréal in 1928, he served as its first president. His skill was recognized outside Canada: admitted to membership in the American College of Surgeons, he was a corresponding member of the Société des Chirurgiens de Paris from 1910 to 1929.

Oscar-Félix Mercier played a major role in bringing modern surgery to the province of Quebec. His efforts to organize operating rooms, introduce aseptic and anaesthetic procedures, install new surgical equipment, and train operating-room nurses enabled Notre-Dame Hospital to provide surgical care of a high quality for the time. He also contributed in a significant way to the teaching of surgery and anaesthesia, by introducing students to new operating methods (such as electrical cautery and local anaesthesia) and to recent theoretical ideas. In short, with the help of a few colleagues, he inspired an important movement to modernize hospital practice in the province of Quebec.

DENIS GOULET and PHILIPPE HUDON

Oscar-Félix Mercier wrote many articles, most of them published in L'Union médicale du Canada (Montréal), for example: "L'anesthésie chirurgicale par la stovaine," 35 (1906): 249–55; "À propos de quelques observations de cures radicales de hernies," 25 (1896): 20–30; "L'art obstétrical à Paris," 19 (1890): 626–31; "Des appendicites," 21 (1892): 617–22; "Du traitement des grands écrasements des membres par l'embaumement," 29 (1900): 831–43; "L'iode, antiseptique chirurgical," 42 (1913): 138–48; and "Le mouvement chirurgical depuis le congrès de Québec," 33 (1904): 412–24.

ANQ-M, CE601-S51, 2 déc. 1866, 4 juin 1895. Arch. de l'Hôpital Notre-Dame (Montréal), Procès-verbaux du bureau médical, 1892–1928; Rapports annuels, 1892–1928. Arch. de l'Institut Pasteur (Paris), Cours de microbie technique, MP 29048 (liste des personnes ayant suivi les cours, 1889–1970). Le Devoir, 27 juill. 1929. Canadian men and women of the time (Morgan; 1898 and 1912). College of Physicians and Surgeons of the Prov. of Quebec, Medical reg. (Montreal), 1897; 1911. "Le docteur Oscar Félix Mercier," La Rev. moderne (Montréal), 10 (1929), no.9: 8. École de Médecine et de Chirurgie de Montréal, Annuaire, 1890–1919. Denis Goulet, Histoire de la faculté de médecine de l'université de Montréal, 1843–1993 (Montréal, 1993). Denis Goulet et al., Histoire de l'hôpital Notre-Dame de Montréal, 1880–1980 (Montréal, 1993). Denis Goulet et Othmar Keel, "Les hommes-relais de la bactériologie en territoire québécois et l'introduction de nouvelles pratiques diagnostiques et thérapeutiques (1890–1920)," RHAF, 46 (1992–93): 417–42. Denis Goulet et André Paradis, Trois siècles d'histoire médicale au Québec; chronologie des institutions et des pratiques (1639–1939) (Montréal, 1992). [Albert] Le Sage, "In memoriam: le professeur Oscar F. Mercier, 1867–1929," L'Union médicale du Canada, 58 (1929): 523–28. Univ. de Montréal, Faculté de médecine, Annuaire, 1920–28.

MEREDITH, Sir HENRY VINCENT, banker and philanthropist; b. 27 Feb. 1850 in London, Upper Canada, son of John Walsingham Cooke Meredith and Sarah Pegler; m. 14 Nov. 1888 Isobel Brenda Allan (d. 1959) in Montreal; they had no children; d. there 24 Feb. 1929 and was buried in Mount Royal Cemetery.

Vincent Meredith was born into a remarkable family of Anglo-Irish immigrants who had come to the Canadas in 1834. Among his father's brothers were William Collis, who would be appointed a chief justice, and Edmund Allen*, who would serve as a senior federal civil servant. Vincent's father became a court clerk and a successful real estate and insurance agent in London. Into "a home rich in cultural elements" were born eight sons and six daughters. The eldest son, WILLIAM RALPH, was to become the provincial Tory leader in 1879. Vincent's other brothers would enjoy success in their professions.

After an initial education at home, Vincent briefly attended the London Collegiate Institute. In May 1867 he joined the Hamilton branch of the Bank of Montreal as a clerk at a salary of $200 per year. Banking in mid-19th-century Canada offered young males the opportunity of attaching themselves to the emerging urban professional class. Starting salaries and conditions – long hours and frequent transfers – were poor, but the prospect of long-term security and social status sustained them. The Bank of Montreal was Canada's oldest and most widely based bank, so Meredith's clerking career saw him posted to branches in Port Hope, Montreal, London, and Simcoe. In 1871 he graduated to teller in Ottawa at a yearly salary of $500 and in 1875 he was appointed an accountant in London at $1,100.

The bank's recognition of Meredith's potential became evident in 1879 when he was brought to the head office in Montreal as assistant inspector. Bank inspectors ensured overall operational integrity; promising employees were appointed inspectors to allow them an intimate knowledge of the bank's entire system. Meredith was made an assistant manager in Montreal in 1887; in 1889 he became a manager at the head office at $5,000 a year. The appointment to Montreal had put him on the doorstep of national commerce and industry and given him an entrée into Anglo-Montreal society. In 1888 he had married Isobel Brenda, the daughter of Montreal steamship magnate Andrew Allan*. They would have no children, but would quickly establish themselves as linchpins of Montreal philanthropy. Meredith joined the Montreal Garrison Artillery Brigade, in which he would rise to command a battery, and he helped found the Montreal Winter Club. In 1894 the Merediths commissioned Montreal architect Edward MAXWELL to build them a Queen-Anne style mansion – Ardvarna – on Pine Avenue.

According to an early-20th-century newspaper,

Meredith

Meredith was "alert, keen and absolutely exacting as to the details of the bank." The erect, military bearing that he would retain to the end of his life gave him an air of authority. He epitomized the values of Canadian banking: integrity and meticulousness. In 1903 he was appointed manager of Montreal's main branch and assistant general manager to Edward Seaborne Clouston*. General managers such as Clouston oversaw the bank's operations and its strategic course. The bank's presidency had generally been bestowed on a Montreal capitalist; presidents Sir George Alexander Drummond* and Richard Bladworth Angus brought railway and manufacturing connections to their often nominal banking duties. Clouston's resignation in November 1911 reflected his chagrin at being passed over for the presidency by Angus; it also opened the way for Meredith's appointment as general manager in December at $30,000.

When Angus retired in 1913, the bank appointed a banker born to be its president – Meredith – at a yearly salary of $40,000. His place as general manager was filled by another seasoned banker, Sir Frederick Williams-Taylor. For the next 14 years the combination of the cautious, retiring Meredith and the urbane, outgoing Williams-Taylor would guide the bank through tumultuous times. Meredith's presidency soon encountered the commercial slump of 1913 and then it would face the unprecedented challenge of a world war. Depression would follow and not until the end of his presidency in 1927 would Canada's economy return to any degree of normality. Meredith's tenure would thus be one of constant adjustment to new circumstances.

The Bank of Montreal grew steadily during Meredith's presidency. From assets of $244,800,000 in 1913, it more than tripled its base to $831,500,000 in 1927. Dividends increased to a steady 14 per cent by the 1920s. Despite problems in revolutionary Mexico, the bank grew internationally as well. Domestic growth was supplemented by amalgamations it initiated with the Bank of British North America (1918), parts of the Colonial Bank (1920), the Merchants' Bank of Canada (1921), and the Molsons Bank (1924). Through these years Meredith sat as president of Royal Trust, the bank's trust company. He was also a director of an array of Montreal-based companies, most notably the Canadian Pacific Railway and Dominion Textile. At the same time he directed his philanthropy to such institutions as McGill University and the Royal Victoria Hospital.

During World War I, Meredith adeptly perpetuated the bank's role as Ottawa's banker and fiscal agent abroad. He held the ear of federal finance minister William Thomas White*. In 1914, for instance, Meredith was pivotal in advising White on wartime monetary arrangements; the Finance Act of 1914 suspended the traditional convertibility of dominion and bank notes into gold and for the first time in Canada introduced the creation of government-backed national credit. With the closure of Canada's capital markets in London, England, the Bank of Montreal facilitated the placing of Canadian war loans in New York and then helped to harness Canadian investors to the national war bond effort. In London, the bank acted as banker to the Canadian military forces in Europe. Closer to home, Meredith spearheaded the bank's donation of a machine-gun battery, named Borden's Motor Machine-Gun Battery, to the Canadian Expeditionary Force. At the same time, he encouraged employees to enlist and ordered that the bank continue to pay their salary for the first six months of military duty. When its retail staff became depleted, he issued instructions that women be taken on as "emergency staff." On 14 Nov. 1916 he was created a baronet for his wartime services to the nation. For her part, Lady Meredith acted as president of the Purple Cross Service for the Care of Wounded and Disabled Horses on the Battlefield.

Peace, Meredith believed, would bring a return to Canada's traditional formula for national growth: the development of natural resources, protected manufacturing, an open-door immigration policy, and reliance on foreign borrowing offset by export earnings. The post-war period, however, refused to fulfil his predictions. Only in the late 1920s did words such as "satisfactory" re-enter his public assessments of Canada's performance.

Meredith's adherence to the economic status quo was echoed in his deeply conservative leadership. In part, his caution was moulded by a realization that as the government's banker, the Bank of Montreal had the most to lose from changes to the structure of Canadian banking. In 1918 the general manager of the Royal Bank of Canada, Edson Loy Pease, had used his stature as president of the Canadian Bankers' Association to champion the idea of a central bank capable of governing the creation – the "rediscount" – of national credit. Sensing that Pease's scheme was a covert attempt to dethrone his bank, Meredith urged White to extend the Finance Act into peacetime; the nation faced too many other post-war challenges to tamper with the way in which national credit was governed, he argued. White heeded this advice, but in the 1920s Canada's lack of an expansive credit mechanism tarnished the credibility of the banking system, particularly in the populist west. When negative sentiments surfaced in 1923 during the revision of the Bank Act, Meredith attacked "the peculiar tenets which regard banking as the instrument of capital and a public menace."

Compulsive caution tainted Meredith's decisions. The amalgamations during his tenure had done little to extend the bank's reach, merely adding branches where the bank was already well rooted. Other banks

732

used mergers and lending policy more aggressively to expand their share of the market. Consequently, the Royal Bank surpassed the Bank of Montreal in assets in 1925, becoming Canada's largest bank. Meredith came to regard Pease with contempt and would not even speak to him.

In 1927, immediately after the bank's annual meeting, the board of directors, possibly concerned over the bank's slipping fortunes, created the position of chairman of the board and appointed Meredith to it, shifting him out of the president's office and installing vice-president Charles Blair Gordon* in his place. Meredith continued to chair the board's executive committee, but in July 1928 he was stricken with cerebral paralysis. He died at home about seven months later. His funeral at Christ Church Cathedral was attended by the city's commercial and political elite. Tributes represented Sir Henry Vincent Meredith as a hybrid of old Canadian financial conservatism and new professional banking. He left bequests totalling $575,000 to the Royal Victoria Hospital, McGill University, and Bishop's College (both academic institutions had conferred honorary degrees on him in 1927) and to two special pension funds for bank employees, one in particular for women employees.

DUNCAN MCDOWALL

Arch., BMO Financial Group (Montreal), Bank circular copybooks, 1914–18; General managers' scrapbooks, 1920–29; Letter and cable copybooks, 1913–18; Sir H. V. Meredith biog. and corr. files; Sir F. W. Taylor biog. file; Staff ledger, L–Mac. BCM-G, RBMB, St Paul's Presbyterian Church (Montreal), 14 Nov. 1888. LAC, MG 26, H; I; MG 27, II, D18. Royal Bank of Canada Arch. (Montreal), RBC 2, 43G PeaE (biog. file); 46A, WA1 (F. T. Walker reminiscence file). Bank of Montreal, *Annual general meeting*, 1913–29. [Archibald Bremner], *City of London, Ontario, Canada: the pioneer period and the London of to-day* (2nd ed., London, 1900; repr. 1967). *Canadian men and women of the time* (Morgan; 1898 and 1912). Merrill Denison, *Canada's first bank: a history of the Bank of Montreal* (2v., Toronto and Montreal, 1966–67), 2. A. B. Jamieson, *Chartered banking in Canada* (Toronto, 1953). "The late Sir Vincent Meredith, bart.," Canadian Bankers' Assoc., *Journal* (Toronto), 36 (1928–29): 211–14. Duncan McDowall, *Quick to the frontier: Canada's Royal Bank* (Toronto, 1993). Donald MacKay, *The Square Mile: merchant princes of Montreal* (Vancouver, 1987). [H.] O. Miller, *A century of western Ontario: the story of London, "The Free Press," and western Ontario, 1849–1949* (Toronto, 1949; repr. Westport, Conn., 1972).

MEREDITH, Sir WILLIAM RALPH, lawyer, politician, judge, and educator; b. 31 March 1840 in Westminster Township, Upper Canada, son of John Walsingham Cooke Meredith and Sarah Pegler; m. 26 June 1862 Mary Holmes in London, Upper Canada, and they had three daughters and one son; d. 21 Aug. 1923 in Montreal and was buried in Toronto.

William Meredith's father, a graduate of Trinity College, Dublin, who studied some law, had been preceded to the Canadas by other members of this notable Anglo-Irish family. He settled on a bush farm in Westminster in 1834. After William's birth, he went to Port Stanley as deputy collector of customs and then to London as market clerk; in 1847 he was appointed clerk there of the Division Court of Middlesex County. This influential position, combined with successes in real estate, loans, and insurance, boosted the economic and social standing of the family, which became an important part of the town's elite. The eldest son among 14 children, William was educated at the London District Grammar School and in 1856 he was articled to lawyer Thomas Scatcherd* of London. Three years later he won a two-year scholarship to the University of Toronto, where he studied law. Called to the bar in 1861, he entered into a partnership with Scatcherd that would last until the latter's death in 1876.

Meredith took on a wide variety of civil and criminal cases and gradually became "the acknowledged leader of the London Bar." In 1871 he was first elected a bencher of the Law Society of Upper Canada. Re-elected on many subsequent occasions, he received more votes than any other lawyer in the 1881 and 1886 polls, results that indicated the esteem in which he was held by his colleagues. He completed the requirements for an LLB from the University of Toronto in 1872 and three years later he was made a QC by the provincial government, an honour that was repeated at the federal level in 1880. In 1876 he had succeeded Scatcherd as London's city solicitor and from 1879 to 1888 he was first president of the Middlesex Law Association. In 1888 he left his practice in London to head the Toronto firm of the late William Alexander Foster*; that same year he became an honorary member of the law faculty of the University of Toronto, which granted him an LLD in 1889.

Not completely satisfied with his legal attainments, in a by-election in 1872 Meredith had succeeded John Carling* as London's representative to the Ontario legislature. There he joined the Conservative caucus on the opposition benches and embraced many of the values held by party leader Matthew Crooks Cameron*. Both men possessed a strong affection for Britain, the empire, and the Church of England, and they often displayed an "aristocratic temper." Still, Meredith's attitude led him to a sense of noblesse oblige that was not present in the more conventional Toryism of Cameron and other provincial Conservatives. In 1874, for example, only Meredith, Simpson McCall (a Conservative), and Daniel John O'Donoghue* (a labour MLA) supported a motion for the unqualified enfranchisement of all males over 21, a measure that most Conservatives and all the Liberals considered too advanced for the times. Such stands have caused some to depict Meredith as a radical, but the appellation seems inappropriate for one who never challenged the basic assumptions of a society from which he derived so many personal benefits. Nevertheless, he was the first clearly defined progressive Conservative in Ontario.

Meredith's tendencies did not prevent him from rising within a caucus thin in talent, and in 1878 Cameron named him deputy leader. Later that year Cameron became a judge and, when the assembly reconvened in January 1879, Meredith was chosen leader without even the formality of a ballot. In the hurried campaign for the election in June, he placed great stress on reducing public expenditure. The Liberal administration of Oliver Mowat* was indicted on some 29 charges of excessive spending. Though retrenchment never again achieved such pre-eminence in Meredith's appeals – he would lead the Conservatives in four subsequent elections (1883, 1886, 1890, and 1894) – it remained a factor in his courting of voters. There were other regular features in Tory campaign literature. Meredith wanted to restore the power over liquor licensing that the province had taken from the municipalities under the Crooks Act of 1876. In addition, he called for a reversion to a non-partisan chief superintendent of education, a position Mowat's Liberals had discarded in favour of a politicized minister of education. Meredith provided ample evidence to show that these moves had done much more for Grit patronage than they had for the public welfare. On one issue he was so conservative that he could be described as reactionary. Sexism was not unusual in the politics of the era, but in 1884 Meredith resisted not only the provincial franchise for women but also the municipal ballot for spinsters and widows and even a government measure to allow females to enter University College in the University of Toronto. In 1892 he sat on the Law Society committee that rejected Clara Brett MARTIN's application to become a lawyer and in the assembly he was the most vocal opponent of the bill introduced by William Douglas Balfour* to require lawyers to interpret the word "person" in the society's statute to include women.

These views were counterbalanced by the progressive component in Meredith's political philosophy. He continued to fight for full male suffrage until it was accepted by the government in 1888, on which occasion the premier acknowledged his pivotal role. In 1884 he had chided Mowat's administration for delaying the payment of annuities promised to many Indians and later in the session he fought unsuccessfully for an extension of the franchise to all adult male natives not living on reserves. The following year he introduced a workmen's compensation bill modelled on British legislation. The Liberals incorporated the measure into one of their own bills in 1886 but Meredith objected to changes that he found too accommodating towards employers. He contended that the legislation should not have exempted corporations with voluntary compensation plans, since it would be impossible to determine whether private schemes could be as fair as the public design. In April 1887 Meredith was again more liberal than the Liberals in his response to the amendment of their factory legislation of 1884. To achieve proper enforcement – the key to success in this sphere – Meredith suggested that an inspector be appointed locally for every county. The government, however, would create only three inspectorships, to be filled by the province, for the whole of Ontario.

Meredith thus developed a balanced and seemingly attractive program, but it did not propel him to power. For one thing the Conservatives were weakly organized. Meredith viewed his job at Queen's Park as a part-time commitment: he saw no need to call caucus meetings, oversee other responsibilities in the assembly, or attend to constituency business. Moreover, throughout his parliamentary career there was the distraction of a full-time legal practice. And to a considerable extent, Meredith's lack of political success was a natural consequence of Mowat's greater skills.

Electorally four main considerations account for the dramatic series of defeats experienced by the Conservatives between 1879 and 1894. First, Mowat's Liberals freely stole many of their proposals. Journalist Hector Willoughby Charlesworth* would later note that "Mowat frequently rode to victory on policies that had originated with his brilliant opponent." Secondly, Meredith's platform held few inducements for rural voters. When he did focus on them, it was usually in a critical way. During the 1886 campaign, for instance, he claimed that it was grossly unjust to grant to farmers' sons voting privileges that were denied to those of urban labourers. Such an approach, however logical and courageous, was politically unwise in a predominantly agricultural society. A third circumstance that cost Meredith votes was his relations with the federal Conservatives under Sir John A. Macdonald*. Meredith hoped for patronage from Ottawa to reward his supporters in Ontario, but little materialized. In addition, the hard line that Macdonald pursued in federal-provincial conflicts, such as the boundary dispute between Ontario and Manitoba, embarrassed Meredith and enabled the Liberals to charge that he was "disloyal" to the province.

Meredith's growing frustration with the national leadership was, in part, responsible for his confrontation with the Roman Catholic Church over separate school rights, which furnishes the fourth reason for his political failure. In the belief that the Catholic vote in Ontario was pivotal, Macdonald forged an alliance with leading clerics, including archbishops John Joseph Lynch* of Toronto and James Vincent Cleary* of Kingston, to bring this bloc into the Tory camp federally. At the same time Mowat courted them to improve his position provincially. An isolated Meredith, who had always objected to the principle of separate schools, agreed with Macdonald that the Catholic vote was essential to political success in Ontario, but increasingly he felt that "humiliating concessions" were being granted to the Catholic minority by the Mowat Liberals.

In 1885, driven by conscience and Macdonald's refusal to respond to his complaints, Meredith launched an attack upon what he saw as the unfair advantages enjoyed by the separate schools. He denounced the Catholics' right to a guaranteed seat on all secondary school boards and the use of unapproved texts in separate schools. Later, he added to his list of grievances the need for compulsory balloting in separate school elections, which clerics had traditionally controlled, and for a more thorough introduction of English as the language of instruction in Ontario's francophone separate schools. Meredith's criticism appeared measured in comparison with the attacks of more extreme antagonists, such as the *Toronto Daily Mail*, but it was sharp enough to draw the wrath of the Catholic leaders. They threw their weight behind the Liberals, thus helping ensure decisive victories in the elections of 1886, 1890, and 1894. In 1891 efforts by the federal Conservatives to draw Meredith off the provincial stage and into the cabinet, to fill the Ontario seat left vacant by Macdonald's death, had been vetoed by justice minister Sir John Sparrow David Thompson*, who, influenced by Catholic bishops in Ontario, found Meredith's position on separate schools unacceptable.

As a result of the election of June 1894, there were no Catholics in the Tory caucus in Toronto. This embarrassing state of affairs, combined with Meredith's disheartening record of defeat, no doubt contributed to his acceptance of an offer from Ottawa to embark on a more promising career, in October, as chief justice of the Common Pleas division of the Ontario High Court of Justice. He had carefully maintained his standing as a lawyer; from 26 Feb. 1894 to 8 October he was corporation counsel for the City of Toronto and nominal head of its legal department. Knighted in 1896, he became chief justice of the province's Court of Appeal in 1913.

Meredith acquired a high reputation and was considered by some to be "the ablest jurist in Ontario." However, after examining 750 of his cases, legal historian R. C. B. Risk has concluded, in part because of their diversity, that Meredith had little opportunity to develop a coherent philosophy of law, except for a firm commitment to the doctrine of strict precedent. He would scour British, American, and Canadian judgements to discover decisions that seemed germane to the case at hand. If conflicting judgements appeared, he favoured the side with the most verdicts.

Throughout the process his personal opinions counted for little: it was a judge's responsibility to apply precedents, not create new ones. Meredith also sought to avoid injecting his views into decisions pertaining to statutes. When working with a law, he tended, impressively, to consider it as a whole along with its history, to determine the intent of the legislators, and to avoid narrow, restrictive interpretation. The statutes he considered most often were the Municipal Act and the Railway Act. With good reason Toronto city lawyer William Johnston would praise him in an obituary as "one of the best versed judges in municipal law."

Within the courtroom Meredith was considered dignified and courteous, but he could also be "severe." At times he appeared irritable and imperious. Barristers who were unprepared or not properly informed about the law often received harsh reprimands. "His genial courtesy," former justice Wallace NESBITT confirmed, "always overbore a slight tendency to explosive indignation at anything which he conceived to be a technical rather than a justice-serving presentation of a case." Meredith revelled in challenging colleagues to meet his exacting standards of legal argument and authority. Respected and affectionately known among his fellow judges as "the Chief," he was a kindly man with "very few intimates" who turned privately to floriculture for recreation.

Despite his refusal to alter law through judicial proceeding, outside the court Meredith did exercise great influence politically, and his legislative and forensic skills were frequently enlisted by various governments. In 1896 and again in 1906 he excelled as a member of Ontario's statutory revision commission. He also emerged as an important educator, having been chosen a senator at the University of Toronto in 1895 and its chancellor in 1900. In the latter position, which he would hold until his death, he was particularly forceful. His conversion of James Pliny Whitney*, his protégé in the legislature and premier from 1905, to the cause of university reform led to legislation in 1906 that modernized the administrative and financial structures of the University of Toronto. Whitney called on Meredith in 1906 to help prepare two other bills: to regulate railways and to establish the Ontario Railway and Municipal Board. The same year he reviewed and encouraged the legislation that initiated the Hydro-Electric Power Commission of Ontario. Whitney clearly valued Meredith's advice, a pragmatic blend of conservative and progressive views. This role culminated in Meredith's appointment in 1910 as a one-man provincial commission to investigate workmen's compensation. The resulting bill of 1914 updated and made much more effective the existing measures in this field. In addition, Meredith, who chaired Toronto's Civic Improvement Committee in 1909–11, was appointed to several other commissions. On the federal level, in 1912 he probed the collapse of the notorious Farmers Bank of Canada and four years later he investigated the awarding of questionable contracts by Ottawa's Shell Committee during World War I. In Ontario in 1919 he looked into police matters and charges concerning the administration of the Ontario Temperance Act; in the latter enquiry his exoneration of licence inspector John Almayne Ayearst was denounced by Liberal leader Herbert Hartley DEWART. In 1921 he served on a committee struck by the United Farmers administration in Ontario to instruct it on the selection of king's counsels. By this time his advice largely transcended partisan considerations.

Meredith remained active until an intestinal ailment, contracted while on holiday in Maine, occasioned his death in Montreal in 1923. Buried in St James' Cemetery in Toronto, he left an estate valued at $133,877, including his home and gardens on Binscarth Road in Rosedale. He was survived by his wife, their three daughters, and seven distinguished brothers, including Sir HENRY VINCENT and Richard Martin, also a chief justice.

Sir W. R. Meredith's main impact was felt in Ontario politics, where he formulated a progressive Conservative tradition which was inherited, and further developed, by Whitney and other Tory leaders. The *éminence grise* of the Whitney regime, he assisted in implementing many of the progressive concepts that he had vainly advocated while in opposition. As a jurist, Meredith was less ideological, but he was highly regarded by his colleagues on the bench as well as by the governments which eagerly sought his advice.

PETER E. PAUL DEMBSKI

LAC, MG 25, G175 (mfm.); MG 26, A, Macdonald to O'Connor, 22 Feb. 1872; Meredith to Macdonald, 29 April 1879, 20 Oct. 1882; Lynch to Macdonald, 9 May 1882; D, Meredith to Thompson, 1 Oct. 1894. London Public Library, London Room (London, Ont.), Hist. ser. scrapbooks; London scrapbooks. *Daily Mail and Empire*, 22 Aug. 1923. *London Free Press*, 29 April 1879. *Mail* (Toronto), 10 Jan. 1879, continued by *Toronto Daily Mail*, 3, 20, 23 Dec. 1886. *Toronto Daily Star*, 22–23 Aug. 1923. F. H. Armstrong, *The Forest City: an illustrated history of London, Canada* ([Northridge, Calif.], 1986). *Canadian album* (Cochrane and Hopkins), vol.1. *Canadian Bar Rev.* (Toronto), 1 (1923): 557–58. *Canadian men and women of the time* (Morgan; 1912). *Cyclopædia of Canadian biog.* (Rose and Charlesworth), vol.1. P. [E. P.] Dembski, "A matter of conscience: the origins of William Ralph Meredith's conflict with Archbishop John Joseph Lynch," *OH*, 73 (1981): 131–44; "Political history from the opposition benches: William Ralph Meredith, Ontario federalist," *OH*, 89 (1997): 199–217; "William Ralph Meredith: leader of the Conservative opposition in Ontario, 1878–1894" (PHD thesis, Univ. of Guelph, Ont., 1977). A. M. Evans, *Sir Oliver Mowat* (Toronto, 1992). C. W. Humphries, *"Honest enough to be bold": the life and times of Sir James Pliny Whitney* (Toronto, 1985). J. R. Miller, *Equal rights: the Jesuits' Estates Act controversy* (Montreal, 1979). *National encyclopedia of Canadian biography*, ed. J. E. Middleton and W. S. Downs (2v., Toronto, 1935–37). Ont., Legislature, "Newspaper Hansard," 1867–86. R. C. B. Risk, "Sir William R. Meredith, C.J.O.: the search for authority," *Dalhousie Law Journal* (Halifax), 7 (1982–83): 713–41. Toronto, City Council, *Minutes of proc.*, 1894: 53, 61, 224; app.A: 51–52, 69. Eric Tucker, *Administering danger in the workplace: the law and politics of occupational health and safety* (Toronto, 1990). *Types of Canadian women . . .* , ed. H. J. Morgan (Toronto, 1903).

MERRILL, FLORA MacDONALD (Denison), dressmaker, writer, innkeeper, social reformer, feminist, and spiritualist; b. 20 Feb. 1867 near Bridgewater (Actinolite), Upper Canada, daughter of George A. Merrill and Elizabeth MacTavish Thompson; m. 12 Aug. 1892 Howard Denison in Detroit, and they had one son, Merrill*; d. 23 May 1921 in Toronto.

Flora MacDonald Merrill Denison lived two lives, one conventional, the other not. As Flora MacDonald (a frequent nom de plume and her maternal grandmother's name), she once wrote, "I have been an interested tenant of Mrs. Denison's body and at times we differ so vastly in our reasoning and conclusions that I have come to believe she and I are two different personalities." Mrs Denison, apparently, was "someone outside myself." This firmly held, and practised, mystical belief complicates any attempt to reconstruct her lives, material and spiritual, especially the early, Merrill years.

Flora's Merrill ancestry included politically respectable loyalists and religiously unorthodox universalists. Her father alternated between universalism and spiritualism; her schoolteacher mother sometimes declared herself a Catholic, sometimes a Methodist. George Merrill, a successful but discontented schoolmaster, tried his hand at prospecting and mining, in association with Billa Flint*, in the wilds of Hastings County, where Flora was born. The venture proved financially disastrous. The family then settled in Belleville, where Merrill probably continued to dream of a mining bonanza, but never gained regular employment. His daughter depicted him as a village intellectual and spiritualist engaging in controversies over religion and science and attempting to create perpetual motion. Alcohol may have been a problem. Elizabeth apparently supported the family. The sixth of eight children, Flora attended school in Belleville and then Picton, dropping out at the age of 15. After a brief stint at schoolteaching that she later described as "little more enticing to me than solitary confinement," she may have attended business school in Belleville, perhaps taught again briefly, worked in Montreal, and then moved to Toronto, employed for a short period at an insurance agency.

The death of her eldest sister, Mary Edwards Merrill, in 1880 was traumatic. Flora would later report that during a period of depression in the mid 1880s her life was transformed by a psychic experience during which her sister materialized and restored her confidence in the future. In 1900 she told Mary's life story in *Mary Melville, the psychic*. Beyond the descriptions of Mary's astonishing psychic powers and advanced mathematical and linguistic genius, the book reveals much about the religious unorthodoxy that Flora had experienced in her early years, leading to her rejection of traditional Christianity, especially the doctrine of total depravity. The evangelists Dwight Lyman Moody and Ira David Sankey make an appearance as does the popular American freethinker Colonel Robert Green Ingersoll, a friend of Walt Whitman who introduced Flora to the poet's work when she heard him speak in 1892. (She may, in fact, have been exposed to Ingersoll earlier, for he had lectured in Belleville in 1880.) The authenticity of the Bible, the validity of such theological doctrines as eternal punishment and the transcendence of God, as well as the meaning of Darwinism are all debated. Mary, her father, and, of course, the author favoured a religion that combined a gospel of social criticism with spiritualism. After Mary's death one of the attending physicians observed, "She did more to make me believe in an existence outside of the body, than did all the sermons I ever listened to. . . . She so often said to me, '. . . poverty should be for none while there is prosperity for any. Caste is the heaviest curse civilization has to carry.'" The Reverend Benjamin Fish Austin*, a prominent Methodist divine recently expelled from his denomination for defending the reality of psychic phenomena, published *Mary Melville*. (Austin had attended Albert College in Belleville with Mary and had shared the platform with Flora at Lily Dale, the spiritualist summer camp in New York State.) He declared the book "in all essential features . . . a genuine biography of a real and wonderful life." Whatever the fictional element of *Mary Melville* (both spiritualists and rationalists performed in 19th-century Belleville and most of the details of Mary Melville's life have been confirmed), the religious and social ideas expressed in the book were ones that guided Flora throughout her career.

Sometime in the mid 1880s Flora moved to Detroit, where she had relatives. There she probably found office work and may also have begun to write. In August 1892 she entered into a form of marriage with Howard Denison, an already married travelling garment salesman. She called him her husband and the union may have been legalized after the death of Howard's wife in 1904. His role in her life is not clear; the relationship would end in 1914. On 23 June 1893, after the Denisons had moved to Toronto, Merrill was born in Detroit, where Flora had gone for the delivery to ensure for her son the personal and political freedom she associated with the United States. Merrill

would become her greatest source of comfort, her intellectual companion and lifelong friend. Since she was a pacifist, it grieved her greatly when he joined the United States Army Ambulance Corps in 1916 but his service in France cemented what Merrill called "the sacred order of the Mother and Son."

Her unconventional marriage and growing attraction to the sexual freedom and democratic ideals found in Whitman's poetry informed an unpublished novel (written with Edmund Ernest SHEPPARD's daughter Hazel Sheppard Wagner) entitled "Flora MacDam's karma or outside of Eden" (1905). It condemned marriage as "another old superstition invented by the church as a source of revenue and also to keep people in subjection to its dogmas," defended free love, and asserted: "Illegitimate! . . . Not a child born under all of nature's wisest regulations, the mutual desire for sexual embrace, should be branded with the blackest word in our vocabulary." Few, even feminist, Canadians shared this radical view of marriage during Denison's lifetime.

In Toronto, Flora entered the dressmaking trade. For the remainder of her life she would be gainfully employed, sometimes in more than one occupation, supporting herself, her child, and perhaps even her husband. In this respect, she practised what she would frequently preach: women's need for financial independence as the basis of genuine equality. In August 1898 she became manager of the custom-dress department of the Robert Simpson Company, a position that required her to design and sew "the swell dresses worn at the Yacht Club ball." Similar costumes would later motivate her demand for "saner dress for women." Her work doubtless also allowed her an opportunity to observe the oppressed condition of the mainly women workers employed in the garment industry. That subject she would soon take up in her contributions to *Saturday Night*, where she criticized the "competitive system . . . [in which] hundreds go under that a few may be on top," and in 1910 she would support the strike by women workers at the T. E. Braime and Company clothing factory in Toronto. In 1905 she left Simpson's to start her own dressmaking business, Denison Costumer, whose success allowed her to support financially the growing women's movement, in which she took an increasingly active role.

Though *Mary Melville* was not explicitly a feminist novel, it did star a young woman who had "knowledge of a higher plane." Perhaps Flora had already begun to read feminist books that she would later refer to – Charlotte Perkins Gilman's *Women and economics* . . . (Boston, 1898) and *The home* . . . (New York, 1903), and Olive Schreiner's *Women and labor* (New York, [1911]). She was also familiar with critiques of traditional marriage and the family by Edward Carpenter and H. G. Wells. Then there were the contacts she made with leaders of the women's movement in Toronto, especially Dr Emily Howard Stowe [Jennings*], her daughter Dr Ann Augusta Stowe* Gullen, and Dr Margaret Blair Gordon, founders of the campaign for woman suffrage. In 1906 she became secretary of the Dominion Women's Enfranchisement Association, which was soon renamed the Canadian Suffrage Association. For a time her home on Carlton Street would serve as headquarters for the CSA, of which she was president from 1911 to 1914. She attended two of the annual world conventions of the International Woman Suffrage Alliance, in Copenhagen in 1906 and Budapest in 1913. She knew and greatly admired Emmeline Pankhurst, the British suffragist leader, who stayed with her during her Canadian tours in 1909 and 1911. In 1913, while visiting the United Kingdom, Denison joined the Women's Social and Political Union and participated in the protest meeting at the London Pavilion where Pankhurst was arrested. Carrie Chapman Catt, president of the National American Woman Suffrage Association, would hire Flora as a full-time paid lecturer in the successful campaign for the franchise in New York State in 1917.

In 1906 Denison gained a popular platform for her feminist advocacy when she began writing a column in the Toronto *World*, run by William Findlay MACLEAN. It appeared first as "Under the Pines," then as "The Open Road towards Democracy," and finally after 1913 as "Stray Leaves from a Suffragette's Notebook." The rights of women evoked her strongest passion. She summed up her claim to equality this way: "A woman's duty and a woman's sphere is just where her capabilities and opportunities lead her." The achievement of equality would make women partners, not opponents of men. "Men need women in politics; women need men in the home," she argued.

The economic and political equality that Denison demanded as a right revealed a feminism that contrasted with the view of the more numerous maternal feminists, who advocated equal suffrage mainly as a defence of the home and family values threatened by industrial and urban society. Denison, as president of the CSA, sat as an ex officio member of the executive of the National Council of Women of Canada, a body that she repeatedly criticized for its temporizing moderation. In 1912 she broke openly with the council over the issue of flogging as a punishment for "procurers." For her, prostitution was a socio-economic issue rather than a moral one. It was not by physical punishment but through social reform that "white slavery" would be abolished. Her stand on this and other issues – her criticism of the tyranny of the home, her support of divorce and birth control, and especially her reluctant defence of the militant tactics of the Women's Social and Political Union – first split the CSA, when the moderates formed the Equal Franchise

League in 1912, and then forced Denison's resignation in 1914. But she continued to campaign. In 1917 she celebrated recent suffragist victories and endorsed Charlotte Perkins Gilman's optimistic assertion that "the immediate hope of the world is in women."

Denison's reform activities were never confined to the suffragist cause. She sympathized with working women and worried about their neglected children, suggesting that women should be paid to stay home. She advocated state intervention to construct "a great hospital home, guaranteeing employment and comfort to all within its gates." "Caste" was "the greatest curse in this world . . . the greatest blessing its abolition," she wrote in 1907, "and when I use the word 'caste' I do so advisedly, because it is comprehensive and far-reaching enough to include the thousand and one evils of state, of church and of social conditions generally." She supported the Canadian Rational Sunday League's campaign in favour of Sunday streetcars and against a ban on Sunday tobogganing. She joined the Progressive Thought Club, to discuss "new thought, scientific and psychical lines." "All theories for social betterment were expounded," she noted, "and advocates of single tax, socialism, spiritualism, theosophy, Christianity, could be heard any Saturday night at Forum Hall." The alternative medical practices of her feminist physician friends, ranging from the laying on of hands to hydrotherapy and electric currents, won her approval. When war broke out in August 1914 she called upon women to oppose it, arguing that "had women stood shoulder to shoulder with men in thinking out world problems this war would never have been." Later in the conflict she supported the campaign for the prohibition of alcohol [*see* Francis Stephens Spence*].

Denison spent the early years of the war in Napanee, working as a dressmaker to pay for her son's education and recoup her finances. But by 1916 the central focus of her life became the Bon Echo Inn at Mazinaw (Massanoga) Lake, which she and her husband had purchased in 1910. "My life's work from now on," she wrote, "will be in propagating the Ideals of Whitman with Bon Echo as a glorious vantage ground." This rustic inn, originally built by a Cleveland dental surgeon as a wilderness retreat from industrial cities, would serve two purposes. Its rental rooms and cabins (one named in honour of Charlotte Perkins Gilman after a 1911 visit) would provide income. More important, Bon Echo would become a memorial to "the great grey poet," the centre of the Whitman Fellowship of Canada, and an "Institution of the Dear Love of Comrades," a phrase that describes the rather vague, democratic, communal, spiritual philosophy that Flora and others drew from the American poet. "Walt Whitman has been the great positive spiritualizing force," the Whitmanites believed, "absolutely refuting the conclusions of materialistic science by including all their findings and infusing them with the divine fire of an immortal soul."

In March 1916 Denison began publishing the *Sunset of Bon Echo* (a total of six issues appeared by May 1920). The magazine combined promotion of the commercial and the Whitmanite goals of the wilderness resort where she employed native people and sometimes dressed in her own version of native costume. "Sunset," she explained, ". . . was an Indian Chief. He first became my friend when Mrs. Denison – then Flora Merrill – taught school in the backwoods." The chief practised "both mental and magnetic healing." Among the visitors to Bon Echo were single-tax cartoonist John Wilson BENGOUGH, Albert Ernest Stafford Smythe*, founder of the Toronto Theosophical Society, Frederic Marlett BELL-SMITH, painter, and James Laughlin Hughes*, educational reformer.

The annual gatherings culminated in the August 1919 celebration of the centennial of Whitman's birth, featuring the dedication of the great rock – "Canada's Gibraltar" – that looms over Mazinaw to "OLD WALT, 1819–1919: dedicated to the democratic ideals of Walt Whitman by Horace Traubel and Flora Mac-Donald." The ageing, ailing Traubel, a biographer and long-time associate of Whitman, travelled from New York for the occasion. He expired two weeks later, the spirit of Old Walt at his deathbed. Flora minutely recorded the struggle to transport Traubel's body south to the railway at Kaladar (Merrill Denison acting as undertaker) and then on to New York for embalming, followed by the funeral there, during which the church caught fire, and burial in Camden, N.J. (Whitman's final resting place).

After the Great War ended, Denison continued the spiritualist and reformist role she had crafted for herself during the first two decades of the century. Her letters to her son often recounted communications with Mary and Old Walt, and her participation in the Association for Psychical Research of Canada. In February 1919 she attended a phenomenal three-hour seance at the Toronto home of Dr Albert Durrant WATSON, author of *The twentieth plane . . .* (Toronto, 1918), where the psychic Louis Benjamin presided. She recorded that "I have sat in hundreds of circles, often with the most remarkable Psychics that any age has produced, but I never sat in one where the dominant note of Love was so pronounced." Lincoln, Ingersoll, Emerson, William Cullen Bryant, and Dr Richard Maurice Bucke* were summoned to attest to Walt Whitman's genius.

So, too, she attended meetings of the Theosophical Society to hear George Herbert Locke*, the chief of the Toronto Public Library, and the People's Forum to hear Robert Henry Halbert, the president of the United Farmers of Ontario. She was a founder of and campaigner for the Ontario section of the Canadian Labor Party. Despite her pessimism about the fate of reform movements in the post-war world, she intended to continue contributing her considerable platform talents to the cause. Though far from an original thinker, she combined practical reform with a mystical utopian vision of "a higher conception of human nature and the brotherhood of man" that was characteristic of many late-Victorian English Canadian regenerators.

Still not restored to full health after a bout with Spanish influenza in autumn 1919, Flora visited Bon Echo during the unseasonably cold, wet spring of 1921. She contracted pneumonia and died on 23 May. Like her feminist mentor, Dr Emily Howard Stowe ("I see no other woman to approach her yet"), she was cremated in Buffalo, doubtless as a demonstration of the superiority of the spiritual over the material life, and the triumph of Flora MacDonald over Mrs Denison.

RAMSAY COOK and MICHÈLE LACOMBE

Flora MacDonald [Merrill] (Denison)'s *Mary Melville, the psychic* was published in Toronto in 1900.

QUA, Merrill Denison fonds. Univ. of Toronto Library, Thomas Fisher Rare Book Library, MS coll. 51 (Flora MacDonald Denison papers). *World* (Toronto), 1906–13. C. L. Bacchi, *Liberation deferred? The ideas of the English-Canadian suffragists, 1877–1918* (Toronto, 1983). Ann Braude, *Radical spirits: spiritualism and women's rights in nineteenth-century America* (Boston, 1989). Ramsay Cook, *The regenerators: social criticism in late Victorian English Canada* (Toronto, 1985). Deborah Gorham, "Flora MacDonald Denison: Canadian feminist," in *A not unreasonable claim: women and reform in Canada, 1880s–1920s*, ed. Linda Kealey (Toronto, 1979), 47–70. Michèle Lacombe, "Songs of the open road: Bon Echo, urban utopians and the cult of nature," *Journal of Canadian Studies* (Peterborough, Ont.), 33 (1998–99), no.2: 152–67; "Theosophy and the Canadian idealist tradition: a preliminary exploration," *Journal of Canadian Studies*, 17 (1982–83), no.2: 100–18. Alex Owen, *The darkened room: women, power, and spiritualism in late nineteenth century England* (London, 1989). Robert Stacey and Stan McMullin, *Massanoga: the art of Bon Echo* (n.p., 1998). *Sunset of Bon Echo* (Toronto), 1 (March 1916–April/ May 1920), nos.1–6.

METCALFE, THOMAS LLEWELLYN, lawyer and judge; b. 21 Feb. 1870 in St Thomas, Ont., son of Thomas Halton Metcalfe, a building contractor, and Elizabeth Hutton; d. unmarried 2 April 1922 in Winnipeg.

Thomas Llewellyn Metcalfe's origins reveal patterns of late-Victorian, middle-class, rural culture that were common to many who made careers as lawyers and judges in Canada before World War I. When he was six or seven years old, his family moved from Ontario to Manitoba, settling in the Oakland district, north of Portage la Prairie. Thomas would live close to his mother, who died in 1914, and his father, who died in 1921, for most of his life. He had three equally successful brothers: George, a Winnipeg businessman, W. E., a physician in Portage la Prairie, and Charles, a businessman, also in Portage la Prairie.

Educated in Portage la Prairie, Metcalfe applied to the Law Society of Manitoba to be a student-at-law at age 16. Despite having no further formal education, he would display, according to an obituary, "a knowledge and a wholly unexpected breadth of reading and learning." On 6 Feb. 1889 he was articled to Winnipeg's most distinguished lawyer, James Albert Manning AIKINS. For reasons unknown, the required five years of articling were then assigned in turn to six other lawyers, mainly in Portage la Prairie, although the last was in Boissevain. After passing two examinations, Metcalfe paid his $100 fee for his call to the Manitoba bar on 13 Jan. 1894. Before the call, however, his father had to post a $400 bond to the Law Society of Manitoba guaranteeing payment of Metcalfe's fees and Metcalfe's obedience to the society's rules. Metcalfe practised civil litigation with Robert Andrew Bonnar, who would specialize in criminal cases, and by 1904 he had formed a partnership with Eliphalet Edwards Sharpe. He was active on behalf of land investors and he regularly lectured on real property at the Manitoba Law School.

His being raised a Presbyterian and his lifelong devotion to amateur sports may have generated in Metcalfe a character that required a commitment to clear rules and the community's enforcement of them. He was an ardent clubman, belonging to lacrosse, duck-hunting, canoe, and golf clubs and he supported local hockey teams. As well, he was a staunch member of the Liberal party, serving as a broker for patronage requests. His networking placed him on numerous royal commissions. Appointed to the commission for revision and consolidation of the statutes of Canada in 1902, he sat until 1907. Two years later he was named to another royal commission, on the condition of the fisheries of Manitoba, Saskatchewan, and Alberta. During 1919–20 he would chair the Winnipeg Electric Railway's board of arbitration.

Appointed directly to the Court of King's Bench of Manitoba on 22 May 1909 at age 39, one of Canada's youngest ever superior court judges, Metcalfe was a legal formalist. "If the laws were unjust his lordship would reiterate [that] to rectify such injustice would only be the prerogative and the duty of the legislature . . . [not] of the judiciary." It was no surprise, then, that in the trial in November and December 1919 of Robert Boyd Russell, a leader of the Winnipeg General Strike [see Mike Sokolowiski*], he enforced all procedural rules to the letter.

Metcalfe presided over the trials of several leaders of Canada's most dramatic labour crisis. The trials of 1919–20 exposed his attitudes, social and legal, beginning with his rudely egalitarian views on women. "When women are taking up special obligations and assuming equal privileges with men . . . ," he argued, "[they] are just as liable to ill treatment in a riot as men and can claim no special protection and are entitled to no sympathy; and if they stand and resist officers of the law they are liable to be cut down." In the Russell case, his charge to a jury of male farmers, brought to Winnipeg as part of a strategy urged by the local, federally employed prosecutor, Alfred Joseph Andrews*, emphasized that "an intention to incite the people to take power into their own hands and to provoke them to tumult and disorder is a seditious intention," citing an unnamed "eminent authority." The jury promptly convicted Russell. On 3 Oct. 1921 Metcalfe moved to the Court of Appeal, perhaps in part as reward for consistent, predictable services to the law and the political order.

Metcalfe died in 1922 at age 52, much younger than either his mother, who died at 78, or his father, who died at 82. The official cause was high blood pressure and arteriosclerosis, but the *Manitoba Free Press*, hardly a strike supporter, insisted that it was the strike trials that led to his final stay in hospital. According to his own correspondence, he may have suffered from chronic illness since at least 1904. Despite 15 years of success at the bar and a judicial income for 13 years, Metcalfe left $46,313 in debts and only $48,194 in assets; at least on paper, he died almost bankrupt. Joseph Thorarinn Thorson, the first dean of the Manitoba Law School and later a judge, recalled Metcalfe as a "renegade" who "drank too much," and had morals that were "not so wonderful," but he conceded that he was "a charming person" and "a very good lawyer."

DeLLOYD J. GUTH and DALE BRAWN

AM, AMLJH, P 1298; C 2374, side B; C 2376, side A; C 2377–78, side B; P 5609, 5612–13, 5616–17. LAC, MG 27, II, D15, 67, 107, 129, 146, 167. *Manitoba Free Press*, 24 Dec. 1919; 12 March, 14 April 1920; 2–3 April 1922. *Manitoba Weekly Free Press*, 17 Aug. 1893. *Winnipeg Free Press*, 3 April 1979. *Canadian men and women of the time* (Morgan; 1912).

MEWBURN, FRANK HAMILTON, surgeon, politician, army officer, and university professor; b. 5 March 1858 in Drummondville (Niagara Falls), Upper Canada, youngest son of Francis Clarke Mewburn and Henrietta Tonge Shotter; m. 14 Dec. 1887 Louise Augusta Nelson in Lethbridge (Alta), and they had two sons and a daughter; d. 29 Jan. 1929 in Edmonton.

Frank H. Mewburn represents the fourth generation of a six-generation medical-military dynasty. His great-grandfather Francis Mewburn was apprenticed as an apothecary in 1765, practised in Whitby in Yorkshire, England, and held a commission in the volunteers when Napoleon threatened invasion. Francis's son John, who studied medicine in London and was in the Peninsular War, immigrated in 1832 to Upper Canada, where he volunteered to help suppress the rebellion of 1837–38. Francis Clarke, John's son and Frank's father, was 15 when the family arrived; following his medical licensure in 1838, he served with the Niagara coloured corps for two years and, during the Fenian raids, in 1866, with the 44th (Welland) Battalion of Infantry. Frank's son Frank Hastings Hamilton, an orthopaedic surgeon, would serve in World War I and his grandson, Robert Hamilton, whose medical studies were interrupted by World War II, would become a psychiatrist. Robert's death in 1977 brought the family's 212-year tradition to a close.

After graduation from McGill College (MD, CM 1881), Frank H. Mewburn served for a year as house surgeon at the Montreal General Hospital. In March 1882 he accepted appointment as house surgeon at the Winnipeg General Hospital, a position that appears to have included all aspects of the hospital's operation. His four years there were not without the occasional controversy brought on by his quick temper and colourful vocabulary, but his work was appreciated; on resigning, he was presented with a gold watch and chain. In March 1885, with the opening salvo of the North-West rebellion, a wing of the building had been taken over as a military base hospital. Here Mewburn gained his first experience as a military surgeon, under James Kerr, and for this service he was awarded the North West Canada Medal.

In December, Mewburn visited Lethbridge on the invitation of Elliott Torrance GALT, manager of the North-Western Coal and Navigation Company Limited, and accepted appointment as its medical officer. On his arrival early in 1886 he was also made acting assistant surgeon to the local detachment of the North-West Mounted Police. Later he became chief medical officer of the Canadian Pacific Railway when it was extended through the Crowsnest Pass. On three occasions (1899, 1900, 1905) he served as mayor of Lethbridge. It was during his 27 years there that Mewburn honed his skill and established his reputation as the premier surgeon of the west. Provided with the most primitive of facilities, he was well suited to the role of a self-made surgeon. He kept up his reading of medical journals. Mewburn's first operation on an aboriginal patient, a Blood Indian from whom he removed a goitre, established his reputation with the native population and led, following similar successes, to his identification as one with special competence in thyroid surgery. He performed his first abdominal operation in 1893 (the drainage of an abscess from a perforated appendix, with the patient surviving) and his first Caesarean section in 1903. From that point, recalled his one-time medical partner Walter Stuart Galbraith, his surgical progress was "continuous." Mewburn was by nature an innovator and although not

dexterous, he was painstaking in his attention to detail and patients' best interests. Those who knew him commented that all who consulted him, rich or poor, aboriginal or European, received the same dedicated care.

In 1913 Mewburn moved to Calgary, where he limited his practice to surgery. At the outbreak of World War I he offered his services to Samuel HUGHES, the minister of militia and defence, who wired back, thanking him while regretting that he was too old. Sydney Chilton Mewburn remembered his cousin's reply: "Reference your wire – go to hell! I am going anyway," and he did. After travelling to London at his own expense, he was taken on strength as a major in the Canadian Army Medical Corps on 1 July 1915. Promoted lieutenant-colonel in 1916, he was posted on 11 April 1917 to the Duchess of Connaught's Canadian Red Cross Hospital (later No.15 Canadian General Hospital) at Taplow, in charge of the surgical division. On the basis of his experience there, he would publish a paper in 1919 on the management of lesions of peripheral nerves. In 1918 he was awarded the Order of the British Empire.

Mewburn's return to surgical practice in Calgary in June 1919 was brief. In 1921 he accepted the founding professorship of surgery at the University of Alberta in Edmonton. Previously students had been required to take their final two years in eastern Canada. His organization of the surgical department and surgical teaching, along with instruction in medicine, enabled the faculty to award its first degrees in 1925. He himself received honorary LLDs from McGill University in 1921 and the University of Alberta the following year. Through the magnetism of his personality and the stories from his past that he wove into his halting presentations in class, the Colonel (a name he did not discourage) became a favourite with his students, who made him an honorary president of their Medical Club and Osler Society. Within his profession, he served as second vice-president of the American College of Surgeons in 1927–28. In January 1929, at age 70, he developed pneumonia after walking home from the university hospital in freezing weather. He died three days later and was buried with full military honours. His name is perpetuated by the Mewburn Medal in Surgery at the University of Alberta and the cairn erected in his honour in 1937 on the grounds of the Galt Hospital in Lethbridge.

Frank H. Mewburn was short (five feet six inches) and of slight build (140 pounds). His dominant feature was his walrus moustache, which gave him a somewhat fierce appearance, but it was offset by his twinkling blue eyes. Many who knew him personally felt compelled to record their observations of a character they respected and loved. He was a study in contrasts. Impatient, irascible, and scathing when faced with what he judged to be carelessness or stupidity, he

741

could be charming, and his humanity and dedication to his patients, profession, and the wider community were never in doubt. He has become a part of the folklore of the old west.

ROBERT A. MACBETH

Frank Hamilton Mewburn wrote a biographical article about his western medical associate and friend George Allan Kennedy*, which was published as "The life and work of Dr. George A. Kennedy" in the Canadian Medical Assoc., *Journal* (Toronto), new ser., 21 (July–December 1929): 327–30. His "Observations on lesions of peripheral nerves; with special reference to pre-operative and post-operative treatment" appeared in Can., Medical Services of the Dept. of Soldiers' Civil Re-establishment and the Board of Pension Commissioners, *Medical Quarterly* (Ottawa), 1 (1919): 279–94.

AM, MG 10, B11, box 15. LAC, RG 150, Acc. 1992–93/166, box 6145–70. McMaster Univ., William Ready Div. of Arch. and Research Coll. (Hamilton, Ont.), ACC, Diocese of Niagara Arch., All Saints' Anglican Church (Niagara Falls, Ont.), RBMB, 4 June 1858. Private arch., R. A. Macbeth (Toronto), Copies of letters of recommendation written in 1883 in relation to Mewburn's application for a position in Winnipeg; Charity Mewburn (Qualicum Beach, B.C.), Papers and memorabilia; R. M. Mewburn (Qualicum Beach), Papers and memorabilia. Univ. of Alta Arch. (Edmonton), Board of governors, annual reports, 1921–22; John James Ower, diaries, 1929. *Examiner* (Charlottetown), 6 Jan. 1888. P. M. Campbell, "Frank Hamilton Mewburn," Calgary Associate Clinic, *Hist. Bull.*, 15 (1950–51): 61–69. *Canadian men and women of the time* (Morgan; 1912). William Canniff, *The medical profession in Upper Canada, 1783–1850 . . .* (Toronto, 1894; repr. 1980), 511–18. F. S. Coulson, "The first surgeon in the west: Frank Hamilton Mewburn (1858–1929)," Calgary Associate Clinic, *Hist. Bull.*, 10 (1945): 120–25. R. B. Deane, "Frank Hamilton Mewburn," Canadian Medical Assoc., *Journal*, new ser., 20 (January–June 1929): 306–8. *Evergreen and Gold* (Edmonton?), [1921–29] (copies in Univ. of Alta Arch.). Joseph Hanaway and Richard Cruess, *McGill medicine* (1v. to date, Montreal and Kingston, Ont., 1996–), 129. H. E. MacDermot, *Sir Thomas Roddick: his work in medicine and public life* (Toronto, 1938), 55. N. T. McPhedran, *Canadian medical schools: two centuries of medical history, 1822 to 1992* (Montreal, 1993), 141–42. H. E. Rawlinson, "Frank Hamilton Mewburn, O.B.E., M.D., C.M., LL.D., lt.-col., C.A.M.C., professor of surgery, University of Alberta, pioneer surgeon," *Canadian Journal of Surgery* (Toronto), 2 (1958–59): 1–5. *Standard dict. of Canadian biog.* (Roberts and Tunnell), vol.1. G. D. Stanley, "Medical pioneering in Alberta: unforgettable incidents in private practice," Calgary Associate Clinic, *Hist. Bull.*, 10: 147–48.

MICKLE, SARA (Sarah), local historian and heritage preservationist; b. 13 June 1853 in Guelph Township, Upper Canada, daughter of Charles Mickle, a farmer and later a lumber merchant, and Ellen Thurtell; d. 2 June 1930 in Toronto.

Sara Mickle must have inherited her great-grandfather's literary disposition. He was William Julius Mickle (Meikle), the Scottish poet and translator of the Portuguese historical epic "Os Lusíadas" by Luís Vaz de Camões. His son, Charles Julius Mickle, immigrated to Canada in 1832, settling north of Guelph, where he established a successful sawmill. Sara was born at Langholm, the house her father had built across the Elora Road from her grandfather's. Shortly after his death in 1879, the family settled in Toronto. The seventh of thirteen children, Sara never married. Having inherited from her father, and later her mother and sister, she dedicated herself to social causes, such as the Hillcrest Convalescent Hospital and St Andrew's Presbyterian Church, both in Toronto. Her greatest passion throughout her life was the preservation of Canada's past.

In March 1898 Mickle was the only woman present when a committee of the Pioneer and Historical Society of the Province of Ontario met to consider ways of widening the association's scope; she moved that the name be changed to the Ontario Historical Society, and two months later it was. She was already involved with the Women's Canadian Historical Society of Toronto, established in 1895 by Sarah Anne Curzon [Vincent*] and Mary Agnes FitzGibbon and now numbering over 200 persons. The society's leaders were socially notable women who claimed descent from "ancestors [who] had taken a . . . prominent part in the making of Canada's history." Like other historical organizations of the period, it promoted, through the collection of documents and relics and the presentation of research about the past, "a unity of national purpose and a high ideal of loyalty and patriotism" that would sustain Canada's "rising status." Mickle contributed as both an organizer and a historian. With FitzGibbon and Lady Edgar [Ridout*] she helped stage a highly successful historical exhibition at Victoria University in 1899, she prepared three calendars on historical themes, and she wrote a number of papers on topics ranging from tombstone inscriptions to historic homes. She was a member of the WCHST executive committee almost continuously from 1897 until her death in 1930, and served the last 15 of those years as president of the society.

Known as "a gifted speaker," she entered the political sphere as an activist for different public causes. Over the first two decades of the 20th century she was a leader in a drawn-out battle to save Toronto's Fort York from urban and commercial encroachment on its territory. When it came under threat in 1905, WCHST rallies were held to raise awareness of the colonial fortress. The following year the society sponsored Saturday lectures at the fort for schoolchildren, an activity that reportedly attracted thousands. Efforts to educate the public were fruitful in 1907, when a by-law that would have permitted the construction of a street railway through the fort grounds was rejected by a solid majority of the city's voters. Nevertheless, historical activists had to remain on their guard. In 1916 Mickle, as president of the WCHST, called for a monument at the fort "to interest and inform the public in the history of the place" and for a proper land survey, which might offer further protection. She was involved again in the 1920s, playing a prominent role in the Committee on the Restoration and Preservation of Old Fort York. With Sir William Dillon OTTER and others, she drafted a pamphlet to "stimulate public interest in [the] value of the Old Fort as a memorial."

But a memorial to what? Why was saving an abandoned colonial fort worth the effort? For Mickle and the WCHST the past was familiar and redolent with the social values that underpinned Canadian society. Indeed, their work was as much about preserving the social and political status quo as it was about preserving historic sites and documents. As the WCHST's annual report asked in 1909, should "the commercial utilitarian element in our city . . . win against the patriotic sentiment and loyal belief in the value of the lessons of our past history"? According to the organization, earlier struggles to maintain ties with the British empire must not be forgotten, particularly in 1910–11 when the Naval Service Bill and reciprocity were being debated in parliament and the daily press. The society supported the war effort, its members assisting in the activities of the Canadian Red Cross and Mickle, in one of her yearly presidential addresses, calling for empire-wide unity. For the same reason, Mickle and the WCHST had joined the OHS and other organizations in a fight against a proposal to erect in Quebec City a memorial to the American major-general Richard Montgomery*, who died while leading an attack on that city in 1775. Petitions were sent over a period of ten years (1898–1908) to the mayor of Quebec, the minister of militia and defence, the governor general, and the king. The notion of placing a monument to a republican invader was repellent to Mickle's group, which described itself in the text of one petition as "a band of women . . . united only by the common bond of patriotism for the study of our country's history, and the preservation of its memorials and for the promotion of loyalty amongst its peoples, especially the children, with the aim of perpetuating the history of those who endured, fought, suffered and died to maintain the supremacy of the British Crown."

Mickle's last major work was the restoration of Colborne Lodge, the 1837 home of artist-architect John George Howard*. He had turned over to the City of Toronto much of the land that became High Park. The lodge in the park's grounds had been a fine and unique structure but by the mid 1920s, when Mickle took the leadership in restoring the house, it had fallen into a "desolate state." She told the mayor that, like other cities, Toronto should have such a place to give citizens "a picture of domestic life long ago." She was tireless in her curatorial efforts, and "never rested until she had had a little talk" with anyone who had ever worked in the house. Her work on the lodge earned her the rare praise of George MacKinnon Wrong*, dean of Canadian historians, who recognized the restoration as "an interesting achievement." His approbation was a significant departure in an era when women's historical efforts were often criticized as amateurish and second-rate.

While Mickle made local history her focus of interest, her goal throughout was to provide Canadians with reminders of their place in something larger: the British empire. Believing that "the need for true patriotism is great," she chose research subjects that demonstrated loyalist values. For her, history was not simply a vocation; it was a public-spirited pursuit and an expression of the desire of her generation of native-born, upper-middle-class women to play a role in the formation of Canadian identity.

DAVID KIMMEL and JANET MIRON

Sara Mickle is the author of "Colborne Lodge" and "The owner of Colborne Lodge" in Women's Canadian Hist. Soc. of Toronto, *Trans.*, no.26 (1927–28): 57–59 and 60–61.

AO, F 1090; F 1139-2, 30 March 1898; F 1180-11, ser.K, file 19; RG 22-305 nos.4569, 23764, 64864; RG 22-318, no.1764. Private arch., David Kimmel (Montreal), [Alan Cane], "Family history and letters: Cane/Armitage/Mickle/Rowe." *Canadian annual rev.*, 1929/30. *Colborne Lodge, High Park, Toronto, Canada, first occupied December 23rd, 1837* ([Toronto, 1951]). S. M. Cook, "Seventy years of history, 1895–1965," Women's Canadian Hist. Soc. of Toronto, *Trans.*, no.29 (1970). *Creating historical memory: English-Canadian women and the work of history*, ed. Beverly Boutilier and Alison Prentice (Vancouver, 1997). "A gifted lady," *Saturday Night*, 21 June 1930: 7. Gerald Killan, *Preserving Ontario's heritage: a history of the Ontario Historical Society* (Ottawa, 1976). Janet Miron, "The Women's Historical Society of Toronto: preserving the 'food of loyalty and the drink of patriotism'" (unpublished paper prepared for York Univ., North York [Toronto], 1996). Cecilia Morgan, "History, nation, and empire: gender and southern Ontario historical societies, 1890–1920s," *CHR*, 82 (2001): 491–528. "The Woman's Canadian Historical Society of Toronto: report of regular monthly meeting, held May 30, '98," *Canadian Home Journal* (Toronto), 4 (1898–99), no.3: 12. *Women of Canada* (Montreal, 1930). Women's Canadian Hist. Soc. of Toronto, *Annual report*, 1896–1930. Donald Wright, "Gender and the professionalization of history in English Canada before 1960," *CHR*, 81 (2000): 29–66.

MILLER, ÉMILE (baptized **Émile-Ladislas**), office holder, geographer, author, professor, and executive secretary; b. 18 Sept. 1884 in Saint-Placide, Que., son of Théophile Miller, a cobbler, and Éléonore (Léonard) Ladouceur; m. 12 July 1908 Albertine Maillé in the Montreal parish of Saint-Jacques, and they had nine children; d. 3 Aug. 1922 in Contrecœur, Que., at the age of 37, while trying to rescue his young son from drowning.

The seventh of thirteen children, Émile Miller attracted attention even in elementary school because of his studiousness and industry, his cheerfulness and penchant for daydreaming, and his passion for reading. Around 1899 the Miller family moved from Saint-Placide to Montreal. At his father's urging, Émile rather reluctantly enrolled in a course in pharmacy, and he obtained his diploma in 1902. Soon after, and without his family's knowledge, he boarded the first ship for Europe. With no financial resources and no clear-cut goal, he found employment as a labourer and set out in search of adventure. In this way he visited England and France.

Having lived through some difficult times, Miller returned to Montreal and went back to regular studies at the École Normale Jacques-Cartier. Soured by life and not really interested in teaching at the elementary level, he got to know Abbé Adélard Desrosiers, the school's vice-principal, who introduced him to the study of geography, a discipline then not much in demand. After completing his studies, Miller got a job in the municipal office of the village of Lorimier (Montreal) in 1906; later he would work in the office of the Montreal city archives. He continued to be interested in geography, and in Montreal in 1912 he published his first book; entitled *Terres et peuples du Canada*, it had a preface by Desrosiers. This volume occupies an important place among Miller's writings and in the geographical field. For the first time, serious questions were being posed about the geography of the country, and the relationship between human beings and their environment was being studied. In 1915 Miller had an article in the *Revue trimestrielle canadienne* (Montréal), entitled "La géographie au service de l'histoire," which emphasized the importance of dialogue between the two disciplines. Along with his writing, he taught classes in geography at the school sponsored by the Council of Arts and Manufactures of the Province of Quebec in Montreal. In 1917 he left the archives to become executive secretary of the Société Saint-Jean-Baptiste in Montreal, a position he would hold until 1922. In 1918, at the urging of this society, he taught public classes in geography at the Monument National and the Union Catholique, among other centres. During the period of his employment, Miller would serve as editor of *Le Courrier de la Société Saint-Jean-Baptiste de Montréal*; first issued in 1921, the journal was to report on the activities of the society's branches. In 1920 he had been appointed to the chair of geography in the new faculty of arts at the Université de Montréal. The following year saw the publication in Montreal of his second volume, *Pour qu'on aime la géographie*, which contained both previously published and unpublished articles. Here Miller took the new approach of geographers in explaining how the environment can be the source of information about methods of colonization and the development of fundamental activities. He was also the author of many articles in various journals, including the *Bulletin* (Québec) of the Geographical Society of Quebec, *L'Action française* (Montréal), and the *Revue trimestrielle canadienne*.

Émile Miller died too young, before he had time to record all he knew, but he was one of the earliest French Canadian geographers, if not indeed the first. Not until French geographer Raoul Blanchard came to teach and to write about French Canada in works published from 1935 to 1952 would interest in geography revive. Miller had made good use of knowledge acquired through reading the great geographers of France and Germany, such as Paul Vidal de La Blache. His explanations sometimes were based on a superficial determinism; nevertheless he had sought to put forward an overview of Canada by linking physical and human geography so as to bring out more clearly the oneness of the country and of the people living in it. After Miller's death, Abbé Desrosiers gathered up his manuscripts and in 1924 he published in Beauceville a *Géographie générale* that would fill a gap in school geography textbooks.

MICHEL BOISVERT

In addition to the publications already mentioned, Émile Miller is the author of *Les armoiries de Montréal* (Montréal, 1920) and *Mon voyage autour du monde* (Montréal, 1923); the latter work was published posthumously by his widow.

ANQ-M, CE606-S11, 1er janv. 1856–27 déc. 1873; CE606-S16, esp. 20 sept. 1884. Univ. Laval (Québec), Laboratoire de Géographie Historique, Arch. de la Soc. de Géographie de Québec. *Le Devoir*, 4 août, 9 sept. 1922. *La Patrie*, 4 août 1922. *La Presse*, 4 août 1922. *Le Soleil*, 4 août 1922. *La Tribune* (Sherbrooke, Qué.), 4 août 1922. Benoît Brouillette, "Un pionnier de la géographie au Canada français," *Rev. canadienne de géographie* (Montréal), 4 (1950), nos.1–2: 94–96. Lionel Groulx, *Mes mémoires* (4v., Montréal, 1970–74), 2. Édouard Montpetit, "Émile Miller," *Rev. trimestrielle canadienne* (Montréal), 8 (1922): 263–66. Christian Morissonneau, *La Société de géographie de Québec, 1877–1970* (Québec, 1971). "Pour qu'on aime la géographie," *Rev. trimestrielle canadienne*, 7 (1921): 510–12. Eugène Rouillard, "Une perte pour la géographie canadienne: M. Émile Miller," Soc. de Géographie de Québec, *Bull.*, 16 (1922): 195. Robert Rumilly, *Histoire de la Société Saint-Jean-Baptiste de Montréal: des patriotes au fleurdelisé, 1834–1948* (Montréal, 1975). Soc. Généalogique Canadienne-Française, *Mariages de la paroisse Saint-Jacques de Montréal (1873–1984)* (13v., Montréal, 1987–90), 10: 25.

MILLS, HARRIET ANN (Roche; Boomer), author and social activist; b. 10 July 1835 in Bishop's Hull, England, second daughter of Thomas Milliken Mills, a solicitor, and Ann Benton; m. first 11 March 1858 Alfred Robert Roche in Staplegrove, England; m. secondly 17 Nov. 1878 Michael Boomer* in New York

City; she had no children; d. 1 March 1921 in London, Ont.

Little is known of Harriet Mills's early life, but she was well educated, most likely by her mother, who found it necessary to take in pupils after being widowed at age 25. Harriet and her sister Mary Louisa came to Canada in 1851 when their mother accepted the principalship of St Cross school at Red River (Man.). In 1857 Harriet and her mother returned to England – Mary Louisa stayed, having married Francis Godschall Johnson*. Mrs Mills took a position at Queen's College in London. Harriet attended classes there, likely until she married Alfred Roche, a geologist who had spent some time in Canada, and moved to Hertfordshire. In 1875 the couple went to the Transvaal to inspect Roche's mining interests; he became ill and died at sea in 1876 on the way home. To help support herself, Harriet produced *On trek in the Transvaal: or, over berg and veldt in South Africa* (London, 1878).

In 1878 she married the Reverend Michael Boomer, principal of Huron College in London, Ont., where she quickly became involved in church and fund-raising activities. To aid the college, for instance, she wrote *Notes from our log in South Africa . . .* (London, Ont., 1880). Widowed again in 1888, she was instrumental that year in establishing the London Convalescent Home and was elected president of its board of management. In October 1893 she attended the founding meeting in Toronto of the National Council of Women of Canada, which would become her main focus; she was a leader at the inaugural meeting on 14 Feb. 1894 of the London Local Council of Women. Presiding over both gatherings was Lady Aberdeen [Marjoribanks*], wife of the governor general and president of the National Council. Harriet visited the vice-regal couple frequently and was proud of her close friendship with them. Lady Aberdeen, in turn, regarded her as "a great feature in our National Council, for her tact & sense of humour has helped us over many a rough place." Harriet was president of the London council from 1897 to 1920, undoubtedly a record among local presidents. A vice-president for Ontario, she attended most annual meetings of the National Council, often presenting motions and papers, and in 1899 she travelled to England for the International Congress of Women.

The concern of Harriet and the London council for health care was evident in many areas. When the city proposed to build a new hospital without a children's wing, Harriet was instrumental in 1898 in securing funding for the children's pavilion at Victoria Hospital, which incorporated the old structure. In 1906 she and the council played a leading role in setting up a branch of the Victorian Order of Nurses, with Harriet as president of its board. In 1919, when the Imperial Order Daughters of the Empire proposed to replace the crowded pavilion with a new war memorial hospital for children, the London council fully supported the fund-raising for the project.

They were proud of their patriotic efforts. In 1900 Harriet had established London's first Red Cross Society to send aid to soldiers in the South African War. The society lapsed but it was revived in 1914 with Lillian, Lady Beck, as president and Harriet as honorary president. During World War I it was responsible for raising almost $1 million. In September 1914 Harriet served as advisory editor of the Belgian Relief Fund issue of the *London Advertiser*. Ever the imperialist, she persuaded the London Board of Education to purchase 5,000 copies of a booklet, *The history of our flag* by Clementina Fessenden [Trenholme*], for distribution.

A firm believer in the education of females, Harriet felt there should be more opportunities for women worldwide. There was a need, she maintained in the National Council's annual report, "to cultivate more and more of the business faculty of which men are supposed to have a monopoly, but of which we women are not bereft." It was especially important that females succeed scholastically and pursue the careers that had opened up for them in the 1900s. The study of domestic science was seen as particularly valuable. Harriet's council exerted pressure on the London school board to introduce it, a goal that was achieved in 1905.

Feminists of the late 19th century believed that it was necessary to have women on school boards since they were the natural educators of children. Harriet logically pointed out to the London board that women had been successful in charitable works and served on boards elsewhere. Thus, in 1898 she was appointed as London's first female trustee; during her three-year term she "learnt woman's hardest lesson – how to be silent." Perhaps she was not entirely successful in this respect since she was not reappointed and the position was allowed to lapse until 1919.

A devout Anglican, she took an active role in many church organizations, including the Mother's Union of Cronyn Memorial Church, the Woman's Auxiliary to the Missionary Society of the Church of England in Canada, and the Women's Christian Association. According to David Williams*, the bishop of Huron, "The inspiration for all her work was her strong faith and loyalty to Jesus Christ."

Harriet Boomer's long years of unselfish service to religious, charitable, and educational causes in London demonstrated that women had a role to play in public affairs, not just in the private sphere. Her forcefulness made enemies, but in her time a woman had to be forceful to be heard. Perhaps her greatest talent was the ability to face all situations, according to the *Advertiser*, "with an indomitable courage, [and] unfailing laughter that kept youth ever bright in her

Mills

heart." She died at age 85 and was buried in Woodland Cemetery.

JOAN KENNEDY

In addition to the works cited, Harriet Ann Boomer is the author of *Little Miss Ellerby and her big elephants: respectfully dedicated to all whom it may concern* ([London, Ont., 188?]), a pamphlet on a juvenile dream that is really a call for united action on reducing parish debt.

AO, RG 22-321, no.15080; RG 80-8-0-826, no.21017. GRO, Reg. of marriages, Taunton, 11 March 1858. London Public Library, London Room (London, Ont.), Materials pertaining to Harriet Boomer. *London Advertiser*, 5 March 1888; 15 Feb. 1894; 2, 4 March 1921. *London Free Press*, 3 Dec. 1897, 8 April 1898, 17 March 1900, 25 Jan.1902, 7 March 1952. F. H. Armstrong, *The Forest City: an illustrated history of London, Canada* (Northridge, Calif., 1986). T. F. Bredin, "The Red River Academy," *Beaver*, outfit 305 (winter 1974): 10–17. *Canadian who's who*, 1910. W. E. Corfield, *To alleviate suffering: the story of Red Cross in London, Canada, 1900–1985* (London, 1985). Joan Kennedy, "The London Local Council of Women and Harriet Ann Boomer" (MA thesis, Univ. of Western Ont., London, 1989). [I. M. Marjoribanks Hamilton-Gordon, Marchioness of] Aberdeen [and Temair], *The Canadian journal of Lady Aberdeen, 1893–1898*, ed. J. T. Saywell (Toronto, 1960). National Council of Women of Canada, *Annual report* ([Ottawa]), 1897. J. R. Sullivan and N. R. Ball, *Growing to serve: a history of Victoria Hospital, London, Ontario* (London, 1985). *Types of Canadian women . . .* , ed. H. J. Morgan (Toronto, 1903).

MILLS, JAMES, educator and office holder; b. 24 Nov. 1840 near Bond Head, Upper Canada, son of John Mills and Ann Stinson; m. 6 July 1869 Jessie Ross (d. 1919) in Cobourg, Ont., and they had five daughters and two sons; d. 4 Dec. 1924 in Ottawa.

The eldest of ten children of parents from County Fermanagh (Northern Ireland), James Mills worked on his father's farm until the age of 20, when he lost his right arm in a threshing machine accident. With physical labour out of the question, he began his education. He went to the Bradford grammar school, graduated in 1868 from Victoria College in Cobourg with the Prince of Wales Medal for proficiency, and became a teacher. In 1871, during his time as classical master at the Cobourg Collegiate Institute, he earned an MA from Victoria. It was at Brantford High School, which he served as principal for six years and raised to collegiate status, that his excellence as an educator became evident. When the position of principal at the Ontario School of Agriculture and Experimental Farm near Guelph became vacant in 1879, the government approached him.

Mills accepted, but the school was a troubled institution: it had had three principals since its founding in 1874 [*see* William Johnston*]. Drawing no respect from the farming community and fractured by a division of responsibility between the experimental farm and the school, it was barely surviving. Mills undertook the job with a great capacity for work – he also taught English literature and political economy and ran the library. After the school's formal incorporation in 1880 as the Ontario Agricultural College and Experimental Farm, by which change Mills became "president," it began a period of growth, due largely to his activism. In speeches and articles he tirelessly promoted agricultural education, especially its introduction into public and normal schools. In 1904, on his retirement and succession by George Christie CREELMAN, the *Farming World and Canadian Farm and Home* (Toronto) would recognize his contribution in safely piloting the OAC "through many and trying difficulties" over a 25-year period. Although Mills had instituted many changes during this time, three accomplishments stand out.

By making the farming community aware of the college's values, Mills won a degree of agrarian support and defused criticism in the agricultural press [*see* William Weld*]. About 1884, at the request of the Council of the Agricultural and Arts Association, he prepared a program of study for farmers' sons. In 1885 he established the Farmers' Institute system, through which experts from the college took information straight to the farmers. In addition, the institute lobbied for the greater recognition of agriculture at Queen's Park, specifically for the creation of a department of agriculture [*see* Charles Alfred Drury*]. Mills would run this system until 1894, when the government took over responsibility. In 1891 he put in place the mechanisms for the travelling dairies conceived by agriculture minister John Dryden*. Mills believed in instruction through experience, but as an educator he emphatically argued, unlike the agrarian press, that farmers needed more than manual training. He championed the merger of scientific and practical agriculture, to which end a degree program had been initiated in 1888 following affiliation with the University of Toronto. One graduate, future premier Ernest Charles Drury*, recalled that Mills "impressed upon us that our part was to go back to the farm and there to become leaders in our communities in the introduction of advanced farming practices."

The second achievement was overcoming the fractured relationship between the college and the experimental farm. When Mills assumed the principalship, William Brown, a professor of agriculture, was in charge of the farm and he reported not to Mills but to the government. Though it tried to give Mills overall responsibility in 1887, the shift was not enforced: Brown's successor, Thomas Shaw, openly ignored the attempt. Mills managed to make this almost impossible situation work; he even collaborated with Shaw in producing a textbook, *The first principles of agriculture* (Toronto, 1890). The issue came to a head in 1893, when, as Mills put it, "the Government finally had the courage to give the President full control" [*see* John Dryden].

Mills's third accomplishment was the establishment of a school of domestic science for young women at the OAC. Interested, as a father of five daughters, in education for women, he had stated as early as 1880 that he had no objection in theory to educating boys and girls together. When Sir William Christopher Macdonald* of Montreal announced that he wished to establish a domestic science school in Ontario, Mills pressed the wealthy philanthropist to endow his college but failed to achieve this goal. Undaunted, he asked Adelaide Sophia Hoodless [Hunter*] and others to intervene, and in 1903 the Macdonald Institute of Home Economics opened its doors.

During his time at the OAC, Mills had many interests, most of which focused on education and science. He belonged to the Guelph Choral Union and the Guelph Scientific Society during the 1880s, and was a member of the Norfolk Street Methodist Church. From 1890 to 1910 he was a regent of Victoria University, which awarded him a LLD in 1892; for 16 years he sat on its senate and on that of the University of Toronto. Elected a fellow of the American Association for the Advancement of Science in 1895, he followed agricultural education internationally and travelled extensively to study colleges in the United States and Europe. In 1899 he was named to the commission formed in Ontario to examine the problem of the San Jose scale insect, which attacked fruit trees [*see* James Fletcher*].

In January 1904 Mills was appointed to the newly created Board of Railway Commissioners in Ottawa [*see* Albert Clements Killam*]. He had little knowledge of transportation and regulatory problems, but it was believed that he could speak for the farming community. He learned as he criss-crossed Canada on hearings. Unafraid to render vigorous dissenting opinions, often based on broad, anti-monopolistic views of the public interest, he served until 1914, when his age forced him to step down. He nonetheless continued to aid the commission unofficially as its librarian and supervisory officer until his death. While living in Ottawa, Mills also took part in reunions of OAC graduates and gave speeches at agricultural events. Beloved by those with any attachment to the college, he died in 1924 and was buried in Guelph.

MARGARET DERRY

James Mills's reports as president of the Ontario Agricultural College and Experimental Farm for the years 1880–1903 appear in Ont., Legislature, *Sessional papers*. An address by Mills, "The Ontario Agricultural College and Experimental Farm for a quarter of a century," was published in the annual report of the Agricultural and Experimental Union of Ontario for 1899, in *Sessional papers*, 1900, no.15: 63–74; other addresses by Mills appear in the reports of the livestock associations of Ontario, in *Sessional papers*, 1910, no.39: 144–45 and 1912, no.39: 40–43.

AO, RG 22-354, no.12003; RG 80-5-0-2, no.1488. Univ. of Guelph Library, Arch. and Special Coll. (Guelph, Ont.), REI, OAC, A0095 (ex-students of OAC, 1874–99); A0852 (Takeo Nomura, corr. concerning N. Kobayashi, 1991–93). *Ottawa Evening Journal*, 5–6, 8 Dec. 1924. Christopher Armstrong and H. V. Nelles, *Monopoly's moment: the organization and regulation of Canadian utilities, 1830–1930* (Philadelphia, 1986). J. E. Bryant, "The Farmers' Institute system of Ontario," *Farming* (Toronto), November 1896: 190–212. *Canadian men and women of the time* (Morgan; 1898 and 1912). *A career of eminent service in education and agriculture, in spite of a serious handicap and many discouraging circumstances: a few facts gleaned from the life and career of James Mills, M.A., LL.D., October, 1917* (Toronto, 1917). *Cyclopædia of Canadian biog.* (Rose and Charlesworth), vol.1. *Farm and Dairy* (Peterborough, Ont.), 19 Jan. 1911: 12; 14 Dec. 1911: 1202. *Farming World and Canadian Farm and Home* (Toronto), 18 Dec. 1900: 372; 15 April 1903: 208; 1 Sept. 1903: 582–83; 1 Feb. 1904: 94–95; 15 Feb. 1904: 135; 1 March 1904: 174; 2 Jan. 1905. D. A. Lawr, "Development of agricultural education in Ontario, 1870–1910" (PHD thesis, Univ. of Toronto, 1972). *O.A.C. Rev.* (Guelph), July 1891; December 1895; November 1900; January 1902; February 1904; January 1905; January, June 1908; December 1909; December 1911; March 1913; March 1915; August 1918; January 1925; June 1928. Ontario agricultural commission, *Report of the commissioners* (4v., Toronto, 1881), 4, app.P: 3–14. A. M. Ross, *The college on the hill: a history of the Ontario Agricultural College, 1874–1974* (Vancouver [and Guelph], 1974). A. M. Ross and T. [A.] Crowley, *The college on the hill: a new history of the Ontario Agricultural College, 1874–1999* (2nd ed., Toronto, 1999).

MILNE, JOHN, manufacturer and politician; b. 22 Jan. 1839 in Aberdeen, Scotland, son of John Milne, a blacksmith, and Elizabeth Mitchell; m. first 3 July 1862 Annie Kendall (d. 1867) in Hamilton, Upper Canada, and they had two sons; m. there secondly 1872 Mary Manson, and they had two sons; d. there 4 March 1922.

John Milne attended public schools in Aberdeen until he was 14, when he left to apprentice as an iron moulder in a local foundry. In 1854 his family immigrated to Canada and settled in Hamilton, where he continued his training in the foundry of Gurneys and Carpenter [*see* Edward Gurney*]. For some time he plied his trade in the United States, following the example of his father, who had moved to Illinois, but in 1860 he returned to Hamilton and began building a career.

Shortly after his first marriage, Milne entered into partnership with Thomas Haggart in a malleable-iron works. In 1864 Milne's former companion in the United States, Charles Stewart, joined forces with William Burrow to form the Hamilton Malleable Iron Works. This venture proved solider than Milne's. He joined the firm as a moulder in 1867 and became a partner in 1872. The three entrepreneurs hit their stride, and business boomed. Burrow, Stewart, and Milne's principal products were castings for harness equipment and saddlery gear such as curry-combs, but quickly their focus shifted to scales and stoves. The firm, which became famous throughout Canada for its Jewel and Victory stoves and ranges, was incorporated as a joint-stock company in 1898, with Milne as president, and by 1910 its factory occupied almost an entire block and employed approximately 300 men. As a result of periodic labour disruptions beginning in the 1870s, Milne, once a unionist, developed strong anti-labour sentiments.

Milne was not satisfied to limit his ambitions to one endeavour. He was adept at forging new business connections to ensure his prosperity. For example, his firm's heavy consumption of iron prompted him to promote the Hamilton Iron and Steel Company in 1893 and then the Hamilton Blast Furnace Company Limited, which commenced operations in December 1895. It amalgamated with Ontario Rolling Mills in 1899 to form Hamilton Steel and Iron. When this firm merged with other companies in 1910 to become the Steel Company of Canada Limited, eventually so crucial to Hamilton's economy [see Robert HOBSON], Milne remained a director. A director as well of Armstrong Cartage, he was president of Grant Spring Brewery, Electric Bond and Share, Premier Trust, and Hamilton Navigation. Instrumental in establishing Hamilton's hydroelectric system, he was one of its first commissioners. In January 1906 he would be appointed to the provincial hydroelectric commission of inquiry [see Sir Adam BECK], where he met resistance from private-power interests in Hamilton. Perhaps his most interesting enterprise was the Pure Milk Company. Established in 1901 with Milne as president, it revealed his shrewdness and ability to capitalize on opportunity. Previously a plethora of small operators had handled the distribution of dairy products in Hamilton. Milne and other businessmen played on public fears of contaminated milk to ensure support for Pure Milk, which had the capital to acquire the latest machinery and technology for sterile processing. Thus Milne combined his indisputable acumen with his sense of community responsibility.

Like many of his contemporaries, Milne was a firm advocate of public libraries as a means of improving the general level of education. He served in various capacities on Hamilton's library board from 1903 to 1921, and was chairman of its building and finance committee in 1911–12, when construction began on a grand new facility. He was credited with influencing the decision of Scottish-born American industrialist Andrew Carnegie to commit $100,000 to the project – Carnegie called him his "fellow-countryman and personal friend." In addition to the library board, Milne

was a member of the Barton masonic lodge, the Commercial Club, and the Twentieth Century Club (a Conservative social club), and he was deeply involved in Knox Presbyterian Church. Best known for his connection with the Hamilton Conservative Association, which he served as president for 23 years, he had become a party supporter in 1876 and was an ardent believer in the National Policy initiated by the government of Sir John A. Macdonald*. According to Milne's obituary in the Hamilton Spectator, "He believed that so long as the United States maintained a high tariff, Canada should enforce strong protection to home industries." Such logic appealed to his self-interest and accorded with his perception of the country's best advantage, and many fellow industrialists shared his point of view. Despite his staunch political affiliation, Milne did not seek public office, choosing instead to work "always in the background, but wielding far more influence than those in the limelight." In December 1915 Prime Minister Sir Robert Laird Borden*, in recognition of his service, appointed him to the Senate. An infrequent contributor, he talked about manufacturing, tariff protection, and, sometimes with references to disruptions at his foundry, the evils of unions. "Labour has now reached such a stage that there is no stopping it," he lamented in April 1920.

Milne's health began to decline in late 1921, and in March 1922 he died of gangrene complicated by pneumonia. Obituaries gave him a great deal of credit for the successful establishment of the steel industry in Hamilton. The Spectator stated baldly that "the existence of the Steel Company of Canada to-day is practically due to the untiring efforts and that spirit of aggressiveness and enterprise which characterized Mr. Milne during his lifetime," while the Hamilton Herald attributed the success of Burrow, Stewart, and Milne mainly to his "energy and business ability." His eulogists can be forgiven for their enthusiasm, since, in Milne's journey from apprentice to respected industrialist and public figure, they had the archetypal rags-to-riches story of a "self-made man who justified faith in Hamilton" and in the promise of Canada.

ANGELA GRAHAM

AO, RG 80-27-2, 82: 90. General Register Office for Scotland (Edinburgh), Aberdeen, reg. of births and baptisms, 22 Jan. 1839. Hamilton Public Library, Special Coll. Dept. (Hamilton, Ont.), Scrapbooks, Herald, vol.M6; Times, vols.B3, L3. Hamilton Herald, 4 March 1922. Hamilton Spectator, 30 Jan., 28 March 1901; 9 July 1910; 2 Dec. 1915; 4 March 1922. Can., Senate, Debates, 27 Feb. 1919; 6, 15 April 1920; 25 May 1921. Canadian annual rev., 1906: 172. CPG, 1918. DHB, vol.1. Hamilton, the Birmingham of Canada (Hamilton, 1893; copy in Hamilton Public Library). Hamilton, the electric city (Hamilton, [1906?]; copy in Hamilton Public Library). William Kilbourn, The elements combined: a history of the Steel Company of Canada (Toronto and Vancouver, 1960). *Magazine of industry and daily times, Hamilton, Ont. – reviewing historically the industrial and financial interests* (souvenir ed., Hamilton, 1910; copy in Hamilton Public Library). B. D. Palmer, *A culture in conflict: skilled workers and industrial capitalism in Hamilton, Ontario, 1860–1914* (Montreal, 1979). *Prominent men of Canada: a collection of persons distinguished in professional and political life, and in the commerce and industry of Canada*, ed. G. M. Adam (Toronto, 1892). *Who's who and why*, 1921.

MINEHAN, LANCELOT (Launcelot) PETER, Roman Catholic priest and social reformer; b. 18 Jan. 1862 in Killaloe (Republic of Ireland), son of Michael Minehan and Hanna Skehan; d. 30 Dec. 1930 in Toronto.

Lancelot Minehan attended All Hallows College in Dublin, where he received the tonsure and minor orders on 10 June 1881. An accident forced him to return to Killaloe and resume his education under the guidance of F. J. McRedmond, the parish priest and vicar general. When he left for Canada in April 1884, McRedmond informed his sponsor, Archbishop John Joseph Lynch* of Toronto, that the young man "has always been as pious and gentle as he is industrious and intelligent. I have no hesitation in forecasting that you will find him in every way an Excellent priest." Minehan would fulfil this prediction and become one of the most successful of the last generation of Irish-born missionary clergy to serve the archdiocese.

In Canada he continued his studies at Lynch's summer home and the Grand Séminaire de Montréal. He was ordained on 20 December and appointed to St Luke's parish in Thornhill, Ont. Barely acclimatized, he threw himself into his work. During his first eight years he was a curate in Thornhill, Brockton (Toronto), Adjala, and Toronto, and a chaplain at the Ontario Reformatory for Boys in Penetanguishene and the Central Prison in Toronto. He worked in Adjala for the flamboyant Father Francis McSpiritt*, who would have demonstrated the power of Irish clergy over their parishioners and the need for mutual loyalty. In 1896, after three years as pastor in Schomberg, Minehan was moved to St Peter's mission church in Toronto, which he organized as a parish with a separate school, a new church, and a rectory. The single blemish on his record appeared in 1903, when he rallied parishioners over Archbishop Denis O'Connor*'s refusal to pay an assistant's salary to his brother, Father James Minehan. Apostolic delegate Donato Sbarretti y Tazza settled the matter, scolding the brothers but instructing O'Connor to pay. Minehan's final posting, in 1914, was to the city's Parkdale area, where he built St Vincent de Paul into a powerhouse of Catholic life, despite wartime impediments. Between the laying of the cornerstone for a church in 1915 and its dedication in 1924, he had a rectory and a school constructed.

Despite his successes, Minehan was never fully satisfied with parochial duty. A forceful preacher, he had discovered early that he was equally at ease as a public speaker and that the press provided an excellent forum in an era when clerics spoke out on social or moral matters. In 1909 the *Globe* claimed Minehan's "priesthood did not cancel his citizenship." He later remarked, "I have never discussed politics from the pulpit, but believe it was my right to do so from the public platform, where all could hear and reply to me." In his many contributions to local newspapers, including the *Catholic Register*, he never shied away from controversy; always courteous, he could be devastatingly blunt and occasionally sarcastic as he defended Catholic teachings. During the Protestant reaction in 1911 to the *Ne Temere* decree on matrimonial law, he delivered a "red-hot sermon" in which, the *Toronto Daily Star* reported, he accused critics of "ignorant and brutal outbursts of bigotry that are a disgrace, not alone to Christianity whose name they usurp, but to humanity itself." To the claim of the Methodist *Christian Guardian* that Catholics in mixed marriages had been commanded to break their vows and abandon their spouses, he replied that such attacks were wilfully or stupidly unjust. He usually left the politically charged separate-school issue to the bishops [*see* Fergus Patrick McEvay*], but the dispute over the qualifications of some teaching nuns and brothers had prompted him in 1906 to write (and thus court unpopularity) that they should have obtained proper certificates in the first place. He further pointed out that separate schools had difficulty attracting qualified teachers because the government denied these schools their fair share of taxes. He later wrote a brilliant critique of Ontario's legislation on taxes.

Minehan was more than an apologist. With a broad range of interests, he fashioned positions as a friend of the poor, a defender of both capital and workers' rights (but an ardent foe of Bolshevism), and a promoter of causes, among them the reform of the civil service and the militia department, wartime conscription, Victory Loans, a Canadian navy, women's suffrage, and Home Rule for Ireland. He supported the formation of the United Church of Canada in 1925 because he believed that, since it would contain most of the country's Protestants, it could facilitate the teaching of religion in public schools. His beliefs carried him into several organizations: he was a vice-president of the Moral and Social Reform Council, a founder of the Parkdale Ratepayers' and Progressive Businessmen's Association and the Neighbourhood Workers' Association, and a director of the Social Service Council of Ontario and the Penny Bank of Ontario, which encouraged thrift among the young. He introduced the first parish-based troop of Boy Scouts in the archdiocese and, alongside his parishioners, worked a plot of land on Yonge Street as an example of urban self-reliance. Minehan's social concerns drew him toward the Social Gospel movement, but with reservation. He found nothing in Salem Goldworth Bland*'s *The new Christianity . . .* (Toronto, 1920), for instance, that had not already been voiced by Pope Leo XIII in the 1890s or by the American bishops in their pastoral letter of 1919.

Central to Minehan's role as a reformer was his prominence in the temperance movement. As a parish priest, he would have dealt with families ruined by alcoholism, but he was realistic enough to know that Prohibition would never prevail in a society where alcohol had always been present. The legacy of hotels with bar rooms had to be tolerated, he believed, but neighbourhood bars with no tradition behind them should be abolished; he worked to reduce with compensation the number of licensed establishments. A vice-president of the Ontario branch of the Dominion Alliance for the Total Suppression of the Liquor Traffic, he joined the wildly popular ban-the-bar movement led by Newton Wesley Rowell*, who became leader of the provincial Liberals in 1911. Minehan's greatest moment in the cause came on 25 June 1914, four days before a provincial election, when he chaired a major rally at Massey Music Hall in Toronto. During his emotional speech to a mainly Protestant audience, he claimed Catholics had suffered the most from the bar-room curse and scathingly referred to Catholic liquor merchants as knifers. The Conservatives retained power, but the campaign for Prohibition found new impetus during the war; in 1916 the government passed the Ontario Temperance Act. When the Conservatives moved to abandon it in 1927 in favour of government control, Minehan re-entered the fray.

The temperance movement had brought him into contact with many of Toronto's leading Protestant clergymen. Theological differences aside, and as long as the Orange lodge was not involved, they worked well together, a relationship that may help explain Minehan's ecumenical spirit. He defended the appointment of Anglican archdeacon Henry John Cody* as minister of education in 1918, he spoke in 1923 at West Presbyterian Church on the "ideals of citizenship" (an address praised by the *Globe* as "another body blow to old prejudices"), and in 1927 he offered the basement of his church to the congregation of Erskine United when it burned.

Lancelot Minehan died unexpectedly of a stroke three years later. Known and respected for his toleration and charity, he was described by Edwin Austin Hardy* of the Community Welfare Council of Ontario "as a man of lovable personality, of strong convictions and of the most devoted zeal in the service of his Lord and Master."

MICHAEL POWER

Lancelot Peter Minehan delivered an address entitled "Civil service reform" to the Empire Club of Canada on 8 Nov. 1906 (Empire Club of Canada, *Speeches* (Toronto), 1906–7: 71–76).

Arch. of the Roman Catholic Archdiocese of Toronto, Clergy biog. and ministry database; Clergy personnel records fonds, Lancelot Minehan file; Rev. E. J. Kelly clergy journals, Minehan entry; L (Lynch papers), AA05.2047; LB (letterbooks), 01.319; ODS (O'Connor – apostolic delegate papers), 05.07, 10, 23, 25(b); 07.10, 13, 21. *Catholic Register* (Toronto), 1906–7, 1917, 1931. *Christian Guardian*, 1911. *Evening Telegram* (Toronto), 1910, 1919, 1924, 1929, 1931. *Globe*, 1909–10, 1914, 1918–20, 1923–24, 1930. *News* (Toronto), 3 Nov. 1906. *Toronto Daily Star*, 1911, 1915–20, 1922–23, 1925, 1927, 1930. Richard Allen, *The social passion: religion and social reform in Canada, 1914–28* (Toronto, 1971; repr. 1990). *Canadian annual rev.*, 1907: 471; 1908: 317–18; 1910: 178; 1911: 326; 1912: 351; 1913: 736; 1914: 445; 1917: 412; 1918: 608; 1919: 237–38. *Canadian men and women of the time* (Morgan; 1912). Kevin Condon, *The Missionary College of All Hallows, 1842–1891* (Dublin, 1986). M. G. McGowan, *The waning of the green: Catholics, the Irish, and identity in Toronto, 1887–1922* (Montreal and Kingston, Ont., 1999). J. S. Moir, "Canadian Protestant reaction to the *Ne Temere* decree," CCHA, *Study Sessions*, 48 (1981): 78–90. *St. Vincent de Paul parish: golden jubilee, 1915–1965* ([Toronto], 1965]).

MONTIZAMBERT, FREDERICK, physician and office holder; b. 3 Feb. 1843 at Quebec, son of Edward Lewis Montizambert, a lawyer, and Lucy Bowen; m. there 15 June 1865 Mary Jane Walker, and they had five daughters and two sons; d. 2 Nov. 1929 in Ottawa.

The Boucher de Montizambert family were direct descendants of Pierre Boucher*, the founder and seigneur of Boucherville. After the conquest they intermarried with influential British families in the colony and gradually became anglicized. Frederick, who used only Montizambert as his surname, was raised in the well-to-do and dominant milieu of the Quebec administrative and judicial upper middle class. His father, having practised his profession as a lawyer, was appointed law clerk to the Legislative Council of Lower Canada in 1862 and the Senate in 1867. His maternal grandfather, Edward Bowen*, had been chief justice of the Superior Court of Lower Canada. Frederick attended the High School of Montreal and, from 1856 to 1859, Upper Canada College in Toronto. Having studied medicine at the Université Laval at Quebec from 1859 to 1861, he set out for Scotland in 1863. He specialized in surgery and obstetrics and began training in clinical medicine at the prestigious medical faculty of the University of Edinburgh. In the winter of 1891 he would spend two months at Johns Hopkins University in Baltimore, Md, studying the bacteria of cholera and other contagious diseases, under the direction of Professor William Henry Welch.

On his return to Quebec in 1865, Montizambert married Mary Jane Walker, whose father, William

Walker, had been a member of the Legislative Council from 1842 to 1863. In 1866 he obtained a position as assistant physician at the quarantine station on Grosse Île in the St Lawrence River, about 33 miles below Quebec. A sturdy man passionately interested in public health, he turned his back on a promising career in private practice and took on the exhausting task of boarding ships and examining their passengers. The quarantine station, which had been opened in 1832 because of a cholera epidemic, had also had to deal with both the massive emigration of Irish fleeing famine and deadly typhus in the late 1840s [see George Mellis Douglas*]. When Montizambert moved there, preparations were under way to cope with another outbreak of cholera.

When Anthony von Iffland* retired as medical director at Grosse Île, Montizambert applied for and in 1869 obtained this important position. At the age of 26, he faced a huge challenge: to put in place a modern, efficient, rapid, and permanent quarantine system where there existed only dilapidated, rudimentary, temporary wooden huts. The task was all the more urgent because Canada, as constituted by confederation, was counting heavily on immigration to populate and develop the country, and at that time a growing number of contagious and increasingly virulent diseases were threatening to come up the St Lawrence with this immigration, now arriving from all over the world.

Over the course of three decades, in spite of petty administrative annoyances and economic and budgetary crises, Montizambert brought Grosse Île to the front rank of North American quarantine stations. The installations were largely rebuilt and compartmentalized, the quarantine regulations were amended, and reception and service were brought into line with the steamship age. Much more important was the fact that, on Montizambert's initiative, the station rapidly and radically altered its scientific approach. From the 1880s, on the heels of major discoveries in microbiology, disinfectants and vaccination put an end to lengthy confinement. In 1892 a bacteriological laboratory was built on the island, enabling bacteria of infectious diseases to be quickly identified. In this way, serious illnesses could be distinguished from ordinary infections that could be treated at Quebec. In 1894, while remaining at Grosse Île, Montizambert was appointed by Ottawa to be superintendent of Canadian quarantine stations. As a result of this appointment, the stations on Lawlor Island near Halifax, Partridge Island in New Brunswick, and William Head on the Pacific coast soon adopted the technical and scientific procedures that had been developed on the St Lawrence.

In 1899, when immigration was becoming heavier and more varied than ever, the federal government considered it urgent to set up, within the Department of Agriculture, a section devoted exclusively to public health. Having spent more than 30 years at Grosse Île, Montizambert was immediately chosen to head this section. In Ottawa, he retained control of the quarantine stations and continued to modernize them. Among his new responsibilities, he took a particular interest in leper hospitals [see Alfred Corbett Smith*]. He played an active part in developing a highly effective treatment for leprosy, which was used in New Brunswick and British Columbia. As an adviser to the government on public health, he submitted many recommendations of all kinds, including a commitment by the federal government to the fight against tuberculosis, inspection of health conditions on passenger trains, and funding of bacteriological laboratories. But there was one project especially dear to his heart: the establishment of a real federal department of health. He shared this idea with the Canadian Medical Association, of which he was president in 1907–8. In 1919, soon after the end of World War I, the government finally granted his wish and created the long-desired department. On the heels of this victory, in 1920, Montizambert retired. Now 77 years old, he had spent 54 consecutive years in the service of public health in Canada. Widowed in 1921, he died in Ottawa in November 1929 at the age of 86.

An energetic, stubborn, and visionary physician who was resolutely bent on action, Frederick Montizambert is not usually recognized by Canadian medical historiography, mainly because he spent his whole career in the rarified atmosphere of the civil service. He tried to get his employers to recognize the professional status (and pay the salary) that he knew he deserved. In other countries – where he made a name for himself by taking part in international colloquiums, among other things – his work as a pathfinder and his experience in the field of public health did, however, bring him many distinctions. In 1891 he was elected president of the American Public Health Association. In 1893 France and Mexico also recognized the international scope of his pioneering work by making him an honorary member of the Société Française d'Hygiène and the National Academy of Medicine of Mexico. He became a companion of the Imperial Service Order in 1903 and a companion of the Order of St Michael and St George in 1916.

ANDRÉ SÉVIGNY

Shortly before his death, Frederick Montizambert wrote a short article, "The story of fifty-four years' quarantine service from 1866 to 1920," Canadian Medical Assoc., *Journal* (Toronto), 16 (1926): 314–19. His other writings, mainly annual reports to the minister of agriculture, are published in Can., Parl., *Sessional papers*, reports of the Dept. of Agriculture.

ANQ-Q, CE301-S61, 5 mars 1843, 15 juin 1865. LAC, MG 24, D16, 48: 38745; MG 26, A: 212656–759; H, 165, 228; MG 28, I, 75, 1(b), file 2.5 (mfm.); MG 29, C101; E18,

5: 75–77, 571–81; 11, file 10; RG 11, B1(a), 298; B2, 905, 1135, 1355, 1593; B2a, 1896; D4, 387, 3966; RG 17, A I, 18, no.1550; 27, no.2837; 46, no.4396; 61, nos.5804, 5843; 65, no.6278; A I.1, 15, files 1201–40; A I.5, 1631; A I.9, 1679; A 13, 1975, nos.1-5; RG 29, 4, nos.191525–26, 225273; 5, nos.126293, 233287; 19, file 10-3-1; RG 32, C2, 191, 683. *Le Droit* (Ottawa), 4 nov. 1929. *Ottawa Citizen*, 4 Nov. 1929. Geoffrey Bilson, "Dr Frederick Montizambert (1843–1929): Canada's first director general of public health," *Medical Hist.* (London), 29 (1985): 386–400. *Canadian men and women of the time* (Morgan; 1912). Le Jeune, *Dictionnaire.* André Sévigny, *Étude polyphasique des aménagements de la Grosse-Île: 1832–1980* (Parcs Canada, Direction des lieux et des parcs hist., Travail inédit, [Ottawa], 1991; *Rapports sur microfiches*, no.477); "Frederick Montizambert, homme-relais de la bactériologie et pionnier de la santé publique au Canada" (copie dactylographiée, Commission des lieux et monuments historiques du Canada, report no.1998-14, Ottawa, 1998), 391–417. Martin Tétreault, "Frederick Montizambert et la quarantaine de Grosse Île, 1869–1899," *Scientia Canadensis* (Thornhill, Ont., and Ottawa), 19 (1995): 5–28. *Who was who . . a companion to "Who's who," containing the biographies of those who died during the period [1897–2000]* (10v. to date and an index, London, 1920–), 3 (*1929–40*): 959.

MORRELL, CHARLOTTE MOUNT BROCK (Schreiber), artist and teacher; b. 21 May 1834 in Colchester, England, eldest daughter of Robert Price Morrell, a Church of England clergyman, and Mary Mount Brock; m. 28 Sept. 1875 Weymouth George Schreiber (d. 5 July 1898) in Witham, Essex, England; they had no children; d. 3 July 1922 in Paignton, England.

Her father's encouragement of her interest in art enabled Charlotte Mount Brock Morrell to study in London in 1850–55 at Carey's School of Art. She also took lessons with John Rogers Herbert and instruction in anatomy from a Mr Scharf. In addition to exhibiting with the Royal Academy of Arts between 1855 and 1874, Charlotte illustrated editions of Edmund Spenser's *The legend of the Knight of the Red Crosse* (London, 1871) and Elizabeth Barrett Browning's *The rhyme of the Duchess May* (London, 1873). In 1875, newly married to her second cousin, Weymouth Schreiber of Toronto, who had three teenaged children, she immigrated to Ontario, locating in Deer Park (Toronto).

Within five years, Charlotte Schreiber's talent was recognized and she had attained a notable position in the province's artistic community. In 1876 she was elected to the Ontario Society of Artists; the following year she was the only woman on the board of the Ontario School of Art and from 1877 to 1880 its sole woman teacher. The first female member of the Royal Canadian Academy of Arts, having been appointed at its founding in 1880, she chose to retire in 1888 rather than resign over its prohibition of women attending meetings. Fearless and forthright, she never lost "the fire and enthusiasm of a young girl" ascribed to her at age 60.

Schreiber's singular achievements as a woman were supported by her ability to produce realistic, popular scenes from literature and everyday life. Paintings of animals, portraits, and romantic, sentimental, and historical depictions were typical. *The croppy boy,* her diploma painting of 1880 for the RCA and her most famous work (now in the National Gallery of Canada), illustrates a tragic moment from an Irish ballad. As a young patriot makes his confession, the priest reveals himself to be a British soldier in disguise, signifying certain death for the youth. Such compelling narrative scenes put Schreiber in the forefront of conventional Victorian aesthetics. She rejected Impressionism. "Every portion of the living body, the parts of a flower, are divinely beautiful," the tall, white-haired artist would explain in an interview in 1895. "It is a joy to paint them as they are in reality." She exhibited with the OSA from 1876 to 1890 and with the Toronto Industrial Exhibition, the Art Association of Montreal, the RCA, and the Women's Art Association of Canada, of which she was a founding member in 1890. She also showed works in American and European exhibitions and continued to illustrate books, among them a simple poetic prayer by Sabine Baring-Gould, *Now the day is over* (Toronto, 1881).

In 1884 the Schreiber family moved to its farm near Springfield (Mississauga) on the Credit River, where Charlotte set up a studio in her home, which she named Mount Woodham. She privately tutored such young artists as George Agnew Reid* and Beatrice Mary Walker, who had married one of her stepsons. Her favourite protégé, and sometime model, was Ernest Thompson Seton*, who would become famous as a naturalist writer and artist. Schreiber was also involved in the local community: she played the organ at St Peter's Anglican Church, helped decorate the sanctuary of a new building, and raised funds through the sale of pet animals and paintings.

In the 1890s Schreiber endured the loss of her two stepdaughters-in-law in childbirth and of her husband. By 1899 she had returned to England and settled in Paignton, where she continued to enjoy a prosperous career, painting until her death at age 88.

MOLLY PULVER UNGAR and VICKY BACH

[The most complete collection of documents pertaining to Charlotte Mount Brock Schreiber is in the possession of Mrs Beatrice Geary of Ottawa, who kindly shared her archive with the authors. This collection includes a pedigree of the Brock family, photographs of the Schreiber family, copies of magazine articles, newspaper clippings, and catalogues, copies of correspondence between Charlotte and Ernest Thompson Seton, and family correspondence about Charlotte. Margaret Fallis's "Charlotte Schreiber, R.C.A., 1834–1922"

(MA thesis, Carleton Univ., Ottawa, 1985) contains a well-researched biography, an exhibition history, and an illustrated catalogue of 83 of Schreiber's works. The website of the National Gallery of Canada (Ottawa) also reproduces some of her work: *www.national.gallery.ca.* M.P.U. and V.B.]

National Gallery of Canada Library and Arch. (Ottawa), Artist file, Schreiber, Charlotte Mount Brock Morrell. *Globe*, 2 March 1895. Thompson Adamson, *175 years of history, 1825–2000: St. Peter's Anglican Church, Erindale*, ed. Shirley Stoppard (Mississauga, Ont., [2000]). Betty Keller, *Black Wolf: the life of Ernest Thompson Seton* (Vancouver, 1984). H. G. Schreiber, "Schreiber pedigree" (typescript, [Toronto], 1960; copy in DCB library).

MORRICE, JAMES WILSON, painter; b. 10 Aug. 1865 in Montreal, son of David Morrice and Annie Stevenson Anderson; d. unmarried 23 Jan. 1924 at the military hospital in Tunis, Tunisia, and was buried there in the cemetery on Taieb Mehiri Avenue (later El Borgel Cemetery).

James Wilson Morrice's family belonged to the wealthy elite of the Montreal merchant bourgeoisie of Scottish origin. Little is known about his childhood. His sister, Annie Mather, remembered that he drew and sculpted at a very early age. From 1878 to 1882 he pursued his secondary education at the Montreal Proprietary School (which became the McTavish School in 1879), where he is believed to have had his first drawing lessons. The earliest known watercolours by Morrice date from 1879 and depict landscapes of the New England shoreline where his family used to spend their summer holidays. After a short stay in Maine during the summer of 1882, Morrice moved to Toronto; he studied there until June 1886, when he obtained a BA from the University of Toronto. He was accepted as a student by the Law Society of Upper Canada in the fall and was called to the Ontario bar three years later, although he would never practise law.

In 1888 Morrice showed two works at the exhibitions of the Royal Canadian Academy of Arts and the Ontario Society of Artists. Thereafter he was a regular participant in Canadian exhibitions and he was often praised by art critics. In 1889 the critic of the Toronto *Week*, for example, wrote, "A new name [to remember] is that of J. W. Morrice, whose style is unique, including sentiment and poetic treatment which will cause us to look for his works in the future." That year he exhibited for the first time at the Art Association of Montreal (later the Montreal Museum of Fine Arts). From 1889 until the end of his life, Morrice dealt with a prestigious Montreal art gallery, William Scott and Sons, which opened in 1859 and remained in business until 1939. This firm would continue to sell Morrice's works after his death and at the auction in 1938 preceding its closing, it put on sale more than 20 of them.

It is not known exactly when Morrice left for Europe, but in 1890 he was in Saint-Malo, France. He lived in Europe until 1924, returning to Canada only temporarily. He seems to have gone first to London, where he moved into a studio at 87 Gloucester Street. In April 1892 the young painter was living in Paris, at 9 Rue Campagne-Première in Montparnasse. During this period he reportedly was a student for a while in the studios of the Académie Julian. He himself said that he had studied with Henri Harpignies, who taught at his studio in the Saint-Germain-des-Prés quarter. Morrice's activities from 1893 to 1895 are obscure. His sketchbooks show that he spent time on the coast of Normandy, in Italy (at Rome, Capri, and Venice), in Holland, and in Belgium. These were the first journeys of the Canadian painter, who throughout his life would travel around Europe while maintaining a pied-à-terre in Paris. He met American artists Maurice Brazil Prendergast, Robert Henri, Édouard Colonna, and William James Glackens, who were living in France.

In February 1896 Morrice moved to Brolles in the forest of Fontainebleau, where he worked with Canadian painter Albert Curtis Williamson. Back in Paris before April, he moved his studio to 34 Rue Notre-Dame-des-Champs. That month he exhibited a painting in the French capital for the first time, at the Salon of the Société Nationale des Beaux-Arts. Early in June he left his new studio to spend part of the summer in Saint-Malo. He would also make a few visits to Cancale. During this period Morrice became friends with Robert Henri, a painter who had a very great influence on his pictorial work at the time. Their friendship continued until the summer of 1900, when Henri returned to the United States. They painted together and criticized each other's work. *Fête foraine, Montmartre* (held at the Hermitage, St Petersburg), painted by Morrice around 1898, is very close to the work done in the same period by the American painter, in its composition and its choice of dark colours set off by highlights. It was probably due to Henri's influence that Morrice began to paint urban scenes.

Morrice was back in Montreal on 28 Nov. 1896, and he likely spent Christmas with his family. On 12 Jan. 1897 he was in Sainte-Anne-de-Beaupré, where he met Canadian painter Maurice Galbraith Cullen*. It was Cullen who opened his eyes to the dazzling light of the Quebec winter. The two artists did their quick studies in oil outdoors in the cold winter at Côte-de-Beaupré. *Sainte-Anne-de-Beaupré* (Montreal Museum of Fine Arts), dated 1897, demonstrates Morrice's talent as a colourist in his use of bright hues. He stayed in the Quebec City region until March, and then returned to Paris by way of Toronto and New York. That fall he travelled to Italy; he also exhibited for the first time at the Royal Glasgow Institute of Fine Arts. In 1898 he moved his studio to 41 Rue Saint-Georges, in the Montmartre quarter in Paris, but until the end of September he lived in Saint-Malo. At the end of March 1899 he went to Charenton, which provided the inspiration for the painting *Charenton washing day* (Art Gallery of Hamilton). At the beginning of October he set up his studio at 45 Quai des Grands-Augustins, where he would remain for more than 15 years. He arrived in Montreal in December to meet his family and then went on to Quebec. In March 1900 he was back in Paris. Morrice regularly sent paintings to Canadian art exhibitions, and on occasion to American ones, including, for the first time, the Pennsylvania Academy of Fine Arts in Philadelphia. In 1910 he won a silver medal at the Pan-American Exposition in Buffalo, N.Y., and was elected an associate of the Société Nationale des Beaux-Arts. He made several visits to Italy in 1901 and 1902, taking a trip during the summer of 1902 with painters Joseph Pennell and Charles Henry Fromuth. There they joined Canadian painters Maurice Cullen, Edmund Montague Morris*, and William BRYMNER. During the Salon of the Société Nationale des Beaux-Arts, critic Henri Marcel noted in *La Gazette des beaux-arts*: "Nomadic Canadian that he is, he wanders from Venice to Brittany, fascinated by the delicate shades of gray on the water at twilight, by the rare colouration sometimes imparted to it by the reflection of a cloud." Morrice showed works in Philadelphia, Pittsburgh, Cincinnati, Ohio, Chicago, Buffalo, St Louis, Mo., and Venice in 1903, as well as for the first time at the Munich Sezession. He became the first Canadian to exhibit at the Venice Biennale. In New York on 16 June 1903, he went on to Montreal and Quebec, and then later in the year to Madrid. He never stopped moving, as his sketchbooks crammed with information about train timetables show.

By now Morrice was a well-known painter. It is not surprising, therefore, that the French government purchased *Quai des Grands-Augustins* (Musée d'Orsay) or that Russian collector Ivan Morozov acquired *Fête foraine, Montmartre* at the Salon of the Société Nationale des Beaux-Arts in 1904. The following year Morrice exhibited in England (London, Manchester, Burnley, and Liverpool), and subsequently in Paris, Venice, and Pittsburgh. Shortly before Christmas he returned to Montreal, where he remained until the end of February 1906. Early in the summer he went to Dieppe, France, and then to Le Pouldu and Concarneau. The painter exhibited for the first time at the Goupil Gallery in London. The next summer he spent some time in Venice before returning to Saint-Malo. In October 1908 he was named vice-president of the jury for the Salon d'Automne in Paris, along with Albert Marquet, Henri Matisse, and Georges Rouault. At Christmas he was back with his family in Montreal. He took advantage of this visit to travel to Quebec City and Montmorency falls. During the summer of 1909 he worked feverishly on the canvases he would present at the Salon d'Automne in Paris. The critics had nothing but praise for him, hailing him as the most talented North American painter. The eminent critic Louis Vauxcelles applauded the subtle and harmonious style of his landscapes and added that in painting, Morrice's "manner is eminently personal." He noted in passing that a number of young artists were trying to imitate him. That year the Canadian government acquired a canvas also entitled *Quai des Grands-Augustins* (National Gallery of Canada).

Morrice went to Montreal to celebrate his parents' golden wedding anniversary on 14 June 1910 but he was back in Paris in the fall. From France he went to London to see the exhibition organized by English critic Roger Eliot Fry, *Manet and the post-Impressionists*, an event marking the first use of the term "post-Impressionist." Morrice was fascinated by the works of Vincent Van Gogh, Paul Gauguin, and Paul Cézanne. In addition to the salons, which he attended regularly, he apparently took an interest in individual shows by other artists such as Pierre Bonnard and Matisse. He spent most of his time in Paris, except for a trip to Boulogne-sur-Mer in the spring of 1911. He exhibited a great deal that year in London, Paris, Toronto, Montreal, Pittsburgh, and Buffalo, and he seemed to be run off his feet. As he himself noted, there were too many exhibitions to which he was sending work. In 1911, as in previous years, Morrice visited his family in Quebec at Christmas, but he left Montreal hastily for Tangier, Morocco, at the end of January. Some Montreal friends are thought to have encouraged him to undertake this first trip to North Africa. Enthused by the landscapes, towns, and people, he painted a great deal, and at the next Salon d'Automne he showed four canvases on Moroccan subjects. In December 1912 he returned to Tangier, where he joined French painters Charles Camoin and Henri Matisse, painting the same subjects as the latter. When he left Morocco in March 1913, Morrice stopped off at Gibraltar and travelled through Spain by way of Toledo.

Morrice went to Cagnes-sur-Mer, near Nice, in the south of France early in 1914, and then headed for Tunis. That year the Arts Club Limited of Montreal held an exhibition of his works. The painter was in Paris in August when war broke out in Europe. He visited London in September and returned to Paris in the course of the autumn. Following the death of his parents, he went to spend Christmas in Montreal. In February 1915 he left Montreal for the West Indies, travelling by way of Washington. In addition to Cuba, he briefly visited Jamaica. Cuba made a profound impression on the painter and he produced luminous canvases. After returning to Paris in May, he was off again almost at once for Bayonne, Carcassonne, and Toulouse. Apparently Morrice did not leave France again until after the war. Since there were no exhibitions or French salons during the hostilities, Morrice showed his works only in Toronto and Montreal. In

1916 the Contemporary Art Society of London purchased *House in Santiago* (Tate Gallery). Morrice moved into a new studio at 23 Quai de la Tournelle in Paris that year.

At the end of 1916 the Canadian government created the Canadian War Memorials Fund, which enabled both Canadian and foreign contemporary artists to paint the activities of Canadian soldiers. In October 1917 Lord Beaverbrook [Aitken*] commissioned Morrice to do *Canadians in the snow* (Canadian War Museum, Ottawa).

After his parents' death Morrice apparently returned less regularly to Canada, but he came back during the winter of 1920–21. He subsequently went to Trinidad, where he did a great deal of painting, especially in watercolours. This visit seems to have renewed his desire to work, since he exhibited three paintings done in Trinidad at the Salon d'Automne in Paris in 1921. When he returned to France, Morrice probably went several times to Cagnes-sur-Mer to see Léa Cadoret and the young Canadian painter John Goodwin Lyman*. He had met Cadoret in Paris around 1898, when she had agreed to pose as a model, and he would remain very attached to her for the rest of his life. He bought a villa for her at Cagnes-sur-Mer in 1922. In January and February of that year he visited Monte-Carlo, Nice, and Corsica. He landed at Algiers the following month and returned to Paris in April. He always carried his sketchbooks with him and, as usual, drew from nature the landscapes he saw. Although his health was eroded by alcohol, Morrice continued to travel. He visited Évian-les-Bains, was hospitalized in Montreux, Switzerland, and then went to Cagnes-sur-Mer to spend Christmas with Cadoret, Lyman, and Brymner. He was in Palermo, Italy, on 14 January and immediately took ship for Tunis. Ravaged by illness, he died there on 23 Jan. 1924 at the age of 58.

The best description of Morrice comes from Matisse: "As a man, he was a true gentleman, a good friend with plenty of wit and humour. He had, as everyone knows, an unfortunate craving for whisky. ... He was a Canadian of Scottish descent, from a rich family, very rich himself, but he did not show it. He was always over hill and dale, a little like a migrating bird but without any fixed landing place." As he travelled, Morrice painted from life small studies in oil and filled his sketchbooks with urban settings, cafés, and genre scenes of landscapes and city buildings with human figures. The painter retained whatever caught his eye, and drew it, sometimes noting variations in colour. Twenty-four of his sketchbooks are held at the Montreal Museum of Fine Arts. These works display a great concern for composition and a wide range of colour. Using his sketches for inspiration, the artist worked in his studio to create full-sized oil canvases. Morrice's style evolved throughout his career, changing from the impasto he employed in the late 1890s to compositions that used the nuances of bare canvas or wood panel in the years that followed.

The landscapes Morrice painted from 1892 to 1894 are characterized by small brush strokes in every direction. During the period 1895–97 he sought to convey atmosphere by patches of colour in the same tonality done with heavier or lighter impasto. His night scenes show the influence of American painter James Abbott McNeill Whistler, as well as that of his friend Robert Henri. In contrast, the works he produced following his trip to Canada in 1897 were done with a palette of bright colours enabling him to paint the luminosity of the Canadian winter. Early in the 20th century, Morrice's work displayed the preoccupation with decorative motifs that the Nabis painters such as Édouard-Jean Vuillard and Pierre Bonnard showed. In the 1910s his work again changed style. The radiance of North Africa and the influence of Matisse led him to adopt a palette of bright colours. His output during his travels in the West Indies in 1915 is enriched by asymmetrical compositions in pure tones. At that time Morrice was employing a very light impasto. He made good use of the bare wood panel or canvas. He took a stylus or the handle of his brush to draw in the fresh paint and incorporated some pencil lines into the painting. His compositions became simpler.

In the course of his career Morrice was more visible on the international scene than any other Canadian painter of the early 20th century. During his lifetime his works appeared in 140 exhibitions held in more than 36 exhibition centres and art galleries in Canada, the United States, England, Scotland, France, Italy, Germany, and Belgium. He attracted attention especially before World War I. Relying on all the large-scale annual exhibitions, he hoped to achieve international recognition for his work.

The continued presence of the works of James Wilson Morrice in all the major exhibitions has brought him fame in art circles in France and Canada. He had a marked influence on Canadian painters, including John Lyman, who wrote in 1909: "Morrice's art is so perfect, so pure, so unadulterated by verisimilitude, the episodical, 'smartness', etc., and refrains so completely from appealing to the literary or the 'fleshy' senses! His work seems to me to be as pure 'painting poetry' as Monet's." That year the critic Louis Vauxcelles named him one of the most important painters of the time and added: "Since the death of James MacNeill Whistler, J. W. Morrice is unquestionably the American painter who has achieved in France and at Paris ... the most notable and well-merited place in the world of art."

NICOLE CLOUTIER

[James Wilson Morrice's works are held by several Canadian museums and private collectors. The main collections

Morrison

are those in the National Gallery of Canada, Ottawa, and the Montreal Museum of Fine Arts. Outside Canada, Morrice's paintings are found in the Musée d'Orsay, Paris, the Hermitage, St Petersburg, and the Tate Gallery, London, among others. The Montreal Museum of Fine Arts has presented two major retrospectives of his works, in 1965 and 1985. N.C.]

ANQ-M, CE601-S120, 3 sept. 1865. Art Gallery of Ontario Research Library and Arch. (Toronto), J. W. Morrice file; Edmund Morris letter-books, 1. Bibliothèque Nationale du Québec (Montréal), MSS 149/2/3 (John Lyman, corr.). Library of Congress (Washington), Manuscript Div., MNC 2796 (C. H. Fromuth, journal); S79-2243 (Robert Henri coll.); S79-35857 (Joseph Pennell fonds). North York Central Library (Toronto), Canadiana Coll., Newton MacTavish coll. Yale Univ. Library, Beinecke Rare Book and MS Library (New Haven, Conn.), Robert Henri, family corr. D. W. Buchanan, *James Wilson Morrice: a biography* (Toronto, 1936). Nicole Cloutier, "Brittany in the work of James Wilson Morrice," *Vie des arts* (Montréal), no.121 (décembre 1985): 21–23, 85; "Deux tableaux de James Wilson Morrice dans la collection Morozov," *Journal of Canadian Art Hist.* (Montreal), 9 (1986): 81–87; *James Wilson Morrice, 1865–1924* (exhibition catalogue, Montreal Museum of Fine Arts, 1985); "Short note; Morrice: 1912," *Journal of Canadian Art Hist.*, 10 (1987): 153–59. Lucie Dorais, *J. W. Morrice* (Ottawa, 1985); "James Wilson Morrice, peintre canadien (1865–1924): les années de formations" (mémoire de MA, univ. de Montréal, 1980). Galeries Simonson, *Catalogue des tableaux et études par James Wilson Morrice* (Paris, 1926). C. C. Hill, *Morrice; a gift to the nation: the G. Blair Laing Collection* (Ottawa, 1992). W. H. Ingram, "Canadian artists abroad," *Canadian Magazine*, 28 (November 1906–April 1907): 218–22. *J. W. Morrice: James Wilson Morrice (1865–1924)* (exhibition catalogue, Montreal Museum of Fine Arts, 1965). G. B. Laing, *Morrice: a great Canadian artist rediscovered* (Toronto, 1984). John Lyman, *Morrice* (Montreal, 1945). Henry Marcel, "Les salons de 1902," *La Gazette des beaux-arts* (Paris), 27 (juin 1902): 472. Micheline Moisan, "Prints and drawings," in *A Montreal collection: gift from Eleanore and David Morrice ...* (Montreal, 1983), 49–63. Sandra Paikowsky, "James Wilson Morrice," in *The dictionary of art*, ed. J. S. Turner *et al.* (34v., New York, 1996), 22: 137–38. Louis Vauxcelles, "The art of J. W. Morrice," *Canadian Magazine*, 34 (November 1909–April 1910): 169–76.

MORRISON, Sir EDWARD WHIPPLE BANCROFT, journalist, militia and army officer, and author; b. 6 July 1867 in London, Ont., third son of Alexander R. Morrison and Jean Campbell; m. 16 Jan. 1911, in New York City, Emma Thacker Kaye (d. 11 Oct. 1936), former wife of Charles Downing Fripp; they had no children; d. 28 May 1925 in Ottawa and was buried there in Beechwood Cemetery.

Edward W. B. Morrison was educated at schools in Galt (Cambridge) and Hamilton, Ont. His first career, beginning in 1888 or 1889, was as a journalist with the *Hamilton Spectator*, where he rose to be city editor. One example of his work was a four-column article in 1896 entitled "Ten thousand islands: camping experiences on the Rocks of Georgian Bay." It described a trip through "the Rocks" from Penetanguishene up the east coast of Georgian Bay for 100 miles or so, an area that had been completely surveyed only a few years before. In keeping with his rather rugged world-view he commented, "It is said that if you scratch a Russian you will find a Tartar, but it is also as true that if you scrape the thin veneer of civilisation on the modern man you find him the same stuff as his aboriginal ancestors."

On 1 July 1898 Morrison joined the *Ottawa Citizen* as its editor-in-chief, and he would remain with this paper until 1913. Replacing Hugh Clark, described a quarter-century later as "not a great editor," Morrison left a better impression on his colleagues. One of them would later characterize him as "a pungent writer, with an uncompromising style, a bonnie fighter in the journalistic field as afterwards he proved himself to be on the field of battle – a man with the most comprehensive knowledge of newspaper work in all its phases," though admittedly this judgement was heavily influenced by hindsight. As an example of his management style, the same colleague recalled that "on Sunday afternoons he used to line us up, not for a symposium on the holy evangels but for a practical talk on the science of gathering news, on literary style and construction and on the fundamental ethics of journalism. He was a stern master in a way and at times he put the subordinate staff over a rough road, but always for our benefit."

Coincidentally, and very much in keeping with his personality, Morrison served as an artillery officer in Canada's militia. He had joined the 4th Field Battery in Hamilton, as a second lieutenant, in May 1897 and then transferred to the 2nd Field Battery in Ottawa in 1898, with the rank of lieutenant. In 1899 he obtained a leave of absence from the *Citizen* to serve in South Africa, where he took part in operations in the Transvaal, the Orange River Colony, and the Cape Colony. After one action in 1900, when he was under the command of Lieutenant-Colonel François-Louis LESSARD, he was among five Canadians to be recommended for a decoration, in his case "for the skill and coolness with which he worked and finally saved his guns" in a hasty retreat. He received the Distinguished Service Order the following year. Morrison described his experiences in a volume entitled *With the guns in South Africa* (1901), providing observations on food, the cold (which came as a surprise to Canadian troops), fellow officers such as Lieutenant John McCrae*, and the nature of operations, especially line of communication work, harassment by Boer commandos, and the occasional battle. The book is, in fact, an excellent source for those interested in the day-to-day life and work of an artillery battery in the South African War. Its last entry encapsulates the military ethos with which Morrison was imbued, reading simply that he had had "a nice time at the war."

After returning from South Africa, Morrison continued to serve as a reservist until 1913, when he joined the Permanent Force as a lieutenant-colonel and director of artillery. With the outbreak of war in 1914 he went overseas with the first contingent of the Canadian Expeditionary Force, in command of the 1st Brigade, Canadian Field Artillery; John McCrae gave him his medical exam. After serving in the second battle of Ypres in April–May 1915, he reported how impressed he was with the coolness of his gunners in engagements that cost the 1st Canadian Division a third of its 18,000 troops. Then came Festubert and Givenchy-lez-La Bassée. Morrison was promoted brigadier-general on 13 Sept. 1915, to command the artillery of the 1st Canadian Division; in October he was appointed to command the 2nd Divisional Artillery. In this capacity he served through the battles of Saint-Eloi (Sint-Elooi), Sanctuary Wood, and Hooge, and through the bloody offensive along the Somme. On 18 Dec. 1916 he was made the general officer commanding the artillery of the Canadian Corps, a position he held during the battles of Vimy Ridge and Hill 70, which proved more successful, and less costly, than previous engagements. On 15 Aug. 1917, after gunners had expended prodigious amounts of ammunition supporting the infantry as it defended newly captured positions against counter-attacks, a staff officer from the British 1st Army noted that its commander was "appalled" at such profligacy. "So are the Germans," was Morrison's reply. He continued to serve as GOC artillery through the battles of Lens and Passchendaele, and the final offensives of 1918. He was promoted major-general on 31 July 1918.

After the war Morrison returned to Canada. He was awarded a KCMG in June 1919. Later that year he became a member of a committee appointed to reorganize the militia [see Sir William Dillon OTTER]; he also became deputy inspector-general of artillery. It fell to him to make the controversial announcement, in February 1920, that 16 artillery officers who had served as brigadiers-general overseas would become artillery brigade commanders in Canada, possibly superseding officers who had remained at home to recruit and train gunners for the battlefields of France and Belgium. Morrison became master-general of the ordnance in 1920 and served as adjutant-general in 1922–23. He retired in 1924 and died in Ottawa the following year.

WILLIAM RAWLING

Morrison's article on the islands of Georgian Bay appears in the *Hamilton Spectator*, 21 Aug. 1896: 5; his *With the guns in South Africa* was published in Hamilton in 1901.

AO, RG 80-8-0-988, no.9403. LAC, RG 150, Acc. 1992–93/166, box 6403–49. *Ottawa Citizen*, 19 Jan. 1911, 28 May 1925. "25 years ago the *Citizen* came under its present ownership and entered evening newspaper field," *Ottawa Citizen*, 25 Nov. 1922. Can., Dept. of Militia and Defence,

Militia list (Ottawa), 1897–1925. *Directory*, Hamilton, 1888/89. G. W. L. Nicholson, *The gunners of Canada; the history of the Royal Regiment of Canadian Artillery* (2v., Toronto, 1967–72). *Standard dict. of Canadian biog.* (Roberts and Tunnell). W. S. Wallace, *Macmillan dictionary of Canadian biography*, ed. W. A. McKay (4th ed., Toronto, [1978]), 597.

MOUNTAIN. *See* SG̲ANISM SM'OOGIT

MOUNT STEPHEN, Baron. *See* STEPHEN

MUNRO, JESSIE KNOX, schoolteacher and missionary; b. 9 Jan. 1861 in Peterborough, Upper Canada, daughter of George Munro, a miller, and Jessie Shearer; d. unmarried 23 March 1923 in Peterborough, Ont.

Jessie K. Munro was raised in a devout Wesleyan Methodist home by stern but loving parents. At age 14 she dedicated her life to Christ during a revival at her church, George Street Methodist in Peterborough. This conversion experience planted a strong desire to devote herself to the service of the Gospel as a missionary. Opposition from her parents prevented Munro from pursuing her vocation immediately. Instead she began to teach at a nearby country school. She subsequently attended the Normal School in Ottawa and in 1882 received her second-class professional certificate. During her teacher training Munro had demonstrated a great capacity for languages and had become fluent in German.

Munro taught in Lakefield, Goderich, and Brighton, but her aspirations to seek a missionary career persisted, and she "covenanted with the Lord" to go to Japan "if He called and opened the way." Shortly thereafter Munro saw an advertisement in the *Christian Guardian* (Toronto) placed by the Woman's Missionary Society seeking a teacher for its school for girls, the Tōyō Eiwa Jo Gakkō, in Tokyo, where the Methodist Church had been working since 1873 [see George Cochran*]. Seeing the advertisement as a sign, Munro immediately applied for the position. Impressed by her credentials and language skills, the missionary society accepted her. She arrived in Japan in the fall of 1888 and enthusiastically began teaching English, the Bible, and western morals to her Japanese students. Munro remained at the school until 1899 when ill health forced her to return to Canada.

In 1904 Munro appealed to the WMS to return to the mission field. That year the society sent her and nurse Retta Edmunds (Edmonds) to Pakan (Alta). The recent settlement of large numbers of Ukrainians in this area had raised concerns particularly among the Methodist and Presbyterian churches that they be Protestantized and assimilated. The Methodists launched their effort (ultimately unsuccessful in winning converts) in 1901, when they sent the medical missionary Charles H. Lawford to Pakan. The task of Munro and Edmunds was to establish a mission to the women and children.

For several months Munro and Edmunds lived in a tent where they conducted Sunday school classes while supervising the construction of the mission station at Wahstao. With the completion of the mission house, they opened a day school for immigrant children, a dispensary, and a clinic and began to offer instruction to Ukrainian women in child care and the domestic arts accompanied by Bible study. Their purpose was to instil the manners and morals of the Protestant Anglo-Canadian home. Ill health again forced Munro to go on furlough two years later. In 1908 she was instrumental in establishing the Home for Ruthenian Girls in Edmonton. Concerned about the plight of young immigrant women who had left their families to find work in the city, Munro hoped the home would provide a moral haven and an uplifting alternative to the "cheap picture shows, low theatres, public dance halls, restaurants of ill-repute" and above all the "Socialistic meetings" where "ignorant men speak against all religions." Poor health forced Munro to retire permanently from mission work in 1909. Thereafter she lived with relatives in Toronto, Lakefield, and finally Peterborough, where she died in 1923.

In many respects Jessie K. Munro was typical of the hundreds of single, well-educated, middle class, and small-town women who pursued careers as missionaries in late 19th and early 20th century Canada. Mission work offered Munro an appealing alternative to the austere and authoritarian home in which she had been raised and enabled her to fulfil the Christian sense of duty implanted by her upbringing. Her career reflected the evangelical imperative to win lost souls for Christ, the ethnocentric desire to "civilize" alien peoples, and the humanitarian concern with the social problems afflicting the disadvantaged that combined at the time to produce a strong missionary impulse within English Canadian Protestantism.

NORMAN KNOWLES

AO, RG 80-8-0-935, no.28269. PAA, UCC, Alberta and Northwest Conference Arch., 75.387, box 12, item 423 (photograph of Munro); Methodist Church (Canada), Woman's Missionary Soc., Alberta branch, minutes of the annual conference, 1904–9. UCC-C, Biog. file; Fonds 15, 78.080C, box 002, 1888, 1904–9; box 007, 1888–99. *Examiner* (Peterborough, Ont.), 24, 26 March 1923. Ethelwyn Chace, *Wahstao memories: letters to Edith Weekes from Ethelwyn Chace recalling pioneer days*, ed. Mrs J. K. Smith (privately published, n.p., n.d.). G. N. Emery, "Methodist missions among the Ukrainians," *Alberta Hist. Rev.* (Calgary), 19 (1971), no.2: 8–19. R. R. Gagan, *A sensitive independence: Canadian Methodist women missionaries in Canada and the Orient, 1881–1925* (Montreal and Kingston, Ont., 1992). Mae Laycock, *Bridges of friendship* (n.p., 1974; copy in UCC-C). *Missionary Outlook* (Toronto), September, December 1904; June 1905; May 1906; July 1909; January 1910. H. L. Platt *et al.*, *The story of the years: a history of the Woman's Missionary Society of the Methodist Church of Canada* (3v., [Toronto], 1908–17). C. I. Rauser, "Clean hearts and clean homes: the work of Methodist women missionaries among Ukrainian immigrants in east-central Alberta, 1904–1925" (MA thesis, Carleton Univ., Ottawa, 1991). Mrs W. E. [Elizabeth] Ross, *Miss Jessie K. Munro* (Toronto, [1923]; copy in Munro's biog. file at UCC-C).

MURRAY, GEORGE HENRY, teacher, lawyer, and politician; b. 7 June 1861 in Grand Narrows, N.S., third son of William Murray and Jane Murray; m. 3 Sept. 1889 Grace Elizabeth Moore (d. 1933) in North Sydney, N.S., and they had three sons; d. 6 Jan. 1929 in Montreal.

Born into a family of shopkeepers of Scottish background, George Murray moved to Sydney Mines shortly after his grandfather's death in 1864 and then to North Sydney in the early 1870s after his widowed mother's remarriage, his father having died in 1867. He attended school in both towns and while still an adolescent, he tried his hand at teaching in Reserve Mines for a year and in Georges River for a term, positions secured no doubt through the influence of his stepfather, John A. H. Rindress, a principal in Sydney Mines. At 16 he moved to Halifax to study law; he returned home to North Sydney to be articled to James H. Hearn between September 1878 and May 1882 and then to Stephen Lowrey Purves until January 1883. After finishing off his formal studies at the Boston University law school, he was admitted to the bar of Nova Scotia later in 1883 and he would maintain a law practice in North Sydney with Daniel Duncan McKenzie until 1896.

As a political aspirant, Murray contested Cape Breton County for the provincial Liberals in 1886 though he did not support Premier William Stevens FIELDING's controversial initiative for the repeal of confederation. Undeterred by his defeat, the next year he made the first of three unsuccessful attempts to win a seat in the House of Commons. He lost to David MacKeen*. The Cape Breton electorate was inclined to support Tory politicians because of Prime Minister Sir John A. Macdonald*'s policy of protectionism, which was considered beneficial for the marketing of the island's coal. The local Conservative majority included Murray's Presbyterian pastor at North Sydney, Isaac Murray*, a man quite willing to use the pulpit to advance his politics. George Murray later claimed that he was the only Liberal in the congregation to persist with this partisan spiritual leader and that he was able to get his own back in 1891 at the baptism of the Murrays' first-born. He deliberately chose that most Liberal of names, Wilfrid Laurier, and enjoyed the preacher's discomfort as he enunciated it over the infant.

Murray's defeats and his pluck brought him to the attention of the Liberal establishment, which embraced him as a promising prospect. In March 1889 Fielding appointed him to the Legislative Council.

Shortly after his second federal defeat, in March 1891, he was reappointed to Nova Scotia's upper house and he joined the Executive Council as a minister without portfolio and government leader in the Legislative Council. As a member of Fielding's cabinet, he worked at exposing the failure of the Conservatives' National Policy to benefit the mining population and he played a pivotal role in the negotiations that led to the organization in 1893 of the Dominion Coal Company, which amalgamated under one management most of the competing mines in Cape Breton [*see* Benjamin Franklin Pearson*].

At the request of the island's Liberal caucus, Murray reluctantly entered the lists for a federal seat again in a by-election on 4 Feb. 1896, this time against Secretary of State Sir Charles Tupper*. It was not a rancorous campaign. The previous year Tupper's son Sir CHARLES HIBBERT, then minister of justice, had expressed the federal government's appreciation of Murray's ability, at least as a lawyer, when he offered him a queen's counsellorship. Murray initially turned down the distinction because of the local Liberals' suspicion of Tory rewards, but his refusal was rejected. In the event, his electoral defeat by Tupper Sr came as no surprise. Notable, however, were two portents: the stand Murray took in favour of the development of local industries to provide a more reliable market for Cape Breton coal and Tupper's prediction that his worthy opponent would have "a brilliant future." In July 1896, after the Conservatives had been defeated and Fielding had joined the cabinet of Wilfrid Laurier*, Murray succeeded his mentor as premier and assumed the portfolio of provincial secretary, which made him responsible for Nova Scotia's finances. In addition, he would function as queen's printer, supervisor of incorporations and statistics, and the link between the cabinet and the departments of agriculture, health, education, and industries and immigration, and, as time went on, such boards as liquor control, utilities management, and workmen's compensation. The succession of 1896 upset longtime Liberal stalwart Attorney General James Wilberforce LONGLEY, but Murray demonstrated his conciliatory nature by keeping him in cabinet and, in appreciation of his own inexperience, by deferring to him on many occasions. The neophyte took his place in the House of Assembly after being acclaimed on 8 August in a by-election in Cape Breton's Victoria County to the seat vacated when Conservative John Lemuel Bethune moved to the House of Commons. Murray's first election as premier, on 20 April 1897, also marked his first personal success at the polls.

According to political scientist J. Murray Beck, "no premier ever started out more auspiciously" than Murray, who benefited from the party organization bequeathed to him by Fielding and, until World War I, generally favourable economic circumstances in the province. Though little more than a Fielding deputy for the first ten years, he remained premier until his retirement in 1923, winning his Victoria seat in five more elections (1901, 1906, 1911, 1916, and 1920). On the basis of his 26½ years of continuous service, he gained distinction as the longest serving leader of a British-style parliamentary government. However, his life was not without its dark side. He suffered a nervous breakdown following the 1901 election, an illness characterized as "gloominess, depression, want of confidence in himself," and he missed most of the 1902 session when he went to the United States for recovery. He was dealt a devastating blow in the spring of 1910, just before the close of the session, when one of his legs had to be amputated above the knee as a result of a blood clot. When he returned for the 1911 session, one Conservative MHA flippantly remarked, "Altho[ugh] he is not all there, there is enough of him to make it interesting for us." Murray overcame his disability by resorting to a cane and artificial leg and the convenience of a chauffeur-driven automobile.

The repeated defeats of the provincial Conservatives were considered to be attributable more to the weakness of the Tory party than to the premier's talents, though Murray's lack of involvement in scandals and known aversion to political chicanery may have helped sustain the Liberal majority. It was also maintained by the composition of the constituencies, which were drawn in such a way that 41.7 per cent of the popular vote in 1901 netted the Conservatives only 2 of 38 seats, and, in 1916, 48.8 per cent translated into 13 of 43 seats. The lacklustre leadership of the Conservatives was another factor, especially after the death of Charles Smith Wilcox* in 1909, though Murray himself could hardly be described as dynamic. Rather, as one Conservative newspaper noted in 1916, "he knows how to play the game."

Within the constraints dictated by the premier's fiscal conservatism and cautious approach, which both contemporaries and scholars have acknowledged, the Murray government contributed to four major areas of provincial life: transportation and communications, practical education, economic development, and social policy. With interprovincial traffic moving over the Intercolonial Railway, the pre-war era was characterized by the development of an intraprovincial railway network. During Murray's first decade as premier, the track mileage more than tripled, from 169 to 617. In 1901 he prided himself on securing from the federal Liberals the railway subsidy of $671,000 for branch lines that the previous Conservative government had refused to pay. In addition, he negotiated an arrangement that year with William MACKENZIE and Donald Mann* for the construction of the Halifax and South Western Railway as part of their much vaunted transcontinental plans [*see* Thomas Robertson*]. Only the eastern shore was left without a line. (The Halifax and Eastern Railway, incorporated in 1906 and opened only in 1916, went inland, with construction stopping at Upper Musquodoboit.) Trains carried passengers around the province in pursuit of work, holidays, and business, and freighted goods for regional markets, replacing unpredictable water transportation and inadequate roads. These lines remained vital until motor vehicles and public highways began to cut into their business.

Although trackage received more attention than roads, Murray's government did encourage the construction of such elements of infrastructure as bridges and culverts out of reinforced concrete and other "durable" materials. A road commissioner was appointed in 1907 and during the next ten years expenditures on roads more than tripled, though, according to custom, spending was often determined more by patronage than by need. Major modernization occurred in 1917 with the abolition of statute labour for road maintenance and the establishment of the first provincial highway board in Canada to supervise rural road construction. Ostensibly a bipartisan board that reported to the Department of Highways created in 1918, the Provincial Highway Board ran into difficulty in 1920 as a result of cost overruns and political manipulation. Murray appointed a royal commission to investigate the charges, which constituted the one public scandal of his premiership. Although the inquiry revealed ample evidence of partisan politics in the operations of the board, the commissioners covered up these findings. The government responded to popular dissatisfaction by revamping the board and, under Alexander Stirling MacMillan* as chair and engineers as the other members, it subsequently pursued a more professional approach to road building. Technical advances also contributed to the expansion of the telephone system, Murray's aim being to extend this modern mode of voice communication to all rural communities, and to the provision of cold storage facilities for the transportation of the fresh produce of both farms and fisheries.

The first decade of the 20th century was characterized by considerable progress in the development of institutions for practical education as Nova Scotia's promoters tried to provide a competitive edge for provincial resources. Murray introduced legislation in 1899 and 1907 that led respectively to the establishment of the Nova Scotia Agricultural College in Truro, to promote more scientific farming methods, and the Nova Scotia Technical College in Halifax, to end the competition for engineering programs among existing colleges and provide support for an industrial economy. Technical studies also included a strong component of adult education to provide, in evening schools across the province, training to upgrade technical and engineering skills and a mining program to replace existing mining schools. By the eve of the war, clerical and homemaking courses had been added for women, the importance of transportation was endorsed through classes in automobile maintenance, and in Halifax a school of navigation was inaugurated. Although a network of vocational secondary schools did not materialize as planned, Murray's support for technical education was interpreted by contemporaries as one of his major contributions. Liberal backbencher Ernest Howard Armstrong* noted in 1908 that Joseph Howe* had given the province constitutional government, Charles Tupper had given it free schools, and Murray had given it technical education.

The major educational initiatives were designed to contribute to resource development and industrialization. The Murray government also intervened directly, and perhaps naively, to promote the interests of capitalists in a period when their activities were characterized by exploitation of labour, watering of stock, influence peddling, hostile mergers, non-resident control, and private speculation at the expense of local advances. Nowhere was this trend more evident than in Cape Breton, where Murray was keen to see development. In 1899 his government authorized the so-called Big Lease in the northern part of the island to a New England consortium, which received highly favourable terms for pulpwood cutting and which, in turn, supported Murray. To help Boston financier Henry Melville WHITNEY establish an iron and coal industry in Cape Breton, the government approved in 1899 a 50 per cent reduction in the coal royalties payable to the province by Dominion Coal. The Dominion Iron and Steel Company Limited, controlled by the same group that had helped form Dominion Coal, developed an eminently suitable new industry, but it bought coal at such a low rate that it was detrimental to the mining industry. In addition, the inexperience of the directors meant that vast amounts of money were wasted in the course of constructing the company's steel mill in Sydney. After Whitney sold out in 1901, both companies were briefly controlled by a syndicate headed by Montreal financier James Ross*. Their separation two years later did not last; in 1910 they were merged into the Dominion Steel Corporation and by 1913 the steelworks was consuming over half of the coal sold in Nova Scotia.

Given the importance of coal royalties – in 1902 mineral dues surpassed the federal subsidy as Nova Scotia's major source of income for the first time – it is not surprising that Murray supported the use of troops during miners' strikes. His concern was normally with the welfare of the resource itself, not with the men. A bill allowing for the recognition of unions, introduced by the opposition during the miners' strike of 1909–10 and supported along with other pro-worker measures by MHA Arthur Samuel Kendall*, the most progressive member of the government, was opposed by Murray. In the Cape Breton strike of 1922 he modified his anti-labour approach only after he had negotiated a return of maintenance men to the mines to prevent their destruction through flooding. Despite his apparent interest in economic development, most historians would now argue that Nova Scotia's coal resources were vastly underutilized and the potential for greater industrialization squandered during Murray's premiership. As mining engineer Francis William Gray commented in 1917, instead of becoming "a metropolis of industry," the province "achieved the status of a mining camp." Nonetheless, at the time Murray promoted an immigration policy out of a sense of urgency, wanting in particular to attract farmers to feed the province's growing industrial population, a campaign which had some success in Britain and the Netherlands.

Although Murray expressed concern for natural resources, he did not support public ownership of the companies that exploited them. Admittedly, in 1909 his cabinet colleague William Thomas Pipes* did guide through an act for a public utilities board to set power, light, and water rates and in 1910 Alexander Kenneth Maclean* moved to strengthen crown lands policy, a sector that had been effectively criticized by Wilcox. But in the contentious realm of hydroelectricity, where the new opposition leader, Charles Elliott Tanner, led the fight for public power, Murray, anxious to promote development, placed his faith in the corporate approach. In 1914 he argued in the assembly that "he would be glad to see private companies come in and develop water powers if the legislature took care that their rights were not exercised in such a way as to be inimical to the public interests." The public interest was sometimes given short shrift, however. The Murray government's support for the merger that led to the formation that year of the Nova Scotia Tramways and Power Company Limited, which was exempt from the authority of the utilities board, alienated the people of Halifax who feared, rightly, that a corrupt corporation would be sustained by unnecessarily high electric rates and tram fares. The government finally established the Nova Scotia Power Commission in 1919 to oversee the development of water-power.

Some of the social legislation enacted by the Murray government and the policy issues it investigated grew out of the industrial expansion that occurred before the war. Concern for the welfare of the industrial worker and his family led to the institution in 1899–1900 of mechanics' lien protection, biweekly and cash payment for miners, and arbitration for mine workers, and the revival of miners' relief societies. In 1910 a workmen's compensation bill was introduced, modelled on British legislation. That same year, after agreeing with a royal commission that an eight-hour day would be injurious to industry, Murray legislated

a work week of no more than 60 hours; he endorsed the eight-hour day only in 1912 for "young" employees. Some of the protections, however, did not stand up in practice. The same acts that required the payment of miners' wages in currency also permitted the check-off of miners' debts, which, according to author Paul MacEwan, had the ironic effect of extending the nefarious truck system to collieries where it had not been in use. In 1922 Murray rejected labour's demand for unemployment insurance and expressed satisfaction with his government's legislative record: "We gave the workmen of this Province the first Arbitration law on this continent. We gave them Relief societies; we abolished the truck system; we abolished the monthly pay and substituted fortnightly; we gave them a modern Workmen's Compensation Act and we inaugurated the Lien law."

Health was another important area for social development. In particular, at a time when tuberculosis was still the great white scourge, the government passed legislation in 1900 for a sanatorium, opened in Kentville in 1904. A combination of interest in health and morals created a vigorous temperance movement, which secured the Nova Scotia Temperance Act in 1910. Stronger than the Canada Temperance Act, it applied to all areas of the province not voluntarily regulated by the provisions of the federal act, with the exception of Halifax, which continued to license the liquor trade until forced to conform with the provincial act in 1916. Although Murray, who enjoyed his drink, was not a prohibitionist and always expressed a preference for a federal solution to the contentious liquor question, he was willing to acknowledge the weight of public opinion. Historian E. R. Forbes has nonetheless interpreted Murray's repeated opposition to prohibition before 1910 as deliberate obstructionism rather than the pragmatic gradualism he claimed to favour. The war provided Murray with a federal solution in 1918, in the form of country-wide prohibition, and in a plebiscite in 1920, a year after the relaxation of the Draconian federal measure, Nova Scotia endorsed a dry status, which would persist through the 1920s.

The Murray years also saw the beginnings of state involvement in child welfare with the creation in 1912 of a superintendency to protect children's interests and the establishment of a juvenile court. For women, there were more promises than action though some progress was made in the area of their rights as citizens. In 1913, and on other occasions, support in the legislature for their eligibility as school board members did not result in the necessary legislation. The provincial suffrage bill of 1917 also went down to defeat, with Murray's blessing though he proclaimed women's enfranchisement to be inevitable. In that year female lawyers became eligible for admission to the bar and in 1918 suffrage for women passed, this time with Murray's support. In 1919 several women were appointed as commissioners of oaths for the first time. The Liberal agenda also included women's welfare. In 1912 seats for young female workers in shops had been mandated and pensions, albeit parsimonious ones, introduced for schoolteachers, the overwhelming majority of whom were women. After the war, a royal commission, appointed in 1920 to examine the hours, wages, and working conditions of women employed in industry, recommended a minimum wage board. A year later the same commissioners, who included a woman, were asked to investigate the need for mothers' allowances. During the turbulent 1920s, however, these measures were not implemented.

For Murray the Great War, in which two of his sons served overseas, was a turning point in many ways. Nova Scotia abandoned its orderly progress to support a mammoth war effort, including large-scale voluntary enlistment, contributions to Belgium and Britain, and war industries. In the process it had also to recover from the devastating Halifax explosion of 1917. Although operating budgets produced a series of deficits between 1913 and 1915 – so much so that in order to make a gift of coal worth $100,000 to the British, the government had to borrow the money from an English bank – the war brought prosperity to many through the introduction of munition plants in the steel towns, a building boom in Halifax, and increased agricultural production to help feed the allies. Provincial efforts to support steel shipbuilding, dating from 1901, materialized with the establishment of a shipyard at Trenton in 1916 and a facility in Halifax two years later. Efforts to bolster the effectiveness of the port of Halifax had already received federal support in 1913 when the Conservative government of Robert Laird Borden* promised $36 million for improvements, including new ocean terminals, railway access to the south end, and adjacent facilities for freight sheds and a grain elevator. Nonetheless, provincial revenues based on coal royalties, succession duties, and the federal subsidy were insufficient by the war period. This situation forced the Murray government to experiment with taxes on corporations, public utilities, land, personal income, theatre tickets, and automobiles. It was with considerable angst that Murray decided to support Borden's Union government in 1917, thereby breaking with his great friend Sir Wilfrid Laurier. His support had limits – considered for the Union cabinet, he apparently refused – but by October 1917 he was solidly behind the Unionist thrust, including the federal candidacy of A. K. Maclean in Halifax. In the realm of federal-provincial relations he was, throughout his career, a steadfast advocate of the right of the Maritimes to compensation for their proprietary interest in the public lands of the central and western provinces, a campaign taken up in 1919 by Liberal MLA James Cranswick Tory in anticipation of the Maritime rights movement.

The post-war landscape revealed the emergence of powerful interest groups and amalgamations, hitherto unknown or ineffective, which turned Murray's "SOUND SAFE SURE" world upside down. They included the farmers, who formed the United Farmers of Nova Scotia in 1920 to provide themselves with a political voice, and the United Mine Workers of America. The UMWA won recognition as the coalminers' sole trade union in 1917–18 and by 1919 it was openly attacking the government's mining policy and advocating political action [*see* Robert DRUMMOND]. Another group was the capitalists who, largely controlled by outside interests, secured provincial incorporation in 1920 of the British Empire Steel Corporation Limited, a flawed amalgamation of the province's coal and steel companies, Halifax Shipyards Limited, and other enterprises. The deteriorating economy could not, however, deliver the excessive profits demanded by the Besco merger (completed in 1921) without resort to reducing the miners' wages. Even in the legislature, the government faced new scrutiny. Organized unemployed men jeered from the gallery in 1922 when Murray, unable to cope with the depression, identified the salvation of Nova Scotia to be economic diversity. "We do not have all our eggs in one basket," he reasoned. And in Nova Scotia's towns and rural settlements, citizen groups, motivated by the Good Roads movement, demanded greater attention to the highways, especially the "wretched" roads of Cape Breton.

As a result of these ominous signs, Murray undertook two strategies to perpetuate Liberal rule. First, he called his final election a year early, in June 1920, to capitalize on what was left of wartime patriotism and head off emerging third-party challenges. Although his surprise tactic worked – the Liberals won 29 of 43 seats – the opposition was now a loosely allied combination of seven United Farmers and four Labour members rather than the Conservatives alone, who could muster only three seats. Second, after succumbing again to debilitating illness, Murray prepared for his retirement as premier by casting about for a successor. Others could see that he was slowing down. His attendance during the legislative session of 1920 was spotty. In 1921 he was too ill to attend at all, except to appear belatedly for his swearing in, and he spent time in a sanatorium in Battle Creek, Mich. With his exit from politics imminent, legislation was passed in 1921 authorizing an annual retirement allowance in recognition of his long service. Much to everyone's surprise he returned for the 1922 session and he resigned the premiership only in January 1923; his resignation of his seat followed in February. Meanwhile, the succession was something of a debacle because the first choice for leader, E. H. Armstrong, then commissioner of public works and mines, indicated his preference for appointment to the Nova Scotia Supreme Court. J. C. Tory, the minister next in line, wanted time to extricate himself from his business commitments at the Sun Life Assurance Company in Montreal. Instead of waiting for the more willing Tory, Murray successfully applied pressure on Armstrong. Tory received the lieutenant governorship of Nova Scotia in 1925, perhaps as compensation. If he had a falling-out with Murray over the matter it did not last long since the Murrays lived in Tory's house in Westmount after they moved to Montreal to be near their family. In 1929 George Murray died of pneumonia at the home of his son Wilfrid. He was buried with United Church rites in Lakeside Cemetery in North Sydney.

No premier could have lasted so long without achieving a remarkable degree of respect. Murray did so on the basis of qualities unusual in a 20th-century politician: honesty, integrity, and modesty. Although his political sense has been described as wily and astute, his approach was open, his character unblemished, and his demeanour friendly. Throughout his career, his conviviality was legendary, extending to late nights spent entertaining his friends at the Halifax Hotel where he resided during the legislative sessions – his wife evidently remained at home in North Sydney and rarely made public appearances – and to frequent encounters with ordinary people in many walks of life. It might be going too far to describe him as a populist, but he manifestly displayed the common touch, practising at the individual level the liberalism he described, at a banquet given for him in 1910, as "the safeguarding of the rights of the masses as against the classes." In 1913 William Arnot Craick noted in *Maclean's* (Toronto) that Murray was known to stop in the street to talk, man to man, to a ditch digger about his work. His willingness to negotiate personally with a cleaner at Province House over her wages became part of her family's lore. These were the kinds of incidents that prompted one colleague, former MHA Edward Mortimer Macdonald*, to claim that Murray "listened to the ordinary citizen who wanted to discuss his personal matters with him with the same care and quiet patience that he might be expected to display with men of great consequence."

Murray was offered many honours in recognition of his service. He declined a knighthood in 1911 and again in 1914, preferring to be "plain George Murray" as the Halifax *Morning Chronicle* put it, but he did accept honorary LLDs from St Francis Xavier College in Antigonish in 1905 and Dalhousie University in Halifax in 1908. His effective leadership for overseas relief during the war was rewarded by decorations from both Belgium (1919) and France (1921). If he had been endowed with greater ambition and better health, he might have been a candidate to succeed Laurier as Liberal Leader, though clearly Fielding

stood in his way and both lacked support in Quebec. In the event, Murray was co-chairman of the national Liberal convention of August 1919, which selected William Lyon Mackenzie King*.

Personally esteemed by all manner of folk, Murray was content to be a mildly progressive, arm's-length politician who left day-to-day administration to the members of government boards and civil servants. A forceful, imaginative, interventionist premier could conceivably have done more to sustain the momentum of Nova Scotia's industrialization and to secure more reliable markets for its products. Moreover, when Murray was caught on the cusp of post-war collapse, he lacked three essentials: political clout in Ottawa, industrial harmony at home, and, despite his decades of experience, a strategy for coping with the adversity caused by local de-industrialization and federal policies that favoured central Canada.

JUDITH FINGARD

[Conventional wisdom has it that Murray destroyed his papers. This sketch depends mainly on four sources: *Canadian annual rev.*, 1901–23; a biographical article, W. A. Craick, "Premier Murray of Nova Scotia: Cape Breton or Pictou are the stamping grounds for leaders of men," *Maclean's* (Toronto), 26 (May–October 1913), no.6: 5–7, 112; the *Morning Chronicle* (Halifax), 7 June 1919; and J. M. Beck, *Politics of Nova Scotia* (2v., Tantallon, N.S., 1985–88), 2. J.F.]

NSARM, MG 1, 1450, no.4; MG 2, 422–541, 784–90(B) (selected items); 707–17; RG 32, M, Cape Breton County, no.64/1889; RG 39, ser.M, 12, file 1; Christina Simmons coll., Helen M. West interviews, May–June 1983. *Halifax Herald*, 7 Jan. 1929. *Morning Chronicle*, 7 Jan. 1929. T. W. Acheson, "The National Policy and the industrialization of the Maritimes, 1880–1910," *Acadiensis* (Fredericton), 1 (1971–72), no.2: 3–28. *Annals, North British Society, Halifax, Nova Scotia, with portraits and biographical notes, 1768–1903*, comp. J. S. Macdonald ([3rd ed.], Halifax, 1905). Christopher Armstrong and H. V. Nelles, "Getting your way in Nova Scotia: 'tweaking' Halifax, 1909–1917," *Acadiensis*, 5 (1975–76), no.2: 105–31. *Canadian men and women of the time* (Morgan; 1898 and 1912). *CPG* 1887, 1897. Margaret Conrad, "Apple blossom time in the Annapolis valley, 1880–1957," *Acadiensis*, 9 (1979–80), no.2: 14–39. G. H. M. Cooper, "Politics and fraud in Nova Scotia road policy: the highways scandal of 1920–1921" (history honours essay, Dalhousie Univ., Halifax, 1983). E. R. Forbes, *The Maritime rights movement, 1919–1927: a study in Canadian regionalism* (Montreal and Kingston, Ont., 1979); "Prohibition and the Social Gospel in Nova Scotia," *Acadiensis*, 1, no.1: 11–36. David Frank, "The Cape Breton coal industry and the rise and fall of the British Empire Steel Corporation," *Acadiensis*, 7 (1977–78), no.1: 3–34; *J. B. McLachlan: a biography* (Toronto, 1999). J. D. Frost, "The aborted British invasion: the case of Swan Hunter Shipbuilders, 1899–1914," Royal Nova Scotia Hist. Soc., *Journal* ([Halifax]), 2 (1999): 40–51. Roselle Green, "The public life of Honorable George H. Murray" (MA thesis, Dalhousie Univ., 1962). Janet Guildford, "Coping with de-industrializization: the Nova Scotia Department of Technical Education, 1907–1930," *Acadiensis*, 16 (1986–87), no.2: 69–84. G. M. Haliburton, *Clansmen of Nova Scotia* (Halifax, 1979). E. M. Macdonald, *Recollections: political and personal* (Toronto, [1938]), 555–59. Paul MacEwan, *Miners and steelworkers: labour in Cape Breton* (Toronto, 1976). Don MacGillivray, "Henry Melville Whitney comes to Cape Breton: the saga of a Gilded Age entrepreneur," *Acadiensis*, 9, no.1: 44–70; "Military aid to the civil power: the Cape Breton experience in the 1920s," *Acadiensis*, 3 (1973–74), no.2: 45–64. Donald Macleod, "Practicality ascendant: the origins and establishment of technical education in Nova Scotia," *Acadiensis*, 15

(1985–86), no.2: 53–92. N.S., House of Assembly, *Debates and proc.*, 1896–1916; *Journal and proc.*, 1896–1923. *Newspaper reference book.* Nova Scotia Liberal Assoc., *Progressive government in Nova Scotia during twenty-nine years of Liberal administration . . .* ([n.p., 1910?]). L. A. Sandberg, "Forest policy in Nova Scotia: the Big Lease, Cape Breton Island, 1899–1960," in *Trouble in the woods: forest policy and social conflict in Nova Scotia and New Brunswick*, ed. L. A. Sandberg (Fredericton, 1992), 65–89. *Standard dict. of Canadian biog.* (Roberts and Tunnell).

MURRAY, MARGARET SMITH. *See* POLSON

N

NAI-KA-WAY-A. *See* NICKAWA, FRANCES

NANTEL, ANTONIN, Roman Catholic priest, teacher, school administrator, and author; b. 17 Sept. 1839 in Saint-Jérôme, Lower Canada, son of Guillaume Nantel, a tanner, and Adélaïde Desjardins; d. 30 July 1929 in Sainte-Thérèse-de-Blainville (Sainte-Thérèse), Que.

In 1851, at the age of 12, Antonin Nantel entered the Petit Séminaire de Sainte-Thérèse, where he would spend virtually all his life. When he was in his sixth year (Rhetoric), his father died. Antonin began to study theology in 1859 and was ordained priest in 1862. That year he joined the faculty of the institution where he had been educated and set up within it the Académie Saint-Charles, named in honour of Charles-Joseph Ducharme*, who had founded the Petit Séminaire. The academy invited the most gifted students of literature to develop their potential through the humanities. By 1863 Nantel had become prefect of studies in the seminary. He published pedagogical writings in the Montreal *Revue canadienne*, and would contribute other articles to *La Semaine religieuse de Montréal*. His *Nouveau cours de langue anglaise selon la méthode d'Ollendorff à l'usage des écoles, académies, pensionnats et collèges*, which he brought out in Montreal, probably in 1864, would go through several editions. His younger brothers Guillaume-Alphonse* and Wilfrid-Bruno*, who were both to have prominent political careers in the Conservative party, also attended the Petit Séminaire de Sainte-Thérèse.

A short man who had an authoritarian personality, Nantel had a vast store of knowledge and his orderly and methodical habits marked him for high office. It was no surprise when he became superior of the Petit Séminaire de Sainte-Thérèse in 1870. A tireless worker, he kept a tight rein on instruction by retaining the office of prefect of studies (until 1873 and again from 1879 to 1883), by continuing to teach courses in

literature, history, and English, and by serving as director of the Académie Saint-Charles. In 1880 Nantel founded the *Annales térésiennes,* the seminary's official organ, which would be published until 1946. This periodical reflected the manifestly Christian vision of things by which Nantel judged all manner of events, the better to instruct his flock about them. He also wrote textbooks, some of which would be accepted as authoritative in educational establishments. In 1881 the college was destroyed by fire. Thanks to the wide support Nantel enjoyed in various influential circles in which many of his former colleagues and students participated, a new building opened in 1883. Nantel would be the seminary's superior until 1886, from 1889 to 1895, and again from 1900 to 1905.

At first glance, Nantel's view of education was a conservative one. He believed in the virtues of classical studies, and wanted to make his students leaders, but even more, convinced Christians and patriots. In 1874 he had accepted the ideas of Pierre-Auguste Leroy* with some enthusiasm. Interested in promoting school reform, Leroy criticized the classical courses for, among other things, not taking pupils' aptitudes into account and for putting too much emphasis on memorization. He recommended that the time devoted to the teaching of Greek and Latin be cut in half, in favour of practical subjects. While not accepting his condemnation of instruction of classical languages, Nantel introduced a program of commercial studies at the Petit Séminaire de Sainte-Thérèse.

Nantel held views similar to those of Joseph-Adolphe Chapleau* and the curé François-Xavier-Antoine Labelle* concerning the social and economic development taking place in northern Quebec. Nantel and Labelle's paths had crossed while they were students at the Petit Séminaire de Sainte-Thérèse and they had become friends in the 1870s. Their warm relationship was based partly on their priestly vocation and attachment to their alma mater, but also on their common desire to contribute to the progress of the north, the advancement of settlers, and the training of leaders. Nantel never missed an opportunity to praise Labelle's work as a colonizer. In 1882, along with his brothers Guillaume-Alphonse and Wilfrid-Bruno, he even founded a colony in Nominingue, where two other Nantel brothers, Jules and Maximien, settled with their families.

The essense of Nantel's political thinking is conveyed in the speech he gave at the celebration organized to mark the consecration of the new college in 1883. "What the church blesses and consecrates, the state respects and protects," he said. Although he was an ultramontane, he did not identify with the "Castors"; he thought that cooperation between church and state gave the latter an area free of clerical intervention. In fact, he believed the state should leave the management of education to the church. In view of the excellence of the elite trained in educational institutions entrusted to the care of religious communities, the state had never, in his opinion, had cause to regret such a division of powers. In all other matters, the superior of the Petit Séminaire de Sainte-Thérèse relied on the leadership of politicians.

By family tradition, by temperament, and clearly by reason of his ecclesiastical status, Nantel's sympathies lay with the Conservative party. In 1872 he corresponded with Louis-Rodrigue Masson*. Like Labelle, however, he was closer to Chapleau; the latter, after his election by acclamation as the MLA for Terrebonne on 12 March 1873, went with Premier Gédéon Ouimet* to Sainte-Thérèse-de-Blainville, where he was warmly received. Chapleau had great admiration for Nantel. For example, when the creation of a bishopric in Saint-Jérôme was under consideration in 1897, Chapleau, who was then lieutenant governor of Quebec, would propose Nantel as an ideal candidate for the mitre. Nantel's discreet political influence, while not as great as Labelle's, had nevertheless been significant. However, the superior of the Petit Séminaire had left participation in party politics to his brothers.

Throughout his life, Nantel had been interested in literature and history. In 1868 he had become a member of the Société Historique de Montréal. The following year, he had published in Montreal *Les fleurs de la poésie canadienne*. In 1877, according to Séraphin Marion*, he was invited to become a member of the Société Littéraire du Canada. In 1905, after completing his final term as superior of the Petit Séminaire, Nantel at the age of 66 set out for France to do further research. He returned to Canada in 1908, having published a scholarly work in Paris that year under the pseudonym of A. Berloin: *La parole humaine: études de philologie nouvelle d'après une langue d'Amérique*. Devoted mainly to the "language of the Algic tribes," this work was reviewed, for the most part favourably, in a number of newspapers. Abbé Camille

Roy*, the future rector of the Université Laval, wrote one of the reviews. Jointly with Benjamin SULTE, Nantel became the senior member of the Société Historique de Montréal in 1919. He was made a Roman prelate in 1923 and received an honorary doctorate of letters from the Université de Montréal the following year. He died at the venerable age of 89.

Antonin Nantel was renowned as a man of letters, but even more as a pedagogue. His writings, especially *La parole humaine*, impressed his contemporaries, yet they soon became dated because they were first and above all for instructional purposes. His work as an educator, on the other hand, left a lasting mark. Although a staunch supporter of classical education based on Christianity, Nantel unhesitatingly adapted his college's curricula to the needs of the developing industrial society, as his introduction of commercial studies and emphasis on the teaching of English show. It was, however, in shaping the future of the Petit Séminaire de Sainte-Thérèse over the greater part of his career that he made his principal contribution to the world of education. He is referred to as the second founder of that institution, which for many years had been the alma mater of much of the elite in the Laurentian region.

SERGE LAURIN

Despite extensive searching, Antonin Nantel's baptismal certificate could not be found. The reader will find articles by Nantel – extracts from the *Annales térésiennes* and from various newspapers and magazines – in his *Pages historiques et littéraires* (Montréal, 1928). Several of Nantel's works are mentioned in the biography; for a more complete list, see Hamel *et al.*, DALFAN, 1022.

Le Devoir, 31 juill., 9 août 1929. L.-P. Audet, "Le Québec à l'Exposition internationale de Paris en 1878," *Cahiers des Dix*, 32 (1967): 125–55. DOLQ, vol.1. Serge Laurin, *Rouge, Bleu: la saga des Prévost et des Nantel: chronique d'un siècle d'histoire politique dans la région des Laurentides* (Sainte-Foy, Qué., 1999). Séraphin Marion, "Origines de l'Institut canadien-français d'Ottawa et de la Société royale du Canada," *Cahiers des Dix*, 39 (1974): 45–84.

NANTON, Sir AUGUSTUS MEREDITH, broker, financier, capitalist, and philanthropist; b. 7 May 1860 in Toronto, son of Daniel Augustus Nanton, a barrister, and Mary Louisa Jarvis, daughter of William Botsford Jarvis*; m. first 7 Dec. 1886 Georgina Hope Hespeler (d. 1887), daughter of William HESPELER, in Galt, Ont., and they had one daughter; m. secondly 17 Nov. 1894 Ethel Constance Clark in Winnipeg, and they had two sons and two daughters who survived infancy; d. 24 April 1925 in Toronto and was buried in Winnipeg.

The death of his alcoholic father forced 13-year-old Augustus Nanton to leave the Toronto Model School to help support his mother and younger brother and sisters. His first position was as an office boy in a real estate firm. Then, through the influence of an uncle, he obtained a junior clerical position at $300 a year in Edmund Boyd OSLER's brokerage firm, Pellatt and Osler. Around 1881 Osler appointed him to look after the accounts of the Aberdeen-based North of Scotland Canadian Mortgage Company Limited, which the firm represented.

In 1882 Osler broke with his partner, Henry Pellatt, and founded, with Herbert Carlyle Hammond, former cashier (general manager) of the Bank of Hamilton, the firm Osler and Hammond. Osler retained the agency of the North of Scotland and kept Nanton with him as its secretary. The following year the partners sent Nanton to Winnipeg on behalf of the Aberdeen company to report on investment opportunities in farm mortgages in the northwest. Nanton's shrewd mind intuitively grasped the opportunities offered by the region to create untold wealth and to further his own ambitions. In 1884 he returned to open a Winnipeg office as a junior partner in the Toronto firm's western branch. Through the agency of Osler, Hammond, and Nanton, the North of Scotland was one of the first companies in the northwest to finance first mortgages, or purchase municipal and school debentures, to any significant extent. Nanton tirelessly promoted the Scottish business and by the end of the first year made £28,629 worth of loans; ten years later capital investment had risen to £315,664 under his management.

Nanton's business in mortgages and debentures was closely bound up with the sale of farm lands and town lots and the encouragement of immigration. From the start Osler, Hammond, and Nanton was the selling agent for the Ontario and Qu'Appelle Land Company Limited and the Canadian Pacific Railway's land-grant bonds. In 1885 the firm undertook the purchase and sale of land scrip but Nanton refused to deal with speculators, saying, "I do not want to buy scrip from dealers and scalpers who rob the half-breeds, but I will buy direct from the Owners at a good price." The firm eventually accumulated the largest scrip account in government records. In the 1880s as well Nanton became involved in the Manitoba Cartage and Warehousing Company, one of the early important businesses in Winnipeg and western Canada. Elected a director within a few years of his arrival there, he became president in June 1891.

About 1890, through Osler's involvement in the financial organization of the Qu'Appelle, Long Lake and Saskatchewan Railroad and Steamboat Company and the Calgary and Edmonton Railway [see James Ross*], Nanton had undertaken responsibility for the promotion and coordination of immigration to and settlement of the lands of these important colonization railways. That same year he became general agent for Elliott Torrance GALT's Alberta Railway and Coal Company of Lethbridge. The following year he established a coal department to wholesale Galt's bitumi-

nous coal. Later he introduced different varieties of American and Canadian coal. When Galt amalgamated the AR&CC with his other companies under one roof in 1904 as the Alberta Railway and Irrigation Company, Osler, Hammond, and Nanton proceeded to purchase all the available shares; in June of the following year Nanton became the ARIC's managing director. His growing prominence in a variety of business activities had been recognized in 1898 when he was elected president of the Winnipeg Board of Trade. That same year he became a director of the Great-West Life Assurance Company [see Jeffry Hall Brock*]. The following January he was made a director of the Winnipeg Electric Street Railway Company (later known as the Winnipeg Electric Railway Company) and appointed to its three-man executive committee.

In 1900 Nanton and several other businessmen, including William Hendrie*, incorporated the Winnipeg Western Land Corporation Limited, which owned land along the line of the Manitoba and North-Western Railway near the Yorkton and Beaver Hills districts (Sask.). The firm also owned considerable acreage in Manitoba's fertile parklands and for many years Nanton was the company's land commissioner in the province. In 1908 he became president of the Canada Saskatchewan Land Company, which had 400,000 acres for sale in Saskatchewan.

To protect Osler, Hammond, and Nanton's considerable investment in mortgages, Nanton had entered the field of fire insurance in 1899. This new departure provided the basis for later expansion into all classes of insurance, excepting life. Next he established a stocks department and a bonds department. In 1903 he became one of the founders of the Winnipeg Stock Exchange, of which he was the first president. It was not until February 1909, however, that formal trading commenced. Since the demand for first mortgages eventually exceeded the North of Scotland's financial resources, Osler, Hammond, and Nanton expanded its agency to include several other loan companies. With increasing amounts of private investment capital coming into the firm from clients in Great Britain and central Canada, Osler and Nanton (Hammond had died in 1909), along with the firm's barrister and two junior Winnipeg partners who had joined the firm in 1908, incorporated the Osler and Nanton Trust Company in 1911.

Through his intimate business association with Osler, who in 1901 had become president of the Dominion Bank, Nanton had been appointed one of the bank's directors in 1907. He became a vice-president in 1919 and on Osler's death in August 1924 he succeeded to the presidency. In 1910 Nanton had been appointed vice-president of the Great-West Life Assurance Company. It was his appointment in 1912 as secretary to the Canadian committee advisory board of the Hudson's Bay Company, however, that clinched his reputation as a dominant figure on the national financial stage. The services of this local committee, composed of a small but select group of mainly western businessman, were initially of a limited scope. Later the London committee of the HBC granted the committee extended authority as its Canadian representative and renamed it simply the Canadian committee to reflect its newly acquired powers. In 1914 Nanton was elected to fill the vacancy on the London committee of the HBC left by the death of Lord Strathcona [Smith*]. With the death in that same year of Sir William Whyte*, a former vice-president of the CPR, whom he had long advised, Nanton assumed Whyte's vacant chairmanship of the HBC's Canadian committee, as well as his place on the CPR's board of directors. Four years later he was appointed to the executive of the CPR's board.

The vigour and intelligence that Nanton exhibited in his business pursuits carried over into his enthusiastic support for the Canadian war effort in defence of the empire and British tradition. With the outbreak of World War I, he joined the national executive of the Canadian Patriotic Fund at the invitation of the governor general, the Duke of Connaught. The organization raised and administered funds for the support of needy dependants of servicemen. He was also president of the Manitoba Patriotic Fund, the only provincial organization to remain independent of the national body. His leadership was a key factor in its success. The money collected and distributed by the Manitoba organization was the largest per capita in the country. Nanton himself generously contributed $1,000 a month. He derived his deepest satisfaction, however, as chairman of the provincial approval committee whose primary purpose was to encourage young men to enlist through assurances that their dependants would be provided for during their absence. The committee did "more towards recruiting . . . than anything else," said Nanton with the profound conviction of one who felt that he was directly participating in the management of what he described as "this most righteous war." For his remarkable contribution he was made a knight bachelor on 13 June 1917. The same skilful management he had shown in this organization had led to his appointment as a member of the first board of governors of the University of Manitoba when that body was created the preceding month.

During the Victory Loan campaigns of 1917, 1918, and 1919, Nanton figured prominently in the mobilization of the country's financial resources. He served on the executive of the Victory Loan Committee of Canada and was chairman of the Manitoba general committee. As the only westerner on the national executive, he helped to organize bond-selling committees in Saskatchewan and Alberta based on the Manitoba organization. The appeal for funds imposed, in his view, an "imperative claim upon every patriotic citizen," and anyone who did not subscribe "ceases to be a good citizen of the Empire." Nanton himself purchased $250,000 worth of bonds in each of the first two campaigns. Systematic canvassing in the prairie provinces raised the astonishing sum of over $246,000,000 in the three campaigns, while Manitoba alone subscribed to $118,000,000. Nanton's biographer, Roderick George MacBeth*, observes that thanks to Nanton's stewardship, westerners "became lenders for the first time in their history."

After the signing of the armistice in November 1918, the threat of a general strike which had been brandished in the summer of 1917 became a reality the following spring. Nanton viewed the Winnipeg General Strike [see Mike Sokolowiski*] as an act of treason and became an influential member of the Citizens' Committee of One Thousand, composed of businessmen who opposed the strike and sought to maintain essential services. His antagonism towards collective bargaining and industrial unionism, fuelled by a vigorous nativist sentiment, went back to 1906 and the violent strike by the workers at the Winnipeg Electric Railway Company and the particularly long and bitter miners' strike at the Galt collieries in Lethbridge [see Frank Henry Sherman*], in which Nanton, as managing director of the ARIC, had been closely involved.

Elected president of the Winnipeg Electric Railway Company in 1919, Nanton anxiously sought to get on with the industrial development of Winnipeg. The company's power project at Great Falls had been suspended in 1916 because of the war. Work resumed in May 1919, but was soon halted because of a shortage of materials and tight money. Construction started again in 1920, when the Manitoba Power Company, organized as a subsidiary of the Winnipeg Electric Railway Company with Nanton as president, took over completion of the generating station. Nationally, Nanton focused his patriotic zeal on the promotion of Canada's industrial and agricultural interests as a member of the executive of the Canadian Reconstruction Association founded in 1918.

Austere and patrician in manner, Nanton was a natural aristocrat who, even before the turn of the century, had accumulated considerable wealth. His sumptuous Winnipeg estate, Kilmorie, conspicuously expressed his commanding position in the community. From junior clerk, Nanton had proved his mettle in one undertaking after another. He eventually became associated with an impressive array of prosperous enterprises in an advisory or active capacity. On the death of Osler, the senior partner, in 1924 Nanton stepped into his shoes as executive head of the firm Osler, Hammond, and Nanton. He owed much to this trusted friend and counsellor, who had taken him under his wing and guided him like a father in the early stages of his career. Between Nanton and Osler there existed a close relationship born of deep respect and admiration that stood, "without a single misunderstanding or dispute," for 40 years. Faced with an important decision, Nanton would always examine the matter from the deeply conservative instincts inherited from his mentor.

Nanton was, above all, a nation builder who aimed to develop the northwest from a region dependent upon central Canada and Great Britain for immigration and development capital to one capable of generating its own wealth. The wider aspirations of his expansionist vision embraced a stable and civilized life stretching across the prairies through the development of town-sites to serve as centres of rural economic life. Winnipeg would become a manufacturing and distribution centre, as well as an important source of capital within the expanding nation. Nanton's sudden death eight months after he assumed the presidency of the Dominion Bank saw the passing of one who had helped lay the foundation of sound financial organization for the development of western Canada.

PETER HANLON

AM, GR 1418, G-1-7-3, MH0035, book 1; MG 14, C85; P 483. Anglican Church of Canada, Diocese of Rupert's Land Arch. (Winnipeg), DRL-84-111, RBMB; 112, RBMB; 129, RBMB. Man., Dept. of Finance, Consumer and Corporate Affairs, Companies office (Winnipeg), Partnership agreements, file no.580, 30 Sept. 1884; index no.83w, 25 June 1902. Private arch., David Nanton (Vancouver), Paul Nanton, "Prairie explosion: setting the pace for Canada" (typescript, 1991). Trinity Anglican Church (Cambridge, Ont.), RBMB, 1874–88: f.204, no.81. Univ. of Aberdeen Library, Dept. of Special Coll. and Arch. (Aberdeen, Scot.), MS 3211/1-84 (North of Scotland Canadian Mortgage Company Limited), Ledgers, nos.2–3; Minutes. *Manitoba Free Press*, 1 May, 1 July 1884; 20 Feb. 1885; 2–3 Feb. 1909; 12 May 1914; 4 June, 8, 17, 26 Nov. 1917; 8, 14 Nov. 1918; 28 Oct. 1919; 13 Aug. 1924. *Monetary Times* (Toronto), 25 July 1919. *Winnipeg Telegram*, 29 Jan. 1910, 13 Feb. 1919. *Winnipeg Tribune*, 26 Feb. 1930. *Canadian annual rev.*, 1919. *The Canadian Patriotic Fund: a record of its activities from 1914 to 1919*, comp. and ed. P. H. Morris ([Ottawa, 1920?]). *London Gazette*, 8 Aug. 1917. R. G. MacBeth, *Sir Augustus Meredith Nanton: a biography* (Toronto, 1931). *Newspaper reference book*. E. B. Osler, *Osler, Hammond, and Nanton Limited: commemorating 65 years of business development in a growing nation* (Winnipeg, [1948]). A. A. den Otter, *Civilizing the west: the Galts and the development of western Canada* (Edmonton, 1982). Osler, Hammond and Nanton, *New homes, free farms in Alberta and Saskatchewan, western Canada* ([Winnipeg, 189?]); *The Qu'Appelle, Long Lake and Saskatchewan Railroad and Steamboat Co. has 1,000,000 acres of odd numbered sections . . .* (Winnipeg, [1891?]).

NAPOLITANO (Neapolitano), ANGELINA, homemaker and convicted murderer; b. *c*. 1883 near Naples (Italy); nothing is known of her baptismal name or parents; m. 1898 Pietro Napolitano; d. in or after 1924.

On the afternoon of Easter Sunday, 16 April 1911, in the upper flat of a house in the immigrant quarter of Sault Ste Marie, Ont., Angelina Napolitano, 28 and pregnant, killed her husband. As he slept, she struck him four times on the neck and head with an axe. After calling a neighbour to tell him what she had done, she waited for the police, hugging the youngest of her four children. Angelina had been born in a rural town near Naples and, following a seven-year stay in New York City, had come to Ontario with Pietro in 1909. They lived first in Thessalon and then moved to the Sault. Two years later Angelina was charged with murder.

At her trial in the town's district court, on 8–9 May 1911, justice Byron Moffatt Britton presided. The crown attorney was Edmund Meredith. Uriah McFadden became Angelina's lawyer only after proceedings began on the 8th and it was revealed that she had no counsel. Court was then adjourned until the next morning so a defence could be prepared. Nine witnesses testified for the crown; Napolitano was the only witness for the defence. She was convicted. The jury recommended clemency but Britton sentenced her to hang – on 9 August, to allow her time to give birth.

Why did Angelina kill Pietro? The evidence strongly suggests that she had become terrified of a violent husband bent on forcing her into prostitution. An underemployed labourer, he had wanted money to build a house. At the trial it was revealed that Angelina's face, neck, and shoulder had been disfigured in November 1910, when he knifed her nine times. Charged with assault, he had received a suspended sentence. The abuse continued, and on the fateful day he had again told Angelina to prostitute herself or, as she put it, "be a bad woman." If she did not have money for him when he woke up, he threatened to beat or kill her.

At the trial McFadden argued that Angelina had been provoked into murder by her husband's abuse, most notably when he had stabbed her the previous year. But the judge ruled such evidence inadmissible, saying that "if anybody injured six months ago could give that as justification or excuse for slaying a person, it would be anarchy complete." In an era before a history of abuse was admissible, Britton's interpretation was reasonable though not generous.

The case produced enormous debate. Among Angelina's critics were bigots who depicted the murder as proof of the danger posed by "foreigners." A columnist quoted in the *Sault Star* drew on contemporary racist stereotypes, calling southern Italians "hot-blooded" foreigners who "are all too ready as it is to use the knife, the pistol, or any other weapon that lies at hand, as a means of redressing real or fancied wrongs." Another article in the paper argued that Angelina deserved to die because she was immoral, making much of the fact that for a brief period when Pietro was out of town she had permitted a man to board with her.

Many people took up her cause, and a campaign was launched to have her sentence commuted to a prison term. A flood of letters and petitions arrived in the office of the federal minister of justice, Sir Allen Bristol Aylesworth*, among them lengthy petitions organized by individuals and groups from Sault Ste Marie, Toronto, New York, New Orleans, and Chicago, as well as England, Austria, and Poland. Italians in the Sault were relatively quiet – the *Sault Star* claimed they were against Angelina – but many in Toronto, Montreal, Chicago, and New York, especially leftists, joined the campaign. So did McFadden and other Anglo-Canadians, including a men's Bible group. Supporters asked the government to acknowledge Angelina's history of abuse and spare her life; a few even demanded a pardon. Some of the loudest voices were those of Canadian, American, and British feminists who, in agitating for the vote, had become seasoned lobbyists. Indeed, the presence of an international women's movement helps account for the sustained publicity the case received. Various feminists stressed that the beatings had constituted sufficient provocation and that Angelina had acted in self-defence. The judge's rejection of this argument, they added, revealed sexist codes. As the suffrage journal *Common Cause* (London) declared, the law and its administration "are both bad" for "they are exclusively masculine."

Other petitioners held Angelina up as a courageous woman who had rid the earth of a lout. "The taking of a corrupt life of her wicked husband was not even murder" but a "dreadful loathsome duty," wrote one woman from England, because it "delivers of the race from loathsome ulcers." "The world," she concluded, "needs such heroines to lift it out of the foul rut in which it lies today," for the "rut of immorality" was "a far worse crime than murder!" Such comments are best understood in the context of the sexual politics of early feminism, which subscribed to popular, though erroneous, stereotypes of the propensity among "foreign" men for violence and sexual immorality.

Some argued that Angelina should be granted clemency to save her unborn child from harm. This reasoning was based on the view, also current at the time, that a foetus could suffer psychological damage because of its mother's agitated state. The Toronto Suffrage Association warned that "every additional hour spent by her [Napolitano] in the condition of terror, anticipating her execution" would "react in a deleterious manner upon her unborn innocent child." (Tragically, the baby would die a few weeks after birth.) Others, including Arthur Cyril Boyce, the MP for Algoma West, even claimed that Angelina's pregnancy had produced temporary insanity – an extreme version of the notion that pregnancy could produce an unbalanced emotional or mental state.

On 14 July 1911 Angelina's sentence was commuted by the federal cabinet to life imprisonment. Eleven years later, on 30 Dec. 1922, she was granted parole from Kingston Penitentiary. From prison she had tried to contact her children, who had been placed in foster homes, but it remains unknown whether she ever saw them again. The trail ends after she left Kingston in the spring of 1924.

FRANCA IACOVETTA

The sources for this article may be found in Karen Dubinsky and Franca Iacovetta, "Murder, womanly virtue, and motherhood: the case of Angelina Napolitano, 1911–1922," *CHR*, 72 (1991): 505–31.

NAULT, ANDRÉ, buffalo hunter, farmer, and captain of the Métis; b. 20 April 1830 in Point Douglas (Winnipeg), son of Amable Nault and Josette (Josephite, Josephte) Lagimodière, known as La Cyprès; grandson of Jean-Baptiste Lagimonière* and Marie-Anne Gaboury*; m. 11 Jan. 1850 Anastasie Landry, and they had 14 children; d. 17 Dec. 1924 in St Vital, Man.

Although André Nault's parents were of French Canadian origin, they had become integrated into the Métis community of the Red River settlement (Man.). As a young man, Nault accompanied his father on buffalo hunts to the Missouri plateau, excelling as a horseman and hunter. He obtained river lot 12 in St Vital and farmed there. On 17 May 1849, at age 19, he supported the Métis drive for free trade at the famous trial of Pierre-Guillaume Sayer* by marching "with a rifle at his shoulder." Judge and historian Louis-Arthur Prud'homme* states that this episode was his apprenticeship as a "defender of the rights and liberties of the country's population."

The first event of the Métis resistance of 1869–70 to the transfer of Rupert's Land to the Canadian government was the stopping of the surveyors on 11 Oct. 1869. Oral history suggests that this event occurred on Nault's river lot in St Vital, but the notebook of surveyor Adam Clark Webbe would seem to indicate that it was on an adjoining lot. Nault's first name is not listed among those of the seven Naults who were present, but the one nicknamed Nanin is assumed to have been him. On the arrival of the surveyors, Nault is said to have gone for his first cousin Métis leader Louis Riel*, who spoke English. It seems likely that Nault played a significant role on this occasion since oral accounts of the event link it to his property.

According to Nault, at a meeting of the Métis on 21 Oct. 1869 Riel ordered him to construct a barrier at St Norbert to prevent the lieutenant governor designate, William McDougall*, from entering the Red River settlement or bringing in arms. Nault had about 250 to 300 men with him. On 1 November he and his brother Benjamin forced McDougall's representatives, Captain Donald Roderick Cameron and Joseph-Alfred-Norbert Provencher*, to return to Pembina (N.Dak.).

Neahkoteah

The following day, under Riel's orders, he and his men captured Upper Fort Garry (Winnipeg) to prevent it from falling into the hands of John Christian Schultz* and his Canadian supporters. From 4 to 23 Dec. 1869 Nault occupied Fort Pembina, the HBC post just north of the international border, to watch the activities of McDougall. When McDougall headed back east, Nault returned to the Red River settlement.

Prud'homme argues that in Riel's provisional government Nault was probably fourth in line of importance after Riel, Ambroise-Dydime LÉPINE, and Elzéar Goulet*. Nault was a member of the court martial that on 3 March 1870 tried Thomas Scott*, an Ontarian captured in mid February. Scott had proved to be a particularly troublesome prisoner and was sentenced to execution. Nault, who commanded the Métis firing squad, would report in 1923 to historian Auguste-Henri de TRÉMAUDAN that Scott "did not believe that we would have the pluck, as he called it, to go the whole length and to shoot him." Scott "would pledge his word to keep the peace in order to be released, then break it as soon as he was free. We had no desire whatever to put him to death, he simply forced us to it."

After troops arrived in August 1870 under the command of Colonel Garnet Joseph Wolseley*, numerous Métis suffered reprisals. In February 1871 Nault was attacked by soldiers at Pembina and left for dead. Prud'homme observed that he carried the scar from this brutal incident until his death. Later in 1871 Nault played a significant role in obtaining information for Riel and the Métis on the movements of William Bernard O'Donoghue*, who had asked Métis leaders, Nault included, for support in attacking Manitoba with a band of Fenians. Nault and Jean-Baptiste Lépine* went to Pembina on 2 October and returned four days later to report that O'Donoghue was planning to attack Fort Pembina before approaching Fort Garry. The Métis under Riel stayed loyal to Canada and did not join O'Donoghue.

In late 1871 Riel suggested the formation of an association of Métis to maintain their influence in the Red River parishes and he looked to Nault as one of the "principal Métis." Nault was named a councillor of the new organization, the Union Saint-Alexandre. Despite the hopes of Métis leaders that their demonstration of loyalty in protecting the colony against the Fenians would help them obtain amnesty for acts carried out during the resistance, they remained disappointed. Nault was arrested in February 1874. He stood trial for the murder of Scott the following November, but the jury was unable to reach a verdict. He was in prison awaiting a second trial when the government of Alexander Mackenzie* granted a full amnesty to all except Riel, A.-D. Lépine, and O'Donoghue in February 1875. His imprisonment left him with heart and lung problems. After his release he returned to his St Vital farm, where he would live until age 94. He took no part in the events of 1885 in Saskatchewan [see Riel], but three of his sons did. He became a member of the Union Nationale Métisse Saint-Joseph du Manitoba, established in 1887 to preserve Métis heritage and culture. An example of his efforts to collect and document Métis history was his donation in 1910 of the original flag of the Union Nationale Métisse to the organization; it is now preserved in the Heritage Centre of the Société Historique de Saint-Boniface. The Métis and francophone communities of Manitoba and André Nault's numerous descendants continue to honour the memory of this man who was an eye-witness to, and participant in, many stirring events.

RUTH SWAN and JANELLE REYNOLDS

Information regarding the flag of the Union Nationale Métisse was given to the authors by Augustine Abraham (Winnipeg) and Agnes Roy (St Vital, Man.) during telephone conversations in the spring of 2001.

AM, MG 3, B18; NR 0157. "The execution of Thomas Scott," ed. A.-H. de Trémaudan, *CHR*, 6 (1925): 222–36. A.-G. Morice, *Dictionnaire historique des Canadiens et des Métis français de l'Ouest* (Québec et Montréal, 1908). L.-A. Prud'homme, "André Nault," RSC, *Trans.*, 3rd ser., 22 (1928), sect.I: 99–111. Louis Riel, *The collected writings of Louis Riel*, ed. G. F. G. Stanley (5v., Edmonton, 1985). N. E. A. Ronaghan, "The Archibald administration in Manitoba – 1870–1872" (PHD thesis, Univ. of Manitoba, Winnipeg, 1986). G. F. G. Stanley, *Louis Riel* (Toronto, 1963). A.-H. de Trémaudan, "Louis Riel and the Fenian raid of 1871," *CHR*, 4 (1923): 132–44.

NEAHKOTEAH (Neakuteuk). *See* NIAQUTIAQ

NEAPOLITANO. *See* NAPOLITANO

NEILL. *See* O'NEILL

NELLIE PIOCHE. *See* CASHMAN, ELLEN

NESBITT, WALLACE, lawyer and judge; b. 13 May 1858 near Holbrook, Upper Canada, son of John W. Nesbitt and Mary Wallace; m. first 1887 Louisa Andrée Plumb, née Elliott (d. 1894); they had no children; m. secondly 1898 Amy Gertrude Beatty, and they had a son; d. 7 April 1930 in Toronto.

Wallace Nesbitt's father, a Scot, immigrated to Canada in 1837 with his Irish wife and settled on a farm in Oxford County. The youngest of 11 children, Wallace was raised there. After attending Woodstock College, he was articled as a law clerk and studied at Osgoode Hall in Toronto, where he won prizes. Following his call to the bar in Hilary term 1881, he practised with his brother John Wallace in Hamilton. In 1883 Britton Bath Osler* persuaded him to join his Toronto firm, McCarthy, Osler, Hoskin, and Creelman. During his nine years there Nesbitt acted in such notable cases as the suit between the Canadian Pacific

Railway and the contracting company of James Conmee*. In 1887 he married the New Orleans–born widow of his one-time partner Thomas Street Plumb, and became the stepfather of two young children.

In 1892 Nesbitt left McCarthy Osler for the firm of William Henry Beatty*, which largely served the Gooderham and Worts business empire. The addition of Nesbitt (who would be named a federal QC in 1896), George Tate BLACKSTOCK, William Renwick Riddell*, and Hugh Edward Rose laid the foundation for the partners' emergence as a top litigation group. By 1898 (the year he married Beatty's daughter), Nesbitt had been involved, according to Henry James Morgan*, in "many important suits" and was "singularly successful" as a jury lawyer. In 1900 he represented the Canadian Copper Company in its opposition to duties on nickel exports [see Andrew Trew Wood*], and within a year he had aligned himself professionally with private companies in the emerging battle over the public ownership of hydroelectric development in Ontario. By 1902, with Beatty spending much of his time running the Gooderham and Worts businesses, David FASKEN had assumed the management of the law firm. This shift does not seem to have sat well with many of its members, and they began to resign. The first to leave was Nesbitt.

On 16 May 1903, at age 45, he was named by Liberal prime minister Sir Wilfrid Laurier* to the Supreme Court of Canada. The appointment represented a break with the patronage appointments of the day since he was both a Conservative and a sound choice. As James G. Snell and Frederick Vaughan say in their history of the court, "Nesbitt had an outstanding reputation as counsel, and his nomination . . . was widely acclaimed." Although he did not have time to produce a significant body of judgements – he would sit for only two years – his decisions, a number of them involving cases of negligence, reflected careful analyses. The support he often won from his fellow judges suggests that he had the respect of the bench, but it was not always mutual – some of his dissents were very critical of the majority.

On 4 Oct. 1905 Nesbitt resigned to return to private practice. He was the second justice to leave that year, Albert Clements Killam* having gone to the Board of Railway Commissioners. Their departures could indicate some unhappiness within the court, but Nesbitt stated simply that he was leaving "for reasons purely private." Perhaps he wanted to assist his father-in-law, who was having a difficult year. George Gooderham* had died in May and Beatty had left his firm to assume the direct leadership of the Gooderham and Worts businesses. Beatty also found himself before the courts over the ownership of some property in northern Ontario, and Nesbitt may well have been asked to come to his aid; he would appear in court on Beatty's behalf in December. Even before his resignation, he

had joined Beatty in business ventures. In June 1905, for example, both were appointed to the board of the Canadian Niagara Power Company, with Beatty becoming president.

Instead of returning to the Beatty firm, however, likely because of the rift with Fasken, Nesbitt rejoined McCarthy Osler and resumed his career as a trial and corporation counsel. One biographical account would note that as a former, and highly regarded, Supreme Court judge, "he took up a unique and enviable position which brought him a large clientèle and ultimately considerable wealth." He acted in many high-profile cases, for example in opposition in 1912 to Ontario Hydro's powers of expropriation and as the nominee in 1918 of Mackenzie, Mann and Company and the Canadian Bank of Commerce in the Canadian Northern Railway arbitration [see Sir William MACKENZIE]. No stranger to the Judicial Committee of the Privy Council in Britain, which he steadfastly defended as Canada's final court of appeal, he continued to argue there, appearing, among other causes, on behalf of the Dominion Iron and Steel Company in the coal case of 1908, for the dominion in a dispute over Quebec marriage law in 1912, and in the long-running reference over the constitutional authority of provinces to incorporate companies with interprovincial or international operations. In 1924 he was named to a commission to consider the Quebec act that had placed the education of Jews under Protestant school boards. In some situations, his corporate and legal interests overlapped; as president of Canadian Niagara Power, he had given way to Ontario Hydro and reached a settlement in 1916.

Since his early years in practice, Nesbitt had been active in the institutions of the legal fraternity. In 1885–86 he was president of the Osgoode Legal and Literary Society. First elected a bencher of the Law Society of Upper Canada in 1906, he became its treasurer (the highest position in the Ontario bar) in 1927; two years later he personally gave it $10,000 in securities to support legal education. In 1928–29 he served as president of the Canadian Bar Association.

Nesbitt found time publicly to address matters of current interest. An opponent of reciprocity with the United States in 1911, he spoke eloquently of the need to strengthen Canada's imperial ties with Britain and its other colonies. One means, he had argued in 1910, was the formation of a permanent imperial council. A Presbyterian, freemason, and keen golfer, clubman, and fisherman, he also took a strong interest in the St John Ambulance Association, which made him a knight of grace for his service as president of its Ontario Council. The tall, bespectacled lawyer possessed a "wide knowledge" of English literature and, in the estimate of British chancellor Lord Sankey, a "genius for friendship."

In the summer of 1929, while at his cottage on

Newcombe

Wawataysee Island in Georgian Bay, Nesbitt suffered a stroke from which he never fully recovered. He died the next year at his home on Warren Road in Toronto and was buried in St James' Cemetery.

C. IAN KYER

Wallace Nesbitt assisted W. H. Beatty in the preparation of *The Boards of Trade General Arbitrations Act (1894) and rules of the Toronto Chamber of Arbitration: with notes and suggestions as to the conduct of a reference* (Toronto, 1894). On his own, Nesbitt published *The Judicial Committee of the Privy Council; a paper presented to the thirty-second annual meeting of the New York State Bar Association, held at the City of Buffalo, on the 28th and 29th of January, 1909* ([Toronto?, 1909?]), *Reciprocity: an address delivered before the Canadian Club, Montreal, December 12th, 1910* ([Montreal?, 1910?]), and *"Our country and its future": speech . . . at the annual banquet of the Chatham Board of Trade, January 9th, 1911* ([Chatham, Ont.?, 1911?]).

AO, RG 22-305, nos.10412, 64362; RG 80-8-0-180, no.22220. *Globe*, 8 April 1930. Christopher Armstrong, *The politics of federalism: Ontario's relations with the federal government, 1867–1942* (Toronto, 1981). *Beatty v. McConnell* (1905), *Ontario Weekly Reporter* (Toronto), 6: 882–85. *Canada Law Journal* (Toronto), 17 (1881): 99. *Canadian annual rev.* Canadian Bar Assoc., *Proc.* (Toronto), 15 (1930): 24–25. *Canadian men and women of the time* (Morgan; 1898 and 1912). Curtis Cole, "McCarthy, Osler, Hoskin, and Creelman, 1882 to 1902: establishing a reputation, building a practice," in *Essays in the history of Canadian law*, ed. D. H. Flaherty *et al.* (8v. to date, Toronto, 1981–), 4 (*Beyond the law: lawyers and business in Canada, 1830 to 1930*, ed. Carol Wilton, 1990): 149-66; *Osler, Hoskin & Harcourt: portrait of a partnership* (Toronto, 1995). G. F. Henderson, "Wallace Nesbitt, K.C.," *Canadian Bar Rev.* (Toronto), 8 (1930): 283–84. "The late Hon. Wallace Nesbitt," *Manitoba Bar News* (Winnipeg), 2 (1929–30), no.9: 4. J. G. Snell and Frederick Vaughan, *The Supreme Court of Canada: history of the institution* ([Toronto], 1985). *Standard dict. of Canadian biog.* (Roberts and Tunnell), 1: 380.

NEWCOMBE, CHARLES FREDERIC, physician, naturalist, and artefact collector; b. 15 Sept. 1851 in Newcastle upon Tyne, England, son of William Lister Newcombe, a railway manager, and Eliza Jane Rymer; m. 6 May 1879 Marian Arnold in Marylebone, London, England, and they had two daughters and four sons; d. 19 Oct. 1924 in Victoria.

Charles Newcombe was raised in Newcastle upon Tyne and studied medicine at the University of Aberdeen. He interned at the West Riding Asylum in Wakefield and graduated MB, CM with distinction in 1873. After a few years as medical officer at the Lancashire County Asylum in Rainhill, near Liverpool, he obtained his MD in 1878.

After their marriage in 1879 the Newcombes moved to Windermere, where Charles practised general medicine. In the early 1880s he visited North America and decided to immigrate. Newcombe, his wife, and their three children settled in Hood River, Oreg., in 1884. There he practised medicine, helped to build his own house, began a fruit farm, and participated in natural history expeditions, collecting specimens of native plants and archaeological artefacts.

In 1889 the family moved to Victoria in search of a milder climate. Newcombe obtained a medical licence for British Columbia and would maintain a general practice for the rest of his life, but he found it difficult to compete with the many established physicians in Victoria. Although not wealthy, he and his wife had inherited some money, which supplemented his income. Shortly after his arrival in Victoria he became an unpaid researcher at the provincial museum [*see* John Fannin*], where he met people with whom he shared interests in botany, geology, marine biology, geography, palaeontology, and anthropology. His passion for these subjects surpassed his interest in the medical profession and other career opportunities.

Following Marian Newcombe's death shortly after childbirth in February 1891, Newcombe travelled to England with his three eldest children, who would remain there for several years. While in England, he pursued studies at the University of London and at the British Museum in various branches of natural history and he purchased modern photographic equipment. He returned alone to Victoria the following year and began to venture further afield, mostly by boat, to pursue his interests in marine biology by dredging for specimens; in addition, he collected fossils and native plants. He was a founding member of the Victoria Natural History Society in 1896.

In 1895, with Francis Kermode* of the provincial museum, Newcombe had travelled by steamer on an expedition to the Kwakiutl community at Alert Bay and to the Queen Charlotte Islands. On this trip he began acquiring anthropological artefacts for his personal collection and he also established a practice of recording detailed field notes. By 1897 he had had a boat specially made for his fieldwork. The *Pelican*, a 24-foot double-ended Columbia River boat, was easy to row and to sail, could be transported by steamer, and permitted independent expeditions to the remotest areas of the coast. That year he returned to the same regions on his first major independent collecting trip. At the request of the provincial government he purchased a Haida totem pole for the Royal Botanic Gardens at Kew (London) and he acquired artefacts for George Mercer Dawson* of the Geological Survey of Canada.

Over the years Newcombe undertook many similar expeditions by boat to isolated locations on the British Columbia coast. Museums in Europe and North America began to commission him to gather natural history specimens. He also found ready buyers in a growing museum market for ethnological artefacts and he avidly competed with other collectors for totem poles, ceremonial masks and regalia, and more utilitarian items. By 1900 he had received commissions from major American museums. Leading American anthropologist Franz Boas* hired him to conduct research on the Haida history of the southern portion of the Queen Charlotte Islands. Newcombe was accompanied on this expedition by assistant Douglas Scholefield and Haida chief Elijah Ninstints. As they rowed and sailed together, Ninstints described the geography and history of his homeland, while Newcombe took notes and photographs, made sketches, and collected specimens. In late 1901 he agreed to work on a full-time basis for the Columbian Museum of Chicago, an arrangement that would last until late 1905. He acquired comprehensive ethnographic collections for displays on the Haida, Kwakiutl, Nootka, and Salish peoples. In 1904 he was commissioned to assemble ethnographic exhibits for the Louisiana Purchase exposition in St Louis that would include a group of Nootka and Kwakiutl cultural performers and artists, as well as a traditional native house, a canoe, and other artefacts purchased and shipped for the event. He eventually developed a web of patrons, clients, and colleagues that extended throughout British Columbia and around the world.

For decades most ethnological artefacts from the northwest coast of Canada were purchased by foreign interests. Newcombe was dismayed that he could not interest provincial and federal governments in the collection and preservation of native artefacts and specimens of natural history. Since his overriding concern was to preserve these items for posterity, he was obliged to deal with American and other foreign institutions. In response to this situation, in 1911 the provincial museum at Victoria hired him as its agent. For four years he travelled throughout the province, compiling a major collection of artefacts. After 1914 his pace began to abate and he turned to researching and writing about the exploration history of the British Columbia coast. After a collecting trip to Alert Bay, he contracted pneumonia and died in 1924.

During a period when many museums were competing to amass anthropological collections from the northwest coast, Newcombe succeeded better than most by developing and maintaining personal relationships with native people, scholars, and museum officials and by travelling where others would not. In the breadth and depth of the anthropological collections he provided various institutions and in the notes he recorded for individual artefacts, he is matched by few other researchers or collectors of the period. Important also are the many photographs he made of First Nations' villages, art works, and people during his expeditions, the best or only visual records of many traditional communities that were soon to change greatly or to disappear. Motivated by the anthropological interest of the time in osteology, he also collected skeletal material. He left a small body of published works, including a few articles and monographs on natural history, botany, and native artefacts.

Charles Newcombe had amassed an extensive personal collection that included thousands of artefacts, botanical specimens, fossils, and samples of marine life, as well as a vast number of photographs, extensive personal correspondence, notebooks, sketches, and a large library. His manuscript material, particularly his correspondence with leading scientific figures, provides insights into the collecting and research activities of his period.

KEVIN NEARY

The province of British Columbia purchased Charles Frederic Newcombe's personal collections from his heirs in 1961; these materials are now at the Royal British Columbia Museum (Victoria) and the BCA (MS-1077). The artefacts and specimens he purchased for others are housed in institutions throughout North America and abroad, including the Royal British Columbia Museum, the Field Museum of Natural Hist. (Chicago), the Canadian Museum of Civilization (Hull, Que.), the Brooklyn Museum of Art (New York), and the Peabody Museum of Archaeology and Ethnology (Cambridge, Mass.).

Newcombe is the author of "Epileptiform seizures in general paralysis," in West Riding Pauper Lunatic Asylum, *Medical reports*, ed. J. C. Browne and H. C. Major (6v., London, 1871–76), 5: 198–226; "Case of locomotor ataxy," *Brain* (London), 2 (1879–80): 134–38; "The Haida Indians," in *Congrès international des américanists, XVᵉ session, tenue à Québec en 1906* (2v., Quebec, 1907), 1: 135–49; *Petroglyphs in British Columbia* ([Victoria?], 1907); *Guide to anthropological collection in the provincial museum* (Victoria, 1909); *The first circumnavigation of Vancouver Island* (Victoria, 1914); "The McGill totem pole," *Ottawa Naturalist*, 32 (1918–19): 99–103; and "The Haida totem pole at the Milwaukee Public Museum," in Milwaukee Public Museum, *Year book* (Milwaukee, Wis.), 1922: 194–97. He co-authored *The sea-lion question in British Columbia* (Ottawa, 1918), was one of the compilers of the British Columbia Provincial Museum's *A preliminary catalogue of the flora of Vancouver and Queen Charlotte islands,* comp. W. R. Carter and C. F. Newcombe (Victoria, 1921), and, with John Forsyth, edited *Menzies' journal of Vancouver's voyage, April to October, 1792* (Victoria, 1923).

Church of Jesus Christ of Latter-day Saints, Geneal. Soc., International geneal. index. *Biographical dictionary of American and Canadian naturalists and environmentalists*, ed. K. B. Sterling *et al.* (Westport, Conn., 1997). *Canadian Field-Naturalist* (Ottawa), 38 (1924): 191–92 (obit.). Douglas Cole, *Captured heritage: the scramble for northwest coast artifacts* (Vancouver and Toronto, 1985). Jean Low, "Dr Charles Frederick Newcombe," *Beaver* (Winnipeg), outfit 312 (1981–82), no.4: 32–39. *Roll of the graduates of the University of Aberdeen, 1956–1970: with supplement, 1860–1955*, comp. Louise Donald and W. S. Macdonald (Aberdeen, Scot., 1982).

NEWHOUSE, SETH (Dayodekane), farmer, Iroquoian traditionalist, and Onondaga chief; b. 27 Jan. 1842 on the Six Nations Reserve, Upper Canada, son of Nicholas Newhouse and Catherine ——; m. first Catherine ——; m. secondly in the early 1890s Lucy Sero, from the Tyendinaga Reserve, Ont., and they had three daughters and a son; d. 11 June 1921 in Tuscarora Township, Ont.

Seth Newhouse's mother was an Onondaga of the Grey Swift clan and his father was a Mohawk. Privileged to attend the Mohawk Institute, he was better educated than many of his peers, competent in both Onondaga and English and an eloquent speaker in Mohawk. Although he was raised a member of the Plymouth Brethren and married Anglicans, he renounced Christianity in favour of the Longhouse religion, a decision that reflected his political beliefs. He took over his father's 45-acre farm near the Grand River, but spent much of his time travelling, recording traditional knowledge at Iroquois reserves in Ontario, Quebec, and New York State.

In the 19th and early 20th centuries, the Six Nations developed new and complex political traditions. The dominant forces were progressivism (associated with Christianity) and conservatism (associated with the Longhouse religion). A reform movement, which existed from the 1860s and sought to establish an elected council, was the most extreme manifestation of the progressive movement. A strong tradition of protest and a belief in the sovereignty of the Grand River Iroquois represented common ground. Newhouse's firm commitment to political independence and cultural preservation ensured his prominence in community affairs.

The 1870s and early 1880s witnessed considerable strife among progressive and conservative chiefs in the Confederacy Council. Newhouse's knowledge of traditional forms and his stature in the community made him an ally of the conservative chiefs. He participated in council as a pine tree chief (an elected, honorary chief) in 1875 and again in 1882–83, but his interest in collecting traditional knowledge and his unpopularity with the progressives would shorten his involvement. In January 1875 and in August 1876, following a serious split, he signed petitions to Indian affairs superintendent David Laird* berating the progressive chiefs and asking for legal recognition of the Iroquois Confederacy. In the 1880s and 1890s he joined in protests over two festering issues, the Haldimand land claim and the Six Nations' losses in the Grand River Navigation Company [see James Winniett*]. In 1882–83 he chaired meetings, recruited for the Six Nations Union Association, and for a time served as its vice-president. He was deposed as a chief by critics in 1884 for "migrating to the United States." The supposed migration, however, was really one of his numerous research trips to upstate New York and Quebec. In subsequent years he co-signed, witnessed, and possibly authored petitions over the land claim and losses grievances, challenged government policy, and asserted the Six Nations' right to self-government.

Newhouse's transcription of the traditional narrative describing the founding of the Iroquois Confederacy was a response to the threat of reform, a defence of the hereditary council, and a result of his lifelong interest in confederacy lore. He had begun collecting information in the 1870s; by 1880 he had completed a small edition of what was to become his "Cosmogony of De-ka-na-wi-da's government." He produced expanded versions in 1885 and 1910. Unable to secure assistance for publishing from the Department of Indian Affairs or the chiefs, who disagreed with his interpretation of council functions, he sent his 1910 manuscript to anthropologist Arthur Caswell Parker of the New York State Museum. Parker combined it with other material, including the code largely prepared by John Arthur Gibson* and accepted by council in 1900, and had the collection published in his museum's *Bulletin* in 1916 as "The constitution of the Five Nations or the Iroquois Book of the Great Law." Newhouse's portion comprised two sections: the legend of Dekanahwideh* (the reputed founder of the confederacy) and his codified laws. Newhouse also worked as an informant with such other anthropologists as Horatio Emmons Hale*, Edward Sapir*, John Napoleon Brinton Hewitt, Alexander Alexandrovich Goldenweiser, and Frederick Wilkerson Waugh.

Seth Newhouse died in 1921 and was buried at Jubilee Methodist Church on lot 7, concession 4, of Tuscarora Township. His life had embodied the political traditions and activism of the Grand River Iroquois and the quiet, determined passion of the scribe.

SCOTT TREVITHICK

Smithsonian Institution, National Anthropological Arch. (Washington), MS 1343 (Constitution of the Confederacy by Dekanawidah, collected and translated from Mohawk by Chief Seth Newhouse, 1898); MS 1359 (Constitution of the Five Nations Indians Confederation, February 1880 [Seth Newhouse version]) (copy at LAC, MG 19, F26); MS 2357 (Iroquoian cosmology, 1896–97 [Newhouse's original dictation]); MS 3489 (Newhouse's text of Handsome Lake religion in Mohawk and typed copy of same by J. N. B. Hewitt); MS 3490 (Mohawk version of the Constitution of the League by Newhouse, 1897. [Other manuscripts in the Smithsonian Institution to which Newhouse contributed are listed on its website (*www.siris.si.edu*).] LAC, RG 10, 624, 796, 1025, 1029, 1949, 2178, 2189, 2284, 2345, 2349, 2353; RG 31, C1, Tuscarora Township, Ont., 1871, div.1: 6; 1901, div.1: 4. "The constitution of the Five Nations or the Iroquois Book of the Great Law," comp. and ed. A. C. Parker, New York State Museum, *Bull.* (Albany, N.Y.), no.184 (1916); reissued as *The constitution of the Five Nations, or, the Iroquois book of the great law*, ed. W. G. Spittal (Ohsweken, Ont., 1991). W. N. Fenton, "Seth Newhouse's traditional history and constitution of the Iroquois Confederacy," American Philosophical Soc., *Proc.* (Philadelphia), 93 (1949): 141–58. A. A.

Goldenweiser, [Review of "The constitution of the Five Nations" (Parker)], *American Anthropologist* (Lancaster, Penn.), new ser., 18 (1916): 431–36; reissued in *The constitution of the Five Nations* (Spittal), 165–69. J. N. B. Hewitt, [Review of "The constitution of the Five Nations" (Parker)], *American Anthropologist*, new ser., 19 (1917): 429–38; reissued in *The constitution of the Five Nations* (Spittal), 169–76; "Iroquoian cosmology," Smithsonian Institution, Bureau of American Ethnology, *Annual report* (Washington), 1899/1900: 127–339. S. R. Trevithick, "Conflicting outlooks: the background to the 1924 deposing of the Six Nations' hereditary council" (MA thesis, Univ. of Calgary, 1998). Sally Weaver, "The Iroquois: the Grand River reserve in the late nineteenth and early twentieth centuries, 1875–1945," in *Aboriginal Ontario: historical perspectives on the First Nations*, ed. E. S. Rogers and D. B. Smith (Toronto, 1994), 213–57; "Seth Newhouse and the Grand River Confederacy at mid-nineteenth century," in *Extending the rafters: interdisciplinary approaches to Iroquoian studies*, ed. M. K. Foster *et al.* (Albany, 1984), 165–82.

NG MON HING (Wen Wuqing in Mandarin), lay missionary, teacher, and Presbyterian minister; b. 25 March 1858 in Chung-lau, Guangdong province (People's Republic of China); m. and had one daughter and two sons; d. 1921 in Canton (Guangzhou).

Born in China, Ng Mon Hing spent the early years of his life in Los Angeles. While aboard ship returning to China, he came into contact with two earnest Christians and the "mission-school teaching was borne in on him." This intense contact resulted in his conversion and he was later baptized in the town of his birth. After a period spent teaching and proselytizing in southern China, he entered the Presbyterian Preachers' Training School in Canton. In 1895 he met the Reverend Alexander Brown Winchester, a Presbyterian minister from Canada who was in China to learn the language. That same year, on Winchester's strong recommendation, the Presbyterian Church in Canada extended a call to Ng as a lay missionary and teacher. On 28 March 1895 Ng arrived in Victoria, where he began a career among the Chinese in Canada that would last almost 25 years. A widower when he arrived, he would later be joined by his son Peter. Like most overseas Chinese, he supported family members in China. On a starting monthly salary of $40 plus $5 for rent, he sent money to an elderly aunt and uncle and to his children in Canton. At his retirement in 1916, his annual salary would be $684.

When Ng arrived in 1895 there were approximately 11,000 Chinese in Canada, most of whom were in British Columbia [*see* CHANG Toy; YIP Sang]. His services as a Cantonese-speaking evangelist were therefore much in demand. In addition to preaching, he held prayer meetings, tended to the sick and elderly, and conducted evening school and Bible classes. On a regular basis he toured Chinatown (Vancouver), visiting businesses, boarding houses, and residences in an effort to attract new followers. His monthly reports made careful note of baptisms and new converts. In the early 20th century there were few Chinese women in Canada and the Presbyterian Church made a special effort to reach out to them. Ng's reports included a meticulous record of the number of women and children who attended church activities. In addition, he collected and sent moneys to China for various causes such as famine relief.

In August 1901 Ng was transferred to Nelson. The following year, when he began to express a desire to return to China, the home mission committee of the Presbyterian Church offered to relocate him in Vancouver. He accepted and by early 1903 had been placed in charge of the Vancouver mission. Over the next four years he divided his time between Vancouver and Victoria. During the summer months, while the mission school in Vancouver was closed, he preached among workers in fish canneries along the coast.

Ng was in a precarious position in the Chinese communities. Those who resisted Christianity saw his presence as an attempt by Canadian officials to monitor and reform their activities. While the Presbyterian Church praised him for his help in the "campaign against Chinese gambling," some of his fellow countrymen responded differently, accusing him in 1902 of collaborating with the police and instigating raids against suspected gambling dens. Fearing for his safety, Ng asked the police for protection. A Vancouver magistrate refused to grant him permission to carry a revolver or a police whistle, but temporarily assigned a white police officer to protect him. Ironically, Ng's nationality made him a target for white Canadians' suspicions. During a routine effort to rid the city of gambling dens, Vancouver police raided his home, seizing money and Chinese-language manuscripts.

In 1906 Ng was asked to transfer to Ontario. He worked mostly in Toronto and at times preached in Hamilton, Ottawa, and other cities with Chinese communities. By 1909, at the request of a group in Vancouver for a Chinese preacher, he had returned to the west coast. In 1913 he was ordained and inducted into St Andrew's Church, becoming the first Chinese minister in the Presbyterian Church in Canada. His ordination had been delayed by his hesitation to remain in Canada. He had often considered retiring to China to live with his children. His son Peter, educated in Vancouver, had returned and by 1911 had a high-ranking government position in Canton.

In 1914, when Ng was 56, his colleagues began to express concern that he no longer possessed the vigour needed to work in the more populous missions. They considered replacing him with a more dynamic preacher. The next year a colleague suggested that he be transferred to Cumberland, but another was worried that he was not strong enough to "endure the necessary privations" of the remote location. In 1916 he resigned from his official duties. He continued to draw a salary and over the next three years he devoted much of his time to aiding church and police efforts to curtail gambling. For reasons that are unclear, he was now reluctant to leave Canada. The Reverend Robert Peter MacKay speculated that his change of heart was due to political upheaval in China. Ng had confided to MacKay that he feared anti-Christian persecution on his return. Ng's superiors were persuaded that his abilities could be put to better use in China. They felt that he was no longer "popular" and hence ineffective, but were uncertain as to how to encourage him to return to China without being "unfair or unkind." According to one co-worker, "The poor man is loath to leave. . . . Meantime the Chinese . . . have had three farewells for him already." When Ng finally departed on 18 Dec. 1919, he had not seen his homeland in 24 years. He continued his missionary work and lived with his son Peter in Canton until his death in 1921.

Ng Mon Hing had served the Chinese communities of western and eastern Canada with diligence. His close contact with English-speaking Canadians, his fluency in English, and his religious mission made him an exceptional Chinese immigrant for his time.

MONA-MARGARET PON

LAC, RG 31, C1, 1901, Victoria, subdist.D, subdiv.6. UCC-C, Fonds 122/12, dossiers 14–15, 72–74, 79–80, 84, 92–93, 119–20, 141. K. J. Anderson, *Vancouver's Chinatown: racial discourse in Canada, 1875–1980* (Montreal and Kingston, Ont., 1991). A. B. Chan, *Gold Mountain: the Chinese in the New World* (Vancouver, 1983). Harry Con *et al.*, *From China to Canada: a history of the Chinese communities in Canada*, ed. Edgar Wickberg (Toronto, 1982; repr. 1988). P. S. Li, *The Chinese in Canada* (Toronto, 1988). R. G. MacBeth, *Our task in Canada* (Toronto, 1912). S. S. Osterhout, *Orientals in Canada: the story of the work of the United Church of Canada with Asiatics in Canada* (Toronto, 1929). N. L. Ward, *Oriental missions in British Columbia* (Westminster [London], 1925). W. P. Ward, "The Oriental immigrant and Canada's Protestant clergy, 1858–1925," *BC Studies* (Vancouver), no.22 (summer 1974): 40–55.

NIAQUTIAQ (Niaqutsiaq, Neahkoteah, Neakuteuk), Inuit trader and post manager; probably b. in the 1880s on the east coast of Baffin Island (Nunavut), son of Iqilarjuq; m. Kowna (Kowdna, Kownang), and they had one adopted son; d. late January 1922 at Kivitoo (Nunavut).

From 1912 to 1922 Niaqutiaq represented the Sabellum Trading Company of London, England, at Kivitoo. His story bears witness to some of the unfortunate circumstances that emerged as Inuit of the eastern Arctic attempted to adapt their socio-economic and cultural traditions to those of western society.

In the late 19th century a number of British whalers increased their trade with the Inuit to offset the rapid decline of the whale population in Davis Strait. A few companies attempted to regularize trade in polar bear, ivory, sealskins, and blubber by appointing Inuit representatives to act as middlemen. Beginning in 1912, the Sabellum Trading Company established several posts along the eastern shore of Baffin Island, including one at Kivitoo where the whalers used to anchor to flense carcasses, bury their dead, and take on fresh water. The management of the trade there was entrusted to Niaqutiaq, who was related by marriage to Angmarlik, the well-known leader at the whaling station on Kekerten Island in Cumberland Sound.

Kivitoo's population was relatively small compared to that of the whaling stations in Cumberland Sound, but by 1920 there were similarities in the commercial operation. Those living at the post were "employed" by Niaqutiaq, in the sense that they received regular food rations and ammunition. Supplies were considered advances on their credit for the furs they traded, often at a much lower price than those brought in from outlying camps. As manager, Niaqutiaq attained inordinate influence and authority over the Inuit, who were entirely dependent upon his goodwill to obtain ammunition, guns, fox traps, tobacco, and other items. As a consequence, "it was customary for them to do his bidding," and they did not question his wisdom.

For the first few years Niaqutiaq is said to have returned an acceptable profit for the company, but World War I intervened and the supply ship did not visit Kivitoo between 1916 and 1920. The Anglican missionaries had departed from Blacklead Island in 1913, and their absence added to the isolation of the community from European influence. With little knowledge or understanding, Niaqutiaq and leaders of other camps began instructing their people on the Christian religion. As anthropologist Marc G. Stevenson suggests, "Many of the roles of shamanistic leadership continued to be played out within the context of Christianity." In Niaqutiaq's case, some of the rituals and taboos of shamanism also resurfaced and were celebrated in the name of Christianity.

In the winter of 1921–22 the Kivitoo community consisted of around 40 men, women, and children. Niaqutiaq and his family had a frame house provided by the company, while the others lived in skin tents covered with snow blocks. Compared to the conditions at neighbouring Padlee (in Merchants Bay), accommodation, equipment, sanitation, clothing, and general health were decidedly inferior. According to police reports, venereal disease introduced by the whalers was still "rampant" at Kivitoo, as evidenced by visible infections and the "number of sterile women and cases of total blindness." As winter approached, Inuit visitors had observed that Niaqutiaq seemed to be suffering from bouts of "mental weakness" and that there were "problems" in the community. They reportedly tried, but were unable, to help.

The festivities on Christmas Day marked the beginning of more serious trouble. According to witnesses, Niaqutiaq suddenly appeared at a dance held in the storehouse, dressed in a white gown, adorned with three-foot angel's wings, and wearing a crown. He first claimed he was an angel, and then later Jesus. Singing and dancing continued long into the night. In the days that followed, he became more demanding and irrational. He appointed two hunters to be his "policemen," to report on those who were "bad" and carry out his punishments. A reign of confusion and charged emotions ensued, as the community spent days at a time without food and with little sleep. There were many sessions of religious instruction, hymn singing, and frenzied dancing, multiple threats at knifepoint, and forced exhibitions of sexual acts. Niaqutiaq warned that disbelievers would be killed. The Inuit became increasingly subservient and frightened. As one woman related later, "My fear of [Niaqutiaq] when he was living was so great that I used to do what he told me to. .... I thought he was God and Jesus."

Derangement eventually led to murder. After failing to restore a blind man's sight by rubbing his eyes, Niaqutiaq declared Mungeuk was "bad" and commanded his policemen to kill him by stabbing him through the heart. The next victim was Semik (Semming), who could not read or write. When his illiteracy did not improve after he was struck three times, Niaqutiaq ordered his execution. This time death was not swift and the policemen fled, fearing they would be victims because they had dared to question Niaqutiaq's orders.

When his own cousin challenged his actions, Niaqutiaq threatened he too would die. Kidlapik lay awake that night, his gun at his side, ready to defend himself and his family. Yet, for reasons unknown, Semik's wife was chosen. Just as Niaqutiaq was about to bludgeon the kneeling woman with a hammer, Kidlapik took aim with his rifle and fatally shot him through the chest, thus ending a month of terror. In the Inuit tradition of allowing kin the right to avenge the murder of a relative, Kidlapik tearfully offered his rifle to Niaqutiaq's widow and others, asking them to take his life. They refused and most thanked him for saving them from certain death.

News of the tragic events spread, reaching the Royal Canadian Mounted Police detachment at Pond Inlet that summer. A year later Kidlapik's brother Peneloo arrived at the RCMP post with a more detailed account. Senior officials agreed that it was a "case of insanity" and that Kidlapik "should be commended" for having defended the community. In March 1924 Corporal Finley McInnes and Constable William MacGregor spent over a month at Kivitoo to record more than 70 typed pages of testimony from nine witnesses. McInnes concluded that the mission-

aries bore a major responsibility for having distributed syllabic Bibles without continued supervision and instruction. To help stabilize the community, he suggested regular police patrols, welfare rations, and education. The investigation also recommended that no further action be taken. Kowna, Niaqutiaq's widow, assumed the position of manager until the Kivitoo post was abandoned in 1926. There were no recurrences of instability.

Additional incidents of fanaticism and "religious insanity" would occur elsewhere in the eastern Arctic. In some cases the police were successful in preventing bloodshed; in others they were not. Meanwhile, the RCMP increased their patrols to outlying camps to provide support where needed and educate the Inuit on Canadian laws.

Seventy-five years later, memories of Niaqutiaq still seemed to haunt the region, with most Inuit reluctant to discuss the incident. For scholars, the Kivitoo murders reflect a dark side of Inuit-Qallunaat relations, one which might have been prevented had there been more financial support for missions, police protection, medical services, and education.

SHELAGH D. GRANT

[Little has been written about Niaqutiaq and the Kivitoo murders. Most of the details described in the present biography were obtained from archival documents and oral history interviews. S.D.G.]

Canadian Heritage, Parks Canada, Western Canada Service Centre, Philip Goldring, "Southeast Baffin historical reports" (1988); North Baffin Oral Hist. Project, Taped interview with Inuit elder Timothy Kadloo (a distant relative of Niaqutiaq), 18 Aug. 1924. LAC, RG 18, 3293, 3667. Private arch., S. D. Grant (Peterborough, Ont.), Pangnirtung Oral Hist. Interviews, Taped interviews with Inuit elders Pauloosie Angmarlik and Etuangat Aksayuk (both distant relatives of Niaqutiaq), 15–18 June 1995. Trent Univ. Arch. (Peterborough), Finley McInnes papers, ser.A, box 1, file 11 (testimony of nine witnesses to the Kevetuk/Kivitoo murders, February–April 1924) [a private collection of papers and photographs now owned by a granddaughter and temporarily housed, with restrictions, in the archives. S.D.G.]. *Arctic whalers, icy seas: narratives of the Davis Strait whale fishery*, ed. W. G. Ross (Toronto, 1985). A. L. Fleming, *Perils of the polar pack: or, the adventures of the Reverend E. W. T. Greenshield, Kt., O.N., of Blacklead Island, Baffin Land* (Toronto, 1932). Philip Goldring, "Inuit economic responses to Euro-American contacts: southeast Baffin Island, 1824–1940," in *Interpreting Canada's north: selected readings*, ed. K. S. Coates and W. R. Morrison (Toronto, 1989), 252–77. S. D. Grant, "Religious fanaticism at Leaf River, Ungava, 1931," *Inuit Studies* ([Quebec]), 21 (1997): 159–88. W. G. Ross, "Whaling, Inuit, and the Arctic islands," in *Interpreting Canada's north*, 235–51. M. G. Stevenson, *Inuit, whalers, and cultural persistence: structure in Cumberland Sound and central Inuit organization* (Toronto, 1997). Gavin White, "Scottish traders to Baffin Island, 1910–1930," *Maritime Hist.* (Tavistock, Eng.), 5 (1977): 34–50.

NICHOL, WALTER CAMERON, journalist, newspaper editor and publisher, and lieutenant governor; b. 15 Oct. 1866 in Goderich, Upper Canada, sixth and youngest son of Robert Ker Addison Nichol, a barrister, and Cynthia Jane Ballard; m. 21 Sept. 1897 Quita Josephine March Moore (d. 1968) in London, Ont., and they had a son and a daughter; d. 19 Dec. 1928 in Victoria.

Although Walter Nichol's paternal grandfather, Lieutenant-Colonel Robert Nichol*, had served with distinction during the War of 1812 and had become a prominent politician, Walter's father did not enjoy much success as a lawyer. Walter received most of his education from his mother while the family lived in Hamilton. At age 12 he worked as a messenger in the law office of Britton Bath Osler*.

In 1881 Nichol became a reporter for the *Hamilton Spectator* under John Robson Cameron. There, he drew simple cartoons and demonstrated his literary skills by writing short poems and skits. He was just 15 when the first issue of *Bicycle* (Hamilton) appeared in September 1882. A small monthly journal devoted to cycling, it was the official organ of the Canadian Wheelmen's Association; Nichol was its editor and contributed humorous fiction. The journal seems to have ceased publication early in 1883. In 1886 Nichol left the *Hamilton Spectator* for Edmund Ernest SHEPPARD's *Evening News* (Toronto). The following year Nichol and Sheppard established a publication devoted to independent political criticism and social, musical, and theatrical commentary that promised to deal with the subjects "in a lighter vein than was habitual in the daily press." With Sheppard as editor and manager, Nichol as assistant editor, and William E. Caiger as advertising manager they launched the weekly *Saturday Night* on 3 December. It was issued on Saturday evening because a municipal by-law prohibited publishing on Sunday. Differences soon arose between Sheppard and his partners, so Nichol and Caiger left to establish a rival, *Life* (Toronto), in February 1888. Under Nichol's editorship it was "a very witty and breezy sheet," as *Saturday Night* would later acknowledge, but it ran for less than a year; the market could not bear two weeklies.

Returning to Hamilton in 1889, Nichol became a reporter for the newly established *Hamilton Herald*. Over the next seven years he rose from reporter to editor-in-chief. In 1896 he moved to London, Ont., where he was a founder of the *News*. The following year, excited by reports of mining booms in western Canada, he left the *News* and travelled to British Columbia. After spending about three months visiting the Kootenay mining district, he became editor of the *Kootenaian* (Kaslo) early in July. In mid August he accepted a post as editor of Hewitt BOSTOCK's weekly *Province* (Victoria), which was modelled upon Henry Du Pré Labouchere's muckraking *Truth* (London, Eng.).

Nichol adopted an aggressive editorial approach. In October 1897 he described the opposing *Daily Colonist* (Victoria) as the "chief mouthpiece" of the administration of Premier John Herbert TURNER, stating that its sole purpose was to "protect the Dunsmuirs [James Dunsmuir*; Robert Dunsmuir*] in the enjoyment of the money-making monopolies which they have secured from hypnotized and venal legislatures." In December, Turner and Attorney General Charles Edward Pooley sued Nichol for libel after he wrote that they were guilty of "improper conduct" in allowing their names to be used to promote public companies in which they were directors. The case would drag on until October 1901, when Nichol would be found not guilty.

In late March 1898 a daily edition of the *Province* started in Vancouver with Nichol as its editor. A year later he claimed that its circulation of over 5,000 was "practically as great as that of all the other daily papers in the province put together." With a loan from Thomas George SHAUGHNESSY, president of the Canadian Pacific Railway, he was able to secure control of the paper in 1901. Although he was a Liberal, his support of the party was not unconditional. Accused of having "turned Tory" in May 1900 when he vehemently opposed the renegade Liberal Joseph MARTIN and supported his Conservative opponents, Nichol explained that he declined to "lend countenance to a person who, masquerading as a Liberal, has left no stone unturned to injure and embarrass the Liberal government both in public and in private."

By 1910 the *Vancouver Daily Province* was the leading newspaper in British Columbia and only the *Manitoba Free Press* (Winnipeg) matched its influence in western Canada. Nichol displayed keen judgement in hiring staff and in later years he delegated most of the writing and editorial tasks to his subordinates while he pursued other business interests, investing in many small and medium-sized companies in western Canada. He served as president of the Pacific Marine Insurance Company and was a director of the Royal Trust Company.

On 24 Dec. 1920 Nichol was appointed lieutenant governor of British Columbia, after Edward Gawler Prior died suddenly. On assuming office, he gave up all active connection with the *Daily Province* and in 1923 he sold controlling interest to William Southam*'s firm for $1,000,000. In office he showed great interest in postgraduate education at the University of British Columbia and in 1925 established a travelling scholarship in French at the Université de Paris. For this gesture he received later that year one of the first honorary degrees conferred by the university and two years later he would be awarded the cross of the Legion of Honour from the French government. Although his term expired in December 1925, he remained in office until late February 1926 when his successor was sworn in. He retired to Miraloma, his country house in Sidney designed by Samuel MAC-LURE. He died in Victoria less than three years later and left an estate worth over $2,700,000, much of it invested in government bonds.

BRAD R. MORRISON and
CHRISTOPHER J. P. HANNA

AO, RG 80-5-0-247, no.9656. BCA, GR-2951, no.1928-09-397085; MS-1320; MS-2700. LAC, RG 31, C1, 1871, Bothwell, Ont., div.1: 46; 1901, Burrard, B.C., subdist.D: 30. *Daily Colonist* (Victoria), 20 Dec. 1928. *Hamilton Herald* (Hamilton, Ont.), 27 Dec. 1920. *Vancouver Daily Province*, 26–27 March 1899; 21 May 1900; 25 Oct. 1901; 28 Nov. 1903; 30 Sept. 1909; 20, 22 Dec. 1928; 7 March 1939. *Vancouver Daily Times*, 20 Dec. 1928, 4 Nov. 1968. *Vancouver Daily World*, 23 Sept., 20–21 Dec. 1897; 25 Oct. 1901; 18 Dec. 1920. *Directories*, Hamilton, 1878–80, 1882–87, 1890–97; London City and Middlesex County, Ont., 1896–98; Toronto, 1888–89; Vancouver, 1908. *Canadian annual rev.*, 1925. *Canadian men and women of the time* (Morgan; 1912). S. W. Jackman, *The men at Cary Castle; a series of portrait sketches of the lieutenant-governors of British Columbia from 1871 to 1971* (Victoria, 1972). Martin Segger, *The buildings of Samuel Maclure: in search of appropriate form* (Victoria, 1986). *Standard dict. of Canadian biog.* (Roberts and Tunnell). *Who's who and why*, 1915/16. *Who's who in western Canada . . .* (Vancouver), 1912–13.

NICHOLLS, FREDERIC THOMAS, businessman, publisher, politician, and office holder; b. 22 Nov. 1855 in London, England, son of Thomas William Nicholls, a silversmith, and Elizabeth Pitkin; m. 29 May 1875 Florence Theresa Mary Graburn (d. 27 April 1909) in Ottawa, and they had four sons and three daughters; d. 25 Oct. 1921 in Toronto.

Little is known of Frederic Nicholls's early years. Obituaries mention that he had been "good at billiards in his youth" and received "some education" in Stuttgart (Germany), though he does not seem to have had any professional training. In 1874 he came to Montreal and shortly thereafter he located in Ottawa; at the time of his marriage to the daughter of an official in the Department of Marine and Fisheries, he was a commission merchant. Ambitious, astute, and a born salesman, in June 1880 he launched the *Industrial World and National Economist*; he remained its manager after his move to Toronto the following year. Retitled the *Canadian Manufacturer and Industrial World* in January 1882, it would continue under his direction until 1894. In 1886 he became secretary of the Ontario Manufacturers' Association (renamed the Canadian Manufacturers' Association later that year) and he held the position until 1891.

During this period the *Canadian Manufacturer* became the official publication of the CMA. In keeping with the association's stance and his own Conservative leanings, Nicholls supported tariff protection to foster industrial growth. About 1886, with Henry Stark Howland*, he opened offices on Front Street called the Permanent Exhibition of Manufacturers and Commercial Exchange. Named a vice-president of the Toronto Press Club in 1889, he returned to the newspaper business in 1895–99 as owner of the *Evening Star*, an acquisition designed to support the Toronto Railway Company and its operation on Sundays. When the CMA was reorganized in 1900, he chaired the committee charged with launching its monthly, *Industrial Canada*.

Nicholls's affiliation with the *Canadian Manufacturer*, the CMA, and the Exchange brought him into contact with leading Toronto businessmen. Looking about for new chances, he decided that the nascent electricity business would be a growth industry [*see* John Joseph WRIGHT]. His organization of a syndicate that included Wilmot Deloui Matthews* led first in 1889 to the Toronto Incandescent Electric Light Company Limited. Managed by Nicholls from his Front Street offices and based on steam generation, it took over Henry Mill Pellatt*'s failing arc-light firm, Toronto Electric Light. In 1891 Nicholls became involved as well in Toronto Construction and Electric Supply. None of these firms developed proprietary products or services – they used franchises from American firms with proven technologies – but the resulting monopoly in the supply of power and lighting united the three men who were to dominate the industry in the city for the next decade: Nicholls, Pellatt, and William MACKENZIE, whose Toronto Railway was the largest consumer of electricity in Ontario.

Nicholls's importance as a link between finance and engineering increased when he assumed management of Canadian General Electric, formed in 1892 to consolidate the Canadian business of Edison General Electric, Edison Electric Light, Thomson-Houston International Electric, and Toronto Construction and Electric Supply. At the same time CGE's head office was moved from Montreal to Toronto, where it supplied generators for the Toronto Railway. Engineer Edward Montague Ashworth remembered Nicholls as his "early idea of a Big Man," whose telephone summonses caused department heads to jump. Although CGE was meant to be an American-controlled subsidiary, its Canadian investors purchased majority control in 1895 and about 1900 Nicholls became second vice-president as well as manager. An eloquent champion of electricity, he was president of the National Electric Light Association of the United States in 1896–97 and brought its annual convention to Niagara Falls, Ont., in 1897.

As a result of his association with Mackenzie in the 1890s, Nicholls emerged as president of many of his railway companies in Canada and, through various syndicators and financiers, an executive officer or director of traction and power companies in South

America and the Caribbean. Through Sir William Cornelius Van Horne* of Montreal, for instance, he joined the group formed to operate the Havana Electric Railway and through Mackenzie he became vice-president in 1900 of São Paulo Tramway, Light and Power and in 1904 of Rio de Janeiro Tramway, Light and Power [*see* Frederick Stark Pearson*]. The following year he would be listed as the president, vice-president, or director of no fewer than 30 companies.

To meet the increasing demand for electricity in Toronto, Nicholls, Pellatt, and Mackenzie looked to Niagara for a vast new supply. In 1902, with Nicholls as manager and first vice-president, they had formed the Electrical Development Company of Ontario Limited, which early the following year secured a franchise from the province for development. Designed by Edward James Lennox*, the company's ornate generating station began sending power to Toronto in 1906. The monopoly over Toronto's electricity market had already led to agitation for public control, however, and that year, through the efforts of Adam BECK and others, the Hydro-Electric Power Commission of Ontario was organized. Considerable ill will emerged between the private companies on the one hand and the City of Toronto, Hydro, and the Niagara Falls Parks Commission on the other. Beck, for instance, refused in 1909 to accept the lowest tender for equipment, from CGE, because he wanted nothing to do with Nicholls. Ultimately, Hydro was ordered to arrange a contract that divided its business between CGE and Westinghouse. In 1922 years of wrangling ended when the hydro commissions of Ontario and Toronto purchased the power assets of Nicholls, Mackenzie, and Pellatt.

Nicholls negotiated a major reorganization of CGE in 1913, when it acquired the manufacturing and sales rights in Canada for the milling and mining equipment of Allis-Chalmers-Bullock (an American company) and formed Canadian Allis-Chalmers. He became president of both Canadian firms, CGE's plant in Peterborough was expanded, the Canada Foundry Company in Toronto was added, and the Stratford Mill Building Company was taken over for the production of some Allis-Chalmers lines. As president of CGE, Nicholls no longer enjoyed the obscurity of working through syndicates, and his hostility to organized labour and his reluctance to cooperate with the Imperial Munitions Board during wartime were exposed. Named a fellow of the Royal Colonial Institute in London in 1911, he was made an honorary lieutenant-colonel in October 1914 and served on the general council of the Canadian Patriotic Fund and the executive committee of the Toronto branch of the Canadian Red Cross Society. His long-time support of the Conservatives stood him in good stead with the government of Sir Robert Laird Borden*, which on 20 Jan. 1917 appointed him to the Senate, where he

chaired a special committee on post-war trade. He continued to run CGE until the spring of 1921, when he stepped down to chair its board. In 1923, after his death, American General Electric repurchased most of CGE's common stock.

An inveterate worker, Nicholls had been accustomed to 16-hour days in the 1880s but he enjoyed more leisure later in life. Readily recognizable by his stockiness, glasses, and moustache, he had a summer home near Shanty Bay on Lake Simcoe and a farm north of Toronto, was apparently an expert rose gardener, and enjoyed the comforts of numerous clubs. In religion, he belonged to the Church of England and served on the boards of Trinity University and Havergal Ladies' College in Toronto and Ridley College in St Catharines. As well, he was a justice of the peace for York County, vice-consul for Liberia from 1887, and consul for Portugal from 1906.

Frederic Nicholls died in October 1921 at his home on St George Street. He had probably known of his cancerous condition: he had had an operation and, in addition to an estate valued at $112,450, he left life-insurance policies worth more than $344,550. By the time of his death, he was a highly regarded spokesperson for the manufacturing and hydroelectric industries.

CHRISTOPHER ANDREAE

Frederic Nicholls's speech of 19 Jan. 1905 to the Empire Club in Toronto was published as *Niagara's power: past, present, prospective* ... ([Toronto?, 1905?], reproduced as CIHM, no.78710). A number of his other speeches are in his *Conservation of Canadian trade* (Toronto, 1918). An oil portrait of Nicholls by Robert Harris* is in the Univ. of Toronto Art Coll.

AO, RG 22-305, nos.21978, 44052; RG 80-5-0-48, no.1678; RG 80-8-0-360, no.2726; RG 80-8-0-804, no.6460. GRO, Reg. of births, Whitechapel (London), 22 Nov. 1855. *Globe*, 26 Oct. 1921. *Monetary Times* (Toronto), 27 Sept. 1913. *Ottawa Free Press*, 31 May 1875. *World* (Toronto), 28 April 1909. E. M. Ashworth, *Toronto Hydro recollections* (Toronto, 1955). Michael Bliss, *A Canadian millionaire: the life and business times of Sir Joseph Flavelle, bart., 1858–1939* (Toronto, 1978). *Canadian annual rev.*, 1901–17. Canadian Manufacturers' Assoc., *The Canadian Manufacturers' Association* ([Toronto, 1890?]); *Souvenir, 1893* (Toronto, 1892). *Canadian men and women of the time* (Morgan; 1898 and 1912). *Cyclopædia of Canadian biog.* (Rose and Charlesworth), vol.3. Merrill Denison, *The people's power: the history of Ontario Hydro* ([Toronto], 1960). *Directory*, Toronto, 1882–1913. *Encyclopaedia of Canadian biography.* ... R. B. Fleming, *The railway king of Canada: Sir William Mackenzie, 1849–1923* (Vancouver, 1991). *Industrial Canada* (Toronto), August, October 1913. Herbert Marshall *et al.*, *Canadian-American industry: a study in international investment* ([Toronto], 1976). Middleton, *Municipality of Toronto*. James Naylor, *The new democracy: challenging the social order in industrial Ontario, 1914–25* (Toronto, 1991). R. T. Naylor, *The history of Canadian business, 1867–1914*

(2v., Toronto, 1975). H. V. Nelles, *The politics of development: forests, mines & hydro-electric power in Ontario, 1849–1941* (Toronto, 1974). Ontario Manufacturers' Assoc., *Report of the proc. of the . . . annual meeting* ([Toronto?]), 1886–91. G. A. Seibel, *Ontario's Niagara parks, 100 years: a history*, ed. O. M. Seibel (Niagara Falls, Ont., 1985).

NICKAWA, FRANCES (baptized **Fanny Beardy**; also known as **Nai-ka-way-a** and **Ny-acka-way-a**) **(Mark)**, Cree performer and recitalist; b. *c.* July 1898, probably in Split Lake (Man.), daughter of Jack or Thomas Beardy and Betsy Necoway (Nickawa); m. 29 Jan. 1927 Arthur Russell Mark in Victoria; they had no children; d. 31 Dec. 1928 in Vancouver.

Frances Nickawa's people had long-standing connections with the fur trade around the major Hudson's Bay Company depot of York Factory (Man.). In the 1890s, however, York Factory lost importance. Around the time of Frances's birth, the Beardys moved inland to Split Lake. Frances's father died soon thereafter. On 2 April 1899 she was baptized by Cree Methodist minister Edward Paupanekis* in St John's (Anglican) Church at Split Lake as Fanny, the daughter of Jack and Betsy Beardy, although her adoptive mother would later refer to her father as Thomas Beardy.

In 1901 a staff member at the Methodist residential school in Norway House circulated her wish to adopt a Native child. The Reverend Charles George Fox, Church of England missionary at Split Lake, brought Fanny, with her mother's consent, to Norway House in October, but by then the teacher had adopted another. However, the school's sewing teacher, Hannah Tindall Riley, to whom Fanny had taken a liking, adopted her. Unmarried, English-born, and in her mid forties, she had joined the staff the previous year. On 25 Dec. 1901, Fox, Betsy Beardy, and Split Lake chief William Kitchekesik (Keche-kesik) signed an adoption agreement. The next month Hannah registered Fanny at the school as Frances Nickawa, using her mother's family name. She would later explain that a colleague had suggested the change because Beardy sounded like a nickname rather than a Native name. Hannah and Frances visited Winnipeg for the General Conference of the Methodist Church of Canada in September 1902. Frances read Psalm 2 to a large gathering in Grace Methodist Church and sang a hymn in Cree. Her self-possession and clear, ringing voice at age four much impressed the audience.

In June 1907 Riley took a position with the Alexandra Orphanage in Vancouver. Frances entered public school, where she experienced racial prejudice for the first time. The Reverend Egerton Ryerson Young, her biographer, would record, "Bravely she would say, 'I'm Indian; I'm Cree to the core, and I'm proud of it.' But her sensitive spirit was constantly harried by ignorant, brutal snobs." Riley left the orphanage in 1910

and she and Frances moved to Port Kells. Neither was in good health; Frances endured several leg operations to treat an injury which had occurred at Norway House. She became a popular soloist and reader at church events. When she was 15, she and Riley moved to South Vancouver. There, she entered elocution contests held by the Woman's Christian Temperance Union and won medals in 1914 and 1916. Studying elocution with theatre director and elocutionist Harold Nelson Shaw, she paid her way with sewing, secretarial service, and dog walking. Shaw was keenly supportive of her talents. The remarkable career of performer Emily Pauline Johnson*, of Mohawk and English origin, who had died in Vancouver in 1913, was surely on his mind. Sometime later he would describe Nickawa as "unusually gifted in the interpretation of the legends and character portrayals of the Indian race, especially those by the late Pauline Johnson."

In January 1919 Nickawa gave her first solo performance at Sixth Avenue Methodist Church in Vancouver. Then, invited to perform at a meeting of the British Columbia Conference in New Westminster, she recited from Johnson and others so effectively that many ministers asked her to visit their churches. In November 1919 she went on a three-month train tour with Riley, giving 18 recitals in cities from Vancouver to Winnipeg. Her style of presentation echoed Johnson's, but she did not compose her own works. The *Manitoba Free Press* described a typical program. First she appeared in a European-style white dress, reciting with "great versatility" pieces ranging from humorous to dramatic. Then she "donned Indian dress" that she had made herself, with "buckskin fringe and strings of gay beads," to recite from Johnson's poetry, Longfellow's *The song of Hiawatha*, and other works.

From September 1920, Nickawa and Riley toured for months at a time. On 24 March 1921 they reached Toronto, where Nickawa won great acclaim. There Ernest M. Sheldrick, musical editor of the *Christian Guardian*, heralded her as "a second Pauline Johnson" and "the embodiment of the Indian of the yesterdays." "A pure-blooded Cree of fine presence," he noted, "she possesses a beautiful speaking voice, which she uses with superb artistry." While in Ontario, she had her portrait painted by John Wycliffe Lowes Forster*.

On 28 July 1921, carrying a strong testimonial from the Toronto Conference, Nickawa and Riley sailed for Britain, where they spent the next year. The Reverend Samuel Dwight Chown*, general superintendent of the Methodist Church of Canada, arranged for her to perform at a large ecumenical conference. Recitals at churches and at the Canadian Club in London drew enthusiastic reviews, enhancing her fame in Canada when she returned in September 1922. In constant demand, she began to give several presentations a week. In February 1923 the Toronto periodical *Saturday Night* featured this "gifted interpreter of the poetry of her race," commending the "exceptional platform success" of this "fullblooded Cree Indian . . . an original Canadian." She received half the proceeds from each performance for income and expenses; the rest went for the support of church work.

Nickawa's only return to her homeland was in the summer of 1923. Methodist missionaries facilitated her travels to Norway House, Oxford House, and Cross Lake, where she performed with great effect, met relatives, and felt a range of emotions. "My life as a child came back slowly at first then . . . like a tornado uprooting all the works of civilization, where can your civilization fit in now? How does it make you feel toward your own people? It was like the tide rushing in on the sands of my life and washing away all signs of civilization that were not founded on Christ, that remained and stronger grew."

In September 1923 Nickawa suffered a breakdown and memory loss. Following a seemingly complete recovery, she and Riley sailed for Australia in March 1924 to undertake a tour; it was warmly received. Rounding the globe, they reached England the next July, where she gave additional performances. After their return to Ontario in December 1925, they again went on tour, recording 57 engagements from March through May 1926. In Vancouver that summer Nickawa met an English businessman, Arthur Russell Mark. They married on 29 Jan. 1927. Mark became her agent and together they resumed her recitals. In Ottawa in May 1928 Nickawa suffered a collapse and returned to Vancouver. After a long illness, she died on 31 December.

Like Johnson and other aboriginal performers of her day, Nickawa faced endless public demands for idealized Indians of yesteryear. She shunned commercialism, using the stage to support Methodist goals for Native missions and aid. Her early death was much mourned; as her biographer wrote, "The light that was in her went out with startling suddenness."

JENNIFER S. H. BROWN

[The author is grateful to the late Harold Egerton Young, of North York (Toronto), for sharing a copy of an unpublished typescript written by his father, Egerton Ryerson Young, probably in the 1930s, entitled "From wigwam to concert platform: the life of Frances Nickawa" (n.p.; copy in the possession of J. S. H. Brown), as well as copies of documents and letters collected by E. R. Young. Most of this material has been deposited in the UCC-C, Fonds 3431. The author would also like to thank R. M. Shirritt-Beaumont, of Winnipeg, for use of his unpublished compilation "Nakawao or Brown family" (updated 27 Sept. 2004), tracing the family back to the early 1800s. In addition, the author would like to acknowledge the assistance provided by Lacey Sanders in obtaining copies of the registration of Nickawa's baptism and her mother's remarriage (Anglican Church of Canada, Diocese of Keewatin Arch. (Keewatin, Ont.), St John's Church (Split Lake, Man.), Reg. of baptisms, 2 April 1899; Reg. of marriages, 13 Nov. 1906). J. W. L. Forster's portrait, *Frances Nickawa (Nyakawaya)*, is held by the Royal Ontario Museum (Toronto). J.S.H.B.]

BCA, GR-2951, no.1928-09-417422; GR-2962, no.1927-09-316920. LAC, RG 10, 4092, file 558902. *Manitoba Free Press*, 6 Dec. 1919. [E. M. Sheldrick], "A second Pauline Johnson: Frances Nickawa," *Christian Guardian*, 6 April 1921: 16. "Frances Nickawa: Cree girl who is a gifted interpreter of the poetry of her race," *Saturday Night*, 3 Feb. 1923: 12. *Voices from Hudson Bay: Cree stories from York Factory*, ed. and comp. Flora Beardy and Robert Coutts (Montreal, 1996).

NITAI'KIHTSIPIMI (One Spot, or One Spotted Horse), leader of the Six Mouths band of Blood Indians; b. *c.* 1848 in what is now southern Alberta, son of Ahksatosi (Good Sun); m. Natsikapawayaki (Double Striker), Pitsiksimatapiaki (Snake Body), Emonisaki (Otter Woman), Sikanaskinaiaki (Black Mouse Woman), and Asayikan; d. January 1928 on the Blood Indian Reserve, Alta.

One Spot's father was a relative of Red Crow [Mékaisto*], leader of the Fish Eaters band, but because he had a large number of followers, he separated in the mid 19th century to form his own band. One Spot became a warrior who was particularly praised for having saved his brother's life. They were involved in a skirmish with some Assiniboin and were retreating to the protection of a hill when the brother was wounded. One Spot stayed with him, shooting at the enemy and keeping them back until the other Blood had secured fortifications on the hill. Then, under the cover of their fire, he helped his brother to safety. His reputation was such that when his father died, One Spot became chief even though he was still in his twenties. He was probably the youngest person, at age 29, to sign Treaty No.7 in 1877.

Although the Six Mouths band had separated from the Fish Eaters, they maintained friendly relations and often camped together. Because of his youthfulness, One Spot was expected by the government to encourage farming and to keep young men from going to war. In 1885 he worked with Red Crow, who was by then the leading head chief of the tribe, to prevent young Blood from going on horse-raiding expeditions during the North-West rebellion. In 1886 Red Crow selected One Spot to travel with him to Ottawa and Brantford, Ont., during a tour provided to "loyal" chiefs. On their return, Indian agent William B. Pocklington wrote of One Spot, "His visit I am satisfied will be very beneficial as he probably has more influence over the young men than many of the others."

In 1887 One Spot accompanied his chief to make a peace treaty with the Assiniboin and Gros Ventre Indians. During negotiations at Fort Belknap (Belknap,

Mont.), he stated, "Red Crow is our head chief and I come next." Because of the attention he was receiving from Red Crow and the Indian agent, One Spot expected to be made head chief of the north camp of the Blood in the late 1880s. When that position went instead to Ksistsikoomina (Thunder Chief), he became embittered and joined with dissidents who were trying to challenge Red Crow's authority. At that time, the Indian agent called him a "Chronic grumbler & jealous of Head Chief."

As he grew older, One Spot withdrew from tribal politics and devoted his attention to ceremonial life. For example, in 1892, he vowed to make an offering to the Sun Spirit to ensure good health for his children and grandchildren. Former Indian agent Robert Nathanial Wilson witnessed the ceremony in which One Spot was painted from head to foot in red ochre, with black spots applied to his cheeks, nose, and chin, and black lines drawn around his wrists and face. After others in his family also were painted, One Spot produced a scarlet blanket decorated with eagle feathers and sage brush which was fastened to a tree and left as an offering.

One Spot's ceremonial dress was a combination of modern and traditional. He wore a tall silk hat, white shirt, government-issue military style coat, and beaded leggings and moccasins. In addition, he had "his face gaudily painted, his hair carefully braided, and ears adorned with ear rings." One Spot lost the use of one eye about the turn of the century, probably because of glaucoma which was prevalent in the tribe, and he became entirely blind a few years later.

As the older chiefs died, One Spot gained prestige because of his role in signing Treaty No.7. As early as 1907 a newspaper described him as a man "who has the distinction of being the only living Indian who signed the treaty of 1877." Because this pact was considered by the Indians to have been made with Queen Victoria herself, One Spot was selected in 1919 to meet her great-grandson the Prince of Wales during his Canadian tour. Although blind and incapacitated by age, One Spot helped fellow chief Mountain Horse to conduct a ceremony which made the prince an honorary chief. One Spot died in the week prior to 20 Jan. 1928 and was buried on the Blood reserve "with full Indian funeral honors."

HUGH A. DEMPSEY

[Details concerning One Spot and the Six Mouths band have been drawn from the author's interviews with Frank Red Crow in May 1954 and with Jack Low Horn on 21 July 1954. H.A.D.]

GA, M 4421, 285–91. LAC, RG 10, 1554: 740–41; 1555: 459; 3875, file 90299. *Calgary Herald*, 7 Aug. 1907, 20 Jan. 1928. *Lethbridge Herald* (Lethbridge, Alta), 4 Oct. 1919. H. A. Dempsey, *Red Crow, warrior chief* (Saskatoon, 1980).

NORTHWAY, JOHN, tailor, merchant, clothing manufacturer, and philanthropist; b. 17 Aug. 1848 at Leat Farm, near Lifton, England, son of Thomas Neathern Northway and Grace Doidge; m. 1 June 1871 Catherine McKay in Embro, Ont., and they had eight children; d. 6 Nov. 1926 in Toronto.

John Northway's father was a poor farmer in Devon; his mother's once prosperous father had fallen into alcoholism and tenancy. John was looked to as the instrument of the family's rehabilitation. A wilful and mischievous boy, he was removed from school at nine and apprenticed to a tailor for nine years, attempting once to cut off his thumb to escape his lot. In search of work in London, he became interested in ladies' tailoring, design, and merchandising. Faced with another long apprenticeship, however, he fled to New York in 1869.

After being robbed and paid for some piecework in worthless Confederate money, he moved in 1870 to Hamilton, Ont., but it, and then Toronto and London, proved little better than New York. Discouraged, he took an assistantship to a tailor in the village of Embro, near Woodstock. The other assistant was Scottish-born Kitty McKay; spirited, intelligent in her trade, and canny in finance, she would play a major role in Northway's success following their marriage. Embro was well positioned for Northway to root himself in Ontario's southwest: his understanding that Cleveland (on the opposite shore of Lake Erie) had eclipsed Toronto in determining the region's fashions gave him an edge.

On a joint salary of $12 weekly, Kitty saved $100, and in April 1873 the Northways opened a tailoring shop in Tilsonburg (Tillsonburg), one of the southwest's most enterprising towns. A Baptist, "Brother John" attached himself to its leaders, especially the dominant Baptists and Liberals. His growing custom led him to add dry goods, and he absorbed the stocks of merchants hit by the depression of the 1870s. His credit rating rose. In 1886 he hired an assistant, Robert Marshall Anderson, who became his partner three years later when he bought a failing store in Orillia and left "R.M." in charge at Tilsonburg. Northway's career centred on taking over ailing firms and turning them around; eventually he held stores at Tilsonburg, Orillia, Simcoe, Ingersoll, St Thomas, Ridgetown, Woodville, Toronto, Chatham, Brantford, Hamilton, and Stratford. He inspected them routinely, shifted his managers to enliven the retailing, convened regular consultations, fixed standards of staffing, purchasing, and merchandising, and skirted brokerage houses by buying in bulk in Europe and the United States, where he also sketched the latest fashions.

In 1893 Northway moved to Toronto in the hope of forming his own brokerage, the Merchant's Import Company. The move was premature, but when good times returned in 1895–96, he displaced the city's only maker of ladies' garments, Alexander and Anderson Limited; in 1898 he built a factory on Wellington Street, John Northway and Son Limited. There he designed and produced Northway mantles, coats, and (beginning in 1908) dresses and skirts, which he sold throughout Canada. He drew in his retail managers by granting them shares in the centralized firm chartered in 1900, the Northway Company Limited. In annual trips to the textile centre of Bradford, he observed the production methods and liberal employee policies of Sir Titus Salt and E. H. Gates and Company, two of Britain's most respected garment manufacturers. Northway's continued to grow. In 1903, on the urging of his partner-managers, he opened a retail outlet at 240–42 Yonge Street in Toronto. Although profits fell during a downturn in 1906–8, the store soon became a flourishing flagship. Because Northway specialized in womenswear, he did not consider himself to be in broad competition with the Eaton's and Simpson's department stores, but his strategy was plain: he countered Eaton's claim of "Big bargains developed by big business" with the "exclusive" quality of Northway's workmanship and fashions and the slogan "Style is a constant study in our designing rooms." By 1911 he was beginning to exhibit a preference for fresh American styling.

Northway's rise led to his appointment to the northern Ontario, wholesale dry goods, and waterfront development committees of the Toronto Board of Trade. The influence of its president, his friend, stockbroker Alfred Ernest Ames*, was also a factor. Northway was named a director of the powerful Imperial Bank of Canada in 1915, and became a member of the Canadian Manufacturers' Association. As is evidenced by trips to Florida, club memberships, and the purchase of a Cadillac and a house in the exclusive Rosedale neighbourhood, he had moved into a different world, and he ruefully recognized it.

With his businesses in good condition by 1910 – two of his sons would become presidents, John Alexander of Northway and Son in 1913 and Arthur Garfield of the Northway Company in 1918 – Northway pursued the education he had been denied as a child. Ill at ease in large gatherings, he recorded that he possessed "knowledge far too limited to appreciate." He began to read widely, religious studies at first and, later, works on the ancient world. In 1912 he and Kitty toured the Mediterranean and the Middle East; Egypt in particular caught his imagination. He made large contributions and endowed scholarships at McMaster, the Baptist university in Toronto, and at Brandon College in Manitoba, where he was counselled by President Howard Primrose Whidden*, a graduate of the liberal Chicago Theological Seminary and later chancellor of McMaster. In 1904 Mary Isabel Northway had married the Reverend Robert James Wilson, whose ministry and socially conscious training at the University of Chicago reinforced his father-in-law's growing theological and social liberalism. During a lengthy recuperation in 1920 from prostate surgery, Northway audited college courses in Florida and California on literature and history, including one on liberalism, socialism, and communism. He was ecstatic when the Tutankhamen finds in Egypt were announced in 1922. Northway had been intellectually and socially awakened.

These new interests led to his rupture with the fundamentalist preaching of Thomas Todhunter Shields* at Jarvis Street Baptist Church. In 1921 he joined the progressive Walmer Road Baptist, the pulpit of John MacNeill. Under the guidance of Whidden, MacNeill, and McMaster's Jones Hughes Farmer, another advocate of the Social Gospel and higher criticism of the Bible, Northway developed greater insight into his responsibilities as an employer. He had always been a benevolent figure, known to all as the Governor; now he added a deeper sense of stewardship. In his last years, despite the increasing pain of his cancer, he devoted himself to the charities of the day, but he paid special heed to his employees and McMaster's students and faculty and took innovative steps for their care. In 1913 he set up a "Special Wages Fund" for ailing and distressed workers in his factory. Four years later an "Employee Benefit Trust Fund" was established for the stores. In 1919, after reviewing the pension schemes of Sir Titus Salt and others, he introduced his own non-contributory plan. (Eaton's would not adopt a plan until 1949.) Northway died in 1926 and was interred in a mausoleum in Mount Pleasant Cemetery; he was survived by his wife, two daughters, and sons Jack and Garfield. From an estate valued at more than $1,816,000, he left a bequest to McMaster for needy theological students and challenged it with a $10,000 gift to initiate a pension plan, which it did.

From an intensive career spent building his own companies, Northway had grown to appreciate a broader world. Recognizing the problems of social reconstruction that followed the downturn of 1906–8 and World War I, he advanced a systematic approach to employee welfare and played no mean part in furthering industrial and business reform in labour matters.

ALAN WILSON

A fuller treatment of John Northway is available in the author's book *John Northway, a blue serge Canadian* (Toronto, 1965). The Northway papers are in the Trent Univ. Arch. (Peterborough, Ont.), 70-003, and a few papers are in the possession of the author.

AO, RG 22-305, no.55736; RG 80-5-0-25, 24: 456.

NY-ACKA-WAY-A. *See* NICKAWA, FRANCES

O

ODELL, ROBERTA ELIZABETH (Tilton), social reformer; b. 20 Sept. 1837 in Whiting, Maine, daughter of Daniel Ingalls Odell and Hannah Elizabeth Peavey; m. 11 Nov. 1858, in Eastport, Maine, John Tilton of Saint John; d. 28 May 1925 in Ottawa and was buried 1 June in Beechwood Cemetery there.

Roberta E. Tilton was an imposing figure of high Victorian Ottawa society. Tall, attractive, and energetic, she was a convincing writer and impressive public speaker in championing women's public role in society, and she helped to forge an enduring female culture through her work in several women's organizations.

She arrived in Ottawa in January 1868, her husband having abandoned his commercial business at Saint John in order to join the federal civil service. Her first known public involvement came in 1878, when she was elected first vice-president of the Ontario Woman's Christian Temperance Union. Three years later she became a founding member of the Ottawa WCTU; she was made president of this body and chair of its Sunday school department, both by acclamation. Devoted to the eradication of alcohol, tobacco, and violence against women and children, the WCTU quickly added to its mission the correction of a host of other social ills. Chief among its goals were the protection of the Christian family unit, the inculcation of a sense of personal and social responsibility in youth through education, and resistance to the hedonism associated with rampant commercialism and secularism.

Tilton was in the forefront of the movement. One of the public projects she promoted in this early period was the establishment of a coffee house in the By Ward Market, where alcoholic refreshments were distressingly bountiful. Even though her husband dismissed the plan as naive, she and her colleagues pushed the initiative through without any help from the WCTU's male advisers. "The ladies had but one mind and one object," she wrote, "to win souls." "Our minds had been fixed on the Master and his love, our object to win souls for Him." Raised in a Unitarian family, Tilton had joined the Church of England at the time of her marriage and her faith was grounded in Anglican evangelicalism. A true believer, she maintained, could aid in another's salvation by forcing a reckoning with sins committed and by creating the means to shun sin in the future.

Like other prominent local and provincial WCTU members, Tilton also served her organization at the dominion level, as superintendent of sabbath observance (1889), treasurer (1892–95), superintendent of soldiers and volunteer camps/militia (1895–97), and official auditor (1898–1901). She had introduced a department of narcotics to the provincial body in 1890 and served as its superintendent until 1891; in 1890 as well she was an Ontario delegate to the annual convention of the Dominion WCTU.

Tilton was also the main founder of the Woman's Auxiliary to the Missionary Society of the Church of England in Canada. She presented her proposal for the new body in April 1885 as the head of a seven-woman delegation to the management board of the church's Domestic and Foreign Missionary Society. In her words, "There are in the Church to-day Marys who have chosen the better part; there are the restless serving Marthas, who only want the opportunity to do something for Jesus; the Magdalens, who tell the story of our blessed Lord's resurrection; the Phoebes, who convey messages of love and Christian greeting; the Tryphenas, and Tryphosas, Dorcases, who are never weary in well doing . . . yes, in the Church of Canada – from Victoria to Sydney – there are women longing to labor more abundantly, to consecrate all their talents to the Lord's work." The board enthusiastically accepted the offer. Tilton was invited to be secretary of the auxiliary in the diocese of Ontario, the first branch to be established [see John Travers Lewis*]. She became corresponding secretary of the WA at the ecclesiastical provincial level when it was formed in 1886, and in 1891 was elected its president, a post she would occupy for a decade. Between 1902 and 1908 she served as president of the dominion auxiliary. Throughout this period she remained active in her diocesan body, where she accepted a number of executive roles. Under Tilton's leadership the WA supported a variety of causes but gradually came to specialize in support of missions and "lady missionaries" and especially in funding the education of missionaries' children who lived far from schools. It became the largest women's association within the Church of England in Canada – at her death it numbered around 70,000 in 3,000 branches – and remains the church's oldest continuous national organization.

When Tilton retired from the executive of the dominion WA in 1908, she was presented with a sizeable cash gift by the grateful organization. She decided to donate the money to support aged women missionaries. The Ottawa diocesan auxiliary, of which she had been a member since the diocese was formed in 1896, further honoured her after her death by the purchase in 1925 of a memorial house in her name as its headquarters. These marks of respect were bestowed in the full knowledge that Tilton had been instrumental in redefining the role of Anglican women. Formerly seen as adjuncts and helpmates in church activities defined for them, women through the auxiliary that Tilton had initiated insisted on their right to identify projects of special significance to other women and to find funding for those projects within their own membership.

Other Anglican women's organizations received the benefit of Tilton's leadership. In April 1889 she had reorganized the Ottawa branch of the Girls' Friendly Society in Canada. Ready and able to use the same strategies she had pioneered in creating, with the WA, a diocesan and ultimately a national organization of older women, she was eager to recreate a structure in which mature Christian women would mentor their younger sisters. Her leadership of the diocesan GFS demonstrates the interlocking nature of women's organizations which so characterized the period. For example, the GFS worked with several organizations in outfitting a room in the Children's Hospital and in providing volunteers and financial aid for the interdenominational mission in Anglesea Square. Its members worked with the Local Council of Women on various projects and benefited from speakers sent by the Young Women's Christian Association, where the director was a friend of Tilton's. Through her involvement with the Anglican diocesan Mothers' Union and Girls' Auxiliary, Tilton further strengthened networks of Christian women. Beyond the church, she was one of the founders of the National Council of Women of Canada, where she was to take a special interest in immigration; at the request of Lady Aberdeen [Marjoribanks*] she represented the GFS at the council's organizing meeting. She sat as well on the executive of the Local Council and of the Orphans' Home of the City of Ottawa, with its Refuge Branch for aged women.

Tilton's husband, John, who had risen to become a deputy minister and had served as commander of the Governor General's Foot Guards, predeceased her in 1914. At some point they had adopted a son, baptized Silas, who had died before reaching manhood. In her journal for 1912 Tilton marked his birthday, noting that, had he been spared, "he would have been married and had children probably & that would have been a great pleasure to us all." "But," she added, "I do not doubt that God did what was best." After a full and dutiful life, she herself died in May 1925. She had earned the commendation to which the WA as a whole aspired: "She hath done what she could, not what she would like to do, nor what others thought she ought to do, but *what she could*." Her life of service is commemorated by the Anglican Church of Canada on 30 May.

SHARON ANNE COOK

Anglican Church of Canada, Diocese of Ottawa Arch., Girls' Friendly Soc. and Ottawa Diocesan Council, minute-book, 1894; General Synod Arch. (Toronto), GS 76-15 (Woman's Auxiliary papers), R. E. Tilton, journals. AO, F 885, MU 8397–98, 8406–7, 8425.10; RG 80-8-0-988, no.9405. LAC, RG 31, C1, 1901, Ottawa, B, 4: 23, no.39 (mfm. at AO). *Ottawa Citizen*, 29 May 1925. Church of England in Canada, Board of Domestic and Foreign Missions, Woman's Auxiliary, *Letter leaflet* (Toronto), November 1896. S. A. Cook, "To 'bear the burdens of others profitably': the changing role of women in the diocese of Ottawa, 1896–1996," in *Anglicanism in the Ottawa valley*, ed. F. A. Peake (Ottawa, 1997), 129–53. Mrs Willoughby Cummings [E. A. McC. Shortt], *Our story: some pages from the history of the Woman's Auxiliary to the Missionary Society of the Church of England in Canada, 1885 to 1929* (Toronto, [1929?]). Key Eliot, "History of the Woman's Auxiliary in Carleton deanery" (typescript, Ottawa, 1957; copy in Anglican Church of Canada, Diocese of Ottawa Arch.). National Council of Women of Canada, *Year book* (Ottawa; Toronto). *Vital statistics from N.B. newspapers* (Johnson), 17, no.864. [L. C. W.], *Sketch of the life and work of Roberta E. Tilton, by one of her first W.A. members* ([Ottawa?], n.d.).

OLIVER, JOHN, farmer, office holder, and politician; b. 31 July 1856 in Hartington, England, son of Robert Oliver and Emma Lomas, a widow; m. 20 June 1886 Elizabeth Woodward in Mud Bay, B.C., and they had five sons and three daughters; d. 17 Aug. 1927 in Victoria.

The eldest of Robert and Emma Oliver's eight children (his mother had a son from her first marriage), John Oliver grew up in an English farming community, where his family eked out a modest living. He left school at age 11 to work in a local lead mine. A few years later, when the mine closed, the Oliver family emigrated to Canada, settling on a farm in Maryborough Township, Ont., in 1870. Five years after their arrival, Emma Oliver contracted rheumatic fever and died. Her death evidently had a significant impact on the family, since members soon began to leave the farm. John stayed in the vicinity for over a year before deciding, at age 20, to travel west. On 5 May 1877 he arrived in Victoria, looking for work. He found it on the mainland of British Columbia with a survey crew of the Canadian Pacific Railway. After a summer of hard labour, he had saved enough money to start a farm, so he pre-empted land in Surrey.

While building a cabin and clearing land, Oliver was drawn to community affairs. He helped to establish a rural school and he petitioned the provincial government for assistance with roads in the recently settled district. At age 26 he was appointed clerk of the municipality; he also served as tax collector and general functionary. In the fall of 1882 he resigned his positions, sold his land, and purchased a farm in Delta. Four years later he married Elizabeth Woodward, a daughter of the local postmaster. They would raise five sons and three daughters, while developing one of the most prosperous farms in the region. Oliver also earnestly applied himself to municipal affairs in Delta. He became a school trustee and a few years later he was elected to the municipal council; he served two terms as reeve.

Although Oliver loved rural life, he had set his sights on higher public office. At age 43, he took a long-contemplated step into provincial politics by running in the election of June 1900. At the time, politics in British Columbia were characterized by intense factionalism and the absence of formal parties. On 28 February Joseph MARTIN had assumed the premiership, though with little support. Surprisingly, Oliver threw his lot in with Martin's forces and campaigned aggressively in Westminster-Delta. On 9 June the Martinites went down to a crushing defeat, electing only 6 members to a house of 38. Oliver experienced his first important political triumph, however, winning in his riding.

Oliver's introduction to the rough-and-tumble of British Columbia politics was neither kind nor gentle. A plain-spoken, rough-hewn man, he was derided as a hayseed by the more urbane and experienced members of the assembly. His unsophisticated clothes, heavy boots, and often crude use of the English language were lampooned by opponents. The Victoria *Week* described him in 1905 as "a good farmer and a weak politician, given to long-winded and very ungrammatical attacks upon anyone who does not agree with him." This criticism did not dampen his spirits; rather, he became even more determined to show that an ordinary man could make a contribution to the democratic process. He studied parliamentary procedure and, over time, he made the transition from municipal to provincial politics, carefully choosing the causes that he championed in the assembly.

During the first decade of the 20th century the province moved towards formal adoption of the party system. By aligning himself with Martin, Oliver had identified himself as a Liberal, in opposition to the government of millionaire coalminer James Dunsmuir*, which was Conservative in all but name. Certainly, Oliver was an anti-establishment figure, yet his own brand of liberalism was shaped by his rural conservative roots. He earned the nickname Honest John for his principled pursuit of a legislative inquiry in 1902–3 into railway land grants that helped to bring down the government of Dunsmuir's successor, Edward Gawler Prior, in June 1903. Richard McBride*, who formed the next government, immediately called an election and announced that it would be the first in British Columbia to be fought along party lines. Even though Oliver had had a falling-out with Martin, there was little doubt that he would campaign as a Liberal. On 3 Oct. 1903 he was returned in Delta with an increased majority. He would serve as part of the Liberal opposition led by James Alexander Macdonald*. McBride became the first premier in British Columbia to hold office under the Conservative banner.

While a member of the opposition, Oliver developed a reputation as a forceful politician. A colourful and folksy figure, he took great pride in his increasing comfort as an MLA and as the opposition's watchdog. Meanwhile, McBride, who held office during a period of economic growth, increased his popularity. His Conservatives were handily re-elected in the provincial election of 2 Feb. 1907. Once again Oliver retained Delta. The Liberal opposition was dispirited by McBride's triumph and lacked the resources to hold a popular government accountable. Even more discouraging was the failure of the federal Liberals to offer any help. In desperation Oliver wrote to Prime Minister Sir Wilfrid Laurier* in June 1909, stating that the provincial Liberal party "would much prefer to fight than to lie down but . . . the latter course appears to be the only one open to us." Oliver sought visits from federal cabinet ministers and, most of all, newspapers with a Liberal bias. "We have an unscrupulous government with a large amount of money at their disposal and with full control of eighty per cent of the newspapers of the Province with an organization in full working order." Laurier responded, but only with words of encouragement, counselling that "it would be a mistake to lose heart."

In the fall of 1909 Macdonald was appointed to the bench, creating a vacancy in the position of provincial Liberal leader. Oliver had emerged as his chief lieutenant and was the obvious choice for the uncoveted post. Reluctant to assume the position, he told Laurier, who had encouraged him to seek the job, that "it is not a desirable thing to fall heir to at this juncture with the prospect of going into a fight crippled and almost helpless." Nevertheless, mounting pressure and the absence of any other candidate compelled him to reconsider. He became leader with insufficient time to prepare for the general election, called for 25 Nov. 1909. A vociferous critic of the government's railway policy, he decided to make it the centrepiece of his campaign. He disapproved of the recently negotiated contract with the Canadian Northern Railway for a line from the Alberta border to Vancouver, arguing that the province was not obliged to assist a private railway and that the details of the contract should have been made public before the election.

The Conservatives, who waged an aggressive campaign, won 38 of the 42 seats. They would face an opposition of two Liberals, Harlan Carey Brewster* and John Jardine, and two Socialists, James Hurst HAWTHORNTHWAITE and Parker Williams. For the first time in almost a decade, Oliver would not sit in the legislature; he lost in the two ridings he had contested, Delta and Victoria. There were reports that $60,000 had been spent to defeat him. Of course, Oliver had not expected to dislodge the Conservatives, but neither had he anticipated a rout and a personal defeat. The day after the election he declared that he was "out of politics for good." As the drubbing was absorbed, however, it was clear that he had not lost his

Oliver

passion for public life. Initially, he returned to his farm and to local affairs in Delta; he was elected a school trustee and later served again as reeve. In the federal election of 1911 he stood as a Liberal in New Westminster. He went down to defeat with the Laurier government.

Early in 1912 McBride called a provincial election. With increased public revenues and little opposition, the Conservatives were poised for another easy victory. In fact, the incumbent in Delta, Conservative Francis James Anderson Mackenzie, pointed to the government's plan to spend $85,000 on public works in the constituency during the forthcoming year, as opposed to the mere $15,000 that had been spent in the last year that Oliver represented the riding. On 28 March 1912 Oliver suffered another political setback and the Liberal party was completely shut out of the legislature. It was difficult to believe that there was a future for the Liberal party in the province. Oliver's political career and dreams of higher public office were seemingly finished.

Within a few years, and after more than a decade in office, the Conservatives started to run out of steam. The provincial economy was unable to sustain rapid levels of growth and headed into a recession as World War I broke out. More troubling for the provincial government were the charges of corruption levelled at it. On 15 Dec. 1915 McBride surprised many by resigning the premiership. He was replaced by the energetic but dour William John Bowser*, who would preside over a sinking ship. In the spring of 1916 two Liberals, including Brewster, the new party leader, won by-elections. When Bowser took his flagging Tories to the polls late in the summer he faced a more organized Liberal party with some new, reformist ideas. On 14 Sept. 1916 Oliver was successful in Dewdney as part of an impressive electoral victory; 36 Liberals, 9 Conservatives, and 2 independents were chosen. The Liberals began a quarter century in which they would be the dominant force in British Columbia's politics.

Oliver was appointed by Brewster, the new premier, to two cabinet positions, agriculture and railways, on 29 November. In both portfolios he applied himself keenly, inspired by the reforming impulse associated with the Liberal victory. Agriculture was a natural choice for him. He took great pride in his understanding of the challenges faced by farmers and he believed that a strong agricultural sector was vital to the province's future. He also concerned himself with the soldiers who would return from the war and wanted to ensure that they would have the opportunity to own and develop farms in rural areas of the province. "Thinking over these problems in the night," wrote his biographer, "an idea occurred to him. He got out of bed, and sitting in his nightshirt . . . he drew up the 'Land Settlement [and Development] Act.'" This landmark legislation, passed in 1917, would be dubbed the "nightshirt" act. Oliver successfully urged the federal government to establish a national policy for the settlement of returning soldiers.

The railway portfolio allowed Oliver to pursue one of his abiding political interests, railway subsidies. His most pressing concern was the fate of the troubled Pacific Great Eastern Railway, a privately promoted scheme closely associated with the Conservative government. The PGER had never fulfilled its objective of establishing a north-south line to serve the province. At one point Oliver went so far as to proclaim in the legislature that he was "not going to become the foster-father of this illegitimate offspring of two unnatural parents. It was a waif left on my doorstep. It was conceived in the sin of political necessity; it was begotten in the iniquity of a half-million dollar campaign fund. I refuse to be the godfather of any such foundling." Despite the declaration, Oliver initiated an investigation into the railway's finances and negotiated its purchase. The criticism he received from the press for his actions made him extremely indignant. He had never evinced a great fondness for the line and he claimed to have "sweat blood" in order to achieve the best possible terms for the province.

Oliver had already established himself as one of Brewster's chief lieutenants when the premier died on 1 March 1918. In the party caucus that followed four days later, Oliver was elected leader of the Liberal party and on 6 March he became premier. He would hold the reins of power, in his distinctively rustic fashion, for almost a decade. He was to retain the agriculture portfolio until April 1918 and the railway portfolio until October 1922. He chose a number of competent ministers to serve in his cabinet; three of them, John Duncan MacLean*, Thomas Dufferin Pattullo*, and John Hart*, would later serve as premiers.

British Columbians seemed comforted by their new, plain-spoken premier, whose personal habits were largely unaffected by the trappings of office. Oliver continued to wear the same old-fashioned tweed suits and heavy boots that had become his trade marks. "Doff your broadcloth and don your overalls," he instructed a large delegation from the province's municipalities soon after assuming office, urging them to assume responsibility for their overspending. He portrayed himself as a man of the people, distrustful of experts and wholly lacking in pretence. This populist style of politics would be his strength and it had great appeal in a province that had grown apprehensive about its future.

When Oliver became premier, World War I was coming to an end. Over the next few years, instead of accepting the government's programs to develop farms, veterans poured into the province's urban and industrial centres. The new premier was sadly disappointed with this result. His government had attempted to deal with the challenges anticipated in the post-war period by introducing social legislation that limited work to an eight-hour day in certain industries, improved working conditions, and provided a minimum wage for women. It moved as well to establish mothers' pensions in 1920, provide maintenance for deserted wives, and improve both health and educational services. Legislation to regulate public utilities and impose controls on the forest industry was also passed. All of these initiatives were based on the belief that direct government intervention was the best way to deal with the problems that beset the province.

The bright burst of reform was insufficient to quell social and economic turmoil, however. To Oliver's chagrin, farmers were agitating against the government, having formed their own political party, the United Farmers of British Columbia, in 1917. The first years of Oliver's premiership were also ones of labour militancy; many workers struck in sympathy with those involved in the Winnipeg General Strike of 1919 [see Mike Sokolowiski*]. In addition to these troubles, the premier acquired some notoriety in the libel case concerning the Dolly Varden mine when he sued the mining company's lawyer for suggesting that he was involved in private land speculation. He eventually won, but was awarded only a token amount in damages. The court decided that Honest John had neither lost his reputation nor suffered from the accusation.

Oliver's leadership of the Liberal party was the subject of criticism. Some Liberals argued that he should have promptly submitted his selection as party leader to the electorate for endorsement. In June 1920 he responded to this pressure, calling an election for 1 December. Women would be casting ballots for the first time in British Columbia and Oliver had been advised that an earlier date in the autumn would be inconvenient for them because it coincided with church fairs and the making of preserves. As it turned out, he had more to worry about than the newly enfranchised women. His government was under attack from resurgent Conservatives and an array of parties and candidates representing labour, farmers, and veterans. His election manifesto asked voters to let the Liberals continue their "safe, sane and progressive administration." The premier focused his campaign on the building of roads to open up the rural areas of the province – a theme that would become a constant feature of politics in British Columbia for the next half century.

The Oliver government barely survived, winning a slim majority, 25 seats out of 47. Under Bowser's aggressive leadership, the Conservatives won 15 seats. Joining them in opposition was a motley group of Labour and independent members. The Liberals' support came primarily from the urban centres. Oliver, who had won in both Delta and Victoria, chose to represent the capital. The election of 1920 signalled

a shift in direction for the Liberal government. The hard-fought campaign had been won by Oliver largely because of the fragmented opposition. Entering a new decade with a tenuous grip on power, he was forced to contend with dissent within his party. Although his cabinet boasted a number of strong ministers, he was criticized as "bossy" and was inclined to function as a one-man government. He suffered resignations, including, in November 1921 that of Mary Ellen Smith [Spear*], the first woman elected to the assembly, and in 1924 that of his finance minister, Hart. The premier fought the Vancouver Liberals' audible mutterings that "Oliver must go." The younger, more urbane forces in the party were clearly tiring of their grandfatherly farmer-premier.

In this hostile environment, Oliver retreated into a careful, almost tentative, mode of governance. The reform impulse associated with the Brewster–Oliver administration dwindled. The 1920s were an economically uncertain decade. Oliver grew even more cautious when it became evident that revenue from resource industries such as forestry could not be counted on to support an expensive agenda of social initiatives. The premier's enthusiasm for reform also diminished because the external challenges to his government increasingly came from the right wing of the political spectrum and from the business community. This situation was highlighted by the formation of a new political force in 1923. Led by Vancouver millionaire Major-General Alexander Duncan McRae* and by Sir Charles Hibbert TUPPER, the Provincial party called for an end to waste in government and the termination of the party system; its interests were those of big business, not the disadvantaged of society. In many other ways the business community expressed its lack of support for the Oliver government. For instance, through 1923 and 1924 the forest industry waged a public battle with the government over its proposals to raise the royalties charged to forest companies. The Timber Industries Council, a powerful lobby group, was eventually able to persuade it to back away from this initiative.

Among the numerous issues that beset Oliver was the liquor question. Through a referendum on 20 Oct. 1920, the province had rejected Prohibition in favour of government-controlled sale of alcohol, although this solution was controversial even within the Liberal party. For example, in 1921 Liberal MLA Henry George Thomas Perry objected to the government profiting from the sale of alcohol, warning that "British Columbia should not become a second Monte Carlo, or the Premier of the Province another Prince of Monaco." The Government Liquor Act, adopted later that year, provided for the sale of alcoholic beverages in government stores, which became known as John Oliver's drug stores, but not in bars or saloons.

The premier managed to keep his party under control and shrugged off the attacks of the combined opposition forces, but his government's prospects appeared bleaker as his term wore on. He had hoped that the return of a Liberal government to Ottawa in 1921, under William Lyon Mackenzie King*, would assist his beleaguered administration. The federal Conservatives had granted scant consideration to his pleas for revisions to railway freight rates. King, although sympathetic, provided little in the way of practical benefit. As Oliver began to contemplate the discomfort of another provincial election campaign, he bravely reported to King, "I am optimistic and if I have to go down, I will go down fighting and with the flag flying."

The lack of favourable reaction from the new Liberal government in Ottawa, combined with intense pressures at home, produced in Oliver the new battle cry "Fight Ottawa." Since the federal government would not assist British Columbia with helpful railway policies or better terms on a range of other issues, Oliver increasingly gave vent to strong words on provincial rights. In moments of sheer frustration, he even went so far as to question his citizenship. "I have never advocated separation, but if the grossly unjust treatment Western Canada is subjected to in favour of Eastern Interests is to be continued indefinitely, then I do not want to call myself a Canadian."

Oliver took this aggressive posture into the provincial election, called for 20 June 1924. It was a bitterly fought contest. Voters were confused and so were the results. After a number of recounts it became clear that the leaders of all three major parties, including Oliver, had been defeated. The Liberals won 23 seats, the Conservatives 17. The Provincial and Labour parties each elected three members and the house would include two independent MLAs as well. With the support of less than a third of the electorate, the Liberals could form a minority government, but the two right-of-centre parties combined had received nearly 54 per cent of the votes cast.

Believing his leadership had provided the key to the Liberal party's bare survival, Oliver stayed on. He won a by-election in Nelson on 23 August and governed by a fragile thread with the support of independent and Labour members of the house. It was hardly a situation to produce vigorous government; in fact, the reform impulse completely faded away. The premier tried to invigorate his party by launching another campaign for lower freight rates. In 1925 he was able to secure a reduction in the rate for grain. This victory enabled him to assist the Liberals in the federal election of 1926. When the Liberal representation from British Columbia in the House of Commons dropped from three in 1925 to one in 1926, it left the premier "very blue."

An improving economy made the last part of the decade somewhat sweeter. Oliver continued his efforts to move construction of the PGER forward against opposition charges of incompetence and corruption, and he survived the royal commission re campaign funds, an investigation in 1927 into allegations that liquor interests had funnelled contributions to the Liberals. In spite of continuing challenges from within his party, he firmly held the reins of leadership. In 1926 he had celebrated his 70th birthday; he was the oldest government leader in Canada. The last session of the legislature with Oliver as premier, which ended on 7 March 1927, was marked by the passage of the Old-age Pension Act. The premier considered it to be among the most important pieces of legislation he had sponsored. In addition to promoting the measure, his party adopted a new program for reform that year, marking a return to the concern for social issues that had characterized Oliver's first mandate. His final year as premier was notably busy. He travelled to Ottawa to lobby the federal government once again on railway issues. He also toured the interior of the province, attending various ceremonies. These activities seemed to take their toll. After he fell ill, his doctors sent him in May 1927 to the Mayo Clinic in Rochester, Minn., where an exploratory operation determined that he had incurable cancer.

John Oliver returned to British Columbia and called a caucus meeting in July, during which he tearfully offered his resignation as party leader and premier. His colleagues refused to accept it, urging him stay on. He agreed, but only on the condition that J. D. MacLean, his long-time lieutenant, be named premier designate. Oliver died in Victoria, aged 71. He lay in state in the legislative chamber that he had dominated for so many years and was given an official funeral. A populist political leader, he had strengthened and consolidated the provincial Liberal party and established a folksy, yet combative style of leadership that would be emulated by British Columbia premiers for generations to come.

DAVID MITCHELL

LAC, MG 26, G; J. *Brief record of the Oliver government* ([Victoria], 1920). *Electoral hist. of B.C.* Robin Fisher and David Mitchell, "Patterns of provincial politics since 1916," in *The Pacific province: a history of British Columbia*, ed. H. J. M. Johnston (Vancouver and Toronto, 1996), 254–72. S. W. Jackman, *Portraits of the premiers: an informal history of British Columbia* (Sydney, B.C., 1969). James Morton, *Honest John Oliver: the life story of the Honourable John Oliver, premier of British Columbia, 1918–1927* (London, 1933). M. A. Ormsby, *British Columbia: a history* ([Toronto], 1958). Martin Robin, *The rush for spoils: the company province, 1871–1933* (Toronto, 1972).

O'NEILL, MARGARET (baptized **Marguerite Neill**), named **Mother Agatha**, teacher and member of the Institute of the Blessed Virgin Mary in America (the Loretto sisters); b. 21 Sept. 1842 in Toronto, daughter of Thomas O'Neill (Neill) and Jane Ash; d. there 4 Feb. 1927.

Margaret O'Neill was a teacher whose devotion to education left a considerable legacy for the Catholic women of Ontario. Little is known about her family background. Married in Toronto in 1836, her parents were Irish; her father, who may have been a labourer, was from Queen's (Laois) County. The widowed Jane O'Neill who was a huckster at the St Lawrence Market in 1862–63 was likely her mother. Five sisters would survive Margaret. She attended the Toronto Normal School between 1861 and 1863, and graduated with a first-class certificate. It was here that she met second master John Herbert Sangster, who is described in an obituary as her mentor. She entered the Institute of the Blessed Virgin Mary in Hamilton on 21 Nov. 1866 and received the habit at Loretto House in Toronto on 6 May 1867, taking the religious name of Agatha. She made her vows on 12 Aug. 1869.

When Margaret entered the Institute it was under the leadership of Mother Teresa [Ellen Dease*]. It had been brought to Toronto to provide education for the daughters of Catholics who could afford private schooling. Along with their select school, the Loretto sisters, as was their custom, set up schools for the less fortunate. In 1874 Mother Teresa established a school in Lindsay, Ont., where young women would be prepared to write the examinations of the provincial Department of Education. Its opening marked the beginning of the Loretto community's involvement in accredited education and represented a significant shift for the Institute. To teach in Lindsay the nuns had to be professionally qualified. Recognized as having the credentials and experience that would allow her to move into a new realm of endeavour, Mother Agatha was one of the nuns chosen. She was highly determined – in early 1875 she lost a hand to blood poisoning but learned to write with her left hand. In 1880 she was sent to Guelph where, as principal, she presided the following year over the first conferral of certificates of matriculation at the Loretto school there. The length of her stay in Guelph is unclear, as are the dates of her teaching assignments elsewhere. She may have been at St Helen's Separate School in Toronto in 1904–5. In 1877 she had participated for the first time in the governance of the community; she was then superior of a house and thus attended the general chapter as a delegate. She took part in the chapters of 1889 and 1910, again as a local superior. In 1901 she was elected a consultrix (assistant) to the mother general and continued in that capacity until 1919.

It was the convergence of Mother Agatha's concern for education and her participation in leadership that allowed her to advance the academic cause of women, both nuns and laywomen. At some point – at least by 1909 – she was given the responsibility of overseeing the educational preparation of the members of the Institute, a task that brought her into correspondence with officials in the Department of Education, notably deputy minister Arthur Hugh Urquhart Colquhoun and superintendent John Seath*. From the time the nuns had gone to Lindsay, the issue of the qualifications of nuns and religious brothers had been generating intense debate [see James Francis WHITE]. Women entering the Institute were expected to teach, frequently before they had been adequately trained. Often the demands of teaching and of religious life combined to make it difficult for them to achieve the level of competence to which they aspired. Mother Agatha fought for her sisters to have time to study, and she is remembered in the community for her stance in this regard.

From 1908 there is evidence that Mother Agatha was also engaged in the community's struggle to establish a college for Catholic women at the University of Toronto. It was during the tenure of Mother General Stanislaus Liddy that Mother Agatha's years of negotiation with the university and the Catholic college there, St Michael's, bore fruit. In October 1911 an agreement was concluded between St Michael's and the two Catholic women's schools in Toronto, Loretto Abbey and St Joseph's Academy, with students to be formally enrolled in St Michael's. Loretto College opened its doors in 1912 with 15 students under Mother Estelle Nolan and the first class graduated in 1915. It was seen as a crowning achievement for the community, particularly for those who cherished a vision of the highest possible education for women. A beneficiary of Mother Agatha's insistence on education was Mother Margarita [Mary Cecilia O'Connor*], the college's dean from 1914 and an outspoken advocate of giving the nuns extended periods of time for study.

In a pamphlet entitled *An old song in new meters*, published in Toronto in 1924 by another member of the Institute, the author mused about the role of women. She agreed with Cardinal James Gibbons, who lamented that "undue stress [had been placed] on the admirable and tender qualities of . . . women" but that sufficient attention had not been given to "the strong and robust points of their character." This could have been written with Mother Agatha in mind. She died at Loretto Abbey in 1927 and was buried in Mount Hope Cemetery. Her strength had been her dedication to education through her community, where she became known as one who "laboured for forty untiring years to advance the certificate and university studies in schools and among the teachers of the Community, undaunted by differing views and oft-recurring obstacles."

BARBARA COOPER

One Spot

AO, RG 2-128-1-2: 15, 24, 34, 48; RG 2-128-4-1; RG 2-128-6-1–2; RG 80-8-0-1050, no.1752. Arch. of the Roman Catholic Archdiocese of Toronto, Religious orders fonds, Loretto sisters (IBVM), University affiliation, 1911–13. Institute of the Blessed Virgin Mary (Loretto) Arch. (Toronto), Loretto College files; Loretto School records, Guelph, Ont., and Lindsay, Ont.; Mother Agatha O'Neill file; Mother Margarita O'Connor, personal papers. St Paul's Roman Catholic Church (Toronto), Reg. of baptisms, 9 Oct. 1842 (mfm. at Arch. of the Roman Catholic Archdiocese of Toronto). *Globe*, 5 Feb. 1927. M. G. A. [Mother Agatha Allison], *An old song in new meters* (Toronto, 1924). E. M. Brewer, *Nuns and the education of American Catholic women, 1860–1920* (Chicago, 1987). Barbara Cooper, "'That we may attain to the end we propose to ourselves': the North American Institute of the Blessed Virgin Mary, 1932–1961" (PHD thesis, York Univ., Toronto, 1989). Sister Mary Aloysius Kerr, *Dictionary of biography of the Institute of the Blessed Virgin Mary in North America: lives of the members of the Institute of the Blessed Virgin Mary in North America from its beginnings in 1847 to 1983* (Toronto, 1984). F. A. Walker, *Catholic education and politics in Ontario* ... (3v., Toronto, 1955–87; vols.1–2 repr. 1976), 3.

ONE SPOT (One Spotted Horse). *See* NITAI'KIHTSIPIMI

OPILIUS ELIAS, Brother. *See* PHANEUF

OSLER, Sir EDMUND BOYD, businessman, politician, and philanthropist; b. 20 Nov. 1845 near Bond Head, Upper Canada, fourth son of the Reverend Featherstone Lake Osler* and Ellen Free Pickton; m. first 1868 Isabella Lammond Smith (d. 1871), and they had two children who died in infancy; m. secondly 3 Sept. 1873 Anne Farquharson Cochran (d. 1910) in Balfour, Aberdeenshire, Scotland, and they had three daughters and three sons; d. 4 Aug. 1924 in Toronto.

Unlike his brothers, Edmund Boyd Osler chose to forgo university and face the world with the education he received from his parents and the grammar school in Dundas, Upper Canada, where his father was the Anglican rector. In the late 1850s, still little more than a boy, he took a job at the Bank of Upper Canada, which was struggling with bad railway and land loans exposed by economic depression. Its demise in 1866 laid bare the price of mismanagement, a lesson Osler carried with him when he joined with fellow employee Henry Pellatt to launch a firm in Toronto that offered stockbroking, investing, and insurance services.

The new partners rode confederation's wave of optimism to some success, and Osler gained a reputation as an enterprising and trustworthy broker. It was likely his standing that attracted a group of promoters trying to establish the Dominion Bank in 1869 and raise $400,000 in capital. When asked to find subscribers, Osler accepted the challenge. He understood the importance of the business connections offered by the Dominion's principal founders, among them Whitby businessman James Holden, and saw too that financing for his own firm might be obtained by cultivating a close relationship with the new bank. His enthusiasm, however, was not enough to raise the capital. The bank's promoters were themselves divided over whether to buy the Royal Canadian Bank, which was in trouble but had established branches and customers, or to build from the ground up. By 1870 the Royal Canadian was off the seller's block and the Dominion's promoters were again searching for capital.

A break appeared when a dispute erupted between William McMaster*, the president of the Canadian Bank of Commerce, and James Austin*, a leading director. Austin resigned and was soon approached by Holden to support the Dominion; by 1871 the bank had opened with Austin as president. Osler became a shareholder but, more important, he was now connected to an influential network of contacts, especially Austin, who was impressed by this aspiring financier and appears to have been his mentor. Osler in turn learned how a sound reputation could win the confidence of nervous investors.

Just as timely for Osler was the combination of large increases in banking capital and the development of an unprecedented level of share issues on the Toronto market. In September 1871 Pellatt and Osler joined the newly reorganized Stock Exchange Association. The firm published weekly stock and bond market reports, which provide some insight into its operations and Osler's milieu. In 1874 the firm was enlarged to include Pellatt's son Henry Mill* and Augustus Meredith NANTON.

During the trading boom of the 1870s Osler built a good business, gradually generated some wealth, and settled into Toronto's elite. He began to associate his name and fund-raising talents with such public causes as the fledgling Hospital for Sick Children, which made him a trustee in 1878. Through much of his early years, it is not hard to imagine, Osler found success partly through his father, who had ties with the city's Anglican establishment. What is certain is that his relationship with Austin flourished. Austin secured a directorship for him at the Dominion Bank after Holden's death in October 1881. The position allowed Osler greater access to bank financing and gave standing to his new brokerage, Osler and Hammond, which he established in 1882 with Herbert Carlyle Hammond, former cashier of the Bank of Hamilton.

Osler's capitalist activities sky-rocketed in the 1880s. He was quick to pursue interests that must have seemed the future of such a large country, especially western land development, railways, and navigational ventures. In 1882, for instance, he was a founder and the managing director of the Ontario and Qu'Appelle Land Company Limited. His first railway undertaking, that same year, was the Winnipeg Street Railway, a scheme largely devised by Austin and his son Albert William*. Osler's job was financing. When he succeeded, interest in his abilities grew in Canada's other commercial centre, Montreal. Soon he was advising George STEPHEN, a member of the syndicate responsible for building the Canadian Pacific Railway. The railway company sold a major portion of its western land grants in 1882 to a group of capitalists headed by Osler and William Bain Scarth*. A founder of the Canada Southern Steamboat Company Limited in 1883, Osler had also begun investing large sums in railway schemes in Ontario, where his expertise and connections brought him the presidency of the Ontario and Quebec Railway. Its takeover by the CPR in 1885 gave him a seat on the board of the transcontinental. Associated with a promising national railway system, he concentrated increasingly on western projects and the development of his Winnipeg branch, Osler, Hammond, and Nanton, which had been launched in 1884 by his protégé A. M. Nanton.

Osler staked the future of his wealth and business on western development and invested in land that promised to appreciate in value when railways reached across the dominion. The CPR's completion in 1885 began the process that Osler envisioned and by 1896, when economic conditions dramatically improved and settlement was made more attractive, Osler began to realize profits from his real estate ventures. Newcomers needed land and an array of financial services, an opportunity not missed by Osler and Hammond, which developed a network that linked British and eastern Canadian investors with western borrowers. The North of Scotland Canadian Mortgage Company Limited, the Canada North-West Land Company, the Dominion Bank, and to a lesser degree the Trusts Corporation of Ontario all facilitated this flow of money. Branches of the Dominion Bank were opened after the turn of the century at points where Osler had business ties, while Osler, Hammond, and Nanton managed institutional investments in western mortgages and debentures. Osler's firm also began offering insurance and serving development more broadly by selling the bonds and debentures of western municipalities to British investors. In addition, a good deal of the firm's business followed the CPR's drive into the Kootenay mining country of British Columbia, as did Osler's private investments. In 1897, for instance, the *Monetary Times* (Toronto) identified him as a prominent shareholder in two stock exchange listings, the War Eagle mine and the Consolidated Cariboo Hydraulic Mining Company, which had its head office in Toronto.

In 1901 Osler became president of the Dominion Bank. He would, however, play almost no role within the Canadian banking system other than giving addresses at annual meetings. Rather, he was a capitalist in banking. On assuming the presidency, he turned over his seat on the stock exchange to his son Francis Gordon, who had joined Osler and Hammond in 1895. Osler Sr nonetheless remained in control of the firm, which continued to concentrate on western business. Having watched the west grow, he was always conscious of the vital role that foreign and eastern investment played in its development. When economic turmoil surfaced in 1907 and slowed progress there, Osler answered western critics of the banks by pointing to very large western loans, which far exceeded bank deposits in the western provinces. In 1913, when prairie farmers and others argued for subsidization of the Canadian Northern Railway, Osler, speaking from a CPR standpoint, denounced any support. Despite his belief in the future of the west, his business ties to Toronto, where he operated increasingly in concert with Wilmot Deloui Matthews*, weakened the currency of his opinion in many western quarters.

Success had brought calls for Osler to enter politics. He answered them for the first time in late 1891, when he joined the Toronto mayoralty race with the support of Goldwin Smith* and a team from the city's establishment. His "silk stocking" candidacy fell flat and he was defeated by Robert John FLEMING. A poor speaker, he had not warmed to popular demands for Sunday streetcars nor evidently, had he comprehended the commitment required because he had conducted his affairs as usual and even travelled to England on business. The observation made in the family history, that he "had little appetite for politics," may help explain this behaviour. At the same time it raises questions about his return to the House of Commons as a Conservative for Toronto West in 1896, the same year he was president of the Board of Trade, and his success in four subsequent contests.

Osler's political ideals are not easily discerned. During the 1896 election, when the Conservatives were divided over the Manitoba school question and party leader Sir Charles Tupper* had embraced remedial legislation to restore the rights of Catholic Manitobans to publicly funded education, Osler opposed Tupper's position. Although he was said to "believe in all Conservative doctrine," he had a streak of independence; he apparently defined his conservatism somewhat differently than the pragmatic side of the party, which expanded the common ground between French and English, Catholic and Protestant. The electoral victory of Wilfrid Laurier*'s Liberals prompted Joseph Wesley Flavelle*, a rising business Titan in Toronto, to suggest a rejuvenation fund for a Conservative party that he thought was falling into serious decline. Osler and the few other prominent Tories canvassed rejected the scheme. One wonders if Osler ever wished he had backed Flavelle's initiative during the 14 years the Tories were in opposition.

Osler

Osler's continued political success leaves many questions unanswered. Like his fellow businessman and Conservative counterpart in Toronto East, Albert Edward KEMP, he was not apt to "overwork Hansard." He was more likely, it seems, to talk in the quiet of parliamentary lounges, avoid fracas in the house, and attend to regional concerns as chairman of the executive committee of the Ontario Conservative Association. Consequently, his tenure in parliament was largely uncontentious and uneventful. Near the end, a newspaper reported "after seventeen years in the House Osler speaks," but this comment is somewhat misleading. In 1901 and 1903 he had tangled with finance minister William Stevens FIELDING over budgets and railways. Osler, who sat on the CPR's executive committee, was himself targeted in the house in 1903–4 as a representative of the undue influence of railways in Canadian politics. As well, he was at the centre of a controversy that would play a small part in the defeat of Laurier's Liberals.

In December 1910 Osler shared the national spotlight with Fielding after the collapse of the Farmers Bank of Canada. Considered by some to be "well fitted" to be minister (had his party been in power), he had been a critic of the bank since its inception. When it applied to the Treasury Board to open for business in 1906, he privately warned Fielding that it was a fraud and that its application should be denied. More alive to the political price of refusing, the minister ignored the warnings of Osler and a good many others. On the bank's failure, he headed for cover and blamed Osler for not giving him more evidence to work with. For Osler and his colleagues the collapse offered a useful tool to undermine the Liberals' business credibility in the debate over reciprocity during the election of 1911. It was Osler's last contest, for he declined to run in 1917; he was 68 and had had reservations about the Union government formed months before by Conservative leader Sir Robert Laird Borden*.

The start of World War I in 1914 had brought financial panic to Canada and a crisis in mortgage financing. The prime minister's office was inundated with calls from across the country, and especially the west, for a moratorium on debts. Osler, afraid that Borden would succumb to the political pressure, reminded him that, since 1912, many British investors with mortgage securities from the west had not received payments and that a moratorium would likely scare off future investment, to the great disadvantage of western development.

By the time the war had broken out, Osler was well known in Toronto for his civic and philanthropic efforts as well as his discreet financial endeavours. He had helped fund the new Toronto General Hospital, and was president (1899–1921) of the Ontario Rifle Association. A major purchaser of art – in 1903 he had bought a large collection of works by Paul Kane* – he was a benefactor of the Art Gallery of Toronto, and in 1912, the year of his knighthood, he had been instrumental in the creation of the Royal Ontario Museum. Osler's cultural tastes are reflected too in the selection of the Toronto architectural firm of Darling and Pearson to design the Dominion Bank's magnificent head office at Yonge and King in 1913–14, and many of its new branch buildings.

In the early months of the war a less impressive side of Osler was revealed by the "German professors issue" at the University of Toronto, where he had been a member of the board of governors since 1906. The sons of a German-born professor at University College took exception to an anti-German speech by their school principal. The protest led two newspapers to demand the dismissal of all three of the university's German-born professors. Osler and his fellow governors concurred but President Robert Alexander Falconer* claimed that they had done no wrong. After a compromise was found, placing the professors on leave, Osler tendered his resignation but it was not accepted.

His reaction in this issue was likely symptomatic of the single-minded determination throughout most of the dominion to defeat the enemy, a spirit that proved more productive, in Osler's case, when applied to war finance. He was a major contributor to the Canadian Patriotic Fund. Through Osler and Hammond, and its Winnipeg branch, dominion bonds were sold to institutional investors, easing the burden of government debt that was piling up in New York. In the west, the firm's influence was also demonstrated in the four Victory Loans campaigns of 1917–19, during which more than $246 million worth of bonds were sold through Osler, Hammond, and Nanton. When the war ended, Osler, one of Toronto's richest men, turned his attention to the economic aftermath and preached a gospel of caution. To each board member of the Dominion Bank he distributed a copy of *Poor Richard's almanack*, Benjamin Franklin's homage to frugality.

Canada had been transformed by the war, and in its wake Canadian businessmen encountered an increasingly hostile public. Many wanted villains to blame for the economic and social woes that had befallen the country; money-men and banks were fair game. As a bank president and a financier who had served the needs of western agriculturalists and municipalities, Osler took offence at allegations that banks were not loaning farmers sufficient money. The fallout from the war made profits unseemly and Osler, like other presidents, found himself in the somewhat uncomfortable position of having to defend the profitability of Canadian banks, a situation that had arisen before the war and grew more pressing after it.

From the porch of Craigleigh, his 13-acre estate in the Rosedale area of Toronto, Osler looked out at a Canada that was very different from the one he had known as a boy and as a young businessman. He understood the changes that had taken place in business. Finance capitalism, in particular, had emerged as a critical component of national development. In 1921, at age 76, Osler retained a high corporate status beyond his bank and Osler and Hammond, as the president of three companies, vice-president of another, and a director of eight.

Within his family circle, his wife had passed away in 1910, and his brothers, Featherston, Britton Bath*, and Sir William*, predeceased him. Sir E. B. Osler died at Craigleigh in 1924. He left an estate worth almost $4 million and a most unusual will. In his final years he had evidently written letters to friends and acquaintances promising money in recognition of their support; a special fund was set up from his estate to cover these obligations. All claimants had to do was present Osler's letter and his promise would be made good.

JOHN A. TURLEY-EWART

[Few primary sources have survived that reveal much about Osler's domestic, business, and political life. Some details have been gleaned from materials in the Toronto Dominion Bank Arch.; the Biog. scrapbooks at the TRL; the Borden papers (MG 26, H) and W. C. Good papers (MG 27, III, C1) at the LAC; and the William S. Fielding papers at the NSARM (MG 2, 422–541, 784–90(B)). J.A.T.-E.]

Mail (Toronto), 25 Sept. 1873. Christopher Armstrong and H. V. Nelles, *The revenge of the Methodist bicycle company: Sunday streetcars and municipal reform in Toronto, 1887–1897* (Toronto, 1977). Michael Bliss, *A Canadian millionaire: the life and business times of Sir Joseph Flavelle, bart., 1858–1939* (Toronto, 1978). A. [C. Boyd] Wilkinson, *Lions in the way: a discursive history of the Oslers* (Toronto, 1956). *Canadian annual rev. Canadian men and women of the time* (Morgan; 1912). *Dominion annual reg.*, 1882–83. J. A. Eagle, *The Canadian Pacific Railway and the development of western Canada, 1896–1914* (Kingston, Ont., 1989). *Encyclopaedia of Canadian biography . . .*, vol.2. R. G. MacBeth, *Sir Augustus Nanton, a biography* (Toronto, 1931). G. P. Marchildon, *Profits and politics: Beaverbrook and the Gilded Age of Canadian finance* (Toronto, 1996). *Ontario and the First World War, 1914–1918; a collection of documents*, ed. and intro. B. M. Wilson (Toronto, 1977). Joseph Schull, *100 years of banking in Canada: a history of the Toronto-Dominion Bank* (Toronto, 1958). O. D. Skelton, *The Dominion Bank, fifty years of banking service, 1871–1921* ([Toronto, 1922]). *Standard dict. of Canadian biog.* (Roberts and Tunnell), vol.1. A. S. Thompson, *Spadina: a story of old Toronto* (Toronto, 1975). J. F. Whiteside, "The Toronto Stock Exchange to 1900: its membership and the development of the share market" (MA thesis, Trent Univ., Peterborough, Ont., 1979). *Who's who in Canada*, 1922.

OTTER, Sir WILLIAM DILLON, militia and army officer; b. 3 Dec. 1843 near the Corners (Clinton), Upper Canada, son of Alfred William Otter and Anna de la Hooke; m. 3 Oct. 1865 Marianne Porter in Toronto, and they had a daughter; d. there 6 May 1929.

Will Otter's paternal grandfather had been a principal of King's College in London, England, and a bishop of Chichester. In 1841 his father came to the Huron Tract in Upper Canada to seek his fortune; he married, failed as a farmer, and used family influence to obtain a position in Goderich with the Canada Company. The eldest of three sons and two daughters, Will was educated at the Goderich grammar school and, following the family's move to Toronto in 1854, at the Model Grammar School and Upper Canada College. His father's financial problems, however, led him as well into the Canada Company as a clerk at age 14.

To Alfred Otter's dismay, Will found an outlet in amateur theatricals and Toronto's working-class, volunteer fire brigade. Formation of volunteer militia companies in the wake of the *Trent* affair in November 1861 [*see* Sir Charles Hastings Doyle*] encouraged Alfred to force his son to join the high-toned Victoria Rifles, a company of the 2nd Battalion of Rifles (Queen's Own Rifles of Toronto), commanded by William Smith Durie*. He was initially rejected because of his humble status and friends, and it took all his father's influence to have him accepted. Though his uniform and fees cost him more than a month's salary, Otter found that military life suited him perfectly. Big, athletic, and handsome, he looked the part; more important, he would recall that "on the first day of my enrolment . . . I became imbued with an ardent desire and love for the order, system and discipline pertaining to and necessary in a military organization." Following the St Albans raid in October 1864 [*see* Gilbert McMicken*], he served full-time with an embodied battalion. That December he became a lieutenant – he was formally gazetted on 19 May 1865 – and on 25 August he was confirmed as adjutant of the Queen's Own. After a winter of alarms and emergency mobilizations, on 2 June 1866 he was one of the raw militiamen who faced a Fenian raid outside Ridgeway [*see* Alfred Booker*]. On the verge of victory, the militia dissolved in panic. It was Otter's first lesson on the true importance of discipline.

On 5 Aug. 1865 Alfred Otter had been fired from the Canada Company, probably for drunkenness. Will, now his family's sole support, continued in the company's employ. Weeks later he was married at St James' Cathedral to Marianne, daughter of James Porter*, Toronto's superintendent of schools. Financially there was no choice for Molly but to begin her married life in the Otter household. Will escaped to the militia and an array of the activities that appealed to Victorian manhood. A founding member of the Toronto Rowing Club in 1865, he stroked the *Edrol* to the 1867 championship against crews from Ottawa, Toronto, and Lachine, Que. That summer he became the founding president and a leading player of the Toronto Lacrosse Club; in 1868 he was elected president of the National

Otter

Lacrosse Association. He was named to the board of the Mechanics' Institute and also became secretary-treasurer of the reorganized Toronto Gymnasium Association and a judge of the Caledonian games. Though he was a poor shot, his organizational ability allowed him to become secretary of the Ontario Rifle Association. As adjutant of the Canadian rifle team at Wimbledon (London) in 1873, he paid his first visit to England and his father's family.

Such activities satisfied Otter's inherited yearning for status, but only the militia met his thirst for regularity and discipline. There he thrived and in 1869 was promoted major; still adjutant of the Queen's Own, he gave it the administrative skills vital for what was as much a social and athletic club as a military unit. Despite shabby uniforms and the collapse of the Toronto drill-shed in March 1870, the battalion increased in size and efficiency. With family responsibilities, debts, and an income of only $1,271 a year, Otter was too poor to aspire to the position of commanding officer, but when the post became vacant in 1875, a year after his promotion to lieutenant-colonel, the officers unanimously selected him.

The fame of the Queen's Own spread. It was called out during the papal jubilee riots of 1875 in Toronto. When Belleville's militia refused to crush Grand Trunk Railway strikers, it travelled from Toronto in bitter weather in January 1877 and did the job. Recreational outings to reviews and sham battles also occurred, but Otter preferred practical field-training – when his men and their employers agreed. In 1880 in Toronto he published *The guide, a manual for the Canadian militia . . .* , a text based on *The soldier's pocket-book for field service* (London, 1869) by Garnet Joseph Wolseley*. Largely ignored until approved in England, Otter's book went through several editions before 1916 and earned him $4,310. It was uncompromising in its insistence on discipline. Some officers, he admitted, believed that severity was inappropriate for militia camps or drill-sheds. "I hold the contrary opinion, . . . the best time to acquire soldierly habits is when quietly parading for weekly drills." Instead of aping British uniforms, etiquette, and snobbery, he wanted the militia to learn from a tough substance of discipline and subordination.

In 1880 Otter's career was at a crossroads. He had done all he could with the Queen's Own; his Canada Company job was stagnant. Militia staff appointments were governed by political patronage. Support for Otter from the Toronto *Globe* was unhelpful, as was backing from Major-General Richard George Amherst Luard*, the tactless British reformer Ottawa had borrowed to command the militia. Would Otter have to settle for being a superintendent in the North-West Mounted Police or a brigade major in Toronto? Victory in the federal election of 1882 persuaded the Conservatives to keep an old promise: creating a tiny

permanent force to run schools for the militia. For the minister, Adolphe-Philippe Caron*, it was a splendid opportunity to reward military-minded political friends, but why not balance the slate with a popular, efficient militia officer? As Otter departed for Wimbledon in June 1883 to command the rifle team, he gave notice to the Canada Company. Late in July he got word from Ottawa of his command of "an Infantry School of Military Instruction" in Toronto at $5.25 a day. After three months' exposure to British military life, he left in October for Canada, where his move from the Queen's Own to the Permanent Force had met with widespread approval. He recruited 100 men and established his school at the New Fort (on the grounds of the present-day Canadian National Exhibition); it opened for instruction in April 1884. Luard's successor, Major-General Frederick Dobson Middleton*, brusquely turned down Otter's offer to lead the Canadian boatmen Britain recruited later that year for its Nile expedition [*see* Frederick Charles Denison*] – the school would be enough.

That decision did not bar Otter from the militia force hurriedly organized to suppress the Métis defiance at Batoche (Sask.) in 1885 [*see* Louis Riel*]. On Friday, 27 March, a telegram ordered him to mobilize 80 men from his school and 500 other militiamen and leave for Winnipeg. By noon on Saturday the soldiers had been selected and they soon seethed with impatience, but Otter, mindful of the ill-equipped men who had gone to Ridgeway, spent the weekend scouring Toronto for winter clothing, snow goggles, and boots. Between Dog Lake and Red Rock in northern Ontario, they trudged overland or huddled in open cars on the intervals of track laid by the still incomplete Canadian Pacific Railway. Despite the goggles, Otter would suffer the after-effects of snow-blindness for the rest of his life. From Winnipeg he moved on to Qu'Appelle (Sask.) and then to Swift Current. There he and his men were supposed to board steamers and go down the South Saskatchewan River to join Middleton at Clark's Crossing, but on 11 April fresh orders came. Panicky appeals from police and settlers at Battleford had gained urgency with the news of the Frog Lake (Alta) massacre [*see* Léon-Adélard Fafard*]. Otter must march to the rescue; his column set off on the 19th. When the troops reached Battleford on the 24th, politicians and journalists praised Otter for covering 180 miles in under six days. Critics complained that if he had attacked on the night of the 23rd, he might have forestalled a final orgy of destruction.

Battleford's citizens demanded revenge and Otter's men agreed. Middleton, his own campaign halted, warned him to stay put but the order came too late. Armed with approval from Edgar Dewdney*, lieutenant governor of the North-West Territories, Otter set out on 31 April with 325 men for the reserve of Plains Cree chief Poundmaker [Pītikwahanapiwīyin*] at

Cut Knife Creek. Upon arriving on 2 May, Otter found the camp gone but, as his force went up Cut Knife Hill, his scouts spotted Indian warriors. A battle ensued. When the natives began flanking the hill, Otter realized that he would have to effect a retreat. It was conducted in textbook fashion with few losses, in part because Poundmaker insisted that there had been enough killing. Otter could rationalize his adventure as a "reconnaissance in force": the Indians had been hurt or they would have pursued. Middleton was not deceived, and Otter's subordinates denounced him as an inept martinet. Others, however, eager for a Canadian-born hero, turned the battle into a triumph; the *Montreal Daily Star* urged "Otterism" as a synonym for merciless repression. Otter next led a futile trek north in search of Big Bear [Mistahimaskwa*] and other leaders of the uprising. Left in the west when most of his men returned, Otter could reflect that the best answer to critics of his British-like military professionalism was that he was Canadian-born. Caron's deputy, Charles-Eugène Panet, took Cut Knife Hill as proof that "Canadians can fight their own battles without foreign help."

Otter reached Toronto in October 1885. The following spring he assumed, in addition to his responsibilities at the infantry school and without extra pay, the duties of deputy adjutant general for Military District No.2 (Toronto and central Ontario). It was the beginning of a long struggle to infect rural militia with his own strict views on obedience and conformity, and to govern issues otherwise managed as patronage, from camp staff to canteen contracts. He persuaded Colonel Sir Casimir Stanislaus Gzowski* to contribute a trophy for the most efficient regiment in camp. In 1891 he helped launch the Canadian Military Institute and secured municipal funding to move Toronto's rifle range from the Garrison Common out to Mimico, thus ending a decade of friction between the militia and Torontonians. The following year Middleton's successor, Major-General Ivor John Caradoc Herbert*, turned the Infantry School Corps into the Canadian Regiment of Infantry. When its four companies gathered for the first time, in 1894 at Lévis, Que., Otter acted as colonel. The next year he would spend six months in England and on the Continent, passing the tests required of a British battalion commander.

At 51, Otter had held the same rank for 20 years and the same salary for 11, and, thanks to his dependent sisters and need to keep up a social position, he was in debt. Earlier, Samuel HUGHES, a militia major and old lacrosse friend, had urged his claims to be adjutant general, the highest position available to a Canadian. But when a vacancy occurred in early 1896, following the retirement of Walker Powell*, Hughes, then a Tory MP, regarded Otter's "grittish proclivities" as a barrier. The Liberals on the other hand suspected him of being a Tory appointee, favoured in April 1896, just before

the federal election, with yet another unpaid title, inspector of infantry. Otter survived the change of government and became an asset to Wilfrid Laurier*'s reform-minded minister of militia and defence, Frederick William Borden*, and to the latest British commander of the Canadian militia, Major-General Edward Thomas Henry HUTTON. Otter was unimpressed by his self-aggrandizing new chief. Though Hutton named him to command a Canadian contingent in the event of war in South Africa, when he finally presented a plan to Borden, Hutton explained that he, not Otter, would command. "You will, I think, be a gainer in the end," he told Otter in September 1899.

He was. The government ignored Hutton's plan and British guidelines. On 13 October Otter was given command of the contingent authorized for South Africa, to be recruited from across Canada and called the 2nd (Special Service) Battalion of the Royal Canadian Regiment of Infantry. Instead of a nominal command, Otter would have a fighting unit. In a frantic two weeks more than a thousand men were enlisted; political squabbles over the appointments of officers continued until the troopship *Sardinian* sailed on 30 October. Determined that his Canadians would acquit themselves like soldiers, Otter began basic training on the decks of this ill-adapted cattle-ship. Used to easy-going militia standards, his subordinates grumbled and acted out regional jealousies.

By the time Otter reached Cape Town on 29 November, he knew how badly the war was going for the British. Sent to Lord Methuen's force on the Modder River, the Canadians were supplanted in action by a veteran British battalion. They endured two more months of drill, marching, and sentry duty at Belmont under the grizzled martinet and a blazing sun. Otter had hoped to use his service to win promotion in the British army but he soon realized that he had little hope against nimble careerists half his age. Instead, as the first Canadian force commander in battle, he found himself overworked, with masters in Ottawa as well as in the field. Hardened by training, the Canadians finally passed muster with Lord Roberts, the British commander, and were sent to join Colonel Horace Lockwood Smith-Dorrien's 19th Brigade.

On 12 Feb. 1900 a train took Otter's battalion to Graspan, where it became part of a plan to trap the army of Boer commander Piet Arnoldus Cronje. Next day the Paardeberg campaign began with a march to Ramdam; of 896 Canadians, 50 dropped out from thirst and heat. More exhausting marches followed, and a few began to appreciate Otter's attempt to prepare them. On the 18th the Canadians reached Paardeberg Drift, crossed the Modder, and advanced on Cronje's defences. Boer rifles soon forced them to seek shelter; in the afternoon, after disparaging the raw colonials, a British battalion attacked through them. The Canadians rose and charged, at a cost of 21 lives, the bloodiest Canadian encounter since the War of 1812. The battle became a siege. On the 27th the Canadians launched a night attack: shooting began, the troops dropped for cover, and a few minutes later most fled to their old trenches. A furious Otter faced the third retreat of his career. On the right, however, the better part of two companies stayed put. As dawn broke the Boers started to surrender. Most imperial soldiers remembered that it was Majuba Day, anniversary of the Boers' humiliating defeat of the British in 1881. The night-time panic forgotten, Otter's Canadians became the ideal symbols of a great victory for the British empire.

More weary marching took the regiment to Bloemfontein, where Roberts planned to rebuild his army. Cold and rain turned the Canadian bivouac into a swamp; eight died in an army-wide epidemic of enteric fever. Seated under a wagon, Otter dealt with a flood of mail from Canada, some of it censuring his harsh discipline. (At home he could count on powerful friends to keep critical letters out of the press.) On 21 April the advance resumed. At Israel's Poort on the 25th, Boer fire drove the battalion's front line to ground. Noting some men slipping back, Otter strode out to stop them. Hardly had he returned when a bullet struck him in the face. He rejoined his battalion on 26 May, in time to lead it at the battle of Doornkop and to march in triumph through Pretoria on 5 June.

By tradition the war should now have been won. Instead, Otter's men faced dispiriting months of guard duty interspersed with futile marches against mounted commandos. Most looked forward to going home when their year was up. Convinced that victory was near, Roberts asked Otter to keep his men a few more weeks. What answer could he give but yes? Many, feeling no such call, went home, armed with a further grievance against their commander. Those who stayed returned as heroes via England, where they were inspected by Queen Victoria on 30 Nov. 1900. Otter's friends in Toronto, determined to flatten his critics, staged a huge banquet for him on 28 December. Governor General Lord Minto [Elliot*] welcomed him as "Canada's best soldier." Otter modestly insisted that, with such excellent material, it had been easy to form "one of the most efficient battalions which tramped the veldt." Earlier the government had changed the Militia Act to allow him and other senior officers to become full colonels (official notice reached Otter in South Africa on 9 October). A CB followed at the end of 1901. His critics were not silenced but they remained anonymous. Once again nationalism served a man who had tried to make Canadians into a good British battalion. "He is a product of the Canadian Militia," declared the *Canadian Military Gazette* (Montreal), "and we should all stand by him and feel proud of him."

Although some Canadians agreed with Sam Hughes that the war had been a triumph of sharpshooting amateurs over blinkered professionals, most believed that active service had made Canadian soldiers as good as the British. Why then should British officers continue to hold key positions in the militia when officers such as Otter were available? The minister, Borden, was sympathetic but cautious and devoutly imperialist, and Otter continued in command of Military District No.2 at a higher salary. With financial advice from Henry Mill Pellatt*, the business-minded commander of the Queen's Own, Otter was never again poor; by 1902 he had $1,000 a year in investment income. In 1901–2 he was part of a committee that adopted the infamous Ross rifle, an achievement he never recorded in his otherwise voluminous personal records.

As in South Africa, Otter's enforcement of discipline and regulations made him unpopular with the largely Conservative officers of central Ontario's militia units. In unrecorded but remembered speeches at reviews and inspections, he attacked the lack of control and subordination in the militia. At 60 he was overage and a Tory victory in 1904 might have ended his career. Instead, he became a beneficiary of amendments to the Militia Act earlier that year, whereby the British general officer commanding was replaced by a militia council in which the senior officer would be chief of the general staff (CGS), and not necessarily British. Eastern Canada was divided into commands and, after an effort to move him to Montreal, Otter took over western Ontario. In a period of such dramatic reform and expansion, his energy and expectations had fuller scope than ever. At the same time the experience of South Africa and the growing threat of war in Europe had fed a British desire to integrate dominion forces. In 1907 an imperial conference agreed to the standardization of doctrine and training. To keep key Canadian positions under its control, the War Office offered Otter a brigade at Aldershot. As he weighed this offer, the death of Brigadier-General Beaufort Henry Vidal* in March 1908 allowed the government to promote its British CGS to the higher post of inspector general and appoint Otter CGS with the rank of brigadier-general. Canadians were delighted. One of their own had been offered a British brigade but had refused it in order to become Canada's top general. Old antagonisms were forgotten in the chorus of praise. Few noted that Otter's predecessor, Major-General Percy Henry Noel Lake*, continued as inspector general and Canada's senior military adviser.

Otter's first task was to organize a vast military review for the celebration of Quebec City's tercentenary. The 12,422 men and 2,134 horses assembled on 24 July 1908 outnumbered the combined forces of Wolfe* and Montcalm*. The assembly was also a climax of military spending. The $1-million annual budget of the 1867–96 period was long forgotten. By 1908–9 the militia department had $6.5 million, with pressure to spend more. However, the prosperity of the Laurier era was running out. At the end of 1908 the Militia Council was told that it had to find $1 million in cuts. The public and the militia clamoured to reduce staff and the Permanent Force rather than summer militia camps. To inspect what defences Canada did have, Otter toured the country in 1909; at Petawawa, Ont., he watched the new Canadian aircraft Baddeck No.1 take off but "did not care to express an opinion." The following year he succeeded Lake as inspector general, an appointment that led to his promotion to acting major-general in November 1910. (A British general became CGS and the government's senior military adviser and no Canadian officer would have this double role until 1920.)

On 10 Oct. 1911 the Conservatives formed a government. As minister of militia, Sam Hughes soon ran foul of the senior British officers. One result was Otter's confirmation as a major-general in July 1912, but almost immediately he heard that he was to be retired on 1 December. Since he was 68 the move was hardly overdue, though he was bitter at being denied a full four-year term as inspector general and the honours that usually marked a distinguished career. His final report, published in January, was a trenchant attack on most of Hughes's policies; in Otter's opinion, militia camps and provisional schools were inadequate, instructors were sometimes unqualified, complacency pervaded the militia, and the Permanent Force was being seriously neglected. Otter was in England when he learned that the governor general, the Duke of Connaught, had prevailed over his ministers and that he would be made a KCB. He was present at Buckingham Palace for his investiture on 11 June 1913.

Back in Canada, Otter was available to speak on military preparedness, as hard times and Hughes's excesses helped drain away an earlier mood of militarism. World war, on 4 Aug. 1914, restored it. Otter felt useless: home guards and the Red Cross Society heard his advice on military needs but ignored it. Lacking direct threats, Canadians turned on the aliens in their midst, forcing the government to intern hundreds of Germans and thousands of Polish and Ukrainian labourers who happened to be Habsburg subjects [see William Perchaluk*]. Minister of Justice Charles Joseph Doherty* summoned Otter to Ottawa on 30 October and invited him to take charge of internment operations. Interrupted only by his wife's death in November, he worked tirelessly, establishing camps from Fort Henry near Kingston, Ont., to Nanaimo, B.C. First-class internees, who could not be expected to work, were distinguished from second-class ones, who would labour at such projects as clearing bush at Kapuskasing, Ont., or developing the national park at Banff, Alta. In addition, Otter consolidated camps, released internees needed for war work, and protected camp commanders who shared his dedication to order.

The post-war anti-Bolshevik panic brought new prisoners to Kapuskasing, and not until the end of 1919 would the last camps be cleared.

In 1919 Otter assumed another chore: heading the reorganization committee formed to combine the old militia regiments and the new units of the Canadian Expeditionary Force. Though most of the work would be done by younger officers, Otter provided experience. He told wrangling colonels of the public feeling that there should be no militia at all. They were unmoved, politicians backed them, and Otter's committee would be blamed for the swollen militia organization that was halved in 1936. He also sat on a committee to choose officers for the Permanent Force. His services ended in June 1920 with three months' pay and virtually no public notice. In 1921 Major-General James Howden MacBrien*, his protégé and post-war CGS, reminded the newly elected Liberal government that Otter had never been transferred to the retired list. The error was graciously remedied on 9 March 1922 by his promotion to general, making him the second Canadian in that rank after Sir Arthur William Currie*. On 7 June 1923 the University of Toronto granted him an honorary LLD at a convocation dominated by returned soldiers. He was declining. On 27 Nov. 1927 veterans of the Queen's Own fêted him at a banquet. For once he was almost incoherent. Early in 1928 he stumbled on a streetcar and broke his ankle; when he seemed ready to walk, he relapsed. On 6 May 1929 his nurses found him dead.

Militia contemporaries called Otter "the Father of the Force." He was its military conscience and disciplinarian and a remorseless critic of its failings. His faith in discipline and order found few echoes among Canadians, but they were qualities that determined victory or defeat. Otter had learned the lesson at Ridgeway.

DESMOND MORTON

Almost all the references for this account can be found in Desmond Morton, *The Canadian general: Sir William Otter* (Toronto, 1974). Otter's papers are in LAC, MG 30, E242. A large collection of scrapbooks, papers, and family bibles is in the possession of the author. The other main secondary sources are Carman Miller, *Painting the map red: Canada and the South African War, 1899–1902* (Montreal and Kingston, Ont., 1993), and S. J. Harris, *Canadian brass: the making of a professional army, 1860–1939* (Toronto, 1988).

OUTRAM, Sir JAMES, Church of England clergyman, mountaineer, author, businessman, militia officer, and Orangeman; b. 13 Oct. 1864 in London, England, eldest son of Sir Francis Boyd Outram and Jane Anne Davidson; m. 17 May 1921 Lillian Mary Balfour in Montreal; they had no children; d. 12 March 1925 in Victoria.

Public distinction marked the family legacy that

Outram

James Outram inherited. His paternal grandfather, Lieutenant-General James Outram, was created a baronet for outstanding service in the Indian Mutiny, and his father also distinguished himself in the military. Outram's clerical career reveals the extent of his own drive. A graduate of Pembroke College, Cambridge (BA 1888, MA 1893), he was ordained deacon in 1889 and priest in 1890. He was curate of Holy Trinity Church in Hampstead (London) and then of Thorpe in Norfolk; from 1896 he was vicar of St Peter's, Ipswich. In 1900 he suffered a mental breakdown from overwork.

Mountain climbing was the cure, and making first ascents of Canadian peaks became Outram's passion. He began with routine climbs in the Swiss Alps and, in 1900 with his brother William, in the Canadian Rocky Mountains, where significant numbers of serious mountaineers had begun climbing for recreation, rather than for professional surveying or scientific work, after the completion of the Canadian Pacific Railway in 1885. Then, during the summers of 1901 and 1902, Outram made spectacular ascents of some of the highest unclimbed peaks in the Rockies. In 1901 he accompanied the CPR-sponsored party of Edward Whymper, the English mountaineer famous for his disastrous first ascent of the pyramid-shaped Matterhorn in Switzerland. Whymper was expected to generate publicity for the CPR by making first ascents, taking photographs, and publishing accounts of his expedition. While he was exploring the Ice River valley and elaborating plans to climb Mount Goodsir, Outram was drawn to the unscaled Mount Assiniboine, at 11,875 feet the highest mountain in the Canadian Rockies south of the CPR. The peak's appeal lay in its dramatic appearance, the technical challenge of its height, and the romantic grandeur associated with its designation as the "Matterhorn of North America." Canadian guide and outfitter Tom Wilson, British climber John Norman Collie, and American climber Walter Dwight Wilcox had already spent years mapping and trail-breaking in the Rockies, and had made numerous attempts to climb Assiniboine. On 3 Sept. 1901, however, it was newcomer James Outram, aided by Banff outfitter Bill Peyto and two Swiss guides, who succeeded.

Outram's accomplishment established his reputation as a serious and ambitious mountaineer. His sudden appearance in the field caused mountaineers who had a much longer history of exploration in the Rockies, and who had hoped to make the first ascent of Assiniboine themselves, to consider him presumptuous as well. This unfavourable impression was reinforced in 1902 when Outram continued to scale some of the highest summits yet conquered in the Rockies, including mounts Columbia (12,298 feet) and Forbes (11,855 feet). A Swiss guide assisted on many of these climbs; on others, Outram joined Collie's party, to the dismay of some members. Outram also spent time with Arthur Oliver Wheeler during his survey of the Selkirk Mountain ranges in British Columbia.

After 1902 Outram disappeared from the field of serious mountaineering as abruptly as he had burst onto it. He made no further climbs of significance, but he continued a keen interest in the sport. He maintained a corresponding membership with the Boston-based Appalachian Mountain Club, and lectured on his climbs to meetings of the American Alpine Club and the Alpine Club of Canada, the latter formed in 1906. He wrote articles on mountaineering and a book, *In the heart of the Canadian Rockies* (London, 1905), an engaging travelogue and history. His writing reveals his sound grasp of mountaineering principles, considerable literary skill, and the fusion of his religious piety and his passion for nature. He hoped his book would draw others to the Rockies to see the "noblest of God's monuments." He became an honorary member of the ACC in 1907, and participated in its mountaineering camps and executive meetings.

From 1908 to 1911 Outram lived in Crescent, Colo. After succeeding to his father's baronetcy in 1912, he moved to Vermilion, Alta, where he became involved in short-lived land development companies. He was too old for overseas duty in World War I, but in 1916–18, with the rank of major, he commanded Vermilion's militia company and served as an instructor in the infantry school at Camp Sarcee in Calgary. In 1920 he settled in Calgary, where he worked at various business-related jobs. During his time there he married an old family friend, the daughter of Joseph Balfour of Athelstone House in Brighton, England, and became a fellow of the Royal Colonial Institute.

Outram was also a dynamic member of the Orange order. He had been initiated into the Vermilion lodge on 13 Oct. 1914, and his numerous positions over the years culminated in terms in 1918–21 as provincial grand master of Alberta. At the Orange convention of March 1919 he took the opportunity to reiterate the order's opposition to both separate schools in Alberta and the use of languages other than English in public discourse. He was provincial grand secretary from 1921, but ill health forced him to resign in August 1924. The next year he went to Victoria, where he died of a stroke and was buried in Royal Oak Burial Park Cemetery.

Outram's impact in Canada revolved around his commitment to Orangeism and his climbing. Outram Memorial Lodge in Calgary and Mount Outram in Alberta are named after him. His published writings and few existing papers usually share credit with fellow climbers for successful ascents, though occasional remarks are self-deprecating to the point of immodesty. Many acquaintances and climbing peers found him aloof and class-conscious, and a number of mountaineers were alienated by his brash, single-minded pursuit of the most prestigious summits in the Rockies. At the same time, his outstanding record of first ascents, and his lecture tours and publications, boosted Canada's image as one of the world's few remaining wildernesses.

SIRI LOUIE

Sir James Outram is the author of "Two traverses" and "The first ascent of Mt. Assiniboine," *Alpine Journal* (London), 19 (1900): 624–25 and 21 (1903): 102–14, as well as the book *In the heart of the Canadian Rockies* (London, 1905).

Jasper-Yellowhead Museum and Arch. (Jasper, Alta), 993.37 (Robson family fonds). Whyte Museum of the Canadian Rockies (Banff, Alta), AC0/19 (A. A. McCoubrey papers); M106 (J. Monroe Thorington fonds), /2, /136, /142, /156 (photocopies); M526 (John Davenall Turner papers); V396 (James Outram fonds). [The Jasper-Yellowhead and Whyte museums both have collections of photographs of or by Outram.] [Review of *In the heart of the Canadian Rockies*], *Athenaeum* (London), 6 Jan. 1906: 13. *Calgary Herald*, 14 March 1925. [Review of *In the heart of the Canadian Rockies*], *Nation* (New York), 14 Dec. 1905: 485. *Times* (London), 19 May 1921, 16 March 1925. Alpine Club of Canada, *Constitution and list of members*, 1907–11, 1920–22. [J.] B. Burke, *A genealogical and heraldic history of the peerage and baronetage . . .* , ed. A. P. Burke (97th ed., London, 1939). *Canadian annual rev.*, 1919: 771. *Canadian men and women of the time* (Morgan; 1912). *Dod's peerage, baronetage, and knightage of Great Britain and Ireland for 1923* (London, 1923). [Review of *In the heart of the Canadian Rockies*], *New York Times Saturday Rev.*, 4 Nov. 1905: 753. R. W. Sandford, *The Canadian Alps: the history of mountaineering in Canada* (Banff, 1990). *Who's who and why*, 1919/20. *Who's who in Canada*, 1922, 1925/26.

P

PAGET, AMELIA ANNE. *See* MCLEAN

PARKHURST, EDWIN RODIE, music and drama critic; b. 3 June 1848 in Walworth (London), England, son of Rodie Parkhurst, a post office clerk, and Phoebe See; d. unmarried 10 June 1924 in Toronto.

Edwin R. Parkhurst's early music training included studies with George Hart, of Hart and Son, a London firm of violin makers. George Hart was not only an excellent violinist; he possessed literary abilities that resulted in an internationally acclaimed book on the violin. It is likely that Parkhurst, only nine years younger, was inspired by Hart's musical talents and literary interests. Albert Ham*, an English-born Toronto musician, recalled that during these years in London Parkhurst played his violin at all important services in the Italian Church in Hatton Garden (St Peter's) and at the Sunday concerts in the Royal Italian Opera House and Her Majesty's Theatre. An obituary claimed in addition that he had been decorated by Emperor Napoleon III for his prowess in fencing in a competition between Britain and France.

Prior to emigrating, Parkhurst worked for the Grand Trunk Railway in London. There is no reason given for his arrival in Canada in 1869 or 1870 to become a stenographer with this company, first in Montreal and later in Toronto. He would continue his interest in swordsmanship, helping to found the Toronto Fencing Club, of which he was secretary for many years. By 1872 he had managed to find work as a reporter with the newly founded Toronto *Mail*, where he received his first assignments to review entertainments. He then became parliamentary reporter in Ottawa for the *Globe* in 1873 and shortly afterward city editor. By 1876 he had returned to the *Mail*, attracted by the offer of becoming music and drama critic, a position he held until 1898 when he retraced his steps to the *Globe* to serve as editor of the *Weekly Globe* and music and drama critic of the daily edition; the latter post he held until his death.

To earn a livelihood as a critic with a daily newspaper, he had to review a large number of events in the city. In addition, he selected articles from other newspapers to be reprinted and determined which performers would receive advance promotion. At least part of the time in the early years he maintained this hectic schedule while living with his brother and sister on the east bank of the Don River, where they managed a market garden and poultry farm. Because the cottage was beyond the city limits, he had to walk several miles to attend performances. Generally, however, he resided at various addresses in the central city, making his routine as critic more manageable. Around 1905 he and his sister would move to a home on D'Arcy Street, which became a regular location for private concerts and for social evenings with local and visiting musicians.

Parkhurst's literary contributions extended beyond the *Mail* and the *Globe*. His articles were also published in the *Canadian Monthly and National Review* (Toronto, 1870s), the *Week* (Toronto, 1880s), *Arcadia* (Montreal, 1892–93), and *Saturday Night* (Toronto, 1909–10). His most important contributions appeared in the *Violin*, which he founded in 1906, possibly acknowledging George Hart's earlier influences. Parkhurst renamed it *Musical Canada* a year later and launched one of the longest runs of a musical journal in Canada. It would appear until 1933, Parkhurst being editor until 1920. His aims for the publication were clear: it was to be "a journal of musical news and comments" about performers and concerts both local and international.

Contemporaries declared Parkhurst to be "the dean of Canadian critics," a distinction earned for several reasons. John Daniel Logan, in a review of Canadian critics, noted that Parkhurst practised a "technico-literary" type of criticism, a blend of technical commentary with "general aesthetic and artistic appeal, spiced with humanized comments on the charms, mannerisms, idiosyncrasies, or personality of a soloist, and on the display of dexterous musicianship." Hector Willoughby Charlesworth*, the Toronto journalist who succeeded Parkhurst as Canada's leading critic, pointed out in 1924 that throughout his career Parkhurst had demonstrated an "ability to deal with technical detail lucidly, and in a manner that the layman could understand." Parkhurst's early reviews that criticized many aspects of performances gave way to a style of writing that encouraged most artists, but still provided clear clues to the reader about the quality of each performance. After Parkhurst's death in 1924, Augustus Stephen VOGT, principal of the Toronto Conservatory of Music and founder of the Toronto Mendelssohn Choir, summed up the views of many performers: "He was one of the most erudite and sympathetic of Canadian critics. To the end he retained his fine literary style, and his critical judgment was at all times highly respected by the profession and by the musical public."

Committed to 19th century values, and personally favouring classical chamber music, Parkhurst was witness to radical changes in musical and theatrical entertainments. These shifts in taste as well as his onerous workload can best be captured by examining a typical month of reviews. During 24 days of "Music and the Drama" columns in the *Globe* of May 1913, he wrote or edited more than 150 items, many of them original commentaries resulting from attending performances. The repertoire included traditional Victorian plays, vaudeville, melodrama, comedy, early film, touring classical artists, and local musicians in concert. Among the people and works featured were Annie Russell and the Old English Comedy Company; Rose Sydell, "Queen of Burlesque," at the Gayety Theatre; the Paulist Choristers of Chicago; the vaudeville *Madame Sherry* at the Grand Opera House; Sheridan's *The rivals* at the Royal Alexandra; and Frank Squire Welsman* and the Toronto Symphony Orchestra. In addition, Parkhurst reprinted commentaries about composers Satie, Debussy, and Schoenberg, all of them still too "contemporary" for Toronto tastes in programming in 1913. Regardless, he felt it important to educate his readers and to print reviews of performances in other major cities, such as a critique of Debussy's "new symphonic poem" (*Printemps*), which had premiered in Paris on 18 April, as well as articles on "music of the future," discussing new rhythms and scales being used by composers. At the same time he continued to edit *Musical Canada*. Parkhurst saw this journal as a pedagogical tool, informing the nation about instruments, styles, and materials relevant to both the amateur and the professional musician. As he had in his newspaper columns, he published articles on contemporary composers and performers.

Described by Charlesworth as "an alert, bright-eyed little man of many interests," Parkhurst made significant contributions to the criticism of music and theatre. Not an avid nationalist, he often failed to promote Canadian composers and writers. But he remained committed to the education of the general public and in all of his reviews never lost sight of his audience. No other living critic in North America could claim the longevity of Parkhurst's career. Although he was dismissed as conservative by some of his peers, other contemporaries recognized that his writings constituted the most substantial record of commentary in Canada for a period spanning nearly a half century.

FREDERICK A. HALL

In addition to his many contributions to newspapers and magazines, Parkhurst compiled and edited *Royal song folio: a collection of standard American vocal gems, with biographical sketches of celebrated composers and vocalists* ([Toronto?], 1886).

AO, RG 22-305, no.50366; RG 80-8-0-949, no.4093. GRO, Reg. of births, St Peter Walworth (Surrey), 3 June 1848. *Globe*, 2 June 1923: 17; 11 June 1924: 11, 13. *Canadian men and women of the time* (Morgan; 1912). H. [W.] Charlesworth, "Music and drama: the death of E. R. Parkhurst," *Saturday Night*, 21 June 1924: 6. *Encyclopedia of music in Canada* (Kallmann et al.). C. L. Hartwell, "*Musical Canada*: a study of music criticism and journalism in an early twentieth century Canadian music periodical" (MA thesis, McMaster Univ., Hamilton, Ont., 1991). Ross Stuart, "The critic as reviewer: E. R. Parkhurst at the Toronto *Mail* and *Globe*, 1876–1924," in *Establishing our boundaries: English-Canadian theatre criticism*, ed. Anton Wagner (Toronto, 1999), 95–106.

PARKIN, Sir GEORGE ROBERT, educator, imperialist, and author; b. 8 Feb. 1846 near Salisbury, N.B., youngest of the 13 children of John Parkin and Elizabeth McLean; m. 9 July 1878, in Fredericton, Annie Connell Fisher (1858–1931), granddaughter of Peter Fisher*, and they had six daughters, two of whom died in infancy, and one son; d. 25 June 1922 in London, England.

George R. Parkin's father was a Yorkshire farmer who had immigrated in 1817; his mother was a Nova Scotian of loyalist descent. In later years Parkin recalled the family's hard struggle on their farm with "little music, few books, [and] not much polished society." Yet his mother gave him a love of literature and he attended school whenever time could be "snatched from the hoeing of potatoes, making hay, [or] chopping wood." These early glimmers of a distant world of learning awakened "a burning desire to <u>know</u> and a longing to see with my own eyes the places one read about – to meet men who wrote books or did things – to get in touch with the world of which the faint echoes only came to one's country life." Parkin followed this desire first to the Normal School at Saint John in 1862 and then to positions in primary schools at Buctouche and on Campobello Island. By 1864 he had saved enough to enrol at the University of New Brunswick in Fredericton, where he imbibed the gospel of mid-Victorian liberalism and progress. He was accepted into Fredericton's polite society, thereby acquiring the social skills he would need in later life. Upon graduating magna cum laude, he taught at the Bathurst Grammar School (1867–71) before his appointment in 1872 as headmaster of the Fredericton Collegiate School, a position he would retain until 1889.

Parkin formed in these years his lifelong conviction that "the degree of civilization attained by any nation" is a direct result of its standard of education and that the teacher has enormous power by forming "the morals and manners of those . . . whose influence for good or bad will be extensively felt." This belief would underpin his later career, not only his work in education but also his public campaigns for imperial unity, social regeneration, and Christian responsibility. During this period as well he perfected his public-speaking techniques in a series of local lectures on history, education, democracy, temperance, and imperial unity. Yet these were also troubled years for Parkin. His careful reading of Thomas Carlyle challenged the liberal notions of his university days and his close friendship with John Medley*, the high-church Anglican bishop of Fredericton, undermined the individualistic, evangelical, Baptist faith of his youth and promoted a more learned, liturgical, and holistic approach to religion. Not knowing which way to turn to reconcile his liberalism and conservatism, or his evangelicalism and Anglicanism, he experienced a nervous breakdown. Medley stepped in and sponsored Parkin for a year at the University of Oxford in 1873–74.

This year set the direction for Parkin's life. As an older student with considerable experience in public speaking, he was a great success at the renowned Oxford Union Society, and he was accorded the unusual honour for a non-degree freshman of being elected its secretary. In a famous debate he defeated the future British prime minister Herbert Henry Asquith, of Balliol College, on the issue of the desirability of imperial unity, Parkin arguing for the affirmative despite the widespread Little Englandism of the time. The attention he received fixed his earlier belief in a united British empire as a force for good in the world. During his Oxford year he also was deeply impressed by Edward Thring, the reforming headmaster of Uppingham School, and saw in Thring's ideals a necessary corrective to the lower standards of pioneer schools in Canada. Thring was equally charmed and, after many years of friendship, assigned Parkin the task of writing his biography. Through Thring, as well as through personal contacts with the brilliant circle at Balliol and through John Ruskin, Parkin was attracted to the idealism that animated much late-19th-century British and Canadian life. Like many of his contemporaries, he accepted idealism as a practical creed rather than a philosophical system, a belief that a moral community in the world would result from the ethical character of citizens moved by a sense of public service rather than by a desire for material gain or individual glory. The creed attracted both liberals and conservatives. Thus in idealism Parkin found a resolution of his earlier struggles. His evangelical energy would now be rechannelled into a lifelong mission to promote the central tenets of Christian idealism in empire, school, church, and society.

Parkin spent the next 15 years teaching in Fredericton. He tried in his own school and in a connected residence he founded to implement Thring's concept of building citizenship through the regimen of residential life and classical education under a committed headmaster. These initial residential experiments were not successful: there were few paying students and the cost of supplies was high. While disappointed, Parkin remained a master teacher. His imaginative classroom methods have been credited with nurturing in these years the Fredericton school of poets led by William Bliss CARMAN and Charles George Douglas Roberts*. In a more opportune setting as headmaster of Toronto's Upper Canada College from 1895 to 1902, Parkin took a moribund institution and, explicitly following Thring's methods, succeeded in making it the premier private school in Canada. He ably raised money, added buildings, hired better masters, and reformed the curriculum, but his core aim was the production of Christian gentlemen. He poured his energy into the headmaster's Sunday evening addresses to the boys and remained convinced that "nothing stamps a school as really great save the power of turning out men of high and noble character."

Parkin's main avenue for the realization of Christian idealism was not the school, however, but the British empire. Throughout his life, but especially during the years 1889–95, he was the leading spokesperson for imperial unity. His campaigns through thousands of speeches and interviews, scores of articles, and several books were very wide-ranging. In the employ of the Imperial Federation League, founded in London in 1884, he left Fredericton to stump across

Parkin

New Zealand and Australia throughout 1889. Bolstered by the reputation he gained there, he settled with his family in England to undertake five years of freelance lecturing and writing for the imperial cause all across Britain, his activities sometimes sponsored by the League, often based on his own personal contacts. His principal manifesto appeared in 1892 as *Imperial federation, the problem of national unity*. That year as well he brought out a school textbook, *Round the empire*, which would sell 200,000 copies and go through four editions by 1919. He also published, in 1893, a large wall map for schools that illustrated the unity of Britain's oceanic empire. He had visited Canada in 1892 to lecture extensively there, and began then his long affiliation with the London *Times*, writing a series of reports on Canadian history and geography (published together as *The great dominion* in 1895).

These were difficult campaigns for Parkin – quite aside from the inadequate financial base on which he operated. Though imperial federation had significant support in Canada, from such advocates as George Taylor Denison and George Monro Grant*, many imperialists there were wary of being too closely tied to, or taxed for, a formally federated British empire, where Britain by force of numbers would dominate. Many British imperialists, on the other hand, felt that the colonies were not paying their fair share of imperial defence and other burdens, and they wanted closer ties and more tax revenues. Parkin tried to bridge these two positions, but controversy arose. There were celebrated disputes with the veteran Canadian politician and high commissioner in Britain, Sir Charles Tupper*, which forced the dissolution of the Imperial Federation League in 1893, and a series of extended attacks on Goldwin Smith*'s anti-imperialism and North American continentalism.

Despite the spiritual motivation of Parkin's imperialism, he did not ignore the practical arguments favouring unity. Influenced by the writings of historian John Robert Seeley and naval theorist Alfred Thayer Mahan, Parkin stressed to the British that, with their oceanic empire, their world position rested on sea power. Given the realities of distance and the dependence of steamships on coal supplies and coaling bases guarded by fortified naval stations, the empire needed to retain, for commerce or defence, the quadrilateral of Australasia, South Africa, Canada, and the United Kingdom, and all the connecting islands and waterways. Without this geopolitical configuration, he presciently forecast, Britain would sink within 50 years into the ranks of the second-class powers before the rising land-based empires of Russia and the United States. To Canadians and Australians, Parkin pointed out that, without the empire, the individual dominions would be battered on the world stage by aggressive superpowers. Self-interest, then,

required unity – and the communications revolution of fast steamships, the telegraph, underseas cables, and connecting railways and canals across an "all-red route" ably defended, combined with a common language, literature, and culture, made unity possible.

Parkin never lost his Canadian orientation, and he naturally articulated at some length Canada's position in a united empire. He sought to enhance his native country's imperial place, especially in the face of an aggressive United States, then perceived to wish for hemispheric economic leadership at least, and perhaps political integration as well. For Parkin, imperial unity did not mean subsuming Canada's interests under those of the British colonial administration; rather it would provide a chance for Canada's fledgling national ambitions to have reasonable scope internationally. Indeed, as the senior dominion, as the geopolitical linchpin in the all-red route, as a nation built on loyalty to the empire, with vast open spaces for immigrants, bountiful natural resources, and a wellspring of racial vigour engendered by a northern climate, Canada was positioned to be the "keystone" of empire. He urged the country to accept its destiny and transform itself from weak colony into strong imperial partner. In Canada he promoted the imperial projects of Sir Sandford Fleming* and others, effectively lobbying for such practical measures to unite the empire as all-red-route telegraph cables, imperial penny postage, productive colonial conferences, and imperial trade preferences. He was especially vocal in pressing in 1899–1902 for the formation of Canadian contingents to fight in the South African War.

The pan-Britannic union that Parkin advocated was not an end in itself, or a means for jingoism, militarism, or financial gain. He viewed it rather as a vehicle for the realization of idealist principles. With imperial power came moral responsibility. In an entirely characteristic speech he noted in 1894 that the Anglo-Saxon race "has temptations of an exceptional kind to yield itself to mere materialism, to forget that the things of the spirit are what endure and conquer in the end." Anglo-Saxons must not "lose the great moral purposes of life in the race for gain." Rather they must view the empire as a means of spiritual regeneration: "The more clearly we realize the growing power, the ever widening influence, the increasing prestige of the empire, the more surely will the thought turn us to self-examination and self-improvement." A strong, united empire would be a stimulant to moral reform of the rulers in Britain and the dominions, then threatened by growing materialism and social declension, and equally to the improvement of subject peoples abroad. In a telling phrase, he saw himself as "a wandering Evangelist of Empire."

Parkin's imperial campaigns eventually won his family moderate prosperity and social respectability. He himself became the confidant of prominent figures both in his native land and abroad. In Canada he had the ear of governors general Lord Aberdeen [Hamilton-Gordon*], Lord Minto [Elliot*], and Lord Grey*; he played a role in the policy decisions of Prime Minister Sir Wilfrid Laurier*, and was an adviser as well to other cabinet ministers and to leading journalists. In England he personally influenced the imperial ideas of Asquith, Lord Rosebery, Lord Milner, Winston Churchill, and Leopold Charles Maurice Stennett Amery, and moved tens of thousands of others to cheering support. His name was coupled by contemporaries with those of Seeley, Rudyard Kipling, and Cecil John Rhodes as the leading advocates of the "new imperialism," and many commentators assigned to him the key role in swaying public opinion to the imperial cause.

Because of his long educational and imperial experience, Parkin was invited by the Rhodes Trust in 1902 to be the first organizing secretary of its scholarship program. Travelling all over the empire and the United States several times before his retirement in 1920, he established the Rhodes scholarships on a permanent and prestigious basis. His English home at Goring became a meeting place for current and former scholars as well as for a host of empire-wide visitors. From this position he continued his speaking and writing on imperial matters, publishing biographies of Sir John A. Macdonald* (1908) and, within a larger account of the scholarships, of Rhodes (1912), both of which not surprisingly emphasized their subjects' imperial virtues. He campaigned vigorously during World War I to keep idealism's lessons front and centre and to build on the imperial unity being demonstrated by the dominions on the battlefields. In 1917–18 the British government asked him to use his contacts from the Rhodes scholarships to lecture all over the United States and attempt to counter anti-British or neutralist sentiment there. After the war he accepted the new definitions of dominion autonomy which evolved from the Paris Peace Conference, for his imperialism had always focused on the moral and spiritual unity of empire, displayed so clearly in the war, rather than on any particular constitutional formula. At the end of his life he devoted more time to the reform of the Church of England, in which he was a prominent lay leader. Many honours came his way: honorary doctorates from several universities, including his beloved Oxford, a CMG in 1898, and a KCMG in 1920.

Parkin's life was significant on several levels. His educational accomplishments, especially at Upper Canada College and with the Rhodes scholarships, have lasted a century. His many imperial campaigns and writings in the pre-1914 period were an important stimulus to the popularity of the new imperialism, which had vast consequences. His view of British imperialism and Canadian nationalism as complementary forces was influential, and his Christian idealism was illustrative of a powerful motivating force for many social and spiritual reforms in the pre-war years. Yet his empire was really a white empire of the mother country and the old dominions and, even within them, of the Anglo-Saxon race. French Canadians, Afrikaners, and the growing number of European immigrants in the dominions, let alone the non-white majorities in the newer colonies of Asia and Africa, could never accept Parkin's racial and cultural formulations. Critics further argued that the empire was a rather incongruous means, with its entrepreneurs and jingoists, to achieve Christian idealist ends. Idealism itself did not long survive the upheavals of the early 20th century.

Although the specific programs Parkin supported have long vanished, the Canadian conservative tradition of which he is part proved more durable. Conservatives of this approach – respectful of history, valuing unity under the crown and service to nation before self, promoting British and Commonwealth ties, wary of American economic integration and popular culture, and shunning materialism and individualism for a sense of community and tradition – have included Parkin's sons-in-law Charles Vincent Massey* and William Lawson Grant*, and his grandson George Parkin Grant*. The latter's *Lament for a nation: the defeat of Canadian nationalism* (Toronto, 1965) explicitly bemoans the passing of his grandfather's vision in the face of American dominance in Canadian culture. Vestiges of Grant's lament (and thus of Parkin's ideal) are still heard in the rhetoric of the federal Conservative and New Democratic parties.

TERRY COOK

[Sir George Robert Parkin's publications include *Imperial federation, the problem of national unity* (London and New York, 1892); *Round the empire; for the use of schools* (London, 1892); *The great dominion: studies of Canada* (London and New York, 1895); *Edward Thring, headmaster of Uppingham School: life, diary and letters* (2v., London and New York, 1898); *Sir John A. Macdonald* (Toronto, 1908); and *The Rhodes scholarships* (Toronto, 1912). A comprehensive bibliography of his works and of the archival sources relevant to his life appears in the author's doctoral dissertation, "'Apostle of empire': Sir George Parkin and imperial federation" (PHD thesis, Queen's Univ., Kingston, Ont., 1977). A selection of the major manuscript collections is listed below. T.C.]

Bodleian Library, Univ. of Oxford, Eng., Viscount Alfred Milner papers (mfm. at LAC, MG 27, II, A3). Durham Univ. Library, Arch. and Special Coll. (Durham, Eng.), GB-0033-GRE (Earl Grey papers), sect.4. LAC, MG 27, II, B1; MG 29, B1; D46; E29; MG 30, D44; D59; D77; MG 32, A1. QUA, Lorne and Edith Pierce coll., Bliss Carman papers. Rhodes House Library, Univ. of Oxford, Rhodes Scholarship Trust, corr. (mfm. at LAC, MG 28, I, 58). Upper Canada College (Toronto), Board of governors and board of trustees, minutes. Carl Berger, *The sense of power; studies in the* ideas of Canadian imperialism, 1867–1914 (Toronto and Buffalo, N.Y., 1970). D. L. Cole, "Canada's 'nationalistic' imperialists," *Journal of Canadian Studies* (Peterborough, Ont.), 5 (1970), no.3: 44–49. Terry Cook, "George R. Parkin and the concept of Britannic Idealism," *Journal of Canadian Studies*, 10 (1975), no.3: 15–31; "A reconstruction of the world: George R. Parkin's British empire map of 1893," *Cartographica* (Toronto), 21 (1984), no.4: 53–65. *DNB*. R. B. Howard, *Upper Canada College, 1829–1979: Colborne's legacy* (Toronto, 1979). John Willison, *Sir George Parkin: a biography* (London, 1929).

PARSONS, GERTRUDE ISABELLA, painter and writer; b. 16 May 1880 in St John's, daughter of Alexander A. Parsons and Maria Raven Thompson; d. there unmarried 27 May 1924.

Gertrude Parsons's family were adherents of the Methodist Church and the church was to have an influential role in her life. She received her early education at a private school operated by Louisa and Sophia Barnes at 217 Gower Street in St John's, and then travelled to England where she studied art, in Liverpool with a Professor Lane and in London with Mrs Hall Neyle. After her return to St John's, she first gained recognition as a painter of portraits and landscapes. She established a portrait studio in St John's and offered art classes. Her work was in demand and displayed throughout the town.

Parsons was also a writer of some acclaim. Her talents were probably encouraged by her father, the first editor of the St John's *Evening Telegram* and a regular contributor to the *Newfoundland Quarterly*. Gertrude's published work was quite small, limited to a short story, "Christmas vision," which appeared in the *Newfoundland Magazine* in 1920, and a novel *Broken links*, published in London in 1923, but it seems to have been well received by the local populace. Set in a small English village, *Broken links* is a tale of lost love, the result of a mischievous prank involving a letter, and the tragic consequences it brings to the hero and heroine. The climax offers an unexpected twist, since the couple do not reunite and live happily ever after. It is well written, with clear and concise prose, a believable story inhabited by credible characters who move the action along at a solid pace. There are strong Methodist influences: morality, punishment for sin, and suffering in this world, with the hope of redemption in the next. Her Victorian education and upbringing are also in evidence.

Parsons was very involved in the work of her local church, Gower Street Methodist. When the Newfoundland branch of the Woman's Missionary Society, a church organization, was formed on 18 Nov. 1915, she was elected secretary of circles and bands, the youth division of the society. Except for 1921–22 she would continue to hold this office until her death. She had considerable success: each year her activity reports indicate steady increases in membership, in

the number of congregations sponsoring circles and bands, and in the amount of money raised. Her contribution was recognized at the 1921 annual meeting when she was presented with a life membership and a gold pin. Parsons had been scheduled to participate in the young people's service at the branch's annual meeting on 28 May 1924, the day after her death. The women delegates to the meeting from all parts of Newfoundland attended her funeral as a body, a further sign of the high esteem in which she was held. A report on her passing in the *Methodist Monthly Greeting* paid tribute to her as "one of the most talented connected with this organization [the WMS]. As an artist, a writer and a most gifted speaker Miss Parsons gave both time and talent most cheerfully to the young people in whom she took such deep interest."

Parsons was in the process of finishing a second novel, set in Newfoundland, at the time of her death. It was never published. Her first novel showed promise. Ironically, the reviewer in the *Daily News* had hoped "that her first volume may not prove the last; and that out of the rich stories of legend, love and life, in which our own Newfoundland abounds, she may find inspiration for many pages in the years to come."

BERTRAM RIGGS

No manuscripts or personal papers of Gertrude Isabella Parsons are known to exist. Her short story, "Christmas vision," appeared in the *Newfoundland Magazine* (St John's), 4 (December 1920): 25–26, and her novel, *Broken links; a story*, was published in London in 1923. The only painting by her that has been found – a portrait of Captain James Moss – hangs in the archives of Gower Street United Church in St John's.

Daily News (St John's), 1 June 1916; 9 June 1917; 6 June 1918; 5–6 June 1919; 2, 4 June 1920; 24 Aug. 1923; 28, 30 May 1924. *Evening Telegram* (St John's), 3 June 1921, 28 May 1924. *Directory*, St John's, 1890. *A history of the Thompson family, by one of its members*, [comp. G. J. A. Thompson] (n.p., 1937). *Methodist Monthly Greeting* (St John's), March 1916, August 1917, July 1918, July 1919, June 1924. *Missionary Outlook* (Toronto), new ser., 39 (1919): 186; 40 (1920): 187; 41 (1921): 165; 42 (1922): 442; 44 (1924): 186.

PATERSON, JOHN ANDREW, lawyer, social reformer, and author; b. 22 June 1846 in Stornoway, Scotland, son of John Paterson and Jane Balfour Allison; m. first 5 Jan. 1876 Christina Dick Riddell in Toronto, and they had three sons and a daughter; m. secondly Mary Allan; d. 13 May 1930 in Toronto.

John Paterson's father was a Presbyterian minister and teacher in Scotland and England and he continued in the ministry after immigrating to Canada with his family in 1858. John was then enrolled at Upper Canada College in Toronto, where he became head boy in 1861. The next year he entered the University of Toronto on a double scholarship in classics and mathematics; he consistently stood first or second in his class. He graduated in 1866 and the following year received his MA while teaching mathematics at Upper Canada College, a post he held for three years. He then decided to use his analytical skills in the study of law. Called to the bar on 26 Nov. 1872, he would practise in Toronto for 57 years.

Throughout his life, Paterson was clearly influenced by his Presbyterian upbringing. He served his congregations, Bay Street (Erskine) in 1872–98 and Bloor Street in 1899–1930, as manager, elder, and Sunday school superintendent. Within the Presbyterian Church in Canada, he attended several general assemblies and sat on many committees and as a senator of Knox College between 1892 and 1925. He was the college's solicitor as early as 1909, when land was being acquired for its new building on St George Street. Active in interdenominational work, he was president of the Ontario Sunday School Association in 1895–96, president of the Ontario Lord's Day Alliance in 1897 (and chair of its committee on law for several years), and chair of the Canadian council of the Laymen's Missionary Movement in 1916. A firm temperance advocate, he took part in the campaign leading up to the Prohibition referendum in Ontario in December 1902 [see Francis Stephens Spence*] and in attempts in 1903 to curb liquor sales. At Bloor Street Church he and assistant pastor Clare Melville Wright prepared a statement for their congregation on the Prohibition plebiscite of 1924. These and other organizations and causes benefited from Paterson's quiet but persuasive legal expertise. Notwithstanding the strength of his Presbyterian roots, he was a leader in the movement to form the United Church of Canada in 1925. He had been vice-president of the General Board of the Presbyterian Church in Canada, and had acted as chair when Daniel Robert Drummond, an opponent of union, resigned shortly before it became a reality.

In politics Paterson identified himself in 1923 as a Liberal in the mould of George Brown*, "as my father was before me, and I have never seen any reason to change my allegiance." One can find evidence that his political, educational, and religious connections helped him in his career. In 1885 a prominent Liberal, James Kirkpatrick Kerr, became the head of his law firm (Kerr, Macdonald, Davidson, and Paterson). From 1900 Paterson was the University of Toronto's solicitor. Named a provincial KC on 27 May 1902, he was soon appointed by John Morison GIBSON, the Liberal attorney general of Ontario, to appear before the Judicial Committee of the Privy Council in England to argue the constitutionality of an 1897 act prohibiting the profanation of the Lord's Day, which had been challenged by the Hamilton Street Railway Company and others. The JCPC found that, in so far as violations of the act were considered criminal, the

statute was unconstitutional since criminal law was a dominion responsibility. Although Paterson was on the losing side, the judgement was an important step in the passage of the federal Lord's Day Act of 1906, for which he had lobbied on behalf of the Lord's Day Alliance. Paterson's abilities were recognized by other administrations as well. In 1912, on behalf of the Conservative government, he successfully had the London and Lake Erie Railway prosecuted under the Ontario Railway Act; the attorney general, however, refused to pay his full bill. In 1921 the United Farmers government called on him to form a commission to inquire into slipshod enforcement of the Ontario Temperance Act by the police magistrate of Dunnville, David Hastings, who resigned as a result. In the private sector his work included many years (1907–25) as lawyer to the North American Life Assurance Company, of which he was also a director. In all his efforts, including his advocacy of life insurance, Paterson saw the goals he sought as steps to alleviate misery brought about by drunkenness, overwork, and poverty.

Paterson's long-standing interest in mathematics had led him in 1890 to join the Astronomical and Physical Society of Toronto (later the Royal Astronomical Society of Canada). In 1892 he published his first paper in its *Transactions*, on stellar evolution, and was elected second vice-president. In this office he accepted many presidential duties owing to the illness or age of incumbents Charles Carpmael* and Larratt William Violett Smith; he served as president in his own right in 1896–97. In 1897, at the Toronto meeting of the British Association for the Advancement of Science, he spoke on the "unification of time." The hope was to get international nautical, civil, and astronomical authorities to agree that the day should start at midnight. The idea appealed to common sense and was promoted by Sir Sandford Fleming*, well known for his efforts to introduce standard-time zones, but traditional practices would prevail until 1925. All told, over a period of 32 years, Paterson wrote 24 reports and popular papers for the astronomical society, most based on lectures he gave. Seven of these were accounts of the lives of well-known astronomers and three concerned astronomy in the work of Tennyson, Shakespeare, and Milton. As Paterson said in 1909, "The muses of Poetry and Urania her sister clasped hands and have in all ages sung to the world the sweet rhymes of mother Nature." He consistently saw the hand of a divine creator in nature, even when he delved into the theory of life on Mars and elsewhere.

Paterson's personal life was marked by several tragedies. His first wife, Tina, died in 1908 after being struck by a cyclist. They had shared many of the same ideals; as well, she had been a recording secretary of the Toronto Local Council of Women and a vice-president of the Women's Art Association of Canada. Two of his sons died young, Harold John in 1904 and Ernest Riddell (the first Rhodes scholar from the University of Toronto) in 1912, and his son-in-law, Saxon Frederick Shenstone, passed away on Christmas Day, 1915, at the age of 37. The last two or three years of his own life were marked by illness.

John A. Paterson was very much a man of his time and circumstances. The causes he championed – missionary work, temperance, and sabbath observance – were all part of the movement to improve morality in Canadian society.

PETER BROUGHTON

Lectures that were given by John Andrew Paterson and reported in the press include "Astronomy and devoutness," *Evening Telegram* (Toronto), 26 Nov. 1924; "Astronomy has no quarrel with spiritual devotees," *Globe*, 26 Nov. 1924; "Discusses theory of life on Mars," *Globe*, 14 Nov. 1923; and "Supposition," *Globe*, 30 Nov. 1921. Articles written by Paterson include "The Privy Council and the Lord's Day Act," *Presbyterian* (Toronto), new ser., 3 (July–December 1903): 379, and "Simon Newcomb – his life and work," Royal Astronomical Soc. of Canada, *Journal* (Toronto), 7 (1913): 389–403.

AO, RG 4-32, 1903, file 1585; 1904, file 911; 1905, file 458; 1908, file 691; 1911, file 716; RG 22-305, nos.7260, 23502, 64760; RG 80-5-0-62, no.12849. Presbyterian Church in Canada Arch. (Toronto), 101/0008 (Knox College, Toronto, legal documents (mortgages, etc.)), 1887–1927; 102/0008 (Knox College, senate, minutes), 1908–27; 1989-4002-1-3 (Erskine Presbyterian Church, Toronto, board of managers and congregational meetings, minutes), 1837–83. UCC-C, 1777, 92.029L, 5-1, 5-2, 7-14, 9-5, 17-2; Biog. file. UTA, A1970-0024/008, vol.10; A1973-0026/357 (69, 79, 82); A1974-0018. Astronomical and Physical Soc. of Toronto, *Trans.*, 1892. *Attorney-General for Ontario v. the Hamilton Street Railway Company and others*, [1903] *Law Reports, Appeal Cases* (London): 524–30. *Canadian annual rev.*, 1902–3, 1907, 1921. *Canadian men and women of the time* (Morgan; 1898 and 1912). Presbyterian Church in Canada, General Assembly, *Acts and proc.* (Toronto), 1891–1925. *The roll of pupils of Upper Canada College, Toronto, January, 1830, to June, 1916*, ed. A. H. Young (Kingston, Ont., 1917). Royal Astronomical Soc. of Canada, *General index to the publications of the Astronomical and Physical Society of Toronto, 1890–1899*, comp. W. E. Harper (Toronto, 1931).

PEARCE, WILLIAM, surveyor, civil engineer, public servant, and statistician; b. 1 Feb. 1848 in Dunwich Township, Upper Canada, son of John Pearce and Elizabeth Moorhouse; brother of John Seabury Pearce*; m. 20 Sept. 1881 Margaret Adolphine Meyer in McKillop Township, Ont., and they had five sons, two of whom died in infancy, and two daughters; d. 3 March 1930 in Calgary.

William Pearce was born on the edge of Upper Canada's settled frontier near Tyrconnell, on Lake Erie. Taken from school at age 12 to help clear the family property, he later returned and eventually enrolled in the engineering course at the University of Toronto, probably in 1868. After a year of study there and three years' apprenticeship with the Toronto engineering firm of Wadsworth and Unwin, he gained certification as an Ontario land surveyor in 1872. The skill he displayed on the complex Thousand Islands survey the following year impressed his senior colleagues, among whom was the dominion surveyor general, John Stoughton Dennis*, who asked Pearce to join his staff for work in Manitoba and the North-West Territories. He thus became a dominion land surveyor in 1874, and in 1875 he was appointed to the board of examiners for dominion land surveyors.

Employed on a series of one-year contracts through the mid 1870s, Pearce was engaged in establishing legal subdivisions in the Winnipeg area, where he gained recognition for his competence in dealing with the difficult and politically charged matter of conflicting Métis land claims [*see* Donald Codd*]. He also helped initiate the meridian, baseline, and township grid surveys that would occupy teams of dominion land surveyors for the next 30 years. It was while involved with these tasks in the Turtle Mountain area in southwestern Manitoba that Pearce took it upon himself to advise his supervisors on land-use policy. Observing the activities of the first wave of homesteaders in the area and what he deemed to be the misappropriation of vital resources by first arrivals, he urged that the government exercise its authority under the Dominion Lands Act of 1872 to reserve large tracts containing scarce timber and water. In Pearce's view, such valuable lands should be held for the use of bona fide farmers rather than surrendered for the private advantage of speculators and a handful of commercial enterprises. It remained his firm conviction throughout his career that it was in the public interest to ensure that lands and resources were developed in a manner benefiting the majority, even if such a policy meant restricting commercial enterprises or the rights of individual property holders. In this regard, Pearce envisaged a degree of government intervention that ran against the laissez-faire spirit that predominated amongst those settling in the west.

The opportunity to carry this point of view into practice was afforded with Pearce's appointment in February 1882 to the position of inspector of dominion lands agencies, which along with the office of commissioner of dominion lands constituted the newly formed Dominion Lands Board within the Department of the Interior. The board's primary responsibilities were to supervise Dominion Lands offices in prairie communities and ensure that there was uniform compliance with the law by local agents, to adjudicate all land disputes, and to advise the government on the development of lands and resources. The board opened its Winnipeg office in March and with characteristic energy Pearce began a series of inspections. The trail of dismissed agents, evicted squatters, and public figures called to account for land speculation that followed soon made him a respected but controversial figure with some powerful enemies, especially Frank Oliver*, owner and editor of the *Edmonton Bulletin*. If Pearce was motivated by a deep sense of mission, he was also inclined to be authoritarian and blunt. There would be times when his insistence on strict compliance had to be curbed by his political masters.

Given the duties of his office, his past experience in Manitoba, and his reputation for meticulous documentation, Pearce was called upon in 1883 to investigate the land claims of settlers and Métis along the North Saskatchewan River between Battleford and Prince Albert (Sask.). His failure to complete this large and complex task before 1885 [*see* Sir David Lewis Macpherson*] was seen by some at the time, and others subsequently, as having been a factor in the North-West rebellion [*see* Louis Riel*]. Following the uprising, Pearce was directed to undertake a comprehensive study of the causes leading up to it and assess the federal government's responsibility. His 1886 report absolving the government of blame did not impress the Liberal opposition. Seen by his opponents as a Conservative, Pearce himself refused to be labelled. In a letter to Clifford SIFTON in 1897, he would declare that, to ensure public trust, he had never cast a vote for any federal, territorial, or municipal candidate or attended a political meeting since the date of his entry into public service.

As construction on the Canadian Pacific Railway advanced into the Rocky Mountains in 1884 and applications for mineral rights to nearby properties began to materialize, Ottawa became convinced that a mining and land boom was about to commence and proposed the establishment of a senior Department of the Interior officer in Calgary whose specific responsibility would be to administer the development of the region's timber and mineral resources. The individual chosen for this new position, superintendent of mines, was William Pearce, who was appointed on 15 May. Already one of a handful of federal civil servants with real power in the west, Pearce emerged now as an even more influential figure. As superintendent, he reported directly to the deputy minister of the interior (until early 1897, Alexander Mackinnon Burgess*) and was almost an independent authority with free rein to exercise his considerable energy and talent over the federal land known as the railway belt, which straddled the CPR's main line from the Red River valley to the Rockies and into British Columbia. It is not hard to understand why Pearce was known to some of his detractors as "Czar of the West." As both a member of the Dominion Lands Board and superintendent of mines, he was responsible not only for administering, but also for formulating, the regulations governing the

future development of resources in the North-West Territories.

Although the redrafting of federal mining regulations occupied Pearce's attention initially, the mining boom failed to materialize and his energies were redirected to other issues. The first of these emerged with competing claims to the newly discovered mineral hot springs near Banff (Alta), claims that Pearce in 1886 was called upon to evaluate. With others, Pearce had concluded that the springs should be retained by the crown, and he had played an important part in having the area set aside in 1885 for public use. Afterwards, using phrasing similar to that found in America's Yellowstone National Park Act of 1872, he drafted the 1887 statute creating Canada's first national park, Rocky Mountains Park. Pearce was subsequently instrumental in setting aside and determining the boundaries of what later became Yoho and Glacier national parks in British Columbia. Anticipating Calgary's future growth, he also set aside St George's and St Patrick's islands, along with the opposite north bank of the Bow River, as future parkland.

As much as Pearce was attracted to the notion of reserving exceptionally scenic areas, he soon came to see water management as a more urgent area of concern. A witness to the severe drought that began in the late 1880s, he became convinced that the future of the prairies was dependent upon the proper distribution of the region's limited water supply. The government should therefore take over the management of this precious resource. Pearce's thoughts in this regard were greatly influenced by his travels in the American west, as well as by the writings of John Wesley Powell, the distinguished head of the United States Geological Survey, and Elwood Mead, America's preeminent authority on irrigation and water law, both of whom advocated government management of water in the arid west.

Believing that most of southern Alberta and western Assiniboia was too dry for cereal agriculture and better suited to grazing, Pearce advised the restriction of homestead settlement in favour of measures that supported the already well-established cattle industry. In 1886 the government, under Pearce's direction, began to set aside for public use select springs and strategic locations along creeks, rivers, and lakefronts. Intended to prevent homesteaders and large cattle companies from denying access to a vital resource, the network of stock-watering reservations established over the following decade was important in helping cattlemen to fend off the initial tide of prairie settlement that followed Clifford Sifton's immigration campaign at the turn of the century.

Managing water in support of the cattle industry was but a preliminary step towards Pearce's real objective, comprehensive government management of the region's entire water supply. While he considered open settlement in the grazing region undesirable, he was aware that there were large tracts of fertile land within the dry belt that were well suited to irrigation. He calculated, however, that the available water was sufficient to irrigate only a fraction of such lands. It therefore seemed obvious to him that continued development of the dry country hinged upon progressive irrigation legislation.

With unrelenting energy, Pearce set about the task of converting community leaders, politicians, and senior federal bureaucrats to the cause. He faced a formidable challenge. It was not so much that irrigation was a hard sell, given the ongoing drought. Rather, it was the nature of the legislative foundation that Pearce wanted to put in place to support it. Instructed by what he had seen in the American west, where a complex patchwork of state and federal laws based upon different water-law doctrines clogged the courts with litigation and made efficient and equitable distribution of water all but impossible, Pearce argued that the key to progressive management lay in vesting the federal government with the ownership of water. This proposal to abolish all private claims to water other than for domestic use flew in the face of the ancient Anglo-Saxon doctrine of riparian rights, was highly controversial, and made Pearce's civil and political masters very nervous. In the end, the continuing drought, an awareness that since the North-West Territories remained sparsely settled there was a moment of opportunity to act before private rights were extensively established, and Pearce's skilful mobilization of regional support pushed his cautious colleagues to move forward. Drafted by Pearce, the North-west Irrigation Act won parliamentary approval in July 1894. It transferred ownership of water throughout the territories to the federal government, enshrined the notion of water as a public resource, privileged community rights over private rights, and enabled federal bureaucrats to manage water in the public interest. Held up by Elwood Mead and other American authorities as a model of enlightened legislation, the act set water management in the Canadian prairie west on a course distinct from practice elsewhere on the continent and it stands as the foundation of contemporary water law in Saskatchewan and Alberta.

Pearce's vision of an irrigated Eden now rested upon the construction of a network of dams, reservoirs, and trunk canals. Unable to convince Ottawa that the government should build this infrastructure, Pearce had initiated discussions with William Cornelius Van Horne*, who headed one of the few private organizations, the CPR, capable of undertaking a project of this scale. Aware that the Canadian government still owed the railway nearly four million acres to fulfil its charter obligations, and that the only significant remaining block of unclaimed prairie was in that portion of the arid district which bordered the

CPR's main line between Medicine Hat (Alta) and Calgary, Pearce seized upon irrigation as the vehicle to enable the railway and the government to resolve the issue. His persistence was instrumental in the transfer to the railway, in August 1903, of more than 3.5 million acres, 2.9 million of which formed a compact area known as the "irrigation block." The CPR began construction on the main canal leading from the Bow River just east of Calgary in 1904, thus launching one of North America's largest irrigation and colonization schemes that included a program of assisted settlement along the lines that Pearce had envisioned. Pearce had also been instrumental in 1896 in enabling Elliott Torrance GALT to consolidate land for irrigation east and south of Lethbridge.

From the outset Pearce understood his irrigation legislation as but an initial step requiring several complementary measures. The most contentious of these called for the creation of a vast forest reserve to protect the headwaters of streams and rivers flowing onto the prairie from the Rocky Mountains. Eventually, in the face of resistance from logging, grazing, and settlement interests, the Foot Hills Forest Reserve (Alta) was established in 1898. Embracing all of the territory from the summit of the Rockies to the prairie and extending northward from the international boundary to the Bow River, this immense reserve, known after 1912 as the Rocky Mountain Forest Reserve, remains a monument to Pearce's foresight.

These achievements aside, the decade following the passage of the North-west Irrigation Act was a difficult one for Pearce. Both the climatic and the political environment conspired to undermine his vision. The weather cycle began to shift almost as soon as the act gained royal assent and years of increased annual rainfall eroded farmers' support for irrigation initiatives. As well, the federal Liberals led by Wilfrid Laurier* came to power in 1896 and Pearce's influence, along with that of his most senior colleagues in the Department of the Interior, gradually declined. He was demoted to chief inspector of surveys in 1901. Eventually, pressure for his dismissal combined with an attractive offer from CPR president Sir Thomas George SHAUGHNESSY led Pearce to leave government service in 1904 and join the railway team designing the huge Bow River irrigation scheme that he had helped to initiate. He could now focus upon what had long been his priority.

Once the irrigation project was well in hand, the CPR called upon Pearce's unrivalled knowledge of prairie lands for a new assignment. He was handed the enormous task of doing a demographic and resource survey of all the territory within the railway's vast land grant while paying particular attention to the millions of acres that remained unsold. Intended as the foundation upon which the railway would plan its spur-line network, this township-by-township survey would take nearly five years to complete and would ultimately help direct the last phase of prairie settlement.

Perhaps in recognition of the immensity of the task ahead, before embarking on the assignment Pearce in 1910 set off on a world tour. Not surprisingly, the focus of his travels was major irrigation projects, including those in Egypt, the Sudan, India, the Philippines, China, Japan, and Australia. The trip, along with his subsequent observation of scores of abandoned homesteads in the dry belt during the course of the CPR survey, reinforced Pearce's conviction that settlement in much of the prairie region hinged upon irrigation. This view was reflected in the work that he did for the economic and development commission in 1916. The influence of his thinking is apparent in the commission's recommendation that the federal government study possible comprehensive irrigation schemes for the semi-arid regions in the west. Pearce had just such a scheme to recommend. Impressed by the scale of the irrigation works he had seen in northern India, he envisioned diverting the North Saskatchewan River to irrigate a nearly 20-million-acre region straddling the Alberta–Saskatchewan border. Coinciding with the return of severe drought, Pearce's scheme gained serious attention. Spurred on by the exodus of settlers from the dry belt, initial topographic surveys demonstrated its feasibility, but the projected cost of $105 million and the return to wet years beginning in 1923 caused momentum to ebb. Pearce remained an advocate, but his voice was lost in the clamour of returning prosperity.

If interest in Pearce's irrigation ideas dwindled, his stature as the region's pre-eminent authority on land and resource development remained undiminished, and his advice and involvement were widely sought. He had earlier influenced Alberta's economic development in another way: as vice-president of the Calgary Petroleum Products Company Limited, he was among the small group of local entrepreneurs responsible for the 1914 Turner valley oil discovery which ultimately transformed his adopted province.

According to his daughter Adolphina Thornton Tassie, Pearce was "a natural pioneer," endowed with "fine health and a powerful physique, capable of unlimited endurance." He was known to his contemporaries as an avid walker and a long-distance snowshoer. He had great intellectual curiosity as well, keeping four encyclopedias in his home. His daughter remembered that he used to tell his children to use a dictionary, sometimes even before they could read. A stalwart of the Church of England in Calgary, he was a member of the Ranchmen's Club there and of the Manitoba Club in Winnipeg. He kept up his professional ties, as first president of the Alberta Land Surveyors' Association and a member of the Engineering Institute of Canada, the Association of Professional Engineers of Alberta, and the Corporation of Land Surveyors of the Province of British Columbia. He was also a fellow of the Royal Geographical Society and served as vice-president of the Canadian Forestry Association. Interested in urban issues, he was president for a time of Calgary's City Planning Commission and honorary president of the Alberta Town Planning and Housing Association.

Pearce retired in 1926 but retained an office at the CPR where he continued to work on projects of interest, including a history of the prairie region in which he had played such a prominent part. He died on 3 March 1930 in his beloved Bow Bend Shack, with its irrigated gardens and fine interior woodwork, at the onset of yet another dry cycle. Though he was not physically present to lead the debate, Pearce's observations, as well as the legislative foundation that he had helped to put in place, would contribute to the framework of discussion for this and each of the droughts that followed. Pearce's initiatives in the establishment of Canada's Rocky Mountain forest and park reserves were similarly far-reaching in their impact. Sent west by the Canadian government to help to build a new nation, William Pearce had built carefully and well.

DAVID BREEN

William Pearce is the author of "Detailed report upon all claims to land and right to participate in the North-West half-breed grant by settlers along the South Saskatchewan and vicinity west of range 26, W. 2nd meridian, being the settlements commonly known as St. Louis de Langevin, St. Laurent or Batoche, and Duck Lake," Can., Parl., *Sessional papers*, 1886, no.8b. He later wrote "Establishment of the national parks in the Rocky and Selkirk mountains: a paper delivered to the Historical Society of Calgary, 16 Dec. 1924," *Calgary Herald*, 27 Dec. 1924: 5, also printed in *Alberta Hist. Rev.* (Calgary), 10 (1962), no.3: 8–27.

AO, RG 80-5-0-98, no.4799. Univ. of Alta Arch. (Edmonton), William Pearce fonds. Assoc. of Ontario Land Surveyors, *Annual report* (Toronto), 1931: 94–97. D. H. Breen, *The Canadian prairie west and the ranching frontier, 1874–1924* (Toronto, 1983). C. S. Burchill, "The origins of Canadian irrigation law," *CHR*, 29 (1948): 353–62. Can., Parl., *Sessional papers*, reports of the Dept. of the Interior, 1880–1905; *Statutes*, 1894, c.30. S. A. Donaldson, "William Pearce: his vision of trees," *Journal of Garden Hist.* (London), 3 (1983): 233–44. D. C. Jones, *Empire of dust: settling and abandoning the prairie dry belt* (Edmonton, 1987). C. S. Kenny, *A treatise on the law of irrigation and water rights . . .* (2nd ed., 4v., San Francisco, Calif., 1912), 1. W. F. Lothian, *A history of Canada's national parks* (4v., Ottawa, 1976–81), 1. Elwood Mead, *Irrigation institutions: a discussion of the economic and legal questions created by the growth of irrigated agriculture in the west* (London, 1903). E. A. Mitchner, "William Pearce and federal government activity in western Canada, 1882–1904" (PHD thesis, Univ. of Alta, 1971); "William Pearce: father of Alberta irrigation" (MA thesis, Univ. of Alta, 1966). A. A. den Otter, *Civilizing the west: the Galts and the development of western Canada* (Edmonton, 1982). A. [T. Pearce] Tassie with C. S. Howard, "Prairie surveys and a prairie surveyor," *Canadian Banker* (Toronto), 60 (1953), no.2: 53–73.

PEASE, EDSON LOY, banker; b. 2 Sept. 1856 in Coteau-Landing (Les Coteaux), Lower Canada, son of Orton Pease and Mary Hare; m. 24 April 1883 Diana Ann Rea in Montreal, and they had two sons, and a daughter who died young; d. 29 Dec. 1930 in Nice, France.

Edson Pease, the 12th of 14 children, was born into the world of the "commercial empire of the St Lawrence." His father, a native of Massachusetts, had immigrated to Lower Canada in 1823. He settled in Coteau-Landing, on the shores of the St Lawrence River, where he prospered as a shoemaker, general merchant, and real estate investor, and served as town treasurer. Pease Street and Pease's Wharf bespoke the family's commercial prowess in the small town. The arterial commerce of the great river shaped Edson's world-view. Since his eldest brother, Charles, had joined his father in the general store, Edson was obliged to seek wider horizons. A boyhood friend, Charles Rudolph Hosmer, had found employment as a telegraph operator with the Grand Trunk Railway. Pease followed the example, joining a telegraph company in Ogdensburg, N.Y., in 1873 or 1874.

Commerce on the St Lawrence River and the technological reach of the telegraph drew Pease out of rural Canada and prepared him for entry into the emerging urban professional class. On 24 April 1875 he joined the Montreal branch of the Toronto-based Canadian Bank of Commerce as a clerk. In 1881 he was promoted to the inspectors' department of the bank. Promising young bankers were made inspectors, a role that required them to police a bank's entire branch system for conformity to the procedures of the head office. Confederation had enabled the disjointed colonial banking systems of British North America to consolidate into a federalized system based on Scottish branch banking. The process was by no means smooth; regionally tied small banks were prone to collapse, often provoked by the narrow base of their business or by the loose regulatory and procedural framework in which they worked.

Typical of this pattern was the Merchants' Bank of Halifax. Since obtaining a federal charter in 1869, it had cautiously built up a network of 25 branches throughout Nova Scotia, New Brunswick, and Prince Edward Island. Bad loans to Nova Scotian steel producers and sugar refiners in the early 1880s and a defalcation in 1882 of its cashier (general manager) had checked the bank's progress [*see* David Hunter Duncan*] and revealed its precarious regional base.

The Merchants' president, Thomas Edward Kenny*, was inclined to aggressive expansion as an anti-dote to regional stagnation. Breadth of operation would induce stability. To pursue this strategy he needed new talent. Accordingly, on 18 Jan. 1883 the bank hired Pease as accountant at its main branch in Halifax at an annual salary of $3,000. Pease's initial task was to implement consistent procedures throughout the bank, thereby preventing further defalcation and ensuring standard loan practices as well as rigorous staff training. Pease soon revealed his true genius – as a strategist of the bank's continental and international expansion and as a progressive innovator of bank procedure.

Pease's innovations met with some resistance from a few of the bank's more conservative directors. In 1887 they opposed his move to open a branch in Montreal in order to place the Merchants' on the doorstep of the westward-oriented national economy. Pease's determination and the backing he received from Kenny helped carry the day. He became the branch's manager, at an annual salary of $3,500. He energetically sought business clients in the city. The St Lawrence Sugar Refining Company Limited, metal fabricator Drummond, McCall and Company [*see* George Edward Drummond*], newspaper proprietor Hugh Graham*, and financier Louis-Joseph Forget* were typical of his early acquisitions. Pease's friendship with Hosmer, now head of the Canadian Pacific Railway's telegraph department, gave him an entrée to the city's commercial elite. Pease also pushed the bank's retail business across the island of Montreal, establishing branches on Rue Notre-Dame and in the emerging affluent suburb of Côte-Saint-Antoine, which would soon become the town of Westmount. Pease struck correspondence agreements with other Canadian and American banks so as to expand the circulation of its notes, hired new staff, including the bank's first French Canadians, and modernized its procedures and facilities, largely along American lines (including spacious, airy bank interiors). Still small in comparison with its large competitors, such as the Bank of Montreal and the Canadian Bank of Commerce, the Merchants' Bank was nonetheless by the late 1890s a national bank, with assets of $17,102,000, 42 branches, and by 1899 a steady seven per cent dividend on common shares.

Success in Montreal fanned Pease's expansionistic instincts. Reluctant to compete with the more established banks in their base of central Canada, he looked to new frontiers. In 1897, egged on by Hosmer, he visited the interior of British Columbia and quickly opened branches in Rossland and Nelson to tap their thriving mining economies. Two years later a branch was established just over the border in the boom town of Republic, Wash., where Montreal firms had mining interests. By 1908 there were 21 branches in British Columbia, coordinated from a regional head office in Vancouver. The bank's experience in financing the movement of Maritime trade in fish, timber, and sugar opened the way to international expansion. Shortly after American troops moved into Havana, Cuba, in 1898, Pease arrived to explore the city. Joined by other Canadian entrepreneurs such as Sir William Cornelius Van Horne* of Montreal and David MacKeen* and Benjamin Franklin Pearson* of Halifax, Pease saw opportunity in post-bellum Cuba. The movement of Cuban sugar to market required forward financing (loans for planting and transportation costs to be repaid on the delivery of sugar to market). In 1899 a branch was opened in New York City to handle the American end of sugar deals. That same year another was established in Havana, followed by a succession of branches in sugar-producing provinces such as Camagüey and Oriente (Santiago de Cuba), usually not far from Van Horne's Cuba Railroad. By 1923 a peak of 65 Cuban branches would be reached. Other branches in the Caribbean and South America included Puerto Rico (1907), Jamaica (1911), Brazil (1919), and Panama (1929). To complement this expansion, Pease directed the opening of branches in the financial centres of Europe: London (1910), Barcelona (1918), and Paris (1919). By 1928 the bank was Canada's leading overseas banker with 121 branches in 28 countries. Such was Pease's instinct for opportunity that in 1919 a branch was even temporarily opened in Vladivostok in revolutionary Siberia, where the Canadian government had sent trade commissioners, sensing possibilities for commerce. Through all this expansion, Pease became an inveterate traveller. Tellers in the bank's main branch at Montreal, for instance, relished the Cuban cigars which he freely distributed on his return from the south.

Pease's orchestration of the bank's expansion out of the Maritimes brought him corporate preferment. In 1899 he was promoted joint general manager, sharing the post with the more conservative David Hunter Duncan, who anchored the Merchants' head office in Halifax. Duncan's retirement at the end of 1899 left Pease in sole command and opened the way to more change. Backed by Kenny, Pease argued that the bank needed a more cosmopolitan image and in 1901 the Merchants' Bank of Halifax became the Royal Bank of Canada (a name reminiscent of the venerable Royal Bank of Scotland). Montreal became the bank's de facto centre of operations with Pease in charge. In 1907 the bank's head office was officially moved to Montreal and Pease joined the board of directors. A year later the bank began adopting North American banking nomenclature to replace the British terminology it had used since its establishment and Pease became a vice-president. Following Kenny's death in 1908, Pease recruited Herbert Samuel Holt*, a successful railway contractor and rising promoter of utilities, to the Royal's presidency. Holt's role was largely titular; he provided the bank with a dynamic image.

Pease was by now the bank's undisputed strategist and senior executive.

Sensing the opportunities of the economic boom during Sir Wilfrid Laurier*'s second term as prime minister, Pease determined to complement the bank's nascent overseas expansion with vigorous national growth. Constrained by the slowness of natural growth (dictated by laborious training of new staff and the expense of head-to-head competition with other banks), Pease opted for an energetic policy of growth by merger. Mergers with smaller, regionally based banks provided two immediate advantages: enhanced regional penetration and the acquisition of reliable, trained staff. Between 1910 and 1925 he engineered five such mergers, all initiated by the Royal. Acquisition of the Union Bank of Halifax in 1910 consolidated the bank's base in the Maritimes. The merger with the Toronto-based Traders' Bank of Canada in 1912 brought strength in Ontario, and the addition in 1917 of the Quebec Bank solidified the Royal's ascendance in Anglo-Quebec commerce. The merger with the Northern Crown Bank in 1918 allowed the Royal to flesh out its network on the prairies. The last and largest merger – with 217 branches of the Union Bank of Canada in 1925 – was conceived by Pease and executed by his successor, Charles Ernest Neill. When called before a committee of the House of Commons in 1913 to justify his bank's aggressive expansion, Holt had read a statement prepared for him by Pease in which he stated that mergers removed "weak banks," enhanced economies of scale, and stabilized national banking. "In union there is strength," he concluded. Pease's policy of mergers vaulted the Royal ahead of its competitors. After the merger with the Union Bank of Canada, the Royal surpassed the Bank of Montreal as Canada's largest bank in terms of both branches (922 by the end of 1925) and assets ($788,000,000). While other banks emulated Pease's strategy, none enjoyed such success in making their operations so solidly national.

Pease's role as the architect of the Royal's forceful evolution was acknowledged in several ways. In 1916 he assumed the title of managing director and chief executive officer of the bank at an annual salary of $45,000. The same year he began a three-year term as the president of the Canadian Bankers' Association. With his usual progressive fervour, he used the office to question the underpinnings of credit creation in Canada. Before World War I, Canadian banks extended credit in the form of their banknotes and loans on the basis of the reserves they held in gold or dominion notes. This process was self-regulating, expansive in good economic times, contractive in recessionary times. The outbreak of war and the suspension of the gold standard disrupted the system. In 1914 Pease and other general managers helped finance minister William Thomas White* fashion temporary state intervention in the creation of credit. The Finance Act of 1914 allowed Ottawa to advance moneys to the commercial banks, thereby facilitating the expansion of credit in abnormal times. Pease favoured extension of the state's ability to "rediscount" commercial bank credit, a mechanism he argued would stimulate post-war recovery. He patterned his suggestion on the newly created federal reserve banks in the United States and first presented it at the annual meeting of the Royal Bank in early 1918 before taking it to the council of the Canadian Bankers' Association and to White later that same year. A CBA committee, advised by Toronto corporate lawyer Zebulon Aiton Lash*, studied the proposition. The idea was stiffly opposed by the Bank of Montreal, which saw in it an end to its long-standing role as the government's banker. Other bankers argued that a government-run central bank would throw the creation of credit open to political manipulation. In 1919 the status quo prevailed and the Finance Act of 1914 was extended into peacetime. When national credit failed catastrophically in the Great Depression and thinking again turned to the need for a central bank, Pease's initiative would be revisited in 1933 during the hearings of the royal commission on banking and currency in Canada.

Pease's aggressive pursuit of corporate expansion and his championing of ideas viewed by most Canadian bankers as iconoclastic indelibly stamped him as an outsider intent on shifting the centre of the Canadian banking establishment. Ill at ease in the stuffy social milieu of Montreal banking, he took a leading role in creating the Mount Bruno Country Club, south of the city. In the 1890s he had joined a property association at Mont Saint-Bruno and by the 1920s had helped to turn it into an exclusive golf and country retreat for the anglophone elite of Montreal who felt unwelcome at the Royal Montreal Golf Club. Pease himself built a large home there in 1922, close to neighbours such as the Birks and Drummond families. Pease was not, in fact, an ardent golfer. He was elected honorary president of the Montreal Amateur Athletic Association in 1910, but had few leisure activities besides cigar smoking and a penchant for practical jokes. His personal and family life was always secondary to his devotion to banking. A Presbyterian by birth, he displayed little interest in religion as an adult. By the 1920s his addiction to the Royal's affairs began to exact its toll. His constitution weakened and his hearing started to fail. The death of his wife in 1922, followed by that of his youngest son in 1923, eroded his family life. In 1922 he resigned his executive functions with the bank, retaining only his vice-presidency and directorship. Nonetheless, he remained an important figure in the bank's affairs, one frequently consulted by Neill, his successor as chief executive officer.

A lifelong Conservative, Pease was a confidant of prominent politicians such as Sir Robert Laird Borden*, Sir William Thomas White, and Richard Bedford Bennett*. Nonetheless, like his colleagues at the head of the other Canadian banks, he downplayed any public demonstration of his sympathies for the Conservatives. His great achievement was to have been seen as a reliable oracle for banking and monetary advice by both Conservative and Liberal finance ministers. In retirement he was wooed by the Liberals. Prime Minister William Lyon Mackenzie King* considered him for a senatorship and the ambassadorship in Washington. In the fall of 1930 Pease left Montreal to winter on the French Riviera. There, the manager of the Royal's Paris branch found him "a lonely, sick man, but lion-hearted withal." Pease insisted that a photograph depicting him with a cigar and tennis racket in hand be dispatched to the head office. After his death in Nice in late December, his body was returned to Canada to be buried high in Mount Royal Cemetery in a plot that overlooked the St Lawrence.

The term "revolutionize" cannot usually be comfortably applied to Canadian banking's careful evolution, but Edson Pease had forced the pace of change more than any other Canadian banker. He had built a regional institution into Canada's leading domestic and international bank and at the same time had provoked broad and prescient discussion about the fundamental tenets of Canadian banking.

DUNCAN MCDOWALL

The Royal Bank of Canada Arch. (Montreal) contains extensive material on Edson Loy Pease's association with the bank from 1883 to 1930. The following records were used in the preparation of this biography: RBC 2, 25 54 1 (corporate personnel); 30G 1–6 (chairman and president files); 43G PeaE (biog. file); 43S PeaE 1–2 (speeches); and 46B (RBC Hist. Project files). Of particular relevance for Pease's campaign to promote a central bank in Canada are the papers of bank executive Solomon Randolph Noble (RBC 2, 29A 3 2, 29A 14, and 29A 17). Additional references to Pease, such as those found in staff reminiscence files and in the *Royal Bank Magazine* (Montreal), may be searched by computer. The archives also holds numerous photographs of Pease.

The papers of Sir Robert Laird Borden (LAC, MG 26, H), Richard Bedford Bennett (LAC, MG 26, K), and Sir William Thomas White (LAC, MG 27, II, D18) contain correspondence with Pease. The Canadian Bankers' Assoc. (Toronto) has materials in its archives relating to Pease's presidency of the association from 1916 to 1919 and on his role in representing the Royal Bank of Canada on its council. For Pease's place in the larger context of Canadian banking, see Z. A. Lash, "The United States Federal Reserve Act and the Canadian banking system, with some contrasts," Canadian Bankers' Assoc., *Journal* (Toronto), 26 (1918–19): 224–44; Duncan McDowall, *Quick to the frontier: Canada's Royal Bank* (Toronto, 1993); and R. C. McIvor, *Canadian monetary, banking and fiscal development* (Toronto, 1958).

ANQ-M, CE601-S115, 24 avril 1883; CE607-S44, 21 sept. 1856. *Canadian men and women of the time* (Morgan; 1912).

PECK, EDMUND JAMES, Church of England missionary, founder of the first permanent mission on Baffin Island (Nunavut), translator, and author; b. 15 April 1850 in Rusholme, near Manchester, England, son of Thomas Peck and Clara Coleman; m. 29 April 1885 Sarah Ann Coleman in Greenwich (London), and they had three children; d. 10 Sept. 1924 in Ottawa.

Born into a devout family of modest means, who moved to Dublin in 1857, Edmund James Peck was the eldest of four children. When his mother died, he had to leave school and go to work in a printing plant though he was only ten years old; his father died three years later. Peck joined the Royal Navy in 1865 and served until 1875. He was a subaltern on numerous ships: the *Ajax*, *Impregnable*, *Caledonia*, *Excellent*, and then *Hector*, on which he found his calling and organized prayer groups. In 1875 he began studying Greek and theology at the Reading Preparatory Institution of the Church Missionary Society [*see* William Duncan*] in Islington (London). In the spring of 1876 Bishop John Horden* of the Anglican diocese of Moosonee was seeking a new recruit for his territory, which covered a good part of Hudson Bay and James Bay. Peck accepted the offer and left England in June 1876, as a missionary trained by the CMS, taking ship on the *Prince of Wales*. During the three-month voyage, he spent his time studying Inuktitut, the language of the Inuit, from textbooks published by the Moravian missionaries who were already established in Greenland and Labrador.

During his first stay among the Inuit (1876–84), Peck dedicated himself to several initiatives. On 1 Sept. 1876 he arrived in Moose Factory (Ont.), a Hudson's Bay Company post where the CMS had established a mission in 1851. He left again almost at once for Little Whale River (Petite Rivière de la Baleine, Que.), another company post farther north, which the expedition reached on 24 October. Convinced that a knowledge of local languages was important for success in evangelization, Peck learned Inuktitut and Cree. At the bishop's request, he even preached a sermon in Cree on 3 Feb. 1878 at Moose Factory, on the occasion of his ordination to the priesthood in the Church of England. Native catechists John and Moses Melucto, Edward Richard, and Adam Lucy helped him greatly in mastering these tongues, as he himself would acknowledge. He adopted the syllabic writing devised for the Ojibwa and Cree languages by Methodist missionary James Evans*, not to adapt it to Inuktitut – a task already accomplished by Horden and the Reverend Edwin Arthur Watkins – but to give new impetus to the work of religious instruction by making

possible a wider circulation of the Gospel texts. In 1877 he distributed catechisms. His *Portions of the Holy Scripture for the use of the Esquimaux on the northern and eastern shores of Hudson's Bay* was published in London in 1878. This first volume was followed in 1881 by *Portions of the Book of Common Prayer: together with hymns, addresses, etc., for the use of the Eskimo of Hudson's Bay* and by *St. Luke's Gospel translated into the language of the Eskimo of Hudson's Bay*. Peck's stay ended in the summer of 1884 with a three-week journey of exploration (from 17 July to 10 August) that took him from Little Whale River to Fort Chimo (Kuujjuaq), where he embarked for England on 5 September.

Peck spent his second stay, from 1885 to 1892, addressing the first challenges. Based in Fort George (Que.), where the Little Whale River mission had been moved in 1886, he now began frequent trips to the surrounding camps to carry out his work as an evangelist. His personal life was also full. He had married while in England, and his three children were born (in 1886, 1889, and 1891) after he returned to live among the Inuit. The missionary had to cut short his stay because of the ill-health of his wife, who found it hard to cope with the isolation.

During his period of rest in England, Peck, who since 1892 had been thinking of extending the range of his mission, found a way of reaching Cumberland Sound free of charge. In 1894 a Scottish shipowner, Crawford Noble, who owned a whaling station in southern Baffin Island, provided passage for him and lay missionary Joseph Calder Parker, on the *Alert*. This was a providential turn of events for Peck, for it finally enabled him to make contact with Inuit who had not yet been evangelized. He and Parker founded the first Anglican mission on Baffin Island on 21 Aug. 1894. The first church, built on Blacklead Island (then home to 171 Inuit), was made of sealskin. Between 1894 and 1905, with other missionaries of the CMS (Edgar William Tyler Greenshield, Julian William Bilby, Charles George Sampson), Peck paid four visits to Cumberland Sound, in 1894–96, 1897–99, 1900–2, and 1903–5. He also made many trips to the neighbouring regions (including Frobisher Bay and Kekerten Island). With the help of the Reverend William Gladstone Walton, he produced many more translations and transcriptions. In 1897 *The four Gospels, translated into the language of the Eskimo of Hudson's Bay* was published in London, where Peck also had a more complete version of *Portions of the Book of Common Prayer* printed in 1900. Encouraged by the success of his evangelizing strategies, especially instruction in writing, he contemplated spreading Christianity much farther north.

At the request of Franz Boas*, Peck endeavoured, notwithstanding his missionary zeal, to collect and translate ethnographic data of high quality, including information about shamanism. Boas would publish this material in *The Eskimo of Baffin Land and Hudson Bay, from notes collected by Capt. George Comer, Capt. James S. Mutch and Rev. E. J. Peck*, a work of two volumes brought out in New York in 1901 and 1907. Peck completed his last transliterations of the Bible between 1895 and 1917. Since 1905 he had held the title of superintendent of missions in the Arctic. Although the CMS had decided in 1903 to withdraw gradually from Canada, Peck spent most of his time in fund-raising to ensure that the work of evangelization would continue on Baffin Island. His main residence was in Ottawa, but he still made a number of limited trips to Hudson Strait in 1909, 1911, 1917, 1918, and 1919, including visits to Lake Harbour (Kimmirut, Nunavut), Wakeham Bay, and Fort Chimo. In 1919 he wrote a grammar and dictionary in Inuktitut. The *Eskimo grammar* (Ottawa, 1919) would go through several reprintings, and the *Eskimo-English dictionary* would be published by Walton in Hamilton, Ont., in 1925. To mark the centenary of the CMS in Rupert's Land in 1920, Peck wrote a pamphlet about the Inuit and the history of the evangelization in the Canadian eastern Arctic entitled *The Eskimo: our brethren of the Arctic*. Meant for a wide readership, it outlined Peck's material and financial needs and was published around 1922, probably in Toronto.

Despite limited technical and financial resources, Edmund James Peck hoped, no matter what the cost, to find solutions to the problem of introducing Christianity among the nomadic Inuit. He remained particularly true to the principles of Henry Venn, the third secretary of the CMS. Thus in Baffin Island, and in what would later become Nunavik, Que., he always organized his catechistical methods around two main poles: the translation and rapid circulation of the Holy Scriptures and, in keeping with the Native Church Policy adopted by the CMS, the training of native converts and leaders. Peck often recruited shamans as the first Inuit ministers, notably the Meluctos, Peter Tulugaqjuaq, and Luke Qillaapik. His peers christened him "the apostle of the Inuit," and the Inuit paid homage to him by naming him Uqammaq, "he who speaks well."

FRÉDÉRIC LAUGRAND

In addition to the works cited above, Edmund James Peck published numerous articles in the *Church Missionary Gleaner* (Toronto) and the *Moosonee and Keewatin Mailbag* (Moosonee, Ont.).

Primary documents concerning Peck are preserved in the Univ. of Birmingham Library, Special Coll. (Birmingham, Eng.), the Church Missionary Soc. Arch., and the Anglican Church of Canada, General Synod Arch. (Toronto), M56/1 (Peck papers). The last collection includes the preliminary version of an autobiography as well as an unpublished biography prepared by Kenn Harper, "Uqarmat: the life of Rev-

erend Edmund James Peck" and a copy of Peck's marriage record. The LAC holds a microfilm copy of the Church Missionary Soc. records relating to Canada (MG 17, B2).

Church of Jesus Christ of Latter-day Saints, Geneal. Soc., International geneal. index. *Apostle to the Inuit; the journals and ethnographic notes of Edmund James Peck: the Baffin years, 1894–1905*, ed. Frédéric Laugrand et al. (Toronto, forthcoming). Karen Evans, "Edmund James Peck: his contribution to Eskimo literacy and publishing," Canadian Church Hist. Soc., *Journal* (Toronto), 26 (1984): 58–68. Kenn Harper, "The early development of Inuktitut syllabic orthography," *Inuit Studies* (Quebec), 9 (1985): 141–62. Frédéric Laugrand, "'Ni vainqueurs, ni vaincus': les premières rencontres entre les chamanes inuit (*angakkuit*) et les missionnaires dans trois régions de l'Arctique canadien," *Anthropologie et Sociétés* (Québec), 21 (1997): 99–123; "Premiers catéchismes et méthodes catéchistiques des missionnaires anglicans et oblats chez les Inuit de l'Arctique de l'Est (1852–1937)," CCHA, *Études d'hist. religieuse*, 64 (1998): 9–29; "*Siqqitiqpuq*: conversion et réception du christianisme par les Inuit de l'Arctique de l'Est canadien (1890–1940)" (thèse de PHD, univ. Laval, Québec, 2000). Arthur Lewis, *The life and work of the Rev. E. J. Peck among the Eskimos* (New York, 1904).

PELLETIER, LOUIS-PHILIPPE (baptized **Louis-Thomas-Godfroi**), lawyer, journalist, newspaper owner, politician, professor, and judge; b. 1 Feb. 1857 in Trois-Pistoles, Lower Canada, son of Thomas-Philippe Pelletier, a merchant and later a legislative councillor, and Caroline Casault, sister of Louis-Napoléon Casault, a politician and future chief justice of the Superior Court of the province of Quebec; m. 11 Jan. 1883 Adèle (Adélaïde) Lelièvre at Quebec; they had no children; d. there 8 Feb. 1921.

Raised in a rather intellectual and conservative family environment, Louis-Philippe Pelletier entered the Collège de Sainte-Anne-de-la-Pocatière at the age of 11, together with his brother Alphonse, who was 13; one of his fellow students was Thomas Chapais*. In 1877 he began his studies in law at the Université Laval in Quebec City. Three years later he obtained his degree "with great distinction," along with the Tessier prize and the gold medal awarded by the governor general, the Marquess of Lorne [Campbell*]; he was articled to Auguste-Réal Angers*, an influential Conservative lawyer with whom he would become friends.

Called to the bar on 17 July 1880, Pelletier embarked upon a long and fruitful career in law. He practised in Quebec City first in the office of Blanchet, Amyot et Pelletier, then in 1889 with the prominent firm Amyot, Pelletier et Fontaine, and in 1903 with Drouin, Pelletier et Baillargeon. In the end he became head of the firm Pelletier, Baillargeon et Alleyn, before being named a judge in 1914. In the meantime, he was appointed a QC on 7 March 1893, was given an honorary doctorate by the Université Laval on 10 June 1902, and was chosen as legal counsel to several banks and firms. He sat on various boards of directors, sometimes even as president, notably of the Canadian Electric Light Company, which used the hydroelectric power of the Chaudière falls, near Quebec City. From 1907 until his death, he was a professor in the faculty of law of the Université Laval.

It was, however, through his political activity on the provincial and federal levels that Pelletier gained renown. In 1885 the Riel affair [*see* Louis Riel*] moved him to side with those who condemned the hanging of the Métis chief, considering it an affront to French Canadians. President of the Club Cartier of Quebec, he resigned from that body and joined the "national alliance" led by Honoré Mercier*, which was made up of dissident Liberals and Conservatives. From 1886 to 1891 Pelletier supported the national program through *La Justice*, a newspaper he founded in January 1886 at Quebec with other National Conservatives. Idealistic and ultramontane, he believed in an alliance reaching beyond partisan lines and private interests which would uphold the fundamental principles of French Canadian society, and he was unrelenting in his efforts to demonstrate the importance of the church in the social fabric. He ran in the provincial election in Témiscouata on 14 Oct. 1886, but was defeated by a Conservative, Georges-Honoré Deschênes*; a candidate again in the federal election of 22 Feb. 1887, he lost in Trois-Rivières to Sir Hector-Louis Langevin* by only 30 votes. To reward him, Mercier, who had become premier, named him to the Legislative Council on 11 May 1888. He thus received the title of honourable and could now participate in the legislative process. Dissatisfied, he managed to switch places with Louis-Napoléon Larochelle*, the MLA for Dorchester, a seat Pelletier won by acclamation in a by-election on 20 December. A crucial period in his career began then. An ordinary backbencher, he was entrusted by Mercier with the task of ensuring that Lieutenant Governor Auguste-Réal Angers cooperated in providing royal assent to bills.

Pelletier again won in Dorchester in the election of 17 June 1890, which gave Mercier's Parti National a comfortable majority. Anxious to put forward his more liberal ideas, Mercier soon found him an obstacle. He publicly rebuffed Pelletier because he expressed reservations about the bill to ensure medical control of insane asylums by the state; then, because *La Justice* did not give unqualified support to the government, he had him removed as editor of the paper early in 1891. Ousted thereby from the Parti National, Pelletier naturally turned to his former party and before long his influence on its ideology and strategies was noticeable. He managed to establish a party newspaper, *Le Matin* (Québec), to counterbalance *L'Électeur*, the organ of the Liberals in Quebec; the paper was published from January to September 1892.

In December 1891 the Baie des Chaleurs scandal led to the downfall of the Mercier government, and the Conservatives under Charles Boucher* de Boucherville took power. At 34, Pelletier, who was known to be hard-working, well informed, and full of fighting spirit, was named secretary and registrar in the new administration as of December; he retained this office under Conservative premier Louis-Olivier TAILLON from 1892 to 1896, and then was attorney general in Edmund James FLYNN's ministry from May 1896 to May 1897. As minister, Pelletier demonstrated his tendency to embrace the ultramontane vision of an orderly management of finances and a minimally interventionist administration; this approach to governing was based on traditional French Canadian values and sought to maintain the status quo for the structures of power and social organization, particularly in areas under the control of religious institutions.

Re-elected on 11 May 1897, despite the Liberal wave that swept across Quebec, Pelletier entered a long period in the opposition. Late in 1904, when Premier Simon-Napoléon Parent* precipitated a provincial election, he backed his party in its decision not to participate. He would try, but without success, to get elected to the provincial, and then to the federal parliament in 1908. Chief organizer of the federal Conservative party for the district of Quebec from 1903, Pelletier gradually let himself be seduced by the nationalist ideas of Henri Bourassa* and the Ligue Nationaliste Canadienne, which had been founded that year by Olivar Asselin* and others. Reconciling Conservative principles with nationalist ideals then became the key that would enable Pelletier to act on the federal scene as an advocate for a form of pan-Canadian nationalism based on traditional values. Through *L'Événement*, of which he was one of the owners from 1902 to 1914 [*see* Louis-Joseph Demers*], he supported the alliance between Bourassa and Frederick Debartzch Monk* and the new Conservative-Nationaliste formation resulting from it in 1910. The newspaper even clearly distanced itself from Conservative leader Robert Laird Borden* with regard to Sir Wilfrid Laurier*'s controversial plan for a naval service; the paper held that the leader "is mistaken, is deluding himself about the dangers to the empire, about Canada's obligations to the mother country." In the federal election of 21 Sept. 1911, which brought the Conservatives to power, Pelletier won in the riding of Quebec as a Conservative with a Nationaliste allegiance. He represented a minority faction within the Borden government, but remained confident of getting along well with the Conservative party from which he had come. Postmaster general from 10 Oct. 1911 to 19 Oct. 1914, Pelletier applied himself to improving rural and regular postal delivery, the various services in post offices, and the working conditions of employees.

Two major questions quickly brought Pelletier into

conflict with those within the Borden government who supported an imperialistic nationalism. Strongly influenced by a type of imperialism extolled by Britain, this nationalist approach showed little sensitivity when it came to the rights and institutions of French Canadians. The issue of protecting the educational rights of Keewatin's francophone Catholic minority emerged in 1912, when part of this large district was to be joined to Manitoba [see George Robson COLDWELL]. Faced with the intransigence of his cabinet colleagues, who refused to put guarantees for the Catholic minority in the act transferring the area to that province, Pelletier had no option but to give in or resign. He chose to accept the negotiations that were going on at the same time with the Manitoba government of Sir Rodmond Palen Roblin* with the objective of obtaining a promise to reduce school taxes for Catholics throughout the province. Then, the Borden government's plan to provide financial aid to the British navy again brought his nationalist convictions into play. A trip to Britain along with Borden in the summer of 1912 convinced him of the threat posed by the Germans and of his slim chances of preventing the adoption of this plan. Again he tried the route of compromise, endeavouring to have every military aid project subjected to a plebiscite, which would make it more acceptable in the eyes of the nationalists. Despite Borden's firm refusal and Monk's resignation on 18 October, Pelletier chose to remain in the cabinet. To some people his decision looked like a definitive abandonment of nationalist ideals. It seems, however, that Pelletier was more the victim of political circumstances militating against advocacy of his ideals and that he preferred to stay to ensure the presence of a nationalist in the cabinet, rather than resign and let the protagonists of the imperialist and Orange ideal retain power by themselves. In October 1914 he submitted his resignation, before being named a judge of the Superior Court for the district of Montreal on 18 November; he was transferred to the Quebec Court of King's Bench on 20 Aug. 1915. He presided, notably, over the trial in April 1920 of Marie-Anne Houde, who was accused of murdering her stepdaughter, Aurore Gagnon*, known as Aurore the martyred child.

Louis-Philippe Pelletier's triple career, which pursued legal, journalistic, and political paths, was impressive although not unusual for its time. It is, however, the period he spent in the federal government that is of particular note, for it illustrates Pelletier's inability to give effect to his nationalist ideals as well as the difficulties he experienced in upholding a French Canadian vision and French Canadian values within a government strongly influenced by imperialist ideology.

DANIÈLE GOULET

[A detailed study of Louis-Philippe Pelletier's political career, including relevant primary and secondary sources, is provided in the author's dissertation "Louis-Philippe Pelletier: un exemple du douloureux mariage du mouvement nationaliste et du Parti conservateur fédéral (1911–1914)" (mémoire de MA, univ. Laval, Québec, 1991). D.G.]

ANQ-Q, CE301-S1, 11 janv. 1883; CE303-S30, 1er févr. 1857.

PELLETIER, PANTALÉON (baptized **Marie-Joseph-Pantaléon**), militia officer, physician, politician, and agent general in London for the province of Quebec; b. 27 July 1860 in Rivière-Ouelle, Lower Canada, son of Joseph Pelletier and Henriette Martin; m. first 24 Jan. 1888 Alice Hudon (d. 1910) at Quebec; m. secondly 1912 Cécile Belleau, widow of Joseph Boivin, in London, England; no children were born of either marriage; d. 19 Oct. 1924 at Quebec.

The eldest son of a prosperous farmer in Rivière-Ouelle, in the Lower St Lawrence region, Pantaléon Pelletier had close relatives from the same locality who had distinguished themselves in politics and the military. They included his uncle Charles-Alphonse-Pantaléon Pelletier* and his first cousin Charles-Antoine-Ernest Gagnon*, both of whom had close ties to Honoré Mercier*, to the Parti National, and then to the Liberal party. They would pass on their political outlook to Pantaléon and open doors for him, thereby helping shape the course of his career.

Pantaléon did the classical program at the Collège de Sainte-Anne-de-la-Pocatière from 1873 to 1882, and subsequently enrolled in the faculty of medicine of the Université Laval at Quebec, where he would pursue his studies until 1887. During this period he enlisted in the 9th Battalion Volunteer Militia Rifles. It was probably through the influence of his uncle Charles-Alphonse-Pantaléon that he was given a commission, as was the latter's son, his cousin Oscar-Charles-Casgrain Pelletier. When the North-West rebellion broke out in March 1885 [see Louis Riel*], the two cousins took part in the campaign, Pantaléon as a first lieutenant in the 7th company of his battalion, which was one of two French Canadian regiments to be involved. Fearing the political repercussions of sending French Canadians into battle against French-speaking Métis, the federal government saw to it that the companies of the 9th Battalion Volunteer Militia Rifles, under the command of Guillaume Amyot*, were based in Calgary and Gleichen, far from the theatre of operations.

In 1887 Pantaléon, who had just obtained a degree in medicine, was appointed assistant surgeon at the Marine and Emigrant Hospital at Quebec, and he retained this position for some time before moving to Sherbrooke. His cousin Charles-Antoine-Ernest Gagnon, who was provincial secretary and registrar in the Mercier cabinet, had probably advised him to settle in that city, knowing he would soon appoint a second coroner there. On 16 Sept. 1889 Pelletier, at the age of 29, did indeed become a coroner for the judicial district of Saint-François, an area with a rapidly growing population, where French Canadians had been in the majority for only a short time. He would hold this post until 1900.

On his arrival in the Eastern Townships (where he would become perfectly bilingual), Pelletier opened an office for private practice in his home on Rue Bowen; he would continue to receive patients there, probably until 1909. He was also involved in the life of the community. As Élie-Joseph-Arthur Auclair would point out in the Sherbrooke newspaper *La Tribune* on 27 Oct. 1924, he was admirably qualified for public life. "Flexible and obliging, yes, but also intelligent and an excellent observer of men and things, that was everyone's view of the popular doctor from east Sherbrooke." The first physician to set up in the city's east end, where working-class and French-speaking people predominated, he was often asked to act as a mediator in labour disputes. In his medical practice Pelletier initially specialized in surgery and gynaecology, fields in which he did further study for six months in 1893 at the New York Polyclinic Medical School and Hospital. He later turned more of his attention to contagious diseases. In 1896 he was appointed medical officer of health for the city of Sherbrooke. The founding of the Sherbrooke Protestant Hospital in 1888 had shown the need to offer the same kind of services to the Catholic population of the Eastern Townships. With this aim in mind, Pelletier, as an original member of the medical board of the Hospice du Sacré-Cœur, in April 1897 helped provide an operating room for the hospice, which established its role as a medical facility. That year he spent six months training in hospitals in Paris, taking courses in microbiology with Émile Roux at the Institut Pasteur [*see* Arthur BERNIER; Oscar-Félix MERCIER]. In addition, he assisted in setting up the Hôpital Général St Vincent de Paul de Sherbrooke, which was opened in 1909.

Pelletier was involved in the organization of the medical profession. In 1890 he was instrumental in founding the Association Médicale du District de Saint-François, whose members included physicians from both French- and English-speaking communities. In 1897 he became one of the three representatives from his district to the Provincial Medical Board of the College of Physicians and Surgeons of the Province of Quebec, and he retained this office until 1904. Pelletier would also campaign for the autonomy of the Quebec medical profession within the Association des Médecins de Langue Française de l'Amérique du Nord. He would become its president in 1908 and would organize its fifth annual convention, which was held in Sherbrooke two years later.

Pelletier's activities in the militia earned him the respect of the English-speaking elite, with whom he associated as a captain and medical officer in the 11th Hussars of Richmond. His prestige increased when his cousin Oscar-Charles-Casgrain Pelletier became the highest-ranking French Canadian officer to serve in the South African War. Pantaléon would also help raise the first French Canadian regiment in the Eastern Townships, the 54th Regiment (Carabiniers de Sherbrooke), which came into being in 1910. The popular physician would be its first commanding officer, with the rank of lieutenant-colonel.

It was probably because he was so well known that Pelletier succeeded, on his first venture into politics, in getting elected for Sherbrooke by a majority of 91 votes in the provincial general election of 7 Dec. 1900. No Liberal had ever before represented this constituency, either provincially or federally. He would be returned by acclamation in the elections of 25 Nov. 1904 and 8 June 1908. Thanks to acquaintances at the highest levels of the Liberal party (and especially to his uncle Charles-Alphonse-Pantaléon), he was able to ensure that his riding enjoyed the patronage of both federal and provincial governments. Sherbrooke's courthouse [*see* Elzéar CHAREST] and armoury, opened respectively in 1906 and 1908, are examples of his influence. His speeches in the house expressed his concerns for the public health movement and for the organization of the medical profession. In 1902 he took a firm stand in favour of strengthening the authority of the Board of Health of the Province of Quebec with respect to vaccination. That year, in a remarkably well-documented speech that anticipated by eight years the recommendations in the report of the royal commission on tuberculosis, he condemned the widespread ignorance about this scourge and called for a program of grants to sanatoriums. In 1903 he would help found the District of St Francis League for the Prevention of Tuberculosis. Pelletier also played an important role in the debate on the Roddick Bill [*see* Sir Thomas George RODDICK], passed by parliament in 1902 as the Canada Medical Act. Although this measure enjoyed broad support within the medical profession, Pelletier considered it a dangerous encroachment on provincial jurisdiction by the federal government. He made every effort to limit its scope, first within the College of Physicians and Surgeons of the Province of Quebec, and then in the Legislative Assembly, where the question was debated in 1903. His vigorous opposition delayed ratification of the federal law by the provincial parliament. On 2 March 1909 Pelletier became speaker of the Legislative Assembly, where he performed his duties with unusual charisma and sound judgement. He replaced Philippe-Honoré Roy, who was being prosecuted [*see* Louis Molleur*].

On 7 Aug. 1911 the government of Sir Lomer GOUIN appointed Pelletier the province's agent general in the United Kingdom of Great Britain and Ireland, an office created shortly before the 1908 election but not yet filled. Hector Fabre* had held a similar position in Paris from 1882 to 1910 (Philippe Roy would take his place until 1912) and in 1914 Godfroy LANGLOIS would be appointed agent general for the province of Quebec in Brussels. In Britain the career of the Sherbrooke physician entered a new phase. Important events in his personal life made the break even more distinct. His wife, Alice Hudon, died in 1910 after a long illness, and in 1912 he married Cécile Belleau (the widow of Joseph Boivin, who had been Mercier's secretary from 1887 to 1890 and under-secretary of the province of Quebec from 1890 to 1909). Pelletier would retain the office in London for the rest of his life. On average he received $25,000 annually, which included a salary of $6,000 and various allowances (for rent, for example). Since some provinces already had an agency in the British capital, his first task was to make Quebec better known, in order to ensure that it would have its fair share of foreign trade and investments. Before World War I, immigration and the promotion of the province's tourist attractions were important aspects of the agency's work. It also was charged with a trade mission. Pelletier's basic objective then became to stimulate the export of goods manufactured in Quebec. He took a particular interest in the sale of agricultural machinery in West Africa, India, and southeastern Asia, where access was facilitated by the policy of imperial preference. He also encouraged Canadian banks to establish branches in these distant parts of the world. The London agency, which opened a year before the one in Paris closed, marked a change in Quebec's external policy, which now began to concentrate on the economy. This initiative would bear fruit as long as the British metropolis maintained its hegemony as a world financial centre. Towards the end of his career, however, Pelletier saw his agency decline in importance, as the United States became the principal market for Quebec exports and the primary source of investment capital.

On 19 Oct. 1924, when he was back in Canada for a visit, Pantaléon Pelletier suffered a stroke as he was going into his daughter-in-law's house on Avenue des Érables at Quebec, and died instantly. In all the fields to which he had been drawn – medical, political, military – he had worked to strengthen the foundations of French Canada. "A patriot in his soul and proud of his race, he defended the rights of his people every inch of the way," Auclair noted a few days after his death. Pelletier had unquestionably played a leading role for francophones in the Eastern Townships. Following in the traditions of his province's Liberal party, he was both a nationalist and a progressive, being firm in his demands, but open to the world, as well as aware of the economic imperatives of industry and dedicated to

the advancement of learning. Therein lay the secret of his success, first in Sherbrooke and then as a representative of the province on the international scene.

PETER SOUTHAM

ANQ-BSLGIM, CE104-S1, 27 juill. 1860. ANQ-Q, CE301-S1, 24 janv. 1888. Arch. de l'Institut Pasteur (Paris), Cours de microbie technique, MP 29048 (liste des personnes ayant suivi les cours, 1889–1970). LAC, RG 31, C1, 1881, Rivière-Ouelle, Qué. *Le Devoir*, 20 oct. 1924. *L'Étoile de l'Est* (Coaticook, Qué.), 22 mai 1890. *La Patrie*, 15 oct. 1886. *Sherbrooke Daily Record* (Sherbrooke, Que.), 21 June 1900; 14 May, 1 Aug. 1903. *La Tribune* (Sherbrooke), 11 oct. 1911; 16 juin, 11 oct. 1913; 15 déc. 1916; 3 août 1923; 20, 27 oct. 1924. [C. A.] Boulton, *Reminiscences of the North-West rebellions, with a record of the raising of her majesty's 100th Regiment in Canada . . .* (Toronto, 1886). [P]. L. H. Camirand, "History of the 54e regiment – Les Carabiniers de Sherbrooke – from the foundation to the First World War" (MA thesis, Bishop's Univ., Lennoxville, Que., 1985). College of Physicians and Surgeons of the Prov. of Quebec, *Medical reg.* (Montreal), 1911. Denis Goulet, *Histoire du Collège des médecins du Québec, 1847–1997* (Montréal, 1997). Jean Hamelin, "Quebec and the outside world, 1867–1967," Que., Bureau of Statistics, *Québec yearbook* (Quebec), 1968–69: 48–52. P.-H. Hudon, *Rivière-Ouelle de la Bouteillerie; 3 siècles de vie* (Ottawa, 1972), 392. Adolphe Michaud, *Généalogie des familles de la Rivière Ouelle, depuis l'origine de la paroisse jusqu'à nos jours* (Québec, 1908). Desmond Morton, *The last war drum: the North-West campaign of 1885* (Toronto, 1972). C. P. [Mulvany], *The history of the North-West rebellion of 1885 . . .* (Toronto, 1885; repr. 1971). Que., Legislative Assembly, *Debates*, 1902–4; Royal commission on tuberculosis, *Report* (Quebec, 1909–10); *Statutes*, 1908, c.11. *Quebec Official Gazette*, 1911: 1528.

PELLETIER, ROMAIN-OCTAVE (baptized **Jean-Romain-Octave**), organist, pianist, notary, professor, and musicographer; b. 9 Sept. 1843 in Montreal, son of Jean-Baptiste-Généreux Peltier, a notary, and Marie-Scholastique Masson; m. 8 June 1869 Athaïs Le Maire in Saint-Benoît (Mirabel), Que., and they had four sons and three daughters; d. 4 March 1927 in Montreal.

Even as a child Romain-Octave Pelletier had an exceptional musical ear. Without having studied music, he began to play the organ and he accompanied hymns and masses. Feeling embarrassed at not being able to read a score set before him, he is said to have learned musical notation in two days and then taken a few lessons from his brother Orphir Peltier*, who was an organist. In large part a self-taught musician, he was appointed organist at the Montreal Roman Catholic cathedral (which would become the basilica of Marie-Reine-du-Monde) in 1860, at the age of 17. He held this position for a few years, and again from 1887 to 1923. Along with his musical activities, he attended the Petit Séminaire de Montréal from 1854 to 1859, and then studied at the Collège Sainte-Marie to become a notary. He obtained his licence in 1864 but practised his profession only briefly. He went against the wishes of his family and the spirit of the times in abandoning this liberal profession to devote himself exclusively to music.

After spending some time, around 1865–67, in Hartford, Conn., where he was hired as organist at the cathedral, Pelletier returned to Montreal. He earned a living by teaching music and as a pianist accompanying a number of performers – among them Frantz Jehin-Prume* – on the concert stage. He also played the organ at the church of Saint-Jacques (probably between 1869 and 1875); there he went against the musical practices of his time by introducing serious sacred music such as the works of Bach, a Protestant composer whose music seemed too austere for Catholic churches. He was thus the moving spirit behind the reform of the repertoire of religious music used in Montreal churches.

In 1869 Pelletier married Athaïs Le Maire, daughter of Félix-Hyacinthe Lemaire*, a notary and legislative councillor, and Luce Barcelo. He went to London two years later to study with George Cooper, the organist at the Chapel Royal. He then moved on to Paris, where he met Camille Saint-Saëns and Charles-Marie Widor, and finally to Brussels to work with Jaak Nikolaas Lemmens. The few months he spent abroad gave him the chance, in particular, to become familiar with the style of French church organists, who used the organ, not simply as an accompaniment, but to play, in turn, preludes, postludes, and versets with the choir. On his return to Montreal he accepted a position as music teacher (vocal music, plainsong, piano, harmonium) at the École Normale Jacques-Cartier, where he taught from 1876 to 1917. From then on the teaching of piano and organ held a central place in his professional activities. He gave private lessons and taught in other institutions as well, including Mont Sainte-Anne in Lachine, which was run by the Sisters of St Anne, and, in Montreal, the Asile Nazareth, the convent of the Sisters of the Holy Names of Jesus and Mary, and the McGill Conservatorium of Music, where he was professor of piano from 1904 to 1907. In 1900, during a second visit to Paris, he met the famous organists Alexandre Guilmant and Eugène Gigout. He was president of the Académie de Musique de Québec for many years (1884–85, 1894–95, 1902–4, 1909–10, and 1915–16). He also inaugurated a number of organs in the province of Quebec, including those in Beauport, Sainte-Marie (in the Beauce), and Varennes.

Romain-Octave Pelletier retired from the cathedral in 1923, and his musical career was crowned two years later with the conferring of an honorary doctorate by the Université de Montréal. He taught music for half a century, and his students included Claude Champagne*, Alfred Laliberté, and Albertine Labrecque

(Morin). A professional musician, he was able to give them a sound and rigorous training. In reforming church music, he was uncompromising in matters of art.

PIERRE VACHON

Although his music was generally improvised, Romain-Octave Pelletier left several not very innovative musical works and a number of theoretical treatises on music. Some of his compositions have been lost; the others are preserved in the Villeneuve collection at the Bibliothèque de Musique de la Univ. de Montréal and in the Music Div. of the LAC. As a musicographer, Pelletier published several instructional works: *Mécanisme du piano, ou, nouvelles études techniques destinées aux élèves avancés* (Québec, [1880?]); *Le toucher du pianiste* (Montréal, 1916; réimpr., 1928) (a summary of lectures given to the nuns of the Congregation of Notre-Dame); *L'étude de la littérature du piano* ([Montréal, 1920?]) (lectures given at Mont Sainte-Anne, in Lachine); *L'art pianistique* (s.l., [1922]); *Guide du professeur de piano par questions et réponses* ([Montréal?], 1925) (prepared for the Sisters of the Holy Names of Jesus and Mary). Around 1881–82 he wrote several articles on the construction and playing of the organ in the *Revue canadienne* (Montréal).

ANQ-M, CE601-S51, 11 sept. 1843; CE606-S9, 8 juin 1869. ANQ-Q, P379-1. *Le Devoir*, 5, 7, 12 mars 1927. *Centenaire de la paroisse St-Jacques de Montréal: église de l'Expo 67, église du métro* ([Montréal?, 1966?]). Jean Cinq-Mars, *Histoire du collège Sainte-Marie de Montréal, 1848–1969* (Montréal, 1998). *Le diocèse de Montréal à la fin du dix-neuvième siècle . . .* (Montréal, 1900). *Encyclopedia of music in Canada* (Kallmann et al.). Olivier Maurault, *Saint-Jacques de Montréal: l'église, la paroisse* (Montréal, 1923). Montreal Urban Community, Planning Dept. of the Territory, *Architecture religieuse* (2v., Montréal, 1981–84), 1 (*Les églises*). Romain Pelletier, "Octave Pelletier, organiste et pédagogue (1843–1927)," *Qui?* (Montréal), 4 (1952–53): 3–24. Pierre Quenneville, "Guillaume Couture (1851–1915): l'éducateur, le directeur artistique et le musicien d'église" (thèse de PHD, univ. de Montréal, 1988).

PERRAULT, JOSEPH-NARCISSE, teacher and school administrator; b. in all likelihood 8 Oct. 1865, son of Narcisse Perrault and Théotiste Perrault; d. unmarried 26 Nov. 1927 in Montreal.

Joseph-Narcisse Perrault studied at the École Normale Jacques-Cartier in Montreal, where he obtained a model school diploma in 1882 and an academic school diploma the following year. He taught for a year in Rivière-Beaudette and then returned to Montreal, finding employment as a teacher at the Maîtrise Saint-Pierre. In 1886 he joined the staff of the Catholic Commercial Academy of Montreal, which was under the jurisdiction of the Roman Catholic Board of School Commissioners of Montreal. This was a prestigious appointment, since the academy, with Urgel-Eugène Archambeault* as principal, was the finest jewel of all the board's schools.

Perrault began his career during a period that was unhappy for Montreal teachers. In the 1870s the Catholic board had built a number of boys' schools, most of which were run by lay teachers. Thus new career opportunities had been created for male teachers and working conditions had been guaranteed them that neither the women teachers in Montreal nor their colleagues in rural schools could hope to enjoy. In the 1880s, however, a declining economy and conservative forces eager to see lay staff replaced by teaching brothers halted the growth in the number of lay teachers, who were virtually threatened with elimination. Hence in 1889 Archambeault, who was also the local superintendent of the Roman Catholic Board of School Commissioners, confided to a teacher seeking employment in one of its schools: "We are being invaded by the religious orders. Three [of them] have come to Montreal in the past two years. . . . A large school will open this fall under the direction of the Brothers of St Gabriel. I tell you this, not to complain about it, . . . but to make you realize that the prospects for lay teachers are not bright."

Perrault soon learned that a teacher's every move was scrutinized in minute detail by principals and school administrators. He encountered his first difficulties in 1893, when Archambeault informed him that his services would not be required for the following school year. He was accused of belonging to the Knights of Labor, a workers' association. Perrault was dumbfounded and explained that he was not a member of it, but that four years earlier he had, like the association, been a keen advocate of the night schools instituted by the government of Honoré Mercier*. Satisfied with this explanation, Archambeault reconsidered his decision and Perrault was able to pursue his career. In the 1890s Perrault was assigned to the École Montcalm, where A.-D. Lacroix was the principal. The two men did not get along well. Lacroix accused him of not respecting his authority, and because he could not tolerate such an attitude, he asked the director of schools to send Perrault back to his previous position. In 1901 Perrault returned to teach at the Catholic Commercial Academy.

Since he was not married, Perrault could devote himself heart and soul to his work. For six years from the end of the 1890s he was president of the Association des Instituteurs du District de Montréal, and from 1900 he was its delegate to the commission administering the teachers' pension fund. His superiors noted his dedication to his students and appreciated his excellence as a pedagogue. Even Lacroix acknowledged that he was a "studious man" whose classes were well prepared, and that "his teaching methods conform to the rules of modern pedagogy." The principals of the schools where he had taught spoke of him also as a good Christian and citizen. These qualities earned him a promotion to the position of principal of the École Montcalm on 10 June 1904, when Lacroix left to become director general of what had become the Montreal Catholic School Commission. Four years later he again followed in Lacroix's footsteps when the commission appointed him the third director general in its history. From 1908 to 1917 Perrault, who was assisted by nine commissioners (three appointed by the archdiocese of Montreal, three by the city of Montreal, and three by the provincial government), would hold the most important office in the Catholic commission at a crucial time in its history. During these years, the commissioners appointed by the city and the government introduced a number of progressive measures, both academic and extra-curricular. These included the creation of nursery schools and the establishment of school savings accounts and of the Œuvre des Grèves, which enabled the children of poor working-class families to attend summer camp. His term of office also spanned a period when Montreal was drawing thousands of non-British immigrants: Jews, Italians, Germans, Poles, Ruthenians, and Chinese. As Perrault pointed out in one of his annual reports, "The emigration of foreigners to a centre as highly populated as Montreal becomes a real problem from the standpoint of languages and the instruction to be given all these children of different nationalities." He took care to recruit women teachers qualified to teach children in their mother tongue, and two schools were built for those from the Italian community.

In addition to the disquiet created by this new situation, Perrault had to contend with certain commissioners who had their sights set on him. At the outset, his appointment as director general brought about a confrontation between two members. From 1913, Pierre-Eugène Lafontaine*, who was an advocate of reform, made no secret of his wish to see Perrault replaced by a less conservative director general, but Perrault managed to win the confidence of the majority of commissioners.

From 1908 to 1915 the Catholic commission annexed half a dozen small school municipalities on the island of Montreal, bringing to 61 the number of schools under its jurisdiction. "These annexations," wrote Perrault in his report for the year 1914–15, "have burdened the Montreal Catholic School Commission with a debt of $820,776. An examination of the books of these school municipalities has shown – in most cases – that their financial administration had been neglected for a long time." At the end of December 1916 the government of Sir Lomer GOUIN yielded to the demands of the Montreal reformers for centralization of the school system and passed a bill providing for the annexation of 23 more school municipalities to the Catholic commission. Montreal was divided into four districts. In each district, the schools – numbering more than 160 in all – were governed by a six-member commission responsible mainly for classroom instruction. The financial administration of the Catholic commission as a whole was the responsibility of a central board composed of seven members. The position of director general was eliminated and Perrault had to submit his resignation. He did, however, become one of the seven members of the central board, which was chaired by Monsignor Émile Roy. As the first teacher to join the Montreal Catholic School Commission, he represented a new class of experienced administrators. In 1919 Commissioner Lafontaine was elected chairman of the central board, becoming the first layman to hold this office. The animosity between him and Perrault was perhaps not unrelated to the former director general's announcement that he would retire at the end of his four-year term of office.

After leaving the commission in 1921, Joseph-Narcisse Perrault went to Europe. He continued to represent the interests of Montreal teachers as their delegate to the administrative commission that managed their pension fund. He died in Montreal on 26 Nov. 1927.

ROBERT GAGNON

BCM-G, RBMS, Notre-Dame de Montréal, 30 nov. 1927. Commission Scolaire de Montréal, Secrétariat Général, Secteur de la gestion des doc. administratifs et des arch., Dossier personnel de J.-N. Perrault, école Montcalm, renseignements sur les professeurs pour l'année scolaire 1889–90; lettres de J.-N. Perrault à MM. les membres de la Commission des écoles catholiques de Montréal, 9 mars 1908, 23 nov. 1915; Fonds U.-E. Archambeault, lettre de U.-E. Archambeault à G. Duhamel, 27 avril 1889; Livre des délibérations des commissaires, 23 nov. 1915; Rapports financiers de la CECM 1914–16. *Le Devoir*, 28 nov. 1927. *La Presse*, 28 nov. 1927. "Diplômes octroyés par l'école normale Jacques-Cartier," *Journal de l'Instruction publique* (Montréal), 2 (1882): 194; 3 (1883): 227. Robert Gagnon, *Histoire de la Commission des écoles catholiques de Montréal; le développement d'un réseau d'écoles publiques en milieu urbain* ([Montréal], 1996), 39–76, 94, 100–18, 128–31; *Histoire de l'école Le Plateau (1856–1996)* ([Montréal], 1997), 13–24. *Notice sur les écoles administrées par la Commission des écoles catholiques de Montréal* (Montréal, 1915), 34.

PERRI, BESSIE. See STARKMAN, BESHA

PERRON, JOSEPH-LÉONIDE, lawyer and politician; b. 24 Sept. 1872 in Saint-Marc, Que., on the Richelieu, son of Léon Perron, a farmer, and Marie-Anne-Eugénie Ducharme; m. 6 June 1898 Berthe Brunet in Montreal, and they had two sons; d. 20 Nov. 1930 in Montreal and was buried 22 November in Notre-Dame-des-Neiges cemetery there.

Joseph-Léonide Perron studied at Collège Sainte-Marie-de-Monnoir in Marieville. He then enrolled at the Montreal branch of the Université Laval to study law, obtaining his LLB in 1892 and his LLM in 1895. On 9 July 1895 he was called to the bar of the province of Quebec. He would be made a KC in 1903 and *bâtonnier* of the Montreal bar for 1922–23.

Perron quickly became one of the most respected lawyers in Montreal. His first partnership, with Raymond Préfontaine*, launched his career and enabled him to attract the attention of influential members of the Liberal party. His next partner was Robert Taschereau, a close relative of Louis-Alexandre Taschereau*, who would be a Liberal premier of Quebec. He also lent his name to organizations and causes that would help him become known. In 1903 he became the promoter of the Compagnie de Publication du Canada in Montreal. He was a member of the council of the Montreal Bar Association in 1907. Two years later, along with fellow lawyer Napoléon-Kemner Laflamme, he appeared for the citizens' committee before the royal commission that was set up to make a general and complete inquiry into the administration of the affairs of the city of Montreal [*see* Lawrence John CANNON]. That year, Premier Sir Lomer GOUIN appointed him to the Catholic committee of the Council of Public Instruction, thereby causing a stir within the organization in view of the suspicions of anticlericalism that hung over him. He would remain a member for the rest of his life.

At Gouin's instigation, Perron ran as the Liberal candidate in a provincial by-election in the constituency of Gaspé in 1910. The seat, which had become vacant when Louis-Joseph Lemieux resigned, was seen as a safe one for getting a strong candidate into parliament. The premier wanted to have a progressive Liberal in the Legislative Assembly to oppose Henri Bourassa* and the Conservatives. Thanks to the popularity of the Gouin government, which promised to build a railway in the Gaspé region, Perron won on 17 February in a riding he hardly knew. For unknown reasons he would not run in the general election of 15 May 1912, but he would be elected by acclamation in the riding of Verchères – his birthplace – in a by-election on 16 October.

In the Legislative Assembly Perron learned to carry out his role as a representative of the Liberal party. In 1911 he supported a bill introduced by Godfroy LANGLOIS to grant the Montreal Tramways Company a monopoly of public transportation on the island. Given his professional activities, Perron became the spokesman of the big companies, in particular the Shawinigan Water and Power Company, the Canada Cement Company, and the Excelsior Life Insurance Company.

Perron was soon an important cog in the Liberal machine, especially for the Montreal region. President since 1914 of the prestigious Montreal Reform Club (where the city's Liberals traditionally met), he increasingly participated in making political decisions concerning the city. This was probably why Gouin on 13 April 1916 appointed him the legislative councillor for the division of Montarville; Perron could now give his full attention to organizing the Liberal campaign in the important metropolitan region. In 1917, when

Perron

Montreal once again found itself deeply in debt, Perron finalized the plan for recovery imposed by the provincial government: amendments to the city's constitution, the annexation of Maisonneuve, and the settlement of the street railway question (in which Perron, as lawyer for the Montreal Tramways Company, was both judge and judged). Despite Mayor Médéric Martin*, whose influence was growing, Perron's vision of Montreal carried the day.

Perron was thus an important figure in the Liberal party. When Gouin retired from provincial politics in 1920, it was only natural that at 47 years of age he should become, along with the attorney general, Louis-Alexandre Taschereau, and the minister of agriculture, Joseph-Édouard CARON, one of the leading candidates to succeed him. Gouin's choice fell on Taschereau, with whom Perron apparently was not on good terms. The two men would have to learn to work together, however. When Taschereau formed his cabinet on 9 July 1920, Perron became minister without portfolio, unofficially responsible for representing Montreal and large corporations. Although he was the only new member in the cabinet, his strong personality, energy, fine personal qualities, and relations with Taschereau gave promise of a prominent career.

Yet the team seemed to work efficiently. Perron even helped Taschereau to draft the bill passed in 1921 that created the Quebec Liquor Commission. When Joseph-Adolphe TESSIER, the minister of roads, was appointed chairman of the Quebec Streams Commission, Perron appeared to be the logical candidate for the vacant post. Already in the cabinet, although without a portfolio, he was seen as the next in line for an important ministry. On 27 Sept. 1921 he became government leader in the Legislative Council and minister of roads. Perron's appointment to this department, which he would leave in 1929, was undoubtedly the high point of his career, and he carried out projects whose lasting importance would greatly enhance his reputation. At the banquet celebrating his appointment, the new minister announced that he intended to build the sections of highways needed to complete the routes from Lévis eastwards to Gaspé and westwards to Saint-Lambert. He also wanted to link Montreal with Sherbrooke to the south, Mont-Laurier to the north, and Ottawa, by way of Hull. This announcement would not only bring contributions to the party coffers – from contractors eager to benefit from this manna from heaven – but would win votes in the regions concerned, proof of Perron's talents as an organizer. In 1922 he announced that responsibility for the major highways would pass from the municipalities to the Department of Roads. He then proceeded to categorize the highways designated as provincial, raised taxes on heavy trucks, and introduced a program of maintenance, repair, and construction. In Perron's view, the new highways were not only useful means for travel, but also attractions for tourists.

Perron's position as a lawyer for large corporations hurt him occasionally. In the 1923 general election the Conservatives would accuse him of corruption because he was both minister of roads and a director of the Canada Cement Company, one of his department's suppliers. Nevertheless, he was able to use his ministerial functions to make electoral gains. In 1922, for example, he had followed Arthur Sauvé*, the leader of the opposition, in order to promise roads wherever the latter was scoring points. Perron used another strategy at meetings. The Liberal MLA of a constituency would claim that the future of his region depended on having a highway and make a request to this effect, addressed to the minister, who would be in the audience. After pretending to think deeply about the question, Perron would stand up and announce that the highway would be built.

But Perron was more than just a skilful actor and electoral manipulator; he also kept his promises. In 1925, for example, he reduced the rate of interest on loans to municipalities for road work from 3 per cent to 2 per cent, a reduction the Conservatives had long been demanding. In the same year he decided that responsibility for colonization roads would be transferred from the Department of Colonization, Mines, and Fisheries to the Department of Roads. He was then in a position to begin his work in the Gaspé region: repairs to the highway between Rimouski and Sainte-Anne-des-Monts, and construction of a road around the Gaspé peninsula from Sainte-Anne-des-Monts to Matapédia, for a total of 190 miles in 1927 and 1928. The number of tourists visiting the Gaspé soared from about 100 in 1927 to 3,500 in 1928. The region finally had a road suitable for motor vehicles and a link to the rest of the province in Highway 126, which for a long time was known as Boulevard Perron (now Highway 132). Elsewhere in the province, the highway between Quebec and La Malbaie had been opened in 1925, and Highway 11 (Route des Laurentides) had been extended the following year from Sainte-Agathe to Mont-Laurier. Always drawn to large-scale projects, Perron even considered instituting a monopoly on the sale of gasoline, which would generate significant revenue for the province at a time when automobiles and foreign tourism were on the increase. He gave up the idea under pressure from industry.

Perron never lost sight of his other duties within the cabinet, including that of political organizer for the Montreal region, a task in which he was assisted by Irénée Vautrin and Fernand Rinfret*. With Taschereau on holiday, it fell to Perron to find the reason for the Liberals' poor performance in the 1923 general election, when they lost ten seats and obtained nearly 15 per cent less of the votes cast than they had in 1919. Refusing to see the party's real organizational problems, he privately blamed, among others, the chair of the Quebec Liquor Commission, who had not allowed ministers to use the organization to buy votes. Commissioned by the premier, in the spring of 1927 Perron relieved the mayor of Montreal, Médéric Martin, of responsibility for the Liberal forces in the constituency of Montréal–Sainte-Marie. In order to avoid a repetition in 1927 of the failures of 1923, Taschereau gave Perron full authority over the political organization of Montreal. In charge of nominations and patronage, he got rid of independent and dissident Liberals, and he succeeded in improving the election results.

Early in 1929, after nearly 20 years as minister of agriculture, Joseph-Édouard Caron left the cabinet and took over the post of vice-chairman of the Quebec Liquor Commission. Many people believed that the time had now come to provide new impetus to agriculture and Taschereau handed this task – to the surprise of many, considering his excellent work in the Department of Roads – to Perron, his most reform-minded minister. Upon taking office, the minister proposed to put in place a program of agricultural self-sufficiency by encouraging the use of new methods of production and marketing, the establishment of agricultural cooperatives, the electrification of the countryside, and the export of produce. He also transformed the Quebec Federated Co-operative into a genuine marketing and exporting organization on a provincial scale, endeavouring to raise agriculture from the level of subsistence farming to that of an industry. The disciples of modernization were enthusiastic when Perron arrived on the scene. Through his dynamism, he wanted to set Quebec agriculture on the path taken by the world leaders.

To justify his new cabinet post, Perron decided to leave behind the placid discussions of the Legislative Council. On 16 Nov. 1929 he was elected MLA for the constituency of Montcalm. The limp response of many Liberals to the attacks of some Conservatives was no doubt the real reason for his return to the Legislative Assembly. Taschereau gave Perron the task of standing up to Camillien Houde*, a fiery Conservative and the new mayor of Montreal, who, since his re-election as MLA for Montréal–Sainte-Marie in 1928, never missed a chance to criticize the government, and especially Perron.

For Perron, 1930 opened on a promising note. First of all, it was in this year that the plans for the Montreal Harbour Bridge (which would become the Pont Jacques-Cartier in 1934) were changed so that access to it would be across property that he reportedly had just bought. But, above all, Perron was preparing to challenge Taschereau, who in the opinion of many had become too conservative for the leadership. He had his eye on nothing less than the office of premier. To this end, he is said to have even taken unofficial control of some of the party's organs. Within the party, he stood

ready to attack Taschereau, with whom his relations were always strained. His supporters were eager to see the struggle begin, and the press was waiting for the signal to start. Then, without notice, Perron went on holiday in the United States. He had suffered an attack of angina pectoris and had just learned from his doctors that his days were numbered. Without letting his family know how serious his condition was, he went quietly back to the ranks and continued his work in his department, as if nothing had happened. He died on 20 Nov. 1930 at the age of 58, at the height of his career.

In Joseph-Léonide Perron, the Liberal party had a supporter and minister whose dynamism, energy, firm opinions, and fighting spirit brought significant reforms to his departments. As the person responsible for the important Montreal region, he was among the most influential organizers, probably second only to the premier himself. His work on the provincial highway system and his reforms in Quebec agriculture made him one of the most important ministers in Taschereau's government.

RENÉ CASTONGUAY

No collection of papers exists for Joseph-Léonide Perron, and archival repositories tell us little about him. There is, however, some information to be found at the LAC, in MG 26, G and at MG 27, III, B4 (Lomer Gouin fonds), and at the ANQ, in the Fonds Louis-Alexandre Taschereau (P350). Historical studies of this period in Quebec's past are very useful, in particular B. L. Vigod, *Quebec before Duplessis: the political career of Louis-Alexandre Taschereau* (Kingston, Ont., and Montreal, 1986), and Conrad Black, *Duplessis* (Toronto, 1977). Robert Lévesque et Robert Migner, *Camillien et les années vingt, suivi de Camillien au goulag: cartographie du houdisme* (Montréal, 1978), shows the animosity that existed between Camillien Houde and Perron when the latter had to return to the Legislative Assembly. More indirectly, Jules Bélanger et al., *Histoire de la Gaspésie* (Montréal, 1981), and J.-G. Genest, *Godbout* (Sillery, Qué., 1996), furnish a number of details as does the reliable Rumilly, *Hist. de la prov. de Québec.*

ANQ-M, CE601-S1, 6 juin 1898; S46, 25 sept. 1872. *Le Devoir*, 20 nov. 1930. *Le Soleil*, 4 févr. 1921. *DPQ*. P. [A.] Dutil, *Devil's advocate: Godfroy Langlois and the politics of liberal progressivism in Laurier's Quebec* (Montreal, 1994). Hector Grenon, *Camillien Houde, raconté par Hector Grenon* ([Montréal], 1979). Hertel La Roque, *Camillien Houde, le p'tit gars de Ste-Marie* (Montréal, 1961). Charles Renaud, *L'imprévisible monsieur Houde* (Montréal, 1964).

PERRY, BESSIE. *See* STARKMAN, BESHA

PETERSON, Sir WILLIAM, classical scholar and university professor and administrator; b. 29 May 1856 in Edinburgh, fifth son of John Peterson, a merchant in Leith (Edinburgh), and Grace Mountford Anderson; m. 8 April 1885 Lisa Ross in London, England, and they had two sons; d. 4 Jan. 1921 in Hampstead Heath (London).

Peterson

William Peterson was entered at the Royal High School in Edinburgh and launched on a brilliant academic career. At the University of Edinburgh he was the youngest graduand of 1875, yet he headed the list with first-class honours in classics. He proceeded with a travelling scholarship to Göttingen (Germany), and then with an open scholarship to Corpus Christi College, Oxford, where he won the Ferguson scholarship in classics and secured a first in classical Moderations and, anomalously, a second in the final examinations. After a brief experience in teaching at Harrow, he was invited back to Edinburgh as assistant professor of humanities and only two years later, in 1882, at age 26, he was appointed principal and professor of classics at the newly opened University College in Dundee. Initially, the college prepared its students for degrees at the University of London; Peterson conducted delicate negotiations and obtained highly satisfactory terms for the affiliation in 1897, two years after his departure, of University College with the University of St Andrews. The University of St Andrews had honoured him with an LLD in 1885.

After 13 years in Dundee, during which he contributed much to the college, Peterson was appointed in 1895 principal of McGill University, Montreal. He had attracted the attention of McGill's chancellor and patron, Sir Donald Alexander Smith*, who was looking for a successor to Sir John William Dawson*. During his 38-year tenure as principal, Dawson had raised McGill from destitution to national and international prominence. McGill's leadership was particularly evident in medicine, law, the sciences, engineering, architecture, and general education. Through its normal school, its provision of Canada-wide matriculation examinations, and its offer of affiliation to colleges with first and second year programs, McGill had made a major contribution to education throughout Canada. Peterson's immense challenge was to maintain and build on this momentum. His inaugural lecture, adumbrating a philosophy of education, showed him well prepared for the task. He said that, in order of teaching, humanistic subjects should precede professional ones and that pure learning should precede applied knowledge, but he also recognized that the development of pure science was attained by responding to the practical needs of life. The university's task, he stated, was to give practical men a sound training in theory and to ensure that theorists kept in touch with practice. Its main goal, however, was to produce good citizens, men and women of character.

These views served him well in his dealings with the McGill faculties, where while not neglecting the humanities he skilfully guided major developments, particularly in the physical sciences, engineering, medicine, law, agriculture, and education. His concern for the sciences was symbolized by his recruiting Ernest Rutherford* in physics. In education his commitment to Dawson's ideals was evidenced in the leading role he took in the Provincial Association of Protestant Teachers (he served as president in 1899), in his encouragement of musical education in elementary schools, and in his editing of *A junior school poetry book* and *A senior school poetry book*, which were both published in New York in 1903 and would be reissued as one work, *A school poetry book,* in 1919. His interest in popular education led him to accept the Canadian editorship of *Nelson's perpetual loose-leaf encyclopedia* . . . (New York, 1917). In 1901 he had supported the establishment by McGill's librarian Charles Henry Gould* of the McLennan Travelling Library, which sent boxes of books to mining and lumber camps and isolated communities from Harbour Grace, Nfld, to Dawson, Y.T. Similarly he encouraged the affiliation with McGill of colleges in Victoria and Vancouver; in 1902 he journeyed west to visit these institutions; both eventually grew into independent universities.

Further afield, Peterson was appointed one of the initial trustees of the Carnegie Foundation for the Advancement of Teaching, established in 1905 to provide annuities to retired professors and to promote higher education. He eventually served as the foundation's chairman and his connection with it took him into the mainstream of American educational developments. The administrators of the parent Carnegie Corporation thought so highly of his contribution that they recognized it in 1919 with a special, unsolicited grant of $1,000,000 to McGill.

Peterson's major preoccupation, however, was the health, and that included the financial health, of the university at home. The other royal university foundations, at Halifax, Fredericton, and Toronto, had all been supported by crown endowments in the form of extensive land grants. In the case of McGill, however, no such grants had been made, on the grounds that James McGill* had already made sufficient provision. When his benevolence was depleted and no supplementary government aid was forthcoming, Dawson had secured the patronage of wealthy benefactors. Here again Peterson proved himself a worthy successor. His major task was to ensure that Smith, William Christopher Macdonald*, William Massey Birks (son of Henry Birks), and a host of others continued their interest in the university. Relationships with Grace Redpath, widow of Montreal industrialist Peter Redpath, and with Smith's heiress, the Baroness Strathcona, both living in England, had to be nurtured and protected. These delicate matters were handled with consummate skill; the Redpath Library and the Royal Victoria College, in particular, owe much to Peterson's diplomacy. Macdonald's major venture into rural education, the establishment of Macdonald College for the advancement of agriculture, domestic economy, and teacher-training, originally intended to be an independent institution, was brought into the McGill fold only by Peterson's personal initiatives and tact.

Despite his heavy responsibilities, in his early years at McGill Peterson maintained his teaching in classics and his own research continued productively until about 1914. In 1901 he had discovered in a private library in England a manuscript of Cicero's orations which provided material for several articles in prestigious journals and for an edition of the Verrine orations, published in 1907. The work was followed by further distinguished publications, around 1910 by Cicero's *Orationes* . . . (Oxford) and in 1914 by a translation of Tacitus's *Dialogus* . . . (London and New York). To the end of his days, Peterson retained a high reputation as a classical scholar.

By reason of his prominent social position, his Anglo-Scottish background, and his family tradition, Peterson took a natural and informed interest in public life. He decried what he saw as an unfortunate divorce of Canadian universities from the conduct of national affairs. In 1911 he invited those who were planning to attend the Congress of the Universities of the Empire in London in 1912 to meet at McGill to consider the congress agenda and to explore the possibility and desirability of speaking from a common concern. This meeting proved to be the founding of the Conference of Canadian Universities, which met again at McGill the following year and, as the National Conference of Canadian Universities (it was renamed in 1916), would become an important institution in Canadian life, especially in World War II and subsequent years. Peterson's own role in the institution was pre-empted by World War I and his retirement and death, but the NCCU and its successors remain an important part of his legacy to Canadian education.

Peterson's many speeches and writings in the pre-war years evidenced his wide range of interests and his predilections. In Canadian politics he was a strong federalist, commenting that "we hear too much of the provinces, and too little of the nation." Consistently, he was also a fervent imperialist, and not surprisingly was frequently attacked in publications supported by Henri Bourassa* and the Ligue Nationaliste Canadienne. His imperialism was enlightened, however. He seems to have envisaged a British Commonwealth of Nations before the term was widely used.

Certainly, when in 1914 war became inevitable, Peterson and the university he led gave Canada and the empire their full, unhesitating support. He encouraged recruiting, worked for wartime charities, and personally visited units composed of McGill students or graduates on the battlefront in France. He continued support at home in Canada through committee work and the raising of funds, and not least through the encouragement of the McGill-led Khaki University of Canada, which worked among the armed forces with conspicuous success. In these years Peterson

asked too much of himself. In January 1919, at yet another charity meeting, he suffered a stroke from which he made little recovery. In April, after 24 years of service, he resigned the principalship and retired to England, where he died in 1921.

Peterson had served McGill, Quebec, and Canada brilliantly, but he never became a Canadian. He was an imperial administrator, selflessly fulfilling his high destiny – like his brothers Franklin, professor of music in Australia, Peter, professor of Sanskrit in India, and Magnus, organist and music teacher in New Zealand. He was created a CMG for his services to Canada and the empire on 17 Sept. 1901 and on 3 June 1915 was made KCMG. Personally, he was unfailingly kind and gracious, but few acquaintances ever penetrated his reserve. He golfed and curled in season moderately and, possessed of a good voice, he enjoyed music, in particular singing old Scottish songs and playing his own accompaniment. His home life was very private. He returned every summer to England, where his two sons were educated and subsequently pursued notable careers. Lady Peterson died in England in 1929. Peterson was one of Britain's greatest gifts to Canada, but he, at least, always knew that he was only on long loan.

S. B. FROST

In addition to the works mentioned in the biography, Sir William Peterson is the author of *Canadian essays and addresses* (London, 1915). A listing of his other published addresses appears in CIHM, *Reg.*

MUA RG 2, c.15–35. *Times* (London), 9 April 1885. W. M. Birks, "McGill's principals since 1900: stories of Peterson, Auckland Geddes, Currie, A. E. Morgan, Lewis Douglas and F. Cyril James," *McGill News* (Montreal), 31, no.4 (summer 1950): 7–12. Augustus Bridle, *Sons of Canada: short studies of characteristic Canadians* (Toronto, 1916). *Canadian men and women of the time* (Morgan; 1912). *DNB.* S. B. Frost, *McGill University: for the advancement of learning* (2v., Montreal, 1980–84); "Salute to Royal Victoria College," *McGilliana* (Montreal), special issue (February 1980): 1–12. Ethel Hurlbatt, "Sir William Peterson, K.C.M.G.," *McGill News*, 12, no.4 (September 1931): 23–26. Cyrus Macmillan, "Sir William Peterson," *McGill News*, 1, no.1 (December 1919): 9, 43. G. [E.] Pilkington, *Speaking with one voice: universities in dialog with government* (Montreal, 1983). J. F. Snell, *Macdonald College of McGill University: a history from 1904–1955* (Montreal, 1963). *Standard dict. of Canadian biog.* (Roberts and Tunnell).

PETTY-FITZMAURICE, HENRY CHARLES KEITH, 5th Marquess of LANSDOWNE, governor general; b. 14 Jan. 1845 in London, England, elder son of Henry Petty-Fitzmaurice and Emily Jane Mercer Elphinstone de Flahault; m. there 8 Nov. 1869 Lady Maud Evelyn Hamilton, and they had two sons and two daughters; d. 3 June 1927 in Clonmel (Republic of Ireland).

Petty-Fitzmaurice

Henry Charles Keith Petty-Fitzmaurice was known as the Earl of Kerry during the three years that his father held the marquessate of Lansdowne. He succeeded to the higher title in 1866, and to the Liberal traditions of his family. Educated at Eton and Balliol, Oxford, the slight, dark-complexioned Lansdowne missed a first class owing to his great interest in sports and life at Oxford. He came early to administrative office: a lord of the Treasury in 1868 under William Ewart Gladstone, under-secretary for war in 1872–74, and under-secretary for India in 1880. He then resigned owing to his dislike of Gladstone's Irish policies; Lansdowne had large estates in Ireland, including a home, Derreen, near Kenmare in County Kerry. By the 1880s a Conservative, he was chosen in May 1883 to succeed the Marquess of Lorne [Campbell*] as governor general of Canada; he was formally appointed on 18 August, arrived at Quebec City on 22 October, and assumed office the following day.

Lansdowne was a highly intelligent and able administrator. With the possible exception of Lord Lisgar [Young*], Prime Minister Sir John A. Macdonald* found him the most perspicacious of the governors he had served before and after confederation. Lansdowne was sensitive to the questions that arose in the Saskatchewan River valley in 1884–85. All for making accommodation with the Métis, he suggested to Macdonald on 9 Aug. 1884 that some means be found of giving employment to certain of their leaders. To Lansdowne's mind, the best place for Louis Riel* might well be on the Council of the North-West Territories. As to the land question [see Gabriel Dumont*], he asked Macdonald, "Would it not be possible to send out a strong commission with powers to deal promptly & ... liberally with these [land] claims?" He also took a great interest in the Canadian Pacific Railway, travelling to the end of steel in September 1885 and riding on horseback across the 47-mile gap in British Columbia between the two railheads. He was to drive the last spike, but weather delayed completion of the line and when he telegraphed Macdonald in October asking if he should return to Ottawa, for the final decision concerning Riel, Macdonald said yes. The last spike was driven instead by Donald Alexander Smith*.

Macdonald and his ministers were struck by Lansdowne's early grasp of the complex, often difficult nature of British-Canadian relations. His diplomatic skills, preparedness, and unexpectedly strong support for Canadian interests were particularly evident in the negotiation of the fisheries treaty with the United States in 1886–87. Fisheries minister George Eulas Foster* was strongly impressed, as was another participant, justice minister John Sparrow David Thompson*, who had liked Lansdowne from the moment they met in 1885.

Despite Lansdowne's aptitude, being an Irish land-lord made him vulnerable. From the time of his arrival he had attracted the ire of Irish nationalists in North America and there were Fenian threats against his life. In 1884, for example, a Fenian from Chicago concealed himself in the winter woods at Rideau Hall for an entire day waiting for Lansdowne to appear. He failed to show, but his son Lord Kerry was skating on a rink nearby; "I could have shot the boy," the Fenian reported, "but my heart failed me."

Lansdowne liked Canada, "its visions of winter, with its clear skies, its exhilarating sports, and within the bright fire of Gatineau logs, with our children and friends gathered round us." He built a summer retreat on the Rivière Cascapédia in the Gaspé, where the salmon fishing thrilled him. But the British government needed him for India, and he left Canada in June 1888 for a six-year term as viceroy. Macdonald would write him from time to time; to one letter Lansdowne replied, on 23 June 1889, "I fancied myself back in my study in Ottawa, listening to your confidences as to House of Commons prospects, & difficulties, unsuspected by the outside world, within the Cabinet."

After India, Lansdowne went home to the British cabinet, where he served as secretary of state for war in 1895–1900. During the South African War, for which he had to sort out Canadian and other colonial offers of troops, he was unjustly criticized for British military failures. A good minister, he took full responsibility and said nothing, though the real fault lay with his military advisers. As foreign secretary from 1900 to 1905, he negotiated the Anglo-Japanese alliance of 1902 and the Entente Cordiale with France in 1904. He revisited Canadian affairs in 1902–4 over the settlement of the Alaska boundary dispute, on which he worked closely with Governor General Lord Minto [Elliot*], who had been his military secretary in Canada. Lansdowne became leader of the Unionist (Conservative) party in the House of Lords in 1903. His pledge, with others, in early August 1914 to bring Unionist support to France's side had the effect of committing cabinet to war. A minister without portfolio in 1915–16, Lansdowne was soon struck by its phenomenal human and financial costs. In a memorandum to cabinet in November 1916, he boldly called for a negotiated peace; on making this sentiment public a year later, he was reproached within and without his party. The veteran servant nonetheless continued to attend the House of Lords. He was devoted to his Irish home, Derreen, which he rebuilt after its destruction by Irish irregulars in the 1922 troubles. He died of a heart attack at the home of his daughter in Ireland, and was buried at Bowood Park, his estate near Calne in England.

Lansdowne could well have matured quietly into a country gentleman; he was a considerable sportsman, a good shot, a rider to hounds, an expert angler. Instead, at an early age he had become a British public official, one of the best of the breed. Perceptive, honest, and hard-working, he was ready to take up responsibility, shoulder consequences, and not blame subordinates. He had that excellent combination of intelligence and patience, joined to a knack for acting at the right time in the right way. His life and its ethos illustrate how and why the British empire succeeded as it did, and lasted so long. The best of the British upper class was very good indeed.

P. B. WAITE

[The Lansdowne papers are under the control of the 8th Marquess of Lansdowne at Bowood, England. In 1963 the sections relevant to Canada were microfilmed; they are in LAC, MG 27, I, B6, together with a few originals. There is a fine run of Lansdowne correspondence in the Sir John A. Macdonald papers, LAC, MG 26, A, vols.84–88. The *DNB* has an extended notice of Lansdowne by his son the 6th Marquess. There is also a good biography of him by [Thomas Wodehouse Legh Newton, 2nd Baron] Newton, *Lord Lansdowne: a biography* (London, 1929). A portrait of Lansdowne hangs in the speaker's office in Canada's House of Commons. P.B.W.]

Times (London), 6 June 1927. D. [G.] Creighton, *John A. Macdonald, the old chieftain* (Toronto, 1955; repr. 1965). *Lord Minto's Canadian papers: a selection of the public and private papers of the fourth Earl of Minto, 1898–1904*, ed. and intro. Paul Stevens and J. T. Saywell (2v., Toronto, 1981–83). Carman Miller, *Painting the map red: Canada and the South African War, 1899–1902* (Montreal and Kingston, Ont., 1993). P. B. Waite, *Canada, 1874–1896: arduous destiny* (Toronto and Montreal, 1971); *The man from Halifax: Sir John Thompson, prime minister* (Toronto, 1985). W. S. Wallace, *The memoirs of the Rt. Hon. Sir George Foster, P.C., G.C.M.G.* (Toronto, 1933).

PEUCHEN, ARTHUR GODFREY, businessman, militia officer, and yachtsman; b. 18 April 1859 in Montreal, son of Godfrey E. Peuchen and Eliza Eleanor Clarke; m. 26 April 1893 Margaret Thomson in Toronto, and they had a daughter and a son; d. there 7 Dec. 1929.

Arthur G. Peuchen's maternal grandfather had been manager of the London, Brighton and South Coast Railway in England. His Prussian father was a railway contractor in South America before he immigrated to Canada in 1850 to work for the Grand Trunk; in 1859 he was a wine merchant. Though born in Montreal, Arthur was raised in Toronto and he attended private schools in Ontario and England. His business career began in Toronto around 1879–80, as a clerk and salesman, and by 1882 he had started to manufacture paint. Moving through various partnerships, he emerged about 1893 as manager of the Canada Paint Company, of which his brother Stanley Cooper was superintendent. Peuchen is said to have been the first manufacturer in Canada to capitalize on pre-mixed, colour-blended paints. Within three years, in Peuchen

and Company, he had also begun to specialize in the production of acetic acid and aceto-based pigment.

To utilize his method of distilling wood alcohol and acetone from hardwood, in 1897 he founded the Standard Chemical Company of Toronto Limited in association with entrepreneur William MACKENZIE, Mackenzie's brother Ewan, Orillia lumberman William Thomson, and others. Standard Chemical opened factories in Ontario at Sault Ste Marie, Fenelon Falls, Deseronto, Longford Mills, South River, Thornbury, and Parry Sound and in Quebec at Fassett, Cookshire, and Mont-Tremblant. In 1909 the firm began making formaldehyde. Two years later it was expanded – Peuchen bought large timber limits in Alberta from Senator Peter McLaren – and reorganized as the Standard Chemical, Iron and Lumber Company.

Peuchen had been a protégé of Toronto financier Henry Mill Pellatt*, who was also a militia officer in the Queen's Own Rifles of Canada. Peuchen joined this regiment at the age of 17; he was promoted second lieutenant in 1888, captain in 1894, and major in 1904. In 1911 he was the marshalling officer in charge of the Indian cavalry in London during the procession for the coronation of King George V. Photographs of him in uniform, with his precisely trimmed beard, present an officer of striking appearance.

A bluff, opinionated millionaire, Peuchen used his success in business and the military as stepping stones in Toronto society. He built a country residence, Woodlands, near Shanty Bay on Lake Simcoe, complete with a marina, tennis courts, and riding stables. The Anglican church and a number of hospital charities enjoyed his support. He was a member of the Albany and Toronto Hunt clubs, among others, and a vice-commodore of the Royal Canadian Yacht Club. His 65-foot yacht, the *Vreda*, regularly captured trophies in Great Lakes regattas.

Peuchen was a seasoned traveller who had crossed the Atlantic at least 40 times. In early 1912 he was in England, where he approached Lord Haldane of the War Office about supplying acetone for making explosives. He booked his return passage on the premier voyage of the *Titanic*. On 14 April it hit an iceberg, but he did not expect it to founder – he left $200,000 in securities in his cabin when he went out to survey the damage. Recognized as an experienced yachtsman, he was ordered by a ship's officer, Charles Herbert Lightoller, into a lifeboat with 20 women and 3 other men. Once in the boat, he did not assert himself, but allowed Robert Hichens, the quartermaster who was at the tiller, to remain there rather than row. The women were terribly uncoordinated. In the end, it was Denver socialite Margaret Brown (later dubbed the Unsinkable Molly Brown) who challenged Hichens and took charge of the boat, which was rescued by the *Carpathia*.

Peuchen was the only Canadian to testify, on 23

Peyasiw-awasis

April, at the American Senate's inquiry into the sinking and the loss of more than 1,500 lives. An impartial, expert witness, he was critical of the seamanship aboard the *Titanic*. Its crew, he said, "was what we would call in yachting terms a scratch crew, brought from different vessels. They might be the best, but they had not been accustomed to working together." In the lifeboat, Hichens had refused his help. He was "swearing a great deal, and was very disagreeable . . . and he told me he was in command," Peuchen testified. "I knew I was perfectly powerless." Back in Toronto, he faced both criticism and praise. Under Edwardian standards, to have survived was judged unbecoming conduct for an officer and a gentleman. The Toronto *Mail and Empire* discredited him as "a man who had to defend himself before the necessity for the defence was apparent." According to another taunt, "He said he was a yachtsman so he could get off the *Titanic*, and if there had been a fire, he would have said he was a fireman." He was nonetheless welcomed back from Washington by his fellow officers in the QOR; on 21 May he was promoted lieutenant-colonel and assumed command of the regiment's 1st Battalion. His reputation from the *Titanic* would be somewhat rehabilitated in 1935 when C. H. Lightoller published his memoirs, in which he wrote that Peuchen had been unfairly criticized for carrying out a direct order.

When World War I broke out in 1914, Peuchen retired from Standard Chemical, which by then had acquired all the companies working in the wood distillation industry in Canada. In November 1915 he stepped down from his militia command. Following the conflict, he lost much of his fortune through bad investments; in December 1918 he was sued by Peter McLaren on an overdue promissory note. He nevertheless retained his house, an apartment in London, and Woodlands, which he would sell in 1928, and he continued to own McLaren Lumber in Alberta and the mill of Prince Albert Lumber in Saskatchewan. During the last years of his life he spent a good deal of time living in Hinton, Alta. Peuchen died in Toronto five weeks after the stock-market crash of 1929, leaving an estate valued at about $67,000. In 1987 his wallet was recovered from the wreck of the *Titanic*; inside were his business card and some streetcar tickets.

ALAN HUSTAK

ANQ-M, CE601-S63, 5 juin 1859. AO, RG 22-305, no.63684; RG 80-5-0-211, no.14413. LAC, RG 31, C1, 1901, Toronto, Ward 2, div.34: 4. *Toronto Daily Star*, 25 March, 26–27 April 1912; 8 Nov. 1915; 8 Feb. 1916; 13 Dec. 1918; 9 Dec. 1929. Hugh Brewster, "Sinking sensation," *Toronto Life* (Toronto), 31 (1997), no.7: 55–65. *Canada Gazette*, 17 Nov. 1888: 864. *Canadian men and women of the time* (Morgan; 1912). *Cyclopædia of Canadian biog.* (Rose and Charlesworth), vol.3. *Directory*, Toronto, 1875–99. *Encyclopaedia of Canadian biography . . .* , vol.2. "Encyclopedia Titanica": *www.encyclopedia-titanica.org*. (consulted 18 June 2004). Alan Hustak, *Titanic: the Canadian story* (Montreal, 1998). *Ontario Gazette* (Toronto), 19 June 1897: 982. "Titanic inquiry project," comp. and ed. Rob Ottmers and Bill Wormstedt: *www.titanicinquiry.org*. (consulted 18 June 2004). U.S., Senate, Committee on commerce, *Titanic disaster*, 62nd Congress, 2nd session, 1912, Senate report 806 (Washington, 1912).

PEYASIW-AWASIS (**Thunderchild**, also known as **Kapitikow**, meaning "the one who makes the sound"), Plains Cree chief; b. 1849, probably along the South Saskatchewan River; m. Mamchwasis and then Ka-kwa; he had several children; d. 29 June 1927 on the Thunderchild Indian Reserve, Sask.

In 1923 the Reverend Edward Ahenakew* recorded Thunderchild's stories of his early life, when his family belonged to the band of Mistawāsis, one of the more important Plains Cree chiefs and the first to sign Treaty No.6 in 1876. The stories tell of buffalo hunts, of hunger when the buffalo disappeared, of raids against the Blackfoot, of sports and entertainment, and of tribal justice and customs. Treaty No.6 marked the end of this existence. Initially, Thunderchild rejected the treaty and joined Big Bear [Mistahimaskwa*] and others who hoped to negotiate better terms. The destruction of the buffalo forced them to change their strategy and in 1879 Thunderchild, who had achieved a certain status and a small following, accepted the treaty. He first appears in treaty paylists as the opening entry in a group of nine families paid at Sounding Lake (Alta) in August 1879.

His band, which spent some time on the reserve of Mōsōmin*, settled permanently on its own reserve west of Battleford (Sask.) in 1883. By early 1884 the Department of Indian Affairs had recognized Thunderchild as a chief. That year, with him setting an example, band members began to farm. At first they were successful, particularly in stock raising, but in the 1890s their progress and size (177 members in 1891) would stall as a result of crop failures, deteriorating health, and departmental policies that limited their market and access to agricultural machinery.

Thunderchild had not played a prominent role in the movement to unite the Cree in 1883–84. When men from the band of Poundmaker [Pītikwahanapiwīyin*] urged him to join them in 1885, he crossed the North Saskatchewan to avoid becoming involved in the unrest. Although hunger eventually forced him to move to Poundmaker's camp, his loyalty during the North-West uprising was subsequently recognized.

Nonetheless, Thunderchild was a tenacious defender of treaty rights and Indian land. In 1889 he refused to transfer ground for a Roman Catholic school on his reserve, arguing that it already had an Anglican school. When a school was built without his permission, he protested for two years to no avail. Finally, flying his treaty flag and wearing his treaty medal, he led his supporters in tearing down the building. Although the Indian department believed that he was within his rights, it eventually pressured him into accepting the school. He was not opposed to education, however. In 1910, when the band was without a school, he argued that it was entitled to one under treaty and that one was essential to the band's advancement. After years of bureaucratic delay, the band itself built a schoolhouse and the department agreed to pay a teacher.

Thunderchild believed that whites and the Cree followed the same God but had been taught different ways of worshipping. He supported traditional religious practices, argued that treaties did not limit his religious rights, and opposed government efforts to outlaw age-old ceremonies. On one occasion he outwitted the Indian agent by gaining the backing of both the Catholic missionary and the Protestant missionary for a Sun Dance. In 1897 he was imprisoned briefly for participating in a Give Away Dance. As late as 1922 he was warned that if he did not stop supporting traditional ceremonies, he would be removed as chief.

The Thunderchild Reserve was on good land, and from 1902 rumours circulated that the band would be moved and the reserve sold to settlers. With both government officials and missionaries urging his band to surrender its land, Thunderchild reluctantly agreed to negotiations in 1908. After three votes his band remained evenly divided on the government's offer. Thunderchild broke the tie, voting to sell the reserve and use the proceeds to purchase another. In 1909 the band moved to a new reserve near Brightsand Lake, but the full implementation of the agreement dragged on until after the chief's death in 1927.

Thunderchild had known the old way of life but he accepted the necessity of change and tried to adapt to the new way. When his efforts met with only the smallest success, he continued to defend his band's rights with the limited resources at his disposal.

ALAN B. MCCULLOUGH

[For assistance on Thunderchild's names, the author thanks Blair Stonechild. A.B.McC.]

LAC, RG 10, 1017; 3563, file 82-11; 3664, file 9834; 3668, file 10644; 3682, file 12628; 3710, files 19550, 19550-4; 3817, file 57562; 3825, file 60511-1, 2; 3964, file 148285; 6294, file 623-1; 7541, file 29105-13; 7626, file 17105-9; 7795, file 29105-9; 9412–13; 9417–19; RG 18, 134, file 189-1897. Edward Ahenakew, *Voices of the Plains Cree*, ed. R. M. Buck (Toronto, 1973). Can., Parl., *Sessional papers*, reports of the Dept. of Indian Affairs, 1880–1925; report of the Indian branch, Dept. of the Interior, 1879. *Canadian annual rev.*, 1927/28. Federation of Saskatchewan Indian Nations (Saskatoon), Research report on the administration of the Thunderchild band lands. Jack Funk, *Outside, the women cried: the story of the surrender by Chief Thun-derchild's band of their reserve near Delmas, Saskatchewan, 1908* (Battleford, Sask., 1989). Robert Jefferson, *Fifty years on the Saskatchewan . . .* (Battleford, 1929). Katherine Pettipas, *"Severing the ties that bind": government repression of indigenous religious ceremonies on the prairies* (Winnipeg, 1994). Blair Stonechild and W. A. Waiser, *Loyal till death: Indians and the North-West rebellion* (Calgary, 1997). J. L. Tobias, "Canada's subjugation of the Plains Cree, 1879–1885," in *Sweet promises: a reader on Indian-white relations in Canada*, ed. J. R. Miller (Toronto, 1991), 212–40.

PHANEUF, JOSEPH-STANISLAS-ZÉPHIRIN, named **Brother Opilius Elias** (like his French-speaking colleagues, he preferred to gallicize his official religious name and signed **Frère Élie**), member of the Brothers of the Christian Schools, educator, and author; b. 27 Dec. 1875 in Salvail, near Saint-Hyacinthe, Que., son of Zéphir Phaneuf, a farmer, and Éliza Chartier; d. 1 Sept. 1929 in Montreal.

Joseph-Stanislas-Zéphirin Phaneuf studied at the Académie Girouard, and afterwards at the Séminaire de Saint-Hyacinthe from 1888 to 1890. He then entered the *juvénat* (which prepared adolescent students before they became novices) run by the Brothers of the Christian Schools at Mont-de-La-Salle in Maisonneuve (Montreal). On 19 March 1892 he donned the habit and took the name of Brother Opilius Elias. Sent first to the scholasticate (March to October 1893), which was also at Mont-de-La-Salle, he subsequently went to the Académie Saint-Jean-Baptiste at Quebec (1893–96), Saint-Jean-d'Iberville (Saint-Jean-sur-Richelieu) (1896 and 1897), and the École Saint-Joseph in Montreal (1897–1903). His superiors assigned him in 1903 to the Collège du Mont-Saint-Louis in Montreal, a bilingual boarding and day school, which was directed at that time by Brother Symphorian Lewis [Stanislas-Alphonse ROBERGE]. Except for one year in Ottawa, in 1904–5, as assistant director of the Académie De-La-Salle, he would spend the rest of his life at Mont-Saint-Louis.

According to his colleagues, Brother Opilius Elias brought to the tasks of teacher and monitor a devotion, courtesy, and perspicacity that readily earned him their respect and the affection of his students. The special interest he took in his school showed in various ways: his painstaking preparation of "Notes historiques sur le Mont-Saint-Louis" from 1910 to 1927, his concern for providing the library with a large collection of Canadiana, and his care in preserving and enriching the Mont-Saint-Louis archives, of which he was temporarily in charge for a few months.

Throughout his career, Brother Opilius Elias took a particular interest in genealogy and history. He published a book on the Casavant family in 1914 and another one on the Phaneuf-Farnsworth family the following year. Twice a winner in the competition of the Société Saint-Jean-Baptiste de Montréal (in 1917 for an article on Pierre Le Moyne* d'Iberville et d'Ardillières, and in 1918 for a narrative entitled "Mathias l'Anglais"), as a writer he focused on the history of French Canada. He helped write the *Histoire du Canada* for the senior course, which was published by his community. He was also the author of biographies and historical accounts under various pseudonyms, including Élie de Salvail, Du Rivage, Des Érables, and Luc. His pieces appeared in such newspapers as *L'Action catholique* (Québec) and *La Presse* (Montréal) (where his "Éphémérides" was a regular feature), and in Montreal magazines such as *Un Canadien errant*, *Le Petit Canadien*, *L'Oiseau bleu*, *Le Pays laurentien*, and the *Revue canadienne*. For a number of years he contributed to his community's publications, among them the *Bulletin du Saint Enfant Jésus* and the *Bulletin des Écoles chrétiennes*. His favourite topics were the great figures of French Canada's history and the customs (especially religious) of the early French Canadians.

Brother Opilius Elias was in the process of revising his major work, *366 anniversaires canadiens*, which revisited the "Éphémérides" published in *La Presse*, when illness struck in the summer of 1929. He died after an operation for acute peritonitis. The obituary in *La Presse* noted that he would be "deeply remembered by all those who knew him as teacher or as historian." His well-documented works recreated an idealized past, centred on New France and its "heroes," especially the religious figures.

NIVE VOISINE

Using his religious name Frère Élie, Joseph-Stanislas-Zéphirin Phaneuf published *La famille Casavant* (Montréal, 1914) and *La famille Phaneuf-Farnsworth: histoire, généalogie, documents, portraits* (Montréal, 1915); *366 anniversaires canadiens* (Montréal, 1930) appeared under the pseudonym Élie de Salvail. Phaneuf is the author of numerous other pieces scattered throughout the newspapers and magazines to which he contributed. From 1910 to 1927 he also prepared "Notes historiques sur le Mont-Saint-Louis"; his contributions appear in volumes 1 (1888–1916) and 2 (1916–27), which are available in the Arch. des Frères des Écoles Chrétiennes du Canada Francophone (Laval, Qué.).

ANQ-M, CE602-S3, 28 déc. 1875. *La Presse*, 3 sept. 1929. *BCF*, 1926. *DOLQ*, 2: 310–13. "F. Opilius Elias," Institut des Frères des Écoles Chrétiennes, *Notices nécrologiques trimestrielles* (Paris), no.127 (juillet–septembre 1929): 131–34. F[rère] Mamès-Irénée [J.-A. Poirier], *Institut des Frères des écoles chrétiennes, district de Montréal: prises d'habit, noviciat de Montréal, 1837–1943* (Sainte-Foy, Qué., 1943). N. S., "Le frère Élie," *Bull. du T. S. Enfant Jésus* (Laval-des-Rapides [Laval], Qué.), 16 (1929–30): 54–55. [Étienne Poitras et Armand Yon], *Un demi-siècle au Mont-Saint-Louis, 1888–1938* (Montréal, 1939).

PICKTHALL, MARJORIE LOWRY CHRISTIE, author and librarian; b. 14 Sept. 1883 in Gunnersbury (London), England, daughter of Arthur Christie Pickthall, a surveyor, and Elizabeth Helen Mary Mallard; d. unmarried 19 April 1922 in Vancouver.

During her childhood in England, Marjorie Pickthall's parents encouraged her artistic talents with gifts of books and lessons in drawing and music. In 1889 or 1890 the family immigrated to Toronto, where her father became a foreman at the city's waterworks and later an electrical draftsman. Following the death of an infant brother in 1894, her parents again bestowed their attention on Marjorie as an only child. Summertimes, which were spent on the Toronto Islands, fostered in her a passion for country walks and habits of close observation. She developed her skills in nature description in the lively diaries she kept throughout her teens. While in the city she attended the Church of England day school on Beverley Street and, from 1899, Bishop Strachan School, where she excelled in composition and formed lasting friendships with other artistic young women. These activities were sometimes interrupted by her delicate health: she was plagued by headaches and later by dental, eye, and back problems.

In 1898, at 15, Pickthall had sold her first story to the Toronto *Globe* for $3. "Two-Ears" is about an Iroquois boy who wants to prove himself a warrior, and is typical of her later fiction: it draws on her imagination or reading about a distant culture and features a male protagonist straining against limits. Pickthall would often use Indian or French Canadian settings for her poetry and prose, as well as the medieval, biblical, and Celtic lore she absorbed from her favourite English poets: William Morris, Dante Gabriel Rossetti, and Fiona Macleod. "Two-Ears" and one of Pickthall's poems won first prizes in the *Daily Mail and Empire*'s writing competition of 1899. In a different response to "Two-Ears," James Cleland Hamilton sent her his pamphlet *Famous Algonquins: Algic legends* (Toronto, 1899), possibly as a corrective to her vilification of this First Nation. "I have 'entered the literary world' with a vengeance," she recorded in her diary on 4 June 1900.

A regular contributor to the "Young people's corner" of the *Mail and Empire*, Pickthall was also invited to write for the *Globe*'s "Circle of young Canada." She won the *Mail and Empire*'s competition again in 1900 with "O keep the world for ever at the dawn," a poem for the new century. With its Canadian inflection of the dream landscapes of late-19th-century aestheticism and its impassioned language and musicality, it attracted the attention of professors whose critical support would ensure Pickthall's lasting reputation. Her rejection of modernism, including Henrik Ibsen's "warped and distorted" work, and futurism's abrasive forms represented continuity with the idealism of the "confederation poets" [*see* Joseph Edmund Collins*] and an alternative to the populist verse of such contemporaries as Robert William Service* and Thomas Robert Edward MacInnes.

Pickthall's career began in earnest when prizes launched her into the magazines. "The greater gift" appeared in July 1903 in the first issue of *East and West* (Toronto), a young people's journal sponsored by the Presbyterian Church. She became a regular contributor; three of her serials would appear in Toronto as books illustrated by Charles William Jefferys*: *Dick's desertion: a boy's adventures in Canadian forests . . .* (1905), *The straight road* (1906), and *Billy's hero; or, The valley of gold* (1908). In a poetry competition in 1904 "The homecomers" had won third prize and the admiration of judge Oscar Pelham Edgar*, a professor at Victoria University in Toronto. He gave advice on her poems, which began appearing steadily in *Acta Victoriana*, and recommended her to the editor of the *University Magazine*, Andrew Macphail* of McGill University in Montreal, who featured her continuously from 1907. In 1913 he published 43 of her poems as *The drift of pinions*, which was successful both commercially and critically.

Not content to trust her literary affairs completely to the paternalistic professors who, she would later remark, "have gotten into a fine mess between 'em" over the publication of *The drift*, Pickthall, starting in 1905, shrewdly used a New York (and later a London) literary agent to place her poetry and fiction in prestigious American periodicals, among them *Century*, *Harper's*, *McClure's*, *Scribner's*, and *Atlantic Monthly*. She did not expect easy rewards from writing poetry. As she wryly noted to friend and fellow poet Helena Coleman on 7 Dec. 1908: "Being a poet in the present state of the market is like saying 'How is your hare-lip today?'" Though most critics have concurred with Archibald McKellar MacMechan* that "her legacy to Canada is a sheaf of true poems," the ambitious Pickthall wrote more fiction during her very productive decade after 1905. Her poetry might be highly praised, but it paid little, while stories fetched as much as $150.

This sum represented four months' salary at Victoria University Library, where Pickthall, with the help of Helena Coleman, obtained work in 1910 as a librarian and research assistant. Her mother's sudden death in February 1910 had devastated her; work, it was believed, would help. In addition, it was necessary for her to earn a steady income. (Marriage never seems to have been a serious consideration.) Back problems and possibly a nervous breakdown in the spring of 1912 obliged her to take a leave of absence.

Later that year, determined to fulfil her dream of travel, Pickthall went to England, where she became part of the lively household of her uncle in Hammersmith (London), Dr Frank Reginald Mallard. With her second cousin Edith Emma Whillier she rented Chalke Cottage near Bowerchalke; she spent her summers there writing, beginning in 1914 with "Poursuite joyeuse," a historical novel. Published first by Meth-

uen in London in 1915 as *Little hearts*, it earned no more than £15. Nor, despite favourable reviews, did it facilitate Pickthall's entry into the London literary world, which she felt was closed to her as a colonial, a situation unaffected by the publication in 1916 of an expanded edition of her poems, *The lamp of poor souls*. Moreover, she was out of touch with the American market.

Pickthall's discouragement over her literary career deepened with her horror at the human costs of World War I. She sought to be useful in the war effort by taking training over the winter of 1915–16 in automobile mechanics. When she did not secure a job as an ambulance or truck driver, she enrolled in a gardening course which lengthened into a summer-long position as part-time secretary to the principal and a part-time market gardener. This experience was the basis for an essay, "Women on the land in England," later published in *East and West*. Subsequently she joined another woman student known only as Long-John in Hampshire's New Forest, where she planned to set a novel. Between March and November 1917 the six-foot-tall Long-John joined her in a financially unsuccessful venture to grow vegetables at Chalke Cottage. One can only speculate as to whether this was an emotionally fulfilled time for Pickthall, whose witty letters reveal a primarily woman-identified woman.

During the winter of 1917–18 Pickthall worked as assistant librarian in the South Kensington Meteorological Office. She was obliged to resign in May 1918 because of eye problems, which the summer at Chalke Cottage did not cure. Nonetheless, she wrote 20 stories between July and December, half of which were sold by January. Another creative burst between September and December 1919 produced a novel ("The bridge: a story of the Great Lakes"), a verse drama (*The wood carver's wife*), and 16 stories. "Canada sick," she set sail from Liverpool on 22 May 1920 on the proceeds of what had been published. With only a week's stop in Toronto, she travelled with a literary friend, Edith Joan Lyttleton, to British Columbia, where she settled in a cabin at Lang Bay, and then in a shack at the summer camp of Isabel Ecclestone Mackay [MACPHERSON] on Boundary Bay. Here she revised "The bridge" and researched another novel, "The beaten man," to be set in the wilderness of British Columbia. Her time with Mackay produced ribald humour as well as literary sparkle. A visit by expatriate novelist Arthur John Arbuthnott Stringer in May 1921 prompted them to attack his recent book, *The wine of life*. "It seems a pity that Canadian writers should make a name in New York's larger world by books of that type," Pickthall wrote Helena Coleman on 12 June. "Isabel Mackay and I are going to do one together which will make *The wine of life* look like coca-cola. It is going to be called 'Life's Envelope.' N.B. & P.S. This is a nawful double entendre. The cover design will have black crêpe-de-chine undies on it."

Published in the *University Magazine* in April 1920, *The wood carver's wife* literalizes the metaphor of killing life to produce art. In this tale, which Pickthall felt was her finest work, a Quebec carver murders his wife's lover in order to have a model for the proper expression of grief for his wooden *pietà*. Here Pickthall's use of synaesthesia conveys her vision of the complex web of human and natural realms, in which masculine containment contrasts with feminine intertwining. "The cedar must have known . . . I should love and carve you so," the sculptor sang to his wife/model. The play was staged at the New Empire Theatre in Montreal in March 1921 and later at Hart House Theatre in Toronto. Audiences responded enthusiastically, as did reviewers, but Pickthall was distressed to learn that the role of the wife had been emphasized over the carver and a native character turned into "a sugary child." This difference points to a general misinterpretation of her work, highlighted by Mackay's preface to the book version of 1922, which notes the close relation of the play's "passions and despairs" to Pickthall's life. Still, the play received amateur productions as recently as 1957. Frustration with the sentimentalization of her work may be what Pickthall had in mind when she railed to Helena Coleman against the contradictions between a "greed for experience plus a slavery to convention": "To me the trying part is being a woman at all . . . what the deuce are you to make of that? – as a woman? As a man, you could go ahead and stir things up *fine*."

Attention to gender might invite a reading of *The bridge* as another critique of male-female relationships. Set on the Toronto Islands, it deals with the failure of a self-centred engineer to take responsibility for the death of his brother and for the love of his wife. Atonement comes through memory and selfless devotion. Pickthall's biographer, Lorne Albert Pierce*, inaptly considers this plot "Balzacian" realism and hails the novel as "a landmark in Canadian fiction" for its "representation of the supreme importance which nature assumes in this country." However, a manuscript reviewer for Hodder and Stoughton, its Canadian publisher in 1922, noted its violation of "the laws of probability." This assessment, Pickthall retorted, showed a lack of knowledge of the "psychological conditions" of the characters. Even the most sympathetic reviewer, poet Alfred Gordon of Montreal, noted problems in characterization. Less the desired "great Canadian novel" than a symbolist treatment of ethical choices along the lines of Joseph Conrad's *Lord Jim*, which Pickthall admired, the novel nonetheless marked a change in her fortunes: the serial rights were sold to *Everybody's Magazine* (New York) for $1,000 and to the *Sphere* (London), and negotiations were initiated on the film rights.

A shift toward greater realism is evident in Pickthall's notes to "can the fantastic" in "The beaten man." She struggled over this novel in Victoria in the winter of 1920–21, had Isabel Mackay read extracts, and rejected five drafts. Despite the change in her treatment, it promised to be about yet another lost man, the forces of "time and memory," and yearning hearts. Taking issue with the observation of British poet Rupert Brooke that there were "no legendary figures to tread our forests," Pickthall planned to show "the possibility of the birth of Canadian legend, the making of the white man's myth," in a plot centring on timber interests and race relations. In the spring of 1921 she travelled by boat up the west coast of Vancouver Island, settling in the remote native community of Clooose; in the summer she took a motor trip through the island's interior. Subsequently a major breakdown led to her confinement in a Victoria nursing home, where she was unable even to attend to business correspondence. After returning to Vancouver in February 1922, she was advised to have surgery for her disc problem, which she underwent successfully on 7 April; she died unexpectedly of an embolism on the 19th. Her death and her funeral at the Church of St Mary the Virgin in Toronto were reported in newspapers across Canada. Pickthall named her father as her executor, but she left her entire estate to her aunt Laura Mallard, in whose home she had written much of her work. She was buried beside her mother in St James' Cemetery.

Pickthall's death overshadowed the publication of *The bridge* and *The wood carver's wife*. Obituaries replaced reviews, with the consequence that her reputation has rested almost entirely upon her early poems, which would form the core of collections published in 1925, 1927, and 1957. In December 1922 the *Boston Evening Transcript* hailed her short stories as the discovery of the year, though generally they were overlooked. Of her more than 200 stories, the 24 published as *Angels' shoes . . .* (London, 1923) failed to sell. Her proposed title, "Devices and desires," might better have attracted readers to these anti-romantic tales. In the best of them, symbolic atmosphere sustains violent incidents involving men in extreme situations.

Most praised for her lyricism, Pickthall has been called "Canada's sweetest voice" and "a singer of spiritual songs," and has been compared in "technical perfection" as a lyricist to both Charles George Douglas Roberts* and William Bliss CARMAN. (Her only explicit pronouncements on poetics had been discussions of prosody in letters to Alfred Gordon, in which she argued against a rigid application of rules of scansion.) Duncan Campbell Scott*, a poet much liked by Pickthall, felt her work was best "overheard," with the "strain of melody" floating from a private world beyond. To a younger poet, Edwin John Pratt*, her poems were most successful in their avoidance of sentimentality in the exploration of pathos. In 1957, however, editor Frederick William Cogswell noted her "obsession with death" and regretted the limitations of the poetic conventions of her day, which tended to the Celtic twilight rather than the Metaphysicals. Her sure sense of rhythm and apt choice of words create sustained moods in her best poems, even though her incantatory Swinburnesque assonance and alliteration, persistent melancholy, double-barrelled epithets, and imagery of precious jewels are dated.

Though her early death may have silenced her, as Pierce believed, "before she had reached the zenith of her powers," it facilitated her canonization in Canadian literary history as it was being written in the 1920s. In dispute was her position: a significant contributor to literature in English? a great Canadian poet? or merely, in Pierce's reassessment of 1943, "first place among the women writers of Canada in her time"? In addition to his biography of 1925, Pierce, her faithful champion, organized an exhibition in 1943, edited a new edition of her poetry, and promoted her placement in school textbooks. "Resurgam," "Père Lalement," and "The bridegroom of Cana," which remained on the Ontario curriculum throughout the 1940s, appealed to the "romantic sensibilities" of the young of that era. The novelist Henry Kreisel, in noting his response to her poems at "an important moment" for him as an immigrant, remembered her as "the first Canadian literary voice I heard." Her reputation suffered a heavy blow in 1952 when Desmond Pacey qualified the period in which she wrote as "the age of brass" and dismissed her work as having "little direct experience of life."

These changing evaluations point to how Pickthall has been situated by both the history of Canadian literature and the historical options available to women writers in her time. Desire was her subject, not death. Recent feminist readings emphasize not so much the facility of her use of classical and biblical mythology but her ability to construct the poetic process in female-centred forms, as in her reworking of the Demeter–Persephone story in "The little fauns to Proserpine" and "Persephone returning to Hades." Feminist criticism has also recognized, in her handling of the theme of imaginative escape from the bondage of the law, an independent, feminine inflection of decadent *fin de siècle* poetics. These readings show Pickthall's work to be more complex than her legacy had hitherto suggested. Certainly her work has received the most sustained critical attention of all the writers of her generation.

BARBARA GODARD

Marjorie Pickthall's papers are in the Alice Rothwell coll. and the Lorne and Edith Pierce coll. at QUA. There is also a substantial Pickthall collection, including numerous photographs, in the Victoria Univ. Library, Toronto.

AO, RG 22-305, nos.45548, 98206; RG 80-2-0-410, no.39545; RG 80-5-0-829, no.22353; RG 80-8-0-180, no.22497; RG 80-8-0-387, no.1961. GRO, Reg. of births, Brentford, 14 Sept. 1883. LAC, RG 31, C1, 1901, Toronto, Ward 5, div.26: 3. St James' Cemetery and Crematorium (Toronto), Burial records, lot 146, sect.I. *Boston Evening Transcript*, 9 Dec. 1922. *Catholic Register* (Toronto), 27 April 1922. *Globe*, 28 April 1922. P. L. Badir, "'So entirely unexpected': the modernist dramaturgy of Marjorie Pickthall's *The wood carver's wife*," *Modern Drama* (Toronto), 43 (2000): 216–45. Sandra Campbell, "'A girl in a book': writing Marjorie Pickthall and Lorne Pierce," *Canadian Poetry* (London, Ont.), no.39 (fall 1996): 80–95. F. [W.] Cogswell, "Marjorie Pickthall," *Fiddlehead* ([Fredericton]), August 1957: 38–39. W. E. Collin, "Marjorie Pickthall, 1883–1922," *Univ. of Toronto Quarterly*, 1 (1931–32): 352–80. Alfred Gordon, "Marjorie Pickthall as artist," *Canadian Bookman* (Toronto), 4 (1922): 157–59. Henry Kreisel, "'Has anyone here heard of Marjorie Pickthall?' Discovering the Canadian literary landscape," *Canadian Literature* (Vancouver), no.100 (spring 1984): 173–80. J. D. Logan, "The genius of Marjorie Pickthall: an analysis of aesthetic paradox," *Canadian Magazine*, 59 (May–October 1922): 154–61; a revised version was published as *Marjorie Pickthall, her poetic genius and art: an appreciation and an analysis of aesthetic paradox* (Halifax, 1922). I. E. Mackay, "Marjorie Pickthall: a memory," in M. L. C. Pickthall, *The wood carver's wife* (Toronto, 1922), 5–7. A. McK. MacMechan, *Headwaters of Canadian literature* (Toronto, 1924; repr. 1974), 221–29. Desmond Pacey, *Creative writing in Canada: a short history of English-Canadian literature* ([rev. ed.], Toronto, 1961); "The poems of Marjorie Pickthall," in his *Essays in Canadian criticism, 1938–1968* (Toronto, 1969), 145–50. Lorne Pierce, *Marjorie Pickthall; a book of remembrance* (Toronto, 1925). E. J. Pratt, "Canadian writers of the past: Marjorie Pickthall," *Canadian Forum* (Toronto), 13 (1932–33): 334–35. D. M. A. Relke, "Demeter's daughter: Marjorie Pickthall and the quest for poetic identity," *Canadian Literature*, no.115 (winter 1987): 28–43. B. K. Sandwell, "The complete Pickthall," *Saturday Night*, 3 April 1937: 11. *Saturday Night*, 29 April 1922. D. C. Scott, "Poetry and progress," *Canadian Magazine*, 60 (November 1923–April 1924): 187–95. Janice Williamson, "Framed by history: Marjorie Pickthall's devices and desire," in *A mazing space: writing Canadian women writing*, ed. Shirley Neuman and Smaro Kamboureli (Edmonton, 1986), 167–78.

PINE, GEORGE. *See* SHINGWAUK, GEORGE

PLAMONDON, JACQUES-ÉDOUARD, notary and public speaker; b. 18 Oct. 1862 at Quebec, son of Jacques Plamondon, a sailor, and Émilie Chalifou; m. 25 May 1891 Marie-Isabelle Simard in Charlesbourg, Que., and they had eight children; d. 13 Oct. 1928 at Quebec and was buried 16 October in the Saint-Charles cemetery there.

Jacques-Édouard Plamondon attended the Petit Séminaire de Québec from 1876 to 1884. He won a number of year-end awards: second prize for excellence in sixth form (Rhetoric) in 1882, second prize in religious education in 1883, and second prize in his final year (Philosophy) in 1884. Following his classical studies, he enrolled in the faculty of law of the

Plamondon

Université Laval, where he obtained his bachelor's degree in 1887. He was accepted into the profession of notary on 6 October of that year and began practising law in Saint-Roch ward in Quebec City. Plamondon certainly was well regarded by his colleagues; he served as inspector of notarial offices from August 1903 until 1918 and he was the author of several theoretical articles in *La Revue de notariat* published in Lévis. Active in public life, he was one of the founders (along with Stanislas-Alfred Lortie* and others) of *La Libre Parole*, a Quebec weekly launched in 1905 which took a nationalist stance and valued the social concerns of the church, just as its French namesake did. Plamondon wrote several political articles for it.

At the turn of the century there was a strong resurgence of anti-Semitism in a number of western countries. The publication of pamphlets and especially such highly publicized trials as those of Alfred Dreyfus in France, Menaham Mendel Beilis in Russia, and Leo Frank in the United States bore witness to a rising hatred of the Jews. At the same time, in the province of Quebec a clerical-nationalist elite was promoting anti-Semitism, to which certain religious, social, and political groups (such as Action Sociale Catholique and the Association Catholique de la Jeunesse Canadienne-Française) were proving receptive. It was in this context that Plamondon, under the auspices of the latter organization's Cercle Charest, gave an anti-Semitic speech on 30 March 1910 at the École du Sacré-Cœur, which was run by the Brothers of the Christian Schools in Saint-Roch parish, Quebec. Quebec was a city with about 75 Jewish families, for the most part active in business. He had been invited by notaries Arthur Duval and Jules Vallerand, who are said even to have suggested the topic for his address. The main lines of his argument were drawn from anti-Semitic French writings, including two works of Édouard Drumont, *La France juive, essai d'histoire contemporaine* and *Le testament d'un antisémite*, which had been published in Paris in 1886 and 1891 respectively, and Maximilien de Lamarque's *Le juif-talmudiste, résumé succinct des croyances et des pratiques dangereuses de la juiverie, présenté à la considération de tous le chrétiens*, which had come out in the French capital in 1888. Plamondon began with the claim that "the Jew, by his beliefs and by his acts, is the enemy of our faith, our lives, our honour, and our property." Much of the address denounced passages from the Talmud, a sacred text of the Jewish tradition which in his view incited hatred of Christians and condoned crimes of the worst kind. Plamondon criticized the Jews for refusing to observe Sunday and urged his listeners, among other things, to stop patronizing their commercial endeavours. The lecture was published in *La Libre Parole* on 16 April; it was later distributed as a pamphlet printed by the newspaper and was entitled

Le juif: conférence donnée au Cercle Charest de l'A.C.J.C., le 30 mars 1910.

In the days after the lecture, there were sharp exchanges in the Quebec press between Catholic newspapers (*La Libre Parole* and *L'Action sociale*) and liberal ones (*La Vigie* and *Le Soleil*). Early in June several young people insulted some Jews by repeating Plamondon's accusations. They also attacked and molested other Jews and broke windows at the synagogue and at the home of Benjamin Ortenberg, a Jewish shopkeeper living at Quebec. Arrests were made and charges laid. Of the seven accused, aged 12 and 13, five were fined.

Louis Lazarovitz, president of the congregation Bais Israel (which included Quebec residents of the Jewish religion), and Ortenberg launched an action for libel against Plamondon as the speaker, and René Leduc as the printer of the pamphlet. Ortenberg retained the services of Lawrence Arthur Dumoulin Cannon*, a future judge of the Supreme Court of Canada. Lazarovitz entrusted his case to three Montreal lawyers, Samuel William Jacobs*, Louis Fitch, and Gui-Casimir Papineau-Couture. The defendants turned to lawyers close to the nationalist movement. Eusèbe Belleau, a professor of law at the Université Laval, who had been chosen *bâtonnier* of the bar in the judicial district of Quebec that year, undertook Plamondon's defence; Joseph-Édouard Bédard, who had adhered to the nationalist program of Henri Bourassa* after leaving the federal Liberal party, represented Leduc. Jules-Alfred Lane acted as consulting counsel; an erstwhile Liberal member of the Legislative Assembly for Québec-Est, he had done battle against Mayor Simon-Napoléon Parent*'s team and reportedly became a municipal councillor for Saint-Roch ward.

The trial was held from 19 to 22 May 1913 and aroused tremendous interest. In his statement, Ortenberg alleged that Plamondon had acted with the intent of causing harm to him and to his co-religionists and compatriots. He claimed damages of $500 for the attack on his honour and the loss of part of his clientele. The lawsuit obviously had a second objective: to prevent other speeches of this nature from being given in a city where Jews constituted only a minority. Since almost all of them were in business, some had reason to fear the effects of the boycott suggested by Plamondon. Called as a witness, Rabbi Herman Abramowitz* was even more explicit about the dangers posed by the spread of anti-Semitic publications; he established a connection between this affair and the trouble Jews experienced in Europe.

Mr Justice Albert Malouin of the Quebec Superior Court for the district of Quebec dismissed the case of Ortenberg and Lazarovitz. Since Plamondon's remarks had been aimed at the Jewish community in general, he had not infringed the rights of a particular individual. This decision was consistent with the case law of the time, when individuals were free in principle to express their views, even if these views were vindictive or, indeed, hateful towards ethnic or religious groups. Only an individual who could prove that he or she had personally been the target of slander or libel and had suffered a loss could sue for damages in his or her own name.

Ortenberg immediately appealed the judgement and the case was heard by a court consisting of the chief justice of Quebec, Horace Archambeault*, and four judges, Norman William Trenholme, Alexander George Cross, Henry George Carroll*, and Louis-Rodolphe Roy. Besides declaring that it was adhering to case law regarding libel, the court acknowledged that members of a community were entitled to sue for libel or slander when that collectivity was small, since individuals in such a group might suffer. On 28 Dec. 1914 the court sentenced the defendants, Plamondon and Leduc, to pay $50 and $25 respectively to Ortenberg.

In February 1919 Jacques-Édouard Plamondon was in the headlines again in connection with the embezzlement of funds from an estate. The judge, convinced that Plamondon had been suffering from mental illness at the time of the offence, ordered him to be confined to the hospital of Saint-Michel-Archange, where he stayed for at least five years. According to a medical report, Plamondon had suffered all his life from a kind of religious fervour. The following September, the Quebec Provincial Board of Notaries revoked his licence. Besides revealing the presence of anti-Semitism in Quebec City, the Plamondon episode also showed the determination of the Jewish community there to fend off attacks by recourse to the judicial system.

SYLVIO NORMAND

The lecture by Jacques-Édouard Plamondon was published under the title *Le juif: conférence donnée au Cercle Charest de l'A.C.J.C., le 30 mars 1910* (Québec, [1910?]).

AC, Québec, État civil, Catholiques, Cimetière Saint-Charles (Québec), 16 oct. 1928. ANQ-Q, CE301-S7, 25 mai 1891; S22, 19 oct. 1862; CN301-S369, 1887–1919; E17, dossier 819 (1919) (versement 1960-01-036/370); dossier 1651 (1924) (versement 1960-01-036/462); dossier 3050 (1921) (versement 1960-01-036/407); TP9, S1, SS5, SSS1, dossier 940 (1914) (Ortenberg *c.* Plamondon) (versement 1960-01-352/157); dossier 941 (1914) (Ortenberg *c.* Leduc) (versement 1960-01-352/157); TP11, S1, SS2, SSS1, dossier 778 (1910) (*Ortenberg c. Plamondon*) (versement 1960-01-053/563); TP12, S1, SS1, SSS1, dossiers 200591–606 (1918–19) (*Le Roi c. Plamondon*) (versement 1960-01-357/186). *Directory*, Quebec and Lévis, 1910. *Dominion Law Reports* (Toronto), 14 (1913). J. Hamelin *et al.*, *La presse québécoise*, 4: 210–11. *Histoire du catholicisme québécois*, sous la dir. de Nive Voisine (2 tomes en 4v. parus, Montréal, 1984–), tome 3, vol.1 (Jean Hamelin et Nicole Gagnon, *Le XXᵉ siècle: 1898–1940*, 1984). Jacques Langlais et David Rome, *Juifs et Québécois français: 200 ans d'histoire commune* (Montréal, 1986). "The Plamondon case and S. W. Jacobs," comp. David Rome, *Canadian Jewish Arch.* (Montreal), no.26 (1982). *Quebec Official Reports: King's Bench* (Quebec), 1915. J.-E. Roy, *Histoire du notariat au Canada depuis la fondation de la colonie jusqu'à nos jours* (4v., Lévis, 1899–1902), 4. Univ. Laval, *Annuaire*, 1884–85.

POLSON, MARGARET SMITH (Murray), social reformer, magazine editor, and founder of the Imperial Order Daughters of the Empire; b. 1 June 1844 in Paisley, Scotland, daughter of Margaret Maclean and William Polson, a starch manufacturer; m. there 20 July 1865 John Clark Murray*, and they had one son and four daughters; d. 27 Jan. 1927 in Montreal.

As a child, Margaret Polson exhibited considerable talent on the piano, but she was not given the opportunity to go abroad for advanced musical studies. She stayed at home and efficiently carried out the duties expected of the eldest daughter in a family of seven children. After her marriage at age 21, she moved to Upper Canada with her husband, who was then professor of philosophy at Queen's College in Kingston. In 1872 he took up a similar appointment at McGill College in Montreal.

Margaret Polson Murray (she frequently signed using both surnames) was soon an active member of several charitable organizations in Montreal. In 1874 she and six other socially conscious women, including Mary McDougall [Cowans*], met to try to help the needy. The outcome of their deliberations was the foundation of the Montreal Young Women's Christian Association the following year. The association's initial objective was to meet young women from the country or abroad at the station or the dock and to "attend to their temporal, moral and spiritual welfare." The need was great and the scope of the work expanded continuously. Murray took on the arduous task of honorary secretary.

Possessing a lively mind and ever-ready for self-improvement, Murray attended lectures of the Montreal Ladies' Educational Association [*see* Anne Molson*]. She arranged a series of instructive entertainments on Saturday afternoons, encouraging others to better themselves. Continuing her musical interests, she helped to establish a choir at St Paul's Presbyterian Church. Her concern for social issues and her writing skills were shown in her contributions to the *Week* (Toronto), in her article "Women's clubs in America," which appeared in the *Nineteenth Century* (London), and in "The housekeeper under protection," published in the *Contemporary Review* (London). Her interest in children was evident when she founded and edited the *Young Canadian* (Montreal). Started in January 1891 and subtitled "an illustrated weekly magazine of patriotism for young Canadians," the journal attracted well-known Canadian authors as contributors on a wide variety of subjects, but it did not last long. Always a staunch supporter of patriotic causes, Murray would lead a brigade of 600 Montreal women to a rally in Dominion Square in August 1914 when the British empire went to war with Germany.

Although Murray was one of seven women who were equally involved in starting the YWCA in Montreal, she was the individual most responsible for the founding of another important and enduring organization. She was in England in 1899 when the first casualties of the South African War became known. She reported that "the whole nation was staggered" but "ablaze with the spirit of giving . . . [in] a perfect stampede of war enthusiasm." She believed that the women of Canada should seize the opportunity "to place themselves in the front rank of colonial patriotism" by forming an organization ready for prompt and united action. Her ardent support for the empire may have been sentimental, but her recognition that there was urgent need for comforts for soldiers, support for their dependants, and care for their graves was eminently pragmatic.

By the time Murray returned to Canada, she had a clear vision of the organization she wanted to establish. She immediately went to work. She had "one or two tentative meetings in her home," and then on 13 Jan. 1900 she sent telegrams to the mayors of major Canadian cities asking, "Will the women of [your city] unite with the women of Montreal in federating as Daughters of the Empire, and inviting the women of Australia and New Zealand to join with them in sending to the Queen an expression of our devotion to the Empire, and an Emergency War Fund, to be expended as Her Majesty shall deem fit." Two days later she outlined her ideas in a press release and gave interviews in Montreal newspapers.

On 1 Feb. 1900 Murray received word that the first local chapter had been formed on 15 January in Fredericton. Twenty-five women attended the meeting she organized in Montreal on 13 February for the founding of a national organization, the Federation of the Daughters of the Empire (its junior branch was named the Children of the Empire), with the motto *Pro regina et patria*. Once again, she chose to become honorary secretary, a strategic position in which she could keep the movement going.

Throughout the summer of 1900, with little help except, in all probability, that of her two unmarried daughters, she performed what she termed "absolutely prodigious work." She drafted a detailed constitution, identified the aims and structure of the organization, and devised special titles for officers, such as queen regent, regent, and standard-bearer. In addition, she set forth advice on how to form chapters, on procedures at meetings, and on projects to undertake. She envisaged a hierarchy of local, provincial, and national chapters in the various colonies with the imperial chapter in the mother country and Queen Victoria as patron. She established the Canadian headquarters in Montreal, but thought that Toronto, with its greater British population, would be more appropriate. By letter and telegram she contacted the wives of notables throughout the empire, secured the support of Lady Minto, wife of Canada's governor-general, Lord Minto [Elliot*], and had the satisfaction of knowing that many chapters were being formed, including some in the United States.

Murray maintained an exhausting tempo during the summer and autumn of 1900. She sent cables, postcards, and as many as 500 letters a day "to well-selected people"; sought patrons of high status; filled orders for badges, cheque books, and copies of the organization's constitution; encouraged the teaching of history in schools and the establishment of prizes and patriotic celebrations for Empire Day; contacted the Department of Indian Affairs so that native women might join; prepared a condensed statement of aims for wide circulation; raised funds; made speeches; organized a huge welcome dinner for returning soldiers; and was determined to "leave no stone unturned."

The care of war graves was one of her vital concerns. To ensure that the graves (Canadian and Boer, especially those in isolated places) were identified and properly tended, she obtained the cooperation of the British War Office and the Cape Town branch of the Guild of Loyal Women of South Africa. The guild promised to identify Canadian graves, and "keep the sacred spots neat, . . . [and] place flowers at Xmas and Easter." In Canada she set up a fund for this purpose with the full knowledge of Lady Minto, Prime Minister Sir Wilfrid Laurier*, and the minister of militia and defence, Frederick William Borden*. War graves, however, became an interest of other organizations and rivalries soon developed among patriots.

In England in 1901 the Victoria League was formed with goals similar to Murray's – to bring the people of the empire together and care for the war graves. The league viewed the work she did for her cause in Britain as an intrusion on its territory. In the summer of 1901 members of the Daughters in Toronto entreated their founder to return to London to strengthen their position. Edith Sarah Louisa Nordheimer [Boulton*], president of the Ontario provincial chapter, sent Murray a telegram urging her to go and "make no concessions." Although reluctant (she had resigned as honorary secretary in February 1901 possibly because of fatigue, but had withdrawn her resignation and was re-elected at the next annual meeting), Murray sailed again to Britain. In typical fashion, she worked vigorously, preparing the way for national chapters in England, Scotland, and Ireland and an imperial chapter in London with herself as secretary. She visited the offices of the Victoria League, where she "was received most delightfully" and affiliation was discussed. On her return to Montreal, however, she was shocked to receive what she later described as an "infamous" letter from the league, accusing her of "breach of faith" and demanding the names and addresses of her contacts in London. The league said it could not "countenance the formation of Branches of the Daughters of the Empire in the United Kingdom, as that would create endless confusion and destroy the whole idea of the Victoria League."

Murray felt what she described as "the keen bitterness of misrepresentation" when the Ontario chapter failed to support her against the league. She also felt betrayed by Lady Minto, who not only publicized the league's accusation but would try to take over her war graves work. Lady Minto had been enthusiastic about Murray's efforts and had agreed to be honorary president of the Daughters and honorary treasurer of the war graves fund. In April 1901 Murray had learned in "speechless amazement" that Lady Minto was recommending that the graves work be postponed until the war was over. The following year, while the war still continued, she was outraged to find that Lady Minto had set up her own Canadian South African Memorial Association and was requesting that donations be sent only to it. In an unbearable "conflict between loyalty and insurrection," Murray dared not speak publicly about her betrayal by the king's representative. She did protest strongly in private, but Lady Minto stood firm and a break in their relationship was inevitable.

Murray was not well after her second trip to England and in October 1901 she had asked the women of the Ontario provincial chapter to assume leadership. They accepted and the Toronto office became the national headquarters. Under the new regime, the organization's name was changed to the Imperial Order Daughters of the Empire, its motto became "One flag, one throne, one empire," its badge was modified, and it was formally incorporated in Ontario. Edith Nordheimer was elected the first national president. Significantly, the ideals, purposes, constitution, and structure Murray had devised remained essentially unchanged. Even the committee on war graves continued its partnership with the Guild of Loyal Women of South Africa.

For a time, relationships between Murray and some of the women in Toronto were strained and there was confusion about her status in the Daughters. Some believed she had severed all ties, but that was not the case. She formed a new Founder's chapter in Montreal, kept up an active correspondence with the national office, and frequently gave advice. Yet open hostility became apparent in 1906 when the standard-bearer of the Hamilton chapter, while acknowledging that Murray was a "wonderfully gifted woman" who had done "stupendous work," published a bitterly critical account of her early activities, accusing her of handing over the organization "in great disorder." Murray protested vigorously and repeatedly to mem-

bers of the national executive but, when they failed once again to support her, she broke her silence. In 1907 she privately published her own version of events in a passionate statement of 94 pages. She detailed the work she had done and described the healthy state of the Daughters (26 chapters established, many more in process) when she passed the head office over to Toronto. Since by that time the Mintos were no longer in Canada, she felt free to expose her feelings about Lady Minto and the Victoria League. Later, to the embarrassment of the national executive, she vindicated herself and even reproached Lady Minto in the pages of *Echoes* (Toronto), the IODE's own journal.

Murray's situation was not properly clarified until after the resignation of Mrs Nordheimer in 1911. In June 1912 she was officially invited to resume her "former position in the Order," and she was later accorded honorary life membership. Her contribution was fully recognized in the elaborately illuminated address presented to her in April 1915 and by the jewelled badge given to her four years later by the primary chapters in Quebec.

On her death in January 1927 tributes arrived from around the world. At that time there were about 650 chapters of the IODE in Canada and some in other parts of the empire, representing a total membership of over 30,000. The IODE was one of the largest, most active, and best-organized women's associations in Canada.

Margaret Polson Murray left a remarkable legacy. She had inspired innumerable women and men with a spirit of patriotism and charity, developed the idea of care for war graves, helped authenticate the participation of women in public life, and encouraged patriotic instruction for children. She bequeathed a vigorous, flexible organization. At the beginning of the 21st century, its mission is more squarely focused on Canada, with particular concern for immigrant and native women. Yet it retains strong links with Britain, its insignia still bears the crown and Union Jack, and it guards the tradition that the wife of the governor general is its patron.

Margaret Polson Murray was buried with her husband in Mount Royal Cemetery, Montreal.

MARGARET GILLETT

Thirty-six issues of the *Young Canadian*, the children's weekly edited by Margaret Smith Polson Murray between 28 Jan. and 30 Sept. 1891, are listed in the CIHM, *Reg.* Murray's publications also include *The Federation of the Daughters of the British Empire and the Children of the Empire (junior branch)* (Montreal, 1900) and *The Daughters of the Empire and the Children of the Empire (junior branch) and the South African Memorial Association: an unwritten chapter of two important imperial movements founded in Montreal, Feb. 1900* (Montreal, 1907).

General Register Office for Scotland (Edinburgh), Abbey (Paisley), reg. of marriages, 20 July 1865. LAC, MG 28, I 8; I 17. MUA, MG 3083. *Gazette* (Montreal), 28 Jan., 3 Feb. 1927. *Montreal Daily Star,* 16 Jan. 1900, 3 Feb. 1927. *Canadian men and women of the time* (Morgan; 1898 and 1912). *Encyclopedia Canadiana,* ed. K. H. Pearson *et al.*([rev. ed.], 10v., Toronto, 1975). Lisa Gaudet, "Nation's mothers, empire's daughters: the Imperial Order Daughters of the Empire, 1920–1930" (MA thesis, Carleton Univ., Ottawa, 1993). D. C. Hamilton, "Origins of the IODE: a Canadian women's movement for God, king and country, 1900–1925" (MA thesis, Univ. of N.B., Fredericton, 1992). [Albert Murray?], "An intimate sketch," *Echoes* (Toronto), March 1927: 5. C. G. Pickles, "Representing twentieth century Canadian colonial identity: the Imperial Order Daughters of the Empire" (PHD thesis, McGill Univ., Montreal, 1996). *Standard dict. of Canadian biog.* (Roberts and Tunnell).

PONTON, JOSEPH-NOÉ (baptized **Joseph-Noé-Hormisdas**), agronomist, professor, and journalist; b. 8 Dec. 1885 in Sainte-Marie-de-Monnoir (Marieville), Que., one of the 14 children of Noé Ponton and Émélie Dandurand; d. unmarried 11 Dec. 1929 in Montreal and was buried on 14 December in Bromptonville, Que.

Joseph-Noé Ponton was only three years old when his father sold his land and bought a woodlot in Brompton Falls (Bromptonville). He experienced the hard life of pioneers and, in order to help with the farm work, in June 1902 he had to give up the commercial course he had begun the previous September at the Séminaire Saint-Charles-Borromée in Sherbrooke. At the age of 20, however, he decided to undertake classical studies at the seminary as a day student, while continuing to work on the farm. On the advice of the head of the Institut Agricole d'Oka, in 1912 he enrolled at the Ontario Agricultural College in Guelph, where he obtained a bachelor's degree in agricultural science three years later. He gained his first professional experience of agronomy while working during the summer for the Ontario Department of Agriculture in the Sudbury region. The French-speaking community there would have liked him to become their permanent agronomist, but he chose to return to his native province.

Ponton held a number of jobs from 1915 to 1920. He was professor at the Institut Agricole d'Oka until 1919, property manager at the farm of Dr Louis de Lotbinière Harwood* in Vaudreuil for a season, and promoter of animal husbandry for the federal Department of Agriculture. According to a former student, he had no great talent for teaching. A man of imposing stature and boundless energy, he was more disposed to be a champion of people's rights. Ponton finally opted for agricultural journalism. In 1920 Auguste Trudel, the manager of the Coopérative Centrale des Agriculteurs de Québec, invited him to take charge of its official publication, *Le Bulletin des agriculteurs.* For nearly two years Ponton carried out his various tasks for the paper, staying in the background while Trudel signed the editorials.

During the summer of 1921 Ponton was asked by the provincial minister of agriculture, Joseph-Édouard CARON, to serve on a committee to study the organization of agricultural education in the Canadian provinces. He refused to sign the report commissioned by the minister, however, on the grounds that it ought rather to be submitted to the Canadian Society of Technical Agriculturists. Furthermore, the deepening agricultural crisis that had followed World War I prompted him to conduct a large-scale, province-wide inquiry into the state of the farming community. More than 40 per cent of those who replied to his questionnaire asserted that they could not afford to buy fodder and commercial feed to keep their herds through the winter. This situation convinced Ponton that it was urgent to set up a system of farm credit, but Caron saw no need for it.

When a federal election was called in the fall of 1921, Ponton had an opportunity to publicize his views. At a banquet in honour of Thomas Alexander Crerar*, the leader of the Progressive party, which had been founded in 1919 by dissident Liberals and farmers' associations in Ontario and western Canada, he was approached by James John Harpell, a printer from Sainte-Anne-de-Bellevue, who suggested that he launch a newspaper for the party in the province of Quebec. Ponton, who for some time had been contemplating starting an independent paper to champion farmers' interests, consulted his friends and his employer. Trudel proposed instead that he purchase the debt-ridden *Bulletin.* The transaction was concluded on 19 October with the approval of the directors of the Coopérative Centrale des Agriculteurs. Ponton's paper became the organ of the Parti Fermier-Progressiste, which was founded on 31 October with the assistance of the 5,000-member Fermiers Unis de Québec, an organization with some 100 local branches, and the Union des Cultivateurs, a professional association formed a few years earlier.

The party nominated 21 candidates in the election. With a platform that included some planks that were very popular in Quebec, such as local processing of natural resources, Canadian independence from Great Britain, and free trade with the United States, the Parti Fermier-Progressiste received 11 per cent of the popular vote, but none of its candidates were successful, whereas 64 Progressives were elected elsewhere in Canada. Liberal propaganda connecting it with the Conservative party, which had been responsible for conscription, contributed to this defeat, but it was handicapped mainly by its rural roots in a province becoming increasingly urbanized, and by the fact that it catered more to the demands of farmers producing for sale rather than subsistence, who were then still a minority in the province's farming community.

The party's electoral failure in Quebec forced Ponton and his colleagues to change their tactics. Now that he had an independent mouthpiece, Ponton began to criticize the agricultural cooperative movement, which agriculture minister Caron had brought under his authority following the merger of the three big federations of cooperatives in 1922. His remarks were often stinging. The minister struck back in *Le Soleil* and *Le Bulletin de la ferme* (Québec), leaping to the defence of the new Quebec Federated Co-operative. Since the farmers were losing control of the cooperatives, Ponton turned his attention to promoting the organization of the farming community on a professional basis, like other social classes. In 1924 he put forward the idea of an agricultural convention to study the possibility of setting up a new professional association for the province's farmers. The convention, held at Quebec on 1 and 2 Oct. 1924, was attended by 2,400 people. A wide-ranging program of reforms was adopted, including agricultural education, the establishment of a system of farm credit, and the organization of local study groups. Laurent Barré*, a farmer backed by Ponton, became the first president of the Union Catholique des Cultivateurs.

Caron resigned himself to accepting the new association, but he tried to convince its members that Ponton's paper was doing a disservice to their cause by constantly criticizing government measures. Some of the stands taken by *Le Bulletin* also irritated prominent members of the clergy. To dispel any misunderstanding, at its 1926 convention Ponton asked the UCC to look to another newspaper for support, and Barré, who was also hostile to the Liberal government, resigned as president. The two men did not abandon their crusade, however.

Caron had been opposed to the creation of the UCC because he suspected its two leaders of wanting to use it as a springboard to enter politics. Rumour had had it that Ponton would be a candidate in the 1921 election, but he had confined himself to the role of campaign organizer for the Parti Fermier-Progressiste. It was not until the end of the UCC convention in 1926 that he showed his political ambitions for the first time. He justified his move by saying that it had become necessary to supplement union activity by parliamentary struggle in order to back the UCC's demands. Ponton and Barré then allied themselves with the Conservatives to fight the government of Louis-Alexandre Taschereau* in the provincial election of 16 May 1927. Ponton ran in Richmond. Despite an effective campaign, they were defeated at the polls. In their view the loss was due to a lack of organization, and they convened a meeting during the next few weeks at which they laid the basis for a new party, the short-lived Action Politique Populaire.

Ponton's entry into active political life alienated a number of Liberal supporters in the farming community, including some leaders of the UCC. His opposition to the proposal for creating a commercial section within it gave rise to other criticisms in the UCC's new organ, *La Terre de chez nous*. For the first time in his career, Ponton saw his leadership challenged. It was at this very point, in December 1929, that he died, at the age of 44, following an attack of nephritis. Agronomist Armand Létourneau, who had met him a month earlier, would write in *La Terre de chez nous* that he had seemed old, tired, and, above all, disillusioned.

Little is known about the influences that shaped Ponton's career. As a very young child he appears to have been profoundly influenced by the study of heroic deeds in Canadian history and also, of course, by his religious education. According to those who were close to him, he believed he had a mission and devoted all his energy to the defence of his ideals. In *Le Bulletin des agriculteurs* he himself described his struggle as a campaign for agricultural renewal. His demands evolved over the years: an increase in the resources allocated to agricultural schools, reform of the agricultural cooperatives, farm credit, diversification of the markets for dairy products by the export of cream to the United States, a reduction in imports of foodstuffs, the improvement of stockyards, and restoration of auctions for dairy products and other produce. He had the pleasure of seeing a number of his ideas incorporated into the program of reforms put forward by Joseph-Léonide PERRON, who succeeded Caron as minister of agriculture. Perron even offered him the position of deputy minister shortly before he died.

Though Joseph-Noé Ponton denied it, the polemic he carried on with Caron was to a large extent a personality conflict. The vehemence with which he criticized the minister's agricultural policy could not fail to draw a belligerent response. Furthermore, the reformer was not always right. The sale of cream to the United States, for instance, did not bring the anticipated results, since the Americans adopted measures to restrict the entry of agricultural produce from Canada, leaving the dairy industry in disarray in part of the Eastern Townships. Despite their differences, Ponton and Caron, who both came from farming backgrounds, were looking for ways to stem the rural exodus and to restore some degree of dignity to those who played an essential role in society without receiving a fair reward for their labour. In the struggle between the two men, Ponton took the high ground by going selflessly to the defence of the weakest who were confronted with a government that he accused of being insensitive to their demands and incompetent in agricultural matters. His former colleagues, including Firmin Létourneau, accorded him the stature of a true hero, the equal of those who had filled his imagination as a child. This is on the whole a fairly accurate portrait, but one that requires some refining. Ponton's great accomplishment was the founding of the Union Catholique des Cultivateurs. He was awarded the gold medal of the Order of Agricultural Merit posthumously in 1961.

JACQUES SAINT-PIERRE

With Firmin Létourneau, Joseph-Noé Ponton published *Album des animaux domestiques: dédié à nos jeunes compatriotes des campagnes* ([Montréal, 1924?]).

ANQ-M, CE602-S21, 9 déc. 1885. *Le Bulletin des agriculteurs* (Montréal), 1920–29. *Le Devoir*, 12 déc. 1929. *La Terre de chez nous* (Montréal), 18 déc. 1929, 9 sept. 1931, 26 févr. 1947. J.-P. Kesteman *et al.*, *Histoire du syndicalisme agricole au Québec: UCC–UPA, 1924–1984* (Montréal, 1984). Nicole Lacelle, *"Le Bulletin des agriculteurs," 1921–1929: les visages d'un journal* (Montréal, [1981?]). Firmin Létourneau, *Histoire de l'agriculture (Canada français)* ([Montréal], 1950). J.-C. Magnan, *Le monde agricole* (Montréal, 1972), 64. Robert Migner, *Quand gronde la révolt verte* (Montréal, 1980). Rumilly, *Hist. de la prov. de Québec*, vols.24–31. Jacques Saint-Pierre, *Histoire de la Coopérative fédérée: l'industrie de la terre* (Québec, 1997).

POPE, Sir JOSEPH, clerk, private secretary, civil servant, and author; b. 16 Aug. 1854 in Charlottetown, elder son of William Henry Pope* and Helen Des-Brisay; m. 15 Oct. 1884 Marie-Louise-Joséphine-Henriette (Minette) Taschereau in Rivière-du-Loup, Que., and they had five sons and a daughter; d. 2 Dec. 1926 in Ottawa.

The family of W. H. Pope had a pleasant house and grounds a mile out of Charlottetown. Most families of his standing sent their children to England to be educated; Joseph went to Prince of Wales College, a local grammar school. When he was ten his father took him on board the *Queen Victoria* to meet the Canadian delegates to the Charlottetown conference. W. H. Pope lived in the style of the upper-middle-class gentry but without the income for it; when he died suddenly in 1879 he left his family largely unprovided for.

A slight, delicate youth not much given to sports, Joseph had been put to work in 1870 as a clerk for Prince Edward Island's treasurer, his grandfather Joseph Pope*. With no experience and atrocious handwriting, he took steps to improve himself. He was good at mathematics and would always have a penchant for astronomy. Through his father he managed in 1872 to get a clerkship in the Merchants' Bank of Canada in Montreal; by 1878 he was working in the Bank of Nova Scotia in Halifax.

After the Conservative victory in the federal election of 1878, his uncle James Colledge Pope* became Sir John A. Macdonald*'s minister of marine and fisheries and the young nephew became the minister's private secretary. Joseph then set to work to learn Pitman shorthand. He needed it. After his father's death, half of his income went to support his mother and sisters. His uncle retired in July 1882 owing to ill health,

and Joseph's friend Frederick White, Macdonald's private secretary and controller of the North-West Mounted Police, found he had too much to do. He recommended Pope to the prime minister. By September Pope had largely taken over White's secretarial responsibilities. All Macdonald's letters had to be done by hand: although typewriters were coming in, Macdonald would not sign a typed letter unless of the most formal character, and then only when he could not avoid it.

Pope's real education in the great world thus began. He had lived in a boarding house on $20 a month, unable to afford the role of a man about town. Now, however, as the prime minister's private secretary, he became something of a personage. Macdonald treated him with great kindness. As early as July 1883 he wrote Pope from his summer home, Les Rochers, in Rivière-du-Loup, "My wife and her brother are off on a spree to Halifax. I wish you were here to keep me company." Each summer from then on Pope was part of Macdonald's entourage. It was in Rivière-du-Loup that Pope met Minette Taschereau, eldest daughter of justice Henri-Thomas Taschereau*, whose wife was a Pacaud from Arthabaskaville (Arthabaska), Que., Wilfrid Laurier*'s stamping ground. Pope's long and close acquaintance with the Lauriers followed. After Laurier became leader of the Liberal opposition in Ottawa in 1887, Lady Macdonald [Susan Agnes Bernard*] was not sure that this relationship should be encouraged, but then she was always more partisan than her husband. Macdonald himself was firm in Pope's defence, having established in his own mind Pope's integrity and discretion. He was glad that Pope had such a friend as the Liberal leader. "Laurier will look after you should you need a friend when I am gone," he told his secretary. On 29 Nov. 1889 Macdonald appointed Pope assistant clerk of the Privy Council, which brought a substantial increase in salary; he would retain this office until 1896. For his part he found the work rich and rewarding, and he loved Macdonald. When Macdonald died in 1891 Pope mourned as for a father.

With Hugh John MACDONALD, Edgar Dewdney*, and Fred White, Pope was a trustee of Macdonald's estate. As the youngest and most vigorous of the group, and the closest to Lady (now Baroness) Macdonald, he became her indispensable guide and financial adviser. She supported his writing her husband's biography and made available to him all correspondence except what was personal to her. She gave him carte blanche as to what he should pen, though in November 1892 she felt constrained to warn him to be careful in writing of Macdonald's political colleague Sir Charles Tupper*. Pope probably did not need the advice: with him the diplomat usually triumphed over the historian. Care, caution, and discretion had always been Pope's strength, and his weakness.

It was the same in his capacity as the effective manager among the trustees of Agnes's financial affairs. Though not badly off, she travelled constantly and worried about money. This uneasiness was the reason for her eventual falling out with Pope. By 1900 she thought her money might be administered more aggressively by a trust company. Pope maintained that Macdonald's arrangements for his widow should be left to stand, so he dragged his feet. The transfer of Agnes's funds to the Royal Trust Company was eventually concluded in 1914 but by that time the breach between Agnes and Pope had become too wide to bridge.

As assistant clerk of the Privy Council, Pope had begun to work with Canadian state papers, in particular those relating to the Bering Sea arbitration between Canada and the United States that took place in Paris in 1893. Technically he was there as secretary to fisheries minister Charles Hibbert TUPPER, the appointed British agent. Also there, as an arbitrator, was Prime Minister Sir John Sparrow David Thompson*. After Thompson's death in 1894 Governor General Lord Aberdeen [Hamilton-Gordon*] called on Mackenzie Bowell* to form a government. Pope had a low estimate of Bowell's talents and thought Aberdeen's judgement deplorable. In late 1895 Tupper Sr was summoned from England to help save the Conservative party from Bowell's follies; he became secretary of state in January 1896 and effectively took charge of the government the following month. He insisted that Pope be appointed under-secretary of state and deputy registrar general in place of Ludger-Aimé Catellier. Traditionally the office had been filled by a French Canadian; Tupper carried his point by taking steps to have a French Canadian succeed an "Englishman" as deputy head of another department. Pope was appointed on 25 April.

After Laurier's electoral victory in June, his position was vulnerable to party pressure. He came to the swearing in of the new government – he was in charge of the Great Seal – and Laurier introduced him to his minister of justice, Sir Oliver Mowat*, as the man who had written Macdonald's biography. At this Mowat said with a smile, "I wish he would write mine." Still, Pope's position was being shot at. The Toronto *Globe* urged a wholesale cleaning out of what it called "Tory Deputy Ministers." On the evening of the day this exhortation appeared, the Popes were dining at the Lauriers'. On entering the drawing room, Minette curtsied before Laurier, exclaiming, "*Ave Caesar Imperator, morituri te salutant.*" Laurier replied, "Why *morituri* [those who are about to die]?" "Ah," he continued after a moment's reflection, "the *Globe*'s rubbish." That is what it remained.

Pope used his position as under-secretary of state to effect some needed changes in the way Canada handled state business. In January 1897 he represented to Laurier the insecure, indeed parlous, way in which Canada's public records were kept. As if to underline his argument, in February a fire in the west block threatened the archival holdings there. The government then appointed a commission of three deputy ministers, including Pope, to examine the state of the public records. Pope's diplomatic skills were well tested – his two colleagues (John Mortimer Courtney* and John Lorn McDougall*) were not speaking to each other – but under his guidance a report emerged in November that all three could agree on. It recommended joining the records branch of the Department of the Secretary of State and the archives branch of the Department of Agriculture, something long sought by Douglas Brymner*, the ageing dominion archivist. Pope's triumph was complete when in 1904 Arthur George Doughty* was appointed to the combined position of dominion archivist and keeper of the records.

In 1899 Laurier had asked Pope to prepare a history of the Alaska boundary question. Named an assistant secretary to the international tribunal formed in 1903, he became the Canadian government's most important expert within the civil service during this long and arduous arbitration. In the course of his work he continually came up against the difficulty of finding current state papers. He found it extremely embarrassing to have to ask the British for copies of papers that were supposed to be in Ottawa, though no one knew where. Pope told Laurier about this problem in 1904, but nothing was done. The question had become more acute by 1908, in which year there were something like 1,600 dispatches from Britain needing action. Laurier would read excerpts in cabinet in order to decide which ministry they would go to. No record of their destinations existed except in Laurier's head.

After the election of 1908, therefore, Pope, Governor General Lord Grey*, and James Bryce, the British ambassador to Washington, combined their efforts to get legislation ready for parliament in 1909 to establish the Department of External Affairs. On 2 June 1909 Pope left the state department to become under-secretary of state for external affairs. His role in this office was, like so much else he did, effective and unobtrusive. He did not want a large staff, but did insist, as a condition of his appointment, that William Henry Walker be brought in from the governor general's office to become his assistant. Walker's grasp of external business, correspondence, and treaties was exceptional, and needed. The primacy claimed by their touchy new minister, Charles Murphy*, which Pope privately resented, was largely nullified by Pope's continued direct access to Laurier. This access could not prevent the new department from being shifted in 1909 out of the east block to the Trafalgar Building five blocks distant, at the corner of Queen and Bank. The move annoyed Lord Grey and dismayed Pope, who found the barber shop and other commercial premises on the ground floor of Canada's Department of External Affairs a distinct lèse-majesté.

In 1911 Pope established a close working relationship with the new Conservative prime minister, Robert Laird Borden*, who, like Laurier, retained real control of external relations. As deputy head Pope handled, in addition to departmental administration, American affairs, trade and tariffs, the consular corps, and such matters of protocol as official visits. On the urging of Grey he was made a KCMG in 1912, the result of his distinguished diplomatic work in Washington on the sealing treaty of 1911 between Canada, Britain, the United States, Japan, and Russia. At this time Pope was perhaps the only high official in Ottawa to whom delicate diplomatic missions could be safely entrusted. In early 1914 Borden gave him the important task of chairing a conference of deputy heads charged with preparing a war book for Canada – a plan for handling the anticipated hostilities in Europe. For Pope, World War I would have great personal significance: four of his sons went to the front as did his sister Cecily Jane Georgina Fane*, a veteran military nurse.

The important changes in Canada's relations with Britain that gradually came on with Borden and the war, Pope found difficult to accept. Over the course of the conflict, on foreign policy and the maturation of Canada's position in imperial affairs, Borden relied more and more on the advice of Loring Cheney Christie*, who had joined the department in 1913. According to its official history, Pope, despite his skill, had become fixed in his handling of external affairs, "not always attentive to new challenges."

Thoroughly loyal, Pope was not given to Canadian nationalism. Indeed, he had always been British in sentiment and thought. His compass, his son Maurice Arthur would later observe, had been set in earlier times. Pope could not adjust it to the polarities of the 1920s. He sided with William Lyon Mackenzie King*'s non-committal response to Britain's astounding call for military support during the Çanak crisis of 1922, but the idea of diplomatic autonomy within a British commonwealth of nations baffled him. In a letter to Maurice his son in 1925 he asked, "How are we going to get on when every member [of the empire] claims an equal status with the rest; where each Dominion shall have . . . not only an army and navy, but also a diplomacy of its own? To my way of thinking such an Empire is an impossibility. I must leave the solution of the problem to younger and more vigorous minds than mine."

In October 1921 Pope's remarkable good health had broken down. A bout of rheumatic fever in the 1870s had left him with a weakened heart, and now the condition started to show itself. A leave of absence in 1921, his first in 43 years of continual public service, failed to restore him and from then on he declined. On 1 April 1925 the consummate bureaucrat retired. He had few hobbies; he used his time to draft his memoirs, which he completed only to 1907. He died on 2 Dec. 1926 and was buried in Beechwood Cemetery in Ottawa.

Pope was the quintessential civil servant – capable, careful, perceptive – but by the 1920s he was felt to be old-fashioned and stiff. Indeed, he had become Ottawa's arbiter of diplomatic niceties and social forms. As the *Ottawa Citizen* observed, under his tutelage correspondence was "carried on with the most exacting propriety." Sir John A. Macdonald's insistence that "forms are things" is a good epitaph for Pope: enshrined in it are the manners and civilization of Macdonald's time that Pope so well exemplified.

P. B. WAITE

[Sir Joseph Pope was a good biographer. He was discreet in *Memoirs of the Right Honourable Sir John Alexander Macdonald, G.C.B., first prime minister of the Dominion of Canada* (2v., Ottawa, [1894]; repr. in 1v., Toronto, 1930) because many of the men who had worked with Macdonald, or fought against him, were still alive. His later biography, *The day of Sir John Macdonald: a chronicle of the first prime minister of the dominion* (Toronto, 1915), was more frank, if much shorter. Pope's other writings include *Jacques Cartier, his life and voyages* (Ottawa, [1890]); *Traditions* (Ottawa, [1891]); and *Sir John A. Macdonald vindicated: a review of the Right Honourable Sir Richard Cartwright's "Reminiscences"* (Toronto, 1912). As Macdonald's literary executor, he published a useful selection of letters, *Correspondence of Sir John Macdonald . . .* (Toronto, 1921). Pope's own papers, including the correspondence of the Macdonald estate, 1891–1922, are in LAC, MG 30, E86.

Pope's life story, edited and completed by his son Maurice Arthur Pope, was published as *Public servant: the memoirs of Sir Joseph Pope* (Toronto, 1960). A well-turned piece of work and a basic foundation for this article, it is composed of two parts: Pope's own memoirs (1857–1907) and his son's biography of the rest of his life (1907–26). The first part was heavily edited, adding nothing and unfortunately eliminating what Maurice A. Pope called matter "merely of private interest." Shorter biographical accounts are found in *Canadian men and women of the time* (Morgan; 1898 and 1912) and *Standard dict. of Canadian biog.* (Roberts and Tunnell). A family tree and history are provided in the introduction to Maurice A. Pope's *Letters from the front, 1914–1919*, ed. Joseph Pope (Toronto, 1993). Louise Reynolds, *Agnes: the biography of Lady Macdonald* (Toronto and Sarasota, Fla, 1979), has much about Pope in its later chapters. For the development of the Department of External Affairs during his time, see John Hilliker and Donald Barry, *Canada's Department of External Affairs* (2v., Montreal and Kingston, Ont., 1990–95). P.B.W.]

PORTER, CHARLES HENRY, musician, educator, composer, and insurance agent; b. 1 Feb. 1856 in

Naugatuck, Conn., son of Charles Henry Porter and Isabelle Carter; m. first 20 July 1887 Louisa Maria Wylde in Halifax; m. secondly Elizabeth Chamberlain; d. 27 Sept. 1929 in New Haven, Conn.

Charles H. Porter was active in the musical life of Halifax as early as 1877. In January that year the first three concerts at the new Academy of Music featured the 150-voice Halifax Musical Union with Porter as conductor. These concerts were well received on the whole, but some reviewers were alarmed by Porter's habit of marking time with his feet. "If he would only keep his feet quiet . . . ," the critic for the *Citizen* said. "Perhaps he does not know how disagreeable it is to the audience to hear his unnecessary stamping."

From 1881 to 1883 and again from 1888 to 1906 Porter served as organist-choirmaster for St Matthew's Presbyterian Church in Halifax. In between, he spent some time studying music in Leipzig (Germany) with Carl Reinecke and Salomon Jadassohn. His work at St Matthew's gave great satisfaction to the session and the board of trustees, whose reports in the 1890s praised his able conduct of "the psalmody of the church" and noted that "under his efficient leadership" the choir had been greatly enlarged and musical services much improved. In 1882 Porter had founded the Orpheus Club, a male choir which he conducted, and about 1890, as pianist, he formed the Leipzig Trio with violinist Heinrich Klingenfeld and cellist Ernst Doering. His brother Samuel had preceded him to Halifax and the two had similar careers. Samuel was a violist with the Haydn Quintette Club and organist-choirmaster at St Paul's Anglican Church. Both taught music as well.

It was in fact as an educator that Porter made what many consider to be his major contribution to the musical life of Halifax: his work as the first director of the Halifax Conservatory of Music. Founded in 1887 in conjunction with the Halifax Ladies' College, the conservatory boasted 240 students by 1890. In addition to serving as director, Porter taught piano and theory, and eventually composition. In 1898 the conservatory affiliated with Dalhousie University, through which it awarded B.MUS. degrees. Porter was among those whom Dalhousie appointed that year to a board of examiners for the degree (he and Frederick Herbert Torrington* of Toronto were responsible for examinations in theory). By the following year the board was apparently no longer considered necessary; success in a series of classes at the conservatory was sufficient to qualify students for the degree. Porter's work was highly regarded by his contemporaries, one of whom commented that he filled the position of director "with unqualified success . . . combining his musical talent with an ability for business, seldom seen in a musician." "He might aptly be called one of the Fathers of Music in Halifax," this observer continued, "for it is through his patient and capable teaching

that Halifax can boast of so many home-reared artists in the piano and organ branches."

Porter had also attracted respect for his musical compositions. He was, according to music historian Helmut Kallmann, a "composer of rank," whose pieces for piano "are reported to suggest Chopin and to be of great difficulty." His works, some of which may have been composed in Leipzig, include Violin sonata op.1 (Kistner, 1886), "Serenade" (G. Schirmer, 1887; words by Charles George Douglas Roberts*), Te Deum in C (G. Schirmer, 1891), a symphony, anthems including "Sing unto the Lord," which was frequently performed at St Matthew's, and song settings such as "Milkmaid's song" (words by Alfred, Lord Tennyson). Some of his compositions were performed at recitals given by the conservatory.

In 1900 Porter resigned as director to become Maritime manager for the Equitable Life Assurance Society of the United States. He remained active as a musician, however, continuing to work at St Matthew's and with the Leipzig Trio and the Orpheus Club. In 1903 he served as associate conductor for the Halifax portion of the Cycle of Musical Festivals of the Dominion of Canada, organized by Charles Albert Edwin HARRISS and presented under the baton of Sir Alexander Campbell Mackenzie. Three years later Porter left Halifax and settled in New Haven, where he served as manager for the Connecticut branch of Equitable Life.

Whether Porter was involved in the musical life of New Haven is not known. He died there of a heart attack in 1929 and was buried in the Union Cemetery at Stratford, Conn. His first wife, Louisa Maria, had died in 1888 after giving birth to a stillborn son. Like Porter, she was a pianist – "one of the most brilliant . . . in this city," according to the Halifax *Morning Herald* – who had studied for a time in Germany. Porter was survived by his second wife, Elizabeth.

NANCY F. VOGAN

Conn., State Dept. of Health, Bureau of vital statistics (New Haven), Medical certificate of death, 28 Sept. 1929. *Evening Mail* (Halifax), 30 Sept. 1929. *Halifax Citizen*, 11 Jan. 1877. *Halifax Herald*, 30 Sept. 1929. *Morning Herald* (Halifax), 2 June 1888. *New Haven Evening Register*, 28 Sept., 4 Oct. 1929. R. C. Buley, *The Equitable Life Assurance Society of the United States, 1859–1964* (2v., New York, 1967). *Conservatory Journal* (Halifax), 1 (1937), no.2. Dalhousie Univ. and College, *Calendar* (Halifax), 1898/99, 1899/1900. *Directory*, New Haven, 1908–29. *Encyclopedia of music in Canada* (Kallmann *et al.*). J. P. Green and N. F. Vogan, *Music education in Canada: a historical account* (Toronto, 1991). Halifax Ladies' College and Conservatory of Music, *Calendar*, 1888/89–1900/1. Helmut Kallmann, *A history of music in Canada, 1534–1914* (Toronto and London, 1960). *Looking backward over two centuries: a short history of St. Matthew's United Church, Halifax, N.S., from the founding of the city to the bicentenary year* (Halifax, 1949). *Musical*

Halifax (Halifax), 1903/4. John Rousmaniere, *The life and times of the Equitable* (New York, 1995). *St. Matthew's Church, Halifax, Nova Scotia: 225th anniversary celebration, November 17–24, 1974 . . .* , comp. M. L. Perry and J. W. Reid (Halifax, 1974). Elizabeth Townsend *et al.*, *A sentinel on the street: St. Matthew's United Church, Halifax, 1749–1999* (Halifax, 1999).

POWELL, ANN JANE (Gray), teacher and social reformer; b. 1 Oct. 1853 in Markham Township, Upper Canada; m. 12 Aug. 1879 Henry Gray (d. 1938) in Princeton, Ont., and they had three daughters and three sons; d. 12 March 1924 in Toronto.

Annie Powell's parents were likely George Powell, a farmer, and Mary Ann Thomas. In the 1860s, after the apparent death of her father, she moved with her mother to Moore Township, on the St Clair River. Educated in Mooretown, she took first prize in reading in the township examinations. She won this distinction on the same day that the battle with the Fenians took place at Ridgeway, 2 June 1866 [*see* John O'Neill*]; consequently the award was long remembered within the family. It was at this competition too that she met Henry Gray, the fellow student who would become her husband. Following her schooling, she moved across the river to St Clair, Mich., where she trained to be a teacher. Granted a first-class certificate, she taught in the country and then in St Clair and Marine City. During this time, she was the organist in her Methodist church.

After her marriage in 1879, she settled in Vankleek Hill, Ont., where her husband had been made principal of the county model school. About 1893 they moved to Toronto. Though Henry was engaged as a public school principal, Annie had given up teaching, no doubt to raise their growing family. An active member in the churches she attended, notably North Parkdale (where she taught Sunday school) and then High Park, she helped organize quarterly official boards and local branches of the Methodist Ladies' Aid and the Woman's Missionary Society. She served as first president of the North Parkdale WMS, established the West District Ladies' Aid in 1913 (and became its first president), and took part in setting up similar bodies in the central and eastern districts of the city. In 1919 she was honoured with a life membership in the Ladies' Aid.

In all her commitments Gray was an unrelenting advocate of temperance. With reference to its traditional symbol, the white ribbon or badge, an obituary would note that "a little white pin was always to be seen on her dress." She participated at all levels of the Woman's Christian Temperance Union in the Toronto region: secretary of the local Gordon union, vice-president (1898–99) and president (1900–11) of the Parkdale union, and first president (1911–22) of the Howard Park union. She particularly encouraged temperance Sundays, which focused on services (usually one a quarter) devoted to the cause. In addition, she worked for the travellers' aid program, another WCTU-supported activity, in which young women seeking work in Toronto were guided to safe lodgings and employment. She was also a superintendent of the journal department for both the Toronto District WCTU and the Parkdale union between 1895 and 1897. This department sought subscribers for the WCTU's *Woman's Journal* (Ottawa) and sometimes submitted information to it on behalf of the union. Between 1905 and 1920 she was superintendent of the department of temperance in sabbath schools of the Ontario WCTU. At the dominion level she was superintendent of the department of Sunday schools from 1920 to 1922. These departments were concerned with supplying temperance literature (leaflets and lesson plans) to Sunday school superintendents in the hope that the materials would be mandated for use by teachers.

Like many WCTU women of her era, Gray was a member of the Royal Templars of Temperance. She belonged to several of its Toronto-area councils and participated at the district, grand, and dominion council levels; among her offices, she was a select councillor for a term and a treasurer for 27 years. Her favourite function was organizing the Templars' medal contests, an activity also run by the WCTU in other parts of the country, with departmental status. Aimed at schoolchildren and temperance youth groups, the medals (or sometimes books or money) were offered for competition in elocution, writing, posters, scrapbooks, and music. At the time of her death, Powell was the Templars' dominion superintendent for medal contests. She had promoted them tirelessly in Toronto, where they were a great success, and her leadership considerably increased their visibility and popularity.

Annie Gray died of pneumonia at the age of 70 in 1924, in her home at 238 Keele Street. She left a strong imprint on both her family and the organizations she had helped sustain. Her daughters all became public-school teachers; two sons became lawyers and one a Methodist minister. In the evangelical feminist language of the time, eulogies lauded her for her skills as a wife and loving mother, as a frugal and efficient household manager, and as a good neighbour and friend. According to the *Canadian White Ribbon Tidings* (London, Ont.), she was admired for her "rigid adherence to duty" and "keen sense of responsibility." Above all, she had impressed those around her with her "Christian optimism" and courage as a "warrior" in the battle against alcohol. Never a lone soldier, she had marched with the temperance army; her favourite poem, recited at her funeral service at High Park Church, was "A band of earnest women." Members of the WCTU who filed past her casket dropped in little white bows while representatives of the Ladies' Aid and other societies quietly deposited tiny flowers. A memorial service was held at the WCTU's Willard Hall in Toronto on 28 March.

SHARON ANNE COOK

AO, F 885, MU 8394.1, 8395, 8396.11, 8397–99, 8404.9–12, 8407–9, 8432–34 (mfm.); RG 80-5-0-84, no.8304; RG 80-8-0-948, no.2217. LAC, RG 31, C1, 1861, Markham Township, Upper Canada, dist.16: 6 (mfm. at AO). *Toronto Daily Star*, 13 March 1924. *Canadian White Ribbon Tidings* (London, Ont.), May 1924: 111 (mfm. in AO, F 885). S. A. Cook, *"Through sunshine and shadow": the Woman's Christian Temperance Union, evangelicalism, and reform in Ontario, 1874–1930* (Montreal and Kingston, Ont., 1995). *Directory*, Toronto, 1894–1914.

PRESSEAULT, *dit* FABIEN. *See* FABIEN

PRÉVOST, ALBERT (baptized **Louis-Elzéar-Albert**), neurologist, forensic pathologist, and professor; b. 5 Aug. 1881 in Montreal, son of Alexis-Édouard-Armand Prévost, a merchant, and Joséphine-Ida Beaudry; m. there 26 Aug. 1909 Thérèse Leduc, and they had four children; d. there 4 July 1926 as a result of an accident.

Albert Prévost grew up in a well-to-do family that had been active in the Montreal business community for two generations. His father and his paternal grandfather, Amable-Cyprien Prévost, owned a number of dry goods stores there. His maternal grandfather, Jean-Baptiste Beaudry, was a merchant, landowner, and banker in Montreal.

In 1895 Prévost began his classical studies at the Collège Sainte-Marie, where one of his classmates was Athanase David*, who would become the provincial secretary. Short, stocky, and of athletic build, Prévost reportedly began to display exceptional ability in sports at that time. After his graduation in June 1903, he enrolled in medicine at the Montreal branch of the Université Laval; he obtained his medical degree "with distinction" four years later. A man of independent means, he went on to Paris to specialize. There he would meet his future wife, the daughter of Joseph Leduc of Montreal, a physician who owned the chain of pharmacies bearing his name. In 1909 he also came across in Paris a boyhood friend with whom he would remain in close touch, Édouard Montpetit*, who later founded the École des Sciences Sociales, Économiques et Politiques at the Université de Montréal.

Prévost's original intention was to obtain a prestigious position as an intern in the hospitals of Paris, as his uncle Dr Azarie Brodeur had earlier done. He quickly discovered, however, that his own field of interest was neurology. Under the guidance of such teachers as Pierre Marie, André Thomas, Joseph Babinski, and especially Jules Déjerine, all former students of the famous Jean-Martin Charcot, Prévost combined clinical observation of patients at the Salpêtrière hospital with laboratory research into the anatomy and physiology of the prime functions of the brain. He also spent some time at the Infirmerie du Dépôt de la Préfecture de Police, studying under psychiatrists Ernest Dupré and Gaëtan Gatian de Clérambault. This work gained him the title of forensic pathologist from the Université de Paris, probably at the end of 1913. He then returned to Montreal, where in February 1914 he joined the staff of the dispensary for diseases of the nervous system at Notre-Dame Hospital. Around the same time he began to take part in the activities of the Société Médicale de Montréal. On 4 May 1914 he also became associate professor of neurology in the faculty of medicine at the Université Laval in Montreal and conducted clinics in diseases of the nervous system at Notre-Dame. During the same period he was appointed consulting physician at the Hôpital Saint-Jean-de-Dieu as well. In addition, he was a member of the medical board of the Institut Bruchési from 1915 to 1924. In 1918 Prévost became head of the neurological department of Notre-Dame Hospital, replacing Georges Villeneuve, who had died that year, and he retained this post for the rest of his life. On 8 April 1918 he was also appointed to the first chair of neurology at the Université Laval in Montreal, with tenure. He quickly gained a reputation as one of the best professors on the faculty, his lectures and theoretical courses being valued as much by students and nurses as by his colleagues. According to Antonio Barbeau, who had studied under him, he was an articulate man, "equally rich in content and in form."

Prévost showed endless devotion to his patients and had an enterprising spirit uncommon among French-speaking physicians at that time. In 1919, realizing that large hospitals were unsuited to the needs of patients suffering from neuroses (nervous conditions increasingly frequent from the time of World War I), Prévost decided to set up a private clinic in the quiet Montreal suburb of Cartierville, near the Rivière des Prairies. This clinic became known as the Sanatorium Prévost. He bought a three-storey house from Raoul-Ovide Grothé, an important Montreal businessman, in 1919 and renovated it at his own expense in order to accommodate ten patients. With the acquisition in 1921 of a dwelling nearby, the property of contractor Félix-Avila Grothé, Prévost could house 23 patients in his sanatorium. Although electrotherapy equipment was installed that year, in keeping with the French theories of the time he used psychotherapy to treat his patients. In this respect the Sanatorium Prévost differed markedly from similar institutions such as the Sanatorium de Trois-Rivières, which had been founded in 1896 by Dr Charles-Numa De Blois, where the primary emphasis was on the use of physical procedures (electrotherapy, hydrotherapy, X-rays, and so forth) to treat depression, drug addiction, and minor psychoses. Under the direction of Charlotte Tassé, the superintendent, and Dr Edgar Langlois, Prévost's first disciple and colleague, this private institution would outlast its founder. After World War II it would become an important teaching centre in the fields of neurology and psychiatry.

As a forensic pathologist, Prévost was frequently called on by the courts. The most famous trial in which he took part as an expert witness was probably that of Marie-Anne Houde, the stepmother of Aurore Gagnon*, known as Aurore the martyred child, in 1920.

In January 1925 Prévost and 18 other French-speaking physicians from Montreal came onto the board of directors of *L'Union médicale du Canada* (Montréal). This new shareholders' group sought to help develop hospital centres and advance university teaching in French Canada, collaborate in the scientific progress of learned societies, and take part in planning the conferences of the Association des Médecins de Langue Française de l'Amérique du Nord, of which Prévost had been a member since 1922. After the reorganization of the board, closer relations arose between French-speaking physicians in Europe and those in Canada. Prévost was getting ready to attend the 30th session of the Congrès Annuel des Médecins Aliénistes et Neurologistes de France et des Pays de Langue Française, which was to be held in Switzerland, in Lausanne and Geneva from 2 to 7 Aug. 1926, when he suffered an accident that would prove fatal.

It seems odd that Prévost wrote very little. Of his papers to the Société Médicale de Montréal, which were sometimes presented in collaboration with colleagues at Notre-Dame, nothing is left except summaries published in *L'Union médicale du Canada*. Undoubtedly Prévost had given clinical descriptions of the principal nervous disorders of organic origin, but he apparently made his main contribution through the tissues he sectioned from the brain or the spinal cord, which made it possible to confirm his diagnoses or those of his colleagues.

Prévost belonged to a number of social clubs, including the Club Saint-Denis, the Cercle Universitaire de Montréal, and the Knights of Columbus. Keen on exercise, he was also a member of the golf club in Laval-sur-le-Lac (Laval) and the Club Chapleau, a private hunting and fishing establishment.

On 4 July 1926 Albert Prévost, who was then at the height of his career, died at the Royal Victoria Hospital in Montreal from the effects of an automobile accident that had occurred the night before on the road between L'Assomption and Saint-Paul-l'Ermite (Le Gardeur). He had been returning from a consultation in Berthier (Berthierville) with Dr D.-Alfred Benoit, who was seriously injured. Prévost's impressive funeral service was attended by many of the leading citizens of Montreal.

GUY GRENIER

Albert Prévost is the author of "Résumé pratique du traitement de la syphilis," *L'Union médicale du Canada* (Montréal), 49 (1920): 612–17.

ANQ-M, CE601-S33, 8 août 1881. Arch. de l'Univ. de Montréal, E 38 (faculté de médecine), procès-verbaux du conseil de la faculté de médecine de l'univ. Laval à Montréal, 1914–18. BCM-G, RBMS, Saint-Louis-de-France (Montréal), 26 août 1909 (mfm.). *Le Devoir*, 5, 10 juill., 25 sept. 1926. *La Presse*, 21 avril 1920; 5, 7 juill. 1926. Antonio Barbeau, "Université de Montréal, chaire de neurologie de la faculté de médecine: leçon inaugurale du professeur Antonio Barbeau," *L'Union médicale du Canada*, 69 (1940): 117–25. E.-P. Benoît, "Nécrologie: Albert Prévost," *L'Union médicale du Canada*, 55 (1926): 465–66. Wilfrid Derome, "Le professeur Albert Prévost," *L'Union médicale du Canada*, 55: 467–70. Jocelyne Dion, *Pavillon Albert-Prévost, 1919–1994: 75 ans* (Montréal, [1994]). J.-E. Dubé, "Nos hôpitaux: le passé, leur évolution, le présent," *L'Union médicale du Canada*, 61 (1932): 148–234. Hôpital Notre-Dame, *Rapport annuel* (Montréal), 1914–26. Madeleine [A.-M. Gleason], "Ceux qui s'en vont . . . ," *La Rev. moderne* (Montréal), 7 (1925–26), no.10: 10. Édouard Montpetit, "Albert Prévost," *Rev. trimestrielle canadienne* (Montréal), 12 (1926): 361–67. Univ. de Montréal, *Annuaire*, 1920–22. Univ. Laval à Montréal, *Annuaire*, 1904–19.

PRICE, Sir WILLIAM, businessman, industrialist, officer, and politician; b. 30 Aug. 1867 in Talcahuano, Chile, son of Henry Ferrier Price, a businessman, and Florence Rogerson; m. 25 Jan. 1894 Amelia Blanche Smith at Quebec, and they had four sons and two daughters; d. 2 Oct. 1924 in Kénogami (Jonquière), Que., and was buried there on 13 Oct. 1924 in the cemetery of St James Anglican Church.

William Price spent his early childhood in Chile, where his father, the son of the late William Price*, an important lumber merchant in Quebec, was a cattle breeder. When he was about five years old, his parents sent him to Canada. He was educated first at Bishop's College, in Lennoxville, Que., and later at St Mark's School in Windsor, England. His classmates nicknamed him Chile Price. In 1885 he embarked on a career in the lumber trade with the Quebec firm of Price Brothers and Company, which was owned by his uncle, Evan John Price*.

From 1885 to 1899 William participated in making the administrative decisions of the firm, which by then owned vast timber limits in many parts of the province. During the last three decades of the 19th century, the company invested in numerous sawmills, which were located at Cap-Chat and Matane in the Gaspé region, Saint-Firmin (Baie-Sainte-Catherine) and Sault-au-Cochon (Forestville) on the north shore of the St Lawrence, Montmagny, Cap-Saint-Ignace, and Trois-Saumons (Saint-Jean-Port-Joli) on the south shore of the St Lawrence, Trois-Pistoles, Saint-Germain-de-Rimouski (Rimouski), Saint-Octave-de-Métis (Grand-Métis), and Le Bic in the lower St Lawrence region, Chicoutimi and Grande-Baie (La Baie) in the Saguenay region, and Saint-Romuald near Lévis.

Evan John Price died in August 1899. By the terms of his will, his nephew William took over the management of Price Brothers and Company, which, because of the decline in shipbuilding and in timber exports at the port of Quebec, had been caught in an economic downturn since the 1880s. Although the company's financial resources were estimated to be between $500,000 and $1 million in July 1900, they had become so shaky that it was on the brink of bankruptcy. That year its principal creditor, the Bank of Montreal, appointed an outside administrator, Robert Ritchie, to represent it and he helped Price to straighten out his firm's affairs.

At the beginning of the century a major change of direction took shape at Price Brothers. While retaining interests in sawmills, Price turned to a new sector: pulp and paper. In 1901 he founded Montmagny Light and Pulp Company and bought the Compagnie de Pulpe de Jonquière. The former, which was equipped with four grinders and four wet machines, could produce nearly 18 tons of pulp a day. This pulp was used to supply the latter company, which had been founded in 1899 by merchants and farmers in Jonquière and specialized in manufacturing cardboard. In 1902, in partnership with Oswald Austin Porritt, who managed the sawmill in Saint-Germain-de-Rimouski, Price founded a joint-stock venture there, the Price-Porritt Pulp and Paper Company. The enterprise, with a capital of $250,000, produced mechanical pulp and cardboard from wood, using hydroelectric resources that it counted on harnessing; it would remain in operation until 1927. He next began a lengthy restructuring of Price Brothers and in 1904 it was incorporated. Price Brothers and Company Limited, with share capital of $2 million and a head office at Quebec, became the parent company of the Compagnie de Pulpe de Jonquière, Montmagny Light and Pulp Company, and Price-Porritt Pulp and Paper Company. The members of its first board of directors were William Price, Henry Edward Price, Robert Ritchie, Gustavus George Stuart, and Andrew Thomson*, all from Quebec City, Edward George Price and Ion Hamilton Benn of London, England, Granger Farwell of Chicago, and William S. Hofstra of New York.

Price continued to operate businesses elsewhere in the province, but from now on most of his industrial activity was carried out in the Saguenay region. Chicoutimi was his main centre of action in this region until 1902, when, as a result of a few misfortunes, he moved his operations to Jonquière. In 1900 there had

been an initial lawsuit over the ownership of the quays located at Chicoutimi, in the basin of the Rivière Saguenay. Built by Price Brothers some 30 years earlier and maintained by them, these quays were considered a waterfront lot belonging to the crown and were sold by the provincial government to the Chicoutimi Pulp Company [see Julien-Édouard-Alfred Dubuc*]. Four years later, the disputes continued with the sale of the sawmill in Chicoutimi, which was immediately demolished by the new owners. Moreover, the Price family's monopoly on the lumber industry in the region [see Evan John Price; William Price] came increasingly under attack from some of the leading citizens of Chicoutimi [see Joseph-Dominique GUAY]. The clashes occurred mainly around 1906, when plans for constructing an aqueduct and electrifying Chicoutimi led to confrontations in the municipal council. Price – who was accused by his detractors of being opposed to progress – did not favour these local initiatives, which threatened to trigger a substantial increase in municipal taxes.

Business was going well, however. In 1905, when its principal trustee, the Bank of Montreal, issued a series of bonds to the value of $1 million, the total assets of Price Brothers were estimated at $4,317,500. Since the beginning of the new century, the firm had made profits estimated at more than $1,200,000. The Prices owned most of the shares: 83.8 per cent in 1907, 83.3 per cent in 1908, and 87 per cent in 1909. Of these family assets, William owned 79.2 per cent in 1907, 78.7 per cent in 1908, and 79.5 per cent in 1909.

The Compagnie de Pulpe de Jonquière had a particularly profitable factory. Equipped with six grinders, it gradually phased out the production of cardboard from mechanical pulp, in favour of producing paper from chemical pulp. A water slide carried the pulp, cardboard, and paper down three miles to the Rivière Saguenay. The factory was powered by its own hydroelectric station, which also served the village of Jonquière. In 1911 it would produce almost equal quantities of pulp and manufactured forest products: 8,000 tons of mechanical pulp, 2,600 tons of sulphite pulp, 6,000 tons of cardboard, and 4,000 tons of paper. It would remain in operation until the end of the 1950s.

In 1910 Price Brothers and Company Limited became Price Brothers Limited and increased its registered capital to $5 million. It specialized increasingly in the production of paper, for a market which the government of Sir Lomer GOUIN hoped to stimulate that year by banning the export of pulpwood taken from crown lands. In 1911 Price Brothers began building a new paper mill, which led the following year to the creation of Kénogami, a municipality that was then estimated to have a population of nearly 4,000. The industry, whose source of electricity was a power station with a capacity of nearly 33,000 horsepower, manufactured 150 tons of paper a day from the time it went into production in December 1912.

Even after investing $2.5 million in infrastructure, Price Brothers estimated its profits at some $460,000 at the end of the fiscal year 1911–12. Its assets were evaluated at $15 million and 85.5 per cent of the $6 million in first-mortgage bonds had already been put on the financial market. Price continued to serve as chairman of the board of directors.

Canada's entry into the war, however, disrupted Price's life. An ardent patriot and imperialist, he had already put in a number of years of military service. He was an officer with the 8th Regiment (Royal Rifles) and had raised two companies during the South African War. Promoted lieutenant-colonel, he was appointed by Samuel HUGHES, the minister of militia and defence, to take charge of all aspects of organizing the camp at Valcartier, near Quebec City. The work began on 10 Aug. 1914, with the electrification of the camp and the construction of an aqueduct, various buildings, and a railway siding. By 25 August, 20,000 soldiers had arrived at the camp, and within two weeks there would be 32,665. As the person in charge of embarking troops and military equipment, Price had to cope with inexperienced staff. Embarkation orders disregarded, congestion in the port of Quebec, and vessels ill-suited to transporting cannons and trucks were some of the factors that led to chaos. On 5 October, when the last of the 31 ships sailed, his nightmare came to an end. His efforts were rewarded with a knighthood on 1 Jan. 1915.

Price now took a personal hand in recruiting and equipping the 171st Infantry Battalion, with which he arrived at the military camp in Witley, England, on 12 Jan. 1917. At the end of the month, after his unit had been disbanded, he became captain of the 4th Battalion of the Canadian Overseas Railway Construction Corps and went across to France. His military duties were purely administrative. In March 1917 he was transferred to the 87th Infantry Battalion (Canadian Grenadier Guards) as supply officer attached to the 4th Division. Suffering from fatigue, he obtained his release from these duties in July 1917. He was sent back to England in September and then returned to Canada.

This long military interlude in Price's life had no negative effect, however, on the fortunes of Price Brothers; its assets were estimated at $19.5 million in 1919 (an increase of $1.4 million over the previous year) and the company recorded a registered capital of $10 million. The Kénogami plant had a daily output of 212 tons of paper, 90 tons of chemical pulp, and 178 tons of mechanical pulp, the one in Jonquière 34.55 tons of paper and 69 tons of mechanical pulp. The factory in Saint-Germain-de-Rimouski produced 10,000 tons of mechanical pulp per year, and the sawmills owned by Price Brothers at that time (in Batiscan,

Montmagny, Cap-Saint-Ignace, Saint-Germain-de-Rimouski, Matane, and Lac-au-Saumon) had an annual output of 30 million feet of lumber, 80,000 railway ties, and several billion cedar shingles.

After a period of consolidation in the 1910s, Price Brothers entered a phase of expansion. In 1920 it increased its registered capital to $60 million. Its projects were huge: the construction of a hydroelectric station at La Grande Décharge of Lac Saint-Jean to supply power for a new pulp and paper mill it planned to build on land that in 1925 would become the town of Riverbend (Alma). Hence in 1920 Price became a minority shareholder (with one-quarter of the shares) in the Quebec Development Company Limited [see Benjamin Alexander SCOTT]; founded in 1913, its majority shareholder was James Buchanan Duke, president of the American Tobacco Company [see Sir Mortimer Barnett DAVIS]. Duke owned the water-power rights on Île Maligne and Price was to obtain, from the government of Louis-Alexandre Taschereau*, who had recently become premier of the province, the necessary permits that would, among other things, let them keep the water level at La Grande Décharge at its maximum height and develop the potential for hydroelectric power. This first step was ratified by an order in council on 7 Dec. 1922.

Price agreed he would transfer 2,850 shares in the Quebec Development Company Limited to Duke, and then buy back 5,950 shares in it for $855,000. In return, the company was to issue an initial bond series of $4 million and undertake the construction of the hydroelectric station, assuming 75 per cent of the cost, with the other 25 per cent to be paid by Price Brothers. It also agreed to supply electricity to the Price Brothers paper mills in the Saguenay region for some 20 years. The work was begun in 1923 and a second series of bonds, to the value of $12 million, had to be issued the following year. The shareholders adopted the corporate name of Duke-Price Power Company Limited, and this firm obtained letters patent in July 1924 with an authorized capital of $1.5 million. The Riverbend plant went into production and the hydroelectric station at Île Maligne began transmitting its first kilowatts in 1925, after the death of Price. In order to sell the electricity produced by this station, Duke-Price Power merged that year with the Aluminium Company of America and its Canadian subsidiary, the Aluminium Company of Canada Limited. These two companies would buy it out in 1926. This transaction would be the first setback in the fortunes of the Price empire, which would thus find its share in the partnership substantially reduced.

Along with his involvement in Price Brothers, Price had fully participated at the beginning of the 20th century in the endeavour to revive the economy of Quebec City. In 1903 he was elected president of the Quebec Chamber of Commerce. Since the late 1890s plans for rail connections had been on the drawing board, with a view to creating a railway terminus of national scale in the old capital. Besides the Great Northern Railway's plan, which was already being carried out [see Richard Reid Dobell*], there were two others, those of the Quebec and James Bay Railway Company and the Trans-Canada Railway Company. Price was a director of both corporations. Unfortunately, in comparison with the Grand Trunk and the Canadian Northern Railway, the proposals of the Quebec City bourgeoisie carried little political weight. The governments of Sir Wilfrid Laurier* and Simon-Napoléon Parent* lost interest in them. Laurier saw them as competing with his intention to construct a new transcontinental link that favoured a different route. As for Parent, he took so long to make up his mind that by 1906 not a single stretch of railway had been built. The projects would be taken over by the Canadian Northern Railway group.

Since 1900 Price had been a director of the Union Bank of Canada [see Andrew Thomson], and Price Brothers had their offices in its building, which had been renovated and enlarged in 1897. In 1908, when he became the bank's vice-president, its balance sheet showed a profit. In the course of that year it opened eight new branches in Saskatchewan, one in Ontario, and one in British Columbia, and it paid the shareholders a dividend of seven per cent – nearly $222,500. Price was also a director of the Quebec Steamship Company, the Guaranteed Pure Milk Company of Quebec Limited, the Quebec Bridge Company, the Quebec Railway, Light and Power Company, Jeffery Hale's Hospital, and the Prudential Trust Company Limited.

Early in the 20th century, Price had, moreover, embarked on a political career. He ran unsuccessfully as a Conservative in the riding of Rimouski in the federal general election of 1904. Four years later he made another attempt in Quebec West. The constituency had been held by his Liberal opponent, William Power, since the death in 1902 of his predecessor, Dobell, and indeed by the Liberals ever since Laurier's first victory in 1896. The election campaign was bitterly contested. Like Rodolphe Forget*, Price was identified with the trusts and millionaire businessmen. His opponents accused him of not using the port infrastructure at Quebec, which he promised nonetheless to develop if elected. Price himself denounced the political inertia of Power in particular and of the federal Liberals in general, who, although they had held the riding for many years, had not managed to develop either a modern port or a railway terminus of national scale. Price won the election by 10 votes, following a judicial recount. His infrequent speeches in the House of Commons dealt with maritime issues (the construction of a building in the port of Vancouver), military matters (the enlargement of the Royal Military Col-

lege of Canada), and railways (the administration of the Intercolonial Railway). From a man eager to put Quebec City back on the road to progress and prosperity, it was hardly a brilliant performance.

In the federal general election of 1911, Price ran in the same riding and faced the same opponent. Once again the Liberals accused him of being a millionaire who took no interest in the economic development of the old capital. He defended himself by pointing out that as an opposition MP his influence was limited. He believed, moreover, that commercial reciprocity with the United States would seriously hurt farmers, industrialists, and working people. The domestic market, developed by means of the National Policy [see Sir Samuel Leonard Tilley*], should, in his opinion, be preserved, as well as economic ties with the mother country, England. In his view, prosperity followed east-west, rather than north-south, lines. This profession of faith, at once Canadian and imperialistic, failed to win him the riding. Power obtained a majority of 91 votes and Price's active political career was over.

Price died on 2 Oct. 1924. While he was in the lumber yard at the Kénogami plant with two engineers, examining a hole left by a cave-in, he had been swept into the Rivière aux Sables by a landslide. His body was found a week later. His sons John Herbert and Arthur Clifford, who were both in their early twenties, succeeded him at the helm of Price Brothers. Although they were responsible in 1929–30 for the construction of the first skyscraper in the old capital, they did not enjoy the financial success their father had. During the depression of the 1930s, Price Brothers was driven to the brink of bankruptcy, and the members of the founding family lost control of it. At the outset of the 21st century, a few of Price's descendants continue to live in the Quebec City region, where they own an inn and two museums, as well as interests in the pulp and paper and lumber industries. What's bred in the bone will come out in the flesh. In 2002 a few relics of the bygone days could still be found: the Price building in the historic quarter and the Price residence on Rue Grande Allée at Quebec, and the monument to William Price (Sir William's grandfather) in Chicoutimi. But other bits of history have disappeared with the passage of time, including the Price Cup, which was awarded in 1911 to the winners of two races, one for sailboats and the other for motor boats. Like their founder, these contests had fitted both the tradition of the 19th century and the modernity of the 20th.

JEAN BENOIT

Information about Sir William Price's activities as a businessman can be found in the *Quebec Official Gazette*, especially for the years 1899–1900, 1902, 1910, 1912, 1919–20, 1923–24, and in the *Pulp and Paper Magazine of Canada*

Price

(Gardenvale, Que.), specifically from 1905 to 1913 and in 1924. The most important source, however, is the Price Brothers fonds (P666) at ANQ-SLSJ (mfm. at ANQ-Q). Of particular interest are S1, SS2, 1.5–1.8; SS3, 20.7; SS7, SSS1, 36.4–36.16; S11, SS1, 283.1; SS2, 284; S14, SS1, SSS1, 288.3, 288.18.

ANQ-Q, CE301-S61, 25 janv. 1894. LAC, RG 150, Acc. 1992–93/166. *Le Devoir*, 3–4 oct. 1924, 28 avril 1926. *Le Progrès du Golfe* (Rimouski, Qué.), 7, 14, 21, 28 oct., 4 nov. 1904. *Quebec Chronicle*, 28, 30 Sept., 7–8, 13, 16, 18–19, 22–24, 27 Oct. 1908; 30 Aug., 6, 11, 16, 18, 21–22 Sept. 1911. *La Semaine commerciale* (Québec), 9 juill. 1897; 1er févr., 30 août 1901; 23 janv., 20 mars, 24 avril, 8 mai 1903; 9, 30 mars 1906; 27 nov. 1908; 1er janv., 3, 9 avril, 8 mai, 11 juin, 2 juill. 1909. *Le Soleil*, 6, 13, 20, 30 oct., 2 nov. 1908; 20, 22 sept. 1911; 10–11, 16, 25, 28 août 1914; 15, 18 févr., 19 avril 1919; 21 juin 1998; 4 oct. 2001. Jules Bélanger *et al.*, *Histoire de la Gaspésie* (Montréal, 1981). Can., House of Commons, *Debates*, 1909–11. *Canadian directory of parl.* (Johnson). *Canadian men and women of the time* (Morgan; 1912). J.-P. Charland et Jacques Saint-Pierre, *Les pâtes et papiers au Québec, 1880–1980: technologies, travail et travailleurs* (Québec, 1990). *Cyclopædia of Canadian biog.* (Rose and Charlesworth), vol.3. *Directory*, Quebec and Lévis, 1900–1, 1906–7. J.-C. Fortin et Antonio Lechasseur, *Histoire du Bas-Saint-Laurent* (Québec, 1993). Camil Girard et Normand Perron, *Histoire du Saguenay–Lac-Saint-Jean* (Québec, 1989). *Histoire de la Côte-du-Sud*, sous la dir. d'Alain Laberge (Québec, 1993). *Histoire de la Côte-Nord*, sous la dir. de Pierre Frenette (Québec, 1996). *Histoire de Lévis-Lotbinière*, sous la dir. de Roch Samson (Québec, 1996). Nicholson, *CEF*. Pierre Poulin, "Déclin portuaire et industrialisation: l'évolution de la bourgeoisie d'affaires de Québec à la fin du XIXe siècle et au début du XXe siècle" (mémoire de MA, univ. Laval, Québec, 1985). *Prominent people of the province of Quebec, 1923–24* (Montreal, n.d.). Que., *Statutes*, 1900, c.73. Bérard Riverin, "La pulperie de Jonquière (1898–1902)," *Saguenayensia* (Chicoutimi, Qué.), 17 (1975): 94–100. Mason Wade, *The French Canadians, 1760–1967* (rev. ed., 2v., Toronto, 1968).

PRICE, WILLIAM HENRY, physician and author; b. 4 or 14 Sept. 1839 in Butternut Ridge (Havelock), N.B., son of William Henry Price and Charlotte Alward; m. 24 Dec. 1873 Catharine Jane Watts in Chicago, and they had two daughters and two sons; d. 8 Sept. 1930 in Phoenix, Ariz.

George Webb Price, the grandfather of William H. Price, was an early settler at Butternut Ridge. He operated a grist mill there as early as 1814. William, however, was apprenticed to medicine under Henry Shaw of Kentville, N.S., and subsequently took formal training at Bowdoin College in Brunswick, Maine, and at the University of the City of New York, from which he graduated in 1865. In that year as well he served briefly as an acting assistant surgeon with the Union army at Nashville, Tenn. He then practised in Prospect Park until 1872 (in which state is unclear, though he is said to have been a member of the Chicago Medical Society in these years), Chicago (1872–76), and New York City (1876–81).

Price was educated according to regular principles, but he accepted many of the therapies of botanic medicine and belonged to the sect of doctors known as eclectics. Though not an aggressive controversialist, he was one of the many practitioners who gathered at Clarendon Hall in New York to observe the outcome of Minneapolis doctor Henry S. Tanner's boast to the regular medical profession of New York in June 1880 that he could survive a 40-day fast. Rotating shifts of observers from both sides of the medical community kept watch over Tanner to ensure his compliance with the challenge. Price took his turn at Tanner's side on the night of 4–5 August, just before the successful completion of the fast on the 7th.

Baby's guide to health (1880), written while Price was in New York, clearly expresses his medical principles. The book belonged to the popular genre of domestic medical literature. It enjoyed its own measure of success, and though self-published was available through the American News Company. Price took issue with the tendency of the physicians appointed to visit the poor in New York to prescribe medicines rather than teach people the general principles for preventing disease. Medical therapeutics were in a state of flux, and Price insisted that the doctor was merely an assistant to nature in matters of health. "It is not the doctor who 'cures,'" he stated, "but it is the laws of *Nature* that only can be entitled to the credit." Price promised a larger work on the same subject but it never appeared.

Price returned home to Butternut Ridge in 1881. He joined the New Brunswick Medical Society and pursued a large practice in the largely rural community. Though in New York he had offered medical advice to patients by mail, it is unknown if he continued this aspect of practice in New Brunswick. He was at least able to blend regular and botanic medicine without disturbing fellow practitioners until his retirement in 1901. He subsequently embarked on hog farming, beginning with 200 pigs. After his wife died in 1913 he moved to Phoenix and lived with his elder daughter, Charlotte.

In religion Price was a Methodist but the rest of his family were Baptists. Following his death in September 1930 he was buried in Forest Lawn Cemetery in Phoenix.

PETER J. MITHAM

William Henry Price is the author of *Baby's guide to health; or, how to promote and preserve the health of babies from the time of birth to the age of two years or more in all seasons and climates* (New York, 1880). An earlier work noted on the title page, *Children's guide to health*, has not been located.

The most detailed obituary of Price appears in the *Kings County Record* (Sussex, N.B.), 26 Sept. 1930: 4. A photograph accompanies the biographical sketch in *Canadian album* (Cochrane and Hopkins), 3: 413.

LAC, RG 31, C1, Havelock, N.B., 1891, dist.16, sub-dist.E, no.2: 23; 1901, dist.18, subdist.E, no.1: 13. *Arizona Republican* (Phoenix), 10 Sept. 1930. *New York Times*, 4 July, 6–7 Aug. 1880. *The descendants of Edmund and Jane (Webb) Price: one of the very early English-speaking couples to settle on the St. John River*, comp. M. F. Amos *et al.* (n.p., 1976), 114–15. *General alumni catalogue of New York University, 1833–1907; medical alumni* (New York, 1908). *General catalogue of Bowdoin College and the Medical School of Maine: a biographical record of alumni and officers, 1794–1950* (sesquicentennial [5th] ed., Brunswick, Maine, 1950).

PROWSE, BENJAMIN CHARLES, merchant and politician; b. 10 Dec. 1862 near Charlottetown, son of William Prowse and Eleanor Eliza Horne; m. first 30 June 1886 Amanda Maud Millner (d. 1928) in Charlottetown, and they had three sons, one of whom died in infancy, and one daughter; m. secondly 9 Jan. 1929 Clara (Clare) Eliza Isabelle MacMillan in Ottawa; d. 22 Feb. 1930 in Charlottetown.

Benjamin C. Prowse attended rural and Charlottetown schools and gained wide practical experience, but his formal education did not extend to the post-secondary level. He began his career in his teens as an employee of W. A. Weeks and Company, a dry goods firm in Charlottetown. In the early 1880s he worked as chief clerk in a men's clothing store owned by his brother Lemuel Ezra, and by 1886 he had become a junior partner.

Known by 1889 as Prowse Brothers, the firm prospered, in part because of an aggressive marketing style. Using sobriquets like "The Wonderful Cheap Men" and "The Farmer's Boys," the Prowses catered to people with middling incomes and rural folk, the latter being a particularly important segment of the Island economy. Customers were drawn by claims that the brothers were "the most wonderful bargain givers on P.E. Island" who "slaughtered [prices] right and left" and by in-store attractions such as bean-counting contests and an exhibition of black bears, mountain sheep, and elk. In 1896, shortly after the store was voted the second most popular dry goods establishment in Charlottetown, in an informal poll at the city's annual fair, Prowse Brothers absorbed the firm ranking third. By then the business had expanded into a wide range of dry goods and occupied one of the most prominent commercial sites in the city. Between 1903 and 1907 a branch store, Prowse Brothers and Crowell, operated in Sydney, N.S. Around 1906 the firm was restructured as a limited stock company with Benjamin as vice-president and general manager. He became president after the death of his brother in December 1925. By 1930 Prowse Brothers was reputed to be one of the largest businesses of its type in the Maritimes. Another firm in which Benjamin was involved was Carter and Company Limited, a stationery and giftware business. One of its incorporators

in 1903, he served as president for a time around World War I.

Benjamin had followed his elder brother into politics, albeit in a less prominent role. Lemuel was returned to the Island's Legislative Assembly in 1893; Benjamin began his political career in 1904 when he was elected a city councillor for Ward 4. An important issue of the day was civic ownership of the electrical utility. Prowse had demonstrated his interest in the generation of electricity as early as 1902 when he was one of the applicants for the incorporation of the Commercial Lighting Company Limited. He seems to have been a supporter of a municipally owned power plant during the election of 1904 but not to have been one of its principal proponents. He eventually backed a settlement for lower rates from the private supplier. He was re-elected in 1906 – again, as in 1904, by a wide margin. These were relatively prosperous times in Charlottetown, and city government was able to make improvements to roads and to water and other services. This increased activity was generally applauded by the public and was linked in the press to the appearance of a better class of municipal political candidate. Prowse was elected mayor in 1908 following a campaign marked by some slanderous accusations on his part. After a term in which the *Patriot* noted that "the affairs of our city have been so successfully and economically managed . . . that there is no opening for criticism," Prowse declined to stand in 1910.

A year later, on 5 May 1911, Prowse was named to the Senate. The vacancy had existed for some time, and commentators focused on the appointee's young age. Some believed that the position had been initially intended for Lemuel, who had served as an MP from 1908, but that Sir Wilfrid Laurier*, perhaps anticipating a difficult federal general election, instead chose to elevate the less politically valuable brother. Although there is evidence to support this story, the press acknowledged that Benjamin was popular, successful, friendly, and politically loyal. Prowse was not particularly noteworthy as a senator, preferring to work quietly behind the scenes. He was credited with advancing the claims of the government of John Alexander Mathieson* for an increase in the province's federal subsidy in 1912 and with gaining tax benefits for Island car dealers in the 1920s.

Prowse had served as a member of the militia from 1878 to 1896, during which time he became a commissioned officer. He was also active in fraternal organizations and enjoyed outdoor pastimes such as bicycling (he rode competitively as a youth), fishing, and shooting. Admired for his "good fellowship and loyalty to his friends," he was regarded as frank and outspoken, with a dislike of cant and hypocrisy, and quietly generous in his charitable endeavours. He was raised a Methodist but seems not to have sought a role of religious leadership. His life, essentially modest, was constructive and successful and balanced the demands of family, business, and public service. He serves as an example of the kind of individual found at the foundations of Island, and Canadian, society in the late 19th and early 20th centuries.

PETER E. RIDER

[The genealogical records at the PARO (P.E.I. Geneal. Soc. coll., family files, Prowse family) provide many of the critical dates for Benjamin Prowse, as well as details concerning his second wife (MacMillan family file). Other collections there include the Prowse family file in the P.E.I. Museum and Heritage Foundation coll. (Acc. 3466, ser.73.100, no.15) and a biographical sketch in the Matheson papers (Acc. 3043/439–40).

Newspapers are important sources for events in Prowse's life. His first marriage was noted in the *Summerside Journal* (Summerside, P.E.I.) on 8 July 1886, his wife's death in the *Charlottetown Guardian* on 14 Feb. 1928, and his second marriage in the *Guardian* on 10 Jan. 1929, and with more extensive coverage, in the Charlottetown *Patriot* and the *Ottawa Citizen* of the same date. Prowse's obituary appeared in the *Guardian* and the *Patriot* on 24 Feb. 1930 and in "Notes by the way" in the *Guardian* the following day. Discussion of his appointment to the Senate may be found in the *Guardian* and the *Patriot* on 5 May 1911, and in the *Examiner* (Charlottetown) on 4 and 5 May 1911. A letter in the Laurier papers (LAC, MG 26, G: 159729–31) records L. E. Prowse's interest in the Senate appointment.

The Atlantic Canada newspaper survey database (available to subscribers on the Canadian Heritage Information Network website, administered through Communications Canada, Ottawa) contains numerous references to Prowse Brothers. The firm's day-book for 1885–86 is preserved at the PARO (Acc. 4327).

Details of Benjamin Prowse's activities in connection with the controversy over city lighting are found in the *Guardian* for 12 July 1904. This and other matters connected with his municipal political career are documented in the Records of the City of Charlottetown (PARO, RG 20), particularly in the council minutes, vols.12–13. Prowse's involvement with the incorporation of the Commercial Lighting Company is recorded in P.E.I., *Acts*, 1902, c.23. The issue of civic street lights is described in H. [T.] Holman, "'A lamp to light their paths': lighting the streets of Charlottetown," in *Gaslights, epidemics and vagabond cows: Charlottetown in the Victorian era*, ed. D. [O.] Baldwin and Thomas Spira (Charlottetown, 1988), 138–52. P.E.R.]

PUGSLEY, WILLIAM, lawyer, businessman, and politician; b. 27 Sept. 1850 in Sussex, N.B., son of William Pugsley and Frances Jane Hayward; m. first 6 Jan. 1876 Frances (Fannie) Jane Parks (d. 1914) in Saint John, and they had three sons and two daughters; m. secondly 1915 Gertrude Macdonald (d. 1963); they had no children; d. 3 March 1925 in Toronto.

William Pugsley was born in the village of Sussex on the Kennebecasis River in Kings County, N.B. He was of loyalist stock. A paternal ancestor had come from England to be one of the earliest settlers on the Croton River in the future state of New York. Pugsley's great-grandfather John Pugsley had fought on the side of the crown in the Revolutionary War and then left the United States to take up residence in the Hammond River valley in Kings County. His paternal grandfather, Daniel, settled in what became Cardwell Parish in the same county and his father, also William, was a farmer near Sussex.

Pugsley received his early education in the local school. At age 15 he left his home to enrol at the University of New Brunswick in Fredericton. He studied mathematics, classics, and English and was awarded many scholarships. In his junior year he was the gold medallist of his class. After three years of university he graduated in 1868 with an honours BA. In 1872 he was admitted to the bar and entered into partnership in Saint John with his brother Gilbert R. Pugsley and John Herbert Crawford. Pugsley was reporter for the New Brunswick Supreme Court for several years and also served as examiner in civil law for the university. The university awarded him a BCL in 1879 and would confer honorary degrees of DCL in 1884 and LLD in 1918. Pugsley was created a QC on 4 Feb. 1891. He built a large and prosperous practice in Saint John and was recognized as a leader of the bar. In 1904 he appeared for the province before the Judicial Committee of the Privy Council, the highest court of the empire, in an unsuccessful case contesting the dominion government's decision, following the 1901 census, to reduce representation in the House of Commons for all the old provinces except Quebec.

In business, Pugsley for some time was the owner-manager of the Saint John *Daily Telegraph* and the Saint John *Evening Times*. He was a principal of the Sussex Land and Stock Company, formed in 1884 to buy, lease, farm, and sell land in the North-West Territories, and was later a strong promoter of the Saskatoon and Western Land Company. A director of Black Consolidated Mines, he also had an interest in railways, including the Edmonton District Railway. For several years he was vice-president of the Qu'Appelle, Long Lake and Saskatchewan Railroad and Steamboat Company and in 1906 he became president. That same year he and his partners sold their rights to all the unclaimed crown land held by the company to David Russell and James Naismith Greenshields* of Montreal. They, in turn, soon sold the capital stock they owned in the company to William MACKENZIE and Donald Mann*, the promoters and builders of the Canadian Northern Railway. Pugsley also acquired and improved a number of commercial properties in Saint John and was a ceaseless advocate of harbour development there.

Pugsley was first elected to the provincial House of Assembly in an 1885 by-election following the death of a Kings County representative, Edwin Arnold Vail*. Re-elected in 1886 and 1890, he served as speaker of the assembly from 1887 to 1889, when Andrew George Blair*, the premier, appointed him solicitor general. In 1892 Pugsley resigned his seat to devote all his time to his law practice. He returned to provincial politics in the 1899 election, standing successfully again in Kings, and the following year, when Lemuel John Tweedie* became premier, he was made attorney general. He was a commanding figure in the rough-and-tumble of New Brunswick politics. Known for his "genial, mild manner," he was, an observer said, "the most imperturbable politician that ever came out of New Brunswick, or any other Province of Canada." To his friends and followers he was Sweet William; to his opponents he was Slippery Bill, a masterful tactician who frustrated them at every turn. Like Blair and Tweedie, Pugsley was of the generation of late-19th-century New Brunswick politicians who, earlier in their careers, had hesitated to align themselves firmly with either of the national parties. Pugsley was said to have backed Sir John A. Macdonald*'s party in the election of 1891, speaking for John Costigan*, a Conservative candidate, and denouncing the Liberals' platform of unrestricted reciprocity. But by the turn of the century Pugsley and the others had declared their allegiance to the Liberal party.

It was a strategic move for the New Brunswickers. The Liberals, in power since 1896, seemed invincible in national politics, Blair was a powerful member of Sir Wilfrid Laurier*'s cabinet, and the Laurier government held the keys to provincial prosperity. Shortly before the federal general election of 1904 Pugsley broke ranks with his former mentor, Blair, who strongly opposed Laurier's transcontinental railway policy. Pugsley believed that the new railway would open opportunities to advance Saint John's development. He told Laurier that the "building of the new Transcontinental line is so entirely in the interest of the country that I feel bound to give it my hearty support." There was a price for this support: the railway terminated at Moncton and Pugsley was lobbying hard to get a connection from there to Saint John so that it could become the freight terminus for the line. "St. John," he emphasized, "is very sensitive on this point." A year later Pugsley drafted the provincial legislation that enabled the New Brunswick government to buy out and take over the unsuccessful Central Railway. The opposition Tories were enraged. They dubbed the Central "Pugsley's sinkhole" and described it as "two streaks of rust connected by a few rotten ties." But for Pugsley the railway could be a building block in a link between Saint John and the Grand Trunk system, whose winter port had long been the city's hated rival, Portland, Maine. Again, in 1905, Pugsley strongly protested to Laurier against the federal government's intention to withdraw support for continuing steamship service between Saint John and the West Indies. It would be "a severe blow to the Party

here," he said. Laurier backed down, leaving the service in place "for the present."

In the provincial legislature the attorney general introduced several mildly progressive social reforms. A 1903 act provided compensation for injured workmen, though it was considered inadequate by labour leaders [see James Leonard SUGRUE]. The next year Pugsley proposed a bill to provide for inspection of factories, exclude labour there for boys and girls under 14, abolish the sweating system, and grant factory workers time off on legal holidays and Saturday afternoons. The measure was, however, withdrawn by the government in favour of a commission of inquiry. In 1906 he had a bill passed admitting women to practise law in New Brunswick on the same terms as men. Then, in 1907, Tweedie was named lieutenant governor of the province and Pugsley succeeded him as premier.

His tenure was brief. Soon after he took office, the Liberal MP for Saint John City and County, Alfred Augustus Stockton*, died and the seat was opened for a by-election. Urged to run, Pugsley resigned his provincial seat and the premiership at the end of May. It was not his first try at national politics. In the 1896 general election he and Daniel J. McLaughlin stood as independent candidates for Saint John to protest a decision a year earlier by George Eulas Foster*, the federal minister of finance, to subsidize Canadian mail steamers that made Portland, not Saint John, their final port of call. They lost. In 1904 Pugsley was involved in the "*La Presse* affair" [see Trefflé Berthiaume*] with David Russell, J. N. Greenshields, Hugh Graham* of the *Montreal Daily Star*, and others. It was a scheme to buy up Liberal newspapers before the general election that year and turn them against Laurier's government. The apparent aim of Russell and his associates was to undo Laurier's Grand Trunk Pacific Railway policy. If they could defeat Laurier, they thought, they could get a new Conservative government to appoint Blair, who had resigned from Laurier's cabinet in 1903 because he was opposed to the transcontinental, as minister of railways and canals. At the same time, hedging his bets in the event that Laurier did win, Russell began to promote Pugsley for a Liberal nomination and eventual appointment to Railways and Canals in a Laurier government. Russell may not have known that Pugsley strongly supported the Grand Trunk policy. It is also doubtful whether Pugsley knew all the twists and turns of Russell's complicated but naive scheme. When he found out, he hurried to Ottawa to reveal the plot to Laurier. That, at least, is what he later claimed had happened. In the end, Laurier forced Blair out of the election campaign and squashed the scheme; Pugsley failed even to get nominated.

Then, early in 1907 Laurier dismissed Henry Robert Emmerson*, New Brunswick's member in cabinet. Both George Robertson, one of the provincial members for Saint John City, and Alfred O. Skinner, president of the New Brunswick Liberal Association, urged Laurier to appoint Pugsley to replace him. Pugsley, Robertson assured Laurier, "will be able to unite every section of the liberal party in this province and lead them to victory at whatever time an election may be held." On 29 August Pugsley was made minister of public works in the Laurier government. The prime minister then learned that the mayor of Saint John, Edward Sears, was going to run against Pugsley in the necessary by-election and firmly squelched his ambitions. "I would urge upon you," he wrote, "the advisability of not giving the enemy the spectacle of division in our ranks." On 18 Sept. 1907 Pugsley was returned to the House of Commons by acclamation.

It was a heady time to be a cabinet minister in Ottawa. The nation was prosperous and building rapidly, with industrial expansion in the east and agricultural development on the prairies. The expenditure on public works more than doubled from $4.7 million in 1900–1 to $11.8 million in 1910–11. Most of the money was spent on harbour and river facilities, dredging, roads and bridges, and public buildings. Two new transcontinental railways were being built to promote growth on the prairies. Between 1901 and 1911 the number of acres under crops there grew from 3.6 million to 17.7 million and wheat production from 55.5 million to 132.1 million bushels. The explosive growth of the wheat and other grain crops created a huge demand for new ships and improved harbours and wharfs on the Great Lakes. Tonnage of cargo from the Lakehead passing through the Welland Canal, mostly grain for export, more than quadrupled. To handle the traffic, the list of harbour development projects undertaken by Pugsley's department on the inland seas grew ever larger during his term of office. The boom times also gave Pugsley a convenient rationale to promote harbour improvements in Saint John. The *Canadian annual review* reported that in the 1908 general election campaign he bragged to his constituents that he had secured $400,000 in Public Works expenditure for wharfs and port development in the city. In 1911, the year of the next general election, work underway there was boosted with another half million dollars for more improvements and the development of terminal facilities for the Grand Trunk Pacific. The grateful business interests of Saint John again returned Pugsley to Ottawa. But nationally, the Liberal party's "reciprocity" campaign was soundly defeated.

In opposition Pugsley and his New Brunswick colleague Frank Broadstreet CARVELL became the twin persecutors of Robert Laird Borden*'s government. While "Fighting Frank" Carvell's weapons were anger, vitriol, and the heavy blows of a broadsword, Pugsley's were the deft, surgical probings of a master courtroom lawyer, always calm, courteous, and reasonable but tactically brilliant and deadly. During the 1913 debate over Borden's Naval Aid Bill, Pugsley masterminded a 72-hour continuous attack against the proposal. The following year Pugsley was the only MP to question any provision of the emergency War Measures Bill. He warned that the suspension of habeas corpus was very dangerous and struck "at the dearest liberties of a British subject." Though a strong supporter of the war effort, Pugsley was a persistent critic of the government's war policy. Samuel HUGHES, the minister of militia and defence, Hughes's crony Lieutenant-Colonel John Wesley Allison, and Hughes's creation the Shell Committee were easy, frequent, and favourite targets. The *Debates* of 1915 are peppered with skirmishes between Pugsley and Hughes. In 1916 Pugsley began his prosecution of Hughes in the debate on the address. Then, on 14 March, he rose in late afternoon and spoke to dinner recess. When debate resumed in the evening, he continued for almost two more hours of devastating criticism of Hughes's, Allison's, and the committee's misdeeds and alleged corruption in the allocation of contracts for boots, binoculars, horses, rifle ammunition, shells, and on and on. Nor was that enough. Just days later he launched another spirited attack on Hughes. Hughes, aware that he was going to be a target that spring, had fled to England. Borden urgently telegraphed him to come home quickly. Hughes stubbornly refused but Pugsley's criticism forced a series of investigations and royal commissions that led to the replacement of the Shell Committee with the Imperial Munitions Board, and, late in 1916, Hughes's dismissal by Borden.

In May 1917 Sir Robert Borden announced that his government would bring in a bill to conscript young Canadians for overseas service. Pugsley rallied behind Laurier's vain attempt to delay and, if possible, defeat the Military Service Bill and the related effort by Borden to form a Union government of both Conservative and Liberal supporters of conscription. In October Pugsley knew that Carvell favoured conscription and was breaking with Laurier. He stayed and reassured his chief that "when happier times arrive, after the war is over, we may all come together again under your leadership." But Pugsley's continuing support of Laurier was costing him political capital at home. F. W. Pearson, acting warden of the Saint John County Council, warned that "the time has arrived when we should express to the Dominion Government our concurrence in any vigorous action that may be taken to secure more men for the defence of the Empire." At the same time Borden was confronted with the dilemma of whom to appoint to his Union government from New Brunswick. John Douglas Hazen*, an original member of Borden's cabinet, was the sitting minister. But naming a Liberal with conscriptionist sympathies such as Pugsley or Carvell would be a major coup. The Saint John Conservatives insisted they would have nothing of Pugsley. Carvell, who had the support of both parties in his Carleton County constituency, got the nod over the pained protests of several prominent New Brunswick Tories. After a plan to send Hazen to Washington as Canada's first diplomatic representative to the United States failed, the former minister of marine and fisheries accepted appointment as chief justice of New Brunswick. Then, on 31 October, the newly appointed lieutenant governor of New Brunswick, Gilbert White Ganong*, suddenly died. Borden approached Pugsley. On 2 November Pugsley informed Laurier that "under the peculiar circumstances now existing I have concluded to avail myself of an opportunity which now offers to retire from politics." Four days later Borden announced Pugsley's appointment as lieutenant governor.

Three years earlier, on 11 May 1914, Fannie Pugsley, William's wife of 38 years and the mother of his two surviving children, had died in Saint John. She had been in failing health since the previous autumn and her death was not unexpected. A year later, in 1915, Pugsley, at age 65, remarried. His second wife was Gertrude Macdonald, a woman from Saint John who lived in Ottawa and had been his private secretary when he was minister of public works. In 1917 they returned to New Brunswick to take up residence in the capital and perform the duties and social obligations of a provincial lieutenant governor. In 1921 Pugsley was asked to run once again as the Liberal candidate for Saint John in the federal general election. He refused. He served out his viceregal term and resigned at the end of February 1923. The following month William Lyon Mackenzie King*, the prime minister, appointed him to a royal commission investigating reparation claims following World War I. On 2 Nov. 1923 Pugsley was seriously ill and entered St Luke's Hospital in Ottawa. An operation followed and then a remarkably quick recovery of his health.

In late February 1925 Pugsley and his wife set out by train for western Canada where he was to continue his work for the reparations commission. They got as far as Toronto, where he was stricken with pneumonia

while staying at the King Edward Hotel. His son John Archer was summoned from New Brunswick but, when William seemed to be recovering at the end of February, he returned home. Then, suddenly, at 11:00 in the evening of 3 March 1925, with Gertrude at his side, Pugsley died. His funeral was on 7 March at St John's Anglican (Stone) Church in Saint John and he was buried there in Fernhill Cemetery.

William Pugsley was just four months shy of 40 years of public service when he died. Throughout his career he was an ardent champion of Saint John, the city he loved. He was no less an advocate of his home province and, like many of his generation, devoted in national politics to currying favours for it. Once aligned with the Liberal party he became a powerful lieutenant to its leader, an able minister of the crown, and a much-feared critic of Sir Robert Borden's government. Only when, as he saw it, the stakes for Canada and for its young men at the front were higher than the interests of the Liberal party did Pugsley abandon his leader and accept Borden's viceregal appointment. Mackenzie King, who gave Pugsley his last assignment, might have sympathized with Pugsley's choice to leave active politics: he too, in 1917, had wavered over conscription before casting his future with Laurier's Liberals.

ROBERT CRAIG BROWN

The main collections of primary material documenting Pugsley's career are held at the LAC: Sir Robert Laird Borden papers (MG 26, H), Sir Wilfrid Laurier papers (MG 26, G), and Department of Public Works fonds (RG 11). Useful newspapers are the *Daily Gleaner* (Fredericton), *Daily Telegraph* (Saint John), *Gazette* (Montreal), *Globe* (Toronto), *Morning Chronicle* (Halifax), *Ottawa Citizen*, *Ottawa Evening Journal*, *Saint John Globe*, *Telegram* (Toronto), *Telegraph-Journal* (Saint John), and *Toronto Daily Star*.

R. C. Brown, *Robert Laird Borden: a biography* (2v., Toronto, 1975–80). R. C. Brown and Ramsay Cook, *Canada, 1896–1921: a nation transformed* (Toronto, 1974). Can., Dominion Bureau of Statistics, *Canada year book* (Ottawa); House of Commons, *Debates*; Parl., *Sessional papers. Canadian annual rev.*, 1901–24/25. A. T. Doyle, *Front benches & back rooms: a story of corruption, muckraking, raw partisanship and intrigue in New Brunswick* (Toronto, 1976). H. G. Thorburn, *Politics in New Brunswick* (Toronto, 1961).

Q

QUIGLEY, HARRY STEPHEN, soldier, aviator, and businessman; b. 3 May 1888 in Toronto, son of Robert John Quigley, a businessman from New Jersey, and Annie Jane Primrose, who was born at Quebec; d.

unmarried 3 Jan. 1929 in Port of Spain (Republic of Trinidad and Tobago).

Harry Quigley, whose father was the founder of the American Watch Case Company of Canada, was raised in Toronto. His parents died prematurely, his mother in 1899 and his father three years later, leaving ten children, several of whom were still very young. Harry and his young brothers and sisters were raised by the eldest of the family, Lillian Primrose. Early in life he began working at various trades – as an accountant, real estate agent, and surveyor.

In 1914 Quigley was in Winnipeg, and when World War I broke out he enrolled in the army. He sailed for England with the 11th Infantry Battalion on 3 October. His courage was soon put to the test in action with the Royal Canadian Engineers (signal corps). He was wounded in the face in May 1915, very likely at the battle of Ypres, and was awarded the Distinguished Conduct Medal. The following January he was promoted lieutenant and in August 1916 he was decorated with the Military Cross. On hearing that the Royal Flying Corps was looking for officers who knew Morse code for its observation units, he obtained a transfer on 30 October and served as an observer with the 9th Squadron and other units. He later learned to fly and in May 1917 he was made a captain. He was serving with the Royal Air Force when the war ended. From his letters to his sister Lillian, it appears that he had persuaded his younger brother Francis Grainger to obtain a transfer to the Royal Air Force as well. Francis was one of the great Canadian aces of World War I, shooting down 34 enemy aircraft. Sadly, just before he was due to return to Canada, he contracted Spanish influenza and he died in 1918, with Harry at his bedside.

Harry put aside his uniform in July 1919, but the battles had left their mark. His experience in the trenches had left him in a state of depression, with a constant nervous tremor, except when stress-related adrenaline provided a stimulant. Like many aviators, he also suffered from partial deafness. Despite the state of his health, his love of flying led him to undertake a new career in the emerging field of civil aviation.

Quigley had some dealings with the Air Board, a federal agency created in June 1919. Its many objectives included the establishment of an aerial forest-patrol and aerial cartography service for the provinces. However, the agency soon became entangled in petty political wrangling, which Quigley found distasteful. Since Price Brothers and Company Limited, located in the Saguenay–Lac-Saint-Jean region [see Sir William PRICE], set up an air service for the same purposes in 1920, he applied for a position and was appointed its chief pilot. Quigley and his team carried on their work from Chicoutimi using two Martinsyde seaplanes. At the end of 1922 Price decided to contract out this operation and Quigley, in order to be in the running, founded the Dominion Aerial Exploration Company. Price, and later the Quebec government, hired him to provide forest-protection, transportation, and photographic services in the Lac-Saint-Jean region and on the north shore of the St Lawrence. Quigley had up to 20 employees in all, including half a dozen pilots and mechanics. He owned two HS-2L seaplanes at the outset, and regularly bought new aircraft; by 1928 he would have five HS-2L seaplanes and two Fairchild monoplanes. In 1926 he moved his main base of operations from Chicoutimi to Trois-Rivières, which was more central and afforded better prospects for contracts. At that time he changed the company's name to Canadian Airways Limited (not to be confused with the company of the same name owned by James Armstrong Richardson*, who in 1930 would buy part of the assets formerly held by Quigley).

Quigley was also a pioneer in the field of air mail. In 1926 one of his seaplanes picked up some mail tied up in a water-tight package and attached to a lifebuoy, which had been thrown overboard from the *Empress of Scotland* off Anticosti Island. After a stop in Rimouski, the package was delivered in Montreal. Because of the many risks involved, this arrangement was soon abandoned. In September 1927 Quigley carried out new experiments for the Post Office Department, but this time the mail was unloaded from a transatlantic liner at the pilot station in Pointe-au-Père and taken westward from there by air. The following year Quigley won the contract to deliver air mail on the Montreal–Toronto line. (A competitor had already obtained the connection to the east.) From then on carrying mail became one of his main activities, and he moved his operations to Pointe-aux-Trembles (Montreal).

Quigley sold his interest in Canadian Airways Limited in October 1928 because his health was deteriorating. He went to the islands of Trinidad and Tobago in hopes of recovery, but died in Port of Spain on 3 January of the following year. His funeral service was held in Toronto.

Harry Quigley came to the world of aviation through the fortunes of war, and he found there a new, adventure-filled life. He defended his country with outstanding zeal and applied the same energy to developing air services for the people of Canada. Despite the brevity of his career, he managed to leave his mark as a pioneer in Canadian civil aviation.

YVES TREMBLAY

Can., Dept. of National Defence, National Defence Headquarters, Directorate of Hist. and Heritage (Ottawa), Canadians in the British flying service, 1914–18, 77/661; Victor Tremblay, "M. Harry Quigley" (typescript, 1961). LAC, RG 150, Acc. 1992–93/166. Private arch., Mrs Joan Page (Waterdown, Ont.), Geneal. of the Quigley family; corr. between H. S. Quigley and his sister Lillian Primrose. Can., Dept. of National Defence, *Report on civil aviation* (Ottawa), 1923–30. F. H. Ellis, *Canada's flying heritage* (Toronto, 1954), 161–62, 239, 313–14, 364. G. A. Mackie, "Aviation suffers severe loss in death of Capt. H. S. Quigley," *Illustrated Canadian Forest and Outdoors* (Montreal), 25 (1929): 51.

Larry Milberry, *Air transport in Canada* (2v., Toronto, 1997), 1. K. M. Molson, *Pioneering in Canadian air transport* ([Winnipeg], 1974). *The official history of the Royal Canadian Air Force* (3v. to date, [Toronto and Ottawa], 1980–), 1; 2. [G. J.] Whitehouse, *Heroes of the sunlit sky* (Garden City, N.Y., 1967), 230–31.

QUINLAN, ANNE, teacher; b. 7 June 1839 in County Tipperary (Republic of Ireland), daughter of William Quinlan and Susan Medill; d. unmarried 18 Feb. 1923 in Chatham, N.B.

Anne Quinlan was the daughter of a Roman Catholic shoemaker and his wife who immigrated from Ireland when she was a child and settled in Chatham. It was then the most populous town in northern New Brunswick and had many residents of Irish extraction. She was educated in its common schools, which were co-educational and non-denominational. One school she attended in the early 1850s was conducted by Davis P. Howe, an independent-minded man of Methodist background from Tipperary. In contrast to most other teachers, he refrained from birching or using other forms of corporal punishment; instead he promoted self-discipline and orderly competition. He encouraged his pupils to respect the learning environment and was one of the few teachers in Chatham who staged money-raising events for their schools.

The experience with Howe may have helped Anne Quinlan decide to become a teacher. In 1856, in her mid teens, she enrolled in the training school in Saint John. The program lasted three months and led to a second-class licence. By February 1857 she was teaching in Chatham. She brought enthusiasm, intelligence, artistic talent, and professionalism to her work and was soon one of the town's most respected educators. Her success may explain why she sometimes had as many as 60 pupils in her classroom. The authorities would not usually divide a class or provide an assistant, so for many years, to make the job manageable, her younger sister Susan helped her on a voluntary basis.

The formation in 1860 of the Catholic diocese of Chatham and the selection of James Rogers* as bishop had a direct impact on education there. Soon after his installation Rogers launched St Michael's Academy for boys, which stimulated public interest in a parallel institution for girls. Because resources were limited, Rogers was unable to act immediately, but in 1862 Anne Quinlan received permission to conduct a school in the Catholic Temperance Hall. Sometimes referred to as St Michael's Female Academy, this de facto Catholic school was officially a common school. When the customary public examinations took place, Chatham's school trustees participated along with the bishop, parents, and others. The compromise the academy represented was mutually beneficial: the trustees were spared the necessity of providing space, and

since Anne Quinlan, as a licensed teacher, was compensated by the province, the diocese was relieved of the cost. All were satisfied with her performance. The Chatham *Gleaner* reported in 1862 that she ran a "very superior" school and in 1865, following a public examination, that "too much praise cannot be given" to the work she was doing with her sister's assistance. Gratitude was also expressed for the musical concerts they staged.

A turning point came in 1871 with the introduction of New Brunswick's Common Schools Act [*see* George Edwin King*], which effectively provided for free, non-sectarian schooling and abolished public support of denominational schools. Catholics objected strenuously but once the act had been proclaimed, Rogers advised that private means should be found for Catholic education. To this end he invited Montreal's Religious Hospitallers of St Joseph, who had established a hospital in Chatham in 1869, to open a girls' school there. After some hesitation they agreed, and they engaged Anne Quinlan to help organize a convent school. St Michael's Academy opened on 2 Oct. 1871 with an enrolment of 30. Although Sister Cesarine Raymond was its designated directress, "Miss Quinlan," whether described as a teacher, head teacher, or principal, was in charge during the 1870s and 1880s. The academy was primarily a day school, but boarders were admitted from the start, and the number of students in each category grew rapidly, reaching more than 200 in total by the late 1880s. In addition to the usual academic subjects, musical and theatrical performance was featured in the curriculum, and the principal was responsive to external requests for special services she and her pupils could provide. They often took part in church events, and when Governor General Lord Dufferin [Blackwood*] visited Chatham in July 1873, the girls provided the "musical and literary entertainment." In the view of the Chatham *Gleaner,* their presentation proved that it was no longer necessary to send young ladies abroad to obtain "a thorough and polite education." In 1877 David George Smith, the Methodist editor of the *Miramichi Advance,* concurred with the community that Miss Quinlan was a highly intelligent teacher and "a lady of no ordinary culture." Even the priests of the diocese sometimes sought her assistance in drafting addresses they had been asked to deliver.

Anne Quinlan had upgraded her teaching credentials at an early date. For many years she was the only member of the St Michael's staff to hold a first-class licence. When an "advanced department" was created around 1880, she became its head, with Sister Margaret Carter as her assistant. She took an interest in the professional development of colleagues in her school and in the public schools of the town and county. For a time in the 1880s she was one of the five members of the management committee of the Northumberland

County Teachers' Institute, which arranged in-service training.

In 1888 Anne Quinlan was still at St Michael's, along with six other teachers (three lay and three religious). However, owing to the onset of an unspecified but "incapacitating infirmity," she soon retired, at around the age of 50. Though her state of health prevented her from ever occupying a full-time position again, it did not render her completely inactive. In 1896 she was appointed to the first Board of School Trustees of the newly incorporated town of Chatham, and she served until 1900. She continued as well to teach privately, in her home and at the Hôtel-Dieu hospital, where she resided for many years prior to her death in 1923. In her obituary in the Chatham *World*, she was described as a woman of "singular nobility of character." Possessed of a "truly Christian spirit," she had accepted with cheerful resignation the limitations her illness had imposed over a span of more than 30 years.

W. D. HAMILTON

Arch. du Diocèse de Bathurst, N.-B., Groupe II/1-1–119 (fonds James Rogers) (mfm. at PANB, MC290, F7652–58).

LAC, RG 31, C1, 1851, 1861, 1871, 1881, 1891, 1901, Chatham, N.B. PANB, RS8, F6777, education, warrants to teachers and inspectors, 1856–59; RS141C5, F18927, no.024755; RS655, petition of Susan Quinlan, 1 March 1866. St Michael's Church (Miramichi, N.B.), Church records. *Gleaner* (Chatham), 24 March 1851; 19 May 1860; 22 Feb., 29 Nov. 1862; 1 Oct. 1864; 8 April, 30 Sept. 1865; 19 July 1873. *Miramichi Advance* (Chatham), 15 Nov. 1877, 1 May 1879, 10 Sept. 1896. *Miramichi Press* (Chatham), 9 July 1969. *North Shore Leader* (Newcastle, N.B.), 23 Feb. 1923. *Union Advocate* (Newcastle), 8 Oct. 1884, 20 Dec. 1899, 31 Jan. 1900. *World* (Chatham), 22 April, 1 Nov. 1882; 22 Oct. 1887; 21 Feb. 1923. *Directory*, New Brunswick, 1865/66. J. A. Fraser, *By favourable winds: a history of Chatham, New Brunswick* ([Chatham], 1975). W. D. Hamilton, *Dictionary of Miramichi biography; biographical sketches of men and women born before 1900 who played a part in public life on the Miramichi: Northumberland County, New Brunswick, Canada* (Saint John, 1997). K. F. C. MacNaughton, *The development of the theory and practice of education in New Brunswick, 1784–1900: a study in historical background*, ed. A. G. Bailey (Fredericton, 1947). N.B., Dept. of Education, *Annual report* (Fredericton). *125 years on the Miramichi: the Religious Hospitallers of St. Joseph, 1869–1994* ([Chatham, 1994]; copy in St Michael's Museum and Geneal. Centre, Miramichi).

R

RAYMOND, WILLIAM ODBER, Church of England clergyman and historian; b. 3 Feb. 1853 in Lower Woodstock, N.B., son of Charles William Raymond and Elizabeth Mary Carman; m. 18 June 1879 Julia Nelson in Saint John, and they had a son and a daughter; d. at midnight 23–24 Nov. 1923 in Toronto.

William Odber Raymond's childhood associations shaped many features of his psychic terrain and his historical interests. Physically, Lower Woodstock lay in a beautiful region distinguished by broad intervale land abutting the Saint John River and graced by tall American elms. Historically, it contained the site of a Maliseet stockade, located at the start of the ancient Amerindian travel route to Passamaquoddy Bay, where the French had established a chapel in 1717 [*see* Jean-Baptiste Loyard*]. Towards the end of the 18th century, Woodstock formed the uppermost point of the original loyalist settlement in the Saint John valley. In religious terms, the neighbourhood was the site of an early New England Company school for native children and a Church of England mission under Frederick Dibblee*. Here Raymond was reared, the product of an extensive connection of Connecticut loyalists who had dominated the legal, religious, administrative, and militia affairs of the region for two generations after settlement, and even in the mid 19th century retained a veneer of public influence and social gentility. Raymond's father, a farmer who was also a militia colonel, lay reader, musician, builder of houses, windmills, and churches, and craftsman of ecclesiastical furniture, personified this *ancien régime*. Raymond himself became its historian.

After graduating in mathematics and science in 1876 with the University of New Brunswick's first honours BA (an earned MA would follow in 1891), he commenced theological study under Bishop John Medley* of Fredericton, who ordained him deacon at the end of 1877 and priest in 1878. Although fragile in health, Raymond passed the first six years of his ministry at the rural mission of Stanley, with occasional forays into lumber camps on the Taxis and Southwest Miramichi rivers. Then in 1884 he took charge of the newly established St Mary's Church in Saint John, where he served for more than three decades.

In the liturgical minefield that was late-19th-century Saint John Anglicanism, Raymond was an uncontroversial recruit to the evangelical cause. Spare and ascetic-looking, he tackled the needs of his rather poor city parish with energy, and in numbers, finances, and building projects it flourished. If the year 1903–4 may be taken as representative, Raymond's ministry embraced many turn-of-the-century Protestant social concerns. He presided at a public meeting to establish a kindergarten for the children of working-class mothers, and soon one was operating in the St Mary's church hall; as president of the Evangelical Alliance, he campaigned for church union and against profanation of the sabbath; he promoted compulsory education and opposed jailing girls for minor offences. In 1908, after fellow city rector John Andrew Richardson* became bishop of Fredericton, he made Raymond archdeacon of Saint John. Prior to his ordination, Raymond had been an ardent member of Woodstock's volunteer artillery. So he took special satisfaction when the St Mary's brass band enlisted en masse during World War I and became the regimental band for the Princess Patricia's Canadian Light Infantry. Vocational success and civic prominence did not bring financial prosperity, however. The Raymonds made ends meet only through the wife's painting lessons and the husband's "literary" productions.

Already in the mid 1860s the juvenile Raymond had been writing prize essays on the history of his neighbourhood, based on interviews with older residents. Years later his first publications were sketches of the loyalist settlements of Kingston (1889) and Woodstock (1891), produced for Anglican parish centennials. Then he turned his MA thesis on the loyalists into a more substantial pamphlet, focusing on the revolution rather than the period of exile. Occasionally, these early publications make the loyalists a text for sermonizing against a "utilitarian" approach to life or for nodding favourably towards imperial federation. At first, Raymond did not refrain from "improving" documentary quotations in a manner common to historical writers of his time. However, in the main he distanced himself from overwrought partisanship, such as he found in the loyalist writings of James Hannay*, and eventually he deplored even the modernization of spelling.

Beginning in the early 1890s, Raymond gained access to the 18th-century manuscript collections that became the basis for his foundational contributions to Maritime historiography, notably the papers of Edward Winslow*, James White, and Ward Chipman* Sr. None was held in a public repository. Indeed, it was from his son's playmates that he purchased documents on the New England Company's outreach to Micmacs (Mi'kmaq) [see Oliver Arnold*] and the sole surviving copy of the Fort Howe treaty of 1778. In a rubbish heap he spotted revolutionary muster rolls and letters on the clamorous politics of loyalist Saint John. Pressed by pastoral duties, Raymond could not aim to turn out book-length monographs. Instead, he wrote literally hundreds of "sketches" and "glimpses" and "incidents" for the press, while making the *Collections* of the New Brunswick Historical Society, the *New Brunswick Magazine,* and *Acadiensis,* all of Saint John, vehicles for documentary editions and essays. Still authoritative are his works on the pre-loyalist settlement of Saint John Harbour from the papers of James Simonds* (1896) and James White (1897, 1899), on pre-loyalist townships in the Saint John valley (1905), on Alexander McNutt* and Planter settlement in peninsular Nova Scotia (1911–12), on loyalist regiments in the revolution (1904), on Benjamin Marston* and the founding of loyalist Port Roseway (Shelburne, N.S.) (1907, 1909), and on Thomas Carleton* (1905, 1914). He collected some of his newspaper articles into an unsatisfactory volume on Saint John valley history in 1905, soon revised and reissued as *The River St. John* (1910).

William Odber Raymond would come to be identified as the quintessential historian of the loyalist generation in New Brunswick. That reputation rests on his massive edition of the *Winslow papers* (1901), a volume that is far more than a cornerstone of Canadian loyalist studies. The vivid world of Edward Winslow and his circle remains the lens through which historians persist in viewing early New Brunswick. Raymond himself was reluctant to take seriously the concerns of those who dissented from this elitist vision, and despite a revolution in loyalist studies pioneered by Esther Clark* Wright's demographic work in the 1950s, most of his academic successors fare no better.

By 1915 the often waspish William Cochrane Milner* could write of Raymond, "No man in Canada has done better work for the country in [the] historical line than he has and got less for it." At Christmas the same year Raymond's health gave way under the strain of war work as chaplain to the 3rd Regiment of Canadian Artillery on Partridge Island in Saint John Harbour. He soon resigned his rectorship and left Saint John to be near his children in Michigan, Vancouver, and finally Toronto. His last letter to his old comrade William Francis Ganong* enjoins a "short" obituary for the Royal Society of Canada (to which he had been elected in 1906); depressed in spirit, he could see only the flaws in his historical labours. But because his academic successors would abandon concern with the native peoples, the French era, and military conflict as old-fashioned, much of Raymond's work on those subjects endures as the authority of first resort. His obituarist for the Royal Society of Canada in 1924 lamented that his passing had left a gap in the world of New Brunswick historiography that no other could fill. So it proved. It would not be until the 1950s that the province found, in William Stewart MacNutt*, another master of the historian's craft. In a sense, however, there never was a successor to William Odber Raymond, the last and best exemplar of the now-superseded genus of historian-amateur. As a collector and editor of documents, his contribution to Maritime historiography is unsurpassed.

D. G. BELL

Reader

[A reliable, convenient source for information about William Odber Raymond's life is the brief, self-effacing autobiographical sketch he included in his *Ancestry of the family of William Odber Raymond, A.D. 1630–1920*, prepared and indexed by R. W. Hale ([Woodstock, N.B., 1983]). Also valuable is the obituary in RSC, *Trans.*, 3rd ser., 18 (1924), proc.: vii–ix. Most of Raymond's transcription books are in LAC, MG 23, D1, ser.1. The L. P. Fisher Library, in Woodstock, has one in its Raymond coll., along with a large portion of Raymond's working library. On departing Saint John in 1916, he deposited his 12 scrapbooks of personal and historical materials with what is now the Saint John Regional Library. A few of Raymond's letters are gathered as S 98–S 98A (Raymond, William Odber coll.) at the N.B. Museum (Saint John); more important ones are in the same institution's W. F. Ganong fonds. W. C. Milner's letter concerning Raymond's historical work, dated 16 Oct. 1915, is in LAC, RG 37, 18. D.G.B.]

Raymond is probably best known for his edition of *Winslow papers, A.D. 1776–1826* (Saint John, 1901). He also wrote *United Empire Loyalists* ([Saint John?, 1893?]). Many of his articles were published in the N.B. Hist. Soc., *Coll.* (Saint John). These include: "Loyalists in arms: a short account of the 'provincial troops' – otherwise known as British American regiments or loyalists corps – that served on the side of the king during the war of the American revolution, A.D. 1775–1783," 2 (1899–1905), no.5: 189–223; "A sketch of the life and administration of General Thomas Carleton, first governor of New Brunswick," 2, no.6: 439–80; "Benjamin Marston of Marblehead, loyalist: his trials and tribulations during the American revolution," 3 (1907–14), no.7: 79–112; "Brigadier General Monckton's expedition to the River Saint John in September, 1758: the beginning of the first permanent settlement of the English on the shores of the St. John harbor: story of old Fort Frederick," 3, no.8: 113–65; and "The founding of Shelburne: Benjamin Marston at Halifax, Shelburne and Miramichi," 3, no.8: 204–77. Raymond also edited several articles for the same publication: "Letters written at Saint John by James Simonds, A.D. 1764–1785," 1 (1894–97), no.2: 160–86; "Selections from the papers and correspondence of James White, esquire, A.D. 1762–1783," 1, no.3: 306–40; "The James White papers continued, A.D. 1781–1788," 2, no.4: 30–72; and "Old townships on the River St. John: papers relating to the St. John's River Society," 2, no.6: 302–57.

Raymond contributed three articles to *Canada and its provinces; a history of the Canadian people and their institutions . . .*, ed. Adam Shortt and A. G. Doughty (23v., Toronto, 1913–17). These are "The Acadian settlements and early history, 1604–1713," 13: 15–66; "New Brunswick: general history, 1758–1867," 13: 127–210; and "New Brunswick: political history, 1867–1912," 14: 403–31.

Raymond published two articles in RSC, *Trans.*, 3rd ser.: "Colonel Alexander McNutt and the pre-loyalist settlements of Nova Scotia," 5 (1911), sect.II: 23–115; 6 (1912), sect.II: 201–15; and "The first governor of New Brunswick and the Acadians of the River Saint John," 8 (1914), sect.II: 415–52. With William Quintard Ketchum, he wrote *Proceedings at the centennial commemoration of the ordination of Rev. Frederick Dibblee* (Saint John, 1891). Collections of some of Raymond's newspaper articles were published in two editions: *Glimpses of the past: history of the River St. John, A.D. 1604–1784* (Saint John, 1905) and *The River St. John: its physical features, legends and history from 1604 to 1784* (Saint John, 1910; abridged ed., ed. J. C. Webster, Sackville, N.B., 1943).

In addition to researching and writing about the history of New Brunswick, Raymond also assisted other historians by editing their work. This is apparent in at least three publications: Walter Bates, *Kingston and the loyalists of the "spring fleet" of A.D. 1783, with reminiscenses of early days in Connecticut: a narrative . . .*, ed. W. O. Raymond (Saint John, 1889; repr. Fredericton, 1980); J. W. Lawrence, *The judges of New Brunswick and their times*, ed. A. A. Stockton and [W. O. Raymond] (Saint John, 1907; repr., intro. D. G. Bell, Fredericton, 1983 [i.e. 1985]); and Peter Fisher, *Sketches of New Brunswick*, notes by W. O. Raymond (Woodstock, 1921).

Daily Telegraph (Saint John), 23 April 1900. *Saint John Globe*, 5 Nov. 1903; 21, 31 Oct. 1904. *St. John Daily Sun* (Saint John), 6 Jan., 25 June, 22 Oct., 7 Dec. 1903; 21 Oct. 1904. D. G. Bell, *Early loyalist Saint John: the origin of New Brunswick politics, 1783–1786* (Fredericton, 1983); "The writings of W. O. Raymond," *New Brunswick Hist. Journal* ([Saint John]), spring 1991. T. R. Millman and A. R. Kelley, *Atlantic Canada to 1900: a history of the Anglican Church* (Toronto, 1983).

READER, JOSEPH, Church of England missionary, Plymouth Brethren evangelist, Indian agent, and author; b. 3 Dec. 1849 in Chilvers Coton (Nuneaton), England, son of William Reader and Mary Ann Hill; m. there 21 April 1874 Marianne Crabb (d. 1924), and they had two sons and one daughter; d. 22 Feb. 1928 in Enderby, B.C.

Little is known of Joseph Reader's early life in England. He attended the Church Missionary Society College in Islington (London) from 1871 to 1874 in preparation for the mission field. On 12 May 1874, three weeks after his wedding, he and his wife, along with William Carpenter Bompas*, the newly ordained bishop of Athabasca, and other Church of England missionaries, sailed from Liverpool. After arriving at New York on 24 May, the party took a train to Fargo (N.Dak.) and a steamer to Winnipeg.

On 11 June 1874 Reader was ordained deacon by Robert Machray*, the bishop of Rupert's Land, in St John's Cathedral, Winnipeg. Soon after, he left for a mission in the Touchwood Hills (Sask.). He returned to Winnipeg the next year and was ordained priest on 16 May 1875. During his rounds preaching to natives, Reader acted as witness to the adhesions of Saulteaux to Treaty No.4 at the Qu'Appelle (The Fishing) Lakes (Sask.) in September. He served the Cree, Assiniboin, Saulteaux, and occasionally the Sioux in the Touchwood Hills until 1880, when the Church Missionary Society transferred him to Devon mission at The Pas (Man.), where the native population was mainly Cree. While there, he became disenchanted with the Church of England and began to question its tenets. Through William Augustus Austin, a surveyor, he learned of the Plymouth Brethren, a fundamentalist millenarian sect, and became attracted to its teachings. On 2 April 1883 he resigned his post as a matter of religious conscience; Machray consequently revoked his licence to officiate as a minister of the Church of England on 9 August.

Soon after his resignation, the deputy superintendent general of the Department of Indian Affairs, Lawrence Vankoughnet, hired Reader as Indian agent for The Pas. He moved to a home and agency office he built at Oonikup (Prospector), near The Pas. To visit each community under his responsibility required about 500 miles of travel. During his years as agent he attempted to spread the beliefs of the Brethren even while he fulfilled his official duties. He attended gatherings of the Brethren and would receive funding from assemblies as far away as London and Los Angeles. Of limited success in his proselytization, he would record 58 baptisms during the period 1898 to 1927. In addition, he translated parts of the Bible into Cree. In 1890 he had imported a printing press and had begun to produce almanacs, primers, and religious material in Cree as well as in English. The Department of Indian Affairs published his Cree and English primer in 1891 and would still distribute it on request 30 years later.

In 1888 the Reverend John Hines, a Church of England missionary, had been appointed to Devon mission. He and Reader travelled to the same native reserves and competed for the same souls. In 1890 Hines wrote to the bishop of Saskatchewan, William Cyprian Pinkham, and then to the Department of Indian Affairs in an attempt to curtail Reader's evangelistic efforts. He claimed that Reader abused his assumed spiritual authority. Branding Reader a heretic, he identified him as the cause of degeneration on the reserves. In addition, he argued that Reader misused his temporal influence as agent, enticing natives to leave the Church of England. The fact that one of Reader's sons had a trading post next to the Indian agency he saw as a conflict of interest and he complained about the perception among the natives that Reader favoured supporters of the Plymouth Brethren with more rations and better supplies. In 1893 the department sided with Reader, defending the right of agents to express such "views on religious matters as the light they possess and their own consciences commend to them as correct." The department believed Reader to be above reproach. It supported him again in 1895, explaining that his "veracity is above question," after a trader filed a complaint charging intimidation and discrimination. The reason Reader left his job as agent in 1898 is unknown.

In 1903 Joseph Reader and his family returned to the Touchwood Hills, where he farmed and continued his ministry. He moved to British Columbia to live with his daughter after his wife's death in 1924 and he died there four years later.

PETER DUECK

Joseph Reader is the author of a manuscript (Sask. Arch. Board (Regina), R-E 3260) that was published as *Brief experiences among the Prairie and Wood Indians of Saskatchewan from 1874 to 1903* (Punnichy, Sask., 1916), and of *The divine mystery; or, the babe that lay in the manger: an answer to modern criticism of the divinity of . . . Jesus Christ* (London, 1924; repr. Niagara-on-the-Lake, Ont., [1980]). He wrote or compiled numerous works in English and Cree and printed many of them himself. Among them are *First reading book for school and families* (Oonikup [Prospector], Man., 1890) [English and Cree in parallel columns]; *Indian child's book: a primer in English and Cree languages* (Ottawa, [1891?]); *Cree almanack/Naheyowawe pesimoo mussinuhikun* (Oonikup), 1891–99 [text in Cree]; *Nikumoowina* (Oonikup, [1891]) [hymnal in Cree syllabic characters], and *Pesimoo mussinuhikun* (Oonikup, [1899?]) [pamphlet in Cree syllabics]. In addition, he translated and printed *The Epistle to the Romans, in the Cree language/Oo mussinuhumakoowinewow Romanuk, naheyowawe keswawinik* (Oonikup, 1897) and *The Epistle to the Galatians in Cree syllabic characters* (Oonikup, [1899]).

AM, HBCA, B.324/a/1–2; B.324/e/4. LAC, RG 10, 3566, file 82, pt.31; 3622, file 4945; 3805, file 51174; 3816, file 56941; 3858, file 80942; 3943, file 121698-28; 6240, file 526-1; RG 31, C1, 1891, Carrot River, [Sask.], and Lake Winnipeg, [Man.], dist.200; 1901, The Pas, [Man.], dist.205, subdiv.43. Private arch., Peter Dueck (Winnipeg), Corr. concerning Joseph Reader; interview with Phil Reader (The Pas), 31 Jan. 2002; May Reader (The Pas), family recollections; Joseph Reader, "The Lord's work: account, 1908–1912" (MS, n.d.). Univ. of Birmingham Library, Special Coll. (Birmingham, Eng.), Church Missionary Soc. Arch., C.1/O (original letters, journals, and papers, incoming), Joseph Reader (mfm. at AM). *The Pas Herald and Mining News*, 18 Jan. 1924, 2 March 1928. Church Missionary Soc., *Register of missionaries (clerical, lay & female), and native clergy, from 1804 to 1904* ([London?, 1905?]). John Hines, *The Red Indians of the plains: thirty years' missionary experience in the Saskatchewan* (Toronto, 1916). Phil Reader, *Oonikup: memoirs of Phil Reader* (The Pas, 1999). Nan Shipley, "Printing press at Oonikup," *Beaver*, outfit 291 (1960–61), no.1: 48–53.

REGIER, PETER, farmer and Mennonite bishop; b. 14 Jan. 1851 in Kalteherberge (Świerznica, Poland), son of Peter Regier and Maria Wiebe; m. first 16 Dec. 1873 Anna Enss (d. 1914), and they had seven daughters and five sons; m. secondly 3 Feb. 1916 in Tiefengrund, Sask., Katharina Wiens, widow of Heinrich Bahnmann and Abraham Dyck; they had no children; d. there 11 April 1925.

The Regiers were an old Mennonite family in West Prussia. Born and raised on the delta of the Vistula (Wisła) River near Danzig (Gdańsk, Poland), Peter Regier became knowledgeable about dyking and raising crops in productive soil that had once been swampland. He began attending school at Altebabke in 1857; in 1863 he transferred to the Rector School at Tiegenhof, east of Danzig. He left two years later since his help was sorely needed on the family farm. In June 1867 his Anabaptist heritage guided him into joining the Fürstenwerder Mennonite Church, where his father was the elder (bishop).

Despite the promises of the Prussian government that Mennonites would be exempt from military service, Regier was drafted in 1872, during the Franco-German War. After two years of service he returned home, bought land at Rückenau in the Elbing (Elbląg) area near Danzig, and began to farm on his own. On 7 Sept. 1879 he was elected as teacher-deacon in the church of the Rosenort group of Mennonites at Rückenau. Ordained teacher-pastor on 18 July 1880, he was elected elder of the Rosenort Church, Elbing District, on 30 Jan. 1887. By 1893 his workload had become oppressive, the economic future of his children lay in doubt, and friends in North America beckoned him to emigrate.

Confident that "God would show the way," the Regiers departed from their home in West Prussia on 8 June 1893 and arrived in the Canadian west, at Gretna, Man., on 1 July. Leaving his family with new friends, who were Bergthaler Mennonites, Peter toured the country as far as Calgary and Edmonton. In exchange for information on the suitability of land for agriculture and settlement, he had free use of the facilities of the Canadian Pacific Railway. He himself purchased S½-18-44-4-W3, in the Saskatchewan River valley southwest of Prince Albert (Sask.), and established a home and farming operation, which became the focal point of a settlement he called Tiefengrund (deep ground). Comprised of relatives and others who joined him in the ensuing years, it developed into a thriving colony of predominantly Mennonite immigrants. In 1896 Regier, always a firm believer in the education of children by competent teachers, initiated the formation of the Tiefengrund Public School District, No.471, and he would serve as its chairman (1896–98) and secretary-treasurer (1899–1900). His log residence was the schoolhouse for several years.

The deeply ingrained spiritual convictions of the settlers dictated as well that an organized congregation be formed. Being an elder, Regier created the Rosenort Church in 1894, and within that body he fostered the formation of several local congregations in the area around Tiefengrund. The first church-house was built in 1896 at Eigenheim, west of Rosthern, where some Mennonite families had settled in 1891. The church at Tiefengrund was erected in 1910. Regier worked unceasingly, travelling by horse and buggy in the summer and by sleigh in the winter, to visit, instruct, and unify widely separated families. The isolation of the Mennonites, on the land and within the mélange of settlers who poured into the west, posed the threat of assimilation and the loss of Anabaptist principles, fates that Regier steadfastly tried to prevent.

Because of the influx of immigrants from all backgrounds into Saskatchewan at the turn of the century, there was also a strong interest in integrating the Rosenort fellowship with other Mennonite congregations, especially those of Manitoba Bergthaler affiliation [see Johann Funk*; Gerhard Wiebe*]. To achieve unity Regier, the progressive visionary but "a weak servant of God," as he regarded himself, organized the historic "Garden Assembly" of Rosenort and Bergthaler delegates in his garden at Tiefengrund on 18 July 1902. The meeting initiated an integration of the articles of faith, principles, and purposes of both religious groups. This collaboration was ratified through the formation of the Konferenz der Mennoniten in Mittlern Kanada (Conference of Mennonites in Middle Canada) on 20–21 July 1903 at the Bergthaler Brethren Church in Hochstadt, Man.

At his request Regier was replaced as elder in 1913 by David Toews. He worked with Toews for some time, and preached his last sermon on 29 Oct. 1922. (In his 43 years of service he had delivered 1,472 sermons.) He remained a steady churchgoer until his sudden death from a heart attack on 1 April 1925. Peter Regier's exemplary life of faith, hard work, and respect for the *tiefen Grund* of his new homeland were rewarded by his becoming a prosperous farmer, a revered churchman, and a good neighbour.

PAUL W. RIEGERT

Mennonite Heritage Centre (Winnipeg), Peter Regier, Tagebüch [Diary], 1851–93. Gerhard Ens and Lawrence Klippenstein, "Die Vorgeschichte der Konferenz der Mennoniten in Kanada," *Bote* (Saskatoon), no.25 (21 June 1978): 1–2. F. H. Epp, *Mennonites in Canada, 1786–1920: the history of a separate people* (Toronto, 1974). Lawrence Klippenstein, "Peter Regier, churchman-farmer (1851–1925)," *Mennonite Historian* ([Winnipeg]), 2 (1976), no.2/3: 1–2. Peter Paetkau and Lawrence Klippenstein, "The Conference of Mennonites in Canada: background and origin," *Mennonite Life* (North Newton, Kans.), 34 (1979), no.4: 4–10. P. W. Riegert, *Deep earth* (Regina, 1996), 1, 9–18; *2005 memories: a history of the Hamburg School District No.2005, Laird, Saskatchewan* (Regina, 1979), 13. *Three score years and ten with God in Tiefengrund Rosenort Mennonite Church, 1910–1980; reaching to its roots, 1893*, ed. Sylvia Regier (Altona, Man., [1980?]). *Through the years with the C. W. Regiers*, comp. W. D. Regier (n.p., 1982), 9–10.

REID, ELIZA ANN. *See* MCINTOSH

REID, JOHN DOWSLEY, doctor, businessman, and politician; b. 1 Jan. 1859 in Prescott, Upper Canada, son of John Reid, a cabinetmaker, and Jane Dowsley; m. 25 Jan. 1899 Ephie Elizabeth Labatt in Hamilton, Ont., and they had a daughter and a son; d. 26 Aug. 1929 near Prescott.

John Dowsley Reid's mother came from a family in the Prescott area; his father, a native of Belfast, entered the customs office in Prescott in 1865, worked for the Edwardsburg Starch Company in nearby Cardinal [see William Thomas Benson*], and became collector of canal tolls there. John was educated in local schools and in 1890 he graduated in medicine from both Queen's College in Kingston and Trinity College in Toronto. He practised for a short time in Cardinal, and in 1906 he would be admitted to the College of Physicians and Surgeons of Ontario. Throughout his life he engaged in business ventures and investment: early in his career he managed Edwardsburg Starch for seven years and the Imperial Starch Company Limited for four.

Reid's principal interest was politics. Shortly after receiving his medical degrees, he was asked by Sir John A. Macdonald* to stand for the Conservatives in Grenville South, which included Prescott and Cardinal. In 1891 he won the seat, which would be renamed Grenville in 1903. An opposition backbencher, he was far from being inconspicuous in party affairs. His managerial skills were soon recognized and he became a key electoral organizer in eastern Ontario. Following party defeats under Sir Charles Tupper* in 1900 and Robert Laird Borden* in 1904 and 1908, Doc Reid, as he was known, joined the small group of malcontents who challenged Borden's leadership in 1910. Some disliked the way Borden was handling the split between French and English Canadian MPs over the naval issue; others were exasperated by his failure to consult the veteran members of caucus when he developed policy. Borden beat them down with a threat to resign. In March 1911, just as the Conservatives were consolidating their opposition to the reciprocity agreement negotiated by Sir Wilfrid Laurier*'s government, the rebels tried again to get rid of Borden but failed, leaving Reid, a Tory journalist noted, "very frightened."

Borden, however, needed him for the general election in September, and Reid responded eagerly. Three days before the contest he reported to Borden that "as to Eastern Ontario . . . I honestly believe everyone we now have is safe." Whereas the Conservatives had won 48 Ontario seats in 1908, they now captured 73, including 20 of the 24 in Reid's charge, and the Conservatives claimed power. Under pressure from Francis Cochrane*, who had taken over from Albert Edward KEMP as chief organizer for Ontario and was about to become minister of railways and canals, Borden rewarded Reid with the Ministry of Customs, but only after a stern lecture on loyalty. Rich in patronage potential, Customs was the third largest ministry after Railways and Canals and the Post Office. More important, in the days before direct taxation, it was responsible for collecting most of the government's revenue.

Over the years Reid's loyalty to his prime minister kept pace with Borden's recognition of his managerial skills. Reid, Cochrane, and Robert Rogers*, the minister of public works, handled the "practical affairs" of the governing party. As one minister after another succumbed to ill health or wartime pressures after 1914, Borden called on Reid to administer the vacated posts. This was especially true of Railways and Canals during Cochrane's physical decline. In 1914 Reid devised the plan and brokered the deal with Sir William MACKENZIE and Sir Donald Mann* that gave the Canadian Northern Railway aid in return for the government's taking 40 per cent of its common stock. Two years later Reid had the Railway Act amended to facilitate the rapid transit of grain. And in 1915 Borden had turned to him to pacify Sir Samuel HUGHES, the minister of militia and defence, when Borden abolished Hughes's Shell Committee and replaced it with the Imperial Munitions Board.

By October 1917, when Reid formally succeeded Cochrane, he had become one of Borden's closest confidants and an ardent conscriptionist. Convinced that the Conservatives could win an election without Liberal support, Reid was sceptical about the need for a coalition, but Borden was determined to fashion a union government and he turned to Reid to help him persuade such western Liberals as Arthur Lewis Watkins SIFTON, James Alexander Calder*, and Thomas Alexander Crerar* to join. When the conscription election finally came, in December, Reid was given overall control of Ontario. He worked, often in uneasy alliance with Newton Wesley Rowell*, the former Ontario Liberal leader who had joined the new Union government, to sort out the claims of conscriptionist Conservatives and Liberals to be candidates. On election day 74 of the province's 82 constituencies returned Unionists, part of the conscriptionist wave that swept over every province but Quebec and changed the face of national politics.

Railways and Canals, in which Reid continued, was a demanding portfolio. He had oversight of the ongoing construction of the Trent Canal and the rebuilding of the Welland Canal, negotiated post-war land settlement plans with the provinces, and carried the Canada Highways Bill in 1919, one of the first cost-sharing programs in dominion-provincial relations [see Archibald William CAMPBELL]. His principal assignments were finishing the nationalization of the Canadian Northern, establishing the new Canadian National Railway Company, and bringing the Grand Trunk and Grand Trunk Pacific railways into the system. In June 1919 Borden, who had just returned from the Paris Peace Conference, discovered that Reid was "in poor health and wished to retire," but he stayed on and acted as the prime minister's eyes and ears in caucus and the House of Commons while Borden, exhausted by his wartime leadership, spent most of the next year away from Ottawa. Often Reid's news was not good. The Union government was collapsing, and in October 1919 Reid reported that "We have two leaders, viz. [Sir George Eulas Foster*] from 3 till 6 pm and [Charles Joseph Doherty*] after that and to put it mildly neither have sufficient influence with the members to hold the House."

Borden stepped down in July 1920. Reid stayed on under Arthur Meighen*, attending to the ongoing negotiation with the Grand Trunk. He resigned his ministry on 20 Sept. 1921; he was 62, had been in the house for almost three decades, and had no desire to face another election. Two days later Meighen appointed him to the Senate, where he was a strong advocate of the formation of the United Church of Canada, an opponent of the Old Age Pensions Bill of Liberal prime minister William Lyon Mackenzie King* in 1926, and a cautionary voice in 1928 over proposals to improve the canal system and exploit the hydroelectric power of the St Lawrence River between Montreal and Kingston. He feared that American interests would take control of both developments.

During his years in the Senate, Reid and his wife lived on River Road near Prescott. A fisherman and hunter, he was a trustee of the local Presbyterian church, a freemason, an Oddfellow, and in 1929 president of the Canadian Pacific Car and Passenger Transfer Company Limited, which ferried trains across the river. In August 1929 he suffered a stroke and died two days later, leaving an estate worth over $636,000; he was buried in the Blue Church cemetery west of Prescott. Thomas H. Blacklock, a Conservative journalist and friend, observed in the Toronto *Daily Mail and Empire* that Doc Reid had "had an almost uncanny prescience in judging Ontario sentiment. . . . He overlooked not the slightest detail in the Ontario Conservative organization, nor anything that might sway the Ontario people."

ROBERT CRAIG BROWN

AO, RG 22-179, no.8735; RG 80-5-0-275, no.16655. LAC, MG 26, H: 3854–56, 7241–42, 40903–04, 62875–81, 70415–17, 157719; Diary; RG 31, C1, 1861, Prescott, Upper Canada, [Ont.]; 1871, Edwardsburg, Ont. UTA, A1973-0026/375(24). *Daily Mail and Empire*, 27 Aug. 1929. *Ottawa Citizen*, 27 Aug. 1929. *Prescott Journal* (Prescott, Ont.), 29 Aug. 1929. R. L. Borden, *Robert Laird Borden: his memoirs*, ed. Henry Borden (2v., Toronto, 1938). R. C. Brown, *Robert Laird Borden, a biography* (2v., Toronto, 1975–80). *Canadian annual rev.*, 1902–27/28. *Canadian directory of parl.* (Johnson). Cardinal, Ont., Council, *A history of Cardinal* ([Cardinal, 1967]). A. W. Currie, *The Grand Trunk Railway of Canada* (Toronto, 1957). John English, *The decline of politics: the Conservatives and the party system, 1901–20* (Toronto, 1977). Roger Graham, *Arthur Meighen: a biography* (3v., Toronto, 1960–65), 1, 2. T. D. Regehr, *The Canadian Northern Railway, pioneer road of the northern prairies, 1895–1918* (Toronto, 1976).

REID, MARY AUGUSTA CATHARINE. *See* HIESTER

REID, Sir WILLIAM DUFF, contractor, railway executive, and developer; b. 20 Nov. 1866 in Sydney (Australia), eldest son of Robert Gillespie Reid* and Harriet Duff; m. 19 March 1894 Minnie Cormack in Kingston, Ont., and they had four sons and one daughter; d. 12 March 1924 in Montreal.

The life of William Duff Reid was encompassed by the activities of his father, a stonemason, bridge builder, and contractor. He was born in Australia only because Robert G. Reid worked there briefly as a stonemason; he left in 1869 when the family moved to his father's home in Scotland. Brought to Canada in 1873 as a consequence of further railway projects undertaken by Reid Sr, he received his education at a variety of public schools in the United States and Canada, including the Galt Collegiate Institute in Ontario. Thereafter his life was absorbed by a succession of family enterprises.

Reid first demonstrated his ability as a builder when he joined his father and Sandford Fleming* in erecting the substructure of the Canadian Pacific Railway bridge at Lachine, Que., in 1885–86. In 1887, with his father and James Isbester, he engaged in the construction of an 86-mile section of the CPR from Algoma Mills (Algoma) to Sault Ste Marie, Ont. Again joining Isbester and Reid, he assisted with a branch of the Intercolonial Railway from Point Tupper to Grand Narrows, N.S., in 1887–90. His greatest achievement, however, was the design, construction, and operation of the Newfoundland Railway, which he supervised from 1890 while his father maintained his principal residence in Montreal. (He was so closely involved in the construction that he lost an eye during a blasting operation in 1891.) He was the primary negotiator for the contract of 1898, by which the government of Sir James Spearman Winter* extended the Reids' operation of the railway for 50 years. On the incorporation in 1901 of the Reid Newfoundland Company Limited, he became vice-president and general manager. When his father died seven years later, having divided his shares amongst his three sons, W. D. assumed the presidency, creating a tension in the family which never subsided.

On the day of his father's funeral in Montreal, W. D. held a private service in his St John's boardroom in the presence of Governor Sir William MacGregor and Lady MacGregor and the heads of departments and employees of the St John's train station. For 15 minutes, work was suspended throughout the railway system. Every train and steamer stopped. This public display of mourning served as a tribute to the accomplishments of Sir R. G. Reid, but it also signalled the newly acquired authority and independence of his son, who was then 41. By this time the Reid industrial empire had expanded into a variety of other activities, including steamer transportation, electric light and power, a trolley system in St John's, and a graving dock. As president, he now sought further opportunities, particularly in developing the timber and mineral resources of the huge land grants the family had acquired in building the railway. By 1911 the company would become, in the words of the Newfoundland journalist Patrick Thomas MCGRATH, "the largest paymaster in the Island to-day, next to the Government itself."

A proponent of confederation with Canada, Reid had devoted his considerable resources to this cause in the elections of 1900 and 1904. The first of these contests was fought in large measure over the desirability of the 1898 contract, which was strongly opposed by Robert BOND, the head of the Liberal party. Despite W. D.'s efforts Bond was successful and in 1901 he forced the Reids to agree to new terms. Four years later the family tried to negotiate a sale of the railway to the government of Newfoundland, but Bond, who had been re-elected in 1904, turned them down. In the election of 1908 Reid backed Bond's rival, Sir Edward Patrick Morris*. When this contest ended in a tie, he again campaigned for Morris, who assumed the prime ministership in 1909 with a policy of creating employment through the building of railway branch lines. Reid subsequently called in his political credit and was rewarded with a contract for six such lines, four of which he completed. With these enterprises in mind, McGrath attributed the apparent progress in the colony to the "transforming genius" of the Reids. But the branch lines proved to be unprofitable and difficult to maintain.

Prior to 1914 Reid was developing a plan for a pulp and paper mill on the Humber River, but it was soon abandoned when war broke out. With costs rising and the construction of the branch lines curtailed, the company began to lose money, and he himself took a hand in the operation of the railway. He was irritable and arbitrary. According to a former employee, "He upset the entire staff with spur of the moment dismissals or promotions and a peculiar system whereby engines were assigned to particular jobs or sections and only certain engines were allowed to handle express trains. . . . Staff turnover was extremely high." Although he was awarded a knighthood in the New Year's honours list of 1916, he sank into a gloom in July of that year when Robert Bruce Reid, his eldest son and heir apparent, was killed at Beaumont-Hamel (Beaumont), France, fighting with the Newfoundland Regiment [see Owen William Steele*].

Facing financial losses and suffering from ill health, in 1917 he was invited by his brothers to abandon the direction of the Reid Newfoundland Company and serve as chairman of the board. He refused. When a meeting of the board was called in December for the purpose of removing him, he hired three Montreal gunmen to snatch the proxy votes secured by his brother Henry Duff Reid, but he failed. With Harry in control of the company, W. D. departed for Montreal, where he had maintained the family residence at 275 Drummond Street. Invalided by his illness, he survived there to see the realization of his plans for the sale of the railway. In 1923 the administration of Prime Minister Sir Richard Anderson Squires* took over the line as part of the final settlement of all questions outstanding between the Reid family and the government of Newfoundland.

RONALD ROMPKEY

[I am grateful for the personal recollections supplied by Ian Job Reid of St John's, a grandson of W. D., during interviews in 1997. Mr Reid also provided access to family papers in his possession. R.R.]

AO, RG 80-5-0-213, no.3979. Canadian Pacific Arch. (Montreal), RG 1 (William Van Horne corr.); RG 2 (T. G. Shaughnessy corr.). Centre for Newfoundland Studies, Arch., Memorial Univ. of Nfld (St John's), Reid papers. New South Wales Registry of Births, Deaths and Marriages (Sydney, Australia), Pioneers index, 1867/99. PANL, MG 17, esp. file 412. *Cadet* (St John's), March 1915: 19–20; March 1916: 9–10. *Canadian Railway and Marine World* (Toronto), [19] (1916): 55–56; 27 (1924): 178. W. J. Chafe, *I've been working on the railroad: memoirs of a railwayman, 1911–1962* (St John's, 1987). *Engineering News and American Contract Journal* (New York), 18 (July–December 1887): 270–72. J. K. Hiller, *The Newfoundland Railway, 1881–1949* (St John's, 1981); "The politics of newsprint: the Newfoundland pulp and paper industry, 1915–1939," *Acadiensis* (Fredericton), 19 (1989–90), no.2: 3–39; "The railway and local politics in Newfoundland, 1870–1901," in *Newfoundland in the nineteenth and twentieth centuries: essays in interpretation*, ed. J. [K.] Hiller and P. [F.] Neary (Toronto, 1980), 123–47. P. T. McGrath, *Newfoundland in 1911: being the coronation year of King George V and the opening of the second decade of the twentieth century* (London, 1911). A. B. Morine, *The railway contract, 1898, and afterwards, 1883–1933* (St John's, 1933). P. B. Motley, "Double tracking of the Canadian Pacific's St. Lawrence River bridge," *Canadian Railway and Marine World*, [17] (1914): 149–56. A. R. Penney, *A history of the Newfoundland Railway* (2v., St John's, 1988–90).

RICHARDSON, HARRY ALDEN, banker; b. 25 May 1862 in Middleboro, Mass.; m. Anne Margaret Macdonald (d. 21 Feb. 1942), and they had two sons and a daughter; d. 18 May 1923 in Toronto.

Raised and educated in Halifax, Harry Alden Richardson spent his entire career with the Bank of Nova Scotia, starting locally at 17. He worked his way up, though how he came to be promoted is unknown. As the bank expanded through the Maritimes, guided by Thomas Fyshe*, Richardson managed branches in Sussex and Newcastle, N.B., Charlottetown, and Yarmouth, N.S., where he dealt with the financial implications of a sea-based economy facing industrialization. His posting in 1900 as manager of the Toronto branch (opened in 1897) coincided with the bank's decision to transfer its head office there from Halifax, to be closer to the opportunities created by booming economic growth in Ontario and the west. Both branch and office occupied space in the Canada Life Assurance Building on King Street until the construction nearby in 1902–4 of separate premises, designed by the firm of Frank DARLING.

Toronto's bankers did not give Richardson or his employer a hearty welcome. Through various creative approaches, he broke their hold on a number of prized customers, including the City of Toronto. After introducing himself to treasurer Richard Theodore Coady, he reportedly said "that he had a good mind to boot the municipal custodian in the classic manner." When a startled Coady asked why, Richardson replied, "Because you have not given us any of your business." Thus was born a fruitful relationship with city hall. Richardson profited as well from the emphasis of general manager Henry Collingwood MCLEOD on transparent accounting. The bank's publication of its audited statements, beginning in 1902 and a first for a Canadian bank, gave Richardson an advantage at a time when bank failures left customers looking for safe repositories. His elevation to general manager in 1910 surprised many, perhaps no one more than assistant general manager Daniel Waters. Richardson proved a contrast to the prickly McLeod, who had not hesitated to spar openly with other bankers during his campaign for government inspection. His humour and grace took the sharp edges off the bank's executive offices. To appease some members of the bank's board of directors, who had become tired of the constant bickering between McLeod and others, Richardson made some concessions to win peace, including ending the publication of the audited statements. He knew how to circulate, as a member of several Toronto clubs as well as St Andrew's Presbyterian Church; keenly aware of the public's perceptions of bankers and failed banks, he displayed simple tastes and personal thrift. During much of his time in Toronto he walked to work in the tan overcoat that became his trade mark, though by 1914 he had acquired a "big car, in which he picked up other bankers to discuss deals and mutual difficulties foisted on the banks by war finance."

Despite their contrasting styles, Richardson shared his predecessor's focus on turning their bank into a national institution. His success would distinguish it from most other banks, which were slow or unable to identify new markets. By 1910 banking was undergoing rapid transformation, with a concentration of capital in central Canada. Extraordinary economic growth brought unbridled optimism, new banks, and the demise of others, run into the ground by venal managers. Inducing shareholders to finance new branches and wooing accounts was a difficult business, but Richardson's interest in expansion began soon after he occupied the general manager's office. At the same time his bank maintained its interests in

the Maritimes – one of his earliest moves was to continue the advancement of funds to Nova Scotia Steel and Coal to thwart a takeover.

To consolidate markets and create a national bank with a strong network, Richardson initiated not just new branches but also mergers and he introduced internal measures to keep his best managers from moving to rival banks or into the lucrative brokerage field. Combination began in 1913, when the Bank of New Brunswick was added. A year later came the Toronto-based Metropolitan Bank. In 1919, in his greatest coup, Richardson persuaded federal finance minister Sir William Thomas White* to allow his bank to buy the Bank of Ottawa. Mergers required cabinet approval, and White was conscious that the disappearance of many banks between 1915 and 1918 had intensified public concern. Richardson told him that the acquisition would put the Bank of Nova Scotia in a better position to provide money for exports – it financed more Winnipeg grain shipments than other banks and was well practised in capitalizing international trade – and thereby buoy up the dollar. White agreed, despite public outcry. Another key to these mergers was Richardson's friendships with the general managers of the other banks, who had all at one time been employed by the Bank of Nova Scotia.

During the war Richardson had placed his services at the dominion's disposal. As advisers to White, he and other senior bankers assisted in the sale of war bonds to the public and played an important role helping the government to manage various fiscal needs and emergencies. Richardson and fellow members of the Canadian Bankers' Association met with White on different occasions to arrange credit for wartime supplies, though in a climate of public hostility to profiteers Richardson was reluctant to have any attention drawn to the banks' commissions. He used his access to White to remedy another problem. His pressure to break the Bank of Montreal's monopoly of government business intensified as this rival accepted the huge sums collected from war loans and other sources. Richardson bluntly told White in 1918 that such large deposits allowed the bank to reduce its rates on commercial loans and that, if Ottawa wanted the banks to share equally in financing exports and government obligations, the preference had to stop. The Bank of Montreal eventually lost its favoured position in the 1920s.

By the war's end, Richardson was a member of White's inner circle of financial advisers, drawn from the top bank managers in the country. A vice-president of the CBA in the early 1920s, he was one of the senior Canadian and American bankers who met in Toronto in July 1922 to discuss areas of possible cooperation as post-war depression had the dominion in a sour mood and looking for new answers to old economic problems. Never comfortable with the steady travel required by his bank's business across Canada and in the Caribbean, by that year he had appointed two assistant general managers and more supervisory officers. However, he did not sail off into retirement as McLeod had done. Apparently troubled by poor health for a good part of his life, he died at age 60 in 1923, still general manager. One bank official was certain that the collapse of sugar prices in the West Indies and fish prices in Newfoundland had contributed to his demise. A friend described him as a man "wrapped up in the bank." It was very much the centre of his life – his outside business involvement appears to have been limited to a directorship with Canada Life. The Bank of Nova Scotia was testament to his success as a banker; his many friends were testament to his character.

JOHN A. TURLEY-EWART

[For a detailed account of sources consulted at the Canadian Bankers' Assoc. Arch. (Toronto), please refer to J. [A.] Turley-Ewart, "Gentleman bankers, politicians and bureaucrats: the history of the Canadian Bankers' Association, 1891–1924" (PHD thesis, Univ. of Toronto, 2000). J.A.T.-E.]

AO, F 977, Mount Pleasant Cemetery, Toronto; RG 22-305, no.48231; RG 80-8-0-910, no.4266. Scotiabank Group Arch. (Toronto), Richardson papers. *Toronto Daily Star*, 18 May 1923. *Canadian annual rev.*, 1916: 361–62; 1920: 57; 1922: 523, 535. H. V. Cann, *Pages from a banker's journal* (n.p., 1933; copy in LAC). J. D. Frost, "The 'nationalization' of the Bank of Nova Scotia, 1880–1910," *Acadiensis* (Fredericton), 12 (1982–83), no.1: 3–38. Joseph Schull and J. D. Gibson, *The Scotiabank story: a history of the Bank of Nova Scotia, 1832–1982* (Toronto, 1982). TRL, *Biog. scrapbooks* (89v., Toronto, 1973; mfm. copy in AO library coll.), 4: 678. *Vital statistics from N.B. newspapers* (Johnson), 81, no.1990.

RICHARDSON, ROBERT LORNE, journalist, newspaper owner and editor, politician, and author; b. 28 June 1860 near Balderson, Upper Canada, son of Joseph Richardson and Harriet Thompson; m. 11 March 1885, in Brockville, Ont., Clara Jane Mallory of Mallorytown, Ont., and they had five daughters, one of whom predeceased him; d. 6 Nov. 1921 in Winnipeg.

The youngest of seven children of a Scottish Presbyterian farmer, Robert Lorne Richardson began life on a rural Ontario farm. He attended school in Balderson and at age 17 followed his second eldest brother to Montreal, where in 1879 he began a career in journalism with the *Montreal Daily Star*. In 1881 he joined the editorial staff of the Toronto *Globe*; he worked there for a year before moving to Winnipeg to participate in the *Sun*'s transformation into a daily paper.

Richardson held the position of city editor with the *Daily Sun* until December 1889, when the paper was bought by the *Manitoba Free Press*; the *Sun* stopped publication in mid January 1890. With his childhood friend Duncan Lloyd McIntyre, he purchased the

Sun's presses and founded the *Winnipeg Daily Tribune*, which began publication in January 1890 as an independent paper, but with the backing of the Liberal party. In June 1903 it would become the *Winnipeg Tribune* and in January 1915, the *Evening Tribune*. As its publisher and editor, Richardson would advocate free trade, government-owned railways, and the abolition of separate schools, increasingly deviating from Liberal policy.

In 1896 Richardson entered politics as the Liberal candidate in the federal riding of Lisgar and he won election on a platform advocating a limited tariff, "for revenue only." Although appointed a government whip, he soon ran foul of his party for opposing the compromise between Prime Minister Wilfrid Laurier* and Manitoba premier Thomas Greenway* on the Manitoba school question. His attacks on the Laurier government's administration of the Yukon and his opposition to the Canadian Pacific Railway soon earned him the enmity of Laurier's western lieutenant, Clifford SIFTON. In 1897–98 Sifton had orchestrated the purchase of the *Free Press* and had transformed it into an influential Liberal organ. Richardson waged an ongoing battle with the *Free Press*.

Ousted from the Liberal caucus for his insubordination, Richardson ran for re-election in 1900 as an independent; he retained his seat with the help of the Manitoba Conservatives, who backed him in return for the *Tribune*'s support. When, early in 1901, the *Tribune* rashly denounced the railway policy of Conservative premier Rodmond Palen Roblin*, the Tories made public details of electoral improprieties committed by Richardson's agents, including the bribing of voters and distribution of alcohol at the polls. Sifton personally absorbed the cost of Richardson's prosecution for these offences. The court annulled Richardson's election in July 1901.

For the remainder of his political career Richardson continued to vacillate in his allegiance. In 1902, after unsuccessfully contesting, as an independent Liberal, the by-election in Lisgar caused by the annulment of his election, he joined other Winnipeg independents to create a short-lived party, the Political Reform Union. As an independent, he lost in Brandon to Sifton in the federal general election of 1904. Sifton had had the constituency's boundaries redrawn to carve up Richardson's base of support. Richardson then campaigned unsuccessfully as a Liberal candidate in Killarney in the Manitoba election of 1907, as an independent Conservative in the Saskatchewan riding of Assiniboia in the federal election of 1908, and as an independent Liberal in a federal by-election in 1912 in Macdonald, a Manitoba constituency. He was finally returned to the House of Commons in 1917 as the radical candidate in Springfield, where he had campaigned in favour of conscription.

Richardson was the author of two novels on rural

Ontario life, *Colin of the ninth concession: a tale of pioneer life in eastern Ontario* (Toronto, 1903) and *The Camerons of Bruce* (Toronto, 1906), both of which had large Canadian sales. One of his most lasting contributions in journalism had been his participation in the founding in 1907 of the Western Associated Press, a cooperative news service, the precursor of the Canadian Press Limited [*see* John Ross Robertson*]. In the spring of 1920 he sold the *Tribune*. He died the next year, following a lengthy illness.

Described by his friend D. L. McIntyre as a man who "refused to allow party or partisan considerations to influence his conduct," Robert Lorne Richardson had cast himself as a populist and a spokesperson for western disaffection. His influence as a politician was blunted, however, by his continually shifting allegiances and by his penchant for placing self-interest ahead of principle. His contribution as a newspaperman – as a central figure in the battle between the *Tribune* and the *Free Press* and in the development of Canadian syndicated news – far outweighed anything he accomplished in the political arena.

THOMAS G. BORESKIE

In addition to the novels mentioned in the biography, Robert Lorne Richardson wrote several brochures about the Canadian west. A list of these is in CIHM, *Reg.*

AM, GR 1662. AO, F 373; RG 80-5-0-135, no.6544. LAC, MG 26, G. *Winnipeg Tribune*, 1890–1921. *Canadian annual rev.*, 1900–29. *Canadian men and women of the time* (Morgan; 1898 and 1912). Ramsay Cook, *The politics of John W. Dafoe and the "Free Press"* (Toronto and Buffalo, N.Y., 1963). CPG, 1896–1919. D. J. Hall, *Clifford Sifton* (2v., Vancouver and London, 1981–85). M. E. Nichols, *(CP): the story of the Canadian Press* (Toronto, 1948). F. H. Schofield, *The story of Manitoba* (3v., Winnipeg, 1913).

RICHER, ARTHUR-JOSEPH (baptized **Joseph-Arthur-Adélard**), physician and professor; b. 16 Nov. 1868 in Saint-Éphrem-d'Upton, Que., son of Damase Richer, a blacksmith, and Célina Lavoie; d. unmarried 26 Feb. 1922 in Sainte-Agathe-des-Monts, Que.

Arthur-Joseph Richer attended the mission school at Sabrevois and became a student in the faculty of medicine of Bishop's College in Montreal in 1888. After graduating in 1892, he enrolled at the New York Postgraduate Medical School. In 1893 he crossed the Atlantic to pursue his studies in France, in particular at the medical faculty of the Université de Paris and at the Institut Pasteur, where he took a keen interest in tuberculosis. He also trained for several months at the École Supérieure de Pharmacie in Paris and at the Laboratoire de Physiologie in the medical faculty of the Université de Paris. During his stay in Europe, Richer made a long study tour, visiting many clinics in Austria, Germany, and Poland. In Cracow (Kraków, Poland) he contracted pulmonary tuberculosis; he

went back to Paris to be treated by his teachers and was confined to bed for six months. When he had recovered, he returned to Canada in 1896 and took up residence in Montreal, where he practised his specialty of phthisical therapy and taught in the faculty of medicine of Bishop's College. He would remain there as professor of physiology, hygiene, and medicine until 1905, when the faculty merged with that of McGill University.

While in Europe, Richer had furthered his knowledge of tuberculosis and the ways of eliminating it. In his opinion the key factor was the sanatorium, which he saw as a place where patients would learn to modify their thinking and daily habits. It was a centre more for training than for treatment. In Paris, Richer had already informed his colleague and friend Sigard Adolphus Knopf of his intention to set one up in Quebec as soon as possible after returning home. Steeped in the theories of two Germans, Hermann Brehmer and Peter Dettweiler, and an American, Edward Livingston Trudeau, as to the therapeutic value of higher altitudes and country living, Richer chose the village of Sainte-Agathe-des-Monts, in the Laurentians, as the site for the first sanatorium in Quebec. It was built with private funds in 1898, less than a year after one had been opened in Ontario in Muskoka [*see* Sir William James GAGE]. His modest institution burned down in 1902, but Richer's initiative was taken up by other groups. Sainte-Agathe-des-Monts became an important treatment centre with the establishment of the Laurentian Sanatorium in 1908, followed by the Mount Sinai Sanatorium, which the Jewish community of Montreal founded in 1912, and, a few years later, by the one set up by the Sisters of Charity of the Hôpital Général of Montreal.

Not discouraged by the misfortune that had befallen his first attempt, Richer advanced the idea of prevention still further by founding in 1905, again in Sainte-Agathe-des-Monts, the Brehmer Rest Preventorium. The first institution of its kind in the Americas, it was intended for persons at risk of or predisposed to tuberculosis, rather than for those suffering from it. As Richer explained in his first annual report, "When we select for treatment convalescents from pneumonia, pleurisy, and typhoid fever, as well as those affected with anaemia, chlorosis and debility, we do so with a definite object in view. Nine-tenths of those affected as above will inevitably become victims of tuberculosis. If they can be treated and trained before they become a prey of the dread scourge, the saving is evident from every viewpoint." The objective, then, was to help people build up their natural resistance. From 1905 until the last years of his life, Richer devoted the greater part of his professional energies to supervising the medical care of the residents at this institution.

The campaign against tuberculosis – the antituberculosis crusade, as it was often termed – had begun in

Canada in the last quarter of the 19th century after Jean-Antoine Villemin in 1865 demonstrated the disease to be contagious and Robert Koch in 1882 identified the microbe causing it. It was necessary, first, to recognize the extent of the disease and to fight against the deep-seated misconception, widely held throughout the 19th century, that tuberculosis was hereditary and incurable. According to the Board of Health of the Province of Quebec, it was responsible for more deaths than all other contagious diseases combined, with an annual mortality rate, from 1896 to 1906, of 192 per 100,000 inhabitants. It was truly considered the scourge to be combated. The federal and provincial governments, however, played only a small direct role at the outset, limiting their involvement to making grants to private endeavours. It was in this context that the National Sanitarium Association was founded in Ontario in 1896, followed in 1901 by the Canadian Association for the Prevention of Tuberculosis and in 1902 by the Montreal League for the Prevention of Consumption and Other Forms of Tuberculosis. Richer was a member of the latter two bodies during their early years. In 1902 he was elected to the executive committee of the Canadian association to represent the province of Quebec along with physicians Emmanuel-Persillier Lachapelle* and Sir William Hales Hingston*. His view of the fight against tuberculosis was well received, and the president of the association announced to the general meeting in April 1902 that "5,000 copies of a brochure by Dr. Richer have been purchased and will be distributed to the various boards of health in the Dominion." A founding member of the Montreal League, Richer was its honorary secretary for a number of years. He held no office in these associations after 1905.

Arthur-Joseph Richer was primarily a specialist who devoted his professional life to the treatment of tuberculosis. Those who knew him described him as a profoundly humane person, liberal in political ideas and highly intelligent. He was loved by his patients and respected by his colleagues, not only in Quebec but outside the province. He died prematurely from an attack of nephritis in 1922 at the age of 53. The legacy he left was the work of a distinguished and learned man, a pioneer in the field of modern phthisical therapy in Canada. His career contributed to the progressive and rational development of public health measures in Canada.

GEORGES DESROSIERS, BENOÎT GAUMER, and OTHMAR KEEL

Arthur-Joseph Richer is the author of the following articles: "On sanatoria: locality and cure," *Canada Medical Record* (Montreal), 27 (1899): 293–97; "L'aspect économique de la question de la tuberculose au Canada," *L'Union médicale du Canada* (Montréal), 32 (1903): 260–63; "Tuberculose pul-

monaire (apyrétique), traitée au moyen des injections de sérum anti-tuberculeux Marmorek," *L'Union médicale du Canada*, 33 (1904): 280–86 (written in collaboration with Louis-Joseph Lemieux); and "The sanatorium and its mission," Canadian Assoc. for the Prevention of Consumption and Other Forms of Tuberculosis, *Trans. of the annual meeting* (Ottawa), 1906, app.13: 86–88.

ANQ-M, CE602-S14, 19 nov. 1868. *Municipal Gazette of Montreal*, 31 Oct. 1904. W. H. Atherton, *Montreal, 1534–1914* (3v., Montreal, 1914), 3. Canadian Assoc. for the Prevention of Tuberculosis, *Annual report* (Ottawa), 1902–19. *Canadian men and women of the time* (Morgan; 1912). Conseil d'Hygiène de la Prov. de Québec, *Rapport* (Québec), 1909: 38–39. C.-A. Daigle, "L'Alliance d'hygiène sociale," *L'Union médicale du Canada*, 34 (1905): 113–19. J.-E. Dubé, "In memoriam: docteur Arthur Joseph Richer," *L'Union médicale du Canada*, 51 (1922): 238–41; "Montréal la plus importante ville du dominion se doit d'être au premier rang dans la lutte antituberculeuse," *L'Union médicale du Canada*, 48 (1919): 572–74. Denis Goulet et André Paradis, *Trois siècles d'histoire médicale au Québec; chronologie des institutions et des pratiques (1639–1939)* (Montréal, 1992), 128–29. J. J. Heagerty, *Four centuries of medical history in Canada and a sketch of the medical history of Newfoundland* (2v., Toronto, 1928), 2: 231. S. A. Knopf, "In memoriam: Arthur J. Richer," *L'Union médicale du Canada*, 51: 235–37; *Tuberculosis as a disease of the masses and how to combat it* (7th ed., New York, 1911). "The Laurentian Sanatorium," *Canada Medical Record*, 27: 339–40. "Medical faculty, University of Bishops College, Montreal," *Canada Medical Record*, 29 (1901): 281. E. H. Milner, *Bishop's medical faculty, Montreal, 1871–1905, including the affiliated dental college, 1896–1905* (Sherbrooke, Que., 1985), 368–69. "Personals," *Canada Medical Record*, 24 (1895–96): 349. Que., Royal commission on tuberculosis, *Report* (Quebec, 1909–10). "University of Bishop's College; faculty of medicine, Montreal," *Canada Medical Record*, 31 (1903), nos.8, 11. G. J. Wherrett, *The miracle of the empty beds: a history of tuberculosis in Canada* (Toronto, 1977), 210.

ROBB, JAMES ALEXANDER, businessman and politician; b. 10 Aug. 1859 in Huntingdon, Lower Canada, son of Alexander Robb, a farmer, and Jenny (Janet) Smith; m. first 11 Sept. 1889 Mary Alma Wattie (d. 1902) in Salaberry-de-Valleyfield, Que., and they had one daughter, who predeceased her father; m. secondly 16 Aug. 1919 Mary Elizabeth Wattie, née Fletcher, in Vancouver; d. 11 Nov. 1929 in Toronto and was buried in Salaberry-de-Valleyfield.

James Robb was educated at Huntingdon Academy until age 16, when he began to work for his uncle in Salaberry-de-Valleyfield as a flour miller's assistant. By the time he was 20 he had become a partner in the firm, named McDonald and Robb. He later became its president and would hold the post until his death. Estimated to be worth only $2,000–$5,000 in 1889, the company was evaluated at $5,000–$10,000 less than ten years later and it would continue to prosper. Later in life Robb would also serve as chief executive of the Montreal wholesale flour business of Bruneau, Currie and Company Limited. In addition to achieving success in business he played an active role in local politics, most notably as mayor of Salaberry-de-Valleyfield from 1906 to 1910 or 1911. A public petition had requested that he assume office in order to put the town's finances in order. During this period he entered federal politics as a Liberal. Beginning in 1908 he won six consecutive mandates. His Huntingdon riding, which became Châteauguay-Huntingdon in 1914, was not a safe Liberal seat. Certainly Robb's chances were improved by his party's popularity in Quebec but his riding had been won by a Conservative immediately before his election and would be won by another shortly after his death. Popular and well known in his constituency, Robb gradually acquired greater responsibilities at Ottawa, being named chief Liberal whip in 1917 and, after the death of Sir Wilfrid Laurier* in 1919, Liberal parliamentary house leader.

In December 1921 the Liberals returned to power in Ottawa. Under William Lyon Mackenzie King*, they had swept all 65 seats in Quebec. Within the Quebec bloc, however, a bitter rivalry divided a Montreal-based group – led by former Quebec premier Sir Lomer GOUIN and defending the interests of big business – and a more populist Quebec City–based group headed by Ernest Lapointe*. Although clearly identified with Gouin's group because of his business interests and his proximity to Montreal, Robb was one of the rare Quebec Liberals to share the confidence and friendship of both factions and he entered cabinet as minister of trade and commerce on 29 December. His most notable accomplishment during the one and a half years he held this portfolio was the negotiation of a trade deal with Australia. From 17 Aug. 1923 to 4 Sept. 1925 he was minister of immigration and colonization, continuing the policies of the period that encouraged white, British settlers to come to Canada. During most of this time he was more preoccupied with his position as acting minister of finance, a role he assumed during the illness of William Stevens FIELDING, than with his position as minister of immigration. His budgets of 1924 and 1925 foreshadowed the economic thrift and political concerns of the four budgets he would present after he officially replaced Fielding.

Robb served as minister of finance from 5 Sept. 1925 to 28 June 1926, when he resigned with King and his cabinet during the King–Byng affair [see King; Julian Hedworth George Byng*]. Shortly afterwards, on 2 July, Arthur Meighen*'s Conservative government was defeated in the house on a legally questionable but politically astute motion which King had asked Robb to introduce concerning the validity of Meighen's government. When the Liberals again took office, Robb was reappointed finance minister on 25 Sept. 1926; he would hold the post until his death in 1929. Robb's budgets, conceived during a period of expanding trade and growing government revenues from moderate tariffs, featured debt reduction, tax cuts, and a general decrease in government spending. Often referred to as prosperity budgets, they were praised by many as responsible and only a few expressed concern that the apparent economic growth was illusory and that the refusal of the government to fund social programs had left many Canadians vulnerable. Presented in Robb's characteristically straightforward style, these budgets contained little that was new or original and simply applied the program of thrift encouraged by King. A comment by Robb to King in 1928 that "good business policies and the national interest require that economy be practised by every department" reflected the content of many letters between the two.

Although King was impressed with Robb's thrift, he often suspected that the minister of finance was over-sympathetic with the economic policies of the Conservative party. "Robb is too Tory and protectionist by instinct and association," King recorded in his diary on 7 March 1925. Robb maintained the reputation and connections he had established as a member of the Gouin high-tariff wing of the Liberal party in the early 1920s. From the time he headed the finance department, however, he proved to be as concerned as King about the political fortunes of the Liberal party and sought to win support for it from those who favoured reduced tariffs. Although he was never interested in the details of political organization, his middle-of-the-road tariff and other policies succeeded not only in satisfying those whom he termed his "manufacturing friends," but also in attracting an important number of low-tariff Progressives. Perhaps a greater limit on Robb's influence in cabinet than his conservative leanings and his identification with Gouin and Fielding was his reputation for relying excessively on the officials in his department. His deputy minister, George Finley O'Halloran, remarked that Robb was "inclined to glance at, rather than read, a long memorandum." Nevertheless, his presence in cabinet was appreciated by the prime minister, who often praised Robb's financial skills and his loyalty to the party.

In the fall of 1929, shortly after the disturbing news of the stock market crash, Robb became seriously ill with pleurisy and he died in November of apoplexy. During his burial service he was praised by many of the mourners as a popular MP respected by all parties. His secretary, Robert Watson Sellar*, noted years later in his memoirs that Robb was "neither an orator nor a ready speaker but he talked sense (in plain and simple English and French) and was an astute and trusted politician who was at his best when reconciling differences."

JOHN MACFARLANE

ANQ-M, CE607-S35, 3 nov. 1859; S72, 11 sept. 1889. BCA, GR-2962. LAC, MG 26, G; I; J (esp. J13); MG 27, III, B10;

MG 31, E5. Can., House of Commons, *Debates*, 1908–29. *CPG*, 1908–29. R. MacG. Dawson and H. B. Neatby, *William Lyon Mackenzie King: a political biography* (3v., Toronto, 1958–76). *Directory*, Montreal, 1929–30. F. W. Gibson, "The cabinet of 1921," in *Cabinet formation and bicultural relations: seven case studies*, ed. F. W. Gibson (Ottawa, 1970), 63–104. J. E. Rea, *T. A. Crerar: a political life* (Montreal, 1997). S. P. Regenstreif, "A threat to leadership: C. A. Dunning and Mackenzie King," *Dalhousie Rev.* (Halifax), 44 (1964–65): 272–89.

ROBERGE, STANISLAS-ALPHONSE, named **Brother Symphorian Lewis** (like his French-speaking colleagues, he preferred to gallicize his official religious name and signed **Frère Symphorien-Louis**), member of the Brothers of the Christian Schools, educator, school administrator, author, and magazine editor; b. 10 April 1848 in Saint-Pierre, Île d'Orléans, Lower Canada, son of Jacques Roberge, a farmer, and Scholastique Côté; d. 25 March 1924 in Montreal.

Stanislas-Alphonse Roberge entered the noviciate of the Brothers of the Christian Schools in Montreal on 24 Sept. 1865 and donned the religious habit on 8 December. He took his final vows on 16 Aug. 1877. In the meantime he had begun his teaching career in 1866 at the parish school of Saint-Joseph in Montreal, where he taught for 14 years. Living conditions were difficult because the school and the community were housed in the church basement. Since the premises were insalubrious the brothers had to move to a better residence in 1870 and to a new school in 1874. As the teacher in charge of the first class (as the final year was called) for a decade, Brother Symphorian Lewis was highly successful. His merit was recognized by commercial firms and business offices, which vied for his best students. In 1880 the new provincial visitor for Canada, Brother Réticius [Louis Gonnet*], chose him as director of the district's junior noviciate (or *juvénat*). Brother Symphorian Lewis's strong personality and his leadership, which were already acknowledged, stood out in a community that had few real teachers. He became the first director of the scholasticate that was established with eight novices on 24 Aug. 1887, in the mother house on Rue Côté in Montreal. Two months later the group moved to the premises known as Mont-de-La-Salle in Maisonneuve (Montreal).

But it was at the Collège du Mont-Saint-Louis, a large boarding school opened in Montreal in 1885, that Brother Symphorian Lewis would make his mark. He went there on 3 Feb. 1890 as assistant director and prefect of discipline and studies for all its senior classes. In 1894 he became its director. The college by then had some 400 boys, mostly boarders, and it provided a three-year preparatory course, beginning in the fourth year of the primary level, which led to either a four-year program of commercial studies or a six-

year science one. Both French- and English-speaking students were accepted and instruction was bilingual. Brother Symphorian Lewis contributed more than anyone else to the stability and flourishing of the new college. It was he who gave Mont-Saint-Louis the distinctive character that would make it one of the finest works of the Brothers of the Christian Schools in Canada. He not only consolidated the educational programs and attracted a growing number of students, but he also made his college better known, with many religious and lay figures being received for visits or special performances.

Highly talented, a tireless worker, and a model of discipline, Brother Symphorian Lewis took on the teaching of literature and philosophy to the students in the senior classes of the science program in addition to his administrative duties. While contributing to the publication of his community's *Leçons de langue française*, he wrote three philosophy textbooks for his students. Until 1920 he was in charge of producing a series of books on Canadian history, and he reputedly was the author of the intermediate and senior history textbooks. Considered by archivist Édouard-Zotique Massicotte* "the most complete, the best organized, and the most interesting" history for schoolchildren, the series emphasizes facts, especially those of a military kind, and puts forward an edifying vision of the past. Widely used in schools in the province of Quebec, it influenced the thinking of several generations of children.

An "inexhaustible poet," according to the authors of *Un demi-siècle au Mont-Saint-Louis*, Brother Symphorian Lewis wrote a long autobiographical poem in verse ("Égypte et terre promise ou la vocation de Paul"), six historical plays (*Colomb dans les fers*, *La découverte du Canada*, *Champlain*, *Maisonneuve*, *Dollard*, *Montcalm ou la trahison*), and three biblical dramas (*Le meurtre de Caïn*, *Joseph*, *Les Macchabées*). He can probably also be credited with writing *La perle de l'océan*. These works were in the main symphonic odes for which he composed both words and music, and most were never published. A number of his plays were put on by the students at his school. He also wrote a collection of poems on the rosary, *Couronne poétique des mystères du rosaire*, and a long epic poem (about 10,000 lines) dedicated to St Jean-Baptiste de La Salle. His poetry flows, but it is often more fluent than lyrical and the alexandrines are sometimes little more than prose. Brother Symphorian Lewis also published *Glanures canadiennes* in Montreal around 1920. His major work, however, is a historical study entitled *Les Frères des écoles chrétiennes au Canada, 1837–1900*, which was brought out in Montreal in 1921. It is based on sound documentation, sometimes supplemented by personal recollections, and it would prove very useful to the authors of *L'œuvre d'un siècle* in 1937.

Robertson

Brother Symphorian Lewis resigned as director of Mont-Saint-Louis in 1914 to become director general of studies for the district of Montreal. He now oversaw instruction in all his community's schools in the district. He still lived at Mont-Saint-Louis, where he continued to teach literature and philosophy. That year he took charge of the *Bulletin du T. S. Enfant Jésus*, which was published by his community. He contributed poems signed Fr. S.-L. almost every month until December 1923, and a few historical articles from time to time. As the person in charge, he collected or composed anonymously the religious stories and edifying accounts that formed the subject-matter of this devotional publication. His qualities as an educator and author were recognized by various awards, including the Ordre des Palmes académiques, conferred by the French government.

Brother Symphorian Lewis was a diabetic, and his health, which began to deteriorate in 1920, declined further towards the end of 1923. He recovered, but on 7 March 1924 he had an unfortunate fall that led rapidly to his death on 25 March. His personality has been well described by the authors of *Un demi-siècle au Mont-Saint-Louis*, who noted that he had "the soul of a religious imbued with piety, a burning patriotism, an open-minded intelligence, a sincere love of young people, rare talents as an organizer, [and] lastly, utter urbanity."

NIVE VOISINE

Most of Brother Symphorian Lewis's poetic and dramatic writings remain unpublished, apart from *Couronne poétique des mystères du rosaire* ([Montréal?, 1905?]), *La découverte du Canada: drame historique en quatre actes, en vers et un tableau (ad libitum) . . .* ([Montréal], 1899), and poems that appear between 1914 and 1923 in the *Bull. du T. S. Enfant Jésus* (Maisonneuve; Laval-des-Rapides [Laval], Qué.); his other works are available in mimeograph or typescript form. His educational and historical writings were published. From 1891 to 1910 he also prepared "Notes historiques sur le Mont-Saint-Louis"; these are held by the Arch. des Frères des Écoles Chrétiennes du Canada Francophone (Laval).

ANQ-Q, CE301-S12, 10 avril 1848. Arch. des Frères des Écoles Chrétiennes du Canada Francophone, "Historique de l'établissement des frères dans la communauté de St-Joseph (Montréal)"; Lettre d'É.-Z. Massicotte au frère Symphorian Lewis, 30 mars 1912; "Notes historiques sur le Mont-Saint-Louis," 1 (1888–1916); 2 (1916–1927); "Notice historique sur le noviciat, la maison-mère et les autres établissements des Frères des écoles chrétiennes au Canada"; "Origine de l'établissement des Frères des écoles chrétiennes, dans la ville de Montréal, au Canada." F. M.-L., "In memoriam," *Bull. du T. S. Enfant Jésus*, 10 (1923–24): 204–5. "F. Symphorian-Lewis," Institut des Frères des Écoles Chrétiennes, *Notices nécrologiques trimestrielles* (Paris), no.102 (janvier-mars 1924): 237–51. *L'œuvre d'un siècle: les Frères des écoles chrétiennes au Canada; centenaire F.E.C.*, sous la dir. du frère Meldas-Cyrille (Montréal, 1937). [Étienne Poitras et Armand Yon], *Un demi-siècle au Mont-Saint-Louis, 1888–* *1938* (Montréal, 1939). Nive Voisine, *Les Frères des écoles chrétiennes au Canada* (3v., Sainte-Foy, Qué., 1987–99), 2.

ROBERTSON, JAMES WILSON, cheese manufacturer, educator, and civil servant; b. 2 Nov. 1857 in Dunlop, Scotland, fourth of the ten children of John Robertson and Mary Wilson; m. 6 May 1896, in Ottawa, Jemima Jane (Jennie) Mather, daughter of John Mather*, and they had a daughter; d. there 19 March 1930.

James W. Robertson's father, a farmer, was also a Church of Scotland evangelist and an activist who worked to enforce school-attendance laws and prevent child labour in mills. James thus grew up in an atmosphere of preaching and social service. His formal education ended at age 14 when he left the Dunlop parish school to be apprenticed to a Glasgow leather firm. In 1875 John Robertson brought his family to Canada and settled on a farm near London, Ont. James went to work in a cheese factory at Ingersoll; he learned so rapidly that by 1884 he was managing eight factories. This success and his acquaintance with MPP Thomas Ballantyne* brought him the post of professor of dairying at the Ontario Agricultural College in Guelph in April 1886. According to William Weld*, editor of the *Farmer's Advocate and Home Magazine* (London, Ont.), a leading agricultural journal, it was remarkable and laudable that he had "been taken from the vat and the churn . . . thus overstepping those who have a college education without practical experience."

In his teaching Robertson combined agricultural theory with practicality – he attended farmers' meetings and listened to their concerns. Applying lessons learned on tours of Denmark and American dairying states, he built a demonstration silo and promoted the use of corn for ensilage, a practice that would allow year-round dairying and improve farmers' incomes. His achievements at the OAC and his speaking ability led to lecture tours, brought offers of employment from American colleges, and attracted the attention of politicians. In 1889, at the meeting of the Dairymen's Association of Ontario in Smiths Falls, Prime Minister Sir John A. Macdonald* was impressed by his advocacy of cold storage to preserve the quality of dairy exports. Robertson was also known to John Carling*, the minister of agriculture, and William Saunders*, head of the government's experimental farm system. Since federal agricultural policy concentrated on settling the west, a program that would appeal to dairy farmers in eastern Canada was politically attractive. Furthermore, tariffs had reduced dairy exports to the United States, and the British market was difficult to penetrate because of the poor reputation of Canadian goods. On 1 Feb. 1890 Robertson became the dominion's first commissioner of agriculture and dairying, under Saunders's supervision, and he moved to Ottawa.

As commissioner, Robertson launched a drive to improve the quality of Canadian dairy products and gain more of the British market. He travelled widely, speaking on ensilage and winter dairying, and set up experimental stations in Ontario, Quebec, and the Maritimes. In the west, where dairying was uncommon, he zealously advocated mixed farming and encouraged cooperative dairying through a program of loans and subsidies. As well, in the mid 1890s he introduced cold-storage facilities to domestic and overseas shipments of butter and cheese. Improved quality and fewer complaints testify to the success of his efforts. His work, in fact, had outgrown the jurisdiction of the Central Experimental Farm and in December 1895 a separate agriculture and dairy branch was created, with Robertson at its head. As his renown grew, he did not hesitate to use the job offers that arose from time to time to promote himself, threatening to quit unless his demands were met. When he did leave the Department of Agriculture, he was its highest-paid employee.

Despite his ambition, Robertson and his wife occupied a "quiet place" in Ottawa's social life. They belonged to St Andrew's Presbyterian Church. Jennie shunned prominence, but when her friend Lady Aberdeen [Marjoribanks*] established the Victorian Order of Nurses in 1897, the Robertsons became involved. James would serve as a governor of the order from 1902 to 1927.

In 1897 Robertson met William Christopher Macdonald* of Montreal, a tobacco magnate with a philanthropic bent. Though they were poles apart in character – Macdonald was retiring, Robertson outgoing and innovative – a common interest in educational reform united the money of one with the vision of the other. Their particular concerns were technical training and elementary education in rural areas. They set up the Macdonald Manual Training Fund in 1899, the same year that Robertson gave $100 as an award for children who grew high-quality seed grain. The gesture fired Macdonald's imagination: in 1900 he gave Robertson $10,000 for prizes. The resulting competitions would lead in 1904 to the formation of the Canadian Seed Growers' Association, of which Robertson became president. The alliance of the two men produced two other influential initiatives: the Macdonald Rural Schools Fund, which promoted manual workshops and school gardens, and the Macdonald Consolidated Schools Project. They were associated as well with Adelaide Sophia Hoodless [Hunter*] in founding the Macdonald Institute of Home Economics at the OAC.

Though Robertson's work with Macdonald consumed much time, he continued as federal agriculture and dairy commissioner. In 1900–2 he had been responsible for sending 90 shiploads of horses, fodder, and food to the British army in South Africa. When some shipments were condemned on arrival in 1902, the War Office blamed Robertson, who in turn faulted Canadian port inspectors and the shippers. The dispute did little damage to his reputation, but it combined with the burden of his normal duties and his involvement with Macdonald to cause a nervous breakdown, followed by a long convalescence in England.

Robertson resigned from the Department of Agriculture on 31 Dec. 1904; on 30 June 1905 he was made a CMG. That same year he became principal of the agricultural college that Macdonald had decided to establish at Sainte-Anne-de-Bellevue, Que. He supervised its construction and for staff he raided the OAC, the experimental farms, and American colleges; the first students were enrolled in 1907. But if Robertson had the skills to get Macdonald College quickly into operation, he was less than the ideal administrator. The faculty was a mixture of self-taught agriculturists and college-educated specialists who often disagreed. Robertson was unable to smooth their relations; his own conflict with one university-trained professor, George Herbert Locke*, resulted in the latter's resignation in 1908. Furthermore, Macdonald wanted to draw students only from eastern Canada, while Robertson believed the college should serve the whole country (his nation-wide interests were reflected in his election in 1909 as president of the Dominion Educational Association). More serious perhaps, his aggressive style came to offend Sir William's sense of propriety. In the fall of 1909, after Robertson had, without authorization, spent funds on extra residential space for students, the college's board of governors limited his spending to $100. Unable to accept this insulting restriction, he tendered his resignation that fall, effective 10 Jan. 1910. Never again would he hold a permanent paid position.

Shortly before leaving, Robertson had been named to the federal Commission of Conservation, and chair of its committee on lands, which was investigating agricultural practices throughout Canada. As well, in June 1910 he was made head of the royal commission on industrial training and technical education, which would occupy him until 1913. The commission championed the cause of vocational education and its report would result in the Technical Education Act of 1919. Grants made to the provinces under this act set a precedent for future federal funding of education [see John Seath*].

During World War I Robertson immersed himself in volunteer work. He helped establish the Ottawa valley branch of the Canadian Red Cross Society in 1915 and chaired its national executive. In 1916 he organized the Canadian committee of the Agricultural Relief of the Allies Fund; from 1916 to 1918 he chaired the advisory committee of Canada's food controller. In the last year of the war he headed the eastern Canada section of the Greater Production Campaign, which collapsed when the government of Sir Robert Laird Borden* revoked the exemption from conscription that had been given to farmers' sons in 1917.

After the war Robertson, then in his sixties, was employed for a time by the Supreme Economic Council at the Paris Peace Conference as Canada's adviser on food for European relief. In 1922 he became chief commissioner of the Boy Scouts of Canada. The following year he was selected to chair the federal royal commission formed to investigate "unrest" among steelworkers at Sydney, N.S.; in 1925 he was a member of a board that attempted conciliation in a Cape Breton mine strike [see William DAVIS]. Throughout the post-war years he also maintained a busy speaking schedule. The recipient of several honorary degrees, in 1928 he was awarded Quebec's Order of Agricultural Merit.

Although Robertson had "a strong rangy body," according to his daughter, Mary Ishbel, in later life his health was not robust. His breakdown in 1902 and recurring stomach illness, which required treatment in an American sanitarium in 1920, may indicate stress-related problems. He died of a ruptured stomach ulcer in 1930 and was buried in Beechwood Cemetery, Ottawa. A year later the OAC established the Robertson Associate Award in his honour. A rural progressive who loved the countryside but lived in cities, he was as responsible as anyone for the growth and modernization of Canada's dairy industry. As an educator, he influenced the curriculum in schools at all levels.

IAN M. STEWART

A "Brief biography" (typescript, 1964) of James Wilson Robertson prepared by his daughter, Mary Ishbel Robertson Currier, is available in Robertson's file at the DCB.

Robertson wrote hundreds of government pamphlets and reports, and many of his articles were printed in the agricultural press. Several of these publications are listed in *Science and technology biblio.* (Richardson and MacDonald). His output also includes "Canadian agriculture and rural education," in *The empire and the century: a series of essays on imperial problems and possibilities*, ed. C. S. Goldman (London, 1905), 385–402. Robertson published only one book, *Conservation of life in rural districts* (New York, 1911), copies of which are in the Univ. of Guelph Library (Guelph, Ont.) and in his papers at the Univ. of B.C. Library, *infra*.

AO, RG 22-354, no.14544; RG 80-5-0-232, no.2604. LAC, RG 17, A I, 617, nos.69943--44, 71588; 1959: 401; 2802. Univ. of B.C. Library, Rare Books and Special Coll. (Vancouver), J. W. Robertson papers. *Farmer's Advocate and Home Magazine* (London, Ont.), December 1886, March 1890. *Ottawa Citizen*, 20 March 1930. Can., Parl., *Sessional papers*, 1891, no.6D: 8; 1896, no.8: xii. *Canadian annual rev.*, 1900–30. *Canadian men and women of the time* (Morgan; 1912). G. C. Church, *An unfailing faith: a history of the Saskatchewan dairy industry* (Regina, 1985). J. M. Gibbon, *The Victorian Order of Nurses for Canada, fiftieth anniversary, 1897–1947* ([Ottawa, 1947]). George Iles, "Dr. Robertson's work for the training of Canadian farmers," *American Rev. of Reviews* (New York), 36 (July–December 1907): 576–84. D. A. Lawr, "The development of Ontario farming, 1870–1914: patterns of growth and change," *OH*, 64 (1972): 239–51. H. R. Neilson, *Macdonald College of McGill University, 1907–1988: a profile of a campus* (Montreal, 1989). *Political appointments and judicial bench* (Coté). A. M. Ross, *The college on the hill: a history of the Ontario Agricultural College, 1874–1974* (Vancouver [and Guelph], 1974). J. F. Snell, *Macdonald College of McGill University: a history from 1904–1955* (Montreal, 1963). *Who's who and why*, 1919/20.

ROBERTSON, LAWRENCE BRUCE, surgeon and army officer; b. 6 Sept. 1885 in Toronto, third son of Alexander James Robertson, a manufacturer's agent, and Julia Dalmage Carry; m. 17 April 1920 Enid Gordon Finley in Montreal, and they had a son and a daughter; d. 24 Feb. 1923 in Toronto.

Of Scottish background, Bruce Robertson was educated at the Toronto Model School, Upper Canada College, University College (BA 1907), and the faculty of medicine of the University of Toronto (MB 1909). After interning in surgery at Toronto's Hospital for Sick Children, of which his uncle John Ross Robertson* was board chairman, he trained for a year and a half in paediatric and orthopaedic surgery at Bellevue Hospital in New York City, and then spent six months as house surgeon at the Children's Hospital in Boston. In 1913 he returned to Toronto as an assistant in both clinical surgery and pathology at Sick Children's as well as a demonstrator in clinical surgery at the university. That year, drawing upon his clinical experience in the United States, he published his first paper, in the American Medical Association's *Journal* (Chicago). Others followed in Canadian and American publications, including an important article in 1915 on blood transfusion in children, written with his hospital colleague Dr Alan Brown*. Here they described the benefits of the new, indirect method of transfusion, by means of syringes and cannulae, that Robertson was using at Sick Children's. (He was also cognizant of the method of transferring blood stored in a cylinder containing an anticoagulant.)

Following the outbreak of World War I, Robertson had enlisted in November 1914 in the Canadian Expeditionary Force, was commissioned a lieutenant, and was posted to the hospital at the training camp on the Toronto exhibition grounds. Located in cow stables, it serviced several dozen patients a day, most of whom had minor illnesses or injuries, but by February 1915 more serious problems were being treated, including cases of pneumonia and meningitis. At the time the Canadian Army Medical Corps's No.2 Casualty Clearing Station was being organized with area officers and medical students from the university. Robertson enrolled for overseas service and embarked from Halifax with the unit on 18 April.

Indirect blood transfusion, which he had learned in

New York and applied in Toronto, helped save thousands of patients in military hospitals at the front. Robertson was the pioneer who introduced the technique to the British army's medical personnel, and through former colleagues also on military service, to other Canadian hospitals overseas. He first used it in the fall of 1915, while posted to No.14 Canadian General Hospital, on soldiers who had received severe shrapnel wounds. The results were published in the *British Medical Journal* (London) some months later. His work in 1916 and 1917, most of it with his original unit, No.2 CCS, was reported in other papers. One, in 1917, included an appreciative note by the consulting surgeon to the British Expeditionary Force, Colonel Charles Gordon Watson, who, confident that the methods of transfusion would improve even more "under the stimulus of war," urged "other surgeons to increased activity in the practice of this life-saving device." Robertson's major paper, "A contribution on blood transfusion in war surgery," was published in *Lancet* (London) in June 1918.

For Robertson transfusion was a means to an end, both to reduce the impact of shock on terribly wounded soldiers, so that he could proceed with the operations that might save their lives, and to facilitate their recovery. He took a keen interest in his patients, imploring them to write to him about their post-operative progress. Dozens did. Lieutenant B. W. A. Massey of the Royal Field Artillery, for example, told Robertson in August 1917 that "I owe most of all to your handling of my amputations and transfusion at the CCS."

In October, because of a shortage of surgeons at the Hospital for Sick Children, President Sir Robert Alexander Falconer* of the University of Toronto requested that Robertson, now a major in the CAMC, be sent home. Following his return in February 1918, he resumed his work at Sick Children's and the university and accepted a posting to the CAMC's Dominion Orthopaedic Hospital in Toronto. At Sick Children's, where he was part of a group of brilliant young surgeons which included William Edward Gallie and David Edwin Robertson, he continued his clinical research, using blood transfusion as a treatment for toxemias in children caused, in many instances, by severe burns. In addition, he followed up on two cases of heavy carbon monoxide poisoning in soldiers he had treated at the front in 1916. In 1920 Robertson married Enid Finley, who had been with the Volunteer Aid Detachment at Hart House at the university. In early February 1923 he had an attack of influenza and was hospitalized. Apparently recovered, he returned to his home and family on Foxbar Road, but on the 17th he was stricken with pneumonia. A week later, at age 37, Bruce Robertson, soldier and surgeon, died.

ROBERT CRAIG BROWN

Lawrence Bruce Robertson's many publications include one article in the American Medical Assoc., *Journal* (Chicago), "Gas bacillus infection – a report of six cases," 61 (July–December 1913): 1624–26; one in the *Arch. of Surgery* (Chicago), "Exsanguination–transfusion: a new therapeutic measure in the treatment of severe toxemias," 9 (1924): 1–15; one in the *Boston Medical and Surgical Journal*, "The significance of the Von Pirquet reaction in surgical tuberculosis in children," 170 (January–[June] 1914): 550–53; two in the *British Medical Journal* (London), "The transfusion of whole blood: a suggestion for its more frequent employment in war surgery" and "Further observations on the results of blood transfusion in war surgery, with special reference to the results in primary haemorrhage . . . with a note by C. G. Watson . . . ," July–December 1916: 38–40 and July–December 1917: 679–83 respectively; three in the Canadian Medical Assoc., *Journal* (Toronto), "Traumatic asphyxia with a report of six cases," "Blood transfusion in infants and young children" (written with Alan Brown), and "Blood transfusion in severe burns in infants and young children: a preliminary report of the treatment of the toxic shock by blood transfusion – with or without preceding exsanguination," 4 (1914): 501–7, 5 (1915): 298–305, and 11 (1921): 744–50 respectively; one written with Gladys Lillian Boyd* in the *Journal of Laboratory and Clinical Medicine* (St Louis, Mo.), "The toxemia of severe superficial burns," 9 (1923–24): 1–14; one in the *Lancet* (London), "A contribution on blood surgery in war surgery," January–June 1918: 759–62; and a collaborative article in *Northwest Medicine* ([Seattle, Wash.]), "Blood transfusion in children: its indications and limitations; from an analysis of 600 cases," 20 (1921): 233–44.

AO, F 1374; RG 22-305, no.46984. LAC, RG 9, III, B2, 3751; 3752: C-3-3; RG 150, Acc. 1992–93/166, box 8363-21. UTA, A1973-0026/382(11). *Gazette* (Montreal), 17, 19 April 1920. H. F. Brewer *et al.*, *Blood transfusion*, ed. Geoffrey Keynes (Bristol, Eng., 1949), 1–40. "Dr. Bruce Robertson," *Canadian Journal of Medicine and Surgery* (Toronto), 53 (January–June 1923): 195–98. N. M. Guiou, *Transfusion: a Canadian surgeon's story in war and in peace* (Yarmouth, N.S., 1985). *History of the Great War based on official documents: medical services; surgery of the war*, ed. Sir W. G. Macpherson *et al.* (London, 1922), 1: chap.5. Geoffrey Keynes, *Blood transfusion* (London, [1922]), chap.7. Sir Andrew Macphail, *Official history of the Canadian forces in the Great War, 1914–19: the medical services* (Ottawa, 1925). Nicholson, *CEF*. A[lexander] Primrose and E. S. Ryerson, "The direct transfusion of blood: its value in haemorrhage and shock in the treatment of the wounded in war," *British Medical Journal*, July–December 1916: 384–86. [William] Rawling, "Providing the gift of life: Canadian medical practitioners and the treatment of shock on the battlefield," *Canadian Military History* (Waterloo, Ont.), 10 (2001), no.1: 7–20. C. L. Starr, "Lawrence Bruce Robertson, B.A., M.B.," Canadian Medical Assoc., *Journal*, 13 (1923): 216–17. "The transfusion of whole blood," *British Medical Journal*, July–December 1917: 695–96. *University of Toronto roll of service, 1914–1918* (Toronto, 1921). *The war book of Upper Canada College, Toronto*, ed. A. H. Young (Toronto, 1923).

ROCHE, HARRIET ANN. *See* MILLS

ROCQUE, OVIDE-ARTHUR, politician, businessman, and office holder; b. 19 Sept. 1847 in Bytown (Ottawa), son of Pierre Rocque and Sophie Normandeau; m. 18 July 1876 Gabrielle Galibert, a native of Milhaud, France, in the church of Sainte-Brigide, Montreal, and they had three sons and three daughters; d. 15 Feb. 1923 in Orleans, Ont.

At the time of Ovide-Arthur Rocque's death, the Ottawa French-language daily *Le Droit* praised him at great length. "The cause of French language rights in Ontario," it declared on page eight, "has just lost one of its most valiant defenders." Four days later, the Montreal daily *Le Devoir* went even further, putting Rocque's obituary on the front page and describing him as "an old fighter" in the French Canadian cause. Between these newspapers' recollections of Rocque and the events of his life, there is, however, a marked difference.

Nothing is known about Rocque's life before 1872, when he was elected an alderman in Ottawa, an office he held until 1876. During his term, he was a member of numerous committees (public works, health, by-laws, court of revision, water supply) and supported, in particular, the construction of sidewalks. He was also one of his ward's two trustees on the separate school board. In 1874 he bought a farm located between the Ottawa River and the village of Orleans. He described himself at that time as a contractor in Ottawa. From 1878 to 1880 he was listed in the city directory as a bread and biscuit baker. Rocque returned to the city council in 1880, but for only a few months since he served as the inspector of markets for the city of Ottawa from 1881 to 1892.

From 1888 to 1903 Rocque was also an industrial inspector for eastern Ontario. The reasons for his appointment are still unclear. His support for the provincial Liberal party, which was reported in newspaper articles at the time of his death, may provide an explanation. As part of his duties under the terms of the Ontario Factories' Act of 1884, Rocque submitted an annual report to the Legislative Assembly on working conditions in the factories and sawmills of eastern Ontario. He noted infractions related to ventilation in workplaces and sanitary facilities, suggested measures for fire prevention, and drew up the list of workplace accidents.

Rocque's chief concern as an inspector, however, was the employment of children as young as 12 and 13 years of age in factories. He considered that this work was injurious to the physical and intellectual development of young people and exposed them to serious moral dangers, such as coarse language and reprehensible sexual conduct, because of the harmful influence of some adults. He did not hesitate to blame the parents of these children, calling them idlers motivated by the lure of gains. Rocque sometimes denounced employers, but he excused them, mentioning that they were led astray by parents who produced false documents to vouch for their children's ages. In order to put an end to child labour, Rocque recommended to the legislature that the minimum legal working age be raised to 14 years for boys and 16 years for girls, a measure adopted in 1893. He was less successful with his suggestion that proof of literacy be required of young people who wanted to work in factories.

Little is known about the extent of Rocque's militancy in support of the rights of French Canadians in Ontario. Since the beginning of the 20th century, growing conflicts between English and French Canadians in the province, especially on matters of religion and education, had led the latter to band together to defend their rights. This experience gave birth to the idea of an association that would unite all Franco-Ontarians. Rocque played a role, although not a leading one, in organizing the convention in January 1910 that would lay the groundwork for it. He displayed a keen enthusiasm for the event, and even confided to the secretary of the organizing committee that he had been trying for several years to set up a provincial association; he also pointed out that the most important issue for francophones was education, and especially securing adequate financing for the schools attended by French Canadians and the establishment of an institution to train French-speaking teachers in Ontario.

As one of the 25 people in charge of preparations for the event, Rocque went on promotional tours of eastern Ontario to arouse enthusiasm for it among French Canadians. The organizers hoped, of course, that this fervour would result in generous financial support. Rocque also became a member of the statistics committee. It fell to him to prepare a quantitative report on the French Canadians in the counties of Glengarry and Stormont that would be submitted to the convention.

When the gathering was held in Ottawa from 18 to 20 Jan. 1910, Rocque and 1,200 delegates supported the formation of the Association Canadienne-Française d'Éducation d'Ontario (ACFEO). In addition to defending and promoting the rights of French Canadians, the ACFEO leaders were given the responsibility for dealing with school system issues. Rocque was a member of the executive committee in 1910–11, and later of the administrative committee, which in fact was the association's management committee. The association was the voice of Franco-Ontarians during the school crisis precipitated by the promulgation of Regulation 17 in 1912, which restricted instruction in French to the first two years of elementary school. Rocque did not play a major role on this occasion, unlike Philippe Landry*, Napoléon-Antoine Belcourt*, Charles Charlebois, and Samuel McCallum Genest*. His daughter Marie-Louise, who was teaching in the Ottawa region, was, however, among those who resisted during this dispute.

There is no further mention of Ovide-Arthur Rocque after 1916, since he had no specific administrative responsibilities in the ACFEO, probably because of his health. He died in 1923, "after a lengthy illness," according to *Le Devoir*.

MARCEL MARTEL

[Information concerning Ovide-Arthur Rocque was taken from a variety of sources, there being no archival collection devoted to him. M.M.]

ANQ-M, CE601-S15, 18 juill. 1876. Arch. paroissiales, Notre-Dame (Ottawa), RBMS, 19 sept. 1847. Centre for Research on French Canadian Culture (Ottawa), C2 (Assoc. Canadienne-Française de l'Ontario, formerly the Assoc. Canadienne-Française d'Éducation de l'Ontario). LAC, RG 31, C1, 1901, Gloucester Township, Ont., div.1: 1 (mfm. at AO). *Le Devoir*, 19 févr. 1923. *Le Droit* (Ottawa), 15 févr. 1923. *Ottawa Evening Journal*, 15 Feb. 1923. *Directory*, Ottawa, 1866–1922. *Historical sketch of the county of Carleton*, ed. C. C. J. Bond (Belleville, Ont., 1971), 176–77 [reprint of the text only of *Illustrated historical atlas of the county of Carleton (including city of Ottawa), Ont.* (Toronto, 1879)]. Ont., Legislature, *Sessional papers* (reports of the minister of agriculture, 1888–1903). Ottawa, City Council, *Minutes*, 1872–76, 1880.

RODDICK, Sir THOMAS GEORGE, surgeon, university professor, militia officer, and politician; b. 30 July 1846 in Harbour Grace, Nfld, son of John Irving Roddick and Emma Jane Martin; m. first 2 Aug. 1880 Urelia Marion Fraser McKinnon (d. 1890) in Montreal; m. secondly 3 Sept. 1906 Amy Redpath in Chislehurst (London), England; no children were born of either marriage; d. 20 Feb. 1923 in Montreal.

Thomas Roddick, one of five children, had a strict Protestant education at the grammar school in Harbour Grace where his father was principal. A promising student, at age 14 he was sent by his father to the Normal School in Truro, N.S. While studying there from 1860 to 1864, he also began to accompany a local physician, Samuel Muir, on his rounds and to assist him in his office. On vacations in Newfoundland, he helped Dr Charles Hugh Renouf, a graduate of the University of Edinburgh. Influenced by these men, he decided to become a physician and to study in Scotland. He stopped in Montreal en route to Edinburgh and had brought with him an introduction to George Edgeworth Fenwick*, a doctor and demonstrator of anatomy at McGill College. While he was visiting Fenwick on 29 June 1864, the Montreal physician received a telegram requesting assistance. A train with 458 passengers had run through an open drawbridge over the Rivière Richelieu near Saint-Hilaire (Mont Saint-Hilaire), plunging cars and passengers into the water. Fenwick took Roddick with him to help. He was so struck with the young man's surgical skills in the face of a major disaster that he persuaded him to abandon his plans for Scotland and to apply to McGill. Roddick graduated in 1868, was first in his class, was valedictorian, and won the Holmes Medal for the highest aggregate marks in the four-year course.

Roddick served as assistant house surgeon at the Montreal General Hospital from 1868 to 1872. His duties were to admit patients, write their histories, assist in operations, and work in the clinic. As house surgeon from 1872 to 1874, he began to have referrals of his own and by 1874 he was well enough established to start a practice. Disturbed by the high rate of surgical infection at the hospital, in 1872 he had made a special trip to Edinburgh to study with Joseph Lister, the discoverer of antisepsis. The following year he was appointed lecturer in hygiene at McGill and in 1874 he became demonstrator in anatomy. His extraordinary surgical talent so impressed the medical faculty that it appointed him professor of clinical surgery in 1875 at age 28.

Roddick's surgical career at the Montreal General had begun in the outpatient clinic in 1874, where he performed only minor surgery. The following year he was promoted full surgeon, but it was not until 1877 that he obtained an indoor appointment, which meant that he could use the operating room and perform major surgery. His operations consisted mostly of amputations, which often resulted in fatal post-operative infections, so much so that he went back to visit Lister in 1877 for retraining in antisepsis. Within two years, with strict adherence to Lister's methods, he reduced his surgical mortality rate due to infection from more than 50 per cent to 3.2 per cent. He was not the first person at McGill to use antiseptic techniques: Robert Craik and others had done so in the previous decade, but had not adhered strictly to Lister's methods, so their results were not as impressive. Through articles and talks at meetings, Roddick became the leading proponent of antisepsis in Canada.

A member of the local militia since 1868, Roddick had been appointed assistant surgeon to the Grand Trunk Railway Brigade and he had served during the Fenian raids of 1870. Later he was placed in command of the University Company of the 1st (Prince of Wales's) Regiment of Volunteer Rifles and by 1885 he was surgeon to the regiment. In March 1885 the Canadian government, in response to the rebellion led by Métis leader Louis Riel*, began to send troops under Major-General Frederick Dobson Middleton* to the North-West Territories to suppress the uprising. On 5 April Roddick was offered the post of deputy surgeon general by the surgeon general of the expedition, Darby Bergin*. He mobilized doctors, nurses, aides, and supplies for the campaign and followed the battles, attending to the wounded. He stayed in the north-west until late August, seeing to the evacuation of casualties by barge and railway and even caring for wounded Métis. Loss of life was minimal during the care and transportation of the injured and Roddick was mentioned in dispatches.

Roddick's reputation began to spread after 1885 and he received numerous appointments, such as the presidency of the Montreal Medico-Chirurgical Society for 1886–88, the professorship in surgery at McGill in 1890, and in the same year the presidency of the Canadian Medical Association. As a member of the original board of governors of the Royal Victoria Hospital in Montreal, set up in 1887, he had advised the project's benefactors, Sir Donald Alexander Smith* and Sir George STEPHEN, on the design of the surgical services. In 1894, soon after the hospital opened, he was appointed chief of surgery. Within one year, once the surgical service was running well, he resigned and was succeeded by James Bell. From 1901 to 1917 he would serve as chairman of the hospital's medical board.

At a meeting of the Canadian Medical Association in 1894 at Saint John, the lack of uniform standards for medical qualification throughout Canada was raised once again and Roddick was made chairman of a committee to investigate the matter. Little did he realize that this appointment would launch him into an 18-year effort to establish a nation-wide standard of medical education and a central system of medical registration in Canada. In 1896, at the request of Prime Minister Sir Charles Tupper*, he ran as a Conservative for election to the House of Commons. He was returned for the Montreal riding of St Antoine and was re-elected in 1900, but did not contest the general election of 1904. He took advantage of his position to promote a bill which became known as the Roddick Bill. Passed in 1902 and officially called the Canada Medical Act, it established the Medical Council of Canada to register all medical graduates in the country. Since education and medical licensing were matters of provincial jurisdiction, the act required ratification by the provincial legislatures before becoming effective. Roddick spent the next few years negotiating with the provincial medical councils over requirements for matriculation, the manner of provincial representation on the dominion council, and a clause to provide special provisions for existing practitioners. In 1911 a revised bill passed the house and by the following year all nine provinces had ratified it. The provinces retained control of pre-medical education and of disciplinary action over doctors. The Medical Council of Canada set examinations for Canadian graduates to qualify for practice anywhere in the dominion. In gratitude for this monumental accomplishment, the Canadian Medical Association elected him honorary president for life in 1912. He served as the first president of the council from 1912 to 1914 and it gave him the first certificate of registration on 1 July 1913.

In Ottawa Roddick had strongly advocated that Newfoundland enter the Dominion of Canada. He supported various projects in the colony, including in 1901 the organization of medical care for the fishing and sealing fleets while at sea. For years he served as president of Montreal's Newfoundland Society, which welcomed Newfoundlanders to the city, and he organized a branch of the Grenfell Mission Society in Montreal to support the work of Wilfred Thomason Grenfell*. In Newfoundland the town of Roddickton and a hospital in Stephenville would be named after him.

As an MP, he also spoke on issues of public health, especially tuberculosis. From 1903 to 1908 he served as vice-president of the Montreal League for the Prevention of Tuberculosis and in 1909 he was appointed to Quebec's royal commission on tuberculosis. Roddick played a prominent role in several other medical organizations. He had helped set up the Canadian branch of the British Medical Association, of which he became president. In 1896–98 he was the first overseas president of the parent organization and he arranged for a meeting of the association in Montreal in 1897, the first outside the British Isles. The meeting was such a huge success that he was elected vice-president for life. He also founded and helped to raise money for an isolation hospital, the Alexandra Hospital in Montreal, and was its president from 1905 to World War I. He held the vice-presidency of the Quebec branch of the Canadian Red Cross in 1896 and was an honorary vice-president of the Victorian Order of Nurses.

In December 1901 Roddick was appointed dean of medicine at McGill. During the next seven years he negotiated more major developments in the faculty than had been seen in the past 72 years. The first problem requiring his negotiating skills was a financial one. Independent of the university, the faculty appointed its members and collected its own fees, but by the turn of the century, with all its bequests and donations having gone for capital expansion, it was running at an annual deficit. By 1903 it was apparent that this situation was going to continue and that the faculty owed a sizeable amount to the university. At Roddick's request, Lord Strathcona [Smith] donated $50,000 to pay the debt, but he strongly suggested that the faculty make arrangements for better financial management. Strathcona was the faculty's major benefactor and Roddick knew that with his eventual passing the faculty would be in even greater trouble. In 1904 he proposed an amalgamation with McGill, which was accomplished the following year, thereby ending 76 years of separate existence.

The second important event during Roddick's term was the establishment of a dental school. The Dental Association of the Province of Quebec had requested that McGill open a dental school many years earlier, but negotiations had failed, so the association had established the Dental College of the Province of Quebec, which affiliated with Bishop's College in 1896. Since by 1903 the school was experiencing difficulty, the Dental Association contacted McGill expressing renewed interest in the establishment of a dental school at the university. In 1904 Bishop's school was accepted in its entirety as the dental faculty of McGill, a department of the faculty of medicine. McGill began teaching dentistry in the autumn of 1905.

The most important development during Roddick's deanship was the request in 1904 from Bishop's medical faculty to amalgamate with McGill. Its school was solvent, and had had 221 graduates since 1872, including Casey Albert Wood*, William Henry Drummond*, and Maude Elizabeth Seymour Abbott*. The merger, completed in 1905, eliminated competition for McGill in the field of English-language medical education in Quebec. There was no room on the staff at McGill for most of the faculty of Bishop's. Students who wanted to graduate with a McGill degree had to start in the first year. Those who did not could continue at McGill and graduate with a degree from Bishop's.

On 15 April 1907 the central portion of the medical faculty's building was destroyed by fire. About 50 per cent of the structure was lost, including part of the medical museum, laboratories, and offices. Roddick felt that incendiarism had to be considered, but an investigation by the fire commission of Montreal failed to reveal any evidence of arson. Roddick, who was to retire in June 1907, agreed to stay on as dean until arrangements were made to continue the medical courses and construct a new building, but he did retire as professor of surgery that year. With the help of funds from Strathcona, construction began and the decision to lengthen the curriculum to five years was finally approved by the university. This important development provided a clinical year for most students, who went into practice without internship. Roddick resigned the deanship in 1908 and in appreciation of his service he was appointed a life governor of McGill.

Additional honours had been conferred on Roddick, among them several honorary degrees: an LLD from Edinburgh in 1898, an LLD from Queen's College, Kingston, in 1903, and a DSC from Oxford in 1904. Others included an honorary fellowship in the Royal College of Surgeons of England in 1900, an honorary membership in the Medical Society of London in 1897, an associate fellowship in the Physicians and Surgeons of Philadelphia in 1898, an honorary fellowship in the American College of Surgeons in 1914, and membership in the Royal Society of Canada in 1914. The crowning honour of his career was a knighthood conferred by King George V in 1914; many considered it long overdue.

The author of 45 publications, including 4 articles on antiseptic surgery which established his reputation, Roddick probably had as great an influence on the practice of medicine in his role as one of the editors of the prestigious *Canada Medical & Surgical Journal* (Montreal) (1882–88) and its successor, the *Montreal Medical Journal* (1888–1903).

Roddick's health began to fail after his deanship.

He had arteriosclerosis with coronary artery disease and took nitroglycerin. He had no specific hobbies or interests apart from medicine, but he and his wife enjoyed travelling. Even this activity was limited after 1914. His last trip to England to receive his knighthood that year was particularly exhausting because of the difficulty getting passage back to Canada once the war had broken out. For a number of years he spent the winter in Florida, but even this custom became too much by the end of the war. Charles Ferdinand Martin, his physician, diagnosed pernicious anaemia with combined system disease, a degeneration of the spinal cord. He gradually deteriorated and he died quietly at home on 20 Feb. 1923.

A punctual man, Sir Thomas Roddick had often discussed with his wife Amy the need for a clock tower at McGill. In 1924 she donated money for the construction of formal gates off Sherbrooke Street with a bell tower at one end. A committee was established, chaired by Sir Herbert Samuel Holt* of Montreal, various designs were considered, and the gates as they are today were constructed; a bell tower on the west side has three clock faces and bells that ring on the quarter-hour. Hundreds of thousands have passed through these gates since their formal opening in 1925.

JOSEPH HANAWAY

The appendix to H. E. MacDermot, *Sir Thomas Roddick: his work in medicine and public life* (Toronto, 1938), includes partial listings of Roddick's contributions to various medical journals and the addresses he gave throughout his career. Additional references can be found in the CIHM, *Reg.* Eighty-three articles by Roddick are listed in the Fichier Medicus quebecensis online database at the Centre Interuniversitaire d'Études Québécoises of the Univ. Laval, Québec, and the Univ. du Québec à Trois-Rivières.

ANQ-M, CE601-S120, 2 août 1880. MUA, RG 38, c.14–16. McGill Univ. Libraries, Dept. of Rare Books and Special Coll., MS coll., MS 659 (T. G. Roddick papers). St Paul's Anglican Church (Harbour Grace, Nfld), Reg. of baptisms, 1775–1916 (copy at PANL). *Le Devoir*, 21 févr. 1923. *Montreal Daily Star*, 4 Sept. 1906, 20 Feb. 1923. *Montreal Gazette*, 30 June 1864, continued as *Gazette*, 16–17 April 1907. *Canadian men and women of the time* (Morgan; 1898 and 1912). *CPG*, 1897–1903. R. B. Kerr, *History of the Medical Council of Canada* (Ottawa, 1979). D. S. Lewis, *Royal Victoria Hospital, 1887–1947* (Montreal, 1969). M. A. Rogers, *A history of the McGill dental school* (Montreal, 1980). *Standard dict. of Canadian biog.* (Roberts and Tunnell). G. D. Thompson, "The Roddick Memorial Gates," *McGill News* (Montreal), 6, no.3 (June 1925): 21–23. *Who's who in Canada*, 1922.

ROGERS, LOUISA. *See* SIMS

ROSENTHAL, BERTHA. *See* LEHMAN

ROSS, WILLIAM GILLIES, businessman, office holder, philanthropist, and sportsman; b. 6 Aug. 1863 in Montreal, fourth of the eight children of Philip Simpson Ross* and Christina Chalmers Dansken; brother of Philip Dansken Ross*; m. 18 Dec. 1888 Ida Elizabeth Millard Babcock in Montreal, and they had three sons and two daughters; d. there 15 April 1929.

On graduating from the High School of Montreal, William Gillies Ross followed his father into accountancy and in 1883 he became a partner in Philip S. Ross, later P. S. Ross and Sons. After several years of auditing, he left the firm to become involved in administration, initially with the Windsor Hotel Company of Montreal, in which he rose from secretary and treasurer to general manager by 1890. Then a revolution in urban transit systems in North America attracted his attention, as electricity began to replace horses. In association with railway engineer James Ross* (no relation) he became involved in the organization and electrification of street railways in Montreal, Saint John, Toronto, Winnipeg, and other cities from about 1892 to 1896. His experience led to his appointment as controller of the Montreal Street Railway Company in 1896. During a strike in May 1903, believing that the workers had no justifiable grievance and that the trams should be kept running, he rode many of them (with revolver in hand, according to one story), helped to preserve order, and gave regular press conferences to report on the status of the various lines. His efforts were applauded by the company, the press, and the public. The *Gazette* remarked on his "nerve, aggressiveness and force," and when he was promoted to managing director several months later he was described by the *Montreal Daily Herald* as "a man who does." He was by no means anti-labour, however; in 1904 he founded the Montreal Street Railway Mutual Benefit Association.

Described by a contemporary as a "man of indefatigable energy, tremendous ability and keen imaginative vision," Ross demonstrated these qualities during seven years as managing director of the Montreal Street Railway. In addition to planning and overseeing the growth of the system and the amalgamation of other street railways on the island of Montreal, he had to cope with the challenge of operating streetcars in winter and the problem of overcrowded cars during rush hours, when conductors had difficulty circulating to collect fares. Ross and his associate Duncan A. L. McDonald designed the pay-as-you-enter streetcar, on which a stationary conductor collected fares as passengers boarded by a single entrance at the rear. The first PAYE car in North America was introduced in Montreal in 1905. Simple as the idea was, it met with opposition, and even derision, in some quarters. Yet when the Canadian concept was introduced to New York and Chicago in 1908 it was called "the greatest single innovation of recent years for the comfort and safety of street railway passengers in the United States." Ross's reputation for skilful and innovative management had already launched him into a wider world of public transit interests. He had been elected president of the Canadian Street Railway Association and of the Street Railway Accountants' Association of America in 1904. Six years later he became the first Canadian to serve as vice-president of the American Street Railway Association.

Ross's growing reputation for organizational ability and business acumen brought him into association with a variety of enterprises. During his business career he served either as president, vice-president, director, managing director, or general manager of 19 firms, including many related to transportation (such as Montreal Tramways Company and Pay-As-You-Enter Car Corporation), several electric companies (Beauharnois Electric Company, Canadian General Electric Company), others involved in resource development (Dominion Iron and Steel Company Limited, Asbestos Corporation of Canada), and a variety of financial and land companies.

One writer observed that "his mind was many-sided and seemingly capable of grappling with many problems simultaneously." Although he presented a calm and cheerful exterior, the diversity and intensity of the work took a toll. When a syndicate headed by Edmund Arthur Robert* secured control of the Montreal Street Railway Company in 1910 with policies that differed fundamentally from his own, he resigned, "to take a well-earned rest" and spend the winter of 1910–11 in Europe. The public clamoured for his return. In 1913 Ross, described by the *Daily Telegraph* as "the one man in Montreal who knows how to run a tramway," accepted a position on the board of the company, now Montreal Tramways.

In 1912 Ross had been named president of the Montreal Harbour Commission, the federally appointed board responsible for the port. It was a heaven-sent opportunity for a man who loved boating and was experienced in transportation. Montreal accommodated both river and ocean ships and, as a place of trans-shipment between the two, it possessed extensive storage facilities, but various factors hindered its development. With his characteristic energy, he set about improving the efficiency of the port, building on the work of predecessors and seeking new ideas. During a three-month trip in 1914 Ross and two colleagues visited 25 ports in Europe and on subsequent trips they toured ports in North America. In Montreal dockside rail services were improved, new warehouses were built, and grain storage facilities were enlarged. By 1918 a contemporary professional journal declared that within a decade Montreal had progressed from "a mere stopping place for ships" to "the front rank of ocean ports." It possessed a buoyed and lighted channel more than 30 feet deep extending 1,000 miles to the sea; it had North America's best system of connecting railways to docks; it stood second to New York among Atlantic seaboard ports in ocean traffic and value of trade; it was the largest grain shipping seaport in the world with the world's largest seaport grain elevator; and it was said to be "the most efficient port in America."

Ross did not hesitate to publicize Montreal's progress and extol its advantages. As president of the commission, he inevitably received much credit for achievements to which many others had contributed in significant ways [see Sir John KENNEDY]. Nonetheless, his organizational abilities were widely recognized. He was elected president of the American Association of Port Authorities in 1916 and re-elected the following year.

In 1911, while Ross was helping to transform Montreal into one of the "foremost ocean ports in the world," friends persuaded him to accept the presidency of the struggling Amalgamated Asbestos Corporation. Despite the pessimistic predictions of many, the enterprise, reorganized the following year as the Asbestos Corporation of Canada, was soon in a strong financial position, with profits rising steadily. Its recovery during more than a decade under his management was called by the *Gazette* "one of the most romantic developments in Canadian mining and industrial history."

Appointed director of naval recruiting for the province of Quebec in 1916, Ross addressed rallies and organized many events in support of the war effort. Serving as president of the Canadian branch of the British Sailors' Relief Fund, he personally donated $10,000 – an amount equal to the contribution of the most generous bank – to get its fund-raising drive started. The money collected – nearly $3,000,000 – was sent to England to benefit navy and merchant-marine sailors and their families. In appreciation of his efforts, the British Navy League made him an honorary vice-president and awarded him its special service decoration. Ross was one of the founders and the first dominion president (1917–19) of the Navy League of Canada. He was also a fund-raiser for the Canadian Patriotic Fund and the Harry Lauder Million Pound Fund for disabled Scottish veterans. In addition, he made many small but generous gestures, such as sending apples to a visiting warship, taking wounded soldiers cruising on his yacht, and dispatching gifts to troops overseas. A president of the St Andrews Society in 1921–22 and a life governor of the Montreal General Hospital, he donated money and property to McGill University and to various institutions and charitable organizations.

Some of the moral principles that guided Ross's life are set out in a small pamphlet which he published and gave to his sons on their 21st birthdays. "The basis of success and happiness in life is character and truthfulness – never depart from them," he wrote. "Take off your coat and make dust in the world," he counselled.

He practised what he preached, raising plenty of dust in street railway operation, port management, asbestos mining, wartime activities, amateur sport, charitable causes, and community affairs. He belonged to dozens of clubs – some social, others related to sports – in Montreal, Ottawa, Quebec, the Eastern Townships, London, and New York. Business affairs had brought Ross into frequent contact with politicians, but he took aim at political office only once, in 1921, when the Conservative candidate in the federal riding of St Antoine withdrew unexpectedly. He was defeated at the polls.

No account of Ross's life would be complete without mentioning his involvement in sport. At age 18 he had joined the Montreal Bicycle Club. He quickly achieved outstanding success in local competitions. When the Canadian Wheelmen's Association held one- and five-mile races in London, Ont., in 1883 for the national championships, Ross won both events. That year he competed in 16 races in Canada and lost only one – a handicap race in which he had the fastest time. At the major American meet in Springfield, Mass., he came third in two events and fourth in two others, at distances ranging from a half-mile to ten miles. When he unexpectedly announced his retirement from competition a year later, a Montreal newspaper regretted the loss of "one of the fastest men in America."

As a young man, Ross had also played for the Britannia Football Club, competed in canoeing, skating, and snowshoe races, and participated in ice-boating, lacrosse, and other recreational activities. Although professional life and a growing family made increasing demands upon his time after 1890, he continued to be active, both as a competitor and as an administrator. He firmly believed in the character-building role of amateur sport and worked to stimulate participation, improve facilities, and expand organizations. He was one of the founders of the Canadian Amateur Skating Association in 1886 and served as its president from 1893 to 1895, in 1905, and perhaps in other years. In 1894 the association organized what he called "the greatest skating meeting ever held in the world" in Montreal. In 1908 he served on the Central Olympic Committee.

In sports as in life, Ross was a determined competitor, a man who, according to the *Herald*, "always does what he has to do with all the power that is in him." Winning was not the only goal, however. Sports brought him in touch with others on a friendly and informal basis. During two decades after 1907 he and his four brothers competed annually in curling and golf, and occasionally in hockey, against five Hodgson brothers. Canada's leading golf magazine considered that there was "nothing more interesting in the realm of amateur sport than these inter-family matches." After the formation of the Canadian Senior Golf Association in 1918, Ross regularly competed in its annual championships, played on Canadian seniors' teams against the United States, and served as a governor of the association. In 1925 he won the seniors' individual championship of the two countries.

William Gillies Ross died in 1929 after an operation. The *Montreal Daily Star* praised "his broad sympathies, his youthful enthusiasms, his quiet manner, and his habitual cordiality."

W. GILLIES ROSS

William Gillies Ross is the author of *Father's advice* (n.p., n.d.), a privately published pamphlet, and "Development of street railways in Canada," *Street Railway Rev.* (Chicago), 11 (1901), no.1: 30–31. He also wrote "Montreal port organization," *Freight Handling and Terminal Engineering* (New York), but nothing more is known about this article (a copy is in the possession of the author).

ANQ-M, CE601-S115, 18 déc. 1888; S120, 6 août 1863. Private arch., W. G. Ross (North Hatley, Que.), 16 scrapbooks of newspaper clippings, articles, and speeches given by the subject; reminiscences. *Daily Telegraph* (Montreal), 5 Aug. 1913. *Gazette* (Montreal), 16 April 1929. *Globe*, 16 April 1929. *Montreal Daily Herald*, 11 Dec. 1903. *Montreal Daily Star*, 15–16 April 1929. Martin Burrell, "The late Mr. W. G. Ross," *Canadian Golfer* ([Brantford, Ont.]), 15 (1929–30): 8–10. *Canadian men and women of the time* (Morgan; 1912). "Eighth annual seniors' tournament," *Canadian Golfer*, 11 (1925–26): 464–77. "The passing of Mr. W. G. Ross," *Canadian Golfer*, 14 (1928–29): 941. *Prominent people of the province of Quebec, 1923–24* (Montreal, n.d.). *The storied province of Quebec; past and present*, ed. W. [C. H.] Wood *et al.*, (5v., Toronto, 1931–32).

ROSVALL, VILJO, railway worker and labour organizer; b. probably 1898, in Finland; d. unmarried November 1929 north of Port Arthur (Thunder Bay), Ont.

Viljo Rosvall came to Canada in the 1920s, one of many socialist or Red Finns fleeing the aftermath of Finland's civil war (January–May 1918), in which he had fought and which had resulted in a victory for the nationalist or White forces. Tough and resilient, he settled in Port Arthur in northwestern Ontario, where there was a substantial community of Finns working in the lumber industries. He is usually described as a maintenance man for the Canadian Pacific Railway, but he also became an organizer for the Lumber Workers' Industrial Union of Canada. By 1929 this union, the most prominent one in the region, was largely Finnish in membership and was dominated by the Communist Party of Canada.

In October 1929 the LWIUC called a strike at Shabaqua, some distance west of Port Arthur. The strike apparently was not going well, so the decision was made to try to extend it to the camps of the Pigeon Timber Company Limited on Onion Lake. The jobber (foreman) there was Leonard A. Mäki, a conservative White Finn known for his hostility to the union. Rosvall and Janne Voutilainen, a trapper who seems to have accompanied him as a guide, set off on 18 November to walk to one of the camps, at the north end of the lake. A few miles short of their destination they came across Mäki and some of his men at a supply depot, preparing for winter cutting operations. Mäki would later claim that he called the two over to warm their hands, warned them about the precarious state of the ice, and last saw them walking up the lake. They were never seen alive again.

From the moment of their disappearance, the Red Finn community was convinced that they had died at the hands of Mäki or his men. An investigation by the Ontario Provincial Police was demanded, and Jacob Laurence Cohen*, a lawyer from the Canadian Labour Defence League in Toronto, was engaged to secure an official inquiry. The OPP conducted a cursory investigation and concluded that the men must have drowned.

On 19 April 1930 the body of Voutilainen was discovered, floating in shallow water at the north end of Onion Lake. Rosvall was found on the 23rd, half a mile away, in a stream described as no more than four feet deep. Rumours spread that both bodies bore marks of violence, and that one or both of them had bullet holes in the head. Autopsies were performed and inquests resulted in similar verdicts: accidental death by drowning. Cohen, who represented the union at Rosvall's inquest, held on 5 May, concluded that "there seemed to be an inclination on the part of the public and official witnesses to minimize any facts which would tend to cause any doubts as to the findings on the doctor's post mortem." Whatever the truth, there can be no doubt that the official verdicts were reached in haste and despite circumstantial evidence that suggests, if it does not prove, foul play. The men had been buried on 28 April in Riverside Cemetery in the largest funeral in Port Arthur's history.

Their deaths came to be seen as a defining moment in the history of the Finnish community at the Lakehead, a symbol of the deep ideological division within that group. Though the LWIUC, and the Finnish Canadian left in general, slid into a period of decline, Rosvall and Voutilainen continued to be hailed as martyrs. In 1992 they were inducted into the Canadian Labour Congress Hall of Fame in North York, Ont.

PETER RAFFO

The author has some recollections, on tape, of relatives and friends of participants in the events surrounding the disappearance and deaths of Rosvall and Voutilainen.

LAC, MG 30, A94, 1, file 10. Lakehead Univ. Arch. (Thunder Bay, Ont.), Thunder Bay Labour Hist. Project, directed by Jean Morrison (taped interviews). Multicultural Hist. Soc. of Ont. (Toronto), Finnish coll. (taped interviews). *Canadan Uutiset* [Canadian News] (Port Arthur [Thunder

Bay]), 28 Nov. 1929; 24 April, 1, 8 May 1930. *Daily Times-Journal* (Fort William [Thunder Bay]), 22 Nov. 1929; 21–23 April, 6 May 1930. *Industrialisti* [Industrialist] (Duluth, Minn.), 27 Oct., 11 Dec. 1929; 30 April 1930. *Metsä-työläinen* [Lumberworker] (Sudbury, Ont.), no.3 (1930); no.7 (1931), no.10 (1932). *News-Chronicle* (Port Arthur), 21, 27 Nov., 18 Dec. 1929; 21–23 April, 6 May 1930. *Vapaus/Liberty* (Sudbury), 16, 18, 27 Nov., 4 Dec. 1929; 21, 28–29 April 1930. Ian Radforth, *Bushworkers and bosses: logging in northern Ontario, 1900–1980* (Toronto, 1987). Satu Repo, "Rosvall and Voutilainen: two union men who never died," *Labour* (St John's), 8/9 (1981–82): 79–102.

ROUILLARD, EUGÈNE (baptized **Nicolas-Olivier-Eugène**), notary, journalist, office holder, author, and geographer; b. 4 June 1851 at Quebec, son of Nicolas Rouillard, a merchant, and Éliza Legris, *dit* Lépine; m. there 10 Jan. 1881 Orpha Myrand, and they had three sons and four daughters; d. there 16 Oct. 1926.

Eugène Rouillard, who was the son of a merchant in Quebec's Lower Town, pursued his classical studies at the Petit Séminaire de Québec from 1860 to 1872. He enrolled in the Université Laval at Quebec in 1872 and graduated three years later with an LLB. On 17 May 1876 he was licensed to practise as a notary, and he would carry on this profession at Quebec until 1884, working as a journalist at the same time. He founded *Le Nouvelliste*, a Conservative daily, on 27 Nov. 1876 and he was its editor-in-chief and co-owner until 23 Oct. 1886, when the paper ceased publication because of a dispute between Rouillard and his business partner, J.-G. Gingras, about its political orientation. Having worked at *Le Canadien* from the end of 1886 until the end of 1888, he became editor-in-chief of *L'Événement*, a position he retained from 1889 until the end of 1891. On 13 Jan. 1892 the Conservative party launched the daily *Le Matin*, through the agency of Louis-Philippe PELLETIER, in anticipation of the coming provincial general election. Rouillard was its sub-editor until it ceased publication on 19 September. He distinguished himself as a journalist by the great variety of subjects he addressed (politics, libraries, the French language, place names) and by his support for the Conservative party. He was the author of nearly 600 newspaper articles.

Rouillard also worked in the civil service. He was a federal government census commissioner in 1881 and 1891 and a civil service examiner from 1882 to 1893. On 14 Oct. 1892 he had been hired by the Quebec provincial government as crown clerk in chancery. Edmund James FLYNN, the commissioner of crown lands, appointed him superintendent of land sales for the eastern section of the province on 3 July 1893. He would hold this office until 1905, when he would become secretary of land sales. On his visits to sparsely inhabited and uninhabited regions, he took an interest in a wide range of subjects related to geogra-

phy, in particular the characteristics of places, natural resources, rivers and means of communication, the potential for colonization, and place names.

In the course of his duties, Rouillard brought out *La colonisation dans les comtés de Témiscouata, Rimouski, Matane, Bonaventure, Gaspé* in 1899, *La colonisation dans les comtés de Dorchester, Bellechasse, Montmagny, L'Islet, Kamouraska* in 1901, and *La Côte nord du Saint-Laurent et le Labrador canadien . . .* in 1908. Published at Quebec, these monographs dealt with the parishes, their people, and their resources (the dairy industry, forestry, roads, rivers). Other works by Rouillard highlighted the province's flourishing wildlife and its hydroelectric potential. As a civil servant, he was involved in lawsuits dealing with territorial issues, zoning (before the term existed), and the use that should or should not be made of land and its management. His work schedule from 3 May 1895 to 27 May 1899 shows the diversity of his duties, the kind of decisions he was called on to make, the advice he had to give on such matters as the sale of public lands, the setting, revision, and arrears of rents, the price of potential water-power, the evaluation of the natural environment (soil and forests), disagreements about waterfront lots, mix-ups in the ownership of a lot, the evaluation of land agents, and encroachment by a railway.

In 1907 Rouillard became the province's representative on the Geographic Board of Canada, which had been set up for the purpose of listing geographical names and making them uniform. His correspondence shows that he would maintain contact with it until 1920. On his initiative, the Quebec Geographical Commission (which came under the Department of Colonization, Mines, and Fisheries) was created by order in council on 15 Nov. 1912. Chair of this commission until 5 Aug. 1915, Rouillard had to find solutions for such problems as chaotic use of official place names, including that of multiple names for the same place or the same one for two places. Among the first rules he set out for spelling place names were: retain those consecrated by long usage, use a hyphen in compound ones, and spell aboriginal names to reflect their pronunciation. The results of his labours were published at Quebec in two significant volumes. The *Dictionnaire des rivières et lacs de la province de Québec*, which came out in 1914 and was reissued in 1925, was intended to determine "in a definitive manner the appropriate spelling of a host of new geographical designations." *Nomenclature des noms géographiques de la province de Québec*, which Rouillard brought out in 1916 in his capacity as secretary general (an office he would hold until 6 March 1920), was the first report of the Quebec Geographical Commission, which would become the Commission de Toponymie in 1977. Before Rouillard, only a handful of works by Joseph Bouchette* and Pierre-Georges

Roy* had been published on the subject of place names.

In 1902 Rouillard was a founding member of the Société du Parler Français au Canada [*see* Stanislas-Alfred Lortie*], for which he wrote *Noms géographiques de la province de Québec et des provinces Maritimes empruntés aux langues sauvages . . .*, which came out at Quebec in 1906. He also wrote many articles for the society's bulletin. He joined the Geographical Society of Quebec in 1907 and became its recording secretary and treasurer the following year. In 1908 he revived its bulletin and, through his dynamic management of the publication, he was able to revitalize the organization, which had been in existence for some 30 years. He would retain both offices in the society for the rest of his life. He also published articles in the *Bulletin des recherches historiques* (Lévis). With 160 magazine articles to his credit, Rouillard in 1915 became a member of the Royal Society of Canada, and he would be president of its French section in 1918. In 1916, six years after receiving the title of *officier d'académie* from the French government, he was granted an honorary doctorate by the Université Laval at Quebec.

Eugène Rouillard suffered an attack of paralysis in December 1919. He soon recovered, but he had a relapse in 1924 and died in 1926, not long after his retirement. A herald of descriptive and applied geography and the author of the first rules of toponymy, he had had a long and fruitful career whose influence was long-lasting. He named many places in the regions of Quebec that were being colonized, and his work on aboriginal place names, published in 1906, would appear in a revised edition in 1999. His contemporaries honoured him for his modesty, his diligence at work, his dedication, his friendliness, his passionate, scientific, and methodical approach, and his love of French Canada and the French language.

LAURENT DESHAIES

[Eugène Rouillard is the author of many books and articles in addition to those mentioned above: *Les bibliothèques populaires* (Québec, 1890); *Our rivers and lakes: fish and game* (Quebec, 1895); *Les premiers almanachs canadiens* (Lévis, Qué., 1898); *The white coal: the water-powers of the province of Quebec* (Quebec, 1909).

A list of Rouillard's works can be found in Joseph Rouillard, "Bio-bibliographie d'Eugène Rouillard, notaire" (mémoire, école de bibliothéconomie, univ. Laval, Québec, 1963). It is relatively complete, but contains errors and omissions, as do Christian Morissonneau, *Index, "Bulletin de la Société de géographie de Québec," 1880–1934; Index, "Bulletin des sociétés de géographie de Québec et de Montréal," 1942–1944* (Sainte-Foy, Qué., [1969]), and Commission de Toponymie, *Bibliographie toponymique du Québec* (2e éd., [Québec], 1987).

Other materials provide more information about Rouillard's work in the area of geographic place names: the Commission de Toponymie du Québec fonds at the ANQ-Q, E51; the Commission de Géographie de Québec fonds, held at the Commission de Toponymie du Québec (Québec), 4230-00-09 (there are indexes and inventories available for this fonds, including minutes and correspondence); a manuscript notebook and some of Rouillard's correspondence between 1895 and 1915 at the Arch. de l'Univ. Laval, P360; and other documents in MCQ-FSQ, SME 2.2/166/34b, 22 févr. 1900; 10/3/36, 2 avril 1902. L.D.]

ANQ-Q, CE301-S1, 5 juin 1851, 10 janv. 1881. *Le Soleil*, 19 oct. 1926. Henri Froidevaux, "L'œuvre de la Commission de géographie de Québec," Soc. de Géographie de Québec, *Bull.* (Québec), 11 (1917): 327–33. Omer Héroux, "In memoriam," Soc. de Géographie de Québec, *Bull.*, 20 (1926): 193–98. Paul Labrecque, "Eugène Rouillard: colonisation et toponymie," *Géographes* (Québec), no.2 (novembre 1992): 68–72. Henri Lanrezac, "À la mémoire de M. Eugène Rouillard," Soc. de Géographie de Québec, *Bull.*, 21 (1927): 86–88. Christian Morissonneau, *La Société de géographie de Québec, 1877–1970* (Québec, 1971). Jean Poirier, *Regards sur les noms de lieux* (Québec, 1982); "75 ans de toponymie," *Le Toponyme* (Québec), 4 (1986–87), no.6: 1–2. P.-G. Roy, "Ouvrages publiés par feu Eugène Rouillard," *BRH*, 33 (1927): 363–64.

ROWELL, SARAH ALICE (Wright), social reformer and editor; b. 4 Dec. 1862 in London Township, Upper Canada, daughter of Joseph Rowell and Nancy Green; m. 26 June 1884 Benjamin Gordon Hobson Wright in London South (London), Ont., and they had four sons; d. 26 June 1930 in London.

Sarah Rowell was strongly influenced in her youth by her father, a farmer from Cumberland, England, who was a Methodist lay preacher and temperance leader, and by her maternal grandmother, a keen and intelligent conversationalist who lived with them. Educated in the village school in Arva, Sarah (known to her family as Sazie) gained some early recognition as a painter and a writer of fiction. She settled in the city of London with her family about 1883, and in 1884 she married Gordon Wright, a native of London Township then in business in Columbus, Ohio. After moving there, she resolved to serve Christ and, accepting a call to mission, began working with black children. In 1886, however, economic hardship forced the Wrights back to London, where Gordon entered the millinery trade – he would eventually set up his own hat company – and they joined Queen's Avenue Church and later First Church (Metropolitan). As Sarah again moved to act on her beliefs, she publicly displayed the strong personality noted by the biographer of her younger brother Newton Wesley*, a lawyer and Methodist activist.

Wright focused her awe-inspiring energies and talents on three organizations with interrelated programs and many common members: the Lord's Day Alliance (of which she was a vice-president), the Missionary Society of the Methodist Church of Canada, and the Woman's Christian Temperance Union. As evidence of her ongoing commitment to mission work, she accepted the presidency of the London Conference branch of the Woman's Missionary Society and for eight years was associate editor of the Methodist Missionary Society's *Missionary Outlook* (Toronto), where her evangelicalism and anti-Catholic sentiments had free rein. Her involvement in the WCTU was even more sustained.

Beginning in 1894, she held the superintendency of the literature department of the London WCTU, which placed temperance materials in public areas such as barber-shops and otherwise arranged for their wide distribution. She also headed the anti-narcotics department, which engineered campaigns against tobacco, illicit substances such as opium, and the overuse of prescription drugs. As well, she worked on a variety of other projects, including the provision of non-alcoholic refreshments at fall fairs. In 1896 she accepted the presidency of the London union, one of the strongest locals in the Ontario WCTU. (The London union would later be named after her.) In this post she exemplified the dutiful, evangelical membership of the WCTU: at her inaugural meeting, on 1 Dec. 1896, she "requested that the first act of this new regime should be one of prayer for Divine Guidance." She continued to take an active role in devotional exercises at all levels of the WCTU and was a key figure in Methodist affairs in London. In 1906, after lectures there on new approaches to biblical criticism, which troubled many, she appealed to the Reverend Albert Carman* for direction on this "perplexing question," but her faith never wavered.

In 1895 her election as recording secretary for the Ontario WCTU had made her an essential executive member, responsible for its detailed annual reports. Between 1897 and 1905 she also took on the tasks of corresponding secretary, a position of great importance since the provincial body was heavily dependent on the mails to exert pressure on public officials. Her marked success in fund-raising throughout the last decade of the 19th century and well into the 20th is reflected in the WCTU journal, *Canadian White Ribbon Tidings* (London). Within the Dominion WCTU, she occupied the positions of vice-president from 1903 and president from 1905 until her death; in recognition of her service she was made a life member of the dominion organization (1903), an honorary life member (1909), and a memorial member (1930). In addition, she was a vice-president of the World's League Against Alcoholism.

To replace the WCTU's defunct periodical, the *Woman's Journal*, Wright had begun the *Canadian White Ribbon Tidings* in 1904 with another WCTU stalwart, May Rowland Thornley of London. Although editorial control was contested by the Ontario and dominion levels, the journal flourished under Wright's able direction as editor, proof-reader,

and business manager. When she became president of the dominion body, she was unable to carry the added burden of producing the paper. Not surprisingly, it proved difficult to find a successor with her range of abilities. In 1906 *Tidings* formally became the journal of the Ontario body and in 1910, during Wright's presidency, the Dominion WCTU launched *Canada's White Ribbon Bulletin* (Ottawa) for the discussion of pan-Canadian issues. In the 1920s Wright would resume her association with *Tidings* as its editor-in-chief.

In all of these capacities, Wright, who excelled as a speaker, stood as an implacable foe of alcohol, tobacco, and domestic violence, one whose talks and writings were laced with feminist and sometimes nativist argument. Like many temperance reformers of her era, she believed the menace of alcohol to be so monumental that the combined forces of several organizations were needed to ensure triumph. Hence, she belonged to many groups and supported even more. A known suffragist, in 1905 she insisted, as a member of the Ontario WCTU, on the municipal enfranchisement of qualified women. She backed the newly formed National Equal Franchise Union in 1914, and spoke that year in Ottawa at the Social Service Congress, which, she concluded, confirmed the link between suffrage, temperance, and the emerging Social Gospel. In November 1926 she was the featured lecturer at a public meeting in Peterborough's Grand Opera House sponsored by the Women's Prohibition Committee; the local WCTU resolved to attend en masse in support of their president. In 1929 she was one of five women appointed to serve on an international advisory council of the World's WCTU, of which she had been named a world memorial member the previous year. In addition to providing temperance leadership, she served as a vice-president of the National Council of Women of Canada and of the Social Service Council of Canada. During the Great War, in which at least one of her sons served overseas, she was first vice-president of the Western Ontario Red Cross, and in 1918 she participated in the Women's War Conference in Ottawa, organized by her brother Newton as chair of the federal War Committee.

Her final years were filled with challenges and unrelenting activity. In 1927, while she was lecturing in British Columbia after the annual meeting of the Dominion WCTU, her husband, also a temperance advocate, died suddenly in London of a heart attack. It was at this meeting that she had lamented the introduction of the controlled sale of liquor in several provinces: "If ever we needed a prayer-hearing, covenant-keeping God, it is now, when our hopes for Canada are for the *Present moment* immersed in a sea of great and almost universal defeat." Unswayed, in June 1930 she addressed numerous audiences during the electoral campaign in New Brunswick, where control had been adopted in 1927; on 24 June she still had the energy to speak to the WCTU branch in Ingersoll, Ont. Two days later she was dead. She was buried from Knox United Church in London.

Sarah Wright had long been regarded by the press as "one of the brightest" of Canadian women. Indeed, she gives evidence of having had a keen intelligence, an exceptionally strong sense of duty, and marked abilities to work with like-minded reformers in many associated causes to good effect.

SHARON ANNE COOK

AO, F 885, MU 8394.1, 8396.11, 8404.9–12, 8440.6–7 (mfm.); Minute-books of selected Ontario Woman's Christian Temperance Union locals (mfm.); RG 22-321, no.20234; RG 80-5-0-127, no.7316; RG 80-8-0-1068, no.21832. LAC, RG 31, C1, 1901, Westminster Township (London South), Ont., div.4: 13 (mfm. at AO). Univ. of Western Ont. Arch., J. J. Talman Regional Coll. (London), Minutes of the London Woman's Christian Temperance Union, 1893–1906. *London Free Press*, 24–25, 28 June 1927; 27 June, 1 July 1930. Richard Allen, *The social passion: religion and social reform in Canada, 1914–28* (Toronto, 1971; repr. 1990). C. L. Bacchi, *Liberation deferred? The ideas of the English-Canadian suffragists, 1877–1918* (Toronto, 1983). *Canadian annual rev.*, 1913: 432. *Canadian men and women of the time* (Morgan; 1912). S. A. Cook, *"Through sunshine and shadow": the Woman's Christian Temperance Union, evangelicalism, and reform in Ontario, 1874–1930* (Montreal and Kingston, Ont., 1995). R. R. Gagan, *A sensitive independence: Canadian Methodist women missionaries in Canada and the Orient, 1881–1925* (Montreal and Kingston, 1992). B. D. Merriman, *The emigrant ancestors of a lieutenant governor of Ontario* ([Toronto], 1993). Margaret Prang, *N. W. Rowell, Ontario nationalist* (Toronto and Buffalo, N.Y., 1975). Mariana Valverde, *The age of light, soap, and water: moral reform in English Canada, 1885–1925* (Toronto, 1991). *Woman's Christian Temperance Union, 1878–1978, London centennial* ([London, 1979?]; copy in Univ. of Western Ont. Arch., J. J. Talman Regional Coll.). *Women of Canada* (Montreal, 1930).

ROY, PAUL-EUGÈNE, professor, Roman Catholic priest, and archbishop; b. 8 Nov. 1859 in Berthier (Berthier-sur-Mer), Lower Canada, son of Benjamin Roy, a farmer, and Desanges Gosselin; d. 20 Feb. 1926 at Quebec.

Paul-Eugène Roy was the seventh in a family of 20 children, five of whom would become priests, including Camille Roy*, the future rector of the Université Laval. He himself enrolled in a commercial course at the Collège de Lévis in the fall of 1872, but he transferred to classical studies at the Petit Séminaire de Québec the next year. After entering the Grand Séminaire de Québec in 1881, he combined teaching rhetoric (the sixth-year program) with studying theology. As a young candidate for the priesthood, he showed great promise, standing first in his class, and on 13 June 1882 the seminary council decided to send him

abroad for further study in arts at the Institut Catholique de Paris and the Sorbonne. He received his licence ès lettres from the latter on 31 Dec. 1884 and embarked for Canada on the following 11 June.

From 1885 to 1890 Roy taught rhetoric at the Petit Séminaire de Québec, where he left many of his handwritten lecture notes. At the same time, he gave extension courses in literature (Latin, French, and Greek) at the Université Laval and contributed to *Le Canada français* (Québec), a periodical published by the university. He was already known for his eloquence, unusual, rich vocabulary, and skill in communication.

Roy was ordained priest on 13 June 1886. While continuing to teach, he ministered as chaplain in the parish of Saint-Zéphirin-de-Stadacona from 1888 to 1890. On 23 June 1888 he was appointed prefect of studies at the Petit Séminaire, but his advancement was blocked in the middle of the 1889–90 academic year. The reason for this abrupt halt is recorded in the seminary's journal of events. Its account of the "academic meeting" of 24 February noted an inappropriate speech in which Roy had apparently made "a very clear allusion condemning the bachelor's bill, and [had done so] in the presence of the Superior and in public." This legislative measure recognized a matriculation diploma as a sufficient prerequisite for the study of law, medicine, or the profession of notary. The hapless orator's apologies were not enough. The seminary's governing council demanded that he resign from his posts and make amends by acknowledging its absolute authority. When the priest refused to accept the second condition, he was dismissed. He had to leave the seminary and head for the United States.

On 11 March 1890 Roy entered a new phase of his life which would span nine years. Appointed curé of the parish of Sainte-Anne, in the diocese of Hartford, Conn., he did his best to gather together the French Canadians scattered across this industrial city and encourage them to retain their mother tongue. To this end he had a church, school, and parish hall built, taught classes for adults, and recruited teaching nuns. During his stay in Hartford, he adopted Blanche Authier, an orphan who would later enter religious life and become a missionary. Their spiritual correspondence would be published in Montreal in 1927.

Roy returned to Quebec on 7 May 1899, having been assigned by the new archbishop, Louis-Nazaire BÉGIN, to raise funds for the Hôtel-Dieu du Sacré-Cœur de Jésus, which was experiencing financial difficulties. As fund-raiser, he made good use of his skills in public speaking and, first and foremost, committed himself to social action for the poor. The year 1901 proved decisive for the direction of his career. Following the boot and shoe workers' strike at Quebec [see Gaudiose HÉBERT], he became one of the first chaplains to their unions, again at the archbishop's request. Bégin entrusted him with the further responsibility of founding the parish of Notre-Dame-de-Jacques-Cartier in Quebec's Saint-Roch ward. Roy served as its curé until 1907, while engaging in various other activities such as preaching on special occasions. He showed a particular devotion to the Sacred Heart, dedicating his parish to it. He also continued to uphold the classic nationalist position of the time: that it was through the church that French Canadians had been able to retain their language and their religion, the distinctive signs which had enabled them to survive as a nation. In 1904 he wrote three chapters of *Le drapeau national des Canadiens français: un choix légitime et populaire*, a work published at Quebec with the aim of getting the symbol of the Sacred Heart added to the French Canadian national flag.

In 1906 Roy became heavily involved in the temperance movement. The crusade was launched in his parish with the cooperation of notary Alphonse Huard, the co-founder and editor of *La Libre Parole* (Québec), and then was extended to the whole diocese by Bégin's pastoral letter of 22 Jan. 1906. As the main preacher for the campaign, Roy wanted to plant the movement's symbolic black cross everywhere. During the third week of January 1907, for example, he preached seven sermons in Saint-Romuald; the following week he gave two in Saint-Gervais, one in Notre-Dame-de-Jacques-Cartier, and another in Saint-Sauveur. At the beginning of February he conducted a triduum (a three-day religious event) in Saint-Agapit, his fourteenth such observance in six months. His influence even extended to other dioceses. Increasingly making his mark as Bégin's right-hand man, on 1 Feb. 1907 he was appointed by the archbishop as his delegate to the founding meeting of the Ligue Antialcoolique de Québec.

It was during this intense campaign that the idea of founding the Action Sociale Catholique took shape. Study sessions, in which Abbé Stanislas-Alfred Lortie*, Abbé Charles-Octave Gagnon, lawyer Adjutor Rivard*, and Roy took part, were held frequently at the presbytery of Notre-Dame-de-Jacques-Cartier, and produced a plan that the four organizers presented to Bégin. The archbishop's pastoral letter of 31 March 1907 created the Action Social Catholique and the Œuvre de la Presse Catholique in his archdiocese. Through its ambitious program, the first organization sought mainly to unite under one banner all the undertakings promoting Catholicism – associations, lectures, congresses, and so on – as well as to encourage new initiatives. The goal of the second was "to further the dissemination of good, wholesome, popular literature through the publication of all kinds of material in magazines, newspapers and pamphlets." The movement, however, was born in controversy. For one thing, the Catholic Church in the diocese of Quebec was more cautious than Roy in its approach to the

social Catholicism initiated by Pope Leo XIII. Priests, especially those at the Séminaire de Québec, were not convinced that social issues required such activism, and they tended to regard the curé of Notre-Dame-de-Jacques-Cartier as overzealous. Then, too, fitting Catholicism into the new social context was also disturbing to the liberal bourgeois elite, who gave this new competition a cool reception.

Upon his appointment as director of the Action Sociale Catholique, Roy said goodbye to his parishioners on Sunday 14 April 1907. Thereafter he gave his full attention to promoting and organizing the new movement. He preached from platforms everywhere and addressed diverse audiences: the bishops' assembly, priests gathered for their annual retreat, students from the Université Laval, members of the Association Catholique de la Jeunesse Canadienne-Française. He recommended numerous forms of action: study groups, lectures and congresses, publications of various kinds, religious associations (the Ligue du Sacré-Cœur, brotherhood of the Third Order of St Francis of Assisi, Sodality of Our Lady, Union Saint-Joseph, Confrérie de la Sainte-Famille, Apostleship of Prayer), associations focused on morality (temperance societies, leagues for protection against salacious books, newspapers, theatres, shows), charitable organizations (St Vincent de Paul societies, mutual aid bodies), workers' and professional groups, and economic organizations (credit unions, cooperatives, farmers' unions). It was only gradually, and mainly from 1909, that the extensive program of study, reflection, teaching, publicity, and social action would fall into place and give direction to the Catholic forces of the archdiocese. The first result was the launching in Quebec on 21 Dec. 1907 of *L'Action sociale* (which would later become *L'Action Catholique*), a daily newspaper that would unquestionably be the ideological instrument with the most far-reaching influence. Not only would it continue to be published until 1973, it would also reach a wide audience, thereby spreading the viewpoint of uncompromising, "integralist" Catholicism for more than 60 years.

On 8 April 1908 Roy was appointed bishop of Eleutheropolis and auxiliary of Quebec by Pope Pius X. On 10 May he was consecrated by Archbishop Bégin and received an honorary doctorate in theology from the Université Laval. He remained director of the Action Sociale Catholique but at the same time took over much of the diocesan administration. Because of his past and his unpredictability, the authorities at the Séminaire de Québec greeted this appointment with some reservation. As a typical representative of a social Catholicism wholly dedicated to establishing the reign of Christ and associated with devotion to the Sacred Heart, Roy adopted *Adveniat regnum tuum* (Thy Kingdom Come) as his motto, and took the Sacred Heart and the cross as his coat of arms.

Roy

The years from 1909 to 1920 would prove decisive in Roy's social ministry. In mid December 1909 a general secretariat for the activities of the Action Sociale Catholique was set up to bring new vitality to the movement; it also ensured cooperation between the various commissions that had been established and the parish committees. The mandate of the latter was to unite the dynamic forces of Catholicism, promote the objectives and activities of the Action Sociale Catholique (especially the Catholic press), and conduct inquiries initiated by the general secretariat. The first parish committee came into being on 26 June 1910 in Saint-Anselme, beginning a series in the archdiocese. During the winter of 1910–11 alone, some 30 parish committees were set up. From its earliest days, under Roy's direction the general secretariat began organizing the first Congrès de Tempérance du Diocèse de Québec. This event took place at Quebec in 1910 and attracted a number of foreign dignitaries who were on their way to the 21st International Eucharistic Congress in Montreal, at which Roy himself would play an active role, presiding over a great rally at the Monument National and delivering the sermon at midnight mass on "the triumphs of the Eucharist."

In 1909 also, because of his exceptional gifts as an orator, Roy became president of the Société du Parler Français au Canada, which had been founded in 1902 by his friends Lortie and Rivard. It was Roy again who would chair the first Congrès de la Langue Française, held at Quebec in 1912 [see Lortie]. On 25 Jan. 1910, recognizing him as a patriotic Christian and champion of French culture in North America, the faculty of arts of the Université Laval conferred on him the title of professor emeritus. That year Roy also became chaplain of the Quebec regional committee of the Association Catholique de la Jeunesse Canadienne-Française, an office he would hold for ten years.

In order to establish a true Christian civilization, Roy put a great deal of effort into the work of the Catholic press, of which L'Action sociale was but one example. In September 1910 he launched Le Croisé (Québec), the monthly liaison bulletin of the Action Sociale Catholique and the black cross, placing it under the patronage of St Michael. On 18 October he founded the Ligue de la Presse Catholique de Langue Française du Canada et des États-Unis, with the aim of bringing together the Catholic press. This body, which would last until the 1920s, would have 31 periodicals under its supervision in 1914. In 1913, with Charles-Octave Gagnon, Roy was assigned to reorganize La Semaine religieuse de Québec, a weekly for both the clergy and Roman Catholics in general. He started a column about the activities of the Action Sociale Catholique in this diocesan publication and changed its title by adding et Bulletin des œuvres de l'Action sociale catholique. During the same period, the Action

Social Catholique's printing press, which had been set up in 1908, also turned out numerous tracts and pamphlets. In 1917 L'Almanach de l'Action sociale catholique (Québec) began publication. Lastly, L'Apôtre (Québec), a monthly for "families that feel the need to take refuge in Christianity," according to its prospectus, would be added to the list in 1919.

On 26 June 1914 Roy became titular archbishop of Seleucia. Just like his manifold appointments, his influence and fields of activity seemed virtually boundless. With Abbé Maxime Fortin*, he worked at organizing Catholic trade unions. On 3 Oct. 1915 he went to Thetford Mines to meet the miners who were being wooed by the international unions, which dominated the labour movement at that time. The following Sunday the Union Catholique de Ouvriers Mineurs de Thetford was founded, under the direction of Abbé Fortin. In 1918 Roy would give his support to the idea of establishing a federation of Catholic unions, an initiative that led to the founding of the Canadian and Catholic Confederation of Labour in 1921. In 1916 he resumed the offensive in favour of temperance, leading a delegation to the legislature to expound to Sir Lomer GOUIN and his colleagues the potential advantages of a province-wide temperance regime, in the process denouncing the fact that some members of the cabinet owned shares in breweries. In 1917 he directed the campaign of the prohibitionists, who eventually won the referendum organized at Quebec City to get the Canada Temperance Act, commonly known as the Scott Act [see Sir Richard William Scott*], applied.

Roy was named coadjutor archbishop of Quebec, with right of succession, on 1 June 1920. The following year, just back from a holiday and rest in Europe, he became the first chairman of the administrative commission of the Séminaire des Missions Étrangères which the provincial episcopate had established in Montreal. He took part in 1922 and 1923 in founding the Hôpital du Saint-Sacrement, which he was bent on making an ecclesiastical institution.

On 17 April 1923, seriously ill with cancer, Roy entered the Hôpital Saint-François d'Assise, where he would remain until his death. His illness did not prevent him from serving as president of the first Congrès Eucharistique Provincial in September 1923. Even though he could not attend the various sessions, he participated in the closing ceremony on the Plains of Abraham. Soon afterwards he gave up the leadership of the Action Sociale Catholique.

Archbishop Bégin died on 18 July 1925 and Roy, despite the state of his health, became archbishop of Quebec. He would run the archdiocese from his hospital room, with Joseph-Alfred Langlois as administrator. During his archepiscopate, which would last only seven months, he wrote a pastoral letter, seven circular letters, and an instruction to the clergy. He was very proud, near the end of his life, to communicate the encyclical *Quas primas*, by which Pope Pius XI proclaimed the universal reign of Christ the King. "We have been intending, from the dawn of our episcopate, to promote and strengthen within our beloved diocesan family the Kingdom of God: *Adveniat regnum tuum*. It is our wish that not only individuals, but all social bodies, should be subject, in full obedience of thought and action, to this sublime kingship," he would write in the circular letter to the clergy dated 18 Jan. 1926. Roy was decorated with the pallium at the consistory of 17 Dec. 1925. He received it on his hospital bed, in a private ceremony, on 10 Jan. 1926, a few days after he had been given the last rites. He died 20 Feb. 1926 at the age of 66.

In Paul-Eugène Roy, as eulogies pointed out at the time of his death, doctrine, teaching, and action were combined. Endowed with remarkable conviction and drive, he embodied the social Catholicism of Quebec at the beginning of the century, a movement that was itself incorporated into the "integralist" strain of Catholicism at that time. He succeeded in providing the Action Sociale Catholique with the organizations, instruments, and workers that defined it and guaranteed its extension. A number of institutions that came into being under his aegis (Catholic unions, cooperatives, hospitals, and so forth) remained active through the century. Roy's vast project, to build a French Roman Catholic nation in North America under the authority of Christ the King, scarcely outlasted him, however. It represented a response from the Roman Catholic Church to the initial industrialization of the province, but did not withstand the shock of the postwar years.

GILLES ROUTHIER

Paul-Eugène Roy published a number of books and articles, among them: *L. A. Olivier* (Lévis, Qué., 1891); "Le règne social du Sacré-Cœur," *Le Messager canadien du Sacré-Cœur* (Montréal), 13 (1904): 248–52, 305–10, 357–63; *L'Action sociale catholique et l'Œuvre de la presse catholique; motifs, programme, organisation, ressources* (Québec, 1907); *Discours religieux et patriotiques* (Québec, 1926); *Apôtres et apostolat* (Québec, 1927); and *D'une âme à une autre: correspondance spirituelle et familière avec une âme consacrée à Dieu* (Montréal, 1927). He is also believed to be the author of *Action sociale catholique et tempérance* (Québec, 1927).

ANQ-Q, CE302-S2, 9 nov. 1859. Arch. de l'archidiocèse de Québec, 20 A (lettres manuscrites des évêques de Québec), IX: 123; 31-18 A (papiers Mgr P.-E. Roy); 61 CD (paroisses), I (Jacques-Cartier): 7; 81 CD (congrégations religieuses féminines), II (Religieuses hospitalières de l'Hôtel-Dieu de Québec): 144. MCQ-DSQ, P7; P10; FSQ, SME 1/MS-34.3, 24 févr.–10 mars 1890; SME 9/151. "La croisade de tempérance," *La Semaine religieuse de Québec*, 9 févr., 11 mai 1907. *Le Devoir*, 22 févr. 1926. "Notre programme," *La Semaine religieuse de Québec*, 18 sept. 1913. Action Sociale

Catholique, *Statuts et règlements de l'Action sociale catholique* (Québec, 1908). *Almanach de l'Action sociale catholique* (Québec), 1 (1917): 18, 40–41; 10 (1926): 35–36; 11 (1927): 10–14. Comité du Drapeau National des Canadiens Français, *Le drapeau national des Canadiens français: un choix légitime et populaire* (Québec, 1904). "Fondation du premier comité paroissial de l'A.S.C.," *Le Croisé* (Québec), 1 (1910–11): 7–9. *Histoire du catholicisme québécois*, sous la dir. de Nive Voisine (2 tomes in 4v. parus, Montréal, 1984–), tome 3, vol.1 (Jean Hamelin et Nicole Gagnon, *Le XXe siècle: 1898–1940*, 1984). *Mandements, lettres pastorales et circulaires des évêques de Québec* (19v. parus, Québec, 1887–), 10: 57–69; 13: 5–77. Sœur Marie-du-Perpétuel-Secours, "Bibliographie de l'œuvre de Sa Grandeur monseigneur Paul-Eugène Roy, 1859–1926, dix-huitième évêque et huitième archevêque de Québec" (mémoire, école de bibliothéconomie, univ. Laval, Québec, 1964). "Monseigneur Roy et les caisses populaires," *Le Croisé*, 1: 155. J.-T. Perron, *Mgr Paul-Eugène Roy: 8ième archevêque et 18ième évêque de Québec; notes biographiques et documentaires* (Québec, 1926). "Le Secrétariat général des œuvres de Québec," *Le Croisé*, 1: 29. "S.G. Mgr Roy à l'Union régionale de Québec," *Le Semeur* (Montréal), 8 (1911–12): 108–11. M. A. Welton, *Un orateur apôtre, Mgr Paul-Eugène Roy, archevêque de Québec (1859–1926)* (Québec, 1941).

RUSSELL, CHARLES MARION, artist; b. 19 March 1864 in St Louis, Mo., son of Charles Silas Russell and Mary Elizabeth Mead; m. 9 Sept. 1896 Nancy Cooper (d. 1940) in Cascade, Mont., and they had one son; d. 24 Oct. 1926 in Great Falls, Mont.

Charlie Russell's father was a partner in a brick manufacturing firm and the family was socially prominent. From an early age, the boy, who struggled in school, dreamed of going west to follow in the footsteps of his grandmother's brothers Charles and William Bent, pioneer western fur traders. In 1880, just before his 16th birthday, his parents let him accompany a sheepman of their acquaintance to Montana Territory. After living with a professional meat hunter, "Kid" Russell in 1882 hired on as night herder on a trail drive to the Judith Basin in central Montana. Over the next 11 years (apart from 1888, when he summered in what is now Alberta), he wrangled horses and cattle during the spring and fall round-ups and gained a local reputation as an amusing story-teller with a knack for drawing the life around him. His 1887 watercolour *Waiting for a chinook*, showing a starving cow surrounded by wolves, summed up a devastating winter on the plains and brought him widespread recognition.

His first visit to Canada was a key event in Russell's life. He rode north from Helena, Mont., with two friends in late May 1888. A job awaited one of them, Philip A. Weinard, who was to take up a position at a ranch southwest of Calgary. But Russell and his other companion, having missed the spring round-up, fished, hunted, and loafed the summer away on a ranch owned by Charles D. M. Blunt. Russell did a few paintings with supplies given him by Blunt and took the opportunity to acquaint himself with the native peoples of the area – Stoney, Sarcee, Blackfoot, Blood, and Peigan. Impressionable and eager to learn, he picked up the rudiments of sign language and absorbed tales of valour from times past. They left a permanent impression on his art, adding to his understanding of cowboy life an abiding interest in Plains Indian culture. Russell returned to Helena in September, leaving behind some sketches, a finished painting of a bear, and, most impressively, an ambitious oil that he gave to Blunt, *Canadian mounted police bringing in Red Indian prisoners*, recording an incident witnessed on the ride north in May. In later paintings and drawings he would honour the mounted police as symbols of justice on the Canadian frontier, a notable subject for an artist who ignored the United States army's role in "winning the west" and sympathized with the Indians in their resistance to white advance.

After his return to Montana, Russell went back to night herding. But in 1893, convinced that the glory days of the open-range cattle industry were over, he turned to art for a living, settling in the town of Cascade, between Helena and Great Falls. There in 1895 he met Nancy ("Mame") Cooper, a 17-year-old whom he married the following year. She proved to have a head for business and drive enough for both of them. They moved to Great Falls in 1897 and together made an impulsive trip north in 1903. Eager to see the last frontier of the northern gold rushes, they set out by train for "Fort Edmonton," only to discover a modern city. Russell was able to sketch a dog train, and he subsequently painted a watercolour titled *The winter packet* (1903) and fashioned a wax group known as *Transport to the northern lights* (c. 1903–5). A more satisfying encounter with his romantic fantasies was provided in November 1908 and the following spring, when he first observed and then participated in two round-ups on Montana's Flathead Reservation of the more than 700 buffalo purchased by the Canadian government for delivery to Alberta. The experience reinvigorated his interest in buffalo and buffalo hunts as artistic subjects.

By then Nancy Russell was her husband's business manager. In 1904 she had persuaded him to make the first in a series of trips to New York. His paintings were already widely familiar through postcards and colour reproductions, and he had his first bronze cast that year. Commissions for illustrations and a major calendar contract followed, contributing to the view that, after Frederic Remington's death in 1909, Russell was North America's premier western artist, an opinion confirmed by a successful, one-man exhibition at New York's Folsom Galleries in 1911. Titled *The west that has passed*, it perfectly conveyed his nostalgic vision of cowboys, Indians, and wildlife in an unfenced land.

The next year Russell exhibited at the first Calgary Stampede, which brought him international attention and new patrons for his art. The show was a great success – 13 of the 20 catalogued paintings sold, three featuring cowboys to Sir Henry Mill Pellatt* of Toronto and four depicting Indians to a titled Englishman – and Russell was back in 1913 to exhibit at a stampede in Winnipeg. Contacts made in Canada led to his only exhibition overseas, at London's Doré Galleries in 1914. He had enjoyed Canadian patronage before. In 1897 William Bleasdell Cameron*, representing an American sportsman's journal, had commissioned six drawings to illustrate his personal memoirs of two months' captivity in the camp of Big Bear [Mistahimaskwa*] following the attack at Frog Lake (Alta) in 1885. Engineer Charles Alexander Magrath* of Lethbridge in 1905 persuaded Russell to paint an oil portraying a pitched battle between Blackfoot, Cree, and Assiniboin fought in the immediate vicinity in 1870 [*see* Jerry Potts*]. Ordinarily, Russell sold generic scenes of Indian and cowboy life to Canadian patrons such as Jimmy Simpson, a Banff outfitter and guide, and William B. Campbell, an Alberta rancher who met Russell at the Winnipeg Stampede in 1913. But after his success in Calgary, he added specifically Canadian content to his repertoire by painting four major mounted police oils, one each year between 1912 and 1915.

The "big four" who had backed the first Calgary Stampede – George LANE, Alfred Ernest Cross*, Patrick Burns*, and Archibald James McLean* – were all connected to the Alberta cattle industry, and Lane became a major patron. When the Russells were lured back to Canada in 1919 for exhibitions at Calgary's "Victory Stampede" and in Saskatoon, Cross bought a cowboy subject, while Burns acquired one of the mounted police oils, *Whiskey smugglers caught with the goods* (1913), and Lane two others, *The queen's war hounds* (1914) and *When law dulls the edge of chance* (1915). The former he eventually donated to the province of Alberta; the latter was presented to the Prince of Wales, who, on an extended Canadian tour, had purchased the ranch next to Lane's Bar U. Rising prices in these years demonstrate Russell's artistic success; by 1920 a single oil commanded $10,000.

His links to the Canadian west took many forms. Between 1906 and 1910 he co-owned a ranch in the Sweet Grass Hills, five miles south of the Canadian border, and often visited southern Alberta, counting many friends among the cattlemen in the area. The Russells wintered in California in 1920, but Russell was always most at home in Montana and Alberta among those who spoke his language. After he died in 1926, A. E. Cross expressed what Russell's passing meant for western Canadians. "You have not only my entire sympathy," he wrote to Nancy Russell, "but the sympathy of all the old cow men in this country." His death would be "a distinct loss, not only to your own Community, the United States, but all the world." Charles M. Russell is still universally known as the "cowboy artist."

BRIAN W. DIPPIE

Private arch., Jim Combs (Great Falls, Mont.), Materials pertaining to C. M. Russell. Taylor Museum, Colorado Springs Fine Arts Center (Colorado Springs, Colo.), Helen and Homer E. Britzman Coll., C.7.159 (A. E. Cross to N. C. Russell, 30 Oct. 1926); E.189 bi (N. C. Russell's annotated copy of *Special exhibition: paintings by Charles M. Russell, at "The Stampede, Calgary, 1912"*); E.346 (*The west that has passed*, exhibition catalogue, Folsom Galleries, New York, 1911). "An artist visitor," *Edmonton Bull.*, 25 Feb. 1903: [3]. *Charlie Russell roundup: essays on America's favorite cowboy artist*, ed. B. W. Dippie (Helena, Mont., 1999). H. A. Dempsey, "Tracking C. M. Russell in Canada, 1888–1889," *Montana: the Magazine of Western Hist.* (Helena), 39 (1989), no.3: 2–15. B. W. Dippie, "Charles M. Russell and the Canadian west," *Alberta Hist.* (Calgary), 52 (2004), no.4: 4–26. [C. M. Russell], *Charles M. Russell, word painter: letters, 1887–1926*, ed. B. W. Dippie (Fort Worth, Tex., 1993). John Taliaferro, *Charles M. Russell: the life and legend of America's cowboy artist* (Boston, 1996).

RUTHERFORD, JOHN GUNION, veterinarian, horse breeder, office holder, editor, politician, and civil servant; b. 25 Dec. 1857 in Mountain Cross, Scotland, son of Robert Rutherford, a United Presbyterian minister, and Agnes Gunion; m. 1887 Edith Boultbee of Ancaster, Ont., and they had three daughters and a son; d. 24 July 1923 in Ottawa.

As a boy, John G. Rutherford attended the parish school in Mountain Cross and the high school in Glasgow. Apprenticed to a bookseller there, he preferred farming. He gained practical experience in the counties of East Lothian and Selkirk, where some of Scotland's best farmers and stockmen could be found; he also studied agriculture at Haddington and Philiphaugh, and later under a private tutor in Edinburgh. After coming to Ontario in September 1875 to join the Hopes, a farming family near Brantford, he continued his agricultural education in 1875–76 at the Ontario School of Agriculture and Experimental Farm in Guelph [*see* William Johnston*], where he won the prize for practical agriculture. Through John Hope, the manager of George Brown*'s Bow Park estate near Brantford, Rutherford was able to find work there over part of this time; he experienced first-hand the presence of bovine tuberculosis in cattle. His interest in this problem would last a lifetime. Drawn to animal science and care, he graduated with honours in 1879 from the Ontario Veterinary College in Toronto.

Rutherford began practising veterinary medicine in Woodstock, where he became involved as well in rearing and selling horses. He shipped many to Britain and imported fine stock for breeding purposes. As a veterinarian, he travelled a great deal: he attended lectures in Europe and the United States, set up Mexico's first veterinary school, and seems to have practised for periods in New York State, Tennessee, and Kentucky.

After returning to Canada in 1884, Rutherford settled in Portage la Prairie, Man. He built up a large veterinary practice and continued in the horse business, with a particular interest in remounts for the British army. In 1885, a year after the Manitoba government had appointed him veterinary inspector, he served in the North-West rebellion as a veterinary officer with the North-West Field Force under Major-General Frederick Dobson Middleton*. While living in Portage la Prairie, he held a number of other positions. He was president of the Veterinary Association of Manitoba (which he had been instrumental in establishing in 1890), the Horse Breeders' Association of Manitoba and the North West Territories, the Manitoba and Lakeside Agricultural Society, the Island Park Racing Association, and the local St Andrew's Society. In addition, he was chairman of the Portage la Prairie General Hospital and edited the *Nor'-West Farmer* (Winnipeg) from 1890 to 1894 and the *Weekly Manitoba Liberal* (Portage la Prairie) from 1896 to 1900.

In 1892 Rutherford was elected as a Liberal for the provincial riding of Lakeside. In the legislature he became chairman of the committee on agriculture. Returned in January 1896, he served for only one session because of his decision to enter dominion politics. He was defeated in the general election in June for the seat of Macdonald, but won there in a by-election in April 1897. During his three years in the House of Commons, he advocated a federal board of railway commissioners and was reported by the *Agricultural Gazette of Canada* (Ottawa) to have been "virtually the author" of the Manitoba Grain Act of 1900. He was defeated in the election of 1900.

In 1901 Rutherford accepted the position offered to him by Canada's chief veterinary inspector, Duncan McNab MCEACHRAN, to inspect Canadian cattle landed in Glasgow. While there he visited many famous cattle operations in Great Britain. On 1 Feb. 1902 he took over from McEachran and agreed to devote all of his time to the inspectorship – McEachran, who ran a veterinary college in Montreal, had served on a part-time basis. With characteristic energy, Rutherford set to work to revitalize the veterinary service of the Department of Agriculture, of which Sydney Arthur FISHER was minister. After reorganizing the health of animals branch, on 19 April 1904 he was named veterinary director-general. In this capacity he established a pathological division and a biological laboratory. From evidence contained in his official reports, Rutherford's scientific grasp of problems was sound, though, like other veterinarians, he could be sceptical of pure bacteriology divorced from

893

commonsensical observation. When he also took over the livestock branch and became dominion livestock commissioner, on 1 July 1906, he was in a position where he could begin to control the spread of animal plagues.

Rutherford was concerned with the containment of such diseases as hog cholera, anthrax, rabies, sheep scab, tuberculosis and contagious abortion in cattle, mange in sheep and cattle, and dourine and glanders in horses. He was successful in stopping the constant infection of Ontario pigs with cholera from the United States. He enforced the use of mallein for the testing of glanders, had reactors slaughtered, and compensated horse owners. In 1904, to get rid of dourine, he set up a program for the quarantine of stock from the United States and for the slaughter of diseased animals. By 1913 both of these horse diseases were under better control as a result of his policies.

But it is Rutherford's work on the eradication of bovine tuberculosis that was his most important contribution. The threat to humans, not cattle, had focused attention on this disease and brought veterinarians into the realm of medical doctors and bacteriologists. (Rutherford claimed to have known of the interrelationship between bovine and human tuberculosis before its announcement in 1882 by Robert Koch, discoverer of the tuberculosis bacilli and the tuberculin for testing.) Rutherford's personal concern, which dated back to his days at Bow Park, had been reinforced when his son died as an infant from tuberculosis contracted from contaminated milk, before the family left Portage la Prairie. His attack was three-pronged, the major thrust being his attempt to control the disease within the nation's herds, as a program initiated by McEachran. It had become apparent by the late 1890s that the testing of general herds, the slaughter of infected cattle, and compensation were simply not feasible in Canada. Programs of this nature had been set up in various American states but had failed and all cost more than the Canadian government could afford. In 1894 McEachran established compulsory testing for imported pure-bred breeding cattle, which were considered the primary vectors. Such stock had to undergo quarantine at government stations; cattle that reacted were destroyed without compensation. Breeders opposed this program. Bovine tuberculosis and its transmission were still not well understood, the test gave ambiguous results, McEachran had acted in an autocratic way, and slaughter caused huge financial hardship. As a result the pure-bred cattle associations repeatedly demanded the cessation of testing. When Koch, in a controversial turnabout in 1901, claimed (wrongly) that the bovine form was not contagious to man, breeders became even more adamant.

Remarkably, Rutherford was able to fashion a climate that allowed for an effective campaign against bovine tuberculosis in pure-bred herds. Socially out-going and possessed of "friendly democratic ways," he was well known to and popular with breeders in Canada and abroad. Pleased when he took over, cattlemen hoped for some relief from testing. Rutherford, however, was just as anxious as McEachran had been to eradicate the disease, so the regulations were not removed. In 1903 he met with the Dominion Cattle Breeders' Association. The cattlemen accepted the testing of imported stock and the slaughter, without compensation, of reactors that displayed clinical symptoms. In return, Rutherford agreed to let breeders keep reactors with no outward signs of the disease, but it would be made clear that the animals potentially were infected: they were required to have a large T punched in the right ear. Later in 1903 a regulation was adopted prohibiting the export of cattle so marked. Rutherford's program was brilliant: it focused the mind of the farming community on the problem as a national issue rather than a matter of personal loss.

The second prong of his attack on bovine tuberculosis was the administration of meat inspection. Tactfully he gained the support of the packing industry in 1907 for a national meat-inspection program though it related only to exports and interprovincial trade. Thirdly, he pressed for tighter municipal standards for milk, but, in part because they were beyond his jurisdiction, he was careful to do so indirectly. "The sale of milk from cows not known to be free of tuberculosis is a crime against society," he stated simply in 1910, "and any community that permits the sale of such milk is an accessory to the crime." Cooperation was the way to success. "The best law ever framed can be made an utter failure by stupid or injurious administration," he reasoned in 1912, "while, on the other hand, the most drastic legislation can be rendered acceptable if enforced with reasonable tact and diplomacy." Federal assistance for municipal control would not become possible until 1914, by which time Rutherford had left the department.

Rutherford's professional standing and his campaign against bovine tuberculosis were considerably enhanced in 1908, when he was appointed an honorary associate of the Royal College of Veterinary Surgeons, went twice to Rome as Canada's delegate to the International Institute of Agriculture, and attended the International Congress on Tuberculosis in Washington, D.C. But it was his presidency of the American Veterinary Medical Association in 1908–9 – an office held by few Canadians – that he recognized as providing a unique opportunity to promote international controls. In 1909, with the support of his future presidential successor, who headed the American Bureau of Animal Husbandry, he was able through the AVMA to set up a Canadian-American commission on bovine tuberculosis. Through this work, if not before, Rutherford undoubtedly became aware of the pioneering research and regulatory organization that had been undertaken by Leonard Pearson of the University of Pennsylvania's veterinary school.

A practising and devoted veterinarian, Rutherford was understandably concerned with the status of his profession. Veterinary medicine had gained much respectability through its attention to bovine tuberculosis and human health. Central to its reputation was the state of professional education. Andrew Smith*, head of the Ontario Veterinary College (by mid 1903 the only veterinary school in Canada after McEachran's had collapsed), had persistently refused to lengthen and enrich the training given there. At the meeting of the Ontario Veterinary Association in Ottawa in 1903, it was agreed that some action should be taken. Two years later Rutherford, as the head of a committee on curriculum revision, drafted proposals for change that included Ontario's takeover of veterinary education and, in the belief that human and animal illnesses were often interconnected, a publicly funded faculty of comparative medicine at the University of Toronto. With characteristic diplomacy, he suggested that Smith be made dean. Although the reforms were not immediately established, the move to upgrade veterinary education and increase government control would gather momentum.

Within his department in Ottawa Rutherford continued his work of administration and promotion. In addition, he wrote at least two bulletins, *The cattle trade of western Canada . . .* (1909) and *Horse breeding and rearing of colts* (1911). He was president of the Civil Service Association of Ottawa from 1909 to 1911. Beyond the civil service, he was a member of the local St Andrew's Society and several recreational clubs, among them the Royal Ottawa Golf Club; he also belonged to the freemasons and the Ancient Order United Workmen. Created a CMG in 1910, he resigned from his departmental positions in May 1911, though at the government's request he continued until 31 March 1912. It is not clear why he stepped down – friction within the Department of Agriculture was put forward in *Farm and Dairy* (Peterborough, Ont.) as a possible reason – but the reaction of the farming community was entirely evident. Praise for his work and dismay at his retirement poured into Ottawa. His service to the livestock industry, however, was certainly not over.

Almost immediately after he had resigned, Sir Thomas George SHAUGHNESSY of the Canadian Pacific Railway, which had just formed a department of natural resources with an animal husbandry branch, hired him to campaign for the improvement of livestock and the extension of mixed farming in the prairie provinces. Rutherford again became a western resident, settling in Edmonton and then Calgary. In 1913 he took full control of the agricultural operations of the CPR when he was appointed its superintendent of agriculture and animal industry. In this position,

which he would hold until 1918, he helped the company carry out work on its experimental farms. His activities, however, were not restricted to the CPR; at times he seemed to be constantly on the move, travelling from one meeting or conference to another. From 1913 to 1919 he was president of the Western Canada Live-Stock Union, an organization he had been instrumental in creating. In addition, he was a president of the Alberta Horse Breeders' Association; a member of Saskatchewan's commission on agricultural and industrial education in 1915, its livestock commission of 1915–18, and the dominion agricultural production commission of 1915–18; chairman of the Manitoba Council of Commerce and Agriculture in 1916; and a vice-chairman of Alberta's Board of Agricultural Education. In 1917, during the wartime conscription crisis, he took a lead in organizing western Liberal support for Sir Robert Laird Borden*. Reputedly he was offered the agriculture portfolio in Borden's Union government but refused on the grounds of ill health. At the end of World War I, he was held in such esteem that cattlemen in Canada had his portrait painted and donated it to the Saddle and Sirloin Club of Chicago for its collection of paintings of luminaries in the livestock world.

Rutherford returned to public service at age 56, when he was appointed on 8 Nov. 1918 to the federal Board of Railway Commissioners. In February he moved back to Ottawa to assume his duties, which would make heavy demands on his grasp of railway operations and his diplomatic skills. His bent for cooperation left him disgusted at times with the self-serving attitudes of applicants to the board as it navigated through complex arguments on post-war rate changes and shipping disputes. Characteristically, he took on other work, including the presidency of the Canadian National Live-Stock Association in 1919. That same year he was named to two federal royal commissions, one on the commercial development of muskox and reindeer herds in the north, the other on horse racing, which he saw as a proven means to control and promote breeding. In recognition of his achievements, the University of Toronto conferred a DVS on him in 1920.

Dr John G. Rutherford died suddenly from Bright's disease at St Luke's Hospital in Ottawa in July 1923. His wife, who was living at their farm near Chilliwack, B.C., was unable to reach the capital in time for his burial in Beechwood Cemetery. More than any other person, Rutherford should be credited with the establishment of a workable program for the eradication of bovine tuberculosis in Canada. The regulations were seemingly limited, with a focus on the international movement of pure-bred stock, virtually no compensation for loss, little interference with general herds, restricted meat inspection, and localized and poorly controlled milk inspection, but they produced

Rutherford

results. Rutherford's system represented an effective plan to contain the disease, a plan that could later be augmented. The program eventually received the full support of the farming community, and triggered changes in the public mind about the need for the better regulation of both meat and milk. Although, at Rutherford's death, the tide against bovine tuberculosis had barely started to turn, Canada's position on the disease was one of the most advanced in the world. In direct contrast was Britain, which made no effort to control the disease until well into the 20th century.

MARGARET DERRY

Reports and addresses by John Gunion Rutherford appear in Can., Parl., *Sessional papers*, 1904, no.15, app.15: 69–92; 1905, no.15: 49–78; 1906, no.15a; 1909, no.15a(2); 1910, no.15, app.17: 103–23; 1911, no.15b; 1912, no.15b; 1913, no.15b, esp.1–34, 106–14, 295–98, 335–47; and in Ont., Legislature, *Sessional papers*, 1904, no.23: 45–47, 183–88; 1907, no.22: 45–48; 1918, no.39: 67–69.

LAC, RG 17, A I, 957, no.142157; 966, no.146882; 1031, no.183471; 1052, no.190827; 1063, nos.192940, 193119; 1162, no.218930. Univ. of Guelph Library, Arch. and Special Coll. (Guelph, Ont.), RE1, OVC, A0219 (C. A. V. Barker, interview with Clive Rogers, 1973); UOG, A0990 ("The 125th anniversary of OVC, 1987"); XAI, MS, A0771 (application of recognition in the Canadian Agricultural Hall of Fame, 1962). *Ottawa Evening Journal*, 24–25, 27 July 1923. *Agricultural Gazette of Canada* (Ottawa), 10 (1923): 455–56. American Veterinary Medical Assoc., *Journal* (Chicago), 63 (April–September 1923): 106–8. C. A. V. Barker and T. A. Crowley, *One voice: a history of the Canadian Veterinary Medical Association* (Ottawa, 1989). *Canadian directory of parl.* (Johnson). *Canadian encyclopedia*, 195–96. *Canadian men and women of the time* (Morgan; 1912). *Cyclopædia of Canadian biog.* (Rose and Charlesworth), vol.3. Margaret Derry, *Ontario's cattle kingdom: purebred breeders and their world, 1870–1920* (Toronto, 2001). *Farm and Dairy* (Peterborough, Ont.), 16 June 1910: 3–4, 11; 30 June 1910: 4; 14 Sept. 1911: 892. *Farming World and Canadian Farm and Home* (Toronto), 1 Aug. 1906: 503–4. *O.A.C. Rev.* (Guelph), March 1905, February 1913, March 1915. B. G. Rosenkrantz, "The trouble with bovine tuberculosis," *Bull. of the Hist. of Medicine* (Baltimore, Md) 59 (1985): 155–75.

RUTHERFORD, WILLIAM JOHN, educator and civil servant; b. 7 Jan. 1868 in Potsdam, N.Y., son of John A. Rutherford and Esther Gray; m. 6 Dec. 1904 Anna Christena Bow in Winchester Township, Ont., and they had two daughters and a son; d. 1 June 1930 in Saskatoon.

In 1878, two years after the death of his Canadian-born mother, William Rutherford moved with his Scottish father and family from upstate New York to a farm in Dundas County, Ont., where he received his primary schooling. He graduated from the collegiate in Morrisburg, taught school for a time, and in 1901 enrolled at the Ontario Agricultural College in Guelph

[*see* James Mills*]. There he served as dean of residence and in 1903 was awarded the bachelor of agricultural science degree. That same year he accepted a professorship in the department of animal husbandry at the Iowa State College of Agriculture and Mechanic Arts in Ames; in 1906 he became professor of agriculture at the Manitoba Agricultural College near Winnipeg.

In November 1908 Rutherford was named deputy commissioner (later deputy minister) of agriculture for Saskatchewan. In this capacity he took a major role in giving shape the following year to the newly established University of Saskatchewan at Saskatoon. His assessment of soil quality was the deciding factor in the selection of land for the campus, which included over 1,000 acres for working and experimental farms. In August 1910 his minister, William Richard Motherwell*, released him to become the university's first dean of agriculture and professor of animal husbandry. Rutherford's initial duties in organizing the college of agriculture consisted of developing its curriculum, advising on facilities and equipment, designing and stocking the working farm, and selecting additional instructors. He chose them with great care, insisting upon strong undergraduate training, research at the graduate level, and practical experience. Nor were moral character and leadership qualities overlooked.

The dean also assumed responsibility for the agricultural extension services previously provided by the province's Department of Agriculture. This work was designed to acquaint farmers with the latest in equipment and practices. Although he supported the application of machinery, he opposed the growing tendency to abandon horses in favour of purely mechanized farming. In addition to ploughing matches and demonstrations, Rutherford oversaw the "Better Farming Train" – a university on rails – which toured rural Saskatchewan annually during the summers of the late 1910s and early 1920s. He was particularly proud of the associate course instituted in 1914 to provide practical, non-degree training for youth seeking careers in farming. When John Walter Grant MacEwan*, who would later join Rutherford's department, visited the province's legislature while attending the Farm Boys' Camp at the Regina exhibition, he was mightily impressed by a speech given by the dean on the topic "The boy increased in wisdom and stature and in favour with God and man." At the university, MacEwan also recalled, Rutherford "knew his students and followed them in rugby and hockey and so on." Though frail-looking and crippled by a boyhood accident, he was himself an ardent curler and lawn bowler in Saskatoon.

Rutherford also undertook to improve the quality of livestock throughout Saskatchewan by importing various breeds of sheep, cattle, and horses, not only for the university but also to make pure-bred sires and dams available to breeders. This program met with great success. Rutherford was particularly noted for the Clydesdale stallions and mares he imported from Scotland, beginning in 1920. These horses and many of their offspring won prizes at Canadian and American expositions (Rutherford himself was a "fearless" judge at major international horse shows). So strong was his fondness for Clydesdales that the Canadian Percheron Horse Breeders' Association accused him of unfair bias in 1919.

Recognized as the founder of agrarian education in Saskatchewan, Rutherford, according to the *Western Producer* (Saskatoon), had a "profound influence in shaping agricultural educational policies throughout the Dominion." His expertise was sought by professional associations, and he was appointed to a number of commissions of inquiry, including the Saskatchewan commissions on agricultural and industrial education (1912), farming conditions (1920), and grain (1928), and the wide-ranging but largely ineffectual federal investigation of the grain trade, including the Winnipeg Grain and Produce Exchange (1923).

In November 1929 Rutherford fell ill with a throat infection. After several recoveries and relapses, he was released from hospital a week before his death. On 1 June 1930 he suffered a fatal haemorrhage of the lungs. His funeral was held in Knox Presbyterian Church on the 5th and he was interred in Saskatoon's Woodlawn Cemetery. Expressions of sympathy, many of them acknowledging debts of gratitude, flooded in to his wife and children and the university. At its first meeting following Rutherford's death, the university's board of governors recognized "his deep sympathy with the children of the farmers in their ambition for a better education; his profound knowledge and understanding of the difficulties which the farmers have faced in their pioneering; his foresight and comprehensive grasp of the large issues involved in the transportation, marketing and financing of Canadian wheat as it moved to the markets of the world; his love of animals and his keen interest in breeding and improvement of livestock; and above all his integrity, sound judgment, loyalty and deep interest in everything pertaining to the well being of his fellow citizens." His son, John Bow, would have a distinguished career with the Dominion Bureau of Statistics and the United Nations. In 1972 W. J. Rutherford was posthumously inducted into the Saskatchewan Hall of Fame.

STANLEY D. HANSON

AO, RG 80-5-0-329, no.17904. Saskatchewan Arch. Board (Saskatoon), Clippings files, biogs. Univ. of Sask. Arch. (Saskatoon), 2001.1 (president's office fonds), file B.99; RG M-1 (board of governors minutes), 14 June 1930. *Leader-Post* (Regina), 2 June 1930. *Saskatoon Star-Phoenix*, 2, 5 June 1930. *Western Producer* (Saskatoon), 13 Feb. 1930. *Canadian annual rev. Canadian men and women of the time* (Morgan; 1912). *Canadian who's who*, 1948. John Hawkes, *The story of Saskatchewan and its people* (3v., Chicago, 1924). Michael Hayden, *Seeking a balance: the University of Saskatchewan, 1907–1982* (Vancouver, 1983). A. [G.] Levine, *The Exchange: 100 years of trading grain in Winnipeg* (Winnipeg, 1987). [J. W.] G. MacEwan, *Heavy horses: highlights of their history* (Saskatoon, 1986); *The sodbusters* (Toronto, [1948]). A. S. Morton, *Saskatchewan: the making of a university* (Toronto, 1959).

RUTTAN, HENRY NORLANDE, engineer, militia officer, and office holder; b. 21 May 1848 in Cobourg, Upper Canada, son of Henry Jones Ruttan and Margaret Pringle; m. 19 Aug. 1871 Andrina Barberie in Dalhousie, N.B., and they had nine children, of whom four sons and two daughters survived infancy; d. 13 Oct. 1925 in Winnipeg.

Henry Ruttan, the eldest of 10 children, was raised in Cornwall and Cobourg, Upper Canada. His paternal grandfather, Henry Ruttan*, had been a militia officer, politician, and inventor. His father was editor of the *Cobourg Star*. In his teens Ruttan quickly established the first of the two occupations that would run as threads throughout the rest of his life, joining the Cobourg Volunteer Militia Rifle Company as a private and graduating from the School of Military Instruction in Kingston at age 18. In 1866 he fought with the militia to repel the Fenian raids [*see* John O'Neill*]; this service would later earn him the Canada General Service Medal.

In 1868 Ruttan began to develop the second aspect of his career when he was hired to work in the engineering department of the Grand Trunk Railway. Within the year, he went to work under Sandford Fleming* as a rodman with the Intercolonial Railway, in charge of the Baie des Chaleurs (N.B./Que.) section. Soon thereafter, he took his discharge from the militia, presumably to concentrate on engineering. In 1874 he transferred to the Canada Pacific Railway (Fleming had been named chief engineer in 1871) and he spent the next two years in charge of a track location party working through the Yellowhead Pass (Alta). In a letter to his wife he describes how he changed by many miles the line of track over the Saskatchewan River from Fleming's original survey without consulting the chief engineer. His status in the railway company is demonstrated by a certificate from David Laird*, superintendent general of Indian affairs, dated 1 May 1875 and placing him second in authority after Fleming to deal with natives while building the line.

Although he left the employ of the Canada Pacific in 1880 and settled in Winnipeg, Ruttan continued to be involved in railway construction. Around 1882 he established a short-lived contracting firm, Ruttan, Rodgers and Company. Two years later the partnership of civil and mining engineers Ruttan and James

Ruttan

Brady announced their interest in railway construction and mining. By 1885, however, Ruttan had formed H. N. Ruttan and Company and Brady was practising on his own. At some point Ruttan also became involved in gold mining at Clearwater Bay (Ont.) as vice-president of the Argyle Mining Company. The first of his lifelong interests had soon re-established itself when in 1883 he became captain of No.2 Company of the 90th (Winnipeg) Battalion of Rifles. In 1885 he fought with his battalion under Major-General Frederick Dobson Middleton* in the North-West rebellion, serving at the battles of Fish Creek and Batoche (Sask.) and in the campaign to capture Big Bear [Mistahimaskwa*]. He returned to Winnipeg and was awarded the North West Canada Medal and clasp.

Ruttan became the first city engineer of Winnipeg in 1885 and remained in office until his retirement in 1914. He soon became known as an efficient and careful engineer. He was keen to improve the city's water supply, arguing for an expansion of the use of artesian wells. He apparently did not see the benefit of going farther afield for an adequate source of water. Indeed, as late as 1910, he was still recommending the expansion of the system, in spite of the inadequacy of artesian wells as a source of supply. Under considerable criticism, the Winnipeg City Council finally agreed to follow the advice of external experts and use Shoal Lake, near the Manitoba–Ontario boundary, for its water supply. With the creation of the Greater Winnipeg Water District, the building of the Shoal Lake aqueduct began in 1913.

Ruttan was interested in developing increased energy sources from water. The city council was enthusiastic about his plan to develop an electric plant on the Assiniboine River. The plan included a proposal to increase the water supply in the Assiniboine River by digging a canal from the river to Lake Manitoba. This canal would also serve to improve inland water transportation. Although they initially supported the plan, the press, the public, and the business community began to criticize it as too costly, so the project was abandoned.

At his retirement in 1914 Ruttan was honoured by a banquet and a significant gift of silver. He had hoped to go overseas during World War I, but was turned down because of his age, 66. In 1887 he had been promoted major. Two years later he was named general officer commanding Military District No.10. In February 1918 he was temporarily replaced as commander of the district, pending an inquiry into the district's administration and into charges of misappropriation of funds. By May several senior officers had been retired and two others relieved of duty. Ruttan was completely exonerated of any blame, but the incident may have influenced his decision to retire from the militia that month.

Henry Norlande Ruttan appears to have been a conscientious individual who served well in the posts he held. He was recognized in both the engineering profession and the military, becoming president of the Canadian Society of Civil Engineers in 1910, for example, and being promoted brigadier-general in 1912, but he does not seem to have had a particular vision for western Canada, a vision that would have set him above the rest.

DAVID R. DYCK

Henry Norlande Ruttan is the author of at least nine engineering reports, all of which are listed in the CIHM, *Reg.* Several of his articles and one of his addresses can be found in the *Science and technology biblio.* (Richardson and Mac-Donald).

AM, MG 14, C52. *Manitoba Free Press*, 9 June 1914, 26 Feb. 1918. *Winnipeg Telegram*, 6 May 1918. A. F. J. Artibise, *Winnipeg: a social history of urban growth, 1874–1914* (Montreal and London, 1975). George Bryce, *A history of Manitoba; its resources and people* (Toronto and Montreal, 1906). *Canadian men and women of the time* (Morgan; 1898). H. N. Ruttan, *A part of the family Ruttan, 1590–1986* (Ottawa, 1986). *Standard dict. of Canadian biog.* (Roberts and Tunnell).

RUTTAN, ROBERT FULFORD, chemist, university professor and administrator, and office holder; b. 15 July 1856 in Newburgh, Upper Canada, son of Dr Allan Ruttan and Caroline Smith; d. unmarried 19 Feb. 1930 in Montreal.

Robert Fulford Ruttan's mother was an ardent churchwoman and she may have named him after Francis Fulford*, who had been enthroned as the first Anglican bishop of Montreal six years before Ruttan's birth. His family moved to Napanee, Upper Canada, around 1863. Ruttan graduated from the local collegiate institute in 1877 and enrolled in the honours course in natural science at the University of Toronto. There he acquired a lifelong enthusiasm for chemistry and biology and obtained a BA in 1881, winning a gold medal.

At that time there were few opportunities in Canada to pursue a career, academic or industrial, in chemistry, so Ruttan registered in medicine at McGill College, Montreal. Apparently he was attracted to this institution because it was his father's alma mater and because of the pre-eminence of Dr William Osler* in the institutes of medicine and of Dr Gilbert Prout Girdwood* in practical chemistry. He graduated MD in 1884, receiving the Sutherland Gold Medal in chemistry and the Morrice scholarship in physiology.

Ruttan never practised medicine. Seeking to perfect his knowledge by postgraduate studies in organic chemistry, he travelled to Europe and spent two years working under August Wilhelm von Hofmann at the University of Berlin. The results of his research were published in several German and Canadian journals. Ruttan would not excel in personal research or in directing the research of others. His friend and colleague Archibald Byron Macallum* ascribed this situation to a lack of time rather than a lack of ability. Rather, Ruttan's main contributions to chemistry were as a teacher and administrator. He had benefited greatly from his exposure to Hofmann's brilliance as lecturer and demonstrator. "As teacher of chemistry," Macallum would later note, Ruttan "had few equals."

Immediately on his return to Canada in 1886 Ruttan was appointed lecturer in chemistry in the faculty of medicine at McGill. He was permitted to supplement his salary by performing water analyses and other tests for outside clients. He became one of the first members of a small group of public analysts who qualified under a recent act of the Canadian government. In 1891 he was promoted professor, and five years later he was elected to the Royal Society of Canada.

Tall, handsome, energetic, and friendly, Ruttan was a leader in the advancements McGill made under principals John William Dawson* and William PETERSON which earned for the institution a worldwide reputation in medicine and to a lesser extent in science, pure and applied. For example, he ensured that chemistry (in the novel form of physiological chemistry or biochemistry) was a strong component of the medical curriculum and that chemistry was at the forefront of postgraduate studies and research. In 1912 the three chemistry programs at McGill in the faculties of medicine, arts, and applied science were amalgamated into one department, with Ruttan as the first director. He would hold the post until 1928. In addition, he served as third director of the Chemistry and Mining Building, supervising non-professional staff and overseeing maintenance, repairs, and improvements. These accomplishments were admired outside McGill as well as at home. He was awarded an honorary D.SC. by the University of Toronto in 1914 and was elected president of the Royal Society of Canada in 1919.

Among Ruttan's ambitions was a desire to have chemistry recognized in Canada as a profession and to ensure that industrial chemistry was provided with the means to be effective across the nation. In 1920 he helped to found the Canadian Institute of Chemistry, incorporated the following year as a society of professionals. As president-elect of the British Society of Chemical Industry (a Canadian section had been formed in 1902), he arranged for it to hold its annual meeting in Montreal in 1921, outside Great Britain for the first time since its founding in 1881.

World War I made evident the need to mobilize the industrial capacity of Canada. Participants in devising ways to achieve this end were the Canadian government, the Canadian Manufacturers' Association, and several universities. After months of deliberation the Honorary Advisory Council for Scientific and Industrial Research was appointed by the government in 1916. Nine years later it was authorized to shorten its name to the National Research Council. Ruttan was one of its original members. Its first administrative chairman was his friend Macallum. He was succeeded in 1921 by Ruttan, who during a short mandate (February to August 1921) managed to get a bill passed in the House of Commons to establish the National Research Institute, a central laboratory whose director would report to the council. Unfortunately the bill was killed in the Senate. Ruttan had had previous experience with government laboratories, having acted on the advisory committee of the Forest Products Laboratories, which opened on the McGill campus in 1913.

These extramural concerns did not deter Ruttan from vigorously discharging his duties at McGill. The 1920s were called the "Golden Age of Chemistry." A number of talented young professors were appointed at McGill, all eager to direct postgraduate research. They included Harold Hibbert*, Frederick Murray Godshall Johnson, Otto Maass*, and George Stafford Whitby. Ruttan, administrator par excellence, served as dean of graduate studies and research from 1924 to 1928.

Ruttan was an accomplished athlete: a cricketer and yachtsman, and later in life, a golfer. (He would be president of the Royal Canadian Golf Association in 1907.) In 1906 he was asked to serve on Canada's first national olympic organization, the Central Olympic Committee. As a young lecturer, he had shared lodgings with Dr John George Adami and Dr Wyatt Galt Johnston*. They led a carefree life and were known as the Three Musketeers. Ruttan enjoyed the company of women, but never married. Bobby, as he was known, had a host of friends and loved to entertain at the University Club or at his apartment on Sherbrooke Street. When he retired after 40 years of service at the end of the 1927–28 session, his colleagues presented him with his portrait (which now hangs in the club) and his students in industrial chemistry gave him a cane. The library-staff room of the chemistry department at McGill University is named in his honour. After an illness lasting several months he died at his residence in 1930.

ROBERT V. V. NICHOLLS

Papers presented by Robert Fulford Ruttan to the Royal Society of Canada can be found in its *Trans.*: 1st ser., 5 (1887), sect. III: 61–74; 10 (1892), sect.III: 35–41; 3rd ser., 9 (1915), sect.III: 1–11; 10 (1916), sect.III: 169–70; 14 (1920), sect.III: xxxv–lvi. Reprints of three articles which he published in medical or scientific journals have been made available on microfiche by the CIHM and are cited in its *Reg.* These and other papers and addresses by Ruttan are listed in the *National union catalog*.

MUA, MG 1062, R. V. V. Nicholls, "Notes for a history of the department of chemistry" (n.d.); MG 3022. *Canadian*

Ryerson

men and women of the time (Morgan; 1912). *Cyclopædia of Canadian biog.* (Rose and Charlesworth), vol.1. RSC, *Trans.*, 3rd ser., 24 (1930), proc.: vii–xi.

RYERSON, GEORGE ANSEL STERLING, physician, teacher, militia and army officer, politician, author, and businessman; b. 21 Jan. 1855 in Toronto, only son of George Ryerson* and Isabella Dorcas Sterling; m. first 14 Nov. 1882 Mary Amelia Crowther (d. 1915) in Toronto, and they had four sons and one daughter; m. secondly 8 June 1916 Elizabeth Van Hook Mann, née Thomas (d. 1924) in Buffalo, N.Y.; they had no children; d. 20 May 1925 in Toronto.

George Sterling Ryerson was born into one of Upper Canada's most renowned families and emerged as an archetypal Toronto Tory. His grandfather Joseph Ryerson had been a distinguished loyalist, and his father, George, brother of the more famous Egerton*, was a notable clergyman who had left the Methodist Episcopal Church in Canada for the millennialist Catholic Apostolic Church, of which he served as head in North America from 1837 to 1872.

George Jr displayed his independence as well as his conservative instincts by opting for membership in the Church of England. He was, however, grateful to his parents for an education that was extraordinary by the standards of the day. After being tutored by William Tassie* at the grammar school in Galt (Cambridge), Ryerson entered Trinity Medical School in Toronto, where he obtained an MB in 1875 (MD 1876). He then undertook further academic work in Edinburgh, Paris, London, Vienna, and Heidelberg, Germany.

Ryerson returned to Toronto in 1880 to begin his practice and soon established himself as a leading oculist. That year he was appointed professor of eye, ear, and throat diseases at Trinity Medical School, launching a teaching career which would continue until 1918. Also in 1880 he became surgeon at the Andrew Mercer Eye and Ear Infirmary in the Toronto General Hospital. Ryerson was responsible for a number of innovations in Canadian medicine such as a recognition of the perils of colour blindness. Nevertheless he regretted "that with the fine training I had had in Europe I did not do any original work in my profession."

One reason for this failure lay in Ryerson's extensive commitments beyond his practice. As a boy of 15 he had enlisted in the militia during the Fenian troubles of 1870. Once he received his medical training he demonstrated an enduring interest in what he called "military medical affairs." Thus he became assistant surgeon to the 10th Battalion of Infantry (Royal Grenadiers) and saw action during the North-West rebellion in 1885 [*see* Darby Bergin*], service that earned him promotion to surgeon the following year. In 1892 he initiated the formation of the Association of Medical Officers of the Canadian Militia, of which he would be elected president in 1908 and

1909. Ryerson was appointed deputy surgeon-general in 1895, and promoted surgeon-major and surgeon–lieutenant-colonel on the same day the following year. On the reserve of officers from 1901, he would be made honorary surgeon-general in 1915 and honorary colonel of the Canadian Army Medical Corps two years later.

In 1892 Ryerson had been appointed an honorary associate of the Order of St John of Jerusalem in England (he would become a knight of grace in 1901); in 1895, under its auspices and with the support of Lieutenant Governor George Airey Kirkpatrick*, he created the St John Ambulance Association in Ontario, an organization he guided as general secretary for 15 years. Ryerson was also instrumental in founding the Canadian Red Cross Society in 1896, became its commissioner to the Canadian forces in South Africa in 1900, and succeeded John Morison GIBSON as its president in 1914. During World War I his experience was again put to use: in 1915 he was sent overseas to investigate the needs of hospitals and make a survey of Red Cross work.

Ryerson shared with many prominent Tories in Toronto a fervent devotion to loyalist origins which caused him in 1896 to launch the United Empire Loyalist Association of Ontario, of which he became second president. For him the loyalists of the American revolution had constituted a natural ruling elite, representing, in historian Moses Coit Tyler's words, a "very considerable portion of the most refined, thoughtful and conscientious people in the colonies." Ryerson sought to bestow the benefits of similar leadership on the provincial electorate when he successfully upheld the Conservative colours in an 1893 by-election in Toronto. Though he was returned for Toronto East in the general election the following year, in the end his political career proved a "disappointment" to himself and others. His elitist bearing was not appreciated in the legislature where in 1897, for example, Premier Arthur Sturgis Hardy* denounced his "very top lofty ideas" about Ontario society. In 1894 Ryerson had been rejected by his caucus as a potential leader in favour of George Frederick Marter*, and four years later he decided not to contest his seat because of illness. An attempt to revive his political career in 1902 saw him embarrassed by a defeat for the Conservative nomination in Toronto North.

Ryerson's aristocratic inclinations found a more favourable response in the upper echelons of British society and he described his participation in Queen Victoria's diamond jubilee in 1897 as the most wonderful day in his life. For him, as for many Canadian Tories, the "perpetual British Empire" was "the mainstay of freedom and civilization throughout the world." Such sentiments often led him into a racist perspective. For example, he viewed North American natives, South African blacks, and European gypsies as "savage peoples." He could also be religiously bigoted, as his prominence in the anti-Catholic Protestant Protective Association during the 1890s clearly revealed.

It was only natural that Ryerson gravitated towards the upper class institutions of Canadian society and he solidified his social standing by membership in such exclusive organizations as the masonic order, the Canadian Military Institute, the Toronto Hunt Club, and the Royal Canadian Yacht Club. He insisted that his sons be educated at Upper Canada College. During his later years he became involved in commercial pursuits which further established him as a successful entrepreneur. When he retired from the medical profession in 1920 he was an affluent man and he withdrew to a large estate, Peaceacres, in Niagara-on-the-Lake. There he wrote his memoirs, which were published in 1924, appropriately by Ryerson Press, as *Looking backward*. Having returned to Toronto to live, he died there the next year of a heart attack following a brief illness.

Ryerson had contributed significantly to the progress of medicine, especially military medicine, in Canada. A paradigm of Toronto Toryism, his political, economic, and social outlook gave him a comfortable life, status, and opportunities for attainments. This outlook was, however, marked by an elitism, rac-

ism, and religious intolerance that lessened his moral stature.

PETER E. PAUL DEMBSKI

George Ansel Sterling Ryerson's publications include *Color blindness in its relation to railway employees and the public* (Toronto, [1889?]); *The after-math of a revolution . . .* (Toronto, 1896); *The soldier and the surgeon* (Toronto, 1899); *Medical and surgical experiences in the South African War . . .* (n.p., [1900?]); and *Looking backward* (Toronto, 1924). An address given by Ryerson in commemoration of the War of 1812 appears in "A century later – Canadian memories of the war . . . ," in *The defended border: Upper Canada and the War of 1812 . . .* , ed. Morris Zaslow and W. B. Turner (Toronto, 1964), 321–24.

LAC, MG 27, II, F6 (photocopies). *Globe*, 15 Nov. 1882, 9 June 1916, 21 May 1925. Can., Dept. of Militia and Defence, *Militia list* (Ottawa), January 1895, October 1899, January 1901, January 1918. *Canada Gazette*, January–June 1895: 1750; January–June 1896: 1655–56. *Canadian album* (Cochrane and Hopkins), 1: 115. *Canadian annual rev.*, 1909, 1911, 1915–16. *Canadian men and women of the time* (Morgan; 1898 and 1912). *CPG*, 1897. P. E. P. Dembski, "William Ralph Meredith: leader of the Conservative opposition in Ontario, 1878–1894" (PHD thesis, Univ. of Guelph, Ont., 1977). G.B., War Office, *The official army list* (London), January 1882. C. W. Humphries, *"Honest enough to be bold": the life and times of Sir James Pliny Whitney* (Toronto, 1985). Ont., Legislature, "Newspaper Hansard," 1894–98. *Who's who and why*, 1921.

S

SAGAWAN. *See* SGANISM SM'OOGIT

SAINT-AMANT, ANNETTE (baptized **Marie-Jeanne-Annie**) **(Frémont)**, teacher and journalist; b. 1 July 1892 in L'Avenir, Que., daughter of Joseph-Charles Saint-Amant and Marie Dionne; m. 26 Dec. 1918 Donatien Frémont* in Prince Albert, Sask., and they had one daughter; d. 4 Aug. 1928 in Winnipeg and was buried in the cemetery of the cathedral in St Boniface (Winnipeg).

Annette Saint-Amant was the granddaughter and daughter of notaries. A native of Deschambault, Lower Canada, her father had moved to L'Avenir, where he began practising his profession in 1884; he was also a writer and the first chronicler of the eastern part of Drummond county. Annette was educated at the convent of the Sisters of the Assumption of the Blessed Virgin Mary in L'Avenir, and then continued her studies with the Ursulines at Quebec in 1907. Eager to obtain a teaching certificate, she enrolled in the École Normale Laval at Quebec as a residential student with the Ursulines in 1908. The following

year she obtained an academic school diploma in French and a model school diploma in English, with great distinction. Unfortunately, for reasons of health she had to enter the sanatorium in Gabriels, N.Y. During her convalescence she occasionally wrote for a number of Montreal newspapers, including *Le Devoir*. She returned to her home province in 1912.

That year Abbé Louis-Pierre GRAVEL, the founder of Gravelbourg, Sask., was desperately seeking teachers for the children of the settlers who had moved into this part of the prairies. Annette and her elder sister Maria answered the call. In August they took the "big coaches" to western Canada, where they were to teach in a rural school near Gravelbourg. They not only devoted themselves to their pupils, but also worked tirelessly in French Canadian organizations, busying themselves with theatre, running competitions, putting on shows, and writing for newspapers.

It was in Saskatchewan that Annette Saint-Amant would meet Donatien Frémont. A native of France, Frémont had arrived in Montreal in 1904 and after 1916 worked in Prince Albert as assistant editor of *Le*

Patriote de l'Ouest. The editor-in-chief at the time, Oblate father Achille-Félix Auclair, had long yearned to have a woman's page in his weekly. After reading some articles by Annette Saint-Amant, he asked Frémont to meet her and persuade her to become editor of this page. On 8 May 1918 Auclair announced that she would be responsible for the column "En famille." "Inspired first of all by patriotic and religious motives," as she explains, "the page will nevertheless be varied and practical" and will not "confine itself to the four walls of the home." On 15 May she also began writing a second column, entitled "Le coin des enfants." As time went by, a deep friendship developed between Donatien and Annette, which was consecrated by the bonds of marriage on 26 Dec. 1918. Their only child, Marie, was born on 2 Dec. 1919.

Le Patriote de l'Ouest was experiencing financial difficulties, however, and in May 1923 it could no longer afford to keep the Frémonts on staff. They left for Manitoba and at the beginning of July Donatien became editor-in-chief of *La Liberté*, a newspaper that had been founded by Archbishop Adélard Langevin* in St Boniface in May 1913. Like the Montreal papers *La Patrie*, *La Presse*, and *Le Devoir*, this weekly already ran a woman's page, with such competent columnists as Gertrude (Emma Gelley) and Jacqueline des Érables (Alice Gagnon). Annette Frémont took charge of this page which, under her direction, was given a new look and improved. On 10 March 1926 she started another page entitled "Le coin des enfants," for which she wrote articles under the pseudonym Mère-Grand. After her death, her sister Paule would continue the column for 18 years. At *La Liberté*, Annette was her husband's right hand, providing advice and writing many anonymous articles, including the column "Livres à lire."

Annette Frémont died on 4 Aug. 1928, at the age of 36, after a long illness. The obituary in *La Liberté* noted that she "possessed to a rare degree the innate gift of being able to offer a useful piece of advice, an original idea, [or] a helpful opinion, in an attractive and natural way." The following year, Donatien collected 37 of her columns in a volume entitled *L'art d'être heureuse*, for which Abbé Lionel Groulx* wrote the preface. For ten years, Annette Frémont had been an important voice for French-speaking women and children in western Canada. She was one of the three or four best women writers of her time. Her husband died in 1967.

MONIQUE HÉBERT

Annette Saint-Amant is the author of *L'art d'être heureuse* (Montréal, 1929; réimpr., Winnipeg, 1931).

ANQ-MBF, CE403-S15, 1er juill. 1892. ANQ-Q, ZQ137, dossiers 359–62. Roman Catholic Chancery Office (Prince Albert, Sask.), Sacred Heart Cathedral, RBMB, 26 Dec. 1918. A.-F. Auclair, "En famille," *Le Patriote de l'Ouest* (Prince Albert), 8 mai 1918. *La Liberté* (Saint-Boniface [Winnipeg]), 1920–26, 8 août 1928, juillet 1993 (special issue). Hélène Chaput, *Donatien Frémont: journaliste de l'Ouest canadien* (Saint-Boniface, 1977). École Normale Laval, *Annuaire* (Québec), 1908–10. Nadia Fahmy-Eid, "La presse féminine au Québec (1890–1920): une pratique culturelle et politique ambivalente," in *Femmes et politique*, sous la dir. de Yolande Cohen (Montréal, 1981), 101–15. Robert Rumilly, *Chefs de file* (Montréal, 1934), 113–21. J.-C. Saint-Amant, *L'Avenir, townships de Durham et de Wickham; notes historiques et traditionnelles, avec précis historique des autres townships du comté de Drummond* (Arthabaskaville [Victoriaville], Qué., 1896).

ST JOHN, THOMAS, seaman, miner, and union organizer; baptized 11 Sept. 1865 in Harbour Main, Nfld, son of James St John and Mary Hunt; m. Alice —— by 1906; last known to have been seen in the period 1920–22.

Thomas St John was born into one of the many Irish Catholic families in the Harbour Main area. His paternal grandfather, John, a native of Tipperary (Republic of Ireland), owned a plantation at Conception Harbour, Nfld, a half interest in a brigantine, and fishing rooms on the Labrador. His father was a sealing captain who worked successfully in partnership with his brothers but the growth in the number of steam vessels eventually forced them, along with many other swoilers (sealers) who used sailing ships, to abandon the seal fishery. Thomas himself went to sea, serving as a mate on merchantmen, and apparently spent time in Bell Island's iron-ore pits, which Canadian capital had developed to supply Nova Scotia's steel industry. He may have been a seasonal worker like many of the island miners, who came largely from the communities around Conception Bay. It is possible too that he found work in the United States.

His appearance on history's stage was brief. On 27 Jan. 1900 he was on the passenger ship *Silvia* when it docked at Halifax en route from New York City to St John's. That summer he led a six-week-long strike on Bell Island. On 11 June miners there struck the Dominion Iron and Steel Company Limited, also known as the Whitney company after its president, Henry Melville WHITNEY. They were indignant that the company, which had begun operations a year earlier, wanted them to work longer for the same pay. They were also offended by their treatment at the hands of the company's managers and foremen, who were from Nova Scotia, a stance that aroused public sympathy for the strike. The miners persuaded the workers at Bell Island's other pit, operated by the Nova Scotia Steel and Coal Company Limited, to join the strike. Together they formed the island's first miners' union, the Wabana Workmen and Laborers' Union, with 1,100 members, and they chose St John as president, Eugene Sheppard as vice-president, and Daniel J. McCarthy as secretary. The union demanded 15 cents an hour for all workers, which represented a five-cent-an-hour increase to match the rate paid at Sydney, N.S., the replacement of the offensive foremen, and the companies' recognition of the miners' committee as the bargaining agent. The companies refused.

St John proved to be an imaginative and meticulous organizer. He quickly established four watches of 300 men each to patrol approaches to the island and to protect company property. These watches allowed him to maintain order among the volatile miners, to know, within minutes, of the arrival of ships with police or strike-breakers, and to monitor the activities of company officials. St John also set up a system whereby the miners allowed no one to leave the island without approval and no one to land without promising not to interfere with the strike. In addition, the strikers appear to have systematically relayed information back and forth between the island and the mainland. St John and the other union leaders maintained morale by organizing parades in which the miners carried banners emblazoned with the slogans "no surrender," "hang her down" (meaning maintain one's place), and "St. John." A "kodaker" (snapshooter), the press reported, even made up buttons featuring a picture of St John. These sold quickly and the miners wore them proudly. Such actions made for an orderly and, initially, effective strike.

The companies responded with strike-breakers, and the government dispatched as many as 52 policemen, a magistrate, and Newfoundland's inspector general of police, John Roche McCowen*, to protect the scabs loading the ore schooners. The government's action did not provoke the miners to violence, but they did become more determined. Their intransigence finally moved the companies to seek the arrest of the leaders. On 12 July, three days after St John and a group of miners had prevented Dominion manager W. S. Grammer and a gang of office hands from unloading a coal schooner, the police charged St John and McCarthy with obstruction and Sheppard with riotous conduct. They pleaded not guilty, but the court remanded them to the penitentiary in St John's for nine days. The arrests, the police protection, and the miners' impoverishment after six weeks without pay broke the strike. On 23 July Edward Michael Jackman*, a merchant tailor and "labor's friend," negotiated an agreement at the Conception Bay community of Kelligrews. The Treaty of Kelligrews, as it became known, gave skilled workers a two-cent-an-hour increase and unskilled workers one cent. The miners also managed to procure the reinstatement of all the strikers, a significant achievement, but there is no indication that the companies recognized the union or acceded to its demands over hours. Thomas St John received a "thunderous ovation" from the miners when he arrived at Bell Island on the 24th to chair a meeting about the settlement. Many miners, including St John, wanted to hold out for a single wage

for all, but the men eventually voted unanimously to return to work at the negotiated rates.

It could be argued that the miners were lucky to have obtained anything given that the government had intervened, that 1900 was an economically poor year, and that the miners were generally only seasonal workers anxious to support their families through the winter. It was no doubt their solidarity, St John's organization, and public support against foreign-owned companies that enabled the miners to make limited gains. The settlement had an immediate impact in the city of St John's, where labourers, who were earning eight cents an hour on average, struck for the Bell Island rates. The historian Briton Cooper Busch has argued that the miners' example also made the sealers more militant during their strike in 1902 [see Simeon Kelloway*].

The details of Thomas St John's life after the strike are sketchy and dependent on personal recollections. Former mineworkers from Bell Island claim that he and other leaders found jobs at the steel plant in Sydney. Manifests for passenger ships between St John's and New York City in 1914 indicate that he had moved to New York and become an American citizen. Members of the St John family who relocated in Glace Bay believe he went to Camden, N.J. Martin Kennedy, who left Newfoundland in 1920 to work in high-steel construction in Camden, boarded until 1922 with Thomas's brother Joe, a dock builder. Although he never met Thomas, or Tombo as he was called, he saw him, and remembers him as a big, tough man, over six feet in height and about 250 pounds, a Roman Catholic, and still a solid unionist.

DUFF SUTHERLAND and JESSIE CHISHOLM

The DCB acknowledges information provided by Steven Neary and Martin Kennedy in interviews held in October 1992.

LAC, RG 76, C: 1(b). National Arch. (G.B.), CO 194/245, no.46. PANL, GN 1/3/A, dispatches 149, 187; GN 5/2/A/9,2, f.572 (1865); GN 9/1, June–August 1900; MG 299; Parish records coll., Roman Catholic Church, Harbour Main, baptisms, no.103. *Daily News* (St John's), 11 Sept. 1899, June–July 1900, 22 March 1906, February 1931. *Evening Herald* (St John's), June–July 1900, March 1906. *Evening Telegram* (St John's), June–July 1900, 21 March 1906, February 1931. *Gazette* (Montreal), July 1900. *Royal Gazette and Newfoundland Advertiser* (St John's), 29 Nov. 1864. *Trade Review* (St John's), June–July 1900. David Alexander, "Newfoundland's traditional economy and development to 1934," in *Newfoundland in the nineteenth and twentieth centuries: essays in interpretation*, ed. J. [K.] Hiller and P. [F.] Neary (Toronto, 1980), 17–39. Addison Bown, *Newspaper history of Bell Island* (2v., n.p., n.d.). J. D. Green, "Miners' unions on Bell Island" (B.COMM. paper, Memorial Univ. of Nfld, St John's, 1968). P. F. Neary, "'Traditional' and 'modern' elements in the social and economic history of Bell Island and Conception Bay," CHA, *Hist. Papers* (1973): 105–36. M. J. Nugent, "Wabana iron mines at Bell Island, Conception Bay," *Adelphian* (St John's), 1 (1904): 94–98.

Saint-Paul

Gail Weir, *The miners of Wabana: the story of the iron ore miners of Bell Island* (St John's, 1989). *Who's who in and from Newfoundland* (St John's), 1927.

SAINT-PAUL. *See* DÉGRÈS

SAM KEE. *See* CHANG TOY

SANFIDELE, FLORENCE. *See* COSTANZO

SAN JI. *See* CHANG TOY

SAUNDERS, DYCE WILLCOCKS, lawyer, cricketer, and Anglican layperson; b. 22 March 1862 in Guelph, Upper Canada, son of Thomas Wilcocks Saunders, a lawyer and police magistrate, and Jemima C. Wilson; m. 12 Sept. 1889 Amy Julia Percival Bréhaut (d. 1927) in Westmount, Que., and they had three sons and three daughters; d. 12 June 1930 in London, England.

Dyce W. Saunders was educated at Trinity College School in Port Hope, Ont., where he played some of his earliest cricket. In 1879 he was captain and wicketkeeper for Trinity's first eleven. Later that year he was admitted into the Law Society of Upper Canada as a student-at-law. Articled with Kingsmill, Cattanach, and Symons in Toronto, he joined this firm after he was called to the bar in Michaelmas term 1884. Saunders would remain with Kingsmill for his entire career, becoming a partner in 1891 and senior partner in 1913. He served as president of the County of York Law Association in 1906–7, was named KC in 1908, and was elected a bencher of the law society on 23 Nov. 1922. Despite such recognition, little is known of his legal work; in 1928 he was appointed to chair a board of arbitration over a wage dispute at the Toronto Transportation Commission.

As a law student, Saunders had lived with his sisters who ran a private school in Yorkville (Toronto). After coming to Toronto, he had continued his interest in cricket, as a wicketkeeper for both the Guelph Cricket Club and the Toronto Cricket Club, his sporting home for over 40 years. Cricket was a gentlemen's sport, the preserve largely of a male elite who supported a code that eschewed professionalism. Contests between local clubs were social affairs; greater importance was attached to international contests, called test matches. Saunders's first international appearance came in 1881 at age 19 against the United States; he went on to play in the annual international match versus the United States 12 times. Between 1885 and 1905 he represented Canada on 20 occasions against teams from America, Ireland, Scotland, and England. In 1887 he and fellow lawyer and TCC member George Goldwin Smith Lindsey assembled an all-star Canadian team for a tour of England, which they chronicled in a book written largely for insiders. The "gentlemen of Canada" had embarked "to learn upon the English cricket fields by the lesson of experience the best features of the good old game." In doing so they hoped to "inaugurate a new era in Canadian Cricket." Saunders, who participated in 17 of the team's 19 matches between 30 June and 27 August (five wins, five loses, nine draws), finished with the second-highest batting average on the squad, 23.58 runs per inning. He would take part in another tour of England in 1922. The "new era" in cricket at home did not happen, however. The continued play of the game for elitist recreation and socialization meant that it would not become widely popular in Canada.

Saunders's reputation was based on both his play as a wicketkeeper, a position of responsibility on the pitch, and his administrative work for cricket. On 28 March 1892 he was one of 34 delegates, all male and most based in Toronto, at the founding meeting there of the Canadian Cricket Association. From 1904 to 1908 he was its president. The association oversaw the J. Ross Robertson Cricket Cup, which recognized the winner of a national competition; in 1911 Saunders was the trustee of this trophy. At his death he was honorary vice-president of the TCC and the Toronto District Cricket Council. By this time, however, the game had declined in the limited popularity it enjoyed. Cricket and international competition were attracting little attention from the sports press as it followed games with broader consumer appeal, such as baseball and hockey, which were often dominated by professional teams.

Outside law and cricket, Saunders's interests included Anglicanism and its educational offshoots. (A Conservative, he was never active politically.) Following his marriage to Amy Bréhaut in 1889, Saunders had settled on Lowther Avenue in Yorkville; for their entire married life they would live in exclusive neighbourhoods in north Toronto. By early 1891 the couple had joined the Anglo-Catholic congregation of St Thomas's Church on Huron Street, where Dyce became a chorister, a representative to synod, and a warden. In this last capacity he was instrumental in 1908 in the construction of a parish hall and the purchase of an adjacent house for use as a rectory. In addition, the church acquired the former residence of Edward Blake*, Humewood, which was converted and opened in 1912 as a maternity home, with Saunders as a trustee. In St Thomas's, a window was donated by the Saunderses in memory of their eldest son, Thomas Brehaut, a lieutenant in the Royal Highlanders of Canada who was killed in action at Sanctuary Wood in Belgium on 16 Oct. 1916. Saunders participated as well in the Missionary Society of the Church of England in Canada and was a member of the national committee of the Laymen's Missionary Movement. From May 1927 until his death he was chancellor of the diocese of Toronto. In education, he was secretary of Bishop Bethune College in Oshawa and a member of the board of governors of Trinity College School (where he led a fund-raising campaign for a new building) and, in Toronto, of the council of Bishop Strachan School and the corporation of Trinity University.

Saunders was in London to argue a case before the Judicial Committee of the Privy Council, and to take in a cricket match, when he died suddenly in June 1930. Following a service there at Grosvenor Chapel on South Audley Street, his remains were cremated; his modest estate was valued at $26,000. On his passing, noted sportswriter William Abraham Hewitt* called the former wicketkeeper the "dean of Canadian cricket." The *Toronto Daily Star* recalled that "in the days when international cricket was played between Canada and the United States, an international team was said not to be complete without him." Despite these accolades, obituaries in Toronto and Guelph newspapers drew more attention to Saunders's legal career and diocesan contributions than to his lifelong involvement with cricket.

RUSSELL FIELD

Dyce Willcocks Saunders is the co-author, with G. G. S. Lindsey, of *Cricket across the sea, or, The wanderings and matches of the gentlemen of Canada, 1887, by two of the vagrants* (Toronto, 1887), reproduced on microfiche by CIHM.

ANQ-M, CE601-S77, 12 sept. 1889. AO, RG 22-305, no.65064; RG 80-27-2, 79: 21. Law Soc. of Upper Canada Arch. (Toronto), 1-1 (Convocation, minutes), 18: 205–6; Ontario bar biog. research project database. *Gazette* (Montreal), 14 Sept. 1889. *Globe*, 14 June 1930. *Guelph Weekly Mercury and Advertiser*, 12, 19 Sept. 1889. *Times* (London), 14, 17 June 1930. *Toronto Daily Star*, 13 June 1930. K. E. Boller, "Canada has colourful cricket history" (typescript, Toronto, 1984; revised 2001; copy available at the Canadian Cricket Assoc., Mississauga, Ont.); "Canadian Cricket Association celebrates centenary, 1892–1992," *Canadian Cricketer* (Toronto), 20 (1992), no.1: 4; "Canadian wicket-keeper Dyce Saunders could bat with the best" (typescript, Toronto, 1983; copy available at the Canadian Cricket Assoc.). *Canada Law Journal* (Toronto), 21 (1885): 27. *Canadian annual rev.*, 1922: 674; 1928–29: 210. David Cooper, "Canadians declare 'It Isn't Cricket': a century of rejection of the imperial game, 1860–1960," *Journal of Sport Hist.* ([Lamont, Pa]), 26 (1999): 51–81. *Directory*, Toronto, 1884–1930. J. E. Hall and R. O. McCulloch, *Sixty years of Canadian cricket* (Toronto, 1895). *Household of God: a parish history of St. Thomas's Church, Toronto*, ed. D. A. Kent (Toronto, 1993). Alan Metcalfe, *Canada learns to play: the emergence of organized sport, 1807–1914* (Toronto, 1987).

SCALLION, JAMES WILLIAM, teacher, farmer, and agrarian leader; b. 14 Feb. 1842 in County Wexford (Republic of Ireland), elder son of William Scallion and Catherine O'Donohue; d. unmarried 24 April 1926 in Virden, Man.

James Scallion immigrated to Upper Canada around 1850 with his family. The Scallions first settled near

Ancaster, but were living in Delaware, Middlesex County, by 1871. After attending the Toronto Normal School in 1867, James taught school for five years before joining his family in Thorold, where he and his brother operated a mercantile business. In 1882 he and his siblings joined the thousands of Ontarians who followed the transcontinental railway to western Canada. They went first to Stonewall, Man., but settled in 1883 in Virden, situated along the main route of the Canadian Pacific Railway in southwestern Manitoba. There they purchased 960 acres and created a prosperous grain and stock-raising farm called The Grange.

By 1900 Manitoba's economy was booming. Farmers were creating huge surpluses of grain for export, but most believed that their prosperity was greatly impeded by high tariffs and the monopoly grain-elevator companies held on the local market. To avoid the high dockage fees exacted by these companies and the low prices they paid, farmers wanted to load boxcars directly and ship their grain themselves. The federal government responded with the Manitoba Grain Act of 1900, which required railway companies to make grain cars available to farmers as requested. Bumper wheat crops in 1901 and 1902 created a severe shortage of cars, however, and farmers believed that elevator companies received precedence. This situation persuaded agriculturists in the North-West Territories to strengthen their voice by forming the first grain growers' association, officially established in January 1902. Scallion joined a committee of agriculturalists from Virden to arrange a special meeting with William Richard Motherwell*, one of the founders of the Territorial Grain Growers' Association. The meeting, held on 7 Jan. 1903, resulted in the formation of the Virden Grain Growers' Association with Scallion as president. Scallion travelled extensively across Manitoba, encouraging other communities to follow Virden's example, until the Manitoba Grain Growers' Association, a provincial organization independent of the territorial organization, was created in Brandon in March 1903. Scallion, chosen president, told the assembly that "40,000 farmers had produced 100,000 bushels of wheat and they should all be wealthy but where was the wealth? Certainly not in the farmers' hands but in the homes of the manufacturers, railway promoters, and grain dealers." In 1904, suffering from impaired hearing, he retired as president; he would remain honorary president for life. He continued to travel to meetings across the province, urging support for the establishment of a cooperative grain company. Formed in 1906 to handle members' grain in competition with private companies, the Grain Growers' Grain Company would evolve into the United Grain Growers Limited in 1917.

In December 1910 Scallion joined other agrarian leaders, such as Ernest Charles Drury*, Robert Sellar*, and James Speakman*, in taking a delegation of over 800 farmers to Ottawa to put their grievances directly before the Canadian government. At the meeting there, Scallion spoke in support of the removal of the high tariff that crippled farmers who were dependent upon imports of agricultural products and implements from the United States. The election of 1911 was fought primarily on the issue of reciprocity with the United States, but the Liberals, whose finance minister, William Stevens FIELDING, had introduced the reciprocity agreement, were defeated. The fact that some prominent Liberals, including Clifford SIFTON, opposed reciprocity heightened farmers' belief that neither political party represented the interests of western farmers.

By the end of World War I farmers were ready to take political action. The national farmers' platform of resolutions first presented in 1910 [see Speakman] was revised in 1918 and farmers were encouraged to vote for candidates who endorsed it. In January 1920 the Manitoba Grain Growers' Association adopted the platform, changed its own name to the United Farmers of Manitoba, and committed itself to political action. Scallion was nominated for the presidency of the new organization, but his name was withdrawn because he was too ill to serve. In 1922 the United Farmers formed the first farmers' government in Manitoba under John Bracken*. That same year the Manitoba Agricultural College honoured Scallion for "his contribution to the social and economic betterment of the farm community." He had taken the first steps in his province to provide farmers with a mechanism for altering the balance of economic power in western Canada.

Near the end of his life, James Scallion and his sister Hannah created two permanent philanthropic endowments, one to support the Virden hospital and the other to maintain the Virden cemetery, where Scallion was buried when he died in 1926.

KAREN NICHOLSON

AO, RG 2-128-1-3; RG 2-128-6-2; RG 2-301-1-3, certificate 2499. LAC, RG 31, C1, 1861, Ancaster, Ont.; 1871, Delaware, Ont.; 1881, Thorold, Ont.; 1891, 1901, Virden, Man. Man., Legislative Library (Winnipeg), Biog. scrapbooks, B8: 73. *Brandon Daily Sun* (Brandon, Man.), 1903–26. *Grain Growers' Guide* (Winnipeg), 1910–26. *Manitoba Free Press*, 1903–26. *Virden Empire-Advance*, 1907–26. Ida Clingan, *The Virden story, 1882–1957: Virden's 75th anniversary celebration, July 21 to 26, 1957* (Virden, 1957). R. D. Colquette, *The first fifty years: a history of the United Grain Growers Limited* (Winnipeg, 1957). F. H. Schofield, *The story of Manitoba* (3v., Winnipeg, 1913). L. A. Wood, *A history of farmers' movements in Canada* (Toronto, 1924; repr., intro. F. J. K. Griezic, Toronto and Buffalo, N.Y., 1975).

SCHREIBER, CHARLOTTE MOUNT BROCK.
See MORRELL

SCOTT, AGNES MARY (Davis), journalist; b. 12 Dec. 1863 in Quebec City, daughter of Allan John Scott and Margaret Cathleen Teresa Heron; m. 29 April 1903 William Patrick Davis in Ottawa, and they had two daughters; d. 19 Nov. 1927 in Paris, France.

As a society reporter in turn-of-the-century Ottawa, Agnes Scott described vice-regal and political society with much the same flair and sense of irony displayed by contemporary writer Sara Jeannette DUNCAN. Scott's witty, well-informed, and often surprisingly daring columns reveal much about the social texture of the capital during the heady early years of Wilfrid Laurier*'s prime ministership. The opening lines of Scott's first piece for Edmund Ernest SHEPPARD's Toronto weekly, *Saturday Night*, in the issue of 13 March 1897, eight months after Laurier's election, illustrate her acerbic style and shrewd appreciation of the realities of power. "'*Le roi est mort, vive le roi*' has been the cry in Ottawa since June 23, and the people who hoped 'those horrid Grits would not get in, as it would ruin Ottawa society' have been the very first to establish an *entente cordiale* with the new-comers."

Scott herself was an integral part of that society. Her father was the youngest brother of the patriarchal Richard William Scott*, Laurier's secretary of state; her mother was a sister of Scott's wife. Yet she was also an outsider. Her father had died young, in 1868, and Agnes grew up in an ambience of shabby gentility in Ottawa's Sandy Hill district, in a ramshackle house that lacked a bathroom and a furnace. A year or so after her mother's death in 1898, she moved in with her uncle. She had the misfortune to be plain looking, though her connections and wit were enough to win her a coveted place in the inner circle of Rideau Hall. The increasing popularity of society reporting, and the opening up of journalism to women, made it possible for her to earn a modest living through writing. Although not professionally ambitious, she supported most of the ideals of the independent "new woman" of the 1890s. "The best men in the land are the men who admire and help," she wrote in 1898 of the newly founded National Council of Women of Canada, which she joined. "It is the man – you know him – who says, 'I don't let my wife do this' and 'I don't let my wife do that!' who is loud in his condemnation of the Council. Beware of him!"

Scott had begun reporting on Ottawa society as early as 1896, with an article for *Lounger* magazine (Ottawa) on a ball given by Lady Aberdeen [Marjoribanks*]. When she formally embarked on a career in journalism, she wrote pseudonymously, in the convention of the era. In *Saturday Night*, for which she prepared freelance columns until June 1902, she was Amaryllis. In the *Ottawa Free Press*, where she was on staff from December 1897 to February 1903, she wrote thrice-weekly as The Marchioness – a nom de plume borrowed, not from any haughty leader of society, but from the cheeky maidservant in Dickens's novel *The old curiosity shop*, described there as "taking a limited view of society through the keyholes of doors." Although she was also a correspondent for the *Montreal Daily Star*, and did occasional pieces for *Saturday Night* on other topics, such as a trip to Paris in 1900, Ottawa was her stock-in-trade.

Some of her best columns poked fun at the rigid social protocols of the times. On 27 April 1897 she wrote in *Saturday Night* of the annual state drawing room held in the Senate Chamber and hosted by Governor General Lord Aberdeen [Hamilton-Gordon*]: "The ordeal of making two very low curtseys gracefully, rising without falling, getting out without turning your back on Her Majesty's representative, is nothing compared to the criticism you know you are undergoing from your friends who have been previously presented and whom you pass as you advance to the throne. Such remarks as 'No, it's not a new gown, only done over,' 'I think she has had it dyed, but am not sure,' 'She ought to try to look more cheerful,' are often heard." Scott was not afraid of chiding the vice-regals. On the annual exhibition of the Royal Canadian Academy of Arts, at the National Gallery of Canada, she observed on 24 Feb. 1900 that it was in a building that also housed Canada's fisheries exhibit. "Almost always, the Governor-General, in his speech on the opening night, alludes to the inadequacy of the place. . . . The Earl of Minto [Elliot*], who does not run to extreme originality in any particular, followed the example of his predecessors and advocated a new building." At least Lady Minto did not "pull his sleeve . . . to offer a suggestion," as Lady Aberdeen had been accustomed to doing when her husband spoke.

Scott hero-worshipped Laurier. In a charming piece on 21 Oct. 1899 she had described a chance encounter with the prime minister on an Ottawa streetcar. "Sir Wilfrid's democratic principles will not allow of his riding in aught else but trams." Far and away her most daring columns touched obliquely on his romantic relationship with the enigmatic Émilie Lavergne [BARTHE], "a brilliant woman called by many the Canadian Lady Chesterfield." (The real Lady Chesterfield had been a close friend of British prime minister Benjamin Disraeli, as Scott took for granted her readers would know.)

For six years she provided sparkling social reportage, seldom equalled in Canada. Although her columns provoked much comment and occasionally outrage, she was always invited back, a pattern which suggests that Ottawa in those days was a more sophisticated capital than is generally supposed. Her career ended abruptly in 1903 when she married Will Davis, a secretary some years her junior, son of a wealthy Ottawa contractor, and a playboy. Though their families had much in common – Irish, Catholic, and Liberal – there is much to suggest that their marriage was

one of convenience. It was certainly unsuccessful. They built a fine house in Sandy Hill and had property in the Thousand Islands; Agnes entertained and found time to research and write papers for the Women's Canadian Historical Society of Ottawa. But on Christmas Eve 1916 Will died suddenly in the apartment where, for years, he had been keeping a mistress.

Agnes stayed on in Ottawa, supported by her husband's estate and the generosity of the Scotts and her father-in-law. Her loose handling of money evidently became an exceedingly sore point between the families. In 1926, by now in straitened financial circumstances, she and her daughters moved to France, where living was cheaper. Briefly, she reinvented herself as a writer, contributing a number of articles to the *Montreal Daily Star*. She died in Paris of poliomyelitis in 1927.

SANDRA GWYN

ANQ-Q, CE301-S98, 14 févr. 1864. AO, RG 22-354, nos.8112, 13347; RG 80-5-0-310, no.5289. LAC, RG 31, C1, 1901, Ottawa, St George's Ward, div.5: 23 (mfm. at AO). *Ottawa Evening Journal*, 21 Nov. 1927. *Ottawa Free Press*, December 1897–February 1903. Sandra Gwyn, *The private capital: ambition and love in the age of Macdonald and Laurier* (Toronto, 1984). National Council of Women of Canada, *Women of Canada: their life and work; compiled . . . for distribution at the Paris international exhibition, 1900* ([Montreal?, 1900]; repr. [Ottawa], 1975), 76. *Saturday Night*, March 1897–July 1902. Lilian Scott Desbarats, *Recollections* (Ottawa, 1957). "The Scotts of Tredinnock: some notes for the eleven grandchildren – some of whom remember their loving grandparents, the house and the gardens," comp. Eileen Scott Morley (typescript, London, 1989). Fraser Sutherland, *The monthly epic: a history of Canadian magazines, 1789–1989* (Toronto, 1989).

SCOTT, BENJAMIN ALEXANDER, clerk, timber contractor, businessman, politician, and militia officer; b. 30 Sept. 1859 at Quebec, son of James George Scott and Mary Ann Green; m. there 1 June 1886, in Notre-Dame cathedral, Joséphine Shehyn, daughter of Joseph Shehyn*, treasurer of the province of Quebec from 1887 to 1891, and they had five sons; d. 14 Dec. 1928 in Montreal.

Benjamin A. Scott's paternal grandfather, a Presbyterian of Scottish ancestry, was born in Newfoundland and settled in Quebec City around 1820. After secondary studies at Quebec High School, young Benjamin assisted his father as an accounting clerk in the two sawmills run by Price Brothers and Company in Chicoutimi from the fall of 1875 until his father's death on 14 March 1885. Scott Sr was manager of both mills; the larger was located at the mouth of the Chicoutimi, employed 300 men, and processed 100,000 sawlogs in 1881, which made it the most substantial establishment of its kind in the region at that time. Scott himself worked there until September 1887.

907

Scott

In 1888 the opening of the Quebec and Lake Saint John Railway, with its terminus at Roberval, made it possible to connect the region with other markets and gave Scott a chance to put to use the experience he had gained in the Price mill. In partnership with the railway's builder, Horace Jansen Beemer*, he sought to take advantage of the region's forest resources and potential for tourism. In 1888 the two men built the Hôtel Roberval in Roberval on the southwest shore of Lac Saint-Jean. Soon tourists from all over the world were coming to the hotel, attracted by such activities as fishing for freshwater salmon (ouananiche). After an extension was added in 1891, the establishment had 257 luxurious, spacious rooms, and offered a multitude of services. The coming of the railway also made it possible to ship lumber to European and American markets, where it was in great demand. Thus in 1888 Scott joined Ross, Beemer and Company, an enterprise founded by James Gibb Ross* and Beemer to exploit the local forest resources. Scott's principal role was that of timber contractor. By autumn an immense two-storey sawmill, 120 feet by 40 feet, was in operation at the outlet of the Rivière Ouiatchouaniche, near the Hôtel Roberval. In 1889 over 11 million feet of boards and planks were shipped to England. To supply the sawmill, Scott, like Ross and Beemer, acquired vast cutting areas along the Mistassini and Péribonka rivers. From 1887 to 1893 his lumber camps produced more than 30 million feet of timber. At the end of the 19th century, his huge timber lands, covering nearly 1,500 square miles, provided employment for 600 men in lumber camps, and 250 others were engaged in rafting timber, working at the sawmill, and shipping. In 1901 Scott purchased the property rights to the mill from Francis Ross*, the brother and heir of J. G. Ross. In 1888 he had obtained from the parish municipality of Roberval a 20-year tax reduction for the sawmill and a 10-year reduction for the hotel.

Although the production of lumber declined in the Saguenay–Lac-Saint-Jean region at the beginning of the 20th century, Scott and his partners found new outlets with the pulp mills, which were supplying the growing market of the newspaper industry. In 1908, despite a fire three years earlier, their sawmill was the largest of its kind in the region. It had a production capacity of 30 million board feet, while the second largest, that of Price Brothers and Company Limited, could supply only 11 million. To carry lumber, settlers, and tourists, Scott and Beemer set up a navigation system linked to the railway. Four steamboats were built between 1888 and 1894. In 1897, in cooperation with the Quebec and Lake Saint John Railway Company, Scott helped found the Société de Colonisation et de Rapatriement du Lac Saint-Jean, which from 1898 to 1905 brought 1,000 people a year to settle in the Lac-Saint-Jean region. Scott acquired two farms to supply his forest enterprises and encourage the establishment of new settlers. The first was an 800-acre farm in Péribonka, which he purchased in 1888, the second a 1,500-acre farm in Mistassini, which he leased in 1897 and bought six years later.

At the end of the first decade of the 20th century, however, the tourist boom in the Lac-Saint-Jean region came to an end. Fire had destroyed one of Scott and Beemer's steamboats in 1907, the Hôtel Roberval in 1908, and Island House, a chalet of some 30 rooms that Beemer had built for fishermen, in 1909. In addition, the sawmill had to be closed in 1910 because of the prohibitive cost of transportation by water; the seasonal nature of navigation also made it unprofitable to transport logs. Some system of communication had to be found that would go right around Lac Saint-Jean and connect with the Quebec and Lake Saint John Railway. Scott consequently formed a partnership in 1911 with some local businessmen, led by Julien-Édouard-Alfred Dubuc*, to found the Roberval and Saguenay Railway Company. The following year a second firm, the Alma and Jonquière Railway Company, was established to extend the network. In the end, the railway did not quite circle the lake. It reached Saint-Félicien in 1917 and Dolbeau in 1927.

Scott's interest in the development of Roberval had also led him to play an important role on the municipal scene. As mayor of the parish municipality of Roberval from 1893 to 1906, a time when it was experiencing rapid growth, he set up committees to improve or create municipal infrastructure (streets, water mains, electric street lighting) and put into effect measures that would attract industries. He presided over the merger of the parish and the village which gave birth to the town of Roberval in 1903, and he was its mayor in 1906 and 1907. During this period he produced a budgetary surplus and he put through council a plan for the construction of a town hall. At the same time, as warden of the county council from 1896 to 1899 and from 1903 to 1905, Scott worked to promote coordination and consultation in the activities of the other municipalities in Lac-Saint-Jean county. He was also one of the founders of the Compagnie Électrique de Roberval in 1897, co-founder of the Compagnie de Téléphone de Roberval in 1898, and owner of the weekly *Le Lac Saint-Jean* (Roberval) from 1907 to 1917. In 1907 he helped establish the Saguenay Chamber of Commerce, where he championed the projects dear to his heart, such as the construction of a dam on the Rivière Grande Décharge at Lac Saint-Jean to facilitate navigation by maintaining the water level of the lake, but also to further his own plans.

Scott was well aware of the potential water-power to be found at the point where Lac Saint-Jean empties into the Rivière Saguenay. On 22 June 1900, through his political connections, he had been able to purchase from the provincial government development rights to a part of the Rivière Grande Décharge, from Île Maligne to Chute-à-Caron, for $6,000. Another concession, downstream from the waterfall, had been granted to Ontario developer Thomas Leopold Willson*, while the American financier Louis Terah Haggin had obtained the part between the island and Lac Saint-Jean. Since substantial capital would have to be invested to develop these energy resources, Scott formed a partnership in 1901 with Haggin and his father. Their goal was major industrial developments, but first they had to be sure they would find purchasers for the electricity that would be generated. In 1913 the American tobacco magnate James Buchanan Duke, who was looking for new sources of energy for his factories, acquired the Haggins' and Willson's concessions, while negotiating an agreement with Scott for the latter's rights. Scott received 25 per cent of the shares of the new Quebec Development Company Limited, which was incorporated that October. Duke and his brother Benjamin Newton were his partners in this enterprise. In return, he had to obtain from the provincial government the right to raise the level of Lac Saint-Jean by building dams. This right was granted in April on condition that the dams be completed within five years and that Scott invest at least a million dollars in the work during this period. Construction was halted, however, by the lack of customers for electricity and by World War I. It was resumed during the 1920s, but Duke then decided to go into partnership with Sir William PRICE and tried to buy up Scott's shares, which Scott refused to sell. There was prolonged litigation before the Superior Court. In the end Scott did not receive the compensation to which his contribution to the company entitled him.

Along with his career as an industrialist and lumber merchant, Scott had also, from the age of 24, shown an interest in the militia. He had obtained a diploma from the Royal School of Artillery on 12 June 1885 and had been promoted to the rank of major on 12 June 1895. He had also received a diploma in cavalry on 4 June 1899. Since there was no regiment in the Saguenay–Lac-Saint-Jean region, Scott and two other officers raised the 18th (Saguenay) Battalion of Infantry, which was given official recognition on 1 Feb. 1900. Consisting of 32 officers and 342 non-commissioned officers and men, plus a band of 24 musicians, the new regiment was commanded by Scott, who received the rank of lieutenant-colonel. He remained in command until 1903. On 1 May 1907 he was given command of the 10th Brigade, which included, besides the 18th (Saguenay) Regiment, the 4th Regiment (Chasseurs Canadiens), the 17th (Lévis) Regiment and the 55th Regiment (Megantic Light Infantry). A number of members of the brigade were called up to serve in the Canadian Expeditionary Corps during World War I, but Scott was not among them. He retired officially from the militia on 31 Jan. 1924, and he was ill at that time. His last years were spent in Montreal. In accordance with his wishes, his ashes were cast into Lac Saint-Jean.

For 35 years Benjamin A. Scott was the leading figure in the development of the Saguenay–Lac-Saint-Jean region. A far-sighted entrepreneur, he had grasped the full economic potential of the hydraulic resources of the Saguenay and of Lac Saint-Jean and he devoted himself to their development with the zeal of a pioneer. The hydroelectric stations of L'Isle-Maligne (Alma) and Chute-à-Caron still bear witness today to the soundness of his views. They have given rise to the construction of paper mills and a large aluminum plant, which in turn have led to the birth of some towns and the growth of others. Scott may rightly be considered the "father" of the industrialization of the Saguenay–Lac-Saint-Jean region. The Commission de Toponymie du Québec named a mountain in his honour on 22 Aug. 2001.

CARL BEAULIEU

ANQ-Q, CE301-S1, 1er juin 1886; S66, 24 nov. 1859. ANQ-SLSJ, P2, S1, D891; P22, Grand ledger of properties, Quebec Development, 1913–15. Arch. de la Ville de Roberval, Qué., Procès-verbaux, 20 juill. 1888: 198–200. Duke Univ. Library (Durham, N.C.), MS Dept., W. R. Perkins papers, J. B. Duke – Canadian papers, 1903–25. LAC, RG 9, II, B4, 4: 296; RG 31, C1, 1861, Quebec City, Saint-Jean ward: f.4922. *Le Colon* (Québec), 10 mars 1938. *Le Lac Saint-Jean* (Roberval), 29 oct. 1903, 11 févr. 1904, 8 avril 1909. Carl Beaulieu, *B. A. Scott, père de l'industrialisation* (Chicoutimi, Qué., 1999). Léonidas Bélanger, "Le lieutenant-colonel B. A. Scott," *Saguenayensia* (Chicoutimi), 15 (1973): 88–92. Raoul Blanchard, *L'est du Canada français, province de Québec* (2v., Montréal et Paris, 1935), 2: 90. Arthur Buies, *La province de Québec* (Québec, 1900), 7–16, 114–15; *La région du Lac Saint-Jean, grenier de la province de Québec* . . . (Québec, 1890), 20. Can., Dép. de l'Intérieur, *La région du Lac-Saint-Jean, le grenier de la province de Québec; guide des colons* (4e éd., [Ottawa], 1908), 13. *Canadian annual rev.*, 1928–29. *Canadian men and women of the time* (Morgan; 1912). Paul Clark, "James Buchanan Duke and the Saguenay region of Canada," in *Rivers of aluminum: the story of the Aluminum Company of Canada* (Montreal, 1964), 158–70. N. S. Crerar, *Historique du développement hydroélectrique du Saguenay* (s.l., 1958), 8. C. M. Johnston, "The historical geography of the Saguenay valley" (MA thesis, McGill Univ., Montreal, 1950), 63. R. G. Le Blanc, "Colonisation et rapatriement au Lac-Saint-Jean (1895–1905)," *RHAF*, 38 (1984–85): 379–408. J.-B. Petit *et al.*, *La vie quotidienne à Chicoutimi au temps des fondateurs; extraits des mémoires de la famille Petit* (2v., Chicoutimi-Nord, Qué., 1994), 1 : 160; 2: 117, 131, 136–37, 212, 229. Qué., Parl., *Doc. de la session*, 1913, réponses aux adresses, no.47: 22; *Statuts*, 1911, c.84. Rossel Vien, *Histoire de Roberval, cœur du Lac-Saint-Jean* ([Chicoutimi, 1955]), *passim*.

SCOTT, DAVID LYNCH, lawyer, militia officer, mayor, and judge; b. 21 Aug. 1845 in Brampton, Upper Canada, son of John Scott, a farmer, and Mary Lynch; m. 19 Nov. 1883 Mary (Minnie) McVittie in Barrie, Ont., and they had two sons and two daughters; d. 26 July 1924 at Cooking Lake, Alta and was buried in Edmonton.

David Lynch Scott's father had immigrated from Scotland about 1817, and his mother was a native of Vermont. Educated at Brampton grammar school, Scott studied law at Osgoode Hall in Toronto and worked in the law office of his brother Alexander Forsyth in Brampton. Called to the bar in 1870, he practised in Brampton and then in Orangeville, which he served as mayor in 1878–80. Scott also saw considerable military service as a young man. He joined the 36th (Peel) Battalion of Infantry as a private during the Fenian invasions of 1866; he reached the rank of lieutenant-colonel in 1879.

In 1882 Scott moved to Regina, where he began his law career as a partner of William Cayley Hamilton, was called to the territorial bar, and served as the town's first mayor in 1884–85. He was the first person enrolled as an advocate in the new Law Society of the North-West Territories on 11 Jan. 1885. That same year he was appointed crown counsel for the district of Western Assiniboia. He began by prosecuting a number of minor crimes in Regina. Following the North-West uprising, during which Scott, as mayor of Regina, had organized a home guard, he undertook his first major work for the crown: as junior counsel in the trials of Louis Riel*, Poundmaker [Pītikwahanapi-wīyin*], Big Bear [Mistahimaskwa*], and others involved in the uprising. Fully committed to the prosecutions, he took depositions in June and July; in court he conducted the examinations of the accused. His performance has been assessed by historians as clumsy, confused, and lacking knowledge of the rules of evidence. The juries, however, found all those tried guilty. Named QC on 23 Oct. 1885, Scott became legal adviser to the lieutenant governor of the territories on 1 July 1887, but he still continued his prosecutorial work and private practice. In 1890 his firm was known as Scott and White and, in 1896, as Scott, Hamilton, and Robinson.

On 28 Sept. 1894, following the death of James Farquharson Macleod*, Scott had been appointed to the Supreme Court of the North-West Territories as a puisne judge for the district of Northern Alberta, seated at Calgary. He had been angling for a judgeship since at least 1887, had appeared frequently before the court, and had gained a reputation, according to the *Regina Leader*, as a man experienced in the real world, possessed of a high moral character and a learned legal mind. But not everyone shared this estimate. Assiniboia West MP Nicholas Flood Davin*, whose political career Scott had tried to derail, dismissed him in 1891 as "a flabby mass of conceited mediocrity."

Though a judge, Scott continued to serve clients in Regina until 1896. In numerous cases from 1894 to 1898 he had to absent himself from the court in banc because he had represented some of the parties at their original trials. In 1907 he joined the Supreme Court of the new province of Alberta. In addition to his court duties in Edmonton, he undertook several judicial investigations, including membership in the royal commission of 1910 on the politically controversial contract of the Alberta and Great Waterways Railway [*see* Arthur Lewis Watkins SIFTON] and an examination in 1914 of the Edmonton police force's handling of vice.

Scott was one of the most active writers of judicial opinions in the history of the Supreme Court between 1894 and 1910. A master of short judgements with incisive summaries of the legal issues, he established major precedents on enforcing city by-laws, expanding the interpretation of legislative enactments, and broadening the discretionary powers of the court in banc to hear all the circumstances of a case. Like his predecessor Macleod, he wrote often of developing a "law of the west," where circumstances unique to prairie life would be allowed as evidence in court regardless of common law precedents to the contrary. The Canadian Pacific Railway, for instance, was made liable for damages arising from sparks causing prairie fires; eastern courts held such ignition as accidental. Scott frequently cited Blackstone on the concept of common law as common custom, and the role of judges in defining it for their region. Preferring selectively appointed justices of the peace and judges, he envisioned a legal culture that, from the lower to the higher courts, would be moulded by a collective vision.

A crisis occurred within the Supreme Court in October 1910 when Horace Harvey* was appointed chief justice of Alberta. Scott's displeasure was marked by his refusal, for the next decade, to sit on appeals in banc, though he continued to sit alone. More controversy arose when separate trial and appellate divisions were created by the Supreme Court acts of 1919–20, which were proclaimed on 15 Sept. 1921. Scott was appointed to head the appellate division and was titled chief justice of Alberta. Harvey, who was made chief of the trial division, claimed that he was still chief justice of Alberta and launched a reference case in the Supreme Court of Canada. It upheld his position, but Scott's appeal to the Judicial Committee of the Privy Council in 1923 was successful. Championed there by Richard Bedford Bennett*, Scott ended his career secure in the belief that he was the premier judge. When he opened his court's spring term on 8 May 1923, Harvey was absent and he did not return to sit in banc until after Scott's death.

Scott had an active social and cultural life. Known for his striking personality, he was a member of the Assiniboia Club in Regina, the Ranchmen's Club in Calgary, and the Edmonton Club. The University of Alberta awarded him an LLD in 1924. An Anglican, he died that year, soon after his court's summer term, at his cottage on Cooking Lake near Edmonton.

LOUIS A. KNAFLA

[Biographical information about David Lynch Scott may be found in *Canadian men and women of the time* (Morgan; 1898 and 1912), *Who's who and why*, 1914, and his obituaries in the *Calgary Herald* and the *Edmonton Journal* for 18 July 1924. Comments by contemporaries are noted by W. F. Bowker, *A consolidation of fifty years of legal writings, 1938–1988*, comp. Marjorie Bowker (Edmonton, 1989), and in an interview on 19 May 1983 with Justice Ronald Martland, Legal Arch. Soc. of Alta (Calgary), 09-00-00 (Calgary Bar Assoc. fonds). A photograph and legal sketch of Scott may be found in L. [A.] Knafla and Richard Klumpenhouwer, *Lords of the western bench: a biographical history of the supreme and district courts of Alberta, 1876–1990* (Calgary, 1997), 163–64. Scrolls of Scott's judicial appointments are in GA, M 722.

A valuable collection of Scott's judical letters and bench-books for 1894–99 and 1902–4, dominated by his trial notes, is found in PAA, PR1969.310. His written decisions on circuit in the northern and southern judicial districts are found in PAA GR1978.235 and GR1979.266. Some of his judgements are noted in the bench-books of judges Horace Harvey and Charles-Borromée Rouleau in PAA PR1968.302. GA, M 517 also contains some of his correspondence and notes on cases.

The major sources for Scott's judicial career are the *Alberta Law Reports* (Toronto), 1907–24 and the *Territories Law Reports* (Toronto), 1894–1906. R. G. Martin discusses many of his decisions in "The common law and the justices of the Supreme Court of the North-West Territories, 1887–1907" (MA thesis, Univ. of Calgary, 1997). His role in the treason trials of 1885 is ably explained by Bob Beal and R. C. Macleod in *Prairie fire: the 1885 North-West rebellion* (Edmonton, 1984), 321–27. (Scott's telegrams on the course of the rebellion are in GA, M 2286.) See also L. H. Thomas, *The struggle for responsible government in the North-West Territories, 1870–97* (Toronto, 1956). L.A.K.]

Calgary Herald, 27 July 1924. *Northern Advance* (Barrie, Ont.), 22 Nov. 1883. *Canadian annual rev.*, 1914, 1924. *Dominion annual reg.*, 1885: 235. C. B. Koester, *Mr. Davin, M.P.: a biography of Nicholas Flood Davin* (Saskatoon, 1980).

SCOTT, HENRI-THOMAS (baptized **Thomas-Henri**), soldier, teacher, pioneer in physical education, journalist, and general merchant; b. 29 May 1880 in Alfred, Prescott County, Ont., son of James Scott, a merchant, and Marie-Louise Lemoyne; grandson of William Henry Scott*, a Scottish Patriote from Saint-Eustache, Que.; d. unmarried 31 May 1926 at Île du Grand Calumet, Que.

One obituary suggests that Henri-Thomas Scott attended school in Ottawa, Saint-Jérôme, Que., and Montreal. When he was about 15, he had his first physical education classes. At the end of his adolescent years, an interest in military life led him to enlist in the 65th Battalion of Rifles (Mount Royal Rifles), and he is regarded as one of the founders of its officers' mess in 1898. His superiors soon recognized his abilities and sent him to study at the infantry school in Saint-Jean, where he obtained a first-class certificate as an infantry instructor. On his return he was promoted to the rank of sergeant-major. At this period the Canadian government was offering a special course in physical education to a representative of each military district in Canada. On the advice of François-Samuel Mackay, lieutenant-colonel of what had become the 65th Regiment of Rifles (Mount Royal Rifles), Scott enrolled at the Royal Military College of Canada in Kingston, Ont., in 1903 as the representative of the military district of Montreal. He obtained a first-class diploma there and was immediately appointed sergeant-major of the 11th Infantry Brigade at the Trois-Rivières camp.

In January 1905, while pursuing his career in the militia, Scott began teaching physical education in Montreal at the École Normale Jacques-Cartier, the Collège Sainte-Marie, and, probably in the same year, the Collège de Saint-Laurent. He favoured the Swedish method, which uses a minimum of equipment. From 1906 to 1908 he also taught the students from the Montreal branch of the Université Laval, the Petit Séminaire de Sainte-Thérèse, the college at Farnham, and the Catholic High School of Montreal, which was attended by Irish students. However, it was Scott's role with the Montreal Catholic School Commission that would establish his reputation. In 1905 the board had given him the assignment of organizing and teaching physical education. His arrival coincided with the rise in Montreal of a reform movement concerned about the ravages of infant mortality and tuberculosis. It was calling for parks, public baths, playgrounds, vacation camps, and a more practical education, better adapted to an industrial and urban society. A pedagogy centred on children's activities was beginning to develop, which also encouraged the practice of physical exercise. Scott began teaching on 16 Oct. 1905. Physical education, however, was still an optional subject and not on the regular timetable. On Saturdays, Scott gave lessons to interested students in the gymnasium which the commission had specially equipped in the Catholic Commercial Academy of Montreal. He organized gymnastics clubs in a number of schools and at the end of November 1906 brought them together in a Ligue des Sociétés de Gymnastique Interscolaires. In 1908–9 he was teacher and supervisor of the teaching done by instructors at ten boys' schools, seven run by lay teachers and the others by religious brothers. He would have liked to see physical education taught in every school and class, but the commission was not so disposed. From 1911 he seems to have used his energies largely in the service of private institutions. On the eve of World War I, he had 2,500 cadets under his command and taught or supervised the teaching of physical education in nearly 30 public and private schools with a total enrolment of more than 4,000 boys. He also gave lessons at Dr Henri Lasnier's Institut de Physiothérapie.

Prominent members of the Roman Catholic Church in Quebec, prompted by the support given to physical education by Pope Pius X in 1905, approved Scott's initiatives. He also received encouragement from the army and from French-speaking members of the liberal professions, business, and industry, as well as from politicians. For several years in succession the Association Saint-Jean-Baptiste de Montréal invited him and his gymnasts to give demonstrations as part of the Saint-Jean festivities. The most unconditional and constant support, however, came from *La Presse*, which gave ample coverage to the activities of his gymnasts. The newspaper even assigned its "Culture physique" columnist, Dr Joseph-Pierre GADBOIS, to promote physical activity, and it published numerous editorials extolling the merits of the "rational gymnastics" taught by Scott. Nevertheless, Scott had to struggle constantly against indifference, prejudice, routine, and conservatism, particularly in educational circles.

To help him with administrative tasks and to ensure that his activities were more widely publicized, Scott founded the Société Nationale de Gymnastique in October 1905. This body hoped to set up gymnastics societies, gymnasiums, and vacation camps throughout the province. The organization also supported the movement for playgrounds. It trained instructors who would spread its principles and methods to schools and colleges. The help it gave to Scott's various initiatives was a major factor in their success.

In June 1907 the second annual school gymnastics tournament managed to attract 500 gymnasts to the Montreal Stadium. Afterwards, more than 70 from seven schools under the Montreal Catholic School Commission, the Petit Séminaire de Sainte-Thérèse, and the Collège de Saint-Laurent boarded the train for Quebec, where a committee had made preparations for their arrival. The gymnasts gave two demonstrations, one at the Quebec Drill Hall, presided over by the lieutenant governor, Sir Louis-Amable Jetté*, on 8 June, and the other for the students and officials of the Université Laval the day after. The event was widely publicized and proved a determining factor in the rapid spread of physical education at Quebec.

The triumph of Scott's gymnasts in Rome in 1908 would make him a hero. To celebrate the 50th anniversary of the ordination of Pius X, the Federation of Catholic Sports Associations in Italy organized an international gymnastics "congress," and *La Presse*

offered to underwrite the cost of sending a team of Scott's best students. Ten boys over the age of 14, most of them from the Collège de Saint-Laurent, were chosen to take part in the event. Belgium, France, Ireland, and Italy were also represented at the tournament, which opened on 23 September on the grounds of the Vatican. On 26 September, in the presence of Pius X, the Canadians were declared the winners. Four days later the pope received them in a private audience, gave them his blessing, and presented them with two boxes of cigars. This papal attention to the small group of boys from Montreal, and their victory, was widely commented on in the press throughout Quebec. On their return, they were welcomed at Quebec and Montreal by crowds estimated at 25,000. The anniversary of this victory would be celebrated for years.

The stellar achievement in Rome encouraged Scott to set up a gymnastics school for women in November 1908. He had been considering it for a long time but had hesitated for fear of offending some people's sensibilities. "The awakening of sympathy" by the success in Rome had overcome his hesitation. In addition, Scott offered, on request, private lessons at home for ladies, who received instruction in riding, tennis, and snowshoeing as well. From 1908 to 1913 he also worked as a journalist for *La Presse*.

In 1911 Scott crossed the Atlantic again with ten of his students to participate in an international "congress" at Nancy, France, of more than 8,000 Catholic gymnasts, the majority of them French. On 31 July, before a crowd of 40,000, the young Montrealers won the international first prize and a number of medals. Following this victory, Scott and his gymnasts, at the invitation of some Belgian organizations, took part in a competition early in August at Diest that brought together 3,000 participants. They left Belgium with gold medals and a certificate of merit. On 8 August they were officially received in London by Lord Strathcona [Smith*], the Canadian high commissioner. Two years later, in September 1913, some of Scott's gymnasts again participated in an international competition in Rome, with 8,000 athletes from 2,000 gymnastics associations. They made a good showing, finishing in second place, and were congratulated by Pope Pius X. After visiting a number of European cities and giving a demonstration of their skill in Ghent, Belgium, they returned to Montreal on 30 September.

In his campaign to provide for the all-round development of young French Canadians, Scott emphasized the need to take part in sports. To increase access, he had received authorization from the Montreal Catholic School Commission in the winter of 1906–7 to build a large open-air skating-rink on the grounds of the Catholic Commercial Academy. In order to ensure some permanence for athletic activities, he worked to set up various clubs. He was also keenly interested in playgrounds. He urged municipal authorities to set them up "in every park," as was common in the United States, and he offered to train instructors. As a member of the Parks and Playgrounds Association of Montreal [see Grace Julia Parker*], he proposed that swimming pools and public markets be converted into gymnasiums during the winter. In the summer of 1910, to improve the lot of children in the city, he became the first francophone in the province to found and run a vacation camp – in Sault-au-Récollet (Montreal), on the banks of the Rivière des Prairies.

While pursuing his career as an educator, Scott continued to rise through the ranks of the military hierarchy. Around 1907, he was made a lieutenant when he was transferred to the 85th Regiment (Régiment de Maisonneuve). From 1905 to 1914 he taught physical education to the men of this regiment as well as to those of the 65th. He spent World War I in Canada as chief recruiting officer of the 57th Infantry Battalion, which was formed on 28 April 1915. In the course of a year, some 1,800 French Canadians enlisted in this unit. Many of them were athletes or students to whom Scott had taught physical education. Appointed major in June 1915, Scott was transferred to the 206th Infantry Battalion on 11 May 1916, which was dissolved within a few months. He subsequently set himself up as a general merchant in Île du Grand Calumet, on a property he had bought with his brother Maurice in 1916. The place soon became a rendezvous for hunters and fishermen, and many prominent people enjoyed his hospitality.

On 31 May 1926 tragedy struck. Henri-Thomas Scott, Joseph Boucher de Labroquerie Taché, chief librarian of the Library of Parliament in Ottawa, and Paul-Émile Bernier, a translator for the Post Office Department, started out on a fishing trip on the Ottawa River. Their canoe overturned and Bernier and Scott were drowned in the rapids. The major's body was recovered on 4 June. And so, the life of the man who can be considered the father of physical education among the francophones of Quebec came to an abrupt end when he was but 46 years old.

GILLES JANSON

[The details for Henri-Thomas Scott's biography were drawn from newspapers, particularly La Presse and Le Devoir. Close to 150 items concerning Scott were found in these two dailies. La Presse was scanned systematically for 1905 to 1910, May to September 1911, and March to October 1913. The obituaries for 1 and 2 June 1926 were also used. Le Devoir was systematically searched between 1910 and 1920. The following newspapers were consulted as well: Le Canada (Montréal), 16 oct., 28 déc. 1907; 2 janv. 1908; 2 juin 1926; Le Droit (Ottawa), 1er–2, 4–5, 7 juin 1926; L'Illustration (Paris), 3 oct. 1908; Le Nationaliste (Montréal), 21 mai, 20 août 1911; 20 avril 1913; La Patrie, 1er–2, 4 juin 1926; Le

Réveil (Montréal), 15 janv. 1916; and Le Soleil, 2 janv., 30 oct. 1908; 19 mai 1909; 18–19, 24, 31 mai, 7–8 juin, 6, 11 juill., 3, 12 août 1911. G.J.]

AO, RG 80-2-0-151, no.28894. Arch. de l'Univ. du Québec à Montréal, 2P (fonds de l'école normale Jacques-Cartier), 2a/17, 2a/26; 2e/4. Commission Scolaire de Montréal, Secrétariat Général, Secteur de la gestion des doc. administratifs et des arch., letters of H.-T. Scott to the director general of the Montreal Catholic School Commission, November 1907, and to the commissioners, 28 Sept. 1909. LAC, RG 150, Acc. 1992–93/166, box 8722. École Normale Jacques-Cartier, Annuaire (Montréal), 1905–6; États de service . . . (Montréal), 1857–1909. Robert Gagnon, Histoire de la Commission des écoles catholiques de Montréal; le développement d'un réseau d'écoles publiques en milieu urbain ([Montréal], 1996), 103–10. Jacques Gouin, William-Henry Scott et sa descendance ou le destin romanesque et tragique d'une famille de rebelles (1799–1944) (Hull, Qué., 1980). Donald Guay, L'éducation physique dans les écoles normales du Québec, 1836–1969 (Montréal, 1969); L'histoire de l'éducation physique au Québec: conceptions et événements (1830–1980) (Chicoutimi, Qué., 1980). Quebec Official Gazette, 1908: 839. Denise Villiard-Bériault, Saint-Laurent: un collège se raconte: 120 ans de collège, 10 ans de cégep (Montréal, 1977), 99–107.

SCOTT, WILLIAM DUNCAN, land agent and civil servant; b. November 1861, likely on the 7th, in Dundas, Upper Canada, son of James Scott, a builder and manufacturer, and Margaret McEwan; d. unmarried 27 Jan. 1925 in Ottawa.

William D. Scott was descended from Scottish Presbyterian pioneers in Dundas. In 1925 the Ottawa Evening Citizen would note that "the old Scott homestead, 'Craigleith,' is one of the beauty spots of the district, comprising 15 acres of undulating garden and orchard." Educated at Dundas High School, Scott began studies to become a lawyer. In 1881 he abandoned this career and went to Manitoba, where he was employed by the Canadian Pacific Railway as a land agent, thus commencing a career of over 40 years in the area of immigration and settlement.

Scott joined the Manitoba immigration office in Toronto as a clerk in January 1889. In October 1890 he was put in charge of Manitoba's immigration program in central and eastern Canada. A slogan used on the letterhead of his office reads, "Help to keep Canadians in Canada." He aggressively promoted the western province in Ontario, Quebec, and the Maritimes, as well as in Michigan, attending dozens of meetings of Farmers' Institutes and farmers' picnics. He had to persuade potential settlers that it was worth their while to purchase land in Manitoba, where free land was largely already taken, rather than seek free homesteads farther west, and also "that in settling in Manitoba they are not leaving civilization, but going into a country with all the advantages of churches, schools, roads, etc." When he met steamers in Halifax and Montreal, he had to counter propaganda amongst prospective immigrants to the effect that there was no work in Manitoba and that they "would freeze in winter."

Clifford SIFTON, minister of the interior in Sir Wilfrid Laurier*'s government, recommended Scott to the minister of agriculture, Sydney Arthur FISHER, for a place on the commission charged with preparing the Canadian exhibit at the universal exposition in Paris in 1900, an appointment made officially from 1 Jan. 1899. Scott was delighted to accept the post, believing, as he told Sifton, "I can do credit to our Western Country and to your Government." The exhibit was a great success, and Scott subsequently promoted Canada at exhibitions in Glasgow, London, Wolverhampton, and Cork. He also supervised the erection of the great arch of Canadian grain in Whitehall for the coronation of Edward VII in 1902. The following year, on 5 January, Sifton appointed him superintendent of immigration in the Department of the Interior. Scott retained this position until 20 Feb. 1919 when he was made assistant deputy minister of the recently created Department of Immigration and Colonization.

The most extensive exposition of Scott's thinking is in his 1913 essay for *Canada and its provinces*, "Immigration and population." Between 1905 and 1911 he was interviewed periodically by the House of Commons standing committee on agriculture and colonization, and here too his ideas sometimes emerge. His statements faithfully reflected the views of the government. Its purpose was to encourage "farmers, farm labourers and domestic servants" from the United States, Great Britain, and northern Europe. In advertising, a major issue was "how Canada may be prominently brought before the countries whose climatic conditions promise a suitable class of settlers for the Dominion." Scott denied an opposition charge in 1905 that Canada was receiving the "offscourings of civilization," insisting that "we are getting a fine class of people." He later pointed out that between 1900 and 1907 Canada received 7,000 more settlers from the British Isles than did the United States. As for "foreigners," the government's policy, Scott assured its critics, was to "try to scatter them as much as possible." Moreover, "we put these foreigners on land that you could not put English-speaking settlers on," on "the poorest land."

In his day Scott was recognized for presiding over the years of record immigration to Canada before World War I, and in particular for the growth of population in the west. Yet more recent writers have associated him with policies of restriction and deportation, especially with strict implementation of the changes to the Immigration Act passed with near-parliamentary unanimity between 1906 and 1910. Indeed, the opposition charged the government with being insufficiently restrictive, and with inadequate inspection of intending immigrants resulting in unnecessarily high levels of deportation. Scott pointed out that policy changes in 1910 were intended to exclude "undesirables," which included the "physically, mentally or morally unfit," those "unlikely to assimilate," and those likely to add to urban congestion. Regulations deliberately impeded immigration from Asia and from southern and eastern Europe. Scott developed the curious argument that the open-door policy of previous years actually had discouraged desirable immigrants who saw that "all and sundry might enter," whereas the new restrictions made Canada attractive to them because they now had confidence "that due care is being exercised in the admission of new settlers." In Scott's opinion, readiness "to assimilate and adopt Canadian customs . . . should be the final test as to the desirability of any class of immigrants." It was essential to sift "'the wheat from the chaff' in the multitudes who seek [Canada's] shores."

In 1911 responsibility for Chinese immigration was moved from the Department of Trade and Commerce to the Department of the Interior, and on 2 October Scott was given the additional task of chief controller of Chinese immigration. As his title implied, the government's purpose was to restrict such immigration, with greater limits on the movement of Chinese immigrants and fewer exemptions from the $500 head tax for those registered in educational institutions, as well as enforcement of the "continuous journey" requirement for intending immigrants [*see* Harnam Kaur*]. Still, the Chinese continued to come in record numbers, so in 1915 the Conservative government of Sir Robert Laird Borden* prohibited arrival at British Columbia ports of artisans and labourers, skilled or unskilled, a measure that dramatically reduced the numbers; only merchants and their families and those attending institutions of higher learning were admitted. This exclusionary policy was formalized by the Liberal administration of William Lyon Mackenzie King* in the Chinese Immigration Act of 1923.

In failing health, Scott retired from the public service on 30 June 1924. The following winter a cold led to pneumonia and other complications which resulted in his death on 27 Jan. 1925. He had been an able and respected civil servant who contributed strongly to the implementation of the immigration policy of the governments of the day, much of it discriminatory on racial grounds, while avoiding controversy. He also was, as obituaries put it, "a man of the most kindly disposition and beloved by all who knew him," who had provided "earnest, anonymous, yet distinguished service."

DAVID J. HALL

William Duncan Scott is the author of "Immigration and population," in *Canada and its provinces: a history of the Canadian people and their institutions . . .* , ed. Adam Shortt and A. G. Doughty (23v., Toronto, 1913–17), 7: 517–90.

LAC, MG 27, II, D15; MG 30, C62. *Globe*, 27 Jan. 1925. *Manitoba Free Press*, 28 Jan. 1925. *Ottawa Citizen*, 27–29 Jan. 1925. *Ottawa Evening Journal*, 27–29 Jan. 1925. Ruth Cameron, "The wheat from the chaff: Canadian restrictive immigration policy, 1905–1911" (MA thesis, Concordia Univ., Montreal, 1976). Can., Dept. of the Secretary of State, *The civil service list of Canada . . .* (Ottawa), 1918; House of Commons, *Journals*, 1905–10/11; Parl., *Sessional papers*, 1904–25. *Canadian men and women of the time* (Morgan; 1912). *Cyclopædia of Canadian biog.* (Rose and Charlesworth), vol.3. Ninette Kelley and Michael Trebilcock, *The making of the mosaic: a history of Canadian immigration policy* (Toronto, 1998). Valerie Knowles, *Strangers at our gates: Canadian immigration and immigration policy, 1540–1997* (rev. ed., Toronto, 1997). P. S. Li, *The Chinese in Canada* (Toronto, 1988). Man., Legislative Assembly, *Sessional papers*, 1889–99. Barbara Roberts, *Whence they came: deportation from Canada, 1900–1935* (Ottawa, 1988).

SEMLIN, CHARLES AUGUSTUS, teacher, miner, packer, hotel owner, rancher, politician, and school trustee; b. 4 Dec. 1836 near Barrie, Upper Canada, son of David Semlin and Susannah Stafford; d. unmarried 2 Nov. 1927 in Cache Creek, B.C.

Charles Semlin was educated at a public school and by private tuition in Barrie; he subsequently became a teacher there. News of the Cariboo gold rush in British Columbia led him to give up his career in central Canada. He travelled to the Pacific coast, arriving in Victoria on 12 June 1862. His career as a miner was neither particularly long nor particularly successful. He prospected and mined for three summers in the Cariboo and then became a packer, carrying supplies between Lillooet and Quesnel.

In the spring of 1865 – evidently en route to the Big Bend of the Columbia River, which at the time was experiencing a gold rush of its own – Semlin came to Cache Creek. It would remain his home for the rest of his life. He soon found work in the area at Ashcroft Manor, managing the roadhouse and adjacent ranch of Clement Francis Cornwall and his brother Henry. Several months later he and a partner, Philip Parke, purchased a roadhouse of their own, Bonaparte House. Their advertisements stressed its strategic location at the junction of the wagon roads north to the Cariboo and east to Savona's Ferry (Savona) and the upper Thompson River. Parke sold out his interest to Wilson Henry Sanford in 1868 and in 1870 Semlin took over Sanford's share. Semlin traded the hotel to James Campbell in 1870, exchanging it for ranch land. He had been acquiring land in the area since 1867 through pre-emption and purchase. He gradually consolidated his holdings into one of the largest ranches in the region, which he would operate as the Dominion Ranch until his death in 1927.

Although Semlin became a successful rancher – the Dominion Ranch carried 15,000 head of cattle and was one of the most notable of the large interior ranches – he also engaged in many activities typical of early European settlers. He was the first postmaster in Cache Creek, for example. In 1873 he successfully lobbied the government for a public boarding school in the interior, so that the region's scattered population of school-age children could receive formal education. As an MLA, he introduced the legislation of 1874 that led to the establishment of the school in Cache Creek and he oversaw its official opening in June.

During its 16-year existence the Central Boarding School attracted a good deal of controversy [*see* John Jessop*]. The choice of Cache Creek over the larger community of Kamloops, the actions of the appointed school board (which comprised Semlin, Parke, Campbell, and C. F. Cornwall), and the conditions at the school all drew critical comment in the press. Semlin staunchly defended the institution, at one point even briefly assuming teaching duties there. It finally shut down in 1890. When a rural school district was created for Cache Creek several years later, Semlin, Parke, and Campbell all served as trustees.

Semlin's career as a politician had begun in 1871, when he was elected in Yale to the inaugural session of the provincial legislature following British Columbia's entry into confederation that year. His election was fortuitous. He and another candidate having tied for third place in the three-member riding, the returning officer allegedly put their names in a hat and declared Semlin elected when his name was drawn. His first years as a politician were not especially notable. He ran unsuccessfully in Yale in the general elections of 1875 and 1878. Then his fortunes improved; he was returned in 1882 and would retain his seat in the general elections of 1886, 1890, 1894, and 1898. He became leader of the opposition after the election of 1894, largely in consequence of Robert Beaven*'s failure to win re-election.

Even sympathetic newspapers noted that Semlin was not particularly effective as leader of the opposition. An affable and easy-going person, he appears to have been uncomfortable in the divisive atmosphere and raucous debate that characterized the legislative sessions of the late 1890s. Complicating matters was the fact that provincial politicians had not yet embraced the party allegiances of the federal arena; for example, both he and Premier John Herbert TURNER were staunch Conservatives. Semlin was really only the titular head of the opposition, since the oppositionists represented all shades of the political spectrum. They were united in their discontent with the Turner government, a fragile base on which to build an effective political force.

By 1897 the land and railway policies of the Turner administration, as well as the actions of individual cabinet ministers such as Charles Edward Pooley and James Baker, were attracting considerable criticism in the national and provincial press. Semlin issued an official opposition platform that summer on behalf of

Semlin

the Provincial party, calling for an electoral redistribution to correct the over-representation of Vancouver Island and the under-representation of the mainland in the assembly, as well as for a reorganization of the civil service, constraints on Asian immigration, and government control of railways. In October 1897 the first gathering of provincial Liberals formulated a similar platform on which to oppose the Turner government. Although the Liberals split over the issue of introducing party lines in the next provincial election, the arrival earlier that year of prominent Manitoba Liberal Joseph Martin had served to give them greater presence.

The Turner government failed to win a clear majority in the election of July 1898, and contested results and delayed polling meant that the exact standings remained in doubt for some time. In a controversial move, Lieutenant Governor Thomas Robert McInnes dismissed Turner and his ministers in early August. He then turned to Beaven and asked him to form a ministry, in spite of the fact that the former premier had failed to win a seat. Beaven was unable to find sufficient support and so McInnes next called on Semlin. Semlin succeeded where Beaven had failed, although Martin had at first been reluctant to serve under him, likely because he hoped to be named leader at a Liberal convention planned for two weeks later in Vancouver. He would then have been well placed to claim the premiership for himself.

Semlin was premier of British Columbia for just 18 months, from 15 Aug. 1898 to 27 Feb. 1900. As many contemporaries later recalled, it was a tempestuous period, in part because of the loose affiliations and informal structures that held political groups together. Uniting such diverse elements would have been a formidable challenge for the most accomplished politician, and Semlin was not a forceful leader. His difficulties also reflected divisions within his cabinet, which included fellow Conservative Francis Lovett Carter-Cotton* as minister of finance and the mercurial Martin as attorney general. The two men detested each other, an animosity that contributed to the disintegration of the government. Semlin's efforts to initiate wide-ranging reforms compounded his problems. Moves such as legislating an eight-hour day for hardrock miners were angrily denounced by mine owners and led to a lengthy and bitter strike (June 1899–February 1900) in the Kootenays. Similarly, the many dismissals that accompanied efforts to purge the civil service of patronage appointments caused heated protests and further eroded government support.

A speech by Attorney General Martin ultimately led to the collapse of the Semlin government. On 20 June 1899, just after the Kootenay miners' strike began, Martin addressed a banquet in Rossland. Irate mine owners in attendance began to heckle. The speech deteriorated into a shouting match and ended in a brawl which had to be broken up by the police. Semlin demanded Martin's resignation, which he tendered only after the caucus had sided with the premier.

When the next legislative session began in January 1900, Martin sat with the opposition. Semlin had not enjoyed a comfortable majority even with Martin in the cabinet; his departure called the government's survival into question. The fatal blow came with the defeat at the end of February of a major government bill concerning electoral redistribution. When Semlin advised Lieutenant Governor McInnes of the defeat, he requested time to see if he could regain the confidence of the house. After several days of negotiations, he found several opposition figures willing to join his ministry. McInnes ignored this development and dismissed the government, calling on Martin to form a ministry. The lieutenant governor's decision created an uproar in the assembly, which responded by passing a motion of no-confidence in Martin. The political situation in British Columbia was degenerating into chaos. Martin could not govern without a popular mandate, which he failed to win in the provincial election of June 1900. McInnes then turned to James Dunsmuir* to form an administration.

Semlin, who had represented Yale since British Columbia entered confederation, did not stand for election in 1900. He later commented that "I felt that I had done my share, and that it was time that younger shoulders were taking up the burdens of public life." He returned briefly to politics, winning a by-election early in 1903, but he opted not to run in the provincial election held that autumn. He campaigned once more, in 1907, but was unsuccessful.

Throughout his time as a politician Semlin had remained active in his community. He was said to have helped to form a local agricultural association in 1888, probably the Inland Agricultural Society of British Columbia of which he was elected president in 1889. He participated in the establishment of the British Columbia Cattlemen's Association in 1889 and he continued to play a role as the ranching industry faced a series of challenges, including greater competition from ranches in neighbouring Alberta, the formation and proliferation of company-owned ranches, and growing numbers of sheep in the area. Semlin followed other pursuits as well. His interest in Canadian history was well known and he served as president of the Yale and Lillooet Pioneer Society for many years. A good speaker, he was often asked to chair meetings or act as master of ceremonies, a role he continued to fill until well into his eighties.

Although known as a lifelong bachelor – even his death certificate lists him as single – Semlin raised a daughter, Mary, and left much of his estate, valued at just over $50,000 and consisting mainly of stock in the Dominion Ranch Limited, to his grandchildren. One account of his life, written after his death by a friend, states that he had adopted the girl. This appears to be contradicted by the census records of 1881, which list Mary's mother, Caroline Williams, a native woman, as living with Semlin and using his surname, but which do not describe them as married.

When Semlin died in 1927, the *Vancouver Daily Province* carried the news on its front page, noting that he was the last surviving member of the province's first legislature. Its editorial columns reflected on this fact, pointing out that Semlin's adult life had spanned the history of the province of British Columbia since its formal creation in 1871. In his own community the local newspaper observed that his grave was next to a cenotaph commemorating European pioneers, "of which the deceased was one of the most beloved."

JEREMY MOUAT

BCA, E/C/Se5, 1879–90, 1896–1904; E/D/Se5, 1901–14; GR-1952, file 1928/2; MS-0700. LAC, RG 14, Parl., E-1, vol.1989, 5th session, 8th Parl., Addresses: For copies of all correspondence between the premier, secretary of state, and the lieutenant-governor of British Columbia, having reference to the dismissal of premiers Turner and Semlin. Univ. of B.C. Library, Rare Books and Special Coll. (Vancouver), Charles Semlin fonds. *British Columbian* (New Westminster), 22 Sept. 1866. R. E. Gosnell, "Prime ministers of B.C., 11: Hon. C. A. Semlin," *Vancouver Daily Province*, 23 May 1921: 18–19. *Mining Review* (Rossland, B.C.), 24 April 1897. *Vancouver Daily Province*, 3, 11, 13 Nov. 1927. J. D. Belshaw, "Provincial politics, 1871–1916," in *The Pacific province: a history of British Columbia*, ed. H. J. M. Johnston (Vancouver and Toronto, 1996), 134–64. Brian Belton, *Bittersweet oasis: a history of Ashcroft; the first 100 years* (Ashcroft, B.C., 1986). John Calam, "An historical survey of boarding schools and public school dormitories in Canada" (MA thesis, Univ. of B.C., 1962). *Canadian men and women of the time* (Morgan; 1898 and 1912). Edith Dobie, "Some aspects of party history in British Columbia, 1871–1903," *Pacific Hist. Rev.* (Berkeley and Los Angeles, Calif.), 1 (1932): 235–51. *Electoral hist. of B.C.* S. W. Jackman, *Portraits of the premiers: an informal history of British Columbia* (Sydney, B.C., 1969). F. H. Johnson, *John Jessop: goldseeker and educator; founder of the British Columbia school system* (Vancouver, 1971). J. B. Kerr, *Biographical dictionary of well-known British Columbians, with a historical sketch* (Vancouver, 1890). E. B. Mercer, "Political groups in British Columbia, 1883–1898" (MA thesis, Univ. of B.C., 1937). W. [R.] Norton, "Cache Creek: the provincial boarding school, 1874–1890," in *Reflections: Thompson valley histories*, ed. W. [R.] Norton and Wilf Schmidt (Kamloops, B.C., 1994), 26–35. B. C. Patenaude, *Golden nuggets: roadhouse portraits along the Cariboo's gold rush trail* (Surrey, B.C., 1998); *Trails to gold* (Victoria, 1995). W. N. Sage, "Federal parties and provincial groups in British Columbia, 1871–1903," *British Columbia Hist. Quarterly* (Victoria), 12 (1948): 151–69. J. T. Saywell, "The McInnes incident in British Columbia (1897–1900), together with a brief survey of the lieutenant-governor's constitutional position in the Dominion of Canada" (BA graduating essay, Univ. of B.C., 1950). E. O. S. Scholefield and F. W. Howay, *British Columbia from the earliest times to the present* (4v., Vancouver, 1914), 4. G. F. G. Stanley, "A 'constitutional crisis' in British Columbia," *Canadian Journal of Economics and Political Science* (Toronto), 21 (1955): 281–92.

SEMMENS, JOHN (he may have been named **Theodore John**), Methodist missionary and school superintendent, Indian agent, inspector for the Department of Indian Affairs, and author; b. 9 Jan. 1850 in St Hilary, Cornwall, England, son of John Semmens and Sarah Hoar; m. first 27 Aug. 1878 Helen Kalista Behimer in Copetown, Ont., and they had seven children; m. secondly 4 Dec. 1907 Elizabeth Cross in Winnipeg; they had no children; d. there 1 Feb. 1921.

A Methodist missionary for 29 years before joining the Department of Indian Affairs in 1901, John Semmens was in the rare position of understanding the aims and policies of both the dominion government and the Methodist Missionary Society. Along with his mother and sister, he had left England in 1860 to join his father at Bruce Mines, Upper Canada. He enrolled in Victoria College, Cobourg, in 1868, but probably did not obtain a degree. In 1870 the Reverend William Morley Punshon* recruited him for a new parish in Walkerville (Windsor). Specially ordained in October 1872, Semmens left immediately for what is now northern Manitoba. The Wesleyan Methodist Conference sent him to Norway House to help the Reverend Egerton Ryerson Young*, who was apparently ill with typhoid fever. Having arrived after a difficult journey over Lake Winnipeg by dog train, Semmens plunged himself into mission life, visiting the Cree and travelling to their hunting camps. He worked closely with Young until his transfer to Headingley, a village west of Winnipeg, in 1873.

In early 1874 Semmens, who wished to work with native people in the north, was sent to open a mission station at Nelson House. He relied heavily on Cree men such as Sandy Harte, Edward Paupanekis*, and William Isbister, an Orkney Cree, to interpret, teach school, and recruit a congregation. Semmens wrote warmly of the Nelson House community and believed his tenure had "resulted in the complete eradication of paganism and a purified society." In 1876 he replaced Young among the Saulteaux at Berens River. From this base he visited outposts at Poplar River, Little Grand Rapids, Fisher River, and Pikangikum (Ont.). He led services, taught in the Berens River Methodist day school, and supported himself by fishing. While he appreciated his well-dressed, orderly congregation of 25, Semmens lamented that the "material . . . was so crude," asserting that the Saulteaux were a hard people, full of the "viciousness of their heathen ways."

In June 1878 the conference transferred Semmens from Berens River. He spent the next six years in mission work at white settlements in Manitoba and Ontario. In June 1884 poverty forced him to request a transfer to Norway House. The conference, unlike parish congregations, paid a regular, and thus secure, salary. While in Norway House he worked with his translator, John C. Sinclair, to transcribe several literary works, such as John Bunyan's *The pilgrim's progress*, and 200 hymns into Cree.

In 1888 Semmens's sons were of school age and he felt that they needed better educational opportunities. He asked to be released from Norway House, in part because he believed that "Indian life was not altogether wholesome.... There was nothing stimulating or uplifting in our surroundings." In June 1888 he went to work in Carberry and later he served in Winnipeg. The Manitoba and North-West Conference elected him secretary in 1891 and president in 1892.

In 1894 the Methodist Board of Missions recommended Semmens to the Department of Indian Affairs for the principalship of the soon-to-open Brandon Industrial School. Accordingly, he secured staff and recruited 38 Cree and Ojibwa children from Brandon, Norway House, and neighbouring missions. He served as superintendent until 1900. He accepted the position of Indian agent for the Berens River agency in April 1901. In 1903 he was transferred to the Clandeboye agency and two years later he became inspector of Indian agencies and schools. In 1908 he was named scrip commissioner with authority to take adhesions to Treaty No.5.

Semmens gave several lectures, wrote magazine articles, and published several small volumes and pamphlets in Cree syllabics, including *The hand-book to Scripture truths* in 1893. In 1884 he had published an account of his work, *The field and the work*. Writing of natives for the *Methodist Magazine*, he lamented that "darkness covers the land and gross darkness the minds of the people. The hereditary deadening influences ... have not yet been eradicated." Yet he was willing to concede that "while we have no desire to paint the Red Man white ... many excellent traits of character are ... associated with Indians." In his ethnocentric and romantic views Semmens was a man of his times, and certainly he was regarded by his contemporaries as an expert in his knowledge and understanding of native people. Nevertheless his harsh judgements of Cree and Ojibwa culture stand out strongly within the missionary literature of the period.

SUSAN GRAY

John Semmens's personal papers, including a copy of his autobiographical *Under the northern lights: notes on personal history* ([Winnipeg?, 1915?]), can be found in UCC, Manitoba and Northwestern Ontario Conference Arch. (Winnipeg), PP34. Semmens published numerous magazine articles, including "The Indian missions of the Methodist Church," *Methodist Magazine* (Toronto and Halifax), 41 (January–June 1895): 128–34; a number were incorporated into his *The field and the work: sketches of missionary life in the far north* (Toronto, 1884). In addition, he is the author of *The hand-book to Scripture truths, or, The way of salvation: words of admonition, counsel, and comfort* [syllabic transcription into Cree], trans. William Isbister, rev. J. [C.] McDougall (Toronto, 1893), and *Trials and triumphs of early Methodism in the great north-west* (2nd ed., Toronto, 1910).

AO, RG 80-5-0-77, no.12093. G. H. Cornish, *Cyclopædia of Methodism in Canada* ... (2v., Toronto and Halifax, 1881–1903). J. H. Riddell, *Methodism in the middle west* (Toronto, 1946).

SEXTON, EDNA MAY WILLISTON. *See* BEST

SGANISM SM'OOGIT (meaning "mountain chief"; also known as **Sagawan**, meaning "sharp tooth," in reference to a mountain at the mouth of the Nass River, B.C., **K'ayax**, and **Mountain**), Nisga'a chief; b. *c.* 1830, probably in Git'iks or Gunwok, B.C.; d. 1928, probably in Kincolith (Gingolx), B.C.

Ancestry and kinship define the social structure of the Nisga'a and other nations of the northwest Pacific coast. Individuals inherit names that determine their place in the kinship networks and in society. In one of the Eagle clan lineages of the Nisga'a Gitxatin tribe, generations of high-ranking men have held one or all of the names Sganism Sm'oogit, Sagawan, and K'ayax, these names changing with their age and rank in society. Since northwest coast peoples reincarnate within their own lineage, these men in reality inherit their own names. The biography of Sganism Sm'oogit then is that of countless generations of individuals who held this name and led this lineage. The lineage was founded by a people who settled at the mouth of the Nass River after the last ice age and, over time, established the villages of Git'iks and Gunwok. Later, others migrated to the region, bringing their distinct histories and forming a complex network of relationships with those already there. Still later, an Eagle clan group of Athapaskan origin which had first settled along Portland Canal and Observatory Inlet joined the group of Sganism Sm'oogit. Finally, around A.D. 500, many groups of both the Eagle and the Wolf clans arrived from the north and one Eagle clan group among them also settled with Sganism Sm'oogit's people.

In the late 18th century, when Euro-Canadian history first intersected with that of the Nisga'a, the Wolf and Eagle clan descendants of these migrating peoples had long been established on the Nass River and active in the trade with interior peoples that had been a vital part of the northwest coast economy for several centuries. When the first European ship arrived in Nass Harbour to barter goods for furs, the Sganism Sm'oogit of the period was well positioned to control access to the ships. He strengthened his ties with Legex [*see* Paul Legaic*], a Tsimshian chief who shared a common ancestry with the last Eagle group to join Sganism Sm'oogit's people. Together they ensured that their sea otter furs would be the first to be traded. To acquire inland furs for exchange, Sganism Sm'oogit drew on his shared ancestry with the Tsetsaut, the Athapaskan people to the north of Portland Canal.

The first Sganism Sm'oogit identified in European history, born about 1830, grew up during a period of intense competition for the wealth to be gained in the declining fur trade economy. He faced attempts to wrest control of the mouth of the Nass from him and the other lineages there, and a decline in the quantity of furs, especially beaver, from Athapaskan sources. In the 1860s lineages of the Eagle, Wolf, and Killer Whale clans vied for the same control of trade along the Nass that the Tsimshian Eagle clan chief Legex exercised over the Skeena River region to the south. The competition for power took form in a race to raise the tallest totem pole on the Nass.

At a feast he hosted in Git'iks around 1860 Sganism Sm'oogit took his names, assumed the rank of chief, and raised the tallest pole on the Pacific coast, thus confirming his wealth and status. Alfred Mountain, in an interview in company with Albert Allen and William Moore, would later describe the feast, explaining that "My uncle made this totem pole at Git'iks . . . as a monument to Gitxhon, Txalaxatk and K'ayax [his predecessors] . . . there was a big quantity of copper shields and goods given away at the time the pole was made.

"It took three days to raise [the pole] and all the people of Laxskiik [Eagle] . . . origin then brought all their wealth such as guns, overcoats, blankets and other valuables [which] were thrown into the hole at the foot of the totem pole.

"[It was] to be erected in the spring just before the arrival of the eulachons when all of the people of the entire Nass were to be invited as well as those of Tongass and Kasaan and messengers were sent to all of these tribes, inviting them to come to the feast of Mountain."

Although only in his thirties, Sganism Sm'oogit had confirmed his lineage's position at the mouth of the Nass. The establishment of the Hudson's Bay Company at Fort Simpson (Lax Kw'alaams) in 1831 had lessened the importance of the mouth of the Nass as a key trading location, but the eulachon fishery there still drew people from up and down the coast and still attracted fur traders. Sganism Sm'oogit continued to trade with his Tsetsaut relations, especially Saanik, a leader at Smailx, at the head of Portland Canal, and he established himself at Knagooli, at the gateway to this lucrative enterprise.

When Robert Tomlinson, a Church of England missionary, moved to Kincolith in 1867, the Wolf clan chief Hlidux saw an opportunity to undercut Sganism Sm'oogit's position. Protected by the missionary and by the navy ships at his disposal, he became Tomlinson's right-hand man at Kincolith, in the heart of Sganism Sm'oogit's territory. He had had his eye on Sganism Sm'oogit's alliance with the Tsetsaut for some time, to the point of killing their leader Saanik in an unsuccessful attempt to force them to trade with him. Hlidux encouraged Tomlinson to visit the Tsetsaut at the head of Portland Canal in the hopes that when William Duncan*, Tomlinson's mentor and counterpart at Metlakatla, visited Kincolith the Tsetsaut would bring their furs to his trading sloop.

As Txalaxatk (Robert Stewart) would explain in 1948, "[Tomlinson] soon learned of [the Tsetsaut] with whom Sagawan had been trading for so long. . . . So he went to this village . . . and saw that there was a great many people there, also they had no canoes and a great deal of furs. So he traded several canoes for some of their furs and then invited them to come to Kincolith, telling them to fetch their furs there, to Mr. Duncan's trading schooner. . . . Tomlinson was accompanied to Smailx by Hlid[u]x, who was his assistant. This man further urged [the new chief] Saanik to move to Kincolith. So bitter became the feelings [of Sagawan toward the new mission and Hlidux] that Sagawan together with his own group moved back to Git'iks."

In spite of Tomlinson's intrusion, Sganism Sm'oogit remained a powerful chief. At the beginning of the 1880s, in protest against Tomlinson's actions, he and other chiefs joined the Methodist mission of the Reverend Alfred Eli Green in Laxgalts'ap. In 1881 Sganism Sm'oogit and some chiefs of this group led the first land claims delegation from the northwest coast, protesting in Victoria against the creation of reserves in British Columbia and the crown's assertion of landownership. In 1885 they published a letter in the Victoria *Daily Colonist* denouncing the inadequacies of the government's land allotments and incursions on their lands.

Because of his status and enormous knowledge of Nisga'a culture, Sganism Sm'oogit was sought out by anthropologists. American Franz Boas*, who visited the Nass region in 1894, and Canadian Marius Barbeau*, during his first visit in 1927, recorded many of the histories of his lineage. Barbeau asked to purchase his famous totem pole, then at risk of falling in the abandoned village of Git'iks. Sganism Sm'oogit's response, "Give me the tombstone of Governor [Sir James Douglas*]; I will give you the totem of my grand-uncles," encapsulates his feelings about the request. He was almost 100 years old when he passed away the following year. He had lived through a period of enormous change. While others resorted to force and alliances with Euro-Canadian institutions, he had remained faithful to his heritage and the dignity of his position.

Little is known about the nephew to whom the title Sganism Sm'oogit passed. As was the custom at the time, he took the English translation of his name as his surname when he was baptized, and became Alfred Mountain. In 1928 he and other nephews of the deceased chief sold the totem pole that had been raised by their uncle to the Royal Ontario Museum in Toronto, where it has been preserved and displayed ever since.

At the beginning of the 21st century, Sganism Sm'oogit (James Robertson) brought the traditions of his ancestors into the political and legal arena. Drawing on "ancestral native law in order to protect ancestral lands," he contested elements of the Nisga'a Final Agreement of 2000, a treaty which excluded lands he and his lineage shared with their Tsetsaut kin. These ancestral traditions, still alive, stretched back to the first Sganism Sm'oogit at the end of the last ice age.

SUSAN MARSDEN

Canadian Museum of Civilization, Arch. (Hull, Que.), Marius Barbeau fonds, folder: I Gwenhoot (original ms), Narrative no.I 122, box 299, f.5; Mss ready for publication ser., folder: The Gwenhoot of Alaska, box 102, f.3, Marius Barbeau, "The Gwenhoot of Alaska in search of a bounteous land" (typescript, Ottawa, 1959); Northwest coast files ser., folder: Gitxatin, B-F-104, box B8, ff.12–13; box B9, f.1. *Daily News* (Prince Rupert, B.C.), 17, 28 June 2002. Marius Barbeau, *Totem poles* (2v., Ottawa, 1950–51), 1. Franz Boas, "Tsimshian mythology," Smithsonian Institution, Bureau of American Ethnology, *Annual report* (Washington), 1909–10: 29–1037. Susan Marsden, *Defending the mouth of the Skeena: perspectives on Tsimshian Tlingit relations* (Prince Rupert, 2000). Susan Marsden and Robert Galois, "The Tsimshian, the Hudson's Bay Company, and the geopolitics of the northwest coast fur trade, 1787–1840," *Canadian Geographer* (Toronto), 39 (1995): 169–83. Peter Murray, *The devil and Mr. Duncan* (Victoria, 1985). E. P. Patterson, *Mission on the Nass: the evangelization of the Nishga (1860–1890)* (Waterloo, Ont., 1982).

SHAKESPEARE, NOAH, labourer, photographer, politician, activist, and civil servant; b. 26 Jan. 1839 in Brierley Hill, England, son of Noah Shakespeare and Hannah Matthews; m. there 26 Dec. 1859 Eliza Jane Pearson (d. 1923), and they had seven children, of whom three sons and one daughter survived infancy; d. 13 May 1921 in Victoria.

Born and raised in the industrial Black Country of Staffordshire, Noah Shakespeare, who claimed a distant relationship to William Shakespeare, began work in a local chain factory at age eight. He returned to school briefly and then worked in an iron-rolling mill until he decided to emigrate in the fall of 1862. Having chosen British Columbia because of glowing accounts of the Cariboo gold rush, he arrived in Victoria on 10 Jan. 1863. He found employment in Nanaimo as a labourer with the Vancouver Coal Mining and Land Company and by working double shifts he was able to pay passage for his wife and son within a

year. The family moved to Victoria in the summer of 1864. There, Shakespeare learned photography from George Robinson Fardon and subsequently managed his photo gallery for a year. By August 1866 he was running another gallery, which he later took over from its absent owner, Charles Gentile. With the exception of a brief interval in 1870, when he worked for journalist and politician Amor De Cosmos* at the *Victoria Daily Standard*, he seems to have continued in photography. Towards the end of his life, he would imply that he had moved quickly into real estate and after 1880 he would identify himself as a manufacturer's agent, but contemporary sources indicate that from 1864 to the late 1870s he was principally a photographer. By 1877 Eliza Jane had opened a "fancy store." An uncommon step for a married woman, her initiative suggests that Shakespeare's income may not have been adequate for the family's needs.

In January 1875 Shakespeare had entered politics when he was acclaimed a city councillor for James Bay Ward. The election of the mayor and many of the councillors had been attributed by some of their opponents to the Chinese vote. In view of his later anti-Chinese activities, Shakespeare's role in helping to defeat a motion in council to disenfranchise Chinese residents in civic elections is ironic. Later in 1875 he initiated a motion to close Chinese brothels in the city. This move may have stemmed from his strong Methodist beliefs or it may have been the beginning of his anti-Chinese platform. Shakespeare ran for council every year from 1876 to 1881, but was successful only in 1878, 1880, and 1881. In the provincial election of 1875 he had run as an independent in suburban Victoria District, but lost to anti-government candidates because of his association with De Cosmos, who had been premier from 1872 to 1874, and with the government of his successor, George Anthony Walkem*.

White working-class hostility towards Chinese immigrants in British Columbia grew in the late 1870s because of fear of their economic competition and professed concern about their morality. Shakespeare, who declared himself an advocate of workingmen, rose to prominence as a leader of the anti-Chinese movement. In August 1878 the Legislative Assembly passed the Chinese Tax Act to enumerate and tax all Chinese residents. Shakespeare was appointed the tax collector in Victoria, on a commission basis. When people refused to pay, he seized their property. The result was a general strike by Chinese workers and shopkeepers in Victoria on 17 Sept. 1878. When Shakespeare's assistant was accused by Tai Sing of illegally seizing and selling his property, justice John Hamilton Gray* of the Supreme Court of British Columbia ruled that the act was *ultra vires* the provincial assembly. The following year the federal government disallowed the act, eliminating any chance of future income from this source.

In October 1878 Shakespeare had assumed leadership of the Workingmen's Protective Association. Formed in Victoria a month earlier, the WPA was an early labour union, with the elimination of Chinese competition its primary goal. Shakespeare expanded the organization to the mainland and used it as a springboard for his political career. Early in 1879 he and the WPA sent a petition with almost 1,500 signatures to parliament, calling for taxation of resident Chinese and the exclusion of new immigrants. In April 1879 he stepped down as president of the declining WPA, but he helped found the Anti-Chinese Association the same year. Its goals were identical and on its behalf he petitioned federal and provincial governments for exclusionary legislation and tried to get Chinese labour barred from work on the proposed transcontinental railway. In spite of varying public support, he persevered.

Shakespeare's rising profile led to his election as mayor of Victoria in January 1882. He acquitted himself well, the high point of his term being the state visit of the governor general, Lord Lorne [Campbell*], later that year. Playing on the growing Sinophobia caused by the influx of Chinese work crews for the Canadian Pacific Railway, Shakespeare, a Conservative, successfully contested one of the two seats for Victoria in the federal election of June 1882. He continued as mayor until the end of his term and when the House of Commons was reconvened in February 1883 he took his seat. The following year he reached his political zenith when he tabled a motion in the commons for a law to prohibit Chinese immigration. It was made necessary, he claimed, by their unfair economic competition and their immorality. His motion was amended and became law in 1885 as the Chinese Immigration Act, introducing the infamous $50 head tax on each Chinese arrival and limiting the number of immigrants per vessel. It did not provide outright exclusion, but it was the culmination of Shakespeare's anti-Chinese activity. Later that year in Victoria he established the Labor Bureau, a union of white labourers to fight Chinese competition. In the 1887 election Shakespeare retained his federal seat, but he resigned it to accept an appointment on 1 Jan. 1888 as postmaster of Victoria, a reward for his loyalty to Conservative prime minister Sir John A. Macdonald*. He held the position until his retirement on 31 March 1914, supervising the rapid growth of postal facilities as the city boomed.

With his election to parliament, Shakespeare had attained a higher social status, demonstrated by his appointment as a justice of the peace in 1883 and by the business opportunities that came his way (he was, for example, an organizer and president of the British Columbia Fire Insurance Company in 1886). He did not become wealthy, but on his appointment as postmaster he was able to commission a new house in a fashionable district. At the same time, Eliza Jane gave up her store.

From the 1860s Shakespeare had been a leader of the temperance movements in Victoria and British Columbia. In 1877 and 1878 he was elected grand chief templar of the Independent Order of Good Templars for British Columbia and the Pacific northwest states. He maintained a lifelong involvement in temperance and in other issues consistent with his Methodist beliefs and the improvement of workingmen. He served as president of the Victoria Mechanics' Institute in 1882, the British Columbia Agricultural Association in 1885, and the Young Men's Christian Association in Victoria in 1886–87, and as a member of the management committee of the British Columbia Protestant Orphans' Home in Victoria at least in 1887 and 1889.

An active Methodist in England, Shakespeare had remained so in Victoria, belonging to Pandora Street Methodist Church until 1885, when he became a trustee for the new Centennial Church. He acted as a local preacher, class leader, steward, and Sunday school superintendent in these congregations, as a delegate to the provincial Methodist conference, and as a director of the Columbian Methodist College. Founder of the provincial branch of the International Sunday School Association, he was its president and later honorary president in the period from about 1900 to 1917. During these years he also played a prominent role in the Victoria branch of the British and Foreign Bible Society.

An atypical "self-made man," Shakespeare had become a member of the social elite not through the conventional route of success in business or industry, but by means of a political career based on his being, in the words of historian Patricia E. Roy, British Columbia's "first professional anti-Chinese agitator." It seems that once he had achieved prosperity and status as postmaster, he abandoned this cause and turned his attention to social issues more consistent with his Methodist beliefs. His period of intense anti-Chinese activism may have been a misguided effort to improve the lot of the white working class or a calculated device to better his own economic and social position. Regardless, he had played a considerable role in defining race and class relations in British Columbia.

JAMIE MORTON

BCA, GR-1052, file 10973; GR-1304, file 182/1921; MS-0254; VF130, frames 0641–65. City of Victoria Arch., CRS1 (council minutes), 25 Aug. 1862–16 April 1884. *Daily Colonist* (Victoria), 1863–1921. *Victoria Daily Times*, 1887–1921, esp. 10 March 1917. H. T. Allen, *Forty years' journey: the temperance movement in British Columbia to 1900* (Victoria, 1981). B.C., Legislative Assembly, *Sessional papers*, 1880: 406. *British Columbia Gazette* (Victoria), 1878–79. *The British Columbia orphans' friend: historical number,* ed. Alexander MacDonald (Victoria, 1914). Can., House of Commons, *Debates*, 1879, 1884–85. *Cyclopædia of Canadian biog.* (Rose and Charlesworth), vol.2. *Directories*, B.C., 1882–85, 1887, 1889; Victoria, 1868–69, 1874. *1881 Canadian census: Vancouver Island*, comp. Peter Baskerville *et al.* (Victoria, 1990). *1891 Canadian census, Victoria, British Columbia*, comp. Eric Sager *et al.* (Victoria, 1991). Valerie Green, *No ordinary people: Victoria's mayors since 1862* (Victoria, 1992). J. B. Kerr, *Biographical dictionary of well-known British Columbians, with a historical sketch* (Vancouver, 1890). "Leading laymen, 4: Mr. N. Shakespeare, Victoria," *Western Methodist Recorder* (Victoria), 1 (1899–1900), no.4: 10. David Mattison, "The Victoria Theatre Photographic Gallery (and the gallery next door)," *British Columbia Hist. News* (Victoria), 14 (1980–81), no.2: 1–14. P. E. Roy, *A white man's province: British Columbia politicians and Chinese and Japanese immigrants, 1858–1914* (Vancouver, 1989). W. P. Ward, *White Canada forever: popular attitudes and public policy toward Orientals in British Columbia* (2nd ed., Montreal and Kingston, Ont., 1990). *Western Methodist Recorder*, 20 (1920–21), no.11: 5. Workingmen's Protective Assoc., *Constitution, by-laws and rules of order . . .* ([Victoria?], 1878).

SHARPE, THOMAS, mason, contractor, and politician; b. 14 March 1866 in County Sligo (Republic of Ireland), son of Mitchell William Sharpe and Jane Johnston; m. 24 May 1888 Mary Jane Cathcart (d. 1922) in Toronto, and they had at least three sons and four daughters; d. 10 May 1929 en route from Winnipeg to Lac du Bonnet, Man.

At age 14 Thomas Sharpe left school to be apprenticed as a mason. On completing his engagement, he became a clerk with the Provincial Bank of Ireland. After a year and a half there, he immigrated to Canada in 1885 and found journeyman's work in Toronto at his original trade. Two years later he started his own company, taking contracts for paving and sidewalks. Early in 1892 he went out of business. Soon afterwards he arrived in Winnipeg, where he worked for a short time as a labourer and then as a bricklayer. He supported his trade's union and in 1892 served on the committee that affiliated it with the American Federation of Labor as a local of the Bricklayers, Masons, and Plasterers' International Union of North America. In 1896 he went once again into contracting. Initially his business depended on contracts for laying the city's first cement sidewalks, but subsequently it expanded into more general contracting and heavy masonry work. By 1901 R. G. Dun and Company judged him a good credit risk with $10,000–20,000 in business assets. In 1905 he accepted his foreman, W. W. College, as a partner and renamed the business Sharpe and College. The firm grew during Winnipeg's boom. In 1911 its assets were estimated at $125,000–200,000 and it received a high credit rating.

The reorganization of Sharpe's company had been necessitated as much by his involvement in municipal politics – two two-year terms as alderman from 1900 to 1903 and three one-year terms as mayor from 1904 to 1906 – as by the increase in his business. He had entered politics with the backing of Winnipeg's wealthiest merchant, James Henry ASHDOWN, who nominated him for alderman. Noted for "his candour and free style" of speech, he frequently took controversial positions.

On the one hand, Sharpe agreed that Winnipeg should undertake its own construction when it could realize savings over tendered work. He urged municipal ownership of utilities and would claim responsibility for the establishment of the city's quarry and asphalt plant. He recognized Winnipeg's minimum wage by-law and he agreed that the city should do business only with those who employed unionized labour. On the other hand, the *Voice*, Winnipeg's labour paper, charged that he simply accepted practices he knew could not be changed. His real sympathies, the *Voice* believed, were revealed in his defence of property qualifications for the municipal franchise.

Sharpe's response to the public protest over prostitution that erupted during his first campaign for the mayoralty demonstrated his selective engagement in some issues. In November 1903 the Winnipeg Ministerial Association, led by Frederic Beal DU VAL, complained that the Winnipeg Police Commission knowingly permitted brothels to operate in the city's west end. Sharpe admitted that, apart from persuading council to take control of the commission when the issue had been first raised by the association two years earlier, he had "paid little attention" to the matter. After his election, he quickly pressed the police to close the brothels in the west end. Despite subsequent charges that the problem continued unabated elsewhere, he defended his record of prosecuting vice.

Similarly, Sharpe became defensive in 1904 when the city's Department of Health reported an increase in typhoid which it attributed to inadequate sewers and waste collection. Sharpe, who had chaired the Board of Works, had campaigned on his record of expanding water and sewer services, so he took the report as a personal attack. He commissioned assessments from two outside experts and conducted his own survey of sanitation systems in large Canadian and American cities. Although the Department of Health's evaluation was confirmed, he could claim leadership on the issue. In 1905 the city's charter was amended to enable it to compel sewer and water connections. Thereafter, with an enlarged health department, increased appropriations for waste removal, and more rigorous enforcement of by-laws, the incidence of typhoid was substantially reduced. Sharpe drew the line at seeking a new source for city water, however, arguing that matters affecting the city's economic development were more important. In 1906 he vigorously and successfully urged voters to approve the necessary appropriation of funds for the city to develop hydroelectric power for manufacturing [*see* Ashdown].

Sharpe was persuaded that municipal governments needed to achieve greater efficiency. Through his service on the executive of the Union of Canadian Municipalities from 1904 to 1906, his attendance at the conference of the National Municipal League of the United States in 1905, and his visits to major North American cities, he was aware of progressive trends elsewhere. In 1905, with the support of the Winnipeg Board of Trade, he proposed that the city establish a board of control, composed of four full-time members who could devote their attentions "in a business-like manner" to municipal affairs. A by-law to this effect passed in 1906.

Sharpe's commitment to corporate efficiency ultimately led to more overt support for business and property interests. When its employees went on strike in late March 1906, the Winnipeg Electric Railway Company hired strike-breakers protected by private detectives. Crowds of sympathizers blocked the streets and threw stones at the streetcars. The company urged Sharpe to call out the militia and on the second day of the strike he agreed. He authorized troops with bayonets and a machine-gun to clear Main Street and was later reported to have called on them to fire above the crowd, only to have the cooler-headed militia commander ignore his order. "Gatling Gun Sharpe," as the *Voice* labelled him, had clearly aligned municipal government with the interests of capital in a way that anticipated the events of the Winnipeg General Strike of 1919 [*see* Mike Sokolowiski*].

Choosing not to run again for mayor, Sharpe returned to business at the end of 1906. About 1912 he dissolved his partnership; he managed on his own the contracting business and various rental properties he had acquired. He continued to be active in fraternal organizations, having for some time belonged to the Independent Order of Foresters, the freemasons, and the Orange lodge, of which he was provincial grand master in 1907–8. In 1924 he served as president of the Winnipeg Conservative Association.

Thomas Sharpe had entered municipal politics at a critical juncture in Winnipeg's history. Population growth had overburdened existing services and taxed the capacity of political institutions to respond to social problems. Supported from the beginning by Winnipeg's business elite, he proposed reforms that adopted the evolving forms of business organization. His populist claims seemed increasingly to have a hollow ring as the city sided in public disputes with capital against labour.

DAVID G. BURLEY

AO, RG 80-5-0-165, no.13833. *Manitoba Free Press*, 6, 12 Dec. 1899; 17 Nov., 5 Dec. 1903; 5 April 1904; 6, 12 Dec. 1905; 11 Jan., 30–31 March, 2 April, 4–5, 18, 29 June 1906; 11 May 1929. *Voice* (Winnipeg) 14, 21 June, 5, 19 July, 16, 30 Aug., 27 Sept., 18 Oct., 29 Nov., 6 Dec. 1901; 24 Oct. 1902; 25 Nov. 1904; 17 Feb. 1905; 6 April, 23 June, 23 Nov. 1906. *Winnipeg Telegram*, 11 Oct. 1901, 27 Sept. 1905, 29 June 1906. *Winnipeg Tribune*, 9 Oct. 1901; 17 Nov. 1903; 11 Jan. 1904; 19, 22 June 1906; 11 May 1929. A. F. J. Artibise, *Winnipeg: a social history of urban growth, 1874–1914* (Montreal and London, 1975). D. J. Bercuson, *Confrontation at Winnipeg: labour, industrial relations, and the general strike* (Montreal and London, 1974). George Bryce, *A history of Manitoba; its resources and people* (Toronto and Montreal, 1906). *Canadian men and women of the time* (Morgan; 1912). *Directories*, Man. and N.W.T., 1892, 1893, 1896; Winnipeg, 1913, 1917, 1920, 1928. *The mercantile agency reference book . . .* (Montreal), 1901, 1911.

SHAUGHNESSY, THOMAS GEORGE, 1st Baron SHAUGHNESSY, railway official; b. 6 Oct. 1853 in Milwaukee, Wis., son of Thomas Shaughnessy, a policeman, and Mary Kennedy; m. 12 Jan. 1880 Elizabeth Bridget Nagle (d. 1937), and they had two sons and three daughters; d. 10 Dec. 1923 in Montreal.

Thomas G. Shaughnessy, the son of Irish Catholic immigrants, was educated in public schools and at the Jesuits' St Aloysius Academy in Milwaukee. He also studied for several months at the Spencerian Business College in that city before entering the service of the Milwaukee and St Paul Railroad at age 16. He served first as a clerk in the purchasing department and then as a bookkeeper in the supply division. In 1874 the railroad extended its service to Chicago and was renamed the Chicago, Milwaukee and St Paul, but popularly it was known simply as the Milwaukee Road.

While employed in relatively low-level jobs, Shaughnessy studied law privately for some time. In 1875 he was the successful candidate in a municipal by-election in Milwaukee's poor and predominantly Irish Catholic Third Ward. He was re-elected several times, serving continuously on the municipal council from 1875 until 1882 and briefly, in 1882, as its president. In 1875 he was made adjutant of the 1st Regiment of the Wisconsin state militia. The following year he sought, unsuccessfully, appointment as clerk of the circuit court.

In 1880 William Cornelius Van Horne* became the general superintendent of the Milwaukee Road and he was soon favourably impressed by Shaughnessy's meticulous but, until then, unspectacular work in the stores department. Van Horne promoted Shaughnessy to the position of purchasing agent. Theft, damage, and the unexplained disappearance of goods, as well as collusion between suppliers and purchasers, were perennial problems for railroads. Shaughnessy and two others were chosen by Van Horne in October 1880 to examine and report on the administrative, security, and accounting procedures in the stores departments of other large railroads. Their report recommended numerous changes, which Shaughnessy, who was appointed storekeeper responsible for all major construction and operating materials and supplies on 1 Jan. 1881, then implemented on the Milwaukee Road.

Van Horne left the Milwaukee Road to become general manager of the fledgling Canadian Pacific Railway on 2 Jan. 1882. He offered Shaughnessy the position of purchasing agent for the entire CPR system. Shaughnessy declined, but when Van Horne returned for a visit in the fall of 1882 he accepted, allegedly over a glass of Milwaukee beer. He began work with the CPR in Montreal that November. The CPR was then in serious financial difficulty. That situation got progressively worse as construction costs mounted and fund-raising efforts by syndicate members, among them George STEPHEN, James Jerome Hill*, and Donald Alexander Smith*, faltered.

One of Shaughnessy's greatest accomplishments was to reduce costs as much as possible. He introduced a tight system of controls and accounting procedures in the ordering and allocation of supplies and he scrutinized all expenditures. Many materials, particularly those needed by construction crews, had to be requested weeks and often months in advance. The company could save substantial sums if materials were ordered to arrive only at the last possible moment and then only in the exact amounts needed. Unused or unneeded supplies were often subject to deterioration and theft while in storage. Shaughnessy had an essentially pessimistic view of human nature, perhaps instilled in him by his father, who had been a policeman and sometime detective in an impoverished district of Milwaukee. While he was active in local politics Shaughnessy himself had seen much evidence of corruption and waste. He was convinced that, given the opportunity, suppliers, contractors, carriers, workers, and anyone else would cheat the company. Constant vigilance was essential. Everything had to be done in accordance with the many rules and regulations he introduced. He delighted in tracing even minor transgressions and then publicly humiliating the perpetrators, usually in writing to ensure that the information became a part of the permanent record. Even the company's most trusted contractors and senior officials were exposed to his wrath if, in their efforts to get necessary work done on time, they paid prices higher than was deemed appropriate or if they failed in any other way to follow his system.

Shaughnessy was a perfectionist. He had a particular compulsion for cleanliness, washing his hands many times a day. Whereas Van Horne ordered mountains moved if they got in the way of his construction program, Shaughnessy was more likely to berate employees about a speck on the dining car cutlery, imperfectly washed passenger cars, a spelling error on

a CPR hotel menu, and, of course, even minute irregularities in any invoice. During the difficult period of construction from 1882 to 1885, he and his staff were exceptionally meticulous, some thought paranoid, when reviewing bills in order to postpone payments as long as possible. They looked for any discrepancy in price, quantity, or quality of material delivered or work done, no matter how insignificant, which might justify delays or substantial reductions in the company's payments. Shaughnessy resorted to and perfected many of the tactics employed by companies teetering on the edge of bankruptcy, paying only the minimum necessary to avoid costly legal battles. In later years he took particular pride in having delayed the payment of millions of dollars and in slashing millions more from bills with which he and his officials found fault.

There were some obvious limits to these tactics. It would not serve the CPR's interest to push good suppliers and contractors into bankruptcy or to alienate them to the point where they would refuse to have further dealings with the company. Shaughnessy therefore collected detailed information on their financial standing and obligations, paying in cash only what they needed to remain in business. For the balance, after all other stalling tactics had been exhausted, he issued notes not immediately negotiable and verbal promises of payment once finances improved. The CPR's interests, as interpreted by him, always came first. He could be exceptionally tough in difficult times, but was more generous when the company's position improved or when alternative opportunities became available for contractors and suppliers.

Shaughnessy's skills earned him a reputation as a stern, humourless, and rigid administrator; they also won him a cherished promotion to assistant general manager in 1885. This position allowed him to impose his meticulous style of management on the operations and expansion of the nearly completed but still chaotic railway. He was not a man without vision. Indeed, like Van Horne, he believed that the CPR must become a multifaceted business empire. At the same time his determination to make the entire system run with clock-like precision provided a perfect counterbalance to Van Horne's visionary enthusiasm.

Financial necessity, if not desperation, had made Shaughnessy's style of management essential in the early years, but after 1888 the fortunes of the company improved. Van Horne became president that year and he and the directors named Shaughnessy assistant president in September 1889. In 1891 Shaughnessy became a director and was elected vice-president. Van Horne gradually assigned almost all administrative responsibilities to Shaughnessy, who succeeded him as president in 1899. The company went on to achieve remarkable success, thanks in part to good management but mainly to the rapid settlement of the Cana-

Shaughnessy

dian prairies [see Sir Clifford SIFTON] and the general improvement in the economy. Prices of its shares, which hit a low of $33 in the mid 1890s, rose to $283 in 1912, though they would decline to $135 before Shaughnessy resigned in 1918. The company operated 7,000 miles of track when he became president in 1899; this would increase to 12,993 miles in 1918. Vast sums were spent in improving the track and rolling stock and in numerous ancillary enterprises.

Shaughnessy was intimately involved in the development of the Canadian Pacific's steamship service. During his presidency newer and larger ships, tugs, barges, and ferries were acquired for service on the Great Lakes, the inland waterways of British Columbia, and the Pacific coast. A profitable steamship service from Vancouver to the Orient had been established in 1891 with three ships forming the Empress Line. This service was significantly improved during the Shaughnessy era by the construction of new Empress ships, which were then the fastest and best equipped on the Pacific. In 1902 Shaughnessy decided the company should establish its own Atlantic service. He took part in the acquisition by the CPR of two Atlantic shipping companies – the Beaver Line and the Allan Line [see Andrew Allan*] in 1903 and 1909 respectively – and in the addition of new ships, including some of the most modern design. The Atlantic service earned only modest profits, but it made the CPR one of the world's major shipowners.

The success of any large transportation system depends on the passengers and freight carried and CPR officials initiated or participated in numerous projects designed to increase traffic. The most important involved the settlement of prairie lands. Vigorous attempts were made to attract settlers who would purchase CPR land and generate freight. Shaughnessy started major irrigation projects which made almost 3,000,000 acres of dry land in southern Alberta much more valuable. He also continued Van Horne's energetic efforts to augment passenger traffic through the promotion of tourism. New CPR hotels were built in Winnipeg, Calgary, and Victoria. Those in Quebec City, Vancouver, Banff, and Lake Louise were substantially enlarged and smaller resort hotels in the Maritimes and several chalets and camps in the mountains were added. All had to meet Shaughnessy's rigorous standards. The Crow's Nest Pass Railway, begun just before Shaughnessy became president, captured the traffic in coal, other minerals, and forest products of southern British Columbia. Several mines and a large smelter at Trail, B.C., had been acquired from American promoters in 1898 and were merged in 1906 to form the CPR-controlled Consolidated Mining and Smelting Company of Canada Limited. Coal was not only an important freight commodity, it powered the steam locomotives, so the company developed important coalmining operations in south-

ern British Columbia. Under Shaughnessy's watch the CPR became a partner in several engineering, steel, rolling stock, locomotive, and other manufacturing companies whose products it needed.

For many years Shaughnessy represented the CPR on the boards of major financial institutions with which it had extensive dealings, including the Bank of Montreal, the Royal Trust Company, the Accident Insurance Company of North America, and the Guarantee Company of North America. He received numerous invitations from friends to invest personally in a variety of ventures. A cautious man, he placed his money in preferred CPR and CPR-related securities. He did not amass the wealth of the great American tycoons or even of some of his fellow CPR directors, but he was almost certainly a millionaire at the time of his death. He loved ceremony and ostentation and was as meticulous about his clothes, personal appearance, and private luxuries as he was about the quality of the service provided by the company. His two great loves were the CPR and his family. He had little interest in philanthropy or social causes.

Shaughnessy was a brilliant administrator who ran one of Canada's largest and most efficient businesses in an effective, but cautious and not very imaginative way. During his administration the CPR, more than any other company, contributed to the building of Canada as a nation. One of the most important services the CPR provided was the transportation of prairie wheat to export markets. The main line made this possible, but it was the massive construction of branch lines and the significant reductions in freight rates during the Shaughnessy years that allowed prairie homesteaders far from the main line to establish successful farms. The railway brought in the coal with which the farmers heated their homes, but it also carried manufactured products and supplies of all kinds, dramatically expanding the economy of western Canada and connecting it with that of central Canada. At the same time, however, it became the primary focus of regional discontent.

The CPR had always been viewed with considerable suspicion in western Canada. It was alleged that the rates charged were too high and that the services of the company were not extended as quickly as they should have been to newly settled areas. Many believed both problems would be alleviated if the CPR was exposed to effective competition. The so-called monopoly clause in the railway's charter had kept rival American lines out of western Canada until 1888, when political agitation in Manitoba [see Thomas Greenway*] resulted in the cancellation of that clause. Subsequently the CPR fought several battles to exclude American railroads. As part of its strategy it retreated from its attempts to invade American territory. This change of policy contributed to Van Horne's resignation as president, but it was offset by the suc-

925

cess of the CPR in beating back efforts by American lines to tap western Canadian traffic. The construction of the line through the Crowsnest Pass was particularly important in securing the traffic of the southern prairies and southern British Columbia.

In 1897, when the CPR was negotiating with the federal government of Sir Wilfrid Laurier* for a subsidy to build the Crow's Nest Pass Railway, pressure from western farmers and their political representatives had led the government to grant the subsidy only if the railway significantly reduced its rates. Under Shaughnessy's administration, the agitation for further rate reductions and more branch lines increased. In 1901, the Manitoba government of Rodmond Palen Roblin* signed an agreement with the promoters of the Canadian Northern Railway, William MACKENZIE and Donald Mann*, to provide substantial guarantees for their railway bonds in return for a significant reduction in freight rates from Manitoba to the Lakehead. The Regina Board of Trade later obtained an extension of those lower rates to its city. To remain competitive the CPR had to match the Canadian Northern's rates. In 1903 Charles Melville Hays* of the Grand Trunk Railway, which was well established in Ontario and Quebec, sought federal assistance to extend its system to the Pacific. It too promised to compete effectively with the CPR.

The federal and provincial governments believed that wherever possible competition between railways should be promoted as a means to ensure better and cheaper service. Railways, however, often enjoyed natural monopolies, particularly in sparsely settled areas, so politicians moved to strengthen government control. The authority of the small railway committee of the Privy Council was greatly expanded with the creation in 1903 of the Board of Railway Commissioners [see Andrew George Blair*], which had legal jurisdiction to settle many of the disputes arising between rival railways and between railways and the general public. It did not initially have the power to set freight rates but, like the Interstate Commerce Commission in the United States, it had the power to order railways to reduce freight rates which unfairly discriminated against some customers. Many in western Canada were convinced that the CPR's ton-mile rates, which were higher there than in central Canada, constituted such discrimination. The CPR argued that the higher western rates were justified by the cost of building and operating the long and expensive line north of Lake Superior. The Board of Railway Commissioners eventually accepted this argument, enunciating it explicitly in 1914.

Shaughnessy tried to deal with the threats of competition prudently. He knew there was not sufficient traffic to justify the construction of two new transcontinental railways or the extension of branch lines into the many sparsely settled parts of the country. Under

his administration the CPR had constructed branches only where they could be justified on sound economic grounds rather than on grandiose promises of future development. When it became clear in July 1903 that Ottawa would assist the rival systems [see Blair], Shaughnessy proposed a radical scheme under which the CPR would sell its expensive but vital line north of Lake Superior to the federal government, which could then double track it and grant running rights to all competitive railways. Shaughnessy was confident the CPR could meet any threat except that posed by rivals enjoying massive government assistance. Under his proposal the subsidies would be sharply reduced and the CPR would no longer be responsible for the operating expenses of the difficult section, though it would retain control over the entire system. Laurier was wary of government ownership and feared that Shaughnessy's proposal would prevent competition. After the Liberals won the election of 1904 the construction of the two new transcontinentals proceeded.

When war broke out in 1914 Shaughnessy gave his full support to the war effort. He organized imperial transport and assisted in the financing of the war effort through loans to the government. Employees were encouraged to enlist. Senior staff were lent to the British and Canadian governments to purchase, organize, and ship supplies overseas. Construction workers were sent to rebuild damaged railways in France and Belgium. The company's largest and fastest ships were requisitioned as transports and auxiliary cruisers and the company's machine shops in Montreal and Winnipeg manufactured munitions and military equipment. Shaughnessy suffered enormous personal loss when one of his two sons, both of whom served overseas, was killed in action in France.

Canada did not need, but it had obtained, three transcontinental railways. All three adopted aggressive competitive tactics. The CPR, which had received federal cash and land subsidies, had a decisive advantage over its rivals, which had obtained only government guarantees for their bonds. Both new transcontinental systems got into serious financial difficulty during World War I. The CPR had the necessary resources to take over parts or all of the other systems, but such a solution was deemed politically unacceptable by the Canadian government. Instead, the federal government moved slowly toward nationalizing them. The CPR's directors, including Shaughnessy, who had resigned as president in 1918 but would continue to serve as chairman of the board until his death, found the notion of competition with a government railway system abhorrent. A state system would be vulnerable to political pressure to offer unreasonably low rates and would then look to the government to cover any deficits. In a desperate effort to thwart such unfair competition, Shaughnessy proposed in August 1921 the sale of the assets of the CPR to the government in exchange for a guaranteed return of interest and principal to the holders of CPR stocks. CPR management – in Shaughnessy's opinion the best anywhere in the world – would then sign a contract to manage the entire system on behalf of the government. This proposal, however, was also rejected by Ottawa. As a result, the CPR was left to manage its operations in the most efficient manner possible. Its profitability was severely limited because it had to compete with the Canadian National Railways (established in 1918 with the merger of the Canadian Northern, the Canadian Government Railways, and other lines), which could offer politically desirable but not necessarily economically viable rail services. Only extensive diversification and the earnings of affiliated companies made it possible for the CPR to retain its overall profitability in the later years of Shaughnessy's presidency.

Failing eyesight had led Shaughnessy to resign from the presidency of the CPR. His frequent visits to Britain and particularly his wartime work had brought him into close contact with leading British politicians, financiers, and businessmen who recognized his administrative talent. They suggested new areas of service to him after surgery resulted in a partial restoration of his eyesight. He had a long-standing interest in the affairs of his ancestors' homeland and became active after the war in opposing the establishment of a republican form of government in Ireland. There were rumours that he might be named governor general of the Irish Free State or be offered some other position in the British government. No appointment was ever made, however. He remained in Canada and continued to work for the CPR until the time of his death, having followed the advice he gave on his deathbed to his successor, Edward Wentworth Beatty*, "Maintain the property. It is a great Canadian property, and a great Canadian enterprise."

Thomas G. Shaughnessy had been made a knight bachelor on 17 Sept. 1901, created a KCVO in 1907, and elevated to the peerage of the United Kingdom as Baron Shaughnessy on 1 Jan. 1916. He suffered a massive heart attack on 9 Dec. 1923 and died the following day. At the pinnacle of his career his identity and that of the CPR seemed inseparable. His achievement did not lie in the conception of grand designs but in the management and execution of an administrative system which carried the CPR to its greatest business success as the country's most important and profitable multifaceted business empire. He could not, however, ward off the encroachments which left the CPR and the country with serious railway problems.

THEODORE D. REGEHR

Canadian Pacific Arch. (Montreal), Incoming corr.; Shaughnessy letter-books. *Globe*, 11 Dec. 1923. Pierre Berton, *The national dream: the great railway, 1871–1881* (Toronto and Montreal, 1970); *The last spike: the great railway, 1881–1885* (Toronto and Montreal, 1971). *The CPR west: the iron road and the making of a nation,* ed. Hugh Dempsey (Vancouver and Toronto, 1984). David Cruise and Alison Griffiths, *Lords of the line* (Markham, Ont., 1988). J. A. Eagle, "Baron Thomas Shaughnessy: the peer that made Milwaukee famous," *Milwaukee Hist.* (Milwaukee, Wis.), 6 (1983), no.1: 28–40; *The Canadian Pacific Railway and the development of western Canada, 1896–1914* (Kingston, Ont., 1989); "Lord Shaughnessy and the railway policies of Sir Robert Borden, 1903–1917" (paper presented at the annual CHA meeting, Montreal, 1972); "Monopoly or competition: the nationalization of the Grand Trunk Railway" (unpublished paper, n.d.; copy in the possession of T. D. Regehr). J. B. Hedges, *Building the Canadian west: the land and colonization policies of the Canadian Pacific Railway* (New York, 1939; repr. 1971). H. A. Innis, *A history of the Canadian Pacific Railway* (Toronto, 1923; repr. Toronto and Buffalo, N.Y., 1971). W. K. Lamb, *History of the Canadian Pacific Railway* (New York and London, 1977). O.[-S.-A.] Lavallée, *Van Horne's road: an illustrated account of the construction and first years of operation of the Canadian Pacific transcontinental railway* (Montreal, 1974). A. A. den Otter, *The philosophy of railways: the transcontinental railway idea in British North America* (Toronto, 1997). G. R. Stevens, *Canadian National Railways* (2v., Toronto and Vancouver, 1960–62).

SHAW, FLORA MADELINE, nurse and educator; b. 15 Jan. 1864 in Perth, Upper Canada, daughter of Henry Dowsley Shaw and Flora Madeline Matheson; d. unmarried 27 Aug. 1927 in Liverpool, England.

An early leader in nursing education in Canada, Flora Madeline Shaw was born into a prominent family. Both of her grandfathers, James Shaw* and Roderick Matheson*, were businessmen and members of the Legislative Council of Upper Canada. An aunt, one of the early graduates in nursing of New York City's Bellevue Hospital, most likely influenced her decision to go into nursing.

In 1894 Shaw entered the nursing school of the Montreal General Hospital, established four years earlier by Gertrude Elizabeth LIVINGSTON, the first such school in the province of Quebec. She graduated in 1896. Because of her evident administrative and teaching abilities, she was appointed second assistant to Livingston, the school's superintendent, and she held the post for three years.

After a short stay as head of a small women's hospital in Boston, Shaw returned to Montreal in 1900 to become Livingston's first assistant. Between 1904 and 1906 she attended Teachers' College at Columbia University, studying teaching in schools of nursing. After other nursing-related work in New York, she once again returned to the Montreal General Hospital, to take charge of a new project introduced there and at the Hospital for Sick Children in Toronto: a program of preliminary instruction for probationary nursing students.

Not content only with teaching and concerned about the professional status of nurses across Canada, Shaw represented the Montreal General Hospital Alumnae Association at the founding meeting of the Canadian National Association of Trained Nurses in 1908, where she was appointed honorary secretary. The following year tuberculosis, a common scourge of nurses at the time, forced her to retire for a while from active work. She spent some time in sanatoriums and later travelled abroad. By 1914 she was a volunteer social worker for the Montreal branch of the Canadian Patriotic Fund.

In 1920, after working on a committee to promote university education for nurses, she was asked to accept the position of director of the McGill School for Graduate Nurses. Until this time nursing education in Canada had been limited to hospital schools. The McGill school offered an eight-month certificate course aimed at creating a cadre of qualified nurses to teach and to take administrative positions in Canadian nursing schools. An eight-month nursing course in public health was also offered.

Shaw took a cautious approach to the development of the school, insisting that, to ensure success, it take on only what it could handle. Thus she argued against adding a two-year degree course until the school was well established. In addition to being responsible for administration, she did most of the teaching on nursing subjects herself. She had taken at her own expense a six-week refresher course at Columbia just before assuming her duties. She was innovative and thorough in her teaching. An ongoing concern of the profession to improve the qualifications of working nurses was concretized under her direction, when extension courses for working nurses in Montreal were jointly sponsored by the school and the Association of Registered Nurses of the Province of Quebec (ARNPQ) between 1923 and 1926. She served as president of the Canadian Association of Nurse Education from 1922 to 1924.

In addition to her pioneering work in nursing education, Shaw played a significant role in improving the professional status of nursing in Canada. As president of the ARNPQ between 1922 and 1926, she was involved in fashioning amendments to its charter. These amendments, passed in 1925, aimed at improving standards for nursing and nursing education in Quebec. In 1926 she was chosen head of the Canadian Nurses' Association. Earlier, she had been asked to preside at a round table held during the 1925 meeting of the International Council of Nurses in Finland. On her way back from a conference of the international council in Geneva in 1927, she fell ill and died in the Liverpool Royal Infirmary.

Shaw was recognized both nationally and interna-

tionally as a leader in nursing education. The Flora Madeline Shaw Chair of Nursing at McGill was established in her memory in 1957.

YOLANDE COHEN and MARYANN FARKAS

MUA, RG 64, c.10, files 19, 22. Édouard Desjardins, *Heritage: history of the nursing profession in Quebec from the Augustinians and Jeanne Mance to Medicare*, trans. Hugh Shaw (Montreal, 1971). H. E. MacDermot, *History of the School of Nursing of the Montreal General Hospital* (Montreal, 1940; repr. 1961). "School for Graduate Nurses," *McGill News* (Montreal), 2, no.1 (December 1920): 16. B. L. Tunis, *In caps and gowns: the story of the School for Graduate Nurses, McGill University, 1920–1964* (Montreal, 1966).

SHEARD, CHARLES, physician, educator, publisher, and politician; b. 15 Feb. 1857 in Toronto, son of Joseph Sheard and Sarah Tuke; m. there 10 July 1884 Virna Stanton, and they had four sons; d. there 7 Feb. 1929.

The son of a builder-architect and future mayor of Toronto, Charles Sheard was raised in the rapidly expanding city of the 1850s and 1860s. After attending Upper Canada College, he enrolled in Trinity Medical School, from which he graduated with an MB in 1878. He then went to Britain and Europe for further training; when he returned to Toronto he was a member of the Royal College of Surgeons of England. Recognized as a leading exponent of scientific medicine and research, he lectured on histology at Trinity from 1880 until its amalgamation in 1903 with the faculty of medicine at the University of Toronto, where he had become a professor of physiology in 1883 and of clinical medicine in 1891. He had received his MD, CM (master of surgery) from Trinity College in 1882. From 1884 to 1905 he was on staff at the Toronto General Hospital; there his innovations included sponsoring the use of the metrotome, a cutting instrument for uterine surgery. As professor of preventive medicine at the university from 1903 to about 1910, he promoted "the science of Sanitation" as a valid medical specialty.

Sheard also established a successful private practice and became involved in medical politics. He was treasurer (1882–83), vice-president (1889), and president (1892) of the Canadian Medical Association and vice-president (1890) of the Ontario Medical Association. In 1887 Sheard and Dr John Lorenzo Davison had taken over publication of the *Canada Lancet*, the country's premier medical journal; Sheard was a co-proprietor until 1893. He thus contributed to the modernization of Canadian medical practice not only through teaching, but also through participation in professional organizations and medical publishing.

Between 1893 and 1910 Sheard had the opportunity to demonstrate his scientific credentials and business skills as Toronto's medical health officer. In 1890, after the resignation of the city's first permanent officer, William Canniff*, he had been part of the committee formed to select Canniff's successor. Its choice, Dr Norman Allen, a young Trinity graduate, lacked the business acumen required for the position and he was dismissed in February 1893. On 17 March Sheard was appointed on a full-time basis to give him time to reorganize the department before he resumed teaching.

During his years in office Sheard introduced Torontonians to the bacteriological phase of the international public health movement. "A scientist to his finger tips," in the estimate of the *Globe*, he improved the city's procedures for handling communicable disease, began the bacterial testing of milk and water supplies, and agitated successfully for improved water and sewage systems. After the department of works was added to his jurisdiction in 1905, he moved to eliminate patronage there; his swift dismissals of incompetent employees earned him accolades from the *Evening Telegram*.

Despite his concern for preventive medicine, Sheard, a social conservative, did not always support demands by reformers for increased government intervention. In 1907, for instance, he opposed calls for medical inspections in schools as a "fad" promoted mainly by women and intended to provide jobs for favoured doctors. Yet the same year he pressed the city's Board of Health to hire, for the first time, a public health nurse to specialize in tuberculin testing and care. In March 1910, fed up with "the many disappointed cliques and influences existent," he resigned as medical health officer. He was persuaded to stay on, however, to deal with an outbreak of typhoid (by chlorinating Toronto's drinking water) and to conclude an inquiry into the Isolation Hospital. He stepped down for good later that year.

By applying his expertise to controlling disease and improving urban services, Sheard had developed the infrastructure on which his successor, Charles John Colwell Orr Hastings*, would build. At the same time, Sheard had been able to continue teaching, and he served as president of the Association of Executive Health Officers of Ontario (1896), as an examiner for the Canadian branch of the Royal Sanitary Institute (1906), as a vice-president of the Toronto League for the Prevention of Tuberculosis (1909–10), and as chair of the Provincial Board of Health (1904–11). He supported professional development through the AEHOO and encouraged the inauguration, at the University of Toronto in 1904, of the diploma in public health, the premier qualification for future generations of Canadian health administrators.

Following his withdrawal from public involvement, Sheard, then in his mid fifties, remained in private practice. He was certainly in comfortable circum-

stances: he enjoyed additional income from real estate holdings that included the valuable commercial block left to him by his father at the northwest corner of Yonge and Adelaide streets. An ardent hunter and fisherman, he belonged to the Ontario Jockey Club, the Church of England, and the Orange order. He lived on Jarvis Street in a prestigious residence designed by his brother Matthew, and owned a cottage with extensive rose gardens on Hanlans Point. His wife was prominent in her own right, as a novelist and poet, and all of their sons, destined for professional careers, attended Upper Canada College.

Throughout his career Sheard combined scientific objectivity with strongly conservative politics. During World War I he returned to public life. Running as a Unionist candidate in Toronto South in the federal election of 1917, he easily defeated labour candidate David Arthur CAREY. In the House of Commons in 1919 he participated in the debate over the bill creating the Department of Health, described by its sponsor, Newton Wesley Rowell*, as "a new departure" in the emphasis it placed "upon the conservation of the health of the people and upon their social welfare." Sheard supported the bill in principle and contributed his professional knowledge, in proposed amendments, to defining the role of the new department. Opposed to unwarranted federal intervention, he argued that it must not infringe on provincial or municipal jurisdictions and must be headed by an effective medical scientist and backed by a bureau of scientific research. In other debates he expressed concern over employment for returned soldiers, applauded the creation of the Civil Service Commission (though he questioned its criteria for appointment), supported demands for funds to dredge Toronto harbour, and advocated stronger legislation on patent and proprietary medicines.

In 1921 Sheard successfully ran for re-election, under the Conservative banner, but he had a much tougher campaign against his well-known Liberal-labour challenger, James Murdock*. Chosen to reply to the Liberals' throne speech of 1922, he did not run in 1925. He died four years later.

Charles Sheard's career represented the transition from doctors as "professional gentlemen" to research scientists. His teaching, in particular, was important for diffusing European knowledge among Canadian practitioners. Likewise, his public service demonstrated the slow evolution from committed amateurs to academically trained medical health officers.

HEATHER MacDOUGALL

Charles Sheard's publications include his presidential address to the Canadian Medical Association, in the *Montreal Medical Journal*, 22 (1893): 293–96; "President's annual address," Assoc. of Executive Health Officers of Ontario, *Report of the annual meeting* (Toronto), 1897: 31–39; "How to prevent outbreaks of infectious diseases among school children and the best methods to adopt tending to limit and suppress these diseases," *Canadian Journal of Medicine and Surgery* (Toronto), 15 (January–June 1904): 153–57; "City of Toronto disposal of sewage and water filtration," Empire Club of Canada, *Addresses* (Toronto), 5 (1907–8): 66–80; and "Disposal of household waste," *Canadian Therapeutist and Sanitary Engineer* (Toronto), 1 (1910): 294–301 (there is a portrait of Sheard opp. p.287). Sheard's reports to Toronto's Board of Health appear in Toronto, City Council, *Minutes of proc.*, 1893–94, 1896–99, 1904, 1907; edited versions of two of the reports were published in Ont., Legislature, *Sessional papers*, reports of the Provincial Board of Health of Ontario, 1895: 135–37 and 1896: 156–57.

AO, RG 22-305, no.61309; RG 80-5-0-131, no.14543. City of Toronto Arch., SC 215 (Paul Bator coll.), Charles Sheard, letter to mayor of Toronto and Board of Control, 22 Sept. 1910. University Health Network Arch. (Toronto), Toronto General Hospital fonds, Board of trustees, minutes of meetings, vols.3 (1880–93)–4 (1894–1904). *Globe*, 17, 20 Nov., 7, 17 Dec. 1917; 11, 22, 24 Oct., 23, 28 Nov., 1, 3, 7 Dec. 1921; 8, 11 Feb. 1929. *Toronto Daily Mail*, 1891, 1893. *Toronto Daily Star*, 24 Oct., 1–2 Dec. 1921; 8 Feb. 1929. P. A. Bator with A. J. Rhodes, *Within reach of everyone: a history of the University of Toronto School of Hygiene and the Connaught Laboratories* (2v., Ottawa, 1990–95). Can., House of Commons, *Debates*, 1918–24. *Canadian men and women of the time* (Morgan; 1912). Heather MacDougall, *Activists and advocates: Toronto's health department, 1883–1983* (Toronto, 1990). Wendy Mitchinson, *The nature of their bodies: women and their doctors in Victorian Canada* (Toronto, 1991). Trinity Medical College, *Annual announcement* (Toronto), 1880/81, 1890/91.

SHEARER, JOHN GEORGE, Presbyterian minister and reformer; b. 9 Aug. 1859 near Bright, Upper Canada, son of John Shearer and Margaret ——; m. 8 Aug. 1883 Elizabeth A. Johnson in Northfield (Northfield Centre), Ont.; they had no children; d. 27 March 1925 in Toronto.

One of the most tireless moral reformers Canada has ever had, John G. Shearer was born to Scottish settlers on a farm in an area of Oxford County known for its evangelical Presbyterianism. He attended the public school in Ratho, the high school in Weston (Toronto), and the collegiate institute in Brantford. He went into teaching but in 1883, following a conversion experience, he decided to enter the Presbyterian ministry. He began preaching in Onondaga, near Brantford, and later worked as a missionary in Fort William (Thunder Bay) and then in Toronto. It was there, as a student at Knox College, that he witnessed the realities of inner-city poverty and vice and began to see city missions as a means to spiritual and moral regeneration. In the *Knox College Monthly* of November 1886, he and a fellow student described mission work in Toronto, with Shearer reviewing the Elizabeth Street mission supported by the Central Presbyterian Church. He graduated from Knox in 1888; ordained on 5 June of that year, he took up parish work in Cale-

donia. During his time there he continued his studies, earning a BA from the University of Toronto in 1889. Two years later he moved to Erskine Presbyterian Church in Hamilton.

Shearer soon became active in nation-wide efforts to keep Canada morally "pure," in which cause he demonstrated tremendous zeal and organizational talent. He was particularly strong in his commitment to the Ontario branch of the Lord's Day Alliance, a group formed in 1888 to secure laws to uphold what it called "the English Sunday." In *The workingmen and the weekly rest day* (Toronto), a pamphlet written about 1896, Shearer attempted to align the interest of labour with Christian moral reform. In 1899 the Presbyterian Church in Canada selected him to convene its committee on sabbath observance and legislation.

The following year Shearer left pastoral work to become the first general secretary of the dominion Lord's Day Alliance, based in Toronto. Its Sabbatarian focus became a pressing concern for evangelical Christianity when decisions by the Judicial Committee of the Privy Council in 1903 and 1905 nullified Sunday laws in Ontario. Shearer provided pressure. In 1903 he had founded a promotional serial in Toronto, the *Lord's Day Advocate*. The Alliance succeeded in its main aim with the passage of the federal Lord's Day Act in 1906, and subsequently devoted its efforts to ensuring the enforcement of the law by local police. In Toronto, for instance, charges under the act constituted the largest group of offences reported in the years before World War I. Many of these charges involved prosecuting Chinese and Jewish vendors, among them vegetable sellers on Spadina Avenue. The Alliance insisted that if Jews wanted to immigrate to Canada, they had to abide by English/Scottish customs regarding Saturdays and Sundays. "A number of Jews in Toronto, at Englehart, and other places, who have found asylums and home comforts in Canada when driven by persecution from other lands," the Alliance noted in its report for 1911, "do not scruple to break our laws while enjoying the protection they afford them."

Sunday observance, temperance, and the fight against prostitution, probably the main three interests of Protestant Canada's moral reform movement, absorbed much of Shearer's time and energy. In 1907, the same year that he had been granted a DD by Knox, he was asked by the Presbyterian General Assembly to head up a department similar to the Methodists' Board of Temperance, Prohibition, and Moral Reform, run by Samuel Dwight Chown*. Leaving the Alliance, Shearer initially set up a standing committee on temperance and other moral and social reforms. The work of this body, which was organized as the Board of Moral and Social Reform in 1908 and renamed the Board of Social Service and Evangelism in 1911, was more evangelical and less influenced by modern approaches to social reform than Chown's. (The Methodists, among other programs, offered courses in sociology and classes in sex hygiene.) To fulfil his mission, Shearer toured the country denouncing red-light districts, obscene literature, and the "demon rum." Such sweeps were characterized less by modern sociological analysis and rescue work than by Shearer's talent for sensationalist revelation and thunderous denunciation, and his undeviating faith in law enforcement and imprisonment. One "vice tour" led him in 1910 to Winnipeg [*see* Frederic Beal DU VAL], where he singled out the involvement of Asians in the so-called white slavery traffic, though the only Chinese uncovered by a subsequent provincial commission on prostitution in Winnipeg were those doing housework in brothels.

On 31 Oct. 1907, in Toronto, Shearer and Thomas Albert Moore*, the social service secretary of the Methodist Church, had founded the interdenominational Moral and Social Reform Council of Canada (renamed the Social Service Council of Canada in 1913). In 1912 Shearer was selected to head one of the council's most active subcommittees, the National Committee for the Suppression of the White Slave Traffic. In this capacity he led lobbies that resulted in criminal-law amendments against prostitution and procurement. He also represented Canada in the international movement against white slavery led by British journalist William Thomas Stead.

Possessed of narrow views, Shearer fit the stereotype of the crusading moralist keen on prohibiting pleasure and oblivious to people's welfare. "Immoral" literature was thus one of his concerns as well. In 1909 the Moral and Social Reform Council joined with Toronto deputy police chief William Stark in successfully lobbying the federal government to strengthen the Criminal Code and consequently to facilitate prosecutions for the sale and distribution of obscene material. In cooperation with his American counterpart Anthony Comstock, Shearer campaigned to enforce the new legislation by targeting such booksellers as Leonard James SKILL of Toronto, who was charged after repeated seizures of his books. Prior to imposing sentence in this case, the judge opined that the most "poisonous" literature originated in France. Shearer was also influential when, in 1911, Toronto police laid charges against several other prominent booksellers, including Albert Britnell, for selling Sir Richard Francis Burton's unexpurgated translation of *Arabian nights' entertainments* and short stories by Guy de Maupassant and Honoré de Balzac – all of which were ordered burned by police magistrate George Taylor DENISON and placed on the list of publications prohibited entry into Canada.

The tenor of Shearer's enforcement efforts in all of these areas is captured in an article he had written for the *Dominion Presbyterian* (Ottawa, etc.) in 1906:

"We may not want to copy the Puritans in every particular, but, in their respect for righteousness, law, order, religion, and the Lord's Day, we could stand a good deal more of Puritanism than we are getting. . . . Let [our] Puritanism be that of the twentieth century – wise, tolerant, gracious, and inflexible . . . let us go ahead in the present crusade unterrified by all the sneering cries of 'Puritanical legislation' raised by cavilling newspapers that would cater to an evil-minded crowd."

Like many of his Presbyterian colleagues, notably George Campbell Pidgeon*, Shearer maintained that evangelism – a fundamental dedication to Jesus – must be accompanied by reform. This linkage, so central to Shearer's theology, was strongly evident in the report he and Thomas Buchanan KILPATRICK wrote on their evangelistic campaign in the Kootenay region of British Columbia in 1909. Their efforts had failed, they concluded, because of strong local disregard for the Lord's Day, the power of liquor and brothels, and the undermining absence of social restraint. According to historian Brian J. Fraser, the campaign "found its most responsive audience among those middle-class community leaders already connected with the church who were seeking to legitimate and defend their moral, social, and religious values in a pioneer community."

By 1912, in the debate within the rising Social Gospel movement over the relation between Christianity and socialism, the puritanism of Shearer's concepts of social welfare was being modified by his increasing progressivism. Shearer's theories of social regeneration were far from original, but when delivered with his customary fire, they conveyed a potent message. He had long argued for his church's involvement in urban problems. In June 1913, at the Presbyterian congress at Massey Music Hall in Toronto, his stirring address on "Redemption of the city" highlighted the hellish impact of urbanization and the need for the social and spiritual reclamation of inner-city folk. Moved by vigorous applause, he asked, "At the peril of the Kingdom of Jesus Christ in Canada, at the peril of the very life of the Church in Canada, shall we neglect to redeem our cities?"

To meet this goal Shearer, through the Board of Social Service and Evangelism, devoted much effort and money to establishing settlement houses in major Canadian cities (starting with St Christopher House in Toronto in 1912), funding local social and moral agencies, and investigating weak police work. Wherever success was achieved, from Halifax to Saskatoon, the much-travelled Shearer was there to trumpet, in the press and public addresses, the eradication of "recognized public vice." Within his own church, however, his demands for increased funding for the board produced a financial crisis in 1913 that led the General Assembly to direct its amalgamation with the Board of Foreign Missions the following year.

Undeterred, in 1914 Shearer and T. A. Moore took leading roles in organizing the seminal Social Service Congress in Ottawa. In his introduction to its published report, Shearer's long-time friend and president of the Social Service Council of Manitoba, Charles William Gordon*, placed at the feet of government and big business the responsibility for the dismal living conditions of many urban and farm dwellers. In 1917 Shearer's membership in the Presbyterian commission on the war, which expressed profound dissatisfaction with conventional religion and intense commitment to social reform, confirmed this vice warrior's dual focus. Two years later he would express sympathy with the United Farmers of Ontario and the participants in the Winnipeg General Strike, a move that likely alienated him from many Presbyterian colleagues and aligned him more with Methodism's progressive sector. In discussing the strike he lamented that "workers had to resort to wrong tactics to secure a correct principle."

The Social Service Council of Canada, which increasingly was Shearer's preferred vehicle for social uplift and for which he worked full-time as general secretary from June 1918, was never a radical organization. It shunned direct association with labour's left wing, and workers were largely indifferent to Presbyterian moralizing. Unlike some Social Gospellers, Shearer refused to consider leaving the church in order to pursue his concerns with wealth and poverty, housing, and working conditions. By 1918 the council's influence and organizational strength were peaking. A federation of leading social-work bodies, it had a full range of representation, including the major religious denominations, agrarian associations, and purity-education and temperance groups. The council's most lasting venture was probably the magazine Shearer founded in 1918, *Social Welfare* (Toronto), Canada's first major publication in the emerging but largely unprofessionalized field of social work. Ever alert to bright recruits, in July 1918 he hired Charlotte Elizabeth Hazeltyne Whitton* as assistant editor and assistant secretary, responsible for handling the council's office in Toronto and liaising with welfare agencies there. Whitton found Shearer, a severely stern man to many, quite amiable – she called him "Mr. Greatheart" – and a hard but understanding taskmaster. After his death in March 1925 and the loss of his sustaining drive, the council seems to have declined to the point of oblivion.

It is not unfair to conclude that the Reverend John G. Shearer had spearheaded the most conservative wing of the social purity/social gospel movement of the early 20th century – conservative theologically, sexually, and racially. Nevertheless, after the war he appeared to move with the times, not just in the direction of the Social Gospel, but also in breaking with the most evangelical wing of Canadian Presbyterianism,

the wing that rejected church union. Shearer distanced himself from many fellow ministers as a result of his belief that moral and social reform could be accomplished best through a union of resources. (The United Church of Canada would come into being in June 1925.) Though Shearer was widely recognized in *Social Welfare* and elsewhere as the dean of social service, the *Presbyterian Record* (Montreal), despite his national prominence, did not even publish an obituary.

MARIANA VALVERDE and S. CRAIG WILSON

AO, RG 22-305, no.52182; RG 80-5-0-114, no.1180. LAC, RG 31, C1, Blandford Township, Ont., 1871, div.2: 40 (mfm. at AO). *Canadian annual rev.*, 1918: 598. *Canadian men and women of the time* (Morgan; 1912). B. J. Fraser, *The social uplifters: Presbyterian progressives and the Social Gospel in Canada, 1875–1915* (Waterloo, Ont., 1988). S. P. Meen, "The battle for the sabbath: the Sabbatarian lobby in Canada, 1890–1912" (PHD thesis, Univ. of B.C., Victoria, 1979). Mariana Valverde, *The age of light, soap, and water: moral reform in English Canada, 1885–1925* (Toronto, 1991).

SHEPPARD, EDMUND ERNEST, journalist and author; b. 29 Sept. 1855 in South Dorchester Township, Elgin County, Upper Canada, only son of Edmund Sheppard and Nancy Bently; m. 8 Oct. 1879 Melissa Culver in Mapleton, Ont., and they had one son and three daughters; d. 6 Nov. 1924 near San Diego, Calif.

In his 1888 novel *Widower Jones*, a melodramatic tale of a prodigal's conflict with his clergyman father, Edmund E. Sheppard described sons of the manse as bad actors, the worst miscreants. He perhaps drew upon personal experience for this and other judgements. Indeed, his whole career (filled as it was with sensational and unorthodox behaviour) might be interpreted as a lifelong rebellion against his own religious upbringing.

Sheppard's father had emigrated from England in 1843. After several years as a teacher and then as a superintendent of schools, he became one of the first Canadian ministers in the Disciples of Christ. Edmund Jr received his early education in the St Thomas area and subsequently began medical studies at Bethany College in West Virginia, an institution which his father had attended before him. He apparently dropped out and headed down to Texas and Mexico, reportedly spending several years as a cowboy and stagecoach driver. After his return to Canada in 1878 he regularly affected the cowboy style: a slouch hat, fine Spanish leather riding boots, string tie, handlebar moustache, and goatee. His penchant for chewing tobacco and strong drink probably also dated from those years in the southwest.

Back in Ontario, he turned to journalism, first in London and St Thomas and then with the *Toronto Daily Mail*, under managing director Christopher William Bunting*. Appointed editor-in-chief of John Riordon*'s newly established Toronto *Evening News* in 1883, he would become its proprietor later that year. There he gathered around him a bold and somewhat Bohemian crew of writers anxious to stir up the complacent Toronto newspaper world. The *News* had two main characteristics: radicalism and sensationalism. In politics it advocated an independent, republican Canada where the elective principle would be applied to virtually all public offices, and church and state would be completely separate. The Knights of Labor, the new trade union that burgeoned briefly in the late 1880s [*see* Alexander Whyte Wright*] and whose intellectual leader, Thomas Phillips Thompson*, acted as assistant editor of the *News*, had the paper's full support. All the employees joined the union and in 1886 marched in the Labour Day procession wearing white plug hats. In 1887, with labour backing, Sheppard contested the Toronto West seat in the dominion parliament, losing narrowly to Frederick Charles Denison*. He was subsequently unsuccessful in campaigns for the provincial legislature (1890) and, running against Robert John FLEMING, for the office of mayor of Toronto (1893).

His paper's sensationalism took a variety of forms. Printed on pink stock, it concentrated on local news, carried mildly salacious gossip, and serialized novels (Sheppard's first fiction, "Dolly," appeared there). Short paragraphs, pungent language, and racy headlines were designed to catch the reader's attention. But sensationalism sometimes had a hard edge. Not surprisingly, given Sheppard's membership in the Orange lodge, the *News* treated Roman Catholics and French Canadians rudely. In 1885 a story written by Louis P. Kribs* cast aspersions on Montreal's 65th Battalion of Rifles (Mount Royal Rifles), suggesting cowardice during the North-West rebellion. Lieutenant-Colonel Joseph-Aldric Ouimet*, the unit's commanding officer and a rising young Conservative MP, brought a libel action against the *News* and its editor. The charge, and Sheppard's efforts first to avoid trial in Montreal and then to resist making the apology demanded by the court for the unfounded story, was a minor *cause célèbre* for over two years. In the end Sheppard lost, apologized, promised to pay a fine and court costs, and, as it turned out, was forced to relinquish control of the financially floundering *News*. The experience doubtless confirmed his francophobia.

As the trial dragged to its finale, Sheppard joined two others, Walter Cameron NICHOL and William E. Caiger, in establishing *Saturday Night*, whose first issue appeared on 3 Dec. 1887. At the new weekly Sheppard put most of his radicalism behind him. Where the *News* had aspired to the role of a "people's paper," *Saturday Night* sought to provide "social intelligence" to a culturally aware, socially conservative readership. During the two decades of Sheppard's edi-

torship – in this period he was also briefly editor of the Toronto *Star* [*see* Sir William James GAGE] – the magazine featured well-written articles on literature, music, art, politics, business, and religion. Sheppard encouraged many young writers, including women such as Kate Eva Yeigh [Westlake*], with whom he had been associated in St Thomas, Agnes Mary SCOTT, and Kathleen Blake Watkins [Catherine Ferguson*], to contribute. In his own regular column (written under the Spanish pseudonym Don), he often questioned received opinions. He especially enjoyed tilting at clerical windmills. During his vigorous campaign for Sunday streetcars in Toronto in the 1890s, he claimed that "the preachers are trying to keep a corner on the Sunday, they are afraid if any other attraction is offered their place of worship will be deserted."

If Sheppard's earlier radicalism subsided at *Saturday Night*, his hostility to French Canadians remained untamed. He repeatedly drew parallels between Canada and the pre–Civil War United States, with Quebec cast in the role of the South. Any attempt to extend the French language beyond the Ottawa River – Canada's Mason-Dixon Line – would be met with force, he contended. For him Quebec was a sink of clerical domination, political corruption, and linguistic aggressiveness. "Why beat about the bush?" he asked rhetorically. "What are we here for? Why did [James Wolfe*] take the trouble to fight with [Louis-Joseph de Montcalm*]? Was is not to conquer Canada? Was it not to make the Anglo-Saxon supreme? . . . We can never become a nation if we continue a dual language." Though the bellicose tone would moderate in later years, Sheppard's ethnocentrism never entirely dissipated.

Despite his repeated criticism of clericalism, Sheppard's writing, Hector Willoughby Charlesworth* observed, frequently had "an underlying religious vein." Certainly that was true of the three unmemorable novels he published in the 1880s. Each one criticized established Christianity, emphasizing the gap between doctrine and action, yet each also displayed sympathy for what Sheppard called "the spirit of Christ's teachings." He apparently shared the theological liberalism so popular among his contemporaries, which inclined some to the Social Gospel. In his case, after ill-health forced his retirement and departure for California in 1906, religious liberalism led down a path to what is sometimes called "mind cure" or "New Thought."

Sheppard's 1915 book, *The thinking universe*, presented a hodgepodge of cultish ideas purporting to demonstrate that Christian Science was the highest stage of religion. Its aim, he wrote, was "to change Man's attitude towards Infinity; to uplift him into a consciousness of being his own Infinity; to stir his Reason into grasping the fact that he is perfectly equipped for every emergency; to point him to the power he has within him to grapple with sickness and sin." The nascent religious liberalism of the writer whom John Wilson BENGOUGH had once called "The Journalistic Cowboy" had, logically enough, reached senescence in the power of positive thinking.

He died, after a lengthy illness, near San Diego, on 6 Nov. 1924.

RAMSAY COOK

Edmund Ernest Sheppard is the author of *Dolly, the young widder up to Felder's* (Toronto, 1886); *Widower Jones, a faithful history of his "loss" and adventures in search of a "companion"; a realistic story of rural life* (Toronto, 1888); *A bad man's sweetheart* (Toronto, 1889); and *The thinking universe; reason as applied to the manifestations of the infinite* (Los Angeles, 1915).

AO, RG 80-5-0-79, no.2197. LAC, RG 31, C1, 1901, Toronto, Ward 3, div.35: 20. *News* (Toronto), 1883–87. Christopher Armstrong and H. V. Nelles, *The revenge of the Methodist bicycle company: Sunday streetcars and municipal reform in Toronto, 1887–1897* (Toronto, 1977). H. [W.] Charlesworth, *Candid chronicles: leaves from the note book of a Canadian journalist* (Toronto, 1925). Ramsay Cook, "An epitaph for Edmund Sheppard and others," in his *Canada, Quebec, and the uses of nationalism* (Toronto, 1986), 175–83. Russell Hahn, "Brainworkers and the Knights of Labor: E. E. Sheppard, Phillips Thompson and the Toronto *News*, 1883–1887," in *Essays in Canadian working class history*, ed. G. S. Kealey and Peter Warrian (Toronto, 1976), 35–57. Paul Rutherford, *A Victorian authority: the daily press in late nineteenth-century Canada* (Toronto, 1982). *Saturday Night*, 1887–1906; 22 Nov. 1924: 2.

SHIRREFF, JENNIE GRAHL HUNTER (baptized **Jane Campbell Hunter**) (**Eddy**), nurse, businesswoman, and philanthropist; b. 14 Feb. 1863 in Chatham, N.B., daughter of John Shirreff, a merchant, and Henrietta Grahl; m. 27 June 1894 Ezra Butler Eddy* in Halifax; they had no children; d. 9 Aug. 1921 in Hull, Que.

Jennie Shirreff did what many young women looking for gainful employment did in the 1880s, she took up nursing. Her mother was from Boston, the family probably had trade connections there, and in 1889 Jennie went to Brookline (a Boston suburb) to train. In 1892 she came to work at the Victoria General Hospital in Halifax as an RN.

It is not known how she met E. B. Eddy. There is a story that when his first wife died in 1893, she went to Hull as his housekeeper, another that she went as companion to Eddy's daughter. A likely explanation is that they met in Halifax, where there was a branch of his lumber and paper company. They were married there in 1894, in the home of J. W. Fraser, a Presbyterian minister, with a wedding breakfast for 25 guests at the Halifax Hotel. She of course moved to Hull with her 66-year-old husband. She was a bright, shrewd woman though it is doubtful whether he relied on her

for business advice since initially she knew little of finance. Eddy's great preoccupation, to keep his firm intact, became her aim too. She consulted her lawyer friend from Chatham days, Richard Bedford Bennett*, who had moved to Calgary in 1897 but seems to have been known to Eddy before his death in 1906.

By then the only living descendant was a young grandson. Under Eddy's will the core of his estate went into a trust, effective until 1916. On reaching his majority the grandson was to receive 250 shares in the company provided he change his name to Eddy, which he did. Jennie Shirreff Eddy abandoned her dower rights under Quebec law in return for 1,259 shares. It seems to have been Eddy's hope that his grandson would take an interest in the business, but by 1916 it was clear he would not, so, on Bennett's advice, Jennie bought out the grandson, thus becoming the majority shareholder. The tenacity of her grasp of the firm was revealed by Eddy lawyer Thomas Patrick Foran, who recorded a meeting about 1919 at which representatives of an American firm made a generous offer for 51 per cent of the stock. She cut them off by saying she intended to keep the Eddy company and name going.

During these years the Quebec government was unhappy over Eddy's will. He had left almost nothing to Catholic institutions in Hull, where his business was located and though he had been its mayor. The eleemosynary institutions he favoured were Protestant and on the Ottawa side. Quebec, in consequence, was prepared to be tough about inheritance tax, but the estate was asset rich and cash thin, and when the government presented a bill for $700,000, Mrs Eddy was taken aback. Beginning in 1908 Bennett became even more important to her in the negotiations over a reasonable settlement. What emerged was a set of instalments. Quebec, however, was not the only interested party. Mrs Eddy lived in the Roxborough Apartments in Ottawa (in a fashion that suggested a life of poverty). When the Ontario government came after her for income tax, she became cross and bought Dunara, Lieutenant-General James Howden MacBrien*'s house in Hull. She moved there in February 1921.

Bennett had tried to draw her away from her penurious style of living, to get her to spend her money pleasurably. The first venture, from which she would derive great satisfaction, was funding a new women's residence for Dalhousie University in Halifax. She knew something of Dalhousie: the Victoria hospital was about a block away, she had developed a considerable respect for the university, and Bennett, a graduate, was on its board of governors. On 20 May 1920 Mrs Eddy offered Dalhousie $300,000 for the residence, a gesture that ranked at the time, along with the gifts of Lillian Frances Treble [Massey*] of Toronto, as one of the largest donations to a university in Canada by a woman. There were terms: the residence was to be called Shirreff Hall, it would be non-denominational (Jennie herself was Presbyterian), and she wanted to approve the architect's plans. In October she came to Halifax, met the female students, and threw a theatre party for all the students, in the midst of which they formally thanked her. In her gracious response, she said she had chosen Dalhousie "because it was the outstanding university of the Maritime Provinces." And she had a philosophy for Shirreff Hall: she did not want a Spartan barracks – she had seen enough as a nurse – but rather a residence with some semblance to the girls' own homes, to round out, as it were, the intellectual training given by the university. She even overruled the architect, Frank DARLING of Toronto, insisting on fireplaces in the public rooms (she knew something of Halifax winters), study rooms on the upper floors, and more light for the library. What emerged was a place that everyone admired, though one Cape Breton girl said in 1923 that it was too rich for her blood.

As the residence was being built in 1921, Jennie Shirreff Eddy was taken ill and underwent surgery at the Ottawa General on 17 February. Whatever her ailment, she was there until June, peritonitis developed, and she died at home in August. Her funeral was attended by representatives of the Ottawa Association for the Blind, various St Andrew's societies, and the Eddy company, including president George Henry Millen; her body was taken to Chatham for interment.

Her will comprehended assets that had increased substantially since E. B. Eddy's death; the estate was valued at more than $3.8 million. Her majority shares went to Bennett and her brother, Joseph Thompson (Harry) Shirreff, then the company's vice-president. McGill University in Montreal was given $200,000 for a chair in industrial chemistry. There was a long argument with Quebec over inheritance tax that turned on the worth of each of her shares. Bennett described Quebec's valuation of $1,600 as "little short of iniquitous"; they settled on $1,000. A warmer legacy existed in Dalhousie's Shirreff Hall and in the memories of those who had known its donor. It is significant that Sturgis Salmon Cushman, a senior manager in the Eddy company, thought highly of her. His granddaughter at age 10 met her and later remembered being impressed with the stylish lady who had spoken to her so pleasantly.

P. B. WAITE

[There do not seem to be any Jennie Shirreff papers, but at one time there must have been an extensive correspondence with R. B. Bennett. Although his papers at the Univ. of N.B. Library, Arch. and Special Coll. Dept. (Fredericton), have nothing directly from her, there is information on her in accession nos.543891, 561564, 580188, 580213, 580553, 581439–67, 581773, 582209, 582295 (also on mfm. at LAC, MG 26, K). Before she died she may have asked Bennett to destroy her letters, possibly because of the slanderous rumour that Bennett's sister Mildred Mariann* was his daughter by Jennie Shirreff. Bennett would have prosecuted but such prosecutions were very difficult since they needed proof of utterance. He explained in 1935 that in 1889, when Mildred was born, he had not even met Jennie Shirreff.

The author is grateful to Evelyn Lucy Wilkinson of Ottawa, the granddaughter of Sturgis Salmon Cushman, a senior manager in the Eddy company, for her recollections. P.B.W.]

Morning Chronicle (Halifax), 29 June 1894, 10 Aug. 1921. *Ottawa Citizen*, 10, 12, 17 Aug. 1921. J. H. Gray, *R. B. Bennett: the Calgary years* (Toronto, 1991). *Vital statistics from N.B. newspapers* (Johnson), 17, no.2881; 69, no.856. P. B. Waite, *The lives of Dalhousie University* (2v., Montreal and Kingston, Ont., 1994–98).

SHORTT, EMILY ANN McCAUSLAND (Cummings), journalist, publicist, social reformer, and office holder; b. 11 May 1851 in Port Hope, Upper Canada, daughter of Isabel Julia Harper and the Reverend Jonathan Shortt*; m. there 27 Sept. 1871 Willoughby Cummings, and they had one daughter; d. 1 Nov. 1930 in Toronto.

As the daughter of the rector of St John the Evangelist, Port Hope, Emily Shortt was born into a life of service to church and community. After her early schooling in Port Hope, she attended Mrs Lucy Simpson's seminary for young ladies in Montreal. In 1871 she married Willoughby Cummings, a Toronto barrister; as a prominent young matron, she would become a leader in Toronto's emerging women's club movement.

Missionary societies were among the most powerful of the first Canadian women's clubs, and Emily Cummings was in the forefront of Anglican missionary outreach as a founding member in 1886 of the Toronto diocesan branch of the Woman's Auxiliary to the Missionary Society of the Church of England in Canada [see Roberta Elizabeth ODELL]. She would hold office in this organization, as recording secretary, corresponding secretary, or vice-president, until her death. In 1890, on behalf of mission work, she made a tour of Indian reservations in British Columbia, Manitoba, and the North-West Territories, which she publicized in a series of articles entitled "Our Indian wards" for the Toronto *Empire* in July and August that year and "A trip through our mission fields" for the *Canadian Church Magazine and Mission News* (Hamilton, Ont.) from November 1890 to June 1891.

Representing Canadian clubwomen, Cummings had gone to Washington in 1888 for the founding meeting of the International Council of Women. Although Cummings was urged to launch a women's council in Canada, the time was not auspicious. In October 1893, however, she assisted the dynamic Lady Aberdeen [Marjoribanks*], wife of Lord Aberdeen [Hamilton-Gordon*], Canada's governor general, in founding the National Council of Women of Canada. Lady Aberdeen had just been elected president of the International Council when it met at the Columbian exposition in Chicago that summer. Cummings was present as special correspondent for the Toronto *Globe* and the *Manitoba Morning Free Press* (Winnipeg). The Chicago fair brought together the three elements, journalism, the National Council, and Lady Aberdeen, that would define the next chapters of Cummings's life.

Her husband's death on 14 Sept. 1892 had jolted Emily out of the conventional life of wife, mother, and volunteer activist; she now needed to earn a living. Her impeccable social connections and her journalistic experience ideally situated her to become the *Globe*'s first society reporter, a position she assumed in 1893 during the editorship of John Stephen WILLISON. As long-time editor Melvin Ormond Hammond would later observe, at first there were "wry faces against such 'horrid and vulgar stuff,'" but Cummings managed the role with sufficient professionalism to establish herself in the editorial department of the *Globe*, the first woman to win such recognition on a Canadian daily. Discretion was crucial; in order to separate her private from her public identity, Cummings adopted the pseudonym Sama, the Japanese word for lady, and might even note in Sama's accounts of society functions that Mrs Willoughby Cummings was among the guests. She occasionally took the opportunity to tilt at the dictates of style, commenting in 1893 that tight lacing for women was worse than footbinding. "One can live without walking," she noted, "but it is still necessary and fashionable to breathe." She would remain with the *Globe* until 1903.

Her career required frequent visits to Ottawa to cover the formal social events of the capital. As a house guest of Lord and Lady Aberdeen and working for a Liberal newspaper, Cummings was the ideal go-between when Lady Aberdeen connived in 1896 to meddle surreptitiously in Canadian politics by encouraging Wilfrid Laurier*'s ambition to become prime minister. Lady Aberdeen rejoiced in Cummings's suitability for the role: "As she is always in communication with me about the Council, her comings & goings will not be considered unnatural & it is well at such a juncture to have some means of communication with the leader of the Opposition."

In common with other women journalists in the heyday of women's clubs, Cummings was both observer and activist. She continued her central role in the National Council of Women, where she served almost continuously as corresponding or recording secretary from 1894 to 1917 and as vice-president from 1910 to 1930. She was active as well in the Toronto Local Council. In 1896 she represented Lady Aberdeen at the International Congress of Women in Boston. When in 1909 Toronto was the setting for the international meeting, Cummings was both organizer and publicist, using her press connections to ensure public attention.

Emily Cummings's career in journalism expanded in 1900 when she became editor of "Woman's Sphere" in the *Canadian Magazine* (Toronto). In the magazine format she was able to branch out into more general social commentary, particularly focusing on questions relating to the education of women. Although she was a member of the British Society of Women Journalists, she was not among the pioneers, such as Katherine Angelina HUGHES and Catherine Coleman [Ferguson*], who founded the Canadian Women's Press Club in 1904 and she did not join until after World War I. Philanthropic rather than professional clubs continued to consume her. She was an original member of the ladies' committee of the Toronto Industrial Exhibition (Canadian National Exhibition) when it began in 1901 and was particularly proud of the Babies' Rest which she established in 1919 to allow mothers to tour the exhibits while their infants were watched by trained nurses. Cummings was also on the executives of the Women's Canadian Historical Society of Toronto [*see* Sara MICKLE], the ladies' committee of the Toronto Technical School, and the Victorian Order of Nurses.

Cummings's labour on behalf of women and social reform was accorded national recognition in 1910. On 1 April the dominion government made her field secretary in the women's department of the old age annuities branch of the Department of Trade and Commerce, at a salary of $1,200. That same year she became the first Canadian woman to receive an honorary degree when King's College in Windsor, N.S., made her a DCL.

When the Great War broke out Cummings, then in her sixties, became chairwoman of the Toronto Women's Patriotic League. For a time she represented the National Council of Women on the National Service Committee, a clearing house for patriotic work, and she was president of the Toronto branch of the Woman's Emergency Corps of Military District No.2, whose aim was to aid recruiting by registering women capable of doing the work of men eligible for active service. In 1918 she was nominated by the dominion government to represent the interests of Canadian women at the Ottawa war conference.

She never abandoned her early involvement with missionary work: she was frequently a delegate to international pan-Anglican conferences; she edited the official newsletter of the Woman's Auxiliary from 1903 until her death, expanding and modernizing it, and for a time she was associate editor of the *Mission World* (Toronto); and around 1919 she became organizing secretary of the women's department of the Anglican "Forward Movement." In the last years of her life Cummings wrote the history of the Woman's Auxiliary: *Our story.*

An exemplary clergyman's daughter to the last, Emily Cummings elevated conventional feminine duties into new public roles in journalism, social reform, and government service. She died in Toronto on 1 Nov. 1930.

MARJORY LANG

In addition to her articles in newspapers and magazines, Emily Shortt Cummings wrote *Our story: some pages from the history of the Woman's Auxiliary to the Missionary Society of the Church of England in Canada, 1885 to 1929* (Toronto, [1929?]).

AO, F 1075-3, [M. O. Hammond], "Ninety years of the *Globe*" (typescript, [1934]), 196; F 1104, Mrs Willoughby Cummings to Mary Bouchier Sanford, 17 Nov. 1897; RG 80-5-0-14: 222. *Globe*, 22 April 1893. Barbara Freeman, "Laced in and let down: women's fashion features in the Canadian dailies of the 1890s" (paper presented at the annual CHA meeting, Victoria, 1990). Sandra Gwyn, *The private capital: ambition and love in the age of Macdonald and Laurier* (Toronto, 1984). Marjory Lang, *Women who made the news: female journalists in Canada, 1880–1945* (Montreal and Kingston, Ont., 1999). [I. M. Marjoribanks Hamilton-Gordon, Marchioness of] Aberdeen [and Temair], *The Canadian journal of Lady Aberdeen, 1893–1898*, ed. J. T. Saywell (Toronto, 1960). National Council of Women of Canada, *Year book* (Ottawa; Toronto), 1894–1930. *Standard dict. of Canadian biog.* (Roberts and Tunnell). V. J. Strong-Boag, *The parliament of women: the National Council of Women of Canada, 1893–1929* (Ottawa, 1976). *These fifty years, 1886–1936: Woman's Auxiliary to the Missionary Society of the Church of England in Canada, and to diocesan missions* ([Toronto, 1936?]).

SIFTON, ARTHUR LEWIS WATKINS, politician, lawyer, and judge; b. 26 Oct. 1858 in St Johns (Arva), Upper Canada, son of John Wright Sifton and Kate Watkins; m. 20 Sept. 1882 Mary Horsman Deering in Cobourg, Ont., and they had one daughter and one son; d. 21 Jan. 1921 in Ottawa.

Arthur Lewis Sifton's father was the son of Anglo-Irish Protestant immigrants to Canada; his mother was born in Ireland and immigrated with her parents. John Wright Sifton was by turn a farmer, a land speculator, an oilman, and a railway contractor. This peripatetic career meant that Arthur was educated in a variety of schools across southern Ontario, including a boys' school at Dundas and the high school in London. The family moved to Manitoba in 1875 to permit J. W. Sifton to take up contracts for telegraph and railway construction in the expanding west. Arthur completed high school in Winnipeg before he and his younger brother, CLIFFORD, were sent in 1876 to Victoria College, a Methodist institution in Cobourg, Ont. Though evidently capable of intellectual brilliance, Arthur was by no means a disciplined student. Rather like his father, he was restless and impulsive, happily skipping

classes while confident of his own ability to pass, choosing to broaden his mind in other ways. His fellow students awarded him a prize for being "intellectually, morally, physically and erratically preeminent in virtue and otherwise, especially otherwise." Following his graduation with a BA in 1880, Arthur began to article in the Winnipeg law office of Albert Monkman, a career path from which he was soon temporarily diverted.

Arthur had inherited from his father a commitment to Methodism and to temperance. Prominent in the Dominion Alliance for the Total Suppression of the Liquor Traffic, J. W. Sifton in 1880 was a leader of a campaign in the federal constituencies of Lisgar and Marquette to bring into effect the local option provisions of the Canada Temperance Act of 1878. Arthur addressed at least 16 meetings in the successful campaign for votes, but the victory eventually was lost to a legal challenge.

In 1881 J. W. Sifton moved to Brandon, hoping to take advantage of the boom in real estate caused by the construction of the Canadian Pacific Railway in western Manitoba. Arthur quickly abandoned his law books and joined his father in the scramble for profits. Though officially he presided over a Brandon branch of Monkman's law firm, he had not qualified for independent practice. In addition to speculating in real estate, he was active in the temperance movement and in organizing a loan company. He also was elected as an alderman to Brandon's first city council, on which he served two terms, in 1882 and 1883. On 20 Sept. 1882 he married Mary H. Deering; their first child, Nellie Louise, would be born the following August. Perhaps the prospect of becoming a father turned his attention to the need to complete his legal training: in the spring of 1883 he passed his barrister's examinations, though not those for attorney, and was called to the Manitoba bar; in June he became a full-fledged partner in his brother's law firm, now Sifton and Sifton. In addition to his service in civic politics, Arthur was elected to the school board, and he was active in the Reform Association, the Brandon Agricultural Society, and the Literary Society of the local Methodist church. Briefly in 1884 he even considered running for mayor, but he concluded that he had insufficient support.

Yet, despite all this success and apparent prospects for the future, in 1885 he removed with his family to Prince Albert (Sask.), dissolving the partnership of Sifton and Sifton. He was made a notary public that year and was enrolled as an advocate in 1886. Why he made the move is unclear. Prince Albert once had had high hopes of being on the main line of the transcontinental railway, but it was facing a more constrained future by 1885, since the CPR was being built far to the south. While making useful political connections and writing for the local newspaper, Sifton found time to earn his MA from Victoria College and his LLB from the University of Toronto, both in 1888. He moved to Calgary, apparently because of his wife's health, the following year. There he established a practice on Stephen Avenue, was appointed QC in 1892, and served at least some time in the office of the city solicitor. He later joined the firm of Sifton, Short, and Stuart and acted as crown prosecutor. In February 1898 his second child, Lewis Raymond St Clair, was born.

During this time his brother had remained in Brandon, building his law practice, speculating successfully in western Manitoba lands, and becoming attorney general of Manitoba in 1891 and minister of the interior in the federal government of Wilfrid Laurier* in November 1896. As interior minister, Clifford was responsible in the cabinet for the whole of western Canada, and in this capacity he relied heavily upon Arthur for advice about the welfare of the Liberal party in the Calgary region and for other services, such as settling a difficult election protest in Prince Albert. Arthur, meanwhile, plied Clifford with suggestions about patronage issues in Calgary and Banff. He did not hesitate to put himself forward. As early as August 1896 he had suggested that the North-West Territories needed a chief justice for its Supreme Court and that a promotion from the existing bench would open up a vacancy for which "there is no one else in the Territories eligible except myself." No court appointment could be made immediately, but Clifford managed from time to time to throw an occasional plum to Arthur, such as a retainer for a coroner's inquest in 1897. Finally, Arthur decided once more to take the plunge into politics, challenging the popular and long-time member for Banff, Dr Robert George BRETT, a Conservative, in the territorial elections of 1898. At first Sifton thought he had won by a majority of 36, but after a series of court challenges to the validity of some of the votes, Brett was declared the victor in 1899 by a margin of two. Sifton in turn successfully protested Brett's election, on the basis of corrupt practices, and he won the ensuing by-election in June 1899. Named president of the Alberta Liberal Association that year, he actively supported the federal Liberals in the dominion election of 1900. The pay for being an MLA was small, however, and Arthur told his brother that the law business, both civil and criminal, was very slow. Clearly he wanted something more remunerative.

Clifford was able to oblige: early in 1901 he chose James Hamilton Ross*, commissioner of public works and treasurer for the North-West Territories, to be Yukon commissioner; on 1 March the territorial premier, Frederick William Gordon Haultain*, appointed Arthur Sifton to succeed Ross. The federal government had granted to the territories full responsible government in 1897; however, the annual federal grant had failed utterly to keep up with the rapid growth of population and demand for facilities and infrastructure there. This problem fuelled a strong demand for provincial autonomy, a movement championed by the Haultain ministry. Arthur Sifton took up the cause as soon as he entered office, asking for supplementary grants to meet unforeseen expenses and then going to Ottawa with Haultain to seek better financial terms and eventual autonomy. He was re-elected with a large majority in 1902.

At this point, yet another career beckoned. As early as September 1901 his brother had proposed the chief justiceship of the territories to him. Arthur had thought it best not to accept, having just taken up his ministerial duties, but made it clear that he would like the post in the long run. He obtained it in January 1903, when the court's first chief justice, Thomas Horace McGuire, retired. Sworn in on the 13th, Sifton occupied the position until 16 Sept. 1907, when he became chief justice of the Supreme Court of the new province of Alberta. As had been the case when he joined the territorial government, his appointment was denounced by the Conservative press as the most crass form of nepotism. The malign hand of Clifford Sifton, rather than merit, was seen to be behind it. Yet Arthur was indeed very able, and took on an exceptionally heavy workload; by July 1903 he was able to tell Clifford, "I like the work better than I anticipated and most people appear to be satisfied now." In recognition of his service the University of Alberta would confer a DCL on him on 13 Oct. 1908.

Although he remained centred in Calgary, Sifton regularly heard cases in the southern territories from Maple Creek (Sask.) west to Cardston and Pincher Creek (Alta), and on occasion went north to Red Deer and Edmonton. Sifton appears to have had a severely practical approach to the law, and there is no indication in studies of his judicial career that he established important new points of law or precedents. He was a difficult personality for lawyers to read: he sat impassively smoking his trademark cigar; some thought him cynical in expression, others sphinx-like. He recorded by hand in notebooks the essence of each case that he heard, along with his decision. He was famed for his "rapid-fire methods" on the bench, frequently offering instant judgements in cases of considerable complexity which might have taken many days to argue. Most common among the cases which he heard in the early years were charges of horse and cattle rustling and other forms of theft, burglary, false pretences, forgery, disputes over money owed, and various other issues concerning property. Typically, cattle rustlers were sentenced to three years' hard labour. Occasional cases of incest, assault, or attempted murder arose, but they were a small fraction of the total. Efficient Sifton may have been. Yet, notes one authority, when his decisions were appealed, "his brethren had difficulty in ruling on them because he rarely provided reasons for his judgments."

Very likely Sifton expected to continue in this position until his retirement. Politics, however, intervened decisively. In February 1909 the premier of Alberta, Alexander Cameron Rutherford*, announced a modestly expansionist policy to encourage the construction of new and branch railway lines; among them was a plan to support the building of the Alberta and Great Waterways Railway northeast from Edmonton to Fort McMurray. On the basis of this policy the Liberal government was re-elected by a large majority in 1909. However, when the new legislature met in February 1910, a scandal concerning the generous financial terms promised to the A&GW exploded with stunning unexpectedness: William Henry Cushing, minister of public works and the representative of Calgary in the cabinet, resigned, followed within a few weeks by William Asbury Buchanan, a minister without portfolio. A significant minority of Liberals supported these ministers. In the interim the attorney general, Charles Wilson CROSS, under attack for his part in the A&GW agreement, also resigned, though he soon returned to the front bench. To try to save his government, Rutherford in mid March appointed a royal commission comprising three justices of the Supreme Court, chaired by Nicholas Du Bois Dominic BECK, to investigate the A&GW contract and the charges of corruption and incompetence. Thereupon the house adjourned until 26 May, when it expected to have a report to consider.

Lieutenant Governor George Hedley Vicars BULYEA, a Liberal partisan who worked closely with Prime Minister Sir Wilfrid Laurier on the matter, realized in February that the divided Liberals would demand "a scapegoat" and that since there was no obvious successor to Rutherford of any strength, salvaging the Liberal government in the province likely would mean seeking a replacement outside the existing legislature. "Possibly Chief Justice only permanent solution," he telegraphed to Laurier in mid March. By 17 May Sifton had agreed; when the house met on the 26th, Bulyea announced Rutherford's resignation, Sifton's appointment as premier, and – to the consternation of the opposition – the prorogation of the legislature, to give Sifton time to select a new cabinet and consolidate his position. C. W. Cross told Laurier, "The result of the acceptance of the Premiership by the Chief Justice is that the family quarrel in the Liberal party here is at an end." At the end of June Sifton and his cabinet were sustained in a series of by-elections, Sifton sitting for the constituency of Vermilion. In addition to his posts as premier and president of the Executive Council, he was provincial treasurer and minister of public works from 1 June 1910 to 4 May 1913 and minister of railways and telephones from 20 Dec. 1911 until his resignation in 1917.

The new premier needed to establish his credentials, first with the divided and somewhat sceptical MLAs, and secondly with the populace at large. He was neither dynamic nor robust: he had had some sort of heart affliction for most of his life, which left him few reserves of energy. This fact was not widely understood, with the result that he often was perceived as lazy. He also spoke far less than most prominent politicians, and was distinctly reserved in public. One historian has described his manner as "glacial and arbitrary." That he had a clear, incisive mind few doubted. With respect to his reputation amongst the public, he was helped by circumstance: Laurier in 1910 made one of his few appearances in the west, and his first extensive sounding of western public opinion in more than 15 years. He invited Sifton to join him for the Alberta leg of his tour; appearing on the platform with the popular prime minister and some of his leading cabinet ministers not only was a statement of solidarity and support from the foremost Liberals in the country, but brought the premier to the attention of his people as no other event could have done. This triumph was followed in 1911 by Sifton's strong endorsement of the federal Liberal policy of reciprocity with the United States. Freer trade with the Americans was highly popular in Alberta, and it gave Arthur Sifton an opportunity to emerge clearly from the shadow of his brother Clifford, who was one of the policy's most formidable opponents.

For many Albertans, however, the major question in local politics was how the premier would extract the province from the mess created by the A&GW contract. Late in 1910 Sifton introduced legislation to wind up the railway company and to seize from the banks the proceeds, totalling some $7,400,000, of the bonds sold on its behalf. He was strongly opposed within his own party by Cross (so much for Cross's sentiments concerning unity in the Liberal family). When the banks refused to turn the money over, the province sued them. Since the province had guaranteed the bonds and interest at five per cent, the bondholders did not suffer, but during the litigation the money was not constructing one foot of railway. At first it looked as though the province might win: in 1911 Charles Allan Stuart of the Supreme Court of Alberta found in its favour; the following year the federal minister of justice, Charles Joseph Doherty*, refused to act on a petition for disallowance of Sifton's legislation, and the Supreme Court in banc dismissed an appeal from Stuart's decision. The Royal Bank of Canada then appealed directly to the Judicial Committee of the Privy Council, which in January 1913 found that the legislation was beyond the powers of the province. What might have been a crushing blow to the government proved not to be so serious. For one thing, late in 1911 Sifton had announced a new and extensive policy of railway construction, including a plan to build an alternative to the A&GW; by the time of the Privy Council decision substantial building had taken place and there was considerable optimism in the province about the future. For another thing, Sifton in 1912 brought Cross into the cabinet as attorney general, thus partially healing the Liberal rift. Finally, the ablest Conservative and de facto leader of the opposition, Richard Bedford Bennett*, had been elected to the federal parliament in 1911. There is little doubt as well that a redistribution (or gerrymander) of seats worked decisively in the government's favour. In the 1913 general election the Liberals took 38 seats, to 18 for the Conservatives.

Yet another reason for the Liberal victory was Sifton's assiduous cultivation of the farm vote. The United Farmers of Alberta [see James Speakman*] was becoming a powerful political pressure group: both the Liberals and the Conservatives were anxious to be seen to be supportive of the farmer. Sifton and his minister of agriculture, Duncan McLean Marshall*, had the advantage of being in power and able to deliver on their promises. The 1913 session of the legislature, just before the election, was called by Liberals the "farmers' session." Three agricultural schools were established, including one in Sifton's riding of Vermilion. The Alberta Farmers Co-operative Elevator Company Limited was incorporated [see Edwin Carswell*], and another act provided for the organization of cooperatives. The Direct Legislation Act introduced referenda and popular initiation of legislation under certain conditions. The historian Lewis Gwynne Thomas notes that these and other acts "all . . . had been foreshadowed in the resolutions of the convention of the U. F. A. in January, 1913." The reality was, according to Thomas, that most Albertans were alienated from, or mistrusted, both traditional parties, and support for the Sifton government was temporary, not deeply rooted. Even fiscal policies were "calculated to avoid giving offence to the agrarian interest."

With the advent of World War I the demands of the UFA only increased. Pressure from the farmers, from other well-organized lobby groups, and from the perceived moral exigencies of war led Sifton to introduce two important, and related, measures: Prohibition and votes for women. A referendum on Prohibition was held in 1915 and was carried by a large majority; the government passed the Liquor Act the next year. Despite the efforts of the UFA and such activists as Emily Gowan Murphy [Ferguson*] and Helen Letitia McClung [Mooney*], Sifton had refused to allow women to vote in the referendum; however, he promised a government measure in 1916 to place "men and women in Alberta on the basis of absolute equality so far as Provincial matters are concerned." Assented to in April that year, the act made Alberta the third province, after Manitoba and Saskatchewan, to grant women the vote.

Another question that concerned Sifton was the issue of provincial control of natural resources, which for the three prairie provinces remained under federal control. He had raised the matter with Laurier in March 1911, and he forwarded his letter to Robert Laird Borden* shortly after the latter became prime minister that fall. In 1913 at a dominion-provincial conference the premiers of Manitoba and Saskatchewan, Sir Rodmond Palen Roblin* and Thomas Walter Scott*, joined with Sifton in asking for a meeting "to consider the transfer to the prairie provinces of the natural resources within these provinces." Despite the fact that Borden had long ago committed himself to transferring control, federal-provincial discussions were unproductive. Nevertheless, Sifton refused to make a public issue of attacking the federal government. He did not believe in east versus west, he noted in a Montreal interview in 1913. Rather, he was reported as saying, he stood for "a Canada united whether on matters of tariff or imperialism." "'We must pull together,' is his motto."

Such views may at least partially explain Sifton's actions in 1917. In June his government was sustained in a provincial election, with 34 Liberals elected against 19 Conservatives and 3 Independents. But by that time a crisis was brewing in federal politics over the related issues of conscription of manpower for overseas military service and the formation of a nonpartisan government to ensure, among other things, that conscription was carried out. The issue severely divided the Liberal party, both nationally and in Alberta, between the unionists, who believed that wholehearted commitment to winning the war must be paramount, and the Laurier loyalists, who agreed with Sir Wilfrid in his opposition to both measures. Early in August, Sifton attended a Liberal convention in Winnipeg, at which he attacked the Borden administration and its war record; coalition under Borden would be impossible. However, the Borden cabinet baulked at the idea of coalition under another leader, and eventually, in early October, Sifton agreed to enter the new Union government. He retired that month as premier of Alberta and was succeeded by Charles Stewart*. Having been sworn in as dominion minister of customs on 12 October, he was elected for the constituency of Medicine Hat in the federal election of 17 December.

During his time in Ottawa Sifton was probably one of the least known members of the government. His declining health reinforced his tendency to be reclusive and speak little; apparently he never walked any distance, but required a car to transport him even the few hundred yards from his apartment in the Château Laurier hotel to the House of Commons. He was deliberately given what were thought to be light portfolios, serving as minister of customs and inland revenue from 18 May 1918 to 1 Sept. 1919, as minister of public works from 3 September to 30 Dec. 1919, and as secretary of state from 31 Dec. 1919. He also served on the war committee of the cabinet and, in 1919–20, as the first chairman of the Air Board, which was designed to establish standards and structures for regulating air traffic in Canada. In none of these positions did he make a great impact, though he did his work with efficiency. Yet his colleagues valued his concise and articulate contributions in council: as Borden later recalled, "Among his colleagues, his rare intellectual power was universally acknowledged; in questions of difficulty, there was no one in whose judgment I placed firmer reliance, while I was head of the Government."

Probably Sifton's greatest contribution came in the behind-the-scenes work he did as a Canadian delegate – along with Borden, C. J. Doherty, and Sir George Eulas Foster* – to the Paris Peace Conference in 1919. He served as vice-chair of the commission on ports, waterways, and railways and represented Canadian interests with respect to the commission on aerial navigation. He also assisted in the preparation of the labour convention, which established the International Labour Organization, and the drafting of regulations governing international flying. His main concern always was to ensure recognition of Canada's equality of status among the nations. He found to his chagrin that constant vigilance was necessary because his country's closest allies, the British and the Americans, were frequently inclined to include Canada in a generic category of the British empire, the interests of which were assumed to be one. Asked to contribute his thoughts for a volume commemorating the peace conference, Sifton wrote, "Canada has no desire in return for or in regard to her sacrifices save that in matters in which she is vitally interested she should be treated as an equal." This position would not be fully acknowledged until the Balfour Declaration of 1926. In the absence of Sir Robert Borden, Sifton and Doherty signed the final form of the peace treaty on 28 June 1919 at Versailles.

Early in 1921 Sifton took leave from his duties for a few days, stating that he required rest and quiet. Unhappily his health became rapidly worse. Then, just when it seemed that there might be hope for improvement, his condition again suddenly deteriorated and he died at home in Ottawa about 8:30 A.M. on 21 Jan. 1921. He was buried there three days later in Beechwood Cemetery. "In him," observed Borden, "the country loses a public servant of the highest ability and of the most conspicuous patriotism."

DAVID J. HALL

[A portrait of Arthur Lewis Watkins Sifton by Victor Albert Long hangs in the Legislative Building in Edmonton.
A. L. W. Sifton left few personal papers. The largest col-

lection is in LAC, MG 27, II, D19, but this material consists almost entirely of official papers relating to his duties as a cabinet minister or his role at the Paris Peace Conference. The other major collection, in the Legal Arch. Soc. of Alberta (Calgary), comprises Sifton's judicial notebooks. There are quite a few letters from Sifton to his brother in the Sir Clifford Sifton papers (LAC, MG 27, II, D15), mostly in the period 1896–1903. There are also useful, if scattered, documents in the Laurier, Borden, and Arthur Meighen papers (LAC, MG 26, G, H, and I).

Sifton's early life has been pieced together largely from accounts in newspapers and standard biographical sources. Several obituaries also cast light on his career. Of the secondary sources, the most valuable is L. G. Thomas, *The Liberal party in Alberta: a history of politics in the province of Alberta, 1905–1921* (Toronto, 1959), which despite its age is the only serious scholarly examination of Sifton's time as premier of Alberta. The entry in L. [A.] Knafla and Richard Klumpenhouwer, *Lords of the western bench: a biographical history of the supreme and district courts of Alberta, 1876–1990* (Calgary, 1997), is most helpful on Sifton's judicial career. D.J.H.]

Univ. of Alta Arch. (Edmonton), file 2315-5 (honorary degree recipients). *Calgary Herald*, November 1898–June 1899 (weekly ed.); 10 Oct. 1914 (daily ed.). *Edmonton Journal*, 10 Oct. 1914. *Manitoba Free Press*, 22 Jan. 1921. *Montreal Daily Star*, 21 Jan. 1921. *Morning Albertan* (Calgary), 12 Oct. 1914. *Ottawa Citizen*, 21 Jan. 1921. *Ottawa Evening Journal*, 21 Jan. 1921. *Standard* (Montreal), 8 Nov. 1913. *Toronto Daily Star*, 21 Jan. 1921. *Alberta in the 20th century: a journalistic history of the province*, [ed. Ted Byfield et al.] (12v., Edmonton, 1991–2003), 2–3. D. R. Babcock, *Alexander Cameron Rutherford: a gentleman of Strathcona* (Calgary, 1989). *Canadian annual rev.*, 1901–21. *Canadian directory of parl.* (Johnson). *Canadian men and women of the time* (Morgan; 1912). *CPG*, 1899–1920. *Cyclopædia of Canadian biog.* (Rose and Charlesworth), vol.3. J. W. Dafoe, *Clifford Sifton in relation to his times* (Toronto, 1931). *Directory of the Council and Legislative Assembly of the North-West Territories, 1876–1905* (Regina, 1970). D. J. Hall, *Clifford Sifton* (2v., Vancouver and London, 1981–85); "T. O. Davis and federal politics in Saskatchewan," *Saskatchewan Hist.* (Saskatoon), 30 (1977): 56–62. J. S. Heard, "The Alberta and Great Waterways Railway dispute, 1909–1913" (MA thesis, Univ. of Alta, 1990). C. C. Lingard, *Territorial government in Canada: the autonomy question in the old North-West Territories* (Toronto, 1946). *The official history of the Royal Canadian Air Force* (3v. to date, [Toronto and Ottawa], 1980–), vol.2 (W. A. B. Douglas, *The creation of a national air force*, 1986). Faye Reineberg Holt, "Women's suffrage in Alberta," *Alberta Hist.* (Calgary), 39 (1991), no.4: 25–31. C. B. Sissons, *A history of Victoria University* (Toronto, 1952). *Standard dict. of Canadian biog.* (Roberts and Tunnell), vol.1. L. H. Thomas, *The struggle for responsible government in the North-West Territories, 1870–97* (Toronto, 1956). Paul Voisey, "The 'votes for women' movement," *Alberta Hist.*, 23 (1975), no.3: 10–23.

SIFTON, Sir CLIFFORD, lawyer, politician, newspaper publisher, and office holder; b. 10 March 1861 in St Johns (Arva), Upper Canada, second son of John Wright Sifton and Kate Watkins; m. 13 Aug.

Sifton

1884, in Winnipeg, Elizabeth Armanella (Arma) Burrows (d. 1925), sister of Theodore Arthur BURROWS, and they had five sons, one of whom predeceased him; d. 17 April 1929 in New York City and was buried in Toronto.

Clifford Sifton represented the second Canadian-born generation of descendants of Anglo-Irish gentry who had settled in Upper Canada in 1818 and 1819. His father, John Wright Sifton, was a farmer and a small oil producer in Lambton County. After Clifford's birth he became a railway contractor in Brant County and later a businessman in London. Throughout his life he was an active and devout Wesleyan Methodist and a prohibitionist. A long-time supporter of the moralistic, crusading politics of George Brown* and Alexander Mackenzie*, John Sifton was rewarded in 1874 by Mackenzie's Liberal government with contracts to build a telegraph line northwest of Winnipeg and two sections of the Canada Pacific Railway, east of Selkirk and west of Port Arthur (Thunder Bay), Ont. The following year he moved his family to Manitoba, where he also farmed and continued to be involved in politics.

Clifford thus was educated in various public schools, at a private boys' school in Dundas, Ont., and at high schools in London and Winnipeg. He graduated at age 15. A boyhood attack of scarlet fever had left him partially deaf, a handicap that would worsen throughout his life. In an effort to overcome the impediment he developed a rigorous self-discipline that would lead to rapid academic advancement and numerous awards. He attended Victoria College in Cobourg, Ont., from 1876 to 1880, graduating the gold medallist of his class. Following two years of articling with the Winnipeg law firm of Samuel Clarke Biggs, he was called to the Manitoba bar in 1882.

Sifton's family had recently moved to the newly created boom town of Brandon and there he established a law practice in which his elder brother, Arthur Lewis Watkins SIFTON, shortly became a partner. Like most lawyers on the Canadian settlement frontier, he developed an expertise in land and homestead law, and he speculated in real estate. He appears, however, to have had little intention of pursuing a career in law; his real avocation from early adulthood was politics.

Such a choice probably came naturally to young Sifton. His father had held minor positions in local politics in Upper Canada and had worked in Mackenzie's campaigns. Since 1878 he had tried, more often with failure than with success, to launch a political career in Manitoba. Clifford's first direct intervention in politics occurred in 1882 when he spoke in support of his father's ill-fated attempt at re-election to the Manitoba legislature. From 1883 to 1885 he was active in the Manitoba and North West Farmers' Union and its successor, the Manitoba and North-West Farmers' Co-operative and Protective Union.

Both were agrarian protest organizations that Liberal politicians used to help establish the Manitoba Liberal party as the voice of western protest against the federal Conservative government of Sir John A. Macdonald* and against what the Liberals believed was Macdonald's "puppet," the provincial government of John Norquay*. The Manitoba Liberals founded a permanent organization in 1885 and nearly defeated the Norquay government in the election of the following year, mainly on the subject of Ottawa's disallowance of provincial railway charters and more broadly on issues of provincial rights. Clifford performed strongly in supporting his father's last, and failed, campaign in 1886.

The momentum lay with the provincial Liberals under Thomas Greenway*. They won a convincing victory in the election of 1888, in which Clifford stood successfully for North Brandon. The election marked the triumph of Manitoba in its long struggle with the federal government, which sought to maintain the Canadian Pacific Railway's monopoly against the province's determination to provide effective competition and reduce freight rates. It also marked what historian William Lewis Morton* called "the triumph of Ontario democracy," the election of a government dominated by newcomers – most from Ontario – and the final rejection of a government that at least had paid lip-service to respecting the population and traditions that pre-dated provincehood in 1870.

No issue so clearly symbolized this change as the Manitoba school question. In 1890 Greenway's government tabled legislation to create a department of education and a system of so-called "national schools" that would be the only system supported by provincial tax dollars. Denominational schools were permitted, but were not to be tax-supported, a condition that would ultimately doom them. Immensely popular, the legislation nonetheless constituted a serious threat to the agreement embedded in the Manitoba Act of 1870 which had sought to enshrine guarantees that the Catholic population would control its own publicly supported school system. French-speaking Catholics viewed their schools as crucial to their cultural survival and worked closely with English-speaking Catholics to oppose the new system. Aided by the federal government, the Catholic minority immediately launched *Barrett v. City of Winnipeg* [*see* John Kelly Barrett*] to challenge the legislation.

Sifton, who had spoken ably in support of the legislation in 1890, was named attorney general of Manitoba on 14 May 1891 and provincial lands commissioner the following day. In May 1892 he also became minister of education. Meanwhile, *Barrett v. City of Winnipeg* had wound its way through the courts. In November 1890 and February 1891 the Manitoba courts had upheld the Public Schools Act of 1890, but in October the Supreme Court of Canada under Chief Justice Sir William Johnston Ritchie* ruled that it violated the minority's rights under the Manitoba Act. Using a brilliant strategy, Sifton arranged to have the Anglicans challenge the Manitoba legislation in light of the Supreme Court's decision. He then appealed both the Catholics' case and the Anglicans' (*Logan v. City of Winnipeg*) to the Judicial Committee of the Privy Council in England. The intent was to emphasize the possibility of fragmentation of the school system should the minority's contention be upheld. On 30 July 1892 the JCPC found in favour of the province.

Early in 1893 the Catholic minority launched another legal challenge. *Brophy and others v. Attorney-General of Manitoba* asked the courts to determine whether the legislation of 1890 adversely affected Catholic rights acquired since 1870 and also whether the federal government had the power to remedy the grievance. When the JCPC ruled early in 1895 that the minority did in fact have an appealable grievance and that the federal government had the power to remedy it, the issue was thrown back into the political arena. Sifton was determined that the public should view any action by Ottawa, not as a moral imperative or a legal requirement, but as a purely political decision calculated to win support in Quebec. The federal government, he told the Manitoba legislature, had no right to interfere with the expressed will of the people of Manitoba. During 1895 he brilliantly outmanoeuvred the federal government of Sir Mackenzie Bowell*, refused requests to compromise, and engineered a provincial election early in 1896. The result was an overwhelming endorsement of the Greenway government. The issue also contributed to the victory of the Liberals under Wilfrid Laurier* in the federal election of June 1896. The two leaders then hammered out the so-called Laurier–Greenway compromise, with Sifton as the dominant figure on the Manitoba side of the negotiations. The settlement provided for limited religious instruction and for bilingual education where ten or more pupils had a native language other than English. Nevertheless, the minority failed entirely to regain either segregation of Catholic pupils or control of their education, which to it were the crucial issues.

Sifton had quickly become a dominant presence in the Greenway government. He successfully pressed the premier to make important changes in the cabinet, devised railway policy, and was the dynamic force that kept the Liberal party organization in fighting trim. During his years in Manitoba politics, recession and depression hampered economic growth. Despite the end of the CPR monopoly in 1888, which allowed for the completion of the Red River Valley Railway and resulted in a slight lowering of freight rates, expansion of the railway system ground to a halt. In 1895 Sifton devised a system of financing railways through provincial government guarantees of the principal and interest on railway bonds. Working with railway contractors Donald Mann* and William MACKENZIE, he arranged for a line into the Dauphin district, the Lake Manitoba Railway, which would be the beginning of the Canadian Northern Railway system. His apparently painless method of financing railways became irresistibly attractive to governments in the boom years of the early 20th century.

Sifton had also gained a reputation in Manitoba as the organizing genius behind the electoral successes of the Greenway government. Every campaign was planned thoroughly and energetically, government propaganda blanketed the constituencies with carefully targeted partisan messages, and everywhere the government aggressively confronted its Conservative "enemy." Sifton's opponents claimed that he did not shy away from questionable tactics – buying votes, supplying liquor, manipulating voters' lists, and the like – but they were never able to substantiate these claims in court.

As his reward for his part in the settlement of the Manitoba school question, Sifton was sworn into Laurier's cabinet as minister of the interior and superintendent general of Indian affairs on 17 Nov. 1896, a few days before the school compromise was officially announced. His new portfolio entailed responsibility for immigration and for the settlement of the prairie west. After moving to Ottawa, Sifton appeared to abandon his western Liberal radicalism and to embrace the principles of John A. Macdonald's policies of national development: protective tariffs, expansion of railways, and settlement of an agricultural population in the west. These policies would give Canada a measure of economic independence and diversify its economy, open new areas to settlement, provide access to untapped resources, and integrate the west into the dominion both as a consumer of domestic manufactures and as a producer of foodstuffs and other natural products in the international market. Sifton also believed that centralizing the administration of these policies would be more efficient than expanding regional or local autonomy. His focus on material development and a strong central government and his belief in the fundamentally British Protestant character of Canada outside Quebec did not incline him to view generously the aspirations of minorities, particularly those of French Canada. In the end he and Laurier viewed the country from quite different perspectives that would prove difficult to reconcile.

The Laurier government took office in propitious times. The domestic economy was recovering, the international economy was expanding, there was new demand in Europe for North American foodstuffs and manufactures, the last waves of emigrants from central and eastern Europe were ready to go abroad, and capitalists from Britain and the United States were prepared to invest unprecedented amounts of money in Canada. Effective methods of agriculture were being developed in the west, and a transportation and service infrastructure was rapidly growing; along with rising prices and lower shipping costs, these factors made farming in the west much more attractive and less risky.

In this context Sifton transformed the immigration branch of the Department of the Interior. Formerly salaried immigration agents suddenly found themselves working for commission, based on the actual number of immigrants settling in the west. The department aggressively sold western Canada: millions of advertisements in various languages were broadcast in Europe; Canada was touted at agricultural fairs; schools in Britain received great quantities of free information about Canada; journalists were given free tours of the west so that they could write about it. Whereas Canadian promotion of immigration from the United States had been largely targeted at repatriation – trying to lure former Canadians back to Canada – Sifton placed the emphasis on attracting agricultural Americans to come to Canada. Tens of thousands responded, searching for large, cheap tracts of land unavailable in the United States or for a block of land for a particular ethnic or religious minority. The government favoured immigrants from the United States because they brought capital, goods, and experience in western farming; moreover, most Canadians viewed them as ethnically compatible. Efforts in Britain were politically necessary, given Canada's heritage, but generally less successful. Only a minority of British immigrants appeared to be interested in the rigours of western farming [*see* Isaac Montgomery Barr*]; others were interested in domestic service or in mainly urban labour. Sifton also worked to encourage settlers from central and eastern Europe. They came in unprecedented numbers [*see* Jósef Olesków*; Peter Vasil'evich VERIGIN] and were generally very successful farmers, although they also created hostility amongst some English-speaking Canadians [*see* Patrick Gammie Laurie*], who saw them as a threat to the ethnic traditions and social values of the majority culture.

Sifton's primary concern was to settle the west with a productive agricultural population: hence his encouragement of American, British, German, Scandinavian, and eastern European farmers. Those whom he believed unlikely to succeed as prairie farmers and therefore more likely to settle in Canadian cities where he feared they would compete with Canadian workers and cause social problems – British city dwellers, southern Europeans, blacks, and Orientals – were not encouraged and were even actively discouraged from coming to Canada. Overall, the annual number of immigrants to Canada rose from 16,835 in 1896 to 55,747 in 1901 and to 141,465 in 1905, though probably less than half of them were intending

to settle in the west. Just as he was interested in attracting agricultural immigrants, Sifton wanted to get them safely located on farms. He greatly increased the survey of western lands, from 1,600,000 acres in 1901 to 12,700,000 acres in 1904. Railway companies were pressured to select the land owing them under land-grant schemes and free up the remaining lands for homesteading. Immigrants were carefully cultivated from the time of their arrival in Canadian ports until they located on a homestead.

Other areas that came under Sifton's jurisdiction were treated in the context of efficiency in achieving the government's overall goals. The Geological Survey of Canada [*see* George Mercer Dawson*; Robert Bell*] was partially reoriented from a largely scientific entity to a body expected to locate mineral deposits and aggressively encourage their exploitation. National parks were developed to attract tourists, but also for other purposes, such as mining. Sifton was instrumental in the negotiation with the CPR's president, William Cornelius Van Horne*, of the contract for the construction of a branch line popularly known as the Crow's Nest Pass Railway [*see* John Duncan McArthur], which linked mining and forest resources into Canada's east-west rail network. The historic Crowsnest Pass agreement passed by parliament in 1897 significantly lowered freight rates on manufactured goods brought into the west, and on grain transported from it to the Lakehead. In addition, Sifton was the strongest advocate in the cabinet of Mackenzie's and Mann's Canadian Northern Railway, enabling it in 1903 to secure its dream of building to transcontinental status, along with the National Transcontinental line favoured by Laurier and a majority of other Liberals. Sifton also was influential in holding the Liberal government to a course of moderate protectionism that steered between the high tariff views of the manufacturers, many Tories and some prominent Liberals and the low tariff, free trade convictions of many Liberals, especially in the west.

Lost in the rush for settlement and economic growth were the native peoples. Sharing the common assumptions of his day about them, Sifton aimed at cutting costs in the administration of the Department of Indian Affairs [*see* Amédée-Emmanuel FORGET] and in native education. He did not believe that native peoples could contribute in a significant way to the material expansion of the nation. In certain cases he permitted his officials to encourage the natives to give up some of their reserve lands for speculation and settlement. He also was responsible in 1899 for approving arrangements for Treaty No.8 [*see* David Laird*; James Andrew Joseph McKenna*; Mostos*], which resulted in the surrender of a large portion of present-day northern Alberta, Saskatchewan, and British Columbia, as well as part of the southern Northwest Territories. This was achieved mainly to allow the safe passage of prospectors heading for the Yukon gold-fields.

Sifton was the minister who had greatest responsibility for the administration of the Yukon territory during the gold rush which originated in 1897. The problems he faced essentially were in three areas: the establishment of civil government; the regulation of the extraction of gold and related taxes or royalties; and the negotiations with the United States over disputed territory and control of trade in the Alaskan panhandle.

The last of these issues affected and complicated the other two. Because the Americans controlled the most readily accessible routes to the Yukon, they were in a position to control trade by making it difficult for Canadian-purchased goods to compete with those purchased in Seattle, Wash., or San Francisco in passing through the panhandle to Canadian territory. Sifton travelled to the disputed region in the fall of 1897 and even went to Washington, D.C., in December to try to sort out the matter. He obtained verbal assurances of American cooperation, but American delays and equivocation precluded a solution and undermined his hopes for an "all-Canadian" route to the Yukon via the Stikine River. Nationalist fervour in both Canada and the United States made it impossible for an Anglo-American joint high commission in 1898–99 to resolve outstanding difficulties between the two countries and, in any event, Sifton was one of the hardliners in the Canadian cabinet, pressing Laurier not to cave in to unsatisfactory American offers. In 1903 Laurier appointed Sifton the British agent in charge of preparing the case for the Alaska Boundary Tribunal. The judicial tribunal consisted of three Americans, one Briton, and two Canadians, Louis-Amable Jetté* and John Douglas Armour (replaced by Allen Bristol Aylesworth* after Armour's death in July 1903). Despite Sifton's vigorous advocacy and enthusiasm, the British – who admittedly had the weaker case – lost on all the crucial decisions. Sifton concluded from the experience that the Americans would not hesitate to use their weight to secure their ends and that the British could not be relied on to defend Canadian interests.

If Canada's freedom to establish civil government and regulate the Yukon trade was constrained by the boundary problem and the strong interest of the United States in the fate of its nationals in the goldfields, it also was limited by ignorance, poor communications, and the demands of patronage. Of the Yukon commissioners (the heads of the territorial government) selected by Sifton in the period before 1905 – James Morrow Walsh*, William Ogilvie, James Hamilton Ross*, and Frederick Tennyson Congdon* – only Ross was a success and his term (1901–2) was cut short by a stroke. Officials appointed by Sifton and his colleagues often were unqualified for their difficult tasks except by political connection and many of them occu-pied themselves with lining their pockets rather than serving the public. Despite the strenuous and repeated efforts of the opposition to link Sifton to alleged corruption in the Yukon, it was unable to prove its charges.

Sifton frequently changed mining regulations, usually because of pressure from the Yukon when officials in Ottawa failed to understand local conditions. The interests of the individualist-adventurer placer miners conflicted with those of capitalists, such as Joseph Whiteside BOYLE and Arthur Newton Christie Treadgold*, who sought large concessions from the government that would justify bringing in heavy equipment to work low-grade ores. Sifton believed that the capitalists would provide greater stability to the Yukon in the long run, but opposition to the concessions, and especially to the huge development proposed in the Treadgold concession, resulted in the failure of that policy before 1905, although in the end Sifton was proven correct.

The Yukon experience was not typical of Sifton's political management. Indeed, he had rapidly acquired a reputation as one of the ablest of Laurier's English-speaking colleagues in the area of manipulation of patronage and management of elections. Instrumental to his success was his purchase of the *Manitoba Free Press* in 1897–98. First under the editorship of Arnott James Magurn and then, from 1901, under the brilliant John Wesley Dafoe*, the paper became a commanding presence in the metropolitan growth of Winnipeg and the expansion of its hinterland from the Lakehead to the Rockies. On one level the paper was a business investment for Sifton and he sought out leading newspapermen such as Dafoe and Edward Hamilton Macklin, the business manager of the *Free Press* from 1900, who shared his vision of the growing potential of western Canada and the opportunities it created for the paper. On another level the paper was a political investment, a weighty voice in support of the Laurier administration, a source of admittedly slanted editorials and news columns for the Liberal newspaper network that Sifton was at pains to establish across the west, and a vital organ at election time. Through the *Free Press* he defended the record of his department and of the Laurier government generally. At the same time, Magurn, and then Dafoe, served as important conduits of information about western conditions. By 1904 there were 35 papers in Manitoba, 22 in the North-West Territories, and 16 in British Columbia on the Liberal patronage list. Although Sifton had a direct financial interest in two or three of them, most were kept in line by the Liberal inclinations of their proprietors and by patronage – usually government advertisements or contracts.

Playing a key role in the Liberal election victories of 1900 and 1904, successful in promoting the development of the west, and plainly carrying great weight in Laurier's cabinet, Sifton astounded the country with his abrupt resignation at the end of February 1905. As he read the education clauses in the bills intended to establish the provinces of Alberta and Saskatchewan, he was convinced that they extended to the Roman Catholic minority privileges beyond those which they then possessed under the territorial government of Premier Frederick William Gordon Haultain*. He believed that the ideal for the new provinces was a single school system which would eliminate denominational differences; since that was politically impossible, he favoured preserving there the situation already existing in the territories, as defined by the territorial ordinances of 1901, which minimized denominational control. Laurier disagreed and refused to compromise on the wording. Eventually, however, Sifton's resignation and the threat of a more widespread rebellion in his cabinet forced him to entrench the status quo. Other factors may have influenced Sifton's decision to resign. He had exhausted himself in the previous election as well as in administration and he had been passed over by Laurier for promotion. There were also allegations that he feared to face charges of corruption or of adultery, although these charges were never substantiated. The fact that his opinion had not been sought, or his advice accepted, on an issue that normally fell under his jurisdiction and on which he was well experienced, is in itself likely sufficient cause for his resignation.

Sifton remained in parliament as a private member until 1911. Laurier made one attempt to lure him back into the cabinet, in 1907. Sifton declined, partly because the prime minister refused to make even minor reforms to his cabinet and partly because he would have been expected to assume responsibility for the exhausting and thankless task of political organization in English-speaking Canada. Outside the cabinet, Sifton seems to have had little or no influence over policy. He appeared rarely in parliament and spoke less. On 31 May 1906 he brilliantly defended his administration as minister of the interior against charges of corruption and on 20 March 1908 he gave a speech urging civil service reform that attracted much attention. At Laurier's request he spearheaded in 1907–8 Canada's interest in participating in the All-Red Line scheme, a plan to provide rapid passenger communication by ships and trains between Britain and her Pacific empire – especially New Zealand and Australia – via Canada (all land parts of the route were coloured red on contemporary maps). Undoubtedly Canada would have benefited significantly from the business generated, which is what attracted Sifton. Australian coolness to the project, however, combined with the prospect that the Panama Canal, then under construction, would soon be completed, undermined the rationale for the scheme and resulted in its being quietly dropped.

The role of backbencher was not congenial to Sifton. He also was growing out of sympathy with the government and seriously considered not running in the general election of 1908. At the last minute he appears to have been persuaded that not to run would be viewed as capitulating to charges of corruption and he worked strongly to salvage the government's organization in Ontario as well as to ensure his own re-election for Brandon. His alienation from the government climaxed in January 1911 when Laurier's minister of finance, William Stevens FIELDING, announced a reciprocity agreement with the United States. The two countries agreed to eliminate tariffs on a wide range of agricultural and fish products, on wood pulp and pulpwood, on a limited number of partly manufactured products, and on barbed wire. They also agreed to a common level of tariff on a further list of products and to reduced tariffs on an additional list. It was not full free trade and it largely left Canadian manufactures protected, but it seemed to go a long way toward free trade and linking the economies of the two countries. Sifton opposed the agreement with a powerful speech in parliament at the end of February. The proposal, he asserted, ran counter to historic efforts to create an east-west trading network and to maintain trade linkages with Britain and the empire, to give Canada not only economic unity, but a measure of independence from the great attraction and dominance of the United States. He decided not to run again for parliament, but did work to link disaffected Liberal businessmen with the Conservative anti-reciprocity campaign and to organize Ontario for the Conservatives. The smashing Tory triumph in the general election in September owed not a little to Sifton's efforts, as Conservative leader Robert Laird Borden* admitted. The extent to which Sifton had abandoned his western free-trade principles was now obvious. His former supporters in Brandon and many of his former Liberal colleagues felt betrayed.

In May 1909 Laurier had appointed Sifton to chair the newly created Commission of Conservation and Borden permitted him to continue until his resignation in November 1918. James WHITE was appointed secretary in 1909; he would become deputy chairman in 1913. The commission was a response to American conservation initiatives under President Theodore Roosevelt and a recognition that conservation required action on the part of Canada and Mexico as well as the United States. Conservation was understood to involve efficient management for ongoing exploitation of resources; in no sense was it preservation. The conservation movement of this period reflected American Progressive ideals of individual and collective action in order to bring about greater economic, social, and political efficiency and to prevent squandering of resources. Sifton embraced these ideals and hoped that as chairman he would be able to make a significant impact. The commission's mandate was to investigate and publicize issues relating to conservation of natural resources and public health; it had neither executive nor administrative powers. Because it trespassed on areas of provincial jurisdiction, it had to be particularly sensitive to provincial concerns. Intended to act at arm's length from government departments, under Sifton it indeed acted quite independently. He established seven committees (forests; lands; minerals; water and water-power; fisheries, game, and fur-bearing animals; public health; press and cooperating organizations), each chaired by a member of the commission and each free to appoint experts and conduct its business as it saw fit. The commission as a whole held meetings once each year, from which its annual reports were generated. Sifton spoke frequently and was an aggressive supporter of its wide range of activities. Only his strength and prestige preserved the commission from ministerial resentment of its independence and discontent among civil servants over what they regarded as its intrusions into their areas of jurisdiction. It was phased out by the government by 1921, a fate that obscured its achievements: many dozens of scientific publications and catalogues of resources, a significant impact on federal and provincial statutes regulating the exploitation of resources, the encouragement of farmers and fishermen, and the growth of public health standards and city planning.

For personal reasons, Sifton, who would be knighted on 1 Jan. 1915, was thoroughly devoted to the war effort from 1914. Four of his sons were in the military and two, Clifford and Wilfred Victor, were wounded and earned the Distinguished Service Order. Sifton helped to arrange the formation and financing of the No.1 Automobile Machine-Gun Brigade (later the 1st Canadian Motor Machine Gun Brigade) and he and his wife spent much of the war in Britain to be closer to their sons. Indeed, he had been out of the country almost a year when he returned in the spring of 1917 to be plunged into the crisis over conscription and the formation of a coalition government. Unhappy with the Borden government's record, not trusting Laurier to pursue an all-out win-the-war policy, and missing the nuances of recent developments in Ottawa, Sifton appeared inconsistent, seeming to side at first with Laurier, who opposed conscription for overseas service, and then with Borden, who was convinced that conscription was essential. He ultimately was instrumental in pulling together pro-conscription western Liberals, including his brother Arthur, Thomas Alexander Crerar*, and James Alexander Calder*, to join with Borden in the Union government. He was equally critical in engineering the Union government's victory in the election of December 1917. It proved to be his last serious involvement in politics. Although his major objective had been to secure a conscriptionist, win-the-war government, he also hoped that the shattering of traditional political loyalties in 1917, added to the upheaval of war, would lead to a new era of reform. The body politic would then be cleansed, he anticipated, and there would result universal suffrage, a reformed civil service, and an end to liquor traffic, slums, and poverty. In this respect, the Union government proved to be a great disappointment to him.

Sifton and his family moved to Toronto in 1919 and during the last decade of his life his public involvement was increasingly marginal. He was deeply mistrusted by Prime Minister William Lyon Mackenzie King* and many Liberals, by the Progressive party (for whom he represented a corrupt past, not a reformed future), and of course by the Conservatives (to whom he was a long-term enemy and a person of unpredictable loyalties). He had some hope that the Progressives, at least as personified by Crerar, would be a reforming influence in Canadian politics, but was disappointed at how they dissipated their early promise. King overcame his dislike of Sifton sufficiently to consult with him periodically and to persuade him to deliver several speeches in the Liberal interest during the election of 1925. King and Sifton shared a belief that Canada should take an isolationist position in the world, moving toward greater independence from Britain to secure her future freedom of action, and through public speeches and interviews with King and Dafoe, Sifton at least reinforced King's policies in this area.

In 1925 Sifton, with his sons, became deeply involved in an effort to revive the fortunes of the Montreal, Ottawa and Georgian Bay Canal Company, which hoped to connect the Ottawa and Mattawa rivers via Lake Nipissing to Georgian Bay in a shorter route for shipping than the Great Lakes and also to develop the hydroelectric potential along the route. The Ontario and Quebec governments, Ontario Hydro, and private hydroelectric power and railway interests combined to pressure the federal government to kill the project in 1927, portraying the Siftons as seeking a monopoly to inflate their already vast fortune.

Sifton's health was in decline and he died of heart failure in New York City, where he had gone to consult a specialist, in 1929. He was buried on 19 April in Mount Pleasant Cemetery in Toronto. His estate, by the highest reckoning, which was that of the Ontario government seeking estate taxes, did not exceed $10 million; the family valued it at about one-third this amount. Either way, much of it was tied up in the value of the *Manitoba Free Press*. Sifton was rich, but not the vastly wealthy robber baron portrayed in the popular press.

Sir Clifford Sifton was, and remains, a controversial figure. He never grasped the legitimate ambitions of French Canadians for equality of status. He was renowned for his mastery of machine politics and

Sims

patronage; charges of corruption – if never proven – dogged his entire career. At the same time he contributed significantly to the success of the Laurier government, to the settlement of western Canada, and to the development of the transportation and other infrastructure necessary for an integrated national economy. He always had a populist streak in his politics and a strong nationalist inclination in dealing with Great Britain and the United States. Perhaps he was not quite a statesman, but he was a politician of great vision and influence.

DAVID J. HALL

[The principal manuscript source for this study is the Sifton papers at LAC, MG 27, II, D15. The collection is substantially complete for Sifton's political career from 1896 to 1905, but is sketchier for his earlier and later life and for his business investments. It contains almost nothing on his private family life or his personal interests. Also of critical importance are the following collections at the LAC: Macdonald papers (MG 26, A), Laurier papers (MG 26, G), Borden papers (MG 26, H), King papers (MG 26, J), and Dafoe papers (MG 30, D45). There is a small collection of Sifton papers at the AM (MG 14, B41), which also houses the important Greenway papers (GR 1662) and Schultz papers (MG 12, E). The Univ. of Man. Libraries, Dept. of Arch. and Special Coll. (Winnipeg), holds the valuable J. W. Dafoe fonds. A selection of letters between Dafoe and Sifton during the last decade of Sifton's life was edited by Ramsay Cook and published as *The Dafoe–Sifton correspondence, 1919–1927* (Altona, Man., 1966).

There are two principal biographies of Sifton. The first is a fine, sympathetic work by his long-time friend and confidant, J. W. Dafoe, *Clifford Sifton in relation to his times* (Toronto, 1931). The other is the author's study, *Clifford Sifton* (2v., Vancouver and London, 1981–85). The second of the two volumes contains a full bibliography, including a list of Sifton's writings. Two more recent works that are important in understanding Sifton's career are Réal Bélanger, *Wilfrid Laurier; quand la politique devient passion* (Québec et Montréal, 1986), and M. F. Girard, *L'écologisme retrouvé: essor et déclin de la Commission de la conservation du Canada: 1909–1921* (Ottawa, 1994). D.J.H.]

SIMS, LOUISA (Rogers), newspaper proprietor; m. James Richard Rogers, and they had a son and a daughter; left Toronto in 1925.

Nothing is known of Louisa Sims's life before she and J. R. Rogers, a London compositor, emigrated from England to East London (Republic of South Africa), where their first child, Frank Arthur James, was born in August 1906. Early in 1910 the family left South Africa, stopped briefly in England, and came on to Toronto, where J. R. Rogers gained employment with the Methodist Book Room. In less than two months tragedy struck. Their son developed a mild case of diphtheria, and, because they lived in a boarding house, they were required to send him to the Isolation Hospital. On 30 June 1910 he died there of complications arising from exposure to scarlet fever and measles. Grief and indignation at the response of medical and civic officials to his concerns about the hospital propelled J. R. Rogers into the public arena. His complaints, once reported in the press, triggered an inquiry. By the time judge John Winchester had reported to city council in late November, exonerating the hospital staff and Charles SHEARD, the city's medical officer of health, Rogers had become an amateur authority on infectious diseases and public health. To draw attention to their crusade, on 29 July 1911 he and Louisa published the first issue of *Jack Canuck*, a biweekly tabloid that unexpectedly found a niche in the Toronto newspaper world, where notions of virtuous journalism held sway. Through the fall of 1911 *Jack Canuck* would run articles on pure water, excessive levels of infant mortality, smallpox vaccinations, the Toronto inquiry, and other investigations conducted by Winchester.

The paper was a family affair, launched "without a dollar of capital. It was edited sometimes in the kitchen, sometimes in the cellar." As a review of "what the public say, do and think," it largely lived up to its motto, Truth and Justice. The first months' issues bristled with allegations of capitalist exploitation (especially of young working women), the betrayal of public trust by civic officials, and calls for reform so passionately felt that R. Rogers (as J. R. signed himself) relinquished the editorship for November 1911, recognizing that "the constant stare of a vacant chair in the home has made us bitter . . . too bitter to render the public service this journal should render." He recovered and set about to create "a wild and earthy weekly," evoking the formula pioneered in London, England, by Henry Du Pré Labouchere's *Truth*. Weekly publication began on 24 Feb. 1912. Louisa was the legal owner and thus the vendor when, buoyed by their success, the Rogerses in October incorporated the Jack Canuck Publishing Company Limited, which bought the paper.

Various local journalists contributed to *Jack Canuck*, notably Harry Milner Wodson. To cultivate a national circulation, Rogers relied on out-of-town stringers, or correspondents, whose use meant some loss of editorial control. Sensationalism was the style, a matter as much of tone as content. Stringers and muckraking both carried the risk of libel action, however, and the Rogerses faced their share. As well, there were the self-styled guardians of public morality, among them the Reverend Thomas Albert Moore*, who occasionally complained to provincial authorities about the paper's corrupting influence. *Jack Canuck* nevertheless attracted a steady cross-class readership. Sales depended heavily on newsboys and news-stands, though subscriptions were encouraged – even the Senate's reading room in Ottawa subscribed. Over the years, there would always be the causes of

948

the moment along with the police-court stories, the personal trivia, the mining-stock tips, and innumerable odds and ends. The appeal to readers for articles or letters – an often contrived and well-worn device to encourage loyalty – may have elicited the infamous racist diatribes against the "Yellow Peril" penned for *Jack Canuck* in 1911–12 by Fred Jarrett. Editorial sympathies, notionally politically independent but resoundingly populist, could waver on particular issues. The most notable instance occurred during the moral panic of 1911–13 over the so-called white slave trade, when the paper printed excerpts from the Reverend John George SHEARER's chapter in *Fighting the traffic in young girls . . .* (Chicago, 1911) but then exposed the book's local promoter, the Reverend Robert B. St Clair, superintendent of the Toronto Vigilance Association. *Jack Canuck* gleefully reported St Clair's trial for publishing obscene material in an attempt to censor a local burlesque show.

From the outset of World War I *Jack Canuck*, ever the crusader against corruption and its attendant, lax government regulation, fought war profiteering. Determined to report first-hand on battlefield conditions for the Canadian forces in France, J. R. Rogers lost his life when the *Lusitania* was torpedoed on 7 May 1915. The paper continued, with Louisa's name discreetly replacing her husband's in the masthead. After the war, she bought a house and lived comfortably with her young daughter, Thelma. Contributors such as cartoonist Jack Newton became mainstays, the paper attracted reputable local and national advertising, and, with its modest market in urban centres throughout Ontario, western Canada, and the northern United States, circulation figures appeared healthy. An average weekly run of 65,000 copies in the immediate post-war period placed the paper well ahead of the prominent *Saturday Night* (Toronto). By 1919 *Jack Canuck* was championing such serious causes as fair employment for veterans. Although it revived its editorial irreverence in the early 1920s, with biting cartoons and moments of vitriolic commentary at election time, the intelligent, focused passion of the pre-war years was gone. Louisa, an admitted arm's-length publisher, was rudely confronted with the truth that print-run did not secure commercial success – the key remained minimizing the return of unsold papers. After a couple of years of "very little" profit, the final issue appeared on 13 Sept. 1924 and a printer's suit for $2,000 forced Jack Canuck Publishing to file for bankruptcy in January 1925. In short order, Louisa sold her house, settled the bankruptcy, and left Toronto, apparently for Florida. As early as August 1926 her solicitors were unable to locate her. Compensation for the loss of her husband was sent in 1931 to a lawyer in Toronto, but there is no conclusive evidence that she was alive at the time.

The brash little paper that Louisa Rogers and her husband had launched in 1911 played a formative role in the emerging culture of English-language tabloid journalism centred in Toronto. The endearing trusting face that *Jack Canuck*, in its quest for Truth and Justice, turned to the world and its transgressions soon seemed dated. But as the tabloid press of each successive era exploited the sordid and the seamy, it battered conventional, class-based notions of privacy and public interest and, as a consequence, contradicted the assumptions of objectivity and news that underlie modern journalistic culture.

SUSAN E. HOUSTON and PATRICK J. CONNOR

Copies of *Jack Canuck* for 1911–12, 1914–17, 1921, and 1923 can be found at the AO. Issues published between 26 May and 23 June 1923 are in the Univ. of Toronto Library, Thomas Fisher Rare Book Library. The City of Toronto Arch. holds *Jack Canuck Illustrated Review of the War: the Harvest* (1914) in the Jack Canuck fonds (SC 251), and issues from 1916 and 1917 are in the Larry Becker collection (fonds 70).

AO, RG 4-32, 1910, interim box 10; 1915, file 753; RG 22-305, no.30063; RG 22-392, box 183, file 6741; RG 22-5800, 1919, nos.1167, 1176, 1635; RG 22-5822, 4, no.18/25; RG 55-1, liber 142: f.93. City of Toronto Arch., RG 1, B-2, box 6 (1910); RG 5, D, box 10, files 3, 5. LAC, RG 117, 37, file 490, case 1606. *Evening Telegram* (Toronto), 11 Feb. 1913, 8 May 1915. *Globe*, 9–10 May 1915. *Hamilton Spectator*, 5 Sept., 7 Nov. 1913. *News* (Toronto), 8, 10 May 1915. *Toronto Daily Star*, 27–29 July 1910. *World* (Toronto), 11 Feb. 1913, 8 May 1915. S. E. Houston, "'A little steam, a little sizzle and a little sleaze': English-language tabloids in the interwar period," Biblio. Soc. of Canada, *Papers* (Toronto), 40 (2002): 37–60. Madge Pon, "Like a Chinese puzzle: the construction of Chinese masculinity in *Jack Canuck*," in *Gender and history in Canada*, ed. Joy Parr and Mark Rosenfeld (Toronto, 1996), 88–100. Dan Schiller, *Objectivity and the news: the public and the rise of commercial journalism* (Philadelphia, 1981). Bill Sloan, *"I watched a wild hog eat my baby!": a colorful history of tabloids and their cultural impact* (Amherst, N.Y., 2001).

SINCLAIR, ALEXANDER MᴀᴄLEAN, Presbyterian minister, author, Gaelic scholar, and educator; b. 1 March 1840 in Glen Bard, N.S., son of John Sinclair and Christy MacLean; m. 1 Aug. 1882 Mary Ann Campbell in Sunny Brae, N.S., and they had four sons and one daughter; d. 14 Feb. 1924 in Hopewell, N.S.

Alexander MacLean Sinclair's parents, both immigrants from Scotland, separated before his birth. Christy Sinclair was a daughter of the renowned Gaelic bard Iain MacGhillEathain* (John MacLean), and the child was apparently named after Alexander MacLean of Coll, who in Scotland had been the bard's patron. Young Alexander was raised by his mother at her parents' home in Glen Bard in a thoroughly Gaelic milieu; he rarely saw his father.

From an early age he attended the local school in Beaver Meadow under the tutelage of Norman Mac-

Donald, who had immigrated to Nova Scotia in 1843. The late Donald Cameron, who was raised in Beaver Meadow, recalled Sinclair telling him in Gaelic that on wintry days in his boyhood he would walk home from school behind his friend William MacDonald, whose large frame – "he had shoulders as wide as a gate" – would shelter him from blowing snow. At the school only English was used and Gaelic was not permitted even during recess. The boy learned to read the language by means of the Lord's Prayer, which he knew by heart in Gaelic.

School was not the only place where young Alexander received his education. "My other teachers," he recalled, "were two near neighbours: John MacDonald, an Taillear Abrach [the Lochaber tailor], and John MacDonald, an Domhnullach Ur [the new MacDonald]. . . . The one could not read at all; the other certainly was not a reader of historical books. But they both had a number of stories of ghosts, strong Highlanders, and clan feuds; they also had bits of old Gaelic songs by heart. I listened to them many a night and became pretty well acquainted with all their lore." In addition to his studies he spent his time in outdoor pursuits: hunting, fishing, trapping, and snaring. "The first money I ever received was from mink skins," he noted in his diary. During these years the family attended religious services at Barneys River (Kenzieville), where the minister was the Reverend Duncan Black Blair, a renowned Gaelic scholar and poet.

By age 15 Sinclair was sufficiently accomplished to be given the charge of 90 students at the schoolhouse in Lochaber, for which he was to receive an annual stipend of $120. In 1856 he began his preparation for the ministry by entering Pictou Academy. He enrolled three years later at the Free Church College in Halifax and in 1861 at the Normal School in Truro, from which he graduated as a teacher. He taught a summer term in 1862 at Canning, where he delivered a lecture on education that was highly acclaimed. In 1863 he entered the Theological Hall of the Presbyterian Church in Halifax and attended courses in chemistry and political economy at Dalhousie College. He was licensed to preach by Blair after a rigorous examination before the Presbytery of Pictou on 2 May 1866. He took up his first charge, Springville and Sunny Brae, on 25 July 1866. He would remain with this congregation, preaching in Gaelic and English, for the next 22 years.

Along with his dedication to the ministry, Sinclair had a lifelong devotion to the Gaelic language. As early as 1862 a ten-stanza Gaelic poem of his had appeared in the Antigonish *Casket* under the signature "A. McG. Sinclair, Gleann-Bard." In 1863 he contributed a biographical account of his grandfather MacLean to the Halifax edition of John Mackenzie's *Sàr-obair nam bàrd Gaelach: or, the beauties of Gaelic poetry, and lives of the Highland bards . . .*

(Glasgow, 1841) that was published by his former teacher, Norman MacDonald. In 1869 he journeyed to Scotland, Ireland, England, and France. In Scotland he met his grandfather's relatives and wrote down from their dictation in Gaelic a considerable amount of genealogical and literary information. His travels there convinced him that those who had emigrated to Canada and their descendants were far better off than those who had stayed in Scotland.

Throughout the 1870s Sinclair continued to collect Gaelic poetry, such as the poem "An adharc [The horn]" by his grandfather which he wrote down in 1873 from the oral recitation of Mary Forbes of Beaver Meadow and which would otherwise have been lost. He also developed an interest in local history. In 1874 he took extensive notes from Finlay Grant of accounts of the early history of the East River region. During this time he worked assiduously on the two important Gaelic manuscripts that his grandfather had brought from Scotland. The first of these was written in the 18th century by Dr Hector Maclean and was given to the bard by Maclean's daughter. It contains some 3,600 lines of poetry, much of which is unknown from other sources. The other manuscript was the bard's own collection, which, according to Sinclair, "contains about 17,700 lines, exclusive of the collector's own poems."

In 1880 Sinclair reissued a collection of the Gaelic hymns of John MacLean and included hymns by Blair, the Reverend James Drummond MacGregor*, and John MacGillivray. The following year he published *Clàrsach na coille* [Harp of the forest], which presents MacLean's secular poetry, both the material composed in Scotland and that written in Nova Scotia, in addition to a few items by other poets, including the bard's son Charles and Sinclair himself. This was the first important collection of Gaelic secular poetry largely composed in Canada. For several years Sinclair conducted a Gaelic-language column in the *Pictou News*. The first sentence of the initial column on 7 Dec. 1883 decries the lack of a Gaelic newspaper in Canada.

In the 1880s Sinclair received offers from a number of congregations and in May 1888 he accepted the pastoral charge of Belfast, P.E.I., where descendants of many of the Selkirk settlers of 1803 [see James Williams*] still kept the Gaelic language and traditions alive. Throughout the following decade and the early years of the 20th century, while attending to his congregation, Sinclair published substantial collections of Gaelic poetry and a number of genealogical studies. These include *Comhchruinneachadh Ghlinn-a-Bhaird: the Glenbard collection of Gaelic poetry* (Charlottetown and Montreal, 1890); *The Gaelic bards from 1411 to [1715]* (Charlottetown, 1890); *The Gaelic bards from 1715 to 1765* (Charlottetown, 1892); *Orain le Iain Lom Mac-Dhomhnaill: poems by*

John Lom MacDonald (Antigonish and Glasgow, 1895); *The Gaelic bards from 1775 to 1825* (Sydney, N.S., 1896); *Na bàird Leathanach: the Maclean bards* (2v., Charlottetown, 1898–1900); *The Clan Gillean* (Charlottetown, 1899); *The Sinclairs of Roslin, Caithness, and Goshen* (Charlottetown, 1901); *Mactalla nan tùr* [Echo of the towers] (Sydney, 1901); *Filidh na coille* [Poet of the forest] . . . (Charlottetown, 1901); *Dain agus orain, le Alasdair Mac-Fhionghain* [Poems and songs, by Alexander MacKinnon] (1902); and *The Gaelic bards from 1825 to 1875* (Sydney, 1904). He also contributed important articles to the *Transactions* of the Gaelic Society of Inverness in Scotland, the *Celtic Review* (Edinburgh) and the *Celtic Monthly* (Glasgow). He published essays in other journals as well and in such newspapers as the *Oban Times* (Oban, Scot.), the *Eastern Chronicle* (New Glasgow, N.S.), the *Presbyterian Witness* (Halifax, etc.), and the *Casket*.

Sinclair retired from his charge in 1906 and returned to Nova Scotia. For several years between 1907 to 1914 he lectured on Gaelic language and literature in the fall semesters at St Francis Xavier College in Antigonish and in the winter semesters at Dalhousie. Manuscript notes of some of his lectures reveal his solid knowledge of comparative Indo-European philology. (Sinclair used the term "Indo-Keltic" just as German philologists used the term "Indo-Germanic.") Among his students at St Francis Xavier were Angus Lewis Macdonald*, later premier of Nova Scotia, and Patrick Joseph Nicholson, who became president of the university and an important supporter of the Gaelic language both there and in his weekly Gaelic article in the *Casket*. Sinclair received an honorary LLD degree from Dalhousie in 1914.

On 14 Feb. 1924, just two weeks before his 84th birthday, Sinclair passed away at his home in Hopewell. He was survived by his wife, whom he had married in an all-Gaelic service more than 40 years earlier, and by all of his five children. He will be remembered as a pioneer in the field of Celtic studies in Nova Scotia and Prince Edward Island. His publications brought to the world nearly all the material in the manuscripts of Dr Hector Maclean and John MacLean. Although modern critics may find fault with the way in which he sometimes "improved" his sources, it should be taken into account that he was a self-made Gaelic scholar who had no formal training in the subject. His promotion of Gaelic language and literature earned for him the respect of contemporary Celtic scholars throughout the world.

KENNETH E. NILSEN

Sinclair's university lecture notes are preserved in the Father Charles Brewer Celtic Coll. at St Francis Xavier Univ. Library, Antigonish, N.S. His collection of the hymns of John MacLean and others was published in Edinburgh as *Dain spioradail. . . . Clàrsach na coille: a collection of Gaelic poetry* was revised and edited by Hector MacDougall and published in Glasgow in 1928 as *The MacLean songster: Clàrsach na coille . . .* ; this edition includes a "Memoir" of Sinclair by his son Donald Maclean. In addition to the works mentioned in the text, Sinclair published "A collection of Gaelic poems" in the *Trans.* of the Gaelic Soc. of Inverness (Inverness, Scot.), 26 (1904–7): 235–62. It should be noted that his volume *Mactalla nan tùr* fills the gap, 1765–75, in his Gaelic bards series.

Casket (Antigonish), 1851–2001. *Morning Herald* (Halifax), 3 Aug. 1882. *Pictou News* (Pictou, N.S.), 1883–86. [Sagart Arisaig (Ronald McGillivray)], *History of Antigonish*, ed. R. A MacLean (2v., [Antigonish], 1976). D. M. Sinclair, "Some family history" (typescript, Halifax, 1979; copy in NSARM Library).

SINCLAIR, DAVID VOLUME, merchant, politician, and temperance advocate; b. 10 June 1864 in Madoc, Upper Canada, eldest son of Peter Sinclair, a harness maker, and Agnes Volume; m. Hettie Miller Reed of Nova Scotia, and they had four daughters and a son; d. 20 Aug. 1922 in Belleville, Ont.

David V. Sinclair moved from Madoc to Belleville in his teens to find employment as a clerk in a dry goods store. He later established his own store, which he was to operate until his death, sometimes with a partner. A kindly employer, he would leave bequests to his staff in his will. In addition, he became extraordinarily active in the community as a member of the Board of Trade, Lions Club, school board, and city council, but he poured most of his enthusiasm into causes related to his Christian faith.

A member of John Street Presbyterian Church, he was for many years superintendent of its Sunday school, as well as clerk of the session, member of the board of managers, and delegate to the General Assembly. His involvement in the Young Men's Christian Association was even greater. Over the years he served in all of its volunteer positions, including that of president; his main contribution seems to have been in the management of its finances.

Not surprisingly, Sinclair was an advocate of Prohibition. In the provincial election of 1914 he ran as an independent temperance candidate in Hastings West but was defeated. Then, in 1921, he was elected president of the leading temperance organization in the province, the Ontario branch of the Dominion Alliance for the Total Suppression of the Liquor Traffic. His election, just years after the branch had brought Prohibition to Ontario, must have seemed a capping moment for this small-city activist, but it was not the success it appeared to be. He had not been prominent within the branch; even close to home his accomplishments were more worthy than significant. Why then would a body that had to deal with important figures, at both the provincial and the federal levels, turn to him? The answer lies within the structure of the branch and the state of its finances.

Like many volunteer organizations, it was dominated by its professional staff, based in Toronto. The key staffer was its combative secretary, the Reverend Benjamin H. Spence, who had held the position since 1907. Under the circumstances it would have taken a strong president to be more than decorative. Members of the executive were additionally out of touch because they met only three or four times a year; those from outside the Toronto–Hamilton region often could not attend. It was difficult too for Sinclair to participate on committees that normally met in Toronto. Moreover, the branch was suffering financial and organizational woes. After Prohibition had been achieved, in 1916, popular support declined. But the costs of maintaining staff and fighting referenda on temperance matters remained high, so that the branch fell into debt. Finally, it had to struggle for place with the rival Ontario Referendum Committee, under the Reverend Andrew Shaw Grant.

By 1921 the branch was thus unattractive to anyone who might be a prominent and forceful candidate for president. (Spence would likely not have encouraged such a candidate.) So it was that Sinclair quietly became president on 24 Feb. 1921, at the branch's annual convention in Toronto. His subsequent impact appears to have been minimal, even during the heated campaign that spring over the referendum on importing liquor into Ontario. The branch continued its decline, and Sinclair's name rarely appears in records of executive or committee meetings. The weak condition of the branch was underscored by the fact that the single name put forward to succeed him as president was nominated without the candidate's permission or knowledge. At the poorly attended convention held a few months after Sinclair's death in August 1922, his name was only briefly mentioned.

David V. Sinclair's obituary in the Belleville *Daily Intelligencer* in August 1922 praises him largely in terms of his service to the local community. This assessment seems fair.

GRAEME DECARIE

AO, F 834, ser.A, files 14–15, 17, 20; RG 22-340, no.6346. YMCA of Belleville, Ont., Records. *Daily Intelligencer* (Belleville), 21–22 Aug. 1922. G. A. Hallowell, *Prohibition in Ontario, 1919–1923* (Ottawa, 1972).

SKILL, LEONARD JAMES, bookseller; b. 15 Dec. 1864 at Camsix Farm, near Felsted, England, fourth of the six children of Charles James Skill, a farmer, and Harriet Eliza Leonard (Lennard); m. 2 Sept. 1895 Minnie Stephens in Woodstock, Ont.; they had no children; d. 6 Jan. 1923 in Toronto.

Raised in England, with an elementary education,

Leonard Skill immigrated to Canada in 1890. An uncle, Henry Herbert Skill, had settled in Cobourg, Ont., in 1883 following his retirement from the British army. Leonard first appears in Toronto directories in 1900. Beginning in 1901 he worked for William Clarke as treasurer and then manager of the Globe Library Club (publishers' agents) and Clarke's publishing and importing business. In early 1905 he opened the Toronto Antiquarian Book Company, with an inventory of some 18,000 rare and second-hand volumes. Skill purchased private libraries, issued monthly catalogues to customers in Canada and the United States, and earned a respectable reputation among the many established politicians, businessmen, and clergy who were his patrons. In addition to the standard antiquarian fare of history, biography, and belles-lettres, the company offered more explicit and "realistic" works, principally translations of Greek, Latin, and modern Continental literature.

In 1907 the bookstore fell under the scrutiny of the Reverend John George SHEARER of Toronto and Anthony Comstock, the famed American vice crusader and postal inspector. Comstock complained frequently that Skill was forwarding immoral literature and advertising through the United States mail. Shipments of books from Skill's Paris suppliers were consequently subjected to repeated confiscations by Canadian postal and customs officials in 1907 and 1908. On 29 June 1909, equipped with a search warrant and reports from Comstock, post-office inspector James Henderson and Toronto morality police seized more than a dozen books, including unexpurgated translations of Balzac, Barbey d'Aurevilly, Brantôme, Flaubert, Hector France, Loti, and Petronius Arbiter, as well as 7,000 catalogues allegedly employing "language manifestly intended to commend them to the prurient mind." Skill and his store manager, John Campbell King, were charged with selling, and posting circulars advertising, literature "tending to corrupt morals."

Represented by Hugh Edward Rose and James Walter Curry respectively, Skill and King pleaded not guilty at the preliminary hearing on 14 July before magistrate Rupert Etherege Kingsford*. Among the witnesses called by prosecutor Herbert Hartley DEWART (filling in for crown attorney John William Seymour Corley) were Henderson, to whom Skill admitted having mailed the catalogues; George Herbert Locke*, head of the Toronto Public Library, who testified the books were "unfit for circulation"; and Arthur Jukes JOHNSON, Toronto's chief coroner, who dismissed Brantôme as "lewd" and Barbey d'Aurevilly as "absolutely foul." The defence argued that the booksellers had no criminal intent and that the books, which possessed more literary merit than others previously accorded the court's sanction, had been sold without restriction for years. The fact that they were published in limited editions, and cost between $20 and $30 in a market where popular writers such as Charles William Gordon* (Ralph Connor) sold for 50 cents, limited their appeal to collectors and prevented their general circulation. Moreover, Curry argued, books which might, if sold to the general public, be deemed objectionable, were not so when placed in the hands of physicians, professionals, or scholars. In the end Kingsford found sufficient evidence to commit Skill and King to trial.

Following several delays, and sensing perhaps that the books were indefensible by contemporary standards, Skill and King changed their pleas to guilty on 20 December. On 3 Jan. 1910 they received a scathing reprimand from judge John Winchester, who maintained that no court could justify having the books read aloud to a jury, the "filth" being so great that "they would never get clear of it, no matter how long they lived." Skill and King were each sentenced to a year in the Central Prison in Toronto.

The federal minister of justice, Allen Bristol Aylesworth*, received applications and petitions urging clemency from more than two dozen prominent businessmen and clergy familiar with the prisoners. He reviewed the books, some of which he deemed to be classics, and discussed the case with provincial attorney general James Joseph Foy. Upon Aylesworth's advice to Governor General Lord Grey*, Skill and King were pardoned and, on 4 March, released. Forced to justify his action in parliament, Aylesworth declared that both men had engaged in "the ordinary legitimate business of respectable book selling" and that, in his judgement as a lawyer, they were not guilty.

The pardons aroused an almost unprecedented degree of outrage among reformers and their political allies. The secular press, led by the Toronto *Globe* in a series of blistering editorials, accused Aylesworth of being "a traitor to private decency and national character" for sanctioning the expression of "the grossest unnatural sensuality." Religious conservatives denounced him for "sodomizing" Canada. Vociferous protests and demands for his resignation were lodged by such groups as the Moral and Social Reform Council of Canada, various Presbyterian, Methodist, and Baptist church bodies, and the Canadian Press Association.

The Reverend James Alexander MACDONALD, editor of the *Globe*, privately warned Sir Wilfrid Laurier* in April that "there is more political gunpowder in this than in almost anything else that has come up of late" and urged that translations of authors such as Brantôme be "absolutely forbidden." In a rare venture into literary criticism, the prime minister argued that Brantôme's object was to provoke mirth, not passion, and his work should not be considered "half so dangerous for youth as some other books of almost daily circulation," including Shakespeare. Did Macdonald,

he wondered, really desire an *index expurgatorius* within the Presbyterian Church?

Despite considerable pressure and embarrassment to the government, Laurier refused to censure or dismiss his friend and minister, while Aylesworth vowed that "if the same thing were to be considered over again, . . . I should act in exactly the way in which I have acted throughout." For his part, Skill soon parted company with his store manager. He renamed his shop the Toronto Book Company in 1911, and continued to own and operate it, apparently without further incident, until he was struck and killed by an automobile in 1923. He was buried in Hillview Cemetery in Woodstock.

Skill's conviction provides a rare glimpse into the mechanisms used to suppress "objectionable" books in early-20th-century Canada. Reform organizations had initiated many such campaigns since the 1890s and typically received the cooperation of authorities, notably the Post Office and Customs departments. The Skill case, however, is memorable for the literary merit of the books involved and the extraordinary controversy it generated following federal intervention.

S. CRAIG WILSON

AO, RG 22-5871, box 2698, S-145–47/1909. LAC, MG 26, G: 170156–59, 170168–69, 170300–7, 170318–21, 170397–402; MG 28, I 327, box 29, Moral and Social Reform Council of Canada, minutes of the annual meeting, 23 Sept. 1910: 20–25 (published as *The release of Skill and King, infra*); RG 31, C1, 1901, Toronto, Ward 6, div.7: 15 (mfm. at AO). *Daily Mail and Empire*, April–May 1910. *Globe*, July 1909, April–May 1910. *World* (Toronto), July 1909, April–May 1910. Can., House of Commons, *Debates*, 1910. *Directory*, Toronto, 1900–23. Moral and Social Reform Council of Canada, Executive Committee, *The release of Skill and King: immoral book vendors . . .* ([Toronto, 1910]; copy in UCC-C). Toronto Antiquarian Book Company, *Catalogue of an interesting collection of miscellaneous books* (Toronto), nos.1 (February 1905)–34 (1909) (copies in Univ. of Toronto Library, Thomas Fisher Rare Book Library).

SLEEMAN, GEORGE, brewer, sportsman, and politician; b. 1 Aug. 1841 in St Davids, Upper Canada, son of John Sleeman and Ann M. Burrows; m. 7 Sept. 1863 Sarah Hill in Guelph, Upper Canada, and they had seven sons and five daughters; d. there 16 Dec. 1926.

John Sleeman immigrated from Cornwall, England, in 1836 and moved to Guelph in 1847. Educated in St Davids and Guelph, George Sleeman always had "big plans" for his father's small Silver Creek Brewery, which he joined in 1859 as general manager. Named a partner in 1865, he increased production by introducing steam power, adding a malthouse, and building a storage cellar; distribution was extended through a sales outlet in Dundas operated by his brother William. He added a porter to his father's ale and sold both at lower prices than their chief competitor, Thomas Holliday's Guelph Brewery.

By 1868, after Sleeman had taken over ownership following his father's return to St Davids, Silver Creek dominated the Guelph market. Sleeman's genius lay in innovation, such as his introduction of bisulphate of soda (a stabilizer and preservative) in 1874 and his invention that year of an attemperator that allowed greater control of the brewing process, lowered labour costs, and enabled him to make lager. As well, he vertically integrated all aspects of production and distribution. By 1890 he was the most highly capitalized brewer in Ontario, with outlets in 15 cities and towns from Sault Ste Marie to Quebec. Such development was enhanced by the province's growing population, the rise in beer consumption from 2.5 gallons per person in 1871 to 5.1 in 1893, and the spread of railways. In 1900 Sleeman, his wife, and three sons incorporated the operation as the Sleeman Brewing and Malting Company Limited.

George Sleeman was just as entrepreneurial in sports. He loved baseball, taking it up as a pitcher for the Maple Leaf Base Ball Club when the game was introduced to Guelph in 1863. The team quickly became a source of civic pride, with hundreds of fans following it to competitions in southern Ontario and the United States [see Thomas Goldie*]. In 1869 the Maple Leafs won the Canadian championship, defeating teams from Ingersoll and Woodstock in a three-day tournament in London. They would remain the dominant team in Ontario for another seven years. As a chief organizer and financial backer of the club – he was elected its president in 1874 – Sleeman was one of the earliest managers to import Americans to play; he kept them happy by giving them a share of the end-of-season surplus. These developments marked the beginning of professional team sports in Canada. Such a strengthened Maple Leaf team won a tournament in 1874 in Watertown, N.Y., which its organizers called "the non-professional championship of the world." Two years later Sleeman began to pay players salaries and encourage others to do the same in the newly formed Canadian Association of Base Ball Players, of which he was president. Ironically, these steps paved the way for the Americanization of the game and the competitive decline of the small-town clubs. After 1886, when Toronto and Hamilton joined the International League, Sleeman's team lost money and was disbanded. In 1999 he would be inducted into the Canadian Baseball Hall of Fame and Museum in recognition of his contributions.

Beyond baseball, Sleeman was prominent in the Guelph Turf Club, the Guelph Bicycle Club, and the Guelph Rifle Association, serving each as president, and he helped found the Royal City Curling Club in 1888. One of the first to link beer to sports, in the 1870s he sponsored (and occasionally pitched for) an amateur baseball team named after his brewery, the Silver Creek Club. He advertised that "Sleeman's lager is the best on the continent" in the turf club's racing programs and donated trophies to the curling club, the rifle association, and the Thanksgiving Day road races.

Ambition, the recognition that sports brought, and the need to protect his market against Prohibition propelled Sleeman into local politics. In 1876 he was elected a councillor for South Ward. When the town became a city in 1880 he was its first mayor, a position he held until 1882 and again in 1892 and 1905–6. As mayor, he contributed to Guelph's growth as an industrial centre and was a strong proponent, during his third term, of bringing Ontario Hydro to Guelph [see Sir Adam BECK]. Though respected as a quiet, efficient financial manager, he could be flamboyantly combative when his business interests were at stake. In 1877, 1885, and 1889 he had led the forces against campaigns that sought to ban the local sale of alcohol. After a resounding victory in the referendum of 1877, the antis paraded behind a float bearing a man dressed as Gambrinus, the Greek god of beer. Sleeman danced along with a broom, proclaiming the sweep of the Prohibitionists out of Wellington County. Such displays, along with sports and politics, were not his only forums for recognition: he was prominent too as an Anglican, a numismatist, and a treasurer of the Oddfellows' Progress Lodge.

Sleeman's civic attachment and love for technology almost cost him his brewery. In 1894, on his own, he started an electric streetcar operation, the Guelph Railway Company, to emulate services installed in Berlin (Kitchener) and Brantford. In its first year he installed five miles of track and though he planned to run the line to other towns, no one else was prepared to invest; the system never realized enough revenue to pay off the costs of construction. In 1902 the banks took over not only the railway but also Sleeman's house and Silver Creek plant. The following year the family started a small, rival operation, the Springbank Brewery. The banks, however, discovered that they could not run the big brewery, now unionized, without him, and in 1906 they sold it back to George Sleeman and Sons Limited. He promptly merged the two breweries and operated them until Prohibition forced him to stop making beer in 1916.

Following an operation for an obstructed bowel, Sleeman died on 16 Dec. 1926, two weeks after the election of a provincial government committed to the controlled sale of alcohol. At the end of a month of frenzied trading in Toronto of brewery and distillery interests, Sleeman's Springbank Brewery Company Limited was sold to a Toronto law firm and a son, Henry Oscar, resumed its operations. In 1933 the company was purchased by the Jockey Club Brewery Limited, and the Sleeman brand was discontinued.

The brewery became inactive in 1939. In 1985 a great-grandson, John Warren Sleeman, reincorporated it and reintroduced Sleeman's Cream Ale, brewed according to George's 19th-century recipe.

BRUCE KIDD

AO, RG 22-318, no.10989; RG 80-8-0-1047, no.36030; RG 80-27-2, 79: 120. Ontario Heritage Foundation (Toronto), Wellington County files, "Baseball in Ontario and the Guelph Maple Leafs." Univ. of Guelph Library, Arch. and Special Coll. (Guelph, Ont.), Sleeman coll. *Guelph Mercury*, 16 Dec. 1926. Gordon Hogarth, "When Maple Leafs first faced curves of pitcher Cummings," *Evening Telegram* (Toronto), 31 Oct. 1923: 31. Lisa Bowes, "George Sleeman and the brewing of baseball in Guelph, 1872–1886," *Historic Guelph: the Royal City* (Guelph), 27 (1987–88): 44–57. *Canadian annual rev.*, 1906. *Canadian men and women of the time* (Morgan; 1912). *Cyclopædia of Canadian biog.* (Rose and Charlesworth), vol.1. B. M. Durtnall, "Brewing beer and ale: working at Sleeman's and Holliday's," *Historic Guelph: the Royal City*, 38 (1999): 35–50. William Humber, *Diamonds of the north: a concise history of baseball in Canada* (Toronto, 1995). L. A. Johnson, *History of Guelph, 1827–1927* (Guelph, 1977). Harold Koch, "George Sleeman as I remember him," Guelph Hist. Soc., *Pubs.* ([Guelph?]), 14 (1974), no.3: 1–2. *Ontario Gazette* (Toronto), 1900: 371. Jarrett Rudy, "Sleeman's: small business in the Ontario brewing industry, 1847–1916" (MA thesis, Univ. of Ottawa, 1994). Tony Shaman, "Guelph's master brewers and mal[t]sters," *Historic Guelph: the Royal City*, 38: 23–32. Sleeman Brewing and Malting, *The family scrapbook* (Toronto, n.d.). "The Sleeman family," Guelph Hist. Soc., *Pubs.*, 14, no.2: 1–2. Steve Thorning, "Streetcars in Guelph: the history of the Guelph Radial Railway," *Historic Guelph: the Royal City*, 22 (1982–83): 4–40.

SMITH. *See also* BELL-SMITH

SMITH, GEORGE ROBERT, mining executive and politician; b. 17 Feb. 1860 in Newark, N.J., son of Benjamin Smith and Mary Ann Codmer; m. 3 March 1886 Isabella Frances Parker in Buckingham, Que., and they had five sons and two daughters; d. 20 Feb. 1922 in Thetford Mines, Que., and was buried in Sherbrooke, Que.

George Robert Smith took commercial courses in Newark and moved to Canada at the age of 16. Soon after his arrival he became interested in the mining industry. He began his career by working in the silver mines near Kingston, Ont. He then managed the mica, graphite, and phosphate mines belonging to William Anderson Allan near Buckingham from 1881 to 1886. From 1886 to 1892 he was a representative of the Ingersoll Rock Drill Company, an American enterprise that had a branch in Montreal during the 1890s. In this capacity he made frequent visits to the mining companies of the Eastern Townships and got to know various owners. His experience there was no doubt what prompted the Englishman John Bell to appoint him manager of his firm, Bell's Asbestos Company, in 1892. Smith now moved to Kingsville (Thetford Mines) and became the first of a long line of Smiths to hold a managerial position in this corporation. Following the purchase of Bell's Asbestos by the American firm of Keasbey and Mattison Company, Smith in 1906 became vice-president and manager of mining operations, positions he held for the rest of his life.

With his enterprising spirit and marked interest in mining, Smith was able to invent and improve equipment that greatly enhanced the reputation of what was commonly known as the Bell Mine, which was considered a leader in new technology. In 1893 it became the first in the world to own an asbestos reduction plant; this innovation was the result of work done by John J. Penhale (who had perfected the technique of milling asbestos for the mines at Black Lake) and extended by Smith. In 1893 and 1894 Smith also developed the notion of underground galleries to facilitate operations during the winter. In 1894 he invented the suction fan, driven by the motor of a steam-powered winch, which separated the fibre from the rock and graded it mechanically. It was an ingenious concept, and one that increased productivity. In 1906 the Bell Mine became one of the first enterprises of its kind to use a steam locomotive, another innovation attributable to Smith's creative genius. During his 30 years in management at the Bell Mine, Smith worked at progressively mechanizing the mining industry and improving its performance. As a result of mechanization 95 per cent of the ore could be milled at the mine itself, a total of about 500 tons a day, by 1894. Under Smith's leadership, the enterprise, which had between 450 and 500 employees, enjoyed a sound financial position and an excellent reputation around the world. The company's exports went mainly to the United States, but at the turn of the century, Great Britain, Belgium, France, and Germany became important customers for the Bell Mine.

Smith was involved in a number of activities related to mining. From 1895 he was one of the principal promoters of what became, in 1898, the Canadian Mining Institute. Founded following the success of the General Mining Association of the Province of Quebec [*see* Benjamin Taylor A. Bell*], it sought to ensure the protection and prosperity of mining companies in Quebec and the rest of Canada. In addition to being co-founder of the institute, Smith was its president from 1906 to 1907. In 1908 he moved to Montreal, where he remained long enough to set up, at the request of his superiors, a plant for manufacturing products made of asbestos (tiles, textiles, packaging material, brake linings). His brother William Henry replaced him at the Bell Mine, and George Robert became vice-president and general manager of the Asbestos Mining and Manufacturing Company, located in Lachine and owned by Keasbey and Mattison Company. In 1912 he had to return to Thetford Mines to supervise the work involved in enlarging the milling plant at the Bell Mine.

Besides devoting himself to professional activities, Smith belonged to a variety of associations, including the exclusive Montreal Club. He also served in the 11th Hussars, a cavalry regiment of the Canadian militia at Richmond, in which he held the rank of major and commanded a squadron until 1908. He spent his rare free time gardening or working at a small farm on his property in Thetford Mines, where he raised domestic animals, including horses, of which he was particularly fond.

Smith also had a career in politics. In the provincial election of 1897 he was returned as the Liberal member for the constituency of Mégantic, with a majority of 267. Since 1878 there had been a number of MLAs from the region, including George Irvine*, Andrew Stuart Johnson, and James King*, who had had an important role in the development of local mining enterprises, serving on their boards and looking out for their interests. Smith was re-elected by acclamation in 1900 and 1904, but was defeated in 1908. During his last term, he worked on the request for incorporation by the town of Thetford Mines. On 5 Jan. 1911 he was appointed legislative councillor for the division of Victoria, an office he retained until his death on 20 Feb. 1922. His funeral service was held in Thetford Mines. Before being interred in the Elmwood Cemetery in Sherbrooke, his coffin travelled more than 60 miles on a train crowded with people who had come to pay him their last respects.

George Robert Smith's appointment as vice-president and manager of the Bell Mine marked the beginning of a long family tradition with the company. From 1892 to 1972 the firm (which became Bell Asbestos Mines Limited in 1936) always had a member of the Smith family as president. The history of this man and his descendants exemplifies the control that Americans and English Canadians had over the asbestos industry in Quebec before it was nationalized by the province in 1978. It also illustrates all the efforts made by these men to develop the mining sector of the economy.

MARYSE BILODEAU

ANQ-O, ZQ127/25, 3 mars 1886. Musée Minéralogique et Minier de Thetford Mines, Qué., G. W. Smith, "La famille Smith et la Bell Asbestos Co. de 1892 à 1971" (texte dactylographié, 1972). *Le Devoir*, 21 févr. 1922. *Montreal Daily Herald*, 4 March 1905. *La Tribune* (Sherbrooke, Qué.), 21, 24 févr. 1922. Romain Dubé *et al.*, *Thetford Mines à ciel ouvert: histoire d'une ville minière, 1892–1992* (Thetford Mines, 1994). [Clément Fortier], *Black Lake: lac d'amiante, 1882–1982* (2v., s.l., 1983–86), 1. G. W. Smith, *Bell Asbestos Mines Ltd., 1878–1967* (n.p., 1968).

SMITH, GEORGE WASHINGTON, barber and news-vendor; b. 15 March 1845 in Charles Town (W.Va), son of Washington Smith and Sydney ——; m. 5 July 1866 Eliza Jane Campbell in Toronto, and they had two daughters and three sons; d. there 24 Dec. 1921.

George Washington Smith immigrated to Canada in 1864 at age 18 or 19, and settled in Toronto. Two years later he and Eliza Jane Campbell, a young black woman from Bowmanville, were married by Baptist minister Thomas Ford Caldicott*. By this time, Smith had already established an entrepreneurial presence, having started out on King Street as a barber. By 1871 he had a shop in the Queen's Hotel on Front Street, in addition to his Colossal Shaving Parlour at King and York streets. An advertisement in the city directory of 1874 promised patrons a "good refreshing bath" and "shampooing, shaving, and hairdressing done with neatness and civility." By this juncture Smith had clearly come into his own; his business was doing so well that he had set up shop at yet another location, the American Hotel at Yonge and Front.

Smith's success set a foundation from which he was able to prosper for some years. Between the mid 1870s and the turn of the century, the *Evening Telegram* would note at his death, he was "well known in downtown business circles." His barber-shops, which appeared at various times on Queen Street and in Union Station, with periodic returns to King Street, were evidently frequented by many of the city's business elite. According to the *Toronto Daily Star*, his economic presence simultaneously enabled him to become "prominent . . . in Toronto's political circles." Though generally a staunch Conservative, he supported Robert John FLEMING, a populist, Liberal-leaning mayor who ran on anti-business platforms that advocated workers' rights and temperance. His campaigns were also infused with undertones of racial and gender equality. Smith's affiliation with the Royal Templars of Temperance as well as his black identity likely drew him to Fleming, even though this position was arguably antithetical to his interests as a businessman. Taking to the stump in support of Fleming on several occasions between 1891 and 1897, Smith earned a reputation as an entertaining and compelling orator. His other associations helped cement his standing: he was a member of the Orange lodge, the Ancient Order of Foresters, and the York Pioneers. Thus, through his various affiliations, he became known as a leader of Toronto's "colored colony."

Despite his success, Smith found himself compelled to give up barbering around 1909 or 1910, likely because he had lost his sight and perhaps because of advancing age. The death in 1907 of his wife, who owned the family home, may also have affected his state of affairs. Eliza left her property to him and four children but stipulated in her will that

George was to take possession only after relinquishing all other claims to her estate. He managed to sustain himself as a newspaper dealer. The status he had enjoyed in earlier years can be gauged from the fact that his stand, at the northwest corner of Queen Street and Spadina Avenue, was, the *Globe* would recall, "the first permitted on the city corners."

Smith met a tragic end. On a cold December night in 1921 he reportedly fell against a hot stove in his news-stand. He was taken to Toronto Western Hospital, where, after 24 hours, he died of "shock following burns," an agonizing death for a blind man of 77 years. He was buried in Mount Pleasant Cemetery. The circumstances surrounding his passing made the city take note – the *Globe*, the *Star*, and the *Telegram* all ran brief chronicles of his life. Probate records indicate that his estate consisted of residential property, real estate, and Victory Bonds with a total value of $2,716.46, a figure that placed him in the ranks of the city's tiny black bourgeoisie. A lifelong Baptist, he left $150 to the Beverley Street Baptist Church.

George Washington Smith's life is intriguing. A relatively obscure figure in Canadian black history, he had nonetheless been known to contemporaries as a leader in Toronto's black community and, later, as a stock figure of sorts at street corners. Further research is needed, however, to determine whether he was widely seen as a leader by members of the black community or whether the mantle was a result of his associations with the city's white elite and the integrationist ethos that characterized much of his life. There is no doubt that, at his peak, Smith had managed to carve out a place for himself at a time when the majority of Toronto's "colored colony" struggled in the face of racial slurs, Jim Crowism, and residential, social, and occupational discrimination.

BARRINGTON WALKER

AO, RG 22-305, nos.19521, 44223; RG 80-2-0-89, no.36343; RG 80-2-0-156, no.41673; RG 80-2-0-226, no.42952; RG 80-8-0-804, no.7475; RG 80-27-2, 67: 1. City of Toronto Arch., RG 5, F, (assessment rolls), sub-ser.1, 1834–1951. *Evening Telegram* (Toronto), 28 Dec. 1891, 27 Dec. 1921. *Globe*, 27 Dec. 1921. *Toronto Daily Star*, 27 Dec. 1921. *Directories*, Ont., 1871; Toronto, 1867–1921.

SMITH, JANET KENNEDY, servant, diarist, and alleged murder victim; b. 25 June 1902 in Perth, Scotland, daughter of Arthur Mitchell Tooner Smith and Johanna Benzies; d. unmarried 26 July 1924 in Point Grey (Vancouver).

Janet Smith is best remembered for her suspicious death and the firestorm of controversy that surrounded it. She was born into a family of modest means in Perth, where her father was a railway fireman. Despite the title later given to her by the press, "the Scottish Nightingale," her ancestry was mixed: her father was of Irish, English, and Scottish descent, her mother was Norwegian. After the family moved to the working-class district of Lambeth (London), when Janet was 11, she finished school and obtained a certificate to be a nursemaid. In January 1923 Doreen and Frederick Lefevre Baker, a Vancouver couple who lived in Kensington, hired her to care for their newborn baby. When F. L. Baker's importing business took the family to Paris, she went with them. In October they returned to Vancouver and Janet Smith, enticed by a monthly salary of $30 and the promise of a return ticket, accompanied them.

They moved into a house in the city's fashionable West End, a location that gave Smith access to nearby Stanley Park, where she often took the baby for strolls. She apparently found it easy to meet members of Vancouver's bachelor community during such excursions, and soon developed relationships that ranged from flirtatious to serious.

The young woman's diary reveals her meditations on her sexuality and romantic adventures. Many entries are decidedly melodramatic: "Heavenly night, immense moon and nobody nice to love me"; others are cryptic: "I suppose I will always play with fire. I expect that is what the fortune teller meant when she said I have the girdle of Venus." Since she meant to return to England, she often scolded herself for leading men along, and seemed to be concerned about remaining a respectable girl. Such writings reveal her to be a more complex figure than the "young Scotswoman of blameless character" that the Vancouver press would later construct.

In May 1924 Smith moved with the Bakers into the home of F. L. Baker's brother, Richard Plunkett, in the elite Shaughnessy Heights neighbourhood of Point Grey (then a separate municipality south of Vancouver). There she worked alongside R. P. Baker's 25-year-old houseboy, Wong Foon Sing. The relationship between Smith and Wong would become the subject of much discussion after her death. Although her friends testified that she feared he would murder her, her diary reveals that Wong gave her intimate presents such as a silk nightdress and that she was well aware of the effect she had on him. She clearly enjoyed the knowledge that men loved her.

On the morning of 26 July 1924 her life came to a sudden end. Her body was found in the basement of the Baker home next to an ironing board. She had a bullet wound through her temple and a revolver lay near her outstretched hand. The Point Grey police also found suspicious burns on her arm and a stain on her finger. The only person in the house when the shooting allegedly occurred was Wong Foon Sing, who later testified that he had heard a noise like a car backfiring and went to the basement, only to find Smith dead. The police concluded that she had committed suicide and the Vancouver coroner, after a hasty inquest, held that she had suffered a "self-inflicted but accidental death."

These conclusions, however, were only the beginning. The unusual chain of events that followed would put the nursemaid's death into the headlines for months. Several of Smith's friends, refusing to believe the finding of suicide, enlisted the aid of Vancouver's United Council of Scottish Societies and Presbyterian church leaders concerned with the moral perils facing immigrant girls. The Scottish Societies sent telegrams to provincial attorney general Alexander Malcolm Manson demanding that the case be reopened. Ultimately it was Vancouver *Star* publisher Victor Wentworth Odlum* who proved to be the primary author of this murder mystery. The scandalous stories that he published about the "puzzling" death and apparent bungling by the police stirred up intense interest, and pointed to Wong Foon Sing as the likely culprit. Other Vancouver papers followed Odlum's lead and made Smith's death a cause célèbre.

Mounting public pressure led to the exhumation of her body on 28 August and a second inquest in September. After a week of sensational testimonies, the jury delivered the anticipated finding: Smith had been murdered. The Scottish Societies thereupon continued to press the government to find the perpetrator. Manson responded by hiring a special prosecutor, Malcolm Bruce Jackson, to determine what had happened to "the girl from the Old Country." The Scottish Societies also lobbied Vancouver MLA Mary Ellen Smith [Spear*] to introduce legislation to prohibit employers from hiring white women and Orientals as servants in the same household. In November Smith introduced the so-called Janet Smith Bill (in fact, an amendment to the Women's and Girls' Protection Act of 1923) but the bill died after Manson concluded that it would likely be found *ultra vires*.

The case largely disappeared from the newspapers until a shocking event occurred in Shaughnessy Heights. On 20 March 1925 a group of men dressed in Ku Klux Klan robes arrived at R. P. Baker's residence and abducted Wong Foon Sing. These men, later identified as operatives hired by the Scottish Societies and some off-duty constables, took Wong to a house where, for six weeks, they tortured him to confess or provide enough information to explain Smith's death. It was later revealed that Manson became aware of Wong's location but did nothing in the hope that the mystery would be solved. His inaction all but ended his promising political career.

On 1 May the kidnappers released Wong but the Point Grey police promptly arrested him for the murder of Janet Smith. He was defended at trial by John Harold Senkler, a prominent lawyer who had been retained by the Chinese Benevolent Association. In October the case was thrown out for lack of evidence, and Wong later returned to China. Three of his kidnappers were imprisoned for their role in the plot but others, including M. B. Jackson, Point Grey reeve James Alexander Paton, and two police commissioners, were acquitted.

By the time of Wong's kidnapping and arrest, other explanations had emerged. The most popular theory was that Smith had been raped and murdered at a "wild party" held at the Baker house by playboy bachelors, who then bribed the police and the coroners. More recently writer Edward Starkins has made the case that F. L. Baker was a drug-smuggler and that his activities played a substantial part in the young woman's demise.

The death of Janet Smith, whether by suicide or murder, remains significant because of the public debate that surrounded it. Popular narratives of the incident speak volumes about the concepts of race, class, gender, and law and order dominant in the British Columbia of the 1920s. The mystery was not mere tabloid fodder but, rather, social drama that led Vancouverites to ask complex questions about their city and province. Janet Smith is buried in Mountain View Cemetery in Vancouver beneath a headstone purchased by the United Council of Scottish Societies.

SCOTT KERWIN

General Register Office for Scotland (Edinburgh), Reg. of births, Perth, 25 June 1902. *Beacon* (Vancouver), December 1924–January 1926. *Dahan Gongbao/Chinese Times* (Vancouver), September 1924–October 1925. *Point Grey Gazette* (Vancouver), August 1924–June 1925. *Vancouver Morning Sun*, 8 Sept. 1924, May–October 1925. *Vancouver Star*, July–December 1924. B.C., Attorney General, *Report of the superintendent of provincial police* (Victoria), 1925. Scott Kerwin, "The Janet Smith Bill of 1924 and the language of race and nation in B.C.," *BC Studies* (Vancouver), no.121 (spring 1999): 83–114; "Re/producing a 'white British Columbia': the meanings of the Janet Smith Bill" (MA thesis, Univ. of B.C., Vancouver, 1996). Sky Lee, *Disappearing moon cafe* (Vancouver, 1990). Martin Robin, *The saga of Red Ryan and other tales of violence from Canada's past* (Saskatoon, 1982), chap.6. Edward Starkins, *Who killed Janet Smith? The 1924 Vancouver killing that remains Canada's most intriguing unsolved murder* (Toronto, 1984). W. P. Ward, *White Canada forever: popular attitudes and public policy toward Orientals in British Columbia* (2nd ed., Montreal and Kingston, Ont., 1990).

SMITH, WILHELMINA. *See* GORDON

SMITH, WILLIAM HARLEY, physician, army officer, and consular agent; b. 23 Dec. 1863 in Toronto, son of Joshua Smith and Alice Berry; m. there 23 Sept. 1890 Isabelle Lucy Emma Gianelli (d. 4 March 1957), and they had two daughters and three sons; d. there 12 Aug. 1929.

Harley Smith's father, a bookkeeper, was a native of Fritton in Suffolk County, England; his mother came from County Cavan (Republic of Ireland). Educated at

Lord Dufferin School and Jarvis Street Collegiate Institute, in 1884 he graduated from the University of Toronto with a BA and a gold medal in languages. (It would become clear from his marriage that he was especially proficient in Italian.) After a period of time teaching in Strathroy, Ont., and Toronto, he attended the Toronto School of Medicine and in 1888 received his MB from the university, with first-class honours in surgery and clinical medicine. A youthful abstainer, he had served in 1887–88 as president of the Toronto Students' Temperance League.

Smith developed a successful private practice in Toronto and became quite active in the city's medical community, though not as a member of the university faculty. In 1898 he was an inspector of "maternity boarding homes." Among his institutional affiliations, Smith, an Anglican, was secretary of the Medical Alumni Association from 1889 to his death, secretary-treasurer of the Toronto Medical Students' Mission Board in 1890–92, a board member of the Victorian Order of Nurses, and honorary treasurer of the medical department of the Church Missionary Society. More significantly, he was a charter fellow (1907) and president (1924–25) of the Toronto Academy of Medicine.

Over the course of his career, Smith's views on the pressing issues of his day in health and medicine were frequently highlighted in the newspapers. Harshly critical of practitioners who were not allopathically trained, he called in 1924 for stronger laws against "those who attempt to practice without preparation." He also cautioned against the rising rate of medical (especially surgical) specialization among physicians in Ontario. General practice, he maintained, "requires more knowledge of human nature and more experience over a wide field of observation." These concerns were typical of the generation trained in the late 19th century, whose professional successors were drawn to the prestige and potential of specialization. At the same time, Smith enthused about medical advances, notably the discovery of the relationship between vitamins and health and hopeful research into the treatment of diabetes. Like many doctors, he was sceptical about the harmful effects of tobacco, noting that alcohol was more dangerous, but he did recommend that those under 20 refrain from smoking in case it triggered some inherited disability during growth. His opinions on alcohol and physical development were consistent with his involvement in the temperance movement and with his philanthropic interests, as a board member of the Canadian Purity-Education Association, vice-president of the Children's Aid Society, and president of the Young Men's Christian Associations of the Provinces of Ontario and Quebec.

Smith's medical career had defined his participation in World War I. He joined the Canadian Army Medical Corps in February 1916 and went overseas in April with the rank of captain. His records reveal that he was a small man – five feet four inches, 125 pounds. Promoted major in October, he served at various hospitals in England and France. Afflicted by neuralgia in his right arm, he returned to Canada in September 1919. Smith's sons had also enlisted; one was killed at Dommiers in France while serving with the French Foreign Legion. Sometime after his return Smith was appointed medical officer to the Toronto Scottish Regiment, a position he held until 1928.

Harley Smith's interest in Europe predated the Great War. His study of languages and his marriage in 1890 to Isabelle Gianelli, daughter of produce dealer and honorary consul Angelo Michel François Gianelli, had drawn him into the Italian community in Toronto. Appointed consular agent there in September 1901, Smith retired in March 1915, when the elevation of the post to a vice-consulate required a native Italian trained in diplomatic service. During that period he often dealt with immigration matters and, with his wife, was active in the cultural activities sponsored by such organizations as the Umberto Primo Benevolent Society; in 1915 Isabelle was on the local committee of the Italian Red Cross Society. In recognition of Harley's duties he was made a chevalier of the Order of the Crown of Italy.

After the war, Smith's interest in Italy continued. He shared his expertise in Italian affairs in the form of several presentations to the Toronto community in the grand settings of the Royal Alexandra Theatre and Massey Music Hall, and in more humble surroundings such as the Anglican Church Home for the elderly on Oxford Street and the Aged Women's and Aged Men's homes on Belmont. During a trip to Italy in 1927, he took part in a service at the tomb of the Unknown Soldier in Rome and interviewed Fascist leader Benito Mussolini. As an unofficial envoy, he helped Mussolini and Ontario premier George Howard Ferguson* exchange greetings. He lauded Il Duce's record in post-war reconstruction and labour policies, and defended him in the face of growing concerns about his handling of the church and Italy's royalty. Like many, Smith saw the Fascists' resistance to the communist threat and their policies of regeneration as signs of a model European state.

Harley Smith died from a heart attack in August 1929, arguably before the worst excesses of Mussolini's regime had become fully evident. Survived by his wife, two sons, and a daughter, he was buried in St James' Cemetery. At his funeral, a friend from student days, the Reverend Henry John Cody*, lamented the loss of "the cheery little doctor who had always some good scheme in hand." Smith's professional views on medicine, his interests in philanthropy, his services in war, and his links to the Italian Canadian community and to Italy had made him a remarkable figure.

JAMES E. MORAN

Snider

AO, RG 22-305, no.62567; RG 80-5-0-192, no.13657; RG 80-8-0-1158, no.6136. LAC, RG 150, Acc. 1992–93/166, box 9051-11. St James' Cemetery and Crematorium (Toronto), Tombstone, lot 109 north sect.8. UTA, A1973-0026/430(63). *Daily Mail and Empire*, 8 Oct. 1924, 19 Sept. 1927, 13 Aug. 1929. *Daily Telegraph* (Toronto), 3 March 1928. *Evening Telegram* (Toronto), 20 Feb. 1926, 16 Jan. 1928. *Globe*, 18 Sept. 1919; 7 May 1924; 23 Jan. 1925; 21 April, 14, 21 July, 17 Sept., 8 Nov. 1927; 28 Jan., 5 Nov. 1928; 13, 15 Aug. 1929. *Toronto Daily Star*, 5 Nov. 1896; 6 Oct. 1898; 19 Dec. 1903; 19 July 1904; 8 Feb. 1905; 12, 22 March, 30 July 1915; 10, 28 Nov. 1922; 7 May, 8–9 Oct. 1924; 6 March 1957. H. B. Anderson, "Harley Smith: for forty-five years secretary of the Medical Alumni Association," *Univ. of Toronto Monthly*, 30 (1929–30): [9]. Can., Parl., *Sessional papers*, 1902, no.29, app.B: 45, 47. *Canadian men and women of the time* (Morgan; 1898 and 1912). *Directory*, Toronto, 1875–1909. Univ. of Toronto, *University of Toronto roll of service, 1914–1918* (Toronto, 1921).

SNIDER, ELIAS WEBER BINGEMAN, miller, manufacturer, and politician; b. 19 June 1842 in Waterloo, Upper Canada, third son of Elias Snider and Hannah Bingeman; m. first 19 April 1864 Nancy Weber (d. 1912) in Preston (Cambridge), Upper Canada, and they had seven sons and four daughters (one son died in infancy); m. secondly 1915 Helen Shoemaker; d. 15 Oct. 1921 in Kitchener, Ont.

E. W. B. Snider left public school at the age of 12 to work on the family farm, but he shared his father's interest in milling and in 1860 began a two-year apprenticeship at the family's flour operation in German Mills (Kitchener). On its completion he became the manager of the mill and in 1864 he made an arrangement with his father to run it on a "shares" basis, which would allow him a measure of the profits. The Sniders expanded their holdings in 1868 to include a small mill at Berlin (Kitchener), but in 1871 Elias Jr set out on his own, purchasing a mill in St Jacobs. There he became the first Canadian to introduce roller milling to the industry. On the advice of John Braun (Brown), a former employee, he purchased a roller system from the Hoerde company of Vienna in 1875. This Walzenstuhle process replaced millstones with a slower but more efficient system of small rollers. The resulting product, which Snider called Walzen flour, represented a dramatic improvement in quality over traditionally milled flour and Snider was able to sell it widely, not only in Ontario but also in eastern Canada, the northeastern United States, and Britain. In 1876 he acquired a second mill, in New Dundee, where he also installed rollers. By the mid 1880s this operation and his Pioneer Roller Flouring Mill in St Jacobs were together producing 250 barrels a day.

The roller milling system was an early example of Snider's fascination with new technology and commercial opportunity. In 1884 he was attracted to the foundry business and purchased a works in Waterloo from Jacob Bricker, which he operated with Bricker's son Levi. Four years later the business was incorporated as the Waterloo Manufacturing Company Limited, with Snider and Absalom Merner, another foundry owner, as the major partners. This firm, of which Snider was president, would become famous for the manufacture of agricultural implements. The company expanded Jacob Bricker's line of threshers and retained his Champion trade mark. It also began to make steam traction engines under the Lion Brand trade name. The 1890s and the ensuing decade were good years for the company in the very competitive agricultural machinery business in Canada. By 1908 it employed 150 men and had 15 travelling salesmen, as well as branch offices in Winnipeg and Regina. Developing technology would restrict its success, however. The introduction of the gasoline tractor led to the replacement of steam as the motive power in agriculture by about 1925. Snider and his firm experimented with a gasoline tractor, but the expense, and American competition, caused them to abandon the project. In the early 1920s, after Snider's death, the introduction of an effective, reasonably priced combine harvester on the prairies threatened the company's future even more; it replaced both the tractor and the thresher, and thereby eliminated Waterloo Manufacturing's main markets. Snider's sons, now in control of the company, sold the firm to Playfair and Company of Toronto in 1927.

From 1881 to 1894 Snider had sat as a Liberal for Waterloo North in the Ontario legislature. He concentrated on expanding municipal powers through his work on municipal assessment and a municipal fire insurance act. Later in his term he became interested in forest preservation and lobbied for the creation of reserves. He would maintain this interest long after leaving politics, publishing an article on the depletion of forests in Waterloo County in the report of the Waterloo Historical Society in 1918. In the federal election of 1896 Snider ran against Conservative Joseph Emm Seagram* in Waterloo North. This was an industrial riding and Snider, though himself a protectionist, bore the cross of the Liberals' freer trade policy. The local Conservative paper called on him to "be a man." "Declare that you will either support [Wilfrid Laurier*] and Free Trade or Joseph Seagram and Protection." The voters preferred Seagram.

Snider experienced success in the manufacturing and milling fields. He also dabbled in railway promotion, with the Waterloo Junction Railway, and the sugar-beet industry. Among his other interests were the Toronto Foundry (later the Anthes Foundry), the Snider Lumber Company of Waterloo Limited, which operated mills at Gravenhurst, and the Canada Felting Company Limited of St Jacobs.

Snider is best known for his role in the introduction of public electricity to Ontario. An early convert to the benefits of electricity, in 1894 he had installed a generator at his mill in St Jacobs which also provided power to homes in the town. In 1900 he joined with Daniel Bechtel Detweiler and Joseph Bingeman to form a company to generate power for mines north of Lake Superior. The Michipicoten Falls Power Company Limited was an early success and convinced Snider of the importance of hydroelectric power for industry. In February 1902 he called upon business and community leaders in the area around Berlin to meet and discuss the most effective way to ensure that power generated at Niagara Falls would be made available to businesses and homes in the province. A subsequent meeting in June struck a committee, chaired by Snider, to consider the matter. Snider and Detweiler, the publicist, researcher, and jack-of-all-trades for the venture, spoke to many municipal and business leaders as well as to the Niagara power companies. At a further meeting in February 1903, attended by delegates from cities and towns throughout southwestern Ontario, it was decided to lobby the provincial government either to build transmission lines as a public work or to allow the municipalities to do so. The government of George William Ross* responded with legislation enabling local governments to proceed and authorizing a commission to establish the feasibility of cooperative municipal power projects. On 12 August Snider became the chair of the Ontario Power Commission, which represented seven municipalities and whose members included London mayor Adam BECK and other leaders. Its report in March 1906 recommended that a cooperative of municipalities construct and operate both a generating and a transmission system for Niagara hydroelectric power. The report was, however, superseded by that of a second commission, appointed in 1905 by the new government of James Pliny Whitney* and chaired by Beck; its recommendation in April 1906 of a provincially owned system carried the day. Four years later Premier Whitney went to Berlin to throw the switch that launched Ontario's hydroelectric system. Snider's role in this development faded from public memory, replaced in great measure by Beck's. In the early 1930s his son William Weber began to lobby the provincial government of George Stewart Henry* to recognize Snider's contribution. This campaign eventually resulted in 1956 in a monument to Snider at St Jacobs and in official recognition from the Hydro-Electric Power Commission of Ontario.

Snider died in 1921 in Kitchener, where he had gone to live after his second marriage. A member of the Evangelical Association, he was laid to rest in the St Jacobs cemetery. He had enjoyed great success in his life by embracing new technology: a new method of milling flour, new machinery for agriculture, and a new system for delivering electricity.

ANDREW THOMSON

E. W. B. Snider's article "Waterloo forests and primitive economics" appears in Waterloo Hist. Soc., *Annual report* (Kitchener, Ont.), 6 (1918): 14–36.

Kitchener Public Library, Rare Books Dept., MC 5.4 (Dan Detweiler papers); MC 6.17 (E. W. B. Snider papers); E. W. B. Snider file. Ontario Agricultural Museum (Milton, Ont.), Waterloo Manufacturing Company coll. *Kitchener Daily Record*, 17 Oct. 1921. John English and Kenneth McLaughlin, *Kitchener: an illustrated history* (Waterloo, 1983). Neil Freeman, "Turn-of-the-century state intervention: creating the Hydro-Electric Power Commission of Ontario, 1906," *OH*, 84 (1992): 171–94. F. L. Leung, *Grist and flour mills in Ontario: from millstones to rollers, 1780s–1880s* (Ottawa, 1981). H. V. Nelles, *The politics of development: forests, mines & hydro-electric power in Ontario, 1849–1941* (Toronto, 1974). Elliott Richmond, "E. W. B. Snider," Waterloo Hist. Soc., *Annual report*, 9 (1921): 183–88. W. A. Schmidt, "The Waterloo Manufacturing Co. Limited," Waterloo Hist. Soc., *Annual report*, 75 (1987): 16–23. H. S. Turner and R. W. Irwin, *Ontario's threshing machine industry: a short history of these pioneer companies and their contribution to Ontario agriculture* (Guelph, Ont., 1974). G. M. Winder, "Following America into corporate capitalism: technology and organization of the Ontario agricultural implements industry to 1930" (PHD thesis, Univ. of Toronto, 1991).

SPENCER, JOSEPH WILLIAM WINTHROP, geologist, teacher, geomorphologist, and author; b. 26 March 1851 in Dundas, Upper Canada, son of Joseph Spencer and Eliza Elenora Coe; nephew of James Spencer*; m. 15 April 1896 Katharine (Kate) Sinclair Thomson in Toronto; they had no children; d. there 9 Oct. 1921.

Joseph William Spencer's great-grandfather Robert Spencer was a loyalist from New Jersey and New York who had served with Butler's Rangers during the American Revolutionary War. Spencer believed that he was related to the Winthrops of Massachusetts and Connecticut, and after he moved to the United States, he added Winthrop to his name, though he generally signed J. W. Spencer. His father, who had founded the Gore grist and paper mills in Dundas, died when he fell from the roof of one of the mill buildings shortly after his son's birth. Young Joseph was educated in Dundas, but in 1867 he and his mother moved to Hamilton, where he worked for two years for druggists T. Bickle and Son. By this time he was already interested in geology and chemistry, in part stimulated by his contact with amateur geologists active in the Hamilton Association, which sought to promote literature, science, and art.

In 1871 Spencer left to study geology at McGill College in Montreal, where he was a student of John William Dawson*. He graduated three years later with first-class honours in the new program of applied science. He then worked for a summer with the Geological Survey of Canada, as assistant to Robert Bell* in Manitoba. Both Dawson and Bell would remain close friends. Unable to find work in Canada, Spencer was briefly employed by Luther G. Emerson, a consultant for the upper Michigan copper mines, in 1875. After returning to Hamilton, he took up a position as science teacher at the Hamilton Collegiate Institute. In the summer of 1877 he travelled to Germany, where he obtained his doctorate at the University of Göttingen with a thesis on the Michigan copper deposits. He was only the second Canadian, after Bernard James Harrington*, to earn a doctorate in geology.

Spencer became professor of geology and chemistry at King's College, in Windsor, N.S., in 1880. Two years later he was appointed to the chair in geology and mineralogy and curator of a new natural history museum at the University of Missouri. He helped to design, build, and equip the museum, but university president Samuel Spahr Laws's plans ran into political and financial troubles, and Spencer lost his position. He joined the University of Georgia in 1888 and became state geologist two years later. He began a geological survey of the northwest part of the state, but soon faced political problems once again since he was more interested in stratigraphy than in gold mining. In 1894 he moved to Washington, D.C., where he worked as a consultant geologist until his return to Canada in 1920. He died in the following year and is buried in the family grave in Dundas.

Spencer's first publication in 1875 dealt with the geology of the Hamilton region. Among other early work to appear in print was a paper on the Michigan copper mines read before the Natural History Society of Montreal in 1876 and published that year in the *Canadian Naturalist* (Montreal) and several on the Palaeozoic geology and fossils of the head of Lake Ontario. His significant research began with his study of preglacial valleys, including the buried Dundas valley, which he originally interpreted as part of an early river system (he called it the Erigan River) draining west through the Lake Erie basin. The work was encouraged by J. Peter Lesley, state geologist of Pennsylvania, whom he had met at a meeting of the American Association for the Advancement of Science, and was published in the *Proceedings* (Philadelphia) of the American Philosophical Society in 1882. Spencer later discovered evidence that the Erigan River had flowed, not up the Grand River and through the Dundas valley, but across the Niagara peninsula west of St Catharines. Further studies convinced him that all the Great Lake basins were originally eroded by a major river system draining east into the St Lawrence valley. He believed the original topography was preglacial and only slightly modified during the ice age.

As far as his teaching duties would allow, Spencer spent the years between 1881 and 1889 working on raised beaches of lakes formed at the end of the ice age ("proglacial lakes"). Many of these beaches were first mapped and named by him. That of the Lake Ontario basin he called the Iroquois beach, described in a paper published in the transactions of the Royal Society of Canada in 1890. By accurate mapping and levelling, Spencer soon discovered that the beaches were no longer level but had been tilted upward towards the north; furthermore, the higher (and therefore older) the beaches, the more they were tilted, a discovery which showed that the tilting was already in operation when the beaches were being formed. Spencer followed Dawson's views about the ice age: he did not believe in the existence of massive ice sheets and attributed phenomena such as boulder clay and striated rocks to the action of floating ice. He therefore did not recognize that tilting of the beaches had been produced by "glacial rebound" (resulting from removal of the load of ice on the crust), but thought it was a widespread, fundamental tectonic process that had affected the whole of eastern North America. He was convinced that the Great Lakes region had stood much higher before the ice age, had been flooded by the sea in more recent times, and had then begun to rise again. Thus he believed that the proglacial lakes were actually marine or brackish, with floating ice, not freshwater lakes dammed by ice sheets, as American contemporaries such as Grove Karl Gilbert and Thomas Chrowder Chamberlin thought. Only in 1910 did Spencer admit (privately) that proglacial lakes were formed by ice-sheet dams, as Gilbert had first proposed in 1871.

Spencer's earliest paper on Niagara Falls was published in 1887. He returned to the area often, even after he moved to the United States, and in 1905 he persuaded Bell, who was acting director of the Geological Survey of Canada, to sponsor a new study of the falls. Published in 1907, it involved a detailed re-survey of the crest line to determine the rate of recession and the first accurate determination of the depth of the river at the whirlpool and just below the falls. His theoretical analysis of the relationship between the rate of erosion and river discharge was criticized by Gilbert in a review published the following year in the journal *Science* (New York). As a result of his incorrect mechanical investigation and flawed study of the drainage history, Spencer's estimates of the age of the falls could not be taken very seriously, even before the era of carbon-14 dating. Nevertheless, the book was generally well received at the time, and the survey data are still valuable.

After Spencer moved to Washington in 1894, he carried out many field investigations in the Caribbean and Central America. His study of the Caribbean islands also revealed evidence of large changes in land elevation, and the discovery of submarine canyons on the western Atlantic continental slope seemed to him further evidence in favour of his theories. Later work has shown that all these phenomena can be explained by agencies unknown in his day, without invoking the immense changes in elevation he proposed.

Joseph William Winthrop Spencer was an original fellow of the Geological Society of America in 1889. Among other honours, in 1919 he received an LLD from the University of Manitoba, which awards the Winthrop Spencer Gold Medal in his memory.

GERARD V. MIDDLETON

[J. W. W. Spencer is the author of more than 100 technical publications, but many were abstracts or republications of material that had appeared elsewhere (a common practice at the time). Two good bibliographical sources which list many of Spencer's works are J. M. Nickles, *Geologic literature on North America, 1785–1918* (2v., Washington, 1923–24), and E. W. Shaw, "Memorial of Joseph William Winthrop Spencer," Geological Soc. of America, *Bull.* (New York), 35 (1924): 25–36. In 1919 Spencer donated his collections and papers to the Univ. of Manitoba Libraries, Dept. of Arch. and Special Coll. (Winnipeg), MSS 30 (Spencer, J. W.), but the papers include no letters. Letters to J. W. Dawson are in MUA, MG 1022; to Robert Bell in LAC, MG 29, B15; and to J. P. Lesley in American Philosophical Soc. Library (Philadelphia), B L56 (J. Peter Lesley papers).

Spencer's best known publication, which summarizes his work not only on the Niagara region but also on the evolution of the Great Lakes basins is *The falls of Niagara: their evolution and varying relations to the Great Lakes; characteristics of the power, and the effects of its diversion* (Ottawa, 1907). For a modern perspective, K. J. Tinkler, "Déjà vu: the downfall of Niagara as a chronometer, 1845–1941," in *Niagara's changing landscapes*, ed. H. J. Gayler (Ottawa, 1994), 81–109, contains a short section on Spencer and discusses his work in relation to other research on Niagara Falls, and K. J. Tinkler *et al.*, "Postglacial recession of Niagara Falls in relation to the Great Lakes," *Quaternary Research* (Orlando, Fla), 42 (1994): 20–29 cites Spencer briefly. G.V.M.]

AO, RG 22-305, no.44167; RG 80-5-0-241, no.490. Univ. of Rochester Library, Dept. of Arch. and Special Coll. (Rochester, N.Y.), A.F16 (Herman LeRoy Fairchild papers, 1869–1943). G. V. Middleton, "J. W. Spencer (1851–1921): his life in Canada and his work on preglacial river valleys," *Geoscience Canada* (St John's), 31 (2004): 49–56; "J. W. Spencer (1851–1921): his life in Missouri and Georgia, and work on proglacial lakes," *Geoscience Canada* (forthcoming); "The Spencers of Dundas" (speech given to the Dundas Valley Hist. Soc. (Dundas, Ont.), 21 April 2004; a copy can be found at *www.unityserve.org/dundashistory/articles/0008.shtml*). Morris Zaslow, *Reading the rocks: the story of the Geological Survey of Canada, 1842–1972* (Toronto and Ottawa, 1975).

SPRINGSTEAD, VELMA AGNES, secretary and athlete; b. 22 Aug. 1906 in Hamilton, Ont., daughter of Margaret Edith Crowe and Bernice Lavelle (Val) Springstead; d. there unmarried 27 March 1927.

Velma Springstead has come to typify the young women who took up sports in the heady post-suffragist years of the early 1920s in industrial cities such as Hamilton, and who established the basis for women's participation ever since. Energetic and cheerful, she worked as secretary to the sales manager of the Tuck-

ett Tobacco Company Limited (founded by George Elias Tuckett*), taught Sunday school at Calvin Presbyterian Church, and studied the piano. But her greatest love was sports. Starting as a teenager, she played softball and basketball for the Hamilton Ladies Club, and regularly won track and field honours in sprinting, hurdling, and high jumping. In 1925 she helped legitimize vigorous competition for Canadian women as a member of the first team ever to compete in international track and field.

That year the all-male Amateur Athletic Union of Canada was invited to send a women's team to London, England, to compete against the national teams of Great Britain and Czechoslovakia. Not wanting to organize it, but unwilling to risk public censure by turning the invitation down, the AAU asked Alexandrine Gibb*, a Toronto brokerage secretary and volunteer sports leader, to select and manage the team. In the hastily convened trials at Varsity Stadium in Toronto on 11 July, Springstead outleaped the Canadian high jump record holder, Innes Bramley, to make the team. Wearing a billowing tunic, she cleared four feet seven inches with the scissors kick.

The trip abroad gave participants the athletic stimulus, broadened horizons, and adventure that often come with international competition, and helped elevate women's sport from obscurity to celebrity. During their journey overseas, via Quebec and Liverpool, the team of ten athletes, Gibb, and a chaperon were fêted by the Canadian government, the Canadian Pacific Railway, and the British organizers and besieged by reporters and photographers.

The British handily won the meet at Stamford Bridge in London on 1 August, and the Czechoslovakians finished second, but the Canadians were "by no means disgraced." Springstead finished third in the high jump and fourth in the hurdles, and infused the entire team with enthusiasm and determination. She was a continual presence around the track, encouraging her teammates and winning over rivals and spectators with her exuberance. Her fellow competitors voted her the Lord Decies Trophy as the all-round athlete of the meet.

The Stamford Bridge experience convinced Gibb and others that Canadian women deserved a permanent place in international sporting competition, but that they would need their own organization to ensure it. As soon as they could, in 1926, they formed the Women's Amateur Athletic Federation of Canada, and began to spread "girls' sports run by girls" across Canada. In 1928, under Gibbs's leadership, the WAAF took the first Canadian women's Olympic team to Amsterdam in association with the AAU.

Though an early favourite for a berth on that team, Springstead never had a chance to compete. In March 1927 she was hospitalized with severe chest pains and died three days later of pneumonia. But her ambition and zest for life continued to inspire the leaders of Canadian women's sports. Following her death the WAAF made health a priority, insisting that participants pass a medical every season and pressing doctors to donate their service to impoverished athletes. The policy became a hallmark of the organization. In 1932 Gibb and the WAAF created the Velma Springstead Trophy to honour the best Canadian female athlete each year. It was to be awarded on the basis of "performance, sportsmanship and behaviour," and exemplified the contribution she had made to Canadian women's sport.

BRUCE KIDD

Canadian athletics, 1832–1992, comp. Bill McNulty and Ted Radcliffe ([Richmond, B.C.], 1992). *DHB*, vol.3. [Alexandrine Gibb?], "Report of the women's athletic team, which competed in international games held at Stamford Bridge, London, Eng., August 1st, 1925," in Canadian Olympic Committee, *Report, 1925 Games held in Chamonix and Paris, France . . .*, comp. J. H. Crocker (n.p., [1925?]). Bruce Kidd, *The struggle for Canadian sport* (Toronto, 1996). N. R. Raine, "Girls invade track and diamond," *Maclean's* (Toronto), 38 (1925), no.16: 12–13, 62–63.

STARKMAN, BESHA (Bessie) (Tobin) (also known as **Bessie Stark, Bessie Perri (Perry)**, and **Rose Cyceno**), organized crime boss; b. 14 April 1889 in Russian Poland, daughter of Shimon (Sam) Starkman and Gello (Gloria) ——; m. 15 Dec. 1907 Harry Tobsen (Tobin) in Toronto, and they had two daughters; about 1913 she entered into a common-law relationship with Rocco Perri*, and they had a child who died shortly after birth; d. 13 Aug. 1930 in Hamilton, Ont.

The Starkman family arrived in Canada sometime around 1900, and settled in the Ward area of downtown Toronto. Legends of Besha Starkman's early life say that she worked as a seamstress in an Eaton's sweatshop. The ambitious young woman found her job and her marriage to Harry Tobin, a Russian who drove for a bakery, frustrating. In 1912 the Tobins rented rooms in their house on Chestnut Street to Rocco Perri, a young immigrant from the Calabria region of Italy. Within a year, Bessie had abandoned her husband, children, and Jewish faith and gone to St Catharines to join Perri, then a labourer on the Welland Canal. By 1916 they were living in Hamilton, where Rocco worked at first as a salesman for a macaroni company; later they ran a small grocery store.

Bessie Perri came to the attention of the police in March 1917, when she was charged under the name Rose Cyceno with keeping a disorderly house. In her defence, she defiantly claimed she was not aware of the activities of her female boarder. She was nonetheless convicted. It was in this case that her characteristic audacity became apparent.

A world of opportunity for organized crime was created by the institution in 1916 of the Ontario Temperance Act, the rejection in 1919 of Prohibition in Quebec, and the expiry of federal controls on the interprovincial movement of liquor. Bootleggers in Ontario had gained valuable experience by the time the United States adopted Prohibition in January 1920. Rocco and Bessie Perri were already taking advantage of the situation in Ontario through a gang made up largely of Calabrians in the Hamilton–Niagara region. Bessie quickly emerged as the gang's head of business and negotiator, the first woman publicly to rise so high in the ranks of organized crime in Canada.

In August 1921 a ruling by a court in Windsor, that there was no Canadian law prohibiting the export of liquor, set the stage for rumrunning on a grand scale. With Ontario still dry, the Perris expanded from the Hamilton–Kitchener–Windsor triangle and sold large amounts of liquor and beer across the province; boxcar loads went to New York State via Niagara and to Detroit and Chicago via Windsor. It was Bessie who placed orders with the distilleries and breweries, laundered the money and handled the bank accounts, dealt with other gangsters on liquor and drug deals, and paid gang members and bribes. Fond of expensive clothing and jewellery, she often displayed a high-handed manner that would alienate members of the Perri mob. In one incident, Rocco promised compensation to the family of a man killed by the police. When the man's uncle appeared to claim the money, she reportedly told him to "go to hell."

Rocco and Bessie Perri took part in a revealing interview with the *Toronto Daily Star* in November 1924. Labelled the "King of the Bootleggers," Rocco did most of the talking, but it was Bessie who guided the interview and interrupted at key points. Her most sensational public appearance was her testimony in March 1927 before the federal royal commission on customs and excise, in reality an investigation of liquor smuggling. Under cross-examination by assistant counsel Robert Louis Calder, she denied any connections to bootlegging and feigned ignorance on many questions, including a number about telephone calls from her home to distilleries. As a result of their testimonies – Rocco had also been examined – and statements in the tax-evasion trial in December of the Gooderham and Worts distilling firm, the Perris were charged with perjury. Likely as part of a plea bargain, the charges against Bessie were dropped when Rocco pleaded guilty; he was sentenced to six months in a reformatory.

The Ontario government's replacement of the temperance act by the Liquor Control Act in June 1927 killed most of the bootleg market. With the liquor business declining, the Perri mob began to expand their drug trade. Apparently Bessie was the leader in making the deals. In June 1929, with hundreds of dollars in her purse, she showed up at a house in Toronto in the midst of a drug raid by the Royal Canadian Mounted Police. With no other evidence, they released her, but her appearance prompted an undercover operation by Sergeant Frank Zaneth [Franco Zanetti*]. At one point she met Zaneth, who was acting as a Chicago drug dealer, in a roadhouse. There was no deal, and the operation went nowhere.

On 13 Aug. 1930 Bessie was killed by shotgun blasts as she and Rocco were leaving the garage of their home. Her funeral on the 17th, the day after the opening in Hamilton of the first British Empire Games, was an unruly scene. Thousands of spectators attempted to break through police lines at the house and later at the small Jewish cemetery south of Hamilton. An investigation by the Ontario Provincial Police concluded that Bessie's arrogance was the probable underlying motive for her murder, but that still left a number of suspects. It was clear she had angered members of the Perri gang by ordering them around and refusing to pay expenses. Three theories emerged: she had been shot by disgruntled members of the gang acting alone, she had broken enough mob customs that Rocco Perri had acquiesced in her murder, and she had reneged on a drug deal with gangsters from Rochester, N.Y., who had shot her. No arrests were made. Her estate went to Rocco and her two married children, Lillian Shime and Gertrude Maidenberg.

The decline of the Perri empire after Bessie's death strongly suggests that it was her skills that had helped the gang become prominent. Although Rocco began living in 1933 with another strong woman, Annie Newman, who helped him revive the fortunes of the gang, it never became as dominant as it had been with Bessie running the business.

ROBIN ROWLAND

A number of police and citizenship files seen by the author are now restricted by access and privacy legislation, and are therefore not listed here.

AO, RG 22-205, no.1615/1930–31; RG 80-5-0-371, no.1121. LAC, RG 18, F-2, 3313 A, file HQ-189-O-1; RG 33-88. *Toronto Daily Star*, 19 Nov. 1924. James Dubro and R. F. Rowland, *King of the mob: Rocco Perri and the women who ran his rackets* (Markham, Ont., 1987).

STATES, WELLINGTON NEY, Baptist clergyman; b. 1 Oct. 1874 in Wolfville, N.S., son of Joab States and Mary Eliza McCulla; m. 4 Dec. 1907 Muriel Viola States in Avonport, N.S., and they had three sons and two daughters; d. 3 May 1927 in Dartmouth, N.S.

W. N. States's paternal ancestor was a freeborn African American refugee from New York who made his way to Saint John in 1783 and later settled in Parrsboro, N.S., which had a large population of black slaves. States's engaging forenames suggest that his great-grandfather McCulla may have been one of the several Waterloo veterans who settled in Nova Scotia

after the end of the Napoleonic Wars in 1815. The youngest child of an interracial marriage, States suffered the loss of both his Anglican mother (in 1880) and his Baptist father (in 1887). Family tradition has it that he was ill-used by his white maternal grandparents, with whom he went to live after his father's death. The following year, aged 14, he ran away to sea.

By 1891 States was a student at Horton Academy in Wolfville, the preparatory school for Acadia University. Leaving the academy in 1895, he went to Annapolis Royal as factotum to the pastor of the local Baptist church, Gilbert James Coulter White, who baptized him and became his mentor. States returned to Horton in 1897, perhaps with a view to university matriculation. He did not attend Acadia, however, but moved on to Halifax, where he joined the African Baptist church on Cornwallis Street and made the acquaintance of lawyer James Robinson Johnston*. They would remain intimate friends until Johnston's murder in 1915.

In 1898 States received a licence to preach from the African Baptist Association. His original intention was to become a foreign missionary but, as this field was an exclusively white preserve, he was sent instead as a home missionary to the pastorless ABA churches of Granville Ferry and Inglewood (near Bridgetown) in Annapolis County. Then in April 1899 States, quite without authorization, took a daring and unilateral step which would render his ministry unique – he became the first black licentiate to be ordained in the Baptist Convention of the Maritime Provinces. For the entire 28 years of his ministry he would be not an African Baptist clergyman but a convention Baptist clergyman who happened to be black and who therefore served only black congregations.

Though the ABA's 1899 annual meeting passed a motion of censure over States's "irregular" ordination, any lingering concerns were soon dispelled by his outstanding personal qualities. Intelligent, articulate, personable, better educated than most of the indigenous black Baptist clergy, and (in historian Robin W. Winks's words) "inordinately handsome," States could not fail to command attention. In August 1902 his standing was confirmed by his election as moderator and his appointment as field missionary, or "evangelist," of the ABA. He would continue to itinerate after he acquired the first of his two major settled pastorates, Second Baptist in New Glasgow, in 1906. No sooner had he taken over Second Baptist than he brought it into the Nova Scotia Eastern Association of the United Baptist Convention of the Maritime Provinces. Throughout his 13 years in New Glasgow, States was between two worlds. New Glasgow was the only town in the industrial heartland of Pictou County where black people were allowed to reside.

States, like the long-serving clerk of the ABA, Peter Evander McKerrow*, was an integrationist, not a separatist. The Eastern Association was the only racially integrated association within the convention. But its liberalism did not mean that the local churches were integrated. Indeed, Second Baptist came into existence in 1903 because black people were not welcome at First Baptist. Though States's views were in the minority among blacks, Second Baptist did not affiliate with the ABA until after he had left the congregation in 1919. By that time the church was part of the Northern Association of the convention, the Eastern Association having divided in 1915.

States's friendship with James R. Johnston, clerk of the ABA in succession to McKerrow, meant that he quickly rose to the top of the association despite being a convention minister. He was three times moderator, in 1902–3, 1914–15, and 1923–24. The devastating loss of Johnston, the black community's paramount leader, during States's second term, was followed by the emergence of a triumvirate consisting of States, the Reverend William Andrew White*, and James Alexander Ross Kinney*, Johnston's successor as clerk, which guided the African Nova Scotian community in the interwar years. If Johnston's murder hastened the descent "to the nadir" (as Winks describes the period), ironically the 65th annual meeting of the ABA in Halifax in September 1918 was States's finest hour. In a move that he supported, the meeting, which was formally opened by the lieutenant governor, resolved to seek statutory incorporation for the ABA (achieved in 1919 as the African United Baptist Association), and States was nominated vice-moderator. During the meeting he reported the formation of a ministerial union, the purpose of which was "to organize the Pastors and Licentiates for more effective efforts, morally, socially and spiritually." He was elected its first president.

Mildly tubercular, States had been prevented in 1917 from going overseas as chaplain of the No.2 Construction Battalion of the Canadian Expeditionary Force (the Black Battalion). It was a crushing blow, since his friendly rival W. A. White went in his place. In 1919, driven from Second Baptist, New Glasgow, by the congregation's inability to pay his salary, States assumed his final pastorate, Victoria Road in Dartmouth, a venerable but also impoverished AUBA church. By 1926 States had, in White's words, "been laid aside, perhaps permanently, by illness." In the spring of 1927, his 53rd year, he succumbed to pneumonia. His widow, who was known to family and friends as Myrtle and who for 30 years was the organizer of the ladies's auxiliary of the AUBA, survived him by 57 years.

W. N. States was the most outstanding African Nova Scotian clergyman of his generation. Quite literally a builder of churches (he was a carpenter), he was also a builder of the African Baptist community. As field missionary, interim pastor, settled pastor, and officer and life member of the AUBA, he served the association not only by leading it in many capacities but also by ministering, at one time or another, to nearly all of its constituent churches. Yet his longest and most productive pastorate was with a newly established congregation which he purposely kept out of the AUBA. For States the church was more Baptist than black, and the needs and interests of the black community were not necessarily best served by an ethnic church association. He strove to preserve the legacy of his friend Johnston, especially in regard to the proposed educational institute which after Johnston's death became the Nova Scotia Home for Colored Children. His own true successor was a fellow native of Wolfville, the Reverend Dr William Pearly Oliver*, who in 1960 became the first AUBA clergyman to be elected president of the white convention.

BARRY CAHILL

[Wellington Ney States was the compiler of *Hymns sung at the services of Rev. W. N. States, evangelist of the African Baptist Association of Nova Scotia, 1903* (Halifax, 1903; reprinted as "Hymns sung at the services (1903)" in vol.1 of *Fire on the water, infra*, 92–96). States's official history of the African Baptist Association, commissioned in 1917, remained unwritten or unfinished, and the history of the ABA has yet to be written. States's few extant papers, including his invaluable commonplace book, are held by his granddaughter, Sherrolyn M. Riley; they form the basis of this article. The only comprehensive secondary source is M. L. Knight, "Wellington Ney States, 1877–1927: life and work with the African United Baptist churches" (M.ED. thesis, St Mary's Univ., Halifax, 1983). The author is grateful to historical demographer David W. States for helping to reconstitute the Reverend States's branch of the extended States family. B.C.]

Baptist Hist. Coll., Acadia Univ. (Wolfville, N.S.), Horton Collegiate Academy, student records, 1879–1910. "The life of Rev. W. N. States," *Clarion* (New Glasgow, N.S.), 6 Sept. 1947. African Baptist Assoc. of N.S., *Minutes* (Halifax), 1898–1929. Fannie Allison *et al.*, *Traditional lifetime stories: a collection of black memories* (2v., Dartmouth, N.S., 1987–90). *The Baptist year book of the Maritime provinces of Canada . . .* (Halifax, etc.), 1898–1905. *Fire on the water: an anthology of black Nova Scotian writing*, ed. G. E. Clarke (2v., Porter's Lake, N.S., 1991–92). A. P. Oliver, *A brief history of the colored Baptists of Nova Scotia, 1782–1953* ([Halifax, 1953]). Donald Thomas, *These fifty years with the Second United Baptist Church* (New Glasgow, 1953). *United Baptist year book* (Saint John), 1906–29. R. W. Winks, *The blacks in Canada: a history* (2nd ed., Montreal and Kingston, Ont., 1997).

STAVELEY, HARRY, architect; b. 21 May 1848 at Quebec, son of Edward Staveley, an architect, and Mary Ann White; m. there 18 Oct. 1876 Barbara Black, and they had three sons and one daughter; d. there 24 July 1925.

Harry Staveley was the second member of a family dynasty who were active as architects in Quebec City from 1845 until 1960. His grandfather Christopher Staveley was an architect, engineer, and surveyor in Leicester, England. His father, Edward, emigrated in 1833 and, after working as an engineer on railway and canal building projects in Baltimore, Md, settled at Quebec in 1844. A year later he went into partnership with Frederick Hacker, an influential British architect who had trained in the London office of John Nash. When Hacker died in 1846, the firm, Hacker and Staveley, was dissolved. Edward then practised on his own before finding a new partner, Gerald George Dunlevie, a surveyor and architect who had been born around 1809 in the West Indies and died sometime after 1883; they formed Staveley and Dunlevie, a firm that lasted from 1851 until 1858. At a time when most of the Irish, British, and American architects who immigrated to Quebec – for example, men like George Browne*, Richard John Cooper, and John Cliff – promptly left to pursue work on important building projects in Montreal, Toronto, or Kingston, Edward Staveley chose to make a career for himself in the city, among the middle-class anglophones who gave him commissions for houses, villas, shops, schools, and churches. His son Harry, who became his next partner, would reap the benefits of his decision to stay.

Harry Staveley studied with Professor Frederick East at Quebec and trained as an architect in his father's firm. In 1863 he was made a partner and it became known as Edward Staveley and Son. By the time of Edward's death nine years later, Harry had begun the productive career that would make him the foremost "Victorian" architect in Quebec City. He was initially influenced by his father, who had adopted a blend of late neoclassicism and Italian Renaissance. The financial elite of the old capital found this image, which was made known by the model books of the American architect Minard Lafever and was widely favoured in Montreal and farther west, reassuring. Harry's work broadened to embrace the formal repertory of historicism more fully. His many cottages, villas, and row houses show the picturesque influence of two Americans, Calvert Vaux and Samuel Sloan. This favourite architect of the anglophone middle class also borrowed stylistic features from the Second Empire. Unlike Joseph-Ferdinand Peachy*, Eugène-Étienne Taché*, Georges-Émile Tanguay, and François-Xavier Berlinguet*, who used elements of this style to re-Gallicize the urban landscape, Staveley confined himself to a rather whimsical interpretation of it, one that was inspired more by the model books of American east coast architects than by the classic French examples. His houses thus add colour to the Grande Allée and to what would become known as the old city, both of them typically French in their austerity and symmetry.

He also designed a number of interesting religious buildings, in fact the only ones in the Quebec City region bearing traces of the ecclesiologist movement that Augustus Welby Northmore Pugin had launched in Great Britain [see Henry Langley*].

Of the four children born to Harry Staveley and Barbara Black, Harry Lorn and Edward Black also pursued careers in architecture. The former worked for the Montreal firm of William Tutin Thomas, but the latter entered his father's business in 1900, and thus the Staveley name would live on in Quebec City. Indeed, Harry's career, which had been extremely productive from 1872 until 1900 while he was working on his own, gained fresh impetus with the arrival of Edward Black. A graduate of McGill University and fully conversant with the latest trends in British architecture, Edward Black put his compositional skill to good use in Staveley and Staveley. In a milieu ossified by the apprenticeship system, the firm was thus able to move beyond the model books and to limit the growing domination of the Quebec scene by architects from Montreal, Toronto, and the United States. Along Chemin Saint-Louis and the extension of the Grande Allée, but also Chemin Sainte-Foy, Avenue des Érables, and Avenue du Parc, the new Montcalm ward became the showplace of the comfortable homes in which Edward Black excelled. The Staveleys' reputation spread beyond the city limits, gaining them the opportunity to build real mansions. Cascade House, erected for Sir William Price at Kénogami (Jonquière), Colin Cathcart Breakey's manor at Breakeyville, and the Hôtel Roberval (in the village of that name), which was owned by Benjamin Alexander Scott and Horace Jansen Beemer*, are fine examples of their work. The firm also tendered successfully for public buildings – fire stations, schools, and hospitals – a market that had hitherto been closed to them.

Staveley and Staveley declined after the death of Harry in 1925. Limited to engaging in "domestic" architecture by difficult economic conditions, the departure of the anglophone entrepreneurial middle class, and the staleness of his architectural idiom, Edward Black retained the name of the family firm until 1936. He retired in 1960 and, a few years later, bequeathed the Staveley family papers to the Archives Nationales du Québec. They include 1,447 drawings and constitute one of the most interesting collections of 19th- and 20th-century architectural designs in Canada.

Luc Noppen

ANQ-Q, CE301-S62, 9 févr. 1862; CE301-S66, 18 oct. 1876; Index BMS, dist. judiciaire de Québec, Metropolitan Church (Québec), 27 juill. 1925; P541. *Gazette* (Montreal), 19 Sept. 1969. *Quebec Chronicle-Telegraph*, 17 Sept. 1969.

Luc Noppen et Marc Grignon, *L'art de l'architecte: trois siè-cles de dessin d'architecture à Québec* (Québec, 1983). S. F. Poulin, "L'architecture résidentielle des Staveley, 1846–1954" (mémoire de MA, univ. Laval, Québec, 1995). A. J. H. Richardson *et al.*, *Quebec City: architects, artisans and builders* (Ottawa, 1984), 507–17. *The storied province of Quebec; past and present*, ed. W. [C. H.] Wood *et al.* (5v., Toronto, 1931–32), 3: 52. *Who's who and why*, 1912.

STEAD, HAY STRAFFORD, artist, HBC clerk, and journalist; b. 26 Oct. 1871 in Lancashire, England, one of the five children of George Strafford Stead and Rachel Agnes ——; m. 4 Nov. 1897 Emily Bertha Earle in Winnipeg; they had no children; d. 19 Feb. 1924 in Montreal and was buried there.

Hay Stead came to Canada with his parents as a boy and arrived in Winnipeg presumably in 1889 with his father, who worked as a civil servant in the provincial legislative buildings. Hay farmed in the Gilbert Plains district of Manitoba, perhaps at about that time. By August 1892 he was living in Winnipeg and working as a clerk in the general office of the Hudson's Bay Company. He left that job in August 1905. From about 1906 until 1922 he worked for the *Manitoba Free Press*, the *Winnipeg Saturday Post*, the *Winnipeg Tele-gram*, and the *Winnipeg Tribune*. He held a variety of posts: journalist, editor, editorial writer, feature writer, illustrator, and editorial cartoonist. He also contrib-uted to other publications, including the Winnipeg entertainment weekly *Town Topics* and *Trail*, a monthly published in Regina.

Stead's practice and promotion of the arts in the west had preceded his career in journalism, his artistic side surfacing while he clerked for the HBC. Through-out his career he participated in cultural, literary, and artistic societies, art education programs, and public art exhibitions – teaching, reading papers, comment-ing on exhibitions, and lending his talents.

A member of the Art and Literature Society, Stead read a paper at one of its meetings in Winnipeg in 1895. That same year local historian, naturalist, and educator George Bryce* sent him to the Manitoba countryside to sketch wild flowers for his textbook *Our Canadian prairies*. Stead painted scenes for the Winnipeg Oper-atic and Dramatic Society the following year. In Octo-ber 1903 he exhibited at Parkin's Studio with the recently established Manitoba Society of Artists. His submission included a watercolour of a fishing boat on a rough sea which a critic in the *Manitoba Free Press* called "especially true to nature, the waves appearing to move as one looks at them." Although the Manitoba Society of Artists had been founded sometime in 1902, it was not until December 1903 that it adopted a con-stitution. Stead was a founding member and its first president. In its first official show he exhibited an oil portrait entitled *A Selkirk native* and small watercolour landscapes. One reviewer singled out *In the Turtle Mountains* and another called Stead's art careful and

clever. His artistic understanding qualified him to cri-tique a loan exhibition displayed in the fine arts section of the Winnipeg Industrial Exhibition of 1904.

At his death Stead was remembered as a "brilliant cartoonist." Although one of his obituaries would claim that his ability as a cartoonist had brought him into the newspaper business, it may have been the public nature of his artistic activities that gained the attention of the *Free Press*. As early as 1905 the paper engaged him to provide watercolours to reproduce as covers for an annual Christmas booklet. During 1907 and 1908 he executed numerous illustrations and car-toons for the *Free Press*; in later years he would work increasingly as an editor. His political cartoons sur-rounding the provincial election of 1907 echoed the content of newspaper editorials opposed to Premier Rodmond Palen Roblin*; some of the editorials may have been his work as well. He also contributed cari-catures of prominent civil servants, businessmen, and professionals for a book produced by the Newspaper Cartoonists' Association of Manitoba, *Manitobans as we see 'em, 1908 and 1909*. Featured in the opening pages along with the other members of the associa-tion, Stead portrays himself as dignified and intro-spective, his collar starched high and rigid. In 1911 he presented to the Western Art Association a paper on caricature, which he defined as "a drawing with the character of the sitter stamped thereon."

In 1912 Stead taught black and white illustration for the Free Art School sponsored by the Western Art Association and the Manitoba Society of Arts and Crafts. That same year the Industrial Bureau appointed him a member of its newly founded fine arts commit-tee. In addition to organizing local and loan exhibi-tions for the bureau's annual fairs, the committee helped to establish the Winnipeg Museum of Fine Arts in 1912 and the Winnipeg School of Art the following year. Stead sat on the committee of management for the school and judged its competition in 1914.

Stead served as temporary curator of the museum, which opened in June 1914 with an exhibit produced by the Western Art Association that featured western Canadian artists who showed "no feeble hankering after old-world atmosphere." Bold oils and water-colours displaying western scenes of buffalo and prairie landscapes made up Stead's contributions, including *Near Pembina highway*, *Prairie sunset*, *The slough trail*, and *Buffalo at Wainwright, Alta*. His waterco-lours *The prairie* and *The canoe* were in the Art Union of Canada's exhibition of January 1915. After that year Stead's presence in the local art community faded except for occasional illustrations and cartoons in the *Telegram*, where he was working primarily as an editor. His work as an editorial cartoonist seems to have drawn him away from artistic societies, or more likely lowered his profile within them. In 1922 he was president of the Winnipeg Press Club; a caricature of him commemorating his service still hangs in the club's meeting room. The following year he moved to Montreal, where he worked as telegraph editor for the *Montreal Daily Star*. He died there after an illness of four months.

A prominent figure in the developing art scene of the Canadian prairie, Stead had displayed western sensibility as a journalist and an artist. His articles in *Trail* were serious and diverse considerations of western environmental, economic, and political topics. The content of his cartoons was regionally interested – deriding, for example, Torontonians in the west. His paintings observed prairie phenomena.

MARCIA STENTZ

Hay Strafford Stead's signed cartoons are the largest existing samples of his art. Only a few of his paintings survive. The Winnipeg Art Gallery's collection includes watercolour scenes of buffalo on the summer prairie dated 1914 and an untitled, undated oil landscape. Undated drawings of the old Prince of Wales Fort (Churchill, Man.) and the second Prince of Wales's Fort and original drawings for cartoons, possibly from the 1920s, are held by the AM.

Stead is the author of the following articles which appeared in the monthly *Trail* (Regina): "The story of half-breed scrip," 2 (1910): 303–11; "The outlet to Hudson Bay," 2: 505–10; "The science of city growth," 3 (1911): 25–33.

AM, HBCA, D.38/53: f.229; D.38/57: ff.396d–97. Man., Dept. of Finance, Consumer and Corporate Affairs, Vital statistics (Winnipeg), no.1897-001170. *Manitoba Free Press*, 13 Oct. 1903; 11 Nov. 1911; 16 Feb., 11, 28 Dec. 1912; 16 Aug. 1913; 6 April 1914; 15 Nov. 1918; 20 Feb. 1924. *Winnipeg Free Press*, 19 Feb. 1972. *Winnipeg Telegram*, 13 Oct., 13 Nov. 1903; 22 July 1904; 20 June, 30 July 1914; 29 Sept. 1917; 18 Nov. 1919. *Winnipeg Town Topics*, 10 Oct., 19 Dec. 1903; 6 Jan., 10 Nov. 1906. *Winnipeg Tribune*, 3 Feb., 2 July, 15 Oct., 5 Nov. 1896; 14 Oct., 17 Dec. 1903; 16 July 1914; 19 Feb. 1924. Marilyn Baker, *The Winnipeg School of Art: the early years* ([Winnipeg], 1984). V. G. Berry, *Vistas of promise, Manitoba, 1874–1919: November 1st, 1987–January 17th, 1988* (exhibition catalogue, Winnipeg Art Gallery, 1987). George Bryce, *Our Canadian prairies: being a description of the most notable plants of Manitoba . . .* (Toronto, [1895]). *Manitobans as we see 'em, 1908 and 1909* (Winnipeg, 1909).

STEPHANSSON, STEPHAN GUDMUNDUR (Stefán Guðmundsson), farmer and poet; b. 3 Oct. 1853 near Víðimýri, Iceland, son of Guðmundur Stefánsson and Guðbjörg Hannesdóttir; m. 28 Aug. 1878 Helga Sigríður Jonsdóttir in Wisconsin, and they had five sons and three daughters; d. 10 Aug. 1927 near Markerville, Alta.

Stefán Guðmundsson was born on a rented farm, Kirkjuhóll, in the northern Icelandic region of Skagafjörður. Educated at home, during his teen years he practised verse making, following old skaldic traditions. If poetry was his avocation, farming was his vocation; in Iceland his work was limited to raising sheep. When he immigrated to the United States in 1873 with his family and a small contingent of Icelanders, American officials, misunderstanding his father's patronymic of Stefánsson, gave the name Stephansson to the entire family. Later in life, Stephan chose to sign his name Stephan G. Stephansson, although he still used his native name of Stefán Guðmundsson among his Icelandic friends. The family settled first in Wisconsin, where Stephan learned the rudiments of tilling the soil and married Helga, his first cousin, in 1878. In 1888, in Garðar (Gardar, N.Dak.), he incurred the wrath of many of his churchgoing countrymen when he helped organize the Hins Islenzka Menningarfelags (Icelandic Cultural Society), a debating club based on the Society for Ethical Culture founded by prominent freethinker Felix Adler in New York City.

A collapse of the grain market forced the family's final move, in 1889, to the Alberta district of the North-West Territories. Stephansson would become a naturalized citizen five years later. Homesteading along the Medicine River north of Calgary, on SW10-T37-R2-W5, he raised cattle and sheep. He was the first secretary of the joint-stock company formed by farmers in 1899 to support a dominion government creamery in nearby Markerville. His reliance on livestock, however, did not preclude his planting of various grains, and in 1900 he was the first member of the Icelandic settlement to harvest rye. In addition to the post he held with the creamery company, he was a justice of the peace and a member of the local school board.

Although Stephansson had written some poetry before moving to Alberta, it was during his years on the Canadian prairies that he honed his craft, marrying traditional Icelandic metre (as well as experimenting with new metres) to the philosophy of the American freethinkers. His long view of history and man's place in it is evident in his poem "Staddur a grothrarstoth" [At the forestry station] of 1917:

Monuments crumble. Works of mind survive
The gales of time. Men's names have shorter life.
Forgetful time may mask where honor's due
But mind's best edifices live and thrive.

Stephansson composed and read mostly at night, and much of his correspondence pertains to literary and intellectual interests. He used verse and prose to criticize the Icelandic Lutheran Church, whose dogma and schisms he viewed as a threat to Icelandic culture. Among others, he sparred with the Reverend Jón Bjarnason*, whom he nonetheless regarded as a true Icelandic nationalist. Another explosive issue for west Icelanders (the designation for those who had come to North America) was World War I. Stephansson was open and vehement in his opposition to it and to Ice-

969

landic Canadian involvement. His *Vígslóða* [The trail of war] is a collection of pacifist poems published in Reykjavík, Iceland, in 1920, only some of which had appeared during the war. Copies sold in Winnipeg brought strong denunciation. Politically he supported the United Farmers of Alberta and he flirted with Marxism, which he viewed as the logical theory of scientific socialism.

Despite controversy, Stephansson was well respected as a poet. Writing only in Icelandic, he excelled at intricate metaphors, wonderful imagery, and neologism. Much of his verse romanticized Iceland and its history; "þó þú langförull legðir" [Song to Iceland] of 1903 has been set to music and is considered an important national song. The narrative "A ferð og flugi" [En route] of 1898, an excellent example of his descriptive ability, tells of the immigrant experience crossing the prairies by train in mid winter:

> The bluish-white tide of the snow had engulphed
>   Each hillock and hollow as well,
> And the frost-haggard trees were like pallid, grey
>   ghosts
>   From the pale, frozen forests of hell.

Other themes include the value of hard work, adversity as challenge, and the transience of life. Much of his verse dwells on the beauty of the Alberta landscape, and in Iceland he became known as Klettafjallaskadið, or the poet of the Rocky Mountains. The first three volumes of his collected works, *Andvökur* [Sleepless nights], were published in 1908–9 in Winnipeg. Stephansson's bitter satire and his use of archaic words and convoluted style generated criticism, but *Andvökur* also brought new exposure and popularity, which led to reading tours of North Dakota, Manitoba, and Saskatchewan in 1908–9 and the west coast in 1913. The greatest honour came in 1917 when the people of Iceland invited him to return for a four-month tour; he was regarded by many there as the best Icelandic poet to have emerged since the 13th century. With the publication of two more volumes in 1923 and a sixth posthumously in 1938, his output fills more than 2,000 pages, making him one of Canada's most prolific poets.

Stephansson suffered a stroke in 1926 and he died at his farm a year later. He was buried in the private Kristinsson cemetery near Markerville. In 1976 Alberta declared his homestead a provincial historic resource.

JANE ROSS

A complete bibliography of the works of Stephan Gudmundur Stephansson can be found in the author's study, written under the name J. W. McCracken, *Stephan G. Stephansson: the poet of the Rocky Mountains* ([Edmonton], 1982). Trans-lated examples of his writings are in [S. G. Stephansson], *Selected prose & poetry*, trans. Kristjana Gunnars (Red Deer, Alta., 1988), and *Selected translations from "Andvökur"*, ed. Jane Ross (Edmonton, 1982).

LAC, RG 15, DIII, 10, 144, f.25 (mfm. at PAA). Private arch., Edwin Stephansson (Markerville, Alta.), Stephan G. Stephansson papers. Univ. of Manitoba Libraries, Elizabeth Dafoe Library (Winnipeg), Icelandic Coll., Stephan G. Stephansson's book coll. Peter Carleton, "Tradition and innovation in twentieth century Icelandic poetry" (PHD thesis, Univ. of California, Berkeley, 1967). F. S. Cawley, "The greatest poet of the western world: Stephan G. Stephansson," *Scandinavian Studies and Notes* (Menasha, Wis.), 15 (1938): 99–109. M[agnús] Einarsson, "Oral tradition and ethnic boundaries: 'West' Icelandic verses and anecdotes," *Canadian Ethnic Studies* (Calgary), 7 (1975), no.2: 19–32. Stefán Einarsson, *A history of Icelandic literature* (New York, 1957). V. J. Eylands, *Lutherans in Canada*, intro. F. C. Fry (Winnipeg, 1945). J. C. F. Hood, *Icelandic church saga* (London, 1946). *Icelandic lyrics: originals and translations*, ed. Richard Beck (Reykjavík, 1930). Skuli Johnson, "Stephan G. Stephansson (1853–1927)," *Icelandic Canadian* (Winnipeg), 9 (1950–51), no.2: 9–12, 44–56. Watson Kirkconnell, "Canada's leading poet: Stephan G. Stephansson (1853–1927)," *Univ. of Toronto Quarterly*, 5 (1935–36): 263–77; *The North American book of Icelandic verse* (New York and Montreal, 1930). W. J. Lindal, *The Icelanders in Canada* (Winnipeg, 1967). Kerry Wood, *The Icelandic-Canadian poet, Stephan Gudmundsson Stephansson, 1853–1927: a tribute* (Red Deer, [1974]).

STEPHEN, GEORGE, 1st Baron MOUNT STEPHEN, businessman, financier, and philanthropist; b. 5 June 1829 near Dufftown, Banffshire, Scotland, son of William Stephen, a carpenter, and Elspet Smith, a crofter's daughter; m. first 8 March 1853 Annie Charlotte Kane (d. 1896) in Woolwich (London), and they had a stillborn child and adopted a daughter; m. secondly 27 Nov. 1897 Gian Tufnell (d. 1933) in Westminster (London), and they had a stillborn child; d. 29 Nov. 1921 in Brocket Hall, Hertfordshire, England.

George Stephen was still an infant when his parents moved to Dufftown, in Banffshire. Educated at the parish school until age 14, he worked briefly at a local hotel and then in Aberdeen as an apprentice to a silk merchant. In 1847 his father and sister immigrated to Montreal. The following year Stephen moved to London, where he worked for a dry goods firm; the remainder of his immediate family went to Montreal. Stephen followed in 1850, after having secured employment with his cousin William Stephen, an importer of dry goods. Within several years Stephen had become the firm's chief buyer. After the death of his cousin in 1862, he took over the business with his youngest brother, Francis. The rapid advance of his career was shown by his election to the Montreal Board of Trade in July 1864. Three years later he sold the dry goods firm to Francis and his partner, Andrew Robertson*.

In 1866 Stephen had established a new firm, George Stephen and Company, which concentrated on the sale and manufacture of woollens and other cloths. He would also act as an agent for textile manufacturers. That year he provided financing to Bennett Rosamond* and his brother William for their tweed mills in Almonte, Upper Canada, and he would be among the incorporators of the Almonte Knitting Company in 1882. By 1866 he had met his cousin Donald Alexander Smith*, a chief factor in the Hudson's Bay Company. The two were to become partners in a myriad of businesses and their careers and fortunes would be closely allied. One of their first investments, in 1868, was the Paton Manufacturing Company of Sherbrooke, a woollen mill built by Andrew Paton*. In 1890 the same partners would acquire the Quebec Worsted Company and, later, a Sherbrooke mill from the firm of Adam Lomas and Son.

By the late 1860s and early 1870s Stephen had become one of the foremost financiers in Montreal. In May 1869 he initiated the recapitalization of the Montreal Rolling Mills Company, a manufacturer of nails and iron bars. He formed a board composed of notables such as Hugh Allan*, Charles John Brydges*, and Edwin Henry King*. The firm would become a leading manufacturer in Saint-Henri (Montreal). A partner in the Sun Mutual Life Insurance Company of Montreal at its incorporation in 1871 [see Mathew Hamilton Gault*], the following year he created the Canada Cotton Manufacturing Company, joining Allan, Smith, Bennett Rosamond, Donald McInnes*, and others in building mills in Cornwall, Ont.

In 1870 Stephen had begun to take an interest in railways, forming the Canada Rolling Stock Company. Smith's convincing tales of the promise of the Canadian northwest encouraged Stephen to attach his name in 1871 and 1873 to two proposals to build lines to Fort Garry (Winnipeg). Although these projects never materialized, his involvement dispels the fable, later circulated by railway executive Sir William Cornelius Van Horne*, that his interest in western railways had been the result of a chance trip from Chicago to St Paul, Minn., in the late 1870s.

A director of the Bank of Montreal since 1871 and vice-president from 1873, Stephen was named president in March 1876. His presidency coincided with a period of economic depression. Nonetheless, the bank maintained its position as Canada's principal consumer and investment bank. Stephen's role was partly ceremonial and partly political, but he was often called on to take an active part in the bank's affairs, travelling to London and New York to meet with leading financiers.

Although he was initially apolitical, Stephen occasionally spoke at public meetings or issued trenchant statements on economic issues. Ostensibly a free trader, as the economic depression of the 1870s deepened he became an advocate of higher tariffs for certain products and of duty exemptions for specialized equipment, such as that used in textile manufacturing or railway construction. By the late 1870s he was increasingly seen as an ally of the Conservatives. After Sir John A. Macdonald* was re-elected prime minister in 1878, textile and rolling mills were among the industries that received favourable treatment under the National Policy. As was the case with other businessmen of his age, Stephen's politics closely followed his economic interests.

In 1877 Smith had introduced Stephen to James Jerome Hill*, a businessman who ran steamboats on the Red River. In August, Stephen visited the unfinished line of the St Paul and Pacific Railroad in Minnesota that Hill sought to purchase and complete to the Canadian border; he was inspired by the prospects. Their meeting led to the establishment of George Stephen and Associates, one of the most profitable partnerships in the history of North American railways. Stephen, Smith, and Hill were joined by Hill's steamboat partner, Norman Wolfred Kittson*. An essential but invisible associate was John Stewart Kennedy, a New York investment banker. The following year Stephen and his partners purchased the line for $5,500,000 in cash and bonds. Unable to obtain financing from London investment banks, Stephen and Smith pledged cash and collateral for their shares, securing short-term financing from the Bank of Montreal. The railway was renamed the St Paul, Minneapolis and Manitoba Railroad, with Stephen as president.

In Montreal's financial community the audacious deal was controversial. It was widely rumoured that Stephen had used his position as president of the Bank of Montreal to obtain loans at preferred rates and with limited collateral. The profits that the company reaped even before the link was established to Winnipeg in December 1878 fuelled these rumours. Stephen's railway enterprises were to be dogged by the press, which closely examined the complicated financial structures for which he would become renowned. He would treat the "scribblers" with contempt, but worried incessantly about their effect on his businesses and reputation.

In the summer of 1880 Stephen began negotiations to secure the contract to build the Canadian Pacific Railway. Using Duncan McIntyre* of the Canada Central Railway as his frontman, he sparred with Macdonald and his minister of railways and canals, Sir Charles Tupper*, over the terms. The final agreement provided the CPR with $25,000,000 in cash, 25,000,000 acres of land west of Winnipeg, and 713 miles of finished railway. The CPR was given tax exemptions, relief on duties for building materials, and a 20-year monopoly prohibiting the construction of railways south of its line in western Canada. When the contract was signed in Ottawa on 21 Oct. 1880, the syndicate comprised Richard Bladworth ANGUS, Stephen, McIntyre, and Hill, as well as Kennedy. Representatives of Morton, Rose and Company, the investment bank led by former finance minister Sir John Rose*, and of Kohn-Reinach et Compagnie, a Franco-German banking house, were also involved. Smith, who had earned Macdonald's animosity, was left off the list, but he would be a substantial shareholder and a valuable assistant to Stephen. The CPR was incorporated on 16 Feb. 1881, with Stephen as president. He immediately resigned from the board of the Bank of Montreal to dedicate himself to the railway.

Stephen miscalculated the time and effort the CPR would require; by November 1881 he admitted it was "assuming dimensions far beyond my calculations." He withdrew from the daily management of the Manitoba line and recalled its vice-president, Angus, to Montreal to assist him with CPR matters. At Hill's suggestion, he hired Van Horne to manage the construction of three major sections. But Hill was unable to persuade the syndicate to abandon the Lake Superior route, which he correctly forecast would be a drag on the CPR in addition to being in direct competition with the Manitoba railway.

The task Stephen faced, of finding additional financing, proved to be as difficult as that of building across 2,000 miles of forest, swamp, rivers, and mountains. The total cost was estimated at $100,000,000, of which at least half had to be secured. Stephen proposed to finance the CPR largely by limiting its ownership to "the smallest possible point," by raising money from a select group of investors, and by providing investors with returns relative to the railway's performance. In so doing, he adopted the model used on the Manitoba line, in which the company would have sufficient funds to reinvest in its line and rolling stock, thereby lowering its operating expenses and building share value. Short-term financing was to be provided by the government grant paid on the completion of each mile of track as well by the revenue from land sales. Stephen's plan was to pattern land settlement along the route, based on the experience of the Manitoba railway, where waves of immigrants had provided the road with passengers and generated freight traffic almost immediately. Both strategies proved to be optimistic. The location of the CPR became the object of speculation, driving land prices to unreasonable levels. Immigrants were not immediately attracted to the prairies, whose fertility had long been the subject of debate. Stephen's schemes to entice settlers from Scotland and Ireland did not get support from the British government, and the HBC, which owned large tracts of land, proved to be a recalcitrant partner in the settlement of the west.

Driven by the need for revenues and an eastern terminus beyond the designated end of the CPR at Cal-lander, near North Bay, Ont., Stephen dedicated much of his time to the acquisition and construction of regional lines in Ontario and Quebec. The syndicate bought the Canada Central in 1881, the western section of the Quebec, Montreal, Ottawa and Occidental in 1882, and the Toronto, Grey and Bruce in 1884. To connect Ottawa to Toronto, it built the Ontario and Quebec Railway. Stephen had personally acquired a large interest in the Credit Valley Railway from George Laidlaw* in 1880 and later incorporated the line into the CPR network. The rapid expansion of the CPR into the territory controlled by the Grand Trunk, under Joseph Hickson*, led to conflict between the two in the 1880s. Under pressure from Macdonald, the CPR and the Grand Trunk put an end to their territorial battles in 1890.

Although Stephen showed considerable tactical skill in creating an eastern network for the CPR, the capital it had required put increasing demands on the syndicate's financial resources. By 1883 the syndicate was showing signs of strain. The CPR had found few investors in the capital markets of London and New York, so Stephen had to borrow against his Manitoba stock and pledge his new Montreal mansion as collateral. Finally he and Smith sold some of their shares in the Manitoba railway in order to meet the CPR's expenses and dividend payments. Hill refused to do the same for fear of losing majority control of the line. He had come to the realization that the CPR would compete fiercely with his own railway for eastbound traffic. He resigned from the CPR board in May 1883, but held on to half of his shares out of loyalty to his partners. Kennedy also left, depressing the CPR stock yet further and making Stephen's increasingly frantic attempts to find capital more difficult.

In the face of the looming crisis, McIntyre resigned in May 1884 and soon after forced the other directors to buy his shares, earning Stephen's lifelong enmity. Stephen had successfully lobbied Macdonald for a bill to guarantee the CPR's dividend payments, due in November 1884, and pay other expenses; the legislation had passed in March. By the beginning of 1885, Stephen, Smith, and Angus had exhausted their collateral. They used the exposure of the Bank of Montreal to the CPR and the threat to the security of the banking system generally as the pretext for a second relief bill. Tupper and MP John Henry Pope* argued convincingly in cabinet in support of the measure. The outbreak of the North-West rebellion [see Louis Riel*] in March 1885 provided ample evidence of the value of a transcontinental link; troops were transported in seven days where it had taken four months in 1870 at the time of the Red River uprising. This situation eased passage of the bill, assented to on 20 July 1885, which provided for a new bond issue that brought the railway enough money to stave off its creditors and complete construction. Stephen was absent when

Smith pounded home the last spike at Craigellachie, B.C., on 7 Nov. 1885.

Whether they had held on out of obstinacy, recklessness, or pride, Stephen, Smith, and Angus were the sole members of the original syndicate to have stayed. The support of Macdonald and his cabinet had proved essential and had provided a counterweight to the CPR's shaky financial foundations. Yet Stephen refused to accept the argument that the CPR owed its existence to the government. He dismissed any attempts to impinge on the railway's freedom and became embroiled in a very public battle of several years' duration with the Manitoba government of Premier John Norquay* over the unpopular monopoly clause. Bowing to public pressure in 1888, the CPR allowed for the construction of branch lines south of its main line, but it wrestled a compensatory payment from the federal government. On this and other issues, Stephen proved himself ill-suited to public debate, his threats and condemnations serving only to fan the flames of discontent. He resigned from the CPR's presidency on 7 Aug. 1888, supporting the appointment of Van Horne as his replacement. He remained a director until 1893, but thereafter showed only sporadic interest in the railway; he reduced his holdings substantially and even encouraged others to follow suit.

As the CPR's first president, Stephen had played politicians ably and his indefatigable pleading had proved effective. He also deployed an extensive network of allies, whom he secured by various means. For instance, Pope, the influential minister, was offered advantageous options on stock in the New Brunswick Railway (also acquired by the CPR). When Hugh John MACDONALD, son of the prime minister, announced his move to Winnipeg to open a law office with a son of Tupper, Stephen immediately offered $5,000 of legal business from the CPR's land department. The extent to which Stephen had acquired the allegiance of Macdonald and his government is hinted at in a letter he wrote to the prime minister in 1890 in which he mentioned that he had personally contributed more than $1,000,000 to the Conservative party since 1882.

If Stephen rued his involvement in the CPR, it was largely because of the toll it took on his own portfolio. His liquidation of a substantial portion of his stake in the Manitoba railway to finance the CPR made him a poorer man than Hill. He also regretted having encouraged his associates to invest in the CPR, knowing that the Manitoba railway was a better opportunity. Although he had resigned the presidency of the Manitoba board in February 1884, he nurtured life-long affection for his first railway venture and for its enterprising president. Hill developed the St Paul, Minneapolis and Manitoba line into the Great Northern Railroad and built his own transcontinental network. It remained Stephen's principal investment and

the source of most of his wealth. In key moments in the expansion of Hill's empire Stephen would prove to be his staunchest ally.

During the mid 1880s Stephen spent more and more time in England. By 1888 he was domiciled there. He had garnered the first of many honours when he was made a baronet on 3 March 1886. In 1891 he was granted a peerage and took the title Baron Mount Stephen from a peak in the Rocky Mountains adjacent to the CPR line. Although he sat regularly in the House of Lords, he never took part in debates or committees. He returned to Canada infrequently, making his last trip in 1894. His support was nonetheless sought by those pursuing higher office in Canada, such as Lord Minto [Elliot*], who acknowledged that he owed his appointment as governor general in 1898 to the influence of Stephen and Garnet Joseph, Lord Wolseley*. From the 1890s onwards, Stephen delegated management of most of his investments in Canada to his brother-in-law Robert Meighen* and his private affairs to his Canadian agent, John Turnbull. His American affairs he left in the hands of lawyer John William Sterling. His English investments were managed by Gaspard Farrer, a partner in Baring Brothers.

In private life Stephen was retiring. He and his first wife had adopted as a young woman Alice Brooke, purportedly the daughter of a Vermont clergyman. Stephen would introduce her to her husband, Henry Stafford Northcote, and would help him secure the position of governor of Bombay. His second wife, Gian Tufnell, 35 years his junior, had been lady-in-waiting to the Duchess of Teck and was a close friend of her daughter, who would become Queen Mary in 1910. The Stephens regularly hosted members of the royal family at Brocket Hall in Hertfordshire, a substantial home with extensive gardens, which they leased from 1893.

A tireless worker, Stephen had only one pastime, salmon fishing. In November 1873 he had bought property at the confluence of the Causapscal and Matapédia rivers in Quebec and acquired leases on fishing rights. He made regular trips there and entertained business partners, friends, and the occasional governor general. A pioneer of sport fishing in the Gaspé peninsula, he introduced many to the sport and to the region, where he became a benefactor. By the 1880s he was seeking other waters to fish. In 1886 he purchased land in Grand-Métis. On a promontory overlooking the Mitis and St Lawrence rivers he built Estevan Lodge. The house, property, and contents cost $73,426. In 1918 he would give the estate to his niece Elsie Reford [Meighen*], who would later transform it into a vast ornamental garden.

In 1883 Stephen had moved into the mansion he built in Montreal. Designed by William Tutin Thomas, the house cost some $600,000. It has been described by architectural historian Arthur John Hampson Richardson as a "one of the real masterpieces of the [Italianate] style in Canada." After Stephen moved to England, the residence was used by his sister Elsie and her husband, Robert Meighen, who acquired it in 1900. It would become the Mount Stephen Club in 1926.

One of the most generous philanthropists of his time, Stephen sought no accolades for his gestures. Although he made ample provision for his 19 nieces and nephews and the relatives of his two wives, he directed much of his wealth towards hospitals. In 1890 he and Smith had acquired the Frothingham estate [see John Frothingham*] in Montreal as the site for the Royal Victoria Hospital and they contributed $500,000 each to its construction. After it opened in 1893, they gave an additional $500,000 each in stock to pay for the building and establish an endowment fund. Stephen also donated a wing to the Montreal General Hospital and made donations to hospitals in Scotland, but he reserved the bulk of his wealth for a single charity, the Prince of Wales Hospital Fund for London (renamed King Edward's Hospital Fund in 1907). Established in 1897, it assisted the voluntary hospitals in the greater London area. Stephen worked closely with the Prince of Wales (later George V) in building the endowment and was its most important benefactor. His total gifts to it amounted to £1,315,000.

Almost completely deaf in his later years, Stephen spent much of his time at Brocket Hall and showed a firm hand and mind until shortly before his death in 1921. He was buried in the graveyard nearby. Although he had given generously to hospitals, it was not because he had had occasion to use them. Blessed with a solid constitution, he had enjoyed remarkable health, not missing a day to illness in over 53 years and never suffering a single headache. At the time of his death, his estate was valued at £1,414,319. He left little to charities or causes in Canada, believing that he had given more to this country than it had given to him.

Unlike his partners and associates Hill, Smith, and Van Horne, Stephen was never accorded a biography by contemporary publicists or authors. The fact that he burned the bulk of his papers before his death and had no children helped to make his story inaccessible. His quiet retirement to England at age 59 had removed him from public attention and the dizzying complexity of his financial transactions made him a less appealing subject than his larger-than-life partners. In addition, his reputation has risen and fallen with that of the CPR. Critics have viewed the railway as a needless extravagance, nationalists have seen it as essential to the creation of a transcontinental nation. Stephen himself was ambivalent. However important he believed the CPR to be to Canada, he was not convinced of its value as a business investment. His with-drawal from it is sometimes interpreted as a slight to Canada and a petulant retreat from a country that had not adequately acknowledged his importance. In fact, he received the highest honour then awarded to a Canadian, a peerage. His rapid withdrawal underscores that he fully comprehended the nature of railroading, where profitability depended more on competent managers than ambitious financiers. In Hill and Van Horne, he was associated with two of the best on the continent.

Historian Donald Grant Creighton* dubbed Stephen "perhaps the greatest creative genius in the whole history of Canadian finance." His phrase nicely captures the ambiguous nature of Stephen's success; creativity in finance is often synonymous with dishonesty. Stephen and the members of his syndicate were assailed at the time as business magnates who manipulated politics, the press, and the financial community to their own gain. The contrast with Stephen's view of himself could not be starker. His gravestone carries the inscription "wise in his benefactions, of stainless integrity." Although he used the complete arsenal employed by financiers to cajole and convince, his chief asset appears to have been his buoyant optimism and his power of persuasion. His obituary in the *Times* (London), penned by associate Gaspard Farrer, ascribed his success to the fact that "he had the gift of instantaneously inspiring confidence and arousing enthusiasm and devotion. . . . In his presence doubt and difficulties vanished and hope and confidence revived."

ALEXANDER REFORD

James Jerome Hill Reference Library (St Paul, Minn.), J. J. Hill papers (mfm. at LAC). LAC, MG 26, A; MG 29, A28, A30; MG 30, D59, 18. Private arch., Alexander Reford (Grand-Métis, Qué.), George Stephen, 1st Baron Mount Stephen, letter-book. *Gazette* (Montreal), 19–20 Aug. 1879. *Globe*, 12 Sept. 1883. *Times* (London), 1 Dec. 1921. Michael Bliss, *Northern enterprise: five centuries of Canadian business* (Toronto, 1987). C. J. Brydges, *The letters of Charles John Brydges, 1883–1889; Hudson's Bay Company land commissioner*, ed. Hartwell Bowsfield, intro. J. E. Rea (Winnipeg, 1981). *Canada Gazette*, 16 Dec. 1871. D. [G.] Creighton, *John A. Macdonald, the old chieftain* (Toronto, 1955; repr. 1965). Merrill Denison, *Canada's first bank: a history of the Bank of Montreal* (2v., Toronto and Montreal, 1966–67). *Dominion annual reg.*, 1879–81, 1885–86. J. A. Eagle, *The Canadian Pacific Railway and the development of western Canada, 1896–1914* (Kingston, Ont., 1989). Ben Forster, *A conjunction of interests: business, politics, and tariffs, 1825–1879* (Toronto, 1986). Heather Gilbert, "A footnote to history: the unaccountable fifth; solution of a Great Northern enigma," *Minn. Hist.* (St Paul), 42 (1971): 175–77; *The life of Lord Mount Stephen . . .* (2v., Aberdeen, Scot., 1965–77); "Mount Stephen: a study in environments," *Northern Scotland* (Aberdeen), 1 (1972), no.2: 177–97. R. D. Lewis, *Manufacturing Montreal: the making of an industrial landscape, 1850 to 1930* (Baltimore, Md, 2000).

Sterling

London Gazette, 26 June 1891. Donna McDonald, Lord Strathcona: a biography of Donald Alexander Smith (Toronto and Oxford, 1996). Albro Martin, James J. Hill and the opening of the northwest (New York, 1976; repr., intro. W. T. White, St Paul, 1991). Keith Morris, The story of Lord Mount Stephen (London, 1922). A. A. den Otter, "The Hudson's Bay Company's prairie transportation problem, 1870–85," in The developing west: essays on Canadian history in honor of Lewis H. Thomas, ed. J. E. Foster (Edmonton, 1983), 25–47; "Transportation and transformation, the Hudson's Bay Company, 1857–1885," Great Plains Quarterly (Lincoln, Nebr.), 3 (1983): 171–85. James Pope-Hennessy, Queen Mary, 1867–1953 (London, [1959]). A. J. H. Richardson et al., Quebec City: architects, artisans and builders (Ottawa, 1984). Types of Canadian women ..., ed. H. J. Morgan (Toronto, 1903). B. J. Young, Promoters and politicians: the north-shore railways in the history of Quebec, 1854–85 (Toronto, 1978).

STERLING, ALICE JANE (Johnson), social reformer; b. 13 Dec. 1839 in Newport, N.S., daughter of John Sterling; m. before 1862 Richard Johnson*, presumably in Nova Scotia, and they had two daughters and two sons; d. 2 Feb. 1921 in Charlottetown.

Little is known of Alice Jane Sterling's life prior to her marriage. Her father, a native of England, had settled in the Windsor area of Nova Scotia, where he is purported to have been a man of some importance. No record remains of when or where Alice received her schooling, but, from an examination of her later involvement in various organizations, she seems to have been well educated. She likely met her future husband in 1860, when he became a Methodist minister in Windsor. Their first child was born in 1862. Richard Johnson had originally studied medicine at Harvard Medical School; he returned to complete his degree in 1864 and graduated the following year. The family then relocated to Charlottetown, where Richard established a practice and a dispensary.

Like many women of her social class, Alice Johnson took an active interest in the welfare of her fellow citizens. She was a founder and first president of the Ladies' Hospital Aid Society, established shortly after the incorporation of the Prince Edward Island Hospital in 1884. The society collected voluntary subscriptions, the sole support for the hospital during its early years, made weekly visits to patients, and arranged lectures, concerts, musical evenings, and skating parties to raise funds for equipment and supplies. By 1897–98 Alice no longer held the presidency.

Although her involvement reflects her support for her husband's work – he was one of the hospital's incorporators and physicians – she also assumed an independent role in other bodies, particularly the Woman's Christian Temperance Union. The first Canadian WCTU had been established in Ontario in 1874 [see Letitia Creighton*] and unions had been formed in Saint John in 1877 and in Halifax about 1878. Prince Edward Island women, however, did not organize until 1890. At that time several locals formed and affiliated themselves with the Maritime WCTU. Alice was instrumental in the organization of locals in both Charlottetown and Summerside, but it was the Charlottetown union that occupied her attention. She was its founding president and continued in the position until at least 1895. Partly on account of her efforts and those of the WCTU, public opinion turned in favour of temperance. In 1900 the legislature passed the Prohibition Act and the Island thus became the first province to ban the sale of alcohol.

Alice's involvement at the regional level had begun when the Island locals joined the Maritime WCTU. At its annual conference in 1890 in Halifax, where she was a delegate for Charlottetown, she was elected vice-president for Prince Edward Island, and was appointed to the committee on resolutions, along with three other women, and as the Island's delegate to the dominion convention to be held in 1891 in Saint John. Re-elected vice-president that year at the Maritime convention in Summerside, she was made a delegate to attend the convention of the World's WCTU in Boston later in 1891. Within three years, in addition to serving as vice-president, she had become superintendent of the Maritime WCTU's department of purity in literature, art, and fashion and recording secretary of its literature committee. Her participation in the Maritime union came to an end in 1895 when a motion was passed at its annual convention to dissolve and allow the three provincial unions to function independently within the dominion union.

Sometime before 1889 Alice Johnson's son William Arthur Sterling had entered his father's drug business in the family home on Kent Street. He was joined in 1893 by his brother, Richard McKay, a graduate pharmacist. A year later Richard Johnson built a modern new house on Prince Street, and Alice lived there after his death in 1903. During the last two decades of her life, she evidently focused her energies on First Methodist Church, of which she was a member. She taught Sunday school from 1902 to 1920, was a vice-president of the Woman's Missionary Society for much of the period from 1901 to 1911, and was president of the Dorcas Society from 1901 to 1917, with breaks in 1908–11 and 1915. When her health began to fail, she assumed a less demanding role; in 1918 she became honorary president of the Dorcas Society. After a two-year illness, she died in the Prince Edward Island Hospital in February 1921 at age 81. She was survived by her son Arthur, then living in Alabama.

Throughout her life, Alice Johnson had demonstrated a moral outlook and commitment to charitable works that were typical of upper-middle-class Protestant women of the era. Until the time of her death, the Charlottetown Guardian noted, she "retained the keen interest of charity and Christian effort to which she had devoted the years of her youth and strength," and she was remembered as "an active worker for every cause that had for its aim the betterment of the community and of the world."

JILL MACMICKEN WILSON

AO, F 834, MU 7278. NSARM, MG 20, 357, item 1; 359, item 3; 360, item 22. *Charlottetown Guardian*, 3–4 Feb. 1921. *Patriot* (Charlottetown), 3 July 1895, 3 Feb. 1921. *Pioneer* (Summerside, P.E.I.), 21 Sept. 1891. First Methodist Church, *Annual report* (Charlottetown), 1897, 1901–21 (mfm. at PARO, Acc. 3295M-4). *A history of the Prince Edward Island Hospital School of Nursing, 1891–1971*, [ed. C. J. Callbeck] (Charlottetown, 1974). Wendy Mitchinson, "The WCTU: 'For God, home and native land'; a study in nineteenth-century feminism," in *A not unreasonable claim: women and reform in Canada, 1880s–1920s*, ed. Linda Kealey (Toronto, 1979), 151–67. *Past and present of Prince Edward Island . . .*, ed. D. A. MacKinnon and A. B. Warburton (Charlottetown, [1906]). Prince Edward Island Hospital, *Annual report* (Charlottetown), 1892–1910 (copies at PARO, Acc. 2594/A, items 31–42). I. L. Rogers, *Charlottetown: the life in its buildings* (Charlottetown, 1983). J. E. Veer, "Feminist forebears: the Woman's Christian Temperance Union in Canada's Maritime provinces, 1875–1900" (PHD thesis, Univ. of N.B., Fredericton, 1994.)

STEVENSON, ALEXANDER PATTERSON, horticulturist and office holder; b. 14 Feb. 1854 in Bannockburn, Scotland; m. 19 Dec. 1877 Catherine Campbell, and they had four daughters and three sons; d. 22 Dec. 1922 in Santa Monica, Calif.

The eldest son in a large Scottish family, Alexander Stevenson was expected to make his own way, so in 1870 he left Scotland for Canada. Experienced in farm work, he spent the next several years as a farm and forestry labourer around Toronto and Markham, Ont. In 1874 he travelled by the Red River route to Manitoba.

Encouraged by people he met to homestead at the edge of the Pembina Hills, midway between the present towns of Morden and Miami, Stevenson immediately began to experiment with fruit growing. The early years were difficult; most of his trees died over winter. His first success was with crab apples and from those he went on to strawberries, standard apples, and other fruit, including pears, mammoth plums, grapes, and black cherries. In spite of grasshopper plagues, he persevered.

Stevenson's success was greatly aided by two factors. First, by 1890 he had obtained stock which had originated in Russia and had come to him from the Iowa State College of Agriculture and Mechanic Arts in Ames, Iowa. Grafting onto this stock, he created new varieties of fruit trees, including the Pine Grove Red apple and the Manitoba plum. The second factor, of equal or greater importance, was his insistence on protection for his trees, in the form of windbreaks and shelter belts. Indeed, his zeal for shelter belts led to his being appointed, at least as early as 1901, tree-plant-ing inspector for the forestry branch of the Department of the Interior, attached to the Forest Nursery Station at Indian Head (Sask.). In this role he lectured extensively in the west on horticultural and forestry matters, becoming so prominent that in 1910 the *Farmer's Advocate and Home Journal* felt it was "safe to say that no man in the Canadian West is more generally known throughout the prairie provinces."

Stevenson was a careful horticulturist. In 1890, for example, he wrote to the *Nor'-West Farmer and Miller* reporting on the results of growing forest-tree seedlings which he had obtained from the experimental farm in Ottawa. He described their survival rates and their measured rates of growth. He operated Pine Grove Nursery, an orchard and nursery, for 37 years, producing especially apples in commercial quantities. In 1909 he sold $500 worth of apples. Two years later his orchard produced 70 barrels and in 1913, 300 barrels. Eventually, he had 25 acres of land producing fruit. He had the best exhibit of apples at the Dry Farming Congress for Alberta, Saskatchewan, and Manitoba held in Lethbridge in 1912 and for it he received a prize of a case of silver valued at $400.

A strong supporter of his community, Nelson, Stevenson served as a school trustee and as an elder of the Presbyterian church. The thriving town disappeared almost overnight in 1881 when the Manitoba South-Western Colonization Railway was constructed a few miles further south, near what became Morden. Stevenson's success and fame in growing fruit in the region led to the establishment of the Dominion Experimental Farm at Morden in 1915. Stevenson had retired two years earlier, however. He turned his nursery over to his sons and moved to Winnipeg. While there, he spent much time at the Manitoba Agricultural College, where his experience was appreciated.

The commitment and careful experimentation of Alexander Stevenson were significant in clearly establishing the fact that good fruit could be grown on the prairies of western Canada. Many prairie residents have benefited from the work of the man who became known as the "Apple King."

DAVID R. DYCK

Alexander Patterson Stevenson's publications include *Growing cherries in Manitoba* ([Winnipeg?], 1914) and *Growing plums in Manitoba* ([Winnipeg?], 1914), as well as various articles on horticulture and sylviculture; a listing is available in *Science and technology biblio.* (Richardson and MacDonald). Several of Stevenson's reports as tree-planting inspector appear in Can., Parl., *Sessional papers*, reports of the Dept. of the Interior, 1902–5.

Farmer's Advocate and Home Journal (Winnipeg), 4 Jan. 1911. *Manitoba Free Press*, 23 Dec. 1922. *Nor'-West Farmer and Miller* (Winnipeg), December 1890. *Winnipeg Tribune*, 31 Aug. 1921. *The hills of home: a history of the municipality of Thompson* (Miami, Man., 1968). [J. W.] G. MacEwan,

Fifty mighty men (Saskatoon, 1958). *Manitoba Agricultural Extension News* (Winnipeg), 3 (1923), no.1: 3–4. Western Canadian Soc. for Horticulture, *Development of horticulture on the Canadian prairies; an historical review*, ed. H. S. Fry (Edmonton, 1986).

STEVENSON, FREDERICK JOSEPH, air force officer and bush pilot; b. 2 Dec. 1896 in Parry Sound, Ont., fourth of the five children of Annie Laurie Quinn and Joseph Stevenson; d. unmarried 3 Jan. 1928 in The Pas, Man.

When Frederick Joseph Stevenson was a young child his father, a superintendent of railway bridge construction, was transferred to Saskatchewan. Stevenson, known as Steve, was a good student, loved baseball, and spent many summers with his father tenting, while his father checked bridges throughout the province. He came to enjoy the outdoors and learned wilderness survival skills which would serve him well as a bush pilot. After high school he worked for the Bank of Hamilton at a branch in Saskatchewan, probably at Vonda, and then one in Winnipeg, where in 1916 he enrolled at Wesley College. Shortly afterwards, he enlisted in the 196th Battalion and was sent to Seaford, England. While in the infantry he was wounded. The lure of Royal Flying Corps aircraft stationed nearby was strong and Stevenson joined the RFC in the summer of 1917. He served with 79 Squadron, flying Sopwith Dolphin fighters. Credited with destroying three observation balloons and 18 enemy aircraft, he was awarded the Distinguished Flying Cross on 3 June 1919, but the citation gave no details as to which of the accomplishments earned him the award. He is also reported to have been awarded the French and the Belgian Croix de Guerre and to have been mentioned in dispatches. He ended the war with the rank of captain.

Unlike most wartime pilots, Stevenson found work as a pilot after the war. First, with the Royal Air Force, he flew delegates and dispatches between London and Paris during the Peace Conference of 1919. He next taught White Russians in the Crimea how to fly. For this service he was awarded the Order of St Stanislaus. In 1920 he joined the Canadian Aircraft Company in Winnipeg, gave exhibitions of aerobatic flying, transported passengers, and barnstormed throughout Manitoba. From 1924 to 1926, with the newly organized Ontario Provincial Air Service, he flew forestry patrols from bases at Sault Ste Marie, Sioux Lookout, and Sudbury. In 1927 he joined James Armstrong Richardson*'s Western Canada Airways. With the new company he made many trips but three operations were considered epic-making and earned him the reputation of being Canada's leading commercial pilot.

The first series of flights was between Cache Lake, Man., at the end of the rail line, and Fort Churchill, during March and April 1927. One of two pilots, Stevenson made 27 round trips in 30 days, flew 6,093 miles, and transported 17,894 pounds of material and 14 men so that exploratory drilling of Fort Churchill's harbour could be undertaken that year. The flights were significant as the first large airlift operation in Canada. They also determined the selection of Fort Churchill as the ocean terminus of the Hudson Bay Railway. The second operation occurred between August and October 1927. Stevenson, flying 12,542 miles in 28 days, transported 23 tons of mining equipment from Cormorant Lake to Cold Lake (northeast of Flin Flon). This operation was the largest freighting contract in North America to that time. More important, it proved to the mining industry that it was more economical to fly in equipment than to pay men to pack it into the bush. During the third trip, in December 1927, Stevenson made a 600-mile return flight from The Pas to Reindeer Lake. Although no details are given in the company's files, likely the importance of this flight was its length and the time of year.

Stevenson's flights helped to establish the usefulness of aircraft in peacetime and in remote areas. At the end of World War I most Canadians looked on flying as a military venture or as a frivolous pastime and saw no use for flying in peacetime. Stevenson helped to change the image of the airplane. He showed how it could open up the north by transporting bulky and heavy freight into distant and generally inaccessible areas. Under the WCA's banner he initiated freighting by air. His pioneering flights were made under primitive conditions; there were often no landing fields, no lighting, no navigation or radio aids, no facilities such as hangars in which to do repairs, and only sketchy maps. In addition, the aircraft were not built to operate in extreme cold and frequently broke down away from base. The pilot, moreover, sat in an open cockpit.

Stevenson was well suited to these pioneer flights, however. His easy-going attitude was ideal for an environment which had no established way of doing things and where each flight was an experiment. Equally important, he was a risk-taker and an innovative thinker, as is evidenced by his tying toboggans to the wheels of his aircraft so that he could land on snow.

On 5 Jan. 1928, after his Fokker Universal aircraft, G-CAGE, had been repaired, he successfully test flew the plane, but crashed while attempting to land and was killed. Pilot error was the cause. His brilliant flying and his contributions to the advancement of aviation were quickly recognized. In 1928 he was posthumously awarded the Harmon Trophy for Canada by the International League of Aviators for the previous year. Also in 1928 Winnipeg's municipal airfield was named Stevenson Aerodrome in his honour. That January the WCA had nominated him, unsuccessfully, for the top Canadian aviation trophy, the McKee Trophy. Seven months later the government of

Manitoba named a northern lake and a river after him. In 1964 the St James–Winnipeg Airport Commission had a bronze bust of him, sculpted by Cecil Richardson, mounted on a pedestal at the airport. In 1973 a Winnipeg school was named in his honour. All of Stevenson's medals are displayed at Winnipeg International Airport.

SHIRLEY RENDER

AM, MG 11, A34; P 3361. Western Canada Aviation Museum (Winnipeg), F. J. Stevenson file. *Winnipeg Free Press*, 19 Oct. 1936, 13 July 1970. *Winnipeg Tribune*, 16 Dec. 1972. Peter Corley-Smith, *Barnstorming to bush flying: British Columbia's aviation pioneers, 1910–1930* (Victoria, 1989). F. H. Ellis, *Canada's flying heritage* (Toronto, 1954; rev. ed., 1961). G. A. Fuller *et al.*, *125 years of Canadian aeronautics: a chronology, 1840–1965* (Willowdale, Ont., 1983). K. M. Molson, *Pioneering in Canadian air transport* ([Winnipeg], 1974). D. F. Parrott, *Harold Farrington, pioneer bush pilot* (Thunder Bay, Ont., 1982). S. L. Render, "Canadian Airways Limited" (MA thesis, Univ. of Man., Winnipeg, 1984). A. G. Sutherland, *Canada's aviation pioneers: 50 years of McKee Trophy winners* (Toronto, 1978). Bruce West, *The firebirds* ([Toronto], 1974).

STEWART, THOMAS, Presbyterian minister, professor, and church administrator; b. 16 Dec. 1855 in West Bay, N.S., fourth son of the Reverend Murdoch Stewart and Catherine McGregor; younger brother of Donald Alexander Stewart* and John Stewart*; m. 10 July 1888 Florence Russell Wetmore in St George, N.B., and they had two daughters; d. 8 Jan. 1923 in Halifax.

In 1843 Thomas Stewart's father, a Presbyterian minister, emigrated from Scotland to Cape Breton Island. Thomas was born into the bosom of the Free Church of Nova Scotia, of which his father was moderator in 1851, and he duly followed him into the ministry. Educated first at Pictou Academy and Dalhousie University (BA 1882), he graduated from the Presbyterian College in Halifax (BD 1884). Licensed by the Presbytery of Halifax in April 1884, he spent the winter session of 1884–85 taking a postgraduate course in the divinity halls of the United Presbyterian Church and the Free Church in Edinburgh. There he came under the influence of Henry Drummond, professor of natural science in the Free Church college and an evangelical theologian whose works harmonized evolution and Christianity and directed Christians to shape their social environment. Stewart also did social work among children in the slums.

Returning to the Synod of the Maritime Provinces, Stewart was ordained by the Presbytery of Saint John in January 1886 and he served briefly as missionary at St George and Pennfield, N.B. In 1887 he was called to Sussex and in 1891 he moved to St James Church in Dartmouth, N.S., where he remained for 17 years. His active pastoral career ended in 1908, when he was appointed professor of church history and practical theology at the Presbyterian College, which granted him a DD that same year. Though he lacked scholarly interests, it was a post for which his formative experiences in Edinburgh had well prepared him. Not only did Stewart, like his father, believe strongly in the need for a learned ministry, he was also a notable evangelical preacher. Throughout his five years as a professor, he was a vigorous exponent of the Social Gospel, which he was chiefly responsible for carrying in the Maritime synod. Writing in *Theologue* (Halifax) in 1911, he challenged the church not to be indifferent to urban poverty of the sort found in Halifax and Sydney, and he urged ministers to take an active interest in parishioners' daily lives. He was joined in this advocacy by two other leading exponents of the Social Gospel in the Maritimes, the Reverend John William Angus Nicholson* of St James Church in Dartmouth and the Reverend William Henry Smith* of St Paul's Church in Fredericton. Their views helped significantly to draw the attention of Maritime Presbyterians to social problems that were perhaps broader in range than those which officially engaged the church's national and regional boards on temperance and moral reform [*see* John George SHEARER].

In 1913 Stewart reluctantly abandoned academic life to accept the post of agent, or treasurer, of the board of trustees of the eastern section of the Presbyterian Church in Canada. He had been offered, and declined, the post on one or two previous occasions. According to historian John S. Moir, the agent acted as secretary of the home and foreign missions committees in the Maritime provinces and of the board of superintendents of the Presbyterian College, and as general treasurer for all church schemes except the Ministers' Widows' and Orphans' Fund. During the nine years he held the post, Stewart became nationally known within the church. He was already mortally ill, apparently with cancer, when elected moderator of the Maritime synod in September 1922; the previous June he had been appointed senior clerk of the General Assembly. He died in January 1923. Had he lived, only his principled opposition to interdenominational church union could have prevented his becoming moderator of the General Assembly, and he, rather than Ephraim Scott*, would likely have been chosen as first moderator of the continuing Presbyterian Church. Unlike many of his closest clerical friends and colleagues, he looked upon the union movement as schismatic.

Though a conservative in theology and ecclesiastical politics, Stewart was an evangelical whose commitment to social justice was rooted in the Scottish liberalism of his father and the Free Church. Another side showed in his obsession with foreign missions, the white man's burden, and jingoistic imperialism that was typical of mainstream Canadian Protestantism, but as a progressive Social Gospeller no senior Presbyterian minister stood in higher esteem than Stewart. "In him," wrote Archibald McKellar Mac-Mechan* in condolence to John Stewart, then dean of medicine at Dalhousie, "I always recognized the quality of steel. He made me think of a drawn sword, something clear, keen, powerful, – a weapon. He belonged to the Church militant. In his intellect, in his preaching, in his standard of faith and morals there was to me always this clearness, this keenness, as of a sword. I knew him chiefly in the pulpit, as a preacher of righteousness, unfaltering, uncompromising."

BARRY CAHILL

[Thomas Stewart's papers, which must have been voluminous, have not survived. Knowledge of his career depends largely on the biographical sketch written shortly after his death by one of his oldest friends, the Reverend George Stephen Carson, and published in the family's memorial volume, *Toward the sunrising and other sermons* (Toronto, 1923). A sermon preached by Stewart in 1921 is reprinted in *History, Church of St. James, Dartmouth, Nova Scotia* ([Dartmouth, 1971?]). B.C.]

Dalhousie Univ. Arch. (Halifax), MS 2-82 (A. McK. MacMechan papers), C906. NSARM, Churches, St James United (Dartmouth), records, 1891–1908 (mfm.). UCC, Maritime Conference Arch. (Sackville, N.B.), Pine Hill Divinity Hall fonds, 1908–23. UCC-C, Biog. file. *Evening Mail* (Halifax), 11 Jan. 1923. *Presbyterian Witness* (Halifax), 1886–1923. E. A. Betts, *Pine Hill Divinity Hall, 1820–1970: a history* (Halifax, 1970). Michael Boudreau, "Strikes, rural decay and socialism: the Presbyterian Church in Nova Scotia grapples with social realities, 1880–1914," in *The contribution of Presbyterianism to the Maritime provinces of Canada*, ed. C. H. H. Scobie and G. A. Rawlyk (Montreal and Kingston, Ont., 1997), 144–59. B. J. Fraser, *The social uplifters: Presbyterian progressives and the Social Gospel in Canada, 1875–1915* (Waterloo, Ont., 1988); "Theology and the Social Gospel among Canadian Presbyterians: a case study," *Studies in Religion* (Waterloo), 8 (1979): 35–46. A. D. MacKinnon, *A history of the Presbyterian Church in Cape Breton* (Antigonish, N.S., 1975). Presbyterian Church in Canada, General Assembly, *Acts and proc.* (Toronto), 1908–23; Synod of the Maritime Provinces, *Minutes* (Halifax, etc.), 1891–1923 (available in UCC, Maritime Conference Arch.). *Presbyterian Record* (Montreal), 1908–23. *Theologue* (Halifax), 1908–19.

STEWART, WILLIAM JAMES, engineer, hydrographic surveyor, and civil servant; b. 23 Jan. 1863 in Ottawa, son of John Stewart and Mary Renney; m. 9 Nov. 1886 Clara Louise Lasher in Cataraqui (Kingston), Ont., and they had two daughters; d. 5 May 1925 in Ottawa.

William J. Stewart was the eldest son of a building contractor and officer in the Ottawa Field Battery. Raised in an Irish Anglican family, he was a goldmedal graduate of both the Ottawa Collegiate Institute (1879) and the Royal Military College of Canada in

Kingston (1883), which emphasized engineering as well as military training. He initially worked in eastern Ontario as a survey engineer for the Department of Railways and Canals and then, in March 1884, he joined the Department of Marine and Fisheries as an assistant to British Admiralty surveyor John George Boulton, who was conducting a hydrographic survey of Georgian Bay. It had been prompted by a mounting loss of lives and shipping, including the steamship *Asia* in 1882. Stewart succeeded Boulton as officer in charge in 1893, though by this time Stewart's fieldwork had extended to the west coast [*see* William Smith*]; his resurvey of Burrard Inlet in 1891 was the first hydrographic survey conducted in salt water by Canadian authorities. To enhance his ability, in 1897 he secured certification as a ship's master on inland waters. With no national geodetic survey to use as a base for hydrography, he reported that same year, he and his crews routinely used transit theodolites, sextants, triangular plotting, soundings from whaleboats or small steamers, and floor sampling. In a typical season, from May to November, about 800 square miles could be sounded.

When the maritime survey functions of Marine and Fisheries, Public Works, and Railways and Canals were united to form the Canadian Hydrographic Service within Marine and Fisheries in 1904, Stewart was appointed chief surveyor. During his tenure, the service published charts, sailing directions, and tide tables that facilitated safe navigation; impressively, Stewart was responsible personally or as a supervisor for producing some 170 charts. Between 1910 and 1922 his branch was part of the Department of the Naval Service, along with the dominion's fledgling navy, fisheries protection, tidal and current survey, and radio-telegraphy.

In 1907 Stewart succeeded William Frederick King* on the International Waterways Commission, later the International Joint Commission [*see* Sir George Christie Gibbons*]. He was involved in delineating the maritime boundary between Canada and the United States. In a related move, the maintenance of the boundary markers in the St Lawrence River and the Great Lakes was placed under his branch. In 1912, the year responsibility for the automatic water-level gauges on the lakes was also transferred, he was made a consulting engineer to the prime minister and the Department of External Affairs on matters relating to the commission. He would be reconfirmed in this position in 1921. The pinnacle of his career was perhaps reached in 1919, when he was asked to advise the British government on international boundaries arising out of the Treaty of Versailles.

A man of medium height and dark complexion, Stewart enjoyed curling but had few other recorded interests. In 1910 he suffered an ailment that left his right arm crippled. He had the reputation of being a demanding and parsimonious officer and a sound mathematician, and he worked closely with W. F. King and Otto Julius KLOTZ of the Dominion Observatory on coastal survey problems. Most of his associational memberships were professional: the oceanography section of the National Committee of Canada (within the International Astronomical Union), the International Geodetic and Geophysical Union, the Engineering Institute of Canada, the American Society of Civil Engineers, the Institute of Civil Engineers of Great Britain, the Geographic Board of Canada, and the Royal Astronomical Society of Canada. He died in May 1925 at the Ottawa Civic Hospital following an emergency operation for gall-bladder cancer, and was buried in Beechwood Cemetery. The *Ottawa Morning Journal* believed he would be remembered as a mathematician and authority on hydrography.

PATRICK BURDEN

William James Stewart is the author of "The Canadian Hydrographic Survey," in British Assoc. for the Advancement of Science, *Handbook of Canada*, ed. Ramsay Wright and James Mavor (Toronto, 1897), 61–66.

AO, RG 80-5-0-141, no.3298; RG 80-8-0-988, no.9305. LAC, RG 25, A-3-a, 1296: file 1921-426; RG 32, C2, 554: file 1863.01.23; RG 48; RG 51; RG 139, 30–31. *Ottawa Morning Journal*, 6 May 1925. Can., Parl., *Sessional papers*, 1892, no.10: 146. *Canadian who's who*, 1910. "Friends of hydrography:" *www.canfoh.org*. (consulted 6 April 2004).

STIRLING, MARION. *See* FAIRWEATHER

STOKES, SUSANNAH AUGUSTA (Maxwell), housewife and laundress; b. 10 March 1805 in Lancaster County, Pa; m. Henry Maxwell, and they had five children; d. 11 Feb. 1923 in Richmond Hill, Ont.

Susannah Stokes was born to free black parents. Orphaned at an early age, she was indentured to a white family, with whom she remained until she reached her majority. The family apparently treated her well and sent her to school, where she learned to read and write. On reaching adulthood, she married and set up a home in Lancaster, possibly in the village of Christiana. Slavery had almost died out in Pennsylvania and the state had become a haven for runaways from the South, but with the passage of the Fugitive Slave Act in 1850, slave-hunters were invested with authority to recapture runaways. Unscrupulous slave-catchers even kidnapped free blacks and dark-skinned whites.

In September 1851 slave-catchers invaded Susannah's village, whose inhabitants put up a fight. This incident was likely the "Christiana resistance," in which Edward Gorsuch and a gang attempted to recapture his runaway slave William Parker and others. The blacks of Christiana fought them off, killing Gorsuch. Although Susannah's name is not mentioned in the documentation of this resistance, the story of her presence in a village that was invaded and defended itself, and her flight from Pennsylvania, fits the narrative, in which several of the "resisters," fearing arrest and imprisonment, fled. In 1855 Susannah's daughter Charlotte Matilda (Tillie) was born in New York State.

By 1858 the Maxwells, like Parker, had come to Upper Canada. At least two of their children were born there. They spent some years in Toronto but, finding work short, they moved north about 1871 to Richmond Hill, where prospects were brighter. Susannah became a laundress, Henry a coal-burner. He soon died, leaving Susannah to support their children. Once her pursuit of employment almost cost her her life. After learning that wages were higher in Markham, she had started walking the seven miles to work there. On her return one evening, a snowstorm battered her into unconsciousness. A dog found her, half dead, and alerted local residents. Perhaps it was after this incident that she opened a laundry business in her home, assisted by her daughters Mary and Tillie. Such a move was one of the many survivalist strategies resorted to by women of Susannah's race, class, and family status.

Susannah evidently joined the Methodist church in Richmond Hill – she is a Wesleyan Methodist in the census of 1871 – but later sources list her as a Presbyterian. Her home was opposite the Presbyterian church on Yonge Street and she was active in its affairs. For a long time, it appears, the Maxwells were the only persons of African descent in Richmond Hill. In 1897 Tillie, who had been in domestic service in Toronto and had not married, rejoined her mother. Eight years later the village celebrated Susannah's 100th birthday at her church; her guests, including judge William Glenholme Falconbridge*, a former villager, gave her $75. By this time all of her children had died except Tillie. Following Tillie's death in 1920, the families she had worked for appear to have provided for Susannah's care.

On 11 Feb. 1923 Susannah herself passed away at the age of 117. Obituaries in Richmond Hill and Toronto newspapers, which differed in some details of her early life, claimed she had been Canada's oldest citizen. She had evidently retained some link with the black community in Toronto because one of the pastors who conducted her funeral service was Richard Amos BALL of Toronto's British Methodist Episcopal Church. Susannah Maxwell had lived through the reigns of six British monarchs, the American Civil War, and World War I. In her residence of over 50 years in Richmond Hill, she saw it evolve from a sleepy hamlet to a thriving town, and was an active participant in its development.

AFUA COOPER

AO, RG 80-8-0-797, no.43303; RG 80-8-0-947, no.38945. LAC, RG 31, C1, 1871, Markham Township, Ont., div.2: 41;

1901, Richmond Hill, Ont., 2. *Globe*, 9 March 1922, 12 Feb. 1923. *Richmond Hill Liberal*, 13 May 1920, 15 Feb. 1923. S. W. Campbell, *The slave catchers: enforcement of the fugitive slave law, 1850–1860* (Chapel Hill, N.C., 1970). *Directory*, York County, Ont., 1871. Jonathan Katz, *Resistance at Christiana: the fugitive slave rebellion, Christiana, Pennsylvania, September 11, 1851: a documentary account* (New York, 1974). R. M. Stamp, *Early days in Richmond Hill: a history of the community to 1930* (Richmond Hill, 1991).

STRANGE, THOMAS BLAND, army and militia officer, rancher, and author; b. 15 Sept. 1831 in Meerut, India, second son of Henry Francis Strange and Maria Letitia Bland; m. first 4 Nov. 1862 Maria Elinor Taylor (d. 1917) in Simla, India, and they had two sons and three daughters who survived to adulthood; m. secondly 1918 Janet Fell, widow of F. C. Ruxton; d. 9 July 1925 in Camberley, England.

Thomas Bland Strange was one of the most colourful of the British army officers who served in Canada in the 19th century. He is most often remembered as commander of the Alberta Field Force during the North-West rebellion, but his ten years as inspector of artillery and warlike stores was arguably a more significant contribution to Canada's military tradition.

Strange was the second son of a family with a long military history; he was born while his father's regiment was stationed in India. Educated at the Edinburgh Academy, a school which specialized in preparing young men to serve the British empire, he absorbed its ideology so fully that he would eventually earn the nickname Jingo Strange. Since the family could not afford the purchase of a commission in a cavalry or infantry regiment for both sons, Thomas was sent to the Royal Military Academy at Woolwich (London) to prepare him for a career in the artillery. After graduating, he was commissioned on 17 Dec. 1851 and soon posted to Gibraltar. Two years later he was promoted first lieutenant and ordered to Jamaica. Desperate efforts to avoid this military backwater failed and Strange not only missed serving in the Crimean War but contracted yellow fever from which he nearly died. He attributed his survival to abstention from alcohol and meat, a regimen he maintained for the rest of his life.

After his recovery he served for a time at Nassau in the Bahamas before returning to England in 1856. His luck was better in 1857 when the next crisis arose. Strange was in the first group of reinforcements rushed to India when the East India Company's Bengal army mutinied. He arrived in Calcutta on 11 Oct. 1857 and proceeded quickly to Benares (Varanasi), the headquarters for suppression of the rebellion. Here he was a willing, if not enthusiastic, participant in the gruesome executions of some mutineers who were tied to the mouths of cannon and literally blown away. More conventional service followed. He did well enough in the months of savage fighting that led up to the fall of Lucknow on 21 March 1858 to receive four mentions in dispatches and promotion to captain in September. He participated in mopping up operations until exhaustion brought on a severe attack of fever. Following his recovery he served in the Punjab for two years. In 1861 he took a six-month leave and embarked on a remarkable walking tour through the Himalayas from Tibet to Kashmir, most of the way on his own. The next year he married Maria Elinor at Simla. Marriage and the imminent arrival of the couple's first child precipitated a return to England.

After a brief period in Ireland, Strange was appointed to the instructional staff at Woolwich. He had always been intensely interested in the latest technological developments in his field and was even more devoted to training his men to the highest possible standard. The Woolwich job suited him perfectly and he did well at it. His skills were recognized in 1869 when he was given the job of training the Artillery Volunteers. He seems to have been highly popular with the citizen soldiers, but an incautious criticism of the obsolete equipment provided to them, published in the *Times*, resulted in disciplinary action. He was nonetheless promoted major in July 1871. His last posting was as an instructor at the School of Gunnery in Shoeburyness.

Strange's limited prospects for advancement are probably one of the reasons that he accepted command in September 1871 of the newly established School of Gunnery at Quebec City (B Battery, Garrison Artillery), which carried with it promotion to the militia rank of lieutenant-colonel. In addition, the following year, he was made an inspector of artillery and warlike stores. These jobs involved organizing Canada's first permanent military units and training the militia gunners now that the new dominion had taken over much of the responsibility for its own defence. Strange's location provided ample scope for his boundless energy and enthusiasm. He was fluent in French and found Quebec City very much to his taste. He was an active member of the Literary and Historical Society of Quebec, organized the public centennial celebrations of the 1775 defeat of the Americans under Richard Montgomery*, and served as master of the Stadacona Hunt Club. When the government decided to switch the artillery school with that at Kingston, Ont., in 1880, Strange reluctantly left Quebec.

While in Kingston, he was promoted colonel in the army in June 1881 and reminded that his 30 years of service were up and he must resign his commission in December. He kept on in his Canadian appointment for another year until he was informed that if he did not leave that job his pension would be cancelled. Strange was 51 and more energetic than most men half his age. Promotion to the honorary rank of major-general did little to remove the bitterness of his forced retirement from work that he loved. He had done a great deal to instil a spirit of professionalism among his amateur gunners and certainly deserves his appellation of "father of the Canadian artillery."

On an inspection trip to the west coast investigating the need to defend the terminus of the Canadian Pacific Railway, Strange had been impressed by the potential of the prairies. In 1882 he acquired a homestead and ranching lease east of Calgary and formed the Military Colonization Company of Canada Limited, which was chartered the next year. His plan was to raise cavalry horses for the British army and to use the ranch to train young Englishmen of good family in the art of stock raising. By 1884 Strange had built a ten-room house and the horses seemed to be thriving, although he complained constantly about theft from the nearby Blackfoot Indian Reserve.

When the North-West rebellion began in the spring of 1885 [see Louis Riel*], the minister of militia and defence, Adolphe-Philippe Caron*, an old friend from Quebec days, asked Strange to organize the defence of the District of Alberta. Strange threw himself into the job with his usual enthusiasm and energy. He put together the Alberta Field Force out of three very green militia battalions along with a few mounted policemen and cowboys. He marched his small unit north to Edmonton and then down the North Saskatchewan River in search of the Cree under Big Bear [Mistahimaskwa*]. After discovering the aftermath of the killings at Frog Lake (Alta), Strange's column continued its pursuit, and there were a few brief skirmishes between the Cree and scouting parties. When the Alberta Field Force finally caught up with Big Bear at Frenchman Butte (Sask.), Strange recognized the strength of the Cree position and refused to allow his inexperienced troops to attack. His professional caution undoubtedly saved many lives.

After the rebellion was over Strange returned to his ranch where a few months later he was kicked by a horse and had his leg badly broken. The ranch was not doing as well as he had hoped and his elder son, Henry Bland Strange, had graduated from the Royal Military College of Canada in Kingston and was now in the Royal Artillery. The War Office had cut off Strange's pension because he had been paid for his services during the rebellion, and he was engaged in a lengthy battle to get it restored. In 1887 he sold the ranch and returned to England. He lived there for the rest of his life apart from some trips abroad as a machine-gun salesman for Hiram Stevens Maxim. Strange remained vigorous and active into the 1920s, publishing an article in the Canadian Defence Quarterly at the age of 93.

The title of Strange's autobiography, Gunner Jingo's jubilee, accurately sums up his character. He was flamboyantly racist and militarist even by the standards of the time. He was also intelligent, courageous, and very good at his chosen profession, and he

played a significant role in imparting a sense of professionalism and technical competence to Canada's first permanent military units.

RODERICK C. MACLEOD

[The best sources for Strange's life and career are his own writings, especially his autobiography, Gunner Jingo's jubilee (London, 1893), which has been reprinted with an introduction by R. C. Macleod ([Edmonton], 1988). Strange's other publications include Artillery retrospect of the last great war, 1870, with its lessons for Canadians (Quebec, 1874); Colonial defensive organization: précis of information concerning the province of Quebec (Quebec, 1876); The military aspect of Canada: a lecture delivered at the Royal United Service Institute (London, [1879?]); and "The father of the Canadian artillery, by 'The Bombardier,'" Canadian Defence Quarterly (Ottawa), 2 (1924–25): 5–9. During his term as inspector of artillery and warlike stores Strange also compiled the Manual for the militia artillery of Canada for the federal Department of Militia and Defence (3 pts., Quebec, 1875–78).

Strange's British army records are to be found in National Arch. (G.B.), WO 76/368, and there is some correspondence with Henry George Hart, compiler of Hart's annual army list, in WO 211/29. His papers in LAC, MG 29, E40 consist almost entirely of copies of telegrams and correspondence relating to the 1885 rebellion. R.C.M.]

Canada Gazette, 25 Nov. 1871: 429–30; 4 Jan. 1873: 593; 10 Feb. 1883: 1309. Dominion annual reg., 1880–81: 356. Hart's annual army list . . . (London), 1880, 1882. G. W. L. Nicholson, The gunners of Canada; the history of the Royal Regiment of Canadian Artillery (2v., Toronto, 1967–72), 1.

STRUTHERS, WILLIAM EUGENE, physician, civil servant, and army officer; b. 17 Nov. 1869 in Kincardine, Ont., fifth child of John Struthers and Anna Christina McLeod; m. first 30 June 1903 Jennie Bennett Brown in Toronto, and they had a son and a daughter; m. there secondly 9 July 1913 Lina Lavanche Rogers*; d. there 20 April 1928.

William Eugene Struthers's Scottish-born father had immigrated to Cape Breton in 1847 and married an islander. In 1855 the family relocated to Bayfield, on Lake Huron south of Kincardine. John Struthers appears to have prospered: in the 1870s he owned a woollen factory in Bayfield. After attending local schools and Goderich collegiate, William secured medical degrees in 1897 from Trinity College (MD, CM) and the University of Toronto (MB). He completed his medical studies in Europe, and for a time in 1901–5 he practised in Lanark, in eastern Ontario. His academic ambition was strong enough to encourage him to take BA degrees in 1904 at both Queen's College in Kingston and Trinity (ad eundem).

In late 1905 Struthers moved to Toronto, where he and Jennie settled at 558 Bathurst Street. Tragically his wife died in 1909 and in 1916 their son would succumb to lockjaw, contracted after he cut his finger while gathering eggs at his uncle's Bayfield farm. In

1910 Toronto's Board of Education instigated medical inspections in schools under the direction of its reformist chief inspector, James Laughlin Hughes*. The overseers of this innovative program, Dr William Belfry Hendry and Dr Helen MacMurchy*, soon resigned over a dispute with Hughes concerning the board's jurisdiction in public health matters. Struthers succeeded them as chief medical inspector in January 1911, thus launching his career in the period's burgeoning public health movement. He immediately took charge of 18 inspectors, 25 nurses, and a dental inspector [see John Gennings Curtis ADAMS].

Struthers's appointment also ushered in a new phase in his private life: he met Lina Rogers, the superintendent of the nurses. She had pioneered acclaimed systems of school nursing in New York City and Pueblo, Colo., and in 1910 had accepted an invitation from John Ross Robertson*, chair of the Hospital for Sick Children, to replicate her efforts in Toronto. Because of her professional relationship to Struthers and wider notions about the impropriety of married women's employment, she resigned on 30 June 1913 to become his wife. The wedding, at High Park Presbyterian Church on 9 July, reportedly caused a sensation since Rogers was "one of the best-known nurses on the continent." The couple shared a commitment to health education and inspection in schools – William Struthers was an early proponent of teaching sex hygiene – and they gave public addresses and published articles in such journals as *Canadian Nurse and Hospital Review*, which Rogers edited for a time, and *Public Health Journal*.

After moving into Struthers's home on Bathurst Street, the newly-weds joined College Street Presbyterian Church. Struthers was prominent in local masonic circles, as a member and sometime master of St Andrew's Lodge, and he belonged to the Oddfellows. Shortly after the beginning of World War I in August 1914, he joined the militia's medical services. In March 1916 he enlisted as a captain in the Canadian Army Medical Corps; he served overseas in 1917–18. While her husband was in the army, Lina boldly opposed the move in 1916 to transfer the school board's medical work to the city's health department and her comprehensive text, *The school nurse*, was published in New York the following year.

In May 1914 the government of Sir James Pliny Whitney* in Ontario had passed the workmen's compensation act, the first Canadian legislation premised on the understanding that recompense for injury should not be contingent on the worker's responsibility. On 14 December, Struthers was appointed first chief medical officer of the Workmen's Compensation Board. Although this position appears to have required less involvement than his work with the school board, he continued to uphold the critical importance of health education and stressed its value

to both the worker and the employer in the prevention of accidents and illness. He would remain in the post until his death at Wellesley Hospital in 1928 from "internal troubles" and influenza. A funeral service at his home was followed by a masonic burial in Mount Pleasant Cemetery. The *Toronto Daily Star* noted that "the doctor was held in such high esteem" that Mrs Struthers's request for no floral tributes went unheeded.

Although overshadowed professionally by his second wife, Struthers had been a pioneering figure in the public health and welfare agencies of early-20th-century Ontario. Under his direction, the medical inspection program of the Board of Education came to be one of the world's most comprehensive, serving 45,000 children within a year of his appointment, and most widely imitated. Similarly, the Workman's Compensation Board served as a prototype for other such agencies throughout North America [see James Leonard SUGRUE]. Struthers's appointments to these agencies signified a key role for health-care professionals in the evolving modern state.

CYNTHIA COMACCHIO

William Eugene Struthers is the author of "Medical inspection of schools in Toronto," *Public Health Journal* (Toronto), 5 (1914): 67–78.

AO, RG 80-5-0-309, no.2372; RG 80-8-0-362, no.6035. LAC, RG 31, C1, 1901, Lanark (village), Ont.: 8 (mfm. at AO); RG 150, Acc. 1992–93/166, box 9392-16. Mount Pleasant Cemetery (Toronto), Tombstone inscription. QUA, Dept. of alumni affairs fonds; Registrar's Office fonds, student registers (mfm.). Toronto Dist. School Board, Museum and Arch. Dept., Toronto Board of Education, Hist. Coll., Board minutes, January 1911, June 1913; Management committee, minute-book, 14 April 1910; Vert. files, biog., L. L. Rogers; W. E. Struthers. UTA, A1973-0026/452(63, 67). *Globe*, 1 July 1903, 21 April 1928. *Toronto Daily Star*, 9, 16 Dec. 1905; 9 July, 4 Oct. 1913; 24 March 1914; 11 Aug. 1916; 20, 23 April 1928; 11 June 1946. *Canadian annual rev.*, 1914–16, 1927–28. Dianne Dodd, "Helen MacMurchy, MD: gender and professional conflict in the medical inspection of Toronto schools, 1910–1911," *OH*, 93 (2001): 127–49. Heather MacDougall, *Activists and advocates: Toronto's health department, 1883–1983* (Toronto, 1990). Ont., Workmen's Compensation Board, *Annual report*, 1914–29. *Ontario medical register* (Toronto), 1901. L. [L.] Rogers Struthers, "Nursing side of medical inspection of schools," *Public Health Journal*, 4 (1913): 147–48. James Struthers, *The limits of affluence: welfare in Ontario, 1920–1970* (Toronto, 1994). Neil Sutherland, *Children in English-Canadian society: framing the twentieth-century consensus* (Toronto, 1976). Toronto Board of Education, *Annual report*, 1911, 1912 ("Medical inspector's reports").

SUGRUE, JAMES LEONARD, carpenter, union organizer, labour leader, and office holder; b. 1 Sept. 1883 in Saint John, son of James Robert Sugrue and Mary Josephine Driscoll; m. there 10 June 1908

Sugrue

Estella Sophia Newman, and they had one son; d. there 24 June 1930.

James L. Sugrue grew up in the Irish working-class environment of west end Saint John. His mother was the daughter of immigrants from County Cork (Republic of Ireland); in 1877 she married James R. Sugrue, an immigrant from Kerry. The latter had become a teacher in the 1860s and taught at St Malachi's School for several decades; "a kindly, amiable man of high ideals and exemplary life," the older Sugrue "had the gift of imparting knowledge and of teaching his boys how to study and progress." Their children included four daughters, one of whom became a teacher and another a stenographer and bookkeeper, and two sons, both of whom entered the city's building trades.

As a young worker in the early years of the century, Sugrue boarded at the family home, now located in the south end. He married Estella Newman in 1908 and they remained lifelong residents of Saint John. Sugrue's elder brother, John, became an officer of the local Bricklayers' and Masons' Union during this period, and James himself began to attract attention among the carpenters. With a long history of independent organization in the 19th century, the Saint John carpenters had joined the American Federation of Labor in October 1901, as Local 919 of the United Brotherhood of Carpenters and Joiners of America. In 1910 Sugrue became financial secretary (and in 1913 business agent) of the local as well as secretary-treasurer of the new Building Trades Council. Before he was 30 Sugrue had also been elected president of the Saint John Trades and Labor Council. Two years later, in 1914, "Jimmie" Sugrue ran as a labour candidate for city commissioner, winning a substantial increase in the labour vote.

Sugrue's rise to prominence as a local union leader coincided with an upsurge in labour activism in Saint John. The carpenters raised their wages to $3 a day in 1911 and in 1913 were the first in their trade in the Maritimes to inaugurate the eight-hour day. Later that year the Labour Day celebrations featured "the most successful labour parade in many years." The extension of unionism to unorganized workers proved more difficult. In 1913 a lock-out of more than 1,000 men at the city's lumber mills lasted from June to September and ended without wage increases or union recognition. The following year the street railway workers also faced employers unwilling to countenance unions. The workers secured a conciliation board under the Industrial Disputes Investigation Act of 1907, naming Sugrue as their representative; he was able to persuade the board to call for recognition of the union and re-employment of its dismissed president, Fred Ramsey. When the company failed to agree, the workers went on strike in July 1914 and shut down public transportation for two days. Thousands of supporters rioted in the streets, overturning streetcars and attacking power installations, before a settlement was reached. For Sugrue, such events demonstrated that the cause of labour was important to the whole community in a major industrial centre such as Saint John. As he had explained in 1912, "In the long run we hope to so improve conditions here that the people won't leave for the west in search of better wages and shorter hours of labor." At the same time, he did not hesitate to call for more assistance from the international unions, reminding organizers that "Montreal is not the eastern extremity of Canada, despite the fact that some of our international executive officers seem to think so." By 1914 Sugrue had succeeded in persuading the Trades and Labor Congress of Canada to hold its annual convention in New Brunswick for the first time.

One of Sugrue's lasting contributions was the organization of a provincial federation of labour, which took place at a time when only British Columbia (1910) and Alberta (1912) had established such bodies. Efforts initiated by the Saint John Trades and Labor Council resulted in a preliminary meeting in September 1912 (which Sugrue did not attend), but the future of the federation was not assured until a more representative gathering took place a year later involving delegates from Saint John, Moncton, Fredericton, and Sackville. In the interim Sugrue had played a leading part in keeping the idea alive; in 1913 he was especially disappointed with the Fair Wage Schedule Act, for which he had lobbied on behalf of the council, and in the pages of the *Eastern Labor News* he argued that the legislative influence of labour could be applied more effectively through a provincial federation. At the organizational meeting on 16 Sept. 1913 Sugrue was elected president of the new federation; he and two other delegates were instructed to prepare a constitution and seek a charter from the TLCC. The first full convention of the New Brunswick Federation of Labor took place in Saint John on 20 Jan. 1914, with about 50 delegates in attendance. Sugrue was elected president, along with Frank Lister, Fredericton, as vice-president and Percy Douglas Ayer, Moncton, as secretary-treasurer. Within the year the federation reported 26 affiliated unions with a membership of 3,000 workers.

With Sugrue as its legislative representative, the federation pursued numerous objectives in Fredericton, including women's suffrage. Increasingly, attention focused on workers' compensation laws, a subject of marked concern to unionized employees on the docks and railways in Saint John and Moncton. The existing Workmen's Compensation for Injuries Act (1903) required workers to go to court to establish employers' liability for workplace accidents; awards were limited to a maximum of $1,500. Despite the election of labour-supported candidates such as Warren Franklin HATHEWAY in 1908, amendments failed to live up to expectations. More advanced legislation adopted by Ontario in 1914 – and in three other provinces in 1915 and 1916 – introduced state-sponsored no-fault insurance programs, backed by mandatory payroll assessments and with benefits administered by a compensation board. Sugrue lobbied provincial politicians for similar legislation, and in 1917 he and Frederick W. Daley of the longshoremen's union were appointed (by a Conservative government) to a royal commission which held hearings throughout the province and reported in favour of a new compensation law. When the bill was introduced (by a Liberal government), labour unions rallied to support it against the opposition of employers. The resulting Workmen's Compensation Act (1918) was considered exemplary progressive legislation at the time, although farmers, fishermen, domestic servants, and workers in the woods were excluded from coverage, and benefits in any claim were limited to a maximum of $3,500. Sugrue himself accepted a salaried position as one of three board members. In its first year of operation, 1919, the board completed consideration of 1,733 claims and approved compensation and pensions amounting to more than $100,000, numbers which increased substantially during the next ten years. Sugrue continued to serve on the board until his death in 1930 at 46 years of age. An apparent heart attack had forced him to reduce activities during the last two years of his life. His widow, who in 1923 had been appointed to a commission of inquiry into mothers' pensions and minimum wages, survived him by 40 years.

The death of Sugrue at such an early age was considered a heavy loss both to organized labour and to provincial society. Described as "not only an able executive but an excellent speaker and a man of ideas," he was remembered as well for his "kindly disposition." Union members in Saint John recalled his occasional musical recitations at labour meetings; a union gathering in his honour featured a variety of musical numbers. Sugrue's respectability was underlined by his participation in the Knights of Columbus, the Children's Aid Society, and other charities; the *New Freeman* eulogized him as "a man who had given freely of his time in all movements for the betterment of the community." In a city with a long history of labour organization in the 19th century, Sugrue promoted the extension of unionization to new groups of workers and collaboration around causes of common concern. While encouraging the transition from occupational loyalty to broader forms of labour solidarity, he remained a consistent supporter of the TLCC and the AFL. As a union leader who became a member of the province's early labour bureaucracy, Sugrue was a pragmatist who believed in mobilizing labour's influence within the existing political and economic structures; his success lends support to the theme of progressivism in the political history of the Maritime

provinces. In promoting the recognition of unions and the enactment of reforms, Sugrue assisted New Brunswick workers and provincial society generally in establishing the regime of industrial legality and social legislation that came to characterize the 20th century.

DAVID FRANK

[The author is grateful to Professor Robert H. Babcock for sharing references from his research in Saint John labour history. D.F.]

Arch. of the Diocese of Saint John, RBMB. PANB, RS6; RS141C5, F18983, no.080270; RS260/D. *Eastern Labor News* (Moncton, N.B.), 1909–13. *Evening Times-Globe* (Saint John), 24, 26 June 1930; 24 Jan. 1931. *New Freeman* (Saint John), 28 June 1930, 31 Jan. 1931. *St. John Standard*, 29–30 March, 5 April 1912; 2 Sept. 1913; 21 Jan., 15 April 1914. *Telegraph-Journal* (Saint John), 25, 27 June 1930. R. H. Babcock, "Blood on the factory floor: the workers' compensation movement in Canada and the United States," in *Social welfare policy in Canada: historical readings*, ed. R. B. Blake and Jeff Keshen (Toronto, 1995), 107–21; "Saint John longshoremen during the rise of Canada's winter port, 1895–1922," *Labour* (St John's), 25 (1990): 15–46; "The Saint John street railwaymen's strike and riot, 1914," *Acadiensis* (Fredericton), 11 (1981–82), no.2: 3–27. *Labour Gazette* (Ottawa), 1 (1900–1)–30 (1930). Ian McKay, "Strikes in the Maritimes, 1901–1914," in *Labour and working-class history in Atlantic Canada: a reader*, ed. David Frank and G. S. Kealey (St John's, 1995), 190–232. G. R. Melvin, *History of New Brunswick Federation of Labour, 1914–1933* (n.p., n.d.). N.B., *Acts*, 1903–30; Workmen's Compensation Board, *Annual report* (Saint John), 1919–30. "Obituary," *Canadian Congress Journal* (Ottawa), 9 (1930), no.7: 29. *Report of proceedings at a conference concerning Workmen's Compensation Act, held at St. John on Thursday and Friday 10th and 11th January, 1924* (n.p., 1924). W. Y. Smith, "Axis of administration: Saint John reformers and bureaucratic centralization in New Brunswick, 1911–1925" (MA thesis, Univ. of N.B., Fredericton, 1984). Trades and Labor Congress of Canada, *Report of the proc. of the annual convention* ([Ottawa]), 18 (1902)–34 (1918).

SULTE, BENJAMIN (baptized **Olivier-Benjamin Vadeboncœur**), journalist, writer, office holder, and historian; b. 17 Sept. 1841 in Trois-Rivières, Lower Canada, son of Benjamin Sulte, *dit* Vadeboncœur, and Marie-Antoinette Lefebvre; m. 3 May 1871 Augustine Parent, daughter of Étienne Parent*, in Ottawa, and they had two children, neither of whom survived; d. 6 Aug. 1923 in Ottawa and was buried on 10 August in Trois-Rivières.

Benjamin Sulte began his studies with the Brothers of the Christian Schools in Trois-Rivières. In October 1847 his father died in a shipwreck near the coast of the Gaspé peninsula; as a consequence, he had to leave school around the age of 10 to provide for his family. He then engaged in different trades: he was, among other things, a clerk in a dry goods shop, clerk in a grocer's shop, bookkeeper for lumber merchants G.-A. Gouin et Compagnie, paymaster on a steamship plying between Trois-Rivières and Montreal, and owner of a shop on a Grand Trunk Railway line under construction from Arthabaskaville (Victoriaville) to Doucet's Landing (Des Ormeaux). A self-taught man, he devoted his free time to reading and study in order to broaden his knowledge. In 1861, at the time of the *Trent* affair [*see* Sir Charles Hastings Doyle*], he joined the militia and he became a sergeant-major some time later. He sought admission to the School of Military Instruction of Quebec, where he is said to have received his captain's certificate. After briefly resuming active service during the campaign against the Fenians, in 1866 he replaced Elzéar Gérin* as editor of *Le Canada*, a Conservative Ottawa newspaper. The following year he was appointed translator in the House of Commons. Then in 1870 Sulte entered the Department of Militia and Defence, where he took charge of correspondence, and in 1889 he became chief clerk. He would hold this office until he retired in 1903.

Sulte came from a modest background. His ancestor Jean Sulte, *dit* Vadebonccœur, a saddler and shoemaker, is thought to have arrived in Canada with the troops of Louis-Joseph de Montcalm*. His son Joseph, Sulte's grandfather, was a carter by trade, and Sulte's father, Benjamin, was a navigator by profession. Sulte's marriage to Augustine Parent introduced him into a circle of men of letters which included his father-in-law, Étienne Parent, a former journalist and MLA, who was under-secretary of state at the time, and his brothers-in-law, Antoine Gérin-Lajoie*, a writer, journalist, and officer holder, and Évariste Gélinas*, a journalist, editor of *La Minerve* (Montréal) from 1861 to 1865, and then office holder. As the years went by, Sulte also wove close ties with intellectuals such as Alfred Garneau, Joseph-Étienne-Eugène Marmette, William Kirby*, and François-Edme Rameau de Saint-Père. The diverse networks he found and cultivated through his correspondence helped round out his cultural knowledge by furthering the exchange of privileged information. They also enabled circulation of material, including unpublished documents, and fostered dissemination of works and recognition of their authors.

Sulte began to write poems and songs for various newspapers around 1860. At the end of this decade, he began publishing at a frenetic rate: *Les Laurentiennes: poésies* (Montréal, 1869), *Histoire de la ville des Trois-Rivières et de ses environs* (Montréal, 1870), *Mélanges d'histoire et de littérature* ([Ottawa], 1876), *Chants nouveaux* ([Ottawa], 1880), and so on. His main work, *Histoire des Canadiens-français, 1608–1880: origine, histoire, religion, guerres, découvertes, colonisation, coutumes, vie domestique, sociale et politique, développement, avenir*, was brought out at Montreal in eight volumes between 1882 and 1884. In it Sulte adopted a point of view different from that of previous writers, taking an interest in the living conditions of ordinary people, an approach well conveyed by the title of the work. Influenced by the realist movement, he examined his sources with a critical eye and did not embrace the received opinion of his predecessors, who exalted the role of religious communities under the French regime. His account provoked many an argument, precisely because of the unflattering portrait he gave of both the Jesuits and Quebec's first bishop, François de Laval*. Sulte thus acquired the reputation of being a historian with liberal ideas. He was also reproached for sliding at times into inappropriate generalizations and for occasionally drawing hasty conclusions. His various works seemed, however, to be better received by anglophones. The quarrels triggered by the publication of *Histoire des Canadiens-français* did not prevent Sulte from continuing to display his convictions openly. An impetuous man, he did not shrink from polemics; in an article published in 1902 he lashed out at Octave Crémazie*, "the Mohammed of the failed patriots," and "the little religion of the *Vive la France*." His outspokenness ruffled the feelings of several contemporaries who glorified the memory of the national poet. There was a general outcry and Sulte barely escaped being expelled from the Institut Canadien-Français of Ottawa. The historian's violent outburst aroused old feelings of rancour and, under the pen of his detractors, he became "the insulter of France, the traitor of his race, and the denigrator of our national figures."

Some distressing events of a private nature cast a shadow over the last years of Sulte's life. In 1912 he separated from his wife. Afterward he lived with his sister Émilie, who joined him in Ottawa. Their life together was not without rough patches and at the end of 1920 he had to move into a room at the Albion Hotel. Loneliness and ill health wore him down. In February 1922 he was taken in by his nephew, Paul-E. Parent, with whom he would stay until his death.

Heavily involved in literary circles, Benjamin Sulte was a member of, notably, the Institut Canadien-Français of Ottawa, the Cercle des Dix in that city, the Société Historique de Montréal, and the Royal Society of Canada. In 1916 the University of Toronto awarded him an honorary LLD. Sulte delivered hundreds of lectures and, according to his contemporaries, was a gifted speaker. The man who had been dubbed the "great stirrer up of history" is remembered as indefatigable and scholarly, a tireless researcher who amassed and compiled notes. He was undoubtedly the most prolific writer of his time, having authored countless articles during his life – more than 3,500 by his own estimate in 1916. His friends recognized his prodigious creativity and celebrated the appearance of Sulte's 100th article, published in the

December 1886 number of the *Revue canadienne* (Montréal), with a literary and historical banquet; the prolific writer in fact wrote all the texts appearing in this issue. Gérard Malchelosse*, who is considered his disciple, collected many of Sulte's articles and published them in Montreal in *Mélanges littéraires* (2 volumes) and *Mélanges historiques* (21 volumes) between 1918 and 1934.

HÉLÈNE MARCOTTE

AO, F 1076, MU 1634. Arch. de l'Univ. de Montréal, P57/58 (fonds Jean Bruchési). Arch. de l'Univ. Laval (Québec), P121 (fonds Gérard-Malchelosse). Arch. du Séminaire de Nicolet, Qué., F045 (fonds Elzéar-Bellemare). Arch. du Séminaire de Trois-Rivières, Qué., 0129-C2 (fonds Marguerite-Marie). Gérard Malchelosse, "Benjamin Sulte et les débuts du journalisme aux Trois-Rivières," *Le Nouvelliste* (Trois-Rivières), 21 juin 1941. "Un autre aspect de la vie de notre historien, B. Sulte," *Le Nouvelliste*, 17 sept. 1941. F.-J. Audet, "Benjamin Sulte," *BRH*, 32 (1926): 337–47. *Cinquante-six ans de vie littéraire: Benjamin Sulte et son œuvre; essai de bibliographie des travaux historiques et littéraires (1860–1916) de ce polygraphe canadien . . .*, Gérard Malchelosse, édit. (Montréal, 1916). Ægidius Fauteux, "Benjamin Sulte," RSC, *Trans.*, 3rd ser., 18 (1924), proc.: iv–vii. Patrice Groulx, "Benjamin Sulte, père de la commémoration," CHA, *Journal*, new ser., 12 (2001): 49–72. Hamel *et al.*, *DALFAN*, 1257–59. Hélène Marcotte, *Benjamin Sulte: cet inlassable semeur d'écrits* (Montréal, 2001). [H. J. Morgan], *The writings of Benjamin Sulte* (Milwaukee, Wis., 1898). "Le premier centenaire de 'La Revue canadienne,'" *Nouvelles Soirées canadiennes* (Montréal), 6 (1887): 544–62. Albert Tessier, "Dans l'intimité de Benjamin Sulte," *Cahiers des Dix*, 21 (1956): 159–77.

SUTHERLAND, HUGH McKAY, lumberman, office holder, politician, and railway promoter; b. 22 Feb. 1843 in New London, P.E.I., son of Donald Sutherland and Euphemia ——; m. first 10 Feb. 1864 Mary Dickie (d. 1875) of Brantford, Upper Canada; m. secondly 10 Dec. 1878 May Banks of Baltimore, Md; m. thirdly 3 Sept. 1921 Constance Margaret Denholm (d. 1925) in Winnipeg; he was survived by two daughters; d. 14 Aug. 1926 in Croydon (London), England, and was buried in Winnipeg.

In 1849 Hugh Sutherland's family moved to Oxford County, Upper Canada, and he attended school there. Afterwards, he worked as a bookkeeper in Ingersoll for lumberman and Liberal politician Adam Oliver*. In 1867, with Oliver and William Cairns Bell, he became a partner in Adam Oliver Company. The following year the company established a planing mill and lumberyard in Orillia. Although the mill and yard were destroyed by fire in 1871 and the partnership was dissolved, Sutherland continued in the lumber business in Orillia; by 1875 he owned a sawmill there.

Sutherland had taken a keen interest in local Liberal politics while in Ingersoll. The victory by the Liberals under Alexander Mackenzie* in the federal election of 1874 brought him an appointment as the superintendent of public works for the North-West Territories, a position he held until the defeat of the Liberals in 1878. While in the west, he unsuccessfully contested the seat of Simcoe East for the Liberals in the Ontario general election of 1875.

Sutherland's term in government service gave him incomparable insights into the rich resources of the west and the transportation facilities needed to exploit and develop them. In 1878 he settled permanently in Winnipeg. He became an exceptionally enthusiastic promoter of western Canada and in the early 1880s participated in the formation of several mining, land, and navigation companies. His most spectacular, but brief, successes came in the lumber business. The phenomenal boom associated with the early construction of the Canadian Pacific Railway created an enormous demand for lumber in Winnipeg in 1881 and 1882. Sutherland obtained numerous timber leases and then built what was allegedly the first large sawmill (with a capacity of 40,000 board feet per day) in Winnipeg and another at Rat Portage (Kenora, Ont.). At the peak of his operations in 1882 he employed 300 men and had recently obtained a timber limit for 64,000 acres of choice pine timber. The collapse of the Winnipeg real estate and housing boom in 1883 severely curtailed his timber operations, however. In 1882, at the height of his business career, he had been elected to the House of Commons for the riding of Selkirk, defeating Stewart Mulvey*, but he lost his bid for re-election to William Bain Scarth* in 1887, when his business affairs were in serious disarray. In parliament he had been an enthusiastic advocate of Manitoba and western Canadian interests, frequently denouncing federal policies which he thought retarded western development.

In the early 1880s Sutherland had also been a promoter of several railway projects. The first was the Manitoba South-Western Colonization Railway, incorporated in 1879, whose objectives were twofold. The early plans of the CPR were to build through Selkirk, bypassing Winnipeg. The Manitoba South-Western, with possible connections to the Northern Pacific Railroad in the United States, was designed to protect Winnipeg's interests. Its second goal was the development of the Souris coalfields, which had allegedly been discovered by Sutherland. The Manitoba South-Western fulfilled both of these objectives when the CPR acquired it in 1884, re-routed the CPR main line through Winnipeg, and assisted in the development of the coalfields.

Sutherland's second railway scheme involved the building of a line from Winnipeg northward to a port on Hudson Bay. Under his tutelage the Winnipeg and Hudson's Bay Railway and Steamship Company was incorporated in 1880, but it faced immediate competition with the Nelson Valley Railway and Transporta-

Sutherland

tion Company, which was also incorporated that year. After some wrangling the two companies were amalgamated in 1883 under Sutherland's leadership. The first 40 miles of the proposed railway was built in 1886, but a financial scandal involving provincial treasurer Alphonse-Alfred-Clément LA RIVIÈRE halted construction before the contractors could be paid.

When prospects of federal aid improved in the 1890s, Donald Mann*, one of the contractors who had built the first 40 miles, used his unsatisfied claims to gain control of the railway. Mann, in partnership with William MACKENZIE, then changed the route and amalgamated the line with others to form the Canadian Northern Railway in December 1898. The loss of his railway marked the end of Sutherland's career as an independent railway promoter. The best he could do, and that only after some hard infighting, was to secure appointment as the Canadian Northern's agent at Winnipeg. Later, he served in other firms controlled by Mackenzie and Mann, as president of the Rainy River Lumber Company (a company he had founded), the Canadian Northern Coal and Ore Dock Company, and the Canadian Northern Prairie Lands Company, and as a director and promoter of several others.

When the financial and railway projects of Mackenzie and Mann collapsed in 1918, Sutherland retired to England. He died there in 1926. He had been actively connected with the development of the Canadian west over a period of more than 40 years. Many of his business ventures prospered, but he failed in the greatest effort of his life, the building of a railway to Hudson Bay. He is, nevertheless, regarded as "the father of the Hudson Bay route." The project was completed only after his death and has been repeatedly threatened with abandonment, but it is still capable of provoking intense political reaction from true believers.

THEODORE D. REGEHR

AO, RG 80-27-2, 1: 150. Man., Dept. of Finance, Consumer and Corporate Affairs, Vital statistics (Winnipeg), no.1921-034353. *Manitoba Free Press*, 16 Aug. 1926. *Canadian directory of parl.* (Johnson). *Canadian men and women of the time* (Morgan; 1912). *CPG*, 1875, 1883, 1887. George Emery, "Adam Oliver, Ingersoll and Thunder Bay district, 1850–82," *OH*, 68 (1976): 25–43. H. A. Fleming, *Canada's Arctic outlet: a history of the Hudson Bay Railway* (Berkeley, Calif., 1957; repr. Westport, Conn., 1978). T. D. Regehr, *The Canadian Northern Railway, pioneer road of the northern prairies, 1895–1918* (Toronto, 1976). G. R. Stevens, *Canadian National Railways* (2v., Toronto and Vancouver, 1960–62).

SUTHERLAND, ROBERT FRANKLIN, lawyer, politician, and judge; b. 5 April 1859 in Newmarket, Upper Canada, son of Donald Sutherland, a storekeeper, and Jane Boddy; m. 4 Sept. 1888 Mary Bartlet in Windsor, Ont., and they had two daughters; d. 23 May 1922 in Toronto.

Of Scottish-Irish parentage, Robert F. Sutherland moved to Windsor when he was 14 and resided with his sister, wife of the pastor of St Andrew's Presbyterian Church. He studied at the Western University of London and the University of Toronto, and was called to the Ontario bar in Easter term 1886, in which year he became a member of the law firm of Cameron and Cleary in Windsor. Appointed a QC in 1898, by 1905 he would be the senior member of Sutherland, Kenning, and Cleary. Besides conducting an extensive court practice, he was active on the city council, the library board, and the cricket field. In his spare time, perhaps with an eye to broader political involvement, he learned to speak French.

When Prime Minister Sir Wilfrid Laurier* visited Windsor on his electoral campaign tour of 1900, the first speaker to welcome him was Sutherland. Only ten days before, he had received the Liberal nomination for Essex North, which had been held by the Liberals since 1891 and which included Windsor, the adjoining border towns, and the rural, mostly French Catholic north half of the county. In addition to lauding Laurier, Sutherland emphasized that, if elected, he would respect all creeds and nationalities. This impartiality became especially important as the campaign wore on. His opponents tarred him with being anti-Catholic and a one-time member of the Protestant Protective Association. He angrily responded that, though a Presbyterian, he had always acted with fairness towards Catholics. While a member of Windsor's council and chairman of its finance committee, he had recommended that the Catholic hospital, the Hôtel Dieu, be excused from paying water rates. For this stand he had been condemned, in his words, as "a half Catholic and a poor Protestant." He further maintained that his refusal to join the PPA had once cost him the mayoralty. Though the association was now defunct, he had reason to worry about the charges against him: in 1900 French-speaking Catholics could sway the election. In the end he easily defeated Solomon White*. His success, and that of Mahlon K. Cowan in Essex South, confirmed that the Liberals, as a coalition of urban Protestants and rural Catholics, could form an enduring political structure in Essex County.

One of the least voluble members of Laurier's government, Sutherland worked diligently to build up his local support. He consulted with Laurier on regional appointments to the Senate. In 1905 he asked the prime minister to back the local bid to have the United States Steel Corporation build a massive plant near Windsor, but Laurier responded that no favouritism could be shown to a particular manufacturer. In parliament Sutherland had the Railway Act amended in 1903 to require railways to drain their properties – a concern in low-lying Essex – and to mount "suitable" cattle guards. His amendments also removed the legal defences used by railways to avoid claims and made them liable for cattle killed by trains. Though he gained popularity among farmers, he did not inspire urban voters. In his only lengthy speech in the House of Commons, in 1902, he had praised the "incidental protection" provided by the government's tariff policies, which, he claimed, were responsible for the industrial growth of the Windsor area. Voters there were not impressed. In the election of November 1904 he lost the city but was re-elected thanks to his rural support.

When the commons convened in January 1905 Sutherland was named speaker. Though his accomplishments were slight, the Windsor *Evening Record* believed "his parliamentary experience brought him many friends and few enemies." Moreover, he kept his local contacts strong. In August, for instance, he advised Windsor's council that the Detroit–Windsor ferry was attempting to renew its licence on terms that favoured the service. Duly warned, the municipality petitioned Ottawa to make sure that the company paid a fee and lowered its rates. After his re-election in 1908, Sutherland declined another term as speaker. On 21 Oct. 1909 he was appointed a puisne judge in the High Court division of the Supreme Court of Ontario.

Sutherland's largely undistinguished career on the bench was punctuated by occasional speaking engagements and cases that attracted mild attention. In 1919, in a referral that hinged on the definition of "public place," he upheld a Toronto magistrate's decision, under the War Measures Act, to fine a workman who had said of the war effort that "the British Parliament was bleeding Canada dry; that King George was just as bad as the Kaiser."

In 1917 the quiet judge had been drawn into the complex, and very political, field of hydroelectric regulation, as a member of the commission set up to determine the amount and price of power to be supplied by the Electrical Development Company of Ontario Limited to the provincial Hydro-Electric Power Commission. The formation of a government by the United Farmers of Ontario in 1919 set the stage for confrontation between Premier Ernest Charles Drury* and the dynamic chairman of Hydro, Sir Adam BECK, over responsibility for the extravagant escalations in its funding and works. To consume its surplus power, it had been planning a system of hydroelectric radial railways. In an effort to neutralize Beck's pressure, in July 1920 Drury appointed a royal commission under Sutherland's chairmanship to examine the project's feasibility.

A year later, in a majority report based on American experience and post-war financial conditions in Ontario, the commission came down against hydro-radials, which, it concluded, would require continual government funding. Moreover, they would compete with the publicly owned Canadian National Railways, their cost could not be justified until an expensive power station at Queenston had been completed and proved to be self-supporting, and with motor vehicles on the rise the government had already embarked on a major road-building program. The commission therefore opposed any provincial guarantees for municipalities seeking to finance hydro-radials. Drury was predictably pleased, but radial advocates in urban centres were incensed. Though the report recommended a municipally controlled system for Toronto, neither its mayor, Thomas Langton Church*, nor York County warden Len Wallace was appeased. Church lambasted Sutherland's commission as a "frame-up."

In May 1922, nine months after rendering this controversial report, Sutherland died at his home on Chestnut Park Road in Toronto. His commission's findings, however, continued to receive scrutiny as the radial issue played itself out. A last-ditch scheme devised by Beck for joint control in Toronto was defeated in the municipal election of January 1923. The following year a second commission appointed by Drury to curb Hydro, headed by Walter Dymond Gregory, substantiated Sutherland's conclusions. Later experience proved that hydro-radials would have been an economic disaster. Even one of their supporters, William Rothwell Plewman, a Toronto alderman, eventually conceded that Sutherland's commission had been right.

PATRICK BRODE

AO, RG 3-5-0-26, 3-5-0-28; RG 22-305, no.45416; RG 80-5-0-158, no.3524. City of Windsor Municipal Arch. (Windsor, Ont.), RG 2, AIV 1/8 (City Council minutes), 14 Aug. 1905. LAC, MG 26, G, Sutherland to Laurier, 26 July 1905; Laurier to Sutherland, 28 July 1905. *Border Cities Star* (Windsor), 24 May 1922. *Evening Record* (Windsor), 20 Oct., 3, 8 Nov. 1900; 26 Oct. 1904; 7 Jan. 1905; 28 Oct. 1909. *Globe*, 17 July 1920, 13 Aug. 1921, 24 May 1922. Can., House of Commons, *Debates*, 25 March 1902, 11 Jan. 1905. *Canadian men and women of the time* (Morgan; 1912). *CPG*, 1905. *Encyclopaedia of Canadian biography . . . ,* vol.3. C. M. Johnston, *E. C. Drury: agrarian idealist* (Toronto, 1986). *The King v. Watson* (1919), *Ontario Weekly Notes* (Toronto), 15: 417–18. Ont., Commission appointed to inquire into hydro-electric railways, *Reports* (Toronto, 1921); also issued in Ont., Legislature, *Sessional papers*, 1922, no.24. W. R. Plewman, *Adam Beck and the Ontario Hydro* (Toronto, 1947).

SYMONDS, HERBERT, Church of England priest, professor, theologian, and author; b. 28 Dec. 1860 in Rickinghall Inferior, England, son of George Symonds, a businessman, and Hannah Wright; m. 27 May 1883 in Bobcaygeon, Ont., Emma Blackhall Boyd, sister of Mossom Martin Boyd*, and they had three sons and four daughters; d. 24 May 1921 in Montreal.

Symonds

Herbert Symonds was educated at Framlingham College in England and, after arriving in Canada in 1881, at Trinity College, Toronto (BA 1886, MA 1887). He also took a postgraduate course in theology at the University of Cambridge. During this period he came under the influence of the Broad Church school of Anglicanism (favouring a liberal interpretation of doctrine) and looked to the writings of such figures as Frederick Denison Maurice and Charles Kingsley of England and Phillips Brooks of the United States for inspiration. He was ordained deacon in 1885 and priest on 6 March 1887 by Arthur Sweatman*, bishop of Toronto. In 1887 he became a fellow of Trinity College and a lecturer there and three years later he was appointed professor of divinity. His Broad Church views accorded ill with the traditional Tractarianism of the college. He upheld the comprehensiveness of Anglicanism and advocated the legitimacy of doctrinal restatement and the adjustment of forms of worship in accordance with the perceived needs of modern discovery. In 1892 he accepted the parish of St Luke, Ashburnham (Peterborough), and in 1901 he was named headmaster of Trinity College School, a prestigious boys' school in Port Hope.

In 1903 Symonds returned to the parochial ministry, becoming vicar of Christ Church Cathedral, Montreal. This was not an easy position. The diocese of Montreal under Archbishop William Bennett Bond* was generally very conservative and it had been convulsed by controversy in 1901 over the liberal teaching of the Reverend Frederick Julius Steen, a professor at the Montreal Diocesan Theological College. Symonds was to find more understanding, although not outright approval, under John Cragg Farthing*, who was elected bishop of Montreal in 1909. Since the rector of Christ Church, John George Norton, was not active in running the parish, most of the parochial responsibilities fell on Symonds. He proved to be a successful and popular incumbent.

Symonds was widely sought after as a speaker in Montreal, elsewhere in English-speaking Quebec and Ontario, and in the United States. He was also actively involved in educational and civic affairs in Montreal. He served as president of the Protestant Board of School Commissioners of the City of Montreal from 1907 to 1912 and was associated with various charitable organizations. He received two honorary degrees, a DD from Queen's College, Kingston, in 1901 and an LLD from McGill University, Montreal, in 1912. In 1918 he helped organize and acted as chairman of the Committee of Sixteen, which sought to combat organized prostitution in Montreal.

Symonds's modernist or Broad Church theology found expression in two particular areas: doctrinal reformulation and inter-church relations. His attempts to rethink the formularies of the Church, and in particular the Nicene and Apostles' creeds, became the focus of endless controversy. He insisted that the teaching of Jesus had to be expressed anew in every age in order to address contemporary concerns and that the traditional formulations should not bind modern thinking. Although his position had wide-reaching implications, attention focused on what was perceived as Symonds's denial of the doctrine of the virgin birth. His views on the matter are not in fact entirely clear, but the controversy that they provoked would prompt demands in 1919 that he be tried for heresy.

Symonds's theological position on inter-church relations is succinctly set out in his Lent letter of 1918, addressed to the congregation of Christ Church. He was then in England visiting the Canadian Expeditionary Force. In this letter he outlined "the main heads of the religious, theological and ecclesiastical needs of our time." He made an "earnest plea for a larger fellowship between Christian people" and felt that "ministers of other Churches than our own should be admitted to our pulpits, and that members of other Churches should be welcomed to our altars." "We must realize," he stated, "that our agreements are far more important than our differences." The letter claimed that his experiences with the army had been central in the formulation of these points, but in fact they were a distillation of views that he had held since the 1890s.

The subject of inter-church relations and union had attracted Symonds early in his career and it was to be one of his major preoccupations. In 1899 he published *Lectures on Christian unity*, the first of many writings on the subject. In 1909 he reluctantly agreed to Bishop Farthing's request that he not publicly invite non-Anglicans to receive communion at the Christmas and Easter services in the cathedral. Farthing refused to attend the services if he did so. Symonds was among a small group of Anglicans who in 1912 presented a memorial to the Canadian house of bishops requesting that Anglican pulpits and altars be opened to non-Anglicans. In 1913 Symonds accepted an invitation to preach at St Giles Presbyterian Church in Montreal. The ensuing furore included an admonition from Farthing and demands that Symonds be tried in a church court. Farthing refused to allow such a trial. The incident was only one of many during his ministry in Montreal. In 1920 there was renewed concern when Symonds attended a service of the Unitarian Church of the Messiah in Montreal. Although Symonds's stand was unacceptable to many Montreal and Canadian Anglicans, it did foreshadow the greater openness of the position adopted by the Lambeth conference of 1920 in its "Appeal to all Christian people," which set forth the Anglican desire for church reunion.

Symonds's actions were practical applications of his view that all English-speaking Protestants were essentially one in faith and that the differences among them were of minor importance. He denied the doctrine of the apostolic succession held by many Anglicans and favoured a federation of Canadian churches. Symonds's position was unusual for most Anglicans and must be seen against the background of the negotiations then in progress that led to the formation of the United Church of Canada in 1925.

Herbert Symonds fell ill on 27 April 1921 while on a speaking tour in Ontario and died almost a month later. He was buried in Mount Royal Cemetery, Montreal. Except as a popular priest, his reputation has faded over the years. Theologically, he has had no lasting influence, partly because he left no systematic body of writing. While many of the questions that he raised are still of importance – such as ecumenism and the interpretation of the creeds – his solutions now seem overly simple and have been largely superseded. As did many modernists in the Anglican and other Protestant churches, Symonds undervalued the importance of doctrine, giving it little weight in his plans for church union or in his preaching and teaching. Still, he was one of the few Canadian representatives of the Anglican Broad Church school and as such deserves to be remembered. His legacy, and that of the modernists, is more one of the spirit than of practical achievement; the willingness to engage in open discussion of theological issues is now more common but is also more firmly grounded in doctrine.

RICHARD VIRR

Herbert Symonds wrote the articles "Church unity" and "The idea of progress" in the *Canadian Churchman* (Toronto), 2 and 9 Nov. 1916 and 19 July 1917, respectively. His publications also include: *Trinity University and university federation: an essay addressed to the council of Trinity University and the members of convocation* ([Peterborough, Ont.], 1894); *Lectures on Christian unity* (Toronto, 1899); *The Anglican Church and the doctrine of apostolic succession* (Montreal, 1907); *The Broad Church: a sermon preached in Christ Church Cathedral, Montreal, December 30th, 1906* (Montreal, 1907); *Religion after the war: a sermon-lecture* (Montreal, 1916); *Lent letter* (n.p., [1918]); and *A spiritual forward movement: an open letter to Rev. Dr. Fraser, principal of the Presbyterian College, Montr[e]al*, which was written sometime between 1918 and his death and likely published in Montreal.

Anglican Church of Canada, Diocese of Montreal Arch., Clergy files, Herbert Symonds; Episcopal journals, James Carmichael, 1907; J. C. Farthing, 1909, 1911, 1913, 1915, 1919–20. Committee of Sixteen, *Preliminary report . . .* ([Montreal], 1918); *Some facts regarding toleration, regulation, segregation and repression of commercialized vice* (Montreal, 1919). J. C. Farthing, *Recollections of the Right Rev. John Cragg Farthing, bishop of Montreal, 1909–1939* ([Montreal, 1946?]). *Herbert Symonds: a memoir* (Montreal, 1921). "The late Rev. Herbert Symonds, D.D., LL.D.," *Montreal Churchman*, 9, no.8 (June 1921): 11.

SYMPHORIAN LEWIS (Symphorien-Louis), Brother. *See* ROBERGE

T

TAILLON, Sir LOUIS-OLIVIER, lawyer, politician, and office holder; b. 26 Sept. 1840 in Saint-Louis-de-Terrebonne (Terrebonne), Lower Canada, son of Aimé Taillon, a farmer, and Josephte Daunais; m. 14 July 1875 in L'Assomption, Que., Georgiana Archambault, widow of Candide Bruneau and daughter of Pierre-Urgel Archambault*, and they had one child, but both mother and child died shortly after the birth in January 1876; d. 25 April 1923 in Montreal.

After studying from 1847 to 1856 at the Collège Masson in Saint-Louis-de-Terrebonne, where his schoolmates included Joseph-Adolphe Chapleau* and Alphonse Desjardins* (1841–1912), Louis-Olivier Taillon resolved to enter the priesthood and he taught at the college for six years before realizing his calling took him elsewhere; he decided to embrace law. He started his clerkship in Montreal in 1862 in the firm Fabre, Lesage et Jetté and finished it under Désiré Girouard*. Admitted to the bar on 6 Nov. 1865, he practised in association with several prominent lawyers, including Sévère Rivard*, François-Xavier-Anselme Trudel*, Fabien Vanasse, Lomer GOUIN, and Siméon

Pagnuelo. His last partnership would be Taillon, Bonin, Morin et Laramée. On 20 Jan. 1882 Taillon was made a QC and in 1892 he was elected *bâtonnier* and a councillor of the bar of Montreal.

Taillon had soon become drawn into politics. Like Rivard and Trudel, he was partial to the ultramontane point of view and he helped to promote and formulate the *Programme catholique* of 1871 [*see* Trudel], which was designed to bring purity to politics and remake the Conservative party to reflect the subordination of politics to the moral teachings of the Roman Catholic Church. A French Canadian nationalist favouring the absolute authority of the pope in matters of faith and discipline, Taillon had advised the bishop of Montreal, Ignace Bourget*, in his dispute with liberal Catholics and particularly with the Sulpicians [*see* Joseph-Alexandre Baile*] in 1867. He received favourable public attention as one of the organizers of the celebrations in 1874 for the 40th anniversary of the Association Saint-Jean-Baptiste de Montréal [*see* Louis-Onésime Loranger*]. The following year, supported by the ultramontanes, including Trudel and Desjardins, he sought election to the Legislative Assembly for Montreal East. He won, but his ultramontane ardour probably kept him from a ministerial position.

In the assembly, Taillon's abilities as a forcible speaker and good debater came to the fore. He was a person of principle, but lacked panache. His baritone voice and patriotic songs made him a banquet favourite. Taillon loved musical evenings and after a particularly difficult day he would return home to play his piano and forget the discords of politics. His charming conversation and enjoyable reminiscences gave great pleasure to countless small gatherings. His long flowing beard, which he pulled alternately with his right and left hand when upset or nervous, became his trade mark. He supported the government of Charles Boucher* de Boucherville and promoted the ultramontane agenda. As an advocate of Bourget, he presented in 1875 the bill to erect in civil law parishes cut out from the former Sulpician parish of Notre-Dame. Boucherville's government had enacted other legislation that year ceding control of education to church leaders.

Taillon backed the government's attempts to make municipalities, such as Montreal, honour their pledges of financial support for the Quebec, Montreal, Ottawa and Occidental Railway. This policy led directly to the so-called *coup d'état* of 2 March 1878, whereby the lieutenant governor, Luc Letellier* de Saint-Just, dismissed the Boucherville government and invited the Liberals under Henri-Gustave Joly* to take office. Although the election of 1 May saw the Liberals gain some ridings and stay in office, Taillon kept his seat. He then worked tirelessly under Chapleau, Boucherville's successor as party leader, to bring the Conservatives to power in October 1879.

Chapleau and Taillon were not always of the same mind, however. Taillon supported the Montreal School of Medicine and Surgery in its fight for independence from the Université Laval [see Thomas-Edmond d'Odet* d'Orsonnens]. A member in 1881 of the administrative committee of the diocese of Montreal which dealt with the presence of the Université Laval in Montreal and a member of the legislative committee which adjudicated the question, he had bitter words with Chapleau over this matter. Nonetheless, he ran in the general election of 1881 under Chapleau's banner and won the largest majority of any candidate. For his work in bringing the Conservatives back into office, his help in by-elections in 1880, and his impressive personal victory, Chapleau proposed him as speaker of the assembly, a position he filled from 8 March 1882 until 27 March 1884, through the administrations of Chapleau and Joseph-Alfred Mousseau*.

When the Mousseau government resigned in January 1884, Taillon accepted the position of attorney general and government leader in the assembly under Premier John Jones Ross* despite his preference for

Louis-Rodrigue Masson* as premier; he acted in this capacity from 23 Jan. 1884 to 25 Jan. 1887. Taillon supported Ross's policy of fiscal restraint and as a legislative tactician he guided the government through the treacherous waters of religious and political disputes. Taillon and Ross became the focus of controversy surrounding the province's response to the North-West rebellion [see Louis Riel*]. They supported the federal government in its decision to allow Riel to hang, much to the anger of many ultramontanes within the Conservative party, but attempted to keep the province at a distance from this decision. Taillon worried that Quebec's intervention in a matter of federal concern would lead to a diminution of provincial power. Honoré Mercier*'s ability to bring nationalists together in defence of Riel dealt a fatal blow to the Ross government in the election of October 1886. Taillon lost in Montreal East, but was elected in Montcalm in December.

In later years Taillon would attribute the electoral defeat of the Ross government not so much to Riel's execution as to the opposition of certain clergy to the government's asylum legislation of 1885. The new policy allowed organizations such as the Roman Catholic Church to run mental asylums, but stipulated that in return for financial contributions from the government a medical board appointed by the state would oversee the institutions and their medical staff [see Edmond-Joseph BOURQUE]. Many bishops and clergy feared this intervention would set a precedent for control of similar facilities such as hospitals and thus fought the legislation with vigour. The state won the battle and resentment festered amongst more strident ultramontanes who desired the financial support of the government without any accountability. Taillon was incorrect, however, to see this issue as key to the Ross government's defeat.

Desperate to remain in power despite their loss in the election, the Conservatives decided that Ross should resign in favour of Taillon; it was thought that he might be able to attract the ultramontanes, who held the balance of power, back into the party fold. The Taillon government took office on 25 Jan. 1887 but failed to gain the support it needed. After losing two votes in the assembly on his choice for speaker, Taillon resigned as premier and Mercier took office on 29 January. The federal Conservatives offered Taillon a place on the Superior Court of Quebec, but, in spite of his protestations to the contrary, Taillon loved politics too much to go to the bench.

As leader of the opposition, Taillon represented Montcalm from 1886 until the general election of 17 June 1890, when he was defeated in the riding of Jacques-Cartier. In addition to attacking Mercier's profligacy, he criticized him for pitting anglophones against francophones through his actions over the Jesuits' Estates Act. During the controversy over the

Baie des Chaleurs Railway, Taillon was merciless in his criticism of the premier. Indeed, this scandal led to the dismissal of Mercier by Lieutenant Governor Auguste-Réal Angers* on 16 Dec. 1891 and to the return of the Conservatives under Boucherville. Taillon assumed the leadership in the assembly and joined the cabinet as a minister without portfolio, and thus without salary. In the general election which followed on 8 March 1892, he won the seat of Chambly, which he would represent until May 1896. When Boucherville resigned in December 1892 because he refused to work under Chapleau, the new lieutenant governor, Taillon was asked to form a government; he did so on 16 Dec. 1892.

A year later, Taillon's character was tested in the assembly. On 28 Dec. 1893 Mercier, who was dying from diabetes, defended his probity before his accusers on the government benches. Looking directly at Taillon across the aisle, he explained that the Conservatives had ruined and dishonoured him. Now they wished to trample his corpse. The governing party had taken all his possessions, but not his honour. He had been acquitted of the charges of corruption against him. In this charged atmosphere, Taillon rose, walked across the aisle, and gave his hand to Mercier. Within a year, Mercier was dead and Taillon's reputation as a decent man remained intact.

As premier, Taillon was an administrator rather than a political leader and his government imposed a hard regime of economy in the aftermath of Mercier's spendthrift government. His reduction of subsidies to railway companies and his tax increases were highly unpopular in Quebec. Like Mercier and Boucherville, Taillon was very supportive of agriculture. The results were promising. Quebec cheese placed in the top categories at the Columbian exposition in Chicago in 1893. That year the Trappists of Oka placed their famous cheese on market. Taillon also followed his immediate predecessors in supporting the timber companies developing the Lac-Saint-Jean region. The critical issue during his tenure was the Hall affair. John Smythe Hall*, the provincial treasurer, did not want to renew a loan the government had obtained from France in 1891. He wished to borrow money through London and through his English-speaking sources in Montreal while Taillon favoured renegotiating with the Crédit Lyonnais and the Banque de Paris et des Pays-Bas. Taillon won this battle, but in the process he lost support from the English-speaking business community and Hall resigned. Taillon held the post of provincial treasurer, as well as the premiership, from 6 Oct. 1894 until his government resigned in 1896.

A question within the jurisdiction of the federal government but one which caused enormous problems for Taillon personally and the federal Conservative party in general was the Manitoba school question

[see Thomas Greenway*]. The failure of the federal Conservatives to conclude this matter led to bitter divisions within the party. In an effort to keep it in power and win the federal general election of June 1896, Taillon resigned as premier on 11 May and joined his colleagues Desjardins, Angers, and Ross in the newly formed government of Sir Charles Tupper* as postmaster general. Taillon and his friends had strong ties with the church and favoured federal legislation to override provincial wishes and restore Catholic schools to Manitoba. They suffered defeat at the hands of Wilfrid Laurier*'s Liberals, however. Taillon lost in Chambly-Verchères and resigned from the cabinet on 8 July. He had never won a provincial election as Conservative leader and he would never win a federal seat.

Following his defeat, Taillon continued to work for the Conservatives. He refused to meet with the apostolic delegate Rafael Merry del Val, whom Rome had sent at Laurier's request, but in opposition to the wishes of most of the Catholic hierarchy, to establish the facts and re-establish peace within the Catholic Church over the Laurier–Greenway agreement, which was designed to resolve the prickly school question. Taillon rejected that settlement as a betrayal of Roman Catholics in Manitoba and spoke against it. He maintained that the Liberals exploited the issue for political gain and that the Liberal leadership generally favoured non-confessional schools. Not surprisingly, he ran, unsuccessfully, in the federal general election of 1900, standing for Bagot. There again he spoke against the agreement out of principle and pledged not to let the matter drop until the population had awakened to the treason of their leaders.

Although he never ran again for a seat in either the provincial legislature or the federal parliament, Taillon continued to support the Conservatives publicly until his death. Like many of them he was ambivalent about the South African War, and he spoke out only to condemn Laurier for sending troops without consulting parliament. Supporting Conservative policy, he spoke in opposition to the establishment of a Canadian navy proposed by the Naval Service Bill in 1910. For his service to the party Robert Laird Borden* appointed him postmaster in Montreal after the Conservative victory in 1911. He held this position until 1915 when he made way for another party stalwart, Joseph-Gédéon-Horace Bergeron. In return, Taillon was made a knight bachelor in the New Year's honours list of 1916. During this period, Taillon offered to write his memoirs if the province would pay for a stenographer. The Liberal government of Sir Lomer Gouin refused and left us all the poorer for that decision. Before the election of 1917 Taillon was appointed president of the French section of the Unionist organization in Quebec and spoke out in an effort to rally French Canadians to conscription.

Tait

Sir Louis-Olivier Taillon came to be regarded as the "grand old man" of the Conservative party. During his long career, he was active in many areas. He served as a commissioner for the Municipal Loan Fund from 1880 to 1882; he was vice-president of the Liberal-Conservative Club of Montreal in the 1890s; he helped to found and was the first president of the Club Lafontaine in 1903; he was prominently identified with the Ligue Antialcoolique de Montréal in 1907; and he was elected a director of the Banque Internationale du Canada in 1911. In 1895, while premier, he had received an honorary DCL from Bishop's College at Lennoxville and in 1901 he received an honorary LLD from the Université Laval at Montreal. Towards the end of his life he gradually lost his sight and by 1922 he had cut off his beard, his political trade mark. A man of slender means, generous with his time and his money, Taillon lived his entire life in humble circumstances and spent his last years in the Institution des Sourdes-Muettes on Rue Saint-Denis in Montreal. A close adviser to Arthur Sauvé*, the leader of the provincial Conservative opposition from 1916 to 1929, he remained active politically behind the scenes until the day he died.

KENNETH MUNRO

Four speeches given by Sir Louis-Olivier Taillon are listed in CIHM, *Reg.*

ANQ-M, CE605-S14, 14 juill. 1875, 27 janv. 1876; CE606-S24, 27 sept. 1840. Arch. de la Chancellerie de l'Archevêché de Montréal, 778.867 (hôpital Saint-Jean-de-Dieu). *Le Devoir,* 26, 28 avril 1923. *Gazette* (Montreal), 25 Jan. 1876, 26 April 1923. Pierre Beullac et Édouard Fabre-Surveyer, *Le centenaire du barreau de Montréal, 1849–1949* (Montréal, 1949). J. D. Borthwick, *History and biographical gazetteer of Montreal to the year 1892* (Montreal, 1892). *Canadian annual rev.*, 1916, 1923. *Canadian men and women of the time* (Morgan; 1898 and 1912). L.-O. David, *Mes contemporains* (Montréal, 1894). Andrée Désilets, *Hector-Louis Langevin, un Père de la Confédération canadienne (1826–1906)* (Québec, 1969). *DPQ.* [Jacqueline] Francœur, *Trente ans rue St-François-Xavier et ailleurs* (Montréal, 1928). Le Jeune, *Dictionnaire.* P.-B. Mignault, "Louis Olivier Taillon," *Les hommes du jour: galerie de portraits contemporains,* L.-H. Taché, édit. (32 sér. en 16v., Montréal, 1890–[94]), 31e sér.: 481–92. *Newspaper reference book.* Rumilly, *Hist. de la prov. de Québec*; *Hist. de Montréal.* George Stewart, "The premiers of Quebec since 1867," *Canadian Magazine,* 8 (1896–97): 289–98.

TAIT. *See also* TEIT

TAIT, JAMES SINCLAIR, physician, politician, office holder, and author; b. 4 March 1849 in Wallace, N.S., son of James Tait and Catherine Sinclair; m. 19 Dec. 1882 Sarah Elizabeth Calkin in St John's, and they had three sons and two daughters, one of whom died in infancy; d. there 5 July 1928.

After attending schools in Wallace and Amherst, N.S., J. Sinclair Tait went to Mount Allison Wesleyan College in Sackville, N.B., from which he graduated in 1877 with a bachelor of science and English literature. Actively involved in student affairs, he had served as business editor of the *Argosy* magazine in 1875 and president of the Eurhetorian Society in 1876–77. This society provided opportunities for public speaking, debating, and literary pursuits, which would serve Tait well in his future endeavours. After graduation – Tait would later obtain a MA from Mount Allison (1891) and a BSC *ad eundem* from Dalhousie in Halifax (1897) – he completed a teacher-training course at the Normal School in Truro, N.S., during the summer of 1877. He spent the next two years teaching in Brigus, Nfld, where he began to study medicine with Dr William Anderson.

Tait had found his vocation. In 1879 he entered medical school at the University of Pennsylvania and he graduated three years later with a first-class honours MD. He returned to Brigus, where he practised until 1885, when he went to Britain to continue his studies. The following year he was licensed by the Royal College of Physicians (London) and the Royal College of Surgeons (Edinburgh). When he returned in 1886, he set up practice in St John's.

It was not long before Tait entered the political arena. In the general election of 1889 he was returned to the House of Assembly as a Liberal in support of Sir William Vallance Whiteway*, in the two-member district of Burin on the south coast. Tait had no previous connection with the area, but parachuting St John's–based candidates into rural districts was common in 19th-century Newfoundland. In 1893 he spearheaded the passage of a bill to regulate the practice of medicine and surgery. The first legislation of its kind in the colony, it led to the establishment of a seven-member medical board [*see* William Munden Allan*]. Tait was re-elected in the contest of 1893, which was quite acrimonious, even by Newfoundland standards. On 6 Jan. 1894, the last possible day for challenges under the Corrupt Practices Act, the Conservatives brought charges of bribery and corruption against 15 of the successful Liberals, including Tait, and against independent member James Murray. Each was found guilty and forced to relinquish his seat, and all except one were barred from future political office. This last penalty was removed by statute the following year, enabling Tait to make an unsuccessful bid to return to the assembly in 1897.

Although Tait's conviction brought his career as an assemblyman to a close, it did not end his partisan involvement. He was the recipient of several patronage appointments, including posts as secretary and registrar of the Newfoundland Medical Board (1894–1909) and membership on the St John's Board of Health (1904–9). As well, he was a public health officer and a visiting surgeon and physician at the St John's General Hospital. His most lucrative appointment was as medical superintendent (1895–97, 1900–7) and resident physician (1902–7) at the Hospital for the Insane in Waterford (St John's).

Tait's first formal involvement with this hospital, which was known as the Newfoundland Asylum until 1899, had occurred in 1890 when he was appointed to a commission of inquiry into its operation under resident physician Henry Hunt Stabb*. Three years later he was made a visiting physician to the hospital. Although he was soon replaced after the Conservatives became the governing party in April 1894, within weeks of the Liberals' return to power in December he was named attendant, or non-resident, physician, a position he had actively pursued. In a letter dated 21 Dec. 1893 to Newfoundland's colonial secretary, Robert BOND, he had sought the appointment at a minimum fixed yearly stipend of $3,000 (the annual salary paid to such professionals as magistrates, teachers, and clergy at the time averaged much less than $1,000). Tait now secured the position but not the salary. With his elevation to the position of medical superintendent on 25 March 1895, however, his emolument was set at $2,000 plus contributions towards his household expenses, which made him one of the highest paid officials on the government's payroll. The construction of an imposing superintendent's residence, on land adjacent to the asylum that had been purchased from Tait during 1896–97, increased his dependence on the public purse and made his position even more lucrative.

Tait's appointment was denounced by Governor Sir John Terence Nicholls O'Brien*, who, in a letter to the British colonial secretary, cited Tait's recent expulsion from the Medical Society of St John's on grounds of unprofessional conduct as sufficient reason to rescind it. (This expulsion, believed to have been in response to Tait's conviction under the Corrupt Practices Act, apparently did not affect his subsequent practice of medicine.) O'Brien's objection had no influence on the governing party. Tait carried out his duties as superintendent until September 1897, when he resigned to become a candidate in that fall's election. The Conservative's victory prevented the defeated Tait from regaining his position at the asylum, which went to Dr Lawrence Edward Keegan, but it did not end his association with the institution. The Liberals were returned to office in 1900 and shortly thereafter the new premier, Bond, reappointed Tait as medical superintendent.

His approach to treatment was guided by his conviction that mental illness was mainly the result of inherited factors, a belief that had gained much credibility in late-19th-century psychiatric pathology. He held little hope for the recovery of most patients; in 1895 he had argued that their incarceration in the asylum was rapidly turning it into "a Home for Incurables rather than a Hospital for the care and cure of the Insane." He advocated that alternative accommodation be found for them and was not averse to transferring them to the local poorhouse. Unlike Keegan, who had implemented an aggressive program of work, Tait believed that this type of occupational therapy was ineffective and fiscally unsound and he cancelled many of Keegan's initiatives when he replaced him in 1900. However, he gradually changed his opinion, acknowledging that some patients did benefit, but he limited work programs to those classified as able-bodied – seldom more than a third of the residents. Tait exercised frugality in the administration of sedatives and the use of physical restraints was common during his superintendence.

Tait's personal and professional conduct was called into question in May 1902 when Miss M. E. Scott, the asylum's matron, made several accusations against him, the most serious of which was causing the death of a patient through lethal injection. He was cleared of any wrongdoing, but when a second inquiry, in 1907 in response to allegations that he was involved in a sexual relationship with one of the female staff, recommended his removal, he submitted his resignation.

Tait had maintained his private practice during his incumbency at the Hospital for the Insane and he now returned to it, though in his later years he would confine himself to consultative work. He had kept abreast of advancements in medicine, studying in Edinburgh, Glasgow, and London, and he received various accreditations, certificates, and licences. In 1896 he was named a fellow of the Royal College of Surgeons (Edinburgh), at the time the only person in Newfoundland with this designation. A writer of some note, he contributed medical articles, essays, and patriotic poems to such local periodicals as the *Newfoundland Quarterly* and the *Cadet*; his pamphlet entitled *Tuberculosis* was published in St John's in 1902. He was elected to the city's municipal council in 1916 and served until 1920. A Methodist and then a member of the United Church of Canada, he died in 1928.

In addition to her role as a homemaker and mother, Tait's wife, who died in 1925, was devoted to community and church work, especially in support of the missionary efforts of Gower Street Methodist Church. Their daughter, Mary Elsinore (Elsie), was a talented musician and holds the distinction of being the first recipient of a degree in music from Mount Allison. She was also a graduate of the Toronto Conservatory of Music and was organist at Gower Street Church for many years. Two sons, Archibald Campbell and Harold Sinclair, followed their father into medicine, while the third, Robert Holland*, opted for a career in law and positions with Newfoundland's information bureaus in the United States. All three served with distinction in World War I, Archibald and Harold with the Royal Army Medical Corps and Robert with the Newfoundland Regiment.

J. Sinclair Tait, in the estimation of historian Patricia O'Brien, "seems to have been a man of small imagination and even smaller humanitarian impulse," particularly in his years as medical superintendent at the Hospital for the Insane. His opposition to innovative therapies and his reliance on antiquated methods reduced his effectiveness as the hospital's administrator and primary caregiver. His removal as superintendent was a direct result of his own misconduct. Yet, his continuing quest for medical knowledge and his large and successful private practice indicate that he was dedicated to his profession and enjoyed the confidence of his patients. He made the most of his term in the assembly by persuading the government to bring structure to the practice of medicine in Newfoundland. As secretary and registrar of the Medical Board for its first 15 years, he was able to ensure that it became the regulating body he had intended.

BERTRAM RIGGS

In addition to his pamphlet, *Tuberculosis*, James Sinclair Tait wrote "Allan Lee," a ballad that was published in *Songs of Newfoundland* (St John's, 1917), 7. Three articles by him appear in the *Newfoundland Quarterly* (St John's) – "Heredity and environment," 1 (1901–2), no.4: 21–24; "The ideal in education," 12 (1912–13), no.1: 6–10; and "The jubilee of years," 11 (1911–12), no.3: 21 – as well as a poem "Britain's call," 14 (1914–15), no.2: 30. Two other poems were printed in the *Cadet* (St John's): "The conflict," December 1917: 23 and "King and empire," December 1918: 1.

Private arch., Bertram Riggs (St John's), E-mail corr. from Cheryl Ennals, Mount Allison Univ. archivist, with information from convocation and commencement programs. *Daily News* (St John's), 20 Nov. 1894, 23 Feb. 1925, 6 July 1928. *Evening Telegram* (St John's), 6 July 1928. *Argosy* (Sackville, N.B.), February 1875, September 1876, October 1877, January 1879, March 1888, February 1893, March 1897. *Births, deaths and marriages in Newfoundland newspapers*, comp. Gert Crosbie (13v., St John's, 1997–99; also available on CD-ROM), 8 (1881–82); 13 (1890). *Canadian men and women of the time* (Morgan; 1912). *Encyclopedia of Nfld* (Smallwood *et al.*), 1: 679–749. Nfld, House of Assembly, *Journal*, 1893–96. Newfoundland Medical Board, *Newfoundland medical register* (n.p.), 1912, 1914. *Newfoundland men . . .*, ed. H. Y. Mott (Concord, N.H., 1894). *Notable events in the history of Newfoundland: six thousand dates of historical and social happenings*, comp. M. A. Devine and M. J. O'Mara (St John's, 1900). Patricia O'Brien, *Out of mind, out of sight: a history of the Waterford Hospital* (St John's, 1989). *Vital statistics from N.B. newspapers* (Johnson), 60 (1882–84). *Who's who and why*, 1914. *Who's who in and from Newfoundland . . .* (St John's), 1927. *Yearbook and almanac of Newfoundland* (St John's), 1887–1929.

TANGUAY, GEORGES-ÉMILE (baptized **George-Elzéar-Émile**), architect; b. 8 Oct. 1858 in Saint-Gervais, Lower Canada, son of Georges Tanguay, a

school inspector, and Angèle Jolivet; m. 10 Aug. 1886 Clara Trudel at Quebec, and they had five sons; d. there 6 Nov. 1923.

After studying at the École Normale Laval at Quebec and serving an apprenticeship with Joseph-Ferdinand Peachy* that began in 1876, Georges-Émile Tanguay set up his own business as an architect at the age of 22. In 1889 he went into partnership with Napoléon-Alfred Vallée, with whom he already shared an office; after Vallée's death in 1898, Tanguay carried on the business in his own name until 1911, when he entered into a new partnership with Jean-Honorius Lebon. After Lebon died, Tanguay et Lebon became known in 1919 as Tanguay et Chênevert; Raoul Chênevert* would retain the firm's name until 1925, two years after Tanguay's death.

In the early years of his career, as a result of his experience with Peachy, Tanguay kept to the formal repertory of the Second Empire, and for a while was part of a movement of builders such as Eugène-Étienne Taché* who were restoring the Gallic character of the provincial capital. In the Saint-Jean and Saint-Roch wards of Quebec City, the houses and shops designed by the young architect helped consolidate an urban landscape inspired by France; for many years, his characteristic mansard roofs and arched windows would serve as a model for other architects. In 1883, however, after spending several weeks in the United States to see the department stores for which the country was becoming well known, Tanguay firmly embraced the modernist idiom. In a capital mired in the French-style historicism of Taché and Peachy, he rapidly outstripped both his teacher and his competitors, such as David Ouellet* and François-Xavier Berlinguet*, who, although they had also been trained through apprenticeship, were rather overwhelmed by the Americanism then gathering momentum. Tanguay assimilated the new trends, whether that of the Chicago School, which he employed extensively in department stores, and or that of art nouveau, which would be introduced at Quebec in the Salon des Dames he designed for the store of Paquet Company Limited in 1906. At a time when growing foreign competition led to the founding in 1890 of the Province of Quebec Association of Architects, an organization inclined to protectionism, Tanguay showed himself at ease with the new architectural programs, as witness his research into forms, that modernized the architectural repertory without abandoning the traditions to which the city of Quebec had become attached.

The most creative period of Tanguay's career began in 1888, on his return from a trip to Europe and Morocco. Before his 40th birthday, he took up two major challenges at Quebec. In 1892 his Pavillon d'Aiguillon, the first clinical wing of the Hôtel-Dieu, was a rival, in the city's urban landscape, of the Château Frontenac, which had been erected that year according to the plans of the American Bruce Price*. Then, two years later, Tanguay's plans for the city hall created a new architectural form fusing the styles of two American architects – the neo-Romanesque of Henry Hobson Richardson and the rationalism of Louis Henri Sullivan – with Second Empire rigid classicism and the fashionable mediaevalism of Frenchman Eugène-Emmanuel Viollet-le-Duc that had left its mark in the city with the rebuilding of its fortifications. It became the first monument in this "municipal style"; all across the city, Tanguay's fire stations and public buildings soon bore witness to this reinvented urban identity.

In the same period, this architect, who in the course of his career would draw up plans for around 40 churches, was revitalizing French Canadian ecclesiastical architecture in the innovative examples of Saint-Ambroise (Loretteville, 1891), Notre-Dame-du-Chemin (Quebec City, 1893), Immaculée-Conception (Montreal, 1896), Sainte-Angèle-de-Saint-Malo (Quebec City, 1900), and others in Ontario, at Alexandria, Cornwall, and Port Arthur (Thunder Bay), as well as in Saskatchewan, at Prince Albert. However, around 1900, Tanguay's architectural knowledge and eclectic approach began to fail him; he could not meet the requirements of the most modern or technologically challenging commissions (factories, hospitals, and other buildings). René-Pamphile Lemay, who had trained in the United States, returned to Quebec in 1896, and it was he, along with men such as Bruce Price, Walter Scott Painter, Harry Edward Prindle, and other "outsiders," who took on these new projects that called for more complex planning and more demanding construction techniques. The problems that Tanguay encountered in 1907 during the erection of the building for the *Daily Telegraph* – "the most modern . . . ever constructed in Quebec City," according to *La Semaine commerciale* (Québec) – and the exasperation of its owner show the context within which the architect would henceforth be obliged to work. As Frank Carrel* wrote to him on 9 Aug. 1909, "Our building, instead of being a credit to Quebec architects and contractors, is a grand spectacle of their inability to put up a satisfactory building, and it is not surprising to me now, that outside architects are being employed for the larger buildings in Quebec."

From this point onwards, Tanguay's success lay in the way he organized his professional practice. Of course he could still rely on the loyalty of numerous clients, among both religious communities and the Liberal establishment, to which he had been brought closer as a result of his contacts with former premier Simon-Napoléon Parent* in the course of the construction of the Quebec city hall during his mayoralty. But it was as a businessman and member (indeed president) of various business associations and of the boards of some ten companies (such as Quebec Power Company, Citadel Brick and Paving Block Company Limited, and Métabetchouan Pulp Company) that Tanguay came to fit an American mould in his style of life, the organization of his work, and his integration into the socio-professional milieu. With a plan that even included opening an office in Trois-Rivières immediately after the fire there in 1908, Tanguay was building a new type of architectural practice. It involved forming consortiums (for example, with the firm of Jean-Omer Marchand*, the first Quebec graduate of the École des Beaux-Arts in Paris) and calling in experts from outside Canada to work under the cover of his own firm's name (the Pittsburgh architect Victor Rigaumont secretly drew up the plans for the Hôpital Laval, for which construction began in 1915). In this manner Tanguay redefined the way he practised his profession in conformity with modern business methods. Ever since the arrival of Jean-Honorius Lebon as an apprentice in 1895, the company, which was located in the building that Tanguay had acquired for his private residence, had been responsible for a growing number of increasingly diverse architectural projects. In 1919 alone, there were plans for more than 20 new buildings in Quebec City on Tanguay's drawing boards; they included a garage, a bank, and a school, as well as various offices, houses, and factories. Five years earlier, the addition of a new apprentice, Raoul Chênevert, a graduate of the École Polytechnique de Montréal, had made it necessary to enlarge his office space and reflected the rapid growth of the company's order book. The seal of Tanguay et Chênevert, symbolizing a new and diverse professional expertise, appeared on the plans of at least 100 projects in Quebec City, which experienced a period of renewal after World War I ended. Some ten schools already bore the sober imprint of Tanguay's classical Beaux-Arts rationalism. This style would soon be followed by art deco, through which Chênevert gave the firm a final renewed vigour.

When Georges-Émile Tanguay died at his residence on Rue d'Aiguillon in 1923, he left a prosperous and well-established business. His son Berchmans, a student at the École Polytechnique who would become an architect, was at his side; his wife was visiting Paris, where their son Georges-Émile was pursuing studies that would lead to his appointment as one of the first professors at the Institute of Music and Dramatic Art of the Province of Quebec in Montreal. President of the Province of Quebec Association of Architects in 1900–1, Tanguay had been, according to biographical sources, "one of the leading architects of the Dominion," as well as "a most distinguished citizen and business man." A short, slight figure of a man with a pale, almost self-effacing expression, he left a legacy of almost 300 buildings and vivid memories among his contemporaries.

In 1974 architect Henriette Barrot, the widow of

Raoul Chênevert, gave the largest collection of architectural archives in Canada to the Université Laval. Transferred to the Archives Nationales du Quebec in 1989, it includes more than 500 separate projects bearing Tanguay's name. These illustrate a period of history in which the character of so many towns was completely transformed and Tanguay made a lasting imprint. Through his work Quebec City acquired a new identity, moving beyond traditional values to enter the modern world.

LUCIE K. MORISSET

[The ANQ-Q holds approximately 550 files (plans, estimates, and other documents) pertaining to Georges-Émile Tanguay in the Raoul Chênevert fonds (P372). A description of these holdings can be found in Geneviève Guimont Bastien *et al.*, *Inventaire des dessins architecturaux aux Archives de l'université Laval* (Ottawa, 1980). The ANQ-Q also has more than 200 notarial instruments relating to Tanguay's architectural works. The projects listed in the biography are documented in CN301-S337, 2 mai 1907; S351, 12 mai 1890, 7 nov. 1891, 25 août 1892, 3 mai 1893; S357, 15 févr. 1892; S377, 5–6, 10–11, 18, 31 déc. 1894; 25 nov., 3 déc. 1895; S381, 29 sept. 1919. Another source of information is Qué., Bureau de la Publicité des Droits, Greffes, J.-É. Boily, 19 juill. 1898; Joseph Sirois, 10 mai 1917, 16 avril 1919; C.-E. Taschereau, 7 déc. 1910; 15 août, 15 sept. 1911.

Although no single book describes Tanguay's work in its entirety, useful sources are Lucie K[oenig] Morisset, "D'un hôtel de ville au style municipal: un monument moderne dans la vieille capitale," in *L'Hôtel de ville de Québec: cent ans d'histoire*, sous la dir. d'Yves Tessier (Québec, 1996), 45–63, and especially the author's more detailed manuscript, "Georges-Émile Tanguay, architecte moderne: pratique de l'architecture et modernité à Québec," which informed part of this biography. Tanguay's church architecture is described in Luc Noppen and Lucie K[oenig] Morisset, *Art et architecture des églises à Québec* ([Québec], 1996); the schools that he produced in the author's "La genèse de l'école de quartier au Québec: histoire typologique d'une architecture scolaire," Soc. for the Study of Architecture in Canada, *Bull.* (Ottawa), 18 (1993): 88–95; his works of commercial architecture in Sylvie Thivierge, "L'architecture commerciale de Québec, 1860–1915" (mémoire de MA, univ. Laval, Québec, 1985); and, lastly, his department stores and working-class homes in Luc Noppen and Lucie K[oenig] Morisset, *L'architecture de Saint-Roch: guide de promenade* ([Québec], 2000). A partial list of Tanguay's works appears in A. J. H. Richardson *et al.*, *Quebec City: architects, artisans and builders* (Ottawa, 1984), 525–26. An analysis of some of them may be found in Luc Noppen *et al.*, *Québec monumental, 1890–1990* (Sillery, Qué., 1990), and *Québec: trois siècles d'architecture* ([Montréal], 1979); in Luc Noppen et Lucie K[oenig] Morisset, *Québec, de roc et de pierres: la capitale en architecture* (Sainte-Foy, Qué., [1998]); and in two of the author's publications: "Flambeau d'une capitale: le parc de l'Exposition provinciale de Québec; projets et réalisation d'un aménagement monumental," Soc. for the Study of Architecture in Canada, *Bull.*, 20 (1995): 61–69 and *Le potentiel monumental du parc de l'Exposition provinciale de Québec . . .* (2v., [Québec], 1994). L.K.M.]

ANQ-Q, CE301-S1, 10 août 1886; CE302-S17, 8 oct. 1858; E6, S8, G.-É. Tanguay. *L'Action catholique* (Québec), 6 nov. 1923. *L'Action sociale* (Québec), 26 mai 1908. *L'Électeur* (Québec), 7 déc. 1888. *L'Événement*, 6 nov. 1923. *Le Journal de Québec*, 28 mars 1883, 10 déc. 1888. *La Minerve*, 24 déc. 1898. *La Semaine commerciale* (Québec), 8 nov. 1907. *Canadian album* (Cochrane and Hopkins), 5: 63. Léon Lortie, *Album biographique des membres du conseil de ville, suivis des principaux officiers et des entrepreneurs du nouvel hôtel de ville de Québec, 1896–97* ([Québec], 1897). *The storied province of Quebec; past and present*, ed. W. [C. H.] Wood *et al.* (5v., Toronto, 1931–32), 3: 63. Benjamin Sulte *et al.*, *A history of Quebec, its resources and its people* (2v., Montreal, 1908), 2: 885–86. *Who's who and why*, 1915/16.

TATE, CAROLINE SARAH. *See* KNOTT

TAYLOR, MARGARET, Lady TAYLOR. *See* VALLANCE

TEIT, JAMES ALEXANDER (until 1884 he spelled his surname **Tait**), store clerk, farmer, hunting guide, ethnographer, author, and political activist; b. 15 April 1864 in Lerwick, Scotland, son of John Tait and Elizabeth Murray; m. first 12 Sept. 1892 Antko (Susannah Lucy) (d. 1899) near Spences Bridge, B.C.; they had no children; m. secondly 15 March 1904 Leonie Josephine Morens (d. 1948) in Spences Bridge, and they had six children; d. 30 Oct. 1922 in Merritt, B.C., and was buried there.

James Teit was born into a merchant family in Lerwick, in the Shetland Islands. His mother had worked as a governess before her marriage. His father was a licensed grocer in Lerwick and a strong promoter of public education; he helped to launch the Anderson Educational Institute, Lerwick's first upper-level public school, in 1868. It was probably from this school that James graduated at age 16.

Following his graduation, James worked first in the family store and then for about a year as a clerk in a Lerwick bank. He also may have spent some months as a commercial fisherman in the North Sea. Sometime in the early 1880s his mother's brother John Murray invited one of his nephews to join him in British Columbia. Murray had established himself in 1859 as a storekeeper and farmer in Cook's Ferry (Spences Bridge), in south central British Columbia. A bachelor, he offered the prospect of an inheritance. The invitation appealed to 19-year-old James, who relinquished his birthright to his younger brother John and arrived at Spences Bridge on 17 March 1884.

At this time James changed the spelling of his surname to Teit. Perhaps influenced by his father's keen interest in Shetland history, he had traced his family roots to Jan Teit, a Norwegian who had settled on the Shetland island of Fetlar in the 12th century. As he would explain in a letter to his uncle Robert Tait in 1905, "[Teit] is the real old original and proper way of spelling the name."

In Spences Bridge, Teit clerked at his uncle's store, supplementing this work with whatever seasonal employment he could find – trapping, farming, and orcharding. Each fall he hunted in remote areas of central and northern British Columbia. His experience would soon enable him to advertise his skills as a guide for big game hunters. Through his uncle he came into close contact with the region's aboriginal peoples, many of whom traded regularly at Murray's establishment. Within three years of his arrival, he was living with Antko, a young Thompson (Nlaka'pamux) woman from Nkaitu'sus, a small native village in the Twaal valley just north of Spences Bridge. On 12 Sept. 1892 they were officially married in her village by Archdeacon Richard Small.

In 1894 the German-American anthropologist Franz Boas* was in British Columbia on an ethnographic field trip. He interrupted his train trip to the coast to spend a night at Spences Bridge. Someone there suggested that he contact Murray, who in turn sent him to find Teit. In a letter to his family on 21 Sept. 1894 Boas described Teit as "a treasure! He knows a great deal about the tribes. I engaged him right away."

Teit was immediately helpful to Boas. Fluent in the Thompson language, he explained to his relatives and friends that Boas wanted to measure and to interview them. Trusting Teit, they all agreed to work with Boas. The following day Teit took Boas on horseback to visit numerous small aboriginal villages in the vicinity. Immediately Boas's attitude to his fieldwork changed. As he explained to his family, "The disagreeable feeling I had that I don't get along with the Indians is slowly wearing off now, and I am hopeful that I will have good results." Before departing for New York City, Boas returned to Spences Bridge in December to undertake more research with Teit. After only two days Boas had measured 123 natives, his greatest accomplishment in any aboriginal community east of the coast, so he was pleased with Teit. He delighted to hear that Teit was well along on a written ethnographic report for him. By spring 1895 Teit had expanded this report to 216 pages, had produced a shorter study of the Nicola (Stuwíxamux), a little-known Athapaskan-speaking group once resident in the Nicola valley, and had assembled and sent to New York a large collection of "articles of ethnological value" from the Spences Bridge region.

Boas's next trip to British Columbia, in June 1897, was funded by Morris Ketchum Jesup, president of the American Museum of Natural History in New York. It was the beginning of a five-year research project known as the Jesup North Pacific Expedition. The goal was to produce a systematic ethnological and archaeological overview of the relations between the indigenous peoples of the Pacific rim of northwestern America and those of northeastern Asia. The JNPE was organized into a number of research teams. The Pacific northwest team consisted of Boas, Americans Harlan Ingersoll Smith, Livingston Farrand, and John Reed Swanton, and British Columbians George Hunt* and Teit.

Throughout the JNPE, Boas relied heavily on Teit. He launched the project at Spences Bridge where, with Teit's assistance, he and his colleagues spent a productive week studying archaeological sites, taking photographs, recording stories and songs, and listening to explanations of designs on woven baskets, jewellery, and masks. Boas also hired Teit to guide his group by packhorse north to Soda Creek and then west to Bella Coola, a trip that took almost seven weeks. Boas made only one more field trip to British Columbia during the JNPE, electing instead to conduct most of his research from his New York base by correspondence with Teit (in the interior) and Hunt (on the coast). Almost weekly these two men mailed him large volumes of written responses to his queries.

During the JNPE, Teit maintained a rigorous field-research and writing schedule which resulted in major publications. Of the 27 JNPE publications in the American Museum of Natural History's *Memoirs* (New York), Teit authored four: "The Thompson Indians of British Columbia" (1900), "The Lillooet Indians" (1906), "The Shuswap" (1909), and "Mythology of the Thompson Indians" (1912). He also contributed indirectly to an additional three. He was a field assistant and consultant (identifying sites, collecting artefacts, and proof-reading reports) for Smith's two archaeological reports of 1899 and 1900 and he supplied many of the primary data featured in Farrand's "Basketry designs of the Salish Indians" (1900). Finally, he facilitated Smith's photographic work at Spences Bridge that formed the core of the *Ethnographical album of the North Pacific coasts of America and Asia* (1900). Teit's productivity for the JNPE, in particular his large synthetic overviews of three individual cultures, stood in contrast to Boas's slim output. Indeed, at least one review of the legacy of the expedition argues that it was Teit's on-the-ground ethnographic work which was largely responsible for the overall success of the project. In every respect Teit surpassed his New York–based colleagues in fulfilling the expedition's goals: in-depth ethnographic studies of individual cultures, comparative analyses of cultural data, a range of field experiences, and large collections of material artefacts.

The JNPE provided Teit with a regular income, an asset after the death of his uncle on 30 March 1896. Murray had left his nephew little more than a piece of property, which Teit sold to pay his uncle's debts, and the old store and its contents. Teit kept the store to house his hunting supplies and ethnographic collections. The building also provided him with space for an office and a venue for holding meetings.

On 2 March 1899 Teit's wife Antko died. He

explained in a letter to Boas that, "as she was a good wife to me and we had lived happily together for over twelve years, I naturally took her demise as a great blow." It may have been the loss of his wife and his uncle within three years that prompted Teit to visit his parents in Lerwick. He departed on 22 Dec. 1901 and sailed from New York after a six-day visit with Boas. On his return he spent about seven days with Boas before arriving in Spences Bridge on 6 July 1902.

In the months that followed, Teit resumed a courtship he had begun earlier with Leonie Josephine Morens, daughter of colonists who had immigrated from the Savoie region of France. On 15 March 1904 in a Roman Catholic ceremony, Teit, almost 40, married 23-year-old Leonie. Although Teit's family was Presbyterian, he had described himself in 1901 as a freethinker. Other than his formal marriages and his friendship with Roman Catholic missionaries such as noted linguist Jean-Marie-Raphaël LE JEUNE, he had little involvement with organized religion. The Teits moved in with Leonie's widowed mother on the family farm near Spences Bridge. Over the next 14 years, they would have six children, each of whom would be given a Norse name. In 1911 Teit would build a home for the family in Spences Bridge, where they would live until they moved to Merritt in 1919.

From 1902 on, as his hunting skills improved, Teit acted as a guide for big game hunters from Europe and the United States. These trips, usually two to three months in duration, supplemented the income he obtained from anthropological research. Less than a decade later the British magazine *Travel and Exploration* would describe him as "the premier guide of the province, with . . . an unrivalled knowledge of the topography of the country . . . , a marvellous instinct for game, and a complete mastery of the various Indian languages." Teit had probably learned target shooting from his father and he was likely already a skilled marksman when he arrived in British Columbia. His expeditions into northern British Columbia brought him into contact with Sekani, Kaska, and Tahltan peoples, some of whom travelled with him.

Meanwhile, throughout the first decade of the 20th century Teit worked steadily for Boas, collecting myths, artefacts, and other ethnological information among the peoples that he knew. He also spent time working on his notes and manuscripts. In September 1904 he guided Homer E. Sargent, a wealthy Chicago consulting engineer, on a sheep-hunting expedition to the Cariboo. During this trip Sargent learned much about Teit's ethnographic work for Boas and in March 1907 he offered to donate funds to it. With this support Teit undertook field research in 1908 and again in spring 1909 in Washington State, Idaho, and Montana among the Salishan- and Sahaptin-speaking peoples. His notes would be published posthumously as "Coeur d'Alene, Flathead and Okanogan Indians" in

the Bureau of American Ethnology's *Annual report* (Washington) for 1927–28 and as *Middle Columbia Salish* (Seattle, 1928). Sargent, a collector of aboriginal artefacts, was particularly interested in basketry and requested that some of his funds be directed towards more acquisitions. In response, Teit began in 1909 to assemble a large British Columbia basket collection, which he deposited in 1910 and 1911 at the Field Museum of Natural History in Chicago, at Sargent's request. His basketry notes, sketches, and photos would be edited by Boas's students Herman Karl Haeberlin (who died part-way through the project) and Helen Heffron Roberts; the resulting publication, "Coiled basketry in British Columbia and surrounding region," would appear in the Bureau of American Ethnology's report for the years 1919 to 1924, published only in 1928. Sargent continued to finance Teit's field research liberally until Teit's death in 1922.

In December 1911 Edward Sapir*, chief of the anthropological division of the Geological Survey of Canada and a student of Boas's, had recommended a systematic study of the Athapaskan-speaking peoples of northern British Columbia and had convinced the director of the survey, Reginald Walter Brock*, that "no better man could be chosen for the position" than Teit. Consequently, Teit was added to the survey's payroll in 1911 on a yearly contract. In 1912 and 1915 he undertook field trips for the survey to the Stikine valley, where he interviewed numerous Tahltan and Kaska people, collected songs and artefacts, and took photographs. He also continued to work intermittently for Boas, doing fieldwork in the Kootenay region in spring 1913 and conducting ongoing research on basketry. In addition, he assembled collections of clothing, tools, and other articles for Charles Frederic NEWCOMBE of the provincial museum. By 1917 Sapir had expressed concern that Teit's work on Boas's projects was interfering with his productivity for the survey. Teit had gathered extensive raw data and artefacts for Sapir, but he had not found time to prepare any material for publication.

There were other demands on Teit's time during the years he worked with Boas and Sapir that affected his anthropological work. Aboriginal leaders all over the province were worried about the future of their peoples, having witnessed large-scale settlement and development in just a few decades, with a loss of their rights to their land base. Because there were so few who could communicate in English, the chiefs were in desperate need of translators to help them argue their position. With his linguistic ability and his ethnographic knowledge, Teit was perfectly placed to take on this role. As he would explain in 1920 to a Senate committee in Ottawa, the Interior Tribes of British Columbia, an alliance of Thompson, Shuswap, and Okanagan leaders, "insisted [in 1909] upon my attending their meetings and helping with their writing. Thus I commenced to act as their secretary and treasurer." He also acted for the Indian Rights Association, an alliance of lower mainland, northern coastal, and Vancouver Island aboriginal groups formed the same year. He spent most of 1910 travelling to reserves throughout the southern interior region to create a liaison between the two groups. By the summer, with Teit's help, the Interior Tribes had produced two important written documents, a declaration and a memorial to Prime Minister Sir Wilfrid Laurier*, outlining its position. This form of political advocacy was in keeping with the anti-state rhetoric that Teit had been following in socialist journals from Vancouver such as the *Western Socialist* and its successor, the *Western Clarion*, between 1902 and 1909.

Teit made several trips to Ottawa with delegations of chiefs to act as translator and lobbyist. The first was in January 1912, when he and nine chiefs representing the Indian Rights Association met with Prime Minister Robert Laird Borden* and members of his cabinet. In July 1912, in response to Borden's appointment of James Andrew Joseph McKenna* as special commissioner of Indian affairs responsible for reaching an agreement with the province about the land question, Teit convened a meeting of about 450 chiefs in Spences Bridge. The agreement McKenna reached with Premier Richard McBride* resulted in the establishment in late March 1913 of the royal commission on Indian affairs for the province of British Columbia. The creation of the McKenna–McBride commission, as it was called, led to further meetings of native leaders at Spences Bridge.

When the Allied Indian Tribes of British Columbia was formed in June 1916 in Vancouver, Teit was selected to serve on its executive committee, along with aboriginal leaders Basil David, John Tetlenitsa, and Peter Kelly*. With Kelly, Teit co-authored the organization's *Statement of the Allied Indian Tribes of British Columbia for the government of British Columbia*, published probably in Vancouver in 1919. The statement rejected the recommendations of the McKenna–McBride commission, which had been published in 1916, especially because they failed to address issues such as land titles and water rights and because they advised that valuable lands be cut off from the reserves and lands of little value added. In 1920 Teit spent from mid March until mid June in Ottawa (with a short trip to British Columbia in mid May), writing letters and lobbying to promote the aboriginal cause. Despite strong opposition from aboriginal peoples, the British Columbia Indian Lands Settlement Act was assented to on Dominion Day 1920, empowering the federal government to implement the recommendations of the royal commission. Two months later Teit was appointed by the federal and provincial governments, along with William Ernest Ditchburn* for the Department of Indian Affairs and

J. W. Clark for British Columbia, to undertake a review of the commission's report. Teit was to represent the aboriginal peoples' interests, a position he agreed to take only with the approval of the chiefs. Just weeks into this work, he became ill with what would be diagnosed as bowel cancer. After a year of rest and treatment, however, he improved and he resumed his work on what became known as the Ditchburn inquiry.

By March 1922, just as he was beginning to write up his report, Teit suffered a relapse. He died seven months later at age 58. His death was a great loss, not only to the anthropological fraternity, but also to aboriginal peoples throughout the province. As Boas commented in his obituary of Teit, "Unceasingly he labored for their welfare and subordinated all other interests, scientific as well as personal, to this work, which he came to consider the most important task of his life." Teit's colleague Peter Kelly was more emphatic on this point, noting in 1953 that "the organization of the Interior Indians fell apart after Teit's death. Not altogether, but it was never the same again."

For many, James Alexander Teit is a minor anthropological figure, remembered at best as Boas's assistant or informant and the author of a number of important ethnographic texts on the plateau peoples of North America. His work as a political advocate is almost entirely unknown. Given his contribution and his legacy (over 2,200 printed pages in 43 published sources and almost 5,000 more in unpublished manuscripts) it is time now to acknowledge him as one of North America's most distinguished anthropologists.

WENDY WICKWIRE

James Alexander Teit is the author of a number of works in addition to those mentioned in the text. A bibliography of his manuscript and published writings can be found in Roderick Sprague, "A bibliography of James A. Teit," *Northwest Anthropological Research Notes* (Moscow, Idaho), 25 (1991): 103–15.

American Museum of Natural Hist., Div. of Anthropology Arch. (New York), Corr., James Teit and Franz Boas, 1894–1902. American Philosophical Soc. (Philadelphia), B B65p (Franz Boas professional papers). Canadian Museum of Civilization (Hull, Que.), Arch., Ethnology records, I-A-236M (Edward Sapir, professional corr.), folder Teit, James A. (1911–22). Private arch., Sigurd Teit (Merritt, B.C.), J. A. Teit, journals, 1897, 1901, 1904, 1908–10, 1912–13, 1920; Teit family papers, photographs, and miscellaneous documents, including copies of documents from the Shetland Arch., Lerwick, Scot. *Shetland Times* (Lerwick), 4 Sept. 1904. J. J. Banks, "Comparative biographies of two British Columbia anthropologists: Charles Hill-Tout and James A. Teit" (MA thesis, Univ. of B.C., Vancouver, 1970). Judith Berman, "'The culture as it appears to the Indian himself': Boas, George Hunt, and the methods of ethnography," in *"Volksgeist" as method and ethic: essays on Boasian ethnography and the German anthropological tradition*, ed. G. W. Stocking (Madison, Wis., 1996), 215–56. [Franz Boas], *The ethnography of Franz Boas*, comp. and ed. R. P.

Tenass

Rohner, intro. R. P. and E. C. Rohner, trans. Hedy Parker (Chicago and London, 1969); "James A. Teit," *Journal of American Folk-Lore* (Lancaster, Pa, and New York), 36 (1923): 102–3. Don Bunyon, "James Teit – pioneer anthropologist," *Heritage West* (Vancouver), 5 (1981), no.3: 21–23. Peter Campbell, "'Not as a white man, not as a sojourner': James A. Teit and the fight for native rights in British Columbia, 1884–1922," *left hist.* (Kingston, Ont.), 2 (1994), no.2: 37–57. Roy Gronneberg, "James Teit – friend of the Indians," *New Shetlander* (Lerwick), 126 (April–June 1978): 28–30. Katharine Howes and Pat Lean, "Commemorating: James Alexander Teit; an interview with Inga Teit Perkin, daughter of noted ethnologist James A. Teit," *Nicola Valley Hist. Quarterly* (Merritt), 2 (1979), no.2: 1, 4. Ira Jacknis, "'The artist himself': the Salish basketry monograph and the beginnings of a Boasian paradigm," in *The early years of native American art history: the politics of scholarship and collecting*, ed. J. C. Berlo (Seattle and Vancouver, 1992), 142–44. Peter Jamieson, "Jimmy Teit of Spence's Bridge, British Columbia," *New Shetlander*, 53 (January–March 1960): 17–20. Pat Lean and Sigurd Teit, "Introduction," *Teit Times* (Merritt), 1 (summer 1995): 1–64. Ralph Maud, *A guide to B.C. Indian myth and legend: a short history of myth-collecting and a survey of published texts* (Vancouver, 1982). R. P. Rohner, "Franz Boas: ethnographer on the northwest coast," in *Pioneers of American anthropology: the uses of biography*, ed. June Helm (Seattle and London, [1966]), 151–247. Frantz Rosenberg, *Big game shooting in British Columbia and Norway* (London, 1928). J. A. Smith, *Widow Smith of Spence's Bridge*, ed. J. M. Campbell *et al.* (Merritt, 1989). W. C. Wickwire, "Beyond Boas? Re-assessing the contribution of 'informant' and 'research assistant', James A. Teit," in *Constructing cultures then and now: the Jesup North Pacific Expedition* (Seattle, forthcoming); "James A. Teit: his contribution to Canadian ethnomusicology," *Canadian Journal of Native Studies* (Brandon, Man.), 8 (1988): 183–204; "'We shall drink from the stream and so shall you': James A. Teit and native resistance in British Columbia, 1908–22," *CHR*, 79 (1998): 199–236. Lincoln Wilbar, "British Columbia for the sportsman," *Travel and Exploration* (London), October 1909: 279.

TENASS, JOHN P., Micmac (Mi'kmaw) chief; b. 12 Sept. 1849 near Richibucto, N.B., son of Peter Tenass and Mary Glinn (Green) of the Richibucto tribe; m. first 1869 Ann Ward (d. 20 Feb. 1915) of the Red Bank band, and they had at least three sons and four daughters; m. secondly 1915 Christine Jones, widow of Lemuel Peter-Paul; d. 24 Dec. 1928 at Red Bank, N.B.

The parents of John P. Tenass were living in the Richibucto area at the time of his birth but they were in Northumberland County in 1855, when their son Francis was baptized. In the census of 1871 John's father, along with his second wife and the younger children of his first marriage, were enumerated in Burnt Church. In 1881 they were at the Eel Ground Indian Reserve on the Northwest Miramichi River, east of Red Bank. Meanwhile, John had married and settled at Red Bank, a place that has been occupied by aboriginals for some 2,500 years.

The Red Bank band was a recognized entity from at least the 1760s, when land in the vicinity of the band's encampments was granted to British immigrants. Hardships befell the native population as a consequence of colonization, but a large reserve was erected at Red Bank and for many years the residents had a significant measure of control over their own affairs. In 1836, however, a rogue named Barnaby Julian became chief. By squandering the band's resources and defying provincial officials, he succeeded in making Red Bank a pariah. In the mid 1840s the officials ceased dealing with him or other representatives and chose instead to regard the residents of Red Bank and Eel Ground as members of a single tribe under the chief of Eel Ground. After confederation the Eel Ground Indians were recognized as a band by the government of Canada but requests from Red Bank for similar recognition were rebuffed for nearly 30 years. During this period disputes arose concerning the once reserved lands on which non-Indians had been living under spurious leases issued by Julian. When the government arranged to sell these lands in the early 1890s without the approval of the band, they raised a clamour that could not be ignored. After much squabbling, the Department of Indian Affairs conceded in 1896 that the Red Bank Indians constituted a distinct band and were entitled to elect their own chief. The victor in the first contest, on 24 Aug. 1896, was John P. Tenass. Dedicated to moving forward rather than brooding over the past, he received all but two of the votes cast.

Unlike several of the elected chiefs at Eel Ground, who had become entangled in internecine disputes [*see* Thomas Barnaby*], Tenass established harmonious relations with almost everyone with whom he was associated, on and off his reserve. His concerns were practical, revolving around timber rights, the acquisition of farm implements, and the establishment of a day school. He first requested a school in 1897, but the district Indian superintendent, William Doherty Carter, opposed the idea on the grounds that there were only a dozen children of school age at Red Bank. When a second election was held, in June 1902, while Tenass was away on a "surveying expedition," he won again. Except for a few years following the election of 1905, which he lost by one vote, he served as chief until 1920; he was then succeeded by his son Mitchell. His dream of establishing a school was realized partially in 1914, when classes were begun, and fully in 1917, when a one-room school was erected.

An important cultural figure at Red Bank, Tenass was concerned that traditional wisdom and craftsmanship be handed down to succeeding generations. When the young American anthropologist Wilson Dallam Wallis began his study of Micmac culture in 1911, he used him as an informant, and his name appears in connection with several of the folk tales and traditions recorded in *The Micmac Indians of eastern Canada*. Tenass died in Red Bank in 1928 and was buried there in the cemetery of St Thomas Roman Catholic Church.

Tenass's daughter Mary Jane and her husband, John Augustine, were the parents of Joseph Michael Augustine, who in the 1970s called the attention of the archaeological community to the significance of the ancient sites at Red Bank. His initiative led to his being granted New Brunswick's distinguished Award for Heritage, and the designation of both the Oxbow site and the Augustine burial mound as national historic sites.

W. D. HAMILTON

The principal facts contained in this sketch are reported and documented in the author's book *The Julian tribe* (Fredericton, 1984). P. [M.] Allen, *Metepenagiag, New Brunswick's oldest village* ([rev. ed.], Fredericton, 1994) was also consulted. John P. Tenass, W. D. Wallis's main host and guide at Red Bank, appears as an informant in W. D. Wallis and Ruth Sawtell Wallis, *The Micmac Indians of eastern Canada* (Minneapolis, Minn., 1955), 408–9, 475, 479.

TESSIER, JOSEPH-ADOLPHE, lawyer, politician, militia officer, and office holder; b. 17 Dec. 1861 in Sainte-Anne-de-la-Pérade, Lower Canada, son of Louis-Gonzague Tessier, a farmer, and Rose de Lima Laquerre; m. 14 Aug. 1888 Marie-Louise-Elmire Guillet in Trois-Rivières, Que., and they had five children, two of whom died in infancy; d. there 4 Nov. 1928.

Born in the old agricultural region of Sainte-Anne-de-la-Pérade, noted for producing public figures, Joseph-Adolphe Tessier began his schooling at the Académie Saint-Cyr in his village. He went on to the Séminaire Saint-Joseph in Trois-Rivières (1876–81), the Université Laval in Montreal, where he studied law (1882–84), and the infantry school at Saint-Jean. Called to the bar on 26 Jan. 1885, he moved to Trois-Rivières, where he practised law, was active in the 86th Infantry Battalion, and associated with the supporters of Honoré Mercier*, a minority group in a city dominated by Bishop Louis-François Laflèche* and his conservative bourgeois allies.

As the 19th century drew to a close, Tessier came under the influence of Jacques Bureau*, a prominent Liberal with whom he would work closely for some 20 years. Carried along by the popularity of Sir Wilfrid Laurier* and inspired by the leadership of Bureau, who was elected MP for Trois-Rivières in 1900, the Liberals in this riding took over power locally at all levels. Tessier now became a key figure, piling up success, honours, and responsibilities: city solicitor (1896–98 and 1901–5), deputy public prosecutor for the judicial district of Trois-Rivières (1900–4), member of the Legislative Assembly for Trois-Rivières (1904–21), lieutenant-colonel of the 86th Regiment (1906–12), and mayor of Trois-Rivières (1913–21).

Entering on his career as an MLA at Quebec on 25 Nov. 1904, Tessier joined erstwhile colleague Lomer GOUIN, and backed him in his fight to take over control of the government led by Liberal Simon-Napoléon Parent*. In Gouin's administration, which held power from 23 March 1905 to 9 July 1920, Tessier served as chair of the private bills committee (1908–12), deputy speaker of the house (1912–14), and minister of highways from 1914. The roads system was one of the premier's priorities and he created the ministry in 1912 because, as he had explained on 10 January, he wanted "to do for the highways, for the roads used by motor vehicles, what was done in the past for the railways." At first, highways were the responsibility of the minister of agriculture but an autonomous department was put in place when Tessier was appointed minister. He would retain this office in the government of Louis-Alexandre Taschereau* from July 1920 until September 1921. At the time of his appointment there were some 10,000 vehicles in the province. When he left seven years later there were six times as many and it was estimated that the ministry had invested $30 million to make 3,500 miles of highway suitable for vehicles. Premier Taschereau, who succeeded Gouin, thought he had inherited "the best highway system in Canada."

While he was in the cabinet, Tessier continued to serve as mayor of Trois-Rivières, which was in the throes of development. His term came at a time of profound change that would transform the Mauricie region from a rural and forested area into a great industrial valley thriving in the era of electricity, pulp, and paper. Tessier thus faced the challenge of turning the old market town of Trois-Rivières into a modern industrial city attuned to the new social and economic realities. The industrial giants that began production there between 1908 and 1921 included the Wabasso Cotton Company Limited [*see* Charles Ross Whitehead*], the Canada Iron Corporation Limited, the Wayagamack Pulp and Paper Company, the Three Rivers Shipyard Company, and the International Power and Paper Company. This tremendous industrial surge was supported by the municipal council, which passed measures favourable to investors: tax credits, loans to companies, the purchase of an industrial development centre, the opening of an "Office for publicity and industry." The industrial expansion brought in its wake a rapid increase in population. From 1909 to 1913 three new parishes were created and three more would be added shortly afterwards. The population doubled in less than 20 years, and these new workers, day-labourers, and small shopkeepers would be faithful to the Liberal party. They would give overwhelming majorities to Tessier in his dual capacity as mayor and member of the assembly, as well as to the Liberal "big boss," the MP Jacques Bureau.

Teyssèdre

There were tensions between the two parliamentarians, however. Observers of the municipal scene, including the newspaper *Le Bien public*, noted Bureau's grip on the Trois-Rivières city council, where it was clear that Mayor Tessier was having difficulty leading his colleagues. Several shady deals turned into scandals. A company belonging to one alderman declared bankruptcy after receiving a loan from the city. Another alderman accepted a commission in a big real estate transaction in which the city had an interest. The same person, who was also the treasurer of Bureau's organization, awarded a contract for a large bond issue to a firm that contributed to the coffers of the Liberals in Trois-Rivières. Late in 1919 a request for an inquiry was submitted to the Superior Court. The judge conducting the inquiry, Louis-Joseph-Alfred Désy, was a former Conservative activist who had clashed with Tessier in the past. He now had an opportunity to dismantle, bit by bit, the foundations of "Rouge power" in Trois-Rivières. Carried out in 1920, his inquiry dealt with eleven different issues involving Mayor Tessier, three sitting aldermen, four former aldermen, and other individuals, including Jacques Bureau. Its report, published in January 1921, drew conclusions damning to the city council, though nothing was proved against the mayor himself. The judge acknowledged that Tessier had been lacking in "circumspection" and had put the city's credit at risk, but that he had in the main acted in good faith. At the age of 59, Tessier now decided to leave active politics. In November 1921 he was appointed chair of the Quebec Streams Commission, a governmental body created in 1910 primarily to regulate the flow of rivers, mainly by constructing dams.

In Trois-Rivières the political battle went on without Tessier. The "populist" Liberal Arthur Bettez would rise to prominence, against the wishes of the old leader Jacques Bureau, and a young Conservative lawyer named Maurice Le Noblet Duplessis* would benefit from the dissension among the Liberals and the discredit brought on them by the Désy inquiry.

Joseph-Adolphe Tessier died in office in 1928. He is regarded as one of the architects of the modern province of Quebec, especially in his native region of Mauricie. He would be remembered in Trois-Rivières for having been effective as a developer, but also for not having managed to put his administration above individual interests.

FRANÇOIS ROY

ANQ-MBF, CE401-S21, 18 déc. 1861; CE401-S48, 14 août 1888. Arch. de la Ville de Trois-Rivières, Qué., Procès-verbaux du conseil municipal, 1913–21; Rapport de l'honorable juge Désy (texte dactylographié, 1921). *Le Bien public* (Trois-Rivières), 1910–21. *L'Éveil* (Trois-Rivières), 1918–19. *Le Journal des Trois-Rivières*, 1890–91. *Le Nouveau Trois-Rivières*, 1908–14. *Le Nouvelliste* (Trois-Rivières), 1920–28. *La Paix* (Trois-Rivières), 1888. *St. Maurice Valley Chronicle* (Trois-Rivières), 1919. *Le Bottin parlementaire du Québec* ([Montréal], 1962). Alain Gamelin et al., *Trois-Rivières illustrée* (Trois-Rivières, 1984). François Roy, "Le crépuscule d'un rouge: J.-A. Tessier, maire de Trois-Rivières et l'enquête Désy de 1920" (mémoire de MA, univ. du Québec à Trois-Rivières, 1989). *RPQ*. Robert Rumilly, *Hist. de la prov. de Québec*, vols.12–17; *Maurice Duplessis et son temps* (2v., Montréal, 1973).

TEYSSÈDRE, ALEXANDRINE, named **Marie-Saint-David**, member of the Sisters of the Presentation of Mary, school administrator, and superior of her order for North America; b. 9 July 1842 in Millau, France, youngest of the five children of Guillaume Teyssèdre, a locksmith, and Marianne Galibert; d. 1 Jan. 1921 in Saint-Hyacinthe, Que., and was buried in the community's cemetery there.

Alexandrine Teyssèdre's father died when she was a child and her mother placed her with the Sisters of the Presentation of Mary in her village when she was about six years old. At the conclusion of her schooling, she became a postulant in this teaching order. Having taken her vows in 1861, she was immediately assigned various duties as a teacher. She came to the attention of her superiors and in 1874 was chosen for their house in Lausanne, Switzerland. Recalled to France two years later, she was immediately selected to go to North America and was sent to Saint-Hyacinthe, where a group of nuns had settled in 1858 after spending two years in Sainte-Marie-de-Monnoir (Marieville) and three in Saint-Hugues.

Soon after her arrival in the summer of 1876, Sister Marie-Saint-David was appointed principal of the community's new boarding school, which had some 80 pupils enrolled that year. The curriculum was based on the one used by the order's schools in France; in addition to reading and writing, the girls studied both sacred and Canadian history, the catechism, French, arithmetic, and geography. In 1879 she was given the position of mistress of novices, which she was to combine with that of assistant to the superior. From 1888, as a result of the rapid growth in the number of sisters in the community and in its activities, she had to confine herself to her duties as assistant. Not long afterwards, both her knees were paralysed by arthritis and, despite the best treatment then available, she was reduced to using crutches. However, the confidence of her community led her to make a pilgrimage to Sainte-Anne-de-Beaupré from which she returned cured on 26 July 1897.

In January 1898 Marie-Saint-David became the fifth superior of the Sisters of the Presentation of Mary for Canada and the United States, assuming the title of mother. She had 20 houses in Quebec and six in the United States under her jurisdiction. A period of expansion commenced which greatly extended the work initiated in 1853 by her predecessors in Quebec and New England. The arrival of some 50 nuns from France provided fresh impetus; they came after the enactment in 1901 of a law requiring unauthorized religious congregations to apply for legal recognition in order to be able to carry on their work in France. Touched by the appeals that the Oblates of Mary Immaculate had been making since the time when Alexandre-Antonin Taché* was consecrated bishop, Mother Marie-Saint-David sent 12 of the sisters to Duck Lake (Sask.) in 1903 to teach in the so-called industrial school run by Father Ovide Charlebois*. It was a favourite project of the mother superior and she visited it five times. She also authorized the founding of two other houses in this part of the country. Between 1900 and 1917, 28 houses were opened, with ten in Quebec, three in Saskatchewan, one in Ontario, and 14 in New England.

From her earliest days in Canada, Marie-Saint-David had studied the school curricula being used in Quebec and had endeavoured to integrate the pedagogical tradition of her order in France with practices in the province. In 1899 she produced an important synthesizing document for her order's schools. At the request of Bishop Alexis-Xyste Bernard of Saint-Hyacinthe, she undertook to organize and build a normal school adjoining the mother house, which opened in September 1912. However, her health, undermined by this arduous task, began to deteriorate.

Weakened by age and illness, Mother Marie-Saint-David was relieved of her duties by the superior general of France on 25 March 1917, after 19 years as superior. She retired to the infirmary of the community and there, in the house to whose influence in Canada and New England she had contributed for nearly 45 years, she died on 1 Jan. 1921. Her keen intelligence and fine personal qualities had won her the esteem of bishops and clergy, as well as of the secular authorities.

MARIE-PAULE R. LaBRÈQUE

[The archives at the mother house of the Sisters of the Presentation of Mary in Saint-Hyacinthe, Que., were lost in the fire of 7 April 1992 that destroyed the building. Despite attempts to reconstruct the records, it is apparent that most of the documents for Mother Marie-Saint-David's tenure as superior have disappeared. It therefore proved necessary to resort to published documents in the preparation of this biography. M.-P.R.LaB.]

Arch. Départementales, Aveyron (Rodez, France), État civil, Millau, 11 juill. 1842. Arch. des Sœurs de la Présentation de Marie, P8.3.2 (mère Saint-David), Doc. pédagogique, 27 mars 1899; "A jubilee story, 1903–1978" (typescript, Duck Lake, Sask., n.d.), 3–4. *Le Courrier de Saint-Hyacinthe*, 8 janv. 1921. [Sœur Sainte-Calixte Bourque], *Sœur Marie Saint-Guibert, 1832–1925: la fondation et les soixante-dix premières années de la Présentation-de-Marie en Amérique* (Saint-Hyacinthe, 1928). *Canada ecclésiastique*, 1898, 1917. M.-J. Ducharme, "Ou nos écoles et le salut . . . ," in *Les Franco-Américains et leurs institutions scolaires*, sous la dir. de Claire Quintal (Worcester, Mass., 1990), 82–105. Guy Laperrière, *Les congrégations religieuses: de la France au Québec, 1880–1914* (2v. parus, Sainte-Foy, Qué., 1996–), 1: 32–33; "'Persécution et exil': la venue au Québec des congrégations françaises, 1900–1914," *RHAF*, 36 (1982–83): 389–411. Sœur Marie-Aimée de Jésus [Éliza Saint-Jacques], *L'enseignement à l'institut de la-Présentation-de-Marie* (Saint-Hyacinthe, 1939). "Notre album de famille: mère Marie Saint-David," *La Rev. présentine* (Saint-Hyacinthe), 8 (1933): 211–14; 9 (1934): 5–8, 81–85, 141–45. *Trois présentines modèles: biographie de vénérée sœur Saint-David* (Avignon, France, 1922).

THOMSON, WILLIAM JAMES, artist; b. 28 May 1857 in Guelph, Upper Canada, son of Charles Thomson and Catharine Stewart; m. 26 June 1889 Jennie Leys (d. 7 Oct. 1922) in Sarnia, Ont., and they had a daughter and two sons, one of whom died in childhood; d. 28 April 1927 in Toronto.

William Thomson's father was a cabinetmaker whose craft took him and his wife from Aberdeenshire, Scotland, to Guelph. The family moved to Toronto in 1860. William was apprenticed to an engraving firm, and in 1882–86 he attended the Ontario School of Art, where he received instruction from William Cruikshank and John Arthur Fraser*. In his early years his focus on engraving vignettes of buildings for business stationery and advertising helped him refine his art. The static quality of his work gave way to etchings with painterly nuancing.

In 1884 Thomson participated in the organization of the Association of Canadian Etchers. The artistic success of its exhibition of international prints the following year was offset by the show's financial failure and the association's demise. Dedicated to printmaking, which established artists' societies initially shunned, Thomson moved on with others in 1886 to create the Toronto Art Students' League, the first society in Canada to further the graphic arts by conducting life classes, exhibitions, and annual publications. Thomson was its treasurer and, in 1890–91, its president. Later he was a member of the Graphic Arts Club, formed in 1903; it too stimulated interest in prints and contributed to what art historian Rosemarie L. Tovell describes as "Canada's etching revival," with reference to such earlier artists as James D. Duncan*.

The collegial benefits and nationalistic flavour of the Students' League and the Arts Club appealed to Thomson, but he was foremost a working artist. In 1886–88 he had been an engraver with Rolph, Smith and Company and in 1890–91 he worked for the *Globe*, covering important trials and other stories. In February 1891, for example, he illustrated iceboats skimming across Toronto Bay, slum conditions in the Ward, and club and gymnastic activities at St Andrew's Institute. He worked as a freelancer usually – for a time his office was next to that of the Students' League in the Imperial Bank Buildings – and within a conducive family. For several years before his death in 1894, his father was a supplier of maple and boxwood for engraving plates. From 1900 to 1913 William headed the Thomson Engraving Company, which employed his younger brothers James Stewart and David Francis and whose services included photo-engraving.

After 1910 wide acclaim came to Thomson through shows at the Canadian National Exhibition and the Winnipeg Museum of Fine Arts, the attention of such connoisseurs as Sir Byron Edmund WALKER and James MAVOR, and purchases by the Art Museum of Toronto and the National Gallery of Canada. His gifts as an engraver on hardwood, steel, and copper placed him in high demand as an instructor and illustrator. He travelled widely in these capacities in the United States and Canada – one dry-point from 1913, *Fisherman's harvest*, is set in Vancouver – and he would remain prolific until his death. Following the motto of the Students' League ("Non clamor sed amor"), he did much of his fine-art work for love, trading his skills for pieces by others and critiquing young artists. In 1916 he was the founding president of the Society of Canadian Painter-Etchers, a largely honorary position since much of his last ten years was spent working in Philadelphia.

Part of Thomson's oeuvre was lost when he donated a quantity of his plates to a munitions drive during World War I. In 1926 he gave his library to the Arts and Letters Club in Toronto, where he also belonged to the freemasons and the Caer Howell Bowling Club. While visiting his son in 1927 he became ill and died at the Toronto General Hospital. Described by the *Globe* as the "dean of Canadian etchers," he was buried beside his wife in Mount Pleasant Cemetery.

ANDREW THOMSON

A collection of William James Thomson's papers and works of art is in the possession of his grandson William D. Thomson of Bath, Ont. Examples of his work for the *Globe* appear in the Saturday editions of 7, 21, and 28 Feb. 1891.

AO, RG 22-305, no.10132; RG 80-5-0-187, no.6199. *Globe*, 30 April 1927. W. G. Colgate, *The Toronto Art Students' League, 1886–1904* (Toronto, 1954). *Dict. of Toronto printers* (Hulse). *Directory*, Toronto, 1884–1923. *The encyclopedia of Canada*, ed. W. S. Wallace (6v., Toronto, [1948]), 6. J. R. Harper, *Early painters and engravers in Canada* (Toronto, 1970). Soc. of Canadian Painter-Etchers, *William J. Thomson, Canada, engraver, 1857–1927 . . .* (Toronto, 1930). R. L. Tovell, *A new class of art: the artist's print in Canadian art, 1877–1920* (Ottawa, 1996).

THUNDERCHILD. *See* PEYASIW-AWASIS

TILTON, ROBERTA ELIZABETH. *See* ODELL

TOBIN, BESHA. *See* STARKMAN

TODD, ALBERT EDWARD, businessman, motoring and tourism promoter, and politician; b. 5 Aug. 1878 in Victoria, son of Jacob Hunter Todd* and Rosanna Wigley; m. 16 March 1910 Ada Beatrice Elvira Seabrook (d. 1968) in Los Angeles, and they had two sons; d. 26 Oct. 1928 in Seattle, Wash.

Bert Todd was born into a privileged situation as the child of a successful wholesale merchant in Victoria. Sent in 1890 to Upper Canada College in Toronto to complete his education, he returned to Victoria four years later to enter the family business, J. H. Todd and Sons, by then an important salmon-canning firm. He remained a principal of the company after his father's death in 1899, but apparently played only a secondary role.

From 1899 to 1904 Todd was a gunner in the No.5 (British Columbia) Garrison Artillery, a militia unit, but this enthusiasm seems to have lost out to the new one of motor tourism. His interest in motoring had started in 1903, when he took his recently purchased White steam car on a day trip over primitive roads to Shawnigan Lake. A founder of the Victoria Motor Club in 1905, he served in 1905–6 as vice-president and in 1912 as president. At various times during the remainder of his life he would be a member or officer of clubs such as the Automobile Club of Southern California, the Victoria Automobile Association, the Island Automobile Association, and the British Columbia Automobile Association.

In 1910 Todd retired from the family firm. Living on income from various assets, he devoted himself to the promotion of highways and tourism, and to civic politics. He initiated a new apartment and commercial development in Victoria, which he would retain until his death. Then he travelled to Los Angeles for his marriage in March to a vivacious 19-year-old, Ada Seabrook, the daughter of a car dealer formerly from Victoria. Before leaving, he requested support from Premier Richard McBride* for the construction of a "Trans-Provincial Highway," but received a non-committal response. The newly-weds set out in a 30-horsepower Cadillac, south to Tijuana, Mexico, and then north to Vancouver on reconnaissance for the proposed Pacific Highway. The story of the trip was submitted to various publications to excite interest in the idea. Later that year Todd was a founder and vice-president of the Seattle-based Pacific Highway Association. He travelled extensively over the next decade to promote the highway and connecting routes from the east, making speeches, lobbying governments, and writing articles. His vision of a unified tourism strategy based on automobile travel in the Pacific northwest and British Columbia led to his promotion in 1915 of the Georgian Circuit route, circling the Strait of Georgia and Puget Sound, and to the formation of the Pacific Northwest Tourist Association in 1917. When the Pacific Highway connecting Vancouver and Tijuana was officially opened in 1923, he was acknowledged as its creator. Todd also promoted the development of Canadian highways, such as the Island Highway connecting Victoria to Nanaimo and points north. He offered cash prizes and medals for various accomplishments in automobile travel on Canadian roads. In 1911 he had been a founder of the Canadian Highway Association, which lobbied governments to construct a transcontinental road. He was also a long-term member and, in 1915, director of the Canadian Good Roads Association.

Todd's promotion of tourism in Victoria and the surrounding region had led to pressure that he enter civic politics. He served as an alderman in 1914–16. In 1914–15 he was the police commissioner and in 1917–18, mayor of Victoria. As alderman and mayor, he advocated lower taxes and balanced budgets, inter-municipal cooperation, and the promotion of industry and tourism. When he rejoined city council in 1920, he concentrated on the Greater Victoria committee, as well as on utilities, particularly the water system. After running unsuccessfully in Victoria City for the Provincial party of Alexander Duncan McRae* in the provincial election of 1924, he remained an alderman until defeated in the civic election of December 1925. Subsequently, he was employed by the city as an industrial commissioner and water consultant until he became ill in 1927.

Active in many boosting organizations in Victoria, Todd had served as vice-president of the local Board of Trade in 1910–11 and he held office later as president of the Associated Boards of Trade of Vancouver Island. He was a director of the Chamber of Commerce in the early 1920s and a central figure in the Victoria and Island Development Association until he resigned in April 1923 (a month after the association was renamed the Victoria and Island Publicity Bureau). A member of Victoria's elite, he belonged to the appropriate clubs, including the Union Club, Pacific Club, Vancouver Club, and Victoria Golf Club, and he was a director of the James Bay Athletic Association. In addition to motoring and tourism, his recreational interests included shooting and fishing. He worshipped in the Church of England.

After his death in Seattle, where he had undergone surgery for a brain tumour, Todd was most recognized in the local press as "Good Roads" Todd for his central role in the development of various highways. This was just one aspect of his enthusiastic vision for Victoria and Vancouver Island. He had also encouraged cooperative strategies of municipal management and promotion. Despite the fact that his social position derived from his family's successful resource-extractive business, he had directed his efforts at building a post-industrial economy for the region based foremost on tourism. His initiatives seem prescient in the Victoria of the early 21st century.

JAMIE MORTON

Albert Edward Todd may have played a role in the preparation of promotional brochures for the organizations in which he was involved. Many of these brochures are available in the library of the BCA. In addition, he wrote numerous letters concerning roads, Victoria's politics, and the promotion of the city and region to the editors of local newspapers. He is also the author of "Good roads and the automobile: Mr. A. E. Todd's Pacific coast international tour," *Pacific Monthly* (Portland, Oreg.), 25 (May 1911): 565–77; an address, *The Pacific Highway . . .* (Seattle, Wash., 1913; copy at BCA); and "British Columbia faces the reconstruction period with confidence," *Industrial Progress and Commercial Record* (Vancouver), 7 (December 1918): 216.

BCA, A/E/G41/T56.2; A/E/G41/T562; E/D/T56; E/D/T56.1 (A. E. Todd clippings file, 1920–25); E/D/T56.1 (A. E. Todd scrapbook, 1910–24); GR-1052, file 16740; GR-1304, files 288/1928–330/1928. City of Victoria Arch., News clippings, A. E. Todd; PR 115 (Todd family coll.). *Daily Colonist* (Victoria), 1909–28. *Victoria Daily Times*, 1909–28. "Alderman Todd," *Sunshine* (Victoria), 17 April 1916: 1–2. Valerie Green, *Excelsior!: the story of the Todd family* (Victoria, 1990); "Good Roads Todd," *British Columbia Hist. News* (Victoria), 24 (1990–91), no.4: 5–7; *No ordinary people: Victoria's mayors since 1862* (Victoria, 1992). G. W. Taylor, *The automobile saga of British Columbia, 1864–1914* (Victoria, 1984). Victoria Motor Club, *Articles of association and by-laws . . .* (Victoria, [1907?]).

TOPLEY, WILLIAM JAMES, photographer and businessman; b. 13 or 27 Feb. 1845 in Montreal, son of John Topley, a saddler and harness maker, and Anna Delia Harrison; m. 15 Aug. 1872 Helena (Nellie) DeCourcy McDonogh in Yorkville (Toronto), and they had two sons and a daughter; d. 16 Nov. 1930 in Vancouver and was buried in Ottawa.

Brought up in Aylmer, Lower Canada, William James Topley was probably introduced to photography by his mother, who in the late 1850s had purchased equipment in Montreal and used it in Aylmer. He began his career as a tintypist and was listed in a directory as an itinerant photographer in Upper Canada in 1863, but he was employed at apprentice wages when he was engaged by William Notman* in Montreal in 1864. He had moved there with his mother and family after his father's death in 1863. His abilities may have later induced Notman to engage his younger brothers Horatio Needham and John George as apprentice photographers.

Notman saw William to be extraordinarily competent not only as a photographer but also, potentially, as a manager. In January 1868, when Topley was 22, Notman put him in charge of his new photographic rooms in Ottawa, the first Notman studio outside Montreal. Located in a purpose-built structure on Wellington Street across from the Parliament Buildings, the studio quickly attracted local patrons and visiting notables such as members of the new dominion parliament. Indeed, the Topley studio took photographs of all the prime ministers from Sir John A.

Topley

Macdonald* to William Lyon Mackenzie King* and of the governors general from Baron Lisgar [Young*] to Lord Grey*. By 1872, when Topley became "proprietor" of the studio, it was attracting over 2,300 sitters each year, a level not exceeded until the beginning of the 20th century.

In 1875 Topley apparently severed his relations with Notman and decided to open a studio under his own name, two blocks away in an opulent Italianate-style building he had constructed at Metcalfe and Queen. Although it included an apartment for Topley and his family, the deepening economic crisis in Canada made the location financially untenable and by 1878 he had moved to the former residence of a dentist at 104 Sparks Street, where he remained until 1888, when he went to 132 Sparks, his final location. The business was probably well established by this time, but he did not purchase a separate residence until the late 1890s.

Notman had opened his Ottawa branch because he saw the city as a growing market. Topley capitalized on this. By the late 1870s he was the official photographer to Governor General Lord Lorne [Campbell*], an association that added lustre to his studio and attracted clientele. Portraits were a major part of Topley's output but his scenic views for the tourist trade, work for businesses and other commissions in Ottawa and across Canada, and a considerable volume for the government constitute tens of thousands of images. His photographs of immigrants arriving at Quebec, done for the Department of the Interior, have become iconic through repeated publication. Outside his studio he used a horse-drawn portable darkroom during the 1870s. His presentation of images changed over time: in the 1860s the vogue had been for cartes de visite and cabinet-sized photographs but by the turn of the century larger prints, mounted on dark-olive-coloured card embossed with the Topley name, were a major product. Like Notman, Topley also produced composite images – large prints created by carefully preconceiving a scene and then photographing the participants at the correct angle and with the right attitude to fit it. Unlike Notman, Topley turned out few of the stereographs that were a mainstay for many 19th-century photographers. With the coming of popular amateur photography, the Topley Studio stocked cameras, film, and other supplies and promoted its photo-finishing and enlargement operations. Sometime about the turn of the century, the Topley Scientific Instruments Company was organized to sell optical devices, surveying equipment, and photostatting machines and to provide support services.

The studio had started in 1868 with a staff of 3, but by 1874 it had expanded to 14 and included photographers, photo-printers, retouchers, and artists (often to prepare composites and scenic backdrops). The subsequent depression led Topley to reduce this number and adoption of the dry-plate process in the 1880s would have improved production efficiency without increasing the staff. During the 1870s he employed his brothers Horatio and John; the former joined the interior department as a photographer in 1887 but the latter remained at the studio until about 1908, when he set up his own operation.

Topley's life appears to have been imbued with an evangelical Christian sensibility. From his earliest days in the capital he was active in the sabbath school movement, in Hull, Ottawa, and elsewhere in the Ottawa valley. By the mid 1870s he was the Sunday school superintendent at Dominion Methodist Church, where he sang in the choir. Active in the Ottawa Bible Society, he was a major force in the Young Men's Christian Association, serving as president in 1871 and 1881 and assuming other directorial duties over the years. He did not, however, limit his community participation to evangelism. He was involved in the Metropolitan Society for the Prevention of Cruelty to Animals, and with his wife contributed to local charities. His sense of compassion is evident in some of his photographs; a portrait of Polly, a female inmate at the Carleton County jail, is particularly affecting. He also sat on the executive of the Fine Arts Association, was a founding member of the Camera Club of Ottawa, had a boat on the Rideau River, and joined in autumn hunting parties.

In 1907 his son, William DeCourcy, took over his studio, but Topley appears to have remained involved, possibly until 1918. By this time it was considerably less significant than it once had been. The importance of portraiture as a photographic art had diminished after 1900 and the number of sittings had declined steeply. The order book ends in 1923, and the business was "discontinued" in July 1926. Topley and his wife, who died in 1927, spent much of their last years in Edmonton with their daughter, Helena Sarah, and son-in-law, Robert C. W. Lett, an employee of the Grand Trunk Pacific Railway who had probably been influential in the naming of Topley, a community on the GTP line in northern British Columbia. W. J. Topley died at Helena's temporary residence in Vancouver in 1930.

ANDREW RODGER

[The Topley studio collection was purchased in 1936 by the Public Archives of Canada (LAC, R639-0-5 (formerly accession 1936-270)) for $3,000 after it had been offered by William DeCourcy Topley in 1926 for $25,000. The collection consists of some 150,000 mainly glass-plate negatives as well as counter-books containing the majority of the images taken by the firm. Second only to the Notman archives, the Topley collection has become one of the most widely used sources of 19th- and early-20th-century photographs in Canada, partly because of the number of portraits of notable figures and in part because of the geographic range, from Quebec to British

Columbia. There is a small amount of manuscript material in this collection, but it relates to the studio; there is nothing on Topley himself. Information about his businesses and private life is scattered throughout the records of his clients, including (at the LAC) such government offices as Agriculture, Interior, and the Geological Survey.

Topley's major published work is *The Ottawa album, containing photographs and advertisements of the principal business houses, hotels and steamboats and local views* (Ottawa, 1875), which includes 61 tipped-in prints. Topley photographs also appeared, mainly in the 1890s, in *Dominion Illustrated* (Montreal), *Lounger* (Ottawa), and *Owl* (Ottawa), among other magazines, as well as in newspapers and sheet music. Selected portraits are reproduced in Public Arch. of Canada, National Photography Coll., *William James Topley: portraits, 1868–1881* . . . ([Ottawa, 1978]). A.R.]

LAC, RG 37, C, 328, 1911; 4 Oct. 1926. *Globe*, 17 Aug. 1872. *Ottawa Citizen*, 8 Nov. 1867, 7 July 1874, 17 Nov. 1930. *Ottawa Free Press*, 2 Feb. 1873. A. A. Gard, *Pioneers of the upper Ottawa and the humors of the valley* . . . (4pts. in 1v., Ottawa, [1906]). *Mitchell's Canada gazetteer and business directory for 1864–65* (Toronto, 1864). S. G. Triggs, *William Notman: the stamp of a studio* (Toronto, 1985).

TOUPIN-FAFARD, MATHILDE (baptized **Marie-Célina-Mathilde**, and known also as **Mathilda**), teacher, Sister of Charity at the Hôpital Général of Montreal, nurse, and school administrator; b. 27 Dec. 1875 in Saint-Cuthbert, Que., daughter of Odilon Toupin, a farmer, and Marie-Célina Fafard; d. 3 Feb. 1925 in Montreal.

After completing her elementary schooling, Mathilde Toupin-Fafard at the age of about 12 entered the boarding school of the Sisters of St Anne in Saint-Cuthbert, from which she graduated "with high honours." She spent only three months at the community's noviciate in Lachine before deciding, at the age of 17, on a teaching career in the village where she was born. She pursued this career until she entered the noviciate of the Sisters of Charity at the Hôpital Général of Montreal on 5 Sept. 1901. The third member of her devout farm family to dedicate her life to the service of the church, she took her final vows on 10 Dec. 1903.

Once in the community, Sister Toupin-Fafard began studying to become a nurse at the school of Notre-Dame Hospital in Montreal, which had been founded in 1897 by her order [*see* Élodie Mailloux*]. After graduating in 1907, she was assigned to the hospital of the Sisters of Charity in Toledo, Ohio. Her zealous care of patients and her great capacity for learning were soon noticed. To further her education, she enrolled in a pharmacy course at Ohio State University in Columbus and she obtained a diploma in June 1915. As a qualified pharmacist, she was appointed in 1916 to the General Hospital in Edmonton and in July 1918 to the Holy Cross Hospital in Calgary.

Sister Toupin-Fafard returned to Montreal at the time of her father's death in 1921. Because of her extensive experience, the director of the community's hospitals, Sister Albertine Pépin-Duckett, chose her as superintendent of nurses at Notre-Dame Hospital. This prestigious position included being head of the training school, a position she would retain until 1924. Through her efforts and her dynamic personality, the school would rank among the top centres in French Canada for hospital training.

In addition to the heavy responsibilities of her daily work at Notre-Dame Hospital, Sister Toupin-Fafard laboured to promote the nursing profession among French Canadian women. She played an important role in the Association of Registered Nurses of the Province of Quebec, which had been founded in 1920, serving as its vice-president from 1922 until her death in 1925. At the time she was the only French Canadian woman on the executive committee. Thanks to her, the official minutes were translated and read in French at meetings, and French Canadian members received notices of meetings and ballots in French. She was actively engaged within the association in drawing up the first curriculum of studies for nurses.

Sister Toupin-Fafard's professional concerns also led her to become a pioneer in nursing education at the university level. In 1923 she became the first director of an advanced course of studies for nurses inaugurated that year at the Université de Montréal. In conjunction with the faculty of medicine and with the support of the university authorities, she organized the courses in public health and dietetics, as well as the first university course for directors of nursing schools. These courses would make an important contribution to establishing professional standards for French-speaking nurses in Quebec, and they would be the starting point for the creation, in 1934, of the Institut Marguerite-d'Youville, an advanced school for nurses which was attached to the Université de Montréal. In 1923 Sister Toupin-Fafard was also the prime mover in the founding of an association of university-trained nurses.

In the same spirit, Sister Toupin-Fafard was involved in January 1924 in launching the magazine *La Veilleuse*. This monthly publication for French-speaking nurses fulfilled the desire to maintain a Christian concept of the profession, while taking scientific progress into account.

A woman of great tact who was highly regarded for her affable manners, Sister Mathilde Toupin-Fafard deserves a place of honour in the annals of the nursing profession in Canada. She helped in a significant way to enhance the prestige of French Canadian nurses and the quality of their training.

LOUISE BIENVENUE

ANQ-M, CE605-S19, 28 déc. 1875. Arch. des Sœurs Grises (Montréal), Dossier de sœur Mathilda Toupin-Fafard, notice biog. "À sa mémoire," *La Veilleuse* (Montréal), 2 (1925),

Tourigny

no.1: 1. Françoise Côté, "75ᵉ anniversaire; jalon important pour les infirmières et infirmiers," *Le Courrier médical* (Montréal), 3, no.9 (26 avril 1983): 20–22. Yolande Cohen, "La contribution des Sœurs de la charité à la modernisation de l'hôpital Notre-Dame, 1880–1940," *CHR*, 77 (1996): 185–220. Yolande Cohen et Éric Vaillancourt, "L'identité professionnelle des infirmières canadiennes-françaises à travers leurs revues (1924–1956)," *RHAF*, 50 (1996–97): 537–70. Édouard Desjardins *et al.*, *Histoire de la profession infirmière au Québec* (Montréal, 1970), 231. Lucie Deslauriers, "Histoire de l'hôpital Notre-Dame de Montréal, 1880–1924" (mémoire de MA, univ. de Montréal, 1984).

TOURIGNY, PAUL (baptized **Napoléon**), merchant, land speculator, farmer, politician, and industrialist; b. 2 Nov. 1852 in Saint-Christophe-d'Arthabaska, Lower Canada, son of Landry Tourigny, a farmer, and Lucie Poirier; m. first 5 May 1874 Alice Lavigne in Saint-Édouard (Bécancour), Que.; m. secondly 2 Sept. 1914 Josephine Laberge, widow of Auguste Laberge, in Montreal; he had at least eight children, of whom four sons and three daughters survived him; d. 31 Jan. 1926 in Victoriaville, Que.

Born into a family that had its origins in the Bécancour region, Paul Tourigny came into the world at an auspicious time. The Grand Trunk Railway was being pushed through on the south shore of the St Lawrence River. The subsequent development of the railway and other means of communication, the implementation of the National Policy in the 1870s, and the economic boom of the late 19th and early 20th centuries laid the foundations for the industrialization of French Canada. The half-century 1875–1925 saw the emergence in Quebec of a francophone capitalist class unlike any seen before. In a single generation men such as Tourigny, born into petty bourgeois families outside metropolitan Quebec and possessing limited education, became industrial captains and political notables.

Tourigny probably went to local schools in Saint-Christophe-d'Arthabaska. Although in 1899 he would belong to the association of former students of the Collège Commercial du Sacré-Cœur, founded in Arthabaskaville (Victoriaville), he most likely never attended the institution; his name is not included in its list of students. In 1875 he moved to nearby Victoriaville, then a burgeoning commercial centre beside the railway, and he soon became involved in commerce and real estate. He acquired a small general store that developed rapidly. When he built his palatial home and business establishment on Victoriaville's commercial artery, it had 100 feet of frontage and included a furniture store and a general store. Around 1908 his son Arthur became involved in the stores, which did a combined yearly business of about $75,000.

From 1875 to 1899 Tourigny had conducted 218 transactions registered by notarial act, most of them concerning land; in a subsequent period, 1903 to 1926, he would complete 199 similar transactions. An avid and successful land speculator, he often sold in short order at two or even three times the price he had paid. For instance, he did not shrink from selling to the Brothers of the Sacred Heart a property he had acquired less than a year earlier at under half the price. His last great real estate venture was his attempt in 1913 to establish with J.-E. Alain a large-scale residential development comprising 1,600 lots, the Parc Victoria. In the 1920s he consolidated his holdings through a series of property transfers and mortgage foreclosures. During most of his life Tourigny also operated a farm and for many years he sat as a member of the Council of Agriculture of the Province of Quebec; in 1907 and 1922 he received the Order of Agricultural Merit.

Tourigny had served as an alderman of Victoriaville from 1890 to 1892; he was elected mayor in 1892. He held office from 1892 to 1899, 1900 to 1905, and 1906 to 1911. In addition, in 1900 he was returned by acclamation as a Liberal to the Legislative Assembly for the riding of Arthabaska. Acclaimed again in 1904, he won a three-way race in 1908 by 1,783 votes, but in 1912 his majority dwindled to 370 votes. He did not contest the general election of 1916. He rarely spoke in the assembly and his brief interventions usually concerned matters which touched him as mayor or businessman. In 1912 he became the first president of the standing committee on industries. His loyalty to his party earned him a nomination to the Legislative Council for the division of Kennebec in 1921.

It was in the industrial sphere that Tourigny's career was most remarkable. Until about 1890 most of the industrial activity in Victoriaville had involved the transformation of natural resources (sawmills, potash production, tanneries, and foundries), enterprises that had been established by English-speaking entrepreneurs with links to Quebec City. In 1894 Tourigny, with Cyrias Thibault and other francophone merchants, founded the Victoriaville Furniture Company Limited with a capitalization of $10,000. The firm made dressers, tables, and sideboards. In 1909 R. G. Dun and Company estimated that it was worth from $35,000 to $50,000. By 1912 it employed 150 people and possessed its own timber limits and sawmills. Despite the prominence of Tourigny's name in Tourigny et Marois, a shoe factory he had established in Quebec City with Alfred-Eugène Marois in 1898, his involvement had been limited to providing $5,000, half of the initial capital. He played no role in the administration of the firm and sold his shares to his partner in 1910. Most of his business endeavours remained concentrated in the Victoriaville region.

When, in 1901, local notables set up the Club de Victoriaville, they saw themselves not as merchants but as industrialists. Tourigny, by this time, was on several boards of directors. He and many of the local businessmen established the Chambre de Commerce du Comté d'Arthabaska two years later. During the first decade of the 20th century Tourigny helped to set up and provided initial capital for a series of companies in the Victoriaville region, most of them manufacturing furniture (chairs, mattresses, and bedsteads that were sold throughout Canada) and a variety of goods for personal consumption (clothing, shoes, and jewellery). In 1909 R. G. Dun and Company estimated that one boot and shoe factory owned by Tourigny was worth between $200,000 and $300,000. About 90 per cent of the capital mobilized to set up these companies had been subscribed by the municipal council, presided over by Tourigny and other members of the same merchant class that directed the firms. The municipality in turn raised the money by issuing bonds that were sold through financial institutions in Montreal. The practice of municipal bonuses, widespread at the time, consisted of outright grants to the companies, forgivable loans, long-term tax holidays (up to 20 years), and in some cases the provision of electricity and water. By the 1920s a new generation of industrial captains had arrived, more ambitious and adventurous than Tourigny. He sold most of his interests in the various firms and there followed a period of reorganization and restructuring.

At his death in 1926, Paul Tourigny possessed only real estate holdings. His business success was not duplicated by his children who, in contrast to their father, benefited from the education and social status that went with being members of the leading family of Victoriaville. Tourigny's will, which would be contested, redistributed his wealth to the poorest members of his family rather than to those of his children who "did not need it." He had also provided for over 550 masses, indicating that he had not forsaken the traditional society from which he had so spectacularly emerged. The merchants and notables of Victoriaville, of whom Tourigny was a prime example, had created the first wave of industrialization in the region, but it did not endure. As his career illustrates, the financial capital of their initial success was transformed into political and social capital. The cultural basis for venture capitalism had yet to emerge.

GARY CALDWELL

ANQ-MBF, CE401-S9, 5 mai 1874; CE402-S2, 3 nov. 1852. BCM-G, RBMS, Saint-Louis-de-France (Montréal), 2 sept. 1914. Bibliothèque de l'Assemblée Nationale (Québec), Service de la recherche, dossiers des parlementaires. *L'Événement*, 2, 5 févr. 1926. *Le Soleil*, 1ᵉʳ févr. 1926. *L'Union des Cantons de l'Est* (Arthabaska [Victoriaville], Qué.), 4, 11 févr. 1926. *Album historique du centenaire de Victoriaville, 1861–1961* (Victoriaville, [1961?]). Alain Bergeron, "Visages du siècle: Paul Tourigny," *L'Union* (Victoriaville), 11 août 1999. Gary Caldwell, "Les industriels francophones: Victoriaville au début du siècle," *Recherches sociographiques* (Québec), 24 (1983): 9–31. Collège Commercial du Sacré-Cœur, *Palmarès du collège commercial du Sacré-Cœur, Arthabaskaville* (Arthabaskaville [Victoriaville], 1898–99). *CPG. DPQ.* J.-C. Falardeau, "L'origine et l'ascension des hommes d'affaires dans la société canadienne-française," *Cahiers internationaux de sociologie* (Paris), 38 (1965): 109–20. P.-A. Linteau, "Quelques réflexions autour de la bourgeoisie québécoise, 1850–1914," *RHAF*, 30 (1976–77): 55–66. *Le patrimoine architectural dans les Bois-Francs*, sous la dir. de Gisèle Beaudet (2v., Arthabaska, 1984), 1 (*Rapport de recherche et circuits architecturaux et historiques Victoriaville–Arthabaska*). Qué., Assemblée Législative, *Débats*, 1900–16. Gustave Turcotte, *Le Conseil législatif de Québec, 1774–1933* (Beauceville, Qué., 1933). *Victoriaville, Québec, Canada, 1913* ([Victoriaville?], 1913).

TOWNSEND, MARGARET (Fox; Jenkins), temperance worker, school trustee, and social reformer; b. 4 Aug. 1843 in Neath, Wales, daughter of Joseph Townsend; m. December 1866 Mr Fox (d. 1876) in Coquimbo, Chile, and they had four children; m. 1879 David Jenkins (d. 1904), a widower with nine children, in Chile; they had three children; of her seven children and nine stepchildren, five boys and five girls survived to adulthood; d. 6 June 1923 in Victoria.

The daughter of a deacon in the Congregational Church in Neath, Margaret Townsend began a career in education when she was indentured as a pupil teacher at age 14. She soon became a fully qualified teacher, but a year in a rural school in Great Britain left her with rheumatic fever. Characteristically, she did not allow the illness to slow her for long; Margaret, later described as a woman of "singular activity, both in the mental and physical sense," went to South America. She had been engaged since 1864 to a Mr Fox, whom she had met in England, and she joined him in Coquimbo, Chile, where they were married shortly after her arrival in December 1866. Margaret opened a school to teach English to the children of Coquimbo.

In 1876 Margaret was left a widow with four young children. Teaching became her main source of income, but after struggling for three years, she "succumbed to an attack of nervous prostration." Perhaps not coincidentally, her health improved with her marriage in 1879 to David Jenkins. She seemed to be following a pattern: hard work led to illness and then recovery through marriage. Although her later work as a pioneer of the women's movement belied this pattern of marrying to regain security, she may have come to believe that women needed more options and independence than she had had. Self-interest would not be her sole motivation for pressing for women's rights. "I consider that women in their public work should lose sight of self," she later said. She seems to have balanced traditional virtues of womanhood such as self-sacrifice, piety, and devotion to motherhood with political and social ideals that attracted her to social reform, women's rights movements, and municipal politics.

1011

Margaret, David, their combined family, and an additional three children born to them set sail for Canada on 30 April 1882. The family's first venture, farming on Salt Spring Island, B.C., failed within a year and they moved to Victoria. She soon applied her formidable energy to various causes.

Between 1883 and 1921 Margaret was a member and office holder of the Welsh Cymmrodorian Society, the ladies' aid committee of the Metropolitan Methodist Church, the Victoria branch of the Women's Conservative Club, the Home Nursing Society, the ladies' auxiliary to the Young Men's Christian Association, and the Women's Canadian Club, of which she was president from 1912 to 1921. The two organizations in which she was most involved, however, were the Woman's Christian Temperance Union and the Local Council of Women. Prompted by a visit from American temperance advocate Frances Elizabeth Caroline Willard, Victoria women met to organize a branch of the WCTU in July 1883. Margaret attended the convention, joined the branch, and became corresponding secretary for the provincial union, established at the same time. She hosted many meetings in her home in 1883 and 1884, and in May 1884 she joined the program committee to plan the second provincial temperance convention to be held the following month. At the June meeting, she was appointed organizer for Vancouver Island. The WCTU put forth a plan to circulate books and tracts, to have articles published in the press, and to urge local organizations to forbid the use of alcohol at their gatherings. Its members tied their role in temperance activities to women's voting rights. In the mid 1880s Margaret and Mrs Anne Cecilia Spofford [McNaughton*] "canvassed the city . . . to get the women of Victoria to vote and thus show their appreciation of the privilege of the [municipal] franchise." In 1887–88 Margaret was vice-president of the provincial WCTU and in 1900 she became president of the Victoria WCTU.

By 1897 Margaret was a member of the Local Council of Women of Victoria and Vancouver Island [see Edith Perrin*], which she would serve as recording secretary from 1904 to 1910 and as vice-president from 1911 to 1914. She became the council's candidate for school trustee in the city election of 1897, promoting "compulsory scientific temperance education." She was Victoria's third female trustee and served in 1897, in 1898, and from 1902 to 1919. In this capacity she visited schools across the country and in 1912 she introduced a special class for mentally challenged children in Victoria schools. She also helped develop domestic science programs. After leaving the school board in 1919 she remained honorary adviser to the domestic science committee. A new public school built in Victoria in 1914 was named the Margaret Jenkins School in recognition of her work. On her retirement in 1921 local women's organiza-

tions hosted a reception attended by 400 women. They paid tribute to her "extraordinary executive abilities, gracious charm and broad vision." Her friend and noted fellow suffragist Emmeline Pankhurst said that in her the Canadian Club had had a president "whose abilities had she been a man – which would have been a great loss to womanhood – would have carried her into any position in the Empire or in Canada." Her granddaughter recalled that even after retiring from public duties Margaret continued to spend many hours visiting hospital-bound war veterans.

Although Margaret Jenkins frequently stated that home and family were her priorities and that a woman's role as a mother was her most important task, she embraced a life of public service in which her children and husband were rarely mentioned. In her 80th year, two years after she had retired, she suffered a heart attack and died at home. The *Daily Colonist* reported that "she will be remembered as one of the most . . . influential figures in the New Woman movement." Her life expressed the contradictions of an era, mixing 19th-century ideals of true womanhood with a public service record that pushed for change and helped launch a "new woman" in the 20th century.

MELANIE BUDDLE

BCA, MS-1961; MS-2227; MS-2818. *Daily Colonist* (Victoria), 1, 4, 6 July 1883; 11 July 1885; 14 May 1897; 16, 26 Oct. 1921; 7 June 1923; 17 Aug. 1971. *Victoria Daily Times*, 6, 19 Oct. 1921; 7 June 1923. Elizabeth Forbes, *Wild roses at their feet: pioneer women of Vancouver Island* ([Victoria], 1971). Lyn Gough, *As wise as serpents: five women & an organization that changed British Columbia, 1883–1939* (Victoria, 1988). *In her own right: selected essays on women's history in B.C.*, ed. Barbara Latham and Cathy Kess (Victoria, 1980). Woman's Christian Temperance Union of British Columbia, *Silver anniversary of the provincial Woman's Christian Temperance Union of British Columbia, 1883–1908* . . . (Victoria, 1908; copy in BCA, Northwest coll.).

TOWNSHEND, Sir CHARLES JAMES, lawyer, politician, judge, and historian; b. 22 March 1844 in Amherst, N.S., son of George Townshend and Elizabeth Lucy Stewart; m. first 23 April 1867 Laura Kinnear (d. 1884) in Amherst, and they had two sons and four daughters; m. there secondly 25 Oct. 1887 Margaret MacFarlane (d. 1928), and they had two sons; d. 16 June 1924 in Wolfville, N.S., and was buried in Amherst.

By blood, outlook, religion, and education, Charles Townshend was a true specimen of the old-regime elite in the Maritimes. His paternal grandfather was William Townshend*, an early collector of customs in Prince Edward Island. His father served as rector of Christ Church, Amherst, for over 60 years, and through his mother, a daughter of judge Alexander

Stewart*, Townshend was connected to the Dickey, Ritchie, and Tupper legal dynasties. A graduate of King's College, Windsor (BA 1863, BCL 1872), Townshend was to sit on its board of governors from 1881 to 1886, become part of the reconstituted "faculty of civil law" in 1890, and act as chancellor from 1912 to 1922. King's would award him an honorary DCL in 1908.

After serving three years of his apprenticeship in Amherst and the final year in Halifax, Townshend was called to the bar in 1866. In 1868 he succeeded to the large Amherst practice of his uncle Senator Robert Barry Dickey. A decade later he admitted his brother John Medley Townshend and his cousin Arthur Rupert Dickey as partners. Amherst in the last quarter of the 19th century was developing a diversified industrial economy, based on nearby coalmines and good rail connections [see Nelson Admiral Rhodes*]. The combination of family prestige, economic growth, and Townshend's own talent would bring him an extensive clientele, including locally based corporations such as the Amherst Boot and Shoe Manufacturing Company, of which he was a promoter and director, and the Cumberland Railway and Coal Company. In 1880 he was created a dominion QC.

In spite of his professional success Townshend was dissatisfied in the early 1880s. Scholarly and reserved, he was temperamentally suited to the judicial role, and as he explained candidly to Premier John Sparrow David Thompson* in 1882, "My tastes and ambition . . . have been to excel in the profession – outside of it – for politics I care nothing, and only went into them, with a view to the Bench." He also began to yearn for horizons larger than Amherst could offer, but his overtures to join Thompson's law firm in Halifax were rebuffed.

Townshend's political career had begun with an unsuccessful attempt to obtain a seat for Cumberland County in the House of Assembly in 1874; he had better luck there in the Conservative sweep of September 1878. As minister without portfolio in the government of Simon Hugh Holmes*, he was notable mainly for drafting the County Incorporation Act of 1879, which ended the antiquated system of local government by the sessions magistrates. Townshend retained his seat after the Conservative rout in 1882, but two years later an arrangement with Cumberland Liberals saw him acclaimed as successor to Sir Charles Tupper*'s seat in the House of Commons [see Thomas Reuben Black*]. Once Thompson became dominion attorney general in 1885, he received a stream of increasingly admonitory letters from Townshend regarding the judgeship that Tupper had allegedly promised him.

On 4 March 1887 Townshend was named to the Supreme Court of Nova Scotia, and he moved to Halifax shortly thereafter. The court was much in need of rehabilitation after a series of mostly indifferent appointments. Thompson's nomination of Townshend was part of his strategy to improve the court through a new emphasis on professional competence. This approach did not render partisan service irrelevant to judicial promotion – it remained fundamental – but it did add a new element to the calculus of patronage; none of Thompson's other four appointees to the Nova Scotia court had held elective office, though all were Conservatives. On 2 Nov. 1907 Prime Minister Sir Wilfrid Laurier* would follow Thompson's lead by elevating Townshend, then the senior judge, to the chief justiceship on the resignation of Sir Robert Linton Weatherbe*, resisting political pressure to promote the junior puisne judge, Liberal Arthur Drysdale. In response to his increasing deafness, Townshend had earlier adopted a rather unbecoming ear trumpet. When he asked his fellow judges how it looked, his colleague Benjamin Russell* observed that "there was no great alacrity in replying, but Mr. Justice Weatherbe was equal to the occasion with the remark: 'What matters it how it looks if it enables you the better to discharge your duty?'" Townshend was made a knight bachelor in 1911 and retired on 10 April 1915; Wallace Nesbit Graham* succeeded him as chief justice. At the end of his life Townshend had the satisfaction of seeing his youngest son, Cecil Wray, take up the legal profession; he graduated from Dalhousie law school in 1923.

During Townshend's tenure a great deal of new federal and provincial legislation was passed. Cases involving temperance regulation, mining law, the power of corporations and municipalities, and legislation relating to married women's property all came before the court with increasing regularity. Townshend was an able jurist and his legal opinions were well respected in the Supreme Court of Canada; his views, however, tended to be conservative. When in parliament he had opposed women's suffrage, and in a number of decisions he gave a restrictive interpretation to Nova Scotia's Married Women's Property Act of 1884 until it was substantially amended in 1898.

If he was best known to contemporaries as a judge, Townshend will be remembered mostly as a historian. His book on the history of the provincial courts of common law and equity marks the first serious institutional study of Nova Scotia courts. Based largely on original documents, it approaches professional historical standards. Townshend also published a book-length study of his grandfather Stewart and several shorter biographies of provincial Supreme Court judges, which are informative but hagiographical in tone.

Townshend delivered the oration at the public celebrations marking the 150th anniversary of representative government in Nova Scotia in 1908, and since that date the commemoration of 1758 has totally eclipsed any celebration of the achievement of responsible

Trask

government. In contrast to early Victorian celebrations, in which representatives of the black and native communities played a part and which sometimes included women, the 1908 event was a white, indeed Anglo-Saxon, male show, constructed to illustrate the superiority of the British race and to bathe provincial institutions in the reflected light of imperial glory. Townshend's imperial bent revealed itself in his private life as well. He insisted that his family descended from the noble Townshends of Norfolk, although the authors of *Burke's peerage* were not convinced; his summer home in Wolfville was named Raynham, after the Townshends' principal manor in England.

Sir Charles Townshend was unusual in being a scion of the old elite who played by the new rules of partisan politics and succeeded. He exploited the economic opportunities of his age as a corporate promoter and business lawyer, and served the public well as a judge, but in his writings and public utterances he adopted an imperialist stance which ultimately veered into nostalgic anglophilia.

PHILIP GIRARD

[There is a small fonds of Townshend papers at NSARM, which features "A short record of the Townshend family," written by Charles James Townshend for his descendants in 1896. Perhaps Townshend's rather severe nature has discouraged biographers: the only published account aside from the standard biographical dictionaries is R. E. Inglis, "Sketches of two chief justices of Nova Scotia," N.S. Hist. Soc., *Coll.* (Halifax), 39 (1977): 107–19. For the political and legal background, P. B. Waite, *The man from Halifax: Sir John Thompson, prime minister* (Toronto, 1985), is indispensable; see also Philip Girard, "The Supreme Court of Nova Scotia, responsible government, and the quest for legitimacy, 1850–1920," *Dalhousie Law Journal* (Halifax), 17 (1994): 430–57.

Townshend's own writings were extensive. His best work, still useful today, is contained in two long articles on the history of Nova Scotia courts which appeared in instalments in the *Canadian Law Times* (Toronto), the first in vol.19 (1899) on the courts of judicature (in fact, restricted to the Inferior Court of Common Pleas and the Supreme Court) and the second in vol.20 (1900) on the Court of Chancery. These articles were published together in 1900 by Carswell of Toronto, under the misleading title *History of the Court of Chancery in Nova Scotia* (Toronto, 1900). Townshend's "Life of Honorable Alexander Stewart, C.B.," appeared in N.S. Hist. Soc., *Coll.*, 15 (1911): 1–114 and was published in book form, probably as a vanity edition, the same year. Townshend's writings include three additional sketches in the *Coll.*: "Memoir of the life of the Honourable William Blowers Bliss," 17 (1913): 23–45; "Jonathan Belcher, first chief justice of Nova Scotia," 18 (1914): 25–57; and his final paper, "The Honourable James McDonald," 20 (1921): 139–53. P.G.]

LAC, MG 26, D, Townshend to Thompson, 11, 14, 19 July 1882; 9 July, 24 Dec. 1886; 1 Jan. 1887; Townshend to A. W. McLellan, 18 Dec. 1886. NSARM, MG 100, 49, no.14; RG 39, ser.M, 2, file 49. *Amherst Gazette* (Amherst, N.S.), 11 March 1887. *Halifax Herald*, 17 June 1924. E. M.

Macdonald, *Recollections, political and personal* (Toronto, [1938?]), 128–29. Benjamin Russell, *Autobiography of Benjamin Russell* (Halifax, 1932), 251–53.

TRASK, CATHERINE (Brown), farmer and homemaker; b. 9 Feb. 1857 in Pilkington Township, Upper Canada, daughter of Charles Trask and Ann French; m. there 9 Jan. 1881 William Brown; d. 26 May 1925 in Peel Township, Ont.

Catherine Trask's parents were English immigrants who settled as tenants in the Pilkington block, northeast of Guelph [*see* Robert Pilkington*]. One of seven children, she was left fatherless at the age of seven when Charles Trask died of appendicitis. In 1865 the children received title to the family farm. Catherine continued to live with her mother, and at age 23 she married William Brown, a Methodist farmer from neighbouring Peel Township. They settled initially in the hamlet of Alma, where William found work in a sawmill. Their first son arrived in 1882, a daughter born the following year died after six months, and a second son was born in 1884. When Catherine became pregnant again two years later, the couple took steps to increase their income.

The value of farmland in many counties in Ontario had started to decline after 1879, but there was still a strong demand for grain threshers, whose work was being altered considerably by the use of movable steam engines. Fascinated with mechanics, William Brown bought a 12-horsepower engine made in Elora. By 1887 he had saved enough money to purchase, in Catherine's name, a 56-acre farm. The following year, when he acquired a better machine, a Champion from the Waterous Engine Works in Brantford [*see* Charles Horatio Waterous*], William sold his possessions to Catherine, subject to a chattel mortgage provided by flax miller John McGowan. Thereafter all of their property would remain in her name, partially as a hedge against legal liability and perhaps because her family had assisted with the finances. Their dealings in the late 1880s marked the beginning of a complicated series of mortgages and debts that continued throughout Catherine's married life. Initially these were contracted locally, but later the couple gained credit from the Metropolitan Bank in Guelph and, through Guelph lawyer Walter Ellis Buckingham, the British Mortgage and Loan Company.

While William was threshing throughout the region, from late summer to the dead of winter, Catherine assumed responsibility for running their own farm, though she disdained the work. Since farm accidents were common, particularly those involving exposed machinery, in 1891 the Browns bought insurance from the Alma court of the Canadian Order of Foresters so that Catherine would receive $1,000 if William were killed. (In a work-related accident, he did lose an eye.) Catherine's early years of marriage were trying in other ways. A third son had died months after she moved to the farm, though two more sons and a daughter would live to maturity. Her first-born shouldered some of the farm work, but he died in 1900. Shortly thereafter the next eldest son, Melvin, moved to the Canadian west in search of cheap land. William's threshing nevertheless paid enough for the couple to add a kitchen to the back of their storey-and-a-half house. By 1906 they were sufficiently well off to subscribe to the local county historical atlas, where their biographical entry boasted of Liberal and Methodist connections and described William as "one of the best threshers in his section." It was Catherine who found comfort in her faith – William was never a regular churchgoer.

On small and middling Ontario farms, children were expected to make a contribution through their labour, but allowance had to be made for differences. No sooner had Melvin Brown returned than his brother Ezra, who had shown an aptitude for mechanics, departed for the west too, and Melvin, whose constitution was not strong, left again to work for a manufacturer. Their departures increased the burden on the youngest son, Cecil, and on daughter Dinah. Cecil's disdain for farm work and his physical weakness so worried his parents that they bought sickness and funeral insurance for him in 1914. Dinah, who picked up the slack on the farm, wanted to join her father in threshing, but he encouraged her to stay home and learn to plough; she demurred and eventually moved to Elora and then to Hamilton as a servant.

Catherine and William had added to their landholdings in 1909 by purchasing a 100-acre farm nearby. This expansion placed them well above the Ontario mean, but refinancing required a much larger mortgage; new threshing equipment was also purchased on credit the following year. Deciding to leave a business where costs were rising appreciably, William, who at various times had sought employment with implement firms in Waterloo and Hamilton and with Canada Flax and Fibre in Alma, applied in 1914 for the caretaking position at the county courthouse in Guelph, but he did not get the job. During World War I inflation hit so severely that the Browns were sometimes unable to pay their grocery bills.

Family circumstances had improved sufficiently by 1919 to allow them to clear the debt on their original farm, but their second property remained encumbered. When Catherine died in 1925 without a will, William became the administrator of her estate. Too old to run the first farm, he turned it over to Cecil, who lacked the ability to make it profitable, and it was sold at auction in 1930. Until his death in 1946, William spent part of each year with Ezra in the west and the remainder with relatives in Ontario.

Catherine Brown's life reveals the heavy labour that farm women undertook in addition to housework and rearing children. Inextricably bound to the life and career of her husband, she testifies to the importance of family and to the resiliency of farmers in a period of economic and technological change in Ontario. Willing to take risks through the assumption of debt and to engage in various occupations, Catherine and William Brown worked as a couple to improve the chances they had inherited.

TERRY CROWLEY

[Family information was kindly supplied to the author in his 1993 interviews with Dinah [Brown] Cripps of Kitchener, Ont., and with Irene [Brown] Allan, Milton and Morley Trask, and Enid Whale, all of Alma, Ont. Additional details were provided by copies of family bible records in the possession of Milton Trask. T.C.]

AO, RG 80-5-0-103, no.12137. Elora Municipal Cemetery (Elora, Ont.), Records. LAC, RG 31, C1, 1871, Pilkington Township, Ont., div.1: 22; 1881, Peel Township, Ont., div.2: 44. Univ. of Guelph Library, Arch. and Special Coll. (Guelph, Ont.), Wellington North Land Registry copy-books, Peel Township: 297–98, 703; XR1 MS A060 (Henry Wissler papers), box 1 (d). Wellington South Land Registry Office (Guelph), Deeds, instrument nos.Y27-11616, Y28-11640, Y34-16409, Y35-16411; Pilkington Township, abstract index to deeds, concession 1, lot 3; reg. of deeds, book 3, no.24401 (27 July 1865) (mfm. at AO). *Historical atlas of the county of Wellington, Ontario* (Toronto, 1906; repr. as *Illustrated historical atlas of Wellington County, Ontario*, Belleville, Ont., 1972). *Threshermen's Rev.* (Detroit and St Joseph, Mich.), April, June 1911.

TRÉMAUDAN, AUGUSTE-HENRI DE, teacher, lawyer, journalist, and man of letters; b. 14 July 1874 in Saint-Jean-Chrysostome (Saint-Chrysostome), Que., son of Auguste de Trémaudan, a farmer, and Jeanne Huet; m. 18 or 19 Feb. 1901 Madeleine Bastien in Montmartre (Sask.), and they had three sons and two daughters; d. 29 Oct. 1929 in Los Angeles.

Auguste-Henri de Trémaudan's family came from Pipriac (dept of Ille-et-Vilaine) in France. His father had been a captain in the French army during the Franco-German war. In 1871 the Trémaudans emigrated to Saint-Jean-Chrysostome, in the province of Quebec, where Auguste-Henri was born three years later. After living there for about ten years, they went back to France and took up residence in Saint-Nazaire, near Nantes. Auguste-Henri attended the Petit Séminaire de Guérande, where he did his classical studies and acquired a good knowledge of English.

In 1893 the family signed a contract with the Société Foncière du Canada, which had been set up in Paris that year to establish a French colony at Montmartre in western Canada, where the Trémaudans settled. Unsuited for farming because of his delicate health, Auguste-Henri studied for a few months at the normal school in Regina. Soon he was giving English lessons to children in Montmartre, where he taught in the primary school until 1902. At the same time he worked as a clerk to familiarize himself with the law. Although not a formal member of the bar, he practised his new profession as a lawyer in Manor from 1902 to 1911, when he left Saskatchewan and moved to The Pas, in Manitoba. There he founded the *Hudson's Bay Herald*, and he remained its editor until 1913, the year he became a member of the Manitoba bar. Around 1914 he moved to St Boniface (Winnipeg), where he would make his home until 1919. During these years, and probably until 1921, he worked for the Winnipeg Trustee Company and wrote for a number of newspapers, sometimes using the pseudonym Prosper Willaume. In October 1915 he also became an editor at *Le Soleil de l'Ouest*, a Liberal weekly published in Winnipeg. When it ceased publication on 2 March 1916, he immediately launched *La Libre Parole* in that city, and he continued to promote the policies of the federal Liberal party and the defence of the French language. He and Albert Dayen, a Frenchman by birth, were co-editors of this weekly until its demise in March 1919. In the period 1916 to 1918 he also gave a few lectures enlivened by history, and some of them were published. From 1919 to 1923 he lived and practised law in Sainte-Rose-du-Lac. He was back in St Boniface in 1923 for a short time, working in the real estate business.

At the beginning of 1924 Trémaudan moved to Los Angeles, where the milder climate was better suited to his failing health. For financial reasons, only one of his sons went with him; the rest of the family joined him a little later. In his new country of adoption, Trémaudan found employment in various places, in particular in law offices. He was also active in the Union Saint-Jean-Baptiste d'Amérique and numerous other organizations to defend the French language.

Although Trémaudan had begun publishing historical works early in the 1920s, his output increased after he moved to the United States. Between 1925 and 1930 (one piece would be published posthumously), he contributed many articles, especially on the history of the Métis, to the *Canadian Historical Review* in Toronto and *Le Canada français* at Quebec. He also wrote a novel and a number of plays, some of which were performed in Montreal and in Los Angeles.

Auguste-Henri de Trémaudan's most important work, however, was probably the *Histoire de la nation métisse dans l'Ouest canadien*. On leaving Canada, he had sold his collection of books and documents on the history of the Canadian west to the Union Nationale Métisse Saint-Joseph du Manitoba. Shortly thereafter, the organization commissioned him to write (as the foreword would put it) "a simple account, as complete as possible, about the deeds of French-Canadian Métis." Trémaudan's collection was returned to him, and he began work in the spring of 1927. The author – who all his life had used his pen to support the cultural and language rights of western Canadian franco-

phones – died of pleurisy before finishing his task. The Union Nationale Métisse Saint-Joseph du Manitoba undertook to write the last chapter, which would appear as an appendix to the volume when it was published at Montreal in 1935.

MICHEL VERRETTE

Auguste-Henri de Trémaudan is the author of several lectures published under the following titles: *Pourquoi nous parlons français* (Winnipeg, 1916); *Les précurseurs* ([s.l., 1916?]); *Le sang français* (Winnipeg, 1918). He also published articles in the *CHR*: "Louis Riel and the Fenian raid of 1871," 4 (1923): 132–44; [Louis Riel], "The execution of Thomas Scott" (edited by Trémaudan), 6 (1925): 222–36; "Letter of Louis Riel and Ambroise Lépine to Lieutenant-Governor Morris, January 3, 1873" (translated and edited by Trémaudan), 7 (1926): 137–60; and a review of *Manitoba* (Paris, 1924) and *La bourrasque* (Paris 1925) by Maurice Constantin-Weyer, 7: 256–59. He contributed two articles as well to *Le Canada français* (Québec): "Les nôtres en Californie," 2ᵉ sér., 18 (1930–31): 107–20, and "Une page de l'histoire de la nation métisse dans l'ouest du Canada," 2ᵉ sér., 16 (1928–29): 7–16. In addition, Trémaudan wrote a novel, *L'île au massacre: roman canadien inédit* (Montréal, 1928), and five plays: *De fil en aiguille: mélodrame canadien-français en 3 actes* (Los Angeles, 1925); *Quand même! pièce canadienne en trois actes* (Montréal, 1928); *Feu follet: comédie dramatique canadienne en quatre actes* (Montréal, 1929); *Petit-Baptiste: comédie héroïque en quatre actes* (Montréal, 1929); and *Pureté: pièce en un acte* (Montréal, [1930]). In addition to his *Histoire de la nation métisse dans l'Ouest canadien*, he published *Hudson Bay road, 1498–1915* (London and Toronto, 1915); *Riel et la naissance du Manitoba* ([Winnipeg], 1921); and *Une page de l'histoire de la nation métisse dans l'ouest du Canada* ([Québec, 1928]).

AM, AVF, A.-H. de Trémaudan. ANQ-M, CE607-S6, 15 juill. 1874. Heritage Centre (Winnipeg), Soc. hist. métisse. LAC, MG 26, G. *La Presse*, 7 nov. 1929. *Biblio. of the prairie prov.* (Peel). Hélène Chaput, *Donatien Frémont: journaliste de l'Ouest canadien* (Saint-Boniface [Winnipeg], 1977). *Cyclopædia of Canadian biog.* (Rose and Charlesworth), vol.3. *Dictionnaire de l'Amérique française; francophonie nord-américaine hors Québec*, Charles Dufresne et al., édit. (Ottawa, 1988), 367. "Les disparus," *BRH*, 36 (1930): 94. Jean Doat, *Anthologie du théâtre québécois* (Québec, 1973). *DOLQ*, vol.2. Lionel Dorge, *Introduction à l'étude des Franco-Manitobains; essai historique et bibliographique* (Saint-Boniface, 1973). Bernard Pénisson, *Henri d'Hellencourt; un journaliste français au Manitoba (1898–1905)* (Saint-Boniface, 1986).

TROUT, JENNY KIDD. *See* GOWANLOCK

TUPPER, Sir CHARLES HIBBERT, lawyer, politician, and author; b. 3 Aug. 1855 in Amherst, N.S., second son of Charles Tupper* and Frances Amelia Morse; m. 9 Sept. 1879 Janet McDonald, daughter of James McDonald*, in Halifax, and they had four sons and three daughters; d. 30 March 1927 in Vancouver.

Charles H. Tupper was educated at King's College

in Windsor, N.S., and at McGill College in Montreal, where he was governor general's scholar. He took his law degree at Harvard University in Cambridge, Mass., in 1876, was called to the bar of Nova Scotia the following year, and in 1881 joined the Halifax law firm of John Sparrow David Thompson* and Wallace Nesbit Graham*, a partnership that would include Robert Laird Borden* when Thompson went to the bench the following year. The son of the federal minister for railways and canals, Tupper was elected to the House of Commons for Pictou in 1882. Prime Minister Sir John A. Macdonald* put him in charge of the Department of Marine and Fisheries in 1888, at 32 years of age the youngest Canadian cabinet minister up to that time.

He entered upon the administration of his department, where he would be ably assisted particularly by deputy minister William Smith*, with the utmost energy and seriousness. A dedicated conservationist, within a year he had offended two interest groups: the lumbermen over his enforcement of rules about sawdust in salmon rivers and east-coast fishermen, who objected to his insistence that lobsters taken be a minimum length of nine and a half inches. "Charly," said Macdonald in a note to Thompson, now minister of justice, "has got the bumptiousness of his father, and should be kept in his place from the start." Tupper would be all right, Thompson assured Macdonald: "He is of good metal, and is the best of his name."

Tupper had a pronounced concern for the well-being of his riding, and that included patronage. Not for nothing was he re-elected in 1887, 1891, 1896, and 1900. Faced with his importunate letters, Macdonald had to remind him in 1889 of his proper responsibilities: "You have not yet been long enough a Minister to learn that every Cabinet Minister must subordinate his duties & his interests to & in his constituency to the general interest of the Dominion."

In 1893 Tupper was named British agent, or research director, in the Bering Sea arbitration in Paris. He did so well that in September he was awarded a KCMG. After the death of Sir John Thompson in 1894, there was some talk of his becoming prime minister, which he was not above encouraging, but the fear then was "too much Tupper" – one in London (where his father was serving as high commissioner), another in Ottawa. So he became minister of justice in the government of Mackenzie Bowell*, though believing that Bowell was not really a fit person as prime minister.

Bowell's inadequacy was abundantly confirmed in his mind early the following year. On 19 March the cabinet accepted Tupper's report on the Manitoba school question [see Thomas Greenway*] as the basis of a remedial order and agreed that a dissolution should follow. Bowell disliked appealing to the people with the heather already ablaze, however, and he decided to postpone everything by having another ses-

sion first. Tupper resigned, telling Bowell, "You cannot, I fear, keep Parliament together long enough to see the end of this fire." No colleagues followed him. The rift was patched up on the strength of Bowell's commitment to remedial legislation if Manitoba failed to restore Catholic rights. In this long story Tupper stands out firmly in support of what the law had decided, but around him on many sides were vacillation and weakness, not least in the prime minister. Bowell's dithering created a more serious problem in January 1896, when Tupper again resigned, this time taking six of his colleagues with him. Some, but not Tupper, came back with the promise that Tupper Sr would become the next prime minister.

After the failure of the remedial bill in April and the dissolution of parliament, Tupper joined his father's government as solicitor general. The administration was defeated in the general election that June, and in 1897 Tupper moved to the west coast to set up practice first in Victoria and then in Vancouver, though he continued to sit as MP for Pictou until 1904. He kept up his political interests until almost the end of his life, remaining in touch with leaders of the Conservative party both in Ottawa and in Vancouver. He objected, however, to some of the Conservatives in British Columbia politics, notably Sir Richard McBride*, premier from 1903 to 1915. His contacts in Nova Scotia were sufficiently important that Borden employed him on a speaking tour there in the federal election of 1911. Another federal politician with whom he was friendly was Richard Bedford Bennett*, elected MP for Calgary in 1911. They shared beliefs in the profligacy of the Borden government's support of the Canadian Northern Railway and the McBride government's even more reckless building of the Pacific Great Eastern from West Vancouver northward to Prince George. In the British Columbia election of 1916 Tupper in fact campaigned for Harlan Carey Brewster*'s Liberals against the Conservatives under McBride's successor, William John Bowser*.

Tupper would frequently send Borden suggestions for appointments and policies that he wanted translated into action, and, being a Tupper, wanted fairly soon. Borden returned soft answers and no action. Tupper thought he was too much the same way with his cabinet. When in 1917 the minister of public works, Robert Rogers*, was accused of corrupt practice in his earlier role as minister of public works in Manitoba, Tupper was so annoyed by Borden's pusillanimity in not dismissing Rogers forthwith that he actually wrote to the opposition leader, Sir Wilfrid Laurier*, to complain.

The 1914–18 war opened a chasm between Tupper and Borden that would never be bridged. What created the final break was Tupper's bitterness at the death of his son Victor Gordon at Vimy Ridge in 1917. Tupper had three sons on the Western Front that year. The other had come back badly wounded in 1915. There were grievances with Borden about all three, but especially about Gordon, for support not given, for promotions not made: "Generals and Colonels . . . might, and did, ask for him as a Staff Officer. But – you know the rest. He had 'no pull'. Had I been Prime Minister and you had worthy sons, I would have struggled to see that the chances were at least offered to them." Tupper's wife, Janet, begged him to suffer and not complain, but in a characteristic reflection he told Borden, "I am not equal to this, nor . . . do I consider it fair to you to conceal my feelings." Tupper also disagreed with Canada's signing the Treaty of Versailles separate from Britain, and he believed the implications of it dangerous. By 1920 his 40-year friendship with Borden was over.

In 1923, with the help of Major-General Alexander Duncan McRae*, Tupper formed a political party to run in the British Columbia election of the following year. He called it the Provincial party, to pull together Conservatives and Liberals "to save the province." In British Columbia, he said, the name Liberal or Conservative was "but the borrowed plumage of men strutting before the electors." The party took only three seats. Tupper continued to work at his law practice, which now included his son Reginald Hibbert. In his spare time he undertook to produce a book about his father, *Supplement to the life and letters of the Rt. Hon. Sir Charles Tupper, bart., KCMG* (Toronto, 1926). It was more hagiographical than its predecessor, and indeed was meant to be.

Sir Charles Hibbert Tupper had the Tupper courage, the Tupper eloquence, and the family concern for the glory of Tupperdom. He was energetic, talented, quick to seize a point, and almost as quick to take offence. He can be said to have been incorruptible, provided it be understood that with Tupper patronage was politics, not a form of corruption. That was the way political business was done in Canada, then and for a long time to come. Tupper contracted pneumonia in March 1927 and died on the 30th at his home in Vancouver. He was interred in Ocean View Burial Park, Burnaby.

P. B. WAITE

[The major manuscript source is the Charles Hibbert Tupper papers at the Univ. of B.C. Library, Rare Books and Special Coll. (Vancouver), a collection which is also available on microfilm at the LAC. There is a rich lode of Tupper's letters in the Sir John A. Macdonald papers (LAC, MG 26, A), vols.286–87 and 529–30. Tupper letters are found as well in the Sir John S. D. Thompson papers (LAC, MG 26, D) and the Sir Mackenzie Bowell papers (LAC, MG 26, E). There is correspondence also in the Sir Charles Tupper papers (LAC, MG 26, F). Obituaries are in the *Ottawa Citizen*, the Montreal *Gazette*, and the *Vancouver Daily Province*, 31 March 1927, and in *Saturday Night*, 9 April 1927. An article on

Tupper's career appears in the *Montreal Standard*, 21 June 1924. A description of certain aspects of Tupper's political life is in F. H. Patterson, "Some incidents in the life of Sir Charles Hibbert Tupper," N.S. Hist. Soc., *Coll.* (Halifax), 35 (1966): 127–62. The most important printed source is [I. M. Marjoribanks Hamilton-Gordon, Marchioness of] Aberdeen [and Temair], *The Canadian journal of Lady Aberdeen, 1893–1898*, ed. J. T. Saywell (Toronto, 1960), with its richly rewarding introduction. Tupper's close relations with Sir John Thompson are discussed in P. B. Waite, *The man from Halifax: Sir John Thompson, prime minister* (Toronto, 1985).

Of other secondary literature there is very little; from the beginning of the *Canadian Periodical Index* (Toronto) in 1920 to 1998, there is only one article, referring marginally to C. H. Tupper – J. A. Russell, "Tupperiana," *Atlantic Advocate* (Fredericton), 53 (1962–63), no.12: 31–34 – and it comprises mostly pictures at that. But it does have an amiable photograph of Tupper aged 18 or 19, as well as one of his sister Emma. Tupper's years in British Columbia are much less well known than his earlier career, but the C. H. Tupper papers give a substantial introduction to them. It is clear from these that the politics of the time exercised Tupper's pugnacious mind, and that his literary activity often took the form of long and detailed letters to the editors of Vancouver and Victoria newspapers in defence of Tupperdom. P.B.W.]

TURGEON, ADÉLARD, lawyer, politician, businessman, and philanthropist; b. 18 Dec. 1863 in Saint-Étienne-de-Beaumont (Beaumont), Lower Canada, son of Damase Turgeon, a sailor, and Christine Turgeon; m. 19 July 1887 Marie-Eugénie Samson in Lévis, Que.; they had no children; d. 14 Nov. 1930 at Quebec and was buried on 17 November in Saint-Étienne-de-Beaumont.

Adélard Turgeon, who was of Norman ancestry, came from a modest background. He attended the Collège de Lévis from 1874 to 1884 and following graduation entered the Université Laval at Quebec. While studying, he articled in the law firm of Isidore-Noël Belleau, Lawrence Stafford, and Eusèbe Belleau. After obtaining his LLB and being called to the bar of the province of Quebec in 1887, he began his career in Lévis with Charles-Albert Lemay. The partners moved to Quebec in 1889, but he left Lemay that year. Turgeon, who would carry on his practice at Quebec until 1917, had other partners over the years: Henry George Carroll* from 1890 to 1897, Arthur Lachance from 1898 to 1906, Ernest Roy (who would also act as his secretary) from 1899 to 1901 and from 1906 to 1917, Auguste Tessier from 1902 to 1903, Michael Joseph Ahern from 1903 to 1906, Roméo Langlais from 1906 to 1917, Oscar-Jules Morin from 1910 to 1916, and François-Xavier Godbout from 1916 to 1917. Turgeon quickly became an important figure in Quebec legal circles and he was made a KC on 26 Aug. 1903.

Like many novice lawyers of his time who had political ambitions, Turgeon took up journalism.

Along with 150 young Liberals, in 1888 he founded *L'Union libérale*, a feisty Quebec weekly that provided them with a training ground for future struggles. The paper, which called for a return to the great principles of liberalism, would cease publication in 1896. Under the pseudonym of Donoso, Turgeon contributed a number of articles to it between 1888 and 1890. He would also be listed as one of the five directors of *Le Soleil* in January 1897, shortly after this newspaper was founded.

Turgeon ran for the Liberals in Bellechasse, the stronghold of Conservative Narcisse-Henri-Édouard Faucher* de Saint-Maurice, in the provincial election of 17 June 1890. He was successful, and he retained his seat in 1892, although the Liberal party lost this election. Like François-Gilbert Miville Dechêne and Jules Tessier, he was among those who stoutly defended the integrity of Premier Honoré Mercier* at a time when it required some courage to do so. Following the Baie des Chaleurs Railway scandal, in which Mercier's government was accused of bribery, the premier was fiercely attacked by the Conservatives, whose powerful political machine he had to face virtually alone. Lieutenant Governor Auguste-Réal Angers*, a former Conservative minister, dismissed him from office on 16 Dec. 1891. Following the general election of 8 March 1892, which came at the end of an aggressive defamatory campaign, Mercier, now ill, abandoned, and ruined, found himself in opposition with 18 MLAs, including Turgeon. The debates at that time contained particularly acrimonious attacks on Mercier, who was even taken to court. During his years on the opposition benches, Turgeon rose a number of times to defend him and his government. The general election of 11 May 1897 returned the Liberals to power under Félix-Gabriel Marchand*. Re-elected, Turgeon was named to the cabinet because of his prominence in the Quebec region and the fighting spirit he had shown while in opposition. He was made commissioner of colonization and mines. Returned by acclamation in 1900, he was offered the same post in Simon-Napoléon Parent*'s cabinet that year. Turgeon refused at first, but then accepted the office, which he would retain until 1901, when he was appointed secretary and registrar; in 1902 he became minister of agriculture. He was again elected by acclamation in 1904. In the Legislative Assembly in the period 1897–1904, he passionately championed the creation of a department of public instruction, and had to face frequent accusations that he was selling public resources to the Americans for a song. Forgoing this revenue (more than $15 million in 1901, according to the census), he told the assembly in 1904, would necessitate direct taxation to finance education, agriculture, and colonization.

The minister seemed headed for a brilliant career. On 27 March 1904 Olivar Asselin*, who knew Turgeon and his colleagues, wrote in the Montreal newspaper *Le Nationaliste* that "Mr Turgeon is virtually the head of the ministry. He has talent [and] ambition. We will judge him by his work." But Turgeon was actively involved in the revolt against Parent and he resigned on 3 Feb. 1905, along with Lomer Gouin, whom he had known at school, and William Alexander Weir. His move was motivated by his sense of personal dignity and, given the discredit into which the Parent government had fallen, by the public interest. He was convinced that Parent had hatched a plot to humiliate them and force them to withdraw. A number of people thought that Turgeon might become premier, amongst them Senator Philippe-Auguste Choquette* (who reportedly supported his appointment) and parliamentarian Godfroy Langlois (who, by contrast, did not look kindly on this possibility). Turgeon was, however, too fond of his peace of mind, his comforts, and his travels, and he was not eager to assume too onerous responsibilities. It was Gouin who took over the office, with Turgeon's support. In 1905 the new premier appointed Turgeon minister of lands, mines, and fisheries and then minister of lands and forests, a position he would retain until 1909.

Turgeon's talents – his eloquence, his breadth of knowledge, his business and administrative sense – were recognized in Ottawa. In 1906 Sir Wilfrid Laurier* offered him a seat in the Senate and Charles Fitzpatrick*'s post as minister of justice and attorney general; he would also be put in charge of the Liberal forces in the Quebec region, which meant, among other things, responsibility for organization and political appointments. Because of Laurier's friendly attitude towards Parent's supporters, Turgeon refused this flattering offer and remained at Quebec to administer the province's public lands. In this capacity, his principal tasks were to open new areas for colonization, create forest reserves, establish tighter control over logging, and fight forest fires more effectively.

At the height of Turgeon's career, what became known as the Abitibi affair occurred. In 1905 the government, which was trying to attract French-speaking immigrants, wanted to establish a Belgian colony in the Abitibi region. The minister of lands and forests was sent as a delegate to the universal exposition held that year in Liège, to extol the province's riches and attract investors. Some 15 financiers showed an interest. The influential Ferdinand-Dieudonné-Henri De L'Épine, Baron De L'Épine, acted as intermediary between a Belgian syndicate and Turgeon. According to the correspondence between De L'Épine's wife and Mme Turgeon, the relationship between the two men took on "an intimate character" during Turgeon's stay in Belgium. The baron filed an application to purchase 200,000 acres of land. The government gave him an option to buy at 70 cents an acre. In the course of discussions there was, however, talk of an additional sum of 30 cents an acre for the election fund. The money was to be paid to the intermediary, who would turn it over to the appropriate party. The negotiations led to an exchange of letters; one of these, from the baron to Turgeon, marked "confidential" and dated 28 Jan. 1906, proved disastrous for the minister, since it confirmed that a contribution had been solicited. Turgeon would assert that he had not received this letter, but rather another one, which did not contain the reference to the election fund. Though he was unable to provide the original, he would maintain that the letter brandished by Baron De L'Épine was a forgery, written after the fact for the purpose of ruining him – which may have been the case.

The affair came to light in 1907 during a libel suit brought against Olivar Asselin by Jean Prévost*, who had recently offered Gouin his resignation as minister of colonization, mines, and fisheries. Asselin was just waiting for this opportunity to expose the Abitibi scandal. Defence counsel Napoléon-Kemner Laflamme, who was advised by Armand La Vergne* and Charles-Alleyn Taschereau, succeeded in grilling Turgeon (who had been called as a witness because the famous letter was addressed to him), but in the end he did not uncover any misappropriation of funds, only instances of negligence and imprudence, and a few suspicions about the Liberal government. *Le Nationaliste*, which had extensively reported on the trial, would not let the matter drop. For weeks, under the byline of Pierre Beaudry (a pseudonym used by Jules Fournier*), it accused Turgeon of perjury. Exasperated, Turgeon sued the newspaper, and this second trial ended with a conviction on 16 Oct. 1907.

Exonerated by the courts, but weary of all the attacks, Turgeon demanded a commission of inquiry. He immediately resigned his seat as MLA for Bellechasse, in order to submit his case to his true judges, the electors, and he pushed Henri Bourassa*, the leader of the Nationalistes, into a trap by challenging him to run against him. How could Bourassa, who had never set foot in this rural constituency, win against one of its own, who knew its every nook and cranny? Bourassa resigned his seat as MP for Labelle and took up the gauntlet. It was a memorable campaign. All the political powers criss-crossed the riding and Turgeon defended himself brilliantly. The municipal council of Saint-Étienne-de-Beaumont supported him. At Gouin's request, Laurier expressed confidence in him.

On 4 November the voters made their choice. Turgeon was re-elected by a majority of 749 votes. Gouin set up the royal commission Turgeon had asked for when he resigned, naming judges François Langelier* and Napoléon Charbonneau to head it. Turgeon, who was called before it, testified that "never, at any time, was there any discussion between the Belgian syndicate, or any of its members, and myself of a con-

tribution that was to be paid into the election campaign fund." Given too narrow a mandate, the commission did not manage to shed any light on the matter. The evidence, which on the whole gives the impression that it was the baron who had lied, remains incomplete.

Turgeon and his party were returned in the general election of 8 June 1908. In a dramatic move, he resigned again. His resignation made it appear that he was running away, since he left the Legislative Assembly one month before Bourassa and La Vergne took their seats there. Many people saw this act as an evasion. On 16 June 1925 *L'Événement* would give health problems as his reason for moving to the Legislative Council, with its calmer atmosphere. Circumstances having changed greatly since 1906, he would gladly have gone to the Senate, to a position of prestige, that, moreover, was in Ottawa, where he could more easily have disappeared from public view. Although Gouin wanted to keep Turgeon in Quebec, he nevertheless contacted Laurier on his behalf, but to no avail. This "tall, handsome figure," he wrote on 3 Aug. 1908, would do honour to Quebec. Two days later Laurier replied that he did not understand why Turgeon wanted to "fade into the background," when, as a minister, he was "in the thick of the fray." The upshot was that Turgeon had to be satisfied with the provincial upper house, where he took his seat on 2 Feb. 1909 at the age of 45. He represented the division of La Vallière and acted as speaker for the remaining 21 years of his life, the longest term ever served in this office.

Turgeon's years in the upper house were happy ones. An art collector who enjoyed reading, receptions, good wine, golf, hunting, and business, the easy-going former minister lived the life of a dilettante. He travelled a good deal in Canada, France, Belgium, and New England. His oratorical skills, his charm, his "aristocratic distinction and his urbanity," as *Le Soleil* would note on 14 Nov. 1930, met with success wherever he went. Turgeon cut a figure as a great lord and, thanks to his annual salary of $5,000 (in 1930) and the money his property is thought to have brought him, he became a philanthropist. For example, he gave $1,000 to the Collège de Lévis and contributed to the fund for erecting historical monuments to Samuel de Champlain* and Octave Crémazie*, among others. When Hector Fabre* died in 1910, Turgeon's name was put forward for the post of Canadian high commissioner in Paris, but Philippe Roy, a senator from Alberta, was chosen instead. It is believed that in 1911 he wanted to succeed Sir Charles-Alphonse-Pantaléon Pelletier* as lieutenant governor of Quebec, but Parent, who was still influential, opposed the appointment. In 1917 he was rumoured to be moving to federal politics.

Along with his political life, Turgeon was involved

in various organizations. In 1907, after strong opposition stemming from rivalry, during this period, between Liberals and Nationalistes, he was elected president of the Société Saint-Jean-Baptiste of Quebec City. He was named to the executive of the Quebec Technical School in 1916. In 1922 he became president of the Conseil Supérieur des Beaux-Arts and founding president of the Commission des Monuments Historiques de la Province de Québec. He was also a member of the National Battlefields Commission. Many honorary titles were awarded him: officer of the Order of Leopold II in 1904, knight of the Legion of Honour in 1904 and officer in 1928, companion of the Order of St Michael and St George in 1906, and commander of the Royal Victorian Order in 1908. On 24 June 1901 France made him an *officier de l'Instruction publique.*

Turgeon also sat on numerous boards of directors. He was president of the Laurentian Water and Power Company, the Frontenac Realty Company, the Nor-Mount Realty Company Limited, and the Quebec Land Company (in which he was active in the division and sale of lots in Limoilou). He was vice-president of Provincial Securities Limited from 1918 to 1926 and of the Quebec Cartage and Transfer Company Limited, and a director of the Quebec Power Company. In 1900 he had been vice-president of the Quebec and Lake Huron Railway Company and he afterwards became a director and shareholder of the St Lawrence and Megantic Railway and the Montreal and James Bay Railway Company, founded in 1902 and 1903 respectively. He had played a key role in the creation of the Quebec and Lake St John Railway [*see* Horace Jansen Beemer*] and he had been instrumental in founding the village of Honfleur (Sainte-Monique) in the Lac Saint-Jean region in 1898. At the beginning of the century, Turgeon put all his political weight behind Alphonse Desjardins* when the *caisses populaires* were being established. The federal government appointed him to a consultative committee to study the proposed St Lawrence canal system, and in 1927 he endorsed the minority report of fellow committee member Beaudry Leman, who recommended that the development of hydroelectric power be put in the hands of the state rather than of private enterprise. In so doing, as Télesphore-Damien Bouchard* would state in the Legislative Assembly in 1935, Turgeon became one of the first defenders of at least partial nationalization of the province's hydroelectric resources.

Turgeon died in office at Quebec on 14 Nov. 1930 at the age of 66 years and 11 months, following a long illness, probably of a pulmonary and respiratory nature. He had often been praised for his ability as speaker, which had been evident from his student days. His eloquence took its inspiration from French politicians and it was often compared to that of Lau-

rier. He was tall, slender, naturally elegant, and haughty in bearing, with wavy hair that was thinning somewhat at the front. He was also a man of culture who enjoyed reading, especially history.

Given the offices he held, Adélard Turgeon played an important role in the political life of his time, but he could have gone further by becoming premier of Quebec or an influential minister in Ottawa. His carelessness and lack of willpower, the laxity of the Liberal government, circumstances, and the political practices of his day made him the whipping boy of the Nationalistes and Conservatives and marred a career that might have been even more brilliant. This highly talented son of Bellechasse in the end was a second-rank political figure, behind Wilfrid Laurier, Henri Bourassa, Lomer Gouin, and Louis-Alexandre Taschereau*.

JOCELYN SAINT-PIERRE

Adélard Turgeon gave many speeches, several of which were published: *Discours de l'hon. M. Lomer Gouin, premier ministre, et de l'hon. M. Adélard Turgeon, ministre des Terres et Forêts, à Longueuil le 22 septembre 1907* (Québec, [1907?]); *Discours prononcé par l'hon. M. Turgeon, ministre des Terres et Forêts, à St-Michel de Bellechasse, le 18 août 1907* ([Québec, 1907?]); *The National Battlefields Commission: Hon. A. Turgeon in the Quebec Legislative Council reviews and explains the progress made in the work: monument to King Edward VII* (Quebec, 1911); *Provincial politics: speeches of Hon. A. Turgeon, minister of lands and forests, delivered at St. Michel of Bellechasse and Longueuil, in August and September, 1907* ([Québec?, 1907?]); *The Roberts case: the judicial and social point of view: speech delivered in the Legislative Council on Wednesday, 22nd November 1922* ([Quebec, 1922?]).

ANQ-Q, CE301-S4, 19 déc. 1863; S100, 19 juill. 1887; P412; P433; P1000, D2348. Arch. de l'Assemblée Nationale (Québec), Commission royale re Abittibi, copie de la preuve, 1907–8; Procès-verbaux des séances, 1908. Arch. du Collège de Lévis, Qué., Corr. entre Wilfrid Laurier et Adélard Turgeon; Fichier des étudiants. Barreau du Québec (Montréal), Tableau de l'ordre des avocats, 1900–1. Bibliothèque de l'Assemblée Nationale (Québec), Service de la recherche, dossiers des parlementaires; Service de la reconstitution des débats, Débats, 1930–31 (texte manuscrit). Cimetière de la Paroisse Saint-Étienne (Beaumont, Qué.), Pierre tombale d'Adélard Turgeon. LAC, MG 26, G (mfm. at ANQ-Q). *Le Devoir*, 14 nov. 1930. *L'Événement*, 20 août, 10 sept., 6–7 juin, 29 oct. 1907; 16 juin 1925. *Le Nationaliste* (Montréal), 27 mars 1904; 9–10, 16, 30 juin, 7, 14, 21, 28 juill., 27 août, 22, 29 sept., 20, 27 oct., 3, 10, 17 nov., 15 déc. 1907; 18 mai 1908; 17 janv., 21 nov. 1909. *La Patrie*, 15 juill.–5 nov. 1907. *Le Soleil*, 27 nov. 1897; 4 oct. 1902; 23 nov., 24 déc. 1904; 17 mai, 26 août 1905; 30 juin 1906; 25 juin, 10 sept., 18, 24, 28 oct., 5 nov. 1907; 24 juill. 1908; 5 févr. 1914; 8 juill. 1916; 8, 28 juin 1922; 7 avril 1928; 14 nov. 1930. *BCF*. Georges Bellerive, *Orateurs canadiens-français aux États-Unis; conférences et discours* (Québec, 1908). C.-M. Boissonnault, *Histoire politique de la province de Québec (1867–1920)* (Québec, 1936). *Canadian album* (Cochrane and Hopkins), vol.2. *Canadian men and women of the time* (Morgan; 1898). P.-A. Choquette, *Un demi-siècle de vie politique* (Montréal, 1936). *Cyclopædia of Canadian biog.* (Rose and Charlesworth), vol.3. *Dîner offert à l'honorable Adélard Turgeon par ses amis de Lévis à l'occasion de son départ pour Québec au Club de la garnison, jeudi, le 26 septembre 1901* (Lévis, 1901). *Directories*, Quebec, 1880–91, 1916–21; Quebec and Levis, 1889–1916. *DPQ*. P. A. Dutil, "The politics of progressivism in Quebec: the Gouin 'coup' revisited," *CHR*, 69 (1988): 441–65. *Encyclopaedia of Canadian biography . . .*, vol.1. J. Hamelin *et al.*, *La presse québécoise*, vols.2–3. Hector Laferté, *Derrière le trône: mémoires d'un parlementaire québécois, 1936–1958*, Gaston Deschênes, édit. (Sillery, Qué., 1998). Charles Langelier, *Souvenirs politiques; récits, études et portraits* (2v., Québec, 1909–12). *"Le Nationaliste" devant la justice de son pays, condamné au maximum de la pénalité; remarques indignées et émues du juge: il regrette de ne pouvoir prononcer une sentence d'emprisonnement* (Québec, [1907?]). *1905, the settler's guide: province of Quebec* (Quebec, 1905). Hélène Pelletier-Baillargeon, *Olivar Asselin et son temps* (2v. parus, [Montréal], 1996–). *Prominent men of Canada: a collection of persons distinguished in professional and political life, and in the commerce and industry of Canada*, ed. G. M. Adam (Toronto, 1892). Qué., Assemblée Législative, *Débats*, 1890, 1892–1909. A.-B. Routhier, *Québec et Lévis à l'aurore du XXᵉ siècle* (Montréal, 1900). P.-G. Roy, *À travers l'histoire de Beaumont* (Lévis, 1943); *Les avocats de la région de Québec* (Lévis, 1936 [i.e. 1937]). Robert Rumilly, *Hist. de la prov. de Québec*; *Honoré Mercier et son temps* (2v., Montréal, 1975). Gustave Turcotte, *Le Conseil législatif de Québec, 1774–1933* (Beauceville, Qué., 1933). Univ. Laval, *Annuaire*, 1885–88. *Un ministre canadien à Mortagne: réception de l'honorable Turgeon, ministre des Terres et Forêts de la province de Québec, par la Société percheronne d'histoire et d'archéologie; Discours de M. Charles Turgeon, professeur à la faculté de droit de l'université de Rennes* (Bellême, France, 1905). J. S. Willison, *Sir Wilfrid Laurier and the Liberal party: a political history* (2v., Toronto, 1903), 2: 34–35.

TURNER, JOHN HERBERT, businessman, politician, and agent general for British Columbia; b. 7 May 1833 in Claydon, Suffolk, England, son of John Turner and Martha ——; m. 1860 Elizabeth Eilbeck (d. 1918) in Whitehaven, England, and they had one son; d. 9 Dec. 1923 in Richmond (London), England.

John Herbert Turner was educated in Whitstable, England, and came to British North America in 1856. He spent two years in Halifax before moving to Charlottetown, where he became a merchant. Moderately successful, he returned to England in 1860 to marry Elizabeth Eilbeck and then brought his wife to Prince Edward Island. News of the gold discoveries in the Cariboo district of British Columbia soon caught his attention. He decided to move to the Pacific coast, and reached Victoria in July 1862. His original plan was to travel to the goldfields and take up mining, but he abandoned the idea shortly after his arrival. Instead, he opted to take advantage of Victoria's booming economy and became a merchant once more, entering into a brief partnership with Jacob Hunter Todd* in the Victoria Produce Market. By late October 1863 the partnership was dissolved.

In 1864 Turner established J. H. Turner and Company, an importing and millinery business, in an imposing building known as London House, on Wharf Street. The venture soon became a success. In 1871, with two London-based men, John Partridge Tunstall, who had been his agent in that city, and Henry Coppinger Beeton, he formed the partnership Turner, Beeton, and Tunstall. When Tunstall left the business in 1878, it became Turner, Beeton and Company, under which name it operated successfully for many years.

Turner played a noteworthy role in Victoria, where he was well known for his genial nature, his attractive home and garden, and his participation in numerous local organizations. Active in the militia for many years, he had helped to form the Vancouver Island Volunteers in 1863. He would retire in 1882 with the rank of lieutenant-colonel. In 1869 the governor in council appointed him to the tariff commission, established to monitor the duties and excise of the colony. Three years later he was named as one of the trustees for the Ogden Point Cemetery, then being planned. Shortly afterwards, he was made a justice of the peace. In 1871 a group of Victoria businessmen had tried publicly to persuade him to stand in the upcoming provincial election, but he declined. By 1876, however, he had entered municipal politics. He was an alderman from 1876 to 1879 and then in 1879 he was acclaimed mayor; he served in that role until 1881, when he retired from municipal politics. While mayor, he also acted as chair of the British Columbia Benevolent Society, the Royal Jubilee Hospital, and the British Columbia Agricultural Association. He left the Pacific coast in June 1882 for an extended stay in England, during which time he represented the province at the International Fisheries Exhibition, held in London the following summer.

Turner entered provincial politics in 1886, winning election in July as one of four members representing Victoria City. Although formal party labels were not then used in British Columbia, he was associated with the governing group; under various leaders it had held power since 1883 and would remain in office until 1898. He was appointed to the cabinet on 8 Aug. 1887, becoming minister of finance and agriculture under Premier Alexander Edmund Batson Davie*. After Davie's death two years later, he continued to hold these portfolios in the cabinets of John Robson* and Theodore Davie*. When Davie resigned in March 1895, Turner became premier. He took office on 4 March and retained the portfolios of finance and agriculture.

Opponents of the governing group bitterly criticized its fiscal management. Throughout the period that Turner was minister of finance (1887–98), the provincial budget was in deficit each year and by the time he left office the gross public debt had climbed to nearly $7,500,000, a sevenfold increase from 1886. The government's generous grants to railway promoters were also denounced and were the reason given by David Williams Higgins* for his resignation as speaker of the house in the spring of 1898. By then, opposition newspapers were condemning what they called "Turnerism." R. Edward Gosnell*, Turner's secretary while he was premier, would define the term in 1921 as "favoritism, a lax civil service, extravagance in expenditure of public moneys, . . . encouragement of speculators and promoters at the expense of public assets, recklessness in railway charters and subventions, lack of definite and comprehensive policies, non-sympathy with labor aspirations, and everything else that might be chargeable against a government, which had been for a long time in power."

Turner was also criticized for using his political position and public profile for private gain. As with other public men of his time, it is difficult to distinguish his political activities from his business interests. He had become involved in new ventures after entering provincial politics. In the late 1880s, for example, he and his brother-in-law had acquired a mining property south of Kamloops. In 1887 they formed the Nicola Mining Company Limited, a London-based company for which they acted as local representatives. Although the business initially attracted favourable publicity, by 1890 it had suspended operations. As minister of finance, Turner had extensive official dealings with the province's London representative, who until 1895 was Beeton, his partner in Turner, Beeton and Company. His most controversial move came in the autumn of 1897, when he and Charles Edward Pooley, a member of his cabinet, agreed to serve on the advisory boards of two British-based companies, the Dawson City (Klondyke) and Dominion Trading Corporation and the Klondyke and Columbian Goldfields Limited, both of which were highly speculative enterprises. Their participation provoked polite disapproval in Britain's financial press and bitter denunciation from British Columbia's opposition newspapers. On 11 Dec. 1897 the Victoria *Province*, for example, dismissed the premier and Pooley as "mere political strumpets," prompting Turner to sue for libel. The subsequent trial, held in January and February 1898, attracted much publicity; Turner's failure to win was a blow to his and his government's credibility.

The Turner administration steadily lost public support in the months leading up to the provincial election of July 1898. The premier and his colleagues could not shake the widely held view that their government was at the beck and call of powerful corpora-

tions and the willing tool of the influential Dunsmuir family [*see* James Dunsmuir*]. They were also criticized for their refusal to ensure equitable political representation for the mainland generally and for the growing city of Vancouver in particular. The Parliament Buildings in Victoria, designed by Francis Mawson Rattenbury* and officially opened in early 1898, were seen as a monument not only to the government's extravagance but also to its support of the interests of Vancouver Island.

The results of the highly controversial election in July seemed to suggest a draw between government and opposition representatives, although numerous protests were launched by defeated candidates and the two-member riding of Cassiar did not go to the polls until a month after the rest of the province. Lieutenant Governor Thomas Robert McInnes nonetheless demanded Turner's resignation. Turner refused and angrily challenged the constitutionality of the move, but ultimately had to accept defeat. He resigned on 8 August and was succeeded by Charles Augustus SEMLIN.

Turner's removal from office brought to an end the Victoria-based political dynasty that had long dominated British Columbia. The defeat also reflected structural changes in the province's economy. The completion of the Canadian Pacific Railway in 1885 had led ultimately to the ascendancy of Vancouver over other coastal cities and by the turn of the 20th century the economic centre of gravity had shifted from Victoria to the mainland. Businesses based in central Canada gradually eclipsed the tightly knit group of Victoria merchants from whose ranks Turner had been recruited.

Turner became leader of the opposition, a post he held until June 1900, when James Dunsmuir won election as premier. Dunsmuir's ministry was in some ways a reprise of the governing group that had held power from 1883 to 1898 and Turner returned to the cabinet on 15 June 1900 to become minister of finance and agriculture once again. By this time he was 67 and perhaps tiring of the province's tumultuous political scene. He resigned on 3 Sept. 1901 in order to assume the post of agent general for British Columbia in England.

On 11 Feb. 1902, shortly after his arrival in London, Turner gave a paper at the Royal Colonial Institute entitled "British Columbia of to-day." He emphasized the province's salubrious climate, its magnificent scenery, and its abundant forest resources, before turning to boast of the many opportunities awaiting the British investor in its mines. These comments raised some eyebrows, for Turner's involvement with speculative mining companies had not been forgotten or entirely forgiven; indeed, his appointment as agent general had generated critical comment in the London press for this reason. During the more than 15 years that he would hold this office, however, his efforts to promote British Columbia would win him respect from many quarters.

As agent general, Turner arranged for many exhibitions of the province's agricultural produce at fairs and shows throughout Britain. In London he left a more permanent symbol of the province with the construction of British Columbia House on Lower Regent Street. Ironically, the formal opening of British Columbia House in late 1915 coincided with Turner's removal from office, to make way for the appointment of Sir Richard McBride*, another recently retired premier. McBride died in August 1917 and Turner once again became agent general; he retired permanently in 1918. He had become a symbolic figure by this time, having taken on such honorary roles as presiding over a dinner held by Canadians in London to celebrate the appointment of Lord Beaverbrook [Aitken*] to the British cabinet, in the spring of 1918.

Six weeks after his 90th birthday, Turner participated in a commemorative tree planting at the graveside of explorer George Vancouver* in Petersham (London), not far from his retirement home in Richmond. The Native Sons of British Columbia had arranged the event, which included the participation of the Prince of Wales as well as delegates from the Vancouver Board of Trade. It was a fitting end to Turner's long association with British Columbia; he died at home less than six months later and was buried in Kensal Green Cemetery.

JEREMY MOUAT

A few speeches and other documents written by John Herbert Turner while he was premier or agent general of British Columbia can be found in the CIHM *Reg.* "British Columbia of to-day," an address he presented to the Royal Colonial Institute, appeared in its *Proc.* (London), 33 (1902): 110–31 and was also published separately in Victoria in 1902.

BCA, GR-0441; GR-1197; MS-0471; MS-0699, box 1, file 1; MS-1130. *Daily Colonist* (Victoria), 11 Dec. 1923. R. E. Gosnell, "Prime ministers of B.C., 10: Hon. J. H. Turner," *Vancouver Daily Province*, 17 May 1921: 12. *Times* (London), 15 July 1898, 5 April 1918. *Vancouver Daily Province*, 19 Oct. 1922. J. D. Belshaw, "Provincial politics, 1871–1916," in *The Pacific province: a history of British Columbia*, ed. H. J. M. Johnston (Vancouver and Toronto, 1996), 134–64. R. E. Cail, *Land, man, and the law: the disposal of crown lands in British Columbia, 1871–1913* (Vancouver, 1974). *Canadian men and women of the time* (Morgan; 1898 and 1912). Edith Dobie, "Some aspects of party history in British Columbia, 1871–1903," *Pacific Hist. Rev.* (Berkeley and Los Angeles, Calif.), 1 (1932): 235–51. *Electoral hist. of B.C.* S. W. Jackman, *Portraits of the premiers: an informal history of British Columbia* (Sydney, B.C., 1969). E. B. Mercer, "Political groups in British Columbia, 1883–1898" (MA thesis, Univ. of B.C., Vancouver, 1937). W. N. Sage, "Federal parties and provincial groups in British Columbia, 1871–1903," *British Columbia Hist. Quarterly* (Victoria), 12 (1948): 151–69. J. T. Saywell,

"The McInnes incident in British Columbia (1897–1900), together with a brief survey of the lieutenant-governor's constitutional position in the Dominion of Canada" (BA thesis, Univ. of B.C., 1950). G. F. G. Stanley, "A 'constitutional crisis' in British Columbia," *Canadian Journal of Economics and Political Science* (Toronto), 21 (1955): 281–92. [J. H. Tunstall], *The life & death of John Henry Tunstall: the letters, diaries & adventures of an itinerant Englishman supplemented with other documents & annotations*, comp. and ed. F. W. Nolan (Albuquerque, N. Mex., [1965]).

TURRIFF, JOHN GILLANDERS, farmer, entrepreneur, politician, and civil servant; b. 14 Dec. 1855 of Scottish Presbyterian ancestry in Petit-Métis (Métis-sur-Mer), Lower Canada, son of Robert Turriff and Jane Gillanders; m. first 1 Oct. 1884 Eva Louise Bartlett-Buchanan (d. 7 Oct. 1897) in Carlyle (Sask.), and they had three daughters and one son; m. secondly 1 March 1900 Catherine Mary Wilson in Chicago; they apparently had no children; d. 10 Nov. 1930 in Ottawa.

Little is known of John G. Turriff's early years. Educated at Petit-Métis and Montreal, he moved to Manitoba in 1878 and homesteaded near Morden. Evidently this experience was not a great success, and he set up as a general merchant and notary public at Carlyle in the North-West Territories, just as settlement was beginning on a substantial scale in the early 1880s. Subsequently he moved to Alameda (Sask.), where he dealt in grain and farm implements and operated a store. In addition, he had stock in a grain merchant business, from which he also drew a salary. From all these sources he made enough to support his family comfortably. Over the years he became involved in a number of milling, mining, and financial businesses; at his death he would be president of the Western Trust Company of Winnipeg.

Elected to the Council of the North-West Territories for Moose Mountain in 1884 and again in 1886, Turriff was a vigorous supporter of territorial rights, particularly the creation of a mostly elective assembly. When the assembly was granted by Ottawa in 1888, Turriff was returned as a Liberal in Souris. He chose not to stand in 1891, but opposed Minister of the Interior Edgar Dewdney* in Assiniboia East in the federal election of that year. Dewdney represented for him the repressive policies of Ottawa. Turriff lost, and provided Liberal leader Wilfrid Laurier* with a frank and perceptive analysis of factors influencing this outcome.

This astute analysis reflected his organizing ability. He met a kindred spirit in Clifford SIFTON, among other things the chief organizing force in Thomas Greenway*'s Liberal government in Manitoba. His admiration for Sifton was revealed in his naming his only son Robert Sifton, and the friendship was mutual and lifelong. After Sifton joined the Laurier government as minister of the interior in 1896, organization amongst Manitoba's provincial Liberals fell on hard times. In late 1897 Sifton recommended Turriff as a man who could bring a new vigour to a tired local government. But Turriff had recently lost his wife, and felt that "it is necessary I should be at home as much as possible." There were other factors: no financial inducement, Sifton's absence, the expectation that his Conservative partners in the grain business would "work against my interests in the Coy," and the fact that he saw himself as "a North Wester" who would lose influence if he worked in Manitoba.

The following year Sifton made Turriff commissioner of dominion lands in the Department of the Interior, his appointment dating from 8 July. No doubt Turriff carried out his duties in adjudicating land claims quite competently. However, his main task was to be a principal organizer for the Liberal party in the prairie west; the great majority of the surviving correspondence between the two men is related to this subject. Early in 1904 Turriff resigned in order to run in Assiniboia East in the upcoming federal election. He was successful, and retained his seat (Assiniboia from 1907) in three subsequent elections, until he was appointed to the Senate on 23 Sept. 1918.

In parliament Turriff never was a prominent leader, but he was an able and active MP and senator. In his early years in the House of Commons he was called upon repeatedly to defend his record, and that of Sifton, with respect to the administration of dominion lands. Even opposition leader Robert Laird Borden* commented after one of Turriff's speeches in 1907 that "he has made a very strong defence."

Turriff also became a champion of western interests. He supported the construction of what became the Hudson Bay Railway and argued for legislation to force railway companies to build within a reasonable time the branch lines for which they held charters. He was a critic of the grain inspection system, and of any tariff increases which would work to the disadvantage of the western farmer. A constant advocate of economy in government, he wanted any wage increases for civil servants tied to longer hours of work. He backed reciprocity in 1911 because "it is the will of the people" and because "a new era of prosperity will dawn for Canada." Denying that there was any urgent need to make a financial contribution to the Royal Navy in 1913, he argued in favour of Laurier's policy of creating a Canadian navy. During World War I he had relatively little to say about the war, but did support calls for Prohibition and for women's suffrage.

Like many Liberals, Turriff by 1916 believed that corruption in the Borden government and its mismanagement of the war effort would result in a Liberal victory if an election was held. Unhappily, on 15 Sept.

1916 his son was killed in the battle of Courcelette; as he despondently told Sifton, "My chief hope in life is gone." Perhaps this loss, as well as the changing circumstances of the war, turned Turriff in the summer of 1917 away from 30 years of loyalty to Laurier, instead to advocate conscription and coalition government. He rejected the Laurier solution of putting conscription to a referendum, believing that it would be beaten and that "there are times when the majority should not rule." Yet his association with the Borden government and the Unionist Liberals in 1917 was reluctant. He did not think that naturalized "enemy aliens" should be deprived of the vote, nor did he agree with special concessions to farmers as a class in the matter of conscription, maintaining that the tribunals set up to adjudicate individual exemptions would recognize the importance of agricultural operations to the war effort.

Borden's appointment of Turriff to the Senate in 1918 was a reward for his support. It was also merciful for Turriff, who had become a pariah among many of his former Liberal friends in the House of Commons. Increasingly, however, Turriff found the government's policies repugnant to his western sensitivities. In 1921 he crossed the floor to sit "as a supporter of the Progressives or Farmers' party." His was a lone voice in the Upper Chamber. The move enabled him to criticize all other parties, though he sided with the Liberals under William Lyon Mackenzie King* more consistently as Progressive fortunes ebbed later in the decade.

Turriff had been in declining health for some years when he died at his Rockcliffe Park home in Ottawa in 1930. The Toronto *Globe* recalled his marked Liberal partisanship when first elected to the House of Commons, but noted that "his views were subsequently modified." "His chief claim to recognition probably was his earnest devotion to the interest of the residents of the Prairie Provinces."

DAVID J. HALL

ANQ-BSLGIM, CE101-S16, 27 févr. 1856. LAC, MG 26, G; J; MG 27, II, D15. *Globe*, 12 Nov. 1930. *Manitoba Free Press*, 11 Oct. 1884, 11–12 Nov. 1930. *Ottawa Citizen*, 3 March 1900, 11 Nov. 1930. *Ottawa Morning Journal*, 11 Nov. 1930. Alameda, Sask., History Committee, *A history of Alameda and district* ([Alameda, 1955]). Can., Dept. of the Secretary of State, *The civil service list of Canada . . .* (Ottawa), 1899; House of Commons, *Debates*, 1905–18; Parl., *Sessional papers*, 1898–1905; Senate, *Debates*, 1919–31. *Canadian directory of parl.* (Johnson). *Canadian men and women of the time* (Morgan; 1912). *CPG*. L. H. Thomas, *The struggle for responsible government in the North-West Territories, 1870–97* (2nd ed., Toronto, 1978).

U

ULOQSAQ (Uluksuk), Copper Inuit hunter, shaman, and convicted murderer; b. *c*. 1887 in the Coppermine district, N.W.T., son of Anerak; he had two wives, Kukiluka (Kuilukak) and Koptana; d. 24 Sept. 1929 at the settlement of Coppermine (Kugluktuk, Nunavut).

The date of Uloqsaq's birth is not known, but at his trial in 1917 it was stated he was about 30. The anthropologist Diamond Jenness*, at whose camp he had stayed in November 1915, reported that he was a prominent shaman who had purchased his powers from a shaman in Bathurst Inlet and could transform himself into a bear, a wolf, or even a European. His guiding spirit appeared as a dog. In March 1915 he had been asked by the Inuit of the Dolphin and Union Strait region to drive away an evil spirit which threatened to destroy them; his dog-spirit drove the evil one out and killed it in the snow. He related to Jenness that as a shaman he had lived underwater for days, brought dead men to life, seen dogs with four tails and white men with mouths on their chests, and turned men and women into wolves and musk oxen.

Late in 1913 two Oblate priests, Jean-Baptiste Rouvière and Guillaume Le Roux, were travelling north towards Coronation Gulf with the intention of winning the Inuit of the Coppermine River region over to Christianity. They had heard that a Church of England missionary was heading there "to sow tares in our fields," and wished to forestall him; the "race for souls" was intense in this era. Sometime in November, near the mouth of the Coppermine, the priests met Uloqsaq and another hunter, Sinnisiak, who agreed to go with them to help with the sleds in return for payment in traps. But when Le Roux, or Ilogoak as he was called, became impatient and angry with the two Inuit – he was apparently short-tempered – they decided that the priests meant to kill them. At Sinnisiak's urging, the Oblates were shot and stabbed, and part of their livers were eaten for ritualistic reasons.

When news of the killings became known to the authorities, a Royal North-West Mounted Police patrol headed by Inspector Charles Deering La Nauze and Corporal Wyndham Valentine Bruce was sent to investigate. The two Inuit surrendered peacefully in May 1916, and willingly gave complete statements. Uloqsaq recalled: "I wanted to speak; Ilogoak put his hand over my mouth. . . . Ilogoak pointed the gun at us. I was afraid and I was crying. . . . Sinnisiak said to me 'We ought to kill these white men before they kill us.'"

This was the second case in which Inuit had killed whites in the Canadian Arctic. In June 1912 two explorers, Harry V. Radford and Thomas George Street, had been murdered in the same area for much

the same reason. The government went no further than a warning then, but in the case of the priests it felt some example had to be made. In August 1917 Sinnisiak, considered the chief perpetrator, was tried in Edmonton for the murder of Rouvière, but was acquitted, probably because the jury thought the priests' foolish treatment of the accused had led to their deaths. Anti-Catholic prejudice may also have been a factor in this acquittal. Both men were then taken to Calgary and, in late August, tried and found guilty of killing Le Roux, the first two Inuit to be convicted of murder by Canadian courts. Their death sentences were immediately commuted to life imprisonment at the police post at Fort Resolution, N.W.T. They were kept there under minimum security for two years, and in 1919 they travelled with the police to help establish a new detachment at Tree River, on the Arctic coast. In 1922 they were permitted to return to their people.

At one time it was believed that Uloqsaq was killed in 1924 by another Inuk because living with Europeans had made him arrogant and bullying, a story that arose out of confusion over Inuit names. Uloqsaq was in fact living at Bernard Harbour in the late 1920s. In 1928 Anglican bishop Archibald Lang Fleming* found him there, destitute and unable to hunt because he had contracted tuberculosis of the spine. He sent Uloqsaq to the church hospital at Aklavik, but since it was unable to provide chronic care, he was taken home to Coppermine in the summer of 1929 on the Hudson's Bay Company ship *Baychimo*. Uloqsaq died there that September, one of the many Inuit who succumbed to the terrible epidemic of tuberculosis then sweeping the region.

WILLIAM R. MORRISON

Can., Parl., *Sessional papers*, report of the Royal North-West Mounted Police, 1916. R. G. Moyles, *British law and Arctic men: the celebrated 1917 murder trials of Sinnisiak and Uluksuk, first Inuit tried under white man's law* (Saskatoon, 1979). W. J. Vanast, "The death of Jennie Kanajuq: tuberculosis, religious competition and cultural conflict in Coppermine, 1929–31," *Inuit Studies* (Quebec), 15 (1991), no.1: 75–104. George Whalley, *The legend of John Hornby* (Toronto, 1962).

URRY, FREDERICK, architect, labour activist, editor, politician, and community leader; b. 6 June 1863 in Sandown, England, son of William Urry, a master mason, and Fanny Spanner; m. 7 July 1891 Eliza Ashmore in Birmingham, England, and they had two sons and a daughter; d. 2 Oct. 1927 in Port Arthur (Thunder Bay), Ont.

Frederick Urry grew up in Birmingham, where he

was articled in and then practised architecture. Along the way he received a strong education in the humanities. A Fabian socialist in outlook, he was active in the Independent Labour party. In 1903 Urry and his wife, the daughter of an "artist-in-oils" whom he had married at an Independent (Congregational) chapel in Birmingham, immigrated to Canada, hoping to find better opportunities for their children. They homesteaded in the Rainy River District of northwest Ontario for three years before moving to the Lakehead, then undergoing spectacular growth due to Canada's wheat boom. Urry opened an architectural practice in Port Arthur, where prosperity had also brought labour unrest and social distress, especially among unorganized workers and the foreign-born. For the rest of his life he would devote himself to ameliorating these problems.

At first Urry attempted to synthesize three distinctive, sometimes opposing, approaches to social betterment: trade unionism, the Social Gospel, and socialism. Initially he found unions in Port Arthur to be in a "lamentable" state. After joining the United Brotherhood of Carpenters and Joiners of America, he became its secretary and was its delegate at the meeting of the Trades and Labor Congress of Canada in Winnipeg in 1907. In April 1908 he founded the Port Arthur Trades and Labor Council and organized a public celebration of the event at his church, St Paul's Presbyterian, with John George SHEARER as key speaker. Its minister, Samuel Crothers Murray, shared Urry's views, and together they organized a lay "Brotherhood" to promote and debate the Social Gospel and the cause of labour. In one discussion Urry would explain that "socialism has for its object the co-operative commonwealth belonging to the whole of the people instead of the competitive system of capitalism."

In September 1908 Urry attended three conferences concerned with social and working conditions in Canada. He represented labour at a meeting in Toronto of the Presbyterian Church's Board of Moral and Social Reform [see Shearer]. Then he attended the founding meeting there of the Ontario section of the Socialist Party of Canada. Later, while in Halifax for the convention of the TLC, he learned of his nomination as the labour-socialist candidate for Thunder Bay and Rainy River in the upcoming federal election. Urry took only eight per cent of the votes, losing to James Conmee*; he also fell out with the SPC over his advocacy of "a fair day's wage" instead of "abolishment of the wage system."

Urry none the less retained labour's esteem. At his initiative the TLC held its convention of 1910 at the Lakehead, with a number of sessions at the Finnish socialist organization's new Labor Temple in Port Arthur, for which Urry had been a building consultant though not the architect. Backed by the labour councils of Port Arthur and Fort William (Thunder Bay), in

1911 he founded the Independent Labor party of "New Ontario," ran as its provincial candidate (and lost), and launched the weekly *Wage-Earner*. He had more electoral success municipally, serving on city council in 1911, 1912, and 1914.

In labour disputes at the Lakehead, Urry often intervened personally or served on boards of conciliation. In 1909 a gun battle in Fort William between Canadian Pacific Railway police and striking, non-unionized freight-handlers, most from Greece and Italy, led to the riot act being read, the militia called out, and regular soldiers brought in from Winnipeg. Now a correspondent for the *Labour Gazette* (Ottawa), the journal of the federal Department of Labour, Urry arranged for the department to appoint a conciliation board. Its decision for the men was a hollow victory since, in 1910, the CPR barred southern Europeans from its employ. In 1912 "Brother Urry" wrote the minority report in a dispute between unionized coal-handlers in Port Arthur and the Canadian Northern Coal and Ore Dock Company. Conciliation failed. Violence and recourse to the militia marked the subsequent walkout and led militant labour organizers to call a general strike. The dispute ended with some concessions for the dockers, thanks to Urry. It was in such situations, his daughter later recalled, that he "would often be called out in the middle of the night. . . . He had a magnetic personality and could quickly take command and quieten the men. The police would be there with drawn revolvers, and there were often shootings and knifings. Mother would be so afraid of something happening to him. The men would never turn on him, but she was afraid a stray bullet might hit him."

In 1913 Urry's conciliatory skills failed to prevent a doomed strike by the street railwaymen's union against the electric railway system of Port Arthur and Fort William. Violence on the part of immigrant sympathizers, the shooting of an onlooker by the police, and the hiring of armed guards led militants to call an abortive sympathy strike. Despite his moderating influence, Urry earned the enmity of civic leaders for being "inflammatory." As well, he clashed with the radical socialists of the Social Democratic Party of Canada over "recognition of the class struggle," its efforts to organize the entire waterfront, and its promotion of a general strike, which Urry saw as a last resort after conciliation had failed. In July 1914 he resigned from the editorship of the *Wage-Earner* and stepped away from labour politics.

When war broke out the following month he withdrew from the trade union movement itself. In 1912 he had denounced jingoism and the arms race; in wartime he differed from labour by becoming "a staunch imperialist." Enamoured of the Royal Navy and an avid sailor, he had instigated and designed Port Arthur's Sailors' Institute, which was built in 1913.

After the war he founded the Port Arthur Navy League and he served for many years on its executive.

Despite his withdrawal from labour, Urry still promoted the welfare of workers. After much professional sacrifice, he found regular work in 1918 as first superintendent of the provincial employment bureau at Port Arthur, a service he had long championed. In 1919 he made representations to the federal royal commission on industrial relations on the unacceptably high cost of living. That year and the next he acted for workers in strikes at the Port Arthur Ship Building Company Limited. Favouring industrial peace over closure of the shipyard, his counsel in 1920 saved jobs but broke the strike. In 1920 too he became president of the Port Arthur Board of Trade, an indication of the growing gulf between him and organized labour.

Besides his labour-related activities, Urry made countless contributions to the community at large. A member of Port Arthur's school board in 1910 and 1923–26, he did much work for it as an architect, often without charge. Concerned about working-class youth, he sat on the board's advisory vocational committee in 1917–19 and was its head in 1923–26. Against some opposition, he agitated successfully for a technical high school and, hoping to win the contract for its design, he resigned from the school board in 1926. The decision to give the job to an engineer specializing in grain-elevator design, Clarence Decatur

Howe*, came as a "terrible shock" to Urry. He served as well as president of the Port Arthur Arts and Letters Club and on the library board and parks commission, and was president of the Thunder Bay Philharmonic Symphony Orchestra for six years before his death.

Frederick Urry left a modest architectural legacy of private dwellings and public buildings, particularly schools. His professional accomplishments, however, had been curtailed by his promotion of "the gospel of brotherly love" and the "co-operative commonwealth."

JEAN MORRISON

[Only six copies of the *Wage-Earner* (Port Arthur [Thunder Bay], Ont.), the labour weekly founded and edited by Urry, have survived. The dates and locations for five of these issues are cited in Jean Morrison, "Frederick Urry: the wage-earner's advocate," Thunder Bay Hist. Museum Soc., *Papers and Records*, 14 (1986): 8–22; a sixth issue (25 April 1913) has since been donated to the museum by the author. Urry also wrote a regular column for the Port Arthur *Evening Chronicle*, of which only a few scattered issues have survived because the paper's back files were destroyed when it was bought out by the *Daily News* in February 1916. J.M.]

GRO, Reg. of births, Ryde (Southampton), 6 June 1863; Reg. of marriages, Birmingham, 7 July 1891. *Daily Times-Journal* (Fort William [Thunder Bay]), 3 Oct. 1927. Jean Morrison, "The organization of labour at Thunder Bay," in *Thunder Bay: from rivalry to unity*, ed. T. J. Tronrud and A. E. Epp (Thunder Bay, 1995), 120–41.

V

VADEBONCŒUR, OLIVIER-BENJAMIN. *See* SULTE, BENJAMIN

VALLANCE, MARGARET (Taylor, Lady Taylor), teacher and social reformer; b. 1 April 1840 in Hamilton, Upper Canada, fourth child of Hugh Vallance, a customs officer, and Ann Waddel, widow of George Liddel; m. there 20 Oct. 1864 Thomas Wardlaw Taylor*, and they had four sons and three daughters; d. 26 Dec. 1922 in Winnipeg and was buried in Hamilton.

Margaret Vallance's mother was a Scottish immigrant who had lost her first husband to cholera soon after landing in Burlington Bay (Hamilton Harbour) in 1832. A year later she married Hugh Vallance, the only local resident who had dared to help the quarantined immigrants. Margaret received a good basic education in a school which emphasized deportment and social graces. At age 16 she lost her father and she had to wait several years before she could enter the Toronto Normal School. After attending in 1863–64,

she graduated with a first-class teaching certificate and obtained a position in Bartonville (Hamilton).

During her teacher training, Vallance had met Thomas Wardlaw Taylor, a widowed Toronto lawyer. A few months later Taylor courted her in Bartonville. After their marriage the couple made their home in Toronto and Margaret Taylor was busy rearing their seven children. In addition, she raised the two surviving children of her husband's first marriage. The wife of a prominent Presbyterian layman, she joined the Woman's Foreign Missionary Society of the Presbyterian Church in Canada [see Marjory Laing*] soon after its formation in Toronto in 1876, despite the demands of a large family.

In 1883 the family moved to Winnipeg, where Taylor's husband became a judge of the Manitoba Court of Queen's Bench. With a few women from various Presbyterian congregations in the city, she founded in 1884 the first auxiliary of the Woman's Foreign Missionary Society in western Canada. Under her guidance, initially as treasurer and then as president, the work grew rapidly. Four years later the Winnipeg auxiliary disbanded in order to form auxiliaries attached to individual congregations. The Winnipeg presbyterial, a regional organization of the society, was formed in 1889 to coordinate the work of the auxiliaries. Taylor "emphatically declined" its presidency, preferring to become one of its four vice-presidents and to continue as president of the Augustine Church auxiliary, a post she had assumed the previous year.

Taylor was also a member of the Christian Women's Union of Winnipeg, a Protestant organization formed in 1883 to undertake work of special significance to women. In January 1885 the union established the Children's Home of Winnipeg and in July Taylor was elected to its board of management. She strongly advocated that this charity be incorporated as a separate entity, a goal achieved in 1887. That year she became one of the union's vice-presidents and president of the home's new board; she continued as president until 1899. She worked closely with the home's secretary, Mrs William H. Culver, and their lengthy association is said to have contributed much to the success of the institution, which would house over 1,200 children in its first 20 years.

The Aberdeen Association was another organization founded and guided by Taylor. The brainchild of Lady Aberdeen [Marjoribanks*], who suggested it at a women's meeting in Winnipeg on 19 Oct. 1890, it was formed within the month to supply instructive and entertaining literature to settlers in the northwest. Taylor would serve as president from its inception in 1890 until she left Winnipeg in 1899. She drafted its regulations and procedures to ensure the regular flow of literature, including religious, agricultural, and scientific periodicals, fashionable magazines, children's books, history, biography, and fiction. By 1896 a national association had been formed; at the height of its activity it would have 16 branches throughout Canada. The Post Office and shipping and railway companies provided free transport. After her return to Ontario, Taylor would deal with the financial problems of the national and local associations caused by the reduction of postal privileges.

From its inception in 1894 Taylor had been an officer of the Winnipeg Local Council of Women, first as its vice-president and from 1896 to 1899 as its second president. The council successfully campaigned for the appointment of police matrons and the improvement of conditions for women prisoners. In 1897 it opened the Girls' Home of Welcome to provide safe accommodation for female immigrants. That same year Taylor's husband was knighted and she became Lady Taylor. Two years later, on his retirement, the couple moved back to Toronto. The minutes of the Winnipeg council indicate that Margaret had inspired affection as well as respect for a job well done.

In 1899 Taylor succeeded Lady Aberdeen as president of the National Council of Women of Canada, an office she would hold until 1902. After the Taylors moved to Hamilton in 1906 she would serve a second term, from 1910 to 1911, following the sudden death of Lady Edgar [Ridout*]. She guided Canada's largest and most powerful women's organization with firmness and tact through a wide range of often controversial and potentially divisive issues, such as temperance and women's suffrage. She successfully opposed suggestions that the council should meet biennially or triennially instead of annually, even though yearly meetings were costly. To address its recurring financial difficulties, she asked for increased funding from affiliates and for prompt and regular payment of annual dues. Responding to a request for assistance in 1900, Taylor and the council shouldered much of the arduous work of developing a fledgling Canadian Red Cross Society of six branches into a strong, 50-branch organization able to cope with the demands of the South African War. During her terms, the council sought answers to the social problems caused by immigration and addressed various social needs: kindergarten classes in the public education system, vacation schools, supervised playgrounds, a women's labour exchange, custodial care of feeble-minded women, water filtration plants, and adequate food inspection laws. Her well-considered contributions to debates on legal matters, including laws to protect women and children, suggest that she benefited from her husband's expertise. During her second term the council undertook a national survey of the legal status of Canadian women to acquire accurate information and to identify areas where women were particularly vulnerable.

Continuing her work for Presbyterian missions, Taylor served on the board of management of the Women's Home Missionary Society, created in 1903, and after its union in 1914 with the Woman's Foreign Missionary Society, on the new joint board of management. At the outbreak of World War I she again immersed herself in Red Cross work, but for reasons of health she was unable to sustain a prolonged effort. By the end of 1914 she was forced to curtail her public activities severely. In 1922 she died peacefully at her daughter's home in Winnipeg. Friends from the National Council remembered her strength, clear thinking, good judgement, and affectionate nature.

Margaret Taylor was an exceptional member of a strong team, whose vision and hard work in the National Council enriched the quality of life in their country by giving women a voice in Canadian society and an enhanced perception of their place within it.

WENDY HEADS

AM, P 2131; P 3586–607. Law Soc. of Upper Canada Arch. (Toronto), T. W. Taylor, "A sketch of the life of Sir Thomas

Vallée

Wardlaw Taylor by his son" (typescript; copy at AM). UCC, Manitoba and Northwestern Ontario Conference Arch. (Winnipeg), Woman's Foreign Missionary Soc., Winnipeg presbyterial, executive minutes, 1889; newpaper clippings. *Manitoba Free Press*, 28 Dec. 1922. Mrs George Bryce [Marion Samuel], "Historical sketch of the charitable institutions of Winnipeg," Man., Hist. and Scientific Soc., *Trans.* (Winnipeg), no.54 (February 1899): 1–31. N. E. S. Griffiths, *The splendid vision: centennial history of the National Council of Women of Canada, 1893–1993* (Ottawa, 1993). Wendy Heads, "The Local Council of Women of Winnipeg, 1894–1920: tradition and transformation" (MA thesis, Univ. of Man., Winnipeg, 1997). National Council of Women of Canada, *Report* (Ottawa; Toronto), 1899–1902, 1910–11; *Retiring president's memorandum . . .* (Hamilton, Ont., 1899). *Pioneer Winnipeg women's work: 1883–1907* ([Winnipeg, 1929?]). Presbyterian Church in Canada, Woman's Foreign Missionary Soc. (Western Div.), *Our jubilee story, 1864–1924* ([Toronto, 1924]). R. L. Shaw, *Proud heritage: a history of the National Council of Women of Canada* (Toronto, 1957). V. J. Strong-Boag, *The parliament of women: the National Council of Women of Canada, 1893–1929* (Ottawa, 1976).

VALLÉE, CHARLES-AMÉDÉE, Papal Zouave, bank manager, and office holder; b. 17 Oct. 1850 in Saint-Roch parish at Quebec, son of Prudent Vallée, a master joiner, and Henriette Cazeau (Casault); brother of Arthur* and Louis-Prudent*; m. there 26 May 1874 Marie-Zoé Marcotte, and they had six children; d. 19 March 1924 in Saint-Gabriel-de-Brandon, Que.

Charles-Amédée Vallée studied at the Collège de Lévis from 1861 to 1864 and then at the Académie Commerciale de Québec. On 16 May 1868, as a youth of 17, he embarked for Italy with the second detachment of Papal Zouaves, who were setting off to defend the Papal States in the face of the threat posed by Giuseppe Garibaldi's troops [see Édouard-André Barnard*]. He was promoted corporal, second class, on 26 March 1870 and quartermaster sergeant, second class, on 1 September. After Rome capitulated, he returned to Quebec in November. Pope Leo XIII would make him a knight of the Order of St Gregory the Great in recognition of his services. Vallée started on a career in the financial sector about 1872. After serving as a clerk in the Banque Nationale at Quebec, of which his father was a director, he became an accountant there. Around 1882 a promotion made him manager of the Montreal branch, a position he held until 1888. During the next two years he worked as a broker and was a member of the Montreal Stock Exchange.

In October 1890 the government of Honoré Mercier*, who was Vallée's close friend, appointed him deputy warden of the common jail in Montreal, known as the Pied-du-Courant. On 18 May 1891 he succeeded to the governorship, his predecessor, Louis Payette, having died on 29 April. The members of the Board of Inspectors of Prisons and Asylums of the Province of Quebec commented enthusiastically on his nomination: "He is, without any doubt, an orga-

nizer of great ability, and his appointment is one of the best which have ever been made."

Vallée would indeed demonstrate not only ability as an administrator, but also professionalism and openmindedness towards new correctional theories, most of which came from Europe. In August 1891 the Montreal jail held 225 inmates and Vallée had a staff of 30 under his orders. He instituted practices that were very different from those of his predecessor. Upon his appointment he began a complete reorganization of the prison staff by dismissing nearly half of the employees in order to remedy problems of all kinds (guards who were often drunk, traffic between guards and prisoners in cigarettes, alcohol, and other items). In their 1891 report the inspectors stated that "the new Governor has transformed the whole building, for the better without doubt, and has introduced a new order of things, which gives to the establishment an entirely new character, and makes of an old tumbledown building, an appropriate local fort, and one which is very ingeniously laid out."

For Vallée, prison was a place for punishing and reforming offenders. The prison governor was therefore no longer a head jailer who made sure that individuals were kept locked up, but rather the penal system's administrator and "practical" thinker. Over the years Vallée produced numerous reports in which he put forward his views on such matters as the importance of solitary confinement in reforming a prisoner, the impossibility of applying this method in a common jail, the question of having prisoners work together at shoemaking, tailoring, carpentry, or sheetmetal work, and the distinction between accused and convicted detainees.

As governor of the Pied-du-Courant prison until 1913, and as a member of the commission charged with preparing and approving plans for the construction of a new common prison (since the Pied-du-Courant was overcrowded), Vallée left a real mark on the history of the Montreal penal system. He was chiefly responsible for the construction of Bordeaux Jail, considered at the time a model prison and ultra modern. To this end, he travelled to Europe and the United States a number of times to visit prisons and penitentiaries and to bring back plans and up-to-date technical, practical, and theoretical information. Designed by architect Jean-Omer Marchand* and built between 1907 and 1912, the building could hold nearly 1,000 inmates.

Charles-Amédée Vallée was governor of Bordeaux Jail from 1913 until he resigned in 1916. Shortly after the war, the provincial government appointed him to the Board of Censors of Moving Pictures. He retired in 1919 and went to live in Saint-Gabriel-de-Brandon, where he died five years later of influenza.

MARIE J. TREMBLAY

ANQ-M, P23. ANQ-Q, CE301-S22, 18 oct. 1850, 26 mai 1874; E17, dossier 1243 (1910) (versement 1960-01-036/271). *Le Devoir*, 20 mars 1924. *Gazette* (Montreal), 20 March 1924. *La Presse*, 20 mars 1924. *Directories*, Montreal, 1888–91; Quebec, 1872–83. René Hardy et Elio Lodolini, *Les Zouaves pontificaux canadiens* (Ottawa, 1976). Que., Parl., S*essional papers*, report of the inspectors of prisons, asylums and public offices of the province of Quebec, 1891–1916.

VARVILLE, JOSEPH-ALPHA. *See* VERVILLE, ALPHONSE

VENNE, JOSEPH, architect; b. 14 June 1858 in Montreal, eldest son of Joseph Venne (Vaine), a carpenter, and Hélène Raymond-Labrosse; m. there 17 Oct. 1882 Philomène Boucher, and they had 11 children, of whom five sons and four daughters lived to adulthood; d. there 9 May 1925.

Although he had been a diligent pupil, Joseph Venne would later describe his studies with the Brothers of the Christian Schools in Montreal as rudimentary, giving him nothing more than a knowledge of grammar and history. Looking back, he would assess their teaching of linear and freehand drawing as weak, and the supply of books and instruments as minimal. When he went to see Henri-Maurice Perrault, a surveyor and architect, in May 1874, with drawings he later considered quite inadequate, he had never seen a T-square. It was only after working persistently for three or four weeks to produce new ones that he was accepted as an apprentice, at a salary of four dollars a month in the first year. His training would last for five years. Perrault was then at the height of his career and was working with Alexander Cowper Hutchison on the construction of the Montreal city hall. In 1880 he turned over management of his firm to his son Maurice*, who went into partnership with Albert Mesnard, the chief draftsman. Even before Perrault and Mesnard invited him to join them as a partner in 1892, Venne was playing an active role in the new company, which did extensive and varied work. Most of their commissions came from the Roman Catholic Church, government agencies, and the French-speaking middle class of the province of Quebec, but there were also some from British Columbia (St Andrew's Cathedral in Victoria, patterned on the church of Saint-Antoine in Longueuil) and from the United States (churches in Boston and Adams, Mass., and in Pawtucket, R.I.).

Venne reportedly was responsible, among other things, for the winning plan for the Université Laval in Montreal (1893–95) and for much of the work on the Monument National (1891–94). In *Marges d'histoire*, Olivier Maurault* affirms that the most beautiful part of the church of Saint-Jacques (1889–91), the façade of the south transept on Rue Sainte-Catherine, was Venne's work, except for a few modifications on

which Mesnard, who was his senior, is believed to have insisted. Venne also drafted the plans for the presbytery (completed in 1895) and the two successive buildings of the church of Sacré-Cœur-de-Jésus in Montreal (it had to be rebuilt after a fire in 1922). In the carved decor of the sacristy are many monograms as well as two faces – thought by some to be those of Venne and his son Émile – placed there as a signature. In this parish, where he had been married and would spend his whole life, Venne was also president of the Sacré-Cœur branch of the Association Saint-Jean-Baptiste de Montréal.

The partnership of Perrault, Mesnard, and Venne was dissolved in 1895; Venne then went into business for himself until 1911, when he took his student Louis Labelle into partnership. In 1923, although ill, he continued to work at his profession with his sons Émile and Adrien, who had been admitted to the Province of Quebec Association of Architects in 1922 and 1923 respectively. From the mid 1890s, his considerable output could be found as far away as Massachusetts (churches in Southbridge and New Bedford).

Since Venne had trained with Perrault and Mesnard in the late Victorian period, his work showed eclectic inspiration and a taste for decors burdened with a style that Gérard Morisset*, in *L'architecture en Nouvelle-France*, would describe as "tasteless complication." He nevertheless developed his art in an original way. In enlarging the parish church of Saint-Enfant-Jésus, in Montreal, whose front wing in the form of a stairway (1903) is its most spectacular feature, he made a very wide transept (1898) forming an octagon at its intersection with the nave – one of the few examples in Quebec of the blending of centred and basilican plans. To match an anterior bell-tower (now truncated and invisible), he added a new campanile on the south wall, at a 45-degree angle to emphasize the overall design. On an unusual and picturesque site, this tower was erected in 1910 to rehouse the bells used at the 21st International Eucharistic Congress, an event at which Venne had made a name for himself as the person in charge of decoration.

In 1899 Venne had constructed the nave of the parish church of Saint-Clément in Viauville ward and in 1913–14 he also built the chancel on the octagonal design he had used previously. This time, however, heavy beams gave a surprisingly vigorous effect to the oblique axes at the juncture of transept and nave. Impressive ceiling coffers emphasized the church's particular geometry and provided additional natural lighting.

In terms of technology, by the end of the 19th century Perrault, Mesnard, and Venne were among the most innovative architects in the use of steel. The iron and glass atrium of the People's Bank (1892–94), inspired by American models, showed how quickly they grasped the latest developments in construction and aesthetics. In 1907 Venne produced the plans for the École Salaberry on Rue Robin, which was built after a deadly fire destroyed Hochelaga School; it reportedly was the Montreal Catholic School Commission's first fireproof building made of concrete.

In addition to practising his profession, Venne made every effort to promote it and help it move ahead. From 1895 to 1899 he taught public courses in construction and architecture at the Monument National under the auspices of the Council of Arts and Manufactures of the Province of Quebec. His many lectures bore witness to his "broad and varied knowledge," as *La Presse* would put it on 3 Sept. 1910. They dealt with such topics as "archaeology," "principles of architectural composition," "internal administration of architectural firms," "aesthetic values of mouldings and contours," and with the buildings he had visited during the course of his travels in Europe, especially Italy. In 1890 he had helped found the Province of Quebec Association of Architects. Venne must have earned the respect of his colleagues, for they elected him to the council in 1893, and named him secretary from 1894 to 1898, second vice-president in 1899, and first vice-president in 1901. Elected president in 1902, in 1912 he became the first person to win this office a second time. From 1906 to 1920 he served almost continuously as examiner for candidates seeking admission to the association. He participated in numerous working groups on subjects as varied as the administration of the association and urban beautification. In 1899 he proposed that a committee on historic monuments be set up to gather information about early architecture. The project materialized in 1909 with the support of the architect William Sutherland Maxwell, brother and partner of EDWARD. In 1911 Venne was a member, along with Joseph-Alcide Chaussé*, of a commission formed to revise the building regulations for the city of Montreal. Several of his plans were displayed in collective exhibitions at the Royal Canadian Academy of Arts in 1882 and 1913, and at the Art Association of Montreal in 1905, 1908, and 1913. With his interest in history, composition, construction, urbanism, and management, Venne was the very model of an accomplished professional.

There were a number of other architects named Venne, beginning with Joseph's two sons, Adrien and Émile. Adrien would also become known as an historian. Émile, who trained at the École des Beaux-Arts in Paris, would teach at the School of Fine Arts in Montreal and the École Polytechnique. Some of Joseph's second and third cousins and grandchildren were also members of the profession; Alphonse Venne*, who would produce an impressive amount of work in the Montreal region, is the best example. Viewed within the framework of all these family ties and business connections, Joseph Venne was at the centre of one of the longest lasting and most outstanding professional networks in the history of Quebec. He left a substantial number of buildings and contributed significantly to the development of the architectural profession in Quebec.

PIERRE-RICHARD BISSON and
JACQUES LACHAPELLE

[The authors wish to express their gratitude to Michel Venne and Michel Allard, a grandson and a great-grandson of Joseph Venne, for family details provided during the course of an interview. P.-R.B. and J.L.]

ANQ-M, CE601-S7, 15 juin 1858, 17 oct. 1882; P124-16, 4 oct. 1894–14 juill. 1908; 17, 1er sept. 1908–7 janv. 1926; 22, 1890–1925; 35. Arch. de la Chancellerie de l'Archevêché de Montréal, 968 (dossier Claude Turmel), 355.122 (extraits des registres paroissiaux relatifs aux bâtiments de la fabrique de la paroisse Saint-Enfant-Jésus). Arch. Nationales (Paris), AJ52 (fonds de l'École nationale supérieure des Beaux-Arts), dossier 308. Arch. Paroissiales, Saint-Clément (Montréal), Plans. "M. Joseph Venne," *La Presse*, 3 sept. 1910: 3. "Montréal va s'embellir d'une nouvelle église," *La Presse*, 22 avril 1911: 16. *La Presse*, 11 mai 1925. W. H. Atherton, *Montreal, 1534–1914* (3v., Montreal, 1914), 3. Soraya Bassil, "Document orientation-concept, résumé critique des recherches et divisions thématiques" (travail dirigé, univ. du Québec à Montréal, 1999). *Canadian album* (Cochrane and Hopkins), 2: 326. *Le diocèse de Montréal à la fin du dix-neuvième siècle . . .* (Montréal, 1900). Olivier Maurault, *Marges d'histoire* (3v., Montréal, 1929–30), 2. Gérard Morisset, *L'architecture en Nouvelle-France* (Québec, 1949).

VERIGIN, PETER VASIL'EVICH, Doukhobor leader; b. 11 July 1859 in Slavianka (Azerbaijan), eighth of the nine children of Vasilii Luk'ianovich Verigin and Anastasiia Vasil'evna Kalmakova; m. 1879 Evdokiia Grigor'evna Kotel'nikova, and they had one son, Peter Petrovich Verigin*; d. 29 Oct. 1924 in Farron, B.C.

Peter Verigin's paternal ancestry is traceable to a family of Old Believers, those who refused to accept the liturgical reforms of the Russian Orthodox Church in the mid 17th century. His mother was the granddaughter of Savelii Kapustin, leader of the Doukhobors from 1802 to 1820 in the Molochnye Vody (Milky Waters) region of what is now southern Ukraine. A Russian Christian sect of uncertain origin, the Doukhobors had come to the attention of tsarist authorities in the 1750s. The name Doukhobor, meaning spirit wrestler, is said to have been attributed to its members in the 1780s by an Orthodox bishop who described them as fighting against the Holy Spirit. The sect adopted the name, claiming to wrestle with and for the spirit of God which dwelt in each believer. It rejected the Orthodox Church and the need for priests, sacraments, and the Bible, since each person could be guided by the spirit within. Doukhobor beliefs were embodied in a collection of orally transmitted teachings, especially psalms and hymns, called the Living Book. During various periods in its history the sect also held pacifist and egalitarian views. Although it refused to recognize any external authority, it looked to its own leaders, who were considered to be divinely chosen. Severely persecuted by the tsarist government, Doukhobors from what are now western Ukraine and southern Russia were resettled in the Milky Waters region in 1802; they were joined by co-religionists from other parts of the Russian empire. The sect prospered in its new home. Starting in 1841, about 4,000 members were again forced into exile, to various parts of the Caucasus Mountains (in present-day Azerbaijan, Georgia, and Turkey).

Fairly well off, the Verigins enjoyed a degree of prominence in the Doukhobor community of the Caucasus. Vasilii ensured that at least his three youngest sons, including Peter, received an elementary education. In 1864, when Peter's cousin Petr Ilarionovich Kalmykov died, his leadership of the Doukhobors devolved to his widow, Luker'ia Vasil'evna Kalmykova. A strong leader, she maintained solidarity among her followers and a working peace with the tsarist authorities. She took notice of Verigin, a handsome and intelligent young man, marking him as one destined for "holy work." In the early 1880s she ordered him to divorce his pregnant wife and summoned him to her personal service. Verigin's intellectual prowess was widely noted by his contemporaries and would be mentioned frequently by later commentators. In 1968 historians George Woodcock* and Ivan Avakumovic, citing an eyewitness, were to describe him as a "powerful personality with a mind that was quick, subtle, and capable, even if it was not profound." His rapid rise in Kalmykova's entourage aroused much resentment. When she died childless in 1886, Verigin was one of the major contenders for the sect's leadership in the unprecedented struggle that ensued. Even though his opponents managed to have him arrested on trumped-up charges in January 1887 and sent into exile late that summer, he was still acknowledged as leader by the vast majority of Doukhobors, who came to be known as the Large Party (estimated at between 5,000 and 7,000 persons); the Smaller Party refused to accept his leadership.

During 15 years of exile, first in Shenkursk, near Archangel (Arkhangel'sk), Russia, and then further north in Kola, near Murmansk, once more in Shenkursk, and finally in the Siberian village of Obdorsk (Salekhard), Verigin underwent a great deal of soul-searching. Influenced by his encounters with exiled revolutionaries and anarchists, as well as by his wide reading, including the works of Count Tolstoy, he laid new emphasis on a long-held Doukhobor tenet that violence, along with other human vices, was to be rejected at all costs. His ideas were conveyed back to the Caucasus by followers who paid him frequent vis-

its and brought him money to supplement his earnings, allowing him some comfort and permitting him to feed the poor. At the end of 1893 he sent his adherents a manifesto. It called on them to refuse military service, divest themselves as much as possible of personal property (thus reviving an earlier tradition of communal holdings), and abstain not only from the consumption of alcohol and tobacco, but also from eating meat. This last directive led to a serious schism of the Large Party into Fasters (*postniki*) and Meat-eaters (*miasniki*). The Meat-eaters, sometimes known as the Middle Party, continued to acknowledge Verigin as their leader, but declined to accept his more radical views. Verigin also called on his flock to practise celibacy during the period of instability (this exhortation would be rescinded on their emigration to Canada). He proposed a new name for the group, the Christian Community of Universal Brotherhood (CCUB), which would become the official name of the Doukhobor community in Canada.

In 1895 Verigin ordered his followers to collect whatever weapons were in their possession and, on 11 July (29 June by the Orthodox calendar), to burn them in a mass demonstration of the sect's rejection of violence. The burning of arms had a practical as well as a symbolic significance. He preferred to see his adherents suffer immediate repression than witness a prolonged conflict with authorities that would be doomed to failure. Several years of persecution by the government ensued; many Doukhobors were exiled to remote villages in the Caucasus, those refusing military service were sent to penal battalions, and others suffered beatings or imprisonment for their beliefs.

During Verigin's exile the Doukhobors' plight had come to the attention of interested outsiders – especially English Quakers – in large part through Verigin's correspondence with Tolstoy, who had come to see in the sect's pacifist, communal, and vegetarian lifestyle a practical embodiment of his own philosophy. Articles published in western papers by Tolstoy and his followers met with a sympathetic response from Prince Kropotkin, a Russian anarchist who had travelled extensively in Canada. Prompted by letters from both Tolstoy and Kropotkin, James MAVOR, a professor of political economy at the University of Toronto, made enquiries of the minister of the interior, Clifford SIFTON, as to the feasibility of bringing the Doukhobors to Canada. As a result of his negotiations, some 7,500 immigrants, mostly members of the Large Party, arrived during the winter and spring of 1899. They were granted homesteads in two colonies in the District of Assiniboia (another one was added later in the District of Saskatchewan). In a letter to Tolstoy on 16 Aug. 1898 Verigin had declared that he was opposed in principle to emigration, but resigned to it if no better option was available. At first prohibited from joining his followers, he was finally allowed to leave Russia in July 1902, when his last term of exile ended.

The months preceding Verigin's coming to Canada were marked by a troublesome incident there. Members of the sect who would later call themselves Freedomites (*Svobodniki*) or Sons of Freedom adopted an extreme interpretation of their leader's call to self-renunciation, turning their farm animals loose and destroying or giving away almost all personal possessions. More than 1,000 set out on a trek from the colonies near Yorkton (Sask.) in search of a place where they could live free of external constraints. In mid November police in Minnedosa, Man., halted the march and returned men, women, and children, some by force, to their settlements.

At his arrival in Winnipeg on 22 Dec. 1902 Verigin was described by a journalist of the city's *Manitoba Free Press* as "a splendid type of his race. Tall and strongly built, and of erect and graceful carriage, he would attract attention among hundreds of good-looking men." His presence had a calming effect on his flock. On 12 Jan. 1903 he explained to Tolstoy that he had defused the trouble the radicals had caused by telling them that their "motives of self-sacrifice ... are legitimate and precious ones, but there is no need to let the children go hungry and cold, so for the time being why not remain with all the rest of the brethren and teach them?" He added that "those with families took this explanation too as a revelation from God." It was not long before his Canadian followers, emphasizing what they perceived as his spiritual strength, began calling him *Gospodnii* (meaning Godly or belonging to the Lord, although frequently mistranslated as Lordly) – a title which had originally been bestowed on him by Luker'ia Kalmykova.

Soon after Verigin's arrival in Canada, he purchased land near the Doukhobor communities and established a village which he named Veregin (Sask.); it would become the group's administrative centre. His ability as a leader was immediately noticeable, as he combined the duties of spiritual leader with the task of managing the community's financial and social development. His pragmatism guided him in the search for compromises with Canadian authorities in matters of Doukhobor rights and responsibilities. The issue of land registration and ownership was particularly thorny. His adherents had settled in 20 small villages and they cultivated the surrounding fields. Under his leadership the number of villages grew to 57. Initially reluctant to register for the land they occupied, his followers agreed to make entries for about 2,700 homesteads, but to hold the land collectively. Verigin encouraged the men to work away from the community; their wages were used to pay the community's debt, acquire the latest agricultural machinery, construct flour- and sawmills, and purchase livestock and supplies that the community could not produce.

Although the government had originally allowed the Doukhobors the privilege of collective ownership, in 1905 Frank Oliver*, the new minister of the interior, faced with increased public pressure to make more land available, demanded the registration of homesteads on an individual basis as a condition to obtaining title. Registration entailed an oath of allegiance to the crown which would obligate members of the sect to take up military service if Canada should ever go to war. Contrary to Verigin's advice, some, called Independent Doukhobors to distinguish them from their Community brethren, had already registered their homesteads as individual farmers and had either taken the oath of allegiance or claimed an exemption similar to that which had been granted to Mennonites, recognizing them as conscientious objectors. Verigin discouraged any contact with the Independents and would even unsuccessfully oppose government recognition of their exemption during World War I.

Disenchanted with the change in official attitude, in 1906 Verigin and several of his key followers went to Moscow to enquire as to the possibility of moving the Doukhobors en masse back to Russia. After a cool reception from tsarist officials and no guarantees of exemption from military service, Verigin was forced to abandon the idea. On his return to Canada he found that since his followers had failed to comply with government regulations, over half of their entries for homesteads had been cancelled and much of the remainder of their land had been vested in the government "for the protection" of the community. He advised his followers to live frugally with what resources remained available to them while he searched for options.

In the summer of 1907 Verigin discovered orchard lands in British Columbia which the Doukhobors could acquire by purchase, a procedure that would obviate the need for an oath of allegiance. The following year four-fifths of his flock left the prairies and followed their leader to a new home in the Kootenays. The remainder, mainly Independent Doukhobors, stayed behind. In 1916 they would establish the Society of Independent Doukhobors under the leadership of Peter George Makaroff.

Verigin's group settled in the Castlegar and Grand Forks districts. Historian Carl J. Tracie speculates that Verigin may have deliberately placed certain Doukhobors in small, scattered communities around Castlegar in order to keep opposing factions, such as agricultural labourers and commercial entrepreneurs, separate from each other and at the same time isolated from English Canadian society, with a view to preventing further fragmentation of the sect. According to Tracie, however, "This distinction only added fuel to the latent uneasiness of the Sons of Freedom about what they saw as the growing materialism of the Orthodox Doukhobors." Their subsequent actions could be interpreted as "an attempt to sharpen and clarify the boundaries between true Doukhoborism and the secular world attempting to compromise it."

Under Verigin's leadership – and guided by his motto, "Toil and peaceful life" – the Doukhobors would prosper in British Columbia and expand their activities, setting up – under the CCUB – sawmills, brick factories, jam factories, and fruit canning and packing plants. While finding orchard farming more compatible with their vegetarian philosophy than cattle-raising on the prairies, Verigin and his followers were by no means freed from conflict with government over land, education, and the registration of vital statistics. One example of contention was British Columbia's Community Regulation Act of 1914, which made the CCUB responsible for non-compliance with government regulations by any of its members.

Verigin's absolute rule over his flock provoked conflict with the provincial authorities, which in turn, combined with the harsh pioneering conditions his followers had endured, caused a certain number to leave. On the other hand, his compromises with various levels of government did not sit well with the radical Freedomites. For example, in 1915 he reached an agreement with Premier William John Bowser* whereby his adherents would allow their children to attend public school and agree to pay school taxes in return for guarantees that there would be no military exercises or religious instruction in the schools. Freedomites resorted to acts of public nudity and arson against the homes, businesses, and schools of Community Doukhobors. The provincial government's failure to respond to Verigin's pleas for protection of Doukhobor property against arson created further tension between the CCUB and the government.

In October 1924 the hatred directed against Verigin from both disaffected CCUB members and Freedomites led to tragedy when a bomb exploded in the train on which he was travelling from Castlegar to Grand Forks. His death was generally viewed as an assassination, although the culprit was never found, and Verigin has continued to live on in Doukhobor memory as a martyr to their ideal of a Christian life. His exalted place among members of an otherwise egalitarian sect made him an unusual and controversial figure, especially in the Canadian context. Endowed with a natural ability for leadership and surpassing his brethren in intellectual achievement and ideological development, he remained one with them in spirit and community of purpose. In addition, his striving for inner development and moral and spiritual self-perfection made him a powerful religious figure.

Perhaps the single most important factor behind Verigin's successful leadership was his pragmatism, his realization of the need to balance the ideal against the feasible. No less significant was his desire and ability to learn. His breadth of vision allowed him to function effectively in the world beyond the Doukhobor community. He was able to draw from it whatever might be beneficial to the Doukhobors and put it to practical use, from his relationship with Tolstoy to the latest farm machinery.

Of course, Verigin was not successful in every undertaking and not all his failures can be attributed simply to unfavourable external circumstances. Some, such as his conflict with his former wife and son, were due to his own human weaknesses. In his typical high-handed manner, he had ordered his wife and son to come to Canada in 1907. When he failed to find any common understanding with them, he had them sent back to Russia. His treatment of them provoked considerable rancour among his wife's relatives and friends in the Saskatchewan colonies.

Verigin also had particular difficulty coming to terms with the Society of Independent Doukhobors. In his attempts to counter their claims to military exemption he had enlisted the aid of the Canadian government, which, of course, went directly against the sect's principles. By today's standards, his methods would be described as authoritarian. Doukhobor leaders long before him had customarily enjoyed absolute command. Verigin accepted this situation as normal and saw no need for change. At the same time, a Doukhobor leader was entrusted with setting a moral example, a charge that he fulfilled significantly better than many of his predecessors.

Some scholars have legitimately questioned Verigin's sincerity. Joshua A. Sanborn, for example, advances the not implausible thesis that Verigin arranged the Doukhobor arms-burning in 1895 specifically to elicit a favourable reaction from Tolstoy. Evidence indicates that Verigin's letters to Tolstoy were, as a rule, carefully crafted. After all, Verigin needed Tolstoy's reputation in support of his cause, just as Tolstoy relied on the Doukhobors for a practical example of his theories opposing the state and state religion and advocating non-violent resistance. The reaction of the Freedomites to Verigin's attempts to reconcile the practical needs of the community with the radical components of his teaching is also worth noting. They concluded that his public appeals for calm were issued only for the benefit of English Canadians and were not intended for his followers. His pleas were interpreted by them as a subliminal encouragement to accelerate their quest for true Doukhoborism. Their actions galvanized public opinion against the Doukhobor community as a whole, alienating needed support. In this way, many of Verigin's decisions and actions, from his original settlement strategy to his compromises with authorities and his fervent appeals for unity and calm, instead of securing the continuity of the Doukhobors' communal way of life, fuelled a series of reactions that hastened its demise.

From an historical perspective, Verigin may be viewed as a leader who attempted – with some degree of success – to unite the two traditional behavioural models established by the first Doukhobor leaders in the 18th century: on the one hand, the leader who counselled compromise with government authority and, on the other, the leader who sought spiritual perfection regardless of the demands of reality. While unmistakably endowed with an exceptional sense of pragmatism, Verigin also unwittingly served as the catalyst for the sect's ultimate fragmentation.

A. A. DONSKOV

The archival sources on Peter Vasil'evich Verigin and the Doukhobor community are numerous and varied. Materials held by the State Museum of the History of Religion (St Petersburg, Russia), especially F.2, inv.7, files 491 and 951, were useful for Verigin's life in Russia and his return visits there. A description of this repository's most pertinent collections can be found in I. V. Tarasova, "Doukhobor materials in the collections of the Museum of Religious History in St. Petersburg," in *Spirit wrestlers: centennial papers in honour of Canada's Doukhobor heritage,* ed. K. J. Tarasoff and R. B. Klymasz (Hull, Que., 1995): 217–32. Significant information from the Russian secret police files is to be found in two publications compiled by John Woodsworth, *Russian archival documents on Canada; the Doukhobors, 1895–1943: annotated, cross-referenced and summarised* (2nd ed., Ottawa, 1997) [text in Russian and English] and *Russian roots and Canadian wings: Russian archival documents on the Doukhobor emigration to Canada,* trans. John Woodsworth ([Manotick, Ont.], 1999) [some text in Russian]. Manuscript and record groups at the LAC which contain important references to the Doukhobor immigration to Canada include the Sir Wilfrid Laurier papers (MG 26, G), John Campbell Hamilton-Gordon, 7th Earl of Aberdeen papers (MG 27, I, B5), James Mavor papers (MG 29, C16), and Sir Andrew Macphail papers (MG 30, D150), the Governor General's Office (RG 7), Department of Justice (RG 13), Parliament (RG 14), Department of the Interior (RG 15) (particularly the records of the dominion lands branch), Royal Canadian Mounted Police (RG 18), External Affairs (RG 25), Labour Canada (RG 27), and Immigration Branch (RG 76), including ships' passenger manifests (C1) as well as file 65101 in volumes 183–86. Additional Mavor papers are located at Univ. of Toronto Library, Thomas Fisher Rare Book Library (MS coll. 119). The most extensive and varied compilation of material concerning Verigin and the Doukhobors is the Doukhobor research coll. at the Univ. of B.C. Library, Rare Books and Special Coll. For many years librarian Jack McIntosh has collected material on the Doukhobors, especially concerning their years in Canada. See his "Update, 1973–1993: excerpts from the Doukhobor bibliography, expanded and updated edition" in *Spirit wrestlers* (*supra*): 187–216. A number of new materials have recently come to light, including the diary of Count Tolstoy's eldest son, published as *Sergej Tolstoy and the Doukhobors: a journey to Canada; a diary and correspondence,* ed. A. [A]. Donskov, comp. Tat'jana Nikiforova, trans. John Woodsworth (Ottawa, 1998) [text in English and Russian]. Much valuable information was obtained from the personal collection of prominent Doukhobor ethnographer Koozma J. Tarasoff (Ottawa). Information on land issues related to the sect

is available from the Saskatchewan Arch. Board (Saskatoon). Also noteworthy are the local materials held by the Selkirk College Library (Castlegar, B.C.), the Tarasoff photo coll. on Doukhobor hist. with an annotated user guide at the BCA, and the Doukhobor coll. at Simon Fraser Univ. Library, Special Coll. and Rare Books (Burnaby, B.C.). A comprehensive introduction to the portrayal of Doukhobors on the Internet may be found in the electronic publication *Canadian Doukhobors on the web: an annotated guide,* prepared by John Woodsworth for the Institute of Canadian Studies at the University of Ottawa.

The letters Verigin exchanged with Tolstoy were published as *Leo Tolstoy–Peter Verigin correspondence,* intro. Lidia Gromova-Opul'skaya, trans. John Woodsworth, ed. A. [A.] Donskov (New York and Ottawa, 1995) [text in Russian and English]. His only published work is *Pis'ma dukhoborcheskago rudovoditelia* [Letters of a Doukhobor leader], ed. V. D. Bonch-Bruevich, intro. V. G. and A. K. Chertkova (Christchurch, Eng., 1901) [text in Russian].

April Bumgardner, "The Doukhobors: history, ideology and the Tolstoy–Verigin relationship" (M.PHIL. thesis, Univ. of Glasgow, 2001). *The Doukhobor centenary in Canada: a multi-disciplinary perspective on their unity and diversity: proceedings of a conference held at the University of Ottawa, 22–24 October 1999,* ed. A. [A.] Donskov *et al.* (Ottawa, 2000). L. A. Ewashen, *Peter V. Verigin, 1859–1924: an appreciation* (Creston, B.C., 1988). S. A. Inikova, *History of the Doukhobors in the archives of Vladimir D. Bonch-Bruevich (1886–1950s): an annotated bibliography,* ed. K. J. Tarasoff (New York and Ottawa, 1999). James Mavor, *My windows on the street of the world* (2v., London and Toronto, 1923). E. H. Oliver, "Peter Verigin," RSC, *Trans.,* 3rd ser., 26 (1932), sect.II: 97–123. J. [A.] Sanborn, "Pacifist politics and peasant politics: Tolstoy and the Doukhobors, 1895–1899," *Canadian Ethnic Studies* (Calgary), 27 (1995), no.3: 52–71. K. J. Tarasoff, *Plakun trava* [Willow-herb]*: the Doukhobors* (Grand Forks, B.C., 1982). United Doukhobor Research Committee, *Report . . . in the matter of clarification of the motivating life concepts and the history of the Doukhobors in Canada . . . ,* comp. and trans. E. A. Popoff (Castlegar, 1997). George Woodcock and Ivan Avakumovic, *The Doukhobors* (Toronto, 1968; repr., Ottawa, 1977).

VERVILLE, ALPHONSE (baptized **Joseph-Alpha Varville**, on 20 Jan. 1930 he gained recognition from the Superior Court of Quebec for the name by which he had always been known), plumber, union leader, and politician; b. 28 Oct. 1864 in the Montreal parish of Notre-Dame-de-Grâce, son of Alfred Varville, a blacksmith, and Pamela Leduc; m. 1 Jan. 1884 Joséphine Mailhot of Saint-Norbert-d'Arthabaska, Que.; they had no children; d. 20 June 1930 in Montreal and was buried there in the cemetery of Le Repos Saint-François-d'Assise on 23 June.

Alphonse Verville attended the parish school in Sault-au-Récollet until he was apprenticed at the age of 14 to a plumber in Montreal. His apprenticeship completed, in 1883 he left for the United States, where he would spend the next ten years. He worked at a number of jobs, including that of foreman in various large workshops in Chicago. The experience he gained in plumbing and installing heating equipment would enable him to set up his own business upon his return to Montreal. Since he joined a union, he also had an opportunity to learn about the American trade union movement.

As soon as he came back in 1893, Verville became involved in the Montreal labour movement. At the end of the 19th century craft unions were growing rapidly in Canada, at the expense of the Knights of Labor and Canadian unions. Although they described themselves as international unions, most of them were North American. The International Association of Journeymen Plumbers, Steamfitters, and Gas Fitters had been active in Canada since 1888. Local 144 in Montreal was created on 22 Sept. 1898. Verville apparently was its founding president, and he remained in office until 1902. On being elected business agent for his union in 1900, he ceased working as a plumber to devote himself full-time to union organizing.

From 1900 Verville rose rapidly within the Quebec and Canadian union hierarchies. Elected to a term as vice-president of the Federated Trades and Labor Council of Montreal in 1900, he served as president from 15 Oct. 1903 until January 1905. Founded in 1897, the council – which officially became the Montreal Trades and Labor Council (MTLC) in 1903 – brought together craft union locals in the Montreal area. Its mandate was to defend the rights of union members at the municipal government level. At the time of Verville's election as the council's president, he held the positions of secretary-treasurer and business agent of the plumbers' union as well, and he was organizer for Canada on behalf of the International Association of Journeymen Plumbers, Steamfitters, and Gas Fitters.

In 1903 Verville was also elected vice-president of the Quebec provincial executive committee of the Trades and Labor Congress of Canada. Founded in 1883 by the Knights of Labor and the craft unions [see Charles March*], the TLC sought primarily to make the federal government aware of the problems of workers, so that it would enact laws favourable to them. On 23 Sept. 1904, at the annual convention of the TLC in Montreal, Verville was elected president. He would retain the office for five successive terms, but refused to stand for re-election at the convention held at Quebec in 1909. A wide variety of issues was dealt with during his presidency, the most significant being working-class political action, which was discussed at the important Victoria convention in 1906 and which would lead to the creation of an independent labour party; strengthening the TLC's stand against immigration; the nationalization of some public utilities, such as railways; and the demand for an eight-hour day for all workers.

Verville ardently supported craft unionism, which emphasized the organization of labour on the basis of the interests of a specific group of workers, namely, skilled tradesmen. Like others backing this strategy, he wanted to improve the material conditions of workers through collective bargaining, but within the capitalist system. To achieve this goal, the unionization of skilled tradesmen was fundamental, since they were the group that could attain the most favourable balance of power with employers. This approach to union activity, which Verville would champion throughout his career, ran counter to that of the Knights of Labor, which wanted, among other things, to organize the working class as a whole, not just skilled tradesmen. It would lead Verville to call for the expulsion of the Knights from the TLC at the convention held in Berlin (Kitchener), Ont., in 1902. In regard to labour relations, Verville promoted conciliation and harmony between capital and labour, with the state intervening as arbitrator in the event of disputes. Lastly, he advocated working-class political action, but of an independent kind, outside the framework of traditional political parties such as the Liberals and the Conservatives. On the other hand, to avoid rifts and dissension among union members, Verville declared his support for the creation of a labour party without official ties to organized labour. At the 1906 convention of the TLC, therefore, he opposed its socialist wing, which wanted workers to join the Socialist Party of Canada. After 1909 Verville continued to attend TLC conventions as a delegate from the plumbers' union. In 1915 he would even be elected to represent the TLC at the Trades Union Congress of Great Britain.

Although Verville favoured the unionization of a privileged group of workers, he also demanded social measures to help the population as a whole. Education was clearly one of his major concerns. When he appeared before the royal commission with respect to the Catholic schools of Montreal, appointed in 1909 by Premier Sir Lomer GOUIN, Verville called for the centralization of the Catholic school boards of the island of Montreal, standard free textbooks, the appointment of a worker to the Catholic Board of School Commissioners of Montreal, and free, compulsory education. A further sign of his interest in education was his acceptance of appointment as secretary-treasurer to the corporation of the Montreal Technical School in May 1912.

In Verville's view the most effective way to improve the working and living conditions of the working class was by lobbying public bodies, a task that could be carried out by trade union organizations such as the MTLC and the TLC, but more direct means, such as political action, could also be used. Hence, while serving as president of these two organizations, he decided to run in the provincial election of 25 Nov. 1904 as the Labour party candidate in Hochelaga. Disappointed with the policies of the Liberal governments of Félix-Gabriel Marchand* and Sir Wilfrid Laurier*, in whom workers had placed high hopes, a group of them from Montreal under the leadership of Joseph-Alphonse Rodier*, a union leader and labour columnist, had founded this party in 1899 to defend the interests of the working class. Taking its inspiration from the British Labour party, its program included measures that then seemed radical to some people: free and compulsory education, abolition of the property qualification for candidates in municipal elections, a law holding employers responsible for accidents in the workplace, and state sickness and old age insurance. Waging an effective campaign, Verville also attacked the trusts and called for the creation by the provincial government of a Quebec department of labour.

Supported by the union organizations of the city and by the newspaper *La Presse*, which called on the public to vote for the labour candidate, Verville benefited from the failure of the weakened Conservative party to field a candidate in the working-class riding of Hochelaga. He gave his Liberal opponent, Jérémie-Louis Décarie, a run for his money, polling 4,123 votes to Décarie's 5,462. Encouraged by this result, Verville returned to the fray in a federal by-election held in February 1906 in the riding of Maisonneuve following the sudden death of cabinet minister Raymond Préfontaine*. Opposing the Liberal candidate Louis-Ovide Grothé, a cigar manufacturer who had incurred the unionists' hatred, Verville won this largely working-class riding by a little more than 1,000 votes. He would be re-elected in Maisonneuve in 1908 and 1911 and Saint-Denis in 1917.

Verville's speeches in the House of Commons dealt mainly with issues related to the field of labour. Faithful to the TLC's program, he vigorously objected to immigration, arguing that the constant arrival of workers in urban centres created pressure to reduce wages. Satisfied with the Immigration Act enacted by the Liberal government in 1910, Verville stopped making speeches on this subject. In 1907 the Canadian parliament had passed the Industrial Disputes Investigation Act, which provided for compulsory conciliation in public utilities and in the mining sector. Although the TLC approved the legislation at its 1907 convention, even before the bill was passed Verville had stated in the house, "I am strongly in favour of that, because I have always advocated a closer connection between capital and labour, that is the only way in which we can avoid strikes." It was, however, on the question of shortening the working day for those employed in public works (then from nine to twelve hours long) that Verville concentrated most of his energy. He introduced his bill on the eight-hour day during the 1906–7 session, but it ended before the measure was given second reading. He renewed his attempt during the next two sessions, with no greater success. During the 1910–11 session the bill finally received third reading, but with substantial amend-

ments that weakened it. Believing that the general principle of his bill was respected, Verville endorsed the new version without consulting the leaders of the TLC, who criticized him severely for this action. The house passed it on 13 Feb. 1911, but ultimately it was rejected by the Senate. Verville's decision to support the amendments was not surprising in view of a statement he had made during the 1906–7 session, in the course of a debate on industrial disputes: "What I want is legislation. Give me bad legislation if you will, but give me legislation, for I would rather have bad legislation than no legislation at all; bad legislation we can amend, but if we have no legislation we cannot improve it." He presented his bill again in 1912 and 1914, under the Conservative government of Robert Laird Borden*, and withdrew it for good in 1914, since it had not reached second reading. During the conscription debate in the spring and summer of 1917, Verville stated that working people did not want conscription, and he predicted there would be a general strike in Canada if this measure was passed.

Despite the repeated promises he had made from the time of his 1904 electoral campaign to remain independent of the "old political parties," Verville soon realized that, as the only labour representative, he was isolated in Ottawa. Because the rigidity of the two-party political system left him little option but to align himself with an existing party, he chose to make common cause with Laurier's Liberals, finding their positions came closest to the interests he was defending. In Montreal labour circles his election had raised high expectations. There was soon criticism and after 1907 it became vicious. While some people were satisfied with what Verville had achieved in Ottawa, others thought he was acting "exactly like a Liberal MP" and was not upholding the Labour party program. To ensure that Verville would be re-elected in the 1908 federal election, Laurier asked his candidate, Victor Gaudet, to withdraw from the race. From then on the Liberal party never ran an accredited candidate against Verville. In 1911 the alliance became official: Verville campaigned in favour of Laurier's cherished policy of commercial reciprocity with the United States, on a Liberal-Labour ticket.

While holding his seat in Ottawa, Verville accepted an appointment to the Administrative Commission of the City of Montreal, which Premier Gouin had set up on 9 Feb. 1918, after the board of commissioners was abolished. The mandate of the five-member commission, which was headed by notary Ernest-Rémi Décary*, was to manage the overall municipal administration and put the city's finances in order. Restricting the powers of the mayor and city council, slashing expenses by dismissing a number of municipal bureaucrats, and increasing the city's powers of taxation, the commission soon became very unpopular with both citizens and elected officials. In view of this situation, the provincial government had to bring the commission's work to an end in 1921, a year before its term was up. Verville's appointment to the commission was not his first position in municipal affairs. In 1916 he had been named to the Montreal Tramways Commission, which was to draw up a new public transport contract between the Montreal Tramways Company and the city of Montreal. His work on the two commissions was sharply criticized by a number of labour activists. One of the criticisms was that he had not upheld the policy of nationalizing public utilities, which was strongly supported by the labour movement. Because of his political conduct, Verville eventually was expelled from the Quebec provincial section of the Canadian Labor Party at its meeting on 1 Dec. 1918.

It was not only the deliberations of the Administrative Commission of the City of Montreal that came to an end in 1921: so did Verville's political career. He chose not to run in the federal election of 6 Dec. 1921. After nine years in retirement, he died on 20 June 1930 in Montreal, at the age of 65, following stomach surgery.

On the whole, Alphonse Verville's political career seems not to have been an unqualified success. Isolated as the only labour MP in Ottawa, he soon joined the Liberal camp, partly because he needed the support of the party in power to get his eight-hour-day bill passed, and partly because the ideas he advanced were consonant with those of the Liberals. Verville's political path was similar to that of other Canadian trade unionists (such as Ralph Smith*, a miner from Nanaimo, B.C.) who were elected under the Labour party's banner early in the 20th century and who would also move to Laurier's Liberals. Disappointed in the position taken by Verville, who had not managed to reconcile working-class expectations with the demands of politics, a number of Labour party activists quit provincial and federal politics at the end of the 1910s in favour of a more active role on the municipal scene. Verville was not solely responsible for this shift. The many defeats suffered by labour candidates in provincial and federal elections, along with the striking victory of carpenter Joseph Ainey* at the board of commissioners of Montreal in 1910 and the abolition of the property qualification in 1912, encouraged this swing to municipal affairs.

ÉRIC LEROUX

ANQ-M, CE601-S6, 29 oct. 1864. *Labor World* (Montreal), 28 June 1930. *People's Voice* (Montreal), 23 Dec. 1905. *BCF*, 1922. Can., House of Commons, *Debates*, 1906–7. Geoffrey Ewen, "International unions and the workers' revolt in Quebec, 1914–1925" (PHD thesis, York Univ., North York [Toronto], 1998). Éric Leroux, "La carrière polyvalente de Gustave Francq, figure marquante du syndicalisme international au Québec (1871–1952)" (thèse de PHD, univ. de Montréal, 1999); "Les syndicats internationaux et la commission royale d'enquête sur l'éducation de 1909–1910," RCHTQ [Regroupement des Chercheurs-Chercheuses en Hist. des Travailleurs et Travailleuses du Québec], *Bull.* (Montréal), 23 (1977), no.1: 5–28. P. K. Malloy, "Alphonse Verville, 'Liberal-Labour' member of parliament, 1906–1914" (MA thesis, Univ. of Ottawa, 1970). Jacques Rouillard, "L'action politique ouvrière au début du 20e siècle," in *Le mouvement ouvrier au Québec*, sous la dir. de Fernand Harvey (Montréal, 1980), 185–213. Trades and Labor Congress of Canada, *Report of the proc. of the annual convention* ([Ottawa]), 16 (1900)–25 (1909).

VÉZINA, GEORGES (baptized **Joseph-Georges-Gonzague**), professional hockey player; b. 21 Jan. 1887 in Chicoutimi, Que., son of Georges Vézina, a baker, and Clara Belley; m. there 3 June 1908 Marie-Adélaïde-Stella Morin, and they had two sons; d. there 27 March 1926.

Georges Vézina studied at the Petit Séminaire de Chicoutimi from 1898 to 1902, leaving after the second year of the commercial course to help his father in his bakery. At the age of 16 he was taken on as goaltender by the Club de Hockey de Chicoutimi. He was familiar with the game, having played street hockey with his friends, but he had never worn skates. Vézina learned quickly. During the 1904–5 season, at an exhibition game between the Montreal Nationals of the Canadian Amateur Hockey League and the Chicoutimi club – a game Vézina's team won – the Nationals' goaltender, Joseph Cattarinich, was impressed by the 18-year-old in the opposing goal. At the end of the 1909–10 season, since he was giving up his position as goaltender for the Canadiens (a club formed in December 1909) to take on other duties with the team, he suggested that Vézina be contacted. To ensure that he would agree to come to Montreal, one of his brothers, who played forward, was also asked to come and practise with the Canadiens for the 1910–11 season. Georges stayed on; his brother went back to Chicoutimi. Hired in December 1910, at a salary of $800 per season (not an unusual figure, since most players received $1,000 or less in those years), he began a brilliant career with the Montreal Canadiens, in both the National Hockey Association of Canada (1911–17) and the National Hockey League (December 1917–25).

The Canadiens, who were known as the Club Athlétique Canadien from November 1910 to the end of the 1915–16 season, were not immediately successful but they continued to make progress, with Vézina invariably in the net. At the end of that season they were NHA champions, and they had to face the Portland Rosebuds of the Pacific Coast Hockey Association in the Stanley Cup playoffs. The Canadiens won them in five games. It would be the first of 24 Stanley Cup victories for the Montreal team up to 1998. One of Vézina's sons was born during the playoffs and he

Vézina

was named Marcel-Stanley in honour of the victory. The following year the Canadiens again won the NHA championship, but in the Stanley Cup playoffs they lost to the Seattle Metropolitans in four games. The same two teams met again in 1919; however, the play-offs could not be completed because many players had come down with Spanish influenza. Joseph Henry Hall, a defenceman for the Canadiens, succumbed to it on 5 April, as did the Canadiens' owner, George Kennedy [KENDALL], on 19 Oct. 1921. The Canadiens resumed their march to victory in 1924, when three teams were competing for the championship. The Canadiens had to play the Calgary Tigers, and then the Vancouver Maroons, to win the Stanley Cup.

The Canadiens began the 1925–26 season with a home game on 28 November against the Pittsburgh Pirates, a new NHL team. At the beginning of the second period, Vézina collapsed on the ice at the Mount Royal arena. He never returned to his team's net. At Chicoutimi, during the night of 26 March 1926, with his family gathered around him, he died of tuberculosis. He was 39 years old.

The most notable feature of Vézina's career was his stamina. From 1911 to 1925 he did not miss a single game for the Montreal Canadiens, and this at a time when teams had only one goaltender in uniform. He played, on average, 21 games during regular seasons, as well as all his team's exhibition games. In 1917 he even competed against the Canadiens in a friendly match to raise money for the war effort; he played on a soldiers' team in order to make the competition more even.

Until the 1920s hockey was played according to the rules of rugby, no forward passes being allowed. The slapshot was still unknown. The goaltender could not make all the moves permitted today. He was not allowed to fall onto the ice to stop the puck, or catch it in his hand, or simply immobilize it. All he could do was hold his stick in both hands and use his body and stick to stop the puck and make it bounce back out of the reach of opposing players. These rules explain why Vézina's career goals-against average – 3.49 – was so high. He was, in fact, one of the best goaltenders in the NHL. Nicknamed "the Chicoutimi Cucumber," he was famous for his composure in the net.

After Vézina's death, the Canadiens' owners, Léo Dandurand, Louis Létourneau, and Joseph Cattarinich, presented a trophy to the NHL in his honour, to be awarded each season to the best goaltender. It was given for the first time in 1927 to George Hainsworth, who had replaced Vézina in the net for the Canadiens. It was subsequently won by other Canadiens goaltenders, including William Ronald Durnan (six times) and Jacques Plante (seven times). Vézina was inducted into the Hockey Hall of Fame in 1945.

MICHEL VIGNEAULT

ANQ-SLSJ, CE201-S2, 22 janv. 1887. Soc. de Généalogie de Québec, Fichier Drouin, Saint-François-Xavier (Chicoutimi, Qué.), 3 juin 1908. *La Patrie*, 16 mars 1926. *La Presse*, 27, 30 mars 1926. *Le Progrès du Saguenay* (Chicoutimi), 30 mars 1926. Dan Diamond and Joseph Romain, *The Hockey Hall of Fame; the official history of the game and its greatest stars* (Toronto, 1988). D'Arcy Jenish, *The Stanley Cup: a hundred years of hockey at its best* (Toronto, 1992). Michael McKinley, *Hockey Hall of Fame legends: the official book* (Toronto, 1993). Charles Mayer, *L'épopée des Canadiens de Georges Vézina à Maurice Richard: 46 ans d'histoire, 1909–1955* (Montréal, 1956). Claude Mouton, *The Montreal Canadiens: an illustrated history of a hockey dynasty* (Toronto, 1987). Andy O'Brien, *Les Canadiens: the story of the Montreal Canadiens* (Montreal, 1972). Séminaire de Chicoutimi, *Annuaire*, 1898–1902. *Total hockey: the official encyclopedia of the National Hockey League*, ed. Dan Diamond et al. (New York, 1998).

VÉZINA, JOSEPH (baptized **François-Joseph**), bandmaster and conductor, professor, organist, and composer; b. 11 June 1849 at Quebec, son of François Vézina, a house painter, and Marie Petitclerc; m. there 24 Sept. 1872 Monique Tardiff, and they had four sons and three daughters; d. there 5 Oct. 1924 and was buried 8 October in Notre-Dame de Belmont cemetery at Sainte-Foy, Que.

Joseph Vézina was given some music lessons by his father, an amateur musician who taught him to play the baritone and the piano, as well as other instruments. He also received six months of instruction in harmony from Calixa Lavallée*. For the rest, Vézina was self-taught. In 1866, at the age of 17, he left the Petit Séminaire de Québec, where he had been a student since 1861, and signed on as a cabin boy on a boat that took him to Europe. During the voyage he felt so painfully homesick that he decided to spend the rest of his life in Quebec City as a professional musician, despite the inherent difficulties in pursuing such a career in the provincial capital.

It was Quebec City's various military ensembles that gave Vézina his first suitable opportunities. In 1866 he enrolled in the School of Military Instruction. The following year he joined the 9th Battalion Volunteer Militia Rifles, playing the baritone in the regimental band, and he would serve as its bandmaster from 1868 to 1879. Over the years he would lead a great many bands; in particular, he founded Notre-Dame de Beauport's in 1874 and those of Montmorency (Beauport) and Charlesbourg in 1875. In addition, he gave lessons in various wind instruments. With a very good ear, an unusual intuitive understanding of music, and a remarkable capacity for work, Vézina brought most of these ensembles to a high level of performance. In 1878, for example, the Notre-Dame de Beauport one took first prize in a competition held at the Victoria Skating Rink in Montreal in which musicians from all across Canada took part. In 1879 Vézina was appointed bandmaster of the Garrison Artillery's B Battery band (which in 1922 became that of the Royal 22nd Regiment). He gave up this position to lead the Saint-Jean-Baptiste de Québec cadet band in 1912.

It was in 1880, during celebrations on Saint-Jean-Baptiste day at the Pavillon des Patineurs in Quebec City, that Vézina conducted the first performance of "O Canada" (with words by Adolphe-Basile Routhier* and music by Calixa Lavallée), which a century later would be chosen officially as the country's national anthem. In the same year he was made a professor of music at the Petit Séminaire de Québec.

Vézina became a member of the Académie de Musique de Québec in 1887 and he would serve as its president in 1914–15. In this period his abilities reportedly were recognized by many leading musical figures of the day, including Carlo Alberto Cappa and Walter Damrosch, both of New York, who are believed to have urged him to move to the United States. But Vézina always refused to leave his native city. The following years were marked by important events. In 1894 and 1896 he conducted the concerts given at the winter carnival, among which the most important was undoubtedly the one held on 27 Jan. 1896 at the Quebec Drill Hall. At this time Vézina also conducted the ensembles that accompanied the famous singer Emma Albani [LAJEUNESSE], notably in her performances of *Casta diva* from Bellini's opera *Norma*, and the *Inflammatus* from Rossini's *Stabat mater*. He became organist for the parish of St Patrick in 1896, a post he would leave in 1912. On 16 Sept. 1901 Vézina conducted a gala concert on Dufferin Terrace on the occasion of a visit by the Duke and Duchess of Cornwall. In June 1902, again at the Quebec Drill Hall, he conducted three concerts held to celebrate the 50th anniversary of the founding of the Université Laval.

These concerts met with success and stirred up enthusiasm. Thus Vézina was invited by three young musicians – Louis-Léonidas Dumas, Joseph Talbot, and his own son, Raoul Vézina – to become the first music director of the Orchestre Symphonique de Québec, which was founded on 3 or 5 Oct. 1902. On 23 Feb. 1903 the orchestra hired some 15 new players, most of whom were professionals and members of either the regimental band or the Septuor Haydn. Known henceforth as the Société Symphonique de Québec – a name retained until 25 June 1942 – this orchestra is the oldest in Canada and it was still performing at the beginning of the 21st century. He quickly built it into an ensemble whose excellence gained national recognition. As early as 1907 the orchestra won first prize in the inaugural music and drama competition organized in Ottawa by Lord Grey*, the governor general of Canada. The judge on that occasion, George Whitefield Chadwick, who was one of the most distinguished composers in the United States and director of the New England Conservatory

of Music in Boston, declared that he was most favourably impressed by the quality of the Société Symphonique de Québec's playing. Critics from Ottawa and elsewhere were unanimously full of praise. The following year Vézina was president of the music committee for the city's tercentennial celebrations, and he conducted several major concerts given by the Société Symphonique de Québec in this connection.

In the course of his 22 years as music director, Vézina led his orchestra to outstanding progress. Until 1914, like the world's great professional ensembles, the Société Symphonique de Québec, which had some 60 musicians, presented subscription concerts; three were given each year in the Auditorium de Québec, a hall inaugurated by Vézina and his orchestra in 1903 that would later become the Théâtre Capitole. The Société Symphonique de Québec also performed at the annual meetings of the Société du Parler Français au Canada [see Stanislas-Alfred Lortie*], an association that lasted until 1946, as well as at many celebrations of a religious or social nature. The orchestra was, moreover, invited to perform in other parts of the country, notably in Ottawa, Montreal, Sherbrooke, and Montmagny.

In 1922 Vézina became one of the first full professors and one of the earliest doctors of music at the École de Musique of the Université Laval, which opened that year with Gustave GAGNON as director. But his teaching career there would be cut short by his death on 5 Oct. 1924. At the age of 75 he had still been a professor at the Petit Séminaire de Québec and conductor of the Société Symphonique de Québec.

Prior to 1900 Vézina had composed many works for military bands, wind ensembles, and symphony orchestras, pieces for various instruments including piano and flute, songs, and a few choral works. He also did a number of arrangements of other composers' works. In later years he would create the musical scores for three comic operas first performed by the Société Symphonique de Québec in 1906, 1910, and 1912 respectively: *Le lauréat* (libretto by Félix-Gabriel Marchand*), *Le rajah* (libretto by Gaston Morelles, pseudonym of Benjamin Michaud), and *Le fétiche* (libretto by Alex Villandray and Louis Fleur, pseudonyms of Alexandre Plante and Antonio Langlais). A fourth lyric work, *La grosse gerbe*, adapted from a poem by Pamphile Le May*, has remained unfinished.

Joseph Vézina was one of the principal forces behind the musical life in the provincial capital for more than half a century. An indefatigable worker, a first-rate organizer, and an exacting, versatile, and undeniably gifted musician, he remains a living presence through his most renowned achievement, the Orchestre Symphonique de Québec, which is now considered one of Canada's leading orchestras.

BERTRAND GUAY

Vigneau

There are documents pertaining to Joseph Vézina in several archival collections. The ANQ-Q holds the Fonds Joseph Vézina (P326) and the Fonds Orchestre symphonique de Québec (P519). The Fonds Joseph Vézina at the Conservatoire de Musique de Québec has manuscript copies of his works. At MCQ-FSQ, information about Vézina will be found in the Journal du séminaire (MS 34) and the Journal du conseil des plumitifs (MS 13) as well as in the series SME 9, which contains some of the subject's letters; also worth consulting is an unclassified musical fonds, which contains scores written by Joseph and his son Raoul.

ANQ-Q, CE301-S1, 4 août 1835, 12 juin 1849, 24 sept. 1872. *Le Devoir*, 6 oct. 1924. Nicole Brown, "Joseph Vézina (1849–1924), vie, œuvre et catalogue" (mémoire de MA, Conservatoire de Musique de Québec, 1994). Vivianne Émond, "'Musique et musiciens à Québec: souvenirs d'un amateur' de Nazaire LeVasseur (1848–1927): étude critique" (mémoire de M.MUS., univ. Laval, Québec, 1986). *Encyclopedia of music in Canada* (Kallmann *et al.*), 1366–67. Bertrand Guay, *Un siècle de symphonie à Québec: l'Orchestre symphonique de Québec, 1902–2002* (Québec, 2002). Odile Magnan, "La musique à Québec, 1908–1918: à travers *l'Action sociale* et *l'Action catholique*" (mémoire de MA, univ. Laval, 1980).

VIGNEAU, PLACIDE, fisherman, schooner captain, lighthouse-keeper, and author; b. 29 Aug. 1842 in Havre-aux-Maisons, Lower Canada, son of Vital Vigneau and Élise Boudreau; m. first 9 Jan. 1865 Louise Cormier in Pointe-aux-Esquimaux (Havre-Saint-Pierre), Lower Canada, and they had one child; m. there secondly 23 Nov. 1869 Victoire Doyle and they had seven children, three of whom reached adulthood; m. thirdly 27 June 1887 Suzanne Chevarie in Natashquan, Que., and they had one child; d. 1 March 1926 in Pointe-aux-Esquimaux.

Little is known about Placide Vigneau's childhood and adolescence, except that he developed his intellectual curiosity thanks to the teachers in his home town on the Îles de la Madeleine. Following in the footsteps of his father, who was of Acadian origin, he learned the trade of deep-sea fishing. In November 1858 his family and a few other people moved from the Îles de la Madeleine to the new village of Pointe-aux-Esquimaux on the north shore of the St Lawrence. A fisherman, labourer, and shipowner, Placide worked with the rest of his family to eke out a living. Aboard his father's schooner, he began as cabin-boy and keeper of the ship's log, and later became its captain. In the spring of 1880, after working on many different crews, he would become the owner of his own schooner, the *Phoenix*.

On arriving in Pointe-aux-Esquimaux, Placide began to keep a journal in which he set down details of everyday life and of the course of his fishing expeditions, in the hope that various events and discussions he had witnessed would not be forgotten. In 1862 he met Louis Ouellet, the first teacher in the village, who became his close friend. Ouellet encouraged him – as

did others – to persevere in his writing project. Throughout his life, Placide would gather masses of information, including songs, statistics, notes about his ancestors, and so on, and he would assemble a collection of books and objects, such as marine charts and artefacts retrieved from shipwrecks. Pierre-Étienne Fortin*, the stipendiary magistrate of fisheries, stopped regularly at Pointe-aux-Esquimaux. He too became a friend of Vigneau, who provided him with information for his annual reports, such as data about the seal, cod, and herring catches. Because of his intellectual abilities, Vigneau held a number of offices in the village: chief cantor at the church, secretary-treasurer of the school, and justice of the peace.

In the mid 1880s declining fish stocks led to such a food shortage that many families were forced to find new ways of earning their living. In the spring of 1892, after exploring numerous different possibilities, Vigneau became the keeper of the lighthouse on Île aux Perroquets, in the Mingan archipelago. This post had become open when the previous keeper, who had held it for only a few months, drowned. In 1912 Vigneau would, in turn, be succeeded by his son Hector. In addition to supervising the lighting mechanisms, his duties included maintaining the buildings and giving aid to sailors.

And so, as he approached the age of 50, Placide Vigneau embarked on a career that would give him more free time. Life on an island also provided the isolation that is sometimes necessary for a writer. Furthermore, Vigneau now began to enjoy relative financial security, with an annual salary of about $600 (from which he had to pay his assistant). While continuing to keep his journal, he wrote about an ever-widening range of subjects, including genealogy, folklore, natural medicines, and linguistics, and set down many accounts of events such as supernatural occurrences, shipwrecks, and visits from scientists. He telegraphed numerous dispatches of a practical nature to the *Family Herald and Weekly Star* in Montreal. By lending his manuscripts, he collaborated, along with Abbé Victor-Alphonse HUARD, Paul Hubert, Bishop Charles Guay, and other authors, in producing works on the history of the north shore of the St Lawrence, the Îles de la Madeleine, and Acadia. For those interested in the history of these regions or in maritime history, Vigneau's work is of immeasurable value.

GUY CÔTÉ

Placide Vigneau is the author of "Histoire ou journal de la Pointe aux Esquimaux," ANQ, *Rapport* ([Québec]), 1968: 5–294; "Les morses dans le golfe Saint-Laurent," *Le Naturaliste canadien* (Québec), 35 (1908): 140–42; *Un pied d'ancre; journal de Placide Vigneau . . .* (Sillery, Qué., 1969); and *Variétés de diverses farces et autres faits ridicules arrivés à la Pointe ou encore à des habitants de la Pointe,*

Guy Côté et Pierre Frenette, compil. ([Baie-Comeau, Qué.], 1996).

ANQ-BSLGIM, P11; ZQ1-S321, 2 oct. 1842. ANQ-CN, CE901-S3, 9 janv. 1865, 23 nov. 1869; CE901-S6, 27 juin 1887; P1; P19; P48; P53. Arch. du Séminaire de Chicoutimi (Chicoutimi, Qué.), C-11 (fonds de l'abbé V.-A. Huard), dossiers 328–31, 333. Antoine Bernard, "Placide Vigneau et la Côte Nord," *L'Évangéline* (Moncton, N.-B.), 29 sept. 1931. *Le Soleil*, 5 mars 1926. *Anthologie de textes littéraires acadiens*, Marguerite Maillet *et al.*, édit. (Moncton, 1979). Georges Arsenault, *Complaintes acadiennes de l'Île-du-Prince-Édouard* ([Montréal], 1980), 119, 123–24, 126–29. René Bélanger, *La Côte Nord dans la littérature; anthologie* (Québec, 1971), 71–75. Antoine Bernard, *Histoire de la survivance acadienne, 1755–1935* (Montréal, 1935), 5, 372–78; *La renaissance acadienne au XXᵉ siècle* (Québec, [1949]). "Capture d'un morse," *Le Naturaliste canadien*, 35: 49–51. Anselme Chiasson, *Les îles de la Madeleine: vie matérielle et sociale de l'en premier* ([Montréal], 1981); *Les légendes des îles de la Madeleine* (2ᵉ éd., Moncton, 1976). Gérard Gallienne, "Placide Vigneau," Soc. Canadienne de Généalogie, *Cahier spécial A* (Québec), janvier 1969: 3–24. Charles Guay, *Lettres sur l'île d'Anticosti à l'honorable Marc-Aurèle Plamondon, juge de la Cour supérieure, en retraite, à Artabaskaville* (Montréal, 1902), 131–40. V.-A. Huard, *Labrador et Anticosti: journal de voyage, histoire, topographie, pêcheurs canadiens et acadiens, indiens montagnais* (Montréal, 1897), 188–89, 253–54. Paul Hubert, *Les îles de la Madeleine et les Madelinots* (Rimouski, Qué., 1926), 11, 111–17, 132–33, 148–52. Chantal Naud, *Chronologie des îles de la Madeleine . . .* (L'Étang-du-Nord, Qué., 1993), 61–62. *La paroisse acadienne de Havre-Saint-Pierre célèbre, dans l'action de grâce, son premier siècle d'histoire, 1857–1957* (s.l., 1957). Carmen Roy, "Les Acadiens de la rive nord du fleuve Saint-Laurent," National Museum of Canada, *Contributions to Anthropology* (Ottawa), 1961–62, part.II: 155–98. Berchmans Scherrer, *Un peu d'histoire: Havre-Saint-Pierre* ([Gallix, Qué., 1996]).

VOGT, AUGUSTUS STEPHEN, organist, choral conductor, music educator, composer, and author; b. 14 Aug. 1861 in Washington, Upper Canada, son of John George Vogt and Marianna Zingg; m. 19 Aug. 1891 Georgia Adelaide McGill (d. 1 Nov. 1922) in Bowmanville, Ont., and they had a daughter and a son; d. 17 Sept. 1926 in Toronto.

Augustus S. Vogt's German father had come to Upper Canada to escape the revolutionary turmoil of 1848. His Swiss mother had immigrated with her parents in the 1830s. Vogt grew up in Elmira, Ont., in a household where the children followed their mother's Lutheranism. Their Roman Catholic father, a hotel-keeper, also built organs, including one locally for St James Lutheran Church, which appointed Augustus organist at age 12. After studying in Hamilton, in 1878 he became organist of First Methodist Church in St Thomas. He completed his musical training at the New England Conservatory of Music, Boston, in 1881–84 and at the Leipzig Conservatory in Germany in 1885–88, during which time the gifted youth composed a prelude and fugue for organ. On his return to

Toronto in 1888, he established himself as organist-choirmaster of the prestigious Jarvis Street Baptist Church, a position he would hold until 1906. His conversion to the Baptist faith may have caused a rift with his father. Active as secretary of a short-lived college of organists in 1889–92 and as a teacher of piano, organ, and theory at the Toronto College of Music [*see* Frederick Herbert Torrington*], in 1892 he secured a similar post at the Toronto Conservatory of Music (Royal Conservatory of Music). He would later be named a fellow of the Royal College of Organists.

Throughout his career, Vogt had to negotiate the politics of Toronto's musical scene. The conservatory tested its own students, and staff who sat as examiners received fees. In the late 1890s Vogt and others opposed the use in Canada of the examinations of the Associated Board of the Royal Academy of Music and the Royal College of Music in London, England. Such external testing was unnecessary, they argued, with much invective and national huffiness over this "traffic in certificates." In response to Vogt's insults, the board's local representative, Samuel Aitken, shot back in 1899 that if the conservatory were to have "sweated" Vogt for half his fees, "he might not now be putting up a new palatial residence in Bloor St." Furthermore, he found it amusing that exception to "foreign" examination should be taken "by a gentleman who spells his name V-O-G-T." Vogt, a self-described "native Canadian and a loyal subject," retorted that the board's president, the Prince of Wales, owned a family name (Saxe-Coburg-Gotha) "which is equally suggestive of such dainties as sauerkraut, limburger and lager." Despite this objection, board examination continued for several more decades.

When a student in Leipzig, Vogt had been a regular listener to the choral singing at the famed Thomaskirche. In Toronto, a stickler for rehearsal, he strove for excellence in the unaccompanied singing of his choir at Jarvis Street Baptist, a standard that enhanced his local reputation as a choral director. In 1894 he founded the Toronto Mendelssohn Choir (now the oldest mixed-voice choir in Canada), and through his work with it he would attract international acclaim. Its initial membership of 75 was drawn largely from his church choir and the repertoire was mostly sung a cappella. At the inaugural concert in the Massey Music Hall on 15 Jan. 1895, there were 167 choristers, of whom 106 were women, all of them unmarried. Among the long-time members was Vogt's wife, whom he had conducted in a choir before their marriage. Vogt broke up the Mendelssohn Choir in 1897 only to reinstate it, astutely, in 1900; under its new constitution it would disband annually and, to keep standards high, each chorister would audition anew. Vogt expanded its repertoire to include works with orchestra and he showcased these pieces in annual festivals, beginning in 1902. The choir collaborated with the Chicago and Pittsburgh orchestras, among others, and its tours in the United States were unprecedented for any Canadian musical organization. The Mendelssohn quickly gained critical acclaim. "Choral music is a branch of the art in which Canadians seem to excel," Vogt explained to the *Musical Times* (London). Ernest Alexander Campbell Mac-Millan* later noted in an appreciation that "the wonderful feeling for musical colour which never failed to appear in Vogt's performances, was compounded of an exceptional sense of rhythm and an almost uncanny sensitiveness to vocal tone."

After a year's trip to Europe, in 1913 Vogt succeeded Edward Fisher* as musical director of the Toronto Conservatory, then situated on College Street. He resigned from the Mendelssohn Choir in 1917 owing to the exigencies of his new duties. As meticulous and visionary in administration as he was in conducting, he enlarged the student base and the number of local centres across Canada for the graded examinations of the conservatory. Vogt himself went west as an examiner until 1921. In 1914 a resident program in performance was introduced. Among the accomplished staff attracted by Vogt was James Healey Willan*, first as head of theory and then as vice-principal. Aided by Sir Byron Edmund WALKER, who chaired the boards of both the conservatory and the University of Toronto, which awarded Vogt a D.MUS. in 1906 – an honour Vogt cherished – he forged a strong liaison with the university, becoming first dean of its faculty of music in 1918 in addition to being principal of the conservatory. Under his tenure, the conservatory became part of the university through provincial legislation in 1919, and in 1924, with university approval, it took over another recognized local school, the Canadian Academy of Music.

Beyond his work as a conductor and administrator, Vogt wrote articles for Edwin Rodie PARKHURST'S *Musical Canada* (Toronto) and for *Musical Life and Arts* (Winnipeg). He was a music critic for *Saturday Night* (Toronto) in the 1890s under the name of Moderato, and he contributed other pieces and letters in 1891, 1912–13, and 1922. His choral compositions included *An Indian lullaby* for women's voices and *Crossing the bar* in 1906 and *The sea* in 1911, and he prepared arrangements of *The Lord's Prayer* and *Rule Britannia*. He is best known for his *Modern pianoforte technique* (Toronto, 1900), his widely used *Standard anthem book* (2v., Toronto, 1894–*c*. 1909), and, with Willan, *School and community song book* (Toronto, 1922).

In 1918 Vogt began suffering from heart problems. Four years later his wife died of breast and liver cancer. He nevertheless carried on with his demanding dual position, but, he told his daughter in August 1926, "the almost deadly nature of my job about kills me." The next month, while suffering from influenza, he died of a heart attack. In 1929 a memorial window commissioned by the Mendelssohn Choir was placed in St Paul's Anglican Church in Toronto, where he had been a member for many years.

GAYNOR G. JONES

AO, RG 22-305, no.55454; RG 80-5-0-188, no.8478; RG 80-8-0-858, no.6219; RG 80-8-0-1018, no.6042. Univ. of Toronto, Faculty of Music, Rare Books and Special Coll., MUS, MSS pam 004 (Vogt papers). UTA, A1973-0026/487(64). *Canadian Statesman* (Bowmanville, Ont.), 19, 26 Aug. 1891. *Globe*, 18 Sept. 1926. *Toronto Daily Star*, 18 Sept. 1926. *An account of the Canadian protest against the introduction into Canada of musical examinations by outside musical examining bodies*, ed. Canadian Protesting Committee (Toronto, 1899). Samuel Aitken, *The case of the Associated Board* ([n.p., 1899?]). *Canadian men and women of the time* (Morgan; 1898 and 1912). *Canadian who's who*, 1910. *Dominion Musical Journal* (Toronto), new ser., 1 (1891–92): 19, 25. *Encyclopedia of music in Canada* (Kallmann et al.), 1378–79. G. G. Jones, "'Exam wars' and the Toronto territorial connection," *Canadian Univ. Music Rev.* (Toronto), 11 (1991), no.2: 51–67. *National encyclopedia of Canadian biography*, ed. J. E. Middleton and W. S. Downs (2v., Toronto, 1935–37). *Saturday Night*, 1891–1926. *Standard dict. of Canadian biog.*(Roberts and Tunnell), vol.1. *Who's who in Canada*, 1925/26.

W

WADE, FREDERICK COATE, newspaper editor, lawyer, office holder, and agent general for British Columbia; b. 26 Feb. 1860 in Bowmanville, Upper Canada, second son of William Wade, a bank clerk, and Harriet Coate; m. 1 Sept. 1886, in Toronto, Edith Mabel Read (d. 1932), daughter of David Breakenridge Read*, and they had a son and a daughter; d. 9 Nov. 1924 in London, England.

A man of keen intellect and brash outspokenness, Frederick Wade received his early education in the public schools of Ottawa and Owen Sound, Ont. In 1879 he entered the BA program at the University of Toronto and he graduated in 1882. While there, he became an editor of the *Varsity*, the student journal. A strong Liberal, he also obtained an editorial position with the party's organ, the *Globe*. In 1883 he began legal studies with David Breakenridge Read. Later that year he moved to Winnipeg and continued his studies, probably with his uncle Charles Rann Wilkes, a lawyer in the city. In February 1884 Wade became a founding member of the Winnipeg Legal Club, which promoted the study of law, public speaking, and essay writing. In 1886 he was made the first president of the Young Liberal Association of Winnipeg, an office to which he was re-elected the following year.

Although Wade had been called to the Manitoba bar in 1886, he did not immediately practise; he became an editorial writer for William Fisher Luxton*'s *Manitoba Free Press*. Wade's first editorial, "The bell wether," depicted the supporters of the Conservative government of John Norquay* as sheep "who did not understand what legislation was about and cared less." The vigorous writings of Wade and Luxton did much to ensure the defeat of the Norquay government in late December 1887 and the arrival of a Liberal administration under Thomas Greenway* in mid January 1888.

Sometime earlier in 1887 Wade had left the *Free Press* to practise law with Wilkes. In one of his first cases he represented the United States in the inquiry into the compensation claims made by trader Jean-Louis Légaré* for provisions he had furnished to the Dakota under Sitting Bull [Ta-tanka I-yotank*]. The following year he joined Archer Evans Stringer Martin* to form Wade and Martin. From 1891 to 1894 he practised with Anson Whealler. In addition, he found time to prepare *The revised statutes of Manitoba, 1891* (Winnipeg, 1892).

Wade devoted much time to developing English-language public education in Manitoba; in 1889 he had served on the Board of Education of Manitoba, the council of the University of Manitoba, and the Winnipeg School Board. With Attorney General Joseph MARTIN, he was a strong defender of the provincial Liberal government's policy in the Manitoba school question [*see* Greenway]. He wrote two pamphlets, *National schools for Manitoba* (Winnipeg, 1892) and *The Manitoba school question* (Winnipeg, 1895), in support of the government's position. In February 1897 he was appointed the commissioner to investigate charges laid against officers of the Stony Mountain Penitentiary. His obituary in the *Province* would claim that his report, dated 1 Sept. 1897, led to "considerable improvement" in conditions there.

On 26 Aug. 1897, in anticipation of the establishment of the Yukon Territory, Wade was nominated registrar of lands by the federal government. He arrived in Dawson in March 1898 and soon became disappointed with the administration of the territory. In a letter to Clifford SIFTON, minister of the interior, he criticized the actions of various government officials. His own conduct as registrar was controversial. In the House of Commons opposition member Sir

Charles Hibbert TUPPER charged that Wade had enriched himself by imposing extra fees for the registration of lands and gold claims. On 7 July 1898 he was dismissed as registrar and appointed legal adviser to the Yukon Council. The following February he was made crown prosecutor. An able lawyer, he handled cases speedily and effectively. After his arrival in Dawson, he had established a private practice with Orange H. Clark and Herbert G. Wilson that was dissolved in May 1899. Wade then formed a partnership with James Allan Aikman and later one with Frederick Tennyson Congdon* that lasted until 1903. In private practice he again found himself in controversy. In 1899 he was severely criticized by local officials when he served as defence counsel for several mining firms that were being prosecuted by him as crown prosecutor. The federal administration responded with an order in council forbidding government officials to engage in private practice.

Wade left the Yukon in July 1901 and travelled abroad for several months. On 23 April 1902 he was appointed a KC. Later that year he became a member of the National Liberal Club of London, England. In early 1903 he was chosen to serve as one of the counsel for the British side in the Alaska boundary dispute [*see* Sir Wilfrid Laurier*]. He spent six months in England working on the case. Although the final decision of the Alaska Boundary Tribunal did not favour Canada, Sifton, who had been appointed British agent to draw up and present the Canadian position, praised his skilful preparation of the case. After moving to Vancouver in the summer of 1904, Wade formed a law partnership with Ernest John Deacon and William Stearne Deacon. In 1909 he established a firm with Whealler, his former partner, and William Garland McQuarrie, which would be known as Wade, Whealler, McQuarrie, and Martin when George Edgar Martin joined in 1911.

In the provincial election of 1909 Wade had been an unsuccessful Liberal candidate for Vancouver City. He dissolved his law partnership in 1912 and became one of the founders of the *Vancouver Sun*, which soon claimed to be "the official organ of the Liberal Party." As its editor and president of its publishing company, he led one of the most effective opposition newspapers in the province during the Conservative regime of Sir Richard McBride* and was noted for his unswerving support of the Liberal party.

In August 1918 Wade was appointed to succeed John Herbert TURNER as agent general of British Columbia in London, England. On his arrival, one of his first actions was to provide beds in British Columbia House for Canadian soldiers on leave. An effective advocate for British Columbia and Canada, he held the position until he died in London from "muscular rheumatism" in 1924.

Frederick Coate Wade believed that one of his most

important accomplishments had been the establishment in 1906 of a fund for the erection of a monument to Major-General James Wolfe* in Greenwich Park (London). The statue would be unveiled in 1930. He had been a competent but controversial journalist, lawyer, and civil servant, whose skills had been best displayed in the case before the Alaska Boundary Tribunal and perhaps worst employed during the Manitoba school question.

BRAD R. MORRISON and
CHRISTOPHER J. P. HANNA

[The authors would like to thank Ronald Greene for his assistance. In addition to the works mentioned in the text, Frederick Coate Wade was the author of numerous pamphlets, some of which originated as lengthy letters to newspapers. A list of these publications can be found in CIHM, *Reg*. B.R.M. and C.J.P.H.]

AO, RG 80-5-0-147, no.14161. BCA, GR-1415, file 10216; GR-2951, no.1932-09-470476; VF155, frames 3013–29. City of Vancouver Arch., Add. MSS 44 (Wade family fonds). LAC, MG 26, G. *Daily Colonist* (Victoria), 14–15 Aug. 1918; 11, 14 Nov. 1924; 6 Aug. 1967 (*Islander Magazine*). *Daily Klondike Nugget* (Dawson, Y.T.), 15 July, 7 Oct., 11 Dec. 1901. *Dawson Daily News* (Dawson), 17 Oct. 1899–22 June 1901. *Klondike Nugget* (Dawson), 27 July 1898; 3 May, 3 June 1899. *Manitoba Free Press*, 12 Feb. 1885, 19 April 1898, 26 June 1909. *Vancouver Daily Province*, 12 April, 13 Aug. 1902; 16–17 June, 17 Sept. 1909; 14 Aug. 1918; 11 Nov. 1924; 20 May 1932; 15 Dec. 1934. *Vancouver Sun*, 14 Aug. 1918, 11 Nov. 1924, 4 March 1958. *Victoria Daily Times*, 10 Jan. 1903, 14 Aug. 1918, 10 Nov. 1924, 2 April 1929. Can., Commission to investigate, inquire into and report upon charges preferred against certain officers and guards connected with the Stony Mountain Penitentiary, *Report* ([Winnipeg?], 1897). *Canada Gazette*, 4 Sept. 1897, 8 May 1902. *Canadian annual rev.*, 1910, 1912. *The Canadian law list* (Toronto), 1906–13. *Canadian men and women of the time* (Morgan; 1912). *Directories*, B.C., 1905; Manitoba, 1888, 1890–91, 1894; Ottawa, 1866, 1870–71; Toronto, 1883; Vancouver, 1908–10, 1912; Winnipeg, 1883–84. D. J. Hall, *Clifford Sifton* (2v., Vancouver and London, 1981–85). D. R. Morrison, *The politics of the Yukon Territory, 1898–1909* (Toronto, 1968). *Newspaper reference book*. C. [L.] Porsild, *Gamblers and dreamers: women, men, and community in the Klondike* (Vancouver, 1998). Jim Wallace, *Forty Mile to Bonanza: the North-West Mounted Police in the Klondike gold rush* (Calgary, 2000). *Who's who in western Canada* ... (Vancouver), 1911. Winnipeg Legal Club, *Constitution* ... (Winnipeg, [1884?]).

WALKER, Sir BYRON EDMUND, banker, philanthropist, and patron of the arts; b. 14 Oct. 1848 near Caledonia, Upper Canada, son of Alfred Edmund Walker and Fanny Murton; m. 5 Nov. 1874 Mary Alexander (d. 1923) in Hamilton, Ont., and they had four sons and three daughters; d. 27 March 1924 in Toronto.

Byron Edmund Walker, born in "the back woods" a half-day's journey south of Hamilton, became a Canadian Medici and one of the most eminent personalities of his generation. He was the eldest son of an unremarkable family, the second of seven children. He claimed to owe his father "whatever qualities I may possess." Alfred Walker was the son of middle-class English immigrants who had settled in the Grand River region in the 1830s. Indifferent health made him unsuited to rural life, and in 1852 he, his wife, and their children moved to Hamilton. A clerk, he never distinguished himself in business but he became a noted amateur geologist and palaeontologist. To his son he transmitted his passion for natural history. "I was taught to appreciate that the truth regarding nature was the divine thing," Walker recalled in 1918, "and that we must learn it so far as it is possible." There was nothing unusual about their interest in fossils; collecting had become a popular pastime in Victorian Canada. What set young Byron apart was his desire to understand how his discoveries explained the world around him. A lack of formal education never impeded him. He was a dedicated autodidact and his inherited spirit of inquiry led him to master a broad array of subjects. Combined with his organizational acumen, ability to influence, and access to powerful individuals, Walker's talents served to develop more aspects of Canadian life than those of any of his contemporaries.

It is principally his contribution to commercial life, however, that remains known. One biographer claims that Walker derived his business skills from his mother. Fanny Murton's parents were also English immigrants of the 1830s, her father, according to Walker's sister Edith, "a gentleman farmer" who had studied law and her mother an educator who "spoke French and Italian fluently, and was the only woman west of Toronto who could play the harpsichord." Mrs Murton ran a private school in Hamilton, and it was there that four-year-old Byron began his schooling. He continued at the Central School, finished after grade 6, and at age 12 prepared to enter teachers' college in Toronto. But doctor's orders prevented him: "I had better run about, and get a little flesh on my bones" was how Walker remembered the directive. Instead, the boy went to work in August 1861 at the exchange office of his uncle John Walter Murton. The previous winter and spring 11 American states had seceded from the Union. Bonds and paper money issued by the United States government as war measures complicated the already complex North American currency situation. Walker's duties included the authentication of coins and notes. Pieces of eight, greenbacks, English silver, and the notes of dozens of failed banks: he handled them all. In 1868 he moved to Montreal to run an exchange firm there, but feeble health (which would plague him for another 20 years) forced him back to Hamilton a few months later to work in the local branch of the recently formed Canadian Bank of Commerce.

The bank had been established in 1867 by Irish-born

merchant William McMaster* and a consortium of Toronto businessmen in reaction to the growing dominance of the Bank of Montreal [see Edwin Henry King*]. Farmers and businessmen in the province needed greater access to credit, and branches of the Commerce were opened in a number of towns. Walker became a discount clerk in Hamilton. An evaluation from 1869 characterizes him as "an invaluable officer, competent in every respect." He rose through the ranks swiftly, becoming chief accountant in Toronto in 1872 and junior agent in New York in 1873. Business failures were commonplace during the depressed 1870s, and Walker appears to have been especially skilled at helping his bank minimize its losses. In 1875 he was sent to Windsor, Ont., to disentangle the Commerce from several sour lumber investments. Later he served as manager at the London (1878–79) and Hamilton (1880–81) branches. As inspector at the head office in Toronto from 1879 to 1880, he introduced the use of telegraphy in multiple-branch banking and implemented printed regulations and operating procedures. Subsequently he reorganized the bank into discrete departments, a measure which anticipated modern business practice.

Also during his Toronto stint Walker produced for McMaster (now a senator) and federal opposition leader Edward Blake* a report on how Canadian banking differed from the American system. The government was in the process of reforming the Bank Act of 1871 after a spate of financial woes. A number of banks had failed during the 1870s and critics began to advocate the United States model of more numerous but smaller local banks (though these were frequently undercapitalized) and centralized control of note circulation. Drawing on his New York experience and his training in an exchange office, Walker compared the two systems and favoured Canadian practices. "We have a system which, while it can be improved in some of its details, is fundamentally sound: our bank issues, owing to the strength and peculiar organization of our Banks, pass at par everywhere in the Dominion . . . and the notes are, from the small number of Banks, well known to the most ignorant of tradesmen, mechanics or agriculturists. No practical fault can be found with our Bank-issue as a circulating medium; . . . if it lacks anything in uniform it possesses a much more important virtue in being elastic." Owing to the structure of Canadian finance, banks were less likely to fail and both borrowers and depositors could be served more securely and conveniently. Partly on the strength of Walker's report, finance minister Sir Samuel Leonard Tilley* proposed a new general bank act in 1880 which effected only minor changes. The system that had evolved since before confederation remained intact, although decennial revisions of the act meant that the chartered banks regularly had, in Walker's words, "to fight for our existence."

His peregrinations continued. In 1881 he began a five-year sojourn in New York, conducting the Commerce's growing role as a foreign-exchange bank. Walker returned to Toronto in autumn 1886 to become general manager. The previous two years are described in the firm's official history as "possibly the most difficult" for the bank. It had suffered through customers' failures in land and timber operations. General manager Walter Nichol Anderson had resigned and Walker was appointed to turn around the company's fortunes. His first task was a thorough re-evaluation of the bank's assets and operations. Several changes were necessary, most significantly an adjustment to its deposits-to-capital ratio. The Commerce's dividends improved markedly as a result, and within ten years Walker had made it the most profitable financial institution in Ontario. Much of this success was due to the program of weekly reports that he implemented in 1889. All branches were required to file a "gossip sheet," which Walker and his staff used in devising the bank's plans and objectives. A distillation of these reports was delivered each year in Walker's address to shareholders. For 35 years financiers and economists in Canada and the United States would benefit from his annual review of the nation's financial and industrial "pulse." It was also during his tenure as general manager that the Commerce began to expand its operations westward with branches in Winnipeg, Vancouver, and Dawson, Y.T., for example, and to build up a presence in the Maritimes.

In January 1907 Walker became president of the bank, succeeding Senator George Albertus Cox*. He would hold the office until his death in 1924, although after 1915 he was no longer chief executive officer. His years were ones of tremendous growth: the company's total assets were $22,000,000 in 1886; by 1915, when John Aird* took the helm, they had increased more than tenfold, as had the number of branches. Walker transformed the bank into a modern corporation with such innovations as a realty company to manage the Commerce's buildings, a pension fund for retired employees, and a bank archives. After 1915 he continued "to dispense optimism and sober reproof," guiding junior officers with wisdom earned in nearly a half-century in the bank's service.

Walker's high position brought him directly into the exclusive circles of Canadian capitalism. These were interconnected groups of entrepreneurs, bankers, and lawyers who to a great extent had succeeded in concentrating control of the nation's financial resources. One such group involved railway promoters William MACKENZIE and Donald Mann*. Their dream of a northern route to the burgeoning west took them several times to the brink of bankruptcy. Walker was their banker, and he continued to extend credit to them despite worries, widespread among politicians and journalists, that the Canadian Northern's recklessness would bring it and the Commerce crashing down. His fidelity to the Northern rested on three things: Mackenzie's friendship, optimism about the potential for profit in the west, and belief in the rightful role of private enterprise to develop Canada clear of government interference. Mackenzie and Mann typified the businessman as nation-builder, and Walker, sharing their vision, gave the bank's unswerving support, as he did with a variety of other development and utilities schemes at home and abroad.

His reputation in business owed as much to his activities apart from the Commerce. He led the bankers' section of the Toronto Board of Trade and was instrumental in founding the Canadian Bankers' Association in 1891 (he would be elected president in 1893 and 1894). His involvement was motivated by his belief that public discourse was too much influenced by journalists who had no expertise in economics. When bank charters were up for renewal in 1890, the newspapers had pressured finance minister George Eulas Foster* to overhaul the current legislation by introducing American-style fixed reserves, a measure favoured as well by Foster's deputy minister, John Mortimer Courtney*, and by imposing a higher degree of state control over inflation. But Canada's laissez-faire bankers were hesitant to relinquish any of their privileges. Acting in concert under the leadership of Walker, Edward Seaborne Clouston* (Bank of Montreal), Thomas Fyshe* (Bank of Nova Scotia), and George Hague (Merchants' Bank of Canada), they were able to preserve their relative independence.

Walker tended to couch his rhetoric in terms of service and development. The branch system, with its handful of chartered banks present from coast to coast, promoted unity and nation-building. Rather than acting out "a compromise between the necessities of the government, arising from war or extravagance, and the commercial requirements of the nation," Canadian bank policy was the result of a "happier condition where the law-maker and the banker have been mainly concerned to give the people the best instrument in aid of commerce that they could devise." The Canadian model had served the country relatively well, and was constantly perfecting itself. For as long as Walker remained involved, the banks maintained most of their rights. Where reforms were introduced – for example, the creation of a bank circulation redemption fund, whereby each bank was obliged to deposit with the government an amount equal to five per cent of its average circulation – they were often prompted by his proposals. Only under the strain of war did the state stray from his advice. The Finance Act of 1914 moved Canadian banking away from its laissez-faire origins, a measure which in some ways prefigured the creation of a central bank in 1935.

Walker also enjoyed an international reputation as a banker. "No name is better known among the banking fraternity than yours," an American colleague told him. In 1913 he was asked to testify before the United States House of Representatives committee on banking, and he frequently addressed foreign audiences on such matters as "Why Canada is against bimetallism," "Banking as a public service," "The relations of banking to business enterprise," and "Abnormal features of American banking." His knowledge of bank history and his economic theories were promulgated in numerous pamphlets and books, among them *A history of banking in Canada*. Known as "the pope of the banking system," Walker often pontificated in defence of financial institutions. "It is the fashion of certain demagogues to speak of bankers and of insurance men as non-producers," he told the International Convention of Life Underwriters in 1918, "but not even the powers of steam and electricity have done more for industry than credit and insurance." Credit did more than pave the way to material prosperity; it was an engine of social uplift.

For his many services to Canada, in 1908 Walker had been made a CVO. Two years later King George V knighted him. Although he had been quiet about his politics – "the interests of the Bank are so extensive that I have found it expedient to keep out of politics," he explained – he had long been a Liberal. In 1911, however, his political aloofness came to an end. The issue was reciprocity, free trade in natural products between Canada and the United States. Canada had prospered under the National Policy of high tariffs on manufactured goods, a creature of Sir John A. Macdonald*'s Conservative government. The Liberal opposition favoured unrestricted reciprocity, but by the time its leader, Wilfrid Laurier*, came to power in 1896, the political and economic usefulness of protectionism had been realized. The Liberal government nevertheless chose to gamble on a policy of free trade in agricultural products, and in January 1911 announced the terms of the Taft–Fielding agreement [see William Stevens FIELDING]. Within a month Canadian businessmen had emerged squarely against the deal: free trade in some products now, they argued, meant unrestricted reciprocity later, a break with the British empire, and eventually annexation.

It was in fact the business community, not the ineffectual Conservative opposition, that led the campaign against Laurier. The most highly organized and nationally prominent anti-reciprocity force was the "Toronto Eighteen," headed by Walker. Described by one historian as "an inter-locking structure of banking, transportation, insurance, manufacturing and other related interests," they unleashed, in the words of another, "a firestorm of anti-American sentiment." They helped create such propaganda bodies as the Canadian National League and the Canadian Home Market Association, published anti-free trade tracts, cartoons, and advertisements, and blanketed the nation with pamphlets publicizing their position. In the general election of September 1911 voters defeated the Liberal government. Walker had been invited by Robert Laird Borden*, leader of the opposition, to run as a Conservative but had declined. However, he advised the new prime minister on a variety of issues during his term. Laurier likely never forgave him. A Toronto newspaper was surprised to find the two seated side by side at a University of Toronto gathering in 1914. The banker quipped, "Well, if Sir Wilfrid does not object I see no reason why I should."

Walker's opposition to reciprocity stemmed from his views on how best to develop Canada's economic position. This small nation could either continue to prosper as a dominion within the empire, he believed, or disappear into the United States. He never liked the way the American economy had taken shape. For example, he denounced the overthrow of founding father Alexander Hamilton's financial system, which he considered sane and intelligent. He also disparaged America's "gross materialism" and tendency to waste. His anti-free trade protest was, therefore, based on "much more than a trade question. . . . The question is between British connection and what has been well called Continentalism." The extent of his anti-Americanism, however, is open to argument. He would tell Canadian audiences they should "save and increase such good qualities as tend to differentiate us from the United States," among them a disdain for "extreme democracy" and suspicion of industrial oligarchy and "machine politics." On the other hand, he told Americans that, while he disliked some features of their country, he greatly admired others. He simply valued Canada's ties to Britain much more and did not think they could be maintained if America's influence grew too strong. Walker was an imperialist, with James MAVOR, Edward Joseph Kylie*, and George MacKinnon Wrong* a member of the Round Table movement, and a believer in the empire as "the greatest political and social enterprise in the history of the world."

It has been suggested that Walker's fight against reciprocity was in part motivated by anti-immigrant sentiment. He was not a hateful man, no more so than any of his contemporaries. He was "proud to feel that Canada was a place where every color and every kind could have an opportunity," but objected to immigrants' seeming hesitance to integrate with British Canadian society. He blamed agricultural settlers in the west for Laurier's departure from protectionism. Immigration itself was not a menace; in fact, Walker understood it to be the catalyst to the economic boom of the century's first decade. Yet he was concerned that Canada had taken in more foreigners than it could absorb. Without proper measures, they could threaten law and order, and indeed seemed to be weakening the imperial tie.

Walker frequently spoke of particular "Canadian

ambitions" and felt that these should be inculcated in newcomers. The alternative was to become too much like the materialistic, polyglot, and potentially unstable United States. "No great nation," he remarked in 1907, "was ever built up solely on the basis of material prosperity," and he insisted that Canadians strive for something greater. This ideal could be attained by cultivating proper tastes and sensibilities and would be aided principally by two things: higher education and the fine arts. To these ends, Walker promoted a wide array of institutions, first among them schools "where the duties of citizenship and the ethical aspects of life are taught in the fullest manner." He was a Toronto Board of Education trustee in 1904, and in 1911 founded the Appleby School in Oakville, Ont.

The University of Toronto benefited most from his efforts. After his return from New York to stay, his family had acquired Long Garth, a large home literally in the university's backyard. In 1890 fire destroyed a good part of the main college building. In addition to witnessing the blaze, Walker was asked by President Sir Daniel Wilson* to head the campaign to raise funds for restoration. His bank donated $1,000 and many local and national businesses followed the example. Subsequently Chancellor Edward Blake asked him to supervise the university's financial situation, and later he worked with Joseph Wesley Flavelle* on the royal commission on the University of Toronto (1905–6), which suggested major changes to funding and management. Shortly before it federated with the university in 1904, Trinity College had made him an honorary DCL and in 1905 the university itself granted him an honorary LLD. He served the university as a trustee (1891–1906), senator (1893–1901), governor (1906–23), and chairman of the board of governors (1910–23), and assumed the office of chancellor upon Sir William Ralph MEREDITH's death in 1923. Walker considered the university to be "the most important institution in Canada apart from the Government itself." In 1918 the minister of education, Henry John Cody*, elaborated on Walker's views: "He believed in the value and power of education in the whole life of the Province and Dominion. Education is at once the key to efficiency and the safeguard of democracy. . . . The universities . . . can render an incalculable service both to the higher life of our people and to the commercial and manufacturing interests of the country."

Among its many recommendations the Flavelle report had proposed a museum for the university. Walker had been advocating such an institution since 1888 when he approached the premier, Oliver Mowat*. He believed that museums afforded the public an opportunity to appreciate the country and the world around them. They would be "shop windows" in which newcomers and Canadians of long standing could understand, at a single glance, the nation's potential. But only in 1909 did the government consent to funding, and not before Walker and Edmund Boyd OSLER had independently raised some money to establish the Royal Ontario Museum. Five years before, Walker had donated his library and his collection of fossils to set the organization in motion.

During their New York years, Walker and his wife had had a rich social life, complete with visits to museums, concert halls, and libraries where they cultivated a love of literature. Their return to Toronto in 1886, therefore, came as a disappointment. The Queen City was growing but it had none of the cultural life of other centres. Nonetheless, its artists and business class aspired to such development. What mainly lacked was leadership. Walker was able to provide the missing element and was unmatched in the range of his accomplishments. For example, local artists had for many years sought an art museum. Painter George Agnew Reid*, president of the Ontario Society of Artists, had been unable to establish a permanent one, but in 1900 Walker joined the cause, raised money privately, set up a board of trustees, and arranged with Harriet Elizabeth Mann Smith and Goldwin Smith* to have their house, the Grange, bequeathed to the Art Museum of Toronto. The Toronto Guild of Civic Art, which adjudicated public art and urban planning schemes, also benefited from his participation.

Walker's involvement in art was more than organizational. He was also a collector, and though his holdings were not as extensive as some, he had extraordinary access to important private collections abroad and knew many artists personally. He advised his friends on building private galleries, and as a result many Canadian collections came to reflect his preference for Dutch interiors and the Barbizon School. He was fondest of Italian art and in 1894 lectured about it at the University of Toronto. In his later years he developed an exquisite collection of Japanese prints (now in the Royal Ontario Museum). His taste in art was cultivated by extensive reading and travelling. He journeyed throughout Europe, spent long periods in England, and visited South America and the Far East.

His cultural activities also took place at the national level. He felt his most important contribution to Canada was the founding in 1905, with historian George M. Wrong and librarian James Bain*, of the Champlain Society, an organization which publishes historical documents. His interest in history also led him to serve the National Battlefields Commission, the Quebec tercentenary committee, and the Historical Manuscripts Commission. During the 1914–18 war Lord Beaverbrook [Aitken*] sought his advice on developing the Canadian War Memorials Fund, and Walker successfully suggested that Canadian artists be commissioned to paint war scenes.

Walker was embroiled in a number of controversies concerning art. One stemmed from his involvement with the National Gallery of Canada. The Royal Canadian Academy of Arts had helped found the gallery in 1880. However, after a quarter-century it was still little more than a repository of diploma works. Artists lobbied for a more complete institution, and in 1907 the government appointed the Advisory Arts Council [see Sydney Arthur FISHER]. Walker became its head in 1910 and in 1913 chairman of the reincorporated National Gallery's board of trustees. Among other tasks he and his colleagues were instructed to build up the national collection. None was an artist, and all came in for criticism, especially Walker because of his very definite likes and dislikes. The most public conflict took place in 1923 when the RCA took strong exception to the National Gallery's selection of a jury which would choose works of art to represent Canada at the British Empire Exhibition. Critic Hector Willoughby Charlesworth* agreed and argued that Walker and gallery director Eric Brown* were wrong to show favouritism to Canadian painters whose work he considered "labored, dull, and unimaginative." Charlesworth called the gallery a "national reproach," echoing MP Charles Murphy* who in 1921 had labelled it "a haven for the special pets of Sir Byron Walker." Despite the criticism, Walker had built a permanent foundation for the gallery, had seen that it survived the war years, and had helped secure relatively generous public funding. Indeed, his death was seen as a loss to the arts in Canada. Walker himself recognized the progress his generation of patrons facilitated: young Canadian painters had begun to "paint our country in moods, colours and atmosphere which cannot be mistaken for anything but Canada"; in a short period, he said in 1923, aesthetic standards had increased to the point that Canada had become much "nearer to the great centres of the world."

Music also benefited from Walker's dedication and acumen. He worked with the Toronto Conservatory of Music and its director, Augustus Stephen VOGT, and arranged the school's affiliation with the university. Particular pleasure he derived from his involvement in the Toronto Mendelssohn Choir, founded by Vogt, which he helped reorganize in 1900. He secured funding for the group and was named its honorary president. He enjoyed travelling with the choir, and in early 1924 was on tour with them in the United States when he contracted pneumonia. Minnie, his wife of nearly 50 years, had just died and Walker coped with his grief by burying himself in his projects. He had begun to work long nights settling the estate of his friend Sir William Mackenzie, and was about to leave for England to attend the British Empire Exhibition when he expired.

Walker admonished students to avoid committing "the historical estimate." He said they should not hold a person in high regard simply "because he accomplished work important for his time"; however, someone whose deeds were "important for all time" was to be valued. Certain of his contemporaries considered Walker to be too powerful and overextended into areas they said he knew little about. He was sometimes seen as "arrogant, domineering, and pretentious." But Walker simply trusted his own judgement and ability. Furthermore, he "had an extraordinary power of creating enthusiasm." In retrospect, the worst his enemies could say about him was that he was "a strong man with a liking for his own way of doing things." "Remember each day," he told the Schoolmen's Club, "that we shall be judged by our children according to the use we have made of the really vast opportunity which fortune has placed in our hands." Clearly he accomplished much, in many fields, at several levels, and in lasting ways.

DAVID KIMMEL

[Many of Walker's addresses were published in professional journals or as pamphlets. A good sampler is *Addresses delivered by Sir Edmund Walker, C.V.O., L.L.D., D.C.L., during the war* ([Toronto], 1919]). *A history of banking in Canada* was originally presented to the Congress of Bankers and Financiers at Chicago on 23 June 1893, and appeared in Canadian Bankers' Assoc., *Journal* (Toronto), 1 (1893–94): 1–25, under the title "Banking in Canada." The *History* went through numerous reissues and revisions, including the Toronto editions of 1899 and 1909. Walker's contribution to the *Dictionary of political economy . . .* , ed. R. H. I. Palgrave (3v., London and New York, 1894–99), on "Canadian banking" also appeared in pamphlet form at Toronto sometime in the 1890s. The majority of Walker's publications have been made available on microfiche by the CIHM and are listed in its *Reg.* A chronological listing of Walker's addresses and publications is available in box 34A, file 3, of his papers at the University of Toronto, *infra.* Also listed in both sources is a pamphlet issued by the Canadian Bank of Commerce under the title *Jubilee of Sir Edmund Walker, C.V.O., L.L.D., D.C.L., 1868–1918* (Toronto, 1918), to commemorate his 50th year of service.

The principal repository of manuscript documents is the Walker papers at Univ. of Toronto Library, Thomas Fisher Rare Book Library (MS coll. 1). The records of the Civic Guild of Toronto (formerly the Toronto Guild of Civic Art) are preserved in TRL, SC. Walker's involvement in the fine arts is documented in archival collections in the research library and archives of the Art Gallery of Ontario, Toronto, and in the B. E. Walker papers and Advisory Arts Council records in the National Gallery of Canada Library, Ottawa. Finally, both the CIBC [Canadian Imperial Bank of Commerce] and the Canadian Bankers' Association possess institutional archives in their head offices in Toronto.

There are three biographies: George P. de T. Glazebrook's commissioned study, *Sir Edmund Walker* (London, 1933); C. W. Colby, "Sir Edmund Walker," *Canadian Banker* (Toronto), 56 (1949): 93–101; and B. R. Marshall, "Sir Edmund Walker, servant of Canada" (MA thesis, Univ. of B.C., Vancouver, 1971). Marshall's dissertation is very good, but is not widely available. Hector Willoughby Charlesworth writes about Walker in *More candid chronicles: further leaves from*

the note book of a Canadian journalist (Toronto, 1928), as does Augustus Bridle in *Sons of Canada: short studies of characteristic Canadians* (Toronto, 1916). The business side of his life can be culled from Victor Ross and A. St L. Trigge, *A history of the Canadian Bank of Commerce, with an account of the other banks which now form part of its organization* (3v., Toronto, 1920–34); R. T. Naylor, *The history of Canadian business, 1867–1914* (2v., Toronto, 1975); and Christopher Armstrong and H. V. Nelles, *Southern exposure: Canadian promoters in Latin America and the Caribbean, 1896–1930* (Toronto, 1988). On Walker's involvement in politics and public life, see the *Canadian annual rev.*, 1901–24, and R. D. Cuff, "The Toronto Eighteen and the election of 1911," *OH*, 58 (1965): 169–80, as well as A. B. McKillop, *Matters of mind: the university in Ontario, 1791–1951* (Toronto, 1994).

K. A. Jordan, *Sir Edmund Walker, print collector: a tribute to Sir Edmund Walker on the seventy-fifth anniversary of the founding of the Art Gallery of Ontario* (exhibition catalogue, Art Gallery of Ontario, 1974), and *Images of eighteenth-century Japan: ukiyoe prints from the Sir Edmund Walker collection, Royal Ontario Museum, Toronto*, comp. David Waterhouse ([Toronto], 1975), discuss Walker the art connoisseur. Maria Tippett, *Art at the service of war: Canada, art and the Great War* (Toronto, 1984) and her *Making culture: English-Canadian institutions and the arts before the Massey commission* (Toronto, 1990), Lovat Dickson, *The museum makers: the story of the Royal Ontario Museum* (Toronto, 1986), and David Kimmel, "Toronto gets a gallery: the origins and development of the city's permanent public art museum," *OH*, 84 (1992): 195–210, survey some of his organizational contributions to Canadian cultural life. The best discussion of Walker's confrontations with critics is found in Ann Davis, "The Wembley controversy in Canadian art," *CHR*, 44 (1973): 48–74. D.K.]

WALLACE, FRANCIS HUSTON, Methodist minister, theologian, educator, and author; b. 5 Sept. 1851 in Ingersoll, Upper Canada, son of Robert Wallace, a Presbyterian minister, and Mary Ann (Marianne) Barker; m. 25 June 1878 Johanna (Joy) Wilson in Metuchen, N.J., and they had five children, of whom two sons and one daughter lived to maturity; d. 2 June 1930 in Toronto.

Francis Huston Wallace was educated in a series of private schools, including Upper Canada College in Toronto, where he was head boy in 1868–69. He enrolled in University College, Toronto, the following year. Although he was not impressed with the quality of teaching, he graduated with a first and a gold medal in classics in 1873 and secured an MA a year later. Wallace and his family had assumed that following graduation he would enter Knox College and become a Presbyterian minister. During his second undergraduate year, however, he became greatly distressed about his spiritual condition and his vocation. He agreed with his father as to the absolute necessity of a conversion experience as the foundation of a truly Christian life, but he was deeply depressed by his failure to achieve it.

Fortunately, at this juncture he was befriended by several perceptive and sympathetic Methodists. Inspired by their counsel and by participation in Methodist services, he eventually felt "his heart strangely warmed," as had John Wesley, and he became "gloriously happy in the joy of salvation." Despite his father's anger and grief, Wallace rejected the Westminster Standards, adopted by the Church of Scotland in 1647, and the prospect of becoming a Presbyterian minister. His Methodist friends quickly decided that he would be a valuable recruit for the Methodist ministry, and with their encouragement, he was accepted as a local preacher in 1873. Nathanael Burwash*, the founding dean of theology at Victoria College in Cobourg, hinted at an eventual appointment in the college. Wallace enrolled in Drew Theological Seminary in Madison, N.J., in 1873. After graduating in 1876, he proceeded to the University of Leipzig, then a leading institution in biblical studies attended by many foreign theological students, where he spent a year. He would return to Germany in 1911–12 to study at the University of Berlin and, in particular, to enrol in the course offered by the eminent and radical church historian Adolf von Harnack, whom he later privately described as a "Unitarian of the highest type."

Wallace was ordained in the Methodist ministry in 1878 and subsequently appointed to pastorates in Peterborough, Toronto, and Cobourg, positions in which he acquired several prominent lay supporters and the friendship of Samuel Sobieski Nelles* and other members of the teaching staff at Victoria College. In 1887 he was appointed professor of New Testament literature and exegesis in Victoria's faculty of theology; he began teaching the following January. Wallace was a member of the faculty until 1920 and its dean from 1900. A respected and committed teacher and administrator, he helped to shape the development of the faculty and the theological outlook of many in the Methodist ministry in Canada, during a period of profound intellectual upheaval – a generation influenced by Darwin's writings, the development of higher criticism in biblical studies, and growing awareness that Christian theology is a transitory construction, as are other forms of human thought. By 1920 Victoria's faculty of theology and the Methodist community in general had come to accept the implications of contemporary biblical scholarship and were probably more distressed by the moral implications of World War I than by arguments about Genesis and prophecy.

At Victoria, from 1892 located in Toronto, this process of adjustment was marked by two controversial incidents and facilitated by Wallace's own approach to biblical studies and his constructive appointments to the faculty. He played no formal part in the first issue, the resignation of his friend and colleague George Coulson Workman* in 1891. He concluded, however, that Workman was a Unitarian and therefore unsuited to instruct Methodist theological students. Again, in 1909 his friend George Jackson, newly appointed professor of English Bible, was threatened with dismissal for stating publicly that the account of creation in Genesis is not a historical one. The dispute was resolved through a statement prepared by John Fletcher McLaughlin, Workman's successor, and signed by the entire faculty of theology. It declared that, "so long as our theological professors maintain their personal vital relation to Christ and Holy Scripture, and adhere to the doctrinal standards of our own church ... they must be left free to do their own work," a position later accepted by the General Conference of the Methodist Church.

A quiet, firm, but tolerant scholar, Wallace believed that the New Testament is "all alive with the experiences, difficulties, struggles, antagonisms, heresies, arguments, appeals, eloquence of the men and times to whom Jesus Christ spake." Historical study enabled Christians better to understand "the living realities of the Bible and of Christian experience." Wisely and perhaps deliberately, he left public controversy to others. His preaching was scholarly and balanced, and he welcomed changes in the role of the church. Wallace did not neglect his duties as a minister. He was a strong advocate of the establishment of the deaconess order in the Methodist Church and an effective supporter of union with the Presbyterian and Congregational churches, achieved in 1925. His home was a hospitable place where he welcomed each generation of students. Above all, he strove to make Victoria's "work in theology equal in scholarship to that of the very best institutions on this continent." He left his colleagues and his students with a "memory of good words and good deeds" that would help constructively to shape the college's role in theological education.

GOLDWIN S. FRENCH

In 1921 Francis Huston Wallace completed "Memories: a family record," an autobiography for his children and their families that was never published. It bears an alternative title, "Memories of the manse, the parsonage, and the college." The UCC-C holds two copies of this work, in fonds 3170. The first leaf of one of them is signed "my own copy F. H. W." Wallace published a number of articles, some pamphlets, and a collection of lectures. These include "Methodist colleges: Drew Seminary," *Canadian Methodist Magazine* (Toronto and Halifax), 9 (January–June 1879): 217–22; "University life in Germany," *Canadian Methodist Magazine*, 17 (January–June 1883): 350–57, 422–31; *Witnesses for Christ, or, a sketch of the history of preaching: lectures delivered under the auspices of the Theological Union of Victoria University, Cobourg, March, 1885* (Toronto, 1885); "The principles, methods and results of the biblical theology of the New Testament," *Acta Victoriana* (Toronto), 19 (1895–96): 93–98, 156–62; *The interpretation of the Apocalypse: a paper read at the Theological Conference of Victo-*

ria University, November, 1902 (Toronto, 1903); and "Our Bible: what it is and how to use it" (typescript, 1923; copy available at UCC-C).

UCC-C, Biog. file; Conference file. R. P. Bowles, "Late Reverend Professor F. H. Wallace: in memoriam . . . ," *New Outlook* (Toronto), 20 Aug. 1930: 809. Michael Gauvreau, *The evangelical century: college and creed in English Canada from the Great Revival to the Great Depression* (Montreal and Kingston, Ont., 1991). D. B. Marshall, *Secularizing the faith: Canadian Protestant clergy and the crisis of belief, 1850–1940* (Toronto, 1992). Margaret Prang, *N. W. Rowell, Ontario nationalist* (Toronto and Buffalo, N.Y., 1975). "Retirement of Dean Wallace," *Acta Victoriana*, 44 (1919–20): 372–75. Tom Sinclair-Faulkner, "Theory divided from practice: the introduction of the higher criticism into Canadian Protestant seminaries," Canadian Soc. of Church Hist., *Papers* (n.p.), 1980 [i.e. 1979]: 33–75.

WALLACE, WILLIAM, police officer; b. 9 March 1867 in County Donegal (Republic of Ireland), son of Samuel Wallace and Sarah McConnell; m. 25 June 1902 Annie Jane McNair in Toronto, and they had two sons; d. there 25 Oct. 1928.

Born in Donegal not far from Londonderry, William Wallace immigrated to Canada in 1886. He was part of an influx of Irish Protestants into Toronto and its police; a large minority in the city, British immigrants were a majority on the police force. Within a few years of joining the department as a patrolman on 1 April 1890, he was promoted to plainclothesman by Detective Alfred Cuddy. He made acting detective in 1903 and full detective six years later. Wallace was not given to a military style of policing, but he was tough. Once, he dared to apprehend three "thugs" in a pawnshop on York Street but he was beaten into unconsciousness, which permanently affected his health.

During World War I, Wallace was on loan to the federal government to monitor aliens, communists, and other radicals. His recommendations to Dominion Police commissioner Sir Arthur Percy Sherwood* and Minister of Justice Charles Joseph Doherty* anticipated Ottawa's anti-radical legislation of 1919. The government asked him to continue his surveillance after the war, but he missed his family and preferred regular detective work, so he returned to Toronto. Detectives, because of their relative autonomy, their aura of glamour, and the perception that they dealt with real crime, were subjected to little public criticism during Wallace's tenure on the force.

In 1919 he became assistant inspector of detectives, under George Guthrie. This was no mere administrative position: Wallace worked long hours, particularly when high-profile investigations arose. His biggest case was the murder in 1921 of druggist Leonard Cecil Sabine by Roy Hotram and William McFadden, who were convicted and hanged. Years of detective work convinced Wallace that criminals were not victims of environment, heredity, or poverty, as social science suggested, but "lazy, selfish, vicious scoundrels."

Wallace was a typical career officer. His community involvement included the freemasons, Erskine Presbyterian (United) Church, and possibly the Orange lodge, whose members dominated Toronto's civic politics and departments. His professional importance stemmed from his participation in the Chief Constables' Association of Canada, a police-lobby organization founded in 1905 which accepted detectives as members. As its secretary-treasurer from 1921 to 1926, he published the proceedings of its annual conventions and the *Canadian Police Bulletin* (Toronto), both valuable sources for the study of the professionalization and ideology of Canadian police.

Through the *Bulletin* and the CCAC's yearly conferences, Wallace reflected the hardline crime-fighting ethos that dominated municipal police circles. At the 1922 conference he gave a speech entitled "Are we encouraging crime by pampering and coddling criminals?" He criticized the rehabilitative approach in criminology and perceived political interference in police work and the administration of criminal justice. In 1923 he spoke out against a bill introduced by an Ontario Independent Labor party MLA, Thomas Tooms, to place municipal police under the control of elective officials rather than boards of police commissioners dominated by appointed officials. Police administration under popular control, he opined, was open to abuse by radical politicians and "parasites" in labour organizations. Wallace also espoused a common belief among detectives: the need to change the federal Identification of Criminals Act to allow the fingerprinting of all persons in lawful custody, not simply those charged with indictable offences. Another pet peeve was the tendency of reformers, religious organizations, and the media to lionize notorious ex-convicts, such as the infamous Norman John (Red) Ryan*, "a plaster hero" in Wallace's estimate.

Wallace was a strong critic of granting leave to convicts under the federal Ticket of Leave Act. His most noteworthy concern, however, was Ontario's Parole Act and its administration. He blamed parole, psychiatry, and the misguided efforts of reformers for the supposed crime wave of the 1920s. Wallace's sustained attacks seriously undermined the work of Alfred Edward Lavell of the Ontario Board of Parole, who first tried to placate Wallace and then appealed over his head to chief constable Samuel James Dickson and judge Emerson Coatsworth of the Toronto Board of Police Commissioners. Wallace used his positions within the Toronto police and the CCAC to discredit Ontario's parole system and prevent its adoption by Manitoba and other provinces. Lavell in turn accused Wallace of misrepresenting rehabilitative efforts and misusing his CCAC office. In 1924 he wrote that the tenacious detective was succeeding in "giving the police the idea that the Ontario Board of Parole is the work of foolish and sentimental fanatics, ineffective, unjust and a menace to the public good."

On 28 Sept. 1928, just weeks before his death, Wallace was appointed chief of detectives. He had recently attended the annual gathering of the International Association of Chiefs of Police, where his conservative views on crime-fighting would have been the norm. He died in the early morning of 25 October at his home on Fern Avenue. Honoured with a full police ceremony and a massive procession, he was buried in Prospect Cemetery. Colleagues noted that he was known within police circles across North America, and as an "outstanding criminologist" and "the most technical Police officer in the country."

GREG MARQUIS

AO, RG 8-54, boxes 6–12; RG 22-305, no.60585; RG 80-5-0-298, no.2049. LAC, RG 13, A2, 231, Wallace to A. P. Sherwood, 22, 30 July 1918; RG 31, C1, 1901, Toronto, Ward 2, div.12: 22 (mfm. at AO). *Globe*, 26 Oct. 1928. *Toronto Daily Star*, 7–11 March 1921, 25–28 Oct. 1928. *Canadian Police Bull.* (Toronto), March 1925, March 1929. Chief Constables' Assoc. of Canada, *Proc. of the annual convention* (Toronto), 1920–30. *Directory*, Toronto, 1891–1928. Greg Marquis, "The early twentieth-century Toronto police institution" (PHD thesis, Queen's Univ., Kingston, Ont., 1987); *Policing Canada's century: a history of the Canadian Association of Chiefs of Police* (Toronto, 1993).

WARBURTON, ALEXANDER BANNERMAN, lawyer, politician, judge, and author; b. 5 April 1852 in Charlottetown, son of James Warburton and Martha C. Green; m. there first 23 Aug. 1883 Helen M. Davies (d. 1884); m. there secondly 26 Oct. 1889 Isabel Cogswell Longworth, daughter of John Longworth*, and they had three daughters; d. there 14 Jan. 1929.

Alexander Bannerman Warburton was born while his father James was a member of Prince Edward Island's first responsible, and reform, government. James had been born in Garryhinch, in the town of Portarlington (Republic of Ireland), and had come to the Island in 1834 to settle in Prince County. A. B. Warburton's given names commemorated Sir Alexander Bannerman*, a lieutenant governor of the Island. He grew up on the family farm in St Eleanors and was a pupil at Summerside Grammar School before attending St Dunstan's College in Charlottetown for two years in the late 1860s. A brilliant pupil, he carried on in 1869 to King's College in Windsor, N.S., where he won the Almon-Welsford prize in his first year for the highest aggregate average; it was also the highest aggregate ever achieved at King's. He won the General Williams prize in engineering as well.

After two years at King's, Warburton enrolled in the University of Edinburgh, where he studied arts and classics. He subsequently attended Walter Wren's school in London before taking his BA at Windsor in 1874. Upon returning to the Island, he was appointed secretary of the Queens County Liberal Association and read law with Louis Henry DAVIES. In 1876 he took a BCL from King's, collecting the Bishop's prize in the process, and then read law with George Baugh Allen at the Inner Temple in London. He was admitted to the bar of the Island in 1879, and would later become associated in practice first with Francis Joseph Conroy and then in turn with Charles Robert Smallwood, Donald Alexander MACKINNON, and D. Edgar Shaw. In 1897 he was appointed a QC. His major early contribution to the law was his collaboration with Francis Longworth Haszard* on a two-volume series of reports on the Island's Supreme Court cases, chiefly those of judge James Horsfield Peters*.

Active in local affairs, Warburton served as secretary-treasurer of the Charlottetown Driving Park and Exhibition Association of Prince Edward Island. An ardent conservationist, in 1884 he managed a project of tree planting in Charlottetown that beautified Queen and Rochford squares. In 1903 he would be appointed to the Island's three-member Forestry Commission, and by 1905 he had joined the Canadian Forestry Association, which he would serve as a provincial vice-president for two terms from 1910 to 1912. A member of St Paul's Anglican Church, he was for many years a delegate to synod. Warburton also acted as a director of the Patriot Publishing Company (which issued the leading Liberal newspaper on the Island) and of the Eastern Assurance Company of Canada. He was a governor of King's College in Windsor, and president of the Liberal Association of West Queens.

In 1890 Warburton ran as a free-trade Liberal candidate for the provincial legislature in Charlottetown, but was defeated. Successful in Queens County, 1st district, in 1891 and 1893, he was re-elected in 1897, when he briefly became leader of the party and premier of the province upon the resignation of Frederick Peters. While premier he struggled with the ongoing problems of finance and dominion-provincial relations without great success. Not even the presence of his former mentor, Sir L. H. Davies, in Ottawa as part of the Liberal government of Sir Wilfrid Laurier* was much help in obtaining assistance for the Island. Warburton's administration did not distinguish itself in any way, and even the biographical sketch he wrote for the 1912 edition of Henry James Morgan*'s *Canadian men and women of the time* does not list any achievements of his premiership. Not surprisingly, in 1898 he stepped down, to be succeeded by Donald Farquharson*. He then took up an appointment as judge of the county court of Kings. Unlike most Island judges, however, Warburton did not give up his political activities. He was mayor of Charlottetown from 1901 to 1904 and a member of the city's Board of School Trustees in 1904. That same year he resigned his seat on the bench and ran unsuccessfully with Lemuel Ezra Prowse as a federal Liberal candidate in Queens.

Warburton had always had scholarly ambitions, and he published several historical and historical-literary studies in the *Prince Edward Island Magazine* and *Acadiensis* in the early 1900s. During the period after his defeat for the House of Commons, he collaborated with D. A. MacKinnon, then lieutenant governor, and others on a history of Prince Edward Island, to which were appended biographical sketches of over 500 prominent Islanders of the past and present. This sort of production was common for most Canadian provinces in the early years of the 20th century. Warburton wrote the opening "Historical sketch," which took the story to 1830 but not beyond. He admitted to difficulty in doing his research. "No complete copies of the early records are to be had on the Island," he noted. "The old newspaper files are very incomplete, and very few of the Journals of the House of Assembly, of the period treated of, are to be found." Warburton relied heavily on the published researches of scholars such as William Francis Ganong* and John Caven. He had access to a few transcripts of off-Island records, but he did not travel to London to examine the Colonial Office files in the Public Record Office. Nor did he make any attempt to improve the Island's historical collecting.

In 1908, standing again in Queens, Warburton was elected to the House of Commons, where he became chair of the committee on public accounts. He did not distinguish himself. His speeches recorded in *Hansard* were infrequent and pedantic. His major honour was to head the parliamentary delegation to the coronation of King George and Queen Mary in 1911, at which time he was presented at Buckingham Palace. He was not re-elected that year or in 1917. In 1920 he was appointed surrogate and judge of probate for the Island, and he served in this capacity until his death.

Warburton in 1923 published *A history of Prince Edward Island from its discovery in 1534 until the departure of Lieutenant-Governor Ready in A.D. 1831*. This work expanded at length on his earlier historical sketch, producing an account limited by the same problems of evidence. Warburton used some transcripts at the Public Archives of Canada, but the book was based largely on contemporary accounts and secondary sources; it thus perpetuated many of the old mistakes of Island historiography. He wrote somewhat apologetically in his preface, "I am well aware that there is much that could be added to this volume, if one could find the scattered material." Nevertheless, the book served until the 1970s as the fullest statement of the early history of the Island and, along

with his court reports, represents Warburton's main claim to distinction.

J. M. BUMSTED

Alexander Bannerman Warburton's writings include his *History of Prince Edward Island*, published in Saint John in 1923, and several articles: "Our educational system," *Prince Edward Island Magazine* (Charlottetown), 2 (1900–1): 279–80; "The sea-cow fishery," *Acadiensis* (Saint John), 3 (1903): 116–19, and *Prince Edward Island Magazine*, 5 (1903–4): 141–45; and "Great epochs in English literature and their causes: a sketch," *Prince Edward Island Magazine and Educational Outlook* (Charlottetown), 6 (1904–5): 212–17. He also collaborated on two publications: *Reports of cases determined in the Supreme Court, Court of Chancery, and Vice Admiralty Court of Prince Edward Island . . .*, comp. with F. L. Haszard (2v., Charlottetown, 1885–86), and *Past and present of Prince Edward Island . . .*, ed. with D. A. MacKinnon (Charlottetown, [1906]).

Charlottetown Guardian, 15 Jan. 1929. *Examiner* (Charlottetown), 23 Aug. 1883, 26 Oct. 1889. *Islander* (Charlottetown), 5 Aug. 1870. *Patriot* (Charlottetown), 15 Jan. 1929. *Canadian directory of parl.* (Johnson). *Canadian men and women of the time* (Morgan; 1912). *Who's who and why*, 1915/16.

WARBURTON, GEORGE AUGUSTUS, YMCA official, prohibitionist, and conservationist; b. 4 Oct. 1859 in Sandford, Somerset, England, son of Samuel Warburton and Elizabeth Jones; m. October 1881 Louise H. Johnson in Port Byron, N.Y., and they had a daughter and two sons; d. 21 Feb. 1929 in Toronto.

In 1869 George Warburton emigrated to the United States with his parents. The family settled in Brockport, N.Y., where George attended school until, as a young teenager, he abandoned formal education and worked with his father, a blacksmith. Soon after, he experienced conversion and served as a Wesleyan lay preacher on weekends, becoming known as "the boy preacher of Central New York." Regretting his earlier refusal to continue in school, Warburton, a man of considerable intellectual ability, educated himself by reading widely.

Warburton's preaching brought him to the attention of the Young Men's Christian Association and he was sent to Newburgh, N.Y., for secretarial training. His long and varied YMCA career began a few months later with his 1880 appointment as general secretary of the association in Watertown. Warburton's accomplishments there soon led to a call to Syracuse, where he served as general secretary from 1881 to 1883. During these years Warburton impressed Cornelius Vanderbilt, who was looking for someone to take charge of New York City's Railroad YMCA. In 1884, at age 25, Warburton became secretary of this association, a position he held for the next quarter century.

Under Warburton's direction the association garnered widespread support from America's leading railways without ever becoming "the child of [the] companies." His efforts on behalf of railway employees included establishment of the Railroad Building and Loan Association. From 1887 to 1908 Warburton's editorship of the monthly *Railroad Men* (New York) extended his influence well beyond the state's boundaries.

By 1909 the board of the Toronto YMCA, which included many of the city's leading financiers and businessmen, was looking for a man who could oversee a major expansion of work in their city. Warburton's record as a fund-raiser, his ability to relate well to captains of industry, and his success in attracting strong laymen to YMCA endeavours made him an ideal candidate. About to turn 50, he was persuaded to relocate to Toronto on the condition that the plans for expansion went ahead.

Within a year of taking over as general secretary of Toronto's Central YMCA, Warburton had helped the association's directors raise over $685,000, a sum that exceeded their goal and made possible the construction of three new YMCA buildings. When the expanded scope of YMCA work in Toronto necessitated creation of a metropolitan organization in 1911, Warburton was put in charge. That same year he supported the decision of Canada's YMCAs to declare their independence from the association's North American organization and establish a separate national entity. In 1913, as the representative of the Toronto body, he was one of Canada's delegates at the World's Conference of the YMCA in Edinburgh. While Warburton served as general secretary of the Metropolitan Toronto YMCA, memberships increased by well over 60 per cent and the city's population by about 40 per cent. The YMCA's rapid expansion owed much to Warburton's fund-raising abilities, initiatives in the field of educational programming, and support for the introduction of an employment agency.

Once war broke out in 1914, Warburton volunteered in a number of patriotic causes, including the Canadian Patriotic Fund and Victory Loan drives. In 1918 he was appointed general director of the national YMCA's Red Triangle Fund campaign. This, the largest appeal the YMCA had ever made in Canada, was carried out across the country over three days in May and raised almost three and a half million dollars. A few months later the Toronto YMCA gave Warburton a four-week leave so that he could, on behalf of the Canadian government, assist in the American YMCA's campaign to raise $175,000,000 for war work. Less than a decade after his arrival in Toronto he had been selected by the federal government to help "strengthen the good relations . . . between Canada and the United States."

Warburton's philanthropic and public service during the 20 years he spent in Canada extended far beyond the YMCA. He served the broader community through his involvement in a range of religious, reform, and charitable organizations. In 1915–16 he had taken a six-month leave from the YMCA to serve as chief organizer of the Citizens' Committee of One Hundred's campaign to get the Ontario government of William Howard Hearst* to outlaw the sale of alcohol in the province, a goal achieved in 1916. Warburton was later asked to take charge of the Dominion Prohibition Committee's federal campaign but, even though the Toronto YMCA agreed to his doing so, time constraints and the "inadvisability of getting involved in political controversies" brought about his withdrawal from this fight early in 1917.

Warburton's impact on Canadian social norms did not stop when ill health forced him to resign from active YMCA service in 1922. In addition to renewed activity in the prohibition movement at the national and provincial levels, he now took on responsibilities in the fight to preserve the country's natural resources, putting his well-honed lobbying skills and networking abilities to work in this cause. A lifelong angler and long-time supporter of fish restocking programs, in 1925 he helped found the Toronto Anglers' Association, which began its operations by sponsoring a survey that documented the ill effects overfishing had already had on one of Canada's natural resources. By 1927, when he became president of the 2,500 member TAA, Warburton was convinced that the political force of a province-wide federation of anglers was needed to bring about government action and he pushed for its creation. His efforts bore fruit early the next year and delegates at the founding convention of the Ontario Federation of Anglers rewarded him with election as president. Under his direction the OFA called upon the government to hire experts to survey the state of the province's fish and wildlife populations and advise on necessary conservation measures. By the time of his death in February 1929 Warburton had alerted Ontarians about the need for conservation and mobilized public opinion in support of this cause.

Patricia Dirks

George A. Warburton was a prolific correspondent and wrote poetry for family and friends. He published two books, *George Alonzo Hall; a tribute to consecrated personality* (New York, 1905) and *A typical general secretary: the life of Edwin F. See* (New York, 1908).

LAC, MG 28, I 95. Y.M.C.A. of Greater Toronto, Minutebook no.3, 1906–18. *Globe*, 22 Feb. 1929. W. [W.] Adair, *Memories of George Warburton* ([New York], n.d.). C. W. Bishop, *The Canadian Y.M.C.A. in the Great War . . .* ([Toronto], 1924). *Canadian annual rev.*, 1910, 1916, 1918. *Canadian men and women of the time* (Morgan; 1912). J. F. Moore, *The story of the Railroad "Y"* (New York, 1930). M. G. Ross, "The Toronto Y.M.C.A. in a changing community, 1864–1940" (MA thesis, Univ. of Toronto, 1947); *The Y.M.C.A. in Canada: the chronicles of a century* (Toronto, 1951).

WARREN, GEORGE STEPHENS (baptized Georges-Étienne), cigar maker, trade union leader, and labour organizer; b. 25 Oct. 1846 in Montreal, son of Étienne Warren and Basilise (?) Boisseau; m. there first 19 April 1873 Élizabeth Chartier, and they had at least eight children; m. there secondly Rose-Anna Cusson; d. there 30 Nov. 1928.

George Stephens Warren was a descendant, through his father, of a Scottish officer who had settled in Nova Scotia; he also had French Canadian roots through his mother and grandmother. His paternal grandparents had established themselves in La Malbaie, but his father, before his first marriage in 1828, had taken up residence in Montreal, where he was a baker by trade. The Warren family spent a few years in Quebec City in the 1850s and then returned to Montreal. When still an adolescent, George fell while sliding on the ice and fractured a leg, which had to be amputated. His disability would not prevent him, however, from being an active man; a popular speaker, he would gesticulate with his crutches to lend emphasis to his words.

Once he had recovered, Warren became an apprentice in a cigar factory, a growing industry in Montreal. In 1866 he went to complete his training in Saratoga (Schuylerville), N.Y. The manufacture of cigars involved skilful rolling of leaf tobacco. It was in the nearby city of Schenectady that Warren was introduced to trade unionism when he joined the Cigar Makers' International Union of America. A few months later he attracted attention and even became a member of the union's executive. Back in Montreal in 1870, he was immediately appointed secretary of the local cigar makers' union, which was affiliated with the CMIUA. This local union disappeared in the turmoil of the severe recession of 1873, but it was re-established the following year and Warren became its president at that time. In 1876 it was dissolved again, its members being unable to find work because of the widespread crisis in the cigar industry. The 1880s proved far more favourable to the growth of trade unionism and in 1880 Warren participated in reorganizing the cigar makers' union; it immediately requested an affiliation charter with the CMIUA, in which it constituted Local 58. He was the local's president in 1886 and 1887, and he even held office as third vice-president of the union's international executive in 1888 and 1889.

The fact that Warren belonged to an international trade union had not prevented him from being an activist within the Knights of Labor, an organization gaining more and more of a foothold in Quebec during the 1880s. Of American origin, it wanted to be open to all workers, not just to those who practised a trade. Quebec's first organizer of the Knights of Labor, Warren in 1883 had taken part in founding Ville-Marie Assembly 3484, which was reserved for francophones

[*see* Olivier-David Benoît*]. He is thought to have established at least 23 assemblies in Quebec. In the 1890s he continued to belong to the assembly while being a member of the CMIUA. As early as 1883, Warren had also attempted to establish an organization that would bring the Montreal unions together and represent them in their dealings with municipal government. His hopes materialized in 1886 with the creation of the Central Trades and Labor Council of Montreal, which brought together the city's unions and Knights of Labor assemblies.

In 1888 Warren was called to testify before the royal commission on the relations of labour and capital regarding transformations in the Montreal cigar industry. He pointed out that cigar makers' salaries had been reduced by almost 50 per cent since the 1870s because of the employment of children in factories. Using moulds invented at the end of the 1860s, these children were able to make 5,500 cigars per day, far more than could a tradesman who meticulously rolled each one of them. He suggested that there be a law like the one in Ontario to limit the number of apprentices according to the number of cigar makers employed in a factory.

While president of his union, Warren had an idea that was to have great appeal: to celebrate Labour Day on the first Monday of September 1886, following the example of what increasingly was being done in American cities after the initial parades held in Toronto and New York in 1882. Eight of the unions in the city responded to his invitation, including the cigar makers' union, whose 350 members participated, carrying a banner with the slogan "Religion et patrie." About 2,000 workers in all, grouped by trade and accompanied by two brass bands, marched through the downtown streets before the crowds lining the route. After the parade, the members' families were transported by boat to Elmwood Grove Park for a picnic, games, and sports competitions. Warren and a few other union leaders took advantage of the occasion to give speeches, encouraging the workers to maintain union solidarity and to vote for the labour candidates in the next elections. The celebration spread across Canada, and the federal government made it a public holiday in 1894. The parade in Montreal became very large-scale at the beginning of the 20th century, but it would disappear in 1953.

Warren represented Ville-Marie Assembly at the meetings of the Trades and Labor Congress of Canada in 1890, 1893, and 1894. In 1890 he was elected to its provincial legislative committee, which was responsible for submitting union workers' grievances concerning labour legislation to the Quebec government. In this forum and in his public pronouncements, he placed particular emphasis on two issues: the banning of child labour and free, public school education.

It is not known what position Warren took in the

conflict that pitted the Knights of Labor against the international unions at the end of the 19th century, but in March 1899 he agreed to work for the American Federation of Labor, which oversaw the international unions. Its president, Samuel Gompers, commissioned him to work as organizer for the district of Montreal. Employed in this position until 1901, he succeeded in setting up unions in Montreal, Quebec City, Saint-Hyacinthe, and Salaberry-de-Valleyfield. In 1903 he championed international unions on the same podium as Joseph-Alphonse Rodier*, Joseph Ainey*, and Alphonse VERVILLE. He subsequently had a more unobtrusive role and he died in 1928 at the age of 82.

According to accounts of the time, George Stephens Warren was an engaging figure by virtue of his enthusiasm and colourful style. A gifted speaker in both French and English and a passionate union activist, he stands among those who through dynamism and devotion laid the foundations of trade unionism in Montreal.

JACQUES ROUILLARD

ANQ-M, CE601-S15, 19 avril 1873; S51, 26 oct. 1846. *Montreal Daily Star*, 21 Nov. 1883; 7 Sept., December 1886; 31 Aug. 1889. *Montreal Herald*, 1 Sept. 1894. *La Patrie*, 18 févr. 1903, 6 déc. 1919. *La Presse*, 6 sept. 1886; 30 nov., 4 déc. 1928; 6 déc. 1930. *Le Repos du travailleur* (Montréal), 1 sept. 1890. Can., Royal commission on the relations of labour and capital in Canada, *Report* (5v. in 6, Ottawa, 1889), *Quebec*, pt.1: 55–60. Charlemagne Rodier, "Le Conseil des métiers et du travail," in *Golden jubilee of the Montreal Trades and Labor Council, 1897–1947* . . . , ed. M.-E. Francq ([Montreal?, 1947?]), 13. Jacques Rouillard, "La fête du Travail à Montréal, expression de la solidarité ouvrière (1886–1964)," RCHTQ [Regroupement des Chercheurs-Chercheuses en Hist. des Travailleurs et Travailleuses du Québec], *Bull.* (Montréal), 22 (1996), no.2: 9–14; *Les syndicats nationaux au Québec, de 1900 à 1930* (Québec, 1979), 33–36, 57, 94, 111.

WATSON, ALBERT DURRANT, physician, astronomer, author, and psychical researcher; b. 8 Jan. 1859 in Dixie (Mississauga), Upper Canada, son of William Youle Watson and Mary Ann Aldred; m. 23 Sept. 1885 Sarah Anne Grimshaw Clare (d. 13 March 1937) in Toronto, and they had two daughters and five sons; d. there 3 May 1926.

Albert Durrant Watson's father and paternal grandparents emigrated from England in 1819 and his maternal grandparents did the same in 1836. According to a Canadian Medical Association obituary, Watson was "of a good family." His father was a reformer in politics and a Methodist in religion. Watson, too, would be active in the Methodist Church of Canada. He was a member of the Euclid Avenue Church in Toronto, the Toronto Conference, the General Conference, the Board of Missions, and the executive of the

Methodist Social Union of Toronto, and he served as treasurer of the church's department of temperance and moral reform. He also conducted a large Bible class for young people. It would be stated in the *Commemorative biographical record of the county of York* (1907) that he was "prominent in the ethical and sociological work of the church." He was founder and president of the Ethological Association of Canada, president of the Canadian Purity-Education Association, "and a recognized teacher and leader in ethical ideals."

Educated first in the schools of Peel County, Watson had studied at the Toronto Normal School and taught for a short period at Malton (Mississauga) and Oakville before turning to the study of medicine. He obtained an MD from Victoria College, Cobourg, in 1883. In 1890 he would receive another, *ad eundem gradum*, from the University of Toronto in recognition of his graduation as a licentiate from the Royal College of Physicians of Edinburgh in 1883. He successfully practised medicine for more than four decades, serving on staff at three hospitals, including Toronto Western.

Among other pursuits, Watson was an avid amateur astronomer. His papers in this field include "The reformation and simplification of the calendar" (1896), "Astronomy in Canada" (1917), and "Astronomy: a cultural avocation" (1918). He had joined the Astronomical and Physical Society of Toronto in 1892; it would develop into the Royal Astronomical Society of Canada, which he served as second and then first vice-president between 1910 and 1915 and as president in 1916 and 1917. In addition, he had many musical and literary interests. During the early decades of the 1900s several of his poems appeared in Methodist and Presbyterian hymnals. In 1908 he wrote an alternative wording for "O Canada" which was widely acclaimed. It is still used in many churches.

In 1908 Watson published *The wing of the wild-bird and other poems*. It was followed by *Love and the universe, The immortals and other poems* (1913), *Heart of the hills (poems)* (1917), *The dream of God (a poem)* (1922), and *Woman: a poem* (1923). Editor Lorne Albert Pierce* of the Ryerson Press, a friend of Watson's, wrote in 1923: "We anticipate a selected edition of his poetry very soon. This ought to establish him securely among the great names of our native literature." *The poetical works of Albert Durrant Watson* appeared the following year. He was strongly influenced by the "confederation poets," including Charles George Douglas Roberts* and William Bliss CARMAN, and echoed their themes of nationalism and romanticism. Like Carman, he was also drawn to mystical subjects.

As a prose author, Watson produced several philosophical studies, including *The sovereignty of ideals* ([1903]), *The sovereignty of character: lessons from the life of Jesus of Nazareth* (1906), and *Three comrades of Jesus* (1919). He wrote the first volume in Pierce's *Makers of Canadian literature* series, on the poet Robert Winkworth Norwood* (1923). Though all reviewers were not so positive, Edwin John Pratt* wrote that the "task of interpretation has been accomplished with insight and refinement." Watson had also collaborated with Pierce in compiling the noted anthology *Our Canadian literature: representative prose and verse* (1922).

While he received recognition for his literary efforts, Watson achieved notoriety through his psychical research. From 1918 to 1920 a series of seances was held by medium Louis Benjamin, usually in the Watson home, with a stenographer present to record the proceedings. Among those present on at least one occasion was Flora MacDonald Denison [MERRILL], like Watson a devotee of Walt Whitman. Watson became president of the Association for Psychical Research of Canada and reported on his study of the seance communications, purportedly dictated by the spirits of departed celebrities, in *The twentieth plane: a psychic revelation* (1918) and *Birth through death, the ethics of the twentieth plane: a revelation received through the psychic consciousness of Louis Benjamin* (1920).

During the first weeks of January 1919 a debate on *The twentieth plane* was held in Toronto newspapers. Author Lucy Maud Montgomery* described the publication in her journal that March as "the book which has made such a sensation in Toronto" (and as "absolute poppycock – utterly unconvincing" despite her own interest in life after death). Watson gained many supporters, but others publicly ridiculed him. He resigned his position as leader of the Bible class. Two years later he dissociated himself from Benjamin, declaring his scepticism about mediums (though reaffirming his belief in the spiritual world), and withdrew from his editorship of the *Twentieth Plane: a Magazine of Psychic Content*. He concluded his study of "spiritual laws and psychic forces" with the publication of *Mediums and mystics . . .* (1923), written in collaboration with Margaret Lawrence, whom he would make his literary executor.

In 1920, in the earliest days of the Baha'i community in Canada, Watson had converted to that faith (as did Lawrence the following year). In the view of Lorne Pierce, "He recognized no national, ecclesiastical or any other frontier, but searched the world through for truth. . . . He sifted the philosophies, the religions and the humanities of the world. . . . No man during this generation in Toronto ever entertained so many strange faces, tongues, sects, systems, enthusiasms, artists, poets, fanatics, sages as he did; no home was more the ante-chamber to the universe."

The literary style epitomized by Watson was eclipsed not long after his death by modern realism, but his dedication to artistic and scientific endeavours will mark his place in Canada's history.

DEBRA BARR and WALTER MEYER ZU ERPEN

All of the subject's works mentioned in the text were published in Toronto, with the exception of *The sovereignty of ideals*, which came out in Westwood, Mass. "The reformation and simplification of the calendar" first appeared in the Astronomical and Physical Soc. of Toronto, *Trans.*, 1896: 59–72, and was reprinted separately the following year. "Astronomy in Canada" and "Astronomy: a cultural avocation" were published in the Royal Astronomical Soc. of Canada, *Journal* (Toronto), 11 (1917): [47]–78 and 12 (1918): [81]–91 respectively, and were also reprinted separately in the same years. Many of these works, and additional poetical works by Watson, have been made available by the CIHM and are listed in its *Reg.* Watson also wrote "The doctor of the future," *Canadian Journal of Medicine and Surgery* (Toronto), 7 (January–June 1900): 311–18 and he published as well in the Baha'i magazine *Star of the West* (Chicago) in 1924 and 1926.

Among the biographical accounts of Watson are *Canadian album* (Cochrane and Hopkins), 1: 105; *Canadian men and women of the time* (Morgan; 1898 and 1912); *Canadian poets*, ed. J. W. Garvin ([rev. ed.], Toronto, 1926), 235–36; *Commemorative biographical record of the county of York . . .* (Toronto, 1907); and L. A. Pierce, *Albert Durrant Watson: an appraisal* (Toronto, 1923 and 1924). Obituaries appear in the *New Outlook* (Toronto), 19 May 1926: 26, the Canadian Medical Assoc., *Journal* (Toronto), new ser., 16 (1926): 991–92, and the Royal Astronomical Soc. of Canada, *Journal*, 20 (1926): 153–57. See also John Colombo, "The Euclid Avenue séances," in his *Haunted Toronto* (Toronto, 1996), 176–79; A. C. Laut, "The poetical works of Albert Durrant Watson," *Christian Guardian*, 26 March 1924: 22–24; L. M. Montgomery [Macdonald], *The selected journals of L. M. Montgomery*, ed. Mary Rubio and Elizabeth Waterston (4v., Toronto, 1985–98), 2: 312; E. J. Pratt, "A new book," *Christian Guardian*, 4 July 1923: 21; and W. C. van den Hoonaard, *The origins of the Bahá'í community of Canada, 1898–1948* (Waterloo, Ont., 1996). Watson's will and death registration are found in AO, RG 22-305, no.54597 and RG 80-8-0-1017, no.3724. His file at UTA, A1973-0026/497(50), includes useful newspaper clippings.

WATSON, Sir DAVID, journalist, newspaper owner, and officer; b. 7 Feb. 1869 at Quebec, only son of William Watson, a rigger of sailing ships, and Jane Grant; m. there 11 Sept. 1893 Mary Ann Browning, and they had three daughters; d. there 19 Feb. 1922.

In 1891, having been educated in public schools in Quebec City, David Watson embarked on a career as a journalist with the *Quebec Morning Chronicle*, which was owned at that time by John Jackman Foote. Ten years later he was appointed general manager of the paper (now the *Quebec Chronicle*). He became general manager of its publisher, the Chronicle Printing Company, in 1906, and he would hold both positions until 1921. Watson unquestionably made a name for himself at the head of the daily. It was highly profitable, as can be seen from the increase in the number of pages over the years and the extensive advertising in them. Politically, he was an independent conservative, and under him the newspaper, on special occasions, could promote the cause of the Conservative party, which was then led by Robert Laird Borden*. In 1909 Watson was a member of the Canadian delegation to the Imperial Press Conference in London, England.

Watson distinguished himself as an accomplished athlete. For several years he was one of the star players in the old capital's hockey club. His passion for amateur sports and his strong personality gave him an entry into the Quebec Athlete Association Company, which he would lead over a long period. At the time of his death, renowned businessman Sir William PRICE would speak of him as a great athlete. Watson also took an early interest in the military, and he would be successful in this sphere as well. He enlisted first as a private in the 8th Royal Rifles, a militia regiment of Quebec City, and then rose through the ranks, obtaining his commission in 1900. Given the rank of lieutenant, he was promoted captain in 1903 and major in 1910. In 1911 he was invited by the federal government to command the company of fusiliers that accompanied the Canadian delegation to the coronation of King George V in England. For this service, he was awarded the Coronation Medal. On 26 Feb. 1912 he took command of his militia regiment with the rank of lieutenant-colonel.

By the beginning of August 1914, Watson was worried about the imminent threat of war in Europe. Wealthy and well known, he enlisted in the first contingent of the Canadian Expeditionary Force at the age of 45. On 22 August he assumed command of the volunteers of the 8th Royal Rifles, which was bound for Valcartier [see Price]. In September he was given command of the 2nd Infantry Battalion of the first contingent of the Canadian Expeditionary Force, a battalion made up of volunteers from eastern Ontario.

After an uneventful crossing in October, the battalion moved into Bustard camp on Salisbury Plain in England with the rest of the Canadian 1st Infantry Brigade. Foul weather made it difficult for Watson's unit to train. After disembarking in France at Le Havre on 11 Feb. 1915, Watson and his men set out for the deserted town of Armentières, which they reached on 17 February. Mightily impressed by the German artillery fire, Watson made an initial tour of the trenches. He was proud when his battalion took its place there officially on 1 March. As he noted in his diary, his unit was responsible for part of "the great line of defences for the Empire."

The 2nd Infantry Battalion showed great courage a few weeks later, in the German attack on Saint-Julien (Sint Juliaan), Belgium. During the second battle of Ypres in the spring of 1915, the Germans tried to take this Flemish village and the surrounding area, which jutted into their lines. They attacked on 22 April. For

the first time in the war, they resorted to poison gas. At 5:00 P.M. they released more than 160 tons of chlorine, which spread panic among the French troops of the 87th (Territorial) Division and the 45th (Algerian) Division. The soldiers of the 45th were on the front line to the left of the positions held by the 3rd Canadian Infantry Brigade. The retreat of the French troops imperilled the Canadian soldiers, leaving their left flank exposed. During this "great and terrible day," as Colonel Archer Fortescue Duguid termed it, the soldiers of the 1st Canadian Division, and in particular those of the 3rd Brigade, showed great heroism in stopping the German advance. The 2nd Battalion was stationed near the village of Wieltje. At 9:00 P.M. it received the order to advance towards Saint-Julien, where it was to take part in operations to check the German thrust. The next day (Friday, 23 April), Watson wrote, "My God! What an awful night we have had. Lost about 200 men & 6 officers of no.1 Coy. . . . They are too embedded in my mind to be ever forgotten." The following day Watson's men stood their ground in their trenches and inflicted "terrible casualties" on the attacking Germans. At 1:55 P.M. the 2nd Battalion received the order to withdraw. According to Captain Richard Douglas Ponton, "Col. Watson's gallantry, in remaining in that exposed position until every man had retired, will never be forgotten." Watson was back at headquarters about 4:00 P.M., "very badly cut up & with less than ½ my battalion." He noted, however, that his unit "saved all our wounded." William Waldie Murray, the 2nd Battalion's official historian, records that the battle of Saint-Julien resulted in the loss of 544 men of all ranks. Only seven of the battalion's 22 officers came through unscathed. Watson had to reorganize his unit, but he was proud of the conduct of his men, who, in his view, comprised "the best Can. Battn."

In June 1915 Samuel HUGHES, the minister of militia and defence, offered Watson an opportunity to go back to Canada and give the troops the benefit of his experiences in the field. He refused point blank, saying that he "would desire nothing better in all the world than a return to Canada but my duty is here with 2nd Battalion who have been so loyal to me." Edwin Alfred Hervey ALDERSON, commander of the 1st Canadian Division, congratulated him on his decision. Watson did accept a promotion, however, and on 30 Aug. 1915 he took command of the 5th Infantry Brigade, with the rank of brigadier-general, as a reward for his battalion's conduct during the second battle of Ypres. When he returned to the front in the spring of 1916, the machine-gunners of his brigade had to endure the terrible ordeal of the battle of the craters at Saint-Éloi (Sint-Elooi), in Belgium, on 5 and 6 April. This engagement, which lasted from 27 March to 16 April, was so named because of the mines exploded by the British under the German lines on the first day, in a vain attempt to recapture the Saint-Éloi salient. It was the 2nd Canadian Division's baptism of fire. All the machine-gunners of the 25th and 26th Infantry battalions were killed, while those of the 22nd (except for two) managed to withdraw to the rear, after a hard-fought hand-to-hand battle with the enemy.

Watson left his brigade on 22 April 1916 and returned to England to take command of the 4th Canadian Division. This was a new one in the Canadian Corps, and a few weeks earlier he had agreed to lead it at the invitation of Hughes. On this occasion, General Alderson (now Sir Edwin Alfred Hervey), mentioned in a letter to Colonel John Wallace Carson (the representative in England of the minister of militia and defence) that Watson "is a good fighting man and gets things done. I think too that he has the moral courage." Watson would command the unit until the end of the war and, as its leader, he would have difficult duties to perform. The 4th Division underwent its initiation in the fall of 1916, when, after the rest of the Canadian Corps had left for the Vimy sector in France, he was ordered to capture Regina Trench. He succeeded in doing so on 11 Nov. 1916, after several weeks of efforts complicated by bad weather conditions.

It was, then, with a body of seasoned troops that Watson set out again within a few days to rejoin the Canadian Corps, which was defending a wide sector between Lens and Arras. On the first day of the battle of Vimy, 9 April 1917, the 4th Canadian Division was given the job of capturing Hill 145 and a nearby height known as the Pimple. Hill 145 was the highest and most strategically important position on the ridge. It was also the best protected, with two lines of defence. As Gerald William Lingen Nicholson, the historian of the Canadian Expeditionary Force, would later note, "It was thus a valuable prize, though the task of attaining it was formidable." The 4th Division took three days to reach its objectives. On 12 April Major-General Watson was able to report, "Mission accomplished!"

Under Watson's command, the division took part next in the battles of Hill 70 (15–25 Aug. 1917) and Passchendaele (26 Oct.–10 Nov. 1917), in Belgium. In 1918 it fought, in France, in the battles of Amiens (8–11 August), Arras (26 August–2 September), and Cambrai (27 September–9 October), the last "the hardest in its career," said Major Charles Bethune Lindsey, a member of Watson's staff. The division captured the town of Denain on 19 Oct. 1918 and it took part in the liberation of Valenciennes in November.

On 21 May 1919 Watson presided over a dinner for 200 members of the 4th Division at the Savoy Hotel in London, England. This last meeting before going home was a source of pride to him. On 1 July 1919, with feelings of relief and joy, he saw his home town once again. "So," his journal noted, "after nearly 5 years of active service, I have returned safe & secure

home again. And after what terrible experiences & what fearful hardships & sufferings." He would scarcely have time to resume his normal activities, however, since he was to die within three years. During that period he carried on his work at the *Quebec Chronicle*, in which he had purchased a majority of shares shortly after his return. He was also chairman of the Quebec Harbour Commission. According to Colonel William Charles Henry Wood*, the war had undermined his health. He had had heavy responsibilities and had shown great concern for the safety and welfare of his troops. For his bravery and distinguished conduct at the front, Watson was awarded the Croix de Guerre by both France and Belgium and was appointed a commander of the Legion of Honour and the Ordre de Léopold. On 4 June 1917 he had been made a CMG and on 1 Jan. 1918 a KCB. Two years earlier he had been honoured with a CB.

Watson was a Presbyterian and he belonged to a number of prestigious societies, including the Garrison Club of Quebec, the St James Club of Montreal, and the Royal Automobile Club of London, England. A member of the masonic St Andrew's Lodge No.6 at Quebec, he became deputy grand master for the District of Quebec and Three Rivers. In 1921 he was a member of the founding council of the Canadian Legion of Veterans and he was granted an honorary DCL by Bishop's College. His business career extended well beyond his work at the *Quebec Chronicle*, since he sat on a number of boards of directors, including those of the Canadian Bankers' Association, Mortgage, Discount and Finance Limited, Davie Shipbuilding and Repairing Company Limited, and the Prudential Trust Company Limited. Nonetheless, he remained a thoroughly modest man, according to Wood.

Murray noted that Watson had left an indelible impression as head of the 2nd Battalion. In his words, "'Davie' Watson became a legend in the Second. Occasionally a martinet, he was never unfair. Stern he was, and it was not always easy for him to unbend; but he was a competent, able commander, and a just one." He was the only regimental commander in the militia to command a division in the Canadian Corps.

JEAN-PIERRE GAGNON

ANQ-Q, CE301-S67, 16 avril 1869, 11 sept. 1893; Index BMS, dist. judiciaire de Québec, Chalmers Free Church (Chalmers-Wesley United Church, Québec), 21 févr. 1922. LAC, MG 30, E69 (mfm.); RG 9, III, A1, vol. 231, file 6-W-4; RG 150, Acc. 1992–93/166, box 10132-13. *Le Devoir*, 20 févr. 1922. *News* (Toronto), 25 Aug. 1915. *Quebec Chronicle*, 20 Feb. 1922. A. F. Duguid, *Official history of the Canadian forces in the Great War, 1914–1919* (only 1v. in 2 pts. [1914–September 1915] was published, Ottawa, 1938). C. B. Lindsey, *The story of the Fourth Canadian Division, 1916–1919* (Aldershot, Eng., [1919]). W. W. Murray, *The* history of the 2nd Canadian Battalion (East. Ontario Regiment), Canadian Expeditionary Force, in the Great War, 1914–1919 ([Ottawa], 1947). Nicholson, CEF. The storied province of Quebec; past and present, ed. W. [C. H.] Wood et al. (5v., Toronto, 1931–32), 3: 22–23.

WEBSTER, ELLA HOBDAY (Bronson), social activist; b. 1 Sept. 1846 in Portsmouth, Va, daughter of Nathan Burnham Webster and Isabella Fish Hobday; m. 8 Sept. 1874 Erskine Henry Bronson in Norfolk, Va, and they had two sons who died as infants and a son and a daughter who survived them; d. 11 Feb. 1925 in Ottawa.

Ella Hobday Webster's father, a cousin of the American politician Daniel Webster, was a prominent southern American educator. Before settling in Ottawa in 1862, Nathan Burnham Webster taught at the Baptist College in Richmond, Va, served as principal of the Military Academy in Portsmouth, and founded and led the Virginia Collegiate Institute in Norfolk. He moved his family to Canada to avoid the Civil War, and remained here until 1869, when he left to establish the Webster Institute in Norfolk.

How Ella Hobday Webster met Erskine Bronson is not known. He was a member of one of Ottawa's most distinguished families, which had made its wealth in the timber trade. After their marriage in Virginia in 1874, Erskine and Ella returned to the Canadian capital. Erskine went on to become a provincial cabinet minister in the government of Oliver Mowat*; Ella was known as a devoted, if sentimental, mother. Her public career began in earnest only after her primary domestic and child-raising duties were behind her. In 1889 she worked with Lady Macdonald [Bernard*] in planning an emigration scheme to bring female domestic servants from Britain. In 1891 she helped Lady Stanley, the wife of the governor general, to arrange some "ambulance lectures," or first-aid courses, and between 1890 and 1892 she served on several informal committees, also with Lady Stanley, to furnish the new nurses' institute building. She was also treasurer for funds raised to provide Ottawa soldiers with comforts during the South African War. A staunch member of St Andrew's Presbyterian Church, she was active in its women's missionary society and sat on a number of committees.

In 1893 Ella Bronson answered a call from Lady Aberdeen [Marjoribanks*] to help establish the National Council of Women of Canada. Although she served as a delegate to several national conventions, she was more consistently involved at the local level, where most of the council's work was centred. Local councils were associated with the national one in a loose federation. Like the missionary societies of the churches, they educated potential female leaders such as Bronson; through them, women learned about the economic and social needs of their community and acquired a network of female contacts; they also provided a legitimate forum from which women could exercise authority and defend the Christian family as they saw it.

A vice-president of the Ottawa Local Council of Women from 1894 until 1911, Bronson served on committees to lobby for the teaching of domestic science in the city's high schools, the creation of a free library system, and the establishment of cottages for consumptives. In 1894 she pioneered the Associated Charities of Ottawa, a scheme intended to coordinate the efforts of various agencies, set standards for recipients of charity, and provide work-placement programs for the unemployed.

The culmination of Ella Bronson's public projects was the foundation and successful operation of the Ottawa Maternity Hospital. With Bronson as president and an all-female board of directors, the hospital opened in 1895, and it functioned until the mid 1920s, when it was absorbed into the Civic Hospital. Much of its funding was raised by Bronson through her contacts in the elites of government and the lumber industry, and she served as its president for nearly 30 years. Fashioned on a new, medical, model of hospital, the Ottawa Maternity Hospital provided obstetrical services to women, most of whom paid a small fee. It eschewed any religious agenda, although it accepted support from church groups, and did not concern itself with its patients' moral purity as some institutions did. Professionalism was stressed, and from 1897 a three-month certification course was offered for nurses from other hospitals. They were educated in post-natal medical and nutritional care for new mothers as well as in pre-natal and obstetrical matters. By the hospital's 25th anniversary in 1920, it had trained 600 nurses, and by its closing it had served more than 10,000 patients. On 3 Feb. 1925 Ella Bronson signed over its property to the city; she took ill the next day and died a week later.

Ella Bronson's contribution to her community, in a private life of duty and kindness and a high-profile public career, was representative of that made by a legion of women who were intent on reshaping society. The Ottawa Journal commemorated her life of engagement when it praised her as "a notable figure, who had given her best in public service." Her husband had predeceased her, and her estate, which was worth about $450,000, was left to family members.

SHARON ANNE COOK

AO, RG 22-354, no.12212-310. Commonwealth of Virginia, Dept. of Health, Div. of vital records (Richmond), Marriage certificate, Norfolk, 8 Sept. 1874. LAC, MG 9, D7-35, 113; MG 27, I, B5, 8–10; MG 28, I 32; I 37, 1–2; III 26, 719. North York Central Library (Toronto), Canadiana Coll., Ontario Geneal. Soc. Library coll., cemetery transcripts, Beechwood Cemetery (Ottawa), sect.50: 44. Ottawa Citizen, October

1899, 12 Feb. 1925. *Ottawa Evening Journal*, October 1896, October 1898, November 1908, May 1909, February 1910, June 1912, December 1918, November 1922, 12 Feb. 1925. *Ottawa Free Press*, June 1899. S. A. Cook, "A helping hand and shelter: Anglo-Protestant social service agencies in Ottawa, 1880–1910" (MA thesis, Carleton Univ., Ottawa, 1987). R. P. Gillis, "E. H. Bronson and corporate capitalism: a study in Canadian business thought and action, 1880–1910" (MA thesis, Queen's Univ., Kingston, Ont., 1975). N. E. S. Griffiths, *The splendid vision: centennial history of the National Council of Women of Canada, 1893–1993* (Ottawa, 1993). Protestant Orphans' Home, *Annual report* (Ottawa), 1864–1925 (copies in City of Ottawa Arch.). [These reports reveal that secondary sources are wrong in claiming Ella Hobday Webster was known for her work with this home; it was her mother-in-law and sister-in-law who were involved in its management. S.A.C.]

WELDON, ISAAC HILLOCK, industrialist; b. 17 Nov. 1874 near Bowmanville, Ont., son of James Weldon and Derenda Rooney, farmers; m. 1905 Georgia Jones of Alexandria, Ind.; they had no children; d. 17 Oct. 1928 in Toronto.

During Isaac H. Weldon's early childhood, his Irish immigrant parents moved with their large family to a farm south of Woodstock, Ont., where he attended high school. He moved to Toronto, apparently to study medicine, but went to work instead with his eldest brother, Thomas Andrew, manager of the office there of the E. B. Eddy Company, a leading maker of fine paper [*see* Ezra Butler Eddy*]. Isaac left the company in 1899 to join Laurentide Paper, a newsprint producer in Grand-Mère, Que., as its North American sales agent; four years later he became sales manager for Burgess Sulphite of New England, which manufactured chemical wood pulp.

In 1909 Weldon teamed up with a handful of American pulp and paper industrialists who, led by his longtime friend Smith Frederick Duncan, owned Bryant Paper of Kalamazoo, Mich. This clique formed the St Lawrence Paper Mills Company in Toronto to take over the fine-paper mill of the bankrupt Cornwall Paper Company at Mille Roches (Long Sault), Ont. Weldon was appointed president, and he and his wife took up residence in Toronto. In 1910 the group, which now included Thomas Weldon, purchased Montrose Paper in Thorold and Barber Paper and Coating Mills in Georgetown [*see* John Roaf Barber*]. The following year Isaac Weldon was a driving force behind the establishment of Interlake Tissue Mills at Merritton (St Catharines), which he would serve as vice-president until his death. Then, in 1913, the group incorporated Provincial Paper Mills under Weldon's presidency to consolidate the operations of St Lawrence, Montrose, and Barber. Weldon would build Provincial into one of Canada's largest producers of book, writing, and coated papers and would carve out a niche for it within the industry.

Although his business affairs were definitely his life's focus – he was a member of the Toronto Board of Trade and the Canadian Manufacturers' Association – he displayed the benevolent streak that also marked many of his contemporaries. A director of the Hospital for Sick Children, he supported the Toronto Playgrounds Association, the Art Gallery of Toronto, and the Boys' Industrial Home in Bowmanville. In his leisure he frequented the National, Granite, Lakeview Golf, and Royal Canadian Yacht clubs, and he maintained a valuable rural property, Summit Farm, north of Richmond Hill. According to one biographer, he was "a man of simple tastes, a delightful and many-sided companion" who possessed a "keen sense of humour" and "showed easy tolerance of the mistakes of others."

Weldon personified his era's progressive business ethos: his strength lay not in technical expertise but in industrial entrepreneurialism. Whereas newsprint, which most of the country's mills manufactured, was sold duty-free in the United States, the fine papers made by Weldon's companies (mainly for books and magazines) were subjected to prohibitive tariffs. This situation forced him to concentrate on the relatively small domestic market, where one of Provincial's clients, Eaton's, needed large supplies of paper for its famous catalogues. To meet the market challenge, Weldon both expanded his product lines and fostered cooperation among producers. He was a co-founder of the Canadian Pulp and Paper Association in 1913, its first vice-president the following year, and president in 1915. In 1918 he took Provincial in as an inaugural member of the Canadian Paper Trade Association, which represented Canada's few fine-paper makers and many of its paper-goods producers, among them W. J. Gage and Company [*see* Sir William James GAGE]. To maximize members' profits and create barriers against potential rivals, it divided the country into sales zones, developed guidelines for standardizing products, and enforced a common sales policy. The upshot was a steady rise in consumption, few new players, and consistent profits.

Vertical integration was another step that Weldon took to consolidate his position. Provincial Paper controlled three converting mills, which turned pulp into paper, but it still purchased its pulp on the open market. To remedy this situation, over the course of 1916–17 Port Arthur Pulp and Paper was incorporated as a subsidiary with Weldon as president and a mill was erected in Port Arthur (Thunder Bay), Ont., to turn spruce into the sulphite pulp required by Provincial's other plants. In 1920 he and his partners incorporated a new Provincial Paper Mills company, of which Weldon continued as president, to combine formally the securities and assets of Provincial and Port Arthur Pulp and Paper.

Isaac Weldon was renowned for his managerial

skills, which he amply demonstrated in his dealings with the Ontario government. Prior to constructing the Port Arthur mill, in 1917 Provincial had applied for a pulpwood limit to support the plant, but it lost in the bidding for the tract. Thwarted in his subsequent efforts to secure a long-term timber supply – the sine qua non for a pulp and paper mill – Weldon tried a different tack in 1920, with the new United Farmers government of Ernest Charles Drury*. Provincial reapplied for another large limit, but this time he exerted pressure by threatening to cut off the supply of paper to magazine publishers if the government did not deliver the tract he wanted. Led by Harold Theodore Gagnier of *Saturday Night* (Toronto), the publishers lobbied Drury to grant Provincial's wish. Provincial concomitantly made a special offer. The Department of Education had traditionally experienced difficulty in purchasing the quantity of paper it needed for textbooks at prices it considered reasonable. Provincial proposed to supply the paper in exchange for the limit. An agreement was signed in July 1921 and thereafter Provincial enjoyed a relationship with the government that ensured it had more than enough timber.

Weldon's association with Provincial ended in 1927, when Dominion Securities of Toronto gained control by purchasing its common stock. By this time he had established himself as one of the pioneers in Canada's modern pulp and paper industry. He died in Toronto in 1928 and was buried in Mount Pleasant Cemetery.

MARK KUHLBERG

AO, F 229-35, box 1, item 5, paper contract, 1914; RG 3-4-0-86; RG 22-305, no.60364; RG 80-8-0-1087, no.6720. LAC, RG 31, C1, 1871, Darlington Township, Ont., div.2: 8. Ont., Ministry of Natural Resources, lands and waters branch, crown land registry (Peterborough, Ont.), Crown land files, files 9457, 11217, 12156, 18284, 61304. *Globe*, 18 Oct. 1928. Canadian Pulp and Paper Assoc., *A handbook of the Canadian pulp and paper industry* (Montreal, 1920). *Directory*, Toronto, 1892–1915. *Pulp and Paper Magazine of Canada* (Gardenvale, Que.), 26 (1928): 1477–78; 27 (January–June 1929), "International number": 67. *Standard dict. of Canadian biog.* (Roberts and Tunnell). *Who's who and why*, 1919/20. *Who's who in Canada*, 1925/26.

WELDON, RICHARD CHAPMAN, educator, lawyer, and politician; b. 19 Jan. 1849 in Sussex Parish, N.B., son of Richard Chapman Weldon and Catherine Geldart; m. first 11 July 1877 Sarah Maria Tuttle (d. 1892) in Stellarton, N.S., and they had four sons and one daughter; m. secondly 28 Dec. 1893 Louisa Frances Hare (d. 1957) in Halifax, and they had two sons and five daughters; d. 26 Nov. 1925 in Dartmouth, N.S.

The Weldons were among the Yorkshire Methodists who settled in the Maritimes in the 18th century. Richard Chapman Weldon and his seven siblings were raised on a farm at Penobsquis, N.B., where he developed into a tall, athletic young man who loved the outdoors. Mount Allison Wesleyan College in Sackville was a natural magnet for a person with Weldon's intellectual leanings. After graduating in 1866 with his BA at age 17, he taught school for two years near Sussex. He would later return to Mount Allison to teach and to obtain his MA in economics (1870). In 1868–69 and 1871–72 he attended Yale College in New Haven, Conn., following in the footsteps of his eldest brother. There he studied constitutional and international law under Richard Henry Dana and Theodore Dwight Woolsey, and graduated with his doctorate in political science in 1872.

Encouraged by his mentors at Yale, Weldon decided to pursue further studies in international law at the Rupert Charles University of Heidelberg in Germany. Adept at languages (he was fluent in German), he soaked up European culture, marvelling at medieval architecture and walking to nearby Mannheim to attend opera rehearsals. Perhaps the cultural diet was too rich: he suffered some kind of breakdown and had to return home in early 1873. This illness incapacitated him until 1875 when he accepted President David ALLISON's offer of a professorship in mathematics and political economy at Mount Allison. The first PHD to join the faculty, he quickly developed a reputation as an excellent teacher in spite of being occasionally obliged to take on subjects as diverse as botany, zoology, and geology in addition to his regular load. Weldon was a firm supporter of university consolidation in the Maritimes, serving as an examiner for the University of Halifax until its collapse in 1881.

Benjamin Russell*, a former fellow student at Mount Allison and a lifelong friend, kept Weldon abreast of the attempts to create a law school in Halifax in the 1870s and early 1880s. These centred on Dalhousie University in spite of its state of near-bankruptcy. The decision of expatriate Nova Scotian philanthropist George Munro* to endow five chairs at Dalhousie allowed these efforts to come to fruition. When Munro wrote to the board of governors in March 1883 offering $40,000 to endow a chair in constitutional and international law, he noted that Weldon had been "recommended by competent judges as most suitable to be at the head of the Law Faculty." Weldon accepted the board's offer, becoming the first full-time professor of law in post-confederation Canada. It may be that a "draft Weldon" movement had begun as early as 1880, when the then professor of mathematics apprenticed himself to a Sackville lawyer. Weldon's articles were recognized by the Nova Scotia Barristers' Society, and he was called to the bar on 9 Dec. 1884.

Modern university legal education was in its infancy

in the 1880s. The Harvard law school had come out of its ante-bellum torpor only with the 1870 appointment of Dean Christopher Columbus Langdell, who clothed legal study with the mantle of a science and insisted on a more interactive and analytical classroom atmosphere. Harvard tended nevertheless to stress the instrumental and practical side of law. Weldon's training drew him to the cultural side, and he included in the curriculum courses in international law, constitutional history, and conflict of laws. The more traditional, professionally oriented subjects were taught by his lieutenant Benjamin Russell and a group of talented members of the Halifax bar, such as Robert Sedgewick* and John Sparrow David Thompson*. Weldon managed to secure the services of John Thomas Bulmer* for a year as founding librarian, and a respectable library of some 5,000 volumes was soon in place. Weldon aired his dreams for the infant institution in his inaugural address, when he encouraged his audience "to build up in this city of Halifax a university with faculties of arts, medicine, applied science and law . . . that shall influence the intellectual life of Canada as Harvard and Yale have influenced the intellectual life of New England."

No sooner was the law school up and running than Weldon launched into a second career as a federal MP. He ran for the Conservatives in the 1887 election in Albert, N.B., where he owned a farm. Law student Richard Bedford Bennett* helped Weldon canvass the county in the 1891 campaign, when he was re-elected. The law-school year was altered to run from September to February so as to accommodate Weldon's absence in Ottawa. This system continued after his defeat in the Liberal sweep of 1896, when Russell in turn became an MP, and continued "through sheer academic inertia" (in the words of John Willis, the historian of the law school) until 1911, seven years after Russell's elevation to the bench.

Weldon displayed an intense interest in public affairs and tried to instil a sense of public service in his students. By today's standards his political career was only modestly productive, but in his own day he was a highly esteemed parliamentarian and at one point was considered as a potential prime minister. He achieved recognition mainly for an 1889 act extending existing extradition legislation to fugitives from countries with which the United Kingdom had no extradition treaty, and expanding the list of crimes for which American fugitives in Canada could be extradited to the United States. The provisions of this act, known to contemporaries as the Weldon Act, remain in today's Extradition Act. In 1894 Weldon was responsible for the passage of a measure providing for the disenfranchisement for seven years of any person found to have sold his vote at a federal election. He himself had been accused of bribing electors in the 1887 and 1891 elections by John Thomas HAWKE, editor of Moncton's Liberal *Daily*

Transcript, but had successfully sued for libel. Something of a gadfly to his own party, Weldon refused to support federal remedial legislation to solve the Manitoba school crisis, and urged upon a reluctant government disallowance of Nova Scotia's 1893 legislation granting extensive rights over provincial coal to Boston industrialist Henry Melville WHITNEY. In early 1896 Weldon was actively involved in a clandestine attempt to find an alternative to Sir Charles Tupper* as a successor to Prime Minister Sir Mackenzie Bowell*. He ran again for parliament, unsuccessfully, in 1900 and 1906.

The law school's success in attracting students from the west coast provided Weldon with some interesting contacts. In 1910 alumnus Richard McBride*, then premier of British Columbia, asked the dean to chair a commission charged with finding a location for the new University of British Columbia. After touring 12 communities, they settled on the Point Grey site. A less successful trip to British Columbia in 1900 had seen Weldon searching for a non-existent mica mine into which he had poured some of the family savings.

Weldon's initial salary of $2,000 was very generous by contemporary standards (the premier of Nova Scotia earned $2,400 in 1883), but it had risen only to $3,000 by the time of his retirement three decades later. Appointed a dominion QC in 1890, he acted as counsel to the firm of Harris, Henry, and Cahan from 1897. Never wealthy, Weldon was nonetheless able to accommodate his large family in two of Dartmouth's stately homes, Lakeside and The Brae, the latter the early Victorian mansion in which he died. The Weldons also spent some years in a gracious home on Inglis Street in Halifax's south end.

It is a fair observation of historian Della Stanley that the school's opening years, "which can be seen as creative and experimental, were followed by a long period of consolidation ending in routine activity and relative stagnancy." During Weldon's later years a new generation of students wanted more hours of instruction, and sought to have courses such as civil procedure and agency law substituted for his courses in constitutional history and international law. Their restiveness was reflected in verse in the Dalhousie *Gazette* in 1914, the year of Weldon's retirement:

I'm familiar with the judgments of all the higher courts,
From the Fourteenth Century Year-Books to Dominion Law Reports;
In general jurisprudence I can give full satisfaction,
But – I don't know what is proper for the conduct of an action.

The bar supported this move to a more professionally oriented curriculum, as did the new dean, Donald Alexander MacRae. His revised curriculum became the standard adopted by the Canadian Bar Association in 1920 and exported to emerging university law schools across the country. The liberal tradition inaugurated by Weldon was not displaced but it was somewhat overshadowed by these developments.

Weldon was the sole full-time professor at the law school during the entire 31 years of his deanship. His working relationship with his half-time colleague Russell – who called Weldon "*dimidium animae meae*, the other half of my soul" – has been compared to that of Langdell and James Barr Ames at Harvard and Albert Venn Dicey and William Martin Geldart at Oxford. The Weldon–Russell team covered what they believed to be the essential curriculum and relied on the Halifax bar to supply the rest. Even then, Weldon was often called upon to fill in gaps: he taught crimes for over a decade, was obliged in 1893 to take on shipping, which he then taught until 1914, and in 1905 added torts to his repertoire – all of these in addition to his "signature" courses. The efforts of Weldon and Russell to conjure up an academic legal education with virtually no resources were nothing short of heroic. If there is an aspect of Weldon's deanship that is open to criticism, it would be the absence of women students at the law school. It is not known whether Weldon actively discouraged women from studying law, but he certainly could not have encouraged them. Nor does it seem that he urged the Nova Scotia Barristers' Society to review its traditional exclusion of women from the profession. It was only in 1915 that the law school admitted its first woman student. Two black students graduated during Weldon's tenure, however, the first being James Robinson Johnston* in 1898.

Given the demands on him as professor and administrator, and those of his political career, it is perhaps not surprising that Weldon left no trace in scholarship. His marked mental deterioration (probably Alzheimer's disease), evident as early as 1906, foreclosed any possibility of academic work after his retirement. Even apart from these impediments, it may be that Weldon had no coherent vision of the Canadian constitution that he felt compelled to set down. In all that has been written about him, and in his political speeches and activities, it is difficult to discern any consistent constitutional theory on his part beyond a basic commitment to federalism and to British rather than American conceptions of law and politics. (Weldon would remain an ardent imperialist and harboured a lifelong suspicion of all things American.) In any case, during the law school's early years the priority had to be on the educational enterprise itself, and on those foundations subsequent deans and faculty members found it easy to erect a scholarly superstructure.

It is as an educator that Weldon is still deservedly remembered, and on this basis that historian P. B. Waite has declared that he was "of all Munro's great gifts to Dalhousie, perhaps . . . the most fruitful one of all." With the encouragement of the local bar, Weldon firmly anchored legal education in a university milieu, creating a model which would radiate across Canada in the 20th century. He lectured in the grand manner rather than employing the newer Socratic method of teaching, and his effect on students was magnetic. They never forgot his combination of intellectual power, impressive demeanour, and personal solicitude, which nourished a potent Weldon mystique that long outlived the dean himself. No doubt his students shared the sense of excitement that comes from being involved in any new and innovative enterprise, but it was Weldon who communicated its significance. He oriented his project around a vision of civic virtue and national service, encouraging his students to look beyond the confines of their community and even their profession. As Premier Angus Lewis Macdonald* would declare on the occasion of the school's 50th anniversary, triumphally fêted in 1933, Weldon had given Dalhousie "not merely a Law School but a breeding ground for public service and public men." The number of graduates who had risen to prominent positions across Canada and abroad in the judiciary, law, politics, and business by that time confirmed the accuracy of Macdonald's eulogy. When Dalhousie opened its new law building in 1966 it was not only inevitable but appropriate that it would be named after the founding dean. On its centenary in 1983, when the law school wished to establish a new prize to honour outstanding accomplishment by a graduate, it created the Weldon Award for Unselfish Public Service. Shortly after the dean's retirement former students had commissioned a portrait of him by Edmund Wyly Grier*. It presides in the foyer, and each new generation of students is introduced to the "Weldon tradition."

PHILIP GIRARD

[Weldon left little in the way of personal papers, though descendants in Halifax retain some memorabilia. The Dalhousie Univ. Arch. contains very little relating to Weldon. The Dalhousie Law School Arch. possesses not much more, but holdings include Weldon's lecture notes from his constitutional history course and the notes of a student, Stephen Edgar March, taken in Weldon's constitutional law course in 1891–92. His discourse at the opening of the law school was published in A. G. Archibald and R. C. Weldon, *The inaugural addresses, &c. delivered at the opening of the law school in connection with Dalhousie University, Halifax, Nova Scotia, at the beginning of the first term in 1883* (Halifax, 1884). Aside from this item and his speeches recorded in Can., House of Commons, *Debates*, 1887–96, which are not extensive, Weldon left no publications, which has only added to his legend. The best treatment of his role at Dalhousie is John Willis, *A history of Dalhousie law school* (Toronto, 1979). Della Stanley provides as complete a biography as we are ever likely to have and examines some of the contradictions in Weldon's life in "Richard Chapman Weldon, 1849–1925: fact, fiction and enigma," *Dalhousie Law Journal*

(Halifax), 12 (1989): 539–66. A sidelight on Weldon's role as a political lobbyist aiming to obtain an exemption from anti-pollution regulations for a sawmill owner in his Albert County constituency is found in Gilbert Allardyce, "'The vexed question of sawdust': river pollution in nineteenth century New Brunswick," *Dalhousie Rev.* (Halifax), 52 (1972): 177–90. For the Dalhousie context, see P. B. Waite, *The lives of Dalhousie University* (2v., Montreal and Kingston, Ont., 1994–98), 1. On Weldon's years at Mount Allison, see J. G. Reid, *Mount Allison University: a history, to 1963* (2v., Toronto, 1984). Benjamin Russell's *Autobiography . . .* (Halifax, 1932) contains several lengthy passages on Weldon, and includes the full text of the tribute he published in the *Evening Mail* (Halifax) at the time of Weldon's retirement. P.G.]

NSARM, RG 39, ser.M, 13, file 11. *Atlantic Weekly* (Dartmouth, N.S.), 2 Feb. 1895. *Dalhousie Gazette* (Halifax), 7 Nov. 1923. *Dartmouth Free Press*, 22 March 1967. *Evening Mail* (Halifax), 27 Nov. 1925. *Halifax Herald*, 27–28 Nov. 1925. *Morning Chronicle* (Halifax), 27 Nov. 1925. *Alumni News* (Halifax), December 1925. Can., *Statutes* (Ottawa), 1889: c.36; 1894: c.14. *Canadian Bar Rev.* (Toronto), 11 (1933): 402–3. J. E. Read, "Jurist and mentor of jurists" [book review], *Canadian Bar Rev.*, 11: 68–69. B[enjamin] Russell, "Richard Chapman Weldon," *Canadian Bar Rev.*, 4 (1926): 197–200.

WELLS, EMMA LUCY (Dickson), novelist; b. 21 Nov. 1854 in Nova Scotia, daughter of Stanford Wells and Alvira ——; m. 11 Jan. 1872 William John Dickson in Truro, N.S., and they had five surviving children; d. 19 March 1926 in Dartmouth, N.S.

Reputedly born in Truro, Emma Wells seems to have spent her early years in Maine and then in Prince Edward Island, where in 1864 her father owned a marble works in Charlottetown. After receiving a common school education on the Island, she moved to Truro with her parents; subsequently, her father was variously described as a "self acting hand loom manufacturer" and a mason. At 17 she married William Dickson, a man ten years her senior, who by 1881 had ceased being a pattern maker and had become a conductor on the Intercolonial Railway. In July 1896 Emma Dickson moved to Halifax. Newspaper notices on the death of her daughter Bertha on 24 Aug. 1897 would suggest that by this time the entire family had relocated.

With the publication in 1895, by William BRIGGS in Toronto, of *Miss Dexie, a romance of the provinces*, a novel written under the pseudonym Stanford Eveleth, Dickson had begun to achieve public attention. Although drawing on the Maine, Halifax, and Prince Edward Island settings of Dickson's own background, *Miss Dexie* bears similarities to Louisa May Alcott's *Little women* in its Civil War time-frame, its independent female protagonist ("One does not need to be born a boy to be of use in this world . . . for in all things that he needs help, I am my father's boy."), its abortive romance with the boy next door, its androgynously named heroine (Dexie for Dexter), and its

stress on a close family circle. However, Dickson introduced her own distinctive touches to these conventions, particularly in her integration into her tale of train travel, Halifax social life, the worship of the Prince Edward Island McDonaldites [*see* Donald McDonald*], and the Victorian redesign of the kitchen. Toronto's *Saturday Night* of 6 April 1895 praised the novel for its "well drawn character" of Miss Dexie, its exposure of selfish behaviour, and its humour (for example, a naive, intoxicated potato farmer from the Island mistakes the train's passenger car for a chapel, the seats for pews, and the conductor for the sexton). Quoting Dickson on 22 June that she had found it necessary to marry off her heroine "as if marriage were the chief end of woman," *Saturday Night* indicated that a sequel was planned if the novel was a success. By the end of November it had reached a third edition and had also been reviewed by the *Toronto Week*, the *Portland Transcript* (Portland, Maine), the *Orillia Packet* (Orillia, Ont.), the *Christian Guardian* (Toronto), and the *Halifax Herald*. Available in cloth at $1.00 and paperback at 50 cents, it continued to be bound by Briggs in runs of 100 paper and 100 cloth until 16 Feb. 1907, when the account was closed.

Dickson's description of a McDonaldite church service forms one of the most colourful sequences of the novel and, according to *Saturday Night*, "brought down upon her head the wrath of the congregation." It was followed on 7 Dec. 1895 by an article in this magazine, "The Jerkers," based on Dickson's visit to a McDonaldite service at Birch Hill, near Pownal, P.E.I., in September. Expressing her disapproval that such evangelical leaping, twirling, and waving was allowed, she none the less created a vivid image of her subjects, writing of one participant, "Turning again, with both arms she salaamed toward the wind-bag in the pulpit, then curveting around she went through the same performance for the benefit of those in the rear, all the while her feet and body being in rhythmical motion." An article on "The new man" in the *Halifax Herald Woman's Extra* on 10 Aug. 1895 had struck an equally acerbic note when Dickson predicted that the "new woman" would prefer single life until such time as the "new man" had evolved enough to ensure both her individuality and her right to make choices about motherhood.

Dickson reputedly wrote children's stories as well as adult fare, but she seems to have disappeared from literary view in the late 1890s. Active in St Paul's Church in Halifax and in charitable pursuits until she became an invalid towards the end of her life, she died in 1926, three years after her husband. Her obituary in the Halifax *Morning Chronicle* described her as "a firm believer in British Israel, and a student of the prophetic writings," but made no mention of her literary output. Yet the lively dialogue, humorous play, and intelligence of her heroine in *Miss Dexie* all reflect her considerable adeptness at writing popular fiction.

GWENDOLYN DAVIES

LAC, RG 31, C1, Truro, N.S., 1871, 1881, 1891; 1901, Halifax, subdist.E, subdiv.4: 7. NSARM, Churches, St Andrew's United (Truro), reg. of marriages, 11 Jan. 1872 (mfm.); St John's Anglican (Truro), reg. of burials, 1897 (mfm.); RG 32, WB, Colchester County, no.29/1872. UCC-C, Fonds 513/1, 83.061C, vols.43–44. *Halifax Herald Woman's Extra*, 10 Aug. 1895. *Morning Chronicle* (Halifax), 19, 22 March 1926. "'A romance of the provinces,' from the *Christian Guardian*, Toronto," *Halifax Herald*, 22 Nov. 1895: 8. *Truro Daily News*, 26 Aug., 1 Nov. 1895; 20 July 1896; 25 Aug. 1897. *Canadian men and women of the time* (Morgan; 1898). M. B. DesBrisay, *History of the county of Lunenburg* (2nd ed., Toronto, 1895; repr. Belleville, Ont., 1980), advertisement, "Some well-known writers of or from the Maritime provinces and their books," in the end-papers. *Directories*, Halifax, 1897/98: 198; 1898/99: 209; 1900–1; N.S., 1871: 376; P.E.I., 1864. *Saturday Night*, 6 April, 22 June, 7 Dec. 1895.

WEN WUQING. *See* NG MON HING

WESTON, GEORGE, baker, businessman, and politician; b. 23 March 1865 in Oswego, N.Y., son of William Weston and Ann ——; m. 3 April 1889 Emma Maud Richards in Toronto, and they had six children, of whom two sons and two daughters survived childhood; d. there 6 April 1924.

As a child – the youngest of seven – George Weston moved with his family to Toronto so that his father, a labourer, might find better work than was available in Oswego. He received a rudimentary education at Wellesley Street School. At age 12 he found employment in the Yonge Street bakery of Charles J. Frogley, where he learned the physically demanding craft of bread-making; some three years later he began work at another bakery, operated by Gilbert H. Bowen. While employed there, the short, lean youth evidently began delivering bread and was introduced to sales and marketing techniques.

In 1882, at 17, Weston purchased two bread routes from Bowen. Through hard work he was able to acquire more; it was on one of his routes that he met Emma Maud Richards, a maid, whom he married. In 1892 he took over Bowen's bakery, then located on Sullivan Street in the Grange area north of Queen. By the mid 1890s it was a moderately successful enterprise. Weston employed several horse-drawn delivery wagons and about 15 people; according to one source, his success stemmed in part from the fact that he paid his employees so little. Around this time he introduced his affordable "homemade" loaf, which became popular among those unable to bake their own bread. Weston promoted value and quality, but as business historian Charles Davies observes, "he had an insider's knowledge of what people would accept and what he could get away with."

Weston astutely recognized that bakeries were undergoing considerable technological change. He was convinced that the future lay not in small, manual operations but in large, mechanized factories that utilized automatic bread-making machines. In 1897 he opened what became known as the Model Bakery on nearby Soho Street. At this point Weston's business took off. With a staff of 40 and a weekly payroll of roughly $350, it produced 3,200 loaves daily. In late 1900 he merged his business with that of John Lawrence Spink, a local grain merchant and mill owner, to form the Model Bakery Company Limited. For unknown reasons the partnership was formally dissolved on 1 Feb. 1907. In 1910 Weston opened a second plant, at Richmond and Peter streets, and a new firm, George Weston Limited, was incorporated that year.

A moderately prosperous businessman, Weston became involved in municipal politics. Between 1910 and 1914 he was an alderman for Ward 4. His campaign advertising in 1912, in which he presented himself as "the business man's candidate," suggests that he believed his commercial acumen could benefit local politics. By 1914, when he declined to run, he was beginning to attract other positions befitting a man of his status, among them seats on the boards of the Victoria Industrial School and the Toronto General Hospital. A devout Methodist, he generously supported the Bathurst Street Church.

In 1911, acting on a plan originally promoted by Niagara-area entrepreneur C. R. Morden to merge several large bakeries into one, Weston and others had formed the Canada Bread Company Limited. Organized and underwritten by Toronto financier Cawthra Mulock*, the enterprise united Weston with Mark Bredin and Henry C. Tomlin of Toronto, William J. Boyd of Winnipeg, and Enoh James Stuart of Montreal. Weston's participation was limited to investment and a directorship. Within two years, under Bredin's management, the company was producing some 3 million pounds per week nation-wide. Canada Bread's profits dropped as a result of supply and price fluctuations during World War I, after which depression and the federal regulation of flour content posed further difficulties for the firm. Still, by early 1919 its two Toronto bakeries alone were producing over 1.6 million pounds of bread each month.

Weston adhered to the agreement among the company's directors not to compete individually against Canada Bread in the manufacture of bread for a period of ten years. His Model Bakery, in fact, had been abandoned by the new company in 1913. He continued, however, to produce biscuits and cakes under the name George Weston Limited at his factory at Richmond and Peter streets. Having travelled to England to learn about biscuit making, he applied this knowledge well and developed a good market. In 1921, after the period of non-competition, he resigned from Canada Bread and began making bread again, with his son Willard Garfield* joining him in George Weston Limited as vice-president. By this time Weston was also active in the affairs of other companies. He was, for example, vice-president of the Permanent Realty Company and a director of the City Dairy Company Limited and the American Sales Book Company Limited.

In March 1924 Weston suffered a severe stroke. He died on 6 April at his home on Palmerston Boulevard and was buried in Mount Pleasant Cemetery. In many respects he was a typical, successful, turn-of-the-century Toronto businessman. Aside from his time in municipal politics, he did not seek public adulation. His belief in hard work, frugality, and Christian morality all contributed to making him representative of his sort. Moreover, his straightforward interest in expansion and surmounting competition, through the formation of Canada Bread, was certainly typical. In building a strong enterprise, he laid the foundations for the food and financial empire established by his son Garfield.

KERRY BADGLEY

A multi-media history of George Weston Limited has been issued by the company on CD-ROM under the title *Weston digital archive 1997* ([Toronto], 1997). The CD, which contains some information about George Weston, largely focuses on the later period of the company.
AO, RG 8-1-1, 5862/1900; RG 22-305, no.49809; RG 55-1-2-B, charter book no.61; RG 80-5-0-174, no.14326. LAC, RG 110, vol.1, bakers' monthly reports, February 1919. *Daily Mail and Empire*, 7 April 1924. *Globe*, 19 Dec. 1900; 23, 30 Dec. 1911; 2 Jan., 24 Dec. 1912; 2 Jan. 1913; 7 April 1924. *Monetary Times* (Toronto), 15 July 1911: 328; 5 Aug. 1911: 630. *Toronto Daily Star*, 7 April 1924. *World* (Toronto), 22 Feb. 1918. Charles Davies, *Bread men: how the Westons built an international empire* (Toronto, 1987). *Directory*, Toronto, 1874–1924. *Industrial Canada* (Toronto), 25 (1924–25): 84.

WETMORE, EDWARD LUDLOW, lawyer, politician, and judge; b. 24 March 1841 in Fredericton, son of Charles Peters Wetmore, a lawyer and clerk of the House of Assembly, and Sarah Burr Ketchum; m. 25 April 1872 Eliza Jane Dickson in Oromocto, N.B., and they had one daughter and two sons; d. 19 Jan. 1922 in Victoria.

Educated at grammar schools in Fredericton and Gagetown, Edward L. Wetmore was granted the BA degree with honours by King's College, Fredericton, in 1859. After studying in the law office of John Campbell Allen*, he was admitted as an attorney in June 1863 and was called to the bar one year later. He practised in Sussex for five years before relocating in Fredericton, where he eventually entered the firm of

John James Fraser* and Edward Byron Winslow, the leading legal office in the capital. Regarded by the *Canadian biographical dictionary* as "one of the foremost men of his age and profession in this part of the province, he being a well-read lawyer, a good logician and an effective speaker," Wetmore would be named a federal QC in 1881.

While carrying on his practice, Wetmore served as deputy clerk of the crown from 1869 to 1882, mayor of Fredericton ("an efficient and popular executive") from 1874 to 1876, a commissioner to revise the statutes of New Brunswick in 1877, and president of the Barristers' Society in 1886 and 1887. From 1884 to 1887 he was a member of the senate of the University of New Brunswick, which would grant him an honorary LLD in 1908. A Conservative in politics, Wetmore had been elected to the House of Assembly for York in 1882 and selected leader of the opposition in 1883. He was defeated in the general election of 1886.

In 1887 Wetmore was appointed a puisne judge of the Supreme Court of the North-West Territories for the district of Eastern Assiniboia and settled in Moosomin (Sask.). Considered by lawyer Charles Coursolles MCCAUL "quite the strongest member of the Court," he gained a reputation as a distinguished jurist, well versed in case law, both criminal and civil, stern but fair, whose emphasis on propriety and punctuality gave dignity to the court. His decisions, expressed in concise and cogent language, were only rarely reversed on appeal. He had a particular interest in civil procedure and his numerous procedural rulings helped shape the administration of justice in the west. In 1944 Hugh Amos Robson*, chief justice of the Manitoba Court of King's Bench and a former attorney general of the North-West Territories, would recall that the prairies of Wetmore's day presented considerable scope for the interpretation and application of laws. In 1889, in *The Queen v. Nan-e-quis-a-ka*, for example, Wetmore was required to rule on the status of marriages according to Indian custom; he concluded that they were valid in the Territories, and the court in banc subsequently supported his view. Wetmore also contributed much to the jurisprudence that emerged on the subject of the Torrens system of land registration, introduced throughout western Canada in the 1880s [see Louis William Coutlée*]. In 1907 he was appointed chief justice of the Supreme Court of Saskatchewan, "to the great satisfaction," in Robson's words, "of not only the bench and bar, but of the whole population." He held the position until his retirement in October 1912.

In addition to attending to his judicial responsibilities, Wetmore chaired the royal commissions to inquire into the "Herchmer Scandals" in 1891–92 [see Lawrence William Herchmer*] and to revise the statutes of Saskatchewan in 1906–9; in 1897–98 he and fellow judge Hugh Richardson* had constituted a commission to consolidate the ordinances of the North-West Territories, and in 1909 he was one of two commissioners appointed to investigate the contracts the Saskatchewan government had signed the previous year with Morang and Company for school readers. In 1907 he had been elected, without a dissenting voice, chancellor of the new University of Saskatchewan in Saskatoon, an office he held until 1917. A stalwart member of the Church of England, Wetmore served as delegate to the Diocesan Church Society, substitute delegate to the synod, and treasurer of the diocese of Qu'Appelle. He was also a third-degree freemason.

After his retirement Wetmore moved to British Columbia. His wife had died in an accident in 1905, the victim of runaway horses, and he lived in Victoria with his daughter Mary Ludlow and her husband, Albert Edward Christie. In 1913 he was named chair of the royal commission on Indian affairs for the province of British Columbia [see James Andrew Joseph McKenna*], and in 1916 he was appointed to a commission to determine whether contracts for roads entered into by the Saskatchewan government were fraudulent in any respect. Wetmore died in 1922 after a long illness, survived by his daughter and sons J. Allen and Valentine H., both then of Vancouver. His funeral was held in St Alban's Church in Moosomin on 25 January and his body was interred beside his wife's in the North Cemetery there.

A grateful University of Saskatchewan had awarded him an honorary DCL in 1919 and, after his death, the board of governors at its meeting of 3 April 1922 placed on record its appreciation of the services the late chief justice had rendered to the province and the university. The board minute, in part, states: "Both enjoy in rich measure the results of his great common sense, his judiciousness and his high sense of public duty in shaping those fundamental traditions which give character and direction to the activities of two of the most influential institutions of the State – the judiciary and the University. . . . during the critical period of selecting a site and adopting policies for the new University, he exercised a large influence in directing public opinion to place the good of the University above all sectarian, political and local interests. His name will ever be associated in our history, with those institutions which establish and foster justice, intelligence, and respect for law in the life of the people of this Province."

STANLEY D. HANSON

PANB (Fredericton), MC 1156. Saskatchewan Arch. Board (Saskatoon), Clippings files, Biogs. Univ. of Sask. Arch. (Saskatoon), RG M-1, 3 April 1922. *Daily Gleaner* (Fredericton), 20 Jan. 1922. *Morning Leader* (Regina), 20 Jan. 1922. W. F. Bowker, "Stipendiary magistrates and Supreme Court of the North-West Territories, 1876–1907," *Alberta Law Rev.* (Edmonton), 26 (1987–88): 245–86. *Canadian biographical dictionary and portrait gallery of eminent and self-made men* (2v., Toronto, 1880–81), 1. *Canadian men and women of the time* (Morgan; 1898). Michael Hayden, *Seeking a balance: the University of Saskatchewan, 1907–1982* (Vancouver, 1983). L. [A.] Knafla and Richard Klumpenhouwer, *Lords of the western bench: a biographical history of the supreme and district courts of Alberta, 1876–1990* (Calgary, 1997). C. C. McCaul, "Precursors of the bench and bar in the western provinces," *Canadian Bar Rev.* (Toronto), 3 (1925): 25–40. *Political appointments and judicial bench* (Coté). *The Queen v. Nan-e-quis-a-ka* (1889), *Territories Law Reports* (Toronto), 1: 211–16. H. A. Robson, "Edward Ludlow Wetmore," *Canadian Bar Rev.* (Ottawa), 22 (1944): 442–49. *Who's who and why*, 1917/18.

WHITE, JAMES, geographer and civil servant; b. 3 Feb. 1863 in Ingersoll, Upper Canada, eldest son of David White, a merchant, and Christina Hendry; m. 12 Oct. 1888 Rachel Waddell in Ottawa, and they had two daughters; d. there 26 Feb. 1928.

Educated first in Ingersoll, James White graduated in 1883 from the Royal Military College of Canada in Kingston. After joining the Geological Survey of Canada in January 1884 as a topographer, he undertook work in the Rocky Mountains, Ontario, and Quebec. Mount White (Alta) was named for him by George Mercer Dawson*, the assistant director of the Ottawa-based GSC. In June 1894 White became the survey's geographer and chief draftsman, in succession to Scott Barlow, son of GSC cartographer Robert Barlow*.

White was promoted in June 1899 to chief geographer in the Department of the Interior, which had begun issuing systematic sectional maps of Canada in 1891. There he accumulated and disseminated a wealth of knowledge: he continued the production of detailed maps – his attempt in 1902 to consolidate government map-making was effectively resisted by the GSC – and wrote or edited valuable books on altitudes, cartography, boundaries, and place-names. He regarded the *Atlas of Canada* ([Ottawa?], 1906), prepared under his direction and one of the world's first national atlases, as his most important technical achievement. He also contributed to the Alaska Boundary Tribunal in 1903 [see Sir Wilfrid Laurier*] and to investigations in 1906–7 of rapid steamship service between Britain and its Pacific possessions via Canada.

The 1900s saw the rise of the environmental conservation movement in North America, and White became one of its key protagonists in Canada. In 1909 the Liberal government of Laurier appointed him secretary of the new Commission of Conservation, chaired by former interior minister Clifford SIFTON. Sifton had enlisted influential businessmen, politicians, and academics as members, but it was White, who became deputy chair in 1913, who must be credited with the daunting task of managing a body that would produce and broadly distribute more than 200 reports from 7 committees (forests; water and water-power; minerals; lands; public health; fisheries, game, and fur-bearing animals; press and cooperating organizations). The commission grew in influence as legislators, academics, and industrialists across the country acted on its recommendations, and as its popular conferences were widely reported. An outspoken administrator, in 1910 White was a strong critic of private power development on the St Lawrence waterways.

During World War I, public opinion shifted from conservation to increased production for the war effort. Sifton's involvement waned and White faced detractors who accused the commission of excessive spending and infringing on the work of other departments. Although White's relationships with colleagues and key ministers deteriorated, he stepped up the activities of the commission, which played a central role in negotiating the Migratory Birds Treaty of 1916. That same year he became the founding chairman of Canada's advisory board on wildlife protection, in which position he established bird sanctuaries at Rocher Percé and Île Bonaventure, Que., and worked for Canadian sovereignty in the Arctic.

Conservative prime minister Arthur Meighen* abolished the commission, on the grounds of duplication, in the spring of 1921, when Canada was battling economic recession. Removed from the federal payroll, White was hired back the following year as a technical adviser to Sir Lomer GOUIN, the minister of justice in the recently elected Liberal administration. He contributed to such important files as the Cayuga claim arbitration and the Labrador boundary dispute but his attempts to revive the commission were unsuccessful.

Throughout his career, White belonged to many scientific and professional organizations. A fellow of the Royal Geographical Society and the Royal Society of Canada, he was a sectional vice-president in the British Association for the Advancement of Science, a president of the RSC's geology section, and chairman of the Geographic Board of Canada in 1927–28. He belonged as well to the National Geographic Society, the Canadian Society of Civil Engineers, and the American Academy of Political and Social Science.

Supporters and critics described White as a bright, ambitious, and single-minded man devoted to the sustainable management of Canada's natural resources. He was known as well as an "indefatigable" worker and researcher whose geographic knowledge of Canada was unsurpassed. An Anglican, he enjoyed travelling, though an early leg fracture restricted his physical activity. He died suddenly at his Ottawa home at age 65.

MICHEL F. GIRARD

James White supervised the preparation of a large number of maps on Canada, many of them listed in the *Catalogue of the*

National Map Collection, Public Archives of Canada, Ottawa, Ontario (16v., Boston, 1976). Among the works that he wrote or compiled are: *The topographical work of the Geological Survey of Canada* ([London, 1897]); *Altitudes in the Dominion of Canada, with a relief map of North America* (Ottawa, 1901); *Dictionary of altitudes in the Dominion of Canada: with a relief map of Canada* (Ottawa, 1903); *Place names in Quebec, Thousand Islands, and northern Canada* ([Ottawa, 1910]); *The North Atlantic fisheries dispute* (Ottawa, 1911); *Place-names in northern Canada* (Ottawa, 1911); *Place-names in Georgian Bay (including the North Channel)* ([Toronto, 1913]); *Boundary disputes and treaties* (Toronto, 1914); *Treaty of 1825: correspondence respecting the boundary between Russian America (Alaska) and British North America* (Ottawa, 1915); *Place-names in the Rocky Mountains between the 49th parallel and the Athabaska River* ([Ottawa], 1916); *Fuels of western Canada and their efficient utilization* (Ottawa, 1918); *Conservation in 1918* (Ottawa, 1919); and *Power in Alberta: water, coal and natural gas* (Ottawa, 1919).

AO, RG 80-5-0-157, no.2434. Christopher Armstrong, *The politics of federalism: Ontario's relations with the federal government, 1867–1942* (Toronto, 1981). *Canadian men and women of the time* (Morgan; 1912). R. P. Gillis and T. R. Roach, *Lost initiatives: Canada's forest industries, forest policy and forest conservation* (Westport, Conn., 1986). M. F. Girard, *L'écologisme retrouvé: essor et déclin de la Commission de la conservation du Canada (1909–1921)* (Ottawa, 1994; contains a detailed bibliography on White, the conservation movement, and the publications of the Commission of Conservation). H. S. Spence, "James White, 1863–1928: a biographical sketch," *OH*, 27 (1931): 543–44. *Standard dict. of Canadian biog.* (Roberts and Tunnell).

WHITE, JAMES FRANCIS, teacher, principal, school inspector, and author; b. 18 Nov. 1857 in Trenton, Upper Canada, son of James White, a shoemaker, and Ellen Maloney; m. 1918 Helen Gertrude Buck in Rochester, N.Y.; they had no children; d. 20 May 1922 in Toronto.

A natural teacher and gifted administrator, James F. White was one of the few lay Roman Catholics of his generation who had a direct and positive influence on separate schools in Ontario. He was as candid about the shortcomings of these schools as he was forthright in recommending solutions. Firm in the belief that Catholics could do much to improve their own schools, he survived the Byzantine politics of Ontario's education bureaucracy by learning how to deal with departmental officials on the one hand and the Catholic hierarchy on the other.

White was the youngest child of Irish parents; one of his sisters became a nun and another a teacher. He went to a separate elementary school, graduated from high school, and, following some private tutoring, enrolled in the Toronto Normal School for the August–December session of 1875. In addition to winning the Dufferin Medal, he earned a first-class provincial certificate, an achievement that guaranteed him a $100 annual bonus from Archbishop John

Joseph Lynch* of Toronto. His early teaching career, which lasted no more than six years, culminated in principalships in Brockville and Lindsay. Outside the classroom, he was a delegate in July 1878 at the convention of separate school teachers in Hamilton, where he was elected recording and corresponding secretary as well as a member of the committees on the convention's constitution and by-laws and on legislation.

In April 1882 the government of Oliver Mowat* appointed White the first provincial inspector of separate schools, in answer to grievances over Protestant inspectors and the lack of consistent professional inspection. After years of intense lobbying, separate school supporters had finally received their own inspector, and a Catholic one at that. White took up residence in Toronto. His appointment, which required him to report directly to the minister, made him the most influential Catholic within the department of education – he was a member of its central committee – and the most powerful lay voice in the separate school camp. His authority would never diminish, even after he gained an assistant (Cornelius Donovan of Hamilton) in 1884.

For his first report, dated December 1882, White travelled from Windsor to the Quebec boundary and as far north as Mattawa. He inspected 135 schools and, though he had another 58 to examine, he felt sufficiently confident to write a detailed analysis. He highlighted a host of ills: the neglect of English in many German and French schools; poor ventilation, lighting, and heating; weak instruction in reading, grammar, and history; indifferent attendance; lack of parental support; and deficient financial support that left many schools, especially in rural areas, struggling to survive. He reserved his harshest criticism for two areas of concern that were to dog him and separate schools well into the 20th century: the uneven certification of teachers and the failure to use the same approved textbooks in all schools.

White advocated normal-school training and certification for all separate school teachers, including those from religious communities. His stand was unpopular because it was often the low-paid and well-liked religious who allowed many urban schools to stay open. He nonetheless argued that it was wrong for trustees to continue hiring teachers with Quebec certificates, which were hardly equal to third-class Ontario certificates. Moreover, regulations adopted in 1879 recognized only those Quebec certificates acquired before confederation. That holders were generally French-speaking religious made White's position all the more unpopular, particularly in the archdiocese of Ottawa, where many French schools had come to depend on religious. Although a model school for training French-speaking teachers was established in Plantagenet in 1890 [see Sir George

William Ross*], evidently as a result of White's recommendations, a crisis erupted in Ottawa in 1892. On the invitation of the French section of the city's separate school board, White wrote a confidential report (later leaked to the press) on the state of its French schools. A scathing indictment of the management and teaching methods of these schools, many run by the Montreal-based Brothers of the Christian Schools, the report was incorporated in the 1895 report of a provincial commission on Ottawa's separate schools. The commissioners praised the work of the teaching sisters but were extremely critical of the Christian Brothers and demanded that they earn Ontario certification. White not only agreed, in his inspector's report of 1895, but he also threatened to recommend the suspension of grants to schools run by the Christian Brothers, who left Ottawa that year and would not return until 1902.

For many years White and other separate school inspectors pleaded unsuccessfully with the Catholic bishops to endorse normal-school training and examination of the religious. White remained keenly interested in the issue following his retirement as an inspector in 1902 and even after the matter was taken out of the inspectors' hands in 1904, when J. D. Grattan, a Catholic teacher and ratepayer, sued the Ottawa board over its decision to hire the Christian Brothers for a school to be built in Notre-Dame parish. Grattan claimed that, since they did not possess Ontario certificates, they were not qualified to teach. The agreement of the High Court of Justice was upheld in 1906 on appeal and, upon reference, by the Judicial Committee of the Privy Council [see Charles Hugh GAUTHIER]. When the government of James Pliny Whitney* was drafting legislation in 1907 on qualification, White privately intervened with the premier. In letters dated 13 and 23 March he suggested a process whereby the religious could obtain certificates with minimal embarrassment and time. His ideas were incorporated.

On the subject of textbooks, White had been no less adamant that all separate schools follow departmental regulations. An abuse of a privilege that allowed boards to choose unauthorized works had led to a confusing variety of texts. From the start White urged an end to such usage. In his report on Ottawa's French schools in 1892, he was disdainful of the Christian Brothers' choice of the De La Salle series of English readers and demanded their removal. When inspecting school children, he used the common-school books instead of those chosen by the bishops, a practice that brought him into conflict with Lynch. The archbishop took White's dislike of the Sadlier's series and the readers favoured by the Christian Brothers as a scandalous insult to episcopal authority, but White was not intimidated. He enjoyed a more constructive relationship with Lynch's successor, John Walsh*, who found no offence in White's opinion in 1891 that "while all are agreed that the reading books for Separate Schools should be Catholic in tone it is no less essential that they be well adapted to teaching purposes." Walsh accepted White's changes in 1895 to the Sadlier's readers and the adoption of the fourth common-school reader for high-school entrance examinations. As a sign of their friendship, the inspector had written "Separate school law and the separate schools of the archdiocese" for *Jubilee volume, 1842–1892: the archdiocese of Toronto and Archbishop Walsh* (Toronto, 1892).

By 1902, when he resigned, White had performed great service to Catholic education in Ontario by forcing public consideration of the contentious problems of teacher certification and textbooks. However, for all his heroic efforts to remind the province of the deplorable state of public financing of separate schools, he was unable to persuade the government to provide more equitable funding. In this failure he did not stand alone – joining him was a long line of bishops, priests, prominent laymen, teachers, and trustees.

On 11 Dec. 1902 White succeeded John Alexander McCabe as principal of the Ottawa Normal School. In addition to managing this large school, he taught the history of education, school management, and English. His workload in 1909 forced him to decline both the invitation of Copp Clark Company to revise the Canadian Catholic readers and the request of Archbishop Fergus Patrick McEvay* of Toronto to compile a Canadian history. In 1913, however, he found time to be secretary of a lay Catholic committee formed to give the Ontario bishops recommendations for the improvement of Catholic secondary schools and colleges. Four years later he remodelled the entire normal school building. White remained principal until his death in 1922 following prostate surgery. He had been ill and had lived in Toronto for the final year of his life, and he was buried there in Mount Hope Cemetery.

A chancellor of the Knights of Columbus, White left bequests to many Catholic organizations and charities. In 1905 he had been awarded an honorary LLD by the University of Ottawa. He had served as president of the literary committee of the Quebec Battlefields Association during the tercentenary celebrations of 1908. Education, however, was his true passion. The Toronto *Globe* wrote that he "was widely known among the teachers of this Province for his accurate scholarship, his devotion to duty, and his great ability as an instructor. He was beloved and admired by all who knew him as a courteous Christian gentleman."

MICHAEL POWER

AO, F 5, MU 3122, White to Whitney, 13, 23 March 1907; RG 22-305, no.6577; RG 22-354, no.10796. Arch. of the Roman Catholic Archdiocese of Toronto, L (Lynch papers), AO20.04, White to Lynch, 21 Dec. 1879; AO30.15, Lynch to White, 30 April 1888; ME (McEvay papers), AE01.92, White to McEvay, 6 Aug. 1909; AE01.93, White to McEvay, 6 Dec. 1909; W (Walsh papers), AB04.25, White to Walsh, 23 Feb. 1895; AD01.11, White to Walsh, 3 Oct. 1891; AD01.17, Walsh to White, 3 Oct. 1895. LAC, RG 31, C1, 1871, Trenton, Ont.: 67–68; 1901, Toronto, Ward 4, div.40: 2 (mfm. at AO). *Catholic Register* (Toronto), 1, 8 June 1922; 9 Jan. 1954. *Globe*, 24 Aug. 1877; 23–25, 29 July 1878; 17 Aug. 1895; 3 Nov. 1906; 22 May 1922. *Ottawa Citizen*, 20, 22 May 1922. *Canadian men and women of the time* (Morgan; 1912). *Documentary history of education in Upper Canada from the passing of the Constitutional Act of 1791 to the close of Rev. Dr. Ryerson's administration of the Education Department in 1876*, ed. J. G. Hodgins (28v., Toronto, 1894–1910), 19: 9–11. *Judicial decisions on denominational schools*, ed. F. G. Carter (Toronto, 1962). Ont., Legislature, *Sessional papers*, 1896, no.1: 6–18; reports of the minister of education, 1882, 1884–85, 1892, 1909, 1921. C. B. Sissons, *Church & state in Canadian education: an historical study* (Toronto, 1959), 62–63. *Toronto Normal School, 1847–1897: jubilee celebration (October 31st, November 1st and 2d, 1897); biographical sketches and names of successful students, 1847 to 1875* (Toronto, 1898). F. A. Walker, *Catholic education and politics in Ontario . . .* (3v., Toronto, 1955–87; vols.1–2 repr. 1976).

WHITNEY, HENRY MELVILLE, entrepreneur; b. 22 Oct. 1839 in Conway, Mass., second of the seven children of James Scollay Whitney and Laurinda (Lucinda) Collins; m. 3 Oct. 1878 Margaret Foster Green in Brookline, Mass., and they had four daughters and one son; d. there 25 Jan. 1923.

Henry Whitney grew up in comfortable circumstances in Conway. He and his brother William Collins (who would become secretary of the navy in Stephen Grover Cleveland's first administration) graduated from Williston Seminary in Easthampton, Mass., in 1859. For the next seven years Henry held a variety of clerical positions, played the cotton market, and concocted schemes to raise sunken vessels during the Civil War; he could now exchange stories about unsuccessful speculations with his father and brother. In 1866 he went to Boston as agent for his father's thriving Metropolitan Steamship Company and he became president of the concern after his father died in 1878. In 1886 he formed the West End Land Company, became over-extended, and linked the firm with the equally new West End Street Railway Company to promote his land development scheme. Whitney absorbed five other street railway systems around Boston and both West End companies proved profitable. The pattern of mergers, corporate linkages, and speculative ventures was established. He began to experiment with electric cars in 1888 to replace the street railway company's 10,000 horses. Frederick Stark Pearson* joined him in 1889 as chief engineer of this firm.

Earlier in 1889 F. S. Pearson had linked up with

Whitney

Benjamin Franklin Pearson*, a promoter of the People's Heat and Light Company Limited in Halifax, which intended to use coal to produce fuel gas for heating and lighting. F. S. Pearson and Whitney were also interested in Nova Scotian coal as a possible source of fuel for Whitney's New England projects. Their group would soon be known in provincial circles as the "Syndicate." One coalmine was quickly purchased and options were obtained on others in the coalfield south of Sydney harbour. Premier William Stevens FIELDING was quite receptive to the idea of combining competing Cape Breton mines in an expanding Nova Scotia coal industry and in 1892 the group was offered an unprecedented 99-year lease at a fixed royalty. Whitney was particularly attractive to the Liberals because his steamships and street railway generators were large consumers of coal. The Syndicate exercised its options, picking up most of the existing collieries in east Cape Breton, along with local players such as John Stewart McLennan* and David MacKeen*.

After the lease had been confirmed by legislation in 1893, the Dominion Coal Company Limited was incorporated on 1 February with Whitney as president, F. S. Pearson as engineer-in-chief, and B. F. Pearson as secretary. Numerous efficiencies and improvements were quickly evident, and within a decade Dominion Coal had 4,000 employees and production had quadrupled. There was also a long list of expensive mistakes and extravagant expenditures. Control was weak, and many of those involved knew nothing about coalmining. Dominion Coal's establishment was accompanied by the issue of a large amount of promotional stock, which took a tumble when Whitney failed to get the American duty on coal eliminated. Speculators had a field day. While B. F. Pearson tried unsuccessfully to drum up markets for coal in, among other places, Newcastle-upon-Tyne, ventures centring on the use of coke in the United States proved more fruitful and a new plan began to take shape. This project, which contemporary observers immediately linked to Dominion Coal when Whitney first announced it in January 1896, was the Massachusetts Pipe Line Gas Company. The company was to purchase gas from the New England Gas and Coke Company, also controlled by Whitney, which in turn would be supplied by Dominion Coal. On 30 Sept. 1897 a contract was signed between New England Gas and Dominion Coal and, despite the American duty, within a couple of years a new plant at Everett, Mass., began to consume large amounts of coal. Unfortunately, this arrangement meant a large missed market at higher prices which almost ruined Dominion Coal and led to the conclusion that the contract had been part of a scheme to enhance the stock value of Whitney's New England gas companies.

Concessions from local government in Cape Breton and the provincial Liberals under Premier George Henry MURRAY, as well as the promise of federal bounties, smoothed the way in June 1899 for the organization of the Dominion Iron and Steel Company Limited, which had been incorporated the previous March. According to Whitney, Sydney offered more advantages for steel making than anywhere else in the world, and the international competition was initially concerned. Whitney became president of the new company and six of his business friends, who had also been on the original Dominion Coal board, joined him as directors. More than the faces were familiar. Reckless and extravagant expenditures, miscalculations, and lack of control, due partly to inexperience, meant that one-third of the initial outlay for construction was wasted. This incompetence left a legacy of high costs, allowing the plant to be profitable only during periods of high prices. A contract between the coal and steel companies brought grief to both. In 1901 it was estimated that 90 per cent of Dominion Coal's production was locked into low-price contracts. The steel company's stock became the sport of speculators. Miners and steelworkers carried their share of the burden through low wages. Halifax had had direct experience of this approach as well. People's Heat and Light, which had been chartered in 1893, featured Whitney as president and B. F. Pearson as secretary. Even though People's had the advantage of low-cost coal, its substandard materials, stock market speculations, and limited experience in industrial development ensured that the company, in the words of Kyle Jolliffe, "collapsed under the heavy weight of its own debts" in less than a decade.

The coal and steel industry that Whitney promoted would employ many thousands throughout the 20th century and left an indelible mark on Cape Breton Island. Although he and his business friends did not have a monopoly on mismanagement, or on dissatisfaction with operating profits, they helped to ensure that the early years of the modern industry in Cape Breton would be difficult ones. The continuing problems led to his early withdrawal from the region; his controlling interest in the coal and steel companies passed to a group headed by Montreal financier James Ross* in 1901. He resigned from the Dominion Coal board in December 1903 and although he continued to be linked with smaller concerns in Cape Breton and remained on the steel board until 1909, his focus was redirected to New England. He was elected president of the Boston Chamber of Commerce in 1904 and made two unsuccessful runs for state office in the next few years, promoting tariff reform and reciprocal trade relations between Canada and the United States.

Whitney was a promoter and a dreamer, with a penchant for mergers and corporate connections. While he may have been, at 10, "a close lad in financial matters," as one account of his early life noted, by 25 he confessed he had disgusted himself with his splendid schemes on paper which proved worthless. His daughter remembered him as a man who loved to develop something but, bored by routine, soon lost interest. Those he left responsible for decision making and day-to-day duties were not always up to the task. It remains unclear just how involved Whitney was in the stock speculation that took place, but his enterprises in Nova Scotia and New England, and their set-up, attracted others whose collective concern was minimal. A personally pleasant and genial individual, with hearing difficulties from childhood, he remained consistent in his later years, continuing to dream, to develop, and to suffer losses. He died of pneumonia at home in Brookline on 25 Jan. 1923. When the estate of "the supposed multi-millionaire," as the *New York Times* had it, was probated there was surprise expressed that it was worth only $1,221.

DON MACGILLIVRAY

T. W. Acheson, "The National Policy and the industrialization of the Maritimes, 1880–1910," in *Atlantic Canada after confederation; the "Acadiensis" reader: volume two*, comp. P. A. Buckner and David Frank (Fredericton, 1985), 176–201. Ron Crawley, "Class conflict and the establishment of the Sydney steel industry, 1899–1904," in *The Island: new perspectives on Cape Breton's history, 1713–1990*, ed. Kenneth Donovan (Fredericton and Sydney, N.S., 1990), 145–86. W. J. A. Donald, *The Canadian iron and steel industry: a study in the economic history of a protected industry* (Boston, 1915). E. A. Forsey, *Economic and social aspects of the Nova Scotia coal industry* (Toronto, 1926). M. D. Hirsch, *William C. Whitney, modern Warwick* (New York, 1948; repr. [Hamden, Conn.], 1969). Kyle Jolliffe, "A saga of Gilded Age entrepreneurship in Halifax: the People's Heat and Light Company Limited, 1893–1902," *Nova Scotia Hist. Rev.* (Halifax), 15 (1995), no.2: 10–25. T. W. Lawson, *Frenzied finance* (New York, 1905). Don MacGillivray, "Henry Melville Whitney comes to Cape Breton: the saga of a Gilded Age entrepreneur," *Acadiensis* (Fredericton), 9 (1979–80), no.1: 44–70. *National cyclopædia of American biography* ... (63v., New York, [etc.], 1892–1984), 10. N.S., House of Assembly, *Debates and proc.*, 13 March 1892: 123–24; *Journal and proc.*, 1893, app.16: 1–8. David Schwartzman, "Mergers in the Nova Scotia coalfields: a history of the Dominion Coal Company, 1893–1940" (PHD thesis, Univ. of Calif., Berkeley, 1953).

WHITTY, GERALD JOSEPH, army officer and veterans' official; b. 25 Aug. 1896 in St John's, son of John Whitty and Catherine Dwyer; d. unmarried 15 Sept. 1924 in nearby Donovans.

The Whittys were of Irish descent and typified rank-and-file Roman Catholic life in the St John's of the period. Gerald (Jerry) Whitty worked for the Reid Newfoundland Company from August 1908 to 24 Dec. 1914, when he enlisted in the Newfoundland Regiment. He trained as a signaller and in September 1915 was sent to Gallipoli (Gelibolu, Turkey). There

he contracted enteric fever and suffered a groin strain. Evacuated first to Malta, he was later sent to England, where he was promoted second lieutenant on 1 Nov. 1916. His enlistment and rise through the ranks highlight the social mobility that the war brought to many young Newfoundlanders and the mobilization of Roman Catholics in a common cause with Protestants. Eventually, the war produced deep social and political divisions in Newfoundland, but it also blurred denominational lines and created new institutions with broad popular appeal. Whitty's life exemplifies these elements.

In June 1917 Whitty went to France. Blown into the Yser Canal in Flanders on 25 July, he suffered eye and nose injuries but remained at the front. In the battle of Cambrai he led a charge on 20 Nov. 1917. He was shot in the shoulder and for his heroism was awarded the Military Cross. In July 1918 he was made acting captain (he had now learned to fly) and on 3 June 1919 he became an officer of the Order of the British Empire (military division).

Whitty arrived back in St John's on 1 July 1919 and was demobilized on the 29th. Like many ex-servicemen, he faced a difficult transition. After disappointing forays to New York and Montreal, he retreated to St John's where he worked temporarily for Reid Newfoundland. On 18 Feb. 1920 he became a member of the Civil Re-establishment Committee, which the Newfoundland government had set up on 25 June 1918 to assist veterans to find their way in civilian life. Eventually, in the late summer of 1920, he found lasting employment as secretary-treasurer (later dominion secretary) of the Great War Veterans' Association of Newfoundland. The GWVA had originated in the Soldiers and Rejected Volunteers Association, formed in St John's on 11 April 1918. On 20 Aug. 1918 this association had refashioned itself along the lines of the Great War Veterans' Association of Canada, established in 1917. The GWVA in both countries was an assertive organization whose brief was written in blood. Whitty's work as secretary-treasurer was multifarious and built upon his work in civil re-establishment. He helped run the poppy campaign, begun in 1921, and edited the *Veteran Magazine*, first published in December 1920. In 1923 he represented the GWVA in London at the first biennial conference of the British Empire Service League.

Two issues dominated the affairs of the GWVA in the early 1920s: the improvement of pensions and the project of a national memorial to honour Newfoundland's war dead. Whitty played a prominent role in both matters. Pensions for veterans and their dependants had been approved by the government in 1917 with payments subject to annual adjustments. When the latter were not forthcoming, the GWVA lobbied hard for redress and made significant gains. The organization was likewise successful in the war memorial project. Under the leadership of former Newfoundland Regiment padre Father Thomas F. Nangle and Whitty, the GWVA conducted a public fund-raising campaign for the monument, which was situated at King's Beach, St John's. Whitty organized the ceremony on 1 July 1924 at which Field-Marshal Earl Haig unveiled the memorial.

Two months later Newfoundland was visited by the Special Service Squadron of the Royal Navy. St John's celebrated the visit appropriately. On the evening of 15 September, while the pleasantries were in progress, Whitty and 13 companions met in a restaurant at Donovans to bid farewell to a friend who was leaving for England. At 11:00 P.M., he, William King, another prominent Newfoundland veteran, and Chief Petty Officer Robert Lovett of HMS *Constance* were standing by the bus that was to take the party back to St John's. Suddenly, a speeding car appeared and struck the three men. Whitty and King were killed instantly, as were four occupants of the car, including two other officers from the *Constance*. The driver was Leonard Reid, the son of the late Sir William Duff REID. In November he would be convicted of manslaughter and sentenced to one year in the penitentiary.

Following the civic triumphs of the unveiling of the National War Memorial and the arrival of the Special Service Squadron, the accident cast a gloom. On 18 September, St John's became a "city of funerals." In the afternoon, following the burial of King in the General Protestant Cemetery, the funeral procession continued to Whitty's residence. From there, a guard of honour from the Catholic Cadet Corps escorted the captain's casket east along Water Street. At the war memorial a short halt was made and wreaths placed. Whitty was buried in Belvedere Cemetery, among the Irish Catholic *prominenti* of St John's, whose ranks, thanks to service in war and its aftermath, he had risen to join. At the graveside, Father Nangle observed that veterans had lost "their best friend and advocate."

MELVIN BAKER and PETER NEARY

The authors are grateful to Mr Gerald Penney of St John's for making available his collection of the *Veteran Magazine* (St John's) for the period 1920–24.

Arch. of the Royal Canadian Legion, Newfoundland and Labrador Command, Branch 56 (St John's), Minute-book of the Soldiers and Rejected Volunteers Assoc., 1918–20. LAC, RG 38, A-2-e, 489: 0-188. PANL, GN 2/39/A, 1921, St John's West (mfm. at Centre for Newfoundland Studies, Memorial Univ. of Nfld, St John's); GN 8/2; MG 592; MG 632. *Daily News* (St John's), 1914–24. *Evening Advocate* (St John's), 1916–24. *Evening Telegram* (St John's), 1914–24. *St. John's Daily Star*, 1918–20. Desmond Morton and Glenn Wright, *Winning the second battle: Canadian veterans and the return to civilian life, 1915–1930* (Toronto, 1987). P. [F.] Neary, "Democracy in Newfoundland: a comment," *Journal of Canadian Studies* (Peterborough, Ont.), 4 (1969), no.1: 37–45; "How Newfoundland veterans became Canadian veterans: a study in bureaucracy and benefit," in *Twentieth-century Newfoundland: explorations*, ed. J. [K.] Hiller and P. [F.] Neary (St John's, 1994), 195–237. Nfld, *Acts*, 1916–24; House of Assembly, *Journal*, 1919, app., "Report of the Civil Re-establishment Committee up to April 26th, 1919." *Newfoundland Quarterly* (St John's), 1914–24. G. W. L. Nicholson, *The fighting Newfoundlander: a history of the Royal Newfoundland Regiment* (St John's, [1964]). P. R. O'Brien, "The Newfoundland Patriotic Association: the administration of the war effort, 1914–1918" (MA thesis, Memorial Univ. of Nfld, 1981).

WILLISON, Sir JOHN STEPHEN, newspaperman, author, and businessman; b. 9 Nov. 1856 near Hills Green, Upper Canada, third child of Stephen Willison, a blacksmith, and Jane Abram; m. first 3 June 1885 Rachel Wood Turner (d. 19 Jan. 1925) in Tiverton, Ont., and they had two sons; m. secondly 10 April 1926 Marjory Jardine Ramsay MacMurchy* in Toronto; d. there 27 May 1927.

After leaving school at 15, John Willison worked as a hired hand in Hills Green and later in the Whitby area near Greenwood, where he impressed the postmaster as "full of ambition." The Toronto *Globe* and Liberal politics fascinated him, as did the library of the Greenwood Mechanics' Institute. In his teens he was the assistant teacher at the local school. He clerked in stores in Stanton and Tiverton, and had his poetry and prose published in newspapers; turning to journalism, he joined the London *Advertiser* in 1881 before following editor John Cameron* to the *Globe* in 1883. Willison reported well enough from the Ontario legislature to be promoted in March 1886 to the Parliamentary Press Gallery in Ottawa, where he was drawn to the Liberals' rising Quebec star, Wilfrid Laurier*. They became friends, with a common love of politics and literature. In June 1887 Edward Blake* gave up the Liberal leadership and Willison boldly supported Laurier, forging a powerful alliance. He told Laurier he would perform "any service" to help the party win Ontario. During the explosive Jesuit estates controversy in 1889, although he loathed the Parti National of Quebec premier Honoré Mercier*, which supported the Liberals, he assured *Globe* readers in a feature article that the Catholic Laurier was "a Liberal in every conviction of his mind."

As part of a restructuring by *Globe* president Robert Jaffray*, Willison, with Laurier's support, replaced Cameron as editor in 1890, though the more experienced, but mercurial, Edward Farrer* took charge of the editorial page. Farrer drew fire during the election of 1891 when the pamphlet he had allegedly written on how Canada could be pressured into union with the United States was leaked to Prime Minister Sir John A. Macdonald*, who delightedly denounced "veiled treason" at the *Globe*. Meanwhile, Willison prevented publication of Blake's condemnation of

Laurier's policy of unrestricted reciprocity until after the election. The Liberals lost (but not disastrously), Farrer departed in July 1892, and Willison's ascendancy at the *Globe* was confirmed.

By the mid 1890s he had assembled a gifted staff of expert editorialists and writers, including the pro-labour radical John Lewis, municipal affairs specialist Thomas Stewart Lyon, and economics analyst Samuel Thomas Wood*. In December 1895 Thomas Charles Patteson, a thorough Tory who had edited the Toronto *Mail* in the 1870s, told Willison that the *Globe* was "certainly now the best paper . . . ever published in Canada. Temperate in its comment, and vigorous in all departments." Patteson was sure that "the converts or waverers made by the *Globe*'s style of comment are ten times as numerous . . . as those made by the old style of polemical writing." Willison's reputation would soar during the election of 1896 as the Liberals found safe footing in trade protection and the case for provincial rights in the controversy over Manitoba's abolition of public funding for Catholic schools [*see* Thomas Greenway*]. Willison opposed any federal interference. Laurier, worried about Catholic Quebec, complained to him in 1895 about his "altogether . . . too absolute" editorials. Willison responded that Ontario "will destroy any party that attempts arbitrary interference with Manitoba." When the governing Tories, under the ageing Sir Charles Tupper*, tried to restore Catholic school rights early in 1896, the *Globe* backed Laurier's proposal of a negotiated compromise. Electoral victory came in June to the Liberals, who tied the Conservatives in Ontario, and the *Globe*'s circulation rose to dizzy heights.

Willison increasingly articulated an imperialist nationalism. In 1888 he had told Laurier that he was "strongly Canada *first*" and he even led the Toronto Young Men's Liberal Club, of which he was president, to vote for Canadian independence. As editor of the *Globe*, however, he moved in high intellectual and social circles that were generally imperialist. In his memoirs he would remember that "no one gave me wiser counsel" than Principal George Monro Grant* of Queen's College in Kingston, who, as the *Globe* put it, promoted "that habit of thought" which saw Canada as a "factor" in the world as part of the British empire. Willison's friendship with George Taylor DENISON, president of the Canadian branch of the British Empire League, was helped by their shared views on corruption and by the new commercial policy the Liberals had adopted in 1893 – "freer" trade with Britain and the United States. In 1896 American tariff pressures caused Willison to conclude, in a speech to the National Club, that Canada would have to "lean upon our Imperial relationships." Then came the party's adroit imperial-preference budget [*see* William Stevens FIELDING] and Laurier's lionization in the summer of 1897 at the celebration of Queen

Victoria's diamond jubilee. Willison told the *Globe* from London in October that Canada was "at last the favorite child of the empire," but a year later he would celebrate the "firmly self-reliant mood" of a nation of destiny. Soon enough, however, imperialism showed its divisive side. In October 1899 war broke out in South Africa between the Boers and Britain. The *Globe* argued that the dominion's dispatch of troops would be "a national declaration of Canada's stake in the British Empire." Privately Willison told the prime minister that "he would either send troops or go out of office." A contingent went, and Laurier was attacked as too imperialist in Quebec and as "not British enough" in Ontario.

Willison's prestige was growing enormously. In March 1900 he was elected president of the Canadian Press Association and in May he became a fellow of the Royal Society of Canada. His *Sir Wilfrid Laurier and the Liberal party: a political history* was published in Toronto in 1903. Sometimes brilliant but devoid of critical analysis, it draws upon *Hansard* and newspapers, and is infused with Willison's detailed knowledge of Liberalism and flattering admiration. He praises Laurier's "patient and courageous resistance to the denationalizing tendencies of racialism, sectarianism, and provincialism." Reviews were commendatory – the *Canadian Magazine* (Toronto) lauded the study as "the greatest biography yet produced in this country." In 1903 Willison was elected an officer of the Canadian Society of Authors and three years later Queen's awarded him an LLD.

Party journalism, however, had begun to frustrate him. He was embarrassed in 1897 when his editorial support for the extension of the Canadian Pacific Railway became linked to efforts by *Globe* proprietors Jaffray and George Albertus Cox* to profit from deals on railway lands in British Columbia. The following year Ontario's Liberal premier, Arthur Sturgis Hardy*, berated him for his even-handed election coverage. In January 1900 a *Globe* manifesto called for an independent railway commission, reform of the Senate and the civil service, and a judicial redistribution of seats in the House of Commons, measures that Laurier criticized as "advanced radicalism." Willison would recall that "as far back as 1897 he said to me 'I wish the Globe would stop urging reforms. Reforms are for Oppositions. It is the business of governments to stay in office.'" When Liberals attacked him for his fair treatment of the Conservatives in the election of 1900, he exploded in a letter to cabinet minister Clifford SIFTON: "Personally I resent the assumption of every Liberal politician that I am his hired man."

Salvation came in the summer of 1902 when Joseph Wesley Flavelle*, the Toronto pork packer and financier, promised to finance a paper in which Willison could express his views without interference. The Toronto *Evening News* was secured, and on 28

November Willison left the *Globe*. His first editorial, which appeared on 19 Jan. 1903, announced "an independent course in politics," but this goal proved elusive. In March, Willison chastised the Ontario Liberals for bribing an opposition MLA to join them, and by early 1905 he had helped hound them from office. Federally the *News* had supported Conservative leader Robert Laird Borden* in 1904 for promoting national ownership as an alternative to Laurier's private-sector project for a second transcontinental railway. Sectarian controversy broke out the following year when Laurier revealed his plan to entrench Catholic separate-school rights for the new provinces to be carved out of the North-West Territories. Willison wanted full provincial autonomy and he had told Laurier so in June 1904: this "was my position on the Manitoba question and I do not see how it is possible to take any other position with respect to the Territories." In March 1905 the *News* denounced the bills creating Alberta and Saskatchewan as "a great betrayal of Liberal principles" and many Liberals agreed, causing the prime minister to compromise. Only religious education within essentially public schools, which had existed under territorial ordinances, was to be tolerated in the new provinces, but Willison was not mollified. He explained to a friend that he had written his book on Laurier largely to celebrate the leader's "devotion to the federal principle and his resolute resistance to clerical interference in education." When Laurier had "turned squarely in the other direction," Willison had been obliged to oppose or "I would have been a joke from one end of the country to the other."

Days of trouble began for the *News* as the populist *Toronto Daily Star* drew even in circulation in 1905 and then surged ahead, draining away much advertising. In 1907 Flavelle put an extra $50,000 into the paper, but financial markets plummeted and he decided he had to sell. Willison could find no other backer. His attacks on William MACKENZIE's Toronto Railway Company and, in the debate over the public ownership of electricity in Ontario [see Sir Adam BECK], his reluctance to abandon private enterprise only brought the *News* discredit. He talked with Laurier about a return to the *Globe* but this could not be sorted out. In 1908 Ontario premier James Pliny Whitney* arranged for the purchase of the *News* by a Tory syndicate led by Francis Cochrane*. Willison would be president and editor, but real control rested with the syndicate. Flavelle's penny-pinching illusions and then the syndicate's demand for slavish partisanship undoubtedly contributed to the paper's weakness and tedious moralizing, along with Willison's tendency to hope against hope that things would improve. The war too may have reduced the ability of the *News* to assemble capital. "I cannot go on as I have gone on for twelve years," Willison told John Dowsley REID in

1916. "We have wasted tens of thousands of dollars by producing a poor paper."

Some outlets for independence had continued. Willison was a highly informed speaker on public affairs, and he remained in demand. He was still a correspondent in Canada for the London *Morning Post*, a position he had been invited to accept in 1905. On the nomination of Governor General Lord Grey* and Laurier, in 1908 he became the Canadian correspondent of the pre-eminent London *Times*. Willison assured Laurier that he would be abstaining there from utterances bearing "partisan interpretation."

A great national crisis arose when American-Canadian negotiations led to the sudden announcement in parliament in January 1911 of a comprehensive agreement on reciprocal trade. Willison, who had embraced moderate protection, recorded in the *Times* on 28 January "an undercurrent of unrest and dissatisfaction in financial and business circles" in Toronto. Within days the *News* articulated the basic case against the agreement. For markets that were possibly illusory, and which the United States could take away, Canada was to "imperil our whole national experiment" by undercutting its east-west rail and financial networks, transcontinental and cross-Atlantic trade, and British investment. "Practically . . . we commercially annex the Canadian West to the United States," the *News* continued, with even the manufacturing sector made hostage. In sum, "we strengthen all the influences towards continentalism and risk the sacrifice both of a young nation and an ancient Empire." Flavelle would tell Willison that the subsequent opposition merely enlarged upon his points. In February, Willison reached out to his unparalleled network of Liberal friends – he worked mainly with Clifford Sifton and banker Sir Byron Edmund WALKER – to put together the "Toronto Eighteen," a group of prominent businessmen who totally rejected the agreement. Willison then went to Ottawa, accompanied by Zebulon Aiton Lash*, one of the 18, to meet with Sifton and Robert Borden to arrange (as Willison recorded) "a basis of co-operation" with the Conservatives. The reciprocity agreement met with filibuster in the commons, and Laurier called an election for September. Willison and Sifton wrote Borden's campaign manifesto using Willison's "parting of the ways" phraseology, and Borden won a majority. In Toronto thousands of revellers surrounded the *News* building crying "Willison, Willison." As 1911 closed, his reputation had never been greater; in the New Year's honours list of 1913 he was awarded a knighthood.

During the early years of Borden's government, Willison worried that Canada's hesitations about naval defence and British delays on trade preferences impeded real progress in the reconciliation of national and imperial dreams. During the "naval scare" in 1909, over Germany's threat to Britain's supremacy, he had supported bipartisan resolutions for the "speedy" beginning of a Canadian navy, though, like other imperialists, he had wanted a special contribution of two Dreadnoughts for Britain. In late 1912 Borden delayed development of a Canadian navy and proposed three Dreadnoughts, but the Liberal Senate refused. Willison would lament the partisanship on both sides. On British resistance to preference, he noted for the *Times* in 1913 Canada's "intense concern," which he also expressed in the London-based imperialist journal the *Round Table*.

After the empire went to war in August 1914, Willison became embattled on several fronts. He and the other Canadian members of the Round Table movement [*see* Edward Joseph Kylie*] insisted that Britain share direction of foreign and defence policy with the matured dominions, thus contradicting the more centralist prescriptions of the movement's London leader, Lionel George Curtis. In Canada, with military victory in doubt in 1916 and voluntary enlistments lagging, pressure built for a union or coalition government. For months the *News* pilloried Laurier as a hostage to the Nationalistes in Quebec and strongly advised Borden not to agree to the union idea. But after meeting with him in February 1917, Willison hinted in the *News* that coalition might be necessary after all. Then, in May, Borden adopted conscription, stirring many English Canadian Liberals, including Ontario leader Newton Wesley Rowell*, to press Laurier to join with Borden. Laurier refused, but Willison, having resigned in June from the *News*, its financial situation beyond salvation, acted for Borden to help bring Rowell aboard. When western Liberals came too [*see* Arthur Lewis Watkins SIFTON], the coalition was constructed. The Union government then sought a mandate. Willison, with Sir Clifford Sifton, wrote Borden's election address of 12 November, and he served as chief coordinator of publicity in the campaign that led to a landslide victory in December.

After 1917 Willison mixed achievements and disappointments. Known for his chairmanship in 1914–16 of the Ontario commission on unemployment, in 1918 he was made head of the Ontario Housing Committee, which unsuccessfully urged federal funding. In addition, on the invitation of business leaders, he served as president of the Canadian Reconstruction Association from 1918 to 1922, but he could not bridge the divisions between business, labour, and agrarian interests. As a member in 1920–21 of the Ontario royal commission on university finances, he felt that the new United Farmers government was not inclined to be generous. Willison himself was a trustee of Queen's University, and a governor of both the University of Toronto and Upper Canada College. At the national level he was at odds in 1918–20 with Borden, who was bent on Canadian autonomy, and in the 1920s with the new Liberal leader, William Lyon

Mackenzie King*, who also opposed imperial policies. As an imperialist nationalist, Willison complained to a friend that "those who hold my view seem to have been deserted." In 1919 his *Reminiscences, political and personal* was published in Toronto. Rich in opinion on journalism and politics, especially before 1900, the book returns in a final chapter ("Laurier and the empire") to imperialist musings. "No one who knew Laurier could believe that he was an Imperialist," Willison stated. He pointed out, however, that the late prime minister had had no quarrel with Britain and noted his work for British preference, his shipment of troops to South Africa, and his belief in Canada's "obligation for naval defence." The autobiography was certainly not as current as Willison's speeches and publications for the Reconstruction Association. Augustus Bridle probably spoke for many when he said in *The masques of Ottawa* (Toronto, 1921) that Willison should "stop writing Reconstruction bulletins and do something of more value to the country, so that the older enthusiasm of men who used to think he was Canada's greatest editor may not altogether die." In 1923 Willison began a biography of Sir George Robert PARKIN and in 1925 he added some chapters to his biography of Laurier. A last hurrah was *Willisons Monthly*, a stylish newsmagazine started that year in Toronto, but with Willison's death in 1927 there was no time to see what lasting impact it could have under his direction.

Compared with Willison's public record, personal information on him and his family is slight. He was an avid clubman and lawn bowler, a Prohibitionist, and a Methodist turned Anglican. Beyond journalism, he had business interests in the 1920s as president of the Municipal Bankers' Corporation Limited, Mortgage, Discount and Finance Limited, and Canadian Rail and Harbour Terminals Limited, as a co-founder with bond-broker Thomas A. Neeley of the financing firm Willison-Neeley Corporation, and as a director of the Western Canada Colonization Association. Willison's first wife had been a founder of the Toronto Ladies' Club in 1904, a councillor of the Imperial Order Daughters of the Empire, and a wartime president of the Canadian National Ladies' Guild for British and Foreign Sailors. Their twin sons both became journalists; one, William Taylor, was killed in France in 1916. Just a year after Willison's remarriage, to Marjory MacMurchy, a former literary editor at the *News* and an accomplished writer, he died of cancer at age 70.

Willison had major champions as well as detractors. Many Liberals could never forgive his turn against Laurier. In July 1927 King told his diary that the editor had been "a tory snob in his behaviour, tho' he had within him qualities that might have made him a truly great man." Writing in the *Dalhousie Review* (Halifax), educationist Arthur Hugh Urquhart Colquhoun remembered "a formidable antagonist and a pillar of strength in the storm. So men of all sorts sought his counsel in an emergency, trusting to his balanced judgment, his unique experience and his incorruptible integrity." Self-educated, very much self-promoting, and widely admired, although he surely faced more criticism, rivalry, and jealousy than uncritical acclaim, Willison rose on the strength of his abilities to become an advocate for major national causes and a close counsellor to Laurier and Borden, astonishingly across the Liberal-Conservative divide and over three decades of rapidly changing conditions, issues, and ideas.

Sir John Willison was one of the most influential English-speaking journalists in Canada in the late 19th and early 20th centuries and a pivotal figure in national political shifts in 1896, 1911, and 1917. With his incisive pen and clear reasoning, he raised the *Globe* to unprecedented prominence. Although he failed to find sustainability for the *News* as a journalist-centred, independent newspaper, he used it effectively as a vehicle for the expression of his large ideas for 14 years. For two highly eventful decades in British-Canadian relations he interpreted Canada brilliantly for the *Times*. His history of Laurier and his *Reminiscences* constituted major literary achievements. In all its facets, his career powerfully touched and expressively reflected the evolution of Canada's nationhood.

RICHARD T. CLIPPINGDALE

Sir John Stephen Willison apparently destroyed virtually all of his private family correspondence, but there are collections of other Willison papers at the AO (F 1083) and the LAC (MG 30, D29). The AO holdings also contain two biographical manuscripts, one an insightful memoir by Lady Willison, the other a long letter to her from historian Jesse Edgar Middleton* that appears to be the text of a speech (presumably by Middleton) to the Canadian Literature Club in Toronto on 1 Oct. 1928. The only published biography is A. H. U. Colquhoun, *Press, politics and people: the life and letters of Sir John Willison, journalist and correspondent of the "Times"* (Toronto, 1935). Rather than an objective analysis, it is an admiring tribute by a friend and journalistic contemporary who allowed Willison to be his own biographer by speaking through his letters. Newspaperman John Wesley Dafoe* characterized it as "a careful blend of biography and quotation."

Willison's publications include: *Agriculture and industry . . .* (Toronto, [1920?]); *Anglo-Saxon amity* ([Toronto?, 1906?]); *The new Canada: a survey of the conditions and problems of the dominion* (London, [1912]); *Partners in peace: the dominion, the empire and the republic* (Toronto, 1923); *The railway question in Canada . . .* (Toronto, [1897]); *Sir George Parkin: a biography* (London, 1929); *Sir Wilfrid Laurier and the Liberal party: a political history* (2v., Toronto, 1903); and *The United States and Canada* (New York, 1908).

AO, RG 80-5-0-132, no.1588; RG 80-8-0-982, no.1347;

RG 80-8-0-1051, no.4037. *Globe & Mail* Library (Toronto), M. O. Hammond, "History of the Globe," ed. H. W. Charlesworth (typescript). LAC, MG 26, G; H; J13, 17 July 1927. QUA, Joseph Flavelle fonds. *Times* Arch. (London, Eng.), New Printing House Square papers, Willison file. *Evening News* (Toronto), 1902–17. *Globe*, 1883–1902, esp. 9 June 1885; 20, 22 Jan. 1925; 10, 12–13 April 1926. *Morning Post* (London, Eng.), 1906–8. *Times* (London), 1908–27. *Toronto Daily Star*, 1905; 26 Oct. 1935. Réal Bélanger, *Wilfrid Laurier; quand la politique devient passion* (Québec et Montréal, 1986). Carl Berger, *The sense of power; studies in the ideas of Canadian imperialism, 1867–1914* (Toronto and Buffalo, N.Y., 1970). Michael Bliss, *A Canadian millionaire: the life and business times of Sir Joseph Flavelle, bart., 1858–1939* (Toronto, 1978). R. C. Brown, *Robert Laird Borden: a biography* (2v., Toronto, 1975–80). R. C. Brown and Ramsay Cook, *Canada, 1896–1921: a nation transformed* (Toronto, 1974). *Canadian annual rev.*, 1902–25/26. H. W. Charlesworth, *Candid chronicles: leaves from the note book of a Canadian journalist* (Toronto, 1925). R. T. Clippingdale, "J. S. Willison and Canadian nationalism, 1886–1902," CHA, *Hist. Papers* (1969): 74–93; "J. S. Willison, political journalist: from liberalism to independence, 1881–1905" (PHD thesis, 2v., Univ. of Toronto, 1970). A. H. U. Colquhoun, "Sir John Willison," *Dalhousie Rev.* (Halifax), 7 (1927–28): 159–62. Ramsay Cook, *The politics of John W. Dafoe and the "Free Press"* (Toronto and Buffalo, 1963). Carman Cumming, *Secret craft: the journalism of Edward Farrer* (Toronto, 1992). J. W. Dafoe, *Clifford Sifton in relation to his times* (Toronto, 1931); *Laurier; a study in Canadian politics* (Toronto, 1922; repr., intro. M. S. Donnelly, 1963). Domino [Augustus Bridle], "A coat of many colours: Sir John Willison," in his *The masques of Ottawa* (Toronto, 1921), 166–72. J. E. Kendle, *The Round Table movement and imperial union* (Toronto and Buffalo, 1975). J. E. Middleton and Fred Landon, *The province of Ontario: a history, 1615–1927* (5v., Toronto, 1927–[28]), 4: 509–10. H. V. Nelles, *The politics of development: forests, mines & hydro-electric power in Ontario, 1849–1941* (Toronto, 1974). Margaret Prang, *N. W. Rowell, Ontario nationalist* (Toronto and Buffalo, 1975). *Round Table* (London), 1910–16. Paul Rutherford, *A Victorian authority: the daily press in late nineteenth-century Canada* (Toronto, 1982). Joseph Schull, *Laurier: the first Canadian* (Toronto, 1965). Minko Sotiron, *From politics to profits: the commercialization of Canadian daily newspapers, 1890–1920* (Montreal and Kingston, 1997). P. B. Waite, *Canada, 1874–1896: arduous destiny* (Toronto and Montreal, 1971). *Who's who in Canada*, 1922.

WILSON, ERASTUS WILLIAM, businessman and officer; b. 1 July 1860 in Belleville, Upper Canada, son of James Wilson, an iron founder, and Mary Ann Dowser; m. 1887 Sara Etta L. Bricker of Berlin (Kitchener), Ont., and they had two sons and one daughter; d. 15 May 1922 in Montreal.

Erastus William Wilson received his early schooling in Belleville and then went on to secondary school in Oshawa. He chose to enter the business world rather than to attend the University of Toronto, where his application had been accepted.

Wilson moved to Montreal in 1882. Two years later

he began working for the Manufacturers' Life Insurance Company [see George Gooderham*], and he would serve as manager of its Montreal office until 1911. After transferring then to the Canada Life Assurance Company, again as manager, he would later be in charge of its operations for the province of Quebec, and he continued in this position for the rest of his life. He would also be a director of Crown Trust Company as well as of Peter Lyall and Sons Construction Company.

In the course of his career, in addition to playing an effective role in the Montreal Board of Trade, Wilson was honoured by appointment as a member for life to the board of directors of the Montreal General Hospital and the Montreal Amateur Athletic Association. He also participated as a mason in the activities of Royal Victoria Lodge No.57, of which he would become a past master. In 1895 he rose to the position of provincial grand director of ceremonies. He belonged to several organizations in the Montreal region: the prestigious St James Club and Mount Royal Club, as well as the Forest and Stream Club. In 1917 the king made him a companion of the Order of St Michael and St George. He would live in Westmount and have a summer residence in Dorval.

Wilson's interest in the military life was evident from the time he came to Montreal in 1882, the year he enlisted as a private in the 3rd Battalion of Rifles (Victoria Rifles of Canada). Probably as a result of the quality of his performance and leadership, he rose through the ranks and obtained an officer's commission in January 1892. He assumed command of the regiment on 25 Sept. 1903, with the rank of lieutenant-colonel, and he relinquished it four years later.

Wilson was promoted colonel on 1 June 1914 with his appointment as acting commander of Military District No.4 (Montreal). When World War I broke out on 4 Aug. 1914, he joined the staff of the minister of militia and defence, Samuel HUGHES, in Valcartier, and in October he accompanied him to England as his orderly officer. On 20 November he took command of Military District No.4. He was made a brigadier-general on 1 Sept. 1915. The following year he was given command of the camp at Valcartier, and in June he was promoted major-general. He resumed command of Military District No.4 in 1917. In the summer of 1918 he went to England and inspected Canadian troops on the front lines with Prime Minister Sir Robert Laird Borden* and the minister of the overseas military forces, Sir Albert Edward KEMP. He returned to Canada in August. When the war ended he asked to be relieved of his duties, but the military authorities persuaded him to remain at his post until the repatriation of the troops had been completed. He finally gave up command of Military District No.4 in October 1919. He died less than three years later, on 15 May 1922, at the age of 61. His two sons had both taken part in World War I. Erastus William had enlisted in the 2nd Canadian Mounted Rifles Brigade and served on its headquarters staff. Bradley Alexander had also joined the Canadian Expeditionary Force.

Wilson made a success of his business and military careers. He even managed to attend to each of them during the war. This was no small task, and he accomplished it at the cost of his health. He performed his wartime duties to the satisfaction of the authorities, as his successive promotions demonstrate. As commander of District No.4, he played a significant role in recruitment. But like many other Montreal businessmen of the time, Wilson did not speak French, and his cultural and social world was an English-speaking one. His lack of sensitivity towards French Canadians hampered his work. He did indeed help Olivar Asselin* in recruiting the 163rd Infantry Battalion, as Rodolphe Lemieux* acknowledged in the House of Commons. On the other hand, on 12 July 1915 he supported the imposition of conscription.

Wilson tried, but failed, to create a strong, vigorous, and active civilian organization in the Montreal area for recruiting French Canadians. For this purpose he got in touch with three soldiers and with three French Canadian civilians, Senator Frédéric-Ligori Béïque*, Sir Alexander LACOSTE, and especially Senator Raoul Dandurand*, but they were unable to respond favourably to his request for assistance. They did not find a francophone priest prepared to take charge of recruiting French-speaking volunteers, as Wilson had hoped, nor were they able to establish a fund similar to that of the Citizen's Recruiting League, an English-language organization set up to promote the recruitment of men willing to enlist in the anglophone battalions operating in Military District No.4. On 14 March 1916 Wilson appointed a Methodist clergyman, the Reverend Charles A. Williams, as chief recruiting agent for his district, claiming that he had been unable to find a French-speaking priest to hold this position. Nonetheless, he might have chosen an officer or a layman instead, as was done in Military District No.5, based at Quebec. Lemieux referred to this ill-considered appointment the following year in the course of the debates on the Military Service Act in the House of Commons. During his time as head of the camp at Valcartier, Wilson could not understand the difficult position of the French Canadian commanders of battalions, who were reduced to the role of recruiting officers. This incomprehension became clear in 1916 in his evaluation of the work of Lieutenant-Colonel Hercule Barré, commander of the 150th Infantry Battalion, and his criticism of Lieutenant-Colonel René-Arthur de La Bruère Girouard, commander of the 178th Infantry Battalion.

In spite of these reservations, it must be acknowledged that Erastus William Wilson was a staunch high-ranking officer, dedicated to the cause of the

Wood

Canadian Expeditionary Force, and, as Lemieux said, in his daily life "a real gentleman."

JEAN-PIERRE GAGNON

LAC, RG 31, C1, 1861, Belleville, [Ont.], dist.1, Sampson Ward: 14; 1871, Oshawa, Ont., div.2: 65–66; RG 150, Acc. 1992–93/166, box 10442-23. *Le Devoir*, 16 mai 1922. J.-P. Gagnon, *Le 22ᵉ bataillon (canadien-français), 1914–1919; étude socio-militaire* (Québec et Ottawa, 1986). Nicholson, *CEF. The storied province of Quebec; past and present*, ed. W. [C. H.] Wood *et al.* (5v., Toronto, 1931–32), 3.

WOOD, JOANNA ELLEN, author; b. 28 Dec. 1867 in Lesmahagow, Scotland, daughter of Robert Wood and Agnes Tod; d. unmarried 1 May 1927 in Detroit.

Hailed as a Canadian Charlotte Brontë on the publication of her first novel in 1894, Joanna, also known as Nelly, Wood was celebrated in an article in the *Canadian Magazine* (Toronto) four years later as one of Canada's "three leading novelists," though "the least familiar." Meteor-like, her career plunged into obscurity after 1902.

Wood was the youngest of 11 children. From a family long established in the isolated Scottish village of Slamannan, her father followed tradition to become a farmer, first as a tenant in Stirlingshire and then at Lesmahagow between 1862 and 1869, a period marked by the death of a number of his children from tuberculosis. In 1869 Robert, Agnes, and five surviving offspring followed the eldest son, William, to Irving, N.Y. They later moved to Ontario, possibly to be closer to Robert's brother John Stanton Wood, who had settled near Guelph. In 1874 Robert purchased The Heights, a large, valuable farm overlooking the Niagara River at Queenston. Once settled, Robert and Agnes Wood became founding members of the Presbyterian church in nearby St Davids.

Reports suggest that Joanna was supported by her brother William, an insurance agent, following her education at the St Catharines Grammar School. Between 1887 and 1901 she was based in New York City, using William's business address there for her mail while she travelled extensively to winter in various American or European cities and summer at Queenston. One of her journeys, to Scotland, enabled her to do research for her last known novel, *Farden Ha'* (London, 1902), set in a Scottish coalmining village with a shaft under the owner's house, as in Lesmahagow.

During a trip to England she had reputedly been presented at court by the sisters of poet Algernon Charles Swinburne, who was said to have been her fiancé. Two essays she wrote for the *Canadian Magazine* in 1901 fuelled these stories, sustained by family legend, but no archival evidence has been found. Moreover, given Swinburne's greater age and homo-

sexual leanings, an engagement is extremely unlikely. In her writing, however, Wood did espouse his aesthetics, with their *fin de siècle* decadence. Like him, she attempted to fuse the sensual with the spiritual through symbolism. Her absence from the Toronto literary scene created a vacuum in which such stories could circulate, mythologizing her within the dominant imperialist nationalism as a leading novelist who, like Charles George Douglas Roberts* and Horatio Gilbert Parker*, the other members of the triumvirate praised in 1898, was a Canadian Cinderella at home in English palaces.

Wood's father had sold The Heights in 1893 to William, who later turned it over to Joanna; in addition, a neighbour bequeathed her an adjoining farm. According to the census of 1901, she lived at The Heights with her widowed mother, a niece, and two lodgers. The *Canadian Magazine*, however, corresponded with her in New York that year. In November 1906 Joanna sold the Queenston property and with her mother rented The Knoll on Regent Street in nearby Niagara-on-the-Lake. Joanna resided there more continuously, joining the Niagara Historical Society in 1907 and giving talks on "Reminiscences of Queenston" and "Impressions of Europe" a year later. In 1914 she was an absentee member of the society, resident in Buffalo, though she continued to visit friends in the Niagara area, among them historian Janet CARNOCHAN and the Woodruffs of St Davids, the family of children's writer Anne Helena Woodruff. In her letters to these friends Wood included poems.

How she had come to be a writer remains a mystery. Quotations in her fiction from the Romantics, Tennyson, Swinburne, and Shakespeare, and from female authors Mme de Staël, George Eliot, Elizabeth Barrett Browning, and Christina Rossetti on the "woman question" (in relation to women's aesthetic and sexual yearnings for transcendence) imply that she was well read. They also connote serious literary ambitions. According to Honora S. Howard in the *Buffalo Illustrated Express* in 1896, Joanna attributed her success to her brother William, her first reader and a severe critic. Apparently on his recommendation she sought a publisher, finding in J. Selwin Tait a sympathetic fellow author who encouraged her to write a novel, which he launched in New York to extravagant praise. His blurb comparing Wood's *The untempered wind* (1894) to Brontë's *Jane Eyre* and Nathaniel Hawthorne's *The scarlet letter* set the terms for subsequent reviews. Her second novel, *Judith Moore* . . . (Toronto), appeared in 1898. Most of her writings, reportedly quite numerous and many of them prizewinners, cannot be located. No trace can be found, for instance, of "The mind of God," which took a $500 award according to the *Canadian Magazine* in 1898. Equally mysterious is the abrupt end to Wood's burst of creative energy. No mention is made of her in the *Cana-

dian Magazine after 1901, not even reviews of *Farden Ha'*, perhaps because she no longer sent news-filled letters to its editor, John Alexander Cooper*.

At the pinnacle of her career in 1901, Wood was the highest paid Canadian fiction writer. Her work was also a critical success, especially her first two novels, though they were praised for different qualities. British reviewers commented that she "has a style," which Americans attacked as overwrought. Characterization was what Canadians admired, along with her innovative "local colour realism," inspired by English novelist Mary Russell Mitford. The *Canadian Magazine*, which praised her depiction of Ontario rural life in *Judith Moore*, later faulted *A daughter of witches . . .* (Toronto, 1900) for its American setting and forecast greater success had she included "local colour in the Canadian country scenes, with which the authoress is so familiar." With her treatment of a Scottish village in *Farden Ha'*, in the tragic manner of Thomas Hardy's Wessex fiction, Wood no longer fit easily into the mythology of the national landscape that had made her the darling of the *Canadian Magazine*.

This tension between cosmopolitanism and regionalism echoes the conflict between boundlessness and constraint in the plots of Wood's novels. They use variations on the love triangle or two-suitors plot common in 19th-century fiction to trace the inward growth of powerful and unconventional heroines confronting the demands of social institutions. Desire, Wood's central theme, is developed through an impressionistic use of landscape to generate powerful symbols. The fallen woman of *The untempered wind*, true to her vow of love, escapes through the night woods from the harassment of the narrow-minded women of Jamestown (likely modelled on Queenston); the diva of *Judith Moore* sings like a lark uncaged in an Ontario orchard, in a reworking of the plot of *Corinne, ou l'Italie* (a de Staël novel), which dramatizes the conflict for women between artistic triumph and romantic fulfilment. These works bow to convention by ending with marriage. Wood's next two novels, *A daughter of witches* and *Farden Ha'*, deal with the disruptive effects of passion on the institution of marriage. The two novellas published in *Tales from Town Topics* (New York) highlight the decadent aspect of Wood's fiction: "A martyr to love" (1897) recounts the adventures of a femme fatale ironically wounded in her heartless conquests, while "Where waters beckon" (1902) draws symbolically on Niagara's whirlpools and local Indian legends as the setting for a dark tale of a woman married off to a madman by her father and later destroyed with her lover, an engineer developing hydroelectricity.

Americans recognized the feminist argument in Wood's critique of patriarchal authority constraining women's desire. However, they made a distinction between the "unconventional theories" in her writing

and her fondness for "feminine frivolities" in her clothing. *Current Literature* (New York) insisted in 1894 that she was no "woman's-righter." In 1896 Honora Howard did not see her as a "new woman" since she supported neither the rational dress movement nor the suffrage movement. Yet Wood's most enthusiastic review, of *Judith Moore* in 1898, came from a "new woman" journalist, Kit Coleman [Ferguson*] of the Toronto *Daily Mail and Empire*. Conversely, Wood's relentless depiction of the persecution of the fallen woman in *The untempered wind* had been condemned as anachronistic and "half-hysteric" – negatively feminine – by another female journalist (possibly Laura Bradshaw Durand) in the Toronto *Globe* in 1894. As Wood confessed to William Kirby*, a Niagara correspondent, this "savage" review hurt because it came from a Canadian, and all the more so because the "poetic flight which smacks of the school-girl composition" attacked by the critic was a quotation from Shelley's "Adonais."

Wood's short stories, in the *New England Magazine* (Boston), the *Canadian Magazine*, the *Christmas Globe* (Toronto), and elsewhere, are divided between controlled ironic renderings of local events centred on strong female characters, and masculine adventure stories from a "Mexican series," which use legend and setting to create atmosphere and suspense. "Unto the third generation," published anonymously in *All the Year Round* (London) in 1890 but attributed to Wood, recounts the effect on a young man of the revelation that his mad mother is locked up in a West Indian house, a topic with similarities to *Jane Eyre*. Among Wood's unlocated stories, "The lynchpin murders" (announced in the Niagara *Times* in 1898) suggests that Wood continued to experiment with new fictional forms until she abruptly stopped publishing in 1902.

According to the Niagara Falls *Evening Review* in 1927, Wood had suffered a nervous breakdown some years before which had compelled her to abandon her writing. She had portrayed such a crisis in *Judith Moore*, invoking the pastoral myth when a stressed prima donna retreats to a village to recover her health and soul. This scenario poses intriguing questions. Was her brother William a hard taskmaster, like Judith's New York manager? Did Joanna choose voluntarily to give up her artistic career, like Judith, in the name of emotional fulfilment? Her last recorded publication is a topical poem, "The man in the ranks," in the *St. Catharines Standard* sometime between 1914 and 1917.

After her mother's death in February 1910, Joanna Wood had resided with her brother William, then a life-insurance agent in New York City and later in Freeport, N.Y. She subsequently spent time with her sisters Mary Glennie in LaSalle, N.Y., and Jessie Maxwell in Detroit, at whose home she died of a stroke on 1 May 1927. She was buried in Fairview Cemetery in Niagara Falls, Ont.

Joanna Wood's concern with women's self-realization and symbolism has stimulated renewed interest in her work by late-20th-century feminist critics. As a result, *The untempered wind* was republished in a centenary edition in Ottawa in 1994.

BARBARA GODARD

Wood's novel *A daughter of witches* was originally serialized in the *Canadian Magazine* (Toronto), 12 (November 1898–April 1899)–13 (May–October 1899). An excerpt from *The untempered wind* was published in *Current Literature* (New York), October 1894: 378 under the title "An inheritance of dishonor: a child's sorrow," and an excerpt from *Judith Moore* entitled "Sam Symmons' great loss" appeared in the *Canadian Magazine*, 10 (November 1897–April 1898): 536–38.

Other stories and articles by Wood which have been located include "Malhalla's revenge" in the *New England Magazine* (Boston), new ser., 12 (March–August 1895): 184–87; and "A mother," "Algernon Charles Swinburne: an appreciation," and "Presentation at court" in the *Canadian Magazine*, 7 (May–October 1896): 558–61 and 17 (May–October 1901): 2–10 and 506–10 respectively. Another story attributed to her, "The land of manana," has not been found.

Reviews of *The untempered wind* appeared in *Current Literature*, October 1894: 298; the *Globe*, 10 Nov. 1894: 9; the New York *Nation*, 30 May 1895: 426; and the Toronto *Week*, 12 Oct. 1894: 1099. *Judith Moore* was reviewed in the *Canadian Magazine*, 10: 460–61; the *Daily Mail and Empire*, 19 March 1898: 4; and the *Nation*, 6 Oct. 1898: 264. Reviews of *A daughter of witches* can be found in the *Canadian Magazine*, 16 (November 1900–April 1901): 91–92 and 388–89; in three London publications – the *Athenæum*, 1 Sept. 1900: 276; the *Bookman*, October 1900: 28; and the *Spectator*, 8 Sept. 1900: 309; and in the New York *Saturday Rev.*, 6 Oct. 1900: 432.

AO, F 1076-A-23. Brock Univ. Library, Special Coll. and Arch. (St Catharines, Ont.), Women's Literary Club of St Catharines Arch., E. M. Stevens, J. E. Wood scrapbook. North York Central Library, Canadiana Coll. (Toronto), J. A. Cooper papers, *Canadian Magazine* files. *Daily Record* (Niagara Falls, Ont.), 2 March 1910: 3. *Evening Review* (Niagara Falls), 3 May 1927. H. S. Howard, "Joanna E. Wood," *Buffalo Illustrated Express* (Buffalo, N.Y.), 26 Dec. 1896: 7. *Niagara Advance* (Niagara-on-the-Lake, Ont.), 28 Aug. 1919. *St. Catharines Standard*, 7 May 1927. *Times* (Niagara-on-the-Lake), 21 Oct. 1898: 5; 14 Feb. 1908: 1; 17 April 1908: 4; 4 March 1910: 1. *Canadian Magazine*, 11 (May–October 1898): 180, 270; 12: 473. *Canadian men and women of the time* (Morgan; 1912). Wendy D'Angelo, "Joanna E. Wood: a 'new woman' and her works" (BA thesis, Dept. of English, York Univ., Toronto, 1987). *Dictionary of literary biography* (317v. to date, Detroit, 1978–), 92 (*Canadian writers, 1890–1920*, ed. W. H. New, 1990). Barbara Godard, "'Petticoat anarchist'?: Joanna Wood, the sex of fiction, the fictive sex," in *Women's writing and the literary institution*, ed. C[laudine] Potvin *et al.* (Edmonton, 1992), 95–125; "A portrait with three faces: the new woman in fiction by Canadian women, 1880–1920," *Literary Criterion* (Bombay), 19

(1984), nos.3–4: 72–92. Carrie MacMillan, "Joanna E. Wood: incendiary women," in *Silenced sextet: six nineteenth-century Canadian women authors*, ed. Carrie MacMillan *et al.* (Montreal and Kingston, Ont., 1992), 169–200. *The Oxford companion to Canadian literature*, ed. Eugene Benson and William Toye (2nd ed., Toronto, 1997). E. M. Stevens, "She's Canada's Charlotte Brontë, but Joanna E. Wood goes unrecognized here," *Early Canadian Life* (Oakville, Ont.), 4 (1980), no.4: B3, B15; "Writers of the Niagara peninsula: Wood, Joanna Ellen," Ontario Geneal. Soc., Niagara peninsula branch, *Notes from Niagara* (St Catharines), 4 (1984), no.2: 6. *Types of Canadian women . . .* , ed. H. J. Morgan (Toronto, 1903).

WOOD, JOSIAH, merchant, industrialist, politician, and lieutenant governor; b. 18 April 1843 in Sackville, N.B., son of Mariner Ayer Wood and Louisa Cynthia Trueman; m. there 14 Jan. 1874 Laura Sophia Trueman (d. 1935), and they had four daughters, one of whom died at birth, and two sons; d. there 13 May 1927.

A native of Dorchester, N.B., Josiah Wood's father established himself as a merchant in Sackville and built a successful wholesale and retail business, which eventually included agricultural, shipbuilding, shipping, and lumbering concerns. By the time of his death in 1875 his firm would be rated the leading commercial enterprise in Sackville with a "pecuniary strength" of $100,000 to $250,000. This considerable economic legacy was matched by the deep Wesleyan Methodist beliefs he passed on to his two sons, who were advised "to read and study the good word of God at least once or twice each day and pray for the holy spirit to accompany the exercise."

At the age of nine, Josiah was enrolled in the Mount Allison Wesleyan Academy in Sackville, and after graduation in 1861 he entered Mount Allison's college branch, where he received his BA in 1863, one of its first two graduates. He began a career in law, but gave it up because of the serious illness of his younger brother, Charles Harmon. In January 1871 M. Wood and Sons was created as a three-way partnership to continue the family business, all of which Josiah inherited on his father's death, Charles having died in the interim. He enlarged the company's operations, emphasizing wholesale sales, purchasing four ships for its fleet, and using the Intercolonial Railway to complement the seaborne trade and import Canadian-made goods. He also engaged in banking, real estate and industrial investment, and railway building.

A wealthy and prominent entrepreneur, Wood was drawn to politics and stood in 1878 for the Westmorland seat in the New Brunswick legislature. Despite family connections with the Liberal Conservatives, he was among the unsuccessful four candidates identified as the "Liberal ticket." He had maintained, however, that he and his colleagues "each will be independent of the other to do as he chooses." His Liberal lapse was soon rectified. At the urging of Conservative senator John Boyd*, who thought him the only man in Westmorland able to defeat the sitting federal Liberal member, Sir Albert James Smith*, and pressed as well by his uncle Acalus Lockwood Palmer, with whom he had studied law, Wood sought and won the Conservative nomination in 1882. Although the possibility of losing her husband, already frequently absent on business, to Ottawa rather disconcerted Laura Wood, it was still her earnest desire "that he shall get his election." In June 1882 her wish was fulfilled when Wood obtained a majority of over 400 votes.

It was the tariff-protection and railway-building policies of the Conservative party that drew Wood into federal politics. He had become a substantial investor in Moncton's emerging industrial base, which profited from the presence of the Intercolonial Railway and the National Policy. With such partners as John Leonard Harris* he raised approximately $1,000,000 to fund enterprises that included a sugar refinery, a gaslight and water company, a cotton mill, and other textile- and metal-manufacturing concerns. Substantial real estate interests in Moncton were matched by the property he controlled in Sackville. Another of his projects was the construction of a railway from Cape Tormentine, on Northumberland Strait, to Sackville, where it would link up with the Intercolonial. When it was launched in 1874 as the New Brunswick and Prince Edward Railway Company, Wood had invested $1,000 out of a total of $66,000. By 1882 he would be president and, with $50,000 in stock, the largest investor.

The railway company failed to meet the conditions of its charter, by which the provincial government promised a subsidy of $5,000 if construction began by 1878 and the line was completed by 1880. Joseph Laurence Black*, one of Westmorland's representatives in the provincial legislature and a shareholder, saw to it that time extensions were granted along with a promise of a reduced subsidy. Federal support was not so easily won, even after the Conservatives under Sir John A. Macdonald* returned to power in 1878. Neighbouring Amherst, N.S., represented in the House of Commons by Charles Tupper*, had its eye on a ship railway across the Chignecto Isthmus [see Henry George Clopper Ketchum*] as well as a conventional line from Amherst to Cape Tormentine. In the end grandiose commitments were made to the ship railway, but the other Amherst line was abandoned and the Sackville railway won federal backing. Wood's intensive lobbying, Tupper's departure from the cabinet, and the determined support of Sir Samuel Leonard Tilley*, New Brunswick's ranking representative in the government, carried the day. The railway received a subsidy of $3,200 a mile in July 1885 as well as a federal commitment to construct a wharf at the Cape Tormentine terminus. Wood was able to report in 1887 that $223,000 of the railway's total cost of $300,000 had been contributed by government.

Linked by a ferry, the railway not only functioned as the major connection to Prince Edward Island but also brought considerable economic benefit to southeastern Westmorland County. These gains, coupled with Moncton's prosperous growth, ensured Wood's re-election, by almost 550 votes in 1887 and over 2,000 in 1891. In the commons he had quickly earned a reputation for speeches that were balanced, well documented, thoughtful, and polite. He rose predictably in defence of Conservative policies, especially the National Policy, which had, he noted, promoted manufacturing in the Maritimes at a time when shipbuilding was in decline and which had created in Canada "a national unity, a national independence, to which we were utter strangers a quarter of a century ago." He also advocated government support for the Canadian Pacific Railway and for its "Short Line" from Montreal to Saint John. Attacked for using his influence as an MP to promote his own railway venture, he unabashedly acknowledged the subsidies provided, which were normal support available to any railway, he explained, and which had been secured without "any undue influence with the Government." His lobbying activities were clearly understated, but they were far from untypical at the time.

What was unusual for a representative of the Maritimes in the House of Commons was Wood's questions concerning the Intercolonial. Built and operated at public expense as a "vital bond of union," the ICR was, he recognized, never intended to be simply a commercial undertaking, but he bemoaned the political patronage linked with it, the increases in freight and passenger mileage that were not matched by increased revenue, and its low rates. By the 1890s he was urging no further extensions of the line, a reduction in its trains and employees, and an increase in rates. Although he did not propose its sale to a private company, he suggested that its operations be truncated through the use of its facilities by the Grand Trunk and the CPR, a proposal that would give these private railways independent access to Maritime seaports. Such a scheme would win Wood little support in Moncton, which housed the headquarters and major shops of the ICR, and perhaps it was just as well that he was spared another election campaign by an appointment to the Senate on 5 Aug. 1895.

In the Senate he was an active participant in debates. He continued his opposition to government ownership and operation of railways, openly acknowledging that in his criticism of the ICR he was "not putting forth the views of the public in the maritime provinces." While generally he praised private railways, he sometimes found government support for them to be excessive or questionable. He had major reservations about the Crowsnest Pass agreement with the CPR, for example, and he totally opposed the Liberal plan to build a second transcontinental railway [*see* Charles Melville Hays*], fearing that the government's obligations might eventually force it to take over the line. On the Manitoba school question he supported "the views of the Roman Catholics" and in 1897 condemned Prime Minister Sir Wilfrid Laurier*'s failure to "carry out the obligations which the highest judicial authority of this empire have declared to be a solemn parliamentary compact." The privileges and role of the Senate were of vital importance to him, and he presented an elaborate case against Senate reform. Yet both senators and MPs were chastised for accepting salary increases. "We are here," Wood argued, "not as paid representatives of the people; we are here, in my opinion, as trustees of the public funds." His own increase was not accepted; instead he allowed the funds to accumulate. Above all, Wood continued to dream that national economic policies could be formulated which would stimulate the growth of the Maritimes. The "eastern section of this Dominion," he believed, could make Canada "one of the greatest manufacturing countries in the world."

Old dreams die hard, and, given Wood's own experiences in the 1880s and 1890s, this one had surprising persistence. One by one almost all the Moncton industries in which he was a partner were bought out, or consolidated and put out of business, by central Canadian competitors as the branch-plant nature of the Maritime economy took hold. He remained active in Sackville utilities companies and, as the town's first mayor from 1904 to 1907, oversaw the purchase of several of these concerns by the town council. In 1904 his son, Herbert Mariner, was made a partner in M. Wood and Sons, but the value of the family business had fallen to between $35,000 and $50,000 by 1905. In 1914 the federal government's purchase, for $270,000, of the renamed New Brunswick and Prince Edward Island Railway, in which Wood had remained the majority owner, probably went a long way towards replenishing the family fortune.

One final honour awaited Wood. With Conservative governments in power both in Ottawa and in Fredericton, he accepted appointment as lieutenant governor of New Brunswick on 6 March 1912. He served until 1917, demonstrating his integrity when, despite pressure from former Conservative friends at the federal and provincial levels, he forced James Kidd FLEMMING to resign as premier in 1914 after two royal commissions found irregularities in his fund-raising.

Throughout his life Wood was a generous supporter of the Methodist Church of Canada. Sackville's Main Street Methodist Church benefited from his work on the board of trustees and the building committee, his financial guidance, and many subscriptions and donations. His beloved alma mater, Mount Allison, was even more in his debt. A member of its board of

regents for more than 40 years, he served as treasurer from 1876 to 1922. He made a $10,000 contribution in the early 1880s, endowed the Josiah Wood chair in classics, financed the excavation of a small lake to enhance the college grounds, and donated the $14,800 he had acquired in deferred senatorial indemnities to fund the Josiah Wood lectureship. In return he was awarded a DCL in 1891 and honoured on the 60th anniversary of his graduation.

Beset by "feeble health" for the last years of his life, Wood died on 13 May 1927 at the age of 84, widely praised for his integrity, strength of character, sound judgement, and breadth of vision. He left an estate worth $178,869.91, of which approximately $90,000 was in bonds, securities, and stocks. Wood's career neatly captures the transition from mercantile to industrial and financial capitalism in the Maritimes and the sometimes inadequate political response to it. Although he survived the transition better than some other capitalists, the region as a whole suffered problems of adjustment that would point to its future lagging rather than leading role within Canada.

W. G. GODFREY

The best primary source collection on Wood is the Wood family papers at PANB, MC 218; also helpful at this institution are the probate records in RS74, nos.1927/3688 and 1935/4393. Holdings at the Mount Allison Univ. Arch. (Sackville, N.B.) include the Wood family fonds (8914 and 9703), the Josiah Wood papers (7843), and Laura [Trueman] Wood's diary (8510).

Chignecto Post (Sackville), 23 May, 13, 20 June 1878, continued as the *Chignecto Post and Borderer*, 9 Feb., 18 May 1882. *Transcript* (Sackville), 9 Feb., 23 March 1882. *Tribune* (Sackville), 9 March 1882; 16 May 1927; 1, 4 April 1935. T. W. Acheson, "The National Policy and the industrialization of the Maritimes, 1880–1910," *Acadiensis* (Fredericton), 1 (1971–72), no.2: 3–28. D. E. Alward, "Down Sackville ways: shipbuilding in a nineteenth century New Brunswick outport" (BA thesis, Mount Allison Univ., 1978). *Biographical review . . . of leading citizens of the province of New Brunswick*, ed. I. A. Jack (Boston, 1900). Can., House of Commons, *Debates*, 1883–96; Senate, *Debates*, 1896–1911. *Canadian biographical dictionary and portrait gallery of eminent and self-made men* (2v., Toronto, 1880–81). A. T. Doyle, *Front benches & back rooms: a story of corruption, muckraking, raw partisanship and intrigue in New Brunswick* (Toronto, 1976); *Heroes of New Brunswick* (Fredericton, 1984). D. [W.] Jobb, "Josiah Wood [1843–1927]: 'A cultured and honoured gentleman of the old school'" (BA thesis, Mount Allison Univ., 1980); "Sackville promotes a railway: the politics of the New Brunswick and Prince Edward Railway, 1872–1886," in *People and place: studies of small town life in the Maritimes*, ed. L. [D.] McCann (Fredericton and Sackville, 1987), 31–56. L. D. McCann, "Metropolitanism and branch businesses in the Maritimes," *Acadiensis*, 13 (1983–84), no.1: 112–25. C. R. McKay, "Investors, government and the CMTR: a study of entrepreneurial failure," *Acadiensis*, 9 (1979–80), no.1: 71–94. *The mercantile agency* reference book ... (Montreal), 1870–1930. W. C. Milner, *History of Sackville, New Brunswick* (Sackville, 1934); "Our lieutenant governors," *Busy East of Canada* (Sackville), 9 (1918–19), no.5: 20–22. *Prominent people of New Brunswick ...*, comp. C. H. McLean ([Saint John], 1937). *Standard dict. of Canadian biog.* (Roberts and Tunnell), vol.1. G. R. Stevens, *Canadian National Railways* (2v., Toronto and Vancouver, 1960–62), 2. *The Wood family, Sackville, N.B.: being a genealogy of the line from Thomas Wood of Rowley, Mass., born about 1634, to Josiah Wood, of Sackville, N.B., born in 1843 ...*, comp. J. A. Kibbe (Warehouse Point, Conn., 1904).

WRIGHT, ADAM HENRY, educator, physician, and office holder; b. 6 April 1846 in Brampton, Upper Canada, son of Henry Wright and Sarah Jane Webb; m. 6 Jan. 1874 Flora Mary Anne Cumming in Trenton, Ont., and they had two sons and three daughters; d. 20 Aug. 1930 in Toronto.

Educated in private schools as a boy, Adam Wright began his long association with the University of Toronto when he attended University College in the 1860s. He was active in athletics, especially football, cricket, tennis, and hockey, and was involved as well in the militia. A lieutenant in the university company of the Queen's Own Rifles, he participated in the action at Ridgeway against the Fenian raiders [*see* Alfred Booker*]. Upon graduation (BA 1866), he spent a number of years teaching high school in Trenton, where he also joined the local artillery battery.

Wright subsequently enrolled at the Toronto School of Medicine. The University of Toronto, which did not offer instruction in medicine at this time, acted only as an examining body, and in 1873 Wright received his MB. He was practising in Colborne – his mother's home town in Northumberland County – when he married in 1874. With an eye to further qualification, he sailed for London, where he took a diploma course and in 1877 was made a member of the Royal College of Surgeons of England.

After his return to Toronto, Wright, partly out of economic necessity, entered various sectors of the medical profession. He joined the staff of the Toronto School of Medicine in 1879, became an editor of the *Canadian Journal of Medical Science* at about the same time (and later of its successor, the *Canadian Practitioner*), was a surgeon at the Toronto General Hospital, and lectured on obstetrics from 1883 to 1886 at Woman's Medical College, of which he was also a director [*see* Emily Howard Jennings*]. First elected as a senator of the University of Toronto in 1885, he joined its re-established faculty of medicine [*see* William Thomas Aikins*] as professor of obstetrics in 1887; the following year he earned his MD.

During the time in the 1890s that Wright was an attending physician at the Burnside Lying-In Hospital, which was part of the TGH, conditions at this maternity hospital improved; the introduction of aseptic procedures during births, for instance, led to a decline in deaths. Though generally conventional in his obstetrical views and practices, Wright did help to advance obstetrics as a distinct field. His own rising status was evident in his election as president of the American Association of Obstetricians and Gynecologists (1890), the Toronto Clinical Society (1897), the Ontario Medical Association (1900), and the Canadian Medical Association (1909). At the University of Toronto he succeeded Uzziel Ogden* in the chair of obstetrics in 1903 and a year later published his *Textbook of obstetrics* (Toronto).

Politically, from 1905 Wright supported the Conservative administration in Ontario of James Pliny Whitney* because of its progressive policies on public health, hospitals, and reformatories. In January 1911 he was made chairman of the Provincial Board of Health. During his tenure, numerous reforms, many initiated by board secretary Dr John William Scott McCullough*, were instituted to improve the administrative structures of public health in Ontario. Among them was a series of amendments to the Public Health Act, especially those in 1912 that strengthened the authority and independence of local medical officers of health. In 1913 the board undertook, for the International Joint Commission [*see* Sir George Christie Gibbons*], an exhaustive examination of water quality along the Ontarian-American boundary. Of considerable importance too, in controlling disease, was the board's approval in 1914 of McCullough's plan to distribute diphtheria antitoxin at low cost, which led to a system of free distribution two years later.

In 1924, at the age of 78, Wright stepped down as chair when the board was disbanded on the formation of the provincial Department of Health. In retirement he continued his recreational interests – golf, fishing, lawn bowling, and curling – pursuits that reflected the athleticism of his student days. He was a member of the Royal Canadian Yacht Club and the Granite Club, of which he had been president in 1891. An Anglican, Wright died in 1930 and was buried in Mount Pleasant Cemetery. He had been followed into medicine by his elder son, Arthur Baldwin.

PAUL ADOLPHUS BATOR

In addition to his textbook, Adam Henry Wright's publications include "Health matters in Ontario" and "Preventive medicine and the family," in *Public Health Journal* (Toronto), 4 (1913): 354–57 and 648–52, respectively; "Medical fees," "Work, fatigue and rest," and "A former epidemic of smallpox in Toronto," in *Canadian Practitioner and Medical Rev.* (Toronto), 41 (1916): 63–65, 42 (1917): 231–36, and 45 (1920): 40–41, respectively; a tribute to former provincial secretary William John Hanna* in *Public Health Journal*, 10 (1919): 270–73; and "The medical schools of Toronto," Canadian Medical Assoc., *Journal* (Toronto), 18 (January–June 1928): 616–20.

Wright

AO, RG 80-5-0-42, no.3540. UTA A1973-0026/527(17). Canadian Medical Assoc., *Journal*, 23 (July–December 1930): 725–26. *Canadian men and women of the time* (Morgan; 1912). Wendy Mitchinson, *The nature of their bodies: women and their doctors in Victorian Canada* (Toronto, 1991). *Who's who and why*, 1921.

WRIGHT, JOHN JOSEPH, electrical engineer; b. 11 Dec. 1847 in Great Yarmouth, England, son of James Wright, a Methodist minister, and Matilda Whittaker; m. 22 June 1874 Jessie Firstbrook in Toronto, and they had six daughters and two sons; d. 1 Feb. 1922 in Newcastle, Ont.

Educated at Shireland Hall in Birmingham, John J. Wright arrived in Toronto in 1870 as a millwright – he later called himself a machinist. In 1874 he married Jessie Firstbrook; her father was a lumber dealer and box maker and some of her brothers were machinists. When Wright went to Philadelphia in 1876, ostensibly to visit the centennial exhibition, he attended lectures on electricity by Elihu Thomson and Edwin James Houston, teachers at the Central High School there and partners in electrical experimentation. He apparently impressed them and entered their employ; he worked on generators and in 1879 helped install North America's first electric-arc street lamp.

Following his return to Toronto in early 1881, Wright, in a back room at the Firstbrook factory, built a trial generator; it powered arc lamps that he had designed and installed in some downtown businesses. Such experimental ventures prompted city council to establish a committee in October 1881 to study the benefits of electric street lighting, but no contracts ensued. One of a number of early electrical entrepreneurs vying for opportunities, in the summer of 1882 Wright opened Toronto's first commercial power station using generators provided by Thomson and Houston and driven by surplus steam from a nearby printing plant. Distribution wires were strung across the rooftops, and in 1884 Wright applied to use the poles of the newly organized Toronto Electric Light Company Limited. Since illumination was required only at night, he sold electric motors to stimulate daytime demand.

In 1883 the Toronto Industrial Exhibition had decided to install an electric railway for demonstration purposes. The directors intended to buy equipment from a Chicago source but, since the price was too high, they settled for an experimental engine built by Thomas Alva Edison and owned by Wright. It proved unable to move any cars. The exhibition tried again in 1884. This time Wright, working for Charles Joseph Van Depoele, a leading American proponent of electric traction, motorized a Grand Trunk flatcar, which performed perfectly. Although newspaper accounts in 1883 and 1884 make no mention of Wright's involvement, he is credited by some with constructing the first electric railway in Canada.

In September 1884 the *Globe* identified him as head of the J. J. Wright Electric Light Company. The city directory of 1885 described him simply as an electrician. His private operations ended in 1886 when he became superintendent (later manager) of the Toronto Electric Light Company, which had acquired a municipal street-light franchise in 1884. Contested by Consumers' Gas and the Toronto Railway Company, the renewal of the franchise in 1894 was tainted with the hint of scandal. The chair of the city's fire and light committee, Alderman William T. Stewart, supposedly suggested that Wright provide $13,000 for distribution to council members. Stewart was tried but the charge was not proved.

Wright's involvement with electrical application illustrates the challenge of working in a field of rapid technological and corporate change. He testified before the Ontario legislature's private bills committee in 1902 that long-distance transmission was impractical and that, in Toronto, steam-driven generating plants were more economical. Although the city received its first electricity from Niagara Falls in 1906, he was still arguing in 1908 that high-voltage lines posed a "grave danger" to farm buildings. Other electrical engineers, such as Robert Alexander Ross* of Montreal, disagreed. Whatever the limits of Wright's know-how, his managerial skills remained valuable, and he stayed with Toronto Electric Light after it became linked in 1908 to William MACKENZIE's large holding company, the Toronto Power Company Limited. In 1910 he was made second vice-president and general consultant. By 1914 he was a consulting engineer with no connection.

A member of the Franklin Institute in Philadelphia, Wright was the first president of the Canadian Electrical Association in 1891–93. He held the office again in 1904, and served on the managing committee of the association until its affiliation in 1911 with the National Electric Light Association in the United States, a step he did not support. In appearance this genial electrical pioneer was a stocky man with a large moustache. An enthusiast "of all kinds of aquatic sports," he belonged to the Royal Canadian Yacht Club and spent many a weekend "speeding" across Lake Ontario, "the central figure of a jolly party." He retired from the electrical industry about 1915, settled in Niagara-on-the-Lake, and moved to Newcastle in 1921. He died the following year and was buried in Mount Pleasant Cemetery in Toronto.

CHRISTOPHER ANDREAE

AO, RG 22-191, no.9526; RG 80-5-0-47, no.11760. GRO, Reg. of births, Great Yarmouth (Norfolk), 11 Dec. 1847. *Canadian Statesman* (Bowmanville, Ont.), 9 Feb. 1922. *Globe*, 12, 17 Sept. 1883; 4, 9, 13 Sept. 1884; 3 Feb. 1922. *Toronto Daily Mail*, 18 Sept. 1883. *Bright lights, big city: the* history of electricity in Toronto (Toronto, 1991). Canadian men and women of the time (Morgan; 1898 and 1912). Canadian National Exhibition, Greater Toronto picture souvenir ([Toronto], 1934). C. W. Condit, The pioneer stage of railroad electrification (Philadelphia, 1977). Merrill Denison, The people's power: the history of Ontario Hydro ([Toronto], 1960). Directory, Toronto, 1873/74–1915. Electrical News (Toronto), 21 (1911), no.7: 73. History of Toronto and county of York, Ontario ... (2v., Toronto, 1885), 1: 385. Middleton, Municipality of Toronto, vol.1: 318.

WRIGHT, SARAH ALICE. See ROWELL

Y

YIP SANG ((Ye Sheng in Mandarin), also known as **Yip Chun Tien (Ye Chuntian)** and **Yip Lin Sang (Ye Linsheng)**; he took the style name **Yip Loy Yiu (Ye Lairao))**, businessman, social reformer, and political activist; b. 6 Sept. 1845 in Shengtang village, Duhu county, Guangdong province (People's Republic of China); m. first Lee Shee (Li Shi); m. secondly Dong Shee (Deng Shi); m. thirdly Wong Shee (Wang Shi); m. fourthly Chin Shee (Jin Shi); he had 19 sons and 4 daughters; d. 20 July 1927 in Vancouver.

The career of Yip Sang illustrates the trans-Pacific family, cultural, and business ties that characterized the lives of most first-generation migrants from China during the 19th and early 20th centuries. He came to North America to escape poverty and unrest at home. His father, the son of a wealthy man, had become impoverished. The family's situation must have worsened when he died during Yip's boyhood. As a teenager Yip lost his mother as well. In 1864, after his older sister had been kidnapped by local bandits, he sold his possessions to buy passage to California. There he worked as a cook, dishwasher, cigar maker, and gold miner. After a time he had saved enough money to return to China for a visit, during which, according to family tradition, he saw a girl he promised himself he would marry. He returned to the United States, once again working as a cook. On his next trip to China he married the girl, who bore his first two children. She died after he went back to North America alone. He accordingly took a second wife. When she proved unable to manage a household, he married for a third time.

Yip came to Canada in 1881 to work on the Cariboo goldfields. Unsuccessful there, he moved to what would become Vancouver and sold coal door to door until he was employed by the Canadian Pacific Railway Supply Company on a construction gang. He became the company's bookkeeper, timekeeper, and paymaster, and eventually its superintendent of Chinese labour. In 1885 he returned to China and took a fourth wife.

In 1888 Yip founded the Wing Sang Company in Vancouver. Like many Chinese firms at this time, Wing Sang engaged in a variety of enterprises. In addition to labour contracting, the company ran a trans-Pacific import and export business, pioneering the export of salt fish to various points on the Pacific rim, including Japan. It also played an important role in forwarding remittances from workers to their families in China and serving as a contact point for correspondence. Yip became the Chinese agent for the Canadian Pacific Railway Company, supplying its railway with construction labourers and its steamships with sailors and fresh produce. By 1908 his company was one of the four largest Chinese companies in Vancouver, with an annual revenue of $50,000 from its import-export business alone and real estate holdings worth over $200,000.

Yip, who became a naturalized British subject in 1891, was one of the most important leaders of Vancouver's Chinese community. He was instrumental in the formation of the Chinese Benevolent Association in Vancouver and the Chinese Board of Trade during the 1890s. These organizations subsequently defended the community from racism, governed its affairs, and established social institutions such as the Chinese hospital and the Chinese public school. Linked to the CPR and fluent in English, Yip also appears to have played a key role as a go-between with the dominant Anglo-European community in British Columbia. He proved to be a major witness for the federal royal commissions headed by the deputy minister of labour, William Lyon Mackenzie King*, in the wake of the anti-Asian riot in Vancouver in 1907. He testified to the decline of the labour-contract system as a result of the increase in the head tax imposed on Chinese immigrants in 1903. Yip also served as a life governor of the Vancouver General Hospital.

Yip played a particularly important role in the formation of the Chinese Empire Reform Association, the first modern Chinese political party, established by reformer Kang Youwei. Kang had fled China and had arrived in Victoria in 1899 en route to England following the failure of the reform movement in China the previous year. Yip Sang sent a close relative, Yip On, to receive Kang. Yip On became the principal organizer of the international association, which sought the establishment of a constitutional monarchy in China, while Yip Sang became president of the Canadian body. Although Kang Youwei had great prestige and was an internationally known figure, it is likely that Yip Sang's business contacts were principally responsible for the spread of the association in the overseas Chinese communities of the Pacific rim and the Americas. Certainly he and Yip On were instrumental in establishing the association's Commercial Corporation, which attracted a great deal of investment from these communities.

In 1901 Yip brought his entire family over from China. He established his three wives, their children, and various other close relatives, along with their servants, in the residence above his store at 51 Dupont (East Pender) Street. When these premises grew too small to accommodate the growing family, he had a six-storey dwelling built at the rear. Yip's grandson Harry Yip remembers that his grandfather established a strict curfew on the building's over 100 residents. At 10:00 P.M. Yip locked the door with the key of which he alone had a copy. Having gone from dire poverty to considerable respectability, he seems to have been determined to preserve his greatest asset, his family.

A firm believer in education, Yip served for ten years as principal of the Aiguo Xuetang, the school established by the Chinese Empire Reform Association in Vancouver about 1902. He insisted that his children be educated in both English and Chinese. He hired private tutors or sent them to the Aiguo Xuetang to ensure their Chinese education. Most also attended provincially controlled public schools and some went on to university. Apparently, with one exception, all of his family's girl house servants also attended school. His daughter Susan was one of the first Chinese Canadian women to attend university, enrolling at the University of British Columbia in 1915. In 1945 Kew Dock Yip, one of his sons, was the first Chinese Canadian to become a member of the bar.

In many ways Yip was ahead of his time. One of the first to seize on the significance of the Chinese reform movement, he appears to have shared Kang Youwei's views on women as well. Not only did he see to the education of his daughters, but as early as 1902, when the married women of Guangdong migrant communities were allowed few activities outside the home – they rarely even appeared in public unescorted by an adult male relative – two of his wives and at least one female relative through marriage were members of the Chinese Empire Reform Women's Association. In other respects, however, Yip, like Kang, was a stern Confucian patriarch. Presumably in an effort to escape succession duties, he bequeathed only token amounts to the 18 sons who survived him. Even though his estate was worth $78,000, he left nothing at all to his daughters.

At the time of his death Yip Sang was one of the foremost members of Canada's Guangdong migrant community. He had played a leading role as a labour contractor, an importer-exporter, and a political and community leader. He had also successfully established the largest Chinese family lineage in Canada, having over 660 living descendants by 1996.

TIMOTHY J. STANLEY

BCA, GR-1415, file 12451. City of Vancouver Arch., Add. MSS 1108 (Yip family and Yip Sang Ltd. fonds). LAC, MG 26, J4. Gordon Clark, "Man honored at family reunion," *Province* (Vancouver), 3 Aug. 1996. Peter McMartin, "The fabulous, overlooked life of Yip Sang," *Toronto Star,* 4 Dec. 1993. Can., Royal commission to investigate methods by which Oriental labourers have been induced to come to Canada, *Report* (Ottawa, 1908). Harry Con *et al.*, *From China to Canada: a history of the Chinese communities in Canada*, ed. Edgar Wickberg (Toronto, 1982; repr. 1988). *Ye Chuntian xiansheng chuanji* [The biography of Mr Ye Chuntian] (Hong Kong, [1973]). Paul Yee, *Saltwater city: an illustrated history of the Chinese in Vancouver* (Vancouver, 1988).

Z

ZIMMERMAN, BENJAMIN, businessman, JP, and community leader; b. 23 July 1862 in Pereiosleve (Pereyaslav-Khmel'nyts'kyy, Ukraine), son of Nathan Zimmerman and Hudel ——; m. 1887 Minnie Schwartz (d. 1929) in Winnipeg, and they had eight sons and one daughter; d. 12 Sept. 1923 in Vancouver and was buried in Winnipeg.

In the wake of pogroms and of social, economic, and political persecution during the early 1880s, thousands of Jews living in the Russian empire immigrated

to North America. Included among the several hundred who settled in Winnipeg in 1882 were Nathan Zimmerman and his family. After working as a labourer on the Canadian Pacific Railway, as did many other Jews who lacked capital, Nathan became a pedlar, probably with his son Benjamin, who was based for several months in Donald, B.C., along the railway's main line. By 1884 Nathan had established a small clothing and dry-goods store on Winnipeg's north Main Street, where other Jewish businessmen were locating. Benjamin assisted his father. Three years later his mother began to manage the store while his father established a pawnbroking business with Benjamin's brother-in-law Joseph (John) Levin (Levine).

By 1890 Benjamin Zimmerman had formed his own peddling company. Five years later he was a jobber specializing in retail clothing and by 1900 he, too, was a pawnbroker, operating the Manchester, London and Liverpool Loan Office at 630–32 Main, where he and his family resided. In 1901 he was described as having Winnipeg's "best known and most reputable loan office" and "a splendid reputation for fair dealing and honest business methods." He made confidential loans on articles of value and was a dealer in new and second-hand goods such as rifles, pistols, and bicycles. Retail jewellery sales increasingly became a mainstay of his business.

During 1903, as a result of his financial success, Zimmerman had a three-storey brick building constructed at 671–73 Main Street to house his business. At various times some of his sons worked in or managed his affairs. Others would form their own firms. By 1910 Zimmerman had a wholesale liquor and cigar firm, managed by his son Norman; his sons Samuel and William N. were running the loans office and the jewellery and pawnbroking business. His family resided in the fashionable southern part of the city. Probably because of the advent of Prohibition in 1916, possibly also because of failing health, Benjamin was no longer in the wholesale liquor business by 1920. In 1922 his son Abraham was the proprietor of Benjamin Zimmerman and Son, jewellers.

In the late 19th and early 20th centuries, Zimmerman was a leader of the growing Jewish community in Winnipeg. In the early 1880s he was president of a small Hebrew congregation, the Anshey Sephard Anshey Russia, and in 1889 he was a founding member of the Shaarey Zedek Synagogue. Later he joined the Rosh Pina Synagogue, established in 1893, and served as president. In 1911 he rejoined the congregation at Shaarey Zedek.

Zimmerman was one of the founders of the earliest Jewish charitable organization in Winnipeg. The Hebrew Benevolent Society, founded in 1884, provided financial assistance to Jewish families and to general community causes as well as job-placement services for Jewish immigrants. In 1900 he was a member of the Jewish committee of the Canadian Patriotic Fund. Following a series of pogroms in eastern Europe, the most infamous of which occurred at Kishinev (Chisinău, Moldova) in May 1903, Zimmerman became a member of the five-man Kishinev relief fund committee established by the major Jewish organizations in Winnipeg. In addition, he served on the executive and the board of directors of the United Hebrew Charities, formed in 1910. Two years later he helped organize the Hebrew Immigration Society of Win-

nipeg. The same year Zimmerman was a founder of the Hebrew Free School. He was also one of the earliest members of Winnipeg Lodge No.650 of the Independent Order of B'nai B'rith and a member of the Oddfellows and of the Ancient Order United Workmen.

Zimmerman's involvement in politics is notable as an example of ethnic political acculturation and because of the influence his positions likely had on other Winnipeg Jewish electors. During the 1890s he alternately supported the Liberal and Conservative parties, but he would become a Conservative after 1900. During the federal election of 1896 he spoke at a meeting of the Hebrew Independent Political Club, which supported Conservative Hugh John MAC-DONALD, probably because the incumbent, Liberal Joseph MARTIN, had made disparaging comments about "Jew peddlers" in the House of Commons. In the absence of a Conservative candidate in the by-election held the following year after the invalidation of Macdonald's election, Zimmerman supported the unsuccessful independent candidate, Edmund Landor Taylor.

In November 1898 Zimmerman was appointed a justice of the peace by the provincial Liberal government of Thomas Greenway*, who wished to rebuild a political bridge to the Jews of Winnipeg. In this capacity, Zimmerman sometimes occupied the bench in the Winnipeg police court, where, one observer commented, "his impartial and judicial decisions earned him the highest respect of all classes of the community." He would remain a JP for almost 25 years.

In the municipal and federal elections of 1904 Zimmerman endorsed Conservative candidates. In March 1908 he was elected by acclamation to the 18-member executive of the Hebrew Conservative Club. During the federal electoral campaign of 1911 he supported the incumbent, Conservative Alexander Haggart, speaking in Yiddish on one occasion against reciprocity with the United States. At a meeting called by Jewish alderman Altar Skaletar in June 1914, he put forward a motion and spoke against the Winnipeg City Council and the Winnipeg Trades and Labor Council for adopting anti-immigration positions during the economic recession of 1912–14.

In order to regain his health – he suffered from Bright's disease – Zimmerman and his wife moved to Vancouver about two months before his death. He was described by the *Manitoba Free Press* as "a prominent figure in Jewish community affairs," and by the daily *Israelite Press* as one of Winnipeg's "most distinguished residents." His tombstone stated simply that he had "devoted his life to Judaism." He was a representative of the hard-working first generation of eastern European Jewish immigrants who became financially successful and integrated into the larger society.

HENRY TRACHTENBERG

Zimmerman

Jewish Hist. Soc. of Western Canada Arch. (Winnipeg), Newspaper database. Man., Legislative Library (Winnipeg), Biog. scrapbooks, B7: 219; B9: 187; M11: 255. Private arch., Henry Trachtenberg (Winnipeg), Telephone interview with Ruth Gotlieb Zimmerman Portigal of Winnipeg, a great-niece of the subject, 1998. "History of the Jews of Winnipeg," *Reform Advocate* (Chicago), special issue, 1914 (mfm. at Man., Legislative Library). *Israelite Press* (Winnipeg), 14 Sept. 1923. *Manitoba Free Press*, 9, 13, 16, 18 July 1892; 1 Dec. 1899; 5, 9 Nov. 1900; 13 Dec. 1904; 20 Sept. 1911; 9–12 Dec. 1912; 16 June 1914; 13 Sept. 1923. *Winnipeg Telegram*, 1, 8 Dec. 1899; 5 Nov. 1900; 21 May 1903; 28, 31 Oct., 1 Nov. 1904; 2 Dec. 1905; 6 March, 11, 25 May 1908; 8 July 1910; 8, 19–20 Sept. 1911; 8 June 1914. *Winnipeg Tribune*, 9, 13, 16 July 1892; 9 June 1896; 23 April 1897; 5, 8 Dec. 1899; 3, 8 Nov. 1900; 1 Nov., 13 Dec. 1904; 6 March 1908; 13 Sept. 1923. A. A. Chiel, *Jewish experiences in early Manitoba* (Winnipeg, 1955); *The Jews in Manitoba: a social history* (Toronto, 1961). *Directory*, Winnipeg, 1893–1923. Harry Gutkin, *Journey into our heritage: the story of the Jewish people in the Canadian west* (Toronto, 1980). *The Jew in Canada: a complete record of Canadian Jewry from the days of the French régime to the present time,* ed. A. D. Hart (Toronto and Montreal, 1926). *Rosh Pina congregation; dedication volume: 1892–1952* (Winnipeg, [1952?]). H. M. Trachtenberg, "The old clo move: anti-Semitism, politics and the Jews of Winnipeg, 1882–1921" (PHD thesis, York Univ., North York [Toronto], 1984). G. G. Weatherhead, *Congregation Shaarey Zedek; one hundred years: 1889–1989* (Winnipeg, 1990).

APPENDIX

Appendix

SHINGWAUK, GEORGE (**Menissino, Menissinowinnini**; also known as **George Pine**), Ojibwa chief; b. 1838 or 1839 at Garden River (Ont.); d. there 13 Feb. 1920.

George Shingwauk was the youngest son of the noted Upper Great Lakes Ojibwa chief Shingwaukonse (Little Pine) (1773–1854), a veteran of the War of 1812 who in 1836 had helped establish Kitigaun Seebee (Garden River), a thriving Ojibwa community on the north shore of St Marys River east of Sault Ste Marie. Shingwauk's native name, Menissino, means "man of the island"; some Ojibwa speakers claim that it also denotes "great warrior" since a man with this name was viewed as capable of maintaining a relationship with powerful spiritual guardians. He eventually assumed the surname Pine, an English translation of Shingwauk, although he remained known locally as Menissino. A much older individual with this native name had accompanied Shingwaukonse to Montreal in 1849 to deliver a speech to Governor Lord Elgin [Bruce*] regarding native land rights. One wonders if this individual could have been Shingwaukonse's son or son-in-law and George Shingwauk a grandson. Oral traditions at Garden River, however, state that George was indeed Shingwaukonse's son and that he had an especially close friendship with his brother John Askin (Erskine) Shingwauk (1836–1919).

Traditions also claim that John Askin's mother, Ogahbageyhequa, Shingwaukonse's fourth and last wife, was a devout Anglican. Since she was George Shingwauk's mother as well, he may have received some schooling as a boy at the Anglican mission at Garden River [see Frederick Augustus O'Meara*]. In addition to Ojibwa, he mastered French but he never gained fluency in English. After becoming a chief, he had to rely on his better educated sons and nephews to act as interpreters, petition writers, and spokesmen when he needed to communicate with outside agencies.

Since the births of John Askin and George Shingwauk occurred so shortly after their parents' conversion to Anglicanism in 1833, during the deaconate of William McMurray*, the boys had respect for the Church of England ingrained in them early, though George Shingwauk later eschewed any form of religious bigotry. He married a Roman Catholic, Cecile Belleau, and strove to maintain harmony between Protestant Ojibwa and the sizeable Catholic Métis contingent who had entered the Garden River community after being driven from their homes at the Sault by non-native settlers. He would transfer this desire for a spirit of unity to his sons, William George Pine and Charles George Pine. At the same time he supported the educational activities of both the Reverend Edward Francis Wilson*, principal of the native residential school (the Shingwauk Industrial Home), and the Reverend Benjamin Fuller, one of his successors. Frequently invited to visit the Shingwauk home and the school for girls (the Wawanosh Home), George Shingwauk gave speeches that stressed the need for native youth to work hard to attain western knowledge and skills while holding on to cherished values that upheld the innate worth of all living things. He viewed western education not as an alternative to Ojibwa culture but as a catalyst for enriching native experience gained in the customary community milieu.

George Shingwauk was first elected as a chief in 1899, at a salary of $100 per annum. By 1900 he was fulfilling roles as a traditional leader and an elected chief. Since Shingwaukonse's death in 1854, positions of leadership had been held by close relatives. His successor, his son Augustan Shingwauk (Ogista, Little Pine), retained the head chiefship until his death in 1890; another son, Henry Buhkwujjenene (Wild Man), held it until his passing in 1900. In 1896 Jarvis Pine, Augustan's eldest son, had become the first chief elected under the federal Indian Act. During his three years in office, George Kabaosa, a grandson of Shingwaukonse, acted as a political spokesman and George Shingwauk and John Askin Shingwauk began assisting with local affairs. For many years the Garden River Reserve retained these two systems of leadership – the traditional mode and the imposed elective type. The community also had to grapple with three thorny issues: native logging rights on the reserve, Sault Ste Marie's covetous interest in the community's land for municipal expansion eastward, and the illegal removal of high-grade gravel.

George Shingwauk retained his elected office until early in 1902, during which time he received encouragement from Indian agent William L. Nichols, an exceptional man who helped the Ojibwa in their campaign to control natural resources by providing funds out of his own pocket. It is possible that Shingwauk had some money of his own to contribute since both he and his brother John Askin logged and farmed, and owned and mined locations in Duncan Township, north of Garden River. Nichols also aided the band in its negotiations with logging firms interested in taking timber off the reserve, among them the Harris Tie and Timber Company, Burton Brothers, and the Echo Bay Lumber Company. George and John Askin Shingwauk thus embarked on complex contract talks. The Department of Indian Affairs in Ottawa eventually became quite stringent about such independent business dealings by natives.

In the band election of 1902 George Shingwauk was ousted by Buhkwujjenene's brother-in-law, an astute political dynamo named Charles Cadotte, although Shingwauk retained his role as traditional chief. Cadotte and his council wrestled with the resource issues previously dealt with by Shingwauk's council, particularly in respect of logging contracts. In September 1902 Cadotte's administration finalized a contract with Burton Brothers to maintain logging berths set out by traditional native fiat, on terms agreed upon by the community but without Ottawa's knowledge. The success of Garden River in such matters gradually encouraged neighbouring Ojibwa communities to emulate its political strategies. It is possible that such victories put Ottawa on its guard, however, since external agencies were clearly at work in the setting of a band election in 1903, only one year into Cadotte's term.

Cadotte proved a capable leader, but he suffered from unwelcome interventions by the local Catholic priest, Gaston-A. Artus SJ. Artus had earlier proved to be of considerable political assistance on resource matters to Chief Jarvis Pine, a Catholic, but, unlike his clerical predecessors, he branded the Anglican Ojibwa leaders as agents of corruption and so alienated some of Cadotte's Protestant followers. The sudden death of Cadotte's main supporter (Joachim Biron) in the midst of the leadership campaign of 1903 also impeded his cause. Backed by his brother-in-law Michael Belleau, his brother John Askin, and two influential Métis, John Corbiere and Theophile Boissoneau, George Shingwauk won by 40 votes. During the campaign he had received support from Protestants and Catholics, despite the fact that Artus unjustly denounced him as an unprogressive politician. This opposition was a hindrance, but George Shingwauk refused to be disheartened.

There were major challenges for Shingwauk's council to surmount, most notably the limitation of encroachments by modern capitalist society. In 1906 the Algoma Advisory Union (the precursor of the Sault Ste Marie Chamber of Commerce) used the Ojibwa's failure to cultivate large prosperous farms as an excuse to petition Prime Minister Sir Wilfrid Laurier* for the expropriation of the Garden River

Reserve. In response, George Shingwauk led a delegation composed of John Askin Shingwauk, Alex Wabanosa, and William J. Pine to Ottawa to present a petition aimed at thwarting the union's plans. Minor victories ensued. After sending additional petitions to Ottawa, the Garden River band received a ruling in 1910 prohibiting the municipal expansion and one in 1914 exempting the Ojibwa from having to contribute labour or funds for the construction or maintenance of a trunk road through their reserve. Further, they secured acceptance of their condition that, should the road cease to be used for public conveyance, the land allowance would revert to the band. Another issue had been settled in 1913 when the Canadian Pacific Railway awarded the community $5,282, less legal costs, for gravel it had taken. Fortified by this partial success – the payment was low – the band would negotiate a better contract in 1914, when George Shingwauk was in his seventies. In this second agreement, which related to a quarry at the Buhkwujjenenewabick (wild man's stone), a trap-rock bluff in the centre of the reserve, the Ojibwa received guarantees of employment, including insurance benefits, and assurance that the boundaries set by the chief would be respected and that the site, when it ceased to be used for quarrying, would revert to the band. Native values pertaining to resource use, notably group ownership, were also preserved. In 1914 and 1915, during World War I, the band rejected a plan to establish a prison farm on 4,000 acres of its territory.

In 1916 George Kabaosa, who had become the most active and daring of Garden River's politicians, won election against George Shingwauk despite his successes. Indian Affairs immediately, and unfairly, branded Kabaosa a troublesome agitator and nullified the result. The politically palatable George Shingwauk then regained the leadership. No firebrand, he had emerged as a gracious and dignified figurehead who saw himself as a loyal subject of the crown, a member of the king's church, and an advocate of continuity and tradition. He nonetheless promoted progressive change within his community. Surreptitiously he encouraged Kabaosa to continue his trenchant complaints against encroachments on native lands and resources. Within Shingwauk's council, younger members learned new ways of defending native prerogatives as the old style of oratory, replete with metaphor, gave way to succinctly worded petitions punctuated with legal terminology. These became necessary as greater interference from government occurred in the years following the war and they helped ensure Shingwauk's retention of power until his death in 1920.

By 1900 George Shingwauk had become one of Garden River's most effective supporters of native rights, as well as an advocate of religious harmony at a time when interdenominational strife threatened to tear some native communities asunder. On his death, the local Indian agent, Alexander D. McNabb, wrote, "The late chief was a good man, I consider [him] the best man on the Garden River reserve, always on the side of justice. . . . [H]e was not an aggressive chief, I always knew he would be found willing to help in all good for the benefit of the Band as a whole." Though at times poor in material goods, he left a rich heritage. His outlook and values were remembered by Ojibwa leaders throughout the Upper Great Lakes district, and his sons and daughters became respected members of the Garden River community. Charles G. Pine was the rector's warden at St John's Anglican Church for many years, as well as a delegate to the Algoma diocesan synod. William G. Pine, who inherited his father's bent for politics, served several terms as chief.

JANET E. CHUTE

Documentary sources include records at St John's Anglican Church (Garden River Reserve) and the letter-books of the Sault Ste Marie Indian agency in AO, D 46 (mfm.).

J. E. Chute, *The legacy of Shingwaukonse: a century of native leadership* (Toronto, 1998).

GENERAL BIBLIOGRAPHY AND
LIST OF ABBREVIATIONS

List of Abbreviations

AC	Archives Civiles	*GPQ*	*Guide parlementaire québécois*
AM	Archives of Manitoba	GRO	General Register Office
AMLJH	Archive of Manitoba Legal-Judicial History	HBCA	Hudson's Bay Company Archives
ANQ	Archives Nationales du Québec	LAC	Library and Archives Canada
AO	Archives of Ontario	MCQ-DSQ	Musée de la Civilisation (Québec), Dépôt du Séminaire de Québec
AVQ	Archives de la Ville de Québec	MCQ-FSQ	Musée de la Civilisation (Québec), Fonds du Séminaire de Québec
BCA	British Columbia Archives		
BCF	*Biographies canadiennes-françaises*	MUA	McGill University Archives
BCM-G	Bibliothèque Centrale de Montréal, Salle Gagnon	NSARM	Nova Scotia Archives and Records Management
BRH	*Le Bulletin des recherches historiques*	*OH*	*Ontario History*
CCHA	Canadian Catholic Historical Association	PAA	Provincial Archives of Alberta
CEF	*Canadian Expeditionary Force*	PANB	Provincial Archives of New Brunswick
CHA	Canadian Historical Association	PANL	Provincial Archives of Newfoundland and Labrador
CHR	*Canadian Historical Review*		
CIHM	Canadian Institute for Historical Microreproductions	PARO	Public Archives and Records Office (Prince Edward Island)
CPG	*Canadian parliamentary guide*	QUA	Queen's University Archives
DAB	*Dictionary of American biography*	RBMB	Register of baptisms, marriages, and burials
DALFAN	*Dictionnaire des auteurs de langue française en Amérique du Nord*	RBMS	Registre des baptêmes, mariages et sépultures
DBC	*Dictionnaire biographique du Canada*	*RHAF*	*Revue d'histoire de l'Amérique française*
DBECC	*Dictionnaire biographique des évêques catholiques du Canada*	*RPQ*	*Répertoire des parlementaires québécois*
DCB	*Dictionary of Canadian biography*	RSC	Royal Society of Canada
DHB	*Dictionary of Hamilton biography*	TRL	Toronto Reference Library
DNB	*Dictionary of national biography*	UCC	United Church of Canada
DNLB	*Dictionary of Newfoundland and Labrador biography*	UTA	University of Toronto Archives
DOLQ	*Dictionnaire des œuvres littéraires du Québec*	VM-DGDA	Ville de Montréal, Division de la Gestion de Documents et des Archives
DPQ	*Dictionnaire des parlementaires du Québec*		
GA	Glenbow Archives		

General Bibliography

The General Bibliography is based on the manuscript, printed, and computerized sources which are most frequently cited, usually in abbreviated form, in the individual bibliographies of volume XV. It is not intended to provide a comprehensive listing of background materials for the history of Canada in the late 19th and early 20th centuries.

Section A describes the principal archival and manuscript collections and is arranged by country. Section B provides a listing of the Canadian newspapers most frequently cited by contributors to the volume. Section C lists various types of published materials: primary printed sources, including publications of the federal and the various provincial governments; reference works, including dictionaries, bibliographies, indexes, and directories; secondary works of the 20th century, including a number of general histories; and the principal journals and the publications of various societies consulted.

A. ARCHIVAL AND MANUSCRIPT COLLECTIONS

CANADA

ARCHIVES CIVILES. *See* QUÉBEC, MINISTÈRE DE LA JUSTICE

ARCHIVES DE LA VILLE DE QUÉBEC. The public service and archives division has prepared several research tools in the form of publications, typescript works, manuscript lists, and databases. In addition to inventories and published catalogues, two other useful sources of information are *État général des Archives de la ville de Québec* (Québec, 1988), written by Renaud Arcand, and *État général des fonds et collections d'archives privées* (Québec, 1997), prepared by Marie-Josée Courchesne.

Series cited in volume XV:
M: Organismes municipaux
    1: Villes, villages et municipalités annexés
        1: Village de Saint-Sauveur
    2: Commission de l'Exposition provinciale
P: Individus et organismes privés
    51: Compagnie limité Dominion Corset
Q: Archives de la ville de Québec
QA: Archives administratives
    5: Ressources financières
QD: Services de développement
    4: Réseau routier et infrastructure
QP: Archives politiques
    1: Conseil de ville

ARCHIVES DU SÉMINAIRE DE QUÉBEC. *See* MUSÉE DE LA CIVILISATION

ARCHIVES JUDICIAIRES. *See* QUÉBEC, MINISTÈRE DE LA JUSTICE

ARCHIVES NATIONALES DU QUÉBEC. The Pistard (Programme informatisé servant au traitement des archives et à la recherche documentaire) database can be consulted on the website of the Archives Nationales du Québec at *www.anq.gouv.qc/cq/conservation/bd.htm*. This database provides descriptions of the fonds and collections in the nine regional centres of the ANQ; the website also has useful online finding aids. Inventories, catalogues, guides, conversion tables, and finding aids on microfiche are available in all of the regional centres.

Series cited in volume XV:
CENTRE RÉGIONAL DE LA CÔTE-NORD (ANQ-CN), Sept-Îles
C: Pouvoir judiciaire, archives civiles
    CE: État civil
    901: Baie-Comeau–Mingan
        S3: Saint-Pierre (Havre-Saint-Pierre)
        S6: Notre-Dame (Natashquan)
        S9: Saint-Patrice-de-la-Rivière-Pentecôte (Rivière-Pentecôte)
        S10: Saint-François-d'Assise (Longue-Pointe)
P: Fonds et collections privés
    1: Bélanger, René
    19: Société historique de Havre-Saint-Pierre Inc.
    48: Vigneau, Placide
    53: Jomphe, Roland

CENTRE RÉGIONAL DE LA MAURICIE ET DU CENTRE-DU-QUÉBEC (ANQ-MBF), Trois-Rivières
C: Pouvoir judiciaire, archives civiles
  CE: État civil
  401: Trois-Rivières
      S9: Saint-Édouard-de-Gentilly (Bécancour)
      S12: Saint-Barthélemy
      S15: Saint-Antoine-de-Padoue (Louise-ville)
      S21: Sainte-Anne-de-la-Pérade (La Pérade)
      S48: L'Immaculée-Conception (Trois-Rivières)
  402: Arthabaska
      S2: Saint-Christophe-d'Arthabaska (Victoriaville)
      S72: Saint-Norbert (Victoriaville)
      S74: Drummondville Protestant Episcopal Congregation
  403: Drummondville
      S11: Saint-Guillaume
      S15: Saint-Pierre-de-Durham (L'Avenir)
      S22: Durham Wesleyan Methodist Church
  CN: Notaires
  401: Trois-Rivières
      S106: Rivard, T.-T.
  TP: Tribunaux provinciaux
      11: Cour supérieure
      S3: Trois-Rivières
      SS2: Matières civiles en général
      SS20: Raisons sociales

CENTRE RÉGIONAL DE L'ESTRIE (ANQ-E), Sherbrooke
C: Pouvoir judiciaire, archives civiles
  CE: État civil
  501: Sherbrooke
      S86: Stanstead Plain Methodist Church
      S93: Shipton Presbyterian Church
  502: Bedford
      S42: Shefford Anglican Church
      S75: Clarenceville Methodist Church

CENTRE RÉGIONAL DE L'OUTAOUAIS (ANQ-O), Hull
P: Fonds et collections privés
  111: De Celles, Alfred-Duclos
  ZQ: Copies
      127: Collection paroisses de l'Outaouais
      25: St Andrew's Presbyterian Church (Buckingham)
      28: Clarendon Methodist Church

CENTRE RÉGIONAL DE MONTRÉAL (ANQ-M)
C: Pouvoir judiciaire, archives civiles
  CE: État civil
  601: Montréal
      S1: Saint-Jacques, cathédrale de Montréal
      S3: Notre-Dame-de-la-Prairie-de-la-Madeleine (La Prairie)
      S4: La Visitation-de-la-Bienheureuse-Vierge-Marie (Montréal)
      S6: Notre-Dame-de-Grâce (Montréal)
      S7: Sacré-Cœur-de-Jésus (Montréal)
      S10: Sainte-Anne (Varennes)
      S15: Sainte-Brigide (Montréal)
      S18: Saint-Constant
      S19: Sainte-Cunégonde (Montréal)
      S22: Sainte-Famille (Boucherville)
      S29: Saint-Henri (Montréal)
      S33: Saint-Jacques-le-Majeur (Montréal)
      S35: Saint-Jean-Baptiste (Montréal)
      S44: Saint-Laurent
      S46: Saint-Marc-de-Cournoyer (Saint-Marc)
      S48: Saint-Martin (Laval)
      S49: Saint-Mathieu (Belœil)
      S50: Saint-Michel (Vaudreuil)
      S51: Notre-Dame de Montréal
      S60: Saint-Vincent-de-Paul (Montréal)
      S63: Christ Church Anglican Cathedral (Montreal)
      S68: St George's Anglican Church (Montreal)
      S77: St Matthias' Anglican Church (Westmount)
      S85: First Baptist Church (Montreal)
      S95: Zion Congregational Church (Montreal)
      S97: Spanish and Portuguese Synagogue (Montreal)
      S105: Mountain Street Methodist Church (Montreal)
      S109: St James Street Methodist Church (Montreal)
      S115: American Presbyterian Church (Montreal)
      S120: Crescent Presbyterian Church (Montreal)
      S126: St Gabriel's Presbyterian Church (Montreal)
      S130: St Paul's Presbyterian Church (Montreal)
      S132: Messiah Unitarian Church (Montreal)
      S150: Wesley Congregational Church (Montreal)
  602: Saint-Hyacinthe

A. ARCHIVAL AND MANUSCRIPT COLLECTIONS

S3: La Présentation-de-la-Sainte-Vierge (Saint-Hyacinthe)
S14: Saint-Éphrem (Upton)
S16: Saint-Hilaire (Mont-Saint-Hilaire)
S21: Sainte-Marie-de-Monnoir (Marieville)
S25: Sainte-Rosalie

603: Sorel
S6: Immaculée-Conception (Saint-Ours)
S7: Saint-Pierre (Sorel)

604: Saint-Jean
S10: Saint-Jean-l'Évangéliste (Saint-Jean-sur-Richelieu)
S14: Saint-Rémi
S32: St John's Methodist Church (Saint-Jean-sur-Richelieu)

605: Joliette
S12: Saint-Roch-de-l'Achigan
S14: L'Assomption
S19: Saint-Cuthbert
S31: Saint-Jacques-de-l'Achigan (Saint-Jacques)
S33: Saint-Paul-l'Ermite (Le Gardeur)
S36: Saint-Liguori

606: Saint-Jérôme
S7: Saint-André-d'Argenteuil
S9: Saint-Benoît (Mirabel)
S11: Saint-Eustache
S16: Saint-Placide
S22: Sainte-Scholastique (Mirabel)
S24: Saint-Louis (Terrebonne)
S25: Sainte-Thérèse-de-Blainville (Sainte-Thérèse)

607: Beauharnois
S6: Saint-Jean-Chrysostome (Saint-Chrysostome)
S7: Saint-Joachim (Châteauguay)
S20: Saint-Urbain-Premier
S35: Huntingdon St Andrew's Presbyterian Church
S44: Hudson Methodist Church
S72: Valleyfield Presbyterian Church

CN: Notaires
601: Montréal
S480: Lighthall, W. F.

P: Fonds et collections privées
23: Vallée, C.-A.
64: Brodeur, L.-P.
76: Lacoste, famille
82: Société Saint-Jean-Baptiste de Montréal
120: Fédération nationale Saint-Jean-Baptiste
124: Ordre des architectes du Québec
133: Fréchette, L.-H.
207: Berthiaume, Trefflé

565: Germain, Nicole
TP: Tribunaux provinciaux
11: Cour supérieure
S2: Montréal
SS2: Matières civiles en général
SS20: Raisons sociales

CENTRE RÉGIONAL DE QUÉBEC (ANQ-Q), Québec
C: Pouvoir judiciaire, archives civiles
CE: État civil
301: Québec
S1: Notre-Dame de Québec
S4: Saint-Étienne (Beaumont)
S6: La Visitation-de-Notre-Dame (Château-Richer)
S7: Saint-Charles-Borromée (Charlesbourg)
S9: Saint-Charles-des-Grondines (Grondines)
S12: Saint-Pierre (île d'Orléans)
S17: Saint-Augustin-de-Desmaures
S19: Saint-Joseph-de-la-Pointe-Lévy (Lévis)
S22: Saint-Roch (Québec)
S25: Saint-Joseph (Deschambault)
S27: Sainte-Brigitte (Sainte-Brigitte-de-Laval)
S53: Saint-Raymond
S61: Quebec Anglican Cathedral Church
S62: Holy Trinity Cathedral (Quebec)
S66: St Andrew's Presbyterian Church (Quebec)
S67: St John's Presbyterian Church (Quebec)
S96: Saint-Sauveur (Québec)
S97: Saint-Jean-Baptiste (Québec)
S98: St Patrick (Quebec)
S100: Notre-Dame-de-la-Victoire (Lévis)
S103: Hôtel-Dieu du Sacré-Cœur de Jésus (Québec)

302: Montmagny
S2: Notre-Dame-de-l'Assomption (Berthier-sur-Mer)
S17: Saint-Gervais
S20: Sainte-Louise-des-Aulnaies (Sainte-Louise)
S25: Saint-Roch-des-Aulnaies

303: Kamouraska
S30: Notre-Dame-des-Neiges (Trois-Pistoles)

304: Charlevoix
S3: Saint-Étienne (La Malbaie)

306: Beauce
S6: Sainte-Claire
S24: Sainte-Marie

CN: Notaires
301: Québec

S292: Angers, É.-J.
S305: Giroux, E.-L.-J.
S336: Auger, Jacques
S337: Bélanger, P.-E.
S351: Labrèque, Cyprien
S357: Leclerc, Louis
S369: Plamondon, J.-É.
S377: Allaire, Joseph
S381: Sirois, L.-P.
CT: Testaments
301: Québec, testaments olographes et licitations
S1: Dossiers
E: Pouvoir exécutif
6: Culture et communication
9: Agriculture
17: Justice
51: Commission de toponymie du Québec
53: Archives nationales du Québec
104: Commission royale d'enquête sur les asiles
d'aliénés
P: Fonds et collections privés
152: Le Vasseur, Nazaire, et Arthur Évanturel
174: Marchand, F.-G.
198: Parent, S.-N.
265: Fortier, René
293: Caron, Ivanhoë
326: Vézina, Joseph
350: Taschereau, L.-A.
372: Chênevert, Raoul
379: Académie de musique de Québec
406: Langlais, J.-A.
412: Société Saint-Jean-Baptiste de Québec,
1842–1966
433: Nor Mount Realty Company
487: La Vergne, Armand
519: Orchestre symphonique de Québec
541: Staveley, famille
569: Papineau, D.-B.
596: Fortier, De La Broquerie
678: Compagnie F.-X. Drolet
734: Flynn, E. J.
P1000: Petits fonds
D2348: Gouin, Sir Lomer
D2396: Duquet, Cyrille
TP: Tribunaux provinciaux
9: Cour d'appel
S1: Québec
SS5: Appels en général
11: Cour supérieure
S1: Québec
SS2: Matières civiles en général
SS10: Index des causes
SS20: Raisons sociales
12: Cour des sessions de la paix
S1: Québec
ZQ: Copies
6: Registres paroissiaux du Québec

S315: Notre-Dame-de-Betsiamites
137: Gravel, famille

CENTRE RÉGIONAL DU BAS-SAINT-LAURENT ET
DE LA GASPÉSIE–ÎLES-DE-LA-MADELEINE (ANQ-
BSLGIM), Rimouski
C: Pouvoir judiciaire, archives civiles
CE: État civil
102: Gaspé
S19: Saint-Michel-de-Percé
104: Kamouraska
S1: Notre-Dame-de-Liesse (Rivière-
Ouelle)
S12: Sainte-Anne (La Pocatière)
S15: Saint-Denis (Kamouraska)
ZQ: Copies
1: Collection registres d'état civil
S321: Sainte-Madeleine (Havre-aux-
Maisons)
P: Fonds et collections privés
11: Hubert, Paul

CENTRE RÉGIONAL DU SAGUENAY–LAC-SAINT-JEAN
(ANQ-SLSJ), Chicoutimi
C: Pouvoir judiciaire, archives civiles
CE: État civil
201: Chicoutimi
S2: Saint-François-Xavier (Chicoutimi)
202: Roberval
S5: Saint-Louis-de-Métabetchouan
(Chambord)
CN: Notaires
201: Chicoutimi
S4: Cloutier, T.-Z.
S5: Gagné, Jean
S9: Belleau, Raymond
S10: Saint-Pierre, G.-A.
P: Fonds et collections privés
2: Société historique du Saguenay
18: Larouche, J.-C.
22: Naud, A.-G.
161: Guay, J.-D.
165: Gosselin, F.-X.
666: Compagnie Price Brothers

ARCHIVES OF MANITOBA, Winnipeg.
Series cited in volume XV:
ATG: Attorney General
25: Winnipeg Surrogate Court
AVF: Archives Vertical Files
A.-H. de Trémaudan
C: Oral history tapes
C 2374: Gordon Campbell interview
C 2376: J. T. Thorsen interview
C 2377–78: Lynne Flett and E. Reeser
interviews
G: Government records

G 393: Surrogate Court, Eastern Judicial District, Winnipeg estate file

G 549: Surrogate Court, Eastern Judicial District, grants of probate

G 1418: Manitoba Hydro General Counsel and Corporate Secretary

G 1662: Executive Council, premier's office files, Thomas Greenway administration

G 8017–18: Public Works – Minister's Office

MG 3: Red River disturbance, North-West rebellion, and related papers

   B: Individuals *re* Red River disturbance, North-West rebellion, and related papers

     18: Nault, André

     19: Lépine, A.-D.

   D: Louis Riel

MG 10: Associations and institutions

   B: Public service and education

     11: Winnipeg General Hospital

   D: Sports

     17: Amateur Athletic Union of Canada, Manitoba section

     26: Shamrock Football Club

MG 11: Industry and commerce

   A: Transportation

     20: Bayne, G. A.

     34: Canadian Airways Limited

MG 12: Lieutenant governors

   E: Schultz, J. C.

   J: Burrows, T. A.

MG 13: Premiers

   G: Roblin, R. P.

MG 14: Public life

   B: Political and judicial figures

     36: Manning, R. A. C.

     41: Sifton, Sir Clifford

     44: Winkler, H. W.

   C: Individuals

     52: Ruttan, H. N.

     74: Harris, J. W.

     85: Nanton, A. M.

NR 0157: Department of Natural Resources – Land surveyor's fieldbooks

P: Private sector records

   192: Political Equality League

   474–77, 485–88: Aikins, Sir J. A. M.

   483: Manitoba Cartage and Warehousing Company Limited

   2131: Middlechurch Home of Winnipeg

   2187–92: Armstrong, J. A. and family

   3361: Paterson, Edith

   3586–607: Council of Women of Winnipeg

   4895, file 2: Lépine, Émile

   5609, 5612–13, 5616–17: Walker, J. S.

HUDSON'S BAY COMPANY ARCHIVES. All records of the Hudson's Bay Company prior to 1870, with the exception of maps, are available on microfilm; microfilming of records for the period 1871–1904, and of the map collection, is in progress. A copy of the microfilm series is available in LAC, MG 20, and a description of its contents is provided in the Public Archives of Canada's *Main entry catalogue and general inventory* (Ottawa, 1987), published on microfiche. The microfilm series is also available through an interlibrary loan program administered by the HBCA; copies of the series list have been deposited in a number of repositories across Canada. The HBCA website (*www.gov.mb.ca/chc/archives/hbca*) contains a brief catalogue of documents available on microfilm as well as online finding aids, in particular, a detailed finding aid for the HBC's trading post records: *www.gov.mb.ca.chc/archives/hbca/resource/post_rec/index.html/*.

Section A: London office records

   A.1/: London minute books

Section B: Post records

   B.290/: Hazelton

   B.324/: Pas Post

Section D: Governor's papers and commissioner's office documents

   D.13–D.18/: Commissioner's outward correspondence

   D.19–D.20/: Commissioner's inward correspondence

   D.21–D.22/: Registers, synopses and indexes of commissioner's inward and outward correspondence

   D.24/: Secretary's files

   D.25–D.26/: Reports and miscellaneous papers

   D.38/: Staff records

   D.44/: Canadian sub-committee records, minutes, draft minutes and working papers

Section E: Private records

   E.6/2: Land register book

   E.218: McLean, W. J.

ARCHIVE OF MANITOBA LEGAL-JUDICIAL HISTORY. In 1996 the Archive of Manitoba Legal History and the Law Society of Manitoba permanently transferred to the Provincial Archives of Manitoba their collections of documents on the understanding that these would form the section Archive of Manitoba Legal-Judicial History within the provincial archives. Materials cited in volume XV form part of series A, which contains files of the members of the Law Society of Manitoba, numbered P1201 to P1354, and series B (Archive of Manitoba Legal History), which is arranged in boxes

P1355 to P1513. Microfilm copies (M) are available where the original documents are still in the possession of the Law Society of Manitoba.

ARCHIVES OF ONTARIO, Toronto. Current collection information and searchable databases are available on the Internet at *www.archives.gov.on.ca*.

Materials cited in volume XV include:
C: Special collections
    C 88: McLaughlin family fonds
D: Diffusion material
    D 46: Sault Ste Marie fonds
    D 217: Township of Kincardine diffusion material
F: Private papers
    F 2: Edward Blake family fonds
    F 5: James Whitney fonds
    F 6: William H. Hearst fonds
    F 8: Howard Ferguson fonds
    F 68: Edmund Bristol fonds
    F 102: J. Castell Hopkins fonds
    F 137: Madawaska Improvement Company fonds
    F 149: William M. Gray fonds
    F 179: Caleb R. Mallory fonds
    F 229: T. Eaton Co. fonds
    F 277: Genealogies collection
    MU 1127: McLean–MacLean
    F 332: William Perkins Bull fonds
    F 373: Tweedsmuir histories collection
    F 719: Laura Elizabeth McCully family fonds
    F 749: Peter C. Larkin scrapbook
    F 775: Miscellaneous collection
    F 834: John Linton fonds
    F 885: Canadian Woman's Christian Temperance Union fonds
    F 975: Edward F. Wilson fonds
    F 977: Ontario Genealogical Society's cemetery recordings collection
    F 978: Church records collection
    F 1009: George T. Denison fonds
    F 1023: Duncan Fraser Macdonald fonds
    F 1027: A. E. Irving fonds
    F 1075: M. O. Hammond fonds
    F 1076: William Kirby fonds
    F 1083: John Willison fonds
    F 1090: Fort York fonds
    F 1104: M. Bourchier Sanford fonds
    F 1138: Niagara Historical Society fonds
    F 1139: Ontario Historical Society fonds
    F 1140: Ontario Society of Artists fonds
    F 1180-11: Women's Canadian Historical Society of Toronto general files
    F 1193: John W. Fisher fonds
    F 1195: Ontario Library Association fonds
    F 1374: L. Bruce Robertson fonds

F 1941: United Counties of Stormont, Dundas and Glengarry fonds
RG: Record Groups – Government records
RG 1: Office of the Commissioner of Crown Lands
    57: Assignments of land grants and sales registered with the commissioner of crown lands
        ser.1: Registers of assignments of land grants and sales
RG 2: Department of Education
    ser.29: Correspondence files of the minister of the Department of Education
    ser.43: Department of Education central registry files
    ser.128: Toronto Normal School student records
    ser.146: Public libraries branch files
    ser.226: Applications for admission to the Ontario Library School
    ser.227: Examination marks of Ontario Library School students
    ser.228: Public Libraries Act working papers
    ser.232: Public libraries financial reports
    ser.301: Registers of first and second class teachers' certificates
    ser.368: Ottawa Normal School student records
    ser.373: Librarianship and library service certificates register, Department of Education
RG 3: Office of the Premier
    ser.4: Premier E. C. Drury correspondence
    ser.5: Premier E. C. Drury office records
RG 4: Office of the Attorney General
    ser.32: Central registry criminal and civil files
RG 8: Department of the Provincial Secretary
    ser.1: Correspondence of the Department of the Provincial Secretary
    ser.5: Correspondence of the provincial secretary
    ser.54: Correspondence of the secretary of the Ontario Board of Parole
RG 10: Ministry of Health
    ser.20: Psychiatric hospitals branch records
RG 22: Court records
    Surrogate courts
    Belleville (Hastings)
        ser.340: Estate files
    Brampton (Peel)
        ser.359: Estate files
    Brockville (Leeds and Grenville)

ser.179: Estate files
Chatham (Kent)
ser.397: Estate files
Cobourg (Northumberland and Durham)
ser.191: Estate files
Guelph (Wellington)
ser.318: Estate files
Hamilton (Wentworth)
ser.205: Estate files
Kingston (Frontenac)
ser.159: Estate files
Kitchener (Waterloo)
ser.214: Estate files
Lindsay (Victoria)
ser.357: Estate files
London (Middlesex)
ser.321: Estate files
Oshawa (Ontario)
ser.264: Estate files
Ottawa (Carleton)
ser.354: Estate files
St Catharines (Lincoln)
ser.235: Estate files
St Thomas (Elgin)
ser.322: Estate files
Sarnia (Lambton)
ser.273: Estate files
Stratford (Perth)
ser.267: Estate files
Toronto (York)
ser.305: Estate files
Windsor (Essex)
ser.311: Estate files
Supreme Court of Ontario
ser.392: Criminal assize clerk, criminal
indictment files
ser.5800: Supreme Court central office,
action files
ser.5822: Supreme Court at Toronto, bankruptcy case files
ser.5871: York County Court of General
Sessions of the Peace, indictment case files
RG 24: Lieutenant Governor's Office
ser.10: Records of Lieutenant Governor
John Morison Gibson
ser.12: Records of Lieutenant Governor
Lionel Herbert Clarke
RG 35: Hydro-Electric Power Commission of
Ontario
RG 55: Companies Division, Consumer and Commercial Relations
ser.1: Company charter-books
ser.17: Expired partnership and sole
proprietorship registrations, pre-
1975
div.33: Middlesex County

div.57: Waterloo County
div.60: City of Toronto
RG 61: Land records
ser.3: Bruce County Land Registry
Office
div.1: Instruments and deeds
RG 63: Office of the Inspector of Asylums, Prisons
and Public Charities
RG 80: Office of the Registrar General
ser.2: Registrations of births and stillbirths
ser.3: Delayed registrations of births
and stillbirths
ser.5: Registrations of marriages
ser.8: Registrations of deaths
ser.24: Original index books to marriage
registrations
ser.27-2: County marriage registers

BIBLIOTHÈQUE CENTRALE DE MONTRÉAL, Salle
Gagnon, Montréal. The Salle Gagnon holds micro-
films acquired by the City of Montreal from the
Drouin Institute of Genealogy. These contain information about baptisms, marriages, and burials of
Catholics and non-Catholics from the Montreal area,
as well as some from Ontario and the United States,
between 1900 and 1940; they are listed in volume
XV with the abbreviation RBMS. Also available is an
index of baptisms, marriages and burials of Catholics
and non-Catholics which covers a good part of the
20th century and mainly the judicial districts of Montreal and Quebec.

BRITISH COLUMBIA ARCHIVES, Victoria. Government records are searchable for the most part on the
BCA website at *www.bcarchives.gov.bc.ca*. Educational records are detailed in *The school record: a
guide to government archives relating to public education in British Columbia, 1852–1946*, comp. P. A.
Dunae (Victoria, [1992]).
Collections cited in volume XV include:
GR: Government records
0216: Cariboo government agency records,
1860–1938
0429: Attorney general, correspondence,
1872–1937
0441: Premiers' records, 1883–1933
0584: Cariboo court records, 1862–1910
0766: Department of Lands and Works, pre-
emption records for west coast land,
1861–86
1052: Victoria Supreme Court, central will registry, probated wills, 1861–1939
1197: Premier John Herbert Turner records,
1893–97
1304: Victoria Supreme Court, probate/estate
files, 1859–1941

1323: Attorney general, correspondence, 1902–37

1372: Colonial correspondence, 1857–72. An artificial series created from the letters inward to departments of the colonial governments of British Columbia and Vancouver Island from both individuals and other government departments. The letters are filed under the names of the senders.

1415: Vancouver Supreme Court, probate/estate files, 1893–1941

1422: New Westminster Supreme Court, probate/estate files, 1881–1943

1438: Registrar of companies files

1440: Lands branch, correspondence files with regard to crown lands, 1872–1918

1676: Government agent, Richfield, 1892–94

1952: Ashcroft Supreme Court, probate/estate files, 1907–90

2025: Matthew Baillie Begbie bench books, 1859–73

2880: Mental health services, patient case files, 1872–1942

2951: Vital Statistics Agency, death registrations, 1872–1984

2962: Vital Statistics Agency, marriage registrations, 1872–1929

3049: Lytton government agency account books, 1858–1900

MS: Manuscripts

0016: Victoria Sealing Company

0054: Crease, Henry Pering Pellew, legal papers, 1853–95

0055: Crease family, private and official correspondence, 1753–1965

0056: Crease family, photocopies of correspondence and miscellaneous papers, 1836–1924

0215: Young Women's Christian Association, 1910–51

0254: Johns, Mrs T. H., "History of Metropolitan Church, Victoria, B.C." (typescript, n.d.)

0303: Tate family, 1852–1933

0471: Premier John Herbert Turner, political correspondence, 1890–1914

0676: LeBourdais, Louis, papers, 1917–45

0699: Bowser, William John, personal and official papers, 1907–49

0700: Laing, F. W., "Colonial farm settlers on the mainland of British Columbia, 1858–1871, with a historical sketch" (typescript, 1939)

1077: Newcombe family, 1870–1955

1130: Turner, John Herbert, correspondence and papers, 1889–92, 1900–1

1320: Nichol, Walter Cameron, scrapbook

1961: Provincial Council of Women records, 1894–1970

2018: E. T. Dodge and Company, New Westminster, freight merchants

2227: Woman's Christian Temperance Union of British Columbia, minute-book, 1880–86

2367: Mackay, Isabel Ecclestone, 1905–33

2561: South Fork Hydraulic and Mining Company records, 1889–1912

2700: Nichol, Quita Josephine [March Moore], papers, 1920–46

2818: Local Council of Women of Victoria records, 1907–81

2879: Crease family collection, 1810–1960

Old Classification

Class A: Early exploration: fur trade
A/E/G41/T56: Todd family
A/E/R54: Robert James Roberts fonds

Class E: Private papers
E/C/B81.3: Brown, James, notes of conversation with Robert Hartley re Cariboo, 1930 (typescript)
E/C/B172.2: Baker, Mrs August, reminiscences, 1929 (typescript)
E/C/Se5: "Old manuscripts," 1879–90, 1896–1904
E/D/L58: Lew, David C., fonds
E/D/M362: Agreement between J. Martin, J. M. Kellie, and Thomas Kidd, 19 Feb. 1900
E/D/T56: Todd, A. E., papers
E/E/C61: Cline, Sperry, "Cataline" (typescript, 1959)
E/E/H85: Hoy, David, reminiscences, 1929 (typescript)
E/E/M311: Manson, William, reminiscences, 1929 (typescript)
E/E/M963: Murray, Alexander, reminiscences (typescript)

Class S: Literature and journalism
S/F/L95: Lowery, R. T., fonds

Other Classifications

Cartographic Records: Plans produced by Samuel Maclure
CM-B308: "Sketch plan for a bungalow for F. S. Hussey, esq. n.d."
CM-B944, sh.1–sh.4: "House for Thos. R. Cusack, esq., cor. Cook and Collinson Sts."
CM-B1641, sh.1–sh.2: "Cary Castle, Belcher St. Victoria, BC" (in collaboration with F. M. Rattenbury)

A. ARCHIVAL AND MANUSCRIPT COLLECTIONS

Vertical Files
>VF36, frames 0941–43: Autobiographical letter by William Henry Curran
>VF42, frames 1197–99: Obituary of Mrs Alice M. Earley
>VF87, frames 0389–578: Maclure family
>VF90, frames 0006–84: Martin, Joseph
>VF130, frames 0641–65: Shakespeare, Noah
>VF155, frames 3013–29: Wade, F. C.

Visual Records Unit
>PDP153–55, PDP161–66, PDP1844, PDP3218, PDP3629, PDP3630, PDP3773: paintings by Samuel Maclure in the British Columbia Archives art collection
>Tarasoff photo collection on Doukhobor history with an annotated user guide

GLENBOW ARCHIVES, Calgary. Descriptions of the archives' holdings are included on the Glenbow website at *www.glenbow.org/lasearch/searmenu.htm*. The online Main Catalogue features links to more detailed finding aids, and, increasingly, scanned documents which can be viewed online.

Materials cited in volume XV:
M: Manuscript collections
>M 131, M 132: Robert George Brett fonds
>M 289: A. E. Cross family fonds
>M 311, M 313, M 3933, M 6017: Richard Burton Deane fonds
>M 320: Edgar Dewdney fonds
>M 353, M 354, M 355, M 356, M 2623, M 3826, M 3943: Bob Edwards fonds
>M 495: Frederick W. G. Haultain fonds
>M 517: John D. Higinbotham fonds
>M 559: Ella Inderwick fonds
>M 651, M 652: George and Elizabeth Lane fonds
>M 722: Scrolls of judicial appointments of David Lynch Scott
>M 927, M 928: Wesley F. Orr fonds
>M 1462: Dixon Brothers fonds
>M 1469, M 1470, M 1471: Great West Saddlery fonds
>M 1749: United Farmers of Alberta fonds
>M 1925: Calgary Bar Association fonds
>M 1931: Law Society of the North West Territories fonds
>M 2286: North-West rebellion fonds
>M 2431, M 2533, M 3748, M 3749, M 3750, M 7899, M 8532: Alberta Railway and Irrigation Company fonds
>M 3983: Alberta Law Society oral history project fonds
>M 4421: Robert Nathaniel Wilson fonds
>M 4843, files 13–14: James Lougheed family fonds

>M 6242: Emilio Picariello fonds
>M 6552: William Edward Cochrane fonds
>M 6840: J. McKinley Cameron fonds
>M 8688: New Walrond Ranche Company Ltd. fonds

Microfilm collections
>Alberta Railway and Irrigation Company
>United Farmers of Alberta
NA: Photographs

LIBRARY AND ARCHIVES CANADA, Ottawa (formerly National Archives of Canada). The collections can be searched on the Internet at *www.collections canada.ca*. ArchiviaNet is the online database that provides access to archival holdings from governmental and private sources.

The LAC's published general guides to the services it offers and to its collections are no longer being updated and researchers are encouraged to use ArchiviaNet. The holdings of the LAC, along with those of over 800 archival repositories in Canada, are now described online at Archives Canada: Canadian Archival Information Network (*www.archives canada.ca*).

Collections cited in the preparation of volume XV include:
Manuscript Division
MG 9: Provincial, local and territorial records
>D: Ontario
>>7: Church records
MG 17: Ecclesiastical archives
>B: Church of England (Anglican Church)
>>2: Church Missionary Society (mfm.)
MG 19: Fur trade and Indians
>F: Indians
>>26: Newhouse, Seth (Da-yo-de-ka-ne) (1842–1921)
MG 23: Late eighteenth-century papers
>D: New Brunswick
>>1: Chipman, Ward (senior and junior)
MG 24: Nineteenth-century pre-confederation papers
>B: North American political figures and events
>>40: Brown, George
>D: Industry, commerce, and finance
>>16: Buchanan, Isaac, and family
MG 25: Genealogy
>G: Genealogy
>>175: Meredith family fonds
MG 26: Papers of the prime ministers
>A: Macdonald, Sir John Alexander
>D: Thompson, Sir John Sparrow David
>E: Bowell, Sir Mackenzie
>F: Tupper, Sir Charles
>G: Laurier, Sir Wilfrid
>H: Borden, Sir Robert Laird
>I: Meighen, Arthur

A. ARCHIVAL AND MANUSCRIPT COLLECTIONS

RG   76: Immigration branch
　　C: Records of entry
　　　　1(a): Quebec
RG   85: Northern Affairs Program
RG   95: Corporations branch
RG 110: Bureau of Competition Policy
RG 117: Office of the Custodian of Enemy Property
RG 125: Supreme Court of Canada
RG 139: Canadian Hydrographic Service
RG 150: Ministry of the Overseas Military Forces of
　　　　Canada
　　　　　　Accession 1992–93/166: Canadian Expe-
　　　　　　ditionary Force personnel files
Documentary Art and Photography Division
　　　　　　120-080260-8: Edmond-Joseph Massicotte
　　　　　　collection
　　　　　　03391: photograph of Edmond-Joseph
　　　　　　Massicotte
　　　　　　PA-27800, 43037, 12295, C-131090:
　　　　　　photographs of Otto Julius Klotz
Literary Manuscript Collection
　　　　　　LMS-0009: Marie-Claire Daveluy
Music Division
　　　　Music Archives
　　　　MUS 10: Emma Albani
　　　　MUS 11: Charles A. E. Harriss
Post offices and postmasters (ArchiviaNet online
database)
R639-0-5 (formerly Accession 1936-270): Topley
Studio fonds

McGill University Archives, Montreal. An
inventory of the various collections of documents
held at McGill University has been published as
Guide to archival resources at McGill University,
comp. Marcel Caya *et al.* (3v., Montreal, 1985). It is
also available on the Internet along with an update
which describes the private fonds acquired between
1985 and 1995: *www.archives.mcgill.ca/resources/
res_guides.htm.*
　　Series cited in volume XV:
Private archives
　　MG 1049: Lochhead, William.
　　MG 1062: Nicholls, R. V. V.
　　MG 3021: Harriss, C. A. E.
　　MG 3022: Ruttan, R. F.
　　MG 3083: Murray, J. C.
　　MG 3099: Livingston, G. E.
Archival records of McGill University
　　RG 2: Office of the Principal and Vice-Chancellor
　　RG 30: Faculty of education
　　RG 38: Faculty of medicine
　　RG 39: Faculty of music
　　RG 43: Macdonald College
　　RG 46: Athletics and physical education
　　RG 49: Public Relations Office
　　RG 64: School of Nursing

RG 96: Montreal General Hospital

Musée de la Civilisation, Québec. In 1995 the
Archives du Séminaire de Québec, one of the components of the Musée de l'Amérique Française, was
attached to the Musée de la Civilisation. In accordance
with the agreement, the archives of the seminary were
regrouped into two large sections: Dépôt du Séminaire
de Québec, for private archives, and Fonds du Séminaire de Québec, for institutional archives. A general
inventory prepared by Marie-Josée Courchesne and
Chantal Michaud has been published as *Plus de trois
siècles d'histoire à découvrir; les archives du séminaire de Québec* (Québec, 1998); it is also available on
the website of the Musée de la Civilisation: *www.mcq.
org/objets/fonds_archives/.*
　　Series cited in volume XV:
Dépôt du séminaire de Québec
　　P7: Roy, P.-E.
　　P10: Roy, Camille
Fonds du séminaire de Québec
　　Séminaire
　　SME: Le séminaire de Québec
　　　　1: La fondation du séminaire de Québec et ses
　　　　　　œuvres
　　　　2: L'administration au séminaire de Québec
　　　　9: L'enseignement supérieur à l'université Laval
　　　　10: Les cérémonies officielles
　　　　13: La collection de manuscrits

National Archives of Canada. *See* **Library
and Archives Canada**

**Nova Scotia Archives and Records Manage-
ment**, Halifax. Collections can be searched on
BosaNova, NSARM's online database at *www.gov.
ns.ca/nsarm.* The database includes both archival
records of the Government of Nova Scotia and private sector archival records of provincial scope or
significance. BosaNova is not yet a complete inventory of NSARM holdings. It is updated regularly.
Also useful is the *Nova Scotia genealogical sources,
county guide series* being published by NSARM (8v.
to date, Halifax, 1988–), which when completed
will contain listings of both published and archival
materials of genealogical interest in the archives for
each of the province's 18 counties and for the city of
Halifax.
　　Materials used in the preparation of volume XV:
Manuscript Groups
MG   1: Personal and family papers
　　　　　　150c: Samuel M. Brookfield miscellaneous
　　　　　　ledger and indexed notebook
　　　　　　1450: W. A. Murray family
　　　　　　1731: James Crosskill Mackintosh fonds
MG   2: Papers of politicians/Records of political
　　　　　　parties

63–223: F. W. Borden fonds
422–541, 784–90(B): W. S. Fielding fonds
707–17: James C. Tory fonds
MG 20: Records of corporate bodies (societies, organizations, etc.)
160: Imperial Order Daughters of the Empire fonds
183, 567: Halifax Ladies' Musical Club fonds
204: Local Council of Women of Halifax fonds, scrapbook
321: Canadian Red Cross Society, Nova Scotia Division fonds
357–60: Nova Scotia Women's Christian Temperance Union fonds
535: Local Council of Women of Halifax fonds, minute-books
MG 100: Miscellaneous manuscripts collection
Government Records
RG 14: Provincial Education Association
RG 21: Department of Mines
RG 32: Vital statistics
M: Marriage licences
WB: Registers of baptisms, marriages, and burials
RG 39: Supreme Court
CO: Colchester County
M: Miscellaneous
HX: Halifax County
M: Miscellaneous
Miscellaneous
Christina Simmons collection, Helen M. West interviews
Pictou (town) Board of School Commissioners, microfilm reference collection, mfm.13278
1990-215/014: Halifax Industries Limited fonds

PROVINCIAL ARCHIVES OF MANITOBA. *See* ARCHIVES OF MANITOBA

PROVINCIAL ARCHIVES OF NEW BRUNSWICK, Fredericton. Information on the manuscript holdings is provided in *A guide to the manuscript collections in the Provincial Archives of New Brunswick*, comp. A. C. Rigby (Fredericton, 1977), although a new classification system has been adopted since its publication and the holdings have significantly increased over the last three decades. Some government records, private records, and cemetery information are indexed or digitized and are available on the Internet at *archives.gnb.ca/Archives*.
The following materials were cited in the preparation of volume XV:
MC: Manuscript collections
80: Family histories database
218: Wood family papers
290: Bathurst Roman Catholic Church:

parish registers, [1846–84]
1156: Graves New Brunswick political biography collection
1246: George Burchill and Sons papers
2495: Cap Pelé Roman Catholic Church: index, [1813–1916]
RS: Record Series
RS6: Executive Council: minutes and orders-in-council
RS8: Executive Council: New Brunswick series
RS68: Northumberland County Probate Court records
RS71: Saint John County Probate Court records
RS74: Westmorland County Probate Court records
RS117: Teachers College records
RS140: Centracare Saint John Inc. records
RS141: New Brunswick vital statistics
RS260: Workplace health, safety, and compensation commission records
RS655: Teachers' petitions and licences
RS657: Grammar, parish, and private school returns

PROVINCIAL ARCHIVES OF NEWFOUNDLAND AND LABRADOR, St John's. Information on the government holdings of the PANL is provided in *A guide to the government records of Newfoundland*, comp. Margaret Chang ([St John's], 1983), and its supplement, *Inventory of the government records collection of the Provincial Archives of Newfoundland and Labrador*, comp. Shelley Smith ([St John's], 1988). A finding aid for the parish records collection is located at *www.gov.nf.ca/panl/par_index.html*. In June 2005 the Provincial Archives moved to a new facility (The Rooms), along with the Provincial Museum of Newfoundland and Labrador and the Art Gallery of Newfoundland and Labrador. The Provincial Archives will still maintain its original website located at *www.gov.nl.ca/panl* but information about the Provincial Archives may also be accessed via The Rooms website: *www.therooms.ca*.
Series cited in volume XV:
GN: Government records of Newfoundland
GN 1: Governor's Office
3/A: Local and miscellaneous correspondence
GN 2: Colonial secretary
5: Special subject files
39/A: Miscellaneous census materials, 1675–1884
GN 5: Court records
2: Supreme Court
GN 8: Office of the Prime Minister
2: Sir Richard Squires papers

GN 9: Executive Council
1: Minute-books
GN 30: Registrar general/Registry of Vital Statistics

MG: Manuscript Groups
MG 17: Reid Newfoundland Company papers
MG 73: Newfoundland Board of Trade correspondence
MG 299: Edward Michael Jackman
MG 592: Great War Veterans' Association, St John's
MG 632: Patriotic Association of Newfoundland
Parish records collection
Methodist/United Church
Roman Catholic Church

PROVINCIAL ARCHIVES OF NOVA SCOTIA. *See* NOVA SCOTIA ARCHIVES AND RECORDS MANAGEMENT

PUBLIC ARCHIVES AND RECORDS OFFICE, Charlottetown. The PARO holds government records and private papers and records deemed to be of lasting historical value. Its website is at *www.edu.pe.ca/paro.*
Collections cited in volume XV include:
Acc. 2320: Charlottetown Camera Club collection
Acc. 2323: George Leard files
Acc. 2594/A:
items 31–42: Annual reports of the Prince Edward Island Hospital, 1892–1910
Acc. 2947: Donald Alexander MacKinnon fonds
Acc. 3043: Matheson fonds
Acc. 3295: Trinity United Church (formerly First Methodist Church), Charlottetown
Acc. 3466: Prince Edward Island Heritage Foundation collection
series 73.100: Prowse family file
Acc. 4327: Prowse Brothers Ltd., day-book
Montague United Church (Montague), Register of baptisms
Parish of Saint-Augustin de Rustico, 1890 census
Prince Edward Island Genealogical Society collection (formerly the Prince Edward Island Heritage Foundation's genealogical division files; transferred to the PARO in 1992)
Family files
St Mary's Roman Catholic Church (Indian River), Register of baptisms

RG 6: Courts
1: Supreme Court fonds
series 3: Trial dockets
subseries 1: Trial docket books
series 19: Legal profession records
subseries 2: Bar admittances
RG 19: Vital statistics
series 3: marriage records
subseries 1: licence cash-books

RG 20: City of Charlottetown records
1–16: city council minutes
RG 25: Premiers
series 25: John Howatt Bell papers

QUÉBEC, MINISTÈRE DE LA JUSTICE, Québec. The Archives Civiles and the Archives Judiciaires of Quebec constitute two separate repositories.

ARCHIVES CIVILES. Following the reform of the Quebec Civil Code, which went into effect in January 1994, the Archives Civiles from the end of the 19th century to the present were transferred to the Direction de l'État Civil, a central repository in Quebec City under the authority of the Ministère de la Justice. This repository holds civil registers, that is to say, certificates of baptism, marriage, and death. Materials are generally moved to the ANQ when the 100-year rule comes into effect.

ARCHIVES JUDICIAIRES. These archives, which are the responsibility of the courts but are in the keeping of the Ministère de la Justice, consist of the records of the various courts as well as documents deposited with them under various laws, such as notarial registers. Generally speaking, documents still current, those of the last five years, remain at the courthouses; semi-active material from the preceding 25 years is located in one of the 12 pre-archival centres organized by the Ministère de la Justice; documents more than 30 years old and those of historical value are placed in the regional centres of the ANQ.
A list of the judicial districts can be found in *Relevé alphabétique des toponymes populaires du Québec*, Commission de toponymie du Québec, compil. (Québec, 1989).

QUEEN'S UNIVERSITY ARCHIVES, Kingston, Ont. Information on the manuscript collections is provided on the Queen's University Archives website, *archives.queensu.ca.*
Materials from the following collections were consulted in the preparation of volume XV:
Bliss Carman fonds
Thomas Alexander Crerar fonds
Merrill Denison fonds
Department of Alumni Affairs fonds
Department of Biology fonds
Joseph Flavelle fonds
Alex MacLennan Gordon fonds
Daniel Miner Gordon fonds
Wilhelmina Gordon fonds
Charles Mair fonds
George William McLaughlin fonds
McLaughlin Carriage Works fonds
Lorne and Edith Pierce collection
Bliss Carman

A. ARCHIVAL AND MANUSCRIPT COLLECTIONS

Isabel Eccleston MacPherson MacKay
Thomas O'Hagan
Marjorie Lowry Christie Pickthall
Alice Rothwell collection
Queen's historical collection
Registrar's Office fonds
Office of the University Secretariat fonds
James Williamson fonds

TORONTO REFERENCE LIBRARY [*tplwpac.tpl. toronto.on.ca*]. Information on the library's manuscript holdings appears in *Guide to the manuscript collection in the Toronto Public Libraries* (Toronto, 1954).

Materials from various collections were consulted for volume XV:

Biographical files
Biographical scrapbooks
Black history file
Civic Guild of Toronto papers
Denison family papers
Special Collections Centre

UNITED CHURCH OF CANADA ARCHIVES [*www. united-church.ca/archives/home.shtm*]. The archives of the United Church includes 19th- and 20th-century archival records of various Canadian Methodist, Presbyterian, Congregational, and Evangelical United Brethren denominations which came together to form the United Church of Canada in 1925. The Central Archives of the United Church is housed at Victoria University, Toronto, along with the university's archives and the records of most conferences, presbyteries, and congregations in Ontario. Records of other Canadian conferences, presbyteries, and congregations are found in the seven regional conference archives of the United Church archives network.

UNITED CHURCH OF CANADA ARCHIVES/VICTORIA UNIVERSITY ARCHIVES, Toronto. Information on the collections is provided in *A record of service: a guide to holdings of the Central Archives of the United Church of Canada*, comp. Ruth Dyck Wilson with P. D. James (Toronto, 1992). An index to local church records is available at *archeion-aao.fis.utoronto.ca/ asearch.html*.

The following United Church fonds were used in the preparation of volume XV:

Fonds 5: Wesleyan Methodist Church in Canada
Fonds 14: Methodist Church (Canada), Missionary Society
Fonds 15: Methodist Church (Canada), Woman's Missionary Society
Fonds 53: British Methodist Episcopal Church of Canada
Fonds 122: Presbyterian Church in Canada, Board of Foreign Missions

Fonds 127: Presbyterian Church in Canada, Women's Missionary Society Western Division
Fonds 513: United Church of Canada Board of Publication collection

Biographical files
Conference files
Local church records
Fonds 1470: Zion United Church (Brantford, Ont.) fonds
Fonds 1777: Bloor Street United Church (Toronto) fonds

Personal papers
Fonds 3170: Francis Huston Wallace
Fonds 3260: Hugh Matheson
Fonds 3270: John MacLean
Fonds 3431: Young family

Photographs

UNIVERSITY OF TORONTO ARCHIVES. The Accessions Database, a searchable database containing accession records of all university and private records held in the University of Toronto Archives, can be found at *www.library.utoronto.ca/utarms*.

Materials used in volume XV:

A: Corporate record accessions
A1967-0007: University of Toronto, office of the president
A1970-0024: University of Toronto, board of governors
A1972-0018: University of Toronto, faculty of forestry, miscellaneous records
A1972-0025: University of Toronto, faculty of forestry, records of the deans
A1973-0026: University of Toronto, department of graduate records. A collection of biographical files on students, graduates, faculty, and staff members.
A1974-0018: Upper Canada College
A1976-0006: University of Toronto, faculty of forestry, text of speeches (including offprints) given by Bernhard Eduard Fernow and Gordon Gunn Cosens
A1976-0025: University of Toronto, department of political economy
A1979-0015: University of Toronto, faculty of forestry, lecture notes of Dr Bernhard Eduard Fernow

B: Private records accessions
B1965-0014: Langton (John) family
B1975-0013: Dale, William

Graduate theses
T1979-0077: University of Toronto, masters theses

VILLE DE MONTRÉAL, DIVISION DE LA GESTION DE DOCUMENTS ET DES ARCHIVES. All of the archival fonds that have been generated by the administration of the City of Montreal are described in *Guide des archives, ville de Montréal* published in Montreal in 1994. A second edition, revised and updated, was published 1997, and a third in 2002; the latter is accessible on the Internet site of the Archives de Montréal, *www2.ville.montreal.qc.ca/archives/archives.htm*. Four hundred fonds have been provided with descriptions that the researcher can follow up in the Réseau de Diffusion des Archives du Québec. Some of them have also been given detailed published descriptions, in the form of file lists.

Series cited in volume XV:
BM2: Collection de la Bibliothèque de Montréal
  S10: Manuscrits catalogués par ordre chronologique
   P: Fonds d'archives privés
    12: Ville de Cartierville
    23: Cité de Saint-Henri
    39: Commission royale d'enquête sur l'administration des affaires de la cité de Montréal
VM: Fonds d'archives institutionnelles
   1: Conseil de ville de Montréal
   6: Service du greffe
  47: Commission de l'aqueduc
  50: Commission des incendies et de l'éclairage

GREAT BRITAIN

GENERAL REGISTER OFFICE, Southport, England. The GRO forms part of the Office for National Statistics, an independent government agency. The GRO also has a presence in central London at the Family Records Centre, which is jointly run by the National Archives. GRO records available at the Family Records Centre include: indexes of births, marriages, and deaths in England and Wales since 1837 up to 18 months ago; indexes of legal adoptions in England and Wales since 1927; and indexes of births, marriages, and deaths of some British citizens abroad since the late 18th century. These indexes are not available on the Internet, but the website *www.gro.gov.uk* provides instructions for obtaining copies of certificates.

NATIONAL ARCHIVES, London, England. The National Archives was formed in April 2003 by joining the Public Record Office and the Historical Manuscripts Commission. The catalogue (formerly PROCAT) is searchable at *www.catalogue.national archives.gov.uk*.

Series consulted in the preparation of volume XV:
Admiralty Office
Royal Marines records
Board of Trade
 Companies Registration Office
  BT 31: Files of dissolved companies
Colonial Office [See *Records of the Colonial Office, Dominions Office, Commonwealth Relations Office and Commonwealth Office*, ed. Anne Thurston (London, 1995), a revised and expanded version of R. B. Pugh, *The records of the Colonial and Dominions offices* (1964).]
 British Columbia
   CO 60: Original correspondence
 Newfoundland
   CO 194: Original correspondence
Home Office
 Census returns
  HO 107: 1841–51
War Office
 Returns
  WO 76: Records of officers' services
 Miscellanea
  WO 211: Private collections: Lieutenant-General Henry George Hart

UNITED STATES

CHURCH OF JESUS CHRIST OF LATTER-DAY SAINTS, GENEALOGICAL SOCIETY, Salt Lake City, Utah. The Family History Library was founded in 1894 to gather genealogical records and assist church members with their family history and genealogical research. The International Genealogical Index (IGI) is a computer file that lists vital information for several hundred million deceased persons from around the world. The IGI, and other of the society's family history databases, can be searched on the Internet at *www.familysearch.org*.

B. NEWSPAPERS

The following Canadian newspapers were particularly useful in the preparation of volume XV. Further details, including additional title variants and locations of copies, are provided in numerous reference sources: for all areas of the country, the National Library of Canada's *Union list of Canadian newspapers on microfiche* (microfiche ed., [Ottawa], 1993) and "Canadian newspapers on microform held by the National Library of Canada," a finding aid available on the LAC's website at *www.collectionscanada.ca/8/*

18/index-e.html; and for the following provinces and territories: *Alberta newspapers, 1880–1982; an historical directory,* comp. G. M. Strathern (Edmonton, 1988); *Union catalogue of British Columbia newspapers,* comp. Hana Komorous and Kenneth Field (microfiche ed., Vancouver, 1987); Manitoba Library Assoc., *Manitoba newspaper checklist with library holdings, 1859–1986* ([Winnipeg], 1986); *New Brunswick newspaper directory, 1783–1988,* comp. H. [C.] Craig (Fredericton, 1989); *Historical directory of Newfoundland and Labrador newspapers, 1807–1987,* comp. Suzanne Ellison (St John's, 1988); *Nova Scotia newspapers: a directory and union list, 1752–1988,* comp. Lynn Murphy *et al.* (2v., Halifax, 1990); *Inventory of Ontario newspapers, 1793–1986,* comp. J. B. Gilchrist (Toronto, 1987) and *Dict. of Toronto printers* (Hulse) [*see* section C]; PARO, "Checklist and historical directory of Prince Edward Island newspapers, 1787–1986," comp. Heather Boylan (photocopied typescript, Charlottetown, 1987); J. Hamelin *et al., La presse québécoise* [*see* section C]; *Historical directory of Saskatchewan newspapers, 1878–1983,* comp. Christine MacDonald (Regina and Saskatoon, 1984); and Yukon Arch., "Checklist of Yukon newspapers, 1898–1905," comp. Amanda Wearmouth (photocopied typescript, [Whitehorse], 1987).

Calgary Herald. 2 July 1885 to the present, under various titles; this one in effect from 13 Feb. 1939.
Christian Guardian. Toronto. 21 Nov. 1829–3 June 1925.
Daily Colonist. Victoria. 31 July 1860–31 Aug. 1980, under various titles.
Daily Mail and Empire. Toronto. 7 Feb. 1895–21 Nov. 1936. Title varies: *Mail and Empire* (from September 1929). See also *Globe.*
Daily News. St John's. 15 Feb. 1894–4 June 1984.
Le Devoir. Montréal. 10 Jan. 1910 to the present.
L'Événement. Québec. 13 May 1867–3 March 1967.
Evening Telegram. St John's. 3 April 1879 to the present.
Evening Telegram. Toronto. 18 April 1876–30 Oct. 1971, under various titles; this one in effect to 19 Feb. 1949.
Gazette. Montreal. 25 Aug. 1785 to the present. Title varies: *Montreal Gazette* (to 1 June 1867).
Globe. Toronto. 5 March 1844–21 Nov. 1936. On 23 Nov. 1936 it merged with the *Mail and Empire* [see *Daily Mail and Empire*] to form the *Globe and Mail,* which continues to the present.

Halifax Herald. 2 Jan. 1892–31 Dec. 1948. Continues the *Morning Herald* (14 Jan. 1875–31 Dec. 1891).
Hamilton Spectator. Hamilton, Ont. 15 July 1846 to the present, under various titles.
Manitoba Free Press. Winnipeg. 6 July 1874 to the present, under various titles, including *Manitoba Morning Free Press* (5 June 1893–26 Jan. 1915) and *Winnipeg Free Press* (2 Dec. 1931 to date).
La Minerve. Montréal. 9 Nov. 1826–27 May 1899.
Montreal Daily Star. 16 Jan. 1869–25 Sept. 1979, under various titles; this one in effect 1877–18 Oct. 1957.
Montreal Gazette. See *Gazette.*
Morning Chronicle. Halifax. 24 Jan. 1844–21 Jan. 1927.
Morning Herald. Halifax. See *Halifax Herald.*
Ottawa Citizen. 22 Feb. 1851 to the present, under various titles.
Ottawa Evening Journal. 10 Dec. 1885–27 Aug. 1980. Title varies: *Ottawa Journal* (from July 1949).
La Patrie. Montréal. 24 Feb. 1879–9 Jan. 1978.
Patriot. Charlottetown. 6 July 1865 to the present, under various titles, including *Patriot* (to 6 April 1881) and *Daily Patriot* (7 April 1881–14 Nov. 1910); issues are available only from 4 July 1867.
La Presse. Montréal. 20 Oct. 1884 to the present.
Saint John Globe. 26 Sept. 1866–15 Jan. 1927.
Le Soleil. Québec. 28 Dec. 1896 to the present.
Toronto Daily Star. 3 Nov. 1892 to the present. Title varies: *Evening Star* (to 24 Jan. 1900); *Toronto Daily Star* (25 Jan. 1900–5 Nov. 1971); subsequently *Toronto Star.*
Vancouver Daily Province. 26 March 1898 to the present, under various titles; this one in effect 20 Jan. 1900–16 Feb. 1952.
Victoria Daily Times. 9 June 1884–30 Aug. 1980.
Winnipeg Free Press. See *Manitoba Free Press.*
Winnipeg Telegram. 3 Feb. 1894–16 Oct. 1920, under various titles; this one in effect from 22 Aug. 1907. Absorbed by the *Winnipeg Tribune* 18 Oct. 1920.
Winnipeg Tribune. 28 Jan. 1890–27 Aug. 1980, under various titles, including *Winnipeg Daily Tribune* (28 Jan. 1890–27 June 1903) and *Winnipeg Tribune* (29 June 1903–6 Jan. 1915 and 30 May 1930–27 Aug. 1980).
World. Toronto. 19 Aug. 1880–9 April 1921.

C. PUBLISHED SOURCES AND THESES

Acadiensis: Journal of the History of the Atlantic Region/Revue de l'histoire de la région atlantique. Fredericton. 1 (1971–72)– .

Alberta: index to registrations of births, marriages and deaths .... Published by the Edmonton branch of the Alberta Genealogical Society. 1 vol.

[*1870 to 1905*] to date. Edmonton, 1995– .

American national biography. Edited by John A[rthur] Garraty *et al.* 24 vols. [to 1995]. New York, 1999. One supplement to date [to 2001]. Edited by Paul Betz *et al.* New York, 2002.

Beaver. Winnipeg. 1 (1920–21)– . Subtitle varies.

Bibliography of Newfoundland. Compiled by Agnes C[ecilia] O'Dea. Edited by Anne Alexander. 2 vols. Toronto, 1986.

A bibliography of the prairie provinces to 1953, with biographical index. Compiled by Bruce Braden Peel. 2nd edition. Toronto and Buffalo, N.Y., 1973. Revised and enlarged edition. Edited by [Ernest] Boyce Ingles *et al.* Toronto, 2003.

Biographies canadiennes-françaises. Ottawa, 1920; Montréal, 1922–84/85. Various editors. Published from 1972/73 with a parallel title, *Who's who in Quebec.*

BRITISH COLUMBIA. Information concerning official publications is available in M. C. Holmes, *Publications of the government of British Columbia, 1871–1947* . . . (Victoria, [1950]).

LEGISLATIVE ASSEMBLY

Journals. Victoria, 1872– .

Sessional papers. Victoria, 1872– . The sessional papers for 1872–75 are included in the *Journals.*

Statutes of the province of British Columbia. Victoria, 1872– .

British Columbia Executive Council appointments, 1871–1986. Compiled by Judith Antonik Bennett and Frederike Verspoor. [Victoria], 1989.

Le Bulletin des recherches historiques. Published usually in Lévis, Qué. 1 (1895)–70 (1968).

Les Cahiers des Dix. Montréal. No.1 (1936)– . Published at Québec from no.36 (1971)– .

CANADA. For details concerning the publications of the government of Canada, *see* O. B. Bishop, *Canadian official publications* (Oxford, 1981), and Marion Villiers Higgins, *Canadian government publications: a manual for librarians* (Chicago, 1935). Information on royal commissions is provided in *Federal royal commissions in Canada, 1867–1966: a checklist,* comp. G. F. Henderson (Toronto, 1967).

Canada Gazette. Ottawa, 1 July 1867– . Bilingual from 1939: *Canada Gazette/La Gazette du Canada.*

HOUSE OF COMMONS/CHAMBRE DES COMMUNES

Debates/Débats. Ottawa, 1867/68– ; official publication begins in 1875. Unofficial reports of the pre-1871 debates are available in scrapbooks at the Library of Parliament ("Scrapbook debates"); these have been microfilmed by the Canadian Library Association ("Parliamentary debates").

Journals/Journaux. Ottawa, 1867/68– .

PARLIAMENT/PARLEMENT

Sessional papers/Documents de la session. Ottawa, 1867/68–1925.

SENATE/SÉNAT

Debates/Débats. Ottawa, 1867/68– ; official publication in English begins in 1871 and in French in 1896. For unofficial reports of the pre-1871 debates, *see* "Parliamentary debates," *supra.*

Statutes/Statuts. Ottawa, 1867/68– . Title varies: *Acts/Actes,* 1873–1951.

Canada, an encyclopædia of the country: the Canadian dominion considered in its historic relations, its natural resources, its material progress, and its national development. Edited by J[ohn] Castell Hopkins. 6 vols. and index. Toronto, 1898–1900.

Le Canada ecclésiastique, almanach annuaire du clergé canadien. Montréal, 1887– . Annual publication with variations in the subtitle. Since 1967 it has appeared with a bilingual title: *Le Canada ecclésiastique/Catholic directory of Canada.*

The Canadian album: men of Canada; or, success by example. . . . Edited by W[illia]m Cochrane and J[ohn] Castell Hopkins. 5 vols. Brantford, Ont., and Toronto, 1891–96. Vols.1–4 were prepared by Cochrane, vol.5 by Hopkins.

The Canadian annual review of public affairs. Toronto. 35 vols. 1901–37/38. Edited by J[ohn] Castell Hopkins, 1901–22. The volume for 1901 was originally published in 1902 as *Morang's annual register of Canadian affairs* and reissued around 1904 as *The Canadian annual review of public affairs, 1901.*

CANADIAN CATHOLIC HISTORICAL ASSOCIATION/ SOCIÉTÉ CANADIENNE D'HISTOIRE DE L'ÉGLISE CATHOLIQUE, Ottawa. Publishes simultaneously a *Report* in English and a *Rapport* in French, the contents of which are entirely different. 1 (1933–34)– . Titles vary. English report: *Study sessions,* 33 (1966)–50 (1983); *Canadian Catholic historical studies,* 51 (1984)–56 (1989); *Historical studies,* 57 (1990)– . French report: *Sessions d'étude,* 33 (1966)–56 (1989); *Études d'histoire religieuse,* 57 (1990)– .

The Canadian directory of parliament, 1867–1967. Edited by J[ames] K[eith] Johnson. Ottawa, 1968.

The Canadian encyclopedia. Edited by James H[arley] Marsh *et al.* 2nd edition. 4 vols. Edmonton, 1988. Also available online at *www.the canadianencyclopedia.com.*

CANADIAN HISTORICAL ASSOCIATION/SOCIÉTÉ HISTORIQUE DU CANADA, Ottawa. *Report of the annual meeting.* . . . 1922– . Title varies: *Annual report,* 1922–24; *Report of the annual meeting . . . /Rapport de l'assemblée annuelle . . . ,* 1951–65; *Historical papers . . . /Communications historiques . . . ,* 1966–89; *Journal/Revue,* new ser., 1 (1990)– .

C. PUBLISHED SOURCES AND THESES

Canadian Historical Review. Toronto. 1 (1920)– .

CANADIAN INSTITUTE FOR HISTORICAL MICRORE-PRODUCTIONS/INSTITUT CANADIEN DE MICRORE-PRODUCTIONS HISTORIQUES, Ottawa. *Canada: the printed record: a bibliographic register with indexes to the microfiche series/Catalogue d'imprimés canadiens: répertoire bibliographique avec index de la collection de microfiches.* Microfiche edition. Ottawa, 1981– . The microfiche collection of Canadiana before 1900, created between 1978 and 2000, contains more than 90,000 titles. In 1997 CIHM began digitizing this collection. Over 8,500 titles are available online at *www.canadiana.org/cihm.*

Canadian Magazine. Toronto. 1 (March–October 1893)–91 (January–April 1939). Title varies: *Canadian Magazine of Politics, Science, Art and Literature* to 63 (May 1924–January 1925); *Canadian,* 88 (July–December 1937)–91.

The Canadian men and women of the time: a handbook of Canadian biography. Edited by Henry James Morgan. Toronto, 1898. 2nd edition. 1912.

The Canadian parliamentary guide. Quebec, 1862–63; Montreal, 1864–74; Ottawa, 1875–1988; Toronto, 1989– . Editor varies. Title varies: *The Canadian parliamentary companion* to 1897. Bilingual from 1982/83: *Canadian parliamentary guide/Guide parlementaire canadien.*

The Canadian who's who. London and Toronto; Toronto. 1910– . No additional/new volume was published until that for 1936/37.

A cyclopædia of Canadian biography. . . . Edited by Geo[rge] Maclean Rose and Hector [Willoughby] Charlesworth. 3 vols. Toronto, 1886–1919. Vols.1–2 were edited by Rose, vol.3 by Charlesworth.

DESJARDINS, JOSEPH. *Guide parlementaire historique de la province de Québec, 1792 à 1902.* Québec, 1902.

Dictionary of American biography. Edited by Allen Johnson *et al.* 20 vols., index, and 2 supps. [to 1940]. New York, 1928–58; reprinted, 22 vols. in 11 and index, [1946?]–58. 10 additional supps. to date [to 1980]. Edited by Edward T[opping] James *et al.* 1973– . *Comprehensive index; complete through supplement ten.* 1996.

Dictionary of Hamilton biography. Edited by Thomas Melville Bailey *et al.* 4 vols. to date [to 1970]. Hamilton, Ont., 1981– .

Dictionary of national biography. Edited by Leslie Stephen and Sidney Lee. 63 vols., 3 supps., and index and epitome [to 1900]. London, 1885–1903; reissued without index, 22 vols., 1908–9. 10 additional supps. to date [to 1990]. Edited by Sidney Lee *et al.* London; Oxford, 1912– . *Missing persons* [additional biographies from the beginning to 1985]. Edited by C[hristine] S[tephanie] Nicholls. Oxford and New York, 1993. New edition. *Oxford*

dictionary of national biography. Edited by H[enry] C[olin] G[ray] Matthew *et al.* 60 vols. and index. Oxford and Toronto, 2004. This is available to subscribers online at *www.oup.com/oxforddnb/info/.*

Dictionary of Newfoundland and Labrador biography. Edited by Robert H. Cuff *et al.* St John's, 1990.

A dictionary of Toronto printers, publishers, booksellers, and the allied trades, 1798–1900. Compiled by Elizabeth Hulse. Toronto, 1982.

Dictionnaire des œuvres littéraires du Québec. Sous la direction de Maurice Lemire *et al.* 7 vols. Montréal, 1978–2003. 2ᵉ édition des vols.1–2, 1980–87.

Dictionnaire des parlementaires du Québec, 1792–1992. Gaston Deschênes *et al.,* compilateurs. Sainte-Foy, Qué., 1993. See also *Répertoire des parlementaires québécois, infra.*

DIRECTORIES. Issued initially as single works, Canadian directories often became regular, usually annual, publications during the 19th century. Because titles within series vary greatly, and editors or compilers frequently change, the directories used in the preparation of volume XV have been cited under the general entry *Directory* and identified by region. Individual titles and publication information are detailed in *Checklist of Canadian directories, 1790–1950,* comp. D. E. Ryder (Ottawa, 1979), and *Canadian directories, 1790–1987: a bibliography and place-name index,* comp. M. E. Bond (3v., Ottawa, 1989).

The dominion annual register and review. . . . [1878–86]. Edited by Henry J[ames] Morgan *et al.* 8 vols. Montreal, etc., 1879–87.

Elections in New Brunswick, 1784–1984/Les élections au Nouveau-Brunswick, 1784–1984. Fredericton, 1984.

Electoral history of British Columbia, 1871–1986. [Victoria, 1988].

An encyclopaedia of Canadian biography: containing brief sketches and steel engravings of Canada's prominent men. 3 vols. Montreal and Toronto, 1904–7.

Encyclopedia of music in Canada. Edited by Helmut Kallmann *et al.* 2nd edition. Toronto, 1992. Also available online at *www.collectionscanada.ca/4/17/.*

Encyclopedia of Newfoundland and Labrador. Edited by Joseph R[oberts] Smallwood *et al.* 5 vols. St John's, 1981–94.

Guide parlementaire québécois. Québec, 1989.

Guide to Canadian ministries since confederation, July 1, 1867–February 1, 1982. [Ottawa], 1982. *Supplement, March 3, 1980–January 15, 1993.* Compiled by Henri Chassé. [Ottawa, 1993.] Also available online at *www.pco-bcp.gc.ca.*

HAMEL, RÉGINALD, *et al. Dictionnaire des auteurs*

de langue française en Amérique du Nord. Montréal, 1989.

HAMELIN, JEAN, *et al. La presse québécoise, des origines à nos jours.* 10 vols. [1764–1975]. Québec, 1973–90. Vols.1–2 [1764–1879] were prepared by André Beaulieu and Jean Hamelin. *Index cumulatifs (tomes I à VII) (1764–1944),* 1987.

KAREL, DAVID. *Dictionnaire des artistes de langue française en Amérique du Nord; peintres, sculpteurs, dessinateurs, graveurs, photographes et orfèvres.* [Québec], 1992.

LEBLANC, JEAN. *Dictionnaire biographique des évêques catholiques du Canada: les diocèses catholiques canadiens des Églises latine et orientales et leurs évêques; repères chronologiques et biographiques, 1658–2002.* Montréal, 2002.

The Legislative Assembly of Nova Scotia, 1758–1983: a biographical directory. Edited by Shirley B[urnham] Elliott. [Halifax], 1984.

Legislators and legislatures of Ontario: a reference guide. Compiled by Debra Forman. 4 vols. [1792–1991]. [Toronto, 1984–92].

LE JEUNE, L[OUIS-MARIE]. *Dictionnaire général de biographie, histoire, littérature, agriculture, commerce, industrie et des arts, sciences, mœurs, coutumes, institutions politiques et religieuses du Canada.* 2 vols. Ottawa, [1931].

LINTEAU, PAUL-ANDRÉ. *Histoire de Montréal depuis la Confédération.* Montréal, 1992.

MANITOBA

    LEGISLATIVE ASSEMBLY/ASSEMBLÉE LÉGISLATIVE

    Journals/Journaux. Winnipeg, 1871– . Published in separate French and English editions until 1889; in English only, 1890–1985; bilingual from 1986. The journals for 1871–1914 include appendices; title varies: "Appendix"/ "Appendice," 1871–85; "Sessional papers"/ Documents de la session," 1886–89; "Sessional papers," 1890–1914.

    Statutes/Statuts. Winnipeg, 1871– . Published in separate English and French editions until 1888/ 89; in English only, 1890–1983, but with some French content after 1980. English title varies: *Acts* from 1890. Bilingual from 1984/85 as *Acts/ Lois.*

MIDDLETON, JESSE EDGAR. *The municipality of Toronto: a history.* 3 vols. Toronto and New York, 1923.

Minding the house: a biographical guide to Prince Edward Island MLAs, 1873–1993. Edited by Blair Weeks. Charlottetown, 2002.

The national union catalog, pre-1956 imprints. . . . 754 vols. London and Chicago, 1968–81.

NEW BRUNSWICK. For a bibliography of New Brunswick government publications, *see* O. B. Bishop, *Publications of the governments of Nova Scotia,*

Prince Edward Island, New Brunswick, 1758–1952 (Ottawa, 1957).

Acts. Saint John or Fredericton, 1786– .

    LEGISLATIVE ASSEMBLY

    Synoptic report of the proceedings. Fredericton, 1893– . Formerly issued in Saint John etc., 1874–92, by the House of Assembly whose name continues to appear on the title-page in 1893–94.

NEWFOUNDLAND. Information on publications of the colonial and provincial governments of Newfoundland appears in the *Biblio. of Nfld* (O'Dea and Alexander), *supra.*

Acts. St John's, 1833– . Title varies: *Statutes* since 1949.

    HOUSE OF ASSEMBLY

    Journal. St John's, 1833–1933. Issued by the unicameral General Assembly, 1843–46. No assemblies took place in 1842 or 1847.

    GENERAL ASSEMBLY

    Proceedings. St John's, 1909–59, except for 1934–48 when no meetings were held. Published under various titles: 1909–24: *Proceedings of the House of Assembly and Legislative Council*; 1925–59: *Proceedings of the House of Assembly.*

"Newspaper Hansard." *See* Ont., Legislature, *Debates, infra.*

The newspaper reference book of Canada; embracing facts and data regarding Canada and biographical sketches of representative Canadian men for use by newspapers. Toronto, 1903.

NICHOLSON, G[ERALD] W[ILLIAM] L[INGEN]. *Canadian Expeditionary Force, 1914–1919: official history of the Canadian army in the First World War.* Corrected 2nd printing. Ottawa, 1964.

NOVA SCOTIA. A bibliography of Nova Scotia government publications is available in O. B. Bishop, *Publications of the governments of Nova Scotia, Prince Edward Island, New Brunswick, 1758–1952* (Ottawa, 1957).

    HOUSE OF ASSEMBLY

    Debates and proceedings. Halifax, 1855–1916. Title varies.

    Journal and proceedings. Halifax, 1761 to the present. This title in effect from 1789.

    LEGISLATIVE COUNCIL

    Debates and proceedings. Halifax, 1858–1922.

    Journal and proceedings. Halifax, 1830–1928.

The statutes of Nova Scotia. Halifax, 1798 to the present. Title varies; this one in effect from 1851/52.

ONTARIO. Further information concerning Ontario government publications is available in the following: O. B. Bishop, *Publications of the government of Ontario, 1867–1900* (Toronto, 1976); H. I. MacTaggart, *Publications of the government of Ontario,*

1901–1955 (Toronto, 1964); *Royal commissions and commissions of inquiry for the provinces of Upper Canada, Canada and Ontario, 1792 to 1991: a checklist of reports*, comp. Dawna Petsche-Wark and Catherine Johnson (Toronto, 1992); and *Select committees of the assemblies of the provinces of Upper Canada, Canada and Ontario, 1792 to 1991: a checklist of reports*, comp. Richard Sage and Aileen Weir (Toronto, 1992).

CHIEF ELECTION OFFICER

A history of the electoral districts, legislatures and ministries of the province of Ontario, 1867–1968. Compiled by Roderick Lewis. Centennial edition. Toronto, [1969]. Originally published as *A statistical history of all the electoral districts of the province of Ontario since 1867*, comp. Roderick Lewis (Toronto, [1960]).

LEGISLATURE

Debates. Toronto, 1867/68– ; official publication begins in 1944. The debates for 1867–1943 were reconstructed from unofficial newspaper reports and made available on microfilm by the AO in 1964 under the title "Newspaper Hansard."

Journals. Toronto, 1867/68–1900.

Sessional papers. Toronto, 1868/69–1948.

Ontario Gazette. Toronto, 7 March 1868– .

Statutes of the province of Ontario. Toronto, 1867/68– .

Ontario History. Toronto. 1 (1899)– ; vols.1–49 (1957) reprinted Millwood, N.Y., 1975. Title varies: Ontario Historical Society, *Papers and Records* to 1946.

Political appointments, parliaments, and the judicial bench in the Dominion of Canada, 1867 to 1895. Edited by N[arcisse]-Omer Coté. Ottawa, 1896. *Supplement . . . 1896 to 1903*. 1903.

PRINCE EDWARD ISLAND. Further information concerning Prince Edward Island government publications is available in O. B. Bishop, *Publications of the governments of Nova Scotia, Prince Edward Island, New Brunswick, 1758–1952* (Ottawa, 1957).

The acts of the General Assembly of Prince Edward Island. Charlottetown, 1790– ; not printed, 1798–1805.

HOUSE OF ASSEMBLY

Debates and proceedings. Charlottetown, 1860–93. Title varies: *The parliamentary reporter; or, debates and proceedings* to 1886.

Journal. Charlottetown, 1788–1893, except 1798–1805 when none were printed. Title varies.

LEGISLATIVE ASSEMBLY

Journal. Charlottetown, 1894– . Title varies.

QUEBEC. For further information on Quebec government publications, see *Répertoire des publications gouvernementales du Québec de 1867 à 1964*, André Beaulieu *et al.*, compil. (Québec, 1968), and Yvon Thériault, *Les publications parlementaires d'hier et d'aujourd'hui* ([2ᵉ éd.], Québec, 1982), also issued in English as *The parliamentary publications, past and present* (1983).

ASSEMBLÉE LÉGISLATIVE/LEGISLATIVE ASSEMBLY

Débats. 1867/68–1967 (continued by the *Débats* of the Assemblée Nationale, 1968–). A semi-official series of debates for the period June 1879–February 1893 was published as *Débats de la législature provinciale de la province de Québec*, G.-A. Desjardins *et al.*, édit. (15v., Québec, 1879–95). Titles and editors vary for the official publication. The *Débats de l'Assemblée législative* for 1867/68–78 and 1893–1962 are being reconstructed from unofficial reports (37v. parus [1867/68–78 and 1893–1927], Marcel Hamelin *et al.*, édit., Québec, 1974–). The reconstruction for the years 1908–32 can be consulted at the following website: *www.assnat.qc.ca.*

Quebec Official Gazette/Gazette officielle de Québec. Bilingual 16 Jan. 1869–1977; issued in French only from 1978.

Statuts de la province de Québec/Statutes of the province of Quebec. 1868– . Title varies. Issued in separate French and English editions until 1941 and from 1978 to 1988; bilingual, 1942–77; French only from 1989.

Répertoire des parlementaires québécois, 1867–1978. Sous la direction d'André Lavoie. Québec, 1980. See also *DPQ, supra.*

A report on Alberta elections, 1905–1982. [Edmonton, 1983].

Les résultats électoraux depuis 1867. Québec, 1990.

Revue d'histoire de l'Amérique française. Montréal. 1 (1947–48)– .

ROY, PIERRE-GEORGES. *Les juges de la province de Québec*. Québec, 1933.

ROYAL SOCIETY OF CANADA/SOCIÉTÉ ROYALE DU CANADA, Ottawa. *Proceedings and Transactions/Mémoires et comptes rendus*. 1st ser., 1 (1882/83)–12 (1894); 2nd ser., 1 (1895)–12 (1906); 3rd ser., 1 (1907)–56 (1962); 4th ser., 1 (1963)–22 (1985); 5th ser., 1 (1986). French title varies: *Délibérations et mémoires* from 4th ser., 10 (1972). Continued as separately issued *Proceedings/Délibérations*, 5th ser., 2 (1987)–4 (1988) and *Transactions/Mémoires*, 6th ser., 1 (1990)–11 (2000). The *Proceedings/Délibérations* and *Transactions/Mémoires* have been published only online since 2001 at *www.rsc.ca.*

RUMILLY, ROBERT. *Histoire de la province de Québec*. 41 vols. Montréal et Paris, 1940–69. 2ᵉ édition des vols.1–9. s.d. 3ᵉ édition des vols.1–6. s.d. Réimpression des vols.1–15 de la 1ʳᵉ édition, Montréal, 1971–80.

——. *Histoire de Montréal*. 5 vols. Montréal, 1970–74.

Saskatchewan executive and legislative directory, 1905–1970. Regina and Saskatoon, 1971. *Supplement, 1964–1977*. Regina and Saskatoon, 1978. An updated version is available online (*www.saskarchives.com/web/services-gov-directory.html*).

Saturday Night. Toronto. 3 Dec. 1887– . Title varies: *Toronto Saturday Night* to 15 July 1911; *Canadian Saturday Night*, August 1962–June/July 1963.

Science and technology in Canadian history: a bibliography of primary sources to 1914. Compiled by R. Alan Richardson and Bertrum H. MacDonald. Microfiche edition. Thornhill, Ont., 1987.

A standard dictionary of Canadian biography: the Canadian who was who. Edited by Charles G[eorge] D[ouglas] Roberts and Arthur L[eonard] Tunnell. 2 vols. Toronto, 1934–38.

UNIVERSITÉ LAVAL, Québec. *Annuaire de l'université Laval*. From the academic year 1856/57 to the present. Title varies: *Annuaire général* from 1932/33; *L'Université Laval* from no.117 (1975–79).

Vital statistics from New Brunswick newspapers.... Compiled by Daniel Fred Johnson. 102 vols. to date [1784–1896]. Saint John, N.B., 1982– . Vols.1–5 [1784–1834] were issued by the New Brunswick Genealogical Society as *New Brunswick vital statistics from newspapers*, comp. D. F. Johnson *et al.* (Fredericton, 1982–84).

WALKINGTON, DOUGLAS. *Ministers of the Presbyterian Church in Canada, 1875–1925*. N.p., 1987.

——. *Methodist ministers in Canada, 1903–1925*. N.p., n.d.

WALLACE, W[ILLIAM] STEWART. *The Macmillan dictionary of Canadian biography*. Edited by W[illiam] A[ngus] McKay. 4th edition. Toronto, 1978.

When was that? A chronological dictionary of important events in Newfoundland down to and including the year 1922; together with an appendix, "St. John's over a century ago," by the late J. W. Withers. Compiled by H[arris] M[unden] Mosdell. St John's, 1923; reprinted 1974.

Who's who and why.... Edited by J. F. Kennedy *et al.* Vancouver, 1912–14; Toronto, 1915/16–1921. Covers Canada and Newfoundland. Subtitle and editor vary.

Who's who in Canada.... Edited by B[arnet] M. Greene *et al.* Toronto, 1922– . Subtitle, publisher, and editor vary. Continues *Who's who and why*.

CONTRIBUTORS

Contributors

ANDREAE, CHRISTOPHER. President, Historica Research Ltd, London, Ontario.
Frederic Thomas Nicholls. John Joseph Wright.

ANDREW, SHEILA. Professor of history, St Thomas University, Fredericton, New Brunswick.
Placide Gaudet. David-Vital Landry.

ARMSTRONG-REYNOLDS, MARILYN. President, Kingsville-Gosfield Heritage Society, Kingsville, Ontario.
William Wilson Hilborn [in collaboration with M. H. Mallott].

ARSENAULT, GEORGES. Animateur de radio à la retraite, Radio-Canada, Charlottetown, Île-du-Prince-Édouard.
Pierre-Paul Arsenault. Joseph Gallant.

AUSTIN, ALVYN J. Adjunct professor of Asian history, Brock University, St Catharines, Ontario.
Jean Isabelle Dow.

AYUKAWA, MICHIKO MIDGE. Independent researcher, Victoria, British Columbia.
Goro Kaburagi.

BACH, VICKY. Chaplaincy nurse, Shalom Village, Hamilton, Ontario.
Frederic Marlett Bell-Smith. Thomas Henry Best. Sir William James Gage. Bellelle Guerin. Frances Mahony (Jeffers; Lovering). Charlotte Mount Brock Morrell (Schreiber). [Biographies written in collaboration with M. P. Ungar.]

BACKHOUSE, CONSTANCE. Distinguished university professor and university research chair, Faculty of Law, University of Ottawa, Ontario.
Clara Brett Martin.

BADGLEY, KERRY. Archivist, Library and Archives Canada, Ottawa, Ontario.
John Douglas Fraser Drummond. Robert Henry Grant. William Egerton Hodgins. Caleb Alvord Mallory. George Weston.

BAKER, MELVIN. Archivist and historian, Memorial University of Newfoundland, St John's, Newfoundland.
John Anderson. Sir Robert Bond [in collaboration with P. Neary]. *Sir Michael Patrick Cashin. Harry Judson Crowe. William Gilbert Gosling. Sir Patrick Thomas McGrath. Gerald Joseph Whitty* [in collaboration with P. Neary].

BAKER, VICTORIA. Senior program officer, Heritage Programs Directorate, Department of Canadian Heritage, Gatineau, Quebec.
William Brymner.

BAKER, WILLIAM M. Professor emeritus of history, University of Lethbridge, Alberta.
Richard Burton Deane.

BALE, GORDON. Professor emeritus of law, Queen's University, Kingston, Ontario.
John Idington.

BALLSTADT, CARL P. Professor emeritus of English, McMaster University, Hamilton, Ontario.
Peter Gilchrist McArthur.

BARMAN, JEAN. Professor of educational studies, University of British Columbia, Vancouver, British Columbia.
William Henry Curran.

BARMAN, RODERICK J. Professor emeritus of history, University of British Columbia, Vancouver, British Columbia.
Jean Caux, known as *Cataline.*

BARR, DEBRA E. Records officer, Royal Roads University, Victoria, British Columbia.
Albert Durrant Watson [in collaboration with W. Meyer zu Erpen].

BARR, ELINOR. Independent researcher, Thunder Bay, Ontario.
Isabel Johnstone.

BARRIÈRE, MIREILLE. Directrice administrative, Société québécoise de recherche en musique, Montréal, Québec.
Georges Alba, known as *Paul Cazeneuve. Eugène Lassalle.*

BASQUE, MAURICE. Directeur, Études acadiennes, Université de Moncton, Nouveau-Brunswick.
Alphée Belliveau.

†BATOR, PAUL ADOLPHUS. Historian, Heritage Programs, Ontario Heritage Foundation, Toronto, Ontario.
John Joseph Mackenzie. Adam Henry Wright.

BEAULIEU, CARL. Historien et éditeur, Les Éditions du Patrimoine inc., Chicoutimi, Québec.
Benjamin Alexander Scott.

BÉGIN, YVES. Étudiant au doctorat en histoire, Université Laval, Québec, et professeur d'histoire, Cégep de Saint-Hyacinthe, Québec.
Louis-Élie Geoffrion.

BÉLAND, MARIO. Conservateur de l'art ancien de 1850 à 1900, Musée national des beaux-arts du Québec, Québec.
Louis Jobin.

BÉLANGER, RÉAL. Directeur général adjoint, *Dictionnaire biographique du Canada/Dictionary of Canadian biography,* et professeur titulaire d'histoire, Université Laval, Québec, Québec.
Émilie Barthe (Lavergne).

BELL, D. G. Professor of colonial law and institutions, University of New Brunswick, Fredericton, New Brunswick.
William Odber Raymond.

BELSHAW, JOHN DOUGLAS. Associate professor of history, University College of the Cariboo, Kamloops, British Columbia.
Hewitt Bostock [in collaboration with E. Duckworth]. *Joseph Guichon.*

CONTRIBUTORS

BENIDICKSON, JAMIE. Associate professor of common law, University of Ottawa, Ontario.
John Rudolphus Booth. Francis Henry Keefer.

BENOIT, JEAN. Chargé de projet, Projet Normetic, Université du Québec (siège social), Québec.
Sir William Price.

BENTLEY, D. M. R. Professor of English, University of Western Ontario, London, Ontario.
William Bliss Carman.

BIENVENUE, LOUISE. Professeure adjointe d'histoire, Université de Sherbrooke, Québec.
Eliza Ann McIntosh (Reid). Mathilde Toupin-Fafard.

BIGGS-CRAFT, KATHERINE N. E. Curator, Saint John Jewish Historical Museum, New Brunswick.
Nathan Green.

BILODEAU, MARYSE. Enseignante d'histoire, École secondaire catholique Marie-Rivier, Kingston, Ontario.
George Robert Smith.

†BISSON, PIERRE-RICHARD. Professeur agrégé d'architecture, Université de Montréal, Québec.
Joseph Venne [in collaboration with J. Lachapelle].

BLAKE, LYNN. Historical geographer, Montgomery, Alabama, U.S.A.
Eugène-Casimir Chirouse. Jean-Marie-Raphaël Le Jeune.

BLISS, MICHAEL. University professor of history, University of Toronto, Ontario.
William Davies.

BOISVERT, ÉRICA. Étudiante à la maîtrise en histoire, Université de Sherbrooke, Québec.
René Fortier [in collaboration with F. Jean].

BOISVERT, MICHEL. Artiste-peintre et galeriste, Baie-Saint-Paul, Québec.
Émile Miller.

BOIVIN, AURÉLIEN. Professeur titulaire de littérature québécoise, Université Laval, Québec, Québec.
Arsène Bessette.

BONVILLE, JEAN DE. Professeur titulaire d'information et de communication, Université Laval, Québec, Québec.
Jules Helbronner.

BORESKIE, THOMAS G. Formerly historian, Manitoba Culture, Heritage and Recreation, Winnipeg, Manitoba.
Robert Lorne Richardson.

BOUCHER, GHISLAINE. Théologienne et auteure, Québec, Québec.
Dina Bélanger, named Marie Sainte-Cécile-de-Rome.

BOUDREAU, MICHAEL. Assistant professor of criminology, St Thomas University, Fredericton, New Brunswick.
Francis Hanrahan.

BRAWN, DALE. Assistant professor of law, Laurentian University, Sudbury, Ontario.
John C. McRae. Thomas Llewellyn Metcalfe [in collaboration with D. J. Guth].

BREEN, DAVID. Professor and head, Department of History, University of British Columbia, Vancouver, British Columbia.
William Pearce.

BRIDGE, KATHRYN. Manager, Access Services, British Columbia Archives, Victoria, British Columbia.
Sarah Lindley (Crease, Lady Crease).

BRISSON, IRÈNE. Professeure d'histoire de la musique et responsable des études, Conservatoire de musique de Québec, Québec.
Nazaire Le Vasseur.

BRODE, PATRICK. Lawyer, Windsor, Ontario.
Robert Franklin Sutherland.

BROUGHTON, PETER. Formerly teacher, Toronto Board of Education, Ontario.
John Andrew Paterson.

BROUWER, RUTH COMPTON. Professor of history, King's College, University of Western Ontario, London, Ontario.
Marion Fairweather (Stirling). Agnes Maule Machar.

BROWN, JENNIFER S. H. Professor of history and Canada Research Chair in Aboriginal Peoples in an Urban and Regional Context, University of Winnipeg, Manitoba.
Frances Nickawa (Mark).

BROWN, ROBERT CRAIG. Professor emeritus of history, University of Toronto, Ontario.
Archibald William Campbell. Frank Broadstreet Carvell. Sir Samuel Hughes. Sir Albert Edward Kemp [in collaboration with J. A. Turley-Ewart]. William Pugsley. John Dowsley Reid. Lawrence Bruce Robertson.

BRUCE, LORNE D. Head, Archival and Special Collections, University of Guelph Library, Ontario.
William Oliver Carson.

BRUCE, MARIAN. Writer and editor, High Bank, Prince Edward Island.
Alexander Anderson.

BRUNET, MANON. Professeure titulaire de français, Université du Québec à Trois-Rivières, Québec.
Félicité Angers, known as Laure Conan.

BUDDLE, MELANIE. Adjunct faculty, Department of History, Trent University, Peterborough, Ontario.
Wenonah Marlatt. Margaret Townsend (Fox; Jenkins).

BUMSTED, J. M. Professor of history, St John's College, University of Manitoba, Winnipeg, Manitoba.
Sir Louis Henry Davies. Alexander Bannerman Warburton.

BURDEN, PATRICK. Chief, Government Archives Division, Library and Archives Canada, Ottawa, Ontario.
William James Stewart.

BURGESS, JOANNE. Professeure d'histoire, Université du Québec à Montréal, Québec.
Sir Mortimer Barnett Davis.

BURLEY, DAVID G. Professor of history, University of Winnipeg, Manitoba.
James Henry Ashdown. Elisha Frederick Hutchings. Thomas Sharpe.

BURR, CHRISTINA. Associate professor of history, University of Windsor, Ontario.
David Arthur Carey.

BUSSIÈRES, ÉDOUARD, S.S.S. Ex-procureur provincial, Congrégation du Très-Saint-Sacrement, Montréal, Québec.
Marie Hébert de La Rousselière, named Marie-Clémentine de Jésus-Hostie.

CAHILL, BARRY. Independent scholar, Halifax, Nova Scotia.
James Wilberforce Longley [in collaboration with P. Girard]. James Crosskill Mackintosh [in collaboration with G. P. Marchildon]. Wellington Ney States. Thomas Stewart.

CALBECK, SCOTT. Producer, Images Film and Video, Toronto, Ontario.
William James Fitzgerald.

CALDWELL, GARY. Independent sociologist, Martinville, Quebec.
Paul (Napoléon) Tourigny.

CONTRIBUTORS

CARTER, SARAH A. Professor of history, University of Calgary, Alberta.
Amelia Anne McLean (Paget).

CASTONGUAY, RENÉ. Chargé de cours en histoire, Université Laval, Québec, Québec.
Louis-Philippe Brodeur. Joseph-Léonide Perron.

CASTONGUAY, STÉPHANE. Titulaire de la Chaire de recherche du Canada en histoire environnementale du Québec, Université du Québec à Trois-Rivières, Québec.
William Lochhead.

CHAGNON, JOANNE. Historienne de l'art, Québec, Québec.
Charles Huot.

CHARBONNEAU, HÉLÈNE. Analyste en gestion de documents et des archives, Ville de Montréal, Québec.
Zéphirin Benoit.

CHISHOLM, JESSIE. Descriptive standards archivist, Provincial Archives of Newfoundland and Labrador, St John's, Newfoundland.
Thomas St John [in collaboration with D. Sutherland].

CHUTE, JANET E. Adjunct professor, Department of Sociology and Anthropology, Mount Saint Vincent University, Halifax, Nova Scotia.
George Shingwauk.

CLAYDEN, STEPHEN R. Curator of botany, New Brunswick Museum, Saint John, New Brunswick.
James Fowler.

CLÉMENT, GABRIEL. Curé, Paroisse Saint-Joseph, Huntingdon, Québec.
Joseph-Médard Emard.

CLIPPINGDALE, RICHARD T. Fellow, School of Canadian Studies, Carleton University, and president, RTC Services, Ottawa.
Sir John Stephen Willison.

CLOUTIER, NICOLE. Historienne de l'art et directrice, Maître d'œuvre de l'histoire inc., Montréal, Québec.
James Wilson Morrice.

COHEN, YOLANDE. Professeure titulaire d'histoire, Université du Québec à Montréal, Québec.
Gertrude Elizabeth (Nora) Livingston. Flora Madeline Shaw [in collaboration with M. Farkas].

COMACCHIO, CYNTHIA. Professor of history, Wilfrid Laurier University, Waterloo, Ontario.
William Eugene Struthers.

COMEAU, GAYLE M. Part-time faculty, Department of History, Glendon College, York University, Toronto, Ontario.
Robert John Fleming. James Grand.

COMEAU, MICHELLE. Chargée de cours en histoire, Université du Québec à Montréal, et chargée de cours en relations industrielles, Université du Québec en Outaouais, Gatineau, Québec.
Marie-Anne Laporte.

CONNOR, PATRICK J. Contract faculty, Department of History, York University, Toronto, Ontario.
Theodore F. Chamberlain. Louisa Sims (Rogers) [in collaboration with S. E. Houston].

COOK, RAMSAY. General editor, *Dictionary of Canadian biography/Dictionnaire biographique du Canada*, University of Toronto, Ontario.
John Wilson Bengough. Flora MacDonald Merrill (Denison) [in collaboration with M. Lacombe]. *Edmund Ernest Sheppard.*

COOK, SHARON ANNE. Professor of education, University of Ottawa, Ontario.
Roberta Elizabeth Odell (Tilton). Ann Jane Powell (Gray). Sarah Alice Rowell (Wright). Ella Hobday Webster (Bronson).

COOK, TERRY. Professor of archival studies, University of Manitoba, Winnipeg, Manitoba.
Sir George Robert Parkin.

COOPER, AFUA. Lecturer in Caribbean studies, Ryerson University, Toronto, Ontario.
Richard Amos Ball. Susannah Augusta Stokes (Maxwell).

COOPER, BARBARA. Teacher, Toronto District School Board, Ontario.
Margaret O'Neill, named Mother Agatha.

CÔTÉ, GUY. Historien, Havre-Saint-Pierre, Québec.
Placide Vigneau.

COURSOL, LUC. Professeur d'histoire, Commission scolaire Pierre-Neveu, Mont-Laurier, Québec.
François-Xavier Brunet.

CRAN, EMILY ELIZABETH. Writer and artist, Tignish, Prince Edward Island.
François-Joseph Buote.

CREIGHTON, PHILIP. Chartered accountant, Toronto, Ontario.
Eliza Jane Creighton (Harvie).

CRERAR, ADAM. Assistant professor of history, Wilfrid Laurier University, Waterloo, Ontario.
John Matheson.

CROSSMAN, KELLY. Associate professor, School for Studies in Art and Culture, Carleton University, Ottawa, Ontario.
Frank Darling.

CROWLEY, TERRY. Professor and chair, Department of History, University of Guelph, Ontario.
Catherine Trask (Brown).

CUFF, HARRY. Formerly professor of education, Memorial University of Newfoundland, St John's, Newfoundland.
James Frederick Bancroft.

CUFF, ROBERT. Heritage consultant, St John's, Newfoundland.
George Frederick Arthur Grimes.

DALE, ANNE CARLYLE. Associate professor of dentistry and curator emeritus, Dental Museum, University of Toronto, Ontario.
John Gennings Curtis Adams.

DANSEREAU, BERNARD. Chargé de cours en histoire, Université du Québec à Montréal et Université de Montréal, et chargé de cours en relations industrielles, Université du Québec en Outaouais, Gatineau, Québec.
Narcisse Arcand.

DAVIES, GWENDOLYN. Dean of graduate studies, associate vice-president (research), and professor of English, University of New Brunswick, Fredericton, New Brunswick.
John Frederic Herbin. Emma Lucy Wells (Dickson).

DEAN, MISAO. Professor of English, University of Victoria, British Columbia.
Sara Jeannette Duncan (Cotes), known as Garth Grafton.

DECARIE, GRAEME. Associate professor of history, Concordia University, Montreal, Quebec.
David Volume Sinclair.

DEGRÂCE, ÉLOI. Archiviste, Sœurs de la Providence, Edmonton, Alberta.
Stanislas-Joseph Doucet.

DEMBSKI, PETER E. PAUL. Independent historian, Waterloo, Ontario.
Jenny Kidd Gowanlock (Trout). Sir William Ralph Meredith. George Ansel Sterling Ryerson.

DEMPSEY, HUGH A. Chief curator emeritus, Glenbow Museum, Calgary, Alberta.
Robert Chambers Edwards. Edward Herbert Maunsell. Nitai'kihtsipimi.

DERRY, MARGARET E. Adjunct professor of history, University of Guelph, and associated scholar, Institute for the History and Philosophy of Science and Technology, University of Toronto, Ontario.
George Christie Creelman. James Mills. John Gunion Rutherford.

DESHAIES, LAURENT. Professeur de géographie à la retraite, Université du Québec à Trois-Rivières, Québec.
Eugène Rouillard.

DESJARDINS, MARC. Directeur des communications, La Financière agricole du Québec, Québec, Québec.
Edmund James Flynn.

DESMEULES, MÉLANIE. Étudiante au doctorat en histoire, Université Laval, Québec, Québec.
Victor-Alphonse Huard.

DESROSIERS, GEORGES. Professeur émérite de médecine sociale et préventive, Université de Montréal, Québec.
Arthur-Joseph Richer [in collaboration with B. Gaumer and O. Keel].

DE SURMONT, JEAN-NICOLAS. Chercheur autonome, Louvain-la-Neuve, Belgique.
Charles Marchand.

DIEUDONNÉ, PATRICK. Maître de conférences d'urbanisme, Institut de géoarchitecture, Université de Bretagne occidentale, Brest, France.
Elzéar Charest.

DIPPIE, BRIAN W. Professor of history, University of Victoria, British Columbia.
Charles Marion Russell.

DIRKS, PATRICIA. Formerly associate professor of history, Brock University, St Catharines, Ontario.
George Augustus Warburton.

DONSKOV, A. A. Professor of modern languages and literatures, University of Ottawa, Ontario.
Peter Vasil'evich Verigin.

DOWBIGGIN, IAN. Professor and chair, Department of History, University of Prince Edward Island, Charlottetown, Prince Edward Island.
Charles Kirk Clarke.

DRUMMOND, ANNE. Independent scholar, Westmount, Quebec.
Sydney Arthur Fisher.

DUCKWORTH, ELISABETH. Museum director, Kamloops Museum and Archives, British Columbia.
Hewitt Bostock [in collaboration with J. D. Belshaw].

DUECK, PETER. Researcher, Mennonite Heritage Centre, Winnipeg, Manitoba.
Joseph Reader.

DUMONT, MICHELINE. Professeure émérite d'histoire, Université de Sherbrooke, Québec.
Julie Bertrand, named Marie de Saint-Basile. Marie Bibeau, named Marie-Anne-de-Jésus. Irène-Mathilde Dégrès, named Saint-Paul. Marie-Louise-Thérèse Lemoine, named Marie-Joseph de Jésus. Aurélie Lesaulnier.

DUNLOP, ALLAN C. Formerly associate provincial archivist, Public Archives of Nova Scotia, Halifax, Nova Scotia.
Robert Maclellan [in collaboration with B. A. Wood].

DUTIL, PATRICE A. Director of research, Institute of Public Administration of Canada, Toronto, Ontario.
Godfroy Langlois.

†DYCK, DAVID R. Formerly professor of history, University of Winnipeg, Manitoba.
Henry Norlande Ruttan. Alexander Patterson Stevenson.

EBER, DOROTHY HARLEY. Researcher and author, Montreal, Quebec.
Mabel Gardiner Hubbard (Bell).

EDMUNDS-FLETT, SHERRY. Executive director, Long-term Inmates Now in the Community, Abbotsford, and doctoral student in history, Simon Fraser University, Burnaby, British Columbia.
Charles Appleby. Joseph Seraphim Fortes.

EDWARDS, GAIL. Instructor in history, Douglas College, New Westminster, British Columbia.
William Henry Collison.

ELLIOTT, MARIE. Formerly administrative assistant, University of Victoria, British Columbia.
Robert Borland. Henry Georgeson.

ELOFSON, WARREN M. Professor of history, University of Calgary, Alberta.
Michael Clark. William Charles James Roper Hull.

ENS, GERHARD J. Associate professor of history, University of Alberta, Edmonton, Alberta.
Ambroise-Dydime Lépine.

EVANS, SIMON M. Adjunct professor of geography, University of Calgary, Alberta.
William Edward Cochrane. George Lane.

EVENDEN, MATTHEW. Assistant professor of geography, University of British Columbia, Vancouver, British Columbia.
William Henry Barker.

FARKAS, MARYANN. Professor of history, Dawson College, Montreal, Quebec.
Flora Madeline Shaw [in collaboration with Y. Cohen].

FAY, TERENCE J., S.J. Lecturer in Christian history, St Augustine's Seminary, Toronto School of Theology, University of Toronto, Ontario.
Edward James Devine.

FERNS, JOHN. Professor of English, McMaster University, Hamilton, Ontario.
John Hornby.

FERNS, THOMAS H. Senior counsel, Dofasco Inc., Hamilton, Ontario.
Sir John Strathearn Hendrie.

FIELD, RUSSELL. Doctoral student in physical education, University of Toronto, Ontario.
Dyce Willcocks Saunders.

FILTEAU, HUGUETTE. Rédactrice-historienne, *Dictionnaire biographique du Canada/Dictionary of Canadian biography*, Université Laval, Québec, Québec.
John Forbes [in collaboration with J. Hamelin].

FINGARD, JUDITH. Adjunct professor of history, Dalhousie University, Halifax, Nova Scotia.
George Henry Murray.

FINKEL, ALVIN. Professor of history, Athabasca University, Alberta.
Charles Wilson Cross.

FITSELL, J. W. Hockey historian and formerly columnist and district editor, *Kingston Whig-Standard*, Ontario.

James George Aylwin Creighton.

FORSTER, BEN. Associate professor and chair, Department of History, University of Western Ontario, London, Ontario.

John Alexander Macdonell (Greenfield).

FOSS, BRIAN. Associate professor of art history, Concordia University, Montreal, Quebec.

Mary Augusta Catharine Hiester (Reid).

FRADET, LOUISE. Chercheure, Québec, Québec.

Jeanne Anctil.

FRANK, DAVID. Professor of history, University of New Brunswick, Fredericton, New Brunswick.

James Leonard Sugrue.

FRASER, BRIAN J. Principal, Tekara Organizational Effectiveness Inc., Vancouver, British Columbia.

Thomas Buchanan Kilpatrick. James Alexander Macdonald.

FRENCH, GOLDWIN S. President emeritus, Victoria University, Toronto, Ontario.

Francis Huston Wallace.

FRENETTE, PIERRE. Professeur d'histoire, Cégep de Baie-Comeau, Québec, et historien consultant, Pointe-Lebel, Québec.

Napoléon-Alexandre Comeau.

FROST, S. B. Formerly director, History of McGill Project, McGill University, Montreal, Quebec.

Sir William Peterson.

FULTON, GORDON W. Director, Historical Services Branch, National Historic Sites, Parks Canada, Gatineau, Quebec.

David Ewart.

FULTON, WENDELL E. Researcher, New Maryland, New Brunswick.

James Kidd Flemming. George Gerald King.

GAGNON, GASTON. Conseiller en patrimoine, Direction du Saguenay–Lac-Saint-Jean, Ministère de la Culture et des Communications, Chicoutimi, Québec.

Joseph-Dominique Guay.

GAGNON, JEAN-PIERRE. Historien et consultant, Gatineau, Québec.

Henri Chassé. Constant Doyon (baptized Paul-Victor-Emmanuel). Sir David Watson. Erastus William Wilson.

GAGNON, ROBERT. Professeur d'histoire, Université du Québec à Montréal, Québec.

Louis-Anthyme Herdt. Joseph-Narcisse Perrault.

GAUMER, BENOÎT. Professeur associé d'administration de la santé, Université de Montréal, Québec.

Arthur-Joseph Richer [in collaboration with G. Desrosiers and O. Keel].

GAUTHIER, RAYMONDE. Professeure associée d'histoire de l'art, Université du Québec à Montréal, Québec.

Louis-Zéphirin Gauthier.

GERUS, OLEH W. Professor of history, University of Manitoba, Winnipeg, Manitoba.

Nestor Dmytriw.

GIBSON, LEE. Formerly researcher and historian, Winnipeg, Manitoba.

Sir James Albert Manning Aikins.

GILBERT, CLAUDE. Agent de recherche, Décanat des études supérieures et de la recherche, Université du Québec à Chicoutimi, Québec.

Elzéar De Lamarre.

GILLETT, MARGARET. William C. Macdonald professor of education emeritus, McGill University, Montreal, Quebec.

Margaret Smith Polson (Murray).

GIRARD, MICHEL F. Director of international affairs, Climate Change Bureau, Environment Canada, Gatineau, Quebec.

James White.

GIRARD, PHILIP. Professor of law, history, and Canadian studies, Dalhousie University, Halifax, Nova Scotia.

James Wilberforce Longley [in collaboration with B. Cahill]. *Sir Charles James Townshend. Richard Chapman Weldon.*

GLENDENNING, BURTON. Formerly manager, Public Service, Provincial Archives of New Brunswick, Fredericton, New Brunswick.

John Percival Burchill.

GODARD, BARBARA. Professor of English, York University, Toronto, Ontario.

Isabel Ecclestone MacPherson (Mackay). Marjorie Lowry Christie Pickthall. Joanna Ellen Wood.

GODFREY, W. G. Stiles-Bennett professor of history, Mount Allison University, Sackville, New Brunswick.

Josiah Wood.

GOLDRING, PHILIP. Ottawa, Ontario.

Kanaka.

GORDON, ALAN. Assistant professor of history, University of Guelph, Ontario.

Edmund James Bristol.

GOSSELIN, LINE. Montréal, Québec.

Joséphine Marchand (Dandurand). Marie-Louise Marmette (Brodeur), known as Louyse de Bienville.

GOULET, DANIÈLE. Chargée de projets, Musée canadien des civilisations, Gatineau, Québec.

Louis-Philippe Pelletier.

GOULET, DENIS. Professeur associé d'histoire, Université de Sherbrooke, Québec.

Arthur Bernier [in collaboration with P. Hudon]. *Joseph-Alphonse Couture* [in collaboration with F. Jean]. *Duncan McNab McEachran* [in collaboration with F. Jean]. *Oscar-Félix Mercier* [in collaboration with P. Hudon].

GRAHAM, ANGELA. Doctoral student in history, McMaster University, Hamilton, Ontario.

Robert Calver Fearman. John Milne.

GRANT, SHELAGH D. Adjunct faculty, Canadian Studies Program, and research associate, Frost Centre for Heritage and Native Studies, Trent University, Peterborough, Ontario.

Niaqutiaq.

GRAUER, LALLY. Associate professor of English, Okanagan University College, Kelowna, British Columbia.

William James McLean.

GRAVEL BERNIER, GHISLAINE. Chargée de cours en littérature française à la retraite, Université Laval, Québec, Québec.

Louis-Pierre Gravel.

GRAY, CAROLYN E. Copyright policy adviser, Publications Ontario, Toronto, Ontario.

Sir John Morison Gibson.

GRAY, SUSAN. Research associate, University of Winnipeg, Manitoba.

John Maclean. John Semmens.

GREENE, RONALD A. Numismatist and historian, Victoria, British Columbia.

Robert Purves McLennan.

GRÉGOIRE, CAROLE. Professeure de littérature musicale, Cégep de Sainte-Foy, Québec.
Damase Lesage.

GRENIER, GUY. Professionnel de recherche, Centre de recherche psychosociale, Hôpital Douglas, Montréal, Québec.
Edmond-Joseph Bourque. Thomas Joseph Workman Burgess. Albert Prévost.

GUAY, BERTRAND. Musicologue, Orchestre symphonique de Québec, Québec.
Joseph Vézina.

GUEST, HAL J. Historical resource consultant, Winnipeg, Manitoba.
Sir Hugh John Macdonald.

GUILDFORD, JANET. Senior research associate, Beach Meadows Research Associates Ltd, Halifax, Nova Scotia.
Sir Charles Frederick Fraser. Alexander Howard MacKay.

GUTH, DELLOYD J. Professor of law and legal history and director, Canadian Legal History Project, University of Manitoba, Winnipeg, Manitoba.
Thomas Llewellyn Metcalfe [in collaboration with D. Brawn].

†GWYN, SANDRA. Journalist and author, Toronto, Ontario.
Agar Stewart Allan Masterton Adamson. Agnes Mary Scott (Davis).

HALE, LINDA L. Instructor in history, Langara College, Vancouver, British Columbia.
Sara Anne Maclure (McLagan).

HALL, DAVID J. Professor emeritus of history, University of Alberta, Edmonton, Alberta.
Robert George Brett. George Hedley Vicars Bulyea. Sir James Alexander Lougheed [in collaboration with D. B. Smith]. *William Duncan Scott. Arthur Lewis Watkins Sifton. Sir Clifford Sifton. John Gillanders Turriff.*

HALL, FREDERICK A. Associate professor of music and associate vice-president (academic), McMaster University, Hamilton, Ontario.
Edwin Rodie Parkhurst.

HAMELIN, DANIELLE. Historian, Parks Canada, Gatineau, Quebec.
William Briggs. Robert Pollock Glasgow.

†HAMELIN, JEAN. Directeur général adjoint, *Dictionnaire biographique du Canada/Dictionary of Canadian biography,* Université Laval, Québec, Québec.
John Forbes [in collaboration with H. Filteau].

HAMILTON, THOMAS. Sessional lecturer in history, University of Prince Edward Island, and senior minister, St Mark's Presbyterian Church, Charlottetown, Prince Edward Island.
Thomas Crawford Brown.

HAMILTON, W. D. Professor emeritus of education, University of New Brunswick, Fredericton, New Brunswick.
Henry A. Braithwaite. Andrew Loggie. Anne Quinlan. John P. Tenass.

HANAWAY, JOSEPH. Clinical assistant professor of neurology, Washington University, and visiting associate professor of neurology, University of Missouri, St Louis, Missouri, U.S.A.
Alexander MacKenzie Torrance Forbes. Sir Thomas George Roddick.

HANLON, PETER. Historian, Winnipeg, Manitoba.

William Forbes Alloway. Sir Augustus Meredith Nanton.

HANNA, CHRISTOPHER J. P. Owner, Alpha Research Corporation, Victoria, British Columbia.
Robert Kelly. Walter Cameron Nichol. Frederick Coate Wade. [Biographies written in collaboration with B. R. Morrison.]

†HANSON, STANLEY D. Formerly university archivist, University of Saskatchewan, Saskatoon, Saskatchewan.
William John Rutherford. Edward Ludlow Wetmore.

HART, ANNE. Honorary research librarian, Queen Elizabeth Library, Memorial University of Newfoundland, St John's, Newfoundland.
Fannie Knowling (McNeil).

HAYTER, CHARLES. Associate professor of radiation oncology, University of Toronto, Ontario.
William Henry Beaufort Aikins.

HEADS, WENDY. College teacher and historian, Pickering, Ontario.
Margaret Vallance (Taylor, Lady Taylor).

†HÉBERT, MONIQUE. Coordinatrice de la Journée nationale des Autochtones, Affaires indiennes et du Nord Canada, Gatineau, Québec.
Annette Saint-Amant (Frémont).

HÉBERT, YVES. Historien consultant, Lévis, Québec.
Joseph-Narcisse Gastonguay.

HERON, CRAIG. Professor of history, York University, Toronto, Ontario.
Sir Frank Wilton Baillie. Cyrus Albert Birge. Robert Hobson.

HISCOCK, PHILIP. Assistant professor of folklore, Memorial University of Newfoundland, St John's, Newfoundland.
John Burke.

HOLMAN, HARRY TINSON. Director, Culture, Heritage and Libraries Division, Department of Community and Cultural Affairs, Charlottetown, Prince Edward Island.
John Howatt Bell. Donald Alexander MacKinnon.

HOULE, JACQUES-ANDRÉ. Violoniste et responsable des livrets, Disques ATMA, Montréal, Québec.
Alfred De Sève.

HOUSTON, SUSAN E. Associate professor emeritus, York University, Toronto, Ontario.
Louisa Sims (Rogers) [in collaboration with P. J. Connor].

HRYNIUK, STELLA. Formerly associate professor of history, University of Manitoba, Winnipeg, Manitoba.
Cyril Genyk.

HUDON, PHILIPPE. Documentaliste et chercheur, Montréal, Québec.
Arthur Bernier. Oscar-Félix Mercier. [Biographies written in collaboration with D. Goulet.]

HUEL, RAYMOND. Professor of history, University of Lethbridge, Alberta.
Henri Grandin.

HULL, JAMES P. Associate professor of history, Okanagan University College, Kelowna, British Columbia.
Bernhard Eduard Fernow.

HUSTAK, ALAN. Journalist, *Gazette,* Montreal, Quebec.
Arthur Godfrey Peuchen.

IACOVETTA, FRANCA. Associate professor of history, University of Toronto, Ontario.
Angelina Napolitano.

IVANY, KATHRYN. Historian, Edmonton, Alberta.
Milton Robbins Jennings.

JANSON, GILLES. Bibliothécaire, Université du Québec à Montréal, Québec.
Joseph-Pierre Gadbois. George Washington Kendall, known as George Kennedy. Henri-Thomas Scott.

JARRELL, RICHARD A. Professor of natural science and history, York University, Toronto, Ontario.
Édouard Deville. Otto Julius Klotz.

JEAN, FRÉDÉRIC. Étudiant au doctorat en études québécoises, Université du Québec à Trois-Rivières, Québec.
Joseph-Alphonse Couture [in collaboration with D. Goulet]. *René Fortier* [in collaboration with É. Boisvert]. *Duncan McNab McEachran* [in collaboration with D. Goulet].

JEDWAB, JACK. Executive director, Association for Canadian Studies, Montreal, Quebec.
Robert Bickerdike.

JONES, GAYNOR G. Associate professor of the history and culture of music, University of Toronto, Ontario.
Augustus Stephen Vogt.

JONES, RICHARD. Professeur d'histoire à la retraite, Université Laval, Québec, Québec.
Sir Lomer Gouin.

KAMINSKI, LEN. Associate professor of social work, University of Manitoba, Winnipeg, Manitoba.
Daniel Salmon Hamilton.

KAREL, DAVID. Professeur titulaire d'histoire, Université Laval, Québec, Québec.
Edmond-Joseph Massicotte.

KEEL, OTHMAR. Professeur titulaire d'histoire, Université de Montréal, Québec.
Arthur-Joseph Richer [in collaboration with G. Desrosiers and B. Gaumer].

KELM, MARY-ELLEN. Associate professor of history, University of Northern British Columbia, Prince George, British Columbia.
Caroline Sarah Knott (Tate).

KENNEDY, JOAN. London, Ontario.
Harriet Ann Mills (Roche; Boomer).

KERR, DONALD CAMERON. Professor emeritus of English, University of Saskatchewan, Saskatoon, Saskatchewan.
James Frederick Cairns.

KERWIN, SCOTT. Lawyer, Borden Ladner Gervais LLP, Vancouver, British Columbia.
Janet Kennedy Smith.

KESHEN, JEFFREY A. Associate professor of history, University of Ottawa, Ontario.
Ernest John Chambers. John Castell Hopkins.

KIDD, BRUCE. Professor and dean, Faculty of Physical Education and Health, University of Toronto, Ontario.
Norton Hervey Crow. Henry John Prescott Wilshere Good. George Sleeman. Velma Agnes Springstead.

KIEFER, NANCY. Project coordinator, Ontario Ministry of Community Safety and Correctional Services, Toronto, Ontario.
Ada Mary Brown (Courtice). Clarence Bartlett Edwards. Robert Mathison.

KIMMEL, DAVID. Montreal, Quebec.
Bertha Lehman (Rosenthal). Sara Mickle [in collaboration with J. Miron]. *Sir Byron Edmund Walker.*

KINNEAR, MARY. Professor of history, University of Manitoba, Winnipeg, Manitoba.
Winona Margaret Flett (Dixon).

KNAFLA, LOUIS A. Professor emeritus of history and director, Socio-Legal Studies, University of Calgary, Alberta.
Charles Frederick Pringle Conybeare. Maitland Stewart McCarthy. Charles Coursolles McCaul. David Lynch Scott.

KNOWLES, NORMAN. Associate professor of history, St Mary's College, Calgary, and adjunct associate professor of history, University of Calgary, Alberta.
George Taylor Denison. Jessie Knox Munro.

KNOWLES, VALERIE. Freelance writer and author, Ottawa, Ontario.
George Henry Ham.

KUHLBERG, MARK. Assistant professor of history, Laurentian University, Sudbury, Ontario.
Isaac Hillock Weldon.

KYER, C. IAN. Lawyer and senior partner, Fasken Martineau DuMoulin LLP, Toronto, Ontario.
Edward Marion Chadwick. David Fasken. Wallace Nesbitt.

LABELLE, RONALD. Ethnologist, Centre d'études acadiennes, Université de Moncton, Nouveau-Brunswick.
Nathalie Melanson (Bourgeois).

LABRÈQUE, MARIE-PAULE R. Historienne, Granby, Québec.
Alexandrine Teyssèdre, named Marie-Saint-David.

LACASSE, GERMAIN. Professeur adjoint d'études cinématographiques, Université de Montréal, Québec.
Henry de Grandsaignes d'Hauterives, Vicomte de Grandsaignes d'Hauterives.

LACHAPELLE, JACQUES. Professeur agrégé d'architecture, Université de Montréal, Québec.
Alexander Francis Dunlop. Joseph Venne [in collaboration with P.-R. Bisson].

LACOMBE, MICHÈLE. Associate professor of Canadian studies, Trent University, Peterborough, Ontario.
Flora MacDonald Merrill (Denison) [in collaboration with R. Cook].

LAMIRANDE, ÉMILIEN. Professeur émérite de sciences des religions, Université d'Ottawa, Ontario.
Damase Dandurand.

†LANDRY, JEAN. Étudiant au doctorat en histoire et chargé de cours en sciences de l'éducation, Université du Québec à Trois-Rivières, Québec.
Laurent-Olivier David.

LANG, MARJORY. Coordinator, Department of History, Langara College, Vancouver, British Columbia.
Emily Ann McCausland Shortt (Cummings).

LAPERRIÈRE, GUY. Professeur d'histoire, Université de Sherbrooke, Québec.
Paul La Rocque.

LAPLANTE, ALCIDE. Bibliothécaire, Séminaire de Saint-Sulpice, Montréal, Québec.
Charles Lecoq.

LAPLANTE, CORINNE. Archiviste régionale, Région Notre-Dame de l'Assomption, Religieuses hospitalières de Saint-Joseph, Bathurst, Nouveau-Brunswick.
Philomène Gendron.

LAROCHE, GINETTE. Historienne de l'art, Charlesbourg, Québec.
Bernard Leonard.

LAROCQUE, COREY. Journalist, *Review*, Niagara Falls, Ontario.
Robert Gray.

LAROUCHE, JEAN-CLAUDE. Président–directeur général, Les Éditions JCL inc., Chicoutimi, Québec.
Alexis Lapointe, known as Alexis le Trotteur.

LARSEN, DAVID. Sales representative, United Library Services, Winnipeg, Manitoba.
Ralph Joseph Horner.

LATHAM, DAVID. Professor of English, York University, Toronto, Ontario.
Charles Mair.

LAUGRAND, FRÉDÉRIC. Professeur agrégé d'anthropologie, Université Laval, Québec, Québec.
Jules Jetté. Edmund James Peck.

LAURIN, SERGE. Professeur d'histoire retraité (à l'enseignement collégial) et historien, Saint-Jérôme, Québec.
Antonin Nantel.

LEBLANC, LEWIS. Vidéothécaire, Radio-Canada, Moncton, Nouveau-Brunswick.
Olivier-Maximin Melanson.

LECHASSEUR, ANTONIO. Directeur, Division des services aux chercheurs, Bibliothèque et Archives Canada, Ottawa, Ontario.
Pierre-Théophile Legaré.

LEFEBVRE, MARIE-THÉRÈSE. Professeure titulaire de musique, Université de Montréal, Québec.
Béatrice La Palme (Issaurel).

LEGER-ANDERSON, ANN. Associate professor of history, University of Regina, Saskatchewan.
Annie Gardner Barr (Brown).

LEMAIRE, MICHEL. Professeur titulaire de littératures, Université d'Ottawa, Ontario.
Albert Lozeau.

LEROUX, ÉRIC. Professeur adjoint de bibliothéconomie et de sciences de l'information, Université de Montréal, Québec.
Alphonse Verville.

LESAGE, GILLES. Directeur général, La Société historique de Saint-Boniface, Manitoba.
Joseph Blain. Zacharie Lacasse.

LEVINE, ALLAN. Teacher of history, St John's–Ravenscourt School, Winnipeg, Manitoba.
Robert Magill.

LOUIE, SIRI. Doctoral student in history, University of Toronto, Ontario.
Sarah Hymas (Bates; Daines). Sir James Outram.

LYON, DEBORAH M. Independent researcher and editor, Winnipeg, Manitoba.
John Walter Harris.

MACBETH, ROBERT A. Professor emeritus of surgery, University of Alberta, Edmonton, Alberta.
Frank Hamilton Mewburn.

MCCARTHY, MARTHA. Historical consultant, Winnipeg, Manitoba.
Lewis Henry Drummond.

MCCULLOUGH, ALAN B. Historical consultant, Ottawa, Ontario.
Sir Cecil Edward Denny. Peyasiw-awasis.

MACDONALD, HEIDI. Assistant professor of history, University of Lethbridge, Alberta.
Mary Connolly, named *Sister Mary Clare.*

MACDOUGALL, HEATHER. Associate professor of history and associate dean of arts, University of Waterloo, Ontario.
Charles Sheard.

MCDOWALL, DUNCAN. Professor of history, Carleton University, Ottawa, Ontario.
Sir Henry Vincent Meredith. Edson Loy Pease.

MACFARLANE, JOHN. Historian, Directorate of History and Heritage, Department of National Defence, Ottawa, Ontario.
François-Louis Lessard. James Alexander Robb.

MCGAHAN, ELIZABETH W. Lecturer in history, University of New Brunswick, Saint John, New Brunswick.
William Munson Jarvis.

†MCGEE, ARLEE HOYT. Archivist, Nurses Association of New Brunswick, Fredericton, New Brunswick.
Sibella Annie Barrington.

MACGILLIVRAY, DON. Associate professor of history, University College of Cape Breton, Sydney, Nova Scotia.
William Davis. Henry Melville Whitney.

MCGOWAN, MARK G. Associate professor of history, University of Toronto, and principal, St Michael's College, Toronto, Ontario.
Alfred Edward Burke. Charles Hugh Gauthier.

MCINNIS, PETER S. Assistant professor of history, St Francis Xavier University, Antigonish, Nova Scotia.
Philip Bennett.

MACK, D. B. Minister, St Andrew's Presbyterian Church, Saint-Lambert, Quebec.
Daniel Miner Gordon.

MCKAY, IAN. Professor of history, Queen's University, Kingston, Ontario.
Robert Drummond.

MACLEOD, RODERICK C. Professor of history, University of Alberta, Edmonton, Alberta.
Sir George Arthur French. Thomas Bland Strange.

MACMICKEN WILSON, JILL. Sessional lecturer in history, University of Prince Edward Island, Charlottetown, Prince Edward Island.
Alice Jane Sterling (Johnson).

†MCMULLEN, LORRAINE. Formerly adjunct professor of English, University of Victoria, British Columbia, and professor emeritus, University of Ottawa, Ontario.
Lily Dougall.

MALAHER, ROSEMARY. Independent researcher, Whistler, British Columbia, and formerly executive director, Manitoba Historical Society, Winnipeg, Manitoba.
James William Armstrong.

MALOTT, MADELINE HILBORN. Kingsville, Ontario.
William Wilson Hilborn [in collaboration with M. Armstrong-Reynolds].

MARCHILDON, GREGORY P. Professor and Canada Research Chair in Public Policy and Economic History, University of Regina, Saskatchewan.
James Crosskill Mackintosh [in collaboration with B. Cahill].

MARCOTTE, HÉLÈNE. Professeure de français, Université du Québec à Trois-Rivières, Québec.
Benjamin Sulte.

MARQUIS, GREG. Associate professor of history, University of New Brunswick, Saint John, New Brunswick.
Henry James Grasett. William Wallace.

MARSDEN, SUSAN. Curator, Museum of Northern British Columbia, Prince Rupert, British Columbia.
Sganism Sm'oogit.

MARSHALL, DAVID B. Associate professor and head, Department of History, University of Calgary, Alberta.
William Dale.

MARTEL, MARCEL. Professeur agrégé d'histoire et titulaire de la chaire Avie Bennett Historica en histoire canadienne, York University, Toronto, Ontario.

Ovide-Arthur Rocque.

MAYBA, I. I. Orthopaedic surgeon, University of Manitoba, Winnipeg, and Manitoba and Health Sciences Centre, Winnipeg, Manitoba.

Gordon Bell. James Wilford Good.

MEYER ZU ERPEN, WALTER. Manager, Corporate Access Initiatives, British Columbia Archives, Victoria, British Columbia.

Albert Durrant Watson [in collaboration with D. E. Barr].

MIDDLETON, GERARD V. Professor emeritus of geology, McMaster University, Hamilton, Ontario.

Joseph William Winthrop Spencer.

MILLARD, J. RODNEY. Assistant professor of history, University of Western Ontario, London, Ontario.

Phelps Johnson. Sir John Kennedy.

MILLER, CARMAN. Professor of history, McGill University, Montreal, Quebec.

William Stevens Fielding. Sir Edward Thomas Henry Hutton.

MILLER, DAVID REED. Associate professor of indigenous studies, First Nations University of Canada, Regina, Saskatchewan.

Matokinajin.

MILLER, PAMELA. History of medicine librarian, Osler Library of the History of Medicine, McGill University, Montreal, Quebec.

David Ross McCord.

MILLER, RANDALL F. Curator of geology and palaeontology and head, Natural Sciences Department, New Brunswick Museum, Saint John, New Brunswick.

George Frederic Matthew.

MILLS, DAVID. Associate professor of history, University of Alberta, Edmonton, Alberta.

Alfred Davis Fidler.

MIRON, JANET. Lecturer in history, Trent University, Peterborough, Ontario, and doctoral student in history, York University, Toronto, Ontario.

Sara Mickle [in collaboration with D. Kimmel].

MITCHELL, DAVID. Vice-president, University Relations, University of Ottawa, Ontario.

John Oliver.

MITHAM, PETER J. Writer and independent researcher, Vancouver, British Columbia.

James Domville. Wilhelmina Gordon (Smith). Warren Franklin Hatheway. William Henry Price.

MOIR, JOHN S. Professor emeritus of history, University of Toronto, Ontario.

William James McKay.

MOIR, MICHAEL B. Director, Corporate Records Systems, and city archivist, City of Toronto, Ontario.

Lionel Herbert Clarke.

MONGRAIN, GUY. Consultant en histoire, Montréal, Québec.

James Carruthers.

MOODY, BARRY M. Professor and head, Department of History and Classics, Acadia University, Wolfville, Nova Scotia.

Minard Wentworth Graves.

MOORE, CHRISTOPHER. Writer and historian, Toronto, Ontario.

Edward Douglas Armour. Newman Wright Hoyles.

MORAN, JAMES E. Assistant professor of history, University of Prince Edward Island, Charlottetown, Prince Edward Island.

William Harley Smith.

MORGAN, CECILIA. Associate professor of theory and policy studies, Ontario Institute for Studies in Education of the University of Toronto, Ontario.

Janet Carnochan.

MORISSET, LUCIE K. Professeure titulaire d'études urbaines et touristiques, Université du Québec à Montréal, Québec.

Georges-Émile Tanguay.

MORNEAU, JOCELYN. Chercheur autonome, Trois-Rivières, Québec.

Augustin Desrosiers.

MORRISON, BRAD R. Historical researcher and writer, Victoria, British Columbia.

Robert Kelly. Walter Cameron Nichol. Frederick Coate Wade. [Biographies written in collaboration with C. J. P. Hanna.]

MORRISON, JEAN. Formerly research historian, Fort William Historical Park, Thunder Bay, Ontario.

Frederick Urry.

MORRISON, WILLIAM R. Professor of history, University of Northern British Columbia, Prince George, British Columbia.

Alikomiak. Uloqsaq.

MORTON, DESMOND. Hiram Mills professor of history, McGill University, Montreal, Quebec.

Sir Edwin Alfred Hervey Alderson. Sir Willoughby Garnons Gwatkin. Sir William Dillon Otter.

MORTON, JAMIE. Instructor in history and sociology, North Island College, Port Alberni, British Columbia.

Noah Shakespeare. Albert Edward Todd.

MOTT, MORRIS. Associate professor of history, Brandon University, Manitoba.

William Wright Breen. Thomas Herman Johnson.

MOUAT, JEREMY. Professor of history, Athabasca University, Alberta.

Charles Augustus Semlin. John Herbert Turner.

MULLALLY, SASHA. Doctoral student in history, University of Toronto, Ontario.

Stephen Rice Jenkins.

MUNRO, KENNETH. Professor of history, University of Alberta, Edmonton, Alberta.

Sir Louis-Olivier Taillon.

MURRAY, DAVID R. Professor of history, University of Guelph, Ontario.

Walter Palmer Archibald.

MYERS, TAMARA. Associate professor of history, University of Winnipeg, Manitoba.

François-Xavier Choquet.

NEARY, KEVIN. President, Traditions Consulting Services Inc., Victoria, British Columbia.

Charles Frederic Newcombe.

NEARY, PETER. Professor of history, University of Western Ontario, London, Ontario.

Sir Robert Bond. Gerald Joseph Whitty. [Biographies written in collaboration with M. Baker.]

NEGODAEFF, MARGARET. Writer, Ottawa, Ontario.

Leonora Annetta Howard (King).

NELLES, H. V. Distinguished research professor of history, York University, Toronto, Ontario.

Sir Adam Beck.

NICHOLLS, ROBERT V. V. Formerly professor of organic

chemistry, McGill University, Montreal, Quebec.
Robert Fulford Ruttan.

NICHOLSON, KAREN. Historian, Historic Resources Branch, Manitoba Culture, Heritage and Tourism, Winnipeg, Manitoba.
James William Scallion.

†NICOLSON, MURRAY W. Lecturer in history, Wilfrid Laurier University, Waterloo, Ontario.
Sarah Hannah Roberta Grier (Coome).

NIGOL, PAUL. Associate lawyer, Burnet, Duckworth, and Palmer LLP, Calgary, Alberta.
Clarence Campbell Chipman.

NILSEN, KENNETH E. Professor of Celtic studies, St Francis Xavier University, Antigonish, Nova Scotia.
Alexander MacLean Sinclair.

NIX, JAMES ERNEST. Formerly minister, United Church of Canada, Mississauga, Ontario.
George Burdon McKean.

NOOTENS, THIERRY. Chercheur postdoctoral en histoire, Université d'Ottawa, Ontario.
Francis McCrea.

NOPPEN, LUC. Titulaire, Chaire de recherche du Canada en patrimoine urbain, Université du Québec à Montréal, Québec.
Harry Staveley.

NORMAND, SYLVIO. Professeur titulaire de droit, Université Laval, Québec, Québec.
Jean-Joseph Beauchamp. Sir Alexandre Lacoste. Jacques-Édouard Plamondon.

Ó SIADHAIL, PÁDRAIG. Associate professor and chair, Department of Irish Studies, St Mary's University, Halifax, Nova Scotia.
Katherine Angelina Hughes.

OTTER, A. A. DEN. Professor of history, Memorial University of Newfoundland, St John's, Newfoundland.
Elliott Torrance Galt.

OTTO, STEPHEN A. Consulting historian, Toronto, Ontario.
Peter Charles Larkin.

†OUELLET, HENRI. Chercheur émérite, Musée canadien de la nature, Ottawa, Ontario.
Charles-Eusèbe Dionne.

PANAYOTIDIS, E. LISA. Assistant professor of education, University of Calgary, Alberta.
James Mavor.

PERIN, ROBERTO. Professeur agrégé d'histoire, York University, Toronto, Ontario.
Louis-Nazaire Bégin.

PILON, HENRI. Archivist, Trinity College Archives, Toronto, Ontario.
Jeanne Lajoie.

POITRAS, CLAIRE. Professeure-chercheure, Institut national de la recherche scientifique – Urbanisation, culture et société, Montréal, Québec.
Édouard Gohier.

PON, MONA-MARGARET. Researcher and writer, Toronto, Ontario.
Ng Mon Hing.

PORSILD, CHARLENE. Director, Research Center, Montana Historical Society, Helena, Montana, U.S.A.
Ellen Cashman.

POWER, MICHAEL. Historian, Welland, Ontario.
Robert Francis Forster. William Richard Harris. William Costello Kennedy. Lancelot Peter Minehan. James Fran-

cis White.

RAFFO, PETER. Sessional lecturer in history, Lakehead University, Thunder Bay, Ontario.
Viljo Rosvall.

RALPH, WAYNE. Author and journalist, White Rock, British Columbia.
William George Barker.

RAMIREZ, BRUNO. Professeur titulaire d'histoire, Université de Montréal, Québec.
Antonio Cordasco.

RAWLING, WILLIAM. Historian, Ottawa, Ontario.
Sir Edward Whipple Bancroft Morrison.

†REA, J. E. Professor of history, University of Manitoba, Winnipeg, Manitoba.
Theodore Arthur Burrows. George Robson Coldwell. Joseph Martin [in collaboration with P. E. Roy].

REANEY, JAMES STEWART. Reporter and columnist, *London Free Press*, London, Ontario.
Victoria Grace Blackburn.

REFORD, ALEXANDER. Director, Reford Gardens, Grand-Métis, Quebec.
Richard Bladworth Angus. George Stephen, 1st Baron Mount Stephen.

REGEHR, THEODORE D. Professor emeritus of history, University of Saskatchewan, Saskatoon, Saskatchewan, and adjunct professor of history, University of Calgary, Alberta.
Edson Joseph Chamberlin. John Duncan McArthur. Sir William Mackenzie. Thomas George Shaughnessy, 1st Baron Shaughnessy. Hugh McKay Sutherland.

REID, JOHN G. Professor of history, St Mary's University, Halifax, Nova Scotia.
David Allison.

REIMER, CHAD. Instructor in history, University College of the Fraser Valley, Chilliwack, British Columbia.
Gordon Charles Davidson.

RENDER, SHIRLEY. Executive director, Western Canada Aviation Museum, Winnipeg, Manitoba.
Frederick Joseph Stevenson.

RENNIE, BRADFORD J. Sessional instructor in history, University of Calgary, Alberta.
Percival Baker. James Bower.

REYNOLDS, JANELLE. Assistant archivist, Still Images Section, Archives of Manitoba, Winnipeg, Manitoba.
André Nault [in collaboration with R. Swan].

RIDER, PETER E. Atlantic provinces historian and curator, Canadian Museum of Civilization, Gatineau, Quebec.
Benjamin Charles Prowse.

†RIEGERT, PAUL W. Professor emeritus of biology, University of Regina, Saskatchewan.
Hugh McKellar. Peter Regier.

RIGGS, BERTRAM. Archivist, Centre for Newfoundland Studies, Memorial University of Newfoundland, St John's, Newfoundland.
Samuel Harris. Gertrude Isabella Parsons. James Sinclair Tait.

ROBERT, MARIO. Analyste en gestion de documents et des archives, Ville de Montréal, Québec.
Lawrence John Cannon.

ROBERTS, DAVID. Scarborough, Ontario.
John Kay Macdonald. Gordon Morton McGregor. Robert McLaughlin.

ROBINSON, IRA. Professor of religion, Concordia University,

CONTRIBUTORS

Montreal, Quebec.

Hyman Meyer Crestohl. Elias Friedlander.

RODGER, ANDREW. Archivist, Art and Photography, Documentary Heritage Collection, Library and Archives Canada, Ottawa, Ontario.

William James Topley.

RODNEY, WILLIAM. Formerly dean of arts, Royal Roads Military College, Victoria, British Columbia.

Joseph Whiteside Boyle.

ROLLMANN, HANS. Professor of religious studies, Memorial University of Newfoundland, St John's, Newfoundland.

Humphrey Pickard Cowperthwaite.

ROMPKEY, RONALD. University research professor of English, Memorial University of Newfoundland, St John's, Newfoundland.

John Mason Little. Sir William Duff Reid.

ROPER, HENRY. Formerly professor of humanities, University of King's College, Halifax, Nova Scotia.

Samuel Manners Brookfield.

ROSS, JANE. Head curator, Cultural Studies, Provincial Museum of Alberta, Edmonton, Alberta.

Stephan Gudmundur Stephansson.

ROSS, W. GILLIES. Professor emeritus of geography, Bishop's University, Lennoxville, Quebec.

William Gillies Ross.

ROUILLARD, JACQUES. Professeur titulaire d'histoire, Université de Montréal, Québec.

Gaudiose Hébert. Zotique Lespérance. Arthur Marois. George Stephens Warren.

ROUTHIER, GILLES. Professeur titulaire de théologie et de sciences religieuses, Université Laval, Québec, Québec.

Paul-Eugène Roy.

ROWLAND, ROBIN. Photo editor and producer, CBC News, and writer, Toronto, Ontario.

Besha Starkman (Tobin).

ROY, FERNANDE. Professeure d'histoire, Université du Québec à Montréal, Québec.

Alfred Duclos De Celles.

ROY, FRANÇOIS. Directeur des communications, Ville de Trois-Rivières, Québec.

Joseph-Adolphe Tessier.

ROY, PATRICIA E. Professor of history, University of Victoria, British Columbia.

Joseph Martin [in collaboration with J. E. Rea].

SAINT-PIERRE, JACQUES. Chercheur autonome, Québec, Québec.

Joseph-Édouard Caron. Guillaume-Narcisse Ducharme. Isidore-Joseph-Amédée Marsan. Joseph-Noé Ponton.

SAINT-PIERRE, JOCELYN. Responsable, Service des archives, de la reconstitution des débats et de la documentation de presse, Direction de la bibliothèque, Assemblée nationale, Québec, Québec.

Adélard Turgeon.

SANDBERG, L. ANDERS. Professor of environmental studies, York University, Toronto, Ontario.

Alfred Dickie.

SANTINK, JOY L. Author, Toronto, Ontario.

Sir John Craig Eaton.

SAUER, ANGELIKA. Associate professor and chair, Department of History and Geography, Texas Lutheran University, Seguin, Texas, U.S.A.

William Hespeler.

SCOLLIE, F. BRENT. Independent researcher, Ottawa, Ontario.

Rufus Allen Burriss.

SEAGER, ALLEN. Associate professor of history, Simon Fraser University, Burnaby, British Columbia.

James Hurst Hawthornthwaite.

SEGGER, MARTIN. Director, Maltwood Art Museum and Gallery, University of Victoria, British Columbia.

Samuel Maclure.

SEMPLE, NEIL. Historian, Toronto, Ontario.

Charles Samuel Eby. Ralph Cecil Horner.

SÉVIGNY, ANDRÉ. Historien, Charny, Québec.

Frederick Montizambert.

SHUTE, DAN. Librarian, Presbyterian College, Montreal, Quebec.

Robert Campbell.

SILVER, A. I. Associate professor of history, University of Toronto, Ontario.

Alphonse-Alfred-Clément La Rivière.

SMITH, DONALD B. Professor of history, University of Calgary, Alberta.

Deskaheh. Sir James Alexander Lougheed [in collaboration with D. J. Hall].

SMITH, GORDON E. Associate professor of music, Queen's University, Kingston, Ontario.

Gustave Gagnon.

SMYTH, ELIZABETH M. Associate professor of curriculum teaching and learning, Ontario Institute for Studies in Education of the University of Toronto, Ontario.

Catherine Anne Campbell, named *Mother Ignatia. Elizabeth Gertrude Lawler.*

SOTIRON, MINKO. Instructor in history, John Abbott College, Sainte-Anne-de-Bellevue, Quebec.

William Findlay Maclean.

SOUTHAM, PETER. Professeur titulaire d'histoire, Université de Sherbrooke, Québec.

Pantaléon Pelletier.

SPEISMAN, STEPHEN A. Director emeritus, Ontario Jewish Archives, Toronto, Ontario.

Moses Bilsky. Henry Dworkin. Isaac Halpern.

SPERDAKOS, SOPHIA. Policy adviser, Law Society of Upper Canada, Toronto, Ontario.

Laura Elizabeth McCully.

STANLEY, TIMOTHY J. Associate professor of education, University of Ottawa, Ontario.

Chang Toy. Lee Mong Kow. David Hung Chang Lew. Yip Sang.

STENTZ, MARCIA. Head, Client Services, Hudson's Bay Company Archives, Archives of Manitoba, Winnipeg, Manitoba.

Hay Strafford Stead.

STEWART, IAN M. Formerly instructor in history, Woodsworth College, University of Toronto, Ontario.

James Wilson Robertson.

†STORTZ, GERALD J. Associate professor of history, St Jerome's University, Waterloo, Ontario.

Thomas Joseph Dowling.

STRANGE, CAROLYN. Director of graduate studies, Centre for Cross-Cultural Research, Australian National University, Canberra, Australia.

Herbert Hartley Dewart.

SURTEES, LAWRENCE. Director of telecommunications research, IDC Canada Ltd, Toronto, Ontario.

Alexander Graham Bell. Arthur Williams McCurdy.
SUTHERLAND, DUFF. Instructor in history, Selkirk College, Castlegar, British Columbia.
Thomas St John [in collaboration with J. Chisholm].
SWAINGER, JONATHAN. Associate professor and chair, History Program, University of Northern British Columbia, Prince George, British Columbia.
Benjamin Franklin English.
SWAN, RUTH. Independent scholar, Swan Heritage Consulting, Winnipeg, Manitoba.
André Nault [in collaboration with J. Reynolds].
SWANICK, ERIC L. Head, Special Collections, W. A. C. Bennett Library, Simon Fraser University, Burnaby, British Columbia.
James Harvie Crocket. John Thomas Hawke.
TASCHEREAU, SYLVIE. Professeure d'histoire, Université du Québec à Trois-Rivières, Québec.
Charles Chaput.
THOMSON, ANDREW. Assistant professor, Wilfrid Laurier University, Waterloo, Ontario.
William Harty. John McClary. Elias Weber Bingeman Snider. William James Thomson.
THORPE, WENDY L. Archivist, Private Sector Archives, Nova Scotia Archives and Records Management, Halifax, Nova Scotia.
Matilda Moore Faulkner (Churchill).
TITLEY, E. BRIAN. Professor of education, University of Lethbridge, Alberta.
Amédée-Emmanuel Forget.
TRACHTENBERG, HENRY. Analyst historian, Historic Resources Branch, Manitoba Culture, Heritage and Tourism, Winnipeg, Manitoba.
Benjamin Zimmerman.
TREMBLAY, MARIE J. Étudiante au doctorat en histoire, Université du Québec à Montréal, Québec.
Charles-Amédée Vallée.
TREMBLAY, ROBERT. Historien, Division de la conservation, Musée des sciences et de la technologie du Canada, Ottawa, Ontario.
Cléophas Fabien.
TREMBLAY, YVES. Historien, Ministère de la Défense nationale, Ottawa, Ontario.
Harry Woodburn Blaylock. Harry Stephen Quigley.
TREVITHICK, SCOTT. Doctoral student and lecturer in history, University of Toronto, Ontario.
Seth Newhouse.
TUCK, ROBERT CRITCHLOW. Canon, St Peter's Cathedral, Charlottetown, Prince Edward Island.
William Lawson Cotton.
TUCKER, ALBERT. Professor emeritus of history, Glendon College, York University, Toronto, Ontario.
Jacob Lewis Englehart.
TURBIDE, NADIA. Coordinator, Music Department, Vanier College, Montreal, Quebec.
Charles Albert Edwin Harriss.
TURLEY-EWART, JOHN A. Deputy comment editor, *National Post*, Toronto, Ontario.
Sir Albert Edward Kemp [in collaboration with R. C. Brown]. *Henry Collingwood McLeod. Sir Edmund Boyd Osler. Harry Alden Richardson.*
UNGAR, MOLLY PULVER. Independent scholar, Montreal, Quebec.
Frederic Marlett Bell-Smith. Thomas Henry Best. Sir Wil-

liam James Gage. Bellelle Guerin. Frances Mahony (Jeffers; Lovering). Charlotte Mount Brock Morrell (Schreiber). [Biographies written in collaboration with V. Bach.]
VACHON, PIERRE. Musicologue, Montréal, Québec.
Emma Lajeunesse (Gye), known as *Emma Albani. Romain-Octave Pelletier.*
VALLIÈRES, MARC. Professeur titulaire d'histoire, Université Laval, Québec, Québec.
Georges-Élie Amyot. François-Xavier Drolet.
VALVERDE, MARIANA. Professor of criminology, University of Toronto, Ontario.
John George Shearer [in collaboration with S. C. Wilson].
VAUGEOIS, DENIS. Historien et éditeur, Sillery, Québec.
Cyrille Duquet.
VERRETTE, MICHEL. Professeur agrégé d'histoire, Collège universitaire de Saint-Boniface, Manitoba.
Auguste-Henri de Trémaudan.
VIGNEAULT, MICHEL. Chargé de cours en kinanthropologie, Université du Québec à Montréal, Québec.
Georges Vézina.
VILLENEUVE, RENÉ. Conservateur de l'art canadien ancien, Musée des beaux-arts du Canada, Ottawa, Ontario.
Henry Birks.
VIRR, RICHARD. Curator of manuscripts, Rare Books and Special Collections Division, McGill University Libraries, Montreal, Quebec.
Herbert Symonds.
VOGAN, NANCY F. Pickard-Bell professor of music, Mount Allison University, Sackville, New Brunswick.
Charles Henry Porter.
VOISINE, NIVE. Professeur émérite d'histoire, Université Laval, Québec, Québec.
Joseph-Stanislas-Zéphirin Phaneuf, named *Brother Opilius Elias. Stanislas-Alphonse Roberge,* named *Brother Symphorian Lewis.*
VON HEYKING, AMY. Assistant professor of elementary education, University of Alberta, Edmonton, Alberta.
Matthew McCauley.
WAGG, SUSAN. Independent architectural historian, Hanover, New Hampshire, U.S.A.
Edward Maxwell.
WAGNER, ROSEMARY. Historian, Kingston, Ontario.
Arthur Jukes Johnson.
WAISER, W. A. Professor of history, University of Saskatchewan, Saskatoon, Saskatchewan.
John Alexander Mackay.
WAITE, P. B. Professor emeritus of history, Dalhousie University, Halifax, Nova Scotia.
Henry Charles Keith Petty-Fitzmaurice, 5th Marquis of Lansdowne. Sir Joseph Pope. Jennie Grahl Hunter Shirreff (Eddy). Sir Charles Hibbert Tupper.
WALKER, BARRINGTON. Assistant professor of history, Queen's University, Kingston, Ontario.
George Washington Smith.
WARDHAUGH, ROBERT A. Assistant professor of history, University of Western Ontario, London, Ontario.
George Reading Crowe. Frederic Beal Du Val. George Frederick Galt.
WATSON, NEIL B. Lawyer, Gorman Gorman Burns and Watson, Calgary, Alberta.
Filumena (Florence) Costanzo (Sanfidele (Lassandro)).
WELWOOD, R. J. Formerly college librarian, Selkirk College, Castlegar, British Columbia.

CONTRIBUTORS

Robert Thornton Lowery.

WHITE, DONNY. Director and curator, Medicine Hat Museum and Art Gallery, Alberta.

John Dixon.

WHITEHEAD, RUTH HOLMES. Curator emeritus, Nova Scotia Museum, Halifax, Nova Scotia.

Jerry Lonecloud.

WICKWIRE, WENDY. Associate professor of history and environmental studies, University of Victoria, British Columbia.

James Alexander Teit.

†WILLIAMS, DAVID RICARDO. Adjunct professor and writer-in-residence, Faculty of Law, University of Victoria, British Columbia.

Eugene Lafleur.

WILLIE, RICHARD A. Vice-president (academic), Concordia University College of Alberta, Edmonton, Alberta.

Nicholas Du Bois Dominic Beck.

WILSON, ALAN. Professor emeritus of history, Trent University, Peterborough, Ontario.

John Northway.

WILSON, S. CRAIG. Doctoral student in law, Osgoode Hall Law School, York University, Toronto, Ontario.

George Tate Blackstock. John George Shearer [in collaboration with M. Valverde]. *Leonard James Skill.*

WOOD, B. ANNE. Formerly associate professor of education, Dalhousie University, Halifax, Nova Scotia.

Robert Maclellan [in collaboration with A. C. Dunlop].

YORKE, LOIS K. Manager, Public Services, Nova Scotia Archives and Records Management, Halifax, Nova Scotia.

Edna May Williston Best (Sexton). Kate Mackintosh.

YOUNG, C. MARY. Independent researcher, Fredericton, New Brunswick.

Loring Woart Bailey.

ZIFF, BRUCE. Professor of law, University of Alberta, Edmonton, Alberta.

Reuben Wells Leonard.

INDEX OF IDENTIFICATIONS

CATEGORIES

Accountants

Agriculture

Architects

Archivists

Armed forces

Artisans

Arts and entertainment

Authors

Blacks

Business

Clerks, secretaries, and stenographers

Collectors, folklorists, and genealogists

Communications

Criminals

Curators

Education

Engineers

Explorers

Fur trade

Hunters, fishermen, and guides

Indigenous peoples

Interpreters and translators

Inventors

Labour activists

Labourers

Legal professions

Librarians

Mariners

Medicine

Miscellaneous

Office holders

Philanthropists

Police

Politicians

Religious

Scientists

Social reformers

Social scientists

Sports

Surveyors

Women

Index of Identifications

Like the network of cross-references within biographies, this index is designed to assist readers in following their interests through the volume. Most of the groupings are by occupation carried on by persons within Canada. This arrangement does not, however, apply to native peoples, who have their own societal organization and structures and whose representatives are listed only under INDIGENOUS PEOPLES, according to the nation or group to which they belonged. Some non-occupational categories have been added to help readers who approach the past from particular perspectives. Thus WOMEN appear in one grouping, as do BLACKS, a reflection of the interest in their history. Readers interested in immigration or in the history of ethnic groups in Canada should consult the first part of the Geographical Index, where subjects are listed by their place of birth.

Some of the occupational categories may require explanation so that users will be better able to find biographies of particular interest. Under AGRICULTURE are to be found a number of groups: developers, including land agents and agricultural leaders and advisers; farmers and managers, whether proprietors or not, who cultivated and supervised agricultural land; horticulturists, specializing in the growing of garden plants, fruits, and vegetables; settlers, who cleared and inhabited new regions; and stockbreeders raising a variety of animals. It should be noted that those who speculated in land are to be found under BUSINESS, Real estate. To shorten the list of office holders in the various jurisdictions, some have been placed under their sphere of activity, whether EDUCATION or MEDICINE. Under MARINERS are included civilian captains, pilots, and navigators; naval officers are a subgroup of ARMED FORCES. Under SOCIAL REFORMERS are to be found those who sought to improve community life, whether socially or politically or from the point of view of education or religion. Although the FUR TRADE might have appeared under BUSINESS, it is given a separate listing for the benefit of readers interested in this aspect of the economy and brings together traders and the administrators of fur-trade companies. Other groups with similarities of function or objective are CLERKS, SECRETARIES, AND STENOGRAPHERS; COLLECTORS, FOLKLORISTS, AND GENEALOGISTS; and HUNTERS, FISHERMEN, AND GUIDES. Individuals who are notable for their exploits, who followed unusual occupations, or who escape easy classification are grouped under MISCELLANEOUS.

Readers following a particular interest may need to refer to more than one grouping. Biographies relevant to the history of town planning, architecture, and the building trades may be listed under ARCHITECTS, ARTISANS, ENGINEERS, LABOURERS, and BUSINESS, Real estate (for building contractors). Those investigating the history of medicine should consult not only MEDICINE but also RELIGIOUS, a category that includes many individuals involved in the founding of hospitals and hospices. Readers pursuing legal history should turn to both LEGAL PROFESSIONS and CRIMINALS.

The DCB/DBC attempts by its assignments to encourage research in new areas as well as familiar ones, but its selection of individuals to receive biographies reflects the survival of documentation and the areas historians have chosen to investigate. The index should not, therefore, be used for quantitative judgements; it is merely a guide to what is contained in volume XV.

ACCOUNTANTS

Birge, Cyrus Albert
Mackintosh, James Crosskill
McLeod, Henry Collingwood
Ross, William Gillies
Yip Sang

AGRICULTURE

Developers

Burke, Alfred Edward
Burriss, Rufus Allen
Fasken, David
Galt, Elliott Torrance
Gastonguay, Joseph-Narcisse
Gravel, Louis-Pierre
Guay, Joseph-Dominique
Lacasse, Zacharie
La Rivière, Alphonse-Alfred-Clément
Nantel, Antonin
Ponton, Joseph-Noé
Scott, Benjamin Alexander
Scott, William Duncan

Farmers and managers

Adams, John Gennings Curtis
Appleby, Charles
Arsenault, Pierre-Paul
Baker, Percival
Barker, William George
Bond, Sir Robert
Borland, Robert
Bower, James
Caron, Joseph-Édouard
Clark, Michael
Curran, William Henry
Dale, William
Deskaheh
Drummond, John Douglas Fraser
Fisher, Sydney Arthur
Fleming, Robert John

Gallant, Joseph
Georgeson, Henry
Grant, Robert Henry
Graves, Minard Wentworth
Guay, Joseph-Dominique
Guichon, Joseph
Hilborn, William Wilson
Horner, Ralph Cecil
Landry, David-Vital
Lane, George
Lépine, Ambroise-Dydime
Lesage, Damase
McArthur, Peter Gilchrist
McCauley, Matthew
McKellar, Hugh
McLennan, Robert Purves
Mallory, Caleb Alvord
Marsan, Isidore-Joseph-Amédée
Matheson, John
Maunsell, Edward Herbert
Maxwell, Edward
Nault, André
Newhouse, Seth
Oliver, John
Ponton, Joseph-Noé
Regier, Peter
Rutherford, John Gunion
Scallion, James William
Stephansson, Stephan Gudmundur
Teit, James Alexander
Tourigny, Paul (Napoléon)
Trask, Catherine (Brown)
Turriff, John Gillanders

Horticulturists

Hilborn, William Wilson
Stevenson, Alexander Patterson

Settlers

Denny, Sir Cecil Edward

Stockbreeders

Baillie, Sir Frank Wilton
Baker, Percival
Beck, Sir Adam
Bostock, Hewitt
Bower, James
Cochrane, William Edward
Davies, William
Dixon, John
Drummond, John Douglas Fraser
English, Benjamin Franklin
Guay, Joseph-Dominique
Guichon, Joseph
Hull, William Charles James Roper
Landry, David-Vital
Lane, George
Lessard, François-Louis
McEachran, Duncan McNab
Maunsell, Edward Herbert
Rutherford, John Gunion
Semlin, Charles Augustus
Strange, Thomas Bland

ARCHITECTS

Charest, Elzéar
Darling, Frank
Dandurand, Damase
Desrosiers, Augustin
Dunlop, Alexander Francis

Ewart, David
Gauthier, Louis-Zéphirin
Maclure, Samuel
Maxwell, Edward

Staveley, Harry
Tanguay, Georges-Émile
Urry, Frederick
Venne, Joseph

ARCHIVISTS

Denny, Sir Cecil Edward

Hughes, Katherine Angelina

Maclean, John

ARMED FORCES

American

Army: soldiers

Jennings, Milton Robbins

British

Air force: officers

Barker, William George
Quigley, Harry Stephen
Stevenson, Frederick Joseph

Army: officers

Alderson, Sir Edwin Alfred Hervey
French, Sir George Arthur
Gwatkin, Sir Willoughby Garnons
Hornby, John
Hutton, Sir Edward Thomas Henry
Strange, Thomas Bland
Whitty, Gerald Joseph

Canadian

Air force: officers

Barker, William George
Gwatkin, Sir Willoughby Garnons

Army: officers

Adamson, Agar Stewart Allan
   Masterton
Alderson, Sir Edwin Alfred Hervey
Burke, Alfred Edward
Chassé, Henri
Crawford Brown, Thomas
Davidson, Gordon Charles
Doyon, Constant (baptized Paul-
   Victor-Emmanuel)

Forbes, Alexander MacKenzie Torrance
Good, James Wilford
Hodgins, William Egerton
Jenkins, Stephen Rice
Lessard, François-Louis
McKean, George Burdon
Mackenzie, John Joseph
Mewburn, Frank Hamilton
Morrison, Sir Edward Whipple
   Bancroft
Otter, Sir William Dillon
Price, Sir William
Quigley, Harry Stephen
Robertson, Lawrence Bruce
Ryerson, George Ansel Sterling
Smith, William Harley
Struthers, William Eugene
Watson, Sir David
Wilson, Erastus William

Army: soldiers

Barker, William George
Hornby, John

Militia: officers

Adamson, Agar Stewart Allan
   Masterton
Blaylock, Harry Woodburn
Boyle, Joseph Whiteside
Carvell, Frank Broadstreet
Chadwick, Edward Marion
Chambers, Ernest John
Chassé, Henri
Denison, George Taylor
Domville, James
French, Sir George Arthur
Gibson, Sir John Morison
Grasett, Henry James
Gwatkin, Sir Willoughby Garnons
Hatheway, Warren Franklin

Hendrie, Sir John Strathearn
Hodgins, William Egerton
Hughes, Sir Samuel
Jarvis, William Munson
Jenkins, Stephen Rice
Leonard, Reuben Wells
Lessard, François-Louis
Le Vasseur, Nazaire
Macdonald, Sir Hugh John
Macdonell (Greenfield), John Alexander
Meredith, Sir Henry Vincent
Morrison, Sir Edward Whipple Bancroft
Otter, Sir William Dillon
Outram, Sir James
Pelletier, Pantaléon
Peuchen, Arthur Godfrey
Price, Sir William
Prowse, Benjamin Charles
Roddick, Sir Thomas George
Ruttan, Henry Norlande
Ryerson, George Ansel Sterling
Scott, Benjamin Alexander
Scott, David Lynch
Scott, Henri-Thomas
Smith, George Robert
Strange, Thomas Bland
Sulte, Benjamin
Tessier, Joseph-Adolphe
Turner, John Herbert
Watson, Sir David
Wilson, Erastus William
Wright, Adam Henry

Militia: militiamen

Barker, William George
Mair, Charles

Papal States

Vallée, Charles-Amédée

ARTISANS

Amyot, Georges-Élie
Ashdown, James Henry
Buote, François-Joseph
Burke, John
Cairns, James Frederick
Drolet, François-Xavier
Duquet, Cyrille

Halpern, Isaac
Hawke, John Thomas
Herbin, John Frederic
Hutchings, Elisha Frederick
Lapointe, Alexis, known as Alexis le
   Trotteur

Mackay, John Alexander
McLennan, Robert Purves
Merrill, Flora MacDonald (Denison)
Northway, John
Sharpe, Thomas

ARTS AND ENTERTAINMENT

AUTHORS

INDEX OF IDENTIFICATIONS

1146

INDEX OF IDENTIFICATIONS

1147

INDEX OF IDENTIFICATIONS

CRIMINALS

CURATORS

1150

EDUCATION

INDEX OF IDENTIFICATIONS

ENGINEERS

EXPLORERS

FUR TRADE

HUNTERS, FISHERMEN, AND GUIDES

Braithwaite, Henry A.
Comeau, Napoléon-Alexandre
Georgeson, Henry

Kanaka
Lonecloud, Jerry
Nault, André

Teit, James Alexander
Vigneau, Placide

INDIGENOUS PEOPLES

Blood

Nitai'kihtsipimi

Cayuga

Deskaheh

Copper Inuit

Uloqsaq

Cree

Nickawa, Frances (Mark)

Inuit

Alikomiak
Kanaka

Niaqutiaq

Métis

Lépine, Ambroise-Dydime
Mackay, John Alexander

Micmac

Lonecloud, Jerry
Tenass, John P.

Nisga'a

Sganism Sm'oogit

Ojibwa

Shingwauk, George (Appendix)

Onondaga

Newhouse, Seth

Plains Cree

Peyasiw-awasis

Santee Sioux

Matokinajin

INTERPRETERS AND TRANSLATORS

Drummond, Lewis Henry
Genyk, Cyril
Helbronner, Jules

Lee Mong Kow
Lew, David Hung Chang
Mackay, John Alexander

McLean, Amelia Anne (Paget)
Peck, Edmund James

INVENTORS

Bell, Alexander Graham
Doucet, Stanislas-Joseph
Duquet, Cyrille

Jobin, Louis
McCurdy, Arthur Williams
McLaughlin, Robert

Sleeman, George
Smith, George Robert

LABOUR ACTIVISTS

Arcand, Narcisse
Bennett, Philip
Carey, David Arthur
Drummond, Robert
Grimes, George Frederick Arthur
Hébert, Gaudiose

Helbronner, Jules
Laporte, Marie-Anne
Lespérance, Zotique
Marois, Arthur
Rosvall, Viljo
St John, Thomas

Shakespeare, Noah
Sugrue, James Leonard
Urry, Frederick
Verville, Alphonse
Warren, George Stephens

INDEX OF IDENTIFICATIONS

LABOURERS

Arcand, Narcisse
Bennett, Philip
Carey, David Arthur
Caux, Jean, known as Cataline
Chang Toy
Cordasco, Antonio
Curran, William Henry
Davis, William
Drummond, Robert
Fabien, Cléophas
Fitzgerald, William James

Fortes, Joseph Seraphim
Georgeson, Henry
Harris, Samuel
Hébert, Gaudiose
Hornby, John
Lapointe, Alexis, known as Alexis le
  Trotteur
Laporte, Marie-Anne
Lespérance, Zotique
Lougheed, Sir James Alexander

Marois, Arthur
Rosvall, Viljo
St John, Thomas
Shakespeare, Noah
Smith, Janet Kennedy
Stokes, Susannah Augusta (Maxwell)
Sugrue, James Leonard
Verville, Alphonse
Warren, George Stephens
Weston, George

LEGAL PROFESSIONS

Judges

Archibald, Walter Palmer
Beck, Nicholas Du Bois Dominic
Brodeur, Louis-Philippe
Cannon, Lawrence John
Choquet, François-Xavier
Davies, Sir Louis Henry
Flynn, Edmund James
Idington, John
Lacoste, Sir Alexandre
Longley, James Wilberforce
McCarthy, Maitland Stewart
Meredith, Sir William Ralph
Metcalfe, Thomas Llewellyn
Nesbitt, Wallace
Pelletier, Louis-Philippe
Scott, David Lynch
Sifton, Arthur Lewis Watkins
Sutherland, Robert Franklin
Townshend, Sir Charles James
Warburton, Alexander Bannerman
Wetmore, Edward Ludlow

Lawyers

Aikins, Sir James Albert Manning
Armour, Edward Douglas
Beauchamp, Jean-Joseph
Beck, Nicholas Du Bois Dominic
Bell, John Howatt
Blackstock, George Tate
Blaylock, Harry Woodburn
Bristol, Edmund James
Brodeur, Louis-Philippe
Cannon, Lawrence John
Carvell, Frank Broadstreet
Chadwick, Edward Marion
Choquet, François-Xavier
Coldwell, George Robson
Conybeare, Charles Frederick Pringle

Creighton, James George Aylwin
Cross, Charles Wilson
David, Laurent-Olivier
Davies, Sir Louis Henry
Denison, George Taylor
Dewart, Herbert Hartley
Fasken, David
Flynn, Edmund James
Forget, Amédée-Emmanuel
Gibson, Sir John Morison
Gouin, Sir Lomer
Hodgins, William Egerton
Hoyles, Newman Wright
Idington, John
Jarvis, William Munson
Johnson, Thomas Herman
Keefer, Francis Henry
Lacoste, Sir Alexandre
Lafleur, Eugene
Longley, James Wilberforce
Lougheed, Sir James Alexander
McCarthy, Maitland Stewart
McCaul, Charles Coursolles
McCord, David Ross
Macdonald, Sir Hugh John
Macdonell (Greenfield), John
  Alexander
MacKinnon, Donald Alexander
Martin, Clara Brett
Martin, Joseph
Meredith, Sir William Ralph
Metcalfe, Thomas Llewellyn
Murray, George Henry
Nesbitt, Wallace
Paterson, John Andrew
Pelletier, Louis-Philippe
Perron, Joseph-Léonide
Pugsley, William
Saunders, Dyce Willcocks
Scott, David Lynch
Sifton, Arthur Lewis Watkins

Sifton, Sir Clifford
Sutherland, Robert Franklin
Taillon, Sir Louis-Olivier
Tessier, Joseph-Adolphe
Townshend, Sir Charles James
Trémaudan, Auguste-Henri de
Tupper, Sir Charles Hibbert
Turgeon, Adélard
Wade, Frederick Coate
Warburton, Alexander Bannerman
Weldon, Richard Chapman
Wetmore, Edward Ludlow

Legal adviser

Lew, David Hung Chang

Magistrates and justices of the peace

Choquet, François-Xavier
Dixon, John
Grant, Robert Henry
Hamilton, Daniel Salmon
Harris, John Walter
Hespeler, William
Macdonald, Sir Hugh John
Macdonald, John Kay
Shakespeare, Noah
Stephansson, Stephan Gudmundur
Turner, John Herbert
Zimmerman, Benjamin

Notaries

Pelletier, Romain-Octave
Plamondon, Jacques-Édouard
Rouillard, Eugène
Sifton, Arthur Lewis Watkins
Turriff, John Gillanders

MISCELLANEOUS

OFFICE HOLDERS

INDEX OF IDENTIFICATIONS

PHILANTHROPISTS

POLICE

Federal government

Deane, Richard Burton
Denny, Sir Cecil Edward
French, Sir George Arthur
Maunsell, Edward Herbert

Provincial and territorial governments

McRae, John C.

Municipal and local governments

Grasett, Henry James
Hanrahan, Francis
McRae, John C.
Ruttan, Henry Norlande
Wallace, William

POLITICIANS

British government

Appointed

Stephen, George, 1st Baron Mount Stephen

Elected

Martin, Joseph

Federal government

Appointed

Bostock, Hewitt
David, Laurent-Olivier
Domville, James
Forget, Amédée-Emmanuel
King, George Gerald
Lacoste, Sir Alexandre
La Rivière, Alphonse-Alfred-Clément
Lougheed, Sir James Alexander
Milne, John
Nicholls, Frederic Thomas
Prowse, Benjamin Charles
Reid, John Dowsley
Taillon, Sir Louis-Olivier
Turriff, John Gillanders
Wood, Josiah

Elected

Aikins, Sir James Albert Manning
Bell, John Howatt
Bickerdike, Robert
Bostock, Hewitt
Bristol, Edmund James
Brodeur, Louis-Philippe
Burrows, Theodore Arthur
Carvell, Frank Broadstreet
Clark, Michael
Cross, Charles Wilson
Davies, Sir Louis Henry
Domville, James
Drummond, John Douglas Fraser

Fielding, William Stevens
Fisher, Sydney Arthur
Flemming, James Kidd
Gouin, Sir Lomer
Harty, William
Hughes, Sir Samuel
Keefer, Francis Henry
Kemp, Sir Albert Edward
Kennedy, William Costello
King, George Gerald
La Rivière, Alphonse-Alfred-Clément
McCarthy, Maitland Stewart
McCrea, Francis
Macdonald, Sir Hugh John
MacKinnon, Donald Alexander
Maclean, William Findlay
Martin, Joseph
Osler, Sir Edmund Boyd
Pelletier, Louis-Philippe
Price, Sir William
Pugsley, William
Reid, John Dowsley
Richardson, Robert Lorne
Robb, James Alexander
Roddick, Sir Thomas George
Rutherford, John Gunion
Shakespeare, Noah
Sheard, Charles
Sifton, Arthur Lewis Watkins
Sifton, Sir Clifford
Sutherland, Hugh McKay
Sutherland, Robert Franklin
Townshend, Sir Charles James
Tupper, Sir Charles Hibbert
Turriff, John Gillanders
Verville, Alphonse
Warburton, Alexander Bannerman
Weldon, Richard Chapman
Wood, Josiah

Provincial and territorial governments

Appointed

Amyot, Georges-Élie

Anderson, John
Bond, Sir Robert
Caron, Joseph-Édouard
Drummond, Robert
Gouin, Sir Lomer
Hespeler, William
Lacoste, Sir Alexandre
McGrath, Sir Patrick Thomas
Murray, George Henry
Pelletier, Louis-Philippe
Perron, Joseph-Léonide
Smith, George Robert
Tourigny, Paul (Napoléon)
Turgeon, Adélard

Elected

Aikins, Sir James Albert Manning
Anderson, John
Armstrong, James William
Beck, Sir Adam
Bell, John Howatt
Bickerdike, Robert
Bond, Sir Robert
Brett, Robert George
Bulyea, George Hedley Vicars
Burchill, John Percival
Burrows, Theodore Arthur
Caron, Joseph-Édouard
Carvell, Frank Broadstreet
Cashin, Sir Michael Patrick
Chamberlain, Theodore F.
Coldwell, George Robson
Cross, Charles Wilson
David, Laurent-Olivier
Davies, Sir Louis Henry
Dewart, Herbert Hartley
Edwards, Robert Chambers
Fielding, William Stevens
Flemming, James Kidd
Flynn, Edmund James
Gouin, Sir Lomer
Grant, Robert Henry
Grimes, George Frederick Arthur
Harty, William
Hatheway, Warren Franklin

INDEX OF IDENTIFICATIONS

RELIGIOUS

INDEX OF IDENTIFICATIONS

SCIENTISTS

SOCIAL REFORMERS

SOCIAL SCIENTISTS

INDEX OF IDENTIFICATIONS

SPORTS

Barker, William George
Beck, Sir Adam
Bell, Gordon
Boyle, Joseph Whiteside
Breen, William Wright
Cairns, James Frederick
Creighton, James George Aylwin
Crow, Norton Hervey
Fidler, Alfred Davis
Fitzgerald, William James
Fortes, Joseph Seraphim

Gadbois, Joseph-Pierre
Galt, George Frederick
Good, Henry John Prescott Wilshere
Hamilton, Daniel Salmon
Kendall, George Washington, known as George Kennedy
Lapointe, Alexis, known as Alexis le Trotteur
McLeod, Henry Collingwood
Outram, Sir James
Peuchen, Arthur Godfrey

Ross, William Gillies
Saunders, Dyce Willcocks
Scott, Henri-Thomas
Sleeman, George
Springstead, Velma Agnes
Stephen, George, 1st Baron Mount Stephen
Vézina, Georges
Watson, Sir David

SURVEYORS

Campbell, Archibald William
Deville, Édouard
Gastonguay, Joseph-Narcisse

Harris, John Walter
Klotz, Otto Julius
Pearce, William

Stewart, William James

WOMEN

Anctil, Jeanne
Angers, Félicité, known as Laure Conan
Barr, Annie Gardner (Brown)
Barrington, Sibella Annie
Barthe, Émilie (Lavergne)
Bélanger, Dina, named Marie Sainte-Cécile-de-Rome
Bertrand, Julie, named Marie de Saint-Basile
Best, Edna May Williston (Sexton)
Bibeau, Marie, named Marie-Anne-de-Jésus
Blackburn, Victoria Grace
Brown, Ada Mary (Courtice)
Campbell, Catherine Anne, named Mother Ignatia
Carnochan, Janet
Cashman, Ellen
Connolly, Mary, named Sister Mary Clare
Costanzo, Filumena (Florence) (Sanfidele (Lassandro))
Creighton, Eliza Jane (Harvie)
Dégrès, Irène-Mathilde, named Saint-Paul
Dougall, Lily
Dow, Jean Isabelle
Duncan, Sara Jeannette (Cotes), known as Garth Grafton
Fairweather, Marion (Stirling)
Faulkner, Matilda Moore (Churchill)

Flett, Winona Margaret (Dixon)
Gendron, Philomène
Gordon, Wilhelmina (Smith)
Gowanlock, Jenny Kidd (Trout)
Grier, Sarah Hannah Roberta (Coome)
Guerin, Bellelle
Hébert de La Rousselière, Marie, named Marie-Clémentine de Jésus-Hostie
Hiester, Mary Augusta Catharine (Reid)
Howard, Leonora Annetta (King)
Hubbard, Mabel Gardiner (Bell)
Hughes, Katherine Angelina
Hymas, Sarah (Bates; Daines)
Johnstone, Isabel
Knott, Caroline Sarah (Tate)
Knowling, Fannie (McNeil)
Lajeunesse, Emma (Gye), known as Emma Albani
Lajoie, Jeanne
La Palme, Béatrice (Issaurel)
Laporte, Marie-Anne
Lawler, Elizabeth Gertrude
Lehman, Bertha (Rosenthal)
Lemoine, Marie-Louise-Thérèse, named Marie-Joseph de Jésus
Lesaulnier, Aurélie
Lindley, Sarah (Crease, Lady Crease)
Livingston, Gertrude Elizabeth (Nora)
McCully, Laura Elizabeth
Machar, Agnes Maule

McIntosh, Eliza Ann (Reid)
Mackintosh, Kate
McLean, Amelia Anne (Paget)
Maclure, Sara Anne (McLagan)
MacPherson, Isabel Ecclestone (Mackay)
Mahony, Frances (Jeffers; Lovering)
Marchand, Joséphine (Dandurand)
Marlatt, Wenonah
Marmette, Marie-Louise (Brodeur), known as Louyse de Bienville
Martin, Clara Brett
Melanson, Nathalie (Bourgeois)
Merrill, Flora MacDonald (Denison)
Mickle, Sara
Mills, Harriet Ann (Roche; Boomer)
Morrell, Charlotte Mount Brock (Schreiber)
Munro, Jessie Knox
Napolitano, Angelina
Nickawa, Frances (Mark)
Odell, Roberta Elizabeth (Tilton)
O'Neill, Margaret, named Mother Agatha
Parsons, Gertrude Isabella
Pickthall, Marjorie Lowry Christie
Polson, Margaret Smith (Murray)
Powell, Ann Jane (Gray)
Quinlan, Anne
Rowell, Sarah Alice (Wright)
Saint-Amant, Annette (Frémont)
Scott, Agnes Mary (Davis)

INDEX OF IDENTIFICATIONS

GEOGRAPHICAL INDEX

CANADA

Alberta

British Columbia
 Mainland
 Queen Charlotte Islands
 Vancouver Island

Manitoba

New Brunswick

Newfoundland and Labrador
 Labrador
 Newfoundland

Northwest Territories

Nova Scotia
 Cape Breton Island
 Mainland

Nunavut

Ontario
 Centre
 East
 Niagara
 North
 Southwest

Prince Edward Island

Quebec
 Bas-Saint-Laurent–Gaspésie–Côte-Nord
 Montréal-Outaouais
 Nord-Ouest–Saguenay–Lac-Saint-Jean–Nord-du-
  Québec
 Québec
 Trois-Rivières–Cantons-de-l'Est

Saskatchewan

Yukon Territory

OTHER COUNTRIES

Algeria
Australia
Azerbaijan
Belgium
Belize
Bermuda
Chile
Democratic Republic of the Congo
Finland
France
Galicia (province of the Austrian empire)
Germany
Greece
Iceland
India
Israel
Italy
Jamaica

Japan
Kenya
Lithuania
Mexico
Netherlands
People's Republic of China
Poland
Republic of Ireland
Romania
Russia
South Africa
Switzerland
Trinidad and Tobago
Turkey
Uganda
Ukraine
United Kingdom
United States of America

ONTARIO

I East
II Centre
III Niagara
IV Southwest
V North

QUEBEC

I Bas-Saint-Laurent–Gaspésie–Côte-Nord
II Québec
III Trois-Rivières–Cantons-de-l'Est
IV Montréal-Outaouais
V Nord-Ouest–Saguenay–Lac-Saint-Jean–
  Nouveau-Québec

Geographical Index

The Geographical Index, in two parts, provides a regional breakdown of subjects of biographies according to place of birth and according to career. Each part has two subsections: Canada and Other Countries.

For the purposes of this index, Canada is represented by the present ten provinces and three territories, listed alphabetically. Five provinces are subdivided. The section Other Countries is based as far as possible on modern political divisions.

Place of birth. This part of the index lists subjects of biographies by their birthplace, whether in Canada or elsewhere. Where only a strong probability of birth in a particular region exists, the name of the subject is followed by a question mark; where no such probability exists, names have not been included. It should be noted that the use of modern political divisions can produce some anachronisms; a person born in Baden appears under Germany. Finally, for certain individuals, places of birth are known only in general terms.

Career. Subjects appear here on the basis of their activity as adults. Places of education, retirement, and death have not been considered. Persons whose functions gave them jurisdiction over several regions, such as a bishop or premier, are listed according to their seat of office, but their activities as described in the biographies have also been taken into consideration. Businessmen appear only in the area of the primary location of their business, unless the biographies indicate active personal involvement in other regions. Explorers are found in the areas they visited. Listed under Other Countries are those Canadians – defined as those born within the present boundaries of Canada or immigrants of more than five years' standing – whose lives took them elsewhere.

PLACE OF BIRTH

Canada

ALBERTA

Nitai'kihtsipimi

BRITISH COLUMBIA

Mainland

Maclure, Samuel
Sganism Sm'oogit

Vancouver Island

Todd, Albert Edward

MANITOBA

Barker, William George
Breen, William Wright

Lépine, Ambroise-Dydime
Marlatt, Wenonah

Nault, André
Nickawa, Frances (Mark)

ONTARIO

SASKATCHEWAN

Other Countries

AUSTRALIA

AZERBAIJAN

BELIZE

BERMUDA

UKRAINE

Dmytriw, Nestor
Dworkin, Henry

Genyk, Cyril

Zimmerman, Benjamin

UNITED KINGDOM

England

Alderson, Sir Edwin Alfred Hervey
Ashdown, James Henry
Bancroft, James Frederick
Barker, William Henry
Bell-Smith, Frederic Marlett
Bostock, Hewitt
Brookfield, Samuel Manners
Chambers, Ernest John
Clark, Michael
Cochrane, William Edward
Conybeare, Charles Frederick Pringle
Dale, William
Davies, William
Davis, William
Denny, Sir Cecil Edward
Good, Henry John Prescott Wilshere
Gwatkin, Sir Willoughby Garnons
Harriss, Charles Albert Edwin
Hawke, John Thomas
Hornby, John
Hull, William Charles James Roper
Hutton, Sir Edward Thomas Henry
Hymas, Sarah (Bates; Daines)
Knott, Caroline Sarah (Tate)
Lindley, Sarah (Crease, Lady Crease)
McKean, George Burdon
Mills, Harriet Ann (Roche; Boomer)
Morrell, Charlotte Mount Brock
   (Schreiber)
Newcombe, Charles Frederic

Nicholls, Frederic Thomas
Northway, John
Oliver, John
Outram, Sir James
Parkhurst, Edwin Rodie
Peck, Edmund James
Petty-Fitzmaurice, Henry Charles Keith,
   5th Marquess of Lansdowne
Pickthall, Marjorie Lowry Christie
Reader, Joseph
Semmens, John
Shakespeare, Noah
Sims, Louisa (Rogers) (?)
Skill, Leonard James
Stead, Hay Strafford
Symonds, Herbert
Turner, John Herbert
Urry, Frederick
Warburton, George Augustus
Wright, John Joseph

Northern Ireland

Briggs, William
Collison, William Henry
Leonard, Bernard
Maclure, Sara Anne (McLagan)
Magill, Robert

Scotland

Anderson, Alexander

Anderson, John
Angus, Richard Bladworth
Bell, Alexander Graham
Brymner, William
Drummond, Robert
Edwards, Robert Chambers
Ewart, David
Georgeson, Henry
Gowanlock, Jenny Kidd (Trout)
Kilpatrick, Thomas Buchanan
Macdonald, John Kay
McEachran, Duncan McNab
Maclean, John
McLean, William James
Mavor, James
Milne, John
Paterson, John Andrew
Peterson, Sir William
Polson, Margaret Smith (Murray)
Robertson, James Wilson
Rutherford, John Gunion
Smith, Janet Kennedy
Stephen, George, 1st Baron Mount
   Stephen
Stevenson, Alexander Patterson
Teit, James Alexander
Wood, Joanna Ellen

Wales

Horner, Ralph Joseph
Townsend, Margaret (Fox; Jenkins)

UNITED STATES OF AMERICA

Bailey, Loring Woart
Burriss, Rufus Allen
Chamberlin, Edson Joseph
Curran, William Henry
Du Val, Frederic Beal
Englehart, Jacob Lewis
English, Benjamin Franklin
Hiester, Mary Augusta Catharine (Reid)
Hopkins, John Castell
Hubbard, Mabel Gardiner (Bell)
Jennings, Milton Robbins

Johnson, Phelps
Lane, George
Lawler, Elizabeth Gertrude
Little, John Mason
Livingston, Gertrude Elizabeth (Nora)
Lonecloud, Jerry
Mahony, Frances (Jeffers; Lovering)
Matokinajin
Odell, Roberta Elizabeth (Tilton)
Porter, Charles Henry
Richardson, Harry Alden

Russell, Charles Marion
Rutherford, William John
Shaughnessy, Thomas George, 1st Baron
   Shaughnessy
Smith, George Robert
Smith, George Washington
Stokes, Susannah Augusta (Maxwell)
Webster, Ella Hobday (Bronson)
Weston, George
Whitney, Henry Melville

CAREER

Canada

ALBERTA

Baker, Percival
Beck, Nicholas Du Bois Dominic
Blain, Joseph
Blaylock, Harry Woodburn
Bower, James
Brett, Robert George
Brymner, William
Bulyea, George Hedley Vicars
Burrows, Theodore Arthur
Clark, Michael
Cochrane, William Edward
Conybeare, Charles Frederick Pringle
Costanzo, Filumena (Florence)
    (Sanfidele (Lassandro))
Cross, Charles Wilson
Deane, Richard Burton
Denny, Sir Cecil Edward
Dmytriw, Nestor
Drummond, Lewis Henry

Edwards, Robert Chambers
Fidler, Alfred Davis
French, Sir George Arthur
Galt, Elliott Torrance
Grandin, Henri
Hornby, John
Hughes, Katherine Angelina
Hull, William Charles James Roper
Hymas, Sarah (Bates; Daines)
Jennings, Milton Robbins
Lane, George
Lougheed, Sir James Alexander
McArthur, John Duncan
McCarthy, Maitland Stewart
McCaul, Charles Coursolles
McCauley, Matthew
McKean, George Burdon
Maclean, John
McLean, William James

Mair, Charles
Maunsell, Edward Herbert
Mewburn, Frank Hamilton
Munro, Jessie Knox
Nitai'kihtsipimi
Outram, Sir James
Pearce, William
Pelletier, Pantaléon
Peuchen, Arthur Godfrey
Peyasiw-awasis
Russell, Charles Marion
Rutherford, John Gunion
Ruttan, Henry Norlande
Scott, David Lynch
Sifton, Arthur Lewis Watkins
Stephansson, Stephan Gudmundur
Strange, Thomas Bland
Toupin-Fafard, Mathilde

BRITISH COLUMBIA

Mainland

Appleby, Charles
Barker, William Henry
Borland, Robert
Bostock, Hewitt
Brymner, William
Cashman, Ellen
Caux, Jean, known as Cataline
Chang Toy
Chirouse, Eugène-Casimir
Collison, William Henry
Costanzo, Filumena (Florence)
    (Sanfidele (Lassandro))
Curran, William Henry
Davidson, Gordon Charles
Denny, Sir Cecil Edward
Eby, Charles Samuel
English, Benjamin Franklin
Fitzgerald, William James
Fortes, Joseph Seraphim
Friedlander, Elias
Georgeson, Henry
Guichon, Joseph
Hull, William Charles James Roper
Kaburagi, Goro
Kelly, Robert

Klotz, Otto Julius
Knott, Caroline Sarah (Tate)
Le Jeune, Jean-Marie-Raphaël
Lew, David Hung Chang
Lindley, Sarah (Crease, Lady Crease)
Lowery, Robert Thornton
McArthur, John Duncan
McCaul, Charles Coursolles
McCauley, Matthew
McLennan, Robert Purves
Maclure, Samuel
Maclure, Sara Anne (McLagan)
MacPherson, Isabel Ecclestone
    (Mackay)
Mair, Charles
Martin, Joseph
Newcombe, Charles Frederic
Ng Mon Hing
Nichol, Walter Cameron
Nickawa, Frances (Mark)
Oliver, John
Outram, Sir James
Pearce, William
Pickthall, Marjorie Lowry Christie
Semlin, Charles Augustus
Sganism Sm'oogit
Smith, Janet Kennedy

Teit, James Alexander
Tupper, Sir Charles Hibbert
Turner, John Herbert
Verigin, Peter Vasil'evich
Wade, Frederick Coate
Yip Sang

Queen Charlotte Islands

Collison, William Henry
Newcombe, Charles Frederic

Vancouver Island

Appleby, Charles
Bostock, Hewitt
Cashman, Ellen
Chang Toy
Curran, William Henry
Friedlander, Elias
Georgeson, Henry
Hawthornthwaite, James Hurst
Knott, Caroline Sarah (Tate)
Lee Mong Kow
Lindley, Sarah (Crease, Lady Crease)
McCurdy, Arthur Williams
McLennan, Robert Purves

Maclure, Samuel
Maclure, Sara Anne (McLagan)
Mair, Charles
Marlatt, Wenonah
Newcombe, Charles Frederic

Ng Mon Hing
Nichol, Walter Cameron
Oliver, John
Pickthall, Marjorie Lowry Christie
Shakespeare, Noah

Todd, Albert Edward
Townsend, Margaret (Fox; Jenkins)
Tupper, Sir Charles Hibbert
Turner, John Herbert

MANITOBA

Aikins, Sir James Albert Manning
Alloway, William Forbes
Armstrong, James William
Ashdown, James Henry
Ball, Richard Amos
Beck, Nicholas Du Bois Dominic
Bell, Gordon
Bell, John Howatt
Blain, Joseph
Breen, William Wright
Brett, Robert George
Burrows, Theodore Arthur
Chamberlin, Edson Joseph
Chipman, Clarence Campbell
Coldwell, George Robson
Crowe, George Reading
Dandurand, Damase
Dmytriw, Nestor
Drummond, Lewis Henry
Du Val, Frederic Beal
Edwards, Robert Chambers
Flett, Winona Margaret (Dixon)
Forget, Amédée-Emmanuel
French, Sir George Arthur
Friedlander, Elias
Galt, George Frederick
Genyk, Cyril
Good, James Wilford

Gordon, Daniel Miner
Ham, George Henry
Hamilton, Daniel Salmon
Harris, John Walter
Hespeler, William
Horner, Ralph Joseph
Hutchings, Elisha Frederick
Jetté, Jules
Johnson, Thomas Herman
Kilpatrick, Thomas Buchanan
Lacasse, Zacharie
La Rivière, Alphonse-Alfred-Clément
Lépine, Ambroise-Dydime
McArthur, John Duncan
McCauley, Matthew
Macdonald, Sir Hugh John
Mackay, John Alexander
McKellar, Hugh
McLean, Amelia Anne (Paget)
Maclean, John
McLean, William James
McLennan, Robert Purves
McLeod, Henry Collingwood
McRae, John C.
Magill, Robert
Mair, Charles
Martin, Joseph
Metcalfe, Thomas Llewellyn

Mewburn, Frank Hamilton
Mills, Harriet Ann (Roche; Boomer)
Nanton, Sir Augustus Meredith
Nault, André
Nickawa, Frances (Mark)
Pearce, William
Reader, Joseph
Richardson, Robert Lorne
Rutherford, John Gunion
Rutherford, William John
Ruttan, Henry Norlande
Saint-Amant, Annette (Frémont)
Scallion, James William
Scott, William Duncan
Semmens, John
Sharpe, Thomas
Sifton, Arthur Lewis Watkins
Sifton, Sir Clifford
Spencer, Joseph William Winthrop
Stead, Hay Strafford
Stevenson, Alexander Patterson
Stevenson, Frederick Joseph
Sutherland, Hugh McKay
Trémaudan, Auguste-Henri de
Turriff, John Gillanders
Vallance, Margaret (Taylor, Lady Taylor)
Wade, Frederick Coate
Zimmerman, Benjamin

NEW BRUNSWICK

Allison, David
Archibald, Walter Palmer
Bailey, Loring Woart
Barrington, Sibella Annie
Belliveau, Alphée
Braithwaite, Henry A.
Buote, François-Joseph
Burchill, John Percival
Carvell, Frank Broadstreet
Cowperthwaite, Humphrey Pickard
Crocket, James Harvie
Domville, James
Doucet, Stanislas-Joseph
Flemming, James Kidd

Fowler, James
Gaudet, Placide
Gendron, Philomène
Gordon, Wilhelmina (Smith)
Green, Nathan
Hatheway, Warren Franklin
Hawke, John Thomas
Jarvis, William Munson
King, George Gerald
Landry, David-Vital
Loggie, Andrew
McKellar, Hugh
Matthew, George Frederic
Melanson, Nathalie (Bourgeois)

Melanson, Olivier-Maximin
Parkin, Sir George Robert
Price, William Henry
Pugsley, William
Quinlan, Anne
Raymond, William Odber
Richardson, Harry Alden
Stewart, Thomas
Sugrue, James Leonard
Tenass, John P.
Weldon, Richard Chapman
Wetmore, Edward Ludlow
Wood, Josiah

ONTARIO

Grandsaignes d'Hauterives, Henry de,
  Vicomte de Grandsaignes
  d'Hauterives
Semmens, John

Centre

Adams, John Gennings Curtis
Adamson, Agar Stewart Allan
  Masterton
Aikins, William Henry Beaufort
Archibald, Walter Palmer
Armour, Edward Douglas
Baillie, Sir Frank Wilton
Ball, Richard Amos
Barker, William George
Beck, Sir Adam
Beck, Nicholas Du Bois Dominic
Bell-Smith, Frederic Marlett
Bengough, John Wilson
Best, Thomas Henry
Birge, Cyrus Albert
Blackstock, George Tate
Booth, John Rudolphus
Briggs, William
Bristol, Edmund James
Brown, Ada Mary (Courtice)
Burgess, Thomas Joseph Workman
Burke, Alfred Edward
Burriss, Rufus Allen
Campbell, Archibald William
Campbell, Catherine Anne, named
  Mother Ignatia
Carey, David Arthur
Carruthers, James
Carson, William Oliver
Chadwick, Edward Marion
Chamberlain, Theodore F.
Clarke, Charles Kirk
Clarke, Lionel Herbert
Crawford Brown, Thomas
Creelman, George Christie
Creighton, Eliza Jane (Harvie)
Crow, Norton Hervey
Dale, William
Darling, Frank
Davies, William
Denison, George Taylor
Dewart, Herbert Hartley
Dixon, John
Dowling, Thomas Joseph
Duncan, Sara Jeannette (Cotes), known
  as Garth Grafton
Dworkin, Henry
Eaton, Sir John Craig
Eby, Charles Samuel
Englehart, Jacob Lewis
Fairweather, Marion (Stirling)
Fasken, David

Fernow, Bernhard Eduard
Fitzgerald, William James
Fleming, Robert John
Forster, Robert Francis
Gage, Sir William James
Galt, George Frederick
Gauthier, Charles Hugh
Gibson, Sir John Morison
Glasgow, Robert Pollock
Good, Henry John Prescott Wilshere
Gowanlock, Jenny Kidd (Trout)
Grand, James
Grasett, Henry James
Grier, Sarah Hannah Roberta (Coome)
Halpern, Isaac
Ham, George Henry
Harris, William Richard
Hawke, John Thomas
Hendrie, Sir John Strathearn
Hiester, Mary Augusta Catharine (Reid)
Hodgins, William Egerton
Hopkins, John Castell
Hoyles, Newman Wright
Hughes, Sir Samuel
Jennings, Milton Robbins
Johnson, Arthur Jukes
Johnson, Phelps
Kemp, Sir Albert Edward
Kennedy, William Costello
Kilpatrick, Thomas Buchanan
Knott, Caroline Sarah (Tate)
Larkin, Peter Charles
Lawler, Elizabeth Gertrude
Lessard, François-Louis
Lochhead, William
Lougheed, Sir James Alexander
McArthur, Peter Gilchrist
McCully, Laura Elizabeth
McCurdy, Arthur Williams
Macdonald, Sir Hugh John
Macdonald, James Alexander
Macdonald, John Kay
Macdonell (Greenfield), John Alexander
McEachran, Duncan McNab
McKay, William James
Mackenzie, John Joseph
Mackenzie, Sir William
McLaughlin, Robert
Maclean, William Findlay
McLeod, Henry Collingwood
Mahony, Frances (Jeffers; Lovering)
Mallory, Caleb Alvord
Martin, Clara Brett
Mathison, Robert
Mavor, James
Meredith, Sir William Ralph
Merrill, Flora MacDonald (Denison)
Mickle, Sara
Mills, James

Minehan, Lancelot Peter
Morrell, Charlotte Mount Brock
  (Schreiber)
Munro, Jessie Knox
Nanton, Sir Augustus Meredith
Nesbitt, Wallace
Ng Mon Hing
Nichol, Walter Cameron
Nicholls, Frederic Thomas
Nickawa, Frances (Mark)
Northway, John
O'Neill, Margaret, named Mother
  Agatha
Osler, Sir Edmund Boyd
Otter, Sir William Dillon
Parkhurst, Edwin Rodie
Parkin, Sir George Robert
Paterson, John Andrew
Peuchen, Arthur Godfrey
Pickthall, Marjorie Lowry Christie
Powell, Ann Jane (Gray)
Richardson, Harry Alden
Richardson, Robert Lorne
Robertson, Lawrence Bruce
Ryerson, George Ansel Sterling
Saunders, Dyce Willcocks
Scott, David Lynch
Scott, William Duncan
Semlin, Charles Augustus
Sheard, Charles
Shearer, John George
Sheppard, Edmund Ernest
Shortt, Emily Ann McCausland
  (Cummings)
Sims, Louisa (Rogers)
Sinclair, David Volume
Skill, Leonard James
Smith, George Washington
Smith, William Harley
Starkman, Besha (Tobin)
Stevenson, Alexander Patterson
Stokes, Susannah Augusta (Maxwell)
Struthers, William Eugene
Sutherland, Hugh McKay
Sutherland, Robert Franklin
Symonds, Herbert
Thomson, William James
Vallance, Margaret (Taylor, Lady Taylor)
Vogt, Augustus Stephen
Wade, Frederick Coate
Walker, Sir Byron Edmund
Wallace, Francis Huston
Wallace, William
Warburton, George Augustus
Watson, Albert Durrant
Weldon, Isaac Hillock
Weston, George
White, James Francis
Willison, Sir John Stephen

PRINCE EDWARD ISLAND

QUEBEC

GEOGRAPHICAL INDEX

SASKATCHEWAN

YUKON TERRITORY

Other Countries

ALGERIA

AUSTRALIA

BELGIUM

Adamson, Agar Stewart Allan
   Masterton
Alderson, Sir Edwin Alfred Hervey
Barker, William George

Davidson, Gordon Charles
Langlois, Godfroy
Morrison, Sir Edward Whipple
   Bancroft

Quigley, Harry Stephen
Robertson, Lawrence Bruce
Watson, Sir David

DEMOCRATIC REPUBLIC OF THE CONGO

Forbes, John

FRANCE

Alderson, Sir Edwin Alfred Hervey
Barker, William George
Blaylock, Harry Woodburn
Chassé, Henri
Davidson, Gordon Charles
Doyon, Constant (baptized Paul-Victor-
   Emmanuel)
Forbes, Alexander MacKenzie Torrance

Good, James Wilford
Huot, Charles
Lajeunesse, Emma (Gye), known as
   Emma Albani
La Palme, Béatrice (Issaurel)
McKean, George Burdon
Morrice, James Wilson
Morrison, Sir Edward Whipple Bancroft

Prévost, Albert
Price, Sir William
Robertson, Lawrence Bruce
Scott, Agnes Mary (Davis)
Smith, William Harley
Watson, Sir David
Whitty, Gerald Joseph

GERMANY

Chassé, Henri

Hespeler, William

Huot, Charles

GREECE

Mackenzie, John Joseph

INDIA

Duncan, Sara Jeannette (Cotes),
   known as Garth Grafton

Fairweather, Marion (Stirling)

Faulkner, Matilda Moore (Churchill)

ISRAEL

Forbes, John

GEOGRAPHICAL INDEX

ITALY

Barker, William George
Burke, Alfred Edward

Lajeunesse, Emma (Gye), known as
Emma Albani

Vallée, Charles-Amédée

JAPAN

Eby, Charles Samuel

Munro, Jessie Knox

KENYA

Forbes, John

MEXICO

Burke, Alfred Edward

PEOPLE'S REPUBLIC OF CHINA

Dow, Jean Isabelle

Howard, Leonora Annetta (King)

Lee Mong Kow

ROMANIA

Boyle, Joseph Whiteside

RUSSIA

Boyle, Joseph Whiteside

Stevenson, Frederick Joseph

SOUTH AFRICA

Alderson, Sir Edwin Alfred Hervey
Lessard, François-Louis

Morrison, Sir Edward Whipple
Bancroft

Otter, Sir William Dillon

GEOGRAPHICAL INDEX

SWITZERLAND

Deskaheh

TURKEY

Whitty, Gerald Joseph

UGANDA

Forbes, John

UNITED KINGDOM

England

Alderson, Sir Edwin Alfred Hervey
Barker, William George
Blaylock, Harry Woodburn
Burke, Alfred Edward
Chassé, Henri
Chipman, Clarence Campbell
Darling, Frank
Deskaheh
Dougall, Lily
Doyon, Constant (baptized Paul-Victor-Emmanuel)
Duncan, Sara Jeannette (Cotes), known as Garth Grafton
Forbes, Alexander MacKenzie Torrance
Forbes, John
Good, James Wilford

Grasett, Henry James
Grier, Sarah Hannah Roberta (Coome)
Harriss, Charles Albert Edwin
Hughes, Katherine Angelina
Kemp, Sir Albert Edward
Lajeunesse, Emma (Gye), known as Emma Albani
La Palme, Béatrice (Issaurel)
Larkin, Peter Charles
McArthur, Peter Gilchrist
McKean, George Burdon
Martin, Joseph
Mewburn, Frank Hamilton
Morrell, Charlotte Mount Brock (Schreiber)
Morrice, James Wilson
Nickawa, Frances (Mark)
Parkin, Sir George Robert

Pelletier, Pantaléon
Pickthall, Marjorie Lowry Christie
Price, Sir William
Quigley, Harry Stephen
Smith, William Harley
Stephen, George, 1st Baron Mount Stephen
Stevenson, Frederick Joseph
Struthers, William Eugene
Turner, John Herbert
Wade, Frederick Coate
Watson, Sir David
Wilson, Erastus William

Scotland

Rutherford, John Gunion

UNITED STATES OF AMERICA

Alba, Georges, known as Paul Cazeneuve
Baker, Percival
Bell, Alexander Graham
Best, Edna May Williston (Sexton)
Bibeau, Marie, named Marie-Anne-de-Jésus
Blackburn, Victoria Grace
Booth, John Rudolphus

Boyle, Joseph Whiteside
Carman, William Bliss
Chipman, Clarence Campbell
Connolly, Mary, named Sister Mary Clare
Creelman, George Christie
Denny, Sir Cecil Edward
De Sève, Alfred
Devine, Edward James

Drummond, Lewis Henry
Duncan, Sara Jeannette (Cotes), known as Garth Grafton
Fairweather, Marion (Stirling)
Fasken, David
Fitzgerald, William James
Forster, Robert Francis
Glasgow, Robert Pollock
Gravel, Louis-Pierre

NOMINAL INDEX

VOLUME I	1000–1700
VOLUME II	1701–1740
VOLUME III	1741–1770
VOLUME IV	1771–1800
VOLUME V	1801–1820
VOLUME VI	1821–1835
VOLUME VII	1836–1850
VOLUME VIII	1851–1860
VOLUME IX	1861–1870
VOLUME X	1871–1880
VOLUME XI	1881–1890
VOLUME XII	1891–1900
VOLUME XIII	1901–1910
VOLUME XIV	1911–1920
VOLUME XV	1921–1930

As of 2005 the following volumes have been published:
volumes I to XV, *Index, volumes I to IV,*
and *Index, volumes I to XII.*

Available in electronic form:

CD-ROM, VOLUMES I to XIV (1000–1920)

ONLINE, VOLUMES I to XIV (1000–1920)
200 BIOGRAPHIES, VOLUME XV (1921–1930)
12 BIOGRAPHIES, POST-1930

Nominal Index

Included in this index are the names of persons mentioned in volume XV. They are listed by their family names, with titles and first names following. Wives are entered under their maiden names with their married names in parentheses. An asterisk indicates that the person has received a biography in a volume already published, or will probably receive one in a subsequent volume. The death date or last floruit date refers the reader to the volume in which the biography will be found. Numerals in bold face indicate the pages on which a biography appears. Titles, variants, and married and religious names are fully cross-referenced.

1195